THE
GOOD
PUB
GUIDE
2020

Trent setters.

Old Empire IPA 5.7%
An authentic recreation of the beer style created for, and enjoyed throughout the Empire.

Pedigree 4.5%
That's George Peard, head brewer when Pedigree was first named.
Bottle conditioned.

61 Deep 3.8%
How deep? 61 metres thereabout. The depth of our fresh water well in Burton.

Saddle Tank 3.8%
Named after the train which brought the hops and malts to the Brewery and then took our beer away.

EPA 3.6%
The stilt walker is actually an original hop picker. In this case Cascade and Styrian hops.

FROM BURTON WITH LOVE

Marston's brewery is the beating heart of Burton-On-Trent. It has been brewing beer in Burton since 1834. We came here for the unique Burton water and settled, becoming interwoven in to the fabric of the town. Burton is to brewing what Detroit is to the American car industry. Burton is to beer what Scotland is to Whisky. Without Burton there would be no Marston's; without Marston's there would be no Burton. We brew beer, that's what we do; this is who we are.

   @marstonsbrewery **marstonsbrewery.co.uk**

THE
GOOD
PUB
GUIDE
2 0 2 0

THE TOP 5,000 PUBS FOR FOOD AND DRINK IN THE UK

Editor: Fiona Stapley

Associate Editor: Patrick Stapley

Managing Editor: Fiona Wright

Editorial Assistant: Sarah Collins

The Good Pub Guide
was founded by Alisdair Aird in 1982

Please send reports on pubs to:

Freepost THE GOOD PUB GUIDE, Random House Publishing,
20 Vauxhall Bridge Road, London SW1V 2SA

or feedback@goodguides.com

or visit our website: www.thegoodpubguide.co.uk

If you would like to advertise in the next edition of The Good Pub Guide,
please email goodpubguide@tbs-ltd.co.uk

10 9 8 7 6 5 4 3 2 1

Published in 2019 by Ebury Press, an imprint of Ebury Publishing

Ebury Press, an imprint of Ebury Publishing
20 Vauxhall Bridge Road,
London, SW1V 2SA

Text © Ebury Publishing 2019
Maps © PerroGraphics 2019
Fiona Stapley has asserted her right to be identified as the author of this Work
in accordance with the Copyright, Designs and Patents Act 1988

www.eburypublishing.co.uk

Penguin
Random House
UK

Penguin Random House is committed to a sustainable future for
our business, our readers and our planet. This book is made from
Forest Stewardship Council® certified paper.

To buy books by your favourite authors and register for offers,
visit www.penguin.co.uk

Typesetter: Integra
Designer: Jerry Goldie Graphic Design
Project manager and copy editor: Cath Phillips
Proofreader: Tamsin Shelton
Good Pub Guide icons: William Collins

Printed and bound in Great Britain by Clays Ltd, Elcograf S.p.A.

ISBN 9781529103724

Contents

RIDLEY INNS

You can be assured of a warm welcome at all of our Ridley Inns – with a broad selection of delicious, high-quality food to suit all tastes and dietary requirements, all home-made and locally-sourced. You'll also find a great selection of drinks including some personally selected real ales.

THE COCK INN, RINGMER

www.cockpub.co.uk
01273 812040
Food Service Times
Monday to Friday: 12-2pm then 6-9:30pm
Saturday: 12-2:30pm & 6-9:30pm
Sunday: 12-8:30pm

THE HIGHLANDS INN, UCKFIELD

www.highlandsinn.co.uk
01825 762989
Food Service Times
Monday to Friday: 12-2:30pm then 6-9:30pm
Saturday: 12-2:30pm & 6-9:30pm (sports bar menu 3-5:30pm)
Sunday: 12-7:30pm

THE HEATHFIELD TAVERN, HEATHFIELD

www.theheathfieldtavern.co.uk
01435 864847
Food Service Times
Monday to Saturday: 12-2:30pm
Sunday: 12-4pm

PUBS & INNS
BUTCOMBE
BREWING CO

Wherever you want your visit to the pub to take you, we've got the venue to fit your bill and make the most of your experience.

From rural landscapes with top quality dining, to live music venues with good old fashioned boozers in between, our eclectic mix of pubs are just the ticket to your perfect outing.

Each pub has its own individuality, fuelled by character and charm, to ensure you have the best experience no matter who you're with.

With pubs across Somerset, Bristol, Bath, Gloucester and Wiltshire, there's something for everyone. So, why not pop in and say hello, we'd love to see you!

Join the Butcombe Loyalty Club and get £5 to spend in any of our managed pubs* today! Head to ButcombeLoyaltyClub.com to register.

butcombe.com

Introduction & The Good Pub Guide Awards 2020

By Fiona Stapley

I started working on the *Good Pub Guide* in 1985 and changes in the pub world since then have been huge. I thought it might be interesting to look back at a few as I step back from the day-to-day running of the guide.

One of the most important changes in the history of pubs was the smoking ban. This came into force on 1 July 2007, following the ban in Scotland, Northern Ireland and Wales 18 months earlier. At first, of course, there were protests condemning the 'nanny state' for forcing this ban, despite all the medical research and evidence showing the dreadful health hazards attached to first- and second-hand smoking. Pubs feared they would face a damaging drop in business as smokers deserted their local boozers, but those small public bars full of fug and male chat quickly became a thing of the past. Lots of pubs adapted by installing smokers' shelters and outdoor heaters, but licensees then realised that by making their pubs smoke-free and turning them into cleaner, brighter places, they had opened up a massive new customer base – women and families with young children who headed to pubs for a meal. This changed many a pub's fortunes.

Eating in pubs

When the first edition of the *Guide* was published in 1983, the sort of food widely available was straightforward pub grub: filled rolls (40p), sandwiches and toasties (from 75p), ploughman's (from 80p), basket meals (£1.35), steak or chicken pies (£1.40), fresh plaice and chips (£1.95), scampi and chips (£2), cold meat salads (£2.50), grilled gammon (£2.80) and steaks (£3.50). If you found an ambitious menu in a smart pub-restaurant, you might be offered such delicacies as champagne pâté, local trout with almonds, seafood pancake or duck à l'orange. But through the 1980s and '90s, the huge growth in foreign travel opened people's eyes to the possibility of there being more to a meal than meat and two veg, and TV cookery programmes and mass-sale cookery books raised people's awareness of what was possible in the kitchen. This is when frozen food producers and the microwave oven came on to the pub scene, resulting in dishes that were new to many customers: meat or vegetarian lasagne, moussaka, chicken kiev or even trout stuffed with lobster. Some pub-goers were delighted by these innovations, but those hoping for real food in a pub disliked dishes coming straight off a freezer-pack lorry that were then described as 'our own special game casserole' or 'home-cooked' – which simply meant a blast in the microwave. We received hundreds of complaints from readers who found the food they were served was tepid, decidedly undercooked or even raw in the middle.

Around the same time, an interesting new development occurred. Ambitious young chefs, often trained in top-class restaurants, started taking on pubs rather than restaurants. This was partly because they liked a pub's more informal surroundings, and partly because a shoestring start-up in a pub made sounder financial sense. Some chefs brought their restaurant style of cooking with them, adding

 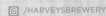

flights of fancy with dishes such as 'salmon digits heavenly dusted in cracked black peppercorns and pan-flashed before being napped with a cream glaze built up with a dash of brandy, a touch of mustard and a scattering of green peppercorns'. Thankfully, this was a short-lived trend – customers found these silly-sounding dishes far too elaborate and they rarely lived up to the menu's great promise.

By the mid 1990s, some sort of rewarding middle ground was found between the use of bought-in freezer packs and food from over-enthusiastic chefs that ranged from proper home-cooking at its most enjoyable to top quality, imaginative, daily specials. It was at this time too that food scares frequently made front-page news – BSE, salmonella in eggs, foot and mouth disease. Customers started questioning what they were eating and where it came from, and chefs began to take a real interest – and pride – in tracking down excellent local suppliers for their meat, vegetables, game and fish. Pubs that have the space now grow their own herbs, vegetables and fruit, keep pigs, chickens and ducks and are keen on the 'nose to tail' approach, wasting virtually nothing.

Nowadays, some of the best and most imaginative food in Britain is found in pubs rather than restaurants. And, of course, flexible all-day food service from breakfast onwards (rather than sticking rigidly to lunch and evening mealtimes only) suits people's modern lifestyles.

Staying overnight

Over the years, mini-breaks have become increasingly popular and, for a few days away, a pub is a delightful place to stay. The changes in this area are enormous. Forget dreary uncomfortable garrets, cheap mattresses, lukewarm water and draughty windows or traipsing down a cold corridor to queue with the publican's family for the bathroom – followed by breakfast in a smoky, uncleaned bar. The very best inns now offer the comfort and facilities of a first class hotel, with the added character and friendly informality of a thriving bar. In this edition, 278 pubs hold one of our Stay Awards, indicating that particular pub is a special place in which to spend the night.

Real ales

Real ales are at the heart of a pub, and without them, you're in a restaurant rather than a proper pub. In recent years there's been a huge increase in the number of small independent breweries, microbreweries and pubs brewing their own beer. And despite all the doom and gloom in the press about people drinking less beer, buying beer from supermarkets to drink at home rather than meeting friends in a pub for a pint, and the market being swamped by the explosion of American-style craft ales, traditional beers served on handpump or tapped from the cask remain a pub's mainstay.

What has changed, of course, are the prices and, as our survey below shows, this varies from county to county throughout Britain. In 1989 the idea of the £1 pint was almost a joke, but it soon became a widespread reality – and by 1991 the average price was £1.10. Today, the average price of a pint of real ale in Britain is £3.79.

There are so many reasons that need to be factored in to explain these increases, and publicans certainly do their very best to absorb price hikes before passing them on to their customers. A third of the cost of a pint is made up of taxes, including beer duties, VAT and business rates. Add to this wage bills (the increase in the national minimum and living wages hit the hospitality business hard) and day-to-day running costs and it's easy to see how prices soon mount up.

Wine in pubs

We scarcely mentioned wine in the first few editions of the *Guide*, and with good reason. It used to be the norm to find a dusty, opened bottle of red languishing on a back shelf alongside some warm, sweetish, oxidising white. Throughout the 1980s, pubs were rather slow to catch on to the possibility that good wine was what customers hoped for – even though wine bars were proving a big draw, women of all ages were coming to pubs for a meal (and choosing wine rather than other drinks) and wine-merchant sales were booming. But move forward ten years, and there was a significant increase in the number of licensees taking a personal and informed interest in the wines they served; even some of the more modest pubs started to have a small but respectable and thoughtful list. It also helped that the technological revolution in keeping opened bottles of wine fresh – from basic vacuum pumps to more sophisticated methods – meant that pubs could safely offer as many different wines by the glass as they wanted, with virtually no risk of them going off. It's now common for a pub to offer at least ten good wines by the glass.

Children in pubs

When the *Guide* started, the proportion of pubs that allowed children inside was so low that we listed them at the back of the book. Family rooms with no access to the bar were the norm, which in reality meant a rather unloved, unattractive and chilly back room away from

the cheerful hubbub of pub life. As the fashion for open-plan pubs spread, those dreary rooms became incorporated into the rest of the building and families felt much more included and part of the action. As one landlord told us, 'There is nothing more pleasant than a large family group out for Sunday lunch, with all generations present – including well behaved children.' But it's here, sadly, that things have not changed. Back in 1985 we organised a survey, asking publicans to give us their views on children in pubs. The answer then was exactly the same as it is now. That while the majority of families behave impeccably, there is still a persistent number who spoil things for everyone else. And if the landlord asks for some control to be shown, he often faces abuse from over-protective parents. It's a challenging and ongoing dilemma to which we can see no easy solution.

Opening hours

In 1988, the government announced plans to liberalise the licensing hours in England and Wales. During the 1914–18 war, licensing hours were strictly curtailed to help wartime production lines, and in spite of gradual extensions since then, they remained remarkably restricted in comparison with most other countries. Broadly speaking, the government planned to allow pubs to open from 11am to 11pm

Monday to Saturday but with no change to the Sunday hours of 12-2pm, 7-10.30pm. But, of course, it was the Sunday opening hours that our readers were finding so restrictive, since Sunday is usually the one day in the week when families can go out for the day to have a pub meal in a relaxed, unhurried atmosphere. It took almost ten years to get to the point where pubs were allowed to stay open throughout Sunday afternoon, if they so wished.

Now, of course, many pubs open all day from breakfast onwards, offering morning coffee, afternoon tea and tapas or nibbles between the main lunch and supper hours.

A few more grumbles

When the book launched, our post bag was full of complaints from readers about two particular dislikes – grubbiness and badly trained staff. Dirt was a serious problem in poorly kept pubs. We were amazed when travelling the country inspecting pubs that so many had visibly poor housekeeping. General drabness, dowdiness, dirty cutlery, crockery and glasses, sticky tables, stained cushions and carpets and, at worst, smelly loos and down-at-heel gardens with uncleared dog mess. And it was not uncommon for a pub to be closed by health inspectors until a kitchen had been thoroughly purged. Customers voted with their feet (particularly women) and clean-ups happened rapidly. It's something you'd rarely find now.

Well trained staff are a matter of pride for most licensees in good pubs because a happy relationship between customers and staff is absolutely vital. We used to (and for some pubs, we still do) get comments such as 'staff knew nothing about the drinks or the food they were serving', 'young staff were more interested in talking to each other than serving me', and staff were 'rude and condescending', 'indifferent and unsmiling', 'unhelpful and disinterested'; landlords were rude, grumpy and even insulting. Though one comment did make us smile: 'there was a very long delay for food (one hour) because we were told they only had one menu and someone else was using it'.

Since we started the *Good Pub Guide* 37 years ago, what has not changed is our enjoyment of a well run pub – they make us happy. They are the hub of a local community where customers from all walks of life and of all ages mix easily and they are run by extraordinary, hard-working licensees who have adapted their establishments to fit in with the needs and whims of our modern lives. We're very lucky to have them.

Drinks: the search for fair prices and top quality

Our national survey of beer prices shows a whopping £1.11 per pint difference in the cost of a pint of ale between Shropshire, the cheapest area at £3.46, and London, the most expensive at £4.57. The average price for a pint in Britain is now £3.79. How does your area rank? Here are the details, in average price order from the cheapest upwards:

Bargain beer
Shropshire, Herefordshire, Northumbria, Yorkshire, Staffordshire
Fair-priced beer
Worcestershire, Northamptonshire, Derbyshire, Leicestershire, Cumbria, Wales, Cheshire, Dorset
Average-priced beer
Lincolnshire, Cambridgeshire, Lancashire, Suffolk, Bedfordshire, Somerset, Devon, Wiltshire, Cornwall, Isle of Wight, Norfolk, Gloucestershire, Essex, Warwickshire, Hampshire
Expensive beer
Buckinghamshire, West Midlands, Oxfordshire, Nottinghamshire, Kent, Hertfordshire, Berkshire, Sussex, Scotland
Top-whack beer
Surrey, London

Oakham began brewing in Rutland in 1993. Their first beer, JHB, was named after Sir Jeffrey Hudson, a 17th-century court dwarf who lived in Oakham and was known as the smallest man from England's smallest county. JHB was soon to win CAMRA's 'Supreme Champion Beer of Great Britain' prize and was followed by other award-winning ales including Bishops Farewell, Citra, Inferno and Scarlet Macaw. They also brew a dozen seasonal choices and craft beer production began in 2014 with Green Devils IPA.

In 1998 they moved to a larger site in a former labour exchange in Peterborough, Cambridgeshire. This became the Brewery Tap (a much loved Main Entry in this *Guide*) with the bar and brewery being divided up by a two-storey glass wall giving fascinating views of the brew plant. As demand rapidly increased and capacity in the pub was reached, a second brewery was opened in the Woodston area of Peterborough. They now supply around 350 outlets and brew 30,000 barrels per year. **Oakham** is our *Brewery of the Year 2020*.

Our Top Ten Beer Pubs are spread across Britain: the **Bhurtpore** in Aston (Cheshire), **Tom Cobley** in Spreyton (Devon), **Fat Cat** in Norwich (Norfolk), **Malt Shovel** in Northampton (Northamptonshire), **Halfway House** at Pitney (Somerset), **Fat Cat** in Ipswich (Suffolk), **Nags Head** in Malvern (Worcestershire), **Maltings** in York (Yorkshire), **Harp** in London and **Guildford Arms** in Edinburgh (Scotland). There's a fantastic range of interesting beers to be found at all of these pubs, but the 32 real ales perfectly kept by the knowledgeable Colin Keatley wins his **Fat Cat** in Norwich our award for *Beer Pub of the Year 2020*.

You'll typically save yourself 43p a pint if you drink at one of the own-brew pubs in this edition of the *Good Pub Guide*. Our Top Ten Own-Brew Pubs are the **Brewery Tap** in Peterborough (Cambridgeshire), **Drunken Duck** near Hawkshead, **Watermill** at Ings and **Beer Hall at Hawkshead Brewery** in Staveley (all Cumbria), **Boot** in Repton (Derbyshire), **Church Inn** at Uppermill (Lancashire), **Grainstore** in Oakham (Leicestershire), **Dipton Mill Inn** at Diptonmill and **Ship** at Newton-by-the-Sea (both Northumbria) and **Gribble Inn** at Oving (Sussex). Our *Own-Brew Pub of the Year 2020* is the **Beer Hall at Hawkshead Brewery** in Staveley.

Of our Main Entry pubs, 357 hold one of our Wine Awards, meaning that they keep a remarkable and carefully chosen wine list. Our Top Ten Wine Pubs are the **Old Bridge Hotel** in Huntingdon (Cambridgeshire), **Acorn** at Evershot (Dorset), **Inn at Whitewell** at Whitewell (Lancashire), **Olive Branch** in Clipsham (Leicestershire), **Luttrell Arms** in Dunster and **Woods** in Dulverton (both Somerset), **Duncombe Arms** at Ellastone (Staffordshire), **Unruly Pig** in Bromeswell and **Crown** in Stoke-by-Nayland (both Suffolk), and **Griffin** in Felinfach (Wales). The generous, spirited and exceptionally knowledgeable Paddy Groves reckons he could put 1,000 wines up on the bar and will open any of them (with a value of up to £100) for just a glass – **Woods** in Dulverton is our *Wine Pub of the Year 2020*.

You can be sure to find a fine range of malt whiskies in our Top Ten Whisky list: **Bhurtpore** in Aston and **Old Harkers Arms** in Chester (both Cheshire), **Acorn** in Evershot (Dorset), **Red Fox** in Thornton Hough (Lancashire), **Black Jug** in Horsham (Sussex), **Pack Horse** in Widdop and **Sandpiper** in Leyburn (both Yorkshire), **Bow Bar** in Edinburgh, **Bon Accord** in Glasgow and **Sligachan Hotel** on the Isle of

Skye (all Scotland). With an extraordinary, 500-strong collection, the **Bon Accord** in Glasgow is our *Whisky Pub of the Year 2020*.

The love-affair with gin continues unabated. All the Brunning & Price pubs keep an extraordinary number of choices and styles, and across Britain new gin distilleries are constantly popping up, with some pubs even opening their own. For their staggering collection of 400-plus gins, the **Cholmondeley Arms** in Cholmondeley (Cheshire) is our *Gin Pub of the Year 2020*.

The best pubs in town and country

We've made a list of our Top Ten Unspoilt Pubs. They are the White Lion at Barthomley (Cheshire), Barley Mow at Kirk Ireton and Flying Childers at Stanton in Peak (both Derbyshire), Square & Compass at Worth Matravers (Dorset), Harrow in Steep (Hampshire), Three Horseshoes in Warham (Norfolk), Crown in Churchill and Halfway House in Pitney (both Somerset), Kings Head in Laxfield (Suffolk) and Olde Mitre in London. **The Kings Head** in Laxfield is our *Unspoilt Pub of the Year 2020*.

A country tavern is exactly what people look for at weekends – particularly if they're away from home. We look for a friendly welcome after a walk, a roaring log fire, comfortable seats in homely surroundings, warming food and a thoughtful choice of drinks. Our Top Ten Country Pubs are the **White Horse** at Hedgerley and **Crown** in Little Missenden (both in Buckinghamshire), **Pheasant** in Burwardsley (Cheshire), **Rugglestone** in Widecombe (Devon), **Brace of Pheasants** in Plush (Dorset), **Royal Oak** at Fritham (Hampshire), **Royal Oak** in Cardington (Shropshire), **Malet Arms** in Newton Tony (Wiltshire), **Fleece** at Bretforton (Worcestershire) and **Harp** in Old Radnor (Wales). A charming inn overlooking the heights of Radnor Forest, with log fires and a characterful bar, and offering comfortable bedrooms with glorious views, the venerable **Harp** in Old Radnor is our *Country Pub of the Year 2020*.

If you're in a town or city, particularly as a stranger, then a welcoming pub is a lovely place to visit. Our Top Ten Town Pubs are the **Lion** in Winchcombe (Gloucestershire), **Wykeham Arms** in Winchester (Hampshire), **Wharf** in Manchester (Lancashire), **Bank House** in King's Lynn (Norfolk), **Victoria** in Durham (Northumbria), **Lion & Pheasant** in Shrewsbury (Shropshire), **Old Green Tree** in Bath (Somerset), **Old Joint Stock** in Birmingham (Warwickshire), **Olde Mitre** in London and **Babbity Bowster** in Glasgow (Scotland). A former tobacco merchant's house with a thoroughly convivial atmosphere, the **Babbity Bowster** in Glasgow is our *Town Pub of the Year 2020*.

Our Top Ten Inns make a few days away from home very special – and with the added bonus of a convivial bar to round off the evening. They are the **Drunken Duck** near Hawkshead (Cumbria), **Rock** at Haytor Vale (Devon), **Kings Head** in Bledington (Gloucestershire), **Wellington Arms** at Baughurst (Hampshire), **Inn at Whitewell** near Whitewell (Lancashire), **Lord Crewe Arms** at Blanchland (Northumbria), **Luttrell Arms** in Dunster (Somerset), **Cat** in West Hoathly (Sussex), **Blue Lion** in East Witton (Yorkshire) and **Griffin** in Felinfach (Wales). With lovely bedrooms in an exceptional place, the **Kings Head** in Bledington is our *Inn of the Year 2020*.

Looking for value and taste

It's tricky to keep food prices down and yet keep meals interesting (rather than just offering sausages and chips). The Top Ten Value

Pubs that have managed this are the **Digby Tap** in Sherborne (Dorset), **Yew Tree** at Lower Wield (Hampshire), **Red Lion** in Preston (Hertfordshire), **Church Inn** at Uppermill (Lancashire), **Dipton Mill Inn** at Diptonmill (Northumbria), **Rose & Crown** in Oxford (Oxfordshire), **Old Castle** in Bridgnorth (Shropshire), **Queen Victoria** at Priddy (Somerset), **Blue Boar** in Aldbourne (Wiltshire) and **Crown & Trumpet** in Broadway (Worcestershire). For its proper main courses and very fair prices, the **Dipton Mill Inn** at Diptonmill is our *Value Pub of the Year 2020*.

For an exceptional meal in convivial surroundings, head for one of our Top Ten Dining Pubs. These are the **Cock** in Hemingford Grey (Cambridgeshire), **Punch Bowl** at Crosthwaite (Cumbria), **Millbrook** in South Pool (Devon), **Wellington Arms** at Baughurst (Hampshire), **Stagg** in Titley (Herefordshire), **Assheton Arms** in Downham (Lancashire), **Luttrell Arms** in Dunster (Somerset), **Horse Guards** in Tillington (Sussex), **Red Lion** in Chisenbury (Wiltshire) and **Shibden Mill** in Halifax (Yorkshire). With exceptional food served in a fine old pub, the **Assheton Arms** in Downham is our *Dining Pub of the Year 2020*.

The best of the very best
Every year we come across fantastic new pubs that range from simple taverns to first class dining pubs. Our Top Ten New Pubs this year are the **Swan** in Marbury (Cheshire), **Boot** in Repton (Derbyshire), **Bull** in Fairford and **Fossebridge Inn** at Fossebridge (both in Gloucestershire), **Blacksmiths** in Clayworth (Nottinghamshire), **Litton** in Litton (Somerset), **Abingdon Arms** in Beckley (Oxfordshire), **Kings Head** in Laxfield (Suffolk), **Hollist Arms** at Lodsworth (Sussex) and **Arrow Mill** at Arrow (Warwickshire). The beautifully refurbished and friendly **Swan** in Marbury is our *New Pub of the Year 2020*.

Behind the best pubs in the country are the landladies and landlords that make them so. Our Top Ten Licensees of the Year are **Philip and Lauren Davison** of the Fox in Peasemore (Berkshire), **Kathryn Horton** of the Ostrich in Newland (Gloucestershire), **Norman and Janet Whittall** of the Three Horseshoes in Little Cowarne (Herefordshire), **Tim Gray** of the Yew Tree in Lower Wield (Hampshire), **Glenn Williams** of the Bell in Tillington (Herefordshire), **Paddy Groves** of Woods in Dulverton (Somerset), **Colin and Teresa Ombler** of the Bell-on-Avon (Warwickshire), **Rob and Liz Allcock** of the Longs Arms in South Wraxall (Wiltshire), **Nigel Stevens** of the Wyvill Arms in Constable Burton (Yorkshire) and the **Key family** of the Nags Head in Usk (Wales). The cheerful, genuinely friendly and hard-working **Nigel Stevens** of the Wyvill Arms in Constable Burton is our *Licensee of the Year 2020*.

To compete in the Pub of the Year category, a pub has to have unanimous enthusiasm from our readers on all aspects of its business – it has to be at the very top of its game. Our Top Ten Pubs are the **Cock** in Hemingford Grey (Cambridgeshire), **Bell** at Horndon-on-the-Hill (Essex), **Kings Head** in Bledington (Gloucestershire), **Inn at Whitewell** in Whitewell (Lancashire), **Olive Branch** in Clipsham (Leicestershire), **Rose & Crown** in Snettisham (Norfolk), **Woods** in Dulverton (Somerset), **Horse Guards** in Tillington (Sussex), **Longs Arms** in South Wraxall (Wiltshire) and **Wyvill Arms** in Constable Burton (Yorkshire). Every aspect of this lovely inn is first class – the **Inn at Whitewell** in Whitewell is our *Pub of the Year 2020*.

Top Ten Pubs 2020

(in county order)

Cock in Hemingford Grey (Cambridgeshire)

Bell at Horndon-on-the-Hill (Essex)

Kings Head in Bledington (Gloucestershire)

Inn at Whitewell in Whitewell (Lancashire)

Olive Branch in Clipsham (Leicestershire)

Rose & Crown in Snettisham (Norfolk)

Woods in Dulverton (Somerset)

Horse Guards in Tillington (Sussex)

Longs Arms in South Wraxall (Wiltshire)

Wyvill Arms in Constable Burton (Yorkshire)

The magic of the Cotswolds

By **Adam Henson**

There's nowhere quite like home and for me that means the Cotswolds. This beautiful, unique region of England, which straddles the southern Midlands and the top end of the West Country, is my birthplace, my workplace and my playground, where I can relax and unwind. I live on the farm my mum and dad moved to in the 1960s and where the British rare breeds on our tourist attraction, the Cotswold Farm Park, have been entertaining visitors for almost 50 years. It's an utterly charming part of the world, but the truth is that the Cotswolds means different things to different people.

For many, the very word conjures up images of attractive, unspoilt villages that look as if they've come straight from the pages of a fairy story. Some think of the soft, undulating hills that rise gently from the river meadows and little tributaries of the Thames up to the broad, open grassland escarpment, while for others it's all about the almost magical qualities of Cotswold stone. It's everywhere! Elegant church towers, magnificent manor houses, humble cottages and hundreds of miles of drystone walls have been built from the honey-coloured oolitic limestone that is the very bedrock of the hills around here. It's all made the Cotswolds a world-famous tourist destination, and probably more recognisable than some of the country's long-established National Parks. But for me there's nothing that can beat a refreshing pint in a characterful Cotswold pub at the end of a hard day's work. And there are plenty to choose from.

The **Eight Bells** in Chipping Campden, Gloucestershire has a special place in the hearts of country lovers. It's situated at the traditional starting point of the Cotswold Way, the 102-mile National Trail that snakes through lovely scenery and skirts around old market towns all the way down to the Roman city of Bath. Over the years, casual walkers, weekend ramblers and serious hikers have all enjoyed the hospitality of the Eight Bells as they steadied themselves and fuelled up before embarking on a day's (or longer) trekking. Horses are big business round here too, with Cheltenham Racecourse, the home of National Hunt racing, right on our doorstep and the whole area dotted with numerous stable yards and gallops. Several pubs cater really well for horse lovers and race-goers, and among the best is my local, the **Hollow Bottom** in the village of Guiting Power.

It's very special to me – and not just because they serve Adam Henson's Rare Breed, the Butcombe pale ale that's made from the malting barley we grow on our farm. Originally called Ye Olde Inn, the pub was renamed because so many people referred to it as the tavern in the hollow at the bottom of the village. The views of the valley from the windows in the bar must be the envy of landlords in less picturesque locations, and even the interior décor is something to write home about. The walls are adorned with beautiful prints and photographs of famous steeplechasers, alongside notable old newspaper cuttings and the occasional lucky horseshoe. So it will come as no surprise to discover that among the pub's former owners are leading trainers Nigel Twiston-Davies and Peter Scudamore. But don't think for a moment that the Hollow Bottom is a pub for racing fans only; it's a friendly and unpretentious place with a menu that includes pub classics as well as plenty of more adventurous and innovative dishes – like pan-seared water buffalo steak!

Not far away, in the nearby hamlet of Ford, is another pub with strong links to the 'sport of kings'. The 16th-century **Plough** sits in a pretty spot opposite the evocatively named Jackdaws Castle, Jonjo O'Neill's impressive racehorse training centre. Drop in to the Plough and your fellow drinkers are likely to include trainers, jockeys and staff from the neighbouring stable yard. It's not just about the range of fine, traditional beers and real ales available at the bar, though, because the B&B accommodation here has a four-diamond rating from both the Heart of England Tourist Board and the AA. The rooms have wooden beams and are situated in a lovely cobblestoned building that's been converted from a hayloft. Meanwhile, over in the restaurant the food is definitely something to shout about and if you come at the right time of year the menu includes several 'must-haves' when asparagus and game are in season.

Food is also front-and-centre at another inn with a long history in the south Cotswolds. The **Weighbridge** on the outskirts of Nailsworth was built beside the old packhorse trail to Bristol, and 200 years ago the innkeeper was not only in charge of the pub but also responsible for collecting the tolls on the turnpike outside (a penny for a horse, thruppence for a score of pigs and tenpence for a herd of cattle)! Today, the Weighbridge is a delightful retreat for drinkers and diners, as well as their dogs, with a big open log fire to keep everyone cosy when the great British weather throws its worst at us. It's the perfect setting if you like good substantial pub grub too, because it's the home of the much loved two-in-one pie: a complete meal with two different fillings under a crumbly shortcrust pastry lid. The recipe is a closely guarded secret and whenever the pub changes hands, it's passed on from one owner to the next with the deeds to the property.

Of course, the Cotswolds region has inspired countless poets, composers and authors, with the most famous writer of them all being Laurie Lee. His best-known book, *Cider with Rosie*, gives a vivid picture of rural life in the Slad valley near

Stroud in the early years of the 20th century. At the heart of Slad village is the **Woolpack**, a cosy, rustic pub that's been serving beer for more than 300 years and where Laurie loved to drink and hold court. There's a lovely timeless atmosphere to the bars, which gives the impression that all the long-ago characters in his renowned book would still recognise the place if they turned up today. To get the very best from your trip to the Woolpack, I'd recommend taking a copy of *Cider with Rosie* with you. If you want to pay your respects to the great man, you won't need to go far – you'll find Laurie's final resting place in the little churchyard opposite the pub. The inscription on the headstone says it all: 'He lies in the valley he loved'. It's easy to see why the Cotswolds evokes such affection – people really do love these hills and valleys that I've known since I was a boy. So whether you're a regular visitor or planning your first excursion, I can guarantee a warm welcome in the Cotswolds and an unforgettable experience.

Adam Henson presents the BBC television series *Countryfile*, often from his 650-hectare farm in the Cotswolds. Adam also presented the BBC's *Lambing Live* with Kate Humble, and has appeared on Radio 4's *On Your Farm* and *Farming Today*. He is the author of three books: *Adam's Farm: My Life on the Land*; the *Sunday Times* bestseller *Like Farmer, Like Son*; and *A Farmer and His Dog*.

Favourite pub Angel, Hetton, Yorkshire.

My favourite pub is one I discovered recently, in the heart of the Yorkshire Dales National Park, where they not only serve great beer but the food is out of this world. I was filming for *Countryfile* with the Angel's Michelin-starred chef Michael Wignall, joining him on a tour of his favourite suppliers in North Yorkshire. And I was lucky enough to stay and dine at the pub, which was a real treat.

Eat, Drink & Sleep

Discover an Individual Inn

Know your grapes

By **Olly Smith**

I love the pub. A pint of local beer always hits the spot and my personal favourite is Harveys Best Bitter, the magnificent brew that flows like rivers of good cheer through my home county of East Sussex. But just like well-kept beer, when a wine list and its bottles are carefully looked after, a glass of vino can be as delicious as any drink from the bar. Here in Britain our wines are rivalling some of the world's best. Our fizz is finally gathering the kind of respect that it deserves – as I've been advocating and personally collecting for the past 20 years. Look out for quality names such as Camel Valley in Cornwall, Hambledon in Hampshire, Breaky Bottom in East Sussex and, indeed, wherever you find yourself, ask if they stock the local bubbly. The zesty styles of our homegrown bubbles are unbeatably refreshing. But that's by no means the whole story. 2018 was our best British vintage ever, with 15 million bottles produced, compared to the usual number of around five million. Quality and quantity are both up and prices remain friendly for our fragrant white Bacchus, which is a thrilling alternative to New Zealand Sauvignon Blanc. Or how about an elegant glass of red from our prime Pinot Noir? English rosés are well worth seeking out too.

But beyond our shores, what should you be looking for to accompany decent pub food? For an all-round white, Italian is the best choice. I know how tempting it can be to stick with what you know, but try grapes like Grillo and Fiano, which are both characterful and quenching. And my top tip is to look for Verdicchio (pronounced 'Ver-dick-ee-oh'). 2018 has produced some sensational quality and value from this grape, which is grown on the Adriatic coast around the Marche. If it's fish and chips or light bites, this is the cool splendour to pour and revel in. For salads, French rosé from Provence is tough to beat, especially with garlic flavours. As for reds in the pub, I'm a fan of styles that are juicy and fruity rather than too rich and savoury: lesser-known grapes such as Austrian Blaufränkisch offer value from off the beaten track, as well as a lighter, silky glass to pair with succulent burgers or pies. And for something a bit richer, while Malbec rightly has its fans, seek out Carménère from Chile for a red with mellow depth and gentle spice. It's the perfect match for a lamb shank or hearty roast. As for curries, the best pairing with a chicken tikka masala is Pinot Gris, which you can pick from Alsace for a lush silky style or New Zealand for something fab and fruity. And with meaty curries like a rogan josh, dive into Rioja – the gentle mellow character of the wine works a charm with those aromatic spices.

Another way to find great wines without blowing the budget is to select wines that remain – inexplicably – out of fashion. Portugal has an amazing range of styles; try a glass of Malmsey from Madeira with your cheeseboard – it tastes like liquid chutney. Greece has long been a favourite of mine for boutique wines that punch way above their price point; if your pub has an adventurous wine list, look for Assyrtiko from Santorini for a turbo-charged zinger of a white or a red Xinomavro, which tastes like a cross between the world's best Barolo and priciest Pinot Noir. And while French classics

tend to have prices to reflect their status, Muscadet remains magically underrated to sip with your shellfish platter and, for a light red at lunchtime, the Beaujolais Crus are some of the world's finest wines that still have fun prices: Morgon, Moulin-à-Vent, Fleurie and the rest. Check the names of the ten Beaujolais Cru and look for them on the wine list.

And finally, hats off to pubs that are taking an increasing pride in the way wine is kept, preserved and served. Temperature is key – when whites are too cold they mute down and when reds are too warm they fall apart. Decanting the wine into a jug or carafe helps open up flavours and aromas and doesn't cost anything except for a few extra seconds of service. And if it were up to me, I'd serve all wines by the glass to give maximum choice to each individual customer (as I do in my Glass House wine bars on board the P&O Cruises fleet). Remember that wine is like books, movies, TV shows and pizzas – we all have our favourite. The best pubs will listen to their customers and recommend the sort of wine that will bring them nothing but delight, and at a price that makes their wallet break into song. Happy sipping and here's to you.

Olly Smith is a multi-award-winning drinks expert and broadcaster. A regular on BBC1's *Saturday Kitchen*, he is also the wine columnist for the *Mail on Sunday*, the author of five boozy books and the presenter of the new Warner Bros TV series *How Beer Changed the World*.

Favourite pub Jolly Sportsman, East Chiltington, East Sussex. I've been going for years and it's the pinnacle of perfection, whether for a cosy winter pint by the fire or a summer sip in the characterful garden. The food year round is, bang for buck, as good as it gets, and the bar snacks are as exotic as they are excellent. You can eat informally, discreetly or, for a bit more of an occasion, the various nooks and settings are faultless. Service is always professional and lives up to the 'jolly' moniker, while the drinks list is sublime – from local wine to a wide range of whisky, beautifully kept beers and carefully chosen cider. In fact, writing all this down is making me wonder why I am not there right now, settling in for a session. Care to join me?

From bar to boardroom: a career in the pub industry

By **Simon Longbottom**

Working in a pub is not something that features in any school's careers advice programme; many people assume that jobs in the sector are mainly for students and part-time workers, or something that people do as a temporary stopgap while in between 'proper' jobs. Those of us who work in pubs and bars know that this couldn't be further from the truth. The pub sector is a thriving industry, full of fantastic opportunities and offering many wide-ranging careers. Anyone with the desire and commitment to succeed has the opportunity to progress from bar to boardroom.

My own experience, and that of many of my colleagues, is testament to that. In 1994, I was working as general manager of a pub called the Old Vicarage in Bournemouth. Twenty years later, in 2014, I was appointed chief executive of Stonegate Pub Company. Our chairman, Ian Payne, also began his career working behind the bar at the age of 19. Our commercial director, Suzanne Baker, and Kate Wilton, operations director for Slug & Lettuce, both started their careers working as waitresses. The experience ignited their interest in, and passion for, the industry. As Kate said recently: 'I got to earn money and have lots of fun; I was hooked!'

The sky's the limit

We currently have 772 pubs and more than 14,500 employees at Stonegate, so we understand the many and varied career opportunities that are available in the industry. Our vision is to deliver award-winning, industry-leading training and development programmes that drive performance improvement and cultural change. We have developed our business to ensure that each and every employee has access to a structured career development path.

We began offering apprenticeships in 2010 and since then have taken on 2,000 apprentices. Our award-winning

Albert's Theory of Progression (ATOP) career development programme underpins our 'Bar to Boardroom' ethos. People are given the opportunity to progress at their own pace from bartender, kitchen porter or commis chef, to team leader, supervisor, assistant manager, general manager, area manager and beyond. For those who want to move on from the pub environment, there are countless opportunities available at head office – purchasing, marketing, IT, human resources, operations, risk management, property (acquisitions and refurbishments), finance – to name but a few.

The Good Pub Guide lists the top 5,000 pubs in the UK. Together, those pubs employ thousands of successful managers and support teams, all of them at different stages of their career and all of them playing a vital role in contributing to each pub's success.

I honestly can't think of a better industry to work in. It's vibrant, varied, challenging, fun, exciting and rewarding on so many levels. The opportunities for career progression really are unlimited!

Simon Longbottom has served as CEO of Stonegate Pub Company since 2014. Prior to that, he spent 26 years within the pub and gaming sector holding a variety of roles including managing director of the leased/tenanted division of Greene King, managing director of Gala Coral's gaming division and senior positions with Mitchells & Butlers and Mill House Inns.

Favourite pub Two Brewers, Clapham High Street, London SW4 7UJ.
The Two Brewers is an award-winning LGBTQ+ venue in Clapham that has been trading for nearly 38 years. It provides a community hub for LGBTQ+ customers, but has an inclusive, welcoming policy, offering a safe place for all to enjoy a night out and to see some high-quality entertainment and top DJs. It's my favourite pub because it personifies everything that Stonegate represents.

What is a Good Pub?

We hear about possible new entries in this *Guide* from our many thousands of correspondents who keep us in touch with pubs they visit – by post, by email at feedback@goodguides.com or via our website, www.thegoodpubguide.co.uk. These might be places they visit regularly (and it's their continued approval that reassures us about keeping a pub as a full entry for another year) or pubs they have discovered on their travels and that perhaps we know nothing about. And it's from these new discoveries that we make up a shortlist, to be considered for possible inclusion as new Main Entries.

What marks a pub out for special attention could be an out of the ordinary choice of drinks – a wide range of real ales (perhaps even brewed by the pub), several hundred whiskies, a remarkable wine list, interesting spirits from small distillers or proper farm ciders and perries. It could be delicious food (often outclassing many restaurants in the area) or even remarkable value meals. Maybe as a place to stay it's pretty special, with lovely bedrooms and obliging service. Or the building itself might be stunning (from golden-stone Georgian houses to part of centuries-old monasteries or extravagant Victorian gin-palaces) or in a stunning setting, amid beautiful countryside or situated by water.

Above all, what makes a good pub is its atmosphere. You should feel at home and genuinely welcomed by the landlord or landlady – it's their influence that can make or break a pub. It follows from this that a lot of ordinary local pubs, perfectly good in their own right, don't earn a place in the *Guide*. What makes them attractive to their regulars could make strangers feel a bit left out.

Another point is that there's not necessarily any link between charm and luxury. A basic unspoilt tavern may be worth travelling miles for, while a too smartly refurbished dining pub may not be worth crossing the street for.

The pubs featured as Main Entries do pay a fee, which helps to cover the *Guide*'s production costs. But no pub can gain an entry simply by paying this fee. Only pubs that have been inspected anonymously, and approved by us, are invited to join.

Using the *Guide*

The Counties

England has been split alphabetically into counties. Each chapter starts by picking out the pubs that are currently doing best in the area, or are specially attractive for one reason or another.

The county boundaries we use are those for the administrative counties (not the old traditional counties, which were changed back in 1976). We have left the new unitary authorities within the counties that they formed part of until their creation in the most recent local government reorganisation. Metropolitan areas have been included in the counties around them – for example, Merseyside in Lancashire. And occasionally we have grouped counties together – for example, Rutland with Leicestershire, and Durham with Northumberland to make Northumbria. If in doubt, check the Contents pages.

Scotland, Wales and London have each been covered in single chapters. Pubs are listed alphabetically (except in London, which is split into Central, East, North, South and West), under the name of the town or village where they are. If the village is so small that you might not find it on a road map, we've listed it under the name of the nearest sizeable village or town. The maps use the same town and village names, and additionally include a few big cities that don't have any listed pubs – for orientation.

We list pubs in their true county, not their postal county. Just once or twice, when the village itself is in one county but the pub is just over the border in the next-door county, we have used the village county, not the pub one.

Star ★

Really outstanding pubs are awarded a star, and in one case two: these are the aristocrats among pubs. The stars do NOT signify extra luxury or specially good food – in fact, some of the pubs that appeal most distinctively and strongly are decidedly basic in terms of food and surroundings. The detailed description of each pub shows what its particular appeal is, and this is what the stars refer to.

Food Award ⓘⓄ

Pubs where food is really outstanding.

Stay Award ⌐⊐

Pubs that are good as places to stay at (obviously, you can't expect the same level of luxury at £60 a head as you'd get for £100 a head). Pubs with bedrooms are marked on the maps as a square.

Wine Award ♀

Pubs with particularly enjoyable wines by the glass – often a good range.

Beer Award ◀

Pubs where the quality of the beer is quite exceptional, or pubs that keep a particularly interesting range of beers in good condition.

Value Award £

This distinguishes pubs that offer really good value food. In all the award-winning pubs, you will find an interesting choice at around £11.

Recommenders

At the end of each Main Entry we include the names of readers who have recently recommended that pub (unless they've asked us not to use their names).

Important note: the description of the pub and the comments on it are our own and not the recommenders'.

Also Worth a Visit

The Also Worth a Visit section at the end of each county chapter includes brief descriptions of pubs that have been recommended by readers in the year before the *Guide* goes to print and that we feel are worthy of inclusion – many of them, indeed, as good in their way as the featured pubs (these are picked out by a star). We have inspected and approved nearly half of these ourselves. All the others are recommended by our reader-reporters. The descriptions of these other pubs, written by us, usually reflect the experience of several different people.

The pubs in Also Worth a Visit may become featured entries in future editions. So do please help us know which are hot prospects for our inspection programme (and which are not!), by reporting on them. There are report forms at the back of the *Guide*, or you can email us at feedback@goodguides.com, or write to us at:

Freepost THE GOOD PUB GUIDE, Random House Publishing, 20 Vauxhall Bridge Road, London SW1V 2SA.

Locating Pubs

To help readers who use digital mapping systems we include a postcode for every pub. Pubs outside London are given a British Grid four-figure map reference. Where a pub is exceptionally difficult to find, we include a six-figure reference in the directions. The Map number (Main Entries only) refers to the maps at the back of the *Guide*.

Motorway Pubs

If a pub is within four or five miles of a motorway junction we give special directions for finding it from the motorway. The special interest lists at the end of the book include a list of these pubs, motorway by motorway.

Prices and Other Factual Details

The *Guide* went to press during the summer of 2019, after each pub was sent a checking sheet to get up-to-date food, drink and bedroom prices and other factual information. By the summer of 2020 prices are bound to have increased, but if you find a significantly different price please let us know.

Breweries or independent chains to which pubs are 'tied' are named at the beginning of the italic-print rubric after each Main Entry. That generally means the pub has to get most if not all its drinks from that brewery or chain. If the brewery is not an independent one but just part of a combine, we name the combine in brackets. When the pub is tied, we have spelled out whether the landlord is a tenant, has the pub on a lease, or is a manager. Tenants and leaseholders of breweries generally have considerably greater freedom to do things their own way, and in particular are allowed to buy drinks including a beer from sources other than their tied brewery.

Free houses are pubs not tied to a brewery. In theory they can shop around, but in practice many free houses have loans from the big brewers, on terms that bind them to sell those breweries' beers. So don't be too surprised to find that so-called free houses may be stocking a range of beers restricted to those from a single brewery.

Real ale is used by us to mean beer that has been maturing naturally in its cask. We do not count as real ale beer that has been pasteurised or filtered to remove its natural yeasts.

Other drinks. We've also looked out particularly for pubs doing enterprising non-alcoholic drinks (including good tea or coffee), interesting spirits (especially malt whiskies), country wines, freshly squeezed juices and good farm ciders.

Bar food usually refers to what is sold in the bar; we do not describe menus that are restricted to a separate restaurant. If we know that a pub serves sandwiches, we say so – if you don't see them mentioned, assume you can't get them. Food listed is an example of the sort of thing you'd find served in the bar on a normal day.

Children. If we don't mention children at all, assume that they are not welcome. All but one or two pubs allow children in their garden if they have one. 'Children welcome' means the pub has told us that it lets them in with no special restrictions. In other cases, we report exactly what arrangements pubs say they make for children. However, we have to note that in readers' experience some pubs make restrictions that they haven't told us about (children allowed only if eating, for example). If you find this, please let us know, so that we can clarify with the pub concerned for the next edition.

The absence of any reference to children in an Also Worth a Visit entry means we don't know either way. Children's Certificates exist, but in practice children are allowed into some part of most pubs in this *Guide* (there is no legal restriction on the movement of children over 14 in any pub). Children under 16 cannot have alcoholic drinks. Children aged 16 and 17 can drink beer, wine or cider with a meal if it is bought by an adult and they are accompanied by an adult.

Dogs. If Main Entry licensees have told us they allow dogs in their pub or bedrooms, we say so; absence of reference to dogs means dogs are not welcome. If you take a dog into a pub you should have it on a lead. We also mention in the text any pub dogs or cats (or indeed other animals) that we've come across ourselves, or heard about from readers.

Parking. If we know there is a problem with parking, we say so; otherwise assume there is a car park.

Credit cards. We say if a pub does not accept them. We also say if we know that a pub tries to retain customers' credit cards while they are eating. This is a reprehensible practice, and if a pub tries it on you, please tell them that all banks and card companies frown on it – and please let us know the pub's name, so that we can warn readers in future editions.

Telephone numbers are given for all pubs if possible.

Opening hours are for summer; we say if we know of differences in winter, or on particular days of the week. In rural areas, many pubs may open rather later and close earlier than their details show (if you come across this, please let us know – with details). Pubs are allowed to stay open all day if licensed to do so. However, outside cities many pubs in England and Wales close during the afternoon. We'd be grateful to hear of any differences from the hours we quote.

Bedroom prices normally include a full english breakfast (if available), VAT and any automatic service charge. If we give just one price, it is the total price for two people sharing a double or twin-bedded room for one night. Prices before the '/' are for single occupancy, prices after it for double.

Meal times. Bar food is commonly served between the hours of 12-2 and 7-9, at least from Monday to Saturday. We spell out the times if they are significantly different. To be sure of a table it's best to book before you go. Sunday hours vary considerably from pub to pub, so it's advisable to check before you leave.

Disabled access. Deliberately, we do not ask pubs about this, as their answers would not give a reliable picture of how easy access is. Instead, we depend on readers' direct experience. If you are able to give us help about this, we would be particularly grateful for your reports.

Website, iPhone and iPad

You can read and search *The Good Pub Guide* via our website (www.thegoodpubguide.co.uk), which includes every pub in this *Guide*. You can also write reviews and let us know about undiscovered gems. The *Guide* is also available as an app for your iPhone or iPad and as an eBook for your Kindle.

Changes during the year – please tell us

Changes are inevitable during the course of the year. Landlords change, and so do their policies. We hope that you will find everything just as we say, but if not please let us know. You can email us at feedback@goodguides.com or use the Report Forms section at the end of the *Guide*.

Editors' acknowledgements

We could not produce the Guide without the huge help we have from the many thousands of readers who report to us on the pubs they visit, often in great detail. Particular thanks to these greatly valued correspondents: Chris and Angela Buckell, John Pritchard, Tony and Wendy Hobden, Susan and John Douglas, Clive and Fran Dutson, Gerry and Rosemary Dobson, Liz Bell, Tracey and Stephen Groves, Ian Herdman, Neil and Angela Huxter, Simon King, Steve Whalley, Michael Butler, Ann and Colin Hunt, Richard Tilbrook, Tony Scott, Richard and Penny Gibbs, Mrs Margo Finlay, Jörg Kasprowski, Edward Mirzoeff, Guy Vowles, Paul Humphreys, David Lamb, Revd R P Tickle, Mike and Mary Carter, Michael Doswell, R K Phillips, Simon Collett-Jones, Peter Meister, Tony and Jill Radnor, Dave Braisted, Sara Fulton and Roger Baker, Dr W I C Clark, Dr and Mrs A K Clarke, Derek and Sylvia Stephenson, Pete and Sarah, John Wooll, Christopher and Elise Way, GSB, Ian Malone, Steve and Claire Harvey, Mike and Eleanor Anderson, John Beeken, Stephen Funnell, M G Hart, David Jackman, Miss B D Picton, Mr and Mrs Richard Osborne, Sheila Topham, Lesley Broadbent, Gordon and Margaret Ormondroyd, Nigel and Jean Eames, Kevin Chesson, Ian Phillips, Christian Mole, Giles and Annie Francis, Robert Wivell, John Coatsworth, Paul Griffiths, Hugh Roberts, Roger and Anne Newbury, John Gibbon, Katharine Cowherd, Audrey Young, Minda and Stanley Alexander, Richard Kennell, R L Borthwick, Derek Stafford, Michael Sargent, I D Barnett, Brian and Anna Marsden, Anthony Bradbury, Gail Plews, David and Judy Robison, MJ, Mark Sheard, Lucien Perring, William and Ann Reid, Martin and Anne Muers, Hunter and Christine Wright, Richard Tingle, Laura Bennett, Mr and Mrs P R Thomas, Dr Simon Barley, David Fowler, David Barras, Jayne Francis, M A Borthwick, M and GR, Christopher Buckmaster, Miss A E Dare, Roy and Gill Payne, Mike and Margaret Banks, W K Wood, John and Hilary Murphy, Ian Cuttle, Margaret and Peter Staples, Guy Smith, Caroline Warwick, Jonathon Caswell, Liz Nicholas, Stuart Norris, Bernice Walsh, Paul Desborough, Penny Shinfield, Sharon Butler, Kim Ryan Skuse, Ammie Thorne, Tim Buckley, Steven Haworth, Colin Gooch, Christopher Warren, Colin and Angela Boocock, Paul Baxter, S G N Bennett, Helene Grygar, David and Stella Martin, Andrew Shaw, Fran Panrucker, Tim and Wendy Lloyd, R&H A-V, Peter Hesketh-Roberts, Hugh Duncan, Nick Hales, Paul Westwood, Malcolm and Pauline Pellatt, Janet and Peter Race, Dr and Mrs J D Abell, Iceman, Peter and Anne Hollindale, Phil and Anne Nash, Adam Bellinger, David and Gill Carrington, Baz Manning, Daniel Nixon, Stephen Shepherd, Robert Lester, Richard and Judy Winn, Gene and Kitty Rankin, MC, Steve Harvey, Mark O'Sullivan, John Kendall, Dr Martin Owton, Chloe and Tim Hodge, B and F A Hannam, John Coatsworth, Jon Neighbour, Demelza Hill, Colin McLachlan, Stephen Saunders, James Corbett, Frosty, Diana and Richard Gibbs, John Hunter Wright, David and Sally Frost, Carl Smith, Stevie Hart, PL, Brian and Margaret Merritt, Gordon and Barbara Illingworth, John Evans, Tom and Ruth Rees, Alan Cowell, Steve Thomas, Edward King, Andrew Bosi, Neil Hammacott, Mrs P R Sykes, Mick and Moira Brummell, Don Humphries, John Harvey, John and Sharon Hancock, Vinnie Grewell, Nick Higgins, Cherry Dainty, Martin Hughes, Dr D J & Mrs S C Walker, Eddie Edwards, Liz and Martin Eldon, Christopher Mobbs, Rod and Chris Pring, Philip Kavanagh, M G Trotter, Mrs P Sumner, Jamie and Sue May, S Holder, Pat and Tony Martin, Max Simons, Roy Shutz, Ian Wilson, Alistair Forsyth, Peter Cole, Clive Adams, Gillian Longman, Julian Richardson, Joe Oakley, Jo Kavaney, Gordon Parry, Susan Robinson, Mrs P Sumner, David Dore, Roy and Lindsey Fentiman, Robert Watt, Mrs J Ekins-Daukes, Mrs Edna Jones, D W Stokes, Franklyn Roberts, Barry Collett, Angela and Steve Heard, R J Herd, David Longhurst, Mr and Mrs J Watkins, E A Eaves, Richard Cole, Patric Curwen, Tony Smaithe, Alan Johnson.

Many thanks, too, to Maria Tegerdine, Hannah Clarke and Zanele Moyo at The Book Service for their cheerful dedication. And particularly to John Holliday of Trade Wind Technology, who built and looks after our all-important database.

Fiona Stapley

ENGLAND

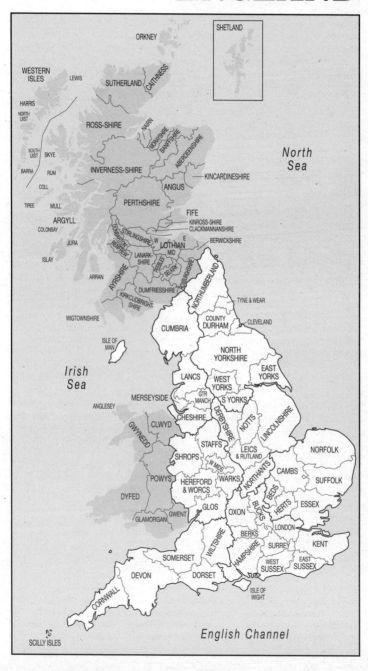

SHETLAND

ORKNEY

WESTERN
ISLES

LEWIS

SUTHERLAND

CAITHNESS

HARRIS

NORTH
UIST

ROSS-SHIRE

NAIRN

MORAYSHIRE

BANFFSHIRE

SOUTH
UIST

SKYE

BARRA

RUM

INVERNESS-SHIRE

ABERDEENSHIRE

COLL

KINCARDINESHIRE

North
Sea

TIREE

MULL

ANGUS

ARGYLL

PERTHSHIRE

COLONSAY

FIFE

JURA

KINROSS-SHIRE

CLACKMANNANSHIRE

ISLAY

STIRLINGSHIRE

W

DUNBARTON

RENFREW

LOTHIAN

E

BERWICKSHIRE

MID

LANARK-
SHIRE

PEEBLES

SELKIRK

ROXBURGHSHIRE

AYRSHIRE

ARRAN

DUMFRIESSHIRE

NORTHUMBERLAND

KIRKCUDBRIGHT-
SHIRE

WIGTOWNSHIRE

TYNE & WEAR

CUMBRIA

COUNTY
DURHAM

CLEVELAND

ISLE OF
MAN

NORTH
YORKSHIRE

Irish
Sea

LANCS

WEST
YORKS

EAST
YORKS

MERSEYSIDE

GTR
MANCH

S YORKS

ANGLESEY

CLWYD

CHESHIRE

DERBYSHIRE

NOTTS

LINCOLNSHIRE

GWYNEDD

STAFFS

LEICS
& RUTLAND

NORFOLK

SHROPS

W MIDS

POWYS

HEREFORD
& WORCS

WARKS

NORTHANTS

CAMBS

SUFFOLK

BEDS

DYFED

GLOS

OXON

BUCKS

HERTS

ESSEX

GWENT

LONDON

GLAMORGAN

WILTSHIRE

BERKS

SURREY

KENT

SOMERSET

HAMPSHIRE

WEST
SUSSEX

EAST
SUSSEX

DEVON

DORSET

ISLE OF
WIGHT

CORNWALL

SCILLY ISLES

English Channel

Bedfordshire

KEY	★ Star Pub	🗯 Top Quality Food	🍺 Great Beer
♀ Good Wines	£ Bargain Meals	🛏 Good Bedrooms	🍴 Serves Food

 **BEDFORD**   TL0550 Map 5

Park ♀

(01234) 273929 – www.theparkbedford.co.uk

Corner of Kimbolton Road (B660) and Park Avenue, out past Bedford Hospital;
MK40 2PA

Civilised and individual oasis – a great asset for the town

A handsome Edwardian building on the outskirts of town, this attractively furnished place has a good bustling atmosphere and a wide mix of customers. There are all sorts of seating areas to choose from, each with appealing décor and thoughtful touches: a more or less conventional bar with heavy beams, panelled dado and leaded lights in big windows, a light and airy conservatory sitting room with easy chairs well spread on a carpet, and an extensive series of softly lit rambling dining areas, carpeted or flagstoned; the airy garden room leads straight outside where a sheltered brick-paved terrace has good timber furniture, some under canopies, and attractive shrubs. Bombardier, Eagle IPA, Marstons Wainwright and Ringwood Razorback on handpump and an excellent choice of wines by the glass; background music.

🍴 All-day enjoyable food includes lunchtime sandwiches and wraps, tapas, warm pigeon salad with crispy chorizo and caramelised apple, prawn cocktail, sweet potato and chickpea curry with coconut rice, beef and mushroom pie with horseradish mash, cider-cured sea trout with samphire, peas and crab broth, lamb belly with courgette, pea and mint risotto, honey-roasted duck breast with cherry sauce, and puddings such as chocolate brownie and vanilla ice-cream and bakewell tart with custard; they also offer brunch (Friday-Sunday 10am-midday). *Benchmark main dish: bubble and squeak with crispy bacon and fried egg £13.50. Two-course evening meal £21.00.*

Little Gems Country Dining Pubs ~ Manager Matt Jackson ~ Real ale ~ Open 10.30am-11.30pm (midnight Thurs, Fri); 9am-midnight Sat; 9am-10.30pm Sun ~ Bar food 12-3, 6-9.30; 10-10 Fri, Sat; 10-8 Sun ~ Restaurant ~ Children in one bar and restaurant ~ Dogs allowed in bar ~ Wi-fi *Recommended by Adam and Natalie Davis, Sandra and Neil White, Edward Edmonton, William Slade, Julie Swift*

IRELAND
TL1341   Map 5

Black Horse 🏮⭐ ♀ 🛏

(01462) 811398 – www.blackhorseireland.com

Off A600 Shefford–Bedford; SG17 5QL

Bedfordshire Dining Pub of the Year

Contemporary décor in old building, excellent food, good wine list and lovely garden with attractive terraces; bedrooms

Attentive, helpful staff welcome you into this 17th-c pub to enjoy the imaginative food and first class choice of drinks. The relaxing bar has inglenook fireplaces, beams in low ceilings and timbering, with Adnams Southwold, Sharps Doom Bar and Woodfordes Wherry on handpump, 25 wines by the glass from a well described list, a dozen malt whiskies, Weston's cider and good coffee from the long green-slate bar counter. There are leather armchairs and comfortable wall seats, a mix of elegant wooden and high-backed leather dining chairs around attractive tables on polished oak boards or sandstone flooring, original artwork and fresh flowers; background music. French windows open from the restaurant on to various terraces with individual furnishings and pretty flowering pots and beds. The chalet-style bedrooms (just across a courtyard in a separate building) are comfortable and well equipped; continental breakfasts are included and taken in your room. The Birch at Woburn is under the same ownership.

🍴 Delicious, seasonal food includes sandwiches, sharing boards, steamed bao bun with crispy pork belly, hoisin sauce, stir-fried vegetables, pickled mooli and sriracha mayonnaise, scallops with bacon crumb, radish and lemon oil, textures of cauliflower (roasted florets, shavings, purée and pickled) with pearl barley, quinoa and crispy kale with truffle oil, steak burger with toppings and french fries, griddled sea bass fillets with chorizo, olive and red pepper salsa, local venison steak with celeriac purée, pickled carrots, crispy shallots and blackberry jus, and puddings such as sticky toffee pear pudding with caramel sauce and vanilla ice-cream and a crème brûlée of the day. *Benchmark main dish: lager-battered fish and chips £14.95. Two-course evening meal £24.95.*

Free house ~ Licensee Darren Campbell ~ Real ale ~ Open 12-3, 6-11; 12-11 Sat; 12-5 Sun ~ Bar food 12-2.15, 6.15-9.45; 12-4.45 Sun ~ Restaurant ~ Children welcome ~ Wi-fi ~ Bedrooms: /£94.95 *Recommended by M G Hart, Graham and Carol Parker, John Gibbon, Beverley and Andy Butcher, William and Sophia Renton, Alison and Tony Livesley, Nicola and Stuart Parsons, Gerry and Rosemary Dobson*

WOBURN
SP9433   Map 4

Birch 🏮⭐ ♀

(01525) 290295 – www.birchwoburn.com

3.5 miles from M1 junction 13; follow Woburn signs via A507 and A4012, right in village then A5130 (Newport Road); MK17 9HX

Well run dining establishment with focus on imaginative food and drinks, plus attentive service

Several individually and elegantly furnished linked rooms here have contemporary décor and furnishings. The upper dining area has high-backed leather or wooden dining chairs around tables on stripped and polished floorboards, and the lower part occupies a light and airy conservatory with a pitched glazed roof, ceramic floor tiles, light coloured furnishings, original artwork and fresh flowers; background music. The bustling bar is similarly furnished and has a few high bar stools against the sleek, smart counter where they serve Adnams Ghost Ship and St Austell Tribute on handpump, 15 good wines by the glass, a dozen malt whiskies and quite a few teas and coffees; background music. There are tables out on a sheltered deck, and in summer the front of the pub has masses of flowering hanging baskets and tubs. This is sister pub to the Black Horse at Ireland.

 Appealing food includes lunchtime baguettes, goats cheese and beetroot arancini with apple purée and parsnip crisps, smoked salmon with chilli-marinated jumbo prawn, lime crème fraîche and shallot, rocket and caper salad, free-range chicken breast with wild mushroom and pea fricassée, duck fat roasted parisienne potatoes and madeira jus, thai-spiced red pepper and butternut squash risotto with pine nuts, confit english pork belly with caramelised apple purée, crackling, honey baked apple, colcannon and cider jus, and puddings such as chocolate and toffee pudding with butterscotch sauce and crème caramel ice-cream and poached pear with mint-infused savarin and vanilla ice-cream. *Benchmark main dish: sea bass fillets with mango salsa £16.95. Two-course evening meal £25.00.*

Free house ~ Licensee Mark Campbell ~ Real ale ~ Open 12-3, 6-11; 12-5 Sun; closed Sun evening, Mon ~ Bar food 12-2.15; 6.15-9.45; 12-4.45 Sun ~ Restaurant ~ Children welcome ~ Wi-fi ~ Pianist or singer some Fri evenings *Recommended by Michael Sargent, Graham and Carol Parker, Sandra and Neil White, Monica and Steph Evans, Rupert and Sandy Newton, Lucy and Giles Gibbon, M and GR*

WOOTTON
Legstraps

TL0046   Map 4

(01234) 854112 – www.thelegstraps.co.uk
Keeley Lane; MK43 9HR

Bustling village pub with a nice range of food from open kitchen, local ales and wines by the glass

Whether you're here for the enjoyable food or just a pint and a chat, the kind staff will make you genuinely welcome. The low-ceilinged bar has an elegant feel with contemporary and comfortable upholstered chairs around all sizes of table, big flagstones, a woodburning stove in a brick fireplace with a leather sofa and box wall seats to either side, and leather-topped stools against the pale planked counter. They keep Sharps Doom Bar and Wychwood Hobgoblin on handpump, good wines by the glass and quite a few gins; background music, TV and board games. The dining rooms have bold paintwork, similar furnishings to the bar, polished bare boards and flower prints on one end wall with butterflies wallpaper on another.

From the open kitchen, the well thought-of modern food includes confit duck leg terrine with honey dressing, pork and chorizo scotch egg with salad, slow-cooked vegetable lasagne, chicken and mushroom pie, sea bass fillet with white wine and grain mustard sauce, tarragon potato croquette and greens, pork tenderloin with dijon dill cream sauce, fondant potato and crackling, garlic, thyme, honey and rosemary lamb rump with carrot purée and kale jus, coffee crème brûlée with cappuccino ice-cream and stout sticky toffee pudding with rum and raisin ice-cream. *Benchmark main dish: beer-battered haddock and triple-cooked chips £15.00. Two-course evening meal £22.50.*

Free house ~ Licensee Ian Craig ~ Real ale ~ Open 12-11; 3-7pm Mon for drinks only; 12-8 Sun; closed one week Jan ~ Bar food 12-9; 12-5 Sun ~ Restaurant ~ Children welcome ~ Dogs allowed in bar ~ Wi-fi *Recommended by Chantelle and Tony Redman, Alice Wright, Belinda Stamp, Sally and David Champion, S and L McPhee*

If you know a pub is ever open all day, please tell us.

Also Worth a Visit in Bedfordshire

Besides the fully inspected pubs, you might like to try these pubs that have been recommended to us and described by readers. Do tell us what you think of them: feedback@goodguides.com

AMPTHILL   TL0337
Albion (01525) 634857
Dunstable Street; MK45 2JT Drinkers' pub with up to 12 well kept ales including local B&T and Everards, real ciders and a perry, no food apart from lunchtime rolls; monthly folk night and other live music; dogs welcome, paved beer garden, open all day. *(Holly and Tim Waite)*

BEDFORD   TL0549
Castle (01234) 353295
Newnham Street; MK40 3JR Modernised 19th-c two-bar pub; Courage Directors, Eagle IPA, Youngs and guests, generous helpings of enjoyable good value pubby food from baguettes up, some themed evenings, friendly helpful service; Mon open mike night; children welcome, no dogs inside at meal times, courtyard garden, five bedrooms, open all day, no evening food weekends. *(Jack Dyer)*

BEDFORD   TL0450
Wellington Arms (01234) 308033
Wellington Street; MK40 2JX Friendly no-frills backstreet local; a dozen well kept ales including Adnams and B&T, real cider/perry and good range of continental beers, wooden tables and chairs on bare boards, lots of brewerania; no food or mobile phones, some live music; seats in backyard, open all day from midday, and perhaps at its best in the evening. *(Jack Dyer)*

BIDDENHAM   TL0249
Three Tuns (01234) 354847
Off A428; MK40 4BD Refurbished part-thatched village dining pub with bar, lounge and restaurant extension; good food (not Sun evening, Mon) from traditional favourites up, well kept Greene King ales and plenty of wines by the glass, friendly service; live music Sun; children welcome, spacious garden with picnic-sets, more contemporary furniture on terrace and decked area, closed Mon lunchtime, otherwise open all day. *(Elise and Charles Mackinlay)*

BLETSOE   TL0157
Falcon (01234) 781222
Rushden Road (A6 N of Bedford); MK44 1QN 17th-c building with comfortable opened-up bar; low beams and joists, seating from cushioned wall/window seats to high-backed settles, woodburner in double-aspect fireplace, snug with sofas and old pews, panelled dining room, popular food from pub standards and burgers up (plenty of gluten-free choices), Bombardier, Courage Directors, Eagle IPA and maybe a guest, decent choice of wines by the glass; background music; children welcome, dogs in bar, decked and paved terrace in lovely big garden down to the Great Ouse, open (and food) all day. *(Ann James)*

BOLNHURST   TL0858
★ **Plough** (01234) 376274
Kimbolton Road; MK44 2EX Stylishly converted Tudor building with thriving atmosphere, charming professional staff and top notch cooking from chef-landlord (must book), Adnams and a couple of interesting guests, over a dozen wines by the glass from good carefully annotated wine list (including organic vintages and plenty of pudding wines), airy dining extension, log fires; children welcome, dogs in bar, attractive tree-shaded garden with decking overlooking pond, remains of old moat, closed Sun evening, Mon and maybe for two weeks after Christmas. *(Peter Andrews, Michael Sargent, Mike Buckingham)*

BROOM   TL1743
Cock (01767) 314411
High Street; from A1 opposite Biggleswade turn-off, follow 'Old Warden 3, Aerodrome 2' signpost, first left signed Broom; SG18 9NA Friendly and unspoilt 19th-c village-green pub; four changing ales tapped from casks by cellar steps off central corridor (no counter), proper cider and enjoyable traditional home-made food, including themed nights and meal deals, original latch doors linking one quietly cosy little room to the next (four in all), low ceilings, stripped panelling, farmhouse tables and chairs on old tiles, open fires, games room with bar billiards and darts; children and dogs welcome, picnic-sets on terrace by back lawn, camping field, open all day, no food Sun evening. *(Jack Dyer)*

CARDINGTON   TL0847
Kings Arms (01234) 838533
The Green; off A603 E of Bedford; MK44 3SP Spacious Mitchells & Butlers village dining pub with refurbished linked areas; extensive choice of enjoyable food from light lunches up including a vegan menu, meal deal Tues and Weds evenings, Sharps Doom Bar and a couple of guests from well stocked bar, helpful friendly service; background music; children and dogs (in bar) welcome, disabled facilities, modern tables and chairs on front terrace, picnic-sets under willows to the side, open (and food) all day. *(Revd R P Tickle)*

CLOPHILL

TL0838

Stone Jug (01525) 860526

N on A6 from A507 roundabout, after 200 metres, second turn on right into backstreet; MK45 4BY Secluded old stone-built local (originally three cottages), cosy and welcoming with traditional old-fashioned atmosphere, well kept Otter, St Austell and a couple of local guests, popular good value pubby lunchtime food (not Sun, Mon), various rooms around L-shaped bar, darts in small games extension; background music; children and dogs welcome, roadside picnic-sets and pretty little back terrace, open all day Fri-Sun, closed Mon lunchtime. *(Sally Hollins)*

FLITTON

TL0535

White Hart (01525) 862022

Village signed off A507; MK45 5EJ Friendly family-managed village dining pub; front bar with dark leather tub chairs around low tables, contemporary leather and chrome seats at pedestal tables, steps down to good-sized, simply furnished back dining area with dark wooden floorboards, a real ale or two such as local B&T, good popular food (booking advised) including afternoon teas; children and dogs (in bar) welcome, neatly kept garden with teak furniture on tree-shaded terrace, 13th-c church next door, open all weekends (Sun till 8pm), closed Mon. *(John Gibbon)*

GREAT BARFORD

TL1351

Anchor (01234) 870364

High Street; off A421; MK44 3LF Open-plan pub by medieval arched bridge and church; good sensibly priced food from snacks up, Eagle IPA, Youngs Bitter and guests kept well, friendly staff, river views from main bar, back restaurant where children allowed; background music; picnic-sets in front looking across to Great Ouse, open (and food) all day weekends. *(Susan and Tim Boyle)*

HARLINGTON

TL0330

Carpenters Arms (01525) 872384

Sundon Road: a mile from M1 junction 12; A5120, first right to Harlington, right in village; LU5 6LS Old low-beamed village local; well kept ales such as Greene King IPA, Marstons Wainwright, Purity Mad Goose and Woodfordes Wherry, generous helpings of enjoyable home-cooked food (not Sun evening), good friendly service, bare boards or carpeted floors, log fires; pool table; children and dogs welcome, open all day Fri-Sun. *(Robert Watt)*

HENLOW

TL1738

Crown (01462) 812433

High Street; SG16 6BS Modernised beamed dining pub with good choice of popular food

including children's menu, well kept Caledonian Deuchars IPA, Courage Directors and a guest, lots of wines by the glass, friendly helpful staff, woodburners (one in inglenook); quiet background music, daily newspapers; terrace and small garden, five well appointed bedrooms in converted stables, open (and food) all day, breakfasts and Sat brunch for non-residents. *(Jack Dyer)*

HENLOW

TL1738

★ Engineers Arms (01462) 812284

A6001 S of Biggleswade; High Street; SG16 6AA Traditional 19th-c village pub with ten well kept changing ales and half a dozen proper ciders/perries, also bottled belgian beers and good choice of wines/gins, helpful knowledgeable staff, snacky food such as rolls; comfortable carpeted front room with old local photographs, various bric-a-brac and nice open fire, smaller tiled inner area and another carpeted one; beer/cider/country wine festivals, music nights, sports TVs; dogs allowed in bar, plenty of outside seating, open all day (till 1am Fri, Sat). *(Stuart Burns)*

HENLOW

TL1738

Five Bells (01462) 811125

High Street; SG16 6AE Long flower-decked pub with busy opened-up bar and restaurant; enjoyable generously served food from extensive reasonably priced menu including bargain OAP weekday lunch, well kept Greene King ales, a guest beer and decent range of wines, friendly helpful staff; children welcome, garden with play area, open all day, food all day Sat, till 7pm Sun. *(John Gibbon)*

HOUGHTON CONQUEST

TL0342

Chequers (01525) 404853

B530 towards Ampthill; MK45 3JP Refurbished roadside country dining pub (Little Gems); enjoyable fairly pubby food from pizzas and burgers up, three real ales and plenty of wines by the glass, friendly helpful service; children welcome, garden with play area, open (and food) all day, weekend brunch from 9am. *(Holly and Tim Waite)*

HOUGHTON CONQUEST

TL0441

Knife & Cleaver (01234) 930789

Between B530 (old A418) and A6, S of Bedford; MK45 3LA Updated and extended 17th-c village dining pub opposite church; good variety of well liked food from separate bar and restaurant menus, extensive choice of wines by the glass including champagne, Bombardier, Eagle IPA and guests, friendly staff; free wi-fi; children welcome, no dogs inside, nine chalet bedrooms arranged around courtyard and garden, good breakfast, free charging of electric cars for guests, open all day from 7.30am for breakfast. *(Charlie)*

We say if we know a pub allows dogs.

HUSBORNE CRAWLEY   SP9635
White Horse   (01525) 280565
Mill Road, just off A507; MK43 0XE
Open-plan village pub arranged around central servery; two real ales and good reasonably priced home-made food (vegetarians and special diets well catered for), friendly attentive staff, beams, wood and quarry-tiled floors, some stripped brickwork and woodburner; live jazz every other Mon, free wi-fi; children and dogs (in bar) welcome, tables outside and lovely hanging baskets, open (and food) all day, till 8pm (6pm) Sun. *(Mary and Douglas McDowell)*

LITTLE GRANSDEN   TL2755
Chequers   (01767) 677348
Main Road; SG19 3DW Welcoming village local in same family for over 60 years and keeping its 1950s feel; simple bar with coal fire, darts and framed historical information about the pub, interesting range of own-brewed Son of Sid ales, step down to cosy snug with another fire and bench seats, comfortable back lounge with fish tank, no food apart from excellent fish and chips Fri evening (must book); open all day Fri, Sat. *(Charlie)*

MILTON BRYAN   SP9730
Red Lion   (01525) 210044
Toddington Road, off B528 S of Woburn; MK17 9HS Refurbished red-brick village dining pub; Greene King ales and a guest, several wines by the glass, cocktails and good range of gins, well liked nicely presented food from bar snacks and sharing boards up, Weds steak night, Thurs burgers, good friendly service, central bar with dining areas either side, beams and open fire; children and dogs welcome, pretty views from big garden, open all day Sat, till 7pm Sun. *(Max Simons)*

NORTHILL   TL1446
★Crown   (01767) 627337
Ickwell Road; off B658 W of Biggleswade; SG18 9AA Popular prettily situated village pub dating from the 17th c; cosy flagstoned bar with copper-topped counter, heavy low beams and bay window seats, woodburner here and in restaurant with modern furniture on light wood floor, steps up to another dining area with exposed brick and high ceiling, good brasserie-style food (not Sun evening) including lunchtime baguettes/panini, Greene King and guests, plenty of wines by the glass, prompt friendly service; soft background music; children welcome, no dogs inside, tables out at front and on sheltered side terrace, more in big back garden with play area, open all day Fri and Sat, till 7pm Sun. *(John Gibbon)*

OAKLEY   TL0053
★Bedford Arms   (01234) 822280
High Street; MK43 7RH 16th-c village inn (sister to the Hare & Hounds in Old Warden); interesting contemporary décor in several interconnected rooms, pubbiest part with wooden furniture on bare boards, flower prints and a woodburner, four cosy, individually decorated rooms lead off, one has farmhouse chairs and a cushioned pew beside a small fireplace, another very much Victorian in style, Eagle IPA and a couple of guests, up to 40 wines by the glass and well regarded food (not Sun evening, Mon), stone-floored dining rooms with tartan-covered seating or wicker chairs, airy conservatory; daily papers, TV, darts and board games; children welcome till 7pm, dogs in bar, pretty garden, open all day (till 8pm Sun). *(Peter Andrews)*

ODELL   SP9657
Bell   (01234) 910850
Off A6 S of Rushden, via Sharnbrook; High Street; MK43 7AS Popular and welcoming thatched village pub; several comfortable low-beamed rooms around central servery, log fire and inglenook woodburner, good reasonably priced home-made food (not Sun evening, booking advised) including Mon steak, Tues pie and Thurs curry nights, well kept Greene King, guest ales and good selection of wines/gins, friendly helpful young staff; children and dogs welcome, big garden backing on to river, handy for Harrold-Odell Country Park, open all day. *(Sally and John Thomas)*

OLD WARDEN   TL1343
Hare & Hounds   (01767) 627225
Village signposted off A600 S of Bedford and B658 W of Biggleswade; SG18 9HQ Sister dining pub to the Bedford Arms at Oakley; four cosy rooms, log fire in one, inglenook woodburner in another, tweed upholstered chairs at light wood tables on stripped wood, tiled or carpeted floors, prints and old photographs including aircraft in the Shuttleworth Collection (just up the road), good food using local ingredients from sharing boards up, Courage Directors, Eagle IPA and guests, several wines by the glass, cocktails, friendly attentive service; background music; children welcome, garden stretching up to pine woods behind, nice thatched village and good local walks, open all day, no food Sun evening. *(Jack Dyer)*

RAVENSDEN   TL0754
★Horse & Jockey   (01234) 772319
Village signed off B660 N of Bedford; pub at Church End, off village road; MK44 2RR Pleasantly modern brick pub decorated in olive greys and deep reds; leather easy chairs in bar with wall of old local photographs, Adnams Southwold, a couple of guests and over 20 wines by the glass, bright dining room with chunky tables and high-backed seats, good food cooked by landlord-chef from shortish but varied menu including weekday set lunch, friendly service; background music, board games,

free wi-fi; children welcome, dogs in bar (limited dining space), modern tables and chairs under parasols on sheltered deck, a few picnic-sets on grass, handsome medieval church next door, open till 6pm Sun, closed Mon. *(Charlie)*

RISELEY   TL0462
Fox & Hounds (01234) 709714
Off A6 from Sharnbrook/Bletsoe roundabout; High Street, just E of Gold Street; MK44 1DT Modernised village pub dating from the 16th c; low beams, stripped boards and imposing stone fireplace, Bombardier, Eagle IPA and a guest, signature flame-grilled steaks cut to weight and other enjoyable food including good value set menu, separate dining room; children and dogs (in bar) welcome, seats out in front and in back garden with terrace, open all day, food all day Sat, till 6pm Sun. *(Elise and Charles Mackinlay)*

SALFORD   SP9339
Swan (01908) 281008
Not far from M1 junction 13 – left off A5140; MK17 8BD Popular Edwardian country dining pub (Peach group); well liked food from sandwiches and deli boards to dry-aged steaks, also fixed-price lunchtime menu Mon-Sat, ales such as Greene King and Hook Norton, good range of wines, gins and cocktails, friendly accommodating staff, updated interior with drinking area to right of central servery, sofas and leather chairs on wood floor, restaurant to left with modern country cottage feel and window view into kitchen; background music; children welcome, dogs in bar, seats out on decking, open (and food) all day. *(Holly and Tim Waite)*

SHEFFORD   TL1439
Brewery Tap (01462) 628448
North Bridge Street; SG17 5DH No-nonsense L-shaped bar notable for its well kept/priced B&T ales brewed nearby and guest beers; bare-boards and low ceiling, beer bottle collection and other breweriana, simple lunchtime rolls, friendly helpful staff; occasional live music, darts and dominoes; children (in family area) and dogs welcome, picnic-sets out behind, open all day. *(Charlie)*

SHILLINGTON   TL1234
Crown (01462) 711667
High Road, S end; SG5 3LP Revamped by same owners as the Chequers at Westoning; emphasis on good food in smart comfortable surroundings from sandwiches, sharing plates and well priced weekday set lunch up, also a cosy bar area serving ales such as Otter and Purity along with excellent range of wines, whiskies and gins, large restaurant/conservatory, cheerful enthusiastic staff; children and dogs welcome, garden tables, open all day, food all day weekends. *(Dr Matt Burleigh)*

SOULDROP   SP9861
Bedford Arms (01234) 781384
Village signposted off A6 Rushden–Bedford; High Street; MK44 1EY Village pub dating from the 17th c; cosy low-beamed bar with snug and alcove, Black Sheep, Greene King IPA and three guests, several wines by the glass, tasty well priced pubby food, cottagey dining area has more low beams, broad floorboards and woodburner in central fireplace, also roomy mansard-ceilinged part with big inglenook; occasional live music, table skittles, shove-ha'penny and darts; children and dogs (in bar) welcome, garden tables, open all day Fri-Sun, closed Mon. *(Jack Dyer)*

STEPPINGLEY   TL0135
French Horn (01525) 721225
Off A507 just N of Flitwick; Church End; MK45 5AU Comfortable dining pub next to church; linked rooms with stippled beams, standing posts and wall timbers, two inglenooks (one with woodburner), eclectic mix of chesterfields, leather armchairs, cushioned antique dining chairs and other new and old furniture on flagstones or bare boards, Greene King IPA and a changing guest, good range of wines by the glass and malt whiskies, well liked freshly made food with french influences, friendly staff, elegant dining room; background music, TV, free wi-fi; children and dogs (in bar) welcome, seats outside overlooking small green, open all day, no food Sun evening, Mon. *(Mary and Douglas McDowell)*

STOTFOLD   TL2136
Fox & Duck (01462) 732434
Arlesey Road; SG5 4HE Welcoming roadside pub-restaurant with light modern interior; good variety of enjoyable generously served food from lunchtime ciabattas and bar snacks up, Greene King IPA, a guest ale and over a dozen wines by the glass, friendly accommodating staff, separate coffee lounge; occasional live music, free wi-fi; children and dogs welcome, big enclosed garden with play area, open (and food) all day. *(Susan and Tim Boyle)*

STUDHAM   TL0215
Bell (01582) 872460
Dunstable Road; LU6 2QG Village pub dating from the 16th c; timbered bar and restaurant, wide choice of food from sandwiches to italian dishes and good value Sun lunch, Greene King, Sharps and guests, decent choice of wines by the glass including champagne, lots of gifts and other items for sale; background music, open mike night every other Weds, quiz Thurs; children and dogs (in bar) welcome, seats out at front and in big back garden with giant blackboard to doodle on, nice country views and good walks, handy for Whipsnade Zoo and the Tree Cathedral (NT), open all day, food all day weekends. *(Sally and John Thomas)*

STUDHAM   TL0215

Red Lion (01582) 872530

Church Road; LU6 2QA Character
community pub with hands-on landlord and
friendly staff; public bar and eating areas
filled with pictures and bits and pieces
collected over many years, house plants,
wood flooring, carpeting and old red and
black tiles, open fire, ales such as Adnams,
Fullers, Greene King and Timothy Taylors,
enjoyable pubby food (not Sun, Mon or Tues
evenings); background music, quiz/curry
night first Tues of month; children and dogs
welcome, green picnic-sets in front under
pretty window boxes, more on side grass,
play house, open all day. *(Elise and Charles
Mackinlay)*

SUTTON   TL2247

★ John O'Gaunt (01767) 260377

*Off B1040 Biggleswade–Potton;
SG19 2NE* Friendly bustling village pub
just up from 14th-c packhorse bridge and
ford: beams and timbering, flagstoned bar
with leather seats and banquettes around
iron-framed tables, open fire, ales such as
Adnams and Woodfordes, local cider and
15 wines by the glass, good food cooked by
landlord-chef including Thurs fish and chips,
dining rooms with mix of furniture on wood
flooring, logburner; background music, free
wi-fi; children and dogs (in bar) welcome,
picnic-sets in sheltered garden, closed Sun
evening, Mon (open lunchtime bank holiday
Mon, then closed Tues). *(John Gibbon)*

TILSWORTH   SP9824

Anchor (01525) 211404

Just off A5 NW of Dunstable; LU7 9PU
Comfortably modernised 19th-c red-brick
village pub now run by welcoming
greek family; popular authentic greek
dishes, Greene King ales, greek wines and
ouzo, cheerful attentive service, dining
conservatory; monthly live music; children
and dogs welcome, picnic-sets in large
garden, open (and food) all day, closed Mon
lunchtime. *(Simon King)*

TOTTERNHOE   SP9721

Cross Keys (01525) 220434

*Off A505 W of A5; Castle Hill Road;
LU6 2DA* Restored thatched and timbered
two-bar pub below remains of a motte and
bailey fort; low beams and cosy furnishings,
good reasonably priced food (not Sun
evening, Mon) from sandwiches up, well kept
Adnams Broadside, Greene King IPA and
guests, dining room; children and dogs (in
bar) welcome, good views from attractive big
garden, plenty of walks nearby, open all day
Fri-Sun. *(Susan and Tim Boyle)*

TURVEY   SP9452

Three Cranes (01234) 881365

Off A428 W of Bedford; MK43 8EP
Renovated stone-built village pub on two
levels, good food (not Sun evening) from
sandwiches and sharing boards to daily
specials, up to five well kept ales, friendly
staff; children and dogs (in bar) welcome,
secluded tree-shaded garden, five bedrooms,
open all day. *(Sarah Hollins)*

TURVEY   SP9352

★ Three Fyshes (01234) 881463

*A428 NW of Bedford; Bridge Street,
W end of village; MK43 8ER* Well
maintained early 17th-c beamed village pub;
big inglenook with woodburner, mix of easy
and upright chairs around tables on tiles
or ancient flagstones, a couple of changing
real ales, decent choice of wines and good
food, friendly staff, carpeted side restaurant;
background music; children and dogs (in
bar) welcome, charming garden with decking
overlooking bridge and mill on the Great
Ouse (note the flood marks), car park further
along the street, open all day, no food Sun
evening, Mon. *(Sarah Hollins)*

WESTONING   SP0332

Chequers (01525) 712967

*Park Road (A5120 N of M1 junction 12);
MK45 5LA* Updated 17th-c thatched village
pub under same owners as the Crown at
Shillington; enjoyable food including good
value set lunch, steak night Weds, seafood
evening Thurs, beers such as Adnams,
Otter and Purity, good choice of wines by
the glass and of other drinks, various teas/
coffees, helpful friendly service, low-beamed
front bar and good-sized stables restaurant;
occasional live music, free wi-fi; children
and dogs welcome, courtyard tables, open
all day from 9am (10am weekends) for
breakfast. *(Charlie)*

WOBURN   SP9433

Bell (01525) 290280

Bedford Street; MK17 9QJ Traditional
and comfortable with small beamed bar and
longer bare-boards dining lounge up steps,
enjoyable good value food, Greene King,
guest beers and several gins, friendly helpful
service; background music; children and dogs
welcome, back terrace, hotel part across busy
road, handy for Woburn Abbey/Safari Park,
open (and food) all day. *(Jack Dyer)*

WOBURN   SP9433

Black Horse (01525) 290210

Bedford Street; MK17 9QB Long and
narrow 18th-c dining pub (Peach group);
enjoyable food from deli boards up including
weekday set menu till 6pm, Weds burger
night and Fri fish, well kept Greene King ales
and a guest, good choice of wines, gins and
cocktails, several bare-boards areas ranging
from bar with old leather settles and coal
fire through more contemporary furnishings,
steps down to pleasant back restaurant;
background music; children in eating areas,
attractive sheltered courtyard, open (and
food) all day. *(Jack Dyer)*

Berkshire

 BRAY   SU9079   Map 2

Crown 🌟 🍷

(01628) 621936 – www.thecrownatbray.co.uk

1.75 miles from M4 junction 9; A308 towards Windsor, then left at Bray signpost on to B3028; High Street; SL6 2AH

Ancient low-beamed pub with open-plan rooms, highly regarded food, real ales and seats in the large garden

There's a friendly little bar in this 16th-c pub with high stools around an equally high table, simple tables and chairs beside an open fire and regulars who drop in for a chat and a drink. Most emphasis is, of course, on dining – which is not surprising given that the owner is Heston Blumenthal. The snug rooms have panelling, heavy old beams (some so low you may have to mind your head), plenty of timbers at elbow height where walls have been knocked through, a second log fire and neatly upholstered dining chairs and cushioned settles. Courage Best and Directors, a beer named for the pub and a quickly changing guest on handpump and around 18 wines by the glass; board games. The garden, complete with an outdoor kitchen and bar, is open from May to September.

🌟 As well as a lunchtime sandwich of the day, the high quality food includes king prawn cocktail, mushroom parfait with pickled onions, a gratin of seasonal vegetables, treacle and ale-cured bacon burger with smoked cheddar, sauce and fries, whole roasted plaice with shrimps and burnt butter, chicken and mushroom pie, pork chop with pancetta, sour onions and violet mustard, and puddings such as rhubarb and custard with caramelised white chocolate and baked vanilla cheesecake with blood orange sorbet and orange liqueur. *Benchmark main dish: beer-battered fish and chips £17.95. Two-course evening meal £33.00.*

Star Pubs & Bars ~ Tenant Matt Larcombe ~ Real ale ~ Open 11.30-11; 11.30-10.30 Sun ~ Bar food 12-2.15, 6-9.15 (9.45 Fri); 12-2.45, 6-9.45; 12-4.45 Sun ~ Children welcome ~ Dogs allowed in bar ~ Wi-fi *Recommended by Simon Collett-Jones, Audrey and Andrew Nichols, Carol and Barry Craddock, Simon Day, Lionel Smith*

 CHAPEL ROW   SU5769   Map 2

Bladebone 🌟 🍷

(0118) 971 4000 – www.thebladebone.com

Centre of village; RG7 6PD

Popular village pub with appealing food, simply furnished bar and dining rooms and seats on terrace and in garden

A hard-working young couple have renovated this red-brick village pub and run it with enthusiasm and good humour. Much emphasis is, of course, placed on the very good, well presented food cooked by Mr Sanderson, but the atmosphere is relaxed and friendly and there's a proper bar for those just wanting a pint and a chat. Furnishings are simple: elegant and more contemporary wooden dining chairs and cushioned window seats around chunky pine tables on bare boards, prints and old black and white photographs of the pub on pale-painted walls, wine bottles lining delft shelves and a couple of open fires. Hook Norton Hooky Gold, Sharps Doom Bar and West Berkshire Good Old Boy on handpump and a dozen wines by the glass; background music. The airy little dining conservatory leads to a terrace with rattan-style furniture and there are more seats on the lawn.

Cooked by the landlord, the thoughtful choice of impressive food includes sandwiches, tempura monkfish and tiger prawns with asian salad, baked camembert with red onion jam, wild mushroom strudel with brie and halloumi, fillet and slow-cooked pork belly with roast apple, dauphinoise potatoes and jus, smoked fish pie topped with gruyère mash, steak in ale pie, slow-braised lamb shank with maple bacon and spiced red cabbage ragoût and sticky sauce, and puddings such as sticky toffee pudding with bourbon toffee sauce and white chocolate and Baileys brûlée; they also offer a two- and three-course set menu (Tuesday-Friday). *Benchmark main dish: scallops gruyère with brioche crumb £18.00. Two-course evening meal £27.00.*

Free house ~ Licensees Richie and Charlotte Sanderson ~ Real ale ~ Open 12-midnight; 12-11 Sun ~ Bar food 12-3, 5.30-9.30; 12-6 Sun ~ Restaurant ~ Children welcome ~ Dogs welcome ~ Wi-fi *Recommended by Matthew and Elisabeth Reeves, Rosie and Marcus Heatherley, Amy Ledbetter, Kerry and Guy Trooper*

CHIEVELEY
SU4574 Map 2

Crab & Boar 🌟 ♉ 🛏

(01635) 247550 – www.crabandboar.com

North Heath, W of village; RG20 8UE

Welcoming inn with imaginative food, a good drinks choice and charming staff; seats outside; lovely bedrooms

A country pub with fine views, this is both stylish and civilised. The interconnecting bars and dining rooms are smartly furnished and one end of the L-shaped bar is light and airy with tall green leather chairs lining a high shelf, a couple of unusual, equally high tables with garden planter bases, a contemporary chandelier and stools lining the shabby-chic counter. Here they keep Bombardier and West Berkshire Good Old Boy on handpump, 12 good wines by the glass and a dozen gins and a dozen malt whiskies. The other end of this bar is cosier, with leather armchairs and sofas facing one another across a low table in front of a woodburning stove; background music and TV. The first room leading off has beams and timbering, tartan-upholstered stall seating and leather banquettes, and framed race tickets on the walls. Dining rooms, linked by timbering and steps, are decorated with old fishing reels, a large boar's head, photos and prints, with an eclectic mix of attractive chairs and tables on bare floorboards or carpet; an end room is just right for a private party. In the garden are elegant metal or teak tables and chairs on gravel and grass; there's also a fountain and an outside bar. Bedrooms are comfortable and well equipped with private courtyards; five even have their own hot tub.

First class modern food includes curried fishcake with tzatziki, wild boar terrine with pumpkin chutney, mushroom risotto with salsa verde, duck tortelli pasta with fried liver, parsnip cream and cocoa nibs, roast chicken with black truffle and smoked chicken pie and tarragon sauce, stone bass with mussels, crispy polenta, jerusalem artichoke and grapes, and puddings such as Valrhona chocolate cake with peanut butter centre, burnt milk ice-cream and salted caramel sauce and custard tart with blackcurrant compote and hibiscus sorbet. *Benchmark main dish: pork three-ways £24.00. Two-course evening meal £25.00.*

Free house ~ Licensee Ed Nelson ~ Real ale ~ Open 12-11 ~ Bar food 12-2, 6.30-9.30; 12-3, 6.30-8.30 Sun ~ Restaurant ~ Children welcome ~ Dogs allowed in bar and bedrooms ~ Wi-fi ~ Bedrooms: /$110 *Recommended by R K Phillips, Mr and Mrs D J Nash, Cecily and Steven Evans, Belinda and Neil Garth, Maria and Henry Lazenby, Holly and Tim Waite, Alan and Linda Blackmore*

CURRIDGE
SU4871 Map 2

Bunk 🌟 🍴 🛏

(01635) 200400 – www.thebunkinn.co.uk

Handy for M4 junction 13, off A34 S; RG18 9DS

Popular pub with attractive bar and dining rooms, good modern food and seats outside; bedrooms

This is an enjoyable and well run pub, and you'll get a genuinely warm welcome from the helpful young staff. The bustling bar has chunky wooden armchairs and a sofa facing one another before an open fire, leather-seated wall banquettes, and farmhouse chairs and stools around pine tables on wide boards. More stools line the counter where they keep Red Rock Devon County, Two Cocks 1643 Cavalier and a changing guest on handpump and good wines by the glass; background music and board games. The candlelit dining room has painted, wooden and high-backed leather chairs around a mix of tables, rustic stable door partitioning, a pale green dado with mirrors and artwork on brick walls above, fresh flowers and little plants in pots; there's also a spacious dining conservatory. Outside, terraces (heated in chilly weather) have tables and chairs and picnic-sets under parasols. Bedrooms are well equipped and comfortable. The pub is well placed for Newbury Racecourse.

🌟 Interesting food includes lunchtime sandwiches, pigeon breast with wild mushroom and jerusalem artichoke fricassée, pickled chicken liver pâté with pickled vegetables, burnt apple and piccalilli chutney, halloumi and mediterranean vegetable kebabs with chips, superfood salad bowl with a choice of toppings, sea bass with saffron potatoes with grilled fennel and salsa vierge, chargrilled cajun chicken with roasted tomatoes and baked field mushroom, himalayan salt-aged steak with a choice of sauce and chips, and puddings such as sticky toffee pudding with vanilla ice-cream and vanilla crème brûlée. *Benchmark main dish: venison shank with black pudding mash and jus £21.00. Two-course evening meal £26.00.*

Upham ~ Real ale ~ Open 7am-midnight; 7.30am-midnight Sat; 8am-11pm Sun; may open at 9am if not busy in winter ~ Bar food 12-9.30; 12-8 Sun; breakfast 7.30-11am (8-11am weekends) ~ Restaurant ~ Well behaved children welcome ~ Dogs allowed in bar and bedrooms ~ Wi-fi ~ Occasional live music ~ Bedrooms: £109/£119 *Recommended by Cliff and Monica Swan, Anna and Mark Evans, Ian Herdman, Christopher Mannings, Geoff and Ann Marston, Douglas Power*

HARE HATCH
SU8077 Map 2

Horse & Groom 🍷 ◗

(0118) 940 3136 – www.brunningandprice.co.uk/horseandgroom

A4 Bath Road W of Maidenhead; RG10 9SB

Spreading pub with attractively furnished, timbered rooms, enjoyable food and seats outside

This stood at one of the old gates into Windsor Forest and dates back 300 years. There are plenty of signs of great age in the interconnected rooms and much of interest too: beams and timbering, a pleasing variety of well spread individual tables and chairs on mahogany-stained boards, oriental rugs and some carpet to soften the acoustics, and open fires in attractive tiled fireplaces. Also, a profusion of mainly old or antique prints and mirrors, book-lined shelves, house plants and daily papers. Well trained, courteous staff serve a splendid range of drinks including a good changing range of 15 wines by the glass, Brakspears Bitter, Marstons Pedigree, Thwaites Lancaster Bomber and Wychwood Hobgoblin on handpump, two farm ciders, 110 gins and 50 malt whiskies; background music and board games. A sheltered back garden has picnic-sets while the front terrace has teak tables and chairs under parasols.

Good, up-to-date food includes sandwiches, potted crab and crayfish with samphire, caper and cucumber salad, butternut squash and mozzarella arancini with butternut squash purée, toasted pumpkin seed pesto and coriander oil, smoked haddock and salmon fishcake with a poached egg and tomato concasse, cumberland sausage with mash and onion gravy, chicken, ham and leek pie with cream sauce, lamb shoulder with dauphinoise potatoes and rosemary gravy, beef with thyme dumplings, horseradish mash and red wine sauce, and puddings such as crème brûlée and lemon posset with blackcurrant granola salad. *Benchmark main dish: steak burger with coleslaw and chips £13.45. Two-course evening meal £21.00.*

Brunning & Price ~ Manager John Nicholson ~ Real ale ~ Open 11.30-11 ~ Bar food 12-9.30 (10 Fri, Sat) ~ Children welcome ~ Dogs allowed in bar ~ Wi-fi *Recommended by John and Mary Warner, D J and P M Taylor, Carol and Barry Craddock, Caroline Sullivan, Miles Green, Susan and John Douglas*

INKPEN

SU3764   Map 2

Crown & Garter 🎖️ 🛏️

(01488) 668325 – www.crownandgarter.co.uk

Inkpen Common: Inkpen signposted with Kintbury off A4; in Kintbury turn left into Inkpen Road, then keep on into Inkpen Common; RG17 9QR

Carefully run country pub with modern touches blending with original features, enjoyable food and seats outside; bedrooms

Tucked away down a country lane, this is a rather fine old brick pub that has been here since 1640. You'll find a friendly welcome and the spreading bar area has wooden stools against the counter where they serve Ramsbury Gold and West Berkshire Good Old Boy and Mr Chubbs on handpump, ten wines by the glass and a dozen malt whiskies; leading off here is a snug area with leather armchairs by an open fire in a raised brick fireplace. Throughout there's an assortment of upholstered dining chairs grouped around simple tables on pale floorboards, cushioned wall seating and armchairs, old suitcases, mirrors and modern artwork on contemporary paintwork and wallpaper that depicts bookcases (in the smart restaurant); background music. The front terrace has seats and tables under parasols. A separate single-storey L-shaped building built around an attractive garden houses the comfortable bedrooms, and there's also a separate coffee shop (which becomes a private dining space in the evening); bike racks. Disabled access.

Well thought-of food includes lunchtime sandwiches, camembert, fig and onion tart with sesame seed dressing, chalk stream trout with truffle honey, yoghurt and caviar, cauliflower steak with nut butter, watercress and pickled cauliflower leaves, beer-battered fish and chips, chicken breast with celeriac purée, portobello mushrooms and sage jus, braised pigs cheeks with creamy polenta, wild mushrooms and ravigote sauce, duck breast with cherries and red wine sauce, and puddings such as custard tart with ginger sorbet and dark chocolate crémeux with hazelnut cream. *Benchmark main dish: proper pies £17.50. Two-course evening meal £23.00.*

Honesty Group ~ Licensee Romilla Arber ~ Real ale ~ Open 11-11 ~ Bar food 12-3, 6.30-9 ~ Restaurant ~ Children welcome ~ Dogs allowed in bar ~ Wi-fi ~ Bedrooms: £105/£130
Recommended by David and Judy Robison, Jim King, Ian Herdman, Angela and Steve Heard, Joe and Belinda Smart, Tom Stone

 KINTBURY   SU3866   Map 2
Dundas Arms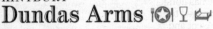
(01488) 658263 – www.dundasarms.co.uk
Village signposted off A4 Newbury–Hungerford about a mile W of Halfway; Station Road – pub just over hump-back canal bridge, at start of village itself; RG17 9UT

Waterside inn between the River Kennet and the Kennet & Avon Canal with plenty of outside seats, newly furnished bar and dining rooms and good choice of food and drinks; stylish bedrooms

Carefully refurbished, this is a handsome early 19th-c inn on a pretty canal islet next to the River Kennet. A riverside terrace and mature garden enjoy the water views and have plenty of seats and tables under large, white parasols; you'd be best to arrive early to bag one. Inside, the simply furnished bar has a counter decorated in old pennies, traditional furniture on bare boards and Ramsbury Gold and a changing local guest on handpump, local cider and 14 wines by the glass served by helpful, friendly staff. There are various dining areas including a main one decorated in classic country style with green panelled walls, decorative tiled flooring and a pretty fireplace, and the Potting Shed with garden tools, little watering cans and books on a dresser and large windows overlooking the garden. Five of the eight contemporary, well appointed riverside bedrooms have their own private terrace.

 Imaginative food using local, seasonal produce includes sandwiches, crab pasta with chilli and coriander salsa, twice-baked cheddar soufflé with pear and hazelnut salad, thyme and parmesan gnocchi with roasted garlic, rocket and salsa verde, chicken, leek and ham pie, moroccan-style sticky lamb with couscous salad, coriander and preserved lemon dressing, thai-spiced hake fillet with coriander rice, pak choi and coconut and ginger sauce, chicken breast with truffle butter, boulangère potatoes and madeira sauce, and puddings such as apple and frangipane tart with vanilla custard and dark chocolate and hazelnut tart with salted caramel ice-cream. *Benchmark main dish: pie of the day £13.50. Two-course evening meal £22.00.*

Free house ~ Licensee Lee Hart ~ Real ale ~ Open 11-11; 12-10 Sun ~ Bar food 12-2.30, 6-9.30; 12-7 Sun ~ Restaurant ~ Children welcome ~ Dogs allowed in bar ~ Wi-fi ~ Bedrooms: /$100 *Recommended by Holly and Tim Waite, Dan and Nicki Barton, Andrea and Philip Crispin, Charlie May*

MAIDENS GREEN   SU9072   Map 2
Winning Post ⌂
(01344) 882242 – www.winningpostwinkfield.co.uk
Follow signs to Winkfield Plain W of Winkfield off A330, then first right; SL4 4SW

18th-c inn with beams and timbering in character rooms, interesting food and drinks choice, friendly feel and seats in garden; bedrooms

At weekends in particular there are lots of chatty locals with their families and dogs here, but as a visitor you'll get just as warm a welcome. It's a gently civilised place with beamed, open-plan rooms connected by timbering (some have crash pads). The main bar area has leather and wood tub chairs around a table in one window, a long cushioned settle in another, and big flagstones and stools by the bar where they keep Otter Bitter and a changing guest on handpump and good wines by the glass. An end room, also with flagstones, has more tub chairs, wall seating and contemporary paintwork on planked walls; TV. The dining rooms are to the left of the bar: one long room has huge wall photos of horses and there are tartan banquettes, cushioned dining chairs around wooden tables on bare boards, a woodburning stove, hanging lanterns and bowler-hat lights. A room to the back of the inn called the Winning Enclosure has horse-racing wall photos and a large raised fireplace. The partly covered terrace has good quality seats and tables. Quiet bedrooms, handy for Ascot and Henley, face the garden.

🍴 Food is good and includes confit duck tart with squash and chestnut, fishcake with poached egg and hollandaise, wild mushroom risotto with cheese, wild boar and apple sausages with mash and puy lentils, braised rabbit with mustard root vegetables and tarragon, scottish salmon with chicory, orange and hazelnuts, ox cheek with ale-braised onions and pickled mushrooms, and puddings such as tonka bean pannacotta with baked figs and apple and blackberry crumble and vanilla ice-cream. *Benchmark main dish: chicken kiev with truffled polenta £17.00. Two-course evening meal £21.50.*

Upham ~ Manager Zach Leach ~ Real ale ~ Open 11am-11.30pm (10.30pm Sun) ~ Bar food 12-9.30; 12-7.30 Sun ~ Restaurant ~ Children welcome ~ Dogs allowed in bar and bedrooms ~ Wi-fi ~ Bedrooms: /£119 *Recommended by Mike Kavaney, Julia and Fiona Barnes, Maria and Henry Lazenby, Martine and Fabio Lockley, Monty Green*

NEWBURY

Newbury 🏵 ⛌ 🍺

SU4767   Map 2

(01635) 49000 ~ www.thenewburypub.co.uk
Bartholomew Street; RG14 5HB

Lively pub with plenty of bar and dining space, rewarding food and regular events

There's always something going on here and a fantastic choice of drinks to boot – the most exciting being gin from their own 137 Gin Distillery (you can buy a bottle to take home with you). Also, a beer named for them (from Greene King), Timothy Taylors Landlord and guests on handpump, 20 malt whiskies, 28 wines (including champagne and sparkling) by the glass, an extensive cocktail list (using their own gin) and a fine range of coffees and teas (including tea grown in Cornwall). There are also lots of different seating areas to suit whatever mood you're in, from a rooftop terrace with a cocktail bar, a pizza oven and an electric folding canopy roof to a downstairs courtyard with seats and tables. The inviting bar has an assortment of wooden dining chairs around sturdy farmhouse and other solid tables on bare boards, comfortable leather sofas, big paintings, church candles and an open fire. Light and airy dining rooms have wall benches and church chairs around more rustic tables on more bare boards, local artwork and an open kitchen; background music and board games. The distillery is also a private dining room for hire.

🍴 Food is very good and the ingredients carefully sourced: smoked beetroot and goats cheese mousse, garlic and rosemary baked camembert, black truffle gnocchi with cheese, butternut squash and mushrooms, chicken caesar salad, burger with toppings and chips, cod loin and tiger prawn, thai red curry, 12-hour haggis-stuffed lamb with celeriac and potato dauphinoise and braised red cabbage purée, plaice with scallops, caper butter and skinny fries, and puddings such as apple and toffee crumble with custard and dark and white chocolate fondant with a poached pear.

Benchmark main dish: pork belly with skin popcorn, carrot and vanilla purée, sticky jus £17.50. Two-course evening meal £23.00.

Greene King ~ Lease Peter Lumber ~ Real ale ~ Open 11.30-11; 5-11 Mon; 11.30am-1am Fri Sat; 11.30-7 Sun; closed Mon lunchtime ~ Bar food 11-3, 5-9; 12-6 Sun ~ Restaurant ~ Children welcome ~ Dogs allowed in bar ~ Wi-fi ~ Open mike every other Thurs evening
Recommended by Katherine Matthews, Millie and Peter Downing, Monty Green, Helena and Trevor Fraser, Melanie and David Lawson

  PEASEMORE   SU4577   Map 2

Fox

(01635) 248480 – www.foxatpeasemore.co.uk
4 miles from M4 junction 13, via Chieveley: keep on through Chieveley to Peasemore, turning left into Hillgreen Lane at small sign to Fox Inn; village also signposted from B4494 Newbury–Wantage; RG20 7JN

Friendly downland pub on top form under its expert licensees

The high standards in this much loved pub never waver and the first class, hands-on Mr and Mrs Davison are always there to offer a genuine welcome to all their customers. The long bare-boards bar has strategically placed high-backed settles (comfort guaranteed by plenty of colourful cushions), a warm woodburning stove in a stripped-brick chimney breast and, for real sybarites, two luxuriously carpeted end areas, one with velour tub armchairs. Friendly, efficient, neatly dressed staff serve West Berkshire Good Old Boy and a couple of changing guests on handpump,16 wines by the glass and summer farm cider; background music. This is downland horse-training country, and picnic-table sets at the front look out to the rolling fields beyond the quiet country lane – on a clear day you can see as far as the Hampshire border hills some 20 miles south. There are more picnic-sets on a smallish sheltered back terrace. They also offer a self-catering apartment. Good surrounding walks.

Pleasing food includes lunchtime sandwiches, salt and pepper popcorn shrimp with sweet chilli mayonnaise, baked camembert for two, venison sausages with mash and onion gravy, vegan mixed bean suet pudding, pork chop with grain mustard gravy, fish pie with cheddar mash, chalk stream trout with chickpea and mushroom cassoulet, and puddings such as profiteroles in warm chocolate sauce and apple and cinnamon crumble tart with custard. *Benchmark main dish: roast lamb rump with rosemary mash and mint lamb gravy £17.95. Two-course evening meal £20.00.*

Free house ~ Licensees Philip and Lauren Davison ~ Real ale ~ Open 12-2.30, 6-11; 12-11 Sat; 12-6 Sun; closed Mon, Tues; two weeks July ~ Bar food 12-2, 6-9; 12-3, 5.30-9 Sat; 12-4 Sun ~ Children welcome ~ Dogs allowed in bar ~ Wi-fi *Recommended by Ian Herdman, Maggie and Matthew Lyons, Tracey and Stephen Groves, Alan Sutton, Jim King, Ian Duncan, Tom Stone*

RUSCOMBE   SU7976   Map 2

Royal Oak

(0118) 934 5190 – www.burattas.co.uk
Ruscombe Lane (B3024 just E of Twyford); RG10 9JN

Wide choice of food at welcoming pub (known locally as Buratta's) with interesting furnishings and paintings and local beer and wine

This place is always on excellent form with plenty of customers and a good, bustling atmosphere – our readers enjoy their visits here very much. The carpeted bars are open-plan but carefully laid out so that each area is fairly snug but still feels part of the action. A good variety of furniture runs from dark oak tables to big chunky pine ones with mixed seating to match; the two sofas facing each other are popular. Contrasting with the old exposed ceiling joists, mostly unframed modern paintings and prints decorate the walls, which are painted in grey and white. Binghams (the brewery is just across the road) Twyford Tipple, Fullers London Pride and a guest from Loddon on handpump, 16 wines by the glass (they stock wines from the village's Stanlake Park vineyard), 14 malt whiskies, six gins and attentive service. Picnic-sets are ranged around a venerable central hawthorn in the garden behind (where there are ducks and chickens); summer barbecues. The pub is on the Henley Arts Trail. Do visit the friendly landlady's antiques and collectables shop, which is open during pub hours.

Popular food includes sandwiches and paninis, sharing platters, chicken liver and gin parfait with orange and cranberry dressing, tempura prawns with sweet chilli dip, thai vegetables with noodles, a pie of the week, lambs kidneys with bacon, mushroom and red wine sauce, venison steak with redcurrant rosemary sauce, sea bass with creamy chive sauce and balsamic tomatoes, rib-eye steak with stilton sauce, and puddings. *Benchmark main dish: monkfish wrapped in parma ham with green peppercorn sauce £15.00. Two-course evening meal £22.00.*

Enterprise ~ Lease Jenny and Stefano Buratta ~ Real ale ~ Open 12-3, 6-11; 12-4 Sun; closed Sun and Mon evenings ~ Bar food 12-2.30, 6.30-9.30; 12-3 Sun ~ Restaurant ~ Children welcome ~ Dogs welcome ~ Wi-fi *Recommended by Stuart and Natalie Granville, Mandy and Gary Redstone, Paul Humphreys, Gail and Frank Hackett, Patti and James Davidson*

SHEFFORD WOODLANDS

SU3673 Map 2

Pheasant 🏠✪ ⚲

(01488) 648284 – www.thepheasant-inn.co.uk
Under 0.5 miles from M4 junction 14 – A338 towards Wantage, first left on B4000; RG17 7AA

Bustling bars, a separate dining room, highly thought-of food and beer and seats outside; bedrooms

The highly rated food, thoughtful choice of drinks and friendly welcome all point to this pub doing particularly well. The various interconnecting bar rooms have been carefully refurbished with contemporary paintwork, lots of antiques and plenty of horse-related prints, photographs and paintings; there are elegant wooden dining chairs and settles around all sorts of tables, big mirrors here and there, leather banquettes and stools, and a warm fire in a little brick fireplace. One snug room has attractively upholstered armchairs and sofas. Drinks include a beer named for the pub (from Banks's), Gritchie English Lore, Marstons Pedigree and Ramsbury Gold on handpump, good wines by the glass from a decent list, 36 gins, 15 vodkas, ten rums, 26 malt whiskies, cocktails and interesting liqueurs. There's also a separate dining room; background music. Seats in the garden have attractive views. The 11 individually decorated and well equipped modern bedrooms are in a separate extension, and breakfasts are tasty.

Enterprising food includes breakfasts (7.30-10.30am), ham hock terrine with a soft boiled quail egg, pickled onions and jerusalem artichoke crisps, mussels with garlic, white wine and cream, twice-baked goats cheese soufflé with charred leeks, spinach and blue cheese sauce, burger with toppings, coleslaw and skinny fries, hake with tarragon polenta chips, samphire, peas and tartare sauce, pork belly with crushed new potatoes, chargrilled hispi cabbage, lardo, spiced pear purée and cider jus, 16oz châteaubriand (to share) with garlic butter, triple-cooked chips and a choice of sauce, and puddings such as apple tarte tatin with caramel sauce and chocolate mousse gateau with chocolate crémeux, toasted hazelnuts and praline cream. *Benchmark main dish: duck breast with offal pastilla, fondant potatoes, pak choi, braised red cabbage and plum sauce £22.00. Two-course evening meal £25.00.*

Free house ~ Licensee Jack Greenall ~ Real ale ~ Open 7.30am-11pm; 8am-11pm Sat; 8am-10.30pm Sun ~ Bar food 12-3, 6-9.30; 12-5, 6-9 Sun ~ Children welcome ~ Dogs allowed in bar and bedrooms ~ Wi-fi ~ Bedrooms: /£115 *Recommended by Mr and Mrs P R Thomas, Dr and Mrs A K Clarke, John Pritchard, Anne and Ben Smith, Julian Richardson, Sophie Ellison*

SONNING   SU7575   Map 2
Bull ⌂

(0118) 969 3901 – www.bullinnsonning.co.uk
Off B478, by church; village signed off A4 E of Reading; RG4 6UP

Attractive spot for pretty timbered inn with plenty of character in old-fashioned bars, friendly staff and good food; bedrooms

Try to visit this 16th-c inn when the wisteria is in bloom and the hanging baskets are at their peak – it's a lovely sight. The two old-fashioned bar rooms have plenty of character: low ceilings and heavy beams, cosy alcoves, leather armchairs and sofas, cushioned antique settles and low wooden chairs on bare boards, and open fireplaces. Fullers HSB and London Pride and a couple of guest ales on handpump served by helpful staff, 16 good wines by the glass, cocktails and a farm cider. The dining room has a mix of wooden chairs and tables, rugs on parquet flooring and shelves of books; TV. The boutique-style bedrooms do get booked up well in advance. If you bear left through the ivy-clad churchyard opposite, then turn left along the bank of the river, you come to a very pretty lock. The Thames Valley Park is close by.

Pleasing food includes lunchtime sandwiches, sharing boards, potted duck with spiced pear chutney, pork belly with seared scallops, pea purée and red wine jus, aubergine, courgette and pepper linguine with basil and chilli breadcrumbs, a pie of the day, hake fillet with sweet potato fondant and crab and avocado salsa, corn-fed chicken with truffle mash, crispy kale and wild mushroom sauce, and puddings such as hot chocolate and caramel fondant with buffalo milk ice-cream and pear, plum and vanilla crumble with crème anglaise. *Benchmark main dish: beer-battered haddock and triple-cooked chips £15.00. Two-course evening meal £23.00.*

Fullers ~ Managers Sian and Jason Smith ~ Real ale ~ Open 10am-11pm; 12-10.30 Sun ~ Bar food 12-9.30 (8.30 Sun); 12-3, 6-9 in winter ~ Restaurant ~ Children welcome ~ Dogs allowed in bar ~ Wi-fi ~ Live local artist and tribute evenings ~ Bedrooms: /£125 *Recommended by Gordon and Patricia Gorringe, Barbara and Phil Bowie, R J Herd, Graham Smart, Rosie and John Moore, Susan and John Douglas*

SWALLOWFIELD   SU7364   Map 2
George & Dragon ⊕ ♀

(0118) 988 4432 – www.georgeanddragonswallowfield.co.uk
Church Road, towards Farley Hill; RG7 1TJ

Busy country pub with enjoyable bar food, real ales, friendly service and seats outside

So popular are the tables here that you'll need to book some time in advance. The various comfortable and easy-going interconnected rooms have plenty of character with beams (some quite low) and standing timbers, a happy mix of nice old dining chairs and settles around individual wooden tables, rugs on flagstones, lit candles, a big log fire and country prints on red or bare brick walls. The attentive and friendly, long-serving licensees keep their ales well – Ringwood Razorback, Sharps Doom Bar and Youngs Bitter on handpump – and also offer quite a few wines by the glass and several gins and whiskies. There are picnic-sets on gravel or paving in the garden. See the pub's website for the enjoyable four-mile walk that starts and ends here.

Top rated food includes lunchtime filled ciabattas, devilled kidneys, salt and pepper squid with piquant mayonnaise, pork and leek sausages with red wine sauce, gratin bayaldi (aubergine, courgette, red and yellow peppers, onion and tomato layers), beer-battered fish and chips, venison medallions with haggis slice, champ and red wine sauce, barbecue baby back ribs with peanut coleslaw, seared tuna steak with mediterranean vegetables, and puddings such as sticky toffee pudding with toffee sauce and lemon posset with mango coulis. *Benchmark main dish: 10oz sirloin steak with a choice of sauce £22.50. Two-course evening meal £24.00.*

Free house ~ Licensee Paul Dailey ~ Real ale ~ Open 12-11 (midnight Sat) ~ Bar food 12-2.30, 7-9.30 ~ Restaurant ~ Children welcome ~ Dogs allowed in bar ~ Wi-fi
Recommended by Susie and Spencer Gray, Catherine and Daniel King, Tony and Jill Radnor, Frances and Hamish Porter, Chloe and Tim Hodge

WOOLHAMPTON
Rowbarge ♀ ◖
SU5766   Map 2

(0118) 971 2213 – www.brunningandprice.co.uk/rowbarge
Station Road; RG7 5SH

Canalside pub with plenty of interest in rambling rooms, six real ales, good quality food and lots of outside seating

Even when it's packed out – which it always is on a sunny day, thanks to its position by the Kennet & Avon Canal – the friendly, efficient young staff keep things running smoothly. Six rambling rooms with beams and timbering are connected by open doorways and knocked-through walls. The décor is gently themed to represent the nearby canal with hundreds of prints and photographs (some of rowing and boats) and oars on the walls, as well as old glass and stone bottles in nooks and crannies, big house plants and fresh flowers, plenty of candles and several open fires; the many large mirrors create an impression of even more space. Throughout there are antique dining chairs around various nice old tables, settles, built-in cushioned wall seating, armchairs, a group of high stools around a huge wooden barrel table, and rugs on polished boards, stone tiles or carpeting. Brunning & Price Traditional Bitter (from St Austell) plus Rowbarge Ruby (named for them from Loddon), Frome Funky Monkey and three quickly changing guest beers on handpump, 20 wines by the glass, 90 gins and 65 malt whiskies; background music and board games. A decked terrace has wooden chairs and tables and you'll find picnic-sets among trees by the water.

Brasserie-style food includes sandwiches, lamb and apricot kofta with cucumber and tomato salad and mint raita, a charcuterie plate with pickles and chutney, beetroot meatballs filled with vegan cheese, butternut squash and tomato sauce, crab and mussel linguine, steak in ale pie, plaice with fennel, chicory and orange salad and white wine sauce, lamb shoulder with carrot and swede mash, dauphinoise potatoes and rosemary gravy, and puddings such as hot waffle with butterscotch sauce and honeycomb ice-cream and chocolate brownie with vanilla ice-cream. *Benchmark main dish: braised lamb shoulder with dauphinoise potatoes, carrot mash and rosemary gravy £17.45. Two-course evening meal £21.00.*

Brunning & Price ~ Manager Steve Butt ~ Real ale ~ Open 10am-11pm; 10am-10.30pm Sun ~ Bar food 10-9.30 (10pm Fri, Sat); 10-9 Sun ~ Restaurant ~ Children welcome ~ Dogs allowed in bar ~ Wi-fi *Recommended by Louise and Simon Peters, Brian and Susan Wylie, Andrew and Michele Revell, Jill and Hugh Bennett*

YATTENDON
SU5574 Map 2

Royal Oak ⭐ 🍷 🛏

(01635) 201325 – www.royaloakyattendon.co.uk

The Square; B4009 NE from Newbury; right at Hampstead Norreys, village signed on left; RG18 0UG

● ●

Berkshire Dining Pub of the Year

Civilised old inn with beamed and panelled rooms, imaginative food and seats in pretty garden; bedrooms

Our readers enjoy staying in the comfortable and attractive bedrooms, all of which overlook the garden or village square; breakfasts are highly rated. The charming bar rooms have beams and panelling, an appealing mix of wooden dining chairs around interesting tables, some half-panelled wall seating, rugs on quarry tiles or wooden floorboards, plenty of prints on brick, cream or red walls, lovely flower arrangements and four log fires; background music and TV. Ales from the local area such as Ramsbury Gold, Ringwood Razorback and a changing guest on handpump are on tip top form; the 12 wines by the glass are well chosen. Under the trellising in the walled back garden are wicker armchairs and tables and they have picnic-sets under parasols at the front; boules. The pub is only ten minutes from Newbury Racecourse, so it can get busy on race days.

🍽⭐ Appetising food includes chicken and sesame yakitori skewers with plum, honey and ginger, crisp soft shell crab with green chilli dressing, pizzas (to take away too), squash and spinach peshwari curry, smoked haddock and leek fishcake with spinach and hollandaise, calves liver and bacon with mustard mash and redcurrant gravy, port-braised shin of beef cottage pie, sea bass with asian greens, soy and sesame, and puddings such as lemon crème brûlée and salted caramel and chocolate truffle tart with roasted hazelnut chantilly; they also offer a two-course weekday lunch menu and proper afternoon tea (must be pre-booked). *Benchmark main dish: lemon and oregano rotisserie chicken with fries £18.00. Two-course evening meal £25.00.*

Free house ~ Licensee Rob McGill ~ Real ale ~ Open 11-11; 12-10.30 Sun ~ Bar food 12-2.30, 6-9.30; 12-3, 6-9.30 Sat; 12-3.30, 6-9 Sun ~ Restaurant ~ Children welcome ~ Dogs welcome ~ Wi-fi ~ Bedrooms: /£99 *Recommended by John Ledbury, Geoffrey Sutton, Brian and Sally Wakeham, Julian Thorpe, Liz and Martin Eldon*

Also Worth a Visit in Berkshire

Besides the fully inspected pubs, you might like to try these pubs that have been recommended to us and described by readers. Do tell us what you think of them: feedback@goodguides.com

---

ALDWORTH SU5579
★ **Bell** (01635) 578272
A329 Reading–Wallingford; left on to B4009 at Streatley; RG8 9SE Unspoilt and unchanging village pub in same family for over 250 years; simply furnished panelled rooms, beams in ochre ceiling, old photographs and ancient one-handed clock, woodburner, glass-panelled hatch serving well kept Arkells, West Berkshire and a monthly guest, Upton cider and nice house wines, good value rolls, ploughman's and winter soup, traditional pub games; no mobile phones or credit cards; well behaved children and dogs welcome, seats in quiet cottagey garden by cricket ground, animals in paddock behind pub, maybe Christmas mummers and summer morris, closed Mon (open lunchtime bank holidays), can get busy weekends. *(Chloe and Tim Hodge)*

ALDWORTH SU5579
Four Points (01635) 578367
B4009 towards Hampstead Norreys; RG8 9RL Attractive 17th-c thatched roadside pub with low beams, standing timbers and panelling, nice fire in bar with more formal seating area to the left and restaurant at back, popular good value

home-cooked food (all day weekends) from baguettes up, bargain lighter lunch deal Mon-Fri, Wadworths 6X and guests, friendly helpful young staff; children and dogs (in bar) welcome, garden over road with play area, open (and food) all day weekends. *(Susan Eccleston)*

ASTON   SU7884
★ **Flower Pot** (01491) 574721
Off A4130 Henley–Maidenhead at top of Remenham Hill; RG9 3DG Roomy red-brick country pub with nice local feel; snug traditional bar and airy back dining area, lots of stuffed fish and other taxidermy, roaring log fire, four well kept ales such as Brakspears and Ringwood, enjoyable reasonably priced food (not Sun evening) from baguettes to fish and game, friendly service; vocal parrot called Paddy; very busy with walkers and families at weekends, dogs allowed in some parts, plenty of picnic-sets in big garden with rural views, Thames nearby, three bedrooms, open all day weekends. *(Susan and John Douglas, D J and P M Taylor)*

BARKHAM   SU7866
Bull (0118) 976 2816
Barkham Road; RG41 4TL Traditional pub run by friendly thai family; opened-up carpeted interior with dining area to one end, half a dozen ales such as Gales, Rebellion, Sharps and Timothy Taylors, popular food including good south-east asian choices and tapas-style bar menu; Mon quiz: children welcome, open all day (till 8pm Sun).
(Darren and Jane Staniforth)

BEECH HILL   SU6964
Elm Tree (0118) 988 3505
3.3 miles from M4 junction 11: A33 towards Basingstoke, turning off into Beech Hill Road after about 2 miles; RG7 2AZ Five rooms (one with blazing fire) and nice rural views especially from more modern barn-style restaurant and conservatory; much enjoyed food from varied menu, prompt friendly service, well kept ales such as Ringwood and Timothy Taylors, good choice of wines by the glass and decent coffee; children and dogs welcome, disabled access/loo, tables on heated front deck with palms, open all day, no food Sun evening. *(Miles Green)*

BEENHAM   SU5868
Six Bells (0118) 971 3368
The Green; RG7 5NX Extended red-brick Victorian village pub with good food from landlord-chef including imaginative additions to standard pub menu, well kept West Berkshire Good Old Boy, Sharps Doom Bar and a guest such as Vale, friendly staff, two bar areas with armchairs and winter fires, dining conservatory; board games; children welcome at lunchtime, four bedrooms, closed Sun evening, Mon lunchtime. *(John Pritchard)*

BISHAM   SU8585
Bull (01628) 898424
Marlow Road; SL7 1RR Old village dining pub with wide choice of good food including weekday bar and restaurant set menus (not Dec), a couple of ales such as Brakspears and Greene King, well chosen wines, friendly helpful service; background music; pleasant garden. *(Mrs P Sumner)*

CHADDLEWORTH   SU4177
Ibex (01488) 638311
Main Street; RG20 7ER Old brick and flint country pub saved from closure by the local community; enjoyable reasonably priced pubby food (not Sun evening, Mon) from sandwiches to good Sun roasts (unlimited veg), Indigenous (brewed in the village) and a couple of guests, friendly accommodating staff; live music and quiz nights, darts; children, muddy boots and paws welcome, tables on sheltered lawn and terrace, two bedrooms, open all day weekends, closed Mon lunchtime. *(Penny and David Shepherd)*

CHARVIL   SU7776
Heron on the Ford (0118) 934 0700
Lands End Lane/Whistley Mill Lane near Old River ford; RG10 0UE Refurbished 1930s Tudor-style pub under new management (was the Lands End); Brakspears beers and enjoyable food from sandwiches up, open-plan bar with log fire, side snug and separate restaurant, helpful friendly service; children welcome, sizeable garden with terrace, open all day weekends (till 6.30pm Sun). *(Paul Humphreys)*

CHEAPSIDE   SU9469
Thatched Tavern (01344) 620874
Off A332/A329, then off B383 at Village Hall sign; SL5 7QG Civilised dining pub with a good deal of character and plenty of room for just a drink; well liked up-to-date food (can be pricey) along with more traditional choices and weekday set lunch, lots of wines by the glass including champagne from extensive list, Fullers London Pride, a beer named for the pub and a guest ale, big inglenook log fire, low beams and polished flagstones in cottagey core, three smart dining rooms off; children welcome, dogs in bar, tables on terrace and attractive sheltered back lawn, handy for Virginia Water, open (and food) all day, busy on Ascot race days. *(Brian and Susan Wylie)*

CHIEVELEY   SU4773
★ **Olde Red Lion** (01635) 248379
Handy for M4 junction 13 via A34 N-bound; Green Lane; RG20 8XB Popular village pub with up to four well kept Arkells beers and good varied choice of generously served food at reasonable prices, welcoming attentive service, low-beamed carpeted bar with log fire, extended back

restaurant; background music, TV; children and dogs welcome, wheelchair accessible throughout, small garden, five bedrooms in separate building, open all day weekends. *(Ian Herdman)*

COOKHAM   SU8985
★ Bel & the Dragon (01628) 521263
High Street (B4447); SL6 9SQ Smartly updated 15th-c inn; heavy beams, log fires and simple country furnishings in two-room front bar and dining area, hand-painted cartoons on pastel walls, more modern bistro-style back restaurant, emphasis on very good food (separate bar and restaurant menus) including weekend brunch, Rebellion IPA and a local guest, plenty of wines by the glass from extensive list, cocktails; children welcome, dogs in bar, well tended garden with tables on paved terrace, play area, five bedrooms, Stanley Spencer Gallery almost opposite, open all day, food all day Sun. *(Theocsbrian)*

COOKHAM   SU8885
★ White Oak (01628) 523043
The Pound (B4447); SL6 9QE Modernised red-brick restauranty pub with highly regarded interesting food including good value set menus, Mon steak night, large back area and several other parts set for eating, front bar serving ales such as Greene King and good range of wines by the glass, friendly efficient service; free wi-fi; children welcome, sheltered back terrace with steps up to white wirework tables on grass, closed Sun evening, otherwise open all day. *(Simon Collett-Jones)*

COOKHAM DEAN   SU8785
★ Jolly Farmer (01628) 482905
Church Road, off Hills Lane; SL6 9PD Refurbished 18th-c pub owned by village consortium; linked beamed rooms with open fires, five well kept ales such as Rebellion and Timothy Taylors, Weston's cider and good choice of wines by the glass, fairly pubby food including wood-fired pizzas, pleasant attentive service; well behaved children and dogs welcome, tables out in front and on side terrace, garden with big play area, open all day. *(Miles Green)*

COOKHAM DEAN   SU8785
Uncle Toms Cabin (01628) 483339
Off A308 Maidenhead–Marlow; Hills Lane, towards Cookham Rise and Cookham; SL6 9NT Welcoming small-roomed local with simple modernised interior; five well kept ales such as Rebellion and Timothy Taylors, plenty of wines by the glass and enjoyable food from lunchtime sandwiches up, low beams (and doorways), wood floors and grey-green panelling, gleaming horsebrasses, open fire; background music, TV; children allowed in eating areas, dogs in bar, seats out at front and in sheltered sloping back garden, peaceful

country setting, open all day Sat, closes 9pm Sun and Mon. *(Tony Scott)*

CRAZIES HILL   SU7980
Horns (0118) 940 6041
Warren Row Road, off A4 towards Cockpole Green, then follow Crazies Hill signs; RG10 8LY Welcoming 16th-c beamed village pub with landlady-chef's good food from lunchtime baguettes and traditional favourites up, Brakspears ales kept well and nice choice of wines by the glass, friendly helpful service, four rooms including raftered barn restaurant; children welcome, dogs in bar, big garden with play area and summer barbecues, open all day Fri and Sat, till 7pm Sun, closed Mon (Tues after bank holiday). *(Paul Humphreys)*

DATCHET   SU9877
Royal Stag (01753) 584231
Not far from M4 junction 5; The Green; SL3 9JH Ancient beamed pub next to church overlooking green; well kept Fullers London Pride and three Windsor & Eton beers, enjoyable food including weekday lunchtime sandwiches, good Sun roasts, friendly staff; Tues quiz; children and dogs welcome, seats outside, open (and food) all day. *(George Sanderson)*

DONNINGTON   SU4770
Fox & Hounds (01635) 40540
Old Oxford Road; RG14 3AP Popular and welcoming family-owned pub (they also run a local butcher's and have a meat raffle every other Sun); well kept Fullers, Sharps and West Berkshire, decent wine range and good generously served food from pub favourites to grills, attentive young staff, dining room around to the left; TV, darts; children and dogs welcome, picnic-sets out in front, handy for M4 (junction 13) and A34, closed Sun evening, Mon, otherwise open all day. *(Ian Herdman)*

EAST GARSTON   SU3676
★ Queens Arms (01488) 648757
3.5 miles from M4 junction 14; A338 and village signposted Great Shefford; RG17 7ET Friendly slate-roofed inn at the heart of racehorse-training country; opened-up bar with antique prints (many jockeys), wheelbacks around well spaced tables on bare boards, well kept Ramsbury, Sharps and a beer badged for them, plenty of wines by the glass, lighter dining area with more prints, good food from sandwiches and traditional choices up (pizzas Sun evening), friendly obliging staff; background music, TV for racing, newspapers including *Racing Post*, free wi-fi; children and dogs (in bar) welcome, seats on sheltered terrace, 12 attractively decorated bedrooms, good surrounding downland walks, fly fishing and shooting can be arranged, open all day; new owners as we went to press so there will be changes. *(Michael Sargent)*

EAST ILSLEY   SU4981
Crown & Horns   (01635) 281545
*Just off A34, about 5 miles N of M4
junction 13; Compton Road; RG20 7LH*
Welcoming brick and tile pub in horse-
training country; rambling beamed rooms
with log fires, enjoyable home-made food
from sandwiches, pizzas and pub favourites
up, Thurs steak night, five real ales and over
a dozen wines by the glass, friendly staff;
background music; children, dogs and muddy
boots welcome, tables in pretty courtyard,
modern bedroom extension, open all day and
busy on Newbury race days. *(Jamie Green)*

EASTBURY   SU3477
Plough   (01488) 71312
Centre of village by stream; RG17 7JN
Popular old whitewashed village dining pub
with very good food from chef-proprietor,
a couple of changing ales and over 40 gins,
friendly efficient staff, open-plan interior
with some modern touches including
large back restaurant, two-way log fire;
children welcome, dogs in bar, tables out
on front deck, open till 4.30pm Sun, closed
Mon. *(Michael Doswell)*

ETON   SU9677
George   (01753) 861797
High Street; SL4 6AF Welcoming 18th-c
corner pub just back from Thames bridge;
traditional beamed interior with settles, pews
and other wooden furniture on bare boards,
open fire, half a dozen Windsor & Eton beers
(tasting trays) from ornately carved oak
counter, ample helpings of enjoyable pubby
food, friendly helpful service; quiz every other
Tues; children and dogs welcome, decked
back terrace with seating booths, eight
bedrooms, open (and food) all day, kitchen
shuts 5pm Sun. *(Kiara Maher)*

FINCHAMPSTEAD   SU7963
Queens Oak   (0118) 996 8567
Church Lane, off B3016; RG40 4LS
Welcoming country pub named for an
oak planted by Queen Victoria on green
opposite; largely open-plan interior with
some updating by present licensees, well
kept Brakspears and other Marstons-related
beers, a dozen wines by the glass and decent
range of other drinks, enjoyable food (all day
weekends) from ciabattas and pub favourites
up; Thurs quiz, some live music; children,
walkers and dogs welcome, good-sized
garden with play area, open all day (till 7pm
Sun). *(Nick Higgins)*

FRILSHAM   SU5573
Pot Kiln   (01635) 201366
*From Yattendon take turning S, opposite
church, follow first Frilsham signpost,
but just after crossing motorway go
straight on towards Bucklebury ignoring
Frilsham signposted right; pub on right
after about 0.5 miles; RG18 0XX*

Tucked-away red-brick country dining pub
with good food including signature local
game; various eating areas and small bare-
boards bar with woodburner, West Berkshire
ales, several wines by the glass and maybe a
couple of real ciders; free wi-fi; children and
dogs welcome, unobstructed views from seats
in big suntrap garden, outside pizza oven,
nice walks in nearby woods, open all day Sat,
till 5pm Sun, closed Tues; refurbishment
and expansion under way as we went to
press. *(Andrew and Michele Revell)*

HAMPSTEAD NORREYS   SU5376
White Hart   (01635) 202248
Church Street; RG18 0TB Friendly and
relaxed low-beamed village pub with three
linked rooms, fireside seating and good-sized
dining area, enjoyable sensibly priced
home-made food from lunchtime baguettes/
ciabattas up, a couple of well kept Greene
King ales and a guest, well chosen wines;
some live music and quiz nights; children
and dogs (in bar) welcome, back terrace
and garden, open all day weekends, closed
Mon. *(Ashley Potter)*

HOLYPORT   SU8977
Belgian Arms   (01628) 634468
*1.5 miles from M4 junction 8/9 via
A308(M), A330; in village turn left
on to big green, then left again at war
memorial; SL6 2JR* Welcoming wisteria-
clad dining pub set back from village green;
opened-up low-ceilinged interior with well
spaced tables on stripped wood floor, good
food from snacks, sharing plates and pub
favourites up, well kept Brakspears and
nice range of wines by the glass, friendly
attentive service; background and live
acoustic music (first Fri of month); children
welcome, attractive garden overlooking pond,
open all day, food all day Sat (brunch from
9am). *(Simon Collett-Jones, Roddy Kane)*

HOLYPORT   SU8977
George   (01628) 628317
*1.5 miles from M4 junction 8/9, via
A308(M)/A330; The Green; SL6 2JL*
Attractive 16th-c village-green pub with
colourful history and plenty of old-world
charm; open-plan low-beamed interior, cosy
and dimly lit, with nice fireplace, good food
from lunchtime baguettes and pub favourites
up, well kept Fullers London Pride, a couple
of Rebellion ales and 16 wines by the glass,
friendly helpful service; background music,
quiz first Mon of month; children and dogs
(in bar) welcome, paved terrace and grassy
beer garden, closed Sun evening, Mon.
(Susan Eccleston)

HUNGERFORD   SU3368
Hungerford Arms   (01488) 682154
*High Street; street parking opposite;
RG17 0NB* Horse-racing themed pub with
open-plan interior stretching back from the
smallish bow-windowed façade; bare boards

and some low beams, open fire at the back, Greene King Old Speckled Hen, Timothy Taylors Landlord and a beer badged for the pub from island servery, decent choice of wines and enjoyable food from sandwiches, wraps and pizzas up, friendly staff; background music, TVs for racing; children welcome, small sheltered back courtyard, open all day. *(Mike and Mary Carter)*

HUNGERFORD   SU3368
John O'Gaunt   (01488) 683535
Bridge Street (A338); RG17 0EG
Welcoming 16th-c town pub with modernised beamed interior; enjoyable generously served food from lunchtime sandwiches/wraps up, six well kept mainly local ales including own microbrews (tasting trays available), good bottled range too and local cider, efficient cheerful service; children and dogs welcome, small sheltered garden, open all day, food all day Sun. *(Monty Green)*

HUNGERFORD   SU3368
Three Swans   (01488) 682721
High Street; RG17 0LZ Refurbished former coaching inn, bright and welcoming, with lower bar serving three well kept ales such as Black Sheep and Ramsbury, Somersby's cider, plenty of wines by the glass and cocktails, good food from snacks and pizzas up, helpful friendly service, large panelled restaurant and coffee shop; children and dogs (in bar) welcome, some tables out at front, more in part-covered courtyard behind, 25 bedrooms open all day from 7am (8am weekends) for breakfast. *(Sally and David Champion)*

HUNGERFORD NEWTOWN   SU3571
Tally Ho   (01488) 682312
A338 just S of M4 junction 14; RG17 0PP Traditional red-brick beamed pub owned by the local community, friendly and welcoming, with good food (not Sun evening) from baguettes to specials and popular Sun lunch, four well kept local ales such as Ramsbury and West Berkshire, proper cider, log fire; occasional music and quiz nights, free wi-fi; children and dogs welcome, a couple of picnic-sets out in front, more tables on side terrace, three bedrooms, open all day. *(Penny and Peter Keevil)*

HURLEY   SU8281
Dew Drop   (01628) 315662
Small yellow sign to pub off A4130 just W; SL6 6RB Old flint and brick pub tucked away in nice woodland setting; shortish choice of food including good lunchtime sandwiches, Brakspears and a guest ale,

two adjoining rooms (one with piano), log fire; free wi-fi; children and dogs welcome, pleasant views from back garden, good local walks, open all day Sat, till 6pm Sun, closed Mon. *(Simon Collett-Jones)*

HURLEY   SU8382
Hurley House   (01628) 568500
A4130 SE, just off A404; SL6 5LH
Elegant up-to-date hotel with informal civilised atmosphere; several different seating areas in big open-plan room including green leather chesterfields grouped in the centre, armchairs in front of a woodburner and some cushioned wall seats, Rebellion IPA, West Berkshire Good Old Boy and good wines by the glass, clubby-feel dining rooms with green button-back leather banquettes and mustard-yellow chairs, candles on tables, highly rated modern food (not Sun evening and not cheap) including set lunch menu, afternoon teas; background music (live Fri evening), board games; children and dogs (in bar) welcome, carefully landscaped gardens, ten comfortable well equipped bedrooms, good breakfast, open all day (till 9pm Sun). *(Susan and John Douglas, Daphne and Robert Staples, Geoff and Ann Marston)*

HURST   SU7973
★Castle   (0118) 934 0034
Church Hill; RG10 0SJ Popular old dining pub next to bowling green and owned by church opposite; very good well presented food (not Sun evening, Mon) from fairly priced varied menu including daily specials (Fri fish night), three well kept changing ales and plenty of wines by the glass, friendly efficient staff, beams, wood floors and old brick nogging, some visible wattle and daub, woodburners; children and dogs (in bar) welcome, picnic-sets out at front behind picket fence and in sunny back garden, open all day weekends, closed Mon lunchtime. *(Paul Humphreys)*

HURST   SU8074
Green Man   (0118) 934 2599
Off A321 just outside village; RG10 0BP Partly 17th-c pub with enjoyable food from sandwiches and baked potatoes up including stone-baked pizzas, well kept Brakspears and a couple of Marstons-related guests, a dozen wines by the glass, friendly service, dark beams and standing timbers, cosy alcoves, wall seats and built-in settles, log fires; children and dogs (in bar) welcome, sheltered terrace, picnic-sets under spreading oak trees in large garden with play area, open (and food) all day. *(Paul Humphreys)*

'Children welcome' means the pub says it lets children inside without any special restriction. If it allows them in, but to restricted areas such as an eating area or family room, we specify this. Some pubs may impose an evening time limit. We do not mention limits after 9pm as we assume children are home by then.

KNOWL HILL   SU8178
Bird in Hand (01628) 826622
A4, handy for M4 junction 8/9; RG10 9UP
Updated Wadworths pub set back from
the road; roomy interior with light beams,
panelling, parquet floor and log fire in main
area, four real ales and enjoyable reasonably
priced food including some specials, pleasant
efficient service, restaurant; background
music, fruit machine; children and dogs
(in bar) welcome, tables on front and back
terraces, bedrooms (some in separate block),
open (and food) all day. *(John Pritchard)*

LAMBOURN   SU3175
Hare (01488) 71386
*aka Hare & Hounds; Lambourn
Woodlands, well S of Lambourn itself
(B4000/Hilldrop Lane); RG17 7SD*
Rambling 17th-c beamed restaurant-pub with
well liked fairly priced food from lunchtime
sandwiches/baguettes to good Sun roasts,
several small linked rooms including a proper
bar with ales such as Ramsbury and Sharps,
friendly efficient service; background music,
TV; children and dogs (in one part) welcome,
garden behind, open all day (till 8pm Sun).
(Michael Sargent)

LITTLEWICK GREEN   SU8379
Cricketers (01628) 822888
*Not far from M4 junction 9; A404(M)
then left on to A4 – village signed on left;
Coronation Road; SL6 3RA* Welcoming
old-fashioned village pub in charming spot
opposite cricket green (can get crowded);
three well kept Badger ales and good choice
of wines by the glass, enjoyable pub food (not
Sun evening) from lunchtime sandwiches
to specials, traditional interior with three
linked rooms, wood and quarry-tiled floors,
huge clock above woodburner in brick
fireplace; background music, TV; children
and dogs welcome, pretty hanging baskets
and a few tables out in front behind picket
fence, open all day. *(Jamie Green)*

MAIDENHEAD   SU8881
15 Queen Street (01628) 623800
Queen Street; SL6 1NB Refurbished bar/
restaurant keeping traditional bare-boards
interior (was the Hand & Flowers); well kept
Brakspears, decent wines and good choice of
other drinks including cocktails, highly rated
food (booking advised) with emphasis on
steaks, also set menu and bottomless brunch,
friendly prompt service; background music,
open all day (till 6pm Sun). *(Max Simons,
Nick Higgins)*

MAIDENHEAD   SU8582
Pinkneys Arms (01628) 630268
Lee Lane, just off A308 N; SL6 6NU
Updated dining pub with good food from
weekly changing menu (can be pricey),
pizzas only Mon and Tues, well kept ales
(mainly Rebellion) and decent wines,
friendly efficient service; outside gents', barn
function room; children and dogs welcome,
big garden, closed Mon lunchtime, otherwise
open all day from midday. *(Nick Higgins)*

MARSH BENHAM   SU4267
Red House (01635) 582017
Off A4 W of Newbury; RG20 8LY
Attractive thatched dining pub with good
imaginative food from french chef-owner, also
lunchtime sandwiches and pub favourites,
fish and chips Thurs, friendly efficient
service, well kept West Berkshire ales and
a guest, lots of wines by the glass, afternoon
teas, roomy bar with wood or flagstone floors,
logburner, separate restaurant, good cheerful
service; background music, monthly quiz;
children and dogs welcome, terrace and
long lawns sloping to River Kennet water
meadows, open (and food) all day. *(David
and Judy Robison, Ian Herdman)*

NEWBURY   SU4766
Catherine Wheel (01635) 569897
Cheap Street; RG14 5DB Popular
Tudor-style pub with mullioned windows,
crenellations and a carriage entrance;
simple furniture on bare boards or stone
tiles, white-painted beams and grey panelled
dados, central fireplace, five well kept ales
along with good selection of craft beers
and real ciders, plenty more in bottles/
cans, also decent wines and good value food
with emphasis on Pieminister pies, friendly
helpful staff; children and dogs welcome,
seats and separate gin bar in back courtyard,
open (and food) all day, kitchen shuts 6pm Sun.
(Pedro Gregory)

NEWBURY   SU4767
Lock Stock & Barrel (01635) 580550
Northbrook Street; RG14 1AA Modern pub
approached down small alleyway and popular
for its canalside (River Kennet) setting;
low ceiling, light wood or slate flooring
and painted panelling, lots of windows
overlooking canal, varied choice of enjoyable
sensibly priced food all day from sandwiches
up, well kept Fullers/Gales beers, efficient
friendly staff; occasional live music, free wi-fi;
children welcome, outside seating including
suntrap roof terrace looking over a series of
locks towards handsome church, moorings,
open all day (till midnight Fri, Sat).
(Brian and Susan Wylie)

OLD WINDSOR   SU9874
Oxford Blue (01753) 861954
*Crimp Hill Road, off B3021 – itself
off A308/A328; SL4 2QY* Refurbished
19th-c restaurant-pub with highly regarded
upscale food (not cheap) from chef-
proprietor, well kept local ales and good
wines (extensive list), friendly professional
service; children and dogs welcome, well
placed with open country views, terrace
tables, open till 6pm Sun, closed Mon,
Tues. *(Charles Welch)*

PALEY STREET   SU8676

★ Royal Oak (01628) 620541

B3024 W; SL6 3JN Attractively modernised
and extended 17th-c restauranty pub owned
by Sir Michael Parkinson and son Nick;
highly regarded british cooking (not cheap)
and most here to eat, good service, dining
room split by brick pillars and timbering with
mix of well spaced wooden tables and leather
chairs on bare boards or flagstones, smallish
informal beamed bar with woodburner,
leather sofas and cricketing prints, Fullers
London Pride and wide choice of wines by
the glass including champagne; background
jazz; children welcome (no pushchairs in
restaurant), seats outside among troughs of
herbs, closed Sun evening. *(Jamie Green)*

PANGBOURNE   SU6376

Elephant (0118) 984 2244

Church Road; RG8 7AR Handsome inn
with decorative elephants of all sizes in
bars, dining room and seating areas; main
bar has flagstone floor, log fire and antler
chandeliers, leather-backed stools around
counter serving West Berkshire, Sharps,
a couple of real ciders and 16 wines by the
glass, good choice of enjoyable food from
lunchtime sandwiches to steaks cooked on
an open fire, afternoon teas, friendly service;
background music; children and dogs (in
bar) welcome, big back garden with giant
chess set and rattan-style sofas on raised
terrace, individually styled bedrooms,
charging point for electric vehicles, open
all day. *(Susan Eccleston)*

READING   SU7173

Alehouse (0118) 950 8119

Broad Street; RG1 2BH No-frills drinkers'
pub with nine well kept quickly changing
ales, craft kegs, lots of different bottled beers
and real ciders/perries; small bare-boards bar
with raised seating area, hundreds of pump
clips on walls and ceiling, corridor to several
appealing panelled rooms, some little more
than alcoves, no food; open all day.
(Monty Green)

READING   SU7273

Fishermans Cottage (0118) 956 0432

*Kennet Side – easiest to walk from Orts
Road, off Kings Road; RG1 3HJ* White-
painted pub tucked away in housing estate
by canalised River Kennet; good food
including tapas and paella, four interesting
changing ales along with various craft beers,
friendly service, modern interior with airy
conservatory; twice-monthly quiz and live
music; children and dogs (at manager's
discretion) welcome, picnic-sets out by
towpath, beach hut-style booths on back
deck, open all day, kitchen closes 7pm Sun
and all Mon. *(Tony Hobden)*

READING   SU7073

Nags Head 07765 880137

Russell Street; RG1 7XD Fairly basic
mock-Tudor drinkers' pub just outside town
centre attracting good mix of customers;
a dozen well kept changing beers and 14
ciders, baguettes and pies (roasts on Sun),
open fire, darts and cribbage; background
and occasional live music, TV for major sports
(busy on Reading FC match days); suntrap
beer garden, open all day. *(Monty Green)*

READING   SU7173

★ Sweeney & Todd (0118) 958 6466

Castle Street; RG1 7RD Pie shop with
popular bar-restaurant behind (little
changed in over 30 years); warren of private
period-feel alcoves and other areas on
various levels, enjoyable home-made food
including their range of good value pies,
cheery service, small bar with four well
kept ales such as Adnams and Hook Norton,
Weston's cider and decent wines; children
welcome in restaurant area, closed Sun
evening and bank holidays, otherwise open
(and food) all day. *(John Pritchard)*

SHINFIELD   SU7368

Black Boy (0118) 988 3116

Shinfield Road (A327); RG2 9BP
Barons group pub well placed for the M4;
contemporary beamed interior with bow-
windowed front bar and spreading back
restaurant, painted half-panelling, some
high tables and lots of booth seating, modern
artwork and a couple of gas woodburners,
three real ales including Greene King and
good range of wines/gins, popular food from
baguettes and sharing plates through burgers
and pub favourites up, friendly helpful staff;
background music; children welcome, no
dogs inside, back terrace with own bar and
various covered seating areas, open all day.
(Darren and Jane Staniforth)

SHINFIELD   SU7367

★ Magpie & Parrot (0118) 988 4130

*2.6 miles from M4 junction 11, via
B3270; A327 just SE of Shinfield on
Arborfield Road; RG2 9EA* Unusual
homely little roadside cottage with two cosy
spic and span bars, warm fire and lots of
bric-a-brac (miniature and historic bottles,
stuffed birds, dozens of model cars, veteran
AA badges and automotive instruments),
Fullers London Pride and a local guest from
small corner counter, weekday lunchtime
snacks and evening fish and chips (Thurs,
Fri); hospitable landlady; no credit cards or
mobile phones; pub dogs (others welcome),
seats on back terrace and marquee on
immaculate lawn, open 12-7.30pm (later once
a month when live jazz), closed Sun evening,
Mon. *(Charles Welch)*

You can send reports directly to us at feedback@goodguides.com

SHURLOCK ROW   SU8374
★**Shurlock Inn**   (0118) 934 9094
Just off B3018 SE of Twyford; The Street;
RG10 0PS Refurbished and extended
17th-c village dining pub (part of the tiny
Rarebreed group – see Plough at Cobham,
Surrey); popular food from bar snacks and
sharing plates up including signature steaks,
well kept ales such as Sharps, Rebellion and
local Stardust, nice wines, interesting gin
range and cocktails, friendly engaging staff,
log fire in double-sided fireplace, restaurant
with open-view kitchen; background music;
children and dogs (in bar) welcome, black
metal furniture on terrace, lawned garden
with picnic-sets and fenced play area, open
(and food) all day, kitchen closes 6.30pm
Sun. *(Penny and David Shepherd)*

SULHAMSTEAD   SU6269
Spring   (0118) 930 3440
Bath Road (A4); RG7 5HP Barn
conversion with spacious bar and balustraded
upstairs dining area under the rafters; good
variety of popular food from interesting
sandwiches up, three real ales including
West Berkshire and nice range of wines by
the glass, friendly efficient staff; children
and dogs (in bar) welcome, plenty of seats
outside, open all day. *(Max Simons)*

SUNNINGHILL   SU9568
Belvedere Arms   (01344) 870931
London Road; SL5 7SB Refurbished
dining pub on edge of Virginia Water and
Windsor Great Park; wide choice of good
interesting food including Weds evening set
menu and weekend brunch, ales such as
Fullers and Sharps, friendly helpful service;
children and dogs welcome, nice outside
seating area with stream, open (and food)
all day. *(Ian Phillips)*

SUNNINGHILL   SU9367
Carpenters Arms   (01344) 622763
Upper Village Road; SL5 7AQ Restauranty
village pub run by french team; good
authentic french country cooking, not
cheap but they do offer a reasonably priced
set lunch (Mon-Sat), nice wines including
house pichets and well kept Sharps Doom
Bar; no children in the evening, terrace
tables, open all day, food all day Sun, booking
recommended. *(John Hunter Wright)*

SUNNINGHILL   SU9367
Dog & Partridge   (01344) 623204
Upper Village Road; SL5 7AQ Bright
contemporary décor and emphasis on
good freshly made food from lunchtime
sandwiches up including some vegan
choices, friendly helpful staff, three real
ales and a good range of wines; background
music; children and dogs welcome, disabled
facilities, part covered courtyard garden with
central fountain, closed Mon, otherwise open
all day, food till 6pm Sun. *(Miles Green)*

THEALE   SU6471
Fox & Hounds   (0118) 930 2295
2 miles from M4 junction 12; follow A4
W, then first left signed for station, over
two roundabouts, then over narrow canal
bridge to Sheffield Bottom; RG7 4BE
Large Wadworths pub with enjoyable
reasonably priced food (not Sun evening)
from baguettes to specials, five well kept
ales, Weston's cider, decent wines and coffee,
friendly efficient service, L-shaped bar with
dividers, traditional mix of furniture on
carpet or bare boards including area with
modern sofas and low tables, two open fires;
pool and darts, Sun quiz; children and dogs
welcome, outside seating at front and sides,
lakeside bird reserve opposite, open all day
Fri-Sun. *(John Pritchard)*

THREE MILE CROSS   SU7167
Swan   (0118) 988 3674
A33 just S of M4 junction 11; Basingstoke
Road; RG7 1AT Smallish traditional pub
built in the 17th c and later a posting house;
four well kept ales including Loddon and
Timothy Taylors, enjoyable fairly standard
home-made food at reasonable prices, friendly
efficient staff, two beamed and panelled bars,
inglenook with hanging black pots, old prints
and some impressive stuffed fish; large well
arranged outside seating area behind, near
Madejski Stadium and very busy on match
days, closed Sun evening, otherwise open
all day. *(John Pritchard)*

WALTHAM ST LAWRENCE   SU8376
★**Bell**   (0118) 934 1788
B3024 E of Twyford; The Street;
RG10 0JJ Welcoming 14th-c village local
with well preserved timbered interior; good
home-made food marked on blackboard from
bar snacks up, cheerful attentive service, five
well kept mainly local beers including Loddon,
up to eight real ciders and plenty of wines by
the glass, also good choice of whiskies; two
compact connecting rooms, another larger
one off entrance hall, warming log fires, daily
newspapers; children and dogs welcome,
pretty back garden with terrace and shady
trees, open all day weekends, no evening food
Sun-Tues. *(Simon Collett-Jones)*

WARGRAVE   SU7878
Bull   (0118) 940 3120
Off A321 Henley–Twyford; High Street;
RG10 8DE Low-beamed 15th-c brick
coaching inn run well by hospitable landlady;
five smallish interconnected rooms, main
bar with inglenook log fire, two dining areas
(one up steps for families), good traditional
home-made food from baguettes up, three
well kept ales including Brakspears Bitter,
friendly attentive staff; background music,
free wi-fi; well behaved dogs welcome, walled
garden behind, four bedrooms, open all day
weekends, no evening food Sun. *(Simon
Collett-Jones)*

WEST ILSLEY

SU4782

Harrow (01635) 281260

Signed off A34 at E Ilsley slip road; RG20 7AR Appealing and welcoming family-run country pub in peaceful spot overlooking cricket pitch and pond; Victorian prints in deep-coloured knocked-through bar, some antique furnishings, log fire, good choice of enjoyable sensibly priced home-made food (not Sun or Mon evenings), well kept Greene King ales and nice selection of wines by the glass, afternoon teas; children in eating areas, dogs allowed in bar, big garden with picnic-sets, more seats on pleasant terrace, handy for Ridgeway walkers, closed Mon lunchtime and maybe early Sun evening if quiet. *(M and GR)*

WHITE WALTHAM

SU8477

★ **Beehive** (01628) 822877

Waltham Road (B3024 W of Maidenhead); SL6 3SH Attractive red-brick village pub popular for landlord-chef's highly regarded food including more affordable bar menu; several comfortably spacious areas with leather chairs around sturdy tables, neat bar has cheerful scatter cushions on built-in wall seats and captain's chairs, Rebellion IPA, Sharps Doom Bar and Timothy Taylors Landlord, 20 wines by the glass, good friendly service, airy restaurant with folding doors on to front terrace overlooking cricket field; children and dogs (in bar) welcome, disabled access/loos, plenty of tables in bigger back garden, open all day Sat, till 6pm Sun. *(Dr and Mrs A K Clarke, DHV, Cecily and Steven Evans)*

WINDSOR

SU9676

Carpenters Arms (01753) 863739

Market Street; SL4 1PB Popular Nicholsons pub rambling around central servery; good choice of well kept ales and several wines by the glass, reasonably priced pubby food from sandwiches up including range of pies, sturdy pub furnishings and Victorian-style décor with two pretty fireplaces, family areas up a few steps, also downstairs beside former tunnel entrance with suits of armour; background music, sports TV; no dogs, tables out on cobbled pedestrian alley opposite castle, no nearby parking, handy for Legoland bus stop, open (and food) all day. *(Penny and David Shepherd)*

WINDSOR

SU9676

Two Brewers (01753) 855426

Park Street; SL4 1LB In shadow of Windsor Castle with three cosy unchanging rooms around central servery, well kept ales such as Fullers London Pride, St Austell Tribute and Sharps Doom Bar, good choice of wines by the glass and enjoyable freshly made food from shortish mid-priced menu (tapas Fri and Sat evenings), friendly service, thriving old-fashioned pub atmosphere, beams, bare boards and open fire, enamel signs, posters and old photographs; background music, daily papers; no children inside, dogs welcome, tables and attractive hanging baskets out by pretty Georgian street next to Windsor Great Park's Long Walk, open all day, kitchen closes 7pm Sun. *(Tony Scott)*

WINDSOR

SU9576

Vansittart Arms (01753) 865988

Vansittart Road; SL4 5DD Friendly three-room Victorian local with cosy corners and open fires, well kept Fullers/Gales beers, big helpings of enjoyable good value home-made food (all day weekends); background music, sports TV, pool, free wi-fi; children and dogs welcome, part-covered beer garden, open all day. *(Nick Higgins)*

WOODSIDE

SU9270

Rose & Crown (01344) 882051

Woodside Road, Winkfield, off A332 Ascot–Windsor; SL4 2DP Attractively updated dining pub; beamed bar with wood flooring and logburner, other areas set for their enjoyable food from sandwiches and pub favourites up including deals and good Sun roasts, attentive friendly service, three well kept ales such as Greene King and Timothy Taylors, lots of wines by the glass; background music; children and dogs (in bar) welcome, tables out at front and in side garden, smallish car park (parking in lane can be tricky), open (and food) all day. *(Simon Collett-Jones)*

WRAYSBURY

TQ0174

George (01784) 482000

Windsor Road (B376); TW19 5DE Beamed dining pub with good fairly priced food from lunchtime sandwiches up (special diets catered for), three real ales and plenty of wines by the glass, friendly helpful service, mix of wooden farmhouse-style furniture on bare boards, wall lanterns and painted half-panelling, armchairs by open fire; background music; children and dogs welcome, decked terrace with modern rattan tables and chairs, open all day, food all day Sun. *(Maggie Lay)*

WRAYSBURY

TQ0074

Perseverance (01784) 482375

High Street; TW19 5DB Welcoming old community village pub ('the Percy'); enjoyable good value home-made food from sandwiches up including weekday set lunch and Weds steak night, well kept Otter Ale and three guests, real cider, decent choice of wines by the glass and interesting selection of gins, friendly helpful staff, beams and log fires (one in inglenook); Thurs quiz, live music Sun afternoon (also twice-monthly open mike night), darts; children till 9pm and dogs welcome, nice back garden with weekend pizza oven, open all day (till 8pm Sun), food all day Sat. *(George Sanderson)*

Buckinghamshire

KEY  ★ Star Pub   📷 Top Quality Food   ☕ Great Beer
   🍷 Good Wines   £ Bargain Meals   🛏 Good Bedrooms   🍴 Serves Food

---

 ADSTOCK   SP7330   Map 4
Old Thatched Inn 📷 🍷 ☕
(01296) 712584 – www.theoldthatchedinn.co.uk
Main Street, off A413; MK18 2JN

Well run dining pub with keen landlord, friendly staff, five real ales and good food

With consistently high standards, this is a pretty thatched place that our readers enjoy very much. The small front bar area has low beams, sofas on flagstones, high bar chairs and an open fire. A dining area leads off with more beams and a mix of pale wooden dining chairs around miscellaneous tables on a stripped wooden floor; background music. Butcombe Bitter, Fullers London Pride, Hook Norton Hooky and Jennings Cumberland on handpump served by the enthusiastic landlord, plus 15 wines by the glass, a dozen malt whiskies and 50 gins; background music. A modern conservatory restaurant at the back has well spaced tables on bare boards, and the sheltered terrace has plenty of tables and chairs under a gazebo. This is an attractive village surrounded by rolling farmland. Disabled access.

📷 Interesting, up-to-date food includes sandwiches, rosemary and garlic-studded baked camembert with home-made chutney, prawn cocktail, potato gnocchi with creamed mushrooms, spinach and peas, cumberland sausage ring with braised red cabbage, cumberland sauce and red wine gravy, sea bream fillet with curried root vegetables, lentils and crispy potatoes, confit leg of duck with oriental noodles, pak choi, spring roll and hoisin sauce, and puddings such as poached pear with vanilla sponge and chocolate sauce. *Benchmark main dish: stuffed braised pork belly with chargrilled cabbage, apple fondant and cider jus £16.50. Two-course evening meal £23.00.*

Free house ~ Licensee Andrew Judge ~ Real ale ~ Open 12-11; 12-10 Sun ~ Bar food 12-2.30, 5-9; 12-8 Sun ~ Restaurant ~ Children welcome ~ Dogs allowed in bar ~ Wi-fi
Recommended by Sophie Ellison, Paul Faraday, Graham and Carol Parker, Jess and George Cowley, Tim and Sarah Smythe-Brown, Penny and David Shepherd

---

 AYLESBURY   SP8113   Map 4
Kings Head ☕
(01296) 718812 – www.kingsheadaylesbury.co.uk
Kings Head Passage (off Bourbon Street), also entrance off Temple Street; no nearby parking except for disabled; HP20 2RW

Fine old town centre pub with civilised atmosphere, good local ales and friendly service

Hidden away behind the shops and offices in a modern town centre, it's quite a surprise to come across a rather special 15th-c building, part of which is a pub and owned by the National Trust; the rest is the tourist information office, an oak-panelled dining room and conference rooms. The Farmers Bar is three timeless rooms that have been restored with careful and unpretentious simplicity: stripped boards, cream walls with minimal decoration, gentle lighting and a variety of seating which includes upholstered sofas and armchairs, cushioned high-backed settles and some simple modern pale dining tables and chairs dotted around. Most of the bar tables are of circular glass, supported on low cask tops. The neat corner counter has Chiltern Pale Ale, Beechwood Bitter, Marble Earl Grey IPA and a couple of guest beers on handpump, 11 wines by the glass, two farm ciders and some interesting bottled beers. Service is friendly and there's no background music or machines. The atmospheric medieval cobbled courtyard (said to be the oldest in England) has teak seats and tables, some beneath a pillared roof; summer barbecues and live events. Disabled access and facilities.

¶❙ Well liked food includes lunchtime sandwiches and baguettes, breaded whitebait with marie rose sauce, sharing platters, curried dhal and coriander burger with coleslaw and chips, sausages of the week with bubble and squeak mash and gravy, lemon and garlic chicken with sautéed potatoes, bacon and savoy cabbage and onions and mushrooms in cream, lamb rump with grain potatoes and red wine and rosemary sauce, and puddings. *Benchmark main dish: beer-battered fish and chips £11.25. Two-course evening meal £18.00.*

Chiltern ~ Manager George Jenkinson ~ Real ale ~ Open 11-11; 12-10.30 Sun ~ Bar food 11.30-3, 5-9 (not Mon or Tues evenings); 11.30-9 Fri, Sat; 12-6 Sun ~ Restaurant ~ Children welcome away from bar ~ Wi-fi *Recommended by Graham and Carol Parker, Robin and Anne Triggs, David and Charlotte Green, James and Sylvia Hewitt*

BEACONSFIELD
White Horse ▿ ☕

SU9490 Map 2

(01494) 360000 – www.brunningandprice.co.uk/whitehorse
London End; HP9 2JD

Bustling town pub with a wide choice of interesting drinks, rewarding food and attractive furnishings

Set in the middle of town, this substantial place usefully opens at 10.30am when they offer teas, hot chocolate and a good selection of coffees. During service time, helpful, friendly staff serve St Austell Brunning & Price Traditional Bitter plus Mad Squirrel Hopfest, Rebellion Roasted Nuts, Redemption Big Chief, Sambrooks Powerhouse Porter and Tring Side Pocket for a Toad on handpump, 20 wines by the glass, 100 gins, 20 brandies and 50 malt whiskies. Life revolves around the bar, and this area and the interlinked dining rooms offer plenty of room for both those wanting just a drink and a chat and others after the fine range of food. There are long, wall banquettes, leather dining and wooden chairs and chesterfield sofas and armchairs on polished boards, rugs or tiles. Horse prints, pictures and photographs line bare brick or painted walls, house plants of varying size are dotted about and shelves of books abound, while open fires and woodburning stoves keep things cosy in winter; board games. A favourite spot is the conservatory towards the back with its skylight and mass of tropical plants interspersed with pretty wicker light fixtures. There are a few tables outside at the front.

¶❙ Good, bistro-style food includes sandwiches, charred mackerel with celeriac remoulade, cucumber and apple, fried pigeon with parsnip purée, kale and game jus, butternut squash tortellini with sunblush tomato dressing, crispy beef salad with sweet chilli sauce, massaman fish and seafood curry with coconut rice, peanuts and sesame pak choi, chicken, leek and ham pie, lamb rump with roasted salsify, jerusalem artichokes and mushroom ketchup, and puddings such as triple chocolate brownie with chocolate sauce and vanilla ice-cream and crème brûlée. *Benchmark main dish: beef bourguignon with horseradish mash £15.25. Two-course evening meal £23.00.*

Brunning & Price ~ Manager Rachel Perry ~ Real ale ~ Open 10.30am-11pm ~ Bar food 12-10; 12-9 Sun ~ Children welcome (but not in the bar after 5pm) ~ Dogs allowed in bar ~ Wi-fi *Recommended by Lionel Smith, David Travis, Beth Aldridge, Ben and Diane Bowie*

BOVINGDON GREEN
SU8386 Map 2

Royal Oak ⭐ 🍷

(01628) 488611 – www.royaloakmarlow.co.uk

0.75 miles N of Marlow, on back road to Frieth signposted off West Street (A4155) in centre; SL7 2JF

Buckinghamshire Dining Pub of the Year

Civilised dining pub with nice little bar, a fine choice of wines by the glass, real ales and imaginative food

Even when really pushed, the staff here remain helpful and impressively efficient. You'll find a fine choice of drinks such as Rebellion IPA on handpump alongside a guest such as Rebellion Roasted Nuts, 33 wines by the glass (including sparkling wine, champagne and pudding wines), 41 gins and 15 malt whiskies – though most customers are here for the excellent food. The low-beamed, cosy snug, closest to the car park, has three small tables and a woodburning stove in an exposed brick fireplace (with a big pile of logs beside it). Several other attractively decorated areas open off the central bar with half-panelled walls variously painted in pale blue, green or cream (the dining room ones are red). Throughout there's a mix of church chairs, stripped wooden tables and chunky wall seats, with rugs on the partly wooden, partly flagstoned floors, co-ordinated cushions and curtains, and a bright, airy feel. Thoughtful extra touches enhance the tone: a bowl of olives on the bar, carefully laid-out newspapers and fresh flowers or candles on the tables. Background music. A sunny terrace with good solid tables leads to an appealing garden with pétanque, ping pong, badminton and swing ball; there's also a smaller side garden and a kitchen herb garden. They have a tipi for private events.

🍴⭐ Delicious modern food includes cuttlefish and octopus stew with smoked paprika and herb crust, goats cheese pannacotta with roast beetroot and parsley dressing, moroccan-style vegetable tagine with tabbouleh and mint yoghurt, local rabbit, cider and bacon pot roast with butternut squash and crispy black pudding croquette, shrimp burger with chilli tartare sauce and sweet potato fries, slow-roast free-range pork belly with shallot mash, buttered kale and local quince compote, and puddings such as milk and white chocolate brownie with sea salt caramel ice-cream and treacle sponge pudding with brown bread ice-cream. *Benchmark main dish: bubble and squeak with oak-smoked bacon, free-range poached egg and hollandaise sauce £13.75. Two-course evening meal £22.00.*

Salisbury Pubs ~ Manager James Molier ~ Real ale ~ Open 11am-midnight; 11-11 Sun ~ Bar food 12-2.30, 6-9.30; 12-3, 6-10 Fri, Sat; 12-9 Sun ~ Restaurant ~ Children welcome ~ Dogs allowed in bar ~ Wi-fi *Recommended by Bramley, Sally and David Champion, Edward and William Johnston, Elizabeth and Peter May*

The star-on-a-plate award, ⭐, distinguishes pubs where the food is of exceptional quality. The knife-and-fork symbol just means the pub serves food.

BRILL
SP6514   Map 4

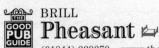

Pheasant 🛏
(01844) 239370 – www.thepheasant.co.uk
Windmill Street; off B4011 Bicester–Long Crendon; HP18 9TG

Long-reaching views, a bustling bar with local ales, attentive staff and tasty food; bedrooms

In warm weather try to bag one of the seats on the decked area or in the garden. The views over the windmill opposite (one of the oldest post windmills still in working order) and into the distance across five counties are wonderful. The interior is more or less open-plan, with a raftered bar area, leather tub seats in front of a woodburner, and a good mix of customers – including chatty, friendly regulars. Fullers London Pride, Timothy Taylors Landlord and Vale Brill Gold on handpump and a dozen wines by the glass are served by charming, attentive staff. Dining areas have high-backed leather or dark wooden chairs, attractively framed prints and books on shelves; background music. Bedrooms are comfortable and two are in the former bakehouse; good nearby walks. Roald Dahl used to drink here, and some of the tales the locals told him were worked into his short stories.

Food is good and includes chicken liver and port parfait with cranberry relish, duo of salmon mousse with caper and beetroot salad, beef and Guinness sausages with mash, onion rings and jus, steak burger with toppings and french fries, vegetable pasta with pesto sauce, prawn curry with rice and poppadums, and puddings such as dark and white chocolate torte with cherry compote and fruit crumble with crème anglaise. *Benchmark main dish: fillet steak with fries and trimmings £19.00. Two-course evening meal £25.00.*

Free house ~ Licensee Marilyn Glover ~ Real ale ~ Open 12-11 (midnight Fri, Sat); 12-10 Sun ~ Bar food 12-2.30, 6-9; 12-5 Sun ~ Children welcome ~ Dogs allowed in bar ~ Wi-fi ~ Bedrooms: $90/$120 *Recommended by John Evans, Neil and Angela Huxter, Gerry and Rosemary Dobson, Graham and Carol Parker, David James, Rupert and Sandy Newton, Thomas Green, Alf and Sally Garner*

BUTLERS CROSS
SP8407   Map 4

Russell Arms 🖈⭐ 🍷 🍺
(01296) 624411 – www.therussellarms.co.uk
Off A4010 S of Aylesbury, at Nash Lee roundabout; or off A413 in Wendover, passing station; Chalkshire Road; HP17 0TS

Brick and flint former coaching inn with good food, local ales, friendly staff and seats on sunny terrace

This is an attractive old pub in a quiet village with access to the Chiltern hills. The simply furnished bar has stools and chairs around polished tables on new pale floorboards, tartan curtains, fresh flowers, an open fire with logs piled high to both sides and a woodburning stove in an inglenook fireplace; there's also a contemporary restaurant area. Well kept Chiltern Beechwood Bitter, Rebellion IPA and Teignworthy Gun Dog on handpump, 11 wines by the glass and artisan gins, all served by welcoming staff; background music and board games. French windows lead to a suntrap terrace with teak furniture and there are steps up to the garden with picnic-sets. This was the servants' quarters for nearby Chequers, the prime minister's country retreat. This is sister pub to the Eight Bells in Long Crendon and Black Boy in Oving.

Using local, seasonal produce the rewarding food includes baked camembert with caramelised onion marmalade, smoked salmon and crème fraîche mousse, pizzas, butternut squash and walnut wellington with roasted mediterranean vegetables and roast tomato sauce, chicken and chorizo pasta with creamy tomato and chilli sauce, thai-style marinated sea bass with stir-fried vegetables, steak, mushroom and Guinness pie, pork chop with bubble and squeak, sautéed cabbage and cider jus, and puddings such as coconut and clotted cream rice pudding with pineapple compote and strawberry cheesecake. *Benchmark main dish: beef or chicken burger with toppings, slaw and skinny fries £14.00. Two-course evening meal £23.00.*

Free house ~ Licensee Paul Mitchell ~ Real ale ~ Open 12-11; 12-6 Sun; closed Mon ~ Bar food 12-9; 12-4 Sun ~ Children welcome ~ Dogs allowed in bar ~ Wi-fi *Recommended by Simon and Sue Lamb, Sally and Brian Turner, Chloe and Tim Hodge, Harvey Brown, Miles Green, Richard Kennell*

FORTY GREEN

SU9291 Map 2

Royal Standard of England

(01494) 673382 – www.rsoe.co.uk

3.5 miles from M40 junction 2, via A40 to Beaconsfield, then follow signs to Forty Green, off B474 0.75 miles N of New Beaconsfield; keep going through village; HP9 1XT

Full of history and character, with fascinating antiques in rambling rooms, and good choice of drinks and food

Trading for nearly 900 years (do read the leaflet documenting its long history), this is an appealing place and the rambling rooms have some fine old features to look out for: huge black ship's timbers, lovely worn floors, carved oak panelling, roaring winter fires with handsomely decorated iron firebacks and cluttered mantelpieces. There's also a massive settle apparently built to fit the curved transom of an Elizabethan ship. Nooks and crannies are filled with a collection of antiques, including rifles, powder-flasks and bugles, ancient pewter and pottery tankards, lots of tarnished brass and copper, needlework samplers and richly coloured stained glass. Belhaven 80/- Ale, Chiltern Pale Ale, Rebellion IPA and Windsor & Eton Conqueror and Guardsman on handpump, a carefully annotated list of bottled beers, 11 malt whiskies, seven gins, farm ciders, perry, somerset brandy and 19 wines by the glass. You can sit outside in a neatly hedged front rose garden or under the shade of a tree; look out for the red gargoyle on the wall facing the car park. The inn is used regularly for filming television programmes such as *Midsomer Murders*.

Traditional, hearty food includes lunchtime baguettes, moules marinière, garlic and rosemary-studded baked camembert, butternut squash and bean burger with pickles and chips, steak and kidney suet pudding, fish pie, liver and bacon with mash and onion gravy, pork belly with bubble and squeak and apple sauce, and puddings such as sticky toffee pudding with caramel sauce and chocolate mousse. *Benchmark main dish: beer-battered fish and chips £14.75. Two-course evening meal £20.00.*

Free house ~ Licensee Matthew O'Keeffe ~ Real ale ~ Open 11-11 ~ Bar food 12-9.30 ~ Children welcome ~ Dogs welcome ~ Wi-fi *Recommended by Selwyn Jones, Mrs Edna Jones, Roy Hoing, Rob Anderson, Mike Swan, Charles Welch, Caroline Sullivan*

FULMER

SU9985   Map 2

Black Horse 🌟◎ ♀

(01753) 663183 – www.theblackhorsefulmer.co.uk

Village signposted off A40 in Gerrards Cross, W of junction with A413; Windmill Road; SL3 6HD

Appealingly reworked dining pub, friendly and relaxed, with up-to-date food, exemplary service and pleasant garden; bedrooms

Usefully open all day, this is an extended 17th-c pub in a charming conservation village. There's a proper bar in the middle and two cosy areas to the left: low black beams, rugs on bare boards, settles and other solid pub furniture and several open log fires. Greene King IPA, Timothy Taylors Landlord and a guest such as St Austell Tribute on handpump, 21 wines by the glass and 22 malt whiskies; staff are friendly and efficient even when pushed. Background music, TV. The main area on the right is set for dining and leads to the good-sized suntrap back terrace where there's a summer barbecue bar. The two bedrooms are stylish and well equipped. The church is next door.

 Some sort of good quality food is served all day from breakfast onwards: crispy squid with sweet chilli mayonnaise, confit pork belly with apple and kohlrabi slaw and apple sauce, sharing boards, wild mushroom risotto with truffle oil, smoky barbecue ribs with coleslaw and skinny fries, smoked haddock fishcake with a poached egg, crispy bacon and hollandaise, chicken korma, confit duck leg with balsamic and bacon lentils, fondant potato and orange jus, and puddings such as passion-fruit crème brûlée and steamed date pudding with banana caramel sauce and vanilla ice-cream. *Benchmark main dish: beer-battered haddock and chips £14.75. Two-course evening meal £20.50.*

Greene King ~ Real ale ~ Open 8.30am-11pm; 12-11 Sun ~ Bar food 8.30am-9.30pm (10pm Sat); 12-7 Sun ~ Restaurant ~ Children welcome ~ Dogs allowed in bar ~ Wi-fi ~ Bedrooms: /£140 *Recommended by R K Phillips, Ian Phillips, Anne and Ben Smith, Andrew and Michele Revell, Luke Morgan, Julian Thorpe*

GRANBOROUGH

SP7625   Map 4

Crown ♀

(01296) 670216 – www.thecrowngranborough.co.uk

Winslow Road; MK18 3NJ

Perfect in good weather with several seating areas and an outside bar, and cosy in winter with open fires

This is an extended former coaching inn with plenty of space for both eating and drinking. The main bar is a long room with painted beams, high chairs at the counter and at elbow tables and a fire at one end; a second bar has leather tub chairs, more painted beams and a comfortable feel. Fullers London Pride, Hook Norton Hooky, Sharps Doom Bar and Vale Brill Gold on handpump, 12 wines by the glass and 50 gins, served by friendly staff. The restaurant is a lovely room with high ceilings and oak beams, farmhouse and other chairs around solid tables on wooden boards and a woodburning stove in a sizeable fireplace; a smaller room is more intimate and similarly furnished; background music. In warm weather you can sit on cushioned rattan-style sofas on the terrace, at wooden tables and chairs under parasols on gravel or at picnic-sets on grass (where there's also a climbing frame); summer barbecues.

Good food uses local, seasonal produce and includes grilled sandwiches, mussels in white wine and cream, black pudding scotch egg with mustard mayonnaise, pea, mint and feta risotto, beer-battered fish and triple-cooked chips, chicken breast with mushroom and bacon tagliatelle and parmesan, slow-cooked beef in red wine sauce with gnocchi, and puddings such as bread and butter pudding with toffee banana ice-cream and chocolate pot with salted caramel base and mandarin jelly; steak night is Tuesday (from 5pm) and they offer Saturday brunch (10.30am-2pm). *Benchmark main dish: slow-cooked duck leg with bubble and squeak £13.95. Two-course evening meal £20.00.*

Free house ~ Licensee Andy Judge ~ Real ale ~ Open 12-11 (5-9 Mon); 12-8 Sun; closed Mon lunchtime ~ Bar food 12-2, 5-9; 10.30-2.30, 5-9 Sat; 12-6 Sun ~ Restaurant ~ Children welcome ~ Dogs allowed in bar ~ Wi-fi *Recommended by Mandy and Gary Redstone, Mick Allen, Graham and Carol Parker, Sally and Lance Oldham, Val and Malcolm Travers*

GREAT MISSENDEN
SP9000 Map 4

Nags Head ★◎⌐

(01494) 862200 – www.nagsheadbucks.com

Old London Road, E – beyond Abbey; HP16 0DG

Well run and pretty inn with beamed bars, an open fire, a good range of drinks and modern cooking; bedrooms

Built as three small cottages in the 15th c, this is a gently civilised pub with creative food. There's a low-beamed area on the left, a loftier part on the right, a mix of small pews, dining chairs and tables on carpet, Quentin Blake prints on cream walls and a log fire in a handsome fireplace. Rebellion IPA and a couple of guests such as Chiltern Beechwood Bitter and Malt Missenden Pale Ale on handpump from the unusual bar counter (the windows behind face the road), 25 wines by the glass from an extensive list, 15 malt whiskies, 20 gins and half a dozen vintage Armagnacs. As well as an outside dining area beneath a pergola, there are seats on the extensive back lawn. Beamed bedrooms are well equipped and comfortable, and the breakfasts are very good. Roald Dahl used this as his local and the Roald Dahl Museum & Story Centre is just a stroll away.

Impressive food includes pork hock wrapped in seaweed leaf with a fried quail egg, piccalilli cream and toast, mushroom feuilletée (puff pastry top) with mushrooms in a calvados cream and julienned vegetables, venison and mushroom pie in red wine jus, crab thermidor with skinny fries, lamb roasted with pine needles, pulled shoulder and pea purée, turkey supreme wrapped in bacon with chestnut jus and barley stuffing parcel, and puddings such as bourbon vanilla crème brûlée and apple and rhubarb tart. *Benchmark main dish: seafood and haddock in saffron cream pie with mozzarella mash topping £17.95. Two-course evening meal £23.50.*

Free house ~ Licensee Adam Michaels ~ Real ale ~ Open 12-11 ~ Bar food 12-2.30, 6.30-9.30; 12-7 Sun ~ Restaurant ~ Children welcome ~ Dogs allowed in bar ~ Wi-fi ~ Bedrooms: £90/£95 *Recommended by Gerry and Rosemary Dobson, Nicola and Holly Lyons, Charlie Stevens, Mark and Sian Edwards, Tom and Lorna Harding*

HEDGERLEY
SU9687 Map 2

White Horse ★ ◀ £

(01753) 643225 – www.thewhitehorsehedgerley.co.uk

2.4 miles from M40 junction 2; at exit roundabout take Slough turn-off following alongside M40; after 1.5 miles turn right at T junction into Village Lane; SL2 3UY

Charming old place with lots of beers, home-made lunchtime food and a cheery mix of customers

You'd never believe that this convivial country gem was so close to suburbia as it feels a world away. The cottagey main bar has plenty of unspoilt character with beams, brasses and exposed brickwork, low wooden tables, standing timbers, jugs, ballcocks and other bric-a-brac, a log fire and a good few leaflets and notices about village events. A little flagstoned public bar on the left has darts, shove-ha'penny and board games. The fine range of real ales might include Rebellion IPA and up to seven daily changing guests, sourced from all over the country and tapped straight from casks kept in a room behind the tiny hatch counter. Their regular bank holiday beer festivals (they can get through about 130 beers at one festival) are highlights of the local calendar. Also, craft ales in kegs or bottles, three farm ciders, 12 wines by the glass, a dozen malt whiskies and winter mulled wine. A canopied extension leads out to the garden where there are tables, lots of hanging baskets and occasional barbecues; a few tables in front of the building overlook the quiet road; disabled access. Good walks nearby and the pub is handy for the Church Wood RSPB reserve.

Lunchtime-only bar food includes good sandwiches, a salad bar with home-cooked quiches and cold meats, changing hot dishes such as soup, sausage or lamb casserole, and proper puddings such as plum sponge and bread and butter pudding. *Benchmark main dish: steak pie £7.95.*

Free house ~ Licensee Kevin Brooker ~ Real ale ~ Open 11-2.30, 5-11; 11-11 Sat; 12-10.30 Sun ~ Bar food 12-2 (2.30 weekends) ~ Children allowed in canopied extension area ~ Dogs allowed in bar ~ Wi-fi *Recommended by Rod Wilson, V Brogden, Roy Hoing, Bob and Melissa Wyatt, Neil Allen, Mike Benton, Professor James Burke*

LITTLE MARLOW   SU8787   Map 2
Queens Head ⭐

(01628) 482927 – www.marlowslittlesecret.co.uk

Village signposted off A4155 E of Marlow near Kings Head; bear right into Pound Lane cul-de-sac; SL7 3SR

Pretty tiled cottage with good food and ales, friendly staff and appealing garden

'A hidden treasure' is how one of our readers describes this charmingly tucked-away country pub. The friendly, unpretentious main bar has simple but comfortable furniture on polished boards and leads back to a sizeable squarish carpeted dining extension with good solid tables. Throughout are old local photographs on cream or maroon walls, panelled dados painted brown or sage, and lighted candles. On the right is a small, quite separate, low-ceilinged public bar with Rebellion IPA and Sharps Doom Bar on handpump, several wines by the glass, quite a range of whiskies and good coffee; neatly dressed efficient staff and unobtrusive background music. On summer days, the front garden (though not large) is a decided plus: sheltered and neatly planted, it has teak tables and quite closely arranged picnic-sets, and white-painted metal furniture in a little wickerwork bower.

Highly rated food includes sandwiches and ciabattas, duck livers with onion jam, seared scallops with honey-roast pork, celeriac and apple, cauliflower steak with halloumi, olives, sautéed potatoes and spiced yoghurt dressing, sea bass fillet with confit fennel and brown shrimp butter, shoulder and rump of lamb with onions, butternut squash and jus, chargrilled rib-eye steak with béarnaise sauce, and puddings such as chocolate fondant with Cointreau ice-cream and lemon tart with raspberry and gin sorbet. *Benchmark main dish: beer-battered haddock and chips £13.00. Two-course evening meal £20.00.*

Punch ~ Lease Daniel O'Sullivan ~ Real ale ~ Open 11-11 ~ Bar food 12-2.30, 6.30-9.30; 12-4, 6.30-9.30 weekends ~ Restaurant ~ Children welcome ~ Dogs allowed in bar ~ Wi-fi
Recommended by Simon Collett-Jones, Alexander and Trish Cutter, Dave Braisted, Martin and Sue Neville, Glen and Patricia Fuller, Alison and Dan Richardson

 LITTLE MISSENDEN   SU9298   Map 4

Crown 🍺 £

(01494) 862571 – www.thecrownlittlemissenden.co.uk
Crown Lane, SE end of village, which is signposted off A413 W of Amersham; HP7 0RD

Long-serving licensees and pubby feel in little country cottage, with several real ales and straightforward food; attractive garden

Coming here is special. It's a traditional brick cottage that's been run by the same lovely family for more than 90 years and they and their loyal bunch of regulars make all visitors feel warmly welcomed. The bustling bars are more spacious than they might first appear – and immaculately kept. There are old red floor tiles on the left, oak parquet on the right, built-in wall seats, studded red leatherette chairs and a few small tables and a winter fire. Otter Bitter and St Austell Tribute with a couple of quickly changing guests on handpump or tapped from the cask, ten farm ciders, summer Pimms, 22 gins and several malt whiskies; darts and board games. A large attractive sheltered garden behind has picnic-sets and other tables, and there are also seats out in front. Bedrooms are in a converted barn (continental breakfasts in your room only). Dogs may be allowed inside if well behaved. No children. The interesting church in the pretty village is well worth a visit.

🍴 Honest lunchtime-only food (not Sunday) includes their famous bucks bite, a big choice of sandwiches with home-made chutney, cornish pasty with baked beans, generous salads and smoked haddock and spring onion or cod and bacon fishcakes with a sweet chilli dip. *Benchmark main dish: pie of the day £9.95.*

Free house ~ Licensees Trevor and Carolyn How ~ Real ale ~ Open 11-2.30, 6-11; 12-4, 7-10.30 Sun ~ Bar food 12-2; not Sun ~ Wi-fi ~ Bedrooms: /£85   *Recommended by Peter and Emma Kelly, Caroline and Oliver Sterling, William and Sophia Renton, Len and Lilly Dowson, Peter and Caroline Waites, Jeff Davies, Tracey and Stephen Groves*

 LONG CRENDON   SP6908   Map 4

Eight Bells 🍺

(01844) 208244 – www.8bellspub.com
High Street, off B4011 N of Thame; car park entrance off Chearsley Road, not 'Village roads only'; HP18 9AL

Good beers and sensibly priced seasonal food in nicely traditional village pub with charming garden

In 1771, this old place got its present name when the church installed three more bells. The little bare-boards bar on the left has Rebellion IPA, XT Four and a guest beer on handpump, 19 wines by the glass, 14 gins and summer cider; service is cheerful. A bigger low-ceilinged room on the right has a log fire, daily papers and a pleasantly haphazard mix of tables and simple seats on ancient red and black tiles; one snug little hidey-hole is devoted to the local morris men who are frequent visitors. Board games, TV (for national sport only) and background music. The small back garden is a joy in summer when there are well spaced picnic-sets among a colourful variety of shrubs and flowers; aunt sally. The interesting old village is known to many from TV's *Midsomer Murders*. Sister pub is the Russell Arms in Butlers Cross and Black Boy in Oving.

🍴 Tasty food includes ciabattas, lots of tapas-style small dishes, pizzas (to take away as well), spiced five-bean and red pepper burger with toppings, sauces and fries, barbecue-glazed baby back ribs with coleslaw and skinny fries, smoked haddock with bubble and squeak, wilted spinach, poached free-range egg and mustard sauce, beef and mushroom stroganoff, confit duck leg with smoky chorizo lentils, and puddings such as chocolate brownie with chocolate sauce and vanilla ice-cream and orange pannacotta with blood orange compote. *Benchmark main dish: beer-battered fish and chips £14.00. Two-course evening meal £22.00.*

Free house ~ Licensee Paul Mitchell ~ Real ale ~ Open 12-11; 12-8 Sun ~ Bar food 12-9; 12-4 Sun ~ Restaurant ~ Children welcome ~ Dogs welcome ~ Wi-fi *Recommended by Gerry and Rosemary Dobson, David Lamb, Peter and Emma Kelly, Brian and Sally Wakeham, Rona Mackinlay*

OVING   SP7821   Map 4

Black Boy

(01296) 641258 – www.theblackboyoving.co.uk

Off A413 N of Aylesbury; HP22 4HN

Village pub with friendly owners, well liked food, local ales and lovely views from spacious garden

Close to the village church, this 16th-c brick and timbered pub is a popular place for both food and drink. The dining rooms and a bar are linked by brick arches with beams, log fires (one in a huge inglenook), wooden chairs around tables of all sizes on bare boards or original black and red tiles, sofas and settles with scatter cushions, books on shelves and various prints and photos on pale walls. Helpful staff serve Chiltern Beechwood Bitter, Rebellion IPA and XT Four on handpump, 11 wines by the glass, farm cider and 12 gins with lots of mixers. Seats and tables on spacious sloping lawns and a raised terrace behind the pub have expansive views of the Vale of Aylesbury; not surprisingly, it's best to arrive early on a sunny day. Sister pubs are the Russell Arms in Butlers Cross and the Eight Bells in Long Crendon.

🍴 Pleasing food includes toasted paninis, lots of little tapas plates, scotch egg with mustard dressing, smoked mackerel fishcake with horseradish cream, pizzas (to take away too), bang bang chicken stir-fry with oriental egg noodles, salmon supreme with potato gratin, sun-dried tomato and caper cream sauce, confit duck leg with parmentier potatoes, red cabbage and blackberry jus, beef and mushroom stroganoff, and puddings such as chocolate brownie with chocolate sauce and crumble of the day. *Benchmark main dish: beer-battered fish and chips £14.00. Two-course evening meal £22.00.*

Free house ~ Licensee Paul Mitchell ~ Real ale ~ Open 12-11; 12-6 Sun; closed Sun evening ~ Bar food 12-9; 12-4 Sun ~ Restaurant ~ Children welcome ~ Dogs welcome ~ Wi-fi *Recommended by Miles Green, Chloe and Tim Hodge, Martine and Fabio Lockley, Peter Pilbeam*

SEER GREEN   SU9691   Map 2

Jolly Cricketers

(01494) 676308 – www.thejollycricketers.co.uk

Chalfont Road, opposite the church; HP9 2YG

Bustling and friendly village pub with cricketing paraphernalia, a thoughtful choice of drinks, enjoyable food and seats on a back terrace

Opposite the village church, this is a welcoming place with a good mix of chatty customers. The two rooms of the parquet-floored bar are divided by a big chimney, with a woodburning stove in each, nice cushioned seats in bow windows, a mix of pale farmhouse and antique dining chairs around wooden and painted tables, candles and fresh flowers, and plenty of old cricketing photos, prints and bats on the walls. The stools at the bar are well used by locals, and friendly, helpful staff serve Rebellion IPA and Vale VPA plus three guests on handpump (they hold regular beer festivals), 16 good wines by the glass, 20 malt whiskies and home-made sloe gin and blackberry vodka; big glass jars of nuts and dried fruit behind the bar, board games, TV and background music. The separate restaurant is similarly furnished and has a tiny cushioned settle, teddy bears in cricket gear, a basket of cricket bats and a chandelier over the table by the window. There's a handsome wisteria at the front and picnic-sets on a back terrace.

Highly regarded food includes devilled potted crab with pickled cucumber, ham, leek and parsley terrine with wholegrain mustard mayonnaise, celeriac and hazelnut risotto with spinach oil, prawn and mussel linguine with chicken, chilli and garlic butter, steak and kidney in Guinness pie, pork belly with black pudding, coriander and potato cake, apple sauce and yuzu, and puddings such as plum and hazelnut crumble with vanilla bean ice-cream and Valrhona chocolate brownie with pistachio ice-cream. *Benchmark main dish: beer-battered fish and chips £16.75. Two-course evening meal £24.00.*

Free house ~ Licensees Amanda and Chris Lillitou ~ Real ale ~ Open 12 (9am Fri)-11.30; 12-midnight Sat; 12-10.30 Sun ~ Bar food 12-2.30, 6.30-9; all day Sat; 12-6 Sun ~ Restaurant ~ Live music last Sun of month from 4.30pm ~ Dogs allowed in bar ~ Wi-fi *Recommended by Maggie and Matthew Lyons, Andy and Louise Ramwell, Pauline and Mark Evans*

SKIRMETT

Frog 🌟 ♈ 🛏

SU7790 Map 2

(01491) 638996 ~ www.thefrogatskirmett.co.uk
From A4155 NE of Henley take Hambleden turn and keep on; or from B482 Stokenchurch–Marlow take Turville turn and keep on; RG9 6TG

Bustling pub with modern cooking, a fine choice of drinks, lovely garden, and nearby walks; bedrooms

In charming Chilterns countryside, this pretty pub is an enjoyable place to stay in comfortable bedrooms with valley views. The public bar is very much the heart of the place, with a winter log fire in the brick fireplace, lots of little framed prints, a cushioned sofa and leather-seated bar stools around a low circular table on the wooden floor, and high bar chairs by the counter; background music. Five Points Pale, Rebellion IPA and a changing guest beer on handpump, 14 wines by the glass (including champagne) and a good choice of malt whiskies; service is friendly and attentive. The two dining rooms are quite different in style – one is light and airy with country kitchen tables and chairs, while the other is more formal with dark red walls, smarter dining chairs and tables and candlelight. Outside, a side gate leads to a lovely garden with a large tree in the middle and unusual five-sided tables that are well placed for attractive valley views. Plenty of nearby hikes (Henley is close by) and the delightful Ibstone windmill is just down the road.

Rewarding food includes lunchtime baguettes, sharing boards, eggs benedict with parma ham, king prawns in tempura batter with chilli jam and sweet chilli noodles, squash stuffed with wild mushrooms, spinach, feta cheese and pumpkin seeds, chicken breast with asparagus, portobello mushrooms, dauphinoise potatoes and rosemary sauce, smoked haddock on colcannon with a poached egg and grain mustard sauce, duck breast with pak choi, rösti potato and orange and Grand Marnier kumquat sauce, and puddings. *Benchmark main dish: liver and bacon with black pudding, colcannon and red wine jus £17.50. Two-course evening meal £22.50.*

Free house ~ Licensees Jim Crowe and Noelle Greene ~ Real ale ~ Open 11.30-3, 6-11; 12-4, 6-10.30 Sun; closed Sun evening Oct-May ~ Bar food 12-2.30, 6.30-9.30; 12-5 winter Sun ~ Restaurant ~ Children welcome ~ Dogs allowed in bar ~ Wi-fi ~ Bedrooms: /£90
Recommended by Richard Kennell, John and Abigail Prescott, Max Simons, Charles and Maddie Bishop, Ted and Mary Bates

Also Worth a Visit in Buckinghamshire

Besides the fully inspected pubs, you might like to try these pubs that have been recommended to us and described by readers. Do tell us what you think of them: feedback@goodguides.com

AMERSHAM SU9597
Elephant & Castle (01494) 721049
High Street; HP7 0DT Twin-gabled local with good value tasty food including sharing plates, stone-baked pizzas and burgers, quick friendly service, three well kept ales such as St Austell from U-shaped counter, low-beams, woodburner in large brick fireplace, conservatory; garden behind, children and dogs welcome, open (and food) all day. *(Anne Taylor)*

AMERSHAM SU9597
Kings Arms (01494) 725722
High Street; HP7 0DJ Picture-postcard timbered inn (dates from the 1400s) in charming street, lots of heavy beams and snug alcoves, big inglenook, Brakspears, Rebellion and a guest, over a dozen wines by the glass and good range of enjoyable food from sandwiches up, afternoon teas, friendly helpful service, restaurant; background music, collection of board games; children and dogs (in bar) welcome, 34 bedrooms, garden behind, open all day, food all day weekends. *(Simon Collett-Jones)*

ASHERIDGE SP9404
Blue Ball (01494) 758305
Braziers End; HP5 2UX Popular little tile-hung country pub with opened-up interior; generous helpings of enjoyable good value food cooked to order including daily specials, well kept Adnams, Fullers, Tring and Youngs, real cider, friendly landlady and staff; children (till 6pm) and dogs welcome, large well maintained back garden, good Chilterns walking country, open all day, no evening food Sun or Mon. *(Brian Smith, Mrs P Sumner, Roy Hoing, David Lamb)*

ASTON ABBOTTS SP8519
Royal Oak (01296) 681262
Off A418 NE of Aylesbury; Wingrave Road; HP22 4LT Welcoming part-thatched beamed pub, up to four real ales and generous helpings of enjoyable reasonably priced food; children welcome, sunny back garden, bedrooms, quite handy for Ascott House (NT). *(David Lamb)*

ASTON CLINTON SP8712
Oak (01296) 630466
Green End Street; HP22 5EU Cosy and attractive part-thatched village pub; well kept Fullers ales and a guest, enjoyable food from snacks up including signature hanging kebabs, friendly attentive service, beams and inglenook log fire; sports TV, free wi-fi; children and dogs welcome, picnic-sets in good-sized garden, open (and food) all day. *(David Lamb)*

ASTWOOD SP9547
Old Swan (01234) 391351
Main Road; MK16 9JS Part thatched 17th-c village pub with warm cosy atmosphere, good food including steaks from the family's butchers, blackboard specials and weekday set menu, well kept Adnams Southwold, Fullers London Pride and Woodfordes Wherry, nice selection of wines, friendly helpful service, beams and gleaming flagstones, inglenook woodburner, separate dining area; children and dogs (in bar) welcome, large garden, closed Sun evening, Mon. *(S Holder, Alan Morris)*

AYLESBURY SP8114
Hop Pole (01296) 482129
Bicester Road; HP19 9AZ Friendly well looked after end of terrace pub brewing its own Aylesbury Brewhouse beers, also guests and traditional cider, enjoyable fairly priced food including sharing plates and grills, back restaurant; regular live music, Tues quiz; seats out at front behind metal fence, open all day Fri-Sun, closed Mon lunchtime. *(Val and Malcolm Travers)*

BEACHAMPTON SP7736
Bell (01908) 418373
Main Street; MK19 6DX Big low-beamed pub with pleasant view down attractive streamside village street; updated bar and

dining area divided by woodburner, popular food including weekday offers, up to four changing ales, good friendly service; children welcome, large garden with paved terrace, open all day (till 8pm Sun). *(Amanda Shipley)*

BEACONSFIELD SU9588
Hope & Champion (01494) 685530
M40, Beaconsfield Services; HP9 2SE
UK's first pub (Wetherspoons) in a motorway service area; spacious modern interior on two floors, five real ales including Sharps Doom Bar and enjoyable food from breakfast on, good fast service; TVs, free wi-fi; children welcome, no dogs inside, disabled access to ground floor only, seats out overlooking lake with fountain, open (and food) all day from 6am. *(William Slade)*

BEACONSFIELD SU9490
Royal Saracens (01494) 674119
1 mile from M40 junction 2; London End (A40); HP9 2JH Former coaching inn with striking timbered façade and well updated open-plan interior; bar area with comfortable seating on wood or tiled floors, massive beams and timbers in one corner, log fires, wide choice of enjoyable food from sandwiches and sharing plates up, well kept ales such as Fullers London Pride and Sharps Doom Bar, craft kegs and plenty of wines by the glass, large back restaurant; children welcome, modern furniture and seating booths in sheltered courtyard, open (and food) all day, busy at weekends when best to book. *(William Slade)*

BLEDLOW SP7702
Lions of Bledlow (01844) 343345
Off B4009 Chinnor–Princes Risborough; Church End; HP27 9PE Great views from bay windows of relaxed take-us-as-you-find-us Chilterns pub; low 16th-c beams, ancient floor tiles, inglenook log fires and a woodburner, five well kept beers and enjoyable food including vegetarian dishes, friendly helpful staff; well behaved children and dogs welcome, picnic-sets out in peaceful sloping garden with sheltered terrace, nice setting and good walks, open all day weekends in summer. *(Lenny and Ruth Walters)*

BLEDLOW RIDGE SU7997
Boot (01494) 481499
Chinnor Road; HP14 4AW Welcoming village pub with fresh modern décor; good food from sandwiches, sharing plates and pub favourites up, well kept Rebellion ales and Sharps Doom Bar, several wines by the glass from extensive list, dining room with exposed rafters and large brick fireplace, friendly service; background music; children and dogs welcome, terrace and sizeable lawned garden, closed Mon, otherwise open all day (till 8pm Sun). *(Alfie Bayliss)*

BOURNE END SU8987
Bounty (01628) 520056
Cock Marsh, actually across the river along the Cookham towpath, but shortest walk – still over 0.25 miles – is from Bourne End, over the railway bridge; SL8 5RG Welcoming take-us-as-you-find-us pub tucked away in outstanding setting on bank of the Thames (accessible only by foot or boat); collection of flags on ceiling and jumble of other bits and pieces, well kept Rebellion ales from boat counter, basic pub food including children's meals, back dining area, darts and bar billiards; background music inside and out; dirty dogs and muddy walkers welcome, picnic-sets with parasols on front terrace, play area to right, open all day in summer (may be boat trips), just weekends in winter and closes early if quiet. *(Tony and Wendy Hobden)*

BRILL SP6513
Pointer (01844) 238339
Church Street; HP18 9RT Carefully restored red-brick pub under newish owners; stylish bar with low beams, windsor chairs, elegant armchairs and sofas, open fires or woodburners in brick fireplaces, a beer named for the pub (brewed by XT), Vale Gravitas and a guest from Rebellion, 11 wines by the glass, a dozen gins and 28 malt whiskies, food can be very good (and pricey), attractive restaurant with open kitchen and high raftered ceiling, french windows to sizeable garden; children and dogs (in bar) welcome, four bedrooms in separate cottage, pretty village (Tolkien based Bree in *The Lord of the Rings* on it), open all day from 8am. *(David James, Jess and George Cowley, David Longhurst)*

BUCKINGHAM SP6933
Villiers (01280) 822444
Castle Street; MK18 1BS Pub part of this large comfortable hotel with own courtyard entrance; big inglenook log fire, panelling and stripped masonry in flagstoned bar, beers from Hook Norton and Black Sheep, reliably good food from shortish menu, afternoon tea, competent friendly staff, sofas and armchairs in more formal front lounges, restaurant with two large tropical fish tanks; background music; children welcome till 9pm, no dogs, terrace tables, open all day. *(Edward Edmonton)*

CHALFONT ST GILES SU9895
Ivy House (01494) 872184
A413 S; HP8 4RS Old brick and flint coaching inn with U-shaped bar, wood or tiled floors, log fire, Fullers ales and a guest

---

If we know a pub has an outdoor play area for children, we mention it.

back beamed and flagstoned restaurant serving tasty home-made food, friendly staff; background and occasional live music, Thurs quiz, free wi-fi; children welcome, some seats out under covered front part by road, pleasant terrace and sloping garden, five comfortable bedrooms, good hearty breakfast, open all day (till 7pm Sun). *(Charles Todd)*

CHEARSLEY   SP7110
Bell (01844) 208077

The Green; HP18 0DJ Cosy traditional thatched and beamed pub on attractive village green; Fullers beers and good wines by the glass, sensibly priced food (not Sun or Mon evenings) from pubby choices up, friendly helpful service, inglenook with big woodburner; quiz (first Sun of month), bingo (first Tues); children in eating area, dogs welcome, plenty of tables in spacious back garden with heated terrace and play area, open all day weekends. *(Karen Osterley)*

CHESHAM   SP9604
Black Horse (01494) 784656

Vale Road, N off A416 in Chesham; HP5 3NS Extended and refurbished black-beamed country pub; well liked traditional food (all day Sat, till 8pm Sun) from sandwiches up, real ales including Bombardier, Courage Directors and Eagle IPA, craft beers and 15 wines by the glass, good friendly service, inglenook log fire; Tues quiz; children and dogs welcome, picnic-sets out in front and on back lawn, closed Mon, otherwise open all day (till 9pm Sun). *(Anne Taylor)*

CHESHAM   SP9501
Queens Head (01494) 778690

Church Street; HP5 1JD Popular corner pub with two traditional beamed bars; scrubbed tables and log fires, Fullers ales and a guest kept well, good thai food along with modest range of pub staples, restaurant, friendly staff and chatty locals; Thurs quiz, sports TV, free wi-fi; children and dogs welcome, tables in small courtyard used by smokers, next to little River Chess, open all day. *(David Allsopp)*

CLIFTON REYNES   SP9051
Robin Hood (01234) 711574

Off back road Emberton–Newton Blossomville; no through road; MK46 5DR Community-owned 16th-c stone-built village pub; well liked food, three real ales and decent wines, good friendly service, dark beams, woodburner in small lounge's inglenook, dining conservatory; bar billiards and darts; children and dogs (in bar) welcome, back garden with terrace and summer barbecues, riverside walks to Olney, closed Mon. *(Nigel Cowdery, Philip Randell)*

COLESHILL   SU9594
★**Harte & Magpies** (01494) 726754

E of village on A355 Amersham–Beaconsfield, by junction with Magpie

Lane; HP7 0LU Busy roadside pub with open-plan interior; collection of pews, high-backed booths and distinctive tables and chairs making for plenty of snug corners, candles in bottles and lots of old patriotic prints, ales such as Chiltern and Rebellion, several wines by the glass and good food from baguettes and pizzas up; children (not live music evenings) and dogs welcome, picnic-sets on terrace by wisteria-draped tree, more tables in big sloping garden with sturdy wooden play area, classic car meeting second Tues of month (Apr-Sept), good surrounding walks, open (and food) all day, Sun till 8pm. *(Edward Edmonton)*

COLNBROOK   TQ0277
Ostrich (01753) 682628

1.25 miles from M4 junction 5 via A4/B3378, then 'village only' road; High Street; SL3 0JZ Historic timbered inn (12th-c origins) with gruesome history – tales of over 60 murders; refurbished interior blending modern furnishings with oak beams and open fireplaces, three Shepherd Neame ales and good choice of wines, enjoyable sensibly priced food from sandwiches and pub favourites up, friendly service, restaurant; children welcome, 11 bedrooms, teak furniture in courtyard, open (and food) all day including breakfast/brunch for non-residents. *(Robin and Ann Triggs)*

CUDDINGTON   SP7311
★**Crown** (01844) 292222

Spurt Street; off A418 Thame–Aylesbury; HP18 0BB Refurbished 17th-c thatched cottage (sister to the Cross Keys at Great Missenden); two low-beamed linked rooms with big inglenook log fire, well kept Fullers and guests and enjoyable fairly priced food from burgers up (special diets catered for), efficient friendly service, two-room back dining area with country kitchen chairs around mix of tables; children and dogs (in bar) welcome; neat side terrace with modern furniture and planters, picnic-sets in front, open all day Fri-Sun, no food Sun evening. *(Paul Humphreys)*

DENHAM   TQ0487
Green Man (01895) 832760

Village Road; next to the Swan; UB9 5BH Welcoming 18th-c red-brick pub in centre of this lovely village; modernised beamed bar with flagstones and log fire, five well kept ales including Rebellion and Sharps, good choice of popular food from baguettes up, cheerful efficient service, conservatory dining extension; free wi-fi; children and well behaved dogs welcome, pretty hanging baskets out at front, sunny back terrace and garden, open all day. *(William Slade)*

DENHAM   TQ0487
★**Swan** (01895) 832085

Village signed from M25 junction 16; UB9 5BH Wisteria-clad Georgian dining pub

(Little Gems group); stylishly furnished bars with nice mix of antique and old-fashioned chairs at solid tables, heavily draped curtains, log fires, Rebellion IPA and a guest, good sensibly priced wine list and decent range of spirits, well liked food (all day Fri-Sun) including blackboard specials and Sat brunch from 9.30am, friendly staff; background music, daily papers, free wi-fi; children and dogs (in bar) welcome, extensive floodlit back garden with sheltered terrace, open all day. *(David and Charlotte Green)*

DINTON   SP7610
Seven Stars   (01296) 749000
Signed off A418 Aylesbury–Thame, near Gibraltar turn-off; Stars Lane; HP17 8UL Pretty 16th-c community-owned pub run by french landlady and popular locally; inglenook bar, beamed lounge and dining room, well kept Fullers, Rebellion and Vale, extensive wine list on two blackboards, consistently good fairly priced food cooked to order from pub staples up (some french influences), friendly service; children welcome, no dogs inside, tables in sheltered garden with terrace, pleasant village, closed Sun evening. *(David Lamb, Graham and Carol Parker, Richard Kennell)*

DORNEY   SU9279
Palmer Arms   (01628) 666612
2.7 miles from M4 junction 7, via B3026; Village Road; SL4 6QW Modernised and extended dining pub in attractive conservation village, good popular food (best to book) from snacks and pub favourites to more restauranty dishes, friendly efficient service, Greene King ales kept well, lots of wines by the glass (interesting list) and good coffee, open fires in civilised front bar and back dining room; background music, daily newspapers; children and dogs (in certain areas) welcome, disabled facilities, terrace overlooking mediterranean-feel garden, enclosed play area, nice riverside walks nearby, open (and food) all day. *(Minda and Stanley Alexander, I D Barnett)*

DORNEY   SU9279
Pineapple   (01628) 662353
Lake End Road: 2.4 miles from M4 junction 7; left on A4 then left on B3026; SL4 6QS Nicely old-fashioned pub handy for Dorney Court (where the first english pineapple was grown in 1661); shiny low Anaglypta ceilings, black-panelled dados, leather chairs around sturdy country tables (one very long, another in big bow window), woodburner and pretty little fireplace, china pineapples and other decorations on shelves in one of three cottagey carpeted linked rooms on left, Fullers London Pride, Sharps Atlantic and a guest, huge variety of signature sandwiches, roasts on Sun; background music, open mike night last Weds of month, games machine; children and dogs welcome, rustic seats on roadside verandah,

round picnic-sets in garden, fairy-lit decking under oak tree, open (and food) all day. *(Alfie Bayliss)*

EASINGTON   SP6810
★Mole & Chicken   (01844) 208387
From B4011 in Long Crendon follow Chearsley, Waddesdon signpost into Carters Lane opposite indian restaurant, then turn left into Chilton Road; HP18 9EY Creeper-clad dining pub with opened-up beamed interior; cream-cushioned farmhouse chairs around oak and pine tables on flagstones or tiles, a couple of dark leather sofas, church candles and good winter log fires, Chiltern ales, several wines by the glass and quite a few malt whiskies from slabby-topped counter; interesting modern food along with more affordable pubby dishes and set menu, good service; background music, free wi-fi; children welcome, no dogs inside, seats on raised terrace and decked area with fine views, simply but elegantly furnished bedrooms, open all day from 7.30am (8am weekends). *(Graham and Carol Parker)*

EMBERTON   SP8849
Bell & Bear   (01234) 711565
Off A509 Olney–Newport Pagnell; High Street; MK46 5DH Old stone-built village pub with good interesting food cooked by landlord-chef including set lunch and tapas-style bar menu (Weds-Sat), four well kept changing ales, craft beers, real cider and good selection of other drinks, friendly efficient staff, bar with log fire and hood skittles, restaurant; well behaved children welcome, muddy boots and dogs in bar, garden tables, open all day Fri-Sun, closed Mon lunchtime, no food Sun evening to Tues lunchtime. *(Donald Allsopp)*

FINGEST   SU7791
★Chequers   (01491) 638335
Off B482 Marlow–Stokenchurch; RG9 6QD Ancient white-shuttered brick and flint pub with unspoilt public bar plus other neatly kept old-fashioned rooms with large open fires, horsebrasses, pewter tankards and pub team photographs, beers from Brakspears and Jennings, traditional cider, decent wines by the glass and several malt whiskies, enjoyable country cooking, smart back dining extension; board games, free wi-fi; children and dogs welcome, tables on terrace and in big beautifully tended garden with fine views over the Hambleden Valley, good walking country and opposite interesting church with unique twin-roofed Norman tower, open all day weekends, closed Mon. *(Amanda Shipley)*

FLACKWELL HEATH   SU8889
Crooked Billet   (01628) 521216
Off A404; Sheepridge Lane; SL7 3SG Steps up to cosily old-fashioned 16th-c pub;

Brakspears and Youngs ales, reasonably priced traditional lunchtime food including sandwiches, charming landlord and friendly staff, eating area spread pleasantly through alcoves, low black beams and good open fire; lovely cottagey garden with nice views (beyond road), walks nearby. *(Robin and Ann Triggs)*

FRIETH SU7990
Prince Albert (01494) 881683
Off B482 SW of High Wycombe; RG9 6PY Cottagey Chilterns local with low black beams and joists, high-backed settles, big black stove in inglenook and log fire in larger area on right, decent lunchtime food from sandwiches up (also Fri and Sat evenings – they ask you to book on Sat), well kept Brakspears ales, friendly service; children and dogs welcome, nicely planted informal side garden with views of woods and fields, good walks, open all day. *(Charles Todd)*

FRIETH SU7990
Yew Tree (01494) 882330
Signed off B482 N of Marlow; RG9 6PJ Brick-built village pub with good food including chargrills and daily specials, real ales such as Chiltern, Loddon, Rebellion and West Berkshire, lots of wines by the glass, helpful personable staff, well presented interior with light coloured beams and timbers, wood floors and log fires, attractive back restaurant, conservatory; background music; children, walkers and dogs (in bar) welcome, tables on front terrace and in garden behind, open all day Sat, till 9pm Sun, closed Mon and Tues. *(Christopher Pick)*

GAWCOTT SP6831
Crown (01280) 822322
Hillesden Road; MK18 4JF Welcoming 16th-c black-beamed village pub; popular good value food including notable fish pie, carvery Weds and Sun, three well kept ales such as Sharps Doom Bar from herringbone brick counter, restaurant area; background and some live music, Sky TV, pool; children and dogs welcome, long back garden with swings, open all day (till 9pm Mon, 10pm Tues), no food Sun evening, Mon. *(William Slade)*

GERRARDS CROSS TQ0089
★Three Oaks (01753) 899016
Austenwood Lane, just NW of junction with Kingsway (B416); SL9 8NL Civilised dining pub facing Austenwood Common; two-room front bar with fireside bookshelves, tartan wing armchairs, sturdy wall settles and comfortable banquettes, well kept Fullers, Rebellion and several

wines by the glass, dining part with three linked rooms, popular highly regarded food including short set menu, Mon steak night, attentive friendly young staff; soft background music, free wi-fi; children welcome, sturdy wooden tables on flagstoned side terrace, open all day. *(John Evans)*

GREAT BRICKHILL SP9029
Red Lion (01525) 261715
Ivy Lane; MK17 9AH Refurbished roadside village pub; enjoyable fairly traditional food including lunchtime sandwiches, real ales from Caledonian and Tring and maybe a local guest, good friendly service, log fire in small bar, restaurant with woodburner; background music, quiz Sun evening; children and dogs (in bar) welcome, lovely views over Buckinghamshire and beyond from enclosed back lawn, closed Mon, open all day weekends, no food Sun evening. *(Val and Malcolm Travers)*

GREAT HAMPDEN SP8401
★Hampden Arms (01494) 488255
W of Great Missenden, off A4128; HP16 9RQ Friendly village pub opposite cricket pitch; comfortably furnished rooms (back one more rustic with big woodburner), well kept Rebellion IPA and a couple of guests, local cider and several wines by the glass from small corner bar, enjoyable reasonably priced pubby food including one or two greek dishes, cheerful efficient service; quiz third Weds of month; children and dogs welcome, seats in tree-sheltered garden, good Hampden Common walks, open all day Sun. *(Amanda Shipley)*

GREAT KINGSHILL SU8798
★Red Lion (01494) 711262
A4128 N of High Wycombe; HP15 6EB Welcoming village pub across from cricket green; contemporary décor and relaxed informal atmosphere, well cooked locally sourced brasserie-style food including fixed-price menu, local beers such as Rebellion and good value wine list, 'lobby' and cosy little flagstoned bar with leather tub chairs by log fire, spacious candlelit dining room; well behaved children welcome, a few seats out at front and behind, closed Sun evening, Mon. *(Anne Taylor)*

GREAT MISSENDEN SP8901
★Cross Keys (01494) 865373
High Street; HP16 0AU Friendly and relaxed village pub dating from the 16th c (sister to the Crown at Cuddington); unspoilt beamed bar divided by standing timbers, traditional furnishings including a high-backed settle, log-effect gas fire in huge fireplace, well kept Fullers ales and often

---

Half pints: by law, a pub should not charge more for half a pint than half the price of a full pint, unless it shows that half-pint price on its price list.

an unusual guest, enjoyable fairly priced food (not Sun evening) from burgers up (special diets catered for), cheerful helpful staff, spacious beamed restaurant; free wi-fi; children and dogs welcome, picnic-sets on back terrace, open all day. *(David and Charlotte Green)*

GREAT MISSENDEN SP8901
George (01494) 865185
High Street; HP16 0BG Recently reopened/refreshed 15th-c drinkers' pub; heavily beamed and timbered split-level interior, medley of circular and small square tables on bare boards or quarry tiles, open fires (one in inglenook), four changing ales, craft beers and real ciders; no food or children; regular live music; dogs welcome, open midday-10pm Fri and Sat, till 9pm Sun, 3-9pm Mon-Thurs. *(Tracey and Stephen Groves)*

HAMBLEDEN SU7886
Stag & Huntsman (01491) 571227
Off A4155 Henley-Marlow; RG9 6RP Friendly brick and flint pub in pretty Chilterns village; chatty locals in busy little bar, built-in cushioned wall seats and simple furniture on bare boards, Rebellion IPA, Sharps Doom Bar and a couple of guests, several wines by the glass, sizeable open-plan room with armchairs by woodburner, dining room with good mix of wooden tables and chairs, hunting prints and other pictures on floral wallpaper, popular food from light meals and sharing plates up; background music, free wi-fi, darts; children and dogs welcome (their springer is Griff), country garden and nice walks nearby, comfortable bedrooms, open all day (may close around 9pm Sun if quiet). *(DHV)*

HUGHENDEN VALLEY SU8697
★Harrow (01494) 564105
Warrendene Road, off A4128 N of High Wycombe; HP14 4LX Small cheerful brick and flint roadside cottage surrounded by Chilterns walks (leave muddy boots in porch); traditionally furnished with tiled-floor bar on left, black beams and joists, woodburner in big fireplace, pewter mugs, country pictures and wall seats, similar but bigger right-hand bar with sizeable dining tables on brick floor, carpeted back dining room, tasty good value pub food (all day Mon-Sat, till 6pm Sun) from sandwiches and baked potatoes up, Fullers London Pride, Rebellion IPA and a guest, quick friendly service; Tues quiz; children and dogs welcome, disabled access, picnic-sets out in front, play area, open all day. *(David Lamb)*

HYDE HEATH SU9300
Plough (01494) 774408
Off B485 Great Missenden-Chesham; HP6 5RW Small prettily placed pub with freshened-up bare-boards bar and carpeted dining extension; Fullers London Pride, a

couple of guest beers and Weston's Old Rosie cider, good choice of popular well priced food, efficient service, real fires and cosy friendly atmosphere; picnic-sets on cricket green opposite, open all day Fri-Sun, closed Mon lunchtime, no food Sun evening-Tues. *(David Lamb)*

ICKFORD SP6407
Rising Sun (01844) 339238
E of Thame; Worminghall Road; HP18 9JD Welcoming thatched local with cosy low-beamed bar, Adnams, Black Sheep, Marstons and a weekly guest, enjoyable reasonably priced home-made food including stone-baked pizzas, log fire; Tues quiz; children, walkers and dogs welcome, pleasant garden with picnic-sets and play area, handy for Waterperry Gardens, open all day Fri-Sun, closed lunchtimes Mon and Tues, no food Sun evening, Mon, Tues. *(David Lamb)*

IVINGHOE SP9416
Rose & Crown (01296) 668472
Vicarage Lane, off B489 opposite church; LU7 9EQ Cosy and welcoming 17th-c red-brick pub; good food at sensible prices from sandwiches up, well kept Sharps, Tring and three local guests, friendly efficient service; children and dogs welcome, a couple of tables out at front, sunny beer garden behind, pleasant village, open all day, no food Sun evening, Mon. *(Andrew Hetherington)*

LACEY GREEN SP8200
Black Horse (01844) 345195
Main Road; HP27 0QU Welcoming two-bar beamed village local; popular good value home-made food (not Sun evening, Mon) from baguettes up, breakfast from 9am Tues-Sat, four real ales including Brakspears and nice choice of wines by the glass, quotations written on walls, inglenook woodburner; darts, sports TV, free wi-fi; children and dogs welcome, picnic-sets in garden with play area and aunt sally, open all day Thurs-Sun, closed Mon lunchtime. *(Roy Hoing)*

LACEY GREEN SP8201
Pink & Lily (01494) 489857
A4010 High Wycombe-Princes Risborough, follow Loosley sign, then Great Hampden, Great Missenden sign; HP27 0RJ Friendly updated 18th-c pub in pretty setting; enjoyable food from lunchtime sandwiches and traditional choices up, four changing mainly local ales and several wines by the glass, pubby furniture and open fire in airy main bar, cosier side areas and conservatory-style extension, small tap room with built-in wall benches on red tiles, framed Rupert Brooke poem about the pub (he used to drink here) and broad inglenook, games room; occasional background music, free wi-fi; children, dogs and muddy walkers welcome, big garden with heated deck, futuristic glass pods, play area and barbecue, open all day. *(Roy Hoing)*

LACEY GREEN   SP8100
Whip (01844) 344060
Pink Road; HP27 0PG Hilltop local with mix of simple traditional furnishings in smallish front bar and larger downstairs dining area, popular generously served pubby food including range of home-made pies, six interesting well kept ales (May beer festival with live music), traditional ciders, friendly helpful staff; background music, Tues quiz, sports TV, free wi-fi; children and dogs welcome, tables in charming sheltered garden looking up to windmill, open all day, no food Sun evening. *(Edward Edmonton)*

LEY HILL   SP9901
★ Swan (01494) 783075
Village signposted off A416 in Chesham; HP5 1UT Friendly well looked-after pub – once three 16th-c cottages; character main bar (some steps) with original features including low beams, standing timbers, antique range and inglenook log fire, nice mix of furniture and collection of old local photographs, St Austell Tribute, Timothy Taylors Landlord and Tring Side Pocket for a Toad, several wines by the glass and tasty reasonably priced food, raftered dining section with french windows to terrace and lawn; children welcome till 9pm, pretty summer hanging baskets and tubs, common opposite with cricket pitch and a nine-hole golf course, closed Sun evening, Mon; for sale as we went to press so may be changes. *(Charles Todd)*

LITTLE MARLOW   SU8788
Kings Head (01628) 476718
Church Road; A4155 about 2 miles E of Marlow; SL7 3RZ Welcoming 16th-c brick pub refurbished under new management; low-beamed bar with traditional furnishings and log fire, well kept Rebellion IPA, Wye Valley HPA and a guest from light-blue panelled counter, separate dining room and lofty garden room also set for eating, generous helpings of enjoyable fairly priced food from shortish but varied menu, friendly helpful staff; children and dogs welcome, a few picnic-sets out at front, big walled garden behind with modern terrace furniture, near the Thames and plenty of nice walks, open (and food) all day, kitchen shuts 6pm Sun. *(Anne Taylor)*

LITTLE MISSENDEN   SU9298
Red Lion (01494) 862876
Off A413 Amersham–Great Missenden; HP7 0QZ Unchanging pretty 17th-c cottage with long-serving landlord; small black-beamed bar, plain seats around elm pub tables, piano squashed into big inglenook beside black kitchen range packed with copper pots, kettles and rack of old guns, little country dining room with pheasant décor, well kept Greene King IPA, Skinners Betty Stogs and Tring Side Pocket for a Toad, fair-priced wines, pubby food; live music Sat; children welcome, dogs in bar, picnic-sets out in front and on grass behind wall, back garden with little bridge over River Misbourne, two bedrooms, open all day Fri-Sun. *(Roy Hoing)*

LITTLEWORTH COMMON   SP9386
Blackwood Arms (01753) 645672
3 miles S of M40 junction 2; Common Lane; SL1 8PP Traditional little 19th-c brick pub tucked away in lovely spot on edge of beechwoods (features in the film *My Week with Marilyn*); sturdy mix of furniture on bare boards, roaring log fire, enjoyable home-made food (not Sun evening) from open sandwiches up, well kept Brakspears and guests (regular beer festivals), interesting selection of wines, friendly accommodating staff; free wi-fi; children and dogs welcome, hitching rail for horses, nice garden and good local walks, closed Mon, otherwise open all day (till 7.30pm Sun). *(Lenny and Ruth Walters)*

LITTLEWORTH COMMON   SU9386
Jolly Woodman (01753) 644350
2 miles from M40 junction 2; off A355; SL1 8PF Lived-in red-brick country pub with three well kept changing ales and generous helpings of reasonably priced home-made food from blackboard menu, rambling multi-level beamed and timbered areas including snug, collection of old tools and other bric-a-brac, central woodburner; children and dogs welcome, small front terrace and nice garden, good site by Burnham Beeches, closed Sun evening, Mon (except for monthly jazz nights – see website), otherwise open all day. *(David Lamb, Frank Price, Margaret and Peter Staples)*

LUDGERSHALL   SP6617
Bull & Butcher (01844) 238094
Off A41 Aylesbury–Bicester; bear left to The Green; HP18 9NZ Nicely old-fashioned country pub under friendly management; bar with low beams in ochre ceiling, pews and wheelback chairs on dark tiles or flagstones, inglenook woodburner, Greene King IPA and Old Speckled Hen plus a guest, enjoyable fairly priced pubby food including weekday set menu (lunchtime/early evening), themed nights and popular Sun lunch (booking advised), back dining room; children and dogs welcome, seats out at front overlooking green with play area, circular walks from the door, open (and food) all day Fri and Sat, till 7pm (6pm) Sun, closed Mon and lunchtime Tues. *(David Lamb)*

MAIDS MORETON   SP7035
Wheatsheaf (01280) 822903
Main Street, just off A413 Towcester–Buckingham; MK18 1QR Attractive 17th-c thatched local; traditional low-beamed bar with bare boards and tiled floors, two inglenooks, four well kept ales including

Tring Side Pocket for a Toad, good fairly pubby food (not Sun evening), friendly service, conservatory restaurant; quiz first Sun of month; dogs allowed in bar, seats on front terrace, hatch service for pleasant enclosed back garden, closed Mon, otherwise open all day. *(Jess and George Cowley)*

MARLOW SU8586
Coach
West Street; SL7 2LS Sister dining pub to Tom Kerridge's Hand & Flowers; very well liked food (tapas-style helpings, no bookings) from open kitchen with rotisserie, good helpful service, compact interior with modern décor, bar area serving up to four changing ales and nice wines by the glass (maybe local fizz) from pewter-topped counter; silent TVs; open all day from 8am for breakfast. *(Simon Collett-Jones)*

MARLOW SU8486
★ Hand & Flowers (01628) 482277
West Street (A4155); SL7 2BP Restaurant-pub owned by celebrity chef Tom Kerridge; nice informal atmosphere in three linked beamed rooms all set for eating, high-backed leather-seated chairs and wall seats around chunky tables, bare boards or flagstones, fresh flowers and candles, first class food (not cheap and must book long in advance), professional service, conservatory bar with four real ales including one named for them, lots of wines by the glass from good list and specialist gins; children welcome, comfortable character bedrooms, Thames walks nearby, closed Sun evening. *(Richard Tilbrook, Simon Collett-Jones)*

MARLOW SU8586
Two Brewers (01628) 484140
St Peter Street, first right off Station Road from double roundabout; SL7 1NQ Red-brick 18th-c beamed pub set just back from the river; fairly pubby food from snacks up including good value lunchtime set menu, four well kept Rebellion ales, Fullers London Pride and a dozen wines by the glass, various dining areas including upstairs room and cellar restaurant; free wi-fi; children and dogs welcome, seats outside, open (and food) all day, kitchen closes 5pm Sun. *(Val and Malcolm Travers)*

MARLOW BOTTOM SU8588
Three Horseshoes (01628) 483109
Signed from Handy Cross roundabout, off M40 junction 4; SL7 3RA Much extended former coaching inn under friendly management; well kept Rebellion ales and enjoyable reasonably priced food including pizzas, beams and log fires, comfortable traditional furnishings on different levels; background music; children and dogs (in bar) welcome, sheltered back garden, good walks nearby, open all day, till 6pm Sun. *(Tracey and Stephen Groves, Roy Hoing)*

MARSWORTH SP9114
Red Lion (01296) 668366
Vicarage Road; off B489 Dunstable–Aylesbury; HP23 4LU Partly thatched 17th-c brick pub close to impressive flight of locks on Grand Union Canal; plain public bar on right with quarry tiles, straightforward furniture and small coal fire, Fullers London Pride and good selection of guests, traditional food at reasonable prices, friendly service, raised ceiling area with leather stools and sofas, multi-level lounge to left and games area (bar billiards, darts and juke box); children and dogs welcome, picnic-sets out in front, back terrace with steps up to sizeable garden, more seats and old stocks on village green opposite, open all day weekends. *(Roy Hoing)*

MILTON KEYNES SP8737
Swan (01908) 679489
Newport Road, Woughton on the Green; MK6 3BS Spacious and picturesque timber-framed Chef & Brewer overlooking village green; beamed interior with good log fires and nice nooks and corners, enjoyable food from their usual extensive menu, Greene King ales and good wine choice; children welcome, plenty of seating in large garden, footpaths to nearby lakes, open (and food) all day. *(Graham and Carol Parker)*

MILTON KEYNES SP8939
★ Swan (01908) 665240
Broughton Road, Milton Keynes village; MK10 9AH Attractive thatched pub with interconnecting rooms mixing original features with contemporary furnishings; main beamed and flagstoned bar with plush armchairs by inglenook, high chairs and tables, cushioned banquette and chunky tables, Bombardier, Youngs Bitter and guests, 30 wines by the glass, good popular food including weekday set menu, helpful friendly young staff, spreading restaurant with open kitchen and doors to outside dining area overlooking garden; free wi-fi; well behaved children welcome, dogs in bar, open (and food) all day, breakfast from 9am. *(Jess and George Cowley)*

MOULSOE SP9141
Carrington Arms (01908) 218050
1.25 miles from M1, junction 14: A509 N, first right signed Moulsoe; Cranfield Road; MK16 0HB Restaurant-pub in former Victorian farmhouse with elegant open-plan interior; good choice of well liked food from pub staples up including chargrilled meats sold by weight from refrigerated display, real ales such as Brakspears, over two dozen wines by the glass from extensive list and good range of whiskies and gins; welcoming helpful staff; children allowed, long pretty garden behind with giant chess set, 16 bedrooms in two adjacent blocks, open all day, food all day weekends. *(Mrs J Ekins-Daukes)*

NEWPORT PAGNELL SP8743
Cannon (01908) 211495
High Street; MK16 8AQ Friendly little bay-windowed drinkers' pub serving four well kept reasonably priced ales; carpeted half-panelled interior with interesting military theme, gas woodburner in central fireplace, room behind for live music and comedy nights; Tues quiz, TV, juke box; seats in small backyard, open all day. *(Anne Taylor)*

NEWTON LONGVILLE SP8431
Crooked Billet (01908) 373936
Off A421 S of Milton Keynes; Westbrook End; MK17 0DF Brick and thatch pub under newish management; comfortably modernised beamed interior with inglenook log fires, good food from pub classics up (they add a service charge), a beer badged for the pub along with Greene King Abbot and two guests, nice wines by the glass and decent choice of other drinks, efficient friendly service; quiz first Mon of month; children and dogs (in bar) welcome, disabled access/loo, plenty of tables in grassy garden, open all day, food till 5pm Sun. *(Simon King)*

NORTH MARSTON SP7722
Pilgrim (01296) 670969
High Street; MK18 3PD Welcoming red-brick pub with comfortably modernised interior, beams, bare boards and woodburner, good food from shortish but varied menu cooked by landlord-chef, some themed nights including turkish and indian, well kept Chiltern, XT and a guest beer, Saxby's cider and decent range of wines by the glass, friendly efficient staff; live music (third Tues of month), quiz (last Tues); sloping back garden with country views over rooftops, interesting village church, open all day Sat, till 8pm Sun, closed Mon and lunchtime Tues. *(Tim Buckley)*

OLNEY SP8851
Bull (01234) 711470
Market Place/High Street; MK46 4EA Former 17th-c coaching inn (Apostrophe group) with spacious well renovated interior; Courage Directors, Eagle IPA, Youngs Bitter and a guest from generously stocked bar, decent choice of enjoyable food from sandwiches and deli boards up, sky-lit dining room with open kitchen, friendly young staff; children and dogs welcome, disabled loo (others upstairs), 12 bedrooms, tables in courtyard and big back garden, open all day from 7am (8am weekends) for breakfast. *(Dr J Barrie Jones)*

OLNEY SP8851
★ Swan (01234) 711111
High Street S; MK46 4AA Cosy little pub with beamed and timbered linked rooms; popular good value food from british tapas through pub favourites and burgers to blackboard specials, set menu deal Mon-Thurs, up to six well kept/priced ales and plenty of wines by the glass from good list, friendly attentive service, cheery log fires, small back bistro dining room (booking advised); courtyard tables, open all day (till 7pm Sun). *(Gerry and Rosemary Dobson, Michael Sargent)*

PENN SU9093
Old Queens Head (01494) 813371
Hammersley Lane/Church Road, off B474 between Penn and Tylers Green; HP10 8EY Stylish old pub with open-plan rooms; well spaced tables and comfortably varied seating on flagstones or broad dark boards, stairs up to attractive two-level raftered dining room, enjoyable food (special diets catered for) including Sat brunch from 9.30am, Greene King ales, lots of wines by the glass and good choice of other drinks including 18 gins, log fire in big fireplace; background music, daily papers, free wi-fi; children and dogs (in bar) welcome, sunny terrace overlooking church, picnic-sets on sheltered L-shaped lawn, beechwood walks close by, open all day. *(Edward Edmonton)*

PENN STREET SU9295
★ Hit or Miss (01494) 713109
Off A404 SW of Amersham, keep on towards Winchmore Hill; HP7 0PX Welcoming traditional village pub; heavily beamed main bar with leather sofas and armchairs on parquet flooring, horsebrasses and open fire, two carpeted rooms with interesting cricketing and chair-making memorabilia, more sofas, wheelback and other dining chairs around pine tables, good interesting food (highish prices) including daily specials, Badger ales; background music, free wi-fi; children and dogs (in certain areas) welcome, picnic-sets on terrace overlooking own cricket pitch, parking over the road, open all day. *(Roy Hoing)*

PENN STREET SU9295
Squirrel (01494) 711291
Off A404 SW of Amersham, opposite the Common; HP7 0PX Sister pub to the nearby Hit or Miss; open-plan flagstoned bar with log fire, comfortable sofas and mix of other furniture, reasonably priced home-made pubby food (not Sun evening, Mon) including range of burgers and good children's meals, up to five well kept ales such as Rebellion, Tring, Vale and XT, various craft beers and a proper cider, quick friendly service, bric-a-brac and cricketing memorabilia (village cricket pitch is opposite), sweets in traditional glass jars; live acoustic music Fri, monthly quiz; dogs welcome, covered outside deck with sofas, logburner and own servery, play area in big back garden, lovely walks nearby, closed Mon lunchtime, otherwise open all day. *(David Lamb, Roy Hoing)*

PRESTWOOD   SP8799

Polecat (01494) 412514

170 Wycombe Road (A4128 N of High Wycombe); HP16 0HJ Major refurbishment for this former 17th-c hunting lodge; low-ceilinged bar, rugs and assorted tables and chairs on bare boards or red tiles, various stuffed animals (white polecats in one cabinet), good open fire, five real ales including Malt and Rebellion, 30 wines by the glass and quite a few gins, good food including wood-fired pizzas and Josper grills, new glass-fronted dining extension with open kitchen; children and dogs (in bar) welcome, terrace and attractive big garden, large play area, open all day from 8am for breakfast. *(Roy Hoing)*

PRINCES RISBOROUGH   SP8104

Red Lion (01844) 344476

Whiteleaf, off A4010; OS Sheet 165 map reference 817043; HP27 0LL Traditional 17th-c family-owned pub in charming village; Sharps Doom Bar and a couple of guests decent wines and good gin selection, enjoyable reasonably priced pubby food including popular steaks, flowers on tables, log fires, friendly efficient service; traditional games in snug; children, walkers and dogs welcome, seats out in front and in garden behind, extensive views over to Oxfordshire, four bedrooms, open all day weekends, closed Mon. *(Alfie Bayliss)*

QUAINTON   SP7420

George & Dragon (01296) 655436

The Green; HP22 4AR Traditional flower-decked brick pub by village green; five well kept mainly local ales, Weston's cider and enjoyable reasonably priced food including blackboard specials and bargain OAP lunch Tues, friendly efficient staff, split-level bar, coffee shop/deli, post office facility Weds; quiz and bingo nights, darts; children welcome, tables outside with good view of windmill, handy for Buckinghamshire Railway Centre, open all day Sat, closed Mon. *(David Lamb, Graham and Carol Parker)*

STOKE GOLDINGTON   SP8348

★ Lamb (01908) 551233

High Street (B526 Newport Pagnell– Northampton); MK16 8NR Chatty village pub with friendly helpful licensees, up to five real ales including Tring, proper ciders and good range of wines, generous helpings of enjoyable home-made food (all day Sat, not Sun evening) from baguettes to good value Sun roasts, lounge with log fire and sheep decorations, two small pleasant dining rooms, darts and table skittles in public bar; may be soft background music, TV; children and dogs welcome, terrace and sheltered garden behind with play equipment, bedrooms in adjacent cottage, closed Mon lunchtime, otherwise open all day (till 7pm Sun). *(William Slade)*

THE LEE   SP8904

★ Cock & Rabbit (01494) 837540

Back roads 2.5 miles N of Great Missenden, E of A413; HP16 9LZ Overlooking village green and run by same friendly italian family for over 25 years; much emphasis on their good italian cooking including popular Weds evening pasta deal, Greene King, Sharps and a beer named for the pub, plush-seated lounge, cosy dining room and larger restaurant; children welcome, dogs in bar, seats on verandah, terraces and lawn, good walks, open all day weekends. *(John Evans, Roy Hoing, David Lamb)*

THE LEE   SP8904

★ Old Swan (01494) 837239

Swan Bottom, back road 0.75 miles N of The Lee; HP16 9NU Friendly tucked-away country pub, mainly 16th-c with attractively furnished linked rooms; heavy beams, flagstones and old quarry tiles, high-backed antique settles and window seats, log fire in inglenook cooking range, good reasonably priced food (not Sun evening, Mon) from sensibly short menu, three real ales including Chiltern and Sharps, several wines by the glass; free wi-fi; children and dogs (in bar) welcome, big, spreading back garden with picnic-sets and contemporary seating around rustic tables, play area, good surrounding walks and cycling routes, open all day Fri and Sat, till 7pm Sun, closed Mon lunchtime. *(David Smith)*

TURVILLE   SU7691

★ Bull & Butcher (01491) 638283

Valley road off A4155 Henley–Marlow at Mill End, past Hambleden and Skirmett; RG9 6QU Popular 16th-c black and white pub in pretty village (famous as film and TV location); two traditional low-beamed rooms with inglenooks, wall settles in tiled-floor bar, deep well incorporated into glass-topped table, Brakspears ales kept well and decent wines by the glass, enjoyable good value food cooked by chef-landlord, friendly staff; background music; children and dogs welcome, seats by fruit trees in attractive garden, good walks (Chiltern Way runs through village), open all day weekends and can get very busy. *(Lorna and Jack Mulgrave)*

WADDESDON   SP7316

Long Dog (01296) 651320

High Street; HP18 0JF Renovated village pub with good food from open-view kitchen including lunchtime baps, friendly accommodating service, well kept ales and nice choice of wines by the glass, bar area with log fire; background music, live jazz every other Tues; children and dogs welcome, tables out front and back, very handy for Waddesdon Manor (NT), open all day, food all day weekends. *(David and Charlotte Green)*

WEEDON   SP8118

★ **Five Elms**   (01296) 641439
Stockaway; HP22 4NL   Cottagey thatched
pub with two welcoming little bars; low
beams and log fires, ample helpings of good
fairly priced food cooked by landlord (best
to book), nice wines, interesting range of
gins and a well kept changing ale, cheerful
helpful service, old photographs and prints,
separate compact dining room; games such
as shove-ha'penny; children welcome (no
under-9s in restaurant); dogs in bar, pretty
hanging baskets and a few picnic-sets out in
front, attractive village, closed Sun evening
and lunchtimes Mon, Tues. *(Alfie Bayliss)*

WEST WYCOMBE   SU8394

George & Dragon   (01494) 535340
*High Street; A40 W of High Wycombe;
HP14 3AB*   Rambling hotel bar in preserved
NT Tudor village; massive beams and sloping
walls, big log fire, three well kept Rebellion
ales along with St Austell Tribute, good range
of wines and enjoyable food from shortish
menu, prompt friendly service; children and
dogs (in bar) welcome, tables in nice garden,
ten bedrooms (magnificent oak staircase),
handy for West Wycombe Park (NT) and the
Hell-Fire Caves, open all day, meals 12-6
Sun. *(Dave Braisted)*

WESTON TURVILLE   SP8510

Chequers   (01296) 613298
Church Lane; HP22 5SJ   Comfortably
updated dining pub tucked away in
attractive part of the village; low 16th-c
beams, flagstones and large log fire, very
good up-to-date food from chef-owner in bar
or restaurant including set lunch, friendly
helpful staff, well kept ales such as Rebellion
and Sharps, wide choice of wines by the
glass; children welcome (under-6s after
4pm), dogs allowed away from dining areas,
tables on large front terrace, closed Sun
evening to Tues lunchtime, otherwise open
all day. *(Peter and Alison Steadman)*

WESTON UNDERWOOD   SP8650

Cowpers Oak   (01234) 711382
*Signed off A509 in Olney; High Street;
MK46 5JS*   Wisteria-clad village pub with
enjoyable home-cooked food from bar snacks
up (special diets catered for), Mon burger
and Tues pie nights, some italian dishes
Sat evening, well kept real ales including
Woodfordes Wherry, several wines by the
glass, friendly helpful staff, beams, painted
panelling and some stripped stone, nice mix
of old-fashioned furnishings, two open fires,
restaurant behind; background music, Mon
quiz; children and dogs (in bar) welcome,
small suntrap front terrace, more tables on
back decking and in big orchard garden,
fenced play area, open all day weekends (till
9pm Sun). *(Edward Edmonton)*

WHELPLEY HILL   SP9501

White Hart   (01442) 833367
Off B4505 Bovington–Chesham; HP5 3RL
Cosy recently refurbished village pub; good
home-made food (till 5pm Sun), well kept
interesting beers and good selection of other
drinks, friendly accommodating service, log
fires; background music; children and dogs
welcome, seats out at front and in big back
garden, nice local walks, open all day, can get
crowded at weekends. *(Charles Todd)*

WINCHMORE HILL   SU9394

Plough   (01494) 259757
The Hill; HP7 0PA   Village pub-restaurant
with good italian food from wood-fired pizzas
up (landlord is from Campania); flagstones,
low beams and open fires, linked dining
area with polished wood floor, real ales and
imported lagers, nice coffee, quick friendly
service, little shop selling italian wines and
other produce; children welcome, tables on
terrace and lawn overlooking green, pleasant
walks nearby, open all day. *(David Lamb)*

WINCHMORE HILL   SU9394

Potters Arms   (01494) 726222
Fagnall Lane; HP7 0PH   Welcoming 17th-c
pub close to the village green; ales such as
Brakspears and Ringwood, enjoyable pubby
food (not Sun evening) from sandwiches and
panini up, thai night Sat, good helpful service,
some black beams, leather sofa and armchairs
by inglenook log fire; popular comedy night
last Thurs of month; children welcome, tables
in fenced front garden, four bedrooms, open
all day Sat, till 7pm Sun. *(David Lamb)*

WINSLOW   SP7627

Bell   (01296) 714091
Market Square; MK18 3AB   Fine old
coaching inn, comfortable and atmospheric,
with reasonably priced food including range
of pies in beamed bar and popular carvery
restaurant, Greene King ales, friendly
welcoming staff, snug with historical photos
and log fire; courtyard tables, 39 bedrooms
(some with four-posters), open all day. *(Val
and Malcolm Travers)*

WOOBURN COMMON   SU9187

★ **Chequers**   (01628) 529575
*From A4094 at Bourne End roundabout,
follow for Wooburn, then into Kiln Lane;
OS Sheet 175 map reference 910870;
HP10 0JQ*   Bustling hotel (former 17th-c
coaching inn) with friendly low-beamed main
bar, second bar to the left and light and airy
restaurant; good range of well liked food
from snacks and sharing plates up, Rebellion
ales, a guest beer and a dozen wines by the
glass from good list, fair range of whiskies
and brandies too, afternoon teas; background
music, TV, free wi-fi; children and dogs (in
bar) welcome, spacious garden set away from
the road, 29 comfortable bedrooms, open (and
food) all day. *(Charles Todd)*

Cambridgeshire

KEY ★ Star Pub 🔘 Top Quality Food 🍺 Great Beer

Ψ Good Wines £ Bargain Meals 🛏 Good Bedrooms 🍴 Serves Food

 BALSHAM   TL5850 Map 5

Black Bull 🔘 Ψ 🍺 🛏

(01223) 893844 – www.blackbull-balsham.co.uk

Village signposted off A11 SW of Newmarket, and off A1307 in Linton; High Street;
CB21 4DJ

Pretty thatched pub with bedroom extension – a good all-rounder –
and with well regarded food, too

Set well back from the village road, this is a handsome black and white
timbered building that our readers enjoy very much. The friendly landlord
offers a warm welcome to all. The beamed bar spreads around a central
servery where they keep Adnams Ghost Ship, Crafty Beers Sauvignon
Blonde, Greene King IPA and Woodfordes Wherry on handpump, 22 wines
by the glass from a good list, 15 malt whiskies, draught lager and interesting
juices. Dividers and standing timbers break up the space, which has an
open fire (with leather sofas in front of it), floorboards and low black beams
in the front part; furniture includes small leatherette-seated dining chairs.
A restaurant extension (in a listed barn) has a high-raftered oak-panelled
roof and a network of standing posts and steel ties. The front terrace has
teak tables and chairs by a long, pleasantly old-fashioned verandah and
there are more seats in a small sheltered back garden. Smart, comfortable
bedrooms are in a neat single-storey extension. This pub has the same good
owners as the Red Lion at Hinxton.

🔘 Particularly good food includes sandwiches, pulled ham hock with pea velouté
and home-made piccalilli, breaded whitebait with lemon mayonnaise, sausage
and mash with cabbage and gravy, root vegetable wellington with sautéed sweet
potatoes, pulled lamb shoulder with pea purée, roast garlic mash and minted jus,
smoked haddock with spinach, mustard sauce and a poached egg, duck breast with
orange-glazed chicory and plum sauce, and puddings such as chocolate délice with
pistachio cream and pear and apple crumble with vanilla ice-cream; they also offer
breakfasts 7.30-9am (8.30-9.30am weekends). *Benchmark main dish: steak in ale pie*
£14.00. Two-course evening meal £22.00.

Free house ~ Licensee Alex Clarke ~ Real ale ~ Open 7.30am (8.30am Sat)-11pm; 8.30am-
10.30pm Sun ~ Bar food 12-2, 6.30-9; 12-2.30, 6.30-9.30 Fri, Sat; 12-3, 6-8 Sun ~ Restaurant ~
Children welcome ~ Dogs allowed in bar and bedrooms ~ Wi-fi ~ Bedrooms: £95/£129
Recommended by Mrs Margo Finlay, Jörg Kasprowski, M and GR, Ben and Diane Bowie, Simon
Sharpe, Jim and Sue James

There are report forms at the back of the book.

CAMBRIDGE
Pint Shop
TL4458 Map 5

(01223) 352293 – www.pintshop.co.uk

Peas Hill; CB2 3PN

Busy, lively, chatty place with fine drinks and food – great fun

A cheerful pub on two floors, this place has a fantastic range of drinks and up-to-date tasty food, which ensures it is always packed with customers of all ages. The bar and dining rooms are simply furnished with wooden tables and chairs and cushioned wall seating on parquet floors, industrial-style lamps hanging from the ceiling and bird prints lining the walls; background music. Efficient, friendly staff keep Kirkstall Black Band Porter, Nene Valley Simple Pleasures, Oakham Citra and a couple of quickly changing guests on handpump, up to 17 craft ales, a good choice of wines and around 100 gins. There are a couple of upstairs dining rooms, similarly decorated, and a split-level, canopy-covered courtyard with chunky picnic-sets and fairy lights. The pub is handy for the Cambridge Arts Theatre and the Corn Exchange. Wheelchair access and loos.

 Particularly good food includes duck and chicken rillettes with pickled vegetables, pork bhaji scotch egg with mango raita, coal-baked flatbreads with toppings such as chilli beef and crispy onions, chargrilled aubergine with chickpea tagine, dukkah and chermoula, spit-roast chicken and chips with garlic butter, whole grilled plaice with cockles, parsley and brown butter, and puddings such as caramelised apple and walnut sponge tart with roasted cinnamon ice-cream and sticky toffee pudding with whipped cream. *Benchmark main dish: chicken masala kebab £12.00. Two-course evening meal £23.00.*

Free house ~ Licensee Richard Holmes ~ Real ale ~ Open 12-11 (midnight Thurs, Fri); 11am-midnight Sat; 11-11 Sun ~ Bar food 12-10 (10.30 Thurs, Fri); 11-10.30 Sat (10 Sun) ~ Restaurant ~ Children welcome ~ Dogs allowed in bar ~ Wi-fi *Recommended by Gary and Marie Miller, Margo and Derek Peters, Graeme and Sally Mendham, Izzy Croker*

ELTON
Crown
TL0894 Map 5

(01832) 280232 – www.crowninnelton.co.uk

Off B671 S of Wansford (A1/A47), and village signposted off A605 Peterborough–Oundle; Duck Street; PE8 6RQ

Pretty pub with interesting food, several real ales, well chosen wines and a friendly atmosphere; stylish bedrooms

Our readers enjoy their visits to this lovely golden-stone thatched pub, with all reports praising the appealing food cooked by the chef-landlord. The softly lit, beamed bar has leather and antique dining chairs around a nice mix of chunky tables on bare boards, an open fire in a stone fireplace and good pictures and pubby ornaments on pastel walls. The beamed main dining area has fresh flowers and candles, and similar tables and chairs on stripped wooden flooring; there's a modern circular dining extension too. High bar chairs against the counter are popular with locals, and they keep a house beer (from Kings Cliffe Brewery), Digfield March Hare, Greene King IPA and Oakham JHB on handpump, well chosen wines by the glass and farm cider; background music and TV. There are tables outside on the front terrace, and Elton Mill and Lock are nearby. Bedrooms are smart, comfortable and well equipped and the breakfasts are especially good. To find the pub (it's on the edge of this charming village), follow the brown sign towards Nassington.

⭐ Highly rewarding food cooked by the landlord includes sandwiches, chicken liver and brandy parfait with red onion marmalade, smoked haddock and home-cured bacon chowder, omelettes, chargrilled halloumi burger with roasted red pepper and grilled courgette and sweet potato fries, steak and mushroom in ale pie, saltmarsh lamb rump with root vegetable and potato gratin and red wine jus, panko-coated plaice with shellfish bisque and crushed, herbed potatoes, and puddings such as spiced apple crumble with clotted cream custard and apple caramel and dark chocolate brownie with chocolate sauce. *Benchmark main dish: pork belly, crispy bacon hash browns, apple purée and cider sauce £17.95. Two-course evening meal £24.00.*

Free house ~ Licensee Marcus Lamb ~ Real ale ~ Open 12-11; 12-9 Sun ~ Bar food 12-2 (3 Sun), 6.30-9; not Sun evening, not Mon except for residents ~ Restaurant ~ Children welcome ~ Dogs allowed in bar ~ Wi-fi ~ Bedrooms: £80/£140 *Recommended by Ian Herdman, Chris and Sophie Baxter, W K Wood, Aly Nicholson, Charlie Stevens, Elise and Charles Mackinlay, James Landor*

HEMINGFORD GREY

TL2970 Map 5

Cock ⭐ � ♣

(01480) 463609 – www.cambscuisine.com/the-cock-hemingford
Village signposted off A14 eastbound, and (via A1096 St Ives road) westbound; High Street; PE28 9BJ

Cambridgeshire Dining Pub of the Year

Imaginative food in pretty pub with extensive wine list, four interesting beers, a bustling atmosphere and a smart restaurant

Many of our readers count this excellent pub as their favourite, and we can quite understand why as it's pretty much faultless in all aspects. Lucky Cambridgeshire. One feature we particularly like in a place that serves first class food is that they've sensibly kept the public bar (on the left) for drinking only: an open woodburning stove on a raised hearth, bar stools, wall seats and a carver, and steps leading down to more seating. Adnams Southwold, Brewsters Hophead and Oldershaw Grantham Stout on handpump, 22 wines by the glass mainly from the Languedoc-Roussillon region, 15 gins (one very local) and Cromwell cider (made in the village). Other bar rooms have white-painted or dark beams and lots of contemporary pale yellow and cream paintwork, church candles, artworks here and there, and a really attractive mix of old wooden dining chairs, settles and tables. In marked contrast, the stylishly rustic restaurant on the right (you must book to be sure of a table) is set for dining, with pale wooden floorboards and another woodburning stove. There are seats and tables among stone troughs and flowers on the terrace and in the neat garden, and pretty hanging baskets. Disabled access. This is a delightful village on the River Ouse. Sister pubs are the Crown & Punchbowl at Horningsea, Three Horseshoes in Madingley and Tickell Arms in Whittlesford (all in Cambridgeshire).

⭐ Delicious food includes sandwiches, glazed pork cheek with pork bonbon, apple, caramelised onion purée and crackling, duck parcel with sweet and sour cucumber and soy and sesame dressing, squash ricotta torte with fennel and potato gratin, lamb, mint and cumin sausages with a choice of sauce, seasonal salad bowl with confit duck or feta, crab and mussel tagliatelle with lemon and parsley gremolata, slow-cooked beef with juniper sauce and dauphinoise potatoes, 9oz sirloin steak with a choice of sauce and chips, and puddings such as damson parfait woth honeycomb and apple and quince sponge and chocolate pot with kirsch-soaked cherries and vanilla ice-cream; they also offer a two- and three-course weekday set lunch. *Benchmark main dish: guinea fowl with braised turnip and leeks, wild mushrooms and red wine sauce £20.00. Two-course evening meal £25.00.*

Free house ~ Licensees Oliver Thain and Richard Bradley ~ Real ale ~ Open 12-3,
6 (5 Fri)-11; 12-11 Sat; 12-10.30 Sun ~ Bar food 12-2.30, 6.30-9; 12-2.30, 6-9.30 Fri, Sat;
12-8 Sun ~ Restaurant ~ Children welcome until evening when must be over 10 (in pub),
over 5 (in restaurant) ~ Dogs allowed in bar ~ Wi-fi *Recommended by Mrs Margo Finlay,
Jörg Kasprowski, Barbara and Phil Bowie, Sarah and David Gibbs, Wendy Halls, Millie and Peter
Downing, Jim King, Ben and Diane Bowie*

HINXTON
TL4945 Map 5

Red Lion 🌟 ♀ 🍺 🛏️

(01799) 530601 – www.redlionhinxton.co.uk

*2 miles off M11 junction 9 northbound; take first exit off A11, A1301 N, then left turn
into village – High Street; a little further from junction 10, via A505 E and A1301 S;
CB10 1QY*

**16th-c pub with friendly staff, interesting bar food, real ales and
a big landscaped garden; comfortable bedrooms**

The low-beamed bar here has a relaxed, friendly atmosphere, oak chairs
and tables on bare boards, two leather chesterfield sofas, an open fire
and an old wall clock. You'll also find their own-label Red & Black Ale (from
the local Nethergate Brewery) plus Adnams Ghost Ship, Woodfordes Wherry
and a guest such as Crafty Beers Sixteen Strides on handpump, 22 wines
by the glass, 15 malt whiskies and first class service. An informal dining
area has high-backed settles, and the smart restaurant (with oak rafters and
traditional dry peg construction) is decorated with various pictures and
assorted clocks. In warm weather, there's plenty of seating outside with teak
tables and chairs on one terrace, huge parasols on a second terrace by the
porch and picnic-sets on grass. There's also a dovecote and nice views of the
village church. This is a fine place to stay in well equipped, pretty bedrooms
in a separate flint and brick building; breakfasts are good. The Imperial War
Museum at Duxford is close by. They also own the Black Bull in Balsham just
up the road.

🌟 Appetising food includes sandwiches, seared scallops with asian slaw, wasabi,
soy, ginger and a honey glaze, pigeon breast with puy lentils and orange, roast
cauliflower with broccoli and butternut squash salad, dukkah and pomegranate,
rolled porchetta stuffed with lemon zest, fennel seeds and chilli, lemon and thyme
flat-iron chicken steak with lemon and honey glaze, lamb rump with pea fricassée,
wild mushrooms and tomato jus, and puddings such as passion-fruit tart with
butternut squash purée and mango sorbet and sticky toffee pudding with
butterscotch sauce. *Benchmark main dish: game pie with red wine jus £14.00.
Two-course evening meal £23.00.*

Free house ~ Licensee Alex Clarke ~ Real ale ~ Open 7.30am (8.30am Sat)-11pm; 8.30am-
10.30pm Sun ~ Bar food 12-2, 6.30-9; 12-2.30, 6.30-9.30 Fri, Sat; 12-3, 6-8 Sun ~ Restaurant ~
Children welcome ~ Dogs allowed in bar and bedrooms ~ Wi-fi ~ Bedrooms: £114/£139
*Recommended by Peter L Harrison, Charlotte and William Mason, Mrs J Ekins-Daukes, Adrian
Buckland, Geoff and Ann Marston, Tony Smaithe*

HORNINGSEA
TL4962 Map 5

Crown & Punchbowl 🌟 ♀ 🛏️

(01223) 860643 – www.cambscuisine.com/the-crown-and-
punchbowl
Just NE of Cambridge; CB25 9JG

**Impressive food and thoughtful drinks choice in carefully refurbished
old inn with seats outside; bedrooms**

Warmly enthusiastic reports on this 17th-c former coaching inn remain the norm here – our readers love it. Original features and character have been maintained and the beamed bar has a woodburning stove in a brick fireplace, leather banquettes and rustic old chairs, stripped boards, terracotta walls and an attractively carved counter where they serve freshly carved ham and home-made pickles. Behind the bar they keep Brewsters Hophead and Milton Pegasus tapped from the cask and 20 wines by the glass (with a focus on the Languedoc-Roussillon region), home-made punches (alcoholic and non-alcoholic), lavender lemonade and local cider. The timbered dining room has leather cushioned chairs around wooden tables on pale boards, wall panelling and candlelight. Another conservatory-style room has large windows and ceramic light fittings (a nod to the village's history as a centre for Roman pottery). There are country seats out in front of the pub, while the five guest bedrooms upstairs are well equipped, light and comfortable. Sister pubs are the Cock at Hemingford Grey, Three Horseshoes in Madingley and Tickell Arms in Whittlesford (all in Cambridgeshire).

 Enticing food includes sandwiches, herb-crusted goats cheese with roasted garlic and tomato, duck parcel with sweet and sour cucumber and soy and sesame dressing, beetroot, walnut and chestnut terrine with roasted pear, earl grey and pear gel, wild mushrooms and mushroom velouté, home-made sausages of the day with mash and onion gravy, a wild game sharing plate with red wine sauce, cod with spiced lentil and pancetta stew, herb dressing and carrot crisps, smoked duck breast with apple and onion confit, red cabbage, potato fondant and cider sauce, and puddings such as cinnamon crème brûlée and cheesecake of the day; they also offer a two- and three-course set weekday lunch. *Benchmark main dish: chicken supreme with kohlrabi rémoulade, crispy potatoes and truffle sauce £16.50. Two-course evening meal £25.00.*

Free house ~ Licensees Oliver Thain and Richard Bradley ~ Real ale ~ Open 12-3, 6 (5 Fri)-11; 12-11 Sat; 12-10.30 Sun ~ Bar food 12-2.30, 6.30-9 (9.30 Fri, Sat); 12-3, 6.30-8.30 Sun ~ Restaurant ~ Children welcome ~ Dogs allowed in bar ~ Wi-fi ~ Bedrooms: /$120
Recommended by M and GR, Mike Benton, David Jackman, Ken and Miriam Day, Scott and Charlotte Havers, Penny and David Shepherd

 HUNTINGDON   TL2471   Map 5
Old Bridge Hotel
(01480) 424300 – www.huntsbridge.com
1 High Street; ring road just off B1044 entering from easternmost A14 slip road; PE29 3TQ

Proper bar in Georgian hotel with a splendid range of drinks, first class service and excellent food; individually styled bedrooms

As a special place to stay, this lovely, civilised hotel, run with thought and great care, has luxurious bedrooms (some overlook the river) and excellent breakfasts. And while much emphasis is naturally on this side of the business, there's a proper little pubby bar at its heart with a wide mix of customers. This has a log fire, comfortable sofas and low wooden tables on polished floorboards, and Adnams Ghost Ship and Nene Valley Blond Session Ale and a guest on handpump. They also have an exceptional wine list (up to 30 by the glass in the bar) and a wine shop where you can taste a selection of wines before you buy. Food is available in the big airy restaurant with floor-to-ceiling windows overlooking the garden, or in the bar/lounge. There are seats and tables on the terrace by the Great Ouse river, and they have their own landing stage.

 Creative food includes sandwiches, pickled mackerel with carrot, caper and cress salad and mustard and honey dressing, carpaccio of beef with celeriac, horseradish and shaved radishes, leek, potato and cheese gratin with wild mushrooms, chargrilled hispi cabbage and beetroot purée, goan fish curry, chicken sausages (boned and stuffed wings, with bacon and garlic and crispy chicken skin), rabbit tortellini with chargrilled king oyster mushroom, venison haunch with root vegetable pie, and puddings such as almond and orange bread and butter pudding with crème anglaise and clotted cream ice-cream and chocolate marquise with caramel liqueur ice-cream. *Benchmark main dish: steak sandwich with caramelised onions and grain mustard with fries £12.95. Two-course evening meal £28.00.*

Huntsbridge ~ Licensee John Hoskins ~ Real ale ~ Open 11am-11.30pm ~ Bar food 11.30-9.15 (10 Fri, Sat) ~ Restaurant ~ Children welcome ~ Dogs allowed in bar and bedrooms ~ Wi-fi ~ Bedrooms: £99/£188 *Recommended by Michael Sargent, Christopher Mannings, Colin McLachlan, Andrew and Nicky Churcher, Claire and Nigel Swanning, Simon and Mary Todd*

KEYSTON
TL0475   Map 5

Pheasant 🏅 🍴 ♟

(01832) 710241 – www.thepheasant-keyston.co.uk

Just off A14 SE of Thrapston; brown sign to pub down village loop road, off B663; PE28 0RE

Smart country dining pub with appealing décor, rewarding food and an attractive garden

This pretty thatched pub was once the village smithy – it's come a long way since then. The main bar has pitched rafters high above, with lower dark beams in side areas. A central serving area has padded stools beside the leather-quilted counter and dark flagstones, with hop bines above the handpumps for Adnams Southwold, Digfield Fools Nook and a guest beer, and 13 wines (including champagne and prosecco) by the glass. Nearby are armchairs, a chesterfield, quite a throne of a seat carved in 17th-c style, other comfortable seats around low tables, and a log fire in a lofty fireplace. The rest of the pub is mostly red-carpeted with dining chairs around a variety of polished tables, large sporting prints, some hunting-scene wallpaper and lighted candles and tea-lights. The attractively planted and well kept garden behind has tables on the lawn and terrace, and there are picnic-sets in front. This is a quiet farming hamlet.

Cooked by the landlord, the modern food includes sandwiches, guinea fowl and free-range pork terrine with celeriac rémoulade, crab linguine with chilli, ginger, parsley, garlic and spring onions, vegetable curry with accompaniments, venison burger with quince jam, goats cheese and chips, whole sole with herb polenta, beetroot, cockles and dill, free-range pork loin with black pudding mash, celeriac, carrots and crackling, veal hash with potato rösti, fried egg, confit garlic and green peppercorn sauce, and puddings such as quince and almond tart with mixed spice ice-cream and star anise parfait with poached rhubarb and brandy snap; they also offer a two- and three-course set lunch and early evening menu. *Benchmark main dish: stuffed rabbit saddle with fondant potato, confit swede, jerusalem artichokes and damson sauce £18.95. Two-course evening meal £28.00.*

Free house ~ Licensee Simon Cadge ~ Real ale ~ Open 12-3, 6-11; 12-midnight Sat; 12-6 Sun; closed Mon; first two weeks Jan ~ Bar food 12-2 (2.30 Fri, Sat), 6.30-9.30; 12-3.30 Sun ~ Restaurant ~ Children welcome ~ Dogs allowed in bar ~ Wi-fi *Recommended by Peter Andrews, Rona Mackinlay, Douglas Power, Dave Braisted, Andrea and Philip Crispin, Katherine and Hugh Markham*

MADINGLEY   TL3960   Map 5

Three Horseshoes

(01954) 210221 – www.cambscuisine.com/three-horseshoes
High Street; off A1303 W of Cambridge; CB23 8AB

Pretty pub with excellent food and wines, charming staff and seats in the garden

---

With light and attractive décor and an easy-going, friendly feel, this thatched pub appeals to a wide mix of customers. It's a bustling and gently civilised place and the bare-boards bar has high-backed cushioned settles and a mix of nice old dining chairs around wooden tables, prints on pale paintwork and a woodburning stove. From the bar counter, friendly, courteous staff serve Adnams Southwold and a changing ale such as Brewsters Hophead on handpump and several good wines by the glass. The airy conservatory restaurant, overlooking the garden, has rattan-style and pale wooden chairs around plain tables on quarry tiles and parquet flooring, a long, brown button-back wall banquette and another woodburning stove. At the front of the building are solid benches and tables, and the sunny back terrace and lawn have picnic-sets and teak tables and chairs. Sister pubs are the Cock in Hemingford Grey, Crown & Punchbowl in Horningsea and Tickell Arms in Whittlesford (all in Cambridgeshire).

Interesting, up-to-date food includes scallops with white bean purée, black pudding and red salsa, goats cheese arancini with arrabiata sauce, garlic-roasted butternut squash with shaved fennel, black olives and almonds, chargrilled corn-fed chicken breast with squash and sage risotto and baked savoy cabbage, herb-crusted hake fillet with lemon roast potatoes and lemongrass butter, slow-cooked beef with dauphinoise potatoes and juniper sauce, and puddings such as caramelised lemon tart with raspberry and thyme sorbet and chocolate pot with kirsch-soaked cherries and vanilla ice-cream; they also offer a two- and three-course set weekday lunch. *Benchmark main dish: local partridge with honey-roasted parsnips and carrots and calvados jus £19.50. Two-course evening meal £26.00.*

Free house ~ Licensee Oliver Thain ~ Real ale ~ Open 12-3, 6 (5.30 Fri)-11; 12-11 Sat; 12-10.30 Sun ~ Bar food 12-2.30, 6.30-9; 12-2.30, 6-9.30 Fri, Sat; 12-8 Sun ~ Restaurant ~ Children welcome ~ Dogs allowed in bar ~ Wi-fi *Recommended by George Sanderson, Melanie and David Lawson, Mrs Margo Finlay, Jörg Kasprowski, M and GR, Suzi Griffin, Patricia and Anton Larkham, James Mackenzie*

PETERBOROUGH   TL1899   Map 5

Brewery Tap ⬤ £

(01733) 358500 – www.thebrewery-tap.com
Opposite Queensgate car park; PE1 2AA

Fantastic range of real ales including their own brews, popular thai food and a lively, friendly atmosphere

---

Deservedly popular (particularly in the evenings), this striking conversion of an old labour exchange is a fine place with particularly good own-brewed ales and thai food. Open-plan and contemporary, it has an expanse of light wood and stone floors and blue-painted iron pillars holding up a steel-corded mezzanine level. Stylish lighting includes steel-meshed wall lights and a giant suspended steel ring with bulbs running around the rim. A band of chequered floor tiles traces the path of the long sculpted pale wood bar counter, which is boldly backed by an impressive display of bottles in a ceiling-high wall of wooden cubes. There's also a comfortable downstairs area, a big-screen TV for sporting events, background music and regular live bands and comedy nights. A two-storey glass wall divides the bar from the brewery, giving fascinating views of the two-barrel brew plan from which they produce their own Oakham Bishops Farewell, Citra, Inferno, JHB and seasonal ales; also, guest ales, quite a few whiskies and several wines by the glass.

🍴 The thai food includes set menus and specials, as well as tom yum soup, chicken, beef, pork, prawn, duck and vegetable curries, stir-fried crispy chilli beef, talay pad cha (prawns, squid and mussels with crushed garlic, chilli and ginger), various noodle dishes, all sorts of salads and stir-fries and five kinds of rice. *Benchmark main dish: pad thai noodles £9.60. Two-course evening meal £20.00.*

Own brew ~ Licensee Jessica Loock ~ Real ale ~ Open 12-11 (1am Fri, 2am Sat); 12-10.30 Sun ~ Bar food 12-2.30, 5.30-10.30; 12-10.30 Fri, Sat; 12-3.30, 5.30-9.30 Sun ~ Restaurant ~ Children welcome during food service times only ~ Dogs allowed in bar ~ Wi-fi ~ Live music Fri, Sat evenings *Recommended by Lorna and Jack Mulgrave, Paddy and Sian O'Leary, Peter and Emma Kelly*

STILLTON
Bell 🍷 🛏
TL1689   Map 5

(01733) 241066 – www.thebellstilton.co.uk
High Street; village signposted from A1 S of Peterborough; PE7 3RA

Fine coaching inn with character bars, popular food, thoughtful drinks choice and seats in a pretty courtyard; bedrooms

Our favourite spot in this lovely 17th-c coaching inn remains the neatly kept right-hand bar which has a great deal of character: bow windows, sturdy upright wooden seats on flagstone floors, a big log fire in a handsome stone fireplace, partly stripped walls with large prints of sailing and winter coaching scenes, and a giant pair of blacksmith's bellows. This room has been opened up with the bistro to create a bar-cum-dining area with a bustling, chatty atmosphere. Digfield Fools Nook, Fullers London Pride, Greene King IPA and Old Speckled Hen and Oakham Bishops Farewell on handpump, several malt whiskies, 15 wines by the glass, 11 gins and farm cider; service is helpful and welcoming. Other rooms include a residents' bar and a restaurant; background music, board games and TV. Through the fine coach arch is a very pretty sheltered courtyard with tables, and a well that dates from Roman times. The bedrooms mix old-world charm with modern facilities and three are on the ground floor overlooking the garden.

🍴 Interesting food (which always includes stilton in a dish or two) includes sandwiches, duck liver parfait with cranberry and orange relish, smoked haddock bake with parmesan and a poached egg, butternut squash filled with red onion and apple with a halloumi topping, chicken breast with goose fat potatoes, red wine jus and carrot purée, cod fillet with chorizo and chickpea cassoulet on linguine, slow-cooked beef with pancetta, celeriac, maple and red wine jus, and puddings such as warm savarin with apple and sultana compote and whipped clotted cream and dark chocolate and coffee délice with salted caramel and Baileys ice-cream. *Benchmark main dish: ham hock with spiced red cabbage £17.00. Two-course evening meal £22.00.*

Free house ~ Licensee Liam McGivern ~ Real ale ~ Open 12-2.30, 5-11; 12-midnight Sat; 12-10.30 Sun ~ Bar food 12-2.15 (2.30 Sat), 6-9; 12-3, 6-8.30 Sun ~ Restaurant ~ Children welcome ~ Wi-fi ~ Bedrooms: £91/£116 *Recommended by Jeff Davies, Lance and Sarah Milligan, M G Hart, Ian Wilson, Ivy and George Goodwill, Susan and Callum Slade, Charles Todd*

The 🍺 symbol shows pubs that keep their beer unusually well,
have a particularly good range or brew their own.

THORNEY   TL2799   Map 5

Dog in a Doublet

(01733) 202256 – www.doginad.co.uk

B1040 towards Thorney; PE6 0RW

Country inn with produce from own farm, tasty food and local ales, friendly service and seats outside; bedrooms

The River Nene and one of the biggest lock gates in Europe are just across the road from here and there are plenty of good nearby walks, making this a fine place for lunch. The bar has sofas, comfortable seats and an open fire and Gun Dog Jacks Spaniels, Pitchfork Puxton Cross and a changing guest on handpump, 15 wines by the glass and three farm ciders. The restaurant leads off and has an open kitchen, solid wooden dining chairs around farmhouse tables, prints on red-painted walls and a monthly live pianist; background music and bar games. A deli counter offers their own produce and treats from further afield too. Outside, there are brightly painted picnic-sets under a gazebo. The eight bedrooms have vaulted ceilings and their own balconies, and they also have a campsite.

Enjoyable food uses free-range eggs, home-grown vegetables and home-reared pigs from their small farm: chicken livers in sherry cream, smoked salmon and roasted pepper pâté, macaroni cheese with truffle, maple and thyme gammon with a duck egg, beer-battered fish and chips, steak with udon noodles, vegetable ribbons, peanuts and herbs, and puddings such as boozy black forest trifle and eton mess; they also offer breakfasts (8.30-10.30am). *Benchmark main dish: short rib burger with toppings and fries £13.00. Two-course evening meal £20.00.*

Free house ~ Licensees John McGinn and Della Mills ~ Real ale ~ Open 12-11; 12-9 Sun ~ Bar food 12-9 ~ Children welcome ~ Dogs allowed in bar and bedrooms ~ Wi-fi ~ Bedrooms: /£65 *Recommended by Charlie Stevens, Lenny and Ruth Walters, Victoria Barry, Donald Allsopp, Edward Nile, Peter Brix*

UFFORD   TF0904   Map 5

White Hart ▪ 🛏

(01780) 740250 – www.whitehartufford.co.uk

Main Street; S on to Ufford Road off B1443 at Bainton, then right; PE9 3BH

Lots of interest in bustling pub, bar and dining rooms, good food and extensive garden; bedrooms

What was a former farm is now a relaxing, welcoming inn with plenty of drinking and dining space. The bar has an easy-going atmosphere, farm tools and chamber-pots, scatter cushions on leather benches, some nice old chairs and tables, a woodburning stove, exposed stone walls and stools against the counter where they serve Grainstore Red Kite, Oakham JHB and a guest ale such as Timothy Taylors Landlord on handpump, 24 wines by the glass and 20 gins. There's also an elegant beamed restaurant and an airy Orangery; background music, board games and TV. In warm weather, the three acres of gardens at the back are a huge bonus – they include a sunken dining area with plenty of chairs and tables, picnic-sets on grass, steps to various peaceful corners and lovely flowers and shrubs. This is a nice place to stay, with four of the comfortable bedrooms in the pub, two in a converted cart shed and six more in the Old Brewery.

Good quality, changing food includes sandwiches, salmon, prawn and chive mousse with cucumber sauce dressing, chicken liver parfait with chutney, butternut squash, mediterranean vegetable and halloumi ragoût with sweet potato purée, burger with toppings, coleslaw and chips, sea bass with crushed new potatoes, king prawns and lemon butter sauce, slow-braised lamb shank in rosemary, garlic, redcurrant and port sauce, and puddings such as Baileys cheesecake with chocolate sauce and glazed lemon tart with raspberry coulis and lemon sorbet. *Benchmark main dish: beef in rich red wine gravy with mash, kale and chantenay carrots £15.95. Two-course evening meal £23.00.*

Free house ~ Licensee Sue Olver ~ Real ale ~ Open 8am-11pm; 8am-midnight Sat; 8am-9pm Sun ~ Bar food 12-2.30, 6-9 (9.30 Fri); 12-9.30 Sat; 12-8 Sun ~ Restaurant ~ Children welcome ~ Dogs allowed in bar and bedrooms ~ Wi-fi ~ Bedrooms: /£95 *Recommended by Caroline Sullivan, Dr Simon Innes, Mike Benton, Cliff and Monica Swan, Neil Allen*

WHITTLESFORD

TL4648 Map 5

Tickell Arms ★ ♦ ♀

(01223) 833025 – www.cambscuisine.com/the-tickell-whittlesford

2.4 miles from M11 junction 10; A505 towards Newmarket, then second turn left signposted Whittlesford; keep on into North Road; CB22 4NZ

Well run dining pub with good enterprising food and pretty garden

Our readers enjoy this pub a great deal, giving plenty of praise to the impressive food, first class service and fine choice of drinks. And there are also some architectural features that are really worth looking at. The L-shaped bar has bentwood stools on floor tiles, ornate cast-iron pillars, a woodburning stove and (under bowler-hatted lampshades over the counter) Brewsters Hophead and Nene Valley Release the Chimps on handpump, 20 fairly priced wines by the glass including champagne, and farm cider. There are also three porcelain handpumps from the era of the legendarily autocratic regime of the Wagner-loving former owner Kim Tickell. Tables in the dining room vary from sturdy to massive, with leather-cushioned bentwood and other dining chairs and one dark pew, and fresh minimalist décor in palest buff. This opens into an even lighter limestone-floored conservatory area, partly divided by a very high-backed ribbed-leather banquette. A side terrace has comfortable tables, and the secluded garden beyond has pergolas and a pond. Sister pubs are the Cock in Hemingford Grey, Crown & Punchbowl at Horningsea and Three Horseshoes in Madingley (all in Cambridgeshire).

Top-rated, up-to-date food includes sandwiches, twice-baked crab and chive soufflé with lemon crème fraîche, samphire and pickled cucumber, pigeon breast with steamed rhubarb, wilted spinach, baby beetroot and thyme sauce, five-spice fried tofu with sweet potato purée, pickled mouli and lemongrass, turmeric and chilli sauce, cod loin with coriander and lentil stew and clam and chilli chowder, and puddings such as lime and bayleaf tart with crème fraîche and candied lime and chocolate mousse with cherry compote, cherry sponge and chocolate crumb; they also offer a two- and three-course set menu (weekday lunchtimes and Sunday-Thursday evenings). *Benchmark main dish: smoked aubergine with aubergine purée, crisp polenta, blackberries and sage £13.50. Two-course evening meal £25.00.*

Free house ~ Licensees Oliver Thain and Max Freeman ~ Real ale ~ Open 12-3, 6-11; 12-11 Sat; 12-10.30 Sun ~ Bar food 12-2.30, 6.30-9; 12-2.30, 6.30-9.30 Fri; 12-3, 6-9.30 Sat; 12-3, 6-8 Sun ~ Restaurant ~ Children must be over 10 in evening pub; over 5 in evening restaurant ~ Dogs allowed in bar ~ Wi-fi *Recommended by Louise and Oliver Redman, Jill and Hugh Bennett, Robert Balchin, Roger Craigen, Vicky Skilton, Adrian Buckland, Gail and Frank Hackett, Sally Harrison, Miranda and Jeff Davidson, Fay Benning*

We include some hotels with a good bar that offers facilities comparable to those of a pub.

Also Worth a Visit in Cambridgeshire

Besides the fully inspected pubs, you might like to try these pubs that have been recommended to us and described by readers. Do tell us what you think of them: feedback@goodguides.com

ABBOTS RIPTON   TL2377
Abbots Elm (01487) 773773
B1090; PE28 2PA Open-plan thatched dining pub reconstructed after major fire; highly rated food from snacks and bar meals to interesting restaurant dishes using locally sourced and home-grown produce, extensive choice of wines by the glass including champagne, three well kept ales, good friendly service; children and dogs welcome, four bedrooms, open all day Sat, till 4pm Sun. *(Mark Morgan)*

BABRAHAM   TL5150
George (01223) 837755
High Street; just off A1307; CB22 3AG Beamed and timbered 18th-c village pub set back from quiet road; decent choice of affordable home-made food from baguettes and pub favourites up, Greene King IPA and a couple of guests, friendly accommodating staff, bare-boards bar, carpeted restaurant and second dining/function room in adjoining barn; live music and quiz nights; children welcome, tables in garden with terrace, open all day. *(Alistair Holdoway)*

BARRINGTON   TL3849
Royal Oak (01223) 870791
Turn off A10 about 3.7 miles SW of M11 junction 11, in Foxton; West Green; CB22 7RZ Rambling thatched Tudor pub with tables out overlooking classic village green; heavy low beams and timbers, mixed furnishings, Greene King IPA and guests, Aspall's and Thatcher's ciders, good wine list and enjoyable food from pub favourites up, friendly helpful service, airy dining conservatory; background music, free wi-fi; children and dogs welcome, classic car club meeting first Fri of month. *(Caroline and Steve Archer)*

BARTLOW   TL5845
Three Hills (01223) 890500
Off Camps Road, signed Ashdon, S Walden; CB21 4PW Attractively updated 17th-c inn; very good well presented food including cheaper bar menu, friendly accommodating service, well kept changing ales, cosy beamed bar, restaurant and snug with log fire; children and dogs welcome, terrace and garden running down to little River Granta, six well appointed bedrooms (four in separate building), picturesque village with interesting Roman barrows nearby (after which the pub is named), closed Sun evening and Mon, otherwise open all day. *(Alexandra and Richard Clay)*

BOURN   TL3256
Willow Tree (01954) 719775
High Street, just off B1046 W of Cambridge; CB23 2SQ Light and airy dining pub with relaxed informal atmosphere despite the cut-glass chandeliers, sprinkling of Louis XVI furniture and profusion of silver-plated candlesticks; restaurant-style cooking (all-day Sun roast till 8pm), Woodfordes and a local guest, well chosen wines and inventive cocktails, friendly staff; live jazz Sun evening; children welcome, smart tables and chairs on back deck, grassed area beyond car park with fruit trees, huge weeping willow and tipi, closed Tues lunchtime, otherwise open all day. *(John Saville)*

BOXWORTH   TL3464
Golden Ball (01954) 267397
High Street; CB23 4LY Attractive partly thatched 16th-c village inn with pitched-roof dining bar, restaurant and small conservatory, emphasis on good fairly priced food from baguettes through pubby choices and grills to blackboard specials, friendly helpful service, well kept Bombardier, Eagle IPA and a guest, 16 wines by the glass and good choice of whiskies and gins; free wi-fi; children welcome, nice garden and heated terrace, pastures behind, ten quiet bedrooms in adjacent block, open all day, food till 7pm Sun. *(Mrs Margo Finlay, Jörg Kasprowski)*

BRAMPTON   TL2170
Black Bull (01480) 457201
Church Road; PE28 4PF 16th-c and later with updated low-ceilinged interior; stripped-wood floor and inglenook woodburner in split-level main bar, restaurant with light wood furniture on tiles, popular well priced pubby food including range of pies, four real ales, friendly efficient staff; free wi-fi; children and dogs (in bar) welcome, garden with play area, open (and food) all day, till 9pm (4pm) Sun. *(Charlie Stevens)*

BRINKLEY   TL6254
Red Lion (01638) 508707
High Street; CB8 0RA Old country pub set back from the road; painted beams, bare boards and inglenook log fire, Woodfordes Wherry and a couple of guests (plans for on-site microbrewery), good sensibly priced food from sandwiches up including some themed nights and Sun brunch, friendly service, restaurant; free wi-fi; children and dogs (in bar) welcome, picnic-sets on lawn, closed Sun evening, Mon and Tues. *(Monica and Steph Evans)*

BROUGHTON   TL2877
★**Crown** (01487) 824428
Off A141 opposite RAF Wyton; Bridge Road; PE28 3AY Attractively tucked-away mansard-roofed dining pub opposite church; fresh airy décor with country pine tables and chairs on stone floors, some leather bucket seats and sofa, good well presented food (special diets catered for) from lunchtime sandwiches and pub favourites up, friendly service, three changing local real ales, restaurant; background music; children and dogs welcome, disabled access and facilities, tables out on big stretch of grass behind, open all day Sun till 6pm, closed Mon. *(Muriel and Spencer Harrop)*

BUCKDEN   TL1967
★**George** (01480) 812300
High Street; PE19 5XA Handsome and stylish hotel (former Georgian coaching inn) with bustling informal bar; fine fan beamwork, bucket chairs on parquet flooring, woodburner in carved stone fireplace, Adnams Southwold and a changing guest from zinc-topped counter, lots of wines including champagne by the glass, teas and coffees, popular brasserie with good modern food served by helpful enthusiastic young staff, also bar meals; background music; children and dogs welcome, tables under large parasols on attractive sheltered terrace with box hedging, 12 charming bedrooms named after famous Georges, smallish car park (free street parking), open all day. *(Michael Sargent)*

BURWELL   TL5867
Anchor (01638) 743970
North Street; CB25 0BA Revamped 18th-c dining pub with good imaginative food cooked by chef-owner, a couple of Greene King ales, a guest beer and plenty of wines by the glass from interesting list, helpful friendly service, restaurant, steps down to snug with books and board games; background music; children welcome till 9pm, dogs in bar, disabled loo, garden backing on to small river, closed Mon and Tues, no food Sun evening. *(Mark Morgan)*

CAMBRIDGE   TL4658
★**Cambridge Blue** (01223) 471680
85 Gwydir Street; CB1 2LG Friendly little backstreet local with a dozen or more interesting ales (some tapped from the cask – regular festivals), also six craft kegs, 200 bottled beers, up to seven ciders and over 70 whiskies, enjoyable well priced home-made food including seasonal specials, extended bar area with lots of breweriana and old advertising signs, attractive conservatory; free wi-fi; children and dogs welcome, seats in back garden bordering cemetery, open all day, food all day weekends when it can get very busy. *(John Harris)*

CAMBRIDGE   TL4459
Castle (01223) 353194
Castle Street; CB3 0AJ Adnams range and interesting guest beers in bare-boards bar and other pleasantly simple rooms including snug and quieter upstairs area, good choice of pub food from sandwiches and snacks to blackboard specials, efficient friendly staff; background music, free wi-fi; children and dogs welcome, part-covered walled back courtyard, open all day and very busy Fri, Sat evenings. *(Monty Green)*

CAMBRIDGE   TL4658
Clarendon Arms (01223) 778272
Clarendon Street; CB1 1JX Welcoming backstreet corner local; pubby furniture on flagstones or bare boards, lots of pictures including local scenes, step down to back bar, Greene King ales and enjoyable home-made food from snacks to Sun roasts, friendly helpful service; free wi-fi; children and dogs welcome, wheelchair access with help, seats in sunny back courtyard, open all day, no food Sun evening. *(John Harris)*

CAMBRIDGE   TL4657
Devonshire Arms (01223) 316610
Devonshire Road; CB1 2BH Welcoming Milton-tied pub with two busy linked bars, their well kept ales and guests, real cider, also great choice of bottled beers, decent wines and a dozen malts, enjoyable good value food (not Sun evening) from sandwiches and pizzas to grills, creaky wood floors, mix of furniture including long narrow refectory tables, architectural prints and steam engine pictures, woodburner in back bar; wheelchair access, handy for the station, open all day. *(Julia and Andrew Blanchett)*

CAMBRIDGE   TL4458
★**Eagle** (01223) 505020
Benet Street; CB2 3QN Once the city's most important coaching inn; rambling rooms with two ancient mullioned windows and the remains of possibly medieval wall paintings, two fireplaces dating from around 1600, lovely worn wooden floors and plenty of pine panelling, dark red ceiling left unpainted since World War II to preserve the signatures of british and american airmen made with Zippo lighters, candle smoke and lipstick, well kept Greene King ales including Eagle DNA (Crick and Watson announced the discovery of DNA's structure here in 1953) and two guests, decent choice of enjoyable food served efficiently considering the crowds; children welcome, disabled facilities, heavy wooden seats in attractive cobbled and galleried courtyard, open all day. *(John Wooll, Tony Scott)*

CAMBRIDGE   TL4558
Elm Tree (01223) 502632
Orchard Street; CB1 1JT Traditional one-bar backstreet drinkers' pub with

welcoming atmosphere; up to ten well kept ales including B&T, wide range of continental bottled beers plus local cider/perry, friendly knowledgeable staff, no food, nice unspoilt interior with breweriana and other memorabilia; some live music; wheelchair access, a few tables out at the side, open all day. *(John Harris)*

CAMBRIDGE TL4559

Fort St George (01223) 354327

Midsummer Common; CB4 1HA Picturesque old pub (reached by foot only) in charming waterside position overlooking ducks, punts and boathouses; good value pubby food including traditional Sun lunch, well kept Greene King ales and decent wines by the glass, cheerful service, interior extended around old-fashioned Tudor core with oars on beams, historic boating photographs and open fire; free wi-fi; children and dogs welcome, wheelchair access via side door, lots of tables outside, open (and food) all day. *(Monty Green)*

CAMBRIDGE TL4558

Free Press (01223) 368337

Prospect Row; CB1 1DU Unspoilt little backstreet pub with interesting décor including old newspaper pages and printing memorabilia (was printshop for a local paper); Greene King IPA, Abbot and Mild plus regularly changing guests, good range of wines by the glass, 25 malt whiskies and lots of gins and rums, tasty good value food, log fire, friendly atmosphere; TV for major sports, board games; children and dogs (in bar) welcome, wheelchair access, small sheltered paved garden behind, open all day. *(John Wooll)*

CAMBRIDGE TL4557

Live & Let Live (01223) 460261

Mawson Road; CB1 2EA Popular backstreet corner pub with friendly relaxed atmosphere; five well kept ales including Nethergate and Oakham, proper cider and over 120 rums, snacky food, panelled interior with sturdy varnished tables on bare boards, some steam railway and brewery memorabilia, old gas light fittings, cribbage and dominoes; dogs welcome, disabled access awkward but possible, closed Weds and Thurs lunchtimes. *(John Harris)*

CAMBRIDGE TL4458

Mill (01223) 311829

Mill Lane; CB2 1RX Fairly compact old pub in picturesque spot overlooking mill pond (punt hire); seven mainly local ales and proper cider from plank-topped servery, reasonably priced food such as burgers, opened-up bar with bare boards, quarry tiles and some exposed brickwork, mix of old and new furniture including pews and banquettes, snug panelled back room; radiogram playing vinyl, Mon quiz, sports TV, free wi-fi; children welcome, open (and food) all day. *(John Wooll)*

CAMBRIDGE TL4458

Mitre (01223) 358403

Bridge Street, opposite St John's College; CB2 1UF Popular Nicholsons pub close to the river and well placed for visiting the colleges; spacious rambling bar on several levels, good selection of well kept ales and reasonably priced wines by the glass, their usual food including range of pies, efficient friendly service; background music, free wi-fi; children welcome, disabled access, open (and food) all day. *(John Saville)*

CAMBRIDGE TL4559

Old Spring (01223) 357228

Ferry Path; car park on Chesterton Road; CB4 1HB Extended Victorian pub, roomy and airy, with enjoyable home-made food from traditional choices up, friendly efficient service, well kept Greene King IPA, Abbot and four guests, plenty of wines by the glass and good coffee, mix of seating including sofas on bare boards, log fires, conservatory; background music; well behaved children welcome, no dogs inside, disabled facilities, seats out at front and on large heated back terrace, open all day, food all day weekends. *(Toby Jones)*

CAMBRIDGE TL4459

★ Punter (01223) 363322

Pound Hill, on corner of A1303 ring road; CB3 0AE Former coaching inn (sister to the Punter in Oxford) with rambling series of informal rooms; pleasing mix of pews, elderly dining chairs and Lloyd Loom on old dark boards, paintings and antique prints, small area down steps with candles on scrubbed tables, Adnams, Mad Squirrel, Oakham and a guest, 15 wines by the glass and ten malt whiskies, interesting fairly priced food from seasonal menu, good friendly service, raftered and flagstoned dining room; background jazz, board games; children and dogs welcome, tables in mainly covered courtyard with another bar/dining area in barn beyond, open all day. *(Martin and Sue Neville, Edward Edmonton, Frances Parsons, Miranda and Jeff Davidson, Buster and Helena Hastings)*

CASTOR TL1298

Prince of Wales Feathers

(01733) 380222 *Peterborough Road, off A47; PE5 7AL* Friendly stone-built local with half a dozen well kept ales including Castor, craft beers and proper cider/perry, good value food cooked by landlady including Thurs steak night, open-plan interior with dining area to the left; Sat live music, Sun quiz, pool, TV; children and dogs welcome, disabled access/loos, attractive front terrace, another at the back with large smokers' shelter, open all day, till late weekends, no food Sun evening. *(Paul Farraday)*

CONINGTON   TL3266
White Swan (01954) 267251
Signed off A14 (was A604) Cambridge–Huntingdon; Elsworth Road; CB23 4LN
Quietly placed 18th-c red-brick country pub; well kept Adnams and guests tapped from the cask, nine wines by the glass and good freshly made food (not Sun evening, Mon, Tues), friendly attentive service, traditional bar with tiled floor and log fire, restaurant extension, some old photographs and local artwork; children and dogs welcome, big front garden with play area, open all day. *(Toby Jones)*

DUXFORD   TL4746
★ John Barleycorn (01223) 832699
Handy for M11 junction 10; right at first roundabout, then left at main village junction into Moorfield Road; CB22 4PP Charming 17th-c thatched and shuttered pub; heavy beams, standing timbers and brick pillars creating alcoves, nice old floor tiles, log fire and all manner of seating including some good antique farmhouse chairs, walls adorned with air force memorabilia, old clocks, china plates, copper pans and plenty of pictures, a couple of Greene King ales and guests such as Sadlers and Wadworths, ten wines by the glass, consistently good food from sandwiches and grazing boards up; background music, free wi-fi; children and dogs (in bar) welcome, easy wheelchair access from back car park, hanging baskets and blue-painted picnic-sets on front gravel, more tables in garden behind, comfortable barn-conversion bedrooms, handy for Imperial War Museum, open all day. *(David Fowler, Catherine and Daniel King, Roy Shutz, Adrian Buckland)*

DUXFORD   TL4745
Plough (01223) 833170
St Peters Street; CB22 4RP Popular early 18th-c thatched pub under new management, clean and bright, with enjoyable home-made lunchtime food, five real ales including Adnams and Everards, also a craft keg, four ciders/perries and good range of gins, friendly helpful service, woodburner in brick fireplace, art exhibitions upstairs; children and dogs welcome, handy for IWM Duxford, open all day. *(Julian Richardson)*

ELLINGTON   TL1671
Mermaid (01480) 891106
High Street; PE28 0AB Popular village dining pub dating in part from the 14th c; highly praised imaginative food (not Sun evening) from owner-chef including interesting tapas menu and plenty for vegetarians/vegans, three changing real ales from brick counter, several wines by the glass (good list), friendly obliging young staff, beams (some hiding coins left by US airmen), country furniture, woodburner, smallish dining rooms; background music (turned off on request); garden overlooking church, no proper car park, open all day weekends (till 8pm Sun), closed Mon. *(Edward Nile)*

ELSWORTH   TL3163
George & Dragon (01954) 267236
Off A14 NW of Cambridge, via Boxworth, or off A428; CB23 8JQ Neatly kept dining pub in same group as the Rose at Stapleford; panelled and carpeted main bar opening on left to slightly elevated dining area with woodburner, garden room overlooking attractive terraces, more formal restaurant on right, wide choice of popular food including speciality fish/seafood, set menus and other deals, Greene King ales, a guest beer and decent range of wines, friendly attentive service; steps down to loos, free wi-fi; children welcome, dogs in bar, open (and food) all day Sun. *(Mrs Margo Finlay, Jörg Kasprowski)*

ELSWORTH   TL3163
Poacher (01954) 267722
Brockley Road; CB23 4JS Welcoming 17th-c thatched and beamed corner local; well kept Woodfordes Wherry and a couple of guests from tiny servery, good reasonably priced traditional food (not Sun evening), friendly service, painted pine furniture on bare boards or tiles, open fire; background and some live music, monthly quiz, TV; children and dogs welcome (they have two huskies), a few picnic-sets out in front, more in back garden, good walks, open all day Sat, until 6pm Sun. *(Charlie Stevens)*

ELTON   TL0893
Black Horse (01832) 280591
Overend; B671 off A605 W of Peterborough and A1(M); PE8 6RU Honey-stone beamed dining pub with nicely updated and opened-up interior; popular generously served food cooked by owner-chef, friendly accommodating service, four real ales including Digfield, Greene King and a beer badged for them, decent wines; children welcome, dogs in bar, terrace and garden with views across to Elton Hall park and village church, open (and food) all day. *(Mark Morgan)*

ELY   TL5479
Cutter (01353) 662713
Annesdale, off Station Road (or walk S along Riverside Walk from Maltings); CB7 4BN Beautifully placed riverside pub with bar, dining lounge and restaurant; enjoyable food from sandwiches and wraps up, friendly helpful service, well kept Sharps, Woodfordes and a guest from boat-shaped counter, nice wines by the glass and decent coffee, good views from window seats and terrace; quiz Mon; children welcome, no dogs inside, moorings, open all day from 10am (food from midday). *(John Saville)*

ELY TL5480
Lamb (01353) 663574
Brook Street (Lynn Road); CB7 4EJ
Good choice of food in popular hotel's
panelled lounge bar or restaurant, friendly
welcoming staff, Greene King ales and
plenty of wines by the glass; children and
dogs welcome, close to cathedral, 37 clean
comfortable bedrooms, good breakfast (for
non-residents too), open (and food) all day.
(Toby Jones)

ETTON TF1406
Golden Pheasant (01733) 252387
*Just off B1443 N of Peterborough, signed
from near N end of A15 bypass;
PE6 7DA* Welcoming former Georgian
farmhouse (a pub since 1964); spacious
bar with open fire, good choice of real ales
and other drinks, well liked food served by
friendly staff, back restaurant; TV; children
welcome, no dogs inside, big tree-sheltered
garden with play area, on Green Wheel cycle
route, closed Sun evening, otherwise open
all day. *(John Harris)*

FEN DRAYTON TL3468
Three Tuns (01954) 230242
*Eastbound on A14, take first exit after
Fenstanton, signed Fen Drayton and
follow to pub; westbound on A14 exit at
junction 27 and follow signs to village
on Cambridge Road; High Street;
CB24 4SJ* Well preserved thatched village
pub with three more-or-less open-plan rooms;
heavy moulded Tudor beams and timbers,
log fires, mix of burgundy cushioned stools,
nice old dining chairs and settles in bar,
red-patterned carpet in dining room, well
kept Greene King IPA, Old Speckled Hen
and a couple of guests, 14 wines by the glass,
good reasonably priced pubby food including
blackboard specials, friendly service; some
quiz and live music nights; children and dogs
(in bar) welcome, back garden with covered
dining area and play equipment, open all
day Fri and Sat, till 6pm Sun, closed Mon.
(B and M Kendall, Michael Butler)

FOWLMERE TL4245
Chequers (01763) 208558
High Street (B1368); SG8 7SR This
popular 16th-c coaching inn was closed for
refurbishment as we went to press; split-
level rooms (one with inglenook), spacious
conservatory and attractive upstairs timbered
dining room; children and dogs have been
welcome, paved terrace and lawn, bedrooms;
reports please. *(Nicola and Holly Lyons)*

GRANTCHESTER TL4355
★ Blue Ball (01223) 846004
Broadway; CB3 9NQ Traditional bare-
boards free house rebuilt in 1900 on site of
much older pub (cellars remain); welcoming
licensees (there's a list of publicans back
to 1767), three real ales such as Adnams

and Woodfordes, Aspall's ciders and decent
choice of wines by the glass, affordably
priced wholesome food, good log fire; some
live music, traditional games including shut
the box and ring the bull, newspapers and
lots of books; children and dogs welcome,
tables on small terrace with lovely views to
Grantchester Meadows, two comfortable
bedrooms, nice village, open all day (till 8pm
Sun). *(Paul Farraday)*

GRANTCHESTER TL4355
Red Lion (01223) 840121
High Street; CB3 9NF Comfortable and
spacious thatched pub with attractively
modernised open areas including pitched-
roof dining room, beams, timbers and
panelling, popular food from shortish varied
menu, well kept ales such as Nene Valley,
Greene King, Oakham and Woodfordes, lots
of wines by the glass and some interesting
gins including Cambridge distilled nearby;
background music; children, dogs and muddy
boots welcome, sheltered terrace and good-
sized lawn with play area, easy walk to river,
open (and food) all day. *(Toby Jones)*

GRANTCHESTER TL4455
Rupert Brooke (01223) 841875
*Broadway; junction Coton Road with
Cambridge–Trumpington Road;
CB3 9NQ* Smartly presented restauranty
pub; contemporary wood-clad extension at
front with big windows, elegant dining chairs
around polished tables on bare boards, back
bar area and two-level restaurant, brasserie-
style food from open kitchen including set
lunch, a couple of real ales and over 20 wines
by the glass, afternoon tea (not Sun), good
friendly service, upstairs club room and roof
terrace; free wi-fi; children and dogs (in
bar) welcome, open all day (till 7pm Sun),
breakfast from 9am Mon-Sat. *(Monica and
Steph Evans)*

GREAT ABINGTON TL5348
Three Tuns (01223) 891467
*Off A1307 Cambridge–Haverhill, and
A11; CB21 6AB* Peacefully set 16th-c
beamed village pub; low-backed settles on
stripped-wood floors, open fires, three well
kept changing ales and good authentic thai
food (traditional roast on Sun), welcoming
landlord and friendly efficient staff; garden
picnic-sets, nine well appointed bedrooms in
modern block, open all day weekends.
(Mark Morgan)

GREAT CHISHILL TL4239
Pheasant (01763) 838535
*Follow Heydon signpost from B1039 in
village; SG8 8SR* Old split-level pub with
beams, timbers, flagstones and open fires,
welcoming friendly staff, a Nethergate house
beer and a couple of guests from herringbone
brick counter, enjoyable food including some
blackboard specials, small dining room;
children and dogs welcome, nice secluded

back garden with small play area and pétanque, open all day weekends, closed Mon lunchtime. *(Caroline and Steve Archer)*

GREAT WILBRAHAM   TL5558
Carpenters Arms (01223) 882093
Off A14 or A11 SW of Newmarket, following The Wilbrahams signposts; High Street; CB21 5JD Village pub dating from the 17th c; traditional low-ceilinged bar on right with straightforward furniture on floor tiles, inglenook woodburner, copper pots and iron tools, bar billiards, own Crafty beers and carefully chosen wines (strong on the Roussillon region), fairly standard home-made food (some french influences) in small carpeted dining area to the left with another big stone fireplace, or in light and airy restaurant extension; children welcome, no dogs inside, attractive homely garden and pretty back courtyard, closed Sun evening, Mon and Tues; for sale, so may be changes. *(Cecily and Steven Evans, Robert and Diana Ringstone, Simon King)*

HADDENHAM   TL4675
Three Kings (01353) 749080
Station Road; CB6 3XD Popular 17th-c village pub; enjoyable home-made food from sandwiches and pub favourites up including good Sun roasts and Thurs curry night, well kept Greene King IPA and guests, friendly welcoming staff, log fire; children and dogs allowed, back courtyard, open all day, food all day weekends. *(John Harris)*

HAIL WESTON   TL1662
Royal Oak (01480) 716712
High Street; just off A45, handy for A1 St Neots bypass; PE19 5JW Picturesque 17th-c thatched pub in pretty village near Grafham Water; cosy interior with beams, flagstones and inglenook log fire, three Adnams ales along with Sharps Doom Bar, enjoyable home-made food including set deal Weds and Thurs, helpful willing service, restaurant; background music (vinyl night third Weds of month), Sun quiz; children and dogs (in bar) welcome, picnic-sets in back garden with sandpit, good circular walks (ask for details), limited parking, closed Mon and Tues, otherwise open all day, no food Sun evening. *(Michael Sargent)*

HARDWICK   TL3758
Blue Lion (01954) 789593
Signed off A428 (was A45) W of Cambridge; Main Street; CB23 7QU Attractive 18th-c split-level dining pub refurbished under new management; good generously served food, can eat in bar or extended dining area with conservatory, three Greene King ales, friendly efficient young staff, white-painted beams and timbers, copper-canopied inglenook; children and dogs welcome, pretty little front garden, more seats on decking and lawn with play area, handy for Wimpole Way walks, open all day Fri-Sun, no food Sun evening. *(Julia and Andrew Blanchett)*

HELPSTON   TF1205
Blue Bell (01733) 252394
Woodgate; off B1443; PE6 7ED Renovated and extended 17th-c stone pub; enjoyable food from sharing plates and pub favourites up, three well kept ales, good range of wines and gins, friendly staff; children and dogs welcome, four bedrooms, open all day weekends, no food Sun evening; John Clare's cottage next door (open Fri, Sat and Mon). *(Toby Jones)*

HEMINGFORD ABBOTS   TL2870
★ Axe & Compass (01480) 463605
High Street; village signposted off A14 W of Cambridge; PE28 9AH Spacious old thatched pub in pretty village; simple, beamed public bar with mate's chairs and stools around wooden tables on ancient floor tiles, two-way fireplace (not in use) into snug, woodburner here and in main room with more beams and standing timbers, tartan-patterned chairs and cushioned wall seats around nice old tables, local photographs, Adnams Lighthouse, Sharps Doom Bar and Timothy Taylors Landlord, local cider and 12 wines by the glass, well liked fairly priced food (all day Sat, not Sun evening, Mon) from pub favourites up, long dining extension; background music (live first Fri of month), quiz Tues, board games; well behaved children and dogs (in bar) welcome, disabled facilities, contemporary furniture on terrace, picnic-sets on grass, fenced play area, river walks, closed Mon lunchtime, otherwise open all day. *(Julian Richardson)*

HEYDON   TL4339
★ King William IV (01763) 838773
Off A505 W of M11 junction 10; SG8 8PW Rambling dimly lit rooms with fascinating rustic jumble (ploughshares, yokes, iron tools, cowbells and so forth) along with copperware and china in nooks and crannies, some tables suspended by chains from beams, central log fire, Fullers, Greene King and Timothy Taylors, good choice of highly rated food including several vegetarian options, helpful staff; background music; children and dogs (in bar) welcome, picnic-sets in back garden with decked area overlooking fields, four

bedrooms in separate building, open (and food) all day weekends. *(Roy Shutz)*

HISTON   TL4363
★ **Red Lion** (01223) 564437
High Street, off Station Road; 3.7 miles from M11 junction 1; CB24 9JD
Impressive choice of draught and bottled beers along with traditional cider/perry (festivals Easter/early Sept); ceiling joists in L-shaped main bar packed with beer mats, pump clips and whisky-water jugs, also fine collection of old brewery advertisements and enamel signs, enjoyable traditional food (not Fri, Sun evenings) including a gluten-free menu, cheerful efficient service, log fires, comfortable brocaded wall seats, matching mate's chairs and pubby tables, extended bar on left (well behaved children allowed here) with darts, TV and huge collection of beer bottles, quiz first Sun of month; mobile phones discouraged, no dogs inside; disabled access/facilities, picnic-sets in neat garden, limited parking, four bedrooms, open all day. *(Caroline and Steve Archer)*

HOUGHTON   TL2772
Three Jolly Butchers
(01480) 463228 *A1123, Wyton; PE28 2AD* Popular 17th-c beamed pub with wide choice of enjoyable home-made food from bar and restaurant menus, friendly accommodating service, well kept ales including Greene King, inglenook woodburner; background and live music, quiz nights, sports TV; well behaved children and dogs (in bar) welcome, covered back terrace with pool table, picnic-sets in large garden down to River Ouse (own moorings), pretty village and handy for Houghton Mill (NT), open (and food) all day, kitchen closes 4pm Sun. *(Mike Kavaney)*

HUNTINGDON   TL2572
King of Belgians (01480) 52030
Main Street, Hartford; PE29 1XU
Traditional and welcoming little 16th-c beamed village local; four well kept changing ales, real cider and popular good value home-made food including stone-baked pizzas in bar or dining lounge; events including live music and quiz nights, charity beer/music festival in May, darts, shut the box and other traditional games, TV for major sports; children and dogs (in bar) welcome, rattan-style furniture on back terrace, open all day (till midnight Fri, Sat). *(Mr Marchant)*

KIMBOLTON   TL0967
New Sun (01480) 860052
High Street; PE28 0HA Pink-painted village pub with cosy low-beamed front lounge, standing timbers and exposed brickwork, comfortable seats by log fire, narrower locals' bar serving Bombardier, Eagle IPA and a guest, several wines by the glass and decent range of gins, well liked food including tapas, friendly service, traditionally

---

furnished dining room and airy conservatory leading to terrace with café-style furniture under giant umbrellas; background music, piano; well behaved children welcome away from bar, dogs allowed in bar, open all day, no food Sun or Mon evenings. *(Peter Andrews, Richard Kennell)*

LEIGHTON BROMSWOLD   TL1175
Green Man (01480) 890238
Signed off A14 Huntingdon–Kettering; PE28 5AW Cosy traditional village pub with origins from the 13th c; four well kept changing ales and enjoyable good value hearty food, friendly long-serving landlady, plenty of unpretentious old-fashioned character with heavy low beams and inglenook log fire; events including live music and quiz nights, northants skittles; children, walkers and dogs welcome, picnic-sets outside, closed Sun evening, Mon. *(Guy Howard)*

LITTLE SHELFORD   TL4551
Navigator (01223) 843901
2.5 miles from M11 junction 11: A10 towards Royston, then left at Hauxton, The Shelfords signpost; CB2 5ES
Attractive little 16th-c village pub with bar and small restaurant; beams, painted panelling and some exposed brickwork, open fire, good authentic thai food, mainstream ales and decent wines, friendly prompt service; children welcome, some picnic-sets outside. *(Charlie Stevens)*

NEWTON   TL4349
★ **Queens Head** (01223) 870436
2.5 miles from M11 junction 11; A10 towards Royston, then left on to B1368; CB22 7PG Lovely traditional unchanging pub run by same welcoming family for many years – lots of loyal customers; peaceful bow-windowed main bar with crooked beams in low ceiling, bare wooden benches and seats built into cream walls, curved high-backed settle, paintings and big log fire, well kept Adnams ales tapped from the cask, farm cider and simple food such as soup and sandwiches, small carpeted saloon, traditional games including table skittles, shove-ha'penny and nine men's morris; children on best behaviour allowed in games room only, dogs welcome, seats out in front by vine trellis. *(Muriel and Spencer Harrap)*

OFFORD D'ARCY   TL2166
Horseshoe (01480) 810293
High Street; PE19 5RH Extended former 17th-c coaching house with two bars and restaurant; emphasis on their good food including popular Sun carvery, Sharps Doom Bar, a couple of guests and well chosen wines, friendly helpful service, beams and inglenooks; children welcome, dogs in snug (not Sun), lawned garden with play area, open all day Sat, till 9pm Sun. *(Elise and Charles Mackinlay)*

ORWELL　　　　　　　　TL3650
Chequers (01223) 207840
Town Green Road; SG8 5QL Village
dining pub with good food (not Tues or Sun
evenings) from pub favourites up including
popular themed nights, well kept ales
and decent choice of wines by the glass,
friendly helpful staff; quiz every other Wed;
children and dogs (in bar) welcome, disabled
facilities, handy for Wimpole Hall (NT), open
all day Fri and Sat, till 8pm Sun, closed Mon.
(Paul Farraday)

PAMPISFORD　　　　　　TL4948
★Chequers (01223) 833220
*2.6 miles from M11 junction 10: A505
E, then village and pub signed off; Town
Lane; CB22 4ER* Traditional neatly kept
old pub with low beams and comfortable
old-fashioned furnishings, booth seating on
pale ceramic tiles in main area, low step
down to bare-boards part, four real ales such
as Greene King IPA and Woodfordes Wherry,
well liked fairly priced pubby food including
Sun carvery, good friendly service; TV, free
wi-fi; children and dogs welcome, picnic-sets
in small garden lit by black streetlamps,
parking can be tricky, open all day (till 4pm
Sun). *(Julian Richardson)*

PETERBOROUGH　　　　TL1998
★Charters (01733) 315700
Town Bridge, S side; PE1 1FP Interesting
conversion of dutch grain barge moored on
River Nene; sizeable timbered bar on lower
deck with up to a dozen real ales including
Oakham (regular beer festivals), restaurant
above serving good value south-east asian
food, lots of wooden tables and pews;
background music, live bands (Fri and Sat
after 10.30pm, Sun from 3.30pm); children
welcome till 9pm, dogs in bar, huge riverside
garden (gets packed in fine weather), open
all day (maybe till 1am Fri, Sat). *(Charlie
Stevens)*

PETERBOROUGH　　　　TL1897
Coalheavers Arms (01733) 565664
Park Street, Woodston; PE2 9BH Friendly
old-fashioned little flagstoned local near
football ground (busy on match days); half
a dozen well kept ales and good range of
bottled beers, traditional cider and several
malt whiskies, basic snacks; Sun quiz, free
wi-fi; dogs welcome, pleasant garden behind,
open all day Fri-Sun, closed lunchtime Mon-
Weds. *(Charlie Stevenson)*

PETERBOROUGH　　　　TL1898
Drapers Arms (01733) 847570
Cowgate; PE1 1LZ Roomy open-plan
Wetherspoons in converted 19th-c draper's;

ten well kept ales and their usual good
value food served all day, prompt friendly
service; TV, free wi-fi; children welcome,
open from 8am and can get very busy Fri, Sat
evenings. *(Charlie Stevenson, Sam Taylor)*

REACH　　　　　　　　TL5666
Dykes End (01638) 743816
*From B1102 follow signpost to
Swaffham Prior and Upware; village
signposted; CB25 0JD* Another change of
management for this 17th-c village pub as we
went to press – reports please.

SPALDWICK　　　　　　TL1372
George (01480) 890293
*Just off A14 W of Huntingdon; PE28
0TD* Former 17th-c village coaching inn with
good food (till 7pm Sun) from bar snacks
up, Timothy Taylors Landlord, Woodfordes
Wherry and a guest, decent wines by the
glass, friendly if not always speedy service,
sofas in beamed bar, larger dining area
including raftered part; children and dogs
(in bar) welcome, seats out behind under
parasols, open all day Fri-Sun. *(Andy Kent)*

ST IVES　　　　　　　TL3171
Oliver Cromwell (01480) 465601
Wellington Street; PE27 5AZ Homely
two-bar pub in little street just back from
the river; enjoyable good value lunchtime
food such as steak and kidney pudding, half
a dozen well kept changing ales, proper
ciders and good choice of wines, friendly
staff; background music (live Thurs), quiz
first Tues of the month (not summer); small
back terrace, open all day. *(Julia and Andrew
Blanchett)*

STAPLEFORD　　　　　TL4651
Rose (01223) 843349
*London Road; M11 junction 11;
CB22 5DG* Comfortable sister dining pub
to the George & Dragon at Elsworth; good
choice of popular fairly pubby food including
set menus and Mon/Tues early bird deal,
three well kept real ales, friendly uniformed
staff, small low-ceilinged lounge with
inglenook woodburner, roomy split-level
dining area; steps up to lavatories; picnic-
sets on back grass, open (and food) all day
weekends. *(Monty Green)*

SUTTON GAULT　　　　TL4279
★Anchor (01353) 778537
*Bury Lane, off High Street (B1381);
CB6 2BD* Charming old inn tucked away
near the river with emphasis on good
imaginative food; stylishly simple with four
heavily timbered rooms, antique settles and
scrubbed pine tables on gently undulating
floors, two log fires, ales such as Milton,

If you report on a pub that's not a featured entry, please tell us any lunchtimes or
evenings when it doesn't serve bar food.

Nethergate, Oldershaw and Three Blind Mice, a dozen wines by the glass; children welcome, seats outside and you can walk along the high embankment (good bird-watching), comfortable well equipped bedrooms, open all day. *(Andy and Rosemary Taylor, M and GR, Richard and Penny Gibbs, Dr W I C Clark, Julie Braeburn)*

SWAFFHAM PRIOR   TL5663

Red Lion (01638) 745483

B1102 NE of Cambridge; High Street; CB5 0LD Comfortable and welcoming 17th-c pub with well kept Batemans and guests, a dozen wines by the glass and enjoyable sensibly priced home-made food (not Sun evening, Mon, Tues lunchtime), OAP weekday set lunch, helpful friendly staff, beams, old quarry tiles and brick fireplace, historic local photographs; quiz third Sun of month, darts, TV; children welcome, picnic-sets in back garden, interesting church and priory, open all day Sat, till 8pm Sun (later on quiz nights), closed lunchtimes Mon and Tues. *(David Bird, M and GR)*

THRIPLOW   TL4346

Green Man (01763) 208855

3 miles from M11 junction 10; A505 towards Royston, then first right; Lower Street; SG8 7RJ Welcoming little roadside pub owned by the village; good food from shortish daily changing menu along with blackboard tapas, four well kept ales and decent wines by the glass, efficient friendly service; free lift home for local evening diners (must book); children and dogs welcome, picnic-sets on small grassy triangle in front, two circular walks from the pub, open (and food) all day. *(John Harris)*

WHITTLESFORD   TL4648

Bees in the Wall (01223) 834289

North Road; handy for M11 junction 10 and IWM Duxford; CB22 4NZ Village-edge local with comfortably worn-in split-level timbered lounge, polished tables and country prints, small tiled public bar with old wall settles, darts, decent good value food from shortish menu, well kept Adnams Lighthouse and one or two guests, open fires; background and live music including folk club second Tues of month, small TV for major sports; children welcome, no dogs, picnic-sets in big paddock-style garden with terrace, bees still in the wall (here since the 1950s), closed all day Mon, lunchtimes Tues-Thurs (and Sat in winter), no food Sun evening or Tues. *(Caroline and Steve Archer)*

Cheshire

ALDFORD
SJ4259 Map 7

Grosvenor Arms ★ ♀

(01244) 620228 – www.brunningandprice.co.uk/grosvenorarms

B5130 Chester–Wrexham; CH3 6HJ

Spacious place with impressive range of drinks, wide-ranging imaginative menu, good service, sun-trap terrace and garden

Part of the Grosvenor Estate, this is a large brick and half-timbered pub with a good mix of customers of all ages. There's a lot of interest and individuality in the spacious cream-painted areas that are sectioned by big knocked-through arches. A variety of floor finishes includes wood, quarry tiles, flagstones, black and white tiles, and the richly coloured turkish rugs look well against these natural materials. Good solid pieces of traditional furniture, plenty of pictures and attractive lighting keep it all cosy. A handsome room has tall bookshelves lining one wall and they keep a good selection of board games. Well trained, attentive staff serve Phoenix Brunning & Price Original, Timothy Taylors Landlord, Weetwood Eastgate and guests such as Big Hand Seren, Salopian Oracle and Timothy Taylors Dark Mild from a fine-looking bar counter, and they offer 20 wines by the glass, more than 80 whiskies, 30 gins and farm cider. The airy terracotta-floored conservatory (lovely on summer evenings) has lots of gigantic low-hanging flowering baskets and chunky pale wood garden furniture. It opens out to a large elegant suntrap terrace and a neat lawn with picnic-sets; the village green is opposite. Disabled access.

Interesting food includes sandwiches, thai crab sesame cakes with asian salad, chilli and lime marmalade, baked camembert with plum and ginger chutney, sweet potato and chickpea pie with beetroot sauce, rosemary and garlic chicken breast with pasta, wild mushroom, bacon and spinach, steak burger with toppings, coleslaw and chips, sea bream with scallops, samphire and grape and white wine sauce, lamb shoulder with dauphinoise potatoes and red cabbage, and puddings such as triple chocolate brownie with chocolate sauce and blackberry compote with yoghurt, lemon curd and granola. *Benchmark main dish: smoked haddock kedgeree with a poached egg £10.50. Two-course evening meal £21.00.*

Brunning & Price ~ Manager Justin Realff ~ Real ale ~ Open 11-11; 12-10.30 Sun ~ Bar food 12-9.30; 12-9 Sun ~ Children welcome ~ Dogs allowed in bar ~ Wi-fi
Recommended by Dr and Mrs A K Clarke, Nik and Gloria Clarke, Julie Swift, Karl and Frieda Bujeya, Mick Allen

---

Pubs close to motorway junctions are listed at the back of the book.

ALLOSTOCK   SJ7271   Map 7

Three Greyhounds Inn 🌟 ♚

(01565) 723455 – www.thethreegreyhoundsinn.co.uk

4.7 miles from M6 junction 18: A54 E then fork left on to B5803 into Holmes Chapel, left at roundabout on to A50 for 2 miles, then left on to B5082 towards Northwich; Holmes Chapel Road; WA16 9JY

Relaxing, civilised and welcoming, with enjoyable food and drink all day

The staff here go out of their way to make you feel welcome and this, combined with a fine choice of drinks and highly regarded food, is why our readers tell us they are 'mightily impressed' by the place. The rooms are linked by open doorways and décor throughout is restful: candles and soft lighting, thick rugs on quarry tiles or bare boards, and dark grey walls (or interesting woven wooden ones made from old brandy barrels) hung with modern black-on-white prints. There's an appealing variety of wooden dining chairs, cushioned wall seats, little stools and plenty of plump purple scatter cushions around all sorts of tables; do note the one made from giant bellows. A smashing choice of drinks includes 15 interesting wines by the glass, over 50 brandies and six local cider brandies, a farm cider and Three Greyhounds Bitter (named for the pub from Weetwood), Byley Bomber, English Ales Black Hound Stout and a couple of guest ales on handpump; unobtrusive background music and board games. Above the old farm barns is a restored private dining and party room called the Old Dog House. The big side lawn has picnic-table sets under parasols, with more tables on a decked side verandah with a Perspex roof. Shakerley Mere nature reserve is just across the road. The pub is owned by Tim Bird and Mary McLaughlin of Cheshire Cat Pubs & Bars.

 Rewarding food includes ham hock terrine with caramelised apple sauce, field mushrooms with shallots, cognac and cream, sharing boards, sweet potato, chickpea and spinach curry, beer-battered haddock and chips, sausages of the day with mash and shallot gravy, calves liver with mash, spinach and onion gravy, pork chop with cheddar, apple and cider sauce, 28-day aged rib-eye steak with a choice of sauce, and puddings such as apple and blackberry crumble with vanilla custard and sticky toffee pudding with rum and raisin ice-cream. *Benchmark main dish: chicken, smoked ham, leek and tarragon pie £13.95. Two-course evening meal £20.00.*

Free house ~ Licensee James Macadam ~ Real ale ~ Open 10.30am-11pm; 10.30-10.30 Sun ~ Bar food 12-9.15 ~ Children welcome until 7pm ~ Dogs allowed in bar ~ Wi-fi
Recommended by Dr and Mrs A K Clarke, Steve Whalley, R Gollin, James and Sylvia Hewitt, John and Claire Masters

ASTON   SJ6146   Map 7

Bhurtpore ★ ♚ 🍴 £

(01270) 780917 – www.bhurtpore.co.uk
Off A530 SW of Nantwich; in village follow Wrenbury signpost; CW5 8DQ

Warm-hearted pub with some unusual artefacts and an excellent range of drinks (especially real ales); big garden

Good curries and a wonderful choice of drinks keep customers coming back to this busy, well run pub on a regular basis. There are around 11 constantly changing real ales from all over the country, which might include Beat New Wave, Heavy Industry 77, Hobsons Postmans Plum Porter, Merlin Merlins Gold, Oakham Citra, Redwillow Weightless Mosaic, Roosters High Tea IPA and International Orange, Salopian Oracle, Thornbridge Kipling and Three Tuns Best. You'll also find dozens of unusual bottled beers and fruit beers, a great many bottled ciders and perries and farm cider, over 100 different whiskies, 100 gins, 20 vodkas, 22 rums, carefully selected soft drinks and a dozen wines by the glass from a good list. The pub name commemorates the 1826 siege of Bhurtpore (a town in India) during which local landowner Sir Stapleton Cotton (later Viscount Combermere) was commander-in-chief. The connection with India also explains some of the quirky artefacts in the carpeted lounge bar – look out for the sunglasses-wearing turbanned figure behind the counter. There are also good local period photographs and some attractive furniture in the comfortable public bar; board games, pool, TV and games machine. Disabled access.

Tasty food includes eight curries plus sandwiches, panko-covered brie with cumberland dressing, breaded cheese and leek cakes, lasagne, steak and kidney in ale pie, braised half lamb shoulder in mint and sherry sauce, chicken breast in creamy stilton and smoked bacon sauce, beer-battered haddock and chips, toulouse sausages with red wine sauce, salmon fillets wrapped in lattice pastry with white wine sauce, and puddings. *Benchmark main dish: chicken and spinach balti £11.50. Two-course evening meal £17.00.*

Free house ~ Licensee Simon George ~ Real ale ~ Open 12-11.30 (midnight Fri, Sat); 12-11 Sun ~ Bar food 12-2, 7-9; 12-9 Fri-Sun ~ Restaurant ~ Children welcome until 8pm ~ Dogs allowed in bar ~ Wi-fi *Recommended by Charles Fraser, Christopher Mannings, Brian and Anna Marsden, Emily and Toby Archer, Christine and Tony Garrett*

BARTHOMLEY
White Lion £

SJ7752 Map 7

(01270) 882242 – www.whitelion-barthomley.co.uk
M6 junction 16, B5078 N towards Alsager, then Barthomley signed on left; CW2 5PG

Timeless 17th-c thatched village tavern with classic period interior, up to half a dozen real ales and good value lunchtime food

If ever there was a perfect respite from the dreary M6, then this timeless and unpretentious pub is it. The bar has a blazing open fire, heavy oak beams dating from Stuart times, attractively moulded black panelling, prints of Cheshire on the walls, latticed windows and uneven wobbly old tables. Up some steps, a second room has another welcoming open fire, more oak panelling, a high-backed winged settle and a paraffin lamp hinged to the wall; shove-ha'penny. Local societies make good use of a third room. Banks's Sunbeam, Jennings Cocker Hoop and Sneck Lifter, Marstons Saddle Tank and Wainwright and a guest beer on handpump and eight wines by the glass served by genuinely friendly staff. The gents' are across an open courtyard. In summer, seats on cobbles outside offer nice views over the pretty village. The early 15th-c red sandstone church of St Bertoline (where you can learn about the Barthomley massacre) is worth a visit.

Traditional lunchtime-only food is good value: sandwiches and baguettes, various hotpots, quiche lorraine, lasagne, sausage and mash with onion gravy, and puddings such as bread and butter pudding. *Benchmark main dish: steak in Guinness pie £8.95.*

Marstons ~ Tenant Katy Hollins ~ Real ale ~ Open 12-11 (10.30 Sun) ~ Bar food 12-2 Mon, Tues; 12-3 Weds-Fri; 12-6 weekends ~ Children welcome away from bar counter ~ Dogs welcome ~ Wi-fi ~ Quiz first Tues of the month *Recommended by John Saville, Andrew Wall, Dr and Mrs A K Clarke, Buster May, Tony Scott, Bridget and Peter Gregson, Paul Scofield*

Bedroom prices include full english breakfast, VAT and any inclusive service charge that we know of.

BOSTOCK GREEN
SJ6769   Map 7

Hayhurst Arms ♈ 🍺

(01606) 541810 – www.brunningandprice.co.uk/hayhurstarms

London Road, Bostock Green; CW10 9JP

Interesting pub with a marvellous range of drinks, a wide choice of rewarding food, friendly staff and seats outside

This former stables and coach house has been cleverly converted and extended. The long main bar is divided into different dining areas by elegant supporting pillars, and it's light and airy throughout: big windows, house plants, bookshelves, standard lamps, metal chandeliers and prints, old photographs and paintings arranged frame-to-frame above wooden dados. The varied dark wooden dining chairs are grouped around tables of all sizes on rugs, quarry tiles, wide floorboards and carpet, and three open fireplaces have big mirrors above them, with hefty leather armchairs to each side. A couple of cosier rooms lead off; background music and board games. Phoenix Brunning & Price Original and Weetwood Eastgate Ale with guests such as Beartown Kodiak Gold, Mobberley Road Runner and Moorhouses Stray Dog on handpump, 25 wines by the glass, 70 malt whiskies and 60 gins; staff are efficient and courteous. The outside terrace is furnished with good quality tables and chairs under parasols, and the village green opposite has swings and a play tractor.

 Enjoyable modern food includes sandwiches, wild mushrooms on toast with spinach, garlic and truffle oil, smoked mackerel rillettes with cucumber and fennel salad, stilton, caramelised red onion and potato pie with carrot purée and redcurrant jus, pork sausages with mash and onion gravy, garlic and tarragon chicken breast with pasta, wild mushrooms and spinach, roasted hake with chorizo and chickpea stew, duck breast with potato fondant, black cherry sauce, sweet potato purée and kale, and puddings such as toasted waffle with glazed pineapple, passion-fruit sauce and coconut ice-cream and dark chocolate, Cointreau and orange trifle. *Benchmark main dish: beer-battered cod and chips £13.75. Two-course evening meal £22.00.*

Brunning & Price ~ Manager Nicola Gow ~ Real ale ~ Open 11-11; 11-10.30 Sun ~ Bar food 12-9.30; 12-10 Fri, Sat; 12-9 Sun ~ Children welcome ~ Dogs allowed in bar ~ Wi-fi
Recommended by Sally and Brian Turner, John and Lorna Chew, Tim and Mary Thomson, Malcolm and Pauline Pellatt

BUNBURY
SJ5658   Map 7

Dysart Arms ♈ 🍺

(01829) 260183 – www.brunningandprice.co.uk/dysart

Bowes Gate Road; village signposted off A51 NW of Nantwich; and from A49 S of Tarporley – coming in this way on northernmost village access road, bear left in village centre; CW6 9PH

Civilised chatty dining pub with thoughtfully laid-out rooms, enjoyable food and a lovely garden with pretty views

On a warm day, you'll need to arrive early if you want to bag one of the sturdy wooden tables on the terrace or a picnic-set on the lawn in the neatly kept and slightly elevated garden; the views of the splendid church at the end of this pretty village and the distant Peckforton Hills are lovely. Although the interior has been opened up, the neatly kept rooms still retain a cottagey feel as they ramble around the pleasantly lit central bar. Each room (some with open fires) is nicely furnished with an appealing variety of well spaced sturdy wooden tables and chairs, a couple of tall filled bookcases and just the right amount of carefully chosen bric-a-brac, properly lit pictures and plants. Flooring ranges from red and black tiles to stripped boards and some carpet. Phoenix Brunning & Price Original and Weetwood Best Bitter with guests such as Facers North Star Porter, Hawkshead Lakeland Gold, Redwillow Headless and Salopian Oracle on handpump, alongside a good selection of 20 wines by the glass, 60 gins and around 40 malt whiskies; background music and board games. Disabled access.

Tempting food includes sandwiches, maple-glazed pork belly with cauliflower purée, apple and caramelised baby onions, crispy baby squid with sweet chilli sauce, butternut squash and sage tortellini with wilted spinach, capers, tomato and lemon, honey-roasted ham and eggs, chicken, ham and leek pie, tandoori-roasted hake with prawn and sesame toast, fennel and cucumber salad and almond pilau rice, lamb shoulder with dauphinoise potatoes, sticky red cabbage and gravy, and puddings such as crème brûlée and dark chocolate and orange tart with passion-fruit sorbet. *Benchmark main dish: local sausages with mash and onion gravy £11.95. Two-course evening meal £22.00.*

Brunning & Price ~ Manager Daniel Rose ~ Real ale ~ Open 10am-11pm ~ Bar food 12-9 (9.30 Sat) ~ Children welcome ~ Dogs allowed in bar ~ Wi-fi *Recommended by Mark Morgan, Simon and Alex Knight, Charles Fraser, Usha and Terri Patel, Anne and Ben Smith*

BURLEYDAM
Combermere Arms

SJ6042   Map 7

(01948) 871223 – www.brunningandprice.co.uk/combermere
A525 Whitchurch–Audlem; SY13 4AT

Roomy and attractive beamed pub successfully mixing a good drinking side with imaginative all-day food

The many rambling, yet intimate-feeling rooms here are attractive and understated. The various nooks and crannies are filled with all sorts of antique cushioned dining chairs around dark wood tables, rugs on wood (some old, some new oak) and stone floors, prints hung frame-to-frame on cream walls, bookshelves and open fires. Friendly, efficient staff serve Phoenix Brunning & Price Original and Weetwood Cheshire Cat Blonde Ale and guests from breweries such as Moorhouses, Plassey, Salopian and Timothy Taylors on handpump, 60 gins, 40 malt whiskies, 15 wines by the glass from an extensive list and two farm ciders; board games and background music. Outside there are good solid wood tables and picnic-sets in a pretty, well tended garden.

Reliably good food includes sandwiches, ham hock and caper croquettes with piccalilli, tempura sea bass fillet with mango and chilli salsa, wild mushroom tortellini with spinach and leek purée, pork and leek sausages with mash and onion gravy, salmon and smoked haddock fishcake with a poached egg and chive sauce, malaysian chicken curry with coconut rice, beef bourguignon with mustard mash and kale, and puddings such as baked cherry and amaretti cheesecake with wild cherry sorbet and clementine marmalade sponge pudding with chocolate sauce. *Benchmark main dish: braised lamb shoulder with dauphinoise potatoes, carrot mash and rosemary gravy £17.45. Two-course evening meal £22.00.*

Brunning & Price ~ Manager Lisa Hares ~ Real ale ~ Open 11.30-11; 12-10.30 Sun ~ Bar food 12-9 (9.30 Fri, Sat) ~ Children welcome ~ Dogs allowed in bar ~ Wi-fi *Recommended by Dan and Belinda Smallbone, Gail and Arthur Roberts, Roger and Anne Newbury, Jack Trussler, Chris Stevenson*

The details at the end of each featured entry start by saying whether the pub is a free house, or if it belongs to a brewery or pub group (which we name).

BURWARDSLEY

SJ5256 Map 7

Pheasant ★ 🍴 ⌷ 🛏

(01829) 770434 – www.thepheasantinn.co.uk

Higher Burwardsley; signposted from Tattenhall (which is itself signposted off A41 S of Chester) and from Harthill (reached by turning off A534 Nantwich–Holt at the Copper Mine); follow pub's signpost up hill from Post Office; OS Sheet 117 map reference 523566; CH3 9PF

●●

Cheshire Dining Pub of the Year

Fantastic views and enjoyable food at this clever conversion of an old heavily beamed inn; good bedrooms

This is a first class all-rounder and our readers enjoy their visits here very much. The attractive low-beamed interior is airy and modern-feeling in parts, and the various separate areas have nice old chairs spread spaciously on wooden floors and a log fire in a huge see-through fireplace; quiet background music and daily newspapers. Friendly, helpful staff serve Storm Bosley Cloud, Weetwood Bitter and Old Dog and a guest such as Pheasant Gold (named for the pub from Oaks) on handpump, 17 wines by the glass, ten malt whiskies and local farm cider. From picnic-sets on the terrace, you can enjoy one of the county's most magnificent views right across the Cheshire plains; on a clear day with the telescope you can see as far as the pier head and cathedrals in Liverpool. Comfortable, character bedrooms are in the main building or an ivy-clad stable wing and make a great base for exploring the area. There are plenty of surrounding walks and the scenic Sandstone Trail along the Peckforton Hills is nearby. Sister pubs are the Fishpool in Delamere and Bears Paw in Warmingham.

 Impressive food includes sandwiches (until 6pm), confit duck leg with blood orange salad and orange dressing, salmon, prawn and haddock fishcakes with lemon and coriander mayonnaise, sharing boards, wild mushroom, tarragon and pecorino cannelloni with shaved truffle, glazed taleggio and rocket salad, chicken caesar salad, steak burger with toppings and chips, cod loin with garlic, spinach, samphire, clams and cockles with caviar and lemon butter sauce, pork saltimbocca, frutti di mare tagliatelle, and puddings such as double chocolate and orange torte with white chocolate ganache and Cointreau ice-cream and caramelised banana sticky toffee pudding with salted caramel and banoffi ice-cream. *Benchmark main dish: steak in ale pie £14.95. Two-course evening meal £22.00.*

Free house ~ Licensee Andrew Nelson ~ Real ale ~ Open 11-11 ~ Bar food 12-9.30 (10 Fri, Sat; 9 Sun) ~ Restaurant ~ Children welcome ~ Dogs welcome ~ Wi-fi ~ Bedrooms: $115/$125 *Recommended by Lesley and Brian Lynn, Gwendoline and Ralph Mason, Richard and Tessa Ibbot, Audrey and Paul Summers, Jacqui and Alan Swan*

CHESTER

SJ4066 Map 7

Albion ★ 🍺 £

(01244) 340345 – www.albioninnchester.co.uk

Albion Street; CH1 1RQ

Strongly traditional pub with comfortable Edwardian décor and captivating World War I memorabilia; pubby food and good drinks

An absorbing collection of World War I memorabilia has been collected throughout the 40 years that the charming Mr and Mrs Mercer have been running this special pub – this is an officially listed site of four war memorials to soldiers from the Cheshire Regiment. The peaceful rooms have large engravings of men leaving for war and similarly moving prints of wounded veterans, as well as flags, advertisements and so on. Also, leatherette and hoop-backed chairs around cast-iron-framed tables, lamps, an open fire in the Edwardian fireplace and dark floral William Morris wallpaper (designed on the first day of World War I). You might even be lucky enough to hear the vintage 1928 Steck pianola being played; there's an attractive side dining room too. The cats Charlie and Rosie appear after food service has finished. There's Sharps Sea Fury and Youngs London Gold on handpump, new world wines, fresh orange juice, organic bottled cider and fruit juice, over 25 malt whiskies and a good selection of rums and gins. Bedrooms are small but comfortable and furnished in keeping with the pub's style (free parking for residents and a bottle of house wine if dining). An attractive way to reach the place is along the city wall, coming down at Newgate/Wolfsgate and walking along Park Street. No children. Please note: if the pub is quiet they may close early, so it's best to ring ahead and check.

The generously served 'trench rations' include club and doorstep sandwiches, corned beef hash with pickled red cabbage, fish pie with cheese topping, boiled gammon and pease pudding with parsley sauce, haggis and tatties, and lambs liver, bacon and onions with cider gravy. *Benchmark main dish: cottage pie £10.70. Two-course evening meal £15.00.*

Punch ~ Lease Mike and Christina Mercer ~ Real ale ~ Open 11-2.30 (3 Sat), 5-11; best to phone for Sun ~ Bar food 12-2.30, 5-8 (8.30 Sat) ~ Dogs allowed in bar ~ 1920s swing monthly ~ Bedrooms: $85/$95 *Recommended by Richard Tilbrook, Nicola and Holly Lyons, Amanda Shipley, Charlie May, Muriel and Spencer Harrop*

CHESTER
Architect ♀ ◖

SJ4066   Map 7

(01244) 353070 – www.brunningandprice.co.uk/architect
Nicholas Street (A5268); CH1 2NX

Busy pub by the racecourse with interesting furnishings and décor, attentive staff, a good choice of drinks and super food

This lively establishment is almost a place of two halves connected by a glass passage. The pubbiest part, with a more bustling feel, is the garden room where they serve Phoenix Brunning & Price Original and Weetwood Eastgate alongside guests such as Heavy Industry Electric Mountain, Purple Moose Snowdonia Ale, Salopian Luminescence, Tatton Blonde and Malt Street Mugger and Titanic Cherry Dark on handpump, a good choice of bottled craft beers, 14 wines by the glass, 74 whiskies, 30 rums, over 100 gins and farm cider. Throughout there are elegant antique dining chairs around a mix of nice old tables on rugs or bare floorboards, hundreds of interesting paintings and prints on grey, blue and teal walls, house plants and flowers on windowsills and mantelpieces, and lots of bookcases. As well as a friendly, easy-going atmosphere, you'll also find open fires and armchairs tucked into cosy nooks, candelabra and big mirrors; background music and board games. Big windows and french doors look over a terrace, where there are plenty of good quality wooden seats and tables under parasols. There are views over the Roodee racecourse.

Well executed modern dishes include sandwiches, satay king prawns, chicken liver pâté with carrot and apricot chutney, butternut squash, barley and spinach nut roast, honey-roasted ham and egg, chicken caesar salad, slow-braised ox cheek ragoût with pasta and parmesan, hake with prosciutto, chorizo, butter bean and spinach cassoulet, glazed duck breast with orange and carrot purée, duck croquette and red wine sauce, and puddings such as rhubarb and apple crumble with vanilla custard and crème brûlée; they also serve afternoon tea (2-5pm, book in advance).

Benchmark main dish: steak burger with toppings, coleslaw and chips £13.45.
Two-course evening meal £20.00.

Brunning & Price ~ Manager Hannah Williams ~ Real ale ~ Open 10.30am-11pm; 10.30am-
11.30pm Fri, Sat; 10.30-10.30 Sun ~ Bar food 12-9.30 (10 Fri, Sat); 12-9 Sun ~ Children
welcome ~ Dogs allowed in bar ~ Wi-fi *Recommended by David Phillips, Richard Tilbrook,*
Steve Whalley, Guy Vowles, Roger and Anne Newbury

CHESTER
Mill £

SJ4166 Map 7

(01244) 350035 – www.millhotel.com
Milton Street; CH1 3NF

**Big hotel with huge range of real ales, good value food and cheery
service in sizeable bar; bedrooms**

A splendid range of up to a dozen real ales on handpump can be found in
this smart, modern hotel. Weetwood Best and Mill Premium (brewed
for them by Coach House) are available all the time, with guests such as
Castle Rock Harvest Pale, Oakham Green Devil IPA and JHB and Phoenix
Double Gold; also, a dozen wines by the glass, two farm ciders and 20 malt
whiskies. You'll find a real mix of customers in the neatly kept bar which
has some exposed brickwork and supporting pillars, slate-effect wallpaper,
contemporary purple/grey upholstered seats around marble-topped tables
on light wooden flooring, and helpful, friendly staff; a glass-walled dining
extension has been added. One comfortable area is reminiscent of a bar on
a cruise liner; quiet background music and unobtrusively placed big-screen
sports TV. Converted from an old mill, the hotel straddles either side of
the Shropshire Union Canal, with a glassed-in bridge connecting the two
sections. Bedrooms are comfortable and rather smart. Disabled access.

There are several different menus, but the bar food includes sandwiches,
whitebait, warm camembert cheese with a sticky onion topping, chicken caesar
salad, roasted vegetable and butternut squash lasagne, rack of ribs with coleslaw, steak
and mushroom in ale pie, gammon and pineapple, and a fish dish of the day. *Benchmark
main dish: beer-battered fish and chips £10.95. Two-course evening meal £16.00.*

Free house ~ Licensee Chris Goulden ~ Real ale ~ Open 11-11 ~ Bar food 11.30-11; 12-10
Sun ~ Restaurant ~ Children welcome ~ Wi-fi ~ Bedrooms: £74/£98
Recommended by Darrell Barton, Alister and Margery Bacon, Lee and Jill Stafford, Neil Allen,
Alf and Sally Garner

CHESTER
Old Harkers Arms ♀ ▰

SJ4166 Map 7

(01244) 344525 – www.brunningandprice.co.uk/harkers
Russell Street, down steps off City Road where it crosses canal; CH3 5AL

**Well run canalside building with a lively atmosphere, fantastic range
of drinks and extremely good food**

The name of this clever conversion of an early Victorian warehouse is
taken from a Mr Harker who once ran a canal-boat chandler's here. And
the pub is right by the Shropshire Union Canal; you can watch the boats
from the tall windows that run the length of the main bar. The striking
industrial interior with its high ceilings is divided into user-friendly spaces
by brick pillars. Walls are covered with old prints hung frame-to-frame,
mixed dark wood furniture is set out in intimate groups on stripped-wood
floors, there's a wall of bookshelves above a leather banquette at one end,
and the attractive lamps lend some cosiness; board games. Cheerful staff

serve Phoenix Brunning & Price Original and Weetwood Cheshire Cat Blonde
Ale with guests such as Castle Rock Harvest Pale, Peerless Oatmeal Stout,
Rudgate Ruby Mild, Salopian Oracle and Spitting Feathers Thirst Quencher
on handpump, 120 malt whiskies, 15 wines from a well described list, 40 gins
and nine farm ciders. Disabled access.

Modern british food includes sandwiches, crispy salt and pepper squid, wild boar
and chorizo meatballs with tomato sauce, roasted squash, sage and cheese quiche
with new potato salad, steak in ale suet pudding, pork sausages with mash and onion
gravy, sea bass fillets with artichoke purée, chorizo hash cake and fennel and samphire
salad, chicken breast with pulled chicken and tarragon croquette and smoked bacon
and wild mushroom sauce, and puddings such as lemon and raspberry pannacotta with
meringue and hot waffle with glazed bananas and banoffi ice-cream. *Benchmark main
dish: lamb shoulder with dauphinoise potatoes and gravy £17.45. Two-course evening
meal £22.00.*

Brunning & Price ~ Manager Paul Jeffery ~ Real ale ~ Open 10.30am-11pm; 10am-11pm Sat,
Sun ~ Bar food 12-9.30; 10.30-9.30 Sat; 10-9 Sun ~ Dogs allowed in bar ~ Wi-fi
Recommended by William Pace, Amy Ledbetter

CHOLMONDELEY

SJ5550 Map 7

Cholmondeley Arms

(01829) 720300 – www.cholmondeleyarms.co.uk
Bickley Moss; A49 5.5 miles N of Whitchurch; SY14 8HN

**Interesting pub with a decent range of real ales and wines,
well presented food and sizeable garden; bedrooms**

An imaginatively converted former schoolhouse, this place has a great
deal to look at. The bar rooms have lofty ceilings and tall Victorian
windows plus huge old radiators and school paraphernalia (hockey sticks,
tennis rackets, trunks and so forth), armchairs by a fire with a massive
stag's head above, big mirrors and all sorts of dining chairs and tables on
warmly coloured rugs over bare boards; fresh flowers, church candles and
background music. As well as an extraordinary number of gins (400 and
counting), you'll find Cholmondeley Best (from Weetwood) plus Merlin The
Wizard, Salopian Shropshire Gold and a guest ale on handpump, 15 wines
by the glass and a farm cider. A sizeable lawn (which drifts off into open
countryside) has plenty of seating and there's more in front overlooking the
quiet road. The bedrooms are in the old headmaster's house opposite and
named after real and fictional teachers; the pictures dotted about actually
did belong to former headmasters. Cholmondeley Castle Gardens are nearby.
Disabled access. The pub is owned by Tim Bird and Mary McLaughlin of
Cheshire Cat Pubs & Bars.

Extremely good food includes sandwiches, devilled lambs kidneys, cider-soused
trout with fennel remoulade, three-grain risotto with toasted pumpkin, toasted
seeds and hazelnut and watercress dressing, glazed gammon steak with a duck egg and
chips, wagyu beef burger with home-made onion rings, caramelised onion chutney and
chips, chicken breast with creamed leek, bacon and spinach sauce, hake with mussels,
sweetcorn and charred leek chowder and root vegetable dauphinoise, and puddings
such as bakewell tart with raspberry ripple ice-cream and salted caramel brownie with
vanilla ice-cream. *Benchmark main dish: steak and kidney pie £13.95. Two-course
evening meal £20.00.*

Free house ~ Licensee Timothy Moody ~ Real ale ~ Open 11-11; 12-11 Sat; 12-10.30 Sun ~
Bar food 12-9.15 (9.45 Fri, Sat); 12-8.45 Sun ~ No under-10s after 7pm ~ Dogs welcome ~
Wi-fi ~ Live music monthly Fri; quiz last Tues of month ~ Bedrooms: £85/£100 *Recommended
by Audrey and Paul Summers, Margo and Derek Peters, Holly and Tim Waite, Claire Adams*

DELAMERE
SJ5667 Map 7

Fishpool ♀ ◖

(01606) 883277 – www.thefishpoolinn.co.uk

Junction A54/B5152 Chester Road/Fishpool Road, a mile W of A49; CW8 2HP

Something for everyone in extensive, interestingly laid-out pub, with a good range of food and drinks served all day

Much thought and style has been brought into play here. The clever layout combines a big, cheerful open main section plus plenty of other snug and intimate smaller areas, and the décor and furnishings are unusual and varied. A lofty central area, partly skylit and full of contented diners, has a row of booths facing the long bar counter, and numerous other tables with banquettes or overstuffed small armchairs on pale floorboards laid with rugs; then comes a conservatory overlooking picnic-sets on a flagstone terrace, and a lawn beyond. Off on two sides are many rooms with much lower ceilings, some with heavy dark beams, some with bright polychrome tile or intricate parquet flooring: William Morris wallpaper here, dusky paintwork or neat bookshelves there, sofas, armchairs, a fire in an old-fashioned open range, lots of old prints and some intriguing objects including carved or painted animal skulls; background music. Weetwood Best, Cheshire Cat Blonde Ale and Eastgate plus a guest named for the pub (from Beartown) on handpump, 13 wines by the glass, 18 malt whiskies, 19 gins and farm cider; unobtrusive background music and upstairs lavatories. Disabled access. Sister pubs are the Pheasant in Burwardsley and the Bears Paw in Warmingham.

 As well as sandwiches (until 6pm), the highly rated food includes moules marinière, chicken liver parfait with apple and rhubarb chutney, vegetable thai green curry, chicken caesar salad, wood-fired pizzas, salmon and haddock fishcakes with lemon and caper mayonnaise and chilli jam, a pie of the week, slow-roasted lamb shoulder with dauphinoise potatoes, honey and thyme roasted vegetables and port wine and redcurrant sauce, and puddings such as double chocolate brownie with chocolate sauce and various knickerbocker glories; they also offer afternoon tea (2.30-5pm; you must book in advance). *Benchmark main dish: slow-cooked beef with thyme rösti potato, creamed savoy cabbage and red wine jus £17.95. Two-course evening meal £22.00.*

Free house ~ Licensee Andrew Nelson ~ Real ale ~ Open 11-11 ~ Bar food 12-9.30 (10 Fri, Sat); 12-9 Sun ~ Restaurant ~ Children welcome ~ Dogs allowed in bar ~ Wi-fi
Recommended by John Harris, Colin and Daniel Gibbs, Jim King, Beverley and Andy Butcher, Patricia and Anton Larkham, Freddie and Sarah Banks

KELSALL
SJ5268 Map 7

Morris Dancer ♀ ◖

(01829) 701680 – www.brunningandprice.co.uk/morrisdancer

Chester Road (A54); CW6 0RS

Attractive renovated pub with thoughtfully furnished bar and dining rooms, a fine choice of drinks, rewarding food and seats outside

Carefully refurbished and extended, this is a village centre pub and the heart of the local community; check the website for regular events. Although the building has been designed to be open-plan with connecting doorways, there are areas that feel more cosy too. One room has a high apex ceiling, a woodburning stove fronted by sturdy red leather armchairs and lined on either side by large bookshelves. Other rooms have open fires, beams and timbering, antique-style dining chairs and cushioned settles around polished tables of many sizes and rugs on polished floorboards. The bare-brick and painted walls are hung with hundreds of prints, paintings and photographs and throughout there are mirrors, house plants and elegant metal chandeliers. Friendly, efficient staff serve Phoenix Brunning & Price Original plus Castle Rock Session IPA, Hawkshead Windermere Pale, Mobberley Road Runner, Severn Brewing Ruby Porter, Tatton Blonde and Weetwood Eastgate Ale on handpump, 20 wines by the glass, 20 malt whiskies and 150 gins; background music and board games. In front of the pub are picnic-sets among pretty flowerbeds with more on a back lawn by a play tractor. The sunny terrace has plenty of wooden chairs and tables under green parasols.

Well executed food includes sandwiches, braised venison, bacon and thyme faggot with mushroom broth, garlic and rosemary-studded camembert with walnut and apple salad, stilton, caramelised red onion and potato pie, local pork sausages with mash and onion gravy, mixed grill, duck breast with carrot purée, fondant potato and cranberry sauce, steak in ale suet pudding, sea trout niçoise with anchovies, egg, new potatoes and mushroom dressing, and puddings such as hot waffle with caramelised bananas and banoffi ice-cream and lemon tart with raspberry sorbet. *Benchmark main dish: braised lamb shoulder with dauphinoise potatoes, carrot mash and rosemary gravy £17.45. Two-course evening meal £21.00.*

Brunning & Price ~ Manager Ryan Martinez ~ Real ale ~ Open 10.30am-11pm; 10.30-10.30 Sun ~ Bar food 10.30-9.30 Mon-Thurs; 10.30-10.30 Fri, Sat; 10.30-9 Sun ~ Restaurant ~ Children welcome ~ Dogs allowed in bar ~ Wi-fi ~ Live music last Sat of month
Recommended by Penny and David Shepherd, Edward and William Johnston, S and L McPhee, Mike Benton

KETTLESHULME
SJ9879 Map 7

Swan ★

(01663) 732943

B5470 Macclesfield–Chapel-en-le-Frith, a mile W of Whaley Bridge; SK23 7QU

Charming 16th-c pub with enjoyable food, good beer and an attractive garden

The fresh fish dishes come in for high praise from our readers in this pretty white cottage, so booking a table in advance is a must. The interior is snug and cosy, with latticed windows, very low dark beams hung with big copper jugs and kettles, timbered walls, antique coaching and other prints and maps, ancient oak settles on a turkish carpet and log fires; the dining room has an open kitchen. Marstons Bitter on handpump with a couple of guest beers such as Hawkshead Windermere Pale and Wincle Waller, ten wines by the glass, 30 gins and a dozen malt whiskies served by courteous, friendly staff. The front terrace has teak tables, while another two-level terrace has further tables and steamer benches under parasols. The pub is handy for walks in the relatively unfrequented north-west part of the Peak District National Park.

As well as tip top fresh fish dishes such as bouillabaisse, smoked haddock kedgeree, dover sole with brown shrimp and caper butter and gurnard with mussels, wild mushrooms, bacon and tarragon fricassée, you'll also find non-fishy choices such as sandwiches, camembert fondue, potted beef with balsamic onion, wild mushroom and truffle oil risotto, beef bourguignon, lamb and apricot tagine, duck breast with sweet and sour morello cherry sauce, and puddings such as orange and treacle sponge and chocolate torte with salted caramel ice-cream. *Benchmark main dish: beer-battered fish and chips £13.95. Two-course evening meal £21.00.*

Free house ~ Licensee Robert Cloughley ~ Real ale ~ Open 12-11 (midnight Sat); 4-8 Mon; 12-8 Sun; closed Mon lunchtime ~ Bar food 12-8.30; 12-4 Sun; no food Mon ~ Restaurant ~

Children welcome ~ Dogs allowed in bar ~ Wi-fi *Recommended by Stuart and Natalie Granville, Chloe and Michael Swettenham, Michael Butler, Kerry and Guy Trooper, Naomi and Andrew Randall, Jamie and Lizzie McEwan*

LOWER PEOVER
SJ7474   Map 7
Bells of Peover

(01565) 722269 – www.thebellsofpeover.com

Just off B5081; The Cobbles; handy for M6 junction 17; WA16 9PZ

Wisteria-covered pub in pretty setting with real ales and interesting food; lots of seating areas in the garden

In a charming spot on a quiet cobbled lane, this is a lovely pub. The various rooms have beams, panelling and open fires that contrast cleverly with contemporary seating ranging from brown leather wall banquettes with scatter cushions to high-backed upholstered or leather dining chairs around an assortment of tables on bare boards; plenty of prints, paintings and mirrors on the walls. Robinsons Cumbria Way, Dizzy Blonde and Unicorn on handpump and several wines by the glass served by helpful, friendly staff; background music. In warm weather, head for the seats on a front terrace overlooking the black and white 14th-c church; there's also rattan-style furniture under a pergola on a side decked area and a spacious lawn with picnic-sets spreading down through trees all the way to a little stream.

A good choice of pleasing food includes lunchtime sandwiches, cashew nut and spinach cannelloni with five-bean salad, peppers, sweet potatoes and scorched goats cheese, burger with toppings, coleslaw and fries, a pie of the day, chicken breast with charred sweetcorn and sweetcorn purée, potato cake and maple jus, lamb rump with dauphinoise potatoes, carrot purée, roast beetroot and lamb and thyme jus, and puddings such as chocolate fondant with pistachio meringue, chocolate mousse and honeycomb ice-cream and caramelised apple and pear crumble with star anise and orange anglaise. *Benchmark main dish: sea bass fillet with roast fennel, celeriac, jerusalem artichoke and lemon butter sauce £16.95. Two-course evening meal £23.00.*

Robinsons ~ Real ale ~ Open 12-11 ~ Bar food 12-9 (9.30 Fri, Sat; 8 Sun) ~ Restaurant ~ Children welcome ~ Wi-fi *Recommended by Steve Whalley, Helene Grygar, Bob and Melissa Wyatt, Chloe and Tim Hodge, Roger and Anne Newbury*

MACCLESFIELD
SJ9271   Map 7
Sutton Hall 🍺

(01260) 253211 – www.brunningandprice.co.uk/suttonhall

Leaving Macclesfield southwards on A523, turn left into Byrons Lane signposted Langley, Wincle, then just before canal viaduct fork right into Bullocks Lane; OS Sheet 118 map reference 925715; SK11 0HE

Historic building set in attractive grounds, with a fine range of drinks and well trained, courteous staff

This particularly well run, ancient place ticks all the boxes. Many of the fine 500-year-old features have been carefully restored and cleverly worked into the fabric of an up-to-date pub. The hall at the heart of the building is especially noteworthy, in particular the entrance space. There's a charming series of rooms (a bar, a library with books on shelves and a raised open fire and dining areas) divided by tall oak timbers: antique oak panelling, warmly coloured rugs on broad flagstones, bare boards and tiles, lots of pictures placed frame-to-frame and two more fires. Background music and board games. The atmosphere is nicely relaxed and a good range of drinks includes Phoenix Brunning & Price Original, Sharps Doom Bar and Wincle

Lord Lucan and guests such as Brightside Odin Blonde, Pennine Amber
Necker and Titanic Plum Porter on handpump, 18 wines by the glass from an
extensive list, 65 malt whiskies and 50 gins; service is attentive and friendly.
The pretty gardens have spaciously laid-out tables (some on their own little
terraces), sloping lawns and fine mature trees.

The tempting food includes sandwiches, satay king prawns with peanuts, garlic
and rosemary-studded baked camembert with walnut and apple salad and
chutney, vegan shepherd's pie, salmon and smoked haddock fishcake with chive and
caper sauce and poached egg, chicken, ham and leek pie with mash and tarragon
and white wine sauce, pollock fillet with tandoori vegetables, sticky coconut rice
and curried sauce, braised lamb shoulder with dauphinoise potatoes and gravy, and
puddings such as hot waffle with caramelised banana and banoffi ice-cream and crème
brûlée. *Benchmark main dish: crispy beef salad with sweet chilli dressing and
cashew nuts £13.95. Two-course evening meal £21.50.*

Brunning & Price ~ Manager Syd Foster ~ Real ale ~ Open 11-11 (10.30 Sun) ~ Bar food
12-9.30 (9 Sun) ~ Restaurant ~ Children welcome ~ Dogs allowed in bar ~ Wi-fi
*Recommended by Gus Swan, Ian Duncan, Brian and Anna Marsden, John Wooll, Peter Pilbeam,
Jacqui and Alan Swan*

MARBURY
Swan ★ ♀ 🍺

SJ5645   Map 7

(01948) 522860 – www.swanatmarbury.co.uk
NNE of Whitchurch; OS Sheet 117 map reference 562457; SY13 4LS

**Carefully renovated village pub with attractive open-plan rooms,
a thoughtful choice of drinks and food served by well-trained staff
and seats on large terrace**

Beautifully refurbished using natural and reclaimed materials, this
handsome village-centre pub reopened in spring 2018. There are two
open-plan dining areas plus an extended Garden Room and a long bar made
from reclaimed school chemistry lab counters – it's all gently civilised,
informal and chatty. Cushioned wooden dining chairs, leather-topped stools,
suede wall seating and long, button-back benches are grouped around nice
old tables on colourful rugs, polished floorboards or tiles, walls are hung
with black and white photos and interesting prints, 2,000 books line shelves
and house plants sit on windowsills. Woodburning stoves keep everything
warm; board games. Friendly, helpful staff serve Beartown Ursa Minor,
Mobberley Road Runner, Stonehouse Station Bitter, Weetwood Southern
Cross and Youngs London Stout on handpump and there are a dozen good
wines by the glass plus wine on tap that they import from France. Outside,
good quality chairs, benches and tables fill a good-sized terrace.

Enterprising modern food includes sandwiches, potted pork with chutney,
curried mussels with toasted beer bread, goats cheese and beetroot, pearl barley
risotto, honey-roast beetroot and candied walnuts, chicken, leek and ham hock pie,
calves liver with charred gem, braised lentils, pancetta, silverskin onions and mash,
lamb dopiaza with crispy shallots, shallot and fennel seed bhaji, turmeric yogurt and
rice, whole plaice with samphire and mussel butter, seaweed and new potatoes and
puddings such as melting chocolate fondant with bayleaf ice-cream and blackberry and
almond frangipane with whipped fromage blanc. *Benchmark main dish: lamb rump
with pancetta and vegetable fricassée £18.95. Two-course evening meal £23.00.*

Free house ~ Licensee Tom Morgan-Wynne ~ Real ale ~ Open 11.30-11; 11.30-10.30 Sun ~
Bar food 12-9.30; 12-9 Sun ~ Restaurant ~ Children welcome ~ Dogs allowed in bar ~ Wi-fi
*Recommended by Brian and Anna Marsden, Patrick and Martine Lawson, Nick and Willow Brown,
Liz and Martin Eldon, Christopher Mobbs*

MOBBERLEY

SJ7879 Map 7

Bulls Head

(01565) 873395 – www.thebullsheadpub.co.uk

Mill Lane; WA16 7HX

Terrific all-rounder with interesting food and drink and plenty of pubby character

A fine range of drinks in this particularly well run, friendly pub includes a beer or two named for the pub plus guests from breweries such as Front Row, Merlin, Storm and Wincle on handpump (useful tasting notes too), 15 wines by the glass, around 100 whiskies and local gins. Several rooms are furnished quite traditionally but with a touch of modernity: an unpretentious mix of wooden tables, cushioned wall seats and chairs on fine old quarry tiles, black and pale grey walls contrasting well with warming red lampshades, and pink bare-brick walls and pale stripped-timber detailing; also, lots of mirrors, hops, candles and open fires. Background music and board games. Dogs get a warm welcome (they're allowed in the snug) with friendly staff dispensing doggie biscuits from a huge jar; a circular walk to and from the pub is mentioned on the website. There are seats outside in the big garden. The pub is owned by Tim Bird and Mary McLaughlin of Cheshire Cat Pubs & Bars.

 Very good food includes sandwiches (until 5pm), corned beef hash cake with crispy bacon and a fried egg, seafood crockpot in a creamy dill and white wine sauce, sharing plates, calves liver, bacon, mash and onion gravy, sweet potato, butternut squash and lentil curry with coconut rice, shepherd's pie with spiced red cabbage, monkfish, king prawn, mussel and cod chowder, chicken breast in mushroom and tarragon sauce with a little chicken pie and rosemary potatoes, and puddings such as dark chocolate brownie with warm chocolate sauce and vanilla ice-cream and banana bread and butter pudding with rum and raisin ice-cream. *Benchmark main dish: steak and kidney pie £13.95. Two-course evening meal £19.00.*

Free house ~ Licensee Barry Lawlor ~ Real ale ~ Open 12-11; 12-10.30 Sun ~ Bar food 12-9.30 (9 Sun) ~ Children welcome but no under-10s after 7pm ~ Dogs allowed in bar ~ Wi-fi ~ Live duo Fri monthly; jazz first Sun of month; quiz last Weds of month (not summer or autumn). *Recommended by Dr and Mrs A K Clarke, R Gollin*

MOBBERLEY

SJ7980 Map 7

Church Inn ★

(01565) 873178 – www.churchinnmobberley.co.uk

Brown sign to pub off B5085 on Wilmslow side of village; Church Lane; WA16 7RD

Nicely traditional, friendly country pub with bags of character; good food and drink

This pretty brick pub is a stylish all-rounder and our readers love it. The small, snug interconnected rooms have all manner of nice old tables and chairs on wide floorboards, low ceilings and plenty of candlelight. The décor in soothing greys and dark green, with some oak-leaf wallpaper, is perked up by a collection of stuffed grouse and their relatives, and a huge variety of pictures; background music. Friendly, efficient young staff serve Mallorys Mobberley Best (George Mallory, lost near Everest's summit in 1924, is remembered in the church with a stained-glass window), and guests such as Brotherhood IPA and Tatton Church Ale-Alujah on handpump, and unusual and rewarding wines, with 12 by the glass. Wine tastings can be booked in the upstairs private dining room (also named after George Mallory) and the award-winning Big Hill gin distillery is in the village. The sunny garden snakes down to an old bowling green with lovely pastoral views and a side courtyard has sturdy tables and benches. They give out a detailed leaflet describing a good four-mile circular walk from the pub, passing sister pub the Bulls Head en route. Dogs are welcomed in the bar with not just a tub of snacks on the counter, but maybe even the offer of a meaty 'beer'. The mainly medieval and Tudor St Wilfrid's Church is opposite. The pub is owned by Tim Bird and Mary McLaughlin of Cheshire Cat Pubs & Bars.

Interesting modern food includes sandwiches, game terrine with date purée and red wine syrup, gin-cured sea trout with orange and tonic jelly, sharing boards, confit chicken leg with puy lentils and pancetta in red wine jus, beetroot gnocchi with avocado purée, pickled beetroot and wilted spinach, lambs liver, crispy bacon, mash and onion gravy, venison burger with toppings and chips, monkfish tail wrapped in parma ham with tomato and red pepper sauce and courgette ribbons, and puddings such as spiced hot chocolate fondant with redcurrant sauce, mincemeat millefeuille and clotted cream ice-cream and clementine tart with candied orange, cranberry gel and tarragon cream. *Benchmark main dish: whole roasted flat fish of the day with sautéed potatoes, peas, bacon and caper butter £15.95. Two-course evening meal £21.00.*

Free house ~ Licensee Simon Umpleby ~ Real ale ~ Open 12-11 (10.30 Sun) ~ Bar food 12-9.15 (9.45 Fri, Sat); 12-8.30 Sun ~ Children welcome but no under-10s after 7pm ~ Dogs allowed in bar ~ Wi-fi *Recommended by Malcolm and Pauline Pellatt, Cliff and Monica Swan, Martine and Fabio Lockley, Julie Braeburn, Edward May*

MOBBERLEY
Roebuck 🏵️ ♀ 🛏️

SJ7879 Map 7

(01565) 873939 – www.roebuckinnmobberley.co.uk
Mill Lane; down hill from sharp bend on B5085 at E edge of 30mph limit; WA16 7HX

Interestingly renovated inn with a good range of drinks, enjoyable food and pretty multi-level garden; boutique-style rustic bedrooms

Refurbished in a quirky and individual style, you'll find old shutters, reclaimed radiators, wood panelling and stripped brickwork, big gilt-edged mirrors, copper cooking pots and red and brick floor tiles. There's an open fire in the bar, chunky leather armchairs, lots of scatter cushions, an old trunk as a table, a two-way woodburner and an eclectic collection of art and photographs. Friendly staff serve Buck Bitter (named for the pub from Weetwood) and Deer Beer (from Dunham Massey) on handpump, a dozen wines and champagne by the glass, and a fine collection of liqueurs and aperitifs. The authentic-looking bistro has pots of herbs and candles in bottles on simple tables, café-style chairs and long leather wall banquettes; background music. To get to the garden you walk through the 'potting shed': upper and lower terraces, gazebos, herb beds and seats that range from rattan or elegant metal chairs to wooden benches and straightforward tables under parasols on decking or flagstones. The front of the building has a mediterranean feel with gnarly olive and standard box trees, flowering window boxes and a couple of benches. Shabby-chic bedrooms have much character and colour and some have log burners; good breakfasts. A walking route is suggested on the website. The pub is owned by Tim Bird and Mary McLaughlin of Cheshire Cat Pubs & Bars.

Appetising food includes pulled chicken, spring onion and carrot spring roll with sweet soy and ginger dipping sauce, gruyère cheese croquettes with spiced tomato and red onion jam, sharing boards, baked cauliflower with ratatouille, onion oil and roast baby potatoes, steak burger with gorgonzola and frites, tempura monkfish with thai sweet and sour sauce, lamb chops with roasted red peppers, bulgar wheat, harissa and yoghurt, and puddings such as crêpes suzette with Grand Marnier syrup and profiteroles filled with raspberry cream with dark chocolate sauce; they also offer brunch daily (9am-noon). *Benchmark main dish: beef bourguignon £18.00. Two-course evening meal £23.00.*

Free house ~ Licensee Chris Sproule ~ Real ale ~ Open 10am-10.30pm; 10am-11pm Sat; 10-10 Sun ~ Bar food 12-3, 6-9.15; 12-9.30 Fri, Sat; 12-8.45 Sun ~ Children welcome but no under-10s after 7pm ~ Dogs allowed in bar ~ Wi-fi ~ Bedrooms: £95/£125 *Recommended by Malcolm and Pauline Pellatt, Dr and Mrs A K Clarke, Martin Cawley, Sylvia and Phillip Spencer, Pauline and Mark Evans, Miranda and Jeff Davidson*

MOTTRAM ST ANDREW
Bulls Head ♀ ◗

SJ8878 Map 7

(01625) 828111 – www.brunningandprice.co.uk/bullshead

A538 Prestbury–Wilmslow; Wilmslow Road/Priest Lane; E side of village; SK10 4QH

Smashing country dining pub with a thoughtful range of drinks and interesting food, plenty of character and well trained staff

Perhaps the star feature here is the dining zone at the far end of the building. Four levels stack up alongside or above one another, each with a distinctive décor and style, from the informality of a sunken area with rugs on a tiled floor, through a comfortable library/dining room to another with an upstairs conservatory feel and the last, with higher windows and more of a special-occasion atmosphere. The rest of the pub has an appealing and abundant mix of old prints and pictures, comfortable seating in great variety, a coal fire in one room, a blazing woodburning stove in a two-way fireplace dividing two other rooms and an antique black kitchen range in yet another. Phoenix Brunning & Price Original and guests such as Epic Beers Hop Gun, Mobberley Maori, Peerless Eureka Blonde and Wincle Sir Philip on handpump, around 20 wines by the glass, 50 malt whiskies, 50 gins and several ciders, and an attractive separate tea-and-coffee station with pretty blue and white china cups, teapots and jugs. Also, background music, daily papers and board games. The lawn has plenty of picnic-sets beneath cocktail parasols. Disabled access.

From a well judged menu the food includes sandwiches, potted poached salmon with horseradish and herb butter and lemon jelly, charcuterie sharing board, thai chicken salad with pak choi, coconut and lime dressing, sweet potato, cauliflower and chickpea tagine with coriander couscous and tempura courgettes, steak burger with toppings, coleslaw and chips, sea bass with a crayfish and chive risotto and pea and ham velouté, beef bourguignon with dijon mustard mash, and puddings such as dark chocolate and caramel tart with caramelised bananas and bread and butter pudding with apricot sauce and clotted cream. *Benchmark main dish: braised lamb shoulder with dauphinoise potatoes and rosemary gravy £17.45. Two-course evening meal £22.00.*

Brunning & Price ~ Manager Ben Coverley ~ Real ale ~ Open 10am-11pm; 9.30am-11pm Sat, Sun ~ Bar food 12-9.30; 9.30-9.30 Sat; 9.30-9 Sun ~ Children welcome ~ Dogs allowed in bar ~ Wi-fi *Recommended by James and Sylvia Hewitt, Lyn and Freddie Roberts, W K Wood, Steve Whalley, Professor James Burke, Sabina and Gerald Grimshaw*

NETHER ALDERLEY
Wizard

SJ8576 Map 7

(01625) 584000 – www.thewizardofedge.co.uk

B5087 Macclesfield Road, opposite Artists Lane; SK10 4UB

Bustling pub with interesting food, real ales, a friendly welcome and relaxed atmosphere

The various rooms here, connected by open doorways, are cleverly done up in a mix of modern rustic and traditional styles. There are beams and open fires, antique dining chairs (some prettily cushioned) and settles around all sorts of tables, rugs on pale floorboards, prints and paintings on contemporary paintwork and decorative items ranging from a grandfather clock to staffordshire dogs and modern lampshades. Merlin The Wizard, Ringwood Razorback and Storm Brain Storm on handpump, 11 wines by the glass and farm cider; background music and board games. There are seats and tables in the sizeable back garden and the pub is just a few minutes from lovely walks along Alderley Edge (a dramatic red sandstone escarpment with fine views). This is part of the Ainscoughs group.

Well thought-of food includes sandwiches, baked camembert with red onion chutney, chicken satay skewers with pickled vegetables, noodle slaw and spicy peanut sauce, Balinese vegetable curry with accompaniments, salmon niçoise, steak in ale pie, duck with cherry jus, dauphinoise potatoes and charred chicory, lamb shank with creamed leeks, braised red cabbage and red wine jus, and puddings such as chocolate brownie with chocolate ice-cream and eton mess. *Benchmark main dish: steak in ale pie £13.95. Two-course evening meal £22.00.*

Free house ~ Licensee Jamie Hurst ~ Real ale ~ Open 12-11; 12-8 Sun ~ Bar food 12-2.45, 6-9; 12-9 Sat; 12-7 Sun ~ Children welcome ~ Dogs welcome ~ Wi-fi *Recommended by Andrew Vincent, Charles and Maddie Bishop, Graham Smart, Brian and Susan Wylie, Mark and Mary Setting*

SANDBACH
Old Hall ♀ 🍺

SJ7560 Map 7

(01270) 758170 – www.brunningandprice.co.uk/oldhall

1.2 miles from M6 junction 17: A534 – ignore first turn into town and take the second – if you reach the roundabout double back; CW11 1AL

Lovely hall-house with plenty of drinking and dining space, six real ales and imaginative food

There are impressive original features in this glorious 17th-c manor house, particularly in the room to the left of the entrance hall. This is much as it's been for centuries, with a Jacobean fireplace, oak panelling and priest's hole, and it leads into the Oak Room, divided by standing timbers into two dining areas with heavy beams, oak flooring and reclaimed panelling. Other rooms in the original building have hefty beams and oak boards, two open fires and a woodburning stove; the cosy snugs are carpeted. The Garden Room is big and bright, with reclaimed quarry tiling and exposed A-frame oak timbering, and opens on to a suntrap back terrace with teak tables and chairs among flowering tubs. Throughout, the walls are covered with countless interesting prints, there's an appealing collection of antique dining chairs and tables of all sizes, and plenty of rugs, bookcases and plants. From the handsome bar counter, efficient and friendly staff serve Phoenix Brunning & Price Original, Timothy Taylors Boltmaker and Three Tuns XXX with guests such as Beartown Bluebeary, Hawkshead Windermere Pale and Redwillow Peerless on handpump, 12 good wines by the glass, 50 malt whiskies and 50 gins; background music, board games. There are picnic-sets provided in front of the building beside rose bushes and clipped box hedging.

Highly enjoyable food includes sandwiches, seared pigeon breast with pearl barley risotto, braised leeks and roast shallots, smoked salmon cheesecake with cucumber, samphire salad and beetroot and horseradish purée, cheshire cheese, potato and onion pie with red wine jus, crispy duck salad with chilli and ginger glazed pineapple, roasted peanuts and soy and orange dressing, chicken breast with thyme fondant potato, sweetcorn purée and sherry sauce, sicilian fish stew with coconut rice, and puddings such as spiced cherry cheesecake with cherry crumble ice-cream and sticky toffee pudding with toffee sauce and vanilla ice-cream; they also offer elevenses during the week (10am-midday). *Benchmark main dish: braised lamb shoulder with dauphinoise potatoes, carrot purée and red wine gravy £17.25. Two-course evening meal £22.00.*

Brunning & Price ~ Manager Hannah Law ~ Real ale ~ Open 10am-11pm; 9.30am-11pm Sat; 9.30am-10.30pm Sun ~ Bar food 12-9.30; 12-9 Sun ~ Restaurant ~ Children welcome ~ Dogs allowed in bar ~ Wi-fi *Recommended by Dr and Mrs A K Clarke, John Harris, Emily and Toby Archer, Hugh Roberts*

 SWETTENHAM   SJ7967   Map 7

Swettenham Arms

(01477) 571284 – www.swettenhamarms.co.uk
Off A54 Congleton–Holmes Chapel or A535 Chelford–Holmes Chapel; CW12 2LF

16th-c country pub in a fine setting with long-serving licensees, shining brasses, five real ales and tempting food

A great deal of care and thought is given to the running of this lovely country pub – and it shows. It's a former nunnery and the three interlinked dark beamed areas are nicely traditional with individual furnishings on bare floorboards or a sweep of fitted turkey carpet. There's also a polished copper bar, three woodburning stoves, plenty of shiny brasses and a variety of old prints including military, hunting, old ships, reproduction Old Masters and so forth. Friendly efficient staff serve a beer named for their dogs, Bootleg Chorlton Pale Ale, Hydes Original Bitter, Moorhouses White Witch and Wincle Rambler on handpump, 14 wines by the glass, 15 malt whiskies and Addlestones cider; background music. Outside at the back there are tables on a lawn that merges into a lavender meadow; croquet and children's games in good weather. They hold classic car and vintage motorbike events in the summer, and can also host civil ceremonies in the grounds or the suite. Do visit the interesting village church which dates in part from the 13th c. You can walk in the pretty surrounding countryside or in the nearby Quinta Arboretum.

Using prime local ingredients, the highly regarded food includes sandwiches and wraps, confit duck and chicken terrine with cumberland sauce, prawn cocktail, spicy thai vegetarian red curry with jasmine rice, chicken stroganoff flamed in brandy, salmon fillet with spring onion mashed potato, pancetta, braised savoy cabbage and a prosecco and chive sauce, game pie in red wine stock, a mixed grill, pork loin stuffed with rosemary and apricot with gratin potatoes, apple sauce and gravy, and puddings such as rhubarb posset with home-made lemon shortbread and chocolate and walnut brownie with warm chocolate sauce. *Benchmark main dish: lemon sole with parmentier potatoes and mushroom, cognac and prawn sauce £17.00. Two-course evening meal £22.00.*

Free house ~ Licensee Frances Cunningham ~ Real ale ~ Open 11.30am-11pm ~ Bar food 12-9 (8 Sun) ~ Restaurant ~ Children welcome ~ Dogs allowed in bar ~ Wi-fi
Recommended by Margaret McDonald, Charles Fraser, George Sanderson, Peter and Emma Kelly, Chloe and Tim Hodge

---

Please keep sending us reports. We rely on readers for news of new discoveries, and particularly for news of changes – however slight – at the fully described pubs: feedback@goodguides.com, or (no stamp needed) Freepost THE GOOD PUB GUIDE, Random House Publishing, 20 Vauxhall Bridge Road, London SW1V 2SA.

THELWALL   SJ6587 Map 7

Little Manor ♀

(01925) 212070 – www.brunningandprice.co.uk/littlemanor

Bell Lane; WA4 2SX

Restored manor house with plenty of room, well kept ales and tasty bistro-style food; seats outside

There's plenty to look at in this big, handsome 17th-c house. Six beamed rooms are linked by open doorways and standing timbers to create plenty of nooks and crannies, and there's so much to attract your attention. Flooring ranges from rugs on bare boards through carpeting to some fine old black and white tiles and an appealing variety of seats includes antique dining chairs around small or large, circular or square tables plus leather armchairs by open fires (note the lovely carved wooden one); background music. Lighting is from metal chandeliers, wall lights and standard lamps, and the décor includes hundreds of intriguing prints and photos, books on shelves and old glass and stone bottles on windowsills and mantelpieces; fresh flowers and house plants too. Phoenix Brunning & Price Original plus Coach House Cromwells Best Bitter, Hawkshead Great White, Mobberley Boom Juice, Prospect Silver Tally and Titanic Plum Porter on handpump, around 20 wines by the glass, 60 gins and 60 whiskies. In fine weather you can sit at the chunky teak chairs and tables on the terrace; some of them are under a heated shelter. Disabled access.

Popular modern food includes sandwiches, king prawns with chilli and garlic, crispy brie with cranberry jam, lamb, leek and potato hash with a free-range fried egg, maple and rosemary-roasted squash with herb and lemon couscous and fennel salad, sticky ginger chicken breast with thai red curry, coconut rice and pak choi, fish pie with french-style peas, 10oz rib-eye steak with dijon and tarragon butter, portobello mushrooms and chips, and puddings such as mixed berry crumble with vanilla custard and chocolate délice with cherry compote and raspberry sorbet. *Benchmark main dish: beer-battered fish and chips £13.75. Two-course evening meal £20.00.*

Brunning & Price ~ Manager Jill Dowling ~ Real ale ~ Open 10.30am-11pm; 10.30-10.30 Sun ~ Bar food 12-9.30 (9 Sun) ~ Children welcome ~ Dogs allowed in bar ~ Wi-fi *Recommended by Steve Whalley, Mandy and Gary Redstone, Alison and Tony Livesley, Monica and Steph Evans, Neil Griffin*

WARMINGHAM   SJ7161 Map 7

Bears Paw ◖ ⌂

(01270) 526317 – www.thebearspaw.co.uk

School Lane; CW11 3QN

Nicely maintained and extensive Victorian inn with enjoyable food, half a dozen real ales and seats outside; bedrooms

Each of the spreading, interlinked bar rooms here have plenty of individual character but we particularly like the two little sitting rooms. These have panelling, fashionable wallpaper, bookshelves and slouchy leather furniture comfortably arranged beside woodburning stoves in magnificent fireplaces; stripped wood flooring and a dado keep it all informal. An eclectic mix of old wooden tables and some nice old carved chairs are well spaced throughout the dining areas, with lofty windows providing a light and airy feel and lots of big pot plants dotted about. There are stools at the long bar counter where cheerful, efficient staff serve Beartown Bears Paw (named for the pub), Bear Ass and Bluebeary and Weetwood Best and Eastgate on handpump, 15 wines by the glass, 17 malt whiskies and local cider; background music. A small front garden by the car park has seats and tables. Bedrooms are well equipped and the breakfasts are very good indeed. Disabled access.This is sister pub to the Pheasant in Burwardsley and the Fishpool at Delamere.

🍴 A fine choice of well regarded food includes sandwiches (until 6pm; not Sunday), moules marinière, mexican-style pork fillet with mango and coriander salsa, woodstone-fired pizzas, vegetable red thai curry, hake fillet with roasted artichokes, black olive tapenade and romesco sauce, slow-cooked beef with colcannon mash and stout sauce, chicken breast with provençale vegetable risotto, charred courgettes, parmesan and mizuna leaf, and puddings such as blueberry and white chocolate cheesecake with raspberry compote and sticky toffee, caramelised banana and date pudding with salted caramel sauce. *Benchmark main dish: burger with toppings and chunky chips £12.95. Two-course evening meal £22.00.*

Free house ~ Licensee Andrew Nelson ~ Real ale ~ Open 11-11 ~ Bar food 12-9.30; 12-10 Fri, Sat;12-9 Sun ~ Restaurant ~ Children welcome ~ Dogs welcome ~ Wi-fi ~ Bedrooms: £95/£105 *Recommended by Karl and Frieda Bujeya, Bob and Melissa Wyatt, Simon Boughey, Miss B D Picton, Kathy Finnigan, Andrew Vincent, William Pace*

WHITELEY GREEN
Windmill 🏠⭐🍷📖
SJ9278 Map 7

(01625) 574222 – www.thewindmill.info
Brown sign to pub off A523 Macclesfield–Poynton, just N of Prestbury; Hole House Lane; SK10 5SJ

Extensive relaxed country dining bar with big sheltered garden and enjoyable food

Most of this pub is given over to dining tables, mainly in a pleasantly informal, painted base/stripped top style, on bare boards; lunch is a particularly popular time to visit. The interior spreads around a big bar counter, its handpumps serving Storm Bosley Cloud and guests from breweries such as Adnams, Macclesfield, Mobberley, Sharps, Storm, Weetwood and Wincle; also, eight wines by the glass served by friendly and helpful staff. One area has several leather sofas and fabric-upholstered easy chairs; another by a log fire in a huge brick fireplace has more easy chairs and a suede sofa; background music. The spreading lawns, surrounded by a belt of young trees, provide plenty of room for well spaced tables and picnic sets, and even a maze to baffle children. Middlewood Way (a sort of linear country park) and Macclesfield Canal (Bridge 25) are just a stroll away.

🏠 Good, pleasing food includes lunchtime sandwiches (not Sunday), duck liver parfait with golden raisin chutney, lamb and mint croquettes with pea and mint purée, butternut squash, pecorino and pine nut strudel with sweet potato fries, haddock, salmon and prawn fish pie in lobster sauce with parmesan mash topping, corn-fed chicken with a pine nut crust, carrot purée, roasted carrots and pesto, slow-cooked lamb shoulder with lamb faggot, baba ganoush and aubergine caviar, and puddings such as honey and buttermilk pannacotta with blackberry granita, crumble and honeycomb and chocolate and orange bread and butter pudding with whisky marmalade, orange syrup and chocolate sauce. *Benchmark main dish: beer-battered fish and chips £11.50. Two-course evening meal £22.00.*

Mitchells & Butlers ~ Lease Peter and Jane Nixon ~ Real ale ~ Open 12-11 ~ Bar food 12-2.30, 5-9; 12-9.30 Sat; 12-7 Sun ~ Restaurant ~ Children welcome ~ Dogs allowed in bar ~ Wi-fi ~ Live acoustic guitar second Fri of month; band night last Fri of month *Recommended by Sandra and Miles Spencer, Belinda and Neil Garth*

It's very helpful if you let us know up-to-date food prices when you report on pubs.

Also Worth a Visit in Cheshire

Besides the fully inspected pubs, you might like to try these pubs that
have been recommended to us and described by readers. Do tell us what
you think of them: feedback@goodguides.com

ALLGREAVE   SU9767
Rose & Crown   (01260) 227232
A54 Congleton–Buxton; SK11 0BJ
Welcoming 18th-c roadside pub in remote
upland spot with good Dane Valley views and
walks; renovated beamed rooms with wood
floors and log fires, much enjoyed local food
from sandwiches to daily specials, half a
dozen well kept ales such as Jennings, Storm
and Wincle from wood-clad servery; children
and dogs welcome, lawned garden taking in
the views, three bedrooms. *(Peter and Emma
Kelly)*

ALPRAHAM   SJ5759
Travellers Rest   (01829) 260523
A51 Nantwich–Chester; CW6 9JA
Timeless four-room country local in same
family for three generations; friendly chatty
atmosphere, well kept Tetleys and Weetwood,
no food, leatherette, wicker and Formica,
some flock wallpaper, fine old brewery
mirrors, darts and dominoes; may be nesting
swallows in outside gents'; dogs welcome,
back bowling green, 'Hat Day' last Sun
before Christmas when locals don unusual
headgear, closed weekday lunchtimes (opens
6.30pm). *(Jack Trussler)*

ASHLEY   SJ7784
Greyhound   (0161) 871 7765
*3 miles S of Altrincham; Cow Lane;
WA15 0QR* Extended red-brick Lees
pub, their well kept ales, decent wines
and good choice of tasty reasonably priced
food including deals, friendly service,
greyhound-theme décor and some old photos
of nearby Tatton Hall (NT), wood floors,
central logburner; fortnightly quiz Tues,
darts; children and dogs (in bar) welcome,
seats out on lawn and terrace, handy for the
station, open (and food) all day. *(Brian and
Anna Marsden)*

AUDLEM   SJ6543
Lord Combermere   (01270) 812277
The Square (A529/A525); CW3 0AQ
Modernised and opened up family-run pub
opposite village church; six well kept ales
such as Greene King, Salopian, Timothy
Taylors and Wincle, generous helpings
of good sensibly priced food catering for
gluten-free diets, friendly helpful staff, sofas,
Vettriano prints, restaurant, music and quiz
nights, sports TV; children welcome, dogs in
bar, front terrace and back garden, handy for
Shropshire Union Canal, open all day (food
all day Fri-Sun). *(Brian and Anna Marsden,
Tony Hobden)*

BARBRIDGE   SJ6156
Barbridge Inn   (01270) 528327
Just off A51 N of Nantwich; CW5 6AY
Spacious open-plan family dining pub by
lively marina at junction of Shropshire Union
and Middlewich canals; enjoyable food from
snacks (good panini) and sharing boards to
steaks, friendly staff, three Weetwood ales
including one rebadged for the pub and one
or two guests, conservatory; background
music; dogs allowed in a couple of areas,
waterside garden with enclosed play area,
moorings, open (and food) all day. *(Dave
Braisted, Tony Hobden, Tom Cosgrove)*

BARTON   SJ4454
★ Cock o' Barton   (01829) 782277
*Barton Road (A534 E of Farndon);
SY14 7HU* Stylish contemporary décor in
bright open skylit bar, cocktails, plenty of
wines by the glass and up to four real ales
including Stonehouse, Fri happy hour till
7pm, good choice of well liked up-to-date
food served by neat courteous staff, beamed
restaurant areas; background music; children
welcome (free main course for them on Sun),
tables in sunken heated inner courtyard with
canopies and modern water feature, picnic-
sets on back lawn, 14 bedrooms, open (and
food) all day from 8am for breakfast.
(Chris Stevenson)

BIRKENHEAD   SJ3386
Refreshment Rooms
(0151) 644 5893   *Bedford Road E;
CH42 1LS* Bow-fronted former 19th-c
refreshment rooms for the Mersey ferry;
three rooms with interesting collection of
old photographs and other memorabilia,
good selection of mainly local ales such
as Brimstage, Peerless and a house beer
from Lees (HMS Conway), Rosie's welsh
cider and a couple of interesting lagers,
good competitively priced home-made food
including set deals, friendly prompt service;
children and dogs welcome, beer garden
at back with play area, open (and food)
all day. *(Daniel King)*

BOLLINGTON   SJ9377
Church House   (01625) 574014
Church Street; SK10 5PY Friendly
traditional village pub on edge of the Peak
District – a good place to start or end a walk;
well liked home-made food including good
value set lunch, efficient friendly service,
well kept Adnams Southwold, Marstons
Wainwright and a guest, nice open fire,
separate dining room; children and clean
dogs welcome, picnic-sets in small beer

garden, five comfortable competitively priced bedrooms, good breakfast, open all day weekends (food all day Sun). *(Jacqui and Alan Swan)*

BOLLINGTON   SJ9377

Holly Bush (01625) 574573

Palmerston Street; SK10 5PW Cosy traditionally refurbished Robinsons pub; their ales and good range of other drinks, enjoyable home-made food from sharing plates up, friendly helpful staff, original panelling, parquet flooring and log fires; fruit machine; children welcome, dogs in bar, open all day, kitchen shuts 7pm Sun. *(Victoria Wood)*

BOLLINGTON   SJ9477

Poachers (01625) 572086

Mill Lane; SK10 5BU Traditional stone-built village local prettily set in good walking area, comfortable and welcoming, with tasty pub food (all day Sun, not Mon) including bargain two-course lunch deal and pie and pint night Weds, well kept Storm, Weetwood and three guests, good range of whiskies/gins, efficient friendly service, log fire and woodburner; quiz second and last Sun of month; children and dogs welcome, sunny back garden, open all day weekends, closed Mon lunchtime. *(Isobel Mackinlay)*

BOLLINGTON   SJ9377

Vale (01625) 575147

Adlington Road; SK10 5JT Welcoming tap for Bollington brewery in 19th-c terrace row; their well kept beers and a couple of guests (tasters offered), real cider/perry, enjoyable food (all day weekends) including range of locally made pies and daily specials, helpful efficient service, interesting photos, newspapers and books, roaring fire; quiz first Sun of month; dogs welcome, picnic-sets in small beer garden just up the road, cricket ground behind, near Middlewood Way and Macclesfield Canal, open all day Fri-Sun. *(Brian and Anna Marsden)*

BROOMEDGE   SJ7086

Jolly Thresher (01925) 752265

Higher Lane; WA13 0RN Spacious well appointed dining pub with enjoyable food including daily specials and good value set lunch (not Dec), well kept Hydes (cheaper Mon), lots of wines by the glass and good choice of other drinks, restaurant and dining conservatory; background music, Tues quiz, free wi-fi; children and dogs (in bar) welcome, disabled access, tables on front terrace and in garden behind, open (and food) all day. *(Lindy Andrews)*

BROXTON   SJ4858

Egerton Arms (01829) 782241

A41/A534 S of Chester; CH3 9JW Large neatly kept mock-Tudor dining pub; old polished furniture on wood or carpeted floors, lots of prints and books, log fires, wide

choice of popular food from sandwiches and pub favourites up, four well kept changing beers and plenty of wines by the glass, efficient friendly staff; children and dogs welcome, wheelchair access, big garden with decking and play area, open all day. *(Celia and Geoff Clay)*

BURTONWOOD   SJ5692

Fiddle i'th' Bag (01925) 225442

3 miles from M62 junction 9, signposted from A49 towards Newton-le-Willows; WA5 4BT Eccentric 19th-c country pub (not to everyone's taste) crammed with bric-a-brac and memorabilia; three well kept changing ales and enjoyable uncomplicated home-made food (cash only), friendly staff and pub cat; may be nostalgic background music; children welcome, open all day weekends. *(Grant Read)*

CHELFORD   SJ8175

★Egerton Arms (01625) 861366

A537 Macclesfield–Knutsford; SK11 9BB Cheerful rambling old village pub; beams and nice mix of furniture including carved settles and a couple of wooden porter's chairs, grandfather clock, Copper Dragon and up to six guests, several wines by the glass, popular food including range of burgers, stone-baked pizzas and signature steaks, restaurant, steps down to little raftered games area with pool, darts and sports TV; background music (live last Fri of month including traditional jazz), quiz last Thurs; children and dogs welcome, picnic-sets on canopied deck and slate terrace, toddlers' play area, adjoining deli/coffee shop, open (and food) all day. *(Lindy Andrews)*

CHESTER   SJ4065

★Bear & Billet (01244) 311886

Lower Bridge Street; CH1 1RU Handsome 17th-c timber and lattice-windowed Market Town Tavern (an inn since the 18th c); Okells beers and three changing guests, belgian/american imports plus good selection of wines and gins, reasonably priced pubby food including range of burgers, efficient service, beamed bar with wood floor and panelling, open fire, scenes of old Chester in back dining part, further rooms above; quiz night and upstairs folk club (both Sun), sports TVs; children and dogs welcome, courtyard seating, open (and food) all day), kitchen closes 7pm Sun. *(Michael Butler)*

CHESTER   SJ4066

Boathouse (01244) 328709

The Groves, off Grosvenor Park Road; on River Dee five-minute walk from centre; CH1 1SD Modernised pub on site of 17th-c boathouse with great River Dee views; well priced pubby food from sandwiches and sharing plates up, Lees ales and decent choice of wines by the glass; Weds quiz, free wi-fi; children welcome, dogs outside only, disabled access/facilities, tables and painted beach huts on paved terrace overlooking the water, little bridge to floating seating area, bedrooms, open (and food) all day. *(Richard Tilbrook)*

CHESTER   SJ4065

★ **Brewery Tap** (01244) 340999

Lower Bridge Street; CH1 1RU Tap for Spitting Feathers brewery in interesting Jacobean building with 18th-c brick façade, steps up to lofty barrel-vaulted bar (former great hall) serving a couple of their well kept ales, five guest beers, a local cider and good choice of wines, hearty home-made food using local suppliers including produce from Spitting Feathers farm (rare-breed pork), pews and other rustic furniture on flagstones, tapestries on walls, large carved red-sandstone fireplace, also smaller plainer room; children and dogs welcome, no wheelchair access, open (and food) all day. *(Peter Pilbeam)*

CHESTER   SJ4166

Cellar (01244) 318950

City Road; CH1 3AE Laid-back Canal Quarter bar with six well kept ales, craft beers and interesting selection of imports, decent wines and cocktails too, happy hour till 9pm weekdays, limited snacky food, basement bar for private functions; sports TVs; closed Mon-Thurs till 3pm, otherwise open noon till late. *(Mark and Sian Edwards)*

CHESTER   SJ4066

Coach House (01244) 351900

Northgate Street; CH1 2HQ Modernised 19th-c coaching inn by town hall and cathedral; comfortable lounge with central bar, well kept Marstons-related beers, decent choice of wines and gins, good fairly priced food including some pub favourites from semi-open kitchen, afternoon teas, prompt friendly service; children and dogs welcome, tables out in front, eight bedrooms, good breakfast, open (and food) all day, kitchen closes 8pm Sun. *(Grant Read)*

CHESTER   SJ4065

Cross Keys (01244) 344460

Duke Street/Lower Bridge Street; CH1 1RU Small Victorian corner pub with ornate interior; dark panelling, etched mirrors and stained-glass windows, button-back leather wall benches and cast-iron tables on bare boards, open fire, well kept Joules ales, a guest beer and good selection of gins, enjoyable sensibly priced pubby food, friendly service, upstairs function room; background music, free wi-fi; no dogs inside, seats out in front, closed Mon and Tues, otherwise open all day. *(Grant Read)*

CHESTER   SJ4066

Olde Boot (01244) 314540

Eastgate Row N; CH1 1LQ Lovely 17th-c Rows building; long narrow bar with heavy beams, dark woodwork, oak flooring and flagstones, old kitchen range in lounge beyond, settles and oak panelling in upper area, well kept/priced Sam Smiths beers, cheerful service and chatty atmosphere; no children. *(Mark and Sian Edwards)*

CHESTER   SJ4066

Pied Bull (01244) 325829

Upper Northgate Street; CH1 2HQ Old beamed and panelled coaching inn with roomy open-plan bar, good own-brewed ales (brewery tours) along with guests and nice wines, enjoyable fairly priced traditional food from sandwiches, baked potatoes and sharing plates up, meal deal including a bottle of wine Mon and Tues, friendly staff and locals, imposing stone fireplace, divided inner dining area; background music; children welcome, tables under parasols on enclosed terrace, handsome Jacobean stairs to 31 bedrooms, open (and food) all day. *(Peter Pilbeam)*

CHESTER   SJ4066

Telfords Warehouse (01244) 390090

Tower Wharf, behind Northgate Street near railway; CH1 4EZ Large converted canal building with half a dozen well kept interesting ales and good variety of fairly priced food from sandwiches and snacks up, friendly efficient young staff, bare boards, exposed brickwork and high ceiling, big wall of windows overlooking the water, some old enamel signs and massive iron winding gear in bar, steps up to heavily beamed area with sofas, artwork and restaurant; late-night live music, bouncers on the door; tables out by canal, open all day (till late Weds-Sun). *(Lindy Andrews)*

CHURCH MINSHULL   SJ6660

Badger (01270) 522348

B5074 Winsford–Nantwich; handy for Shropshire Union Canal, Middlewich branch; CW5 6DY Opened-up and modernised 18th-c coaching inn next to church in pretty village; good food from sharing boards and pub favourites up, well kept ales such as Tatton, Titanic and Weetwood, Thatcher's cider, interesting range of wines and spirits, friendly helpful staff, bar with old quarry tiles and two-way woodburner, lounge/dining area leading to conservatory; background music, free wi-fi; children and dogs (in bar) welcome, paved terrace with rattan-style furniture, five bedrooms, good breakfast, open (and food) all day. *(Tony Hobden)*

COMBERBACH   SJ6477

Spinner & Bergamot

(01606) 891307 *Warrington Road; CW9 6AY* Comfortable 18th-c beamed village pub named after two racehorses; good home-made food (smaller helpings available for some main courses), well kept Robinsons ales and nice choice of wines, pitched-ceiling timber dining extension, two-room carpeted lounge and tiled-floor public bar where dogs allowed, log fires; unobtrusive background music, sports TV; children welcome, small verandah, picnic-sets on sloping lawn, bowling green, open all day (food all day Sun till 7.30pm). *(Heather and Richard Jones)*

CONGLETON SJ8659
Horseshoe (01260) 272205
Fence Lane, Newbold Astbury, between A34 and A527 S; CW12 3NL Former 18th-c coaching inn set in peaceful countryside; three small blue-carpeted rooms with decorative plates, copper and brass and other knick-knacks (some on delft shelves), mix of seating including plush banquettes and iron-base tables, log fire, well kept predominantly Robinsons ales, popular hearty home-made food at reasonable prices including good daily specials, friendly staff and locals; children welcome, no dogs, rustic garden furniture, adventure play area, good walks. *(Celia and Geoff Clay)*

CONGLETON SJ8662
Young Pretender (01260) 273277
Lawton Street; CW12 1RS Same ownership as the Old Dancer (Wilmslow) and Treacle Tap (Macclesfield); one-room former shop divided into smaller areas with local artwork on display, half a dozen well kept interesting ales and good selection of international draught/bottled beers, enjoyable food from snacks up including range of locally made pies; various events such as Sun quiz, games evenings and DJ night third Fri of month; children (till 8pm) and dogs welcome, open (and food) all day. *(Nik and Gloria Clarke)*

COTEBROOK SJ5765
Alvanley Arms (01829) 760200
A49/B5152 N of Tarporley; CW6 9DS Welcoming roadside coaching inn, 17th-c behind its flower-decked Georgian façade, with updated beamed rooms, Robinsons ales, several wines by the glass and good choice of other drinks, well liked fairly priced food from pubby menu, friendly helpful service; background music, free wi-fi; children welcome, disabled access, garden with deck and large pond, pleasant walks, seven comfortable bedrooms, good breakfast, open (and food) all day. *(Daniel King)*

COTEBROOK SJ5765
★ Fox & Barrel (01829) 760529
A49 NE of Tarporley; CW6 9DZ This popular old beamed pub (former Main Entry) was closed for refurbishment under new owners as we went to press – reports please.

CREWE SJ7055
Borough Arms (01270) 748189
Earle Street; CW1 2BG Drinkers' pub with up to ten well kept changing ales (maybe own microbrews), also good choice of continental beers and a couple of real ciders, friendly staff and regulars, two small

rooms off central bar and downstairs lounge; occasional sports TV; picnic-sets on back terrace and lawn, open all day Fri-Sun, closed lunchtime other days. *(Richard Tingle)*

CREWE SJ7055
Hops (01270) 211100
Prince Albert Street; CW1 2DF Friendly and relaxed belgian café-bar on two floors; huge range of continental bottled beers (some also on draught), half a dozen interesting ales and good range of ciders, snacky lunchtime food (Weds-Sat), proper coffee; children and dogs welcome, disabled access/loo, seats out at front, closed Mon lunchtime, otherwise open all day. *(Sarah Roberts)*

DISLEY SJ9784
White Lion (01663) 762800
Buxton Road (A6); SK12 2HA Welcoming pub at east end of village; up to nine well kept changing ales and enjoyable food (not Mon) including good home-made pies, friendly efficient staff; quiz nights; dogs welcome in one part (food for them too), closed Mon lunchtime, otherwise open (and food) all day. *(Jim Tucker)*

EATON SJ8765
★ Plough (01260) 280207
A536 Congleton–Macclesfield; CW12 2NH Cosy and welcoming village pub with beams, leaded windows and exposed brickwork, cushioned wooden wall seats and comfortable armchairs, woodburner in big stone fireplace, three real ales such as Bombardier and Hydes, ten wines by the glass from decent list and over 20 malt whiskies; well liked food including sandwiches and good value set lunch (Mon-Thurs), friendly efficient staff, heavily raftered barn function room (moved here from Wales); background music (live Thurs), board games and occasional TV, free wi-fi; children and dogs (in bar) welcome, disabled access, big tree-lined garden with tables set for dining on covered deck, fine views of Peak District fringes, appealingly designed bedrooms in converted stable block, open (and food) all day. *(Steve Whalley)*

FADDILEY SJ5852
Thatch (01270) 524223
A534 Wrexham–Nantwich; CW5 8JE Attractive thatched and timbered dining pub; low beams and open fires, raised room to right of bar, back barn-style dining room, Salopian Shropshire Gold, Timothy Taylors Landlord and a guest, popular traditional food from lunchtime sandwiches up, friendly helpful service; background music, free wi-fi; children and dogs (in bar and snug) welcome, nice country garden with play area, open all day. *(Simon Roberts)*

GAWSWORTH SJ8869
★ Harrington Arms (01260) 223325
Off A536; Congleton Road/Church Lane; SK11 9RJ This unspoilt three-storey

building is still part of a working farm; low 17th-c beams, tiled and flagstoned floors, snug corners and log fires, counter in narrow space on right serving Robinsons ales, a guest beer and good selection of wines and whiskies, several unpretentious rooms off with old settles and eclectic mix of tables and chairs, lots of pictures on red or pale painted walls, well liked hearty food from hot and cold sandwiches to daily specials, friendly relaxed atmosphere; background music (live folk Fri), free wi-fi; children and dogs (in bar) welcome, benches out on small front cobbled area, more seats in garden overlooking fields, lane leads to one of Cheshire's prettiest villages, open all day weekends. *(Michael Butler)*

GOOSTREY   SJ7770
Crown (01477) 532128
Off A50 and A535; CW4 8PE Extended and opened-up 18th-c red-brick village pub refurbished under present management; beams and open fires, small conservatory, good choice of enjoyable fairly pubby food including bargain lunch menu, up to five well kept Marstons-related ales, lots of wines by the glass, cocktails, friendly efficient service from young aproned staff; children and dogs welcome, picnic-sets outside, close to Jodrell Bank, open (and food) all day. *(Heather and Richard Jones)*

GRAPPENHALL   SJ6386
Parr Arms (01925) 212120
Near M6 junction 20 – A50 towards Warrington, left after 1.5 miles; Church Lane; WA4 3EP Black-beamed pub in picture-postcard setting with picnic-sets out on cobbles by church, more tables on small canopied back terrace; enjoyable reasonably priced food from sandwiches and baked potatoes to chargrills, also blackboard specials, well kept Robinsons and good range of other drinks from central bar, friendly service, log fires; children and dogs (in one area) welcome, open (and food) all day. *(Daniel King)*

GREAT BUDWORTH   SJ6677
★George & Dragon (01606) 892650
Signed off A559 NE of Northwich; High Street opposite church; CW9 6HF Characterful building dating from 1722 (front part is 19th-c) in delightful village; Lees ales kept well and plenty of wines by the glass, good choice of enjoyable home-made food from sandwiches and pub favourites to specials, dark panelled bar with log fire, grandfather clock and leather button-back banquettes, back area more restauranty with wood floors and exposed brickwork, tables around central woodburner, some stuffed animals and hunting memorabilia; children and dogs (in bar) welcome, picnic-sets outside, open (and food) all day. *(Chris Stevenson)*

HAUGHTON MOSS   SJ5855
Nags Head (01829) 260265
Off A49 S of Tarporley; CW6 9RN Extended black and white beamed pub under new management; spacious updated interior including oak-framed conservatory, well kept ales such as Weetwood and over 20 wines by the glass, enjoyable food from lunchtime sandwiches, sharing plates and pizzas up, friendly service; children and dogs welcome, nice garden with rattan tables and chairs under parasols, bowling green, open (and food) all day. *(Mark and Sian Edwards)*

KNUTSFORD   SJ7776
Dun Cow (01565) 633093
Chelford Road; outskirts of Knutsford towards Macclesfield; WA16 8RH Comfortably opened-up country dining pub arranged around central servery; modern décor with cosy alcoves and log fires, popular sensibly priced food (smaller helpings available for some dishes) from sandwiches/ciabattas to daily specials, well kept Robinsons ales, friendly caring service; children and dogs welcome, good disabled access, tables on paved front and back terraces, open (and food) all day. *(Tom Cosgrove, R Gollin)*

KNUTSFORD   SJ7578
Lord Eldon (01565) 652261
Tatton Street, off A50 at White Bear roundabout; WA16 6AD Traditional red-brick former coaching inn with four comfortable rooms (much bigger inside than it looks), friendly staff and locals, beams, brasses, old pictures and large open fire, well kept Tetleys and a couple of guests, no food; music and quiz nights, darts; dogs welcome, back garden but no car park, handy for Tatton Park (NT), open all day. *(Jack Trussler)*

KNUTSFORD   SJ7578
Rose & Crown (01565) 652366
King Street; WA16 6DT Beamed and panelled 17th-c inn; very well liked food from sandwiches and sharing plates up, changing ales, plenty of wines by the glass and some interesting gins, afternoon tea, good friendly service, log fires in cosy bar and restaurant; live acoustic music Sun evening; children and dogs (in bar) welcome, outside bar and terrace, nine bedrooms, open (and food) all day. *(Martin Cawley)*

LANGLEY   SJ9471
★Leather's Smithy (01260) 252313
Off A523 S of Macclesfield; OS Sheet 118 map reference 952715; SK11 0NE Isolated stone-built pub in fine walking country next to reservoir; well kept Theakstons and two or three guests, lots of whiskies, good food (including vegan options) from sandwiches to blackboard specials, efficient friendly service, flagstoned bar and carpeted dining areas, beams, log fire

and interesting local prints/photographs; unobtrusive background music; children welcome, no dogs inside but muddy boots allowed in bar, picnic-sets in garden behind and on grass opposite, lovely views, open all day Sat, till 8pm Sun, closed Mon evening. *(Peter and Emma Kelly)*

LITTLE BUDWORTH   SJ5867
Cabbage Hall (01829) 760292
Forest Road (A49); CW6 9ES Restauranty pub (part of the Pesto chain) specialising in good tapas-style italian food (piattini), drinkers catered for in comfortable bar with real ales and decent wines by the glass, also italian-style afternoon teas, efficient friendly staff; children welcome, garden tables, open (and food) all day. *(Grant Read)*

LITTLE BUDWORTH   SJ5965
Egerton Arms (01829) 760424
Pinfold Lane; CW6 9BS Welcoming 18th-c family-run country free house with up to six well kept mainly local ales (beer festivals), good selection of bottled beers and interesting cocktails (two-for-one Fri), enjoyable home-made food including wood-fired pizzas and range of burgers; weekend live music; children and dogs welcome, seats out in front and in nice garden behind overlooking cricket pitch, walks from the door, handy for Oulton Park racetrack, closed Sun evening, Mon (except bank holidays), otherwise open all day (from 3pm Tues, Weds, Thurs in winter). *(Brian and Anna Marsden, Alan Johnson)*

LITTLE LEIGH   SJ6076
Holly Bush (01606) 853196
A49 just S of A533; CW8 4QY Brick and timbered 17th-c thatched pub; good choice of enjoyable well priced food including several vegetarian options, very friendly helpful staff, Tetleys and a couple of mainstream guests, bar with open fire, restaurant extension; Sun quiz; children welcome, no dogs inside, wheelchair access, courtyard tables and garden with play area, 14 bedrooms in converted back barn, open all day weekends (food all day Sun). *(Celia and Geoff Clay)*

LOWER WHITLEY   SJ6178
Chetwode Arms (01925) 640044
Just off A49, handy for M56 junction 10; Street Lane; WA4 4EN Rambling low-beamed dining pub dating from the 17th c; good food including range of exotic meats cooked on a hot stone, welcoming efficient service, solid furnishings all clean and polished, small front bar with warm open fire, four real ales and good wines by the glass; well behaved children allowed (under-10s eat free early evening), limited wheelchair access, tables outside along with tipi and own bowling green, open from 5.30pm (12-9pm Sun), closed Mon. *(Isobel Mackinlay)*

LYMM   SJ7087
Barn Owl (01925) 752020
Agden Wharf, Warrington Lane (just off B5159 E); WA13 0SW Popular comfortably extended pub in nice setting by Bridgewater Canal; Marstons Lancaster Bomber and Wainwright, Thwaites Original plus three guests, decent wines by the glass and some interesting gins, good choice of affordably priced traditional food including weekday OAP menu and Sun carvery, efficient service even when busy, friendly atmosphere; children and dogs (in one part) welcome, disabled facilities, moorings (space for one narrowboat), open all day. *(Heather and Richard Jones)*

LYMM   SJ6886
Church Green (01925) 752068
Higher Lane; WA13 0AP Popular dining pub owned by celebrity chef Aiden Byrne; food can be very good from restauranty dishes to more affordable pubby choices, also children's menu, Caledonian and a guest beer, carefully chosen wines and interesting gins, various dining areas including conservatory; background music; disabled access/loos, pretty garden with heated side deck, open (and food) all day, breakfast from 10am (9am weekends), kitchen shuts 7pm Sun. *(Jacqui and Alan Swan)*

MACCLESFIELD   SJ9173
Snow Goose (01625) 619299
Sunderland Street; SK11 6HN Quirky laid-back bar with feel of an alpine ski lodge; well kept ales such as Storm, several craft beers and good range of wines, shortish choice of food such as hotdogs and hotpots, bare-boards interior on three levels, woodburners, local artwork for sale, piano; background and live music, board games; children and dogs welcome, balcony overlooking back garden, open all day and can get very busy. *(Jim Tucker)*

MACCLESFIELD   SJ9173
Treacle Tap (01625) 615938
Sunderland Street; SK11 6JL Simply furnished little bare-boards bar in former shop (same owners as the Young Pretender in Congleton and Old Dancer in Wilmslow); three interesting mainly local ales and good selection of bottled beers (particularly belgian and german), other drinks too, short menu including meat/cheese platters, tasty local pies and a vegan option; regular events such as Sun quiz, foreign language evenings, photography club and a stitch'n'bitch night; children welcome till 8pm, open (and food) all day Fri-Sun, from 4pm other days. *(Lindy Andrews)*

NANTWICH   SJ6452
★**Black Lion** (01270) 628711
Welsh Row; CW5 5ED Cosy old black and white pub with plenty of character,

beams, timbered brickwork, bare boards and stone floors, open fire, good food (not Sun evening, Mon) from shortish fairly pubby menu, four well kept Weetwood ales and two or three guests, good friendly service, upstairs rooms with old wooden tables and leather sofas on undulating floors; children welcome, dogs in courtyard Hop Room only in the evening, open all day weekends when can get very busy, closed Mon lunchtime. *(Tony Hobden)*

NANTWICH   SJ6552
Vine (01270) 619055
Hospital Street; CW5 5RP Black and white fronted pub dating from the 17th c; modernised interior stretching far back with steps and quiet corners, woodburner, four well kept ales including Hydes (cheaper Mon), nine wines by the glass and popular good value food from fairly pubby menu (some vegan choices), friendly staff and locals, raised seating areas; background music, sports TVs, darts; children and dogs welcome, small sunny outside seating area behind, open all day, food till 6pm Sun. *(Sarah Roberts)*

NESTON   SJ2976
Harp (0151) 336 6980
Quayside, SW of Little Neston; keep on along track at end of Marshlands Road; CH64 0TB Tucked-away little two-room country local; five well kept ales such as Holts and Timothy Taylors, decent choice of bottled beers, wines by the glass and some good malt whiskies, enjoyable simple pub food (not Sun evening) including Tues curry night, log fire, pale quarry tiles and simple furnishings, interesting old photographs, hatch servery to lounge; children and dogs allowed, garden behind and picnic-sets up on front grassy bank facing Dee Marshes, glorious sunsets with wild calls of wading birds, good walks, open all day. *(Peter and Emma Kelly)*

NORLEY   SJ5772
Tigers Head (01928) 788309
Pytchleys Hollow; WA6 8NT Friendly little village local near Delamere Forest; enjoyable good value home-made food (evening deals), well kept Weetwood and four guests, over 30 gins including their own Second Son; tap room and lounge, upstairs skittle alley/function room; pool, darts, sports TV; children and dogs welcome, some seating out in front, more on paved terrace behind, bowling green, open all day Fri and Sat, till 9pm Sun and Mon, closed lunchtimes Mon-Thurs. *(Chris Stevenson)*

PARKGATE   SJ2778
Boathouse (0151) 336 4187
Village signed off A540; CH64 6RN Popular 1920s black and white timbered pub with attractive linked rooms; good choice of enjoyable food from

sandwiches and snacks up, cheerful if not always speedy service, well kept Hydes and guests (cheaper on Mon), several wines by the glass, big conservatory with great views to Wales over silted Dee estuary (RSPB reserve), may be egrets and kestrels; children and dogs (in bar) welcome, seats out on decking, open (and food) all day. *(Mark and Sian Edwards)*

PARKGATE   SJ2778
Ship (0151) 336 3931
The Parade; CH64 6SA Far-reaching estuary views from hotel's bow-windowed bar; well kept Brimstage Trappers Hat and guests, several wines by the glass, over 50 whiskies and interesting range of gins, good reasonably priced home-cooked food including sandwiches (until 5pm), daily specials and popular Sun roasts, friendly service, log fire; children welcome, no dogs inside, a few tables out at front and to the side, 25 bedrooms, open (and food) all day. *(David and Leone Lawson)*

PEOVER HEATH   SJ7973
★ **Dog** (01625) 861421
Wellbank Lane; the pub is often listed under Over Peover instead; WA16 8UP Well renovated traditional country pub with intimate rooms (sister to the Ship at Styal); good variety of popular generously served food, five ales including Weetwood, decent choice of wines by the glass and malt whiskies, friendly efficient staff; children welcome, dogs in tap room, picnic-sets out at front and in pretty back garden, can walk from here to the Jodrell Bank Discovery Centre and Arboretum, six bedrooms, open (and food) all day. *(Sarah Roberts)*

POYNTON   SJ9283
Cask Tavern (01625) 875157
Park Lane; SK12 1RE Popular refurbished Bollington pub with five of their well kept ales and a guest, craft beers, real ciders and several wines by the glass including draught prosecco, friendly staff, some snacky food; fortnightly Mon quiz; children and dogs allowed, open all day Fri-Sun, from 4pm other days. *(Nik and Gloria Clarke)*

STYAL   SJ8383
Ship (01625) 444888
B5166 near Ringway Airport; SK9 4JE Busy 17th-c beamed pub under same ownership as the Dog at Peover Heath; good variety of well liked food including popular Sun lunch, ales such as Dunham Massey, Timothy Taylors and Weetwood, plenty of wines by the glass, friendly helpful service, lots of alcoves and snugs, some stripped brickwork and painted panelling, open fire; children welcome, seats out at front and on back terrace, attractive NT village with good walks on the doorstep, open (and food) all day. *(Isobel Mackinlay)*

SUTTON
SJ9469

★**Ryles Arms** (01260) 252244

Hollin Lane, Higher Sutton; SK11 0NN
Popular dining pub in fine countryside; very
good food from extensive menu including
signature grills, ales such as Black Sheep and
Wincle, decent wines and several whiskies,
pleasant décor, hill-view dining room with
french windows to terrace; children welcome,
good bedrooms in converted barn, open all
day. *(Grant Read)*

SUTTON
SJ9273

Sutton Gamekeeper (01260) 252000

Hollin Lane; SK11 0HL Updated beamed
village pub with good freshly made food from
interestingly varied menu (best to book),
Dunham Massey, Wincle and a guest, good
friendly service, warm open fire; children
welcome, well behaved dogs in bar, metal
furniture in fenced garden behind, closed
Mon (except bank holidays), otherwise open
all day till 10pm, food all day weekends (till
7pm Sun). *(Simon Roberts)*

WESTON
SJ7352

White Lion (01270) 587011

*Not far from M6 junction 16, via A500;
CW2 5NA* Refurbished 17th-c black and
white inn; low-beamed lounge bar with
slate floor, standing timbers and inglenook
woodburner, three well kept ales including
Salopian and good selection of wines, popular
well presented food from sandwiches and
sharing boards up, restaurant and cocktail
bar, good helpful service; background music;
children allowed in eating areas, dogs in bar,
lovely garden with bowling green (not owned
by the pub), 17 comfortable bedrooms, open
all day. *(Jacqui and Alan Swan)*

WHITEGATE
SJ6268

Plough (01606) 889455

*Beauty Bank, Foxwist Green; OS Sheet
118 map reference 624684; off A556 just
W of Northwich, or A54 W of Winsford;
CW8 2BP* Comfortable country pub with bar
and extended dining area; good home-made
food (best to book) from panini and baked
potatoes up, cheerful efficient service, four
well kept Robinsons ales and plenty of wines
by the glass; background music, free wi-fi; no
under-14s inside, well behaved dogs allowed
in tap room, disabled access, picnic-sets

out at front and in back garden, colourful
window boxes and hanging baskets, popular
walks nearby, open (and food) all day.
(Chris Stevenson)

WILMSLOW
SJ8481

Old Dancer (01625) 530775

Grove Street; SK9 1DR Mock Tudor-
fronted pub on pedestrianised street (sister
pubs are Young Pretender in Congleton and
Treacle Tap in Macclesfield); bare-boards
interior with simple wooden furniture and
padded wall benches, some striking murals,
five well kept changing local ales, ten craft
beers and a proper cider, decent coffee
and good value food from sandwiches and
bar snacks up, friendly staff, second bar/
function room upstairs (not always open);
regular events including music and film
nights, traditional games, newspapers, free
wi-fi; children and dogs welcome, seats out
in front, open all day (till 1am Fri, Sat).
(Daniel King)

WINCLE
SJ9665

★**Ship** (01260) 227217

*Village signposted off A54 Congleton–
Buxton; SK11 0QE* Friendly 16th-c stone-
built country pub; bare-boards bar leading to
carpeted dining room, old stables area with
flagstones, beams, woodburner and open
fire, good generously served food (not Sun
evening) from varied well priced menu, three
Lees ales and several wines by the glass,
quick attentive service; children and dogs
welcome, tables in small side garden, good
Dane Valley walks, open all day. *(Roger and
Donna Huggins)*

WRENBURY
SJ5947

Dusty Miller (01270) 780537

*Cholmondeley Road; village signed from
A530 Nantwich–Whitchurch; CW5 8HG*
Converted 19th-c corn mill with fine
canal views from terrace and series of tall
glazed arches in bar; spacious feel with
banquettes, oak settles and wheelback chairs
around mix of tables, old lift hoist up under
the rafters, Robinsons beers, proper cider
and good food (all day weekends) from varied
interesting menu, friendly staff; background
music, free wi-fi; children and dogs welcome,
disabled access/loos, farm shop, closed Mon,
otherwise open all day. *(Brian and Anna
Marsden)*

Cornwall

KEY ⭐ Star Pub 🍽 Top Quality Food ☕ Great Beer
🍷 Good Wines £ Bargain Meals 🛏 Good Bedrooms 🍴 Serves Food

 ANTONY   SX4054 Map 1

Carew Arms 🍽 🍷

(01752) 814440 – carewarms.com

Off A374; PL11 3AB

**Renovated village pub with imaginative food, well kept ales,
good wines by the glass and downstairs farm shop**

The bar and dining rooms here are interconnected with wide floorboards,
painted farmhouse and other sturdy chairs around rustic wooden tables,
wide stripped floorboards and immaculate pale paintwork; décor is minimal
and includes a few pieces of artwork dotted about. There's also an open fire.
High chairs line the bar counter (and the tables here are reserved for those
wanting just a drink and a chat) where they keep Exeter Avocet, St Austell
Tribute and Skinners Betty Stogs on handpump and ten wines by the glass
served by courteous staff. Downstairs is a store-cum-farm-shop with a small
café at one end (and a woodburning stove) and they've an upstairs loft room
for private hire.

🍽 Highly regarded food using local, seasonal produce includes local king scallops
with smoked bacon lardons, spring onions and garlic butter, chicken liver
pâté with red onion marmalade, spicy veg and five-bean burger with halloumi, garlic
mayonnaise and horseradish ketchup, beer-battered haddock and chips, chicken
supreme with parmesan, wild mushroom, tarragon and green onion risotto, calves
liver with bacon, red wine, caramelised red onion and veal jus, local rib-eye steak with
trimmings and chips, and puddings. *Benchmark main dish: luxury fish pie £14.95.
Two-course evening meal £21.00.*

Free house ~ Licensee Tremayne Carew Pole ~ Real ale ~ Open 12-11 ~ Bar food 12-2.30
(5 Sun), 6-9; not Mon evening ~ Restaurant ~ Children welcome ~ Dogs allowed in bar ~
Wi-fi ~ Quiz first Sun of month *Recommended by Catherine and Daniel King, George and Alison
Bishop, Trish and Karl Soloman, Martine and Fabio Lockley*

 BOSCASTLE   SX0991 Map 1

Cobweb

(01840) 250278 – www.cobwebinn.com

B3263, just E of harbour; PL35 0HE

Plenty of interest in cheerful pub, several real ales and friendly staff

Serving as an off-licence in the early 18th c, this is now a bustling village
pub close to the tiny, steeply cut harbour. The two interesting bars have
quite a mix of seats (from settles and carved chairs to more pubby furniture),

heavy beams hung with hundreds of bottles and jugs, lots of pictures of bygone years, and cosy log fires; the atmosphere is lively, especially at peak times. They keep four real ales such as St Austell Tribute, Tintagel Harbour Special and a guest beer on handpump, decent wines by the glass, a local cider and a dozen malt whiskies; games machine, darts and pool. The restaurant is upstairs; background music. There are picnic-sets and benches outside, some under cover; dogs must be kept on a lead. A self-catering apartment is for rent.

Well liked food includes sandwiches and baguettes, whitebait with a citrus dip, chicken liver and brandy pâté, seafood medley salad, vegetarian chilli with sour cream and rice, home-cooked ham and eggs, pizzas, a curry of the day, local sausages with mash and caramelised onion gravy, beer-battered fish and chips, lamb chops with redcurrant and red wine jus, mixed grill, and puddings. *Benchmark main dish: steak in ale pie £10.95. Two-course evening meal £16.00.*

Free house ~ Licensee Adrian Bright ~ Real ale ~ Open 10.30am-11pm (midnight Sat); 12-11 Sun ~ Bar food 11.30-2.30, 5.15-9 (9.30 weekends); may serve food all day in peak summer ~ Restaurant ~ Children welcome ~ Dogs allowed in bar ~ Wi-fi ~ Live music Sat evenings from 9.30pm *Recommended by Andrew Vincent, John Sargeant, Christine and Tony Garrett, Chris Stevenson*

CONSTANTINE
Trengilly Wartha ♀ ⌂
SW7328   Map 1

(01326) 340332 – www.trengilly.co.uk

Nancenoy; A3083 S of Helston, signposted Gweek near RNAS Culdrose, then fork right after Gweek; OS Sheet 204 map reference 731282; TR11 5RP

Well run inn surrounded by big gardens with a friendly welcome for all, and popular food and drink; bedrooms

An unexpected find down these steep narrow lanes, this is a bustling country inn not far from the Helford River. It's run by long-serving, helpful owners and the long, low-beamed main bar has a sociable feel (especially in the evening when locals drop in), all sorts of tables, chairs and settles, a woodburning stove, lots of pump clips, and cricket team photos and bats on the walls. Penzance Potion No 9, Sharps Doom Bar and a changing guest beer on handpump, lots of wines by the glass, 80 malt whiskies and 11 gins. Leading off the bar is the conservatory family room and there's also a cosy bistro. The six acres of gardens are well worth a wander and offer plenty of seats and picnic-sets under large parasols. Cottagey bedrooms are comfortable, breakfasts highly regarded and there are good nearby walks.

Food is good and includes lunchtime sandwiches (the seasonal crab is popular), beer-battered prawns with sweet chilli dip, chicken liver pâté with home-made chutney, caramelised onion and cheddar frittata, fish medley (three fillets of fish with pesto sauce and dauphinoise potatoes), hungarian goulash, pork and apple sausages with mustard mash and onion gravy, local sirloin steak with trimmings and chips, and puddings that include local ice-cream. *Benchmark main dish: steak and mushroom in ale pie £14.50. Two-course evening meal £20.00.*

Free house ~ Licensees Will and Lisa Lea ~ Real ale ~ Open 11-3, 6-11; 11-11 Sat; 12-11 Sun ~ Bar food 12-2.15, 6.30-9.30 ~ Restaurant ~ Children welcome ~ Dogs allowed in bar and bedrooms ~ Wi-fi ~ Live music Weds and Sun evenings ~ Bedrooms: £77/£84 *Recommended by Sophie and James Collier, Sandra and Miles Spencer, Andrew and Ruth Simmonds, Simon Cotterell, Fiona and Gavin May*

We say if we know a pub has background music.

DEVORAN
SW7938 Map 1

Old Quay

(01872) 863142 – www.theoldquayinn.co.uk

Devoran from new Carnon Cross roundabout A39 Truro–Falmouth, left on old road, right at mini roundabout; TR3 6NE

Light and airy bar rooms in friendly pub with four real ales, good wine, imaginative food and seats on pretty back terraces

As this charming pub is just up the hill from Devoran Quay, you can arrive by boat – provided the tide is right; many other customers are walkers, cyclists and even horse riders. It's just 50 metres from the coast-to-coast Portreath to Devoran Mineral Tramways cycle path. The easy-going, roomy bar has an interesting 'woodburner' set halfway up one wall, a cushioned window seat, wall settles and a few bar stools around just three tables on stripped boards, and bar chairs by the counter. Black Sheep, Sharps Atlantic and Doom Bar and Skinners Betty Stogs on handpump and good wines by the glass (including prosecco). Off to the left is an airy room with pictures by local artists (for sale), built-in cushioned wall seating, plush stools and a couple of big tables on the dark slate floor. To the other side of the bar is another light room with more settles and farmhouse chairs, attractive blue and white striped cushions and more sailing photographs; darts and board games. As well as benches outside at the front looking down through the trees to the water, there's a series of snug little back terraces with picnic-sets and chairs and tables. Nearby parking is limited unless you arrive early. Wheelchair access through a side door. Please note, they no longer have bedrooms.

 Good quality food using local produce includes lunchtime sandwiches, pulled ham hock with crispy parma ham and pea velouté, smoked mackerel pâté, butternut squash crumble topped with goats cheese, burgers with toppings and triple-cooked chips, honey, lemon and thyme chicken with glazed vegetables and crispy roast potatoes, mussel and prawn tagliatelle, local sirloin steak with trimmings and peppercorn sauce, and puddings such as Baileys crème brûlée and chocolate fondant with vanilla ice-cream. *Benchmark main dish: beer-battered cod and chips £12.95. Two-course evening meal £20.00.*

Punch ~ Tenants John and Hannah Calland ~ Real ale ~ Open 11-11 ~ Bar food 12-3, 6-9 ~ Restaurant ~ Children welcome ~ Dogs welcome ~ Wi-fi *Recommended by Sally Harrison, Liz and Mike Newton, Ian Herdman, Len and Lilly Dowson, Thomas Green, Peter Pilbeam*

GURNARDS HEAD
SW4337 Map 1

Gurnards Head Hotel

(01736) 796928 – www.gurnardshead.co.uk

B3306 Zennor–St Just; TR26 3DE

Interesting inn with lots of wines by the glass, good inventive food and wild surrounding walks; comfortable bedrooms

If you stay in the comfortable, well appointed bedrooms in this informally civilised inn, you'll have fine views of the rugged moors or the Atlantic ocean just 500 metres away. The bars and dining areas are painted in bold, strong colours with work by local artists on the walls, open fires, books on shelves, fresh flowers and all manner of wooden dining chairs and tables and sofas on stripped boards or rugs. Firebrand West Coast IPA, Granite Rock Penryn Company and St Austell Tribute on handpump, 14 wines by the glass or carafe and a couple of farm ciders; background music, darts and board games. The large, enclosed back garden has plenty of seats.

Disabled access on ground floor only. This is under the same ownership as the Old Coastguard in Mousehole (also in Cornwall) and the Griffin at Felinfach (Wales).

 Impressive seasonal food includes smoked fish croquette with tartare sauce, pickled beetroot with shallots, hazelnuts and goats curd salad, potato gnocchi with smoked onion, stilton, pied de mouton mushrooms, sprouting broccoli and almonds, ray wing with caper and anchovy dressing on crushed potatoes, beef rump with Marmite butter, stilton, hazelnuts and gherkins, and puddings such as carrot cake with mascarpone, salt caramel, pecan, orange and cinnamon ice-cream and strawberry parfait with yoghurt and lime sorbet. *Benchmark main dish: lamb breast with charred gem, wild garlic, anchovies and capers £19.00. Two-course evening meal £26.00.*

Free house ~ Licensees Charles and Edmund Inkin ~ Real ale ~ Open 10am-11pm; closed first week Dec ~ Bar food 12-2.30, 6 (6.30 Sun)-9 ~ Restaurant ~ Children welcome ~ Dogs allowed in bar and bedrooms ~ Wi-fi ~ Bedrooms: £105/£130 *Recommended by Neil Turner, Angela and Steve Heard, Caroline and Peter Bryant, Andy and Louise Ramwell*

HALSETOWN
SW5038   Map 1

Halsetown Inn
(01736) 795583 – www.halsetowninn.co.uk
B3311 SW of St Ives; TR26 3NA

Quirky little stone pub with local ale and wine suppliers and interesting food

The easy-going atmosphere and chatty mix of customers – along with some inventive food – appeals to our readers who drop in here on a regular basis. As well as a snug bar (liked by locals for a pint and a chat), there are simply furnished dining areas with an old range and a woodburning stove, an eclectic collection of wooden dining chairs and mismatched tables on quarry tiles, cushioned settles, candles and fresh flowers. Artwork and murals are bold and contemporary, with many of the pieces created by local artists. Skinners Betty Stogs and a guest such as St Austell Tribute on handpump, 12 wines by the glass, a dozen malt whiskies, 35 gins and cider; background jazz. The front terrace has a few picnic-sets. It's important to the licensees that they run the pub with environmental awareness (they use green energy and recycle as much as possible) and are strongly committed to local producers, who range from farmers and fishermen to the local tea plantation.

Good, contemporary food includes local crab beignets with pear and chilli chutney, wild mushroom arancini with parmesan cream and truffle, mushroom and aubergine curry with cardamom rice, honey-glazed ham with a duck egg and grilled pineapple, duck breast with salt-baked celeriac, confit leg bonbon and pickled blackberry jus, roasted cod with cauliflower, pickled apple, brown shrimps and caper brown butter, and puddings such as caramel baked apple with salted almond ice-cream and sticky ginger pudding with toffee sauce. *Benchmark main dish: fresh fish dish of the day £16.50. Two-course evening meal £21.00.*

Free house ~ Licensee Natalie Edmunds ~ Real ale ~ Open 12-2, 5-11; 12-11 Sat, Sun ~ Bar food 12-2, 6-9; 12-3 Sun ~ Restaurant ~ Children welcome ~ Dogs welcome ~ Wi-fi *Recommended by Greta and Gavin Craddock, Sabina and Gerald Grimshaw, Diana and Richard Gibbs, Daphne and Robert Staples*

'Children welcome' means the pub says it lets children inside without any special restriction. If it allows them in, but to restricted areas such as an eating area or family room, we specify this. Some pubs may impose an evening time limit. We do not mention limits after 9pm as we assume children are home by then.

HELFORD

SW7526 Map 1

Shipwrights Arms

(01326) 231235 – www.shipwrightshelford.co.uk

Off B3293 SE of Helston, via Mawgan; TR12 6JX

17th-c waterside inn with seats on terraces, attractively decorated bars, friendly service and tasty food

This thatched pub's lovely position is a big draw in summer, with a view of the beautiful wooded creek (at its best at high tide) and seats on various terraces that drop down to the water's edge. You can moor at their pontoon and get a foot-ferry from Helford Passage. The bars have quite a nautical theme, with old navigation lamps, ship models, boat wallpaper, appropriate artworks and even the odd figurehead; antique pine and oak furniture sits on slate or bare-boarded floors and cushioned window seats have pretty cushions. Stools line the counter where they keep St Austell Tribute and a couple of guests such as Skinners Porthleven and St Austell Proper Job on handpump, 14 wines by the glass, 14 gins and ten malt whiskies; there's an open fire in winter. Good surrounding walks include a long-distance coast path that goes right past the front door.

Good food includes sandwiches (until 3pm), local scallops with black pudding, peas and truffle purée, pork, duck, pistachio and cranberry terrine with onion chutney, tarragon gnocchi with wild mushrooms, artichoke hearts, sun-dried tomatoes and a white wine and basil pesto cream sauce, cajun chicken burger with toppings, beer-battered haddock and chips, braised lamb shank with dauphinoise potatoes, chantenay carrots and mint gravy, and puddings such as dark chocolate brownie with dark chocolate sauce and lemon posset with raspberry jelly; their outside pizza oven is much used in warm weather. *Benchmark main dish: goan seafood curry £16.00. Two-course evening meal £22.00.*

Free house ~ Licensees Roger and Laura Fergus ~ Real ale ~ Open 11-11; 12-5 Sun in winter ~ Bar food 12-3, 6-9; not Sun evening in winter ~ Restaurant ~ Children welcome ~ Dogs welcome ~ Wi-fi ~ Live music most Sun afternoons *Recommended by Robert and Diana Ringstone, Greta and Gavin Craddock, Usha and Terri Patel, Helena and Trevor Fraser, Katherine and Hugh Markham*

HELSTON

SW6522 Map 1

Halzephron

(01326) 240406 – www.halzephron-inn.co.uk

Gunwalloe, village about 4 miles S but not marked on many road maps; look for brown sign on A3083 alongside perimeter fence of RNAS Culdrose; TR12 7QB

Bustling pub in lovely spot with tasty bar food, local beers and good nearby walks; bedrooms

This makes a perfect lunch break after a visit to nearby Church Cove with its sandy beach or to Gunwalloe fishing cove just 300 metres away. The bar and dining areas are neatly kept and have an informal, friendly atmosphere, some fishing memorabilia, comfortable seating, a warm winter fire in a woodburning stove and a good range of drinks: Sharps Doom Bar and Skinners Porthleven on handpump, nine wines by the glass, 40 malt whiskies and summer farm cider. The dining gallery seats up to 30 people; board games. Picnic-sets outside look across National Trust fields and countryside. The pretty bedrooms have country views and there are lovely coastal walks in both directions. Disabled access.

🍴 Popular food includes lunchtime sandwiches and ploughman's plus seafood chowder laced with cream, breaded brie with cumberland dipping sauce, butternut squash and leek pie, local sausages with grain mustard mash and onion gravy, local crab in creamy thermidor sauce topped with cheese, duck breast with cherry and brandy sauce and roasted pine nuts, pork medallions with black pudding in creamy garlic and rosemary sauce, 12oz sirloin steak with rustic chips and onion rings, and puddings. *Benchmark main dish: daily fresh fish dish £14.95. Two-course evening meal £23.00.*

Free house ~ Licensee Claire Murray ~ Real ale ~ Open 11-11; 12-10.30 Sun ~ Bar food 12-2.30, 6-9 ~ Restaurant ~ Children welcome ~ Dogs allowed in bar and bedrooms ~ Wi-fi ~ Weekly quiz Tues evening ~ Bedrooms: £65/£100 *Recommended by Guy Henderson, Andrew and Michele Revell, Marianne and Peter Stevens, Jeremy Snaithe*

 LANLIVERY   SX0759   Map 1

Crown 🛏

(01208) 872707 – www.thecrowninncornwall.co.uk

Signposted off A390 Lostwithiel–St Austell (tricky to find from other directions); PL30 5BT

Chatty atmosphere in nice old pub, with traditional rooms and well liked food and drink; bedrooms

A pretty white-painted long house with a lot of character, this dates in part back to the 12th c. A good mix of customers includes both visitors and locals and the main bar has a woodburning stove in a huge fireplace, traditional settles on big flagstones, church and other wooden chairs around all sorts of tables, old Cornwall photographs and boarded ceilings with beams. Sharps Doom Bar and Skinners Betty Stogs plus a guest such as Harbour IPA on handpump, several wines by the glass and local cider. A couple of other rooms have high-backed black leather dining chairs and built-in cushioned pews, there's another (smaller) woodburning stove and a simply furnished conservatory; darts. The porch has a huge well with a glass top and the quiet, pretty garden has picnic-sets. The bedrooms (in separate buildings) are clean and comfortable and overlook the rustic garden; breakfasts are good. The Eden Project is a ten-minute drive away.

🍴 Pleasing food includes lunchtime sandwiches, chicken liver parfait with red onion chutney, meze sharing plate, broad bean, baby corn and spinach risotto with fruity red pepper reduction, burger with toppings, coleslaw and chips, slow-roast pork belly with garlic and thyme potatoes and red wine gravy, beef cobbler with a thyme and cheddar scone, red snapper fillet with lemon and dill butter, venison steak with beetroot and fruit jus, and puddings. *Benchmark main dish: chicken breast on chorizo risotto with chilli, lime and coriander dressing £12.50. Two-course evening meal £19.00.*

Free house ~ Licensee Nigel Wakeham ~ Real ale ~ Open 11.30-11; 12-10.30 Sun ~ Bar food 12-2.30, 6-9 ~ Restaurant ~ Children welcome ~ Dogs allowed in bar and bedrooms ~ Wi-fi ~ Bedrooms: /£99 *Recommended by Adam and Natalie Davis, Belinda and Neil Garth, Brian and Susan Wylie, Alexandra and Richard Clay*

 LONGROCK   SW5031   Map 1

Mexico Inn

(01736) 710625 – www.themexicoinn.co.uk

Riverside; old coast road Penzance–Marazion; TR20 8JB

Granite-stone pub with rustic charm, seasonal food cooked by both licensees and a merry atmosphere

Our readers are quick to praise this cheerful pub for its chatty, easy-going atmosphere, genuine welcome and enjoyable home-cooked food. The open-plan rooms include one with leather tub chairs and a chesterfield sofa around a woodburning stove, as well as dining rooms with wheelback and wooden chairs around nice antique tables on bare boards, bold aqua-green and orange paintwork, bookshelves, and stools against the counter where they serve Cornish Crown Causeway, St Austell Harlequin and Skinners Lushingtons on handpump, several wines by the glass, local gin, farm cider and home-made pink lemonade and ginger beer; background music, darts and board games. At the front are a few picnic-sets and the extended back garden has a terrace and a large area growing herbs; there are more seats available here too.

Cooked by two enthusiastic chefs, the good, high quality food includes salt and pepper tempura king prawns, duck, mushroom and red wine risotto with parmesan, crispy polenta with roasted beetroot, caramelised mushrooms, goats cheese and salsa verde, glazed ham with new potatoes, roasted celeriac, poached egg and parsley sauce, brisket and ale burger with toppings, pickles and chips, ling goan-style curry with rice and poppadum, and puddings such as chocolate brownie with hot chocolate sauce and baked apple and almond crumble with crème anglaise. *Benchmark main dish: venison and pork belly bolognese £13.75. Two-course evening meal £20.00.*

Free house ~ Licensee Tom Symons ~ Real ale ~ No credit cards ~ Open 11.30-11.30 (midnight Fri, Sat); 12-11 Sun ~ Bar food 12-2, 6-9; 12-2.45, 5.30-8 Sun ~ Restaurant ~ Children welcome ~ Dogs allowed in bar ~ Wi-fi ~ Regular live bands; quiz Thurs evening
Recommended by David Appleyard, Millie and Peter Downing, Stephen Bradley, Tony Smaithe, Geoffrey Sutton, Andrew and Michele Revell

LOSTWITHIEL
SX1059 Map 1

Globe ♈ ◗

(01208) 872501 – www.globeinn.com
North Street (close to medieval bridge); PL22 0EG

Traditional local with interesting food and drink, friendly staff and suntrap back courtyard

With pleasing food, good drinks and welcoming staff, you'll quickly feel at home here. The unassuming and friendly bar, which is long and narrow, has a mix of pubby tables and seats, local photographs on pale blue plank panelling at one end and nice, mainly local prints (for sale) on walls above a coal-effect stove at the snug inner end; there's also a small front alcove. The ornately carved bar counter, with comfortable leatherette stools, dispenses Sharps Atlantic and Own and Skinners Betty Stogs on handpump, ten reasonably priced wines by the glass, 20 malt whiskies and two local ciders; background music, darts, board games and TV. The sheltered back courtyard is not large but has some attractive and unusual plants, and is a real suntrap (with an extendable awning and outside heaters). You can park in several of the nearby streets or the (free) town car park. The 13th-c church is worth a look and the ancient river bridge, a few metres away, is lovely.

From a seasonal menu, the reliably good food includes moules marinière, prawn cocktail, vegetarian roast with red onion, mushrooms and port sauce, gammon with pineapple and a free-range egg, chilli con carne, sausages with mash and onion gravy, a pie of the week, slow-roasted lamb with mash and gravy, and puddings such as ginger and black treacle sponge and caramel apple pie with local clotted cream. *Benchmark main dish: fresh fish dish of the day £12.95. Two-course evening meal £21.50.*

Free house ~ Licensee William Erwin ~ Real ale ~ Open 12-11 (midnight Fri, Sat) ~
Bar food 12-9; maybe 12-2, 6.30-8.30 out of season ~ Restaurant ~ Children welcome ~
Dogs allowed in bar ~ Wi-fi ~ Live music alternate Fri evenings ~ Bedrooms: /£70
Recommended by Sheila Topham, R K Phillips, Vibekke Böhl, Len and Lilly Dowson, Peter Brix,
Daphne and Robert Staples, Buster May

 MOUSEHOLE   SW4726   Map 1

Old Coastguard 🌟 ♉ 🛏

(01736) 731222 – www.oldcoastguardhotel.co.uk
The Parade (edge of village, Newlyn coast road); TR19 6PR

Lovely position for civilised inn with an easy-going atmosphere,
good choice of wines and first rate food; bedrooms

On the edge of an old fishing village, this is a well run inn with comfortable
bedrooms that have views out over St Michael's Mount and the Lizard;
breakfasts are highly thought of. The bar rooms have boldly coloured walls
hung with paintings of sailing boats and local scenes, stripped floorboards
and an atmosphere of informal but civilised comfort. The Upper Deck houses
the bar and the restaurant, with a nice mix of antique dining chairs around
oak and distressed pine tables, lamps on big barrel tables and chairs to either
side of the log fire, topped by a vast bressumer beam. St Austell Tribute and
a guest such as Padstow Windjammer on handpump, 14 wines by the glass
or carafe, a big choice of gins, vodkas and whiskies, a farm cider and a good
choice of soft drinks. The Lower Deck has glass windows running the length
of the building, several deep sofas and armchairs, and shelves of books
and games; background music. A rather special garden has tropical palms
and dracaena, a path leading down to rock pools, and seats on the terrace
looking over the sea. Disabled access. This is sister pub to the Gurnards
Head (also Cornwall) and the Griffin at Felinfach (Wales).

 From a well judged menu the modern food includes confit rabbit leg and
chargrilled loin with caesar salad and a soft egg, cured scallops with pickled
rhubarb, fennel and roe, grana padano gnocchi with roasted shallot, cauliflower, raisins
and sage, tempura courgette flower with english feta, spring vegetables and a duck egg,
hake and octopus with cannellini bean and seaweed broth and nduja mayonnaise, lamb
rump with olive oil potatoes, peas, sweetbreads, mint and spinach, and puddings such as
crème brûlée and marmalade iced parfait with dark chocolate. *Benchmark main dish:*
fish stew with aioli £14.50. Two-course evening meal £23.00.

Free house ~ Licensees Charles and Edmund Inkin ~ Real ale ~ Open 8am-11pm; closed
one week Jan ~ Bar food 12.30-2.30, 6.30-9.15 ~ Restaurant ~ Children welcome ~ Dogs
allowed in bar and bedrooms ~ Wi-fi ~ Live music last Sun of month ~ Bedrooms: £105/£140
Recommended by Miranda and Jeff Davidson, Michael Sargent, John and Mary Warner, Elise and
Charles Mackinlay, Harvey Brown

MYLOR BRIDGE   SW8137   Map 1

Pandora ♉

(01326) 372678 – www.pandorainn.com
Restronguet Passage: from A39 in Penryn, take turning signposted Mylor Church,
Mylor Bridge, Flushing and go straight through Mylor Bridge following Restronguet
Passage signs; or from A39 further N, at or near Perranarworthal, take turning
signposted Mylor, Restronguet, then follow Restronguet Weir signs, but turn left down
hill at Restronguet Passage sign; TR11 5ST

Idyllically placed waterside inn with lots of atmosphere in beamed
and flagstoned rooms, and all-day food

As well as driving to this perfectly placed pub, you can reach it by walking along the estuary among avenues of wild flowers or arrive (as some customers do) by boat; in fine weather you can sit with your drink on the long floating pontoon and watch children crabbing. Inside, rambling, interconnected rooms have low beams, beautifully polished big flagstones and three large log fires in high hearths (to protect them against tidal floods); also, cosy alcoves, cushioned built-in wall seats and pubby tables and chairs, maps, yacht pictures, oars and ships' wheels; church candles help with the lighting. There's also a back cabin bar with pale farmhouse chairs, high-backed settles and a model galleon in a big glass cabinet. St Austell HSD, Proper Job, Trelawny and Tribute on handpump, 17 wines by the glass and 18 malt whiskies. Upstairs, the attractive dining room has exposed oak vaulting, dark tables and chairs on pale oak flooring and large brass bells and lanterns. Because of the pub's popularity, parking is extremely difficult at peak times; wheelchair access.

As well as sandwiches (until 5pm), the popular all-day food includes local mussels with cream, ginger, honey and spring onions, crayfish salad with rosemary croutons and avocado mayonnaise, halloumi burger with toppings and chips, streaky bacon-wrapped chicken breast with chorizo dauphinoise and mushroom cream, slow-cooked pork belly with sweet potato purée, creamy cabbage and spiced reduction, and puddings such as caramel pannacotta with cookie crumb and raspberry and gin sorbet and chocolate and orange brioche bread and butter pudding with vanilla custard. *Benchmark main dish: fish pie £13.75. Two-course evening meal £20.00.*

St Austell ~ Tenant John Milan ~ Real ale ~ Open 10.30am-11pm ~ Bar food 12-9.30 ~ Restaurant ~ Children welcome ~ Dogs allowed in bar ~ Wi-fi *Recommended by Franklyn Roberts, Martine and Lawrence Sanders, Justine and Neil Bonnett, Adrian Johnson, Steve Whalley, Matilda and Gerald Thoms*

PENZANCE
Turks Head
SW4730   Map 1

(01736) 363093 – www.turksheadpenzance.co.uk
At top of main street, by big domed building turn left down Chapel Street; TR18 4AF

Bustling atmosphere in well run pub with popular food and beer

A cheerful, honest local that appeals just as much to visitors too. The bar has old flat irons, jugs and so forth hanging from the beams, pottery above the wood-effect panelling, wall seats and tables and a couple of elbow-rests around central pillars; background music and board games. Sharps Doom Bar, Skinners Betty Stogs and a couple of guests on handpump, ten wines by the glass, a dozen gins and 12 malt whiskies. The suntrap back garden has big urns of flowers, seats under a giant parasol and a barbecue. There's been a Turks Head here for over 700 years – though most of the original building was destroyed by a Spanish raiding party in the 16th c.

 Pleasing food includes sandwiches, prawn cocktail, bouillabaisse, red lentil, mediterranean vegetable and butternut squash moussaka, gammon and egg, pork and leek sausages with red wine and red onion gravy, lemon chicken on roasted red pepper, chorizo and chickpea stew, burger with toppings and skin-on chips, seafood pie, slow-roasted lamb shoulder on spiced couscous with apricot compote, and puddings. *Benchmark main dish: beer-battered fish and chips £12.95. Two-course evening meal £18.00.*

Punch ~ Lease Jonathan and Helen Gibbard ~ Real ale ~ Open 11.30am-midnight; 12-11 Sun ~ Bar food 12-2.30, 6-10 ~ Restaurant ~ Children welcome ~ Dogs welcome ~ Wi-fi *Recommended by Alan Johnson, Paul Faraday, Ivy and George Goodwill, Simon and Alex Knight, Greta and Gavin Craddock, Alison and Michael Harper*

POLGOOTH

SW9950 Map 1

Polgooth Inn 🍺

(01726) 74089 – www.polgoothinn.co.uk

Well signed off A390 W of St Austell; Ricketts Lane; PL26 7DA

Welcoming pub with plenty of space for eating and drinking, cornish ales, well liked food and seats on big front terrace

In a little village not far from the Lost Gardens of Heligan is this spacious old pub with high quality food. The spreading, linked rooms have dark beams and timbering, open fires and woodburning stoves. Seating ranges from high-backed settles to tartan upholstered dining chairs, banquettes to nice farmhouse seats (all around wooden tables on carpet), and there are old agricultural tools and photos on painted or exposed-stone walls. St Austell Cornish Best, HSD, Proper Job, Tribute and a seasonal guest on handpump, good wines by the glass and a gin menu. A dining extension with country kitchen furniture has a modern woodburner against a black brick wall, contemporary lighting and french doors to the terrace. They have picnic-sets arranged on grass (some under an awning), separate dining booths and a kitchen garden where you'll find home-grown herbs and salad and free-range chickens.

 Using own-grown produce, the interesting food includes sandwiches, scallops with roasted parsnip purée and bacon lardons, port-soaked chicken liver parfait with brown sugar and fennel seed onion chutney, pakora and halloumi burger with mint salsa and rustic-style chips, giant smoked haddock fishcake with a soft poached egg and hollandaise, steak, tattie and turnip pie, burritos with different fillings and red cabbage coleslaw, chicken curry, fresh crab salad, and puddings such as lemon and raspberry millefeuille and sticky toffee pudding with toffee sauce and clotted cream; they also offer breakfasts (7.30-10am Friday and Saturday). *Benchmark main dish: barbecue brisket of beef with coleslaw and chips £16.50. Two-course evening meal £21.50.*

St Austell ~ Tenants Alex and Tanya Williams ~ Real ale ~ Open 10am-11pm; 7.30am-midnight Fri, Sat ~ Bar food 12-9.30 ~ Restaurant ~ Children welcome ~ Dogs allowed in bar ~ Wi-fi ~ Live music summer Sun afternoons *Recommended by David and Charlotte Green, Isobel Mackinlay, Colin and Daniel Gibbs, William Slade, Helena and Trevor Fraser*

POLKERRIS

SX0952 Map 1

Rashleigh 🍺

(01726) 813991 – www.therashleighinnpolkerris.co.uk

Signposted off A3082 Fowey–St Austell; PL24 2TL

Lovely beachside spot with sizeable sun terrace, five real ales and quite a choice of food

Although things have changed completely since this was once a fishermen's tavern, nothing can take away the splendid view from the front terrace which stretches right away to the far side of St Austell and Mevagissey bays. Inside, the bar has comfortably cushioned chairs around dark wooden tables at the front, and similar furnishings, local photographs and a winter log fire at the back. Padstow Padstow Pride, Sharps and Betty Stogs and guests from Dartmoor, Sharps and Tintagel on handpump plus nine wines by the glass, two farm ciders and organic soft drinks; background music. All the tables in the restaurant have a sea view. There's plenty of parking in either the pub's own car park or the large village one. A fine beach with a restored jetty is a few steps away, as is the local section of the South West Coast Path (renowned for its striking scenery).

Changing food includes lunchtime sandwiches, moules marinière, whitebait with garlic mayonnaise, vegetarian goan-style curry, a proper steak pie with mash and gravy, summer fresh crab salad, fillet of ling with chorizo and chickpea stew, grilled flounder with garlic butter, and puddings such as chocolate fudge cake and sticky toffee pudding with clotted cream or ice-cream. *Benchmark main dish: beer-battered fresh fish and chips £12.00. Two-course evening meal £19.00.*

Free house ~ Licensees Jon and Samantha Spode ~ Real ale ~ Open 11-11 (10 winter) ~ Bar food 12-3, 6-9; summer snacks 3-5 ~ Restaurant ~ Children welcome ~ Dogs allowed in bar *Recommended by Ian Herdman, Serena and Adam Furber, Geoff and Ann Marston, Patti and James Davidson, Sally and David Champion*

POLPERRO
SX2050   Map 1
Blue Peter
(01503) 272743 – www.thebluepeterinn.com
Quay Road; PL13 2QZ

Friendly pub overlooking harbour with fishing paraphernalia, real ales and carefully prepared food

An atmospheric little pub right by the busy harbour, this is as enjoyable and as popular as ever. Traditional furnishings include a small winged settle and a polished pew, wooden flooring, fishing regalia, photographs and pictures by local artists, lots of candles and a solid wood bar counter. St Austell Tribute and Sharps Own plus up to three guests from Cornish or Devon breweries on handpump and a growing choice of gins and rums served by the helpful, long-serving licensees. One window seat looks down on the harbour, while another looks out past rocks to the sea. Background music and board games. There are seats on the terrace outside and more in an amphitheatre-style area upstairs. The pub gets crowded at peak time and families must use the upstairs room only.

 Food is reasonably priced and includes sandwiches (the crab is popular), crab bruschetta with lime and yoghurt dressing, chicken liver pâté with red onion chutney, chickpea and vegetable burger with sweet chilli dipping sauce, tempura-style fish and chips, honey and cider roasted ham with eggs and pineapple chutney, fresh fish dish of the day, a pie of the day, chicken tikka with minted rice, and puddings. *Benchmark main dish: seafood platter £18.75. Two-course evening meal £20.00.*

Free house ~ Licensees Steve and Caroline Steadman/Rob and Rebecca Hawkes ~ Real ale ~ Open 11-11; 12-10.30 Sun ~ Bar food 12-2.30, 6-8.30; 12-9 in high season ~ Children in upstairs family room only ~ Dogs welcome ~ Wi-fi ~ Live music Fri, Sat 9pm; Sun 3pm *Recommended by Colin Gooch, Anne Roots, Ian Herdman, Vibekke Böhl, Sally and David Champion, Max Simons, Len and Lilly Dowson*

PORT ISAAC
SX0080   Map 1
Port Gaverne Inn
(01208) 880244 – www.portgavernehotel.co.uk
Port Gaverne signposted from Port Isaac and from B3314 E of Pendoggett; PL29 3SQ

Bustling small hotel with a proper bar and real ales, well liked food in several dining areas and seats in the garden; bedrooms

After blowing the cobwebs away on a walk along the splendid and usually bracing surrounding clifftops, many come here for lunch. The chatty bar has low beams, flagstones and carpeting, some exposed stone, a big log fire and St Austell Proper Job and Tribute, Skinners Betty Stogs and Timothy Taylors Landlord on handpump, 20 wines by the glass, 40 gins,

30 malt whiskies and farm cider. The lounge has some interesting old local photographs. You can eat in the bar or in the 'Captain's Cabin', which is a little room where everything is shrunk to scale (old oak chest, model sailing ship, even the prints on the white stone walls). There are seats and tables under parasols at the front, with more in the terraced garden. The individually furnished and comfortable bedrooms have plenty of character, though the stairs up to most of them are fairly steep (staff will carry your luggage). This is a lovely spot just back from the sea.

🍴 Good quality food includes duck and chicken liver parfait with fig and apple jam, dressed local crab with brown crab mayonnaise and grapefruit, squash risotto with ricotta, toasted seeds, pickled walnut and black truffle cream, roast chicken with chestnut-stuffed leg, anchovy and lemon, plaice with brown shrimps, seaweed and lime butter, dry-aged local steaks with garlic snails, and puddings such as earl grey crème brûlée with dark chocolate sorbet and red wine pear and passion-fruit cheesecake with caramelised white chocolate banana and passion-fruit sorbet. *Benchmark main dish: tandoor-spiced monkfish with aubergine and tamarind, cashews and samphire pakora £22.00. Two-course evening meal £23.00.*

Free house ~ Licensee Jackie Barnard ~ Real ale ~ Open 11-11 ~ Bar food 12-2.30, 5-9.30 ~ Restaurant ~ Children welcome ~ Dogs welcome ~ Wi-fi ~ Bedrooms: /£170 *Recommended by Selwyn Jones, Abigail Slater, Nigel Morton, Celia and Rupert Lemming, Charlie May, Diana and Richard Gibbs*

PORTHLEVEN
Ship

SW6225 Map 1

(01326) 564204 – www.theshipinnporthleven.co.uk
Mount Pleasant Road (harbour) off B3304; TR13 9JS

Welcoming harbourside pub with fantastic views, pubby furnishings, real ales and tasty food and seats on terrace

On a stormy night, this friendly old fishermen's pub is just the place to sit in snug warmth and watch the boats and birds blowing across the harbour. In kinder weather, there are tables in the terraced garden that make the most of the sea view, and the harbour is interestingly floodlit. Both the bustling bar and dining room share these views. There are open fires in stone fireplaces, quite a mix of chairs and tables on flagstones or bare boards, beer mats and brasses on the ceiling and walls, and various lamps and pennants. Sharps Cornish Coaster and Doom Bar, Skinners Porthleven and changing guests such as Penzance Brisons Bitter and Tintagel Harbour Special on handpump, farm cider and eight wines by the glass; background music. They also have a cosy, traditionally furnished and separate function room.

🍴 Home-cooked food includes sandwiches, crispy ham hock bites with pickled vegetables and mustard mayonnaise, fish goujons with sweet chilli sauce, chestnut mushroom, new potato, halloumi and feta bake, fresh fish and chips with pea purée, cajun chicken, beef or vegetarian burgers with toppings and coleslaw, mussels in creamy leek and cider sauce with fries, chargrilled sirloin steak with chimichurri, and puddings. *Benchmark main dish: fish pie £13.50. Two-course evening meal £20.00.*

Free house ~ Licensee Christian Waite ~ Real ale ~ Open 11am-midnight ~ Bar food 12-2.30, 6-9; no food Sun evening Jan-Mar ~ Well behaved children welcome away from bar ~ Dogs welcome ~ Wi-fi ~ Occasional live music *Recommended by Alan Johnson, Guy Henderson, Matthew and Elisabeth Reeves, Barry and Daphne Gregson*

If we know a featured-entry pub does sandwiches, we always say so – if they're not mentioned, you'll have to assume you can't get one.

ST IVES

SW5441   Map 1

Queens 🛏

(01736) 796468 – www.queenshotelstives.com

High Street; TR26 1RR

Bustling inn with a spacious bar, open fire, real ales and tasty food; bedrooms

---

Plenty of regulars and visitors crowd into the bar here to enjoy the local ales and popular food – and it's handy for the harbour too. The open-plan, spreading bar has a relaxed atmosphere, all sorts of wooden chairs around scrubbed tables on bare floorboards, tartan banquettes on either side of the Victorian fireplace, a wall of barometers above a leather chesterfield sofa and some brown leather armchairs; also, fresh flowers and candles on tables and on the mantelpiece above the open fire. Red-painted bar chairs line the white marble-topped counter where they serve St Austell Proper Job and Tribute on handpump, eight wines by the glass (including a local one), a good choice of gins and rums and farm cider; background music, board games and TV for sports events. Bedrooms are attractive, airy and simply furnished, with cornish artwork on the walls and some period furniture. The window boxes and hanging baskets are quite a sight in summer.

 From a seasonal menu, good food includes sandwiches (until 3pm), mussels in white wine, cream and garlic, chicken liver pâté with chutney, vegetable lasagne, pulled pork burger with relish, onion rings and chips, honey-roast ham and free-range eggs, local sausages with mash and onion gravy, cottage pie, rib-eye steak with a choice of sauce, and puddings such as sticky toffee pudding with clotted cream and apple, raisin and cinnamon crumble with vanilla ice-cream. *Benchmark main dish: beef stew with dumplings £12.00. Two-course evening meal £18.00.*

St Austell ~ Tenant Neythan Hayes ~ Real ale ~ Open 11-11 ~ Bar food 12-3, 6-9; 12-9 Sun ~ Children welcome ~ Dogs allowed in bar ~ Wi-fi ~ Live music Weds and Sat in summer ~ Bedrooms: £139/£179 *Recommended by Julian Richardson, Hilary and Neil Christopher, Pauline and Mark Evans, Peter Brix, Nick Higgins*

ST MAWGAN

SW8765   Map 1

Falcon

(01637) 860225 – www.thefalconinnstmawgan.co.uk

NE of Newquay, off B3276 or A3059; TR8 4EP

Friendly, creeper-covered stone inn with a cosy, simply furnished bar and dining room and seats in spacious garden; bedrooms

---

A traditional old pub in an attractive village with a good choice of drinks and popular food, this is favoured by a wide mix of customers. The bar has a log fire in the big fireplace, farmhouse chairs and cushioned wheelbacks around an assortment of tables on patterned carpet, antique coaching prints and falcon pictures, and stools against the counter where friendly staff serve Dartmoor Jail Ale and Legend and a guest on handpump, several wines by the glass and 30 gins and 30 malt whiskies; background music and darts. A compact stone-floored dining room is similarly furnished. The pretty garden has a wishing well, a cobbled front courtyard and a lawn with picnic-sets. Bedrooms are comfortable.

 Well regarded food includes lunchtime sandwiches, baked garlic and rosemary-studded camembert with red onion marmalade, crispy sweet chilli beef with asian-style salad, sweet potato gnocchi with cauliflower steak, vine tomatoes and ratatouille, ham and eggs, sausages and mash with bacon shards, crispy shallots and gravy, curry of the day, confit lamb leg with sweetcorn macaroni cheese and gremolata, hake with crushed new potatoes, gazpacho and tomato concasse, and puddings. *Benchmark main dish: pie of the day £12.95. Two-course evening meal £20.00.*

Free house ~ Licensees Steph and Jaimey Lomax ~ Real ale ~ Open 11-3, 5.30-11; 11am-midnight Fri, Sat; 12-11 Sun ~ Bar food 12-2, 6-9 ~ Restaurant ~ Children welcome away from the bar ~ Dogs allowed in bar ~ Wi-fi ~ Bedrooms: £65/£95 *Recommended by Philip J Alderton, Edward Nile, Peter Brix, Toby Jones, R J Herd, Belinda Stamp, Belinda May*

ST MERRYN
Cornish Arms
SW8874 Map 1

(01841) 532700 – www.rickstein.com/eat-with-us/the-cornish-arms
Churchtown (B3276 towards Padstow); PL28 8ND

Bustling pub with plenty of space in bar and dining rooms, real ales, popular food, friendly service and seats outside

The main door here leads into a sizeable informal area with a pool table and plenty of cushioned wall seating; to the left, a light, airy dining room overlooks the terrace. There's an upright modern woodburner, photographs of the sea and former games teams, and pale wooden dining chairs around tables on quarry tiles. This leads to two more linked rooms with ceiling joists; the first has pubby furniture on huge flagstones while the end room has more cushioned wall seating, contemporary seats and tables and parquet flooring. There's also a dining room to the back. St Austell Proper Job, Trelawny and Tribute on handpump, 12 wines by the glass, a local gin and a farm cider, friendly service, background music, board games and TV. The window boxes are pretty and there are picnic-sets on a side terrace and on grass. Disabled access.

Quite a choice of seasonal food includes sandwiches, local sardines with bacon and oatmeal, guinea fowl terrine, maple-roasted pumpkin with dukkah and feta cheese, goan seafood curry, lancashire hotpot, ham and egg, burger with toppings, chipotle and chips, chicken piri-piri with coleslaw and aioli, scampi in a basket, local rump steak with tomato, shallot and thyme salad, and puddings such as treacle tart with clotted cream and sticky toffee pudding. *Benchmark main dish: beer-battered cod and chips £14.95. Two-course evening meal £21.50.*

St Austell ~ Tenant Siebe Richards ~ Real ale ~ Open 11.30-11 ~ Bar food 12-3, 5-9 ~ Children welcome ~ Dogs welcome ~ Wi-fi *Recommended by Colin and Daniel Gibbs, Fiona and Jack Henderson, Elizabeth and Andrew Harvey, Naomi and Andrew Randall*

ST TUDY
St Tudy Inn
SX0676 Map 1

(01208) 850656 – www.sttudyinn.com
Off A391 near Wadebridge; PL30 3NN

Cornwall Dining Pub of the Year

Well run pub with several bars and dining rooms, good wines by the glass, first class food and seats outside

Of course, customers are here to enjoy the imaginative food cooked by the landlady, but they also keep a good choice of drinks such as St Austell Tribute and a beer named for the pub (from Padstow) on handpump, 25 wines by the glass and a couple of ciders. It's welcoming and attractive and the main bar has a leather armchair beside a log fire in a raised fireplace (fairy lights on the bressumer beam), beer-cask seats, chairs and cushioned window seats by a mix of tables on floor slates, and stools at the wooden counter. The dining rooms are relaxed and informal with dark farmhouse, wheelback and elegant wooden chairs and tables on bare boards or rugs, a second fireplace, fresh flowers and candlelight; background music. There are picnic-sets under parasols at the front and more seats in the garden.

 Excellent contemporary food includes baked figs with honey, thyme and ticklemore goats cheese, local mussels with saffron, spinach and cream, wild garlic, parmesan and butter risotto, beer-battered haddock and rustic chips, honey-glazed baked ham with free-range eggs, monkfish tails with rosemary focaccia crumb, citrus mayonnaise and fries, lamb curry with spinach, yoghurt and rice, and puddings such as pannacotta with passion fruit and shortbread and chocolate mousse with vanilla seed ice-cream. *Benchmark main dish: fish stew £14.00. Two-course evening meal £30.00.*

Free house ~ Licensee Emily Scott ~ Real ale ~ Open 11am-midnight; 11-6 Sun; closed Mon ~ Bar food 12-2.30, 6.30-9; not Sun evening ~ Restaurant ~ Children welcome ~ Dogs allowed in bar ~ Wi-fi *Recommended by Gordon and Patricia Gorringe, Simon and Sue Lamb, Rosie and John Moore, Sophia and Hamish Greenfield, Matilda and Gerald Thoms*

TREBURLEY   SX3477   Map 1
Springer Spaniel
(01579) 370424 – www.thespringerspaniel.co.uk
A388 Callington–Launceston; PL15 9NS

Cosy pub with highly popular food, friendly staff and a genuine welcome for all

There's a good mix of both locals and holiday-makers in this bustling 18th-c pub which makes the atmosphere cheerful and chatty. The bar has beams, antlers and a few copper pans on an exposed stone wall above a woodburning stove, books on shelves, pictures of springer spaniels, a rather fine high-backed settle and other country kitchen chairs and tables and old parquet flooring. Dartmoor Jail Ale and St Austells Tribute plus a local guest on handpump, ten good wines by the glass (including sparkling), home-made cocktails and a growing collection of gins; background music. A dining room has more bookcases, candles and similar tables and chairs, and stairs lead up to the main restaurant; a second woodburner is set into a slate wall with a stag's head above it. Outside in the small enclosed, paved garden are picnic-sets.

 Well regarded food includes sandwiches, fennel-cured trout with horseradish yoghurt, black pudding scotch egg with burnt apple gel, wild mushroom risotto with truffle oil, burger with toppings, onion rings and fries, ham hock terrine with pineapple and an egg, pine-smoked pork belly with parsnip and miso purée, sea bream with brown shrimps and butter sauce, lamb rump with smoked bacon lentils and baby gem, and puddings such as textures of chocolate and orange with orange sorbet and sticky toffee pudding with banana and honeycomb. *Benchmark main dish: beer-battered fish and chips £14.00. Two-course evening meal £20.50.*

Free house ~ Licensee Victoria Martin ~ Real ale ~ Open 12-3, 5-11.30; 12-11.30 Fri-Sun ~ Bar food 12-3, 6-9 (tapas 3-6); 12-9 Sun (roast until 4) ~ Restaurant ~ Children welcome ~ Dogs allowed in bar ~ Wi-fi *Recommended by Hazel Hyde, Richard and Tessa Ibbot, Nick Higgins, Sandra Morgan, Jack Trussler*

We say if we know a pub allows dogs.

TREVAUNANCE COVE

Driftwood Spars 🍺 🛏️

SW7251   Map 1

(01872) 552428 – www.driftwoodspars.co.uk

Off B3285 in St Agnes; Quay Road; TR5 0RT

Friendly inn with plenty of history, own microbrewery, a wide range of other drinks and popular food; nearby beach; bedrooms

The fine choice of drinks here, served by knowledgeable, friendly staff, includes their own-brewed Driftwood Spars ales and guests from breweries such as Atlantic, Firebrand and Harbour on handpump (they hold three beer festivals a year), plus 20 malt whiskies, 15 rums, 30 gins and several wines by the glass. Three small bars are timbered with massive ships' spars (the masts of great sailing ships, many of which were wrecked along this coast), and furnishings include dark wooden farmhouse and tub chairs and settles around tables of different sizes, padded stools by the counter, old ship prints, lots of nautical and wreck memorabilia and woodburning stoves; table football. It's said that an old smugglers' tunnel leads from behind the bar up through the cliff. The modern dining room overlooks the cove. Bedrooms are attractive and comfortable and some have fine views. The summer hanging baskets are pretty and there are seats in the garden. Being close to a dramatic cove and beach, it can get pretty busy at peak times. Disabled access.

A good choice of food includes sandwiches, crispy whitebait with lemon mayonnaise, garlic and rosemary-studded baked brie with red onion jam, potato rösti with a poached egg, smoked cheese sauce, wilted spinach and rémoulade, local sausages with mash and red wine gravy, burger with toppings, coleslaw and ale mayonnaise, hake with parmentier potatoes and cider, leek and mussel velouté, confit duck with pickled red cabbage, garlic mash and star anise jus, and puddings such as chocolate brownie with vanilla bean ice-cream and maple and pecan tart with butterscotch ice-cream. *Benchmark main dish: beer-battered fish and chips £13.50. Two-course evening meal £20.00.*

Own brew ~ Licensee Louise Treseder ~ Real ale ~ Open 11-11; 11am-midnight Sat ~ Bar food 12-2.30, 6-9; 12-8 Sun ~ Restaurant ~ Children welcome away from main bar ~ Dogs allowed in bar and bedrooms ~ Wi-fi ~ Live music last Sat evening of month ~ Bedrooms: £55/£165 *Recommended by Nicola and Holly Lyons, Daniel King, Charles Todd, Edward May, Simon Day*

Also Worth a Visit in Cornwall

Besides the fully inspected pubs, you might like to try these pubs that have been recommended to us and described by readers. Do tell us what you think of them: feedback@goodguides.com

ALTARNUN SX2280
Kings Head (01566) 86241
Five Lanes; PL15 7RX Old mansard-roofed beamed village pub; two or three west country ales and generous helpings of reasonably priced pubby food from sandwiches up including popular Sun carvery, carpeted lounge set for dining with big log fire, slate floor restaurant and public bar with another fire, friendly staff and ghost of former landlady Peggy Bray; background music; children and dogs welcome, picnic-sets on front terrace and in small raised garden, comfortable bedrooms, big breakfast, open (and food) all day, handy for A30. *(Peter and Emma Kelly)*

ALTARNUN SX2083
★ **Rising Sun** (01566) 86636
NW; village signed off A39 just W of A395 junction; PL15 7SN Tucked-away 16th-c pub with traditionally furnished L-shaped main bar, low beams, slate flagstones and coal fires, well kept Penpont St Nonnas, Skinners Lushingtons and guests, real cider and nice wines by the glass, highly rated food including local seafood and daily

specials, good crab sandwiches too, efficient friendly service, restaurant; background music, pool, free wi-fi; well behaved children and dogs (in bar) welcome, seats on suntrap terrace and in garden, pétanque, camping field, nice village with beautiful church, open all day weekends. *(Peter and Emma Kelly)*

BLISLAND   SX1073
★ **Blisland Inn** (01208) 850739
Village signposted off A30 and B3266 NE of Bodmin; PL30 4JF Traditional old-fashioned local with convivial landlord (usually in shorts) and friendly staff; six well kept west country ales (some tapped from the cask) including two badged for the pub from Sharps, also proper cider and fruit wines, generous helpings of pubby food cooked by landlady, beams and ceiling covered in pump clips and collection of mugs, beer-related posters and other memorabilia, carpeted lounge with several barometers, toby jugs on beams, also a family room with pool and table skittles; background and regular live music; dogs welcome, picnic-sets out on front grass overlooking village green, close to Camel Trail cycle path, open all day (till midnight Sat), no food Sun evening. *(Malcolm and Madeline Ashton)*

BODINNICK   SX1352
Old Ferry (01726) 870237
Across the water from Fowey; coming by road, to avoid the ferry queue, turn left as you go downhill – car park on left before pub; PL23 1LX Welcoming 17th-c inn just up from the river with lovely views from terrace, dining room and some of its 12 comfortable bedrooms; traditional bar with nautical memorabilia, old photographs and woodburner, back room hewn into the rock, well kept Sharps ales and at least one guest, nice wines, good food from lunchtime sandwiches up including daily specials and children's menu, friendly french landlord and helpful staff; free wi-fi; good circular walks, lane by pub in front of ferry slipway is extremely steep and parking limited, open (and food) all day. *(Ian Herdman)*

BODMIN   SX0767
Hole in the Wall (01208) 72397
Crockwell Street; PL31 2DS Former debtors' prison with masses of bric-a-brac including old rifles, pistols and swords (note the stuffed lion), beams and arched 18th-c stonework, small coal fire, well kept Butcombe, Sharps and guests, local cider and enjoyable food including tapas, friendly staff and regulars, upstairs dining/function room; Thurs quiz; children and dogs welcome, well planted courtyard garden with small stream, open all day. *(Chris Stevenson)*

BOSCASTLE   SX0990
★ **Napoleon** (01840) 250204
High Street, top of village; PL35 0BD Welcoming 16th-c thick-walled cottage at the top of this steep quaint village (fine views halfway up); cosy rooms on different levels, slate floors, oak beams and log fires, interesting Napoleon prints and lots of knick-knacks, good food including daily specials in bar areas or small restaurant, well kept St Austell ales tapped from the cask, Healey's cider and decent wines; traditional games; background music (live Fri, sing-along Tues), free wi-fi; children and dogs welcome, small covered terrace and large sheltered garden, open (and food) all day. *(Andrew Vincent)*

BOSCASTLE   SX0991
Wellington (01840) 250202
Harbour; PL35 0AQ Old hotel's long beamed and carpeted bar, good varied choice of fairly priced food including vegan menu (other special diets catered for), cornish ales kept well, nice coffee and cream teas, roaring log fire, upstairs gallery area and separate evening restaurant with more upmarket menu; Weds folk night, quiz first Mon of month; children and dogs (in bar) welcome, big secluded garden, bedrooms and apartments in adjacent mill, Museum of Witchcraft and Magic nearby, open all day. *(Andrew Vincent)*

CADGWITH   SW7214
★ **Cadgwith Cove Inn** (01326) 290513
Down very narrow lane off A3083 S of Helston; no nearby parking; TR12 7JX Friendly little pub in fishing cove with lovely walks in either direction; simply furnished front rooms with bench seating on parquet, log fire, local photos and nautical memorabilia, big back bar with huge fish mural, well kept Otter, Sharps, Skinners and a guest from Atlantic, popular food including local fish/seafood (can be pricey); background music, folk night Tues, local singers (sea shanties) Fri, TV, darts and board games; children and dogs welcome, front terrace overlooking old fishermen's sheds, comfortable bedrooms with sea views, coastal walks, open all day. *(Adrian Johnson)*

CALSTOCK   SX4368
Tamar (01822) 832487
The Quay; PL18 9QA Cheerful and relaxed 17th-c local opposite the Tamar and its imposing viaduct; painted beams, dark stripped stone, flagstones and bare boards, more modern back dining room, good straightforward food and well kept west country ales including Sharps Doom Bar, summer cream teas, reasonable prices and friendly prompt service; some live music, sports TV; children (away from bar) and well behaved dogs welcome, nicely furnished terrace, hilly walk or ferry to Cotehele (NT), open all day in summer, all day Fri-Sun winter. *(Dave Braisted)*

CHAPEL AMBLE   SW9975
Maltsters Arms (01208) 812473
Off A39 NE of Wadebridge; PL27 6EU

Country pub-restaurant with good food including set lunch offer (Weds-Fri) and Sun lunchtime carvery, friendly accommodating staff, ales such as Sharps Doom Bar, Weston's cider, beams, stripped stone and painted half-panelling, woodburner, modern back extension; music and quiz nights; children and dogs (on slate-floored area) welcome, seats outside. *(Donald Allsopp)*

CHARLESTOWN SX0351
Harbourside (01726) 67955
Part of Pier House Hotel; PL25 3NJ
Glass-fronted split-level warehouse conversion alongside the refurbished Pier House Hotel (also worth a visit); great spot looking over classic little harbour and its historic sailing ships; St Austell ales and guests, popular reasonably priced food including sandwiches and pizzas, friendly efficient service; live music every other Sat, sports TVs, pool; children and dogs welcome, interesting film-set conservation village with shipwreck museum, good walks, parking away from pub, open (and food) all day. *(David Phillips, Ian Herdman)*

CHARLESTOWN SX0351
Rashleigh Arms (01726) 73635
Charlestown Road; PL25 3NJ Modernised early 19th-c inn with public bar, lounge and dining area; five well kept St Austell ales, three guests and good wine choice, popular fairly priced food including Tues curry night, quick friendly service; background music, sports TV, free wi-fi; children welcome, dogs in bar, disabled facilities, front terrace and garden with picnic-sets, eight bedrooms (some with sea views), ten more in nearby Georgian house, Grade II listed car park (site of old coal storage yards), short walk to attractive harbour with tall ships, open (and food) all day. *(Max Simons)*

COMFORD SW7339
Fox & Hounds (01209) 820251
Comford; A393/B3298; TR16 6AX
Rambling low-beamed roadside pub; stripped stone and painted panelling, rugs on flagstones, mix of old and new furniture, woodburners, good range of well liked freshly made food from pub favourites up including daily specials and Sun carvery, well kept St Austell ales, efficient friendly service; background music, pool and darts; children and dogs (in bar) welcome, disabled facilities, nice floral displays at front, picnic-sets in back garden, open all day weekends. *(Sophia and Hamish Greenfield)*

COVERACK SW7818
Paris (01326) 280258
The Cove; TR12 6SX Comfortable Edwardian seaside inn above harbour in beautiful fishing village; carpeted L-shaped bar serving well kept St Austell ales and Healey's cider, large relaxed dining room with white tablecloths and spectacular bay

views, wide choice of enjoyable food from sandwiches to good fresh fish, Sun lunchtime carvery, helpful cheery staff, model of namesake ship (wrecked nearby in 1899); popular Weds quiz, pool, free wi-fi; children and dogs welcome, more sea views from garden and six bedrooms, limited parking. *(E A Eaves)*

CRACKINGTON HAVEN SX1496
Coombe Barton (01840) 230345
Off A39 Bude–Camelford; EX23 0JG
Extended old inn in beautiful setting overlooking splendid sandy bay (fine sunsets); much enjoyed food from shortish fairly priced menu (booking advised), four rotating cornish ales and good choice of other drinks, efficient friendly service; background and some live music, quiz nights, sports TV, pool and darts; children welcome, dogs in bar, picnic-sets on side terrace, lovely cliff walks, roomy bedrooms, open all day. *(Andrew Low)*

CROWS NEST SX2669
Crows Nest (01579) 345930
Signed off B3264 N of Liskeard;
OS Sheet 201 map reference 263692;
PL14 5JQ Characterful and welcoming little 17th-c pub under newish management; well kept St Austell ales, decent wines and good home-made food including Thurs steak night, bowed beams hung with stirrups, brasses and so forth, exposed stonework and big log fire, chatty locals; outside loos; children and dogs welcome, picnic-sets on terrace by quiet lane, handy for Bodmin Moor walks, open all day weekends, closed Tues. *(Sally and Colin Allen)*

CUBERT SW7857
★Smugglers Den (01637) 830209
Off A3075 S of Newquay; TR8 5PY Big open-plan 16th-c thatched pub tucked away in small hamlet; enjoyable locally sourced food and up to four beers from barrel-fronted counter, several wines by the glass, friendly staff, neat ranks of tables, dim lighting, stripped stone and heavy beam and plank ceilings, west country pictures and seafaring memorabilia, steps down to part with huge inglenook, another step to big side dining room, also a little snug area with woodburner and leather armchairs; background and occasional live music; children and dogs welcome, small front courtyard and terrace (both decked) with nice country views, sloping lawn and play area, camping opposite, open all day. *(R K Phillips)*

DULOE SX2358
Plough (01503) 262556
B3254 N of Looe; PL14 4PN Popular restauranty pub with three country-chic linked dining rooms all with woodburners, dark polished slate floors, a mix of pews and other seats, good food using locally sourced produce (must book weekends),

well kept St Austell, Sharps and summer
guests, Cornish Orchards' cider and seven
wines by the glass, friendly helpful service;
unobtrusive background music; children and
dogs welcome, picnic-sets out by road, closed
Tues lunchtime. (Anne Roots)

EDMONTON   SW9672
★**Quarryman** (01208) 816444
Off A39 just W of Wadebridge bypass;
PL27 7JA Welcoming busy family-run pub
adjoining small separately owned holiday
courtyard complex; three-room beamed bar
with interesting decorations including old
sporting memorabilia, enjoyable food from
short but varied menu, well kept ales such as
Exeter, Padstow and Skinners, decent wines
by the glass, efficient friendly service; sports
TV; well behaved children and dogs (on
slate-floored area) allowed, disabled access
(upstairs lavatories), picnic-sets in front and
courtyard behind, self-catering apartment,
open all day. (Geoff and Anne Marston)

EGLOSHAYLE   SX0071
Earl of St Vincent (01208) 814807
Off A389, just outside Wadebridge;
PL27 6HT Pretty flower-decked beamed
dining pub with over 200 working antique
clocks (many chiming), also golfing
memorabilia, art deco ornaments, old
pictures and rich furnishings, enjoyable
home-made food from sandwiches to
steaks, St Austell ales and Healey's cider;
background music, outside loos; well behaved
children allowed, no dogs inside, lovely
garden. (Serena and Adam Furber)

FALMOUTH   SW8032
Beerwolf (01326) 618474
Bells Court (opposite Marks & Spencer);
TR11 3AZ Stairs up to intriguing old
pub-cum-bookshop hidden down little alley
in centre of town; a former working men's
club with raftered ceilings and eclectic mix
of furniture on bare boards, good range
of well kept changing beers and ciders,
decent coffee, no food but can bring your
own, friendly laid-back atmosphere; games
including table tennis and pinball, free wi-fi;
children and dogs welcome, a few picnic-sets
outside, open all day. (Max Simons)

FALMOUTH   SW8033
Boathouse (01326) 315425
Trevethan Hill/Webber Hill; TR11 2AG
Two-level pub with buoyant local atmosphere,
four well kept changing beers featuring
some smaller cornish brewers, good range
of other drinks and enjoyable home-made
food including fresh fish/seafood, friendly
service; background and live music; children
(till 8.30pm) and dogs (in bar) welcome,
tables outside, upper deck with awning and
fantastic harbour views, closed weekday
lunchtimes in winter, otherwise open
all day. (Max Simons)

FALMOUTH   SW8132
★**Chain Locker** (01326) 311085
Custom House Quay; TR11 3HH
Refurbished 16th-c pub in fine spot by
inner harbour; St Austell ales, guest beers
and nice wines by the glass, good food
from sandwiches and sharing plates to
fresh local fish/seafood, friendly efficient
young staff, bare boards and flagstones in
nautically themed bar with plenty to look at,
woodburners, upstairs restaurant (they have
a lift) with two balconies taking in the views;
background music, Tues quiz, fruit machine;
well behaved children and dogs (in bar)
welcome, quayside tables under parasols,
six well appointed boutique bedrooms, open
all day from 8am. (Adrian Johnson, E A Eaves,
Steve Whalley)

FALMOUTH   SW8033
★**Chintz Symposium** (01326) 617550
High Street/Brewery Yard; TR11 2BY
Upstairs bar with Alice in Wonderland-
inspired décor, welcoming and relaxed and
run by two brothers; wood floors, rafters,
comfortable plain furniture and hot little
stove, plenty of quirky features including
pitched ceiling decorated with patchwork
of wallpaper and prints, a gold room hidden
behind a bookcase and loos with dinosaur
and circus-tent themes; a couple of changing
local ales, plenty of bottled beers, Healey's
cider and 15 wines by the glass from carefully
chosen list, also good range of spirits (some
cornish ones), cheese and charcuterie
boards, friendly service; live music and
other events, board games; children and
dogs (theirs is Pig) welcome, roof terrace,
open all day weekends, from 5pm Mon-Fri,
3pm weekends; the Hand craft beer bar is
below. (Max Simons, Amanda Shipley)

FALMOUTH   SW8132
Front (01326) 212168
Custom House Quay; TR11 3JT
Welcoming bare-boards quayside
drinkers' pub; great changing selection of
well kept ales, some tapped from the cask
from hop-strewn barrel-fronted counter, also
foreign beers and ciders/perries, friendly
knowledgeable staff, no food but can bring
your own (fish and chip shop above), good
mix of customers; seats outside, open all day.
(Max Simons)

FALMOUTH   SW8032
Seven Stars (01326) 312111
The Moor (centre); TR11 3QA Quirky
17th-c local, unchanging, unsmart and not for
everybody; friendly atmosphere with chatty
regulars, up to six well kept ales tapped
from the cask including Bass, Sharps and
Skinners, quiet back snug; no food or mobile
phones; dogs welcome, corridor hatch
serving roadside courtyard, open all day.
(Amanda Shipley)

FALMOUTH
Working Boat (01326) 314283   SW8032
Greenbank Quay, off Stratton Place; TR11 2SP Part of the Greenbank Hotel set down by one of the up-river piers (town centre is a brisk ten minutes' walk); interior on varying levels with big windows overlooking the water, dark green walls and stripped plank wainscoting, some nautical touches and many interesting Falmouth pictures, black-tile or board floors, tables with candles in bottles, St Austell, Skinners and a couple of other real ales, decent wines by the glass and good fairly priced food, friendly efficient service; background music, quiz nights; tables out overlooking the natural harbour, another good bar and restaurant in the hotel, open all day. *(Max Simons)*

FLUSHING
Royal Standard (01326) 374250   SW8033
Off A393 at Penryn (or foot-ferry from Falmouth); St Peters Hill; TR11 5TP Compact pub just back from the waterfront with bistro-bar feel; good fairly priced food from blackboard menu, well kept local ales and decent wines by the glass, friendly helpful staff; background and live music; children and dogs welcome, picnic-sets on small front terrace, garden behind with harbour views, open all day. *(Adrian Johnson)*

FLUSHING
Seven Stars (01326) 374373   SW8033
Trefusis Road; TR11 5TY Old-style waterside pub with welcoming local atmosphere; good selection of well kept ales (tasting trays available), pubby food including Mon evening fish and chips, coal fire, separate dining room; darts and pool; children and dogs welcome, pavement picnic-sets, great views of Falmouth (foot-ferry across), open all day. *(Sally and Colin Allen)*

FOWEY
★ **King of Prussia** (01726) 833694   SX1251
Town Quay; PL23 1AT Handsome quayside building with roomy upstairs bar, bay windows looking over harbour to Polruan, good food from ciabattas and sharing plates up including specials, St Austell ales and sensibly priced wines, friendly helpful staff, side restaurant; background music, free wi-fi; children and dogs welcome, partly enclosed outside seating area, six pleasant bedrooms (all with views), open all day. *(Mark and Sian Edwards)*

FOWEY
Lugger (01726) 833435   SX1251
Fore Street; PL23 1AH Centrally placed St Austell pub with good mix of locals and visitors (can get very busy); up to three of their well kept ales in spotless front bar with nautical memorabilia, small back dining area, generous helpings of enjoyable good value food including local fish, friendly helpful staff; children and dogs welcome, pavement tables, open all day. *(Patti and James Davidson)*

FOWEY
Ship (01726) 832230   SX1251
Trafalgar Square; PL23 1AZ Bustling 16th-c beamed pub with open fire in bare-boards bar, maritime prints, nauticalia and other bits and pieces, St Austell ales and good wines by the glass, steps up to dining room with big stained-glass window, popular food from sandwiches and pub favourites up; background music; children and dogs welcome, bedrooms (some oak-panelled), open all day. *(Charlie May)*

GERRANS
Royal Standard (01872) 580271   SW8735
The Square; TR2 5EB Friendly little local (less touristy than nearby Plume of Feathers in Portscatho); narrow doorways linking plainly furnished carpeted rooms, a couple of well kept cornish ales, Sharps cider and Skinners lager, short choice of well chosen wines, enjoyable pub food from sandwiches to local fish, old photographs on white plaster or black boarded walls, brass shell cases and kitchen utensils, woodburner; children welcome away from bar, disabled access, sunny beer garden, opposite interesting 15th-c church (rebuilt in 19th c after fire), self-catering apartment; for sale, so could be changes. *(Theocsbrian)*

GOLANT
Fishermans Arms (01726) 832453   SX1254
Fore Street (B3269); PL23 1LN Partly flagstoned small waterside local with lovely views across River Fowey from front bar and terrace; good value generous pubby food and up to four well kept west country ales, friendly service, log fire, interesting old photographs; fortnightly quiz Tues; children and dogs welcome, pleasant garden, open all day in summer (all day Fri-Sun, closed Mon in winter). *(Ian Herdman)*

GRAMPOUND
Dolphin (01726) 882435   SW9348
A390 St Austell–Truro; TR2 4RR Friendly St Austell pub with their well kept ales and decent choice of wines, good generous pub food (not Mon), two-level bar with black beams and some panelling, polished wood or carpeted floors, pubby furniture with a few high-backed settles, pictures of old Grampound, woodburner, darts, pool, TV; children welcome, dogs in bar and garden, wheelchair access from car park, beer garden, good smokery opposite, handy for Trewithen House and Gardens, closed Mon lunchtime; for sale as we went to press, so things may change. *(Max Simons)*

GWEEK   SW7026
Black Swan (01326) 221502
*Village signed from A394 at Edgcumbe;
TR12 6TU* Welcoming village pub with
large open-plan beamed bar, woodburner in
big stone fireplace, well kept ales such as
St Austell and Skinners, enjoyable reasonably
priced food from sandwiches and light
meals up, good friendly service, roomy back
restaurant; live music, monthly quiz, pool, TV;
children and dogs welcome, picnic-sets out
at the side, short walk from seal sanctuary,
four bedrooms, open all day. *(Geoff and Anne
Marston)*

HELFORD PASSAGE   SW7626
★ Ferryboat (01326) 250625
Signed from B3291; TR11 5LB Busy old
pub in lovely position by sandy beach (can
book seats on terrace in advance); bar with
farmhouse and blue-painted kitchen chairs,
built-in cushioned wall seats and stripped
tables on grey slates, woodburner, St Austell
Proper Job, Tribute and a guest, real cider
and a dozen wines by the glass, good food
including local fish/seafood, friendly service,
arched doorway to games room with pool and
darts; some live music, free wi-fi; children
and dogs (in bar) welcome, summer ferry
from Helford village across the water, can
also hire small boats and arrange fishing
trips, walk down from car park is quite steep,
open (and food) all day. *(Adrian Johnson)*

HELSTON   SW6527
★ Blue Anchor (01326) 562821
Coinagehall Street; TR13 8EL Many love
this no-nonsense, highly individual, 15th-c
thatched pub; quaint rooms off corridor,
flagstones, stripped stone, low beams and
well worn furniture, ancient back brewhouse
still producing distinctive Spingo ales
including Middle, a very strong Special and
Bragget made with honey and herbs, no food
but can bring your own (good pasty shop
nearby), family room, traditional games
and skittle alley, friendly local atmosphere;
regular live music, Mon quiz; dogs on leads
welcome, back garden with own bar, four
bedrooms in house next door, generous
breakfast, open all day. *(Peter Johnson)*

HESSENFORD   SX3057
Copley Arms (01503) 240209
A387 Looe–Torpoint; PL11 3HJ Friendly
17th-c village pub popular with passing
tourists; focus on enjoyable reasonably
priced food from bar snacks to grills in
linked carpeted areas, well kept St Austell
ales and nice choice of wines, variety of teas
and coffee, log fires, tables in cosy booths in
one part, sofas and easy chairs in another;
background and some live music, Thurs quiz;
children and dogs (in bar) welcome, a few
roadside picnic-sets by small River Seaton,
fenced play area, five bedrooms, open all day.
(Chris Stevenson)

HOLYWELL   SW7658
Treguth (01637) 830248
*Signed from Cubert, SW of Newquay;
TR8 5PP* Ancient whitewashed stone
and thatch pub near large beach; cosy
low-beamed carpeted bar with big stone
fireplace, bigger dining room at back, three
west country ales and popular food cooked
by landlord-chef, friendly service; regular
live music, Weds quiz, pool; children and
dogs welcome, handy for campsites and
popular with holidaymakers, open all day
weekends. *(Andrew Vincent)*

KINGSAND   SX4350
Devonport (01752) 822869
The Cleave; PL10 1NF Lovely bay views
from front bar of this popular pub; well kept
changing local ales and ciders, good food
from french chef-landlord including fish/
seafood (excellent Fowey mussels), nice
sandwiches and afternoon cream teas too,
friendly efficient service even at busy times,
light airy modern décor, warming log fire;
occasional live music, free wi-fi; children
and dogs welcome, tables out by sea wall, closed
Tues during school term time, otherwise open
all day. *(Banjax64)*

LAMORNA   SW4424
Lamorna Wink (01736) 731566
Off B3315 SW of Penzance; TR19 6XH
Cleanly updated 18th-c granite pub with
great collection of nauticalia; bar with pale
wood furniture on slate floor, upholstered
wall benches and woodburner, dining room
with another woodburner, well kept Skinners
and enjoyable good value food from shortish
menu; children welcome, no dogs inside,
picnic-sets and play area outside, short
stroll to beautiful cove and good coast walks,
closed Sun evening; for sale as we went to
press, so may be changes. *(Donald Allsopp)*

LANIVET   SX0364
Lanivet Inn (01208) 831212
Truro Road; PL30 5ET Welcoming old
stone pub with long L-shaped bar, dining end
with woodburner and generous helpings of
popular good value food (best to book) from
sandwiches/wraps to daily specials, St Austell
ales and guests, friendly efficient service;
background and live music, fortnightly quiz
Tues, pool, darts and TV; children and dogs
(in bar) welcome, seats out at front and in
fenced garden, handy for Saints Way trail,
unusual pub sign recalling days when village
supplied bamboo to London Zoo's pandas,
open all day weekends. *(Sally and Colin Allen)*

LELANT   SW5436
Watermill (01736) 757912
Lelant Downs; A3074 S; TR27 6LQ
Mill-conversion family dining pub; working
waterwheel behind with gearing in dark-
beamed central bar opening into brighter
airy front extension, upstairs restaurant,

Sharps Doom Bar, Skinners Betty Stogs and a guest, decent choice of good reasonably priced food including daily specials, helpful friendly staff; Weds quiz, free wi-fi; dogs welcome downstairs, good-sized pretty streamside garden, open all day. *(Alan Johnson)*

LIZARD   SW7012
Top House (01326) 290974
A3083; TR12 7NQ Comfortable pub with friendly staff and regulars; tasty food from sandwiches and snacks up including fresh fish, four well kept St Austell ales, local sea pictures (some RNLI photographs), shipwreck relics and serpentine craftwork, warm log fire; TV, darts and pool; children and dogs (in bar) welcome, disabled access, sheltered terrace, eight bedrooms in adjoining building (three with sea views), good coastal walks, open (and food) all day in summer, food all day weekends in winter. *(Amanda Shipley)*

LIZARD   SW7012
Witchball (01326) 290662
Lighthouse Road; TR12 7NJ Small friendly beamed pub popular with locals and visitors (booking recommended in season), good food from sandwiches and pizzas to fresh fish/seafood, well kept ales such as Cornish Chough, St Austell and Skinners, cornish cider, cheerful helpful staff; Sat quiz; children and dogs welcome, front terrace, open all day summer, closed winter lunchtimes Mon-Wed. *(Adrian Johnson)*

LOSTWITHIEL   SX1059
Earl of Chatham (01208) 872269
Grenville Road; PL22 0EP Traditional 16th-c split-level pub with beams, bare stone walls and open woodburner, generous helpings of enjoyable home-made food including popular Sun lunch, St Austell ales and nice choice of wines, friendly staff; children and dogs welcome, terrace picnic-sets, bedrooms, open all day. *(Mark and Sian Edwards)*

LOSTWITHIEL   SX1059
Royal Oak (01208) 872552
Duke Street; PL22 0AG Welcoming old pub with bar, lounge and evening dining area, open fires, St Austell Tribute, Sharps Doom Bar and guests, traditional cider, several wines by the glass and a gin menu, good generously served pub food including Sun carvery, amiable helpful staff; background and Fri live music, free wi-fi; children welcome, dogs in bar, terrace picnic-sets under large willow, six comfortable clean bedrooms, open all day. *(Charlie.May)*

LUDGVAN   SW5033
White Hart (01736) 740175
Off A30 Penzance–Hayle at Crowlas; TR20 8EY Ancient stone-built village pub, friendly and welcoming, with well kept ales

such as Sharps and Skinners and enjoyable home-made food including blackboard specials, small unspoilt beamed rooms with wood and stone floors, nooks and crannies, woodburners; background and summer live music, quiz first Weds of month; children and dogs welcome, back garden with decked area, interesting church next door, open all day in summer (closed weekday lunchtimes in winter). *(Chris Stevenson)*

MANACCAN   SW7624
New Inn (01326) 231301
Down hill signed to Gillan and St Keverne; TR12 6HA Refurbished part-thatched community-owned pub in attractive village setting; opened-up bar area with painted beam-and-plank ceiling, exposed stonework and blue/grey half-panelling, cushioned wall benches and other fairly traditional furniture on flagstones, log fire, garden room opening on to small terrace, up to three well kept changing ales (often Dartmoor Legend), good home-cooked local food served by friendly staff; children and dogs welcome, open all day Fri-Sun, evening meals only Fri and Sat out of season. *(Christopher Mobbs, Pam Luddington, Hilary Flunder)*

MARAZION   SW5130
Godolphin Arms (01736) 888510
West End; TR17 0EN Revamped and extended former coaching inn with wonderful views across to St Michael's Mount; light contemporary décor and modern furnishings, well liked food from sandwiches and sharing plates up, St Austell and Skinners ales, lots of wines by the glass and good coffee, friendly staff; children welcome, beachside terrace and upper deck, ten stylish bedrooms (most with sea view, some with balconies), good breakfast, open all day from 8am. *(Michael Sargent)*

MARAZION   SW5130
Kings Arms (01736) 710291
The Square; TR17 0AP Old one-bar pub in small square, comfortable, cosy and welcoming with warm woodburner, good well presented food (best to book) including local fish from regularly changing menu, well kept St Austell ales, friendly helpful staff; Tues quiz; children and dogs welcome, sunny picnic-sets out in front, open all day. *(Alan Johnson)*

MAWGAN   SW7025
Ship (01326) 221240
Churchfield, signed off Higher Lane; TR12 6AD Former 18th-c courthouse in nice setting near Helford River on the Lizard peninsula; high-ceiling bare-boards bar with woodburner in stone fireplace, end snug and raised eating area, emphasis on landlord's good food including local fish/seafood and seasonal game (best to book), takeaway fish and chips Tues, well kept ales and decent

wine list, cheerful helpful young staff; well behaved children and dogs welcome, garden picnic-sets, closed lunchtimes and all day Sun, Mon. *(Roger Burton)*

MAWNAN SMITH   SW7728
Red Lion (01326) 250026
W of Falmouth, off former B3291 Penryn–Gweek; The Square; TR11 5EP Old thatched and beamed pub with cosy series of dimly lit rooms including raftered bar; enjoyable food from light lunches to daily specials, friendly helpful service, well kept ales such as Bath Gem, St Austell Tribute and Skinners Betty Stogs, plenty of wines by the glass and good selection of rums, woodburner in huge stone fireplace, country and marine pictures, stoneware bottles/flagons and some other bric-a-brac; children (away from bar) and dogs welcome, disabled access, picnic-sets outside, handy for Glendurgan (NT) and Trebah gardens, open all day. *(Graeme and Sally Mendham)*

MENHERION   SX2862
Golden Lion (01209) 860332
Top of village by reservoir; TR16 6NW Tucked-away little stone dining pub in nice spot by Stithians Reservoir; beamed bar and snug, woodburner, well kept St Austell ales, decent wines by the glass and local gin, good choice of tasty well presented food, friendly welcoming staff, restaurant with lake view; children and dogs welcome, wheelchair access using ramps, disabled loo, attractive garden with play area, good walks, camping, open (and food) all day. *(Peter Johnson)*

METHERELL   SX4069
Carpenters Arms (01579) 351148
Follow Honicombe sign from St Anns Chapel just W of Gunnislake A390; Lower Metherell; PL17 8BJ Steps up to heavily black-beamed village local; huge polished flagstones and massive stone walls in cosy bar, carpeted lounge/dining area, three well kept ales such as St Austell, Sharps and Timothy Taylors Landlord, good reasonably priced food (not lunchtimes Mon-Thurs) cooked by landlord including stone-baked pizzas Mon and Fri evenings, friendly staff and regulars; live music, free wi-fi; children and dogs welcome, front terrace, farmers' market and brunch first Sat of month, handy for Cotehele (NT), open all day Fri-Sun, from 2pm other days. *(Patti and James Davidson)*

MEVAGISSEY   SX0144
★**Fountain** (01726) 842320
Cliff Street, down alley by Post Office; PL26 6QH Popular low-beamed fishermen's pub; slate floor, some stripped stone and a welcoming coal fire, old local pictures, well kept St Austell ales and good reasonably

priced food including local fish/seafood, friendly staff, back bar with glass-topped pit (the remains of an old fish-oil press), small upstairs evening restaurant; children and dogs welcome, pretty frontage with picnic-sets, three bedrooms, open all day in summer. *(Max Simons)*

MEVAGISSEY   SX0144
Kings Arms (01726) 843904
Fore Street; PL26 6UQ Small unpretentious pub tucked away behind the harbour; four well kept cornish ales and nice wines from slabby-topped wooden counter, much enjoyed interesting food (shortish changing menu) cooked by chef-landlord, own-baked bread and pasties, May lobster festival, good friendly service; background and maybe some acoustic live music, board games; children and dogs welcome (pub cats), opening times can vary. *(Chris Stevenson)*

MEVAGISSEY   SX0144
Ship (01726) 843324
Fore Street, near harbour; PL26 6UQ 16th-c pub with interesting alcove areas in big open-plan bar, low beams and flagstones, nautical décor, woodburner, fairly priced pubby food (small helpings available) from sandwiches to good fresh fish, well kept St Austell ales, cheery uniformed staff; background and some live music, Tues quiz, games machines, pool; children and dogs (in the bar) welcome, five bedrooms, open all day (food all day in summer). *(R K Phillips)*

MITCHELL   SW8554
★**Plume of Feathers** (01872) 510387
Off A30 Bodmin–Redruth, by A3076 junction; take southwards road then first right; TR8 5AX Popular 16th-c coaching inn with appealing contemporary décor; several linked bar and dining rooms, stripped beams and standing timbers, local artwork on pastel walls, painted dados and two open fires, good food from sandwiches up with some emphasis on fish, Sharps, Skinners and St Austell ales, several wines by the glass, impressive dining conservatory with central olive tree; background music; children (away from bar) and dogs welcome, picnic-sets under parasols in well planted garden areas, comfortable stable-conversion bedrooms, open all day from 8am. *(R J Herd, GSB, R K Phillips)*

MITHIAN   SW7450
★**Miners Arms** (01872) 552375
Off B3285 E of St Agnes; TR5 0QF Cosy old stone-built pub with traditional small rooms and passages, pubby furnishings and open fires, fine old wall painting of Elizabeth I in back bar, good choice of popular reasonably priced food from sandwiches/

baked potatoes up, St Austell, Sharps and Skinners kept well, friendly helpful staff; background music, board games; children and dogs (in bar areas) welcome, seating in sheltered front cobbled forecourt, back terrace and garden, open (and food) all day. *(Amanda Shipley)*

MORWENSTOW   SS2015
Bush (01288) 331242
Signed off A39 N of Kilkhampton; Crosstown; EX23 9SR 13th-c beamed pub in fine spot near coastal walks and surfing beaches; character bar with traditional pubby furniture on flagstones, horse tack and copper/brass knick-knacks, woodburner in stone fireplace, two St Austell ales and a guest, real cider and several wines by the glass, reasonably priced pubby food from sandwiches up, friendly staff, various dining rooms, one in modern raftered extension overlooking garden; background and some live music, fortnightly quiz Weds; children and dogs (in bar) welcome, picnic-sets and thatched cabanas on lawn, play area, bedrooms with sea views and a self-catering cottage, open (and food) all day. *(Malcolm and Madeline Ashton, Dennis and Doreen Haward)*

MOUSEHOLE   SW4626
★ Ship (01736) 731234
Harbourside; TR19 6QX Busy harbourside pub with opened-up main bar; black beams and panelling, built-in wooden wall benches and stools around low tables on granite flagstones, sailors' fancy ropework, cosy open fire. St Austell ales and several wines by the glass, straightforward pubby food; maybe background music, free wi-fi; children and dogs (in bar) welcome, bedrooms above or in next-door cottage (some overlooking sea), best to park at top of this pretty village and walk down (traffic in summer can be a nightmare), Christmas harbour lights also worth a look, open all day. *(Alan Johnson, Harriet, Michael Sargent)*

NEWLYN   SW4629
★ Tolcarne (01736) 363074
Tolcarne Place; TR18 5PR Simply updated 17th-c quayside pub with highly rated food from chef-landlord, much emphasis on local fish/seafood (menu changes daily) and must book, friendly efficient service, St Austell Tribute, Skinners Betty Stogs and maybe a local microbrew; live jazz Sun lunchtime; children and dogs welcome, terrace (harbour wall cuts off view), good parking. *(Jan)*

NEWQUAY   SW8061
Fort (01637) 875700
Fore Street; TR7 1HA Massive pub in magnificent setting high above surfing beach and small harbour; full St Austell range and decent food from sandwiches and baked potatoes up, friendly staff coping well at busy times, modernised open-plan areas with solid

furnishings from country kitchen tables and chairs to comfy sofas, soft lighting, games part with two pool tables, excellent indoor children's play area; great views from long glass-walled side section and sizeable garden with multi-level terrace and further play areas, open (and food) all day. *(Alan Johnson, Tony Scott)*

NEWQUAY   SW8061
Lewinnick Lodge (01637) 878117
Pentire headland, off Pentire Road; TR7 1QD Modern flint-walled bar-restaurant built into bluff above the sea – big picture windows for the terrific views; light airy bar with wicker seating, three or four well kept ales and plenty of wines by the glass, spreading dining areas with contemporary furnishings on light oak flooring, popular bistro-style food from shortish menu, pleasant relaxed atmosphere; children and dogs (in bar) welcome, modern seats and tables on terraces making most of the stunning Atlantic views, ten bedrooms, open all day; same management as the Plume of Feathers in Mitchell. *(Sally and Colin Allen)*

NEWTOWN   SW7423
Prince of Wales (01326) 231247
The one off B3293, SE of Helston; TR12 6DP Flower-decked stone pub in tucked-away hamlet on the Lizard peninsula; beamed bar with pubby furniture on slate floor, woodburner, small restaurant, cornish ales such as Penzance and St Austell, good well presented food cooked to order from shortish menu, friendly helpful service; darts; children and dogs welcome, picnic-sets on back gravel terrace and lawn, bedrooms and camping, open all day Sun, closed Mon lunchtime; for sale as we went to press, so may be changes. *(Paul and Karen Cornock)*

PADSTOW   SW9175
★ Golden Lion (01841) 532797
Lanadwell Street; PL28 8AN Old inn dating from the 14th c; cheerful black-beamed locals' bar and high-raftered back lounge with plush banquettes, well kept Sharps Doom Bar, Skinners Betty Stogs and a guest, good range of gins, enjoyable generously served food including reasonably priced bar lunches, evening steaks and fresh fish, popular Sun lunch, friendly helpful staff, coal fire and woodburner; pool in family area, background music, sports TV; dogs welcome, colourful floral displays at front, terrace tables behind, three good bedrooms, open all day (no food Sun evening). *(GSB)*

PADSTOW   SW9175
Harbour Inn (01841) 533148
Strand Street; PL28 8BU Attractive old-school pub just back from the harbour and a quieter alternative; long room with nautical bric-a-brac, pubby furnishings including some high-backed settles, comfy sofas in front area, piano and woodburner, well kept

St Austell ales and enjoyable generously served traditional food, friendly helpful staff; children and dogs welcome, open all day. *(Serena and Adam Furber)*

PADSTOW   SW9175
Shipwrights (01841) 532451
North Quay; PL28 8AF Long brick-built quayside pub with open-plan beamed and flagstoned bar; St Austell ales, decent wines and good food from lunchtime sandwiches and sharing plates up, friendly staff, further upstairs eating area; background music, pool, TVs and fruit machine; children and dogs welcome, a few tables out by the water, more in back suntrap garden, open all day. *(M A Borthwick)*

PAUL   SW4627
Kings Arms (01736) 731224
Mousehole Lane, opposite church; TR19 6TZ Refurbished beamed local with cosy bustling atmosphere, enjoyable sensibly priced pub food from sandwiches, baked potatoes and basket meals up, well kept St Austell ales, Healey's cider and good selection of gins; live music including Tues bluegrass; children welcome, dogs in one bar, a few picnic-sets out in front, five bedrooms, open all day in summer. *(Celia and Robert Lemming)*

PELYNT   SX2054
Jubilee (01503) 220312
B3359 NW of Looe; PL13 2JZ Beamed 16th-c village inn; enjoyable locally sourced food from sandwiches up, well kept St Austell ales, Healey's cider and decent range of other drinks including cornish rum and gin, spotless interior with interesting Queen Victoria mementoes (pub renamed in 1897 to celebrate her diamond jubilee), some handsome antique furnishings, log fires under copper canopies, separate bar with winter pool table and darts; children and dogs (not in restaurant) welcome, disabled facilities, large terrace, 11 comfortable bedrooms, open all day (food all day in summer, all day weekends in winter). *(Gary and Diane Amer)*

PENDEEN   SW3834
North (01736) 788417
B3306, opposite the school; TR19 7DN Friendly little creeper-clad village pub set back from the road; well kept St Austell ales and popular food including range of curries and good Sun roasts, single bar with interesting tin-mining memorabilia, upstairs restaurant looking over fields to the sea; children and dogs welcome, boules in big back garden, bedrooms and camping, good walks, open all day. *(Steve and Claire Harvey)*

PENDOGGETT   SX0279
Cornish Arms (01208) 880335
B3314; PL30 3HH Old beamed coaching inn dating from the 16th c; traditional oak

settles on front bar's polished slate floor, well kept Sharps ales, a guest beer and several wines by the glass from good list, around 100 gins, enjoyable home-made food including sandwiches/panini, interesting burgers and two-course light lunch deal (Mon-Fri), friendly efficient service, dining room and proper back locals' bar with woodburner; children and dogs welcome, disabled access, distant sea view from terrace, seven bedrooms, open all day. *(Andrew Low, Michael Akin)*

PENELEWEY   SW8140
★ Punch Bowl & Ladle
(01872) 862237 *B3289; TR3 6QY* Thatched dining pub dating from the 15th c; very enjoyable freshly made food from sandwiches to daily specials, four St Austell ales, Healey's cider and good wine and whisky selection, helpful friendly service, dark beams, some white-painted stone walls and oak panelling, rustic bric-a-brac and big sofas, steps down to lounge/dining area, restaurant; soft background music, quiz second and fourth Sun of month, free wi-fi; children (away from bar) and dogs welcome, wheelchair access (not from small side terrace), handy for Trelissick Garden (NT), open all day. *(Max Simons)*

PENZANCE   SW4730
Admiral Benbow (01736) 363448
Chapel Street; TR18 4AF Wonderfully quirky two-floor pub packed with interesting nautical paraphernalia and full of atmosphere; St Austell Proper Job, Sharps Doom Bar and a guest such as Treens, local Polgoon cider and good selection of gins and other spirits, enjoyable pubby food from shortish menu, friendly staff, cosy corners and log fire, downstairs restaurant in captain's cabin style, second bar upstairs and nice view from back room; unobtrusive background music; children welcome, dogs in some areas (theirs is Sir Cloudesley), open all day. *(Mark and Sian Edwards)*

PENZANCE   SW4730
Bath (01736) 331940
Cornwall Terrace; TR18 4HL Friendly well looked-after pub tucked away behind the seafront; linked rooms (bigger than it looks) with beams, some panelling and old photographs of Penzance, good range of beers, no food; pool, darts, sports TV, fruit machine; children (till 9pm) and dogs welcome, delightful sunny beer garden, open all day weekends. *(Steve and Claire Harvey)*

PENZANCE   SW4730
Crown (01736) 351070
Victoria Square, Bread Street; TR18 2EP Friendly little backstreet corner local with neat bar and back snug, own Cornish Crown beers and several wines by the glass, no food but can bring your own; live acoustic music

Mon, quiz Tues, board games; children and dogs welcome, a few seats out in front, open all day. *(Sophia and Hamish Greenfield)*

PENZANCE SW4729
Dolphin (01736) 364106
Quay Street, opposite harbour after swing-bridge; TR18 4BD Old stone-built pub with enjoyable good value food including fresh fish, up to four well kept St Austell ales and good wines by the glass, roomy bar on different levels, nautical memorabilia and three resident ghosts; pool and darts; children and dogs welcome, pavement picnic-sets, three comfortable bedrooms with sea/harbour views, no car park (public one not far away), handy for Scillies ferry, open (and food) all day. *(Andrew Vincent)*

PERRANARWORTHAL SW7738
Norway (01872) 864241
A39 Truro–Penryn; TR3 7NU Large beamed pub with half a dozen linked areas, good choice of food including daily specials and Sun carvery, St Austell ales and several wines by the glass, cream teas, good friendly service, open fires, panelling and mix of furniture on slate flagstones, restaurant; background music, quiz nights, free wi-fi; children and dogs welcome, tables outside, four comfortable bedrooms, good breakfast, open (and food) all day. *(Amanda Shipley)*

PERRANUTHNOE SW5329
★Victoria (01736) 710309
Signed off A394 Penzance–Helston; TR20 9NP Village pub with attractively furnished L-shaped bar, exposed joists, cosy corners and woodburner, Monty's Growler (named after the pub dog) from Cornish Crown, Sharps Doom Bar and weekly guests, over ten wines by the glass and good food cooked by landlord, separate restaurant; background music, board games; children and dogs (in bar) welcome, tables in tiered garden, South West Coast Path nearby, cosy bedrooms, closed Sun evening (and Mon, Tues in winter). *(Sophie and James Collier, Sally and Brian Turner, Sally and David Champion, Millie and Peter Downing)*

PERRANWELL STATION SW7739
Royal Oak (01872) 863175
Village signposted off A393 Redruth–Falmouth and A39 Falmouth–Truro; TR3 7PX Traditional chatty village pub; carpeted black-beamed bar with paintings by local artists, candlelit tables in snug room behind, big fireplace, St Austell Proper Job, Sharps Doom Bar, Skinners Lushingtons and a guest, proper cider and several wines by the glass, hearty helpings of enjoyable home-cooked food including specials, good friendly service; free wi-fi; children and dogs (in bar) welcome, picnic-sets out at front, more seats in back garden, good surrounding walks, open all day weekends. *(Celia and Robert Lemming)*

PHILLEIGH SW8739
★Roseland (01872) 580254
Between A3078 and B3289, NE of St Mawes just E of King Harry Ferry; TR2 5NB In small hamlet handy for the King Harry Ferry and Trelissick Garden (NT); two cosy black-beamed bar rooms, one with flagstones, the other carpeted, wheelbacks and built-in red cushioned seats, horsebrasses, interesting old photographs and some framed giant beetles, woodburner, tiny lower area liked by locals, side restaurant too, well kept Skinners Betty Stogs, Sharps Doom Bar and a guest, nice wines by the glass and enjoyable home-made food, friendly helpful service; folk night first Weds of month (not summer), free wi-fi; children and dogs (in bar) welcome, seats on pretty paved front terrace, may open all day weekends in high season. *(Graeme and Sally Mendham)*

POLPERRO SX2051
Crumplehorn Mill (01503) 272348
Top of village near main car park; PL13 2RJ Converted mill and farmhouse keeping beams, flagstones and some stripped stone, snug lower bar leading to long main room with cosy end eating area, well kept cornish ales, wide choice of popular food from snacks to blackboard specials (booking advised), friendly efficient service, log fire; children and dogs welcome, outside seating and working mill wheel, bedrooms and self-catering apartments, open all day. *(Mark and Sian Edwards)*

POLPERRO SX2050
Three Pilchards (01503) 272233
Quay Road; PL13 2QZ Small low-beamed local behind fish quay; generous helpings of reasonably priced food from baguettes to good fresh fish, well kept St Austell Tribute, up to four guest beers and decent wines by the glass, efficient obliging service even when busy, lots of black woodwork, dim lighting, simple furnishings, open fire in big stone fireplace; weekend live music; children and dogs welcome, lovely views from terrace up steep steps with own bar, open all day. *(Chris Stevenson)*

POLRUAN SX1250
Lugger (01726) 870007
The Quay; back roads off A390 in Lostwithiel, or foot-ferry from Fowey; PL23 1PA Popular waterside pub under newish management; steps up to cosy beamed bar with open fire and woodburner, well kept St Austell ales and enjoyable fairly pubby food including specials and Sun carvery, friendly efficient service, restaurant on upper level; children, dogs and boots welcome, not suitable for wheelchairs, good local walks, limited nearby parking (steep hill to main car park), open all day. *(Marianne and Peter Stevens)*

PORT ISAAC SW9980

⭐ **Golden Lion** (01208) 880336

Fore Street; PL29 3RB Popular well positioned 18th-c pub keeping friendly local atmosphere in simply furnished old rooms; bar and snug with open fire, window seats and balcony tables looking down on rocky harbour and lifeboat slip far below, upstairs restaurant, enjoyable food including good local fish, well kept St Austell ales from well stocked bar, amiable helpful staff; background music, pool, darts; children and dogs welcome, dramatic cliff walks, open all day. *(Charlie May)*

PORTHALLOW SW7923

Five Pilchards (01326) 280256

SE of Helston; B3293 to St Keverne, then village signed; TR12 6PP Sturdy old-fashioned stone-built local in secluded cove right by shingle beach; lots of salvaged nautical gear, interesting shipwreck memorabilia and model boats, woodburner, four real ales such as St Austell, Bays, Dartmoor and Exeter, a nearby cider and enjoyable reasonably priced food including local fish, friendly chatty staff, conservatory; children and dogs welcome, seats out in sheltered yard, sea-view bedrooms, open all day Sun, closed in winter Mon lunchtime and Tues. *(Graeme and Sally Mendham)*

PORTHLEVEN SW6325

Atlantic (01326) 562439

Peverell Terrace; TR13 9DZ Friendly buzzy pub in great setting above the harbour; good value tasty food including bargain OAP lunch (Mon, Weds, Fri) and other deals, ales such as St Austell and Skinners from boat-shaped counter, Weston's cider, big open-plan lounge with well spaced seating and cosier alcoves, good log fire in granite fireplace, carpeted dining room with trompe l'oeil murals; live music/entertainment Sat evening, Mon quiz, TV for major sports, darts, free wi-fi; children and dogs welcome, lovely bay views from raised front terrace, open all day. *(Chris Stevenson)*

PORTHLEVEN SW6225

Harbour Inn (01326) 334128

Commercial Road; TR13 9JB Large neatly kept pub-hotel in outstanding harbourside setting; expansive lounge and bar with dining area off, big public bar, well kept St Austell ales and good range of fairly pubby food from snacks and sharing boards up, well organised friendly service; unobtrusive background music (live Sat), Thurs quiz, free wi-fi; children and dogs (in bar) welcome, picnic-sets on spacious quayside terrace, 15 well equipped bedrooms (some with harbour view), good breakfast, open (and food) all day. *(Max Simons)*

PORTHTOWAN SW6948

⭐ **Blue** (01209) 890329

Beach Road, East Cliff; car park (fee in season) advised; TR4 8AW Popular easy-going bar (not a traditional pub) by stunning beach attracting customers of all ages; big picture windows looking across terrace to huge expanse of sand and sea, wicker and white chairs around pale tables on grey-painted floorboards, cream or orange walls, ceiling fans and some large ferns, ales from St Austell, Sharps and Skinners, several wines by the glass, cocktails and shots, various coffees, hot chocolates and teas, all-day summer food from 10am brunch on including nachos with toppings, burgers and stone-baked pizzas; background music (live Sat evening), free wi-fi; children and dogs welcome, open all day (till midnight Fri, Sat), closed evenings out of season and may shut all Jan and some of Feb. *(Peter and Emma Kelly)*

PORTLOE SW9339

Ship (01872) 501356

At top of village; TR2 5RA Cheerful traditional local in charming fishing village; L-shaped bar with tankards hanging from beams, nautical bric-a-brac, local memorabilia and beer bottle collection, straightforward pubby tables and chairs on carpet, open fire, St Austell ales, cider/perry and six wines by the glass, generously served food from shortish menu; background music, sports TV, darts, free wi-fi; children and dogs (in bar) welcome, sloping streamside garden across road, comfortable bedrooms, beach close by. *(Andrew Vincent)*

PORTREATH SW6545

Portreath Arms (01209) 842259

The Square; by B3300/B3301 N of Redruth; TR16 4LA Modernised family-owned Victorian hotel; good food including specials and themed nights in bar or restaurant, friendly attentive service, beers such as Bays, St Austell and Skinners, local cider and good range of other drinks; quiz first Sun of month, some live music, sports TV, pool; children and dogs welcome, seven bedrooms, well placed for coastal walks, open all day. *(Mr and Mrs R G Spiller)*

PORTSCATHO SW8735

Plume of Feathers (01872) 580321

The Square; TR2 5HW Largely stripped-stone coastal village pub with some sea-related bric-a-brac and pictures in two comfortable linked areas, also small side bar and separate restaurant, St Austell ales and enjoyable reasonably priced pubby food, friendly staff; background music, free wi-fi; children, dogs and boots welcome, disabled access (steps to restaurant and gents'),

---

If you know a pub is ever open all day, please tell us.

picnic-sets out under awning, lovely coast walks, open all day in summer (and other times if busy). *(Sally and Colin Allen)*

ROCK SW9375
Mariners *(01208) 863679*
Rock Road; PL27 6LD This popular modern dining pub with lovely estuary views had just changed hands as we went to press, so it's too early to gauge feedback; light spacious bar with slate flooring and bare stone or painted walls, contemporary metal chairs and wall seats around pale wood-topped tables, Sharps ales, similarly furnished upstairs restaurant with balcony; children and dogs have been welcome, seats on front terrace (or can sit on sea wall). *(Patti and James Davidson)*

RUAN LANIHORNE SW8942
★ Kings Head *(01872) 501263*
Village signed off A3078 St Mawes Road; TR2 5NX Country pub in quiet hamlet with interesting church nearby; relaxed small bar with log fire, Skinners and a guest, maybe farm cider, very well liked food especially local fish/seafood, dining area to the right divided in two, lots of china cups hanging from ceiling joists, cabinet filled with old bottles, hunting prints and cartoons, separate restaurant to the left; background music; well behaved children allowed in dining areas, dogs in bar only, terrace across road and nice lower beer garden, walks along Fal estuary, closed winter Sun evening and Mon. *(Sophia and Hamish Greenfield)*

SENNEN COVE SW3526
Old Success *(01736) 871232*
Cove Hill; Cove Road off A30; TR19 7DG Glorious Whitesand Bay view from the terraced garden or inside this seaside hotel; beamed bar with lifeboat and other nautical memorabilia, log fire, St Austell ales from plank-fronted servery, generally well liked food including fresh local fish; background and some live music; children and dogs welcome, 14 comfortable bedrooms, four self-catering apartments, popular with surfers, open all day. *(Tony Scott)*

ST BREWARD SX0977
Old Inn *(01208) 850711*
Off B3266 S of Camelford; Churchtown; PL30 4PP Broad slate flagstones, low oak beams, stripped stonework and two massive granite fireplaces dating from the 11th c, ales such as Sharps and Tintagel, proper ciders and several wines by the glass, enjoyable good value food including popular Sun carvery, roomy extended restaurant with tables out on deck; background music, darts, pool, free wi-fi; children and dogs welcome, moorland behind (cattle and sheep wander into the village), open all day in summer. *(Max Simons)*

ST DOMINICK SX4067
Who'd Have Thought It
(01579) 350214 Off A388 S of Callington; PL12 6TG Large comfortable country pub with popular reasonably priced home-made food (booking advised) including gluten-free and vegan choices, well kept St Austell ales, a guest beer and good value wine list, friendly competent service, superb Tamar views especially from conservatory, beams and open fire; live music and quiz nights; children and dogs (in bar) welcome, garden tables, handy for Cotehele (NT), open all day. *(John Evans)*

ST EWE SW9746
Crown *(01726) 843322*
Pub signed from Kestle and Polmassick; PL26 6EY Tucked-away 16th-c village pub with thoroughly traditional décor; low black-painted beams, big slate flagstones and carpet, two fireplaces decorated with shiny horsebrasses, china in glazed corner cupboards, wheelback chairs, pews and a splendid high-backed settle, four St Austell ales kept well and good value food from light dishes up, also bargain OAP lunch Fri, back overflow dining room up steps; children and dogs welcome, disabled access/facilities, handy for Lost Gardens of Heligan. *(Jamie Taylor)*

ST ISSEY SW9271
Ring o' Bells *(01841) 540251*
A389 Wadebridge–Padstow; Churchtown; PL27 7QA Traditional slate-clad 18th-c village pub with open fire at one end of beamed bar, pool table the other, well kept Courage Best, St Austell Tribute, Sharps Doom Bar and Skinners Betty Stogs, good choice of wines and whiskies, friendly service, enjoyable sensibly priced food (own vegetables and pork) in long narrow side dining room; live music; children and dogs welcome, decked courtyard with pretty hanging baskets and tubs, three bedrooms, car park across road, open all day weekends and can get packed in summer, closed weekday lunchtimes. *(Charlie May)*

ST IVES SW5140
Golden Lion *(01736) 797935*
Market Place, next to church; TR26 1RZ Refurbished 19th-c two-room pub with friendly relaxed atmosphere, Skinners Betty Stogs and guests, proper ciders and enjoyable good value pubby food from sandwiches and baked potatoes up; live music and summer quiz nights, sports TV; children and dogs welcome, beer garden behind, open all day. *(Chris Stevenson)*

ST IVES SW5140
Lifeboat *(01736) 794123*
Wharf Road; TR26 1LF Thriving family-friendly quayside pub with decent choice

of generously served food from snacks up including fish/seafood, well kept St Austell ales, friendly busy staff, spacious modernised interior with harbour-view tables and cosier corners, nautical theme including lifeboat pictures, log fire; background music, sports TV, darts; no dogs inside, disabled access/ facilities, newly added bedrooms, open (and food) all day, breakfast from 8am. *(Dave Chapman)*

ST IVES   SW5441
Pedn Olva (01736) 796222
The Warren; TR26 2EA Hotel rather than pub perched on rocky outcrop with fine views of sea and Porthminster beach (especially from tables on roof terrace); roomy bar with well kept St Austell ales and good food, separate restaurant, efficient friendly service; 30 comfortable bedrooms, open (and food) all day. *(Alan Johnson)*

ST IVES   SW5140
★**Sloop** (01736) 796584
The Wharf; TR26 1LP Busy low-beamed, panelled and flagstoned harbourside inn; St Ives School pictures and attractive portrait drawings in front bar, atmospheric dimly lit corners, booth seating in back bar, good choice of food from sandwiches and baguettes to lots of fresh local fish, quick friendly service, well kept Sharps, real cider and an own-label gin, upstairs evening restaurant; background and live music, TV; children in eating area, beach view from roof terrace and seats out on cobbles, handy for Tate gallery, bedrooms (some in separate buildings), open all day (breakfast from 9am). *(Alan Johnson, Dave Chapman, Tony Scott)*

ST IVES   SW5140
Union (01736) 796486
Fore Street; TR26 1AB Popular and friendly low-beamed local, roomy but cosy, with good value food from sandwiches to local fish, buy two steaks and get a free bottle of house wine, well kept Sharps Doom Bar, a guest beer and Healey's cider, small hot fire, leather sofas on carpet, dark woodwork and masses of old ship photographs; background and live music; dogs welcome, open all day. *(Alan Johnson)*

ST JUST IN PENWITH   SW3731
Kings Arms (01736) 788545
Market Square; TR19 7HF Friendly pub with three separate carpeted areas; granite walls, beamed and boarded ceilings, open fire, shortish menu of good home-made food (not Sun evening in winter), well kept St Austell ales and decent coffee; background

music, Weds quiz, free wi-fi; children and dogs welcome, tables out in front, open all day. *(Alan Johnson, M G Hart)*

ST JUST IN PENWITH   SW3731
★**Star** (01736) 788767
Fore Street; TR19 7LL Low-beamed two-room local with friendly landlord and relaxed informal atmosphere; five well kept St Austell ales, no food (can bring your own lunchtime sandwiches or pasties), dimly lit main bar with old mining photographs on dark walls, ceiling covered in flags, coal fire; nostalgic juke box, live celtic music Mon, open mike Thurs, darts and euchre; tables in attractive backyard with smokers' shelter, open all day. *(Sally and Colin Allen)*

ST KEW   SX0276
★**St Kew Inn** (01208) 841259
Village signposted from A39 NE of Wadebridge; PL30 3HB Popular 15th-c beamed pub next to village church; unchanging slate-floored bar with fire in old black range, two dining areas including neat restaurant with stone walls, winged high-back settles and other traditional furniture on tartan carpet, another log fire in stone fireplace, St Austell ales from cask and handpump, gin menu, well liked food (not Sun evening in winter) from lunchtime baguettes to good Sun lunch, friendly efficient service; live music every other Fri; children away from bar and dogs welcome, pretty flowering tubs and baskets outside, picnic-sets in garden over road, open all day in summer. *(Penny Shinfield)*

ST MAWES   SW8433
Idle Rocks (01326) 270771
Tredenham Road; TR2 5AN Civilised waterfront hotel by edge of harbour; pleasant small bar area and separate lounge, two-tier restaurant looking on to terrace and sea, Sharps Doom Bar (bottled beers only in winter) and decent wines by the glass, good food from bar snacks up, friendly helpful staff; well behaved dogs (but no small children) allowed on sun terrace, smallish bedrooms overlooking the water are the best bet, open all day. *(R K Phillips)*

ST MAWES   SW8433
★**Rising Sun** (01326) 270233
The Square; TR2 5DJ Light and airy pub across road from harbour wall; bar on right with end woodburner and sea-view bow window, rugs on stripped wood and a few dining tables, sizeable carpeted left-hand bar and conservatory, well prepared tasty food from local fish to good steaks, cream teas, well kept St Austell ales and nice

---

If you stay overnight in an inn or hotel, they are allowed to serve you an alcoholic drink at any hour of the day or night.

wines by the glass, friendly young staff, buzzy atmosphere; background music, free wi-fi; children and dogs welcome, awkward wheelchair access, picnic-sets on sunny front terrace, comfortable bedrooms, open (and food) all day. *(Serena and Adam Furber)*

ST MAWES   SW8533
St Mawes Hotel (01326) 270170
Marine Parade; TR2 5DN Harbourside hotel's relaxed bar-restaurant; bare boards and simple furnishings, woodburner, enjoyable food from small plates and pizzas up, St Austell Tribute and a summer guest, nice wines and good italian coffee, more room upstairs with sofas, scatter-cushion wall seats and second woodburner, small balcony overlooking the sea, friendly helpful staff; children welcome, a few tables out in front, good if not cheap bedrooms (lovely views), open all day. *(Amanda Shipley)*

TIDEFORD   SX3459
Rod & Line (01752) 851912
Church Road; PL12 5HW Small old-fashioned rustic local set back from the road up steps; St Austell and Skinners kept well, nice food including good fresh fish/seafood from blackboard menus, friendly helpful service, angling theme with rods etc and other bric-a-brac, low-bowed ceiling, settles, good log fire; live music, darts and shove-ha'penny; children and dogs welcome, tables outside, three new well appointed bedrooms, open all day. *(Peter Woods)*

TINTAGEL   SX0588
Olde Malthouse (01840) 770461
Fore Street; PL34 0DA Refurbished 14th-c beamed pub under newish management; inglenook bar and restaurant; good food (booking advised) and three well kept local ales including Tintagel, friendly helpful service; children and dogs welcome, tables on roadside terrace, seven bedrooms, nice walks, open all day, no evening food Sun-Tues. *(Graeme and Sally Mendham)*

TOWAN CROSS   SW4078
Victory (01209) 890359
Off B3277; TR4 8BN Welcoming roadside local, comfortable and relaxed, with four real ales including St Austell and Skinners, generous helpings of enjoyable well priced food and good helpful service, open-plan interior with nice unfussy country décor, conservatory; pool and euchre; children and dogs welcome, beer garden, camping, handy for good uncrowded beaches, open all day. *(Patti and James Davidson)*

TREBARWITH   SX0585
Port William (01840) 770230
Trebarwith Strand; PL34 0HB Lovely seaside setting with glorious views and sunsets, waterside picnic-sets across road and on covered terrace, maritime memorabilia and log fires inside, enjoyable

food from sandwiches and baked potatoes to daily specials (they may ask to swipe a card before you eat), St Austell ales; background music; children and dogs welcome, eight well equipped comfortable bedrooms, open all day. *(John Ledbury)*

TREEN   SW3923
★**Logan Rock** (01736) 810495
Just off B3315 Penzance–Land's End; TR19 6LG Cosy traditional low-beamed bar with good log fire, well kept St Austell ales and tasty pub food from sandwiches and pasties to nice steaks, small back snug with collection of cricketing memorabilia (welcoming landlady eminent in county's cricket association), family room (no under-14s in bar); dogs welcome on leads, pretty split-level garden behind with covered area, good coast walks including to Logan Rock itself, handy for Minack Theatre, open all day in season and can get very busy. *(Donald Allsopp)*

TREGADILLETT   SX2983
★**Eliot Arms** (01566) 772051
Village signposted off A30 at junction with A395, W end of Launceston bypass; PL15 7EU Creeper-covered pub with series of small rooms, interesting collections including 72 antique clocks, 700 snuffs and hundreds of horsebrasses, also barometers, old prints and shelves of books/china, fine mix of furniture on Delabole slate from high-backed settles and chaises longues to more modern seats, open fires, well kept St Austell Tribute, Wadworths 6X and a scottish house beer, big helpings of enjoyable pubby food, friendly staff and chatty locals; background music, darts, games machine; children and dogs welcome, outside seating front and back, lovely hanging baskets and tubs, two bedrooms, open all day. *(Peter Andrews)*

TREGONY   SW9244
Kings Arms (01872) 530202
Fore Street (B3287); TR2 5RW Light and airy 16th-c village coaching inn; long traditional main bar and two beamed and panelled front dining areas, St Austell ales, Healey's cider/perry and nice wines, enjoyable sensibly priced pub food using local produce, tea and coffee, prompt service and friendly chatty atmosphere, two fireplaces, one with huge cornish range, pubby furniture on carpet or flagstones, old team photographs, back games room; children and dogs welcome, disabled access, tables in pleasant suntrap garden. *(Max Simons)*

TREMATON   SX3960
Crooked Inn (01752) 848177
Off A38 just W of Saltash; PL12 4RZ Friendly family-run inn down long drive; open-plan bar with lower lounge leading to conservatory (lovely views), beams, straightforward furnishings and log fire, cornish ales and decent wines by the

glass, good choice of popular freshly made food from doorstep sandwiches to daily specials, Sun lunchtime carvery, helpful service; children and dogs welcome, terrace overlooking garden and valley, play area, roaming ducks and geese, 15 bedrooms, open all day. *(John Evans)*

TRURO   SW8244

★**Old Ale House** (01872) 271122
Quay Street; TR1 2HD City-centre tap for Skinners brewery, five of their ales plus guests (some from casks behind bar), lots of craft beers, west country ciders and several wines by the glass including country ones, no food (can bring your own), good cheerful service, dimly lit beamed bar with engaging mix of furnishings, sawdust on the floor, beer mats on walls and ceiling, some interesting 1920s bric-a-brac and life-size cutout of Betty Stogs, daily newspapers and free monkey nuts, upstairs room with table football; juke box, live music Mon and Sat evenings; children (away from bar) and dogs welcome, open all day (till 1am Sat). *(Alan Johnson)*

TRURO   SW8245

Rising Sun (01872) 240003
Mitchell Hill; TR1 1ED Comfortably opened-up spit-level dining pub up steep hill from town centre; highly praised food (not Sun evening) cooked by chef-owner, Skinners beers along with Fullers London Pride and a guest, well chosen wines and interesting selection of whiskies and gins, helpful friendly staff; children and dogs (in bar) welcome, back courtyard, parking can be tricky, closed Mon in winter, otherwise open all day. *(Mathias Sexton)*

TYWARDREATH   SX0854

New Inn (01726) 813901
Off A3082; Fore Street; PL24 2QP Welcoming 18th-c local in nice village setting; St Austell ales and guests including Bass tapped from the cask, good food in back restaurant and conservatory, friendly relaxed atmosphere; some live music; children and dogs welcome, large secluded garden behind with play area, open all day. *(Andrew Vincent)*

WAINHOUSE CORNER   SX1895

Old Wainhouse (01840) 230711
A39; EX23 0BA Popular roadside pub under new management; main flagstoned bar with attractive built-in settle and stripped rustic farmhouse chairs around mix of tables, beams hung with old tools, horse tack, copper pans and so forth, large woodburner,

simpler room off and dining room with high-backed chairs around pale wooden tables and another woodburner, Sharps beers, enjoyable food including Thurs steak night; pool and darts; children and dogs (in bar) welcome, picnic-sets on side grass, bedrooms looking towards the sea, South West Coast Path close by, open all day. *(R K Phillips, Andrew Low)*

WATERGATE BAY   SW8464

Beach Hut (01637) 860877
B3276 coast road N of Newquay; TR8 4AA Great views from bustling modern beach bar appealing to customers of all ages; planked walls, cushioned wicker and cane armchairs around scrubbed wooden tables, corner snugs with banquettes and tile-topped tables, weathered stripped-wood floor and unusual sloping bleached-board ceiling, big windows and doors opening to glass-fronted deck with retractable roof, three real ales including Skinners, decent wines by the glass and lots of coffees and teas, enjoyable modern food served by friendly young staff; background music; dogs welcome in bar, easy wheelchair access, open all day from 9am (10.30am-5pm in winter). *(Mark and Sian Edwards)*

ZELAH   SW8151

Hawkins Arms (01872) 540339
A30; TR4 9HU Homely 18th-c beamed local with up to four well kept ales such as Bays, St Austell and Skinners, tasty generously served food from sandwiches to blackboard specials, friendly staff, woodburner in stone fireplace, restaurant; occasional live music and quiz nights; children and dogs welcome, back and side terraces, three bedrooms. *(Donald Allsopp)*

ZENNOR   SW4538

★**Tinners Arms** (01736) 796927
B3306 W of St Ives; TR26 3BY Character pub attracting good mix of locals and visitors; long unspoilt bar, granite walls, flagstones and stripped pine, real fire each end, well kept St Austell, Skinners and a house beer (Zennor Mermaid) from Sharps, cornish cider, sensibly priced wines and decent coffee, good food from sandwiches to fresh local fish, back dining room, polite helpful staff; Thurs folk night; children, muddy boots and dogs welcome, tables in small suntrap courtyard, lovely windswept setting near coast path and church with its 15th-c carved mermaid bench, bedrooms in building next door, good breakfast, open all day. *(Neil Turner, Andrew Low, Steve and Claire Harvey)*

A star symbol before the name of a pub shows exceptional character and appeal. It doesn't mean extra comfort. Even quite a basic pub can win a star, if it's individual enough.

ISLES OF SCILLY

ST AGNES   SV8808
★ **Turks Head** (01720) 422434
The Quay; TR22 0PL One of the UK's most
beautifully placed pubs with idyllic sea and
island views from garden terrace – can get
packed on fine days; enjoyable food from
freshly made pasties (must be ordered by
11am) to local fish, well kept ales including
a house beer from St Austell, proper cider,
friendly licensees and good cheerful young
staff, nautical memorabilia in beamed
and flagstoned bar, carpeted dining room;
children and dogs welcome, closed in winter,
otherwise open all day. *(Nigel Morton, R J
Herd, Ian Herdman)*

ST MARTIN'S   SV9116
Seven Stones (01720) 423777
*Lower Town above Lawrence's Flats;
TR25 0QW* Stunning location and sea and
islands views from this long single-storey
stone building (the island's only pub);
welcoming atmosphere and enjoyable food
from sandwiches to local fish, well kept
St Austell, Sharps and Skinners, five wines
by the glass; some film and live music nights;
children and dogs allowed, lots of terrace
tables, wonderful walks, open all day in
summer (Weds, Fri and Sat evenings, all
day Sun till early evening in winter).
(Ian Herdman, Tony Scott)

ST MARY'S   SV9010
Atlantic Inn (01720) 422323
*The Strand; next to but independent
from Atlantic Hotel; TR21 0HY* Spreading
and hospitable dark bar with well kept
St Austell ales and popular pubby food
including children's menu, sea-view
restaurant, low beams, hanging boat and
other nauticalia, mix of locals and tourists –
busy evenings, quieter on sunny lunchtimes;
background and live music, pool, darts,
games machines, free wi-fi; dogs welcome
in bar, attractive raised verandah with
wide views over harbour, bedrooms in
adjacent hotel. *(Ian Herdman)*

ST MARY'S   SV9010
Mermaid (01720) 422701
The Bank; TR21 0HY Splendid picture-

window views across town beach and harbour
from back restaurant extension, dimly lit
bar with lots of seafaring relics and ceiling
flags, woodburner, steps down to second bar
with stone floor and boat counter, enjoyable
sensibly priced food including children's
choices, Sun carvery, well kept Ales of
Scilly, Sharps and Skinners, friendly staff;
background and some live music, pool, fruit
machine; dogs welcome in bars, open all
day and packed Weds and Fri when the gigs
(rowing boats) race. *(Ian Herdman)*

ST MARY'S   SV9110
Old Town Inn (01720) 422301
Old Town; TR21 0NN Nice local feel
in welcoming light bar and big back
dining area, wood floors and panelling,
good freshly made food (not Mon-Weds
in winter) from changing menu, efficient
service even at busy times, up to four real
ales including a house IPA and Sharps
Doom Bar, great range of ciders; monthly
folk club and other live music, cinema
in back function room, pool and darts;
children and dogs welcome, wheelchair
access, tables in garden behind, three
courtyard bedrooms, handy for airport,
open all day in season, closed weekday
lunchtimes in winter). *(Ian Herdman)*

TRESCO   SV8815
★ **New Inn** (01720) 423006
New Grimsby; TR24 0QG Handy for
ferries and close to the famous gardens;
main bar with comfortable sofas,
banquettes, planked partition seating
and farmhouse tables and chairs, a few
standing timbers, boat pictures, collection
of old telescopes and model yacht, pavilion
extension with wicker seats on blue-painted
floors, Ales of Scilly and Skinners, a dozen
good wines by the glass, quite a choice
of spirits and several coffees, enjoyable
not especially cheap food including daily
specials, friendly young staff; background
music, board games, darts and pool;
children and dogs (in bar) welcome,
seats on flower-filled sea-view terrace,
16 bedrooms, heated swimming pool, open
all day in summer (all day Sun in winter, but
closed Mon, Tues lunchtime and Weds).
(R J Herd, Ian Herdman, Bernard Stradling)

Cumbria

 AMBLESIDE   NY3704 Map 9

Golden Rule 🍺

(015394) 32257 – www.goldenrule-ambleside.co.uk

Smithy Brow; follow Kirkstone Pass signpost from A591 on N side of town; LA22 9AS

Simple town tavern with a cosy, relaxed atmosphere and real ales

This is very much an honest Lakeland local where little has changed over the years, which is just how regular customers like it. The bar area has built-in wall seats around cast-iron-framed tables (one with a local map set into its top), horsebrasses on black beams, assorted pictures on the walls, a welcoming winter fire and a relaxed atmosphere. Robinsons Cumbria Way, Dizzy Blonde, Double Hop, Trooper and Wizard on handpump and Weston's cider; they also offer various teas and good coffee all day. A brass measuring rule hangs above the bar (hence the pub's name). There's also a back room with TV (not much used), a room on the left with darts and a games machine, and another room, down a couple of steps on the right, with lots of seating. The backyard has benches and a covered heated area, and the window boxes are especially colourful. There's no car park. Disabled access.

 The scotch eggs and pies (if they have them) run out fast, so don't assume you will get something to eat.

Robinsons ~ Tenant John Lockley ~ Real ale ~ Open 11am-midnight ~ Children welcome away from bar before 9pm ~ Dogs welcome ~ Wi-fi *Recommended by Arthur and Sarah Hedgcock, Abigail Slater, Mike and Eleanor Anderson*

 AMBLESIDE   NY3703 Map 9

Wateredge Inn 🍷 🛏

(015394) 32332 – www.wateredgehotel.co.uk

Borrans Road, off A591; LA22 0EP

Lakeside inn with plenty of room both inside and out, six ales on handpump and enjoyable all-day food; good bedrooms

Once found, our readers tend to return here regularly. It's in a lovely setting at the tip of Lake Windermere and the stylish and comfortable bedrooms have fine views; if you want one of the picnic-sets in the garden close to the water, you'll have to arrive early on a warm day – they also have their own moorings. The bustling, modernised bar has big picture windows, leather tub chairs around wooden tables on flagstones and several different areas leading off with exposed-stone or wood-panelled walls and interesting old photographs and paintings. A cosy and much favoured room has beams and timbering, sofas, armchairs and an open fire. Real ales on handpump include Bombardier and Burning Gold, Jennings Cumberland and Sneck Lifter, Marstons EPA and Pedigree and a guest from Tirril, and they offer nine wines by the glass, 15 gins, ten malt whiskies and quite a choice of coffees. Background music and board games. Disabled access.

All-day food is of high quality: sandwiches, chunky fish chowder, chicken liver parfait with orange and thyme butter and cumberland sauce, five-bean chilli with sour cream, cheese and tortilla chips, cumberland sausage with root vegetables and sautéed potatoes, chicken parmigiana, 16oz gammon steak with caramelised pineapple and a free-range egg, minted lamb rump with chargrilled aubergines, crushed rosemary and garlic infused sweet potatoes and redcurrant and port sauce, swordfish steak on chive mash and lemon and basil sauce, and puddings such as bread and butter pudding and salted caramel chocolate profiteroles with hot chocolate sauce. *Benchmark main dish: beer-battered fish and chips £13.75. Two-course evening meal £20.00.*

Free house ~ Licensee Derek Cowap ~ Real ale ~ Open 11-11 ~ Bar food 12-4.30, 5.30-8.30; 12-3.30, 5.30-8.30 in winter ~ Children welcome ~ Dogs allowed in bar and bedrooms ~ Wi-fi ~ Live music Fri evenings ~ Bedrooms: £75/£140 *Recommended by John and Sylvia Harrop, Kerry and Guy Trooper, Edward Edmonton, Steve Whalley, Jo Garnett, Alison and Michael Harper, Andrew Vincent*

BASSENTHWAITE LAKE   NY1930 Map 9

Pheasant ★ ⭐ ♇ 🛏

(017687) 76234 – www.the-pheasant.co.uk
Follow Pheasant Inn sign at N end of dual carriageway stretch of A66 by Bassenthwaite Lake; CA13 9YE

Delightful little bar in smart hotel, with enjoyable bar food and a fine range of drinks; comfortable bedrooms

To make the most of the beautiful scenery and endless surrounding walks, many customers use the well equipped, pretty bedrooms here as a base. So it's a pleasant surprise to find a properly pubby, old-fashioned bar at the heart of the place. This has mellow polished walls, cushioned oak settles, rush-seat chairs and library seats, and hunting prints and photographs. Black Sheep, Coniston Bluebird Bitter and Cumbrian Legendary Loweswater Gold on handpump, 16 good wines by the glass from a fine list, 80 malt whiskies and ten gins and ten vodkas all served by friendly, knowledgeable staff. There's a bistro at the front, a formal restaurant at the back overlooking the garden, and several comfortable lounges with log fires, beautiful flower arrangements, fine parquet flooring, antiques and plants. The garden has seats and tables and is surrounded by attractive woodland.

Very good food can be eaten in the bar, bistro or lounges at lunchtime, and in the bistro and restaurant only in the evening: lunchtime sandwiches, seafood gratin, chicken and duck liver pâté with apple and cider chutney, meze platter, sweet potato and celeriac hotpot with garlic and almond butter, beer-battered haddock and chips, trio of sausages with onion marmalade and red wine jus, braised venison with champ potato, carrot and swede mash and red wine jus, and puddings; they also offer a two- and three-course set menu (not Saturday, not Sunday lunchtime). *Benchmark main dish: shepherd's pie £13.95. Two-course evening meal £20.00.*

Free house ~ Licensee Matthew Wylie ~ Real ale ~ Open 11.30-11; 12-11 Sat ~ Bar food 12-2.30, 6-9 ~ Restaurant ~ Children welcome but must be over 8 in bedrooms ~ Dogs allowed in bar and bedrooms ~ Wi-fi ~ Bedrooms: £105/£120 *Recommended by Martin Day, Dr D J & Mrs S C Walker, Patricia and Gordon Thompson, Susan and Tim Boyle, Louise and Anton Parsons*

BOWNESS-ON-WINDERMERE
Hole in t' Wall

SD4096 Map 9

(015394) 43488 – www.newhallinn.robinsonsbrewery.com

Fallbarrow Road, off St Martins Parade; LA23 3DH

Lively and unchanging town local with popular ales and friendly staff

Full of interest and character, this is the sort of place where both locals and visitors mingle easily. There's plenty to look at in the character bar and the split-level rooms have beams, stripped stone and flagstones, lots of country knick-knacks and old pictures, and a splendid log fire beneath a vast slate mantelpiece; the upper room has some noteworthy plasterwork. Robinsons Dizzy Blonde, Hartleys XB and Unicorn plus a couple of guest beers on handpump, 23 malt whiskies, a dozen gins and 11 vodkas; juke box in the bottom bar. The small flagstoned front courtyard has sheltered picnic-sets and outdoor heaters.

 Bar food includes pâté of the day, scampi and chips, steak in ale or fish pies, a daily curry, steak with trimmings, and puddings such as chocolate sponge and sticky toffee pudding. *Benchmark main dish: lamb with mint and spices with red wine jus £12.00. Two-course evening meal £19.00.*

Robinsons ~ Tenant Susan Burnet ~ Real ale ~ Open 11-11; 11am-11.30pm Fri, Sat; 12-11 Sun ~ Bar food 12-2.30, 6-8.30; 12-8 Fri, Sat; 12-5 Sun ~ Children welcome ~ Live music Fri and every other Sun Easter-Christmas *Recommended by Darrell Barton, Mick Allen, Emma Scofield, Sandra Morgan, Alf Wright, Alice Wright*

BRIGSTEER
Wheatsheaf ♀

SD4889 Map 9

(015395) 68938 – www.thewheatsheafbrigsteer.co.uk

Off Brigsteer Brow; LA8 8AN

Bustling pub with interestingly furnished and decorated rooms, a good choice of food and drink, and seats outside; luxury bunkhouse bedrooms

Tucked away in the Lyth Valley, this is a well run pub with an easy-going atmosphere. The bar has a two-way log fire, carved wooden stools against the counter and Bowness Bay Swan Blonde, Hawkshead Bitter, Marstons Wainwright and a guest beer such as Eden Fuggle on handpump, 16 wines by the glass and eight malt whiskies. There's an appealing variety of cushioned dining chairs, carved and boxed settles and window seats set around an array of tables on either flagstones or floorboards, walls with pale-painted woodwork or wallpaper hung with animal and bird sketches, cartoons or interesting clock faces, and lighting that is both old-fashioned and contemporary. Outside there are seats and tables along the front of the building and picnic-sets on raised terracing. Their luxury bunkhouse (half a mile up the road) has five ensuite rooms and fine country views; breakfasts are hearty.

Generous helpings of tasty food includes salt and pepper squid with miso mayonnaise, goats cheese soufflé with shallot and beetroot salad, sharing boards, pizzas and topped flatbreads, sweet potato, lentil and chickpea curry, local sausages with sage mash and caramelised red onion gravy, fish pie, free-range chicken, bacon and smoked stilton salad with croutons, grapes and crispy onions in honey and mustard dressing, and puddings such as cheesecake of the day and salted dark chocolate and amaretto mousse with peanut butter ice-cream. *Benchmark main dish: 12-hour braised beef £13.95. Two-course evening meal £20.00.*

Individual Inns ~ Managers Nicki and Tom Roberts ~ Real ale ~ Open 10am-11pm ~
Bar food 12-2.30, 5.30-9; 12-7.30 Sun ~ Restaurant ~ Children welcome ~ Dogs allowed in
bar ~ Wi-fi ~ Bedrooms: /£100 *Recommended by Susan and Tim Boyle, Liz and Mike Newton,
Peter Andrews, Steve Whalley, David Appleyard, David and Charlotte Green, Matt and Hayley Jacob*

BROUGHTON MILLS
Blacksmiths Arms

SD2190   Map 9

(01229) 716824 – www.theblacksmithsarms.com
Off A593 N of Broughton-in-Furness; LA20 6AX

Charming small pub with rewarding food, local beers and open fires

The four small rooms in this friendly little pub have a relaxed, friendly
atmosphere and are simply but attractively decorated; three have original
beams, slate floors and warm log fires. Three real ales such as Barngates
Cracker, Cross Bay Halo and a local guest on handpump, nine wines by the
glass, 11 malt whiskies and summer farm cider; darts, board games and
dominoes. The hanging baskets and tubs of flowers in front of the building are
very pretty in summer, and there are seats and tables under parasols on the
front terrace. The surrounding countryside is lovely and walks are peaceful.

Enjoyable food includes lunchtime sandwiches, pigeon breast with cauliflower
purée, candied apple, peanut crumbs and garlic, beetroot-cured salmon with
crispy capers and beetroot jam, spiced aubergine tagine with apricot and rocket salad
and garlic-roasted potatoes, chargrilled chicken with parmentier potatoes, carrot purée
and chicken jus, honey-roast ham and poached eggs with home-made chutney, warm
salad of shredded confit duck leg with hoisin sauce, cod loin with white wine and chive
sauce and fondant potato, and puddings such as seville orange posset with raspberry
jelly and dark chocolate torte with berry coulis and vanilla ice-cream. *Benchmark
main dish: slow-braised minted lamb shoulder with roasted root vegetables and
dauphinoise potatoes £15.50. Two-course evening meal £22.50.*

Free house ~ Licensees Mike and Sophie Lane ~ Real ale ~ Open 12-2.30, 5-11; 12-11 Sat;
12-10.30 Sun; closed Mon (except bank holidays) ~ Bar food 12-2, 6-9; not Mon ~ Restaurant
~ Children welcome ~ Dogs welcome ~ Wi-fi *Recommended by Helene Grygar, Peter Andrews,
Elise and Charles Mackinlay, Diana and Richard Gibbs, Liz and Martin Eldon*

CARLETON
Cross Keys

NY5329   Map 9

(01768) 865588 – www.thecrosskeyspenrith.co.uk
A686, off A66 roundabout at Penrith; CA11 8TP

**Friendly refurbished pub with several connected seating areas,
real ales and popular food**

There's quite a bustle of customers here, especially at lunchtime when
lovers of the outdoors pile in. The beamed main bar has a friendly feel,
pubby tables and chairs on light wooden floorboards, modern metal wall
lights and pictures on bare stone walls, and Tirril 1823 and a guest such
as Wychwood Dirty Tackle on handpump. Steps lead down to a small
area with high bar stools around a high drinking table and then upstairs
to the restaurant: a light, airy room with big windows, large wrought-iron
candelabras hanging from the vaulted ceiling, solid pale wooden tables and
chairs, and doors leading to a verandah. At the far end of the main bar, there
are yet another couple of small connected bar rooms with darts, games
machine, pool, juke box and dominoes; TV and background music. There are
views of the fells from the garden. This is under the same ownership as the
Highland Drove in Great Salkeld.

Seasonally changing food includes ham terrine with apple chutney, prawn cocktail, sharing platters, feta cheese and spinach strudel with confit tomatoes and provençale sauce, cumberland sausages with mash and gravy, beer-battered haddock and chips, lamb rump with black pudding mash, roasted root vegetables and red wine sauce, 10oz gammon steak with fresh pineapple and fried eggs, and puddings. *Benchmark main dish: steak in ale pie £13.00. Two-course evening meal £20.00.*

Free house ~ Licensee Paul Newton ~ Real ale ~ Open 12-2.30, 5pm-1am; 12pm-2am Sat; 12pm-1am Sun ~ Bar food 12-2.30, 6-9 (8.30 Sun); 12-2.30, 5.30-9 Fri, Sat ~ Restaurant ~ Children welcome ~ Dogs allowed in bar ~ Wi-fi *Recommended by Jacqui and Alan Swan, Caroline and Peter Bryant, Chloe and Tim Hodge, Nicola and Holly Lyons, Simon Day*

 CARTMEL FELL   SD4189   Map 9

Masons Arms

(015395) 68486 ~ www.masonsarmsstrawberrybank.co.uk

Strawberry Bank, a few miles S of Windermere between A592 and A5074; perhaps the simplest way to find the pub is to go uphill W from Bowland Bridge (which is signposted off A5074) towards Newby Bridge and keep right, then left at the staggered crossroads – it's then on your right, below Gummer's How; OS Sheet 97 map reference 413895; LA11 6NW

Wonderful views, beamed bar with plenty of character, interesting food and a good choice of ales and wines; self-catering cottages and apartments

From the windows inside and from the rustic benches and tables on the heated and covered terrace you can enjoy stunning views over the Winster Valley to the woods below Whitbarrow Scar. The main bar has plenty of character, with low black beams in the bowed ceiling, and country chairs and plain wooden tables on polished flagstones. A small lounge has oak tables and settles to match its fine Jacobean panelling. There's also a plain little room beyond the serving counter with pictures and a fire in an open range, a family room with the atmosphere of an old parlour, and an upstairs dining room; background music and board games. Hawkshead Bitter, Marstons Wainwright and Ulverston Flying Elephants on handpump, quite a few foreign bottled beers, 14 wines by the glass, nine malt whiskies, 16 gins and farm cider; service is friendly and helpful. They offer stylish and comfortable self-catering cottages and apartments.

As well as hot and cold lunchtime sandwiches (until 6pm weekends), the reliably good food includes baked camembert topped with mulled wine poached pears and walnuts, smoked salmon with crispy potato rösti, poached egg and guacamole, potato gnocchi with a spiced butternut squash, spinach and feta bake, a pie of the day, beer-battered fresh haddock and chips, crispy pork belly with mash and a casserole of chorizo, white beans, carrots and savoy cabbage, duck breast and crispy confit duck leg with blackberry and port jus, braised red cabbage and celeriac purée, and puddings such as baked coconut rice pudding with rum and tropical fruit minestrone and crumble of the day with vanilla ice-cream and custard. *Benchmark main dish: slow-cooked lamb shoulder with cumberland glaze, garlic and rosemary jus and pot-roasted vegetables £18.95. Two-course evening meal £24.00.*

Individual Inns ~ Managers John and Diane Taylor ~ Real ale ~ Open 11-11; 12-10.30 Sun ~ Bar food 12-2.30, 6-9; 12-9 weekends ~ Restaurant ~ Children welcome ~ Dogs allowed in bar ~ Wi-fi *Recommended by John Evans, Hugh Roberts, Christian Mole, Kim Holt, Alister and Margery Bacon, Charlotte and William Mason, Claire Adams*

We accept no free drinks or meals and inspections are anonymous.

CLIFTON

NY5326   Map 9

George & Dragon 🌟 ♈ 🛏

(01768) 865381 – www.georgeanddragonclifton.co.uk

A6; near M6 junction 40; CA10 2ER

Former coaching inn with local ales, well chosen wines, smashing food and seats outside; smart bedrooms

---

The attractive bars and sizeable restaurant here are civilised and friendly. The relaxed reception room has bright rugs on flagstones, leather chairs around a low table in front of an open fire, and a table in a private nook to one side of the reception desk. The main bar area, through wrought-iron gates, has more cheerful rugs, assorted wooden farmhouse chairs and tables, grey panelling topped with yellow-painted walls, photographs of the Estate and of the family with hunting dogs, various sheep and fell pictures and some high bar stools by the bar counter. Eden Gold, Hawkshead Bitter and a changing guest beer such as Cumberland Great Corby Blonde on handpump, 20 wines by the glass from a well chosen list and interesting local liqueurs; background music and TV. To the left of the entrance, the sizeable restaurant consists of four open-plan rooms: there are plenty of old pews and church chairs around tables set for dining, a woodburning stove and a contemporary open kitchen. Outside, chunky tables and chairs are set in a decoratively paved front area and in a high-walled enclosed suntrap courtyard. Bedrooms are stylish and comfortable and breakfasts very good. Partial disabled access.

 Using produce grown in their garden at Askham Hall and Estate game, the impressive food includes lunchtime sandwiches, twice-baked cheese and spring onion soufflé with chive cream, hot and sour king prawn broth with a steamed dumpling, mushroom bourguignon with smoked potatoes, rare-breed sausages with mash and onion gravy, cod with butter bean, chorizo, mussel and red pepper stew, red deer and blue cheese steamed pudding, côte de boeuf (for two people) with dauphinoise potatoes, shallots, pancetta and red wine jus, and puddings such as dark chocolate fondant with caramelised banana and banana ice-cream and crumble of the day with custard; they also offer breakfasts (8-9.30am; champagne optional). *Benchmark main dish: rare-breed burger with toppings, coleslaw and dripping chips £14.00. Two-course evening meal £24.00.*

Free house ~ Licensee Charles Lowther ~ Real ale ~ Open 12-11 ~ Bar food 12-2.30, 6-9; breakfast 8-9.30am. ~ Restaurant ~ Children welcome ~ Dogs allowed in bar and bedrooms ~ Wi-fi ~ Bedrooms: £90/£100 *Recommended by Simon and Sue Lamb, Sophie and James Collier, Rupert and Sandy Newton, David and Charlotte Emslie, Michael Bayer*

CONISTON

SD3098   Map 9

Sun 🍴 🛏

(015394) 41248 – www.thesunconiston.com

Signed left off A593 at the bridge; LA21 8HQ

Extended old pub with a lively bar, plenty of dining space, a fine choice of real ales, well liked food and seats outside; comfortable bedrooms

---

The cheerful bar here has up to eight real ales on handpump: Coniston Bluebird Bitter and Premium XB, Cross Bay Sunset Blonde, Cumbrian Legendary Grasmoor Dark Ale and Loweswater Gold and frequent guests from other local brewers including Fell, Hardknott, Hawkshead and Ulverston. Also, ten wines by the glass, 20 malt whiskies, several gins and farm cider; service is friendly. There are beams and timbers, exposed stone walls, flagstones and a Victorian-style range – as well as cask seats, old settles and cast-iron-framed tables, quite a few Donald Campbell photographs (this was his HQ during his final attempt on the world water-speed record) and a good mix of customers (often with their dogs). Above the bar is another room with extra seating, more pictures, pool, darts and a TV for sport, and beyond that is a sizeable lounge. A big dining conservatory houses a daytime café. This is a fine spot and the dramatic mountain views are shared by seats and tables on the terrace and in the big tree-sheltered garden, as well as by the quiet and comfortable bedrooms.

Rewarding food includes lunchtime rolls and sandwiches, haggis and black pudding fritters, honey and coriander chicken kebab with a dip, mediterranean vegetable and pesto tart, beer-battered fish and chips, slow-braised lamb with mint marinade and red wine jus, sea bass on prawn, pea and parmesan risotto, and puddings such as chocolate brownie and crumble of the day. *Benchmark main dish: burger with toppings and chips £13.00. Two-course evening meal £20.00.*

Free house ~ Licensee Alan Piper ~ Real ale ~ Open 11-11 ~ Bar food 12-3, 5.30-8.30 ~ Restaurant ~ Children welcome ~ Dogs allowed in bar and bedrooms ~ Wi-fi ~ Bedrooms: £65/£95 *Recommended by David and Charlotte Green, David Appleyard, Peter Pilbeam, Edward May*

CROSTHWAITE
SD4491 Map 9

Punch Bowl ⓘ ⓘ ♀ ⌂

(015395) 68237 ~ www.the-punchbowl.co.uk
Village signed off A5074 SE of Windermere; LA8 8HR

Cumbria Dining Pub of the Year

Smart dining pub with a proper bar and other elegant rooms, a fine wine list, impressive food and friendly staff; stylish bedrooms

Of course, many customers come to this civilised place for the excellent food but there is a proper public bar too, and plenty of chatty locals. This bar has rafters, a couple of eye-catching rugs on flagstones, bar stools by the slate-topped counter, Barngates Tag Lag, Bowness Bay Swan Blonde and Marstons Wainwright on handpump, 15 wines (including champagne and prosecco) by the glass, 15 malt whiskies and local damson gin. To the right are two linked carpeted and beamed rooms with well spaced country pine furniture of varying sizes (including a big refectory table), and walls that are painted in restrained neutral tones with an attractive assortment of prints; winter log fire, woodburning stove, lots of fresh flowers and daily papers. On the left, the wooden-floored, light and airy restaurant area has comfortable high-backed leather dining chairs; background music. Tables and seats on a terrace are stepped into the hillside and overlook the pretty Lyth Valley. Bedrooms are lovely and well equipped and breakfasts first class.

 Delicious food includes lunchtime sandwiches, twice-baked lancashire cheese soufflé, scallops en croûte, honey-roasted root vegetables with crispy goats cheese, chicken breast with camembert ravioli, pak choi and oyster mushrooms, smoked haddock with grain mustard sauce and a poached egg, venison with beetroot and green peppercorn sauce, beef medallions with rösti potato and pink peppercorn sauce, cod loin with mussels, leek, pancetta and creamed potatoes, and puddings such as whisky pannacotta with honeycomb and blackberry sorbet and lemon tart with home-grown damson sorbet. *Benchmark main dish: roast cod loin with Morecambe Bay shrimps, leeks and pancetta £18.95. Two-course evening meal £26.00.*

Free house ~ Licensee Richard Rose ~ Real ale ~ Open 11-11; 12-11 Sun ~ Bar food 12-4, 6-9 ~ Restaurant ~ Children welcome ~ Dogs allowed in bar ~ Wi-fi ~ Bedrooms: £95/£135

Recommended by Christian Mole, Peter and Caroline Waites, Audrey and Andrew Nichols, John and Sylvia Harrop, Colin McLachlan, Richard I, Patti and James Davidson, Nicola and Stuart Parsons

ELTERWATER
Britannia
NY3204 Map 9

(015394) 37210 – www.thebritanniainn.com
Off B5343; LA22 9HP

Much loved inn surrounded by wonderful walks and scenery, with up to eight real ales and well liked food; bedrooms

A long-standing favourite with our readers, this is an unpretentious and rather special place in spectacular scenery and with walks of every gradient right from the front door. It does get packed out at peak times, but the friendly, efficient staff still find time to make you feel welcomed. The small front bar has beams and a couple of window seats that look across to Elterwater through the trees, while the small back bar is traditionally furnished: thick slate walls, winter coal fires, oak benches, settles, windsor chairs and a big old rocking chair. A beer named for the pub – Britannia Special (from Coniston) – plus Coniston Bluebird Bitter, Cumberland Corby Ale and guests such as Jennings Neddy Boggle and Sneck Lifter and Langdale Blonde on handpump, and 12 malt whiskies. The lounge is comfortable, and there's also a hall and dining room. Plenty of seats outside, and visiting dancers (morris and step and garland) perform in summer. Bedrooms are warm and charming.

 Reliably good food is usefully served all day and includes sandwiches and rolls, breaded brie with red onion marmalade, mackerel, salmon and trout fishcakes with garlic mayonnaise, wild and button mushroom stroganoff in creamy brandy and mustard sauce, cumberland sausage and mash with onion gravy, chicken, ham and leek pie, sea bass with crab mayonnaise and radish and avocado salad, and puddings such as crème brûlée of the day and dark chocolate and mixed berry tart with blackcurrant ice-cream. *Benchmark main dish: slow-braised lamb in mint and spices with red wine gravy £15.95. Two-course evening meal £22.00.*

Free house ~ Licensee Andrew Parker ~ Real ale ~ Open 10.30am-11pm ~ Bar food 12-5, 6-9 ~ Restaurant ~ Children welcome ~ Dogs welcome ~ Wi-fi ~ Bedrooms: $100/$110
Recommended by Tina and David Woods-Taylor, Margaret and Peter Staples, John and Sylvia Harrop, Audrey and Paul Summers, Mr and Mrs Richard Osborne

GREAT SALKELD
Highland Drove
NY5536 Map 10

(01768) 898349 – www.highlanddroveinnpenrith.co.uk
B6412, off A686 NE of Penrith; CA11 9NA

Cheerful pub with good food and fair choice of drinks, and fine views from the upstairs verandah; bedrooms

A father and son team keep this bustling pub spic and span, and there's always a good mix of regulars and visitors. The chatty main bar has sandstone flooring, stone walls, cushioned wheelback chairs around a mix of tables and an open fire in a raised stone fireplace. The downstairs eating area has more cushioned dining chairs around wooden tables on pale wooden floorboards, stone walls and ceiling joists, and a two-way fire in a raised stone fireplace that separates this room from the coffee lounge with its comfortable leather chairs and sofas. It's best to book to be sure of a table in the upstairs restaurant. Theakstons Black Bull and a guest such as Banks's Sunbeam on handpump, a dozen wines by the glass and 28 malt whiskies; background music, darts, pool and dominoes. The lovely views over the Eden Valley and the Pennines are best enjoyed from seats on the upstairs verandah; there are also seats on the back terrace. Bedrooms are comfortable and breakfasts are hearty. This is under the same ownership as the Cross Keys in Carleton.

 Generous helpings of well regarded food includes sharing platters, chicken and ham hock terrine with tarragon mayonnaise, beetroot and whisky-cured salmon with prawns in lobster marie rose sauce, vegetarian moussaka, cumberland sausage with mash and onion gravy, lamb rump with potato rösti, honey-roasted carrots and parsnips with a mint-infused reduction, hake fillet with red pepper relish and crushed new potatoes, and puddings such as seasonal berry crème brûlée and sticky toffee pudding with toffee sauce and vanilla ice-cream. *Benchmark main dish: pie of the day £13.00. Two-course evening meal £20.00.*

Free house ~ Licensees Donald and Paul Newton ~ Real ale ~ Open 12-3, 6-1am; 12-1am Sat; 12-1am Sun; closed Mon lunchtime ~ Bar food 12-2, 6-9; 12-2, 6-8.30 Sun ~ Restaurant ~ Children welcome ~ Dogs allowed in bar ~ Wi-fi ~ Bedrooms: £60/£90 *Recommended by John Evans, Ian Herdman, Andrew Lawson, Shona and Jimmy McDuff, Margo and Derek Stapley, Karl and Frieda Bujeya*

HAWKSHEAD   NY3501   Map 9
Drunken Duck

(015394) 36347 – www.drunkenduckinn.co.uk

Barngates; the pub is signposted from B5286 Hawkshead–Ambleside, opposite the Outgate Inn and from north first right after the wooded caravan site; LA22 0NG

Stylish little bar, several restaurant areas, own-brewed beers and bar meals as well as innovative restaurant choices; stunning views and lovely bedrooms

As always, our readers love coming here. It's civilised but friendly and relaxed and both the food and the bedrooms are first class. At lunchtime, the smart little bar draws in those exploring the area. The star attraction then are their own-brewed ales on handpump from the Barngates brewery, including Brathay Gold, Cat Nap, Cracker Ale, Goodhews Dry Stout, Pale, Red Bull Terrier, Tag Lag and Vienna, plus their own weiss beer. They also offer 16 wines by the glass (including pudding wines) from a fine list, 25 malt whiskies and 17 gins (including ones to which they add their own botanicals). There are leather bar stools by the slate-topped counter, leather club chairs, beams and oak floorboards, and old Lake District photographs on the walls. The three restaurant areas are elegant and the new lounge area is a huge success offering morning coffee, afternoon tea, cocktails and so forth. Sit at the wooden tables and benches on grass opposite the building for spectacular views across the fells, and if you come in spring or summer the flowering bulbs are lovely. Please note: dogs are allowed in the bar only.

Food is first class and from the brunch menu (8.30am-3.30pm) there might be cauliflower and ale pastie with grape chutney, maple-glazed cornbread with braised beans, crispy corn, yoghurt and hazelnuts, eggs benedict with bacon, pork burger with apple and chorizo butter and a curry bowl to share; also, beef brisket ravioli with mushroom sauce and pickled shallots, confit sea trout with salt-baked kohlrabi and chives, pumpkin, mushroom and sage suet pudding, and puddings such as chocolate fondant with peanuts and salted caramel ice-cream and brûléed lemon and orange cake with pineapple and vanilla ice-cream. *Benchmark main dish: duck breast and thigh with wonton and rhubarb, chilli and ginger broth £23.00. Two-course evening meal £30.00.*

Own brew ~ Licensee Steph Barton ~ Real ale ~ Open 11.30-11; 12-10.30 Sun ~ Bar food 8.30-3.30, 6-9; 8.30-4 Sun ~ Restaurant ~ Children welcome ~ Dogs allowed in bar ~ Wi-fi ~ Live music Sun afternoon ~ Bedrooms: £94/£125 *Recommended by Colin McLachlan, Elspeth Macdonald, Dan and Belinda Smallbone, Ian Wilson*

 INGS   SD4498   Map 9

Watermill

(01539) 821309 – www.watermillinn.co.uk
Just off A591 E of Windermere; LA8 9PY

Bustling, cleverly converted pub with fantastic range of real ales including own brews; bedrooms

The ten real ales on handpump in this former woodmill and joiner's shop continue to draw in many cheerful customers. The range includes their own brews Watermill A Bit'er Ruff, Bad Dog, Black Beard, Collie Wobbles, Dogth Vader, Golden Retriever, Isle of Dogs, Windermere Blonde, Shih Tzu Faced and guests such as Coniston Bluebird, Cumbrian Legendary Loweswater Gold and Theakstons Old Peculier. Also, a choice of foreign bottled beers and quite a few malt whiskies. The two cleverly converted bars have woodburning stoves, and the Riverside Bar (where dogs are allowed) backs on to the River Gowan and has low-beamed ceilings, flagstones, a darts area and views into the brewery. The Smithy Bar has leather-backed seats, carpentry memorabilia and a sunny conservatory with views of the surrounding hills. The two outside seating areas take in the views and the sound of the river. Bedrooms are dog-friendly and two have balconies; breakfasts are hearty. Disabled access.

Traditional food served all day includes hot and cold sandwiches (until 5pm), black pudding stack with crispy bacon, a poached egg and creamy mustard sauce, chicken liver pâté with cumberland sauce, chicken caesar salad, spinach and ricotta tortellini in tomato, pesto and cream sauce, beer-battered haddock and chips, local game casserole, fish pie, lamb hotpot, 21-day aged sirloin steak with a choice of sauce, and puddings such as hot chocolate fudge cake with vanilla ice-cream and apple crumble with custard. *Benchmark main dish: beef in ale pie £12.95. Two-course evening meal £29.00.*

Own brew ~ Licensee Brian Coulthwaite ~ Real ale ~ Open 11.15-11; 11.15-10.30 Sun ~ Bar food 12-9 ~ Children welcome ~ Dogs allowed in bar and bedrooms ~ Wi-fi ~ Storytelling first Tues of month ~ Bedrooms: £49/£89 *Recommended by Denis and Margaret Kilner, Sam Cole, Rona Mackinlay, Douglas Power, Val and Malcolm Travers*

 KIRKBY LONSDALE   SD6178   Map 7

Sun

(015242) 71965 – www.sun-inn.info
Market Street (B6254); LA6 2AU

White-painted stone inn on cobbled alley with character bar, local ales and good wines and enjoyable food; lovely bedrooms

This is a particularly pretty village surrounded by fells including the Langdale Pikes flanking the Dungeon Ghyll Force waterfall. The inn backs on to the churchyard and dates back to the 17th c and there's plenty of history to the place. The rambling beamed bar has flagstones and stripped oak boards, pews, armchairs and cosy window seats, paintings on cream walls and a woodburning stove. Hawkshead Bitter, Kirkby Lonsdale Monumental Blonde and Marstons Wainwright on handpump served by helpful, friendly staff. There are a couple of dining rooms (one is red-walled) with a two-way woodburning stove and leather banquettes; background music. Bedrooms are attractive, comfortable and warm and several are dog-friendly; dogs get a welcome pack and they offer dog walking and sitting too. Disabled access. Turner stayed here in 1818 when painting the picture known as 'Ruskin's View'. Thursday is market day.

First class food using the best local seasonal produce includes lunchtime sandwiches, whitebait with salsa verde and citrus salad, gin-cured salmon with cucumber, dill and salmon roe, mushroom risotto with pickled onions, cumberland sausages with horseradish mash and black pepper jus, beer-battered fish and chips, 8oz rib-eye steak with onion rings, chips and peppercorn sauce, and puddings such as dark chocolate mousse with quince sorbet and pumpkin and rapeseed cake with honey ice-cream. *Benchmark main dish: slow-cooked pork belly with roasted root vegetables and cider sauce £14.25. Two-course evening meal £22.50.*

Free house ~ Licensees Jenny and Iain Black ~ Real ale ~ Open 10.30am-11pm; 11-11 Sun; closed Mon lunchtime ~ Bar food 12-3, 6.30-9; snacks 3-6.30 ~ Restaurant ~ Children welcome ~ Dogs allowed in bar and bedrooms ~ Wi-fi ~ Bedrooms: $97.50/$115
Recommended by Christopher May, Richard and Tessa Ibbot, Margaret McDonald, Jeremy Snow, David and Charlotte Green

LANGDALE
NY2806   Map 9
Old Dungeon Ghyll 🍺 £
(015394) 37272 – www.odg.co.uk
B5343; LA22 9JY

Honest place in lovely position with real ales, traditional food and fine surrounding walks; bedrooms

A friendly, straightforward local, this is the perfect place for damp walkers and climbers. It's at the heart of the Great Langdale Valley and surrounded by fells including the Langdale Pikes flanking the Dungeon Ghyll Force waterfall. There's no need to remove boots or muddy trousers as you can sit on seats in old cattle stalls by the big warming fire and enjoy the fine choice of six real ales on handpump: Cumbrian Legendary Esthwaite Bitter and Loweswater Gold, Hawkshead Bitter and Windermere Pale, Jennings Cumberland and Theakston Old Peculier. Farm cider and several malt whiskies. It's a good place to stay, with warm bedrooms, a plush residents' lounge and highly rated breakfasts. It may get lively on a Saturday night (there's a popular National Trust campsite opposite).

Generous helpings of tasty food includes their own bread and cakes, lunchtime sandwiches, home-made soup, vegetable lasagne, chilli con carne, a changing curry, gammon and free-range eggs, cumberland sausage with mash and onion gravy, slow-cooked lamb henry, and puddings. *Benchmark main dish: pie of the day £7.95. Two-course evening meal £18.00.*

Free house ~ Licensee Neil Walmsley ~ Real ale ~ Open 11-11 (10.30 Sun) ~ Bar food 12-9 ~ Restaurant ~ Children welcome ~ Dogs allowed in bar and bedrooms ~ Wi-fi ~ Bedrooms: $58/$116 *Recommended by Charles Fraser, Lenny and Ruth Walters, Tony Smaithe, Peter Barratt, Julie Braeburn*

'Children welcome' means the pub says it lets children inside without any special restriction. If it allows them in, but to restricted areas such as an eating area or family room, we specify this. Places with separate restaurants often let children use them, and hotels usually let children into public areas such as lounges. Some pubs impose an evening time limit – let us know if you find one earlier than 9pm.

LEVENS

SD4987 Map 9

Strickland Arms ♀ 🍺

(015395) 61010 ~ www.thestricklandarms.com

4 miles from M6 junction 36, via A590; just off A590, by Sizergh Castle gates; LA8 8DZ

Friendly, open-plan pub with popular food, local ales and a fine setting; seats outside

The entrance to Sizergh Castle (owned by the National Trust) is opposite, so lunchtimes can get busy here; it's best to book a table in advance. The atmosphere is friendly and gently civilised and the bar on the right has oriental rugs on flagstones, a log fire, Bowness Bay Swan Blonde, Cross Bay Halo, Pennine Hair of the Dog and Wychwood Hobgoblin Gold on handpump, several malt whiskies and nine wines by the glass. On the left are polished boards and another log fire, and throughout there's a nice mix of sturdy country furniture, candles on tables, hunting scenes and other old prints on the walls, curtains in heavy fabric and some staffordshire china ornaments. Two of the dining rooms are upstairs; background music and board games. The flagstoned front terrace has plenty of tables and chairs, and picnic-sets are arranged on a grassy area; disabled access and facilities. The pub is part of the Ainscoughs group.

 Rewarding food includes lunchtime sandwiches, salt and pepper chicken wings, black pudding stack with bacon, cheese, poached egg and mushrooms, wild mushroom risotto with creamy sauce, burger with toppings and chips, cumberland sausage with mash and gravy, rack of lamb with red wine jus and dauphinoise potatoes, lancashire hotpot, hake wrapped in parma ham with a prawn and white wine sauce and lyonnaise potatoes, and puddings such as banoffi pie and double chocolate brownie with chocolate sauce. *Benchmark main dish: pie of the day £14.00. Two-course evening meal £20.00.*

Free house ~ Licensee Michael Redmond ~ Real ale ~ Open 12-11; 12-midnight Sat; 12-10 Sun; 12-3, 5-11 in winter ~ Bar food 12-9 (8 Sun); 12-3, 6-8.30 weekdays in winter ~ Children welcome ~ Dogs welcome ~ Wi-fi *Recommended by Steve Whalley, Daniel King, Gary and Marie Miller, Charlotte and William Mason, Darrell Barton*

LITTLE LANGDALE

NY3103 Map 9

Three Shires 🍺 🛏

(015394) 37215 ~ www.threeshiresinn.co.uk

From A593 3 miles W of Ambleside take small road signposted The Langdales, Wrynose Pass; then bear left at first fork; LA22 9NZ

Fine valley views from seats on the terrace, local ales, quite a choice of food and good service; comfortable bedrooms

The pub's name relates to the three shires that are the historical counties of Cumberland, Westmorland and Lancashire, which meet at the top of nearby Wrynose Pass. Our readers continue to praise both the genuine welcome and reliably high standards here, and the comfortably extended back bar is where most of them head for first: stripped timbers and a stripped beam-and-joist ceiling, green Lakeland stone and William Morris patterned wallpaper, antique oak carved settles, country kitchen chairs and stools on big dark slate flagstones and cumbrian photographs. Five real ales on handpump include Bowness Bay Swan Blonde, Coniston Old Man Ale, Cumbrian Legendary Langdale, Hawkshead Bitter and a changing guest, and they also have over 50 malt whiskies, a wide choice of gins including local ones and a decent wine list. The front restaurant is furnished with chunky leather dining chairs around solid tables on wood flooring, and a snug leads off here; the residents' lounge has leather sofas and an open fire. Background music, TV and board games. The views from seats on the terrace down over the valley to the partly wooded hills below are stunning; there are more seats on a neat lawn behind the car park, backed by a small oak wood, and award-winning summer hanging baskets. The pretty bedrooms have a fine outlook. Disabled access to public rooms (not to bedrooms).

As well as lunchtime sandwiches, the enjoyable food includes tempura cod cheeks with asian-style vegetables, black pudding with a poached egg and mustard cream, macaroni cheese with truffle, a curry of the day, spiced mutton stew with lemon couscous and pomegranate, pheasant with roasted artichokes, creamed cabbage and bacon, monkfish with salt-baked swede, clam and leek broth and sea herbs, and puddings such as chocolate orange tart and apple and nashi pear crumble. *Benchmark main dish: chicken and leek pie £14.50. Two-course evening meal £25.00.*

Free house ~ Licensee Anthony Guthrie ~ Real ale ~ Open 11-10 (10.30 Sat); check winter opening hours on website; closed Jan ~ Bar food 12-2, 6-8.30 ~ Restaurant ~ Children welcome ~ Dogs allowed in bar ~ Wi-fi ~ Bedrooms: £99/£128 *Recommended by Tina and David Woods-Taylor, Margaret and Peter Staples, Jamie and Lizzie McEwan, Charlie and Mark Todd*

LOWESWATER
Kirkstile Inn 🍺 🛏

NY1421 Map 9

(01900) 85219 – www.kirkstile.com

From B5289 follow signs to Loweswater Lake; OS Sheet 89 map reference 140210; CA13 0RU

Fine location for this well run, popular inn with busy bar, own-brewed beers, good food and friendly welcome; bedrooms

This is a well run, extremely popular 16th-c inn, surrounded by stunning walks. The main bar has a cosy atmosphere thanks to a roaring log fire, plus low beams and carpeting, comfortably cushioned small settles and pews, partly stripped stone walls, board games and a slate shove-ha'penny board. As well as their own-brewed Cumbrian Legendary Esthwaite Bitter, Langdale, Loweswater Gold, Vanilla Oatmeal Stout and a seasonal guest on handpump, they keep nine wines by the glass and 20 malt whiskies; staff are kind and efficient. The stunning views of the peaks can be enjoyed from picnic-sets on the lawn, from the very attractive covered verandah in front of the building and from the windows in one of the rooms off the bar. Bedrooms are comfortable and breakfasts are especially good. Dogs are allowed only in the bar and not during evening food service.

Rewarding food includes sandwiches, locally smoked salmon with horseradish and chive pannacotta and cumberland, mustard and caper dressing, breaded goats cheese with almond, pear and sunblush tomato salad, feta, spinach and roasted vegetable cakes with cumberland, mustard and honey, pork tenderloin with pancetta, chorizo, orange jus and goats cheese bonbon, teriyaki salmon with sesame, pak choi, sweet chilli and tempura sweet potatoes, and puddings such as chocolate bavarois with orange curd and chocolate sauce and cheesecake of the day with vanilla cream. *Benchmark main dish: steak in ale pie £13.50. Two-course evening meal £21.00.*

Own brew ~ Licensee Roger Humphreys ~ Real ale ~ Open 11-11 ~ Bar food 12-2, 6-9; light bites 2-4.30 ~ Restaurant ~ Children welcome ~ Dogs allowed in bar ~ Wi-fi ~ Bedrooms: £63.50/£121 *Recommended by Ian and Rose Lock, Margaret and Peter Staples, Sally and Colin Allen, Caroline and Peter Bryant, Edward May, Richard Tilbrook*

LUPTON
Plough

SO5581   Map 7

(015395) 67700 – www.theploughatlupton.co.uk

A65, near M6 junction 36; LA6 1PJ

Smart inn with civilised bar rooms, a good choice of drinks, interesting food and seats outside; fine bedrooms

---

The comfortable, attractive and well equipped bedrooms here (most are dog-friendly) make a perfect base for exploring the local area. Stylish and congenial, the spreading open-plan bars have beams, a nice mix of antique dining chairs and tables, comfortable leather sofas and armchairs in front of large woodburning stoves, prints on pink and grey-painted walls, rugs on wooden floors, fresh flowers and daily papers; background music and board games. High bar stools sit beside the counter where neatly dressed, helpful staff serve Copper Dragon 13 Steps, Kirkby Lonsdale Monumental, Marstons Wainwright and Settle Jericho Blonde on handpump, 13 wines by the glass, ten gins and local vodka; background music and board games. Outside, rustic wooden tables and chairs under parasols are set behind a granite-topped wall, with more in the back garden.

 Excellent, imaginative food includes sandwiches (until 5pm; not Sunday), spiced game pâté with fig and cinnamon chutney, smoked salmon mousse ballotine with horseradish and beetroot, wild mushroom risotto with irish regato cheese and white truffle oil, beef and onion in stout pie, buttered and poached chicken supreme with roasted salsify, artichoke purée and fondant potato, sea bass fillet with giant couscous, caramelised endive, cauliflower purée, spiced vinaigrette and coriander, and puddings such as sour cherry pavlova with pistachio and chantilly cream and prune and ginger pudding with toffee sauce and vanilla ice-cream; they also offer afternoon tea (must book 24 hours in advance; 12-5 weekdays; 3-5 Saturday). *Benchmark main dish: duck breast with carrot purée, glazed beetroot, dauphinoise potatoes and red wine jus £17.50. Two-course evening meal £23.00.*

Free house ~ Licensee Paul Spencer ~ Real ale ~ Open 11-11; 11-10.30 Sun ~ Bar food 12-9 ~ Restaurant ~ Children welcome ~ Dogs allowed in bar and bedrooms ~ Wi-fi ~ Bedrooms: $85/$120 *Recommended by Nick and Meriel Cox, Andrea and Philip Crispin, Mark and Mary Setting, Hilary Forrest*

NEAR SAWREY
Tower Bank Arms

SD3795   Map 9

(015394) 36334 – www.towerbankarms.com

B5285 towards the Windermere ferry; LA22 0LF

Well run pub with several real ales, well regarded bar food and a friendly welcome; nice bedrooms

---

Immortalised in *The Tale of Jemima Puddle-Duck*, this friendly, busy pub backs on to Beatrix Potter's farm. The low-beamed main bar has plenty of rustic charm with a rough slate floor, game and fowl pictures, a grandfather clock, a log fire and fresh flowers; there's also a separate restaurant. Barngates Tag Lag, Cumbrian Legendary Loweswater Gold and Hawkshead Bitter and Brodies Prime on handpump, ten wines by the glass, 14 malt whiskies and seven farm ciders; board games and darts. There are pleasant views of the wooded Claife Heights from seats in the extended garden. The pretty bedrooms have a country outlook; breakfasts are good.

Popular food includes lunchtime sandwiches, potted chicken liver and pistachio pâté with cumberland sauce, crayfish tails with marie rose sauce, gnocchi with wilted spinach and mushrooms in creamy tarragon sauce, cumberland sausage with caramelised red onion gravy and apple and sage mash, chicken with tarragon, red wine, mushroom and onion sauce and rösti potatoes, beer-battered haddock with chips, pork medallions with brandy, green peppercorn and sage cream, bubble and squeak and apple fritter, and puddings such as chocolate brownie with berries and vanilla ice-cream and raspberry eton mess. *Benchmark main dish: beef in ale stew £13.75. Two-course evening meal £20.15.*

Free house ~ Licensee Anthony Hutton ~ Real ale ~ Open 12-11; 12-10.30 Sun; closed Mon Nov-early Feb, Mon-Thurs one week Dec/Jan ~ Bar food 12-2, 6-8 ~ Restaurant ~ Children welcome ~ Dogs allowed in bar and bedrooms ~ Wi-fi ~ Bedrooms: /£98 *Recommended by Selwyn Jones, Adam Jones, Diana and Richard Gibbs, Patrick and Martine Lawson, Andrew and Nicky Churcher*

RAVENSTONEDALE NY7203 Map 10

Black Swan 🟊◐⮐

(015396) 23204 – www.blackswanhotel.com
Just off A685 SW of Kirkby Stephen; CA17 4NG

Bustling hotel with thriving bar, several real ales, enjoyable food and good surrounding walks; comfortable bedrooms

There are walks straight from the front door here and they have leaflets describing some of the routes; many customers then come to this well run inn for lunch. The popular U-shaped bar has hops on the gantry, quite a few original period features, stripped-stone walls, high wooden stools by the counter, a comfortable tweed banquette, various dining chairs and little stools around a mix of tables and fresh flowers; the cosy small lounge has armchairs and an open fire. You can eat in the bar or in two separate restaurants. Friendly, helpful staff serve Black Sheep Bitter and four guests from breweries such as Hawkshead, Kirkby Lonsdale, Pennine and Tirril on handpump, 11 wines by the glass, more than 30 malt whiskies, 25 gins and a good choice of fruit juices and pressés; background music, TV, darts, board games, newspapers and magazines. The tree-sheltered streamside garden across the road has picnic-sets. Bedrooms are well appointed and very comfortable (some have disabled access, others are dog-friendly) and breakfasts are excellent. Disabled access.

🍴 Imaginative food includes sandwiches, game terrine with apricot chutney, venison tartare with truffle mayonnaise, mushrooms and hazelnuts, celeriac rösti with stilton, pickled apple, walnuts and poached egg, chicken with pancetta, mushrooms, chestnuts and tarragon sauce, cod loin with artichokes, mussels and almond vinaigrette, pork and octopus with chorizo, lentils and grilled sweetcorn, rib-eye steak with pepper sauce and chips, and puddings such as lemon tart with blackcurrant and poppy seed crème fraîche and chocolate truffle with miso caramel and popcorn cream. *Benchmark main dish: rump and shoulder of lamb with onion and mint pesto £23.00. Two-course evening meal £22.00.*

Free house ~ Licensee Louise Dinnes ~ Real ale ~ Open 7.30am-midnight ~ Bar food 12-3, 5-9; 12-4, 5-9 Sun; snacks all day ~ Restaurant ~ Children welcome ~ Dogs allowed in bar and bedrooms ~ Wi-fi ~ Bedrooms: £95/£110 *Recommended by Neil and Angela Huxter, Jacqui and Alan Swan, Margo and Derek Peters, Sophia and Hamish Greenfield, Caroline and Peter Bryant*

Please tell us if any pub deserves to be upgraded to a featured entry – and why: feedback@goodguides.com, or (no stamp needed) Freepost THE GOOD PUB GUIDE, Random House Publishing, 20 Vauxhall Bridge Road, London SW1V 2SA.

STAVELEY   SD4798   Map 10

Beer Hall at Hawkshead Brewery ◀

(01539) 825260 – www.hawksheadbrewery.co.uk
Staveley Mill Yard, Back Lane; LA8 9LR

Hawkshead Brewery showcase plus a huge choice of bottled beers, brewery memorabilia and tasty food

From 14 handpumps, knowledgeable, friendly staff serve the full range of Hawkshead Brewery ales. These include Bitter, Brodies Prime, Dry Stone Stout, Lakeland Gold, Lakeland Lager, Red, Session IPA, Windermere Pale and seasonal beers; they hold regular beer festivals. Also, 40 bottled beers, 30 gins and 23 whiskies with an emphasis on independent producers. It's a spacious and modern glass-fronted building and the main bar is on two levels with the lower level dominated by the stainless-steel fermenting vessels. There are high-backed chairs around light wooden tables, benches beside long tables and nice dark leather sofas around low tables (all on oak floorboards); a couple of walls are almost entirely covered with artistic photos of barley, hops and the brewing process. You can buy T-shirts, branded glasses and polypins and there are brewery tours. Parking can be tricky at peak times.

As well as quite a few bar bites and sliders, the popular food includes fries with different toppings, macaroni cheese with parmesan crumbs and truffle oil, venison chilli with sour cream and toasted pitta, and puddings such as sticky toffee pudding with caramel sauce and vanilla ice-cream and malted milk pannacotta with stout cake. *Benchmark main dish: giant yorkshire pudding filled with ale-braised beef £7.50. Two-course evening meal £13.50.*

Own brew ~ Licensee James Taylor ~ Real ale ~ Open 12-7 Mon-Thurs; 12-11 Fri, Sat; 12-8 Sun ~ Bar food 12-3 Mon-Thurs; 12-8.30 Fri, Sat; 12-6 Sun; hours may be extended during school holidays ~ Children welcome ~ Dogs allowed in bar ~ Wi-fi ~ Open mike night Sun from 5pm; folk club second Fri of month; band night three nights a month 8pm
Recommended by John and Delia Franks, Colin and Daniel Gibbs, Douglas Power, David Travis, Penny and David Shepherd, Nick Higgins

STAVELEY   SD4797   Map 9

Eagle & Child ◀ £ ⇔

(01539) 821320 – www.eaglechildinn.co.uk
Kendal Road; just off A591 Windermere–Kendal; LA8 9LP

Friendly inn with a good range of local beers and enjoyable food; bedrooms

This is a popular lunch spot for walkers, so it's best to book a table in advance. The bar has a chatty, cheerful atmosphere and plenty of separate parts furnished with pews, banquettes, bow-window seats and high-backed dining chairs around polished dark tables; there's a log fire beneath an impressive mantelbeam in the L-shaped flagstoned main area. Also, police truncheons and walking sticks, some nice photographs and interesting prints, a delft shelf of bric-a-brac, a few farm tools and another log fire. Five regularly changing ales come from breweries such as Barngates, Bowness Bay, Coniston, Cumbrian Legendary, Hawkshead and Jennings on handpump, several wines by the glass, 25 malt whiskies, 30 gins and farm cider; background music. A barn-themed dining room upstairs has its own bar for functions. The sheltered garden by the River Kent has picnic-sets under parasols, with more on a good-sized back terrace and a second garden behind. Bedrooms are comfortable and the breakfasts very generous. This is a lovely spot with enjoyable walks that fan out from the recreation ground just across the road.

Well regarded food includes sandwiches, home-breaded brie with cumberland sauce, smoked salmon pâté with toast, cheese, leek and potato pie, beer-battered fresh haddock and chips, cumberland sausage with mash and caramelised onion gravy, cajun chicken caesar salad, gammon with egg and pineapple, sirloin steak with beer-battered onion rings and a choice of sauce, and puddings such as apple crumble and chocolate fudge cake with custard or ice-cream. *Benchmark main dish: moroccan-style lamb with spices, honey, lemon and sweet potato £12.95. Two-course evening meal £18.00.*

Free house ~ Licensees Richard and Denise Coleman ~ Real ale ~ Open 11.30-11 (11.30 Sat); 12-10.30 Sun ~ Bar food 12-2.30, 6-9; 12-9 weekends ~ Restaurant ~ Children welcome ~ Dogs allowed in bar ~ Wi-fi ~ Bedrooms: £90/£95 *Recommended by Tina and David Woods-Taylor, George and Alison Bishop, Sandra King, Chris Stevenson, John and Mary Warner, Julie Braeburn*

STONETHWAITE   NY2513 Map 9

Langstrath 🍺 🛏

(017687) 77239 – www.thelangstrath.com
Off B5289 S of Derwentwater; CA12 5XG

Nice little place in a lovely spot, popular food with a modern twist, real ales and good wines, and seats outside; bedrooms

The comfortable, warm bedrooms here are just right as a base for a walking holiday and both the Cumbrian Way and the Coast to Coast path are close by. It's a friendly and civilised small inn and the neat, simple bar (at its pubbiest at lunchtime) has a welcoming log fire in a big stone fireplace, rustic tables, plain chairs and cushioned wall seats, and walking cartoons and attractive Lakeland mountain photographs on its textured white walls. Jennings Cocker Hoop, Keswick Gold, Marstons Wainwright and a changing guest on handpump, 25 malt whiskies and several wines by the glass; background music. The restaurant has fine views and there's a cosy residents' lounge too (in what was the original 16th-c cottage). Outside, a big sycamore shelters several picnic-sets that look up to Eagle Crag. Disabled access (not to bedrooms).

Reliably good food includes sandwiches, chicken liver pâté with cumberland and port sauce, locally smoked trout fillet with lemon and dill crème fraîche, sweet potato and black bean burger with whisky barbecue sauce and cajun potato wedges, cumberland sausage with mustard mash and blue cheese and port sauce, slow-cooked lamb shoulder with rosemary and red wine jus, a fresh fish dish of the day, chicken, mushroom and chorizo suet pudding with white wine and leek sauce, and puddings. *Benchmark main dish: steak in ale pie £16.00. Two-course evening meal £25.00.*

Free house ~ Licensees Guy and Jacqui Frazer-Hollins ~ Real ale ~ Open 12-10.30; closed Mon, all Dec, Jan ~ Bar food 12-4.30, 6-8.30 ~ Restaurant ~ Children welcome but not in bedrooms ~ Dogs allowed in bar ~ Wi-fi ~ Bedrooms: /£130 *Recommended by Martin Day, Gwendoline and Ralph Mason, Mark and Mary Setting, Claire Adams, Ian Wilson, Liz and Mike Newton, Max Simons*

If we don't specify bar meal times for a featured entry, these are normally 12-2 and 7-9; we do show times if they are markedly different.

TALKIN NY5457 Map 10

Blacksmiths Arms ♀ ⇐

(016977) 3452 – www.blacksmithstalkin.co.uk

Village signposted from B6413 S of Brampton; CA8 1LE

**Neatly kept and welcoming, tasty bar food, several real ales
and fine nearby walks; bedrooms**

Surrounded by good walks in attractive countryside, this extended former
blacksmiths has warm open fires and a genuine welcome. Several
neatly kept, traditionally furnished bars include a lounge on the right with
upholstered banquettes and wheelback chairs around dark wooden tables
on patterned red carpeting, with country prints and other pictures on the
walls. The restaurant is to the left and there's also a long lounge opposite
the bar, with a step up to another room at the back. Black Sheep, Cumbrian
Legendary Loweswater Gold and Hawkshead Bitter and Fullers London
Pride on handpump, 20 wines by the glass, 40 malt whiskies and ten gins;
background music, darts and board games. A couple of picnic-sets are placed
outside the front door with more in the back garden. The cottagey bedrooms
are comfortable and the breakfasts good. Disabled access.

Honest food includes sandwiches, black pudding bonbons with peppercorn dipping
sauce, duck spring rolls with soy dip, vegetable curry, beef stroganoff, liver and
bacon casserole with mash, chicken and leek pie, salmon fillet with white wine sauce,
8oz rump steak with onion rings and chips, and puddings. *Benchmark main dish:
beer-battered haddock and chips £9.95. Two-course evening meal £15.00.*

Free house ~ Licensees Donald and Anne Jackson ~ Real ale ~ Open 12-midnight ~ Bar
food 12-2, 6-9 ~ Restaurant ~ Children welcome ~ Wi-fi ~ Bedrooms: £60/£80 *Recommended
by Philip J Alderton, Robert and Diana Myers, Dave Braisted, Peter Pilbeam, Scott and Charlotte
Havers, Daniel King*

THRELKELD NY3225 Map 9

Horse & Farrier £ ⇐

(017687) 79688 – www.horseandfarrier.com

A66 Penrith–Keswick; CA12 4SQ

**Well run and friendly inn with good food and drinks and lovely nearby
walks; bedrooms**

Newly refurbished, this is a popular 17th-c Lakeland pub with attractive,
comfortable bedrooms and fine walks straight from the doorstep. The
linked rooms have beams, a mix of wooden and prettily upholstered dining
chairs around polished tables on bare boards, open fires, a woodburning
stove and a handsome old range, prints on freshly painted walls and a partly
stripped-stone restaurant. Jennings Bitter, Cumberland and Sneck Lifter
and a couple of guests from Tirril on handpump, several wines by the glass
and efficient, friendly service; background music. There are picnic-sets out
to the side of the building and in the garden and fine views towards the
Helvellyn range.

Well regarded food includes sandwiches, prawn cocktail, breaded garlic
mushrooms with garlic mayonnaise, spinach and ricotta ravioli with roasted
squash, sage and hazelnut butter, steak in ale pie, cumberland sausage with spring
onion mash and onion, thyme and ale gravy, chicken breast stuffed with sun-dried
tomato and spinach, wrapped in bacon with fennel risotto and cep mushroom cream
sauce, beef daube on mustard mash with red wine jus, swordfish marinated in paprika
and garlic with jerk-spiced rice and chilli, lime and mango dressing, and puddings

such as creme egg chocolate tart and spiced bread and butter pudding with vanilla ice-cream. *Benchmark main dish: beer-battered fish and chips £12.95. Two-course evening meal £20.00.*

Jennings (Marstons) ~ Lease David Arkley ~ Real ale ~ Open 8am-midnight ~ Bar food 12-9 ~ Restaurant ~ Children welcome ~ Dogs allowed in bar ~ Wi-fi ~ Bedrooms: £68/£125
Recommended by Tina and David Woods-Taylor, Denise Courtney, Miles Green, George Sanderson, Belinda Stamp, Sandra and Nigel Brown, Margaret and Peter Staples

TIRRIL
Queens Head

NY5026 Map 10

(01768) 863219 – www.queensheadinn.co.uk
B5320, not far from M6 junction 40; CA10 2JF

Dating from 1719 with two bars, real ales, tasty food and seats outside; bedrooms

After visiting Dalemain House and Garden at Dacre or nearby Ullswater, many customers come to this 18th-c inn to enjoy their speciality pies. The oldest parts of the main bar have original flagstones and floorboards, low beams and black panelling, and there are nice little tables and chairs on either side of the inglenook fireplace (always lit in winter). Another bar to the right of the entrance has pews and chairs around sizeable tables on a wooden floor, and candles in the fireplace, while the back locals' bar has heavy beams and a pool table; they have three dining rooms too. Robinsons Cumbria Way, Dizzy Blonde and a guest or two on handpump and several wines by the glass. Outside there are picnic-sets at the front, and modern chairs and tables under cover on the back terrace. The hard-working licensees also run the Pie Mill (you can eat their pies here) and the village shop.

 As well as their eight pies, the well liked food includes lunchtime sandwiches and omelettes, black pudding and haggis stack with a poached egg and beetroot chutney, creamy garlic mushrooms and crispy bacon, roasted mediterranean vegetable lasagne, cumberland sausages with mash and gravy, burgers (chicken and chorizo, pork and brie, chilli beef) with toppings, coleslaw and chips, salmon fillet with parsley butter, chicken breast with stilton and cream sauce, and puddings such as fruit pie with custard and chocolate sponge with chocolate sauce; they also offer an early bird two-course menu (5-6pm). *Benchmark main dish: pies £11.95. Two-course evening meal £18.00.*

Robinsons ~ Tenants Margaret and Jim Hodge ~ Real ale ~ Open 11-11; 11am-11.30pm Sat; 12-10 Sun ~ Bar food 12-2.30, 5-8.30 ~ Restaurant ~ Children welcome ~ Dogs allowed in bar and bedrooms ~ Wi-fi ~ Bedrooms: £50/£80 *Recommended by Tina and David Woods-Taylor, Pauline and Mark Evans, Paul Faraday, Mike Swan, Jo Garnett, Toby Jones*

ULVERSTON
Bay Horse ♀ ⇐

SD3177 Map 7

(01229) 583972 – www.thebayhorsehotel.co.uk
Canal Foot signposted off A590, then wend your way past the huge Glaxo factory; LA12 9EL

Civilised waterside hotel with lunchtime bar food, three real ales and a fine choice of wines; smart bedrooms

Lunchtime is when you'll find the newly wallpapered bar here at its most informal, and there's a relaxed atmosphere despite its smart furnishings: cushioned teak dining chairs, paisley-patterned built-in wall banquettes, glossy hardwood traditional tables, a huge stone horse's head, black beams and props, and lots of horsebrasses. Magazines are dotted about, there's an open fire in the handsomely marbled, grey slate fireplace and decently reproduced background music; board games. Kind, helpful staff serve Jennings Cumberland and Wychwood Hobgoblin on handpump, 16 wines by the glass (including champagne and prosecco) from a carefully chosen, interesting list and 15 malt whiskies. The conservatory restaurant has lovely views over Morecambe Bay and the terrace has plenty of seats and tables. This is a fine place to stay and the newly refurbished bedrooms have french windows that open out to a panoramic view of the Leven estuary (the bird life is wonderful); breakfasts are excellent.

Using the best local, seasonal produce the well thought-of food includes a formal evening menu plus lunchtime choices such as hot and cold sandwiches, chicken, ham and pistachio nut terrine with gooseberry and juniper purée, smoked salmon with buttered treacle bread and sweet and sour mayonnaise, butternut squash stuffed with mushroom and herb quinoa and mixed pepper and red onion salad, beef and mushroom in Guinness casserole with white pudding mash, chicken in coconut milk with lime and ginger with grilled pancetta and pineapple, calamari and king prawns with chilli, lemon and garlic, and puddings such as chocolate crème brûlée and bananas baked with apricot, vanilla, rum and raisin and served with cinnamon cream; they also offer afternoon tea. *Benchmark main dish: crab and salmon fishcakes with white wine and fresh herb cream sauce £19.95. Two-course evening meal £27.50.*

Free house ~ Licensee Robert Lyons ~ Real ale ~ Open 11-11; 11-10.30 Sun ~ Bar food 12-2 (3 in summer), 7-8.30 ~ Restaurant ~ Children welcome at lunchtime, must be over 9 in bedrooms ~ Dogs allowed in bar and bedrooms ~ Wi-fi ~ Bedrooms: $95/$120 *Recommended by Sally and Brian Turner, Barry and Daphne Gregson, Mike Benton, W K Wood, Patricia and Anton Larkham, Patti and James Davidson*

WINSTER
Brown Horse 🍺 🛏

SD4193 Map 9

(015394) 43443 – www.thebrownhorseinn.co.uk
A5074 S of Windermere; LA23 3NR

Traditional inn with character bar and dining room, own-brewed ales, tasty varied food and seats outside; bedrooms

The valley in which this former coaching inn sits is very pretty and the surrounding walks are enjoyable. The chatty beamed and flagstoned bar has church pews, a lovely tall settle and mate's chairs around a mix of tables, while the candlelit dining room has a medley of painted and antique chairs and tables, old skis, carpet beaters, hunting horns and antlers. The fine choice of drinks includes Handsome Top Knot, Marstons Wainwright, Winster Valley Lakes Blonde and a guest beer on handpump plus several wines by the glass, quite a few malt whiskies and an extraordinary list of 180 gins from all over the world with 13 different tonics to mix with them; background music, board games and TV. The gents' is upstairs. There are seats outside among flowering tubs, with more on a raised terrace. Bedrooms are thoughtfully furnished and four in the annexe have their own outside seating area.

As well as lunchtime sandwiches, the interesting food includes potted game with red onion marmalade, crispy chicken skin and pheasant popcorn, haggis and black pudding wellington with whisky cream, wild mushroom and spinach risotto with herb oil, steak and kidney pudding, lamb shank with mash and greens, hake fillet with a soft poached egg, crispy kale and chive butter sauce, 30-day aged rib-eye steak with a choice of sauce, and puddings such as lemon and vanilla cheesecake with berry gel and chocolate sticky toffee pudding with caramel ice-cream and toffee sauce.

Benchmark main dish: curried cod with lentil dhal and crispy cauliflower £17.50.
Two-course evening meal £25.00.

Free house ~ Licensees Craig and Shaun Edmondson ~ Real ale ~ Open 10am-11pm;
10am-10.30pm Sun ~ Bar food 12-2.30 (3 weekends), 6-9 ~ Restaurant ~ Children welcome
~ Dogs allowed in bar ~ Wi-fi ~ Bedrooms: £95/£115 *Recommended by Barry, Alexandra and*
Richard Clay, Tim and Sarah Smythe-Brown, James and Sylvia Hewitt, Anne and Ben Smith,
Mike Benton

WITHERSLACK
Derby Arms

SD4482 Map 10

(015395) 52207 – www.thederbyarms.co.uk
Just off A590; LA11 6RH

Bustling country inn with well kept ales, good food and wine and a genuine welcome; bedrooms

The six real ales on handpump here might include Fell Milk Stout, Bowness
Bay Swan Blonde, Cumbrian Legendary Loweswater Gold, Ennerdale
English Pride and Handsome Top Knot and they also offer 11 wines by the
glass and 22 malt whiskies. The main bar has sporting prints on pale grey
walls, elegant old dining chairs and tables on large rugs over floorboards,
and an open fire. A larger room to the right is similarly furnished (with the
addition of some cushioned pews) and has local prints, another open fire,
and alcoves in the back wall full of bristol blue glass, ornate plates and
staffordshire dogs and figurines. Large windows lighten the rooms, helped at
night by candles in brass candlesticks; background music, TV and pool. There
are two additional rooms; one has dark red walls, a red velvet sofa, sporting
prints and a handsome mirror over the fireplace. Bedrooms are fairly priced
and there's plenty to do nearby – Sizergh Castle (National Trust), Levens Hall
and good walks around the Southern Lakes and Dales. This is part of the
Ainscoughs group.

Food includes lunchtime sandwiches, chicken liver pâté with red onion marmalade,
mini rack of barbecue ribs, gnocchi with broccoli, blue cheese, candied walnuts
and salad, beer-battered haddock and chips, burger with toppings and chips, cumberland
sausage with mash and gravy, lamb curry, and puddings such as toffee apple crumble and
ice-cream and double chocolate brownie with chocolate sauce. *Benchmark main dish:*
steak in ale pie £13.95. Two-course evening meal £22.50.

Free house ~ Licensee Jamie King ~ Real ale ~ Open 12-11.30 (midnight Sat) ~ Bar food 12-
2.30, 5.30-8.30; 12-3, 5.30-9 in summer; 12-9 Sat ~ Children welcome ~ Dogs allowed in bar ~
Wi-fi ~ Live music twice a month Sat evening ~ Bedrooms: /£80 *Recommended by Nicholas and*
Lucy Sage, Alan and Alice Morgan, Paul Walker, Peter Pilbeam, Mike Benton, Edward May

Also Worth a Visit in Cumbria

Besides the fully inspected pubs, you might like to try these pubs that
have been recommended to us and described by readers. Do tell us what
you think of them: feedback@goodguides.com

ALLITHWAITE SD3876
Pheasant (015395) 32239
B5277; LA11 7RQ Welcoming family-run
pub on village outskirts; enjoyable freshly
cooked food including blackboard specials
and good Sun roasts, smaller appetites and
special diets catered for, well kept Cumbrian

Legendary Loweswater Gold, Tetleys Bitter
and up to three guests, friendly efficient
service, traditional bar with log fire, two
dining areas off; Thurs quiz; children
welcome (not in conservatory), dogs in bar,
outside tables on deck with Humphrey Head
and Morecambe Bay views, open (and food)
all day. *(James Tilley, Michael Butler)*

ALSTON   NY7146
Angel (01434) 381363
Front Street; CA9 3HU Simple 17th-c inn
on steep cobbled street of this charming
small Pennine market town; mainly local
ales and generously served food including
daily specials, reasonable prices, timbers,
traditional furnishings and open fires,
friendly atmosphere; children and dogs
welcome, tables in sheltered back garden,
four bedrooms. *(Simon Day)*

AMBLESIDE   NY4008
★ Kirkstone Pass Inn (015394) 33888
A592 N of Troutbeck; LA22 9LQ Historic
inn (Lakeland's highest pub) set in wonderful
rugged scenery; flagstones, stripped stone
and dark beams, lots of old photographs and
bric-a-brac, open fires, enjoyable good value
pubby food and well kept changing cumbrian
ales, hot drinks, friendly efficient service; soft
background music, daily newspapers; well
behaved children and dogs welcome, tables
outside with stunning views to Windermere,
bedrooms, bunkhouse and camping
field, open all day in summer (till 6pm Sun),
phone for winter hours. *(Denis and Margaret
Kilner)*

APPLEBY   NY6819
★ Royal Oak (01768) 351463
B6542/Bongate; CA16 6UN Attractive
old beamed and timbered coaching inn on
edge of town; popular generously served food
including early bird and OAP deals, some
themed nights, well kept Black Sheep and
one or two local guests, friendly efficient
young staff, log fire in panelled bar, lounge
with easy chairs and carved settle, traditional
snug and restaurant; background music, TV;
children and dogs welcome (menus for both),
terrace tables, 11 bedrooms and self-catering
cottage, good breakfast, open all day from 8am.
(J H Bell, Margaret and Peter Staples)

ASKHAM   NY5123
Punch Bowl (01931) 712443
*4.5 miles from M6 junction 40;
CA10 2PF* Attractive 18th-c village pub
on edge of green opposite Askham Hall;
spacious beamed main bar, locals' bar, snug
lounge and dining room, open fires, well
kept Hawkshead and guests, decent choice
of enjoyable food (all day weekends) from
pub standards up, friendly staff; children and
dogs welcome, picnic-sets out in front and
on small raised terrace, six bedrooms, open
all day. *(Martin Day)*

ASKHAM   NY5123
Queens Head (01931) 712350
*Lower Green; off A6 or B5320 S of
Penrith; CA10 2PF* 17th-c beamed village
pub recently bought and refurbished by the
Askham Hall Estate (sister to the George
& Dragon at Clifton – see Main Entries);
reports please. *(Maria and Henry Lazenby)*

BAMPTON GRANGE   NY5218
★ Crown & Mitre (01931) 713225
Opposite church; CA10 2QR Old inn set
in attractive country hamlet (*Withnail and I*
was filmed around here); opened-up bar with
comfortable modern décor and nice log fire,
separate dining room, popular good quality
home-made evening food from pub favourites
up, three well kept changing local ales (two
in winter), friendly staff; children and dogs
welcome, good walks from the door, eight
bedrooms, shut lunchtimes (open from 5pm),
winter hours may vary. *(Miles Green)*

BARBON   SD6282
Barbon Inn (015242) 76233
*Off A683 Kirkby Lonsdale–Sedbergh;
LA6 2LJ* Charmingly set 17th-c fell-foot
village inn; comfortable old world interior, log
fires (one in range), some sofas, armchairs
and antique carved settles, a couple of local
ales and nice selection of wines, decent food
from bar meals up, restaurant, friendly staff
and regulars; children and dogs welcome,
wheelchair access (ladies' loo is upstairs),
sheltered pretty garden and terrace, good
walks, ten bedrooms, open (and food)
all day weekends; for sale as we went to
press. *(Nicola and Holly Lyons)*

BASSENTHWAITE   NY2332
Sun (017687) 76439
Off A591 N of Keswick; CA12 4QP
White-rendered 17th-c village pub; rambling
bar with low black beams and blazing
winter fires in two stone fireplaces, built-in
wall seats and heavy wooden tables, two
Jennings ales and a guest, generous food
served by friendly staff, cosy dining room;
children and dogs welcome, terrace with
views of the fells and Skiddaw, open all day
Sun, from 4pm other days. *(Louise and Anton
Parsons)*

BEETHAM   SD4979
Wheatsheaf (015395) 64652
*Village (and inn) signed off A6 S
of Milnthorpe; LA7 7AL* Striking old
building with fine black and white timbered
cornerpiece; opened-up recently refurbished
interior with wood floors, stained-glass
windows and back open fire, three well kept
changing local ales, 20 wines by the glass
and good range of whiskies and other spirits,
enjoyable food including daily specials,
friendly helpful service; background music,
quiz first Thurs of month; children and dogs
welcome, plenty of surrounding walks, pretty
14th-c church opposite, four bedrooms, open
(and food) all day. *(Max Simons)*

BOOT   NY1701
Boot Inn (019467) 23711
*Aka Burnmoor; signed just off the
Wrynose/Hardknott Pass road;
CA19 1TG* Beamed country inn with
Robinsons ales, decent wines and enjoyable

home-made food including daily specials, friendly helpful staff, blazing log fire in bare-boards bar, conservatory; children and dogs welcome, garden with play area, lovely surroundings and walks, nine bedrooms, open (and food) all day. *(Jeff Davies)*

BOOT   NY1701
★ **Brook House** (019467) 23288
From Ambleside, W of Hardknott Pass; CA19 1TG Lovely views and walks from this friendly family-run country inn; good sensibly priced food from sandwiches to specials, up to ten well kept ales such as Barngates, Cumbrian Legendary, Hawkshead and Yates, Weston's cider/perry, decent wines and over 180 whiskies, relaxed comfortable raftered bar with log fire and stuffed animals, smaller plush snug, peaceful separate restaurant; Sun quiz; children and dogs welcome, tables on flagstoned terrace, eight reasonably priced bedrooms, good breakfast (for nearby campers too), mountain weather reports, excellent drying room, handy for Eskdale miniature railway terminus, open all day. *(George Sanderson)*

BOOT   NY1901
Woolpack (019467) 23230
Bleabeck, midway between Boot and Hardknott Pass; CA19 1TH Last pub before the Hardknott Pass; warm welcoming atmosphere in main walkers' bar, also an evening restaurant (Fri, Sat), good home-made food including tapas-style dishes, wood-fired pizzas, steaks and daily specials, up to eight well kept ales, real cider and vast range of vodkas and gins; regular events such as live music, Apr sausage and cider festival and June beer festival, pool room, big-screen sports TV; children and dogs welcome, mountain-view garden with play area, eight bedrooms, open (and food) all day. *(George Sanderson)*

BOUTH   SD3285
★ **White Hart** (01229) 861229
Village signed off A590 near Haverthwaite; LA12 8JB Cheerful old inn with popular generously served food, six well kept mainly local ales and 25 malt whiskies, friendly service, sloping ceilings and floors, old local photographs, farm tools and stuffed animals, collection of long-stemmed clay pipes, two woodburners; background music; children and dogs (in one part of bar) welcome, tables out at back, playground opposite and fine surrounding walks, five comfortable bedrooms, adjoining self-catering cottage, open all day, food all day Sun. *(Michael Butler)*

BOWLAND BRIDGE   SD4189
★ **Hare & Hounds** (015395) 68785
Signed from A5074; LA11 6NN Fine valley views from this quietly placed 17th-c inn; little bar with hop-strung beams and

woodburner, well kept ales including a house beer from Tirril (Hare of the Dog), local farm cider and a dozen wines by the glass, good sensibly priced food from sandwiches and pubby dishes up, other attractively furnished rooms with mix of tables and chairs on black slate or old pine boards, numerous hunting prints on painted or stripped-stone walls; background music, board games, daily papers and free wi-fi; children and dogs (in bar) welcome, front terrace with teak furniture under parasols, more seats in spacious side garden, comfortable bedrooms, open all day, food all day weekends. *(Helene Grygar, Geoff Owen, Gerry and Pam Pollard, Gail and Frank Hackett)*

BOWNESS-ON-
WINDERMERE   SD4096
Royal Oak (015394) 43970
Brantfell Road; LA23 3EG Family-run inn handy for the steamer pier; interconnecting bar, dining room and big games room, old photographs and bric-a-brac, open fire, well kept ales such as Coniston, Jennings, Sharps, Timothy Taylors and Tetleys, generous reasonably priced pub food from baguettes to specials, friendly efficient service; pool, darts and TV; children and dogs welcome, tables out in front, eight bedrooms, open (and food) all day. *(Ben and Jenny Settle)*

BRAITHWAITE   NY2323
Royal Oak (017687) 78533
B5292 at top of village; CA12 5SY Refurbished village pub with warm welcoming atmosphere; four well kept Jennings ales and hearty helpings of good value traditional food (smaller servings available) including recommended steaks, efficient helpful service, large L-shaped beamed bar, restaurant; background music, TV, board games; children welcome, no dogs at mealtimes, ten bedrooms, open all day. *(Mike and Eleanor Anderson)*

BROUGHTON-IN-
FURNESS   SD2187
Black Cock (01229) 716529
Princes Street; LA20 6HQ Cosy low-beamed pub dating from 16th c; up to five real ales and good home-cooked food including daily specials, friendly efficient service, log fire; some live music; children and dogs welcome, picnic-sets out in front and in attractive courtyard, five simple clean bedrooms, open all day. *(Shona and Jimmy McDuff)*

BROUGHTON-IN-
FURNESS   SD2187
Manor Arms (01229) 716286
The Square; LA20 6HY Friendly end-of-terrace drinkers' pub on quiet sloping square; up to eight well kept changing ales and good choice of ciders, flagstoned front bar with nice bow-window seat, two log fires, old photographs and chiming clocks, limited food

such as rolls; pool, board games, free wi-fi; children and dogs allowed, bedrooms, open all day. *(Freddie and Sarah Banks)*

BUTTERMERE · NY1716
Bridge Hotel (017687) 70252
Just off B5289 SW of Keswick; CA13 9UZ Welcoming and popular with walkers, hotel-like in feel but with two traditional comfortable beamed bars (dogs allowed in one), four well kept cumbrian ales and good food, more upmarket menu in evening dining room; free wi-fi; children welcome, fell views from brick terrace, 21 bedrooms and six self-catering apartments, open (and food) all day. *(Jeff Davies)*

CARTMEL · SD3778
Cavendish Arms (015395) 36240
Cavendish Street, off the Square; LA11 6QA Former coaching inn with simply furnished open-plan bar, hop-strung beams and roaring log fire (even on cooler summer evenings), three or four well kept ales including one named for them, several wines by the glass and good range of gins, friendly staff, enjoyable fairly traditional food from lunchtime ciabattas up, restaurant; children welcome, dogs in bar, tables out in front and behind by stream (must pay in advance if you eat out here), nice village with notable priory church, racecourse and good walks, ten bedrooms – three more above their shop in the square, open (and food) all day. *(Hugh Roberts)*

CARTMEL · SD3778
Kings Arms (015395) 33246
The Square; LA11 6QB Bustling 18th-c pub close to the priory; cosy beamed rooms with flagstones and bare boards, log fires, nice mix of furniture including easy chairs and comfortable sofas, Hawkshead ales and a guest, cocktails, enjoyable food from sharing boards, pizzas and burgers up, friendly service; live weekend bands (pub open till 1am then), free wi-fi; children and dogs welcome, seats outside facing the lovely square, open (and food) all day. *(Nicola and Nigel Matthews)*

CARTMEL · SD3778
★Royal Oak (015395) 36259
The Square; LA11 6QB Low-beamed flagstoned inn under same management as the Kings Arms next door; long rustic tables, settles, leather easy chairs and big log fire, cosy nooks, good value food including pub favourites, home-made pizzas, pasta and grills, local ales such as Cumbrian Legendary, Hawkshead and Unsworth's Yard, good choice of wines, welcoming helpful staff; background and weekend live music, two sports TVs, free wi-fi; children and dogs welcome, some seats out in square, nice big riverside garden behind with heated terrace and marquee, four neat bedrooms, open (and food) all day. *(Michael Butler)*

CASTERTON · SD6379
★Pheasant (015242) 71230
A683; LA6 2RX Welcoming 18th-c family-run inn with neatly furnished beamed rooms; highly regarded attractively presented food from imaginative menu, also lunchtime sandwiches and one or two pub favourites, well kept ales including a house beer brewed by Tirril, nice wines and several malt whiskies, friendly helpful staff, arched and panelled restaurant; background music, free wi-fi; children and dogs welcome, a few roadside seats, more in pleasant garden with Vale of Lune views, near church with notable Pre-Raphaelite stained glass and paintings, ten comfortable bedrooms, closed Mon, otherwise open all day; for sale, so may be changes. *(Derek Stafford)*

CASTLE CARROCK · NY5455
Duke of Cumberland
(01228) 670341 *Geltsdale Road; CA8 9LU* Popular and welcoming stone-built village-green pub; updated interior with upholstered wall benches and mix of pubby furniture on stone floor, open fire, dining area with old farmhouse tables and chairs, two local ales and good food (all day weekends) including a couple of curries; children and dogs (theirs is Poppy) welcome, sunny picnic-sets out at front, self-catering apartment, good walks nearby, closed Tues, otherwise open all day (best to check winter hours). *(Marcus Byron)*

COCKERMOUTH · NY1230
Castle Bar (01900) 829904
Market Place; CA13 9NQ Busy 16th-c pub on three floors; beams, timbers and other original features mixing with modern furnishings, five well kept local beers such as Cumbrian Legendary and Jennings (cheaper 3-7pm Mon-Fri, all day Sun), Weston's cider, enjoyable home-made food including good value Sun roasts in upstairs dining room or in any of the three ground-floor areas, efficient service from friendly young staff; sports TV; children welcome, dogs downstairs, seats on sunny back tiered terrace, open all day. *(Mike and Eleanor Anderson)*

CONISTON · SD3097
Black Bull (015394) 41335/41668
Yewdale Road (A593); LA21 8DU Bustling 17th-c beamed inn brewing its own good Coniston beers; back area (liked by walkers and their dogs) with slate floor, more comfortable carpeted front part with log fire and Donald Campbell memorabilia, enjoyable food including daily specials, friendly helpful staff, lounge with Old Man of Coniston big toe (large piece of stone in the wall), restaurant; they may ask for a credit card if you run a tab; children welcome, plenty of seats in former coachyard, 15 bedrooms, open (and food) all day from 10am, parking not easy at peak times. *(Julian Thorpe)*

CROOK   SD4695
Sun (01539) 821351
B5284 Kendal–Bowness; LA8 8LA
Welcoming end-of-terrace country pub;
low-beamed bar with dining areas off, stone,
wood and carpeted floors, log fires, enjoyable
traditional food from sandwiches up
including specials and weekday early evening
deal (not winter), two or three changing
ales; occasional live music; children welcome
(games for them), dogs and muddy boots in
some parts, seats out at front by road, open
all day Fri and Sat, till 9pm Sun, closed Tues.
(Nicola and Holly Lyons)

DENT   SD7086
George & Dragon (015396) 25256
Main Street; LA10 5QL Two-bar corner
tap for Dent Brewery in cobbled street; their
full range kept well plus a guest and real
cider, old panelling, partitioned tables and
open fires, enjoyable food from snacks up,
friendly young staff, steps down to restaurant,
games room with pool and juke box; sports
TV, free wi-fi; children, walkers and dogs
welcome, ten bedrooms, lovely village, open
all day. *(Charles and Maddie Bishop)*

DUFTON   NY6825
Stag (017683) 51608
*Village signed from A66 at Appleby;
CA16 6DB* Traditional little 18th-c pub by
pretty village's green; good reasonably priced
home-made food and interesting range of
well kept changing beers, two log fires, one
in splendid early Victorian kitchen range in
main bar, room off to the left, dining room;
quiz every other Thurs, darts; children,
walkers and dogs welcome, tables out at front
and in back garden with lovely hill views,
handy for Pennine Way, self-catering cottage,
open all day weekends, closed weekday
lunchtimes. *(George Sanderson)*

ENNERDALE BRIDGE   NY0716
Fox & Hounds (01946) 861373
High Street; CA23 3AR Popular village
pub with updated beamed interior, bare
boards and quarry tiles, upholstered wall
benches and wheelback chairs around pubby
tables, woodburners, local Ennerdale and up
to four other well kept cumbrian ales, tasty
reasonably priced home-made food including
some vegetarian/vegan choices, friendly staff;
children and dogs welcome, picnic-sets in
streamside garden, three spacious bedrooms,
handy for walkers on Coast to Coast path,
open (and food) all day in summer.
(Jeff Davies)

ENNERDALE BRIDGE   NY0615
Shepherds Arms (01946) 861249
Off A5086 E of Egremont; CA23 3AR
Friendly well placed walkers' inn
by car-free dale; bar with log fire and
woodburner, up to five local beers and good
generously served home-made food, can

provide packed lunches, panelled dining
room and conservatory; board games, free
wi-fi; children and dogs welcome, seats
outside by beck, eight bedrooms, good
breakfast. *(Simon Day)*

ESKDALE GREEN   NY1200
Bower House (019467) 23244
0.5 miles W of Eskdale Green; CA19 1TD
Comfortably modernised 17th-c stone inn
extended around beamed core; four regional
ales and enjoyable hearty food (all day
weekends) in bar or biggish restaurant, log
fires, friendly atmosphere; Sun quiz, free
wi-fi; children and dogs welcome, play area
in sheltered garden, charming spot by cricket
field with great view of Muncaster Fell, good
walks, 20 bedrooms (some in converted
barn), open all day. *(Charles and Maddie
Bishop)*

FAR SAWREY   SD3795
Cuckoo Brow (015394) 43425
B5285 N of village; LA22 0LQ
Renovated 300-year-old coaching house in
lovely setting; opened-up bar with wood
floors and central woodburner, steps down
to former stables with tables in stalls,
harnesses on rough white walls, even
water troughs and mangers, four well kept
changing local ales and hearty food served
by friendly helpful staff; background music,
free wi-fi; children, walkers and dogs
welcome, seats on nice front lawn,
14 bedrooms, open (and food) all day.
(Shona and Jimmy McDuff)

FAUGH   NY5054
String of Horses (01228) 670297
*S of village, on left as you go downhill;
CA8 9EG* Welcoming 17th-c coaching inn
with cosy communicating beamed rooms;
log fires, oak panelling and some interesting
carved furniture, tasty traditional food
alongside latin american/mexican dishes,
well kept local beers such as Allendale and
nice house wines, restaurant; background
music, sports TV, free wi-fi; children
welcome, no dogs, a few picnic-sets out
in front, 11 comfortable bedrooms, good
breakfast, closed lunchtimes and all day
Mon. *(Louise and Anton Parsons)*

FOXFIELD   SD2085
★ Prince of Wales (01229) 716238
Opposite station; LA20 6BX
Unpretentious, popular and cheery; half
a dozen good changing ales including
some bargains brewed here, bottled
imports and real cider too, huge helpings
of enjoyable home-made food (lots of
unusual pasties), character landlord and
good friendly service, hot coal fire; live
music second/fourth Weds of month, pub
games including bar billiards, daily papers
and beer-related reading matter; children
and dogs welcome, four reasonably priced
bedrooms, open all day Fri-Sun, from

2.45pm Wed and Thurs, closed Mon, Tues; may be new people taking over as we went to press. *(Nicola and Holly Lyons)*

GLENRIDDING   NY3816
Travellers Rest (017684) 82298
Back of main car park, at the top of the road; CA11 0QQ Friendly low-beamed and panelled two-bar pub, good straightforward food and well kept ales such as Hesket Newmarket and Jennings, simple yet comfortable pubby décor, old local photographs, real fire; Ullswater views from terrace picnic-sets, children, walkers and dogs welcome (nearest pub to Helvellyn), open (and food) all day in summer. *(Tina and David Woods-Taylor)*

GOSFORTH   NY0703
Gosforth Hall (019467) 25322
Off A595 and unclassified road to Wasdale; CA20 1AZ Friendly well run Jacobean inn with interesting history; beamed and carpeted bar (popular with locals), fine plaster coat of arms above woodburner, lounge/reception area with huge fireplace, four changing regional ales and enjoyable home-made food including good range of pies, restaurant; children and dogs welcome, nice big side garden, 22 bedrooms (some in new extension), open all day. *(Penny and David Shepherd)*

GRASMERE   NY3406
Travellers Rest (015394) 35604
A591 just N; LA22 9RR Welcoming 16th-c roadside coaching inn with attractive creeper-clad exterior; traditional linked rooms, settles, padded benches and other pubby furniture on flagstone or wood floors, old local photographs and open fires, well kept Jennings ales, good selection of wines and enjoyable reasonably priced food including steak menu and specials, friendly helpful service; background music, pool, steps up to gents'; children, walkers and dogs welcome, seats outside with fell views, ten bedrooms, open (and food) all day. *(Ian and Rose Lock)*

GRASMERE   NY3307
Tweedies (015394) 35300
Part of Dale Lodge Hotel; LA22 9SW Lively properly pubby atmosphere in big square hotel bar; wide choice of well kept beers on tap and in bottles, proper cider/perry and plenty of wines by the glass too, good service, traditional décor with hundreds of beer mats on display, log fire, sturdy furnishings in adjoining flagstoned dining room serving good hearty food including children's choices, also separate restaurant; weekend live music, Sept beer/music festival; walkers and dogs welcome, picnic-sets out in large pleasant garden, comfortable well equipped bedrooms, open (and food) all day. *(Mr and Mrs Richard Osborne)*

GREYSTOKE   NY4430
Boot & Shoe (017684) 83343
By village green, off B5288; CA11 0TP Cosy 17th-c two-bar pub in pretty 'Tarzan' village; low ceilings, exposed brickwork and dark woodwork, good generously served traditional food including blackboard specials, well kept Black Sheep and local microbrews, bustling friendly atmosphere; Thurs quiz, live music; children welcome till 8pm, dogs in bar, seats out at front and in back garden, on national cycle route, four bedrooms, open all day. *(Freddie and Sarah Banks)*

HARTSOP   NY4013
Brotherswater Inn (017684) 82239
On Kirkstone Pass Road, S of Patterdale; CA11 0NZ Cosy well run walkers' and campers' pub in magnificent setting at the bottom of Kirkstone Pass; good local ales and enjoyable sensibly priced food served by friendly helpful staff, beautiful fell views across the lake from picture windows and terrace tables; children and dogs welcome, six bedrooms, bunkhouse and campsite, open all day (from 8am for breakfast). *(Tina and David Woods-Taylor)*

HAWESWATER   NY4914
Haweswater (01931) 713235
Lakeside Road; CA10 2RP Remote 1930s hotel in commanding position overlooking reservoir; plenty of art deco detail in refurbished bar/bistro and separate evening restaurant, open fires, enjoyable food from pub favourites up, no handpulled ales (bottles only), friendly efficient service; children and dogs (in bar) welcome, attractive gardens with red squirrels and wonderful views, on Wainwright's Coast to Coast path, 17 bedrooms, open (and food) all day. *(Hugh Roberts)*

HAWKSHEAD   SD3598
Kings Arms (015394) 36372
The Square; LA22 0NZ Old inn with low ceilings, traditional pubby furnishings and log fire, well stocked bar serving local ales such as Cumbrian Legendary and Hawkshead, good variety of enjoyable food from lunchtime sandwiches to daily specials, quick service, side dining area; background music, free wi-fi; children and dogs (in bar) welcome, terrace overlooking central square of this lovely Elizabethan village, bedrooms, self-catering cottages nearby, free fishing permits for residents on Esthwaite Water, open all day till midnight. *(David Pickering)*

HAWKSHEAD   SD3598
Queens Head (015394) 36271
Main Street; LA22 0NS Black and white timbered pub in this charming village; low-ceilinged flagstoned bar with heavy bowed black beams, dark panelling and open fire, snug little room off and several eating areas,

Robinsons ales, a guest beer and good range of other drinks, enjoyable food from pub favourites and pizzas up, friendly helpful staff; background music and TV; children and dogs welcome, seats outside and pretty window boxes, 13 bedrooms, self-catering cottage, open all day. *(George Sanderson)*

HAWKSHEAD   SD3598
Red Lion (015394) 36213
Main Street; LA22 0NS Friendly old inn with well kept local ales including Hawkshead and good food from shortish menu, recent refurbishment under new owners keeping original panelling and log fire; sports TVs; dogs welcome, bedrooms (some sloping floors), open all day.
(George Sanderson)

HAWKSHEAD   SD3598
Sun (015394) 36236
Main Street; LA22 0NT Steps up to welcoming 17th-c beamed inn; Hawkshead, Jennings and a couple of guests, decent wines and extensive range of gins, popular fairly priced food from lunchtime sandwiches up, sizeable restaurant; live music, TV; children and dogs (in bar) welcome, tables out in small front courtyard, eight bedrooms, open all day, food all day Sun.
(David Pickering)

HESKET NEWMARKET   NY3438
Old Crown (016974) 78288
Village signed off B5299 in Caldbeck; CA7 8JG Straightforward cooperative-owned local in attractive village; small bar with bric-a-brac, mountaineering kit and pictures, woodburner, good Hesket Newmarket beers brewed in barn behind (can book tours), hearty home-made food (not Mon), reasonable prices and friendly service, dining room and garden room; folk night Mon, juke box, pool, darts and board games; children and dogs welcome, lovely walking country away from Lake District crowds (near Cumbria Way), open all day Fri-Sun, closed lunchtimes other days.
(Dr Geoff Butts)

KENDAL   SD5192
Riflemans Arms (01539) 241470
Greenside; LA9 4LD Old-fashioned local in village-green setting on edge of town, friendly regulars and staff, Greene King Abbot, Timothy Taylors Landlord and guests, no food; Thurs folk night, Sun quiz, pool and darts (regular matches); children and dogs welcome, closed lunchtimes Mon-Thurs, otherwise open all day. *(Hugh Roberts)*

KESWICK   NY2623
Dog & Gun (017687) 73463
Lake Road; off top end of Market Square; CA12 5BT Smartly furnished beamed town pub; button-back leather banquettes, stools and small round tables on light wood flooring, collection of striking mountain

photographs, reasonably priced hearty food including signature goulash (served in two sizes), a house beer from Keswick (Woof & Bang), Cumbrian Legendary, Theakstons and five guests, friendly helpful staff, log fire; occasional quiz nights, poker Weds; children till 9.30pm and dogs welcome, beer garden, open (and food) all day, can get very busy in season. *(Margaret and Peter Staples)*

KESWICK   NY2623
George (017687) 72076
St Johns Street; CA12 5AZ Handsome 17th-c coaching inn with open-plan main bar and attractive dark-panelled side room; old-fashioned settles and modern banquettes under black beams, log fires, four Jennings ales and a couple of guests kept well, ten wines by the glass, generous home-made food including signature cow pie and gluten-free dishes, friendly helpful service, restaurant; background music, daily papers; children welcome in eating areas, dogs in bar, 12 bedrooms, open all day. *(Andrew Vincent)*

KESWICK   NY2624
Inn on the Square 0800 840 1247
Market Square; CA12 5JF Hotel with contemporary scandinavian-influenced décor; enjoyable food in front and back bars or steakhouse restaurant, good choice of wines and cocktails, well kept ales such as Keswick, efficient friendly service; children and dogs (in bar areas) welcome, 34 bedrooms, open all day. *(Andrew Vincent)*

KESWICK   NY2624
Pheasant (017687) 72219
Crosthwaite Road (A66, 1 mile out); CA12 5PP Small 17th-c beamed roadside local; good choice of popular home-made food at reasonable prices, well kept Jennings and guests, efficient friendly service, open fire, dining room; children (if eating) and dogs (in bar) welcome, a few picnic-sets out at front, beer garden up steps behind, bedrooms, near ancient church of St Kentigern, open all day.
(Nick and Meriel Cox)

KESWICK   NY2623
Royal Oak (017687) 74584
Main Street; CA12 5HZ Refurbished 18th-c coaching house; Thwaites ales, decent wines and good choice of popular food, friendly service; children and dogs welcome, comfortable bedrooms, open (and food) all day.
(Andrew Vincent)

KESWICK   NY2421
Swinside Inn (017687) 78253
Newlands Valley, just SW; CA12 5UE Updated 18th-c pub in peaceful valley setting; two bars and various dining areas, open fires, well kept ales including one named for them (Double Sunset), good reasonably priced pubby food from lunchtime sandwiches up, friendly helpful staff; background music, free wi-fi; children and

dogs (in some parts) welcome, tables in garden and on upper and lower terraces with fine views across to the high crags and fells around Rosedale Pike, six bedrooms, big breakfast, open all day. *(Tina and David Woods-Taylor, Richard Tilbrook)*

KIRKBY LONSDALE   SD6178

Orange Tree (01524) 271716

Fairbank B6254; LA6 2BD Family-run inn acting as tap for Kirkby Lonsdale brewery, well kept guest ales too, a real cider and good choice of wines and bottled belgian beers, carpeted beamed bar with central wooden servery, sporting cartoons and old range, hearty reasonably priced food in back dining room, efficient young staff; background music, pool and darts; children and dogs welcome, comfortable bedrooms (some in building next door), open all day. *(Steve Whalley)*

KIRKOSWALD   NY5641

Fetherston Arms (01768) 898284

The Square; CA10 1DQ Busy old stone inn with cosy bar and various dining areas; enjoyable food at reasonable prices including good home-made pies, interesting range of well kept changing beers, friendly helpful staff; children and dogs welcome, bedrooms, nice Eden Valley village. *(Ben and Jenny Settle)*

LANGDALE   NY2906

Sticklebarn (015394) 37356

By car park for Stickle Ghyll; LA22 9JU Glorious views from this roomy and busy Langdale Valley walkers'/climbers' bar owned and run by the NT; up to five well kept changing ales and a real cider, shortish choice of enjoyable home-made food (some meat from next-door farm), mountaineering photographs, two woodburners; background music (live Sat in season), films shown Tues in upstairs function room, quiz Sun; children, dogs and boots welcome, big terrace with inner verandah, outside pizza oven and fire pit, open (and food) all day, shuts in winter at 6pm (9pm weekends). *(Nicola and Nigel Matthews)*

LEVENS   SD4885

Hare & Hounds (015395) 60004

Off A590; LA8 8PN Welcoming 16th-c village pub handy for Sizergh Castle (NT); five well kept changing local ales and good home-made pub food including burgers and pizzas, partly panelled low-beamed lounge bar, front tap room with open fire and further seating down steps, also a barn dining room; Weds winter quiz; children, walkers and dogs welcome, disabled loo, good views from front terrace, four bedrooms, open (and food) all day. *(Mr and Mrs Richard Osborne)*

LINDALE   SD4180

★**Royal Oak** (015395) 32882

The Gill; LA11 6LX Nicely presented open-plan village pub with three distinct areas; very good freshly made food (best to book) including chargrills and weekly specials, friendly helpful staff, well kept Robinsons ales, Weston's Stowford Press cider and good range of wines; children welcome, small garden behind, open all day Fri-Sun, closed lunchtime Mon and Tues. *(Michael Butler)*

LORTON   NY1526

★**Wheatsheaf** (01900) 85199

B5289 Buttermere–Cockermouth; CA13 9UW Good local atmosphere in neatly furnished bar with two log fires and vibrant coloured walls, Jennings ales, regularly changing guests and several good value wines, popular home-made food (all day Sun) from sandwiches up, smallish restaurant (best to book), affable hard-working landlord and friendly staff; children and dogs welcome, tables out behind and campsite, open all day Fri-Sun. *(Charles and Maddie Bishop)*

LOW HESKET   NY4646

Rose & Crown (01697) 473346

A6 Carlisle–Penrith; CA4 0HG Welcoming 18th-c coaching inn with split-level interior; enjoyable home-made food including vegetarian menu, Jennings Bitter and guests, good service, pitched-roof dining room with railway memorabilia and central oak tree; background music, TV; children welcome, closed Mon and lunchtimes apart from Sun. *(Max Simons)*

MELMERBY   NY6137

Shepherds (01768) 889064

A686 Penrith–Alston; CA10 1HF Comfortable and welcoming 18th-c split-level country pub under newish management; beamed and flagstoned bar with woodburner, barn dining room, good food cooked by landlord-chef including themed nights, three well kept ales such as Allendale, Hawkshead and Tirril; children and dogs welcome, a few tables out at front, closed Mon, Tues and lunchtimes Weds-Fri. *(A J and R J Allen)*

MUNGRISDALE   NY3630

Mill Inn (017687) 79632

Off A66 Penrith–Keswick, 1 mile W of A5091 Ullswater turn-off; CA11 0XR Part 17th-c pub in fine setting below fells with wonderful surrounding walks; neatly kept bar with old millstone built into counter, traditional dark wood furnishings, hunting pictures and woodburner in stone fireplace, well kept Robinsons ales and good range of malt whiskies, enjoyable traditional food

---

Virtually all pubs in this book sell wine by the glass. We mention wines if they are a cut above the average.

from lunchtime sandwiches/rarebits up, friendly staff, separate dining room; darts and dominoes, pool in winter; children and dogs welcome, wheelchair access, seats in garden by river, six bedrooms, open (and food) all day. *(Mark Millon)*

NETHER WASDALE   NY1204
★**Strands** (01946) 726237
SW of Wast Water; CA20 1ET Lovely spot below the remote high fells around Wast Water; own-brew beers and popular good value food from changing menu, well cared-for high-beamed main bar with woodburner, smaller public bar with pool and table football, separate dining room, pleasant staff and relaxed friendly atmosphere; background and occasional live music; children and dogs welcome, neat garden with terrace and belvedere, 14 bedrooms, good breakfast, open all day. *(George Sanderson)*

NEWBIGGIN   NY5649
Blue Bell (01768) 896615
B6413; CA8 9DH Small L-shaped village pub, friendly and unpretentious, with a changing local ale and enjoyable pubby food cooked by landlady, fireplace on right with woodburner; darts and pool; children welcome, good Eden Valley walks, closed weekday lunchtimes. *(Julian Thorpe)*

NEWBY BRIDGE   SD3686
★**Swan** (015395) 31681
Just off A590; LA12 8NB Substantial hotel (extended 17th-c coaching house) in lovely setting by River Leven and its fine old bridge; busy low-ceilinged bar with scrubbed tables on bare boards, cheerful upholstered dining chairs and window seats, decorative plates around log fire in small iron fireplace, stools against counter serving ales such as Jennings, Cumbrian Legendary and Marstons, good popular food from varied menu, more space and another log fire towards the back, main hotel also has a sizeable restaurant; background music; children (till 7pm) and dogs (in bar) welcome, iron-work tables and chairs on riverside terrace, well equipped contemporary bedrooms plus luxury cottages, open (and food) all day. *(John Evans, Cecily and Steven Evans, Derek Stafford)*

PAPCASTLE   NY1131
Belle Vue (01900) 821388
Belle Vue; CA13 0NT Revamped beamed corner pub-restaurant (former Spotted Pig) under new management; good well presented food including deals, cumbrian ales such as Jennings, decent wines and interesting selection of whiskies and gins, friendly helpful service; background music; children welcome, closed Tues. *(Alan Eaves)*

PATTERDALE   NY3915
White Lion (017684) 82214
A592 opposite village shop; CA11 0NW Tall narrow roadside inn with ready market of walkers and climbers (can get very busy especially in season); large helpings of enjoyable pub food and well kept beers such as Marstons and Theakstons, friendly hard-working staff, traditional flagstoned bar, open fires; children and dogs welcome, seven bedrooms (five ensuite), open (and food) all day. *(Tina and David Woods-Taylor)*

RAVENSTONEDALE   NY7401
Fat Lamb (015396) 23242
Crossbank; A683 Sedbergh–Kirkby Stephen; CA17 4LL Isolated inn surrounded by great scenery and lovely walks; comfortable old-fashioned feel, pews in beamed bar with fire in traditional black range, interesting local photographs and bird plates, propeller from 1930s biplane over servery, good choice of enjoyable food from sharing boards to daily specials, can eat in bar or separate dining room (less character), well kept Black Sheep or Pennine, decent wines and around 60 malt whiskies, friendly helpful staff; background music; children and dogs welcome, disabled facilities, tables out by nature reserve pastures, 12 bedrooms, open all day, food all day weekends. *(Nicola and Nigel Matthews)*

RAVENSTONEDALE   NY7204
★**Kings Head** (015396) 23050
Pub visible from A685 W of Kirkby Stephen; CA17 4NH Sizeable riverside inn with opened-up beamed rooms, rugs on big flagstones and attractive array of wooden chairs and cushioned settles, prints on grey-painted walls, double-sided woodburner and another log fire in raised fireplace, similarly furnished dining room, Theakstons Best, a couple of guests and eight wines by the glass, popular interesting food, friendly staff, games room with darts and local photographs; background music; children and dogs (in bar) welcome, picnic-sets by the river in fenced-off area, comfortable clean bedrooms, good surrounding walks, open (and food) all day; for sale, so may be changes. *(Mr and Mrs P R Thomas)*

ROSTHWAITE   NY2514
Scafell (017687) 77208
B5289 S of Keswick; CA12 5XB 19th-c hotel's big tile-floored back bar useful for walkers; weather forecast board and blazing log fire, up to five well kept local ales in season, 60 malt whiskies and enjoyable food from sandwiches up, afternoon teas, also cocktail bar/sun lounge and dining room, friendly helpful staff; background music,

---

pool; children and dogs welcome, tables out overlooking beck, 23 contemporary bedrooms, open all day. *(Brian and Anna Marsden)*

RYDAL   NY3606
Glen Rothay Hotel (015394) 34500
A591 Ambleside–Grasmere; LA22 9LR
Small 17th-c roadside hotel with cosy back Badger Bar, copper-topped tables, stools and benches, lots of interesting local prints, up to five well kept changing ales and varied choice of locally sourced food from good sandwiches up, nice coffee, beamed and panelled dining lounge with open fire, restaurant, friendly efficient service; unusual loos cut into the rock; children, walkers and dogs welcome, tables in pretty garden (resident badgers are fed at dusk), eight comfortable bedrooms, good breakfast, handy for William Wordsworth's house at Rydal Mount, open all day.
(John and Sylvia Harrop)

SANDFORD   NY7316
Sandford Arms (01768) 351121
Village and pub signposted just off A66 W of Brough; CA16 6NR Neatly modernised former 18th-c farmhouse in peaceful village; good choice of enjoyable food served by friendly helpful staff, L-shaped part-carpeted main bar with stripped beams and stonework, well kept ales such as Black Sheep, comfortable raised and balustraded eating area, more formal dining room and second flagstoned bar, woodburner; background music; children and dogs welcome, seats in front garden and covered courtyard, five bedrooms, closed Tues and lunchtime Weds. *(Miles Green)*

SANTON BRIDGE   NY1101
Bridge Inn (019467) 26221
Off A595 at Holmrook or Gosforth; CA19 1UX Old inn set in charming riverside spot with fell views; bustling beamed and timbered bar, some booths around stripped-pine tables, log fire, four well kept ales such as Jennings, enjoyable food (booking advised) including blackboard specials and Sun carvery, friendly helpful staff, separate dining room and small reception hall with open fire; background music, newspapers and free wi-fi, World's Biggest Liar competition (Nov); children and dogs (in bar) welcome, seats outside by quiet road, plenty of walks, 16 bedrooms, open (and food) all day, breakfast for non-residents. *(Freddie and Sarah Banks)*

SATTERTHWAITE   SD3392
Eagles Head (01229) 860237
S edge of village; LA12 8LN Nice little pub prettily placed on edge of beautiful Grizedale Forest (visitor centre nearby); low black beams and comfortable furnishings, antlers, horsebrasses, decorative plates and other odds and ends, old tiled floor,

woodburner, four well kept changing cumbrian ales, popular pubby food from shortish menu including good home-made pies, friendly welcoming staff; occasional live music, local artwork for sale; children, dogs and muddy boots welcome, picnic-sets in attractive tree-shaded courtyard garden, open all day in summer, closed Weds in winter. *(Charles Welch)*

SCALES   NY3426
White Horse (017687) 79883
A66 W of Penrith; CA12 4SY Traditional Lakeland pub in lovely setting below Blencathra; log fire in flagstoned beamed bar, little snug and another room with black range, three local ales and good pubby food (all day weekends); board games, free wi-fi; children and dogs welcome, picnic-sets out in front, bunkhouse, open all day. *(Jimmy)*

SEATHWAITE   SD2295
Newfield Inn (01229) 716208
Duddon Valley, near Ulpha (not Seathwaite in Borrowdale); LA20 6ED Friendly 16th-c whitewashed stone cottage in quiet country setting; bar with unusual slate floor and interesting pictures, woodburner, four well kept changing local beers and good reasonably priced home-made food from sandwiches up; children and dogs welcome, tables in nice garden with hill views and play area, good walks, open (and food) all day. *(Mrs Edna Jones)*

SEDBERGH   SD6592
Black Bull (015396) 20264
Main Street; LA10 5BL Old coaching inn stylishly refurbished under present management; highly rated food using local suppliers from bar snacks and pubby choices up (more restauranty evening menu with some asian influences), well chosen wines, ales such as Black Sheep along with craft kegs, friendly helpful staff, wood flooring, some exposed stonework and reclaimed timber cladding, large photographs of local landscapes, banquettes and logburners; children welcome, sunny garden behind, 18 comfortable modern bedrooms named after fells, good breakfast, open all day.
(Maria and Hugh Lazonby)

SEDBERGH   SD6592
Dalesman (01539) 621183
Main Street; LA10 5BN Stone-built corner inn with three modernised linked rooms; good freshly made food from sandwiches and stone-baked pizzas up, friendly prompt service, five well kept local ales, plenty of wines by the glass and good range of other drinks, stripped stone and beams, central woodburner; background music; children welcome, no dogs inside, chunky picnic-sets out in front by road, five bedrooms and a self-catering cottage, open (and food) all day, breakfast/brunch from 8am. *(Miles Green)*

TORVER   SD2894
Church House (015394) 49159
A593/A5084 S of Coniston; LA21 8AZ
Friendly 14th-c coaching house; pubby
bar with heavy beams (some painted),
straightforward tables and chairs on slate
floors, Lakeland bric-a-brac and big log
fire in sizeable stone fireplace, enjoyable
home-made food (all day weekends)
from sandwiches and sharing plates up,
four changing ales and seven wines by
the glass from barrel-fronted counter,
comfortable lounge and separate dining
room; occasional live music; children and
dogs (in bar) welcome, lawned garden,
four bedrooms and two bunk rooms, also
standing for five caravans/motor homes,
good nearby walks to Lake Coniston, open
all day. *(Julian Thorpe)*

TORVER   SD2894
Wilson Arms (015394) 41237
A593; LA21 8BB Old family-run roadside
inn with adjoining deli; beams, nice log fire
and one or two modern touches, well kept
cumbrian ales and good locally sourced
food cooked to order in bar or dining room,
friendly service; free wi-fi; children and dogs
welcome, hill views (including Old Man of
Coniston) from tables in large garden, seven
bedrooms and three holiday cottages, open
(and food) all day. *(Julian Thorpe)*

TROUTBECK   NY4103
Mortal Man (015394) 33193
*A592 N of Windermere; Upper Road;
LA23 1PL* Popular 17th-c lakeland inn;
beamed and partly panelled bar with cosy
room off, log fires, well kept local ales
including a house beer from Hawkshead,
several wines by the glass and well liked
food in bar and picture-window restaurant;
folk night Sun, open mike Tues, quiz Weds,
storytelling Thurs, free wi-fi; children and
dogs welcome, great views from sunny
garden, lovely village and surrounding walks,
bedrooms, open (and food) all day.
(Charles and Maddie Bishop)

TROUTBECK   NY4103
★ Queens Head (015394) 32404
A592 N of Windermere; LA23 1PW
Popular 17th-c beamed coaching inn well
restored after devastating 2014 fire; some
original features remain such as the four-
poster bar and stone fireplaces, but generally
an airier feel with good quality oak furniture
on wood and flagstoned floors, enjoyable
sensibly priced food from hot or cold
sandwiches and pub favourites up, well kept
Robinsons ales, a dozen wines by the glass
and good selection of whiskies/gins, friendly
efficient service; background music; children,
walkers and dogs welcome, seats outside
with fine views across to Applethwaite Moors,
ten comfortably refurbished bedrooms
(some in barn opposite), open (and food) all

day, kitchen shuts 7pm Sun. *(Hugh Roberts,
Margaret and Peter Staples, Christian Mole,
Graham and Elizabeth Hargreaves)*

TROUTBECK   NY3827
Troutbeck Inn (017684) 83635
A5091/A66; CA11 0SJ Former railway
hotel with small bar, lounge and log-fire
restaurant, a couple of Jennings ales and
good food from pub standards up, efficient
friendly service; children and dogs (in
bar) welcome, seven bedrooms plus three
self-catering cottages in converted stables,
open all day weekends, from 2.30pm
weekdays, winter hours may differ.
(Andrew Vincent)

ULDALE   NY2436
Snooty Fox (016973) 71479
*Village signed off B5299 W of Caldbeck;
CA7 1HA* Comfortable and welcoming
two-bar village inn; ample helpings of good
quality home-cooked food (not Weds) using
local ingredients, up to four well kept
changing ales including a summer brew
named for the pub, decent selection of
whiskies, friendly attentive staff, fox hunting
memorabilia; winter pool table, free wi-fi;
children welcome in dining areas, dogs in
snug, nice location with garden at back,
three bedrooms, closed lunchtimes apart
from Sun. *(Ben and Jenny Settle)*

ULVERSTON   SD2878
★ Farmers (01229) 584469
Market Place; LA12 7BA Convivial
refurbished town pub opposite the market
cross; front bar with comfortable leather
armchairs and sofas, original fireplace,
Cumberland Legendary Loweswater Gold
and three quickly changing guests, a dozen
wines by the glass, good varied choice of
popular fair-priced food from baguettes and
deli boards up, cocktail bar leading to big
raftered dining area with seating booths on
either side (children here only); background
music, Thurs quiz; colourful hanging baskets
and tubs on front terrace warmed by a
fire pit, Thurs and Sat market days (pub
very busy then), self-catering apartments/
cottages nearby, open all day from 9am for
breakfast. *(Michael Butler)*

ULVERSTON   SD2878
Mill (01229) 581384
Mill Street; LA12 7EB Converted 19th-c
flour mill on three floors; ground-floor bar
with huge waterwheel behind glass, mix of
furniture including leather armchairs and
sofas on wood floor, warming logburners,
around ten real ales including Lancaster
(brewery owns the pub), good wines and
fine array of whiskies, gins and brandies,
spiral stairs up to restaurant and second bar
with terrace, very good well presented food
from sandwiches and snacks up, evening
cocktail lounge on top floor (Fri, Sat),
friendly efficient young staff; live music and

quiz nights; children and dogs welcome, open all day. *(Chris Taylor)*

UNDERBARROW
SD4692

Black Labrador (015395) 68234

From centre of Kendal at town hall, turn left into Beast Banks signed for Underbarrow, then follow Underbarrow Road; LA8 8HQ Friendly village local with open-plan beamed bar, mix of furniture including leather sofas on stone floor, woodburner, well kept Hawkshead and local guests, good choice of enjoyable freshly prepared food from snacks and deli boards up, new dining extension; free wi-fi; children and dogs welcome, picnic-sets and covered balcony outside, handy for walkers, closed Tues. *(Hugh Roberts)*

WASDALE HEAD
NY1807

Wasdale Head Inn (019467) 26229

NE of Wast Water; CA20 1EX Mountain hotel worth knowing for its stunning fellside setting; roomy walkers' bar with welcoming fire, several local ales and good choice of wines, ample helpings of enjoyable pubby food; residents' bar, lounge and panelled restaurant; children and dogs welcome, several tables outside, nine bedrooms, self-catering apartments in converted barn and camping, open all day. *(Michael Butler)*

WETHERAL
NY4654

Wheatsheaf (01228) 560686

Handy for M6 junctions 42/43; CA4 8HD Popular 19th-c pub in pretty village; three well kept local ales and enjoyable home-made food including daily specials, good friendly service; Tues quiz, sports TV; children and dogs welcome, picnic-sets in small garden, open all day, no food Mon, Tues. *(Charles Welch)*

WHITEHAVEN
NX9718

Gin & Beer It (01946) 329354

Market Place; CA28 7JB Friendly and relaxed little bar with six craft beers (many more in bottles and cans), over 50 gins and decent range of wines by the glass, nice cheese/charcuterie boards, eclectic mix of furniture on original tiled floor, exposed stone and wood-clad walls; unobtrusive background music, board games; dogs welcome, closed Sun-Tues and lunchtimes. *(Sharon Butler)*

WINDERMERE
SD4198

★**Crafty Baa** (015394) 88002

Victoria Street, beside the Queens; LA23 1AB Small atmospheric bar with great selection of craft beers on tap and in bottles (listed on blackboards), good range of other drinks too including decent coffee, enjoyable food from snacks to more substantial cheese and charcuterie combinations served on slates, friendly knowledgeable staff, rustic décor with bare boards, exposed stone walls and log fire, recycled materials and plenty of quirky touches, lots more room upstairs and in new cosy extension serving real ales and pies; background and live music; dogs welcome (theirs is Henry), a few seats out at front, open (and food) all day. *(Penny and David Shepherd)*

WREAY
NY4349

Plough (016974) 75770

Village signed from A6 N of Low Hesket; CA4 0RL Welcoming 18th-c beamed pub in pretty village; modernised split-level interior with pine tables and chairs on wood or flagstone floors, some exposed stonework, woodburner, good choice of enjoyable freshly prepared food (not Mon) including specials, well kept Hawkshead and a couple of guests from brick-fronted canopied bar, efficient friendly service; Mon quiz; children welcome, closed Mon lunchtime and Tues. *(Julian Thorpe)*

YANWATH
NY5128

Gate Inn (01768) 862386

2.25 miles from M6 junction 40; A66 towards Brough, then right on A6, right on B5320, then follow village signpost; CA10 2LF Cheerful family now running this 17th-c pub and you're sure of a friendly welcome; cosy bar with country pine and dark wood furniture, lots of brasses on beams, nightlights on tables, woodburner in attractive stone inglenook, real ales such as Black Sheep and Eden, Weston's cider and decent wines by the glass, good food cooked by landlord-chef including daily specials, restaurant with oak floor, panelling and another woodburner; background music, board games; children and dogs welcome (their jack russell is Rocky), terrace and garden tables under parasols, closed Tues, Weds. *(Graham and Elizabeth Hargreaves, Simon and Sue Lamb)*

Derbyshire

BRADWELL

Samuel Fox 🍴★ 🍷 🛏

SK1782 Map 7

(01433) 621562 – www.samuelfox.co.uk

B6049; S33 9JT

Friendly pub in the Hope Valley with real ales and fine food, good service and neat bar; comfortable bedrooms

One of the main draws here is, of course, the modern british food cooked by the landlord – though plenty of customers drop in for a pint and a chat after walking in the surrounding Peak District National Park. The open-plan bar and interlinked dining room have red and dogtooth upholstered tub chairs grouped around tables on striped carpet or wooden flooring, country scenes hang on papered walls above a grey dado, curtains are neatly swagged and there are several open brick fireplaces. Intrepid Blonde and Pennine Best Bitter on handpump, 15 wines by the glass from a good list, and a farm cider served by helpful, courteous staff. The neat restaurant is similarly furnished but with red plush dining chairs. At the front of the building, cream metal seats are arranged around small ornamental trees and there are some wooden seats too. Bedrooms are carefully furnished and quiet. No dogs inside. Wheelchair access.

🍴 The chef-landlord cooks the excellent food: lunchtime choices such as 'boozy bunny' salami with pickles and toast, goats cheese salad with amaretto and roasted butternut squash, chickpea fritters with beetroot aioli and hummus, and fillet of bream on a ragoût of mussels, saffron potatoes and root vegetables, and evening dishes such as scorched cured sea trout with fennel and orange, chicken breast with colcannon, cauliflower and chorizo and feather blade of beef with a fricassée of mushrooms and shallots with red wine sauce, and puddings such as coconut rum-infused pannacotta with mango and passion fruit and white chocolate cheesecake with rhubarb and pistachios. Please note, you can book lunchtime food in advance Wednesday to Saturday; they also offer a two- and three-course early bird menu (6-7pm weekdays and Saturday) and a two- and three-course evening menu. *Benchmark main dish: pork belly with cauliflower, chorizo and cider sauce £19.00. Two-course evening meal £29.00.*

Free house ~ Licensee James Duckett ~ Real ale ~ Open 6-11 Weds-Sat; 1-4 Sun; closed Mon, Tues (except for residents); lunchtimes except Sun; first two weeks Jan ~ Bar food 6-9 Weds-Sat; 1-4 Sun ~ Restaurant ~ Children welcome ~ Wi-fi ~ Bedrooms: /£135
Recommended by Diana and Bertie Farr, Alan and Linda Blackmore, Molly and Stewart Lindsay, Brian Dunn, Colin and Daniel Gibbs, Geoff and Ann Marston, Alexandra and Richard Clay, Miles Green

CHELMORTON

SK1170 Map 7

Church Inn ◀ £ ⇔

(01298) 85319 – www.thechurchinn.co.uk

Village signposted off A5270, between A6 and A515 SE of Buxton; keep on up through village towards church; SK17 9SL

Cosy, convivial inn beautifully set in High Peak walking country, with good value food and well kept ales

As ever, we only get warm praise from our readers on all aspects of this charming inn. The hands-on, long-serving licensees keep the chatty, low-ceilinged bar spic and span with its open fire and built-in cushioned benches and simple chairs around polished cast-iron-framed tables (a couple still with their squeaky sewing treadles). Shelves of books, Tiffany-style lamps and house plants in the curtained windows, atmospheric Dales photographs and prints, and a coal-effect stove in the stripped-stone end wall all add a cosy feel. Abbeydale Moonshine, Marstons Pedigree and Saddle Tank and a couple of guests on handpump and ten wines by the glass; darts in a tile-floored games area on the left and board games. The inn is opposite a mainly 18th-c church and is prettily tucked into woodland with fine views over the village and hills beyond from good teak tables on a two-level terrace.

Tasty food includes sandwiches, prawn cocktail, black pudding fritters with spicy home-made chutney, mixed bean chilli, lasagne, chicken breast in stilton sauce, beef casserole with dumplings, salmon fillet with white wine and prawn sauce, sirloin steak with onion rings and chips, and puddings. *Benchmark main dish: rabbit pie £13.95. Two-course evening meal £20.00.*

Free house ~ Licensees Julie and Justin Satur ~ Real ale ~ Open 12-3, 6-11; 12-11 Sat; 12-10.30 Sun ~ Bar food 12-2.30, 6-8.30; 12-8.30 Fri-Sun ~ Restaurant ~ Children welcome ~ Dogs allowed in bar ~ Wi-fi *Recommended by Rob Yates, Jim King, Charles Welch, Jo Garnett, Mike Swan, Harvey Brown*

CHINLEY

SK0382 Map 7

Old Hall ★ ◀ ⇔

(01663) 750529 – www.old-hall-inn.co.uk

Village signposted off A6 (very sharp turn) E of New Mills; also off A624 N of Chapel-en-le-Frith; Whitehough Head Lane, off B6062; SK23 6EJ

Fine range of ales and ciders in splendid building with lots to look at and good country food; comfortable bedrooms

Even if you're just dropping in for a drink, do take a peek at the surprisingly grand dining room with its great stone chimney soaring into high eaves, refectory tables on a parquet floor, lovely old mullioned windows and a splendid minstrels' gallery. The warm bar (basically four small friendly rooms opened into a single area tucked behind a massive central chimney) contains open fires, broad flagstones, red patterned carpet, sturdy country tables and a couple of long pews and various other seats. Marstons Wainwright and guests from breweries such as Abbeydale, Kelham Island, Marble, Peak, Phoenix, Storm, Thornbridge, Whim and Wincle on handpump, as well as some interesting lagers on tap, 20 malt whiskies, 40 gins and six cask ciders, a rare range of bottled ciders and around 50 bottled (mostly belgian) beers. They hold a beer festival with music in September. Also, around a dozen new world wines by the glass and friendly, helpful service. The pretty walled garden has picnic-sets under sycamore trees. Some of the attractive bedrooms look over the garden and there are also a couple of self-catering cottages.

Rewarding food includes sandwiches, scallops with black pudding and jerusalem artichoke, crispy chicken thigh with carrot salad and quail eggs, white onion risotto with caramelised onion purée, burger with toppings, coleslaw and triple-cooked chips, smoked bacon, pork and sage sausages with mash and red wine gravy, lancashire hotpot, duck breast with dauphinoise potatoes, beetroot and chard, hake with broad beans, bacon and charred baby gem, and puddings such as toffee crème brûlée and fruit and nut chocolate brownie with Hilly Billy ice-cream. *Benchmark main dish: steak in ale pudding £14.00. Two-course evening meal £20.00.*

Free house ~ Licensee Daniel Capper ~ Real ale ~ Open 12-11 (midnight Sat) ~ Bar food 12-2, 5-9 (9.30 Fri, Sat); 12-7.30 Sun ~ Restaurant ~ Children welcome ~ Dogs allowed in bar ~ Wi-fi ~ Bedrooms: £79/£110 *Recommended by David and Doreen Beattie, Gordon and Patricia Gorringe, Lorna and Jeff Mason, Malcolm and Pauline Pellatt, Edward May*

FENNY BENTLEY
SK1750 Map 7

Coach & Horses

(01335) 350246 – www.coachandhorsesfennybentley.co.uk
A515 N of Ashbourne; DE6 1LB

Cosy inn with pretty country furnishings, roaring open fires and food all day

The traditional interior here has all the trappings you'd expect of a 17th-c country coaching inn, from roaring log fires, exposed brick hearths and flagstone floors to black beams hung with pewter mugs, and hand-made pine furniture that includes wall settles with floral-print cushions. There's also a conservatory dining room and a cosy front dining room. Marstons Pedigree and a changing guest on handpump, a couple of farm ciders and seven wines by the glass; the landlord is knowledgeable about malt whiskies and he stocks around two dozen; quiet background music. A side garden by an elder tree (with views across fields) has seats and tables, and there are modern tables and chairs under cocktail parasols on a front roadside terrace. It's a short walk from the Tissington Trail, a popular cycling/walking path along a former railway line (best joined at the nearby picture-book village of Tissington). No dogs allowed inside.

 Well thought-of food includes chicken liver pâté with red onion marmalade, sharing deli board, wild mushroom stroganoff, gammon with egg or pineapple, sea bass on crushed potatoes with prawn and lemon butter, chicken breast stuffed with haggis and whisky and black pepper sauce, sirloin steak with onion rings, chips and a choice of sauce, barnsley lamb chop with port, redcurrant and rosemary sauce, and puddings such as lemon meringue roulade and honeycomb and vanilla cheesecake. *Benchmark main dish: lamb casserole £12.95. Two-course evening meal £20.00.*

Free house ~ Licensees John and Matthew Dawson ~ Real ale ~ Open 11-11; 12-10.30 Sun ~ Bar food 12-9 ~ Restaurant ~ Children welcome ~ Wi-fi *Recommended by David and Leone Lawson, Frank and Marcia Pelling, Frances Parsons, Nicola and Holly Lyons*

GREAT LONGSTONE
SK1971 Map 7

Crispin

(01629) 640237 – www.thecrispingreatlongstone.co.uk
Main Street; village signed from A6020, N of Ashford in the Water; DE45 1TZ

Spotlessly kept pub with emphasis on good, fair-priced food

As this is open all day, customers enjoying the beautiful surrounding countryside drop in and out for refreshment. Décor throughout is traditional: brass or copper implements, decorative plates, horsebrasses on beams in the red ceiling, cushioned built-in wall benches and upholstered chairs and stools around polished tables on red carpet – and a warming fire. A corner area (with a woodburning stove) is snugly partitioned off and there's a separate, more formal dining room on the right; darts, board games and maybe faint background music. Robinsons Dizzy Blonde, Trooper and Unicorn, Thornbridge Jaipur IPA and a guest beer on handpump, Weston's Old Rosie cider and quite a choice of wines and whiskies. In warm weather there are seats in the garden and picnic-sets out in front (one under a heated canopy) set well back above the quiet lane. Disabled access.

🍴 Pubby food includes a two- and three-course lunchtime deal plus sandwiches, omelettes, home-made pies, beer-battered fish and chips, chilli con carne, curries, fish pie, dressed crab, steaks from the local butcher, and puddings. *Benchmark main dish: steak and kidney pie £13.95. Two-course evening meal £20.00.*

Robinsons ~ Tenant Paul Rowlinson ~ Real ale ~ Open 12-3, 6-11; 12-11 Sat; 12-10.30 Sun ~ Bar food 12-2.30, 6-9 ~ Restaurant ~ Children welcome ~ Dogs welcome ~ Wi-fi
Recommended by Andrew Wall, Toby Jones, Patricia Healey, Mike and Sarah Abbot, Victoria and James Sargeant, Sophie Ellison

HASSOP
SK2272 Map 7

Old Eyre Arms
(01629) 640390 – www.oldeyrearms.co.uk
B6001 N of Bakewell; DE45 1NS

Comfortable old farmhouse with long-serving owners, decent food and beer, and pretty views from the garden

In summer, the hanging baskets in front of this 17th-c coaching inn are lovely and the delightful garden (with its gurgling fountain) looks straight out to fine Peak District countryside. The low-ceilinged beamed rooms are snug and cosy with log fires and traditional furnishings that include cushioned oak settles, comfortable plush chairs, a longcase clock, old pictures and lots of brass and copper. The tap room, snug and lounge are similarly decorated with cushioned oak benches, old pictures and an impressive collection of brass and copper; the tap room also has a fine display of teapots. Abbeydale Deception, Peak Chatsworth Gold and Swift Nick, Sheffield Crucible Best and Thornbridge Crackendale and Lord Marples on handpump, good wines by the glass, ten gins, 20 malt whiskies and farm cider; background music. Above the stone fireplace in the lounge is a painting of the Eyre coat of arms. Chatsworth House and Haddon Hall are both close by, as is the Monsal Trail cycling/walking path.

🍴 A good choice of food includes twice-baked goats cheese soufflé, treacle-cured salmon with soda bread, vegetable risotto, local sausages and mash with onion gravy, slow-cooked shoulder of lamb, shepherd's pie, burger with toppings and onion rings, chicken kiev with coleslaw and frites, and puddings such as pear and chocolate crumble and bakewell tart with crème fraîche. *Benchmark main dish: lobster and crayfish ravioli with lobster bisque £14.50. Two-course evening meal £21.00.*

Free house ~ Licensees Sian Faxton and Lee Burgin ~ Real ale ~ Open 12-11 ~ Bar food 12-3, 6-9; 12-9 Sun ~ Children welcome ~ Dogs welcome ~ Wi-fi
Recommended by Colin and Daniel Gibbs, Caroline Prescott, Nicola and Stuart Parsons, Brian and Susan Wylie, Lenny and Ruth Walters

---

Bedroom prices are for high summer. Even then you may get reductions for more than one night, or (outside tourist areas) weekends. Winter special rates are common, and many inns reduce bedroom prices if you have a full evening meal.

HATHERSAGE

SK2380 Map 7

Plough 🌟 ◑ ♀ 🛏

(01433) 650319 – www.theploughinn-hathersage.co.uk

Leadmill; B6001 towards Bakewell; S32 1BA

• •

Derbyshire Dining Pub of the Year

Comfortable dining pub with well presented food, beer and wine and seats in a waterside garden; bedrooms

This is an immaculately kept 16th-c inn in the Peak District National Park, with cosy and traditionally furnished rooms. There are bright tartan and oriental patterned carpets, rows of dark wooden chairs and tables plus a very long banquette, three woodburning stoves and terracotta walls hung with decorative plates. The neat dining room is slightly more formal. Abbeydale Moonshine, Bradfield Yorkshire Farmer and Timothy Taylors Landlord on handpump, 25 wines by the glass from a good list and 20 malt whiskies; quiet background music. The seats on the terrace have wonderful valley views and the nine-acre grounds are on the banks of the River Derwent where the pretty garden slopes down to the water. Well equipped bedrooms are in a barn conversion. Disabled access.

 As well as hot and cold sandwiches (until 5.30pm), the first class food includes ham hock and blue cheese terrine with fig and apple chutney, partridge breast with a parsnip tart, roast salsify and chestnuts, pizzas, mushroom and nut wellington with home-made mushroom ketchup, king prawn pasta with garlic, chilli and parsley butter, bacon-wrapped chicken breast with a cassoulet of cannellini beans, kale and smoked bacon velouté, turbot with a fricassée of jerusalem artichokes, porcini and truffle sauce, beef bourguignon with mustard mash and honey-roast parsnips, and puddings such as rhubarb and custard pannacotta and chocolate cake with boozy cherries and black cherry sorbet. *Benchmark main dish: 10oz rib-eye steak £23.00. Two-course evening meal £24.00.*

Free house ~ Licensees Bob, Cynthia and Elliott Emery ~ Real ale ~ Open 11-11; 12-10.30 Sun ~ Bar food 11.30-9 ~ Restaurant ~ Children welcome ~ Dogs welcome ~ Wi-fi ~ Bedrooms: $85/$130 *Recommended by Audrey and Paul Summers, Penny and David Shepherd, Christopher Mannings, Geoff and Ann Marston, Rona Mackinlay, Roy and Lindsey Fentiman*

HAYFIELD

SK0387 Map 7

Royal 🛏

(01663) 742721 – www.theroyalathayfield.com

Market Street; SK22 2EP

Big, bustling inn with fine panelled rooms, friendly service and thoughtful choice of drinks and food; bedrooms

After wandering around this attractive village, come here for lunch. The oak-panelled bar and lounge areas have open fires, a fine collection of seats from long settles with pretty scatter cushions through elegant upholstered dining chairs to tub chairs and chesterfields, and an assortment of solid tables on rugs and flagstones; house plants and daily papers as well. Howard Town Twenty Trees, Marstons Lancaster Bomber and Wainwright, Peak Bakewell Best Bitter and Wincle Lord Lucan on handpump, 11 wines by the glass, ten malt whiskies and two farm ciders; background music, TV and board games. Bedrooms are well appointed and comfortable and make an excellent base for exploring the Peak District; breakfasts are good too.

Pleasing food includes sandwiches (until 5pm), creamy garlic mushrooms on toasted ciabatta, salmon and spring onion fishcake with celeriac rémoulade, chicken satay with peanut sauce and sticky rice, sharing plates, macaroni cheese, a curry and a pie of the day, gammon with egg or pineapple fritter, salmon with lemon and chive butter, 10oz sirloin steak with peppercorn sauce, and puddings such as bakewell tart and a cheesecake of the day; steak night is Wednesday. *Benchmark main dish: steak in ale pie £11.95. Two-course evening meal £16.00.*

Free house ~ Licensees Mark and Lisa Miller ~ Real ale ~ Open 11-11 (11.30 Sat); 11-10.30 Sun ~ Bar food 12-8.30 (9 Sat); 12-7 Sun ~ Children welcome ~ Dogs allowed in bar ~ Wi-fi ~ Bedrooms: £65/£85 *Recommended by David and Doreen Beattie, Monica and Steph Evans, Max and Steph Warren, Bridget and Peter Gregson, John and Claire Masters*

KIRK IRETON
SK2650   Map 7
Barley Mow
(01335) 370306
Village signed off B5023 S of Wirksworth; DE6 3JP

Welcoming old inn that focuses on real ale and conversation; bedrooms

Since it first became an inn nearly 270 years ago, this handsome Jacobean stone house has changed little and it's been run by the same kindly landlady for over 40 years. The small main bar is relaxed and pubby with chatty locals, a roaring coal fire, antique settles on tiles or built into panelling, four slate-topped tables and shuttered mullioned windows. Another room has built-in cushioned pews on oak parquet and a small woodburning stove; a third has more pews, low beams and big landscape prints. In casks behind a modest wooden counter are five well kept ales including Whim Hartington IPA and four guests from breweries such as Abbeydale, Blue Monkey, Burton Bridge, Peak, Shardlow, Storm and Thornbridge; french wines and farm cider too. There are two pub dogs; the newfoundland is confined but does not like other dogs on her patch. Outside you'll find a good-sized garden, a couple of benches at the front and a shop in what used to be the stable. Bedrooms are comfortable, and readers enjoy the good breakfasts served in the stone-flagged kitchen. Clean dogs may be allowed in bedrooms, but not at breakfast; they must be kept on a lead at all times. This hilltop village is very pretty and within walking distance of Carsington Water.

 Very inexpensive filled rolls – at lunchtime only – are the only food.

Free house ~ Licensee Mary Short ~ Real ale ~ No credit cards ~ Open 12-2, 7-11 (10.30 Sun) ~ Bar food lunchtime rolls only ~ Well behaved, supervised children lunchtime only ~ Dogs allowed in bar ~ Bedrooms: £45/£65 *Recommended by Luke Morgan, Maddie Purvis, Belinda and Neil Garth, Chris and Sophie Baxter, Mike and Eleanor Anderson*

OVER HADDON
SK2066   Map 7
Lathkil
(01629) 812501 – www.lathkil.co.uk
Village and inn signposted from B5055 just SW of Bakewell; DE45 1JE

Traditional pub with long-serving owners (they've been here 38 years), super views, a good range of beers and well liked food; bedrooms

The warm, comfortable bedrooms here are used as a base to explore the Peak District National Park; breakfasts are hearty. On the right as you enter, an airy room has a nice fire in an attractively carved fireplace, old-fashioned settles with upholstered cushions, chairs, black beams, a delft shelf of blue and white plates and some original prints and photographs. On the left, the sunny spacious dining area doubles as an evening restaurant and there's a woodburning stove. Peak Swift Nick and Whim Hartington Bitter with guests such as Bradfield Farmers Blonde, Kelham Island Easy Rider and Raw Brown Cow on handpump, a reasonable range of wines (including mulled wine and prosecco), 40 gins and a decent selection of malt whiskies; they hold a beer, cider and gin festival in September. Background music, darts, TV and board games. Dogs are welcome, but muddy boots must be left in the lobby. The views are spectacular and can be enjoyed from seats in the walled garden and from windows in the bar.

Food is buffet-style at lunchtime and includes filled rolls, salads, a vegetarian dish, lasagne and venison casserole; evening choices might be whole mini camembert with pear chutney, calamari with garlic aioli, stilton and vegetable crumble, a pie of the day, chicken breast in tomato and mascarpone sauce with crispy chorizo, smoked haddock and mozzarella fishcakes with chive mayonnaise, sirloin steak with chips and a choice of sauce, and puddings. *Benchmark main dish: venison and blackberry casserole £10.25. Two-course evening meal £21.00.*

Free house ~ Licensee Alice Grigor-Taylor ~ Real ale ~ Open 11-11; 12-10.30 Sun ~ Bar food 12-2 (2.30 weekends), 6.30-8.30 ~ Restaurant ~ Children welcome ~ Dogs allowed in bar and bedrooms ~ Wi-fi ~ Bedrooms: £65/£99 *Recommended by John Arnold, Peter and Emma Kelly, Martine and Fabio Lockley, David Appleyard, Miles Green*

REPTON
Boot 🍺 ⛱

SK3027 Map 7

(01283) 346047 – www.thebootatrepton.co.uk
Boot Hill; DE65 6FT

Refurbished village pub with simply furnished bar and dining rooms, well regarded food, own-brews and seats outside; bedrooms

This carefully restored 17th-c inn is a big hit with our readers. The bustling bar has beams and bare floorboards, high stools around equally high wooden tables, plush chairs and cushioned benches, and a good range of drinks that includes their own-brewed Boot Beer: Beast, Bitter, Clod Hopper, ESB, IPA, Repton Cross and Tuffers Old Boots. Also, a guest from another changing brewery and several wines by the glass served by friendly, efficient young staff. There's a dining room with antique-style chairs and tables and big doors that open on to the courtyard, plus a second room down a couple of steps with a woodburning stove. The split-level walled garden has wooden chairs and tables under parasols. Bedrooms are light and airy, comfortable and attractively furnished.

Interesting food includes breakfasts (8-11am weekdays, 8-10.30am weekends), smoked salmon pâté with caper jam and pickled cucumber, linguine with basil pesto, ricotta and toasted hazelnuts, pulled pork burger with pickles and skin-on fries, pie of the day, corn-fed chicken breast stuffed with black garlic with parmesan arancini, lemon purée and onion sauce, sea trout with braised red lentils and curried shellfish sauce, dry-aged steak of the day with caesar salad and triple-cooked chips, and puddings such as bakewell tart with clotted cream ice-cream and dark chocolate ganache with passion-fruit curd and sorbet and peanut granola; they also offer a two- and three-course set lunch. *Benchmark main dish: fish dish of the day £17.00. Two-course evening meal £22.00.*

Free house ~ Licensee John Archer ~ Real ale ~ Open 8am-11pm ~ Bar food 12-2.30, 6-9 ~
Restaurant ~ Children welcome ~ Dogs allowed in bar ~ Wi-fi ~ Bedrooms: /£90
Recommended by Stephen Shepherd, Dave Skipp, Geoff and Ann Marston, Douglas Power,
Julian Thorpe

STANTON IN PEAK   SK2364 Map 7

Flying Childers ◼ £

(01629) 636333 – www.flyingchilders.com
Village signposted from B6056 S of Bakewell; Main Road; DE4 2LW

**Top notch beer and inexpensive simple bar lunches in a warm-hearted,
unspoilt pub; a delight**

Evolved from several stone cottages, this cottagey pub is in a beautiful
steep stone village and is named after an unbeatable racehorse of the
early 18th c. A snug little right-hand bar is the best place to enjoy your
Bombardier and guests from breweries such as Castle Rock, Matlock Wolds
Farm and Welbeck Abbey on handpump, and several wines by the glass.
This bar was virtually built for chat with its dark beam-and-plank ceiling,
dark wall settles, single pew, plain tables, a hot coal and log fire, a few team
photographs, dominoes and cribbage; background music. There's a bigger,
equally unpretentious bar on the left. As well as seats out in front, there
are picnic-sets in the well tended back garden. The surrounding walks are
marvellous and both walkers and their dogs are warmly welcomed; they
keep doggie treats behind the bar. Now that there is no longer a village shop,
the pub does sell some produce.

 Simple lunchtime-only food includes filled rolls and toasties, home-made soups
and weekend dishes such as rabbit casserole, home-made vegetarian burger,
local sausages, and home-made cake and bakewell pudding. *Benchmark main dish:
large bowl of soup £4.60.*

Free house ~ Licensees Richard and Sophie Wood ~ Real ale ~ No credit cards ~
Open 12-2 (3 weekends), 7-11; closed Mon and Tues lunchtimes ~ Bar food 12-2 ~
Children in top end of bar only ~ Dogs allowed in bar ~ Wi-fi *Recommended by Brian and*
Anna Marsden, Edward May, Barry and Daphne Gregson, Lorna and Jack Mulgrave, Jeremy
Snow, Max Simons

WOOLLEY MOOR   SK3661 Map 7

White Horse ⊙ ⏰ ♀ ⇖

(01246) 590319 – www.thewhitehorsewoolleymoor.co.uk
Badger Lane, off B6014 Matlock–Clay Cross; DE55 6FG

**Attractive old dining pub in pretty countryside with good food
and drinks; bedrooms**

Ogston Reservoir is just a couple of minutes' drive away, so many
customers here are walkers. The pub is neat and uncluttered, and
the bar, snug and dining room have wooden dining chairs and tables,
stools and leather sofas on flagstone or wooden floors, a woodburning
stove (in the bar), an open fire (in the dining room) and boldly patterned
curtains and blinds. Peak Bakewell Best Bitter and Chatsworth Gold
and a guest such as Dancing Duck Ay Up on handpump, nine gins
and 13 wines by the glass. In the front garden you'll find picnic-sets
under parasols on gravel and boules. The contemporary, well equipped
bedroom suites each have a private balcony and floor-to-ceiling windows
that give splendid views over the Amber Valley.

🍴⭐ Extremely good food includes scallops with black pudding, home-cured bacon and cauliflower purée, korean fried chicken with asian slaw, bean cassoulet with baba ganoush and flatbread, chicken breast with boulangère potatoes, charred onions and jus, salmon with noodles and ginger and coriander dressing, venison steak with parmentier potatoes and red wine sauce, and puddings such as mango parfait and coconut sorbet and meringue with caramelised lemon curd and lemon ice-cream. *Benchmark main dish: pork belly with spring onion mash and smoked bacon sauce £14.95. Two-course evening meal £20.00.*

Free house ~ Licensees David and Melanie Boulby ~ Real ale ~ Open 12-3, 6-11; 12-4 Sun; closed first three weeks Jan ~ Bar food 12-1.45, 6-8.45; 12-4 Sun ~ Restaurant ~ Children welcome ~ Wi-fi ~ Bedrooms: £139/£149 *Recommended by Derek and Sylvia Stephenson, Alistair Forsyth, Jo Garnett, Dr Simon Innes, Lindy Andrews, Harvey Brown*

Also Worth a Visit in Derbyshire

Besides the fully inspected pubs, you might like to try these pubs that have been recommended to us and described by readers. Do tell us what you think of them: feedback@goodguides.com

ALDERWASLEY SK3153
Bear (01629) 822585
Left off A6 at Ambergate on to Holly Lane (turns into Jackass Lane) then right at end (staggered crossroads); DE56 2RD Unspoilt country inn with beamed cottagey rooms, one with large glass chandelier over assorted tables and chairs, another with tartan-covered wall banquettes and double-sided woodburner, other décor includes staffordshire china ornaments, old paintings/engravings and a grandfather clock, Timothy Taylors Landlord, Thornbridge Jaipur and guests, also own-brew Invader, several wines by the glass (decent list) and malt whiskies, enjoyable traditional food including good Sun carvery; children and dogs (in bar) welcome, seats in lovely garden with fine views, eight bedrooms and two self-catering cottages, open all day, food all day Fri-Sun. *(Peter and Emma Kelly)*

ASHBOURNE SK1846
Smiths Tavern (01335) 300809
St John Street, bottom of marketplace; DE6 1GH Traditional little pub stretching back from heavily black-beamed bar through lounge to light and airy end room, up to seven well kept Marstons-related ales plus a weekend guest (tasting glasses available) and over 30 whiskies, friendly knowledgeable staff, good pork pies; darts; children (until 9pm) and dogs welcome, open all day. *(Cliff and Monica Swan)*

ASHFORD IN THE WATER SK1969
Ashford Arms (01629) 812725
Off A6 NW of Bakewell; Church Street (B6465, off A6020); DE45 1QB Attractive 18th-c inn set in pretty village; decent reasonably priced food including OAP weekday lunch, well kept Black Sheep and two local guests, nice wines, restaurant and dining conservatory; free wi-fi; children and dogs welcome, plenty of tables outside, eight comfortable bedrooms, open all day Sun (food till 6pm). *(Jim King)*

ASHFORD IN THE WATER SK1969
⭐**Bulls Head** (01629) 812931
Off A6 NW of Bakewell; Church Street (B6465, off A6020); DE45 1QB Traditional 17th-c pub in attractive unspoilt village run by same family since 1953; cosy two-room beamed and carpeted bar with fires, one or two character gothic seats, spindleback and wheelback chairs around cast-iron-framed tables, local photographs and country prints on cream walls, four Robinsons ales and good choice of traditional food (not Tues evening), friendly efficient service; background music, daily papers; children and dogs welcome, overshoes for walkers, hardwood tables and benches in front and in good-sized garden behind with boules and Jenga, open all day weekends in summer. *(John and Delia Franks)*

ASHOVER SK3462
⭐**Old Poets Corner** (01246) 590888
Butts Road (B6036, off A632 Matlock–Chesterfield); S45 0EW Friendly unpretentious local in character village; easy-going bar with mix of chairs and pews, open fire, small room off and french door to tiny balcony, own-brewed Ashover ales and guests (beer festivals Mar and Oct), belgian beers, 12 ciders and good range of fruit wines and malt whiskies, straightforward food at fair prices, dining room; background and regular live music (mainly acoustic), quiz Weds; children (away from bar) and dogs welcome, wheelchair access/disabled loo, attractive bedrooms, holiday cottage sleeping up to eight, open all day, food all day Sat. *(Julie and Andrew Blanchett)*

ASTON-UPON-TRENT   SK4129

Malt (01332) 799116

M1 junction 24A on to A50, village signed left near Shardlow; The Green (one-way street); DE72 2AA Comfortably modernised village pub with enjoyable good value food (not Sun evening), well kept Bass, Marstons Pedigree, Sharps Doom Bar and three guests, friendly atmosphere; some live music, TV; children and dogs welcome, back terrace, open all day. *(Greta and Gavin Craddock)*

BAMFORD   SK2083

Anglers Rest (01433) 659317

A6013/Taggs Knoll; S33 0BQ Friendly community-owned pub with five good local beers and tasty home-made food including Tues pizza night and Fri evening fish and chips, also has a café and post office; some live music, quiz Weds, free wi-fi; children, walkers and dogs welcome, open all day, full menu served Weds evening to 5pm Sun. *(Charlie Stevens)*

BEELEY   SK2667

Devonshire Arms (01629) 733259

B6012, off A6 Matlock–Bakewell; DE4 2NR Lovely 18th-c stone coaching inn in attractive Peak District village near Chatsworth House; original part with black beams, flagstones, stripped stone and cheerful log fires, contrasting ultra-modern bistro/conservatory, up to five well kept changing ales, several wines by the glass and nice range of malt whiskies, generally well liked food (can be pricey) including some pub standards; background music; children welcome, dogs in bar and some of the 18 bedrooms, open all day. *(Frank and Marcia Pelling)*

BELPER   SK3349

Bulls Head (01773) 828898

Belper Lane End; DE56 2DL New management and refurbishment for this spacious beamed village pub; well kept Bass, Dancing Duck and Sharps, good fairly traditional food at reasonable prices from sandwiches/baguettes up, friendly attentive staff, main bar with comfy leather sofas, woodburner in snug, gin/cocktail bar and garden room; acoustic live music; children and dogs (in some parts) welcome, terrace seating, closed Mon lunchtime, otherwise open all day, no food Sun evening, Mon. *(Mike and Sarah Abbot)*

BIRCHOVER   SK2362

Druid (01629) 650424

Off B5056; Main Street; DE4 2BL New owners and redecoration for this hospitable 17th-c stone pub at edge of village; traditional quarry-tiled bar with two woodburners, dining areas either side plus more modern downstairs restaurant and newly opened upstairs space, good well presented food from seasonal menu (special diets catered for) using local suppliers along with own lamb, eggs and honey, five changing ales, Aspall's cider and eight wines by the glass, friendly service; background music, free wi-fi; children and dogs welcome, tables out in front on two levels, good area for walks, Nine Ladies stone circle nearby, open all day Fri and Sat, till 8pm Sun, closed Mon and Tues (hours may be extended in high season). *(Brian and Anna Marsden)*

BIRCHOVER   SK2362

Red Lion (01629) 650363

Main Street; DE4 2BN Welcoming early 18th-c stone-built pub; good value wholesome food including some italian influences (landlord is sardinian), Sun lunchtime carvery, they also make their own cheese and have a deli next door, Birchover ales (brewed here) and four ciders, glass-covered well inside, woodburners; acoustic music sessions and quiz nights; children and dogs welcome, nice rural views from outside seats, open all day Sat, till 8pm Sun, closed Mon, Tues and lunchtimes Weds-Fri. *(Brian and Anna Marsden)*

BONSALL   SK2758

★ **Barley Mow** (01629) 825685

Off A5012 W of Cromford; The Dale; DE4 2AY One-room stone-built local with friendly buoyant atmosphere; beams, pubby furnishings and woodburner, pictures and plenty of bric-a-brac, own Chickenfoot ales, local guests and real ciders, hearty helpings of good value popular food from short daily changing menu (be prepared to share a table); live music Fri and Sat, outside loos; children and dogs welcome, nice little front terrace, events such as hen racing and world record-breaking day, walks from the pub, camping, open all day weekends, closed Mon and lunchtimes Tues-Fri. *(Nick Sharpe)*

BONSALL   SK2758

Kings Head (01629) 822703

Yeoman Street; DE4 2AA Welcoming 17th-c stone-built village local with two cosy beamed rooms; pubby furniture including cushioned wall benches on carpet or tiles, various knick-knacks and china, woodburners, three Batemans ales and enjoyable good value home-made food, restaurant; live music, darts; children and dogs welcome (pub dog is Barney), seats out at front and in back courtyard, handy for Limestone Way and other walks, open all day weekends, closed Mon and Tues lunchtimes. *(Patricia and Anton Larkham)*

BRACKENFIELD   SK3658

Plough (01629) 534437

A615 Matlock–Alfreton, about a mile NW of Wessington; DE55 6DD Modernised 16th-c former farmhouse in lovely setting; three-level beamed bar with cheerful log-effect gas fire, three well kept ales, plenty of wines by the glass and decent range of gins, good popular food including blackboard specials and daily deals, appealing lower-level restaurant extension, friendly attentive staff; background music; children welcome, large neatly kept gardens with terrace, closed Mon, otherwise open all day (food till 5.30pm Sun). *(Paul and Sonia Broadgate, M and GR)*

BRADWELL   SK1781
Bowling Green (01433) 620450
*Smalldale, off B6049 at Gore Lane/
Townend; S33 9JQ* Popular and welcoming 16th-c village local with bar, restaurant and garden room extension; good choice of enjoyable reasonably priced pubby food including Sun carvery, well kept ales such as Abbeydale, Adnams and Bradfield, log fires; children and dogs (in bar) welcome, lovely views from garden, bedrooms in separate building, open all day. *(Nick Sharpe)*

BRASSINGTON   SK2354
★ Olde Gate (01629) 540448
*Village signed off B5056 and B5035
NE of Ashbourne; DE4 4HJ* Wonderfully unspoilt place – like stepping back in time; mullioned windows, 17th-c kitchen range with copper pots, old wall clock, rush-seated chairs and antique settles, beams hung with pewter mugs and shelves lined with embossed Doulton stoneware flagons, also a panelled Georgian room and, to the left of a small hatch-served lobby, a cosy beamed room with stripped settles, scrubbed tables and an open fire under a huge mantelbeam, Marstons, Thwaites and a guest, enjoyable fairly traditional food along with a vegetarian menu; cribbage and dominoes; well behaved children welcome, dogs in bar, benches in small front yard, garden with tables looking out over pastures, open all day Fri-Sun, closed Mon lunchtime, no food Sun evening. *(Cliff and Monica Swan)*

BRETTON   SK2078
★ Barrel (01433) 630856
*Signposted from Foolow, which itself is
signposted from A623 just E of junction
with B6465 to Bakewell; can also be
reached from either the B6049 at Great
Hucklow, or the B6001 via Abney, from
Leadmill just S of Hathersage; S32 5QD*
Recently extended inn on edge of isolated ridge with fine views (on a clear day you can see five counties); stubs of massive knocked-through walls divide the rooms into several spic and span areas, the cosy oak-beamed bar has gleaming copper and brass, patterned carpet and warming fire, ales from Marstons and Wychwood, real cider, several wines by the glass and

28 malt whiskies, enjoyable traditional food served by friendly staff; background music; well behaved children welcome, no dogs inside, seats on front roadside terrace and in courtyard garden, good walks, comfortable well appointed bedrooms, open all day, food all day Sun. *(Brian and Anna Marsden)*

BUXTON   SK0573
Gilberts (01298) 214071
*High Street, on edge of Market Place;
SK17 6ET* Relaxed bar in former shop; solid rustic tables and chairs and some red leather chesterfields on bare boards, modern artwork and pendant lighting, woodburner, tractor-seat stools at corrugated-iron-fronted counter serving two or three well kept ales and a traditional cider, generous helpings of good freshly made food from sandwiches and sharing boards up, reasonable prices, friendly helpful staff; background and live music, free wi-fi; children and dogs (theirs is Bruce) welcome, enclosed back terrace, open all day from 9am for breakfast. *(David H Bennett)*

BUXTON   SK0573
Old Sun (01298) 937986
High Street; SK17 6HA Updated 17th-c coaching inn with several cosy linked areas; half a dozen well kept Marstons-related beers, good choice of wines by the glass and decent coffee, generous helpings of enjoyable home-made food including Tues pizza night, Thurs pie & pint and Fri fish, friendly accommodating staff, low beams, panelling, bare boards and flagstones, old local photographs, open fire and woodburner; background music, alternating quiz/open mike night Weds; children (till 9pm) and dogs welcome, tables out at front and in back garden with pizza oven, open all day, food all day weekends. *(Barry Collett)*

BUXTON   SK0573
Tap House (01298) 214085
*Old Court House, George Street;
SK17 6AT* Buxton brewery tap with their cask and craft range plus guests, also good selection of bottled beers, wines and spirits, tasty well priced food including some cooked in smoker, various interesting teas and coffees, friendly knowledgeable staff; daily newspapers; children and dogs welcome, a few seats outside, open (and food) all day. *(Paul Moore)*

BUXWORTH   SK0282
Navigation (01663) 732072
*S of village towards Silkhill, off B6062;
SK23 7NE* Inn by restored Bugsworth canal basin; half a dozen ales including Marstons and Timothy Taylors, good value

---

Cribbage is a card game using a block of wood with holes for matchsticks or special pins to score with; regulars in cribbage pubs are usually happy to teach strangers how to play.

pubby food from sandwiches up, linked low-ceilinged rooms, canalia, brassware and old photographs, open fires, games room with pool and darts; background and live music, free wi-fi; children (away from main bar), walkers and dogs welcome, disabled access, tables on sunken flagstoned terrace, six bedrooms, open (and food) all day. *(David and Doreen Beattie)*

CALVER   SK2374
Derwentwater Arms (01433) 639211
In centre, bear left from Main Street into Folds Head; Low Side; S32 3XQ Elevated stone-built village pub with big windows looking over to cricket pitch; good fairly priced food (all day Sun) from pies, pizzas and pub favourites to daily specials, three well kept ales including Bass and Bradfield, friendly helpful service; children, walkers and dogs (in bar) welcome, terraces on slopes below (disabled access from back car park), next-door holiday cottage, open all day. *(Jill and Dick Archer)*

CASTLETON   SK1582
★ **Olde Nags Head** (01433) 620248
Cross Street (A6187); S33 8WH Small solidly built hotel dating from the 17th c; interesting antique oak furniture and coal fire in civilised beamed and flagstoned bar, adjoining snug with leather sofas, steps down to restaurant, well kept Bradfield Farmers Blonde, Sharps Doom Bar and several guests, nice coffee and good fairly priced pubby food including burgers and pizzas, friendly helpful staff; quiz Fri, live music Sat; children and dogs (in bar) welcome, nine comfortable bedrooms, good breakfast, open all day. *(David Hunt, Paul Humphreys)*

CHESTERFIELD   SK3670
Rose & Crown (01246) 563750
Old Road; S40 2QT Popular Brampton Brewery pub with their full range plus Everards and two changing guests, no food apart from Sun roasts, friendly helpful staff, spacious traditional refurbishment with leather banquettes, panelling, wood or carpeted floors, brewery memorabilia and cast-iron Victorian fireplace, cosy snug area; Tues quiz, trad jazz first Sun of month, free wi-fi; tables outside, closed till 3pm Mon and Tues, otherwise open all day. *(John Harris)*

CHINLEY   SK0482
Paper Mill (01663) 750529
Whitehough Head Lane; SK23 6EJ Under same management as next door Old Hall (see Main Entries); good selection of ales and craft kegs, plenty of bottled belgian beers and couple of ciders, simple bar snacks along with good home-made pizzas (Thurs-Sun), also pop-up street-food kitchens, good choice of teas and coffees, friendly helpful staff, flagstones, woodburners and open fire, local artwork for sale; TV for major sports; children and dogs welcome, seats out at

front and on split-level back terrace, plenty of good local walks, four bedrooms, open from 2pm Sat, 1pm Sun, closed weekday lunchtimes. *(John and Delia Franks)*

CLOWNE   SK4975
Heist (01246) 819044
Mill Street; S43 4JN Craft beer bar in former Victorian schoolhouse; split-level interior with pitched roof, brick walls and simple furnishings, half a dozen changing beers (including their own), plenty more in bottles and cans, real ciders, decent wines and good range of gins, friendly knowledgeable service, some food such as pizzas; seats out in front, closed Mon. *(Julie and Andrew Blanchett)*

CRICH   SK3454
Cliff (01773) 852444
Cromford Road, Town End; DE4 5DP Unpretentious little two-room roadside pub; well kept ales such as Blue Monkey, Buxton, Dancing Duck and Sharps, generous helpings of good value straightforward food (not weekend evenings or Mon), friendly staff and regulars, two woodburners; quiz first Thurs of the month, some live music, free wi-fi; children and dogs welcome, great views and walks, handy for National Tramway Museum, open all day weekends, closed weekday lunchtimes. *(Jill and Dick Archer)*

CROWDECOTE   SK1065
Packhorse (01298) 83618
B5055 W of Bakewell; SK17 0DB Small three-room 16th-c pub in lovely setting, welcoming landlord and staff, good reasonably priced home-made food from weekday light bites and sandwiches up, four well kept changing ales, split-level interior with brick or carpeted floors, stripped-stone walls, open fire and two woodburners; Thurs quiz, pool and darts; children and dogs welcome, tables out behind, beautiful views and a popular walking route, closed Mon, Tues. *(Frank and Marcia Pelling)*

DERBY   SK3635
Alexandra (01332) 293993
Siddals Road; DE1 2QE Imposing Victorian pub with two simple rooms; traditional furnishings on bare boards or carpet, railway prints and memorabilia, well kept Castle Rock and several quickly changing microbrewery guests, lots of continental bottled beers with more on tap, snack food such as pork pies and cobs; background music; children and dogs welcome, nicely planted backyard, 1960s locomotive cab in car park, four bedrooms, open all day. *(Peter and Emma Kelly)*

DERBY   SK3635
Brunswick (01332) 290677
Railway Terrace; close to Derby Midland Station; DE1 2RU One of Britain's oldest railwaymen's pubs; up to 16 real ales

including Everards and selection from own microbrewery, craft kegs, real ciders and good choice of bottled beers too, bargain food from generous sandwiches and snacks up, high-ceilinged panelled bar, snug with coal fire, chatty front parlour, interesting old train photographs and prints; live jazz upstairs first Thurs of month, darts, TV, games machine, free wi-fi; dogs welcome, walled beer garden behind, open all day, no food Sun evening, Mon and Tues evening, limited choice on Derby County home match days.
(Dr J Barrie Jones)

DERBY   SK3536
Dog & Moon (01332) 986966
Sadler Gate; DE1 3NF Friendly place in pedestrianised street; good range of real ales and craft beers from well stocked bar (plenty of gins), chatty knowledgeable staff, enjoyable food perfect for sharing including platters, cheeseboards and a variety of home-made scotch eggs, simple décor with lots of exposed brick and timber; background and regular live music, comedy and quiz nights; terrace behind, closed Mon and lunchtime Tues, otherwise open all day (till late Fri, Sat). *(John Harris)*

DERBY   SK3435
Exeter Arms (01332) 605323
Exeter Place; DE1 2EU Victorian survivor amid 1930s apartment blocks and car parks; extended into next-door cottage, but keeping its traditional character including tiled-floor snug with curved wall benches and polished open range, friendly staff, well kept Dancing Duck, Marstons and two guests, good all-day food from varied menu; quiz Mon, summer live music Sat in small garden with outside bar (beer festivals), children and dogs welcome, open all day (till midnight Fri, Sat). *(John Harris)*

DERBY   SK3534
Falstaff (01332) 342902
Silver Hill Road, off Normanton Road; DE23 6UJ Big Victorian red-brick corner pub (aka the Folly) brewing its own good value ales, two friendly bars with interesting collection of memorabilia including brewerania, games room; children (till 6pm) and dogs welcome, outside seating area, open all day. *(John Harris)*

DERBY   SK3436
Five Lamps (01332) 348730
Duffield Road; DE1 3BH Corner pub with opened-up but well divided interior around central servery, wood-strip or carpeted floors, panelling, leather button-back bench seats

and small balustraded raised section, over a dozen well kept ales such as Bass, Everards, Oakham and Peak along with a house beer from Derby, real ciders, decent good value pubby food (not Sun evening); background music, TV; a few picnic-sets out in front, more on decked terrace, open all day (till midnight Fri, Sat). *(John Harris)*

DERBY   SK3536
Olde Dolphin (01332) 267711
Queen Street; DE1 3DL Quaint 16th-c timber-framed pub just below cathedral; four small dark unpretentious rooms including appealing snug, big bowed black beams, shiny panelling, opaque leaded windows, lantern lights and coal fires, half a dozen well kept predominantly mainstream ales, reasonably priced bar food and upstairs evening restaurant (Thurs-Sat); quiz and live music nights; children welcome if eating, dogs in bar, sizeable outside area for drinkers/smokers, open all day. *(John Harris)*

DERBY   SK3335
Rowditch (01332) 343123
Uttoxeter New Road (A516); DE22 3LL Popular character local with own microbrewery (well kept Marstons Pedigree and guests too), friendly landlord, two bars and attractive little snug on right, coal fire; no children, dogs welcome at weekends, pleasant back garden, closed weekday lunchtimes. *(John Harris)*

DERBY   SK3536
Silk Mill (01332) 365439
Full Street; DE1 3AF 1920s pub with central bar, lounge and skylit dining area, banquettes, cushioned stools and cast-iron-framed tables on wood floors, open fires, one or two quirky touches such as fish wallpaper, a stuffed crocodile and antler chandelier, good choice of real ales and ciders, several wines by the glass, enjoyable food (all day weekdays, till 8pm Sun) from sandwiches and sharing boards up, friendly service; daily newspapers and free wi-fi; open all day.
(John Harris)

DERBY   SK3536
Tap (01332) 366283
Derwent Street/Exeter Place; DE1 2ED 19th-c Derby Brewing Co pub (aka Royal Standard) with unusual bowed end; ten real ales including five of their own from curved brick counter, lots of bottled imports and good selection of other drinks, knowledgeable staff, decent good value food (all day Sat, till 3pm Sun) from sandwiches and pizzas up, open-plan bare-boards interior

---

Real ale may be served from handpumps, electric pumps (not just the on-off switches used for keg beer) or – common in Scotland – tall taps called founts (pronounced 'fonts') where a separate pump pushes the beer up under air pressure.

with two high-ceilinged drinking areas, more room upstairs and roof terrace overlooking the Derwent; open all day (till 1am Fri, Sat). *(Jim King)*

EARL STERNDALE   SK0966
★ **Quiet Woman** (01298) 83211
Village signed off B5053 S of Buxton; SK17 0BU Old-fashioned unchanging country local in lovely Peak District countryside; simple beamed interior with plain furniture on quarry tiles, china ornaments and coal fire, well kept Marstons and guests, own-label bottled beers (available in gift packs), good pork pies; family room with pool, skittles and darts; no dogs inside, picnic-sets out in front along with budgies, hens, ducks and donkeys, you can buy free-range eggs, local poetry books and even hay, good hikes across nearby Dove Valley towards Longnor and Hollinsclough, small campsite next door with caravan for hire. *(Alexandra and Richard Clay)*

EDALE   SK1285
Old Nags Head (01433) 670291
Off A625 E of Chapel-en-le-Frith; Grindsbrook Booth; S33 7ZD Relaxed well used traditional pub at start of Pennine Way; good value food from sandwiches up including Sun carvery, a beer named for them plus three other well kept local ales, log fire, flagstoned area for booted walkers, airy back family room; background music, TV, pool and darts, Sept beer barrel race; dogs welcome, front terrace and garden, two self-catering cottages, open (and food) all day in summer, closed Mon and Tues in winter, can get very busy weekends. *(Frank and Marcia Pelling)*

ELMTON   SK5073
★ **Elm Tree** (01909) 721261
Off B6417 S of Clowne; S80 4LS Popular competently run country pub with landlord-chef's good fairly traditional food including weekday set lunch and afternoon teas, gluten-free and other special diets catered for, well kept Black Sheep and a guest, several ciders and wide range of wines, friendly obliging service even when busy, stripped stone and panelling, log fire, back barn restaurant (mainly for functions); children and dogs (in bar) welcome, garden tables, play area, closed Tues, otherwise open (and food) all day, till around 8pm (6pm) Sun. *(Derek and Sylvia Stephenson)*

EYAM   SK2276
Miners Arms (01433) 630853
Off A632 Chesterfield to Chapel-en-le-Frith; Water Lane; S32 5RG Three-roomed 17th-c beamed inn with enjoyable food (not Sun evening, Mon lunchtime) from sandwiches up, Greene King and Theakstons ales, friendly efficient service; TV, background music, free wi-fi; children,

walkers and dogs welcome, picnic-sets out at front and in back garden, nice walks nearby especially below Froggatt Edge, seven bedrooms, open all day. *(Paul Humphreys, Michael Butler)*

FOOLOW   SK1976
★ **Bulls Head** (01433) 630873
Village signposted off A623 Baslow–Tideswell; S32 5QR Friendly pub in pretty upland village by green; simply furnished flagstone bar with interesting collection of photographs, real ales including a house beer from Peak, over 30 malt whiskies and well liked food from sandwiches up (more elaborate choices Sat evening), step down to former stables with high ceiling joists, stripped stone and woodburner, sedate partly panelled dining room with plates on delft shelves; background music; children, walkers and dogs welcome, side picnic-sets with nice views, paths from here out over rolling pasture enclosed by dry-stone walls, three bedrooms, open (and food) all day weekends, closed Mon. *(Jill and Dick Archer)*

FROGGATT EDGE   SK2476
★ **Chequers** (01433) 630231
A625, off A623 N of Bakewell; S32 3ZJ Roadside dining pub surrounded by lovely countryside; opened-up bar and eating areas, cushioned settles, farmhouse and captain's chairs around mix of tables, antique prints, longcase clock and woodburner, good interesting food (all day weekends) along with more traditional choices, home-made chutneys and preserves for sale, Bradfield, Peak and a guest ale, several wines by the glass, friendly helpful staff; background music; children welcome, no dogs inside, garden with Froggatt Edge escarpment up through woods behind, six comfortable clean bedrooms, good breakfast, open all day. *(Graham and Elizabeth Hargreaves)*

GLOSSOP   SK0394
Star (01457) 853072
Howard Street; SK13 7DD Unpretentious corner alehouse opposite the station; four well kept changing ales along with Weston's Old Rosie cider, no food, traditional layout including flagstoned tap room with hatch service, old local photographs; dogs welcome, open all day from 2pm (noon Sat, Sun). *(Amanda Shipley)*

GRINDLEFORD   SK2378
Sir William (01433) 630303
B6001, opposite war memorial; S32 2HS Popular pub-hotel under welcoming management; good freshly made food from sandwiches up, Greene King ales and guests, friendly helpful service, restaurant; Sun quiz, free wi-fi; children, walkers and dogs (in a couple of areas) welcome, splendid view especially from terrace, eight comfortable bedrooms, open all day. *(D J and P M Taylor)*

HARDWICK HALL   SK4663

★**Hardwick Inn** (01246) 850245

Quite handy for M1 junction 29; S44 5QJ Popular golden-stone pub dating from the 15th c at south park gate of Hardwick Hall (NT); several endearingly old-fashioned linked rooms including proper bar, open fires, fine range of some 220 malt whiskies and plenty of wines by the glass, well kept Black Sheep, Peak, Theakstons and a house beer (Bess of Hardwick) from Brampton, wide range of good reasonably priced bar food plus carvery restaurant, long-serving licensees (in same family for three generations), efficient friendly staff; unobtrusive background music; children allowed away from bar areas, dogs in one part, tables out at front and in pleasant back garden, open (and food) all day. *(Ian Herdman)*

HATHERSAGE   SK2381

Bank House (01433) 449060

Main Road, centre of village; S32 1BB Busy recently opened restaurant-bar in converted bank; popular food from mediterranean-influenced menu including tapas and pizzas, extensive range of wines, gins and cocktails, a craft beer on handpump with plenty more in bottles, cheerful efficient service, ground-floor bar, restaurant upstairs; open all day, weekend brunch from 10am. *(Neil Ingoe)*

HATHERSAGE   SK2381

★**Scotsmans Pack** (01433) 650253

School Lane, off A6187; S32 1BZ Friendly bustling inn equally popular with drinkers and diners; dark panelled rooms with lots of knick-knacks, upholstered stools and dining chairs, cushioned wall seats and assortment of tables, woodburner, five well kept Marstons-related ales, a dozen wines by the glass and good food from pub standards up, cream teas; background and some live music, quiz and bingo night Thurs, TV, darts; picnic-sets on terrace overlooking trout stream, plenty of surrounding walks, five bedrooms, open all day. *(John Harris)*

HAYFIELD   SK0388

Lantern Pike (01663) 747590

Glossop Road (A624 N) at Little Hayfield, just N of Hayfield; SK22 2NG Popular old roadside pub; traditional bar with warm fire and a few photos of the original *Coronation Street* cast (many were regulars along with series creator Tony Warren who based his characters on the locals), Timothy Taylors Landlord and a guest, decent pubby food; background and live music, free wi-fi; children welcome, tables on stone-walled terrace looking over towards Lantern Pike, plenty of surrounding walks on windswept moors, five bedrooms, open all day weekends, closed Mon. *(Greta and Gavin Craddock)*

HAYFIELD   SK0387

Pack Horse (01663) 749126

Off A624 Glossop to Chapel-en-le-Frith; Market Street; SK22 2EP Modernised stone-built pub under welcoming licensees; good interesting food from landlord-chef using local suppliers including themed night last Fri of month, four well kept ales and decent choice of wines and gins, opened-up interior with some cosy areas, woodburners; background music, Weds quiz; children, walkers and dogs welcome, disabled access, a few picnic-sets out at front, closed Mon (except bank holidays when shuts Tues), otherwise open all day. *(Julie and Andrew Blanchett)*

HOGNASTON   SK2350

★**Red Lion** (01335) 370396

Off B5035 Ashbourne–Wirksworth; DE6 1PR Traditional 17th-c village inn with open-plan beamed bar; attractive mix of old tables, curved settles and other seats on ancient flagstones, three fires, Marstons Pedigree and guests, nice wines by the glass and good well presented home-made food from shortish menu, friendly service, dining conservatory; children and dogs welcome, picnic-sets in field behind, boules, handy for Carsington Water, three good bedrooms, big breakfast, open all day Sun (food till 7pm). *(John Harris)*

HOLBROOK   SK3645

Dead Poets (01332) 780301

Chapel Street; village signed off A6 S of Belper; DE56 0TQ Friendly drinkers' local under new management; up to nine real ales, traditional ciders and good range of other drinks, lunchtime bar food such as cobs and pies, simple cottagey décor with beams, stripped-stone walls and broad flagstones, high-backed settles forming booths, big log fire, plenty of tucked-away corners, woodburner in snug, well behaved children allowed in conservatory; background music; dogs welcome, seats out at back, open all day Thurs-Sun. *(Jill and Dick Archer)*

HOPE   SK1783

★**Cheshire Cheese** (01433) 620381

Off A6187, towards Edale; S33 6ZF 16th-c traditional stone inn with snug oak-beamed rooms on different levels; open fires, red carpets or stone floors, straightforward furnishings and gleaming brasses, up to five real ales such as Abbeydale, Bradfield and Peak, 12 malt whiskies and enjoyable food from sandwiches and pub favourites up, friendly service; Weds quiz, folk night first and third Thurs of month; children and dogs welcome, good local walks in the summits of Lose Hill and Win Hill or the cave district around Castleton, four bedrooms, limited parking, open all day weekends in summer, closed Mon. *(Patricia and Anton Larkham)*

HOPE SK1783
Old Hall (01433) 620160
Market Place, A625; S33 6RH Traditional 16th-c stone coaching inn; good pubby food from sandwiches to specials, five well kept real ales including Theakstons (beer festivals) and over 100 malt whiskies, friendly helpful staff, tea room; children and dogs (not in restaurant) welcome, sunny terrace, five comfortable bedrooms, open (and food) all day, breakfast from 8am. *(Revd R P Tickle)*

HORSLEY WOODHOUSE SK3944
Old Oak (01332) 881299
Main Street (A609 Belper–Ilkeston); DE7 6AW Busy roadside local linked to nearby Bottle Brook and Leadmill microbreweries, their ales and guests plus weekend back bar with another eight well priced beers tapped from the cask, farm ciders too, basic snacks (can also bring your own food), beamed rooms with blazing coal fires; occasional live music; children and dogs welcome, hatch service to covered courtyard tables, nice views, open all day weekends, closed weekday lunchtimes till 4pm. *(Nick Sharpe)*

HURDLOW SK1265
★ Royal Oak (01298) 83288
Monyash–Longnor Road, just off A515 S of Buxton; SK17 9QJ Bustling pub in rural spot near High Peak Trail; two-room beamed bar with open fire, copper kettles, bed warming pans, horsebrasses and so forth, straightforward pubby chairs and tables, ales such as Peak, Sharps, Whim and Wincle, two proper ciders and seven wines by the glass, good food including range of pies, friendly efficient service, dining room with traditional furniture on bare boards and another open fire, flagstoned cellar room perfect for a large group of diners; background music; children and dogs welcome, tables in terraced garden, self-catering barn with bunk bedrooms, campsite, open (and food) all day. *(John McKenzie, Gerry and Rosemary Dobson)*

ILKESTON SK4742
Dewdrop (0115) 932 9684
Station Street, Ilkeston junction, off A6096; DE7 5TE Large Victorian red-brick corner local in old industrial area, not strong on bar comfort but popular for its well kept beers (up to eight) such as Acorn, Blue Monkey and Oakham, simple bar snacks, back lounge with fire and piano, connecting lobby to front public bar with pool, darts and TV, some Barnes Wallis memorabilia; children and dogs welcome, sheltered outside seating at back, walks by former Nottingham Canal, open all day weekends, closed weekday lunchtimes. *(Mike and Sarah Abbot)*

ILKESTON SK4641
Spanish Bar (0115) 930 8666
South Street; DE7 5QJ Busy bar with half

a dozen well kept/priced ales, traditional ciders and bottled belgian beers, friendly efficient staff, evening overspill room; Tues quiz, weekend live music, sports TV, free wi-fi; dogs welcome, small back garden and skittle alley, open all day. *(Jill and Dick Archer)*

INGLEBY SK3427
John Thompson (01332) 862469
NW of Melbourne; turn off A514 at Swarkestone Bridge or in Stanton by Bridge; can also be reached from Ticknall (or from Repton on B5008); DE73 7HW Own beers from the longest established microbrewery in the UK; comfortable neatly kept lounge with beams, old settles, button-back leather seats and sturdy oak tables, antique prints and paintings, log-effect gas fire, a couple of smaller cosier rooms off, simple good value lunchtime food including carvery, piano, TV and games in conservatory; background music, free wi-fi; children welcome till 9pm, dogs in bar and conservatory, seats on lawns or partly covered terrace, pretty surrounding countryside, self-catering chalets, open all day weekends, closed Mon. *(Amanda Shipley)*

KING'S NEWTON SK3826
Hardinge Arms (01332) 863808
Not far from M1 junction 23A, via A453 to Isley, then off Melbourne/Wilson Road; Main Street; DE73 8BX Bright spacious old pub with enjoyable bar and evening restaurant food, well kept local ales and good range of wines, quick friendly service, chunky low beams, brick, wood and flagstone floors, woodburner; Sun quiz; children welcome in eating areas, handy for Donington Park and East Midlands Airport, bedrooms in converted stables, open all day Thurs-Sun, from 3pm other days. *(John Harris)*

LADYBOWER RESERVOIR SK1986
Ladybower Inn (01433) 651241
A57 Sheffield–Glossop, just E of junction with A6013; S33 0AX Batemans pub handy for the huge nearby reservoir; their ales and a couple of guests, enjoyable pubby food from sandwiches up, friendly service, various traditionally furnished carpeted areas with cast-iron fireplaces, Lancaster Bomber pictures recalling the Dambusters' practice runs on the reservoir; background music, darts, free wi-fi; children and dogs (in bar) welcome, picnic-sets out at front, annexe bedrooms, open (and food) all day. *(Charlie Stevens)*

LADYBOWER RESERVOIR SK2084
★ Yorkshire Bridge (01433) 651361
A6013 N of Bamford; S33 0AZ Busy inn a short stroll from Ladybower dam and close to Derwent and Howden reservoirs; beamed bar with woodburner, wheelbacks and other chairs around mix of tables on patterned carpet, copper items, china plates

and various photographs and paintings, other areas including airy garden room with fine valley views, ales such as Acorn, Bradfield, High Peak and Kelham Island, nine wines by the glass, generous helpings of popular pub food from sandwiches to grills, friendly service; background music, free wi-fi; children welcome, no dogs at mealtimes, picnic-sets in paved courtyard, 14 comfortable bedrooms, lovely surrounding walks, open all day, food all day weekends. *(Alexandra and Richard Clay)*

LANGLEY MILL   SK4248
Thorn Tree   (01773) 768675
Woodlinkin, Nottingham Road; NG16 4HG
Updated roadside restaurant/pub (part of the Georges Tradition group) with great views over rolling country, good choice of enjoyable reasonably priced food including signature fish and chips and grills, three local ales, attentive friendly service, conservatory and deck taking in the view; children and dogs welcome, beer garden, open (and food) all day. *(John and Delia Franks)*

LEES   SK2637
Cow   (01332) 824297
Just off Langley Common–Longford Road, off B5020 W of Derby; DE6 5BE
Well reworked 19th-c beamed village pub/restaurant (sister to the Cock at Mugginton); good fairly priced food including range of tapas-style dishes, a beer named for them, guest ales and good range of other drinks, friendly helpful service; background music, TV; children and dogs welcome, 12 boutique bedrooms, open all day, food all day Sun till 8pm. *(Peter and Emma Kelly)*

LITTLE LONGSTONE   SK1971
Packhorse   (01629) 640471
Off A6 NW of Bakewell via Monsal Dale; DE45 1NN Long low building with three comfortable linked rooms; beams, open fires and pine tables on flagstones, well kept ales including Black Sheep and Thornbridge, good generously served home-made food from daily changing blackboard using fresh local produce (booking advised), affordably priced wine list, friendly accommodating service; Thurs quiz; children, dogs and hikers welcome (on Monsal Trail), terrace in steep little back garden, open (and food) all day weekends. *(Frances Gibbs)*

LITTON   SK1675
Red Lion   (01298) 871458
Village signposted off A623, between B6465 and B6049 junctions; also signposted off B6049; SK17 8QU
Welcoming traditional village pub; two linked front rooms with low beams, panelling and

open fires, bigger stripped-stone back room, four well kept interesting ales and enjoyable home-made food from sandwiches to daily specials; dogs allowed, seats and tables in front with more on village green, good dales walks nearby, open (and food) all day. *(Brian and Anna Marsden)*

LULLINGTON   SK2513
Colvile Arms   (01827) 373212
Off A444 S of Burton; Main Street; DE12 8EG Popular 18th-c brick-built village pub; high-backed settles in simple panelled bar, cosy comfortable beamed lounge, well kept Bass, Marstons Pedigree and two guests, over 30 gins, no food except cobs, pleasant friendly atmosphere; background music, free wi-fi; children welcome till 7.30pm, dogs in bar, picnic-sets on sheltered back lawn, closed lunchtimes apart from Sun. *(Lenny and Ruth Walters)*

MAKENEY   SK3544
★ **Holly Bush**   (01332) 841729
From A6 heading N after Duffield, take first right after crossing River Derwent, then first left; DE56 0RX Unspoilt 17th-c two-bar village pub (former farmhouse); beams and black panelling, tiled and flagstone floors, three blazing fires, one in old-fashioned range by snug's curved high-backed settle, well kept changing ales (some served from jugs), craft beers and real cider, enjoyable lunchtime food from rolls and pork pies up, lobby with hatch service; beer festivals and occasional live music; children, walkers and dogs welcome, picnic-sets outside, open all day. *(Jim King)*

MARSTON MONTGOMERY   SK1338
Crown   (01889) 591430
On corner of Thurvaston Road and Barway; DE6 2FF Welcoming red-brick beamed village pub, clean and bright, with popular good value food, three real ales including Marstons Pedigree and several wines by the glass, friendly helpful staff, restaurant; some live music; children and dogs welcome, disabled access, terrace tables, seven good bedrooms, open (and food) all day, kitchen closes 7pm Sun. *(John Peter)*

MATLOCK   SK2960
Moca   (01629) 583973
Dale Road; DE4 3LT Light café-style bar with half a dozen or so well kept local beers and snacky lunchtime food, friendly knowledgeable staff, chunky pine furniture on bare boards, black and white photographs of musicians/bands; can fill up as not large; dogs welcome, back terrace, open all day. *(John Harris, Jim King)*

Post Office address codings confusingly give the impression that a few pubs are in Derbyshire, when they're really in Cheshire (which is where we list them).

MATLOCK
SK2960
Thorn Tree
(01629) 580295
Jackson Road, Matlock Bank; DE4 3JQ
Superb valley views to Riber Castle from this
homely little 19th-c stone-built local; Bass,
Greene King, Nottingham, Timothy Taylors
and guests, simple well cooked food (Tues-Fri
lunchtimes till 1.30pm, Sun 5-6.30pm, Weds
pie night), friendly staff and regulars; free
wi-fi; children and dogs welcome, tables
outside taking in the view, open all day
Fri-Sun, closed Mon lunchtime. *(Jim King)*

MAYFIELD
SK1444
★ Rose & Crown
(01335) 342498
*Main Road (B5032 off A52 W of
Ashbourne); DE6 2JT* Welcoming dining
pub with good attractively presented food
cooked by owner-chef, reasonable prices,
well kept Marstons Pedigree and nice range
of good value wines, efficient friendly service,
woodburner in beamed bar, restaurant;
children welcome, no dogs inside, terrace
tables under parasols, local walks, three
bedrooms, closed Sun evening, Mon and
Tues, food served 12-1.30pm, 6.30-8.30pm
(no lunchtime meals Weds, Thurs).
(Lenny and Ruth Walters)

MIDDLE HANDLEY
SK4078
Devonshire Arms
(01246) 434800
Off B6052 NE of Chesterfield; S21 5RN
Welcoming 18th-c village dining pub under
newish management; freshly updated modern
décor in opened-up bar and restaurant
areas, enjoyable food from sandwiches,
sharing dishes and pub favourites to burgers
and steaks, three real ales including one
badged for them, a dozen wines and good
choice of gins and cocktails, friendly helpful
service; background and some live music;
children and dogs (in bar) welcome, tables
on front and side terraces, play area, seven
refurbished bedrooms, open (and food) all
day, kitchen closes 7pm Sun. *(Greta and
Gavin Craddock)*

MILLERS DALE
SK1473
Anglers Rest
(01298) 871323
*Just down Litton Lane; pub is PH on
OS Sheet 119 map reference 142734;
SK17 8SN* Creeper-clad pub in lovely quiet
riverside setting; two bars and dining room,
log fires, Bradfield, Kelham Island and a
couple of guests, enjoyable uncomplicated
food at reasonable prices, cheery helpful
service; darts and pool; children welcome,
muddy boots and dogs in public bar,
wonderful gorge views and river walks (on
the Monsal Trail), self-catering apartment,
open all day, all day Sat, till 8pm Sun.
(Charlie Stevens)

MILLTOWN
SK3561
Miners Arms
(01246) 590218
*Off B6036 SE of Ashover; Oakstedge
Lane; S45 0HA* Spotless stone dining pub

with good freshly made food from well priced
daily changing blackboard menu (booking
advised), nice wines and one changing real
ale, log fires; children welcome, no dogs
inside, attractive country walks from the
door, closed Sun evening-Weds (open Weds
in Dec). *(Patricia and Anton Larkham)*

MILTON
SK3126
Swan
(01283) 704072
Just E of Repton; DE65 6EF Welcoming
flower-decked village pub under newish
family management; well kept Bass and
guests, nice range of gins and enjoyable
food including range of home-made
pies, complimentary cheese board Sun,
comfortable homely atmosphere; children
and dogs (in bar) welcome, garden behind,
open all day weekends, from 5pm other days.
(Amanda Shipley)

MONYASH
SK1566
★ Bulls Head
(01629) 812372
B5055 W of Bakewell; DE45 1JH
Rambling stone pub with high-ceilinged
rooms, straightforward traditional
furnishings including plush stools lined along
bar, horse pictures and a shelf of china, log
fire, four real ales such as Black Sheep and
Peak, restaurant with high-backed dining
chairs on heated stone floor, popular pubby
food (all day weekends) from sandwiches and
baked potatoes up, friendly service, small
back room with darts, board games and pool;
background music; children and dogs (in
bar) welcome, plenty of picnic-sets under
parasols in big garden, gate leading to well
equipped public play area, good surrounding
walks, open all day in high summer, all day
Fri-Sun other times. *(Mike and Sarah Abbot)*

MOORWOOD MOOR
SK3656
White Hart
(01629) 534888
*Inns Lane; village signed from South
Wingfield; DE55 7NU* Welcoming country
inn with good seasonal food in bar and
restaurant, helpful attentive staff, well kept
Sharps Doom Bar, Timothy Taylors Landlord
and a couple of local guests; children and
dogs welcome, disabled access/loos, tables
on attractive heated terrace, ten modern
bedrooms, open (and food) all day, kitchen
closes 6.45pm Sun. *(Derek and Sylvia
Stephenson)*

MUGGINTON
SK2843
Cock
(01773) 550703
*Bullhurst Lane; N of Weston Underwood;
DE6 4PJ* Sister pub to the Cow at Lees with
nicely renovated traditional bar areas, beams
and panelling, lots of pictures, old quarry
tiles and cosy woodburners, steps down to
large glass-fronted modern extension with
mezzanine floor, good popular food from bar
snacks, through pub favourites and some
asian choices to chargrills, also separate
vegan and gluten-free menus, half a dozen
well kept ales, craft beers and good range

of other drinks, efficient friendly service; children and dogs welcome, wheelchair access, plenty of tables in attractive walled gardens, outside summer bar, car park with electric charging points, good local walks, open all day, food all day Sun till 7pm. *(Lenny and Ruth Walters)*

NEW MILLS   SJ9886
Fox (0161) 427 1634
Brook Bottom Road; SK22 3AY Tucked-away old-fashioned country local in good walking area at end of single-track road; Robinsons ales and good value pub food (no credit cards), log fire; darts and pool; children and dogs welcome, plenty of tables outside, open all day Fri-Sun. *(Charlie Stevens)*

NEW MILLS   SK0086
Pack Horse (01663) 742365
Mellor Road; SK22 4QQ Popular and friendly stone-built country inn with lovely views across broad Sett Valley to Kinder Scout; Tetleys and three guests kept well, good quality food in traditional log-fire bar and restaurant; children welcome, no dogs inside, terrace and garden on different levels, 12 well equipped clean bedrooms, open (and food) all day. *(Peter Sutton)*

NEWTON SOLNEY   SK2825
Brickmakers Arms 07525 220103
Main Street (B5008 NE of Burton); DE15 0SJ Friendly end-of-terrace beamed pub owned by Burton Bridge Brewery; four of their well kept ales and a couple of guests including Timothy Taylors Landlord, real ciders and plenty of bottled beers, no food, two rooms off bar, one with original panelling and delft shelf displaying jugs and plates, pubby furniture, built-in wall seats and coal fires, area with books; Mon quiz, free wi-fi; dogs welcome, tables on terrace, open all day weekends (from 1pm Sat), closed lunchtimes during the week. *(Simon Abbott)*

OCKBROOK   SK4236
Royal Oak (01332) 662378
Off B6096 just outside Spondon; Green Lane; DE72 3SE 18th-c village local run by same friendly family since 1953; good value honest food (not Sun evening) from good lunchtime cobs to steaks, well kept Bass and three interesting guests, real cider; tile-floored tap room, carpeted snug, inner bar with Victorian prints, larger and lighter side room, nice old settle in entrance corridor, open fires; darts and dominoes, some live music; children welcome, dogs in the evening, disabled access, sheltered cottage

garden and cobbled front courtyard, separate play area, open all day Fri-Sun. *(Nick Sharpe)*

OLD BRAMPTON   SK3171
Fox & Goose (01246) 566335
Off A619 Chesterfield–Baslow at Wadshelf; S42 7JJ Fine panoramic views from this restored 14th-c pub; character beamed bar with traditional pubby furniture on large flagstones, woodburner in big stone fireplace, Black Sheep, Bradwell, Peak and a couple of guests, a dozen wines by the glass (regular wine tasting evenings), snug with more heavy beams, comfortable seating and small fire, good interesting food from sandwiches, derbyshire tapas and sharing plates up, separate dining room and orangery restaurant taking in the views; children and dogs (in bar) welcome, tables under parasols on decked and terraced areas, open all day Thurs-Sat, till 6pm Sun, closed Mon-Weds. *(Lucy and Giles Gibbon, Brian and Susan Wylie, Diane Abbot)*

OSMASTON   SK1943
Shoulder of Mutton (01335) 342371
Off A52 SE of Ashbourne; DE6 1LW Beamed red-brick pub incorporating post office/shop; Marstons Pedigree and a guest or two, generous helpings of enjoyable home-made food (all day weekends) from sandwiches up, good friendly service; free wi-fi; children welcome, no dogs inside, picnic-sets in attractive garden (farmland views), peaceful pretty village with thatched cottages, duck pond and good surrounding walks, open all day. *(Martin Day, Simon Bather)*

PARWICH   SK1854
Sycamore (01335) 390212
By church; DE6 1QL Welcoming old village pub (some refurbishment); flagstoned bar with upholstered wall benches and woodburner, Robinsons ales, good reasonably priced home-made food including themed nights, efficient friendly service, a couple of back dining rooms, pub also houses the village shop; darts, free wi-fi; children and dogs welcome, picnic-sets in small front courtyard, more on side grass, good walks, open all day weekends. *(R L Borthwick)*

PILSLEY   SK2371
★**Devonshire Arms** (01246) 565405
Village signposted off A619 W of Baslow, and pub just below B6048; High Street; DE45 1UL Civilised little country inn on the Chatsworth Estate; gentle contemporary slant with wood-floored bar and several fairly compact areas off (each with own

---

A star symbol before the name of a pub shows exceptional character and appeal. It doesn't mean extra comfort. And it's nothing to do with exceptional food quality, Even quite a basic pub can win a star, if it's individual enough.

character – some steps), log fires in stone fireplaces, comfortable seating and big modern paintings, three well kept Peak ales, a cider such as Lilley's and several wines by the glass, enjoyable food from lunchtime sandwiches up using Estate produce, friendly staff; children and dogs welcome, a few picnic-sets out at front, charging point for electric vehicles in car park, Chatsworth farm shop at the top of lane, bedrooms (some with four-posters), open all day. *(Alexandra and Richard Clay)*

REPTON   SK3026
Bulls Head (01283) 704422
High Street; DE65 6GF Lively village pub (can get packed) with interesting décor in various interconnecting bars; beams and pillars, mix of wooden dining chairs, settles, built-in wall seats and squashy sofas on bare boards or flagstones, driftwood sculptures, animal hides and an arty bull's head, log fires, ales such as Marstons Pedigree, lots of bottled beers and ciders, also good selection of wines, gins and cocktails, popular food including wood-fired pizzas and range of grilled yakitori sticks, cheerful staff, upstairs restaurant; background music, free wi-fi; children and dogs (in bar) welcome, sizeable heated terrace with neatly set tables and chairs under big parasols, open (and some food) all day. *(Jim King)*

RIPLEY   SK3950
Talbot Taphouse (01773) 742382
Butterley Hill; DE5 3LT Traditional drinkers pub with eight well kept changing ales, traditional ciders, and good selection of draught belgian and bottled beers, friendly knowledgeable staff, long narrow panelled room with comfortable chairs, open fire in brick fireplace; some live music, sports TV; open all day Fri-Sun, from 2pm other days. *(Frank and Marcia Pelling)*

ROWSLEY   SK2565
★**Peacock** (01629) 733518
Bakewell Road; DE4 2EB Civilised 17th-c country hotel (former manor house); comfortable seating in spacious modern lounge, inner bar with log fire, bare stone walls and some Robert 'Mouseman' Thompson furniture, very good if not cheap food from lunchtime sandwiches to restaurant meals, Peak ales, nice wines and well served coffee, pleasant helpful staff; attractive riverside gardens, trout fishing, 15 good bedrooms. *(Mike and Sarah Abbot)*

SHARDLOW   SK4430
Malt Shovel (01332) 792066
3.5 miles from M1 junction 24, via A6 towards Derby; The Wharf; DE72 2HG Welcoming canalside pub in late 18th-c former maltings; interesting odd-angled layout with cosy corners and steps down to snug, Marstons Pedigree and a beer badged for the pub, very good value tasty food from

sandwiches and baked potatoes up including popular breakfasts, evening meals Weds and Thurs (thai) only, quick friendly service, beams, panelling and central open fire; live music Sun, free wi-fi; children and dogs welcome, lots of terrace tables by Trent & Mersey Canal, pretty hanging baskets, open all day. *(Frank and Marcia Pelling)*

SHARDLOW   SK4429
Old Crown (01332) 792392
Off A50 just W of M1 junction 24; Cavendish Bridge, E of village; DE72 2HL Good value pub with half a dozen well kept Marstons-related ales and decent choice of malt whiskies, traditional food (all day Sat, not Sun evening, Mon or Fri evening) from sandwiches/baguettes up including Thurs steak night and bargain Sun lunch, beams with masses of jugs and mugs, walls covered with other bric-a-brac and breweriana, big inglenook; quiz Mon, fortnightly live music Tues; children and dogs welcome, garden with play area, open all day. *(Sean Lavers)*

SHELDON   SK1768
★**Cock & Pullet** (01629) 814292
Village signed off A6 just W of Ashford; DE45 1QS Charming no-frills village pub with low beams, exposed stonework, flagstones and open fire, cheerful mismatch of furnishings, large collection of clocks and various representations of poultry (some stuffed), well kept Sharps Doom Bar, Timothy Taylors Landlord and a guest such as Peak, tasty pub food from shortish menu including popular Sun roasts, reasonable prices and friendly efficient service; quiet background music, pool and TV in plainer public bar; children and dogs welcome, seats and water feature on pleasant back terrace, pretty village just off the Limestone Way and popular all year with walkers, clean bedrooms, open all day. *(Julie and Andrew Blanchett)*

SHIRLEY   SK2141
Saracens Head (01335) 360330
Church Lane; DE6 3AS Modernised late 18th-c dining pub in attractive village; good range of well presented blackboard food from pubby choices to more expensive restaurant-style dishes, four Greene King ales, decent wines and speciality coffees, simple country-style dining furniture and two pretty working art nouveau fireplaces; background music; children and dogs (in bar area) welcome, pub cat is Billy, picnic-sets out in front and on back terrace, open all day Sun. *(Charlie Stevens)*

SOUTH WINGFIELD   SK3755
Old Yew Tree (01773) 833626
B5035 W of Alfreton; Manor Road; DE55 7NH Friendly 16th-c village pub with good reasonably priced home-made food (not Sun evening) including lunchtime/early

evening deal, Bass, a local guest (maybe two at weekends) and a proper cider, log fire, beams and carved panelling, separate restaurant area; Sat music, Weds quiz, TV, free wi-fi; children, walkers and dogs welcome, some rattan-style furniture out at the side, open all day Fri-Sun, closed Mon and Tues lunchtimes. *(Sean Lavers)*

SUTTON CUM DUCKMANTON   SK4371
Arkwright Arms (01246) 232053
A632 Bolsover–Chesterfield; S44 5JG
Friendly and relaxed mock-Tudor pub with bar, pool room (dogs allowed here) and dining room, all with real fires, good choice of well priced food (not Sun evening), up to 16 changing ales (always one from Raw), ten real ciders and four perries (beer/cider festivals Easter/Aug bank holidays); TV, games machine; children welcome, seats out at front and on side terrace, open all day. *(Derek and Sylvia Stephenson)*

THORPE   SK1650
Old Dog (01335) 350990
Spend Lane/Wintercroft Lane; DE6 2AT
Popular bistro-style village pub (former 18th-c coaching inn) with good food from sensibly short menu including burgers and hot dogs, four well kept changing ales often from smaller breweries, friendly prompt service, candlelit tables on flagstones, woodburners; background music; children, walkers and dogs welcome, covered eating area outside, handy for Dovedale and Tissington Trail, closed Mon, otherwise open all day, food all day weekends (till 7pm Sun). *(Brian and Anna Marsden)*

TICKNALL   SK3523
Wheel (01332) 865168
Main Street (A514); DE73 7JZ Corner pub under new management; contemporary décor in bar and upstairs restaurant, enjoyable mediterranean food including tapas, a couple of real ales, friendly staff; children welcome, outside area with café tables on raised deck, near entrance to Calke Abbey (NT). *(Brian Boyland)*

TIDESWELL   SK1575
Star (01298) 872725
High Street; SK17 8LD Friendly little village pub with three well kept Marstons-related ales, enjoyable traditional food and reasonably priced wine list, quick cheerful service, four compact rooms including lounge with woodburner and dining room; Thurs quiz, darts and dominoes; children welcome, dogs in front bar, closed lunchtime apart from Sun, no food Mon-Weds. *(David Hunt)*

UPPER LANGWITH   SK5169
Devonshire (01623) 747777
Rectory Road; NG20 9RF Popular dining pub with several cosy modernised areas; highly rated food (best to book) from

lunchtime sandwiches and pub favourites up including a vegan menu, well kept Sharps Doom Bar and three guests, decent wines, friendly attentive service; children and dogs (in bar) welcome, easy disabled access, a few picnic-sets out at front, open all day (till 7pm Sun). *(Sean Lavers)*

WARDLOW   SK1875
★ Three Stags Heads (01298) 872268
Wardlow Mires; A623/B6465; SK17 8RW
Basic unchanging pub (17th-c longhouse) of great individuality; old country furniture on flagstones, heating from cast-iron kitchen ranges, old photographs, long-serving plain-talking landlord, locals in favourite corners, well kept Abbeydale ales including a strong house beer (Black Lurcher), proper cider and lots of bottled beers, simple food on home-made plates (licensees are potters and have a small gallery), may be free roast chestnuts or cheese on the bar, folk music Sun afternoon; no credit cards or mobile phones; well behaved children and dogs welcome (resident lurchers), hill views from front terrace, good walking country, only open Fri evening and all day weekends. *(Peter and Emma Kelly)*

WHITTINGTON MOOR   SK3873
Derby Tup (01246) 269835
Sheffield Road; B6057 just S of A61 roundabout; S41 8LS Popular Castle Rock local with their ales along with Pigeon Fishers (landlord owns the brewery) and several guests, also craft beers, up to seven ciders and good range of other drinks; coal fire, simple furniture and lots of standing room, two side snugs; live music including jam session last Mon of month; dogs welcome, seats out on small back deck, open all day Fri and Sat, from 2pm Sun, closed Mon-Thurs lunchtimes. *(Cliff and Monica Swan)*

WILLINGTON   SK2928
Dragon (01283) 704795
The Green; DE65 6BP Renovated and extended pub backing on to Trent & Mersey Canal; good choice of enjoyable well prepared food from sandwiches to grills, vegan/vegetarian menu and weekday set deal (not Fri evening), microbrews from sister pub the Boot at Repton (see Main Entries), guest beers and good selection of other drinks including 27 wines by the glass, range of coffees and teas; some live music, sports TV, free wi-fi; children and dogs (not in restaurant) welcome, picnic-sets out overlooking canal (moorings), bedrooms in attached cottage, open (and food) all day, breakfast from 8am. *(Nick Sharpe)*

WINSTER   SK2460
★ Bowling Green (01629) 650219
East Bank, by Market House (NT); DE4 2DS Traditional old stone pub with good chatty atmosphere, character

long-serving landlord and welcoming staff, enjoyable generously served food including popular pies, at least three well kept changing local ales and good selection of whiskies, end log fire, dining area and family conservatory (dogs allowed here too); nice village with good surrounding walks, closed Mon, Tues and lunchtimes apart from Sun. *(Brian and Anna Marsden)*

WINSTER SK2360

Miners Standard (01629) 650279

Bank Top (B5056 above village); DE4 2DR Simply furnished 17th-c stone local, friendly and relaxed, with bar, snug and restaurant, well kept ales such as Bass, Greene King and Marstons, good value pub food (not Sun evening) including some vegetarian/vegan choices, big woodburner, lead mining photographs and minerals, lots of brass, a backwards clock and ancient

well; background music; children (away from bar) and dogs welcome, attractive view from garden, campsite next door, interesting stone-built village below, open all day. *(Amanda Shipley)*

YEAVELEY SK1840

Yeaveley Arms (01335) 330700

On byroad S of Ashbourne; DE6 2DT Recently refurbished village pub with good food (not Sun evening) from fairly traditional menu, well kept ales such as Fullers London Pride, Marstons Pedigree and Timothy Taylors Landlord, good whisky/gin selection, helpful attentive service, slate-floor bar with two-way woodburner, separate restaurant; quirky gents' loo; children and dogs (in bar) welcome, a few picnic-sets out at front overlooking church, more behind, open all day Fri-Sun, closed lunchtimes Mon and Tues. *(Charlie Stevens)*

Devon

BRANSCOMBE   SY1888 Map 1
Fountain Head 🍺

(01297) 680359 – www.fountainheadinn.com

Upper village; W of Branscombe at Street; EX12 3BG

Friendly, unspoilt pub with local beers and tasty, fair priced food

Dating back to the 14th c and steadfastedly old-fashioned, this fine old place is set down a narrow winding lane close to the church. The room on the left was once a smithy and has forge tools and horseshoes on high oak beams, cushioned pews and mate's chairs, and a log fire in the original raised hearth with its tall central chimney. There's Branscombe Vale Branoc, Golden Fiddle and Summa That on handpump, two local ciders and eight wines by the glass. On the right, an irregularly shaped snug room has another log fire, a white-painted plank ceiling with an unusual carved ceiling rose, brown-varnished panelling, a flagstone floor and local artwork for sale; darts and board games. You can sit outside on the front loggia and terrace listening to the little stream gurgling beneath the flagstoned path; barbecues and spit roasts may be held on Sunday evening from 6pm (end July-early September). Good coastal walks.

🍴 Well liked food includes sandwiches and toasties plus home-cured trout with pickled cucumber, dill and caper salad with horseradish mascarpone, ham hock, bacon and chicken terrine with piccalilli, home-cooked honey-roast ham and eggs, cauliflower cheese with crusty bread, lasagne, fresh fish dish of the day, chicken and ham with ginger, honey and mango salad, venison pie, 10oz rump steak with chips, and puddings. *Benchmark main dish: beer-battered fish and chips £12.00. Two-course evening meal £19.00.*

Free house ~ Licensee Jon Woodley ~ Real ale ~ Open 10-3, 6-11; 12-10.30 Sun ~ Bar food 12-2, 6.30 (7 Sun)-9 ~ Restaurant ~ Children welcome away from main bar area ~ Dogs welcome *Recommended by Roger and Donna Huggins, Thomas Green, Peter Pilbeam, Dr and Mrs J D Abell, Dr Martin Owton, Alfie Bayliss, Diane Abbot*

BUCKLAND MONACHORUM   SX4968 Map 1
Drake Manor 🍺 £ 🛏

(01822) 853892 – www.drakemanorinn.co.uk

Off A386 via Crapstone, just S of Yelverton roundabout; PL20 7NA

Nice small village pub with snug rooms, popular food, quite a choice of drinks and pretty back garden; bedrooms

Our readers are extremely fond of this charming little pub and many come here on a regular basis. It's run by a friendly, long-serving landlady who continues to offer comfortable bedrooms and enjoyable, very fair value food. The heavily beamed public bar on the left has a chatty, easy-going feel, brocade-cushioned wall seats, prints of the village from 1905 onwards, horse tack and a few ship badges and a woodburning stove in a very big stone fireplace; a small door leads to a low-beamed cubbyhole. The snug Drakes Bar has beams hung with tiny cups and big brass keys, a woodburning stove in another stone fireplace, horsebrasses and stirrups, and a mix of seats and tables (note the fine high-backed stripped-pine settle with hood). On the right is a small beamed dining room with settles and tables on flagstones. Darts and board games. Dartmoor Jail Ale, Exeter Avocet and Sharps Doom Bar on handpump, ten wines by the glass, a dozen malt whiskies, 15 gins and three farm ciders; darts and board games. There are picnic-sets in the prettily planted and sheltered back garden and the front floral displays are much admired; morris men perform regularly in summer. They also offer an attractive self-catering apartment. Buckland Abbey (National Trust) is close by.

Good value food using home-reared pork and honey from their own bees includes lunchtime baguettes and ploughman's, ham hock terrine with celeriac slaw and pickled vegetables, whitebait with tartare sauce, butternut squash and caramelised onion tart with spinach, feta and honey-roast nut salad, gammon and free-range eggs, fritto misto with fries, pie of the day, beer-battered fish of the day with chips, chicken curry, lamb rump with fondant potatoes and port jus, hake fillet with lyonnaise potatoes and caper and lemon butter, and puddings such as chocolate fondant with raspberry coulis and sorbet, and millionaire's cheesecake with vanilla ice-cream. *Benchmark main dish: pie of the day £13.00. Two-course evening meal £20.00.*

Punch ~ Lease Mandy Robinson ~ Real ale ~ Open 11.30-2.30, 6-11; 11.30-11.30 Fri, Sat; 12-11 Sun ~ Bar food 12-2, 6.30-9.30; 12-2.30, 6-9.30 Sat; 12-2.30, 6.30-9 Sun ~ Restaurant ~ Children welcome ~ Dogs allowed in bar ~ Wi-fi ~ Bedrooms: £80/£100
Recommended by Glen and Patricia Fuller, Freddie and Sarah Banks, Camilla and Jose Ferrera, John Evans, Mr and Mrs J Watkins, John D'Silva, Cliff and Monica Swan, Alister and Margery Bacon, Elizabeth and Andrew Harvey, Fiona and Jack Henderson, Colin McLachlan

CHAGFORD

SX7087   Map 1

Three Crowns 🛏

(01647) 433444 – www.threecrowns-chagford.co.uk
High Street; TQ13 8AJ

Stylish bar and lounges in ancient inn, conservatory restaurant and good food and drinks; smart bedrooms

Ancient and modern features blend cleverly together here with massive beams and standing timbers, huge fireplaces with wood fires (lit all year), exposed stone walls, flagstones and mullioned windows, and a contemporary dining room with a glazed atrium. The bar areas have leather armchairs and stools, built-in panelled wall seats and a few leather tub chairs. St Austell Proper Job and Tribute on handpump, 20 wines by the glass and 21 gins served by friendly, efficient staff. Throughout the building are antique prints, photographs and polished copper kettles, pots and warming pans; background music and board games. Sturdy tables and chairs are placed among box topiary in the south-facing courtyard garden. Bedrooms are stylish and well appointed and blend character with modern design. Parking is limited to superior rooms only but there's also a nearby pay-and-display car park. Muddy boots and dogs are welcome.

Rewarding food includes sandwiches, duck liver parfait with crostini, smoked salmon and mackerel fishcake with niçoise salad, sharing platters, wild mushroom risotto with mascarpone, trio of sausages and chive mash with onion gravy, chicken breast with tenderstem broccoli purée, black garlic and potato fondant, lamb rump with confit shallots, artichokes and jus, sea bass with samphire, carrot purée and garlic mash, and puddings such as chocolate délice with raspberry sorbet and fruit crumble with clotted cream. *Benchmark main dish: beer-battered fish and chips £13.00. Two-course evening meal £20.00.*

St Austell ~ Managers John Milan and Steve Bellman ~ Real ale ~ Open 10am-11pm; 10am-midnight Fri, Sat ~ Bar food 12-9 (9.30 Sat); 8-10am breakfast, 10am-midday snacks; 2.30-6 sandwiches and cream teas ~ Restaurant ~ Children welcome ~ Dogs allowed in bar ~ Wi-fi ~ Bedrooms: £90/£110 *Recommended by Catherine and Daniel King, Charlie and Mark Todd, Dr Martin Owton, Sandra and Michael Smith, Rosie and John Moore, Ian Herdman*

COCKWOOD
Anchor 🍺

SX9780 Map 1

(01626) 890203 – www.anchorinncockwood.com
Off, but visible from, A379 Exeter–Torbay, after Starcross; EX6 8RA

Very popular dining pub specialising in seafood (other choices available), with up to six real ales

Particularly on a sunny day, the position here really comes into its own with much prized tables on the sheltered front terrace looking over the small harbour with its bobbing boats, swans and ducks. Inside, there are several small, low-ceilinged, rambling rooms with black panelling and good-sized tables in various nooks, a snug with a cheerful winter coal fire, and an extension made up of mainly reclaimed timber and decorated with over 300 ship emblems, brass and copper lamps and nautical knick-knacks. Five real ales on handpump include Dartmoor Jail Ale, Otter Ale and St Austell Tribute with a couple of guests (they hold beer festivals at Easter and Halloween), eight wines by the glass, 16 gins and 20 malt whiskies; background music, darts, cards and board games.

Although the food majors on fresh fish and seafood, they offer non-fishy choices too: crab and brandy soup, scallops with sweet mango purée, sharing platters, vegetarian sausages with creamed potatoes, steak in ale pie, duo of fish and shellfish in a hot, spicy tomato sauce, chicken breast on mushrooms and shallots with peppers and leeks, slow-roast pork belly stuffed with cream cheese and sage with cumberland sauce and grain mustard mash, a seafood platter, and puddings such as sticky toffee pudding and chocolate and salted caramel tart. *Benchmark main dish: mussels with a choice of 18 different sauces £15.95. Two-course evening meal £22.95.*

Heavitree ~ Lease Malcolm and Katherine Protheroe, Scott Hellier ~ Real ale ~ Open 11-11; 11.30-10.30 Sun ~ Bar food 12-9 ~ Restaurant ~ Children welcome if seated and away from bar ~ Dogs allowed in bar *Recommended by Lauren and Dan Frazer, Richard and Tessa Ibbot, Patricia Hawkins, Graeme and Sally Mendham, Nick Higgins*

COLEFORD
New Inn 🍴⭐ ⭐ 🛏

SS7701 Map 1

(01363) 84242 – www.thenewinncoleford.co.uk
Just off A377 Crediton–Barnstaple; EX17 5BZ

Ancient thatched inn with hospitable owners, good food and real ales; bedrooms

Customers have been welcomed here since the 13th c, so it must be one of the oldest 'new' inns around. You'll be sure of a cheerful greeting from the hands-on licensees – and from Captain, the chatty Amazon blue parrot too – and there are always plenty of chatty regulars. The U-shaped, thatched building has the servery in the 'angle' with interestingly furnished areas leading off it: ancient and modern settles, cushioned stone wall seats, some character tables (a pheasant worked into the grain of one) and carved dressers and chests. Also, paraffin lamps, antique prints on the white walls, landscape-decorated plates on one beam and pewter tankards on another. Otter Ale and Sharps Doom Bar with a guest such as the local Hunters Half Bore or Shepherd Neame Spitfire on handpump, local cider, 16 wines by the glass and a dozen malt whiskies; background music, darts and board games. There are chairs and tables on decking beneath a pruned willow tree by the babbling stream, and more in a covered dining area. Bedrooms are peaceful and comfortable and the breakfasts are very good indeed.

Quite a choice of good food includes venison and pork terrine with cranberry and orange compote, fillets of smoked salmon, smoked trout and smoked mackerel with smoked mackerel pâté, aubergine and sweet potato moussaka with tomato and onion passata and feta, chicken fillet with crème fraîche, wholegrain mustard and tarragon sauce and charlotte potatoes, slow-cooked lamb shank with red wine, pink peppercorn and mushroom sauce, orange pepper-dusted cod with dauphinoise potatoes and citrus butter sauce on roasted fennel, confit duck leg on a duck liver and orange croûte with cider sauce, and puddings such as treacle tart with custard and caramel and praline roulade with fudge nuggets. *Benchmark main dish: luxury fish pie £13.95. Two-course evening meal £21.00.*

Free house ~ Licensees Carole and George Cowie ~ Real ale ~ Open 12-3, 6-11 (10.30 Sun) ~ Bar food 12-2, 6.30-9 ~ Restaurant ~ Children welcome ~ Dogs allowed in bar ~ Wi-fi ~ Quiz mid-month Sun evening; hog roasts May, July, Oct ~ Bedrooms: £72/£95
Recommended by John Ledbury, I D Barnett, Geoffrey Sutton, Sandra King, Jim and Sue James

DALWOOD
ST2400   Map 1

Tuckers Arms 🌟

(01404) 881342 – www.thetuckersarms.co.uk
Village signposted off A35 Axminster–Honiton; keep on past village; EX13 7EG

13th-c thatched inn with friendly, hard-working licensees, real ales and interesting bar food

After the church, this cream-washed and thatched medieval longhouse is the oldest building in the parish. You'll find a genuine welcome from good-humoured staff and the flagstoned bar is kept warm by a big inglenook log fireplace; it's very cosy. Also, heavy beams, traditional furnishings including assorted dining chairs, window seats and wall settles, numerous horsebrasses and a cheerful, bustling atmosphere. The back bar has an enormous collection of miniature bottles and there's also a more formal dining room; lots of copper implements and platters. Branscombe Vale Branoc, Exeter Avocet and Otter Bitter on handpump, several wines by the glass and up to 20 malt whiskies; background music and a double skittle alley. There are seats in the garden. The colourful summer window boxes, hanging baskets and tubs are really pretty and the pub is surrounded by narrow high-hedged lanes and hilly pasture countryside.

Extremely good food includes lunchtime sandwiches, potted crab, pâté of the day, pumpkin and sage ravioli, local moules marinière, steak in ale pie, lamb rump with redcurrant and rosemary gravy, pork belly with apricot, cider and raisin chutney, beer-battered fish and chips, and puddings such as butterscotch and ginger pudding with salted caramel ice-cream and lemon meringue pie. *Benchmark main dish: fisherman's platter £10.50. Two-course evening meal £19.50.*

Free house ~ Licensee Tracey McGowan ~ Real ale ~ Open 11.30-3, 6.30-11.30 ~ Bar food 12-2, 6.30-9 ~ Restaurant ~ Well behaved children in restaurant ~ Dogs allowed in bar ~ Wi-fi ~ Bedrooms: $45/$69.50 *Recommended by Diana and Bertie Farr, Edward May, Alexandra and Richard Clay, Richard and Penny Gibbs, Belinda Stamp*

EXETER
Fat Pig

SX9192   Map 1

(01392) 437217 – www.fatpig-exeter.co.uk
John Street; EX1 1BL

Enthusiastically run pub with own-brew beers, home-distilled spirits, big-flavoured food and a buoyant atmosphere

This is a great pub with a lively, cheerful feel, high quality food and a fine choice of drinks. The big-windowed bar is simply furnished: elegant stools against a mahogany counter, more stools and long cushioned pews by sturdy pale wooden tables on bare boards, an open fire in a pretty fireplace, blackboards listing food choices and lots of mirrors. As well as their own-brewed Fat Pig Ham 69 and Phat Nancys IPA and a changing guest on handpump, you'll find good wines by the glass, around 100 malt whiskies and their own Exeter Distillery gins (they have three), vodka and apple pie moonshine. There's also a red-painted and red quarry-tiled conservatory with a happy jumble of hops and house plants, books and old stone bottles on shelves, more mirrors and long benches and settles with scatter cushions around rustic tables.

Robust and extremely good using local game, beef from local farms and making their own sausages and black pudding, the food includes treacle-cured salmon with pickled cucumber, baked mackerel with horseradish and pickles, potato gnocchi with wild mushrooms, courgettes and cream, slow-cooked and pulled chipotle beef, breaded pork chop with creamed cabbage and bacon, and puddings such as apple and rhubarb frangipane tart and chocolate and mint pudding. *Benchmark main dish: crispy smoked lamb shoulder with rosemary potatoes and harissa yoghurt £18.00. Two-course evening meal £22.00.*

Free house ~ Licensee Paul Timewell ~ Real ale ~ Open 5-11pm; 4-midnight Fri; 12-midnight Sat; 12-5 Sun ~ Bar food 5-9; 12-9 Sat; 12-4 Sun ~ Restaurant ~ Children allowed Sun lunchtime only ~ Dogs welcome ~ Wi-fi *Recommended by Roger and Donna Huggins, Philip J Alderton, Sophie and James Collier, Derek Stafford, Gerry and Pam Pollard, Beth Aldridge*

FROGMORE
Globe ⌑

SX7742   Map 1

(01548) 531351 – www.theglobeinn.co.uk
A379 E of Kingsbridge; TQ7 2NR

Extended and neatly refurbished inn with bar and several dining areas, real ales, popular food and seats outside; warm bedrooms

This is a lovely area to explore and the surrounding South Hams countryside is very appealing, so it makes sense to stay in the well equipped, comfortable bedrooms here – and breakfasts are generous. The neatly kept bar has a double-sided woodburner with horsebrass-decorated stone pillars on either side, another fireplace filled with logs, cushioned settles, chunky farmhouse chairs and built-in wall seats around a mix of tables on wooden flooring, and a copper diving helmet. Attentive staff serve Otter Ale, Skinners Betty Stogs and South Hams Eddystone on handpump and several wines by the glass. The slate-floored games room has a pool table and darts. There's also a comfortable lounge with an open fire, cushioned dining chairs and tables on red carpeting, a big leather sofa, a model yacht and a large yacht painting – spot the clever mural of a log pile. Teak tables and chairs sit on the back terrace, with steps leading up to another level with picnic-sets; the summer window boxes are most attractive.

🍴 Food is well regarded and includes mushroom bruschetta with creamy white wine sauce, smoked salmon and haddock fishcakes with dill, lemon and horseradish, pizzas, burger with toppings, sauce and chips, crab, squid and prawn linguine with lime, chilli and coriander, steak in ale pie, a curry of the day, chicken with pepper, mushroom and cream sauce, 10oz rib-eye steak with a choice of sauce, and puddings such as white chocolate cheesecake with fruit compote and treacle tart with clotted cream. *Benchmark main dish: seafood pancake £14.95. Two-course evening meal £20.50.*

Free house ~ Licensees John and Lynda Horsley ~ Real ale ~ Open 12-11 (10.30 Sun); mid Sept-end June 12-2.30, 6-11 (6.30-10.30 Sun in winter); closed Mon lunchtime in winter ~ Bar food 12-2, 6-9 ~ Restaurant ~ Children welcome ~ Dogs allowed in bar and bedrooms ~ Wi-fi ~ Jazz alternate Weds evening; folk first Tues and third Thurs of month ~ Bedrooms: £75/£90 *Recommended by Freddie and Sarah Banks, Geoff and Ann Marston, Paul Farraday, Jane Rigby*

GEORGEHAM
Rock 🏅♟   SS4639 Map 1

(01271) 890322 – www.therockinn.biz
Rock Hill, above village; EX33 1JW

Beamed pub with smashing food, five real ales, plenty of room inside and out and a relaxed atmosphere

Our readers enjoy their visits to this friendly old pub, citing the very good food and five real ales as highlights. The big bustling bar is divided in two by a step. The pubby top part has half-planked walls, an open woodburning stove in a stone fireplace and captain's and farmhouse chairs around wooden tables on quarry tiles; the lower area has panelled wall seats, some built-in settles forming a cosy booth, old local photographs and ancient flat irons. Leading off here is a red-carpeted dining room with attractive black and white photographs of North Devon folk. Helpful young staff serve Exmoor Gold, St Austell Tribute, Sharps Doom Bar and Timothy Taylors Landlord on handpump and more than a dozen wines by the glass; background music and board games. The light and airy back dining conservatory has high-backed wooden or modern dining chairs around tables under a vine, with a little terrace beyond. There are picnic-sets at the front beside pretty hanging baskets and tubs; wheelchair access.

🍴 Rewarding food includes french-style mussels, thai crab cakes with sweet chilli sauce and asian salad, sharing platters, wild mushroom and blue cheese tortellini with white wine and tarragon sauce, spanish burger (chorizo and beef) with manchego, serrano and aioli, chicken curry, local sausages with mash and red onion gravy, hickory smoked barbecue ribs with slaw, sea bass fillet with salmon and crayfish risotto, 10oz rib-eye steak with handcut chips and garlic mushrooms, and puddings such as marshmallow and fresh fruit skewers with chocolate sauce and sticky toffee pudding with butterscotch sauce. *Benchmark main dish: linguine with clams, chilli and garlic £16.95. Two-course evening meal £21.00.*

Star Pubs & Bars ~ Lease Daniel Craddock ~ Real ale ~ Open 11am-11.30pm (midnight Sat); 12-11.30 Sun ~ Bar food 12-2.30, 6-9; 12-8.30 Sun ~ Restaurant ~ Children welcome ~ Dogs allowed in bar ~ Wi-fi *Recommended by John Wilson, Vibekke Böhl, Cecily and Steven Evans, Neal Griffith, Mike Benton, Andrew and Michele Revell, Edward May*

HAYTOR VALE   SX7777 Map 1

Rock ★ 🏅 🍷 🛏

(01364) 661305 – www.rock-inn.co.uk

Haytor signposted off B3387 just W of Bovey Tracey, on good moorland road to Widecombe; TQ13 9XP

Smart Dartmoor inn with lovely food, real ales and seats in pretty garden; comfortable bedrooms

Cleverly appealing to casual lunchtime customers (many are walkers from Dartmoor National Park) as well as those expecting a more formal evening meal and comfortable overnight stay, this is an especially well run and civilised inn. The two neatly kept, linked, partly panelled bar rooms have lots of dark wood and red plush, polished antique tables with candles and fresh flowers, old-fashioned prints and decorative plates, and warming winter log fires (the main fireplace has a fine Stuart fireback). Dartmoor Jail Ale and Exeter Avocet on handpump, 15 wines (plus champagne and sparkling rosé) by the glass and 20 malt whiskies. There's also a light and spacious dining room in the lower part of the inn and a residents' lounge. The large, pretty garden opposite has some seats, with more on the little terrace next to the pub. Beamed bedrooms are smart (with either garden or moor views) and are highly regarded by our readers, and breakfasts are excellent. You can park at the back of the building. Dogs are allowed in the conservatory area and in some bedrooms.

🏅 First class food includes sandwiches, beetroot-cured salmon with horseradish and dill, quail with confit leg, fried quail egg, pearl barley and red wine jus, wild garlic risotto with parmesan and white truffle oil, lamb and rosemary burger with mint mayonnaise and chips, roast cod with crab croquette, avocado purée, shaved fennel and lemon oil, lamb rump with lamb pithivier, smoked aubergine and red wine jus, and puddings such as tonka bean cheesecake and amaretto ice-cream and chocolate marquise with soaked cherries and cherry sorbet; they also offer a two- and three-course lunch menu. *Benchmark main dish: rib-eye steak with roast cherry tomatoes and chips £22.95. Two-course evening meal £22.00.*

Free house ~ Licensee Christopher Graves ~ Real ale ~ Open 11-11; 11-10.30 Sun ~ Bar food 12-2, 7-9 (8.30 Sun) ~ Restaurant ~ Children welcome away from main bar ~ Dogs allowed in bedrooms ~ Wi-fi ~ Bedrooms: £80/£110 *Recommended by Dr and Mrs A K Clarke, Richard Cole, Maggie and Matthew Lyons, David and Charlotte Green, Matt and Hayley Jacob, Peter and Caroline Waites, Andrew Laurence*

HORNDON   SX5280 Map 1

Elephants Nest 🍺 £ 🛏

(01822) 810273 – www.elephantsnest.co.uk

If coming from Okehampton on A386, turn left at Mary Tavy Inn, then left after about 0.5 miles; pub signposted beside Mary Tavy Inn, then Horndon signposted; on OS Sheet it's named as the New Inn; PL19 9NQ

Off the beaten track with some interesting original features, real ales and changing food; good bedrooms

A remote old inn on the lower slopes of Dartmoor and once three isolated miners' cottages, this makes a good base for exploring the area. Bedrooms are attractively furnished and comfortable and breakfasts are particularly good. The friendly main bar has lots of beer pump clips on the beams, high bar chairs by the bar counter, Dartmoor Jail Ale, Palmers IPA and St Austell Proper Job on handpump, a couple of farm ciders, ten wines by the glass and 15 malt whiskies. Two other rooms have an assortment of wooden dining chairs around a mix of tables, and throughout there are bare stone walls, flagstones, horsebrasses and three woodburning stoves. When the weather is warm, the spreading, pretty garden (with an area reserved only for adults) really comes into its own, with picnic-sets under parasols and views across dry-stone walls to pastures and rougher moorland above.

Enjoyable food includes lunchtime baguettes, pork terrine with pickles and cumberland sauce, seafood salad, braised ox cheek with mushroom risotto, cumberland sausage with mash and onion gravy, goat, lemongrass and coconut curry with accompaniments, king prawns in olive oil, garlic, chilli and white wine, lamb shank with minted peas and bacon, duck breast with creamed leeks and madeira sauce, and puddings such as treacle tart with clotted cream and lemon posset with blueberry compote. *Benchmark main dish: steak and kidney pudding £16.95. Two-course evening meal £22.00.*

Free house ~ Licensee Hugh Cook ~ Real ale ~ Open 12-3, 6.30-11 (10.30 Sun) ~ Bar food 12-2.15 (3 Sun), 6.30-9 ~ Restaurant ~ Children welcome away from bar ~ Dogs welcome ~ Wi-fi ~ Bedrooms: £100/£120 *Recommended by Stephen Shepherd, William Slade, Julie Swift, Christopher Mannings, Peter Barrett, Andrew and Michele Revell, Colin McLachlan*

 IDDESLEIGH
Duke of York 🛏

SS5608   Map 1

(01837) 810253 – www.dukeofyorkdevon.co.uk
B3217 Exbourne–Dolton; EX19 8BG

15th-c thatched local with tasty food and a fair choice of drinks; bedrooms

If you enjoy simple, honest pubs you'll feel at home here, though it's not to everyone's taste. The unspoilt bar has plenty of chatty locals, rocking chairs, cushioned benches built into the wall's black-painted wooden dado, stripped tables and other simple country furnishings, banknotes pinned to beams, and a large open fireplace. Bays Topsail, Otter Bitter and a guest ale tapped from the cask, several wines by the glass and three farm ciders. It can get pretty cramped at peak times. The dining room has a huge inglenook fireplace. Through a small coach arch is a little back garden with some picnic-sets. Bedrooms are clean but old-fashioned (and some may have no lock on the door); three are in the pub, with three more just a minute's walk away. Michael Morpurgo, author of *War Horse*, got the inspiration to write his novel after talking to World War I veteran Wilfred Ellis in front of the fire here over 30 years ago.

Bar food includes sandwiches, salt and pepper squid with sweet chilli dip, garlic mushrooms with stilton topping, vegetable chilli, home-cooked ham and eggs, chicken and bacon lasagne, local sausages with mash and onion gravy, scampi with home-made tartare sauce, slow-roasted pork belly with apple and cider sauce, beer-battered fish and chips, and puddings. *Benchmark main dish: steak and kidney pudding £13.55. Two-course evening meal £17.00.*

Free house ~ Licensee John Pittam ~ Real ale ~ Open 11-11 (midnight Sat) ~ Bar food 12-9.30; no food 3-5pm Mon-Weds in winter ~ Restaurant ~ Children welcome ~ Dogs allowed in bar and bedrooms ~ Wi-fi ~ Bedrooms: £60/£80 *Recommended by Peter Pilbeam, Len and Lilly Dowson, Ian Cuttle, Lindy Andrews, Frank and Marcia Pelling, David Appleyard*

KINGSBRIDGE   SX7344   Map 1

Dodbrooke Inn 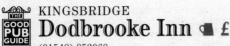 £

(01548) 852068

Church Street, Dodbrooke (parking some way off); TQ7 1DB

Bustling local with friendly licensees, chatty locals and well regarded food and drink

The friendly, long-serving licensees have been at the helm here for 32 years. You'll get a genuine welcome and as it's a small terraced pub in a quiet residential area there are lots of chatty regulars. The traditional bar has built-in cushioned stall seats and plush cushioned stools around pubby tables, some horse tack, local photographs and china jugs, a log fire and an easy-going atmosphere. Bass, Dartmoor IPA and Sharps Doom Bar on handpump, local cider and eight wines by the glass. You can sit in the covered courtyard, which might be candlelit in warm weather.

Fair value food includes sandwiches, deep-fried whitebait with tartare sauce, scallops with crispy bacon, ham and egg, beef stroganoff, sausage in a basket, minted lamb shank, popular steaks, and puddings. *Benchmark main dish: beer-battered fish and chips £9.75. Two-course evening meal £15.00.*

Free house ~ Licensees Michael and Jill Dyson ~ Real ale ~ Open 12-2, 5.30-11; 12-2, 7-10.30 Sun; closed Mon-Weds lunchtimes ~ Bar food 12-1.30, 5.30-8.30 ~ Children welcome if over 5 ~ Wi-fi *Recommended by Alf and Sally Garner, Charlie Stevens, Peter Brix, Edward May, Brian and Sally Wakeham*

POSTBRIDGE   SX6780   Map 1

Warren House

(01822) 880208 – www.warrenhouseinn.co.uk

B3212 0.75 miles NE of Postbridge; PL20 6TA

Isolated 18th-c pub, ideal for a drink or meal after a moorland hike

A perfect pub after a damp walk on Dartmoor, this is a straightforward and honest place with proper character. The cosy bar has simple furnishings such as easy chairs and settles beneath the beamed ochre ceiling, old pictures of the inn on partly panelled stone walls and dim lighting (powered by the pub's own generator); one of the open fires is said to have been kept alight since 1845. There's also a family room. There's Otter Ale plus guests such as Roam Sound Bitter and Summerskills Start Point on handpump, local farm cider and malt whiskies. The picnic-sets on both sides of the road have moorland views.

Bar food includes lunchtime ploughman's and baked potatoes, pasties, breaded king prawns with garlic dip, steak in ale pie, ricotta and spinach cannelloni, ham and chips, spanish-style lamb in sherry, cajun chicken with a dip and fries, smoked haddock and spring onion fishcakes, steaks with trimmings, and puddings. *Benchmark main dish: rabbit pie £13.50. Two-course evening meal £18.00.*

Free house ~ Licensee Peter Parsons ~ Real ale ~ Open 11-10; 12-10 Sun; 11-3 Mon, Tues in winter ~ Bar food 12-9; 12-8.30 Sun; 12-2.30 Mon, Tues in winter ~ Restaurant ~ Children in family room only ~ Dogs allowed in bar *Recommended by Anne Taylor, Colin and Daniel Gibbs, John Evans, Colin McLachlan*

If we don't specify bar meal times for a featured entry, these are normally 12-2 and 7-9; we do show times if they are markedly different.

RATTERY
Church House

SX7461 Map 1

(01364) 642220 – www.thechurchhouseinn.co.uk

Village signposted from A385 W of Totnes, and A38 S of Buckfastleigh; TQ10 9LD

Ancient place with friendly licensees, a good range of drinks, well regarded bar food and seats in the garden

This is one of Britain's oldest pubs, so there's lots to look at while enjoying a pint. Parts of the original building, dating from around 1030, still survive – look out for the spiral stone steps behind a little stone doorway on the left. The rooms have a lot of character: massive oak beams and standing timbers in the open-plan bar, large fireplaces (one with a cosy nook partitioned around it), traditional pubby chairs and tables, some window seats, and prints and horsebrasses on plain white walls. There's also a dining room, a lounge and a separate restaurant with a courtyard garden that's equipped with smart seats and tables under big parasols. Dartmoor Jail Ale, Exeter Avocet and Otter Bitter on handpump, 19 malt whiskies and a dozen wines by the glass. At the front of the building are picnic-sets with more on a large hedged-in lawn; the summer hanging baskets are pretty.

 Popular, seasonal food includes lunchtime sandwiches, ham hock terrine with piccalilli, venison carpaccio with truffle and parmesan, sharing boards, spinach and ricotta ravioli with spinach and basil pesto and parmesan, local sausages with mash and gravy, free-range chicken breast with fondant potato and wild mushroom jus, megrim sole with chorizo and caper dressing, rack of lamb with caramelised cauliflower and mint jus, and puddings. *Benchmark main dish: pork belly with wholegrain mustard mash and cider jus £15.50. Two-course evening meal £21.00.*

Free house ~ Licensees John and William Edwards ~ Real ale ~ Open 11.45-11; closed Mon mid Sept-July ~ Bar food 12-2.30, 6-9 ~ Restaurant ~ Children welcome ~ Dogs allowed in bar ~ Wi-fi *Recommended by John Evans, Andrew Low, Stuart and Natalie Granville, George and Alison Bishop, Richard Cole, Hugh Roberts, Dr and Mrs A K Clarke*

SANDFORD
Lamb

SS8202 Map 1

(01363) 773676 – www.lambinnsandford.co.uk

The Square; EX17 4LW

16th-c inn with good food, thoughtful choice of drinks and seats in garden; well equipped bedrooms

You'll find a wide mix of customers in the linked beamed bar and dining areas here and the atmosphere is friendly and chatty. The bar has red leather sofas beside a log fire, cushioned window seats, a settle and various dining chairs round a few tables on patterned carpet. Branscombe Vale Branoc and Powderkeg Speak Easy Translatlantic Pale with guests such as Dartmoor Jail Ale and Exmoor Antler on handpump, ten wines by the glass, four farm ciders, 20 gins (most are local) and 20 malt whiskies. The dining area has a woodburning stove, a cushioned wall pew, all manner of nice old wooden dining chairs and tables and quite a few mirrors. There's also a Tap Room with board games. The cobbled, three-level garden has fairy lights and rustic seats and tables, and beyond the hedge are some picnic-sets on grass. Bedrooms are comfortable, modern and well equipped. Nearby parking is at a premium, but the village car park is just a few minutes' walk up the small lane to the right.

🍴 Enjoyable food includes lunchtime ciabatta rolls, scallops with chorizo and red pepper, roast chicken thigh with pork bonbon and blue cheese mousse, broccoli and blue cheese tart with pepper purée and pickles, burgers with toppings and chips, duck breast with fondant potato and star anise, local lamb rack with dauphinoise potatoes and jus, 10oz rib-eye steak with garlic butter and chips, and puddings such as raspberry brûlée with blackberry buttercream and sticky toffee pudding with salted caramel ice-cream. *Benchmark main dish: fresh fish dish of the day £16.95. Two-course evening meal £21.00.*

Free house ~ Licensee Nick Silk ~ Real ale ~ Open 9am-11pm (midnight Sat); 9am-10.30pm Sun ~ Bar food 12-2.15, 6.30-9 ~ Restaurant ~ Children welcome ~ Dogs welcome ~ Wi-fi ~ Live music monthly; cinema twice a month; see website ~ Bedrooms: /£75 *Recommended by Abigail Slater, Douglas Power, Belinda Stamp, Kerry and Guy Trooper, Mary and Douglas McDowell*

SOUTH POOL

SX7740   Map 1

Millbrook 🌟🍷

(01548) 531581 – www.millbrookinnsouthpool.co.uk

Off A379 E of Kingsbridge; TQ7 2RW

Devon Dining Pub of the Year

Delightful village local by the Salcombe estuary with local ales, very good food and a warm welcome for all

Southpool Creek is only a few moments' stroll away from where this charming, tiny pub has mooring facilities for visiting yachts and small boats. Seats on the outside terrace overlook the water. The small main bar has a log fire in an inglenook fireplace, a couple of settles and a blanket box on turkey rugs, and stools against the counter where they keep Salcombe Lifesaver, South Hams Wild Blonde and Timothy Taylors Landlord on handpump, 20 wines by the glass, eight malt whiskies, eight rums and a couple of local farm ciders; daily papers, darts and board games. A dining area to the right has a woodburning stove, settles and wheelback chairs around scrubbed wooden tables, and stone and cream walls decorated with maps. This leads to another small dining area and there's also a simply furnished Top Bar. They also offer an apartment (which can be on a self-catering basis). A Land Rover Defender can pick up customers from the nearby ferry. It does get a bit crowded at weekends.

🌟 Excellent food using the best local, seasonal produce includes tandoori-crusted scallops with parsnip purée and seaweed, pork liver parfait with apple purée, apple dusted crackling and crispy hogs pudding, roasted skate wing with chorizo vinaigrette, charred broccoli and jerusalem artichoke, trio of lamb with hedgerow-foraged pesto, potato fondant and pea and broad bean fricassée, seared calves liver with bone marrow mash and caramelised onion fritters, and puddings such as singapore gin sling upside-down cake with limoncello curd and frozen Cointreau yoghurt and spiced poached pear with candied nut crumble, smoked pear coulis and sorbet. *Benchmark main dish: burger with home-made sauce and chips £12.00. Two-course evening meal £27.00.*

Free house ~ Licensees Charlie and Tess Baker ~ Real ale ~ Open 12-11 ~ Bar food 12-2, 6-9; hot snacks all day ~ Restaurant ~ Children welcome but not in bedrooms ~ Dogs allowed in bar ~ Wi-fi ~ Live music alternate Sunday afternoons ~ Bedrooms: /£150 *Recommended by Megan and William Stapley, Sophie and James Collier, Barry and Daphne Gregson, Helene Grygar*

Virtually all pubs in this book sell wine by the glass. We mention wines if they are a cut above the average.

SOUTH ZEAL
SX6593 Map 1

Oxenham Arms 🛏

(01837) 840244 – www.theoxenhamarms.com

Off A30/A382; EX20 2JT

Wonderful 15th-c inn with lots of history, character bars, real ales, enjoyable food and big garden; bedrooms

This ancient place is just the spot to unwind after the busy A30. First licensed in 1477, it was built to combat the pagan power of the Neolithic standing stone that still forms part of the wall in the room behind the bar (there's actually 20 feet of stone below the floor). The heavily beamed and partly panelled front bar has elegant mullioned windows and Stuart fireplaces, all sorts of chairs and built-in wall seats with scatter cushions around low oak tables on bare floorboards, and bar stools against the counter where friendly staff serve Merry Monk (named for them from Dartmoor), Dartmoor Jail Ale and Teignworthy Gun Dog on handpump; also, seven wines by the glass, 70 malt whiskies, 25 ports, local mead and three farm ciders. A small room has beams, wheelback chairs around polished tables, decorative plates and another open fire. The four-acre garden is reached up imposing curved stone steps and has plenty of seats and fine views – plus more tables under parasols out in front. Some of the bedrooms have four-poster beds; Charles Dickens, snowed up one winter, wrote a lot of *The Pickwick Papers* here. You can walk straight from the door on to the moor and they provide details of walking tours.

 Popular food includes ham hock and parsley terrine with piccalilli, mussels with garlic, cream and parsley, sharing boards, mushroom, leek and blue cheese pie, trio of local sausages with mustard mash and greens, minute steak with fries and a choice of sauce, cod loin with lemon and thyme, braised chicory and warm herb dressing, duck breast with parmentier potatoes, carrot and coriander purée and duck sauce, and puddings such as vanilla pannacotta with strawberry and blueberry compote and chocolate tart with raspberry sorbet. *Benchmark main dish: steak in ale pie £12.95. Two-course evening meal £20.50.*

Free house ~ Licensees Simon and Lyn Powell ~ Real ale ~ Open 11-11 ~ Bar food 12-3, 6-8.30; cream teas in afternoon ~ Restaurant ~ Children welcome ~ Dogs allowed in bar ~ Wi-fi ~ Bedrooms: /£108 *Recommended by Gerry and Pam Pollard, Liz and Mike Newton, Dr Martin Owton, Adrian Johnson, Helene Grygar*

SPREYTON
SX6996 Map 1

Tom Cobley 🍺

(01647) 231314 – www.tomcobleytavern.co.uk

Dragdown Hill; W out of village; EX17 5AL

Huge range of quickly changing real ales and ciders, and wide choice of food in friendly, busy village pub

Up to 14 real ales – well kept on handpump or tapped from the cask – change quickly here and include Dartmoor Jail Ale, Exeter 'fraidNot, Holsworthy Tamar Black, Otter Ale, Plain Inncognito, St Austell Tribute and Teignworthy Gun Dog; also, up to 14 farm ciders and perries. The comfortable bar has traditional furnishings, an open fire and local photographs and country scenes on the walls, and you can be sure of a genuine welcome from the hospitable landlord and his cheerful staff. A large back dining room has beams and similar décor. There are picnic-sets in the garden and more out in front by the quiet street. Several of the comfortable bedrooms have Dartmoor views. Disabled access.

Good quality, traditional food includes lunchtime sandwiches, pasties, omelettes and brunch, plus chicken liver pâté with caramelised onion chutney, prawn cocktail, sweet potato and spinach curry, lamb and mint suet pudding, lambs liver with bacon and onion gravy, thai prawn and cod fishcakes with chips, cottage pie, chicken curry, gammon with egg and pineapple, duck with home-made orange sauce, mixed grill, and puddings. *Benchmark main dish: steak in ale pie £10.95. Two-course evening meal £20.00.*

Free house ~ Licensees Roger and Carol Cudlip ~ Real ale ~ Open 12-3, 6-11 (midnight Fri, Sat); 12-4, 7-11 Sun; closed Mon lunchtime ~ Bar food 12-2, 7-9 ~ Restaurant ~ Children welcome ~ Dogs allowed in bar and bedrooms ~ Bedrooms: £60/$100
Recommended by Steve Watson, Ian Herdman, Selwyn Jones, Audrey and Andrew Nichols, David and Leone Lawson, Colin and Daniel Gibbs

 TIPTON ST JOHN   SY0991   Map 1
Golden Lion
(01404) 812881 – www.goldenliontipton.co.uk
Pub signed off B3176 Sidmouth–Ottery St Mary; EX10 0AA

Busy village pub with three real ales, well liked food and plenty of seats in the attractive garden

You'll need to book a table in advance if you wish to enjoy the good food cooked by Mr Teissier in this bustling, neatly kept pub. The main bar, split into two, has a comfortable, relaxed atmosphere, as does the back snug. Throughout are paintings by west country artists, art deco prints, Tiffany lamps and copper pots and kettles. A few tables are kept for those just wanting a pint and a chat. Otter Ale and Bitter and Sharps Doom Bar on handpump, ten wines by the glass and several gins; background music. There are seats on the terracotta-walled terrace with outside heaters and grapevines and more seats on the grass edged by pretty flowering borders. Dog walkers may use a verandah.

The tempting food cooked by the chef-landlord includes lunchtime sandwiches and ploughman's, crayfish salad with lime and garlic mayonnaise, vegetable lasagne, home-cooked ham and egg, steak and kidney pudding, beer-battered cod and chips, steak frites, duck breast with oriental plum sauce, slow-roasted lamb shanks, and puddings such as crème brûlée and boozy chocolate pot. *Benchmark main dish: fish soup £9.00. Two-course evening meal £23.00.*

Heavitree ~ Tenants François and Michelle Teissier ~ Real ale ~ Open 12-2.30, 6-10; 12-3 Sun; closed Sun evening, Mon ~ Bar food 12-2, 6.15-7.30 (8 Fri, Sat) ~ Children welcome *Recommended by Claire Adams, Rosie and John Moore, Charles Todd, Diane Abbot, Susan and Callum Slade*

TOTNES   SX8059   Map 1
Steam Packet 🛏
(01803) 863880 – www.steampacketinn.co.uk
St Peters Quay, on W bank (ie not on Steam Packet Quay); TQ9 5EW

Quayside pub with an attractive layout, friendly staff, good food and seats overlooking the water

There's plenty of room here for both eating and drinking and the three distinct bar areas have polished floorboards, bare stone and brick walls, half-panelling and delft shelving and open fires. There are built-in wall seats, dark wooden chairs and leather-topped stools around traditional tables and a comfortable sofa with scatter cushions beside shelves of books. Friendly, efficient staff, who cope well at peak times, serve Dartmoor Legend, Roam Tavy Best Bitter, Salcombe Seahorse and Sharps Doom Bar on handpump, several wines by the glass and farm cider; background music and TV. There's also a conservatory restaurant. At the front, seats under big parasols on the terrace overlook the River Dart; it's best to arrive early on a sunny day. Bedrooms are light, airy and comfortable with spotless, up-to-date bathrooms.

Food is popular and includes breakfasts (8-10.30am weekdays; 8.30-10.30am weekends), sandwiches (until 6pm), chestnut mushroom and gruyère tart, chicken, apricot and pancetta terrine, crab and king prawn linguine, cajun chicken burger with fries, roast pork belly with black pudding mash, apple and ginger purée, crackling shard and cider gravy, thai green fish, prawn and coconut curry, and puddings. *Benchmark main dish: beer-battered fish and chips £13.00. Two-course evening meal £21.50.*

Buccaneer Holdings ~ Manager Ian Durrant ~ Real ale ~ Open 8.30am-11pm ~ Bar food 12-9 (8 Sun) ~ Restaurant ~ Children welcome ~ Dogs allowed in bar ~ Wi-fi ~ Bedrooms: /£140 *Recommended by Peter and Alison Steadman, Max and Steph Warren, Mike Swan, Rob Anderson, Gus Swan, Jo Garnett, Julian Richardson*

WIDECOMBE
SX7276   Map 1

Rugglestone

(01364) 621327 – www.rugglestoneinn.co.uk
Village at end of B3387; pub just S – turn left at church and NT church house, OS Sheet 191 map reference 720765; TQ13 7TF

Charming local with a couple of bars, cheerful customers, friendly staff, four real ales and traditional pub food

Just the place to refuel after enjoying one of the surrounding Dartmoor walks, this remains a tucked-away little gem. The unspoilt bar has just four tables, a few window and wall seats, a one-person pew built into the corner beside a nice old stone fireplace (with a woodburner) and a good mix of customers. The rudimentary bar counter dispenses Bays Gold, Dartmoor Legend, Exeter Avocet and a beer named for the pub (from Teignworthy) tapped from the cask; local farm cider and a decent small wine list. The room on the right is slightly bigger and lighter in feel, with beams, another stone fireplace, stripped-pine tables and a built-in wall bench; there's also a small dining room. To reach the picnic-sets in the garden you have to cross a bridge over a little moorland stream. Disabled access but no disabled loos. They have a holiday cottage to rent.

Traditional food includes sandwiches, chicken liver pâté, local potted crab, cheese and spinach cannelloni, home-cooked ham and eggs, fish pie, spicy meatballs in tomato sauce topped with cheese, smoked trout salad with home-made coleslaw, lasagne, and puddings. *Benchmark main dish: steak and stilton pie £12.00. Two-course evening meal £18.00.*

Free house ~ Licensees Richard and Vicki Palmer ~ Real ale ~ Open 11.30-3, 6.30-11; 11.30-3, 5-11.30 Fri; 11.30-11.30 Sat; 12-11 Sun ~ Bar food 12-2, 6.30-9 ~ Restaurant ~ Children allowed away from bar area ~ Dogs welcome *Recommended by Roger and Donna Huggins, Melanie and David Lawson, Moira and Jon Weller, Susan and Callum Slade, Frank and Marcia Pelling, Colin McLachlan*

Real ale may be served from handpumps, electric pumps (not just the on-off switches used for keg beer) or – common in Scotland – tall taps called founts (pronounced 'fonts') where a separate pump pushes the beer up under air pressure.

Also Worth a Visit in Devon

Besides the fully inspected pubs, you might like to try these pubs that have been recommended to us and described by readers. Do tell us what you think of them: feedback@goodguides.com

ABBOTSKERSWELL SX8568

Court Farm (01626) 361866

Wilton Way; look for the church tower; TQ12 5NY Attractive neatly extended 17th-c longhouse tucked away in picturesque hamlet; various rooms off long beamed and paved main bar, good mix of furnishings, woodburners, well priced popular food (worth booking) including weekday lunchtime bargains, friendly helpful service, Bass, Otter and other beers, farm cider and decent wines; background music, pool and darts; children and dogs (in bar) welcome, picnic-sets in pretty lawned garden, open all day, food all day Thurs-Sun. *(Chris Stevenson)*

APPLEDORE SS4630

Beaver (01237) 474822

Irsha Street; EX39 1RY Relaxed, well run harbourside pub with lovely estuary view from popular raised dining area; enjoyable reasonably priced food especially fresh local fish, prompt friendly service, good choice of west country ales, farm cider, decent house wines and great range of whiskies; background music and some live music, quiz Weds, pool in smaller games room, TV; children and dogs (in bar) welcome, disabled access (but no nearby parking), tables on small sheltered water-view terrace. *(Alan and Alice Morgan)*

APPLEDORE SS4630

Royal George (01237) 424138

Irsha Street; EX39 1RY Waterside dining pub refurbished under new owners; local beers, plenty of wines by the glass and good reasonably priced food from daily changing menu including fresh fish, friendly staff, superb estuary views from dining room and upstairs restaurant with balcony; children and dogs (downstairs) welcome, picturesque street sloping to the sea, a few picnic-sets out at front, four comfortably revamped bedrooms, open all day. *(Chris Sallnow)*

ASHILL ST0811

Ashill Inn (01884) 840506

M5 junction 27, follow signs to Willand, then left to Uffculme and Craddock on B3440; Ashill signed to left; pub in centre of village; EX15 3NL Popular 19th-c village pub, cosy and friendly, with well kept local ales and highly rated home-cooked food including daily specials (booking advised), reasonable prices, black beams, woodburner in stone fireplace, modern dining extension overlooking small garden; some live music, darts and skittles, TV; children welcome, closed Mon lunchtime, no food Sun evening/Mon. *(Jane and Philip Saunders)*

ASHPRINGTON SX8157

Durant Arms (01803) 732240

Off A381 S of Totnes; TQ9 7UP Traditional 18th-c village inn; enjoyable home-cooked food and three well kept ales including Noss Beer Works, good friendly service, slate-floored bar with stag's head above woodburner, china on delft shelf, other connecting rooms; occasional live music; children, walkers and dogs welcome, three bedrooms, open all day weekends, may close Mon in winter. *(Ben and Jenny Settle)*

AVONWICK SX6958

★ **Turtley Corn Mill** (01364) 646100

0.5 miles off A38 roundabout at SW end of South Brent bypass; TQ10 9ES Converted watermill with series of linked areas; mix of wooden dining chairs and chunky tables on oriental rugs or dark flagstones, fat church candles, various prints and some framed 78rpm discs, woodburners, big windows looking out over grounds, Dartmoor, Otter and guests, nine wines by the glass and 30 malt whiskies, wide choice of brasserie-style food, friendly service; free wi-fi; children and dogs (in bar) welcome, extensive garden with well spaced picnic-sets, giant chess set and small lake, six bedrooms, open (and food) all day from 9am for breakfast. *(Rosie and Marcus Heatherley)*

AXMOUTH SY2591

Harbour Inn (01297) 20371

B3172 Seaton–Axminster; EX12 4AF Ancient thatched pub by estuary; updated heavily beamed bar rooms with bare boards, flagstones and some stripped-stone walls, huge inglenook, lots of model boats, old pictures, photographs and accounts of shipwrecks, other partitioned dining/seating areas including carpeted part with armchairs by woodburner, Badger ales and several wines by the glass, enjoyable food from sharing boards up; background music, Weds quiz; children and dogs (in bar) welcome, modern furniture on terrace, picnic-sets on grass, open (and food) all day. *(Barbara Brown)*

AYLESBEARE SY0490

Halfway (01395) 232273

A3052 Exeter–Sidmouth, junction with B3180; EX5 2JP Modernised roadside dining pub (same owners as the Bowd in Sidmouth); well cooked food from fairly priced pub favourites up including home-made american-style burgers, good fresh fish/seafood and lunchtime carvery, well kept Otter Bitter and Greene King Abbot, efficient friendly service, Dartmoor views from restaurant/conservatory and raised outside seating area; children and dogs (in bar) welcome, open all day Sun, closed Tues in winter. *(Joy Griffiths)*

BAMPTON   SS9522
★**Swan** (01398) 332248
Station Road; EX16 9NG Popular, well run beamed village inn with spacious bare-boards bar, woodburners in two inglenooks, three changing west country beers, nice wines and fine choice of gins, very good food from interesting varied menu (both licensees are chefs), efficient friendly service; children and dogs welcome, well appointed bedrooms, big breakfast, closed Mon lunchtime otherwise open all day, no food Mon or third Sun evening of month. *(Jeff Jordan)*

BANTHAM   SX6643
★**Sloop** (01548) 560489
Off A379/B3197 NW of Kingsbridge; TQ7 3AJ Welcoming 14th-c split-level pub close to fine beach and walks, popular and relaxed, with good mix of customers in black-beamed stripped-stone bar, country tables and chairs on flagstones, blazing woodburner, well kept St Austell Tribute, Proper Job and a guest, several wines by the glass and very nice food from sandwiches to good fresh fish, courteous helpful service, restaurant; background music; children and dogs (in bar) welcome, seats out at back, six bedrooms (a couple with sea views), open all day in summer. *(Jane Durrant)*

BEER   ST2289
Anchor (01297) 20386
Fore Street; EX12 3ET Sea-view inn with good choice of enjoyable food including local fish, Greene King, Otter and good value wines, open-plan interior with large eating area, friendly staff; background music, sports TV, fruit machine, free wi-fi; children well looked after, dogs welcome in bar, lots of tables in clifftop garden over road, six reasonably priced bedrooms, open (and food) all day. *(Nicola and Holly Lyons)*

BEESANDS   SX8140
Cricket (01548) 580215
About 3 miles S of A379, from Chillington; in village turn right along foreshore road; TQ7 2EN Pub-restaurant with pebbly Start Bay beach just over the sea wall; light airy new england-style décor with dark wood or leather chairs around chunky tables, stripped-wood flooring by the bar, carpet in the restaurant, some nautical bits and pieces including model boats, relaxed chatty atmosphere with a few tables kept for drinkers, Otter and St Austell ales, local cider and 14 wines by the glass, generally well liked food with emphasis on fish/seafood, can be expensive; background radio, TVs, free wi-fi; children

and dogs (in bar) welcome, wheelchair access/loo, picnic-sets by sea wall, seven attractive bedrooms (some overlooking the sea), South West Coast Path runs through the village, open all day, food all day in high summer. *(Chris Stevenson)*

BELSTONE   SX6129
Tors (01837) 840689
A mile off A30; EX20 1QZ Popular small Victorian granite pub-hotel in peaceful Dartmoor-edge village, family-run and welcoming, with long carpeted bar divided by settles, well kept ales such as Dartmoor and Teignworthy, over 60 malt whiskies and good choice of wines, enjoyable food from baguettes to specials, cheerful prompt service, restaurant; live music; children welcome and dogs (they have their own), disabled access, seats out on nearby grassy area overlooking valley, good walks, bedrooms, open all day weekends. *(Mike Benton)*

BISHOP'S TAWTON   SS5629
★**Chichester Arms** (01271) 343945
Signed off A377 outside Barnstaple; East Street; EX32 0DQ Friendly 15th-c cob and thatch pub serving generous helpings of good well priced food from sandwiches/baguettes to fresh local fish, quick obliging service even when crowded, St Austell Tribute, Bombardier and a guest, decent wines, heavy low beams, large stone fireplace, restaurant; free wi-fi; children and dogs welcome, awkward disabled access but staff very helpful, picnic-sets on front terrace and in back garden, open all day. *(Neal Griffith)*

BOVEY TRACEY   SX8178
Cromwell Arms (01626) 833473
Fore Street; TQ13 9AE Welcoming 17th-c beamed inn with several areas including separate restaurant, popular good value food and up to five St Austell ales; quiz Tues, open mike first Thurs of the month, games machines, free wi-fi; children and dogs (in bar) welcome, disabled access/loos, small garden with decking and pergola, 14 bedrooms, open all day. *(Jill and Dick Archer)*

BRAMPFORD SPEKE   SX9298
Lazy Toad (01392) 841591
Off A377 N of Exeter; EX5 5DP 18th-c local with convivial licensees mainly concentrating on private events now (they only offer cold bar snacks); linked rooms with beams, standing timbers and slate floors, pubby furnishings and log fire, Exeter County Best, Hanlons Yellowhammer and several wines by the glass; tables in courtyard (once used by the local farrier and wheelwright) and in walled garden, charming village of thatched cottages, good walks beside the River Exe and Devonshire Heartland Way, open Tues-Sat lunchtimes, Thurs-Sat evenings, closed Mon. *(Rosie and Marcus Heatherley)*

BRANSCOMBE   SY2088
Masons Arms (01297) 680300
*Main Street; signed off A3052
Sidmouth–Seaton, then bear left into
village; EX12 3DJ* Popular old pub near
the sea in pretty village; rambling bar with
ancient ships' beams, comfortable seats on
slate floors and log fire in massive hearth,
St Austell Proper Job, Tribute and guests, ten
wines by the glass, enjoyable fairly traditional
food including some vegetarian options and
daily specials, afternoon cream teas, friendly
helpful staff, second bar with two-way
woodburner and stripped pine, two smartly
furnished dining rooms; free wi-fi; children
and dogs (in bars) welcome, quiet flower-
filled front terrace with thatched-roof tables,
side garden, neat comfortable bedrooms
(some in converted cottages), open all
day and can get very busy at peak times.
*(Joy Griffiths, Dr A J and Mrs B A Tompsett,
Dr Martin Owton)*

BRATTON CLOVELLY   SX4691
Clovelly (01837) 871447
*From S (A30), turn left at church,
pub is on the right; EX20 4JZ* Friendly
18th-c village pub with cosy bar and two
dining rooms; generous helpings of popular
reasonably priced traditional food including
specials, well kept Dartmoor, Sharps and a
guest, cheerful staff, games room; may be live
jazz second Mon of month; children and dogs
welcome, 17th-c wall paintings in Norman
church, open all day weekends. *(Tim and
Holly Waite)*

BRAYFORD   SS7235
★ Poltimore Arms 07969 356278
*Yarde Down; 3 miles towards
Simonsbath; EX36 3HA* Ivy-clad 17th-c
beamed pub – so remote it generates its
own electricity, and water is from a spring;
good home-made evening food Thurs-Sat,
also Sun lunchtime (best to book), two or
three changing ales tapped from the cask,
friendly helpful staff, traditional furnishings,
woodburner in inglenook, two attractive
restaurant areas separated by another
woodburner, good country views; free wi-fi;
children and dogs (in bar) welcome, picnic-
sets in side garden, shop and gallery, open
all day. *(Robin and Anna Triggs)*

BRENDON   SS7547
★ Rockford Inn (01598) 741214
*Rockford; Lynton–Simonsbath Road, off
B3223; EX35 6PT* Homely and welcoming
little 17th-c beamed inn surrounded by
fine Exmoor walks and scenery; neatly
linked rooms with cushioned settles, wall
seats and other straightforward furniture,
country prints and horse tack, open fires,
good helpings of enjoyable sensibly priced
pubby food (not Mon lunchtime), a couple
of well kept ales such as Clearwater and
Cotleigh tapped from the cask, Addlestone's

and Thatcher's ciders, decent wines by the
glass, lots of pump clips and toby jugs behind
counter; background music, board games;
children and dogs (in bar) welcome, seats
across the road overlooking East Lyn river,
seven well appointed bedrooms, open all day.
(Ian Herdman)

BRENDON   SS7648
Staghunters (01598) 741222
Leedford Lane; EX35 6PS Idyllically
set family-run hotel with gardens by East
Lyn river, can get packed, though quiet
out of season; good choice of enjoyable
reasonably priced food, up to six well kept
ales such as Exmoor and St Austell, real
cider, friendly efficient staff, bar with
woodburner, restaurant; children, walkers
and dogs welcome, riverside tables, 14 good
value bedrooms, open all day weekends (and
weekdays if busy). *(Rupert and Sandy Newton)*

BRIXHAM   SX9256
New Quay (01803) 883290
King Street; TQ5 9TW Early 18th-c pub
tucked down side street; well kept changing
west country beers and ciders from board-
fronted servery, good range of wines by the
glass and gins, friendly helpful staff, beam
and plank ceiling, spindleback chairs and
mix of old tables on slate tiles, warming
woodburner, fairly traditional menu using
fresh local produce, upstairs restaurant with
another woodburner and old town views; no
children under 10, dogs welcome in bar, open
all day Sun in summer, closed Mon-Weds and
till 5.30pm Thurs-Sat. *(Charles Welch)*

BROADCLYST   SX9997
New Inn (01392) 461312
Wimple Road; EX5 3BX Friendly
former 17th-c farmhouse with stripped
brickwork, boarded ceiling, low doorways
and log fires, enjoyable reasonably priced
pubby food, Dartmoor, Hanlons, Otter and
Sharps, restaurant; skittle alley; children and
dogs welcome, garden with play area, open
all day. *(Jane and Philip Saunders)*

BROADHEMBURY   ST1004
Drewe Arms (01404) 841267
*Off A373 Cullompton–Honiton;
EX14 3NF* Extended partly thatched
pub dating from the 15th c; carved beams
and handsome stone-mullioned windows,
woodburner and open fire, modernised bar
area, five well kept local ales and seven wines
by the glass, enjoyable pubby food (not Sun
evening, Mon), friendly helpful service, skittle
alley; children and dogs (in bar) welcome,
terrace seats, more up steps on tree-shaded
lawn, nice setting near church in pretty
village, open all day. *(Ben and Jenny Settle)*

BROADHEMPSTON   SX8066
Monks Retreat (01803) 812203
The Square; TQ9 6BN Old pub next to the
village school; black beams, wood floors and

logburner in huge stone fireplace, cheerful welcoming staff, Dartmoor ales and enjoyable sensibly priced home-made food including daily specials, OAP lunch Tues and fish and chips Weds evening, steps to sizeable dining area, also new oak-framed dining extension; dogs welcome, bedrooms, closed Mon lunchtime, no food Sun evening or Mon; for sale, so may be changes. *(Chris Stevenson)*

BUCKFAST SX7467
Abbey Inn (01364) 642343
Buckfast Road, off B3380; TQ11 0EA Lovely position perched on bank of River Dart; partly panelled bar with woodburner, three St Austell ales and Healey's cider, enjoyable reasonably priced pubby food from sandwiches, baguettes and pizzas up, Sun carvery, big dining room with more panelling and river views; background music, free wi-fi; well behaved children and dogs (in bar) welcome, terrace and bedrooms overlooking the water, open all day. *(Mike Benton)*

BUCKLAND BREWER SS4220
★Coach & Horses (01237) 451395
Village signposted off A388 S of Monkleigh; OS Sheet 190 map reference 423206; EX39 5LU Friendly 13th-c thatched pub with heavily beamed bar (mind your head), comfortable seats, handsome antique settle and inglenook woodburner, smaller lounge with another inglenook log fire, Exmoor Gold, Otter Ale and Sharps Doom Bar, local ciders and several wines by the glass, decent food including home-made curries, small back games room (darts and pool) and skittle alley/function room; background music, occasional sports TV, games machine, free wi-fi; children and dogs (in bar) welcome, picnic-sets on front terrace and in side garden, holiday cottage next door, closed Mon and Tues lunchtimes in winter. *(Alan and Linda Blackmore)*

BUTTERLEIGH SS9708
Butterleigh Inn (01884) 855433
Off A396 in Bickleigh; EX15 1PN Traditional heavy-beamed country pub, friendly and relaxed with good mix of customers, enjoyable reasonably priced pubby food (not Mon) from baguettes up, Sun carvery, four well kept ales such as Cotleigh, Dartmoor, Hanlons and Otter, real ciders and good choice of wines, unspoilt lived-in interior with two big fireplaces, back dining room; free wi-fi; children and dogs welcome, picnic-sets in large garden, four comfortable bedrooms, closed Sun evening, Mon lunchtime. *(Philip Kingsbury)*

CADELEIGH SS9107
★Cadeleigh Arms (01884) 855238
Village signed off A3072 W of junction with A396 Tiverton–Exeter at Bickleigh; EX16 8HP Attractive and friendly old pub owned by the local community; well kept Exeter Avocet, Hanlons Yellowhammer

and a guest, Sandford Orchards cider, good locally sourced food (not Sun evening) from regularly changing menu, carpeted room on left with bay-window seat and ornamental stove, flagstoned room to the right with high-backed settles and log fire in big fireplace, valley views from airy dining room down a couple of steps; background music, skittle alley; children and dogs welcome, tables on sunny terrace and gently sloping lawn, closed Mon lunchtime. *(Alan and Alice Morgan)*

CALIFORNIA CROSS SX7053
California (01548) 821449
Brown sign to pub off A3121 S of A38 junction; PL21 0SG Neatly kept 18th-c or older beamed dining pub; red carpets, panelling and stripped stone, plates on delft shelving and other bits and pieces, log fire, good choice of enjoyable food from baguettes to steaks in bar and family area, popular Sun lunch (best to book), separate evening restaurant (Weds-Sun) and small snug, St Austell Tribute, Sharps Doom Bar and a local guest, traditional cider and decent wines by the glass, good friendly service; background music, free wi-fi; dogs welcome, attractive garden and back terrace, open all day. *(Jill and Dick Archer)*

CHAGFORD SX6987
Chagford (01647) 433109
Mill Street; TQ13 8AW Former coaching inn just off market square; main bar/dining room with understated modern décor; blue-painted half-panelling, mix of furniture including pine settles forming booths, local artwork, fresh flowers and woodburner, good food from changing menu featuring locally farmed Dexter beef, well kept ales such as Butcombe, Dartmoor and Otter, Symonds's and Thatcher's ciders, nice wines and proper coffee, friendly helpful staff; background music; children and dogs welcome, walled courtyard garden behind, three comfortable annexe bedrooms; still for sale, so may be changes. *(Michael Longman)*

CHAGFORD SX7087
Ring o' Bells (01647) 432466
Off A382; TQ13 8AH Welcoming old shuttered pub with good mix of locals and visitors; beamed and panelled bar, four well kept ales including Dartmoor and enjoyable home-made food at fair prices, friendly attentive service, woodburner in big fireplace; some live music, free wi-fi; well behaved children and dogs welcome, sunny walled garden behind, nearby moorland walks, four comfortable spotless bedrooms, good breakfast, open all day. *(Rupert and Sandy Newton)*

CHALLACOMBE SS6941
Black Venus (01598) 763251
B3358 Blackmoor Gate–Simonsbath; EX31 4TT Welcoming 16th-c low-beamed pub; two or three well kept changing ales,

Thatcher's cider and decent wines by the glass, enjoyable fairly priced food from sandwiches to popular Sun lunch, helpful chatty staff, pews and comfortable chairs, woodburner and big fireplace, roomy attractive dining area, games room with pool and darts; free wi-fi; children and dogs welcome, garden play area, lovely countryside and good walks from the door, open all day in summer. *(Tony and Jill Radnor)*

CHERITON BISHOP   SX7792
★ **Old Thatch Inn** (01647) 24204
Off A30; EX6 6JH Attractive thatched village pub with welcoming relaxed atmosphere; rambling beamed bar separated by big stone fireplace, Otter, Dartmoor and a couple of guests, ciders such as Sandford's, good freshly prepared food including range of burgers, efficient friendly service, restaurant; free wi-fi; children and dogs welcome, nice sheltered garden, open all day, no food Sun evening, Mon, Tues; for sale as we went to press, so may be changes. *(Barbara Brown)*

CHERITON FITZPAINE   SS8706
★ **Ring of Bells** (01363) 860111
Off Barton Close, signed to village centre; EX17 4JG Renovated 14th-c thatched and beamed country pub; very good food cooked by landlord-chef including set menus (popular Tues auberge night), ales such as Branscombe Vale, Exe Valley and Teignworthy, local cider, friendly efficient service; children and dogs welcome (pub dog is Ruben), self-catering cottage, closed Mon, no food Sun evening. *(Nick Borst-Smith)*

CHILLINGTON   SX7942
Bear & Blacksmiths (01548) 581171
A379 E of Kingsbridge; TQ7 2LD Old refurbished pub with clean modern interior; landlord-chef's good food using local produce including some from own farm, three well kept ales, friendly helpful staff; children and dogs (in bar) welcome, tables on back terrace. *(Chris Stevenson)*

CHITTLEHAMPTON   SS6325
Bell (01769) 540368
Signed off B3227 S Molton–Umberleigh; EX37 9QL Family-run village inn on edge of square opposite historic church; decoratively tiled entrance to high-ceilinged bar with half-panelling and magnolia walls, lots of old photographs, animal heads and antlers, wooden pubby furniture, tasty good value home-made food from sandwiches and pub favourites up, ales such as Cotleigh and Exmoor, real ciders including local Winkleigh's, outstanding range of whiskies and over 50 gins, cheerful hard-working young staff; children (away from bar) and dogs welcome, ramp for wheelchairs, disabled loos, shaded circular picnic-sets

on front cobbles, nice sunny garden behind, three bedrooms, open all day Fri-Sun. *(Mike Benton)*

CHRISTOW   SX8385
★ **Teign House** (01647) 252286
Teign Valley Road (B3193); EX6 7PL Former farmhouse in country setting; very good freshly made food from pub favourites up, also an asian menu, three well kept local ales, cider and nice wines, friendly helpful staff, open fire in beamed bar, dining room; some live music; well behaved children and dogs welcome, garden and camping field, open all day. *(Charles Welch)*

CHUDLEIGH   SX8679
Bishop Lacey (01626) 854585
Fore Street, just off A38; TQ13 0HY Old low-beamed former church house; three well kept west country beers and enjoyable reasonably priced home-made food, cheerful obliging staff, two bars, log fire; children and dogs welcome, open all day. *(Donald Allsopp)*

CHULMLEIGH   SS6814
Red Lion (01769) 580384
East Street; EX18 7DD Nicely updated 17th-c coaching inn with beams and open fires, enjoyable fairly priced food including range of burgers and pizzas, St Austell, Sharps and a guest, friendly helpful service; background music (live every other Sat), darts; children welcome, five bedrooms, open all day Fri-Sun, closed Mon lunchtime. *(Tim and Holly Waite)*

CHURCHSTOW   SX7145
Church House (01548) 852237
A379 NW of Kingsbridge; TQ7 3QW Attractive building dating from the 13th c; heavy black beams and stripped stonework, high-backed settle and other traditional furniture, copper pans hanging above woodburner in big inglenook, glass-covered well in one part, good home-made food including vegetarian options, summer pizzas and monthly curry night, St Austell ales and decent wines, friendly helpful staff; live folk evening first Thurs of the month, games such as table skittles in conservatory; children and dogs (not in restaurant) welcome, tables on big sunny terrace, closed out of season Sun evening, Mon. *(Helen and Brian Edgeley, Yvonne Knapman)*

CLAYHIDON   ST1615
Half Moon (01823) 680291
On main road through village; EX15 3TJ Attractive old village pub with warm friendly atmosphere; good choice of popular home-made food from sharing boards up, well kept Otter and a couple of guests, Healey's cider, good wine list, comfortable bar with inglenook log fire; some live music; children

---

We accept no free drinks or meals and inspections are anonymous.

and dogs welcome, picnic-sets in tiered garden over road, lovely valley views, closed Sun evening, Mon. *(Guy Vowles)*

CLOVELLY SS3124
Red Lion (01237) 431237
The Quay; EX39 5TF Rambling 18th-c building in lovely position on curving quay below spectacular cliffs; beams, flagstones, log fire and interesting local photographs in character back bar (dogs allowed here), well kept Country Life and Sharps, enjoyable food including good value set lunch, efficient service, upstairs restaurant; occasional live music; children and dogs welcome, 11 attractive bedrooms (six more in Sail Loft annexe), own car park for residents and diners, open all day. *(Robin and Anna Triggs)*

CLYST HYDON ST0201
Five Bells (01884) 277288
W of village, just off B3176 not far from M5 junction 28; EX15 2NT Thatched and beamed dining pub (former 16th-c farmhouse); smartly updated interior with several different areas including raised dining part, assorted tables and chairs on wood or slate floors, woodburner in large stone fireplace, good food from pub favourites up, efficient friendly service, beers such as Butcombe and Otter, Sandford Orchard's cider and a dozen wines by the glass; children welcome, dogs in bar, disabled access/loo, cottagey garden with country views. *(Mr and Mrs Richard Osborne)*

CLYST ST GEORGE SX9888
St George & Dragon (01392) 876121
Topsham Road/A376, at roundabout; EX3 0QJ Spaciously extended open-plan Vintage Inn; low beams and some secluded corners, log fires, St Austell Tribute, Sharps Doom Bar and good choice of wines by the glass, their popular reasonably priced food, good service; children and dogs welcome, bedrooms in adjoining Innkeepers Lodge, open all day. *(Roger and Donna Huggins)*

CLYST ST MARY SX9791
Half Moon (01392) 873515
Under a mile from M5 junction 30 via A376; EX5 1BR Popular old beamed pub near disused 12th-c bridge over the River Clyst; good home-made food at reasonable prices including daily specials (best to book), many dishes available in smaller helpings, well kept ales such as Otter and decent choice of wines by the glass, friendly helpful staff, bar and separate lounge/dining area, stone floors, some red plush seating and log fire; quiz or bingo night Sun; children and dogs welcome, disabled access, open all day Fri-Sun. *(Roger and Donna Huggins)*

COCKWOOD SX9780
★ **Ship** (01626) 890373
Off A379 N of Dawlish; EX6 8NU Comfortable traditional 17th-c pub set back from the estuary and harbour – gets very busy in season; good food including some fish specials, five ales such as Dartmoor and St Austell, friendly staff and locals, partitioned beamed bar with big log fire and ancient oven, decorative plates and seafaring memorabilia, small restaurant; background music; children and dogs welcome, nice steep-sided garden, open all day, food all day Sun. *(Charles Welch)*

COMBE MARTIN SS5846
Pack o' Cards (01271) 882300
High Street; EX34 0ET Unusual 'house of cards' building constructed in the late 17th c to celebrate a substantial gambling win – four floors, 13 rooms and 52 windows; snug bar area and various side rooms, three real ales such as Exmoor, St Austell and Wickwar, decent wines by the glass and good range of well liked food including children's choices and all-day Sun carvery, cream teas, friendly helpful service even at busy times, restaurant; dogs welcome, pretty riverside garden with play area, six comfortable bedrooms, generous breakfast, open all day. *(Mike Benton)*

COMBEINTEIGNHEAD SX9071
Wild Goose (01626) 872241
Off unclassified coast road Newton Abbot–Shaldon, up hill in village; TQ12 4RA Friendly 17th-c family-run pub; spacious back lounge with beams and agricultural bits and pieces on the walls, five west country ales and good freshly made food including daily specials, big fireplace in front bar, more beams, standing timbers and some flagstones, step down to area with another large fireplace, further cosy room with tub chairs; background and occasional live music, Sun quiz, TV projector for major sports; children and dogs welcome, nice country views from back garden, closed Mon. *(Chloe and Tim Hodge)*

COUNTISBURY SS7449
Blue Ball (01598) 741263
A39, E of Lynton; EX35 6NE Welcoming heavy-beamed roadside pub in lovely rural setting; good range of generous local food in bar and restaurant, three or four real ales including Exmoor and one badged for them, decent wines and proper ciders, log fires; background music, TV, free wi-fi; children, walkers and dogs welcome, views from terrace tables, good nearby cliff walks (pub provides details of circular routes), comfortable bedrooms, open all day, food all day in summer. *(Mike Benton)*

CREDITON SS8300
Crediton Inn (01363) 772882
Mill Street (follow Tiverton sign); EX17 1EZ Small friendly local (the 'Kirton') under long-serving landlady; well kept Hanlons Yellowhammer and up to nine quickly changing guests (Nov beer festival),

cheap well prepared weekend food, home-made scotch eggs at other times, back games room/skittle alley; free wi-fi; open all day Mon-Sat. *(Penny and David Shepherd)*

CROYDE   SS4439
Manor House Inn (01271) 890241
St Marys Road, off B3231 NW of Braunton; EX33 1PG Friendly family pub with good choice of enjoyable food from lunchtime sandwiches to blackboard specials, also some asian dishes (thai chef), three well kept west country ales, cream teas, cheerful efficient service, spacious bar, restaurant and dining conservatory; background and live music, sports TV, games end with pool and darts, skittle alley; free wi-fi; dogs welcome in bar, disabled facilities, attractive terraced garden with big play area, open all day. *(Chris Stevenson)*

CROYDE   SS4439
Thatch (01271) 890349
B3231 NW of Braunton; Hobbs Hill; EX33 1LZ Lively thatched pub near great surfing beaches (can get packed in summer); rambling and roomy with beams and open fire, settles and other good seating, enjoyable pubby food from sandwiches and baked potatoes up, well kept changing local ales, morning coffee, teas, cheerful young staff, smart restaurant with dressers and lots of china; background and live music; children in eating areas, dogs in bar, flower-filled suntrap terraces and large gardens shared with neighbouring Billy Budds, good play area, simple clean bedrooms above the pub and nearby, self-catering cottage, open (and food) all day. *(Mike Handley)*

CULMSTOCK   ST1013
Culm Valley (01884) 840354
B3391, off A38 E of M5 junction 27; EX15 3JJ Friendly 18th-c pub with good choice of food from varied menu, four real ales including Otter, local cider and plenty of wines by the glass, country-style décor with hotchpotch of furniture, rugs on wood floors and some interesting bits and pieces, small front conservatory; occasional live music, free wi-fi; children and dogs (in bar) welcome, totem pole outside, tables on raised grassed area (former railway platform) overlooking River Culm and old stone bridge, open all day Fri-Sun. *(Chloe and Tim Hodge)*

DARTINGTON   SX7861
★Cott (01803) 863777
Cott signed off A385 W of Totnes, opposite A384 turn-off; TQ9 6HE Long 14th-c thatched pub with heavy beams, flagstones, nice mix of old furniture and two inglenooks (one with big woodburner), good locally sourced home-made food from traditional choices up in bar and restaurant, three well kept ales including local Hunters and Greene King, Ashridge cider, nice wines by the glass, friendly efficient service; live

music Sun; children and dogs welcome, wheelchair access (with help to restaurant), picnic-sets in garden and on pretty terrace, five comfortable bedrooms, open all day. *(Mike and Mary Carter)*

DARTMOUTH   SX8751
★Cherub (01803) 832571
Higher Street; walk along riverfront, right into Hauley Road and up steps at end; TQ6 9RB Ancient building (Dartmouth's oldest) with two heavily timbered upper floors jettying over the street, many original features including oak beams, leaded lights and big stone fireplace, bustling bar serving up to six well kept ales such as Exeter, South Hams and a house beer brewed by St Austell, enjoyable sensibly priced food from pub favourites to blackboard specials, efficient friendly service, low-ceilinged upstairs restaurant; background music; children welcome (no pushchairs), dogs in bar, open all day. *(Richard Tilbrook)*

DARTMOUTH   SX8751
Floating Bridge (01803) 832354
Opposite Upper Ferry; Coombe Road (A379); TQ6 9PQ Popular pub in lovely quayside spot; bar with lots of stools by windows making most of waterside view, black and white photographs of local boating scenes, St Austell Tribute, Sharps Doom Bar and guests, several wines by the glass, enjoyable pubby food including daily specials, bare-boards dining room with leather-backed chairs around wooden tables; children and dogs (in bar) welcome, pretty window boxes, seats out by the river looking at busy ferry crossing, more on sizeable roof terrace, open (and food) all day. *(David Hastings)*

DARTMOUTH   SX8751
★Royal Castle Hotel (01803) 833033
The Quay; TQ6 9PS Much character and many original features in this 17th-c waterside hotel; the two ground-floor bars are quite different: the oak-beamed Galleon bar (on right) has a log fire in a Tudor fireplace, some fine antiques and maritime pieces and plenty of chatty locals; the Harbour Bar (to left of flagstoned entrance hall) is contemporary and rather smart, with big-screen TV and live acoustic music on Thurs, four real ales including Dartmoor, Otter and Sharps, 28 wines by the glass and well liked food from lunchtime sandwiches and bar meals up, the Grill Room restaurant overlooks the river and has a Sun carvery; children welcome, dogs in bars and stylish bedrooms, open (and food) all day from 8am. *(David Hastings, Tony Scott)*

DITTISHAM   SX8654
★Ferry Boat (01803) 722368
Manor Street; best to park in village car park and walk down (quite steep); TQ6 0EX Cheerful riverside pub with lively mix of customers; beamed bar with log fires

and straightforward pubby furniture, lots of boating bits and pieces, tide times chalked on wall, flags on ceiling, picture-window view of the Dart, at least three real ales such as Otter and Sharps, a dozen wines by the glass and good range of tasty home-made food including pie of the day and various curries, efficient service; background and some live music, quiz night Thurs; children and dogs welcome, moorings for visiting boats on adjacent pontoon and bell to summon ferry, good walks, open (and food) all day. *(Mike Handley)*

DODDISCOMBSLEIGH   SX8586
⭐ **Nobody Inn** (01647) 252394
Off B3193; EX6 7PS Atmospheric old country inn, same owners as the Spoken in Exmouth; beamed lounge with handsomely carved antique settles, windsor and wheelback chairs around all sorts of wooden tables, guns and hunting prints in snug area by one of the big inglenooks, a beer named for the pub from Branscombe Vale and a couple of guests, three real ciders, 30 wines by the glass from extensive list and around 270 malt whiskies, good food from shortish changing menu, friendly service, more formal restaurant; children welcome away from main bar (no under-5s in restaurant), dogs allowed in bar, pretty garden with rural views, local church worth a visit for its fine medieval stained glass, bedrooms, open all day. *(S G N Bennett)*

DREWSTEIGNTON   SX7390
Drewe Arms (01647) 281409
Off A30 NW of Moretonhampstead; EX6 6QN Pretty thatched village pub under welcoming licensees; unspoilt room on left with basic wooden wall benches, stools and tables, original serving hatch, ales such as Dartmoor and Otter from tap room casks, local cider, enjoyable sensibly priced pubby food from sandwiches to daily specials, two dining areas, one with Rayburn and history of Britain's longest serving landlady (Mabel Mudge), another with woodburner, darts and board games, some live music in back Long Room; free wi-fi; children and dogs welcome, good local walks and handy for Castle Drogo (NT), open all day Sun (no evening food then). *(Roger and Donna Huggins, Ian Herdman)*

DUNSFORD   SX8189
Royal Oak (01647) 252256
Signed from Moretonhampstead; EX6 7DA Friendly comfortably worn-in village pub; generous helpings of traditional home-made food at reasonable prices, well kept ales such as Dartmoor and Greene King, local cider, airy lounge with woodburner and view from sunny bay, simple dining room, steps down to pool room; background and some live music; children and dogs (on leads) welcome, sheltered tiered garden with

play area, various animals including donkeys, miniature ponies and alpacas, good value bedrooms in converted barn. *(Rupert and Sandy Newton)*

EAST ALLINGTON   SX7648
Fortescue Arms (01548) 521215
Village signed off A381 Totnes–Kingsbridge, S of A3122 junction; TQ9 7RA Pretty 19th-c wisteria-clad village pub; two-room bar with mix of tables and chairs on black slate floor, half-panelling and open fire, St Austell and Dartmoor ales, eight wines by the glass, spacious restaurant with high-backed dining chairs around pine tables and another fire in stone fireplace, enjoyable well priced traditional food cooked by landlord-chef including separate vegetarian/vegan evening menu, warm friendly service; background and occasional live music, free wi-fi; children welcome, dogs in bar (food for them), wheelchair access, tables out at front with more on sheltered terrace, closed Mon and lunchtime Tues. *(M Towers)*

EAST BUDLEIGH   SY0684
Sir Walter Raleigh (01395) 442510
High Street; EX9 7ED Friendly little 16th-c low-beamed village local; well kept changing west country beers and good traditional food, restaurant down step; children and dogs welcome, parking some way off, wonderful medieval bench carvings in nearby church, handy too for Bicton Park Botanical Gardens. *(Jill and Dick Archer)*

EAST DOWN   SS5941
Pyne Arms (01271) 850055
Off A39 Barnstaple–Lynton near Arlington; EX31 4LX Welcoming old pub tucked away in small hamlet; cosy carpeted bar with lots of alcoves, woodburner, good well presented food from traditional choices up, Exmoor, St Austell and a guest, nice choice of wines, flagstoned area with sofas, conservatory; background music, free wi-fi; children and dogs welcome, small enclosed garden, good walks and handy for Arlington Court (NT), three comfortable bedrooms, open all day weekends, closed Mon lunchtime. *(Barbara Brown)*

EAST PRAWLE   SX7836
Pigs Nose (01548) 511209
Prawle Green; TQ7 2BY Quirky 16th-c three-room pub, lots of interesting bric-a-brac and pictures, mix of old furniture with jars of wild flowers and candles on tables, low beams, flagstones and open fire, local ales tapped from the cask, farm ciders and enjoyable simple food including range of pies, small family area with unusual toys, pool and darts; background music, hall for live bands (landlord was 1960s tour manager); friendly pub dogs (others welcome and menu for them), tables outside, pleasant spot on village green. *(Donald Allsopp)*

EXETER   SX9390
Double Locks (01392) 256947
Canal Banks, Alphington, via Marsh Barton Industrial Estate; EX2 6LT Unsmart, individual and remotely located by ship canal; Youngs and local guests, farm cider in summer, bar food (not Sun evening); background and some live music; children and dogs welcome, seats out on grass or decking with distant view to city and cathedral (nice towpath walk out), big play area, camping, open all day. *(Mike Benton)*

EXETER   SX9292
Georges Meeting House
(01392) 454250 *South Street; EX1 1ED* Interesting Wetherspoons in grand former 18th-c chapel; bare-boards interior with three-sided gallery, stained glass and tall pulpit at one end, eight real ales from long counter, their usual good value food; children welcome, tables in attractive side garden under parasols, open all day from 8am. *(Roger and Donna Huggins)*

EXETER   SX9292
★ Hour Glass (01392) 258722
Melbourne Street; off B3015 Topsham Road; EX2 4AU Old-fashioned bow-cornered pub tucked away in surviving Georgian part above the quay; good inventive food including vegetarian choices from shortish regularly changing menu, up to five well kept local ales (usually one from Otter) and extensive range of wines and spirits, friendly relaxed atmosphere, beams, bare boards and mix of furnishings, assorted pictures on dark red walls and various odds and ends including a stuffed badger, open fire in small brick fireplace; background and live music; children (away from bar) and dogs welcome (resident cats), open all day weekends, closed Mon lunchtime. *(Roger and Donna Huggins, Andy Nash)*

EXETER   SX9192
Mill on the Exe (01392) 214464
Bonhay Road (A377); EX4 3AB Former paper mill in good spot by pedestrian bridge over weir; spacious spread-up interior on two floors (each with bar), bare boards, old bricks, beams and timbers, four well kept ales including St Austell, good house wines and popular food from snacks and sharing boards up, all-day Sun carvery, large airy conservatory with feature raised fire, friendly atmosphere; children and dogs welcome, river views from balcony tables, spiral stairs down to waterside garden (summer barbecues), 11 bedrooms in attached hotel side, open (and food) all day. *(Nick and Meriel Cox)*

EXETER   SX9292
Old Fire House (01392) 277279
New North Road; EX4 4EP Relaxed city-centre pub in Georgian building behind high arched wrought-iron gates; arranged over three floors with dimly lit beamed rooms and simple furniture, up to ten real ales from casks behind bar, several ciders and good choice of bottled beers and wines, bargain food including late-night pizzas; background music, live weekends and popular with young crowd (modest admission charge Fri, Sat night), Mon quiz; children welcome until 5pm, picnic-sets in front courtyard, open all day till late (3am Thurs-Sat). *(Roger and Donna Huggins)*

EXETER   SX9292
White Hart (01392) 279897
South Street; EX1 1EE Rambling 15th-c inn close to the cathedral; various bars with heavy beams, oak flooring and some nice furnishings, inner cobbled courtyard, Marstons-related ales and good choice of reasonably priced food including deals and Sun carvery, friendly helpful staff; background music; children welcome, 65 bedrooms (40 in back extension), open all day. *(Mike Benton)*

EXMINSTER   SX9686
★ Turf Hotel (01392) 833128
From A379 S of village, follow the signs to the Swans Nest, then continue to end of track, by gates; park and walk right along canal towpath – nearly a mile; EX6 8EE Remote but popular waterside pub reached by 20-minute towpath walk, cycle ride or 60-seater boat from Topsham quay (15-minute trip); several little rooms – end one with slate floor, pine walls, built-in seats and woodburner, simple room along corridor serving devonshire ales, local cider/juices and ten wines by the glass, interesting locally sourced food, friendly staff; background music, board games; children and dogs welcome, big garden with picnic-sets and summer barbecues, arrive early for a seat in fine weather, bedrooms and a yurt for hire, good breakfast, open all day in summer (best to check other times). *(D W Stokes, Chris Mills)*

EXMOUTH   SY0080
Bicton Inn (01395) 272589
Bicton Street; EX8 2RU Traditional 19th-c backstreet corner local with friendly buoyant atmosphere, up to eight well kept ales and a proper cider, no food; regular live music including folk nights, pool, darts and other pub games; children and dogs welcome, open all day. *(Chloe and Tim Hodge)*

EXMOUTH   SX9980
Grapevine (01395) 222208
Victoria Road; EX8 1DL Popular red-brick corner pub on fringe of town centre; light and spacious with mix of wooden tables and seating on bare boards, own Crossed Anchors beers plus changing west country guests, plenty of bottled imports and nice choice of

wines by the glass, tasty american diner-style food from open kitchen, friendly service and relaxed atmosphere; background music, live bands Fri and Sat, free wi-fi; children and dogs welcome, open (and food) all day. *(Theocsbrian)*

EXMOUTH SY0080
Spoken (01395) 265228
Strand; EX8 1AL Relaxed corner bar under same ownership as the Nobody Inn at Doddiscombsleigh; quirky interior with eclectic mix of tables and chairs on wood floor, over 1,000 spirits including own gin, good selection of other drinks and popular food from breakfast on, friendly knowledgeable staff; pavement seats, children welcome, open all day from 10am. *(Alan and Linda Blackmore)*

EXTON SX9886
Puffing Billy (01392) 877888
Station Road/Exton Lane; EX3 0PR Attractively opened-up dining pub with light spacious interior; flagstones and woodburner in pitched-ceiling bar area, restaurant part with wood-strip flooring and second woodburner in two-way fireplace, some painted tables and chairs and upholstered wall benches, good food from sharing plates and pub favourites up, beers such as Bath, Bays and Otter, good selection of wines and gins, friendly attentive service; background music, quiz first Mon of month; children and dogs (in bar) welcome, tables out at front by road and on paved side terrace, handy for Exe Estuary cycle trail. *(Alan and Alice Morgan)*

GOODLEIGH SS5934
New Inn (01271) 342488
Goodleigh Road; EX32 7LX Small village pub under welcoming long-serving licensees; low-beamed hop-hung bar with chatty locals on bar stools, well kept Sharps Doom Bar and a guest, wide blackboard choice of good reasonably priced food cooked by landlady including local game, log fire; children and dogs welcome, closed Tues and lunchtime Weds. *(Tony and Jill Radnor)*

HARBERTON SX7758
★Church House (01803) 840231
Off A381 S of Totnes; next to church; TQ9 7SF Ancient village inn (dates to the 13th c) with unusually long bar; blackened beams, medieval latticed glass and oak panelling, attractive 17th- and 18th-c pews and settles, woodburner in big inglenook, well kept ales, local cider and ten wines by the glass, good fairly priced food (just pizzas Sun evening), friendly efficient service, separate dining room; quiz and live music nights; children and dogs welcome, sunny walled back garden, comfortable bedrooms, open all day Sun till 9pm, closed Mon and Tues lunchtimes. *(Donald Allsopp)*

HATHERLEIGH SS5404
Tally Ho (01837) 810306
Market Street (A386); EX20 3JN Friendly and relaxed old pub with own beers from back brewery plus a couple of guests; attractive heavy-beamed and timbered linked rooms, sturdy furnishings, big log fire and woodburner, good food from ciabattas up, restaurant, busy Tues market day (beer slightly cheaper then); background music, open mike night third Weds of month, darts; children and dogs welcome, tables in nice sheltered garden, three good value bedrooms, open all day. *(Robin and Anna Triggs)*

HEMYOCK ST1313
Catherine Wheel (01823) 680224
Cornhill; EX15 3RQ Popular and friendly village pub with bar, lounge and restaurant; Otter and Sharps Doom Bar, Thatcher's cider and plenty of wines by the glass, good food (not Sun evening, Mon) from varied menu, fresh flowers on tables, leather sofas by woodburner, efficient service; Sun quiz, darts, pool and skittle alley, free wi-fi; children and dogs welcome, closed Mon lunchtime. *(Guy Vowles)*

HONITON SY1198
★Holt (01404) 47707
High Street, W end; EX14 1LA Charming bustling little pub run by two brothers, relaxed and informal, with just one room downstairs, chunky tables and chairs on slate flooring, shelves of books and coal-effect woodburner, full range of Otter beers (the family founded the brewery), bigger brighter upstairs dining room with similar furniture on pale floorboards, extremely good and inventive food, well chosen wine list, friendly efficient service; cookery classes and some live music; well behaved children welcome, dogs in bar, closed Sun, Mon. *(Revd R P Tickle)*

HOPE COVE SX6740
Hope & Anchor (01548) 561294
Tucked away by car park; TQ7 3HQ Seaside inn on two floors; open kitchen serving decent choice of popular food from sharing plates to local fish, St Austell ales and a west country guest, several wines by the glass, helpful amiable young staff, flagstones and bare boards, two woodburners, dining room views to Burgh Island; background music, free wi-fi; children and dogs welcome, more sea views from tables on decked balcony and terrace, 11 bedrooms, open (and food) all day from 8am for breakfast. *(Helen and Brian Edgeley, Ben and Anthea Carter)*

HORNS CROSS SS3823
★Hoops (01237) 451222
A39 Clovelly–Bideford, W of village; EX39 5DL Pretty thatched and beamed inn dating from the 13th c, friendly and

relaxed, with traditionally furnished bar, log fires in sizeable fireplaces and some standing timbers and partitioning, more formal restaurant with attractive mix of tables and chairs, some panelling, exposed stone and another open fire, St Austell Tribute and a guest, over a dozen wines by the glass, generous helpings of enjoyable fairly straightforward food using local suppliers, cream teas, welcoming helpful staff; may be background music; children and dogs allowed, picnic-sets under parasols in enclosed courtyard, more seats on terrace and in two acres of gardens, 13 well equipped bedrooms, open (and food) all day. *(Dennis and Doreen Haward)*

HORSEBRIDGE
SX4074

★ **Royal** (01822) 870214

Off A384 Tavistock–Launceston; PL19 8PJ Ancient dimly lit local with dark half-panelling, scrubbed tables on slate floors, log fires and interesting bric-a-brac, well kept Otter, St Austell and Skinners direct from the cask, real cider and good reasonably priced food, friendly service; no children in the evening, dogs welcome, picnic-sets on front and side terraces and in big garden, quiet rustic spot by lovely old Tamar bridge, popular with walkers and cyclists. *(Ben and Jenny Settle)*

IDE
SX9090

Huntsman (01392) 272779

High Street; EX2 9RN Welcoming thatched and beamed country pub; enjoyable fairly pubby food from baguettes and sharing boards up (more evening choice), two sittings for Sun lunch, Butcombe, Exeter and Sharps, friendly attentive service; children and dogs welcome, picnic-sets in pleasant garden, open all day Fri-Sun, no food Sun evening. *(Charles Welch)*

IDE
SX8990

Poachers (01392) 273847

3 miles from M5 junction 31, via A30; High Street; EX2 9RW Cosy beamed pub in quaint village; Branscombe Vale Branoc and five changing west country guests from ornate curved wooden bar, enjoyable home-made food, mismatched old chairs and sofas, various pictures and odds and ends, big log fire, restaurant; occasional quiz, free wi-fi; dogs welcome (they have a boxer), tables in pleasant garden with barbecue, open (and food) all day, till late Fri, Sat. *(Jill and Dick Archer)*

IDEFORD
SX8977

★ **Royal Oak** (01626) 852274

2 miles off A380; TQ13 0AY Unpretentious little 16th-c thatched and flagstoned village pub; a couple of changing local ales and generous helpings of tasty well priced pubby food, navy theme including interesting Nelson and Churchill memorabilia, beams, panelling and big open

fireplace; children and dogs welcome, tables out at front and by car park over road, closed Mon lunchtime. *(Alan and Alice Morgan)*

ILFRACOMBE
SS5247

George & Dragon (01271) 863851

Fore Street; EX34 9ED One of the oldest pubs here (14th c) and handy for the harbour; clean and comfortable with friendly local atmosphere, ales such as Exmoor and Sharps, decent wines and traditional food including local fish, black beams, stripped stone and open fireplaces, lots of ornaments, china etc; background and some live music, Tues quiz, no mobile phones; children and dogs welcome, open all day and can get very busy weekends. *(Dave Braisted)*

ILFRACOMBE
SS5247

Ship & Pilot (01271) 316085

Broad Street, off harbour; EX34 9EE Updated blue-painted pub near harbour attracting friendly mix of regulars and visitors; four well kept beers from Bath and St Austell, real cider and several gins, enjoyable home-cooked food, good service; sports TV; children and dogs welcome, some tables outside, two bedrooms, open all day. *(Chris Stevenson)*

ILSINGTON
SX7876

Carpenters Arms (01364) 661629

Old Town Hill next to the church; TQ13 9RG Welcoming little 18th-c village pub under newish management; L-shaped room with painted beams and hefty flagstones, comfortable seats by woodburner in large stone fireplace, country-style tables and chairs, enjoyable fairly traditional food including stone-baked pizzas, three west country ales tapped from the cask; children, walkers and dogs welcome, tables on pretty front terrace, good surrounding walks, open all day weekends, closed Mon lunchtime. *(Rosie and Marcus Heatherley)*

INSTOW
SS4730

Boat House (01271) 861292

Marine Parade; EX39 4JJ Popular recently revamped bar-restaurant by huge tidal beach with views across to Appledore; enjoyable food from light lunches up including fish/seafood specials, well kept west country ales and decent wines by the glass, friendly prompt service; good roof terrace; children and dogs welcome, disabled facilities, open all day. *(Mike Benton)*

KENN
SX9285

Ley Arms (01392) 832341

Signed off A380 just S of Exeter; EX6 7UW Rambling old thatched dining pub in quiet spot near the church; good range of popular well presented/priced food using local produce including blackboard specials, smaller appetites and special diets catered for, well kept west country ales and decent range of wines, friendly helpful staff, beams, exposed stonework and polished granite flagstones, log fires, restaurant and garden room; children and dogs (theirs is Reggie) welcome, terrace tables under parasols, open all day, food all day weekends. *(M J Winterton)*

KENNFORD   SX9186
Seven Stars (01392) 834887
Centre of village; EX6 7TR Updated little village pub with three west country beers and good food including pies and takeaway pizzas, friendly atmosphere; quiz last Tues of month, open mike night first Fri, pool, darts and sports TV; children and dogs welcome, closed Mon lunchtime, otherwise open all day. *(Charles Welch)*

KILMINGTON   SY2698
New Inn (01297) 33376
Signed off Gammons Hill; EX13 7SF Thatched local (originally three 14th-c cottages), friendly and welcoming, with good reasonably priced food including popular Sun roasts, well kept Palmers ales; skittle alley and boules court, monthly quiz; children and dogs welcome, disabled access/loo (steps in one part), large garden with tree-shaded areas, closed Mon lunchtime, no food Sun evening, Mon. *(Jill and Dick Archer)*

KILMINGTON   SY2798
★Old Inn (01297) 32096
A35; EX13 7RB Bustling 16th-c thatched and beamed pub on edge of the village; well kept ales such as Branscombe Vale and Otter, decent choice of wines and enjoyable pubby food including daily specials, welcoming attentive service, small character front bar with traditional games (there's also a skittle alley), inglenook log fire in back lounge, small restaurant; beer/cider festivals and some live music; children and dogs welcome, wheelchair access, terrace and lawned area, open all day from 8am. *(Tony and Jill Radnor)*

KING'S NYMPTON   SS6819
★Grove (01769) 580406
Off B3226 SW of South Molton; EX37 9ST Welcoming 17th-c thatched pub in remote conservation village; beamed bar with lots of bookmarks hanging from the ceiling, simple pubby furnishings on flagstones, bare stone walls and a log fire, four well kept country ales, half a dozen ciders, over 30 wines (including champagne) by the glass and some 65 malt whiskies, very good home-cooked food (not Sun evening) including daily specials, Tues night fish and chips, restaurant; darts and board games, free wi-fi; well behaved children and dogs welcome, self-catering cottage, nice surrounding walks, closed Mon. *(John Ledbury)*

KINGSKERSWELL   SX8666
★Bickley Mill (01803) 873201
Bickley Road, follow Maddacombe Road from village, under new ring road,

W of Kingskerswell; TQ12 5LN Restored 13th-c mill tucked away in lovely countryside; rambling beamed rooms with open fires and rugs on wood floors, variety of seating from rustic chairs and settles to sofas piled with cushions, modern art and black and white photos on stone walls, good well presented food including pub favourites from sensibly priced menu, a couple of Bays ales and 14 wines by the glass, cheer helpful service; monthly jazz Sun lunchtime, free wi-fi; children and dogs (in bar) welcome, seats on big terrace, also a subtropical hillside garden, well appointed modern bedrooms, good breakfast, open all day. *(Mike and Mary Carter)*

KINGSTON   SX6347
Dolphin (01548) 810314
Off B3392 S of Modbury (can also be reached from A379 W of Modbury); TQ7 4QE Peaceful and friendly 16th-c inn with knocked-through beamed rooms; traditional furniture on red carpeting, open fire, woodburner in inglenook fireplace, Butcombe and Dartmoor and a couple of guests, a farm cider, straightforward food; Mon darts, occasional live music; children and dogs welcome, seats in garden, pretty tubs and summer window boxes, quiet village with several tracks leading down to the sea, three bedrooms in building across road, open all day weekends. *(Robin and Anna Triggs)*

LAKE   SX5288
Bearslake (01837) 861334
A386 just S of Sourton; EX20 4HQ Rambling thatch and stone pub (former longhouse dating from the 13th c); leather sofas on crazy-paved slate floor at one end, other beamed rooms with stripped stone walls, woodburners, toby jugs, farm tools and traps, ales such as Otter and Teignworthy, decent wines and enjoyable food from separate bar and restaurant menus; quiz nights; children and dogs welcome, large sheltered streamside garden, Dartmoor walks, six comfortable bedrooms, closed Sun evening, otherwise open all day. *(Donald Allsopp)*

LANDSCOVE   SX7766
Live & Let Live (01803) 762663
SE end of village by Methodist chapel; TQ13 7LZ Friendly open-plan village local refurbished under current owners; good food and well kept ales such as Bays and Dartmoor, beams, exposed stonework and log fire; children and dogs welcome, tables on small front terrace and in little orchard across lane, good walks, bedrooms, closed Mon (and maybe Sun evening in winter). *(Ben and Jenny Settle)*

LIFTON   SX3885
Arundell Arms (01566) 784666
Fore Street; PL16 0AA Good imaginative food in substantial country-house fishing

hotel including set lunch, warmly welcoming and individual, with professional service, good choice of wines by the glass, morning coffee and afternoon tea; also adjacent Courthouse bar, complete with original cells, serving enjoyable fairly priced pubby food (not Sun evening, Mon) along with daily specials and children's meals, well kept Dartmoor Jail Ale and St Austell Tribute, darts and some live music; 25 bedrooms, useful A30 stop. *(Peter Andrews)*

LOWER ASHTON   SX8484
Manor Inn (01647) 252304
Ashton signposted off B3193 N of Chudleigh; EX6 7QL Friendly well run country pub with good quality reasonably priced food including lunchtime set menu and daily specials, well kept ales such as Dartmoor, Otter and St Austell, good choice of wines; open fires in both bars, back restaurant in converted smithy; children and dogs welcome, disabled access, garden picnic-sets with nice rural outlook, open all day Sun (no evening food then), closed Mon. *(Jane and Philip Saunders)*

LUPPITT   ST1606
★ Luppitt Inn (01404) 891613
Back roads N of Honiton; EX14 4RT Unspoilt basic farmhouse pub tucked away in lovely countryside, an amazing survivor, run by chatty veteran landlady with help from her granddaughter; corner servery and single table in tiny bar, another room (not much bigger) with fireplace and darts, cheap Otter tapped from a polypin, intriguing metal puzzles made by a neighbour, no food or music, lavatories across the yard; only open Thurs–Sat from 7.30pm. *(Robin and Anna Triggs)*

LUSTLEIGH   SX7881
★ Cleave (01647) 277223
Off A382 Bovey Tracey– Moretonhampstead; TQ13 9TJ Busy thatched pub in lovely Dartmoor National Park village; low-ceilinged beamed bar with granite walls and log fire, attractive antique high-backed settles, cushioned wall seats and wheelbacks on red patterned carpet, Dartmoor, Otter and a guest, good variety of enjoyable home-cooked food, efficient friendly service, back room (formerly the old station waiting room) converted to light airy bistro with pale wooden furniture on wood-strip floor, doors to outside eating area; children and dogs (in bar) welcome, more seats in sheltered garden, good circular walks, shuts around 6pm Sun, otherwise open (and food) all day. *(Nicola and Holly Lyons)*

LUTON   SX9076
★ Elizabethan (01626) 775425
Haldon Moor; TQ13 0BL Popular tucked-away low-beamed dining pub (once owned by Elizabeth I, but much altered); wide choice of good well presented food including

daily specials, two well kept ales and several reasonably priced wines by the glass, friendly attentive service; children and dogs (in bar) welcome, pretty front garden, open all day Sun. *(Mike Benton)*

LYDFORD   SX5184
★ Castle Inn (01822) 820241
Off A386 Okehampton–Tavistock; EX20 4BH Pink-painted Tudor inn next to the castle and church; traditional twin bars with big slate flagstones, bowed low beams and granite walls, high-backed settles and four inglenook log fires, notable stained-glass door and plenty of bits and pieces to look at; hearty helpings of popular well priced food, St Austell ales, guest beers and good wine selection, friendly helpful service, restaurant; free wi-fi; children and dogs welcome in certain areas, wheelchair access, seats out at front and in sheltered back garden, lovely NT river gorge nearby, eight bedrooms, open all day. *(Eddie Edwards)*

LYDFORD   SX5285
Dartmoor Inn (01822) 820221
Downton, A386; EX20 4AY Gently civilised inn, more restaurant-with-rooms and at its most informal at lunchtime with walkers from Dartmoor National Park; cheerful small bar with log fire, Otter Ale, St Austell Tribute and nice wines by the glass, good interesting food in several linked dining rooms with stylish contemporary décor; children and dogs (in bar) welcome, three well equipped pretty bedrooms (each with its own sitting area), best to check website for opening times. *(Alan and Linda Blackmore)*

LYMPSTONE   SX9984
Redwing (01395) 222156
Church Road; EX8 5JT Modernised dining pub not far from the church; comfortable seating on oak or black slate floors, well kept local beers such as Hanlons and St Austell, wide range of wines by the glass and good freshly made food from ciabattas and pub favourites up, friendly attentive service, converted loft restaurant; children and dogs (in bar) welcome, terrace tables, attractive unspoilt village, open all day weekends. *(Alan and Alice Morgan)*

LYMPSTONE   SX9884
Swan (01395) 270403
The Strand, by station entrance; EX8 5ET Old beamed pub with enjoyable home-made food including local fish and bargain weekday set lunch, split-level dining area with big log fire, Hanlons Yellowhammer and four other west country ales, short but well chosen wine list; occasional live music, pool, free wi-fi; children welcome, picnic-sets out at front, popular with cyclists (bike racks provided), shore walks, open all day. *(Barbara Brown)*

LYNMOUTH   SS7249
Rising Sun (01598) 753223
Harbourside; EX35 6EG Nice old pub
in wonderful position overlooking harbour;
beamed and stripped-stone bar bustling
with locals and tourists, good fire, three
Exmoor ales and a guest, popular food
from comprehensive menu (emphasis on
fish), upmarket hotel side with attractive
restaurant; background music; well behaved
children (till 7.30pm) and dogs (in bar)
welcome, gardens behind, bedrooms in
cottagey old thatched building, parking
expensive during the day and scarce at night,
open all day. *(Chris Stevenson)*

LYNTON   SS7248
Beggars Roost (01598) 753645
Manor Hotel; EX35 6LD Stone-
built country pub with friendly relaxed
atmosphere; enjoyable freshly made food
and well kept ales including Exmoor and
a house beer brewed by Marstons, helpful
cheerful staff; children and dogs welcome,
good bedrooms in hotel side, also camping
next door, closed Jan, otherwise open all
day. *(Robin and Anna Triggs)*

LYNTON   SS7148
Cottage Inn (01598) 753496
B3234 just S; EX35 6NR Interesting
place run by friendly licensees; wide choice
of craft beers including own Fatbelly range,
authentic evening thai food (cooked by
landlady) along with traditional Sun roasts,
churchy Victorian windows, beamed and
carpeted bar with woodburner, dining room
overlooking West Lyn gorge; June music/
beer festival; children and dogs welcome,
footbridge to wooded NT walks up to
Watersmeet, bedrooms. *(Richard and
Penny Gibbs)*

LYNTON   SS6548
Hunters (01598) 763230
*Pub well signed off A39 W of Lynton;
EX31 4PY* Large Edwardian country inn set
in superb Heddon Valley position down very
steep hill by NT information centre; two bars
one with woodburner, up to six ales including
Exmoor and Heddon Valley (brewed for them
locally), good range of other drinks and
enjoyable well priced food from fairly pubby
menu, efficient friendly service, dining room
overlooking back garden; quiz and music
nights, pool, board games, free wi-fi; children
and dogs welcome, four-acre grounds
(roaming peacocks), great walks including
to the sea, ten bedrooms, open all day.
(Therese Sjogren)

MARLDON   SX8663
★Church House (01803) 558279
Off A380 NW of Paignton; TQ3 1SL
Pleasant village pub dating from the 15th c;
spreading bar with woodburner, unusual
windows and some beams, dark pine and

other dining chairs around solid tables; four
real ales such as Dartmoor and Teignworthy,
local cider, 16 wines by the glass and ten
malt whiskies, other rooms including two
restaurants (one in old barn), interesting
much liked food, good service; background
music, board games, free wi-fi; children
and dogs (in bar) welcome, picnic-sets on
three carefully maintained grassy terraces
behind. *(Mike and Mary Carter)*

MARSH   ST2510
Flintlock (01460) 234403
*Pub signed just off A303 Ilminster–
Honiton; EX14 9AJ* Comfortable neatly
maintained dining pub popular for its good
value blackboard food including Sun lunches,
special diets catered for, well kept Butcombe
and Otter, decent choice of wines, friendly
accommodating service, woodburner in stone
inglenook, beams and mainly stripped stone
walls, copper and brass; background music,
free wi-fi; children welcome, dogs in garden
only, closed Mon. *(Penny and David Shepherd)*

MEAVY   SX5467
★Royal Oak (01822) 852944
Off B3212 E of Yelverton; PL20 6PJ
Partly 15th-c pub taking its name from the
800-year-old oak on green opposite; heavy
beamed L-shaped bar with pews, red plush
banquettes, old agricultural prints and
church pictures, smaller locals' bar with
flagstones and big open-hearth fireplace,
separate dining room, good reasonably priced
food served by friendly staff, four well kept
ales including Dartmoor, farm ciders, a dozen
wines by the glass and several malt whiskies;
background music, board games; children
and dogs (in bar) welcome, picnic-sets out in
front and on the green, pretty Dartmoor-edge
village, open all day. *(Charles Welch)*

MEETH   SS5408
★Bull & Dragon (01837) 811742
A386 Hatherleigh–Torrington; EX20 3EP
Welcoming 15th-c beamed and thatched
village pub; large open bar with inglenook
woodburner, well kept ales such as Exmoor
and Otter, good reasonably priced home-
made food from shortish menu plus some
blackboard specials (booking advised),
charming helpful staff; children and dogs
welcome, at end of Tarka Trail cycle route,
closed Sun evening and Mon. *(Rosie and
Marcus Heatherley)*

MILTON COMBE   SX4865
Who'd A Thought It (01822) 853313
*Village signed off A386 S of Yelverton;
PL20 6HP* Attractive 16th-c whitewashed
pub; black-panelled bar with some
interesting bits and pieces, traditional
furniture and woodburner, two separate
dining areas, good home-made food from
varied menu including set deal, friendly
efficient staff, four well kept ales, real cider
and decent choice of wines; background and

some live music; children and dogs welcome, a few tables out in front, more in back beer garden with stream, two bedrooms in converted hayloft, open all day Sun, closed Mon lunchtime. *(Lindsay Blaney)*

MOLLAND   SS8028
London (01769) 550269
Village signed off B3227 E of South Molton; EX36 3NG Proper Exmoor inn at its busiest in the shooting season; two small linked rooms by old-fashioned central servery, local stag-hunting pictures, cushioned benches and plain chairs around rough stripped trestle tables, Exmoor Ale, attractive beamed room on left with famous stag story on the wall, panelled dining room on right with big curved settle by fireplace (good hunting and gamebird prints), enjoyable home-made food using fresh local produce including seasonal game (not Sun evening, no credit cards), small hall with stuffed animals; fine Victorian lavatories; children and dogs welcome, picnic-sets in cottagey garden, untouched early 18th-c box pews in church next door, two bedrooms, closed Mon lunchtime. *(Charles Welch)*

MONKLEIGH   SS4520
Bell (01805) 938285
A388; EX39 5JS Welcoming thatched and beamed 17th-c village pub with carpeted bar and small restaurant; well kept Dartmoor and a couple of guests, enjoyable reasonably priced food including daily specials, themed evenings and Sun carvery, friendly staff; background music, quiz nights and occasional live music, darts; children (till 9pm) and dogs welcome, wheelchair access, garden with raised deck, views and good walks, closed Mon. *(Jill and Dick Archer)*

MORCHARD BISHOP   SS7607
London Inn (01363) 877222
Signed off A377 Crediton–Barnstaple; EX17 6NW Prettily placed 16th-c village coaching inn run by mother and daughter team, thriving local atmosphere, good generous home-made food (best to book weekends), Fullers London Pride and a local guest, helpful friendly service, low-beamed open-plan carpeted bar with woodburner in large fireplace, small dining room; pool, darts and skittles; children and dogs welcome, closed Mon lunchtime.
(Alan and Alice Morgan)

MORELEIGH   SX7652
New Inn (01548) 821326
B3207, off A381 Kingsbridge–Totnes in Stanborough; TQ9 7JH Cosy old-fashioned country local with friendly landlady (same family has run it for several decades); large helpings of enjoyable home-made food at reasonable prices including good steaks, Timothy Taylors Landlord tapped from the cask and a weekend guest, character old

furniture, nice pictures and good inglenook log fire; opens from 6.30pm (12-2.30, 7-10.30 Sun). *(Tim and Holly Waite)*

NEWTON ABBOT   SX8671
Olde Cider Bar (01626) 354221
East Street; TQ12 2LD Basic old-fashioned cider house with plenty of atmosphere; around 30 interesting reasonably priced ciders (some very strong), a couple of perries, more in bottles, good country wines from the cask too, baguettes, pasties etc, friendly staff, stools made from cask staves, barrel seats and wall benches, flagstones and bare boards; regular live folk music, small back games room with bar billiards; dogs welcome, terrace tables, open all day.
(Chris Stevenson)

NEWTON ABBOT   SX8468
Two Mile Oak (01803) 812411
A381 2 miles S, at Denbury/ Kingskerswell crossroads; TQ12 6DF Appealing two-bar beamed coaching inn; black panelling, traditional furnishings and candlelit alcoves, inglenook and woodburners, well kept Bass, Dartmoor and Otter tapped from the cask, nine wines by the glass, enjoyable well priced pubby food from sandwiches and baked potatoes up (special diets catered for), decent coffee, cheerful staff; background music; quiz last Tues of month; children and dogs welcome, round picnic-sets on terrace and lawn, open all day.
(Chris Stevenson)

NEWTON FERRERS   SX5447
Dolphin (01752) 872007
Riverside Road East; Newton Hill off Church Park (B3186) then left; PL8 1AE Shuttered 18th-c pub in attractive setting (friendly new owners and some refurbishment); L-shaped bar with a few low beams, slate floors and open fire, well kept ales and good food cooked by landlord-chef, children welcome, terraces over lane looking down on River Yealm and yachts, can get packed in summer, parking limited. *(Ben and Jenny Settle)*

NEWTON ST CYRES   SX8798
Beer Engine (01392) 851282
Off A377 towards Thorverton; EX5 5AX Former 19th-c railway hotel brewing its own beers since the 1980s; good home-made food including specials and popular Sun lunch, log fire in bar; children and dogs welcome, seats on decked verandah, steps down to garden, open all day, food all day Sun. *(Roger and Donna Huggins)*

NEWTON TRACEY   SS5226
Hunters (01271) 858339
B3232 Barnstaple–Torrington; EX31 3PL Extended 15th-c pub with massive low beams and two inglenooks, popular reasonably priced food from pub standards up including choices for smaller

appetites, well kept St Austell Tribute and Sharps Doom Bar, decent wines, friendly service, skittle alley/overflow dining area; soft background music; children and dogs welcome, disabled access using ramp, tables on small terrace behind, open all day weekends, food all day Sun till 7.45pm. *(Penny and David Shepherd)*

NOMANSLAND   SS8313
Mount Pleasant (01884) 860271
*B3137 Tiverton–South Molton;
EX16 8NN* Informal country local with good mix of customers; huge fireplaces in long low-beamed main bar, happy mismatch of simple well worn furniture, candles on tables, country pictures, well kept ales such as Cotleigh, Exmoor and Sharps, several wines by the glass, Weston's cider, good range of enjoyable freshly cooked food (special diets catered for), friendly attentive service, cosy dining room in former smithy with original forge, darts in public bar; background music; well behaved children and dogs welcome, back garden with play area, open (and food) all day. *(Nicola and Holly Lyons)*

NORTH BOVEY   SX7483
Ring of Bells (01647) 440375
Off A382/B3212 SW of Moretonhampstead; TQ13 8RB Popular 13th-c thatched inn restored after 2016 fire; low beams, bulgy walls and brick floors, woodburners (one in inglenook), much liked food at fair prices from lunchtime sandwiches and traditional choices up, cask-tapped ales such as Dartmoor and Teignworthy, real cider and a dozen wines by the glass from good list, helpful friendly staff; quiz nights; children and dogs (in bar) welcome, picnic-sets and flower-filled troughs out at front, pretty Dartmoor village with lovely tree-covered green, good walks, five attractively refurbished bedrooms, open all day. *(Mike Benton)*

NOSS MAYO   SX5447
★ Ship (01752) 872387
*Off A379 via B3186, E of Plymouth;
PL8 1EW* Charming setting overlooking inlet and visiting boats (can get crowded in good weather); thick-walled bars with bare boards and log fires, four well kept ales such as Dartmoor and Noss Beer Works, good choice of wines and malt whiskies, popular food from varied menu, friendly efficient service, lots of local pictures and charts, books, newspapers and board games, restaurant upstairs; children and dogs (downstairs) welcome, plenty of seats on heated waterside terrace, parking restricted at high tide, open (and food) all day. *(Alan and Linda Blackmore)*

OKEHAMPTON   SX5895
Fountain (01837) 53532
Fore Street (just off A30); EX20 1AP Well run and welcoming former coaching

inn; good food from snacks to daily specials, Sun carvery, three or four well kept ales including Dartmoor and Sharps (cheaper Fri afternoon), cocktails, two bars and a restaurant; skittle alley; children and dogs welcome, seats out on decking, six bedrooms, open all day. *(Jamie and Sue May)*

OTTERY ST MARY   SY0995
Volunteer (01404) 814060
Broad Street; EX11 1BZ Welcoming early 19th-c pub; traditional front bar with darts and open fire, four real ales tapped from the cask including Otter, more contemporary restaurant behind, good reasonably priced home-made food (not Sun evening), friendly service; upstairs loos; open all day. *(Charles Welch)*

PARKHAM   SS3821
★ Bell (01237) 451201
Rectory Lane; EX39 5PL Thatched village pub reopened after devastating fire; three sympathetically renovated linked rooms (one on lower level), beams and standing timbers, cob walls, pubby furniture on slate or red patterned carpet, brass, copper and old photographs, grandfather clock, two woodburners and a range (they cook Sun roasts in it), well kept Dartmoor, Otter and Ringwood, 30 gins and a dozen malt whiskies, good reasonably priced home-made food; darts, free wi-fi; well behaved children welcome, dogs in bar, disabled access/loo, picnic-sets on covered back terrace with fairy lights, open (and food) all day Sun. *(Kim Ryan Skuse)*

PARRACOMBE   SS6644
★ Fox & Goose (01598) 763239
*Off A39 Blackmoor Gate–Lynton;
EX31 4PE* Popular and welcoming Victorian pub with linked rooms; hunting and farming memorabilia and interesting old photographs, well kept Cotleigh, Bath and a guest, Winkleigh's cider and several wines by the glass, good variety of well cooked generously served food from blackboard menus including local fish and game, also takeaway pizzas, friendly helpful staff, log fire, separate dining room; children and dogs welcome, wheelchair access with help, small front verandah, riverside terrace and garden room, four bedrooms, open all day in summer. *(John Gilbert)*

PAYHEMBURY   ST0801
Six Bells (01404) 841261
Village signed from A373; leave A30 at Honiton; EX14 3HR Welcoming 17th-c village local; good range of well kept beers such as Dartmoor and Sharps, generous helpings of reasonably priced home-made food from sandwiches to specials, friendly helpful service, restaurant; skittle alley, pool; children and dogs (in bar) welcome, open all day Fri-Sun, closed Mon lunchtime, no food Sun evening, Mon. *(Colin Bateman)*

PETER TAVY   SX5177

★ **Peter Tavy Inn** (01822) 810348

Off A386 near Mary Tavy, N of Tavistock; PL19 9NN Old stone village inn tucked away at end of small lane; bustling low-beamed bar with high-backed settles on black flagstones, mullioned windows, good log fire in big stone fireplace, snug dining area with carved wooden chairs, hops on beams and various pictures, up to five well kept west country ales, Winkleigh's cider and good wine/whisky choice, well liked food from varied menu including OAP lunch (not Sun) and early evening deal, friendly efficient service, separate restaurant; children, walkers and dogs welcome, picnic-sets in pretty garden, peaceful moorland views, open all day weekends. *(Helen and Brian Edgeley, Peter Andrews, Stephen Shepherd, Neil Hammacott)*

PLYMOUTH   SX4953

Bridge (01752) 403888

Shaw Way, Mount Batten; PL9 9XH Modern two-storey bar-restaurant with terrace and balcony overlooking busy Yacht Haven Marina; enjoyable food from sandwiches and pub favourites up, St Austell Tribute, Sharps Doom Bar and nice range of wines by the glass, impressive fish tank upstairs; children welcome, well behaved dogs downstairs, open all day from 9am for breakfast. *(Jane and Philip Saunders)*

PLYMOUTH   SX4854

Dolphin (01752) 660876

Barbican; PL1 2LS Unpretentious drinkers' pub with buoyant chatty atmosphere; good range of well kept cask-tapped ales including Bass and St Austell, open fire, Beryl Cook paintings (even one of the friendly landlord), no food but can bring your own; dogs welcome, open all day. *(Gavin and Helle May, Dr and Mrs A K Clarke)*

PLYMOUTH   SX4755

Fortescue (01752) 660673

Mutley Plain; PL4 6JQ Traditional Victorian corner local with nine well kept mostly changing ales and good range of traditional ciders, no food apart from Sun lunch, cellar bar/function room; Sun quiz, Weds poker night, TV, fruit machine; dogs welcome, seats on raised back terrace, open all day. *(Chris Stevenson)*

PLYMPTON   SX5455

Brook (01752) 297604

Longbrook Street; PL7 1ND Popular community pub with enjoyable sensibly priced home-made food and well kept local beers, good friendly service, separate coffee lounge; regular live music and other events, pool; children (till 9pm) and dogs welcome, garden picnic-sets, open all day till 9.30pm (10.30pm weekends), bar snacks only Sun evening. *(John Evans)*

PLYMTREE   ST0502

Blacksmiths Arms (01884) 277474

Near church; EX15 2JU Friendly 19th-c beamed and carpeted village pub; good reasonably priced food cooked by landlord, three well kept changing local ales and decent choice of wines by the glass; pool room and skittle alley; children welcome, dogs on leads (their leonberger is called Jagermeister), garden with boules and play area, open all day Sat, till 4pm Sun, closed Mon, lunchtimes Tues-Fri. *(Colin Bateman)*

PUSEHILL   SS4228

Pig on the Hill (01237) 459222

Off B3226 near Westward Ho!; EX39 5AH Extensively revamped restauranty pub (originally a cowshed); good choice of highly enjoyable, well presented food (must book ahead), friendly helpful service, Country Life and local guests, games room with skittle alley; background music; children and dogs (in bar) welcome, disabled facilities, good views from terrace tables and picnic-sets on grass, play area, boules, three self-catering cabins, open all day. *(Mike Benton)*

RACKENFORD   SS8518

Stag (01884) 881755

Pub signed off A361 NW of Tiverton; EX16 8DT Well restored 12th-c thatched pub with ancient cobbled 'tunnel' entry passage between massive walls; three changing local ales, real ciders and interesting gin range, good freshly made food using local ingredients including own pork and lamb, low beams and some 17th-c panelling with witches' marks, eclectic mix of antique and contemporary furniture including long oak refectory table and fine high-backed settles either side of inglenook, cosy room with sofas and another inglenook, bar area with polished concrete floor and glass-covered well; skittle alley in function room; children and dogs welcome, disabled access/loo, back terrace, closed Sun evening, Mon and Tues. *(Malcolm Axtell)*

RINGMORE   SX6545

Journeys End (01548) 810205

Signed off B3392 at Pickwick Inn, St Anns Chapel, near Bigbury; best to park opposite church; TQ7 4HL Ancient village inn (dates from the 13th c) with friendly chatty atmosphere; character panelled lounge and other linked rooms, four local ales tapped from the cask, real cider, seven wines by the glass and well executed/presented food including some thai dishes from good shortish menu (best to book in summer), log fires, family dining conservatory with board games; dogs welcome throughout, garden with picnic-sets on gravel, old-fashioned street lights and decked area, attractive setting near thatched cottages and not far from the sea, open all day weekends (no food Sun evening), closed Mon. *(Jane and Philip Saunders)*

ROBOROUGH SS5717
New Inn (01805) 603247
Off B3217 N of Winkleigh; EX19 8SY
Tucked-away 16th-c thatched village pub, cheerful and busy, with well kept local ales, great range of ciders, several wines by the glass and 40 or so gins, enjoyable fairly priced food from varied menu, beamed bar with woodburner, tiny back room leading up to restaurant, friendly helpful staff; children and dogs welcome, seats on sunny front terrace, open all day Fri-Sun, closed lunchtimes Mon, Tues. *(Alan and Alice Morgan)*

ROCKBEARE SY0195
★ **Jack in the Green** (01404) 822240
Signed from A30 bypass E of Exeter; EX5 2EE Neat welcoming dining pub (most customers here to eat) run well by long-serving owner; first class food from interesting menu including excellent puddings, good friendly service, carpeted dining rooms with old hunting/shooting photographs and high-backed leather chairs around dark tables, big woodburner, also airy restaurant and club-like ante-room with two-way stove, comfortable sofas in flagstoned lounge bar, ales such as Butcombe, Otter and Sharps, local cider, a dozen wines by the glass (over 100 by the bottle); background music; well behaved children welcome, no dogs inside, disabled facilities, plenty of seats in courtyard, open all day Sun, closed 25 Dec-5 Jan, quite handy for M5. *(John Evans)*

SALCOMBE SX7439
Fortescue (01548) 842868
Union Street, end of Fore Street; TQ8 8BZ Linked rooms with painted beams and half-panelling, rugs and pine furniture on quarry tiles, old local photographs and some stuffed fish, woodburners, decent pubby food including stone-baked pizzas, well kept ales such as Otter, Salcombe and Sharps, public bar with parquet floor, booth seating, games, TVs and machines; children welcome, courtyard picnic-sets, three bedrooms, open (and food) all day. *(Alan and Alice Morgan)*

SALCOMBE SX7439
★ **Victoria** (01548) 842604
Fore Street; TQ8 8BU Bustling town centre pub with traditionally furnished beamed bar, huge flagstones and open fire in big stone fireplace, two well kept St Austell ales, a beer named for the pub and a guest, several wines including champagne by the glass, a prosecco menu and around 25 gins,

enjoyable food from good crab sandwiches up, other dining/drinking areas have stripped floorboards and nautical décor, more room upstairs; free wi-fi; children and dogs (in bar) welcome, pretty summer window boxes and large tiered back garden with play area, chickens and budgies, quirky but comfortable Hobbit House bedrooms, no breakfasts (cafés and restaurants nearby), open (and food) all day. *(Roger and Donna Huggins, Chris Wraith)*

SAMPFORD COURTENAY SS6300
New Inn (01837) 82247
B3072 Crediton–Holsworthy; EX20 2TB Thatched 16th-c pub in picturesque village; good food from landlord-chef including daily specials and a vegan menu, local ales tapped from the cask, proper cider and good range of wines and gins, relaxed friendly atmosphere, beams and log fires; quiz second and last Weds of month; children and dogs (in bar) welcome, garden picnic-sets. *(Tim and Holly Waite)*

SANDY PARK SX7189
Sandy Park Inn (01647) 432114
A382 Whiddon Down–Moretonhampstead; TQ13 8JW Hospitable little 17th-c thatched and beamed inn; cosy bar with wall settles and log fire, small dining room on left and inner snug, well kept Exeter Avocet, Dartmoor IPA and Otter Bitter, enjoyable simple food including range of pies, good friendly service; some acoustic live music; children and dogs welcome, nice back garden with country views, open all day Sun, otherwise from 4pm. *(Rosie and Marcus Heatherley)*

SHALDON SX9372
Clifford Arms (01626) 872311
Fore Street; TQ14 0DE Attractive 18th-c open-plan pub on two levels; clean and bright, with good range of blackboard food including Weds-Sat evening set menu, cream teas, up to four mainly local ales, lots of wines by the glass and cocktails, low beams and stone walls, wood or carpeted floors, log fire; regular live jazz; children over 5 welcome, café-style seating on front terrace, decked area behind with palms, pleasant seaside village, closed Sun evening, Mon and Tues, otherwise open all day from 8.30am. *(Ben and Jenny Settle)*

SHALDON SX9371
Ness House (01626) 873480
Ness Drive; TQ14 0HP Georgian hotel on Ness headland overlooking Teign estuary and well worth knowing for its position; comfortable two-room bar with mixed furniture on bare boards, log fire, Badger ales and decent wines by the glass, popular food in restaurant or small conservatory, afternoon teas; free wi-fi; children welcome, no dogs, disabled facilities, terrace with lovely views, picnic-sets in back garden, nine bedrooms, open all day. *(Charles Welch)*

SHEBBEAR   SS4309
Devils Stone Inn (01409) 281210
*Off A3072 or A388 NE of Holsworthy;
EX21 5RU* Neatly kept 17th-c beamed
village pub reputed to be one of England's
most haunted; seats in front of open
woodburner, long L-shaped pew and second
smaller one, flagstone floors, St Austell
Tribute and a couple of local guests, decent
wines and enjoyable food in dining room
across corridor, plain back games room with
pool and darts; children and dogs welcome
(they have a rottweiler), picnic-sets on front
terrace and in garden behind, next to actual
Devil's Stone (turned by villagers on 5 Nov to
keep the devil at bay), eight bedrooms (steep
stairs to some), open all day Sun, closed Weds
lunchtime; for sale as we went to press, so
may be changes. *(Mark Chamberlain)*

SHEEPWASH   SS4806
Half Moon (01409) 231376
*Off A3072 Holsworthy–Hatherleigh at
Highampton; EX21 5NE* Ancient inn
loved by anglers for its 7 miles of River
Torridge fishing (salmon, sea and brown
trout); simply furnished main bar, lots of
beams, log fire in big fireplace, well kept
ales such as Otter, St Austell and Sharps,
several wines by the glass and tasty food from
shortish sensibly priced menu (some gluten-
free options), friendly service, separate
extended dining room; children and dogs
welcome, 11 bedrooms (four in converted
stables), tiny Dartmoor village off the beaten
track, open all day. *(Steven Holmes)*

SIDBURY   SY1496
Hare & Hounds (01404) 41760
*3 miles N of Sidbury, at Putts Corner;
A375 towards Honiton, crossroads with
B3174; EX10 0QQ* Large roadside pub
popular for its highly thought-of daily carvery;
spreading rooms with two log fires, heavy
beams, red plush dining chairs, window seats
and leather sofas around plenty of tables on
carpet or bare boards, Otter and St Austell
ales tapped from the cask, eight wines by the
glass, newer dining extension with central
fire; children welcome (no under-12s in bar),
dogs in bar only, tables on decked area and in
big garden with lovely views down Sid Valley
to the sea, open (and food) all day. *(Joe and
Belinda Smart, Ivy and George Goodwill)*

SIDFORD   SY1389
Blue Ball (01395) 514062
A3052 just N of Sidmouth; EX10 9QL
Handsome thatched pub in same friendly
family for over 100 years; central bar with
three main areas each with log fire, pale
beams, nice mix of wooden dining chairs
around circular tables on patterned carpet,
prints, horsebrasses and plenty of bric-a-
brac, well kept Bass, Otter, St Austell and
Sharps, enjoyable bar food, chatty public
bar; background music, board games, darts

and skittle alley; children and dogs welcome,
flower-filled garden, terrace and smokers'
gazebo, coastal walks close by, bedrooms,
open all day. *(Roger and Donna Huggins)*

SIDMOUTH   ST1287
Anchor (01395) 514129
Old Fore Street; EX10 8LP Welcoming
family-run pub popular for its fresh fish and
other good value food, well kept Caledonian
ales including one named for them, decent
choice of wines, good friendly service, large
carpeted L-shaped room with nautical
pictures and aquarium, steps down to
restaurant; darts; tables out in front, more
in back beer garden with stage for live acts,
open (and food) all day. *(Roger and Donna
Huggins, Dave Braisted)*

SIDMOUTH   SY1090
Bowd (01395) 513328
Junction B3176/A3052; EX10 0ND
Popular thatched and beamed dining pub
(sister to Halfway in Aylesbeare) with
enjoyable sensibly priced food (all day Sun)
including daily carvery, a couple of Otter ales
and Sharps Doom Bar, friendly helpful staff,
spacious flagstoned interior with standing
timbers and alcoves; children and dogs
welcome, plenty of seats in big garden, play
area, open all day. *(Roger and Donna Huggins)*

SIDMOUTH   SY1287
Dukes (01395) 513320
Esplanade; EX10 8AR More brasserie
than pub, but long bar on left serves
Branscombe Vale and a couple of guests,
good food specialising in local fish (best to
book in the evening), friendly efficient young
staff, linked areas including conservatory
and flagstoned eating area (once a chapel),
smart contemporary décor; big-screen TV,
daily papers; children welcome, disabled
facilities, prom-view terrace tables, bedrooms
in adjoining Elizabeth Hotel, open (and food)
all day (may be summer queues). *(Roger and
Donna Huggins)*

SIDMOUTH   SY1287
★ Swan (01395) 512849
York Street; EX10 8BY Cheerful old-
fashioned town-centre local, well kept
Youngs ales and enjoyable good value
blackboard food from sandwiches up, friendly
helpful staff, lounge bar with interesting
pictures and memorabilia, darts and
woodburner in bigger light and airy public
bar with boarded walls and ceilings, daily
newspapers, separate carpeted dining area;
no under-14s, dogs welcome, flower-filled
garden with smokers' area, open all day.
(Roger and Donna Huggins)

SILVERTON   SS9503
Lamb (01392) 860272
Fore Street; EX5 4HZ Traditional
flagstoned local run well by friendly landlord;
well kept Otter and a couple of guests tapped

from stillage casks, inexpensive home-made pubby food including specials, separate eating area; quiz nights and other events, darts, skittle alley, free wi-fi; children and dogs welcome, handy for Killerton (NT), open all day weekends. *(Charlie Jones)*

SLAPTON   SX8245
Queens Arms (01548) 580800
Junction Sands Road and Prospect Hill; TQ7 2PN Smartly kept one-room village local with friendly staff and regulars, good value well balanced menu cooked by landlord, four real ales including Dartmoor and Otter, snug comfortable corners, roaring log fire, fascinating World War II photos and scrapbooks; children and dogs welcome, lots of tables in lovely suntrap stepped garden, parking can be tricky at weekends. *(Nick and Meriel Cox)*

SLAPTON   SX8245
★Tower (01548) 580216
Church Road off Prospect Hill; TQ7 2PN Close to some fine beaches and backed by Slapton Ley nature reserve, this old inn has a low-beamed bar with settles, armchairs and scrubbed oak tables on flagstones or bare boards, log fires, three or four well kept west country ales including one badged for them from St Austell, local cider and decent wines by the glass, good interesting food cooked by french chef from lunchtime sandwiches up, friendly accommodating service; free wi-fi; children and dogs (in bar) welcome, wheelchair access to dining area (but not to lavatories), picnic-sets in pretty back garden overlooked by ivy-covered ruins of 14th-c chantry, comfortable bedrooms reached by external stone staircase, good breakfast, lane up to the pub is very narrow and parking can be tricky particularly at peak times, closed Sun evening and first two weeks of Jan. *(Chris Stevenson)*

SOURTON   SX5390
★Highwayman (01837) 861243
A386, S of junction with A30; EX20 4HN Unique place – a quirky fantasy of dimly lit stonework and flagstone-floored burrows and alcoves, all sorts of things to look at, one room a make-believe galleon; a couple of well kept local ales, proper cider and maybe organic wines, lunchtime sandwiches, home-made pasties and platters (evening food mainly for residents), friendly chatty service; nostalgic background music, open mike nights, poetry evenings; children allowed in certain areas, outside fairy-tale pumpkin house and an old-lady-who-lived-in-a-shoe, period bedrooms with four-posters and half-testers. *(Jane and Philip Saunders)*

STICKLEPATH   SX6494
★Devonshire (01837) 840626
Off A30 at Whiddon Down or Okehampton; EX20 2NW Welcoming old-fashioned 16th-c thatched village local next

to Finch Foundry museum (NT); low-beamed slate-floor bar with big log fire, longcase clock and easy-going old furnishings, stuffed animal heads, key collection, sofa in small snug, well kept low-priced ales tapped from the cask, farm cider, good value sandwiches, soup and home-made pasties from the Aga, games room, lively folk night first Sun of month; £1 fine for using mobile phone; dogs welcome, wheelchair access from car park, good walks, open all day Fri, Sat, closed Sun evening. *(Mike Benton)*

STOKE FLEMING   SX8648
Green Dragon (01803) 770238
Church Street; TQ6 0PX Village local freshened up under present friendly management; beamed and flagstoned interior with open fire, well kept ales such as St Austell and Bath, decent wines by the glass and enjoyable home-made food; background music; children and dogs welcome, tables on front terrace, small garden behind with play area, handy for coast path, best to check opening and food times. *(David Hastings, Richard Tilbrook)*

STOKE GABRIEL   SX8457
Church House (01803) 782384
Off A385 just W of junction with A3022; Church Walk; TQ9 6SD Popular and welcoming early 14th-c pub; lounge bar with fine medieval beam-and-plank ceiling, black oak partition wall, window seats cut into thick butter-coloured walls, woodburner in huge fireplace, look out for the ancient mummified cat, well kept Bass, Sharps Doom Bar and a guest, enjoyable good value food, also little locals' bar; background music, Sun quiz; well behaved children and dogs welcome, picnic-sets on small front terrace, old stocks (pub used to incorporate the village courthouse), limited parking, open all day. *(Robin and Anna Triggs)*

STOKENHAM   SX8042
Tradesmans Arms (01548) 580996
Just off A379 Dartmouth–Kingsbridge; TQ7 2SZ Picturesque partly thatched 14th-c pub; traditional low-beamed cottagey interior with log fire, well kept west country beers and decent wine list, good locally sourced food from lunchtime sandwiches to blackboard specials (booking advised), friendly attentive service, restaurant; children and dogs welcome, seats over lane on raised area looking down on village green, four nice bedrooms (they also have a self-catering apartment nearby), good breakfast. *(Charles Welch)*

TAVISTOCK   SX4874
★Cornish Arms (01822) 612145
West Street; PL19 8AN Chef-owner's highly regarded upscale pub food is a real draw here, can eat in bar or elegant dining room, comfortable seating and real fires, four well kept St Austell ales, good friendly service;

children and dogs welcome, tables on split-level terrace, seven well appointed individual bedrooms, open all day. *(Keith Smith, Stephen Shepherd, Neil Hammacott)*

TEIGNMOUTH
SX9372

Olde Jolly Sailor (01626) 772864

Set back from Northumberland Place; TQ14 8DE Town's oldest pub (said to date from the 12th c), comfortable low-ceilinged interior with stripped-stone walls, various nooks and crannies, well kept Otter Ale, Sharps Doom Bar and a couple of guests, generous helpings of tasty pub food (all day weekends), friendly welcoming staff; live music including Mon jazz, sports TV, free wi-fi; children and dogs welcome, seats in front courtyard, more behind with estuary views, open all day. *(Philip Kingsbury)*

TEIGNMOUTH
SX9372

Ship (01626) 772674

Queen Street; TQ14 8BY Quayside pub with lovely estuary views from terrace picnic-sets; good reasonably priced food especially simply cooked local fish/seafood, five real ales including Bass, Otter and St Austell from brick-faced counter, bare boards bar with woodburner, back gallery restaurant; music festivals May/Aug; children and dogs welcome, open all day. *(Roger and Donna Huggins)*

THORVERTON
SS9202

Thorverton Arms (01392) 860205

Village signed off A396 Exeter–Tiverton; EX5 5NS Spacious former coaching inn with five adjoining areas including log-fire bar and restaurant, uncomplicated well cooked food at affordable prices (good fish and chips), Butcombe and a couple of other beers, friendly helpful staff; quiz second Wed of month, live music, pool; children and dogs (in bar) welcome, wisteria-draped terrace and sunny garden, pleasant village, six comfortable bedrooms, good breakfast, open all day weekends, closed Sun evening and lunchtimes Mon, Tues. *(Chloe and Tim Hodge)*

THURLESTONE
SX6743

Village Inn (01548) 563525

Part of Thurlestone Hotel; TQ7 3NN Updated 16th-c pub attached to family-run hotel; wide choice of well liked food from open sandwiches and other snacks up, local beers and plenty of wines by the glass, friendly attentive service; background music, quiz Tues, free wi-fi; children and dogs welcome, picnic-sets out at front, handy for coast path, open all day weekends and in high season. *(Helen and Brian Edgeley)*

TOPSHAM
SX9688

★Bridge Inn (01392) 873862

2.5 miles from M5 junction 30: Topsham signposted from exit roundabout; in Topsham follow signpost (A376) Exmouth, on the Elmgrove Road,

into Bridge Hill; EX3 0QQ Very special old drinkers' pub (former 16th-c maltings painted a distinctive pink), in landlady's family for five generations and quite unchanging and unspoilt; small characterful rooms and snugs, traditional furniture including a nice high-backed settle, woodburner, the 'bar' is landlady's front parlour (as notice on the door politely reminds customers), up to nine well kept ales tapped from the cask, simple food including good ploughman's, friendly staff and locals; live folk and blues, no background music, mobile phones or credit cards; children and dogs welcome, picnic-sets overlooking weir. *(Charles Smith)*

TOPSHAM
SX9687

★Globe (01392) 873471

Fore Street; 2 miles from M5 junction 30; EX3 0HR Handsome carefully renovated former coaching inn blending original features with up-to-date touches; red-painted panelling in beamed bar hung with old prints, armchairs in a corner and suede tub and pubby chairs around dark tables on bare boards, small brick fireplace, second tartan-carpeted bar has pale panelling, traditional furniture and woodburner, St Austell ales and several wines by the glass, good choice of enjoyable food from breakfast on, another log fire and huge candlesticks in elegant dining room; free wi-fi; children and dogs (in bar) welcome, large terrace with parasol-shaded tables, individually decorated modern bedrooms, open (and food) all day. *(Adrian Johnson, Roger and Donna Huggins, Dr and Mrs A K Clarke, Hugh Roberts, Guy Vowles)*

TOPSHAM
SX9688

Passage House (01392) 873653

Ferry Road, off main street; EX3 0JN Relaxed 18th-c pub just back from the estuary shore; traditional black-beamed bar and slate-floored lower dining area, very good food (booking advised) from ciabattas to local fish, several well kept west country ales, decent wines and some interesting gins, friendly attentive service; Tues quiz, free wi-fi; children and dogs welcome, picnic-sets on terrace looking over moorings to nature reserve (lovely at sunset), open (and food) all day. *(Richard Tilbrook, Roger and Donna Huggins, The Rogue)*

TORBRYAN
SX8266

★Old Church House (01803) 812372

Pub signed off A381; TQ12 5UR Character 13th-c former farmhouse with attractive bar (popular with locals), benches built into fine panelling, settle and other seats by big log fire, Hunters and a couple of guests, proper cider, several wines by the glass and around 35 malt whiskies, good variety of well liked wholesome food from baguettes up, cheerful helpful staff, discreetly lit lounges, one with a splendid deep Tudor inglenook; background and occasional live music; free wi-fi; children and dogs (in bar) welcome, bedrooms, good breakfast; closed Mon lunchtime, otherwise open all day. *(Nick and Meriel Cox)*

TORCROSS   SX8242
Start Bay (01548) 580553
A379 S of Dartmouth; TQ7 2TQ
More fish and chip restaurant than pub, but does sell Otter and St Austell, local wine and cider; very much set out for eating and exceptionally busy at peak times, staff cope well and food is generous and sensibly priced; wheelback chairs around dark tables, country pictures, some photographs of storms buffeting the building, winter coal fire, small drinking area by counter, large family room; no dogs during meal times, seats outside (highly prized) looking over pebble beach and wildlife lagoon, open all day.
(Charles Langton)

TORQUAY   SX9265
★ Cary Arms (01803) 327110
Beach Road: off B3199 Babbacombe Road, via Babbacombe Downs Road; turn steeply down near Babbacombe Theatre; TQ1 3LX Charming higgledy-piggledy hotel reached down a tortuously steep lane (pay and display parking at bottom for non-residents); small, glass-enclosed entrance room with large ship lanterns and cleats, beamed grotto-effect bar overlooking the sea, rough pink granite walls, alcoves, hobbit-style leather chairs around carved wooden tables, slate or bare-board floors, woodburner, Bays, Hanlons and Otter, two local ciders and nine good wines by the glass, enjoyable if not particularly cheap food; free wi-fi; children and dogs (in bar) welcome, plenty of outside seating on various terraces, outside bar, barbecue and pizza oven, steps down to quay with six mooring spaces, boutique-style bedrooms, self-catering cottages (glorious views) and chic beach huts and shore suites, open all day. *(Alan Sutton)*

TORQUAY   SX9166
Crown & Sceptre (01803) 328290
Petitor Road, St Marychurch; TQ1 4QA Friendly two-bar local (in same family for over 40 years) with eight well kept ales such as Butcombe, Courage, Dartmoor, Hanlons, Harveys and Otter, three proper ciders and basic good value lunchtime food (not Mon, Tues), interesting naval memorabilia and chamber-pot collection; regular live music including Tues jazz and Fri folk; children and dogs welcome, sunny deck and garden. *(Alan and Linda Blackmore)*

TORQUAY   SX9163
Hole in the Wall (01803) 200755
Park Lane, opposite clock tower; TQ1 2AU Ancient two-bar local tucked away near harbour; enjoyable reasonably

priced pubby food including good fresh fish, seven well kept ales such as St Austell, Butcombe, Otter and Sharps, real cider, good friendly service, smooth cobbled floors, low beams and alcoves, lots of nautical brassware, ship models and old local photographs, restaurant/function room; live music; children and dogs welcome, some seats in alley out at front, open all day and can get very busy at weekends. *(Roger and Donna Huggins, Tony Scott)*

TORRINGTON   SS4919
Black Horse (01805) 622121
High Street; EX38 8HN Popular twin-gabled former coaching inn; beams hung with stirrups in smallish bar, solid furniture and woodburner, lounge with striking ancient oak partition wall, back restaurant, five well kept ales including Courage and St Austell, generous helpings of tasty home-made food served by friendly staff; background music, darts and shove-ha'penny; children and dogs welcome, disabled access, three bedrooms, open all day. *(Jill and Dick Archer)*

TOTNES   SX8060
Albert (01803) 863214
Bridgetown; TQ9 5AD Unpretentious slate-hung pub near the river, small bar and two other rooms, low beams, flagstones, panelling, some old settles and lots of knick-knacks, friendly landlord brewing his own good Bridgetown ales, real cider and plenty of whiskies, honest reasonably priced pub food, friendly local atmosphere; quiz and music nights, darts, free wi-fi, no dogs (theirs is Albert), paved beer garden behind.
(Chris Stevenson)

TOTNES   SX7960
Bay Horse (01803) 862088
Cistern Street; TQ9 5SP Welcoming traditional two-bar inn dating from the 15th c; half a dozen well kept ales including New Lion, ciders such as Sandford Orchards, simple lunchtime food; background and regular live music including good Sun jazz; children and dogs (on leads) welcome, nice garden behind, three bedrooms, good breakfast, open all day. *(Chris Stevenson)*

TOTNES   SX8060
★ Royal Seven Stars (01803) 862125
Fore Street, The Plains; TQ9 5DD Handsome, well run hotel across from River Dart; companionable bar to left of interesting entrance hall, open fire, button-back banquettes and cushioned chairs around circular tables, stools against counter serving New Lion (brewery in town), Dartmoor, Salcombe, Sharps and a guest, real cider, carefully chosen wines (22 by the glass) and interesting gins, dining rooms with lots to look at, good food from sandwiches and pub favourites up; background music, TV; children welcome, dogs in bar and bedrooms, disabled access, covered tables out at front among

box-planted troughs, open (and food) all day from 8am. *(Sophie and James Collier, Alan and Linda Blackmore, George Sanderson)*

TUCKENHAY   SX8156
Maltsters Arms (01803) 732350
Ashprington Road, off A381 from Totnes; TQ9 7EQ Popular old pub (once owned by celebrity chef Keith Floyd) in lovely quiet spot by wooded Bow Creek; good food from bar snacks to fresh fish specials, well kept Bays and three west country guests, local ciders and great range of wines by the glass, friendly service, creek-view restaurant; background music, live music, free wi-fi; children and dogs welcome, waterside terrace with open-air bar, pontoon for visiting boats, six bedrooms (three with river views), open all day, food all day Fri-Sun during summer school holidays.
(Nicola and Holly Lyons)

TYTHERLEIGH   ST3103
Tytherleigh Arms (01460) 20214
A358 Chard–Axminster; EX13 7BE Modernised village dining pub dating from the 16th c; highly praised imaginative cooking (also some cheaper pubby dishes), ales such as Branscombe and Otter, well chosen wines, friendly professional service, bare boards bar with log fire, restaurant; well behaved children welcome (no under-5s in the evening), dogs allowed in bar, six comfortable bedrooms in converted stables, closed Sun evening out of season. *(A E Forbes)*

UFFCULME   ST0612
George (01884) 842556
Commercial Road; EX15 3EB Cleanly modernised former 18th-c coaching inn under welcoming new owners; enjoyable home-made food from monthly changing menu including daily specials, well kept west country beers, decent wines and good selection of gins, friendly service, log fire; courtyard seating, handy for M5 (junction 27), open all day Fri and Sat, till 8pm Sun, closed Mon and lunchtime Tues. *(Ben and Jenny Settle)*

UGBOROUGH   SX6755
Anchor (01752) 690388
Off A3121; PL21 0NG New management for this 17th-c beamed inn; bar with open fire, comfortable armchairs and dining chairs around mix of tables on wood floor, stools against planked counter serving Sharps Doom Bar, a guest beer and several wines by the glass, well regarded food, two-level restaurant with rattan dining chairs and wooden tables on flagstones in one part, more traditional dark wooden

furniture in lower area, woodburner in big fireplace; background music, TV and board games; children and dogs (in bar) welcome, ten comfortable individually furnished bedrooms (four in courtyard cabins), open all day. *(M J Winterton, John Evans, Julie and Andrew Blanchett)*

UGBOROUGH   SX6755
Ship (01752) 892565
Off A3121 SE of Ivybridge; PL21 0NS Friendly dining pub extended from cosy 16th-c flagstoned core; well divided open-plan eating areas a step down from neat bar with woodburner, good food from bar meals up including blackboard specials (plenty of fish), well kept Palmers, St Austell and a local guest, nice house wines, cheerful chatty staff; background music; children and dogs (in bar) welcome, tables out in front, shuts Mon afternoon, otherwise open all day. *(Andrew Low)*

UPOTTERY   ST2007
Sidmouth Arms (01404) 861252
Near the church; EX14 9PN Attractive 18th-c pub in pleasant village setting, roomy and comfortable, with helpful friendly staff, a couple of well kept Otter beers and a guest, proper cider, enjoyable good value traditional food; children and dogs welcome, small outside area, open (and food) all day. *(Bob and Margaret Holder, Roger and Donna Huggins, Joy Jones)*

WEARE GIFFARD   SS4722
Cyder Press (01237) 425517
Tavern Gardens; EX39 4QR Welcoming village local with amiable landlord; impressive range of ciders, four real ales including a house beer from Clearwater and some interesting gins, enjoyable fairly priced home-made food (Weds-Sat and Sun lunchtime), black beams and timbers, inglenook woodburner; Tues folk night, Fri darts, monthly quiz; children (till 8.30pm) and dogs welcome, seats outside, beautiful countryside and handy for Tarka Trail, bedrooms, closed Mon and Tues lunchtimes, otherwise open all day (shuts Weds-Fri afternoons in winter). *(Jane and Philip Saunders)*

WELCOMBE   SS2317
Old Smithy (01288) 331305
Signed off A39 S of Hartland; EX39 6HG Cosy thatched and low-beamed country pub; open-plan bar with mix of wooden chairs at scrubbed pine tables, quirky 1960/70s retro decor; fairy lights and open fires, well kept local ales, traditional ciders and popular pubby food, good friendly service, more room upstairs; background and live music

---

If you report on a pub that's not a featured entry, please tell us any lunchtimes or evenings when it doesn't serve bar food.

including Mon folk night, quiz and pizza Thurs, various games, free wi-fi; children and dogs welcome, lovely garden and setting by narrow lane leading eventually to attractive rocky cove, bunkhouse, closed Sun evening and lunchtimes Mon, Tues. *(Malcolm and Madeline Ashton)*

WEMBURY   SX5349
Odd Wheel (01752) 863052
Knighton Road; PL9 0JD Popular modernised village pub with five well kept west country ales and good fairly traditional food from sandwiches/ciabattas up, reasonable prices including set lunch Mon-Fri, friendly helpful service, back restaurant; pool, darts, sports TV, free wi-fi; children and dogs (in bar) welcome, seats out on decking, fenced play area, open (and food) all day weekends. *(Colin Stubbs)*

WESTON   ST1400
Otter (01404) 42594
Off A373, or A30 at W end of Honiton bypass; EX14 3NZ Big busy family pub with heavy low beams; good choice of enjoyable reasonably priced food (best to book) including menu for smaller appetites and two-for-one deals, carvery Thurs and Sun lunchtimes, cheerful helpful staff, well kept Otter ales and a guest, carpeted opened-up interior with good log fire; background music, pool; dogs allowed in one area, disabled access, picnic-sets on big lawn leading to River Otter, open (and food) all day. *(Barbara Brown)*

WIDECOMBE   SX7176
Old Inn (01364) 621207
B3387 W of Bovey Tracey; TQ13 7TA Busy dining pub with spacious beamed interior; enjoyable fairly standard food at reasonable prices, well kept Badger, Dartmoor and a guest; Weston's cider, good friendly service, side conservatory with large central woodburner; children and dogs (in bar) welcome, nice garden with water features and pleasant terrace, wandering ducks and chickens, great walks from this pretty moorland village, Widecombe Fair second Tues of Sept, open (and food) all day, kitchen closes 5.30pm Sun. *(Dave Statham)*

WONSON   SX6789
Northmore Arms No phone
Between Throwleigh and Gidleigh; EX20 2JA Proper traditional old pub set in beautiful remote walking country; two simple old-fashioned rooms, log fire and woodburner, low beams and stripped stone, well kept ales such as Dartmoor tapped from the cask, farm cider and decent house wines, good

reasonably priced food including popular Sun lunch; walkers and dogs welcome, tables in garden; seeking a new licensee as we went to press, and opening times limited. *(Chris Stevenson)*

WOODBURY SALTERTON   SY0189
Diggers Rest (01395) 232375
3.5 miles from M5 junction 30: A3052 towards Sidmouth, village signposted on right about 0.5 miles after Clyst St Mary; also signposted from B3179 SE of Exeter; EX5 1PQ Welcoming 500-year-old thatched and beamed village pub; main bar with antique furniture and open fire, two Otter ales, a local guest and several wines by the glass, tasty pub food (not Sun evening) from lunchtime sandwiches up, modern extension opening on to garden; background music; children and dogs welcome, ramp provided for wheelchair access, pretty window boxes and flowering baskets, fine walks around Woodbury Common and in surrounding Otter Valley, open all day Sun. *(Clare Holmes)*

YEALMPTON   SX5851
Rose & Crown (01752) 880223
A379 Kingsbridge–Plymouth; PL8 2EB Central bar counter, all dark wood and heavy brass, leather-seated stools and mix of furnishings on stripped-wood floors, comfy sofa by woodburner, emphasis on popular bar and restaurant food, friendly attentive service, three St Austell ales, a dozen wines by the glass and decent coffee; children and dogs (bar area) welcome, tables in walled garden with pond, also a lawned area, eight well appointed bedrooms in separate building, open (and food) all day. *(Keith Smith)*

LUNDY

LUNDY   SS1344
★Marisco (01271) 870870
Get there by ferry (Bideford and Ilfracombe) or helicopter (Hartland Point); EX39 2LY One of England's most isolated pubs, yet surprisingly busy most nights; great setting, steep trudge up from landing stage, galleried interior with lifebelts and shipwreck salvage, open fire, two St Austell ales named for the island and its spring water on tap, Weston's cider and reasonably priced house wines, good basic food using Lundy produce, friendly staff, books and games; no mobile phones; children welcome, tables outside, souvenir shop doubling as general store for the island's few residents, open (and food) all day from breakfast on. *(Chloe and Tim Hodge)*

Dorset

KEY	★ Star Pub	🍽 Top Quality Food	🍺 Great Beer
	♀ Good Wines	£ Bargain Meals	🛏 Good Bedrooms	🍴 Serves Food

ASKERSWELL   SY5393 Map 2
Spyway Inn £ 🛏
(01308) 485250 – www.thespywayinn.com
Off A35 Bridport–Dorchester; DT2 9EP

Popular inn with welcoming owners, attractive décor, real ales and fine views; bedrooms

A simple country local, this was once a smugglers' lookout. The unspoilt little rooms have cushioned wall and window seats, a few tub chairs, old photos of the pub, jugs hanging from beams and a Rayburn – a bonus on chilly days. Otter Bitter and a guest from Cerne Abbas or Copper Street on handpump and nine wines by the glass. The dining area has oak beams and timber uprights, quite a mix of tables and chairs, some horse tack and a woodburning stove. Two smaller rooms lead off from here. There are lovely views of the downs and coast from seats on the back terrace and in the garden. Comfortable, light bedrooms look over the grounds and breakfasts are enjoyable. The steep lane outside continues up Eggardon Hill, one of the highest points in the region.

🍴 Pleasing food includes lunchtime sandwiches, potted rainbow trout with cucumber pickle, devilled chicken liver pâté with onion marmalade, butternut squash and mixed vegetables with a nut and seed filling topped with cream cheese and sultanas, local sausages with mash and onion gravy, jamaican-spiced jerk chicken with coriander salsa, lambs liver in seville orange sauce, moroccan-style hake fillet with butter bean and tomato stew, daily pies, and puddings such as chocolate brownie with vanilla ice-cream and apple cake with custard. *Benchmark main dish: malaysian king prawn curry £16.00. Two-course evening meal £20.00.*

Free house ~ Licensee Mark Watson ~ Real ale ~ Open 12-3, 6-11; closed Mon ~ Bar food 12-2.30, 6-8.30 ~ Restaurant ~ Children welcome ~ Dogs allowed in bar ~ Wi-fi ~ Bedrooms: £60/£90 *Recommended by Pete and Sarah, Scott and Charlotte Havers, John and Delia Franks, Rob Anderson, Ben and Jenny Settle*

BURTON BRADSTOCK   SY4889 Map 1
Three Horseshoes
(01308) 897259 – www.threehorseshoesburtonbradstock.co.uk
Mill Street; DT6 4QZ

Well placed and thatched village inn with traditional furnishings, a friendly welcome and good food and drink

As this welcoming thatched pub is only a few minutes away from a lovely, sandy beach, it's pretty popular at peak times; our readers enjoy their visits. The bar has sofas in bow windows, a nice mix of old dining chairs around wooden tables on floor slates, built-in cushioned wall seats, button-back armchairs by the woodburning stove, some high, mustard-coloured chairs around equally high tables and stools against the stone bar counter. Walls and beams are decorated with bird prints, horsebrasses, mirrors and some farming implements, and there's also a similarly furnished dining room. Well kept Palmers Copper, Dorset Gold, IPA, Tally Ho, 200 and seasonal guests on handpump and a dozen wines (including prosecco) by the glass; background music and board games. At the front of the building are some rustic tables and chairs, while the back garden has a terrace and plenty of picnic-sets.

Good value, enjoyable food cooked by the landlord includes lunchtime sandwiches, beef tataki with onion ponzu and japanese mayonnaise, king scallops with cauliflower purée, cauliflower beignet and black pudding, roast beetroot and butternut squash tart with onion marmalade, pomegranate and quinoa, local pork sausages with spring onion mash and shallot and ale jus, lamb rump with wild mushrooms and spinach and redcurrant jus, teriyaki-glazed duck breast with stir-fried vegetables and chilli and cashews, and puddings such as apple crumble and custard and sticky toffee pudding with bourbon sauce and clotted cream. *Benchmark main dish: indonesian seafood coconut curry £16.00. Two-course evening meal £21.00.*

Palmers ~ Tenants Jaap and Hannah Schep ~ Real ale ~ Open 12-11(10 Sun); 12-3, 5-11 weekdays in winter ~ Bar food 12-9; 12-3 Sun; 12-2, 6-9 weekdays in winter ~ Restaurant ~ Children welcome ~ Dogs allowed in bar ~ Wi-fi *Recommended by Pete and Sarah, Darrell Barton, Charlotte and William Mason, Gwendoline and Ralph Mason, Barry Gibb, Heather and Richard Jones, Nicola and Holly Lyons, Matt and Hayley Jacob*

CERNE ABBAS
ST6601   Map 2
New Inn 🌟 ♿ ♟ 🛏

(01300) 341274 – www.thenewinncerneabbas.co.uk
Long Street; DT2 7JF

Handsome former coaching inn with character bar and two dining rooms, friendly licensees, local ales and inventive food; fine bedrooms

There's plenty of history and original features here (it was built as a guest house for the nearby Benedictine abbey) including heavy oak beams, mullioned windows and a pump and mounting block in the former coachyard. The bar has a solid oak counter, an attractive mix of old dining tables and chairs on slate or polished wooden floors, settles built into various nooks and crannies and a woodburner in the opened-up Yorkstone fireplace. Palmers Copper, Dorset Gold, IPA and 200 on handpump, ten wines by the glass, several malt whiskies and local cider. The dining room is furnished in a similar style; background music. There are seats on the terrace and picnic-sets beneath mature fruit trees or parasols in the back garden. Bedrooms are smart and well equipped and located in either the charming 16th-c main building or a converted stable block. You can walk from the chocolate-box pretty village to the prehistoric Cerne Abbas Giant chalk carving and then on to other villages.

Interesting food includes lunchtime sandwiches, pig cheek and cider terrine with apricot and pear chutney, brown shrimp, smoked haddock and roe fishcake with shellfish sauce, spelt and barley risotto with salt-baked celeriac and beetroot, a pie of the day, duck leg, toulouse sausage, root vegetable and truffle cassoulet, smoked hake with sautéed potatoes, butternut squash and dill oil, and puddings such as hazelnut roulade with cinnamon nougat, hazelnut brittle and fig ice-cream and clementine pannacotta with orange crisp. *Benchmark main dish: fresh fish dish of the day £17.00. Two-course evening meal £22.50.*

Palmers ~ Tenant Julian Dove ~ Real ale ~ Open 12-11 (10 Sun) ~ Bar food 12-2.30, 7-9; 12-2.30, 6.30-9 Fri, Sat; 12-3, 7-8.30 Sun ~ Restaurant ~ Children welcome ~ Dogs allowed in bar and bedrooms ~ Wi-fi ~ Occasional live music on Sun afternoons in courtyard ~ Bedrooms: £90/£120 *Recommended by S G N Bennett, Tracey and Stephen Groves, Christopher Mannings, Dr and Mrs A K Clarke, Matthew and Elisabeth Reeves, Jack Trussler, Liz and Martin Eldon, Sophia and Hamish Greenfield*

CHETNOLE   ST6008   Map 2

Chetnole Inn 🛏

(01935) 872337 – www.thechetnoleinn.co.uk

Village signed off A37 S of Yeovil; DT9 6NU

Attractive country pub with beams and huge flagstones, real ales, popular food and seats in the back garden; bedrooms

Our readers enjoy their visits to this friendly, well run pub, praising the comfortable bedrooms overlooking an old church and the tempting food. The beamed bar has a relaxed country kitchen feel with wheelback chairs and pine tables on huge flagstones and a woodburning stove. Butcombe Rare Breed, Wriggle Valley Golden Bear and a guest beer on handpump and around ten wines by the glass. Popular with locals, the snug has a leather sofa near another woodburner and stools against the counter; dogs are allowed in here. More wheelback chairs around pale wooden tables can be found in the airy dining room, along with stripped floorboards and a small open fire. At the back, a delightful garden has picnic-sets and a view over fields. The surrounding countryside is lovely.

A thoughtful choice of interesting food includes lunchtime sandwiches, mussels and clams in cheese and mustard sauce topped with breadcrumbs with skinny fries, gin and beetroot home-cured salmon with horseradish cream and blinis, a fish board, mushroom stroganoff with saffron basmati, burger with toppings, coleslaw and fries, guinea fowl breast with swede purée, roasted celeriac and creamy mustard sauce, venison loin on sautéed leeks with potato galette and wild mushroom jus, and puddings such as chocolate and hazelnut brownie with dark chocolate sauce and ice-cream and vanilla bean crème brûlée. *Benchmark main dish: fillet steak cooked on granite slab at your table £23.00. Two-course evening meal £19.50.*

Free house ~ Licensees Simon and Maria Hudson ~ Real ale ~ Open 11-3, 6-11; 11-11 Sat; 12-4 Sun ~ Bar food 12-2, 6.30-9; not Sun evening ~ Restaurant ~ Children welcome ~ Dogs allowed in bar ~ Wi-fi ~ Bedrooms: £80/£105 *Recommended by Nick and Meriel Cox, Philip J Alderton, Selwyn Jones, Frank and Marcia Pelling, Martin and Anne Terry, Holly and Tim Waite, Martin and Sue Neville*

CHIDEOCK   SY4191   Map 1

Anchor 🛏

(01297) 489215 – www.theanchorinnseatown.co.uk

Off A35 from Chideock; DT6 6JU

Stunning spot for carefully renovated inn, lots of character, well kept ales and popular food and seats on front terrace; light, airy bedrooms

What really distinguishes this thoughtfully refurbished old pub is its splendid position, almost straddling the South West Coast Path and nestling beneath the 617-ft Golden Cap pinnacle. Inside, there's plenty of character in the three smallish, light rooms: padded wall seating, nice old wooden chairs and stools around scrubbed tables on bare boards, a couple of woodburning stoves (one under a huge bressumer beam), tilley lamps, model ships and lots of historic photographs of the pub, the area and locals. From the wood-panelled bar they serve Palmers Copper, Dorset Gold, IPA and 200 on handpump, seven wines by the glass, 25 gins, over 35 rums and cocktails; background music. Attractive, airy bedrooms overlook the sea and are decorated with nautical touches using driftwood and ropework. In warm weather, the seats and tables on the spacious front terrace are much prized. You can park for free in front of the pub or across the road for £4 (refundable against a spend of £20 or more in the pub).

Highly thought-of food includes filled rolls, twice-baked smoked cheese soufflé with waldorf salad, scallops with pea and mint velouté, black pudding crumb and air-dried ham crisps, sharing platters, chickpea and beetroot burger with red onion marmalade, slaw and yoghurt, fish pie, guinea fowl breast with liquorice-infused leeks, salsify, oyster mushrooms and shallot purée, and puddings such as tiramisu with boozy cherries and chantilly cream-filled profiteroles with salted caramel sauce. *Benchmark main dish: vinegar and sea herb battered fish and chips £15.00. Two-course evening meal £20.00.*

Palmers ~ Tenant Paul Wiscombe ~ Real ale ~ Open 10am-11pm ~ Bar food 12-9 ~ Children welcome ~ Dogs allowed in bar ~ Wi-fi ~ Bedrooms: £155/£170 *Recommended by Lyn and Freddie Roberts, Ian Duncan, Heather and Richard Jones, Alan and Linda Blackmore, Nicola and Stuart Parsons*

CHURCH KNOWLE
New Inn ♀

SY9381 Map 2

(01929) 480357 – www.newinn-churchknowle.co.uk
Village signed off A351 N of Corfe Castle; BH20 5NQ

Bustling pub with plenty of seating in various rooms, open fires, a thoughtful choice of drinks, good food and a friendly landlord

In a pretty little village, this partly thatched 16th-c inn was once part of a working farm and is run by friendly, cheerful people. The main bar has an open fire in a stone fireplace, high-backed black leather dining chairs and cushioned wall settles around heavy rustic tables on red patterned carpet and quite a few stools against the counter; there's an interesting glass cabinet full of old medicine boxes and tins and quite a few horsebrasses. Ringwood Razorback, Sharps Doom Bar and a summer guest on handpump, six wines by the glass and farm cider; there's a wineshack from which you can choose your own wines, and also a wide choice of teas, coffees and local soft drinks. A similarly furnished dining room leads off here. There are picnic-sets on the lawn and a campsite, and the ruins of Corfe Castle (National Trust) are close by. The pub is popular with walkers using the nearby Dorset Coast Path.

Popular, seasonal food includes daily fresh fish dishes (best to order lobster, dover sole or skate wings in advance), sandwiches, cheddar or blue cheese soufflé, crispy duck salad, nut roast with vegetarian gravy, home-cooked ham and eggs, shepherd's pie, lambs liver and bacon, slow-roast pork belly on black pudding with creamed potato and apple sauce, 28-day aged steaks with trimmings, and puddings such as spotted dick with custard and white chocolate pannacotta with raspberry compote. *Benchmark main dish: roast of the day £12.00. Two-course evening meal £20.00.*

Punch ~ Tenants Maurice and Matthew Estop ~ Real ale ~ Open 10-3, 6 (5 in summer)-11 (10 in winter); 12-3, 6-10 Sun ~ Bar food 12-2.15, 6-9; 12-3, 5-9.15 Sun ~ Restaurant ~ Children welcome ~ Wi-fi *Recommended by Sally and Colin Allen, Charlie and Mark Todd, Alan Barnley, Belinda Stamp, Alfie Bayliss*

EVERSHOT

ST5704 Map 2

Acorn

(01935) 83228 – www.acorn-inn.co.uk

Off A37 S of Yeovil; DT2 0JW

• •

Dorset Dining Pub of the Year

Nice old place in a pretty village with character rooms, log fires and knick-knacks and friendly licensees; bedrooms

A 400-year-old inn and particularly well run, our readers enjoy their visits here. The public bar, popular locally, has a log fire, lots of beer mats on beams, big flagstones and high chairs against the counter where they serve Dorset Jurassic and a guest on handpump, 28 wines by the glass, 30 gins (including a gin of the month) and over 100 malt whiskies. A second bar has comfortable beige leather wall banquettes and little stools around tables set with fresh flowers, and a turkish rug on nice old quarry tiles. This leads to a bistro-style dining room with ladder-back chairs around oak tables; the slightly more formal restaurant is similarly furnished. There's also a comfortable lounge with armchairs, board games and shelves of books and a skittle alley. Throughout are open fires, wood panelling, pretty knick-knacks, all manner of copper and brass items, water jugs, wall prints and photographs; background music, TV, board games and darts. A walled garden has picnic-sets under a fine beech tree. Each of the attractive bedrooms is individually decorated and has a Thomas Hardy theme; the inn is immortalised as the Sow & Acorn in Thomas Hardy's *Tess of the D'Urbervilles*. Guests can use the spa facilities at the nearby Summer Lodge hotel. Numerous nearby walks.

 A thoughtful choice of good food includes mackerel and smoked salmon terrine with orange and fennel chutney, open lasagne of confit rabbit, leeks and wild mushrooms with rosemary jus, antipasti sharing platter, crispy buffalo mozzarella stuffed arancini with mediterranean vegetables, spinach and wild garlic velouté and roasted cherry tomatoes, honey and ginger roasted free-range chicken on wild mushroom risotto with red wine jus, trio of pork (braised cheek, slow-roasted belly, loin wrapped in smoked bacon) with sage creamed potatoes and madeira reduction, and puddings such as custard tart with poached rhubarb, coconut crumble, yoghurt ice-cream and rhubarb crisp and baked vanilla cheesecake with candied orange, marmalade and cranberries. *Benchmark main dish: burger with toppings, coleslaw and triple-cooked chips £15.00. Two-course evening meal £25.00.*

Free house ~ Licensee Natalie Legg ~ Real ale ~ Open 11-11; 12-10.30 Sun ~ Bar food 12-2, 7-9 ~ Restaurant ~ Children welcome ~ Dogs welcome ~ Wi-fi ~ Bedrooms: £115/£125
Recommended by Clive and Fran Dutson, Tracey and Stephen Groves, S G N Bennett, Isobel Mackinlay, Monty Green, Mike and Sarah Abbot, Celia and Geoff Clay

FARNHAM

ST9515 Map 2

Museum

(01725) 516261 – www.museuminn.co.uk
Village signposted off A354 Blandford Forum–Salisbury; DT11 8DE

Partly thatched smart inn with appealing rooms, brasserie-style food, real ales and fine wines, and seats outside; comfortable bedrooms

The brasserie-style food remains a big draw here – as do the attractive bedrooms. There's a proper small bar with beams, flagstones, a big inglenook fireplace and quite an assortment of dining chairs around plain or painted wooden tables. Stools line the counter where friendly staff serve

Flack Manor Double Drop, Waylands Sixpenny 6d Best Bitter and Wychwood Hobgoblin Gold on handpump, ten wines by the glass, 20 malt whiskies, 30 gins and local spirits and ciders. Leading off here is a simply but attractively furnished dining room with cushioned window seats, a long dark leather button-back wall seat, similar chairs and tables on bare floorboards and quite a few photographs on patterned wallpaper. A quiet lounge has armchairs around a low table in front of an open fire, books on shelves and board games. Outside, the terrace has cushioned seats and tables under parasols. Four bedrooms are in the main building, the remaining four in converted stables, and they also have a large thatched self-catering cottage.

Rewarding, modern food includes crab, chilli and spring onion cake with crispy, soft shell crab, pickled mouli and dashi, cured pigeon breast with celeriac rémoulade, pickled kohlrabi and beetroot dressing, gnocchi with celeriac purée, purple sprouting broccoli and goats curd, a pie of the day with champ mash and red wine sauce, duck breast with duck faggot, roasted carrots and parisienne potatoes, cod fillet with baby leek, mussel and squid broth, saffron potatoes and saffron aioli, and puddings such as turkish delight, pistachio and raspberry millefeuille with vanilla cream and irish coffee cheesecake with chocolate ganache and salted popcorn. *Benchmark main dish: local pork belly with glazed pig cheek, fondant potato, pickled beetroot £18.95. Two-course evening meal £23.00.*

Free house ~ Licensee Paolo Corgiolu ~ Real ale ~ Open 12-11 (10.30 Sun) ~ Bar food 12-2.30, 6-9 (9.30 Fri); 12-9.30 Sat; 12-8 Sun ~ Restaurant Fri and Sat evening, Sun lunch ~ Children welcome ~ Dogs allowed in bar and bedrooms ~ Wi-fi ~ Bedrooms: /£120
Recommended by Philip J Alderton, Dr Simon Innes, Joe and Belinda Smart, Mungo Shipley, Peter Pilbeam

KINGSTON
Scott Arms

SY9579 Map 2

(01929) 480270 – www.thescottarms.com
West Street (B3069); BH20 5LH

Magnificent views from a large garden, rambling character rooms, real ales and interesting food and an easy-going atmosphere; bedrooms

The views of Corfe Castle (National Trust) and the Purbeck Hills from the well kept garden (which has rustic-style seating and an outside summer kitchen) are quite magnificent, and this is a lovely spot to relax after a walk. The bar areas and dining room are on several levels with stripped stone and brickwork, flagstones and bare boards, beams and high rafters, seats ranging from sofas and easy chairs through all manner of wooden chairs around tables of varying sizes, and open fires; stairs lead up from the bar to a small minstrels' gallery-like area with sofas facing one another across a table. Dorset Durdle Door and Jurassic and a guest such as Waylands Sixpenny 6d Best Bitter on handpump, 11 wines by the glass and local cider; background music and board games. The four bedrooms are attractively decorated.

As well as a summer jerk shack for caribbean food (the landlady is Jamaican), the varied food includes sandwiches, clam chowder with lemon and dill, mushrooms on toast with tarragon and truffle, sharing boards, moroccan-style vegetable stew with apricots, preserved lemon, almonds and harissa yoghurt, local sausages with mash and gravy, serrano ham-wrapped pork tenderloin with cider and sage jus, free-range chicken with creamy wild mushroom sauce and dauphinoise potatoes, and puddings such as chocolate torte and sticky toffee pudding. *Benchmark main dish: burger with toppings, onion rings and chips £14.95. Two-course evening meal £22.00.*

Greene King ~ Lease Ian, Simon and Cynthia Coppack ~ Real ale ~ Open 11-10 (11 Sat) ~ Bar food 12-2.30, 6-8.30; 12-8.30 weekends ~ Children welcome ~ Dogs allowed in bar ~

Wi-fi ~ Bedrooms: £110/£120 *Recommended by M G Hart, Nick Sharpe, John Harris, Simon Pyle, Jamie and Lizzie McEwan, Stuart and Natalie Granville, Catherine and Daniel King*

MIDDLEMARSH   ST6607   Map 2
Hunters Moon ⌒

(01963) 210966 – www.hunters-moon.org.uk
A352 Sherborne–Dorchester; DT9 5QN

Plenty of bric-a-brac in several linked areas, reasonably priced food and quite a choice of drinks; comfortable bedrooms

The convivial, hands-on licensees work hard to create a relaxed, friendly atmosphere here – for customers as well as their dogs (who are also allowed in the bedrooms for a small charge). The beamed bar rooms are filled with a great variety of tables and chairs on red patterned carpet, an array of ornaments from horsebrasses and horse tack to pretty little tea cups hanging from beams, and lighting in the form of converted oil lamps; the atmosphere is properly pubby. Booths are formed by some attractively cushioned settles, walls are of exposed brick, stone and some panelling and there are three log fires (one in a capacious inglenook); background music, children's books and toys and board games. Butcombe Bitter, Ringwood Best and a local guest on handpump, farm cider and 16 wines by the glass. A neat lawn has picnic-sets, including some circular ones.

 Popular food includes lunchtime sandwiches, king prawns in garlic and chilli sauce, chicken liver pâté with onion chutney, mixed bean, lime and coriander chilli with crème fraîche, a pie of the day, beer-battered cod and chips, chicken breast in creamy white wine and garlic sauce, pork steaks in cider and thyme gravy, steaks with a choice of sauce, and puddings such as banoffi pie with toffee sauce and blackberry bakewell tart with berry purée and clotted cream ice-cream. *Benchmark main dish: chicken in barbecue sauce with bacon and cheese £15.00. Two-course evening meal £21.00.*

Enterprise ~ Lease Dean and Emma Mortimer ~ Real ale ~ Open 10.30-2.30, 6 (5 Fri)-11; 10.30am-11pm Sat; 10.30-10.30 Sun ~ Bar food 12-2, 6-9; all day weekends ~ Children welcome ~ Dogs welcome ~ Wi-fi ~ Bedrooms: £65/£75 *Recommended by Sandra and Neil White, Sally and Lance Oldham, Louise and Oliver Redman, Maria and Henry Lazenby, Nik and Gloria Clarke*

NETTLECOMBE   SY5195   Map 2
Marquis of Lorne ◀

(01308) 485236 – www.themarquisoflorne.co.uk
Off A3066 Bridport–Beaminster, via West Milton; DT6 3SY

Attractive country pub with enjoyable food and drink, friendly licensees and seats in big garden; bedrooms

In warm weather, the big mature garden behind this former farmhouse really comes into its own with its pretty herbaceous borders, picnic-sets under apple trees and a rustic-style play area. Inside, the comfortable, bustling main bar has a log fire, mahogany panelling, old prints and photographs and neatly matching chairs and tables. Two dining areas lead off, the smaller of which has another log fire. A wooden-floored snug (liked by locals) has board games, table skittles and background music, and they keep Palmers Copper, Dorset Gold and IPA on handpump, with ten wines by the glass from a decent list and ten gins. Eggardon Hill, the site of one of Dorset's most famous Iron Age hill forts, is within walking distance.

Pleasing food includes duck liver pâté with spiced pears, scallops and black pudding with garlic and parsley cream, vegetable lasagne with lovage pesto, mustard and brown sugar baked ham and eggs, pork tenderloin wrapped in serrano ham on flageolet bean and spinach ragoût with blue cheese mousse, sticky beef on indonesian-style salad, sea bass with creamed prawn velouté, and puddings such as crème brûlée and steamed raspberry and coconut pudding with custard. *Benchmark main dish: lambs liver and bacon with mustard-battered onions and mash £13.00. Two-course evening meal £20.00.*

Palmers ~ Tenants Stephen and Tracey Brady ~ Real ale ~ Open 12-2.30, 6-11 ~ Bar.food 12-2, 6-9 ~ Restaurant ~ Children welcome ~ Dogs allowed in bar ~ Wi-fi ~ Bedrooms: £85/£95 *Recommended by Jason Caulkin, Scott and Charlotte Havers, Mark Morgan, Alice Wright, John Harris, Rob Anderson*

PLUSH

ST7102 Map 2

Brace of Pheasants 🌟 🍷 🛏

(01300) 348357 – www.braceofpheasants.co.uk
Village signposted from B3143 N of Dorchester at Piddletrenthide; DT2 7RQ

16th-c thatched pub with friendly service, popular food and pleasant garden; comfortable bedrooms

You'll find this old thatched cottage tucked away down narrow, country lanes. It's just the place for spending a weekend in attractive and comfortable bedrooms; our readers enjoy the annexe ones which are spotlessly kept and have their own little terrace. Breakfasts are first class. The beamed bar has windsor chairs around good solid tables on patterned carpeting, a few standing timbers and a huge heavy-beamed inglenook at one end with a good warming log fire at the other. Cerne Abbas Ale and a guest such as Flack Manor Double Drop are tapped from the cask and they offer a fine choice of wines with 20 by the glass and two proper farm ciders. A decent-sized garden includes a terrace and a lawn sloping up towards a rockery. There's a bridleway behind the building that leads to the left of the woods and over to Church Hill.

Particularly good food from a daily changing menu includes crab, leek and saffron tartlet, marinated thai beef spring rolls with crunchy coriander salad and sweet chilli sauce, warm goats cheese salad with croutons, beetroot, walnuts and potato salad, loin of hake with parsley sauce, duck breast with caramelised orange and madeira sauce and potato rösti, garlic and herb venison steak with port and redcurrant sauce and confit garlic mash, and puddings such as spotted dick with custard and 'angel tower' (meringue, lemon curd, ice-cream and passion-fruit coulis. *Benchmark main dish: liver and bacon £12.95. Two-course evening meal £20.00.*

Free house ~ Licensees Phil and Carol Bennett ~ Real ale ~ Open 12-3, 7-11 (10.30 Sun) ~ Bar food 12-2.30, 7-9 ~ Children welcome ~ Dogs allowed in bar ~ Wi-fi ~ Bedrooms: £89/£99 *Recommended by Colin and Pat Honey, Alan Johnson, Sandra and Neil White, Ian Malone, Scott and Charlotte Havers, David and Charlotte Green, Nicola and Stuart Parsons, Pete and Sarah*

SHAFTESBURY

ST8622 Map 2

Grosvenor Arms 🛏

(01747) 850580 – www.grosvenorarms.co.uk
High Street; SP7 8JA

Relaxed hotel with a cheerful bar, several dining areas, enjoyable food and local ales, and seats in a courtyard; bedrooms

Handy for the town centre, this place is much enjoyed by our readers. The civilised back bar has cheerful cushions on sofas and armchairs, cushioned settles, a woodburning stove, antlers on partly panelled walls, a coir and wood floor, and a few high chairs against the counter where they serve Otter Bitter and a guest such as Wriggle Valley Golden Bear on handpump and 20 wines by the glass; service is friendly and helpful. A conservatory area (looking over a central courtyard with a fountain surrounded by metal and wood-slat chairs and tables) links this bar with several spreading dining rooms. There's a bistro-like area, a restaurant with brown leather dining chairs and tables on a wood floor, a small end room with bookcase wallpaper and another little dining room at the front. Bedrooms are comfortable and up to date.

Well regarded food includes ciabatta sandwiches, smoked ham hock terrine with apple and gherkin salsa, crab cakes with pickled shallots, celeriac rémoulade and lemon and dill, sharing platters, wood-fired pizzas, gnocchi with wild mushroom ragoût, baked ricotta, beetroot and spinach, flat-iron chicken tikka with raita, potato bhaji, butternut dhal, coriander and lime, hake fillet with café de paris butter, polenta, cavolo nero and salsify, dry-aged steaks with a choice of sauce, and puddings such as salted caramel and chocolate tart with cherry sorbet and yoghurt pannacotta with rhubarb, honey and almond crumble. *Benchmark main dish: burger with toppings and chips £13.50. Two-course evening meal £23.50.*

Free house ~ Licensee Kirsty Schmidt ~ Real ale ~ Open 11-11; 11-10.30 Sun ~ Bar food 9am-11pm (10.30 Sun) ~ Restaurant ~ Children welcome ~ Dogs allowed in bar and bedrooms ~ Wi-fi ~ Bedrooms: /£95 *Recommended by Justine and Neil Bonnett, Ivy and George Goodwill, Sally and Lance Oldham, Andy and Louise Ramwell, Dan and Nicki Barton*

SHERBORNE

ST6316   Map 2

Digby Tap 🍺 £
(01935) 813148
Cooks Lane; park in Digby Road and walk round corner; DT9 3NS

Regularly changing ales in simple alehouse, open all day with very inexpensive beer and food

A fine example of an old-fashioned town pub, you'll find customers from all walks of life enjoying the well kept beers and marvellously cheap food. The atmosphere is lively, chatty and warmly welcoming and the straightforward flagstoned bar with its cosy corners is full of understated character. The small games room has a pool table and a quiz machine, and there's also a TV room; mobile phones are banned. The splendid choice of beers on handpump includes Cerne Abbas Ale, Goffs Jouster, Otter Bitter and Slaters Western American Pale Ale. Also, several wines by the glass and a choice of malt whiskies. Beautiful Sherborne Abbey is just a stroll away.

Generous helpings of extraordinarily good value, straightforward lunchtime food includes sandwiches and toasties, three-egg omelettes, sausages with free-range eggs, beef chilli, burgers and specials such as fish pie, sausage casserole and a mixed grill. *Benchmark main dish: liver and bacon £6.00.*

Free house ~ Licensees Oliver Wilson and Nick Whigham ~ Real ale ~ No credit cards ~ Open 11-11; 12-11 Sun ~ Bar food 12-2; not Sun ~ Children welcome until 6pm ~ Dogs allowed in bar ~ Wi-fi *Recommended by Simon and Sue Lamb, Chloe and Michael Swettenham, Dr and Mrs A K Clarke, Heather and Richard Jones, Sophia and Hamish Greenfield, Caroline and Peter Bryant*

We say if we know a pub allows dogs.

WEST STOUR
ST7822   Map 2

Ship 🌟 🍸 🍺 🛏

(01747) 838640 – www.shipinn-dorset.com

A30 W of Shaftesbury; SP8 5RP

Civilised and pleasantly updated roadside dining inn offering a wide range of food and ales; bedrooms

A very welcoming pub with a smart but relaxed feel and a cheerful, convivial landlord. The neatly kept rooms include a smallish but airy bar on the left with cream décor, a mix of chunky farmhouse furniture on dark boards and big sash windows that look beyond the road and car park to rolling pastures. The smaller flagstoned public bar has a good log fire and low ceilings. Bass, Butcombe Original and Otter Bitter on handpump, 13 wines by the glass, 19 gins, a dozen malt whiskies and five farm ciders. During their summer beer festival they showcase a dozen beers and ten ciders, all from the west country. On the right, two carpeted dining rooms with stripped pine dado, stone walls and shutters are similarly furnished in a pleasantly informal style, and have attractive contemporary prints of cows; TV, numerous board games and background music. The bedlington terriers are called Douglas and Elliot. The garden behind the pub is lovely, and the bedrooms are appealing and comfortable with pastoral views; breakfasts are particularly good. Rewarding surrounding walks.

 Highly enjoyable food includes lunchtime sandwiches, scallops with beetroot cream and herb crème fraîche, pigeon breast in red wine sauce with carrot and carraway purée and game chips, spinach and ricotta tortellini with herb and garlic cream, cod supreme with asparagus velouté, parmentier potatoes and crispy capers, corn-fed chicken supreme with cauliflower purée and bacon and cabbage, slow-roast pork belly with black pudding potato croquettes and apple ketchup, and puddings such as rhubarb posset and jelly and passion fruit and vanilla cheesecake with clotted cream ice-cream. *Benchmark main dish: luxury fish pie £13.95. Two-course evening meal £20.00.*

Free house ~ Licensee Gavin Griggs ~ Real ale ~ Open 12-3, 6-11.30; 12-10.30 Sat, Sun ~ Bar food 12-2.30, 6-9; not Sun evening ~ Restaurant ~ Children welcome ~ Dogs allowed in bar ~ Wi-fi ~ Bedrooms: £65/£95 *Recommended by Edward Mirzoeff, M G Hart, Robert Watt, Simon and Alex Knight, Diana and Richard Gibbs, Simon and Mary Todd, David and Charlotte Emslie*

WEYMOUTH
SY6878   Map 2

Red Lion 🍺 £

(01305) 786940 – www.theredlionweymouth.co.uk

Hope Square; DT4 8TR

Bustling place with sunny terrace, a smashing range of drinks, tasty food and lots to look at

This is the nearest pub to Weymouth RNLI and features numerous pictures and artefacts relating to the lifeboat crews and their boats. They keep a marvellous choice of drinks that includes Dorset Jurassic, Lifeboat Bitter (named for the pub with 10p per pint going towards the RNLI), St Austell Tribute and a changing guest on handpump, a dozen wines by the glass, 40 gins and 120 rums (with a rum 'bible' to explain them all). The refurbished bare-boards interior, kept cosy with candles, has a cheerful, lively atmosphere, all manner of wooden chairs and tables, cushioned wall seats, some unusual maroon-cushioned high benches beside equally high tables, the odd armchair here and there, and plenty of bric-a-brac on stripped-brick walls. Some nice contemporary touches include the woven timber wall and loads of mirrors wittily overlapped; daily papers, board games and background music. Plenty of seats outside stay warmed by the sun well into the evening.

As well as lunchtime sandwiches, the well regarded food includes smoked mackerel pâté, crispy fish taco with avocado purée, pickled red onion, shredded carrot and spicy aioli, sharing plates, vegetarian pie topped with sweet potato mash, local sausages and mash with onion gravy, beer-battered haddock and chips, seafood burger with wasabi mayonnaise and celeriac rémoulade, steak in ale pie, pork belly with mustard mash, braised red cabbage and calvados sauce, and puddings such as chocolate brownie with vanilla ice-cream and date sticky toffee pudding with rum and raisin ice-cream. *Benchmark main dish: seafood board for four £26.95 per head. Two-course evening meal £21.00.*

Free house ~ Licensee Brian McLaughlin ~ Real ale ~ Open 12-11 (10.30 Sun) ~ Bar food 12-9 (8 Sun) ~ Children welcome until 7pm ~ Wi-fi ~ Live music outside Sun 2pm in summer *Recommended by David Bird, Alf and Sally Garner, Dave Chapman, Nicholas and Lucy Sage, Patricia and Gordon Tucker, Belinda and Neil Garth*

WIMBORNE MINSTER   SZ0199   Map 2
Green Man £
(01202) 881021 – www.greenmanwimborne.com
Victoria Road, at junction with West Street (B3082/B3073); BH21 1EN

Cosy, warm-hearted town tavern with well liked food and Wadworths ales

Everyone is welcomed here – even dogs damp from a walk (who are offered a biscuit or two). It's a cheerful, bustling place and the small linked areas have some timbering, tartan banquettes, wheelback and farmhouse chairs around pubby tables on parquet flooring or carpet, some William Morris-style wallpaper, horsebrasses and a high shelf of stone bottles. The bar features a woodburning stove and high chairs line the counter where friendly staff keep Wadworths 6X, IPA and Swordfish on handpump and a farm cider. Darts, a silenced games machine and juke box; the Barn houses a pool table. In summer, the award-winning flowering tubs, hanging baskets and window boxes are quite amazing and there are more on the heated back terrace.

Food is served 10am-4pm and as well as popular breakfasts, there are also sandwiches and baguettes, chicken caesar salad, vegetarian burger with coleslaw and chips, all-day brunch, sausages and mash with onion gravy, gammon and eggs, and daily specials. *Benchmark main dish: beer-battered fish and chips £8.50.*

Wadworths ~ Tenants Katherine Twinn and Scott Valenti ~ Real ale ~ Open 10-11; 11-11 Mon; 10-midnight Fri, Sat; 10am-10.30pm Sun ~ Bar food 11-4 Mon; 10-4 Tues-Sun ~ Restaurant ~ Children welcome until 7pm ~ Dogs allowed in bar ~ Wi-fi ~ Quiz Thurs; live music weekends *Recommended by Thomas Green, Freddie and Sarah Banks, Edward May, Dr and Mrs A K Clarke, Gus Swan, Caroline Prescott*

WORTH MATRAVERS   SY9777   Map 2
Square & Compass
(01929) 439229 – www.squareandcompasspub.co.uk
At fork of both roads signposted to village from B3069; BH19 3LF

Unchanging country tavern with masses of character, in the same family for many years; lovely sea views and fine nearby walks

Our readers love this honest, unspoilt gem, and the long-serving family who run it (they've now been here over 100 years) are warmly friendly and hospitable to all. A couple of simple rooms have straightforward furniture on flagstones and wooden benches around the walls, a woodburning stove, a stuffed albino badger and a loyal crowd of chatty locals. Cotleigh Tawny Owl, Hattie Browns HBA and Moonlite and a couple of quickly changing guests tapped from the cask, and home-produced and ten other farm ciders are passed through the two serving hatches to customers in the drinking corridor; also, 20 malt whiskies. From the local stone benches out in front there's a fantastic view over the village rooftops down to the sea. There may be free-roaming chickens and other birds clucking around and the small (free) museum exhibits local fossils and artefacts, mostly collected by the current landlord and his father. Wonderful walks lead to some exciting switchback sections of the coast path above St Aldhelm's Head and Chapman's Pool – you'll need to park in the public car park (£2 honesty box) 100 metres along the Corfe Castle road.

Bar food consists of home-made pasties and pies.

Free house ~ Licensees Charlie Newman and Kevin Hunt ~ Real ale ~ No credit cards ~ Open 12-11 ~ Bar food all day ~ Children welcome ~ Dogs welcome ~ Live music weekend evenings *Recommended by S G N Bennett, Sally and Brian Turner, Dave Chapman, Robert Watt, Simon Pyle, Tony Scott, Nina Reynolds*

Also Worth a Visit in Dorset

Besides the fully inspected pubs, you might like to try these pubs that have been recommended to us and described by readers. Do tell us what you think of them: feedback@goodguides.com

BLANDFORD FORUM   ST8806
Crown (01258) 456626
West Street; DT11 7AJ Civilised brick-built Georgian hotel on edge of town; spacious well patronised bar/dining area including snug with leather armchairs and roaring fire, full range of Badger ales from nearby brewery, numerous wines by the glass, cocktails, teas and coffee, good food from sandwiches and small plates up, separate restaurant; children welcome, dogs in bar, tables on big terrace with formal garden beyond, 27 refurbished bedrooms, open (and food) all day. *(David and Sally Cullen)*

BOURNEMOUTH   SZ1092
Cricketers Arms (01202) 551589
Windham Road; BH1 4RN Well preserved Victorian pub near the station; separate public and lounge bars, tiled fireplaces and lots of dark wood, etched windows and stained glass, Fullers London Pride and two quickly changing guests, food weekend lunchtimes only from limited menu; folk night second and fourth Mon of the month, free wi-fi; children and dogs

welcome, picnic-sets out in front, open all day. *(Dr and Mrs A K Clarke)*

BOURNEMOUTH   SZ0891
Goat & Tricycle (01202) 314220
West Hill Road; BH2 5PF Interesting Edwardian local (two former pubs knocked together) with rambling split-level interior; Wadworths ales and guests from pillared bar's impressive rank of ten handpumps, real cider, reasonably priced pubby food, friendly staff; background music, Sun quiz, free wi-fi; no under-18s, dogs welcome, good disabled access, part-covered yard, open (and food) all day. *(Ian Herdman)*

BOURTON   ST7731
★ **White Lion** (01747) 840866
High Street, off old A303 E of Wincanton; SP8 5AT 18th-c coaching inn with beamed bar and dining room; bare boards, flagstones, stripped stone and half-panelling, medley of old wooden tables and chairs, church candles and inglenook log fire, Otter Amber, a couple of guest beers and several wines by the glass, well regarded food; background and live music including opera; children and dogs

Post Office address codings confusingly give the impression that some pubs are in Dorset, when they're really in Somerset (which is where we list them).

welcome, back terrace and raised lawn with picnic-sets, comfortable bedrooms, handy for Stourhead (NT), open all day. *(Julia Swift)*

BRIDPORT   SY4692
George (01308) 423187
South Street; DT6 3NQ Relaxed and welcoming old town pub; good food from open kitchen cooked by landlord-chef including daily specials, well kept Palmers and decent wines by the glass, attentive friendly service; children and dogs (in bar) welcome, disabled facilities, open all day (from 10am for brunch on Sat market day), closed Sun evening. *(Peter Brix)*

BRIDPORT   SY4692
Ropemakers (01308) 421255
West Street; DT6 3QP Long rambling town-centre pub with lots of pictures and memorabilia, well kept Palmers ales and enjoyable home-made food from sandwiches up (they cater for special diets), good friendly service; regular weekend live music, Tues quiz, free wi-fi; children and dogs welcome, tables in back courtyard, open all day except Sun evening. *(Peter Brix)*

BRIDPORT   SY4692
★Stable (01308) 459922
At the back of the Bull Hotel; DT6 3LF Not a pub in any sense, but this lively cider/pizza bar is great fun and popular with customers of all ages; lofty barn-like room with rough planked walls and ceiling, big steel columns, two long rows of pale wooden tables flanked by wide benches, steps up to raised end area with cushioned red wall benches, over 80 ciders (tasting boards), St Austell Proper Job and six wines by the glass, good hand-made pizzas and other food such as pies, vegan menu, upstairs room (not always open); background music, free wi-fi; children and dogs welcome, terrace seating, open (and food) all day. *(Peter Brix, Julia Swift)*

BRIDPORT   SY4692
Tiger (01308) 427543
Barrack Street, off South Street; DT6 3LY Cheerful and attractive open-plan Victorian beamed pub with Sharps Doom Bar and five quickly changing guests, real ciders, no food except breakfast for residents; skittle alley, darts, sports TV, free wi-fi; dogs welcome, seats in heated courtyard, six bedrooms, open all day. *(Cliff and Monica Swift)*

BUCKHORN WESTON   ST7524
Stapleton Arms (01963) 370396
Church Hill; off A30 Shaftesbury–Sherborne via Kington Magna; SP8 5HS Handsome Georgian inn under new management; large bar with sofas in front of fine stone fireplace, mix of other seating on flagstones or bare boards including farmhouse and chapel chairs around scrubbed tables, horsey pictures on green

walls, ales such as Plain and St Austell, real cider and good range of other drinks, enjoyable food from traditional choices up, separate elegantly furnished candlelit restaurant; some live music, free wi-fi; children and dogs (in bar) welcome, seats out at front and in charming back garden, boules court, good nearby walks, four comfortable well equipped bedrooms, open (and food) all day Thurs-Sun. *(Alec and Susan Hamilton)*

BUCKLAND NEWTON   ST6804
Gaggle of Geese (01300) 345249
Locketts Lane; E end of village; DT2 7BS Victorian country pub reopened/refurbished under present management; Sharps Doom Bar and other well kept west country beers, good home-made food from sandwiches up, log-fire in bar, separate restaurant; live music and quiz nights, skittle alley; children and dogs welcome, big garden with terrace, orchard and pizza oven, camping, closed Mon, otherwise open (and food) all day, till 8pm (5pm) Sun. *(Sophie Ellison)*

BURTON BRADSTOCK   SY4889
Anchor (01308) 897228
B3157 SE of Bridport; DT6 4QF Friendly helpful staff in pricey but good seafood restaurant, other local food including nice steaks, village pub part too with blackboard choices from baguettes up, ales such as Dorset, St Austell and Sharps, decent wines by the glass and several malt whiskies; live music second Sun of month, games including table skittles; children and dogs (in bar) welcome, two bedrooms, open all day. *(Helene Grygar)*

CERNE ABBAS   ST6601
Royal Oak (01300) 341797
Long Street; DT2 7JG Creeper-clad 16th-c thatched village-centre pub; low black beams, flagstones and rustic memorabilia, nice log fire, well kept ales including local Cerne Abbas, good home-made food from lunchtime sandwiches to daily specials, friendly helpful service; some live music; children and dogs welcome, small back garden, open all day Fri-Sun, may close Tues in winter. *(Nick and Meriel Cox, Tony Scott)*

CHEDINGTON   ST4805
Winyards Gap (01935) 891244
A356 Dorchester–Crewkerne; DT8 3HY Attractive dining pub surrounded by NT land with spectacular view over Parrett Valley into Somerset; enjoyable food including Sun carvery, four well kept changing ales, local ciders, friendly helpful service, bar with woodburner, steps down to restaurant, skittle alley/dining room; children and dogs welcome, tables on front lawn under parasols, good walks, comfortable bedrooms and self-catering, open all day weekends, may close Mon in winter. *(Charlie Stevens)*

CHIDEOCK
SY4292
George (01297) 489419
A35 Bridport–Lyme Regis; DT6 6JD
Welcoming thatched pub with cosy low-beamed rooms; well kept Palmers ales, real cider and popular straightforward food from shortish menu (also some daily specials), good service, warm log fires; background and some live music, monthly quiz; children and dogs welcome (pub dog is Ramsey), pretty walled garden with terrace and wood-fired pizza oven, open all day Sun.
(Colin and Pat Honey)

CHILD OKEFORD
ST8213
Saxon (01258) 860310
Signed off A350 Blandford–Shaftesbury and A357 Blandford–Sherborne; Gold Hill; DT11 8HD Welcoming early 18th-c village pub; snug bar with log fire and two dining rooms, Butcombe, Otter and guests, nice choice of wines and enjoyable reasonably priced home-made food from changing blackboard menu, efficient friendly service; children and dogs (in bar) welcome, attractive back garden, good walks on Neolithic Hambledon Hill, four comfortable bedrooms. *(Lenny and Ruth Walters)*

CHRISTCHURCH
SZ1593
Rising Sun (01202) 486122
Purewell; BH23 1EJ Comfortably modernised old pub specialising in good authentic thai food, L-shaped bar serving Flack Manor Double Drop, Sharps Doom Bar and good choice of wines by the glass, pleasant helpful young staff; terrace with palms and black rattan furniture under large umbrellas, open all day.
(William and Sophie Renton)

CORFE CASTLE
SY9681
Castle Inn (01929) 480208
East Street; BH20 5EE Welcoming little two-room pub mentioned in Hardy's *The Hand of Ethelberta*; up to three real ales and popular generously served food including Fri fish night, special diets catered for, accommodating friendly service, heavy black beams with fairy lights, exposed stone walls, flagstones and woodburner; background music; children welcome, no dogs inside, back terrace and big sunny garden with mature trees, steam train views, open all day. *(Peter Brix)*

CORFE CASTLE
SY9682
Greyhound (01929) 480205
A351; The Square; BH20 5EZ Bustling picturesque old pub in centre of this tourist village; three small low-ceilinged panelled rooms, steps and corridors, well kept ales such as Palmers, Ringwood and Sharps, local cider and good range of other drinks, nice food (they add a service charge) from ciabattas, light dishes and pizzas up, friendly staff coping well at busy times, traditional games including Purbeck longboard shove-ha'penny, family room; background and weekend live music; dogs welcome, garden with large decked area, great views of castle and countryside, pretty courtyard opening on to castle bridge, open (and food) all day, best to book in summer. *(Peter and Anne Hollindale, Dave Chapman, D J and P M Taylor, Tony Scott)*

CORSCOMBE
ST5205
Fox (01935) 892381
Towards Halstock: Hight Street into Fudge Street, L into Court Lane, L into Court Hill; DT2 0NS Thatched and rose-clad 16th-c country pub; beams, flagstones, built-in settles and log fires, well liked food using seasonal local produce, three well kept west country ales, friendly efficient young staff, conservatory; regular live music, darts; children and dogs welcome (their labrador is Ruby), streamside lawn across lane, annexe bedroom (no breakfast), open all day Sun, closed Mon and Tues. *(Marianne and Peter Stevens)*

CRANBORNE
SU0513
Inn at Cranborne (01725) 551249
Wimborne Street (B3078 N of Wimborne); BH21 5PP New licensees were taking over this attractive 16th-c village pub as we went to press – so could be changes; rambling bars with heavy beams and standing timbers, main one has built-in wall seats and assorted chairs on parquet or flagstones, inglenook woodburner, Badger ales and decent selection of other drinks, food has been good, back dining areas with similar furnishings and another woodburner; tables on gravel terrace and lawn, comfortable well equipped bedrooms, has opened all day. *(David and Charlotte Green)*

DEWLISH
SY7798
Oak (01258) 837352
Off A354 Dorchester–Blandford Forum; DT2 7ND Welcoming red-brick village pub; two or three well kept local ales and enjoyable good value food including specials and popular Sun lunch, friendly helpful service, woodburner and open fire in bar, small dining room; winter quiz; children welcome, good-sized garden behind, two bedrooms and self-catering cottage, open (and food) all day. *(Charlie Stevens)*

DORCHESTER
SY6990
Blue Raddle (01305) 267762
Church Street, near central short-stay car park; DT1 1JN Cheery pubby atmosphere in long carpeted and partly panelled bar, well kept ales such as Cerne Abbas, Dartmoor, Otter and St Austell, local ciders, good wines and coffee, enjoyable simple home-made lunchtime food (not Sun, Mon, Tues), evenings Thurs-Sat, efficient friendly service (they don't accept credit/debit cards), coal-effect gas fires; background and live folk music (Weds

fortnightly), darts and cribbage teams; no under-14s, dogs welcome, good disabled access apart from one step, closed Mon lunchtime. *(David and Doreen Beattie, Clive and Fran Dutson, Dr and Mrs A K Clarke)*

EAST CHALDON SY7983
Sailors Return (01305) 854441
Village signposted from A352 Wareham–Dorchester; from village green, follow Dorchester, Weymouth signpost; note that the village is also known as Chaldon Herring; OS Sheet 194 map reference 790834; DT2 8DN Thatched village pub with five well kept ales such as Palmers, Otter and Ringwood, Thatcher's Gold cider and good food from short fairly pubby menu plus daily specials, Weds pie night, friendly attentive service, flagstoned bar and various dining areas; Tues winter quiz; children welcome, dogs in bar (no food in bar Fri evening), picnic-sets out at front and in side garden, useful for coast path, open all day weekends, closed Mon. *(Lenny and Ruth Walters)*

EAST MORDEN SY9194
★**Cock & Bottle** (01929) 459238
B3075 W of Poole; DT7 7DL Popular extended dining pub with wide choice of good food including specials (best to book), separate traditional bar with open fire, well kept Badger ales and nice selection of wines by the glass, efficient cheerful service; children and dogs allowed in certain areas, outside seating and pleasant pastoral outlook, closed Sun evening. *(Sally and Lance Oldham)*

EAST STOUR ST8123
Kings Arms (01747) 838325
A30, 2 miles E of village; The Common; SP8 5NB Extended dining pub with popular generously served food from scottish landlord-chef including bargain lunch menu and all-day Sun carvery (best to book), St Austell Tribute, Sharps Doom Bar and a guest, decent wines and good selection of malt whiskies, friendly efficient staff, open fire in bar, airy dining area with light wood furniture, scottish pictures and Burns quotes; gentle background music; children and dogs (in bar) welcome, good disabled access, picnic-sets in big garden, bluebell walks nearby, three bedrooms, open all day Sun. *(Roy Hoing, R C Hastings)*

FIDDLEFORD ST8013
Fiddleford Inn (01258) 472886
A357 Sturminster Newton–Blandford Forum; DT10 2BX Beamed roadside pub with three linked areas; modern charcoal paintwork blending with traditional furnishings, old flagstones, carpets and some exposed stone and brick, two-way woodburner, well kept ales including one badged for the pub, good traditional food from shortish menu, special diets catered for, friendly young staff; children and dogs welcome, big fenced garden, four bedrooms, open (and food) all day, kitchen closes 6.30pm Sun. *(Glen and Patricia Fuller)*

FONTMELL MAGNA ST8616
Fontmell (01747) 811441
A350 S of Shaftesbury; SP7 0PA Imposing dining pub with rooms, much emphasis on the enterprising modern cooking, but also some more straightforward cheaper dishes (own rare breed pork), good wine list, a house beer (Sibeth) from Keystone and two west country guests, small bar area with comfy sofas and easy chairs, restaurant overlooking fast-flowing stream that runs under the building; garden across road with two wood-fired pizza ovens, six comfortable well appointed bedrooms, open all day from 9am (10am Sun). *(Edward Mirzoeff, Nicola and Stuart Parsons, Gail and Frank Hackett, Alison and Tony Livesley, Andrew Wall)*

GILLINGHAM ST7926
Buffalo (01747) 823759
Off B3081 at Wyke 1 mile NW of Gillingham, pub 100 metres on left; SP8 4NJ Welcoming family-run Badger local; two linked bars and restaurant serving generous helpings of good well priced italian food (best to book), friendly attentive service; background and some live music; children welcome, back terrace by car park, open till 7pm Sun, closed Mon lunchtime. *(Edward Mirzoeff)*

HINTON ST MARY ST7816
White Horse (01258) 472723
Just off B3092 a mile N of Sturminster; DT10 1NA Welcoming traditional little village pub dating from the early 17th c; good varied choice of food including wood-fired pizzas and fresh local fish/seafood (best to book), own-brew beers and decent house wines, unusual inglenook fireplace in cheerful bar, extended dining room; children, walkers and dogs welcome, picnic-sets in small well maintained garden, attractive setting, closed Sun evening, all day Mon and Tues evening (no food Tues lunchtime). *(Dan and Nicki Barton)*

HOLT SU0304
Old Inn (01202) 883029
Holt Lane; beside the church; BH21 7DJ Updated red-brick Badger dining pub, their

---

A star symbol before the name of a pub shows exceptional character and appeal. It doesn't mean extra comfort. Even quite a basic pub can win a star, if it's individual enough.

ales kept well and good range of wines and gins, tasty food including wood-fired pizzas and Mon steak night, quick friendly service, mix of pubby furniture on wood-strip floors, beams and log fire; children and dogs welcome, picnic-sets on front terrace, more tables in part-covered back garden, open all day weekends. *(Councillor Stephen Chappell, David and Sally Cullen)*

HURN SZ1397
Avon Causeway (01202) 482714
Village signed off A338, then follow Avon, Sopley, Matchams sign; BH23 6AS Comfortable and roomy hotel/dining pub with enjoyable food from sandwiches and pub favourites up, well kept Wadworths ales, helpful staff, interesting railway decorations and coach restaurant (used for functions) by former 1870s station platform; children and dogs welcome, disabled access, nice garden (some road noise) with play area, 12 good value bedrooms, near Bournemouth Airport (2 weeks' free parking if you stay before or after you fly), open all day, food all day Sun. *(Peter Brix)*

IBBERTON ST7807
Ibberton (01258) 817956
Village W of Blandford Forum; DT11 0EN Welcoming 16th-c village pub in beautiful spot under Bulbarrow Hill; refurbished beamed and flagstoned bar with inglenook woodburner, three local beers and Dorset Orchards' cider from brick-faced servery, popular good value food including traditional choices, friendly helpful staff, two dining areas (one carpeted, the other where dogs allowed); children welcome, picnic-sets in front/side garden with stream, enjoyable walks, closed Mon, Tues and Sun evening. *(Alan Morris)*

LANGTON MATRAVERS SY9978
Kings Arms (01929) 422979
High Street; BH19 3HA Friendly old-fashioned village local; ancient flagstoned corridor to bar, simple rooms off, one with a fine fireplace made from local marble, beers including Ringwood and enjoyable good value pubby food, cheerful helpful staff, splendid antique Purbeck longboard shove-ha'penny; children and dogs welcome, sunny picnic-sets outside, good walks including to Dancing Ledge, open all day. *(Sally and Lance Oldham)*

LYME REGIS SY3492
Cellar 59 (01297) 445086
Broad Street; DT7 3QF Two-room flagstoned bar down steps; up to 14 real ales/craft kegs chalked on blackboard including their own Gyle 59 unfined beers, tasting trays available, friendly knowledgeable staff, tapas-style platters (vegetarians and vegans catered for), shop above selling wide range of bottled beers; outside seating area, open all day (may shut Mon, Tues in winter). *(Nicola and Stuart Parsons)*

LYME REGIS SY3391
Cobb Arms (01297) 443242
Marine Parade, Monmouth Beach; DT7 3JF Spacious place with well kept Palmers ales, decent wines and good choice of reasonably priced freshly cooked food (gluten-free options available), cream teas, quick service, a couple of sofas, ship pictures and marine fish tank, open fire; pool, juke box, TVs; children and dogs welcome, disabled access (one step up from road), tables on small back terrace, well located next to harbour, beach and coastal walk, three bedrooms, open all day. *(Alan Johnson, Karl Lehmann, Tony Scott)*

LYME REGIS SY3391
Harbour Inn (01297) 442299
Marine Parade; DT7 3JF More eating than pubby atmosphere; generally very well liked food from lunchtime sandwiches to local fish/seafood (not particularly cheap, booking advised in season), special diets catered for, Otter and St Austell ales, good choice of wines by the glass, tea and coffee, friendly service, clean-cut modern décor keeping some original flagstones and stone walls (lively acoustic), paintings for sale, sea views from front windows; background and occasional live music; dogs welcome, disabled access from street, tables on verandah and beachside terrace, open all day except Sun evening in winter. *(Guy Vowles)*

LYME REGIS SY3492
Pilot Boat (01297) 443157
Bridge Street; DT7 3QA Smart modern refurbishment for this popular bow-fronted pub near the waterfront; Palmers ales, good choice of wines by the glass and cocktails, enjoyable food from sandwiches, home-made pizzas and pubby choices up, can eat in bar or separate restaurant with open kitchen, helpful friendly staff; Weds live music, Thurs quiz; children and dogs welcome, roof terrace, three boutique bedrooms (one with sea view), open (and food) all day from 8am. *(Nicola and Stuart Parsons)*

LYME REGIS SY3492
Volunteer (01297) 442214
Top of Broad Street (A3052 towards Exeter); DT7 3QE Cosy old-fashioned pub with long low-ceilinged bar, nice mix of customers (can get crowded), a well kept house beer from Branscombe Vale tapped from the cask and west country guests, enjoyable modestly priced food in dining lounge (children allowed here), friendly young staff, roaring fires; dogs welcome, open all day. *(Roger and Donna Huggins)*

MARNHULL ST7719
Blackmore Vale (01258) 820701
Burton Street, via Church Hill off B3092; DT10 1JJ Welcoming old stone-built village

pub reopened after two-year closure; three well kept ales and decent food including Fri fish and chips, opened-up beamed and flagstoned bar with woodburner, more flagstones and oak flooring in cosy smaller bar with log fire; occasional live music, no mobile phones; walkers and dogs welcome, garden tables, open all day Sat, till 7pm Sun, closed Mon. *(Nick Chambers)*

MARNHULL
ST7818
Crown (01258) 820224
About 3 miles N of Sturminster Newton; Crown Road; DT10 1LN Part-thatched inn dating from the 16th c (the Pure Drop in Hardy's *Tess of the D'Urbervilles*); linked rooms with oak beams, huge flagstones or bare boards, log fire in big stone hearth in oldest part, more modern furnishings and carpet elsewhere, Badger ales, plenty of wines by the glass and over 50 gins, enjoyable generously served food including Sun carvery, special diets catered for, good friendly service, restaurant; children welcome, peaceful enclosed garden, six bedrooms, open all day. *(Holly and Tim Waite)*

MARTINSTOWN
SY6488
Brewers Arms (01305) 889361
Burnside (B3159); DT2 9LB Friendly family-run village pub (former 19th-c school) with attractively updated interior; good reasonably priced home-made food from lunchtime baguettes to specials, vegan/vegetarian options and popular Tues curry night, well kept Palmers and Sharps, separate restaurant; Weds quiz and some live music; children and dogs welcome, picnic-sets out at front and in courtyard, historic sheepwash nearby (start of the annual plastic duck race), good local walks, two bedrooms, closed Sun evening, Mon. *(David and Charlotte Green)*

MILTON ABBAS
ST8001
Hambro Arms (01258) 880233
Signed off A354 SW of Blandford; DT11 0BP Nicely updated beamed pub in beautiful late 18th-c thatched village; bar, lounge and restaurant, well kept local ales and decent choice of wines, good restaurant food including one or two pub favourites (they cater for special diets), efficient friendly service; children welcome, dogs in bar, tables on front terrace, four bedrooms, open (and food) all day. *(Peter Brix)*

MOTCOMBE
ST8426
Coppleridge (01747) 851980
Signed from The Street, follow to Mere/ Gillingham; SP7 9HW Welcoming country inn (former 18th-c farmhouse) with traditional bar and various dining rooms, good home-made food from ciabattas and pub favourites up including some imaginative choices, Thurs steak night, ales such as Butcombe and decent wines by the glass, friendly helpful staff; children welcome,

dogs in bar and garden room, ten spacious courtyard bedrooms, barn function room (popular wedding venue), 15-acre grounds with play area and two tennis courts, lovely views over Dorset countryside, open all day. *(Michael Doswell)*

NORDEN HEATH
SY94834
Halfway (01929) 480402
A351 Wareham–Corfe Castle; BH20 5DU Cosily laid-out partly thatched 16th-c beamed pub; Badger beers, nice wines by the glass and enjoyable freshly cooked food including children's and vegetarian choices, good friendly service, front rooms with flagstones, stripped stone and woodburners, snug little side area, pitched-ceiling back room; dogs welcome, picnic-sets on paved terrace and lawn, good nearby walks, open all day, food all day during school holidays. *(David Bird)*

OSMINGTON MILLS
SY7381
Smugglers (01305) 833125
Off A353 NE of Weymouth; DT3 6HF Old partly thatched family-oriented inn set down from the road; well extended, with cosy dimly lit timber-divided areas, woodburners, old local pictures, Badger ales, guest beers and several wines by the glass, food generally good, service friendly and helpful; dogs welcome, picnic-sets on crazy paving by little stream, thatched summer bar, play area, lovely sea views from car park (parking charge refunded at bar), useful for coast path, four bedrooms, open (and food) all day. *(D W Stokes, Matthew, Dave Chapman, Tony Scott)*

PAMPHILL
ST9900
★Vine (01202) 882259
Off B3082 on NW edge of Wimborne: turn on to Cowgrove Hill at Cowgrove sign, then left up Vine Hill; BH21 4EE Simple old-fashioned place run by same family for three generations and part of Kingston Lacy Estate (NT); two tiny bars with coal-effect gas fire, handful of tables and seats on lino, local photographs and notices on painted panelling, narrow wooden stairs up to room with darts, a couple of real ales, local cider and foreign bottled beers, lunchtime bar snacks; quiet background music, no credit cards, outside lavatories; children (away from bar) and dogs welcome, verandah with grapevine, sheltered gravel terrace and grassy area, Sept pumpkin and conkers festival. *(Lenny and Ruth Walters)*

PIDDLEHINTON
SY7197
Thimble (01300) 348270
High Street (B3143); DT2 7TD Spacious recently renovated thatched pub with log fires and deep glassed-over well in low-beamed core; good freshly made food catering for special diets from baguettes up including range of burgers, well kept Palmers ales, friendly welcoming staff; background and live music, free wi-fi; children and dogs

(in bar) welcome, disabled facilities, valley views from garden with stream, open (and food) all day. *(Marianne and Peter Stevens)*

POOLE SZ0391
Bermuda Triangle (01202) 748087
Parr Street, Lower Parkstone (just off A35 at Ashley Cross); BH14 0JY Quirky 19th-c bare-boards local on different levels; four well kept changing ales, two or three good continental lagers and many other beers from around the world, friendly staff, no food, dark panelling, snug old corners and lots of nautical and other bric-a-brac; background and some live music; no children and a bit too steppy for disabled access, new decked seating area outside, open all day Fri-Sun. *(Dan and Nicki Barton)*

POOLE SZ0190
Poole Arms (01202) 673450
Town Quay; BH15 1HJ Friendly 17th-c waterfront pub looking over harbour to Brownsea Island; one comfortably old-fashioned room with boarded ceiling and nautical prints, popular much enjoyed food (predominantly fresh fish/seafood) at fair prices, four well kept ales such as Ringwood and St Austell, good service; outside gents'; no children, picnic-sets in front of the handsome green-tiled façade, almost next door to the Portsmouth Hoy, open all day. *(Simon King)*

POOLE SZ0090
Portsmouth Hoy (01202) 673517
The Quay; BH15 1HJ Harbourside pub with views to Brownsea Island; old-world atmosphere with dark wood, beams and bare boards, well kept Badger ales and decent food including fresh fish, friendly service; children and dogs welcome, outside tables shared with the Poole Arms, open all day. *(Charlie Stevens)*

POOLE SZ0090
Rope & Anchor (01202) 675677
Sarum Street; BH15 1JW Split-level Wadworths pub next to Poole Museum; good food including fresh fish, well kept beers and some nice wines by the glass, friendly accommodating staff; background music (live Fri), daily papers, free wi-fi; children and dogs welcome, seats on back terrace, open (and food) all day. *(Cliff and Monica Swift)*

PORTLAND SY6873
Cove House (01305) 820895
Follow Chiswell signposts – pub is at NW corner of Portland; DT5 1AW Low-beamed traditional 18th-c pub in superb position, effectively built into sea defences just above the end of Chesil Beach, great views from three-room bay windows; Sharps Doom Bar and other well kept beers, good freshly cooked food including blackboard fish specials (booking advised), friendly efficient service, steep steps down

to gents'; background music, folk night Thurs; children and dogs welcome, tables out by seawall, open all day, no food Sun evening. *(David and Doreen Beattie, M G Hart)*

PORTLAND SY6872
George (01305) 820011
Reforne; DT5 2AP Cheery 17th-c stone-built local (one of Portland's oldest buildings); small beamed rooms with low doorways, some tables carved with names of generations of sailors and quarrymen, interesting prints and mementoes, log fires, well kept Greene King Abbot, guest beers and real ciders, enjoyable pubby food from baguettes and toasties up; weekend live music, darts; children and dogs welcome, picnic-sets in walled back garden, closed till 3pm Mon and Tues, otherwise open all day. *(Heather Feakins)*

POWERSTOCK SY5196
Three Horseshoes (01308) 485328
Off A3066 Beaminster–Bridport via West Milton; DT6 3TF Tucked-away village pub with cheerful cosy bar, stripped panelling, windsor and mate's chairs around assorted tables on bare boards, Palmers ales and several wines by the glass, good freshly made food including specials; children and dogs welcome, picnic-sets on back terrace with garden and country views, good surrounding walks, three comfortable bedrooms, closed Sun evening, Mon lunchtime. *(Peter Brix)*

PUDDLETOWN SY7594
Blue Vinny (01305) 848228
The Moor; DT2 8TE Large modernised village pub with beamed oak-floor bar and restaurant, good choice of highly regarded well presented food from lunchtime baguettes up (booking advised), special diets catered for, well kept Sharps Doom Bar and a couple of guests, friendly helpful young staff; children welcome, dogs in one part, terrace overlooking garden with play area, open all day Fri-Sun, no food Sun evening. *(Roger White)*

PUNCKNOWLE SY5388
Crown (01308) 897711
Off B3157 Bridport–Abbotsbury; DT2 9BN Welcoming 16th-c thatched inn continuing well under new family management; enjoyable pubby food from sandwiches up, Palmers ales and decent choice of wines by the glass, beams and inglenook log fires; children and dogs (in bar) welcome, disabled facilities, valley views from peaceful pretty back garden, good walks, two bedrooms, open all day Sat, till 6pm Sun, closed Mon. *(Helene Grygar, Pete and Sarah)*

SANDFORD ORCAS ST6220
★ Mitre (01963) 220271
Off B3148 and B3145 N of Sherborne; DT9 4RU Thriving tucked-away country

local with welcoming long-serving licensees; three well kept changing ales and proper ciders, wholesome home-made food (not Mon) from good soup and sandwiches up, flagstones, log fires and fresh flowers, small bar and larger pleasantly homely dining area; occasional open mike nights, games including shove-ha'penny and dominoes; children and dogs welcome, pretty back garden with terrace, good local walks (on Macmillan Way and Monarch's Way), closed Mon lunchtime. *(David and Charlotte Green)*

SHAPWICK   ST9301
Anchor (01258) 857269
Off A350 Blandford–Poole; West Street; DT11 9LB Welcoming red-brick Victorian pub owned by village consortium; popular freshly made food (booking advised) including blackboard specials, vegan and other diets catered for, Sharps Doom Bar and a couple of guests, real cider, good friendly service, scrubbed pine tables on wood floors, pastel walls and open fires; children and dogs welcome, tables out in front, more in attractive back garden with terrace, handy for Kingston Lacy (NT), closed Sun evening, Mon, otherwise open all day. *(Frances and Hamish Potter)*

STOBOROUGH   SY9286
Kings Arms (01929) 552705
B3075 S of Wareham; Corfe Road opposite petrol station; BH20 5AB Popular part-thatched 17th-c village pub, well kept Isle of Purbeck, Ringwood and up to three guests, good fairly priced food in bar and restaurant from snacks and pub favourites up including some interesting specials, cheerful efficient staff; children and dogs welcome, disabled access/loos, flower-decked terrace and garden with play area, views over marshes to River Frome, open all day during summer school holidays (all day Fri-Sun at other times). *(Kristin Warry)*

STOKE ABBOTT   ST4500
★ New Inn (01308) 868333
Off B3162 and B3163 2 miles W of Beaminster; DT8 3JW Welcoming 17th-c pub in unspoilt thatched village with nice surrounding walks; well kept Palmers ales and good home-cooked local food including daily specials, woodburner in big inglenook, beams, brasses and copper, some handsome panelling, flagstoned dining room; children and dogs (in bar) welcome, wheelchair access, two attractive gardens, street fair third Sat in July, closed Sun evening, all Mon and Tues lunchtime. *(Dan and Nicki Barton)*

STOURPAINE   ST8609
White Horse (01258) 453535
Shaston Road; A350 NW of Blandford; DT11 8TA Traditional country local extended from early 18th-c core (originally two cottages); popular fairly pubby food including OAP deal, five well kept ales,

traditional cider and over 70 gins, good friendly service, open-plan layout with scrubbed pine tables on bare boards, woodburners, games part with pool, also incorporates post office and shop; quiz first Mon of month, regular live music; well behaved children welcome, dogs in bar, seats out at front and on back deck, open all day, no food Mon evening. *(Holly and Tim Waite)*

STOURTON CAUNDLE   ST7115
Trooper (01963) 362405
Village signed off A30 E of Milborne Port; DT10 2JW Pretty little stone-built pub in lovely village setting (Enid Blyton's house opposite); friendly staff and atmosphere, a couple of well kept changing beers (their microbrewery is currently closed), a real cider and good range of gins, food Weds and Fri (fish and chips) evenings only, tiny low-ceilinged bar, stripped-stone dining room, darts, dominoes and shove-ha'penny, skittle alley, outside gents'; background music, folk night second Sun of month; children, walkers and dogs welcome, a few picnic-sets out in front, pleasant side garden, bunkhouse and camping, closed Mon and lunchtimes apart from Sun. *(Peter Brix)*

STRATTON   SY6593
Saxon Arms (01305) 260020
Off A37 NW of Dorchester; The Square; DT2 9WG Traditional (though recently built) flint-and-thatch local; spacious open-plan interior with light oak tables and comfortable settles on flagstones or carpet, log fire, well kept Butcombe, Timothy Taylors Landlord and two guests, good value wines, tasty generously served food including deli boards and good choice of specials, pleasant efficient service, large comfortable dining section on right; background music, traditional games; children and dogs welcome, terrace tables overlooking village green, open (and food) all day Fri-Sun. *(Glen and Patricia Fuller)*

STUDLAND   SZ0382
Bankes Arms (01929) 450225
Off B3351, Isle of Purbeck; Manor Road; BH19 3AU Creeper-clad stone pub in very popular spot above fine beach, outstanding country, sea and cliff views from huge garden over road with lots of seating; comfortably basic big bar with raised drinking area, beams, flagstones and good log fire, several real ales including own Isle of Purbeck (Aug beer festival), local cider, decent wines by the glass and fairly pubby blackboard food served quickly by young staff; darts and pool in side area; background music, machines, sports TV; over-8s and dogs welcome, just off coast path near to Old Harry Rocks, can get very busy on summer weekends and parking complicated (NT car park), ten bedrooms (Studland Bay views from front ones), open (and food) all day. *(Dave Chapman)*

STURMINSTER MARSHALL SY9499
Golden Fox (01258) 857217
A350; BH21 4AQ Roadside country pub with popular good value food catering for special diets, up to three real ales such as Dartmoor, Hop Back and Sixpenny, friendly helpful service, long comfortable beamed and panelled bar with log fire; games machines; children and dogs (in bar) welcome, terrace seating, open all day Fri-Sun, closed Tues. *(Charlie Stevens)*

STURMINSTER NEWTON ST7813
Bull (01258) 472435
A357, S of centre; DT10 2BS Cosy thatched and beamed 15th-c pub, well kept Badger ales and enjoyable good value home-made food, friendly helpful staff, log fires; children and dogs welcome, roadside picnic-sets, more in small back garden, closed Sun evening, Mon, otherwise open all day. *(David and Charlotte Green)*

SWANAGE SZ0278
Red Lion (01929) 423533
High Street; BH19 2LY Popular and unpretentious low-beamed local with great choice of ciders and up to six well kept ales such as Otter, Ringwood, Sharps and Timothy Taylors, good value food including Weds curry night and Fri steak night, quick friendly service, brasses around log fire, restaurant; background and some live music, pool, darts and fruit machine; children welcome till 9pm, picnic-sets in garden with part-covered terrace, bedrooms in former back coach house, open all day. *(Charlie Stevens)*

SYDLING ST NICHOLAS SY6399
Greyhound (01300) 341303
Off A37 N of Dorchester; High Street; DT2 9PD Former coaching inn with beamed and flagstoned serving area, woodburner in brick fireplace, hops above counter, three well kept changing ales and a couple of proper ciders, carpeted bar with Portland stone fireplace, painted panelling and exposed stonework, popular food including good value set lunch, friendly welcoming staff, covered well in cosy dining room, flagstoned conservatory; children and dogs (in bar) welcome, picnic-sets in little front garden, six comfortable bedrooms, open all day Sun. *(Lenny and Ruth Walters)*

TARRANT MONKTON ST9408
★ Langton Arms (01258) 830225
Village signposted from A354, then head for church; DT11 8RX Bustling thatched pub in picturesque spot next to 15th-c church; high-backed dining chairs around wooden tables on flagstones, a cushioned window seat and a few high chairs against light oak counter, Flack Manor Double Drop and guests, real cider and decent choice of wines and whiskies, popular food using meat from own farm, two connecting beamed dining rooms with cushioned wooden chairs around white-clothed tables, airy conservatory; background music, board games, skittle alley; children and dogs (in bar) welcome, seats out at front and in back garden with play area, bedrooms in brick buildings around courtyard and in neighbouring cottage, open all day, food all day weekends. *(Sally and Lance Oldham)*

TOLPUDDLE SY7994
Martyrs (01305) 848249
Former A35 W of Bere Regis; DT2 7ES 1920s village dining pub with enjoyable home-made food including Mon curry, Fri fish and chips and Sun carvery, two or three Badger ales, friendly accommodating staff, opened-up bare-boards interior; background and live music, children welcome, good disabled access, small front terrace and garden behind, open (and food) all day. *(Holly and Tim Waite)*

TRENT ST5818
★ Rose & Crown (01935) 850776
Opposite the church; DT9 4SL Partly thatched pub across from lovely church; cosy little right-hand bar with sofas in front of open fire, bigger bar opposite has old wooden tables and chairs on quarry tiles, Wadworths ales, a guest beer and 20 wines by the glass, good food from lunchtime sandwiches and pub favourites to well presented restaurant dishes, attentive friendly service, two other interconnected rooms with pews, grandfather clock and more fireplaces, simply furnished back dining room; board games, free wi-fi; children and dogs welcome, parasol-shaded tables in back garden with fine views, pretty bedrooms in converted byre, excellent breakfast, open all day. *(Christine and Tony Garrett, Lyn and Freddie Roberts)*

UPLODERS SY5093
Crown (01308) 485356
Signed off A35 E of Bridport; DT6 4NU Attractive stone-built village pub; log fires, dark low beams, flagstones and mix of old furniture including stripped pine, grandfather clock, good fairly traditional home-made food using local suppliers, curry evenings, three Palmers ales; background music; children and dogs (in bar) welcome, tables in pretty two-tier garden, closed Mon. *(Dan and Nicki Barton)*

WAREHAM SY9287
Kings Arms (01929) 552503
North Street (A351, N end of town); BH20 4AD Traditional thatched town local; five well kept changing ales, real cider and decent good value pubby food (till 6pm Sun), friendly staff, back serving counter and two bars off flagstoned central corridor, beams and inglenook log fire, carpeted dining room to the right, another at the back; some live music, free wi-fi; children and dogs welcome,

steps up to garden behind with circular picnic-sets and smokers' shelter, open all day. *(William and Sophie Renton)*

WAREHAM   SY9287
Old Granary (01929) 552010
The Quay; BH20 4LP Fine old brick building in good riverside position – can get very busy; beamed snug by entrance opening into main bar with brick walls and new oak standing timbers, Badger ales and good wines by the glass, enjoyable fairly standard food at reasonable prices, friendly young staff, restaurant area with connecting rooms, also upstairs river-view dining room; quiet background music; children and dogs (in bar) welcome, seats out overlooking the water and on covered roof terrace, boats for hire over bridge, limited nearby parking, open all day from 9am (10am Sun), food served from brunch on. *(D J and P M Taylor)*

WAREHAM   SY9287
Quay Inn (01929) 552735
The Quay; BH20 4LP Comfortable 18th-c pub in great waterside position; enjoyable food including pubby choices and cook-your-own meat on a hot stone, well kept Isle of Purbeck, Ringwood and Timothy Taylors, friendly attentive service, two open fires (one gas); weekend live music; children and dogs welcome, terrace area and picnic-sets out on quay (boat trips), market day Sat, three bedrooms, parking nearby can be difficult, open all day. *(Robert Watt)*

WAREHAM FOREST   SY9089
Silent Woman (01929) 552909
Wareham–Bere Regis; Bere Road; BH20 7PA Long neatly kept dining pub divided by doorways and standing timbers; good choice of enjoyable food including daily specials, Badger ales kept well and plenty of wines by the glass, friendly helpful young staff, traditional furnishings, farm tools and stripped masonry; background music; no children inside, dogs welcome, wheelchair access, plenty of picnic-sets outside including a covered area, walks nearby, opening times vary during the year and it's a popular wedding venue, so best to check it's open. *(Glen and Patricia Fuller)*

WAYTOWN   SY4797
Hare & Hounds (01308) 488203
Between B3162 and A3066 N of Bridport; DT6 5LQ Attractive 18th-c country local up and down steps; friendly staff and regulars, well kept Palmers tapped from the cask, local cider, and generous helpings of enjoyable good value food (not

Sun evening) including popular Sun lunch, open fire, two small cottagey rooms and pretty dining room; children and dogs welcome, lovely Brit Valley views from sizeable well maintained garden with play area. *(Matthew and Elisbeth Reeves)*

WEST BAY   SY4690
★ West Bay (01308) 422444
Station Road; DT6 4EW Informal inn with views to the sea and emphasis on fresh fish dishes (best to book); fairly simple front part with bare boards, coal-effect gas fire and a mix of maritime and nostalgic prints, cosier carpeted dining area, Palmers ales and a seasonal guest, eight wines by the glass; background music, 100-year-old skittle alley; dogs welcome, tables in side and larger back garden, quiet, comfortable bedrooms; open all day in summer; the two unspoilt beaches either side of the busy little harbour are much visited since the *Broadchurch* TV series was filmed here. *(Dr and Mrs J D Abell, Roger and Donna Huggins, Andrew Low)*

WEST BEXINGTON   SY5386
Manor Hotel (01308) 897660
Off B3157 SE of Bridport; Beach Road; DT2 9DF Relaxing quietly set hotel with long history and fine sea views; good choice of enjoyable food (highish prices) in beamed cellar bar, flagstoned restaurant or Victorian-style conservatory, well kept Otter, Thatcher's cider and several wines by the glass; children welcome, dogs on leads (not in restaurant), charming well kept garden, close to Chesil Beach, 13 bedrooms. *(Dan and Nicki Barton)*

WEST KNIGHTON   SY7387
New Inn (01305) 852349
Off A352 E of Dorchester; DT2 8PE Extended country pub with carpeted bar and restaurant; good home-made food using local produce including daily specials and Sun carvery, special diets catered for, a couple of real ales such as Palmers , friendly efficient staff; skittle alley, pool, free wi-fi; children welcome, dogs in bar, pleasant setting on edge of quiet village with farmland views, eight bedrooms, good breakfast, open all day Sun. *(Sally and Lance Oldham)*

WEST LULWORTH   SY8280
Lulworth Cove (01929) 400333
Main Road; BH20 5RQ Modernised inn with good range of enjoyable reasonably priced food from baguettes up, well kept Badger ales and several wines by the glass, friendly staff, seaside theme bar with bare boards and painted panelling; free wi-fi; children and dogs welcome, picnic-sets on

---

Please tell us if the décor, atmosphere, food or drink at a pub is different from our description. We rely on readers' reports to keep us up to date: feedback@goodguides.com, or (no stamp needed) Freepost THE GOOD PUB GUIDE, Random House Publishing, 20 Vauxhall Bridge Road, London SW1V 2SA.

sizeable terrace, short stroll down to cove, 12 bedrooms (some with sea-view balcony), open (and food) all day and can get very busy. *(Dave Chapman)*

WEST STAFFORD   SY7289
Wise Man (01305) 261970
Signed off A352 Dorchester–Wareham; DT2 8AG Modernised 16th-c thatched and beamed pub near Hardy's Cottage (NT); open-plan interior with flagstone and wood floors, logburner, good food from imaginative varied menu, well kept Butcombe, Fullers and Timothy Taylors, decent choice of wines by the glass, friendly staff; children and dogs welcome, disabled facilities, plenty of seats outside, lovely walks nearby, open all day Sat, till 6.30pm Sun. *(Marianne and Peter Stevens)*

WEYMOUTH   SY6778
Boot 07809 440772
High West Street; DT4 8JH Friendly unspoilt old local near the harbour; beams, bare boards, panelling, hooded stone-mullioned windows and coal fires, cosy gently sloping snug, ten well kept ales including Ringwood and other Marstons-related beers (tasting trays available), real cider and good selection of malt whiskies, no food apart from pork pies and pickled eggs (regulars bring own food on Sun to share); live music Tues, quiz Weds; free wi-fi; disabled access, pavement tables, open all day. *(William and Sophie Renton)*

WEYMOUTH   SY6779
Handmade Pie & Ale House (01305) 459342
Queen Street; DT4 7HZ Friendly and relaxed place opposite the station; wide range of good home-made pies plus other food, six well kept changing ales and plenty of ciders, more dining space in upstairs raftered room; children welcome, open (and food) all day. *(Charlie Stevens)*

WEYMOUTH   SY6878
Nothe Tavern (01305) 787300
Barrack Road; DT4 8TZ Updated 19th-c red-brick pub a short walk from the busy harbour area; enjoyable food from lunchtime sandwiches and bar snacks up including daily specials, some vegan choices and weekend breakfasts, Brakspears, Ringwood and a dozen wines by the glass, friendly efficient service, restaurant with harbour and more distant sea views; children and dogs (in bar) welcome, more views from terrace, near

Nothe Fort, open all day, food all day Sun till 7pm. *(David and Doreen Beattie, Tony Scott)*

WIMBORNE MINSTER   SZ0199
Minster Arms (01202) 840700
West Street; BH21 1JS Updated candlelit corner pub with log fires, leather sofas and an assortment of tables and chairs on wood floors, three real ales and extensive choice of wines by the glass, well liked food from varied menu, friendly service; live music Thurs; children and dogs welcome, courtyard area with heaters, comfortable modern bedrooms, open (and food) all day. *(Charlie Stevens)*

WIMBORNE MINSTER   SU0100
Olive Branch (01202) 884686
East Borough, just off Hanham Road (B3073, just E of its junction with B3078); BH21 1PF Handsome townhouse with various opened-up dining areas, one with beams and view into kitchen, another more canteen-like with long tables and padded benches, popular food from range of small plates through burgers up, special diets catered for, relaxed atmosphere, Badger beers in comfortable panelled bar with woodburner, also a coffee bar; mediterranean-style garden, open all day from 8am for breakfast. *(Cliff and Monica Swift)*

WINTERBORNE STICKLAND   ST8304
Crown (01258) 881042
North Street; DT11 0NJ Popular thatched and beamed village pub improved under present welcoming management; two rooms separated by servery, smaller one with inglenook woodburner, well kept Marstons-related ales including Ringwood, proper cider and good freshly made food at sensible prices; children and dogs welcome, pretty back terrace and steps up to lawned area with village view, open all day, till 7pm Sun. *(Nick Chambers)*

WINTERBORNE WHITECHURCH   ST8300
Milton Arms (01258) 880431
A354 Blandford–Dorchester; DT11 0HW Modernised village pub under new ownership; good sensibly priced food and three well kept beers, friendly helpful staff; children and dogs welcome, closed Sun evening, otherwise open all day. *(Holly and Tim Waite)*

Essex

CHRISHALL
TL4439 Map 5

Red Cow 🍺 🛏

(01763) 838792 – www.theredcow.com

High Street; off B1039 Wendens Ambo–Great Chishill; SG8 8RN

Thatched 16th-c pub with beamed rooms, four real ales, well liked food and seats in appealing garden; bedrooms

Five, airy, attractive and comfortable bedrooms have been opened up in a restored, thatched barn here and readers have been quick to voice their enthusiasm. A bustling, well run local, there's a neat and friendly bar and dining room with heavy beams and timbers, a woodburning stove and an open fire, all sorts of wooden dining chairs around tables of every size on bare floorboards, and a comfortable sofa and armchairs. Adnams Southwold and Woodfordes Wherry plus two guest beers such as Greene King Old Speckled Hen and Timothy Taylors Landlord on handpump, eight wines by the glass, Aspall's cider and cocktails; they hold a music and beer festival in May. Terraces have picnic-sets and the garden is pretty. Walkers enjoy the nearby Icknield Way, coming here for refreshment afterwards.

🍴 Pleasing food includes lunchtime paninis, chicken liver pâté with red onion jam, prawn cocktail, caramelised red onion and mozzarella tarte tatin with spinach and watercress dressing, burger with toppings, coleslaw and chips, home-roasted honeyed gammon and free-range eggs, sausages with herby mash and gravy, a fresh fish dish of the day, steaks with a choice of sauce, and puddings such as mixed berry and marshmallow pavlova and chocolate brownies with rum chocolate sauce. *Benchmark main dish: pie of the day £14.00. Two-course evening meal £25.00.*

Free house ~ Licensees Toby and Alexis Didier Serre ~ Real ale ~ Open 12-3, 6 (5.30 Fri)-midnight; 12-midnight Sat; 12-10 Sun; closed Mon lunchtime ~ Bar food 12-2, 6-9; 12-2.30, 6-9 Sat; 12-3.30 Sun ~ Restaurant ~ Children welcome ~ Dogs allowed in bar ~ Wi-fi ~ Live music Fri evenings and some Sun afternoons ~ Bedrooms: £110/£130
Recommended by David Jackman, Serena and Adam Furber, Carol and Barry Craddock, Geoff and Ann Marston, Beverley and Andy Butcher

FEERING
TL8720 Map 5

Sun 🍺

(01376) 570442 – www.suninnfeering.co.uk

Just off A12 Kelvedon bypass; Feering Hill (B1024 just W of Feering proper); CO5 9NH

Striking 16th-c pub with six real ales, popular food and pleasant garden

With its handsome frontage and bustling atmosphere, this is a well run pub with a good mix of customers. The busy slate-floored bar has an easy-going feel and two big woodburning stoves (one in the huge central inglenook fireplace, another by an antique winged settle on the left). Throughout there are handsomely carved black beams and timbers galore, and attractive wildflower murals in a frieze above the central timber divider. The beers on handpump include Shepherd Neame Bishops Finger, Master Brew, Spitfire Gold and Whitstable Bay Pale plus a guest such as Isla Vale Hopping Mad, and they hold summer and winter beer festivals; also, 13 wines by the glass, ten malt whiskies and 21 gins served by cheerful staff. A brick-paved back courtyard has tables, heaters and a shelter, and tall trees shade green picnic-sets in the garden beyond. The pub has its own small car park through an archway in the middle of the adjoining terraced houses.

A wide choice of food includes lemon and black pepper sole goujons with smoked eel tartare, raised game pie with pickled vegetables and tomato and chilli chutney, vegetable tagine with couscous and citrus yoghurt, honey and mustard glazed ham and free-range eggs, venison loin with celeriac two-ways, braised potatoes, chestnuts and venison sauce, ox cheek with creamed chive potatoes, baby onions, mushrooms and pancetta, and puddings such as chocolate millionaire brownie with caramel, shortbread and toffee ice-cream and blackberry and apple lattice tart with crème anglaise. *Benchmark main dish: beef, mushroom and stilton pie £13.50. Two-course evening meal £21.00.*

Shepherd Neame ~ Tenant Andy Howard ~ Real ale ~ Open 12-3, 5.30-11; 12-3, 5.30-midnight Fri, Sat; 12-10.30 Sun ~ Bar food 12-2.30, 6-9 (9.30 Fri, Sat); 12-8 Sun ~ Well behaved children welcome ~ Dogs welcome ~ Wi-fi *Recommended by David Twitchett, Trevor and Michele Street*

FULLER STREET
Square & Compasses ⭐ 🍺

TL7416 Map 5

(01245) 361477 – www.thesquareandcompasses.co.uk

Back road Great Leighs–Hatfield Peverel; CM3 2BB

Attractive surroundings, with two woodburning stoves, three ales and enjoyable food

'A really great country pub' and 'perfect after walking the Essex Way' are just two positive reports from readers; there's a small extension for walkers and their dogs. The L-shaped beamed bar has two woodburning stoves in inglenook fireplaces, and friendly staff serve Crouch Vale Brewers Gold and Maldon Drop of Nelsons Blood and Pucks Folly tapped from the cask, 23 wines by the glass, three farm ciders and home-made elderflower and lemon cordial; background jazz. The carpeted dining room features shelves of bottles and decanters against timbered walls, and an appealing variety of dining chairs around dark wooden tables set with linen napkins. Tables out in front on decking offer gentle country views.

Tasty food from a seasonal menu includes lunchtime sandwiches, game terrine wrapped in smoked bacon with beetroot relish, scallops with pea purée and truffle-infused oil, fennel and carrot cheesecake with potato salad, local sausages with spring onion mash and onion gravy, burger with toppings and chips, cod fillet with couscous and tomato and coriander sauce, local lamb chump with rosemary-roasted crushed potatoes and red wine and thyme sauce, 28-day aged sirloin steak with celeriac dauphinoise and smoked bacon sauce, and puddings such as lemon tart with lemon syrup and spotted dick and custard. *Benchmark main dish: steak in ale pie £13.95. Two-course evening meal £21.00.*

Free house ~ Licensee Victor Roome ~ Real ale ~ Open 11.30-11; 12-11.30 Sat; 12-11 Sun ~ Bar food 12-2 (2.30 Sat), 6.30-9.30; 12-5.45 Sun ~ Restaurant ~ Well behaved children welcome ~ Dogs allowed in bar *Recommended by Ian Wilson, Patricia Healey, Andrew and Ruth Simmonds, Mrs Margo Finlay, Jörg Kasprowski, Rob Anderson, Anne and Ben Smith, Sabina and Gerald Grimshaw*

FYFIELD
TL5706 Map 5

Queens Head ⭐ ♀

(01277) 899231 – www.queensheadfyfield.co.uk
Corner of B184 and Queen Street; CM5 0RY

Friendly old pub with seats in riverside garden, a good choice of drinks and highly regarded food

It's the enterprising food that our readers favour the most here. The compact, low-beamed, L-shaped bar has exposed timbers, pretty lamps on nice sturdy elm tables and comfortable seating from wall banquettes to attractive, unusual high-backed chairs, some in a snug little side booth. In summer, two facing fireplaces have church candles instead of a fire; background music. Adnams Southwold and Ghost Ship and Franklins Citra IPA on handpump and seven good wines by the glass. The upstairs restaurant is more formal. At weekends when this place is usefully open all day, customers tend to arrive early in warm weather in order to bag a seat in the prettily planted back garden, which runs down to the sleepy River Roding.

⭐ Imaginative food includes scotch egg with mustard sauce, tagliatelle with clams, tomatoes, garlic and chilli, seared cauliflower with sweet potato purée, green tomato vinaigrette, chickpeas and paprika hazelnuts, john dory with roast chicken sauce, crispy chicken skin, shimeji mushrooms and spring onions, rack and belly of lamb with boulangère potatoes, celeriac fondant and salsa verde, steaks with a choice of sauce and triple-cooked chips, and puddings such as chocolate mousse with chantilly cream and praline soufflé with butterscotch sauce and roast hazelnut ice-cream; they also offer a two- and three-course set menu (not Saturday evening or Sunday). *Benchmark main dish: steak and kidney pudding £17.00. Two-course evening meal £22.00.*

Free house ~ Licensee Daniel Lamprecht ~ Real ale ~ Open 11-4, 6-11; 11-11 Sat; 12-7 Sun; closed Mon (except bank holidays when open 12-7); Tues after a bank holiday ~ Bar food 12-2.30 (4 Sat), 6.30-9.30; 12-6 Sun ~ Restaurant ~ Children welcome away from bar ~ Wi-fi *Recommended by Claire Adams, David and Leone Lawson, Beth Aldridge, Nicholas and Maddy Trainer, Alan and Linda Blackmore*

GOLDHANGER
TL9008 Map 5

Chequers 🍺

(01621) 788203 – www.thechequersgoldhanger.co.uk
Church Street; off B1026 E of Heybridge; CM9 8AS

Cheerful and neatly kept pub with six real ales, traditional furnishings, friendly staff and tasty food

You'll quickly be made to feel at home in this friendly pub – by the locals as well as the licensees. A nice old corridor with red and black floor tiles leads to six rambling rooms. These include a spacious lounge with dark beams, black panelling and a huge sash window overlooking the graveyard, a traditional dining room with bare boards and carpeting and a games room with bar billiards; woodburning stove, open fires, TV and background music. Adnams Ghost Ship, Exeter Avocet, Marstons Lancaster Bomber, Ringwood Old Thumper, Sharps Atlantic and Woodfordes Wherry on handpump, and they hold spring and autumn beer festivals. Also, 16 wines by the glass, ten malt whiskies and several farm ciders. There are picnic-sets under umbrellas in the courtyard with its grapevine. Do take a look at the fine old church next door.

Rewarding food includes sandwiches, duck and orange pâté with cumberland sauce, tempura-battered prawns and sticky chicken skewers with creamy dill dip, macaroni cheese and spinach bake, ham and free-range eggs, burger with toppings, coleslaw and chips, smoked haddock and spring onion fishcakes with horseradish dip, lamb and mint pudding, jamaican jerk sirloin steak with thai prawns and chilli mayonnaise dip, and puddings such as lemon meringue pie and chocolate pot. *Benchmark main dish: steak in stout pie £12.25. Two-course evening meal £19.00.*

Punch ~ Lease Philip Glover and Dominic Davies ~ Real ale ~ Open 11-11; 12-11 Sun ~ Bar food 12-3, 6.30-9; not Sun evening or Mon bank holiday evening ~ Restaurant ~ Children welcome except in tap room ~ Dogs allowed in bar ~ Wi-fi *Recommended by Dan and Belinda Smallbone, John and Mary Warner, Amy Ledbetter, Chloe and Tim Hodge*

HORNDON-ON-THE-HILL

TQ6783 Map 3

Bell 🌟 ♉ 🍺 🛋

(01375) 642463 – www.bell-inn.co.uk

M25 junction 30 into A13, then left after 7 miles on to B1007, village signposted from here; SS17 8LD

Essex Dining Pub of the Year

Lovely historic pub with fine food and a very good range of drinks; lovely bedrooms

This is a first class all-rounder and we get nothing but glowing reports on it from our readers. It's been run by the same friendly family for more than 80 years, and they treat it and their customers with great care and respect. The heavily beamed, panelled bar maintains a strongly pubby appearance with high-backed antique settles and benches, rugs on flagstones and highly polished oak floorboards, and an open log fire. Look out for the curious collection of dried hot-cross buns hanging along a beam in the saloon bar – the first was put there in 1906 to mark the day (a Good Friday) that Jack Turnell became licensee. The timbered restaurant has numerous old copper pots and pans hanging from beams. An impressive range of drinks includes Crouch Vale Brewers Gold, Greene King IPA, Leigh on Sea Cockle Row Spit and Renown and Sharps Doom Bar on handpump, 24 gins and over 114 well chosen wines (16 by the glass). Two giant umbrellas cover the courtyard, which has very pretty hanging baskets in summer. Centuries ago, many important medieval dignitaries would have stayed here as it was the last inn before travellers heading south could ford the Thames at Highams Causeway. Today, it remains a special place to stay with individually styled, thoughtfully equipped bedrooms of all sizes, from large and grand to small and cosy.

Impressive food includes sandwiches, paprika monkfish with orange curd, pink grapefruit and fennel salad, pork, apple and mustard spring roll with artichoke purée and sautéed black pudding, lemon and goats cheese crispy ravioli with broccoli purée and nut brown butter, lamb chop with merguez sausage, mushrooms and jus, beer-battered whiting with gherkin mayonnaise, calves liver and bacon with pearl barley and caramelised onions, duck breast with sautéed rainbow chard, charred clementines, pickled blackberries and jus, and puddings such as orange and mint pannacotta with macerated berries and cherry ice-cream and white chocolate and raisin bread and butter pudding with caramelised bananas and vanilla ice-cream. *Benchmark main dish: 28-day aged rib-eye with charred chicory, pickled shallots and caesar dressing £29.95. Two-course evening meal £26.95.*

Free house ~ Licensee John Vereker ~ Real ale ~ Open 11-11; 12-10.30 Sun ~ Bar food 12-1.45, 6.30 (6 Sat)-10; 12-2.30, 7-9.45 Sun ~ Restaurant ~ Children welcome ~ Dogs allowed in bar and bedrooms ~ Wi-fi ~ Bedrooms: /£100 *Recommended by Gwendoline and Ralph Mason, Christopher May; Nick and Willow Brown, Andrew and Nicky Churcher, Jeremy Snaithe, Susan and Callum Slade*

HOWE STREET
Green Man 🍴⭐🍷
TL6914 Map 5

(01245) 408820 – www.galvingreenman.com

Just off A130 N of Chelmsford; CM3 1BG

Sizeable pub with up-to-date extensions, plenty of natural light, three real ales, first class food, friendly staff and big garden

Food plays a major part here, which isn't surprising since the place is owned by the Galvin brothers – both exceptional chefs. But if you just want a drink and a chat, there's a cosy, timber-framed bar with proper character: flagstones or bare boards, an open fire, leather-topped stools, a button-back brown leather chesterfield, nice old wooden chairs around circular tables, a cushioned window seat and photos and prints on ochre walls. Also, Adnams Ghost Ship and Trumans Runner on handpump, good wines by the glass, several malt whiskies, organic cider and a non-alcoholic juice of the day. Staff are attentive, friendly and helpful. The high-raftered dining rooms are divided by a two-way woodburning stove in a large brick fireplace. Big windows and glass doors provide plenty of natural light and the contemporary furnishings include modern lighting, and dark painted cushioned dining chairs and long button-back leather banquettes on either pale floorboards or flagstones; background music and TV. The 1.5 acres of garden, with the River Chelmer running along the bottom, has black metal furniture on a terrace and picnic-sets on grass.

🍴⭐ Inventive food includes sandwiches, ham hock and chicken terrine with plum chutney, whipped smoked cod roe with crispy chicken skin, radish and croutons, roast aubergine with charred spring onions, cumin yoghurt and smoked tomatoes, pie of the day, guinea fowl with tarragon consommé, herb gnocchi, baby turnips and chestnut mushrooms, wood-roasted stone bass with apple dashi, pak choi and prawn wonton, beef châteaubriand (for two) with red wine jus and french fries, and puddings such as Valrhona chocolate fondant with pistachio ice-cream and salted caramel tart with almond milk ice-cream. *Benchmark main dish: burger with toppings and roast onion mayonnaise £16.50. Two-course evening meal £23.00.*

Galvin Pub Company ~ Licensees Chris and Jeff Galvin ~ Real ale ~ Open 11am-11.30pm; 11-9 Sun ~ Bar food 12-2.30, 6-9 (9.30 Thurs); 12-2.30, 5.30-10.30 Fri, Sat; 11.30-6 Sun ~ Restaurant ~ Children welcome ~ Dogs allowed in bar ~ Wi-fi *Recommended by Mrs Margo Finlay, Jörg Kasprowski, Trish and Karl Soloman, Bob and Melissa Wyatt, Neil Allen*

HULLBRIDGE
Anchor 🍴⭐🍷
TQ8195 Map 5

(01702) 230777 – www.theanchorhullbridge.co.uk

Ferry Road; SS5 6ND

Big riverside pub with seats by the water, orangery-style restaurant, a good selection of drinks, up-to-date décor and modern british food

Acres of countryside and a nature reserve surround this light and airy pub, and its waterfront position is lovely. The décor and furnishings are contemporary and the bar is friendly (as are the efficient staff) and relaxed; they keep Fullers London Pride, Leigh on Sea Six Little Ships and a guest ale on handpump, good wines by the glass and plenty of cocktails; background music. There are sofas, curved banquettes and black leather wall seats on wooden floorboards and high chairs by the counter used by chatty locals. The focus is probably on the restaurant with its floor-to-ceiling windows, pale leather dining chairs around wooden tables on more wooden floors and very tall button-back banquettes; the open kitchen keeps things lively. Circular picnic-sets under parasols on grass are right by the River Crouch and chrome and wicker seats on terraces also look over the water.

Well executed contemporary food includes sandwiches, eggs benedict, lemon and chilli calamari with harissa mayonnaise, portobello mushroom cottage pie, Josper-grilled bacon steak with free-range eggs, build your own salads with a choice of toppings, beer-battered fish and chips, 12-hour cider-roasted pork belly with apple purée, crackling and gravy, sea bass with peppers, sweet potato hash and pumpkin seed pesto, Josper-cooked steaks with fries and a choice of sauces, and puddings such as lemon posset with lemon curd and a brandy snap and white chocolate cheesecake with ginger caramel ice-cream. *Benchmark main dish: burger with toppings £14.00. Two-course evening meal £23.50.*

Oakman Inns & Restaurants ~ Manager Charlotte Claxton ~ Real ale ~ Open 11-11 (midnight Sat); 11-10.30 Sun ~ Bar food 11-10 (9 Sun) ~ Restaurant ~ Dogs allowed in bar ~ Wi-fi *Recommended by David and Charlotte Green, David and Leone Lawson, John and Delia Franks, Matthew and Elisabeth Reeves, Jill and Hugh Bennett*

LITTLE WALDEN
Crown 🍺 £ 🛏

TL5441 Map 5

(01799) 522475 – www.thecrownlittlewalden.co.uk
B1052 N of Saffron Walden; CB10 1XA

Bustling old pub with a warming log fire, hearty food and real ales; bedrooms

Staying overnight here means you can explore the area in comfort; breakfasts are excellent too. Very much the heart of the local community with a genuine welcome from the staff, this 18th-c cottage has a friendly, chatty atmosphere. The low-ceilinged rooms have traditional furnishings, floral curtains, bare boards or navy carpeting, cosy warm fires and an unusual walk-through fireplace. A higgledy-piggledy mix of chairs ranges from high-backed pews to little cushioned armchairs spaced around a good variety of closely arranged tables, mostly big, some stripped. A small red-tiled room on the right has two small tables. Three changing beers such as Adnams Broadside, Greene King Abbot and Woodfordes Wherry and a guest ale are tapped straight from casks racked up behind the bar; TV. Tables on the terrace have views over the tranquil surrounding countryside. Disabled access.

Good quality food includes baguettes, creamy garlic mushrooms, devilled whitebait, four-cheese ravioli, lasagne, smoked halibut, salmon and crayfish salad, honey-roast ham and eggs, pork fillet in spicy cajun sauce, chicken curry, and puddings such as eton mess and treacle pudding with custard. *Benchmark main dish: steak and mushroom pie £11.00. Two-course evening meal £18.50.*

Free house ~ Licensee Colin Hayling ~ Real ale ~ Open 11.30-2.30, 6-11; 12-11 Sun ~ Bar food 12-2, 7 ; 12-3.30 Sun ~ Restaurant ~ Children welcome ~ Dogs welcome ~ Wi-fi ~ Jazz Weds evening ~ Bedrooms: /$80 *Recommended by David Twitchett, Sara Fulton, Roger Baker, Adrian Buckland, Julia and Fiona Barnes, Cliff and Monica Swan, Charlie May*

If we know a pub has an outdoor play area for children, we mention it.

LITTLEY GREEN
Compasses

TL6917 Map 5

(01245) 362308 – www.compasseslittleygreen.co.uk

Village signposted off B1417 Felsted road in Hartoft End (opposite former Ridleys Brewery), about a mile N of junction with B1008 (former A130); CM3 1BU

Charming brick tavern – a prime example of what is now an all too rare breed; bedrooms

This is a classic, East Anglian, traditional country local. The friendly bar has brown-painted panelling and wall benches, plain chairs and tables on quarry tiles, and chat and laughter rather than piped music as the backdrop. There's a piano, darts and board games in one side room, and decorative mugs hanging from beams in another. A fine range of ales includes Bishop Nick Ridleys Rite (brewed in Braintree by the landlord's brother) as well as guests such as Bishop Nick Dark Times, Crouch Vale Essex Boys Best Bitter, Mourne Mountains Red Trail and Oakham Dragon in Bavaria tapped from casks in a half cellar. In summer and at Christmas they hold beer festivals featuring dozens of beers, alongside events that may include vintage ploughing in the field opposite. Also, constantly changing ciders from Biddenden, Carter's, Millwhites, Orchard Pig and so forth, and eight wines by the glass. Picnic-sets sit out on the sheltered garden to the side and back, with a couple of long tables on the front cobbles by the quiet lane. Bedrooms are in a modern block next to the pub.

A big blackboard shows the day's range of huffers: big rolls with a hearty range of hot or cold fillings. They also serve ploughman's, baked potatoes and sensibly priced dishes such as chicken liver pâté, a changing curry, fresh fish dishes, gammon and egg, and rib-eye steak. *Benchmark main dish: beer-battered cod and chips £10.00. Two-course evening meal £17.00.*

Free house ~ Licensee Jocelyn Ridley ~ Real ale ~ Open 12-3, 5.30-11.30; 12-11.30 Thurs-Sun ~ Bar food 12-2.30, 6.30-9.30; 12-2.30, 6-9.30 Fri; 12-4, 6-9.30 Sat; 12-8.30 Sun ~ Children welcome ~ Dogs welcome ~ Wi-fi ~ Live folk music every third Mon of the month ~ Bedrooms: /£85 *Recommended by David Jackman, David Twitchett, Alf and Sally Garner, Glen and Patricia Fuller, Roy and Lindsey Fentiman, Charlie May*

SOUTH HANNINGFIELD
Old Windmill ♀

TQ7497 Map 5

(01268) 712280 – www.brunningandprice.co.uk/oldwindmill

Off A130 S of Chelmsford; CM3 8HT

Extensive, invitingly converted pub with interesting food and a good range of drinks

This has been a pub since 1799 – but it's changed a great deal recently. A forest of stripped standing timbers and open doorways have created cosy, rambling areas throughout with an agreeable mix of highly polished old tables and chairs, frame-to-frame pictures on cream walls, woodburning stoves and big pot plants. Deep green or dark red dado and a few old rugs dotted on the polished wood floors provide splashes of colour; other areas are more subdued with beige carpeting. Attentive young staff serve St Austell Brunning & Price Traditional Bitter and guests from breweries such as Crouch Vale, Leigh on Sea, Mighty Oak and Nethergate on handpump, a dozen wines by the glass, 70 malt whiskies and a good range of spirits; background music. A back terrace has tables and chairs under parasols and there are picnic-sets on the lawn and a few more seats out in front.

🍴 Good, modern food includes sandwiches, potted smoked mackerel with cucumber jelly, charcuterie board for sharing, butternut squash, spinach, lentil and stilton pie, cumberland sausages with mash and onion gravy, crispy beef salad with sweet chilli dressing and cashew nuts, tandoori cod with spinach and red onion dhal and mussel curry sauce, steak and kidney pudding, duck breast with fondant potato, celeriac purée and blackberry jus, and puddings such as lemon meringue pie with raspberry sorbet and warm waffle with grilled pineapple, coconut rum syrup and coconut ice-cream. *Benchmark main dish: pie of the day £14.00. Two-course evening meal £21.00.*

Brunning & Price ~ Manager Nick Bryant ~ Real ale ~ Open 11.30-11; 12-10.30 Sun ~ Bar food 12-9 (9.30 Fri, Sat) ~ Restaurant ~ Children welcome ~ Dogs allowed in bar ~ Wi-fi *Recommended by John Saville, David Twitchett, Heather and Richard Jones, Gus Swan, Caroline Prescott*

Also Worth a Visit in Essex

Besides the fully inspected pubs, you might like to try these pubs that have been recommended to us and described by readers. Do tell us what you think of them: feedback@goodguides.com

ARDLEIGH   TM0429
⋆**Wooden Fender** (01206) 230466
A137 towards Colchester; CO7 7PA
Extended old pub (former 17th-c staging post) with beams and log fires; good freshly made food from sharing plates through grills to daily specials, Greene King and guests, decent wines, friendly attentive service; children welcome in large dining area, dogs in bar, good-sized garden with play area, open all day Fri and Sat, till 9pm Sun, breakfast 7.30-11am Weds-Sun. *(David Roberts)*

ARKESDEN   TL4834
Axe & Compasses (01799) 550272
Off B1038; CB11 4EX Comfortable part-thatched pub now run by two brothers; original part dating back to 1650 with low ceilings, original floor tiles and open fire in brick fireplace, upholstered chairs, cushioned wall seats and settles, Greene King IPA and Old Speckled Hen plus a guest, good choice of wines and malt whiskies, well liked food (not Sun evening) in converted stables with photographs of the pub and surrounding area, friendly efficient service; occasional live music; children welcome, benches out at front, more seats on side terrace, lovely village. *(Christopher and Elise Way)*

AYTHORPE RODING   TL5915
Axe & Compasses (01279) 876648
B184 S of Dunmow; CM6 1PP Attractive weatherboarded and part-thatched roadside pub, neatly kept and cosy, with beams, stripped brickwork and pale wood floors, modern furnishings, original part (on the left) has a two-way fireplace marking off a snug raftered dining area, popular food from light lunches up including deals and themed nights, special diets catered for, Fullers ale plus two guests and 13 wines by the glass; background and some live music, monthly

quiz, board games; small back garden with stylish modern furniture, views across fields to windmill, open (and food) all day from 9am for breakfast. *(Donald Allsopp)*

BELCHAMP ST PAUL   TL7942
Half Moon (01787) 277402
Cole Green; CO10 7DP Quaint recently rethatched 16th-c beamed pub overlooking village green; good reasonably priced home-made food (not Sun evening, Mon) from varied menu, well kept Greene King IPA and guests, decent wines by the glass, friendly helpful staff, snug carpeted interior with woodburner, restaurant; Aug beer/music festival; children welcome, no dogs inside, tables out in front and in back garden, open all day weekends. *(Mrs Margo Finlay, Jörg Kasprowski)*

BIRCHANGER   TL5122
⋆**Three Willows** (01279) 815913
Under a mile from M11 junction 8: A120 towards Bishop's Stortford, then almost immediately right to Birchanger Village; don't be waylaid earlier by the Birchanger Services signpost; CM23 5QR Welcoming village dining pub under newish management; spacious carpeted bar with lots of cricketing memorabilia, well furnished smaller lounge, Greene King ales and good fairly traditional food cooked by landlord-chef including plenty of fresh fish, efficient friendly young staff; children welcome, dogs allowed in bar, picnic-sets out in front and on lawn behind (some motorway and Stansted Airport noise), play area, open all day Sat, till 7pm Sun. *(Ian Prince, Mrs Margo Finlay, Jörg Kasprowski)*

BISHOPS GREEN   TL6317
Spotted Dog (01245) 231598
High Easter Road; CM6 1NF Pretty 18th-c thatched pub-restaurant in quiet rural

hamlet; very good food cooked by landlord-chef including more affordable set menu (not Fri, Sat evenings or Sun lunchtime), friendly attentive staff, Greene King IPA and a guest, contemporary beamed interior with high-backed leather chairs at well spaced tables; background music; children welcome, rattan-style furniture out behind picket fence, closed Sun evening, Mon. *(Bob and Melissa Wyatt)*

BOREHAM   TL7409
Lion (01245) 394900
Main Road; CM3 3JA Stylish roadside bistro-bar with rooms; popular affordably priced food from snacks to daily specials, no bookings so may have to queue at busy times, several wines by the glass, bottled beers and up to six well kept changing ales, efficient friendly staff, conservatory; monthly comedy club; children welcome, no dogs inside, 23 comfortable bedrooms, open all day, food all day weekends. *(Tina and David Woods-Taylor)*

BOREHAM   TL7509
Six Bells (01245) 467232
Main Road (B1137); CM3 3JE Family dining pub with several linked areas including inglenook bar, good affordably priced home-cooked food (smaller appetites and gluten-free diets catered for), well kept Greene King ales and a guest, polite helpful staff; no dogs inside, play area in good-sized garden, open (and food) all day weekends. *(Tina and David Woods-Taylor)*

BRAINTREE   TL7421
King William IV (01376) 567755
London Road; CM77 7PU Small friendly drinkers' local with two simple bars, up to five real ales tapped from the cask including own Moody Goose brews, also proper ciders/perries and some unusual lagers, no food apart from snacks; folk night third Sun of month; well behaved children and dogs welcome, picnic-sets in big garden, open all day Fri-Sun, from 3pm other days. *(Mark Crossley, Robert Kennedy)*

BRENTWOOD   TQ6195
Rose (01277) 218809
Chelmsford Road (A1023), Shenfield; CM15 8RN Updated beamed and timbered dining pub serving good fairly priced food (booking advised) from breakfast on, a couple of real ales including one badged for them and plenty of wines by the glass, friendly attentive young staff, cosy interior with woodburners and separate restaurant; children welcome, no dogs inside, terrace tables (some under cover), open all day from 8am (midday Sun). *(Mrs Margo Finlay, Jörg Kasprowski)*

BURNHAM-ON-CROUCH   TQ9596
Ship (01621) 785057
High Street; CM0 8AA Relaxed 18th-c dining pub with good fairly priced food from

imaginative snacks up, fish Fri, unlimited prosecco lunch Sat, local beers plus guests such as Harveys, decent wines and cocktails (happy hour 6.30-8.30pm Fri, Sat), friendly helpful staff, bare-boards bar with blue-painted panelling and woodburner; background music; children welcome, some pavement seating, three comfortable boutique-style bedrooms, open (and food) all day. *(Martin Day)*

BURNHAM-ON-CROUCH   TQ9495
White Harte (01621) 782106
The Quay; CM0 8AS Cosy old-fashioned 17th-c hotel on water's edge overlooking yacht-filled River Crouch; partly carpeted bars with down-to-earth charm, assorted nautical bric-a-brac and hardware, other traditionally furnished high-ceilinged rooms with sea pictures on brown panelled or stripped brick walls, cushioned seats around oak tables, enormous winter log fire, beers from Adnams and Crouch Vale, generally well liked food; children and dogs allowed, outside seating jettied over the water, 19 bedrooms (eight with river view), open all day. *(Elisabeth and Bill Humphries)*

BURTON END   TL5323
Ash (01279) 814841
Just N of Stansted Airport; CM24 8UQ Thatched 17th-c country pub; well kept ales including Greene King IPA and a beer badged for them, decent range of wines by the glass, enjoyable generously served food from lunchtime sandwiches and pubby choices up, friendly staff, black beams and timbers, quarry tiled floors, woodburner, pitched-roof dining extension; monthly quiz and charity events, sports TV, free wi-fi; children welcome, tables out on deck and grass, open (and food) all day. *(Kelly James)*

CASTLE HEDINGHAM   TL7835
Bell (01787) 460350
St James Street B1058; CO9 3EJ Beamed and timbered three-bar pub dating from the 15th c, unpretentious, unspoilt and run by the same family since the late 1960s; Adnams, Mighty Oak and guests tapped from the cask (July beer festival), popular pubby food along with turkish specials, good friendly service; background and live music including lunchtime jazz last Sun of month, quiz Sun evening; dogs welcome, children away from public bar, garden with hops and covered area, well placed for Hedingham Castle, open all day Fri-Sun. *(Millie and Peter Downing)*

CHATHAM GREEN   TL7115
Windmill (01245) 910910
Chatham Green, pub signed from A131; CM3 3LE Beamed and timbered country dining pub; good attractively presented food from chef-landlord, well chosen wine list, cocktails and a couple of ales such as Greene King and Maldon, friendly helpful

staff, cushioned wooden chairs around sturdy tables on bare boards or tartan carpet, some rustic bric-a-brac, log fires; children and dogs welcome, tables out at front, plans for bedrooms in adjacent stub of former windmill, open all day Fri and Sat, till 9pm Sun, closed Mon, Tues and lunchtimes Weds, Thurs. *(Neil Allen)*

CHELMSFORD   TL7006
Orange Tree   (01245) 262664
Lower Anchor Street; CM2 0AS Bargain lunchtime bar food (also evenings Thurs-Sat) in traditional two-room brick local, eight well kept ales (some tapped from the cask) including Adnams, Dark Star and Mighty Oak, efficient service; Tues charity quiz, sports TV; dogs welcome in public bar, back terrace, handy for county cricket ground and can get very busy on match days, open all day. *(Jeff Davies)*

CHIGWELL ROW   TQ4693
Two Brewers   (020) 8501 1313
Lambourne Road; IG7 6ET Spacious Home Counties pub with welcoming relaxed atmosphere; assortment of tables and chairs and wall banquettes on flagstones or bare boards, heavy draped curtains, lots of pictures, photos and gilt-edged mirrors, two-way fireplace, good choice of real ales and wines by the glass, popular food from varied menu; children and dogs welcome, nice three-mile circular walk from the door, open (and food) all day. *(Nicholas and Maddy Trainer)*

CLAVERING   TL4832
★ Cricketers   (01799) 550442
B1038 Newport–Buntingford; CB11 4QT Busy dining pub with plenty of old-fashioned charm, inventive food and signed cookbooks by Jamie Oliver (his parents own it); main area with very low beams and big open fireplace, bays of deep purple button-backed banquettes and padded leather chairs on dark floorboards, split-level back part with carpeted dining areas and some big copper and brass pans on dark beams and timbers, three Adnams and Nethergate beers and 19 wines by the glass; background music, free wi-fi; children welcome, attractive front terrace with rattan-style chairs around teak tables, bedrooms, handy for Stansted Airport, open all day from 7am, food all day Sun. *(Donald Allsopp)*

COLCHESTER   TL9924
Fat Cat   (01206) 577990
Butt Road/Alexandra Road; CO3 3BZ Small sister pub to the Ipswich and Norwich Fat Cats; eight well kept ales (including

their own) and wide range of other beers all marked up on blackboard, enjoyable inexpensive food (not Mon-Weds), friendly helpful staff; beer festivals, Sun quiz, sports TV; children (until 5pm weekends only) and dogs welcome, open all day (no food Sun evening, Mon, Tues). *(David Roberts)*

COLCHESTER   TL9925
Three Wise Monkeys
(01206) 543014 *High Street; CO1 1DN* Popular centrally located bar on several levels; ground floor serves half a dozen changing ales, 15 craft beers and good selection of other drinks including cocktails, enjoyable food from well priced american smokehouse menu, prompt friendly service, another bar/dining area upstairs and above that a live music/comedy venue, there's also a weekend gin bar in the cellar; open (and food) all day, shuts 1am Fri, Sat. *(Hannah Clarke)*

DANBURY   TL7805
Bakers Arms   (01245) 227300
Maldon Road; CM3 4QH Pink-painted roadside pub with pleasant informal atmosphere; well kept ales such as Adnams and Sharps (May beer festival), enjoyable food (not Sun evening or lunchtimes Mon, Tues) including pizzas and four sizes of fish and chips, welcoming cheerful staff; children and dogs allowed (they have a mastiff and great dane), picnic-sets in back garden, open all day (till 8pm Sun). *(Bridget and Peter Gregson)*

DEBDEN   TL5533
Plough   (01799) 541899
High Street; CB11 3LE Welcoming village pub doing well under hard-working licensees, beer/music festivals, live music some weekends, monthly pub quiz third Weds; good freshly made food from landlord-chef including daily specials, special diets catered for, up to four well kept local ales and decent wines, cheerful helpful service, restaurant, log fire; children and dogs (in bar) welcome, fair-sized garden behind, open all day Fri-Sun, closed Mon and lunchtime Tues. *(Bob and Melissa Wyatt)*

DEDHAM   TM0533
Sun   (01206) 323351
High Street (B2109); CO7 6DF Tudor coaching inn opposite church; well kept Adnams, Crouch Vale and two guests, Aspall's cider, impressive wine selection (many by the glass/carafe), varied italian-influenced menu, afternoon teas, historic panelled interior with high carved beams, handsome furnishings and splendid fireplaces, split-

level dining room; background music, TV; children and dogs (in bar) welcome, picnic-sets on quiet back lawn with mature trees and view of church, characterful panelled bedrooms, good Flatford Mill walk, open all day, breakfast for non-residents 8.15-9.45am Fri-Sun. (*Charles Todd*)

DUNMOW   TL6222
Angel & Harp (01371) 859259
Church Road, Church End; B1057 signposted to Finchingfield/The Bardfields, off B184 N of town; CM6 2AD
Comfortable old place with linked rooms rambling around through standing timbers and doorways, mix of seating including armchairs, sofas and banquettes, stools each side of free-standing zinc 'counter' serving Nethergate, guest beers and 11 wines by the glass, good range of popular food, substantial brick fireplace and some fine old floor tiles in low-ceilinged main area, steps up to interesting raftered room with one huge table, also attractive extension with glass wall overlooking flagstoned courtyard and grassed area beyond; background music, quiz last Weds of month, free wi-fi; children and dogs (in bar) welcome, open (and food) all day from 9am. (*David Twitchett*)

DUTON HILL   TL6026
Three Horseshoes (01371) 870681
Off B184 Dunmow–Thaxted, 3 miles N of Dunmow; CM6 2DX Friendly traditional village local; well kept Mighty Oak and a couple of guests (late May Bank Holiday beer festival), central fire in main bar, aged armchairs by another fireplace in homely left-hand parlour, lots of interesting memorabilia, small public bar with darts and pool, no food; dogs welcome, old enamel signs out at front, garden with pond and views, closed lunchtimes Mon-Thurs. (*Neil Allen*)

EARLS COLNE   TL8528
Lion (01787) 226823
High Street; CO6 2PA Restored village pub dating from the 15th c; mediterranean-style menu from tapas and wood-fired pizzas up, well kept changing beers and interesting wines (choose a bottle from their small shop to drink in or take away), friendly service; children and dogs welcome, courtyard tables, open (and food) all day from 9am (10.30am Sun) for breakfast. (*Greta and Gavin Craddock*)

EPPING FOREST   TL4501
Forest Gate (01992) 572312
Bell Common; CM16 4DZ Friendly open-plan pub dating from the 17th c and run by the same family for over 50 years; beams, flagstones and panelling, big woodburner,

well kept Adnams and guests from brick-faced bar, inexpensive pubby food (they also have a smart upmarket restaurant next door); darts; children and dogs welcome, tables on front lawn popular with walkers, four bedrooms in separate building, open all day. (*Donald Allsopp*)

FINCHINGFIELD   TL6832
Fox (01371) 810151
The Green; CM7 4JX Pargeted 16th-c building overlooking village duck pond; spacious beamed bar with exposed brickwork and central fireplace, flowers on tables, up to four changing local ales and good choice of wines by the glass, popular pubby food (not Sun evening) including lunchtime sandwiches, afternoon teas (must be pre-booked, not Sun), friendly helpful staff; background and some live music; children and dogs welcome, hanging baskets and picnic-sets in front, open all day. (*Mrs Margo Finlay, Jörg Kasprowski, Tony Scott*)

FINGRINGHOE   TM0220
Whalebone (01206) 729307
Off A134 just S of Colchester centre, or B1025; CO5 7BG Old village dining pub with airy country-chic rooms; cream-painted tables on oak floors, fresh flowers and log fire, good varied choice of food from sandwiches and wraps up, four well kept beers including Adnams, friendly helpful staff, barn function room; background music; children and dogs welcome, charming back garden with peaceful valley view, front terrace, handy for Fingringhoe Wick nature reserve, open all day Sat, till 6pm Sun. (*Kelly James*)

GESTINGTHORPE   TL8138
★ Pheasant (01787) 461196
Off B1058; CO9 3AU Civilised country pub with old-fashioned character in small opened-up beamed rooms; settles and mix of other furniture on bare boards, books and china platters on shelves, woodburners in nice brick fireplaces, Adnams Southwold, a house beer from Woodfordes and an occasional guest, nine wines by the glass, good food using local and some home-grown produce including daily specials; children and dogs (in bar) welcome, seats outside under parasols with views over fields, five stylish bedrooms, closed Mon and lunchtimes Tues-Thurs, they also take days off Jan-May – so best to phone or check website. (*Sally Harrison*)

GOSFIELD   TL7829
Kings Head (01787) 474016
The Street; CO9 1TP Tudor village pub recently refurbished and improved under new owners; beams, standing timbers and other

original features, main bar with handsome brick fireplace, three real ales such as Bishop Nick, Sharps and Woodfordes, good sensibly priced food (not Sun evening, Mon) from baguettes up, efficient friendly service, well spaced tables in dining area opening into carpeted conservatory; some live music and quiz nights; children welcome, terrace picnic-sets, open all day. *(Tracey Lewis)*

GREAT BARDFIELD TL6730
Vine (01371) 811822
Vine Street; CM7 4SR Red-brick Victorian dining pub with highly rated well presented food from pub staples to monthly tasting menus, real ales such as Greene King, extensive wine list and some unusual gins, friendly helpful service, light airy décor with roaring log fire; children welcome, picnic-sets in good-sized garden (Aug beer festival), interesting village with links to notable artists, open all day. *(Nicholas and Maddy Trainer)*

GREAT BROMLEY TM0824
Court House (01206) 250322
Harwich Road/Frating Road; CO7 7JG Popular modernised roadside pub; carpeted bar with white-painted beams, good reasonably priced pubby food from lunchtime sandwiches up, well kept changing ales, friendly efficient service, restaurant and tea room; children welcome, bedrooms (some in motel-style building), closed Sun and Mon evenings, otherwise open all day. *(Mrs Margo Finlay, Jörg Kasprowski)*

GREAT BROMLEY TM0627
Great Bromley Cross
(01206) 621772
Ardleigh Road, just off A120 Colchester–Harwich; CO7 7TL Welcoming updated community-owned country pub on crossroads; a couple of well kept ales such as Bishop Nick and Colchester, various gins and cocktails, low-priced food served Fri evening and on their regular events nights (live music, quizzes and so forth); Weds morning post office, library and coffee shop; children and dogs welcome, open Sun 12-3pm, closed Mon, Tues and lunchtimes Thurs-Sat. *(Lesley Broadbent)*

GREAT CHESTERFORD TL5142
Crown & Thistle (01799) 530278
1.5 miles from M11 junction 9A; pub signposted off B184, in High Street; CB10 1PL Refurbished old building under friendly management; decorative plasterwork inside and out, particularly around the early 16th-c inglenook, low-ceilinged area by bar serving ales such as Adnams, Fullers and Woodfordes, enjoyable thai food in long handsomely proportioned dining room; children, walkers and dogs (in bar) welcome, picnic-sets out at front, more tables in suntrap back courtyard, closed Sun evening. *(Mrs Margo Finlay, Jörg Kasprowski)*

GREAT CHESTERFORD TL5142
Plough (01799) 531651
Off M11/A11 via B184; High Street; CB10 1PL Updated and extended 18th-c pub in peaceful village; popular fairly traditional food from sandwiches up including Mon fish and chips and Fri steak nights, Greene King ales and good range of other drinks, friendly attentive service, timbered pitch-roof bar connecting to three restaurant areas; background music; children and dogs welcome, attractive well maintained garden, open all day Fri-Sun, food all day Sat, till 6pm Sun. *(Mrs Margo Finlay, Jörg Kasprowski)*

GREAT EASTON TL6126
Green Man (01371) 852285
Mill End Green; pub signed 2 miles N of Dunmow, off B184 towards Lindsell; CM6 2DN Popular well looked-after country dining pub down long winding lane; linked beamed rooms including bar with log fire, good food (best to book weekends) from pub favourites and tapas up, real ales such as Adnams, Greene King and Sharps, decent wines by the glass and cocktails, friendly helpful service; background music; children welcome, dogs in bar, good-sized garden with terrace and play area, closed Mon, otherwise open all day (till around 7.30pm Sun). *(Mrs Margo Finlay, Jörg Kasprowski)*

GREAT HENNY TL8738
Henny Swan (01787) 267953
Henny Street; CO10 7LS Welcoming dining pub in great location on River Stour; well kept Adnams and a couple of guests, proper cider and plenty of wines by the glass, good food from separate bar and restaurant menus (booking advised), friendly efficient service; background music (live third Sun of month); children allowed in restaurant till 8pm, dogs in bar and lounge, disabled loos, terrace and waterside garden, may be summer boat trips, open (and food) all day, restaurant closed Mon. *(Charles Todd)*

GREAT WARLEY STREET TQ5890
Thatchers Arms (01277) 233535
Warley Road; CM13 3HU Old pub across from small village green; decent food from sandwiches and baked potatoes up, real ales including one badged for them, friendly young staff, red-carpeted black-beamed interior; may be background music; children, walkers and dogs welcome, picnic-sets outside, closed Mon, otherwise open all day (till midnight Fri, Sat), food all day Sat, till 5pm Sun. *(Eddie Edwards)*

HARWICH TM2632
Alma (01255) 318681
Kings Head Street; CO12 3EE Popular old seafarers' local just back from the quayside; highly rated food (best to book) from sharing plates up including good fresh

fish/seafood, special diets catered for, well kept Adnams and good range of other beers, proper ciders and decent wines, friendly service; live music Fri, maybe a shanty group first Mon of month, quiz every other Tues; children and dogs welcome, cosy back courtyard, six bedrooms, open (and food) all day. *(Jeff Davies)*

HASTINGWOOD   TL4807

★ **Rainbow & Dove** (01279) 415419

0.5 miles from M11 junction 7;
CM17 9JX Pleasantly traditional low-beamed country pub dating from the 11th c (originally a small farmhouse) with three cosy rooms; built-in cushioned wall seats and mate's chairs around pubby tables, some stripped stonework, woodburner in original fireplace, three or four well kept changing ales, good choice of wines by the glass and enjoyable fairly priced food from sandwiches to popular Sun roasts, breakfast from 9am Sat, friendly helpful staff, barn function room; background music; children and dogs welcome, tables out under parasols, smallholding with rare-breed pigs, goats and chickens (own sausages and eggs), closed Sun and Mon evenings. *(Sally Harrison)*

HATFIELD BROAD OAK   TL5416

★ **Dukes Head** (01279) 718598

B183 Hatfield Heath–Takeley; High
Street; CM22 7HH Relaxed well run dining pub with various rambling seating areas; solid wooden chairs around chunky stripped tables, comfortable armchairs and sofas, cheerful prints on cream walls, woodburner, Greene King IPA, Sharps Doom Bar and Timothy Taylors Landlord, 20 wines by the glass from good list, well regarded food served by cheerful staff; background music and board games; children welcome, dogs in bar (pub dogs are Sam and Zac), picnic-sets at front corner of building which has some nice pargeting, teak tables under parasols on sheltered back terrace, open all day, food all day Sat, till 6pm Sun; for sale as we went to press, so may be changes. *(Jacqui and Alan Swan)*

HATFIELD HEATH   TL5115

Thatchers (01279) 730270

Stortford Road (A1005); CM22 7DU Thatched and weatherboarded 16th-c dining pub at end of large green; good food from short but varied menu, well kept Greene King IPA, St Austell Tribute and two guests from long counter, several wines by the glass, friendly attentive service, inglenook woodburner, beams, some copper and brass and old local photographs; background music; children in back dining area, no dogs

inside, tables out in front behind picket fence, open (and food) all day, till 9pm (6pm) Sun. *(Gail Plews)*

HENHAM   TL5428

Cock (01279) 850347

Church End; CM22 6AN Old timbered building striking good balance between community local and dining pub; enjoyable well priced home-made food from fairly pubby menu, Greene King IPA, a beer from Saffron (brewed in the village) and Sharps Doom Bar, decent wines, restaurant with leather-backed chairs on wood floor, good open fires; quiz first Mon of month, sports TV in snug; children and dogs welcome, seats out at front and in tree-shaded garden behind, open all day Fri and Sat, till 7pm Sun. *(Elisabeth and Bill Humphreys)*

HOWLETT END   TL5834

White Hart (01799) 599030

Thaxted Road (B184 SE of Saffron
Walden); CB10 2UZ Comfortable and well run pub-restaurant; two smartly set modern dining rooms either side of small bar, good generously served food from sandwiches and pubby choices up, a real ale such as Nethergate and nice choice of wines, friendly helpful service; children welcome, terrace and large garden, closed Sun evening, Mon (open bank holiday lunchtime). *(Frances Parsons)*

KIRBY LE SOKEN   TM2221

Ship (01255) 679149

B1034 Thorpe–Walton; CO13 0DT Refurbished 17th-c beamed pub with wide choice of enjoyable good value bar and restaurant food (all day Sat, till 5pm Sun), six real ales and a dozen ciders, friendly helpful service; children and dogs (in bar) welcome, disabled facilities, picnic-sets and flowers on fenced front terrace, garden and covered area behind, open all day. *(Adrian Johnson)*

LANGHAM   TM0232

Shepherd (01206) 272711

Moor Road/High Street; CO4 5NR Roomy 1920s village pub on crossroads; L-shaped bar with areas off, wood floors and painted half-panelling, large OS map covering one wall, comfortable sofas, woodburner, well kept beers such as Adnams, plenty of wines by the glass and good selection of other drinks, enjoyable fairly priced food including set menu (Mon-Sat), Sun roasts, efficient friendly service; occasional quiz and live music nights; children and dogs (in bar) welcome, side garden, open all day, food all day Sat, till 5pm Sun, not Mon. *(David Roberts)*

Real ale may be served from handpumps, electric pumps (not just the on-off switches used for keg beer) or – common in Scotland – tall taps called founts (pronounced 'fonts') where a separate pump pushes the beer up under air pressure.

LEIGH-ON-SEA   TQ8385
★**Crooked Billet** (01702) 480289
High Street; SS9 2EP Steps up to homely old pub with waterfront views from big bay windows, packed on busy summer days when queues likely; half a dozen ales including Adnams and Sharps, enjoyable standard Nicholsons menu, log fires, beams, panelled dado and bare boards, local fishing pictures and bric-a-brac; background music; children welcome, dogs outside only, side garden and terrace, seawall seating over road shared with Osborne's good shellfish stall (plastic glasses for outside), pay-and-display parking by flyover, open (and food) all day. *(Nicholas and Maddy Trainer)*

LITTLE BRAXTED   TL8413
Green Man (01621) 891659
Kelvedon Road; signed off B1389; OS Sheet 168 map reference 848133; CM8 3LB Compact cream-painted village pub opposite tiny green; modern décor with old beams and log fires, enjoyable reasonably priced traditional food from sandwiches and baked potatoes up, OAP set menu and other deals, special diets catered for, Greene King ales and a guest, Aspall's cider, friendly helpful staff; children, walkers and dogs welcome, picnic-sets out at front and in pleasant sheltered garden, five-mile circular walk from pub, open all day Sat, till 7pm Sun, closed Mon evening. *(Donald Allsopp)*

LITTLE BROMLEY   TM1028
Haywain (01206) 390004
Bentley Road; CO11 2PL Popular 18th-c roadside pub; carpeted/flagstoned interior with various cosy areas leading off main bar, beams, exposed brickwork, painted wainscoting and open fires, well kept Adnams and a couple of guests, enjoyable food from snacks to lava rock grills, friendly helpful service; children, walkers and dogs welcome, small side garden, closed Sun evening to Tues, otherwise open (and food) all day, breakfast from 9.30am Fri-Sat. *(Bob and Melissa Wyatt)*

LITTLE TOTHAM   TL8811
Swan (01621) 331713
School Road; CM9 8LB Welcoming little village local with half a dozen well kept ales tapped from the cask, farm ciders/perry and good straightforward lunchtime food; low 17th-c beams and log fire, back dining area, games bar with darts; live music and quiz nights, June beer festival; children, walkers and dogs welcome, disabled access, front lawned garden and small terrace, open all day. *(Sally Harrison)*

LITTLE WALTHAM   TL7013
White Hart (01245) 360205
The Street; CM3 3NY Handsome village pub with contemporary open-plan rooms; wood, slate and tartan-carpeted floors, seating from woven cane chairs through wall banquettes and cushioned window seats to upholstered armchairs, fireplaces (some piled high with logs), metal deer heads, antler chandeliers and candles in tall glass lanterns, Adnams, Nethergate and guests, Weston's cider and good wines by the glass, wide choice of popular reasonably priced food from sandwiches and snacks up including deals, efficient friendly service; free wi-fi; children and dogs (in bar) welcome, garden with cheerfully coloured metal chairs and parasols along with rattan-style seating and picnic-sets, open (and food) all day from 9am breakfast on. *(David Jackman)*

LOUGHTON   TQ4296
Victoria (020) 8508 1779
Smarts Lane; IG10 4BP Chatty and welcoming flower-decked Victorian local; panelled bare-boards bar with small raised end dining area, five real ales including Sharps Doom Bar and Timothy Taylors Landlord, decent range of whiskies and good helpings of enjoyable home-made food from blackboard menu; children and dogs welcome, pleasant well maintained front garden, Epping Forest walks, open all day. *(Charles Todd)*

MARGARETTING TYE   TL6801
★**White Hart** (01277) 840478
From B1002 (just S of A12/A414 junction) follow Maldon Road for 1.3 miles, then turn right immediately after river bridge, into Swan Lane, keeping on for 0.7 miles; The Tye; CM4 9JX Bustling country pub with open-plan but cottagey bars; dark timbers and painted wainscoting, mix of old wooden tables and chairs, woodburner with deer's head above, Adnams Broadside, Southwold and up to three guests tapped from the cask, 14 wines by the glass and 30 gins, enjoyable food from sandwiches and pub staples up, neat carpeted conservatory; background music, summer beer/music festivals, darts and board games; well behaved children welcome, dogs in bar, picnic-sets and fenced duck pond outside, nice rural views, comfortable bedrooms, closed Mon, otherwise open (and food) all day. *(David Twitchett, Louise and Oliver Redman, Sylvia and Phillip Spencer)*

MATCHING GREEN   TL5310
Chequers (01279) 731276
Off Downhall Road; CM17 0PZ Lively red-brick Victorian pub-restaurant in picturesque village; good traditional and mediterranean-style food from lunchtime ciabattas and sharing plates up, also more affordable fixed-price weekday lunch, friendly helpful staff dressed in black, nice wines from comprehensive list, cocktails and well kept ales including Greene King; background music and occasional cabaret/tribute nights; disabled facilities, quiet spot

overlooking large green, good local walks, open all day Fri-Sun, closed Mon except bank holidays. *(Jim King)*

MATCHING TYE   TL5111
Fox (01279) 731335
The Green; CM17 0QS Long 18th-c village pub opposite tiny green; decent range of popular well priced food, Greene King IPA, Shepherd Neame Spitfire and a guest, friendly welcoming staff, various areas including beamed restaurant and raftered barn room, comfortable dark wood furniture, brasses, woodburners; regular live music and quiz nights, TV; children welcome, 12 bedrooms, open all day Sun. *(Jeff Davies)*

MESSING   TL8919
★ Old Crown (01621) 815575
Signed off B1022 and B1023; Lodge Road; CO5 9TU Bustling late 17th-c village pub near fine church; convivial carpeted bar with wheelback and farmhouse chairs around part-painted tables, open fire, ales such as Adnams and Crouch Vale, a dozen wines by the glass including champagne, highly regarded interesting food (not Sun evening), cheerful helpful service, two-room restaurant with white-painted chairs and rustic tables on bare boards, boating pictures on canary yellow or modern papered walls, another open fire; children and dogs (in bar) welcome, picnic-sets under parasols in back garden, more seats in front, deli behind the pub selling good local produce, open all day (till 8.30pm Sun). *(David Twitchett, Noel Privett)*

MILL GREEN   TL6401
Viper (01277) 352010
The Common; from Fryerning (which is signposted off N-bound A12 Ingatestone bypass) follow Writtle signposts; CM4 0PT Unpretentious country local tucked away in wooded area; cosy unchanging rooms with spindleback and country kitchen chairs around neat little tables, tapestried wall seats and log fire, the fairly basic tap room is even simpler with parquet floor and coal fire, beyond is another room with sensibly placed darts; two beers named for the pub plus guests, Weston's cider/perry, straightforward lunchtime food; Easter and Aug beer/music festivals; children (at one end of bar) and dogs welcome, pretty garden (mass of summer colour) and lots of hanging baskets and window boxes, some seats on lawn, open all day (busy with walkers and cyclists weekends). *(Neil Allen)*

MISTLEY   TM1131
★ Thorn (01206) 392821
High Street (B1352 E of Manningtree); CO11 1HE Popular for american chef-landlady's good food (especially seafood), but there's also a friendly welcome if you just want a drink or coffee; high black beams give a clue to the building's age (Matthew

Hopkins, the notorious 17th-c witchfinder general, based himself here), décor, though, is crisply up to date – bentwood chairs and mixed dining tables on terracotta tiles around central bar, cream walls above blue dado, colourful modern artwork, end brick fireplace with woodburner; newspapers and magazines, cookery classes; front pavement tables looking across to Robert Adam's swan fountain, interesting waterside village, 12 well appointed comfortable bedrooms (some in separate building), open all day. *(Dr K Nesbitt)*

MOUNT BURES   TL9031
Thatchers Arms (01787) 227460
Off B1508, Hall Road; CO8 5AT Modernised country pub with good food cooked to order from lunchtime rolls to daily specials, four well kept ales including Adnams and Crouch Vale, cheerful helpful staff; background and some live music occasional theatre and quiz nights, bar billiards; children and dogs welcome, picnic-sets out behind with peaceful Stour Valley views, closed Mon, otherwise open all day (till 9pm Sun). *(Bridget and Peter Gregson)*

NORTH SHOEBURY   TQ9286
Angel (01702) 589600
Parsons Corner; SS3 8UD Timbered and partly thatched 17th-c pub by busy roundabout; Greene King and a couple of guests, popular food including daily specials and a vegan menu, small quarry-tiled entrance bar flanked by tartan-carpeted dining rooms, steps up to back bar with wood floor and some old local pictures, woodburner; background music, free wi-fi; children and dogs allowed in certain areas, disabled facilities, seats out at front, open all day. *(Donald Allsopp)*

PAGLESHAM   TQ9492
Plough & Sail (01702) 258242
East End; SS4 2EQ Relaxed 17th-c weatherboarded dining pub in pretty country spot; popular fairly traditional food at affordable prices, well kept local ales, decent house wines, friendly service, low black beams and big log fires, pine tables, lots of brasses and pictures; background music; children welcome, front picnic-sets and attractive side garden, open all day Sun. *(Jeff Davies)*

PELDON   TL9916
Plough (01206) 735808
Lower Road; CO5 7QR Welcoming little weatherboarded village pub with a couple of real ales such as Adnams and Greene King, decent wines by the glass and good choice of enjoyable food, cheerful service, beams and woodburners, cosy restaurant; children and dogs welcome (their friendly victorian bulldog is Ponto), picnic-sets in back garden, shuts around 8pm Mon and Sun, also closed Mon lunchtime. *(Jim King)*

PELDON   TM0015
Rose (01206) 735373
*B1025 Colchester–Mersea (do not turn
left to Peldon village); CO5 7QJ* Popular
and friendly 14th-c inn with dark bowed
beams, standing timbers and little leaded-
light windows, some antique mahogany and
padded leather wall banquettes, arched brick
fireplace, a couple of Adnams ales along with
Sharps Doom Bar, several wines by the glass
and well liked home-made food (not Sun
evening), cosy restaurant plus contrasting
airy garden room; children (away from bar)
and dogs welcome, plenty of seats in spacious
garden with pretty pond, comfortable
country-style bedrooms, open all day.
(M G Hart)

PLESHEY   TL6614
Leather Bottle (01245) 237291
The Street; CM3 1HG Quaint little
two-room local in nice village with good
walks nearby; ales such as Greene King,
Harveys, Sharps and Skinners, enjoyable
home-made food, friendly helpful staff,
low ceilings and log fires; children and
dogs welcome, garden with play area,
open all day. *(Eddie Edwards)*

PURLEIGH   TL8401
Bell (01621) 828348
*Off B1010 E of Danbury, by church
at top of hill; CM3 6QJ* Cosy rambling
beamed and timbered pub with fine views
over the marshes and Blackwater estuary;
bare boards, hops and brasses, inglenook
log fire, well kept ales such as Adnams
and Mighty Oak, plenty of wines by the
glass (some local), good sensibly priced
home-made food including specials, friendly
staff; cinema and local art exhibitions in
adjoining barn; children welcome, picnic-sets
on side grass, good walks (St Peter's Way),
closed Sun evening, Mon (except bank
holidays). *(Charles Todd)*

RIDGEWELL   TL7340
White Horse (01440) 785532
*Mill Road (A1017 Haverhill–Halstead);
CO9 4SG* Comfortable beamed village
pub with up to four well kept changing ales
(some tapped from the cask), real ciders
and decent wines by the glass, enjoyable
food including lunchtime set menu, friendly
service; background music, free wi-fi; well
behaved children welcome, no dogs, tables
out on terrace, modern bedroom block with
good disabled access, closed Mon lunchtime,
otherwise open all day, no food Sun
evening. *(Millie and Peter Downing)*

SAFFRON WALDEN   TL5338
★ **Eight Bells** (01799) 522790
*Bridge Street; B184 towards
Cambridge; CB10 1BU* Handsome Tudor
pub with open-plan beamed bar; leather
armchairs, chesterfield sofas and old
wooden settles on bare boards, coal-effect
gas fire in brick fireplace, interesting old
photographs, three real ales including
Woodfordes Wherry, ten wines by the glass
and several malt whiskies, good inventive
food (they add a service charge), splendidly
raftered and timbered back dining
barn with dark modern furniture and
upholstered wall banquettes, woodburner;
background music, free wi-fi; children and
dogs (in bar) welcome, garden with raised
deck, nice walks nearby and handy for
Audley End (EH), open (and food) all day,
kitchen closes 6pm Sun. *(Michael Sargent,
Adrian Buckland)*

SAFFRON WALDEN   TL5338
Kings Arms (01799) 522768
Market Hill; CB10 1HQ Steps up to chatty
town centre pub close to market square;
five well kept ales and generous helpings
of reasonably priced lunchtime food from
sandwiches up, traditional multi-room
interior on different levels, cosy open fire
in back room; live music and quiz nights;
children and dogs welcome, sunny beer
garden behind, open all day. *(David and
Gill Carrington)*

SAFFRON WALDEN   TL5438
Old English Gentleman
(01799) 523595 *Gold Street; CB10 1EJ*
Busy 19th-c red-brick pub in centre of
town; bare boards, panelling and log fires,
plenty of inviting nooks and crannies, well
kept Adnams and guests, plenty of wines
by the glass and good choice of enjoyable
lunchtime only food from sandwiches and
deli boards up, Sun roasts, friendly staff;
background music, TV; children welcome,
part-covered heated terrace with modern
furniture, open all day (till 1am Fri, Sat).
(Sally Harrison)

SOUTHEND   TQ8885
Pipe of Port (01702) 614606
Tylers Avenue, off High Street; SS1 1JN
Cellar bar/wine merchants (not strictly a
pub) with plenty of atmosphere, sawdust
and candlelight, well liked food including
signature pies and steaks, good value
set menu (Mon-Thurs), excellent range
of affordably priced wines and other
drinks from craft beers to cocktails,
friendly knowledgeable staff; regular wine
tasting evenings; closed Sun and bank
holidays. *(David Roberts)*

SOUTHMINSTER   TQ9699
Station Arms (01621) 772225
Station Road; CM0 7EW Popular little
weatherboarded local; unpretentious
L-shaped bar with bare boards and panelling,
well kept Adnams Southwold and several
guests, Weston's cider, friendly chatty
atmosphere; live blues third Sat of month,
darts; back courtyard with barn, open all day
weekends (from 2pm Sat). *(Kelly James)*

STANSTED TL5125
Dog & Duck (01279) 812047
Lower Street; CM24 8LR Down-to-earth weatherboarded village pub run by friendly hard-working licensees; traditional beamed and carpeted lounge bar with well kept Greene King ales and guests, four different dining areas for their enjoyable reasonably priced food including good vegetarian choices and two-course OAP menu; live music, quiz nights and other events, sports TV; children and dogs (in public bar) welcome, seats out on small front deck and in back garden, open (and food) all day, kitchen shuts 5pm Sun. *(Mrs Margo Finlay, Jörg Kasprowski, Chris Allen)*

STOCK TQ6998
Bakers Arms (01277) 840423
Common Road, just off B1007 Chelmsford–Billericay; CM4 9NF Popular open-plan beamed pub with good home-made food including mediterranean influences, friendly attentive service, four real ales such as Crouch Vale and Greene King, airy dining room with french windows to enclosed terrace, more seats out at front and in side garden; children welcome, open all day (food all day Fri-Sun). *(Deborah Lammiman)*

STOCK TQ6999
★ Hoop (01277) 841137
B1007; from A12 Chelmsford bypass take Galleywood, Billericay turn-off; CM4 9BD Cheerful weatherboarded pub with open-plan bar; beams and standing timbers (hinting at the original layout when it was three weavers' cottages), pubby tables and chairs, well kept Adnams and guests (beer/cider festival end of May), dining room up in the eaves with open fire in big brick-walled fireplace, popular food (not Sun evening); children and dogs welcome in certain parts, picnic-sets and covered seating area in large sheltered back garden prettily bordered with flowers, limited parking, open all day. *(Simon and Sue Lamb, Adam and Natalie Davis)*

STOW MARIES TQ8399
★ Prince of Wales (01621) 828971
B1012 between South Woodham Ferrers and Cold Norton Posters; CM3 6SA Friendly atmosphere in this traditional weatherboarded pub; several little unspoilt low-ceilinged rooms, bare boards and log fires, conservatory dining area, half a dozen widely sourced changing ales, bottled/draught belgian beers including fruit ones and a couple of ciders, enjoyable food (all day Sun) with some interesting specials, Thurs pizzas

from wood-fired oven; live jazz (third Fri of month); children in family room, terrace and garden tables, maybe summer barbecues, four good bedrooms in converted stable, open all day. *(Bridget and Peter Gregson)*

THEYDON BOIS TQ4598
Bull (01992) 812145
Station Approach; CM16 7HR Cosy beamed pub dating from the 17th c; polished wood and carpeted floors, log fire, three well kept ales including Bombardier, several wines by the glass and good home-made food from sandwiches to blackboard specials (booking advised, particularly weekends), friendly staff; sports TV; children and dogs (in bar) welcome, paved beer garden, open all day, food all day Thurs-Sat, kitchen closed Sun evening. *(Jeff Davies)*

TOOT HILL TL5102
Green Man (01992) 522255
Off A113 in Stanford Rivers, S of Ongar, or A414 W of Ongar; CM5 9SD Traditional village pub refurbished to a good standard; large bar with comfortable seating and big log fire, three separate eating areas, Greene King IPA, a guest beer and several wines by the glass, good food from bar snacks up including several fish dishes, attentive friendly service; children and dogs welcome, attractive courtyard garden at front, four bedrooms, open all day. *(Mrs Margo Finlay, Jörg Kasprowski)*

UPSHIRE TL4100
Horseshoes (01992) 712745
Horseshoe Hill, E of Waltham Abbey; EN9 3SN Welcoming Victorian village pub with small bar area and dining room; good food cooked by chef-landlord with some emphasis on fish, well kept McMullens beers, friendly helpful staff; children and dogs (in bar) welcome, garden overlooking Lea Valley, more tables out in front, good walks, open all day, no evening food Sun or Mon. *(Gail Plews)*

WENDENS AMBO TL5136
★ Bell (01799) 540382
B1039 W of village; CB11 4JY Cottagey local with cheery bustle in low-ceilinged bars; brasses on ancient timbers, wheelback chairs at neat tables, winter log fire, Adnams, Oakham, Woodfordes and a guest, real ciders and ten wines by the glass, well liked food (not Sun night), pizza van Thurs evening; background music, free wi-fi; children and dogs welcome, three-acre garden with seats under parasols on paved terrace, pond leading to River Uttle, woodland walk and timber play area, open all day. *(Sarah Fox)*

A star before the name of a pub shows exceptional quality. It means most people (after reading the report to see just why the star has been won) would think a special trip worthwhile.

WICKHAM ST PAUL   TL8336

★**Victory** (01787) 269364

SW of Sudbury; The Green; CO9 2PT
Old village dining pub by cricket green,
attractive and spacious, with varied choice
of well liked food served by friendly efficient
staff, Adnams and guests from brick-faced
counter, beams and timbers, leather sofas and
armchairs, inglenook woodburner; background
music, pool and darts; children welcome, dogs
in public bar, picnic-sets in neat front garden,
open all day Fri-Sun, closed Mon, no food Sun
evening. *(Jerry Stevenson)*

WIDDINGTON   TL5331

★**Fleur de Lys** (01799) 543280

*Signed off B1383 N of Stansted;
CB11 3SG* Welcoming unpretentious
low-beamed and timbered village pub;
enjoyable locally sourced food (not Sun
evening, Mon, Tues) in bar and dining room
from sandwiches to very good (if pricey)
steaks, OAP set lunch Weds and Thurs, well
kept Adnams, Woodfordes and a couple of
guests chosen by the regulars, decent wines,
efficient friendly service, dim lighting, tiled
and wood floors, inglenook log fire; pool and
other games in back bar; children and dogs
welcome, picnic-sets in pretty garden, open
all day Fri and Sat, till 7.30pm Sun, closed Mon
and Tues lunchtimes. *(Mrs Margo Finlay,
Jörg Kasprowski)*

WIVENHOE   TM0321

Black Buoy (01206) 822425

Off A133; CO7 9BS Village pub owned
by local consortium; open-plan partly
timbered bare-boards bar; well kept ales
such as Colchester, Mighty Oak and Red
Fox, a craft keg, Aspall's cider and several
wines by the glass, good sensibly priced
home-made food (not Sun evening) from
lunchtime sandwiches to daily specials,
cheerful service, open fires, upper dining
area glimpsing river over roofs; well
behaved children and dogs allowed in
certain areas, seats out on brick terrace,
two smart bedrooms up steep staircase,
open all day. *(Frances Parson)*

WOODHAM MORTIMER   TL8104

Hurdlemakers Arms

(01245) 225169 *Post Office Road;
CM9 6ST* Small quietly placed traditional
country local with low ceilings and
timbered walls, five well kept changing ales
(beer festivals) and good choice of ciders,
generous helpings of enjoyable food from
varied menu (special diets catered for),
friendly service; children and dogs welcome,
large garden with picnic-sets among
trees and shrubs, play area and summer
barbecues, open all day (till 9pm Sun),
food all day weekends (till 7.30pm Sun).
(Steve Harding)

Gloucestershire

BARNSLEY
SP0705 Map 4

Village Pub

(01285) 740421 – www.thevillagepub.co.uk

B4425 Cirencester–Burford; GL7 5EF

Bustling pub with interesting food, a good choice of drinks and seats in the back courtyard; bedrooms

This place is at the heart of a lovely Cotswold village, so you'll usually find a chatty group of locals in for a pint and a chat – this makes the atmosphere friendly and relaxed. Low-ceilinged bar rooms are smart and contemporary with pale paintwork, flagstones and oak floorboards, heavy swagged curtains, plush chairs, stools and window settles around polished candlelit tables, three open fireplaces and country magazines and newspapers. Wickwar Cotswold Way and Wye Valley Butty Bach and HPA on handpump, an extensive wine list with a dozen by the glass and up to six farm ciders in summer; background music. The sheltered back courtyard has solid wooden furniture under parasols, outdoor heaters and its own servery. Bedrooms are individually decorated and extremely comfortable and breakfasts are particularly good.

Rewarding food includes ham hock terrine with piccalilli, thai-style crab cakes with lemon mayonnaise, mushroom and butternut squash linguine with pesto, burger with toppings, bacon jam and chips, chicken kiev with truffle mash and green beans, fish pie in thermidor sauce, lamb rump with dauphinoise potatoes and spiced carrot purée, and puddings such as hibiscus pannacotta with mixed berries and double chocolate torte with vanilla ice-cream. *Benchmark main dish: barnsley chop with cherry tomatoes, olives and creamed potato £20.00. Two-course evening meal £23.00.*

Free house ~ Licensee Michael Mella ~ Real ale ~ Open 11-11; 11-10.30 Sun ~ Bar food 12-2.30, 6-9.30 (10 Fri); 12-3, 6-10 Sat; 12-9 Sun ~ Children welcome ~ Dogs allowed in bar ~ Wi-fi ~ Bedrooms: /£149 *Recommended by Mrs Zara Elliott, Guy Vowles, Mike and Mary Carter, Tracey and Stephen Groves, Caroline and Peter Bryant, Charlie May*

BLEDINGTON
SP2422 Map 4

Kings Head

(01608) 658365 – www.kingsheadinn.net

B4450 The Green; OX7 6XQ

Gloucestershire Dining Pub of the Year

16th-c inn with atmospheric furnishings, super wines by the glass, real ales and delicious food; smart bedrooms

This is a lovely place to stay with cosy rooms above the inn itself and more spacious ones in a courtyard; breakfasts are particularly good and the setting (opposite the green in a tranquil village) is most attractive. The friendly, bustling main bar is where most people head for first: ancient beams and other atmospheric furnishings (high-backed wooden settles, gate-leg or pedestal tables), a warming log fire in a stone inglenook, fine old flagstones and sporting memorabilia relating to rugby, racing, cricket and hunting. To the left, a drinking area has built-in wall benches, stools and dining chairs around wooden tables, rugs on bare boards and a woodburning stove. Attentive, welcoming staff serve Hook Norton Hooky and guests from breweries such as Butcombe, Prescott, Purity and Wye Valley on handpump, a super wine list with ten by the glass, 20 malt whiskies and an extensive gin collection; background music, board games and cards. There are seats out in front and rattan-style armchairs around tables in the pretty back courtyard garden with a pagoda; maybe free-range bantams and ducks. The same professional licensees also run the Swan at Swinbrook (in Oxfordshire).

 Local, organic produce is used for the impressive food which includes open sandwiches, pigeon breast with sour cherries, chicory, parmesan crumb and pigeon jus, grilled sardines on toast with café de paris butter, sharing boards, wild mushroom and spinach tagliatelle with shallot cream and white truffle oil, burger of the day with skinny chips, pork cutlet with star anise and carrot purée, salami, sprout flowers and jus, fillet of stone bass with smoked pancetta and sun-dried tomatoes, pickled red onions and samphire, and puddings such as chocolate tart with orange compote and caramelised banana millefeuille with salted caramel ice-cream. *Benchmark main dish: beer-battered fish and chips £14.00. Two-course evening meal £22.00.*

Free house ~ Licensees Nicola and Archie Orr-Ewing ~ Real ale ~ Open 11-11 ~ Bar food 12-2, 6.30-9; 12-2.30, 6-9.30 Fri, Sat; 12-3, 6.30-9 Sun ~ Restaurant ~ Children welcome ~ Dogs allowed in bar ~ Wi-fi ~ Bedrooms: £90/£110 *Recommended by Guy Vowles, Tracey and Stephen Groves, Liz Bell, Brian and Sally Wakeham, Elise and Charles Mackinlay, Helene Grygar*

BOURTON-ON-THE-HILL
Horse & Groom

SP1732 Map 4

(01386) 700413 – www.horseandgroom.info
A44 W of Moreton-in-Marsh; GL56 9AQ

Georgian inn with quite a choice of drinks and lovely views from seats outside; bedrooms

A handsome old place, this has fine country views from the large back garden where there are plenty of seats under parasols. Inside, the pubby bar is light, airy and simply furnished with a pleasing mix of farmhouse and other wooden chairs, settles, cushioned wall and window seats and tables on bare boards and a woodburning stove in a stone fireplace. Brakspears Bitter, Wye Valley Butty Bach and a changing guest on handpump, good wines by the glass, maybe a local farm cider and local gin. There are plenty of original features throughout; background music. Dining areas spread off from here, again with an attractive variety of dining chairs and rustic tables, rugs, snug little corners, an open fire and pale-painted or exposed stone walls. Bedrooms are individually styled. It's best to arrive early to be sure of a space in the smallish car park. Batsford Arboretum is not far away.

Seasonal food includes soused mackerel with treacle yoghurt, fennel and seaweed powder, mushrooms on toast with a crispy egg, goats cheese and vegetable pie with braised red cabbage, smoked salmon and brown shrimp, caper and fennel salad with bloody mary dressing, burger with toppings, tandoori aioli and chips, cod with mussels, fennel, bacon and white wine sauce, rib-eye steak with béarnaise sauce and chunky chips, and puddings such as dark chocolate fondant with salted caramel ice-cream and sticky toffee pudding with vanilla ice-cream. *Benchmark main dish: beer-battered fresh fish and chips £14.00. Two-course evening meal £21.00.*

Free house ~ Licensee Abbie Davies ~ Real ale ~ Open 12-11 ~ Bar food 12-3, 6-9 (8.30 Sun) ~ Restaurant ~ Children welcome ~ Dogs allowed in bar and bedrooms ~ Wi-fi ~ Bedrooms: /$120 *Recommended by Philip Chesington, Patricia and Gordon Tucker, Martine and Lawrence Sanders, Paul Faraday, Richard Tilbrook*

BROCKHAMPTON
SP0322 Map 4
Craven Arms 🍽️⭐ 🍺

(01242) 820410 – www.thecravenarms.co.uk

Village signposted off A436 Andoversford–Naunton – look out for inn sign at head of lane in village; can also be reached from A40 Andoversford–Cheltenham via Whittington and Syreford; GL54 5XQ

Friendly village pub with tasty bar food, real ales and seats in a big garden; bedrooms

Once you've found this enjoyable, family-run country pub, you'll be back! The character bars have low beams, roughly coursed thick stone walls and partly slate and partly wooden floors, and the atmosphere is chatty and easy-going. And although it's largely been opened out to give a sizeable eating area off the bar servery, there's a feeling of several communicating rooms. What was a smaller lower bar has been enlarged to include a second bar counter. Throughout the furniture is mainly pine, with comfortable leather sofas, wall settles and tub chairs; also, farming implements, hand-presses, an open fire and a woodburning stove. Attentive staff serve Bristol Beer Factory Fortitude, Prescott Hill Climb and Stroud Organic Pale Ale on handpump, eight wines by the glass and a farm cider; board games. Sliding doors now connect the restaurant with the large garden, with its lovely views and plenty of seats. The bedrooms are attractively decorated and comfortable. You can walk around the surrounding fields and beyond.

🍴⭐ Pleasing food using only british produce is cooked by the landlady's son and includes baguettes, gin-cured salmon with pickled vegetables, wild mushroom arancini with tarragon purée, ham and egg, chicken in a basket, a vegan choice such as potato linguine, jerusalem artichokes, kale, caramelised onions and pine nut sauce, venison stew with creamy mash, hake fillet with braised puy lentils, celeriac purée, samphire and herb dressing, lamb rump with dauphinoise potatoes, beetroot purée, roasted root vegetables and jus, and puddings such as chocolate tart with hazelnut and rose ice-cream and cashew and vanilla cheesecake with rhubarb compote. *Benchmark main dish: pork belly with pressed squash, creamed leeks, apple, crackling and jus £16.50. Two-course evening meal £21.50.*

Free house ~ Licensee Barbara Price ~ Real ale ~ Open 12-3, 6-11; 12-11 Sat; 12-5 Sun; closed Sun evening, Mon, Tues ~ Bar food 12-2 (2.30 Sat), 6.30-9; 12-3 Sun ~ Restaurant ~ Children welcome ~ Dogs allowed in bar ~ Wi-fi ~ Bedrooms: /$90 *Recommended by Helene Grygar, Guy Vowles, Patrick and Martine Lawson, Brian and Margaret Merritt, Richard Tilbrook*

CHEDWORTH
SP0512 Map 4
Seven Tuns 🍷

(01285) 720630 – www.seventuns.co.uk

Village signposted off A429 NE of Cirencester; then take second signposted right turn and bear left towards church; GL54 4AE

Bustling, enjoyable little pub with good food and wine, several real ales and seats outside

New owners have completely refurbished this 17th-c village pub and customers are delighted. What was the upstairs skittle alley is now a rather smart restaurant with an interesting menu. The downstairs linked rooms have original character with flagstone and wooden floors, restored furniture along with newer comfortable seating, and woodburning stoves. Goffs Winter Ale, Hook Norton Hooky, Otter Bitter and guests from Clavell & Hind and Old Dairy on handpump, 17 wines by the glass from a large and thoughtful list, 28 malt whiskies, and farm cider served by friendly, helpful staff; board games. You can sit outside at the front and back of the building; boules. Disabled access. Nearby walks are good but most people are keen to visit the nearby Roman villa (National Trust).

Quite a choice of well regarded food includes summer sandwiches, home-smoked salmon with beetroot and dill, pork, red wine and fennel sausage with pickles, pumpkin suet pudding with bubble and squeak, wagyu burger with toppings, home-made ketchup and chips, fish stew with tomato, saffron and rouille, veal schnitzel with garlic and parmesan, glazed pork belly with mustard sauce and herb potatoes, and puddings such as chocolate terrine with honeycomb and praline sauce, and rhubarb posset with poached and jellied rhubarb. *Benchmark main dish: calves liver with pancetta, greens and mash £14.00. Two-course evening meal £23.00.*

Youngs ~ Tenant Simon Willson-White ~ Real ale ~ Open 11-11 (midnight Sat) ~ Bar food 12-3, 6-9.30; 12-9.30 Sat; 12-4, 6-9 Sun ~ Restaurant ~ Children welcome ~ Dogs allowed in bar *Recommended by Richard Tilbrook, Tom and Noelle Straiton, Sam Cole, Naomi and Andrew Randall, Edward Mirzoeff, Barbara Brown, Ian Duncan, Jim King*

CHELTENHAM
Old Courthouse ♀ ◀

SO9422   Map 4

(01242) 500930 – www.brunningandprice.co.uk/oldcourthouse
County Court Road; GL50 1HB

Stunning conversion of a former courthouse on two levels with a fine choice of drinks and food

This rather grand, Italianate-style former courthouse has been carefully converted into a lovely two-storey pub. On the ground floor, what was the waiting room is now a big bar with cushioned wooden dining chairs around dark tables on rugs or parquet flooring, a central group of high chairs around equally high tables, a long, green leather button-back banquette stretching down one wall, lots of paintings and armchairs in front of open fires; background music and board games. Friendly young staff serve St Austell Brunning & Price Traditional Bitter plus guests from breweries such as Bespoke, Cotswold Lion, Goffs, Hop Shed, Milestone, Purity and Sadlers on handpump, 23 wines by the glass, 60 rums, 70 malt whiskies and 160 gins. Leading off here are two small dining rooms with more open fires: one with blue décor and tartan-upholstered chairs and the other with lots of horse-racing prints and a dark red button-back leather wall banquette. At the top of the stairs, you pass under a vast chandelier to get to the handsome main courtroom. The raised, panelled seating area, largely unaltered, is surrounded by paintings of judges and looks down on a dining room with elegant marble pillars, leather chairs and wall seats, more paintings and a second bar counter. Throughout are the group's trademark bookshelves, house plants and church candles. Outside, a few tables and chairs are set out on the front pavement.

Appealing food includes sandwiches, pulled pork croquettes with barbecue sauce, red cabbage and green chilli coleslaw, scallops with ham hock fritters, cauliflower purée and lemon dressing, thai green vegetable curry with sticky coconut rice and tempura okra, mussels with bacon, leeks and cider and frites, steak in ale pie, braised lamb shoulder with dauphinoise potatoes, carrot and swede mash and rosemary gravy, king prawn and chorizo salad with gazpacho dressing, and puddings such as crème brûlée and triple chocolate brownie with chocolate sauce. *Benchmark main dish: steak burger with toppings and chips £13.45. Two-course evening meal £22.00.*

Brunning & Price ~ Manager Dale Allison ~ Real ale ~ Open 10.30am-11pm; 10.30am-midnight Fri, Sat; 10.30-10.30 Sun ~ Bar food 12-9.30; 12-10 Fri, Sat; 12-9 Sun ~ Children welcome ~ Dogs allowed in bar ~ Wi-fi ~ Live bands every other Fri evening
Recommended by Alister and Margery Bacon, Lorna and Jeff Mason, Ben and Jenny Settle, Guy Vowles, Mark Morgan, Martin and Joanne Sharp

CHELTENHAM   SO9624   Map 4
Royal Oak
(01242) 522344 – www.royal-oak-prestbury.co.uk
Off B4348 just N; The Burgage, Prestbury; GL52 3DL

Bustling pub with popular food, several real ales and wine by the glass, and seats in the sheltered garden

As the closest pub to Cheltenham Racecourse, this 16th-c inn does get pretty busy on race days. The congenial low-beamed bar has polished brasses, a comfortable mix of seating including chapel chairs on parquet flooring, some interesting pictures on the ochre walls and a woodburning stove in a stone fireplace. Helpful staff keep Butcombe Adam Hensons Rare Breed and Original plus two changing guest beers from breweries such as Bespoke and Liberation on handpump and seven wines by the glass; background music. Dining room tables are nicely spaced so that you don't feel crowded, and the skittle alley doubles as a function room. There are picnic-sets under parasols on the terrace and in a sheltered garden.

Good quality food includes lunchtime sandwiches, confit duck leg croquettes with pickled carrots and fennel and tarragon mayonnaise, potted smoked trout with new potatoes and horseradish and cucumber chutney, wild mushroom, ricotta and mozzarella lasagne with pickled fennel salad, toad in the hole with champ mash and onion gravy, ham with free-range eggs and pineapple, daily fresh fish and lobster bisque pie, crispy pork belly with roasted turnips and apples, black pudding mash and cider sauce, and puddings such as apple and rhubarb crumble with vanilla custard and dark chocolate brownie with toffee popcorn and salted caramel ice-cream. *Benchmark main dish: lamb wellington £19.00. Two-course evening meal £20.00.*

Butcombe ~ Manager Thomas Wright ~ Real ale ~ Open 11-11; 12-10.30 Sun ~ Bar food 12-2, 6-9; 12-9 Fri, Sat; 12-8 Sun ~ Restaurant ~ Children welcome ~ Dogs allowed in bar ~ Wi-fi *Recommended by Dr and Mrs H J Field, Nick and Meriel Cox, Dr and Mrs A K Clarke, Tony Poole, Charlie Stevens, Richard and Tessa Ibbot, Max Simons*

COOMBE HILL   SO8926   Map 4
Gloucester Old Spot ★ 🏵 🍺
(01242) 680321 – www.thegloucesteroldspot.co.uk
Exit M5 junction 11 and use satnav GL51 9SY; access from junction 10 is restricted; GL51 9SY

Interestingly furnished country pub with much character, good ales and likeable food

You'll get a warm welcome from helpful, friendly staff here and the place manages to retain the feel of a country local, despite being close to Cheltenham. The quarry-tiled beamed bar has chapel chairs and other seats around assorted tables (including one in a bow-windowed alcove) and opens into a lighter, partly panelled area with cushioned settles and stripped kitchen tables. Purity Mad Goose, Timothy Taylors Landlord and Wye Valley HPA on handpump, eight decent wines by the glass and four farm ciders including their own-brand medium sweet perry are served by young, friendly staff. Decoration is in unobtrusive good taste, with winter log fires. A handsome baronial-style separate dining room (once a hunting lodge to nearby Boddington Manor) has similar country furniture, high stripped-brick walls, dark flagstones and candlelight; background music. Outside, there are chunky benches and tables under parasols on a terrace, with some oak barrel tables on brickwork and pretty flowers in vintage buckets and baskets; heaters for cooler weather and a new smoker for smoked meats, fish and other treats. They hope to develop hook-ups for motorhomes.

Popular food includes filled rolls, charred pork and pepper satay skewer with asian-style slaw and crushed cashews, cheese soufflé with cream and nutmeg, roasted beetroot, goats cheese and spinach wellington with basil and almond pesto, burger with toppings, celeriac slaw and triple-cooked chips, lamb and rosemary meatballs with chorizo and romesco ragoût, pasta and parmesan, confit duck leg with smoked pork belly lardons, baby gem and mint salsa, and puddings; they also offer a two-course weekday lunch menu. *Benchmark main dish: pork belly with mustard and cider cream reduction £13.95. Two-course evening meal £20.00.*

Free house ~ Licensees Simon and Kate Daws ~ Real ale ~ Open 10am-11pm (midnight-early May-Sept); 10-10 Sun ~ Bar food 12-2 (2.30 Sat), 6-9; 12-8 Sun ~ Restaurant ~ Children welcome ~ Dogs allowed in bar ~ Wi-fi *Recommended by M G Hart, John Copple, Mike and Mary Carter, Clive and Fran Dutson, Dr and Mrs A K Clarke, Gordon and Margaret Ormondroyd*

COWLEY
Green Dragon 🌟 🛏

SO9714   Map 4

(01242) 870271 – www.green-dragon-inn.co.uk

Off A435 S of Cheltenham at Elkstone, Cockleford sign; OS Sheet 163 map reference 970142; GL53 9NW

Inn dating from 1643 with character bars, separate restaurant, popular food, real ales and seats on terraces; bedrooms

So busy is this attractive and well run stone-fronted country pub that you must book ahead to guarantee a table. The two beamed bars have a good mix of customers, plenty of character and a cosy, nicely old-fashioned feel; big flagstones, wooden floorboards, candlelit tables and winter log fires in two stone fireplaces. The furniture and the bar itself in the upper Mouse Bar were made by Robert 'Mouseman' Thompson craftsmen and have little mice running over the hand-carved tables, chairs and mantelpiece; there's also a small upstairs restaurant. Friendly staff keep a good range of drinks such as Hook Norton Old Hooky, Sharps Doom Bar and a guest such as Butcombe Bitter on handpump, ten wines by the glass, ten gins and ten malt whiskies; background music and a separate skittle alley. Bedrooms are comfortable and breakfasts are generous. The outside terraces have lots of seats and tables. Disabled access but not to bedrooms.

High quality food includes sandwiches, camembert and fig tartlet with spicy red onion marmalade, pork and mushroom pâté with home-made chutney, cheesy beetroot and bean pie with stilton cream sauce, free-range chicken with succotash (sweetcorn, cannellini beans, onions, chilli and cream), grilled whole plaice with toasted almonds, lemon and butter, chargrilled pork loin steak with smoked bacon, oregano and white wine cream sauce, steak and kidney suet pudding, and puddings such as ginger sponge with custard and crème brûlée. *Benchmark main dish: garlic and marjoram crispy duck with apple and cider brandy sauce £19.95. Two-course evening meal £25.00.*

Buccaneer Holdings ~ Managers Simon and Nicky Haly ~ Real ale ~ Open 11-11; 12-10.30
Sun ~ Bar food 12-2.30 (3 Sat), 6-10; 12-3.30, 6-9 Sun ~ Restaurant ~ Children welcome ~
Dogs allowed in bar ~ Wi-fi ~ Bedrooms: £80/£105 *Recommended by Dr and Mrs A K Clarke,*
Richard Tilbrook, Dr A J and Mrs B A Tompsett, Guy Vowles, Andrea and Philip Crispin,
Wendi Johns

DIDMARTON   ST8187   Map 2
Kings Arms ♀ ⌂

(01454) 238245 – www.kingsarmsdidmarton.co.uk

A433 Tetbury road; GL9 1DT

**Bustling pub with enjoyable food, a good choice of drinks,
and pleasant back garden; bedrooms**

Several knocked-through beamed bar rooms in this former coaching inn
work their way around a big servery (where there are high chairs and
stools against the counter), with grey-painted half-panelling, armchairs
by a log fire in a stone fireplace, settles and window seats with scatter
cushions, bare boards here and flagstones and rugs there, and a mix of
farmhouse chairs and benches around wooden tables of all shapes and sizes.
Church candles on shelves or in lanterns, antlers, prints and fresh flowers
create interest. There's also a restaurant with another open fire. Flying
Monk Elmers, Otter Amber and Ringwood Boondoggle and Razorback on
handpump, 19 wines by the glass and nine gins; darts. There are plenty of
seats and picnic-sets in the pleasant back garden. Bedrooms are individually
furnished and comfortable and they also have self-catering cottages
in a converted barn and stable block. The pub is handy for Westonbirt
Arboretum. Disabled access.

Highly regarded food includes cauliflower bhaji with spiced chickpea purée,
cucumber yoghurt and pickled mushrooms, home hot-smoked salmon with wasabi,
crème fraîche, tapioca crisp and pickled cucumber, tarragon gnocchi, squash and
balsamic rocket, burger with toppings, bacon ketchup and smoked mayonnaise, pork
medley (belly, cheek and tenderloin) with carrot quinoa and parsnip croquette, cod with
braised lentils, king oyster mushrooms and dauphinoise potatoes, and puddings such
as rhubarb mousse with poached rhubarb, polenta sponge and yoghurt ice-cream and
cappuccino pannacotta with coffee amaretto gel and a chocolate doughnut. *Benchmark
main dish: duo of duck (glazed breast, confit croquette) with mouli fondant, pak choi
and soy jus £17.95. Two-course evening meal £22.00.*

Free house ~ Licensee Mark Birchall ~ Real ale ~ Open 11-11; 11-10 Sun ~ Bar food 12-2.30,
6-9; 12-3, 6-8 Sun ~ Restaurant ~ Children welcome ~ Dogs allowed in bar and bedrooms ~
Wi-fi ~ Bedrooms: £70/£140 *Recommended by Dan and Belinda Smallbone, Julian Richardson,
B and F A Hannam, Dr and Mrs A K Clarke, Trish and Karl Soloman, Nicola and Stuart Parsons,
Rupert and Sandy Newton*

DURSLEY   ST7598   Map 4
Old Spot ◗

(01453) 542870 – www.oldspotinn.co.uk

Hill Road; by bus station; GL11 4JQ

**Unassuming and cheery town pub with a fine range of ales,
regular beer festivals and good value lunchtime food**

A splendid choice of drinks in this bustling town local includes up to seven
real ales on handpump such as Uley Old Ric and a guest from Uley plus
Harveys Best, Otter Bright, St Austell Trelawney and Wye Valley HPA; they
also hold an annual beer festival and there are 20 malt whiskies, 40 gins,

three farm ciders, half a dozen wines by the glass and artisan spirits. Staff are enthusiastic and helpful. The front door opens into a deep-pink small room with a lively mix of customers, stools on shiny quarry tiles beside a pine-boarded bar counter and old enamel beer signs on the walls and ceiling. Another little room leads off on the left towards the garden and a room to the right has lots of wooden benches and tables, with plenty of porcine paraphernalia throughout. The heated and covered garden has benches and parasols. Wheelchair access but no disabled loos.

Reasonably priced lunchtime food includes doorstep sandwiches, smoked mackerel pâté, twice-baked goats cheese soufflé, cauliflower, squash and lentil curry, home-baked ham and eggs, burger with toppings and chips, chicken, leek and cider pie, sweet chilli beef with stir-fried vegetables and noodles, pork in a creamy apple and cider sauce, and puddings such as double chocolate brownie with raspberry coulis and fruit crumble with custard. *Benchmark main dish: pork and apple sausages with creamed leeks and gravy £11.00. Two-course evening meal £18.00.*

Free house ~ Licensee Ellie Sainty ~ Real ale ~ Open 12-11 ~ Bar food 12-3 ~ Children in family room ~ Dogs allowed in bar ~ Wi-fi ~ Live music twice a month *Recommended by Kerry and Guy Trooper, Angela and Steve Heard, Monty Green, Maria and Henry Lazenby, Elisabeth and Bill Humphries*

EASTINGTON
SO7705 Map 4

Old Badger

(01453) 822892 – www.oldbadgerinn.co.uk
Alkerton Road, a mile from M5 junction 13; GL10 3AT

Friendly, traditionally furnished pub with plenty to look at, five real ales, tasty food and seats in attractive garden

A good choice of popular food makes this old-fashioned and friendly pub the perfect break from the M5. The split-level connected rooms have two open fires, traditional furnishings such as built-in planked and cushioned wall seats, settles and farmhouse chairs around all sorts of tables, quarry tiles and floorboards, and an informal atmosphere. There are stone bottles, bookshelves, breweriana on red or cream walls and even a stuffed badger. Flying Monk Elmers, Moles Best, Uley Hogshead, Wickwar Cotswold Way and Wye Valley Butty Bach on handpump alongside ten wines by the glass, a dozen malt whiskies and farm cider; they hold beer and cider festivals with local musicians and also run brewery trips. The nicely landscaped garden has benches and picnic-sets on a terrace and a lawn and under a covered gazebo; the flowering tubs and window boxes are pretty. Wheelchair access to the top bar/dining area only; disabled loos are shared with baby-changing facilities.

Likeable food includes lunchtime baguettes, salt and pepper squid with tartare sauce, a sharing meze board, vegetable and bean chilli with couscous, burger with toppings, coleslaw and chips, king prawn and crab linguine, pork chop with grain mustard sauce and mash, crispy duck in ginger, coconut and lemongrass sauce with peanut noodles, and puddings such as chocolate and salted caramel brownie with ice-cream and poached pear and ginger pudding with almond milk custard. *Benchmark main dish: beer-battered fish and chips £13.00. Two-course evening meal £19.00.*

~ Manager Anthony Pask ~ Real ale ~ Open 12-11.30 ~ Bar food 12-2.30, 6-9; 12-3 Sun ~ Children welcome away from bar area ~ Dogs welcome ~ Wi-fi ~ Live music monthly Fri or Sat *Recommended by Chris and Angela Buckell, Guy Vowles, Charlie and Mark Todd, Dr and Mrs A K Clarke, Nick Sharpe, Alfie Bayliss, Peter Pilbeam*

EASTLEACH TURVILLE   SP1905   Map 4

Victoria

(01367) 850277 – www.thevictoriainneastleach.co.uk

Off A361 S of Burford; GL7 3NQ

Traditional stone pub in village with simply furnished bars, Arkells ales and decent food

Although this place dates back to the early 18th c, it wasn't until 1856 that somebody had the idea of turning it into an inn. The open-plan low-ceilinged rooms cluster around the central servery, with cushioned window seats, leather armchairs and wheelbacks in the bar and more wheelbacks and cushioned settles in the dining room where there's a log fire. Well kept Arkells 3B and a changing guest and seven wines by the glass are served by friendly staff; background music and board games. Seats and tables under parasols and picnic-sets at the front overlook the picturesque village (which is famous for its spring daffodils). Disabled access but no loos. There are enjoyable surrounding walks.

 Cooked by the landlord, the pleasing food includes sandwiches, game rillettes with onion marmalade, smoked haddock, cheese and hollandaise gratin, butternut squash, red onion, goats cheese and walnut tart, venison stew with dauphinoise potatoes, stone bass with creamed leeks, spinach and mash, breaded pheasant with red cabbage slaw, organic pork chop with apple sauce and pancetta, sirloin steak with béarnaise sauce and fries, and puddings such as chocolate pot and bread and butter pudding with clotted cream ice-cream. *Benchmark main dish: beer-battered haddock and chips £12.50. Two-course evening meal £20.00.*

Arkells ~ Tenants Tom and Maya Gabbitas ~ Real ale ~ Open 11-11 ~ Bar food 12-2.30 (3 weekends), 6.30-9; not Sun or Mon evenings ~ Restaurant ~ Children welcome ~ Dogs welcome ~ Wi-fi ~ Live music (check website) *Recommended by Helene Grygar, Donald Allsopp, Susan and Callum Slade, Lorna and Jack Musgrave, R K Phillips, Heather and Richard Jones, Amy Ledbetter, Graeme and Sally Mendham*

EBRINGTON   SP1839   Map 4

Ebrington Arms

(01386) 593223 – www.theebringtonarms.co.uk

Off B4035 E of Chipping Campden or A429 N of Moreton-in-Marsh; GL55 6NH

Nice old pub in attractive village with own-brewed ales, thoughtful choice of food and seats in the garden; bedrooms

The three venerable oak trees after which this old stone pub was once named still stand outside by the village green. The character bar and dining room have beams, a log fire in a fine inglenook fireplace and a woodburning stove in a second fireplace (the ironwork is original) with armchairs beside it. Also, an airy bow-window seat, ladder-back and farmhouse chairs and cushioned settles on old flagstones or bare boards, and fresh flowers and church candles. Their three own-brewed Yubberton ales are Yubby Bitter, Yubby Goldie and the seasonal Yawnie Bitter on handpump alongside local guests such as North Cotswold Moreton Mild, Otter Bitter and Wye Valley Dorothy Goodbodys Wholesome Stout, good wines from a thoughtful list (with notes), nine gins, farm cider and winter mulled wine. Board games, bagatelle, shut the box and dominoes. An arched stone wall shelters seats and tables under parasols on the terrace and picnic-sets line the lawn. Well equipped, country-style bedrooms are very comfortable and breakfasts are good. As only three tables in the bar are for owners with dogs, it's best to book in advance. Hidcote (National Trust) and Kiftsgate Court

Gardens are both nearby. This is sister pub to the Killingworth Castle in Wootton (in Oxfordshire).

 Interesting food includes as much organic produce as possible: beef with tartare confit egg yolk, roasted garlic mayonnaise and thai shallots, confit trout with dill crème fraîche, roasted beetroot and crispy skin, leek and tarragon risotto, beer-battered haddock and chips, venison burger with toppings, onion rings and chips, duck breast with pommes anna and star anise purée, whole plaice with beurre noisette, sautéed potatoes and crispy capers, and puddings such as banana parfait with chocolate mousse and peanut brittle and honey pannacotta with rhubarb and granola. They also offer a two- and three-course weekday lunch. *Benchmark main dish: organic pork chop with butternut squash and thyme purée, potato rösti and cider and mustard sauce £25.00. Two-course evening meal £25.00.*

Free house ~ Licensees Claire and Jim Alexander ~ Real ale ~ Open 9am-11pm ~ Bar food 12-2, 6-9 (9.30 Fri); 12-3.30; 6-9.30 Sat; 12-3.30, 6-8.30 Sun ~ Restaurant ~ Children welcome ~ Dogs allowed in bar ~ Wi-fi ~ Folk night first Mon of the month ~ Bedrooms: /£130 *Recommended by Ian Herdman, Martin and Sue Neville, Mike and Mary Carter, Gordon and Margaret Ormondroyd*

FAIRFORD
Bull 🛏️
SP1501   Map 4

(01285) 712535 – www.thebullhotelfairford.co.uk
Market Place; GL7 4AA

Fine renovation of an old coaching inn with character bars and dining rooms and a thoughtful choice of good food and drink; bedrooms

From the outside, this handsome former coaching inn looks just as it has done for hundreds of years. Inside, though, all has changed. Original features blend cleverly with up-to-date touches that manage to hold on to the historic character. There are beams and timbering, bare stone walls and antique tables and dining chairs on top of rugs and wide floorboards – all mixed in with bold wallpaper, strong-coloured paintwork and bright scatter cushions. The room to the right of the entrance has vintage armchairs and a sofa in front of an open fire, and opposite are two bar rooms with chapel chairs and settles, seats in a bow window and a vast bull's head above another open fire. You'll find other rooms up small staircases and through open doorways until you reach the dining rooms – one clad with reclaimed boards lined with large skulls and seating that consists of long button-back wall banquettes and modern dining chairs. Arkells 3B, Hoperation IPA and Wiltshire Gold on handpump, several wines by the glass, a dozen gins and 13 malt whiskies; background music and board games. At the front are rustic tables and benches with more seats in a courtyard garden. Bedrooms are neat, comfortable and contemporary and breakfasts are well regarded. Disabled access. Do visit the church which has Britain's only set of intact medieval stained-glass windows. Sister pubs are the Five Alls in Filkins and Plough at Kelmscott (Oxfordshire).

Good, enjoyable food includes lunchtime sandwiches, chicken and duck liver pâté with onion chutney, venison carpaccio with parmesan and orange and juniper dressing, pizzas, wild mushroom risotto with wilted spinach, steak and kidney pie, fillet of sea bream with pea purée and salsa verde, chicken breast with sprout flowers, gnocchi and pancetta, flat-iron steak with pink peppercorn sauce, and puddings such as apple and pear crumble with vanilla ice-cream and white chocolate and raspberry cheesecake; they also offer breakfasts, morning coffee and afternoon tea to non-residents. *Benchmark main dish: braised blade of beef £16.50. Two-course evening meal £22.00.*

Arkells ~ Tenant Steve Cook ~ Real ale ~ Open 12-11 (midnight Sat); 12-10.30 Sun ~ Bar food 12-2.30, 6-9.30; 12-3, 6-8.30 Sun ~ Restaurant ~ Children welcome ~ Dogs allowed in bar and bedrooms ~ Wi-fi ~ Bedrooms: £75/£120 *Recommended by James and Sylvia Hewitt, Audrey and Paul Summers, Neil Allen, Alexander and Trish Gendall*

FOSSEBRIDGE   SP0711   Map 4

Fossebridge Inn ⌂

(01285) 720721 – www.innatfossebridge.co.uk

A429 Cirencester to Stow-on-the-Wold; GL54 3JS

Handsome stone building in large, riverside grounds with character bars, a thoughtful choice of food and drinks and friendly welcome; pretty bedrooms

This is a rather special place and our readers have been warmly enthusiastic about their recent visits. It's a lovely 17th-c former coaching inn with welcoming licensees at the helm and a cheerful mix of both locals and visitors. Stone arches divide the two original beamed bar rooms which have both a woodburning stove and a log fire, stripped-stone walls hung with copper implements and all sorts of nice old chairs, settles and cushioned wall and window seats around pale wooden tables on polished flagstones or bare boards. Butcombe Gold and Original, Clavell & Hind Coachman, Wadworths 6X and a beer named for the pub on handpump and 11 wines by the glass; background music and board games. The four acres of gardens include lawns running down to the River Coln, a huge lake and plenty of picnic-sets under parasols. Bedrooms are individually furnished in a country style with modern bathrooms – and breakfasts are highly rated. As well as a two-mile circular meander from the grounds you can walk up the River Coln valley in glorious countryside. Chedworth Roman Villa (National Trust) is not far away.

Good, enjoyable food includes breakfasts for non-residents (8.30-10am) and afternoon teas (3-5.30pm), plus sandwiches, prawn cocktail, honey-baked goats cheese salad with pine nuts, wild mushroom and basil tagliatelle with mascarpone cream sauce, sausages of the day with mash and red onion gravy, chicken curry with mango chutney and poppadums, sea bass with creamy white wine and parsley sauce, 10oz rib-eye steak with coleslaw and chips, and puddings such as double chocolate brownie and apple and blackberry pie and custard. *Benchmark main dish: old family recipe cottage pie plus jug of gravy £12.50. Two-course evening meal £21.00.*

Free house ~ Licensee Dee Ludlow ~ Real ale ~ Open 12-11 ~ Bar food 12-8 ~ Children welcome ~ Dogs welcome ~ Wi-fi ~ Bedrooms: £85/£145 *Recommended by Guy Vowles, James and Sylvia Hewitt, Sally Harrison, Patti and James Davidson, Sally and Lance Oldham*

GLOUCESTER   SO8318   Map 4

Café René ◀

(01452) 309340 – www.caferene.co.uk

Southgate Street; best to park in Blackfriars car park (Ladybellegate Street) and walk through passageway – pub entrance is just across road; GL1 1TP

Interestingly placed bar with fair value food all day, and good choice of drinks

Dating back to the 17th c and certainly different to many other places in our *Guide*, this has a subterranean feel, with black beams, dim lighting and no windows – plus stripped brick and timbering and an internal floodlit well with water trickling down into its depths. There's quite a choice of drinks: the long bar counter is made of dozens of big casks, and they keep four changing real ales tapped from the cask, such as Blue Monkey

Evolution, Farr Brew The Best Bitter, Wickwar Falling Star and Wychwood Hobgoblin, plus farm ciders and a good choice of wines by the glass (decoration consists mainly of great banks of empty wine bottles). Service remains friendly and efficient even when really pushed. One antique panelled high-backed settle joins the usual pub tables and wheelback chairs on carpet, and there's a sizeable dining area on the right. Well reproduced background music, a silenced games machine and big-screen TV (for rugby only). They have regular live music and hold a popular rhythm and blues festival at the end of July. There are plenty of picnic-sets under parasols out by the churchyard. To get here you walk down a flagstoned passageway beside the partly Norman church of St Mary de Crypt.

Some sort of food is served all day: lunchtime sandwiches and wraps, prawn cocktail, organic chicken liver pâté with cranberry sauce, tomato, cream cheese and basil linguine with garlic bread, chicken caesar salad, trio of sausages with wholegrain mustard mash and red onion gravy, whole rack of baby ribs in barbecue sauce, caribbean-style lamb with gungo pea rice, mango chutney and cucumber raita, chargrilled mixed grill, salmon fillet with lemon, prawn and caper butter, and puddings such as lemon tart and chocolate fudge cake. *Benchmark main dish: burger with toppings, home-made salsa and chips £9.50. Two-course evening meal £16.00.*

Free house ~ Licensee Paul Soden ~ Real ale ~ Open 11am-midnight (later Fri, Sat) ~ Bar food 12-9.30 ~ Restaurant ~ Wi-fi ~ Live music Weds and Fri evenings
Recommended by Julian Richardson, Mark Morgan, Trevor and Michele Street, Maddie Purvis, Daphne and Robert Staples

KILCOT

Kilcot Inn 🛏

SO6925 Map 4

(01989) 720707 – www.kilcotinn.com
2.3 miles from M50 junction 3; B4221 towards Newent; GL18 1NG

Attractively reworked small country inn, kind staff, enjoyable local food and drink; bedrooms

This is a nice place to stay in light, airy and comfortable bedrooms and our readers praise the breakfasts. The open-plan bar and dining areas have stripped beams, bare boards and dark flagstones, sunny bay-window seats, homely armchairs by one of the two warm woodburning stoves, tables with padded dining chairs and daily papers. Stools line the brick counter where the hard-working landlord and his staff serve Marstons EPA and Ringwood Razorback and Wye Valley Butty Bach on handpump, four draught ciders and perry (with more by the bottle), 20 malt whiskies, local wine and organic fruit juice; TV and maybe background music. The outside dining area has tables and chunky benches under thatched parasols next to a rose garden and there's also a children's play area; at the front are picnic-sets under cocktail-style parasols. There's a smart shed for bicycle storage.

They keep bees and grow herbs for their popular food which includes breakfasts (9-10.30am) and lunchtime sandwiches plus pork terrine with piccalilli, juniper-cured gravadlax with gin, watermelon and dill, spinach gnocchi with nasturtium pesto, baby vegetables and herbs, duck with whisky, black pudding and celeriac, pork belly with parsnip purée, fermented pears and jus, sea bream with wild garlic, turmeric and plum, braised lamb with roast onion, pancetta and kefir mash, and puddings such as pine pannacotta with orange and cardamon ice-cream and gingerbread with lemon and honey sorbet; they also offer a two- and three-course menu. *Benchmark main dish: beef brisket £16.95. Two-course evening meal £25.00.*

Free house ~ Licensee Mark Lawrence ~ Real ale ~ Open 11-11; 12-10 Sun; 12-5.30 Sun in winter ~ Bar food 12-2.30, 6-9; 12-3.30 Sun ~ Restaurant ~ Children welcome ~ Dogs allowed in bar ~ Wi-fi ~ Live music second Sat of month ~ Bedrooms: £85/£95

Recommended by S Holder, Len and Lilly Dowson, Bridget and Peter Gregson, Nicola and Holly Lyons, David and Charlotte Green, Frank and Marcia Pelling

LOWER SLAUGHTER
Slaughters Country Inn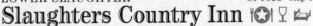
SP1622 Map 4

(01451) 822143 – www.theslaughtersinn.co.uk

Village signposted off A429 Bourton-on-the-Water to Stow-on-the-Wold; GL54 2HS

Comfortable streamside inn with enticing food, real ales, attractive dining bar and fine grounds; smart bedrooms

This is such a lovely setting right by the River Eye, and the handsome stone building also has spacious grounds with tables and chairs under parasols on terraces and lawns that sweep down to the water. The spreading bar area has several low-beamed linked rooms with well spaced tables on polished flagstones, a variety of seats from simple chairs to soft sofas and warm log fires. You'll also find mullioned windows, shelves of board games, a few carefully placed landscape pictures or stuffed fish and an air of understated refinement. Service is first class. Brakspears Bitter and Wychwood Hobgoblin on handpump, and a dozen good wines by the glass. The smart evening restaurant looks over the lawn and the sheep pasture beyond. Bedrooms are comfortable and stylish and make a good base for exploring the area; some are in the main house, some across the courtyard.

 Tempting food includes ham hock terrine with piccalilli purée, salmon and dill roulade with caviar and charred cucumber, risotto of sweet potato and kale, local sausages with crispy shallots and gravy, moules marinière, blade of beef with horseradish mash and parsnips, chicken supreme with mushrooms, quinoa and pancetta, chargrilled steak with house fries and a choice of sauce, and puddings such as chocolate and Horlicks mousse with vanilla ice-cream and clementine crème brûlée. *Benchmark main dish: beer-battered fish and chips £15.50. Two-course evening meal £23.00.*

Free house ~ Licensee Stuart Hodges ~ Real ale ~ Open 10am-11pm ~ Bar food 12-3, 6.30-9; afternoon tea 3-5.30 ~ Restaurant ~ Children welcome ~ Dogs allowed in bar and bedrooms ~ Wi-fi ~ Bedrooms: /£190 *Recommended by Nick and Meriel Cox, Richard Tilbrook, Susan and Tim Boyle, Sally Harrison, Brian and Sally Wakeham, Thomas Green*

MEYSEY HAMPTON
Masons Arms
SU1199 Map 4

(01285) 850164 – www.masonsarmsmeyseyhampton.com

Just off A417 Cirencester–Lechlade; High Street; GL7 5JT

Lovely old village pub, carefully renovated with old and new features blending well and enjoyable drinks and food; comfortable bedrooms

'This pub never disappoints' says one reader with enthusiasm – and many others agree. It's a beautifully refurbished 17th-c village inn and the bar has heavy old beams, an open fire, country paintings and a collection of clock faces on contemporary paintwork, a cushioned window seat and church chairs around scrubbed tables, and stools against the counter. The interconnected dining areas are furnished with more church chairs plus high-backed wooden ones and built-in cushioned seats on bare floorboards, modern artwork on Cotswold stone or painted walls, and a woodburning stove. Welcoming and helpful staff serve Arkells 3B and Wiltshire Gold on handpump, 15 gins and good wines by the glass; background music, darts and board games. There are seats outside on the village green. The spotless bedrooms are stylish, up to date and well appointed and overlook the village, farm or manor house. Partial disabled access.

From a quickly changing menu, the enterprising food includes sandwiches, wild mushroom and truffle risotto, plaice goujons with tartare sauce, sweet potato, aubergine and spinach curry, chicken, ham and leek pie, beer-battered fish and chips, honey and mustard glazed ham and eggs, beef casserole with horseradish mash, roast cod with white bean purée and gremolata, and puddings such as nougat parfait and mixed fruit crumble. *Benchmark main dish: burger with toppings and chips £12.00. Two-course evening meal £20.00.*

Arkells ~ Licensee Paul Fallows ~ Real ale ~ Open 7.15-3, 5-11; 12-11 Sat; 12-10 Sun ~ Bar food 12-2, 6-9; 12-8 Sun ~ Restaurant ~ Children welcome ~ Dogs allowed in bar and bedrooms ~ Wi-fi ~ Bedrooms: £95/£105 *Recommended by Sara Fulton, Roger Baker, Sandra and Miles Spencer, Alexander and Trish Cutter, Guy Vowles, Buster and Helena Hastings, Julie and Andrew Blanchett, Liz Bell*

NAILSWORTH
Weighbridge 🏅🍷

(01453) 832520 – www.weighbridgeinn.co.uk
B4014 towards Tetbury; GL6 9AL

Bustling pub with cosy old-fashioned bar rooms, a fine choice of drinks and food, friendly service and sheltered garden

As ever, we hear nothing but praise for the famous two-in-one pies here. The relaxed bar with its good choice of drinks and the warm welcome from helpful staff are cherries on top of the cake. Three cosily old-fashioned rooms have open fires, stripped-stone walls and antique settles, country chairs and window seats. The black-beamed ceiling of the lounge bar is thickly festooned with black ironware – sheep shears, gin traps, lamps and a large collection of keys, many from the old Longfords Mill opposite the pub. Upstairs is a raftered hayloft with an engaging mix of rustic tables. Wadworths 6X and guest beers such as Clavell & Hind Blunderbuss, Prescott Hill Climb and Uley Old Spot Prize Strong Ale on handpump, 18 wines (and champagne and prosecco) by the glass, farm cider, 12 malt whiskies and 20 gins. A sheltered landscaped garden at the back has picnic-sets under umbrellas. Good disabled access and facilities.

 The renowned two-in-one pies (also available for home baking) come in a divided bowl – one half contains the filling of your choice (perhaps steak, kidney and stout, salmon in cream sauce, or root vegetables with beans and pulses in tomato sauce) with a pastry topping, the other half with home-made cauliflower cheese (or broccoli mornay or root vegetables). Also, lunchtime paninis and baked potatoes, breaded brie wedges with cranberry sauce, pâté of the day, baked gnocchi in herby tomato sauce, home-cooked ham and eggs, stew with dumplings, fish pie, and puddings such as dark chocolate mousse and sticky toffee pudding. *Benchmark main dish: two-in-one pies £12.95. Two-course evening meal £19.00.*

Free house ~ Licensee Mary Parsons ~ Real ale ~ Open 12-10.30 (11 Fri, Sat); closes 10pm Mon-Thurs in winter ~ Bar food 12-8.30 (9 Fri, Sat) ~ Restaurant ~ Children welcome in upstairs dining room ~ Dogs welcome *Recommended by Tom and Ruth Rees, Julia and Fiona Barnes, Lauren and Dan Frazer, Dr and Mrs A K Clarke, Sandra Morgan, Colin and Daniel Gibbs, Jim and Sue James*

NEWLAND
Ostrich 🏅🍷🍺

(01594) 833260 – www.theostrichinn.com
Off B4228 in Coleford; or can be reached from the A466 in Redbrook, by turn-off at the England–Wales border – keep bearing right; GL16 8NP

Super range of beers in welcoming country pub, with spacious bar, open fire and good interesting food

Whether you're a regular or a customer passing through, you'll receive a genuine welcome from the charming landlady of this gently civilised pub. It's mostly 16th-c and the low-ceilinged bar is spacious but cosily traditional, with a chatty, relaxed atmosphere, a roaring log fire, creaky floors, window shutters, candles in bottles on the tables, miners' lamps on uneven walls, and comfortable furnishings that include cushioned window seats, wall settles and rod-backed country kitchen chairs. The fine choice of eight real ales on handpump includes Adnams Southwold, Cotswold Lion Best in Show, Fat Cat Wild Cat, Otter Bitter, RCH Pitchfork, Timothy Taylors Landlord and Wye Valley Butty Bach and HPA; also, several wines by the glass, a couple of farm ciders and a good range of soft drinks. Newspapers to read, perhaps quiet background jazz and board games. The walled garden has seats and tables, with more out in front. The church opposite, known as the Cathedral of the Forest for its unusual size, is worth a visit.

 Pleasing food includes ham hock terrine with piccalilli, creamy crab claw with lemon risotto, three-cheese tart with sun-dried tomatoes and basil, wild boar sausages with dauphinoise potatoes and red wine gravy, beef in ale pie, pork ribs in a tangy sauce with garlic bread, corn-fed chicken with roasted red pepper and basil risotto in white wine and cream, trout fillet with lobster and lime cream sauce on linguine, lamb wellington with fennel duxelles and madeira sauce, and puddings. *Benchmark main dish: salmon and spinach fishcakes with parsley sauce £13.50. Two-course evening meal £20.00.*

Free house ~ Licensee Kathryn Horton ~ Real ale ~ Open 12-3, 6.30 (6 Sat)-11; 12-4, 6.30-10.30 Sun ~ Bar food 12-2.30, 6.30 (6 Sat)-9.30 ~ Restaurant ~ Children welcome ~ Dogs allowed in bar *Recommended by Clive and Fran Dutson, Andrew and Michele Revell, David and Leone Lawson, Nik and Gloria Clarke, Louise and Oliver Redman, Jill and Hugh Bennett*

NORTHLEACH
SP1114 Map 4

Wheatsheaf 🟊 ♀ 🛏

(01451) 860244 – www.cotswoldswheatsheaf.com
West End; the inn is on your left as you come in following the sign off A429, just SW of the junction with A40; GL54 3EZ

Attractive stone inn with contemporary food, real ales and a relaxed atmosphere; stylish bedrooms

After strolling around this lovely little market town, do come here as it's open all day. The airy, big-windowed linked rooms have three open fires, high ceilings and antique and contemporary artwork. There's an attractive mix of dining chairs, big leather button-back settles and stools around wooden tables, with flagstones in the central bar and wooden floors laid with turkish rugs in the dining rooms. Butcombe Bitter, Stroud Budding and a guest such as Church Farm Pale Ale on handpump, a dozen wines by the glass from a fantastic list of around 300 and local cider; background music and TV. The pretty back garden has plenty of seats. Bedrooms are comfortable and individually styled and breakfasts are much enjoyed. Dogs are genuinely welcomed and they even keep a jar of pigs' ears behind the bar especially for them.

 Food is good and offered all day from breakfast (8-10am) plus devilled kidneys on sourdough toast, gin-cured chalk stream trout with avocado, cucumber and salmon caviar, roast squash risotto with crispy taleggio with cavolo nero and chestnuts, confit pork belly with celeriac pureé, haggis and black pudding, lemon sole with samphire, capers and beurre noisette, calves liver with bacon, sage and onions, crab linguine with fennel and chilli butter, and puddings such as crème brûlée and sticky date pudding with salted caramel sauce. *Benchmark main dish: dry-aged steaks (minimum 30 days) with french fries £16.50. Two-course evening meal £22.00.*

Free house ~ Licensee Chris Connor ~ Real ale ~ Open 8am-11pm ~ Bar food 12-3, 6-9.30; 12-3.45, 6-9 Sun ~ Restaurant ~ Children welcome ~ Dogs welcome ~ Wi-fi ~ Bedrooms: /£140 *Recommended by Mark Mullins, Guy Vowles, Cliff and Monica Swan, Simon Day, Christine and Tony Garrett, James and Sylvia Hewitt*

 OLDBURY-ON-SEVERN ST6092 Map 2

Anchor ♀ 🍺 £

(01454) 413331 – www.anchorinn-oldbury.co.uk

Village signposted from B4061; BS35 1QA

Friendly country pub with tasty bar food, a thoughtful range of drinks and a pretty garden with hanging baskets

They keep a fine choice of drinks here, all served by hard-working, attentive staff. There might be Bass, Butcombe Bitter and St Austell Tribute on handpump, 11 wines by the glass, three farm ciders, 30 gins and 60 malt whiskies with helpful tasting notes. A neat lounge has black beams and stonework, cushioned window seats and a range of other wooden chairs, gate-leg tables, oil paintings of local scenes and a big log fire. The Village Bar has old and farming photographs on the walls, and there's a contemporary dining room towards the back of the building. In summer, the attractive garden is a real bonus with pretty hanging baskets and window boxes, and seats beneath parasols or trees; pétanque. You can walk from the pub to the River Severn and then along numerous footpaths and bridleways. There's wheelchair access to the dining room and a disabled lavatory. Nearby St Arilda's Church is interesting, set on an odd little knoll.

Highly thought-of food includes ciabattas, crayfish mayonnaise with lemon and capers, grilled halloumi and pesto with marinated artichokes, rocket and basil, sharing platters, goats cheese and red onion marmalade filo tart, burger with toppings, slaw and fries, ham and free-range eggs, venison and pheasant sausages with mash and red wine jus, chicken breast with mushroom and brandy sauce with dauphinoise potatoes, kashmiri lamb curry, minute steak with chilli butter and fries, and puddings such as chocolate brownie with chocolate sauce and salted caramel ice-cream and crème caramel. *Benchmark main dish: fish pie £12.95. Two-course evening meal £18.00.*

Free house ~ Licensees Michael Dowdeswell and Mark Sorrell ~ Real ale ~ Open 11.30-2.30, 6-10.30; 11.30-11 Sat; 12-10 Sun ~ Bar food 12-2 (2.30 Sat), 6-9; 12-3, 6-8 Sun ~ Restaurant ~ Children welcome but no under-12s in bar or lounge ~ Dogs allowed in bar ~ Bedrooms: £60/£85 *Recommended by Ian Wilson, Chris and Angela Buckell, Chloe and Michael Swettenham, Margaret McDonald, Miranda and Jeff Davidson, Donald Allsopp*

 PAXFORD SP1837 Map 4

Churchill Arms ⭐ ♀ 🛏

(01386) 593159 – www.churchillarms.co

B4479, SE of Chipping Campden; GL55 6XH

Super food and drinks in golden-stone inn, attractive furnishings and seats outside; well equipped bedrooms

To make the most of this 17th-c village dining pub, you should enjoy the first rate food then stay overnight in the stylish boutique bedrooms; breakfasts are good and hearty. The attractively updated, open-plan interior has painted beams and panelling, flagstone and wooden floors, a woodburner in an inglenook fireplace, cushioned settles and window seats and a medley of cushioned wooden dining chairs around pale tables, and big country photographs. Friendly, efficient staff serve Purity Mad Goose and Pure UBU and Winston (named for them from North Cotswold) on handpump and several wines from a good list. There are picnic-sets on a small front area and more seats in the gravelled back courtyard. Nice surrounding walks.

High class food from a sensibly short menu and cooked by the chef-owner includes seared tuna with avocado and soy dressing, ham hock and chicken terrine with piccalilli, asparagus with herb gnocchi, poached egg and wild garlic mayonnaise, sea trout with ton kha gai, pak choi and clams, calves liver with confit bacon, cider onions, mustard dressing and mash, beef wellington with truffle mash (for two people), and puddings such as dark chocolate and salted caramel tart with mascarpone and crème caramel with blackberries. *Benchmark main dish: pork T-bone with lyonnaise potatoes, crispy onions, caramelised apple and pork jus £17.95. Two-course evening meal £24.00.*

Enterprise ~ Tenant Nick Deverell-Smith ~ Real ale ~ Open 12-11 ~ Bar food 12-3, 6-9; 12-8 Sun ~ Restaurant ~ Children welcome ~ Dogs allowed in bar ~ Wi-fi ~ Bedrooms: /£120
Recommended by Martin Day, Andrew and Nicky Churcher, Patrick and Martine Lawson, Matilda and Gerald Thoms

SELSLEY

SO8303   Map 4

Bell 🌟 🍽 ♀

(01453) 753801 – www.thebellinnselsley.com
Bell Lane; GL5 5JY

First rate food and a good drinks choice in golden-stone inn with friendly service and seats overlooking valley

If you're after a weekend break, come to this attractively updated 16th-c village pub with its comfortable couple of bedrooms and fine walks along the Cotswold Way and on Selsley Common. Inside, three interconnected rooms have beams, a woodburning stove and an open fire and all manner of chairs and tables on wood-strip floors. Stroud Budding, Wickwar BOB and a beer named for the pub on handpump, several wines by the glass including champagne, 18 malt whiskies and 100 gins – and service is friendly and helpful. The pub dog is called Bacchus. There's a garden room dining extension with retractable glass doors on to the terrace where picnic-sets enjoy spreading valley views.

The landlord cooks the well presented food, which includes lunchtime sandwiches, pressed ham hock terrine with chicken liver parfait and piccalilli, peppered venison carpaccio with smoked mayonnaise, glazed leek, gruyère and tarragon fregola with crispy shallots, salmon with samphire, brown shrimps in cherry tomato butter sauce, free-range chicken with celeriac, potato and mustard croquette, charred leek and tarragon jus, loin of local roe deer with mushroom purée, roasted tomatoes and wild garlic, and puddings such as white chocolate mousse with blood orange and honeycomb and peanut butter parfait with caramelised bananas, banana bread and toffee. *Benchmark main dish: beer-battered fish and chips £14.00. Two-course evening meal £23.00.*

Free house ~ Licensees Mark Payne and Sarah Natts ~ Real ale ~ Open 11-11; 11-8 Sun; 11-3, 5-11 Mon-Thurs in winter; closed Sun evening ~ Bar food 12-2.30, 6-9; 12-3.30 Sun ~ Restaurant ~ Children welcome ~ Dogs welcome ~ Wi-fi ~ Bedrooms: £90/£95 *Recommended by Tom and Ruth Rees, David and Charlotte Green, Charles Welch, Susan and Tim Boyle, John and Abigail Prescott, Adam Jones*

SHEEPSCOMBE

SO8910 Map 4

Butchers Arms £

(01452) 812113 – www.butchers-arms.co.uk

Village signed off B4070 NE of Stroud; or A46 N of Painswick (but narrow lanes); GL6 7RH

Cheerful pub with open fire and woodburner, plenty to look at, several real ales and enjoyable food; fine views

Our readers enjoy their visits here very much, praising all aspects of the place. The bar has farmhouse chairs and stools around scrubbed tables, two big bay windows with cushioned seats, low beams clad with horsebrasses, and flooring that's half parquet and half old quarry tiles. Also, delft shelves lined with china, brass and copper cups, lamps and blow torches (there's even a pitchfork) and walls decorated with hunting prints and photos of the village and surrounding area. Leading off here is a high-ceilinged room with exposed-stone walls hung with maps of local walks (there are many) and wheelback and mate's chairs around tables on bare boards. A cosy snug area has historic photos of the village and the area and a log-effect gas fire. Prescott Hill Climb, Quantock QPA and St Austell Proper Job on handpump, 12 wines by the glass and farm ciders; daily papers. The view over the lovely steep beechwood valley is terrific, and the seats outside make the most of it. Apparently, this area was once a royal hunting ground for King Henry VIII.

 Popular food includes sandwiches, deep-fried, breaded whitebait with tartare sauce, chicken liver and port pâté with spiced plum chutney, sharing platters, mediterranean vegetable gratin with feta, pork, apple and sage sausages with grain mustard mash and onion gravy, cod, salmon and dill fishcakes with lemon mayonnaise, lambs liver and bacon, slow-cooked pork belly with celeriac mash, roasted carrots and apple and rosemary jus, and puddings. *Benchmark main dish: burger with toppings, coleslaw and chips £12.00. Two-course evening meal £19.00.*

Free house ~ Licensees Mark and Sharon Tallents ~ Real ale ~ Open 11.30-3, 6.30-11; 11.30-11 Sat; 12-10 Sun ~ Bar food 12-2.30, 6.30-9.30; 12-9.30 Sat; 12-6 Sun ~ Restaurant ~ Children welcome ~ Dogs allowed in bar ~ Wi-fi *Recommended by Richard Tilbrook, Dr and Mrs A K Clarke, Guy Vowles, Mike and Sarah Abbot, Bridget and Peter Gregson, Amy and Luke Buchanan*

STOW-ON-THE-WOLD

SP1925 Map 4

Porch House 🏨 ⭐ 🍷 🛏

(01451) 870048 – www.porch-house.co.uk

Digbeth Street; GL54 1BN

Fine old character inn with carefully refurbished bars and dining areas, and imaginative food; comfortable bedrooms

Although mainly 17th-c, some striking features and parts of great antiquity here include thousand-year-old timbers (there was some sort of inn on the site in 947). The bar areas have beams (some hop-draped), big flagstones or bare floorboards, exposed stone walls and open fireplaces; background music and board games. Also, all sorts of cushioned wooden and upholstered chairs, little stools and settles with scatter cushions around myriad tables, church candles and lanterns, books on shelves, stone bottles on windowsills and a woodburning stove. The cosy snug is similarly furnished but also has sofas and armchairs. A beer named for the pub (from Brakspears) plus Brakspears Bitter and a couple of guests on handpump and good wines by the glass and ten gins. There's a dining room with upholstered, high-backed chairs (some with striking blue cushions), and also a conservatory. A raised terrace has rattan chairs and cushioned wall benches around rustic tables intermingled with more contemporary seats. Bedrooms are individually designed and stylish and breakfasts particularly good. This is a lovely small town to explore.

Carefully crafted food includes ham hock and pea terrine with confit pig fritter, grape mustard mayonnaise and pickled vegetables, juniper-cured smoked salmon with fennel seed, grapefruit and squid ink tapioca crisp, goats cheese and red pepper ravioli with rocket and lemon pesto, rare-breed burger with toppings and triple-cooked chips, smoked haddock, chive and sweet potato fishcakes with french-style peas, lardons and hollandaise, chicken kiev ballotine with parmentier potatoes and tomato and thyme dressing, and puddings such as treacle tart with raspberry compote and milk ice-cream and vanilla crème brûlée. *Benchmark main dish: parma ham-wrapped monkfish with ratte potatoes and chive vinaigrette £17.95. Two-course evening meal £22.00.*

Free house ~ Licensee Nicky Dedra ~ Real ale ~ Open 8am-11pm (10.30pm Sun) ~ Bar food 12-3, 6-9.30; 12-8.30 Sun ~ Restaurant ~ Children welcome ~ Dogs allowed in bar and bedrooms ~ Wi-fi ~ Bedrooms: /£99 *Recommended by Helene Grygar, Mike and Mary Carter, Abigail Slater, John and Lorna Chew, Frank Price, Simon Collett-Jones, Brian and Susan Wylie, Gerry and Pam Pollard, Andy and Louise Ramwell*

TETBURY
ST8494 Map 4

Gumstool 🍴 ♀ 🛏

(01666) 890391 – www.calcotmanor.co.uk
Part of Calcot Manor Hotel; A4135 W of town, just E of junction with A46; GL8 8YJ

Civilised bar with relaxed atmosphere, super choice of drinks and enjoyable food; bedrooms

With a great deal of civilised comfort and style, this is a well run bar-brasserie attached to the very smart Calcot Manor Hotel. The thoughtfully divided, stylish layout gives your table the feeling of having a snug area more or less to itself, without losing the friendly atmosphere of plenty going on around you. There are flagstones, elegant wooden dining chairs and tables, well chosen pictures and drawings and wooden 'stag's head and antlers' on mushroom-coloured walls, leather tub armchairs and stools and a neat row of copper cooking pans above the blazing log fire. From the long counter lined with modern chairs, they keep Butcombe Bitter and Wickwar BOB on handpump, two dozen interesting wines by the glass and several malt whiskies; background music. The slightly sunken front courtyard has a few picnic-sets. Westonbirt Arboretum is not far away.

Exceptional food includes salt and pepper calamari with sweet chilli mayonnaise, twice-baked cheddar cheese soufflé, butternut squash and sage risotto with truffle, pork and sage sausages with mash, crispy shallots and onion gravy, chicken supreme with pancetta, dauphinoise potatoes and wild mushrooms, lamb shank shepherd's pie, sea bream with samphire, roast salsify and tarragon and mustard cream, and puddings such as raspberry bakewell tart and bread and butter pudding with toffee sauce and vanilla ice-cream. *Benchmark main dish: pork belly with mustard mash and roast apple £18.00. Two-course evening meal £25.00.*

Free house ~ Licensees Paul Sadler and Richard Ball ~ Real ale ~ Open 12-11 ~ Bar food 12-2 (2.30 Sat), 6-9.30; 12-4, 6-9 Sun ~ Children welcome ~ Wi-fi ~ Bedrooms: £194/£219 *Recommended by Stuart and Natalie Granville, Moira and Jon Weller, Bernard Stradling, Diana and Richard Gibbs, Patrick and Martine Lawson, Matilda and Gerald Thoms*

Pubs close to motorway junctions are listed at the back of the book.

WESTON SUBEDGE

SP1241   Map 4

Seagrave Arms ♀ ⇔

(01386) 840192 – www.seagravearms.com

B4632; GL55 6QH

Golden-stone inn with friendly staff and enjoyable food; contemporary bedrooms

The Cotswold Way is nearby and as many of the well equipped, modern bedrooms (either in the main house or in the converted stables) allow dogs, this fine old place makes a good weekend base; breakfasts are good and hearty. There's plenty of character here, especially in the cosy little bar: ancient flagstones, half-panelled walls, an open fire, padded window seats and a chatty, informal atmosphere. 14 wines (plus prosecco and champagne) by the glass, served by helpful, friendly staff; background music, TV and board games. The two dining rooms have an appealing mix of wooden chairs and tables on floorboards. Outside, there are wicker chairs and tables on neat gravel at the front of the building and more seats in the back garden.

 Contemporary food includes lunchtime sandwiches, sea bass with charred fennel and chervil, caramelised onion soufflé with gruyère sauce, butternut squash risotto with puffed rice, goats curd and smoked almonds, honey-glazed ham and duck egg, beer-braised beef cheek with salt-baked celeriac, onion and an oyster, seaweed-poached cod with cauliflower, sea herbs, curry and mussels, and 30-day aged local sirloin with café de paris butter and triple-cooked chips, and puddings such as salted caramel parfait with bitter chocolate, beer caramel and parsnip, and muscovado cheesecake with forced rhubarb, puff pastry and ginger. *Benchmark main dish: hay-smoked hogget, turnips, ewes milk, potato terrine and monks beard £22.00. Two-course evening meal £25.00.*

Free house ~ Licensee Simon Cheese ~ Real ale ~ Open 12-11; 12-9 Sun ~ Bar food 12-2.30, 6-9; 12-8 Sun ~ Restaurant ~ Children welcome ~ Dogs allowed in bar and bedrooms ~ Wi-fi ~ Bedrooms: /£150 *Recommended by Lee and Jill Stafford, Jennifer and Nicholas Thompson, Jim and Sue James, Elizabeth and Peter May, Jeff Davies*

WINCHCOMBE

SP0228   Map 4

Lion ★◎ ♀ ⇔

(01242) 603300 – www.thelionwinchcombe.co.uk

North Street; GL54 5PS

Historic inn in fine town with drinking and dining spaces in character rooms, and seats on pretty terraces; warm, TV-free bedrooms

It's all very stylish here with plenty of customers, rustic-chic furnishings and a friendly, bustling atmosphere. The bar and dining areas have exposed golden-stone walls or portraits and gilt-edged mirrors on pale paintwork, armchairs, scatter cushions on wall seats, stools and elegant wooden dining chairs around mixed tables on flagstones, jugs of fresh flowers and plenty of big stubby candles. Marstons EPA, Prescott Hill Climb, Wye Valley Butty Bach and a changing guest on handpump, ten good wines by the glass, 20 gins and ten malt whiskies served by smiling, courteous staff; daily papers, board games, TV and background music. Wood and metal seats and tables sit on various terraced areas among shrubs and climbers and there are more seats on grass. Bedrooms are individually decorated in a country style; two have their own staircases and one is in a converted hayloft. Sudeley Castle is within walking distance and Cheltenham Racecourse is nearby.

◎ Interesting food includes lunchtime sandwiches, potted duck and ham rillettes with gherkins, cured mackerel with yuzu gel, compressed cucumbers and fennel, vegetable gnocchi with herb pesto and parmesan, pie of the day, venison sausages with colcannon mash and onion gravy, slow-cooked sticky pork belly with pigs head fritter, carrot and kohlrabi, cod loin with mussels, potato chowder and sea vegetables, and puddings such as chocolate tart with candied walnuts and pear sorbet and apple tarte tatin and muscovado ice-cream. *Benchmark main dish: Torbay sole with seaweed butter, brown shrimps and ratte potatoes £22.00. Two-course evening meal £25.00.*

Free house ~ Licensee Luke Buckle ~ Real ale ~ Open 8.30am-11pm ~ Bar food 12-3, 6-9 ~ Restaurant ~ Children welcome ~ Dogs allowed in bar and bedrooms ~ Wi-fi ~ Bedrooms: /£135 *Recommended by Richard Tilbrook, Joe and Belinda Smart, Liz and Martin Eldon, Jill and Dick Archer*

Also Worth a Visit in Gloucestershire

Besides the fully inspected pubs, you might like to try these pubs that have been recommended to us and described by readers. Do tell us what you think of them: feedback@goodguides.com

ALDSWORTH   SP1510
Sherborne Arms   (01451) 844346
B4425 Burford–Cirencester; GL54 3RB
Rural pub (former 17th-c stone farmhouse) set down from the road and run by same family since 1984; enjoyable good value home-made food (can offer smaller helpings on some dishes), two or three changing ales and proper cider, friendly service, beams, stripped stone and log fire, smallish bar and big dining area, conservatory, games/function room; background music, film night first Mon of month; children and dogs welcome, disabled access, pleasant front garden with smokers' shelter, closed Sun evening, Mon (except bank holidays). *(Maria and Henry Lazonby)*

AMBERLEY   SO8401
Amberley Inn   (01453) 872565
Steeply off A46 Stroud–Nailsworth – gentler approach from N Nailsworth; GL5 5AF Popular well located old stone inn with beautiful views and good local walks; two comfortable bars, snug and a more formal restaurant, well kept Stroud ales, nice wines and enjoyable locally sourced food from bar snacks up (special diets catered for), friendly helpful staff; children and dogs (in bar) welcome, side terrace and back garden, 11 bedrooms. *(Anne Taylor)*

AMBERLEY   SO8401
Black Horse   (01453) 872556
Off A46 Stroud–Nailsworth to Amberley; left after Amberley Inn, left at war memorial; Littleworth; best to park by war memorial and walk down; GL5 5AL Two-bar pub with spectacular valley views from small conservatory and terraced garden; mix of pine furniture on wood and slate floors, exposed stone walls, modern artwork and two woodburners, up to five real ales, Weston's cider and good range of whiskies and gins, enjoyable fairly traditional food (not Sun evening) at reasonable prices including Fri evening deals, nice staff; children, walkers and dogs welcome, wheelchair access (highish step by gate), outside gents', picnic-sets on front grass, more in split-level back garden, parking can be tricky, open all day (till 9pm Sun). *(Daniel King)*

AMPNEY CRUCIS   SP0701
Crown of Crucis   (01285) 851806
A417 E of Cirencester; GL7 5RS Comfortably modernised roadside inn with spacious split-level bar, beams and log fires, good choice of enjoyable food including competitively priced dish of the day (weekday lunchtimes), Sharps Doom Bar, a guest beer and decent choice of wines, friendly helpful service; children and dogs welcome, disabled facilities, tables out by Ampney Brook with wooden bridge over to cricket pitch, handy for Palladian Way walkers, quiet courtyard bedrooms, good breakfast, open (and food) all day. *(Dr A J and Mrs B A Tompsett)*

ANDOVERSFORD   SP0219
Royal Oak   (01242) 821426
Signed just off A40; Gloucester Road; GL54 4HR Cosy 17th-c beamed village pub, popular locally with lots of stripped stone, galleried raised dining room beyond big central open fire, well kept ales including Otter and over a dozen wines by the glass, good sensibly priced food from sandwiches and various burgers up, friendly welcoming staff; games end with pool and darts; children and dogs welcome, tables on back terrace, open all day. *(Tim Senn)*

APPERLEY   SO8627
Farmers Arms   (01452) 780886
Lower Apperley (B4213); GL19 4DR Popular extended country pub again under new management; beams, big open fire and spacious split-level dining area, Wadworths ales, several wines by the glass and good home-made food, friendly helpful staff;

children and dogs welcome, picnic-sets on terrace and in garden with nice rural views, own chickens and pigs, open all day. *(Theocsbrian, Katharine Cowherd)*

ARLINGHAM   SO7110
Red Lion (01452) 740700
High Street; GL2 7JH Old village corner pub owned by the local community; good food from lunchtime sandwiches and pub favourites up, Uley Bitter and guests, friendly staff, updated interior with wood and carpeted floors, some beams and two woodburners; children and dogs welcome, picnic-sets out by the road, good circular walks (not far from the River Severn), closed Mon lunchtime, otherwise open all day, food all day Sat, till 6pm Sun, not Mon. *(Liz and Martin Eldon)*

ASHLEWORTH QUAY   SO8125
Boat (01452) 700272
Ashleworth signposted off A417 N of Gloucester; quay signed from village; GL19 4HZ Tiny unpretentious old pub in lovely spot on the banks of the Severn; front parlour with mats on flagstones, built-in settle by scrubbed deal table, elderly chairs next to old-fashioned kitchen range, cribbage and dominoes, back quarry-tiled dining room with fireplace and a cosy snug, up to ten mostly local ales and great range of ciders, simple food such as basket meals and burgers; live music and beer/cider festivals; children, dogs and muddy boots welcome, tricky for wheelchairs (friendly staff will help), sunny crazy-paved front courtyard, more seats to the side and on grass by river, moorings, near interesting 15th-c tithe barn (NT), open all day in summer apart from Mon lunchtime (all day Fri-Sun, closed Mon in winter). *(Daniel King)*

AUST   ST5788
Boars Head (01454) 632278
0.5 miles from M48 junction 1, off Avonmouth Road; BS35 4AX Cream-painted 17th-c village pub under new management; Marstons-related ales, decent wines and well liked food, linked rooms and alcoves, beams, some stripped stone, flagstones and big fireplaces; children and dogs (in bar) welcome, wheelchair access, attractive sheltered garden with covered area for smokers, convenient for the 'old' Severn bridge. *(Chris and Angela Buckell)*

AVENING   ST8898
Bell (01453) 836422
High Street; GL8 8NF Welcoming whitewashed country pub with proper locals' bar and separate dining area, well kept ales

including Timothy Taylors and Wickwar, good authentic indian food (takeaways available); quiz first Sat of month, sports TV; children, walkers and dogs welcome, a few picnic-sets out at front, open all day weekends, from 5.30pm other days, no food Mon. *(Jon Neighbour)*

AVENING   ST8897
Queen Matilda (01453) 350305
B4014 Tetbury–Nailsworth; GL8 8NT Welcoming traditional stone-built village pub; enjoyable fairly pubby food cooked by landlord-chef including blackboard specials, some authentic thai curries and popular Sun roasts, three changing ales, good range of gins and decent wines, helpful friendly service, wood floors, exposed stonework, open fire and woodburner; quiz last Thurs of month; children and dogs welcome, a few picnic-sets out at front, more in grassy back garden, three comfortable barn-conversion bedrooms, good breakfast, closed Sun evening, Mon and lunchtimes (except Sun). *(Jon Neighbour)*

AYLBURTON   SO6101
Cross (01594) 842823
High Street; GL15 6DE Popular village pub under new management; enjoyable fair-priced traditional food, ales such as Butcombe and several wines by the glass, friendly helpful staff, open-plan split-level flagstoned bar, beams, modern furniture alongside high-backed settles, woodburners in large stone fireplaces, high-raftered dining room; children and dogs welcome, wheelchair access from car park, pleasant garden with play area, open all day Fri-Sun. *(Liz and Martin Eldon)*

BIBURY   SP1006
★Catherine Wheel (01285) 740250
Arlington; B4425 NE of Cirencester; GL7 5ND Attractive old dining pub in beautiful Cotswold village; enjoyable freshly made food (best to book weekends) from sandwiches and pizzas up including good local trout, well kept Hook Norton Hooky and a couple of guests, Weston's cider, cheerful attentive young staff, open-plan main bar and smaller back rooms, low beams, stripped stone and log fires, raftered dining room; children and dogs welcome, picnic-sets in front and in good-sized garden, handy for country and riverside walks, four bedrooms in separate building, open (and some food) all day. *(Guy Vowles)*

BISHOP'S NORTON   SO8425
Red Lion (01452) 730935
Wainlode Lane; GL2 9LW Isolated red-brick pub on picturesque bend of the

---

Cribbage is a card game using a block of wood with holes for matchsticks or special pins to score with; regulars in cribbage pubs are usually happy to teach strangers how to play.

River Severn (prone to flooding); ales such as Butcombe and Wye Valley, proper cider and decent range of wines, gins and whiskies, enjoyable food (all day Sat, not Sun evening) from sandwiches and sharing boards up; bar to the left of entrance, two snugs to the right, stripped-wood floors, blue/grey dados and woodburners in brick fireplaces, pubby furniture including pews, old photos and agricultural posters; background music (turned down/off on request), TV, free wi-fi; children welcome, wheelchair access using portable ramp (friendly staff will help), picnic-sets on cobbled frontage, riverside garden across narrow road, adjacent campsite, good walks, open all day Fri and Sat, till 9pm Sun. *(Martin and Joanne Sharp)*

BLAISDON   SO7016
Red Hart (01452) 830477
Village signposted off A4136 just SW of junction with A40 W of Gloucester; OS Sheet 162 map reference 703169; GL17 0AH Bustling village pub with plenty to look at in flagstoned main bar and attractive carpeted restaurant: woodworking and farming tools on magnolia walls and hanging from beams, old photographs of prize farm stock, a framed inventory of the pub in 1903 and lots of books, pot plants and some interesting prints, candles on traditional tables, cushioned wall and window seats, well kept ales including Otter, real cider and ten wines by the glass, popular food from sandwiches and traditional choices up; background music, board games, free wi-fi; children welcome (family dining part), dogs in bar, wheelchair access, picnic-sets on terrace and in garden with play area, pretty summer window boxes, good surrounding walks, little church nearby worth a visit. *(Dr A J and Mrs B A Tompsett, Wendi Johns, Clive and Fran Dutson)*

BLOCKLEY   SP1635
Great Western Arms
(01386) 700362 *Station Road (B4479); GL56 9DT* Simple little beamed pub under new management; well kept Hook Norton ales, decent wines by the glass and good home-made food from varied menu, friendly efficient service, comfortable bar where dogs allowed, dining room; children welcome, paved terrace with lovely valley view, attractive village, open (and food) all day. *(Maria Birch, Martin Day)*

BRIMPSFIELD   SO9413
★ **Golden Heart** (01242) 870261
Nettleton Bottom (not shown on road maps, so instead we list the pub under the name of the nearby village); on A417 N of the Brimpsfield turning northbound; GL4 8LA Traditional old roadside inn with low-ceilinged bar divided into five cosy areas; log fire in huge inglenook, exposed stone walls and wood panelling, well worn built-in settles and other old-fashioned furnishings, brass items, typewriters and banknotes, parlour on right with decorative fireplace leading into further room, well kept Brakspears with guests such as Jennings, Stroud and Wychwood, several wines by the glass, popular sensibly priced food from extensive blackboard menu including several vegetarian/vegan options, friendly efficient staff; children and dogs welcome, seats and tables on suntrap terrace with pleasant valley views, nearby walks, open all day. *(Richard Tilbrook)*

BROAD CAMPDEN   SP1537
★ **Bakers Arms** (01386) 840515
Village signed from B4081 in Chipping Campden; GL55 6UR Beamed 17th-c stone pub in delightful Cotswold village; tiny character bar with stripped-stone walls and inglenook woodburner, half a dozen well kept ales such as North Cotswold, Stanway, Wickwar and Wye Valley, simply furnished dining room serving popular pubby food (not Sun evening, Mon) plus blackboard specials; folk night last Weds of month, darts and board games; children (away from bar) and dogs (in bar) welcome, picnic-sets on terraces and in back garden, good nearby walks, open all day weekends, closed Mon lunchtime. *(Martin Day)*

BROADWELL   SP2027
Fox (01451) 870909
Off A429, 2 miles N of Stow-on-the-Wold; GL56 0UF Atmospheric golden-stone pub set above broad village green; traditional furnishings in beamed bar with flagstones, stripped-stone walls and log fire, well kept/priced Donnington BB and SBA, good selection of wines and much enjoyed home-cooked food from shortish reasonably priced menu, friendly attentive staff, opened-up dining area; background music, darts and dominoes; children and dogs (in bar) welcome, picnic-sets on gravel in sizeable back garden, aunt sally, paddock for camping (ring for details), open all day weekends, no food Sun evening. *(Asad Noorani, Alun and Jennifer Evans)*

BROCKWEIR   SO5301
Brockweir Inn (01291) 689548
Signed just off A466 Chepstow–Monmouth; NP16 7NG Welcoming unpretentious country local set just back from the River Wye; beams and stripped stonework, quarry tiles, sturdy settles and woodburner, nice snug with parquet floor and open fire, up to four well kept local ales, three ciders and enjoyable home-cooked food at reasonable prices, small back dining area and room upstairs 'Devil's Pulpit' (games and books); occasional live music and quiz nights; children and dogs welcome, little walled garden with clay oven, good walks, open till 6pm Sun, closed Mon and lunchtime Tues. *(Charles and Maddie Bishop)*

BUSSAGE SO8804
Ram (01453) 883163
At Eastcombe, take The Ridgeway and first right The Ridge; pub is 500 metres on left; GL6 8BB Tucked-away Cotswold-stone local with roomy opened-up interior; good pubby food (not Sun evening) from lunchtime sandwiches to daily specials, well kept Bath, Butcombe, Greene King and St Austell, varied choice of wines, friendly helpful staff; soft background music, free wi-fi; children and dogs (in bar) welcome, a few picnic-sets outside, good nearby walks, open all day Fri, Sat, till 8pm Sun. *(Celia and Geoff Clay)*

CAMP SO9111
Fostons Ash (01452) 863262
B4070 Birdlip–Stroud, junction with Calf Way; GL6 7ES Open-plan dining pub continuing well under new owners; good sensibly priced food from varied menu, three well kept ales and nice range of wines by the glass, amiable helpful staff; background music; children and dogs welcome, rustic tables in attractive garden with part-covered terrace and play area, good walks, open all day (food all day Sun). *(Richard Tilbrook)*

CHARLTON KINGS SO9620
Royal (01242) 228937
Horsefair, opposite church; GL53 8JH Large 19th-c pub with clean modern décor; good food (all day weekends) in bar or dining conservatory, several well kept ales (tasting trays available) and decent wines, prompt friendly service; live music and quiz nights; children and dogs welcome, picnic-sets in garden overlooking church, open all day. *(Alf and Sally Garner)*

CHEDWORTH SP0608
Hare & Hounds (01285) 720288
Fosse Cross – A429 N of Cirencester, some way from village; GL54 4NN Rambling stone-built restauranty pub with very good food cooked by italian chef-owner including lunchtime set menu, a couple of well kept local ales and nice wines, friendly efficient service, low beams and wood and flagstoned floors, soft lighting, cosy corners and little side rooms, two big log fires, small conservatory; children welcome, disabled access/facilities, ten courtyard bedrooms. *(Richard Tilbrook)*

CHELTENHAM SO9421
Jolly Brewmaster (01242) 772261
Painswick Road; GL50 2EZ Popular convivial local with seven well kept changing ales and six ciders, friendly obliging young staff, open-plan linked areas around big semicircular counter, log fire; dogs welcome, coachyard tables, open from 2.30pm (midday Sat, Sun). *(Ian Duncan)*

CHELTENHAM SO9522
Old Restoration (01242) 522792
High Street; GL50 1DX Refurbished 17th-c beamed pub; extensive range of real ales and craft beers including Butcombe, enjoyable fair-priced food from sandwiches to good Sun roasts, friendly helpful staff, open fires, games room with darts, table football and retro video games; children (away from bar) and dogs welcome, open (and food) all day, from 9.30am weekends. *(Sabine and Gerald Grimshaw)*

CHELTENHAM SO9624
Plough (01242) 361506
Mill Street, Prestbury; GL52 3BG Convivial thatched and beamed village local tucked away behind church; comfortable little front lounge with brick fireplace, upholstered wall benches in flagstoned back tap room, old local photographs and a grandfather clock by big log fire, corridor hatch serving two or three changing ales from stillage casks and proper ciders, enjoyable good value food including range of Pieminister pies, friendly service; may be live folk music Thurs; children and dogs welcome, picnic-sets in big back garden with own bar, play area and boules, open all day, no food Sun evening. *(Ian Duncan)*

CHELTENHAM SO9422
Railway (01242) 522925
New Street; GL50 3QL Relaxed backstreet pub serving good authentic thai food, Ringwood and other Marstons-related beers and decent selection of wines and gins, friendly helpful staff; Thurs quiz; children and dogs welcome, part-covered terrace garden, open all day Fri-Sun, from 4.30pm other days. *(Guy Vowles)*

CHELTENHAM SO9522
Sandford Park (01242) 571022
High Street; GL50 1DZ Former nightclub converted to a popular pub; three bar areas and upstairs function room, up to nine well kept changing ales along with craft and continental beers, several ciders and good value home-cooked food from tapas up (not Sun evening, Mon lunchtime), friendly staff; Sun quiz, bar billiards; large back garden, open all day. *(Maria and Henry Lazonby)*

CHIPPING CAMPDEN SP1539
★ Eight Bells (01386) 840371
Church Street (one-way – entrance off B4035); GL55 6JG Lovely historic inn with cheerful bustling atmosphere; candlelit

---

Post Office address codings confusingly give the impression that some pubs are in Gloucestershire, when they're really in Warwickshire (which is where we list them).

bar areas with massive timbers and beams, stripped-stone walls and log fires, cushioned pews, sofas and solid dark wood furniture on broad flagstones, ales such as Hook Norton, Goffs, Purity and Wye Valley from fine oak counter, also a couple of real ciders and seven wines by the glass, good food including lunchtime doorstep sandwiches, glass panel in dining room reveals church passage used by Catholic priests escaping the Roundheads; background music, board games, free wi-fi; well behaved children (not in bar after 7pm) and dogs (in bar) welcome, large terraced garden with striking views of almshouses and church, attractive comfortable bedrooms, good breakfast, open all day. *(Michael Sargent, John and Sharon Hanceck)*

CHIPPING CAMPDEN   SP1539
Kings   (01386) 840256
High Street; GL55 6AW Eclectic décor in 18th-c hotel's bar-brasserie and separate restaurant, good food from lunchtime sandwiches and pubby dishes to more upmarket choices, friendly attentive service, well kept Hook Norton Hooky and good choice of wines by the glass (can be pricey), afternoon teas, daily papers and nice log fire; secluded back garden with picnic-sets and terrace tables, 12 comfortable bedrooms, open all day. *(Celia and Geoff Clay)*

CHIPPING CAMPDEN   SP1539
Noel Arms   (01386) 840317
High Street; GL55 6AT Handsome 16th-c inn with beamed and stripped-stone bar, nice food from sandwiches to steaks, some good curries too from sri lankan chef (curry night last Thurs of month), well kept Hook Norton, local guests and good choice of wines by the glass, friendly efficient staff, coffee bar (from 9am), conservatory and separate restaurant; lunchtime jazz first Sun of month; children and dogs welcome, sunny courtyard tables, 28 well appointed bedrooms, good breakfast, open all day. *(Dave Braisted)*

CHIPPING SODBURY   ST7282
Horseshoe   07780 505563
High Street; BS37 6AP Welcoming unpretentious little pub in former stationers' making most of the space; seven well kept ales and six ciders, low priced pubby lunchtime food (not Sun, Mon), curry night Weds, otherwise rolls at the bar, comfortable sofas and settles, another intimate room upstairs; occasional live music, sports TV; dogs welcome, small pretty garden behind, open all day (till midnight weekends). *(Roger and Donna Huggins)*

CIRENCESTER   SP0202
Corinium   (01285) 659711
Dollar Street/Gloucester Street; GL7 2DG

Civilised and comfortable Georgian-fronted hotel (originally a 16th-c wool merchant's house); bar with good mix of tables on wood or flagstone floors, leather bucket seats by woodburner in stone fireplace, enjoyable fairly priced food from sandwiches to daily specials, three well kept local ales and decent wines, cheerful helpful young staff, restaurant; entrance through charming courtyard, wheelchair access with help, picnic-sets in attractive walled garden, 15 bedrooms. *(Theocsbrian)*

CIRENCESTER   SP0103
Drillmans Arms   (01285) 653892
Gloucester Road, Stratton; GL7 2JY Unpretentious two-room roadside local with welcoming long-serving landlady; well kept Sharps Doom Bar and three quickly changing guests, basic lunchtime food (not Tues), low beams and woodburner; skittle alley, darts and pool; dogs welcome, tables out by small front car park, open all day Sat. *(Richard Tilbrook)*

CIRENCESTER   SP0202
Fleece   (01285) 658507
Market Place; GL7 2NZ Carefully renovated old inn with various bars, lounges and airy dining areas; bare boards, contemporary pale paintwork, plenty of prints and fresh flowers, Thwaites ales and guests such as Cotswold Lion and Flying Monk, several wines by the glass and good selection of coffees and teas, well liked food from generous sandwiches up served by efficient courteous staff; children and dogs (in bar) welcome, terrace with white metal tables and chairs under parasols, attractive well equipped bedrooms, hearty breakfast, open (and food) all day. *(Michael Sargent, Roger and Donna Huggins)*

CIRENCESTER   SP0202
Golden Cross   (01285) 652137
Black Jack Street, between church and Corinium Museum; GL7 2AA Bustling backstreet coaching inn with long thin bar, snug and skylit restaurant, enjoyable food at sensible prices including Sat brunch, well kept Arkells and good range of wines and whiskies, friendly service; occasional live music, sports TV; children and dogs welcome, rattan-style furniture in sunny courtyard garden, bedrooms, open all day (Sun till 9.30pm). *(Martin and Joanne Sharp)*

CIRENCESTER   SP0201
Marlborough Arms   (01285) 651474
Sheep Street; GL7 1QW Busy bare-boards drinkers' pub with eight well kept ales including Box Steam and North Cotswold, also proper ciders and continental draught/bottled beers, friendly staff and good mix of

---

It's very helpful if you let us know up-to-date food prices when you report on pubs.

customers, brewery memorabilia, pump clips and shelves of bottles, open fire; live music and quiz nights, sports TV, board games; enclosed back courtyard, open all day. *(Beth Aldridge)*

COATES SO9600
Tunnel House (01285) 770702
Follow Tarlton signs (right then left) from village, pub up rough track on right after railway bridge; OS Sheet 163 map reference 965005; GL7 6PW Character bow-fronted stone pub by entrance to derelict canal tunnel; rambling rooms with beams, exposed stonework and flagstones, good mix of furnishings and plenty to look at including old enamel signs, railway lamps, stuffed animals, even an upside-down card table fixed to the ceiling (complete with cards and drinks), sofas by log fire, Box Steam, Bristol Beer Factory, Butcombe and Timothy Taylors, ciders such as Sandford Orchards, nine wines by the glass, happy hour 4-7pm Mon-Fri, enjoyable pubby food (not Sun evening) from baguettes to daily specials, good friendly service, more conventional dining extension and back conservatory; background music, free wi-fi; children and dogs welcome, disabled access/loos, impressive views from front terrace, big garden down to the canal, good nearby walks, open all day. *(Kim Adams, Tom and Ruth Rees, Guy Vowles)*

COLESBOURNE SO9913
Colesbourne Inn (01242) 870376
A435 Cirencester–Cheltenham; GL53 9NP Gabled 19th-c roadside coaching inn; decent choice of popular food from sandwiches and sharing boards up, smaller appetites and gluten-free diets catered for, well kept Wadworths ales and plenty of wines by the glass, friendly service, linked partly panelled rooms, log fires, comfortable mix of settles, softly padded seats and leather sofas, candlelit back dining room; background music, TV; dogs welcome, views from attractive back garden and terrace, nine bedrooms in converted stables, good breakfast (for non-residents too), open (and food) all day. *(Richard Tilbrook, Christian Mole)*

CROMHALL ST6990
Royal Oak (01454) 430993
Tortworth Road; GL12 8AD Spacious old country pub under helpful friendly licensees; varied choice of popular reasonably priced food including set lunch and gluten-free menu, Butcombe and a couple of guests such as Bristol Beer Factory and Wickwar, good wine list, interesting split-level interior with log fires (one in inglenook), table built around illuminated medieval well in restaurant; children and dogs (in bar) welcome, wheelchair access to most areas, picnic-sets on paved terrace and grass, open all day. *(Ian Herdman)*

DYMOCK SO6931
Beauchamp Arms (01531) 890266
B4215; GL18 2AQ Friendly parish-owned village pub with well kept changing ales, local ciders and good value traditional food, cheerful helpful staff, three smallish rooms, log fire; children and dogs welcome, pleasant little garden with pond, nearby walks among daffodils and bluebells, church with corner devoted to the Dymock Poets, closed Mon, no food Sun evening. *(Daniel King)*

ELKSTONE SO9610
Highwayman (01285) 821221
Beechpike; A417 6 miles N of Cirencester; GL53 9PL Interesting 16th-c building with rambling interior; low beams, stripped stone and log fires, cosy alcoves, antique settles among more modern furnishings, good home-made food (gluten-free options) from lunchtime sandwiches up, Arkells beers and decent wines by the glass, friendly service; free wi-fi; children and dogs welcome, disabled access, outside play area, closed Sun evening, Mon. *(Monica and Steph Evans)*

EWEN SU0097
Wild Duck (01285) 770310
Off A429 S of Cirencester; GL7 6BY Character 16th-c village inn (former cottages and barns for Ewen Manor) now owned by the Lucky Onion group; old stone path to entrance with unusual duck clock up on right, dimly lit interior with appealing nooks and crannies, dark hop-strung beams, scrubbed pine tables on wood floors, crimson walls and antique furnishings, open fires including one in handsome Elizabethan fireplace, good if not particularly cheap food from varied changing menu (service charge added), six real ales including Butcombe, Sharps and Stroud, good selection of wines by the glass from extensive list; occasional live music and comedy nights; children and dogs welcome, currently no wheelchair access, tables under parasols in heated courtyard and garden, Thames Path not far away, bedrooms planned, open all day. *(Anne Taylor)*

FORD SP0829
★ Plough (01386) 584215
B4077 Stow–Alderton; GL54 5RU 16th-c pub opposite famous stables and popular with the local horse-racing fraternity; beamed and stripped-stone bar with racing prints and photos, old settles and benches around big tables on uneven flagstones, oak tables in snug alcove, open fires and woodburners, Donnington BB and SBA, eight wines by the glass and a dozen malt whiskies, generous helpings of good reasonably priced food, charming service; background music, TV (for the races), free wi-fi, darts; children and dogs (in bar) welcome, picnic-sets and pretty hanging baskets in front, large garden

behind with play fort, comfortable clean bedrooms (some with views of the gallops), Cotswold Farm Park nearby, open all day from 9am, food all day Fri-Sun, gets packed on race days. *(Helene Grygar, Dave Braisted, Katharina Cowherd, M and GR)*

FORTHAMPTON   SO8731

Lower Lode Inn (01684) 293224

At the end of Bishop's Walk by river; GL19 4RE Brick-built 15th-c coaching inn with River Severn moorings and plenty of waterside tables (prone to winter flooding); beams, flagstones and traditional seating, woodburners, enjoyable reasonably priced pubby food including summer Sun carvery, half a dozen well kept interesting beers, friendly helpful staff, restaurant, back pool room; children and dogs welcome, disabled facilities, four bedrooms and campsite, summer ferry from Lower Lode Lane, open (and food) all day in season, closed lunchtimes Mon-Thurs in winter. *(Theocsbrian)*

FRAMPTON COTTERELL   ST6681

Globe (01454) 778286

Church Road; BS36 2AB Popular white-painted pub next to church; large knocked-through bar-dining area with black beams and some stripped stone, usual furniture on parquet or carpet, woodburner in old fireplace, five well kept ales including Butcombe, Fullers and St Austell, Thatcher's ciders and well chosen wine list, enjoyable fairly priced pubby food, attentive friendly staff; background music, Tues quiz; children and dogs welcome, wheelchair access via side door, disabled/baby changing facilities, big grassy garden with play area and smokers' gazebo, on Frome Valley Walkway, open all day. *(Charles and Maddie Bishop)*

FRAMPTON MANSELL   SO9202

★**Crown** (01285) 760601

Brown sign to pub off A491 Cirencester–Stroud; GL6 8JG Welcoming 17th-c country pub (former cider house) with pretty outlook; enjoyable food including daily specials, Butcombe, Sharps, Stroud, Uley and a guest, three ciders and good choice of wines, friendly helpful young staff, stripped stone and heavy beams, rugs on bare boards, two log fires and a woodburner, restaurant; various events including notable bonfire-night fireworks; children and dogs welcome, disabled access, picnic-sets in sunny front garden, 12 bedrooms in separate block, open all day from midday, food all day Sun. *(David Bird)*

FRAMPTON ON SEVERN   SO7407

Three Horseshoes (01452) 742100

The Green (B4071, handy for M5 junction 13, via A38); GL2 7DY Cheerfully unpretentious 18th-c pub by splendid green; welcoming staff and locals, well kept Sharps, Timothy Taylors and Uley

from small counter, proper ciders/perry too, good value home-made food including speciality pies; lived-in interior with parquet flooring, cushioned wall seats and open fire in large brick fireplace, quieter back lounge/dining room; folk nights, darts; children, walkers and dogs welcome, wheelchair access, picnic-sets out in front, garden behind with two boules pitches, views over River Severn to Forest of Dean, parking can be tricky (narrow road), open all day weekends. *(Monica and Steph Evans)*

FROCESTER   SO7831

Frocester George (01453) 828683

Peter Street; GL10 3TQ Large refurbished Quality Inns pub on crossroads, bare-boards bar with modern furniture, light wood dados and big bay windows, some repro animal prints and oil-lamp fittings on off-white walls, warm woodburner in old fireplace, ales such as Moles, Otter and Sharps, decent choice of ciders and extensive range of gins, good food from bar snacks and pub favourites to restaurant dishes, pleasant prompt service, can eat in bar, back annexe or restaurant; children and dogs welcome, wheelchair access via back door, part-covered courtyard, ten well equipped comfortable bedrooms, open (and food) all day. *(Chris and Angela Buckell)*

GLASSHOUSE   SO7121

★**Glasshouse Inn** (01452) 830529

Off A40 just W of A4136; GL17 0NN Much extended beamed red-brick pub with series of small linked rooms; tiled or flagstoned floors, ochre walls and boarded ceilings, appealing old-fashioned and antique furnishings, hunting pictures and taxidermy, cavernous black hearth with old iron pots etc, well kept ales including cask-tapped Butcombe and Sharps, Weston's cider, good reasonably priced wines, some interesting malt whiskies and a couple of decent gins, enjoyable home-made food from sandwiches and basket meals up (no bookings except Sun lunch), good friendly service, large flagstoned dining conservatory; background music; no under-14s (in bars) or dogs, good disabled access (but no loos), rustic furniture in neat garden with interesting topiary, flower-decked cider presses and lovely hanging baskets, nearby paths up wooded May Hill (NT), three self-catering lodges, closed Sun evening. *(Chris and Angela Buckell)*

GLOUCESTER   SO8318

Fountain (01452) 522562

Westgate Street; GL1 2NW Tucked-away 17th-c pub off pedestrianised street; well kept ales such as Bristol Beer Factory, Butcombe, Dartmoor, St Austell and Thwaites, a couple of craft beers, Thatcher's and Weston's ciders and a modestly priced wine list, good value pubby food from sandwiches and basket meals up, friendly chatty staff, open-plan carpeted bar with woodburner in handsome stone fireplace, some black beams and dark varnished dados, pubby furniture and built-in wall benches; background music; children and dogs welcome, disabled access/loos, flower-filled courtyard with big gates to Berkeley Street, handy for cathedral, open all day (food all day Fri and Sat, till 5pm Sun). *(Bernard Stradling)*

GLOUCESTER SO8218

Lord High Constable of England
(01452) 302890

Llanthony Warehouse, Llanthony Road; GL1 2EH Busy Wetherspoons on east side of the docks; spacious and comfortable with high raftered ceiling, good range of real ales and craft beers, their usual well priced food, efficient service; TVs, free wi-fi; children welcome, outside area overlooking canal, open all day from 8am. *(Liz and Martin Eldon)*

GREAT RISSINGTON SP1917

★Lamb (01451) 820388

Turn off A40 W of Burford to the Barringtons; keep straight on past Great Barrington until Great Rissington is signed on left; GL54 2LP Cotswold-stone village inn dating from the 18th c, bar with pubby furnishings including padded wall benches and sewing-machine tables on strip-wood floor, woodburner, leather chairs against counter serving well kept Brakspears, Wychwood Hobgoblin and a beer badged for the pub, decent wines by the glass and good choice of gins/malt whiskies, second woodburner in restaurant with collection of old agricultural tools, well liked interesting food along with sandwiches and a few pub standards, Weds steak day, friendly prompt service; background music, TV, free wi-fi; children, walkers and dogs (in bar) welcome, seats in sheltered hillside garden where Wellington bomber crashed in 1943 (see plaque and memorabilia), attractive circular walk, 13 bedrooms (four in converted outbuildings), open all day. *(Richard Tilbrook, Maria Birch, Simon Collett-Jones, Guy Vowles)*

GRETTON SP0130

Royal Oak (01242) 604999

Off B4077 E of Tewkesbury; GL54 5EP Renovated old golden-stone country pub; bar with painted kitchen chairs, leather tub seats and pale wooden tables on bare boards or flagstones, open fires, airy dining room and conservatory, candelabras, antlers and big central woodburner, ales such as Goffs, Purity, Ringwood, St Austell and Wye Valley, plenty of wines by the glass, popular food from pub favourites to specials; background music; children and dogs (in bar) welcome, wheelchair access (not to raised dining room), seats on back terrace with views over village to Dumbleton Hills and Malverns, play area and bookable tennis court, GWR steam trains run along bottom of garden in summer, open all day, food till 7.30pm Sun. *(Dr A J and Mrs B A Tompsett, Guy Vowles)*

GUITING POWER SP0924

★Farmers Arms (01451) 850358

Fosseway (A429); GL54 5TZ Nicely old-fashioned with stripped stone, flagstones, lots of pictures and woodburner, well kept/priced Donnington BB and SBA, wide blackboard choice of good honest food cooked by landlord including notable rabbit pie and reasonably priced Sun roasts, welcoming prompt service, carpeted back dining part; games area with darts, dominoes, cribbage and pool, skittle alley; children welcome, garden with quoits, lovely village and good surrounding walks, bedrooms. *(Richard Tilbrook)*

GUITING POWER SP0924

★Hollow Bottom (01451) 850392

Village signposted off B4068 SW of Stow-on-the-Wold (still called A436 on many maps); GL54 5UX Cosy old cottage popular with the racing fraternity; opened-up beamed bar with wooden flooring, horse-racing pictures and woodburner in unusual pillared stone fireplace, Greene ales, several wines by the glass and 15 malt whiskies, enjoyable food from wraps, sharing boards and pizzas up, pleasant attentive service, flagstoned dining areas with exposed stone walls, built-in cushioned wall seats and medley of tables; background music, TVs for racing, free wi-fi; children and dogs (in bar) welcome, back garden has a decked area, heaters, fire pit and own thatched bar, views towards sloping fields and good nearby walks, five comfortable bedrooms (two in annexe), open (and food) all day from 9am. *(Michael Sargent, Helene Grygar, Richard Tilbrook)*

HAM ST6898

Salutation (01453) 810284

On main road through village; GL13 9QH Welcoming unpretentious three-room country local; brasses on beams, horse and hunt pictures on Artex walls, high-backed settles, bench seats and other pubby furniture on tiled floors, six well kept local ales including own-brewed Tileys, 11 real ciders/perries and good range of

---

A star symbol before the name of a pub shows exceptional character and appeal. It doesn't mean extra comfort. And it's nothing to do with exceptional food quality, for which there's a separate star-on-a-plate symbol. Even quite a basic pub can win a star, if it's individual enough.

bottled beers, limited choice of simple low-priced lunchtime food such as ham, egg and chips (own pigs, hens and potatoes), more ambitious weekend menus; folk night first Thurs of month and other live music, traditional games including shove-ha'penny, skittle alley, free wi-fi; children and dogs welcome, wheelchair access (some tight doorways), grassy beer garden overlooking water meadows, handy for Berkeley Castle, open all day weekends, closed Mon lunchtime. *(Chris and Angela Buckell)*

HANHAM ST6470
Chequers (0117) 329 1711
Hanham Mills; BS15 3NU Popular pub in lovely spot overlooking River Avon; enjoyable food from sandwiches and sharing plates up including Weds steak night and Fri fish and chips, Youngs ales, guest beers and interesting wines (plenty by the glass), efficient cheerful service, spacious up-to-date interior with various partitioned areas including snug with woodburner and comfortable seating by low tables, river views from large windows in flagstone and wood-floored bar/dining area, connecting carpeted restaurant; background music, Mon quiz; children and dogs welcome, disabled access/loo, tables on riverside terrace, moorings, open (and food) all day.
(Chris and Angela Buckell)

HARTPURY SO7924
Royal Exchange (01452) 700273
A417 Gloucester–Ledbury; GL19 3BW Comfortable 19th-c country pub under same ownership as the Red Lion at Bishop's Norton and Swan in Staunton; modernised opened-up interior, flagstones, bare boards and carpet, two-way woodburner, popular reasonably priced food (all day Sat, not Sun evening) from sandwiches and sharing plates to chargrills and specials, Weds curry night, Wye Valley ales and guests, local cider/perry; quiz first Mon of month, sports TV; children and dogs (in bar) welcome, fine views from garden with terrace and covered deck, open all day Fri-Sun. *(Theocsbrian)*

HAWKESBURY UPTON ST7786
★**Beaufort Arms** (01454) 238217
High Street; GL9 1AU Unpretentious 17th-c pub in historic village; welcoming landlord and friendly chatty atmosphere, up to five well kept changing local ales and good range of ciders, popular pubby food (all available to take away), extended dining lounge on right with central woodburner, interesting brewery memorabilia and old local photographs, darts and skittles in bigger stripped-brick bare-boards bar with glass-topped well; free wi-fi; well behaved children allowed, dogs in bar, disabled access/loos/parking, picnic-sets in grassed beer garden, on Cotswold Way and handy for Badminton Horse Trials, open all day.
(Chris and Angela Buckell)

HILLESLEY ST7689
Fleece (01453) 520003
Hawkesbury Road/Chapel Lane; GL12 7RD Comfortably updated old stone-roofed pub owned by the local community; up to seven well kept mainly local ales, good wines by the glass and decent range of gins, enjoyable good value food including specials, friendly chatty staff and locals, bar with mix of pubby furniture, cushioned benches and wall seats, woodburner, steps down to dining room and snug; some live acoustic music; children, walkers and dogs welcome (leave muddy boots in porch), wheelchair access to bar only, back garden with play area and smokers' shelter, small village in lovely countryside near Cotswold Way, closed till 4.30pm Mon, Tues, otherwise open all day.
(Charles and Maddie Bishop)

HINTON DYRHAM ST7376
★**Bull** (0117) 937 2332
2.4 miles from M4 junction 18; A46 towards Bath, then first right (opposite the Crown); SN14 8HG Welcoming 17th-c stone pub in nice setting; main bar with two huge fireplaces, low beams, oak settles and pews on ancient flagstones, stripped-stone back area and simply furnished carpeted restaurant, good food from pub standards to specials (pork from own pigs), well kept Wadworths ales; background music; children and dogs welcome, difficult wheelchair access (steps at front, but staff willing to help), seats on front balcony and in sizeable sheltered upper garden with play equipment, well placed for Dyrham Park (NT), open all day weekends (food till 6pm Sun).
(Alf and Sally Garner)

IRON ACTON ST6883
Lamb (01454) 228265
B4058/9 Bristol–Chipping Sodbury; BS37 9UZ Welcoming 17th-c former coaching house: well stocked bar serving ales such as Flying Monk and Wickwar, competitively priced wines and interesting gins, enjoyable good value food including lunchtime/early evening BOGOF deal, prompt pleasant service, low-ceilinged carpeted bar with dark varnished dados, rough-plastered cream walls and pubby furniture, woodburners in huge stone fireplaces; unobtrusive background music, Mon quiz, pool and darts; children and dogs welcome, wheelchair access, picnic-sets on front terrace and in large grassy garden behind, open all day. *(Chris and Angela Buckell)*

KEMBLE ST9899
Thames Head (01285) 770259
A433 Cirencester–Tetbury; GL7 6NZ Roadside pub with opened-up modernised interior around central servery; faux black beams, stripped-stone walls and some rough-boarded dados/wall seats, fairly rustic furniture on tartan carpet, shelves of books,

stoneware jugs and a bust of Old Father Thames, intriguing little front alcove, two open fires, enjoyable fairly priced food, well kept Arkells and good value wines, friendly attentive staff; background music, free wi-fi, skittle alley; children and dogs (in bar area) welcome, wheelchair access using ramp, disabled loo, tables outside, four simple bedrooms in converted stables, good breakfast, walk (crossing railway line) to nearby Thames source, open (and food) all day. *(Sara Fulton, Roger Baker)*

KILKENNY   SP0118
Kilkeney Inn (01242) 820341
A436, 1 mile W of Andoversford; GL54 4LN Spacious beamed pub (originally five stone cottages); stripped-stone and some plank-clad walls, wheelback, tub and leather dining chairs around tables on slate, wood or carpeted floors, open fire and woodburner, conservatory, ales such as Bombardier and Youngs, Weston's cider and decent wines by the glass, well liked food from owner-chef including signature 'slow-cooked' dishes, gluten-free diets catered for, good friendly service; background music; children welcome, wheelchair access from car park, tables out at front with lovely Cotswold views, more seating in back garden, one well appointed bedroom, closed Sun evening, Mon. *(Anne Taylor)*

KINETON   SP0926
Halfway House (01451) 850344
Signed from B4068 and B4077 W of Stow-on-the-Wold; GL54 5UG Welcoming 17th-c beamed village inn with enjoyable food including good burgers, well kept Donnington BB and SBA, Addlestone's cider and decent wines, separate dining area, log fire; pool and darts; children and dogs welcome, picnic-sets in sheltered back garden with pergola, good walks, bedrooms, open (and some food) all day. *(James and Sylvia Hewitt)*

KNOCKDOWN   ST8388
Holford Arms (01454) 238669
A433; GL8 8QY Welcoming 16th-c beamed pub; bare-stone walls, flagstone or wood floors, leather sofas, armchairs and cushioned wall/window seats, candles on old dining tables, two woodburners (one in huge stone fireplace), cask-tapped ales including own Knockdown brews, also own Sherston's cider and apple juice, good wine list, enjoyable food from sandwiches up using local and home-grown produce, Mon steak night and Weds thai, pleasant helpful service; background and live music (bluegrass Fri), skittle alley; children and dogs welcome, wheelchair access (no disabled loos), picnic sets in side and back gardens, outside summer bar, six bedrooms, camping/glamping, handy for Westonbirt Arboretum, Highgrove and Badminton Horse Trials, open all day weekends, from 4pm weekdays. *(Guy Vowles)*

LEIGHTERTON   ST8290
★ Royal Oak (01666) 890250
Village signposted off A46 S of Nailsworth; GL8 8UN Handsome early 18th-c mullion-windowed village pub; rambling beamed bar with two log fires, stripped stonework and pastel paintwork, mix of furniture including country pine, candles and fresh flowers on tables, ales such as Flying Monk, Uley and Wye Valley, traditional cider and several wines by the glass, very good food from interesting varied menu including some pub favourites and popular Sun lunch, helpful friendly service; children and dogs welcome, disabled access, sheltered side courtyard with teak and metal furniture, surrounding walks (on Monarch's Way) and handy for Westonbirt Arboretum, closed Sun evening, Mon. *(Michael Doswell, Dr and Mrs A K Clarke)*

LITTLETON-UPON-SEVERN   ST5989
★ White Hart (01454) 412275
3.5 miles from M48 junction 1; BS35 1NR Sympathetically updated 17th-c farmhouse with three main rooms; nice mix of country furnishings, flagstones at front, huge tiles at the back, log fires (loveseat in inglenook), well kept Youngs ales and guests, good range of other drinks including their own cider, popular food cooked by landlord from bar snacks and traditional choices to more adventurous specials, efficient service (may ask for a credit card before you eat); children (family dining room) and dogs welcome, wheelchair access, tables on front lawn looking over fields to the river, more behind in big orchard garden with roaming chickens and geese, walks from the door, open all day, food all day weekends. *(R G Marshall, Chris and Angela Buckell)*

LONGBOROUGH   SP1729
Coach & Horses (01451) 830325
Ganborough Road; GL56 0QU Traditional little 17th-c stone local with up to three well kept/priced Donnington ales, Thatcher's cider and enjoyable good value pub food including basket meals, friendly landlord and staff, leather armchairs on flagstones, inglenook woodburner, darts, dominoes and cribbage; background music, quiz last Sun of month; children and dogs welcome, tables out at front looking down on stone cross and pretty village, two simple clean bedrooms, handy for Sezincote house and gardens, open all day Fri-Sun. *(Ian Duncan)*

LONGFORD   SO8320
Queens Head (01452) 301882
Tewkesbury Road (A38 just N of Gloucester); GL2 9EJ Partly timber-framed roadside dining pub; linked areas with attractive clubby décor including flagstoned bar area, generous helpings of very popular sensibly priced food (booking

advised), Sharps and Wye Valley ales, good choice of wines and gins, efficient friendly service; no under-12s, open all day weekends. *(Richard Tilbrook, Mike and Mary Carter)*

LONGHOPE SO6720
Farmers Boy (01452) 470105
Boxbush, Ross Road; A40 outside village; GL17 0LP Popular roadside country pub extended around 17th-c core; a couple of Greene King ales and enjoyable range of food including signature pies, friendly service, beams, exposed stonework and wood floors, some bric-a-brac and logburner, steps down to restaurant and garden room with old well; background music, monthly tribute bands, TV; children and dogs (in bar) welcome, picnic-sets in pleasant garden, eight courtyard bedrooms, open all day. *(Louise and Oliver Redman)*

LOWER ODDINGTON SP2326
★Fox (01451) 870555
Signed off A436; GL56 0UR Attractively presented 16th-c creeper-clad inn with emphasis on their excellent food (can be pricey and must book), top notch service too, Hook Norton and a guest such as Ringwood, Robinson's cider and well chosen wines (16 by the glass), series of relaxed country-style flagstoned rooms with assorted chairs around pine tables, candles and fresh flowers, log fires including inglenook woodburner; background music; children and dogs (in bar) welcome, tables under parasols at front, enclosed cottagey back garden and heated terrace, pretty village, three comfortable bedrooms. *(Richard Tilbrook)*

LOWER SWELL SP1725
Golden Ball (01451) 833886
B4068 W of Stow-on-the-Wold; GL54 1LF Unassuming 17th-c stone-built village local surrounded by good walks; well kept Donnington ales (the attractive brewery is nearby), Addlestone's cider and well prepared/priced pubby food cooked by landlord-chef including charolais beef from the family farm, good friendly service, neatly kept beamed interior with some cosy nooks, woodburner; background music, sports TV, darts; children and dogs welcome, small garden and raised deck/balcony, aunt sally, open all day weekends, no food Sun evening. *(Richard Tilbrook)*

MARSHFIELD ST7773
★Catherine Wheel (01225) 892220
High Street; signed off A420 Bristol–Chippenham; SN14 8LR Attractive Georgian-fronted building in unspoilt village; high-ceilinged bare-stone front part with medley of settles, chairs and stripped tables, charming dining room with impressive open fireplace, cottagey beamed back area warmed by woodburners, well kept Butcombe, Fullers London Pride and a local guest, interesting

wines and other drinks, enjoyable sensibly priced food from pub favourites up; darts and dominoes, live music last Thurs of month, free wi-fi; well behaved children and dogs welcome, wheelchair access with help, flower-decked backyard, three bedrooms, open all day. *(Dr and Mrs A K Clarke)*

MAYSHILL ST6882
New Inn (01454) 773161
Badminton Road (A432 Frampton Cotterell–Yate); BS36 2NT Popular largely 17th-c coaching inn with two comfortably carpeted bar rooms leading to restaurant, good choice of enjoyable generously served pub food at fair prices, friendly staff, three well kept changing ales, Weston's cider and decent wines by the glass, log fire; children and dogs welcome, garden with play area, open all day Fri-Sun, food all day weekends. *(Celia and Geoff Clay)*

MICKLETON SP1543
★Kings Arms (01386) 438257
B4632 (ex A46); GL55 6RT Popular 18th-c honey-stone pub; good often imaginative food from lunchtime sandwiches to daily specials, real ales such as Bombardier, proper cider and several wines by the glass from interesting list, friendly helpful staff, atmospheric open-plan beamed lounge with nice mix of comfortable chairs, soft lighting and good log fire, small locals' bar; background music, free wi-fi; children and dogs welcome, circular picnic-sets under parasols in courtyard, more tables in sizeable garden, attractive village, handy for Hidcote (NT) and Kiftsgate Court Gardens, open all day. *(Katherine Matthews)*

MINCHINHAMPTON SO8500
Old Lodge (01453) 832047
Nailsworth–Brimscombe – on common, fork left at pub's sign; OS Sheet 162 map reference 853008; GL6 9AQ Welcoming dining pub (former golf clubhouse and now part of the Cotswold Food Club group); civilised modern bistro feel with wood floors and stripped-stone walls, good food from pub favourites up, decent wines by the glass and four well kept changing beers, friendly helpful service; children and dogs (in bar) welcome, tables on neat lawn looking over NT common with grazing cows and horses, six bedrooms, open all day (food all day weekends). *(Guy Vowles)*

MINCHINHAMPTON SO8801
Ragged Cot (01453) 884643
Cirencester Road; NE of town; GL6 8PE Attractively updated 17th-c Cotswold stone inn; front bar with open fire one end woodburner the other, cushioned window seats and painted pine tables on wood-strip floor, connecting rooms including airy pitched-ceiling restaurant overlooking the garden, emphasis on their well liked (if not especially cheap) food from one or two pub

favourites up, a beer badged for the pub along with Ringwood Razorback and a guest, decent range of wines; children and dogs welcome, outside café called 'the Shed', nine well appointed bedrooms. *(Beth Aldridge)*

MISERDEN — SO9308
Carpenters Arms (01285) 821283
Off B4070 NE of Stroud; GL6 7JA Welcoming traditional 17th-c country pub (used in the 2015 BBC adaptation of *Cider with Rosie*) with opened-up low-beamed bar; stripped-stone walls, log fire and woodburner, some interesting old photographs, Wye Valley Butty Bach, HPA and a guest, fine range of ciders and decent wines, generous helpings of popular reasonably priced food cooked by landlord using local/home-grown produce including good vegetarian choices, also breakfast from 9am and afternoon teas, friendly helpful staff; Weds folk night, quiz Thurs; children and dogs welcome, seats out in front and to the side, popular with walkers and handy for Miserden Park, open (and food) all day, kitchen closes 7pm Sun. *(Richard Tilbrook)*

MORETON-IN-MARSH — SP2032
Black Bear (01608) 652992
High Street; GL56 0AX Friendly beamed and stripped-stone corner pub; bustling wood-floor bar with sports TVs and a couple of carved bears either side of log fire, well kept/priced Donnington ales, decent wines by the glass and good food from sensibly short changing menu, woodburner and light wood furniture in airy dining room; children welcome, open (and food) all day, kitchen closes 4pm Sun. *(Richard Tilbrook)*

MORETON-IN-MARSH — SP2032
Inn on the Marsh (01608) 650709
Stow Road, next to duck pond; GL56 0DW Stone-built roadside pub with comfortable beamed bar; inglenook woodburner and some dutch influences to the décor, chef-landlady is dutch and cooks some good value national dishes alongside pub favourites, well kept Marstons-related beers and guests, cheerful welcoming staff, modern conservatory restaurant; background music from vintage vinyl or maybe landlord playing his guitar; children and dogs welcome, seats at front and in back garden, closed Mon lunchtime. *(James and Sylvia Hewitt)*

MORETON-IN-MARSH — SP2032
Redesdale Arms (01608) 650308
High Street; GL56 0AW Relaxed 17th-c hotel (former coaching inn); alcoves and big stone fireplace in comfortable solidly furnished panelled bar on right, darts in flagstoned public bar, three well kept ales, decent wines and coffee, enjoyable food from breakfast on served by courteous helpful staff, spacious child-friendly back brasserie and dining conservatory; background

music, TVs, games machine; heated floodlit courtyard, 34 comfortable bedrooms (newer ones in mews), open all day from 8am. *(Katharine Cowherd)*

MORETON-IN-MARSH — SP2032
White Hart Royal (01608) 650731
High Street; GL56 0BA Substantial 17th-c coaching inn with Charles I connection; cosy beamed quarry-tiled bar with fine inglenook and nice old furniture, adjacent smarter panelled room with Georgian feel, separate lounge and restaurant, Hook Norton and a guest ale, good choice of wines, well liked food from sandwiches and pub favourites up including children's choices, friendly service; background music; courtyard tables, 28 bedrooms, good breakfast, open all day. *(Louise and Oliver Redman)*

NAILSWORTH — ST8499
Britannia (01453) 832501
Cossack Square; GL6 0DG Large open-plan pub (part of the small Cotswold Food Club chain) in former manor house; popular bistro food including stone-baked pizzas (best to book evenings), friendly helpful service, well kept Hook Norton, Wadworths and guests, good choice of wines by the glass, big log fire; children welcome, picnic-sets in front garden, open all day (food all day weekends). *(Tom and Ruth Rees)*

NAILSWORTH — ST8499
Egypt Mill (01453) 833449
Off A46; heading N towards Stroud, first right after roundabout, then left; GL6 0AE Converted 16th-c mill with working waterwheels; split-level brick and stone floor bar, stripped beams and some hefty ironwork in comfortable carpeted lounge, seating ranging from elegant dining chairs to cushioned wall seats and sofas, well kept ales, a dozen wines by the glass and enjoyable reasonably priced food including vegetarian/vegan options, good friendly service; background music; children welcome, plenty of tables in floodlit garden overlooking millpond, well equipped bedrooms (some with fine beams and timbering), open (and food) all day. *(Tom and Ruth Rees)*

NAUNTON — SP1123
★ Black Horse (01451) 850565
Off B4068 W of Stow-on-the-Wold; GL54 3AD Welcoming locals' pub with well kept/priced Donnington BB and SBA, Weston's cider and popular home-made food from traditional favourites to daily specials such as seasonal game, bargain set menu Mon evening (must book), friendly efficient service, black beams, stripped stone, flagstones and log fire, dining room; background music, darts and dominoes; children and dogs welcome, small seating area outside, charming village and fine Cotswold walks (walking groups asked to

pre-order food), open all day Fri-Sun.
(Dr A J and Mrs B A Tompsett, Richard Tilbrook, Margaret and Peter Staples, Guy Vowles)

NETHER WESTCOTE   SP2220

★**Feathered Nest** (01993) 833030
Off A424 Burford to Stow-on-the-Wold; OX7 6SD Civilised former malthouse with largely stripped-stone bar up a few stairs, low beams and dark flagstones, carved settle among other carefully chosen furniture, saddle stools at counter serving Purity ales and 24 wines by the glass (impressive list), high-raftered room leads off with sofas by vast log fire, smart two-level dining rooms, very good food and service; background music, TV; children and dogs (in bar) welcome, teak tables and wicker armchairs on paved terrace, heated shelter and spreading lawn bounded by floodlit trees, Evenlode Valley beyond, well equipped individually decorated bedrooms, good breakfast, closed Mon-Weds, two weeks Feb, two weeks July and one week Oct, otherwise open all day (till 9pm Sun).
(Jacqui and Alan Swan, Louise and Oliver Redman, Bernard Stradling)

NIBLEY   ST6982

Swan (01454) 312290
Badminton Road; BS37 5JF Part of small local pub group, friendly and relaxed, with good food from snacks to daily specials, Bath, Butcombe and Cotswold Spring, real cider and over a dozen wines by the glass, good service, modernised interior with fireside leather sofas one side, dining tables the other, separate restaurant; background music; children and dogs (in bar) welcome, garden picnic-sets, open all day.
(Anne Taylor)

NORTH CERNEY   SP0208

★**Bathurst Arms** (01285) 832150
A435 Cirencester–Cheltenham; GL7 7BZ Handsome 17th-c inn with beamed and panelled bar, attractive medley of old tables and chairs on flagstones, window seats and fireplace at each end (one is huge and has an open woodburner), oak-floored room leading off, Butcombe Bitter, St Austell Tribute and a guest, good wines by the glass and well liked food, restaurant with another woodburner; children and dogs (in bar) welcome, plenty of seats in attractively landscaped garden with River Chun running through it, lovely church opposite and handy for Cerney House Gardens, well appointed bedrooms, open all day (till 8pm Sun in winter). *(Giles and Annie Francis, Lyn and Freddie Roberts, Alexander and Trish Cutter, Guy Vowles)*

NORTH NIBLEY   ST7596

New Inn (01453) 543659
E of village itself; Waterley Bottom; GL11 6EF Former cider house in secluded rural setting popular with walkers; up to three well kept local beers served from antique pumps, fine range of ciders/perries (more in bottles) and enjoyable food from lunchtime sandwiches and ploughman's up, lounge bar with cushioned windsor chairs and high-backed settles, partly stripped-stone walls, simple cosy public bar (no children here after 6pm), cider festivals and other events (maybe local mummers); no credit cards; dogs welcome, hitching rail and trough for horses, picnic-sets and swings on lawn, covered decked area, two bedrooms, open all day weekends, closed Mon lunchtime (evening too in winter). *(Ian Duncan)*

OLD DOWN   ST6187

★**Fox** (01454) 412507
3.9 miles from M5 junction 15/16; A38 towards Gloucester, then Old Down signposted; turn left into Inner Down; BS32 4PR Tucked-away yet popular family-owned country pub; six well kept ales such as Bath, Butcombe, Fullers and Sharps, Thatcher's cider and several wines by the glass, good reasonably priced traditional food (not Sun evening) from baguettes up, low beams, carpeted, wood or flagstone floors, log fire, plain modern wooden furniture, dark green faux leather wall seats in bar, snug family room; live music first Sat of month; dogs welcome, good disabled access (no loos), front and back gardens, long verandah with grapevine, play area, open all day Sun. *(Chris and Angela Buckell, Roger and Donna Huggins)*

OLD SODBURY   ST7581

Dog (01454) 312006
3 miles from M4 junction 18, via A46 and A432; The Hill (a busy road); BS37 6LZ Welcoming old pub with popular two-level carpeted bar, low beams, stripped stone and open fire, good reasonably priced food from sandwiches and baked potatoes to fresh fish and steaks, Sharps Doom Bar and three Wickwar ales kept well, friendly attentive young staff; children and dogs welcome, handy for Cotswold Way walkers, nice big garden with paved terrace, four annexe bedrooms, open all day. *(Guy Vowles, Dr and Mrs A K Clarke)*

PAINSWICK   SO8609

Falcon (01452) 814222
New Street; GL6 6UN Handsome stone-built inn dating from the 16th c; sympathetically updated open-plan layout with bar and two dining areas, good, popular food including daily specials, four well kept beers and good choice of fairly priced wines by the glass, friendly young staff; occasional live music; children and dogs welcome, 12 comfortable bedrooms, opposite churchyard famous for its 99 yews. *(Dr J Barrie Jones)*

PARKEND   SO6107

Fountain (01594) 562189
Just off B4234; GL15 4JD 18th-c village inn by terminus of restored Dean Forest

Railway; well kept ales such as Hillside, Greene King and Wye Valley, Severn and Weston's ciders, wines in glass-sized bottles, enjoyable reasonably priced home-made food including Sun carvery and OAP weekday lunch deal, prompt service from friendly young staff, assorted chairs and settles in two linked carpeted rooms, pale wood panelling, old tools, bric-a-brac, photographs and framed local history information, open fire; quiz and live music nights; children, walkers and dogs welcome, wheelchair access using ramps, disabled loo, grassy streamside beer garden, seven bedrooms and bunkhouse, open all day Sat. *(Chris and Angela Buckell)*

PARKEND   SO6308
Rising Sun (01594) 562008
Off B4431; GL15 4HN Perched on wooded hillside and approached by roughish single-track drive – popular with walkers and cyclists; open-plan carpeted bar with modern pub furniture, Wickwar BOB, several guests and real ciders, well priced straightforward food from sandwiches and baked potatoes up, friendly service, lounge/games area (pool and machines); children and dogs welcome, wheelchair access with help, views from balcony and terrace tables under umbrellas, big woodside garden with play area and duck pond, self-catering accommodation, open (and food) all day. *(Celia and Geoff Clay)*

PILNING   ST5684
Plough (01454) 632556
Handy for M5 junction 17 via B4055 and Station Road; Pilning Street; BS35 4JJ Fairly remote but thriving roadside local much extended over the years; Wadworths ales and Thatcher's ciders, good value pubby food including children's and OAPs' menus, cheerful efficient young staff, flagstone floors in the oldest part, polished wood and carpet elsewhere, dados and some old advertising pictures, log fires; live music and karaoke nights, pool and darts; dogs welcome (pub labrador is Bruiser), wheelchair access/loos, picnic-sets out at front and in large paddock with fenced-in play area, open all day, no food Sun evening. *(Chris and Angela Buckell)*

POULTON   SP1001
Falcon (01285) 850878
London Road; GL7 5HN Popular bistro-feel village dining pub with highly regarded food from chef-owner including good value set lunch, well kept Hook Norton Old Hooky, a local guest beer and nice wines by the glass, friendly attentive service, neat modern interior with some old black beams, relaxed easy-going atmosphere; background music; well behaved children welcome, closed Sun evening, Mon. *(Daniel King)*

QUENINGTON   SP1404
Keepers Arms (01285) 750349
Church Road; GL7 5BL Community local in pretty Cotswold village; cosy and comfortable,

with stripped stone, low beams and log fires, friendly helpful landlord and staff, good fairly priced food in bar and restaurant from changing menu including daily specials, three well kept beers, a dozen wines by the glass and interesting range of gins; quiz first Thurs of month; dogs welcome (their border collies are Denzil and Doris), picnic-sets out in front, three bedrooms, closed Mon and Tues lunchtimes, no evening food Sun-Tues. *(Giles and Annie Francis)*

SALFORD HILL   SP2629
Greedy Goose (01608) 646551
Junction A44/A436, near Chastleton; GL56 0SP Old roadside country dining pub with contemporary interior; enjoyable food from sandwiches and stone-baked pizzas up, three North Cotswolds ales, friendly staff; children and dogs welcome, seats out at front and in back decked/gravelled area, campsite including wooden pods, open all day. *(Graeme and Sally Medham)*

SAPPERTON   SO9403
★ Bell (01285) 760298
Village signposted from A419 Stroud–Cirencester; OS Sheet 163 map reference 948033; GL7 6LE Welcoming 250-year-old pub-restaurant with cosy connecting rooms around central bar; beams and exposed stonework, flagstone, wood and quarry-tiled floors, log fires, four well kept ales, plenty of wines by the glass and good choice of other drinks, much liked food (not Sun evening) from sandwiches, sharing boards and pub favourites to more ambitious choices, friendly knowledgeable service; children and dogs welcome, seats out in front and in back courtyard garden, tethering for horses, plenty of surrounding walks, closed Mon in winter, otherwise open all day (till 8pm Sun). *(Helene Grygar, Tom and Ruth Rees, Tim Senn, R J Herd, Richard Sanderson, Gail Plews)*

SAPPERTON   SO9303
Daneway Inn (01285) 760297
Daneway; off A419 Stroud–Cirencester; GL7 6LN Quietly tucked-away 18th-c whitewashed pub; three linked rooms with bare boards or carpet, woodburner in amazing floor-to-ceiling carved oak dutch fireplace, also an inglenook, up to four Wadworths ales including a summer elderflower beer (Rare Find, named for the Large Blue butterfly found here), traditional cider/perry and enjoyable home-made food at fair prices, friendly staff, traditional games such as shove-ha'penny and ring the bull; quiz last Mon of month; children and dogs welcome, tricky wheelchair access (there are disabled loos), terrace tables and lovely sloping lawn, good walks by disused canal with tunnel to Coates, surrounding nature reserves, campsite with shepherd's hut, open (and food) all day except Sun when kitchen closes 4-6pm. *(Liz and Martin Eldon)*

SHIPTON MOYNE   ST8989
★ **Cat & Custard Pot** (01666) 880249
*Off B4040 Malmesbury–Bristol; The
Street; GL8 8PN* Refurbished and extended
early 18th-c pub in picturesque village; three
real ales such as Flying Monk, Hook Norton
and Wickwar, local ciders and interesting
selection of whiskies and gins, decent wines
by the glass too, good freshly made food at
sensible prices including range of burgers,
deceptively spacious inside with several
dining areas, beams and bric-a-brac, hunting
prints, cosy back snug, two-way woodburner;
children, walkers and dogs welcome, front
wheelchair access to most areas, disabled
loos, picnic-sets in small front garden,
handy for Beaufort Polo Club, Highgrove
and Westonbirt Arboretum, six comfortable
bedrooms, open all day weekends, no food
Sun evening. *(Chris and Angela Buckell,
Giles and Annie Francis)*

SHURDINGTON   SO8318
Bell (01242) 862245
A46 just S of Cheltenham; GL3 4PB
Friendly early 19th-c village pub with
well liked fairly traditional food (some
mediterranean influences) from lunchtime
sandwiches up, Weds steak night, several
local ales and good wines by the glass,
attentive helpful staff, conservatory looking
over cricket field; live music last Sat of
month; children and dogs welcome, adjacent
playground, open all day, no food Sun
evening. *(Dr A J and Mrs B A Tompsett)*

SLAD   SO8707
Woolpack (01452) 813429
B4070 Stroud–Birdlip; GL6 7QA Popular
early 19th-c hillside village pub with lovely
valley views; four unspoilt little connecting
rooms, interesting photographs including
some of Laurie Lee who was a regular (his
books for sale), log fire, good imaginative
food (highish prices) along with pub
favourites, pizzas served Mon night, well
kept Uley ales and guests, local farm cider/
perry and decent wines by the glass,
friendly prompt service; some live music;
children, walkers and dogs welcome, nice
garden taking in the view, open all day
(till 1am Fri, Sat), no food Sun evening,
Mon lunchtime. *(Roger and Anne Mallard,
Guy Vowles)*

SLIMBRIDGE   SO7204
★ **Tudor Arms** (01453) 890306
*Shepherds Patch; off A38 towards
Slimbridge Wetlands Centre; GL2 7BP*

Much extended red-brick roadside pub just
back from canal swing bridge; welcoming and
popular with six mainly local ales, similar
number of ciders/perries and good wines
by the glass, also some interesting whiskies
and gins such as Seven Swans and welsh
Penderyn, enjoyable well priced pubby food
including basket meals, daily specials and
weekday two-course lunch deal, prompt
friendly service, linked areas with wood,
flagstone or carpeted floors, some leather
chairs and settles, comfortable dining room,
conservatory; darts, pool and skittle alley;
children and dogs (in back bar) welcome,
disabled access/loos, tables on part-shaded
terrace, boat trips, 16 annexe bedrooms,
caravan site off car park, open (and food)
all day. *(Chris and Angela Buckell, Dr A J and
Mrs B A Tompsett)*

SNOWSHILL   SP0933
Snowshill Arms (01386) 852653
Opposite village green; WR12 7JU
Unpretentious country pub in honeypot
village – so no shortage of customers;
well kept Donnington ales and reasonably
priced straightforward (but tasty) food from
sandwiches up, prompt friendly service,
beams, log fire, stripped stone and neat
array of tables, charming village views from
bow windows, local photographs; skittle
alley; children and dogs welcome, big back
garden with stream and play area, handy
for Snowshill Manor (NT), lavender farm
and Cotswold Way walks. *(Charles and
Maddie Bishop)*

SOMERFORD KEYNES   SU0195
Bakers Arms (01285) 861298
On main street through village; GL7 6DN
Pretty little 17th-c stone-built pub with
catslide roof; four well kept ales, seven wines
by the glass and enjoyable traditional food
including range of burgers and Thurs steak
night, lots of pine tables in two linked areas,
fire in big stone fireplace; children and dogs
welcome, seats out at front and in garden
with play area, lovely village, handy for
Cotswold Water Park, open (and food)
all day except Sun when shuts at 6pm.
(Louise and Oliver Redman)

SOUTHROP   SP2003
★ **Swan** (01367) 850205
Off A361 Lechlade–Burford; GL7 3NU
Creeper-clad 17th-c pub in pretty village and
part of the Thyme company on the Southrop
Manor Estate; chatty gently civilised bar
with simple tables and chairs on flagstones,
open fire, stools at counter serving ales such

'Children welcome' means the pub says it lets children inside without any special
restriction. If it allows them in, but to restricted areas such as an eating area or family
room, we specify this. Places with separate restaurants often let children use them,
and hotels usually let children into public areas such as lounges. Some pubs impose
an evening time limit – let us know if you find one earlier than 9pm.

as Cotswold Lion, Hillside, North Cotswold and Stroud, up to 15 wines by the glass from well chosen list, good imaginative food using Estate produce, helpful staff, two low-ceilinged dining rooms with tweed-upholstered chairs around nice mix of tables, cushions on settles, rugs on flagstones, fresh flowers, candles and open fires; background music, TV, board games and skittle alley; children and dogs welcome, picnic-sets out at front, elegant metal furniture in sheltered walled garden, bedrooms, open all day. *(Cecily and Steven Evans)*

STANTON SP0634

★ **Mount** (01386) 584316
Village signposted off B4632 SW of Broadway; keep on past village on no-through road up hill, bear left; WR12 7NE Popular 17th-c pub with lovely views over village towards the welsh mountains; heavy beams in low ceilings, flagstones and inglenook log fire, well kept Donnington ales, good wines by the glass and much enjoyed food from baguettes to daily specials, prompt friendly service despite the crowds, picture-window restaurant taking in the view; darts and board games, free wi-fi; well behaved children and dogs welcome, wheelchair access via side door (no disabled loos), attractive terraced gardens, paddock across lane, good walks (Cotswold Way and Wyche Way nearby), closed Sun evening (and Mon in winter). *(S Holder, Dr A J and Mrs B A Tompsett, Guy Vowles, Chris and Angela Buckell, R J Herd)*

STAUNTON SO7829

Swan (01452) 840323
Ledbury Road (A417), on mini roundabout; GL19 3QA Village pub owned by local farming family (they also have the Red Lion at Bishop's Norton and Royal Exchange in Hartpury); enjoyable well priced food from sandwiches up including set lunch Weds-Sat, ales such as Butcombe and Wye Valley, Weston's cider, bar with sofas and woodburner, spacious restaurant and modern conservatory, attached barn for functions; occasional quiz nights, free wi-fi; children and dogs welcome, pretty garden, open all day Fri-Sun, closed Mon lunchtime, no evening food Sun. *(James and Sylvia Hewitt)*

STAUNTON SO5412

White Horse (01594) 834001
A4136; GL16 8PA Village pub on edge of Forest of Dean close to welsh border, welcoming and relaxed, with good freshly prepared food in bar or restaurant including popular Sun lunch, well kept local ales and ciders, friendly helpful service; small shop; children and dogs welcome, disabled access, picnic-sets in good-sized garden with glamping pods, open all day Sat, till 9pm Sun, closed Mon. *(Beth Aldridge)*

STAVERTON SO9024

House in the Tree (01242) 680241
Haydon (B4063 W of Cheltenham); GL51 0TQ Friendly old beamed and partly thatched pub; five real ales including Dartmoor, Otter and Sharps, traditional cider and decent wine list, well liked generously served food from baguettes to daily specials, good helpful service, rambling linked areas, open fires; children and dogs welcome, plenty of tables in garden with good play area and pets corner, handy for M5 (junction 10), open all day, food all day Sat, till 6pm Sun. *(Anne Taylor)*

STOW-ON-THE-WOLD SP1925

Bell (01451) 870916
Park Street; A436 E of centre; GL54 1AJ Modernised creeper-clad dining pub with enjoyable food from breakfasts and bar snacks up, lots of wines by the glass including champagne, well kept Youngs and a guest such as Purity, can eat in beamed and flagstoned bar with woodburner, or connecting dining areas; live acoustic music Sun evening, quiz Tues; children and dogs welcome, picnic-sets outside, five well equipped bedrooms, eight more in nearby townhouse, open (and food) all day from 8am. *(Simon Collett-Jones)*

STOW-ON-THE-WOLD SP1925

Queens Head (01451) 830563
The Square; GL54 1AB Traditional old Donnington pub under new management; overlooking the market square; their well kept/priced beers along with good well cooked pubby food, friendly chatty staff and buoyant atmosphere, stripped-stone front lounge, heavily beamed and flagstoned back bar with high-backed settles, coal-effect fire; background music; children (not in front bar) and dogs welcome, tables in attractive sunny back courtyard, open all day. *(Richard Tilbrook, Martin Day)*

STOW-ON-THE-WOLD SP1925

Talbot (01451) 870934
The Square; GL54 1BQ Relaxed one-bar pub in good position on market square; light airy décor with wood-clad walls and easy chairs by log fire, well liked/priced food from sandwiches and sharing plates to grills, Wadworths ales, real cider and several wines by the glass, upstairs function room (and lavatories); background and live (Fri) music, free wi-fi; children and dogs welcome, a few courtyard tables, open all day (till 6pm Sun); some refurbishment planned as we went to press. *(I D Barnett)*

STROUD SO8505

Ale House (01453) 755447
John Street; GL5 2HA Fine range of well kept beers and ciders/perries (third-of-a-pint tasting glasses available), enjoyable food including signature curries and good value

Sun lunch, main high-ceilinged part with sofa by big open fire, other rooms off; live music and quiz nights; well behaved children and dogs welcome, small side courtyard with café-style tables and chairs, farmers' market Sat, open all day Fri-Sun. *(Guy Vowles)*

SWINEFORD ST6969
Swan (0117) 932 3101
A431, right on the Somerset border; BS30 6LN Popular 19th-c roadside pub, well kept Bath and St Austell ales, local ciders, decent wines and good range of spirits including Penderyn welsh whisky and Tarquin cornish gin, enjoyable food from lunchtime sandwiches up, efficient friendly staff, updated interior with quarry tiles and light wood floors, pastel walls and bluey-green panelling, raised back dining area, open fire; background music; children and dogs welcome, wheelchair access to main bar, picnic-sets out at front and in large grassy garden with play area, open all day, food all day weekends. *(Tom and Ruth Rees, Chris and Angela Buckell)*

TETBURY ST8893
Close (01666) 502272
Long Street; GL8 8AQ Old stone hotel's contemporary bar, comfortable and stylish with blazing log fire, enjoyable food from sandwiches up, also brasserie and more formal dining room, coffee and afternoon teas, charming staff; children welcome, tables in lovely garden behind, open all day. *(Celia and Geoff Clay)*

★ TETBURY ST8993
Royal Oak (01666) 500021
Cirencester Road; GL8 8EY Carefully renovated golden-stone inn; rambling open-plan bar with several snug areas and roaring log fire, variety of chairs around dark tables on wide floorboards, built-in green leather wall seats and a few elbow tables, six real ales including Moor from handsome carved counter, also traditional cider, ten wines by the glass and interesting spirits, upstairs dining room with fine raftered ceiling, dark polished furniture on more wide floorboards, fresh flowers and candles, good food (not Sun evening) including a vegan menu, friendly helpful service; background and some live music, free wi-fi; children welcome till 8pm (unless in restaurant), dogs in bar, disabled access/loos, tables under parasols on terraces and lawn, maybe Airstream trailer for mexican street food in summer, good boutique bedrooms across cobbled courtyard (book well ahead), woodland walks from the door, open all day. *(Chris and Angela Buckell, Nicky Michaels, Peter Harrison)*

TETBURY ST8993
Snooty Fox (01666) 502436
Market Place; GL8 8DD High-ceilinged stripped-stone hotel lounge serving four well kept local ales, a real cider and good house

wines, enjoyable all-day bar food including breakfasts for non-residents (9-11.30am) and afternoon teas (3-5.30pm), leather sofas and elegant fireplace, nice side room and anteroom, restaurant; background music; children and dogs welcome, a few sheltered tables out in front, 12 bedrooms. *(Martin and Joanne Sharp)*

TEWKESBURY SO8932
Nottingham Arms (01684) 276346
High Street; GL20 5JU Popular old black and white-fronted local under new management; bare-boards timbered bar with ales such as St Austell, Sharps and Wye Valley, enjoyable home-made food at reasonable prices including good Sun lunch, friendly service, back dining room; Sun live music, Thurs quiz; children and dogs welcome, open all day. *(Dr J Barrie Jones)*

TEWKESBURY SO8932
Royal Hop Pole (01684) 274039
Church Street; GL20 5RT Wetherspoons conversion of old inn (some parts dating from the 15th c); their usual value-minded all-day food and drink, good speedy service; free wi-fi; terrace seating and lovely garden leading down to river, 28 bedrooms, open from 7am. *(Theocsbrian, Dr J Barrie Jones)*

TEWKESBURY SO8932
Theoc House (01684) 296562
Barton Street; GL20 5PY Old pub now more like a café/wine bar but with local ales, good range of reasonably priced food including tapas and all-day brunch, enthusiastic young staff, spacious split-level interior, books and board games; monthly live jazz, quiz night Sun, free wi-fi; children and dogs welcome, open (and food) all day from 8.30am breakfast. *(Beth Alridge)*

TODDINGTON SP0432
Pheasant (01242) 621271
A46 Broadway–Winchcombe, junction with A438 and B4077; GL54 5DT Large stone-built roadside pub with modern open-plan interior; tartan carpets, blue panelled dados and log fire, Donnington ales and generous helpings of enjoyable good value food, friendly attentive staff; children and dogs (in bar area) welcome, picnic-sets outside, handy for preserved Gloucestershire Warwickshire Steam Railway station, open all day, breakfast (10-11am, not Mon), no food Sun evening. *(Martin and Joanne Sharp)*

TOLLDOWN ST7577
Crown (01225) 891166
1 mile from M4 junction 18 – A46 towards Bath; SN14 8HZ Cosy heavy-beamed stone pub on crossroads; most here for the good food (all day Sun) from sandwiches and pub favourites to more upmarket choices, special diets also catered for, efficient welcoming staff, Wadworths ales, Thatcher's cider, plenty of wines by the glass

and some decent gins, warm log fires, candles on pine tables, wood, coir and quarry-tiled floors, animal prints on green rough plaster walls, some bare stonework; children and dogs (in bar) welcome, disabled access/loos, sunny beer garden, nine bedrooms in building behind, handy for Dyrham Park (NT), open all day. *(Chris and Angela Buckell, Dr and Mrs A K Clarke, Hugh Maclean)*

ULEY ST7998
Old Crown (01453) 860502
The Green; GL11 5SN Unspoilt 17th-c pub prettily set by village green just off Cotswold Way; long narrow room with settles and pews on bare boards, step up to partitioned-off lounge, five well kept local ales including Uley, decent wines by the glass and small choice of well liked pubby food from baguettes up, friendly service, open fire; children and dogs welcome, a few picnic-sets in front and attractive garden behind, four bedrooms, open all day. *(Daniel King)*

UPPER ODDINGTON SP2225
★ Horse & Groom (01451) 830584
Village signposted from A436 E of Stow-on-the-Wold; GL56 0XH Welcoming 16th-c Cotswold-stone village inn; beamed bar with stripped-stone walls and inglenook log fire, three real ales including Wye Valley, local cider and plenty of wines by the glass, popular well cooked food from sensibly short but varied menu, can eat in bar, comfortable lounge or restaurant; background music, free wi-fi; children and dogs (in bar) welcome, tables under parasols on terrace and in garden, bedrooms in main building and 'cottage', good breakfast, open all day. *(Nigel and Sue Foster)*

UPTON CHEYNEY ST6969
Upton Inn (0117) 932 4489
Village signed off A431 at Bitton; BS30 6LY Friendly 18th-c stone-built village pub; bar with wood or carpeted floors, two dining areas, one with woodburner in huge stone fireplace, the other with white panelling and pictures of old Bath, enjoyable home-made food from snacks up, well kept Badger ales, Thatcher's and Weston's ciders, pleasant hard-working staff; background music; children welcome, wheelchair access from back door, disabled loo (shared with ladies'), views of the Avon Valley from front terrace, open all day. *(Chris and Angela Buckell, Tom and Ruth Rees)*

WESTONBIRT ST8690
★ Hare & Hounds (01666) 881000
A433 SW of Tetbury; GL8 8QL Substantial roadside hotel with separate entrance to pub; much liked food from snacks and sharing boards up, well kept regional ales such as Cotswold and Wadworths, interesting ciders, lots of wines by the glass and good gin/whisky/rum selection (some locally distilled), coffee and

afternoon teas, prompt polite service from uniformed staff, two bar areas and series of interconnecting rooms with polished wood floors, various pictures (including hares and hounds) and woodburner in two-way fireplace, more formal restaurant; background music; children welcome, muddy boots and dogs (there's a menu for them) in bar, disabled access/loos/parking, shaded wicker tables on front paved terrace, pleasant gardens, 42 bedrooms (some in outbuildings), convenient for the Arboretum, open all day and gets very busy (especially weekend lunchtimes). *(Chris and Angela Buckell)*

WHITECROFT SO6005
Miners Arms (01594) 562483
B4234 N of Lydney; GL15 4PE Popular local under friendly new management; up to five changing ales, traditional cider and enjoyable sensibly priced food from lunchtime sandwiches up, rooms on either side of bar, woodburner and open fire, conservatory; background and some live music including jazz, skittle alley; children and dogs welcome, disabled access/loos, gardens front and back (one with stream), good local walks and well placed for steam railway, self-catering cottage, open all day. *(Chris and Angela Buckell)*

WILLERSEY SP1039
Bell (01386) 858405
B4632 Cheltenham–Stratford, near Broadway; WR12 7PJ Imposing neatly modernised 17th-c stone inn overlooking village green and duck pond; popular home-made food from sandwiches and bar meals up, Purity UBU and Mad Goose, prompt friendly service; children welcome, dogs in bar, lots of tables in big garden, good local walks (Cotswold Way), five bedrooms in outbuildings, open all day weekends. *(Charles and Maddie Bishop)*

WINCHCOMBE SP0228
Corner Cupboard (01242) 602303
Gloucester Street; GL54 5LX Attractive old golden-stone pub with enjoyable food (all day weekends) including range of curries in back dining room, four well kept ales such as Fullers, Sharps, Wickwar and Wye Valley, decent wines by the glass; comfortable stripped-stone lounge bar with heavy-beamed Tudor core, traditional hatch-service lobby, small side room with woodburner in massive stone fireplace; sports TV; children and dogs welcome, tables in back garden, handy for nearby Gloucestershire Warwickshire Steam Railway, open all day, food all day weekends. *(Dr A J and Mrs B A Tompsett)*

WINCHCOMBE SP0228
White Hart (01242) 602359
High Street (B4632); GL54 5LJ 16th-c inn with big windows looking out over village street, mix of chairs and small settles around

pine tables on bare boards, well kept ales such as Goffs, Otter and Sharps, wine shop at back (corkage added if you buy to drink on premises), also good choice by the glass, generally well liked food including specials, afternoon teas, good friendly service, separate restaurant; children and dogs (in bar and bedrooms) welcome, open all day from 8am for breakfast. *(Caroline and Peter Bryant)*

WITHINGTON   SP0315
Mill Inn (01242) 890204
Off A436 or A40; GL54 4BE Idyllic streamside setting for this mossy-roofed old stone inn, plenty of character with nice nooks and corners, beams, wood or flagstone floors, two inglenook log fires and woodburner, well kept/priced Sam Smiths tapped from the cask and ample helpings of traditional food including basket meals,

four dining rooms, cheerful staff; children and dogs welcome, picnic-sets in big garden, splendid walks, open all day Fri-Sun in summer (all day Sat, closed Sun evening in winter), shut Mon lunchtime. *(Richard Tilbrook)*

WOOLASTON COMMON   SO5900
Rising Sun (01594) 529282
Village signed off A48 Lydney–Chepstow; GL15 6NU Traditional 17th-c stone village pub on fringe of Forest of Dean; generous helpings of good home-made food (some choices available in smaller servings), well kept Marstons Pedigree, Wye Valley Bitter and a guest, friendly service; quiz Weds; children and dogs welcome, seats out at front and in large back garden, open all day during summer school holidays, otherwise all day Fri-Sun, closed Mon lunchtime. *(Monica and Steph Evans)*

Hampshire

AMPORT
Hawk Inn 🛏

SU2944 Map 2

(01264) 710371 – www.hawkinnamport.co.uk

Off A303 at Thruxton interchange; at Andover end of village just before Monxton;
SP11 8AE

**Relaxed rambling pub with contemporary furnishings, helpful staff
and well thought-of food; bedrooms**

Our favourite spot for a relaxed drink and a chat in this rambling pub is
the comfortable front bar. This is open-plan and modern, with brown
leather armchairs and plush grey sofas by a low table, sisal matting on bare
boards and a log fire in a brick fireplace. To the left, a tucked-away snug
room has horse-racing photographs, shelves of books and a TV. Two dining
areas have smart window blinds, black leather cushioned wall seating and
elegant wooden chairs (some carved) around pale tables, big oil paintings on
pale walls above a grey dado, and a woodburning stove; background music
and board games. Black-topped stools line the counter, where courteous
staff serve Nethergate Priory Mild on handpump and quite a few wines by
the glass. A sunny sandstone front terrace has picnic-sets looking across the
lane to more seating on grass that leads down to Pill Hill Brook. Bedrooms
are comfortable, stylish and up to date and breakfasts are good. The famous
Hawk Conservancy Trust is just down the road.

Food is good and includes venison scotch egg with apple and black pudding purée
and celeriac rémoulade, salted cod croquettes with crab mayonnaise, sharing
boards, roasted butternut squash linguine with shiitake mushrooms and creamy onion
and coconut purée, sausages of the day with onion gravy, confit duck leg with roasted
garlic mash, orange and thyme and braised red cabbage, a pie of the day, skate wings
with chorizo and new potatoes and parsley and butter sauce, and puddings. *Benchmark
main dish: burger with toppings, coleslaw and fries £14.50. Two-course evening
meal £22.00.*

Upham ~ Manager Ryan Blandford ~ Real ale ~ Open 7.30am-11pm; 8.30am-11pm Sat;
8.30am-10.30pm Sun ~ Bar food 12-2.30, 6-9 (9.30 Fri, Sat) ~ Children welcome ~ Dogs
welcome ~ Wi-fi ~ Live music monthly ~ Bedrooms: /£100 *Recommended by Chloe and
Michael Swettenham, Mick Allen, Christopher and Elise Way*

'Children welcome' means the pub says it lets children inside without any special
restriction. If it allows them in, but to restricted areas such as an eating area or family
room, we specify this. Some pubs may impose an evening time limit. We do not mention
limits after 9pm as we assume children are home by then.

BANK
SU2806 Map 2

Oak

(023) 8028 2350 – www.oakinnlyndhurst.co.uk

Signposted just off A35 SW of Lyndhurst; SO43 7FD

Busy New Forest pub with friendly, efficient staff, popular food and interesting décor

There's always quite a mix of customers here, and as it's tucked away they tend to be walkers, cyclists and horse-riders. The L-shaped bar has bay windows with built-in red-cushioned seats, and two or three little pine-panelled booths with small built-in tables and bench seats. The rest of the bare-boarded bar has low beams and joists, candles in brass holders on a row of stripped old and newer blond tables set against the wall and all manner of bric-a-brac: fishing rods, spears, a boomerang, old ski poles, brass platters, heavy knives and guns. There are cushioned milk churns along the bar counter and little red lanterns among hop bines above the bar. Fullers London Pride and two weekly changing guests on handpump and 14 wines by the glass; background music. A pleasant side garden has picnic-sets and long tables and benches by big yew trees.

 Quite a choice of food includes lunchtime sandwiches, smoked mackerel pâté with ale chutney, black pudding and leek croquettes with apple ketchup, sharing boards, gnocchi with mozzarella, peas, shallots and broccoli and pine nut pesto, burger with toppings and triple-cooked chips, salmon, chorizo and butter bean casserole, duck breast with caramelised shallots, fondant potato and red wine jus, hot smoked salmon niçoise salad with olives and a quail egg, and puddings such as bakewell tart and crème anglaise, chocolate brownie with peanut brittle, salted caramel and buffalo milk ice-cream. *Benchmark main dish: beer-battered haddock and triple-cooked chips £13.50. Two-course evening meal £20.00.*

Fullers ~ Manager Matt England ~ Real ale ~ Open 11.30-11; 12-10.30 Sun ~ Bar food 12-5, 6-9 (8 Sun) ~ Children welcome during food service ~ Dogs allowed in bar ~ Wi-fi
Recommended by Katharine Cowherd, John Evans, Fiona and Jack Henderson

BAUGHURST
SU5860 Map 2

Wellington Arms

(0118) 982 0110 – www.thewellingtonarms.com

Baughurst Road, S of village; RG26 5LP

Hampshire Dining Pub of the Year

Delightful little country pub-with-rooms with hands-on, hard-working owners, exceptional cooking and a friendly welcome; character bedrooms

The wonderful food receives constant admiration from our readers, but this charming, immaculately kept and pretty little spot is also a lovely place to stay with four deeply comfortable and very well equipped bedrooms; breakfasts are first class. A thoughtful choice of drinks includes Longdog Bunny Chaser and West Berkshire Good Old Boy on handpump, 12 wines by the glass from a smashing list, farm ciders, good aperitifs and home-made elderflower cordial; background music. The dining room is attractively decorated with an assortment of cushioned oak dining chairs around a mix of polished tables on terracotta tiles, pretty blinds, brass candlesticks, flowers and windowsills stacked with cookery books. The garden has colourful herbaceous borders, teak tables and chairs under parasols as well as some picnic-sets.

From a daily changing, sensibly short menu using their own vegetables, home-reared livestock, honey from their bees and other very carefully sourced produce – and cooked by the chef-landlord – the exceptional food includes pheasant, rabbit and pork terrine with spiced apple chutney, salad with hand-picked crab, avocado, shoots and leaves and marie rose sauce, potato gnocchi with garlic, caramelised butternut squash, walnuts, sage and parmesan, lamb in white wine and rosemary pie with mash, roast cod fillet with preserved lemon crust, sautéed samphire and puy lentils, chargrilled pork chop on sticky red cabbage with parsnip crisps, and puddings such as eton mess and chocolate squidgy pudding with stem ginger ice-cream; they also offer a two- and three-course lunch. *Benchmark main dish: twice-baked cheese soufflé £11.00. Two-course evening meal £30.00.*

Free house ~ Licensees Simon Page and Jason King ~ Real ale ~ Open 9-3, 6-10 (11 Sat); 9-5 Sun ~ Bar food 12-1.30, 6.30-8; 12-1.30, 6-9 Fri, Sat; 12-3 Sun ~ Children allowed weekend lunchtimes ~ Dogs welcome ~ Wi-fi ~ Bedrooms: /£125
Recommended by Mrs P Sumner, Alexandra and Richard Clay, Melanie and David Lawson, Christopher and Elise Way, Diana and Richard Gibbs, Andrew and Nicky Churcher

BEAULIEU
SU3902 Map 2

Montagu Arms

(01590) 614986 – www.montaguarmshotel.co.uk
Almost opposite Palace House; SO42 7ZL

Separate Monty's Bar, open for both drinks and food

If you come to this picturesque village at the heart of the New Forest, drop into Monty's Bar. It's attached to the civilised Montagu Arms hotel, but does have its own entrance and is usefully open all day. This simply furnished bar has panelling, bare floorboards, bay windows and a mix of pale tables surrounded by tartan-cushioned dining chairs; winter log fire. Stools line the bar counter where they keep Ringwood Best and Fortyniner and a seasonal guest on handpump and several wines by the glass, served by cheerful, helpful bar staff. Across the entrance hall is a smarter panelled dining room. Do visit the hotel's tucked-away back garden – it's really quite charming in warm weather.

 Using produce grown in their kitchen garden, the popular food includes sandwiches, seared scallops with celeriac purée, salt-baked celeriac, apple foam and bacon crumb, chicken and game terrine with pickled red cabbage, a vegetarian dish of the day, chicken caesar salad, fish pie, lamb of the day with dauphinoise potatoes and jus, duck breast with orange and carrot purée, duck fat hash browns, honey-roasted hazelnuts and ginger beer glaze, and puddings such as chocolate tart with brandy cream and seville orange soufflé. *Benchmark main dish: burger with toppings, slaw and fries £15.95. Two-course evening meal £22.00.*

Free house ~ Licensee Andrew Nightingale ~ Real ale ~ Open 11-3, 6-11.30; 11am-11.30pm Sat, Sun ~ Bar food 12-2.30, 6.30-9 ~ Restaurant ~ Children welcome ~ Dogs allowed in bar ~ Wi-fi ~ Bedrooms: $174/$229 *Recommended by Maggie and Matthew Lyons, Susan and Tim Boyle, Mary Joyce, Andrea and Philip Crispin, Caroline Prescott, Nicola and Stuart Parsons*

BRANSGORE
SZ1997 Map 2

Three Tuns 🍴⭐🍷🛏

(01425) 672232 – www.threetunsinn.com
Village signposted off A35 and off B3347 N of Christchurch; Ringwood Road, opposite church; BH23 8JH

17th-c inn with proper old-fashioned bar with good beers, a civilised main dining area and inventive food

Now a free house and brewing their own Three Tuns ales, this pretty thatched pub is much enjoyed in summer with its lovely hanging baskets, picnic-sets on an attractive and extensive, shrub-sheltered terrace and more tables on the grass looking over pony paddocks; pétanque. Inside, on the right, is a separate traditional regulars' bar that seems almost taller than it is wide, with an impressive log-effect stove in a stripped-brick hearth, some shiny black panelling and individualistic pubby furnishings. The friendly, helpful licensees keep their own Three Tuns beers, Exmoor Gold, Otter Amber, Purity Pure Gold, Ringwood Best Bitter and Fortyniner and two or three quickly changing guests on handpump (they also hold a beer festival in September) plus a farm cider and a dozen wines by the glass. A roomy, low-ceilinged and carpeted main area has a fireside 'codgers' corner', as well as a good mix of comfortably cushioned low chairs around a variety of dining tables. The Grade II listed barn is popular for parties – and they hold a civil ceremonies licence. Disabled access and newly refurbished disabled loo.

Creative food includes sandwiches, oysters with raspberry vinegar and shallot dressing, truffle salami, truffle custard, veal jelly and apple rémoulade, vegetable and halloumi espetada (on skewers) with cheese custard and garlic bread, pork sausages with haricot beans in tomato sauce, calves liver and bacon with mash and onion jus, roast halibut on crab risotto with mango and lemon gel and red pepper essence, moroccan-style lamb with confit lemon, and puddings such as banana and chestnut pavlova with caramel sauce and chocolate salami with cherry sandwich. *Benchmark main dish: slow-roasted pork with compressed apple and cider and mustard sauce £16.00. Two-course evening meal £25.00.*

Free house ~ Licensee Nigel Glenister ~ Real ale ~ Open 11-11; 12-10.30 Sun ~ Bar food 12-2.15, 6-9.15; 12-9.15 weekends and bank holidays ~ Restaurant ~ Children welcome ~ Dogs allowed in bar ~ Wi-fi *Recommended by Dr Martin Owton, M G Hart, Buster and Helena Hastings, Sophie Ellison, Patricia and Gordon Thompson, Matt and Hayley Jacob*

CADNAM

SU2913 Map 2

White Hart ♀ ▥

(023) 8081 2277 – www.brunningandprice.co.uk/whitehartcadnam
Old Romsey Road, handy for M27 junction 1; SO40 2NP

New Forest pub with busy bar and dining rooms, a warm welcome, good choice of drinks and tasty food

There's always a good mixed crowd of customers in this smartly extended pub, all keen to enjoy the interesting food and drinks. There's a cosy area with a woodburning stove in a nice old brick fireplace, rugs and comfortable leather armchairs; background music and board games. Various dining rooms lead off with more rugs on carpet or tiles, all manner of cushioned dining chairs and wooden tables, frame-to-frame country pictures and photographs on pale walls above painted wooden dados, house plants on windowsills, mirrors and elegant metal chandeliers. The bar has an open fire, stools and tables on parquet flooring and from the long curved counter, St Austell Brunning & Price Traditional Bitter, Flack Manor Double Drop and Hedge Hop, Hop Back Crop Circle and Minstrel and Itchen Valley Watercress Best on handpump, farm ciders, good wines by the glass and cocktails; staff are helpful and friendly. The back terrace and garden have plenty of chairs and tables and there's a children's play area with a painted tractor.

Imaginative food includes sandwiches, wild mushroom arancini with truffle mayonnaise, scallops with cauliflower purée, black pudding fritters and apple dressing, butternut squash risotto with toasted hazelnuts and crispy sage, steak burger with toppings, coleslaw and chips, fish pie with french-style peas, braised lamb shoulder with dauphinoise potatoes, carrot mash and gravy, malaysian fish curry with sticky coconut rice, and puddings such as triple chocolate brownie with chocolate sauce and boozy cherry meringue roulade with mango sorbet. *Benchmark main dish: honey-roasted ham with free-range eggs £11.95. Two-course evening meal £21.00.*

Brunning & Price ~ Manager Steve Butt ~ Real ale ~ Open 9am-11.30pm ~ Bar food 12-9.30; 12-10 Fri, Sat; 12-9 Sun ~ Restaurant ~ Children welcome ~ Dogs allowed in bar ~ Wi-fi
Recommended by Tim and Mary Thomson, Mick Allen, Alister and Margery Bacon, Nicholas and Lucy Sage, Maggie and Stevan Hollis, Diana and Bertie Farr

DROXFORD
SU6018   Map 2

Bakers Arms

(01489) 877533 – www.thebakersarmsdroxford.com
High Street; A32 5 miles N of Wickham; SO32 3PA

Welcoming, opened-up and friendly pub with good beers, cosy corners and interesting cooking

As the brewery is only a mile away from this cheerful pub, the Bowman Swift One and Wallops Wood are in perfect condition. They also keep a guest such as Ringwood Old Thumper on handpump, local cider and ten wines by the glass from a short, carefully chosen list. The pub is attractively laid out with the central L-shaped, open-plan bar as the main focus. Well spaced tables on carpet or neat bare boards are spread about with low leather chesterfields and an assortment of comfortably cushioned chairs at one end; a dark panelled dado, dark beams and joists and a modicum of country oddments emphasise the freshness of the crisp white paintwork. A good log fire, an easy-going atmosphere and board games. To one side, with a separate entrance, is the village post office. There are picnic-sets outside. The walks along and around the nearby River Meon are lovely.

A wide choice of well regarded food includes baguettes and gluten-free wraps, whole baked camembert with chutney, hot smoked trout with horseradish pannacotta with pickled cucumber, red cabbage and shiitake mushroom bolognese with brown rice pasta and pecans, home-cooked ham and free-range eggs, chicken breast with pasta in a creamy wild mushroom sauce, crab thermidor with skinny fries, pork fillet with bubble and squeak and chorizo cream sauce, local steaks with dripping chips, and puddings such as chocolate and fudge brownie with butterscotch ice-cream and rhubarb bakewell tart with clotted cream. *Benchmark main dish: wagyu beef burger with slaw and skinny fries £14.75. Two-course evening meal £22.00.*

Free house ~ Licensees Adam and Anna Cordery ~ Real ale ~ Open 11.45-2.30 (3 Sat), 6-11; 12-6 Sun ~ Bar food 12-2, 6-9 (9.30 Fri); 12-2.30, 6-9.30 Sat; 11.45-5 Sun ~ Children welcome ~ Dogs welcome ~ Wi-fi *Recommended by Sandra and Neil White, Nicola and Stuart Parsons, Louise and Anton Parsons, Len and Lilly Dowson, Alison and Michael Harper*

EVERSLEY
SU7762   Map 2

Tally Ho ♀ 🍺

(01189) 732134 – www.brunningandprice.co.uk/tallyho
Fleet Hill; RG27 0RR

Attractive pub with a busy bar and popular dining rooms, a good drinks list and rewarding food and seats outside

An extended former farmhouse this has lots of room both inside and out. The main bar area, which is genuinely dog-friendly, has a few beams and standing timbers, wooden dining chairs and built-in window seats on rugs, bare boards and quarry tiles, house plants and glass bottles on windowsills and stubby candles. By the main door is a giant bellows made up as a table for newspapers and another window seat that's backed by guidebooks. One dining room leads off and two others have unusual slatted wooden walls, more large windows, a raised fireplace, similar tables and chairs on carpet or parquet flooring and a great many prints, cartoons and photographs on pale-painted walls. St Austell Brunning & Price Traditional Bitter plus guest beers from breweries such as Flack Manor, Longdog, Sambrook, Timothy Taylors and West Berkshire on handpump, 21 wines by the glass and around 55 gins; background music. There are plenty of picnic-sets under white parasols on a lawn, with a few wooden tables and chairs by the front door.

Popular food includes sandwiches, seared scallops with black pudding fritters, cauliflower purée and lemon dressing, confit duck leg croquettes with asian salad and plum sauce, thai green vegetable curry with coconut rice, pork and leek sausages with mash and onion gravy, smoked haddock and salmon fishcakes with dill mayonnaise and tomato and spring onion salad, jamaican jerk chicken with mango slaw, cider-braised pork belly with butternut squash purée and sage and onion croquette, and puddings such as dark chocolate tart with orange sorbet and crème brûlée. *Benchmark main dish: crispy beef salad with sweet chilli sauce and cashews £13.95. Two-course evening meal £21.00.*

Brunning & Price ~ Manager Jamie Rensch ~ Real ale ~ Open 10am-midnight; 12-10 Sun ~ Bar food 12-9; 12-9.30 Fri, Sat ~ Restaurant ~ Children welcome ~ Dogs allowed in bar ~ Wi-fi *Recommended by Patricia and Gordon Tucker, Barbara and Phil Bowie, Gary and Marie Miller, Philip Chesington, Lenny and Ruth Walters*

FACCOMBE

SU3958 Map 2

Jack Russell 🏠⭐ 🍷 🛏️

(01264) 737315 ~ www.thejackrussellinn.com

Signed from A343 Newbury–Andover; SP11 0DS

Spacious, brick-built pub with contemporary and old-style furnishings in bar and dining rooms, up-to-date food, friendly service and seats outside; bedrooms

You'll find two resident dogs, Barnie and Betty, and sika and white fallow deer at this sizeable, tucked-away country pub, and your dog will be made welcome in both the pub and some of the comfortable bedrooms (which are in a separate building); lots of surrounding walks. The main door leads to a small entrance room with armchairs and an open fire and this in turn leads into the bar. Here, there's an informal, almost club-like feel with leather button-back wall seats, panelled walls inlaid with A-Z cartoon characters, and kitchen chairs and stools on black and white floor tiles. Cheerful, efficient young staff serve Ramsbury Gold, Ringwood Razorback and West Berkshire Good Old Boy on handpump and quite a few wines from a thoughtful list; background music and TV. The grey-panelled dining area, split up by blue-painted wooden partitions, is furnished with mustard-coloured leather banquettes and chunky wooden chairs around a mix of tables on parquet flooring, and has another open fire, bunches of dried flowers and contemporary ceiling lights. A bigger back restaurant has pale button-back sofas and white-painted chairs around wooden tables on carpet. Throughout there are china plates and china dogs as well as books and board games on delft shelving. The garden has plenty of seats and tables and a pond. Disabled access.

Imaginative food includes sandwiches, moules marinière with home-made bread, game and foie gras terrine with bacon and red onion jam, wild mushroom and tarragon risotto with truffle oil, beer-battered haddock with triple-cooked chips, lamb rump with ratatouille, dauphinoise potatoes and rosemary and thyme jus, pistachio-crusted sea bass with clams, samphire, beetroot risotto and salsa verde, confit pork belly with rhubarb and ginger compote and chorizo pommes anna, and puddings such as chocolate fondant with chocolate sauce and salted caramel ice-cream and vanilla crème brûlée with poached rhubarb. *Benchmark main dish: pie of the day with truffle mash £15.00. Two-course evening meal £24.00.*

Free house ~ Licensee Ross Nicol ~ Real ale ~ Open 11-11; 11-10 Sun ~ Bar food 12-3, 6-9 (9.30 Fri, Sat); 12-7 Sun ~ Children welcome ~ Dogs allowed in bar and bedrooms ~ Wi-fi ~ Bedrooms: £120/£160 *Recommended by Ian Herdman, Chloe and Michael Swettenham, Belinda Stamp, David and Judy Robison, Ivy and George Goodwill, Sarah Roberts, Patrick and Emma Stephenson*

FREEFOLK
SU4848 Map 2

Watership Down ♀ 🍺 🛏
(01256) 892254 – www.watershipdowninn.com
Freefolk Priors, N of B3400 Whitchurch–Overton; brown sign to pub; RG28 7NJ

Cosy bar and open-plan dining rooms, five real ales, good food and pretty garden; bedrooms

At the foot of the North Wessex Downs stands this attractively refurbished old country inn. The wood-floored bar has stools by a pale oak counter, high stools next to an elbow shelf and five real ales on handpump sourced from within a 30-mile radius. These include Bowman Swift One, Flowerpots Bitter, Itchen Valley Hampshire Rose, Stonehenge Sign of Spring and West Berkshire Good Old Boy; several good wines by the glass. Leading off here are two connected dining rooms with mate's chairs (some draped with animal skins) around chunky tables on more bare boards or old brickwork, and a woodburning stove in a raised fireplace; throughout, plants line the windowsills, and modern art and photos hang on pale paintwork above a grey-green dado. A conservatory with high-backed, cushioned wicker chairs around solid tables on floor tiles leads to a two-tiered terrace with seats and tables under big parasols. The large lawn has plenty of picnic-sets and views over the River Test Valley. Seven bedrooms (named after characters from the novel *Watership Down*) are airy and pretty and look across the countryside.

Enjoyable food includes sandwiches, twice-baked cheese soufflé with sticky fig relish, seared scallops with smoked pancetta lardons and vanilla butternut squash purée, mildly spiced mixed vegetable and coconut curry, chicken, bacon and wild mushroom linguine in creamy tarragon and parmesan sauce, local venison steak with sweet and sour red cabbage, blackberries, mushrooms and port jus, slow-cooked ox cheeks in red wine sauce with horseradish mash, and puddings such as lemon and lime tart with blood orange sorbet and baked apple sticky toffee pudding with roasted pecan and maple syrup sauce and vanilla bean ice-cream. *Benchmark main dish: beer-battered haddock with minted pea purée £14.00. Two-course evening meal £22.00.*

Free house ~ Licensee Philip Denée ~ Real ale ~ Open 12-3, 6-11; 12-11.30 Fri, Sat; 12-9.30 Sun ~ Bar food 12-2.30 (3 Sat), 6.30-9; not Sun or Mon evenings ~ Restaurant ~ Children welcome ~ Dogs allowed in bar ~ Wi-fi ~ Bedrooms: /£110 *Recommended by Sally and Brian Turner, Alf and Sally Garner, Jess and George Cowley, David Appleyard, Jane Rigby, Miranda and Jeff Davidson*

FRITHAM
SU2314 Map 2

Royal Oak 🍺
(023) 8081 2606 – www.royaloakfritham.co.uk
Village signed from M27 junction 1; SO43 7HJ

Rural New Forest spot with traditional rooms, log fires, up to seven real ales and simple lunchtime food

This delightful and charming thatched pub is part of a working farm, so there are ponies and pigs out on the green in front and plenty of livestock nearby. The three quite unchanging and neatly kept rooms are straightforward but full of proper traditional character, with black beams, prints and pictures involving local characters on the white walls, restored panelling, antique wheelback, spindleback and other old chairs and stools with colourful seats around solid tables on oak floors, and two roaring log fires. The back bar has books; darts and board games. Up to seven real ales are tapped from the cask including one named for the pub (from Bowman), Branscombe Vale Branoc, Flack Manor Double Drop, Hop Back Summer Lightning, Ringwood Best and Stonehenge Danish Dynamite. Also, nine wines by the glass (mulled wine in winter), 14 country wines, local cider and a September beer festival; service remains friendly and efficient even when the pub is packed (which it often is). Summer barbecues may be held in the neatly kept big garden, which has a marquee for poor weather and a pétanque pitch. They have three shepherd's huts to rent for overnight stays. Dogs are welcome but must be on a lead. Disabled access.

Good value, limited food – served at lunchtime only – consists of wholesome winter soup, a particularly good pork pie, quiche and sausages. *Benchmark main dish: ploughman's £8.50.*

Free house ~ Licensees Neil and Pauline McCulloch ~ Real ale ~ Open 11-11; 12-10.30 Sun; 11-3, 5.30-11 weekdays in winter ~ Bar food 12-2.30 (3 weekends) ~ Children welcome ~ Dogs welcome *Recommended by Ann and Colin Hunt, Peter Meister, David and Judy Robison, Gerry and Pam Pollard, Holly and Tim Waite*

HIGHCLERE
Yew Tree 🍷 🛏

SU4358 Map 2

(01635) 253360 – www.theyewtree.co.uk

Hollington Cross; RG20 9SE

Friendly country inn with character rooms, a good choice of drinks, enjoyable food and seats in garden; bedrooms

With Highclere Castle so nearby, this 17th-c inn does get its fair share of *Downton Abbey* fans at peak times. The main door opens into a heavy-beamed character bar with leather tub chairs and a leather sofa in front of a two-way fireplace housing a chiminea stove, and stools and high chairs against the counter (church candles in chunky candlesticks to either side). Ringwood Boondoggle and West Berkshire Good Old Boy on handpump and good wines by the glass, served by friendly, helpful staff. Leading off to the left is a room with antlers and stuffed squirrels on the mantelpiece above an inglenook fireplace, books piled on shelves, a pale button-back leather window seat, a mix of wooden and painted dining chairs around nice old tables on red and black tiles or carpet and, at one end, a tartan and leather wall banquette; background music and board games. Dining rooms to the left of the bar, divided by hefty timbers, have high-backed tartan seating creating booths and more wooden or painted chairs around a mix of tables on flagstones or sisal carpet. Doors lead to the garden where there's an outside bar and a variety of elegant metal and teak seats and tables either on gravel or raised decking. Well equipped and comfortable bedrooms (two on the ground floor) are named after trees; breakfasts are good.

Highly popular food includes venison carpaccio with truffle aioli, black pepper crisps and sauerkraut, gin-cured trout with charred cucumber and horseradish, beetroot risotto with parmesan crisps and pickled golden beetroot, guinea fowl breast with jerusalem artichoke foam and cream sauce, monkfish wrapped in parma ham with carrot purée and spiced parmentier potatoes, a trio of pork with black pudding, mash, apple and jus, rib-eye steak with a choice of sauce, and puddings such as treacle tart with vanilla ice-cream and passion-fruit pannacotta with pineapple; they also offer a two- and three-course set menu. *Benchmark main dish: roasted cauliflower with truffle crumb and watercress pesto £12.00. Two-course evening meal £20.50.*

Free house ~ Licensee Kiran Shukla ~ Real ale ~ Open 8am-11pm ~ Bar food 12-2.30, 6-9 ~ Children welcome ~ Dogs welcome ~ Wi-fi ~ Bedrooms: /£120 *Recommended by Richard Kennell, Darren and Jane Staniforth, David and Judy Robison, Andrew Wall, Nicola and Nigel Matthews, Moira and John Wheeler*

HOOK
Hogget

SU7153 Map 2

(01256) 763009 – www.thehogget.co.uk
1.1 miles from M3 junction 5; A287 N, at junction with A30 (car park just before traffic lights); RG27 9JJ

Well run and accommodating pub giving all-round good value

Both the A30 and M3 are nearby, so lunchtime here can be busy. It's a chatty pub with a friendly atmosphere and the various comfortable rooms ramble around the central servery, providing plenty of space for all. The wallpaper, lighting and carpet pattern, plus high-backed stools and bar tables on the right at the back, give an easy-going and homely feel – as does the way the layout provides several smallish distinct areas. Ringwood Fortyniner and Razorback and Wychwood Hobgoblin on handpump, 14 wines by the glass plus prosecco and plenty of neatly dressed staff; daily papers, background music and books (often cookery books) on shelves. A sizeable terrace has sturdy tables and chairs, including some in a heated covered area.

Tasty food includes sandwiches, calamari with aioli and lemon, creamy stilton mushrooms on toast, spaghetti with roasted peppers, sprouting broccoli, chilli and lemon, chicken and bacon caesar salad, prawn and crayfish risotto with leeks, garlic and parmesan, hot and sticky barbecue pork spare ribs with coleslaw, chilli con carne, lamb and apricot tagine with saffron and coriander couscous, and puddings such as cheesecake of the day and chocolate brownie with vanilla ice-cream. *Benchmark main dish: burger with toppings £11.00. Two-course evening meal £19.00.*

Marstons ~ Lease Tom and Laura Faulkner ~ Real ale ~ Open 12-3, 6-11; 12-11 Sat; 12-7 Sun ~ Bar food 12-2.30, 6.30-9; 12-9 Sat; 12-6 Sun ~ Restaurant ~ Children welcome but not after 7pm Fri, Sat ~ Dogs allowed in bar ~ Wi-fi *Recommended by Mary and Douglas McDowell, Kerry and Guy Trooper, Angela and Steve Heard, Frances Parsons, Susan Eccleston, Edward Nile*

HURSLEY
Kings Head ♀ 🍺 🛏

SU4225 Map 2

(01962) 775208 – www.kingsheadhursley.co.uk
A3090 Winchester–Romsey; SO21 2JW

Creeper-covered pub with interestingly furnished rooms, well kept ales, good wines and enjoyable food; lovely bedrooms

Bedrooms here (named after previous owners of the Hursley Estate) are thoughtfully equipped and comfortable with original fireplaces and antiques. Turning to the left inside the door is a bar with a cushioned and shuttered window seat, high-backed plush green chairs and chunky leather stools around scrubbed tables on black floor slates, one high table with equally high chairs, and a raised fireplace with church candles on the mantelpiece above. Stools line the S-shaped, grey-painted counter where they serve Palmers Copper Ale, Ringwood Razorback and Sharps Doom

Bar on handpump, 21 wines by the glass, 40 gins and ten malt whiskies; background music, daily papers and board games. A character lower room has a rather fine brick wall, a woodburning stove and wall banquettes with leather and tartan upholstery, and cushioned settles on floorboards. You can hire out the atmospheric downstairs skittle alley. There are seats and tables in the smart courtyard garden, plus parasols and heaters. The ancient village church is opposite.

 Pleasing food includes lunchtime flatbreads with toppings, sharing boards, local venison salami with beetroot sorbet, trio of prawns with marie rose sauce and bloody mary salsa, butternut squash gnocchi with sorrel, mushrooms, local bocconcini, tomato and basil, sausages with bubble and squeak and eggs, lemon sole meunière with brown shrimp black butter, confit pork belly char siu with spiced noodles, pak choi and crispy skin, and puddings such as peanut butter parfait with praline and butterscotch and passion-fruit pannacotta with pineapple flower. *Benchmark main dish: beer-battered fish and chips £14.75. Two-course evening meal £21.00.*

Free house ~ Licensee Liam Chamberlain ~ Real ale ~ Open 11-11 ~ Bar food 12-3, 6-9.30 ~ Restaurant ~ Children welcome ~ Dogs allowed in bar and bedrooms ~ Wi-fi ~ Bedrooms: /£100 *Recommended by Andrew Lawson, Donald Allsopp, Toby Jones, Christopher and Elise Way, Jack and Hilary Burton, Liz and Martin Eldon, Tim King*

HURSTBOURNE TARRANT
SU3853 Map 2

George & Dragon 🎯 🍷 🛏

(01264) 736277 ~ www.georgeanddragon.com
The Square (A343); SP11 0AA

15th-c coaching inn with local ales, particularly good food and wine, and seats on a terrace; bedrooms

There are plenty of original features in this carefully renovated inn and the beamed bar is at the heart of things. There's a leather chesterfield and a couple of large upholstered pouffes on quarry tiles in front of a woodburning stove and stools against the counter. Here, helpful, convivial staff keep Betteridges HBT (named for the pub – the brewery is just a few yards away), Penton Park The Duke and West Berkshire Mr Swifts Pale Ale on handpump and 16 wines by the glass (also served by the carafe) from a carefully chosen list; it's all very relaxed and friendly. Carpeted dining areas have mate's chairs and wheelbacks, cushioned banquettes line cosy window alcoves and a second woodburner is fronted by button-back armchairs. There are seats and tables on a small secluded terrace, and nine comfortable, quiet bedrooms. This is a pretty village surrounding by walking country.

⭐ High quality food includes tapas dishes such as crispy scallop roe with wasabi pearls and tapioca and chicken terrine with confit fennel plus halibut with passion fruit, lambs lettuce and crouton, goats curd with carrot fondant and hazelnut pesto, gnocchi with cheese, leek cream, truffle and grilled broccoli, monkfish with oysters, broccoli and mussel broth, lamb rump with goats cheese, pine nuts and mint, salt-aged rib-eye steak with bordelaise butter and triple-cooked chips, and puddings such as custard tart with smoked brown sugar ice-cream and whipped ruby chocolate cheesecake with blackberry sorbet. *Benchmark main dish: burger with toppings and fries £15.00. Two-course evening meal £23.00.*

Free house ~ Licensee Patrick Vaughan-Fowler ~ Real ale ~ Open 8am-11pm (10pm Sun) ~ Bar food 12-2.30, 6-9; 12-3, 6-9.30 Fri, Sat; 12-3, 6-8 Sun ~ Children welcome ~ Dogs allowed in bar ~ Wi-fi ~ Bedrooms: £75/£90 *Recommended by Freddie and Sarah Banks, Alexandra and Richard Clay, Sandra and Michael Smith, Julie and Andrew Blanchett, Nick Sharpe*

LITTLETON

SU4532 Map 2

Running Horse 🌟 ⌨

(01962) 880218 – www.runninghorseinn.co.uk

Main Road; village signed off B3049 NW of Winchester; SO22 6QS

Carefully renovated country pub with several dining areas, woodburning stove in the bar, enjoyable food and cabana in garden; pretty bedrooms

Staff here are courteous and friendly and the atmosphere is chatty and easy-going. Spreading dining areas, gently refurbished in 2019, are attractively furnished with an appealing variety of chairs and tables on big flagstones or bare boards. Also, button-backed banquettes in a panelled alcove, an unusual wine-bottle ceiling light, old books on rustic bookshelves and big mirrors. A brick fireplace holds a woodburning stove, and leather-topped stools line the bar counter where they keep three real ales including Moles Best, Red Cat Prowler Pale and a changing guest on handpump, 14 wines by the glass and a farm cider. The front and back terraces have seats and tables and there are picnic-sets on the back grass by a spreading sycamore, and a popular cabana with cushioned seats. Bedrooms are attractive and breakfasts are good.

 Good quality, popular food includes sandwiches, twice-baked cheese soufflé with red onion marmalade, moules marinière, sharing boards, vegetable kedgeree with curry velouté and a soft boiled egg, a pie of the day, roast cod with white bean cassoulet and pickled fennel, chicken supreme with wild mushrooms and dauphinoise potatoes, venison haunch with butternut fondant, red cabbage and jus, and puddings such as dark chocolate cheesecake with peanut butter ice-cream and apple and blackberry crumble with mascarpone ice-cream. *Benchmark main dish: calves liver with crispy bacon and onion jus £14.95. Two-course evening meal £21.00.*

Upham ~ Licensee Jack Fuller ~ Real ale ~ Open 11-11; 12-10.30 Sun ~ Bar food 12-2.30, 6-9 (9.30 Fri, Sat); 12-8 Sun ~ Restaurant ~ Children welcome ~ Dogs allowed in bar and bedrooms ~ Wi-fi ~ Bedrooms: /£119 *Recommended by Lyn and Freddie Roberts, Frances and Hamish Potter, Christopher and Elise Way, Jamie and Lizzie McEwan, Gail and Arthur Roberts*

LONGSTOCK

SU3537 Map 2

Peat Spade 🌟 ♀

(01264) 810612 – www.peatspadeinn.co.uk

Off A30 on W edge of Stockbridge; SO20 6DR

Former coaching inn with imaginative food, real ales and some sporting décor; bedrooms

A pint and a meal is just what tired walkers from the Test Way are after here, as are fishermen from the world famous River Test just 100 metres away – and the atmosphere is chatty and relaxed. It's best to book a table in advance. The bars have plenty of hunting and fishing pictures and prints and the odd stuffed fish on green walls and several old wine bottles dotted here and there. Both the bar and dining room have attractive windows, an interesting mix of dining chairs around miscellaneous tables on bare boards and candlelight. Bowman Swift One, Crafty Dunsfold Best and Otter Bitter on handpump, 12 wines by the glass, 19 gins and 28 malt whiskies; background music, TV and board games. Seating on the terrace or in the garden ranges from modern rattan-style through traditional wooden chairs and tables to a sunken area with wall seats around a fire pit. This is a pretty village worth a visit.

Interesting contemporary food includes lunchtime sandwiches, seared scallops with ox cheek croquettes and tarragon and chive beurre blanc, chicken liver parfait with spiced tomato chutney, sharing platters, halloumi salad with fig, beetroot, pecan and avocado with honey and mustard dressing, calves liver and bacon with caramelised onions, mash and onion gravy, dry-aged beef burger with wild mushrooms, truffle mayonnaise and fries, fillet of bream with feta, edamame beans, courgettes and tomato sauce, and puddings such as caramelised orange tart with toast ice-cream and blackberry mousse cake with blackberry curd and blackberry sorbet. *Benchmark main dish: duo of pork (confit and belly) with prune and armagnac sauce £15.00. Two-course evening meal £21.00.*

Upham ~ Manager Shelly Dias ~ Real ale ~ Open 8am-11pm; 9am-11pm Sat; 9am-10.30pm Sun ~ Bar food 12-2.30, 6.30-9; 12-2.30, 6-9 Fri, Sat; 12-8 Sun; pizza oven all day ~ Restaurant ~ Children welcome ~ Dogs allowed in bar and bedrooms ~ Wi-fi ~ Bedrooms: /£124 *Recommended by Miss B D Picton, Cecily and Steven Evans, Sally and Brian Turner, Richard Wilton, John and Delia Franks, Jim King, Martine and Lawrence Sanders*

LOWER FROYLE
SU7643   Map 2

Anchor ♀ 🛏

(01420) 23261 – www.anchorinnatlowerfroyle.co.uk
Village signposted N of A31 W of Bentley; GU34 4NA

Plenty to look at in smart country pub, real ales and good wines; bedrooms

With comfortable bedrooms and lovely surrounding walks, this stylish pub is tucked away in the countryside. There are low beams, standing timbers and log fires, candlelight, flagstones in the bar itself and stripped wood floors elsewhere, sofas and armchairs dotted here and there, and a mix of attractive tables and dining chairs. Throughout are all sorts of interesting knick-knacks, books, copper items, horsebrasses and lots of pictures and prints on contemporary paintwork. High bar chairs line the counter where they keep Ringwood Razorback and Triple fff Altons Pride and Moondance on handpump, nice wines by the glass and a growing gin collection; background music and board games. Chawton Cottage (Jane Austen's house) is a ten-minute drive away.

Cooked with flair, the food includes lunchtime sandwiches, ham hock and chicken terrine with piccalilli and carrot purée, peppered mackerel fishcake with horseradish granita, pumpkin potato cake with teriyaki cauliflower, fried egg and sage oil, burger with toppings, bacon jam and skinny fries, cod wrapped in parma ham with squid ink linguine, scampi, caper salsa and hazelnuts, ballotine of chicken with romanesco and mushroom velouté, and puddings such as caramel tart with rhubarb sorbet and banoffi cheesecake with malt ice-cream. *Benchmark main dish: beer-battered fish and chips £15.00. Two-course evening meal £23.00.*

Free house ~ Licensee Lee Hart ~ Real ale ~ Open 11-10.45; 11-11 Sat; 11-9 Sun ~ Bar food 12-2.45, 6.30-8.45 ~ Restaurant ~ Children welcome ~ Dogs allowed in bar and bedrooms ~ Wi-fi ~ Bedrooms: £110/£200 *Recommended by Lorna and Jeff Mason, John and Delia Franks, Isobel Mackinlay, Tony and Jill Radnor, Robin and Anne Triggs, Alison and Dan Richardson, Andrew Wall, Len and Lilly Dowson*

LOWER WIELD
SU6339   Map 2

Yew Tree

(01256) 389224 – www.the-yewtree.org.uk
Turn off A339 NW of Alton at 'Medstead, Bentworth 1' signpost, then follow village signposts; or off B3046 S of Basingstoke, signposted from Preston Candover; SO24 9RX

Bustling country pub with a charming landlord, relaxed atmosphere and super choice of wines and food; sizeable garden

As ever, you can be sure of a genuinely warm welcome from the hard-working, hands-on landlord in this particularly well run pub. A small flagstoned bar area on the left has pictures above a stripped-brick dado, a ticking clock and a log fire. There's carpet around to the right of the serving counter (with a couple of stylish wrought-iron bar chairs), and miscellaneous chairs and mixed tables are spread throughout. Drinks include 15 wines by the glass from a well chosen list (with summer rosé and Louis Jadot burgundies), local cider, a beer named for the pub (from Bowman) and Longdog Bunny Chaser on handpump and local Silverback gin. Outside, the front terrace has solid tables and chunky seats, a sizeable side garden has picnic-sets and there are pleasant views; the cricket field is across the quiet lane and there are walks nearby. Disabled access.

Reasonably priced, highly regarded food includes sandwiches, smoked trout, caper and horseradish mousse, gorgonzola and crispy bacon salad, sri lankan sweet and sour aubergine, cashew, pineapple and chickpea curry, pork and leek sausages with onion gravy and parsley mash, venison burger with toppings and chips, cumin-topped hake with korma cream sauce, duck leg confit with teriyaki and star anise sauce on sesame noodles, beef fillet stroganoff, and puddings such as cherry chocolate biscuit cake and apricot, toffee and white chocolate bread and butter pudding. *Benchmark main dish: half shoulder of lamb with bacon and leek bubble and squeak and rosemary jus £14.95. Two-course evening meal £17.50.*

Free house ~ Licensee Tim Gray ~ Real ale ~ Open 12-3, 6-11; 12-10.30 Sun; closed Mon; first two weeks Jan ~ Bar food 12-2, 6.30-9 ~ Children welcome ~ Dogs allowed in bar ~ Wi-fi *Recommended by Ann and Colin Hunt, Sandra and Neil White, John and Lorna Chew, Caroline Sullivan, Katherine Matthews, Hilary and Neil Christopher*

LYMINGTON
Mayflower 🍺

SZ3394 Map 2

(01590) 672160 – www.themayflowerlymington.co.uk
Kings Saltern Road; SO41 3QD

Renovated inn with nautical décor, plenty of drinking and dining space, good food and drink and seats in garden; bedrooms

This well run pub is extremely busy at peak times, when it's best to book a table. Full of cheerful customers, the high-ceilinged front rooms have built-in wall seats and leather-seated dining chairs around dark wooden tables, candles and fresh flowers, patterned wallpaper or turquoise paintwork and logs piled neatly into the fireplace. Mayflower Bitter (named for the pub from Marstons) and a guest such as Flack Manor Double Drop on handpump and several wines by the glass served by cheerful, efficient young staff. At the back, two rooms have similar seats and tables, model yachts and big modern lanterns, yachting photographs on planked walls, books and a raised woodburning stove; background music and TV. You can walk from here out on to the covered terrace and then down steps to the lawn with its heavy rustic tables and benches. The airy bedrooms have nautical touches and some overlook the coast. The pub is right by the Marina.

Pleasing food includes crayfish cocktail with spiced bloody mary dressing, asian beef salad with cashews, toasted sesame seeds, chilli, rocket and asian-style dressing, mushroom wellington with spinach, field mushroom and root vegetables, pie of the day, seafood tagliatelle, slow-roast pork belly with spiced apple purée, cavolo nero and black pudding hash, rib-eye steak with a choice of sauce and chunky chips, and puddings such as hot chocolate fondant with orange sorbet and banana sticky toffee pudding with salted caramel ice-cream. *Benchmark main dish: hake with local crab and lobster bisque £18.50. Two-course evening meal £22.00.*

Free house ~ Licensee Gary Grant ~ Real ale ~ Open 12-11 (midnight Sat); 12-10 Sun ~ Bar food 12-3, 6-9 ; 12-9 Sat; 12-8 Sun ~ Restaurant ~ Children welcome ~ Dogs allowed in bar and bedrooms ~ Wi-fi ~ Bedrooms: /£200 *Recommended by Gavin and Helle May, Anne Taylor, Edward Nile, Harvey Brown, Jasmine Voos, Alice Wright, Malcolm Stapley*

MATTINGLEY   SU7357   Map 2
Leather Bottle 🍷 🍺

(0118) 932 6371 – www.brunningandprice.co.uk/leatherbottle

3 miles from M3 junction 5; in Hook, turn right-and-left on to B3349 Reading Road (former A32); RG27 8JU

Charming village inn with plenty of room in rambling areas, a fine choice of drinks and food and seats in garden

This is a little brick cottage with a lot of character. Open doorways and standing timbers connect the many small beamed rooms, which have rugs on nice old parquet floors and flagstones, built-in cushioned wooden wall settles, upholstered banquettes and old-style dining chairs and stools around polished tables (each set with flowers and a candle). There are open fires and a woodburning stove, mirrors, prints and antique photographs on the walls and glass bottles and house plants lining the windowsills. Friendly, helpful and efficient staff serve St Austell Brunning & Price Traditional Bitter plus guests from breweries such as Andwell, Triple fff, Windsor & Eton and XT on handpump, 21 wines by the glass, over 44 gins and 31 whiskies; background music. Outside are wooden chairs and tables under green parasols, picnic-sets on grass and the company's trademark play tractor.

 Appealing food includes sandwiches, crumbed cod cheeks with smoked chorizo jam, seaweed salad and lemon dressing, garlic and rosemary-studded camembert with chutney, cauliflower and chickpea curry with charred aubergine and spiced tomato sauce, pork and leek sausages with mash and onion gravy, steak in ale pie, sea trout with pickled beetroot, orange gel and horseradish crème fraîche, chicken burger with crispy mozzarella, chorizo, chipotle mayonnaise and skin-on chips, rib-eye steak with tarragon and dijon butter, and puddings such as crème brûlée and boozy cherry meringue roulade with cherry sorbet. *Benchmark main dish: lamb shoulder with dauphinoise potatoes and rosemary jus £17.95. Two-course evening meal £23.00.*

Brunning & Price ~ Manager Gary Davis ~ Real ale ~ Open 11-11; 11-10 Sun ~ Bar food 12-9.30 ~ Children welcome ~ Dogs allowed in bar ~ Wi-fi *Recommended by Patricia Hawkins, Ian Duncan, Carol and Barry Craddock, Geoffrey Sutton, Sandra and Nigel Brown, Valerie Sayer*

NORTH WARNBOROUGH   SU7352   Map 2
Mill House 🍷 🍺

(01256) 702953 – www.brunningandprice.co.uk/millhouse

A mile from M3 junction 5: A287 towards Farnham, then right (brown sign to pub) on to B3349 Hook Road; RG29 1ET

Sizeable raftered mill with an attractive layout, modern food, good choice of drinks and lovely waterside terraces

The M3 is close by – so this converted mill makes a fine spot for lunch. There are several linked areas on the main upper floor with its heavy beams, plenty of well spaced tables in a variety of sizes and styles, rugs on polished boards or beige carpet, coal-effect gas fires in pretty fireplaces and a profusion of often interesting pictures. A section of floor is glazed to reveal the rushing water and mill wheel below, and a galleried section on the left looks down into a dining room, given a more formal feel by panelling. St Austell Brunning & Price Traditional Bitter plus guests such as Andwell Spring Magic, Ascot Racecard, Longdog Lamplight Porter, Old Pie Factory Pie in the Sky and Weltons Sussex Pride on handpump, a fine range of 40 malt whiskies, 20 wines by the glass, 100 gins and local farm cider; background music and board games. At the back is an extensive garden with lots of solid tables and chairs on terraces, picnic-sets on grass and attractive landscaping around the sizeable millpond; a couple of swings too.

Rewarding food includes beetroot-cured salmon with orange, pickled cucumber and horseradish cream, barbecue chicken wings, stilton, onion and potato pie, crispy beef salad with sweet chilli sauce and cashews, salmon and smoked haddock fishcake with a poached egg and chive and caper sauce, chicken caesar salad, steak burger with toppings, coleslaw and chips, and puddings such as cherry and almond tart with sour cherry sorbet and sticky toffee pudding with toffee sauce. *Benchmark main dish: braised lamb shoulder with dauphinoise potatoes and rosemary gravy £17.45. Two-course evening meal £21.00.*

Brunning & Price ~ Lease Ellie Moore ~ Real ale ~ Open 11-11; 12-10.30 Sun ~ Bar food 12-9.30; 12-10 Fri, Sat; 12-8 Sun ~ Restaurant ~ Children welcome ~ Dogs allowed in bar ~ Wi-fi *Recommended by Ian Wilson, Professor James Burke, Gus Swan, Mark Hamill, William Pace*

PETERSFIELD

SU7227 Map 2

Trooper 🏵 🍺 🛏

(01730) 827293 – www.trooperinn.com

From A32 (look for staggered crossroads) take turning to Froxfield and Steep; pub 3 miles down on left in big dip; GU32 1BD

Courteous landlord, popular food, decent drinks, persian knick-knacks and local artists' work; attractive bedrooms

A charming landlord and his friendly, well trained staff will take good care of you here. The convivial bar has a log fire in a stone fireplace, all sorts of cushioned dining chairs around dark wooden tables, old film star photos, paintings by local artists (for sale), little persian knick-knacks, several ogival mirrors, lit candles and fresh flowers. Ringwood Best and a couple of guests from breweries such as Cotleigh, Crafty and Youngs on handpump, seven wines by the glass, a dozen gins and seven malt whiskies. There's also a sun room with lovely downland views, carefully chosen background music, board games, newspapers and magazines. The attractive raftered restaurant has french windows to a paved terrace with views across the open countryside, and there are lots of picnic-sets on an upper lawn. Bedrooms are neatly kept and the breakfasts are very good. Surrounding walks are lovely. The horse rail in the car park is reserved 'for horses, camels and local livestock'.

Rewarding food includes kiln-smoked salmon with dill and mustard sauce, chicken liver and brandy pâté with chutney, smoky aubergine bake with garlic ciabatta, scampi with fries, cheese burger with bacon jam and fries, pork with sage and onion gravy, sirloin steak with peppercorn sauce and chunky chips, and puddings such as chocolate brownie with clotted cream ice-cream and clementine polenta cake. *Benchmark main dish: slow-cooked lamb shank with mint and honey £16.00. Two-course evening meal £20.00.*

Free house ~ Licensee Hassan Matini ~ Real ale ~ Open 12-3, 6-11; 12-4 Sun; closed Sun evening, Mon-Thurs lunchtimes (except bank holidays when open Mon lunchtime but closed evening) ~ Bar food 12-2, 6.30-9; 12-2.30 Sun ~ Restaurant ~ Children welcome ~ Dogs allowed in bar ~ Wi-fi ~ Bedrooms: £69/£99 *Recommended by Christopher and Elise Way, Julian Richardson, Patti and James Davidson, Amanda Shipley, Brian and Sally Wakeham, Edward Nile*

PORTSMOUTH

SZ6399 Map 2

Old Customs House £

(023) 9283 2333 – www.theoldcustomshouse.com

Vernon Buildings, Gunwharf Quays; follow brown signs to Gunwharf Quays car park; PO1 3TY

Well converted historic building in a prime waterfront development with real ales and well liked food

Shoppers using the extensive modern waterside complex of which this lovely Grade I listed, 18th-c former customs house is part come here for lunch regularly; it might be worth booking a table in advance. The big-windowed high-ceilinged rooms have nautical prints and photographs on pastel walls, coal-effect gas fires, nice unobtrusive lighting and well padded chairs around sturdy tables of varying sizes on bare boards; the sunny entrance area has leather sofas. Broad stairs lead up to a carpeted restaurant with similar décor. Fullers ESB, Gales HSB, London Pride and Seafarers and a couple of changing guests on handpump, a decent range of wines by the glass and good coffees and teas. Staff are efficient and the background music well reproduced. Picnic-sets out in front are just metres from the water; the bar has disabled access and facilities. The graceful Spinnaker Tower (170 metres high with spectacular views from its observation decks) is just around the corner.

Popular food includes bar nibbles such as smoked salmon scotch egg and tempura king prawns with japanese mayonnaise plus sandwiches, sharing platters, macaroni cheese, steak and mushroom in ale pie, chicken kiev with mash, burger with toppings and triple-cooked chips, tea and hop-smoked haddock with bacon and leek carbonara, dry-aged rib-eye steak with béarnaise sauce, and puddings such as knickerbocker glory and treacle tart with buffalo milk vanilla ice-cream. *Benchmark main dish: fish pie £16.00. Two-course evening meal £21.00.*

Fullers ~ Manager Marc Duvauchelle ~ Real ale ~ Open 9.30am-11pm; 9.30am-midnight Fri, Sat; 9.30am-10.30pm Sun ~ Bar food 9.30am-9pm; 9.30-9.30 Sat; 9.30-8 Sun ~ Children welcome ~ Dogs allowed in bar ~ Wi-fi *Recommended by Miss A E Dare, Tony Scott, Neil Allen, Charlie May, John Harris, Rona Mackinlay, David Longhurst*

ROCKBOURNE

SU1118 Map 2

Rose & Thistle

(01725) 518236 – www.roseandthistle.co.uk

Signed off B3078 Fordingbridge–Cranborne; SP6 3NL

Homely cottage with hands-on landlord and friendly staff, informal bars, real ales and good food, and seats in garden

Previously, this thatched pub was two 16th-c cottages and there are some nice old features including beams, timbers and flagstones. The cosy bar has homely dining chairs, stools and benches around a mix of old pubby tables, Butcombe Gold, Sharps Doom Bar and a changing local ale such as Flack Manor Double Drop on handpump, eight wines by the glass and Black Rat cider; background music and board games. The restaurant has a log fire in each of its two rooms (one in a big brick inglenook), old engravings and cricket prints and an informal and relaxed atmosphere; background music and board games. There are benches and tables under lovely hanging baskets at the front of the building, with picnic-sets under parasols on grass; good nearby walks. This is a pretty village on the edge of the New Forest and the Roman Villa is nearby.

Well regarded food includes lunchtime sandwiches, smoked pancetta and oyster mushroom salad with garlic croutons and a poached egg, twice-baked cheese soufflé, roasted red pepper and halloumi burger with chipotle mayonnaise, slow-roasted ham hock with honey and orange glaze on braised fennel and thyme, confit rare-breed pork belly with sweet potato purée, black pudding croquette, apple sauce and red wine jus, and puddings such as vanilla pannacotta and chocolate and cherry brownie with ice-cream; they also offer a two- and three-course set menu. *Benchmark main dish: steak and kidney suet pudding £15.95. Two-course evening meal £23.00.*

Free house ~ Licensee Chris Chester-Sterne ~ Real ale ~ Open 11-3, 5-10.30; 11-10.30 Sat; 12-6 Sun ~ Bar food 12-2.15, 7-9.15; 12-2.15 Sun ~ Children welcome ~ Dogs allowed in bar ~ Wi-fi *Recommended by Patricia and Gordon Thompson, Mike and Sarah Abbot, Mike Swan, Robert and Diana Myers, Ian Duncan, Christopher Mannings*

ST MARY BOURNE
SU4250 Map 2
Bourne Valley 🍷 🛏
(01264) 738361 – www.bournevalleyinn.com
Upper Link (B3048); SP11 6BT

Bustling country inn with plenty of space, an easy-going atmosphere and enjoyable food and drink; good bedrooms

Although popular locally, plenty of visitors find their way here too, and all are welcomed. The bar areas have sofas, all manner of wooden dining chairs and tables on coir or bare boards, empty wine bottles lining shelves and windowsills, and a warm log fire. Palmers Copper Ale, Ramsbury Gold, Sharps Atlantic and West Berkshire Mr Chubbs on handpump and lots of wines by the glass served by helpful, friendly staff; background music, board games and TV. There's also a deli counter for coffee and cake, afternoon tea and picnic hampers. A large barn extension, complete with rafters and beams, rustic partitioning and movable shelves made from crates, has big tables surrounded by leather, cushioned and upholstered chairs, more coir carpeting, a second open fire and doors that lead out to a terrace with picnic-sets and other seating. Bedrooms are comfortable and up to date and are named after local lakes, brooks and rivers. Good nearby walks.

 Contemporary food includes sandwiches, smoked haddock fishcake with a poached egg and pea purée, confit duck leg terrine with crispy skin, raspberry and pickled fennel, chicken caesar salad, linguine with slow-roasted tomato and chilli sauce topped with parmesan, a pie of the day, herb-crusted cod with cauliflower purée and confit chicken wings, crispy lamb breast with caponata and savoy cabbage, and puddings such as dark chocolate torte with peanut butter salted caramel ice-cream and gooseberry tart with gooseberry jam and vanilla ice-cream. *Benchmark main dish: burger with toppings and fries £13.50. Two-course evening meal £22.00.*

Free house ~ Licensee Clare Cunningham ~ Real ale ~ Open 11-11 ~ Bar food 12-2.45, 6-9; 12-3, 6-9 weekends ~ Children welcome ~ Dogs welcome ~ Wi-fi ~ Bedrooms: /£95 *Recommended by Nicholas and Maddy Trainer, Millie and Peter Downing, Simon Pyle, Charlie May, Belinda Stamp*

STEEP
SU7525 Map 2
Harrow 🍺 £
(01730) 262685 – www.theharrowinnsteep.co.uk
Take Midhurst exit from Petersfield bypass, at exit roundabout take first left towards Midhurst, then first turning on left opposite garage, and left again at Sheet church; follow over dual-carriageway bridge to pub; GU32 2DA

Unchanging, simple place with long-serving landladies, beers tapped from the cask, unfussy food and cottage garden; no children inside

Happily for all of us, this little country gem remains as unspoilt as ever. There's no pandering to modern methods – no credit cards, no waitress service, no restaurant, no music and the rose-covered loos are outside. The same family have run it for 87 years and everything revolves around village chat. Adverts for logs sit next to calendars of local views (on sale in support of local charities) and news of various quirky competitions. The small public bar has hops and dried flowers (replaced every year) hanging from the beams, built-in wall benches on the tiled floor, stripped-pine wallboards, a good log fire in the big inglenook and wild flowers on scrubbed deal tables; dominoes. Bowman Swift One, Dark Star Hophead, Flack Manor Double Drop, Hop Back GFB, Langham Hip Hop and Ringwood Best are tapped straight from casks behind the counter, and they have local wine and apple juice; staff are polite and friendly, even when under pressure. The big garden has seats on paved areas surrounded by cottage garden flowers and fruit trees. The Petersfield bypass doesn't intrude much on this idyll, though you'll need to follow the directions above to find the pub. No children inside and dogs must be on leads. They sell honesty-box flowers outside for Macmillan nurses. Wheelchair access but no disabled loos.

Honest food includes sandwiches, hearty soups, salads, hot scotch egg, quiches, and puddings such as lemon crunch cheesecake and winter treacle tart. *Benchmark main dish: ploughman's £11.50. Two-course evening meal £17.00.*

Free house ~ Licensees Claire and Denise McCutcheon ~ Real ale ~ No credit cards ~ Open 12-2.30, 6-11; 11-3, 6-11 Sat; 12-3, 7-10.30 Sun; closed Sun evening in winter ~ Bar food 12-2, 7-9; not Sun evening ~ Dogs allowed in bar *Recommended by Ian Wilson, Ann and Colin Hunt, Tony and Jill Radnor, Tim Everitt, Serena and Adam Furber*

SWANWICK   SU5109   Map 2

Navigator

(01489) 572123 – www.thenavigatorswanwick.co.uk
Handy for M27 junction 9 – A27, by Bursledon Bridge; SO31 7EB

Bustling inn with cosy bar and plenty of dining space, helpful staff, popular food and local ales and seats outside; bedrooms

This substantial and carefully extended place is opposite Swanwick Marina on the peaceful River Hamble; in warm weather there are plenty of seats under large parasols, though no water views. The cosy bar has leather sofas by the open fire, church candles and fresh flowers, stools lining the bleached wooden bar counter and slate flooring and bare boards. Langham Arapaho and Best and a guest from breweries such as Ascot and Bowmans on handpump and good wines by the glass; background music. Dining rooms have painted wall seats with colourful cushions, wall banquettes, cushioned wooden chairs around dark tables, woodstrip walls and yachting and lighthouse photographs; an airy, conservatory-style dining area is much in demand with raffia-style chairs and pale tables on more bare boards. Bedrooms are attractively decorated, smart and comfortable.

Well thought-of food includes lunchtime sandwiches, potted slow-cooked pork belly with spiced apple chutney, chalk stream trout and king prawn roll with wild garlic mayonnaise, vegan curry with rice and naan bread, burger with toppings, coleslaw and fries, pancetta-wrapped chicken breast with wild garlic and chilli rösti and madeira cream, sea bass fillets with fennel and watercress salad and sauce vierge, 28-day aged rib-eye steak with chips and a choice of sauce, and puddings such as coconut rice pudding with pineapple and chilli salsa and caramel cheesecake with a fruit biscuit base and honeycomb ice cream. *Benchmark main dish: sea bass fillets with fennel and watercress salad and sauce vierge £18.50. Two-course evening meal £22.00.*

Upham ~ Manager Nick Hall ~ Real ale ~ Open 7.30am-11pm; 8am-midnight Sat; 8am-10.30pm Sun ~ Bar food 12-9.30 (10 Fri, Sat); 12-9 Sun ~ Restaurant ~ Children welcome ~ Dogs allowed in bar and bedrooms ~ Wi-fi ~ Bedrooms: /£99 *Recommended by Amy and Luke Buchanan, Trish and Karl Soloman, Sally and David Champion, Jane and Philip Saunders*

 TOTFORD   SU5737   Map 2

Woolpack

(01962) 734184 – www.thewoolpackinn.co.uk
B3046 Basingstoke–Alresford; SO24 9TJ

Carefully refurbished rooms, plenty of character, first class food and drink and seats outside; lovely bedrooms

This is a charming flint and brick pub with an interesting mix of contemporary and old-fashioned décor. The bar has an easy-going atmosphere, leather button-back armchairs, little stools and wooden chairs around a mix of tables on wide floorboards, and high chairs against the counter where they offer Andwell Resolute, Palmers Copper Ale and Red Cat Prowler Pale on handpump, 15 wines by the glass and a rather special bloody mary. Leading off here is a dining room with flagstones and carpet, a raised fireplace with guns, bellows and other country knick-knacks above it, and chunky tables and chairs. Throughout the other rooms are rugs on flagstones, exposed brick and stone work, a few bits of timbering and beamery, church candles, lots of photographs, some cosy booth seating and high-back upholstered dining chairs and leather wall seats around a mix of tables. The pool table converts into a dining table when they're really busy; background music, TV and board games. Outside, on the terrace, on gravel and on grass are teak tables and chairs and picnic-sets under parasols, and distant views. The bedrooms, named after game birds, are extremely comfortable and well equipped. Plenty of surrounding walks in the Candover Valley.

Top class cooking includes cured chalk stream trout with smoked avocado purée, salt beef scotch egg with spiced tomato mayonnaise, pea and broad bean risotto with mascarpone, burger with toppings, wild garlic mayonnaise and fries, free-range chicken milanese with creamed spinach, fried egg and truffle, crusted sea bream with courgette and basil purée, pickled vegetables and smoked almonds, and puddings such as treacle tart with clotted cream ice-cream and banana bread and caramelised banana with banoffi mousse. *Benchmark main dish: lamb loin with pea and wild garlic purée and spring onion mash £26.00. Two-course evening meal £22.00.*

Free house ~ Licensee James Waterhouse ~ Real ale ~ Open 11-11; 12-10.30 Sun ~ Bar food 12-3 (3 Sat), 6.30-9; 12-3.30, 5.30-8 Sun ~ Restaurant ~ Children welcome ~ Dogs welcome ~ Wi-fi ~ Bedrooms: /£110 *Recommended by Amy and Luke Buchanan, Matthew and Elisabeth Reeves, Hilary and Neil Christopher, Jacqui and Alan Swan, Julian Richardson*

WINCHESTER   SU4829   Map 2

Wykeham Arms

(01962) 853834 – www.wykehamarmswinchester.co.uk
Kingsgate Street (Kingsgate Arch and College Street are now closed to traffic; there is access via Canon Street); SO23 9PE

Tucked-away pub with lots to look at, several real ales, many wines by the glass and highly thought-of food; pretty bedrooms

With so much to see and do in the town and nearby, why not stay in the lovely bedrooms here; some have four-posters, the two-level suite has its own sitting room, and breakfasts are first class. A series of bustling rooms have all sorts of interesting collections and three log fires, as well as 19th-c oak desks retired from Winchester College, kitchen chairs, deal tables with candles and big windows with swagged curtains. A snug room at the back, known as the Jameson Room (after the late landlord, Graeme Jameson), is decorated with a set of Ronald Searle 'Winespeak' prints. A second room is panelled. Fullers HSB, London Pride and Spring Sprinter, Gales Seafarers and a guest such as Flowepots Goodens Gold on handpump, 25 wines by the glass, 29 malt whiskies, a couple of farm ciders and quite a few ports and sherries; the tea list is pretty special. There are tables on a covered back terrace and in a small courtyard.

🍴 Excellent food includes sandwiches, chicken terrine with sweetcorn purée and bacon granola, cured salmon, crab and avocado mousse with pickled beetroot, potato gnocchi with carrot purée, salted baked beetroot, celeriac and parsnip, beer-battered haddock with triple-cooked chips, haggis, neeps and tatties with peppercorn sauce, lemon sole with mussel velouté, samphire and jerusalem artichoke, 24oz dry-aged sirloin steak with peppercorn sauce, and puddings such as dark chocolate torte with chocolate sauce and vanilla ice-cream and popcorn cheesecake with dulce de leche and salted caramel ice-cream. *Benchmark main dish: shepherds pie £12.50. Two-course evening meal £20.50.*

Fullers ~ Manager Jon Howard ~ Real ale ~ Open 11-11 (10.30 Sun) ~ Bar food 12-3, 6-9.30; 12-8 Sun ~ Restaurant ~ Children over 8 allowed at lunchtime ~ Dogs allowed in bar and bedrooms ~ Wi-fi ~ Bedrooms: £100/£149 *Recommended by Christopher and Elise Way, Philip J Alderton, Ann and Colin Hunt, Julie Swift, Bridget and Peter Gregson, Elise and Charles Mackinlay*

Also Worth a Visit in Hampshire

Besides the fully inspected pubs, you might like to try these pubs that have been recommended to us and described by readers. Do tell us what you think of them: feedback@goodguides.com

ALRESFORD   SU5832
Bell (01962) 732429
West Street; SO24 9AT Comfortable Georgian coaching inn with popular food including weekday fixed-price menu, up to five well kept changing ales and extensive choice of wines by the glass, bare-boards interior with scrubbed tables and log fire, hops and trophy heads (including a moose) in bar, separate smallish dining room; children and dogs welcome (resident spaniels Freddie and Teddy), attractive sunny back courtyard, six bedrooms, open all day (till 6pm Sun). *(Ann and Colin Hunt, Neil and Angela Huxter)*

ALRESFORD   SU5831
Cricketers (01962) 732463
Jacklyns Lane; SO24 9LW Large pebble-dashed corner pub with modernised interior; good sensibly priced food (all day weekends) including two-course lunchtime/early evening deal, well kept beers and decent choice of wines by the glass, welcoming attentive staff, cricketing memorabilia and woodburner, separate dining area; monthly live music; children and dogs (in bar) welcome, good size garden with covered terrace, pizza oven and play area, open all day. *(Helen and Brian Edgeley)*

ALRESFORD   SU5832
Globe (01962) 733118
Bottom of Broad Street (B3046) where parking is limited; SO24 9DB Popular and welcoming old tile-hung pub (former coaching inn); enjoyable food (all day Sun) including weekday lunchtime/early evening deal, real ales such as Otter and more than 20 wines by the glass, friendly staff; children and dogs welcome, nice garden overlooking Alresford Pond, good riverside walks, open all day. *(David and Judy Robison)*

ALRESFORD   SU5832
Horse & Groom (01962) 734809
Broad Street; town signed off A31 bypass; SO24 9AQ Comfortable attractively updated Fullers pub with roomy well divided interior; their well kept ales and a local guest, enjoyable food from fairly compact but varied menu, friendly young staff, pale beams (some supported by iron

pillars), exposed brickwork and log fires, bow window seats and a few stepped levels, back restaurant area; background and some live music, fortnightly quiz, daily newspapers, free wi-fi; children and well behaved dogs welcome, small enclosed back terrace, open all day, food all day Sun till 7pm. *(Karl and Frieda Bujeya)*

ALRESFORD
SU5832

Swan (01962) 732302

West Street; SO24 9AD Long narrow bar in 18th-c hotel (former coaching inn); painted panelling and some rustic stall seating, well kept ales such as Itchen Valley, Sharps and Triple fff, decent wines, tea and coffee, popular reasonably priced food including breakfast (until 10.30am) and Sun roasts, efficient friendly service, two dining rooms (one more formal); children welcome, café-style table on terrace, 22 bedrooms, open all day. *(Charles Todd)*

AMPFIELD
SU4023

★ **White Horse** (01794) 368356

A3090 Winchester–Romsey; SO51 9BQ Snug low-beamed front bar with candles and soft lighting, inglenook log fire and comfortable country furnishings, spreading beamed dining area behind, well kept Greene King, guest ales and several wines by the glass, good food including all-day snacks, efficient service, locals' bar with another inglenook; background music; children and dogs welcome, pergola-covered terrace and high-hedged garden with plenty of picnic-sets, cricket green beyond, good walks in Ampfield Woods and handy for Hillier Gardens, open all day. *(Joy Griffiths)*

ARFORD
SU8236

Crown (01428) 288090

Off B3002 W of Hindhead; GU35 8BT This popular low-beamed dining pub was closed for refurbishment as we went to press – reports please.

BARTON STACEY
SU4341

Swan (01962) 760470

Village signed off A303; SO21 3RL Beamed coaching inn with good affordably priced pubby food (not Sun evening, Mon) from lunchtime sandwiches up, three well kept ales, friendly owners and helpful young staff, bar with brick and timber walls, light wood flooring and inglenook log fire, back restaurant; board games, free wi-fi; children and dogs welcome, picnic-sets on front gravel and lawn, open all day Sat, till 6pm Sun, closed Mon. *(Susan and Tim Boyle)*

BEAUWORTH
SU5624

Milbury's (01962) 771248

Off A272 Winchester–Petersfield; SO24 0PB Traditional 17th-c tile-hung

country pub; beams, panelling and stripped stone, inglenook log fire (even on cooler summer days), massive 17th-c treadmill for much older incredibly deep well, galleried area, three changing ales and enjoyable reasonably priced simple food; skittle alley; children (in eating areas) and dogs welcome, garden with fine downland views, good walks, regular classic car meetings including TVR, two bedrooms, closed Sun and Mon evenings. *(Richard Tilbrook)*

BENTLEY
SU7844

Star (01420) 23184

Centre of village on old A31; GU10 5LW Welcoming little early 19th-c village pub; good reasonably priced food (smaller helpings available) cooked by landlady including Weds steak night, Sharps Doom Bar, Triple fff Moondance and a guest, eight wines by the glass from decent list, good service, open fire in brick fireplace, restaurant; quiz second Mon of the month, newspapers, free wi-fi; children and dogs welcome, garden with thatched gazebos, open all day, food all day Sun till 7pm. *(Patricia Healey)*

BENTWORTH
SU6740

Sun (01420) 562338

Well Lane, off Station Road; signed Shaldon/Alton; GU34 5JT Creeper-clad 17th-c country tavern; unspoilt little beamed rooms with scrubbed deal tables, high-backed settles, pews and wheelback chairs on bare boards or brick floor, candles on tables, various pictures and knick-knacks, three log fires, good range of local real ales and enjoyable attractively presented food from shortish menu, friendly service; children and dogs welcome, seats out at front and in back garden, open (and food) all day Sun. *(Tony and Jill Radnor, S G N Bennett)*

BISHOP'S SUTTON
SU6031

Ship (01962) 732863

B3047, on Alton side of Alresford; SO24 0AQ Old village corner dining pub revamped under present management; good food from pub favourites up including daily specials, three well kept changing ales, helpful friendly service, two-level bar with rugs on bare boards, woodburner, back dining room; children and dogs welcome, tables in garden, good walks and handy for Watercress Line, open all day Fri and Sat, till 7pm Sun, closed Mon. *(Helen and Brian Edgeley)*

BISHOP'S WALTHAM
SU5517

Barleycorn (01489) 892712

Lower Basingwell Street; SO32 1AJ Traditional 18th-c two-bar village local; popular generously served pub food at reasonable prices, good friendly service, well kept Greene King ales, a guest beer and decent wines, beams and some low ceiling

---

We say if we know a pub has background music.

panelling, open fires; well behaved children and dogs welcome, large garden and back smokers' area, open all day. *(Pat Holmes)*

BISHOP'S WALTHAM   SU5517
Crown   (01489) 893350
The Square; SO32 1AF Spacious and attractively updated 16th-c beamed coaching inn; Fullers/Gales beers and popular fairly priced food from sandwiches to daily specials, cheerful helpful staff, bar area on the left with bare boards, comfortable seating and log fire, split-level dining room to the right with three further fireplaces; background music; children and dogs welcome, courtyard tables, opposite entrance to palace ruins, eight good bedrooms, open all day from 8.30am, food all day Fri-Sun. *(Ann and Colin Hunt)*

BOLDRE   SZ3198
★ Red Lion   (01590) 673177
Off A337 N of Lymington; SO41 8NE Relaxed New Forest-edge dining pub with five black-beamed rooms and three log fires; pews, sturdy cushioned dining chairs and tapestried stools, rural landscapes on rough-cast walls, other rustic bits and pieces including copper and brass pans, a heavy horse harness and some ferocious-looking traps, old cooking range in cosy bar, well kept Ringwood and guests, very good home-made food from varied menu (worth booking), friendly service; dogs welcome, opposite village green with seats out among flowering tubs and hanging baskets, more tables in back garden, self-catering apartment, open all day Sun. *(Malcolm Phillips)*

BRAISHFIELD   SU3724
Wheatsheaf   (01794) 368652
Village signposted off A3090 on NW edge of Romsey; SO51 0QE Friendly bay-windowed pub with four well kept beers and tasty home-cooked food, beams and cosy log fire; background music (live Thurs), sports TV, pool; children and dogs welcome, garden with play area and nice views, woodland walks nearby, close to Hillier Gardens, open all day. *(Joe and Belinda Smart)*

BRAMBRIDGE   SU4721
Dog & Crook   (01962) 712129
Near M3 junction 12, via B3335; Church Lane; SO50 6HZ Bustling 18th-c pub with beamed bar and cosy dining room; enjoyable home-made food including separate gluten-free menu and Weds steak night, four real ales such as Bowman and Timothy Taylors, several wines by the glass, friendly service; background music, TV, fortnightly quiz Thurs; children and dogs welcome, disabled access/loos, garden with

covered deck, Itchen Way walks nearby, open all day Fri-Sun. *(Simon Sharpe)*

BRAMDEAN   SU6127
Fox   (01962) 771363
A272 Winchester–Petersfield; SO24 0LP Popular and welcoming 17th-c part-weatherboarded roadside pub; open-plan bar with black beams and log fires, well kept Sharps Doom Bar and guests, real ciders and several wines by the glass, ample helpings of good fairly traditional home-made food from sandwiches and sharing boards up, cheerful helpful staff; quiz first Mon of month; children and dogs welcome, walled-in terraced area and spacious lawn under fruit trees, three shepherd's huts, good surrounding walks, open (and food) all day Fri-Sun, kitchen closes 7pm Sun. *(Richard Tilbrook, Reg Robertson)*

BREAMORE   SU1517
Bat & Ball   (01725) 512252
Salisbury Road; SP6 2EA Dutch-gabled, red-brick roadside pub with two linked bar areas and restaurant; well kept Ringwood ales and enjoyable reasonably priced food, friendly service; regular live music; children and dogs welcome, pleasant side garden (summer barbecues), Avon fishing and walks (lovely ones up by church and stately Breamore House), open (and food) all day. *(John Harris)*

BROCKENHURST   SU3002
Huntsman   (01590) 622225
Lyndhurst Road (A337); SO42 7RH Large modernised roadside inn; popular food from sandwiches and sharing plates up including wood-fired pizzas and chargrilled steaks, friendly service, three or four real ales such as Ringwood, cocktails and plenty of wines by the glass, coffee bar; skittle alley; children and dogs (in bar) welcome, decent-sized garden with part-covered terrace, 13 well appointed bedrooms, open (and food) all day. *(Richard Elliott)*

BROOK   SU2714
Bell   (023) 8081 2214
B3079/B3078, handy for M27 junction 1; SO43 7HE Really a hotel with golf club, but has neat flagstoned bar with lovely 18th-c inglenook fire, well kept ales such as Flack Manor, Ringwood and Wychwood, good cider, plenty of wines by the glass and extensive range of gins, nice food too from snacks up, afternoon teas (perhaps with a glass of house champagne), helpful friendly uniformed staff, attractive restaurant; children and dogs (in bar) welcome, picnic-sets in big garden, delightful village, 28 comfortable bedrooms, open all day. *(Miss B D Picton)*

Half pints: by law, a pub should not charge more for half a pint than half the price of a full pint, unless it shows that half-pint price on its price list.

BROOK   SU2713
★**Green Dragon** (023) 8081 3359
*B3078 NW of Cadnam, just off M27
junction 1; SO43 7HE* Thatched New
Forest dining pub dating from the 15th c;
popular food from usual favourites to
blackboard specials, well kept Wadworths
ales and good range of wines by the glass,
friendly helpful staff, linked areas with
beams, log fires and traditional furnishings,
lots of pictures and other bits and pieces
including some old leather 'bends' showing
brand marks of forest graziers; children
and dogs (not in restaurant) welcome,
disabled access from car park, attractive
small terrace, garden with play area and
paddocks beyond, picturesque village,
open all day. *(PL)*

BROUGHTON   SU3032
Tally Ho (01794) 301280
*High Street, opposite church; signed off
A30 Stockbridge–Salisbury; SO20 8AA*
Welcoming pub with light airy bar and
separate eating area, four well kept ales
including Ringwood and a house beer brewed
in the village, good food from pub favourites
up (more elaborate evening choice), friendly
service; quiz and pizza nights; children
welcome, charming secluded back garden,
good walks, open all day. *(Ann and Colin Hunt,
Brian and Margaret Merritt)*

BUCKLERS HARD   SU4000
Master Builders House
(01590) 616253 *M27 junction 2
follow signs to Beaulieu, turn left on
to B3056, then left to Bucklers Hard;
SO42 7XB* Sizeable red-brick hotel in
lovely spot overlooking river; character
main bar with heavy beams, log fire and
simple furnishings, rugs on wood floor,
mullioned windows, interesting list of
shipbuilders dating from 18th c, ales such
as Ringwood Best and Sharps Doom Bar,
decent wine list, stairs down to room with
fireplace at each end, enjoyable bar and
restaurant food from sandwiches and
pizzas up, afternoon teas, prompt friendly
service; children and dogs welcome,
picnic-sets on stepped terrace, small gate
at bottom of garden for waterside walks,
summer barbecues, 26 bedrooms, open
(and food) all day. *(Ian Phillips)*

BURGHCLERE   SU4660
Carpenters Arms (01635) 278251
Harts Lane, off A34; RG20 9JY
Welcoming little village pub (some recent
refurbishment) with enjoyable reasonably
priced food and well kept Arkells beers,
helpful friendly service, good country
views (Watership Down) from conservatory
and terrace, log fire; background music;
children, walkers and dogs welcome, handy
for Sandham Memorial Chapel (NT) with its
Stanley Spencer murals and Highclere Castle,

eight comfortable annexe bedrooms, open
all day, no food Sun evening. *(Patric Curwen,
David and Judy Robison)*

BURLEY   SU2103
Queens Head (01425) 403423
*The Cross; back road Ringwood–
Lymington; BH24 4AB* Large brick and
tile Chef & Brewer dating partly from the
17th c; several updated rambling rooms, open
fire, good choice of enjoyable reasonably
priced food (order at bar) including deals,
Greene King and local guests, helpful friendly
staff; background music, fruit machine;
children and dogs (in one area) welcome,
plenty of space outside, car parking fee
refunded at bar, pub and New Forest village
can get packed in summer, open all day.
(Tony Scott)

BURLEY   SU2202
White Buck (01425) 402264
*Bisterne Close; 0.7 miles E, OS Sheet 195
map reference 223028; BH24 4AZ* Lovely
New Forest setting for this well run 19th-c
mock-Tudor hotel; Fullers ales in long bar
with two-way log fire at either end, seats in
big bow window, comfortable part-panelled
shooting-theme snug and spacious well
divided dining area on different levels, good
attractively presented food (some prices
on the high side) and nice wines, helpful
personable staff; background music, free
wi-fi; children and dogs welcome, terraces
and spacious lawn, excellent walks towards
Burley itself and over Mill Lawn, good
bedrooms, open all day. *(David and Sally Frost,
Mr and Mrs D J Nash)*

CHALTON   SU7316
Red Lion (023) 9259 2246
Off A3 Petersfield–Horndean; PO8 0BG
Largely extended timber and thatch country
dining pub; interesting old core around
inglenook (dates to the 12th c and has been
a pub since the 1400s); well kept Fullers/
Gales beers and a guest, popular food (all
day weekends) from sandwiches and pub
favourites up, friendly helpful service, back
restaurant; children and dogs welcome,
disabled access and facilities, nice views
from neat rows of picnic-sets on rectangular
lawn by large car park, good walks, nearby
church also worth a visit and handy for
Queen Elizabeth Country Park, open all day.
(Ann and Colin Hunt)

CHAWTON   SU7037
Greyfriar (01420) 83841
*Off A31/A32 S of Alton; Winchester
Road; GU34 1SB* Tile-hung beamed dining
pub opposite Jane Austen's House Museum;
enjoyable food (not Sun evening) from
lunchtime sandwiches and bar snacks up,
Fullers ales, guest beers and good selection
of gins, welcoming relaxed atmosphere with
comfortable seating and sturdy pine tables
in neat linked areas, open fire in restaurant

end; children and dogs welcome, small garden with terrace, good nearby walks, open all day. *(Ann and Colin Hunt, Tony and Jill Radnor)*

CHERITON   SU5828
★ **Flower Pots** (01962) 771318
Off B3046 towards Beauworth and Winchester; OS Sheet 185 map reference 581282; SO24 0QQ Unspoilt 19th-c red-brick country local in same family since 1968; three or four very good value cask-tapped ales from on-site brewery, enjoyable reasonably priced home-made food (not Sun evening, Mon) including generous baps, range of casseroles and popular Weds curry night, cheerful welcoming staff, extended public bar with painted brick walls, tiled floor, open fire and glass-covered well, another straightforward but homely room with country pictures and small log fire; no under-13s, dogs welcome, seats on pretty front and back lawns (some under apple trees), vintage motorcycles Weds lunchtime, good local walks. *(Tony and Jill Radnor, Ann and Colin Hunt, David and Judy Robison)*

CHILBOLTON   SU3939
Abbots Mitre (01264) 860348
Off A3051 S of Andover; SO20 6BA Traditional 19th-c brick-built village pub; five well kept local ales and decent wines by the glass, popular food from sandwiches and pubby choices up including daily specials, friendly service; children and dogs (in bar) welcome, wheelchair access, picnic-sets outside, River Test and other walks (circular one from the pub), open (and food) all day. *(David and Judy Robison)*

CRONDALL   SU7948
Plume of Feathers (01252) 850245
The Borough; GU10 5NT Attractive 15th-c brick and timber pub in picturesque village; good range of popular generously served food from standards up, friendly helpful staff, well kept Greene King, some unusual guest beers and nice wines by the glass, beams and dark wood, red carpet, prints on cream walls, restaurant with log fire in big brick fireplace; soft background music, free wi-fi; children welcome, picnic-sets in back terrace garden (bookable barbecues), three bedrooms, open all day Sun. *(Sarah Little)*

CROOKHAM   SU7952
Exchequer (01252) 615336
Crondall Road; GU51 5SU Welcoming smartly presented dining pub (part of the Red Mist group – Royal Exchange at Lindford, Wheatsheaf in Farnham, Surrey, etc); popular food (all day weekends) from sandwiches and sharing boards to blackboard specials, Mon burger night, can eat in bar or restaurant, four well kept ales, cider and lager from local Hogs Back, also good choice of wines by the glass and interesting gins/cocktails, pleasant hard-working young staff,

cosy woodburner, daily newspapers; children and dogs welcome, rattan-style furniture on split-level terrace, near Basingstoke Canal, open all day Fri and Sat, till 9.30pm Sun. *(Simon King)*

DUMMER   SU5846
Queen (01256) 397367
Under a mile from M3 junction 7; take Dummer slip road; RG25 2AD Comfortable well divided beamed pub with lots of softly lit alcoves; Courage, Fullers and a guest, decent choice of wines by the glass and popular food from lunchtime sandwiches and light dishes up, friendly service, big log fire, pictures of the Queen and some steeplechase prints; background music, free wi-fi; children welcome in restaurant, picnic-sets under parasols on terrace and in back garden, attractive village with ancient church, open all day. *(Susan and Tim Boyle)*

DUNBRIDGE   SU3126
Mill Arms (01794) 340355
Barley Hill (B3084); SO51 0LF Much extended 18th-c coaching inn opposite station; welcoming informal atmosphere in spacious high-ceilinged rooms, scrubbed pine tables, farmhouse chairs and several sofas on oak or flagstone floors, two log fires, local ales such as Flack Manor, enjoyable food, dining conservatory; darts and two skittle alleys; children and dogs (in bar) welcome, big garden, plenty of walks in surrounding Test Valley, six comfortable bedrooms, open all day (till 6pm Sun). *(Alison and Tony Livesey)*

DUNDRIDGE   SU5718
★ **Hampshire Bowman** (01489) 892940
Off B3035 towards Droxford, Swanmore, then right at Bishop's Waltham signpost; SO32 1GD Chatty mix of customers at this homely relaxed country pub; five well kept local ales tapped from the cask (beer festival last weekend in July), ten or more traditional ciders and good value food (all day Fri-Sun) from generous sandwiches and hearty pub dishes to specials, good cheerful service, stable bar and cosy unassuming original one; mobile phones discouraged; children and dogs welcome, tables on terrace and peaceful lawn, play equipment, hitching post for horses, popular with walkers and cyclists, open all day. *(Ann and Colin Hunt)*

DURLEY   SU5116
Farmers Home (01489) 860457
B3354 and B2177; Heathen Street/Curdridge Road; SO32 2BT Comfortable red-brick beamed country pub, spacious but cosy, with two-bay dining area and restaurant, enjoyable food including good steaks and popular Sun lunch, friendly service, room for drinkers too with decent wines by the glass and three well kept ales including Gales and Ringwood, woodburner; children and dogs (in bar) welcome, large

garden with pergola and play area, nice walks, open (and food) all day. *(Lyn and Freddie Roberts)*

DURLEY   SU5217
★ **Robin Hood** (01489) 860229
Durley Street, just off B2177 Bishop's Waltham–Winchester – brown signs to pub; SO32 2AA Quirky open-plan beamed pub with popular well prepared food from varied blackboard menu (order at bar), a house beer from Greene King and a couple of guests, nice wines, good friendly service, log fire and leather sofas in bare-boards bar, dining area with stone floors and mix of old pine tables and chairs, bookcase door to loos; background music; children and dogs welcome, disabled facilities, decked terrace (barbecues) and garden with play area, country views, open all day Sun. *(Jan Sutton)*

EAST BOLDRE   SU3700
Turf Cutters Arms (01590) 612331
Main Road; SO42 7WL Small dimly lit 18th-c New Forest local behind white picket fence; lots of beams and pictures, nicely worn-in furnishings on bare boards and flagstones, log fire, enjoyable home-made food from ciabattas up (worth booking evenings/weekends), well kept Ringwood ales and a guest, friendly helpful service and chatty relaxed atmosphere; children and dogs welcome, picnic-sets in large back garden, enjoyable heathland walks, bedrooms in nearby converted barn; open all day. *(Martyn Stringer)*

EAST END   SZ3696
★ **East End Arms** (01590) 626223
Back road Lymington–Beaulieu, parallel to B3054; SO41 5SY Simple friendly pub (owned by former Dire Straits bass guitarist); unfussy bar with chatty locals and log fire, Ringwood Best or Fortyniner and several wines by the glass, enjoyable freshly made food (not Sun evening) served by cheerful helpful staff, attractive dining room; occasional live music, free wi-fi; children and dogs (in bar) welcome, picnic-sets in terraced garden, pretty cottagey bedrooms, open all day July-Sept (all day Fri-Sun other times). *(Anne and Ben Smith)*

EAST MEON   SU6822
Olde George (01730) 823481
Church Street; signed off A272 W of Petersfield, and off A32 in West Meon; GU32 1NH Atmospheric heavy-beamed village inn with good choice of well liked food including vegetarian and gluten-free options, Badger ales and decent selection of wines by the glass, cosy areas around central brick counter, inglenook log fires; children and dogs welcome, nice back terrace, five bedrooms, good breakfast, pretty village with fine church and surrounding walks, open all day Sun. *(Charles Welch)*

EASTLEIGH   SU4519
Steam Town Brewery
(023) 8235 9139 *Bishopstoke Road/ Dutton Lane; SO50 6AD* New brewpub with four or five of their beers along with guest ales and 16 craft kegs, also three ciders, decent wines and around 40 gins, good range of chargrilled burgers, friendly knowledgeable staff, industrial-style bare-boards interior with some reclaimed materials including factory light fittings, old train seats and a servery made from the side of a railway carriage; regular live music; children and dogs (in bar) welcome, open all day, food all day Sat, till 6pm Sun. *(Steve White)*

EASTON   SU5132
Chestnut Horse (01962) 779257
3.6 miles from M3 junction 9: A33 towards Kings Worthy, then B3047 towards Itchen Abbas; Easton then signposted on right – bear left in village; SO21 1EG Comfortable 16th-c pub in pretty village of thatched cottages; open-plan but with a series of cosy separate areas, log fires, black beams and joists hung with jugs, mugs and chamber-pots, three Badger ales, plenty of wines by the glass and good selection of whiskies and gins, well liked food including home-made pizzas, Mon steak night and other offers, attentive friendly staff; background music; children and dogs (in bar) welcome, seats and tables on smallish sheltered decked area, summer tubs and baskets, walks in Itchen Valley, open all day Fri-Sun, food all day Sun. *(Katharine Cowherd, David and Judy Robison)*

ECCHINSWELL   SU4959
Royal Oak (01635) 297355
Ecchinswell Road; RG20 4UH Cosy and welcoming whitewashed village pub; bar with open fire, window seats and plush-topped stools around tables on wood floor, second room with another fire and airy dining room with country kitchen chairs and mix of tables on light boards, three well kept ales and enjoyable fair value food, good friendly service; children welcome, picnic-sets on front terrace behind picket fence, more in large back garden running down to stream. *(David and Judy Robison)*

EMERY DOWN   SU2808
★ **New Forest Inn** (023) 8028 4690
Village signed off A35 just W of Lyndhurst; SO43 7DY Well run 18th-c weatherboarded village pub in one of the best parts of the New Forest for walking; good sensibly priced home-made food including vegetarian choices, daily specials and popular Sun roasts (should book), friendly helpful uniformed staff, Ringwood and guests, real cider and several wines by the glass, coffee and tea; attractive softly lit separate areas on varying levels, each with

own character, old pine and oak furniture, milk churn stools by bar, hunting prints and two log fires; background music; children and dogs welcome, covered terrace and nice little three-tier garden, four good value simple bedrooms, open (and food) all day, can get very busy weekends. *(Sara Fulton, Roger Baker, Wendi Johns)*

EMSWORTH   SU7405
Blue Bell (01243) 373394
South Street; PO10 7EG Friendly and relaxed little 1940s red-brick pub close to the quay; old-fashioned lived-in interior with nautical and other memorabilia, good choice of popular reasonably priced home-made food with emphasis on local produce including fresh fish (best to book), bar nibbles Sun lunchtime, well kept Sharps Doom Bar and a couple of guests such as Emsworth from brick and timber servery, helpful amiable staff; TV, daily newspapers; dogs welcome, seats on small front and side terraces, Sun market in adjacent car park, open all day. *(Ann and Colin Hunt, Dom Escott, Tony Hobden)*

EMSWORTH   SU7405
Coal Exchange (01243) 375866
Ships Quay, South Street; PO10 7EG Friendly little L-shaped Victorian local near harbour; well kept Fullers/Gales beers and guests, good value home-made lunchtime food (evenings Tues-Thurs including Weds pizza night), simple low-ceilinged bar with fire at each end; live music, free wi-fi; children and dogs welcome, tables outside and smokers' shelter, handy for Wayfarers Walk and Solent Way, open all day Fri-Sun. *(Tony Hobden, Tony Scott)*

EMSWORTH   SU7505
Lord Raglan (01243) 372587
Queen Street; PO10 7BJ Traditional 18th-c flint pub with wide choice of enjoyable home-made food from daily changing menu, well kept Fullers/Gales beers, good friendly service, log fire, restaurant; live music Sun evening, free wi-fi; dogs welcome, pleasant waterside garden behind, open all day weekends. *(Pat Holmes)*

EVERTON   SZ2994
Crown (01590) 642655
Old Christchurch Road; pub signed just off A337 W of Lymington; SO41 0JJ Quietly set restaurant-pub on edge of New Forest; highly thought-of food cooked by landlord-chef including daily specials, friendly service, Greene King, Ringwood and a guest, decent wines at sensible prices, two attractive dining rooms off tiled-floor bar, log fires; children welcome, wheelchair access

possible, picnic-sets on front terrace behind picket fence and in small back garden, closed Mon. *(Kevin Adams)*

EXTON   SU6120
★ Shoe (01489) 877526
Village signposted from A32 NE of Bishop's Waltham; SO32 3NT Popular brick-built country dining pub on South Downs Way; three linked rooms with log fires, good well presented food (best to book) from traditional favourites to more imaginative restaurant-style dishes including fresh fish and seasonal game, well kept Wadworths ales and a guest, several wines by the glass including local sparkling, good service from friendly young staff; children and dogs welcome, disabled facilities, seats under parasols at front, more in garden across lane overlooking River Meon (ice-cream shack summer weekends), open all day weekends. *(Sarah Little)*

FAREHAM   SU5705
Castle in the Air (01329) 280320
Old Gosport Road; PO16 0XH Open-plan Greene King pub by tidal Fareham Creek; their beers and guests kept well, enjoyable sensibly priced food including deals, good friendly service, flagstones and bare boards, big brick fireplace; live music and quiz nights; children and dogs welcome, terrace seating, open (and food) all day. *(Ann and Colin Hunt)*

FAREHAM   SU5806
Cob & Pen (01329) 221624
Wallington Shore Road, not far from M27 junction 11; PO16 8SL Cheerful old corner local near Wallington River; four well kept ales including Hop Back, St Austell and Sharps, enjoyable well priced home-made food from sandwiches to specials, log fire; some live music, TV, darts; children and dogs welcome, large garden with play area and summer barbecues, open all day, no food Sun evening and winter Mon. *(Alison and Tony Livesey)*

FARNBOROUGH   SU8756
★ Prince of Wales (01252) 545578
Rectory Road, near station; GU14 8AL Ten well kept ales including five quickly changing guests at this friendly Victorian local, three small linked areas with exposed brickwork, carpet or wood floors, open fire and some antiquey touches, generous lunchtime pubby food at reasonable prices, also Mon curry night and Fri evening fish, good friendly service; quiz first Sun of month, some live music; well behaved children and dogs welcome, a few picnic-sets on front

---

If you stay overnight in an inn or hotel, they are allowed to serve you an alcoholic drink at any hour of the day or night.

pavement, more seating on back terrace with smokers' gazebo, open all day Fri-Sun. *(Tony Hobden)*

FAWLEY SU4603
Jolly Sailor (023) 8089 1305
Ashlett Creek, off B3053; SO45 1DT Cottagey waterside pub near small boatyard and sailing club; good value straightforward bar food, Ringwood Best and a guest, cheerful service, mixed pubby furnishings on bare boards, raised log fire, second bar with darts and pool; children and dogs welcome, tables outside looking past creek's yachts and boats to busy shipping channel, good shore walks, well placed for Rothschild rhododendron gardens at Exbury, open all day, no food Sun evening, Mon. *(Helen Peterston)*

FINCHDEAN SU7312
George (023) 9241 2257
Centre of village; PO8 0AU Red-brick village pub dating from the 18th c; traditional beamed front bar, back dining area with conservatory, enjoyable fairly priced food (all day Sat, till 8pm Sun) from sandwiches and basket meals up, well kept mainstream ales such as Black Sheep, Sharps and Timothy Taylors, good friendly service; some live music; children and dogs (in bar) welcome, picnic-sets out in front and in garden behind, good nearby walks, open all day till 10pm (midnight Fri, Sat). *(Ann and Colin Hunt)*

FROGHAM SU1712
Foresters Arms (01425) 652294
Abbotswell Road; SP6 2JA Updated New Forest pub (part of the Little Pub Group); enjoyable good value food from lunchtime baguettes up, well kept Wadworths ales and a guest, good friendly service, cosy rustic-chic interior with rugs on wood or flagstone floors, woodburners in brick fireplaces, pale green panelling, mix of old and new furniture including settles and pews, antlers and grandfather clock; monthly quiz; children, walkers and dogs (in bar) welcome, picnic-sets out at front under pergola and on lawn, maybe ponies and donkeys, open all day weekends. *(Peter and Anne Hollindale, David and Judy Robison)*

GOODWORTH CLATFORD SU3642
Royal Oak (01264) 324105
Longstock Road; SP11 7QY Comfortably modern L-shaped bar with ales such as Flack Manor and Ringwood, nice wines by the glass and good pubby food from sandwiches up, friendly efficient staff; children welcome, picnic-sets in pretty dell-like garden, attractive Test Valley village and pleasant River Anton walks, closed Sun evening. *(David and Judy Robison)*

GOSPORT SZ6198
Fighting Cocks (023) 9252 9885
Clayhall Road, Alverstoke; PO12 2AJ Welcoming modernised local in residential area; Wadworths ales and good choice of enjoyable pubby food at sensible prices including Sat breakfast from 9.30am, friendly helpful service, bar with some booth seating and upholstered wall benches, skylit dining room; Sun quiz, darts, TV, fruit machine; children and dogs in bar (welcome), big garden with play equipment, handy for Stokes Bay beaches, open all day, no food Sun evening. *(Ann and Colin Hunt)*

GOSPORT SZ6100
Queens 07974 031671
Queens Road; PO12 1LG Classic bare-boards corner local with six real ales such as Fallen Acorn, Ringwood and Youngs kept in top condition by long-serving no-nonsense landlady, popular Oct beer festival, three areas off bar, good log fire in interesting carved fireplace, sensibly placed darts, TV for major sports; children allowed Sat afternoon only, no dogs, open all day Sat, closed lunchtimes Mon-Thurs. *(Ann and Colin Hunt)*

GRAYSHOTT SU8735
Fox & Pelican (01428) 604757
Headley Road; GU26 6LG Large village pub with enjoyable food from sandwiches up, Fullers/Gales beers and a guest, friendly service, linked areas with comfortable seating on wood or carpeted floors, open fire in large fireplace, dining conservatory; background and some live music, quiz Thurs, sports TV, games machines; children and dogs welcome, wheelchair access, tables on paved terrace and lawn, fenced play area, open all day, food all day Fri and Sat, till 6pm Sun. *(John and Bernadette Elliott)*

GREYWELL SU7151
Fox & Goose (01256) 702062
Near M3 junction 5; A287 towards Odiham, then first right to village; RG29 1BY Welcoming two-bar village pub popular with locals and walkers; traditional interior with country kitchen furniture and open fire, enjoyable home-made pubby food from good lunchtime sandwiches/baguettes up, three well kept ales including Sharps Doom Bar; open mike night third Mon of month; children and dogs welcome, good-sized back garden and camping field, River Whitewater and Basingstoke Canal walks, open all day. *(D J and P M Taylor)*

GRIGGS GREEN SU8231
Deers Hut (01428) 724406
Off A3 S of Hindhead; GU30 7PD Popular old country pub with horseshoe bar and several rustically furnished dining areas; good if slightly pricey food (service charge added) from baguettes and pub staples to daily specials, Sharps Doom Bar, Youngs Bitter and a couple of guests, good choice of other drinks, friendly young staff; children welcome, attractive woodland setting with picnic-sets on front terrace and green, handy

for Shipwrights Way walkers, classic car event (Father's Day), open all day. *(Jim and Sue James)*

HAMBLE   SU4806

Bugle (023) 8045 3000

3 miles from M27 junction 8; SO31 4HA
Bustling little 16th-c village pub just back from the River Hamble; beamed and timbered rooms with flagstones and polished boards, woodburner in fine brick fireplace, bar stools along herringbone-brick and timber counter, a beer named for the pub from Itchen Valley plus a couple of guests (often Flack Manor), well liked food (all day Sun); background music, TV; children and dogs (in bar) welcome, picnic-sets on small raised front terrace with boat views, open all day. *(Ted and Mary Bates)*

HAMBLE   SU4806

King & Queen (023) 8045 4247

3 miles from M27 junction 8; High Street; SO31 4HA Popular with locals and visiting yachtsmen, this cheerful bustling pub has a simply furnished bar with log fire at one end, three changing ales, good wines, cocktails and some 30 different rums, steps down to two small dining rooms serving generous helpings of enjoyable food from sandwiches and pizzas up; children and dogs welcome, planked tables and picnic-sets in sunny front garden, open all day. *(Ted and Mary Bates)*

HAMBLE   SU4806

Victory (023) 8045 3105

High Street; SO31 4HA Split-level 18th-c red-brick pub with four well kept ales and enjoyable reasonably priced bar food including popular Sun lunch, cheerful welcoming staff, nautical theme including Battle of Trafalgar mural, beams and half-panelling, wood, flagstone and carpeted floors; live music, sports TV; children and dogs welcome, terrace picnic-sets, open all day. *(Ted and Mary Bates, Pat Holmes)*

HAMBLEDON   SU6716

★**Bat & Ball** (023) 9263 2692

Broadhalfpenny Down; about 2 miles E towards Clanfield; PO8 0UB Extended dining pub opposite historic cricket pitch; log fires and comfortable modern furnishings in three linked rooms, lots of cricketing memorabilia (the game's rules are said to have been written here), Fullers ales and enjoyable food from well priced snacks up, panelled restaurant; free wi-fi; children and dogs welcome, tables on front terrace, garden behind with lovely downs views, good walks, open (and food) all day. *(Ann and Colin Hunt)*

HAVANT   SU7106

Old House At Home

(023) 9248 3464 *South Street; PO9 1DA*
Black and white 17th-c pub next to church;

modernised two-bar interior with low beams and nice rambling alcovey feel, enjoyable sensibly priced food from sandwiches and baked potatoes up, steak night Weds, Fullers/Gales beers including seasonals, friendly service; Tues quiz, juke box (some live music), sports TV, fruit machines; children (in smaller bar) and dogs welcome, pretty jettied frontage with hanging baskets, tables and smokers' shelter in back garden, open all day, food all day Fri and Sat, till 5pm Sun. *(Tony and Wendy Hobden, Ann and Colin Hunt)*

HAVANT   SU7106

Robin Hood (023) 9248 2779

Homewell; PO9 1EE Traditional 18th-c pub tucked away opposite church; opened-up bar with beams and log fires, well kept Fullers/Gales ales tapped from the cask, tasty simple lunchtime food, friendly service; Tues quiz, sports TV; dogs welcome, seats in small back garden, open all day. *(Brian Lintern, Ann and Colin Hunt)*

HAVANT   SU7206

Wheelwrights Arms (023) 9247 6502

Emsworth Road; PO9 2SN Sizeable stylishly decorated Victorian pub; five well kept beers, decent wine list and enjoyable pubby food from snacks and sharing plates up, OAP lunch deal Mon-Fri, friendly service; background and some live music, quiz night (Havant a Clue) first and third Weds of month; children and dogs welcome, shaded tables out at front and in courtyard garden behind, open all day, food all day Fri-Sun. *(Dr and Mrs J D Abell)*

HAWKLEY   SU7429

Hawkley Inn (01730) 827205

Off B3006 near A3 junction; Pococks Lane; GU33 6NE Traditional tile-hung village pub with seven well kept mainly local ales from central bar, open fires (large moose head above one), rugs on flagstones, old pine tables and assorted chairs, popular home-made food from pub favourites up, friendly staff; children and dogs welcome, covered seating area at front, picnic-sets in big back garden, useful for walkers on Hangers Way, six comfortable bedrooms, open all day weekends, no food Sun evening. *(David and Judy Robison)*

HAYLING ISLAND   SU7201

Maypole (023) 9246 3670

Havant Road; PO11 0PS Sizeable two-bar 1930s roadside local; good reasonably priced home-made pub food including Fri fish night, Fullers/Gales beers kept well, friendly service, parquet floors and polished panelling, plenty of good seating, open fires; Thurs quiz, darts; children and dogs welcome, garden picnic-sets and play equipment, closed Sun evening. *(John Harris)*

HAZELEY   SU7459
Shoulder of Mutton (0118) 932 6272
*Red Hill; pub signed from B3011;
RG27 8NB* 18th-c dining pub with good
range of fairly priced food including some
pasta dishes, selection of real ales served
from brick and timbered servery, friendly
helpful staff, log fires; children and
dogs welcome, terrace and garden with
attractive views across meadows, closes
7pm Sun. *(Tony and Jill Radnor)*

HECKFIELD   SU7260
New Inn (0118) 932 6374
*B3349 Hook–Reading (former A32);
RG27 0LE* Rambling open-plan dining
pub with good reasonably priced food (all
day weekends) from sandwiches and baked
potatoes up, well kept Badger ales and
good choice of wines and whiskies, efficient
friendly service, attractive layout with some
traditional furniture in original core, two
log fires, restaurant; quiz last Thurs of the
month; children welcome, good-sized heated
terrace, 16 bedrooms in extension, open
all day. *(Darren and Jane Staniforth)*

HERRIARD   SS6744
Fur & Feathers (01256) 510510
*Pub signed just off A339 Basingstoke–
Alton; RG25 2PN* Light and airy Victorian
country pub with highly regarded food from
sharing plates and a burger menu up, four
well kept changing ales and good choice of
wines and gins, selection of cuban cigars
too, friendly efficient staff, smallish bar
with dining areas either side, pine furniture
on stripped-wood flooring, painted half-
panelling, two woodburners; background
music; children welcome, garden behind with
paved terrace, closed Mon, otherwise open
all day (till 6pm Sun). *(Jan Sutton)*

HORDLE   SZ2996
★Mill at Gordleton (01590) 682219
Silver Street; SO41 6DJ Charming
tucked-away country inn; small panelled
bar to the right with leather armchairs and
Victorian-style mahogany dining chairs
on parquet flooring, pretty corner china
cupboard and electric woodburner, three
well kept real ales, 16 good wines by the
glass and 15 malt whiskies, also cosy lounge
with open fire, spacious second bar and
sizeable beamed restaurant extension, food
can be good including more affordable set
menus, afternoon teas; background music,
free wi-fi; children and dogs (in front bar)
welcome, lovely gardens with extensive series
of interestingly planted areas, sculptures
and several ponds, plenty of places to sit
including main waterside terrace, good

nearby walks, 12 comfortable individually
furnished bedrooms, open all day. *(Mr and
Mrs D J Nash, Christopher and Elise Way)*

HORSEBRIDGE   SU3430
John O'Gaunt (01794) 388644
*Off A3057 Romsey–Andover, just SW
of Kings Somborne; SO20 6PU* Neatly
refurbished River Test village pub; L-shaped
bar with mix of furniture including armchairs
on bare boards, light wood dados, book
wallpaper either side of woodburner, popular
good value home-made food from baguettes
up, Ringwood Razorback and three guests,
a couple of real ciders and good selection
of gins, friendly helpful service; children,
walkers and dogs welcome, seats outside,
open all day, food all day weekends.
(Ann and Colin Hunt)

HOUGHTON   SU3432
Boot (01794) 388310
*Village signposted off A30 in
Stockbridge; SO20 6LH* Well maintained
country pub with cheery log-fire bar and
more formal dining room; well kept real ales
such as Flack Manor, Otter and Ringwood,
Weston's and Thatcher's ciders and a dozen
wines by the glass, good bar and restaurant
food (not Sun or Mon evening) from
baguettes to blackboard specials; children
and dogs welcome, picnic-sets out in front
and in spacious tranquil garden by lovely
(unfenced) stretch of River Test, outside
summer grill, opposite Test Way walking/
cycling path. *(Joe and Belinda Smart)*

KEYHAVEN   SZ3091
★Gun (01590) 642391
Keyhaven Road; SO41 0TP Busy rambling
17th-c pub looking over boatyard and sea to
Isle of Wight; low-beamed bar with nautical
bric-a-brac and plenty of character (less
in family rooms and conservatory), good
fairly standard food including nice crab
sandwiches, well kept ales such as Ringwood,
Sharps and Timothy Taylors tapped from the
cask, Weston's cider, lots of malt whiskies,
prompt service from helpful young staff; bar
billiards; tables out in front and in big back
garden with swings and fish pond, you can
stroll down to small harbour and walk to
Hurst Castle, open all day Sat, closed Sun
evening. *(David and Judy Robison)*

KINGSCLERE   SU5258
Bel & Dragon (01635) 299342
Swan Street; RG20 5PP Attractively
updated 15th-c beamed village inn, emphasis
on dining with well liked bar and restaurant
food including Josper grills, weekend brunch,
three real ales, cocktails and good selection
of wines by the glass including champagne,

A star symbol before the name of a pub shows exceptional character and appeal.
It doesn't mean extra comfort. Even quite a basic pub can win a star,
if it's individual enough.

friendly helpful staff; children welcome, nine bedrooms, good surrounding walks, open all day, food all day Sun. *(Anne and Ben Smith)*

LANGSTONE SU7104

★**Royal Oak** (023) 9248 3125

Off A3023 just before Hayling Island bridge; Langstone High Street; PO9 1RY Charmingly placed waterside dining pub overlooking tidal inlet and ancient wadeway to Hayling Island – boats at high tide, wading birds when it goes out; four Greene King ales and good choice of wines by the glass, reasonably priced pubby food from sandwiches up, spacious flagstoned bar and linked dining areas, log fire; children welcome in restaurant, dogs in bar, nice garden with pond, good coast paths nearby, open (and food) all day from 10am. *(Tony Scott)*

LASHAM SU6742

Royal Oak (01256) 381750

Beside church; pub signed from A339; GU34 5SJ Refurbished fairly tucked-away dining pub gaining good reputation under present licensees; much liked affordably priced food from pub standards up including weekday set lunch, three well kept local ales, friendly welcoming service, pristine interior with flagstoned bar and separate wood-floored restaurant; quiz third Thurs of month; children and dogs welcome, nice quiet garden by church, attractive village and good surrounding walks, open all day weekends, closed Mon. *(Tony and Jill Radnor, Tony and Wendy Hobden)*

LINDFORD SU8036

Royal Exchange (01420) 488118

Liphook Road; GU35 0NX Red Mist pub with spacious bar and light modern dining room; enjoyable food from sandwiches and sharing boards to specials, four real ales including a house beer from Tilford, craft beers, plenty of wines by the glass and interesting selection of gins; children and dogs welcome, seats outside, open all day Fri-Sun, food all day Sun. *(Karl and Frieda Bujeya)*

LINWOOD SU1910

High Corner (01425) 473973

Signed from A338 via Moyles Court, and from A31; BH24 3QY Big rambling pub in splendid New Forest position at end of track; various areas including original log-fire bar, big back extensions for the summer crowds, nicely partitioned restaurant and lounge with verandah, good helpings of popular home-made food, well kept Wadworths ales and Weston's cider, friendly staff; children and dogs welcome, horses too (stables and paddock available), extensive wooded garden with play area, seven comfortable bedrooms, open all day in summer (all day weekends other times). *(Patricia Healey)*

LIPHOOK SU8330

Links Tavern (01428) 723773

Portsmouth Road; GU30 7EF Spacious Fullers pub with comfortably modernised interior, plenty of connecting rooms and intimate spaces, four of their ales and wide choice of wines by the glass, enjoyable food from sandwiches and sharing boards up, friendly service; some live music, free wi-fi; children welcome, picnic-sets on surrounding terraces and lawn, smokers' gazebo, pleasant woodland and lakeside walks at Foley Manor, open all day, food all day weekends. *(John and Bernadette Elliott)*

LISS SU7826

Jolly Drover (01730) 893137

London Road, Hill Brow; B2070 S of town, near B3006 junction; GU33 7QL Traditional 19th-c pub under long-serving licensees; neat carpeted beamed bar with a couple of chesterfields in front of brick inglenook, Sharps Doom Bar, Timothy Taylors Landlord and a dozen wines by the glass, generous helpings of enjoyable fairly priced food (puddings particularly good), friendly helpful service, two back dining sections; free wi-fi; children welcome, teak furniture on terrace, picnic-sets on lawn, six barn-conversion bedrooms, closed Sun evening. *(Tony and Wendy Hobden)*

LITTLE LONDON SU6259

Plough (01256) 850628

Silchester Road, off A340 N of Basingstoke; RG26 5EP Tucked-away local, cosy and unspoilt, with log fires, low beams and mixed furnishings on brick or tiled floors (watch the step), well kept Otter, Ringwood and interesting guests tapped from the cask, good value baguettes, no credit cards; bar billiards and darts; dogs welcome, attractive garden, handy for Pamber Forest and Calleva Roman remains, open all day. *(Charles Todd)*

LONG SUTTON SU7447

Four Horseshoes (01256) 862488

Signed off B3349 S of Hook; RG29 1TA Welcoming unpretentious country pub with loyal band of regulars; open plan with black beams and two log fires, long-serving landlord cooking uncomplicated bargain food such as lancashire hotpot and fish and chips, friendly landlady serving Palmers and maybe a guest ale; monthly quiz and jazz nights; children and dogs welcome, disabled access, small glazed-in front verandah, picnic-sets and play area on grass over road, pétanque, bedrooms with country views, closed Sun evening, Mon lunchtime. *(Tony and Jill Radnor)*

LYMINGTON SZ3295

Angel & Blue Pig (01590) 672050

High Street; SO41 9AP Busy town-centre Georgian inn; cosy right-hand room with comfortable sofas and armchairs, rugs on bare boards and an open fire, flagstoned area and two beamed rooms to the left of the entrance with old range in brick fireplace, large boar's head and lots of books, back bar has some nice old leather armchairs by woodburner, four real ales including a house beer from Ringwood, 16 wines by the glass and cocktails, enjoyable brasserie-style food; live music second Fri of month; children and dogs (in bar) welcome, terrace with seats under blue parasols, 14 stylish modern bedrooms, open (and food) all day. *(Jim and Sue James)*

LYMINGTON   SZ3293
Chequers (01590) 673415
Ridgeway Lane, Lower Woodside – dead end just S of A337 roundabout W of Lymington, by White Hart; SO41 8AH Old beamed pub with enjoyable food from traditional favourites up (smaller helpings available), Ringwood ales and good wines by the glass, bare boards and quarry tiles, mix of furniture including spindleback chairs, wall pews and country pine tables, yacht-racing pictures, woodburner; well behaved children and dogs welcome, tables and summer marquee in neat walled back garden, good walks and handy for bird-watching on Pennington Marshes, open all day, food all day weekends. *(Jim and Sue James)*

LYMINGTON   SZ3295
Kings Head (01590) 672709
Quay Hill; SO41 3AR Dimly lit old pub in steep cobbled lane of smart small shops; well kept Fullers, Ringwood, Timothy Taylors and a couple of guests, several wines by the glass and enjoyable uncomplicated food from sandwiches up, nice mix of old-fashioned furnishings in rambling beamed rooms, log fire and woodburner; background music, daily papers; children and dogs welcome, sunny little courtyard behind, open all day and can get very busy (food all day weekends). *(John Harris)*

LYMINGTON   SZ3295
Monkey House (01590) 676754
Southampton Road (A337); SO41 9HA Updated beamed dining pub with good variety of well liked sensibly priced food from open sandwiches up, five well kept local ales and a dozen wines by the glass, pleasant helpful staff, two rooms divided by a couple of steps, lower one with high pitched ceiling, log fires; background and Sun live music, TV; children and dogs welcome, tables on paved terrace and grass, two bedrooms, open all day, food all day Sun. *(Mr and Mrs D J Nash)*

LYNDHURST   SU2908
Fox & Hounds (023) 8028 2098
High Street; SO43 7BG Big busy low-beamed former coaching inn, comfortable and much modernised with good food including Tues burger night, well kept Fullers/Gales beers and plenty of wines by the glass, cheerful efficient service, rambling opened-up interior with exposed brick and standing timbers, rugs on wood floors, log fires; regular live music, Mon quiz, free wi-fi; children and dogs welcome, disabled facilities, murals and old enamel signs in paved courtyard garden, open all day, food all day weekends. *(John Beeken, Richard Elliott)*

LYNDHURST   SU2908
Waterloo Arms (023) 8028 2113
Pikes Hill, just off A337 N; SO43 7AS Thatched 17th-c New Forest pub with low beams, stripped-brick walls and log fire, three regular beers and large selection of ciders, enjoyable well priced pubby food including blackboard specials, friendly staff, comfortable bar and roomy back dining area; live music Sun; children and dogs welcome, terrace and nice big garden, open (and food) all day. *(Mrs P Sumner)*

MAPLEDURWELL   SU6851
★ Gamekeepers (01256) 322038
Off A30, not far from M3 junction 6; RG25 2LU Dark-beamed dining pub with good upmarket food from regularly changing blackboard menu (not cheap and they add a service charge), also some pubby choices and lunchtime baguettes, welcoming helpful landlord and friendly efficient staff, three well kept local ales including Andwell, good coffee, a few sofas in flagstoned and panelled core, well spaced tables in large dining room; background music, TV; children and dogs (in bar) welcome, terrace and garden, lovely thatched village with duck pond, good walks, open all day weekends. *(Frances Parsons)*

MARCHWOOD   SU3809
Pilgrim (023) 8086 7752
Hythe Road, off A326 at Twiggs Lane; SO40 4WU Picturesque thatched pub (originally three 18th-c cottages) with enjoyable sensibly priced food from lunchtime sandwiches up, well kept Fullers/Gales beers and decent wines, friendly helpful staff, open fires; children and dogs welcome, tree-lined garden with circular picnic-sets, 14 stylish bedrooms in building across car park, open all day. *(Lyn and Freddie Roberts)*

MEONSTOKE   SU6120
Bucks Head (01489) 877313
Village signed just off A32 N of Droxford; SO32 3NA Opened-up tile-hung pub in lovely village setting with ducks on pretty little River Meon; stone floors and log fires, popular food from sandwiches to blackboard specials, three well kept ales including Greene King, good friendly service; children and dogs welcome, small walled gardens either side, one overlooking river, good walks, five bedrooms, open all day Sat, till 6pm Sun. *(Ann and Colin Hunt, Patric Curwen)*

MILFORD-ON-SEA   SZ2891
Beach House   (01590) 643044
Park Lane; SO41 0PT Civilised well
placed Victorian hotel-dining pub owned by
Hall & Woodhouse; restored oak-panelled
interior with plenty of fine original features,
entrance hall bar serving Badger First Gold,
Tanglefoot and a guest, nice wines by the
glass and enjoyable sensibly priced food from
lunchtime sandwiches and sharing boards to
specials, friendly helpful service, magnificent
views from dining room (note the arty stags
heads) and terrace; children welcome, dogs
in bar, grounds down to the Solent looking
out to the Needles, 15 bedrooms, open (and
food) all day. *(Katharine Cowherd, David and
Sally Frost, David and Judy Robison)*

MINSTEAD   SU2810
★Trusty Servant   (023) 8081 2137
*Just off A31, not far from M27
junction 1; SO43 7FY* Attractive 19th-c
red-brick dining pub in pretty New Forest
hamlet with wandering cattle and ponies and
plenty of easy walks; two-room bare-boards
bar and big dining room, local pictures and
hunting-themed prints, open fires, well
kept ales such as Flack Manor, Ringwood
and Sharps, several wines by the glass, good
popular food from doorstep sandwiches to
pub favourites to local game, friendly helpful
staff; children and dogs welcome, terrace
and big sloping garden, interesting church
where Sir Arthur Conan Doyle is buried, five
bedrooms, open (and food) all day. *(Peter
Meister, David and Judy Robison, Tony Scott)*

NEW CHERITON   SU5827
★Hinton Arms   (01962) 771252
A272 near B3046 junction; SO24 0NH
Popular neatly kept country pub with
cheerful accommodating landlord and
friendly staff, three or four real ales including
a house beer from Bowman, decent wines
by the glass, large helpings of enjoyable
pub food from sandwiches to daily specials,
sporting pictures and memorabilia; TV
lounge; well behaved children and dogs
welcome, terrace and big garden, lots of
colourful tubs and hanging baskets, very
handy for Hinton Ampner House (NT).
(Ann and Colin Hunt, M and GR)

NORTH GORLEY   SU1611
Royal Oak   (01425) 652244
*Ringwood Road; village signed off A338
S of Fordingbridge; SP6 2PB* Modernised
17th-c thatched and beamed New Forest pub;
three well kept ales including Ringwood, a
dozen wines by the glass/carafe and decent
range of gins, good popular food (not Sun
evening) from pub favourites up, attentive
friendly service, children and dogs welcome,
seats out at front behind picket fence and
in back garden, big duck pond over road,
closed Mon, otherwise open all day till
10pm (8pm Sun). *(Anne and Ben Smith)*

NORTH WALTHAM   SU5645
★Fox   (01256) 397288
*3 miles from M3 junction 7: A30
southwards, then turn right at second
North Waltham turn, just after
Wheatsheaf; pub also signed from village
centre; RG25 2BE* Well run traditional
flint pub with low-ceilinged bar; Andwell,
Brakspears, West Berkshire and a guest,
Aspall's cider (many more in bottles)
and good range of wines and whiskies,
padded country kitchen chairs on parquet
floor, poultry prints above dark dado, big
woodburner, good food from sandwiches/
baguettes to daily specials, larger separate
dining room with high-backed leather chairs
and blue tartan carpet; free wi-fi; children
and dogs (in bar) welcome, picnic-sets under
parasols in colourful garden with pergola
walkway, pretty window boxes and hanging
baskets, nice walks including one to Jane
Austen's church at Steventon, open all day.
(Michael and Margaret Cross)

OVERTON   SU5149
★White Hart   (01256) 771431
London Road; RG25 3NW Handsome 500-
year-old beamed inn with some contemporary
touches; cosy bar with open fire, carved
counter serving well kept beers, a dozen
wines by the glass and cocktails, two-level
dining room with a central woodburner and
there's another room with cushioned wall
seating, interesting up-to-date food including
lunchtime sandwiches; live music first Fri of
month, free wi-fi; children and dogs (in bar)
welcome, suntrap garden (heated awning
for cooler days), comfortable bedrooms in
converted stable block, handy for Laverstoke
Mill (home to Bombay Sapphire distillery),
open all day. *(Jess and George Cowley)*

OVINGTON   SU5631
Bush   (01962) 732764
Off A31 W of Alresford; SO24 0RE
Popular 17th-c country pub in charming
spot with streamside garden; low-ceilinged
bar, high-backed settles, pews and lots of
old pictures, log fire, well kept Wadworths
ales and good choice of wines by the glass,
enjoyable food from sandwiches and sharing
boards up, friendly service; free wi-fi;
children and dogs welcome, good local
walks, open all day weekends, food all
day Sun. *(David and Judy Robison)*

OWER   SU3216
Mortimer Arms   (023) 8081 4379
*Romsey Road, by M27 junction 2;
SO51 6AF* Pub-hotel under same ownership
as the New Forest Inn at Emery Down; cosy
informal bar with tables around three-sided
servery, more formal restaurant, well kept
ales such as Ringwood, a dozen wines by
the glass and some interesting gins, good
food from bar snacks and sharing plates to
specials, welcoming helpful service; events

such as themed food weeks and quiz nights; children (till 7pm in bar) and dogs welcome, picnic-sets in enclosed garden, handy for Paultons theme park, 14 bedrooms, good breakfast, open (and food) all day. *(Sara Fulton, Roger Baker)*

PETERSFIELD   SU7423

Square Brewery (01730) 264291

The Square; GU32 3HJ Cheerful town-centre pub in modern-rustic style; three well kept Fullers ales and a guest, decent choice of wines and enjoyable sensibly priced food including good lunchtime sandwiches, wood floors, painted panelling and central woodburner; background music (live bands weekends), monthly quiz first and third Thurs of month, free wi-fi; children and dogs welcome, seats out overlooking the square and in covered courtyard behind, open all day, no evening food Sat or Sun. *(Richard Kennell)*

PETERSFIELD   SU7129

White Horse (01420) 588387

Up on an old downs road about halfway between Steep and East Tisted, near Priors Dean – OS Sheet 186 or 197 map reference 715290; GU32 1DA New tenants for this unspoilt country pub (aka the Pub With No Name); two charming candlelit parlour rooms with open fires, oak settles and a mix of dark wooden dining chairs around nice old tables, smarter beamed dining room, Fullers and guests from eight handpumps, local ciders and a fairly pubby menu including sandwiches; children and dogs (in bar) welcome, some rustic seats outside and camping facilities, open all day. *(Christopher and Elise Way)*

PHOENIX GREEN   SU7555

Phoenix (01252) 842484

London Road, A30 W of Hartley Wintney; RG27 8RT Beamed 18th-c pub with timber dividers, rugs on bare boards and big end inglenook, good freshly made food from varied daily changing menu including speciality dry-aged steaks, four well kept ales, a couple of real ciders and 16 wines by the glass, good friendly service, back dining room; children and dogs (in bar) welcome, pleasant outlook from sunny garden, open all day. *(M G Trotter)*

PILLEY   SZ3298

★ **Fleur de Lys** (01590) 672158

Off A337 Brockenhurst–Lymington; Pilley Street; SO41 5QG Attractive thatched and beamed village pub with

11th-c origins; highly regarded restaurant-y food from shortish menu (booking advised), Courage Directors, Sharps Doom Bar and a guest, good wines, friendly helpful service, inglenook log fires; well behaved children and dogs welcome, pretty garden with old well, good forest and heathland walks, open all day Sat, till 6pm Sun, closed Mon. *(Mr and Mrs D J Nash)*

PORTSMOUTH   SU6400

Brewhouse & Kitchen

(023) 9289 1340 *Guildhall Walk next to Theatre Royal; PO1 2DD* Popular mock-Tudor pub visibly brewing its own good beers, also decent choice of well priced food from sandwiches and small plates up, friendly helpful staff; children welcome, open (and food) all day. *(Frances Parsons)*

PORTSMOUTH   SZ6399

Bridge Tavern (023) 9275 2992

East Street, Camber Dock; PO1 2JJ Maritime theme and good harbour views; flagstones, bare boards and lots of dark wood, comfortable furnishings, Fullers ales and a dozen wines by the glass, generous helpings of good sensibly priced food including plenty of fish dishes, upstairs dining rooms (more modern and airy); children welcome, painted picnic-sets on waterside terrace, open all day and busy with diners at weekends (kitchen closes 5pm Sun). *(Pat Holmes)*

PORTSMOUTH   SU6706

George (023) 9222 1079

Portsdown Hill Road, Widley; PO6 1BE Comfortable one-bar Georgian pub with friendly local feel (despite being surrounded by busy roads); seven well kept ales and good range of gins, popular pubby food including good ploughman's, helpful pleasant staff; live music Tues, quiz every other Sun; dogs welcome, picnic-sets on side terrace, views of Hayling Island, Portsmouth and Isle of Wight, hill walks across the road, open all day, closed (food) evenings. *(Jan Sutton)*

PORTSMOUTH   SU6501

George (023) 9275 3885

Queen Street, near dockyard entrance; PO1 3HU Spotless old inn (Grade I listed) with two rooms (one set for dining), log fire, glass-covered well and maritime pictures, well kept Greene King Abbot, Sharps Atlantic and Doom Bar, well priced food (not Sun evening, Mon lunchtime) from sandwiches up, good friendly service; eight bedrooms, handy for dockyard and HMS *Victory*, open all day. *(Ann and Colin Hunt)*

PORTSMOUTH   SZ6399
Pembroke (023) 9282 3961
Pembroke Road; PO1 2NR Traditional
well run corner local with good buoyant
atmosphere, comfortable and unspoilt under
long-serving licensees, Bass, Fullers London
Pride and Greene King Abbot from L-shaped
bar, simple cheap food including fresh rolls,
coal-effect gas fire; monthly live music,
darts; dogs welcome, open all day (break
5-7pm every other Sun when there's a quiz
night). *(Charles Welch)*

PORTSMOUTH   SU6300
Ship Anson (023) 9282 4152
*Victory Road, The Hard (opposite
Esplanade Station, Portsea); PO1 3DT*
No-frills mock-Tudor pub close to dockyard
entrance, spacious and comfortable, with
well kept Greene King ales and a guest,
generous pub food at bargain prices, also
coffee and cakes, buoyant local atmosphere;
fruit machines, sports TVs; children welcome,
seats outside overlooking ferry port, very
handy for HMS *Victory*, open (and food)
all day. *(John Harris, Charles Welch)*

PORTSMOUTH   SZ6299
Still & West (023) 9282 1567
Bath Square, Old Portsmouth; PO1 2JL
Great location with superb views of narrow
harbour mouth and across to Isle of Wight,
especially from glazed-in panoramic upper
family area and waterfront terrace; nautical
bar with fireside sofas, Fullers ales and good
choice of wines by the glass, enjoyable all-day
food from sandwiches and sharing plates
to good fish dishes; background music, free
wi-fi; dogs welcome in bar, handy for Historic
Dockyard, nearby pay-and-display parking,
open from 10am (11.30am Sun). *(Colin Gooch,
Jess and George Cowley)*

RINGWOOD   SU1504
Railway (01425) 473701
Hightown Road; BH24 1NQ Traditional
two-bar Victorian local with up to four
well kept changing ales (usually one from
nearby Ringwood), enjoyable home-made
food including range of burgers, also vegan/
vegetarian menu, friendly service; Thurs
quiz, darts; children and dogs welcome, nice
enclosed garden with play area, vegetable
patch, ducks and chickens, open all day.
(Simon Sharpe)

ROMSEY   SU3521
Old House At Home (01794) 513175
Love Lane; SO51 8DE Attractive
17th-c thatched pub surrounded by new
development; friendly and bustling, with
comfortable low-beamed interior, wide
choice of freshly made sensibly priced bar
food including popular Sun lunch, well kept
Fullers/Gales beers and a guest, cheerful
service; regular folk sessions; children
and dogs (in bar) welcome, split-level

back terrace, open all day (no food Sun
evening). *(Ted and Mary Bates)*

ROMSEY   SU3520
Three Tuns (01794) 512639
*Middlebridge Street (but car park signed
straight off A27 bypass); SO51 8HL*
Good well presented food is the star at this
old village pub but they do keep four beers
including Flack Manor, local cider and
11 wines by the glass; bar with cushioned
bow-window seat, dark wooden tables on
flagstones, beer mats pinned to the walls
and church candles in fireplace, dining areas
either side, one with a huge stuffed fish over
another fireplace, the other with prints on
yellow walls above a black dado, a few rugs
scattered around, heavy beams and antler
chandeliers; background music, board games,
free wi-fi; children and dogs welcome, back
terrace with picnic-sets under parasols, more
seats in front by the tiny street, open all day.
(Ted and Mary Bates)

ROTHERWICK   SU7156
Coach & Horses (01256) 768976
*Signed from B3349 N of Hook; also quite
handy for M3 junction 5; RG27 9BG*
Friendly 17th-c pub with traditional
beamed front rooms, well kept Badger ales
and good choice of popular reasonably
priced pubby food including specials,
cheerful accommodating staff, log fire and
woodburners, newer back dining area;
open mike night first Weds of month, quiz
fourth Tues; children, dogs and muddy boots
welcome, tables out at front behind picket
fence and on back terrace overlooking fields,
pretty flower tubs and hanging baskets, good
walks, open all day Sat, till 6pm Sun, closed
Mon (except bank holidays). *(Darren and
Jane Staniforth)*

ROTHERWICK   SU7156
Falcon (01256) 765422
*Off B3349 N of Hook, not far from M3
junction 5; RG27 9BL* Welcoming open-
plan country pub; good freshly made food,
well kept ales and decent selection of wines
and gins, friendly efficient service, rustic
tables and comfy sofas in bare-boards bar,
flagstoned dining area, log fires; quiz and live
music nights, free wi-fi; children and dogs
welcome (resident black labrador), disabled
access, tables out in front and in back
garden, open all day, food all day Sun.
(Charles Todd)

SELBORNE   SU7433
Selborne Arms (01420) 511247
High Street; GU34 3JR Old-fashioned
17th-c beamed village pub; character tables,
pews and deep settles made from casks on
antique boards, good range of local ales and
popular food from lunchtime baguettes up,
big log fire, carpeted dining room with local
photographs; quiz and live music nights;
children welcome, no dogs inside, garden

with arbour and terrace heated by logburner, orchard and play area, zigzag path up the Hanger, handy for Gilbert White's House, open all day weekends. *(Ann and Colin Hunt)*

SHEDFIELD SU5613
Samuels Rest (01329) 832213
Upper Church Road (signed off B2177); SO32 2JB Cosy village local overlooking cricket pitch; well kept Wadworths ales and generous helpings of enjoyable sensibly priced home-made food, nice eating area away from bar, conservatory; some live music including folk night third Weds of month, pool and darts, free wi-fi; children and dogs (in bar) welcome, aviary with parrots, good sized garden, lovely church nearby, open all day, food all day weekends (till about 6pm Sun). *(Ann and Colin Hunt)*

SHEDFIELD SU5513
Wheatsheaf (01329) 833024
A334 Wickham–Botley; SO32 2JG Friendly extended traditional local; well kept/priced Flowerpots and guests tapped from the cask, proper cider, short sensible choice of enjoyable bargain lunches (evening food Tues and Weds), good service; live music Sat, darts; children and dogs (in bar) welcome, nice little back garden, handy for Wickham Vineyard, open all day. *(Ann and Colin Hunt)*

SHERFIELD ENGLISH SU3022
Hatchet (01794) 322487
Romsey Road; SO51 6FP Beamed and panelled 18th-c pub with good choice of popular fairly priced food including two-for-one steak deal (Tues, Thurs evenings), four well kept ales and good wine choice, friendly hard-working staff, long bar with cosy area down steps, woodburner, more steps up to second bar with darts, TV and juke box; monthly quiz; children and dogs (on leads) welcome, outside seating on two levels, play area, open all day weekends. *(Holly and Tim Waite)*

SOBERTON SU6116
White Lion (01489) 877346
School Hill; signed off A32 S of Droxford; SO32 3PF Attractive unchanging 17th-c pub in nice spot opposite raised village green; enjoyable home-made food from baguettes up, four well kept ales including Bowman and Sharps, good range of wines by the glass, friendly efficient service, low-ceilinged bar with built-in wall seats and open fire, separate small restaurant; children and dogs welcome, sheltered garden and suntrap terrace, good walks nearby, stable-conversion bedrooms, open all day, food all day Sun. *(Ann and Colin Hunt)*

SOPLEY SZ1596
Woolpack (01425) 672252
B3347 N of Christchurch; BH23 7AX Pretty 17th-c thatched and beamed pub with rambling open-plan bar; well kept Ringwood Razorback, Sharps Doom Bar and a guest, Thatcher's cider and good choice of wines by the glass, enjoyable traditional food such as cod and chips served in newspaper, daily specials and range of sandwiches/wraps, modern dining conservatory overlooking weir; children and dogs (menu for them) welcome, terrace and charming garden with weeping willows, duck stream and footbridges, open (and food) all day. *(David and Sally Frost)*

SOUTHAMPTON SU4314
Butchers Hook (023) 8178 2280
Manor Farm Road; SO18 1NN One-room micro-pub in former Bitterne Park butchers (some original features remain including tiling); changing cask and keg beers from scaffold stillage (no bar), good bottled range too and real cider, friendly helpful service, no food (can bring your own); board games; well behaved dogs welcome, a few bench seats out in front, closed Mon, Tues and lunchtimes Weds-Fri, open all day Sat from 1pm, Sun from 2pm, gets packed at busy times. *(Anne and Ben Smith)*

SOUTHAMPTON SU4111
★**Duke of Wellington** (023) 8033 9222
Bugle Street (or walk along city wall from Bar Gate); SO14 2AH Striking timber-framed building dating from the 14th c (cellars even older); heavy beams and fine log fire, up to eight well kept Wadworths ales (tasting trays available), plenty of wines by the glass and good fairly priced food, friendly helpful service; background music (live jazz Fri), free wi-fi; children welcome, sunny streetside picnic-sets, handy for Tudor House & Garden, open all day. *(Pat Holmes, Anne and Ben Smith)*

SOUTHAMPTON SU4213
Rockstone (023) 8063 7256
Onslow Road; SO14 0JL Popular relaxed place with well liked generous food from signature burgers to street food (booking advised), good variety of real ales, craft beers and ciders from well stocked bar, friendly hard-working staff; some live music; children welcome, seats out at front, open (and food) all day (till 1am Sat). *(Pat Holmes)*

SOUTHAMPTON SU4313
South Western Arms
(023) 8032 4542 *Adelaide Road, by St Denys station; SO17 2HW* Friendly easy-going corner local under newish management; ten well kept changing ales

---

Real ale to us means beer that has matured naturally in its cask – not pressurised or filtered. We name all real ales stocked.

and good choice of bottled beers, pizza van Weds-Sat evenings, bare boards, exposed brickwork and lots of woodwork, old range; darts, pool and table football in upper gallery, some live music; dogs welcome, picnic-sets in walled beer garden with passing trains, open all day. *(Anne and Ben Smith)*

SOUTHAMPTON   SU4213
White Star (023) 8082 1990
Oxford Street; SO14 3DJ Modernised opened-up bar with crescent-shaped banquettes, panelling and open fires, wood or stone floors, comfortable sofas and armchairs in secluded alcoves by south-facing windows, bistro-style dining area serving good up-to-date food along with pub favourites, Fullers ales and nice choice of wines by the glass, efficient attentive staff; background music; sunny pavement tables on pedestrianised street, 13 boutique bedrooms, open all day from 7am (8.30am weekends) for breakfast. *(Pat Holmes, Charles Welch)*

SOUTHSEA   SZ6699
Artillery Arms (023) 9273 3610
Hester Road; PO4 8HB Traditional two-bar Victorian backstreet local; half a dozen well kept ales including Triple fff, no food apart from rolls on match days (near Fratton Park), friendly atmosphere; Mon quiz, sports TV, pool and darts; children and dogs welcome, garden with play equipment, open all day. *(Tony Scott)*

SOUTHSEA   SZ6498
Belle Isle (023) 9282 0515
Osbourne Road; PO5 3LR Café-bar-restaurant in former shop, informal and relaxed, with interesting continental-feel décor, three real ales, international bottled beers, cocktails and eclectic blackboard menu, decent coffee too; background music; children welcome, a few seats out at front under awning, open all day. *(Jim and Sue James)*

SOUTHSEA   SZ6698
Eastney Tavern (023) 9282 6246
Cromwell Road; PO4 9PN Bow-fronted corner pub just off the seafront, spacious and comfortable, with various eating areas (plenty of room for drinkers too), popular good value food including Weds burger night and Thurs curry (reduced menu Mon), Sharps Doom Bar and a couple of local guests, decent choice of wines by the glass, good cheerful service; Tues quiz, live music last Fri of the month, sports TV; children and dogs welcome, seats in courtyard garden, nearby parking difficult, open all day. *(Jan Sutton)*

SOUTHSEA   SZ6499
★Hole in the Wall (023) 9229 8085
Great Southsea Street; PO5 3BY Friendly unspoilt little local in old part of town, six interesting well kept/priced ales including

Flowerpots Goodens Gold, four craft kegs and good range of bottled beers, real cider/perry, speciality local sausages and other simple good value food (evenings Tues-Sat, lunchtime Fri), nicely worn boards, dark pews and panelling, old photographs and prints, hundreds of pump clips on ceiling, little snug behind the bar and sweet shop; Oct beer festival; dogs welcome, small outside area at front with benches, side garden, open all day from 4pm (noon Fri, 2pm Sat and Sun). *(Ann and Colin Hunt)*

SOUTHSEA   SZ6499
King Street Tavern (023) 9307 3568
King Street; PO5 4EH Victorian corner pub in attractive conservation area with fine tiled façade; four well kept Wadworths ales and a couple of guests, craft kegs and two proper ciders, enjoyable good value food from smokehouse/barbecue menu, friendly atmosphere; live music including irish folk session every other Thurs, big-screen sports TV; children welcome, courtyard tables, open all day Fri and Sat, till 7pm Sun, closed lunchtimes Mon, Tues (and Weds in winter). *(Jan Sutton)*

SOUTHSEA   SZ6498
Meat & Barrel (023) 9217 6291
Palmerston Road; PO5 3PT Sizeable bar-restaurant under same ownership as Southsea's Belle Isle; fine range of real ales and craft beers, tasters offered by friendly knowledgeable staff, enjoyable food including range of burgers and various sausage and mash combinations; children welcome, open all day. *(John Harris)*

SOUTHSEA   SZ6499
Wine Vaults (023) 9286 4712
Albert Road, opposite King's Theatre; PO5 2SF Bustling Fullers pub with several chatty rooms on different floors; main panelled bar with long plain counter and pubby furniture on bare boards, seven well kept ales and decent choice of food including pizzas and range of burgers, good service, separate restaurant; background music, live jazz or folk every other Tues, sports TV, table football; children welcome, dogs in bar, smokers' roof terrace, open (and food) all day. *(Ann and Colin Hunt, Jess and George Cowley)*

SOUTHWICK   SU6208
Golden Lion (023) 9221 0437
High Street; just off B2177 on Portsdown Hill; PO17 6EB Spotless two-bar 16th-c beamed pub (where Eisenhower and Montgomery came before D-Day) under welcoming ebullient landlord; up to seven well kept local ales including two from Suthwyk using barley from surrounding fields, four ciders and a dozen wines by the glass, good locally sourced home-made food (not Sun or Mon evenings) from snacks up in bar and dining room, cosy lounge with

sofas and log fire; live music including Tues jazz; good outside loos; children and dogs welcome, picnic-sets on side grass, picturesque Estate village with scenic walks, next to Southwick Brewhouse shop/museum (over 250 bottled beers), open all day Sat, till 7pm Sun. *(Ann and Colin Hunt, Penny and Peter Keevil, Paula Allen)*

SPARSHOLT   SU4331
Plough (01962) 776353
Village signposted off B3049 (Winchester–Stockbridge), a little W of Winchester; SO21 2NW Neatly kept dining pub under newish ownership; main bar with interesting mix of wooden tables and farmhouse or upholstered chairs, old farm tools on walls and ceiling, Wadworths ales and good choice of wines by the glass, generally well regarded food from blackboard menu, dining tables on the left looking over fields to woodland; children and dogs welcome, disabled access/facilities, plenty of seats on terrace and lawn, play fort, open all day. *(Joe and Belinda Smart)*

STOCKBRIDGE   SU3535
Greyhound (01264) 810833
High Street; SO20 6EY Civilised inn-restaurant with highly regarded interesting food, not cheap but they do offer a good value set lunch, three real ales including a house beer from Ringwood, nice choice of wines and whiskies, friendly efficient staff, log fires each end of bay-windowed bar (restaurant to the right), dark low beams, scrubbed old tables on woodstrip floor, evening candles; children and dogs allowed, charming Test-side garden behind, ten bedrooms, good walks and fly fishing, open all day. *(Richard Kennell)*

STOCKBRIDGE   SU3535
Three Cups (01264) 810527
High Street; SO20 6HB Lovely low-beamed building dating from 1500, updated and added to yet keeping country inn feel; some emphasis on dining with lots of set tables, but also high-backed settles and rustic bric-a-brac, three well kept ales and nice wines by the glass, enjoyable food from shortish menu including one or two pub favourites, friendly if not always prompt service, back 'orangery' restaurant extension; children and dogs welcome, charming streamside garden with vine-covered terrace, eight bedrooms (back ones quieter), open all day. *(Edward Mirzoeff, D J and P M Taylor)*

STOCKBRIDGE   SU3535
White Hart (01264) 810663
High Street; A272/A3057 roundabout; SO20 6HF Spacious village-edge pub with pleasantly busy divided beamed bar, attractive décor with antique prints, oak pews and other seats around pine tables, decent choice of enjoyable food from bar snacks to daily specials, well kept

Fullers/Gales beers, good friendly service, comfortable restaurant with open fire (children allowed); dogs in bar, terrace tables and nice garden, 24 bedrooms (ten recently added), open (and food) all day. *(Edward Mirzoeff, David and Judy Robison)*

SWANMORE   SU5716
Brickmakers (01489) 890954
Church Road; SO32 2PA Large 1920s pub in centre of village, friendly and relaxed, with four well kept ales, decent wines and good food cooked by landlord-chef including popular Sun roasts and OAP weekday lunch deal, cheerful efficient service, leather sofas by log fire, pitched-roof dining area with local artwork; Tues quiz, some live music; children and dogs welcome (pub dog is Rosie), garden with raised deck, nearby walks, open (and food) all day. *(Ann and Colin Hunt)*

SWANMORE   SU5815
Rising Sun (01489) 896663
Droxford Road; signed off A32 N of Wickham and B2177 S of Bishop's Waltham, at Hillpound E of village centre; SO32 2PS Welcoming 17th-c brick coaching inn; low-beamed carpeted bar, comfortable seating by log fire, pleasant roomier dining area with brick barrel vaulting in one part, a house beer from Flack Manor along with Flowerpots Goodens Gold and a local guest, good range of wines by the glass and enjoyable reasonably priced home-cooked food including daily specials, friendly speedy service; children and dogs (in bar) welcome, picnic-sets on side grass with play area, King's Way long-distance path nearby, closed Sun evening. *(Ann and Colin Hunt)*

SWAY   SZ2898
Hare & Hounds (01590) 682404
Durns Town, just off B3055 SW of Brockenhurst; SO41 6AL Comfortable New Forest family dining pub with hearty helpings of home-cooked food including daily specials, well kept ales such as Itchen Valley, Ringwood and Timothy Taylors, good friendly service, some low beams and central log fire; background music, Sun quiz; children and dogs welcome, picnic-sets and play frame in neatly kept garden, open all day. *(Lyn and Freddie Roberts)*

TICHBORNE   SU5730
★Tichborne Arms (01962) 733760
Signed off B3047; SO24 0NA Welcoming old-fashioned thatched pub (rebuilt in the 1930s) at the edge of this quiet little village; half-panelled bare-boards bar with interesting pictures and other odds and ends, candlelit pine tables and raised woodburner, four regular beers including Palmers and local guests tapped from cooled casks, real cider, good fairly traditional home-made food (not Sun or Mon evenings, booking advised), friendly attentive service, locals' bar with piano, darts and open fire; children and

dogs welcome, sheltered terrace and large peaceful garden with water meadow views, close to Wayfarers Walk and Itchen Way, open all day Sat, till 7.30pm Sun. *(Tony and Jill Radnor, David and Judy Robison)*

TITCHFIELD SU5305
Queens Head (01329) 842154
High Street; off A27 near Fareham; PO14 4AQ Welcoming early 17th-c family-run pub with enjoyable home-made food and four well kept changing ales; cosy bar with old local pictures, window seats and warm winter fire in central brick fireplace, small dining room; Sun quiz, function room for nostalgic dinner-dance and theatre nights; children welcome, picnic-sets in prettily planted backyard, pleasant conservation village near nature reserve, walks to coast, open all day. *(John Harris)*

TITCHFIELD SU5405
Wheatsheaf (01329) 842965
East Street; off A27 near Fareham; PO14 4AD Welcoming old pub with small bow-windowed front bar and large back restaurant extension, good food including small-plates menu, Tues steak night and popular Sun roasts, five well kept ales such as Flowerpots and Palmers, log fires; background music; terrace tables behind, open all day, food all day Sat, till 7pm Sun. *(Ann and Colin Hunt, John Harris)*

TWYFORD SU4824
★ ### Bugle (01962) 714888
B3355/Park Lane; SO21 1QT Modern dining pub with good enterprising food (highish prices) from daily changing menu, also lunchtime sandwiches and snacks, well kept ales such as Bowman and Flowerpots, nice wines by the glass, attentive friendly young staff; background music; children and dogs (in bar) welcome, seats on attractive verandah, good walks nearby, three country-style bedrooms, open all day, no food Sun evening. *(David and Judy Robison)*

TWYFORD SU4824
Phoenix (01962) 713322
High Street (B3335); SO21 1RF Cheerful open-plan local with raised dining area and big inglenook log fire, jovial long-serving landlord and friendly attentive staff, eight well kept ales including Greene King, good value wines and big helpings of enjoyable food from reasonably priced traditional menu; background music, sports TV, quiz nights, skittle alley; children welcome, side terraces, open all day in summer. *(Ann and Colin Hunt)*

UPHAM SU5320
Brushmakers Arms (01489) 860231
Shoe Lane; village signed from Winchester–Bishop's Waltham downs road, and from B2177; SO32 1JJ Welcoming low-beamed village pub;

L-shaped bar divided by central woodburner, cushioned settles and chairs around mix of tables, various brushes (once made here) and related paraphernalia, little back snug, enjoyable locally sourced home-made food, Bowman, Flack Manor, Flowerpots and a guest, good choice of wines; quiz first Weds of month, folk session third Sun (from 5pm); children and dogs welcome, big garden with picnic-sets on sheltered terrace and tree-shaded lawn, good nearby walks, open all day weekends, closed Mon lunchtime. *(Ann and Colin Hunt)*

UPPER CLATFORD SU3543
Crook & Shears (01264) 361543
Off A343 S of Andover, via Foundry Road; SP11 7QL Cosy and welcoming 17th-c thatched pub; well kept Otter and Ringwood ales, Thatcher's cider and reasonably priced traditional food (not Sun evening, Mon) from baguettes to enjoyable Sun roasts, also Tues steak night, friendly attentive service, open fires and woodburner, small dining room, back skittle alley with own bar; children and dogs welcome, pleasant secluded garden behind, closed Mon lunchtime. *(Ted and Mary Bates)*

UPPER FARRINGDON SU7135
Rose & Crown (01420) 587001
Off A32 S of Alton; Crows Lane – follow Church, Selborne, Liss signpost; GU34 3ED Early 19th-c tile-hung village pub freshened up under welcoming new management; L-shaped bar with bare boards and log fire, local ales, plenty of wines by the glass and nice range of gins, good food (not Sun evening) from pub favourites up including Mon steak night, friendly helpful service, back dining room; children and dogs welcome wide views from attractive garden, open all day Sat, till 9pm Sun. *(Tony and Jill Radnor)*

UPTON SU3555
Crown (01264) 736044
N of Hurstbourne Tarrant, off A343; SP11 0JS Popular old country pub with good imaginative food from bar snacks up, two or three changing regional ales and well chosen wines by the glass including english fizz, friendly helpful service, nice log fire, coffee lounge, restaurant and conservatory, also recently added farm shop; children and dogs (in bar) welcome, small garden and terrace, closed Mon and Tues, otherwise open all day, weekend brunch from 10am. *(Pat Holmes)*

UPTON GREY SU6948
Hoddington Arms (01256) 862371
Signed off B3349 S of Hook; Bidden Road; RG25 2RL Nicely updated 18th-c beamed pub; good food from varied menu (not Sun evening), three well kept ales and ten wines by the glass, friendly staff; events including live music, movie nights and beer/

cider festivals; children and dogs welcome, big enclosed garden with terrace, quiet pretty village with interesting Gertrude Jekyll garden, good walking/cycling, open all day Fri-Sun. *(Sarah Little)*

VERNHAM DEAN   SU3456
George (01264) 737279
Centre of village; SP11 0JY Rambling open-plan 17th-c beamed and timbered pub with notable eyebrow windows, some exposed brick and flint, inglenook log fire, well kept Flack Manor, Greene King, Hop Back and a guest, popular home-made food (not Sun evening) including range of smaller lunchtime dishes, good friendly service; children and dogs welcome, pretty garden behind, lovely thatched village and fine walks, open all day (Sun till 6pm). *(David and Judy Robison)*

WALHAMPTON   SZ3396
Walhampton Arms (01590) 673113
B3054 NE of Lymington; aka Walhampton Inn; SO41 5RE Large comfortable Georgian-style family roadhouse handy for Isle of Wight ferry; popular well priced food including carvery (Sun and Mon) in raftered former stables and two adjoining areas, pleasant lounge, Ringwood and Flack Manor ales and traditional cider, cheerful helpful staff; quiz nights; attractive courtyard, good walks, open (and food) all day. *(Helen Peterston)*

WALTHAM CHASE   SU5614
Black Dog (01329) 832316
Winchester Road; SO32 2LX Old brick-built country pub with low-ceilinged carpeted front bar, three well kept Greene King ales and a guest, over a dozen wines by the glass and enjoyable well priced food (all day Sun) from baguettes and basket meals up including weekday offers, cheerful helpful service, log fires, extended back restaurant; some live music, sports TV; children and dogs welcome, tables under parasols in good-sized neatly kept garden with deck, play area and colourful hanging baskets, open all day weekends. *(Joy Griffiths, Ann and Colin Hunt)*

WELL   SU7646
★ ### Chequers (01256) 862605
Off A287 via Crondall, or A31 via Froyle and Lower Froyle; RG29 1TL Appealing low-beamed country dining pub; very good restaurant-style food (some quite pricey) including fresh fish/seafood, also brasserie menu and lunchtime sandwiches, Badger ales kept well and good choice of wines, wood floors, panelling and log fires; free wi-fi; bench seating on vine-covered front terrace, spacious back garden overlooking fields, open (and food) all day. *(Patricia Healey)*

WEST MEON   SU6424
★ ### Thomas Lord (01730) 829244
High Street; GU32 1LN Named after founder of Lord's Cricket Ground, so lots of cricketing memorabilia – even stuffed squirrels playing the game in cabinet above counter; bar has leather chesterfield and armchairs by log fire, animal-hide stools, wooden chairs and corner settles on parquet, half a dozen well kept ales including Crafty, 13 wines by the glass and good quality food using local produce (own vegetables and eggs), small similarly furnished room off with antlers above fireplace, slightly more formal restaurant and snug with big photo mural of local countryside; background music, board games, free wi-fi; children and dogs (in bar) welcome, picnic-sets in sizeable garden with pizza oven and barbecue, open all day. *(Christopher and Elise Way)*

WEST TYTHERLEY   SU2730
Black Horse (01794) 340308
North Lane; SP5 1NF Compact unspoilt village local with welcoming chatty atmosphere; traditional beamed bar with a couple of long tables, woodburner in big fireplace, four mainly local ales and a real cider, nicely set dining area serving enjoyable reasonably priced food including good Sun roasts; quiz last Thurs of month, skittle alley; children, walkers and dogs welcome, open all day Sun till 7pm, closed Mon. *(Simon Sharpes)*

WHERWELL   SU3839
Mayfly (01264) 860283
Testcombe (over by Fullerton, not in Wherwell itself); A3057 SE of Andover, between B3420 turn-off and Leckford where road crosses River Test; OS Sheet 185 map reference 382390; SO20 6AX Busy red-brick pub in wonderful spot overlooking fast-flowing River Test; spacious beamed and carpeted bar with fishing paraphernalia, rustic pub furnishings and woodburner, well kept Fullers ales and extensive range of wines by the glass, popular food (must book for a good table) from sandwiches up, amiable staff coping well with the crowds, conservatory; background music; well behaved children and dogs welcome, plenty of riverside picnic-sets on terrace and grass, open (and food) all day. *(Ian Herdman, Edward Mirzoeff)*

WHERWELL   SU3840
White Lion (01264) 860317
B3420; SP11 7JF Early 17th-c multi-level beamed village inn, popular and friendly, with good choice of enjoyable food including signature pies and daily specials, well kept Sharps, Timothy Taylors and a local guest,

---

If we know a pub has an outdoor play area for children, we mention it.

ciders such as Orchard Pig and several wines by the glass, cheery helpful staff, open fire, comfy leather sofas and armchairs, dining rooms either side of bar; background music; well behaved children and dogs welcome, teak furniture in sunny courtyard, Test Way walks, three bedrooms, open all day Sat, till 9pm Sun, closed Mon (apart from bank holidays). *(Ann and Colin Hunt, Edward Mirzoeff)*

WICKHAM   SU5711
Greens   (01329) 833197
The Square, at junction with A334; PO17 5JQ Civilised restaurantry place with clean-cut modern décor, small bar with leather sofa and armchairs on light wood floor, extensive wine choice and a couple of real ales, obliging young staff, step down to split-level balustraded dining areas with good imaginative food along with more traditional choices and lunchtime set menu; background music; children welcome if eating, pleasant lawn overlooking water meadows, closed Sun evening, Mon. *(Simon Sharpe)*

WINCHESTER   SU4829
Bishop on the Bridge
(01962) 855111   *High Street/Bridge Street; SO23 9JX* Popular 19th-c red-brick Fullers pub by the River Itchen; their well kept beers (not cheap) and enjoyable food from sandwiches to daily specials, good friendly service, opened up traditional bare-boards interior; free wi-fi; children and dogs welcome, nice back terrace overlooking the river, open all day. *(Tony Scott)*

WINCHESTER   SU4828
★Black Boy   (01962) 861754
B3403 off M3 junction 10 towards city, then left into Wharf Hill; no nearby daytime parking – 220 metres from car park on B3403; SO23 9NQ Wonderfully eccentric décor at this chatty old-fashioned pub, floor-to-ceiling books, lots of big clocks, mobiles made of wine bottles or spectacles, variety of stuffed animals including a baboon, donkey and dachshund, two open fires, orange-painted room with big oriental rugs on red floorboards, also a barn room with open hayloft, five well kept local ales, real cider and good selection of gins (weekend gin bar), decent straightforward home-made food (not Sun evening, Mon) from sandwiches up, cheerful service; table football and board games; supervised children and dogs welcome, slate tables out in front and seats on attractive secluded terrace, ten bedrooms in adjoining building, open all day. *(Ann and Colin Hunt)*

WINCHESTER   SU4829
Golden Lion   (01962) 865512
Alresford Road; SO23 0JZ Welcoming 1930s flower-decked pub on outskirts; generous helpings of enjoyable food from standard choices up (they cater for special diets including vegan), well kept Wadworths beers and ten wines by the glass, friendly attentive service, comfortable interior with modern back conservatory overlooking garden; live bluegrass last Tues of the month; children and dogs welcome, open all day Sun. *(Peter Hesketh-Roberts)*

WINCHESTER   SU4830
Hyde Tavern   (01962) 862592
Hyde Street (B3047); SO23 7DY Cosy 15th-c gabled pub with friendly chatty atmosphere in two wonderfully old-fashioned bars, well kept ales and a couple of proper ciders, no food (can bring your own), open fire; regular live music including folk nights, storytelling and writers' workshops, quiz first Sun of month, Father's Day beer festival; steps down to cellar bar and secluded garden, open all day weekends, shut weekdays till 5pm. *(Ann and Colin Hunt)*

WINCHESTER   SU4829
★Old Vine   (01962) 854616
Great Minster Street; SO23 9HA Popular big-windowed town bar with four well kept ales including local Alfreds, plenty of wines by the glass and decent range of whiskies, high beams and worn oak boards, larger dining side and modern conservatory (young children here only), good variety of food from sandwiches and pub staples up, efficient friendly service even though busy; background music; dogs welcome in bar, wheelchair accessible using ramp (no access to lavatories), by cathedral with a few pavement seats, more tables in partly covered back terrace, charming bedrooms, open all day. *(Jess and George Cowley)*

WINCHESTER   SU4728
Queen   (01962) 853898
Kingsgate Road; SO23 9PG Cottagey twin-gabled pub in attractive setting opposite College cricket ground; cosy interior with bare boards and log fire, up to ten well kept beers including own brews (tasting trays available), enjoyable sensibly priced home-made food from sandwiches, bar snacks and sharing plates up, good friendly service, step to restaurant; May beer/cider/music festival; children and dogs (in bar) welcome, paved front terrace and large garden behind, open all day. *(Tony and Jill Radnor, Jess and George Cowley)*

WINCHESTER   SU4729
St James   (01962) 861288
Romsey Road; SO22 5BE Smallish corner pub (Little Pub Group) with attractively refurbished split-level interior; bare boards and flagstones, pews and wheelback chairs by scrubbed pine tables, some leather armchairs, painted panelling and a Victorian fireplace, plenty of pictures and other odds and ends, Wadworths ales, craft beers and good selection of wines by the glass,

enjoyable food from sharing plates up including Mon burger night and Weds pie night, weekend brunch, gluten-free diets catered for, good friendly service; background and some live music, quiz Tues; children and dogs welcome, pleasant little terrace behind, open all day. *(Pat Holmes)*

WINCHESTER   SU4829
Willow Tree   (01962) 877255
Durngate Terrace; no adjacent weekday daytime parking, but Durngate car park is around corner in North Walls; a mile from M3 junction 9, by Easton Lane into city; SO23 8QX Popular 19th-c riverside pub; cosy pubby bar to the left with open fire, larger smarter restaurant to the right, well liked food from sandwiches and snacks up, four changing ales, well priced cocktails

and several wines by the glass, friendly staff; Weds quiz, Thurs live music; children and dogs welcome, lovely waterside garden (summer wood-fired pizzas), Winnall Moors nature reserve over the road, closed Sun evening, Mon, otherwise open all day. *(Ann and Colin Hunt)*

WOOTTON   SZ2497
Rising Sun   (01425) 610360
Bashley Common Road; BH25 5SF Busy well run New Forest pub; good fairly pubby food from light dishes to daily specials, efficient friendly service, five real ales including Flack Manor and Greene King, wide range of wines; children and dogs welcome, large garden with good adventure playground, roaming ponies, open (and food) all day. *(David and Sally Frost)*

Herefordshire

KEY ★ Star Pub  Top Quality Food 🍺 Great Beer
🍷 Good Wines £ Bargain Meals 🛏 Good Bedrooms 🍴 Serves Food

CAREY   SO5631 Map 4

Cottage of Content 🛏

(01432) 840242 – www.cottageofcontent.co.uk

*Village signposted from good back road betweeen Ross-on-Wye and Hereford E of A49,
through Hoarwithy; HR2 6NG*

**Country furnishings in a friendly rustic cottage with interesting food,
real ales and seats on terraces; bedrooms**

A medieval cottage in a tranquil spot near the River Wye, this has much
unspoilt character. There's a multitude of beams, country furnishings
such as stripped-pine kitchen chairs, long pews beside one big table and
various old-fashioned tables on flagstones or bare boards and genuinely
welcoming staff. Hobsons Best and Wye Valley Butty Bach on handpump,
seven wines by the glass, a gin list and local cider and perry during the
summer. Outside, picnic-sets can be found either on the flower-filled front
terrace or in the rural-feeling garden at the back. Bedrooms are quiet and
the breakfasts are good.

Highly thought-of food cooked by the landlord includes a tapas menu (5.30-9pm
Friday) plus sandwiches, serrano ham and broad bean risotto with minted crème
fraîche and smoked paprika almonds, crispy salt and pepper squid with cucumber
and lime salad and chilli jam, spice-crusted tofu with miso-glazed aubergine, griddled
kohlrabi, sesame dressing and coconut rice, a fish dish of the day, venison steak with
celeriac, tomato and pine nuts, dauphinoise potatoes and red wine and juniper jus,
duck breast with hasselback potatoes, roasted root vegetables and peppercorn, whisky
and raisin jus, and puddings such as cherry bakewell trifle and rhubarb and gingernut
cheesecake with rhubarb wafers. *Benchmark main dish: treacle-cured beef with
horseradish mash, wild mushroom and stilton pudding and jus £18.50. Two-course
evening meal £23.00.*

Free house ~ Licensees Richard and Helen Moore ~ Real ale ~ Open 12-2.30, 6.30 (6 Weds)-
10.30; 12-2.30, 6.30 (5.30 Fri)-11 Sat; 12-3 Sun; closed Sun evening, Mon, winter Tues ~
Bar food 12-2, 6.30-9; 12-2 Sun ~ Restaurant ~ Children welcome ~ Dogs allowed in bar ~
Bedrooms: $65/$85 *Recommended by Mike and Mary Carter, Barry Collett, Andrew Lawson,
Anne Taylor, John and Claire Masters, Karl and Frieda Bujeya, Scott and Charlotte Havers*

EARDISLEY   SO3149 Map 6

Tram £

(01544) 327251 – www.thetraminn.co.uk

Corner of A4111 and Woodseaves Road; HR3 6PG

Character pub with a lively mix of customers and good food and beer

Highly regarded food and well kept ales continue to draw people to this handsome old pub. The beamed bar on the left has local character, especially in the cosy back section behind sturdy standing timbers. Here, regulars congregate on the bare boards by the counter, which serves Hobsons Best, Wye Valley Butty Bach and a guest such as Bespoke Saved by the Bell on handpump and three local organic ciders. Elsewhere there are antique red and ochre floor tiles, a handful of nicely worn tables and chairs, a pair of long cushioned pews enclosing one much longer table, a high-backed settle, old country pictures, interesting tram prints and a couple of pictorial Wye maps. There's a small dining room on the right, a games room (with pool and darts) in a converted brewhouse and a covered terrace; background music. The outside gents' is extremely stylish. A sizeable, neatly planted garden has picnic-sets on the lawn; pétanque. The famous black and white village is a big draw too. Wheelchair access to the restaurant but no disabled loos.

Quite a choice of reliably good food includes baguettes, chicken and pork pâté with home-made chutney, grilled field mushrooms with a cheese rarebit filling, beetroot, carrot and caramelised onion tart with red onion marmalade, honey-baked ham and free-range eggs, beer-battered hake and chips, free-range chicken with chorizo and chive stuffing and tomato, basil and spinach pasta with parmesan, 28-day aged sirloin steak with a choice of sauce, and puddings such as chocolate and caramel torte with honeycomb ice-cream and pear and almond frangipane tart. *Benchmark main dish: steak in ale pie £10.00. Two-course evening meal £17.00.*

Free house ~ Licensee James Wood ~ Real ale ~ Open 12-3, 6-midnight; 12-4, 7-10.30 Sun; closed Mon except bank holidays ~ Bar food 12-3, 6-9; 12-3 Sun; not Sun evening or Mon ~ Restaurant ~ Children welcome ~ Dogs allowed in bar ~ Wi-fi *Recommended by Guy Vowles, Susan and Callum Slade, M and GR, Alan and Linda Blackmore, Jill and Hugh Bennett*

KILPECK   SO4430   Map 6
Kilpeck Inn ♀
(01981) 570464 – www.kilpeckinn.com
Village and church signposted off A465 SW of Hereford; HR2 9DN

Imaginatively extended country inn in fascinating and peaceful village; bedrooms

This neatly refurbished eco-minded country inn has been the centre of village life for over 250 years – and that remains the same today. The beamed, flagstoned bar rambles happily around to provide several tempting corners, with an antique high-backed settle in one and high stools around a matching chest-high table in another. This opens into two cosily linked dining rooms on the left, with high panelled wainscoting. Ledbury Dr Rudi's Extra Pale and Wye Valley Butty Bach on handpump, seven wines by the glass, a gin list (including local ones) and farm cider; background music. The neat back grass has picnic-sets. The light and airy bedrooms are comfortable and breakfasts are good. Do visit the ruins of Kilpeck Castle and the unique Romanesque church; there are also plenty of good surrounding walks including along the Offa's Dyke Path.

The landlord cooks the interesting food including sandwiches, venison croquettes with redcurrant and chilli jam, mussels, pancetta, sage and cider cream sauce, ricotta gnudi with vegetables, sage butter and parmesan, burger with toppings and rosemary salted chips, free-range chicken with cauliflower cheese purée, celeriac, balsamic shallots and thyme jus, smoked haddock fillet with mustard mash, baby spinach and poached duck egg, lamb shank with tomato, rosemary and butter beans, and puddings such as rhubarb crème brûlée and apricot-glazed brioche bread and butter pudding. *Benchmark main dish: rack of lamb with wild garlic and pine nut crust, fondant potato and rosemary jus £18.00. Two-course evening meal £22.00.*

Free house ~ Licensee Ross Williams ~ Real ale ~ Open 12-3, 5.30-11; 12-11 Sat; 12-5
Sun; closed Sun evening, Mon lunchtime ~ Bar food 12-2 (2.30 Sat), 6.30-9; 12-3.30
Sun ~ Restaurant ~ Children welcome ~ Dogs allowed in bar ~ Wi-fi ~ Bedrooms:
£90/£100 *Recommended by Colin and Daniel Gibbs, Charles Welch, Mrs J Ekins-Daukes,
Celia and Geoff Clay, Sylvia and Phillip Spencer, Margaret McDonald*

LITTLE COWARNE   SO6050   Map 4
Three Horseshoes �
(01885) 400276 – www.threehorseshoes.co.uk
Pub signposted off A465 SW of Bromyard; towards Ullingswick; HR7 4RQ

**Long-serving licensees and friendly staff in bustling country pub
with good food and drink; bedrooms**

A place to return to again and again, and run by lovely hands-on owners
who've been here for over 30 years. The L-shaped, quarry-tiled middle
bar has hop-draped beams, upholstered settles, wooden chairs and tables,
old local photographs above a woodburning stove, and local guidebooks.
Opening off one side is the garden room with wicker armchairs around
tables, and views over an outdoor seating area; leading off the other side is
the games room, with pool, darts and cribbage. Wye Valley Bitter, Butty Bach
and HPA on handpump, local Oliver's cider and perry and Robinsons cider,
ten wines by the glass and home-made elderflower cordial. A popular Sunday
lunchtime carvery is offered in the stripped-stone, raftered and spacious
restaurant extension. There are well sited tables and chairs on the terrace
and in the neat, prettily planted garden. Bedrooms are reached by outside
stairs. Disabled access.

Using some home-grown produce and making all their own chutneys, pickles and
jams, the well thought-of food includes lunchtime sandwiches, prawn and haddock
smokies, devilled lambs kidneys, goats cheese, leek, celery, apple and walnut filo parcel,
chicken breast with cider and mushroom sauce, roasted sea bass fillets with chive
butter sauce, pheasant breast with orange and wholegrain mustard sauce, sirloin steak
with pepper sauce, and puddings; Friday is fish and chips night. *Benchmark main dish:
steak in ale pie £14.00. Two-course evening meal £24.00.*

Free house ~ Licensees Norman and Janet Whittall ~ Real ale ~ Open 11-3, 6.30-11; 12-4
Sun; closed Sun evening, Tues ~ Bar food 12-2, 6.30-9.30 ~ Restaurant ~ Children welcome
~ Dogs allowed in bar ~ Wi-fi ~ Bedrooms: £45/£90 *Recommended by Dr and Mrs H J Field,
Geoff and Ann Marston, Alf and Sally Garner, Joanna Burke, Graham Kelly, Francis and Mandy
Robertson, Julian Richardson, John Sargeant*

MICHAELCHURCH ESCLEY   SO3133   Map 6
Bridge Inn 🛏
(01981) 510646 – www.thebridgeinnmichaelchurch.co.uk
Off back road SE of Hay-on-Wye, along Escley Brook valley; HR2 0JW

**Character riverside inn with woodburning stoves in bar and dining
rooms, local drinks, hearty food and seats by the water; bedrooms**

You can sit outside this remote inn in warm weather – tucked away down
a steep lane in an attractive valley – and watch ducks and maybe brown
trout on the river. The bar is homely and easy-going, with hops on dark
beams, pine pews and dining chairs around rustic tables, a big woodburning
stove and Wye Valley Butty Bach and HPA on handpump, good wines by
the glass, local cider and their own gin served by the friendly landlord.
Background music and board games; pétanque. Two dining areas, with
contemporary paintwork, have local artwork on the walls. The bedrooms in

the 16th-c farmhouse (one minute's walk away) are warm and comfortable and there's a cosy sitting room too; they also have two yurts for hire and a riverside campsite with hard-standing sites and electric hook-ups. Disabled access.

🍴 Reliably good food includes gin-cured salmon with crispy jerusalem artichokes, crème fraîche and dill oil, free-range chicken liver parfait with apple and raisin chutney, beetroot and horseradish arancini with salt-baked beetroot, bitter leaves and warm goats cheese sauce, a pie of the day, venison burger with curried mayonnaise and chips, cornish ling with chorizo, chickpea and wild garlic cassoulet, and puddings such as tonka bean crème brûlée and chocolate mousse with salted caramel and honeycomb. *Benchmark main dish: local steak £22.00. Two-course evening meal £20.00.*

Free house ~ Licensee Glyn Bufton ~ Real ale ~ Open 12-3, 5.30-11; 12-midnight Sat; 12-10 Sun; closed winter Mon; 13 Jan-5 Feb ~ Bar food 12-2.30, 5.30-8.30 (9.30 Fri); 12-3, 5.30-9.30 Sat; 12-4, 5.30-8.30 Sun ~ Restaurant ~ Children welcome ~ Dogs allowed in bar ~ Wi-fi ~ Bedrooms: £70/£100 *Recommended by Philip J Alderton, Martine and Lawrence Sanders, Trevor and Michele Street, Geoffrey Sutton, Daniel King, Lauren and Dan Frazer, Paul Scofield*

ROSS-ON-WYE
Kings Head 🛏

SO5924 Map 6

(01989) 763174 – www.kingshead.co.uk
High Street (B4260); HR9 5HL

Welcoming bar in well run market-town hotel with real ales and tasty food; good bedrooms

The comfortable bedrooms in this partly 14th-c inn have a lot of character with beams and wonky floors, as well as good bathrooms and excellent breakfasts. The little beamed and panelled bar on the right has traditional pub furnishings, including comfortably padded bar seats and an antique cushioned box settle, stripped floorboards and a couple of black leather armchairs by a log-effect fire. Wye Valley Bitter, Butty Bach and HPA on handpump, three farm ciders, 16 gins, 15 malt whiskies and several wines by the glass at sensible prices. The beamed lounge bar on the left, also with bare boards, has some timbering, soft leather armchairs, padded bucket seats and shelves of books, and there's also a big carpeted dining room; background music, TV and board games. A sheltered back courtyard has plenty of contemporary tables and chairs for warm weather.

🍴 Appetising food includes prawn and avocado tian with mango salsa, a plate of smoked fish, sharing boards, wild mushroom, spinach and blue cheese gnocchi, pie of the day, salmon fillet with samphire and mixed pepper risotto with flame-roasted red pepper sauce, duo of local pork (sesame-glazed tenderloin and marinated belly) with shallot and thyme purée, wholegrain mustard mash and lime and chilli dressing, and puddings such as chocolate mousse with peanut crumb and pistachio ice-cream and lemon and cardamom posset with coconut crunch. *Benchmark main dish: duck breast with celeriac and sage fondant, carrot crisps and honey and orange jus £17.50. Two-course evening meal £22.00.*

Free house ~ Licensee James Vidler ~ Real ale ~ Open 11-11; 12-10.30 Sun ~ Bar food 12-2, 5.30-9 ~ Restaurant ~ Children welcome ~ Dogs allowed in bar and bedrooms ~ Wi-fi ~ Bedrooms: £70/£90 *Recommended by Richard and Tessa Ibbot, Peter and Emma Kelly, A E Forbes, Monty Green, Martine and Lawrence Sanders*

Virtually all pubs in this book sell wine by the glass. We mention wines if they are a cut above the average.

SYMONDS YAT

SO5616 Map 4

Saracens Head 🍺 🛏

(01600) 890435 – www.saracensheadinn.co.uk

Symonds Yat E; HR9 6JL

Lovely riverside spot with seats on waterside terraces, a fine range of drinks and interesting food; comfortable bedrooms

Eight of the nine up-to-date, light bedrooms here look over the river and a boathouse annex has two more contemporary rooms; breakfasts are hearty. The flagstoned bar has plenty of chatty customers creating a buoyant atmosphere plus Sharps Doom Bar, Wye Valley Butty Bach and HPA and guests such as Kingstone Llandogo Trow, Ledbury Gold and Swan Gold on handpump, 13 wines by the glass, 40 vodkas, 20 malt whiskies and several ciders; TV, background music and board games. A cosy lounge and a modernised bare-boards dining room have fine old photos of the area and fresh flowers in jugs. There are lots of seats on terraces beside the River Wye; best to get here early in warm weather to bag one. Plenty of walks in the nearby Forest of Dean. An alternative way to reach the inn is via the little hand-ferry (pulled by one of the staff). Disabled access to the bar and terrace.

Well regarded food includes sandwiches and baguettes, tempura soft shell crab with pak choi and chilli jam, goats cheese soufflé with beetroot purée, moroccan-spiced bean burger with toppings, crème fraîche and chips, stone bass with tempura prawns, romesco sauce and dauphinoise potatoes, duck breast with black garlic purée and fondant potato, lamb rump with boulangère potatoes and salsa verde, and puddings. *Benchmark main dish: steak pie £14.95. Two-course evening meal £21.00.*

Free house ~ Licensees P K and C J Rollinson ~ Real ale ~ Open 11-11; 11-10.30 Sun ~ Bar food 12-2.30, 6.30-9 ~ Restaurant ~ Children welcome but not in bedrooms ~ Dogs allowed in bar ~ Wi-fi ~ Bedrooms: £65/£100 *Recommended by Mr and Mrs D J Nash, Lauren and Dan Frazer, Robert and Diana Myers, Kate Moran, Christine and Tony Garrett, Julian Richardson*

TILLINGTON

SO4645 Map 6

Bell 🍺

(01432) 760395 – www.thebelltillington.com

Off A4110 NW of Hereford; HR4 8LE

Relaxed and friendly pub with a snug character bar opening into civilised dining areas – good value

Mr Williams comes in for special praise from our readers for his hard-working and hands-on approach and the way he welcomes all his customers, no matter how busy things are. The snug parquet-floored bar on the left has assorted bucket armchairs around low, chunky, mahogany-coloured tables, brightly cushioned wall benches, team photographs and shelves of books; the black beams are strung with dried hops. Swan Gold and Wye Valley Bitter and Butty Bach on handpump, cider made on site, six wines by the glass and locally produced spirits from Chase, all served by notably cheerful staff; daily papers, background music and board games. The bar opens into a comfortable bare-boards dining lounge with stripy plush banquettes and a coal fire. Beyond that is a pitched-ceiling restaurant area with more banquettes and big country prints; through slatted blinds you can see a sunken terrace with contemporary tables, and a garden with teak tables, picnic-sets and a play area. Disabled access.

🍴 The standard of food is high and includes open sandwiches, breaded brie with red onion chutney, tempura prawns with chilli, lime dip, sweet potato and spinach curry with ginger rice, marinated chicken and goats cheese salad, lamb rump with dauphinoise potatoes and jus, sesame-glazed duck breast with vegetable stir-fry, salmon fillet with dijon parmesan crust and baby herb-roast potatoes, and puddings such as chocolate and salted caramel tart and lemon posset. *Benchmark main dish: steak in ale pie £13.50. Two-course evening meal £20.00.*

Free house ~ Licensee Glenn Williams ~ Real ale ~ Open 12-10.30; 12-11 Sat; 12-9 Sun ~ Bar food 12-2.30, 6-9; all day Fri, Sat; 12-3 Sun ~ Restaurant ~ Children welcome ~ Dogs allowed in bar ~ Wi-fi *Recommended by Sandra and Miles Spencer, Belinda and Neil Garth, Lindy Andrews, Nicholas and Maddy Trainer, Alison and Michael Harper, Dave Braisted*

TITLEY
SO3359   Map 6
Stagg ⭐ ♡ 🛏
(01544) 230221 – www.thestagg.co.uk

B4355 N of Kington; HR5 3RL

• •

Herefordshire Dining Pub of the Year

Exceptional food in three dining rooms, real ales and a fine choice of other drinks, and seats in the two-acre garden; comfortable bedrooms

'There's not one aspect of this little gem that isn't wonderful' says one of our readers – and we have to agree. And while, of course, most people are here to dine, there is a pubby and convivial little bar with friendly, chatty locals and a good choice of drinks. As well as a gently civilised atmosphere, furnishings are deliberately simple: high-backed elegant wooden or leather dining chairs around a medley of tables on bare boards, candlelight and (in the bar) 200 jugs hanging from the ceiling. Courteous, warmly welcoming staff serve Ledbury Gold and Wye Valley Butty Bach on handpump, 18 house wines by the glass (plus a carefully chosen bin list), interesting soft drinks, a long list of enterprising cocktails and mocktails, local cider and perry, 16 local gins and several whiskies. The two-acre garden has seats on a terrace and a croquet lawn. Bedrooms are either above the pub or in a Georgian vicarage four minutes' walk away; super breakfasts. The inn is surrounded by good walking country and is handy for the Offa's Dyke Path.

🍴 They use their own eggs and home-grown vegetables and fruit (when available) for the delicious food, which includes sandwiches on home-made ciabatta bread, scallops with celeriac, apple and hazelnuts, local snails with parsley purée, ham, mushroom and garlic croutons, a couple of pubby choices such as pork sausages with mash and onion rings, roast cauliflower with cauliflower purée and cauliflower couscous, curry oil and parmentier potatoes, cod fillet with fennel, shrimps, parsley and lemon butter, lamb rump and slow-cooked shoulder with jerusalem artichokes and dauphinoise potatoes, beef fillet with mushroom purée, red wine shallots and chips, and puddings such as three crème brûlées (vanilla, coffee and cardamom) and pedro ximénez sherry cheesecake with coffee ice-cream and prunes. *Benchmark main dish: crispy duck leg with spiced rhubarb and fondant potato £13.50. Two-course evening meal £25.00.*

Free house ~ Licensees Steve and Nicola Reynolds ~ Real ale ~ Open 12-3, 6.30-11; 12-3.45 Sun; closed Sun evening; Mon, Tues, one week Feb, one week June, two weeks Nov ~ Bar food 12-2, 6.30-9; 12-2.45 Sun ~ Restaurant ~ Children welcome ~ Dogs allowed in bar and bedrooms ~ Wi-fi ~ Bedrooms: £90/£110 *Recommended by Guy Vowles, Paul Cooper, Andrew and Nicky Churcher, Matilda and Gerald Thoms, Claire and Nigel Swanning, Lindy Andrews*

We accept no free drinks or meals and inspections are anonymous.

UPPER COLWALL

SO7643 Map 4

Chase

(01684) 540276 – www.thechaseinnmalvern.co.uk

Chase Road, brown sign to pub off B4218 Malvern–Colwall, first left after hilltop on bend going W; WR13 6DJ

Gorgeous sunset views from nicely traditional tavern's garden, good drinks and traditional food

If you visit this cheerful country pub on a clear day, you'll be rewarded with a view across Herefordshire and even as far as the Black Mountains and the Brecon Beacons; the seats and tables on a steep series of small, pretty terraces behind the pub make the most of this outlook. The bars have a companionable atmosphere, a great variety of seats (from a wooden-legged tractor seat to a carved pew) and tables, an old black kitchen range and plenty of decorations – china mugs, blue-glass flasks, lots of small pictures. Four well kept ales are tapped from the cask, such as Bathams Best, Courage Directors and a couple of guests such as Brains Rev James and Pershore Pale Ale, and friendly staff also serve six wines by the glass, 15 gins, six malt whiskies and a farm cider; board games. Good surrounding walks.

 Good quality food includes sriracha king prawns with mango salsa, creamy garlic mushrooms on toasted ciabatta, butternut squash, lentil, mixed bean and chickpea stew, honey-mustard roast ham and eggs, chicken bourguignon with creamed potatoes, sea bass fillet with honey roast chantenay carrots, sautéed potatoes and creamy white wine sauce, local sirloin steak with peppercorn sauce and chips, and puddings. *Benchmark main dish: beer-battered fish and chips £13.90. Two-course evening meal £21.00.*

Free house ~ Licensee Duncan Ironmonger ~ Real ale ~ Open 12-3, 5-11; 12-11 Sat; 12-10.30 Sun ~ Bar food 12-2 (2.30 weekends), 6.30-9 ~ Children welcome ~ Dogs allowed in bar ~ Wi-fi *Recommended by Patricia and Gordon Thompson, Nicholas and Maddy Trainer, Richard Kennell, Simon Day, Emily and Toby Archer*

WOOLHOPE

SO6135 Map 4

Butchers Arms

(01432) 860281 – www.butchersarmswoolhope.com

Off B4224 in Fownhope; HR1 4RF

Pleasant half-timbered inn in peaceful setting, with an inviting garden, interesting food and a fine choice of real ales

This is a friendly place in lovely countryside with picnic-sets in a pretty, streamside garden. Inside, the bar has very low beams, built-in cushioned wall seats, farmhouse chairs and stools around a mix of old tables (some set for dining) on carpet, paintings by local artists on cream walls and a woodburning stove in a big fireplace; there's also a little beamed dining room, similarly furnished. Ledbury Gold, Wye Valley Bitter and Butty Bach and a local guest ale on handpump, six wines by the glass from a good list, 14 malt whiskies and a couple of farm ciders. The parrot is called Max. To really appreciate the surroundings, turn left as you come out of the pub and take the tiny left-hand road at the end of the car park; this turns into a track and then a path, and the view from the top of the hill is quite something (if you ask, the pub will provide a map).

 Good food includes crispy haggis fritters with beetroot relish, pigeon with black pudding and smoked bacon in barbecue sauce, vegetable and chickpea thai curry, pheasant, tarragon and smoked bacon burger with toppings and chips, sea bass fillets in cherry tomato and basil sauce with dauphinoise potatoes, pork tenderloin wrapped in smoked bacon with black pudding, elderflower sausage, apple sauce and gravy, beef fillet medallions in mushrooms, whisky and cream, and puddings such as black cherry cheesecake and amaretto pannacotta with almond brittle. *Benchmark main dish: lambs liver and bacon with onion rings and mash £13.95. Two-course evening meal £20.00.*

Free house ~ Licensee Stephen Bull ~ Real ale ~ Open 11-3, 6-11; 11-4 Sun; closed Sun evening, Mon except bank holidays, Tues ~ Bar food 12-2.30, 6-9; 12-2.30 Sun ~ Restaurant ~ Children welcome ~ Dogs allowed in bar ~ Wi-fi *Recommended by Glen and Patricia Fuller, Peter and Alison Steadman, Amy Ledbetter, Harvey Brown, Ian Duncan, David and Charlotte Green*

WOOLHOPE
Crown

SO6135   Map 4

(01432) 860468 – www.thecrowninn.pub
Village signposted off B4224 in Fownhope; HR1 4QP

Chatty village local with fine range of local ciders and perries, and popular food

Cider lovers should head for this cheerful, honest pub. The landlord makes four ciders (and keeps a couple of guests too) and serves around two dozen bottled ciders and perrys from within a 15-mile radius; they also hold a May Day Bank Holiday festival with live music, beer, cider and perry. Also, Ledbury Bitter and Wye Valley Butty Bach and HPA on handpump and several wines by the glass. The bar has painted farmhouse and other wooden chairs, upholstered settles and rustic tables on wooden flooring, an open fire and two woodburning stoves, some standing timbers and stools against the bar counter; background music, darts and board games. In summer, there's a bar in the lovely big garden, which has a fire pit and a particularly comfortable smokers' shelter equipped with cushions and darts; marvellous views. Disabled access.

Pleasing food includes sandwiches, rabbit terrine with garlic and oregano focaccia, twice-baked mature cheddar soufflé with black garlic and wild mushroom sauce, goats cheese and flat mushroom stack with red onion marmalade, beer-battered hake and chips, cider-braised ham with duck eggs and bean chutney, hickory-smoked venison burger with toppings and french fries, pork belly with kibbled onion mash, caramelised apple and rioja jus, and puddings such as caramel and vanilla sundae with chocolate honeycomb crumble and elderflower and thyme parfait. *Benchmark main dish: lamb rump with dauphinoise potatoes and mint jus £18.00. Two-course evening meal £20.00.*

Free house ~ Licensee Matt Slocombe ~ Real ale ~ Open 12-3, 5-10.30; 12-11.30 Sat; 12-10 Sun ~ Bar food 12-2, 6-9; 12-3 Sun ~ Restaurant ~ Children welcome ~ Dogs allowed in bar ~ Wi-fi *Recommended by Robert and Diana Ringstone, Charlotte and William Mason, Katherine Matthews, Mike Swan, Audrey and Paul Summers*

Please tell us if the décor, atmosphere, food or drink at a pub is different from our description. We rely on readers' reports to keep us up to date: feedback@goodguides.com, or (no stamp needed) Freepost THE GOOD PUB GUIDE, Random House Publishing, 20 Vauxhall Bridge Road, London SW1V 2SA.

Also Worth a Visit in Herefordshire

Besides the fully inspected pubs, you might like to try these pubs that have been recommended to us and described by readers. Do tell us what you think of them: feedback@goodguides.com

ALMELEY   SO3351
Bells (01544) 327216
Off A480, A4111 or A4112 S of Kington;
HR3 6LF Welcoming old country local;
original jug-and-bottle entry lobby and
carpeted beamed bar with woodburner,
second bar has been converted into village
shop/deli; a couple of well kept changing
ales, traditional cider/perry and good
honest home-made food (not evenings) from
sandwiches up; children and dogs welcome,
garden with decked area and boules, on
Wyche Way long distance path, open all day
weekends. *(Chris)*

AYMESTREY   SO4265
★ **Riverside Inn** (01568) 708440
A4110, at N end of village, W of
Leominster; HR6 9ST Black and white
inn with terrace and tree-sheltered garden
making most of lovely waterside spot by
ancient stone bridge over the Lugg; cosy
rambling beamed interior with some antique
furniture alongside stripped country kitchen
tables, warm fires, well kept Hobsons,
Wye Valley and a guest, local ciders and
well chosen wines by the glass, very good
imaginative food from chef-patron using
local rare-breed meat and own fruit and
vegetables (bar snacks only Sun evening),
friendly helpful staff; quiet background
music; children welcome, dogs in bar, lovely
circular walks, nine well appointed bedrooms
including three new garden rooms, fly fishing
for residents, good breakfast, closed Mon
lunchtime, otherwise open all day. *(Dr and*
Mrs H J Field, Clive and Fran Dutson)

BISHOPS FROME   SO6648
Green Dragon (01885) 490607
Just off B4214 Bromyard–Ledbury;
WR6 5BP Welcoming early 17th-c village
pub; four linked rooms with unspoilt rustic
feel, beams, flagstones and log fires (one in
fine inglenook), half a dozen ales, real ciders
and enjoyable traditional food (Tues-Sat
evenings and Sun lunchtime); children and
dogs welcome, tiered garden with smokers'
shelter, on Herefordshire Trail, closed
weekday lunchtimes, open all day Sat.
(Mark Morgan)

BODENHAM   SO5454
Englands Gate (01568) 797286
On A417 at Bodenham turn-off, about
6 miles S of Leominster; HR1 3HU
Attractive black and white 16th-c coaching
inn; rambling interior with beams and joists
in low ceilings around a vast central stone
chimneypiece, sturdy timber props, exposed
stonework and well worn flagstones (one or
two steps), Hobsons, Wye Valley and a guest,
local cider and generally well liked food
from lunchtime sandwiches up including
themed nights, friendly staff; background
and occasional live music, monthly quiz,
July beer/cider/sausage festival; children
welcome, dogs in bar, tables under parasols
on terrace and in pleasant garden, modern
bedrooms in converted coach house next
door, open all day. *(Simon Day)*

BOSBURY   SO6943
Bell (01531) 640285
B4220 N of Ledbury; HR8 1PX Timbered
village pub opposite the church; log fires
in both bars, Otter, Wye Valley and a guest,
three ciders and good choice of wines by the
glass, dining area serving popular sensibly
priced traditional food (not Sun evening,
Mon, Tues) including Sun carvery, friendly
staff; pool and darts; children and dogs
welcome, large garden with covered terrace
and play equipment, open all day Sun till
9pm, closed lunchtimes Mon-Thurs.
(Rose and Marcus Heatherley)

BRINGSTY COMMON   SO6954
Live & Let Live (01886) 821462
Off A44 Knightwick–Bromyard 1.5
miles W of Whitbourne turn; take track
southwards at Black Cat inn sign,
bearing right at fork; WR6 5UW Bustling
17th-c timber and thatch cottage (former
cider house); cosy flagstoned bar with log fire
in cavernous stone fireplace, earthenware
jugs hanging from low beams, old casks built
into hop-strung counter serving three well
kept ales including Wye Valley Butty Bach,
local ciders/apple juice and decent wines by
the glass, enjoyable fairly traditional food
served by friendly staff, two dining rooms
upstairs under steep rafters; children and
dogs welcome, glass-topped well and big
wooden hogshead used as terrace tables,
peaceful country views from picnic-sets and
rustic benches in former orchard, handy for
Brockhampton Estate (NT), open all day
Sat, till 6pm Sun, closed Mon.
(Lee and Jill Stafford)

BROMYARD DOWNS   SO6755
★ **Royal Oak** (01885) 482585
Just NE of Bromyard; pub signed
off A44; HR7 4QP Beautifully placed
low-beamed 18th-c pub with wide views;
open-plan carpeted and flagstoned bar,
log fire and woodburner, dining room with
huge bay window, well kept Malvern Hills,
Purity and Woods, real cider, enjoyable
food (special diets catered for) including

daily specials, friendly helpful service; background music, pool and darts; children, walkers and dogs welcome, nice garden with front terrace and play area, closed Sun evening, Mon (open all day bank holiday weekends). *(Mike Benton)*

CANON PYON
SO4648
Nags Head *(01432) 830725*
A4110; HR4 8NY Welcoming 17th-c timbered roadside pub; beamed bar with log fire, flagstoned restaurant and tearoom, three well kept changing ales and popular good value food from bar snacks up, pleasant attentive service; darts; children and dogs (in bar) welcome, extensive garden with play area, open all day Sat, till 5pm Sun, closed Mon and lunchtime Tues.
(Liz and Martin Eldon)

CLIFFORD
SO2445
Castlefields *(01497) 831554*
B4350 N of Hay-on-Wye; HR3 5HB Rebuilt and enlarged family pub retaining some old features including a glass-covered well; generous helpings of popular good value food and a couple of changing ales, friendly helpful staff, wood or carpeted floors, two-way stone fireplace with woodburner, restaurant; pool, darts and various community-based events; lovely country views, camping, open and food all day weekends (till 4pm Sun), closed Mon, Tues.
(Simon Day)

CLODOCK
SO3227
Cornewall Arms *(01873) 860677*
N of Walterstone; HR2 0PD Wonderfully old-fashioned survivor in remote hamlet by historic church facing the Black Mountains; friendly stable-door bar with log fire each end, a few mats and comfortable armchairs on stone floor, lots of ornaments and knick-knacks, photos of past village events and other pictures, books for sale, games including darts and devil among the tailors, bottled Wye Valley and cider, no food or credit cards; dogs welcome, open all day weekends, closed weekday lunchtimes. *(Mark Morgan)*

COLWALL
SO7440
★ **Wellington** *(01684) 540269*
A449 Malvern–Ledbury; WR13 6HW Welcoming roadside country pub; highly thought-of food from bar snacks and standards to imaginative restaurant dishes, well kept Goffs Tournament, a couple of guests and nice wines by the glass, friendly helpful landlord and staff, comfortably lived-in two-level beamed bar with red patterned carpet and quarry tiles, some built-in settles including unusual high-backed one framing a window, woodburner and open fire, spacious relaxed back dining area; occasional live music, daily newspapers; children and dogs welcome, nice views from picnic-sets on grass above car park, good

local walks, closed evenings Sun and bank holiday Mon (shut all day Aug Bank Holiday Mon). *(Sylvia and Phillip Spencer)*

DORSTONE
SO3141
★ **Pandy** *(01981) 550273*
Pub signed off B4348 E of Hay-on-Wye; HR3 6AN Ancient inn (12th-c origins) by village green; traditional rooms with low beams, stout timbers and worn flagstones, various alcoves and vast fireplace, several woodburners, Sharps Doom Bar, Wye Valley Butty Bach and a house beer from Grey Trees, local cider, enjoyable reasonably priced food (not Sun evening) from changing blackboard menu; children and dogs (in bar) welcome, side garden with picnic-sets and play area, four good bedrooms in purpose-built timber lodge (now run independently, but breakfast in the pub), closed Mon lunchtime, otherwise open all day (till 9.30pm Sun), in winter closed lunchtime Mon-Thurs. *(Peter Meister)*

EWYAS HAROLD
SO3828
Temple Bar *(01981) 240423*
Village centre signed from B4347; HR2 0EU Popular creeper-clad Georgian inn run by welcoming family; good freshly made food from bar meals to interesting evening restaurant dishes, Wye Valley Butty Bach, HPA and a guest, local cider, modernised interior keeping original oak beams, flagstones and log fire; children and dogs (in bar) welcome, disabled access, three comfortable bedrooms, hearty breakfast, open all day weekends, no evening food Sun, Mon or Tues. *(Charles Duncan)*

GARWAY
SO4622
Garway Moon *(01600) 750270*
Centre of village, opposite the green; HR2 8RQ Attractive 18th-c pub in pretty location overlooking common; decent food (not Mon) served by friendly staff, well kept ales such as Butcombe, Kingstone and Wye Valley, proper ciders, beams and exposed stonework, woodburner in inglenook, restaurant; children, dogs and muddy boots welcome, garden with terrace and play area, three bedrooms, open all day weekends, closed lunchtimes Mon and Tues.
(Mark Morgan)

GOODRICH
SO5719
Hostelrie *(01600) 890241*
Pub signed from B4229, S of village; HR9 6HX Unusual village inn with turreted Victorian gothic façade; three well kept Wye Valley ales and decent choice of wines from brick and timber servery, sandwiches, pub favourites and other enjoyable food including blackboard specials and Mon curry night, can eat in bar or restaurant, good friendly service, traditionally updated and softly lit with painted panelling, beams and stripped stonework; children, dogs and muddy boots welcome, picnic-sets in attractive garden, bedrooms, near Goodrich Castle and Wye

Valley Walk, open all day Fri-Sun, closed Mon lunchtime. *(Clive and Fran Dutson)*

GORSLEY SO6726
Roadmaker (01989) 720352
0.5 miles from M50 junction 3; village signposted from exit – B4221; HR9 7SW Popular 19th-c village pub run by group of retired gurkhas; large carpeted lounge bar with central log fire, good nepalese food here and in evening restaurant, also Sun roasts and other english choices, well kept ales such as Butcombe, efficient courteous service; quiz first Sun of month; children welcome, no dogs, terrace with water feature, open all day. *(Larry and Val Brown)*

HAMPTON BISHOP SO5538
Bunch of Carrots (01432) 870237
B4224; HR1 4JR Spacious beamed country pub by River Wye; good daily carvery and choice of other pubby food (all day weekends), cheerful efficient service, well kept Wye Valley Butty Bach, Sharps Doom Bar and a couple of guests, local cider and a dozen wines by the glass, traditional dimly lit bar area with wood and flagstone floors, woodburner, airy restaurant; children and dogs welcome, disabled access/loo, garden with play area, open all day. *(Gordon and Barbara Illingworth)*

HAREWOOD END SO5227
Harewood End Inn (01989) 730637
A49 Hereford to Ross-on-Wye; HR2 8JT Roadside pub in two connecting buildings; compact bar and a couple of bare-boards dining rooms, high-backed chairs around scrubbed-top tables, interesting collection of enamel signs on panelled walls, open fire, good choice of enjoyable home-made food from lunchtime sandwiches to grills including signature Harewood burger, three well kept ales and decent choice of wines, welcoming attentive staff; quiz last Sun of month, pool, darts and TV, free wi-fi; children and dogs welcome, nice garden and local walks, five bedrooms, closed Mon.
(Harry Longford)

HEREFORD SO5139
Barrels (01432) 274968
St Owen Street; HR1 2JQ Friendly 18th-c coaching inn popular with good mix of customers; former home to the Wye Valley brewery and up to seven of their very well kept/priced ales from barrel-built counter (beer/music festival end Aug), Thatcher's cider, cheerful efficient staff, no food; live jazz first Mon of month, Thurs quiz, juke box, sports TV, pool and darts; dogs welcome, partly covered courtyard behind, open all day. *(Peter Meister)*

HEREFORD SO5040
Beer in Hand 07543 327548
Eign Street, next to church; HR4 0AP Friendly micropub with good range of cask and keg beers including local Odyssey from temperature-controlled stillage, more in bottles and decent selection of other drinks, snacky food such as pork pies and pickled eggs, evening pizzas Thurs-Sat, enthusiastic knowledgeable staff, wooden tables and chairs down each side of simple front room, part-divided back part with sofas and benches, some barrel tables in bar area with pump clips decorating the ceiling; quiz first Weds of month, board games, dogs welcome, narrow side terrace, open all day Fri and Sat, from 3pm Sun and 5pm other days. *(Peter Meister)*

HEREFORD SO5039
Lichfield Vaults (01432) 266821
Church Street; HR1 2LR A pub since the 18th c in picturesque pedestrianised area near cathedral; dark panelling, some stripped brick and exposed joists, impressive plasterwork in large-windowed front room, traditionally furnished with dark pews, cushioned pub chairs and a couple of heavily padded benches, hot coal stove, charming cypriot landlord and friendly staff, six well kept ales such as Butcombe, Caledonian and Sharps, enjoyable lunchtime food from sandwiches up including greek dishes and good Sun roasts; faint background music, live blues/rock last Sun afternoon of month, TV for sports (particularly rugby), games machines, daily papers; children and dogs welcome, picnic-sets in pleasant back courtyard, open all day. *(Peter Meister)*

HOARWITHY SO5429
New Harp (01432) 840900
Off A49 Hereford to Ross-on-Wye; HR2 6QH Open-plan village dining pub with cheery bustling atmosphere; good well presented local food from chef-landlord, friendly helpful service, ales such as Wye Valley, Ledbury and Otter, Weston's cider (maybe their own organic cider in summer), pine tables on slate tiles, bay-window seats and half-panelling, screened-off dining area with light wood furniture, a couple of woodburners; background and some live music, sports TV; children, walkers and dogs welcome, pretty tree-sheltered garden with stream, picnic-sets and decked area, little shop and Mon morning post office, unusual italianate Victorian church nearby, open all day. *(Barry Collett)*

KINGSLAND SO4461
★Corners (01568) 708385
B4360 NW of Leominster, corner of Lugg Green Road; HR6 9RY Comfortably updated, partly black and white 16th-c village inn with snug nooks and corners; log fires, low beams, dark red plasterwork and some stripped brickwork, bow-window seat and leather armchairs in softly lit carpeted bar, well kept Hobsons, Wye Valley and decent selection of wines, big side dining room in converted hay loft with rafters and huge

window, enjoyable reasonably priced food from pubby choices up including meal deals, cheerful attentive service; children welcome, no garden, comfortable bedrooms in modern block behind. *(Lee and Jill Stafford)*

KINGTON SO3056

★ **Olde Tavern** (01544) 231945
Victoria Road, just off A44 opposite B4355 – follow sign to 'Town Centre, Hospital, Cattle Market'; pub on right opposite Elizabeth Road, no inn sign but 'Estd 1767' notice; HR5 3BX Gloriously old-fashioned with hatch-served side room opening off small plain parlour and public bar, plenty of dark brown woodwork, big windows, settles and other antique furniture on bare floors, gas fire, old local pictures, china, pewter and curios, four well kept local ales such as Hobsons and Ludlow, Weston's cider, generous helpings of enjoyable home-made food (Thurs-Sun), friendly atmosphere; children and dogs welcome, little yard at back, open all day weekends, closed weekday lunchtimes. *(Caroline and Oliver Sterling)*

KINGTON SO2956

Oxford Arms (01544) 230322
Duke Street; HR5 3DR Traditional old-fashioned beamed inn; woodburners in main bar on left and dining area to the right, smaller lounge with sofas and armchairs, real ales such as Hobsons (beer festivals), good reasonably priced home-made food including Weds curry and Thurs steak nights, good friendly service; some live music, pool and darts; children and dogs welcome, terrace picnic-sets, clean comfortable bedrooms, open all day weekends, closed Mon and lunchtimes Tues-Fri. *(Charles Duncan)*

KINGTON SO2956

Royal Oak (01544) 231864
Church Street; HR5 3BE Welcoming 17th-c pub under new landlady; enjoyable home-made food including good value Sun carvery, well kept Timothy Taylors Landlord and Wye Valley HPA, bar with darts and open fire, separate dining room; children and dogs welcome, big back garden with (summer barbecues and live music), handy for Offa's Dyke walkers, three neat simple bedrooms, open all day weekends, closed weekday lunchtimes, no evening food Sun or Tues. *(Jill and High Bennett)*

LEDBURY SO7137

★ **Feathers** (01531) 635266
High Street (A417); HR8 1DS Handsome black and white Tudor hotel with convivial bar-brasserie, locals at one end with hop-covered beams, stripped panelling and stools against counter serving Fullers London Pride, a couple of guest beers and extensive range of other drinks including cocktails, main part for diners with flowers on tables, comfortable bays of banquettes and other seats, log fire, much enjoyed food from sharing plates

and pub classics up, charming professional service, afternoon teas in sedate front lounge with another fire; children and dogs (in bar) welcome, tables under parasols on sheltered back terrace (lots of pots and hanging baskets), stylish bedrooms, good breakfast, open all day. *(Simon Glover, Gary and Marie Miller, Neal Griffith)*

LEDBURY SO7137

★ **Prince of Wales** (01531) 632250
Church Lane; narrow passage from Town Hall; HR8 1DL Friendly old black and white local prettily tucked away down narrow cobbled alley; seven well kept ales, foreign draught/bottled beers and real cider, knowledgeable staff, decent uncomplicated low-priced food from sandwiches up, beams, nooks and crannies and shelves of books, long back room; background music, live blues Thurs night and Sun afternoon, folk session Weds evening; dogs welcome, a couple of tables in flower-filled backyard, open all day. *(Harry Longford)*

LEDBURY SO7137

Seven Stars (01531) 635800
Homend (High Street); HR8 1BN 16th-c beamed and timbered pub with well liked fairly straightforward food (all day weekends) using produce from own farm, also a vegan menu, three well kept ales including Shepherd Neame, friendly helpful staff, bar area with comfortable seating and cosy woodburner, dining room behind; free wi-fi; children and dogs welcome, disabled access, walled back terrace, three bedrooms, open all day. *(Mike Benton)*

LEDBURY SO7137

Talbot (01531) 632963
New Street; HR8 2DX Comfortable 16th-c black and white fronted coaching inn; carpeted log-fire bar with Wadworths ales and guests, plenty of wines by the glass and good fairly traditional food from sharing boards and lunchtime sandwiches up, gluten-free menu, friendly efficient service, oak-panelled dining room; courtyard tables, 13 bedrooms (six in converted stables), good breakfast, open all day. *(Mike Benton)*

LEINTWARDINE SO4073

Lion (01547) 540203
High Street; SY7 0JZ Restored inn beautifully situated by packhorse bridge over River Teme; helpful efficient staff and friendly atmosphere, good well presented food from varied menu including some imaginative choices (can be pricey), Tues steak night, restaurant and two separate bars (both with woodburners), well kept beers such as Ludlow and Wye Valley, afternoon teas; children welcome, safely fenced riverside garden with play area, eight attractive bedrooms, can arrange fishing trips, open all day (may shut early Sun in winter). *(Rosie and Marcus Heatherley)*

LEINTWARDINE   SO4073
★**Sun** (01547) 540705
Rosemary Lane, just off A4113; SY7 0LP
Interesting 19th-c time warp: benches and
farmhouse tables by coal fire in brick-floored
front bar (dogs welcome here), three well
kept ales including Hobsons tapped from the
cask (Aug beer festival), another fire in snug
carpeted parlour, pork pies and perhaps a
lunchtime ploughman's (can bring food from
adjacent fish and chip shop), friendly staff
and cheery locals; open mike night last Fri of
month; new pavilion-style extension at back
with bar and garden room, open all day.
(Sylvia and Phillip Spencer)

LEOMINSTER   SO4959
★**Grape Vaults** (01568) 611404
Broad Street; HR6 8BS Popular and
friendly little two-room character pub; half
a dozen well kept ales including Ludlow and
tasty good value traditional food (no credit
cards – ATM opposite), good cheerful service,
two coal fires, beams and stripped woodwork,
original dark high-backed settles and round
copper-topped tables on bare boards, old
local prints and posters, bottle collection,
shelves of books in snug; live music Sun
afternoon, occasional quiz nights, free
wi-fi; dogs welcome, open all day, no food
Sun evening. *(Larry and Val Brown)*

LINTON   SO6525
Alma (01989) 720355
On main road through village; HR9 7RY
Cheerful village local with up to five well
kept ales, Weston's cider and several wines by
the glass, enjoyable pub food (not Sun, Mon)
including specials, friendly service, front bar
with open fire, restaurant, pool in small back
room; monthly quiz and open mike nights,
also June music festival; children and dogs
welcome, good-sized garden behind with
nice views, closed Mon lunchtime.
(Charles Duncan)

LUGWARDINE   SO5441
Crown & Anchor (01432) 850630
*Just off A438 E of Hereford; Cotts
Lane; HR1 4AB* Cottagey timbered pub
dating from the 18th c; ample helpings of
enjoyable reasonably priced food, well kept
Wye Valley and a guest, decent wines, good
friendly service, various smallish opened-up
rooms, inglenook log fire; children and dogs
(in bar) welcome, seats in front and back
gardens, open all day weekends, food till
7pm Sun. *(Simon Day)*

MUCH DEWCHURCH   SO4831
Black Swan (01981) 540295
*B4348 Ross-on-Wye to Hay-on-Wye;
HR2 8DJ* Roomy attractive beamed pub
(partly 14th-c) with welcoming long-serving
landlady; well kept Timothy Taylors Landlord
and local guests, Weston's cider, decent wines
and enjoyable straightforward home-made

food using local produce, log fires in cosy well
worn bar and lounge/eating area, pool room
with darts, TV and juke box; Thurs folk night;
children and dogs welcome, seats on front
terrace, open all day Sun. *(Mark Morgan)*

MUCH MARCLE   SO6634
Royal Oak (01531) 660300
*On A449 Ross-on-Wye to Ledbury;
HR8 2ND* New management for this
roadside country dining pub with lovely
views; good food from snacks and pub
favourites up, meal deals Mon-Weds, well
kept Brakspears and Marstons Pedigree,
friendly service, smallish bare-boards bar
area, various dining sections including library
room and large back function room; tribute
bands and other live music, skittle alley;
children and dogs (in bar) welcome, garden
and terrace seating, two bedrooms, open all
day in summer. *(Dr A J and Mrs B A Tompsett)*

PEMBRIDGE   SO3958
New Inn (01544) 388427
Market Square (A44); HR6 9DZ Timeless
ancient inn overlooking small black and
white town's church; unpretentious three-
room bar with antique settles, beams, worn
flagstones and impressive inglenook, well
kept changing ales, traditional cider and
generous helpings of popular good value
food including notable game pie, friendly
service, quiet little family dining room; some
live folk music, traditional games; no dogs
inside, unsuitable for wheelchairs and loos
downstairs. *(Dave Braisted, R K Phillips)*

PETERSTOW   SO5524
Red Lion (01989)730546
A49 W of Ross-on-Wye; HR9 6LH
Roadside country pub with much enjoyed
food cooked by landlord-chef (sensible prices
and smaller appetites catered for), four
well kept ales, Weston's cider, friendly staff,
open-plan with large dining area and modern
conservatory, log fires; quiz first Mon of
month; children and dogs welcome, back
play area, open all day, except 3-6pm Sun.
(Colin and Daniel Gibbs)

PRESTON   SO3841
Yew Tree (01981) 500359
Village W of Hereford; HR2 9JT Small
tucked-away pub handy for River Wye; simple
and welcoming, with a changing ale tapped
from the cask and real cider, good value
home-made food including Fri steak night,
beams and woodburner; some live music,
pool, free wi-fi; children and dogs welcome,
bunkhouse, open all day weekends.
(Caroline and Oliver Sterling)

ROSS-ON-WYE   SO6024
White Lion (01989) 562785
Wilton Lane; HR9 6AQ Friendly riverside
pub dating from 1650; well kept Wye Valley
and a couple of guests, enjoyable traditional
food (not Sun evening) from sandwiches up,

good service, big fireplace in carpeted bar, stone-walled gaol restaurant (building once a police station); quiz second Thurs of month, free wi-fi; children and dogs welcome, lots of tables in garden and on terrace overlooking the Wye and historic bridge, bedrooms and camping, open all day. *(Liz and Mark Eldon)*

SELLACK SO5526

★**Loughpool** (01989) 730888

Off A49; HR9 6LX Cottagey black and white country pub – some modernisation but keeping character; bars with beams and standing timbers, rustic furniture on flagstones, open fire and woodburner, well kept Wye Valley ales and a guest, local farm ciders/perries and several wines by the glass, landlord-chef's good attractively presented food from interesting menu including daily specials, back restaurant, friendly attentive service; well behaved children and dogs (in bar) allowed, garden tables under parasols, good surrounding walks, closed Sun evening, Mon. *(Martin Hartog)*

STAPLOW SO6941

Oak (01531) 640954

Bromyard Road (B4214); HR8 1NP Popular roadside village pub with two snug bar areas; beams, flagstones and woodburners, four real ales and good choice of wines, open-kitchen restaurant serving good food from lunchtime sandwiches/ciabattas up, cheerful helpful service; occasional live music; children and dogs welcome, garden picnic-sets, four comfortable bedrooms, open all day. *(Clive and Fran Dutson)*

STAUNTON-ON-WYE SO3844

Portway (01981) 500474

A438 Hereford to Hay-on-Wye, by Monnington turn; HR4 7NH Comfortable 16th-c beamed inn with good choice of popular well priced food, ales such as Ludlow, Sharps and Wye Valley, several wines by the glass, log-fire bar, lounge and restaurant; background music, TV, pool; children and dogs welcome, picnic-sets in sizeable garden among fruit trees, nine bedrooms, open all day. *(Lee and Jill Stafford)*

STOCKTON CROSS SO5161

Stockton Cross Inn (01568) 612509

Kimbolton; A4112, off A49 just N of Leominster; HR6 0HD Renovated half-timbered 16th-c drovers' inn; heavily beamed interior with inglenook woodburner, Wye Valley ales and guests, good choice of wines/gins and popular food (best to book) from daily changing menu, friendly accommodating staff; quiz third Tues of

month; children and dogs welcome, picnic-sets in front garden and on gravel back terrace, handy for Berrington Hall (NT), closed Mon, otherwise open all day, no food Sun evening. *(Mike and Mary Carter)*

SUTTON ST NICHOLAS SO5345

Golden Cross (01432) 880274

Corner of Ridgeway Road; HR1 3AZ Popular modernised pub with enjoyable good value food from ciabattas up, Wye Valley Butty Bach and two regularly changing guests from stone-fronted counter, good friendly service, clean décor, some breweriana, relaxed upstairs restaurant; weekend live music, juke box, pool and darts; children and dogs welcome, disabled facilities, no-smoking garden behind, pretty village and good surrounding walks, open all day Fri-Sun. *(Audrey and Peter Summers)*

TRUMPET SO6639

Trumpet Inn (01531) 670277

Corner A413 and A438; HR8 2RA Modernised black and white timbered pub dating from the 15th c; well kept Wadworths ales and plenty of wines by the glass, popular food from sandwiches up (some mains available in smaller helpings), efficient service, carpeted interior with beams, stripped brickwork and log fires, restaurant; free wi-fi; children and dogs (in bar) welcome, tables in big garden behind, campsite with hard standings, open all day, food all day Sat, till 5pm Sun. *(R K Phillips)*

UPPER SAPEY SO6863

Baiting House (01886) 853201

B4203 Bromyard–Great Witley; WR6 6XT Refurbished 19th-c country inn; two bars with flagstone and wood-strip flooring, woodburners, very good food from lunchtime ciabattas up including two- and three-course set lunch, five well kept ales such as Hobsons and Wye Valley, local ciders, several wines by the glass and good selection of gins, friendly attentive service, restaurant; separate room for pool, darts and sports TV; children welcome, dogs in one bar and snug, disabled access, picnic-sets on brick terrace (summer pizza oven) and raised lawn, six comfortable well appointed bedrooms, open all day (closed Mon, Tues lunchtimes), no food Sun evening, Mon. *(Colin and Daniel Gibbs)*

UPTON BISHOP SO6326

★**Moody Cow** (01989) 780470

B4221 E of Ross-on-Wye; HR9 7TT Popular tucked-away dining pub with modern rustic décor; sandstone walls, slate floor and woodburner in L-shaped bar, biggish raftered

Post Office address codings confusingly give the impression that a few pubs are in Herefordshire when they're really in Gloucestershire or even Wales (which is where we list them).

restaurant and second more intimate eating area, highly regarded freshly made food from changing menu (can be pricey), three well kept changing ales and decent wines including some local ones, friendly service; children and dogs (treats for them) welcome, garden growing own fruit/vegetables, closed Sun evening, Mon and Tues. *(Mike and Mary Carter, Guy Vowles)*

WALFORD   SO5820
★ **Mill Race** (01989) 562891
B4234 Ross-on-Wye to Lydney; HR9 5QS
Whitewashed village pub with distinctive row of high arched windows; comfortable leather armchairs and sofas on flagstones, photographs of local countryside, some stripped stonework and a two-way woodburner; Wye Valley ales, real cider and plenty of wines by the glass, well liked food from sandwiches and pub standards up, separate compact dining room; background music; children and dogs (in bar) welcome, terrace with views towards Goodrich Castle, more tables in garden, good nearby walks, open all day Sat, till 6pm Sun, closed Mon and Tues. *(Clive and Fran Dutson, Guy Vowles, Mike and Mary Carter)*

WALTERSTONE   SO3424
★ **Carpenters Arms** (01873) 890353
Follow Walterstone signs off A465; HR2 0DX Charming unspoilt stone cottage with unchanging traditional rooms (known locally as the Gluepot – once you're in you don't want to leave); beams, broad polished flagstones, a roaring fire in gleaming black range warming ancient settles against stripped-stone walls, Wadworths 6X and a guest tapped from the cask, enjoyable straightforward food in snug main dining room with mahogany tables and oak corner cupboards, another little dining area with old oak tables and church pews on more flagstones; no credit cards, outside loos are cold but in character; children welcome.
(Liz and Martin Eldon)

WELLINGTON HEATH   SO7140
Farmers Arms (01531) 634776
Off B4214 just N of Ledbury – pub signed right, from top of village; Horse Road; HR8 1LS Roomy open-plan beamed pub with enjoyable food (booking advised) including daily specials and various themed nights, Otter, Wye Valley Butty Bach and a guest, friendly staff; free wi-fi; children and dogs welcome, picnic-sets on paved terrace, good walking country, open all day weekends, closed Mon (except bank holidays 12-5.30pm) and Tues lunchtime. *(Charles Duncan)*

WEOBLEY   SO4051
Salutation (01544) 318443
Off A4112 SW of Leominster; HR4 8SJ

Old beamed and timbered inn at top of delightful village green; enjoyable food cooked by chef-landlord from bar snacks up including set lunch/early evening deal, well kept Hobsons, Wye Valley and a local guest, Robinson's cider, friendly helpful service, bar and various dining areas, inglenook log fires; quiz/curry night first Weds of month; children welcome, sheltered back terrace, three bedrooms, good breakfast, open all day.
(Simon Day)

WESTON-UNDER-
PENYARD   SO6323
Weston Cross Inn (01989) 562759
A40 E of Ross; HR9 7NU Creeper-clad 19th-c roadside pub with good choice of enjoyable well priced food in bar or restaurant, Bass, Otter and a guest, Weston's cider, friendly helpful staff; children, walkers and dogs welcome, good-sized garden with plenty of picnic-sets and play area, open all day Sat, limited menu Sun evening.
(Caroline and Oliver Sterling)

WHITBOURNE   SO7156
Live & Let Live (01886) 822276
Off A44 Bromyard–Worcester at Wheatsheaf; WR6 5SP Welcoming pub on southern edge of the village; good freshly made food (not Sun evening) from blackboard menu including interesting specials, well kept ales such as Ludlow and Wye Valley, friendly helpful staff, beams and nice log fire, big-windowed restaurant; quiz second Sun of month; children welcome, garden with country views, open all day weekends, closed Mon lunchtime.
(Liz and Martin Eldon)

WIGMORE   SO4168
Oak (01568) 770424
Ford Street; HR6 9UJ Restored 16th-c coaching inn mixing original features with contemporary décor; highly regarded imaginative food (not Sun evening), Hobsons and guests, real cider and nice wines by the glass, good friendly service; children and dogs (in one part) welcome, two bedrooms, open all day Sun till 8pm, closed Mon, Tues and lunchtimes Weds-Sat.
(Lee and Jill Stafford)

WINFORTON   SO2946
Sun (01544) 327677
A438; HR3 6EA Welcoming village pub with enjoyable freshly cooked food (not Sun evening) including a couple of specials, Wye Valley beers and Robinson's cider, country-style beamed areas either side of central servery, stripped stone and woodburners; children and dogs welcome, garden picnic-sets, bedrooms, open all day weekends, closed Mon.
(Charles Duncan)

Hertfordshire

KEY ★ Star Pub | 🌟 Top Quality Food | 🍺 Great Beer
🍷 Good Wines | £ Bargain Meals | 🛏 Good Bedrooms | 🍴 Serves Food

---

ARDELEY
Jolly Waggoner
TL3027 Map 5

(01438) 861350 – www.jollywaggoner.co.uk
Off B1037 NE of Stevenage; SG2 7AH

Extended cottage in pretty village, homely bar and smarter restaurant, good food and well kept ales and seats in garden

'I wish this was our local' says one of our readers wistfully – and many others agree. A cottagey, beamed, 16th-c pub owned by Church Farm opposite, it has lots of nooks and corners and is traditionally furnished with horsebrasses along the bressumer beam above the log fire, some tartan-upholstered armchairs and high chairs against the counter; darts and background music. Friendly staff serve Adnams Southwold and a couple of guests from breweries such as Greene King and Leighton Buzzard on handpump, 15 wines by the glass and their own Old Vodka distilled on site at the farm. The restaurant, extended into the cottage next door, has high-backed dark leather dining chairs around white-clothed tables and modern prints on dark green walls. There are picnic-sets on gravel and in the lawned garden. This is a pretty, tucked-away village with thatched cottages around the green. Disabled access.

🍴 Pleasing food using their own farm produce includes warm goats cheese salad, duck and orange pâté with chutney, macaroni cheese, trio of sausages with mash and gravy, chicken with lemon and parsley pesto on pasta, beer-battered fish and chips with home-made tartare sauce, rare-breed steak with onion rings and chips, sea bass with lemon, caper and dill risotto, and puddings such as chocolate brownie with ice-cream and fruit crumble and custard. *Benchmark main dish: slow-braised lamb with dumplings £14.75. Two-course evening meal £20.00.*

Free house ~ Licensee Lesley Lamb ~ Real ale ~ Open 12-11; 12-10 Sun; 12-9 Mon, Tues in winter ~ Bar food 12-2.30, 6-9; 12-9 Sat; 12-6 Sun ~ Restaurant ~ Children welcome ~ Dogs allowed in bar ~ Wi-fi *Recommended by Rosie and John Moore, David Appleyard, Victoria and James Sargeant, Mark and Mary Setting, Gail and Frank Hackett*

BARNET
Duke of York 🍷 🍺
TQ2599 Map 5

(020) 8440 4674 – www.brunningandprice.co.uk/dukeofyork
Barnet Road (A1000); EN5 4SG

Big place with reasonably priced bistro-style food and nice garden

This is a rather grand building and open doorways and stairs cleverly divide up the spreading rooms, while big windows and mirrors keep everything light and airy. There's a relaxed atmosphere and an eclectic mix of furniture on tiled or wooden flooring, hundreds of prints and photos on cream walls, fireplaces and thoughtful touches such as table lamps, books, rugs, fresh flowers and pot plants; background music. Served from an impressive counter by friendly staff, the fine range of drinks includes St Austell Brunning & Price Traditional Bitter plus guests from breweries such as Leighton Buzzard, Redemption, Sambrooks, Tring, Twickenham and Weltons on handpump, 20 wines by the glass, 30 gins and a large choice of whiskies. The garden is particularly attractive, with a range of seats, tables and picnic-sets on a tree-surrounded terrace and lawn, and a tractor in the popular play area.

Brasserie-style food includes sandwiches, scallops with crispy ham fritters and pea purée, a charcuterie board to share, maple and rosemary-roasted squash with herb and lemon quinoa and fennel salad, salmon and smoked haddock fishcake with a poached egg and chive and caper sauce, steak burger with toppings, coleslaw and chips, chicken, ham and leek pie, slow-braised lamb shoulder with dauphinoise potatoes and gravy, and puddings such as hot waffle with glazed banana, toffee sauce and honeycomb ice-cream and raspberry and almond tart with custard. *Benchmark main dish: beer-battered cod and chips £13.95. Two-course evening meal £21.00.*

Brunning & Price ~ Real ale ~ Open 11-11 (10.30 Sun) ~ Bar food 12-9 (9.30 Thurs-Sat) ~ Restaurant ~ Children welcome ~ Dogs allowed in bar ~ Wi-fi *Recommended by Justine and Neil Bonnett, Rob Anderson, Mrs Margo Finlay, Jörg Kasprowski, Greta and Gavin Craddock, Melanie and David Lawson*

COTTERED
Bull

TL3229   Map 5

(01763) 281243 – www.thebullcottered.co.uk
A507 W of Buntingford; SG9 9QP

Busy dining pub in nice village, attractive bar rooms with an easy-going feel, several ales, interesting food and seats in sizeable garden

There's a pretty view of a row of charming thatched cottages from seats in front of this well run village pub, and more seats in the big attractive back garden. The interconnected bar and dining rooms have bare boards, contemporary paintwork, a woodburning stove and a log-effect gas fire, all sorts of upholstered or cushioned dining chairs around dark wooden tables, tartan armchairs and button-back banquettes. Also, fresh flowers, candles in big white lanterns, country prints above wooden dados and stone bottles and carpentry planes. Greene King IPA and Abbot on handpump and nine decent wines served by helpful staff.

Popular food includes sandwiches, fried brie on warm port sauce, smoked salmon and prawn parcel, burger with toppings and a choice of sauce, mustard and calvados braised ham with a truffled duck egg, fillet of salmon with cheese and sunblush tomato sauce, calves liver with sage and bacon, pork belly with roasted baby onions and jus, and puddings. *Benchmark main dish: sea bass fillet with chilli, ginger, garlic and soy sauce £18.95. Two-course evening meal £23.00.*

Greene King ~ Tenant Darren Perkins ~ Real ale ~ Open 11-3, 6.30-11; 12-10.30 Sun ~ Bar food 12-2, 6.30-9; 12-3.30, 6-8.30 Sun ~ Restaurant ~ Children welcome but no highchairs or changing facilities ~ Wi-fi *Recommended by Mrs Margo Finlay, Jörg Kasprowski, Alan and Angela Scouller, John and Delia Franks, Nik and Gloria Clarke, Jamie Green*

Pubs close to motorway junctions are listed at the back of the book.

FLAUNDEN

GOOD PUB GUIDE

Bricklayers Arms ★ � ♀

TL0101 Map 5

(01442) 833322 – www.bricklayersarms.com

4 miles from M25 junction 18; village signposted off A41 – from village centre follow Boxmoor, Bovingdon road and turn right at Belsize, Watford signpost into Hogpits Bottom; HP3 0PH

• •
Hertfordshire Dining Pub of the Year
• •

Cosy country restaurant with fairly elaborate food; very good wine list

Dating from the 18th c and tucked away down winding lanes, this low brick and tiled pub is a civilised place for an excellent meal. It's mainly open-plan with stubs of knocked-through oak-timbered walls indicating the original room layout, and the well refurbished low-beamed bar is snug and comfortable, with a roaring log fire in winter. Stools line the brick counter where attentive staff keep Paradigm Heads Up, Tring Side Pocket for a Toad and a changing guest on handpump, an extensive wine list with 20 by the glass and a good choice of spirits; background music. In summer, the terrace and beautifully kept old-fashioned garden have seats and tables. Just up the Belsize road, a path on the left leads through delightful woods to a forested area around Hollow Hedge. The pub is just 15 minutes by car from the Warner Bros Studios where the Harry Potter films were made; you can tour the studios but must book in advance. Please note: dogs are allowed in the bar, but not on Sundays.

 First class food includes duck liver parfait with roasted pistachios and pear and white wine chutney, white crab meat with home-smoked salmon, chive cream and blinis, courgette, pea and celeriac risotto with melted cheese, ballotine of chicken and roasted red peppers with a poppy seed crust and tomato cream, pork tenderloin wrapped in bacon with apple and hazelnut jus, roasted red mullet fillets with citrus beurre blanc, 21-day aged fillet of local beef with green peppercorn-flavoured brandy cream sauce, and puddings such as hazelnut 'Bounty' tonka and white chocolate cream with coconut ice-cream and lemon and meringue slice on a biscuit base with blackcurrant sorbet. *Benchmark main dish: duck breast and confit leg with fig jus £19.95. Two-course evening meal £25.00.*

Free house ~ Licensee Alvin Michaels ~ Real ale ~ Open 12-11.30 (midnight Sat); 12-8.30 Sun ~ Bar food 12-2.30, 6.15-9.30; 12-7 Sun and bank holidays ~ Restaurant ~ Children welcome ~ Dogs allowed in bar ~ Wi-fi *Recommended by Andrea Shorey, Peter and Jan Humphreys, Andy and Rosemary Taylor, Matthew and Elisabeth Reeves, David Longhurst, Karl and Frieda Bujeya, Moira and John Wheeler, Daniel King*

FRITHSDEN

GOOD PUB GUIDE

Alford Arms ★ ♬ ♀

TL0109 Map 5

(01442) 864480 – www.alfordarmsfrithsden.co.uk

A4146 from Hemel Hempstead to Water End, then second left (after Red Lion) signed Frithsden, then left at T junction, then right after 0.25 miles; HP1 3DD

Thriving dining pub with a chic interior, good food from imaginative menu and a thoughtful wine list

Many customers combine a walk in the lovely surrounding National Trust woodland with a meal in this pretty Victorian pub. The elegant, understated interior has simple prints on pale cream walls, with blocks picked out in rich heritage colours, and an appealing mix of antique furniture from Georgian chairs to old commode stands on bare boards and patterned quarry tiles. A good mix of both drinkers and diners creates a cheerful atmosphere, and helpful staff serve Sharps Doom Bar and guest ales such as 3 Brewers Classic English Ale, Farr Brew Chief Jester and Tring Side Pocket for a Toad on handpump, 31 wines by the glass (including two sparkling ones), 20 gins and 24 whiskies and bourbons; background jazz and darts. There are plenty of tables outside.

Creative food includes pigeon, venison and wild boar terrine with apple chutney, smoked paprika braised octopus with red pepper piperade, indian-spiced caramelised onion and spinach risotto with bocconcini, pork and leek sausages with creamy mash and wholegrain mustard gravy, mullet fillet with chorizo and clam puy lentil stew, confit free-range pork belly with smoked ham hock and toulouse sausage cassoulet, ale-braised beef rib and bone marrow suet pudding with honey-roast parsnips, and puddings such as white chocolate and marsala tart with local elderberry sorbet and warm spiced banana cake with toffee sauce and banana mousse. *Benchmark main dish: bubble and squeak with oak-smoked bacon, free-range poached egg and hollandaise sauce £13.75. Two-course evening meal £21.00.*

Salisbury Pubs ~ Lease Darren Johnston ~ Real ale ~ Open 11-11; 12-10.30 Sun ~ Bar food 12-2.30, 6.30-9.30; 12-3, 6-10 Fri, Sat; 12-9 Sun ~ Restaurant ~ Children welcome ~ Dogs allowed in bar ~ Wi-fi *Recommended by Peter and Jan Humphreys, Audrey and Andrew Nichols, Patricia and Gordon Thompson, Professor James Burke, Ian Duncan*

HERTFORD HEATH
TL3510   Map 5

College Arms 🍽️⭐ ♈

(01992) 558856 – www.thecollegearmshertfordheath.com
London Road; B1197; SG13 7PW

Light and airy rooms with contemporary furnishings, friendly service, good, interesting food and real ales; seats outside

Once found, our readers tend to come back to this civilised pub on a regular basis. The bar has long cushioned wall seats and pale leather dining chairs around tables on rugs or wooden floorboards, and a modern bar counter where attentive staff serve quickly changing ales such as Ringwood Boondoggle and Wadworths Dirty Rucker on handpump and 20 wines by the glass; background music. Another area has more long wall seats and an open fireplace piled with logs, plus there's a charming little room with brown leather armchairs, a couple of cushioned pews, a woodburning stove in an old brick fireplace, hunting-themed wallpaper and another rug on floorboards. The elegant, partly carpeted dining room contains a real mix of antique-style dining chairs and tables. On the back terrace are tables, seats and a long wooden bench among flowering pots.

Well executed food includes sandwiches, ham hock and caper terrine with fruit loaf, moules marinière, wild mushroom and spinach risotto with truffle oil, a pie of the day, burger with toppings, slaw and fries, chicken supreme with fondant potato, kale and madeira jus, catalan fish stew, venison steak with horseradish mash and juniper and redcurrant jus, and puddings such as apple and cinnamon cheesecake and warm banana sponge with caramelised banana and caramel sauce. *Benchmark main dish: beer-battered fish and chips £14.50. Two-course evening meal £20.50.*

Punch ~ Lease Andy Lilley ~ Real ale ~ Open 12-11 (midnight Fri); 9.30am-midnight Sat; 9.30am-8pm Sun ~ Bar food 12-3, 6-9; 12-9.30 Fri; 9.30-9.30 Sat; 9.30-6 Sun ~ Restaurant ~ Children welcome ~ Dogs allowed in bar ~ Wi-fi *Recommended by David Hunt, Lorna and Jack Musgrave, Chantelle and Tony Redman, John Gibbon, Sandra Morgan, Charlie May*

The star-on-a-plate award, 🍽️⭐, distinguishes pubs where the food is of exceptional quality. The knife-and-fork symbol just means the pub serves food.

POTTERS CROUCH
Holly Bush  £

TL1105 Map 5

(01727) 851792 – www.thehollybushpub.co.uk

2.25 miles from M25 junction 21A: A405 towards St Albans, then first left, then after a mile turn left (ie away from Chiswell Green), then at T junction turn right into Blunts Lane; can also be reached fairly quickly, with a good map, from M1 junctions 6 and 8; AL2 3NN

Neat pub with gleaming furniture, well kept Fullers beers, good value food and an attractive garden

If you want to escape the traffic-laden M25 for some peace and quiet, head for this neatly kept, popular pub. The long, stepped bar has particularly well kept Fullers ESB, London Pride, Seafarers and a Fullers seasonal beer on handpump and several wines by the glass. There are quite a few antique dressers (several filled with plates), a number of comfortably cushioned settles, a fox's mask, some antlers, a fine old clock with a lovely chime, daily papers and (on the right as you enter) a big fireplace. In the evening, neatly placed candles cast glimmering light over darkly varnished tables, all sporting fresh flowers. The fenced-off back garden has plenty of sturdy picnic-sets on a lawn surrounded by handsome trees.

Rewarding food includes sandwiches and platters, brussels pâté with apple and ale chutney, smoked salmon with lemon crème fraîche, wild mushroom, asparagus and cream and white wine pie, chicken breast or beef burgers with toppings, coleslaw and chips, ham and eggs, lamb koftas with feta cheese, pitta bread and tzatziki, smoked haddock fishcakes with roasted vine tomatoes, chilli con carne, and puddings such as chocolate brownie with ice-cream and cinnamon-dusted belgian waffle with maple syrup. *Benchmark main dish: steak in ale pie £13.50. Two-course evening meal £20.00.*

Fullers ~ Tenants Steven and Vanessa Williams ~ Real ale ~ Open 12-2.30, 6-11; 12-3, 7-10 Sun ~ Bar food 12-2 (2.30 Sun), 6-9; not Sun-Tues evenings ~ Children welcome
Recommended by Charles Todd, Jane Rigby, Paul Farraday, Max and Steph Warren, Peter and Emma Kelly

PRESTON
Red Lion  £

TL1824 Map 5

(01462) 459585 – www.theredlionpreston.co.uk
Village signposted off B656 S of Hitchin; The Green; SG4 7UD

Homely village local with changing beers, fair-priced food and neat colourful garden

In 1982, this became the first pub in the country to be owned by the local community, and they've never looked back. It's busy and cheerful and the main room on the left, with grey wainscoting, has sturdy, well varnished furniture including padded country kitchen chairs and cast-iron-framed tables on patterned carpet, a generous window seat, fox hunting prints and a log fire in a brick fireplace. The somewhat smaller room on the right has steeplechase prints, varnished plank panelling and brocaded bar stools on flagstones around the servery; background music, darts and dominoes. Fullers London Pride and Tring Side Pocket for a Toad with guests such as Butcombe Original, Oakham JHB and Wolf in Sheeps Clothing on handpump, five farm ciders, seven wines by the glass (including an english house wine), a perry and winter mulled wine. A few picnic-sets on grass at the front face lime trees on the peaceful village green opposite, while the pergola-covered back terrace and good-sized sheltered garden with its colourful herbaceous border have seats and picnic-sets (some shade is provided by a tall ash tree).

400 | HERTFORDSHIRE

🍴 Traditional food includes sandwiches, prawns in garlic and chilli, parma ham with parmesan salad, wild mushroom, stilton and broccoli crumble, rabbit ragoût with pasta, malaysian chicken curry, chilli con carne, moussaka, moules frites, and puddings such as crème brûlée and chocolate fudge cake. *Benchmark main dish: fish pie £12.50. Two-course evening meal £19.00.*

Free house ~ Licensee Raymond Lambe ~ Real ale ~ Open 12-2.30, 5.30-11; 12-midnight Sat; 12-10.30 Sun; 12-4, 7-10.30 Sun in winter ~ Bar food 12-2, 6.30-8.30; not Sun evening, Mon ~ Children welcome ~ Dogs welcome ~ Wi-fi *Recommended by Alan and Angela Scouller, Sophie Ellison, Miranda and Jeff Davidson, Tracey and Stephen Groves, Lindy Andrews, William Pace, Charles Welch*

REDBOURN   TL1011   Map 5

Cricketers 🍺

(01582) 620612 – www.thecricketersofredbourn.co.uk

3.2 miles from M1 junction 9; A5183 signed Redbourn/St Albans, at second roundabout follow B487 for Hemel Hempstead, first right into Chequer Lane, then third right into East Common; AL3 7ND

Good food and beer in attractively updated pub with a bar and two restaurants

A heart-of-the-village pub that's well run and extremely popular. The relaxed front bar is decorated in country style: comfortable tub chairs, cushioned bench seating and high-backed bar stools on pale brown carpet, and a woodburning stove. Four quickly changing ales on handpump include St Austell Tribute and Tring Side Pocket for a Toad with guests such as Sharps Doom Bar and Tring Blinkers, 16 wines by the glass, farm cider, 18 gins and ten malt whiskies; background music. This bar leads back into an attractive, comfortably refurbished and unusually shaped modern restaurant; there's also an upstairs contemporary restaurant for private parties or functions. A side garden has plenty of seating and summer barbecues. Redbourn Common is opposite and many other walking and cycling opportunites surround the place. They can help with information on the Redbourn village museum next door.

🍴 A wide choice of well liked food includes confit lamb with tabbouleh salad (spring onions, cherry tomatoes and feta cheese), ham hock terrine with piccalilli, roasted baby aubergine and marinated tofu with quinoa and sunblush tomato purée, cumberland sausage with mash and onion gravy, chicken supreme wrapped in pancetta and stuffed with asparagus, sun-dried tomatoes and blue cheese, cod with wild rice and pak choi, soy sauce, sesame oil, ginger and chilli, 28-day aged fillet steak with peppercorn sauce, and puddings such as lavender, honey and lemon brulée tart with fresh blueberries and rhubarb, stem ginger and orange crumble with crème anglaise; they also offer a two- and three-course set menu. *Benchmark main dish: herb-crusted rack of lamb with dauphinoise potatoes £18.50. Two-course evening meal £24.00.*

Free house ~ Licensees Colin and Debbie Baxter ~ Real ale ~ Open 12-11 (midnight Sat); 12-10.30 Sun ~ Bar food 12-3, 6-9; 12-4 Sun ~ Restaurant ~ Children welcome ~ Dogs allowed in bar ~ Wi-fi *Recommended by Richard Kennell, Rosie and John Moore, Rob Anderson, John Gibbon, John and Claire Masters, Lorna and Jack Mulgrave, Patrick and Emma Stephenson*

'Children welcome' means the pub says it lets children inside without any special restriction. If it allows them in, but to restricted areas such as an eating area or family room, we specify this. Places with separate restaurants often let children use them, and hotels usually let children into public areas such as lounges. Some pubs impose an evening time limit – let us know if you find one earlier than 9pm.

SARRATT
TQ0499 Map 5

Cricketers ♀

(01923) 270877 – www.brunningandprice.co.uk/cricketers

The Green; WD3 6AS

Plenty to look at in rambling rooms, up to six real ales, nice wines, enjoyable food and friendly staff; seats outside

It's really worth wandering about this sizeable place (which has just been gently redecorated) before you decide where you want to sit as the interlinked rooms have numerous little snugs and alcoves. There are all manner of antique dining chairs and tables on rugs or stripped floorboards, comfortable armchairs or tub seats, cushioned pews, wall seats and two open fires in raised fireplaces; decoration includes cricketing memorabilia, fresh flowers, large plants and church candles. The drinks selection includes St Austell Brunning & Price Traditional Bitter plus guests from local breweries such as Chiltern, Malt, Paradigm (brewed in the village) and Tring on handpump, good wines by the glass, 30 gins and 50 malt whiskies; background music and board games. Several sets of french windows open on to the back terrace where there are tables and chairs, with picnic-sets on grass next to a colourfully painted tractor. This is a pleasant village setting overlooking the green and duck pond.

Interesting modern food includes sandwiches, smoked salmon with horseradish yoghurt and gin jelly, five-spiced duck leg with spring onion, cucumber, sweet chilli sauce and pancakes, sweet potato, cauliflower, almond and chickpea tagine with couscous and tempura broccoli, chicken caesar salad with anchovies, honey-roasted ham and eggs, sicilian fish stew, duck breast with potato gnocchi, roasted beetroot and beetroot purée, and puddings such as triple chocolate brownie with chocolate sauce and sticky toffee pudding with toffee sauce. *Benchmark main dish: braised lamb shoulder with dauphinoise potatoes and rosemary gravy £17.95. Two-course evening meal £22.00.*

Brunning & Price ~ Manager Simon Walsh ~ Real ale ~ Open 10am-11pm (10.30pm Sun) ~ Bar food 12-9.30; 12-9 Sun ~ Restaurant ~ Children welcome ~ Dogs allowed in bar ~ Wi-fi
Recommended by Glen and Patricia Fuller, Max and Steph Warren, Daniel King, Richard Kennell, Geoff and Ann Marston, John Harris, Martin Jones

ST ALBANS
TL1308 Map 5

Prae Wood Arms ♀

(01727) 229090 – www.brunningandprice.co.uk/praewoodarms

Garden House Lane; AL3 6JZ

Spreading manor house in extensive grounds, with interestingly furnished rooms, plenty to look at, a fine range of drinks and modern food

The five open fires here certainly keep this large and rather gracious pub warm in winter. The various chatty interconnected bar and dining areas have antique-style dining chairs and tables of every size and shape on bare boards, parquet and carpet, pale-painted walls that are hung with portraits, prints and huge mirrors, and elegant metal or glass chandeliers. Also, lots of books on shelves and house plants and stone and glass bottles on windowsills. Wooden stools line the counter where friendly, courteous young staff serve St Austell Brunning & Price Traditional Bitter with guests such as Adnams Mosaic, BrewDog Punk IPA, Timothy Taylors Landlord and Tring Side Pocket for a Toad on handpump, 18 wines by the glass and 100 gins; background music and board games. The loos are upstairs. In the extensive grounds, there's a partly covered big stone terrace with lots of good quality tables and chairs under green parasols, picnic-sets on grass and lawns that slope down to the River Ver at the bottom.

🍴 A wide choice of modern food includes sandwiches, teriyaki king prawns with tamari and ginger dressing, braised ox cheek pie with roasted cauliflower, carrot purée and deep-fried kale, butternut squash tortellini with sunblush tomato and caper dressing, pork and leek sausages with mash and onion gravy, steak burger with toppings, coleslaw and chips, confit duck leg with baby vegetables, chickpea and sweet potato cassoulet, sea trout with tomato salsa, baby spinach, fennel and gnocchi, braised shoulder of lamb with dauphinoise potatoes, carrot mash and rosemary gravy, and puddings such as crème brûlée and sticky toffee pudding with toffee sauce. *Benchmark main dish: beer-battered fish and chips £13.95. Two-course evening meal £23.00.*

Brunning & Price ~ Manager Rebecca Hall ~ Real ale ~ Open 11.30am-11pm ~ Bar food 12-9.30; 12-10 Fri, Sat; 12-9 Sun ~ Children welcome ~ Dogs allowed in bar ~ Wi-fi
Recommended by Alice Wright, Sylvia and Phillip Spencer, Richard Kennell, Audrey and Paul Summers, Cliff and Monica Swan, Sandra Morgan, Nick Higgins

WATTON-AT-STONE   TL3019   Map 5
Bull
(01920) 831032 – www.thebullwatton.co.uk
High Street; SG14 3SB

Bustling old pub with beamed rooms, candlelight and fresh flowers, real ales served by friendly staff and enjoyable food

Customers tend to gravitate towards the huge inglenook fireplace in the middle of this 15th-c pub – especially on chillier days. The main bar has a relaxed atmosphere created by friendly staff, fresh flowers, contemporary paintwork, a leather button-back chesterfield and armchairs, solid dark wooden dining chairs and plush-topped stools around tables on bare boards and a leather banquette beside a landscape-patterned wall. Adnams Ghost Ship, Sharps Doom Bar and a quickly changing guest on handpump, 15 gins, good wines by the glass and a cocktail list; background music and TV. Near the entrance are some high bar chairs along counters by the windows; from here, it's a step up to a cosy room with just four tables, decorative logs in a fireplace, books on shelves, board games and an old typewriter. At the other end of the building is an elegantly furnished dining room (part-carpeted and part-slate floored). Outside, a covered terrace has seats and tables, there are picnic-sets on grass plus a small well equipped play area. This is a pretty village.

🍴 Highly thought-of food includes lunchtime sandwiches, salt and pepper squid with chilli sauce, box-baked, garlic aned rosemary-studded camembert with red onion marmalade, lentil and spinach shepherds pie, steak and kidney pudding, pad thai (chicken with rice noodles, bean sprouts, chilli, spring onions, coriander, fresh lime and a plum and mirin dressing), cheesy haddock smokies, and puddings such as Oreo cheesecake with mint chocolate ice-cream and buttermilk and peach pannacotta. *Benchmark main dish: burger with toppings, bloody mary salsa and straw fries £13.95. Two-course evening meal £21.00.*

Star Pubs & Bars ~ Lease Alastair and Anna Bramley ~ Real ale ~ Open 9.30am-11pm; 12-9 Sun ~ Restaurant ~ Children welcome ~ Dogs allowed in bar ~ Wi-fi *Recommended by Ron and June Buckler, Rosie and John Moore, Sylvia and Phillip Spencer, John Gibbon, Lorna and Jack Mulgrave, Patrick and Emma Stephenson*

We say if we know a pub has background music.

Also Worth a Visit in Hertfordshire

Besides the fully inspected pubs, you might like to try these pubs that have been recommended to us and described by readers. Do tell us what you think of them: feedback@goodguides.com

ALDBURY SP9612

Greyhound (01442) 851228

Stocks Road; village signed from A4251 Tring–Berkhamsted, and from B4506; HP23 5RT Picturesque village pub with some signs of real age inside; inglenook in cosy traditional beamed bar, more contemporary area with leather chairs, airy oak-floored back restaurant with wicker seats at big tables, Badger ales and a dozen wines by the glass, generally well liked food from lunchtime sandwiches, sharing plates and pubby choices up, set menu Mon-Thurs; children welcome, dogs in bar, front benches facing green with whipping post, stocks and duck pond, suntrap gravel courtyard, eight bedrooms (some in newer building behind), open all day, food all day weekends (till 4.30pm Sun). *(Alf Wright)*

ALDBURY SP9612

★**Valiant Trooper** (01442) 851203

Trooper Road (towards Aldbury Common); off B4506 N of Berkhamsted; HP23 5RW Cheery traditional 17th-c village pub; appealing beamed bar with red and black floor tiles, built-in wall benches, a pew and small dining chairs around country tables, two further rooms (one with inglenook) and back barn restaurant, enjoyable generously served food (all day Sat, not Sun or Mon evenings), Chiltern, Tring and three guests, five ciders and plenty of wines by the glass, friendly helpful staff; background music, free wi-fi; children and dogs (in bar) welcome, enclosed garden with wooden adventure playground, well placed for Ashridge Estate beechwoods, open all day. *(Sandra Morgan)*

ALDENHAM TQ1498

Round Bush (01923) 855532

Roundbush Lane; WD25 8BG Cheery and bustling traditional village pub with plenty of atmosphere; two front rooms and back restaurant, popular generously served food at fair prices, well kept ales such as Courage Directors, Eagle IPA and St Austell Tribute, friendly efficient staff; quiz first Mon of month, occasional live music, darts; children, walkers and dogs welcome, big enclosed garden with play area, open (and food) all day. *(Peter and Emma Kelly)*

ALLENS GREEN TL4517

Queens Head (01279) 723393

Village signed from West Road, Sawbridgeworth; CM21 0LS Friendly semi-detached village drinkers' pub owned by the local community; four well kept beers including Fullers (many more third weekend of the month and on bank holiday beer festivals), also good range of ciders/perries, straightforward reasonably priced food; live music; dogs welcome, large garden, open all day weekends, closed lunchtimes Mon and Tues. *(Nigel Lusby)*

ASHWELL TL2639

★**Bushel & Strike** (01462) 742394

Off A507 just E of A1(M) junction 10, N of Baldock, via Newnham; Mill Street opposite church, via Gardiners Lane (car park down Swan Lane); SG7 5LY Smartly modernised 19th-c village dining pub (originally a brewery); highly regarded attractively presented food from chef-landlord's interesting menus including set choices and occasional themed nights, half a dozen real ales and nice selection of wines by the glass, friendly helpful young staff in aprons; children and dogs welcome, wheelchair access, picnic-sets on lawn and small terrace with view of church, open all day, food till 6pm Sun. *(John Walker)*

ASHWELL TL2739

Three Tuns (01462) 743131

Off A505 NE of Baldock; High Street; SG7 5NL Attractively refurbished 18th-c red-brick inn; well liked food including weekday two-course lunch deal, lounge bar with upholstered chairs on woodstrip flooring, blue-painted dado and woodburner, cask and craft beers, a dozen wines by the glass and good selection of gins, cheerful helpful service, partitioned dining room with cushioned wooden dining chairs around mix of tables, open fire in big fireplace; background music; children and dogs (in bar) welcome, terrace and large garden with apple trees, three comfortable bedrooms, charming village, open all day, food all day Sat, till 5pm Sun. *(Melanie and David Lawson)*

AYOT ST LAWRENCE TL1916

Brocket Arms (01438) 820250

Off B651 N of St Albans; AL6 9BT Attractive 14th-c country inn with low beams and inglenook log fires, entrance corridor with bar on left and dining room to the right, good traditional food (special diets catered for), friendly helpful staff, six real ales such as Greene King, Nethergate and Sharps, wide choice of wines by the glass; live music including jazz and open mike nights, quiz second Sun of the month; children welcome, dogs in bar, nice suntrap walled garden with play area, handy for George Bernard Shaw's house (Shaw's Corner – NT), six comfortable bedrooms, open all day, no food Sun evening. *(Simon King, John Gibbon)*

BALDOCK   TL2433
Orange Tree (01462) 892341
Norton Road; SG7 5AW Unpretentious old two-bar pub with up to 13 well kept ales including three from Greene King four real ciders and large selection of whiskies, good value home-made food (all day Sat, till 4pm Sun) including range of pies and local sausages, friendly helpful staff; quiz Tues, folk club Weds, sports TV; children, dogs and muddy boots welcome, garden with play area, open all day Thurs-Sun. *(M G Hart, John Gibbon)*

BARKWAY   TL3834
Tally Ho (01763) 848071
London Road (B1368); SG8 8EX Little village-edge pub with clean modern décor; mix of wooden furniture on light boarded floor, log fire in central brick fireplace, four changing ales including Dark Star and good range of other drinks (happy hour 4-7pm Fri, Sat), limited menu of sandwiches, soup and bar snacks (may be fish and chip van or pop-up restaurants), friendly efficient staff; quiz second Weds of month; children welcome, decked seating area at front, picnic-sets and weeping willow in garden beyond car park, open all day (till 7pm Sun). *(John and Claire Master)*

BENINGTON   TL3023
Bell (01438) 869827
Town Lane; just past Post Office, towards Stevenage; SG2 7LA Traditional 16th-c pub in very pretty village; local beers such as Buntingford and enjoyable caribbean food (licensees are from Trinidad), low beams, sloping walls and big inglenook; occasional folk nights and other events; big garden with country views, handy for Benington Lordship Gardens, open all day Sun (food till 6pm), closed Mon, Tues and Wed lunchtimes. *(Eric Barnes)*

BERKHAMSTED   SP9907
Boat (01422) 877152
Gravel Path, by bridge; HP4 2EF Cheerfully refurbished open-plan Fullers dining pub in attractive canalside setting (can get packed in fine weather); their ales kept well and guests, good choice of wines by the glass, cocktails, popular food from weekday lunchtime sandwiches and small plates to daily specials, mix of seating including padded stools and leather chesterfields on mainly parquet flooring, painted panelling and contemporary artwork, a couple of Victorian fireplaces; background music, live jazz Sun afternoon; children and

dogs welcome, french windows to paved terrace overlooking towpath and canal, moorings, open (and food) all day. *(Alison and Michael Harper)*

BERKHAMSTED   SP9807
Highwayman (01442) 285480
High Street; HP4 1AQ Bustling town pub (owned by the White Brasserie Company) with plenty of room for both drinkers and diners; relaxed bar with big windows overlooking the street, upholstered and leather chairs around all sorts of tables, lots of church candles in stubby holders, Sharps, Timothy Taylors and a guest such as Tring, over 20 wines by the glass and well liked modern food from interesting french-influenced menu, cheerful helpful young staff, steps down to expansive dining room with dark green leather wall seats and cushioned chairs at barley-twist tables; monthly live music, sports TV, free wi-fi; children and dogs (in bar) welcome, back terraced garden, open (and food) all day. *(Peter and Jan Humphreys, Simon King)*

BERKHAMSTED   SP9907
Rising Sun (01442) 864913
George Street; HP4 2EG Victorian canalside pub known locally as the Riser; five well kept ales including one badged for them from Tring, up to 30 ciders/perries (four beer/cider festivals a year) and interesting range of spirits, two very small traditional rooms with a few basic chairs and tables, coal fire, snuff and cigars for sale, no food apart from substantial ploughman's, friendly service; background music, Thurs quiz; children and dogs welcome, chairs out by canal and well worn seating in covered side beer garden, colourful hanging baskets, open all day. *(Louise and Oliver Redman)*

BRAUGHING   TL3925
Axe & Compass (01920) 821610
Just off B1368; The Street; SG11 2QR Nice country pub in pretty village with ford; enjoyable freshly prepared food (all day Sat, till 5.30pm Sun) from varied menu, own-baked bread, well kept ales including Harveys and several wines by the glass, friendly uniformed staff, mix of furnishings on wood floors in two roomy bars, lots of old local photographs, log fires, restaurant with little shop selling home-made chutney and relish; well behaved children and dogs welcome, garden overlooking playing field, outside bar, open all day. *(Ian Duncan)*

BRAUGHING   TL3925
Brown Bear (01920) 822157
Just off B1368; The Street; SG11 2QF Steps up to traditional little low-beamed

---

We include some hotels with a good bar that offers facilities comparable to those of a pub.

pub with inglenook bar; up to four well kept changing ales and enjoyable home-cooked pubby food (not Tues) from ciabattas to good fish and chips, friendly staff, dining room with another good fire; Thurs quiz, occasional live music, games including darts, dominoes and shove-ha'penny; tricky disabled access, picnic-sets in garden behind with pizza oven, barbecue and pétanque, attractive village, closed Mon, otherwise open all day (till 6pm Sun). *(Ian Duncan)*

BRAUGHING   TL3925
Golden Fleece   (01920) 823555
Green End (B1368); SG11 2PE 17th-c village dining pub with good food (special diets catered for) from chef-landlady including some imaginative choices, popular tapas night last Weds of the month and curry evenings, Adnams Southwold and local guests, plenty of wines by the glass, cheerful service, bare-boards bar and two dining rooms, beams, timbers and good log fire, pictures for sale; quiz nights, July wheelbarrow race; children welcome, circular picnic-sets out at front, back garden with metal furniture on split-level paved terrace, play area, open all day weekends (food till 6pm Sun). *(Mrs Margo Finlay, Jörg Kasprowski)*

BRICKET WOOD   TL1302
Gate   (01923) 678944
Station Road/Smug Oak Lane; AL2 3PW Popular family pub with good sensibly priced home-cooked food including british tapas, ales such as Bombardier, Eagle IPA and Youngs, friendly service, bar with log fire and side dining area; quiz Mon, free wi-fi; dogs welcome, garden (summer barbecues), open all day, no food Sun evening. *(Audrey and Paul Summers)*

BURNHAM GREEN   TL2516
White Horse   (01438) 798100
Off B1000 N of Welwyn; Whitehorse Lane; AL6 0HA Well supported village-green dining pub; mix of modern and traditional rustic décor including attractive 17th-c beamed core, good food (not Mon and Tues evenings in winter) from varied menu, McMullens ales, friendly obliging service; monthly quiz; children and dogs (in bar) welcome, good-sized pretty garden behind with duck pond and play area, open all day (till 6pm Sun). *(Mrs Margo Finlay, Jörg Kasprowski)*

BUSHEY   TQ1394
Horse & Chains   (020) 8421 9907
High Street; WD23 1BL Comfortably modernised pub with enjoyable bar food from sandwiches and sharing plates up, also separate restaurant menu, themed nights and Sun brunch, well kept ales and good choice of wines by the glass, efficient friendly service, woodburner in big inglenook, kitchen view from compact dining room; children and dogs welcome, open (and food) all day. *(Alf Wright)*

BUSHEY   TQ1395
King Stag   (020) 8950 2988
Bournehall Road; WD23 3EH Popular mock-Tudor Victorian pub tucked away in residential street; opened-up bare-boards interior, good choice of local beers along with a Greene King house ale, enjoyable food including weekday set lunch, Mon burger night and Weds steaks, friendly helpful service; variety of events; children and dogs welcome (menus for both), picnic-sets in back beer garden, open all day. *(James Reiff, Jim Craig-Grat)*

BUSHEY   TQ1395
Swan   (020) 8950 2256
Park Road; turning off A411; WD23 3EE Homely atmosphere in this traditional single-room terraced pub; well kept Black Sheep, Greene King, Timothy Taylors and Youngs, some snacky food, old photos and other memorabilia, coal fires; sports TVs, darts and board games; beer garden behind (outside ladies' loo), open all day. *(Jim Craig-Grat)*

CHAPMORE END   TL3216
Woodman   (01920) 463339
Off B158 Wadesmill–Bengeo; pub signed 300 metres W of A602 roundabout; OS Sheet 166 map reference 328164; SG12 0HF Early Victorian local in peaceful country hamlet; plain seats around stripped pub tables, floor tiles or broad bare boards, working period fireplaces, two well kept ales and guests poured from the cask, thai and tapas menus Weds-Sat evenings and Sun lunchtime, friendly staff, conservatory; children and dogs welcome, picnic-sets out in front under a couple of walnut trees, bigger back garden with fenced play area and boules, maybe summer Sun barbecues, closed Mon lunchtime, otherwise open all day. *(Eric Barnes)*

CHIPPERFIELD   TL0400
Cart & Horses   (01923) 263763
Quickmoor Lane/Common Wood; WD4 9BA Smallish 18th-c wisteria-clad pub popular for its enjoyable generously served food including bargain specials, two or three well kept changing ales and good choice of wines by the glass, friendly staff; children and dogs welcome, picnic-sets in big garden with marquee and play area, nice surrounding countryside and walks, open all day. *(Sandra Morgan)*

CHORLEYWOOD   TQ0294
Land of Liberty, Peace & Plenty   (01923) 282226
Long Lane, Heronsgate, just off M25 junction 17; WD3 5BS Traditional 19th-c drinkers' pub in leafy outskirts; half a dozen well kept interesting ales and good choice of ciders/perries, snacky food such as pasties,

simple layout, darts, skittles and board games; background jazz, TV (on request), no mobile phones or children inside; dogs welcome, garden with pavilion, open all day. *(Cliff and Monica Swan)*

CHORLEYWOOD   TQ0295
Stag (01923) 282090
Long Lane, Heronsgate, just off M25 junction 17; WD3 5BT Open-plan Edwardian dining pub with good varied choice of food from sandwiches and tapas up, well kept McMullens ales and several wines by the glass, friendly attentive service, bar and eating areas extending into conservatory, woodburner in raised hearth; daily papers, free wi-fi; children and dogs welcome, tables on back lawn, open all day, food all day Weds-Sun. *(Richard Kennell)*

CHORLEYWOOD   TQ0396
White Horse (01923) 283033
A404 just off M25 junction 18; WD3 5SD Black-beamed roadside pub with good food such as pizzas, tapas and panini, Greene King ales, friendly helpful staff, big log fire; sports TV; children and dogs (in bar) welcome, small back terrace, open all day. *(Jeff Tilley)*

COLNEY HEATH   TL2007
Plough (01727) 823720
Sleapshyde; handy for A1(M) junction 3; A414 towards St Albans, double back at first roundabout then turn left; AL4 0SE Refurbished part-thatched 17th-c dining pub; good interesting food from snacks up including vegan choices, four real ales, three proper ciders and wide selection of wines and gins, attentive friendly service, cosy low-beamed interior with two fireplaces; children and dogs welcome, front and back terraces, picnic-sets on lawn overlooking fields, open all day, no evening food Sun or Mon. *(Andrew Seib)*

ESSENDON   TL2608
Candlestick (01707) 261322
West End Lane; AL9 6BA Peacefully located country pub run by father and son team; enjoyable pubby food, three well kept beers and several wines by the glass, relaxed friendly atmosphere, comfortable clean interior with faux black timbers, wood and carpeted floors and log fires; quiz nights, TV; children and dogs welcome, plenty of seats outside, good walks, closed Mon and Tues, otherwise open all day, Sun till 8pm (food until 5pm). *(John Gibbon)*

FLAUNDEN   TL0100
Green Dragon (01442) 832269
Flaunden Hill; HP3 0PP Comfortable and chatty 17th-c beamed pub; partly panelled extended lounge, back restaurant and traditional little tap bar, log fire, popular good value food (not Mon), Fullers, St Austell and Youngs, friendly helpful service; background music, darts and other pub

games; children and dogs welcome, hitching rail for horses, well looked after garden with smokers' shelter, pretty village, only a short diversion from Chess Valley Walk, closed Sun evening and Mon lunchtime, otherwise open all day. *(Ian Duncan)*

GILSTON   TL4313
Plume of Feathers (01279) 424154
Pye Corner; CM20 2RD Old beamed corner pub with decent choice of well priced food (all day Fri and Sat, till 7pm Sun) including cook-your-own meat on a volcanic rock, Courage Best, Adnams Broadside and local guests, Weston's cider and maybe a mulled winter one, good choice of wines by the glass, friendly if not always speedy service, carpeted interior with brass-hooded log fire; background music, free wi-fi; children welcome, seats on terrace and fenced grassy area with play equipment. *(Cliff and Monica Swan)*

GREAT AMWELL   TL3712
George IV (01920) 870039
St Johns Lane; SG12 9SW Pleasant 19th-c brick pub in pretty spot by church; good well presented food cooked by owner-chef from interesting snacks and pub staples up, occasional themed evenings, can eat in log-fire bar or back restaurant, well kept beers such as Adnams and Greene King, good choice of wines and gins, friendly helpful staff, flowers and candles on tables; quiz last Tues of month; attractive outside seating areas front and back, River Lea nearby, open all day Sat, till 6pm Sun, closed Mon (except 12-6pm bank holidays). *(Mrs Margo Finlay, Jörg Kasprowski)*

GREAT HORMEAD   TL4030
Three Tuns (01763) 289405
B1038/Horseshoe Hill; SG9 0NT Old thatched and timbered country pub-restaurant in lovely surroundings; enjoyable home-made food including blackboard specials, Adnams and a couple of guests, good choice of wines by the glass and local gin, small linked areas, huge inglenook with another great hearth behind, back conservatory extension; monthly quiz, free wi-fi; children, walkers and dogs welcome, nice secure garden, open all day Sun till 7pm, closed Mon apart from bank holidays. *(Paul Farraday)*

HALLS GREEN   TL2728
Rising Sun (01462) 790487
NW of Stevenage; from A1(M) junction 9 follow Weston signs off B197, then left in village, right by duck pond; SG4 7DR Welcoming 18th-c beamed and carpeted country pub; enjoyable good value traditional food (not Sun evening or Mon) in bar or conservatory restaurant, well kept McMullens ales, friendly helpful service, woodburner and open fire; children and dogs (in bar) welcome, disabled access, big

garden with terrace, boules and plenty for kids including swings and playhouse, closed Mon, otherwise open all day. *(Jeff Tilley)*

HATFIELD TL2308
Eight Bells (01707) 272477
Park Street, Old Hatfield; AL9 5AX
Attractive old beamed pub (two buildings knocked together) with Charles Dickens association; small rooms on different levels, wood floors and open fire, three well kept ales including Sharps, good value lunchtime food; background music (live Tues, Sat), games machine, free wi-fi; children and dogs welcome, tables in backyard, open all day Fri-Sun, closed Mon. *(Ivy and George Goodwill)*

HATFIELD TL2108
Harpsfield Hall (01707) 265840
Parkhouse Court, off Comet Way (A1001); AL10 9RQ Newly built aviation-theme Wetherspoons with large hangar-like interior; interesting décor using some old aircraft parts including a seating booth made from a jet engine housing, good range of beers and other drinks from long servery with time-zoned clocks in aeroplane windows, their usual good value food, friendly staff; TVs, free wi-fi; children welcome, disabled access, tables on paved terrace, open all day from 8am. *(John Gibbon)*

HATFIELD TL2308
Horse & Groom (01707) 264765
Park Street, Old Hatfield; AL9 5AT
Friendly old town local with up to half a dozen well kept ales (beer festivals) and good value pubby lunchtime food, also Fri thai night and Tues and Sat suppers (free if you buy a pint), dark beams and good winter fire, old local photographs, darts and dominoes; quiz Thurs, sports TV; dogs welcome, a few tables out behind, handy for Hatfield House, open all day. *(Ivy and George Goodwill)*

HEMEL HEMPSTEAD TL0411
Crown & Sceptre (01442) 234660
Bridens Camp; leaving on A4146, right at Flamstead/Markyate sign opposite Red Lion; HP2 6EY Traditional rambling pub, welcoming and relaxed, with well kept Greene King ales and several guests, generous helpings of good reasonably priced pubby food including Tues pie night, cheerful efficient staff, dining room with woodburner; children allowed, dogs in outside bar/games room, picnic-sets at front and in pleasant garden, good walks, open all day weekends, no food Sun evening. *(Peter and Jan Humphreys)*

HEMEL HEMPSTEAD TL0604
Paper Mill (01442) 288800
Stationers Place, Apsley; HP3 9RH
Recently built canalside pub on site of former paper mill; spacious open-plan interior with upstairs restaurant, Fullers ales and a couple of guests (usually local), food from sandwiches and sharing plates up, friendly staff, log fire; Mon quiz and live music nights, free wi-fi; children welcome, tables out on balcony and by the water, open (and food) all day. *(Ian Duncan)*

HERTFORD TL3212
Old Barge (01992) 581871
The Folly; SG14 1QD Red-brick bay-windowed pub by River Lee Navigation canal; clean quaint interior arranged around central bar, wood and flagstone floors, some black beams and log fire, well kept Marstons-related beers and three guests, real ciders/perry and enjoyable reasonably priced food (not Sun evening) from sandwiches up, friendly staff; background music, Sun quiz, games machines; children and dogs (in one part of bar) welcome, a few tables out in front, more to the side, open all day. *(John and Claire Master)*

HERTFORD TL3212
Old Cross Tavern (01992) 583133
St Andrew Street; SG14 1JA Chatty old red-brick pub popular for its half a dozen particularly well kept daily changing ales including own microbrews, also bottled belgian beers and Aspall's cider, some snacky food such as pork pies, friendly staff and cosy relaxed atmosphere, open fires; May and Oct beer festivals, dogs welcome, small back terrace, open all day weekends, from 4.30pm other days. *(Ian Duncan)*

HERTFORD TL3212
Salisbury Arms (01992) 583091
Fore Street; SG14 1BZ Rambling 18th-c pub-hotel with three bars and smart restaurant; well kept McMullens ales, plenty of wines by the glass and good fairly priced food from sandwiches up, afternoon teas, efficient cheerful service, splendid Jacobean staircase to bedrooms; children welcome, open all day. *(John and Claire Master)*

HERTFORD HEATH TL3511
Goat (01992) 535788
Vicarage Causeway; SG13 7RT Popular 16th-c low-beamed pub facing village green; generous helpings of enjoyable fair-priced food including deals, Greene King IPA and a couple of guests, friendly helpful staff, restaurant; quiz last Thurs of month, classic

---

Please tell us if any pub deserves to be upgraded to a featured entry – and why: feedback@goodguides.com, or (no stamp needed) Freepost THE GOOD PUB GUIDE, Random House Publishing, 20 Vauxhall Bridge Road, London SW1V 2SA.

car meeting first Sun; children and dogs (in lower bar) welcome, picnic-sets out at front, open all day, no food Sun evening. *(Richard Kennell)*

HIGH WYCH   TL4614
Rising Sun (01279) 724099
Signed off A1184 Harlow–Sawbridgeworth; CM21 0HZ Opened-up 19th-c red-brick village local; up to five well kept ales such as Courage, Mighty Oak and Oakham tapped from the cask, friendly staff and regulars, woodburner, no food; live music and monthly quiz nights, darts; walkers and dogs welcome, small side garden, closed lunchtimes Tues and Thurs. *(Jeff Tilley)*

HITCHIN   TL1828
Half Moon (01462) 453010
Queen Street; SG4 9TZ Tucked-away local freshened up under present friendly licensees; up to ten well kept ales (beer festivals Apr and Oct) and good value pubby food from sandwiches up; quiz first Tues of month, some live music; children (till 8pm) and dogs welcome, back garden with terrace, open all day (till 1am Fri, Sat), kitchen closed Sun evening, Mon. *(Sandra Morgan)*

HITCHIN   TL5122
Victoria (01462) 432682
Ickleford Road, at roundabout; SG5 1TJ Popular wedge-shaped Victorian corner local; Greene King ales and three guests, enjoyable reasonably priced lunchtime food (also Mon and Fri evenings); events including beer festivals, live music and quiz nights, barn function room; children welcome, seats in sunny beer garden, open all day. *(Peter and Emma Kelly)*

HUNSDON   TL4114
Fox & Hounds (01279) 843999
High Street; SG12 8NJ Village dining pub with good enterprising food from chef-landlord, not cheap but they do offer a weekday set menu, Adnams Southwold, a local guest and wide choice of wines by the glass, beams, panelling and fireside leather sofas, more formal restaurant with period furniture, bookcase door to lavatories; children welcome, dogs in bar, heated covered terrace, closed Sun evening, Mon. *(Mrs Margo Finlay, Jörg Kasprowski)*

LEY GREEN   TL1624
Plough (01438) 871394
Plough Lane, Kings Walden; SG4 8LA Small brick-built rural local, plain and old-fashioned, with chatty regulars, two well kept Greene King ales and a guest, simple low-priced food; live music including Tues folk session, free wi-fi; children and dogs

welcome, big informal garden with peaceful views, good walks nearby, camping, closed lunchtimes Mon and Tues, otherwise open all day. *(Louise and Oliver Redman)*

LITTLE HADHAM   TL4322
Nags Head (01279) 771555
Hadham Ford, towards Much Hadham; SG11 2AX Popular and welcoming 16th-c country dining pub with small linked black-beamed rooms; enjoyable food from snacks to daily specials including good Sun roasts, close-set tables in cosy bar with three regular ales and decent wines, restaurant down a couple of steps; occasional quiz nights; children welcome in eating areas, no dogs inside, tables out at front and in pleasant garden behind, open all day Sun till around 9pm. *(Eric Barnes)*

LONG MARSTON   SP8915
Queens Head (01296) 668368
Tring Road; HP23 4QL Welcoming beamed village local with enjoyable good value food from pub favourites up, well kept beers including Tring Side Pocket for a Toad, helpful friendly service, open fire; children welcome, seats on terrace, good walks nearby, two bedrooms in annexe, open all day weekends, closed weekday lunchtimes, no food Sun evening and Mon-Weds. *(Audrey and Paul Summers)*

MARSWORTH   SP9114
Anglers Retreat (01442) 822250
Startops End; HP23 4LJ Homely unpretentious pub near Tring Reservoirs and Grand Union Canal; smallish L-shaped angler-theme bar with stuffed fish and live parrot (Rosie), four well kept ales including Tring Side Pocket for a Toad, wide choice of good value food from baguettes up, Mon pizza night, friendly welcoming staff; Thurs live music, Sun poker, outside gents'; children, walkers and dogs welcome, side garden with tables under parasols, duck pond, aviary and an old tractor, bedrooms (some in separate building), open all day. *(Roy Hoing)*

NUTHAMPSTEAD   TL4134
★Woodman (01763) 848328
Off B1368 S of Barkway; SG8 8NB Tucked-away thatched and weatherboarded village pub under long-serving family; 17th-c low beams/timbers and inglenook log fire, Buntingford, Greene King and Woodfordes tapped from the cask, enjoyable home-made food (not Sun evening) from traditional choices up, friendly service, dining extension, interesting USAF memorabilia and outside memorial (near World War II airfield); children in family room with play area, dogs in bar, benches out overlooking tranquil

lane, two comfortable bedrooms, closed Mon, otherwise open all day (till 7pm Sun). *(Louise and Oliver Redman)*

PIRTON   TL1431
Motte & Bailey (01462) 712730
Great Green; SG5 3QD Welcoming village-green pub refurbished under new owners; enjoyable food from shortish menu including themed nights, real ales such as Adnams, Nethergate and Woodfordes, good selection of wines and gins, friendly helpful service; live music and quiz nights; children and dogs welcome, picnic-sets out at front behind picket fence, more in back garden with play equipment, good surrounding walks, open all day, no food Sun evening. *(Rupert Hennen)*

POTTEN END   TL0108
Martins Pond (01442) 864318
The Green; HP4 2QQ Refurbished 19th-c brick dining pub facing village green and pond; popular freshly prepared food from sandwiches up, well kept Vale beers, several wines by the glass and decent range of gins, friendly attentive staff, conservatory; children and dogs (in bar) welcome, smallish paved garden to the side, circular walks from the door, open all day, food all day weekends. *(Paul Farraday)*

REDBOURN   TL1011
Hollybush (01582) 792423
Church End; AL3 7DU Picturesque pub dating from the 16th c run by father and son team; black-beamed lounge with big brick fireplace and heavy wooden doors, larger area with some built-in settles, Brakspears and two guests, enjoyable reasonably priced pubby food (not Sun evening) from sandwiches and basket meals up, friendly accommodating service; some live music, darts; children and dogs (in bar) welcome, picnic-sets in pleasant sunny garden (distant M1 noise), pretty spot near medieval church, open all day. *(Sandra Morgan)*

REDCOATS GREEN   TL2026
Farmhouse (01438) 729500
Stevenage Road; SG4 7JR Large 15th-c tile-faced building (part of the Anglian Country Inns group) set in four-acre grounds; good food from shortish but varied menu (can be pricey), also fixed-price lunch and afternoon teas, plenty of wines by the glass including champagne, Adnams Southwold, friendly helpful staff, conservatory restaurant; children and dogs (in bar) welcome, 30 bedrooms (most in converted outbuildings), open all day, no food Sun evening. *(Jeff Tilley)*

RICKMANSWORTH   TQ0594
Feathers (01923) 770081
Church Street; WD3 1DJ Old pub quietly set off the high street next to St Mary's Church; beams, panelling and soft lighting, well kept ales such as Fullers London Pride,

good wine list and varied choice of freshly prepared food from sandwiches up, friendly young staff coping well at busy times; children allowed till 8pm, dogs in one side of the bar, picnic-sets out behind, open (and food) all day. *(Ian Duncan)*

RICKMANSWORTH   TQ0592
Rose & Crown (01923) 773826
Woodcock Hill/Harefield Road, off A404 E of Rickmansworth at Batchworth; WD3 1PP Wisteria-clad 17th-c country dining pub; enjoyable traditional home-cooked food including range of burgers and gluten-free menu, well kept Fullers London Pride and a guest, friendly young staff, airy dining room and conservatory, low beams and open fires; quiz and live music nights; children and dogs welcome, large peaceful garden with views, open all day (till 8pm Sun). *(Ian Duncan)*

RIDGE   TL2100
Old Guinea (01707) 660894
Crossoaks Lane; EN6 3LH Welcoming modernised country pub with good pizzeria alongside traditional bar; two regular ales including St Austell Tribute, nice italian wines and proper coffee, open fire; children and dogs (in bar) welcome, large garden with far-reaching views, open all day (food till 10pm). *(Peter and Emma Kelly)*

ROYSTON   TL3540
Old Bull (01763) 242003
High Street; SG8 9AW Coaching inn dating from the 16th c with bow-fronted Georgian façade; roomy high-beamed bar, exposed timbers and handsome fireplaces, plenty of tables and some easy chairs on wood floor, dining area with wall-sized photographs of old Royston, enjoyable pubby food including Sun carvery, well kept Greene King ales, a guest beer and several wines by the glass, helpful pleasant service; background music, live folk second and last Fri of month, daily newspapers; children and dogs (in bar) welcome, suntrap courtyard, 11 bedrooms, open all day from 8am (till 1am Fri, Sat). *(John Pritchard)*

RUSHDEN   TL3031
Moon & Stars (01763) 288330
Mill End; off A507 about a mile W of Cottered; SG9 0TA New management for this cottagey low-beamed pub in peaceful country setting; well liked/priced food in bar or small dining room, three real ales including Greene King, friendly service; children and dogs welcome, large back garden, closed Sun evening, Mon. *(Colin and Daniel Gibbs)*

SARRATT   TQ0499
★**Boot** (01923) 262247
The Green; WD3 6BL Early 18th-c dining pub with good food (all day Sat, not Sun evening) from lunchtime sandwiches and

sharing plates up, weekend breakfast (9.30-11.30am), also tapas and pizzas Fri and Sat evening, three well kept ales and good choice of wines by the glass, friendly young staff, rambling bar with unusual inglenook, restaurant extension; children and (in some parts) dogs welcome, good-sized garden with polytunnel growing own produce, pleasant spot facing green, handy for Chess Valley walks, open all day. *(Audrey and Paul Summers)*

SARRATT   TQ0498

Cock (01923) 282908

Church End: a very pretty approach is via North Hill, a lane N off A404, just under a mile W of A405; WD3 6HH Comfortably traditional 17th-c pub; latched back door opening directly into homely tiled snug with cluster of bar stools, vaulted ceiling and original bread oven, archway through to partly oak-panelled lounge with lovely inglenook log fire, red plush chairs at oak tables, lots of interesting artefacts and several namesake pictures of cockerels, Badger ales and decent choice of enjoyable food (not Sun evening) including OAP deal, carpeted restaurant in converted barn; background and live music, free wi-fi; children and dogs (in bar) welcome, picnic-sets out at front looking over quiet lane towards churchyard, more on sheltered lawn and terrace with open country views, play area, open all day. *(Melanie and David Lawson)*

ST ALBANS   TL1406

Fighting Cocks (01727) 869152 ·

Abbey Mill Lane; through abbey gateway – you can drive down; AL3 4HE Ancient octagonal building by River Ver; enjoyable pubby food (not Sun evening) cooked by landlord-chef, decent wines and up to nine well kept ales, friendly service (may be a wait at busy times), sunken Stuart cockfighting pit (now a dining area), low heavy beams, panelling and copper-canopied inglenook; some live music, darts and board games; children and dogs welcome, attractive public park beyond garden, open all day. *(Tony Scott)*

ST ALBANS   TL1406

Garibaldi (01727) 894745

Albert Street; left turn down Holywell Hill past White Hart – car park left at end; AL1 1RT Civilised little Victorian backstreet local with well kept Fullers/Gales beers and a guest, good wines by the glass and popular Sun roasts (no other food), friendly staff; live music, sports TV, free wi-fi; children and dogs welcome, picnic-sets on enclosed terrace, lots of window boxes and flowering tubs, open all day (from 2.30pm Mon, 1pm Tues-Thurs, noon Fri-Sun). *(Simon King)*

ST ALBANS   TL1506

Great Northern (01727) 730867

London Road; AL1 1PQ Welcoming nicely updated roadside pub; good attractively presented food from sensibly short regularly changing menus including early evening set deal (useful for next-door cinema), four well kept beers including Black Sheep, good selection of wines and gins, efficient friendly service; terrace tables, open all day Fri-Sun, closed lunchtimes other days, no food Sun evening, Mon. *(Tom Savory)*

ST ALBANS   TL1507

Mermaid (01727) 845700

Hatfield Road; AL1 3RL Bay-windowed pub with several seating areas (including window seats) arranged around central servery, six well kept ales, 15 ciders/perries and good selection of bottled beers, friendly knowledgeable staff, small menu serving Pieminister pies and some other food; background and live music, sports TV, darts; beer garden behind, open all day. *(Tony Scott)*

ST ALBANS   TL1307

Six Bells (01727) 856945

St Michaels Street; AL3 4SH Rambling old pub with half a dozen well kept beers including Oakham, Timothy Taylors and Tring, reasonably priced home-made pubby food (not Sun evening) from lunchtime sandwiches up, cheerful helpful staff, low beams and timbers, log fire, quieter panelled dining room; some live music; children and dogs welcome, small back garden, handy for Verulamium Museum, open all day. *(Tony Scott)*

ST ALBANS   TL1407

Verulam Arms (01727) 836004

Lower Dagnall Street; AL3 4QE Quirky pub run by team of hunters and gatherers – they use wild game, fruit and fungi for their interesting food, brew their own beer and make liqueurs using foraged ingredients (you can buy tickets to join them on their foraging walks); simple furnishings include scrubbed tables and old dining chairs on bare boards, fireplaces with big gilt-edged mirrors above, a few prints on sage green paintwork, large blackboards listing daily specials; well behaved children and dogs welcome, gravelled garden with brightly painted picnic-sets and a heated awning clad in hops and grapes, open all day, till 9pm Sun. *(Kevin Chesson, Gary and Marie Miller, Gail and Arthur Roberts, Simon King)*

Post Office address codings confusingly give the impression that some pubs are in Hertfordshire, when they're really in Bedfordshire, Buckinghamshire or Cambridgeshire (which is where we list them).

ST ALBANS   TL1406
White Hart Tap (01727) 860974
Keyfield, round corner from Garibaldi;
AL1 1QJ Friendly 19th-c corner local with
seven well kept ales (maybe one from on-site
microbrewery), decent choice of wines by the
glass and reasonably priced home-made food
(all day Sat and Sun); Weds quiz; children
and dogs welcome, picnic-sets outside, open
all day. *(Ian Duncan)*

THERFIELD   TL3337
Fox & Duck (01763) 287246
Signed off A10 S of Royston; The Green;
SG8 9PN Open-plan 19th-c bay-windowed
pub in peaceful village setting with picnic-
sets on small front green; good food (not Sun
evening) from pub favourites up, Greene King
and a couple of guests, friendly helpful staff,
country chairs and sturdy stripped-top tables
on stone flooring, smaller bare boarded area
on left with darts, carpeted back restaurant;
children and dogs welcome, garden behind
with gate to park (play equipment), pleasant
walks nearby, open all day weekends,
closed Mon. *(Audrey and Peter Summers)*

TRING   SP9211
Kings Arms (01442) 823318
King Street; by junction with Queen
Street (which is off B4635 Western
Road – continuation of High Street);
HP23 6BE Cheerful backstreet pub built
in the 1830s; five well kept ales including
Tring, real cider and decent choice of malt
whiskies and gins, good value food (not Sun
evening) from pub favourites up including
daily specials, special diets catered for, stools
around cast-iron tables, cushioned pews,
some pine panelling and two warm coal
fires (unusually below windows), separate
courtyard restaurant (Fri-Sun); darts, free
wi-fi; children till 8.30pm, no dogs inside,
open all day weekends from 10am for
breakfast. *(Paul Farraday)*

TRING   SP9211
Robin Hood (01442) 824912
Brook Street (B486); HP23 5ED
Welcoming traditional local with four Fullers/
Gales beers and a couple of guests kept well,
good value pubby food (all day Sat), pop-up
thai restaurant June evening, friendly service,
several well cared-for smallish linked areas,
main bar with banquettes and traditional
tables and chairs on bare boards or carpet,
conservatory with woodburner; background
music, Weds quiz, free wi-fi; children
welcome, dogs in bar, small back terrace,
public car park nearby, open all day.
(Alison and Michael Harper)

WESTMILL   TL3626
Sword Inn Hand (01763) 271356
Village signed off A10 S of Buntingford;
SG9 9LQ Beamed 14th-c colour-washed
pub in pretty village next to church; good

food in bar and pitched-ceiling dining room
from snacks to evening specials, cheerful
attentive service, Greene King IPA and a
guest from brick-faced counter, pine tables
on bare boards or tiles, log fires; children
and dogs (in one part of bar) welcome, attractive
outside seating area, four comfortable
bedrooms in outbuilding, open all day Fri,
Sat, closed Sun evening. *(Sandra Morgan)*

WHEATHAMPSTEAD   TL1716
Cross Keys (01582) 832165
Off B651 at Gustard Wood 1.5 miles
N; AL4 8LA Friendly 17th-c brick pub
attractively placed in rolling wooded
countryside; enjoyable reasonably priced
pubby food (not Sun-Tues evenings) in bar
and beamed restaurant including good
Sun roasts, four well kept ales such as
Adnams and Greene King, inglenook log
fire; quiz second Mon of month; children,
walkers and dogs welcome, picnic-sets
in large garden with play area, three
bedrooms, open all day weekends.
(John and Claire Master)

WIGGINTON   SP9310
Greyhound (01442) 824631
Just S of Tring; HP23 6EH Friendly
village pub with good well presented food
from varied menu including daily specials,
four real ales and decent choice of wines,
warm efficient service, woodburner in
bare-boards bar, polished tables and leather
chairs in connecting carpeted dining rooms;
children and dogs welcome, back garden
with fenced play area, handy for Ridgeway
walks, three bedrooms, open (and food) all
day apart from Sun when kitchen closes at
5pm. *(Peter and Jan Humphreys, Malcolm and*
Sue Scott, Mrs P Sumner)

WILDHILL   TL2606
Woodman (01707) 642618
Off B158 Brookmans Park–Essendon;
AL9 6EA Simple tucked-away country local
with friendly staff and regulars, two well
kept Greene King ales and four guests, real
cider, open-plan bar with log fire, two smaller
back rooms (one with TV), straightforward
weekday bar lunches (not Sun); darts, free
wi-fi; children and dogs welcome, plenty of
seating in big garden. *(Eric Barnes)*

WILLIAN   TL2230
Fox (01462) 480233
A1(M) junction 9; A6141 W towards
Letchworth then first left; SG6 2AE
Contemporary dining pub with pale wood
tables and chairs on stripped boards or big
ceramic tiles, paintings by local artists, good
inventive food along with more traditional
choices including sandwiches, Adnams,
Fullers and three guests, good wine list
(14 by the glass), attentive friendly young
staff; background music, summer beer
festival, TV; children and dogs (in bar)
welcome, side terrace with smart tables

under parasols, picnic-sets in good-sized back garden below handsome 14th-c church tower, eight bedrooms, open all day. *(John Gibbon)*

WILSTONE   SP9014
Half Moon (01442) 826410
Tring Road, off B489; HP23 4PD Popular old village pub, clean and comfortable, with good value pubby food from sandwiches/panini up (best to book), well kept ales such as Malt, Sharps and Tring, friendly efficient staff, big log fire, low beams, old local pictures and lots of brasses; may be background radio, games including Scrabble, dominoes and darts, free wi-fi; children and dogs welcome, some seats out in front and in good-sized back garden, handy for Grand Union Canal walks, open all day, no evening food Sun or Mon. *(Roy Hoing)*

WINKWELL   TL0206
Three Horseshoes (01442) 862585
Just off A4251 Hemel–Berkhamsted; Pouchers End Lane, just over canal swing bridge; HP1 2RZ 16th-c pub worth knowing for its charming setting by unusual swing bridge over Grand Union Canal; low-beamed three-room core with inglenooks, traditional furniture including settles, a few sofas, ales such as Bombardier and Courage Directors, good selection of wines by the glass, food from british tapas to burgers (they may ask to keep a credit card while you eat), bay-windowed extension overlooking canal; background music, comedy and quiz nights; children welcome, picnic-sets out by the water, open (and food) all day. *(Peter and Emma Kelly)*

Isle of Wight

 BEMBRIDGE   SZ6487 Map 2

Spinnaker 🛏

(01983) 873572 – www.thespinnakeriow.co.uk

Steyne Road; PO35 5UH

**Bustling refurbished inn with plenty of dining and drinking space,
a friendly atmosphere and local ales; bedrooms**

This attractively refurbished Edwardian inn has various bars, lounges
and dining rooms all interconnected by open doorways – yet with each
one retaining its individuality. There's an interesting mix of upholstered
dining chairs and tables on wooden floors, armchairs and sofas in
front of log fires and a woodburner, some bold paintwork and plenty
of photographs and nautical memorabilia. Goddards Fuggle-Dee-Dum,
Marstons EPA and St Austell Tribute on handpump, several wines by the
glass and a growing gin collection. Bedrooms are comfortable and the
breakfasts are well regarded. This is sister pub to the island's Boathouse
in Seaview, Fishbourne Inn in Fishbourne and New Inn in Shalfleet – all
belong to the Inns of Distinction group.

🍴 Using local produce, the good choice of food includes sandwiches (until 6pm),
garlic-studded camembert with caramelised red onion marmalade, whitebait with
citrus crème fraîche, spiced butternut squash and beetroot salad with a soft boiled egg,
garlic croutons and red pepper balsamic dressing, beer-battered fish of the day, breaded
chicken breast with garlic and chorizo butter and potato salsa, salmon wellington with
lemon and dill cream, and puddings. *Benchmark main dish: lamb rump with minted
pea purée, potato croquette and rosemary jus £17.25. Two-course evening meal £21.00.*

Free house ~ Licensee Martin Bullock ~ Real ale ~ Open 11-10.30; 11-11 Sat ~ Bar food 12-9
~ Children welcome ~ Dogs allowed in bar ~ Wi-fi ~ Live music Sun afternoon in July/Aug
~ Bedrooms: $114/$134 *Recommended by Nik and Gloria Clarke, Julie Swift, Karl and Frieda
Bujeya, Greta and Gavin Craddock, Shona and Jimmy McDuff*

 FISHBOURNE   SZ5592 Map 2

Fishbourne Inn 🛏

(01983) 882823 – www.thefishbourne.co.uk

*From Portsmouth car ferry turn left into Fishbourne Lane (no-through road);
PO33 4EU*

**Attractively furnished pub with a contemporary feel, real ales,
plenty of wines by the glass and all-day food; bedrooms**

Offering some sort of food all day, this attractive half-timbered pub is also handy for the Wightlink ferry terminal. The open-plan bar has tartan-upholstered built-in wall seats and wooden chairs on slate flooring, a woodburning stove with a huge mirror above it and stools against the counter where friendly staff serve Fullers Seafarer, Timothy Taylors Landlord and a guest from Goddards on handpump and a dozen wines by the glass; leading off here is a comfortable, beamed lounge area with leather sofas, large pouffes, a couple of button-back armchairs and a flatscreen TV. There's also a bare-boards room with several clocks and a smart, airy dining room with high-backed black leather chairs around all sorts of tables, chandeliers and house plants. The outside seating areas have picnic-sets and contemporary tables and chairs. Bedrooms are comfortable and breakfasts are good. Disabled access but no loo. The inn is handy for the Wightlink ferry terminal. This is sister pub to the Boathouse in Seaview, Spinnaker at Bembridge and New Inn at Shalfleet.

Pleasing food includes sandwiches (until 6pm), local crab, fennel and orange salad with citrus dressing, pulled pork croquettes with celeriac purée and apple sauce, wild mushroom and spinach linguine with creamy pesto sauce and parmesan, trio of local sausages with wholegrain mustard and chive mash and gravy, sea bass fillet with mediterranean-style vegetables, parmentier potatoes and chorizo, duck breast with a port glaze and dauphinoise potatoes, and puddings such as lemon tart with fruit coulis and raspberry sorbet and white chocolate crème brûlée. *Benchmark main dish: crisp cod loin with local crab risotto £13.50. Two-course evening meal £20.00.*

Inns of Distinction ~ Lease Martin Bullock ~ Real ale ~ Open 10am-11pm; 10am-10.30pm Sun ~ Bar food 11-9.30 ~ Restaurant ~ Children welcome ~ Dogs allowed in bar ~ Wi-fi ~ Live music Sun afternoon July/Aug ~ Bedrooms: /$134 *Recommended by Sally and Brian Turner, Lenny and Ruth Walters, Claire Adams, Paddy and Sian O'Leary, Bob and Melissa Wyatt*

GODSHILL   SZ5281   Map 2

Taverners ⭐ ♀ 🍺

(01983) 840707 – www.thetavernersgodshill.co.uk
High Street (A3020); PO38 3HZ

Isle of Wight Dining Pub of the Year

Well run, friendly country pub with local ales, food cooked by the landlord, a relaxed atmosphere and seats in garden

Bigger than it looks from outside, this cheerful 17th-c whitewashed pub has plenty of room for drinking and dining. The little bar has an open fire, a couple of button-back leather armchairs, plush stools around a few tables and high chairs against the brick counter where friendly staff serve ales from Goddards, Sharps and a beer named for the pub from Yates on handpump, ten wines by the glass and interesting home-made liqueurs. The dining areas have a two-way open fire as well as a woodburning stove, chapel, mate's and wheelback chairs around scrubbed country kitchen tables on flagstones, bare boards and nice old bricks. Mirrors and old local photographs hang on walls and wine decanters and horsebrasses sit on mantelpieces. The garden has seats and tables on a terrace and on grass, there's a children's play area and vegetable patches. A shop sells home-made and local produce. The pub is handy for the Model Village.

Good food using home-grown and other local produce and cooked by the landlord includes baps, potted shrimps on toast, chicken liver pâté with onion marmalade, triple-cheese macaroni with cherry tomatoes and garlic bread, shredded ham hock salad with new potatoes, egg and creamy mustard dressing, 10oz 21-day aged rump steak with béarnaise sauce and chips, local black bream fillet with lemon, caper and tomato butter, new potatoes and spinach, salt-roasted pork with faggot and celeriac purée, and puddings such as pear and almond tart and sticky toffee and date pudding. *Benchmark main dish: beer-battered fish and chips £13.25. Two-course evening meal £20.00.*

Free house ~ Licensee Roger Sergent ~ Real ale ~ Open 11-11; 11-5 Sun ~ Bar food 12-2.45, 6-8.45 (9.15 Fri, Sat); no food Sun evening ~ Restaurant ~ Children welcome ~ Dogs allowed in bar *Recommended by Steve Whalley, Martine and Lawrence Sanders, Paul Faraday, Charlie May, Colin and Daniel Gibbs*

SEAVIEW
Boathouse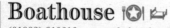

SZ5992 Map 2

(01983) 810616 – www.theboathouseiow.co.uk
On B3330 Ryde–Seaview; PO34 5AW

Contemporary décor in well run pub with real ales, quite a choice of food, a friendly welcome and seats outside; bedrooms

Picnic-sets and other seats under parasols on the terrace here have fine views of the sea, as the beach is just across the road. Some of the bedrooms also look over the water. It's an extended, blue-painted Victorian pub and the appealing interior has a bar with built-in wall seats, armchairs and leather pouffes, a large model yacht on the mantelpiece above a woodburning stove with a huge neat stack of logs beside it, and Ringwood Fortyniner, Sharps Doom Bar and a guest from Goddards on handpump, several gins and 11 wines by the glass; background music. The dining rooms have elegant wooden and high-backed black leather dining chairs, portraits on pale blue walls and an ornate mirror over an open fire; one of these rooms has a dinghy (complete with oars) leaning against the wall. Throughout, the paintwork is light and fresh and there's a mix of polished bare boards, flagstones and carpet. This is sister pub to the Fishbourne Inn at Fishbourne, Swan at Beambridge and New Inn at Shalfleet.

 Well regarded food includes sandwiches (until 6pm), garlic, herb and lemon prawns, parma ham-wrapped asparagus with hollandaise sauce topped with a poached egg, halloumi and root vegetable tart with spiced quinoa and roast chickpea salad, honey and dijon mustard glazed ham with a fried duck egg and cider apple jelly, scampi and chips, lamb loin with artichoke purée, potato and aubergine terrine with a port reduction, halibut with a nut crust, cauliflower champ and cockle sauce, and puddings such as crème brûlée with berries and strawberry shortbread cheesecake. *Benchmark main dish: crab ravioli with smoked salmon mousse and crab bisque £14.25. Two-course evening meal £19.00.*

Inns of Distinction ~ Lease Martin Bullock ~ Real ale ~ Open 10am-11pm; 10am-10.30pm Sun ~ Bar food 12-2.30, 6-9 (9.30 Fri, Sat) ~ Restaurant ~ Children welcome ~ Dogs allowed in bar ~ Wi-fi ~ Live music Sun afternoon July/Aug ~ Bedrooms: £114/£134
Recommended by Dave Chapman, Sandra and Michael Smith, Monty Green, Jill and Dick Archer, Barbara Brown, Mike Benton

SHALFLEET
New Inn

SZ4089 Map 2

(01983) 531314 – www.thenew-inn.co.uk
A3054 Newport–Yarmouth; PO30 4NS

Bustling pub with cheerful bar, local ales and popular food

This is an 18th-c former fishermen's haunt near the quay and still popular with visiting sailors. The rambling rooms have plenty of character with log fires, boarded ceilings and scrubbed pine tables on flagstone or carpeted floors. Friendly staff keep a beer named for the pub (from Goddards), Hook

Norton Old Hooky and a guest ale on handpump, a growing gin collection and several wines by the glass; background music. The pub has recently joined the Inns of Distinction group.

🍴 Well liked food includes lunchtime sandwiches, potted shrimp crumpet with gherkins and parsley, pea and broad bean scotch egg, butternut squash, bean and red pepper ragoût with pasta, garlic and rosemary-marinated chicken and chorizo risotto with spinach and mushrooms, local beer-battered fish of the day, 12-hour braised lamb shoulder, shepherd's pie, local rump steak with trimmings and chips, and puddings such as cheesecake of the day and peaches poached in Grand Marnier syrup with chantilly cream. *Benchmark main dish: seafood sharing platter for two £60.00. Two-course evening meal £21.00.*

Inns of Distinction ~ Licensee Martin Bullock ~ Real ale ~ Open 12-10.30; 11-11 Sat; 11-10.30 Sun ~ Bar food 12-2.30, 6-9 (9.30 Fri, Sat) ~ Children welcome ~ Dogs allowed in bar ~ Wi-fi *Recommended by Mike and Sarah Abbot, Patricia and Gordon Thompson, Barry and Daphne Gregson, Caroline and Peter Bryant, Nik and Gloria Clarke*

Also Worth a Visit on the Isle of Wight

Besides the fully inspected pubs, you might like to try these pubs that have been recommended to us and described by readers. Do tell us what you think of them: feedback@goodguides.com

ARRETON   SZ5386
White Lion (01983) 528479
A3056 Newport–Sandown; PO30 3AA
White-painted roadside pub (former coaching inn); beamed bar with stripped-wood floor and comfortable seats by log fire, Sharps Doom Bar, Timothy Taylors Landlord and a guest, several wines by the glass, good choice of well liked food, friendly attentive staff, restaurant; children, walkers and dogs welcome, pleasant terrace with view up to ancient church, nice walks, open all day. *(Gary Newley)*

BEMBRIDGE   SZ6488
Pilot Boat (01983) 872077
Station Road/Kings Road; PO35 5NN
Harbourside pub shaped like a boat – even has portholes; good food from sandwiches to local seafood, well kept Goddards and guests, friendly staff, restaurant area with woodburner and local artwork for sale; sports TV, darts; children and dogs welcome, disabled access, tables out overlooking the water or in two pleasant courtyards behind, well placed for coast walks, five redecorated bedrooms (overnight cycle storage), open all day. *(William Pace)*

BONCHURCH   SZ5778
★Bonchurch Inn (01983) 852611
Bonchurch Shute; from A3055 E of Ventnor turn down to Old Bonchurch; opposite Leconfield Hotel; PO38 1NU
Quirky former stables with restaurant run by welcoming italian family (here since 1984); congenial bar with narrow-planked ship's decking and old-fashioned steamer-style seats, a couple of ales such as Bombardier

tapped from the cask, decent wine list, popular bar food and good italian dishes, charming helpful service; background music, darts, shove-ha'penny and other games; children and dogs welcome, delightful continental-feel courtyard (parking here can be tricky), holiday flat. *(Steph Manton)*

CARISBROOKE   SZ4687
★Blacksmiths (01983) 529263
B3401 1.5 miles W; PO30 5SS Hillside pub under same owners as the Pointer at Newchurch; airy bare-boards dining extension with superb Solent views, popular food from sandwiches and pub favourites up (all day Sat, till 6pm Sun), scrubbed tables in neat beamed and flagstoned front bar serving Yates, a couple of guests and good choice of wines by the glass; children, dogs and walkers welcome (Tennyson Trail nearby), more views from terrace and garden down steps, play equipment, open all day. *(Jack and Hilary Burton)*

COWES   SZ4995
Duke of York (01983) 295171
Mill Hill Road; PO31 7BT Welcoming inn usefully situated near the high street and ferry; well kept ales such as Sharps and Yates, real cider and good choice of popular generously served pub food, lots of nautical bits and pieces; free wi-fi; children and dogs welcome, bedrooms, open all day. *(Gary Newley)*

COWES   SZ4996
Globe (01983) 506053
The Parade; PO31 7QJ Modernised bar-restaurant worth knowing for its waterfront location, great Solent views from balcony and

roof terrace with own bar; Goddards Island
Pride, Ringwood Fortyniner and a guest from
well stocked downstairs bar with big-screen
sports TV and pool, popular smokehouse
menu, also weekend brunch and Sun carvery,
efficient friendly service, upstairs dining
room; children welcome (not on roof terrace),
open all day, food all day weekends.
(Richard Tilbrook, Dr and Mrs J D Abell)

COWES   SZ5094
Lifeboat (01983) 292711
*Britannia Way, East Cowes Marina;
PO32 6UB* Modern bar-restaurant at the
heart of the marina with great views from
waterside terrace; popular good value food
including daily specials, ales such as Fullers
and Goddards, decent wine list, friendly
efficient staff; sports TV; children and dogs
welcome, open (and food) all day.
(Richard Tilbrook)

CULVER DOWN   SZ6385
Culver Haven (01983) 406107
*Seaward end, near Yarborough
Monument; PO36 8QT* Superb Channel
views from this isolated clifftop pub, clean
and modern, with popular fairly priced home-
made food, well kept changing ales such as
Goddards, Timothy Taylors and Wadworths,
several wines by the glass and decent coffee,
friendly service, big restaurant; children and
dogs welcome, small terrace, good walks.
(Dave Chapman)

FRESHWATER   SZ3487
★ Red Lion (01983) 754925
*Church Place; from A3055 at E end
of village by Freshwater Garage mini
roundabout follow Yarmouth signpost,
then take first real right turn signed to
Parish Church; PO40 9BP* Bay-windowed
red-brick pub on quiet village street; well
kept St Austell Proper Job, three guest beers
and several wines by the glass, popular
well priced food from changing blackboard
menu (booking advised), efficient friendly
young staff, open-plan bar with country-style
furnishings on flagstones or bare boards,
woodburner; well behaved children and dogs
welcome, a couple of picnic-sets out at front
with view of church, more tables in back
garden, good walking on nearby Freshwater
Way, open all day. *(Gary Newley)*

GURNARD   SZ4796
Woodvale (01983) 292037
Princes Esplanade; PO31 8LE Large 1930s
inn with splendid picture-window views of
the Solent (great sunsets); good choice of
food from sandwiches and baguettes to daily
specials, Fullers London Pride, Ringwood
Fortyniner and a couple of guests, plenty of
wines by the glass, friendly staff; weekend live
music, Mon quiz; children and dogs welcome,
garden with terrace and summer barbecues,
five bedrooms, open all day, food all day
weekends. *(Nicola and Holly Lyons)*

HAVENSTREET   SZ5590
White Hart (01983) 883485
*Off A3054 Newport–Ryde; Main Road;
PO33 4DP* Old brick and stone village pub
with good choice of popular food (special
diets catered for) from sandwiches up,
Ringwood and Goddards ales, friendly
efficient service, cosy log-fire bar and
carpeted dining area; children and dogs
welcome, tables in secluded garden
behind, open all day, food all day Sun.
(Jack and Hilary Burton)

HULVERSTONE   SZ3984
★ Sun (01983) 741124
B3399; PO30 4EH Lovely sea views
from this pretty thatched pub; low-
ceilinged bar with character furniture
(including a fine old settle) on flagstones
or bare boards, brick and stone walls,
horsebrasses and ironwork around
woodburner, ales such as Courage,
Hancocks and Sharps, ten wines by
the glass, and enjoyable pubby food,
traditionally furnished dining room with
big windows taking in the view; weekly live
music; children and dogs welcome, picnic-
sets in split-level cottagey garden, open
(and food) all day. *(Tony and Jill Radnor)*

NEWCHURCH   SZ5685
★ Pointer (01983) 865202
High Street; PO36 0NN Well run
old two-room pub by Norman church;
generous helpings of good fairly priced
local food including blackboard specials
(booking advised in season), well kept
Fullers ales and a guest, friendly attentive
service; children and dogs welcome, views
from pleasant back garden, boules, open
(and food) all day. *(S Holder)*

NEWPORT   SZ5089
Bargemans Rest (01983) 525828
Little London; PO30 5BS Quayside
pub with spreading bare-boards interior
packed with nautical memorabilia; good
choice of generous reasonably priced pubby
food including vegetarian and gluten-free
options, Goddards, Ringwood and four guests;
frequent live music, free wi-fi; children (away
from bar) and dogs welcome, part-covered
terrace overlooking River Medina, handy for
Quay Arts Centre, open (and food) all day.
(William Pace)

NEWPORT   SZ4989
Newport Ale House 07708 018051
Holyrood Street; PO30 5AZ Steps up to
intimate one-room pub with friendly chatty
atmosphere; stools and leatherette bucket
chairs on bare boards, half-panelling and
some striking wallpaper, five well kept
changing ales tapped from the cask by
knowledgeable landlord, pies, rolls and
sandwiches; regular live music, darts; dogs
welcome, open all day. *(William Pace)*

NINGWOOD   SZ3989
★**Horse & Groom** (01983) 760672
A3054 Newport-Yarmouth, a mile
W of Shalfleet; PO30 4NW Roomy carefully
extended pub liked by families; comfortable
leather sofas grouped around low tables on
flagstones, sturdy tables and chairs well
spaced for relaxed dining, winter log fire,
Ringwood Best, a couple of guest beers and
a dozen wines by the glass, good freshly
made food (smaller appetites catered for),
friendly welcoming staff; background music,
games machine, board games, free wi-fi; dogs
allowed in bar, garden with well equipped
play area including bouncy castle and crazy
golf, nearby walks, open all day from 9am
for breakfast. *(Penny and Peter Keevil)*

NITON   SZ5075
★**Buddle** (01983) 730243
St Catherine's Road, Undercliff;
off A3055 just S of village, towards
St Catherine's Point; PO38 2NE 16th-c
former smugglers' haunt with character
traditional bar rooms; heavy black beams,
captain's chairs, wheelbacks and cushioned
wall seats around solid wooden tables, big
flagstones or carpeted floors, open fire in
a broad stone fireplace with a huge black
oak mantelbeam, a beer named for the
pub plus Fullers London Pride, Goddards
Fuggle-Dee-Dum and Sharps Atlantic,
11 wines by the glass and a couple of farm
ciders, enjoyable food including good fresh
fish; background music, free wi-fi; children
and dogs welcome, picnic-sets on two stone
terraces and in neatly kept sloping garden
looking down to the sea, coast path nearby,
open (and food) all day. *(Dave Chapman,
Selwyn Jones, Sheila Topham)*

NORTHWOOD   SZ4983
Travellers Joy (01983) 298024
Off B3325 S of Cowes; PO31 8LS
Friendly pub with simple contemporary
interior; several well kept ales and enjoyable
reasonably priced food from sandwiches
and pubby choices to daily specials, long bar
with log fire, dining conservatory, pool room;
Sun quiz and some live music; children,
walkers and dogs welcome, garden with
pétanque and play area, open all day.
(Glen and Patricia Fuller)

SANDOWN   SZ5984
Castle (01983) 403169
Fitzroy Street; PO36 8HY Friendly red-
brick local serving six well kept beers such
as Goddards, Shepherd Neame, Wadworths
and Wychwood, carpeted interior with log
fire and bric-a-brac (notable Halloween
decorations); Sun quiz, darts, TV and fruit

machine; children and dogs (theirs is Max)
welcome, colourful back terrace, open
all day. *(Andrew Bosi)*

SEAVIEW   SZ6291
Seaview Hotel (01983) 612711
High Street; off B3330 Ryde–Bembridge;
PO34 5EX Small civilised but relaxed
Victorian hotel; traditional wood furnishings,
seafaring paraphernalia and log fire in pubby
bare-boards bar, comfortable more refined
front bar (like a naval wardroom), three well
kept ales including Goddards, eight wines by
the glass from good list and well executed
pub food, also first class upscale set menu
in separate restaurant, pleasant helpful
staff; background music; children welcome,
dogs in bar, sea glimpses from tables on tiny
front terrace, 13 bedrooms (seven in modern
back annexe), self-catering cottage, good
breakfast, open all day. *(Steph Manton)*

SHANKLIN   SZ5881
★**Fishermans Cottage** (01983) 863882
Bottom of Shanklin Chine; PO37 6BN
Early 19th-c thatched cottage in terrific
setting tucked into the cliffs on Appley
beach, steep zigzag walk down beautiful
chine; two cosy little rooms with low beams,
flagstones and stripped-stone walls, old local
pictures, fireplace with two-tier mantelpiece,
Fullers London Pride and a couple of Island
beers, good value pub food including plenty
of fish, friendly staff; background and some
live music; children and dogs welcome, sun-
soaked terrace overlooking sea, lovely walk
to Luccombe, open all day in summer, but
may shut early in bad weather, also closed
much of winter (best to check times).
(Dave Chapman)

SHANKLIN   SZ5881
Steamer (01983) 862641
Esplanade; PO37 6BS Busy nautically
themed beachfront bar (fun for holiday
families); good choice of enjoyable well
priced food from snacks to daily specials,
ales such as Goddards, Ringwood and Yates,
friendly hard-working staff, mix of seating
including cushioned pews and leather sofas
on quarry tiles; live music most weekends;
fine sea views from part-covered two-tier
terrace, eight bedrooms, open all day.
(Dave Chapman)

ST HELENS   SZ6289
Vine (01983) 872337
Upper Green Road; PO33 1UJ Victorian
red-brick local overlooking large village
green; enjoyable home-cooked food (all day
Sat, Sun) including stone-baked pizzas, well
kept Sharps and guests, cheerful helpful
staff; weekend live music, Weds quiz, pool

We mention bottled beers and spirits only if there is something unusual about them
– imported belgian real ales, say, or dozens of malt whiskies; so do please let us know
about them in your reports.

and darts, free wi-fi; children and dogs welcome, some seats out in front, play area across road, open all day. *(William Pace)*

VENTNOR SZ5677

Perks (01983) 857446

High Street; PO38 1LT Popular little bar packed with interesting memorabilia behind shop-window front; well kept ales including Bass and good range of wines, enjoyable well priced home-made lunchtime food from sandwiches and baked potatoes up, bargain OAP two-course lunch (evening food Fri and Sat only), fast friendly service; dogs welcome, open all day. *(Glen and Patricia Fuller)*

VENTNOR SZ5677

★Spyglass (01983) 855338

Esplanade, SW end; road down is very steep and twisty, and parking nearby can be difficult – best to use pay-and-display (free in winter) about 100 metres up the road; PO38 1JX Perched above the beach with fascinating jumble of seafaring memorabilia in snug quarry-tiled interior; Ringwood ales and guests, good choice of wines and popular food including fish/seafood dishes (good crab sandwiches), friendly helpful service; background music, live daily in summer; children welcome, dogs and muddy boots in bar, sea-wall terrace with lovely views, coast walk towards the Botanic Garden, heftier hikes on to St Boniface Down and towards the eerie shell of Appuldurcombe House, four sea-view bedrooms, open (and food) all day. *(Dave Chapman)*

VENTNOR SZ5677

Volunteer (01983) 852537

Victoria Street; PO38 1ES Welcoming one-room local under same management as nearby Perks; five well kept changing ales (always one from an Isle of Wight brewery)

and a real cider, renovated interior with bare boards and carpet, upholstered pews, farmhouse chairs and cast-iron-framed tables, some military and Ventnor brewery memorabilia, Victorian tiled fireplace (electric fire); simple home-made food including sandwiches; background music, darts and the local game of rings; dogs welcome, no children, open all day. *(Kevin Upton)*

WHITWELL SZ5277

White Horse (01983) 730375

High Street; PO38 2PY Extended 15th-c pub with popular good value food from pub staples to daily specials (booking advised), four well kept changing ales, good friendly service, carpeted beamed bar with exposed stonework, restaurant; Mon quiz, pool, darts and traditional rings game; children and dogs welcome, picnic-sets among fruit trees in big garden with play area, open all day, food all day weekends. *(Glen and Patricia Fuller)*

YARMOUTH SZ3589

Bugle (01983) 760272

The Square; PO41 0NS Old coaching house with long frontage and several linked rooms; chesterfields by open fire in low-ceilinged panelled lounge, farmhouse-style furniture in dining areas, books on shelves (and book wallpaper), restaurant with high-backed leather chairs around mix of tables on bare boards or carpet, generous helpings of enjoyable pub food including daily fresh fish, quick cheerful service, traditionally furnished bar with five real ales such as Courage and Sharps, Thatcher's cider, conservatory; background music; children and dogs welcome, picnic-sets and lots of hanging baskets in large courtyard garden, seven bedrooms, handy for ferry, open (and some food) all day. *(Sheila Topham)*

Kent

BIDDENDEN
TQ8238 Map 3

Three Chimneys 🍽️ 🍷 🛏️

(01580) 291472 – www.thethreechimneys.co.uk

Off A262 at pub sign, a mile W of village; TN27 8LW

Pubby beamed rooms of considerable individuality, log fires, imaginative food and big, pretty garden; well appointed bedrooms

If you're visiting the gardens at nearby Sissinghurst (National Trust), come to this lovely old inn for lunch. The small, low-beamed bar and dining rooms are civilised but informal with plenty of character. They're simply done out with plain wooden furniture and old settles on flagstones and coir matting, some harness and sporting prints on the stripped-brick walls and good log fires. Adnams Southwold, Harveys Best and a changing weekly guest beer tapped from the cask, 14 wines plus sparkling wine and champagne by the glass from a good list, local Biddenden's cider and nine malt whiskies; background music in the restaurant and cards. A candlelit bare-boards restaurant has rustic décor and french windows that open into an extended conservatory looking over seats in the pretty garden, where raised beds contain herbs and other produce for the kitchen. At the front of the building is an enclosed open-air dining courtyard. Five comfortable bedrooms each have their own terrace and there's also a holiday cottage available for rent.

🍽️ Highly thought-of food includes salmon and smoked haddock fishcakes with tartare sauce, pigeon breast with celeriac purée and blackberries, moroccan-style couscous with spiced aubergine, courgette and tomato ragoût with grilled halloumi, pork and sage sausages with creamed potatoes and port and red onion gravy, duck breast with parmentier potatoes and onion and thyme purée, salmon fillet on roasted sweet potatoes with spiced pumpkin purée and pomegranate, slow-braised ox cheeks in red wine with savoy cabbage and pancetta, and puddings such as dark chocolate délice on praline base with pistachio ice-cream and vanilla pannacotta with raspberry coulis. *Benchmark main dish: rack of lamb with dauphinoise potatoes and rich jus £19.95. Two-course evening meal £27.50.*

Free house ~ Licensee Craig Smith ~ Real ale ~ Open 11.30-11 ~ Bar food 12-9 (9.30 Sat) ~ Restaurant ~ Children welcome ~ Dogs allowed in bar ~ Wi-fi ~ Bedrooms: /£140
Recommended by Alan Cowell, Ian Clifton, Martin Day

CHIDDINGSTONE CAUSEWAY TQ5146 Map 3

Little Brown Jug

(01892) 870318 – www.thelittlebrownjug.co.uk

B2027; TN11 8JJ

Bustling pub with interconnected bar and dining rooms, open fires, four real ales and enjoyable food; seats outside

Surrounded by rolling countryside, this pub is pretty busy at peak times, meaning it's sensible to book a table. The beamed front bar has rugs on bare boards or tiled floors, a roaring log fire, leather chesterfield sofas and chunky stools in one corner and high chairs against the carved counter where helpful, efficient staff serve Larkins Traditional and guests from local breweries such as Tonbridge and Westerham on handpump and 22 wines by the glass; background music and board games. Throughout, various dining areas merge together with open doorways and timbering, and there's all manner of cushioned wooden dining chairs, wall seats and settles with scatter cushions around polished dark wood or rustic tables, and more open fires. Also, hundreds of prints, framed old cigarette cards, maps and photos on painted walls, books on shelves, house plants, old stone bottles and candles on windowsills and big mirrors. A terrace has seats and tables, there are picnic-sets on grass and a children's play area; you can hire the 'dining huts' for £25, but you must book in advance.

 A wide choice of food includes jackfruit spring rolls with hoisin and peanut dipping sauce, field mushrooms in parsley and garlic butter, macaroni cheese with garlic bread, home-cooked gammon and free-range eggs, pork and leek sausages with mash and onion gravy, a pie and a roast of the day, moules frites, duck breast with carrot and sweet potato purée, fondant potato and red wine reduction, and puddings such as strawberry and white chocolate mousse and salted caramel tart with clotted cream. *Benchmark main dish: beer-battered fish and chips £11.95. Two-course evening meal £20.00.*

Whiting & Hammond ~ Lease Laura Colvin ~ Real ale ~ Open 10am-11pm; 9am-11pm Sat; 9am-11pm Sun ~ Bar food 12-9.30; 12-9 Sun ~ Restaurant ~ Children welcome ~ Dogs allowed in bar ~ Wi-fi *Recommended by Christian Mole, Neil Allen, Nik and Gloria Clarke, Miles Green, Tony Scott, Gerry and Pam Pollard, Alfie Bayliss*

CHIPSTEAD TQ5056 Map 3

George & Dragon

(01732) 779019 – www.georgeanddragonchipstead.com

Near M25 junction 5; 39 High Street; TN13 2RW

Enjoyable pub with enthusiastic staff, simple furnishings, inventive cooking and seats in the garden

We like this pub and are glad that our readers do too, all commenting on the slightly quirky décor and bustling and easy-going atmosphere. The simply furnished bar has leather armchairs and chesterfields, some plain tables and benches, wide floorboards, a small open fire and high chairs at the counter where they keep Westerham George's Marvellous Medicine and Grasshopper Kentish Bitter plus a changing guest on handpump, 13 wines by the glass, a good choice of spirits and lots of teas and coffees; background music. You can eat at plain wooden tables in a grey panelled area with an open fire or in the smarter knocked-through dining room. This has standing timbers in the middle, a fire at each end and shiny, dark wooden chairs and tables on floorboards; there are standard lamps, stag heads, a reel-to-reel tape recorder, quite a few mirrors and various deli items for sale. Several seating areas outside have good quality tables and chairs under parasols, picnic-sets on decking and deckchairs and more picnic-sets on grass.

 Using home-reared pigs, free-range eggs and other local produce, the rewarding, hearty food includes sandwiches, king prawns in harissa butter, pork, rabbit and pistachio terrine with chutney and pickles, wild garlic and spinach risotto with parmesan, burger with toppings, dijon mustard and tarragon mayonnaise and chips, chicken breast stuffed with sunblush tomato and mozzarella with greens and basil oil, cod fillet with spinach and lemon butter sauce, seared venison haunch with jerusalem artichokes and truffle, and puddings. *Benchmark main dish: steak sandwich £11.50. Two-course evening meal £21.00.*

Free house ~ Licensee Ben James ~ Real ale ~ Open 12-11 (10.30 Sun) ~ Bar food 12-3 (4 Sat), 6-9.30; 12-4, 6-8.30 Sun ~ Restaurant ~ Children welcome ~ Dogs allowed in bar ~ Wi-fi *Recommended by Colin McLachlan, Philip Chesington, Samuel and Melissa Turnbull, Naomi and Andrew Randall, Charlie Stevens*

FORDWICH
George & Dragon 🍷 🍺
TR1759 Map 3

(01227) 710661 – www.brunningandprice.co.uk/georgeanddragon
Off A28 at Sturry; CT2 0BX

15th-c pub with a good choice of drinks, enjoyable food and well trained staff

On the banks of the River Stour in Britain's smallest town stands this handsome old place. There are spreading character rooms, steps up and down, with beams, timbers and open fires and floors ranging from carpet or tiled and flagstoned to polished boards topped with rugs. You'll find an assortment of nice old chairs and tables (one a giant bellows), button-back leather armchairs, plush banquettes and little stools, and the décor includes hundreds of prints and paintings, bookshelves, large mirrors, house plants and tankards. Friendly, helpful staff serve St Austell Brunning & Price Traditional Bitter plus guests such as Canterbury Ales The Millers Ale, Harveys Wild Hop and Westerham Spirit of Kent on handpump, 15 wines by the glass, 34 whiskies and 49 gins. The lawn has plenty of picnic-sets plus their hallmark play tractor. Disabled car park, access and loos. Howletts Wild Animal Park is nearby.

High quality food includes sandwiches, potted crab and crayfish with samphire, caper and cucumber salad, charcuterie sharing board, five-bean and sweet potato chilli with guacamole and lime crème fraîche, honey-roast ham and eggs, steak burger with toppings, coleslaw and chips, chicken breast with thyme, spaghetti vegetables, chorizo croquette and lemon sauce, salmon and smoked haddock fishcake with a poached egg, beef bourguignon with mustard mash, and puddings such as triple chocolate brownie with chocolate sauce and crème brûlée. *Benchmark main dish: braised lamb shoulder with dauphinoise potatoes and red wine jus £17.95. Two-course evening meal £22.00.*

Brunning & Price ~ Manager Diana Larfi ~ Real ale ~ Open 10am-11pm; 10am-10.30pm Sun ~ Bar food 12-9; 12-9.30 Fri, Sat ~ Restaurant ~ Children welcome ~ Dogs allowed in bar ~ Wi-fi *Recommended by Sarah Roberts, Susan Eccleston, Anne Taylor, Patrick and Emma Stephenson*

Real ale may be served from handpumps, electric pumps (not just the on-off switches used for keg beer) or – common in Scotland – tall taps called founts (pronounced 'fonts') where a separate pump pushes the beer up under air pressure.

ICKHAM   TR2258 Map 3

Duke William 🛏

(01227) 721308 – www.thedukewilliamickham.com

Off A257 E of Canterbury; The Street; CT3 1QP

Friendly pub with character rooms, good food and ales and seats in pretty garden; bedrooms

Our readers enjoy their visits to this well run, gently civilised village pub. The spreading bar has huge oak beams and stripped joists, seats that range from country kitchen to cushioned settles with animal skin throws, all manner of tables on stripped wooden floors and a log fire with a low barrel table in front of it. Friendly staff serve McCanns Harry Hop, Old Dairy Gold Top and Romney Modern British on handpump, eight wines by the glass and a good choice of gins and whiskies. The low-ceilinged dining room is similarly furnished and a conservatory looks over the garden and fields beyond. Throughout, paintwork is contemporary, tables are set with fresh flowers and candles in stone bottles and there are interesting paintings, prints and china plates on the walls; background music and board games. Modern seats and tables are set under parasols on the partly covered terrace, with picnic-sets and a children's play area on grass. Bedrooms (named after the owner's culinary heroes) are attractively and simply furnished and breakfasts are generous.

 Food is good and includes smoked chicken terrine with lardons and leek mayonnaise, moules marinière, caramelised cauliflower spelt with cauliflower crisps and truffle, honey and mustard glazed ham with triple-cooked chips, free-range chicken breast with brown butter celeriac and red wine and caper jus, chargrilled pork cutlet with gnocchi and mushroom and tomato ragoût, and puddings such as rhubarb baked alaska and warm banana bread with toffee sauce and clotted cream. *Benchmark main dish: barnsley chop with caponata and green sauce £17.50. Two-course evening meal £22.00.*

Free house ~ Licensee Mark Sargeant ~ Real ale ~ Open 12-11; 11-midnight Sat; 11-10.30 Sun ~ Bar food 12-3, 6-9; 12-3, 6.30-9.30 Sat; 12-5 Sun ~ Restaurant ~ Live music monthly (check website) ~ Dogs allowed in bar ~ Wi-fi ~ Bedrooms: /£120 *Recommended by Gerry and Pam Pollard, Alison and Tony Livesley, Claire Adams, Deborah and Duncan Walliams, Peter and Emma Kelly*

LANGTON GREEN   TQ5439 Map 3

Hare 🍷 🍺

(01892) 862419 – www.brunningandprice.co.uk/hare

A264 W of Tunbridge Wells; TN3 0JA

Edwardian pub with lots to look at, a fine choice of drinks and imaginative food

Enterprising food and a wide range of drinks keep interested customers coming back here on a regular basis. The high-ceilinged rooms are light and airy with rugs on bare boards, built-in wall seats, stools and old-style wooden tables and chairs, dark dados below pale-painted walls covered in old photographs and prints, romantic pastels and a huge collection of chamber-pots hanging from beams; background radio and board games. Cheerfully efficient young staff serve Greene King IPA and Old Speckled Hen plus guests such as Bath Gem and Bedlam Benchmark on handpump, 20 wines by the glass, 59 malt whiskies, 42 gins and a farm cider. French windows open on to a big terrace with pleasant views of the tree-ringed village green. Parking in front of the pub is limited, but you can park in the lane to one side.

Contemporary food includes sandwiches, venison, bacon and thyme faggot with parsnip purée, smoked salmon with spiced avocado purée, shaved fennel and radish, stilton, caramelised red onion and potato pie with redcurrant jus, steak burger with toppings, coleslaw and chips, pork and leek sausages with mash and onion gravy, chicken, ham and leek pie, crispy beef salad with sweet chilli sauce and cashews, smoked haddock, cod, king prawn, mussel and bacon chowder with sweetcorn dumplings, and puddings such as apple and mixed berry crumble with custard and sticky toffee pudding with toffee sauce. *Benchmark main dish: braised lamb shoulder with dauphinoise potatoes and rosemary and red wine gravy £17.95. Two-course evening meal £20.00.*

Brunning & Price ~ Manager Rebecca Bowen ~ Real ale ~ Open 11-11; 11-midnight Fri, Sat; 11-10.30 Sun ~ Bar food 12-9.30; 12-10 Fri, Sat; 12-9 Sun ~ Children welcome ~ Dogs allowed in bar ~ Wi-fi *Recommended by Gerry and Rosemary Dobson, Pauline and Mark Evans, Rob Anderson, Monica and Steph Evans, Emily and Toby Archer, Richard and Penny Gibbs*

MEOPHAM
Cricketers

TQ6364 Map 3

(01474) 812163 – www.thecricketersinn.co.uk
Wrotham Road (A227); DA13 0QA

Popular village pub with friendly staff, plenty to look at, several real ales, good wines and well thought-of food

Opposite the village green, this is a busy pub with a wide mix of customers. Head for the front bar if it's just a drink you want, where you'll find cushioned wall settles, a mix of old-style wooden dining chairs and tables, a raised fireplace, newspapers to read and Caledonian Deuchars IPA and guests such as Bexley Session Golden Ale, Fullers London Pride and Tonbridge Coppernob and Countryman on handpump and around a dozen wines by the glass. Staff are hard-working and helpful. Glass partitioning separates an end room, which has bookshelves either side of another fireplace, rugs on bare floorboards and big house plants. Down steps to one side of the bar is a sizeable dining room with another raised fireplace and similar chairs and tables on more rugs and boards. Throughout there are frame-to-frame photos, prints and paintings, and church candles on each table; background music. Doors in the end family room open to sizeable outdoor seating areas (overlooking the windmill) with contemporary black rattan-style seats under parasols; there are a few seats out in front too.

Tasty food includes sandwiches, jackfruit spring rolls with hoisin and peanut butter dipping sauce, goats cheese pannacotta with port and onion jam bonbon, tofu and lentil curry, free-range piri-piri chicken with guacamole and skinny fries, corned beef hash with bubble and squeak, a fried egg and home-made baked beans, a roast and a pie of the day, pork and leek sausages with mash and onion gravy, moules marinière, 21-day aged fillet steak with a choice of sauce and skinny chips, and puddings such as chocolate brownie with chocolate sauce and american cheesecake with fruit compote. *Benchmark main dish: beer-battered cod and chips £11.95. Two-course evening meal £20.00.*

Whiting & Hammond ~ Manager Duke Chidgey ~ Real ale ~ Open 9am-11pm; 9am-midnight Fri, Sat ~ Bar food 12-9.30 (9 Sun) ~ Restaurant ~ Children welcome ~ Dogs allowed in bar ~ Wi-fi *Recommended by Mick Allen, Louise and Simon Peters, Daniel King, Bridget and Peter Gregson, Ben and Diane Bowie, Kate Moran*

The details at the end of each featured entry start by saying whether the pub is a free house, or if it belongs to a brewery or pub group (which we name).

PENSHURST
Bottle House ⭐️ ♟ 🍷

TQ5142 Map 3

(01892) 870306 – www.thebottlehouseinnpenshurst.co.uk

Coldharbour Lane; leaving Penshurst SW on B2188 turn right at Smarts Hill signpost, then bear right towards Chiddingstone and Cowden; keep straight on; TN11 8ET

Country pub with friendly service, a good choice of drinks, tasty food and sunny terrace; nearby walks

Although the open-plan rooms in this tile-hung old country pub are all connected, there are plenty of nooks and crannies and standing timbers that give a sense of being separate and yet part of the chatty, bustling atmosphere. Pine wall boards and bar stools are ranged along the timber-clad copper-topped counter where they keep Larkins Traditional and Tonbridge Coppernob on handpump, 20 wines by the glass from a good list and local gin. There's also a hotchpotch of wooden tables (with fresh flowers and candles), fairly closely spaced chairs on dark boards or coir, a woodburning stove and photographs of the pub and local scenes; background music. Some walls are of stripped stone. The sunny, brick-paved terrace has teak chairs and tables under parasols, and olive trees in white pots. Good nearby walks.

Pleasing food includes sandwiches, crispy whitebait with pickled samphire and lemon dill mayonnaise, pulled pork with coconut and chilli broth and coriander noodles, vegetable and chickpea wellington with creamed spinach, chicken breast with celeriac purée and butternut squash and puy lentils, indonesian beef curry with spicy rice, garlic and ginger marinated swordfish steak with seared chicory and herby new potatoes, and puddings such as custard cream cheesecake and sticky toffee pudding with toffee sauce. *Benchmark main dish: slow-roasted pork belly with creamed cabbage and bacon and apple and cider jus £15.95. Two-course evening meal £22.00.*

Free house ~ Licensee Paul Hammond ~ Real ale ~ Open 11-11; 11-10.30 Sun ~ Bar food 12-10; 12-9 Sun and bank holidays ~ Restaurant ~ Children welcome ~ Dogs allowed in bar ~ Wi-fi *Recommended by Trevor and Michele Street, Buster and Helena Hastings, Martin Day, Andy and Rosemary Taylor, Sally and David Champion, Gerry and Rosemary Dobson*

PLUCKLEY
Dering Arms ⭐️ ♟ 🍷 🛏

TQ9243 Map 3

(01233) 840371 – www.deringarms.com

Pluckley station, which is signposted from B2077; or follow Station Road (left turn off Smarden Road in centre of Pluckley) for about 1.3 miles S, through Pluckley Thorne; TN27 0RR

Interesting building with stylish main bar, carefully chosen wines, three ales and good fresh fish dishes; bedrooms

To make the most of this well run, handsome inn, why not stay overnight in the comfortable bedrooms; breakfasts are highly regarded. Built as a hunting lodge on the Dering Estate, it has an imposing frontage, mullioned arched windows and dutch gables. The high-ceilinged, stylishly plain main bar has a solid country feel with a variety of wooden furniture on flagstones, a roaring log fire in a big fireplace, country prints and some fishing rods. The smaller half-panelled back bar has similar dark wood furnishings, plus an extension with a woodburning stove, comfortable armchairs, sofas and a grand piano; board games. A beer named for the pub from Goachers and Goachers Gold Star Ale on handpump, 11 good wines by the glass from a fine list, local cider, 30 malt whiskies and 20 cognacs. Classic car meetings (the long-serving landlord James has a couple of classic motors) are held here on the second Sunday of the month.

First class fish and shellfish are the stars here, though they do offer non-fishy choices too: interesting tapas, crayfish tails with chilli and lime beurre noisette, duck rillettes with ciabatta toast, whole crab salad, guinea fowl casseroled in sherry and tarragon sauce, confit duck with bubble and squeak potato cake and black cherry and ginger sauce, leg of lamb steak with peppers, black olives and saffron on couscous, scallops with basil spaghetti and saffron sauce, and puddings such as apple, sultana and calvados tart with vanilla ice-cream and sticky toffee pudding with warm walnut sauce. *Benchmark main dish: sea bass fillets with minted leeks and bacon and saffron sauce £15.95. Two-course evening meal £22.50.*

Free house ~ Licensee James Buss ~ Real ale ~ Open 11.30-3.30, 6-11; 12-4 Sun; closed Sun evening, Mon ~ Bar food 12-2.30, 6.30-9; 12-3 Sun ~ Restaurant ~ Children welcome ~ Dogs allowed in bar ~ Bedrooms: £85/£95 *Recommended by Belinda and Neil Garth, Susie and Spencer Gray, Edward Nile, Elise and Charles Mackinlay, Sandra and Michael Smith*

SEVENOAKS   TQ5055   Map 3
Kings Head ⏀
(01732) 452081 – www.kingsheadbesselsgreen.co.uk
Bessels Green; A25 W, just off A21; TN13 2QA

Bustling pub with open-plan character rooms, quite a choice of ales, good food and seats in garden

The little bar here is always full of chatty customers keen to try the six real ales on handpump, such as Dark Star Hophead, Old Dairy Blue Top, Pig & Porter Ashburnham and Skylarking, St Austell Proper Job and Tonbridge Coppernob – plus a dozen wines by the glass; a dog-friendly and attractive small room with a two-way open fire leads off here. Spreading dining areas have a wide mix of cushioned dining chairs, button-back wall seats and settles with scatter cushions around rustic or dark wooden tables on bare-board or tile floors. Also, open fires, frame-to-frame prints, old photos and maps on painted walls, house plants, church candles and old bottles on windowsills, and bookshelves; background music. Outside there are teak tables and chairs on a terrace, picnic-sets on grass and one or two circular 'dining huts' (bookable in advance for £25).

Rewarding food includes sandwiches, marinated buffalo wings in hot sauce with sour cream and chives, chicken liver parfait with apple and sultana chutney, three-cheese macaroni with garlic ciabatta, salmon, cod and horseradish fishcake on creamed spinach with a poached egg and hollandaise sauce, pork and leek sausages with onion gravy and mash, a pie of the day, 28-day aged sirloin steak with a choice of sauce, and puddings such as spotted dick and custard and banoffi pie with caramel ice-cream. *Benchmark main dish: slow-cooked corned beef hash with bubble and squeak, fried egg and home-made baked beans £13.95. Two-course evening meal £22.00.*

Whiting & Hammond ~ Manager Rob Locke ~ Real ale ~ Open 10am-11pm; 10am-midnight Sat; 11-10.30 Sun ~ Bar food 12-9.30 (9 Sun); breakfast 9-11.30am Fri and weekends ~ Children welcome ~ Dogs allowed in bar ~ Wi-fi *Recommended by Gene and Kitty Rankin, Sylvia and Phillip Spencer, Joe and Belinda Smart, Carol and Barry Craddock, Beverley and Andy Butcher, William and Sophia Renton*

SEVENOAKS   TQ5352   Map 3
White Hart ⏀
(01732) 452022 – www.brunningandprice.co.uk/whitehart
Tonbridge Road (A225 S, past Knole); TN13 1SG

Well run coaching inn with lots to look at in character rooms, rewarding food and friendly, helpful staff

There's a lot to look at in the many atmospheric rooms here, connected by open doorways and steps. You'll find log fires and woodburners, antique-style chairs and tables, rugs and bare floorboards and hundreds of prints and old photographs of local scenes or schools on cream-painted walls. Fresh flowers, house plants and candles too. Friendly, efficient staff serve St Austell Brunning & Price Traditional Bitter, Harveys Best and Old Dairy Blue Top plus guests from breweries such as Empire, Harveys, Timothy Taylors, Tonbridge and Westerham on handpump, 20 good wines by the glass, 50 malt whiskies and a farm cider; daily papers, board games. At the front of the building are picnic-sets under parasols, with wooden benches and chairs around tables under more parasols on the back terrace.

High quality cooking includes sandwiches, five-spiced duck leg with spring onion, cucumber, hoisin sauce and pancakes, scallops with butternut squash purée, soused apple, quinoa and crisp pancetta, cauliflower, chickpea and pepper jalfrezi with almond pilaf rice and sweet potato bhaji, steak burger with toppings, coleslaw and chips, pork tenderloin with creamy bacon and spring onion mash, crackling and cider jus, smoked haddock, cod, king prawn, mussel and bacon chowder with sweetcorn dumplings, crispy beef salad with sweet chilli sauce and cashews, and puddings such as dark chocolate, Cointreau and orange trifle and crème brûlée. *Benchmark main dish: chicken, ham and leek pie with tarragon cream sauce £14.95. Two-course evening meal £22.00.*

Brunning & Price ~ Manager Tom Dennis ~ Real ale ~ Open 11.30-11; 12-11 Sun ~ Bar food 12-9.30; 12-10 Fri, Sat; 12-9 Sun ~ Children welcome away from bar until 7pm ~ Dogs allowed in bar ~ Wi-fi *Recommended by Tony R, Martin Day, Mike Buckingham, Alan Cowell, Gerry and Rosemary Dobson, Adam Jones, Jacqui and Alan Swan, Professor James Burke, Sandra Hollies, Penny and David Shepherd*

SHIPBOURNE

Chaser ♀

TQ5952 Map 3

(01732) 810360 – www.thechaser.co.uk
Stumble Hill (A227 N of Tonbridge); TN11 9PE

Busy country pub with rambling rooms and interesting décor, log fires, good choice of drinks, enjoyable food and seats outside

Our readers enjoy their visits here very much, all citing the genuine welcome, buzzing atmosphere and thoughtful choice of food and drink. The comfortably opened-up bar and dining areas have an eclectic mix of solid wood tables (each set with a church candle) surrounded by prettily cushioned dining chairs, stripped wooden floors and several roaring log fires. Frame-to-frame pictures, maps and old photos line the walls above pine wainscoting, house plants and antique glass bottles are placed on windowsills, and rows of books sit on shelves. Courteous staff serve Greene King IPA, Larkins Traditional, Tonbridge Coppernob and a guest from Bexley on handpump, 14 good wines by the glass and 20 malt whiskies; background music and board games. A striking, school chapel-like room at the back has wooden panelling and a high, timber-vaulted ceiling. French windows open on to an enclosed central courtyard with wicker-style tables and chairs on large flagstones and plants in wall pots; this has a retractable awning and a woodburning stove and creates extra family dining space. A side garden with hedges and shrubs has picnic-sets and is overlooked by the church. You can use the small back car park or park in the lane opposite by the green-cum-common; local walks.

Enterprising food includes sandwiches, baked camembert studded with garlic and rosemary with cranberry sauce, sweet chilli squid with asian salad, vegetarian lasagne, honey mustard ham with free-range eggs, minced beef and onion pie, venison and root vegetable casserole with creamy mash, fish stew, duck breast with stir-fried vegetables, hoisin sauce and noodles, and puddings such as chocolate fondant with chocolate sauce and home-made sweet pancakes with berry compote and vanilla ice-cream. *Benchmark main dish: half shoulder of local lamb with dauphinoise potatoes and redcurrant and mint gravy £20.95. Two-course evening meal £22.00.*

Whiting & Hammond ~ Manager Duke Chidgey ~ Real ale ~ Open 10am-11pm; 9am-11pm Thurs-Sat; 9am-10pm Sun ~ Bar food 12-9.30; 9am-9.30pm Thurs-Sat; 9-9 Sun ~ Children welcome ~ Dogs allowed in bar ~ Wi-fi *Recommended by Ian Phillips, Gene and Kitty Rankin, Mark Hamill, Buster and Helena Hastings, Angela and Steve Heard, Paddy and Sian O'Leary*

STALISFIELD GREEN   TQ9552 Map 3
Plough 🌟 🍺 🛏
(01795) 890256 – www.theploughinnstalisfield.co.uk
Off A252 in Charing; ME13 0HY

●●●

Kent Dining Pub of the Year

Ancient country pub with rambling rooms, open fires, interesting local ales and smashing food; bedrooms

Individually designed, split-level suites have been opened up in a renovated barn here; they offer good views and breakfasts are tasty. The relaxed hop-draped bar and dining rooms ramble around, up and down, with open fires in brick fireplaces, interesting pictures, books on shelves, farmhouse and other nice old dining chairs around a mix of pine or dark wood tables on bare boards, and the odd milk churn dotted about; background music. Four Old Dairy ales on handpump, 14 wines by the glass, 26 gins, 14 malt whiskies, six local ciders and 13 rums. There are picnic-sets on a simple terrace overlooking the village green below. They now offer certified camping and caravan sites.

🌟 Imaginative food using the best local produce and cooked by the landlord includes lunchtime rolls, prawn cocktail with whisky marie rose and avocado purée, ham hock and chorizo terrine with celeriac rémoulade, beef burger and slow-cooked sticky chipotle pork belly with smoked cheese and chips, pie of the day, 28-day dry-aged steak with a choice of sauce and triple-cooked chips, seasonal daily specials, and puddings such as coffee burnt cream with almond biscotti and poached pear and ginger parkin with butterscotch sauce. *Benchmark main dish: slow-cooked pork belly with spring onion mash and spiced plum £16.00. Two-course evening meal £24.00.*

Free house ~ Licensees Richard and Marianne Baker ~ Real ale ~ Open 12-3, 5-11; 12-11 Sat; 12-6 Sun; closed Mon ~ Bar food 12-1.45, 6-8.45; 12-2.30, 6-8.45 Sat; 12-3.30 Sun ~ Restaurant ~ Children welcome ~ Dogs allowed in bar and bedrooms ~ Live entertainment (see website) ~ Bedrooms: £110/£120 *Recommended by Ivy and George Goodwill, Mike and Sarah Abbot, Pauline and Mark Evans, Susan and Callum Slade, Barry and Daphne Gregson, Patricia and Gordon Thompson*

STONE IN OXNEY   TQ9428 Map 3
Ferry 🍺
(01233) 758246 – www.oxneyferry.com
Appledore Road; signed from Tenterden Road (B2080); TN30 7JY

Bustling small pub with character rooms, candlelight, open fires, real ales and popular food

In a lovely marshland setting, this pretty 17th-c cottage has plenty of room for both drinkers and diners. The chatty main bar has hop-draped painted beams, a green dado and stools against the counter where they serve a beer named for the pub (from Goachers), Harveys Best, Sharps Doom Bar and a guest such as Cellar Head IPA on handpump, ten wines by the glass, farm ciders and 24 gins. To the right is a cosy eating area with wheelback chairs and a banquette around a few long tables, and a log fire in an inglenook with candles in wall sconces on either side. To the left of the main door is a dining area with big blackboards on red walls, a woodburning stove beneath a large bressumer beam and high-backed, light wooden dining chairs around assorted tables; up a couple of steps, a smarter dining area has modern chandeliers. Throughout there are wooden floors, all sorts of pictures and framed maps, a stuffed fish, beer flagons, an old musket and various brasses. Background music, TV, darts and pool in the games room. In warm weather, the tables and benches on the front terrace and seats in the back garden are much prized; a river runs along the bottom and the sunsets can be lovely. Disabled access in the bar and on the terrace.

Tempting food includes rosemary-infused baked baby camembert with onion marmalade, moules marinière, creamy mushroom and tarragon linguine, buttermilk chicken burger with spicy coleslaw and sweet potato fries, pork fillet with smoked apple mash and cider mustard sauce, glazed duck breast with parmentier potatoes, chargrilled chicory and sage and orange sauce, guinea fowl breast with wild mushrooms and mushroom jus and sautéed new potatoes, and puddings such as lemon and lime cheesecake and treacle sponge pudding with custard. *Benchmark main dish: steak and chorizo burger with toppings and dripping chips £14.45. Two-course evening meal £21.00.*

Free house ~ Licensee Paul Withers Green ~ Real ale ~ Open 11-11; 12-10 Sun ~ Bar food 12-3, 6-9; 11-9 Sat; 12-8 Sun ~ Restaurant ~ Children welcome ~ Dogs allowed in bar ~ Wi-fi
Recommended by Helene Grygar, Miranda and Jeff Davidson, David Appleyard, Sophie Ellison, Mark Morgan, Andrew Vincent, Julian Richardson

TUNBRIDGE WELLS
Sankeys ♀ 🍺
TQ5839 Map 3

(01892) 511422 – www.sankeys.co.uk
Mount Ephraim (A26 just N of junction with A267); TN4 8AA

Pubby bar, real ales, decent food and relaxed feel; downstairs brasserie (wonderful fish and shellfish) and seats on sunny back terrace

The interesting choice of drinks in this street-level bar, plus the cheerful, easy-going atmosphere, continue to draw in keen customers. Harveys Best, Larkins Traditional and a local guest are well kept on handpump and there's a constantly changing range of craft beers, fruit beers, lagers and ciders, 16 wines by the glass and an extensive range of spirits – all served by helpful staff. Comfortably worn leather sofas and pews sit around all sorts of tables on bare boards, and do note the particularly fine collection of rare enamel signs and antique brewery mirrors plus old prints, framed cigarette cards and lots of old wine bottles and soda siphons. There's a big flatscreen TV (for rugby only), background music and board games. Downstairs is a sizeable function room with french windows that lead out to an inviting suntrap deck.

Good value, tasty food includes sandwiches, snacks such as cockles, local butcher chipolatas, rock oysters and salt and pepper calamari, fish soup with rouille, honey goats cheese gratin with candied walnuts, burger with toppings and chips, cajun chicken with chipotle sauce and salsa, thai beef salad with chilli and lime leaves, cornish cock crabs, seared sea bass fillet with a poached egg and smoked hollandaise, seafood paella, and puddings. *Benchmark main dish: cornish lobsters £20.00. Two-course evening meal £25.00.*

Free house ~ Licensee Matthew Sankey ~ Real ale ~ Open 12-11 ~ Bar food 12-3, 6-10; 12-10 Sat; 12-6 Sun ~ Restaurant ~ Children welcome ~ Dogs welcome ~ Wi-fi *Recommended by Richard and Penny Gibbs, Stuart and Natalie Granville, Catherine and Daniel King, Patricia and Gordon Tucker*

ULCOMBE   TQ8550   Map 3

Pepper Box

(01622) 842558 ~ www.thepepperboxinn.co.uk

Fairbourne Heath; signposted from A20 in Harrietsham, or follow Ulcombe signpost from A20, then turn left at crossroads with sign to pub, then right at next minor crossroads; ME17 1LP

Friendly country pub with a fine log fire, well liked food, fair choice of drinks and seats in a pretty garden

The position here – nicely placed on high ground above the Weald – is very restful, and in warm weather the hop-covered terrace and shrub-filled garden are just the place to relax after a walk along the nearby Greensand Way footpath. The homely bar has attentive and convivial licensees, standing timbers and a few low beams (some hung with hops), copper kettles and pans on windowsills, and nice horsebrasses on the fireplace's bressumer beam; two leather sofas are set beside the splendid inglenook fireplace with its lovely log fire. A side area, furnished more functionally for eating, extends into the opened-up beamed dining room with a range in another inglenook and more horsebrasses. Shepherd Neame Master Brew and guests such as Shepherd Neame Spitfire and Whitstable Bay Pale Ale on handpump and 15 wines by the glass; background music. The village church is worth a look.

 Enjoyable food includes lunchtime sandwiches, scallop gratin with parmesan breadcrumb, sloe gin pigeon with blackberry dressing, portobello mushrooms stuffed with spinach and gorgonzola with a parsley crumb, a pie of the day, chicken curry with coconut cream, duck breast with apple and calvados sauce and boulangère potatoes, steak and kidney pudding, salmon fillet with braised lettuce, peas, samphire and crab, and puddings such as crème brûlée of the day and warm treacle and stem ginger tart with custard. *Benchmark main dish: moules frites £13.50. Two-course evening meal £21.00.*

Shepherd Neame ~ Tenant Sophie Pemble ~ Real ale ~ Open 11-3, 6-11; 12-5 Sun ~ Bar food 12-2.15, 6.30-9.30; 12-3 Sun ~ Restaurant ~ Children over 10 only ~ Dogs allowed in bar ~ Wi-fi *Recommended by Martin Day, Sophie Ellison, Victoria and James Sargeant, Justine and Neil Bonnett, Nick Higgins, Jill and Hugh Bennett*

WHITSTABLE   TR1066   Map 3

Pearsons Arms ♀

(01227) 773133 ~ www.pearsonsarmswhitstable.co.uk

Sea Wall off Oxford Street after road splits into one-way system; public parking on left as road divides; CT5 1BT

Seaside pub with an emphasis on imaginative food, several local ales and good mix of customers

You'll find a thoughtful range of drinks and interesting food in this beachside pub, where's plenty of space for enjoying both. The two front bars are divided by a central chimney: cushioned settles, captain's chairs and leather armchairs on a stripped-wood floor, driftwood walls and big flower arrangements on the bar counter. Courteous staff serve Pearsons Arms (named for them from Adnams), Ramsgate Gadds Seasider and Sharps Doom Bar on handpump plus 14 good wines by the glass and an extensive list of cocktails; background music. A cosy lower room has a bookcase mural and a couple of big chesterfields and dining chairs around plain tables on a stone floor. Up a couple of flights of stairs, the restaurant (overlooking the water) has mushroom-coloured paintwork, contemporary wallpaper, more driftwood and church chairs and pine tables on nice wide floorboards.

Highly regarded food includes sandwiches, crab, ginger and chive spring roll with spiced fresh mango chutney, confit free-range chicken terrine with piccalilli, beetroot with braised puy lentils, salsify, charred tenderstem and toasted almonds, beef bourguignon, dover sole with caper and lemon brown butter, lamb rump with pea, broad bean and feta ragoût and salsa verde, fish pie, hot chocolate and orange fondant with marmalade ice-cream and sticky toffee pudding with caramelised banana and butterscotch sauce; they also offer a two- and three-course weekday set lunch. *Benchmark main dish: beer-battered fish and triple-cooked chips £16.00. Two-course evening meal £25.00.*

Enterprise ~ Lease Jake Alder ~ Real ale ~ Open 12-midnight (11 Sun) ~ Bar food 12-8; bar food 12-3, 5-9 ~ Restaurant ~ Children welcome ~ Dogs allowed in bar ~ Wi-fi ~ Live music evenings Sun and Tues *Recommended by JJ, Jacqui and Alan Swan, Graeme and Sally Mendham, Beverley and Andy Butcher, Alison and Dan Richardson, Alfie Bayliss, Beth Aldridge*

WINGHAM

Dog 🍴⭐ 🍷 🛏   TR2457 Map 3

(01227) 720339 – www.thedog.co.uk
Canterbury Road (A257); CT3 1BB

Hands-on licensees in handsome old pub with first class food, local ales, friendly staff and seats on terrace; bedrooms

Contemporary touches in this medieval inn have been thought out with care, so they blend easily with the heavy beams and nice old brickwork. The carpeted bar has a woodburning stove in an inglenook fireplace with armchairs grouped around in front, more armchairs against the walls, a cushioned window seat, dog motifs on the back of leather chairs and a white-painted piano; dotted about are fabric dogs, dog cartoons and prints on grey paintwork, pub games and daily papers. Swivelling wooden stools line the counter where they keep Harveys Best and a guest beer on handpump and nice wines by the glass; background music and board games. One part of the dining room has metal and animal-hide chairs and upholstered wall banquettes around wooden tables on wide floorboards, a few animal-hide stools by the bar and an open fire. An airy second room has a woodburning stove, high-backed tartan or leather chairs around more tables on flagstones and plants on windowsills. Outside on the terrace are grey or white up-to-date chairs and tables and a gazebo. They have eight stylish, well equipped and individually styled bedrooms and breakfasts are particularly good.

Good, enterprising food includes sandwiches, soy and ginger-cured salmon, pickled cockles, wasabi and sesame, braised ox cheek with cauliflower purée and crispy shallot, caramelised onion and blue cheese suet pudding with truffle cream sauce, supreme of chicken with ham croquette, fondant potato and sweetcorn, chalk stream trout with smoked mussels, pancetta and soft herb risotto, duck breast, potato rösti, pak choi, cucumber and cherries, and puddings such as treacle tart with blood orange sorbet and pistachio crumble and chocolate fondant with peanut butter ice-cream. *Benchmark main dish: lamb rump with garlic risotto and pancetta £23.00. Two-course evening meal £30.00.*

Free house ~ Licensee Marc Brigden ~ Real ale ~ Open 11-11; 11-9 Sun ~ Bar food 12-2, 6-9; 12-5 Sun ~ Restaurant ~ Children welcome ~ Dogs welcome ~ Wi-fi ~ Bedrooms: $80/$100 *Recommended by Katharine Cowherd, Belinda and Neil Garth, Charlotte and William Mason, Diana and Bertie Farr, Graham Kirby, Miranda and Jeff Davidson, Buster May, Julie and Andrew Blanchett, Guy Henderson*

WYE
Kings Head

TR0546 Map 3

(01233) 812418 – www.kingsheadwye.com

Church Street; TN25 5BN

Busy pub in handsome high street with good food, ales and wines by the glass – and bright bedrooms

A former Victorian coaching inn, this is popular with our readers and, once found, tends to become a regular haunt. The chatty, informal bare-boards bar is divided by a two-way log fire, with a long brown button-back wall banquette in one part and armchairs beside the fire on the other side by a glass-topped trunk table. Other furnishings include comfortable chairs around all sorts of tables and pale-painted high chairs beside the counter where they keep Black Sheep and Shepherd Neame Whitstable Bay Pale Ale on handpump and 13 good wines by the glass, plus an array of olives, cakes, home-made pork crackling and so forth; a dresser is lined with local jams, honey, gin and flavoured olive oils for sale. The dining room has one long wall banquette and painted kitchen chairs around pine tables, with an open fire at one end. Throughout there are rustic boarded walls, church candles, photographs of the local area, daily papers and background jazz. A small courtyard has a few tables and chairs, and the bedrooms are airy and simply furnished. Disabled access.

As well as breakfasts (8-11am), the highly regarded food includes lunchtime sandwiches and omelettes, wild boar and chorizo scotch egg with piccalilli, clams with pancetta, white wine, cream and garlic, asparagus tart with basil and pine nut pesto, crab and smoked salmon salad with chilli and lime crème fraîche, home-smoked cod and chorizo fishcake with a poached egg and hollandaise sauce, burgers with toppings and skinny fries, a pasta dish of the day, lamb kebabs with harissa hummus and mint and cucumber yoghurt, and puddings such as ginger cheesecake with poached rhubarb and chocolate délice with orange chocolate soil and salted caramel ice-cream. *Benchmark main dish: chicken breast with pancetta and mushrooms £16.00. Two-course evening meal £20.00.*

Shepherd Neame ~ Tenant Scott Richardson ~ Real ale ~ Open 8am-11pm Weds-Sat; 8am-10pm Sun-Tues; 8am-10pm Sun ~ Bar food 12-3, 6-9; all day weekends (till 5pm Sun) ~ Restaurant ~ Children welcome ~ Dogs allowed in bar and bedrooms ~ Wi-fi ~ Bedrooms: /£65 *Recommended by Richard Kennell, Frances Parsons, Celia and Geoff Clay, Matt and Hayley Jacob, Andy and Louise Ramwell, Elise and Charles Mackinlay, John and Abigail Prescott*

Also Worth a Visit in Kent

Besides the fully inspected pubs, you might like to try these pubs that have been recommended to us and described by readers. Do tell us what you think of them: feedback@goodguides.com

APPLEDORE   TQ9529
Black Lion (01233) 758206
The Street; TN26 2BU Bustling 1930s brick pub in attractive village; good generously served food (special diets catered for) including lamb from Romney Marsh and local fish, Goachers and four guests, Biddenden cider, welcoming helpful staff, partitioned back eating area, log fire; background music, events such as bank holiday hog roasts; children welcome, tables out at front under

parasols, good Military Canal walks, open all day, food all day Fri-Sun. *(Julie Swift)*

BARHAM   TR2050
Duke of Cumberland
(01227) 831396 *The Street; CT4 6NY*
Open-plan pub close to village green; enjoyable home cooking including good Sun roasts, well kept Harveys, Greene King, Black Sheep and a guest, friendly staff, plain tables and chairs on bare boards or flagstones, hops and log fire; quiz second Tues of month,

board games and darts; children welcome, dogs in bar, garden with boules and play area, three bedrooms, handy for A2, open all day, food all day weekends. *(Jill and Hugh Bennett)*

BEARSTED TQ8055
Oak on the Green (01622) 737976
The Street; ME14 4EJ Well run dining pub with friendly bustling atmosphere (sister to the Old Mill at Kennington); two hop-festooned bar areas with bare boards and half-panelling, wide choice of home-made food including range of burgers and some mexican dishes, Harveys Best and three guests, restaurant; they also own the smaller fish restaurant next door (closed Sun evening, Mon); children and dogs (in bar) welcome, disabled access, seats out at front under big umbrellas, open (and food) all day. *(Eddie Edwards)*

BENENDEN TQ8032
★ Bull (01580) 240054
The Street; by village green; TN17 4DE Relaxed informal atmosphere in bare-boards or dark terracotta-tiled rooms, pleasing mix of furniture, church candles on tables, log fire in brick inglenook, ales such as Dark Star, Harveys and Larkins from carved wooden counter, Biddenden cider, more formal dining room, tasty generously served food (not Sun evening) including speciality pies and popular Sun carvery, friendly helpful staff; background music (live Sun afternoon 5-7pm); children and dogs (in bar) welcome, picnic-sets out in front behind white picket fence, back garden, open all day. *(V Brogden)*

BETHERSDEN TQ9240
George (01233) 820235
The Street; TN26 3AG Tile-hung village local with good buoyant atmosphere; well kept Harveys, St Austell and two guests, generous sensibly priced food including good value carvery (Sun, Weds), large public bar with open fire, smaller lounge next to dining area; pool, free wi-fi; children and dogs welcome, open all day, no food Sun evening, Mon lunchtime. *(Paddy and Sian O'Leary)*

BIDBOROUGH TQ5643
★ Kentish Hare (01892) 525709
Bidborough Ridge; TN3 0XB Good imaginative food at this popular dining pub including set menus; leather armchairs around open fire in main bar, unusual stools made of corks, bookcase wallpaper, a house beer from Tonbridge along with Harveys and a guest, 30 wines by the glass and good choice of other drinks, modern two-way woodburner in cosy middle room, second bar with seating booths and airy back restaurant with view into kitchen; background music, free wi-fi; children welcome (under-5s eat free), dogs allowed in some areas, contemporary tables and chairs on deck overlooking lower terrace, open all day Sat,

closed Sun evening, Mon. *(Martin Day, Tony and Rosemary Swainson)*

BODSHAM TR1045
Timber Batts (01233) 750083
Following Bodsham, Wye sign off B2068 keep right at unsigned fork after about 1.5 miles; TN25 5JQ Eccentric old rural pub under family ownership; traditional beamed bar with inglenook log fire, eclectic mix of furniture and masses of quirky bits and pieces including lots of taxidermy, three kentish ales and four ciders, some evening food (Thurs-Sat) including Fri pizzas; live music and DJ nights, bar billiards, pinball, board games; children and dogs welcome, lovely views over wide-spreading valley from garden with wandering chickens, camping, working forge next door (landlord is a blacksmith), closed Mon-Weds, open from 4pm Thurs and Fri, all day Sat, till 7pm Sun. *(Lindy Andrews)*

BOUGH BEECH TQ4846
Wheatsheaf (01732) 700100
B2027, S of reservoir; TN8 7NU Attractive 14th-c pub with emphasis on food including children's meals, three Westerham ales along with Harveys and good choice of wines, beams and timbering, bare boards and log fires (one in a huge fireplace), high ceilinged dining room, more tables upstairs; dogs welcome, nice outside seating area and good walks including circular one around Bough Beech Reservoir, open all day (till 9pm Sun). *(Martin Day)*

BOUGHTON ALUPH TR0247
Flying Horse (01233) 620914
Boughton Lees, just off A251 N of Ashford; TN25 4HH Interesting old pub overlooking village cricket pitch; beams, panelling and inglenooks, stone-arched window and ancient glass-covered well, enjoyable food from sandwiches to grills including Tues burger night and Weds steaks, Fullers London Pride, Harveys Best and guests; background music, TV; children and dogs welcome, tables out at front and in spacious back garden, bedrooms, open all day from 8am for breakfast. *(Paul Humphreys)*

BOXLEY TQ7758
Kings Arms (01622) 755177
1.75 miles from M20 junction 7; opposite church; ME14 3DR Cosy dining pub in pretty village at foot of the downs; largely 16th/17th-c, with good choice of popular food from lunchtime baguettes to weekly specials, four well kept ales including Fullers and Harveys, welcoming helpful service, spic-and-span interior with low black beams, red chesterfields by big brick fireplace; background music, monthly quiz; children and dogs welcome, picnic-sets and play area in nice garden, good local walks, open (and food) all day. *(Dave Braisted, Lewis Canning)*

BOYDEN GATE   TR2265
Gate Inn (01227) 860498
Off A299 Herne Bay–Ramsgate signed
for Hillboro', Reculver, then left to
Chislet; Chislet also signed off A28
Canterbury–Margate at Upstreet – keep
right on to Boyden; CT3 4EB Rustic
beamed pub with unpretentious quarry-tiled
bar rooms; cushioned pews around character
tables, attractively etched windows, old
local photographs and double-aspect log
fire, Shepherd Neame and occasional guest
from tap room casks, popular sensibly priced
home-made food from doorstep sandwiches
to specials (must book weekends),
bare-boards restaurant in former bakery,
woodburner; children and dogs (in bar)
welcome, sheltered garden bounded by two
streams, ducks and chickens, open all day
weekends, no food Sun night. *(Buster May)*

BRASTED   TQ4654
Stanhope Arms (01959) 561970
Church Road; TN16 1HZ Welcoming old
red-brick village pub next to the church;
six real ales including Greene King and
well liked pubby food (not Sun evening,
Mon, limited choice Tues), good service,
cosy traditional bar with darts, bright
cheerful restaurant with white tablecloths
and napkins; children and dogs welcome
(resident labradors), summer barbecues
and bat and trap in back garden, closed
Mon lunchtime, otherwise open all day.
(Martin Day)

BRENCHLEY   TQ6841
★Halfway House (01892) 722526
Horsmonden Road; TN12 7AX Beamed
18th-c inn with attractive mix of rustic and
traditional furnishings on bare boards, old
farm tools and other bric-a-brac, two log
fires, friendly welcoming staff, up to a dozen
well kept changing ales tapped from the
cask (bank holiday beer/cider festivals end
of May, Aug); enjoyable traditional home-
made food including popular Sun roasts,
two eating areas; quiz every other Weds;
children and dogs welcome, picnic-sets and
play area in big garden, summer barbecues,
two bedrooms, open all day, no food Sun
evening. *(Victoria and James Sargeant)*

BROADSTAIRS   TR3967
Charles Dickens (01843) 600160
Victoria Parade; CT10 1QS Centrally
placed with big busy bar; decent choice of
beers and wines, popular food from snacks
to good local fish/seafood, breakfast from
10am (9am weekends), upstairs restaurant
with fine sea views; Sat live music, sports TV;
children welcome, tables out overlooking

Viking Bay, almost next door to Dickens
House Museum, open all day. *(John Wooll)*

BROADSTAIRS   TR3868
Four Candles 07947 062063
Sowell Street; CT10 2AT Quirky, much
enjoyed one-room micropub in former shop;
good selection of local beers chalked on
blackboard including own brews, kentish
ciders and wines, high tables and stools on
sawdust floor, bucket lightshades and various
odds and ends including pitchfork handles
(the famous *Two Ronnies* sketch was inspired
by a Broadstairs ironmonger), local cheese
and pork pies, friendly chatty atmosphere;
closed weekday lunchtimes, open all day Sat.
(Peter Meister)

BROADSTAIRS   TR3967
★Tartar Frigate (01843) 862013
Harbour Street, by quay; CT10 1EU
Flint-faced harbourside pub dating
from the 18th c; pleasantly old-fashioned
bar with interesting local photographs
and fishing memorabilia, hanging pots and
brasses, log fire, well kept ales such as
Ramsgate, lunchtime bar food (Mon-Sat) and
very good fish/seafood in popular upstairs
restaurant with fine Viking Bay views, also
good value four-course Sun lunch with
two sittings 12.30pm and 3.30pm, friendly
hospitable staff; background and weekly live
music including Weds folk session; open all
day, no food Sun evening. *(Tom and Ruth Rees)*

BROOKLAND   TQ9724
Woolpack (01797) 344321
On A259 from Rye, turn right signposted
Midley where main road bends sharp
left, just after Walland Marsh; OS Sheet
189 map reference 977244; TN29 9TJ
15th-c cottage in heart of Romney Marsh;
lovely uneven brick floor in ancient entrance
lobby, quarry-tiled main bar with low beams
(thought to have come from local wrecks)
and massive inglenook, carpeted dining room,
generous helpings of enjoyable reasonably
priced home-made food from sandwiches and
baked potatoes up, Shepherd Neame ales;
may be background radio; children welcome,
picnic-sets in good-sized gardens, summer
barbecues, good local walks, open (and food)
all day weekends. *(Nick Morgan)*

BURMARSH   TR1032
Shepherd & Crook (01303) 872336
Shear Way, next to church; TN29 0JJ
Traditional 16th-c marshside village local
with smuggling history; three well kept
changing ales, good straightforward home-
made food at reasonable prices including
deals and gluten-free options, friendly
service, interesting photographs and blow

If you report on a pub that's not a featured entry, please tell us any lunchtimes
or evenings when it doesn't serve bar food.

lamp collection, open fire; bar games such as ring the bull; children and dogs welcome, seats on side terrace, closed Mon (except bank holidays), otherwise open all day (Sun till 6pm). *(Andy and Rosemary Taylor)*

CANTERBURY   TR1458
Dolphin (01227) 455963
St Radigunds Street; CT1 2AA
Busy modernised dining pub with plenty of tables in light spacious bar; enjoyable fairly traditional home-made food from baguettes to popular Sun roast, Sharps Doom Bar, Timothy Taylors Landlord and guests, nice wines including some country ones, friendly staff, bric-a-brac on delft shelf, board games, flagstoned conservatory; free wi-fi; children welcome, dogs at management's discretion, disabled access, picnic-sets in good-sized back garden, open all day (food all day Sat).
(Louise and Anton Parsons)

CANTERBURY   TR1457
Foundry (01227) 455899
Stour Street; CT1 2NR This backstreet brewpub has recently moved to new premises just around the corner; Canterbury Brewers beers from visible microbrewery plus local guests (tasting trays available), they also make their own cider and spirits, decent food (till 6pm Sun, Mon) from sandwiches and sharing plates up including range of home-made pies and chargrills, helpful cheerful staff; children welcome, no dogs, disabled access/loo, open all day (till midnight Fri, Sat). *(Bob Ott)*

CANTERBURY   TR1557
Lady Luck (01227) 763298
St Peters Street; CT1 2BQ Quirky rock 'n' roll bar with music-themed decor; real ales such as Sharps Doom Bar, craft beers and good selection of other drinks including a rum menu, enjoyable home-cooked food with plenty for vegetarians/vegans, good friendly service; regular live bands and DJs, juke box, pool, daily newspaper and board games; a couple of pavement tables, more seats in beer garden behind, open all day (till 2am Fri, Sat), food served till 7pm (3pm Sun). *(Eddie Edwards)*

CANTERBURY   TR1558
New Inn (01227) 464584
Havelock Street; CT1 1NP Friendly little Victorian terraced local not far from the city centre; seven well kept changing ales (tasters offered), a proper cider and good range of whiskies, bare-boards bar with woodburner, modern back conservatory, no food; juke box and various games; dogs welcome, seats in garden behind, nearby parking can be difficult, open all day Fri-Sun. *(Nick Higgins)*

CANTERBURY   TR1457
Parrot (01227) 454170
Church Lane – the one off St Radigunds Street, 100 metres E of St Radigunds car park; CT1 2AG Ancient heavy-beamed pub tucked down narrow part-cobbled street; wood and flagstone floors, stripped masonry, hops and three log fires, up to six real ales including Shepherd Neame, good food from open sandwiches up, extensive wine list, friendly service, upstairs vaulted function room; children welcome, nicely laid out courtyard with central barbecue, open all day from midday, food all day Thurs-Sun. *(I D Barnett)*

CANTERBURY   TR1457
White Hart (01227) 765091
Worthgate Place, opposite tree-shaded square off Castle Street; CT1 2QX Popular little pub with friendly atmosphere; Shepherd Neame ales and enjoyable well priced food cooked by landlady including some italian dishes, opened up bare-boards interior with woodburner in side room; quiz nights; children and dogs welcome, large garden behind (one of very few in the city), open (and food) all day. *(Nick Higgins)*

CAPEL   TQ6444
Dovecote (01892) 835966
Alders Road, SE of Tonbridge; TN12 6SU Cosy pub in nice country surroundings with open fire, beams and some stripped brickwork, up to six cask-tapped ales including Harveys, enjoyable well priced food (not Sun evening, Mon) from pitched-ceiling dining end, friendly helpful staff; live acoustic music Mon, quiz every other Weds; well behaved children allowed, dogs in bar (not at food times), lots of picnic-sets in back garden with terrace and play area, bat and trap, open all day Sun, closed Mon lunchtime. *(Bob and Melissa Wyatt)*

CHARING   TQ9551
Bowl (01233) 712256
Egg Hill Road; TN27 0HG Popular 16th-c pub high on the downs (near Pilgrims Way) run by father and daughter; beamed bare-boards bar with inglenook log fire, tusky boar's head behind dark-panelled counter serving good kentish beers such as Ramsgate Gadds, carpeted dining area, enjoyable fairly priced food (all day Sat, till 5pm Sun) from lunchtime sandwiches/baguettes up including range of burgers, friendly helpful service; July beer/cider/cocktail festival with live music; children and dogs welcome, chunky picnic-sets on heated front terrace, more tables in big lawned garden, good local walks, six bedrooms, open all day. *(Sandra Hollies)*

CHARTHAM   TR1054
Artichoke (01227) 738316
Rottington Street; CT4 7JQ Attractive timbered pub (dates from the 15th c); generous helpings of enjoyable reasonably priced pub food (till 5pm Sun) from sandwiches and baked potatoes up, well

kept Shepherd Neame ales, good service, carpeted log-fire bar, dining area with light wood tables (one built around a glass-topped well); quiz last Thurs of the month, darts and bat and trap; children welcome, picnic-sets in back garden, closed Mon lunchtime, otherwise open all day. *(Julie Swift)*

CHIDDINGSTONE CAUSEWAY   TQ5247
Greyhound   (01892) 870275
Charcott, off back road to Weald; TN11 8LG Red-brick village pub; well kept Larkins and a couple of guests, Dudda's Tun cider and good range of gins, enjoyable home-made food at reasonable prices (some produce from own farm), log fire; children, walkers and dogs welcome, picnic-sets out in front and in side garden, closed Mon, otherwise open all day (till 8pm Sun), no food Sun evening. *(Martin Day)*

CHIDDINGSTONE HOATH   TQ4943
★ Rock   (01892) 870296
Hoath Corner on back road Chiddingstone–Cowden; OS Sheet 188 map reference 497431; TN8 7BS Welcoming and bustling little tile-hung cottage with undulating brick floor, simple furnishings and woodburner in fine brick inglenook, some quirky touches such as curtains made from beer mats, well kept Larkins (brewed close by) and good home-made food (not Sun evening) from varied menu including specials, large stuffed bull's head for ring the bull, up a step to smaller room with long wooden settle by nice table; walkers and dogs welcome, picnic-sets out in front and on back lawn, open all day (till 8pm Sun). *(Richard and Penny Gibbs, Tony Scott)*

CHILHAM   TR0653
★ White Horse   (01227) 730355
The Square; CT4 8BY 15th-c pub in picturesque village square; handsome ceiling beams and massive fireplace with lancastrian rose carved in the mantel beam, chunky light oak furniture on pale wood flooring and more traditional pubby furniture on quarry tiles, three well kept ales (Aug beer/cider festival), enjoyable varied food (all day Sat, not Sun evening), amiable helpful service; live music and quiz nights, free wi-fi; children welcome, dogs in bar, handy for the castle, open all day. *(Louise and Anton Parsons)*

CHILLENDEN   TR2653
★ Griffins Head   (01304) 840325
SE end of village; 2 miles E of Aylesham; CT3 1PS Attractive 14th-c beamed and timbered pub surrounded by nice countryside; gently upscale local atmosphere in two bars and flagstoned back dining room, big log fire, full range of Shepherd Neame ales, good wine list and decent choice of popular home-made food, attentive friendly service; no under-8s, dogs welcome, summer

weekend barbecues in pretty garden, vintage car meetings first Sun of the month, shuts 5pm Sun, otherwise open all day. *(Claire Adams)*

CHIPSTEAD   TQ4956
★ Bricklayers Arms   (01732) 743424
Chevening Road; TN13 2RZ Attractive flower-decked pub (originally three cottages) overlooking lake and green, relaxed chatty atmosphere, well kept Harveys from casks behind long counter, good choice of popular fairly priced food (not Sun evening) from baguettes up including Mon steak night and Fri fish, cheerful helpful service, heavily beamed flagstoned bar with open fire and fine racehorse painting, larger back restaurant; Tues quiz and monthly live music; children and dogs welcome, disabled access/loo, seats out in front, open all day. *(Alan Cowell, Martin Day, David Jackman, Tony Scott)*

CONYER QUAY   TQ9664
Ship   (01795) 520881
Conyer Road; ME9 9HR Renovated and extended 18th-c creekside pub owned by adjacent Swale Marina; bare boards and open fires, enjoyable home-cooked food including weekend breakfast from 10am, three changing ales; children and dogs welcome, useful for boaters, walkers (on Saxon Shore Way) and birders, seats out at front, open all day weekends (till 9.30pm Sun). *(Jill and Hugh Bennett)*

COWDEN   TQ4640
Fountain   (01342) 850528
Off A264 and B2026; High Street; TN8 7JG Good fairly priced food from sandwiches up in attractive tile-hung village pub; steep steps up to bar with well kept Harveys and decent wines by the glass, friendly helpful staff, beams, half-panelling and old photographs, good log fire, mix of tables in adjoining room, woodburner in small back dining area, conservatory; background music, quiz first Thurs of month; children, walkers and dogs welcome, picnic-sets on small terrace and lawn, pretty village, open all day Sun but no evening food. *(Tony Scott)*

COWDEN   TQ4642
★ Queens Arms   (01342) 850598
Cowden Pound; junction B2026 with Markbeech Road; TN8 5NP Friendly little Victorian time warp known as Elsie's after former long-serving landlady – present local owner has thankfully kept things much the same; two simple unpretentious rooms with open fires, a well kept/priced ale from Larkins, no food, darts, shove-ha'penny and other traditional games, piano; folk music (second and third Tues of month and some Sats), morris dancers and Christmas mummers; dogs welcome, open 5-10.30pm Mon, Tue, 5-7.30pm Weds, Thurs, 5-9pm

Fri, 5-7.30pm Sat (longer if there is live music), 12-3pm Sun. *(Nick Morgan)*

DARGATE
TR0761
Dove (01227) 751085
Village signposted from A299; ME13 9HB Tucked-away 19th-c restauranty pub refurbished under new management; first class food (not Sun evening) cooked by chef-owner including set menus, Shepherd Neame ales and good wines by the glass, friendly efficient service, stripped-wood tables on bare boards, some blue half-panelling and old pictures of the pub, woodburner in brick fireplace; children, walkers and dogs welcome, sheltered garden, open all day Fri and Sat, till 6pm Sun, closed Mon. *(Victoria and James Sargeant)*

DARTFORD
TQ5272
Horse & Groom (01322) 290056
Leyton Cross Road; DA2 7AP Refurbished pub next to Dartford Heath with large bar and restaurant extension; six mainly local ales, a dozen wines by the glass and good food from regularly changing menu including some pub favourites, friendly service; free wi-fi, children welcome, open all day, food all day Fri-Sun. *(Simon Day)*

DARTFORD
TQ5473
Malt Shovel (01322) 224381
Darenth Road; DA1 1LP Cheerful 17th-c waney-boarded pub with two bars and conservatory; well kept Youngs, St Austell and a guest, several wines by the glass and good reasonably priced food (not Sun evening, Mon or Tues) from sandwiches and sharing plates up, friendly helpful staff; Mon quiz, some live music including folk night second Sun of month, free wi-fi; children and dogs welcome, tables on paved part-covered terrace, closed Mon lunchtime, otherwise open all day. *(Simon Day)*

DEAL
TR3751
Berry (01304) 362411
Canada Road; CT14 7EQ Small no-frills local opposite old Royal Marine barracks; welcoming enthusiastic landlord serving up to 11 well kept ales including Dark Star and Harveys (tasting notes on slates, regular beer festivals), kentish farm cider and perry, no food, L-shaped carpeted bar with coal fire; quiz second Fri of month, darts teams, pool and some live music; dogs welcome, small vine-covered back terrace, open all day (from 3pm Tues). *(Lindy Andrews)*

DEAL
TR3752
Bohemian (01304) 361939
Beach Street opposite pier; CT14 6HY Seafront bar with five real ales and good choice of bottled beers, extensive range of spirits too including 170 gins, popular traditional home-made food, friendly helpful staff, L-shaped room with mismatched furniture (some découpage tables), polished wood floor, lots of pictures, mirrors, signs and other odds and ends, sofas and weekend papers, similar décor in upstairs cocktail bar with good sea views; background music; children and dogs welcome, sunny split-level deck behind and heated smokers' gazebo, open all day and can get very busy (particularly weekends). *(Lindy Andrews)*

DEAL
TR3752
Just Reproach 07432 413226
King Street; CT14 6HX Popular and genuinely welcoming micropub in former corner shop; simple drinking room with sturdy tables on bare boards, stools and cushioned benches, friendly knowledgeable service from father and daughter team, three or four changing small brewery ales tapped from the cask, also real ciders and some organic wines, locally made cheese, friendly chatty atmosphere; no mobile phones (fine for using them); dogs welcome, closed Sun evening. *(Lindy Andrews)*

DEAL
TR3753
Prince Albert (01304) 375425
Middle Street; CT14 6LW Compact 19th-c corner pub in conservation area; bowed entrance doors, etched-glass windows and fairly ornate interior with assorted bric-a-brac, three changing local ales, popular food (Weds-Sat evenings) and Sun carvery in back dining area, friendly staff; dogs welcome, small garden behind, bedrooms, closed lunchtimes except Sun. *(Julie Swift)*

DEAL
TR3752
Royal (01304) 375555
Beach Street; CT14 6JD Popular early 18th-c hotel right on the seafront; light and comfortable with plenty of casual drinkers in pubby bar, Shepherd Neame ales and good choice of enjoyable well priced food from sandwiches to fresh fish, friendly uniformed staff, restaurant; children and dogs (in bar) welcome, terrace overlooking the beach, 18 bedrooms (some with sea-view balconies), open (and food) all day from 8am. *(Nick Higgins, Julie Swift)*

DEAL
TR3753
Ship (01304) 372222
Middle Street; CT14 6JZ Traditional dimly lit two-room local in historic maritime quarter; five well kept/priced ales including Dark Star and Ramsgate served by friendly staff, no food, bare boards and lots of dark woodwork, stripped brick and local ship and wreck pictures, evening candles, cosy panelled back bar, open fire and woodburner; dogs welcome, small pretty walled garden, open all day. *(Lindy Andrews)*

DOVER
TR3241
Blakes (01304) 202194
Castle Street; CT16 1PJ Small flagstoned cellar bar down steep steps; brick and flint walls, dim lighting, woodburner, Adnams

and six changing guests, farm ciders/perries, several wines by the glass and over 50 malt whiskies, good bar food from sandwiches up, panelled carpeted upstairs restaurant, friendly staff; well behaved children welcome, dogs in bar, side garden and suntrap back terrace, four bedrooms, open (and food) all day. *(Buster May)*

DUNGENESS TR0916
Pilot (01797) 320314
Battery Road; TN29 9NJ Single-storey, mid 20th-c seaside café-bar by shingle beach; well kept ales such as Adnams and Sharps, decent choice of good value food from nice sandwiches to fish and chips, friendly efficient service (even when packed), open-plan interior divided into three areas, dark plank panelling (including the slightly curved ceiling), lighter front part overlooking beach, prints and local memorabilia, books for sale (proceeds to RNLI); background music, free wi-fi; children welcome, picnic-sets in side garden, open all day till 10pm (9pm Sun). *(Simon Day)*

DUNKS GREEN TQ6152
★ **Kentish Rifleman** (01732) 810727
Dunks Green Road; TN11 9RU Relaxing Tudor country pub with bare-boards bar and two carpeted dining areas; various rifles and guns on low beams, cosy log fire, well kept ales such as Harveys, Tonbridge, Westerham and Whitstable, enjoyable reasonably priced food from light meals to popular Sun roasts, Tues pie and pint deal, friendly efficient staff; children and dogs welcome, tables in pretty garden with well, good walks from the door, one bedroom, open all day Fri-Sun, no food Sun or Mon evenings. *(Hugh Roberts)*

EAST PECKHAM TQ6548
Man of Kent (01622) 871345
Tonbridge Road; TN12 5LA Traditional tile-hung pub dating from the 16th c; low black beams, mix of pubby furniture on carpet or slate tiles, fresh flowers, big two-way woodburner in central fireplace, ales such as Harveys, Sharps, Timothy Taylors and Tonbridge, enjoyable well priced home-made food (all day Sat, not Sun evening); children welcome, terrace seating by River Bourne, nearby walks, open all day. *(Charlie Parker)*

EASTLING TQ9656
Carpenters Arms (01795) 890234
Off A251 S of M2 junction 6, via Painters Forstal; The Street; ME13 0AZ Partly 14th-c red-brick village pub; well kept Shepherd Neame ales and good reasonably priced pubby food from sandwiches and various ploughman's to daily specials, friendly attentive service, big log fires front and back, oak beams and mix of old and new furniture on brick or bare-boards floors, vintage photographs of the pub and surroundings; some live music; children welcome, paved terrace with rattan-style

furniture, open all day Sat, closed Mon. *(David Harries, John Hunter Wright)*

EGERTON TQ9047
Barrow House (01233) 756599
The Street; TN27 9DJ Stylishly refurbished 16th-c weatherboarded pub under same ownership as the Milk House at Sissinghurst; back bar with high beams and light stone floor, inglenook log fire (plastered canopy has signatures of World War II airmen), main bar with more beams and timber partitions, attractive wooden counter serving well kept ales such as Harvey's and Dark Star and good choice of wines, enjoyable food from snacks and sharing plates up, two-room restaurant with bare boards, painted tables and antler chandeliers, friendly staff; background and some live music; children, walkers and dogs welcome, disabled access via garden, three comfortable bedrooms, open all day from 9am. *(Caroline Prescott)*

FAVERSHAM TR0161
Bear (01795) 532668
Market Place; ME13 7AG Traditional late Victorian Shepherd Neame pub (back part dates from the 16th c); their ales kept well and occasional guests, enjoyable low-priced pubby food (not Fri-Sun evenings), friendly relaxed atmosphere, locals' front bar, snug and back dining lounge (all off side corridor); quiz last Mon of month, darts, free wi-fi; a couple of pavement tables, open all day. *(Simon Day)*

FAVERSHAM TR0160
Elephant (01795) 590157
The Mall; ME13 8JN Traditional town ale house, friendly and chatty, with four or five good changing ales mainly from smaller kent brewers, maybe a local cider too, no food (can bring your own), single bare-boards bar with central log fire and cosy seating areas, dim lighting; juke box and some live music; children and dogs welcome, peaceful suntrap back garden with pond, open all day Sat, till 7pm Sun, from 3pm weekdays, closed Mon. *(Nick Higgins)*

FAVERSHAM TR0161
Sun (01795) 535098
West Street; ME13 7JE Rambling 15th-c pub in pedestrianised street; unpretentious feel in small low-ceilinged partly panelled rooms, one with big inglenook, well kept Shepherd Neame ales and enjoyable food (not Sun evening) from sandwiches and pub favourites up, smart restaurant attached; background and live music (Fri), free wi-fi; wheelchair access negotiating small step, pleasant back courtyard, eight bedrooms, open all day from 8am for breakfast. *(Graham Kirby)*

FINGLESHAM TR3353
★ **Crown** (01304) 612555
Just off A258 Sandwich–Deal; The Street; CT14 0NA Neatly kept low-beamed

country local dating from the 16th c; good value generous home-made food from usual pub dishes to interesting specials, friendly helpful service, Dark Star and a couple of guests, softly lit split-level carpeted bar with stripped stone and inglenook log fire, two attractive dining rooms; children and dogs welcome, lovely big garden with play area and bat and trap, campsite with five hook-ups, open all day Fri-Sun. *(Alexandra and Richard Clay)*

FOLKESTONE
TR2336
British Lion (01303) 251478
The Bayle, near churchyard; CT20 1SQ Popular 18th-c flower-decked pub nestling behind parish church; comfortable and cosy, with four well kept ales and a couple of real ciders, big helpings of good value traditional food, friendly helpful service; children welcome, tables out in small yard, open all day Sun. *(Lindy Andrews)*

FORDCOMBE
TQ5240
Chafford Arms (01892) 740267
B2188, off A264 W of Langton Green; TN3 0SA Picturesque 19th-c tile-hung pub; real ales including Harveys and Larkins, good selection of wines and enjoyable food from sandwiches and baguettes to imaginative specials, helpful friendly staff, comfortable lounge bar, dining room and locals' bar where dogs allowed, three woodburners; children welcome (menu for them), picnic-sets on front terrace and in attractive sheltered back garden with Weald views, 1930s telephone box in car park, closed Sun evening, Mon, otherwise open (and food) all day. *(Andy and Rosemary Taylor)*

FORDWICH
TR1859
★ **Fordwich Arms** (01227) 710444
Off A28 in Sturry; CT2 0DB Interesting 1930s red-brick building by the River Stour (the much older pub burnt down); most customers here for young chef-landlord's excellent modern food (not Sun evening, Mon), but still drinkers in the long parquet-floored bar where they serve four real ales and good wines by the glass, courteous friendly staff, simply furnished panelled back dining room with open fire; background music; children and dogs welcome, tables on side lawn and riverside terrace, the town hall opposite is thought to be England's oldest, closed Mon, otherwise open all day. *(Tony Scott)*

FRITTENDEN
TQ8141
Bell & Jorrocks (01580) 852415
Corner of Biddenden Road/The Street; TN17 2EJ Simple 18th-c tile-hung village local; well kept Black Sheep, Harveys and a couple of guests (Easter weekend beer festival), Weston's and Thatcher's ciders, good home-made food (not Sun evening, Mon, Tues), friendly welcoming atmosphere, beamed interior with propeller from german

bomber above fireplace; regular live music and other events, sports TV, kentish darts; children and dogs welcome, closed Mon and Tues lunchtimes till 3pm, otherwise open all day. *(Claire Adams)*

GOODNESTONE
TR2554
Fitzwalter Arms (01304) 840303
The Street; NB this is in E Kent not the other Goodnestone; CT3 1PJ Old lattice-windowed brick-built village pub; rustic beamed bar with wood floor and open fire, Shepherd Neame ales, enjoyable reasonably priced pubby food (beer and burger Weds, steak night Sat), helpful cheerful service, carpeted dining room with another fire; darts; well behaved children and dogs welcome, terrace with steps up to peaceful garden, lovely church next door and close to Goodnestone Park Gardens, three bedrooms (steep stairs), closed Mon lunchtime in winter, otherwise open all day, no evening food Sun or Mon. *(Jill and Hugh Bennett)*

GOUDHURST
TQ7037
Green Cross (01580) 211200
East off A21 on to A262 (Station Road); TN17 1HA Although they may major on excellent fish and shellfish here, there is a properly pubby little two-roomed front bar with a chatty atmosphere, Harveys Best and half a dozen wines by the glass; hop-draped beams, stripped floorboards and dark wooden furnishings, wine bottles on windowsills, brass jugs on a mantelshelf above the fire, more formal main back dining room; background music; children and dogs (in bar) welcome, small side terrace, closed Sun evening. *(Emily and Toby Archer, Richard and Penny Gibbs, Audrey and Paul Summers)*

GOUDHURST
TQ7237
Star & Eagle (01580) 211512
High Street; TN17 1AL Steps up to striking medieval inn next to the church; settles and Jacobean-style seats in old-fashioned carpeted areas on different levels, beams and log fires, good choice of enjoyable food including some spanish influences, well kept ales such as Brakspears and Harveys, afternoon teas, friendly service, restaurant; occasional live music; children welcome, no dogs inside, tables out at back with lovely views, attractive village, 11 character bedrooms, good breakfast, open all day. *(Nick Morgan)*

GOUDHURST
TQ7037
Vine (01580) 211105
High Street; TN17 1AG White-painted 17th-c tile-hung village pub; four updated linked rooms (steps down to two on left), mix of old wooden tables and chairs on bare boards, some half-panelling and exposed timbers, various pictures, old photographs and a large boar's head, woodburner in brick

fireplace, Harveys Best, two changing guests and several wines by the glass including english sparkling, decent choice of enjoyable mid-priced food from pub favourites to interesting specials, upstairs grill room and cocktail lounge; background music, free wi-fi; children and dogs (in bar) welcome, picnic-sets out at front around olive tree, enclosed gravel terrace behind, closed Mon, otherwise open all day. *(Sandra Hollies)*

GROOMBRIDGE   TQ5337

★**Crown** (01892) 864742

B2110; TN3 9QH Charming tile-hung wealden inn with snug low-beamed bar; old tables on worn flagstones, panelling, bric-a-brac, fire in sizeable brick inglenook, well kept Harveys, Larkins and a guest, enjoyable pubby food (all day Sat, till 5pm Sun) from lunchtime sandwiches up including plenty of gluten-free options, good friendly service, refurbished two-room restaurant with smaller inglenook; background music, free wi-fi; children and dogs (in bar) welcome, tables on narrow brick terrace overlooking steep green, more seats in garden behind, four bedrooms, handy for Groombridge Place gardens, open all day Sat, till 9pm Sun. *(Martin Day, John Hunter Wright, Chloe Jones)*

HAWKHURST   TQ7531

★**Great House** (01580) 753119

Gills Green; pub signed off A229 N; TN18 5EJ Stylish white-weatherboarded restaur019 pub (part of the Elite Pubs group); good variety of well liked if not always cheap food, ales such as Harveys, Old Dairy and Sharps from marble counter, polite efficient service, sofas, armchairs and bright scatter cushions in chatty bar, stools against counter used by locals, dark wood dining tables and smartly upholstered chairs on slate floor beside log fire, steps down to airy dining room with doors out to garden; background music and some live music; children and dogs (in bar) welcome, open all day (food all day weekends). *(Nicky Menzies, David Jackman)*

HAWKHURST   TQ7630

Queens (01580) 754233

Rye Road (A268 E); TN18 4EY Fine Georgian-fronted pub (building actually dates from the 16th c) set back from the road; main bar with heavy beams and bare boards, some high modern chairs and barrel tables, armchairs either side of inglenook woodburner, dining area and cosy snug, well liked food from bar meals up, ales such as Old Dairy, Rockin' Robin and Sharps, decent wines by the glass, good friendly service, separate restaurant to left of entrance with another inglenook; background music; children welcome, tables out in front, seven bedrooms including family rooms, open all day, breakfast for non-residents. *(Charlie Parker)*

HEAVERHAM   TQ5758

Chequers (01732) 670266

Watery Lane; TN15 6NP Attractive 16th-c beamed country pub; well kept Shepherd Neame ales, decent wines by the glass and enjoyable fairly traditional food at sensible prices, friendly helpful service, public bar with open fire, inglenook woodburner in dining area, old timbered barn for functions; children and dogs welcome, big garden, good North Downs walks, closed Mon, otherwise open all day, no food Sun evening. *(Martin Day)*

HERNE   TR1865

Butchers Arms (01227) 371000

Herne Street (A291); CT6 7HL The UK's first micropub (converted from a butchers in 2005); up to half a dozen well kept changing ales including Adnams and Old Dairy tapped from backroom casks, tasters offered by friendly former motorbike-racing landlord, just a couple of benches and butcher's-block tables (seats for about ten), lots of bric-a-brac; dogs welcome, disabled access, tables out under awning, open 12-1.30pm, 6-9pm, closed Sun evening. *(Buster May)*

HERNHILL   TR0660

Red Lion (01227) 751207

Off A299 via Dargate, or A2 via Boughton Street and Staple Street; ME13 9JR Pretty Tudor pub by church and attractive village green, some refurbishment but keeping character; densely beamed with antique-style tables and chairs on flagstones or parquet, log fires, fairly traditional food from sharing boards up, well kept ales such as Sharps and Shepherd Neame, decent wines, friendly helpful staff, upstairs restaurant; background and some live music; children and dogs welcome, seats in front and in big garden, open all day. *(Victoria and James Sargeant)*

HEVER   TQ4743

Greyhound (01732) 862221

Uckfield Lane; TN8 7LJ Fully restored 19th-c country pub with good popular food from sandwiches up, three well kept ales including Harveys, friendly efficient service, restaurant; handy for Hever Castle, five comfortable bedrooms, closed Mon lunchtime in Nov, no food Sun evening in winter. *(Nick Higgins)*

HEVER   TQ4744

Henry VIII (01732) 862457

By gates of Hever Castle; TN8 7NH Predominantly 17th-c with heavy beams, wide floorboards, some fine oak panelling and inglenook fireplace, Henry VIII touches to décor, emphasis on enjoyable fairly priced food from pubby choices up, well kept Shepherd Neame ales, friendly efficient staff, restaurant; children and dogs welcome, outside covered area with a couple of leather sofas, steps down to deck and pondside lawn, closed Mon, otherwise normally open all day (but best to check), food till 6pm Sun. *(Tina and David Woods-Taylor, Tony Scott)*

HODSOLL STREET TQ6263
Green Man (01732) 823575
Signed off A227 S of Meopham; turn right in village; TN15 7LE Friendly family-run village pub with traditional furnishings in neat mainly carpeted rooms around central bar; painted half-panelling, old framed photographs and woodburner in standalone fireplace, Harveys, Sharps, Timothy Taylors and a guest, wide choice of enjoyable blackboard food from sandwiches/baguettes up including popular two-course weekday lunch deal; background music (live Sun), quiz Mon, free wi-fi; children and dogs welcome, picnic-sets in front overlooking small green, more tables and climbing frame on back lawn, open (and food) all day Fri-Sun. *(Paddy and Sian O'Leary)*

HOLLINGBOURNE TQ8455
Dirty Habit (01622) 880880
B2163, off A20; ME17 1UW Ancient dimly lit beamed pub in same Elite Pubs group as the Great House in Hawkhurst, Gun at Gun Hill (Sussex) etc; ales such as Harveys and Shepherd Neame, several wines by the glass and popular food including seasonal offers, armchairs and stools on slate floor in main bar area, panelled end room with mix of tables and chairs, low-beamed dining room and a further raftered eating area with brick floor and woodburner; children welcome, good outside shelter with armchairs and sofas, on North Downs Way and handy for Leeds Castle, open all day. *(Tony Holland)*

HOLLINGBOURNE TQ8354
★ Windmill (01622) 889000
M20 junction 8, A20 towards Lenham then left on to B2163 – Eyhorne Street; ME17 1TR Most people here for the impressive food, but there's a small back bar serving Sharps, a guest such as local Musket and up to 15 wines by the glass; light and airy main room with white-painted beams, animal skins on bare boards and log fire in low inglenook, mix of furniture including armchairs, heavy settles with scatter cushions, red leather banquette and dark wood dining tables and chairs, two further dining rooms (steps up to one), candles and fresh flowers; background music (live Sun), free wi-fi; children and dogs (in bar) welcome, back garden with play area and summer barbecues, open all day. *(Miss A E Dare)*

IDE HILL TQ4851
Cock (01732) 750310
Off B2042 SW of Sevenoaks; TN14 6JN Pretty village-green local dating from the

15th c, chatty and friendly, with two bars (steps between), well kept Greene King ales and a beer badged for them, enjoyable good value traditional food including notable steak and kidney pudding, decent affordably priced wine list, cosy in winter with inglenook log fire; children and dogs welcome, picnic-sets out at front, handy for Chartwell and Emmetts Garden (both NT), nice walks nearby, open all day. *(Julie Swift)*

IGHTHAM TQ5956
George & Dragon (01732) 882440
The Street, A227; TN15 9HH Ancient half-timbered pub with spacious modernised interior; enjoyable food from pub favourites up including daily specials and weekday set menu, well kept Shepherd Neame ales and decent wines, friendly staff, sofas among other furnishings in long main bar, heavy-beamed end room, woodburner and open fires, restaurant; children and dogs welcome, back terrace by car park, handy for Ightham Mote (NT), good walks, open all day from 10am for breakfast, food till 7pm Sun. *(Martin Day)*

IGHTHAM COMMON TQ5955
Old House (01732) 886077
Redwell, S of village; OS Sheet 188 map reference 591559; TN15 9EE Basic unchanging two-room country local tucked down narrow lane (no inn sign); beams, bare bricks and big inglenook log fire, half a dozen interesting changing ales from tap room casks, good selection of whiskies and gins, no food; darts; dogs welcome, closed weekday lunchtimes (opens 7pm) and may shut early if quiet. *(Martin Day)*

KENNINGTON TR0245
Old Mill (01223) 661000
Mill Lane; TN25 4DZ Updated and much extended early 19th-c dining pub (same owners as the Oak on the Green at Bearsted); good choice of popular food from sandwiches and snacks up, well kept ales and nice selection of wines, friendly helpful service; children welcome, plenty of terrace and garden seating, open (and food) all day. *(Paul Humphreys)*

KINGSDOWN TR3748
Kings Head (01304) 373915
Upper Street; CT14 8BJ Tucked-away split-level local with two cosy bars and L-shaped extension; black timbers, lots of old photographs on faded cream walls, woodburner, three real ales and popular reasonably priced food including blackboard specials and children's menu, friendly landlord and staff; background and occasional live music , a few vintage amusement machines and darts; dogs

---

It's very helpful if you let us know up-to-date food prices when you report on pubs.

welcome, small side garden, skittle alley, open all day Sun, closed weekdays till 5pm. *(Beverley and Andy Butcher)*

KINGSTON   TR2051
Black Robin (01227) 830230
Elham Valley Road, off A2 S of Canterbury at Barham signpost; CT4 6HS 18th-c pub named after a notorious highwayman who was hanged nearby; kentish ales and good helpings of enjoyable home-made food from shortish menu (can eat in bar or back restaurant extension), stone-baked pizzas to take away; background and live music including some established folk artists, sports TV, free wi-fi; children and dogs welcome, disabled access, seats out on decking, open all day (till 6pm Sun). *(Claire Adams)*

LADDINGFORD   TQ6848
Chequers (01622) 871266
The Street; ME18 6BP Friendly old beamed and weatherboarded village pub; good sensibly priced food from sandwiches and sharing boards up, some themed nights, well kept Adnams Southwold and three guests; events including ale and cheese festival Apr/May; children and dogs welcome, big garden with play area, shetland ponies in paddock, Medway walks nearby, one bedroom, open all day weekends.
(David Travis)

LEEDS   TQ8253
George (01622) 861314
Lower Street; ME17 1RN Welcoming 17th-c tile-hung village pub; Shepherd Neame ales and good choice of enjoyable pubby food from blackboard menu including range of fajitas; sports TV, fruit machine; children and dogs welcome, picnic-sets out at front and in good-sized garden up steps, covered dining terrace, handy for Leeds Castle, open (and food) all day, kitchen closes 6pm Sun.
(Eddie Edwards)

LEIGH   TQ5446
Fleur de Lis (01732) 832283
High Street; TN11 8RL Modernised and opened-up brick pub in former 1855 cottage row; well kept ales such as Timothy Taylors, Tonbridge and Whitstable along with a house beer (4 Jays) from Greene King, good fairly priced food including blackboard specials, friendly attentive staff; sports TV; children and dogs welcome, rattan furniture on back terrace, open all day Fri-Sun. *(Peter Meister)*

LEIGH   TQ5646
Plough (01732) 832149
Powder Mill Lane/Leigh Road, off B2027 NW of Tonbridge; TN11 9AJ Attractive opened-up Tudor country pub; lattice windows, hop-strung beams and parquet flooring, some cushioned pews and farmhouse chairs, massive grate in two-way inglenook, well kept Tonbridge Coppernob

and up to three local guests, popular home-cooked food, friendly helpful staff, small flagstoned room behind servery with old mangle and darts; quiz third Thurs of month; children and dogs welcome, picnic-sets in garden with play area, old barn for weddings and other functions, open all day Sun till 9pm, closed Mon-Weds. *(Lindy Andrews)*

LINTON   TQ7550
Bull (01622) 743612
Linton Hill (A229 S of Maidstone); ME17 4AW Comfortably modernised 17th-c dining pub; good choice of food from sandwiches and light dishes to pub favourites and grills, popular Sun carvery, fine fireplace in nice old beamed bar, carpeted restaurant, well kept Shepherd Neame ales, friendly efficient service; children and dogs (in bar) welcome, side garden overlooking church, splendid far-reaching views from back decking, two gazebos, open (and food) all day. *(Debbie Kemp)*

LITTLE CHART   TQ9446
Swan (01233) 840011
The Street; TN27 0QB Attractive 15th-c village pub with notable arched Dering windows, open fires and clean fresh décor in unspoilt front bar and good-sized dining area, flowers on tables, enjoyable home-made food (not Sun evening), well kept beers and decent wines by the glass, friendly staff; Weds quiz; children and dogs (in bar) welcome, nice riverside garden, closed Mon, otherwise open all day. *(Paddy and Sian O'Leary)*

LOWER HARDRES   TR1453
Granville (01227) 700402
Faussett Hill, Street End; B2068 S of Canterbury; CT4 7AL Spacious pub with contemporary furnishings in several linked areas, one with unusual central fire under large conical hood, also a proper public bar with farmhouse chairs, settles and woodburner, enjoyable food from baguettes and pub favourites to more restaurant dishes, good value set lunch and other deals, up to three Shepherd Neame ales including Master Brew, 13 wines by the glass; background music, artwork for sale; children and dogs welcome, seats on small sunny terrace and in garden under large spreading tree, open all day.
(Bob and Melissa Wyatt)

LUDDESDOWNE   TQ6667
★Cock (01474) 814208
Henley Street, N of village – OS Sheet 177 map reference 664672; off A227 in Meopham, or A228 in Cuxton; DA13 0XB Early 18th-c country pub under long-serving no-nonsense landlord; at least seven well kept ales such as Adnams, Goachers, Harveys and St Austell, also some good german beers, snacky bar food, rugs on bare boards in bay-windowed lounge, beams and panelling, quarry-tiled locals'

bar with settles, cask tables and other pubby furnishings, aircraft pictures, beer mats and bric-a-brac from stuffed animals to model cars, woodburners, back dining conservatory; music quiz fourth Mon of month, bar billiards and darts; no children inside or on part-covered heated back terrace, dogs welcome, big secure garden, good walks, open all day Fri-Sun, from 4pm other days. *(Graham Kirby)*

LYNSTED   TQ9460
Black Lion (01795) 521229
The Street; ME9 0RJ Welcoming early 17th-c village pub; well kept Goachers and good freshly made pubby food (all day Sat, not Sun evening) including blackboard specials, settles and old tables on bare boards, log fires; some live music, pool; children and dogs welcome, well tended garden with play area, open all day. *(Nick Morgan)*

MARDEN   TQ7547
Stile Bridge (01622) 831236
Staplehurst Road (A229); TN12 9BH Friendly roadside pub with five well kept ales including Dark Star and Goachers, also lots of bottled beers, real ciders and extensive range of gins, good traditional food (not Sun evening); regular live music; dogs welcome in bar, back garden and terrace, open all day. *(Andy and Rosemary Taylor)*

MARKBEECH   TQ4742
Kentish Horse (01342) 850493
Off B2026 Hartfield–Edenbridge; TN8 5NT Attractive village pub (originally three cottages) next to the church, friendly and welcoming, with three well kept ales including Harveys and Larkins from brick counter, good value traditional food (not Sun or Mon evenings), friendly helpful staff, black beams and log fire in long carpeted bar, restaurant with pubby furniture and woodburner in large brick fireplace, french windows to terrace; folk night second Sun of the month; children welcome, picnic-sets and fenced play area in big garden, nice views, open all day. *(Tony Scott)*

MARTIN   TR3347
Lantern (01304) 852276
Off A258 Dover–Deal; The Street; CT15 5JL Pretty 17th-c brick pub (originally two farmworker's cottages) in lovely setting; small refurbished bar with low beams, stripped brick and cosy corners, extensive range of craft beers and real ales from copper-topped counter, decent wines by the glass including prosecco on tap, cocktails, enjoyable food from traditional choices up, friendly helpful service, soft lighting, log fires; background and some acoustic live music, other events such as book club and wine tasting, shop selling home-made and local produce; children and dogs welcome, some tables out at front, more in good-sized

back garden with big play house, open all day in summer, all day Fri-Sun winter. *(Louise and Anton Parsons)*

MATFIELD   TQ6642
★ **Poet at Matfield** (01892) 722416
Maidstone Road; TN12 7JH Civilised 17th-c beamed pub-restaurant named for Siegfried Sassoon who was born nearby; highly regarded modern cooking from south african chef-patron including tasting menus (evenings Weds, Thurs) and very good value set menu (Tues-Sat lunch, Tues-Thurs dinner), ales such as Harveys and Westerham, well chosen wines and some interesting gins, friendly professional service; garden with barbecue, closed Sun evening and Mon, otherwise open all day. *(Caroline Prescott)*

MATFIELD   TQ6541
Star (01892) 725458
Maidstone Road (B2160); TN12 7JR Creeper-clad pub close to the village duck pond; beamed and bare-boards front bar with real ales such as Harveys, enjoyable food (not Sun evening) including signature home-made pies, friendly service, restaurant in older back part with inglenook woodburner; quiz third Thurs of month, occasional live music; picnic-sets on gravel terrace, open all day. *(Gene and Kitty Rankin)*

MERSHAM   TR0438
Farriers Arms (01233) 720444
The Forstal/Flood Street; TN25 6NU Large early 17th-c pub owned by the local community; beers from on-site microbrewery including seasonal ales, decent choice of wines and enjoyable home-made food from bar snacks to daily specials, friendly staff, opened-up interior with beams and log fires, restaurant; July beer festival; children and dogs welcome, pretty streamside garden behind with pleasant country views, open all day. *(Alexandra and Richard Clay)*

NEWENDEN   TQ8327
White Hart (01797) 252166
Rye Road (A268); TN18 5PN Popular 16th-c weatherboarded local; long low-beamed bar with big stone fireplace, dining areas off serving enjoyable reasonably priced pub food including good Sun roasts, well kept Harveys, Rother Valley and guests (July beer/cider festival), friendly helpful young staff, back games area with pool; background music, quiz nights, sports TV; children and dogs welcome, boules in large garden, near river (boat trips to NT's Bodiam Castle), six bedrooms, open all day. *(Paddy and Sian O'Leary)*

NORTHBOURNE   TR3352
Hare & Hounds (01304) 369188
Off A256 or A258 near Dover; The Street; CT14 0LG Welcoming 17th-c village pub with well kept Harveys, a guest beer

and good choice of wines from brick-faced servery, decent pubby food, bare-boards and flagstoned bar separated by a couple of archways, nice log fire; children and dogs welcome, paved terrace and garden with play area, open all day Thurs-Sun. *(Claire Adams)*

OARE   TR0163
★**Shipwrights Arms** (01795) 590088
S shore of Oare Creek, E of village; signed from Oare Road/Ham Road junction in Faversham; ME13 7TU Remote marshland tavern with plenty of character; three dark simple little bars separated by standing timbers, wood partitions and narrow door arches, medley of seats from tapestry-cushioned stools to black panelled built-in settles forming booths, flags and boating pennants on ceiling, wind gauge above main door (takes reading from chimney), up to six kentish beers tapped from the cask (pewter tankards over counter), simple home-cooked food lunchtime only; children (away from bar area) and dogs welcome, large garden with bat and trap, path along Oare Creek to Swale estuary, lots of surrounding bird life, closed Mon. *(Nick Higgins)*

OARE   TR0063
Three Mariners (01795) 533633
Church Road; ME13 0QA Comfortable simply restored 18th-c pub with good food including fresh fish and evening set menu, Shepherd Neame ales and plenty of wines by the glass, beams, bare boards and log fire; children and dogs (in bar) welcome, attractive garden overlooking Faversham Creek, good walks, open all day (till 9pm Sun). *(Jill and Hugh Bennett)*

PAINTERS FORSTAL   TQ9958
Alma (01795) 533835
Signed off A2 at Ospringe; ME13 0DU Welcoming weatherboarded and timbered village local, homely and tidy, with well kept Shepherd Neame ales, decent wines and good value home cooking including notable steak and kidney pudding, Tues lunchtime set deal, helpful service; children and dogs (in bar) welcome, picnic-sets in small enclosed garden, play area over the road, campsite nearby, no food Sun evening. *(Julie Swift)*

PEMBURY   TQ6240
Camden Arms (01892) 822012
High Street (The Green); TN2 4PH Substantial tile-hung inn opposite village green; good generously served food from extensive reasonably priced menu, Sun carvery, well kept ales such as Harveys and decent choice of other beers and wines, friendly welcoming staff, large opened-up central bar with smaller dining rooms off, beams, bare boards and flagstones, various bits and pieces including landlord's remarkable collection of Dinky Toys; children

and dogs welcome, tables on covered paved terrace, picnic-sets on lawn, 15 bedrooms some with four-posters, open (and food) all day. *(Nigel and Jean Eames)*

PENSHURST   TQ5241
★**Spotted Dog** (01892) 870253
Smarts Hill, off B2188 S; TN11 8EP Quaint weatherboarded pub first licensed in 1520; heavy low beams and timbers, attractive moulded panelling, big inglenook fireplace, hops, horsebrasses and lots of country pictures, traditional furniture on bare boards or carpet, Harveys, Larkins, Tonbridge and Youngs, several wines by the glass, popular pubby food (not Sun evening); free wi-fi; children and dogs (in bar) welcome, terrace seating on several levels with good views over miles of countryside, open all day (till 10pm Sun). *(Tony Scott)*

PETT BOTTOM   TR1652
Duck (01227) 830354
Off B2068 S of Canterbury, via Lower Hardres; CT4 5PB Popular tile-hung pub in attractive downland spot; long bare-boards bar with scrubbed tables, pine-panelling and two log fires, good food cooked by landlord-chef including weekday set lunch, friendly attentive service, two or three well kept beers and good wine choice; children and dogs welcome, seats and old well out in front, garden behind where Ian Fleming used to make notes for his James Bond books (see blue plaque), camping nearby, closed Mon. *(Victoria and James Sargeant)*

PETTERIDGE   TQ6640
Hopbine (01892) 722561
Petteridge Lane; NE of village; TN12 7NE Unspoilt tiled and weatherboarded cottage in quiet hamlet; two small rooms separated by an open fire, traditional pubby furniture, hops and horsebrasses, well kept Long Man, Tonbridge and a guest, proper cider and enjoyable good value home-made food including wood-fired pizzas (two-for-one deal Weds), themed evenings, friendly staff, steps up to simple back part with brick fireplace; dogs welcome, outside gents'; terrace seating, open all day Fri-Sun, no food Mon, Tues. *(Gene and Kitty Rankin)*

PLUCKLEY   TQ9144
Rose & Crown (01233) 840048
Mundy Bois – spelled Monday Boys on some maps – off Smarden Road SW of village centre; TN27 0ST Popular 17th-c tile-hung pub with good food (all day Sat and Sun) from snacks to daily specials, three well kept beers including Harveys and Whitstable, friendly attentive service, main bar with massive inglenook, small snug and restaurant; background music, beer/music festival Aug; children and dogs (in bar) welcome, pretty garden and terrace with views, play area, open all day. *(Miss A E Dare)*

RAMSGATE   TR3764
Artillery Arms   (01843) 853202
West Cliff Road; CT11 9JS Old-fashioned little corner local on two levels, chatty and welcoming, with half a dozen well kept interesting beers and enjoyable food (all day weekends), artillery prints/memorabilia and fine listed windows depicting Napoleonic scenes; dogs welcome, wheelchair access, open all day. *(Andy and Rosemary Taylor)*

RAMSGATE   TR3764
Conqueror   07890 203282
Grange Road/St Mildreds Road; CT11 9LR Cosy single-room micropub in former corner shop; welcoming enthusiastic landlord serving three changing ales direct from the cask, also local cider and apple juice, friendly chatty atmosphere, large windows and old photos of eponymous cross-channel paddle steamer; dogs welcome, closed Sun evening, Mon. *(Charlie Parker)*

ROCHESTER   TQ7468
Coopers Arms   (01634) 404298
St Margarets Street; ME1 1TL Ancient jettied building behind the cathedral; cosily unpretentious with two comfortable beamed bars, low-priced pub food and good range of well kept beers, list of landlords back to 1543 and ghostly tales of a walled-up monk (mannequin marks the spot); live music (Sun) and quiz nights; tables in attractive courtyard, open all day. *(Martin Day)*

ROLVENDEN   TQ8431
Bull   (01580) 241212
Regent Street; TN17 4PB Welcoming tile-hung cottage with woodburner in fine brick inglenook, high-backed dining chairs around rustic tables on stripped boards, built-in panelled wall seats, well kept Harveys and Old Dairy, enjoyable food (not Sun evening in winter) from pub favourites and pizzas up, pale oak tables in dining room; background music; children and dogs (in bar) welcome, picnic-sets behind picket fence at front and side, more seats in sizeable back garden, open all day, till 7pm Sun. *(Alan Cowell)*

ROLVENDEN LAYNE   TQ8530
Ewe & Lamb   (01580) 241837
Maytham Road; TN17 4NP Tile-hung village pub under newish management; beams, bare boards and log fires, three real ales including Harveys and over 30 gins, good home-made food including light lunch menu, daily specials and Sun carvery, good friendly service, back restaurant; some live music; children, walkers and dogs welcome, seats out at front behind picket fence, not much parking, open (and food) all day. *(Richard and Penny Gibbs)*

SANDGATE   TR2035
Ship   (01303) 248525
High Street; CT20 3AH Long narrow corner pub with traditional nautical-theme bar and dining area at front and modern conservatory restaurant behind overlooking the sea, half a dozen cask-tapped ales including Dark Star, Greene King and Hop Back, real cider, decent wines and good range of gins, popular food with emphasis on local fish/seafood, affable long-serving landlord and friendly efficient staff; more good sea views from roof terrace and bedrooms, open all day. *(Richard Kennell)*

SANDWICH   TR3358
Crispin   (01304) 621967
High Street; CT13 9EA Welcoming 15th-c corner pub next to medieval barbican and toll bridge; long timbered main room divided by open fire, four well kept ales including a house beer from local Mad Cat, good authentic caribbean food along with more traditional choices; some live music; children and dogs welcome, seats out overlooking river, open all day, no food Sun evening. *(Tony Scott)*

SARRE   TR2564
Crown   (01843) 847808
Ramsgate Road (A253) off A28; CT7 0LF Historic 15th-c inn (Grade I listed) sandwiched between two main roads; front bar and other rambling rooms including restaurant, beams and log fires, well kept Shepherd Neame ales and decent fairly priced wines, own cherry brandy (pub known locally as the Cherry Brandy House), generous helpings of enjoyable locally sourced food from sandwiches up, good friendly service; children welcome, side garden (traffic noise), comfortable surprisingly quiet bedrooms, open all day. *(Daniel King)*

SEASALTER   TR0864
★ Sportsman   (01227) 273370
Faversham Road, off B2040; CT5 4BP Informal restauranty pub just inside seawall – rather unprepossessing from outside but surprisingly light and airy; imaginative modern cooking using plenty of seafood (not Sun evening, Mon, must book and not cheap), good wine choice including english and a couple of well kept Shepherd Neame ales, knowledgeable landlord and friendly staff; two plain linked rooms and long conservatory, scrubbed pine tables, wheelback and basket-weave dining chairs on wood floor, local artwork; children welcome, plastic glasses for outside, wide views over marshland with grazing sheep and (from seawall) across to Sheppey, small

---

Half pints: by law, a pub should not charge more for half a pint than half the price of a full pint, unless it shows that half-pint price on its price list.

caravan park one side, wood chalets the other, open all day Sun till 10pm. *(Glenn Tilbrook, Caroline Prescott)*

SEVENOAKS   TQ5555
★**Bucks Head** (01732) 761330
Godden Green, just E; TN15 0JJ
Welcoming and relaxed old flower-decked pub with neatly kept bar and restaurant area, good freshly cooked blackboard food from baguettes to Sun roasts, well kept Shepherd Neame and a guest, beams, panelling and splendid inglenooks; children and dogs welcome, front terrace overlooking informal green and duck pond, pretty back garden with mature trees, pergola and views over quiet country behind Knole (NT), popular with walkers, closed Mon except bank holidays. *(Claire Adams)*

SEVENOAKS   TQ5355
Halfway House (01732) 463667
2.5 miles from M25 junction 5; TN13 2JD Nicely updated old roadside pub with friendly staff and regulars; good competitively priced food from sensibly short blackboard menu, three changing ales, local wines and some interesting flavoured vodkas, upper bar with record deck and LPs (can bring your own), some live music too including ukulele club every other Mon; handy for the station, parking can be tricky, open all day. *(Martin Day)*

SHADOXHURST   TQ9737
Kings Head (01233) 732243
Woodchurch Road; TN26 1LQ Old family-run pub with clean updated interior; good value enjoyable food in bar and separate restaurant including blackboard specials, well kept Shepherd Neame and guests, friendly efficient staff, stripped pine tables on bare boards or quarry tiles, various bits and pieces including china, copper and brass, vintage photos and old horse tack, log fires; games area with pool, quiz last Sun of month; children and dogs welcome, tables on front terrace and in garden behind with play area, closed Sun evening, Mon. *(Beverley and Andy Butcher)*

SHOREHAM   TQ5161
Kings Arms (01959) 523100
Church Street; TN14 7SJ
Part-weatherboarded 16th-c pub in quaint unspoilt village close to the River Darent; cosy and unpretentious, with generous helpings of good honest food including Fri fish and chips, two or three well kept beers such as Bombardier and Greene King, friendly helpful staff, log fire, plates and brasses, small restaurant area; children welcome, no dogs, picnic-sets outside (some under cover), note the ostler's box (compete with mannequin) at the front, good local walks, open all day, no evening food Sun-Tues. *(Mike Buckingham)*

SHOREHAM   TQ5261
Olde George (01959) 522017
Church Street; TN14 7RY Traditional 16th-c pub opposite the church; low beams, uneven floors and a cosy fires, two or three well kept changing ales and enjoyable pubby food including bargain OAP lunch (Thurs), friendly attentive service, carpeted dining area to one side; children, walkers and dogs welcome, picnic-sets by road, open all day. *(Louise and Anton Parsons)*

SHOREHAM   TQ5161
Two Brewers (01959) 522800
High Street; TN14 7TD Busy rather smart family-run pub with two stylishly modernised beamed rooms, back part more restauranty; good freshly made food from varied menu, can be pricey but they also do a set lunch, well kept kentish ales and nice wines from carefully chosen list, afternoon teas; friendly attentive staff, snug areas with comfortable seating, two woodburners; children welcome, trees in planters and a couple of benches out in front behind picket fence, café-style tables on small Astroturf deck, near the Shoreham Cross and good walks, closed Sun evening, Mon and Tues. *(B and M Kendall)*

SISSINGHURST   TQ7937
★**Milk House** (01580) 720200
The Street; TN17 2JG Bustling village inn near Sissinghurst Castle Garden (NT); bar on right with grey-painted beams and handsome Tudor fireplace fronted by plush sofas, wicker-faced counter serving Dark Star, Harveys and a local guest, real cider, 14 wines by the glass and good range of gins and whiskies, restaurant to the left with small room off (perfect for a private party), good popular food including pizzas from outside oven; background music, daily papers, free wi-fi; children and dogs (in bar) welcome, large side terrace with sturdy furniture under green parasols, garden picnic-sets and children's play hut by fenced-in pond, comfortable well equipped bedrooms, open all day from 9am. *(Caroline Prescott)*

SMARDEN   TQ8642
Bell (01233) 770283
From Smarden follow Water Lane (between church and Chequers pub), then left at T junction; or from A274 take unsignposted turn E a mile N of B2077 to Smarden; TN27 8PW Old brick and tile country pub with series of cosy beamed rooms, enjoyable food from traditional choices up, Shepherd Neame ales and decent range of wines, good friendly service; picnic-sets in garden with own bar, closed Mon, otherwise open all day. *(Sandra Hollies)*

SNARGATE   TQ9928
★**Red Lion** (01797) 344648
B2080 Appledore–Brenzett; TN29 9UQ Unchanging 16th-c pub in same family

for over 100 years; simple old-fashioned charm in three timeless little rooms with original cream wall panelling, heavy beams in sagging ceilings, dark pine Victorian farmhouse chairs on bare boards, an old piano and coal fire, local cider and four or five ales including Goachers tapped from casks behind unusual free-standing marble-topped counter, no food, bar snacks, traditional games like toad in the hole, nine men's morris and table skittles, friendly staff; children in family room, dogs in bar, outdoor lavatories, cottage garden, closed Mon evening. *(Bob and Melissa Wyatt)*

SPELDHURST   TQ5541
★ **George & Dragon**   (01892) 863125
Village signed from A264 W of Tunbridge Wells; TN3 0NN Handsome pub based around a 13th-c manorial hall (lovely original features); entrance lobby with half-panelled room to the right, wheelback and other dining chairs, cushioned wall pew, small pictures and horsebrasses, doorway to another dining room with similar furnishings and second inglenook, bar to left of entrance has woodburner in small fireplace, high-winged cushioned settles and other wooden furniture on stripped-wood floor, good range of well liked food from baguettes up, obliging friendly service, Harveys, Larkins and a guest, several wines by the glass, raftered upstairs restaurant with fine king post; background music, free wi-fi; children and dogs (in bar) welcome, teak furniture on front gravel terrace, covered back area and lower terrace with 200-year-old olive tree, open all day, no food Sun evening. *(Adrian Johnson, Mrs J Ekins-Daukes, Robert David Craine)*

ST MARY IN THE MARSH   TR0627
Star   (01797) 362139
Opposite church; TN29 0BX Remote fairly down-to-earth pub with Tudor origins; popular food (not Sun evening, Mon) from sandwiches and baked potatoes up, five well kept ales including Shepherd Neame and Youngs from brick-faced counter, friendly service, inglenook woodburner; live music nights; children and dogs welcome, tables in nice garden, beamed bedrooms with Romney Marsh views, lovely setting opposite ancient church (where Edith Nesbit, author of *The Railway Children*, is buried), popular with walkers and cyclists, open all day. *(Jill and Hugh Bennett)*

STAPLEHURST   TQ7846
Lord Raglan   (01622) 843747
About 1.5 miles from town centre towards Maidstone, turn right off A229 into Chart Hill Road opposite Chart Cars; OS Sheet 188 map reference 785472; TN12 0DE Country pub with cosy chatty area around narrow counter, hop-strung low beams, big log fire and woodburner, mix of comfortably worn dark wood furniture, Goachers, Harveys and

a guest, farm cider and perry, well liked reasonably priced home-cooked food, good wine list; children and dogs welcome, wheelchair access, tables on terrace and in the side orchard, Aug bank holiday onion festival, closed Sun. *(Sandra Hollies)*

STODMARSH   TR2160
★ **Red Lion**   (01227) 721339
High Street; off A257 just E of Canterbury; CT3 4BA Tucked-away pub close to Stodmarsh National Nature Reserve; bar rooms with country kitchen furniture, plenty of candles and big log fire, Greene King IPA and a guest tapped from the cask, Kentish Pip cider and eight wines by the glass, good food including Weds pie night, friendly helpful staff; background music, piano; children and dogs (in bar) welcome, tables in back garden, bedrooms, open all day summer, closed Sun evening, Mon in winter. *(Nick Morgan)*

SUNDRIDGE   TQ4855
White Horse   (01959) 561198
Main Road; TN14 6EQ Refurbished open-plan village pub under new management; decent range of well liked food from sandwiches up including range of burgers, three real ales such as Adnams Southwold and Timothy Taylors Landlord, several wines by the glass, good friendly service, log fires and low beams, comfortable seating on wood floors; live music and quiz nights, children welcome, dogs in bar area, picnic-sets under parasols on fenced lawn, open all day, no food Sun evening. *(Beverley and Andy Butcher)*

SUTTON VALENCE   TQ8050
Plough   (01622) 842555
Sutton Road (A274), Langley; ME17 3LX Refurbished roadside dining pub; main bar painted in shades of grey with mix of wooden and copper-topped tables, side bar and candlelit dining extension behind with view into kitchen, well kept Harveys, local Rockin' Robin and a guest, several wines by the glass, happy hours Mon-Fri, enjoyable food from sandwiches and bar snacks to restauranty choices, friendly relaxed atmosphere; live music Fri; children and dogs welcome, tables and vintage plough out at front behind picket fence, open all day (Sun till 10pm). *(Victoria and James Sargeant)*

TENTERDEN   TQ8833
White Lion   (01580) 765077
High Street; TN30 6BD Comfortably updated beamed and timbered 16th-c inn behind Georgian façade; popular food including Josper grills and pizzas from open kitchen, mainly local ales and a beer badged for them, good choice of other drinks, big log fire, friendly helpful staff; background music, free wi-fi; heated terrace overlooking street, comfortable well equipped bedrooms, open (and food) all day. *(Richard Tilbrook)*

TEYNHAM TQ9661
Plough (01795) 521348
Lewson Street; ME9 9JJ Picturesque 13th-c weatherboarded pub in quiet village; unpretentious split-level interior with low hop-strung beams and inglenook woodburner, friendly staff and atmosphere, Shepherd Neame ales, decent wines and enjoyable home-made food including popular Sun roasts; some live music, resident parrot called Bob; children and dogs welcome, front terrace behind picket fence, large well kept back garden with play area overlooking meadow, closed Sun evening, Mon. *(John Hunter Wright)*

TUDELEY TQ6145
Poacher & Partridge
(01732) 358934 *Hartlake Road; TN11 0PH* Renovated in smart country style by Elite Pubs (Great House in Hawkhurst, Dirty Habit at Hollingbourne etc); light interior with feature pizza oven, wide range of food including daily specials, Tues steak night, ales such as Sharps Doom Bar and Timothy Taylors Landlord, good choice of wines by the glass; live music including some afternoon jazz; children and dogs welcome, outside bar and grill, play area, nearby interesting church with Chagall stained glass (note roof paintings at pub's entrance), circular walks (leaflets provided), open (and food) all day. *(Nicky Menzies)*

TUNBRIDGE WELLS TQ5839
Black Pig (01892) 523030
Grove Hill Road; TN1 1RZ Refurbished dining pub under newish ownership; long narrow bare-boards bar with woodburner at one end, steps up to cosy room with bookshelves and Victorian fireplace, Harveys Best, Brakspears Oxford Gold and good wines by the glass, popular food from varied often interesting menu, grey panelled restaurant with kitchen view, private dining rooms upstairs; children welcome, teak furniture on back gravel terrace, handy for the station, open all day, no food Sun evening. *(Anne Taylor, James Cranwell)*

TUNBRIDGE WELLS TQ5837
Bull (01892) 263489
Frant Road; TN2 5LH Friendly 19th-c pub towards the southern outskirts of town; two modernised linked areas with one or two quirky touches, chunky pine tables and kitchen chairs on stripped-wood floor, a couple of leather sofas by open fire, well kept Shepherd Neame and good food cooked by chef-landlord from shortish menu (not Sun evening, Mon); children (till 8.30pm) and dogs welcome, seats out on fenced

roadside terrace, closed Mon lunchtime, otherwise open all day, no food Sun evening, Tues. *(James Cranwell)*

UNDERRIVER TQ5552
★White Rock (01732) 833112
SE of Sevenoaks, off B245; TN15 0SB Attractive village pub with good food from pubby choices up (all day weekends, best to book), friendly helpful service, well kept Harveys, Tonbridge and a beer badged for them, decent wines, beams, bare boards and stripped brickwork in cosy original part with adjacent dining area, another bar in modern extension with woodburner; background and some live music, darts, pool; children welcome, dogs may be allowed but do ask first, small front garden, back terrace and large lawn with boules and bat and trap, pretty churchyard, good walks nearby, open all day in summer, all day weekends winter. *(Ian Phillips, Martin Day)*

UPNOR TQ7671
Ship (01634) 290553
Upnor Road, Lower Upnor; ME2 4UY Smallish mock-Tudor pub overlooking the Medway and boats; good home cooking including fish specials, Courage Best, Shepherd Neame Master Brew and guests, friendly staff, carpeted interior with marine knick-knacks; children and dogs welcome, picnic-sets out at front and in garden behind, open all day. *(Louise and Anton Parsons)*

UPPER UPNOR TQ7570
Tudor Rose (01634) 714175
Off A228 N of Strood; High Street; ME2 4XG 16th-c pub down narrow cobbled street just back from the river and next to Upnor Castle (best to use village car park at top); cosy beamed rooms with mix of old furniture and some nautical bits and pieces, Shepherd Neame ales and an occasional guest, popular pubby food (not Sun evening) from baguettes up, good friendly service; free wi-fi; children welcome, seats out at front made from an old boat, large enclosed garden behind with arbour, open all day, till 8pm Sun. *(Nick Higgins)*

WAREHORNE TQ9832
★Woolpack (01233) 732900
Off B2067 near Hamstreet; TN26 2LL Part-weatherboarded 16th-c dining pub under same ownership as the Globe in Rye (Sussex); interesting interior with various connecting areas, beams, inglenook fire and woodburner, brick and quarry-tiled floors, walls (some boarded) hung with prints, old photographs, hops and ornate mirrors, lots of other bits and pieces including farming implements, fishing rods, oars and a boar's

---

If you stay overnight in an inn or hotel, they are allowed to serve you an alcoholic drink at any hour of the day or night.

head, candles on tables, four well kept regional ales direct from the cask, local cider and good wines by the glass, much liked food including daily specials (no bookings so best to arrive early), helpful service and friendly easy-going atmosphere; background jazz; children and dogs welcome, rows of outside seating overlooking quiet lane and 15th-c church, five comfortable quirky bedrooms, open all day. *(Peter Meister, Bill)*

WEALD   TQ5250
★**Windmill** (01732) 463330

Windmill Road; TN14 6PN Popular and friendly village pub with six well kept ales including Goachers, local ciders and good fair-priced food (not Sun evening, Mon) from interestingly varied menu, attentive helpful service, traditional hop-strung interior with etched windows and two fires, mix of seating including old pews and carved settles by candlelit tables, jugs and bottles on delft shelves, snug dining area; live music, darts; children and dogs welcome, easy wheelchair access, nice quiet back garden, closed Mon lunchtime, otherwise open all day.
(Alexandra and Richard Clay)

WEST MALLING   TQ6757
Scared Crow (01732) 840408

Offham Road; ME19 6RB Cosy brick-built pub with good mexican food along with pizzas and more traditional choices, well kept Adnams ales, friendly helpful service; background and some live music; children welcome, nice back garden, open all day Sun. *(Malcolm and Jane Levitt)*

WEST PECKHAM   TQ6452
Swan on the Green (01622) 812271

Off A26/B2016 W of Maidstone; ME18 5JW Attractively placed brick and weatherboarded pub facing village cricket green; own-brewed Swan beers in relaxed open-plan beamed bar, stripped brickwork, bare boards and mixed furnishings, two-way log fire, enjoyable freshly made food (not Sun, Mon evenings) from varied menu, friendly efficient service; children and dogs welcome, next to interesting part-Saxon church, good walks including Greensand Way, shuts at 9.30pm Sun and Mon, and may close early other evenings if quiet. *(Paddy and Sian O'Leary)*

WESTBERE   TR1862
Old Yew Tree (01227) 710501

Just off A18 Canterbury–Margate; CT2 0HH Heavily beamed 14th-c pub in pretty village; simply furnished bare-boards bar with inglenook log fire, good reasonably priced food from varied menu including Thurs pie and pint deal, Shepherd Neame Master Brew and a guest, friendly helpful staff, quiz first Weds of the month, open mike last Weds; picnic-sets in garden behind, open all day weekends, closed Mon. *(Buster May)*

WESTGATE-ON-SEA   TR3270
Bake & Alehouse 07913 368787

Off St Mildreds Road down alley by cinema; CT8 8RE Friendly micropub in former bakery; simple little bare-boards room with a few tables (expect to share when busy), five well kept interesting ales tapped from the cask, real ciders (maybe a warm winter one – Monks Delight), kentish wines, local cheese, sausage rolls and pork pies, friendly chatty atmosphere; closed Sun evening, shuts around 9pm other days.
(Bob and Melissa Wyatt)

WHITSTABLE   TR1066
Black Dog

High Street; CT5 1BB Quirky micropub (former deli) with five changing ales and several artisan ciders tapped from the back room, friendly staff may offer tasters, snacky food, narrow dimly lit Victorian-feel bar with high tables and benches along two sides, intriguing mix of pictures and other bits and pieces on green walls, prominent chandelier suspended from red ceiling; eclectic background music and occasional folk sessions; open all day. *(Julie Swift)*

WHITSTABLE   TR1066
Old Neptune (01227) 272262

Marine Terrace; CT5 1EJ Great view over Swale estuary from this popular unpretentious weatherboarded pub set right on the beach (rebuilt after being washed away in 1897 storm); Harveys, Shepherd Neame and a guest, reasonably priced lunchtime food from shortish menu including decent fish and chips, friendly young staff; weekend live music; children and dogs welcome, picnic-sets on the shingle (plastic glasses out here and occasional barbecues), fine sunsets, can get very busy in summer, open all day. *(Shane A Still)*

WHITSTABLE   TR1066
Smack Inn (01227) 772910

Middle Wall next to Baptist church; CT5 1BJ Small Victorian backstreet local away from the tourist trail; two Shepherd Neame ales and shortish choice of enjoyable low-priced food including burgers and fish and chips, cheerful helpful staff, cosy interior arranged around central servery, panelling, stripped brickwork and log fire; regular live music, often in beach-themed back garden (barbecues); children and dogs welcome, open all day. *(Sandra Hollies)*

WICKHAMBREAUX   TR2258
Rose (01227) 721763

The Green; CT3 1RQ Attractive 16th-c and partly older pub in nice spot across green from church and watermill; enjoyable home-made food, Greene King IPA and two guests (May/Aug beer festivals), local ciders on rotation, friendly helpful staff, small bare-boards bar with log fire in big fireplace, dining area beyond standing timbers with woodburner, hop-strung beams, panelling and stripped brick; children and dogs welcome, enclosed side garden and small courtyard, open (and food) all day, kitchen closes 4pm Sun. *(Daniel King)*

WILLESBOROUGH STREET
TR0341

Blacksmiths Arms (01233) 623975

The Street; TN24 0NA Beamed village pub dating in part from the 17th c; Fullers London Pride and a couple of guests, good traditional home-cooked food from sandwiches and snacks up, daily blackboard specials, friendly service, open fires including inglenook; children and dogs welcome, picnic-sets in good-sized garden with play area, handy for M20 (junction 10), open all day, no food Sun evening. *(Nick Higgins)*

WROTHAM
TQ6159

Bull (01732) 789800

1.7 miles from M20, junction 2 – Wrotham signed; TN15 7RF Restored 14th-c coaching inn with large beamed bar and separate restaurant, matching tables and chairs throughout, enjoyable food from pubby dishes up including a smokehouse/barbecue menu, real ales such as Dark Star, craft kegs and good wine list, friendly efficient service; Fri live music; children welcome, 11 comfortable bedrooms, open all day, food all day weekends. *(Mike Buckingham)*

WYE
TR0546

New Flying Horse (01233) 812297

Upper Bridge Street; TN25 5AN 17th-c Shepherd Neame inn with beams and inglenook; enjoyable food including fixed-price menu in bar and restaurant, friendly accommodating staff; Sun quiz, occasional live music, free wi-fi; children welcome, good-sized pretty garden with play area and miniature thatched pub (a former Chelsea Flower Show exhibit), nine bedrooms (some in converted stables), open (and food) all day, breakfast from 8am for non-residents. *(Buster May)*

WYE
TR0446

Tickled Trout (01233) 812227

Signed off A28 NE of Ashford; TN25 5EB Popular summer family pub by River Stour; rustic-style carpeted bar with beams, stripped brickwork, stained-glass partitions and open fire, spacious conservatory/restaurant, ales such as Canterbury and Sharps, kentish ciders and several wines by the glass, friendly helpful staff; quiz nights, live music first Sun of month; children and dogs welcome, tables on terrace and riverside lawn, open (and food) all day. *(Buster May, Claire Adams)*

YALDING
TQ6950

Walnut Tree (01622) 814266

B2010 SW of Maidstone; ME18 6JB Old timbered village pub under new ownership; split-level main bar with fine old settles, a long cushioned mahogany bench and mix of dining chairs on brick or carpeted floors, candles in bottles on chunky wooden tables, interesting old photographs, big inglenook log fire, up to five real ales such as Adnams, Harveys and Tonbridge, good food from bar meals to more inventive restaurant dishes, Sun carvery, friendly prompt service, attractive raftered dining room; background and live music (every other Fri); children and dogs (in bar) welcome, paved back terrace, open (and food) all day, kitchen closes 6pm Sun. *(Nigel and Jean Eames, Jan Gibbons)*

Lancashire

with Greater Manchester, Merseyside and Wirral

KEY	★ Star Pub	🍴 Top Quality Food	🍺 Great Beer
🍷 Good Wines	£ Bargain Meals	🛏 Good Bedrooms	🍴 Serves Food

BASHALL EAVES   SD6943 Map 7
Red Pump 🍴 🛏
(01254) 826227 – www.theredpumpinn.co.uk
NW of Clitheroe, off B6478 or B6243; BB7 3DA

**Beautifully placed pub with a cosy bar and first class food
in contemporary, inviting dining rooms; bedrooms**

There are lovely views of Pendle Hill and Longridge Fell from the seats on the front terrace and the newly landscaped garden; the comfortable and individually decorated bedrooms share the same splendid country views. As well as glamping yurts, they're adding a couple of luxury shepherd's huts. Two inviting dining rooms and a cosy, traditional central bar have bookshelves, cushioned settles and wheelbacks on flagstones, and log fires, and the convivial licensees create a cheerful, friendly atmosphere. Three regional beers on handpump change weekly and might include a beer named for the pub, Copper Dragon Scotts 1816 and a changing guest, plus 11 wines by the glass, 15 gins and ten whiskies; background music. There are good walks in the surrounding Forest of Bowland area and fishing on the nearby River Hodder. Disabled access.

🍴 Food is particularly good and includes all-day pizzas (in fine weather) from a new outdoor wood-fired oven and slowly matured steaks from grass-fed cattle plus sandwiches, black and white pudding fritters with mustard mayonnaise, trout and leek terrine with watercress and sour cream, chicken in creamy coconut and lemongrass pie, rare-breed pork belly with sticky barbecue sauce, foraged wild garlic and dauphinoise potatoes, slow-roasted veal shin with polenta and celeriac, seafood sharing platter, herb-crusted lamb cutlets with lyonnaise potatoes and red wine jus, and puddings; they also offer a two- and three-course menu. *Benchmark main dish: chargrilled 40-day aged steak £25.00. Two-course evening meal £20.00.*

Free house ~ Licensees Frances and Jonathan Gledhill ~ Real ale ~ Open 12-10; 12-11 Fri, Sat; 12-8.30 Sun; closed Mon, Tues; first two weeks Jan ~ Bar food 12-2, 6-8.30 (9 Fri, Sat); 12-5.30 Sun ~ Restaurant ~ Children welcome ~ Dogs allowed in bar and bedrooms ~ Wi-fi ~ Bedrooms: £70/£95 *Recommended by Mr and Mrs P R Thomas, Patricia and Gordon Thompson, Nicholas and Maddy Trainer, David Heath, Lyn and Freddie Roberts, Caroline and Steve Archer*

'Children welcome' means the pub says it lets children inside without any special restriction. If it allows them in, but to restricted areas such as an eating area or family room, we specify this. Some pubs may impose an evening time limit. We do not mention limits after 9pm as we assume children are home by then.

BAY HORSE

SD4952 Map 7

Bay Horse 🔯 🛏

(01524) 791204 – www.bayhorseinn.com

1.2 miles from M6 junction 33: A6 southwards, then off on left; LA2 0HR

18th-c former coaching inn with log fires, comfortable bar and restaurant, well regarded food, local ales and friendly staff

Many customers come to this gently civilised and family-owned place for a good meal and it's handy for the nearby M6. There's a series of small, rambling linked rooms and the cosily pubby beamed bar has cushioned wall banquettes in bay windows, lamps on windowsills and a good log fire. Bowland Hen Harrier and Moorhouses Pendle Witches Brew on handpump, ten wines by the glass, ten malt whiskies and 20 gins served by friendly, efficient staff. The dining room has a woodburning stove and lovely views over the garden – where there are plenty of seats and tables. Disabled access.

🍽 Cooked by the chef-owner, the highly regarded food includes sandwiches, treacle salmon with fennel and orange salad, beetroot mayonnaise and crispy egg, venison and pistachio terrine with pickled walnuts and preserved cherries, aubergines and roasted tomatoes with wheat, spelt, haricot beans, toasted yeast and parsley, duck legs with red wine lentils, kale and sautéed potatoes, hake fillet with parsnip purée, bacon and brown crab sauce, and puddings such as chocolate torte with caramel ice-cream and vanilla pannacotta with honeyed figs and blackberries. *Benchmark main dish: chicken breast with haggis and creamy grain mustard and whisky sauce £18.75. Two-course evening meal £25.00.*

Free house ~ Licensee Craig Wilkinson ~ Real ale ~ Open 12-3, 6-11; 12-3, 6-10 Sun; closed Mon, Tues; one week Jan, one week Nov ~ Bar food 12-2, 6-9; 12-3, 6-8 Sun ~ Restaurant ~ Children welcome ~ Dogs allowed in bar *Recommended by Jim and Sue James, Andrew and Ruth Simmonds, Nigel Havers, Bob and Melissa Wyatt, Graeme and Sally Mendham, Claire Adams*

BISPHAM GREEN

SD4813 Map 7

Eagle & Child 🔯 ♉ 🍺

(01257) 462297 – www.eagleandchildbispham.co.uk

Maltkiln Lane (Parbold–Croston road), off B5246); L40 3SG

Civilised pub with antiques, enterprising food, an interesting range of beers and appealing rustic garden

Our readers really enjoy their visits to this well-run all-rounder. The largely open-plan bar is carefully furnished with several handsomely carved antique oak settles (the finest made in part, it seems, from a 16th-c wedding bedhead), a mix of small old oak chairs, an attractive oak coffer, old hunting prints and engravings and hop-draped low beams. Also, red walls, coir matting, oriental rugs on ancient flagstones in front of a fine old stone fireplace and counter; the pub dogs are called Beryl, Betty, Brenda and Rolo. Friendly young staff serve Hawkshead Windermere Pale, Marstons Wainwright, Moorhouses White Witch and Thwaites Original on handpump, farm cider, ten wines by the glass, 25 gins and around 30 malt whiskies. A popular beer festival is usually held on the early May Bank Holiday weekend. The spacious garden has a well tended but unconventional bowling green; beyond is a wild area that's home to crested newts and moorhens. A handsome side barn houses a shop selling interesting wines and pottery, plus a proper butcher and a deli. This is part of the Ainscoughs group. Disabled access.

🍽 High quality food includes sandwiches, marinated mackerel fillet with beetroot and tonic jelly, Morecambe Bay shrimps with asparagus and crispy duck egg, wild mushroom risotto with parmesan, local sausage and black pudding with beer-battered onion rings, rich onion gravy and mash, chicken breast with pesto, brie and pea risotto, pork fillet and haggis wellington with whisky sauce, and puddings such as vanilla and passion-fruit cheesecake and duo of chocolate mousse (dark chocolate with orange and chilli and white chocolate) with blackcurrant sauce. *Benchmark main dish: beer-battered fish and chips £12.95. Two-course evening meal £17.00.*

Free house ~ Licensee Peter Robinson ~ Real ale ~ Open 11-11; 11-10.30 Sun ~ Bar food 12-2, 5.30-8.30 (9 Fri); 12-9 Sat; 12-8 Sun ~ Children welcome ~ Dogs welcome ~ Wi-fi ~ Live music last Fri evening of the month; quiz Mon evening *Recommended by Angela and Steve Heard, Katherine Matthews, Patricia Healey, Beth Aldridge, Julian Richardson, Heather and Richard Jones*

DOWNHAM
SD7844   Map 7

Assheton Arms 🏅 ♟ 🛏

(01200) 441227 – www.asshetonarms.com

Off A59 NE of Clitheroe, via Chatburn; BB7 4BJ

Lancashire Dining Pub of the Year

Traditional country inn with plenty of dining and drinking space, a friendly welcome, several real ales and creative food; bedrooms

The exceptional food in this fine old place remains one of the main draws, but plenty of customers do come for just a pint and a chat. A small front bar, with a hatch to the kitchen, has tweed-upholstered armchairs and stools on large flagstones around a single table, a woodburning stove surrounded by logs, and drawings of dogs and hunting prints on grey-green walls. Off to the right, a wood-panelled partition creates a cosy area where there are similarly cushioned pews and nice old chairs around various tables on a rug-covered wooden floor, and a couple of window chairs. The main bar, up a couple of steps, has old photographs of the pub and village on pale walls and a marble bar counter where they serve Hawkshead Lakeland Gold, Marstons Wainwright and a guest beer on handpump, a dozen wines by the glass and farm cider. Background music and board games. Staff are helpful and attentive. A two-level restaurant has carpet or wooden flooring, two fireplaces (one with a woodburning stove, the other with a lovely old kitchen range) and hunting prints. Picnic-sets and tables and chairs enjoy far-reaching views. The lovely, comfortable bedrooms (once a post office and two cottages) make an excellent base for exploring the area. Do note the lovely church opposite. This is part of the Seafood Pub Company.

Imaginative food includes pigeon breast with lentil dhal, pickled beetroot and pigeon leg bhaji, sticky soy and treacle pigs cheeks with artichoke purée, queen scallops and granny smith apple, beetroot and blue cheese gnocchi with celeriac, roasted beets and smoked almonds, crab and chilli linguine with charred lime, beef curry with thai roti bread and lemon and ginger fried rice, miso-glazed salmon with sweet potato purée, baby pak choi, scallop and crab wontons, soy and sesame, venison haunch with pearl barley, roasted onions, crispy bacon and pickled blackberries, and puddings such as chocolate délice with tangerine jelly centre and caramel and hazelnut crumb and locally sourced fruit crumble with custard. *Benchmark main dish: venison and pheasant pie with dandelion and burdock gravy £13.95. Two-course evening meal £23.00.*

Free house ~ Licensee Jocelyn Neve ~ Real ale ~ Open 12-11; 12-midnight Sat; 12-10.30 Sun ~ Bar food 12-9; 12-10 Fri, Sat; 12-8 Sun ~ Restaurant ~ Children welcome ~ Dogs allowed in bar ~ Wi-fi *Recommended by W K Wood, Nicola and Stuart Parsons, Maggie and Matthew Lyons, Paul Walker, Sorren Maclean, Emily and Toby Archer, Ted and Mary Bates, Sylvia and Phillip Spencer, Mike and Sarah Abbot*

FORMBY

SD3109 Map 7

Sparrowhawk ♀ ◖

(01704) 882350 – www.brunningandprice.co.uk/sparrowhawk

Southport Old Road; brown sign to pub just off A565 Formby bypass, S edge of Ainsdale; L37 0AB

Light and airy pub with interesting décor, good food and drinks choices and wooded grounds

A rather grand conversion of an old hotel, this has all the styling of a well run Brunning & Price pub. The nicely proportioned open-plan rooms, spreading out from the central bar, have plenty of interest: attractive prints on pastel walls, church candles, flowers, snug leather fireside armchairs in library corners and seats and tables with rugs on dark boards by big bow windows. There's also a comfortably carpeted conservatory dining room; background music. Happy, friendly young staff serve 21 wines by the glass, 89 malt whiskies, 49 gins and Phoenix Brunning & Price Original, Salopian Oracle, Titanic Plum Porter and three guests on handpump. Five acres of woods and parkland surround the pub and a flagstoned side terrace has sturdy tables, with picnic-table sets on lawns by a set of swings and an old Fergie tractor. A walk from the pub to coastal nature reserves might just yield red squirrels, still hanging on in this area.

A wide choice of food includes sandwiches, smoked salmon with spiced avocado purée, shaved fennel and radish, lamb, leek and potato hash cake with fried free-range egg, sweet potato, cauliflower, almond and chickpea tagine with couscous, steak burger with toppings, coleslaw and chips, sea bream with crab and dill potato cake, cherry vine tomatoes and clam salsa, braised lamb shoulder with dauphinoise potatoes and gravy, chicken breast with seasonal risotto, and puddings such as crème brûlée and sticky toffee pudding with toffee sauce and vanilla ice-cream. *Benchmark main dish: crispy beef salad with sweet chilli dressing and cashew nuts £14.95. Two-course evening meal £21.50.*

Brunning & Price ~ Manager Iain Hendry ~ Real ale ~ Open 10am-11pm; 9am-11pm Sat; 9am-10.30pm Sun ~ Bar food 10am (9am Sat)-9.30pm; 9-9 Sun ~ Children welcome ~ Dogs allowed in bar ~ Wi-fi *Recommended by Mrs S Wilson-Sproat, Darrell Barton, George and Alison Bishop, Steve Whalley, Matilda and Gerald Thoms, Dave Sutton, Diane Abbott, Sophia and Hamish Greenfield*

GREAT MITTON

SD7138 Map 7

Aspinall Arms ♀ ◖

(01254) 826555 – www.brunningandprice.co.uk/aspinallarms

B6246 NW of Whalley; BB7 9PQ

Cleverly refurbished and extended riverside pub with cheerful helpful service and a fine choice of drinks and food

R ight in the heart of the Ribble Valley and on the banks of the river, you'll find a good mix of customers dropping in and out all day here. The various rambling rooms have seating that ranges from attractively cushioned old-style dining chairs through brass-studded leather ones to big armchairs and sofas around an assortment of dark tables. Floors are flagstoned, carpeted or wooden and topped with rugs, while the pale-painted or bare stone walls are hung with an extensive collection of prints and local photographs. Dotted about are large mirrors, house plants, stone bottles and bookshelves and there are both open fires and a woodburning stove. From the central servery, knowledgeable staff serve Phoenix Brunning & Price Original and Moorhouses Aspinall Witch (named for the pub) with guests such as Moorhouses Black Cat, Saltaire Blonde, Settle Jericho Blonde and Timothy Taylors Golden Best on handpump, 15 wines by the glass, 50 gins, an amazing 150 malt whiskies and a farm cider; background music and board games. Plenty of chairs and tables on a terrace and lots of picnic-sets on grass make the most of the waterside position.

Up-to-date food includes sandwiches, ham hock fritters with parsley, pineapple salsa and chicory salad, crispy baby squid with sweet chilli sauce, honey and mustard, cheese, potato and onion pie, pork sausages with mash and onion gravy, thai chicken salad with asian leaves and mango, coconut and lime dressing, duck breast with duck hash cake and black cherry sauce, sea bream with sautéed potatoes and lemon beurre blanc, and puddings such as hot waffle with warm blueberries and blackcurrant and liquorice ice-cream and triple chocolate brownie with chocolate sauce. *Benchmark main dish: steak in ale pie £14.50. Two-course evening meal £22.00.*

Brunning & Price ~ Manager Susanne Engalmann ~ Real ale ~ Open 10.30am-11pm; 10.30-10.30 Sun ~ Bar food 12-9.30 (9 Sun) ~ Restaurant ~ Children welcome ~ Dogs allowed in bar ~ Wi-fi *Recommended by W K Wood, John and Sylvia Harrop, Shona and Jimmy McDuff, Nicola and Stuart Parsons, Andy and Louise Ramwell*

MANCHESTER
SJ8297 Map 7

Wharf ♀ ◖

(0161) 220 2960 – www.brunningandprice.co.uk/thewharf
Blantyre Street/Slate Wharf; M15 4SW

Big wharf-like pub with large terrace overlooking the water and a fine range of drinks and food

The most pubby part of this huge, open-plan place is downstairs, where you'll find a friendly, informal atmosphere and groups of high tables and chairs. The more formal restaurant is upstairs. Throughout there's an appealing variety of dining chairs around dark wooden tables on rugs and shiny floorboards, hundreds of interesting prints and posters on bare brick or painted walls, old stone bottles, church candles and house plants on windowsills and tables, plus bookshelves, armchairs and large mirrors over open fires. Efficient, hard-working staff serve Phoenix Brunning & Price Original and Weetwood Cheshire Cat plus up to seven quickly changing guest ales on handpump from breweries such as Beartown, Brightside, Epic Beers, Moorhouses, Rudgate and Titanic, as well as farm cider, 16 wines by the glass, 60 gins and over 50 malt whiskies. The large front terrace has plenty of wood and chrome tables and chairs around a fountain, and picnic-sets overlooking the canal basin.

A wide range of popular food includes sandwiches, chicken liver pâté with Vimto chutney, king prawns with chorizo and chipotle sauce, butternut squash, stilton and lentil pie with port gravy, leek and pork sausages with onion gravy, malaysian fish stew, chicken breast with pasta, spinach, wild mushroom and parmesan sauce, five-spice glazed duck breast with creamed cabbage, fondant potato and red wine jus, braised lamb shoulder with dauphinoise potatoes and gravy, and puddings such as triple chocolate brownie with chocolate sauce and crème brûlée. *Benchmark main dish: beer-battered fish and chips £13.95. Two-course evening meal £20.00.*

Brunning & Price ~ Manager Natasha Metcalfe ~ Real ale ~ Open 12-11; 12-midnight Sat; 12-10.30 Sun ~ Bar food 10-9.30; 10-10 Fri, Sat; 10-9 Sun ~ Restaurant ~ Children welcome ~ Dogs allowed in bar ~ Wi-fi ~ Live music Fri evening *Recommended by Brian and Anna Marsden, William Pace, Lenny and Ruth Walters, Shona and Jimmy McDuff, Rosie and John Moore, David and Charlotte Green*

You can send reports directly to us at feedback@goodguides.com

MELLOR

SD6530 Map 7

Millstone 🍺 🛏

(01254) 813333 – www.millstonemellor.co.uk

The Mellor near Blackburn; Mellor Lane; BB2 7JR

Smart, popular dining pub with rewarding food, real ales and seats outside; bedrooms

A handsome and neatly kept 18th-c stone coaching inn, this has a central bar with extensive panelling on both sides, with Thwaites Original and guests such as Marstons Wainwright and Thwaites Nutty Black on handpump and a dozen wines by the glass, served by friendly staff. Both here and in the dining rooms there are elegant painted wooden and attractively upholstered modern dining chairs and button-back wall seats around polished tables on carpet or parquet flooring. Also, several log fires, books on shelves, mirrors, flowers on tables and attractive prints on pale paintwork; background music. A side terrace has seats and tables under parasols. Bedrooms are well equipped and comfortable (some are in a separate block across the car park) and breakfasts are good. Disabled access.

 Good, popular food includes sandwiches, crayfish cocktail with red chicory, fennel, avocado and micro-herb salad, duck spring rolls with sticky plum sauce, sharing platters, roasted pumpkin, squash and beetroot gnocchi with garlic and spinach cream and parmesan, tandoori chicken with saag aloo potatoes, onion bhaji and raita, cod loin with cockle and pea velouté and salt and vinegar mash, saddle of local lamb with dauphinoise potatoes, ratatouille and rosemary and shallot jus, and puddings such as pecan nut pie with salted caramel ice-cream and chocolate fondant with gingerbread ice-cream. *Benchmark main dish: steak and kidney in ale pudding £12.50. Two-course evening meal £22.00.*

Thwaites ~ Manager Tim Parker ~ Real ale ~ Open 7am-11pm; 8am-11pm Sat, Sun ~ Bar food 12-9.30 (9 Sun) ~ Restaurant ~ Children welcome ~ Dogs allowed in bar ~ Wi-fi ~ Bedrooms: /$89 *Recommended by Dr D J & Mrs S C Walker, Beverley and Andy Butcher, Martine and Fabio Lockley, Edward Edmonton, Paul Walker, Julia and Fiona Barnes, Jill and Hugh Bennett*

NETHER BURROW

SD6175 Map 7

Highwayman 🍷

(01524) 273338 – www.highwaymaninn.co.uk

A683 S of Kirkby Lonsdale; LA6 2RJ

Large and skilfully refurbished old stone house with country interior, serving carefully sourced food; attractive gardens

Both the food and drink in this substantial 17th-c stone pub are highly regarded and there's always a friendly mix of customers. The stylishly simple flagstoned interior is nicely divided into intimate corners, with a couple of large log fires, wooden, leather-seated or tartan chairs around dark tables, button-back or leather wall banquettes and a bustling atmosphere. There are some big photos on the walls and interesting modern lighting. Phoenix Brunning & Price Original plus Hawkshead Red, Kirkby Lonsdale Tiffin Gold, Lancaster Black and Moorhouses Pendle Witches Brew on handpump, ten wines by the glass, 28 gins and 27 whiskies served by friendly, efficient staff; background music amd TV. French windows open out to a big terrace and lovely gardens with smart rattan-style furniture. The surrounding Lune Valley countryside is very pretty.

 Pleasing food using seasonal, local produce includes sandwiches, scallops with crab and lemon fritters and pea purée, shredded ham hock and pork belly terrine with pistachios, orange and piccalilli, sweet potato, cauliflower, almond and chickpea tagine with couscous and deep-fried courgettes, crispy beef salad with sweet chilli sauce, roasted cashew nuts and lotus root crisp, lancashire hotpot with pickled red cabbage, bream with capers, samphire and wild garlic butter, and puddings such as raspberry cheesecake with raspberry ripple ice-cream and bread and butter pudding with apricots and clotted cream. *Benchmark main dish: braised lamb shoulder with roast potatoes and gravy £17.45. Two-course evening meal £21.00.*

Brunning & Price ~ Manager Sean Parker ~ Real ale ~ Open 10am-11pm; 10am-11pm Sat; 10am-10.30pm Sun ~ Bar food 12-9; 12-10 Fri, Sat ~ Restaurant ~ Children welcome ~ Dogs allowed in bar ~ Wi-fi *Recommended by Sandra and Neil White, Catherine and Daniel King, Audrey and Paul Summers, Charlie May, Margaret McDonald, Sandra and Michael Smith*

PLEASINGTON
SD6528 Map 7

Clog & Billycock ♀ ☙

(01254) 201163 – www.brunningandprice.co.uk/clogandbillycock
Village signposted off A677 Preston New Road on W edge of Blackburn; Billinge End Road; BB2 6QB

Wide range of good food and drink in appealing and well run stone-built village pub

A carefully extended stone inn, this is now under the Brunning & Price umbrella and some changes have been made to the décor. Several light and airy rooms run together with flagstoned floors, high ceilings with beams and joists and pale grey walls above a grey dado. There are laden bookshelves, mirrors, prints and pictures on pale painted walls, big house plants, wooden, plush upholstered or leather chairs and tartan banquettes around simple wooden tables, and an open fire and a fine old range. Helpful, friendly young staff serve Phoenix Brunning & Price Original and guests from breweries such as Bowland, Hawkshead, Moorhouses, Three B's and Timothy Taylors on handpump, eight wines by the glass, 40 rums, 50 malt whiskies and 60 gins; background music and board games. The small garden has an awning-covered terrace with benches, seats and tables and a fire pit. Disabled access.

Interesting food includes sandwiches, camembert studded with rosemary and garlic, smoked mackerel rillettes with cucumber and fennel salad, cauliflower, chickpea and pepper jalfrezi with almond pilau rice and sweet potato bhaji, steak burger with toppings, coleslaw and chips, fish pie with french-style peas, herb-marinated chicken breast with crushed potato and chorizo cake and saffron and lemon dressing, harissa lamb and couscous salad with feta cheese, pomegranate and mint falafels, and puddings such as lemon cheesecake with blackcurrant compote and triple chocolate brownie with chocolate sauce. *Benchmark main dish: cheese and onion pie with tomato salad £12.95. Two-course evening meal £20.00.*

Brunning & Price ~ Manager Rob Broadbent ~ Real ale ~ Open 10am-11pm; 10am-11pm Sat; 10am-10.30pm Sun ~ Bar food 12-9; 12-10 Fri, Sat ~ Children welcome ~ Dogs allowed in bar ~ Wi-fi *Recommended by Monica and Steph Evans, Serena and Adam Furber, W K Wood, Robert and Diana Myers, Mark and Sian Edwards, Geoff and Ann Marston*

PRESTON
SD5634 Map 7

Haighton Manor ♀ ☙

(01772) 706350 – www.brunningandprice.co.uk/haightonmanor
Haighton Green Lane, Haighton; PR2 5SQ

Rather grand stone building surrounded by lawns and countryside with thoughtful drinks and food choice, and seats outside

They offer a fine choice of drinks and good, modern cooking in this lovely 17th-c place and customers pop in and out all day. The big bustling bar has an open fire, wooden chairs around a large farmhouse kitchen table, elegant metal chandeliers and stools against the counter where cheerful staff serve Phoenix Brunning & Price Original plus guests such as Epic PG Steam, Hawkshead Bitter, Lancaster Blonde, Moorhouses Black Cat and Timothy Taylors Landlord on handpump, over 50 gins and 50 malt whiskies and ten farm ciders; board games. Various open-plan rooms lead off here with rugs on wooden floors, wall-to-wall prints, photographs and mirrors on pale walls above painted dados, more open fires, antique-style cushioned dining chairs around dark tables, and house plants and candles. One cosy character room has armchairs and chesterfield sofas on flagstones and exposed stone walls, and there's a big, carpeted conservatory dining extension. Good quality chairs, benches and tables under parasols are set out on a terrace surrounded by lawns (on which there's a trademark tractor for children); pleasant country views. Disabled access.

Appealing food includes sandwiches, fried lamb sweetbreads with watermelon, edamame beans and crispy wontons, teriyaki king prawns with tamari and ginger dressing, maple-roasted squash with herb and lemon quinoa and fennel salad, crispy beef salad with asian leaves, fresh chillis and cashew nuts, fish pie with french-style peas, chicken breast with wild garlic, pea and broad bean risotto, steak burger with toppings, coleslaw and chips, rump steak with dijon and tarragon butter, and puddings such as apple and rhubarb crumble with custard and sticky toffee pudding with toffee sauce. *Benchmark main dish: braised lamb shoulder with dauphinoise potatoes and gravy £17.25. Two-course evening meal £22.50.*

Brunning & Price ~ Licensee Chris Humphries ~ Real ale ~ Open 11-11; 11-10.30 Sun ~ Bar food 12-9.30; 12-10 Fri, Sat; 12-9 Sun ~ Children welcome ~ Dogs allowed in bar ~ Wi-fi
Recommended by Steve Whalley, W K Wood, John Perry, Gwendoline and Ralph Mason, Amanda Shipley, Rosie and Marcus Heatherley, Nicola and Holly Lyons

SAWLEY   SD7746 Map 7
Spread Eagle 🛏

(01200) 441202 – www.spreadeaglesawley.co.uk
Village signed just off A59 NE of Clitheroe; BB7 4NH

Nicely refurbished pub with quite a choice of food, riverside restaurant and four real ales; bedrooms

It's a real treat to come here, and our readers enjoy their visits very much. A well run attractive old coaching inn, the bar rooms have a pleasing mix of nice old and quirky modern furniture (anything from an old settle and pine tables to up-to-date low chairs upholstered in animal print fabric) all set off well by the grey rustic stone floor. Low ceilings, cosy sectioning, a warming fire and cottagey windows keep it feeling intimate. The dining areas are more formal, with modern stripes and a bookshelf mural; background music and board games. Young, efficient and friendly staff serve a beer named for the pub (from Bowland), Dark Horse Hetton Pale Ale, Marstons Wainwright and Moorhouses White Witch on handpump and several wines by the glass. Bedrooms are individually furnished and comfortable and breakfasts are good. Do visit the nearby 12th-c cistercian abbey or take an exhilarating walk in the Forest of Bowland.

High quality food includes sandwiches, pressed ham hock, caper and apple terrine with celeriac remoulade and quince jelly, beetroot-cured salmon on horseradish cream with potato salad and beetroot relish, sharing platters, spicy chickpea and cauliflower tagine with pearl couscous and dried fruit, cumberland sausage with mash and onion gravy, cod fillet with asparagus, black pudding, potato purée and chive cream, pork fillet with apple, cider and parsley velouté, mash and crisp puff pastry, and puddings such as vanilla pannacotta with aniseed blackcurrants and white chocolate tart with caramelised oranges, orange curd and dark chocolate sorbet. *Benchmark main dish: mussels in cream and cider with fries and garlic mayonnaise £13.95. Two-course evening meal £20.00.*

Individual Inns ~ Managers Greig and Natalie Barns ~ Real ale ~ Open 12-11; 12-10 Sun ~ Bar food 12-2, 5.30-9; 12-2, 6-9.30 Sat; 12-7 Sun ~ Restaurant ~ Children welcome ~ Dogs allowed in bar and bedrooms ~ Wi-fi ~ Jazz first Sun of month ~ Bedrooms: £92/$150
Recommended by Andy Dawson, Sue and Paul Green, John and Sylvia Harrop, David Heath, Michael Butler

THORNTON HOUGH

Red Fox ♀ ▦

SJ2979 Map 7

(0151) 353 2920 – www.brunningandprice.co.uk/redfox
Liverpool Road; CH64 7TL

Sizeable spreading pub with a fine choice of beers, wines, gins and whiskies, courteous staff serving enjoyable food and large back garden

Friendly, cheerful staff serve a fantastic range of drinks that includes Phoenix Brunning & Price Original plus guests such as Brightside Amarillo, Conwy West Coast Pale Ale, Cwrw Ial Limestone Cowboy, Hopback Crop Circle, Lancaster Black and Red and Oakham Inferno on handpump, 16 wines by the glass, 156 malt whiskies, 145 gins and ten farm ciders. The spacious main bar is reached up stairs from the entrance: big central pillars divide the room into smaller areas with high stools and tables in the middle, dark wooden tables and chairs to each side and deep leather armchairs and fender seats next to the large fireplace. This leads into a long, airy, carpeted dining room with two rows of painted iron supports, hefty leather and wood chairs around highly polished tables and a raised fire pit; doors from here lead out to a terrace. Two additional dining rooms are similarly furnished, one with an elegant chandelier hanging from a fine moulded ceiling. Throughout there are photographs, prints and pictures covering the walls, big plants, stone bottles and shelves of books; background music and board games. You reach the pub along a drive surrounded by lawns and pleasant country views. At the back of the building there are terraces with good quality wooden chairs and tables under parasols, and steps down to picnic-sets around a fountain. Disabled access.

Well presented food includes sandwiches, corned beef hash cake with poached egg and brown sauce, deep-fried brie with pickled cranberries and candied pecan salad, wild mushroom tortellini with spinach and leek purée, roast artichokes and mushroom glaze, chicken, ham and leek pie, sea bass with chorizo butter and paprika potatoes, venison and wild mushroom ragoût with pasta, vietnamese pork belly salad with pickled ginger and peanuts, and puddings such as crème brûlée and hot waffle with chocolate fudge sauce and banana ice-cream. *Benchmark main dish: beer-battered fish and chips £13.75. Two-course evening meal £21.00.*

Brunning & Price ~ Manager David Green ~ Real ale ~ Open 10am-11pm; 10am-10.30pm Sun ~ Bar food 12-10 ~ Restaurant ~ Children welcome ~ Dogs allowed in bar ~ Wi-fi
Recommended by Christine and Tony Garrett, Frances and Hamish Potter

---

Bedroom prices are for high summer. Even then you may get reductions for more than one night, or (outside tourist areas) weekends. Winter special rates are common, and many inns reduce bedroom prices if you have a full evening meal.

UPPERMILL   SD0006   Map 7

Church Inn

(01457) 820902 – www.churchinnsaddleworth.co.uk

From the main street (A607), look out for the sign for Saddleworth Church,
and turn off up this steep narrow lane – keep on up; OL3 6LW

**Community pub with big range of own-brew beers at unbeatable
bargain prices and tasty food; children very welcome**

You'll always find a cheerful crowd of happy customers here – despite
its remote setting – all keen to try the wonderful own-brewed ales and
incredible value food. The big, unspoilt, L-shaped main bar has a cheerful,
friendly atmosphere, high beams and some stripped stone, settles, pews, a
good individual mix of chairs, lots of attractive prints, staffordshire and other
china on a high delft shelf, jugs, brasses and so forth. They keep up to 11 of
their own Saddleworth beers – though if the water levels from the spring
aren't high enough for brewing, they bring in guests such as Black Sheep
and Copper Dragon. Some of their own seasonal ales are named after the
licensee's children, only appearing around their birthdays; two home-brewed
lagers on tap too. TV (for sporting events) and unobtrusive background
music. A conservatory opens on to the terrace. The local bellringers arrive
on Wednesdays to practise with a set of handbells kept here, and anyone
can join the morris dancing on Thursdays. Children enjoy the menagerie
of animals; dogs are made to feel very welcome.

Honest, fair priced food includes sandwiches, prawn cocktail, spicy chicken
wings with a choice of dip, vegetable fajita with two wraps, sour cream, salsa and
guacamole, full english breakfast, scampi and chips, gammon and egg, steak and kidney
pudding, poached cod with parsley sauce, lamb shank in minted gravy, mixed grill, and
puddings such as hot chocolate fudge cake and cheesecake of the day. *Benchmark
main dish: steak and mushroom in ale pie £10.50. Two-course evening meal £17.00.*

Own brew ~ Licensee Christine Taylor ~ Real ale ~ Open midday-midnight Mon-Fri, Sun;
midday-1am Fri, Sat~ Bar food 12-3, 5-9; 12-9.30 Fri, Sat; 12-9 Sun and bank holidays ~
Restaurant ~ Children welcome ~ Dogs allowed in bar ~ Wi-fi *Recommended by Chloe and
Michael Swettenham, Amy and Luke Buchanan, Kate Moran, Colin and Daniel Gibbs, Buster and
Helena Hastings, Jim and Sue James*

WHITEWELL   SD6546   Map 7

Inn at Whitewell ★

(01200) 448222 – www.innatwhitewell.com

*Most easily reached by B6246 from Whalley; road through Dunsop Bridge from B6478
is also good; BB7 3AT*

**Rather grand old house with smartly pubby atmosphere, top quality
food, exceptional wine list, real ales and professional, friendly
service; luxury bedrooms**

Reports on this elegant manor house remain as warm and enthusiastic
as ever – it's a very special place. Many of our readers stay in the lovely
bedrooms (several have open fires) which are individually furnished and
have beautifully restored bathrooms; breakfasts are excellent. The civilised
bar rooms have handsome old wood furnishings, including antique settles,
oak gate-leg tables and sonorous clocks, set off beautifully against powder
blue walls neatly hung with big appealing prints. The pubby main bar has
roaring log fires in attractive stone fireplaces and heavy curtains on sturdy
wooden rails; one area has a selection of newspapers and magazines, local
maps and guidebooks. There's a piano for anyone who wants to play, and

board games. Early evening sees a cheerful bustle that later settles to a more tranquil and relaxing atmosphere. Drinks include a marvellous wine list of around 230 wines with 21 by the glass (reception has a good wine shop), 24 whiskies, eight gins, organic ginger beer, lemonade, fruit juices and Black Sheep, Moorhouses Blond Witch, Timothy Taylors Landlord and Tirril Ullswater Blonde on handpump. The inn is set high on the banks of the River Hodder with spectacular views down the valley into the heart of the Forest of Bowland; the riverside bar and adjacent terrace make the most of this outlook. They own several miles of trout, salmon and sea trout fishing on the River Hodder; picnic hamper on request. Limited disabled access.

Delicious food uses the best local produce and includes lunchtime sandwiches, potted crab with avocado purée and cucumber pickle, warm chicken liver salad with artichoke hearts, cherry tomatoes and savoury dressing, cheese and onion pie, local sausages with champ, a fried egg and caramelised onion jus, corn-fed chicken breast with bubble and squeak potato cake, celeriac purée and red wine jus, fresh fish dish of the day, pork loin chop with black pudding bonbons, savoy cabbage and mustard seed potato cake, parsnip purée and apple sauce, and home-made puddings. *Benchmark main dish: fish pie £13.00. Two-course evening meal £20.00.*

Free house ~ Licensee Charles Bowman ~ Real ale ~ Open 11am-midnight; 11am-midnight Sat; 11am-midnight Sun ~ Bar food 12-2, 7.30-9.30 ~ Restaurant ~ Children welcome ~ Dogs welcome ~ Wi-fi ~ Bedrooms: £99/£137 *Recommended by John and Sylvia Harrop, Bill Braithwaite, Alan and Alice Morgan, Paul Walker, Steve Whalley, Matilda and Gerald Thoms, Patrick and Martine Lawson, Nick and Willow Brown*

WORSLEY   SD7401   Map 7
Worsley Old Hall ♀ ◖

(0161) 703 8706 – www.brunningandprice.co.uk/worsleyoldhall
A mile from M60 junction 13: A575 Walkden Road, then after roundabout take first left into Worsley Park; M28 2QT

Very handsomely converted landmark building, now a welcoming pub scoring high on all counts

This grand and civilised place is open and serves food all day, so customers from the nearby M60 make a beeline for it. The lovely, original architectural features include a gracefully arched inglenook and matching window alcove, handsome staircase, heavy beams and glowing mahogany panelling. The relaxed and chatty main area spreads generously around the feature central bar, where swift, friendly staff serve 17 good wines by the glass, more than 100 malt whiskies and 38 gins. Also, Phoenix Brunning & Price Original, Timothy Taylors Landlord and a beer named for the pub (from Facers) plus guests from breweries such as Beartown, Castle Rock, Dunscar, Howard Town, Inveralmond and Lancaster on handpump. There's also the usual abundance of well chosen prints, fireside armchairs and a wide collection of cushioned dining chairs and wooden tables, and rugs on oak parquet; board games and background music. On a sunny day, the seats and tables on the big flagstoned back terrace behind are quickly snapped up; there's also a barbecue area, a neat lawn beyond the fountain with picnic-table sets and views over the golf course. Worsley Bridgewater Canal heritage area is a ten-minute walk away and RHS Garden Bridgewater (the largest gardening project in Europe) will open in 2020.

Interesting food includes sandwiches, five-spice duck leg with spring onion, cucumber, hoisin sauce and pancakes, wild mushroom arancini, beetroot burger with skinny fries, guacamole and red cabbage slaw, cumberland sausages with mash and onion gravy, grilled whole trout with crab and herb butter, slow-braised ox ragoût with tomatoes, pasta and parmesan, sticky ginger chicken with thai red curry, coconut rice and pak choi, and puddings such as crème brûlée and sticky toffee pudding with toffee sauce. *Benchmark main dish: harissa-spiced lamb rump with tomato and cumin sauce, cauliflower couscous and marinated apricots £17.95. Two-course evening meal £22.00.*

Brunning & Price ~ Manager Ryan Maguire ~ Real ale ~ Open 10am-11pm; 10am-10.30pm Sun ~ Bar food 10-10; 10-9.30 Sun ~ Restaurant ~ Children welcome ~ Dogs allowed in bar ~ Wi-fi *Recommended by Michael Butler, Donald Allsopp, Barry and Daphne Gregson, Scott and Charlotte Havers, Steve Whalley, Belinda Stamp, Jim King, Harvey Brown*

Also Worth a Visit in Lancashire

Besides the fully inspected pubs, you might like to try these pubs that have been recommended to us and described by readers. Do tell us what you think of them: feedback@goodguides.com

BARLEY   SD8240
★ **Barley Mow** (01282) 690868
Barley Lane; BB12 9JX Bars and dining rooms reminiscent of a hunting lodge; animal hide chairs and cushions, antlers and stuffed animals including a big boar's head, exposed-stone, cream-coloured or planked walls, woodburners (one in a raised two-sided fireplace), long rustic wall seats and mix of other furniture on carpet, bare boards or flagstones, Moorhouses, Thwaites and Timothy Taylors, eight wines by the glass and well liked hearty food; background music (live last Fri of month), TV, board games, free wi-fi; children and dogs (in bar) welcome, comfortable bedrooms, open (and food) all day. *(Ruth May)*

BARLEY   SD8240
Pendle (01282) 614808
Barley Lane; BB12 9JX Friendly 1930s stone pub in shadow of Pendle Hill; three cosy rooms, two log fires and six well kept regional ales including Moorhouses, popular good value pubby food (all day weekends) using local produce (lamb from family farm), conservatory; fortnightly quiz, free wi-fi; children and dogs welcome, picnic-sets on strip of lawn at front, small fenced play area across road by stream, lovely village and good walking country, bedrooms, open all day Fri-Sun. *(Ruth May)*

BARNSTON   SJ2783
★ **Fox & Hounds** (0151) 648 7685
3 miles from M53 junction 3: A552 towards Woodchurch, then left on A551; CH61 1BW Early 20th-c pub refurbished and extended under present management; local Brimstage, Theakstons and guests, over 60 malt whiskies, 40 gins and plenty of wines by the glass from extensive list, good home-made food including popular Sun lunch, roomy lounge with wood flooring and open fire, sizeable new conservatory and garden room, also small traditional locals' bar and snug where dogs allowed; free wi-fi; children

welcome, courtyard behind with teak furniture and heated smokers' shelter, open (and food) all day. *(Paul Humphreys)*

BARTON   SD5137
Sparling (01772) 860830
A6 N of Broughton; PR3 5AA Contemporary dining pub with enjoyable food including set deals, real ales such as Marstons Wainwright and good choice of wines by the glass, roomy bar with comfortable sofas and other seats, plenty of tables in linked areas off, wood and flagstone floors, modern fireplaces; free wi-fi; children welcome, handy for M6, open all day weekends. *(Lionel Smith)*

BELMONT   SD6715
Black Dog (01204) 811218
Church Street (A675); BL7 8AB Nicely set Holts pub with enjoyable traditional food including deals, well kept beers and friendly staff, various modernised areas (some slightly raised), pubby furnishings including banquettes on light wood or carpeted floors, a couple of coal fires, picture-window dining extension; children and dogs (in bar) welcome, seats outside with moorland views over village, part-covered courtyard behind, good walks, three bedrooms, open (and food) all day. *(Simon and Alex Knight)*

BLACKBURN   SD6525
Oyster & Otter (01254) 203200
1.8 miles from M65 junction 3: A674 towards Blackburn, turn right at Feniscowles mini roundabout, signposted to Darwen and Tockholes, into Livesey Branch Road; BB2 5DQ Distinctive clapboard and stone building in modern new england style; open-plan interior with cushioned dining booths by big windows on one side, other cosy seating areas divided by shoulder-high walls and large central hearth, end part with comfy sofas, good food including signature fish/seafood from open kitchen, Marstons Wainwright, a guest ale and a dozen wines by the glass; background

music, free wi-fi; children welcome, seats on decking above road, open (and food) all day. *(Tim North)*

BOLTON
SD7112
Brewery Tap (01204) 302837
Belmont Road; BL1 7AN Two-room corner tap for Bank Top, their full range kept well and a guest, knowledgeable friendly staff, no food; quiet background music, free wi-fi; children (until 7pm) and dogs welcome, disabled access, seats outside, open all day. *(John and Claire Masters)*

BRINDLE
SD5924
★Cavendish Arms (01254) 852912
3 miles from M6 junction 29, via A6 and B5256 (Sandy Lane); PR6 8NG Traditional beamed village pub (dates from the 15th c) on corner adjacent to church; cosy snugs with open fires, stained-glass windows depicting the Battle of Brunanburh, carpets throughout, four Marstons-related ales and good inexpensive home-made food including Thurs specials and Fri fish, friendly helpful service, back dining room; Tues quiz; children and dogs (in tap room) welcome, heated canopied terrace with water feature, more tables in side garden, good walks, open (and food) all day weekends, closed lunchtimes Mon and Tues (no food those days or lunchtime Weds). *(Francis and Mandy Robertson)*

BROUGHTON
SD4838
Plough at Eaves (01772) 690233
A6 N through Broughton, first left into Station Lane under a mile after traffic lights, then left after 1.5 miles, Eaves Lane; PR4 0BJ Pleasantly unpretentious old country tavern with two homely beamed bars; three well kept ales including Thwaites and good choice of enjoyable reasonably priced food, friendly accommodating service, lattice windows and traditional furnishings, old guns over woodburner in one room, log fire in dining bar with conservatory; background music; children welcome, front terrace and spacious side/back garden, well equipped play area, open all day Fri-Sun. *(Peter and Emma Kelly)*

BURY
SD8313
Trackside (0161) 764 6461
East Lancashire Railway station, Bolton Street; BL9 0EY Welcoming busy station bar by East Lancs steam railway; bright, airy and clean with ten real ales including a house beer from local Outstanding, also bottled imports, real ciders and great range of whiskies, enjoyable lunchtime food (not Mon, Tues); folk night last Thurs of month;

children (till 7pm) and dogs welcome, platform tables under canopy, open all day. *(P A Lord)*

CARNFORTH
SD5173
Longlands (01524) 781256
Tewitfield, about 2 miles N; A6070, off A6; LA6 1JH Popular family-run village inn; good food in bar and airy restaurant from pub favourites and pizzas up, four local beers, helpful friendly staff; live music; children and dogs welcome, bedrooms and self-catering cottages, Lancaster Canal and M6 nearby, open all day. *(Geoff and Anne Marston)*

CHATBURN
SD7644
Brown Cow (01200) 440736
Bridge Road; BB7 4AW Welcoming village pub refurbished under present management; opened-up interior with separate dining room, good well priced home-made food including weekly specials, Marstons Wainwright and three guests, friendly helpful service; children and dogs (in bar area) welcome, wheelchair access (ramp provided) and disabled loo (others upstairs), back garden with flagstone terrace, closed Mon, otherwise open all day, food all day weekends. *(Matthew and Elisabeth Reeves)*

CHEADLE
SJ8588
James Watts (0161) 428 3361
High Street (A560); SK8 1AX Newly refurbished mock-Tudor pub owned by Hydes; fine range of cask and craft beers plus 50 or more in bottles (all marked on little blackboard panels), good choice of wines and other drinks too, food from snacks to various sharing combinations served on slates, friendly helpful staff; live acoustic music Mon and Thurs, quiz Tues; back terrace, open (and food) all day (till midnight Fri, Sat). *(Lyn and Freddie Roberts)*

CHEADLE HULME
SJ8785
Church Inn (0161) 485 1897
Ravenoak Road (A5149 SE); SK8 7EG Popular old family-run pub with good food from varied menu including set deals, well kept Robinsons beers and nice selection of wines by the glass, gleaming brass on panelled walls, warming coal fire, back restaurant; live music most Sun evenings; children welcome, seats outside (some under cover), car park across road, open all day. *(Michael Butler)*

CLAUGHTON
SD5666
★Fenwick Arms (01524) 221157
A683 Kirkby Lonsdale–Lancaster; LA2 9LA Civilised 250-year-old black and white pub in Lune Valley, mainly popular for its food including good fish/seafood;

All *Guide* inspections are anonymous. Anyone claiming to be a *Good Pub Guide* inspector is a fraud. Please let us know.

smartly updated with white-painted beams in wonky ceilings, open fires (one in a black range) and painted panelling, upholstered and antique-style dining chairs around mix of tables on carpet or bare boards, window seats with scatter cushions, Marstons Wainwright, Timothy Taylors Landlord and a guest, several wines by the glass and a good choice of spirits, efficient friendly staff; background music, free wi-fi; children and dogs (in bar) welcome, picnic-sets on front terrace, nine comfortable modern bedrooms, open (and food) all day. *(John and Sylvia Harrop)*

CLITHEROE   SD7441
Holmes Mill (01200) 407120
Greenacre Street; BB7 1EB Conversion of town's last working cotton mill; cavernous industrial interior keeping some of the old machinery, lovely flagged floor and plenty of recycled fixtures and fittings, walls fitted with leather benches and scrubbed plank tables, sturdy canteen chairs and high-backed stools elsewhere, vast U-shaped counter serving 24 real ales including six from Bowland (brewery visible behind glass partitions), good selection of enjoyable food including grills, also has a café and boutique hotel; background and some live music; picnic-sets outside along with covered seating in shipping containers, open (and food) all day, till 8pm Sun. *(Tim North)*

CLITHEROE   SD7441
New Inn (01200) 423312
Parson Lane; BB7 2JN Traditional old-fashioned local with ten or more well kept ales including Coach House and Moorhouses from central bar, friendly knowledgeable staff, cosy rooms with log fires; fortnightly irish session (Sun afternoon) and other live music; dogs welcome, seats out at front and back, camping, open all day. *(Francis and Mandy Robertson)*

COLNE   SD8940
Black Lane Ends (01282) 863070
Skipton Old Road, Foulridge; BB8 7EP Country pub tucked away in quiet lane; generous helpings of good sensibly priced food, three well kept real ales including Timothy Taylors Landlord and decent wine choice, cheerful attentive staff, long bar with spindleback chairs, padded wall benches and scrubbed tables, large fireplace partially separating small dining room with cast-iron range; children welcome, play area in back garden, nice views towards Wycoller from terrace, handy for canal and reservoir walks, open (and food) all day. *(Professor Simon Burke)*

DELPH   SD9809
Royal Oak (01457) 874460
Off A6052 about 100 metres W of White Lion, turn up steep Lodge Lane and keep on up into Broad Lane; OL3 5TX Welcoming traditional 18th-c pub in steep winding lane opposite old moorland church, great views of surrounding valleys; real fires in three small rooms, comfortable solid furniture, four well kept ales including Millstone and Moorhouses, no food; closed Mon, Tues and lunchtimes apart from Sun when open 12-6pm. *(Shona and Jimmy McDuff)*

DENSHAW   SD9710
Printers Arms (01457) 874248
Oldham Road; OL3 5SN Above Oldham in shadow of Saddleworth Moor; modernised interior with small log-fire bar and three other rooms, popular good value food including bargain set menu (12-5pm Mon-Fri), Black Sheep and Timothy Taylors Golden Best, several wines by the glass, friendly staff; children welcome, lovely views from two-tier beer garden, open (and food) all day. *(Lionel Smith)*

DENSHAW   SD9711
Rams Head (01457) 874802
2 miles from M62 junction 22; A672 towards Oldham, pub N of village; OL3 5UN Sweeping moorland views from this popular roadside dining pub (don't be put off by the rather austere exterior); good food (all day weekends) including seasonal game and seafood, ales such as Timothy Taylors kept well and several wines by the glass, friendly service, four thick-walled little rooms, beam-and-plank ceilings, panelling, oak settles and built-in benches, log fires, coffee shop and adjacent delicatessen selling local produce; soft background music; children welcome, closed Mon and Tues. *(Michael Butler)*

DENTON   SJ9395
Lowes Arms (0161) 336 3064
Hyde Road (A57); M34 3FF Thriving 19th-c pub with own Westwood beers and local guests such as Crossbay, jovial community-spirited landlord and helpful friendly staff, reasonably priced food including daily specials, bar with pool and darts, restaurant; children and dogs welcome, tables outside, smokers' shelter, open all day. *(Peter and Emma Kelly)*

DIGGLE   SE0007
Diggle (01457) 872741
Village signed off A670 just N of Dobcross; OL3 5JZ Sturdy four-square hillside pub (new management) in quiet spot just below the moors overlooking Standedge Canal tunnel; good value food (till 7pm Sun, not Mon) from sandwiches and snacks up, well kept ales such as Black Sheep, Millstone and Timothy Taylors, helpful staff; free wi-fi;

We say if we know a pub allows dogs.

children and dogs welcome, disabled access, picnic-sets out among trees, four bedrooms, closed Mon lunchtime, otherwise open all day. *(Colin and Daniel Gibbs)*

DOLPHINHOLME   SD5153
Fleece (01524) 791233
A couple of miles from M6 junction 33; W of village; Chipping Lane/Anyon Road; LA2 9AQ Extensively renovated old stone inn (parts date from the 16th c); various rooms including black-beamed bar with rugs on flagstones and log fire with unusual copper canopy, four well kept regularly changing ales and decent wines by the glass, popular sensibly priced food (not Mon), friendly efficient service, dining lounge with some modern booth seating and sofas in front of woodburner, little shop selling local produce; children and dogs welcome, modern rattan-style furniture on terrace with Trough of Bowland views, nine comfortable well appointed bedrooms, good breakfast, closed Mon lunchtime, otherwise open all day. *(Simon and Alex Knight)*

DUNHAM TOWN   SJ7488
Axe & Cleaver (0161) 928 3391
School Lane; WA14 4SE Big 19th-c country house converted into spacious open-plan Chef & Brewer; good value popular food from light lunchtime choices and sharing plates up (best to book Sun lunch), three well kept ales, friendly service; children welcome, garden picnic-sets, handy for nearby Dunham Massey (NT), open (and food) all day. *(Ruth May)*

DUNHAM TOWN   SJ7288
Vine (0161) 928 3275
Barns Lane, Dunham Massey; WA14 5RU Tucked-away (but busy) old-fashioned village local with friendly staff and regulars; well kept/priced Sam Smiths ales and several ciders, enjoyable generously served food (not Sun evening, Mon), cosy bar and other smallish rooms, coal fires in brick fireplaces; children and dogs welcome, picnic-sets in good-sized garden, handy for Dunham Massey (NT), open all day. *(Steve Whalley)*

EDENFIELD   SD7919
Coach (01706) 825000
Market Street; BL0 0HJ Updated and extended 19th-c dining pub; good food from lunchtime sandwiches up, three real ales, over a dozen wines by the glass and good range of gins, friendly young staff; free wi-fi; children and dogs (in bar) welcome, disabled access/facilities, a few tables on front pavement, open (and food) all day. *(David Appleyard)*

EGERTON   SD7015
Cross Guns (01204) 291204)
Blackburn Road (A666); BL7 9TR Recently renovated 18th-c stone pub below

the moors; spacious cleanly updated interior with beams, standing timbers, bare boards and exposed stone walls, two snug areas to the right with woodburners, bar constructed from salvaged beams serving four well kept/priced ales such as Brightside, Dunscar and Moorhouses, over a dozen wines by the glass and good choice of other drinks, popular food from lunchtime sandwiches and pub favourites up including some interesting choices, restaurant extending into old stables, friendly staff; children welcome, narrow fenced front terrace with dog shower, open all day, food till 7pm Sun. *(Steve Whalley)*

FENCE   SD8237
Fence Gate (01282) 618101
2.6 miles from M65 junction 13; Wheatley Lane Road, just off A6068 W; BB12 9EE Imposing 18th-c dining inn with good choice of enjoyable food, five real ales and several wines by the glass, friendly service, panelled bar with pewter counter and woodburner in large stone fireplace, contemporary brasserie plus various function rooms, look out for their display of over 600 gins; background and regular live music; children welcome, rattan-style furniture out at front, 24 bedrooms, open all day. *(Tim North)*

FENCE   SD8237
★**White Swan** (01282) 611773
Wheatley Lane; BB12 9QA Whitewashed village dining pub with comfortably renovated Victorian-style interior; highly regarded imaginative food (not cheap) from short daily changing menu, good friendly service, four well kept Timothy Taylors ales from curved polished wood servery, nice wines, own infused spirits and good coffee, old pictures of the pub, some antlers and stuffed animal heads, wall lights and chandeliers, fireplace at each end; children welcome, outside seating on two levels with chunky wooden tables, open all day, no food Sun evening, Mon. *(W K Wood)*

GISBURN   SD8248
White Bull (01200) 415805
Main Street (A59); BB7 4HE Modernised roadside pub with opened-up dining areas either side of entrance, more room further back to right of bar; taupe-painted walls and stone-effect wallpaper, mix of dark furniture on polished wood or flagstone floors, some whitewashed beams and standing timbers, enjoyable food (not Mon) from sandwiches, sharing boards and pub standards up, Weds steak night, well kept ales from semi-circular counter with cherry wood top, friendly service; children and dogs (in one section) welcome, narrow access to large back car park, grassy beer garden, eight comfortable bedrooms, closed Mon lunchtime. *(Michael Butler)*

GOOSNARGH
SD5636
Stags Head (01772) 861536
Whittingham Lane (B5269); PR3 2AU
Old roadside dining pub extensively
refurbished under present owners; good
range of popular freshly made food at fair
prices, friendly helpful service, ales such as
Caledonian Deuchars IPA and Theakstons
Best, lots of separate areas including
pitched-roof restaurant, open fires; Thurs
quiz, board games, TV; children, walkers and
dogs welcome, tables out in pleasant garden
with fenced play area, open (and food)
all day. *(Peter Pilbeam)*

GREAT ECCLESTON
SD4240
★ Farmers Arms (01995) 672018
Halsall Square (just off A586); PR3 0YE
Popular attractively refurbished country
pub not far from Fylde Coast and Blackpool;
smart dining areas, on two floors, with
painted panelled walls and eclectic
collection of seating on carpet or polished
boards, woodburners in stone fireplaces, ales
such as Marstons Wainwright and Timothy
Taylors Boltmaker, good choice of wines/
gins and highly regarded food with emphasis
on fish/seafood and grills, cheerful attentive
service; free wi-fi; children and dogs (in bar)
welcome, teak furniture on sheltered terrace,
open (and food) all day. *(Frank and Joan
Carruthers, Stephen Hampson)*

GREAT HARWOOD
SD7332
Royal (01254) 876237
Station Road; BB6 7BA Popular Victorian
local with half a dozen well kept changing
ales and generous helpings of enjoyable pub
food, friendly staff; some live music, pool
and darts; children welcome, partly covered
terrace, open all day. *(Colin and Daniel Gibbs)*

GREAT MITTON
SD7139
Three Fishes (01254) 826888
*Mitton Road (B6246, off A59 NW of
Whalley); BB7 9PQ* This popular village
pub (previous Main Entry) was being
refurbished by new owners (Brunning &
Price) as we went to press – reports please.

GREENFIELD
SD9904
King William IV (01457) 873933
Chew Valley Road (A669); OL3 7DD
Welcoming 19th-c village pub with eight
well kept ales including local Greenfield
and Millstone, enjoyable home-made food
(not Mon, Tues or lunchtimes Weds, Thurs),
helpful, friendly staff; Mon quiz, sports TV,
free wi-fi; children and dogs welcome, tables
on walled front terrace, open all day.
(Martin and Joanne Sharp)

GREENFIELD
SD9904
Railway Hotel (01457) 872307
*Shaw Hall Bank Road, opposite station;
OL3 7JZ* Friendly four-room stone pub with
half a dozen well kept mainly local ales, no
food, old local photographs and open fire; live
music Thurs, Fri and Sun, sports TV, upstairs
games bar with darts and pool; children and
dogs welcome, disabled access, good views
from beer garden, closed Mon, otherwise
open all day. *(Thomas Green)*

HESWALL
SJ2782
Jug & Bottle (0151) 342 5535
Mount Avenue; CH60 4RH Nicely updated
Victorian building with views through trees
of the Dee estuary and welsh mountains
beyond; good-sized bar with wood and
flagstone floors, open fire, dining rooms off,
half a dozen well kept ales including Brains,
Brimstage and a house beer from Coach
House, lots of wines by the glass, good choice
of popular fairly priced food from sandwiches
and sharing plates up, friendly attentive staff;
children and dogs welcome, teak furniture
on front deck and surrounding garden,
six bedrooms, open (and food) all day.
(Iain Bignold, Robert Tarbath)

HURST GREEN
SD6837
★ Shireburn Arms (01254) 826678
*Whalley Road (B6243 Clitheroe–
Goosnargh); BB7 9QJ* Welcoming 17th-c
hotel with peaceful Ribble Valley views from
big airy restaurant and neatly kept garden;
food from sandwiches and traditional dishes
to daily specials, leather armchairs, sofas and
log fire in beamed and flagstoned lounge bar
with linked dining area, two well kept ales
and several wines by the glass; occasional
live music, daily papers; children and dogs
welcome, pretty Tolkien walk from here,
22 comfortable bedrooms, open all day from
8am for coffee, food all day weekends.
(Simon and Alex Knight)

HYDE
SJ9595
Sportsman (0161) 368 5000
Mottram Road; SK14 2NN Welcoming
Victorian local with Rossendale ales and
lots of changing guests (frequent beer
festivals), bargain bar food including Weds
curry and Thurs steak nights, also popular
upstairs cuban restaurant, bare boards and
open fires, pub games; children and dogs
welcome, back terrace with heated
smokers' shelter, open all day.
(Francis and Mandy Robertson)

INGLETON
SD6972
Masons Arms (01524) 242040
New Road (A65); LA6 3HL Welcoming
roadside village inn; stools and upholstered
chairs around mix of pubby tables on wood-
strip flooring, tartan-carpeted dining end
with woodburner, generous helpings of tasty
straightforward food from lunchtime hot or
cold sandwiches up (more evening choice),
well kept ales such as Sharps and four guests,
decent wine list with half a dozen by the
glass, good friendly service; children and
dogs welcome, three bedrooms, open (and
some food) all day. *(Peter Pilbeam)*

IRBY
SJ2586

★ **Irby Mill** (0151) 604 0194

Mill Lane, off Greasby Road; CH49 3NT
Converted miller's sandstone cottage
(original windmill demolished 1898);
friendly and welcoming, with eight well
kept ales including Caledonian Deuchars
IPA, good choice of wines by the glass and
ample helpings of popular reasonably priced
food from sandwiches up, efficient service,
two low-beamed traditional flagstoned
rooms and extended carpeted dining area,
log fire, interesting old photographs and
history; children and dogs welcome, tables
on terraces and revamped side area, good
local walks, open (and food) all day, gets
crowded evenings/weekends when parking
limited. *(Matthew and Elisabeth Reeves)*

LANCASTER
SD4761

Borough (01524) 64170

Dalton Square; LA1 1PP Civilised and
popular city-centre pub; high ceilinged bar
rooms with chandeliers, leather chesterfields
and elbow tables on bare boards, some
stained-glass partitioning, eight real ales and
lots of bottled beers, big dining room with
booths along one side, decent food including
daily specials and deals; upstairs comedy
night Sun; children and dogs welcome, nice
little enclosed back garden, bedrooms, open
(and food) all day from 8am. *(Thomas Green)*

LANCASTER
SD4761

Sun (01524) 66006

Church Street; LA1 1ET Hotel bar with ten
well kept ales including five from Lancaster,
plenty of continental beers and good choice
of wines by the glass too, popular food from
sandwiches, sharing boards and pub staples
up, exposed stonework, panelling and several
fireplaces, conservatory; background music,
TV; children welcome away from servery,
tables on walled and paved terrace,
16 comfortable bedrooms, open all day
(till 1am Fri, Sat). *(Chris Taylor)*

LANCASTER
SD4761

Water Witch (01524) 63828

*Parking in Aldcliffe Road behind
Royal Lancaster Infirmary, off A6;
LA1 1SU* Attractive conversion of 18th-c
canalside stables; flagstones, stripped stone,
rafters and pitch-pine panelling, half a dozen
well kept changing ales, extensive choice of
fairly traditional food from sandwiches and
deli boards up including weekday lunch deal,
upstairs restaurant; Weds open mike night,
Thurs quiz, free wi-fi; children welcome
in eating areas, picnic-sets out by water,
moorings, open (and food) all day.
(Thomas Green)

LANESHAW BRIDGE
SD9141

Alma (01282) 857830

*Emmott Lane, off A6068 E of Colne;
BB8 7EG* Attractively renovated 18th-c inn

with popular food, several wines by the glass
and good choice of real ales, friendly helpful
staff, flagstoned bar and part-panelled lounge
with rugs on bare boards, open fires, large
garden room extension; background music;
well behaved children and dogs welcome,
nine comfortable well appointed bedrooms,
open (and food) all day, breakfast for non-
residents. *(Ruth May)*

LITTLE ECCLESTON
SD4240

★ **Cartford** (01995) 670166

*Cartford Lane, off A586 Garstang–
Blackpool, by toll bridge; PR3 0YP*
Riverside coaching inn with unusual
four-level layout combining traditional
and contemporary elements, four real ales
including a house beer (Giddy Kipper)
from Moorhouses, speciality bottled beers,
11 wines by the glass and interesting range
of gins and whiskies, highly regarded
imaginative food plus some pub favourites,
restaurant, on-site shop and delicatessen;
children welcome (no under-10s after 8pm),
garden tables looking out over tidal River
Wyre (crossed by toll bridge), individually
decorated bedrooms and two new studio
cabins, closed Mon lunchtime, otherwise
open all day, food all day Sun. *(Peter and
Emma Kelly)*

LITTLEBOROUGH
SD9517

Moorcock (01706) 378156

Halifax Road (A58); OL15 0LD Long
roadside inn high on the moors with far-
reaching views; good food from sandwiches
and pub favourites up in flagstoned bar
or restaurant, four well kept beers; sports
TV; terrace tables taking in the view, seven
comfortable reasonably priced bedrooms,
open all day, food all day Fri-Sun, kitchen
closed lunchtimes Mon-Weds. *(Robert Wivell)*

LIVERPOOL
SJ3489

Baltic Fleet (0151) 709 3116

Wapping, near Albert Dock; L1 8DQ
Unusual bow-fronted pub with six interesting
beers including Wapping (brewed in the
cellar), real ciders and several wines by the
glass, simple well cooked/priced lunchtime
food such as traditional scouse, bare
boards, big arched windows, simple mix of
furnishings and some nautical paraphernalia,
fires in parlour and snug; background music,
TV; children welcome in eating areas, dogs
in bar, back terrace, open all day. *(Anthony
Barnes, Dr and Mrs A K Clarke, Michael Butler)*

LIVERPOOL
SJ3589

Belvedere (0151) 709 0303

Sugnall Street; L7 7EB Unspoilt little
19th-c two-room pub with friendly chatty
atmosphere, original features including
etched glass and coal fires, four well kept
changing ales such as Melwood and Salopian,
good selection of bottled beers, real cider
and fine choice of gins; dogs welcome, open
all day. *(Colin and Daniel Gibbs)*

LIVERPOOL   SJ3589
Cracke (0151) 709 4171
Rice Street; L1 9BB Friendly unchanging
local with five well kept ales including
Phoenix and Thwaites, traditional cider, no
food, small unspoilt bar with bare boards and
bench seats, snug and a bigger back room
with unusual Beatles diorama, local artwork
and some photos of John Lennon who used
to drink here; juke box, sports TV; picnic-sets
in sizeable tree-shaded back garden, open
all day and popular with tourists.
(Dr and Mrs A K Clarke)

LIVERPOOL   SJ3590
Crown (0151) 707 6027
Lime Street; L1 1JQ Well preserved (if a
little worn around the edges) art nouveau
showpiece; fine tiled fireplace and copper
bar front, dark leather banquettes, panelling
and splendid moulded ceiling, smaller back
room with another good fireplace, impressive
staircase sweeping up under cupola to
handsome area with ornate windows, eight
real ales and good choice of bottled beers,
wide range of reasonably priced pubby food
including deals; sports TV, fruit machine; very
handy for the station, open all day from 8am
for breakfast. *(Dr and Mrs A K Clarke)*

LIVERPOOL   SJ3490
Dead Crafty Beer 07977 228918
*Dale Street opposite the old magistrates'
court; L2 5TF* Craft beer bar with 20 on
tap and over 150 in bottles, tasters offered by
friendly knowledgeable staff, compact fairly
basic interior with bare boards and exposed
brickwork, bar made from flight cases; unisex
loos downstairs; dogs allowed, open all day
Fri-Sun, closed lunchtimes Mon-Thurs.
(Dr and Mrs A K Clarke)

LIVERPOOL   SJ3589
Dispensary (0151) 709 2160
Renshaw Street; L1 2SP Small busy
central pub worth knowing for its very well
kept changing beers (up to ten), good choice
of bottled imports too, no food, bare boards
and polished panelling, wonderful etched
windows, comfortable raised back bar with
fireplace (not used), some Victorian medical
artefacts; background music, silent TVs,
notices on house rules; open all day (till
midnight Fri, Sat). *(Dr and Mrs A K Clarke,
Colin and Daniel Gibbs)*

LIVERPOOL   SJ3490
Doctor Duncan (0151) 709 5100
St Johns Lane; L1 1HF Victorian pub
with several rooms including impressive
back area with pillared and vaulted tiled
ceiling, open fires and various apothecary
cabinets, five well kept ales and good value

pubby food, friendly helpful service; beer
garden, open all day. *(Dave Braisted)*

LIVERPOOL   SJ3589
Fly in the Loaf (0151) 708 0817
Hardman Street; L1 9AS Market Town
Tavern in former bakery; well kept Okells,
guest ales and several foreign beers from
long counter, also good selection of wines
and cocktails, decent food including
bar snacks and pizzas, efficient friendly
service, panelling and some raised sections;
background music, sports TV; disabled loos
(others upstairs along with function room),
open all day, till midnight Fri, Sat.
(Dave Braisted, Dr and Mrs A K Clarke)

LIVERPOOL   SJ3490
Hole In Ye Wall (0151) 227 3809
Off Dale Street; L2 2AW Character 18th-c
pub (the city's oldest) with thriving local
atmosphere in high-beamed panelled bar;
half a dozen changing ales fed by gravity from
upstairs (no cellar as pub is on Quaker burial
site), extensive gin range, baguettes, pies,
burgers and so forth, friendly staff, plenty of
woodwork, stained glass and old Liverpool
photographs, coal-effect gas fire in unusual
brass-canopied fireplace; live music evenings
Mon, Fri and Sat, traditional sing-along Sun,
sports TV, fruit machine; children allowed
till 5pm, no dogs, open all day.
(Dr and Mrs A K Clarke)

LIVERPOOL   SJ3490
Lion Tavern (0151) 236 9768
Moorfields, off Tithebarn Street; L2 2BP
Beautifully preserved ornate Victorian corner
pub; sparkling etched glass, big mirrors,
panelling and tilework, serving hatches in
central bar, two small back lounges one
with fine glass dome, eight changing beers
and extensive range of whiskies, simple
reasonably priced lunchtime food including
good pork pies, friendly staff; sports TV, free
wi-fi; open all day. *(Colin and Daniel Gibbs)*

LIVERPOOL   SJ3590
Ma Egerton's Stage Door
(0151) 345 3525 *Pudsey Street, opposite
side entrance to Lime Street station;
L1 1JA* Victorian pub behind the Empire
Theatre named after former long-serving
landlady/theatrical agent; refurbished but
keeping old-fashioned character with green
leather button-back banquettes (note the
bell pushes), swagged curtains, wood floors,
panelling and a small period fireplace, lots
of celebrity pictures and other memorabilia,
a couple of changing ales and enjoyable food
including sharing plates and popular pizzas,
friendly staff; Mon quiz, Fri sing-along, bingo
last Thurs of month; open all day.
(Dr and Mrs A K Clarke)

If you know a pub is ever open all day, please tell us.

LIVERPOOL SJ3589
Peter Kavanaghs (0151) 709 3443
Egerton Street, off Catherine Street;
L8 7LY Character Victorian pub popular
with locals and students; interesting décor
in several small rooms, old-world murals,
stained glass and all kinds of bric-a-brac (lots
hanging from ceiling), piano, wooden settles
and real fires, well kept Greene King Abbot
and guests, friendly licensees; free wi-fi;
open all day (till 1am Fri, Sat).
(Colin and Daniel Gibbs)

LIVERPOOL SJ3589
Philharmonic Dining Rooms (0151) 707 2837
36 Hope Street; corner of Hardman
Street; L1 9BX Beautifully preserved
Victorian pub with wonderful period detail;
centrepiece mosaic-faced counter, heavily
carved and polished mahogany partitions
radiating out under intricate plasterwork
ceiling, main hall with stained glass of
Boer War heroes Baden-Powell and Lord
Roberts, rich panelling, mosaic floor and
copper panels of musicians above fireplace,
other areas including two side rooms called
Brahms and Liszt, the original Adamant
gents' is also worth a look, ten real ales,
several wines by the glass and decent choice
of malt whiskies, fair-priced food; background
music and machines; children welcome
till 7pm, open (and food) all day.
(Anthony Barnes, Dr and Mrs A K Clarke)

LIVERPOOL SJ3589
Roscoe Head (0151) 709 4365
Roscoe Street; L1 2SX Unassuming old
local with cosy bar, snug and two other
spotless unspoilt little rooms; well kept
Tetleys Bitter, Timothy Taylors Landlord
and four guests (tasting trays available),
friendly staff and regulars, lunchtime pies
and sandwiches (not weekends), interesting
memorabilia; Tues quiz and traditional games
such as crib, free wi-fi; open all day.
(Thomas Green)

LIVERPOOL SJ3490
Ship & Mitre (0151) 236 0859
Dale Street; L2 2JH Friendly local with
fine art deco exterior and ship-like interior;
up to a dozen unusual changing ales (many
beer festivals), real ciders and over 70
bottled beers, decent choice of good value
food (all day Fri-Sun) such as wraps, burgers
and all-day breakfast, upstairs function room
with original 1930s décor; well behaved
children (till 7pm) and dogs welcome,
open all day. *(Peter and Emma Kelly)*

LIVERPOOL SJ3490
★Thomas Rigbys (0151) 236 3269
Dale Street; L2 2EZ Spacious three-
room Victorian pub; main bare-boards bar
with iron pillars supporting sturdy beams,
panelling and stained glass, Okells ales and

guests from long counter, also good range of
imported draught/bottled beers and several
gins, back Nelson Room with impressive
fireplace and an oak-panelled dining parlour
where children allowed, enjoyable reasonably
priced pubby food till early evening, efficient
service; sports TV; disabled access (although
some steps and downstairs lavatories), seats
in big courtyard, open all day. *(Fintan Hayes)*

LONGRIDGE SD6137
Corporation Arms (01772) 782644
Lower Road (B6243); PR3 2YJ Updated
18th-c roadside inn next to reservoir;
good range of popular home-cooked food
generously served and reasonably priced,
four well kept changing ales, plenty of wines
by the glass, cheerful service and good
welcoming atmosphere in three small linked
rooms and restaurant; children welcome,
five comfortable bedrooms, closed Mon,
otherwise open (and food) all day.
(Martin and Joanne Sharp)

LONGRIDGE SD6038
★Derby Arms (01772) 782370
Chipping Road, Thornley; 1.5 miles N
of Longridge on back road to Chipping;
PR3 2NB Creeper-clad village pub with
attractively updated bar and connecting
dining rooms, wide floorboards or grey
carpet, woodburner and open fire, assorted
seating including high-backed chairs, settles
with scatter cushions, wall banquettes
and leather-topped stools, Copper Dragon,
Thwaites and Timothy Taylors from stylish
oak-planked servery, nice selection of
wines by the glass too, good food including
chargrills and daily fish specials, cheerful
helpful service; free wi-fi; children and
dogs (in bar) welcome, good quality
furniture on front terrace behind picket
fence, comfortable modern bedrooms,
open (and food) all day, breakfast for non-
residents. *(Bryan, William and Ann Reid)*

LONGRIDGE SD6037
New Drop (01254) 878338
Higher Road, Longridge Fell, parallel to
B6243 Longridge–Clitheroe; PR3 2YX
Pleasant modernised dining pub in lovely
moors-edge country overlooking Ribble
Valley; good choice of reasonably priced
food, decent wines and three well kept
ales such as Black Sheep, friendly service;
children welcome, open all day Sun,
closed Mon. *(Paul Walker)*

LYDGATE SD9704
★White Hart (01457) 872566
Stockport Road; Lydgate not marked
on some maps and not the one near
Todmorden; take A669 Oldham–
Saddleworth, right at brow of hill to
A6050 after almost 2.5 miles; OL4 4JJ
Smart up-to-date dining pub overlooking
Pennine moors; mix of locals (in bar or
simpler end rooms) and diners in elegant

brasserie with smartly dressed staff, highly regarded if not cheap food, Lees, Timothy Taylors and a guest beer, 16 wines by the glass, old beams and exposed stonework contrasting with deep red or purple walls and modern artwork, open fires; children welcome, dogs in bar, picnic-sets on back lawn making most of position, 12 bedrooms, open all day. *(Professor Simon Burke)*

LYTHAM SD3627

★ **Taps** (01253) 736226
A584 S of Blackpool; Henry Street – in centre, one street in from West Beach; FY8 5LE Popular town pub just a couple of minutes from the beach; ten well kept ales including Greene King and a couple of proper ciders, simple good value lunchtime food (not Sun), friendly efficient staff, open-plan bar with wood or tiled floor, stripped brickwork and open fires (summer air-conditioning), dining area leading through to sunny terrace; quiz Mon, TV for major sports, darts, fruit machine; children allowed till 7.30pm, small garden, parking nearby difficult (best to use West Beach car park on seafront, free Sun), open all day. *(Steve Whalley, Dr J Barrie Jones, Michael Butler)*

MANCHESTER SJ8498

Angel (0161) 833 4786
Angel Street, off Rochdale Road; M4 4BR Friendly place on edge of the Northern Quarter; good value home-made food, ten well kept ales including one badged for them, bottled beers and a couple of ciders/ perries, piano in bare-boards bar, smaller upstairs restaurant with two log fires and local artwork; free wi-fi; children (till 8pm) and dogs welcome, back beer garden, open all day. *(Francis and Mandy Robertson)*

MANCHESTER SJ8398

Ape & Apple (0161) 839 9624
John Dalton Street; M2 6HQ Large open-plan pub with four well kept/priced Holts ales, guest beers and traditional bar food including deals, comfortable seating on bare boards, carpet or tiles, lots of old prints and posters, upstairs restaurant/ function room, friendly atmosphere; Mon salsa dancing and Weds comedy night, juke box, games machines, free wi-fi; children and dogs welcome, disabled access, central courtyard and roof terrace, open all day (till 9pm Sun). *(Dr and Mrs A K Clarke)*

MANCHESTER SJ8397

★ **Britons Protection** (0161) 236 5895
Great Bridgewater Street, corner of Lower Mosley Street; M1 5LE Lively unpretentious pub with rambling rooms

and notable tiled murals of 1819 Peterloo Massacre (took place nearby); plush little front bar with tiled floor, glossy brown and russet wall tiles, solid woodwork and ornate red and gold ceiling, two cosy inner lounges, both served by hatch, eight real ales including one named for the pub from massive counter with heated footrail, also over 300 malt whiskies, straightforward lunchtime food Mon-Fri; occasional storytelling and live music, free wi-fi; children till 7pm, tables in enclosed back garden, handy for Bridgewater Hall concerts, open all day (very busy lunchtime and weekends). *(Dr and Mrs A K Clarke)*

MANCHESTER SJ8498

Castle (0161) 237 9485
Oldham Street, about 200 metres from Piccadilly, on right; M4 1LE Restored 18th-c pub run well by former *Coronation Street* actor; simple traditional front bar, small snug, Robinsons ales and guests from fine bank of handpumps, Weston's Old Rosie cider; juke box, back room for regular live music and other events, overspill space upstairs; nice tilework outside, open all day till late. *(Dr and Mrs A K Clarke)*

MANCHESTER SJ8497

Circus Tavern (0161) 236 5818
Portland Street; M1 4GX Traditional little two-room local; friendly staff serving well kept Robinsons and Tetleys from tiny corridor bar (or may be table service), leatherette wall benches and panelling, back room with football memorabilia and period fireplace; sports TV; open all day and can get crowded. *(Mike and Eleanor Anderson)*

MANCHESTER SJ8398

City Arms (0161) 236 4610
Kennedy Street, off St Peters Square; M2 4BQ Friendly old-fashioned two-bar local sandwiched between two other pubs; eight well kept quickly changing ales, belgian bottled beers and decent range of whiskies and gins, simple weekday lunchtime food, bare boards, panelling and button-back banquettes, coal fires; quiet background music, sports TV, darts and dominoes; wheelchair access but steps down to back lounge, open all day (till 8pm Sun). *(Thomas Green)*

MANCHESTER SJ8397

Dukes 92 (0161) 839 8642
Castle Street, below the bottom end of Deansgate; M3 4LZ Friendly informal atmosphere in refurbished former stables overlooking canal basin; modern furnishings on light tiled floor, exposed brickwork, stairs

---

A star symbol before the name of a pub shows exceptional character and appeal. It doesn't mean extra comfort. And it's nothing to do with exceptional food quality. Even quite a basic pub can win a star, if it's individual enough.

up to stylish gallery bar leading to roof terrace, a couple of local ales such as Seven Bro7hers, decent wines and wide range of spirits (happy-hour cocktails Mon-Thurs), good food choice from bar snacks and pizzas up; background music, DJs Fri and Sat, live music Sun; children welcome till 8.30pm, no dogs inside, waterside tables on big terrace with outside bar/kitchen, open (and food) all day (till 1am Fri, Sat). *(Dr and Mrs A K Clarke)*

MANCHESTER SJ8194
Font (0161) 871 2022
Manchester Road, Chorlton; M21 9PG
Relaxed split-level bar with eight changing ales, 16 craft kegs and extensive range of bottled beers, also traditional ciders and fair-priced cocktails, enjoyable food from sandwiches and wraps to burgers and burritos; weekend DJs, free wi-fi; children (till 8pm) and dogs welcome, seats out at front behind railings, open (and food) all day (till 1am Fri, Sat), popular with students. *(Thomas Green)*

MANCHESTER SJ8397
Knott Bar (0161) 839 9229
Deansgate; M3 4LY Modern glass-fronted café-bar under railway arch by Castlefield heritage site; eight well kept changing ales, also lots of craft beers and continental imports, pizza-based menu; background music; children welcome until 8pm, upstairs balcony overlooking Rochdale Canal (dogs allowed here), open (and food) all day.
(Dr and Mrs A K Clarke)

MANCHESTER SJ8497
Lass o' Gowrie (0161) 273 5822
36 Charles Street; off Oxford Road; M1 7DB Traditional tile-fronted side-street local refurbished a few years ago but keeping Victorian character; big-windowed bar with cosy room off, wood floors and stripped brickwork, pendant lighting, various pictures including black and white photos of old Manchester, three well kept Greene King ales plus local guests, simple bargain food such as home-made pies, friendly service; Thurs quiz, some live music; balcony overlooking River Medlock, open all day. *(David Appleyard)*

MANCHESTER SJ8499
★**Marble Arch** (0161) 832 5914
Rochdale Road (A664), Ancoats; centre of Gould Street, just E of Victoria station; M4 4HY Cheery pub with fine listed Victorian interior; long narrow bar with high ceiling, extensive glazed brickwork, marble and tiling, sloping mosaic floor and frieze advertising various drinks, old stone bottles on shelves, real ales including their own Marble beers (brewery visible from windows in back dining room – tours by arrangement), well liked home-made food including separate cheese menu; background music; children welcome, small garden, open (and food) all day. *(David Appleyard)*

MANCHESTER SJ8398
★**Mr Thomas's Chop House**
(0161) 832 2245 *Cross Street; M2 7AR* Interesting late 19th-c pub with well preserved original features; generously served food including signature corned beef hash, ales such as Black Sheep and Holts, decent wines by the glass; front bar with panelling, old gas lamp fittings and framed cartoons, stools at wall and window shelves, back green-tiled eating areas have rows of tables on black and white Victorian tiles, archways and high ceilings; seats out at back, open (and food) all day. *(Thomas Green)*

MANCHESTER SJ8298
New Oxford (0161) 832 7082
Bexley Square, Salford; M3 6DB Red-brick Victorian corner pub with up to 18 well kept changing ales (chalked on blackboard), plus extensive range of draught and bottled continental beers, real ciders too, light airy feel in small front bar and back room, coal fire, low-priced basic food; open mike and quiz nights, monthly beer festivals, juke box, free wi-fi; café-style seating out in square, open all day. *(Thomas Green)*

MANCHESTER SJ8398
★**Oast House** (0161) 829 3830
Crown Square, Springfields; M3 3AY Quirky mock-up of a kentish oast house surrounded by modern high-rises; lofty rustic interior with bare boards, timbers and plenty of tables, good selection of draught and bottled beers, wines and cocktails, enjoyable fairly priced food from deli boards to barbecues and rotisserie grills, friendly helpful young staff, busy cheerful atmosphere; background and nightly live music; children welcome, spacious outside seating area, open all day (till 2am Fri, Sat).
(Lionel Smith)

MANCHESTER SJ8398
Old Wellington (016) 839 5179
Cathedral Gates, off Exchange Square; M3 1SW Tudor pub moved from Old Shambles Square during redevelopment; open-plan with original flagstones, panelling and gnarled timbers, small bar and dining area, restaurant and further bar on two floors above, half a dozen real ales (not cheap) and decent food from Nicholson's menu including range of pies, good friendly service; background music; children welcome, lots of tables out overlooking Exchange Square, open all day. *(Richard Tilbrook)*

MANCHESTER SJ8397
★**Peveril of the Peak** (0161) 236 6364
Great Bridgewater Street; M1 5JQ Vivid art nouveau external tilework and three sturdily furnished old-fashioned bare-boards rooms, interesting pictures, lots of mahogany, mirrors and stained or frosted glass, log fire, four changing ales from central servery,

cheap basic lunchtime food; background music, TV, table football and pool; dogs welcome, pavement tables, open all day. *(Dr and Mrs A K Clarke)*

MANCHESTER   SJ8498
Port Street Beer House
(0161) 237 9949 *Port Street; M1 2EQ* Former shop in Northern Quarter backstreet; fantastic range of draught and bottled craft beers along with well kept changing ales, knowledgeable staff, no food, can get very busy but more room upstairs; events such as 'meet the brewer' and 'tap takeovers'; open all day. *(Lionel Smith)*

MANCHESTER   SJ8397
Rain Bar (0161) 235 6500
Great Bridgewater Street; M1 5JG Bare boards and lots of woodwork in former umbrella works, Lees ales and plenty of wines by the glass, good choice of enjoyable fair value food from sandwiches to grills, friendly relaxed atmosphere, nooks and corners, coal fire in small snug, large upstairs bar/ function room; background music; good back terrace overlooking Rochdale Canal, handy for Bridgewater Hall, open (and food) all day, shuts 8pm Sun. *(Dr and Mrs A K Clarke)*

MANCHESTER   SJ8398
Sams Chop House (0161) 834 3210
Back Pool Fold, Chapel Walks; M2 1HN Downstairs dining pub (offshoot from Mr Thomas's Chop House) with original Victorian décor; british food served by formal waiters such as steak and kidney pudding, corned beef hash and various grills, weekend brunch, well kept Lees beers and good wine choice, a former haunt of LS Lowry (a bronze statue of him sits contemplatively at the bar), back restaurant with black and white tiled floor; background music, sports TV; children welcome, some pavement tables, open all day. *(Thomas Green)*

MANCHESTER   SJ8498
Smithfield (0161) 819 2767
Swan Street; M4 5JZ Simply presented pub on edge of the Northern Quarter owned by Blackjack brewery, their ales and guests from six handpumps, also a dozen craft kegs, real cider and good selection of spirits, straightforward food such as sausages and pies, three main areas with vintage mismatched furniture on wood floors; occasional live music, traditional games including darts, shove-ha'penny and table skittles; dogs welcome, open all day weekends, from 4pm Mon, 2pm Tues-Fri. *(Thomas Green)*

MARPLE   SJ9389
Hare & Hounds (0161) 427 0293
Dooley Lane (A627 W); SK6 7EJ Well run dining pub above River Goyt with modern layout and décor; big helpings of tasty traditional food at reasonable prices

---

from sandwiches up, Hydes ales and a guest, friendly service; background music; well behaved children welcome, outside seating, open (and food) all day. *(Michael Butler)*

MARPLE   SJ9588
Ring o' Bells (0161) 427 2300
Church Lane; by Macclesfield Canal, bridge 2; SK6 7AY Popular old-fashioned canalside local with assorted memorabilia in four linked rooms; well kept Robinsons ales and good reasonably priced food (all day weekends); quiz nights and some live music including brass bands in the waterside garden; children welcome, dogs at licensees' discretion, own narrowboat, one bedroom, open all day. *(Lyn and Freddie Roberts)*

MARPLE BRIDGE   SJ9889
Hare & Hounds (0161) 427 4042
Mill Brow; from end of Town Street in centre turn left up Hollins Lane and keep on uphill; SK6 5LW Comfortable, civilised and well run stone-built country pub in lovely spot; good modern cooking including a grazing menu and popular Sun lunch, well kept Robinsons ales and nice wines, quite small inside (can get crowded), log fires; children and dogs (in bar) welcome, garden behind, open all day weekends (food till 7pm Sun), closed lunchtimes Mon-Thurs. *(John and Claire Masters)*

MELLOR   SJ9888
Devonshire Arms (0161) 427 2563
This is the Mellor near Marple; village signed from A626 at Marple Bridge; left to Town Street before bridge; Longhurst Lane; SK6 5PP Freshly revamped Robinsons pub with well kept ales, decent range of wines by the glass and enjoyable fair priced pubby food from sandwiches and sharing plates up, good friendly service; children and dogs (in bar) welcome, garden with large part-covered pergola, open all day. *(Roger Yates)*

MORECAMBE   SD4264
Midland Grand Plaza
(01524) 424000 *Marine Road W; LA4 4BZ* Classic art deco hotel in splendid seafront position; comfortable if unorthodox contemporary furnishings in spacious sea-view Rotunda Bar, rather pricey but enjoyable food from interesting lancashire tapas to restaurant meals (popular and very good afternoon tea), good service; wide variety of events including 1930s vintage festival (Sept), free wi-fi; children welcome, 44 bedrooms, open all day. *(Simon and Alex Knight)*

NEWTON   SD6950
★ Parkers Arms (01200) 446236
B6478 7 miles N of Clitheroe; BB7 3DY Welcoming arch-windowed pub on edge of village; good locally sourced seasonal food from lunchtime sandwiches (home-baked

bread) to imaginative specials, can eat in bar or restaurant, two changing ales, nice range of wines and decent coffee, pale green and cream walls, old oak boards or flagstones, upholstered window seats and open fires; children and well behaved dogs welcome, disabled access, lovely views from picnic-sets on front lawn, two bedrooms, closed Mon, Tues. *(Steve Whalley)*

PARBOLD   SD4911
Windmill (01257) 462935
Mill Lane; WN8 7NW Opened-up and modernised beamed pub next to village windmill and facing Leeds & Liverpool Canal; mix of furniture on flagstone or oak floors including settles and some interesting carved chairs, candles on tables, animal prints on walls, good open fire, five well kept ales (some from own microbrewery), several wines by the glass and enjoyable food from pub favourites up, friendly young staff; Tues quiz; children and dogs (in snug) welcome, too many steps for wheelchairs, seats out in front behind railing and on back paved terrace, good local walks, open all day, food all day weekends. *(Steve Whalley)*

PRESTON   SD5329
Black Horse (01772) 204855
Friargate; PR1 2EJ Listed ornate Victorian pub in pedestrianised street; splendid mosaic-tiled main bar serving eight well kept ales (Robinsons and guests), friendly helpful staff, panelling, stained glass and old local photographs, open fires, two quiet cosy snugs, mirrored back area and upstairs function room; no food or children; open all day from 10.30am (midday Sun). *(Peter Pilbeam)*

RABY   SJ3179
★Wheatsheaf (0151) 336 3416
Raby Mere Road, The Green; from A540 heading S from Heswall, turn left into Upper Raby Road, village about a mile further; CH63 4JH Up to nine well kept ales in pretty 17th-c black and white thatched pub, simply furnished rambling rooms with homely feel, cosy central bar and nice snug formed by antique settles around fine old fireplace, small coal fire in more spacious room, well liked reasonably priced bar food including good range of sandwiches/toasties, à la carte menu in large former cowshed restaurant, good friendly service, conservatory; children welcome, dogs in bar, picnic-sets on terrace and in pleasant back garden, open all day and gets very busy at weekends, no food Sun or Mon evenings. *(Steve Whalley)*

RAMSBOTTOM   SD8016
Eagle & Child (01706) 557181
Whalley Road (A56); BL0 0DL Friendly refurbished roadside pub; generally well liked food from fairly ambitious menu using locally sourced produce including own

vegetables, well kept Thwaites ales, real cider and decent choice of wines by the glass, good service; children welcome, orangery dining extension and interesting garden with valley views over roof tops to Holcombe Moor and Peel Tower, five owl-themed bedrooms (two with balconies), open all day Fri and Sat, till 7pm Sun. *(Matthew and Elisabeth Reeves)*

RAMSBOTTOM   SD8017
★Fishermans Retreat (01706) 825314
Twine Valley Park/Fishery signed off A56 N of Bury at Shuttleworth; Bye Road; BL0 0HH Remote yet busy pub-restaurant with highly regarded food (can be pricey) using produce from surrounding Estate and trout lakes (they can arrange fishing); mountain lodge-feel bar with beams and bare stone walls, five well kept ales including Copper Dragon, Moorhouses, Timothy Taylors and Thwaites, over 300 malt whiskies and good wine list, small family dining room and restaurant extension, helpful friendly staff; a few picnic-sets outside with lovely valley views, closed Mon, otherwise open (and food) all day. *(Ruth May)*

RAMSBOTTOM   SD7816
Major (01706) 826777
Bolton Street; BL0 9JA Whitewashed end-of-terrace stone local with two carpeted bars, banquettes and other pubby furniture, old local pictures, two-way woodburner; Bank Top Flat Cap, St Austell Tribute and three guests, enjoyable inexpensive home-made food with some choices available in smaller helpings, friendly helpful staff; sports TVs, pool, fruit machine; dogs welcome, beer garden behind, open all day, food all day Sat, till 6pm Sun. *(Ruth May)*

RAWTENSTALL   SD8213
Buffer Stops (0161) 764 7790
Bury Road; in East Lancashire Railway station; BB4 6EH Platform bar at Rawtenstall heritage station; five well kept ales including Outstanding Piston Broke, real cider/perry and selection of bottled beers, snacky food and pies, popular with locals and railway enthusiasts, good friendly service; quiz night first and third Weds of month; children (in former waiting room) and dogs welcome, platform tables, open all day. *(P A Lord)*

RILEY GREEN   SD6225
★Royal Oak (01254) 201445
A675/A6061; PR5 0SL Refurbished and extended old four-room pub (former coaching inn); popular freshly made food (all day Sat and Sun) from pizzas, burgers and pub favourites up, friendly efficient staff, well kept Marstons, Thwaites and a guest from well stocked bar, low beams, ancient stripped stone and log fires, lots of nooks and crannies, comfortable dining rooms; children

and dogs (in bar) welcome, picnic-sets at front and in side beer garden, short walk from Leeds & Liverpool Canal, footpath to Hoghton Tower, open all day. *(W K Wood, Jan Gould)*

ROCHDALE   SD8913
Baum (01706) 352186
Toad Lane (off Hunters Lane) next to the Rochdale Pioneers (Co-op) Museum; OL12 0NU Welcoming pub with plenty of old-fashioned charm in surviving cobbled street (new management but no major changes); seven well kept ales and lots of international bottled beers, good value food all day (Sun till 6pm) from lunchtime sandwiches up, cheerful young staff, bare boards, old advertising signs, conservatory; free wi-fi; children and dogs welcome, garden behind with pétanque, open all day (till midnight Fri, Sat). *(Martin and Joanne Sharp)*

ROMILEY   SJ9390
Platform 1 (0161) 406 8686
Stockport Road next to station; SK6 4BN Red-brick Victorian pub with airy opened-up interior; six mostly local ales including a well priced house beer, good value pubby food from sandwiches up, carpeted upstairs restaurant called Platform 2; occasional live music; children welcome, small decked seating area outside, open (and food) all day, kitchen closes 7pm Sun. *(David Appleyard)*

SALESBURY   SD6732
Bonny Inn (01254) 248467
B6245 Ribchester–Wilpshire; BB1 9HQ Cleanly refurbished and opened up with light airy bar and split-level carpeted dining room, popular freshly made food including blackboard specials, Thwaites ales and several wines by the glass, good service, back conservatory with fine Ribble Valley views; children and dogs (in bar) welcome, sturdy picnic-sets out in front under awning, more seats and views on terrace behind, open all day, food all day Sun. *(Tim North)*

SCARISBRICK   SD4011
Heatons Bridge Inn (01704) 840549
Heatons Bridge Road; L40 8JG Pretty 19th-c pub by bridge over Leeds & Liverpool Canal (popular with boaters); good value home-made food (not Sun evening, Mon, Tues), well kept Black Cat and two guests, friendly welcoming staff, four traditional cosy areas and dining room; Tues quiz, free wi-fi; children and dogs welcome, pretty hanging baskets, garden with play area and World War II pillbox (pub hosts two vintage military vehicle events during the year), open all day. *(Professor Simon Burke)*

SILVERDALE   SD4675
Royal (01524) 702608
Emesgate Lane; LA5 0RA Refurbished village-centre pub with smallish parquet-floored bar, three local ales from light wood counter, sofa and armchairs by woodburner in stone fireplace, good reasonably priced food including breakfast from 10.30am, steak night Thurs, friendly helpful service, small front conservatory and upstairs dining room; daily newspapers, sports TV, free wi-fi; children welcome, no dogs inside, picnic-sets on terrace, two self-catering cottages, open all day, food all day weekends. *(Shona and Jimmy McDuff)*

STALYBRIDGE   SJ9598
Station Buffet (0161) 303 0007
The Station, Rassbottom Street; SK15 1RF Charming little Victorian buffet bar; period advertisements, old photographs of the station and other railway memorabilia on wood-panelled and red walls, fire below etched-glass mirror, six quickly rotating beers, two proper ciders, seven wines by glass and ten malt whiskies, straightforward low-priced food, newish conservatory and extension into former ladies' waiting room and part of the stationmaster's quarters with original ornate ceilings; free wi-fi; children and dogs welcome, open (and food) all day. *(Thomas Green)*

STOCKPORT   SJ8990
★ Arden Arms (0161) 480 2185
Millgate Street/Corporation Street, opposite pay car park; SK1 2LX Cheerful Victorian pub in handsome dark-brick building; several well preserved high-ceilinged rooms off island bar (one tiny old-fashioned snug accessed through servery), tiling, panelling and two coal fires, sensibly priced lunchtime food from sandwiches to specials (also Thurs-Sat evenings), half a dozen well kept Robinsons ales, friendly efficient service; background and live music including Mon jazz, Tues quiz, free wi-fi; children and dogs welcome, tables in courtyard with smokers' shelter, open all day. *(John Wooll)*

STOCKPORT   SJ8990
Crown (0161) 429 6948
Heaton Lane, Heaton Norris; SK4 1AR Busy but welcoming partly open-plan Victorian pub popular for its well kept changing ales (up to 11), also bottled beers and real cider, three cosy lounge areas off bar, bargain lunchtime food; frequent live music, pool and darts; dogs welcome, tables in cobbled courtyard, huge viaduct soaring above, open all day. *(David Appleyard)*

STOCKPORT   SJ8890
Magnet (0161) 429 6287
Wellington Road North; SK4 1HJ Busy pub with 14 changing ales including Watts from on-site brewery, real cider, pizza van Fri evenings; pool, darts and juke box; children (till 8pm) and dogs welcome, beer garden with two raised terraces, open all day Fri-Sun, from 4pm other days. *(David Appleyard)*

STOCKPORT   SJ8990
Swan With Two Necks
(0161) 480 2341 *Princes Street; SK1 1RY*
Traditional narrow pub with welcoming
local atmosphere; front panelled bar, room
behind with button-back wall benches, stone
fireplace and skylight, drinking corridor, well
kept Robinsons ales and decent lunchtime
food (not Sun, Mon) from sandwiches up;
children and dogs welcome, small outside
area, open all day Fri-Sat. *(David Appleyard,
Ruth May)*

TATHAM   SD6169
Tatham Bridge Inn (01524) 221326
*B6480, off A683 Lancaster–Kirkby
Lonsdale; LA2 8NL* Popular 17th-c pub
with cosy low-beamed bar; well kept ales
such as Tetleys and good range of enjoyable
fair-priced food, friendly helpful staff,
restaurant with woodburner; children and
well behaved dogs welcome, large garden,
camping, open all day except Weds and
Thurs when closed 2-5pm. *(Geoff and
Anne Marston)*

TOCKHOLES   SD6623
Black Bull (01254) 581381
*Between Tockholes and Blackburn;
BB3 0LL* Welcoming 19th-c country
pub on crossroads high above Blackburn;
home to the Three B's Brewery with their
good beers including Black Bull Bitter
from brick-fronted counter (tasting trays
available), no food, neat opened-up interior
with dark blue patterned carpet and leaf
wallpaper, cushioned wall seats and high-
backed chairs, woodburner, snug to left of
entrance with another fire; background
music; seats outside (some under cover
– including summerhouse), good views,
open all day weekends, otherwise from
4pm, closed Mon, Tues. *(Andy and
Rosemary Taylor)*

TOCKHOLES   SD6621
Royal (01254) 705373
*Signed off A6062 S of Blackburn, and
off A675; Tockholes Road; BB3 0PA*
Friendly old pub with unpretentious little
rooms and big open fires, four well kept ales
from tiny back servery, well priced pubby
food including some blackboard specials
and Weds steak night; some live music, free
wi-fi; children, walkers and dogs welcome,
big garden with views from sheltered
terrace, good walks including to Darwen
Tower, closed Mon, otherwise open all day.
(John and Claire Masters)

TODMORDEN   SD9324
The Pub (01706) 812145
Lower part of Brook Street; OL14 5AJ
Micropub/gin bar with cosy rustic décor;

half a dozen well kept interesting ales from
plank-faced servery and over 30 gins, helpful
chatty staff, stools and window seats by small
round tables, more room and loos upstairs;
open all day till 9pm (10pm Thurs, 11pm Fri,
Sat). *(Jennifer Fairbanks)*

TUNSTALL   SD6073
★ Lunesdale Arms (01524) 236191
A683 S of Kirkby Lonsdale; LA6 2QN
Attractive and stylishly refurbished 17th-c
dining pub; opened-up interior with bar,
split-level restaurant and snooker room, lots
of modern artwork, Marstons Wainwright
and Timothy Taylors Landlord, good
range of wines and gins, highly regarded
mediterranean-influenced food (best to
book), friendly efficient service; children and
dogs (in bar) welcome, pretty Lune Valley
village, church has Brontë associations, open
all day, food all day weekends. *(Beth Aldridge)*

WADDINGTON   SD7243
Higher Buck (01200) 423226
The Square; BB7 3HZ Welcoming pub
in picturesque village; smartly modernised
open-plan interior with airy new england feel
and nice mix of seating, good food including
pub favourites (all day Sun till 8pm), well
kept Thwaites from pine servery, good
friendly service; background music; children
and dogs welcome, tables out on front
cobbles and in small back courtyard, seven
attractively refurbished bedrooms, open
all day. *(Mike Bird)*

WADDINGTON   SD7243
★ Lower Buck (01200) 423342
Edisford Road; BB7 3HU Old stone village
pub tucked away behind the church; four
smartly presented little rooms, each with
a warming coal fire, thriving front bar with
scrubbed tables, large rug on bare boards and
some stained-glass panelling, five well kept
real ales including Bowland, Moorhouses and
Timothy Taylors, several wines by the glass
and enjoyable reasonably priced food from
sandwiches up, friendly helpful service; daily
newspapers; children and dogs welcome,
picnic-sets out on front cobbles and in the
sunny back garden, good Ribble Valley walks
nearby, open all day. *(Ruth May)*

WADDINGTON   SD7243
★ Waddington Arms (01200) 423262
*Clitheroe Road (B6478 N of Clitheroe);
BB7 3HP* Character inn with four linked
bars, left one snuggest with blazing
woodburner in huge fireplace, other low-
beamed rooms have fine oak settles, chunky
stripped-pine tables and lots to look at
including antique and modern prints and
vintage motor-racing posters, tasty food,
well kept Moorhouses and four guests, good
choice of wines by the glass and a dozen

malt whiskies; children and dogs welcome, seats out at front looking over to village church, also two-level back terrace and neat tree-sheltered lawn, comfortable bedrooms, good walks in nearby Forest of Bowland, open all day. *(Paul Walker)*

WEST BRADFORD SD7444
Three Millstones (01200) 443339
Waddington Road; BB7 4SX Attractive old building, but more restaurant than pub, with all tables laid for owner-chef's highly praised food including weekday set menu, four comfortable linked areas, beams, timbers and warming fires in two grand fireplaces, a couple of well kept local beers and good selection of wines, friendly efficient service; five bedrooms in new block, closed Sun evening, Mon, Tues. *(Thomas Green)*

WEST KIRBY SJ2186
White Lion (0151) 625 9037
Grange Road (A540); CH48 4EE Friendly proper pub in interesting 18th-c sandstone building; several small beamed areas on different levels, Black Sheep, and a couple of quickly changing guests, good value simple bar lunches (not Sun), coal stove; Mon quiz night; no children, steep steps up to attractive secluded back garden with fish pond, parking in residential side streets, open all day. *(Peter and Emma Kelly)*

WHALLEY SD7336
★Swan (01254) 822195
King Street; BB7 9SN Modernised 17th-c former coaching inn with friendly staff and good mix of customers in spacious bar; a couple of Bowland ales plus Timothy Taylors Landlord, enjoyable food from fairly standard menu, further room with leather sofas and armchairs on bare boards; background music; children and dogs welcome, picnic-sets on back terrace and on grass strips by car park, six bedrooms, open (and food) all day. *(Tim North)*

WHEATLEY LANE SD8338
★Sparrowhawk (01282) 603034
Wheatley Lane Road; towards E end of village road, which runs N of and parallel to A6068; one way to reach it is to follow Fence signpost, then turn off at Barrowford signpost; BB12 9QG Comfortably civilised 1930s feel in imposing black and white pub; oak panelling, parquet flooring and leather tub chairs, domed stained-glass skylight, six well kept ales including Reedley Hallows from cushioned leatherette counter, nice wines by the glass and good food from sandwiches and light lunches up, friendly young staff; background and live music; children and dogs (in bar) welcome, heavy wooden tables on spacious front terrace with good views to the moors beyond Nelson and Colne, open all day. *(David Appleyard)*

WISWELL SD7437
★Freemasons Arms (01254) 822218
Village signposted off A671 and A59 NE of Whalley; pub on Vicarage Fold, a gravelled pedestrian passage between Pendleton Road and Old Back Lane in village centre (don't expect to park very close); BB7 9DF Civilised dining pub with three linked rooms; antique sporting prints on cream or pastel walls, rugs on polished flagstones, carved oak settles and variety of chairs around handsome stripped or salvaged tables, candles and log fires, ales such as Bowland and Reedley Hallows, well chosen wines and highly regarded imaginative food (all day Sun till 6pm), efficient friendly service from uniformed staff, more rooms upstairs; children and dogs (in bar) welcome, flagstoned front terrace with heaters and awning, open all day weekends, closed Mon, Tues and maybe first two weeks of Jan. *(Matthew and Elisabeth Reeves)*

WOODFORD SJ8882
Davenport Arms (0161) 439 2435
A5102 Wilmslow–Poynton; SK7 1PS Popular red-brick country local (aka the Thief's Neck) run by same family since 1932; well kept Robinsons ales and enjoyable lunchtime food from snacks up (evening menu Fri and Sat), friendly service, snug rooms arranged around central bar, log fires; sports TV; children and dogs welcome, tables on front terrace and in nice back garden with play area, open all day. *(John and Claire Masters)*

WRIGHTINGTON SD5011
Rigbye Arms (01257) 462354
3 miles from M6 junction 27; off A5209 via Robin Hood Lane and left into High Moor Lane; WN6 9QB 17th-c dining pub in attractive moorland setting, welcoming and relaxed, with wide choice of good sensibly priced food including game menu and Thurs steak night, hot and cold sandwiches too, well kept Timothy Taylors and two guests, decent wines, several carpeted rooms including cosy tap room, open fires, separate evening restaurant (Weds-Sat, booking required); free wi-fi; children welcome, garden and bowling green, regular car club meetings, open (and food) all day Sun. *(Martin and Joanne Sharp)*

WRIGHTINGTON BAR SD5313
Corner House (01257) 451400
B5250, N of M6 junction 27; WN6 9SE Opened-up 19th-c corner pub-restaurant; good food (all day weekends) from traditional to more upscale choices, also meal deals and daily specials, a couple of local ales and good quality wines, plenty of tables in different modernised areas; children and dogs welcome, seats outside, monthly vintage/classic car meetings, open all day. *(Lyn and Freddie Roberts)*

Leicestershire

and Rutland

KEY  Star Pub   Top Quality Food   Great Beer

Good Wines   £ Bargain Meals   Good Bedrooms   Serves Food

 BREEDON ON THE HILL   SK4022   Map 7

Three Horseshoes

(01332) 695129 – www.thehorseshoes.com

Main Street (A453); DE73 8AN

**Comfortable pub with friendly licensees and emphasis
on popular food**

Opposite a quaint little conical village lock-up stands this nicely restored and well run 18th-c dining pub. There's a stylishly simple feel to the clean-cut bar with its heavy worn flagstones, green walls and ceilings, a log fire, pubby tables and a dark wood counter. You'll find Marstons Pedigree and Timothy Taylors Landlord on handpump and decent house wines. Beyond the bar is a dining room with maroon walls, dark pews and tables, while a two-room dining area on the right has a comfortably civilised and chatty feel with big antique tables set quite closely together on coir matting, and colourful modern country prints and antique engravings on canary yellow walls. Even at lunchtime there are lit candles in elegant modern holders. The farm shop sells their own and other local produce: eggs, jams, meat, smoked foods and chocolates. The hillside church is interesting to visit and can be seen for miles around. Disabled access.

Enjoyable food includes chicken liver pâté with fruit chutney, grilled goats cheese with sun-dried tomato pesto, roast vegetable and chickpea casserole, beef hotpot with yorkshire pudding, chicken breast with stilton amd mushrooms, braised lamb shank in rosemary and garlic with parsnip mash, cod with butter beans, black pudding and spinach, beef fillet with peppercorn sauce and chips, and puddings. *Benchmark main dish: beer-battered fish and chips £12.50. Two-course evening meal £20.00.*

Free house ~ Licensees Ian Davison, Jennie Ison, Stuart Marson ~ Real ale ~ Open 12-2, 5.30-10; 12-3.30 Sun; closed Sun evening, Mon ~ Bar food 12-2, 5.30-9; 12-3.30 Sun ~ Restaurant ~ Children welcome ~ Dogs allowed in bar ~ Wi-fi *Recommended by Malcolm Phillips, Usha and Terri Patel, Graham Lovis, Jasmine Voos, Peter Brix, Harvey Brown, Shona and Jimmy McDuff*

CLIPSHAM

SK9716 Map 8

Olive Branch ★ 🌟 ⚍ 🍺 🛏

(01780) 410355 – www.theolivebranchpub.com

Take B668/Stretton exit off A1 N of Stamford; Clipsham signposted E from exit roundabout; LE15 7SH

Leicestershire Dining Pub of the Year

A special place for a drink, a meal or an overnight stay; bedrooms

Our readers, once again, give warmly enthusiastic praise on all aspects of this lovely inn. Once labourers' cottages, the various small and attractive bar rooms have a remarkably unstuffy feel, with dark joists and beams, rustic furniture, an interesting mix of pictures (some by local artists), candles on tables and a cosy log fire in a stone inglenook fireplace; background music, bar billiards and board games. There's a beer named for the pub (from Grainstore) and local Round Corner Lazars on handpump, an enticing wine list (with at least 25 by the glass or carafe), a thoughtful choice of spirits and cocktails (they make their own using seasonal ingredients) and several british and continental bottled beers. Service is efficient and genuinely friendly. Outside, tables, chairs and big plant pots sit on a pretty little terrace, with seating on the neat lawn, sheltered in the crook of the two low buildings. A renovated Georgian property across the road from the main pub houses the individually decorated, restful bedrooms, and breakfasts are delicious. The wine shop also sells their own jams and chutneys, you can order individual dishes to take away and they can even organise food for a dinner party at home. Disabled access.

 The chef-landlord cooks the inspired food: tea-smoked duck with charred chicory and blood orange salad, cider-cured trout with citrus crème fraîche, apple and watercress, cauliflower and spinach curry with almonds, raisins and jasmine rice, honey-baked bacon with sweet potato chips and fried duck egg, corn-fed chicken with tarragon gnocchi, wild mushrooms and madeira sauce, turbot with cockle risotto, parsley oil and coriander, and puddings such as warm treacle tart with clotted cream and glazed lemon tart with raspberry sorbet; they also offer a two- and three-course set lunch. *Benchmark main dish: local lamb rump with dauphinoise potatoes, wild garlic and sheeps milk curd and lamb jus £23.50. Two-course evening meal £30.00.*

Free house ~ Licensees Sean Hope and Ben Jones ~ Real ale ~ Open 12-3, 6-11; 12-11 Sat; 12-10.30 Sun ~ Bar food 12-2, 6.30-9.30; 12-2.30, 6.30-9.30 Sat; 12-3, 7-9 Sun ~ Restaurant ~ Children welcome ~ Dogs allowed in bar and bedrooms ~ Wi-fi ~ Bedrooms: £117.50/£135
Recommended by Sophie and James Collier, Abigail Slater, Naomi and Andrew Randall, Louise and Simon Peters, Peter Andrews, Sally Wright, Ted and Mary Bates, Caroline Sullivan, Donald Allsopp

GREETHAM

SK9314 Map 7

Wheatsheaf 🌟 ⚍

(01572) 812325 – www.wheatsheaf-greetham.co.uk

B668 Stretton–Cottesmore; LE15 7NP

Friendly stone pub with interesting food, real ales, a dozen wines and seats in front and back gardens

Hands-on, hard-working Mr and Mrs Craddock continue to make all their customers feel at home and warmly welcomed. There's always a happy, friendly atmosphere and the linked L-shaped rooms have two wood-burning stoves, traditional settles and cushioned captain's chairs around tables of varying sizes, and Brewsters Hophead, Grainstore Steelback IPA and Greene King IPA on handpump, a dozen wines by the glass, 30 gins and home-made cordials; you must book a table in advance for the restaurant. A games room has TV, darts, pool, board games and background music. The pub dogs are a dachshund and a labradoodle, and visiting dogs are welcome in the bar. There are chunky picnic-sets on the front lawn and more seats on a back terrace by a pretty stream with a duck house; pétanque. They sell their own pickles, chutneys and chocolates. There's a ramp for wheelchairs.

The landlady cooks the highly regarded food, which includes lunchtime sandwiches (using home-baked bread), whole baked camembert with apricot chutney, pigeon and chicken liver pâté with onion confit, twice-baked cheese soufflé with leeks, gressingham duck breast with cured ham dauphinoise and red wine sauce, tiger prawns with garlic, parsley and lemon, pork belly with puy lentils, hispi cabbage and mustard sauce, and puddings such as passion-fruit crème brûlée and drunken chocolate cake with vanilla ice-cream; they also offer a two- and three-course menu. *Benchmark main dish: bavette steak with chips, red wine and tarragon butter £18.50. Two-course evening meal £22.00.*

Punch ~ Lease Scott and Carol Craddock ~ Real ale ~ Open 12-3, 6-11; 12-11 Fri, Sat; 12-10 (8 in winter) Sun; closed Mon except bank holidays; first two weeks Jan ~ Bar food 12-2 (2.15 Sat), 6.30-9; 12-2.45 Sun ~ Restaurant ~ Children welcome ~ Dogs allowed in bar ~ Wi-fi *Recommended by Michael and Jenny Back, Glen and Patricia Fuller, Peter and Alison Steadman, Michael Butler, Hilary and Neil Christopher, Helena and Trevor Fraser, Valerie Sayer*

OAKHAM
Grainstore 🍺 £

SK8509   Map 4

(01572) 770065 – www.grainstorebrewery.com
Station Road, off A606; LE15 6RE

Super own-brewed beers in a former Victorian grain store, cheerful customers and pubby food

You can book online for a tour of the rather special brewery in its converted railway grain warehouse (though not on Friday or Saturday evenings). Following the traditional tower system of production, the beer is brewed on the upper floors of the building directly above the down-to-earth bar; during working hours, you'll hear the busy noises of the brewery rumbling overhead. The ten own-brews are served traditionally on handpump at the left end of the bar counter and through swan necks with sparklers on the right: Cooking, Rutland Osprey, Rutland Panther, Ten Fifty, Triple B and a seasonal ale plus beer takeaways, and they hold a beer festival (with over 80 real ales and live music) on the August Bank Holiday weekend. There's also a farm cider, several wines by the glass and 15 malt whiskies. Décor is plain and functional, with well worn wide floorboards, bare ceiling boards above massive joists supported by red metal pillars, a long brick-built bar counter with cast-iron stools, tall cask tables and simple elm chairs; games machine, darts, board games, giant Jenga and bottle-walking. In summer, the huge glass doors are pulled back, opening on to a terrace furnished with picnic-sets. Disabled access.

Popular food includes weekend breakfasts (9-11.30am) plus sandwiches, crispy salt and pepper squid with chilli and lime dip, ham hock terrine with piccalilli, sharing platters, pasta with goats cheese, red peppers, tomato and basil oil, beer-battered haddock and chips, gammon with onion rings and fried eggs, warm teriyaki beef or chickens strips, bacon and parmesan salads, mixed grill, and puddings. *Benchmark main dish: burger with toppings, coleslaw and fries £11.95. Two-course evening meal £18.00.*

Own brew ~ Licensee Peter Atkinson ~ Real ale ~ Open 11-11; 9am-midnight Sat; 9am-11pm Sun ~ Bar food 12-3, 6-9; 9-9 Sat; 9-4 Sun ~ Children welcome ~ Dogs welcome ~ Wi-fi ~

Live music, comedy nights and open mike (see website for details) *Recommended by Richard Tilbrook, Barry Collett, Matt and Hayley Jacob, Beth Aldridge, Anne and Ben Smith, Guy Henderson*

OAKHAM
SK8608 Map 4
Lord Nelson ★ ♀ ◧
(01572) 868340 – www.kneadpubs.co.uk/the-lord-nelson
Market Place; LE15 6DT

Splendidly restored and full of interest, usefully open all day, real ales and ciders and well liked food

It's worth having a good look around this handsome old building before you decide where to sit as there are over half a dozen rooms spread over two floors, giving plenty of companionable places for chatty relaxation. There are cushioned church pews, leather elbow chairs, long oak settles, sofas, armchairs or, to watch the passing scene, a big bow-window seat; carpet, bare boards and ancient red and black tiles plus William Morris wallpaper. There's plenty to look at too, from intriguing antique *Police News* and other prints (plenty of Nelson, of course) to the collections of mullers, copper kettles and other homely bric-a-brac in the heavy-beamed former kitchen with its Aga. Fullers London Pride and Oakham JHB with guest ales such as Black Sheep, Caledonian Dr Bobs Magic Potion and Second Line Brewing Medley on handpump; also 13 gins with half a dozen tonics, four farm ciders and 18 wines by the glass. Background music, TV and board games. Disabled access.

 Tasty food includes ciabattas, nibbles such as pigs in blankets with rosemary potatoes and camembert with chutney, sharing boards, sweet potato, chickpea and spinach curry, beef in ale pie, chargrilled chicken with parmesan bonbons, crispy parma ham, soft boiled egg, caesar salad and croutons, harissa lamb tacos with sour cream, pineapple salsa and guacamole, beer-battered haddock and chips, lambs liver and bacon, and puddings such as lemon cheesecake with berry compote and banoffi ripple sundae. *Benchmark main dish: pizzas with different toppings £12.00. Two-course evening meal £22.00.*

Knead Pubs ~ Manager Lee Jones ~ Real ale ~ Open 9am-11.30pm ~ Bar food 12-2.30, 6-9; 9-9 Sat; 9-8 Sun ~ Children welcome ~ Dogs welcome ~ Wi-fi *Recommended by Michael Butler, Barry Collett, Gail and Arthur Roberts, Robin and Anne Triggs, Gerry and Rosemary Dobson, Rosie and Marcus Heatherley, James and Becky Plath, Simon King*

PEGGS GREEN
SK4117 Map 7
New Inn £
(01530) 222293 – www.thenewinnpeggsgreen.co.uk
Signposted off A512 Ashby–Shepshed at roundabout, then turn immediately left down Zion Hill towards Newbold; pub is 100 metres on the right, with car park on opposite side of road; LE67 8JE

Intriguing bric-a-brac in unspoilt pub, friendly welcome, well liked food at fair prices and real ales; cottagey garden

The same friendly family have run this cheerful pub since 1978 and they've collected an extraordinary amount of bric-a-brac that covers almost every inch of the walls and ceilings in the two cosy tiled front rooms. The little room on the left, a bit like an old kitchen parlour (called the Cabin), has china on the mantelpiece, lots of prints and photographs, three old cast-iron tables, wooden stools and a small stripped kitchen table. The room to the right has attractive stripped panelling and more appealing bric-a-brac. The small back 'Best' room is good for private meetings and doubles as a gift shop selling pottery, glass and cards plus home-made gifts (which sell for charity). Fullers London Pride, Marstons Pedigree and a quickly changing guest beer on handpump; background music and board games. There are plenty of seats in front of the pub, with more in the peaceful back garden. Do check the unusual opening and food service times carefully.

There's a visiting fish and chip van on Monday evening and a pizza van on Wednesday evening (you can eat both in the pub); Tuesday is pie night; chips and toppings are on offer on Friday nights, and filled rolls on Friday and Saturday lunchtimes; Sunday brunch (10-3) is for open toasties. Filled cobs are always available.

Enterprise ~ Lease Maria Christina Kell ~ Real ale ~ Open 5.30-11 Mon-Thurs; 12-2.30, 5.30-11 Fri; 12-3, 6.30-11 Sat; 10-3, 7-10.30 Sun; closed lunchtimes Mon-Thurs ~ Bar food 5.30-9 Mon, Weds, Thurs; 6-8 Tues; 12-2, 7-10 Fri; 12-2 Sat; 10-2 Sun ~ Well behaved children welcome ~ Dogs allowed in bar ~ Wi-fi ~ Live folk club second Mon of the month; open mike monthly (see website) *Recommended by Colin and Daniel Gibbs, Andrew Wall, Rob Anderson, Anne and Ben Smith, Shona and Jimmy McDuff, Brian and Sally Wakeham, Edward Nile*

SILEBY   SK6015 Map 7

White Swan
(01509) 814832 – www.whiteswansileby.co.uk

Off A6 or A607 N of Leicester; in centre turn into King Street (opposite church), then after mini roundabout turn right at Post Office signpost into Swan Street; LE12 7NW

Exemplary town local, a boon to its chatty regulars, with tasty home cooking and a friendly welcome

Walkers from Cossington Meadows and boaters moored at Sileby Marine are fond of this honest local – run for over 30 years by Mrs Miller. It has all the touches that mark the best of between-the-wars estate pub design, such as an art deco-tiled lobby, polychrome-tiled fireplaces, a shiny red Anaglypta ceiling and a comfortable layout of linked but separate areas including a small restaurant (lined with books). Packed with bric-a-brac from bizarre hats to decorative plates and lots of prints, it quickly draws you in thanks to the genuinely bright and cheerful welcome. No real ales but they do keep six wines by the glass. Mrs Miller also runs a highly successful outside catering business for domestic and business meals.

Fair priced food includes prawn cocktail, spicy chicken goujons with garlic mayonnaise, mushroom, brie and cranberry parcel with vegetarian gravy, burgers with toppings and fries, beef bourguignon, chicken breast with mediterranean vegetables in tomato and garlic sauce, linguine with king prawns, lemongrass, chilli and garlic, duck breast with marmalade and whisky glaze, cod fillet and scallops in creamy white wine sauce, and puddings such as toffee ice-cream with hot chocolate sauce and eton mess. *Benchmark main dish: beef cobbler £13.75. Two-course evening meal £18.00.*

Free house ~ Licensee Theresa Miller ~ Open 6-10 Tues-Sat; 6-11 Sat; 12-3.30 Sun ~ Bar food 6-8.30 Tues-Sat; 12-1.30 Sun ~ Restaurant ~ Children welcome ~ Dogs allowed in bar ~ Wi-fi *Recommended by Julia and Fiona Barnes, Mark Morgan, Alfie Bayliss, Peter Pilbeam, Chloe and Tim Hodge*

A star symbol after the name of a pub shows exceptional character and appeal. It doesn't mean extra comfort. And it's nothing to do with exceptional food quality, for which there's a separate star-on-a-plate symbol. Even quite a basic pub can win a star, if it's individual enough.

SUTTON CHENEY
SK4100 Map 4

Hercules Revived 🕮✩ ♟

(01455) 699336 – www.herculesrevived.co.uk

Off A447 3 miles S of Market Bosworth; CV13 0AG

Attractively furnished bar and upstairs dining rooms, highly regarded food, real ales and helpful staff

An 18th-c former coaching inn, this is just as welcoming to those popping in for a pint and a chat as it is for diners expecting an enjoyable meal. The long bar has a relaxed, chatty atmosphere, brown leather wall seating with attractive scatter cushions, upholstered brown and white checked or plain wooden church chairs around various tables, rugs on wooden flooring, fresh flowers, prints and ornamental plates on creamy yellow walls and a big open fire; background music. There are high leather chairs against the rough hewn counter, where they serve Church End What the Foxs Hat and Sharps Doom Bar on handpump and ten wines by the glass. Upstairs, each of the interlinked, grey-carpeted dining rooms has its own colour scheme and tartan dining chairs around dark wooden tables; one wall is a giant map of the area. Picnic-sets under parasols on the little back terrace have views across a meadow to the local church. Dogs are allowed in the downstairs area.

 Appealing food includes madeira-creamed garlic mushrooms on toast, smoked and poached salmon with beetroot gravadlax and herb mayonnaise, smoked paprika and pepper arancini with chargrilled vegetables and tomato salsa, burgers with toppings and chips, lightly soda-battered fish and chips, 10oz rib-eye steak with a choice of sauce, cod with prawns, capers, tomatoes and lemon and chive-crushed potatoes, and puddings such as strawberry cheesecake with strawberry salad and vanilla ice-cream and date and sticky toffee pudding. *Benchmark main dish: slow-roasted pork belly with wild mushroom and tarragon sausage and bacon and red wine jus £16.95. Two-course evening meal £23.45.*

Free house ~ Licensee Oliver Warner ~ Real ale ~ Open 12-3.30, 6-11; 12-11 Sat; 12-5 Sun ~ Bar food 12-2.30, 6-9; 12-4 Sun ~ Restaurant ~ Children welcome ~ Dogs allowed in bar
Recommended by Celia Caulkin, David and Charlotte Green, John and Delia Franks, Charles and Maddie Bishop, Alison and Michael Harper, Lindy Andrews

SWITHLAND
SK5512 Map 7

Griffin 🍺

(01509) 890535 – www.griffininnswithland.co.uk

Main Street; between A6 and B5330, between Loughborough and Leicester; LE12 8TJ

A good mix of cheerful customers and well thought-of food in a well run, busy pub

In a quiet tucked-away village in the heart of Charnwood Forest, this attractive stone-built pub is handy for Bradgate Country Park and walks in Swithland Woods. The three beamed communicating rooms are cosy and traditional with some panelling, leather armchairs and sofas, cushioned wall seating, a woodburner, a nice mix of wooden tables and chairs and lots of bird prints. Stools line the counter where Everards Original, Sunchaser and Tiger and a couple of changing guests such as Bath Gem and Everards Tubby are well kept on handpump plus a couple of farm ciders, several malt whiskies and wines by the glass from a good list; background music. The terrace, screened by plants, has wicker seats and there are more seats in the streamside garden overlooking open fields, as well as painted picnic-sets outside the Old Stables. They also have a café/deli selling local produce and artisan products. Good wheelchair access and disabled facilities.

Popular food includes baguettes, ham hock terrine with burnt apple purée, creamy garlic mushrooms on toasted ciabatta, mexican-style halloumi salad with lime dressing and flatbreads, pie of the day, trio of local sausages with mash and onion gravy, moules frites, sri lankan pork curry, cannon of lamb with fondant potato, pea purée and port jus, and puddings such as mocha pannacotta with pistachio crumb and chocolate orange torte with vanilla ice-cream. *Benchmark main dish: paella with king prawns, chicken, squid, mussels and chorizo £13.95. Two-course evening meal £20.00.*

Everards ~ Tenant John Cooledge ~ Real ale ~ Open 12-11 (10.30 Sun) ~ Bar food 12-2.30, 5.30-9 (9.30 Fri); 12-9.30 Sat; 12-8 Sun ~ Restaurant ~ Children welcome ~ Dogs allowed in bar ~ Wi-fi *Recommended by Audrey and Andrew Nichols, Nicholas and Lucy Sage, Peter and Emma Kelly, Edward Nile, Justine and Neil Bonnett, Susan Eccleston, Peter Pilbeam*

WING SK8902 Map 4

Kings Arms

(01572) 737634 – www.thekingsarms-wing.co.uk

Village signposted off A6003 S of Oakham; Top Street; LE15 8SE

Former farmhouse with big log fires, super choice of wines by the glass and good modern cooking; bedrooms

The neatly kept and inviting long main bar here has two large log fires (one in a copper-canopied central hearth), various nooks and crannies, nice old low beams and stripped stone, and flagstone or wood-strip floors. Friendly, helpful staff serve almost three dozen wines by the glass, as well as Black Sheep, Courage Directors, Grainstore Cooking and Skinners Betty Stogs on handpump, 30 wines by the glass, 12 gins, 14 malt whiskies and 11 home-made hedgerow liqueurs; dominoes and cards. There are seats out in front, and more in the sunny yew-sheltered garden. If you stay here you can choose between the Old Bake House (the village's former bakery) or Orchard House (just up their private drive); both have well equipped, pretty rooms, and breakfasts are particularly good. The car park has plenty of space. Do visit the medieval turf maze just up the road and it's only a couple of miles to one of England's two osprey hotspots.

Using produce from their own smokehouse, home-baked bread and home-made pickles, chutneys, preserves and so forth, the particularly good food includes cobs, mussels in crayfish bisque with herbs and cognac, smokehouse platter, butternut squash and sage risotto with parmesan, game sausages with braised red cabbage, roasted apples and red wine gravy, monkfish and sautéed wild mushrooms in dill and tarragon cream, pancetta-wrapped venison steak and venison salami with thyme rösti and port sauce, and puddings such as vanilla crème brûlée and chocolate mousse with berries and chocolate brittle; they also offer a two- and three-course set lunch. *Benchmark main dish: pork and leek pie £16.00. Two-course evening meal £22.00.*

Free house ~ Licensee David Goss ~ Real ale ~ Open 12-3, 6.30-10; 12-3, 6-midnight Sat; 12-3 Sun; closed Mon lunchtime ~ Bar food 12-2, 6.30-8.30; 12-2, 6.30-9 Fri, Sat; 12-2 Sun ~ Restaurant ~ Children welcome but must be seated and eating ~ Dogs allowed in bar and bedrooms ~ Wi-fi ~ Bedrooms: £75/£100 *Recommended by Peter Andrews, Martin Day, Neil Tipler, Diane Abbott, Jack Trussler, Jeremy Snaithe, Alan and Alice Morgan*

Bedroom prices are for high summer. Even then you may get reductions for more than one night, or (outside tourist areas) weekends. Winter special rates are common, and many inns reduce bedroom prices if you have a full evening meal.

Also Worth a Visit in Leicestershire

Besides the fully inspected pubs, you might like to try these pubs that have been recommended to us and described by readers. Do tell us what you think of them: feedback@goodguides.com

---

AB KETTLEBY   SK7519
Sugar Loaf (01664) 822473
Nottingham Road (A606 NW of Melton);
LE14 3JB Beamed roadside pub with
modern open-plan bar; wooden tables and
chairs on tartan carpet, old prints and
photographs, wood-strip end with coal-effect
gas fire, airy dining conservatory, enjoyable
reasonably priced pubby food from baguettes
and light lunches to daily specials, Weds pie
and pudding night, ales such as Sharps Doom
Bar, welcoming attentive service; background
and occasional live music, TV, free wi-fi,
darts; children welcome, no dogs inside, seats
on small side terrace and grass, open (and
food) all day. *(Laura and Dan Frazer)*

ASHBY-DE-LA-ZOUCH   SK3516
Tap at No 76 No phone
Market Street; LE65 1AP High-street
micropub in former tea rooms; fine range
of ales and craft beers including Tollgate
(tasting trays available), proper ciders and
several wines by the glass, friendly helpful
staff, cosy interior with wall benches and
high tables on light wood floor, pendant
lighting and good woodburner, some old
beams and a back skylit area, snacky food
such as pork pies; open all day weekends,
closed Mon and lunchtimes Tues-Fri.
(Lindy Andrews)

BARROWDEN   SK9400
Exeter Arms (01572) 747365
Main Street, just off A47 Uppingham–
Peterborough; LE15 8EQ Welcoming
family-run former coaching inn; open-
plan bar with beams, stripped stone and
woodburner, ales such as Grainstore, Greene
King and Oakham from long central counter,
enjoyable food from sandwiches and pubby
choices up including two-course lunch deal
Weds-Fri, friendly helpful service; quiz first
Thurs of month, open mike third Thurs;
children and dogs welcome, picnic sets on
narrow front terrace with lovely views over
village green and Welland Valley, more tables
and boules in large garden behind, good
local walks, three bedrooms, closed Sun
evening, Mon and lunchtime Tues.
(Mike and Margaret Banks)

BELMESTHORPE   TF0410
Blue Bell (01780) 763859
Village signposted off A16 just E of
Stamford; PE9 4JG Cottagey 17th-c
stone pub in attractive remote hamlet; good
keenly priced home-made food and decent
range of well kept ales such as Grainstore

and Oakham, friendly welcoming staff,
comfortable dining areas either side of
central bar, beams and huge inglenook;
children and dogs welcome, seats in
garden, open all day weekends, closed
Mon lunchtime. *(Barry Collett)*

BOTCHESTON   SK4804
Greyhound (01455) 824421
Main Street, off B5380 E of Desford;
LE9 9FF Welcoming beamed village pub
(originally three cottages) recently reopened
and refurbished under new owners; good
reasonably priced home-made food from
sandwiches and sharing plates up, Tues curry
night, Marstons-related ales and decent
choice of wines and gins, friendly attentive
service; Mon quiz, skittle alley; children and
dogs (in bar) welcome, garden with play
area, open all day Fri and Sat, till 7pm Sun,
closed Mon lunchtime, no food Sun evening,
Mon. *(Jim King)*

BRANSTON   SK8129
Wheel (01476) 870376
Main Street near the church; NG32 1RU
Beamed 18th-c ironstone village pub;
enjoyable food from sandwiches up including
lunchtime/early evening deal and Tues
evening tapas, three well kept changing ales
(May beer festival) from central servery,
proper cider and a dozen wines by the
glass, friendly staff, woodburner and open
fires; background and occasional live music,
skittle alley; children welcome, dogs in bar,
attractive garden, splendid countryside near
Belvoir Castle, open all day (till 8pm Sun),
closed Mon in winter. *(Guy Henderson)*

BRAUNSTON   SK8306
Blue Ball (01572) 722135
Off A606 in Oakham; Cedar Street
opposite church; LE15 8QS Pretty 17th-c
thatched and beamed dining pub with good
food (not Sun evening) from light lunches
up, well kept ales including Marstons EPA
and one badged for them, decent choice of
wines, friendly welcoming staff, log fires,
leather furniture and country pine in linked
rooms, small conservatory; monthly jazz Sun
lunchtime, free wi-fi; children and dogs (in
bar) welcome, painted furniture on decking,
attractive village, open all day Sat, till 8pm
Sun, closed Mon. *(Barry Collett)*

BRAUNSTON   SK8306
Old Plough (01572) 722714
Off A606 in Oakham; Church Street;
LE15 8QT Comfortably opened-up black-
beamed village local; four well kept ales,

craft beers and good range of gins, happy hour Mon-Thurs 3-7pm, enjoyable food (not Sun evening) from ciabattas to grills, log fire, back dining conservatory; children, dogs and muddy boots welcome, tables in sheltered back garden with pétanque, five bedrooms, open all day. *(Barry Collett)*

BRUNTINGTHORPE   SP6089
⋆**Joiners Arms**   (0116) 247 8258
Off A5199 S of Leicester: Church Walk/Cross Street; LE17 5QH More restaurant than pub with most of the two beamed rooms set for eating, drinkers have area by small light oak bar with open fire; civilised relaxed atmosphere, candles on tables, elegant dining chairs and big flower arrangements, first class imaginative food served by efficient friendly staff, cheaper set menu option Mon-Sat lunchtimes/ Tues evening, plenty of wines by the glass including champagne, one mainstream ale such as Greene King or Sharps; picnic-sets in front, closed Sun evening, Mon. *(Sandra Morgan)*

BUCKMINSTER   SK8822
Tollemache Arms (01476) 860477
B676 Colsterworth–Melton Mowbray; Main Street; NG33 5SA 19th-c country dining inn with popular food from pub favourites up in bar or restaurant, OAP lunch Thurs and other deals; boarded floors in linked areas with mix of wooden furniture including some small hand-made pews, armchairs by open fire in bar, leather sofas in library room off restaurant, Grainstore, Oakham and a guest, good choice of wines by the glass and several malt whiskies; background music, TV, free wi-fi; children and dogs (in bar) welcome, plenty of teak tables and chairs in sizeable garden, bedrooms, lovely village and handy for A1, open (and food) all day Sat, till 5pm Sun, closed Mon. *(Beth Aldridge)*

BURBAGE   SP4492
Anchor (01455) 636107
Church Street; LE10 2DA Popular nautically themed pub (locals call it the Yacht Club) with opened-up interior; beams, woodburners and some red plush, well kept Marstons-related ales, friendly staff, no food (maybe cobs on the bar); weekly live music, Sun winter quiz, sports TV; dogs welcome, circular picnic-sets in sunken garden behind, pleasant village, open all day. *(Matt Francis)*

BURTON OVERY   SP6797
Bell (0116) 259 2365
Main Street; LE8 9DL This popular 1930s pub was still for sale as we went to press, so may be changes; open-plan L-shaped bar with comfortable sofas and log fire, ales such as Timothy Taylors and Woodfordes Wherry, good choice of well liked/priced blackboard food (not Mon) from lunchtime sandwiches up; friendly service, separate dining room

used mainly for larger parties; well behaved children and dogs welcome, nice garden and lovely village, open all day weekends, closed lunchtimes Mon and Tues. *(R King)*

CALDECOTT   SP8693
Plough (01536) 770284
Main Street; LE16 8RS Welcoming pub in attractive ironstone village; carpeted bar with banquettes and small tables leading to spacious eating area, log fires, four well kept changing beers, real ciders and wide range of popular inexpensive food including blackboard specials, prompt service; children and dogs welcome, good-sized garden at back, bedrooms and self-catering apartments, closed weekday lunchtimes. *(Matt and Hayley Jacob)*

COLEORTON   SK4016
Angel (01530) 834742
The Moor; LE67 8GB Friendly and homely with good range of enjoyable reasonably priced food (all day Sun) including carvery and blackboard specials, well kept beers such as Marstons Pedigree, hospitable attentive staff, beams and open fire; children welcome, tables outside, open all day Sun. *(John Evans)*

COLEORTON   SK4117
⋆**George** (01530) 834639
Loughborough Road (A512 E); LE67 8HF Traditional and homely with well divided beamed bar, scatter-cushioned pews and wall seats, church candles on tables, dark panelled dado with local photographs above, shelves of books, leather sofa and tartan-upholstered tub chairs by woodburner, ales such as Leatherbritches, Marstons and Purple Cow, several wines by the glass and decent choice of popular food from sharing slates and light lunches up, friendly attentive staff, bigger room on left with another woodburner and plenty to look at; background music, free wi-fi; well behaved children welcome, dogs in bar, wheelchair access via side door ramp, disabled loo, spreading back garden with sturdy furniture and country views, play area, open all day Sat, till 8pm Sun, closed Mon. *(Malcolm and Pauline Pellatt)*

CROXTON KERRIAL   SK8329
Geese & Fountain (01476) 870350
A607 SW of Grantham; NG32 1QR Modernised 17th-c coaching inn with five real ales such as Grainstore, Oldershaw and Pheasantry, several craft beers and extensive bottled range, also organic wines and some interesting spirits, wide choice of food from sandwiches and pizzas up, big open-plan beamed bar with log fire, dining room and garden room; occasional live music, darts; children, walkers and dogs welcome, secure bike racks for cyclists, inner courtyard and sloping garden with views, seven good bedrooms in separate block, open all day summer, best to check winter hours. *(Ian Herdman)*

DADLINGTON   SP4097
Dog & Hedgehog   (01455) 213151
The Green, opposite church; CV13 6JB
Popular red-brick village dining pub with
good choice of food including well liked Sun
lunch, friendly staff and hands-on character
landlord, rebadged ales from brewers such
as Quartz and Tunnel, nice wines, restaurant;
children and dogs welcome, garden looking
down to Ashby-de-la-Zouch Canal, closed
Sun evening, otherwise open all day.
(Guy Henderson)

DISEWORTH   SK4524
Plough   (01332) 810333
*Near East Midlands Airport and M1
junction 23A; DE74 2QJ* Extended 16th-c
beamed pub with well kept ales such as
Bass, Marstons and Timothy Taylors, low-
priced traditional food (not Sun evening),
friendly staff, bar and spacious well divided
restaurant, log fires; children and dogs
welcome, large paved terrace with steps up
to lawn, handy for Donington Park race track,
open all day. *(James Landor)*

EXTON   SK9211
Fox & Hounds   (01572) 812403
*The Green; signed off A606 Stamford–
Oakham; LE15 8AP* Handsome 17th-c inn
facing small village green; high-ceilinged
candlelit lounge with comfortable seating
and big stone fireplace, well cooked/
presented food here or in more formal
restaurant, Grainstore, Greene King and
a guest, nice wines by the glass, attentive
service; soft background music; children
welcome, dogs in bar, sheltered walled
garden overlooking pretty paddocks, four
refurbished bedrooms, handy for Rutland
Water and the gardens at Barnsdale, closed
Mon, otherwise open all day, till 9pm Sun.
(Mrs D A Thatcher)

FOXTON   SP6989
Foxton Locks   (0116) 279 1515
*Foxton Locks, off A6 3 miles NW of
Market Harborough (park by bridge
60/62 and walk); LE16 7RA* Busy place in
great canalside setting at foot of spectacular
flight of locks; large comfortably reworked
L-shaped bar, popular pubby food including
Sun carvery, converted boathouse for snacks
(not always open), well kept ales including
Theakstons and one named for the pub;
some live music, free wi-fi; children and
dogs welcome, glassed-in dining 'terrace'
overlooking the water, steps down to fenced
waterside lawn, good walks, open (and
food) all day. *(Mike and Margaret Banks,
Tony Hobden)*

GADDESBY   SK6813
Cheney Arms   (01664) 840260
Rearsby Lane; LE7 4XE Friendly red-
brick country pub set back from the road; bar
with bare-boards and terracotta-tiled floor,
well kept Everards and guests from brick-
faced servery, open fires including inglenook
in more formal dining room, big helpings of
reasonably priced food (not Sun evening,
Mon) from good lunchtime baguettes up,
Weds pie night; sports TV, free wi-fi; children
welcome, disabled access, walled back
garden with smokers' shelter, lovely medieval
church nearby, four bedrooms, closed Mon
lunchtime, otherwise open all day.
(Paul Scofield)

GILMORTON   SP5787
Grey Goose   (01455) 552555
Lutterworth Road; LE17 5PN Popular
bar-restaurant with good range of enjoyable
freshly made food including lunchtime/early
evening weekday set menu and Sun carvery,
ales such as Sharps Doom Bar and several
wines by the glass, good friendly staff coping
well at busy times, light contemporary
décor, stylish wood and metal bar stools
mixing with comfortable sofas and armchairs,
woodburner in stripped-brick fireplace;
modern furniture on terrace, closed Sun
evening, otherwise open all day.
(Beth Aldridge)

GLASTON   SK8900
Old Pheasant   (01572) 822326
*A47 Leicester–Peterborough, E of
Uppingham; LE15 9BP* Attractive much
extended stone inn under newish ownership;
beamed bar with inglenook log fire, three
real ales including Grainstore and Timothy
Taylors from central brick servery, enjoyable
good value food (till 6pm Sun), friendly
helpful service, steps up to restaurant; bar
billiards; children and dogs welcome, picnic-
sets on sheltered terrace, bedrooms, open
all day. *(Mervyn Walker)*

GREETHAM   SK9214
Plough   (01572) 813613
B668 Stretton–Cottesmore; LE15 7NJ
Traditional village pub, comfortable and
welcoming, with good home-made food
including weekday deals, breakfast Sat from
9.30am, can eat in cosy lounge or fire-divided
restaurant, Grainstore, Timothy Taylors and
guests, helpful friendly service; children and
dogs welcome, garden behind, good local
walks and not far from Rutland Water, open
all day. *(James Landor)*

GRIMSTON   SK6821
Black Horse   (01664) 812358
*Off A6006 W of Melton Mowbray; Main
Street; LE14 3BZ* Steps up to popular old
village-green pub on two levels; welcoming
licensees and friendly locals, well kept
Adnams, Marstons and a couple of guests,
decent wines, fairly priced traditional food
from baguettes to blackboard specials, open
fire; darts; children welcome, pétanque in
back garden, attractive village with stocks
and 13th-c church, closed Sun evening.
(M and GR)

GUMLEY   SP6890
Bell (0116) 279 0126
NW of Market Harborough; Main Street; LE16 7RU Friendly beamed village local; L-shaped bar with two log fires, Timothy Taylors Landlord, Woodfordes Wherry and guests, nine wines by the glass, fair-priced food including steak nights (Mon, Weds) and set evening deal (Tues, Thurs); sports TV; children and dogs welcome, terrace garden with pond, local walks and cycle routes, open (and food) all day weekends.
(Tony Hobden)

HALLATON   SP7896
Bewicke Arms (01858) 555734
On Eastgate, opposite village sign; LE16 8UB Attractive 18th-c thatched dining pub; good interesting food from sensibly short menu using local ingredients, three changing ales, proper cider and well chosen wines, bar dining areas and restaurant, log fires and woodburners, memorabilia from ancient inter-village bottle-kicking match (still held on Easter Mon); children and dogs welcome, disabled facilities, big terrace overlooking paddock, play area, three bedrooms in converted stables, café and shop, open all day.
(Brian and Sally Wakeham)

HARBY   SK7531
Nags Head (01949) 869629
Main Street; LE14 4BN Popular old beamed pub in interesting Vale of Belvoir village; good pubby food including burger menu, Tues evening deal and themed nights, Jennings Cumberland, Marstons Wainwright and a guest, friendly service, four comfortable linked rooms with real fires; live music first Fri of month and bank holidays, quiz last Thurs, sports TV, free wi-fi; picnic-sets in large garden, open all day Fri-Sun, closed Mon lunchtime. *(Beth Aldridge)*

HINCKLEY   SP4293
Railway (01455) 612399
Station Road; LE10 1AP Friendly chatty pub owned by Steamin' Billy, their ales and guests from seven pumps, also draught continentals and real cider, sensibly priced food including Thurs pie night, friendly young staff; Sun quiz, Weds lunchtime jazz, darts; dogs welcome, beer garden behind, open all day and handy for the station.
(Matt and Hayley Jacob)

HOBY   SK6717
Blue Bell (01664) 434247
Main Street; LE14 3DT Attractive well run thatched pub; good range of popular realistically priced food (smaller appetites and special diets catered for) including Mon set deal, friendly attentive uniformed staff, four well kept Everards ales and two guests, lots of wines by the glass, teas/coffees, open-plan and airy with beams, comfortable traditional furniture, old local photographs; background music, skittle alley and darts; children, walkers and dogs welcome, picnic-sets in valley-view garden with boules, open all day, food all day weekends. *(Paul Scofield)*

HOUGHTON ON THE HILL SK6703
Old Black Horse (0116) 241 3486
Main Street (just off A47 Leicester–Uppingham); LE7 9GD Welcoming modernised village pub with enjoyable home-made food (not Sun evening, Mon) including weekday set lunch and Tues steak night, well kept Everards, decent wines by the glass and good range of other drinks, opened up split-level interior divided into distinct areas, mix of bare boards, tiles and carpet, some painted panelling, woodburner and open fire; background music and occasional live music, quiz nights; children and dogs (in bar) welcome, attractive big garden with rural views, open all day Fri-Sun, closed Mon lunchtime.
(Mike and Margaret Banks)

HUNGARTON   SK6907
Black Boy (0116) 259 5410
Main Street; LE7 9JR Large partly divided restaurant bar with open fire; well priced food cooked to order by landlord-chef (weekend booking advised) including various themed nights, three changing ales, cheerful staff; background music; children welcome, picnic-sets on decking, closed Sun evening, Mon. *(James Landor)*

ILLSTON ON THE HILL   SP7099
★ Fox & Goose (0116) 259 6340
Main Street, off B6047 Market Harborough–Melton Mowbray; LE7 9EG Village pub under same ownership as the Foxton Locks at Foxton; two rooms keeping traditional feel with hunting pictures and assorted oddments including some stuffed animals, woodburner and open fire, well kept Everards, a guest beer and decent choice of other drinks, popular good quality home-made food (not Sun evening, Mon, Tues) from lunchtime huffers up, cheerful helpful staff; children, walkers and dogs (in bar) welcome, disabled access, outside seating at front and side, Sept onion competition, open all day Weds-Sat, till 9pm Sun, closed Mon lunchtime. *(R L Borthwick)*

KNIPTON   SK8231
Manners Arms (01476) 879222
Signed off A607 Grantham–Melton Mowbray; Croxton Road; NG32 1RH Handsome Georgian hunting lodge reworked as comfortable country inn; bare-boards bar with log fire, four well kept ales such as Castle Rock and Everards, nice choice of wines by the glass and reasonably priced food, sizeable restaurant with attractive conservatory; background music; children and dogs welcome, terrace with ornamental pool, lovely views over

pretty village, ten comfortable individually furnished bedrooms, open all day. *(Melanie and David Lawson)*

KNOSSINGTON   SK8008
Fox & Hounds (01664) 452129
Off A606 W of Oakham; Somerby Road; LE15 8LY Attractive 18th-c ivy-clad village dining pub; beamed bar with log fire and cosy eating areas, well liked food (best to book) from traditional choices to blackboard specials, Fullers London Pride, attentive friendly service; children (over 8) and dogs welcome, big back garden, closed Sun evening, Mon and lunchtimes Tues-Sat. *(Sandra Morgan)*

LANGHAM   SK8411
Wheatsheaf (01572) 869105
Burley Road/Bridge Street; LE15 7HY Popular and relaxed village pub; central bar flanked by eating areas, four real ales including Fullers London Pride and Greene King Abbot, over 150 gins and good generously served home-made food including a vegetarian/vegan menu, friendly helpful staff; children and dogs welcome, seats on pleasant flower-decked terrace, closed lunchtimes Mon and Tues, otherwise open all day, food all day Sun. *(Barry Collett)*

LEICESTER   SK5804
Blue Boar (0116) 319 6230
Millstone Lane; LE1 5JN Single room micropub with fine range of interesting beers on tap and in bottles including a house ale from Leatherbritches, also proper ciders and a dozen wines by the glass, some snacky food such as cobs and cheese boards, friendly helpful staff, barrel tables, keg stools and bench seats on bare boards, half-panelled walls with old Leicester maps, cellar visible through glass doors behind counter; dogs welcome, open all day. *(Richard Tingle)*

LEICESTER   SK5804
Globe (0116) 253 9492
Silver Street; LE1 5EU Original character and lots of woodwork in partitioned areas off central bar; bare boards and some Victorian mosaic flooring, mirrors and working gas lamps, four Everards ales, three guests and a couple of real ciders, over a dozen wines by the glass, friendly staff, well priced food from bar snacks up including deals, function room upstairs; background music (not in snug); children and dogs welcome, metal café-style tables out in front, open all day. *(Matt England)*

LEICESTER   SK5803
Kings Head (0116) 254 8240
King Street; LE1 6RL Small drinkers' pub under friendly new management; ten well kept ales including Black Country, craft beers, a couple of proper ciders and good gin range, no food apart from cobs, log fire; Thurs

quiz, sports TV, newspapers and board games; raised back terrace, near rugby ground and crowded on match days, open all day. *(John Salter, Matt England, Richard Tingle)*

LEICESTER   SK5804
★ Rutland & Derby Arms
(0116) 262 3299 *Millstone Lane; nearby metered parking; LE1 5JN* Neatly kept modern town bar with open-plan interior; long counter serving Everards and guests, 20 wines by the glass and good range of malt whiskies and other drinks, well liked food including pizzas and some german-influenced dishes, good service from smartly dressed staff; background and live music, Mon quiz, annual St Patrick's Day Guinness and oyster festival, sports TV, free wi-fi; children welcome, sunny courtyard with tables under parasols, more seats on upper terrace, closed Sun, otherwise open (and food) all day, till 1am Fri, Sat. *(Richard Tingle)*

LEICESTER   SK5804
Salmon (0116) 253 2301
Butt Close Lane, near bus station; LE1 4QA Small tucked-away Victorian corner pub with U-shaped bar, well kept Black Country ales, guest beers and a couple of ciders from 12 handpumps, simple food including bargain Sun lunch, friendly staff; sports TV; suntrap terrace, open all day. *(John Salter)*

LITTLE BOWDEN   SP7386
Cherry Tree (01858) 463525
Kettering Road; edge of Market Harborough, near supermarket roundabout; LE16 8AE Refurbished traditional thatched and beamed pub with two bars, dining room and games room (darts, skittles and sports TV), well kept Everards, guest ales and enjoyable low-priced food from baguettes and basket meals up, cheerful efficient service; children and dogs welcome, two gardens, one with play area, the other for adults only, near 12th-c church, open all day Fri-Sun, no food Sun or Mon evenings. *(John Salter)*

LONG WHATTON   SK4823
★ Royal Oak (01509) 843694
The Green; LE12 5DB Compact smartly updated village dining pub with good well presented modern food along with pub favourites, set menu choices and Sun pie night, well kept ales such as Charnwood and St Austell, nice wines by the glass from extensive list, friendly efficient staff; comfortable spotless bedrooms in separate building, good breakfast, handy for East Midlands Airport, open all day. *(Michael Doswell)*

LYDDINGTON   SP8797
★ Marquess of Exeter (01572) 822477
Main Street; LE15 9LT Busy pub named after the Burghley family who have long

owned this charming village (Burghley House is about 15 miles away); spacious open-plan areas with beams and exposed stonework, mix of tables and chairs, leather sofas, pine chests and old barrels on flagstone or wood floors, several open fires, Ringwood Boondoggle, a Marstons beer named for the pub and around a dozen wines by the glass, good food cooked by landlord-chef; children and dogs (in bar) welcome, picnic-sets on terrace, more seats in tree-sheltered gardens, attractive comfortable bedrooms, open all day. *(Richard Kennell, Louise and Oliver Redman)*

LYDDINGTON   SP8796
★**Old White Hart** (01572) 821703
Village signed off A6003 N of Corby; LE15 9LR Popular and welcoming 17th-c inn across from small green; two cosy linked bars with log fires and heavy beams, cushioned wall benches and simple wooden furniture on tiled floors, some fine hunting prints, Greene King IPA and a guest, good food (not Sun evening in winter) including own sausages and cured meats (long-serving landlord is a butcher), half-price offer Mon-Thurs and other deals, efficient obliging service, attractive restaurant and small conservatory with rugs on strip-wood floors; children welcome, seats by heaters in pretty walled garden (dogs welcome here), eight floodlit boules pitches, well placed for Bede House (EH) and good nearby walks, 20 bedrooms (six in nearby building), open all day (may be a break Sun afternoon). *(Mr and Mrs D J Nash, Peter Andrews)*

MANTON   SK8704
Horse & Jockey (01572) 737335
St Marys Road; LE15 8SU Welcoming early 19th-c pub under same ownership as the Fox at North Luffenham; updated low-beamed interior with modern furniture on wood or stone floors, logburner, well kept ales such as Grainstore and Greene King plus a house beer (Fall at the First), decent fairly priced food from baguettes to blackboard specials, cheery service; background music; children and dogs welcome, picnic-sets out at front and on paved terrace, colourful tubs and hanging baskets, nice location on Rutland Water cycle route (racks provided), open all day in summer (all day Fri, Sat, till 7pm Sun in winter). *(Mike and Margaret Banks, Barry Collett)*

MARKET HARBOROUGH   SP7387
Beerhouse (01858) 465317
St Marys Road; LE16 7DX Micropub tucked away behind fish and chip shop; a dozen real ales tapped from stillage, plenty of craft kegs and a couple of real ciders, friendly knowledgeable staff, no food (can bring your own), simple interior with connecting rooms; Mon quiz, some live music and comedy nights, free wi-fi; dogs welcome, a few picnic-sets outside, closed lunchtimes Mon and Weds, all day Tues, otherwise open all day. *(John Salter, Tony Hobden)*

MARKET OVERTON   SK8816
Black Bull (01572) 767677
Opposite the church; LE15 7PW Attractive low-beamed thatch and stone pub dating from the 17th c; good home-made food (booking advised) from pub staples up in long carpeted bar and two separate dining areas, woodburner, banquettes and sofas, well kept local ales along with some craft beers, friendly welcoming staff; quiz night last Thurs of month, free wi-fi; children and dogs welcome, tables out in front by small carp pool, pretty village well placed for Rutland Water, two bedrooms, open till 6pm Sun, closed Mon. *(Barry Collett)*

MEDBOURNE   SP7992
★**Nevill Arms** (01858) 565288
B664 Market Harborough–Uppingham; LE16 8EE Handsome stone-built Victorian inn facing stream and little footbridge; good bar and restaurant food served by friendly helpful staff, well kept ales including St Austell, craft kegs and good choice of wines by the glass, carpeted bar with beams and mullion windows, two woodburners (one in stone inglenook), modernised restaurant with banquettes and light wood furniture on white tiles; children and dogs (in bar) welcome, streamside picnic-sets, back terrace and stable-conversion café (8.30am-5pm), ten bedrooms, open all day. *(Sandra Morgan)*

MELTON MOWBRAY   SK7519
Anne of Cleves (01664) 481336
Burton Street, by St Mary's church; LE13 1AE Monks' chantry dating from the 14th c and gifted to Anne of Cleves by Henry VIII; heavy beams, flagstones and mullioned windows, tapestries, swords and other bits and pieces on ochre walls, chunky tables, character chairs and settles, log fire, well kept Everards and guests, decent wines and generously served food, small end dining room; background music, free wi-fi; children and dogs welcome, tables in pretty little walled garden, open all day. *(Dr and Mrs A K Clarke, Tracky Cropper)*

MELTON MOWBRAY   SK7518
Boat (01664) 500969
Burton Street; LE13 1AF Chatty and welcoming local with three well kept beers including Adnams and over 40 malt whiskies, no food, bar with panelling and open fire in range, another fire (not often used) in

---

We say if we know a pub has background music.

snug; quiz nights and darts; dogs welcome, handy for the station, open all day Thurs-Sun (Fri from 2pm), closed lunchtimes Mon and Weds. *(Mark Morgan)*

MOUNTSORREL   SK5715
Swan (0116) 230 2340
Loughborough Road, off A6; LE12 7AT Former coaching inn with split-level interior; log fires, old flagstones and stripped-stone walls, good well priced food (best to book evenings) including monthly themed nights, friendly efficient staff, well kept ales such as Black Sheep and good choice of wines, neat dining areas; dogs welcome in bar, pretty walled back garden down to canalised River Soar, open all day weekends.
(Laura and Dan Frazer)

MOWSLEY   SP6488
Staff of Life (0116) 240 2359
Village signposted off A5199 S of Leicester; Main Street; LE17 6NT Gabled village pub with roomy fairly traditional bar; high-backed settles on flagstones, wicker chairs on shiny wood floor and stools around unusual circular counter, woodburner, ales such as Black Sheep, Exmoor and Wadworths, a dozen wines by the glass and decent whisky choice, well liked food from interesting mid-priced menu, also set evening deal Weds-Fri; background music; well behaved children welcome (no under-12s Fri and Sat nights), no dogs, seats out in front and on nice leaf-shaded deck, open Sun till 7pm, closed Mon (including bank holidays) and weekday lunchtimes. *(Mike and Margaret Banks)*

NEWBOLD VERDON   SK4402
Windmill (01455) 824433
Brascote, via B582 (off A447 Hinckley–Coalville); LE9 9LE Modernised roadside country pub based on former mill house; cobbled back way into open-plan two-part bar, comfortable seats by woodburner, split-level restaurant with painted pine furniture and pitched ceiling, good food (not Sun evening) from baguettes up including set menus and themed nights, Greene King ales and guests, friendly efficient staff; background music; children welcome (they eat for free weekdays 12-1pm, 6-7pm), dogs in bar, picnic-sets in long narrow garden, open all day Sat, till 7pm Sun. *(R L Borthwick)*

NORTH LUFFENHAM   SK9303
★**Fox** (01780) 720991
Pinfold Lane; LE15 8LE Sister pub to the Horse & Jockey at Manton; flagstoned bar with woodburner, four well kept ales and several wines by the glass from light wood servery, lounge with comfortable seating on wood floor, exposed stone walls and another woodburner, good quality food including pub favourites, spacious modern dining room, friendly prompt service; darts and TV upstairs; children and dogs welcome, large planters and picnic-sets under parasols on

paved terrace, pretty village, open all day weekends, closed Mon lunchtime.
(Barry Collett, Colin McLachlan)

OADBY   SK6202
★**Cow & Plough** (0116) 272 0852
Gartree Road (B667 N of centre); LE2 2FB Converted farm buildings with extraordinary collection of brewery memorabilia in two dark back rooms – enamel signs and mirrors advertising long-forgotten beers, an aged brass cash register, furnishings and fittings salvaged from pubs and churches (there's some splendid stained glass behind the counter), own Steamin' Billy beers and several guests, two real ciders and a dozen malt whiskies, good generously served pubby food plus some interesting specials (booking essential weekends), long front extension and conservatory; background music, live jazz Weds lunchtime, TV, darts and board games, free wi-fi; children and dogs (in bars and garden) welcome, picnic-sets in the old yard, open all day, no food Sun evening.
(Mike and Margaret Banks)

OAKHAM   SK8508
Admiral Hornblower
(01572) 723004 *High Street; LE15 6AS* Attractive pub-hotel in former 17th-c farmhouse with several differently decorated areas; good imaginative food at sensible prices from interesting sandwiches and sharing boards up, also some pub favourites (with a twist) and good value set menus, special diets catered for, three well kept ales, efficient friendly service; children and dogs welcome, seats out at front behind railings and in terrace garden, ten bedrooms, substantial breakfast, open all day, food all day Sun, weekend brunch from 9am.
(Richard Tilbrook, Michael Butler)

OAKHAM   SK8508
Wheatsheaf (01572) 723458
Northgate; Church Street end; LE15 6QS Attractive and popular 17th-c local near church; well kept Everards and guests, good selection of wines by the glass and generous pubby food including specials, cheerful comfortable bar with open fires, quieter lounge, back conservatory; some live music; pretty suntrap courtyard, open all day Fri-Sun. *(Barry Collett)*

OLD DALBY   SK6723
★**Crown** (01664) 820320
Debdale Hill; LE14 3LF Extended and cleverly revamped 17th-c creeper-clad pub (sister to Curzon Arms in Woodhouse Eaves and Windmill in Wymeswold); cosy rustic rooms in original part, plenty of reclaimed wood, nice old floorboards, flagstones and eclectic collection of old and new furniture, shelves of books, advertising mirrors, even a stuffed hare holding a shotgun; Charnwood Vixen and guests, three ciders, 14 wines by

the glass and cocktails, popular interesting food along with more traditional choices and good value set menu; background and some live music, quiz last Tues of month, darts and board games; children welcome, dogs in bar, partly covered garden room leading to sunny terrace and lawn, open all day Fri-Sun, food till 6pm Sun. *(Michael Butler)*

QUENIBOROUGH
SK6412

Britannia (0116) 260 5675

Main Street; LE7 3DB Welcoming beamed village pub with good choice of popular food including traditional favourites, pizzas and various pasta dishes, Mon steak night and Tues pie deal, well kept ales such as Adnams, Belvoir, Sharps and Timothy Taylors, 16 wines by the glass and a dozen gins, friendly helpful service, restaurant; Sun quiz; children and dogs welcome, picnic-sets out at front and in heated beer garden open (and food) all day. *(Mike and Margaret Banks)*

REDMILE
SK7935

★**Windmill** (01949) 842281

Off A52 Grantham–Nottingham; Main Street; NG13 0GA Old village pub with snug low-beamed bar, sofas, easy chairs and log fire in large raised hearth, comfortable roomier dining areas with woodburners, good food including lunchtime set menu, three well kept changing ales and nice choice of wines by the glass, efficient friendly young staff; some pictures of 1980s TV series *Auf Wiedersehen Pet* being filmed here; children, walkers and dogs welcome, sizeable front terrace, open all day Fri, Sat, till 6.30pm Sun, closed Mon. *(Phil and Jane Hodson)*

ROTHLEY
SK5812

Woodmans Stroke (0116) 230 2785

Church Street; LE7 7PD Family-run 18th-c thatched pub (aka Woodies); good value weekday lunchtime food from sandwiches up (order at the bar), well kept changing ales and nice wines by the glass, friendly staff, beams and settles in front rooms, open fire, old local photographs and rugby/cricket memorabilia; sports TV; pretty hanging baskets and attractive garden with heated terrace and pétanque, open all day Sat. *(Barry Collett)*

RYHALL
TF0310

Wicked Witch (01780) 763649

Bridge Street; PE9 4HH Village dining pub with highly regarded upmarket food cooked by chef-owner from weekly changing set menu, also occasional themed evenings; two dining areas and comfortable bar serving Banks's Mansfield and maybe a guest,

nice wines, good friendly service; children welcome till 7pm, tables in back garden, closed Sun evening, Mon. *(Sandra Morgan)*

SADDINGTON
SP6591

Queens Head (0116) 240 2536

S of Leicester between A5199 (ex A50) and A6; Main Street; LE8 0QH Welcoming village pub with well kept Everards, a couple of guest beers and nice wines by the glass (Fri happy hour 6-10pm), good attractively presented food (all day Sat, till 7pm Sun), clean interior on different levels, country and reservoir views from dining conservatory and sloping terrace; free wi-fi; children welcome, garden with play area, farm shop (11.30am-4.30pm), closed afternoons Mon and Tues, otherwise open all day. *(Tony Hobden)*

SEATON
SP9098

★**George & Dragon** (01572) 747418

Main Street; LE15 9HU Newish management and refurbishment for this cosy 17th-c stone pub; split-level interior with bar (former bakery) and separate restaurant, Bass, Grainstore and a beer badged for them, highly praised food from short but interesting menu including good Sun lunch, attentive friendly service; children and dogs (in bar) welcome, rattan-style tables and chairs on paved terrace, unspoilt hilltop village with good views of Harringworth Viaduct, three bedrooms, closed lunchtimes Mon and Tues, otherwise open all day, no food Sun evening. *(Paul Scofield)*

SHARNFORD
SP4891

Bricklayers (01455) 271799

Leicester Road; LE10 3PP Welcoming 18th-c beamed and timbered village pub; big main bar, side lounge with woodburner and dining room in newer extension, beers such as Bombardier and Greene King, decent choice of enjoyable reasonably priced pub food including Weds burgers, Thurs tapas/pizza night and popular Sun lunch (should book), friendly efficient staff; children welcome, garden, handy for Fosse Meadows nature park, open all day Fri-Sun. *(R L Borthwick)*

SHAWELL
SP5480

White Swan (01788) 860357

Main Street; village signed down declassified road (ex A427) off A5/A426 roundabout – turn right in village; not far from M6 junction 1; LE17 6AG Attractive little 17th-c beamed dining pub with clean contemporary interior; good interesting food from landlord-chef along with some pub staples, local Dow Bridge ales

---

and guests, lots of wines by the glass (wine tasting evenings and champagne breakfast Sat); children welcome, closed Sun evening, otherwise open all day. *(Brian and Sally Wakeham)*

SHEARSBY   SP6290
Chandlers Arms (0116) 247 8384
Fenny Lane, off A50 Leicester–Northampton; LE17 6PL Comfortable old creeper-clad pub in attractive village; six well kept ales including Dow Bridge, a summer cider and good value pubby food along with range of 'sizzling' dishes; background music, table skittles; children welcome, secluded raised garden overlooking green, open Sun till 7pm, closed Mon and lunchtimes Tues-Thurs.
(Melanie and David Lawson)

SHEPSHED   SK4618
Horse (01509) 507006
Ashby Road; handy for M1 junction 23; LE12 9EF Modernised and extended pub with emphasis on dining; popular well presented food from sandwiches up, cheerful attentive service, real ales such as Greene King Abbot and good choice of other drinks; some live music and quiz nights; children welcome, dogs in bar, garden and terrace with pizza oven, six courtyard bedrooms, open all day, no food Sun evening.
(Gerry and Rosemary Dobson)

SOMERBY   SK7710
★**Stilton Cheese** (01664) 454394
High Street; off A606 Oakham–Melton Mowbray, via Cold Overton, or Leesthorpe and Pickwell; LE14 2QB Welcoming old ironstone pub with beamed bar/lounge; comfortable furnishings on red patterned carpets, country prints, plates and copper pots, stuffed badger and pike, open fire, Grainstore, Marstons and three guests, 30 malt whiskies, good reasonably priced pubby food along with daily specials, restaurant; children and walkers welcome, no dogs (there's a friendly pub cat), seats on terrace, peaceful setting on edge of pretty village. *(Mike and Margaret Banks, R L Borthwick)*

SOUTH LUFFENHAM   SK9401
★**Coach House** (01780) 720166
Stamford Road (A6121); LE15 8NT Old roadside inn under mother and son team (he cooks); stripped-stone and flagstoned bar, scatter cushions on short pews, log fire, four real ales including Greene King and Sharps, plenty of wines by the glass and much liked food from lunchtime sandwiches and pub favourites to upscale restaurant choices, friendly efficient service, separate snug with neat built-in seating, smarter more modern dining room; children and dogs (in bar) welcome, small back deck, seven bedrooms, open all day Sun till 9pm, closed Mon lunchtime. *(Faye Stephens)*

SPROXTON   SK8524
Crown (01476) 861608
Coston Road; LE14 4QB Friendly fairly compact 19th-c stone-built inn; good reasonably priced food cooked by landlady, well kept changing ales and nice wines by the glass, light airy bar with woodburner, lounge area and restaurant; children and dogs (in bar) welcome, sunny courtyard, attractive village and good local walks, three bedrooms, open all day Fri-Sun, closed lunchtimes Mon-Thurs. *(James Landor)*

STRETTON   SK9415
★**Jackson Stops** (01780) 410237
Rookery Lane; a mile or less off A1, at B668 (Oakham) exit; follow village sign, turning off Clipsham Road into Manor Road, pub on left; LE15 7RA. Attractive thatched former farmhouse with plenty of character; meandering rooms filled with period features, black-beamed country bar with wall timbering, coal fires and elderly settle on worn tile and brick floor, a couple of Grainstore ales, eight wines by the glass and ten malt whiskies, smarter airy room to the right with mix of ancient and modern tables on dark blue carpet, corner fire, two dining rooms, one with stripped-stone walls and old open cooking range, much liked food including deals, friendly service; rare nurdling bench (a game involving old pennies), background music; children and dogs (in bar) welcome, closed Sun evening, Mon. *(Ian Prince, Barry Collett)*

THORPE LANGTON   SP7492
★**Bakers Arms** (01858) 545201
Off B6047 N of Market Harborough; LE16 7TS Civilised thatched restauranty pub with small bar; very good imaginative food (must book) from regularly changing menu including several fish/seafood dishes, set menu Sat lunchtime, cottagey beamed linked areas and stylishly simple country décor, a well kept ale from Langton (brewed in the village) and good wines by the glass, friendly licensees and efficient service; no under-12s or dogs, picnic-sets in back garden with country views, closed Sun evening, Mon and weekday lunchtimes.
(Gerry and Rosemary Dobson)

THRUSSINGTON   SK6415
Star (01664) 424220
Village signposted off A46 N of Syston; The Green; LE7 4UH Neatly modernised 18th-c village inn; L-shaped bar with low stripped beams, broad floorboards and inglenook woodburner, unusual double-sided high-backed settle, Belvoir Star Bitter, a couple of guests and 14 wines by the glass, steps up to skylit dining room with banquettes and high-backed chairs, popular pubby food including lunchtime sandwiches; background music, Sun quiz, TV, free wi-fi; children and dogs (in bar)

welcome, side garden and flagstoned terrace, nine bedrooms, open all day from 8am for breakfast. *(Jim King)*

UPPER HAMBLETON SK8907

Finchs Arms (01572) 756575

Off A606; Oakham Road; LE15 8TL 17th-c stone inn on Rutland Water peninsula; beamed and flagstoned bar with log fires and old settles, five real ales such as Castle Rock and Grainstore, good selection of wines by the glass including champagne, modern back restaurant opening on to spacious hillside terrace with lovely views over the water, well liked food from ciabattas and sharing boards up, also set menus and afternoon teas; children and dogs (in bar) welcome, good surrounding walks, ten bedrooms (four with reservoir views), open all day, food all day Sun. *(Martin Day)*

UPPINGHAM SP8699

Falcon (01572) 823535

High Street East; LE15 9PY Quietly refined old coaching inn, welcoming and relaxed, with oak-panelled bar, spacious nicely furnished lounge and restaurant, big windows overlooking market square, roaring log fire, good food (not Sun evening) from bar snacks up, three Grainstore ales, efficient friendly service; some live folk and jazz; children and dogs (in bar) welcome, back garden with terrace, bedrooms (some in converted stable block), open all day. *(Martin Day, Barry Collett)*

UPPINGHAM SP8699

Vaults (01572) 823259

Market Place next to church; LE15 9QH Attractive old pub with compact modernised interior; popular reasonably priced traditional food along with pizzas, two Greene King ales, Marstons Pedigree, Theakstons Lightfoot and a house beer from Grainstore, several wines by the glass, friendly service, two pleasant little upstairs dining rooms; background music, sports TVs; children and dogs welcome, tables out overlooking picturesque square, four bedrooms (booking from nearby Falcon Hotel), open all day. *(Guy Henderson)*

WALTHAM ON THE WOLDS SK8024

Royal Horseshoes (01664) 464346

Melton Road (A607); LE14 4AJ Attractive sympathetically restored stone and thatch pub in centre of village; good varied choice of generous affordably priced blackboard food, well kept Castle Rock, Marstons, Sharps and three guests, interesting wine list and some 30 gins, two main rooms with beams and open fires; darts;

children welcome, no dogs inside, courtyard tables, good value comfortable bedrooms in annexe, hearty breakfast, open all day weekends. *(Beth Aldridge)*

WELHAM SP7692

Old Red Lion (01858) 565253

Off B664 Market Harborough–Uppingham; Main Street; LE16 7UJ Popular comfortably updated corner dining pub (part of the King Henry's Taverns group); beamed rooms, some on different levels, including unusual barrel-vaulted back area, leather sofas by log fire, Fullers London Pride and Greene King IPA, nice selection of wines, decent coffee and extensive choice of enjoyable fairly conventional food including steaks and Sun carvery; children and walkers welcome (ramblers menu), no dogs, open (and food) all day. *(Mike and Margaret Banks)*

WHITWICK SK4316

Three Horseshoes (01530) 837311

Leicester Road; LE67 5GN Unpretentious and unchanging brick local known locally as Polly's (no proper pub sign so easy to miss); long quarry-tiled bar with old wooden benches and open fires, tiny snug to the right, well kept Bass and Marstons Pedigree, no food; piano, darts, dominoes and cards; outside loos, open all day Sun. *(Melanie and David Lawson)*

WOODHOUSE EAVES SK5214

★Curzon Arms (01509) 890377

Maplewell Road; LE12 8QZ Cheerful old beamed pub in pretty Charnwood Forest village (same group as the Crown at Old Dalby, Windmill at Wymeswold etc); popular food (not Sun evening) from lunchtime sandwiches and pub favourites up, also Weds steak night and weekday lunchtime/early evening set menu, Sharps Doom Bar, Timothy Taylors Landlord and a couple of guests, several wines by the glass and range of cocktails, good friendly service, attractive up-to-date décor in linked areas; background music, Tues quiz, TV, free wi-fi; children, walkers and dogs welcome, ramp for wheelchairs, good-sized front lawn and terrace, open all day Fri-Sun. *(James Landor)*

WOODHOUSE EAVES SK5313

Wheatsheaf (01509) 890320

Brand Hill; turn right into Main Street, off B591 S of Loughborough; LE12 8SS Brick and stone wisteria-clad country pub with pretty window boxes and tubs; traditionally furnished beamed bar areas with open fires, some black and white motor-racing photographs, dining rooms with wheelback or high-back chairs around

---

If you report on a pub that's not a featured entry, please tell us any lunchtimes or evenings when it doesn't serve bar food.

country pine tables, ales such as Adnams, Charnwood, Fullers and Timothy Taylors, several wines by the glass and generally well liked food, friendly service; children and dogs (in bar) welcome, seats outside in courtyard under parasols, open all day Sat, closed Sun evening. *(James Landor, Jim King)*

WYMESWOLD SK6023
Windmill (01509) 881313
Brook Street; LE12 6TT Bustling side-street village pub in same group as the Crown at Old Dalby and Curzon Arms in Woodhouse Eaves; enjoyable home-made food (not Sun evening) from lunchtime snacks up including set menus and Tues steak night, three well kept rotating ales; quiz last Sun of month, acoustic music second Mon; children welcome, dogs in bar, back garden with decked area, open all day Fri- Sun. *(Matt and Hayley Jacob)*

WYMONDHAM SK8518
Berkeley Arms (01572) 787587
Main Street; LE14 2AG Golden-stone beamed village inn under new welcoming owners; Greene King IPA and a couple of guests such as Grainstore and Oakham, Lilley's cider and several wines by the glass, enjoyable freshly made food (not Sun evening) served by friendly accommodating staff, comfortable seating by log fire, dining areas with red floor tiles or bare boards; children and dogs (in bar) welcome, seats out at front, good surrounding walks. *(Michael Butler, Barry Collett)*

Lincolnshire

BARNOLDBY LE BECK
TA2303 Map 8

Ship 🎯 🍷

(01472) 822308 – www.the-shipinn.com
Village signposted off A18 Louth-Grimsby; DN37 0BG

Tranquil refined dining pub with plenty to look at

Do wander around this charming village and then come here for lunch.
There's a marvellous collection of Edwardian and Victorian bric-a-brac,
including stand-up telephones, violins, a horn gramophone, a bowler and top
hats, old racquets, riding crops and hockey sticks. Heavy dark-ringed drapes
swathe the windows and the furnishings fit in well, with pretty cushions on
comfortable Lloyd Loom-style chairs, heavily stuffed gold plush Victorian-
looking chairs on a new rust-coloured carpet and a warming winter coal fire.
Axhome Cleethorpes Pale Ale, Batemans XB and Black Sheep on handpump,
eight malt whiskies and good wines by the glass; background music. The
fenced-off sunny area behind has hanging baskets and a few picnic-sets
under parasols. Disabled access.

🎯 Appealing food includes sandwiches, smoked mackerel pâté with horseradish
cream, crispy squid and king prawns with chargrilled spring onion and chilli
with soy dipping sauce, mushroom, spinach and thyme risotto with parmesan, beef
in ale pie, sea bass fillets with honey and orange glaze and warm potato, lentil and
watercress salad, pancetta-wrapped pork loin with sage mash and apple and thyme jus,
hake fillet with dauphinoise potatoes and white wine and lemon velouté, and puddings
such as lemon meringue cheesecake with lemon curd and tiramisu with chocolate
mousse. *Benchmark main dish: beer-battered haddock and chips £11.95. Two-course
evening meal £22.00.*

Free house ~ Licensee Michele Robinson ~ Real ale ~ Open 12-3, 6-11; 12-5 Sun; closed Sun
evening, Mon ~ Bar food 12-2, 6-9; 12-4 Sun ~ Restaurant ~ Children welcome ~ Wi-fi
*Recommended by Peter and Anne Hollindale, Lindy Andrews, Susan Eccleston, Tom Stone,
Mike and Sarah Abbot, Daniel King, Lorna and Jack Mulgrave*

BASTON
TF1113 Map 8

White Horse 🎯 🍷 🍺

(01778) 560923 – www.thewhitehorsebaston.co.uk
Church Street; PE6 9PE

**Refurbished village pub with four real ales, welcoming staff
and good, popular food**

A friendly family runs this blue-painted 18th-c pub and customers come from far and wide for both the impressive food and the wide choice of drinks. It's been interestingly renovated using reclaimed farm materials that include the bricks in the bay window, the boards in the ceiling, some of the beams and the huge piece of sycamore that acts as the counter in the snug bar. The main bar has built-in wall seats with scatter cushions, windsor and farmhouse chairs and stools around all sorts of tables on wooden flooring, a woodburning stove in a brick fireplace (with big logs piled into another) and horse-related items on pale paintwork; background music, darts, TV and board games. The dining area is similarly furnished. Stools line the blue-painted counter where they keep Adnams Southwold, Oakham JHB and a couple of guests from Grainstore and Timothy Taylors on handpump, 12 wines by the glass, 20 gins and 14 malt whiskies; the resident springer spaniel is called Audrey. There are seats and tables on a side terrace.

 First class food includes sandwiches, confit duck terrine with blackberry ketchup, black treacle-cured salmon with sweet and sour rhubarb, beetroot and carrot burger with tomato chutney and chips, local sausages with mash and onion gravy, a smokehouse platter, chicken breast with chickpea and lentil tagine, fresh fish dish of the day, beef ragoût with basil and pesto pasta, venison loin with swede fondant, chicory and pear, rib-eye steak with a choice of sauce, and puddings such as dark chocolate nemesis with chocolate sorbet and apple tarte tatin with spiced parsnip sorbet. *Benchmark main dish: burger with toppings and chips £13.25. Two-course evening meal £20.00.*

Free house ~ Licensees Ben Larter and Germaine Stribling ~ Real ale ~ Open 4-11 Mon, Tues; 12-11 Wed-Fri; 9.30am-midnight Sat; 9.30am-10.30pm Sun; closed lunchtimes Mon and Tues ~ Bar food 5.30-9 Tues; 12-2.30, 5.30-9 Wed-Sat; 12-6 Sun; no food Mon ~ Restaurant ~ Children welcome until 9pm ~ Dogs allowed in bar ~ Wi-fi *Recommended by Colin and Angela Boocock, Alison and Dan Richardson, Beverley and Andy Butcher, Patricia and Anton Larkham, Beth Aldridge*

GREAT LIMBER

New Inn 🌟 ♟ ⌨

TA1308   Map 8

(01469) 569998 – www.thenewinngreatlimber.co.uk
High Street; DN37 8JL

Rather grand with an easy-going atmosphere, marvellous food, fine wines and large back garden; bedrooms

A handsome place with a good mix of regulars and visitors, this has everything going for it. The impressive food is a huge draw, but there's also a proper working bar with a wide choice of drinks, quiz evenings and a darts board. The bar has windsor chairs, red button-back wall seats, some upholstered tub chairs and oak tables on pale floorboards, neatly stacked logs on either side of one fireplace and shelves of books by another, and chairs against the counter where efficient, friendly staff serve a regular from Timothy Taylors with guests from Greene King and Tetleys on handpump and a dozen wines by the glass. A snug little corner has a curved high-backed wall seat just right for a small group. The dining room is split into two, with cushioned wooden chairs in one part and comfortable red chairs and long wall seats with pretty scatter cushions in another. Throughout, the walls are hung with modern art, black and white photos and big mirrors; background music and TV. The landscaped back garden has both picnic-sets and tables and chairs. Bedrooms are quiet and comfortable and breakfasts are highly regarded.

 Interesting food uses produce from the Brocklesby Estate (to which this pub belongs) and includes local haddock fishcakes with tartare sauce, chicken liver parfait with chutney, vegetable pasty, free-range chicken with pressed leg and triple-cooked chips, gammon fritter with roasted pineapple and fried egg, confit duck leg with white bean stew, pork loin with glazed cheek, apple tarte tatin and confit onion, and puddings such as chocolate and orange tart with orange purée and banana ice-cream and sticky toffee pudding with toffee sauce and crème anglaise. *Benchmark main dish: lamb shoulder pie £16.50. Two-course evening meal £19.00.*

Free house ~ Licensee Lewis Phillips ~ Real ale ~ Open 4.30-10 Mon; 12-11.30 Tue-Fri; 11.30-11 Sat; 11.30-10 Sun; closed Mon lunchtime except bank holidays ~ Bar food 12-2, 6-9; 12-3.30 Sun; not Sun evening, Mon lunchtime ~ Restaurant ~ Children welcome ~ Dogs allowed in bar and bedrooms ~ Wi-fi ~ Bedrooms: /£99 *Recommended by Philip J Alderton, Susan and Tim Boyle, Celia and Rupert Lemming, Stewart Dalziel, Penny and David Shepherd, Simon and Alex Knight*

HEIGHINGTON
TF0369   Map 8

Butcher & Beast 🍺

(01522) 790386 – www.butcherandbeast.co.uk
High Street; LN4 1JS

Traditional village pub with pubby food, thoughtful choice of drinks, pubby food and a pretty garden by a stream

The terrific range of drinks chosen by the hands-on, hard-working licensees here includes half a dozen real ales such as Batemans XB, XXXB and Salem Porter, Oakham Green Devil IPA and Timothy Taylors Landlord on handpump, two farm ciders, eight wines by the glass, 30 gins and 20 malt whiskies. The simply decorated bar has a thriving atmosphere, button-back wall banquettes, pubby furnishings and stools along the counter, while the Snug has red-cushioned wall settles and high-backed wooden dining chairs. A beamed and extended dining room is neatly set with an attractive medley of wooden or painted chairs around chunky tables on floorboards, and there's a woodburning stove; throughout, the cream or yellow walls are hung with old village photos and country pictures. Award-winning hanging baskets and tubs make a delightful show in summer and picnic-sets line a lawn that runs down to a stream.

Tasty food includes creamy garlic mushrooms on toast with a blue cheese crumb, crispy chicken goujons with barbecue sauce, pumpkin, red onion and cranberry tagine, a curry of the day, home-baked ham and egg, chicken in a creamy apricot and stilton sauce, burger with toppings and relish, fillet of beef and mushroom stroganoff, and puddings such as chocolate brownie fudge cake and sticky toffee pudding with toffee sauce. *Benchmark main dish: steak in ale pie £11.95. Two-course evening meal £20.00.*

Batemans ~ Tenants Mal and Diane Gray ~ Real ale ~ Open 12-11; 12-10.30 Sun ~ Bar food 12-2, 5-8; 10-2, 5-9 Fri, Sat; 12-6 Sun ~ Restaurant ~ Children welcome away from bar ~ Dogs allowed in bar ~ Wi-fi *Recommended by Neil Allen, Usha and Terri Patel, Sandra Morgan, James and Sylvia Hewitt, William Pace, Caroline and Steve Archer*

HOUGH-ON-THE-HILL
SK9246   Map 8

Brownlow Arms 🏠 ♨ ♀ 🛏

(01400) 250234 – www.thebrownlowarms.com
High Road; NG32 2AZ

Lincolnshire Dining Pub of the Year

Refined country house with beamed bar, real ales, imaginative food and graceful terrace; bedrooms

It's such a delight to find yourself here after the tedious A1. The comfortable and warmly welcoming bar has beams, plenty of panelling, some exposed brickwork, local prints and scenes, a large mirror, and a pile of logs beside a big fireplace. Seating includes elegant, stylishly mismatched upholstered armchairs, and the carefully arranged furnishings give the impression of several separate and cosy areas. Served by impeccably polite staff, the ales on handpump are Timothy Taylors Landlord and Wadworths 6X, there are ten wines by the glass and 15 malt whiskies; background music. Bedrooms are well equipped and comfortable and the breakfasts are very good.

Delicious food includes sandwiches, oak-smoked salmon mousse with tomato concasse and streaky bacon crisp, confit duck spring roll with plum and ginger purée and crunchy vegetable ribbons, moroccan-spiced cauliflower, carrot and fennel with spiced chickpeas, sweet potato hummus, cauliflower couscous and yoghurt, slow-roast pork belly with black pudding, caramelised apples and jus, duck breast with golden raisin purée, boulangère potatoes and red wine jus, seafood linguine with lemon and parsley, and puddings such as chocolate brownie with chocolate sauce and vanilla crème brûlée with passion-fruit coulis. *Benchmark main dish: cashew, chilli and coriander sea bream with tom yum broth £19.25. Two-course evening meal £26.00.*

Free house ~ Licensee Paul L Willoughby ~ Real ale ~ Open 12-2.30, 6-11; 12-3.30 Sun; closed Sun evening, Mon, Tues lunchtime ~ Bar food 12-2, 6.30-9; 12-2.30 Sun ~ Restaurant ~ Wi-fi ~ Bedrooms: $80/$130 *Recommended by Dr K Nesbitt, Ian Herdman, Melanie and David Lawson, Emily and Toby Archer, M and GR, Alister and Margery Bacon, Gail and Arthur Roberts*

INGHAM   SK9483 Map 8
Inn on the Green 🌟

(01522) 730354 – www.innonthegreeningham.co.uk

The Green; LN1 2XT

Nicely modernised place serving thoughtfully prepared food and with a happy atmosphere

The appetising food here continues to draw in many customers, while locals head for the chatty bar. This is informal and pubby with a log fire, and caring staff who serve Milestone Welsh Dragons, Oldershaw Mosaic Blonde, Pheasantry Best Bitter and Sharps Doom Bar on handpump, a dozen wines by the glass, 18 malt whiskies, 35 gins and home-made cordials; several tables may also be occupied by those enjoying the tasty food. The beamed and timbered dining room is spread over two floors, with lots of exposed brickwork, local prints and a warm winter fire; do book ahead to be sure of a table. The lounge between these rooms has leather sofas and background music and a bar counter where you can buy home-made jams, marmalade and chutney. There are attractive views across the village green. Dogs are allowed in the bar outside of food service times.

Tempting food includes sandwiches, salmon and chive fishcakes with sweet chilli jam, pâté of the day with red onion marmalade, seasonal vegetarian risotto of the day, local sausages with spring onion mash and onion gravy, burger with toppings and fries, thai-style tiger prawns with noodles, chicken tikka masala, crispy duck leg with sweet and sour beetroot, guinea fowl breast with chorizo meatballs and rice cakes, and puddings such as pineapple upside-down cake with piña colada ice-cream and Baileys crème brûlée; they also offer breakfast (9-10.30am) on the last Saturday of the month and a takeaway menu (12-8 Tuesday-Sunday). *Benchmark main dish: braised blade of beef with bubble and squeak and jus £16.00. Two-course evening meal £20.00.*

Free house ~ Licensees Andrew Cafferkey and Sarah Sharpe ~ Real ale ~ Open 12-11; 12-10.30 Sun; closed Mon ~ Bar food 12-8.30; 3-8 Tues pies only; 12-7 Sun ~ Restaurant ~

Children welcome ~ Wi-fi *Recommended by Anne and Ben Smith, Jill and Hugh Bennett, Sabina and Gerald Grimshaw, Melanie and David Lawson, James Allsopp, Geoffrey Sutton*

KIRKBY LA THORPE

TF0945 Map 8

Queens Head £

(01529) 305743 – www.thequeensheadinn.com

Village and pub signposted off A17, just E of Sleaford, then turn right into Boston Road cul-de-sac; NG34 9NU

Reliable dining pub very popular for its good food and helpful, efficient service

This is a highly regarded local, but visitors love it too. It's gently traditional and neatly comfortable with open fires, elaborate flower arrangements and plenty of courteous dark-waistcoated staff, and the carpeted bar has stools along the counter, button-back banquettes, sofas and captain's chairs around shiny dark tables. The smart, beamed restaurant has high-backed, orange-upholstered dining chairs around linen-set tables on carpet, heavy curtains and a woodburning stove; there's also a popular dining conservatory. Nice decorative touches take in thoughtful lighting, big prints, china plates on delft shelves and handsome longcase clocks (it's quite something when they all chime at midday). Batemans XB and XXXB and a changing guest on handpump; background music. Easy disabled access.

First class food cooked by the landlord includes lunchtime sandwiches and omelettes, pigeon breast with black pudding fritters and walnut dressing, king scallops with ratatouille and balsamic glaze, butternut squash and spinach curry with home-made naan bread, lambs liver with onions and bacon on mash, dark sugar and mustard roast ham with free-range eggs, venison loin with truffle mash, crispy shallots and red wine sauce, cod loin with horseradish-crushed potatoes and bacon jus, and puddings such as duo of chocolate torte and white chocolate brûlée and sticky ginger and date pudding with clotted cream and vanilla custard. *Benchmark main dish: steak in ale pie £10.95. Two-course evening meal £18.00.*

Free house ~ Licensee John Clark ~ Real ale ~ Open 12-3, 6-11; 12-3, 6-midnight Sat; 12-10.30 Sun ~ Bar food 12-2.30, 6-9.30; 12-8.30 Sun ~ Restaurant ~ Children welcome ~ Dogs allowed in bar *Recommended by Peter and Emma Kelly, Christopher Mannings, Derek and Sylvia Stephenson, Elizabeth and Peter May, Jeremy Snaithe, Nick Higgins*

STAMFORD

TF0306 Map 8

George of Stamford 🔯 ⏐ 🛏

(01780) 750750 – www.georgehotelofstamford.com

High Street, St Martins (B1081 S of centre, not the quite different central pedestrianised High Street); PE9 2LB

Lovely coaching inn with traditional bar, several dining areas and lounges, excellent staff and top class food and drink; bedrooms

This wonderful place was built in 1597 for Lord Burghley (whose splendid nearby Elizabethan house is well worth visiting) and it has plenty of genuine character. The most pubby part is the little York Bar at the front. It offers Adnams Broadside, Black Sheep and Grainstore Triple B on handpump alongside 20 wines from an exceptional list and 30 malt whiskies; food here is simple. The atmosphere throughout remains gently civilised and yet informal, and service is first class. The various areas are furnished with all manner of seats from leather, cane and antique wicker to soft sofas and easy chairs, and there's a room to suit every occasion. The central lounge is particularly striking with sturdy timbers, broad flagstones, heavy beams and massive stonework. Service is professional yet friendly. There's an amazing oak-panelled restaurant (jacket required) and a less formal Garden Room restaurant, which has well spaced furniture on herringbone glazed bricks around a central tropical planting. Seats in the charming cobbled courtyard are highly prized and the immaculately kept walled garden is beautifully planted; there are also sunken lawns and croquet. Bedrooms are individually and thoughtfully decorated and breakfasts are splendid. Disabled access.

The simplest food option is the York Bar snack menu with sandwiches (their toasties are especially good), a proper ploughman's and a plate of smoked salmon with capers. Excellent food in the restaurants includes moules marinière, sautéed mushrooms with crispy pancetta, tarragon and crème fraîche on sourdough, half lobster with mild chilli sauce on spaghetti, calves liver with parsley mash and red onion marmalade, organic chicken with truffle-braised leeks and crispy skin, lamb cutlets with rosemary and garlic breadcrumbs, parmentier potatoes, ratatouille and salsa verde, and puddings from their famous trolley such as dark chocolate tart with orange sorbet and baked alaska. *Benchmark main dish: sirloin steak sandwich £14.85. Two-course evening meal £30.00.*

Free house ~ Licensee Paul Reseigh ~ Real ale ~ Open 11-11 ~ Bar food all day ~ Restaurants ~ Children welcome ~ Dogs allowed in bar and bedrooms ~ Wi-fi ~ Bedrooms: $135/$225 *Recommended by Martin Day, William and Sophia Renton, Brian and Sally Wakeham, James and Becky Plath, Sally Harrison, Caroline Sullivan*

STAMFORD
TF0307 Map 8

Tobie Norris

(01780) 753800 – www.kneadpubs.co.uk/the-tobie-norris
St Pauls Street; PE9 2BE

A warren of ancient rooms, a good period atmosphere, a fine choice of drinks, enjoyable food and seats outside

This has been beautifully restored, making the best of the building's great age. A charming series of small, characterful rooms have worn flagstones, meticulously stripped stonework, a huge hearth for the woodburning stove in one room, and steeply pitched rafters in one of the two upstairs rooms. There's a wide variety of furnishings from pews and wall settles to comfortable armchairs, and a handsomely panelled shrine to Nelson and the Battle of Trafalgar. Attentive, friendly staff serve Fullers London Pride, Oakham JHB and guests such as Framework Brewery Summit Pale Ale, Grainstore Ten Fifty and St Austell Tribute on handpump, farm cider and 19 wines by the glass; board games and TV. A snug end conservatory opens out to a narrow but sunny two-level courtyard with seats and tables.

Enjoyable food includes focaccia sandwiches and pizza wraps, sharing boards, beetroot and goats cheese tortellini with beetroot purée and salsa verde, crab benedict, wasabi duck with spring onion and lemongrass potato rösti, sautéed mushrooms, ginger and orange carrot, crispy seaweed and plum and red wine sauce, indian-style burger with sag aloo and sweet onion bhaji, beer-battered fish and chips, chicken in a box (poussin with yorkshire pudding, pigs in blankets and duck fat potatoes), and puddings such as chocolate melting pot for two with strawberries, doughballs and marshmallows and lemon cheesecake with raspberry sorbet. *Benchmark main dish: stone-baked pizzas with a choice of toppings £10.95. Two-course evening meal £19.00.*

Knead Pubs ~ Licensee Matthew Williamson ~ Real ale ~ Open 10am-11pm; 10am-midnight Fri, Sat; 11-11 Sun ~ Bar food 12-2.30, 6-9; 12-9.30 Fri, Sat; 12-8 Sun ~ Children welcome until 8pm ~ Dogs welcome ~ Wi-fi *Recommended by John Saville, Elizabeth and Andrew Harvey, Anna and Mark Evans, Ted and Mary Bates, Justine and Neil Bonnett, David Appleyard, Lorna and Jack Mulgrave*

WOOLSTHORPE

SK8334   Map 8

Chequers 🍴⭐ 🍷

(01476) 870701 – www.chequersinn.net

Woolsthorpe near Belvoir, signposted off A52 or A607 W of Grantham; NG32 1LU

Interesting food in comfortably relaxed inn with good drinks and appealing castle views from outside tables; bedrooms

A friendly former coaching inn, dating in part back to 1640, this makes a good base for exploring the lovely Vale of Belvoir – the comfortable bedrooms are in converted stables next door. The heavily beamed main bar has two big tables (one a massive oak construction), a comfortable mix of seating including some handsome leather chairs and banquettes, and a huge boar's head above a good log fire in the big brick fireplace. Among cartoons on the wall are some of the illustrated claret bottle labels from the series commissioned from famous artists. There are more leather seats in a dining area on the left and a corridor leads to the light and airy extended main restaurant and then to another bar; background music. Gloucester Cascade, Greene King Abbot and Ruddles County and Pheasantry Single Hop on handpump, 30 wines by the glass, 50 malt whiskies, around 20 gins, a seasonal cocktail list and a farm cider. There are good quality teak tables, chairs and benches outside and, beyond these, some picnic-sets on the edge of the pub's cricket field, with views of Belvoir Castle.

🍴⭐ Well executed food includes escabeche of tuna fillet with aubergine purée and lemon gel, twice-baked local cheese soufflé with pear and walnut salad, sweet potato and mozzarella burger with toppings and chips, pie of the day, grilled fresh fish of the day with herb butter, local sausages with mash and onion gravy, chicken supreme with black pudding pommes anna and calvados cream sauce, sea bream with basil gnocchi, arrabiata sauce and chargrilled vegetables, and puddings such as chocolate fondant and baked alaska. *Benchmark main dish: rib of beef with trimmings for two £50.00. Two-course evening meal £20.00.*

Free house ~ Licensee Justin Chad ~ Real ale ~ Open 12-11; 12-midnight Sat; 12-10.30 Sun ~ Bar food 12-2.30, 6-9.30; 12-8.30 Sun and bank holidays ~ Restaurant ~ Children welcome ~ Dogs allowed in bar and bedrooms ~ Wi-fi ~ Bedrooms: /£90 *Recommended by Elisabeth and Bill Humphries, Alison and Michael Harper, Edward Nile, William Pace, Jacqui and Alan Swan, Jo Garnett*

Also Worth a Visit in Lincolnshire

Besides the fully inspected pubs, you might like to try these pubs that have been recommended to us and described by readers. Do tell us what you think of them: feedback@goodguides.com

ALLINGTON   SK8540
★**Welby Arms** (01400) 281361
The Green; off A1 at N end of Grantham bypass; NG32 2EA Friendly well run village inn; large simply furnished bar divided by stone archway, beams and joists, log fires (one in attractive arched brick fireplace), comfortable plush wall banquettes and stools, up to six changing ales, over 20 wines by the glass and plenty of malt whiskies, good popular food including blackboard specials, reasonable prices, can eat in bar or back dining lounge; background music; children welcome, tables in walled courtyard with pretty flower baskets, picnic-sets on front lawn, comfortable bedrooms, open all day weekends. *(James and Sylvia Hewitt)*

ASLACKBY   TF0830
Robin Hood & Little John
(01778) 440681 *A15 Bourne–Sleaford; NG34 0HL* Old mansard-roofed roadside country pub; split-level bar with beams, flagstones and woodburners, popular traditional food including vegetarian and gluten-free choices, daily specials and two-course deal Mon-Thurs, Greene King Abbot and guests, friendly staff, separate more modern oak-floored restaurant; children and

dogs (in bar) welcome, tricky wheelchair access, three-level terrace, open (and food) all day weekends. *(Sally Harrison)*

BARHOLM   TF0810
Five Horseshoes   (01778) 560238
W of Market Deeping; village signed from A15 Langtoft; PE9 4RA Welcoming old-fashioned village local, cosy and comfortable, with beams, rustic bric-a-brac and log fire, half a dozen well kept ales such as Adnams, Oakham and Woodfordes, good range of wines, Fri and Sat pizzas, occasional Sun barbecues; pool room with TV, some live music; children and dogs welcome, garden and shady arbour, play area, open all day weekends (from 1pm Sat), closed weekday lunchtimes. *(Ian Tanner)*

BASSINGHAM   SK9160
Five Bells   (01522) 788269
High Street; LN5 9JZ Cheerful old red-brick pub with well liked food including good value lunchtime set menu (Mon-Thurs) and steak nights (Weds, Thurs), Greene King ales and good range of brandies, efficient friendly service, bare-boards interior with hop-draped beams, country furniture and cosy log fires, lots of brass and bric-a-brac, an old well in one part; well behaved children and dogs welcome, a few tables out in front fenced from the road, open all day (food till 7pm Sun). *(Charles and Maddie Bishop)*

BELCHFORD   TF2975
★ Blue Bell   (01507) 533602
Village signed off A153 Horncastle–Louth; LN9 6LQ Popular 18th-c dining pub with cosy comfortable bar, Batemans XB and guests, Thatcher's cider, good traditional and modern food (best to book), efficient friendly service, restaurant; children and dogs welcome, picnic-sets in terraced back garden, useful base for Wolds walks and Viking Way (remove muddy boots), open all day Sun, closed Mon evening; for sale last we heard. *(Lenny and Ruth Walters)*

BICKER   TF2237
Red Lion   (01775) 821200
A52 NE of Donnington; PE20 3EF Nicely decorated 17th-c village pub; enjoyable home-made food including set lunch and popular Sun carvery, also a 'Lincolnshire tapas' menu, friendly helpful service, Courage Directors and a guest, bowed beams (some painted), exposed brickwork and half panelling, wood and flagstone floors, logburners, part-raftered restaurant; quiz first Weds of month; children welcome, no dogs inside, rattan-style furniture on brick terrace with pergola, lawned garden, open all day Sun till 7pm, closed Mon, Tues. *(Caroline and Steve Archer)*

BILLINGBOROUGH   TF1134
★ Fortescue Arms   (01529) 240228
B1177, off A52 Grantham–Boston; NG34 0QB Beamed village pub with old stonework, exposed brick, panelling and big see-through fireplace in carpeted rooms, tables in bay windows overlooking high street, well kept ales such as St Austell and Sharps, enjoyable home-made food including occasional themed nights, good friendly service even at busy times, Victorian prints, brass and copper, a stuffed badger and pheasant, dining rooms at each end; free wi-fi; children and dogs welcome, picnic-sets and rattan-style furniture in sheltered courtyard with flowering tubs, useful big car park, open all day weekends, closed Mon lunchtime. *(Silas Davidson)*

BOSTON   TF3244
Mill   (01205) 352874
Spilsby Road (A16); PE21 9QN Roadside pub run by friendly italian landlord, reasonably priced food (not Tues) including some italian choices and blackboard specials, Batemans XB and a guest; children welcome, tables out in front, open all day. *(Sally Harrison)*

BOURNE   TF0920
★ Smiths   (01778) 426819
North Street; PE10 9AE Cleverly converted grocery store arranged over three floors; warren of interconnecting rooms with woodburners and open fires, walls hung with vintage enamel signs and mirrors, assorted items such as tilley lamps, pots, pans and cauldrons even an old butcher's bike, Fullers London Pride, Oakham JHB and guests, nice wines by the glass and a dozen gins, good choice of enjoyable food; background music, TV and games machine; children and dogs welcome, enclosed courtyard with metal tables and chairs, picnic-sets on grass and play area, open all day. *(Martine and Fabio Lockley, Heather and Richard Jones)*

BURTON COGGLES   SK9725
Cholmeley Arms   (01476) 550225
Village Street; NG33 4JS Three well kept changing ales in small beamed pubby bar with warm fire, generous helpings of good reasonably priced home-made food (not Sun evening), friendly accommodating staff, restaurant; children welcome till 8pm, dogs at licensees' discretion, farm shop, four comfortable modern bedrooms in separate building overlooking garden, convenient for the A1, open all day weekends. *(Lenny and Ruth Walters)*

Virtually all pubs in this book sell wine by the glass. We mention wines if they are a cut above the average.

CASTLE BYTHAM   SK9818
Castle Inn   (01780) 411223
*Off A1 Stamford–Grantham, or B1176;
NG33 4RZ* Friendly 17th-c beamed village
pub; enjoyable pubby food and three well
kept changing ales, fire in inglenook range
(some food cooked here); events including
quiz and karaoke nights; children and dogs
welcome, disabled access, tables on back
terrace, open all day. *(James and Sylvia
Hewitt)*

CAYTHORPE   SK9348
Red Lion   (01400) 272632
*Signed just off A607 N of Grantham;
High Street; NG32 3DN* Popular 17th-c
village pub; good fairly traditional home-
made food (not Sun evening) including
lunchtime deals (Weds-Fri) and Tues
evening fish and chips, friendly helpful
staff, well kept Adnams, a guest beer and
sensibly priced wines, bare-boards bar with
light wood counter, black beams and roaring
fire, modern restaurant; back terrace by car
park, open all day Sun, closed Mon.
(Harvey Ford)

CHAPEL ST LEONARDS   TF5672
Admiral Benbow   (01754) 871847
The Promenade; PE24 5BQ Small bare-
boards beach bar in former shelter; ales
including Black Sheep, foreign bottled beers
and decent range of other drinks, sandwiches
and snacks, friendly staff, cushioned bench
seats, stools and barrel tables, lots of bric-a-
brac and nautical memorabilia on planked
walls and ceiling; free wi-fi; children and
dogs welcome, picnic-sets out on mock-up
galleon, great sea views, open when the flag
is flying, usually all day summer (all Fri-Sun
winter), but best to check website.
(Mike and Sarah Abbot)

CLAYPOLE   SK8449
Five Bells   (01636) 626561
Main Street; NG23 5BJ Friendly brick-
built village pub with good-sized beamed
bar and smaller dining area beyond servery,
well kept Tetleys and mainly local guests,
a couple of ciders, enjoyable reasonably
priced home-made food including range of
burgers and daily specials; pool and darts;
children welcome, dogs in bar, grassy back
garden with play area, four bedrooms, closed
lunchtimes Mon and Tues, otherwise open
all day. *(Jim and Sue James)*

CLEETHORPES   TA3009
No 2 Refreshment Room
07905 375587 *Station Approach beneath
the clock tower; DN35 8AX* Small
comfortable station bar with well kept
Hancocks HB, Rudgate Ruby Mild, Sharps
Doom Bar and guests, real cider too, friendly
staff, interesting old pictures of the station,
historical books on trains and the local area,
no food apart from free Sun evening buffet;

tables out under heaters, open all day from
7.30am (9am Sun). *(Margaret McDonald)*

CLEETHORPES   TA3008
Nottingham House   (01472) 505150
Sea View Street; DN35 8EU Seafront pub
with lively main bar, lounge and snug, seven
well kept ales including Tetleys Mild, Timothy
Taylors Landlord and Oakham Citra, Weston's
ciders, good reasonably priced food (not Mon,
Tues) from sandwiches and pub favourites up
in bar or upstairs restaurant, helpful friendly
staff; regular live music, annual winter beer
festival; children and dogs (in bar) welcome,
bedrooms, good breakfast, open all day.
(Margaret McDonald)

CLEETHORPES   TA3108
★**Willys**   (01472) 602145
*Highcliff Road; south promenade;
DN35 8RQ* Popular mock-Tudor seafront
pub enjoying panoramic Humber views;
open-plan interior with tiled floor and
painted brick walls, own good ales from
visible microbrewery, also changing guests
and belgian beers, enjoyable home-made
bar lunches at bargain prices, good mix of
customers; children welcome, no dogs at food
times, a few tables out on the prom, open all
day (till 2am Fri, Sat). *(Margaret McDonald)*

COLEBY   SK9760
Bell   (01522) 813778
*Village signed off A607 S of Lincoln,
turn right and right into Far Lane at
church; LN5 0AH* Restaurantly pub with
very good food from owner-chef including
early bird menu (Weds-Fri), welcoming
staff, well kept Timothy Taylors and several
wines by the glass (not cheap), bar and
three dining areas; children over 8 welcome,
terrace tables, village on Viking Way with
lovely fenland views, three bedrooms, open
evenings Weds-Sat and lunchtime Sun.
(Silas Davidson)

DONINGTON ON BAIN   TF2382
Black Horse   (01507) 343640
*Main Road; between A153 and A157, SW
of Louth; LN11 9TJ* Welcoming roadside
village inn with two carpeted bars (back
one with low beams) and restaurant, open
fires and woodburner; good locally sourced
food cooked by landlord-chef including
daily specials, well kept changing ales and
proper cider, games room with pool, darts
and dominoes; children and dogs (in bars)
welcome, picnic-sets in back garden, eight
motel-style bedrooms, on Viking Way and
handy for Cadwell Park race circuit, closed
Mon lunchtime, Tues. *(Jim and Sue James)*

FOSDYKE   TF3132
Ship   (01205) 260764
Moulton Washway; A17; PE12 6LH
Useful roadside pub close to the River
Welland; popular reasonably priced food
from varied menu, also Sun carvery

(two lunchtime sittings), a couple of Adnams beers and Batemans XB, friendly staff, boaty décor with quarry tiles, blue wainscotting and woodburner; children and dogs welcome, garden tables, open all day. *(Sally and Lance Oldham)*

FULBECK SK9450

Hare & Hounds (01400) 272322

The Green (A607 Leadenham–Grantham); NG32 3JJ Converted 17th-c maltings overlooking attractive village green; modernised linked areas, easy chairs by bar's woodburner, highly regarded food from pub favourites up, friendly attentive service, four well kept ales and an affordable wine list, raftered upstairs function room; no dogs inside, terrace seating, eight good bedrooms in adjacent barn conversion, generous breakfast, open all day Sun till 8pm (food till 7pm). *(James and Sylvia Hewitt)*

GAINSBOROUGH SK8189

Eight Jolly Brewers (01427) 611022

Ship Court, Silver Street; DN21 2DW Small drinkers' pub in former warehouse; eight interesting real ales, traditional cider and plenty of bottled beers, friendly welcoming staff and locals, beams and bare brick, more room upstairs; live music Thurs; seats outside, open all day. *(Lorna and Jack Mulgrave)*

GRASBY TA0804

Cross Keys (01652) 628247

Brigg Road; DN38 6AQ Welcoming country pub with lovely wolds views (Lincoln Cathedral visible on a clear day); very good well presented/priced food from bar snacks and pub staples up (special diets catered for), bargain OAP menu 12-6pm Mon-Fri, well kept ales and good range of other drinks, cheerful efficient service; Tues quiz, live music some weekends, sports TV; children and dogs welcome, garden behind, handy for Viking Way walkers, open (and food) all day, kitchen closes 6.30pm Sun, 7pm Mon. *(Nick Barker)*

GREAT GONERBY SK8938

Recruiting Sargeant (01476) 562238

High Street; NG31 8JP Friendly village pub with popular good value food cooked to order from lunchtime baguettes up, well kept Everards ales, comfortable back restaurant (separate menu); TV; children and dogs (in bar) welcome, disabled access/loo, open all day Fri-Sun, no evening food Sun-Tues, handy for A1. *(Mike and Margaret Banks)*

HEALING TA2110

Pig & Whistle (01472) 884544

Healing Manor, Stallingborough Road; DN41 7QF Pub attached to the Healing Manor Hotel; good food from bar meals up (cooked in the hotel kitchen), real ales including a house beer from local

Axholme, extensive wine list and some 40 gins; children and dogs welcome (menus for both), 36-acre grounds, open (and food) all day. *(Harvey Ford)*

KIRKBY ON BAIN TF2462

★ Ebrington Arms (01526) 354560

Main Street; LN10 6YT Popular village pub with good value traditional food (not Mon, booking advised) and half a dozen well kept ales such as Adnams, Sharps and Timothy Taylors, friendly staff, beer mats on low 16th-c beams, carpets and banquettes, open fire, restaurant behind; background music, darts; children and dogs welcome, wheelchair access, tables out in front by road, lawn to the side with play equipment, campsite next door, closed Mon lunchtime. *(David Jackman)*

KIRMINGTON TA1011

Marrowbone & Cleaver

(01652) 688335 *High Street; DN39 6YZ* Friendly 19th-c local owned by British motorcycle racer/presenter Guy Martin and his sister; enjoyable good value home-made food (all day Sun) from sandwiches to blackboard specials, three well kept ales including a house beer from Batemans and Sharps Doom Bar, carpeted bar with log fire, flying and racing memorabilia, snug, dining conservatory; live music last Sat of month, TV and darts; children welcome, picnic-sets on side lawn, open all day.
(Charles and Maddie Bishop)

LEADENHAM SK9552

George (01400) 272251

Off A17 Newark–Sleaford; High Street; LN5 0PN Former coaching inn with comfortable old-fashioned two-room bar; well kept ales, several wines by the glass and remarkable range of over 700 whiskies, good choice of enjoyable food from fairly pubby menu, Sun carvery, friendly helpful service, restaurant; events including live music and comedy nights; children and dogs welcome, outside seating, six annexe bedrooms, open all day. *(Sally Harrison)*

LINCOLN SK9871

Dog & Bone (01522) 522403

John Street; LN2 5BH Comfortable and welcoming backstreet local with well kept Batemans, several guest beers and real cider, log fires, various things to look at including collection of valve radios, local artwork and exchange-library of recent fiction; background and live music, beer festivals; dogs welcome, picnic-sets on back terrace, open all day weekends, from 4.30pm other days (3.30pm Fri). *(Silas Davidson)*

LINCOLN SK9771

Jolly Brewer (01522) 528583

Broadgate; LN2 5AQ Popular no-frills pub with unusual art deco interior; half a dozen well kept ales such as Welbeck Abbey, real cider and decent range of other drinks, friendly staff; regular live music including Weds open mike night, darts; back courtyard with covered area, open all day. *(Silas Davidson)*

LINCOLN   TF0854
Red Lion (01526) 321686
North Street, Digby; LN4 3LY Welcoming family-run village pub; comfortable beamed front bar, restaurant and a couple of other snug dining areas, good reasonably priced food cooked by chef-landlady including some vegetarian/vegan options, Weds steak night, four changing ales, helpful friendly service; Sun quiz, pool and darts; children welcome, closed Mon and lunchtime Tues, no food Sun evening. *(Jim King)*

LINCOLN   SK9771
Strugglers (01522) 535023
Westgate; LN1 3BG Cosily worn-in beer lovers' haunt tucked beneath the castle walls, built in 1841 and once run by the local hangman (note the pub sign); half a dozen or more well kept ales, bare boards throughout with lots of knick-knacks and pump clips, two open fires (one in back snug); some live acoustic music; no children inside, dogs welcome, steps down to sunny back courtyard with heated canopy, open all day (till 1am Fri, Sat). *(Silas Davidson)*

LINCOLN   SK9771
Victoria (01522) 541000
Union Road; LN1 3BJ Old-fashioned local just outside the castle gates; simply furnished tiled front lounge with pictures of Queen Victoria, coal fire, half a dozen well kept ales including Batemans and Castle Rock, foreign draught/bottled beers and real cider, basic lunchtime food, friendly knowledgeable staff and good mix of customers (gets especially busy at lunchtime and later in the evening); live music Sat; children and dogs welcome, seats on heated terrace, play area, good castle views, open all day till midnight (1am Fri, Sat). *(David Hunt)*

LINCOLN   SK9771
Widow Cullens Well (01522) 523020
Steep Hill; just below cathedral; LN2 1LU Ancient reworked building on two floors (upstairs open to the rafters); well kept/priced Sam Smiths beers and good value pubby food including children's choices, chatty mix of customers (busy evenings and weekends), friendly service, beams, stone walls and log fire, back extension with namesake well; dogs welcome, terrace seating, open all day. *(Tracey and Stephen Groves)*

LINCOLN   SK9771
★Wig & Mitre (01522) 535190
Steep Hill; just below cathedral; LN2 1LU Civilised café-style dining pub with attractive period features and plenty of character; big-windowed downstairs bar, beams and exposed stone walls, pews and Gothic furniture on

oak boards, comfortable sofas in carpeted back area, quieter upstairs dining room with views of castle walls and cathedral, antique prints and caricatures of lawyers/clerics, well liked food from breakfast on including good value set menus, extensive choice of wines by the glass from good list, Everards Tiger and guests such as Oakham, friendly service; children and dogs welcome, open 8.30am-midnight. *(Jim King)*

LONG BENNINGTON   SK8344
Reindeer (01400) 281382
Just off A1 N of Grantham – S end of village, opposite school; NG23 5DJ Cleanly refurbished 17th-c roadside pub; enjoyable fair value food (not Sun evening) from snacks and pub favourites to daily specials, three real ales including Timothy Taylors Landlord, friendly staff, low painted beams, log fire in stone fireplace; background music; children and dogs welcome, white picnic-sets on fenced front terrace, open all day. *(James and Sylvia Hewitt)*

LONG BENNINGTON   SK8344
Royal Oak (01400) 281332
Main Road; just off A1 N of Grantham; NG23 5DJ Popular local with spacious open-plan bar serving Marstons ales, several wines by the glass and good sensibly priced home-made food including specials and popular Sun roasts, friendly helpful staff; children welcome, seats out in front and in big back garden with play area, path for customers to river, open all day Tues-Sat, till 7.30pm Sun, 6pm Mon. *(Lenny and Ruth Walters)*

MARKET DEEPING   TF1310
Bull (01778) 343320
Market Place; PE6 8EA Refurbished and extended under present management, but the heavy-beamed medieval Dugout Bar remains, flagstone and oak floors, woodburner in original stone fireplace, well kept Everards and guests, generous helpings of enjoyable reasonably priced food served promptly by friendly staff; children welcome, beer garden with own bar in converted stable, play area, open all day from 8am for breakfast. *(Caroline and Steve Archer)*

MARKET RASEN   TF1089
Aston Arms (01673) 842313
Market Place; LN8 3HL Popular market-square pub serving generous helpings of inexpensive food, John Smiths, Theakstons and a guest, friendly staff, beamed bar, lounge and games area; children and well behaved dogs welcome, side terrace, open all day. *(Margaret McDonald)*

NORTON DISNEY   SK8859
Green Man (01522) 789804
Main Street, off A46 Newark–Lincoln; LN6 9JU Old beamed village pub-restaurant; highly rated food from

chef-landlord (booking advised) including pub standards and daily specials, Black Sheep and a guest, friendly, helpful staff, opened-up modernised interior; children welcome, tables out in front and in spacious back garden, closed Mon and Tues. *(Silas Davidson)*

PINCHBECK
TF2326
Ship (01775) 711746
Northgate; PE11 3SE Popular thatched and beamed riverside pub; cosy split-level bar with warm woodburner, four real ales and enjoyable generously served food, friendly helpful staff, restaurant; traditional games such as shove-ha'penny; children and dogs welcome, tables out on decking, open all day Sat, closed Sun evening, Mon. *(Sally Harrison)*

REVESBY
TF2961
Red Lion (01507) 568665
A155 Mareham–Spilsby; PE22 7NU Former 19th-c red-brick coaching inn set back from the road; ample helpings of enjoyable home-made food from reasonably priced pubby menu, Sun carvery, can eat in comfortable lounge bar with open fire or separate dining room, well kept Batemans ales; games area with pool; children welcome, tables out at front and on large side lawn, four bedrooms, open all day. *(Lenny and Ruth Walters)*

SCAMPTON
SK9579
Dambusters (01522) 731333
High Street; LN1 2SD Welcoming pub with several beamed rooms around central bar; masses of interesting Dambusters and other RAF memorabilia, generous helpings of reasonably priced straightforward food (not Sun evening) from shortish menu, also home-made chutneys, pâté and biscuits for sale, six interesting ales including own microbrews (ceiling covered in beer mats), short list of well chosen wines, pews and chairs around tables on wood floor, log fire in big two-way brick fireplace, more formal seating at back; children and dogs welcome (their black labrador is Bomber), very near Red Arrows runway viewpoint, closed Mon, otherwise open all day (till 7.30pm Sun). *(Lorna and Jack Mulgrave)*

SKENDLEBY
TF4369
Blacksmiths Arms (01754) 890662
Off A158 about 10 miles NW of Skegness; PE23 4QE Cottagey-fronted 17th-c pub under newish management; refurbished cosy two-room bar, low beams and log fire, view into the cellar from servery, a couple of real ales and enjoyable sensibly priced food served by friendly staff, back dining extension with deep well; children welcome, wolds views from back garden, has closed Sun evening, Mon lunchtime. *(Miranda and Jeff Davidson)*

SKILLINGTON
SK8925
Cross Swords (01476) 861132
The Square; NG33 5HB Welcoming 19th-c stone pub on crossroads in delightful village; good sensibly priced food from new owners and well kept ales such as Batemans and Timothy Taylors; background music; children and dogs welcome (they have a jack russell), three annexe bedrooms, open all day Sat, closed Mon. *(Jim and Sue James)*

SOUTH FERRIBY
SE9921
Hope & Anchor (01652) 635334
Sluice Road (A1077); DN18 6JQ Refurbished nautical-theme pub; bar, snug and back dining area with wide views over confluence of Rivers Ancholme and Humber (plenty for bird-watchers), popular locally sourced food (not Sun evening) from pub standards to more restauranty choices including 40-day aged steaks (not cheap), Theakstons and two guests, several wines by the glass including champagne, good friendly service; children and dogs welcome, disabled access/loos, outside tables, closed Mon, otherwise open all day. *(Sally Harrison)*

SOUTH RAUCEBY
TF0245
Bustard (01529) 488250
Main Street; NG34 8QG Modernised 19th-c stone-built pub with good food from shortish but varied menu (can be pricey, early evening discount on some dishes), well kept Batemans, Loxley and a house beer called Cheeky Bustard (actually Batemans XB), plenty of wines by the glass, friendly efficient staff, flagstoned bar with log fire, steps up to bare-stone restaurant (former stables); live jazz third Weds of month; children welcome, no dogs inside, attractive sheltered garden, open all day Sat, closed Sun evening, Mon. *(James and Sylvia Hewitt)*

SOUTH WITHAM
SK9219
Angel (01572) 768302
Church Street; NG33 5PJ Old stone pub next to the village church; good value pubby food cooked by co-owner/chef including Mon burger night, OAP lunch (Tues, Thurs) and popular Sun carvery, well kept Black Sheep, Bombardier and a guest, happy hour 5-7pm; sports TV; dogs welcome, open all day (Mon from 4pm), handy for A1. *(Sally and Lance Oldham)*

SPALDING
TF2422
Priors Oven 07972 192750
Sheep Market; PE11 1BH Friendly well run micropub in ancient building (former bakery); small octagonal room with vaulted ceiling, island bar serving up to six well kept changing ales and local cider, no food apart from jars of nuts, spiral stairs up to loos and comfortable lounge with period fireplace; open all day. *(Dr J Barrie Jones)*

STAMFORD — TF0207
All Saints Brewery – Melbourn Brothers (01780) 752186

All Saints Street; PE9 2PA Well reworked old building (core is a medieval hall) with warren of rooms on three floors; upstairs bar serving bottled fruit beers from adjacent early 19th-c brewery and low-priced Sam Smiths on handpump, food from pub favourites up including set deals and good vegetarian options, ground-floor dining area with log fire and woodburner, top floor with leather sofas and wing chairs; children and dogs welcome, picnic-sets in cobbled courtyard, brewery tours, open all day. *(Margaret McDonald)*

STAMFORD — TF0306
★ Bull & Swan (01780) 766412

High Street, St Martins; PE9 2LJ Handsome former staging post with three traditional linked rooms; low beams and bare boards, portraits on stone or painted walls, several open fires and good mix of seating including high-backed settles, leather banquettes and bow-window seats, Adnams Southwold, Sharps Doom Bar and guests, 20 wines by the glass and 30 malt whiskies, well liked food from panini and sharing boards up, helpful staff; background music, free wi-fi; children and dogs welcome, tables in back coachyard with pizza shed, character bedrooms named after animals, open all day. *(Miranda and Jeff Davidson)*

STAMFORD — TF0207
Crown (01780) 763136

All Saints Place; PE9 2AG Substantial well modernised stone-built hotel in same small group as the Tobie Norris (also in Stamford, see Main Entries); good choice of popular food using local produce (some from their own farm), prompt friendly service, well kept ales such as Fullers, Oakham and Timothy Taylors (can be pricey), lots of wines by the glass and cocktails, decent coffee and afternoon teas, spacious main bar with long leather-cushioned counter, substantial pillars, step up to more traditional flagstoned area with stripped stone and armchairs, restaurant; background music, free wi-fi; well behaved children and dogs allowed, seats in back courtyard, 28 comfortable bedrooms (some in separate townhouse), good breakfast, open (and food) all day. *(Gerry and Rosemary Dobson, Martin Day)*

STAMFORD — TF0207
Jolly Brewer (01780) 755141

Foundry Road; PE9 2PP Welcoming unpretentious 19th-c stone pub; six well kept ales including own Bakers Dozen, traditional cider and wide range of interesting whiskies (some from India and Japan), low-priced simple food (weekday lunchtimes and Fri evenings), open fire in brick fireplace; regular beer festivals and fortnightly Sun quiz, sports TV, pool, darts and other games; dogs welcome, picnic-sets out at front, open all day. *(Miranda and Jeff Davidson)*

STOW — SK8881
Cross Keys (01427) 788314

Stow Park Road; B1241 NW of Lincoln; LN1 2DD Village dining pub close to interesting Saxon minster church; bar with painted half-panelling, bottles and decorative china on delft shelving, woodburner, well kept local ales and good food cooked by chef-landlord including daily specials, friendly attentive service, restaurant; quiz nights and cooking demonstrations; children welcome, open all day weekends, closed Mon and Tues. *(Peter and Anne Hollindale)*

SURFLEET — TF2528
Mermaid (01775) 680275

B1356 (Gosberton Road), just off A16 N of Spalding; PE11 4AB Two high-ceilinged carpeted rooms, huge sash windows, banquettes, captain's chairs and spindlebacks, Adnams and a couple of guests, good choice of fairly standard food including monthly themed night, restaurant; background music; children welcome, pretty terraced garden with summer bar and seats under thatched parasols, play area walled from River Glen, moorings, four bedrooms, closed Mon. *(Silas Davidson)*

TATTERSHALL THORPE — TF2159
Blue Bell (01526) 342206

Thorpe Road; B1192 Coningsby–Woodhall Spa; LN4 4PE Ancient low-beamed pub (said to date from the 13th c) with friendly cosy atmosphere; RAF memorabilia including airmen's signatures on the ceiling (pub was used by the Dambusters), big open fire, three well kept ales (one badged for the pub), nice wines and enjoyable well priced pubby food, small dining room; some live music; garden tables, bedrooms, closed Sun evening, Mon. *(Mike and Sarah Abbot)*

TETFORD — TF3374
White Hart (01507) 533255

East Road, off A158 E of Horncastle; LN9 6QQ Friendly bay-windowed village pub dating from the 16th c; pleasant bar with curved-back settles and slabby elm tables on red tiles, inglenook log fire, Bombardier, Brains Rev James and a couple of guests, good value generous pubby food, other areas including village shop; live music Thurs; children and dogs welcome, sheltered back lawn, bedrooms; open all day weekends, from 3.30pm weekdays. *(Harvey Ford)*

THEDDLETHORPE ALL SAINTS — TF4787
★ Kings Head (01507) 339798

Pub signposted off A1031 N of Maplethorpe; Mill Road; LN12 1PB Welcoming 16th-c thatched pub; carpeted two-room front lounge with very low ceiling, brass platters on timbered walls, antique dining chairs and tables, easy chairs by log fire, central bar (more low beams) serving well kept ales such as Batemans and a local cider, coal fire with side oven, shelves of books, stuffed owls and country pictures, long dining room, good local food from sandwiches and sharing plates to steaks and fresh Grimsby fish, popular Sun roasts; children and dogs welcome, one or two picnic-sets in front area, more on lawn, self-catering apartment, open all day weekends, closed Mon and lunchtime Tues (all day Tues in winter). *(Jack Faulkner)*

THREEKINGHAM   TF0836
Three Kings (01529) 240249
Just off A52 12 miles E of Grantham; Saltersway; NG34 0AU Former coaching inn with big entrance hall, fire and pubby furniture in comfortable beamed lounge, also a panelled restaurant and bigger dining/function room, good choice of enjoyable home-made food including Thurs steak night, Bass, Timothy Taylors Landlord and guests; Weds quiz; children and dogs (in bar) welcome, sunny paved terrace and small lawned area, various car club meetings, closed Mon. *(Tom Gray)*

WAINFLEET   TF5058
★Batemans Brewery (01754) 880317
Mill Lane, off A52 via B1195; PE24 4JE Circular bar in brewery's ivy-covered windmill tower; Batemans ales in top condition, czech and belgian beers on tap too, ground-floor dining area with cheap food including baguettes and a few pubby dishes, popular Sun carvery, old pub games (more outside), lots of brewery memorabilia and plenty for families to enjoy; no dogs inside, entertaining brewery tours and shop, tables on terrace and grass, bar open 11.30am-4pm, bistro 12-2pm, seasonal hours for brewery tours and shop. *(Charles and Maddie Bishop)*

WASHINGBOROUGH   TF0170
Ferry Boat (01522) 790794
High Street; LN4 1AZ Friendly old village pub with enjoyable traditional food including good value two-course weekday lunch, a couple of ales such as Adnams and Sharps; high-raftered central bar with low-beamed areas off including restaurant, bare-stone and stripped-brick walls, mix of furniture on wood floors, open fire; background and some live music, Weds quiz, games part with

pool, darts and TV; children and dogs (in bar) welcome, beer garden, good river walks nearby, open all day. *(Sally Harrison)*

WEST DEEPING   TF1009
Red Lion (01778) 347190
King Street; PE6 9HP Stone-built pub with long low-beamed bar, four well kept ales including Fullers London Pride and often local Hopshackle, popular freshly made food from baguettes up including weekday evening deal, back dining extension; occasional live music, quiz last Tues of month, free wi-fi; children welcome, no dogs inside, tables in back garden with terrace and fenced play area, vintage car/motorcycle meetings, open till 4pm Sun, closed Mon. *(Lenny and Ruth Walters)*

WILSFORD   TF0043
Plough (01400) 230304
Main Street; NG32 3NS Traditional old two-bar village pub next to church; beams and open fires, a couple of real ales, nice range of wines and good choice of well presented bar food (till 6pm Sun), pleasant friendly service, dining conservatory; pool and other games in adjoining room; children welcome, small walled back garden, good local walks, open all day Fri and Sun, closed Mon. *(Caroline and Steve Archer)*

WITHAM ON THE HILL   TF0516
Six Bells (01778) 590360
Village signed from A6121, SW of Bourne; PE10 0JH Well restored Edwardian stone inn with smart comfortable bar; popular food including wood-fired pizzas and Weds 'auberge supper', three well kept ales, good friendly service; children and dogs welcome, rattan-style furniture on front terrace, nice village, three bedrooms, good breakfast, open all day Sat. *(Margaret McDonald)*

WOODHALL SPA   TF1963
Village Limits (01526) 353312
Stixwould Road; LN10 6UJ Modernised country pub-restaurant on village outskirts; good locally sourced food cooked by landlord-chef from pub standards up, well kept Batemans XB and a beer badged for the pub from local Horncastle, friendly service, banquettes in smallish beamed bar, dining room with light wood furniture on wood-strip floor; children welcome, eight courtyard bedrooms, good views from garden, closed Mon lunchtime. *(Harvey Ford)*

Post Office address codings confusingly give the impression that a few pubs are in Lincolnshire, when they're really in Cambridgeshire (which is where we list them).

Norfolk

KEY ★ Star Pub 🍽 Top Quality Food 🍺 Great Beer
🍷 Good Wines £ Bargain Meals 🛏 Good Bedrooms 🍴 Serves Food

BAWBURGH   TG1508 Map 5

Kings Head 🍽 🍷 🛏

(01603) 744977 ~ www.kingsheadbawburgh.co.uk
Harts Lane; A47 just W of Norwich then B1108; NR9 3LS

Busy, small-roomed pub with five real ales, good wines by the glass, interesting food and friendly service; bedrooms

Impressive food, helpful and friendly service and an enjoyable place to stay too, it's no wonder our readers favour this little spot so much. Dating from the 17th c, it has much character and the small rooms have plenty of low beams and standing timbers, leather sofas and an attractive assortment of old dining chairs and tables on wood-strip floors; also, a knocked-through open fire and a couple of woodburning stoves in the restaurant areas. Adnams Broadside and Lighthouse and a couple of changing guests on handpump, 11 wines by the glass, 20 gins (including five local ones) and eight malt whiskies; background music. There are seats in the garden and the pub is opposite a little green. The six bedrooms are comfortable and pretty, and there are also two self-catering apartments available. Portable disabled ramp but no loos.

🍽 Top notch food includes sandwiches, scallops with almond and curry butter, cauliflower purée and roasted florets, smoked haddock kedgeree with spinach and a poached egg, spiced falafel burger with grilled halloumi, beetroot and apple slaw and skinny fries, honey-roast ham with a fried duck egg, sea bass with confit squid, squid ink risotto and roasted baby fennel, lamb rump with pea and mint purée, parmentier potatoes and mint jus, and puddings such as coconut parfait with poached Malibu pineapple, granola bar and pineapple salsa and millionaire's tart with butterscotch ice-cream. *Benchmark main dish: beer-battered fish and chips £15.00. Two-course evening meal £22.00.*

Free house ~ Licensee Anton Wimmer ~ Real ale ~ Open 11-11 ~ Bar food 12-2, 5.30-9; 12-3, 5.30-8 Sun ~ Restaurant ~ Children welcome ~ Dogs allowed in bar ~ Wi-fi ~ Bedrooms: £90/£110 *Recommended by John Evans, John and Mary Warner, Molly and Stewart Lindsay, Nick Sharpe, John Harris, Carol and Barry Craddock*

BLAKENEY   TG0243 Map 8

White Horse 🍷 🛏

(01263) 740574 ~ www.adnams.co.uk/locations/the-white-horse
Off A149 W of Sheringham; High Street; NR25 7AL

Friendly, popular inn with several bars and airy conservatory, local ales, well liked food and seats outside; charming bedrooms

Both locals and holidaymakers enjoy this busy little place with its chatty and convivial atmosphere. The long, split-level bar has high chairs by the counter, button-back seats along the walls, simple dining chairs and tartan-upholstered armchairs around pine-topped tables and Adnams Broadside, Ghost Ship and Southwold and a guest beer on handpump, a dozen wines by the glass and six malt whiskies; background music and board games. The airy dining conservatory has modern art on planked walls, white rattan armchairs with colourful scatter cushions around pale-topped tables on floor tiles and big ceiling lanterns. A breakfast room is similarly furnished to the bar and there's a cosy lounge with sofas and armchairs in front of a small woodburning stove. In a suntrap walled side terrace you'll find black rattan-style furniture under large parasols. Some of the contemporary, attractive and comfortable bedrooms have views of the coastal marshes; breakfasts are highly rated. Dogs are allowed in one bedroom.

A wide choice of good food includes lunchtime sandwiches (not Sunday), baked baby camembert with onion marmalade, local crab with celeriac rémoulade, compressed watermelon and lemon gel, sweet potato and chickpea harissa stew with chargrilled broccoli, courgette greek yoghurt fritter and tzatziki, cottage pie, southern fried chicken fillet burger with lemon mayonnaise and gruyère, seared salmon fillet with smoked haddock and cockle chowder and beer bread, lamb loin with pulled lamb, potato croquette and smoked celeriac purée, and puddings. *Benchmark main dish: pork tenderloin with colcannon potatoes, crispy pork cheek and apple purée £19.00. Two-course evening meal £22.00.*

Adnams ~ Tenant Nick Attfield ~ Real ale ~ Open 11-11; 11-10.30 Sun ~ Bar food 12-2.30, 6-9; 12-2.30, 6-8.30 Sun ~ Restaurant ~ Children welcome ~ Dogs allowed in bar ~ Wi-fi ~ Bedrooms: $89/$114 *Recommended by Cliff and Monica Swan, Andrew Vincent, Samuel and Melissa Turnbull, Edward and William Johnston, Simon Sharpe, Elizabeth and Peter May*

BURSTON

Crown 🌟 🍺

TM1383   Map 5

(01379) 741257 – www.burstoncrown.com

Village signposted off A140 N of Scole; Mill Road; IP22 5TW

Friendly, relaxed village pub usefully open all day, with a warm welcome, real ales and well liked bar food

The best place to sit in the heavily beamed, quarry-tiled bar room on a cold day is on the comfortably cushioned sofas in front of a woodburning stove in a huge brick fireplace; there are also stools by a low chunky wooden table, and newspapers and magazines. The public bar on the left has a nice long table and panelled settle on an old brick floor in one alcove, a pool table, and more tables and chairs towards the back near a dartboard. Both rooms are hung with paintings by local artists. Adnams Broadside and Southwold and guests such as Oakham Citra and Scarlet Macaw, Star Wing Spire Light, Three Blind Mice Nothing Rhymes with Orange and Winters Golden on handpump or tapped from the cask, ten wines by the glass and seven malt whiskies; background music, board games, dominoes and cards. The simply furnished, beamed dining room has another big brick fireplace. Outside, there are seats and tables on a terrace and in the secluded garden, and a play area for children.

Rewarding food cooked by the landlord includes sandwiches, chicken liver parfait with white port and juniper berries and red onion marmalade, crab cakes with pineapple salsa, spinach and cream cheese pancakes topped with cheddar, goan cod cheek curry with stir-fried mangetout, veal escalope with caper and ham cream sauce and parmentier potatoes, chilli chicken ramen with soba noodles, bean shoots and spring onions, 10oz rib-eye steak with horseradish and chive butter, and puddings such as chocolate pot with raspberry coulis and sticky toffee pudding with butterscotch sauce. *Benchmark main dish: pie of the week £14.00. Two-course evening meal £20.00.*

Free house ~ Licensees Bev and Steve Kembery ~ Real ale ~ Open 12-11; 12-10.30 Sun ~ Bar food 12-2, 6.30-9; 12-4 Sun; no food Sun evening, Mon ~ Restaurant ~ Children welcome ~ Dogs allowed in bar ~ Wi-fi ~ Live music, plays, art festival (see website for details)
Recommended by Heather and Richard Jones, Graeme and Sally Mendham, Caroline Sullivan, Melanie and David Lawson, Lucy and Giles Gibbon

CASTLE ACRE
TF8115   Map 8

Ostrich

(01760) 755398 – http://ostrichcastleacre.com
Stocks Green; PE32 2AE

Friendly old village pub with some fine architecture, real ales and tasty food; bedrooms

In this former coaching inn dating back in part to the 16th c, you'll be able to pick out some interesting features, such as original masonry, beams and trusses. The L-shaped, low-ceilinged front bar (on two levels) has a woodburning stove in a huge fireplace, lots of wheelback chairs and cushioned pews around pubby tables on a wood-strip floor and gold patterned wallpaper; there's a step up to an area in front of the bar counter where there are similar seats and tables and a log fire in a brick fireplace. Helpful staff serve Adnams Ghost Ship, Black Sheep and Greene King Abbot and IPA on handpump, around a dozen wines by the glass and several malt whiskies; background music, darts and board games. There's a separate dining room with another brick fireplace. The sheltered garden has picnic-sets under parasols and the inn faces the tree-lined village green. Bedrooms are warm and comfortable. Nearby are the remains of a Norman castle and a cluniac priory (English Heritage).

Pleasing food includes lunchtime ciabattas, confit smoked duck with beetroot and egg salad, seared scallops with roasted red onions, pancetta and fondue sauce, sharing platters, roast artichoke, chicory and halloumi salad, pizzas with lots of toppings, poached haddock topped with a poached egg, asparagus and cheese sauce, confit duck leg with carrot purée and honey-roast parsnips and sweet potatoes, gammon with pineapple, sirloin steak with red onion marmalade and chips, and puddings such as hot chocolate fondant with vanilla ice-cream and rhubarb and strawberry cheesecake. *Benchmark main dish: slow-cooked pork belly and maple beef with sautéed cabbage and bacon £18.50. Two-course evening meal £22.00.*

Greene King ~ Tenant Carl Wade ~ Real ale ~ Open 10am-10.30pm; 10am-11.30pm Sat, Sun ~ Bar food 12-3, 6-9; 12-3, 6-10 Sat ~ Restaurant ~ Children welcome ~ Dogs allowed in bar ~ Wi-fi ~ Bedrooms: £75/£85 *Recommended by Bruce White, Elisabeth and Bill Humphries, Thomas Green, Paddy and Sian O'Leary, Andrea and Philip Crispin*

GREAT MASSINGHAM
TF7922   Map 8

Dabbling Duck 🏮⭐🍺

(01485) 520827 – www.thedabblingduck.co.uk
Off A148 King's Lynn–Fakenham; Abbey Road; PE32 2HN

Unassuming from the outside but with character bars, real ales and interesting food; comfortable bedrooms

If the weather is warm you can sit on the front terrace here and take in the pleasant setting (the village green and big duck ponds are opposite); there are also seats and a play area in the enclosed back garden. The cosy bars have leather sofas and armchairs, a mix of antique wooden dining tables and chairs on flagstones or stripped wooden floors, a very high-backed settle, 18th- and 19th-c quirky prints and cartoons, and plenty of beams and standing timbers; the three woodburning stoves are put to good use in winter. At the back of the pub is the Blenheim room, just right for a private group, and there's also a candlelit dining room. Adnams Broadside and Ghost Ship and Woodfordes Wherry and Nelsons Revenge on handpump and a dozen wines by the glass, served from a bar counter made of great slabs of polished tree trunk; background music, TV, darts and board games. Nine bedrooms are named after famous local sportsmen and airmen from the World War II air base in Massingham. Wheelchair access.

High quality food includes sandwiches, pheasant tacos with salsa verde, pink onions and avocado, seared tuna steak with kimchi, edamame beans and miso orange dressing, cauliflower burger with toppings, slaw and fries, beer-battered cod with dripping chips, chicken curry, rib-eye steak with chimichurri dressing and chips, and puddings such as pear and apple gateau with brown butter pear and brown butter ice-cream and sticky toffee pudding with milk ice-cream and toffee sauce. *Benchmark main dish: rare-breed burger with toppings and dripping chips £13.50. Two-course evening meal £21.00.*

Free house ~ Licensee Dominic Symington ~ Real ale ~ Open 8am-11pm ~ Bar food 12-9 ~ Restaurant ~ Children welcome ~ Dogs allowed in bar and bedrooms ~ Wi-fi ~ Bedrooms: /£110 *Recommended by Tracey and Stephen Groves, William Pace, Camilla and Jose Ferrera, Christopher and Elise Way, Millie and Peter Downing, Elise and Charles Mackinlay, Peter and Alison Steadman*

HOLKHAM TF8943 Map 8

Victoria ♀ ⇔

(01328) 711008 – www.victoriaatholkham.co.uk
A149 near Holkham Hall; NR23 1RG

Smart, handsome inn with pubby bar, plenty of character dining space, thoughtful choice of drinks, friendly staff and enjoyable food; bedrooms

As this well run pub is just across the road from the vast stretches of Holkham Beach it does get packed at peak times – so you must arrive early then. The atmosphere is gently upmarket yet informal, staff are helpful and the choice of wine and food is good. A proper bare-boards bar to the left of the main door is popular locally and serves Fullers London Pride, Woodfordes Wherry and a couple of guest beers on handpump and 20 wines by the glass; background music, TV, darts and board games. The spreading dining and sitting area has an appealing variety of antique-style dining chairs and tables on rugs and stripped floorboards, antlers and antique guns, and sofas by a big log fire. An airy conservatory dining room, decorated in pale beige, leads out to a back terrace with green-painted furniture; in summer the outside bar and seafood shack is much used. Some of the stylish bedrooms (a few are dog-friendly) have views of the sea, and breakfasts are good and generous.

High quality food includes breakfasts (8-10am) plus ham hock terrine with piccalilli, scallops, black pudding, bacon and apple, mushroom and toasted pecan risotto, lambs liver with mustard mash and caramelised onion jus, salmon with mousseline and asparagus sauce, chicken supreme with tomato, chorizo and vegetable broth, sea bass and squid with baby gem, pea and herb fricassée, and puddings such as pineapple fritters with crisp apple sorbet and chocolate biscuit cake with cranberry compote. *Benchmark main dish: beer-battered fish and chips £14.75. Two-course evening meal £21.00.*

Free house ~ Licensee Lord Coke ~ Real ale ~ Open 8am-11pm; 8am-10.30pm Sun ~ Bar food 12-2.30, 6.30-9; bar snacks 12-6 ~ Restaurant ~ Children welcome ~ Dogs welcome ~ Wi-fi ~ Bedrooms: £135/£195 *Recommended by David Jackman, Tim and Mary Thomson, Richard and Penny Gibbs, Susan and Tim Boyle, Sally and Lance Oldham, Nicola and Stuart Parsons*

KING'S LYNN

TF6119   Map 8

Bank House 🏅 ♟ 🛏

(01553) 660492 – www.thebankhouse.co.uk

Kings Staithe Square via Boat Street and along the quay in one-way system; PE30 1RD

Georgian bar-brasserie with plenty of history and character, airy rooms, real ales and imaginative food from breakfast onwards; bedrooms

Helpfully open and serving some kind of food all day, this well run place was the first site in 1780 for what became Barclays Bank. The various stylish rooms include the elegant bar (once the bank manager's office) with sofas and armchairs, a log fire with fender seating, Adnams Southwold, Barsham Bitter Old Bustard and a guest beer on handpump, 18 wines by the glass, 58 gins, 14 whiskies, interesting vodkas, cocktails and a farm cider; background music. The restaurant has antique chairs and tables on bare boards, an airy brasserie has sofas and armchairs around low tables and a big brick fireplace, and two other areas (one with fine panelling, the other with a half-size billiards table) have more open fires. The atmosphere throughout is gently civilised but easy-going and service is helpful and courteous. An outside area, flanked by magnificent wrought-iron gates, has fire pits for warmth on chillier evenings, and the riverside terrace (lovely sunsets) has an open-air cocktail bar in summer. Most of the charming bedrooms overlook the river and breakfasts are first class. This is a splendid quayside spot and the Corn Exchange theatre and arts centre is just five minutes away. Sister pub is the Rose & Crown in Snettisham.

A fine choice of interesting food includes sandwiches, smoked salmon bonbon with kale slaw and ponzu dressing, pork and black pudding terrine with orange purée and crispy shallots, sharing platters, chickpea, broccoli, cherry tomato, cashew, goji berry and pomegranate salad, moules frites, slow-cooked lamb shoulder with celeriac fondant, warm apple and red cabbage chutney and creamed brussels sprouts, duck breast with hasselback potatoes, sautéed baby turnips, pancetta and maple syrup, and puddings such as lemon tart with gin-infused cucumber, lemon curd ice-cream and burnt lemon powder and rum-soaked sultana and white chocolate bread and butter pudding with crème anglaise. *Benchmark main dish: steak burger with toppings and fries £14.00. Two-course evening meal £24.00.*

Free house ~ Licensee Michael Baldwin ~ Real ale ~ Open 11-11; 11-10 Sun ~ Bar food 12-9.30 (8.30 Sun) ~ Restaurant ~ Children welcome ~ Dogs allowed in bar and bedrooms ~ Wi-fi ~ Bedrooms: £95/£115 *Recommended by Dr J Barrie Jones, James Tilley, Scott and Charlotte Havers, Alison and Michael Harper, John Wooll*

Post Office address codings confusingly give the impression that a few pubs are in Norfolk, when they're really in Cambridgeshire or Suffolk (which is where we list them).

LARLING

TL9889 Map 5

Angel 🍺 🛏

(01953) 717963 – www.angel-larling.co.uk

From A11 Thetford–Attleborough, take B1111 turn-off and follow pub signs; NR16 2QU

Good-natured, chatty atmosphere in busy pub with several real ales and tasty bar food; bedrooms

It's busy here in warm weather, when customers visiting Peter Beales Roses or enjoying the lovely surrounding walks arrive for refreshment. The pub has been run by the same friendly family since 1913 and they still have the original visitors' books from 1897 to 1909. The comfortable 1930s-style lounge on the right has squared panelling, cushioned wheelback chairs, a nice long cushioned panelled corner settle and some good solid tables for eating; also, a collection of whisky-water jugs on a delft shelf over the big brick fireplace, a woodburning stove, a couple of copper kettles and some hunting prints. Adnams Southwold and four guests from breweries such as Crouch Vale, Oakham, Orkney and Swannay on handpump, ten wines by the glass, 100 malt whiskies, 50 gins and a farm cider; they hold an August beer festival with more than 100 real ales and ciders, live music and a barbecue. The quarry-tiled, black-beamed public bar has a good local feel, with a juke box, games machine, board games and background music. There's a neat grass area behind the car park with picnic-sets around a big fairy-lit apple tree and a fenced play area. Five bedrooms are attractive and comfortable and their four-acre meadow is used as a caravan and camping site from March to October.

 Honest food includes sandwiches, chicken liver pâté with chutney, prawn cocktail, sweet pepper and mushroom lasagne, burger with toppings and chips, grilled whole trout with parsley butter and lemon, gammon with egg or pineapple, chicken and mushroom stroganoff, salmon and prawn pasta topped with cheese and breadcrumbs, rack of barbecue pork ribs, mixed grill, and puddings such as treacle tart and bread and butter pudding. *Benchmark main dish: steak and kidney pie £11.95. Two-course evening meal £20.00.*

Free house ~ Licensee Andrew Stammers ~ Real ale ~ Open 10.30am-11pm; 10.30-10.30 Sun ~ Bar food 12-9.30; 12-10 Fri, Sat ~ Restaurant ~ Children welcome ~ Wi-fi ~ Bedrooms: £60/£90 *Recommended by Colin and Daniel Gibbs, Adrian Buckland, Nicola and Stuart Parsons, Geoff and Ann Marston, Rosie and Marcus Heatherley*

MORSTON

TG0043 Map 8

Anchor 🍴⭐ 🍷

(01263) 741392 – www.morstonanchor.co.uk

A149 Salthouse–Stiffkey; The Street; NR25 7AA

Quite a choice of rooms filled with bric-a-brac and prints, real ales and pleasing food

Our readers enjoy their visits to this cosy pub in a small seaside village. Three traditional rooms on the right offer a friendly atmosphere and have straightforward seats and tables on original wooden floors, coal fires, local 1950s beach photographs and lots of prints and bric-a-brac. Adnams Ghost Ship, local Winters Golden and Woodfordes Wherry on handpump, 20 wines by the glass and 25 gins; background music, darts and board games. The contemporary airy extension on the left, with comfortable benches and tables, leads into the more formal restaurant where local art is displayed on the walls. You can sit outside at the front of the building.

If parking is tricky at the pub, there's an off-road overflow around the corner and a National Trust car park five minutes' walk away. The surrounding area is wonderful for bird-watching and walking, and you can book seal-spotting trips here.

Reliably good food includes lunchtime sandwiches, twice-baked cheese soufflé with onion jam, smoked haddock scotch eggs with curry sauce, crab aioli with parsley and wild garlic risotto, crispy buttermilk chicken with sriracha mayonnaise and triple-cooked chips, burger with toppings, slaw and fries, beer-battered haddock and chips, 28-day aged rib-eye steak with black garlic butter, and puddings such as cinnamon doughnuts with rhubarb jam and vanilla custard and dark chocolate crémeux with salted caramel and peanut butter ice-cream. *Benchmark main dish: hake with mussel sauce, cauliflower and capers £17.00. Two-course evening meal £22.00.*

Free house ~ Licensees Harry Farrow and Rowan Glennie ~ Real ale ~ Open 9am-11pm; 9am-10pm Sun ~ Bar food 12-3, 6-9 ~ Restaurant ~ Children welcome ~ Dogs allowed in bar ~ Wi-fi *Recommended by David Eberlin, D and NF, Tracey and Stephen Groves, Tony Scott, Tim and Wendy Lloyd, Monty Green, Caroline and Peter Bryant*

NORWICH
Fat Cat 🍺

TG2109   Map 5

(01603) 624364 – www.fatcatpub.co.uk
West End Street; on foot from city centre (1 mile) turn R down Nelson Street off Dereham Road; NR2 4NA

A place of pilgrimage for beer lovers and open all day; lunchtime rolls and pies

A visit to this cheerful town pub is an absolute must for real ale lovers. The knowledgeable Mr Keatley and his hospitable staff can help guide you through the extraordinary choice of 32 perfectly kept and quickly changing beers. On handpump or tapped from the cask in a stillroom behind the bar – big windows reveal all – are their own beers (Fat Cat Bitter, Honey Ale, Marmalade Cat, Tom Cat and Wild Cat), as well as guests such as Adnams Mosaic, Colchester Drizzle, Crouch Vale Yakima Gold, Dark Star American Pale Ale, Fullers ESB, Greene King Abbot, Oakham Bishops Farewell and Citra, Thornbridge Jaipur and Timothy Taylors Landlord – and many more choices from across the country. You'll also find imported draught beers and lagers, over 50 bottled beers from around the world, ten malt whiskies, ten rums and 20 ciders and perries. The no-nonsense furnishings include plain scrubbed pine tables and simple solid seats, lots of brewery memorabilia, bric-a-brac and stained glass; board games. There are tables outside. No children.

Bar food consists of filled rolls and good pies at lunchtime (not Sunday).

Own brew ~ Licensee Colin Keatley ~ Real ale ~ Open 12-11; 11-midnight Sat ~ Bar food filled rolls available until sold out; not Sun ~ No children inside ~ Dogs allowed in bar ~ Wi-fi *Recommended by Richard and Penny Gibbs, Daniel King, Matthew and Elisabeth Reeves, Christine and Tony Garrett*

Please tell us if the décor, atmosphere, food or drink at a pub is different
from our description. We rely on readers' reports to keep us up to date:
feedback@goodguides.com, or (no stamp needed)
Freepost THE GOOD PUB GUIDE, Random House Publishing,
20 Vauxhall Bridge Road, London SW1V 2SA.

SALTHOUSE

TG0743   Map 8

Dun Cow

(01263) 740467 – www.salthouseduncow.com

A149 Blakeney–Sheringham (Purdy Street, junction with Bard Hill); NR25 7XA

Cheerful village pub, a good all-rounder with enterprising food

Our readers enjoy this bustling pub very much and return here on a regular basis. The flint-walled bar consists of a pair of high-raftered rooms opened up into one area, with stone tiles around the counter where regulars congregate, and a carpeted seating area with a fireplace at each end. Also, scrubbed tables, one very high-backed settle, country kitchen chairs and elegant little red-padded dining chairs, with big sailing ship and other prints. Adnams Ghost Ship, Norfolk Brewhouse Moon Gazer Golden Ale and Amber Ale and Woodfordes Wherry on handpump, 19 wines by the glass and 14 malt whiskies. Bedrooms are self-catering. Picnic-sets on the front grass look out towards the sea and there are more seats in a sheltered back courtyard as well as an orchard garden beyond.

With quite an emphasis on fresh fish, the very good food includes sandwiches (until 5pm), salt and pepper squid with chilli and garlic, rare fresh tuna tempura with wasabi and soy, shakshuka (pepper, chickpea and tomato stew with cumin, chilli, baked eggs and pizza bread), fresh fish dish of the day, steak in ale pie, quiche of the day, crispy buttermilk chicken burger with toppings, coleslaw and fries, fresh local crab linguine with chilli, mint and lime, and puddings such as treacle tart and custard and flourless orange and almond cake with clotted cream. *Benchmark main dish: côte de boeuf for two £55.00. Two-course evening meal £21.00.*

Punch ~ Lease Daniel Goff ~ Real ale ~ Open 11.30-11 ~ Bar food 12-9 ~ Children welcome ~ Dogs welcome ~ Wi-fi *Recommended by D and NF, Roy Hoing, Neil and Angela Huxter, Richard Tilbrook, M G Hart, Clive and Fran Dutson*

SNETTISHAM

TF6834   Map 8

Rose & Crown

(01485) 541382 – www.roseandcrownsnettisham.co.uk

Village signposted from A149 King's Lynn–Hunstanton just N of Sandringham; coming in on the B1440 from the roundabout just N of village, take first left into Old Church Road; PE31 7LX

Norfolk Dining Pub of the Year

Particularly well run inn with log fires and interesting furnishings, imaginative food, a fine range of drinks and stylish seating on heated terrace; well equipped bedrooms

Not surprisingly, this lovely old inn is a favourite with so many customers. All aspects remain first class, from the well trained, friendly staff to the fine range of drinks and excellent food and on to the stylish bedrooms. The two main bars have distinct character and simple charm, with an open fire and woodburning stove, old quarry tiles or coir flooring, cushioned wall seating and wooden tables and chairs, candles on mantelpieces and daily papers. There are stools against the bar where locals enjoy Adnams Broadside and Southwold, Greene King Old Speckled Hen and Woodfordes Wherry on handpump; also, a dozen wines by the glass, around 20 gins (including local ones), seasonal cocktails and jugs of sangria, local cider and fresh fruit juices. A small wood-floored back room has old sports equipment, the landlord's sporting trophies and photos of the pub-sponsored village cricket team. The civilised little restaurant (decorated in soft greys) has cushions and picture mounts with splashes of bright green and cream candles in antique brass candlesticks. At the back of the building, two rooms make up the bustling Garden Room, with sofas, wooden farmhouse and white-painted dining chairs around a mix of tables, church candles in large lanterns, striped blinds and doors that lead to the pretty walled garden. Here there are plenty of contemporary seats and tables underneath cream parasols, outdoor heaters, herbaceous borders and a wooden galleon-shaped climbing structure for children. Bedrooms are spacious and individually decorated and breakfasts very good. Disabled lavatories and wheelchair ramp. This is sister pub to the Bank House in King's Lynn.

Impressive food using the best local produce includes sandwiches, roast figs, lamb's lettuce and walnut salad with cranberry dressing, prawn and crayfish cocktail, sharing platters, wild garlic risotto with courgette, spinach, pine nuts and parmesan, burger with toppings, onion rings and fries, crab pasta with cherry tomatoes, lemon, capers and parsley, dashi-seasoned hake with seafood velouté, saffron potatoes and charred gem, corn-fed chicken with fried halloumi and warm vegetable salad, and puddings such as apple and berry crumble with crème anglaise and roasted pineapple with star anise, cinnamon and frozen yoghurt. *Benchmark main dish: beer-battered haddock and chips £14.50. Two-course evening meal £22.50.*

Free house ~ Licensee Anthony Goodrich ~ Real ale ~ Open 11-11; 11-10.30 Sun ~ Bar food 12-9.30; 12-8.30 Sun ~ Restaurant ~ Children welcome ~ Dogs allowed in bar and bedrooms ~ Wi-fi ~ Bedrooms: £100/£120 *Recommended by Dr K Nesbitt, D and NF, John Wooll, Roy Hoing, Christopher and Elise Way, Tracey and Stephen Groves, Derek and Sylvia Stephenson, Peter Cole*

THORNHAM
TF7343 Map 8
Lifeboat 🍺 🛏
(01485) 512236 – www.lifeboatinnthornham.com
A149 by Orange Tree, then first left; PE36 6LT

White-painted, traditional inn with bars and dining rooms, real ales, popular food and super surrounding walks; bedrooms

There's a great deal of character in the rambling rooms here and plenty of space for eating and drinking. The main bar has beams, big lamps, brass and copper jugs and pans, cushioned window seats, chairs and settles around dark sturdy tables on quarry tiles and a woodburning stove; the antique penny-in-the-hole game is hidden under a bench cushion. A second bar, favoured by locals, is smaller, with some fine carving around the counter. Greene King Abbot and IPA, Norfolk Brewhouse Moon Gazer Amber Ale and Woodfordes Mardlers Mild and Wherry on handpump, good wines by the glass and nine gins; background music and board games. The formal entrance hall has sofas and fender seats by a big open fire, there's another room with more sofas and a cylindrical woodburner and also a simply furnished dining room. A quarry-tiled conservatory (used for eating) has fairy lights and steps that lead up to the back garden with grey-painted picnic-sets and a couple of cabanas; out in front are more picnic-sets. Bedrooms are warm and comfortable and you can walk from here to the salt marshes which are about a mile away.

Good quality food includes sandwiches, deep-fried brie with chilli jam, prawn cocktail, pea and feta risotto with crispy onions, home-cooked ham and eggs, roast chicken caesar salad, fresh local crab salad, burger with toppings, coleslaw and skinny fries, sea bass with dill butter and crushed new potatoes, rump steak with peppercorn sauce, and puddings such as triple chocolate brownie with chocolate ice-cream and sticky toffee pudding with caramel sauce. *Benchmark main dish: beer-battered fish and chips £16.00. Two-course evening meal £23.00.*

Punch ~ Tenant Ewen Thomson ~ Real ale ~ Open 11-11 ~ Bar food 12-9 ~ Restaurant ~ Children welcome ~ Dogs allowed in bar and bedrooms ~ Wi-fi ~ Bedrooms: /£145
Recommended by David Brown, Andrew Clark, Tracey and Stephen Groves, Melanie and David Lawson

 THORNHAM   TF7343   Map 8

Orange Tree

(01485) 512213 – www.theorangetreethornham.co.uk
Church Street/A149; PE36 6LY

Nice combination of friendly bar and modern dining, plus suntrap garden; bedrooms

Many customers enjoy staying in the well equipped, comfortable and up-to-date rooms here; you can choose between the Courtyard, Old Bakery annexe and Manor Lodge, and breakfasts are good. The sizeable pubby bar has white-painted beams, red leather chesterfields in front of a log fire, and flowery upholstered or leather and wooden dining chairs and plush wall seats around a mix of tables on wooden or quarry-tiled floors. Black Sheep, Woodfordes Wherry and a guest beer on handpump, 37 wines by the glass, 19 gins and a farm cider; background music and flatscreen TV. A little dining room leads off here with silver décor, buddha heads and candles, and the two-part restaurant is simple and contemporary in style. The front garden is pretty with lavender beds and climbing roses, lots of picnic-sets under parasols, outdoor heaters and a small smart corner pavilion. At the back of the building is a second outdoor area with children's play equipment. Lovely walks all around. They're kind to dogs and have a doggie menu plus snacks.

Rewarding food includes sandwiches, chicken satay with puffed wild rice and spring onion, ham hock terrine with pickled wild mushrooms and tarragon aioli, sharing platters, vegetable red thai curry, corn-fed chicken with fondant potato, bread sauce purée, compressed apples and chicken emulsion, halibut with tarragon gnocchi, sautéed wild mushroom and citrus beurre blanc, 15-hour smoked rack of ribs with kohlrabi slaw and fries, and puddings such as chocolate brownie with chocolate sauce and vanilla ice-cream and banana split with toffee sauce, Caramac and granola. *Benchmark main dish: 48-hour home-smoked brisket burger with toppings, bourbon sauce and fries £15.45. Two-course evening meal £24.50.*

Punch ~ Lease Mark Goode ~ Real ale ~ Open 11-11; 12-10.30 Sun ~ Bar food 12-3, 6-9; all day weekends ~ Restaurant ~ Children welcome ~ Dogs allowed in bar and bedrooms ~ Wi-fi ~ Bedrooms: £85/£110 *Recommended by Tracey and Stephen Groves, W K Wood, Gail and Arthur Roberts, Jamie and Lizzie McEwan, Martin Day, Nick and Willow Brown, Sophia and Hamish Greenfield, Jeremy Snaithe*

THORPE MARKET   TG2434   Map 8

Gunton Arms

(01263) 832010 – www.theguntonarms.co.uk
Cromer Road; NR11 8TZ

Impressive place with an easy-going atmosphere, open fires and antiques, real ales, interesting food and friendly staff; bedrooms

There aren't many places in this *Guide* that are reached through a 1,000-acre deer park! Nor many that are in such a grand country house. But it's part of the fun and certainly rather individual. Through a large entrance hall is the simply furnished bar with dark pubby chairs and tables on a wooden floor, a log fire, a long settle beside a pool table, and high stools against the mahogany counter where they serve Adnams Broadside and Southwold,

Woodfordes Wherry and a guest beer on handpump, 13 wines by the glass, 16 malt whiskies and two ciders; staff are chatty and helpful. Heavy curtains line an open doorway into a dining room, where vast antlers hang above a big log fire (they often cook over this) and there are straightforward chairs around scrubbed tables on stone tiles. A lounge, with comfortable old leather armchairs and a sofa on a fine rug in front of yet another log fire, has genuine antiques and standard lamps. The restaurant is more formal with candles and napery, and there are also two homely sitting rooms for hotel residents. Many of the walls are painted dark red and hung with assorted artwork and large mirrors; background music, darts, TV and board games. The lovely bedrooms have many original fittings, but no TV.

Robust food using Estate produce includes sandwiches (until 5pm), prawn and local crab salad with cucumber noodles and saffron aioli, pork belly with apple and peashoots, their own venison sausages with mash and onion gravy, chicken, bacon and leek pie, slow-roast lamb shoulder with bubble and squeak, sea trout fillet with sea-shore vegetables and brown shrimps, well hung steaks cooked over the open fire with béarnaise sauce, cod fillet with creamed leeks, peas and bacon, and puddings such as chocolate truffle torte with griottine cherries and treacle tart with clotted cream. *Benchmark main dish: venison stew £16.00. Two-course evening meal £23.00.*

Free house ~ Licensee Simone Baker ~ Real ale ~ Open 12-11; 12-10.30 Sun ~ Bar food 12-3, 6-10 (9 Sun) ~ Restaurant ~ Children welcome ~ Dogs allowed in bar and bedrooms ~ Wi-fi ~ Bedrooms: /£130 *Recommended by David Twitchett, Bob and Melissa Wyatt, Ben and Jenny Settle, Tracey and Stephen Groves, Mark and Mary Setting, Alison and Graeme Spicer, Matilda and Gerald Thoms*

WARHAM
Three Horseshoes ⚑

TF9441 Map 8

(01328) 710547 – www.warhamhorseshoes.co.uk
Warham All Saints; village signed from A149 Wells-next-the-Sea to Blakeney, and from B1105 S of Wells; NR23 1NL

Renovated old pub with straightforward furnishings, gaslight in some rooms, friendly service, tasty food and seats in garden; bedrooms

You'll find plenty of charm in the unspoilt bar rooms of this old-fashioned pub. Some of them are gaslit and have panelling and painted roughcast walls hung with china plates and royalist photographs, padded leather or upholstered wall seats and kitchen chairs around rustic pine tables on quarry tiles and several Victorian fireplaces. Adnams Ghost Ship and Woodfordes Wherry on handpump and 12 wines by the glass served through a hatch by friendly staff; darts, dominoes, shove-ha'penny, cards and board games. There's a courtyard garden with flower tubs, a terrace with metal chairs and tables and lawns with picnic-sets. Four stylish, comfortable bedrooms are next door in what was the post office.

Traditional food includes filled rolls, potted prawns with lemon mayonnaise, cheese croquettes with chilli jam, vegetable chilli with nachos and sour cream, sausages with mash and onion gravy, lamb burger with bacon and tzatziki, beer-battered fish and chips, and puddings such as dark chocolate mousse with butterscotch sauce and pink prosecco jelly with raspberry sorbet. *Benchmark main dish: pie of the day £12.00. Two-course evening meal £19.00.*

Free house ~ Licensees Victoria and James Hadley ~ Real ale ~ Open 11-11; 12-10.30 Sun ~ Bar food 12-2.30, 6-9; 12-9 Sat; 12-8 Sun ~ Children welcome ~ Dogs welcome ~ Wi-fi ~ Bedrooms: £120/£140 *Recommended by John Utley, Alison and Dan Richardson, Amanda Shipley, Sally and Lance Oldham, Richard and Penny Gibbs, Belinda Stamp*

WELLS-NEXT-THE-SEA   TF9143   Map 8

Crown 🏆⭐🛏️

(01328) 710209 – www.crownhotelnorfolk.co.uk

The Buttlands; NR23 1EX

Handsome white-painted inn with a friendly informal bar, local ales, good modern food and elegant restaurant; bedrooms

There's a good mix of drinkers and diners in this smart old coaching inn and plenty of different rooms to choose from. The rambling bar is on several levels with beams and standing timbers, grey-painted planked wall seats and leather dining chairs on stripped boards, with Adnams Fat Sprat and Jack Brand Mosaic Pale Ale and a beer named for the pub on handpump and good wines by the glass. An airy dining room (there's also a more formal restaurant) has rugs on floorboards, armchairs and sofas, painted farmhouse and other chairs, lots of books on shelves, boating paintings and large cow horns on pale-painted walls, and several woodburning stoves. There are seats and tables outside. Bedrooms are smart, comfortable and well equipped (and dogs can stay in some of them). Disabled access.

Good, modern food cooked by the chef-owner includes lunchtime sandwiches, crab spring roll with sweet chilli mayonnaise, braised beef hash with a poached egg and tomato and thyme jus, black quinoa, roast red onions, broccoli, cashew nuts and tomatoes topped with crumbled feta, cod fillet on parsnip and chilli risotto with tempura soft shell crab and crushed peas, pork, apple and sage burger with red onion marmalade and sweet potato fries, lamb belly with apricot stuffing, braised red cabbage, fried gnocchi and red wine jus, and puddings such as baked alaska with raspberry coulis and chocolate and nut brownie with vanilla ice-cream. *Benchmark main dish: battered haddock goujons with chips £11.95. Two-course evening meal £22.00.*

Flying Kiwi Inns ~ Licensee Chris Coubrough ~ Real ale ~ Open 11-11; 12-10.30 Sun ~ Bar food 12-2.30, 6-9; 12-9 Sun ~ Restaurant ~ Children welcome ~ Dogs allowed in bar and bedrooms ~ Wi-fi ~ Bedrooms: £145/£235 *Recommended by Thomas Green, Charlie Stevens, Freddie and Sarah Banks, John Wooll, Charles Fraser, Sophia and Hamish Greenfield, Ben and Jenny Settle*

WOLTERTON   TG1732   Map 8

Saracens Head 🏆⭐🛏️

(01263) 768909 – www.saracenshead-norfolk.co.uk

Wolterton; Erpingham signed off A140 N of Aylsham, on through Calthorpe; NR11 7LZ

Remote inn with stylish bars and dining room and seats in courtyard; good bedrooms

Built as a coaching inn for Lord Walpole's Estate and reached down country lanes, this is a gently civilised place with a friendly atmosphere. The two-room bar is simple but stylish with high ceilings, light terracotta walls and tall windows with cream and gold curtains – all lending a feeling of space, though it's not large. There's a mix of seats from built-in wall settles to wicker fireside chairs, as well as log fires and flowers. Courteous staff serve Woodfordes Wherry and a changing guest such as Panther Red Panther on handpump and several wines by the glass. The windows look on to a charming old-fashioned gravel stableyard with plenty of chairs, benches and tables. A pretty six-table parlour on the right has another big log fire. Bedrooms are comfortable and up to date.

🍴⭐ Top rated food includes chicken, bacon and pistachio terrine with red onion marmalade, grilled fresh mackerel with lime, chilli and soy dip, beetroot and parsnip hash cakes with a poached egg, savoury cheesecake with roasted squash, baby tomatoes and basil, guinea fowl breast with sage and onion stuffing and celeriac and apple purée, herb-crusted cod fillet with parsnip mash and lemon and white wine sauce, slow-cooked local pork belly with white bean, tomato and chorizo stew, and puddings such as vanilla pannacotta with raspberry sorbet and boozy cherries and bakewell tart with custard. *Benchmark main dish: roast local lamb with red onion tarte tatin with fondant potato and red wine jus £18.50. Two-course evening meal £23.00.*

Free house ~ Licensees Tim and Janie Elwes ~ Real ale ~ Open 11-3, 6-10.30; closed Sun evening in winter ~ Bar food 12-2, 6-8.30; 12-2, 6.30-8 Mon; 12.30-2.30, 6.30-8 Sun ~ Restaurant ~ Children welcome ~ Dogs allowed in bar and bedrooms ~ Wi-fi ~ Bedrooms: £75/£110 *Recommended by Brian and Sally Wakeham, Alison and Graeme Spicer, Chloe and Tim Hodge, Karl and Frieda Bujeya, Charlie May, Beth Aldridge*

WOODBASTWICK
TG3214 Map 8

Fur & Feather 🍺

(01603) 720003 – www.thefurandfeather.co.uk

Off B1140 E of Norwich; NR13 6HQ

Full range of first class Woodfordes brewery ales, friendly service and popular bar food

Of course, the ale here is perfectly kept as Woodfordes brewery is just next door. It's a charming place converted from a row of thatched cottage buildings in a lovely Estate village. Efficient, helpful staff dispense Bure Gold, Nelsons Revenge, Norfolk Nog, Reedlighter and Wherry, plus two guests, all tapped from the cask; also, a dozen wines by the glass and 12 malt whiskies. The style and atmosphere are not what you'd expect of a brewery tap – it's set out more like a comfortable and roomy dining pub with wooden chairs and tables on tiles or carpeting, plus sofas and armchairs; background music. There are seats and tables in the pleasant garden where they keep chickens. You can also visit the brewery shop (and if you eat here, you get a ten per cent discount voucher for the shop).

🍴 Good food includes sandwiches (until 5pm), spiced jerk chicken with coleslaw, local cheese and mushroom bruschetta, vegetarian tart of the day, local sausages and mash with caramelised onion gravy, beer-battered fish and chips, beef and kidney pudding, sea bass with camomile tea sauce, honey-glazed pork loin with bubble and squeak, sirloin steak with onion rings, chips and a choice of sauce, and puddings such as lemon tart with fruit compote and fudge brownie with ice-cream. *Benchmark main dish: pie of the day £13.95. Two-course evening meal £20.00.*

Woodfordes ~ Tenant Daniel Pratt ~ Real ale ~ Open 10am-11pm ~ Bar food 12-2.30, 5.30-8.30; all day in high season ~ Restaurant ~ Children welcome ~ Dogs allowed in bar ~ Wi-fi *Recommended by Dave & Sue, Matthew and Elisabeth Reeves, Christopher May, Elise and Charles Mackinlay, Mark Morgan, Jasmine Voos, Richard and Tessa Ibbot*

'Children welcome' means the pub says it lets children inside without any special restriction. If it allows them in, but to restricted areas such as an eating area or family room, we specify this. Places with separate restaurants often let children use them, and hotels usually let children into public areas such as lounges. Some pubs impose an evening time limit – let us know if you find one earlier than 9pm.

Also Worth a Visit in Norfolk

Besides the fully inspected pubs, you might like to try these pubs that have been recommended to us and described by readers. Do tell us what you think of them: feedback@goodguides.com

AYLMERTON TG1840
Roman Camp (01263) 838291
Holt Road (A148); NR11 8QD Large 19th-c mock-Tudor roadside inn – some recent refurbishment; comfortable panelled bar, cosy sitting room off with warm fire and light airy dining room, decent choice of enjoyable sensibly priced food from sandwiches up, well kept Adnams, Greene King and guests such as Humpty Dumpty, friendly helpful service from uniformed staff; free wi-fi; children welcome, attractive sheltered garden behind with sunny terraces and pond, 16 well appointed bedrooms, substantial breakfast, open (and food) all day. *(Ian Herdman)*

AYLSHAM TG1926
★ Black Boys (01263) 732122
Market Place; off B1145; NR11 6EH Small friendly hotel with imposing Georgian façade; informal open-plan beamed bar with comfortable seating and plenty of tables on carpet or bare boards, popular generously served food from snacks up including good Sun roasts, Adnams, guest ales and 25 wines by the glass, friendly attentive staff coping well at busy times; children and dogs welcome, seats in front by marketplace, more behind, eight bedrooms, big cooked breakfast from 8am, open all day, food all day Fri-Sun. *(John Wooll, M G Hart)*

BANNINGHAM TG2129
★ Crown (01263) 733534
Colby Road; opposite church by village green; NR11 7DY Welcoming 17th-c beamed pub in same family for 28 years; good choice of popular food (they're helpful with gluten-free diets), well kept Greene King, local guest ales and decent wines, friendly efficient service, log fires and woodburners; events including annual jazz festival and winter quiz nights (last Tues of month), TV, free wi-fi; children and dogs welcome, disabled access, open (and food) all day weekends. *(David Twitchett)*

BARTON BENDISH TF7105
Berney Arms (01366) 347995
Off A1122 W of Swaffham; Church Road; PE33 9GF Attractive dining pub in quiet village; good freshly made food from pub favourites to more inventive dishes including good value set lunch, Adnams ales, two guests and several wines by the glass, afternoon teas, restaurant; children and dogs (in bar) welcome, nice garden with gazebos and unusual church tower slide, good bedrooms in converted stables and forge (also two in main building), open all day, food all day Sun. *(Chloe and Guy Hodge)*

BINHAM TF9839
Chequers (01328) 830297
B1388 SW of Blakeney; NR21 0AL Long low-beamed 17th-c local away from the bustle of the coastal pubs; comfortable bar with coal fires at each end, Adnams Southwold, Norfolk Brewhouse Moon Gazer Golden and guests, enjoyable pub food at reasonable prices, friendly staff; various games; children and dogs welcome, picnic-sets in front and on back grass, interesting village with huge priory church, open all day weekends. *(David Jackman)*

BLAKENEY TG0243
Kings Arms (01263) 740341
West Gate Street; NR25 7NQ A stroll from the harbour to this chatty 18th-c pub; three simple low-ceilinged connecting rooms and airy garden room, Woodfordes and guests, generous wholesome food from breakfast on; children and dogs welcome, big garden, seven bedrooms, open (and food) all day from 9.30am (midday Sun). *(Paddy and Sian O'Leary)*

BLICKLING TG1728
Bucks Arms (01263) 732133
B1354 NW of Aylsham; NR11 6NF Handsome Jacobean inn well placed by gates to Blickling Hall (NT); small proper bar, dining lounge with woodburner and smarter more formal restaurant with another fire, Adnams and a guest such as Wolf, several wines by the glass and substantial helpings of enjoyable pub food, good friendly service; background music; children and dogs welcome, tables out on lawn, excellent walks nearby, three bedrooms, open all day, food all day Sun. *(David Twitchett, Tracey and Stephen Groves)*

BODHAM STREET TG1240
Red Hart (01263) 588270
The Street; NR25 6AD Old family-run village pub with well liked fairly traditional home-cooked food from lunchtime ciabattas up, three real ales, friendly helpful service; occasional live music and quiz nights, sports TV, pool, free wi-fi; children and dogs welcome (menus for both), garden picnic-sets, open all day. *(Peter and Emma Kelly)*

BRAMERTON TG2905
Waters Edge (01508) 538005
Mill Hill, N of village, by river; NR14 7ED Clean modern pub-restaurant in great spot overlooking bend of River Yare;

popular if not especially cheap food including daily specials (booking recommended in summer), ales such as Adnams and Woodfordes, plenty of wines by the glass, efficient friendly service; free wi-fi; children welcome, wheelchair access, circular picnic-sets on waterside deck, moorings, open all day in summer, closed Mon and Tues in winter. *(Julie Swift)*

BRANCASTER   TF7743
Ship (01485) 210333
London Street (A149); PE31 8AP Popular roadside inn under new management; compact bar with built-in cushioned and planked wall seats, four local ales and plenty of wines by the glass from oak counter, several dining areas, well liked food from lunchtime sandwiches up, friendly helpful staff, contemporary paintwork throughout, nice mix of furniture on rugs and bare boards, bookcases, shipping memorabilia and lots of prints, woodburner; background music; children and dogs welcome, gravelled seating area with circular picnic-sets out by car park, nine attractive well equipped bedrooms, open all day, food all day Sun. *(Millie and Peter Downing)*

BRANCASTER STAITHE   TF7944
★ Jolly Sailors (01485) 210314
Main Road (A149); PE31 8BJ Unpretentious pub set in prime bird-watching area on edge of NT dunes and salt flats; chatty mix of locals and visitors in simply furnished bars, wheelbacks, settles and cushioned benches around mix of tables on quarry tiles, photographs and local maps on the walls, woodburner, their own Brancaster ales (brewery not on site) and local guests, several wines by the glass, sizeable back dining room with popular food including pizzas (prices reasonable for the area), cheerful staff coping well at busy times (may ask for a card if running a tab); children and dogs welcome, plenty of picnic-sets and play equipment in peaceful back garden, ice-cream hut in summer, vine-covered terrace, open all day (food all day in season). *(Ian Herdman, Euan Blundell, Neil and Angela Huxter)*

BRANCASTER STAITHE   TF8044
★ White Horse (01485) 210262
A149 E of Hunstanton; PE31 8BY Popular restauranty place, but does have proper informal front bar serving own Brancaster beers (also in bottles), guest ales, lots of wines by the glass (including local rosé) and good range of gins, log fire, pine furniture, historical photographs and bar billiards, middle part with comfortable sofas and newspapers, splendid views over tidal marshes from airy dining conservatory and raised lounge, good bar and restaurant food including tapas and plenty of fish, friendly efficient staff (may ask for a credit card if running a tab); children and dogs (in

bar) welcome, seats on sun deck enjoying the view, more under cover on heated front terrace, 15 nice bedrooms, coast path at bottom of garden, open (and bar food) all day, breakfast from 9am. *(Tracey and Stephen Groves, W K Wood, Roy Hoing, Ian Herdman, Neil and Angela Huxter)*

BRISLEY   TF9521
Brisley Bell (01362) 705024
B1145; The Green; NR20 5DW Refurbished 17th-c pub in good spot on edge of sheep-grazed common (one of England's biggest); friendly atmosphere, various areas ranging from cosy beamed snug with large open fire to airy garden room, well liked interesting food (not Sun evening) including set lunch, Adnams and local guests, nice wines and decent range of other drinks (norfolk whisky/gin), friendly efficient service; events such as live music, charity auctions and quiz nights; children and dogs welcome, terrace and good-sized garden, bedrooms in converted outbuildings, closed Mon, otherwise open all day. *(Gina Foster, Christopher and Elise Way)*

BROCKDISH   TM2179
Old Kings Head (01379) 668843
The Street; IP21 4JY Light and airy old pub at centre of village; several well kept changing ales, decent wines by the glass and over 100 gins, enjoyable food with Italian slant including good pizzas, friendly helpful staff, L-shaped beamed bar with comfortable leather sofa, tub chairs, pews and scrubbed wooden tables on bare boards, log fire, steps up to smaller seating area, café serving good coffee and cakes, maybe local artwork for sale; live music nights; popular with Angles Way walkers, dogs welcome in bar, a few tables out at the side, closed Mon, otherwise open (and food) all day, shuts 9pm Sun. *(Sarah Roberts)*

BROOKE   TM2899
Kings Head (01508) 550335
Norwich Road (B1332); NR15 1AB Welcoming 17th-c village pub with enjoyable food from traditional choices up including regular themed evenings, four real ales and excellent choice of wines by the glass, maybe a Norfolk whisky, light and airy bare-boards bar with log fire, eating area up a step; occasional quiz and live music nights, free wi-fi; children and dogs welcome, tables in sheltered garden, open all day (from 9.30am weekends for breakfast). *(Mat)*

BROOME   TM3591
Artichoke (01986) 893325
Yarmouth Road; NR35 2NZ Unpretentious split-level roadside pub with up to ten well kept ales (some from tap room casks) including Adnams, belgian fruit beers and excellent selection of whiskies, good traditional home-made food in bar or dining room, friendly helpful staff, wood

and flagstone floors, log fire in big fireplace; dogs welcome, garden picnic-sets, smokers' shelter, good walks nearby, closed Mon otherwise open all day. *(Kim Holt)*

BURNHAM MARKET   TF8342
Hoste (01328) 738777
The Green (B1155); PE31 8HD Stylish hotel's character front bar with informal chatty atmosphere; leather dining chairs, settles and armchairs, wood-effect flooring, farming implements and cartoons on the walls, woodburner, well kept ales including Woodfordes, Aspall's cider, 25 wines by the glass from extensive list and several malt whiskies, enjoyable if not cheap food including lunchtime sandwiches, afternoon teas, elegant dining areas, bustling conservatory and smart airy back restaurant; children and dogs (in bar) welcome, attractive garden, luxurious bedrooms, open all day from 9am. *(David Jackman, D and NF, Tracey and Stephen Groves)*

BURNHAM MARKET   TF8342
Nelson (01328) 738321
Creake Road; PE31 8EN Dining pub with nice food from sandwiches and pub favourites to more ambitious dishes in bar and restaurant, pleasant efficient staff, well kept Adnams Ghost Ship, Woodfordes Wherry and guests from pale wood servery, extensive wine list, L-shaped bar with leather sofas and armchairs, local artwork for sale; children and dogs welcome, terrace picnic-sets under parasols, seven bedrooms (two in converted outbuilding), open all day. *(Tony Scott)*

BURNHAM OVERY
STAITHE   TF8444
★ ## Hero (01328) 738334
Wells Road (A149); PE31 8JE Spacious refurbished roadside pub (sister to the Anchor at Morston – see Main Entries); good choice of well liked often inventive food from sandwiches and snacks up (booking advised), three real ales such as Adnams and Grain, decent wines and interesting range of gins, friendly young staff, large bar and separate pitched-ceiling restaurant, woodburners; children and dogs welcome, terrace seating front and back, bedrooms, open all day from 9am. *(Roy Hoing)*

CHEDGRAVE   TM3699
White Horse (01508) 520250
Norwich Road; NR14 6ND Welcoming pub with five well kept ales such as Adnams and Timothy Taylors, decent wines by the glass and good choice of sensibly priced food (all day Sun) including a 'healthy options' menu and themed nights, friendly attentive staff, log fire and sofas in bar, restaurant, occasional steak nights; some live music, comedy nights, pool and darts; children and dogs welcome, garden picnic-sets, open all day. *(Max and Steph Warren)*

COCKLEY CLEY   TF7904
Twenty Churchwardens
(01760) 721439 *Off A1065 S of Swaffham; PE37 8AN* Informal pub in converted school next to church; two well kept Adnams ales and enjoyable well-priced food including home-made pies, three linked beamed rooms, good open fire; no credit cards; children and dogs (particularly) welcome, tiny unspoilt village. *(Lyn and Freddie Roberts)*

COLTISHALL   TG2719
Kings Head (01603) 737426
Wroxham Road (B1354); NR12 7EA Dining pub close to River Bure and moorings; imaginative food from owner-chef (especially fish/seafood), also bar snacks, lunchtime set menu and children's choices, well kept Adnams and two guests, good wines by the glass, open fire, fishing nets and stuffed fish including a monster pike; background music; no dogs, seats outside (noisy road), four bedrooms, open (and food) all day Sun. *(Neil Allen)*

COLTON   TG1009
Norfolk Lurcher (01603) 880794
Village signed from A47 at Blind Lane, W of Easton; NR9 5DG Family-run barn conversion in small village; friendly relaxed atmosphere in large comfortable beamed bar, some old enamel signs and other memorabilia, woodburner, four well kept changing local ales, decent wines and fine range of whiskies, good food including extensive specials board and vegetarian choices, restaurant, monthly jazz nights; children and dogs welcome (friendly pub dog is Alfie), terrace and big garden with lake, eight bedrooms, shuts 9pm Sun and Tues lunchtime. *(Liz Nicholas, Daniel Nixon)*

CONGHAM   TF7123
Anvil (01485) 600625
St Andrews Lane; PE32 1DU Tucked-away modern country pub with welcoming licensees; wide choice of generously served home-made food (smaller helpings available) including good value Sun carvery, quick friendly service, three or more well kept ales (at least one local); live music and quiz nights; children welcome, no dogs inside, picnic-sets in small walled front garden, campsite, closed Mon, otherwise open all day. *(Gus Swan)*

CROMER   TG2242
Red Lion (01263) 514964
Off A149; Tucker Street/Brook Street; NR27 9HD Substantial Victorian hotel with elevated views over the sea and pier; original features including panelling and open fires, up to six well kept local ales, a couple of ciders and decent wines in bustling bare-boards flint-walled bar, good food from sandwiches and sharing plates up, efficient

friendly service, spacious restaurant and conservatory; background music; children and dogs welcome, disabled access/loos, tables in back courtyard, 14 comfortable bedrooms (some with great view), open all day. *(Tina and David Woods-Taylor, Revd R P Tickle, Dr J Barrie Jones)*

DEREHAM TF9813
George (01362) 696801
Swaffham Road; NR19 2AZ Welcoming 18th-c inn/restaurant; enjoyable generously served food at fair prices including popular Fri steak night and some themed evenings, monthly cookery demonstrations, Adnams and Woodfordes ales, friendly helpful staff, panelled interior with decent sized bar, dining room and conservatory; children and dogs welcome, heated terrace, seven bedrooms (two in annexe), open all day. *(Lucy and Giles Gibson)*

DERSINGHAM TF6930
Coach & Horses (01485) 540391
Manor Road; PE31 6LN Friendly local with well kept Woodfordes Wherry, a couple of guest beers and enjoyable food including daily specials, cheerful efficient service, bar and back dining room; Thurs quiz, some live music; children and dogs (in bar) welcome, painted picnic-sets in garden with play area and pétanque, three bedrooms, open all day, no food Sun evening. *(Tracey and Stephen Groves)*

DERSINGHAM TF6930
Feathers (01485) 540768
B1440 towards Sandringham; Manor Road; PE31 6LN Jacobean carrstone inn (once part of the Sandringham Estate); two adjoining bars (main one with big open fire), well kept Adnams, Woodfordes and a guest, good value food including OAP lunch deal Mon-Fri, friendly helpful service, back dining room; background music; children and dogs welcome (there's a pub dog), large garden with play area, function room in converted stables, six bedrooms, open all day, food all day weekends. *(David Jackman)*

EAST RUDHAM TF8228
★ **Crown** (01485) 528530
A148 W of Fakenham; The Green; PE31 8RD Civilised open-plan beamed pub by village green; main room with log fire at one end, wooden and brown leather dining chairs around mixed tables on rugs and stripped boards, Adnams, Black Sheep, Woodfordes and a guest, 20 wines by the glass, decent choice of enjoyable food from sandwiches up, friendly service, pubbier part with built-in cushioned seats and high chairs against handsome slate-topped counter, lower snug towards the back and upstairs dining room with high-pitched ceiling and woodburner; children and dogs welcome, partial wheelchair access (no disabled loos), seats under parasols on front gravelled

terrace, comfortable bedrooms, open all day, food all day Sun. *(David Jackman, Barbara Brown, Jill and Dick Archer, Max Simons, Derek and Sylvia Stephenson, Tracey and Stephen Groves)*

EDGEFIELD TG0934
Pigs (01263) 587634
Norwich Road; B1149 S of Holt; NR24 2RL Popular country pub with rooms; Adnams, Greene King, Woodfordes and a house beer brewed by Wolf tapped from casks in tiled-floor bar, dining areas either side, one split into stalls by standing timbers and low brick walls, the other light and airy with white-painted floorboards, some interesting artwork, good variety of well liked food (all day Sun) including norfolk tapas, games room with pool and table football, also children's playroom; background music; dogs allowed in bar, good wheelchair access, rustic furniture on big covered front terrace, adventure playground, boules, ten bedrooms (seven with spa facilities including sauna and outside bath), open all day from 8am (breakfast for non-residents). *(Tracey and Stephen Groves)*

ELSING TG0516
Mermaid (01362) 637640
Church Road; NR20 3EA Welcoming 17th-c pub in quiet little village; L-shaped carpeted bar with woodburner, well kept Adnams, Woodfordes and guests tapped from the cask, enjoyable home-made food including range of pies and suet puddings (signature steak and kidney roly-poly), indian and thai curries also available, Tues steak night, friendly helpful service; pool and other games such as dominoes and shut the box, free wi-fi; children and dogs welcome, disabled facilities, handy for walkers on Wensum Way, nice garden, 14th-c church opposite with interesting brasses, closed Mon lunchtime. *(Lucy and Giles Gibson)*

GELDESTON TM3991
Wherry (01508) 518371
The Street; NR34 0LB Welcoming little red-brick village pub with enjoyable home-made food including bargain OAP lunch (Mon, Weds, Thurs), well kept Adnams and decent wines by the glass, tea room (Fri-Sun till 4pm); quiz second Thurs of month; children and dogs welcome, pleasant garden, good walks and handy for Rowan Craft Marina, afternoon break Mon-Weds, otherwise open all day, food till 6pm Sun. *(M J Winterton)*

GREAT BIRCHAM TF7632
Kings Head (01485) 578265
B1155, S end of village (called and signed Bircham locally); PE31 6RJ Handsome Edwardian hotel with cheerful little bar; comfortable sofas, tub chairs and log fire, three well kept local ales such as Woodfordes, good range of wines, whiskies

and over 80 gins, lounge areas and airy modern restaurant with varied choice of much liked food, friendly helpful staff; background music, free wi-fi; children and dogs welcome, tables out at front and in back garden with nice country views, 12 comfortable bedrooms, open all day, food all day during summer school holidays. *(David Jackman)*

GREAT CRESSINGHAM TF8401
★ **Windmill** (01760) 756232
Village signed off A1065-S of Swaffham; Water End; IP25 6NN Shuttered red-brick inn with interesting pictures and bric-a-brac in warren of rambling linked rooms, plenty of cosy corners; wide choice of tasty food from sandwiches to chargrills, a house beer (Windy Miller) brewed by Purity along with Adnams, Greene King and two guests, good choice of wines by the glass and extensive range of whiskies/gins, friendly efficient staff; background music, big sports TV in side snug, games room with pool and other pub games; children and dogs welcome, picnic-sets and good play area in large garden, caravan parking, 15 bedrooms, open all day from 7.30am for breakfast. *(Brian Glozier)*

HAPPISBURGH TG3831
Hill House (01692) 650004
By village church; NR12 0PW Comfortable traditional village pub with Arthur Conan Doyle association; heavy-beamed bar with woodburner in brick inglenook, half a dozen well kept ales including own Dancing Men brews, good reasonably priced food from sandwiches and baguettes up, Sun carvery, friendly landlord and separate restaurant in converted stables; pool and darts; children and dogs welcome, tables out front and back, bedrooms (one in former signal box), nice setting near the sea, open all day. *(Revd R P Tickle)*

HARPLEY TF7825
Rose & Crown (01485) 521807
Off A148 Fakenham–King's Lynn; Nethergate Street; PE31 6TW Old village pub run well by friendly licensees; good generously served home-made food including popular Sun roasts, well kept Woodfordes Wherry and guests, Aspall's cider, modernised interior with open fires; free wi-fi; children and dogs welcome, picnic-sets in garden, open (and food) all day. *(David Jackman)*

HEYDON TG1127
★ **Earle Arms** (01263) 587376
Off B1149; NR11 6AD Popular old dutch-gabled pub overlooking green and church in delightfully unspoilt Estate village; well kept Adnams, Woodfordes and a guest, food

from varied if not extensive menu using local fish and meat (gluten-free choices marked), decent wine list, old-fashioned candlelit bar with racing prints, some stuffed animals and good log fire, more formal dining room; free wi-fi; children and dogs welcome, picnic-sets in small cottagey back garden, open all day Sun (no evening food then), closed Mon. *(John Rooney)*

HICKLING TG4123
Greyhound (01692) 598306
The Green; NR12 0YA Popular little village pub with welcoming long-serving landlord; enjoyable fairly pubby food in bar and neat restaurant, three or four well kept ales including Adnams, local cider, nice open fire; sports TV, free wi-fi; well behaved children and dogs welcome, seats out at front and in pretty back garden with covered terrace, handy for Hickling Broad and nature reserve, open all day but may shut early if quiet. *(Roy Hoing, Peter and Anne Hollindale)*

HILBOROUGH TF8200
Swan (01760) 756380
Brandon Road (A1065); IP26 5BW Welcoming early 18th-c pub with good quality food including interesting blackboard specials and Sun carvery, also a gluten-free menu, up to four well kept beers and sensibly priced wine list, pleasant helpful staff, small back restaurant; free wi-fi; children and dogs (in bar) welcome, picnic-sets on sheltered lawn, eight bedrooms, open all day, food all day Fri-Sun. *(Beth Aldridge)*

HINGHAM TG0202
White Hart (01953) 850214
Market Place, just off B1108 W of Norwich; NR9 4AF Georgian-fronted coaching inn with character rooms arranged over two floors; beams and standing timbers, stripped floorboards with oriental rugs, mix of furniture including comfortable sofas in quiet corners, lots of prints and photographs, woodburners, galleried long room up steps from main bar with egyptian frieze, upstairs dining/function room, good choice of enjoyable food including british tapas, four real ales, lots of wines by the glass and cocktails; background music, bar billiards; children welcome, dogs downstairs, modern benches and seats in gravelled courtyard, pretty village with huge 14th-c church, five refurbished bedrooms, open all day, food all day weekends. *(Gus Swan)*

HOLME-NEXT-THE-SEA TF7043
White Horse (01485) 525512
Kirkgate Street; PE36 6LH Attractive old-fashioned place with warm log fires and lots of nooks and crannies; ample choice of enjoyable inexpensive food including local

---

Real ale to us means beer that has matured naturally in its cask – not pressurised or filtered. We name all real ales stocked.

fish, friendly efficient service, Adnams, Greene King and decent wines, side extension; children and dogs welcome, small back garden, more seats out in front and on lawn opposite, play area, open all day. *(John Wooll)*

HOLT
TG0738

Feathers (01263) 712318

Market Place; NR25 6BW Relaxed hotel with popular locals' bar comfortably extended around original panelled area, open fire, antiques in attractive entrance/reception area, good choice of enjoyable fairly priced food including blackboard specials, Wed thai and Thurs curry nights, friendly accommodating service, Greene King ales and decent wines, good coffee, restaurant and dining conservatory; background music; children and dogs (in bar) welcome, 14 comfortable bedrooms, open all day. *(John Evans)*

HONINGHAM
TG1011

Honingham Buck (01603) 880393

Just off A47 W of Norwich; The Street; NR9 5BL Picturesque and smartly renovated 16th-c pub; beamed and timbered bar with flagstones and inglenook woodburner, Lacons beers and plenty of wines by the glass including champagne, very good imaginative food from unusual snacks up, friendly attentive service, comfortable restaurant with upholstered chairs and banquettes; children welcome, seats on sheltered lawn, eight clean modern bedrooms in converted outbuildings, open all day, food all day Sun till 7pm. *(Dr Peter Crawshaw)*

HORSEY
TG4622

★Nelson Head (01493) 393378

Off B1159; The Street; NR29 4AD Red-brick country pub, nicely tucked away and unspoilt, with impressive range of beers (some tapped from the cask), proper ciders and good sensibly priced bar food from sandwiches and snacks to daily specials, friendly chatty staff, log fire and lots of interesting bric-a-brac including various guns, small side dining room; quiet background music; children welcome, well behaved dogs in bar, outside seating (some in field opposite), good coast walks (seals), open all day, no food Sun evening in winter. *(Alison and Graeme Spicer)*

HORSTEAD
TG2619

Recruiting Sergeant (01603) 737077

B1150 just S of Coltishall; NR12 7EE Light, airy and spacious roadside pub – busy and well run; good generously served food from wraps and jacket potatoes up including ample fish choice (booking recommended), efficient welcoming staff, up to half a dozen changing ales such as Adnams, Greene King, Timothy Taylors and Woodfordes, over 25 wines by the glass, big open fire; children and dogs welcome, terrace and garden

tables, variety of local walks, five comfortable bedrooms, open all day, breakfasts from 8am (9am weekends). *(Tony and Jill Radnor)*

HUNWORTH
TG0735

Bell (01263) 711151

Signed off B roads S of Holt; NR24 2AA Renovated 18th-c beamed pub (known locally as the Hunny Bell) under same ownership as the Duck at Stanhoe; neat bar with country chairs around wooden tables, stone floor and woodburner, cosy snug and high-raftered restaurant, enjoyable food from sandwiches and pubby choices to more restauranty dishes cooked by landlord-chef, five real ales such as Greene King, Woodfordes and Yetmans, friendly helpful service; children and dogs welcome, wheelchair access, tables on terrace overlooking village green, more seats in garden among fruit trees, open all day, food all day Sun. *(Lyn and Freddie Roberts)*

ITTERINGHAM
TG1430

★Walpole Arms (01263) 587258

Village signposted off B1354 NW of Aylsham; NR11 7AR 18th-c country pub owned by local farming family; beamed and timbered open-plan bar with woodburner, stripped-brick walls and cushioned wooden dining chairs around dark tables on red carpet, Adnams Grain, Norfolk Brewhouse Moon Gazer and a guest from Woodfordes, several wines by the glass and quite a few gins, very good modern cooking using local ingredients (some from the farm), airy restaurant; live jazz some summer evenings; children and dogs (in bar) welcome, vine-covered terrace and two-acre landscaped garden, handy for Blickling Hall (NT), open all day Sat, closed Sun evening. *(David Twitchett, Patricia and Gordon Tucker; Alan and Linda Blackmore, Clive and Fran Dutson)*

KING'S LYNN
TF6120

Crown & Mitre (01553) 774669

Ferry Street; PE30 1LJ Old-fashioned unchanging pub in great riverside spot; lots of interesting naval and nautical memorabilia, up to six well kept ales and good value straightforward home-made food, river-view back conservatory; no credit cards; well behaved children and dogs allowed, quayside tables; may be for sale. *(John Wooll)*

KING'S LYNN
TF6119

Goldings (01553) 602388

Saturday Market Place; PE30 5DQ Corner bar-restaurant-café dating from the 18th c (former Wenns hotel); clean-cut modern décor with light wood furnishings, pastel shades and pendant lighting, enjoyable reasonably priced food from traditional choices up, good selection of beers and other drinks including 25 gins, happy hour 5-7pm, relaxed friendly atmosphere; next-door deli; children and dogs welcome, six bedrooms named after former licensees, open (and food) all day from 8am for breakfast. *(John Wooll, Jess Marlow)*

KING'S LYNN   TF6119
Marriotts Warehouse
(01553) 818500
South Quay; PE30 5DT Bar-restaurant-café in converted 16th-c brick and stone warehouse; well priced food from lunchtime sandwiches and light dishes up (greater evening choice), good range of wines, three real ales, cocktails, small upstairs bar with river views; children welcome, quayside tables, open all day from 10am.
(Dr J Barrie Jones)

LESSINGHAM   TG3928
Star (01692) 580510
School Road; NR12 0DN Popular little pub on outskirts of village; low ceilings and inglenook woodburner, local ales and ample helpings of enjoyable reasonably priced food, warm friendly service, small back restaurant; children and dogs welcome, good-sized garden, two bedrooms in building behind, closed Mon, no food Sun evening. *(Roy Hoing)*

LETHERINGSETT   TG0638
Kings Head (01263) 712691
A148 (Holt Road) W of Holt; NR25 7AR Country house-style dining inn under same ownership as the Jolly Sailors in Brancaster; rugs on quarry tiles, hunting/coaching prints and open fires, own Brancaster beer along with Adnams, Norfolk Brewhouse Moon Gazer and Woodfordes, food from good sandwiches and pubby choices up, skylit bare-boards dining room with built-in wall seating, farm tools on cream-painted flint and cob walls, back area under partly pitched ceiling with painted rafters; background music, sports TV, free wi-fi; children and dogs welcome, picnic-sets out at front and in big garden with play area, four bedrooms, open all day. *(M and GR, James Tilley, Clive and Fran Dutson)*

LYNG   TG0617
Fox (01603) 872316
The Street; NR9 5AL Old beamed village pub with several linked areas and separate restaurant; ample helpings of good inexpensive home-made food including Mon street-food menu, Tues steak night and midweek two-course lunch deal, ales such as Adnams and Woodfordes, friendly staff; pool and giant chessboard in one part; children and dogs (in front bar) welcome, enclosed garden with view of church, open all day in summer apart from Mon lunchtime.
(Chloe and Guy Hodge)

MARSHAM   TG1924
Plough (01263) 735000
Old Norwich Road; NR10 5PS Welcoming 18th-c inn with open-plan split-level bar; enjoyable food using local produce (special diets catered for) including good value set lunch, Adnams Southwold and a couple of guests, friendly helpful staff; free wi-fi; children welcome, dogs in garden only, comfortable bedrooms, lock-up for bicycles, open all day. *(Peter and Emma Kelly)*

MUNDFORD   TL8093
Crown (01842) 878233
Off A1065 Thetford–Swaffham; Crown Road; IP26 5HQ Unassuming 17th-c pub with heavy beams, huge fireplace and interesting local memorabilia, ales such as Courage Directors and Woodfordes Wherry, over 50 malt whiskies, enjoyable generously served food at sensible prices, friendly staff, spiral iron stairs to two restaurant areas (larger one has separate entrance accessible to wheelchairs), locals' bar with sports TV; children and dogs welcome, back terrace and garden with wishing well, bedrooms (some in adjoining building), also self-catering accommodation, open all day. *(Beth Aldridge)*

NEATISHEAD   TG3421
White Horse (01692) 630828
The Street; NR12 8AD Multi-roomed red-brick village pub (sister to the Lion at Thurne); open fire in traditional quarry-tiled bar with unusual beer-glass lights hanging from ceiling, pump clips decorating the walls, good selection of cask and keg beers (some brewed here) and plenty of other drinks including a house gin infused with hops, generally well liked food from ciabattas up, modern galleried restaurant extension with view into microbrewery; quiz nights and some live music, TV, darts; children and dogs (in main bar) welcome, small courtyard behind, popular with boaters (mooring nearby), open all day. *(Simon King)*

NEW BUCKENHAM   TM0890
Inn on the Green (01953) 860172
Chapel Street; NR16 2BB Modern renovation of late Victorian red-brick pub by little green close to the Kings Head; emphasis on good freshly prepared food from pub favourites to more restauranty dishes including blackboard specials, well kept ales and good selection of wines, pleasant efficient staff; children (away from bar) and dogs (in bar) welcome, terrace tables, handy for Banham Zoo, closed Mon.
(Paul Farraday)

NEW BUCKENHAM   TM0890
Kings Head (01953) 861247
Market Place; NR16 2AN Family-run 17th-c pub by small green opposite medieval market cross; ales such as Adnams Southwold and generous helpings of popular reasonably priced pubby food (booking advised), helpful service, modern open-plan bar with beams and inglenook, big back dining area; pool, free wi-fi; five bedrooms, open all day.
(Millie and Peter Downing)

NORTH CREAKE   TF8538
Jolly Farmers (01328) 738185
Burnham Road; NR21 9JW Former
coaching inn in charming flintstone village;
main bar with large open fire in brick
fireplace, mix of farmhouse and high-backed
leather dining chairs around scrubbed pine
tables on quarry tiles, Adnams Broadside,
Woodfordes Wherry and a guest or two, 11
wines by the glass and a dozen malt whiskies,
smaller bar with pews and woodburner,
another in dining room (no food as we went
to press); children and dogs welcome, plenty
of seats on terrace, self-catering cottage,
closed Sun evening, Mon and Tues.
(Bridget and Peter Gregson)

NORTH TUDDENHAM   TG0413
Lodge (01362) 638466
Off A47; NR20 3DJ Popular modernised
dining pub; good sensibly priced food from
traditional choices up including burger
menu and various sizzling dishes, Weds steak
night, local beers (just one in winter) such
as Woodfordes Reedlighter, friendly attentive
service; monthly quiz; children and dogs (in
bar) welcome, tables outside (some on deck),
closed Sun evening and Mon, otherwise open
(and food) all day. *(Victoria Hunt)*

NORTHREPPS   TG2439
Foundry Arms (01263) 579256
Church Street; NR27 0AA Welcoming
village pub with good reasonably priced
traditional food (not Sun evening) from
generous sandwiches up, well kept
Woodfordes Wherry and a couple of guests,
decent choice of wines, good friendly service,
woodburner, smallish comfortable restaurant;
pool and darts in separate area; children and
dogs welcome, picnic-sets in back garden,
open all day. *(Tina and David Woods-Taylor)*

NORWICH   TG2309
Adam & Eve (01603) 667423
*Bishopgate; follow Palace Street from
Tombland, N of cathedral; NR3 1RZ*
Ancient pub dating from at least 1240 when
used by workmen building the cathedral,
has a Saxon well beneath the lower bar floor
and striking dutch gables (added in 14th and
15th c); old-fashioned small bars with tiled or
parquet floors, cushioned benches built into
partly panelled walls and some antique high-
backed settles, three well kept ales such as
Adnams, Greene King and Wolf, Aspall's cider
and around 40 malt whiskies, traditional
pubby food (not Sun evening) from baguettes
up, friendly service; background music;
children allowed in snug till 7pm, no dogs
inside, picnic-sets out among pretty tubs and

hanging baskets, open all day, closed 25, 26
Dec, 1 Jan. *(Tracey and Stephen Groves)*

NORWICH   TG2408
Coach & Horses (01603) 477077
Thorpe Road; NR1 1BA Light and airy
tap for Chalk Hill brewery (tours available),
standard food from baguettes up including
lunch deals and Sat brunch, friendly staff,
L-shaped bare-boards bar with open fire,
pleasant back dining area; sports TVs, gets
very busy on home match days; disabled
access possible (not to lavatories), front
terrace, open all day. *(Lucy and Giles Gibson)*

NORWICH   TG2210
Duke of Wellington (01603) 441182
Waterloo Road; NR3 1EG Rambling corner
local with huge range of well kept quickly
changing ales including Fullers, Oakham
and Wolf, many served from tap room casks,
foreign bottled beers too, no food apart from
sausage rolls and pies (can bring your own)
and weekend summer barbecue, real fire;
live music and quiz nights, Aug and Oct beer
festivals, traditional games, free wi-fi; well
behaved dogs welcome, nice back terrace,
open all day. *(Neil Allen)*

NORWICH   TG2308
Edith Cavell (01603) 765813
Tombland/Princes Street; NR3 1HF
Corner pub-restaurant named after the
gallant World War I Norfolk nurse; popular
fairly priced food from sandwiches to good
steaks cooked on hot rocks, three real ales
including a house beer from Wolf, helpful
helpful service, smallish bar, upstairs
restaurant (and loos); diagonally across
from Erpingham Gate leading into cathedral
green, open all day (till 1am Fri, Sat).
(Lucy and Giles Gibson)

NORWICH   TG2310
Fat Cat Tap (01603) 413153
Lawson Road; NR3 4LF This 1970s
shed-like building is home to the Fat Cat
brewery and sister pub to the Fat Cat (see
Main Entries); good buzzy atmosphere, their
ales and up to 12 guests along with draught
continentals, lots of bottled beers and eight
or more local ciders/perries, no food apart
from chips (with or without toppings) and
cheeseboards, can also bring your own;
regular live music and quiz nights; dogs
welcome, children till 6pm, seats out front
and back, open all day. *(Jamie McClennan)*

NORWICH   TG2309
★ Kings Head (01603) 620468
Magdalen Street; NR3 1JE Traditional
Victorian local with good friendly atmosphere

A star symbol before the name of a pub shows exceptional character and appeal.
It doesn't mean extra comfort. Even quite a basic pub can win a star,
if it's individual enough.

in two simply furnished bare-boards bars (front one is tiny), a dozen very well kept changing regional ales, good choice of imported beers and a local cider, no food except pork pies; bar billiards in back bar, free wi-fi; dogs welcome, open all day. *(Neil Allen)*

NORWICH TG2208

Plough (01603) 661384

St Benedicts Street; NR2 4AR Small city-centre pub owned by Grain, their ales and guests kept well, good wines and cocktails, food limited to sausage pie, cheeseboards and summer barbecues, simply updated split-level interior with bare boards and open fire; background music; good spacious beer garden behind, open all day. *(Neil Allen)*

NORWICH TG2308

Ribs of Beef (01603) 619517

Wensum Street, S side of Fye Bridge; NR3 1HY Comfortable and welcoming riverside pub; nine real ales including Oakham, four traditional ciders and good wine choice, generous well priced lunchtime food (also Weds-Fri evenings), quick cheerful service, traditional carpeted bar with river views, smaller downstairs room; Sun live music, quiz every other Thurs, sports TV; children welcome, seats out on narrow waterside terrace, open all day. *(Lucy and Giles Gibson)*

NORWICH TG2308

St Andrews Brew House

(01603) 305995 *St Andrews Street; NR2 4TP* Interesting place visibly brewing its own good beers (can tour the brewery), also plenty of guest ales, craft kegs and bottled beers, utilitarian bare-boards interior with exposed ducting, rough masonry walls and eclectic mix of seating including some button-back booths, popular sensibly priced food from british tapas and sharing boards up, busy efficient staff, upstairs function room; background music, Weds quiz, sports TV; children and dogs welcome, pavement tables, open all day. *(Richard Tilbrook)*

NORWICH TG2309

Wig & Pen (01603) 625891

St Martins Palace Plain; NR3 1RN Popular 17th-c beamed pub opposite cathedral close; half a dozen well kept local ales including Adnams, Humpty Dumpty and Woodfordes, well priced wines and good value food from sandwiches up, prompt friendly service; background music, sports TVs, spring beer festival; metal café-style furniture out at front, open all day (till 6.30pm Sun). *(Revd R P Tickle)*

OLD HUNSTANTON TF6842

Lodge (01485) 532896

Old Hunstanton Road (A149); PE36 6HX Old red-brick roadside pub with clean contemporary décor; popular food in bar or restaurant from pizzas and pub favourites up, well kept local beers and good choice of wines by the glass, friendly helpful staff, plenty of seating on wood floors including booths and sofas by woodburner; sports TV, occasional live music; children and dogs (in bar) welcome, tables on covered terrace and small lawn, 16 good bedrooms, open all day. *(Gus Swan)*

OVERSTRAND TG2440

Sea Marge (01263) 579579

High Street; NR27 0AB Substantial half-timbered sea-view hotel (former Edwardian country house) with separate entrance to spacious bar; enjoyable food from ciabattas to local seafood including weekday deal (till 6pm) on some main courses, real ales and decent wines by the glass, panelled restaurant (more upmarket menu); children welcome, dogs in some areas, five-acre grounds with terraced lawns down to clifftop and steep steps to coast path and beach, 26 comfortable bedrooms, open (and bar food) all day. *(Mark Morgan)*

OVERSTRAND TG2440

White Horse (01263) 579237

High Street; NR27 0AB Comfortably modernised red-brick pub with good choice of well liked food in bar, dining room or barn restaurant (also used for functions), up to five well kept regional ales, friendly attentive staff; background music, silent sports TV, pool; children and dogs welcome, picnic-sets out in front, more in garden behind with play equipment (may be bouncy castle), short walk to beach, eight bedrooms, open all day from 8am. *(Mark Morgan)*

OXBOROUGH TF7401

★ Bedingfeld Arms (01366) 328300

Near church; PE33 9PS Attractively furnished Georgian dining inn peacefully set opposite Oxburgh Hall (NT); wood-floored bar with green leather chesterfields, tub chairs and window seats, open fire in marble fireplace with gilt mirror above, fresh flowers and candles, long counter serving Adnams Broadside, Woodfordes Reedlighter and a guest, ten wines by the glass, airy dining room has high-backed chairs around antique tables, wall seats with scatter cushions and bird prints on pale grey walls, good food from lunchtime sandwiches up; background music, TV for major sports, free wi-fi; well behaved children welcome, dogs in bar, covered verandah extension, more seats in garden with view of church, nine bedrooms (five in coach-house annexe), good breakfasts, open all day, food all day Sun. *(Tracey and Stephen Groves)*

RINGSTEAD TF7040

Gin Trap (01485) 525264

Village signed off A149 near Hunstanton; OS Sheet 132 map reference 707403; PE36 5JU Attractive 17th-c village pub (former coaching inn); original beamed bar with woodburner, farmhouse and mate's chairs around solid pine tables on bare boards, yellow tartan window seats, pub photos on walls, horse tack and coach lamps, Adnams, Greene King, Woodfordes and guests, several wines by the glass and extensive range of gins (one named for the pub), decent choice of food served by friendly staff; step up to quarry-tiled room with conservatory beyond, character back snug with red-painted walls and nice old floor tiles; children and dogs (in bar) welcome, picnic-sets and play area in back garden, more seats out in front, handy for Peddars Way, comfortable well equipped bedrooms (some in adjacent building), open all day. *(Paul Scofield, David Jackman, Tracey and Stephen Groves)*

ROYDON   TF7022
Three Horseshoes (01485) 600666
The Roydon near King's Lynn; Lynn Road; PE32 1AQ Updated brick and stone village pub under same ownership as nearby Congham Hall Hotel; pleasant pastel décor with simple wood furniture, stone-floor bar and split-level part-carpeted restaurant, woodburner in each, popular home-made food including good steaks from reasonably priced blackboard menu, OAP set lunch Mon-Fri, Greene King IPA and a couple of guests, friendly helpful staff; children and dogs (in bar) welcome, tables out at front, open all day, food all day weekends. *(John Wooll, David Jackman)*

SCULTHORPE   TF8930
★**Sculthorpe Mill** (01328) 856161
Inn signed off A148 W of Fakenham, opposite village; NR21 9QG Welcoming dining pub in rebuilt 18th-c mill, appealing riverside setting with seats out under weeping willows and in attractive garden behind; light, airy and relaxed with leather sofas and sturdy tables in bar/dining area, good reasonably priced food from sandwiches to daily specials, attentive service, Greene King ales and good house wines, upstairs restaurant; background music, free wi-fi; six comfortable bedrooms, open all day in summer (all day weekends in winter). *(John Wooll)*

SEDGEFORD   TF7036
King William IV (01485) 571765
B1454, off A149 King's Lynn–Hunstanton; PE36 5LU Homely inn handy for beaches and bird-watching; bar and dining areas decorated with paintings of north Norfolk coast, high-backed dark leather dining chairs around pine tables on slate tiles, log fires, Adnams, Greene King and Woodfordes, ten wines by the glass and well liked food from pub favourites up including blackboard specials; magazines and daily papers; children welcome (no under-4s in main restaurant after 6.30pm), dogs allowed

in bar and a couple of the bedrooms, seats on terrace and under parasols on grass, also an attractive covered dining area surrounded by flowering tubs, closed Mon lunchtime, otherwise open all day. *(Alison and Graeme Spicer)*

SHERINGHAM   TG1543
Crown (01263) 823213
East Cliff; NR26 8BQ Comfortable 1930s bay-windowed pub in good position overlooking the Wash; five well kept ales including Adnams, Greene King and Sharps, decent choice of enjoyable reasonably priced pubby food, three connecting areas with panelling and some exposed brickwork, upholstered wall benches and other traditional furniture on patterned carpet; background and live music, Mon quiz, darts, TVs and fruit machine; children and dogs welcome, lots of picnic-sets on sea-view terrace, next to the Mo Museum, open (and food) all day except Sun when kitchen closes at 5pm. *(John Evans, David and Gill Carrington)*

SHERINGHAM   TG1543
Lobster (01263) 822716
High Street; NR26 8JP Almost on seafront and popular with both locals and tourists; friendly panelled bar with log fire and seafaring décor, wide range of ales including Adnams, Greene King and Woodfordes, two or three ciders and decent wines by the glass, generous reasonably priced bar food from good sandwiches up, restaurant with seasonal seafood including lobster and crab; some live music; children and dogs welcome, bedrooms, open all day. *(Martin Day)*

SHOULDHAM   TF6708
Kings Arms (01366) 347410
The Green; PE33 0BY Traditional 17th-c pub on village green; beams and flagstones, exposed-stone or red-painted walls hung with prints, homely mix of dining chairs and tables, a leather button-back sofa and inglenook woodburner, well kept ales such as Adnams, Beeston and Grain tapped from the cask, local cider, ten wines by the glass and decent range of gins and malt whiskies, enjoyable food (not Sun evening, Mon) including good Sun roasts, also has a café staffed by volunteers selling village-baked cakes and scones; background and live music; children and dogs (in bar) welcome, painted picnic-sets on grass, classic car/motorcycle meetings first Sun of month, closed Mon lunchtime, otherwise open all day. *(Amy Ledbetter, David Jackman)*

SOUTHREPPS   TG2536
★**Vernon Arms** (01263) 833355
Church Street; NR11 8NP Popular old-fashioned brick and cobble village pub, welcoming and relaxed, with good home-made food (booking advised), friendly helpful staff, well kept Adnams, Greene

King, Woodfordes and a guest, decent choice of wines and malt whiskies, big log fire; darts and pool, occasional live music; tables outside, children, dogs and muddy boots welcome, open all day, no evening food Sun or Mon. *(Chloe and Guy Hodge)*

STANHOE TF8037

★ **Duck** (01485) 518330

B1155 Docking–Burnham Market; PE31 8QD Smart pub with emphasis on good imaginative food (sister to Bell at Hunworth); little entrance bar with cushioned Edwardian-style chairs around wooden tables on dark slate floor, stools against fine slab-topped counter serving Adnams, Elgoods and a dozen wines by the glass, woodburner in small area off, two dining rooms with scatter-cushion wall seats, scrubbed tables and local seascapes; free wi-fi; children and dogs (in bar) welcome, disabled access/loo, tables out on front gravel and under fruit tree in small garden, there's also a garden room with fairy lights and candles, comfortable well appointed bedrooms, good breakfast, open all day, food all day Sun. *(Roy Hoing, David Jackman, Christopher and Elise Way)*

STIFFKEY TF9643

Red Lion (01328) 830552

A149 Wells–Blakeney; NR23 1AJ Popular old village pub; main bar with tiled floor and inglenook woodburner, cushioned pews and other pubby seats, Woodfordes ales, a dozen wines by the glass and some local gins, well liked food (all day weekends) from pubby choices to local fish/shellfish, friendly service, two back dining rooms, one a flint-walled conservatory; children and dogs welcome, big partly covered gravelled courtyard, more tables on covered deck, ten bedrooms in modern block with own balconies or terraces, nearby coastal walks, open all day. *(Tracey and Stephen Groves, Clive and Fran Dutson)*

STOW BARDOLPH TF6205

Hare Arms (01366) 382229

Just off A10 N of Downham Market; PE34 3HT Popular modernised village pub; bare-boards bar with traditional pub furnishings and log fire, Greene King ales and a couple of well kept guests, ten wines by the glass, generous helpings of enjoyable good value food (all day Sun) from sandwiches up, three dining areas including converted coach house; children welcome in some parts, no dogs inside, plenty of seats in front and back gardens, maybe wandering peacocks, Church Farm Rare Breeds Centre nearby, open (and food) all day weekends. *(Tracey and Stephen Groves)*

SURLINGHAM TG3107

Ferry House (01508) 538659

Ferry Road: far end by river; NR14 7AR Welcoming unpretentious pub by River Yare;

well kept regional ales and hearty helpings of good inexpensive home-made food from baguettes up, helpful accommodating service, central woodburner in brick fireplace; some live music; children and dogs welcome, very busy with boats and visitors in summer (free mooring), picnic-sets on waterside lawn, handy for RSPB reserve, open (and food) all day. *(Denis and Margaret Kilner)*

THOMPSON TL9296

Chequers (01953) 483360

Griston Road, off A1075 S of Watton; IP24 1PX Picturesque 16th-c thatched dining pub tucked away in attractive setting; enjoyable food including bargain weekday lunch offer and regular themed nights, ales such as Greene King and Woodfordes, friendly atmosphere, series of quaint rooms with low beams, inglenooks and some stripped brickwork; children and dogs (in bar) welcome, seats out in front and in back garden with swing, bedroom block, open (and food) all day Sun. *(Beth Aldridge)*

THORNHAM TF7343

Chequers (01485) 512229

High Street (A149); PE36 6LY Updated 16th-c roadside inn under same owners as the nearby Lifeboat (see Main Entries); two front bar rooms with pale-painted beams, wooden chairs or cube seats around mix of wooden tables on carpet or painted floorboards, some local photographs, open fire, a few stools at counter serving two local ales and decent wines by the glass, well liked food from norfolk tapas and pizzas up, cosy room off with sofas, armchairs and woodburner, modern back dining room; children and dogs welcome, painted picnic-sets out at front, more seating in back courtyard garden with a couple of cabanas, 11 comfortable modern bedrooms, open all day. *(Julie Swift)*

THURNE TG4016

Lion (01692) 671806

The Street; NR29 3AP Revamped Victorian villa at end of Thurne Dyke – popular with boaters; good choice of real ales, craft kegs and proper ciders, several wines by the glass and some 20 gins including a house one infused with hops, happy hour 5-7pm (4-7pm weekends), enjoyable fair priced food from burgers and pizzas to specials, two-course set lunch Mon-Fri, friendly efficient service, sizeable restaurant; monthly quiz and some live music; children and dogs (in bar areas) welcome, grounds with play area, plenty of moorings (fee charged from 4pm), open all day. *(Simon King)*

TUNSTEAD TG2921

Horse & Groom (01603) 737555

Granary Way off Market Street; NR12 8AH Welcoming thatched village pub with modernised beamed interior; enjoyable fairly priced food from pub favourites up including Thurs curry night and Fri fish and chips, well kept changing local beers and good selection of gins, cheerful helpful staff; darts team Mon, quiz Tues, live acoustic music Weds; children and dogs welcome, open all day, no food Sun evening. *(Jonathon Caswell)*

WALSINGHAM   TF9336
Black Lion (01328) 820235
Friday Market Place; NR22 6DB Attractively renovated beamed village inn dating from the 15th c; nice mix of old furniture on flagstones or quarry tiles, shelves of books, farming tools and other bits and pieces including a tandem on one wall, woodburners and open fire, tractor-seat stools by counter serving well kept Adnams, Woodfordes, a guest ale and a dozen wines by the glass, good traditional home-made food, friendly service; background and some live music; children and dogs welcome, a few tables out at front, more on little terrace with old well, six comfortable bedrooms, open all day. *(Revd R P Tickle)*

WALSINGHAM   TF9336
Bull (01328) 820333
Common Place/Shire Hall Plain; NR22 6BP Quirky pub in pilgrimage village; lived-in bar with shelves of curious knick-knacks, pictures of archbishops and clerical visiting cards, a half-size statue of Charlie Chaplin, even a mirror ball in one part, three well kept changing ales and tasty reasonably priced food (not weekend evenings), roaring fire, typewriter in snug, old-fashioned cash register in the gents'; TV, free wi-fi; children welcome, courtyard and attractive flowery terrace by village square, dovecote stuffed with plastic lobsters and crabs, outside games room, nice snowdrop walk in nearby abbey garden, bedrooms, open all day. *(Max and Steph Warren)*

WEASENHAM ST PETER   TF8522
Fox & Hounds (01328) 838868
A1065 Fakenham–Swaffham; The Green; PE32 2TD Traditional 18th-c beamed local well run by friendly family; bar and two dining areas (one with inglenook woodburner), three changing ales and good reasonably priced home-made food (not Sun evening), pubby furniture and carpets throughout, brasses and lots of military prints; children welcome, big well maintained garden and terrace, closed Mon. *(Peter and Emma Kelly)*

WELLS-NEXT-THE-SEA   TF9143
Albatros 07979 087228
The Quay; NR23 1AT Bar on 1899 quayside clipper, charts and other nautical memorabilia, Woodfordes ales served from the cask, dutch food including speciality pancakes, seats on deck with good views of harbour and tidal marshes; regular live music; children welcome, no good for disabled visitors, cabin accommodation with shared showers, open all day. *(Dr J Barrie Jones)*

WELLS-NEXT-THE-SEA   TF9143
Bowling Green (01328) 710100
Church Street; NR23 1JB Welcoming 17th-c pub in quiet spot on outskirts; Greene King, Woodfordes and a guest, generous helpings of reasonably priced traditional food including bargain OAP lunch Tues, L-shaped bar with corner settles, flagstone and brick floor, two woodburners, raised dining end; children and dogs welcome, sunny back terrace, two bedrooms in converted barn, also self-catering accommodation, open all day. *(Paul Farraday)*

WELLS-NEXT-THE-SEA   TF9143
Edinburgh (01328) 710120
Station Road/Church Street; NR23 1AE Traditional 19th-c pub near main shopping area; three well kept ales and good home-made food including blackboard specials, open fire, sizeable restaurant, also 'lifeboat' dining room decorated in RNLI colours; background music, free wi-fi; children and dogs welcome, disabled access, courtyard with heated smokers' shelter, three bedrooms, open all day. *(Paul Farraday)*

WELLS-NEXT-THE-SEA   TF9143
★Globe (01328) 710206
The Buttlands; NR23 1EU Handsome blue-painted Georgian inn on elegant square, a short walk from the quay; plenty of space and nice atmosphere in opened-up contemporary rooms, tables on oak boards, big bay windows, well kept Adnams beers, thoughtful wine choice and enjoyable food from lunchtime ciabattas up, good friendly service; background and some live music; children and dogs welcome, attractive courtyard with pale flagstones, more seats at front overlooking green, 18 bedrooms (some in courtyard annexe) and nearby holiday house, open all day (breakfast for non-residents). *(Tracey and Stephen Groves, Dr J Barrie Jones, Tim Willson)*

WEST ACRE   TF7815
Stag (01760) 755395
Low Road; PE32 1TR Small family-run local with three or more well kept changing ales in appealing unpretentious bar, good value home-made food including set Sun lunch, neat dining room; quiz third Sun of month; attractive spot in quiet village, closed Mon. *(Millie and Peter Downing)*

WEYBOURNE   TG1143
Ship (01263) 588721
A149 W of Sheringham; The Street; NR25 7SZ Popular traditional 19th-c village pub; three well kept changing ales, decent wine choice and over 150 gins, big bar with pubby furniture and woodburner, two dining rooms, good reasonably priced home-made

food (should book weekends) from lunchtime sandwiches through pub favourites to local fish/seafood; background music, monthly quiz, free wi-fi; well behaved children welcome, dogs in bar, seats out at front and in nice side garden handy for Muckleburgh military vehicle museum, open all day in season, no food Sun evening. *(Roy Hoing)*

WIVETON   TG0442
★**Wiveton Bell** (01263) 740101
Blakeney Road; NR25 7TL Busy pub very popular for its top notch food but also welcoming drinkers; mainly open-plan with some fine old beams, log fire and attractive mix of furniture on stripped-wood flooring, sizeable dining conservatory, ales such as Norfolk Brewhouse Moon Gazer, Woodfordes and Yetmans, a dozen wines by the glass, friendly attentive service; children and dogs (in bar) welcome, picnic-sets on front grass looking across to church, stylish wicker furniture on decked areas behind, well equipped character bedrooms (three have small terraces), also a self-catering cottage, open all day. *(Dr K Nesbitt, Roy Hoing, Tim and Wendy Lloyd, Freddie and Sarah Banks)*

WYMONDHAM   TG1001
★**Green Dragon** (01953) 607907
Church Street; NR18 0PH Picturesque heavily timbered medieval pub with plenty of character; small beamed bar and snug, bigger dining area, interesting pictures, log fire under Tudor mantelpiece, five well kept changing ales (beer/cider festival May) and over 50 whiskies, generous helpings of popular good value food (best to book) including daily specials and gluten-free menu, friendly helpful staff, upstairs function room; quiz Thurs, open mike night third Sun of month, ukulele group third Tues; children and dogs welcome, garden behind with raised deck, near glorious 12th-c abbey church, open all day (food all day Fri-Sun). *(Lyn and Freddie Roberts)*

Northamptonshire

KEY	★ Star Pub	🍴⭐ Top Quality Food	🍺 Great Beer
🍷 Good Wines	£ Bargain Meals	🛏 Good Bedrooms	🍴 Serves Food

FARTHINGHOE   SP5339   Map 4

Fox 🛏

(01295) 713965 – www.foxfarthinghoe.co.uk

Just off A422 Brackley–Banbury; Baker Street; NN13 5PH

Bustling stone inn with a neat bar and dining rooms, tasty food, helpful service and seats in the garden; bedrooms

It would be best to book a table in advance here as it's very popular. A stylish, golden-stone pub with a friendly, hands-on landlord, the dark beamed bar has stools and a log fire in a stripped-stone fireplace, with Youngs Bitter and a couple of guests from Marstons on handpump, nine wines by the glass and a good choice of gins. The dining areas have seats ranging from leather tub chairs to banquettes, cushioned wall seats with scatter cushions and quite a range of wooden dining chairs, all arranged around rustic wooden tables; pastel walls are hung with mirrors and country prints. Background music. The terrace and lawn have picnic-sets under a giant parasol. Bedrooms in an adjoining barn conversion are quiet and comfortable; one is suitable for disabled customers.

🍴 Pleasing food includes chicken caesar salad, braised meatballs in garlic and tomato sauce, sharing boards, chickpea curry, salmon salad with chilli and lemon dressing, home-roasted ham and duck eggs, sausages with mash and onion gravy, breaded plaice and chips, cajun chicken with ratatouille and dauphinoise potatoes, barbecue ribs with coleslaw and chips, 10oz sirloin steak with a choice of sauce, and puddings such as chocolate fondant with vanilla ice-cream and passion-fruit and mango cheesecake. *Benchmark main dish: burger with toppings, coleslaw and chips £12.00. Two-course evening meal £19.00.*

Charles Wells ~ Lease Neil Bellingham ~ Real ale ~ Open 12-3, 6-10; 12-11 Fri, Sat; 12-10 Sun ~ Bar food 12-2.30, 6-9; 12-9 Sat; 12-8 Sun ~ Restaurant ~ Children welcome ~ Dogs allowed in bar ~ Wi-fi ~ Bedrooms: /£75 *Recommended by Gerry and Rosemary Dobson, Julie Swift, John and Claire Masters, Edward Nile, Daniel King, Julia and Fiona Barnes, Frances and Hamish Porter*

FARTHINGSTONE   SP6155   Map 4

Kings Arms 🍺 £

(01327) 361604

Off A5 SE of Daventry; village signed from Litchborough; NN12 8EZ

Individual place with cosy traditional interior, carefully prepared food and lovely garden

Plenty of chatty customers create a cheerful, relaxed atmosphere in this charming little pub. The cosy flagstoned bar has a huge log fire, comfortable homely sofas and armchairs near the entrance, whisky-water jugs hanging from oak beams, and lots of pictures and decorative plates on the walls. A games room at the far end has darts, dominoes, cribbage, table skittles and board games. The ever-changing beers are kept in top condition and might include Butcombe Bitter, Gloucester Gold, Harveys Best and Woodfordes Wherry on handpump; also Weston's Old Rosie cider and a short but decent wine list. Look out for the interesting newspaper-influenced décor in the outside gents'. The handsome gargoyled stone exterior is nicely weathered and very pretty in summer when the hanging baskets are at their best. There are seats on a tranquil terrace among plant-filled, painted tractor tyres and recycled art, and they've recorded over 200 species of moth and 20 different butterflies. This is a picturesque village and enjoyable walks nearby include the Knightley Way. It's worth ringing ahead to check the opening and food times.

Served at weekend lunchtimes only, popular food includes sandwiches, filled yorkshire puddings, cassoulets, stews, and puddings such as gingerbread pudding and meringues. *Benchmark main dish: meat/fish/mixed platters £13.00.*

Free house ~ Licensees Paul and Denise Egerton ~ Real ale ~ Open 7-11 Tues-Thurs; 6.30-11.30 Fri; 12-11.30 Sat; 12-5, 9-11 Sun; closed Mon, weekday lunchtimes ~ Bar food 12-2.15 or so weekends; maybe evening snacks ~ Children welcome ~ Dogs allowed in bar ~ Wi-fi ~ Live music occasional Sat *Recommended by Mark and Mary Setting, Colin Humphreys, Jack Trussler, Sandra King, Dave Sutton, Simon Sharpe, Jamie Green*

FOTHERINGHAY
Falcon 🏮✪ ♟

TL0593   Map 5

(01832) 226254 – www.thefalcon-inn.co.uk
Village signposted off A605 on Peterborough side of Oundle; PE8 5HZ

Upmarket dining pub with a good range of drinks and modern british food, and attractive garden

Comfortably civilised and warmly welcoming, this appealing place is run by a hands-on landlady. There are winter log fires in stone fireplaces, fresh flowers, cushioned slatback armchairs, bucket chairs and comfortably cushioned window seats and bare floorboards. The Orangery restaurant opens on to a charming lavender-surrounded terrace with lovely views of the huge church behind and of the attractively planted garden; plenty of seats under parasols. The thriving little locals' tap bar has a fine choice of drinks including Fullers London Pride, Greene King IPA and a guest from local breweries such as Digfield, Kings Cliffe, Nobbys and Oakham on handpump, 16 good wines by the glass and eight malt whiskies; darts team and board games. This is a lovely village (Richard III was born here) with plenty of moorings on the River Nene; the ruins of Fotheringhay Castle, where Mary, Queen of Scots was executed, is nearby.

Well liked food includes sandwiches, chicken liver pâté with chutney, prawn cocktail, smoked cheese, leek and mushroom filo basket with garlic potatoes, local baked ham and eggs, pie of the day, oriental duck salad with coriander dressing, calves liver with onion and bacon gravy, rib-eye steak with chips and a choice of sauce, and puddings such as warm chocolate brownie with vanilla ice-cream and fruit cheesecake with cream; they also offer a two- and three-course set menu (not Saturday evening or Sunday lunchtime). *Benchmark main dish: smoked haddock and cheddar fishcakes £14.00. Two-course evening meal £21.00.*

Free house ~ Licensee Sally Facer ~ Real ale ~ Open 12-11; 12-10.30 Sun; 12-4.30 in winter ~ Bar food 12-2, 6-9; 12-3 Sun (12-3, 5.30-8 May-Sept) ~ Restaurant ~ Children welcome ~ Dogs allowed in bar ~ Wi-fi *Recommended by Ian Herdman, Peter Andrews, Emily and Toby Archer, Deborah and Duncan Walliams, Frances and Hamish Porter, David Longhurst, Peter and Emma Kelly*

 GREAT BRINGTON   SP6664   Map 4

Althorp Coaching Inn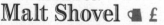

(01604) 770651 – www.althorp-coaching-inn.co.uk

Off A428 NW of Northampton, near Althorp Hall; until recently known as the Fox & Hounds; NN7 4JA

Northamptonshire Dining Pub of the Year

Friendly golden-stone thatched pub with some fine architectural features, tasty popular food, well kept real ales and sheltered garden

There are plenty of happy customers here keen to enjoy the thoughtful choice of food and drink. The ancient bar has all the traditional features you'd wish for, from a dog or two sprawled by the huge log fire to old beams, sagging joists and an appealing mix of country chairs and tables (set with fresh flowers) on broad flagstones and bare boards; background music. There are snug alcoves, nooks and crannies with some stripped-pine shutters and panelling, two fine log fires and an eclectic medley of bric-a-brac from farming implements to an old clocking-in machine and country pictures. Greene King Abbot and IPA, Phipps India Pale Ale, St Austell Tribute and Sharps Doom Bar on handpump; also, eight wines by the glass, a dozen malt whiskies and farm cider. A function room is located in a converted stable block next to the lovely cobbled and paved courtyard (also accessible by the old coaching entrance) with sheltered tables and tubs of flowers; more seating is available in the charming garden.

 Highly enjoyable food includes sandwiches, moules marinière, goats cheese and walnut salad, three-bean chilli with rice, pie of the day, hot chicken and bacon salad with honey and mustard dressing, sea bass with parmentier potatoes, lamb shank in red wine sauce, and puddings such as chocolate brownie with ice-cream and fresh fruit pavlova. *Benchmark main dish: beer haddock and chips £11.95. Two-course evening meal £20.00.*

Free house ~ Licensee Michael Krempels ~ Real ale ~ Open 11-11; 11-midnight Sat; 11-10 Sun ~ Bar food 12-3, 6-9; 12-9 Sat; 12-7 Sun ~ Restaurant ~ Children welcome ~ Dogs allowed in bar ~ Wi-fi ~ Mon quiz *Recommended by Alistair Forsyth, Peter Andrews, Francis and Mandy Robertson, Patti and James Davidson*

NORTHAMPTON   SP7559   Map 4

Malt Shovel £

(01604) 234212 – www.maltshoveltavern.com

Bridge Street (approach road from M1 junction 15); no parking in nearby street, best to park in Morrisons central car park, far end – passage past Europcar straight to back entrance; NN1 1QF

Friendly, well run real ale pub with bargain lunches and over a dozen varied beers

Knowledgeable, enthusiastic staff in this bustling tavern keep their 13 real ales in tip top condition and there's a wonderful choice of other drinks too. From a battery of handpumps lined up on the long counter, regulars might include Hook Norton Old Hooky, Nethergate Melford Mild,

Oakham Bishops Farewell and JHB and Phipps NBC India Pale Ale, with seven quickly changing guests including Dent Kamikaze, Island Yachtsmans Ale, Milestone Honey Porter, Nethergate Augustinian and Essex Border, Purity Longhorn and Pure UBU. They also stock belgian draught and bottled beers, 25 malt whiskies, 15 rums, 17 vodkas, 50 gins and Cheddar Valley and Weston's Old Rosie farm ciders; regular beer festivals. The pub is also home to quite an extensive collection of carefully chosen brewing memorabilia – look out for the rare Northampton Brewery Company star, displayed outside the pub, and some high-mounted ancient beer engines; darts, daily papers and background music. The secluded back yard is furnished with tables and chairs and a smokers' shelter; disabled facilities.

🍴 Lunchtime-only food includes doorstep sandwiches, sharing platters, filled baked potatoes, shepherd's pie, lambs liver and bacon casserole, fish or meat pies and casseroles. *Benchmark main dish: cottage pie £7.00.*

Free house ~ Licensees Scott Whyment, Kirsty Bowen ~ Real ale ~ Open 11.30-11; 12-10.30 Sun ~ Bar food 12-3; 12-4 weekends ~ Well behaved children welcome in bar ~ Dogs allowed in bar ~ Wi-fi ~ Blues music Weds evening *Recommended by Dr J Barrie Jones, Jess and George Cowley, Bob and Melissa Wyatt, Sabina and Gerald Grimshaw, Simon Day, Emma Scofield*

Also Worth a Visit in Northamptonshire

Besides the fully inspected pubs, you might like to try these pubs that have been recommended to us and described by readers. Do tell us what you think of them: feedback@goodguides.com

ABTHORPE SP6446
★**New Inn** (01327) 857306
Signed from A43 at first roundabout S of A5; Silver Street; NN12 8QR Traditional partly thatched country local run by cheery farming family; fairly basic rambling bar with dining area down a couple of steps, beams, stripped stone and inglenook woodburner; four well kept Hook Norton beers, Weston's cider and good pubby food (not Sun evening, Mon) using local produce including own meat; open mike night second Sun of month, quiz last Sun, darts and table skittles, free wi-fi; children, dogs and muddy boots welcome, garden tables, bedrooms in converted barn (short walk across fields), open all day Fri-Sun, closed lunchtimes Mon and Tues. *(Simon and Alex Knight)*

ARTHINGWORTH SP7581
Bulls Head (01858) 525637
Kelmarsh Road, just above A14 by A508 junction; pub signed from A14; LE16 8JZ Steps up to much extended black-beamed pub with various seating areas in L-shaped bar, pubby furniture and upholstered banquettes on patterned carpet, woodburner, well kept Adnams and a couple of guests (May beer festival), enjoyable good value food, efficient cheery service, restaurant; background music, TV, darts and skittles, free wi-fi; wheelchair access (from behind) and disabled loos, terrace picnic-sets, eight bedrooms in separate block, handy for Kelmarsh Hall, open all day weekends (food till 7.30pm Sun). *(Jimmy Clark)*

ASHBY ST LEDGERS SP5768
Olde Coach House (01788) 890349
Main Street; 4 miles from M1 junction 18; A5 S to Kilsby, then A361 S towards Daventry; village also signed off A5 N of Weedon; CV23 8UN Handsome former farmhouse with opened-up right-hand bar, stools against counter serving Bombardier, Marstons Pedigree and a monthly guest, 16 wines by the glass, several informal dining areas (food can be good), hunting pictures, large mirrors and an original old stove in one part; background music and TV; children welcome, dogs in bar, modern tables and chairs out in front, dining courtyard and back garden with picnic-sets among shrubs and trees, well equipped contemporary bedrooms (11 in converted stables), interesting church and the nearby manor house was once owned by one of the Gunpowder plotters, open all day, food till 8pm Sun. *(Pauline and Mark Evans, Sylvia and Phillip Spencer, Susan and John Douglas)*

AYNHO SP5133
Cartwright (01869) 811885
Croughton Road (B4100); handy for M40 junction 10; OX17 3BE Welcoming 16th-c coaching inn with linked areas; contemporary furniture on wood or tiled floors, some exposed stone walls, leather sofas by big log fire in small bar, two real ales, nice wines and good coffee, popular well presented food including set deals, friendly helpful staff; background music, TV, daily papers and free wi-fi; children welcome,

a few seats in pretty corner of part-cobbled coachyard, 21 bedrooms, good breakfast, pleasant village with apricot trees growing against old cottage walls, open all day. *(Ian and Sally Duncan)*

AYNHO   SP4932
★**Great Western Arms**
(01869) 338288 *On B4031 1.5 miles E of Deddington, 0.75 miles W of Aynho, adjacent to Oxford Canal and Old Aynho station; OX17 3BP* Attractive old creeper-clad pub with series of cosy linked rooms; fine solid country tables on broad flagstones, golden stripped-stone walls, two-way woodburner, well kept Hook Norton and guests, good wines by the glass and good food cooked by landlord-chef from pubby choices up (separate gluten-free menu), friendly attentive young staff, elegant dining area on right, extensive GWR collection including steam locomotive photographs; background music; children and dogs welcome, white cast-iron furniture in back former stable courtyard, moorings on Oxford Canal and nearby marina, four bedrooms, open all day, food all day Sun. *(Robert Watt, Darren and Jane Staniforth, Michael Sargent)*

BADBY   SP5558
Windmill (01327) 311070
Village signposted off A361 Daventry–Banbury; NN11 3AN Attractive 17th-c thatched and beamed village pub; flagstoned bar with tiled fireplace in huge inglenook, another log fire in adjoining snug, three mainstream ales and a regional guest, good food from interesting varied menu including daily specials, welcoming helpful staff, back restaurant extension; background music, free wi-fi; children and dogs welcome, picnic-sets out at front by small green, nice walks (Badby bluebell woods close by), eight bedrooms, open all day in summer, all day weekends winter. *(Nick Steadman)*

BARNWELL   TL0584
Montagu Arms (01832) 273726
Off A605 S of Oundle, then fork right at Thurning/Hemington sign; PE8 5PH Attractive old stone pub in pleasant streamside village; two well kept Digfield ales (brewed close by) and a couple of guests, real ciders and 11 wines by the glass, happy hour Mon 6-7pm, good food including Weds evening two-course deal, cheerful staff, low beams, flagstones and log fire, back dining room, conservatory and cellar bar; children and dogs welcome, big garden with play area, enjoyable walks, open all day Fri-Sun. *(Katherine Matthews)*

BRAYBROOKE   SP7684
Swan (01858) 462754
Griffin Road; LE16 8LH Thatched pub with popular sensibly priced food (not Sun evening) from sandwiches and pub favourites up, friendly attentive staff, Everards ales and

good choice of other drinks (happy hour Fri 5.30-7pm), fireside sofas, soft lighting, beams and some exposed brickwork, restaurant; background music, quiz second Tues of month; children and dogs welcome, disabled facilities, pretty hedged garden with covered terrace, open all day Sat, closed Mon. *(Mr and Mrs D J Nash)*

BRIXWORTH   SP7470
Coach & Horses (01604) 880329
Harborough Road, just off A508 N of Northampton; NN6 9BX Welcoming early 18th-c thatched and beamed pub; enjoyable food from fairly straightforward menu plus more adventurous specials including seasonal game, lunchtime and early evening set deals, well kept Marstons-related ales, prompt friendly service, log-fire bar with small dining area off, back lounge; tables on gravelled terrace behind, bedrooms in converted outbuildings, charming village with famous Saxon church, open (and food) all day Sun. *(Gerry and Rosemary Dobson)*

CHACOMBE   SP4943
George & Dragon (01295) 711500
Handy for M40 junction 11, via A361; Silver Street; OX17 2JR Welcoming 17th-c pub with beams, flagstones, panelling and bare stone walls, two inglenook woodburners and deep glass-covered well, good popular food (not Sun evening) in three dining areas including various deals, Everards ales and a guest from brass-topped counter, several wines by the glass; background music, charity quiz first Sun of month; children and dogs (in bar) welcome, picnic-sets on suntrap terrace, pretty village with interesting church, open all day. *(Jimmy Clark)*

CHAPEL BRAMPTON   SP7366
★**Brampton Halt** (01604) 842676
Pitsford Road, off A5199 N of Northampton; NN6 8BA Popular well laid out McManus pub on Northampton & Lamport Railway (which is open some weekends) in much extended former stationmaster's house; railway memorabilia and train theme throughout, wide choice of enjoyable food from sandwiches to blackboard specials, meal deal Mon-Thurs, half a dozen well kept ales including Fullers, Sharps and Timothy Taylors (beer festivals), plenty of wines by the glass and good range of other drinks, cheerful attentive service even when very busy, large restaurant; background music, TV in bar; children welcome, no dogs inside, lots of tables in big garden with awnings and heaters, summer barbecues and marquee, attractive views over small lake, Nene Way walks, open (and food) all day. *(Gerry and Rosemary Dobson, Revd R P Tickle)*

CHARLTON   SP5235
Rose & Crown (01295) 811317
Main Street; OX17 3DP Cosy 17th-c thatched village pub under welcoming

family management; enjoyable reasonably priced home-made food and well kept ales such as Greene King and Timothy Taylors, good friendly service, beams and stripped stone, nice log fire; children, walkers and dogs welcome, back garden with picnic-sets and wisteria arbour, Cherwell Valley views, open all day Fri and Sat, till 6pm Sun, closed Mon. *(Ian and Sally Duncan)*

CLIPSTON   SP7181
Bulls Head (01858) 525268
B4036 S of Market Harborough; LE16 9RT Welcoming village pub with popular good value food (not Mon) served in bar and restaurant, Everards ales and up to five guests, log fire and heavy beams (coins inserted by World War II airmen); background music, Tues quiz, TV; children and dogs welcome, terrace tables, three comfortable bedrooms, open all day weekends, closed Mon lunchtime.
(Mike and Margaret Banks)

COGENHOE   SP8360
Royal Oak (01604) 890922
Whiston Road; NN7 1NJ Modernised beamed village pub with very good food (best to book) from varied menu including summer wood-fired pizzas, three real ales such as Hook Norton Hooky and St Austell Tribute, friendly helpful staff, open fire in bar, smallish restaurant; children welcome, picnic-sets on part-covered deck, steps down to garden with play area, open all day Fri and Sat, till 7.30pm Sun, closed Mon.
(Alan Sutton)

COLLINGTREE   SP7555
Wooden Walls of Old England (01604) 760641
1.2 miles from M1 junction 15; High Street; NN4 0NE Cosy thatch and stone village pub dating from the 15th c and named as a tribute to the navy; four well kept ales and good choice of wines by the glass, generous helpings of reasonably priced home-made food (not Sun evening, Mon), friendly staff, beams and open fire, northamptonshire skittles in one room; background music, sports TV, free wi-fi; children welcome, big back garden with part-covered terrace, closed Mon lunchtime, otherwise open all day. *(Simon and Alex Knight)*

COLLYWESTON   SK9902
★ **Collyweston Slater** (01780) 444288
The Drove (A43); PE9 3PQ Roomy 17th-c main road inn with good popular pub food including themed evenings, well kept Everards ales and decent selection of wines, friendly service, contemporary interior with brown leather sofas and easy chairs, smart

modern two-part dining room plus some more informal areas, one with raised woodburner in dividing wall, beams, stripped stone and mix of dark flagstones, bare boards and carpeting; background music, TV, darts; children welcome, dogs in bar areas, teak furniture on flagstoned terrace, boules, three bedrooms, open all day, no food Sun evening. *(Colin McLachlan)*

COSGROVE   SP7942
Barley Mow (01908) 562957
The Stocks; MK19 7JD Friendly old village pub close to Grand Union Canal; well kept Everards ales and a guest, decent range of wines and enjoyable reasonably priced home-made food, beamed interior with various connecting areas, dark furniture on carpet or light stone floors, some half-panelling, two-way woodburner in stone fireplace; occasional live music, TV, free wi-fi; children and dogs welcome, tables on terrace and lawn down to the canal, open all day, food all day weekends. *(Frances and Hamish Porter)*

CRICK   SP5872
★ **Red Lion** (01788) 822342
1 mile from M1 junction 18; in centre of village off A428; NN6 7TX Nicely worn-in stone and thatch coaching inn run by same family since 1979; charming traditional low-ceilinged bar with lots of old horsebrasses (some rare) and tiny log stove in big inglenook, straightforward low-priced lunchtime food, more elaborate evening menu (not Sun) including popular steaks, plenty for vegetarians too, Adnams Southwold, Bombardier and a guest, good friendly service, quiz last Sun of month, free wi-fi; children (under-12s lunchtime only) and dogs welcome, picnic-sets on terrace and in Perspex-covered coachyard with pretty hanging baskets. *(Ian and Sally Duncan)*

CRICK   SP5872
Wheatsheaf (01788) 823824
Main Road (A428, handy for M1 junction 18); NN6 7TU Ironstone pub with comfortable log-fire bar and large smartly furnished back restaurant, five well kept ales including one badged for them, good selection of ciders, wines and gins, popular food including bargain OAP set deal (Mon-Sat till 5pm), friendly efficient service; occasional live music and quiz nights; children and dogs (in bar) welcome, bedrooms, open (and food) all day. *(Clive and Fran Dutson, Tony Hobden)*

CULWORTH   SP5447
Red Lion (01295) 760050
Off B4525 NE of Banbury; OX17 2BD Nicely restored 18th-c beamed dining pub at

---

We checked prices with the pubs as we went to press in summer 2019.
They should hold until around spring 2020.

end of stone terrace; cosy and comfortable, with much liked food (must book) including good Sun roasts, attentive but not intrusive service from welcoming staff, up to four real ales and decent choice of wines; lovely garden behind, open all day Sun, closed Mon and Tues. *(Paul Humphreys)*

DUDDINGTON   SK9800
Royal Oak (01780) 444267
High Street, just off A43; PE9 3QE Stone-built inn on edge of pretty village; modern bar area with leather sofas and chairs on flagstones, panelling and log fire, three real ales from brick servery, restaurant with stone walls, wood floor and light oak furniture, decent food from pub favourites up including set menu (Mon-Thurs), gluten-free and vegan diets catered for; background music; children welcome, disabled facilities, tables on small grassy area at front, six bedrooms, open all day Fri-Sun.
(Charles Fraser)

EAST HADDON   SP6668
Red Lion (01604) 770223
High Street; village signposted off A428 (turn right in village) and off A50 N of Northampton; NN6 8BU Elegant golden-stone thatched hotel with sizeable dining room, log-fire lounge and bar, emphasis on their well presented fairly priced food from pub favourites to more restauranty choices, most tables set for dining, but they do keep Courage Directors, Youngs Bitter and offer around a dozen wines by the glass, efficient friendly service; background music; children welcome, attractive grounds including walled side garden, seven comfortable bedrooms, good breakfast, open all day, food all day weekends. *(Gerry and Rosemary Dobson, Alan Sutton)*

EASTON ON THE HILL   TF0104
Blue Bell (01780) 763003
High Street; PE9 3LR Stone-built village pub with good italian food (not Sun evening, Mon), three or four changing ales including Grainstore and plenty of wines by the glass, friendly italian licensees and staff, restaurant; some live music, pool and TV in games area, May beer festival; children and dogs welcome, picnic-sets in sheltered garden behind, open all day Sun, closed Mon. *(Colin McLachlan)*

EASTON ON THE HILL   TF0104
★Exeter Arms (01780) 756321
Stamford Road (A43); PE9 3NS Renovated 18th-c pub with friendly easy-going atmosphere; country-feel bar with cushioned captain's chairs, wall/window seats and copper pans above woodburner, tractor seats by counter serving several wines by the glass and ales such as Shepherd Neame and local Stoney Ford, good food (not Sun evening) from varied menu, pizzas in summer, restaurant and airy orangery

opening on to sunken terrace; free wi-fi; children and dogs (in bar) welcome, picnic-sets on lawn, light comfortable bedrooms, open all day, no food Sun evening.
(Jimmy Clark)

EYDON   SP5450
Royal Oak (01327) 263167
Lime Avenue; village signed off A361 Daventry–Banbury, and from B4525; NN11 3PG Interestingly laid-out 300-year-old ironstone pub, some lovely period features including fine flagstone floors and leaded windows, small cosy snug on right with cushioned benches built into alcoves, seats in bow window, inglenook log fire, long corridor-like central bar linking three other small characterful rooms, Sharps Doom Bar, Youngs Bitter and a guest, enjoyable food from pub favourites up (just evenings Fri-Sat and Sun lunchtime), friendly staff; children and dogs welcome, terrace seating, open all day Sat, closed lunchtimes Mon and Tues.
(Nick Steadman)

GRAFTON REGIS   SP7546
★White Hart (01908) 542123
A508 S of Northampton; NN12 7SR Thatched roadside dining pub with several linked rooms; good home-cooked food from lunchtime baguettes to daily specials, popular Sun roasts (best to book), Greene King Abbot and IPA, Aspall's cider and nice wines by the glass, friendly helpful staff coping well when busy, restaurant with open fire; background music; children and dogs welcome (they have a couple of boxers and a parrot), terrace tables and gazebo in good-sized garden, self-catering cottage, closed Mon. *(Luke Barnes)*

GREAT BILLING   SP8162
Elwes Arms (01604) 407521
High Street; NN3 9DT Thatched and low-beamed 16th-c village pub with two bars (steps between); wide choice of good value tasty food including weekday lunch deal, Adnams, Sharps and Wychwood Hobgoblin, friendly service, pleasant dining room where children allowed; background music, cosy Thurs and Sun, open mike night first Weds of month, sports TV, darts, free wi-fi; no dogs, garden tables and nice covered decked terrace, play area, open all day, food all day Sat and till 5pm Sun. *(Alan Sutton)*

GREAT OXENDON   SP7383
★George (01858) 452286
A508 S of Market Harborough; LE16 8NA Modernised well run pub under same owners as the Joiners Arms at Bruntingthorpe (Leicestershire); small back bar with two Langton ales and a craft beer, all other areas for dining/pre-dining with bistro-style décor, very good well presented food from shortish but varied menu including a few specials, also good value three-course menu (Mon-Sat lunchtime, Mon evening), prompt friendly

service from well turned out staff; children welcome, no dogs inside, paved terrace overlooking garden, eight bedrooms (four in annexe), open all day. *(Gerry and Rosemary Dobson, Mike and Margaret Banks)*

HACKLETON   SP8054
White Hart (01604) 870271
B526 SE of Northampton; NN7 2AD Comfortably traditional 18th-c country pub; enjoyable sensibly priced food from pub favourites up, Fullers London Pride, Greene King IPA and a guest, friendly helpful staff, flagstoned bar with log fire, dining area up steps, beams, stripped stone and brickwork, deep illuminated well; background music, sports TV, pool and hood skittles; well behaved children and dogs welcome, disabled access, picnic-sets in sunny garden, open all day, no food Sun evening. *(Katherine Matthews)*

HARRINGTON   SP7780
Tollemache Arms (01536) 711770
High Street; off A508 S of Market Harborough; NN6 9NU Pretty thatched and beamed Tudor pub under same ownership as the Red Lion at East Haddon; enjoyable food including sharing boards, pizzas and burgers, well kept Bombardier, Eagle IPA and three guests, good choice of wines by the glass, cocktails and a local artisan gin, friendly attentive staff; children and dogs (in bar) welcome, back garden with country views and play area, lovely quiet ironstone village, handy for Carpetbagger Aviation Museum, open all day weekends (till 9pm Sun). *(Alan Sutton, M and GR)*

HIGHAM FERRERS   SP9668
Griffin (01933) 312612
High Street; NN10 8BW Welcoming 17th-c pub-restaurant (bigger than it looks) with enjoyable food including fresh fish and popular Sun carvery (till 3.30pm), five well kept rotating ales and good selection of wines and malt whiskies, comfortable front bar with log fire (note the stools), smart back restaurant and dining conservatory, friendly relaxed atmosphere; free wi-fi; tables on heated terrace, open all day Fri-Sun. *(Revd R P Tickle)*

HINTON-IN-THE-HEDGES   SP5536
Crewe Arms (01280) 705801
Off A43 W of Brackley; NN13 5NF Stone-built village pub dating from the 15th c; enjoyable home-made food (not Sun evening) including vegetarian/vegan choices and monthly tapas evening, well kept Hook Norton Hooky, a beer named for the pub and a couple of guests, decent wines and over 20 gins, good friendly service, log fires; quiz every other Mon, film nights, free wi-fi; children and dogs welcome, picnic-sets in garden, two comfortable bothy bedrooms, open all day summer (all day Fri-Sun, from 4pm other days in winter). *(Peter Andrews)*

KETTERING   SP8778
Alexandra Arms (01536) 522730
Victoria Street; NN16 0BU Backstreet pub with up to 15 quickly changing ales kept well by knowledgeable landlord; basic opened-up bar with pump clips covering walls and ceiling, some snacky food, darts, hood skittles and TV in back games room; quiz night Weds; dogs welcome, a couple of picnic-sets out in front, small beer garden with benches behind, open all day (from 2pm Mon-Thurs). *(Julian and Fiona Barnes)*

KILSBY   SP5671
★ George (01788) 822229
2.5 miles from M1 junction 18: A428 towards Daventry, left on to A5 – pub off on right at roundabout; CV23 8YE Welcoming pub handy for the motorway (shuts 3-5.30pm); wood-panelled lounge with plush banquettes and coal-effect gas stove opening into smarter comfortably furnished area, proper old-fashioned public bar, well kept Adnams, Fullers, Timothy Taylors and a guest, fine range of malt whiskies, enjoyable good value home-made food including daily specials and themed evenings; Sun quiz, free-play pool tables, darts, TV, free wi-fi; children welcome if eating, dogs in bar, garden picnic-sets, six bedrooms. *(Nick Steadman)*

KINGS SUTTON   SP4936
White Horse (01295) 812440
The Square; OX17 3RF Attractively updated Cotswold-stone pub; low beams, flagstone and wood floors, open fire, highly rated creative cooking from chef-landlord along with some more pubby choices and good value set lunch, well kept Brakspears and Jennings, 16 wines by the glass, gin bar with over 40 varieties and cocktails, good friendly service; children and dogs (in bar) welcome, wheelchair access, front picnic-sets looking over village green to striking church, closed Mon, otherwise open all day. *(Jimmy Clark)*

KISLINGBURY   SP6959
Cromwell Cottage (01604) 830288
High Street; NN7 4AG Sizeable dining pub tucked away near River Nene; comfortable modernised bar/lounge with some beams and open fire, civil war themed pictures, maps and a large mural on one wall, smart dining room, popular food (booking advised) from snacks to specials including weekend brunch from 9am, well kept changing ales and nice wines, friendly staff; no dogs, plenty of seats on paved terrace, open (and food) all day. *(Simon and Alex Knight)*

KISLINGBURY   SP6959
Sun (01604) 833571
Off A45 W of Northampton; Mill Road; NN7 4BB Welcoming thatch and ironstone village pub; Greene King IPA, St Austell Tribute and a guest, enjoyable fairly

traditional food including pizzas and some vegetarian/vegan options, L-shaped bar-lounge and small separate dining area; quiz last Sun of month and occasional live music, sports TV, dominoes, board games, free wi-fi; children welcome, no dogs inside, disabled access, a few picnic-sets out at front, open all day weekends, no food Sun evening, Mon or lunchtime Tues. *(Ian and Sally Duncan)*

LITCHBOROUGH SP6353
Old Red Lion (01327) 830064
Banbury Road, just off former B4525 Banbury–Northampton; opposite church; NN12 8JF Attractive beamed pub with four cosy rooms; flagstoned bar with woodburner in big inglenook, three real ales such as Grainstore, Great Oakley and Merrimen, enjoyable reasonably priced pubby food (not Mon), friendly relaxed atmosphere, barn-conversion restaurant at back; table skittles, darts; children and dogs welcome, popular with walkers, terrace seating, open all day Sat, till 9pm Sun, from 2.30pm other days (4pm Mon). *(Charles Fraser)*

LITTLE BRINGTON SP6663
★Saracens Head (01604) 770640
4.5 miles from M1 junction 16, first right off A45 to Daventry; also signed off A428; Main Street; NN7 4HS Friendly old village pub freshened up and continuing well under new owners; good food from interesting varied menu (booking advised), well kept ales including Timothy Taylors Landlord, a dozen wines by the glass and 18 gins, helpful efficient service, roomy U-shaped beamed bar with woodburner, tartan carpeted book-lined dining room; children welcome, dogs in bar (resident lurcher is Ellie), disabled access, picnic-sets and rattan-style furniture out on gravel, country views and nearby walks, handy for Althorp House and Holdenby House, open all day, no food Sun evening. *(Cliff Wyatt)*

LITTLE HARROWDEN SP8671
Lamb (01933) 673300
Orlingbury Road/Kings Lane – off A509 or A43 S of Kettering; NN9 5BH Popular 17th-c pub in delightful village; split-level carpeted lounge bar with brasses on beams and log fire, dining area, good promptly served food including OAP lunch deal, three real ales and sensibly priced wine list; games room with hood skittles, background music, free wi-fi; children welcome, small raised terrace and garden, open all day weekends, no food Sun evening. *(Frances and Hamish Porter)*

LITTLE HOUGHTON SP8059
Four Pears (01604) 890900
Bedford Road, off A428 E of Northampton; NN7 1AB Modernised pub owned by four local couples (hence the name); three well kept ales, several wines by the glass and decent coffee, enjoyable

food (not Sun evening) from light dishes to daily specials, friendly service, good-sized bar, comfortable lounge with woodburner and separate restaurant; children and dogs welcome, spacious outside courtyard area, parking can be tricky (no car park, narrow village street), open all day from noon. *(Gerry and Rosemary Dobson)*

LODDINGTON SP8178
Hare (01536) 710337
Main Street; NN14 1LA Welcoming 17th-c stone-built dining pub with modernised interior; good fairly priced home-made food from baguettes up, five well kept ales such as Greene King, Gun Dog and Sharps; background music, TV, Sun quiz; children and dogs welcome, picnic-sets on front lawn, open all day weekends, closed Mon. *(Mike and Margaret Banks)*

LOWICK SP9780
Snooty Fox (01832) 733434
Off A6116 Corby–Raunds; NN14 3BH Solidly built 17th-c village pub under new family management; spacious lounge bar with woodburner in sizeable fireplace, stripped stone and handsomely moulded dark oak beams, leather sofas and easy chairs on big terracotta tiles, carved counter serving two well kept changing ales and a dozen wines by the glass, more formal dining rooms with chunky tables on pale wood floor, enjoyable food from pub favourites and pizzas up (some produce from own allotment), friendly helpful service; children and dogs (in bar) welcome, picnic-sets on front grass, play area, open all day weekends, closed Mon. *(Peter Andrews, Gerry and Rosemary Dobson, Clive and Fran Dutson)*

MAIDWELL SP7477
Stag (01604) 686700
Harborough Road (A508 N of Northampton); a mile from A14 junction 2; NN6 9JA Beamed dining pub with woodburner in pubby part by bar, extensive eating areas; good value traditional food served by friendly if not always speedy staff, well kept often local ales and good choice of other drinks; background music, sports TV, free wi-fi; children and dogs (in bar) welcome, disabled facilities, picnic-sets on back terrace, good-sized sloping garden beyond, five bedrooms, not far from splendid Palladian Kelmarsh Hall and park, open all day Fri and Sun. *(Mike and Margaret Banks, Gerry and Rosemary Dobson)*

MOULTON SP7866
Telegraph (01604) 648228
West Street; NN3 7SB Welcoming old village pub with good popular food from sandwiches and pizzas up, well kept Fullers, Sharps and a couple of guests, log fire in bar, back restaurant extension; children welcome, open (and food) all day Fri and Sat, till 9pm (5pm) Sun. *(Ian and Sally Duncan)*

NETHER HEYFORD   SP6658
Olde Sun (01327) 340164
1.75 miles from M1 junction 16; village signposted left off A45 westbound; Middle Street; NN7 3LL Popular village pub (some recent refurbishment) with small atmospheric linked rooms; beams and low ceilings, rugs on parquet, red tiles or flagstones (steps between some areas), big inglenook log fire, assorted bric-a-brac including brassware, railway memorabilia, advertising signs and World War II posters, nice old cash till in one part, Banks's, Greene King and two guests, good range of gins and enjoyable well priced food from sandwiches and baguettes up, takeaway fish and chips Fri, games room with hood skittles and darts; background music, quiz night second Sun of month; children and dogs welcome, old farm equipment outside, open all day, no food Sun evening, Mon. *(Laura Bennett)*

NORTHAMPTON   SP7560
Albion Brewery Bar (01604) 946606
Kingswell Street; NN1 1PR Tap for revived 19th-c Albion Brewery (visible through glass partition, tours available); half a dozen Phipps ales in top condition plus a guest and local cider, also their own Kingswell gins, bar food Tues-Sun, friendly staff, pitched-ceiling bar with big windows and reclaimed fittings (many from closed Phipps pubs), traditional games including northamptonshire skittles and bar billiards; live music (upstairs concert venue still planned); children and dogs welcome, disabled access/loo, open all day Fri and Sat, closed Sun evening, Mon lunchtime. *(Jess and George Cowley)*

NORTHAMPTON   SP7261
Hopping Hare (01604) 580090
Harlestone Road (A428), New Duston; NN5 6PF Spacious Edwardian pub-restaurant-hotel on edge of housing estate, contemporary and comfortable, with good well presented food from lunchtime sandwiches and pub favourites to more pricey restaurant dishes, lunchtime/early evening set menu Mon-Thurs, three well kept ales and a dozen wines by the glass including champagne, prompt friendly service; background music, daily newspapers, free wi-fi; children welcome, tables out on deck, 20 comfortable modern bedrooms, good breakfast, open (and food) all day. *(Gerry and Rosemary Dobson)*

NORTHAMPTON   SP7560
Lamplighter (01604) 631125
Overstone Road; NN1 3JS Welcoming Victorian corner pub in the Mounts area attracting good mix of customers; wide choice of draught and bottled beers (beer festivals), well priced generously served food including range of burgers, good vegetarian options and popular Sun roasts; regular live music (open mike Mon), quiz Weds; children

welcome if eating, picnic-sets in heated courtyard, open (and food) all day. *(Michael Domeney)*

NORTHAMPTON   SP7661
Olde England (01604) 603799
Kettering Road, near the racecourse; NN1 4BP Quirky conversion of Victorian corner shop over three floors (steepish stairs to upper level and down to cellar bar), ground-floor room with assorted tables and chairs on bare boards, 20 changing ales and similar number of ciders served from hatch on stairs, lots of pictures with medieval or Arthurian themes, plus the odd banner, boar's head and suit of armour, cheap food with more extensive choice weekends when pub at its busiest, friendly staff and broad mix of customers; cards and board games; children and dogs welcome, open all day Fri-Sun, closed lunchtimes other days. *(Jimmy Clark)*

NORTHAMPTON   SP7660
Princess Alexandra (01604) 245485
Alexandra Road; NN1 5QP Revamped backstreet pub (near the town centre) calling itself a Craft Beer & Alehouse; spacious relaxed bars with pleasing modern décor, recycled timber, exposed brickwork and woodburner, wide range of changing beers and some interesting ciders, tasters offered by friendly knowledgeable staff, shortish menu including snacks and pizzas; children and dogs welcome, small garden behind, parking nearby can be difficult, closed Mon-Weds lunchtime, otherwise open all day (till 1am Fri, Sat). *(Jimmy Clark)*

NORTHAMPTON   SP7560
Wig & Pen (01604) 622178
St Giles Street; NN1 1JA Long L-shaped beamed room with bar running most of its length; up to a dozen well kept ales (tasters offered) including Adnams, Fullers and Greene King, traditional ciders and good choice of bottled beers, whiskies and gins, generous helpings of reasonably priced pub food (not weekend evenings) from sandwiches and snacks up, friendly young staff; summer Tues jazz and other live music, weekend DJs, sports TVs; split-level walled garden behind, handy for Guildhall and Derngate Theatre, open all day (till 1.30am Fri, Sat) and busy on Saints rugby days. *(Michael Domeney, Dr J Barrie Jones, Nigel and Sue Foster)*

OLD   SP7873
White Horse (01604) 781297
Walgrave Road, N of Northampton between A43 and A508; NN6 9QX Popular and welcoming village pub; good sensibly priced food from shortish menu along with some interesting specials (booking advised), three well kept changing ales, craft beers, proper ciders and decent wines by the glass, friendly if not always fast

service, additional dining area upstairs; quiz night first Thurs of month, live music last Fri, free wi-fi; well behaved children and dogs welcome, garden and deck overlooking 13th-c church, outside pizza oven, open all day Fri and Sat, till 7pm Sun, closed Mon. *(Gerry and Rosemary Dobson, Pete Newton)*

OUNDLE   TL0388
Ship (01832) 586934
West Street; PE8 4EF Bustling down-to-earth pub run by two brothers; heavily beamed lounge to left of central corridor, cosy areas with mix of leather and other seats, sturdy tables and log fire in stone inglenook, well kept Brewsters, Nene Valley, Sharps and Timothy Taylors, eight wines by the glass and fair value pubby food (not Sun evening), charming panelled snug at one end, also refurbished bistro bar and terrace bar with pool, darts and sports TV; background and some live music, free wi-fi; children and dogs welcome, series of small covered terraces (lit at night), 14 bedrooms, open all day. *(Katherine Matthews)*

OUNDLE   TL0388
Talbot (01832) 273621
New Street; PE8 4EA Hotel in handsome former merchant's house; various rooms including comfortably modernised bar serving a couple of real ales such as Digfield, enjoyable food from sandwiches and sharing plates up, good helpful service, restaurant; children welcome, seats in courtyard and garden, 40 bedrooms, open (and food) all day, breakfast from 7am. *(Nick Steadman)*

RAVENSTHORPE   SP6670
Chequers (01604) 770379
Chequers Lane; NN6 8ER Cosy old creeper-clad brick pub set among modern residential development; L-shaped bar and restaurant, well kept ales including Oakham and Thwaites, good choice of enjoyable reasonably priced food from light snacks to steaks and daily specials, banquettes, cushioned pews and sturdy tables, coal-effect fire; children and dogs welcome, partly covered side terrace, play area and separate building for northamptonshire skittles, handy for Ravensthorpe Reservoir and Coton Manor Garden, open all day weekends. *(Charles Fraser)*

ROCKINGHAM   SP8691
Sondes Arms (01536) 772193
Main Street; LE16 8TG Refurbished 16th-c pub under same owners as the Thornhill Arms at Rushton; cleanly updated beamed interior with wood and stone floors, modern furnishings and woodburner, popular good value home-made food including bargain set menus (Mon-Fri, Sat lunchtime) and carvery (Weds evening, Sun), four real ales, helpful friendly staff; children and dogs welcome, courtyard picnic-sets, attractive views of castle and church, lovely village

(except for traffic), open (and food) all day Sun, closed Mon evening Jan and Feb. *(Mike and Margaret Banks)*

RUSHDEN   SP9566
Station Bar (01933) 318988
Station Approach; NN10 0AW Not a pub but part of station HQ of Rushden Historical Transport Society (non-members can sign in for £1); bar in former ladies' waiting room with gas lighting, enamel signs and railway memorabilia, seven ales including Dark Star and Phipps, tea and coffee, filled rolls and perhaps some hot food, friendly staff; also museum and summer train rides, table skittles in a Royal Mail carriage; outside benches, open all day weekends, closed weekday lunchtimes. *(Ian and Sally Duncan)*

RUSHTON   SP8483
Thornhill Arms (01536) 710251
Station Road; NN14 1RL Busy family-run dining pub opposite lovely village's cricket green; enjoyable food (booking advised) including keenly priced set menu (weekday evenings, Sat lunchtime) and carvery (Sun, Mon evening), gluten-free menu too, up to four well kept ales such as Black Sheep and Sharps, smart high-beamed back restaurant and several other neatly laid-out dining areas, open fire; children welcome, garden with decked area, open (and food) all day Sun. *(Mike and Margaret Banks)*

SHUTLANGER   SP7249
Plough (01604) 864644
Main Road, off A43 N of Towcester; NN12 7RU Revamped dining pub with excellent food presented with real flair (booking advised), three real ales including St Austell Tribute, good choice of wines by the glass, cocktails (weekday happy hour 5-7pm), efficient friendly service; painted picnic-sets on gravel terrace, nearby walks (dogs allowed in the bar), closed Mon and Tues, otherwise open all day (Sun till 9pm, food till 4.30pm). *(Alan Sutton)*

SPRATTON   SP7170
Kings Head (01604) 847351
Brixworth Road, off A5199 N of Northampton; NN6 8HH Combination of brasserie, bar and coffee shop; pale flagstones and ancient stripped stonework mixing well with handsome new wood flooring and up-to-date décor, leather chesterfields, an antique settle and café chairs around stripped tables, woodburner in brick fireplace, Shepherd Neame Spitfire, a changing beer from Grainstore and eight wines by the glass, decent range of gins and cocktails, good popular food from light lunches up; background music, free wi-fi; children and dogs (in bar) welcome, back courtyard with modern tables and chairs, open all day Fri-Sun, no food Sun evening (coffee shop from 8.30am-5pm, closed Sun). *(Alan Sutton)*

STANWICK   SP9871
Duke of Wellington (01933) 622452
Church Street; NN9 6PS Welcoming 19th-c stone pub next to the church; fresh contemporary décor in split level interior, good well presented food (not Sun evening) from lunchtime sandwiches and pub favourites up including vegan choices, real ales such as Greene King Abbot and IPA, craft beers and decent range of wines; background and occasional live music, Weds quiz; children welcome, picnic-sets out at front under parasols, more behind, open all day (till 10pm Mon-Thurs, 11pm Fri, Sat, 9pm Sun). *(Peter Andrews)*

STAVERTON   SP5461
Countryman (01327) 311815
Daventry Road (A425); NN11 6JH Beamed and carpeted dining pub with popular food from shortish menu including some interesting vegetarian choices, Bombardier, Phipps and a guest, bar divided by brick pillars, restaurant; background music; children and dogs welcome, disabled access, tables out at front and in small garden behind, open (and food) all day Sun. *(Julian and Fiona Barnes)*

STOKE BRUERNE   SP7449
Boat (01604) 862428
3.5 miles from M1 junction 15 – A508 towards Stony Stratford, then signed on right; Bridge Road; NN12 7SB Long thatched pub (run by the same family since 1887) in picturesque canalside spot; traditional flagstoned bar with open fire, half a dozen well kept Marstons-related ales and maybe a local guest, Thatcher's cider, enjoyable fairly standard food at reasonable prices from baguettes up, friendly service, more modern central-pillared back bar and bistro, comfortable upstairs bookable restaurant with separate menu (closed Mon, Sun evening); background music, northamptonshire skittles; children and dogs welcome, disabled facilities, tables out by towpath opposite canal museum, shop for boaters and trips on own narrowboat, open all day and can get very busy in summer, especially weekends when parking nearby difficult, open all day from 9am for breakfast. *(Revd R P Tickle)*

STOKE DOYLE   TL0286
★ Shuckburgh Arms (01832) 272339
Village signed (down Stoke Hill) from SW edge of Oundle; PE8 5TG Relaxed 17th-c pub in quiet hamlet; four traditional rooms with some modern touches, low black beams in bowed ceilings, pictures on pastel walls, lots of pale tables on wood or carpeted floors, stylish art deco seats and elegant dining chairs, inglenook woodburner, well kept ales such as Nene Valley and Black Sheep from granite-top bar, well selected wines and popular sensibly priced food

including Thurs steak night, helpful attentive staff; soft background music; children welcome, disabled access/loos, garden with decked area and play frame, bedrooms in separate modern block, closed Sun evening, Mon. *(Peter Andrews)*

SUDBOROUGH   SP9682
Vane Arms (01832) 730033
Off A6116; Main Street; NN14 3BX Old thatched pub in pretty village; low beams, stripped stonework and inglenook fires, well kept Everards Tiger and guests, enjoyable freshly cooked food served by friendly staff, restaurant; free wi-fi; children and well behaved dogs (in bar) welcome, disabled loo, terrace tables, three bedrooms in nearby building, closed Sun evening. *(Jimmy Clark)*

SULGRAVE   SP5545
★ Star (01295) 760389
Manor Road; E of Banbury, signed off B4525; OX17 2SA Handsome creeper-clad inn under newish family management; woodburner in fine inglenook, working shutters, old doors and flagstones, mix of antique, vintage and retro furniture, polished copper and brass, Hook Norton ales, several wines by the glass and enjoyable food from short but varied menu, friendly service, dining room with working range, snug in former farmhouse kitchen; children and dogs welcome, back garden where aunt sally is played, short walk to Sulgrave Manor (George Washington's ancestral home), three bedrooms named after racehorses, closed Sun evening, Mon. *(John Pritchard)*

THORNBY   SP6675
★ Red Lion (01604) 740238
Welford Road; A5199 Northampton–Leicester; NN6 8SJ Popular old village pub with interesting range of well kept/priced changing ales, very good home-cooked food (not Sun evening, Mon) from standards up including notable steak and stilton pie, smaller helpings available for some lunchtime dishes, prompt friendly service, beams and log fire, lots of old local photographs, back dining area; children and dogs welcome, garden with picnic-sets, accommodation in converted barn, open all day weekends when can get very busy (booking advised), closed Mon lunchtime. *(Mike and Margaret Banks, Gerry and Rosemary Dobson)*

THORPE MANDEVILLE   SP5344
★ Three Conies (01295) 711025
Off B4525 E of Banbury; OX17 2EX Attractive and welcoming 17th-c ironstone pub; well kept Hook Norton ales and good choice of enjoyable locally sourced food (not Sun evening, Mon), beamed bar with some stripped stone, mix of old tables and comfortable seating on bare boards, log fires, large dining room; background and live music, quiz first Tues of month, TV, hood

skittles; children and dogs welcome, disabled facilities, tables out in front, more behind on decking and lawn, closed lunchtimes Mon and Tues, otherwise open all day. *(Katherine Matthews)*

TOWCESTER SP7047

Folly (01327) 354031

A5 S, opposite racecourse; NN12 6LB Early 18th-c thatched and beamed dining pub with highly rated food (booking advised) including more affordable set lunch, good selection of wines and a couple of well kept local beers such as Towcester Mill, friendly efficient staff, small bar with steps up to dining area; children (till 8pm) and dogs (in bar) welcome, tables out at back, open all day Sun till 9pm, closed Mon. *(Gerry and Rosemary Dobson)*

TOWCESTER SP6948

Towcester Mill (01327) 437060

Chantry Lane; NN12 6YY Old mill tucked away behind market square surrounded by redevelopment; nice little bare-boards bar acting as tap for on-site brewery (tours available – book ahead), seven ales including a couple of guests, also good range of ciders, friendly knowledgeable staff; live music, comedy and quiz nights in upstairs room; dogs welcome, garden behind with seats by mill race and pond, closed lunchtimes Mon-Fri, and shuts at 8pm Sun and Mon. *(Matt Stevens)*

TURWESTON SP6037

Stratton Arms (01280) 704956

E of crossroads in village; pub itself just inside Buckinghamshire; NN13 5JX Friendly chatty local in picturesque village; five well kept ales including Otter and good choice of other drinks, enjoyable reasonably priced traditional food (Weds-Sun lunchtimes, Weds-Sat evenings), low ceilings and two log fires, small restaurant; background music, sports TV; children and dogs welcome, large pleasant garden by Great Ouse with barbecue and play area, camping, open all day, till 7pm Sun. *(Katherine Matthews)*

TWYWELL SP9578

Old Friar (01832) 732625

Lower Street, off A14 W of Thrapston; NN14 3AH Welcoming pub with enjoyable food including set lunch menu and Sun carvery, Greene King and a couple of guests, modernised split-level interior with beams and some exposed stonework; children and dogs (in bar) welcome, garden with good play area, open (and food) all day weekends. *(Mike and Margaret Banks)*

UPPER BODDINGTON SP4853

Plough (01327) 260364

Warwick Road; NN11 6DH 18th-c thatched village inn keeping much of its original character; small beamed and

flagstoned bar, lobby with old local photos, four real ales including Greene King and Shepherd Neame, a dozen wines by the glass and enjoyable fairly traditional food in restaurant, snug or intimate 'Doll's Parlour' named after former veteran landlady, friendly efficient service, woodburners; quiz first Sun of month, occasional live music and beer festivals, free wi-fi; children and dogs welcome, five bedrooms (some sharing bathroom), open all day weekends, no food Sun evening. *(Matt Stevens)*

WALGRAVE SP8072

Royal Oak (01604) 781248

Zion Hill, off A43 Northampton– Kettering; NN6 9PN Welcoming old stone-built village local; good fairly priced food including set lunch menu and daily specials, well kept Adnams, Greene King and three guests, decent wines, friendly prompt service, long three-part carpeted beamed bar, small lounge and back restaurant extension; live music and quiz nights, sports TV, darts and northamptonshire skittles; children welcome, no dogs inside, small garden with play area, open all day Sun. *(Mike and Margaret Banks, Gerry and Rosemary Dobson, Alan Sutton)*

WELFORD SP6480

Wharf Inn (01858) 575075

Pub just over Leicestershire border; NN6 6JQ Spacious castellated Georgian folly in delightful setting by two Grand Union Canal marinas; six well kept ales such as Grainstore, Marstons and Oakham in unpretentious pub, popular reasonably priced food (all day Sun) including good steak and kidney pudding and daily specials, helpful friendly service, pleasant dining section; children and dogs welcome, wheelchair access (portable ramps) and disabled loo, large waterside garden and enjoyable local walks, four bedrooms, open all day. *(Mike and Margaret Banks, Tony Hobden)*

WELLINGBOROUGH SP8867

Coach & Horses (01933) 441848

Oxford Street; NN8 4HY L-shaped bar adorned with breweriana including hundreds of pump clips fixed to the beams; a dozen well kept changing ales, ten craft beers, 15 ciders and 80 gins, good value pubby food including speciality pies, friendly staff, comfortable cosy atmosphere with open fire; sports TV; no children but dogs welcome, disabled access, beer garden, open all day (till 6pm Sun, 9pm Mon), no food Sun evening, Mon or Tues. *(Tony and Wendy Hobden)*

WELTON SP5866

White Horse (01327) 702820

Off A361/B4036 N of Daventry; behind church, High Street; NN11 2JP Beamed 17th-c village pub on different levels; well kept Purity, Oakham, Sharps and a couple of guests, local cider and nice house wines, reasonably priced food (not Sun evening, Mon, Tues) including good value steak deal Weds-Sat, roasts only on Sun, woodburners, separate games bar with darts and skittles, small dining room; fortnightly Sun quiz and some live music; children and dogs welcome in one part, attractive garden and terrace, open all day Fri-Sun, closed Mon and Tues lunchtimes. *(Ian and Sally Duncan)*

WESTON   SP5846
Crown (01295) 760310
The Weston N of Brackley; Helmdon Road; NN12 8PX Handsome 16th-c stone-built inn (ex-farmhouse); updated interior with log fires, painted beams and exposed stone walls, Hook Norton Hooky, Sharps Doom Bar and Towcester Mill Race, well liked food from sandwiches and good value pubby dishes to more restauranty choices, Weds fish night, good friendly service; children and dogs welcome, five bedrooms, attractive village handy for Canons Ashby (NT) and Sulgrave Manor, closed Sun evening and lunchtimes Mon, Tues. *(Jimmy Clark)*

WHITTLEBURY   SP6943
Fox & Hounds (01327) 858048
High Street; NN12 8XJ Double-fronted

19th-c village bar-restaurant; modern interior with wood flooring and comfy stylish seating, four well kept ales, nice selection of wines and good well presented food from sandwiches and sharing boards up (separate bar and restaurant menus), friendly helpful service; children and dogs welcome, picnic-sets on suntrap gravel terrace, handy for Silverstone, open all day weekends, closed Mon. *(Matt Stevens)*

YARDLEY HASTINGS   SP8656
★ **Rose & Crown** (01604) 696276
Just off A428 Bedford–Northampton; NN7 1EX Spacious and popular 18th-c dining pub in pretty village; flagstones, beams, stripped stonework and quiet corners, step up to big comfortable dining room, flowers on tables, good well presented food from interesting changing menu along with bar snacks and pubby choices, efficient friendly young staff, six well kept ales including a house beer from local Hart Family, four ciders and decent range of wines; background and occasional live music, daily newspapers; children welcome till 9pm, dogs in bar, tables under parasols in split-level garden, boules, open all day (from 5pm Mon). *(Frances and Hamish Porter)*

Northumbria

(County Durham, Northumberland and Tyneside)

KEY ★ Star Pub 🍽 Top Quality Food 🍺 Great Beer

🍷 Good Wines £ Bargain Meals 🛏 Good Bedrooms 🍴 Serves Food

BARRASFORD

Barrasford Arms 🍽

(01434) 681237 – www.barrasfordarms.co.uk

Village signposted off A6079 N of Hexham; NE48 4AA

**Good local atmosphere in friendly bar, smarter dining rooms,
rewarding food and drinks and seats outside; bedrooms**

You can be sure of a warm welcome from the hard-working, hands-on
licensees of this sandstone inn. The traditional, bustling bar has a log
fire, old photos and bric-a-brac and ales such as First & Last Equinox and
High House Farm Auld Hemp on handpump, seven wines by the glass, local
gins and five malt whiskies. Two dining rooms have either upholstered and
striped or leather high-backed chairs around wooden tables; one has wall
seating at the end of the room and the other has a stone chimneybreast hung
with guns and copper pans; background music, TV, darts and board games.
A new decking area makes the most of the fine views, while the warm,
comfortable bedrooms make the perfect base for exploring nearby Hadrian's
Wall; breakfasts are highly rated. There's a new storage area set aside for
cyclists and fishermen – and good fishing can be found on the North Tyne
River just 100 metres away.

🍽 The landlord cooks the highly regarded food: sandwiches, black pudding scotch
egg with apple purée and celeriac rémoulade, confit pork belly terrine with
caramelised onion and cranberry chutney, maple-roast vegetable tart with rocket and
sage butter sauce, hake and chips, chicken breast with fondant potato, confit carrot and
red wine jus, local pheasant with bacon croquette and whisky cream, lambs liver with
bacon, pomme purée and crispy onion rings, and puddings such as chocolate orange
terrine with salted caramel and hazelnut praline and Baileys crème brûlée; they also
offer a two- and three-course set lunch. *Benchmark main dish: rib-eye steak with
onion rings, peppercorn sauce and chips £22.00. Two-course evening meal £22.00.*

Free house ~ Licensees Michael and Victoria Eames ~ Real ale ~ Open 12-11; closed Mon ~
Bar food 12-2, 6-8.30; 12-3 ~ Restaurant ~ Children welcome ~ Wi-fi ~ Bedrooms: £75/£95
*Recommended by Michael Doswell, Richard and Tessa Ibbot, Robert and Diana Myers, Julia and
Fiona Barnes*

A star after the name of a pub shows exceptional quality. It means most people
(after reading the report to see just why the star has been won) would think a special
trip worthwhile.

BLANCHLAND
NY9650 Map 10

Lord Crewe Arms ★ 🎯 🍷 🍴 🛏

(01434) 675469 – www.lordcrewearmsblanchland.co.uk

B6306 S of Hexham; DH8 9SP

Wonderful historic building, with unique Crypt bar, cosy dining rooms and spacious character restaurant; comfortable, well equipped bedrooms

Locals, walkers and those enjoying the rather smart (yet informal) restaurant all mingle easily here, welcomed by the genuinely friendly and helpful staff. It was built as a guest house in 1235 for the neighbouring premonstratensian monastery and the architecture is remarkable. The Crypt bar is a medieval vaulted room sculpted by thick stone walls, lit by candlelight and with family crests on the ceiling. There are high wooden stools by wall shelves and against the armour-plated counter, cushioned settles and plush stools around a few little tables, with Hadrian Border Tyneside Blonde, Wylam Red Kite and Lord Crewe Brew (named for the pub from Wylam) on handpump, 14 wines by the glass, ten malt whiskies and a farm cider; background music and board games. One character sitting area has a leather sofa and two big tartan armchairs on flagstones in front of a large open fire, while the grand restaurant features a fine old wooden floor, cushioned wall seating and leather-cushioned dining chairs around oak-topped tables, fresh flowers, antlers on the walls and a large central candelabra. It's a real treat to stay in the bedrooms, which range from cosy to luxury suites; breakfast is excellent. Derwent Reservoir is nearby.

First class food includes sandwiches, salt-aged steak tartare with an egg yolk, chicken terrine with piccalilli, ricotta gnocchi with squash, kale and cheese, mutton haggis and sausage on toast with crispy egg and spinach, fish pie with whipped potato, chicken breast with haggis and sausage patty, leeks and mustard cream sauce, halibut fillet with dill hollandaise, salt-aged lamb loin with baked shallots and caper butter, and puddings such as chocolate fondant and raspberry bakewell pudding. *Benchmark main dish: chargrilled picanha (rump) steak with garlic butter and fries £15.00. Two-course evening meal £24.00.*

Free house ~ Licensee Tommy Mark ~ Real ale ~ Open 7am-midnight ~ Bar food 12-2.30, 6-9; 12-3, 6-9 Sat; 12-3.30, 6.30-8.30 Sun ~ Restaurant ~ Children welcome ~ Dogs allowed in bar and bedrooms ~ Wi-fi ~ Bedrooms: /£147 *Recommended by Peter Meister, Paul Faraday, Andrew and Michele Revell, Buster and Helena Hastings, Rob Anderson, Bill Braithwaite, Nicholas and Maddy Trainer*

COTHERSTONE
NZ0119 Map 10

Fox & Hounds 🛏

(01833) 650241 – www.cotherstonefox.co.uk

B6277; DL12 9PF

Bustling Georgian inn with good food, real ales and quite a few wines by the glass; bedrooms

This is a genuine country pub with warmly welcoming and helpful licensees. The cheerful, simply furnished beamed bar has a partly wooden floor (elsewhere it's carpeted), a good winter log fire, thickly cushioned wall seats and local photographs and country pictures in various alcoves and recesses. There's Black Sheep Ram Tackle, Pennine Hair of the Dog and Tirril 1823 on handpump, alongside seven wines by the glass and over 20 gins and malt whiskies. There are seats outside on a terrace and quoits. The bright, clean and comfortable bedrooms make a good base for exploring the area; fine surrounding walks. Disabled access.

As well as fresh fish delivered daily, the pleasing food includes sandwiches, warm bacon, cheese and red apple salad, baked pot of prawns, leeks and mushrooms in cream cheese with a herb crust, french vegetable bake, gammon steak with tomato and cheese melt, lambs liver with mustard mash, crispy bacon and rich gravy, steak and black pudding in ale pie, beer-battered haddock and chips, and puddings such as chocolate cream crunch and sticky toffee pudding. *Benchmark main dish: cheese-filled chicken with bacon and creamy leek sauce £11.80. Two-course evening meal £20.00.*

Free house ~ Licensee Nichola Swinburn ~ Real ale ~ Open 12-3, 6-11; 12-3, 6-midnight Sat; closed Mon-Weds lunchtimes Nov-Easter ~ Bar food 12-2, 6-8.30; 12-2, 6-9 Fri, Sat ~ Restaurant ~ Children welcome ~ Dogs allowed in bar and bedrooms ~ Wi-fi ~ Bedrooms: $50/$90 *Recommended by Trevor and Michele Street, Anne and Ben Smith, Mungo Shipley, Elise and Charles Mackinlay, Phoebe Peacock*

CRASTER
NU2519 Map 10

Jolly Fisherman

(01665) 576461 – www.thejollyfishermancraster.co.uk
Off B1339, NE of Alnwick; NE66 3TR

Stunning views, very good food and plenty of seasonal visitors

A simple place, this is lifted right out of the ordinary by its lovely position overlooking the harbour and out to sea and by the friendly welcome. The seats and tables in the garden have the same view and get snapped up pretty quickly on a warm day. The busy bar has a warming winter fire, leather button-back wall banquettes and upholstered and wooden dining chairs around hefty tables on bare boards, a few stools scattered here and there, and photographs and paintings in gilt-edged frames; background music. Black Sheep, Mordue Workie Ticket, Timothy Taylors Landlord and a changing guest on handpump are served by helpful staff. From big windows in the upstairs dining room you look down on the water. They have a couple of fishermen's cottages and an apartment for rent, as well as a café and gift shop opposite the pub. This is a fine base for walkers and the route from here along the cliff to ruined Dunstanburgh Castle (English Heritage) is popular.

 Tasty food includes sandwiches, their famous crab soup, omelette arnold bennett, burger with toppings and chips, smoked haddock and salmon fishcakes with tartare sauce, grilled squid with chickpeas, pancetta and herb salad, venison or rib-eye steaks with beef dripping chips, asian-spiced hake with cauliflower purée, bhaji and bombay potatoes, and puddings such as double chocolate cheesecake and lemon posset. *Benchmark main dish: fish platter £17.00. Two-course evening meal £21.00.*

Punch ~ Lease David Whitehead ~ Real ale ~ Open 11-11; 12-10.30 Sun ~ Bar food 11-3, 5.30-8.30; 12-7 Sun; closed Mon evening in winter ~ Restaurant ~ Children welcome ~ Dogs allowed in bar ~ Wi-fi *Recommended by Margaret and Peter Staples, John and Sylvia Harrop, Darren and Jane Staniforth, Tracey and Stephen Groves, WAH*

DIPTONMILL
NY9261 Map 10

Dipton Mill Inn 🍷 🍺 £

(01434) 606577 – www.diptonmill.co.uk
Dipton Mill Road, S of Hexham; village signed from B6306; NE46 1YA

Own-brew beers from on-site microbrewery, good value bar food and waterside terrace

The fine choice of drinks here includes beers from their family-owned Hexhamshire Brewery. Well kept on handpump these are Blackhall English Stout, Devils Elbow, Devils Water, Shire Bitter and Whapweasel. Also, 11 wines by the glass, 18 malt whiskies and a guest cider. This is a quaint little country pub and the neatly kept snug bar has genuine character, dark ply panelling, low ceilings, red furnishings, a dark red carpet and two welcoming open fires. The garden is peaceful and pretty with attractive planting and seats on grass by a restored mill stream. Hexham Racecourse is not far away and there are also woodland walks nearby.

 Remarkable value food includes chicken liver pâté, smoked salmon and prawns, cheese and onion flan, chicken breast with sherry sauce, lambs liver and sausages, haddock in tomato and basil sauce, steak and kidney pie, and puddings such as apple crumble and syrup sponge and custard. *Benchmark main dish: mince and dumplings £7.95. Two-course evening meal £14.00.*

Own brew ~ Licensee Mark Brooker ~ Real ale ~ Open 12-2.30, 6-11; 12-3 Sun ~ Bar food 12-2, 6-8.30; 12-2 Sun ~ Children welcome ~ Wi-fi *Recommended by Martine and Colin Fresher, Sally and Brian Turner, Jill and Hugh Bennett, Caroline and Peter Bryant, Nik and Gloria Clarke*

DURHAM
NZ2742 Map 10

Victoria 🍺

(0191) 386 5269 – www.victoriainn-durhamcity.co.uk
Hallgarth Street (A177, near Dunelm House); DH1 3AS

Unchanging and neatly kept Victorian pub with royal memorabilia, cheerful locals and well kept regional ales; bedrooms

The original Victorian décor is still in place here and the immaculately kept inn remains charming and unspoilt – just how the long-serving owners like it. Three small rooms, leading off a central bar, have mahogany, etched and cut glass and mirrors, colourful William Morris wallpaper over a high panelled dado, some maroon plush seats in little booths, leatherette wall seats and long narrow drinkers' tables. Also, coal fires in handsome iron and tile fireplaces, photographs and articles showing a real pride in the pub, lots of period prints and engravings of Queen Victoria, and staffordshire figurines of her and the Prince Consort. Big Lamp Lamp Light, Durham White Stout, Fyne Jarl and Wylam Gold Tankard on handpump, over 35 irish whiskeys, 60 scottish malts and fair priced house wines; dominoes. Attractive bedrooms, hearty breakfasts and free off-street parking make this little gem perfect for exploring the city's castle and cathedral. Credit cards are accepted only for accommodation. No food.

Free house ~ Licensee Michael Webster ~ Real ale ~ No credit cards ~ Open 11.45-11; 12-10.30 Sun ~ Children welcome ~ Dogs welcome ~ Bedrooms: £70/£88 *Recommended by William Pace, Caroline Sullivan, Sophie Ellison, Carol and Barry Craddock, Margaret McDonald, Miles Green*

GILSLAND
NY6366 Map 10

Samson 🍺

(016977) 47880 – www.thesamson.co.uk
B6318, E end of village; CA8 7DR

Friendly village pub in wonderful countryside, with cheerful atmosphere in cosy bar, local ales and enjoyable food; bedrooms

Three farmers run this charming and busy pub that's just 30 metres from the Hadrian's Wall Path and on Hadrian's Cycleway. The chatty bar has woodburning stoves, cushioned settles, traditional chairs and stools around sewing machine-treadle and other pubby tables on red-patterned carpeting, swagged curtains, and plush stools at the carved wooden counter. Allendale Golden Plover and Muckle Tickle on handpump and several wines by the glass served by friendly staff; throughout the year they hold quiz nights, themed evenings and live music events. In the dining room are beige tartan-upholstered chairs around white-clothed tables on wide floorboards and prints on red or yellow walls. There are picnic-sets on the back lawn, and warm and attractive bedrooms that make a good base for exploring the area. They also run Willowford Farm B&B just outside the village.

They use their own produce for the popular food: twice-baked cheddar soufflé, chicken liver and smoked bacon pâté with redcurrant, orange and port, and chilli jelly, mixed mushroom risotto with chestnut and onion topping, steak in ale pie, gammon and free-range eggs, local sausages with mash and caramelised onion gravy, chicken breast in cheese sauce topped with bacon and mozzarella crumb, and puddings such as apple and coconut crumble with custard and creamy armagnac parfait served with their own fig compôte. *Benchmark main dish: salmon, cod and smoked haddock pie £12.45. Two-course evening meal £20.00.*

Free house ~ Licensees Liam McNulty and Lauren Harrison ~ Real ale ~ Open 12-10.30 ~ Bar food 12-2.30, 6-8.30 ~ Children welcome ~ Dogs allowed in bar ~ Wi-fi ~ Acoustic night second Sun of month ~ Bedrooms: /£90 *Recommended by Serena and Adam Furber, Geoff and Ann Marston, Beverley and Andy Butcher, Patti and James Davidson, Dan and Nicki Barton, Peter and Alison Steadman*

HEDLEY ON THE HILL
Feathers 🌟 🍷 🍺

NZ0759   Map 10

(01661) 843607 – www.thefeathers.net

Village signposted from New Ridley, which is signposted from B6309 N of Consett; OS Sheet 88 map reference 078592; NE43 7SW

Northumbria Dining Pub of the Year

Hilltop tavern with imaginative food, interesting beers from small breweries and a friendly welcome

Hard-working, hands-on licensees keep everything just right here and the pub is very much the heart of the local community. Tiny but very well run and welcoming, there are two neat, homely bars with open fires, tankard-hung beams, stripped stonework, solid furniture including settles, and old black and white photographs of local places and farm and country workers. Allendale Wagtail Best Bitter, Mordue Workie Ticket and a couple of guest beers on handpump, as well as a wide range of farm ciders, 30 wines by the glass, 30 malt whiskies, home-flavoured gins and home-produced cordials. They regularly hold wine and beer evenings, festivals and other events (see the website for details); dominoes and board games. The picnic-sets at the front are a nice place to sit and watch the world drift by.

First class food using only the best, carefully sourced local produce from artisan producers and farmers includes home-cured rare-breed ox tongue pastrami with potato salad and pickled beetroot, baked duck egg with morel mushrooms, wild garlic and cream, roast cauliflower steak with warm cracked wheat, roasted tomato and pepper sauce, beer-battered fish and chips, rabbit, cider and wild mushroom pie, local roast mallard with marmalade and Cointreau and celeriac purée, slow-cooked rare-breed lamb with braised spelt, leeks, carrots and mint, and puddings such as almond and orange sponge with vanilla custard and dark chocolate brownie with candied walnuts and vanilla ice-cream. *Benchmark main dish: roe deer wellington with port and redcurrant jelly sauce and dauphinoise potatoes £21.00. Two-course evening meal £21.00.*

Free house ~ Licensees Rhian Cradock and Helen Greer ~ Real ale ~ Open 6-10.30 Mon, Weds; 12-11.30 Thur-Sun; closed Mon and Weds lunchtimes, all day Tues ~ Bar food 6-8.30

Weds; 12-2.30, 6-8.30 Thurs-Sat; 12-4.30 Sun ~ Children welcome ~ Wi-fi *Recommended by Chris and Sophie Baxter, Martine and Colin Fresher, Melanie and David Lawson, Helena and Trevor Fraser, Andrew and Michele Revell*

NEWTON
NZ0364 Map 10

Duke of Wellington

(01661) 844446 – www.thedukeofwellingtoninn.co.uk

Off A69 E of Corbridge; NE43 7UL

Big stone pub with modern and traditional furnishings, well kept ales, good wines by the glass and highly thought-of food; bedrooms

This well run inn is part of an attractive farming hamlet. Our readers head for the bustling bar with its leather chesterfields, built-in cushioned wall seats, farmhouse chairs and tables on honey-coloured flagstones, a woodburning stove with a shelf of books to one side, and rustic stools against the counter. They serve Greene King IPA, Hadrian Border Tyneside Blonde, High House Farm Nels Best and Mordue Panda Frog Panarillo on handpump, a dozen wines by the glass and a good choice of malt whiskies and gins; TV, darts, board games and daily papers. The L-shaped restaurant has elegant tartan-upholstered and wood dining chairs around pale tables on bare boards, modern art on exposed stone walls, and french windows that lead out to the terrace. Paintwork throughout is contemporary. In fine weather, the seats on the back terrace have lovely views across the Tyne Valley. The comfortable and well equipped bedrooms (several are dog-friendly) are popular with those exploring the area; breakfasts are hearty.

 Creative food includes breakfasts (8-10am), mackerel with white chocolate, horseradish and beetroot, braised pork cheek with sultana ragoût, grain mustard croquette, braised leeks and caraway jus, pie of the day, truffled mushroom arancini with pea purée, salt-baked beetroot and charred corn, steak burger with toppings, slaw and fries, halibut with prawns, braised fennel and sea vegetables, duck breast with pistachio sponge, apricots and baby vegetables, and puddings such as rocky road fondant with white chocolate, chocolate fudge ice-cream, marshmallows and almond praline and black cherry bakewell tart with vanilla mousse. *Benchmark main dish: lamb loin with lamb suet pudding and wild garlic £20.00. Two-course evening meal £22.00.*

Free house ~ Licensee Rob Harris ~ Real ale ~ Open 8am-11.30pm ~ Bar food 12-9; 12-5 Sun ~ Restaurant ~ Children welcome ~ Dogs allowed in bar ~ Wi-fi ~ Quiz alternate Mon evenings ~ Bedrooms: £100/£140 *Recommended by Claire and Emma Braithwaite, Katherine and Hugh Markham, John Harris, Andy and Louise Ramwell, Katherine Matthews, Lionel Smith*

NEWTON-BY-THE-SEA
NU2424 Map 10

Ship

(01665) 576262 – www.shipinnnewton.co.uk

Low Newton-by-the-Sea, signed off B1339 N of Alnwick; NE66 3EL

In a charming square with good simple food and own-brew beers; best to check winter opening times

If you're lucky enough to be here in warm weather, you can make the best of the lovely position. Tables outside this row of converted fishermen's cottages look across the sloping village green and down to the sea and you can walk from here along the massive stretch of empty, beautiful beach with views all the way to Dunstanburgh Castle (English Heritage). Inside, the plainly furnished but cosy bare-boards bar on the right has nautical charts on dark pink walls, while another simple room on the left has beams, hop bines, some bright modern pictures on stripped-stone walls and a woodburning stove in a stone fireplace. They brew their own beers and usually have four on handpump at any one time from a choice of 26 – maybe Ship Inn Dolly Daydream, Indian Summer and a seasonal guest as well as a guest from another brewery; also 14 malt whiskies and half a dozen wines by the glass. There's darts and dominoes. It can get extremely busy at peak times, so it's best to book in advance, and there might be a queue for the bar. There's no nearby parking from May to September, but there is a car park up the hill.

 Good quality food includes sandwiches, kipper pâté, local hand-picked crab with salad, pasta with pesto, cheese and tomatoes, chicken with chorizo and chickpea stew, cod fillet with crispy pancetta and pea mash, rib-eye steak with onion marmalade and crushed herbed potatoes, and puddings such as lime posset and rhubarb and custard tart. *Benchmark main dish: ploughman's £8.95. Two-course evening meal £20.00.*

Own brew ~ Licensee Christine Forsyth ~ Real ale ~ Open 11-11; 12-10 Sun; 11-5 Mon-Weds; 12-5 Sun in winter ~ Bar food 12-2.30, 7-8; not Sun-Tues evenings ~ Well behaved children welcome ~ Dogs welcome ~ Wi-fi ~ Live music (check website) *Recommended by Tracey and Stephen Groves, WAH, Martine and Fabio Lockley, Alison and Dan Richardson, Freddie and Sarah Banks*

ROMALDKIRK
Rose & Crown ★ ◉ � NY9922 Map 10
(01833) 650213 – www.rose-and-crown.co.uk
Just off B6277; DL12 9EB

18th-c coaching inn with accomplished cooking, attentive service and a fine choice of drinks; boutique-style bedrooms

This is a lovely, handsome old inn and our readers enjoy their visits very much. The beamed bar area has old-fashioned seats facing a warming log fire, a Jacobean oak settle, a grandfather clock, brass hunting horns and old farm tools and black and white pictures of Romaldkirk on the walls. Black Sheep, Marstons Wainwright and Village Brewer White Boar Bitter on handpump, seven wines by the glass from a good list, 20 malt whiskies and 16 gins. Another room has elegant pale oak country chairs and stools by a woodburning stove and there's an oak-panelled restaurant; background music. Picnic-sets line the front terrace facing the village green where you can still see the original stocks and water pump. If you stay in the comfortable, well equipped bedrooms (in the main building, the courtyard or Monk's Cottage), the owners provide an in-house guide for days out exploring the area, and a *Walking in Teesdale* book. Disabled access. The village church is interesting and the exceptional Bowes Museum and High Force waterfall are both nearby.

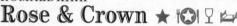 Impressive food includes sandwiches, goats cheese mousse with red wine-poached pear and red wine syrup, tempura cod and prawns with sweet chilli sauce, sharing platters, roast nut, root vegetable and red wine wellington with red wine and thyme jus, cumberland sausage with savoy cabbage and bacon, champ mash, anise carrots and onion gravy, lamb loin with braised shoulder, lamb bonbon, mint pesto and jus, lemon sole with salsa verde and sautéed potatoes, and puddings such as vanilla rice pudding with roasted pear purée and dark chocolate crémeux with kendal mint cake ice-cream. *Benchmark main dish: local estate venison pie £18.00. Two-course evening meal £25.00.*

Free house ~ Licensee Cheryl Robinson ~ Real ale ~ Open 11-11 ~ Bar food 12-2.30, 6-8.30 ~ Restaurant ~ Children welcome until 8pm ~ Dogs allowed in bar and bedrooms ~ Wi-fi ~ Bedrooms: £130/£140 *Recommended by Ian Herdman, Caroline and Steve Archer, WAH, John and Claire Masters, Peter and Emma Kelly, Naomi and Andrew Randall*

SEAHOUSES

NU2232   Map 10

Olde Ship ★ ◪ £ ⇔

(01665) 720200 – www.seahouses.co.uk

Just off B1340, towards harbour; NE68 7RD

Lots of atmosphere and maritime memorabilia in busy little inn, with views across harbour to Farne Islands; bedrooms

You'll find a rich assemblage of nautical bits and pieces in the unchanging and old-fashioned bar here: such as lots of shiny brass fittings, ships' instruments and equipment, a knotted anchor made by local fishermen, sea pictures and model ships (including fine ones of the North Sunderland lifeboat and the Seahouses' *Grace Darling* lifeboat). There's also a model of the *Forfarshire*, the paddle steamer that local heroine Grace Darling went to rescue in 1838 (you can read more of the story in the pub), and even the ship's nameboard. An anemometer takes wind-speed readings from the top of the chimney. It's all gently lit by stained-glass sea-picture windows, lantern lights and a winter open fire. Simple furnishings include built-in leatherette pews around one end, stools and cast-iron tables. Black Sheep, Born in the Borders Game Bird, Courage Directors, Greene King Old Speckled Hen and Ruddles County, Hadrian Border Farne Island Pale Ale and Theakstons Best Bitter on handpump (summer guests too), eight wines by the glass from a good wine list, 30 gins and 55 malt whiskies; background music and TV. The battlemented side terrace (you'll also find fishing memorabilia out here) and one window in the sun lounge look across the harbour to the Farne Islands (as do some bedrooms). If you find yourself here as dusk falls, the beam of the Longstones lighthouse shining across the fading evening sky is a charming sight. The pub is not really suitable for children, though there is a little family room, and children are welcome on the terrace (as are walkers). You can book boat trips to the Farne Islands at the harbour, and there are bracing coastal walks, notably to Bamburgh, the birthplace of Grace Darling.

🍴 Tasty food includes sandwiches, duck and orange pâté, salt and pepper squid with garlic mayonnaise, vegetable lasagne, fresh crab salad, gammon with egg and pineapple, barbecue spare ribs with chips, chicken and mushroom casserole, sirloin steak with onion rings, mushrooms and peppercorn sauce, and puddings such as lemon meringue pie and rum and raisin pudding. *Benchmark main dish: beer-battered fish and chips £9.75. Two-course evening meal £16.00.*

Free house ~ Licensees Judith Glen and David Swan ~ Real ale ~ Open 11-11; 12-11 Sun ~ Bar food 12-2.30, 7-8.30 ~ Restaurant ~ Children allowed in lounge and dining room if eating, but must be over 10 in bedrooms ~ Wi-fi ~ Bedrooms: £50/£100 *Recommended by Margaret and Peter Staples, Tracey and Stephen Groves, Monica and Steph Evans, Mark and Mary Setting, Emily and Toby Archer, Peter Pilbeam*

STANNERSBURN

NY7286   Map 10

Pheasant £ ⇔

(01434) 240382 – www.thepheasantinn.com

Kielder Water road signposted off B6320 in Bellingham; NE48 1DD

Friendly village inn with quite a mix of customers, homely bar food and streamside garden; bedrooms

In a quiet valley surrounded by forests, and not far from Kielder Water, is this family-run former farmhouse. The low-beamed lounge has ranks of old local photographs on stripped stone and panelling, brightly polished surfaces, shiny brasses, dark wooden pubby tables and chairs and

upholstered stools ranged along the counter; there are several open fires.
A separate public bar is simpler and opens into another snug seating area
with beams and panelling. The friendly licensees and courteous staff serve
Timothy Taylors Landlord and a couple of guests such as Allendale Wayfarer
and Wylam Cascade on handpump, several wines by the glass, 40 malt
whiskies and a couple of farm ciders. There are picnic-sets in the streamside
garden, plus a pony paddock. Bedrooms are comfortable, breakfasts are
good and they have a self-catering cottage as well.

Enjoyable food includes sweet marinated herrings, chicken liver parfait with
apple and ginger chutney, vegetarian dish of the day, game and mushroom pie,
moroccan-style cod with roasted vegetable couscous, chicken breast filled with cream
cheese and sun-dried tomatoes wrapped in parma ham, sole, monkfish or sea bass
grilled with herb butter or a light cream sauce, and puddings such as orange and treacle
tart and lime and lemon cheesecake. *Benchmark main dish: slow-roast shoulder of
local lamb with rosemary and redcurrant £12.95. Two-course evening meal £21.00.*

Free house ~ Licensees Walter and Robin Kershaw ~ Real ale ~ Open 12-3, 6-midnight;
closed Mon and Tues Nov-Feb ~ Bar food 12-2, 6-8 ~ Restaurant ~ Children welcome ~
Dogs allowed in bedrooms ~ Wi-fi ~ Bedrooms: $80/$110 *Recommended by Elise and Charles
Mackinlay, Alfie Bayliss, WAH, John Harris, Mike Swan, Toby Jones, Charles Welch*

WARK

NY8676 Map 10

Battlesteads 🍺 🛏

(01434) 230209 – www.battlesteads.com
B6320 N of Hexham; NE48 3LS

**Eco pub with good local ales, fair value interesting food and a relaxed
atmosphere; comfortable bedrooms**

The nicely restored, low-beamed, carpeted bar here has a woodburning
stove with a traditional oak surround, comfortable, tartan-upholstered
seats and easy chairs and some high chairs around an equally high table.
You'll find a good range of drinks: 12 wines by the glass, 25 malt whiskies,
35 gins and a farm cider, plus Fyne Jarl and Hadrian Border Secret Kingdom
with a couple of guests such as Oakham Citra and Sonnet 43 Abolition on
handpump. Service is excellent; background music and TV. There's also
a restaurant, a spacious conservatory and tables on the terrace and they're
licensed to hold civil marriages. Some of the ground-floor bedrooms
have disabled access. The owners are extremely conscientious about the
environment and gently weave their beliefs into every aspect of the business;
they grow their own produce (and have their own mushroom farm), have
a charging point in the car park for electric cars and use a biomass boiler.

Highly regarded food includes sandwiches, smoked hake scampi with wild
garlic mayonnaise, coronation chicken salad, home-grown shiitake and oyster
mushrooms with tagliatelle, pesto and cheese, local rabbit casserole with mash, herb-
crusted salmon with roasted home-grown vegetables, calves liver potato gratin with
sage and thyme, duck breast with gin-infused orange sauce, mini shepherd's pie with
lamb cutlet and haggis bonbons, and puddings such as blackcurrant cheesecake and
chocolate brownie with warm chocolate sauce. *Benchmark main dish: braised beef
cheek with mash and rich jus £13.95. Two-course evening meal £22.00.*

Free house ~ Licensees Richard and Dee Slade ~ Real ale ~ Open 11.30-11.30 ~ Bar food
12-3, 6.30-9 ~ Restaurant ~ Children welcome ~ Dogs allowed in bar and bedrooms ~ Wi-fi
~ Bedrooms: $70/$120 *Recommended by Peter Smith and Judith Brown, Michael and Sarah
Lockley, Rosie and Marcus Heatherley, Liz and Martin Eldon, Sophia and Hamish Greenfield,
Mary and Nigel Joyce*

WINSTON

NZ1416   Map 10

Bridgewater Arms 🍴⭐ 🍷

(01325) 730302 – www.thebridgewaterarms.com

B6274, just off A67 Darlington–Barnard Castle; DL2 3RN

Former school house with quite a choice of appealing food, three real ales and seats outside

Many customers come to this carefully converted Victorian school house to enjoy the rewarding food, but they also keep Brakspears Bitter, Rudgate Jorvik Blonde and a guest beer on handpump, a dozen wines by the glass and 12 malt whiskies. The high-ceilinged bar has an informal, friendly atmosphere, an open log fire, cushioned settles and chairs, a wall lined with bookcases and high chairs against the counter. Two restaurant rooms have high-backed black leather dining chairs around clothed tables on stripped wooden flooring or tartan carpet, wine bottles lining a delft shelf and various prints and pictures on pale yellow walls. There are some picnic-sets at the front. Do stroll down to the fine 18th-century bridge across the River Tees as it's really worth a look.

🍴 Fish and shellfish play a big part in the food here: warm salad of crab, langoustine and spring onion thermidor, mussels with shallots, garlic, tarragon and cream, monkfish on bacon with curried prawn risotto, and grilled seafood platter. They also offer cheddar and spinach soufflé, confit duck leg with wild garlic mash and red wine sauce, roast venison loin with wild mushrooms, pancetta and carrots, lamb rack with leek and potato cake and rosemary gravy, and puddings such as tiramisu with coffee ice-cream and saffron-poached pear with brandy snap basket and lemongrass ice-cream. *Benchmark main dish: wild sea bass with king scallops, stir-fried green vegetables and lime crème fraîche £25.00. Two-course evening meal £23.00.*

Free house ~ Licensee Paul Grundy ~ Real ale ~ Open 12-3, 6-close; closed Sun, Mon ~ Bar food 12-2, 6-9 ~ Restaurant ~ Well behaved children welcome ~ Wi-fi *Recommended by Julie Braeburn, Rona Mackinlay, Christopher Mannings, Helena and Trevor Fraser, James Allsopp*

Also Worth a Visit in Northumbria

Besides the fully inspected pubs, you might like to try these pubs that have been recommended to us and described by readers. Do tell us what you think of them: feedback@goodguides.com

ACOMB

NY9366

Miners Arms (01434) 603909
Main Street; NE46 4PW Friendly little 18th-c village pub; good value traditional food (not Sun evening, Mon) including weekday set menu and popular Sun roasts, Wylam, Yates and guests, carpeted bar with comfortable settles and huge fire in stone fireplace, back dining area; quiz last Thurs of month; children and dogs welcome, a couple of tables out in front, more in back courtyard, open all day weekends, closed weekday lunchtimes. *(David Travis)*

ALLENDALE

NY8355

Golden Lion (01434) 683225
Market Place; NE47 9BD Friendly 18th-c two-room pub; beers from on-site microbrewery along with guests such as Timothy Taylors Landlord, enjoyable traditional food at reasonable prices, can eat in bar or upstairs restaurant, games area with pool and darts; regular live music; children and dogs welcome, Allendale Fair first weekend of June, New Year's Eve flaming barrel procession, open all day (till late Fri, Sat). *(Peter Meister)*

ALNMOUTH

NU2410

⭐ **Red Lion** (01665) 830584
Northumberland Street; NE66 2RJ Friendly 18th-c coaching inn with peaceful sheltered garden and raised deck giving wide views over the Aln estuary; black beams, classic leather wall banquettes and window seats in pleasant relaxed bar, old local photographs on dark mahogany brown panelling, cheerful fires, four well kept ales (Oct beer festival), half a dozen wines by the glass and popular fairly pubby food from sandwiches up, stripped-brick restaurant

with flagstones and woodburner; background and monthly live music, Tues quiz, free wi-fi; children and dogs (in bar) welcome, comfortable well equipped bedrooms, open all day. *(Miles Green)*

ALNWICK   NU1813
John Bull (01665) 602055

Howick Street; NE66 1UY Chatty drinkers' pub – essentially the front room of an early 19th-c terraced house; good selection of well kept changing ales, real cider and lots of bottled belgian beers, also over 100 malt whiskies; Sat cheese club, live music every other Mon, darts and dominoes; small beer garden, closed weekday lunchtimes.
(Amy and Luke Buchanan)

ALNWICK   NU1913
Market Tavern (01665) 602759

Fenkle Street; NE66 1HW Refurbished split-level pub in central position; popular fairly priced food including good steaks, well kept ales such as Black Sheep, Weston's cider and decent wines by the glass, friendly helpful service; background and occasional live music, TV, free wi-fi; children and dogs welcome, six bedrooms, open all day.
(Jim Trood)

ALNWICK   NU1813
Plough (01665) 602395

Bondgate Without; NE66 1PN Smart contemporary pub-cum-boutique hotel in Victorian stone building (under same management as the Jolly Fisherman at Craster – see Main Entries); Timothy Taylors Landlord and a guest, several wines by the glass and extensive range of gins, good food (not Sun evening) in bar, bistro or upstairs restaurant, friendly helpful staff; children and dogs welcome, pleasant streetside raised terrace, seven bedrooms, open all day.
(Amy and Luke Buchanan)

ALNWICK   NU1813
Tanners Arms (01665) 602553

Hotspur Place; NE66 1QF Welcoming little drinkers' pub with five well kept local ales and a decent glass of wine; flagstones and stripped stone, warm woodburner, plush stools and wall benches, small tree in the centre of the room; juke box and some live acoustic music, TV; dogs welcome, open all day weekends, closed weekday lunchtimes. *(Amy and Luke Buchanan)*

ANICK   NY9565
★ Rat (01434) 602814

Village signposted NE of A69/A695 Hexham junction; NE46 4LN Popular country pub with cosy traditional bar; coal fire in kitchen range, cottagey knick-knacks such as floral chamber-pots hanging from beams, china and glassware on a delft shelf, six well kept ales, real cider, a dozen wines by the glass, good well presented interesting food (not Sun evening), efficient service,

conservatory; background music, free wi-fi; children welcome, charming garden with dovecote, statues and lovely North Tyne Valley views, limited parking (you can park around the village green), open all day. *(WAH)*

AYCLIFFE   NZ2822
★ County (01325) 312273

The Green, Aycliffe; just off A1(M) junction 59, off A167 at West Terrace and then right to village green; DL5 6LX Smart inn with comfortable open-plan rooms; seating from cushioned dining chairs to tartan banquettes, stripy carpets, painted ceiling joists and log fires, highly regarded imaginative food in minimalist wood-floored restaurant, three real ales, a craft beer and 11 wines by the glass, friendly service; free wi-fi; children welcome, no dogs inside, metal tables and chairs out at front facing green, seven attractive bedrooms, open all day, food all day Sun till 6pm. *(Alistair Forsyth)*

BAMBURGH   NU1834
Castle (01668) 214616

Front Street; NE69 7BW Well cared-for comfortably old-fashioned pub with generous helpings of reasonably priced food from good crab sandwiches to daily specials, friendly efficient service, well kept local ales and decent house wines, cheery part-panelled bar and expanded dining area, open fires (one in old range); free wi-fi; children welcome, no dogs inside, circular picnic-sets in nice beer garden, open (and food) all day.
(Margaret and Peter Staples, Revd Michael Vockins, Tracey and Stephen Groves)

BAMBURGH   NU1834
Lord Crewe Arms (01668) 214243

Front Street; NE69 7BL Small early 17th-c hotel prettily set in charming coastal village dominated by Norman castle; bar and restaurant (Wynding Inn) with painted joists and panelling, bare stone walls and light wood floor, warm woodburner, a couple of well kept local ales and a craft beer, good varied menu from lunchtime sandwiches up, friendly helpful staff; children and dogs (in one area) welcome, sheltered garden with castle view, short walk from splendid sandy beach, seven comfortable bedrooms, open all day. *(Barry Collett)*

BARDON MILL   NY7566
Twice Brewed (01434) 344534

Military Road (B6318 NE of Hexham); NE47 7AN Large busy inn well placed for fell-walkers and major Hadrian's Wall sites; up to half a dozen ales including some from on-site microbrewery, they also distil their own spirits, good value home-cooked food from sandwiches/panini up, cheerful helpful service, woodburners, artwork for sale; children and dogs welcome, disabled access, picnic-sets in back garden, 18 bedrooms, open (and food) all day. *(Peter Meister)*

BEADNELL   NU2229
Beadnell Towers (01665) 721211
The Wynding, off B1340; NE67 5AY
This popular pub-hotel was about to reopen after major refurbishment as we went to press – reports please.

BEAMISH   NZ2154
Beamish Hall (01207) 233733
NE of Stanley, off A6076; DH9 0YB
Converted stone-built stables in courtyard at back of hotel; popular and family-friendly (can get crowded), with five or six beers from own microbrewery (tours available), decent wines and enjoyable food from light lunches up, uniformed staff; regular events such as live music, barbecues and a summer festival; plenty of seats outside, big play area, open (and food) all day. *(Peter Smith and Judith Brown)*

BEAMISH   NZ2055
Black Horse (01207) 232569
Red Row (off Beamishburn Road NW, near A6076); OS Sheet 88 map reference 205541; DH9 0RW Late 17th-c country dining pub with contemporary/rustic interior; heritage colours blending with beams, flagstones and some exposed stonework, enjoyable food (not Sun evening) from sandwiches and pub favourites up, themed nights including asian (Weds) and steak (Thurs), half a dozen well kept changing beers and decent wines by the glass, afternoon teas, friendly attentive staff, cosy fire-warmed front room extending to light spacious dining area with central bar, another dining room upstairs, airy conservatory; children welcome, dogs in bar, restful views from big paved terrace, more tables on grass, open all day from 9am for breakfast. *(Peter Smith and Judith Brown)*

BERWICK-UPON-TWEED   NT9952
Barrels (01289) 308013
Bridge Street; TD15 1ES Small friendly pub with interesting collection of pop memorabilia and other bric-a-brac, some eccentric furniture too including a barber's chair in bare-boards front bar, well kept Anarchy Blonde Star, four guests and range of foreign bottled beers, snacky food, red banquettes in back room; regular live acoustic sessions (often in basement bar) and good quality background music; children and dogs welcome, open all day. *(Tony Scott)*

CATTON   NY8257
★Crown (01434) 618351
B6295, off A686 S of Haydon Bridge; NE47 9QS Welcoming 18th-c village pub in good walking country; inner bar with stripped stone and bare boards, dark tables, mate's chairs and a traditional settle, good log fire, Allendale beers and enjoyable home-cooked blackboard food, efficient staff, extension

with folding glass doors opening on to small garden, lovely Allen Valley views; folk night Thurs, quiz every other Tues, bar billiards; children and dogs welcome, open (and food) all day Sat, till 6pm Sun, from 5pm weekdays. *(Lucy and Giles Gibbon)*

CHATTON   NU0528
Percy Arms (01668) 215244
B6348 E of Wooler; NE66 5PS Sympathetically updated stone-built country inn (same owners as the Northumberland Arms at Felton); good well presented food from standard dishes up in flagstoned log-fire bar or light panelled dining room (booking advised), six well kept ales, good whisky and gin choice, friendly helpful staff, open fire and woodburner; darts; children and dogs (in bar) welcome, picnic-sets on small front lawn, five well appointed bedrooms, good breakfast, quiet village with sweeping views of the Cheviot Hills, open (and food) all day. *(John and Sylvia Harrop, Tracey and Stephen Groves, Gordon and Margaret Ormondroyd)*

CONSETT   NZ1150
Travellers Rest (01207) 507555
Forster Street; DH8 7JU Renovated brick-built pub on two floors; bare-boards bar with farmhouse furniture, woodburner in big fireplace, good pubby food including blackboard specials and Weds burger deal, three changing ales, friendly attentive staff, upstairs galleried dining area; jukebox and TV, free wi-fi; children welcome, paved beer garden behind, open all day.
(Mathew Cartmell)

CORBRIDGE   NY9964
★Angel (01434) 632119
Main Street; NE45 5LA Imposing coaching inn at end of broad street in this attractive old town; best sense of building's age in separate lounge with oak panelling and a big stone fireplace, also look out for the fine 17th-c arched doorway in left-hand porch; airy modern bar serving six local ales including a Wylam house beer, Weston's cider; 19 wines by the glass and numerous gins and malt whiskies, good food from varied menu, dining lounge and raftered restaurant; background music, daily newspapers; children and dogs (in bar) welcome, heated tables out at front under parasols, comfortable bedrooms, car parking for residents, so best to use the free car park on the other side of the bridge (just five minutes away), open (and food) all day. *(Susan and John Douglas, Andrea and Philip Crispin)*

CORBRIDGE   NY9864
Black Bull (01434) 632261
Middle Street; NE45 5AT Rambling 18th-c beamed pub with four linked rooms; mix of traditional pub furniture including leather banquettes, wood, flagstone or carpeted floors, log fires (one in open hearth with

gleaming copper canopy), ceramic collection in front room and information about Hadrian's Wall, decent reasonably priced pubby food, three Greene King ales, a guest beer and good choice of wines by the glass, efficient cheery service; children welcome, no dogs, seats out on two-level terrace, open all day. (Elise and Charles Mackinlay)

CORNHILL-ON-TWEED   NT8539
Collingwood Arms   (01890) 882424
Main Street; TD12 4UH Comfortably updated Georgian stone hotel; nice little bar with decent wines, around 25 malt whiskies and a couple of well kept local ales, good reasonably priced food in adjoining dining room or more pricey restaurant, friendly helpful staff, open fires; free wi-fi; children and dogs (in bar) welcome, tables out in lovely grounds, local fishing and shooting, 15 well appointed bedrooms (named after ships from the Battle of Trafalgar), good breakfast, open all day. (David Travis)

CROOKHAM   NT9138
Blue Bell   (01890) 820789
Pallinsburn; A697 Wooler–Cornhill; TD12 4SH Welcoming 18th-c roadside country pub; enjoyable freshly prepared food, three well kept ales and good selection of gins, friendly attentive service; dogs welcome in bar, comfortable clean bedrooms, good breakfast, open all day Fri–Sun. (Tom Stone)

DARLINGTON   NZ2814
Number Twenty 2   (01325) 354590
Coniscliffe Road; DL3 7RG Long narrow Victorian pub with high ceiling, wood and carpeted floors and some exposed brickwork, up to 13 quickly changing ales (tasters offered) including own Village Brewer range, draught continentals and 20 wines by the glass, they also have an in-house distillery, snacky lunchtime food, good friendly service; open from 4pm Mon and Tues, all day Weds–Sat, 2–7pm Sun. (Freddie and Sarah Banks)

DINNINGTON   NZ2073
White Swan   (01661) 872869
Prestwick Road; NE13 7AG Large open-plan pub-restaurant popular for its wide range of good value food including gluten-free menu, reasonably priced wines and a well kept changing ale, efficient friendly service even at busy times; background music (children's menu till 5.30pm), no dogs inside, disabled facilities, orangery and attractive garden with pond, handy for Newcastle Airport, open all day Sun till 6pm. (Celia and Rupert Lemming)

DUNSTAN   NU2419
Cottage   (01665) 576658
Off B1339 Alnmouth–Embleton; NE66 3SZ Comfortable single-storey beamed inn; enjoyable reasonably priced food from sandwiches/panini to daily specials, up

to three well kept ales such as Hadrian & Border, restaurant and conservatory; live music, quiz nights, free wi-fi; children and dogs welcome, attractive garden with covered terrace and play area, ten bedrooms, open all day. (Dr Simon Innes)

DURHAM   NZ2742
Dun Cow   (0191) 386 9219
Old Elvet; DH1 3HN Unchanging backstreet pub in pretty 16th-c black and white timbered cottage; tiny chatty front bar with wall benches, corridor to long narrow back lounge, three well kept ales including Black Sheep and simple good value food (not Sun evening), friendly staff; background and occasional live music, Mon quiz, free wi-fi; children welcome, no dogs, open all day. (Miles Green)

DURHAM   NZ2742
Head of Steam   (0191) 383 2173
Reform Place, North Road; DH1 4RZ Hidden-away pub close to the River Wear; modern open-plan interior on two floors, well stocked bar serving good range of changing ales, craft kegs, real ciders and plenty of bottled continental beers, competitively priced food including burgers and pizzas; background music (live upstairs); dogs welcome, outside tables, open (and food) all day. (Peter Smith and Judith Brown)

DURHAM   NZ2642
Old Elm Tree   (0191) 386 4621
Crossgate; DH1 4PS Friendly old pub on steep hill across from the castle; two-room main bar and small lounge up steps, half a dozen well kept beers including Wychwood Hobgoblin (occasional beer festivals), reasonably priced home-made food, open fires, live folk music and quiz nights; dogs welcome, small back terrace, open all day. (Miles Green)

DURHAM   NZ2742
Shakespeare   (0191) 340 9438
Saddler Street; DH1 3NU Friendly refurbished 19th-c brick pub (bigger inside than it looks); fairly compact front bar incorporating former snug, larger back lounge and an upstairs spirits bar, well kept Caledonian Deuchars IPA, Fullers London Pride and two guests, pubby lunchtime food; children (till 5pm) and dogs welcome, convenient for castle, cathedral and river, can get crowded (particularly weekends), open all day. (Miles Green)

DURHAM   NZ2742
Swan & Three Cygnets
(0191) 384 0242   Elvet Bridge; DH1 3AG Victorian pub in good bridge-end spot high above the river, city views from big windows and terrace; bargain lunchtime food and Sam Smiths ales, helpful friendly young staff, popular with locals and students; open all day. (David Appleyard)

EACHWICK
NZ1069

Plough (01661) 853555

Stamfordham Road (extension of B6324), S of village; NE18 0BG Large refurbished stone inn tucked away in remote countryside; open-plan split-level lounge with comfortable furniture including sofas, tub and wing-back chairs on wood or carpeted floors, good choice of enjoyable food from snacks to specials, also evening chinese menu, two well kept changing ales and fairly priced wines, separate restaurant; outside seating, three bedrooms, open all day Fri and Sat, till 5pm Sun, closed Mon, Tues. *(Patricia Hawkins)*

EARSDON
NZ3273

★ **Beehive** (0191) 252 9352

Hartley Lane; NE25 0SZ Popular well run 18th-c country pub with cosy linked rooms; low painted beams, soft lighting, woodburners and one or two quirky touches, three well kept hatch-served ales (tasting trays available), good fairly priced home-made food (best to book weekends) from sandwiches, light dishes and sharing boards up, friendly service; background and some live music, TVs; children welcome, dogs in one area, picnic-sets out overlooking fields, summer bar and separate family garden with play area, open (and food) all day, till 8pm (6pm) Sun. *(Andrew Lawson)*

EDMUNDBYERS
NZ0150

Punch Bowl (01207) 255545

B6278; DH8 9NL Small village's community local; three well kept ales and good choice of reasonably priced food including daily specials, friendly service; TV, free wi-fi; children and dogs (in bar) welcome, fishing on nearby Derwent Reservoir (permits from the pub), six updated bedrooms, good breakfast, open (and food) all day. *(Celia and Rupert Lemming)*

EGLINGHAM
NU1019

★ **Tankerville Arms** (01665) 578444

B6346 Alnwick–Wooler; NE66 2TX Traditional 19th-c stone inn with contemporary touches and cosy friendly atmosphere; beams, bare boards and some stripped stonework, banquettes and warm fires, well kept Hadrian Border and a guest, good wines, enjoyable nicely presented food from shortish menu, raftered split-level restaurant; free wi-fi; children, walkers and dogs welcome, lovely country views from back garden, attractive village, three bedrooms, closed lunchtimes Mon, Tues, otherwise open (and food) all day. *(Andrew Lawson)*

ELLINGHAM
NU1625

Pack Horse (01665) 589292

Signed off A1 N of Alnwick; NE67 5HA Stone-built pub in peaceful rural village; masses of jugs hanging from beams in flagstoned bar, a long settle and upholstered stools around traditional tables, log fire, Black Sheep, Timothy Taylors and a guest from local Rigg & Furrow, good food (not Sun evening) using own produce including home-reared meat, bare-boards snug with stag's head above large stone fireplace, restaurant divided into two with high-backed chairs around pale tables on tartan carpet; background music, open mike night last Sun evening of month; children and dogs (in bar) welcome, picnic-sets in enclosed garden, pretty bedrooms, open all day in summer. *(GSB, Michael Doswell, WAH, Gordon and Margaret Ormondroyd)*

EMBLETON
NU2322

Dunstanburgh Castle Hotel

(01665) 576111 *B1339; NE66 3UN* Comfortable hotel in attractive spot near magnificent coastline; good choice of enjoyable bar and restaurant food using local meat and fish, good vegetarian options too, efficient friendly service, local ales and decent wines, two lounges for coffee with open fires; children welcome, seats in nice garden, good for Embleton Bay and Dunstanburgh Castle (EH), bedrooms and self-catering cottages, open all day. *(David Travis)*

EMBLETON
NU2322

Greys (01665) 576983

Stanley Terrace off WT Stead Road, turn at the Blue Bell; NE66 3UY Welcoming pub with carpeted bar and cottagey back dining room; enjoyable home-made food including good crab sandwiches, well kept regional beers such as Hadrian Border and Wylam; juke box, sports TV; children and dogs welcome, small walled back garden with village views from raised deck, open all day. *(David Travis)*

ESH
NZ1944

Cross Keys (0191) 373 1279

Front Street; DH7 9QR Friendly 18th-c beamed village local; hearty helpings of good well priced food (not Sun evening) including blackboard specials, Big Lamp, Black Sheep and guests, afternoon teas; children welcome, colourful hanging baskets out at front, good country views from behind, closed Mon, otherwise open all day (but may shut if quiet). *(Victoria and James Sargeant)*

FELTON
NU1800

Northumberland Arms

(01670) 787370 *West Thirston; B6345, off A1 N of Morpeth; NE65 9EE* Stylish 19th-c inn across road from River Coquet (same owners as the Percy Arms in Chatton); roomy open-plan lounge bar with beams, exposed stone/brickwork and nice mix of furnishings including big sofas on flagstones, woodburner, bare-boards restaurant with mix of light wood tables, good sensibly priced food from bar snacks and standard dishes up (best to book), bread from their own bakery, three or four well kept mainly local beers and nice wines by the glass, friendly service; children welcome, dogs in bar, six good bedrooms, open (and food) all day. *(R L Borthwick)*

FROSTERLEY   NZ0236
★ **Black Bull** (01388) 527784

Just off A689 W of centre; DL13 2SL Unique in having its very own peal of bells (licensee is a campanologist); great atmosphere in three interesting traditional beamed and flagstoned rooms with coal fires (one in old range), landlord's own good photographs and three grandfather clocks, four well kept local ales, traditional cider/ perry and carefully chosen wines, good range of malt whiskies too, highly rated food using local and organic ingredients (best to book evenings and Sun lunch), friendly helpful staff; some acoustic live music; well behaved children and dogs welcome, attractive no-smoking terrace with wood-fired bread oven and old railway furnishings (opposite steam line station), closed Sun evening to Thurs, otherwise open all day. *(John Saville)*

GATESHEAD   NZ2563
Central (0191) 478 2543

Half Moon Lane; NE8 2AN Unusual 19th-c wedge-shaped pub (Grade II listed) restored by the Head of Steam group; well preserved features including notable buffet bar, great choice of changing local ales, real ciders and lots of bottled beers, low-priced food from short menu, upstairs function rooms and roof terrace; some live music; dogs welcome, open all day (till midnight Fri, Sat). *(Tom Stone)*

GRETA BRIDGE   NZ0813
★ **Morritt** (01833) 627232

Hotel signposted off A66 W of Scotch Corner; DL12 9SE Striking 17th-c country house hotel popular for weddings and the like; pubby bar with big windsor armchairs and sturdy oak settles around traditional cast-iron-framed tables, open fires and remarkable 1946 mural of Dickensian characters by JTY Gilroy (known for his Guinness adverts), big windows looking on to extensive lawn, three real ales including Black Sheep and Timothy Taylors, 19 wines by the glass from extensive list, enjoyable bar and restaurant food, afternoon teas, friendly staff; background music; children and dogs (in bar and bedrooms) welcome, attractively laid-out split-level garden with teak tables and play area, open all day. *(Barry Collett)*

HALTWHISTLE   NY7166
Milecastle Inn (01434) 321372

Military Road; B6318 NE – OS Sheet 86 map reference 715660; NE49 9NN Sturdy stone-built pub on remote moorland road running alongside Hadrian's Wall; small carpeted rooms off beamed bar, brasses, prints and two log fires, up to three well kept ales (maybe just Big Lamp Prince Bishop

in winter), popular home-made food (best to book weekends), friendly helpful service, small comfortable restaurant; children welcome, no dogs inside, tables and benches in big sheltered garden with stunning views, two self-catering cottages next door, open (and food) all day in summer. *(Peter Meister)*

HART   NZ4634
White Hart (01429) 265468

Just off A179 W of Hartlepool; Front Street; TS27 3AW End-of-terrace pub with ship's figurehead outside; fires in both bars (one in old range), enjoyable fairly traditional food (not Sun evening), two changing ales; children welcome, no dogs inside, open all day. *(Edward May)*

HAYDON BRIDGE   NY8364
General Havelock (01434) 684376

Off A69 Corbridge–Haltwhistle; B6319 (Ratcliffe Road); NE47 6ER Old darkly painted pub, a short stroll upstream from Haydon Bridge itself; L-shaped bar with open fire, piano and some Philip Larkin memorabilia, two well kept ales, decent choice of wines by the glass and enjoyable generously served food, stripped-stone barn dining room; children and dogs (in bar) welcome, terrace with fine South Tyne river views, closed Mon lunchtime. *(Miles Green)*

HEXHAM   NY9464
Heart of Northumberland (01434) 608013 *Market Street; NE46 3NS* Renovated old local with Timothy Taylors Landlord and four guests kept well, also craft beers, proper ciders and plenty of wines by the glass, well cooked reasonably priced food from pub favourites up, good cheerful service, traditional furniture on bare boards, some blue-painted panelling and exposed stonework, woodburner in big fireplace; live music Tues; children and dogs welcome, small outside seating area behind, open (and food) all day including brunch from 11am. *(GSB, Martin Day)*

HIGH HESLEDEN   NZ4538
Ship (01429) 836453

Off A19 via B1281; TS27 4QD Popular Victorian inn with seven well kept changing ales and good food cooked by landlady (some interesting specials), sailing ship models including big one hanging with lanterns from boarded ceiling, log fire; sea views over farmland from garden, six bedrooms in modern block, open all day Sun till 8pm, closed Mon and lunchtimes Tues-Fri. *(Justine and Neil Bonnett)*

HOLWICK   NY9126
Strathmore Arms (01833) 640362

Back road up Teesdale from Middleton; DL12 0NJ Attractive and welcoming old stone-built country pub in beautiful scenery just off Pennine Way; four well kept ales

and several real ciders, good low-priced traditional food, beams, flagstones and open fire; live music Fri, quiz first Weds of month, pool, free wi-fi; well behaved dogs welcome, popular with walkers, four bedrooms, closed Tues, otherwise open all day.
(David Appleyard)

HOLY ISLAND   NU1241
Crown & Anchor (01289) 389215
Causeway passable only at low tide, check times (01289) 330733; TD15 2RX
Simply updated pub-restaurant by the priory; three well kept Hadrian Border ales including gluten-free Grainger, good range of whiskies and gins and enjoyable food from changing blackboard menu cooked by landlord-chef, cosy bar with coal fire, more roomy back dining room; children and dogs (in bar) welcome, disabled access/loo, picnic-sets in grassy garden with lovely views, four bedrooms, open all day, food till 6pm Sun.
(Dr Simon Innes)

HOLY ISLAND   NU1241
Ship (01289) 389311
Marygate; TD15 2SJ Well positioned and busy in season; beamed bar with wood floors, stone walls and maritime memorabilia, big stove, steps down to carpeted lounge/dining area, popular pubby menu including fish/seafood (good crab sandwiches), Holy Island Blessed Bitter badged for them by Hadrian Border plus one or two guests, also 30 malt whiskies and their own gin; background music; children welcome and usually dogs (but do ask first), sheltered sunny garden, four bedrooms, may close at quiet times.
(Tracey and Stephen Groves, Roger and Donna Huggins, Ian Wilson)

HORSLEY   NZ0965
Lion & Lamb (01661) 852952
B6528, just off A69 Newcastle–Hexham; NE15 0NS Friendly 18th-c former coaching inn under newish management (some refurbishment); main beamed and flagstoned bar with scrubbed tables, stripped stone and open fire, mainly local beers and popular good value food, attentive service, bareboards restaurant; monthly quiz and some live music; children welcome, Tyne views from attractive sunny garden with terrace and play area, open all day.   *(Amy and Luke Buchanan)*

HURWORTH-ON-TEES   NZ2814
★ **Bay Horse** (01325) 720663
Church Row; DL2 2AQ Popular dining pub (best to book, particularly weekends) with very good imaginative food, quite pricey but they do offer a fixed-price alternative (lunchtimes Mon-Sat, evenings Mon-Thurs), also vegetarian menu and children's meals, three well kept changing ales, extensive wine

list, efficient friendly young staff, sizeable bar with good open fire, restaurant, and another dining room upstairs; seats on back terrace and in well tended walled garden, charming village by River Tees, open all day.
(Michael Doswell)

HURWORTH-ON-TEES   NZ3110
Otter & Fish (01325) 720019
Off A167 S of Darlington; Strait Lane; DL2 2AH Pleasant village setting across road from the Tees; up-to-date open-plan layout with flagstones and stripped wood, open fires and church candles, nice mix of dining furniture, comfortable armchairs and sofas by bar, popular well presented local food including set deals and decent vegetarian and children's choices (best to book especially weekends), friendly helpful staff, two changing ales and several wines by the glass; closed Sun evening.
(Andrew Lawson)

KNARSDALE   NY6754
Kirkstyle (01434) 381559
Signed off A689; CA8 7PB Welcoming 18th-c country pub in lovely spot looking over South Tyne Valley to hills beyond; enjoyable reasonably priced food including range of sausages and some interesting specials, well kept Yates, dining room, games area with darts and pool; children and dogs welcome, handy for Pennine Way, South Tyne Trail and South Tynedale Railway (Lintley terminus), closed Sun evening, Mon lunchtime, all day Tues and Weds (might be shut at 9pm if quiet), no food Mon.   *(Patricia Hawkins)*

LANGDON BECK   NY8531
Langdon Beck Hotel
(01833) 622267 *B6277 Middleton–Alston; DL12 0XP* Isolated unpretentious inn with two cosy bars and spacious lounge; good choice of enjoyable generous food using local Teesdale beef and lamb, ales such as Great North Eastern Rivet Catcher and Marstons Wainwright, friendly helpful staff, interesting rock collection in 'geology room'; events such as Easter 'egg jarping' and late May beer festival; children and dogs welcome, wonderful fell views from garden, well placed for walks including Pennine Way; seven bedrooms (some sharing bathrooms), open all day, closed Mon in winter.
(Miles Green)

LANGLEY ON TYNE   NY8160
Carts Bog Inn (01434) 684338
A686 S, junction B6305; NE47 5NW Isolated 18th-c moorside pub; heavy beams and stripped-stone walls, spindleback chairs around mix of tables on red carpet, old photographs and nice open fire, enjoyable generously served food from sandwiches up including signature Bog Pie (steak and

---

There are report forms at the back of the book.

mushroom suet pudding) and popular Sun lunch (best to book), two or three well kept local ales, friendly efficient young staff; pool and darts in games room; children and dogs welcome, picnic-sets in large garden with views, open all day weekends, closed Mon, Tues. *(David Travis)*

LESBURY   NU2311
★ **Coach** (01665) 830865

B1339; NE66 3PP Picturesque stone pub at heart of pretty village; low-beamed rooms with pubby furniture on tartan carpet, dark leather stools by counter serving well kept Timothy Taylors Landlord and a guest, snug off to left with sofas and armchairs, small dining room and restaurant both with woodburners, popular good value home-made food including daily specials, friendly staff; background music; children and dogs (not in restaurant) welcome, picnic-sets on front terrace and in back garden, lovely flowering tubs and baskets, handy for Alnwick Castle, open (and food) all day in summer, closed afternoons in winter and no food Sun evening. *(Gordon and Margaret Ormondroyd)*

LONG NEWTON   NZ3716
Vane (01642) 580401

Darlington Road; TS21 1DB Restored 19th-c pub popular for landlord-chef's good food from pub favourites to imaginative restaurant dishes, lunchtime/early evening set menu, Black Sheep and a couple of guests, warm friendly service, solid dark dining tables and chairs, upholstered banquettes, cosy bar with log fire; background music, Sun quiz; children and dogs (in bar) welcome, picnic-sets in garden with far-reaching views across fields, three bedrooms, open all day Sun, closed Mon and lunchtime Tues, no food Sun evening. *(Justine and Neil Bonnett)*

LONGFRAMLINGTON   NU1301
Granby (01665) 570228

Front Street; NE65 8DP Welcoming old coaching inn run by same family for three generations; highly regarded food cooked by chef-landlord from well executed pub favourites to creative restaurant dishes, also good value set lunch and afternoon teas, one well kept real ale and several malt whiskies, comfortable traditional beamed interior with bar, lounge and small restaurant; children welcome, no dogs, five bedrooms, open (and food) all day. *(Andrew Lawson)*

LONGFRAMLINGTON   NU1301
Village Inn (01665) 570268

Just off A697; Front Street; NE65 8AD Friendly 18th-c stone inn arranged into three distinct areas; tasty freshly prepared pub food including good Sun carvery, own-brewed VIP beers along with local guests; comfortable bedrooms and self-catering cabins (just outside the village), open all day. *(Andy and Louise Ramwell)*

LONGHORSLEY   NZ1494
Shoulder of Mutton (01670) 788236

East Road; A697 N of Morpeth; NE65 8SY Comfortable bar and restaurant with good choice of enjoyable reasonably priced food from lunchtime baguettes up, weekday deals and popular Sun carvery till 6pm (must book), three real ales, good selection of other drinks, friendly staff; background music, TV, fruit machine; children and dogs (in bar) welcome, picnic-sets in back garden, two bedrooms, open all day, food all day Fri-Sun. *(Tom Stone)*

LUCKER   NU1530
Apple (01668) 213824

Off A1 N of Morpeth; NE70 7JH Updated old stone-built pub in tiny village; very good food from pub favourites, burgers and chargrills to more upmarket choices, real ales including a house beer from Alnwick and nice wines, friendly engaging staff, woodburner in bar's large fireplace, stripped wood floors and some exposed stonework, modern furnishings, roomy big-windowed dining area; children and dogs welcome, wheelchair access, circular picnic-sets on decking, two comfortable bedrooms, good breakfast, closed Sun evening, otherwise open all day. *(Gordon and Margaret Ormondroyd)*

MAIDEN LAW   NZ1749
Three Horseshoes (01207) 520900

A6067 N of Lanchester; DH7 0QT Spacious roadside dining pub; enjoyable good value food from varied menu including several vegetarian options, pie night Tues, Mexican evening Weds, neatly kept open-plan interior with central beamed and quarry-tiled bar, mix of high-backed cane chairs, leatherette sofas and tub chairs, two-way woodburner, conservatory; children welcome, disabled parking and wheelchair access, garden with play area, open all day Sat, till 5pm Sun, closed Mon. *(Julie Swift)*

MICKLETON   NY9724
★ **Crown** (01833) 640381

B6277; DL12 0JZ Bustling pub under friendly hands-on licensees; simply furnished bars and dining areas, cushioned settles, upholstered leather and wooden dining chairs around all sorts of tables on polished boards, country prints and photographs, woodburner flanked by two leather armchairs, a couple of Marstons-related beers including Wainwright, several wines by the glass and good food from lunchtime sandwiches and pub favourites to more restauranty choices; children and dogs welcome, rustic picnic-sets in garden with fine country views, one bedroom and campsite, closed Mon-Weds, otherwise open (and food) all day, kitchen closes 4pm Sun. *(GSB)*

MIDDLETON   NZ0685
Ox (01670) 772634
Village signed off B6343, W of Hartburn;
NE61 4QZ Welcoming unpretentious
Georgian country pub in small tucked-away
village; a couple of well kept local ales
and tasty straightforward home-made food
(served Fri-Sun lunchtime); children and
dogs welcome, seats outside, handy for
Wallington (NT), open all day Sun, from
4.30pm other days. *(Miles Green)*

MIDDLETON ONE ROW   NZ3612
Devonport (01325) 332255
The Front; DL2 1AS Spacious recently
refurbished 18th-c pub/hotel under same
ownership as the Bay Horse at Hurworth-on-
Tees; stone and wooden floors, open fires,
some distinctive pictures on fashionable
grey-green walls and a dog-friendly bar,
enjoyable fairly pubby food, three real ales
and good selection of wines and spirits, warm
welcoming service; beer garden and sunny
terrace, attractive spot facing village green,
eight comfortable bedrooms with up-to-
date bathrooms, good breakfast, handy for
Teesside Airport. *(Michael Doswell)*

MILFIELD   NT9333
Red Lion (01668) 216224
Main Road (A697 Wooler–Cornhill);
NE71 6JD Comfortable and welcoming
18th-c coaching inn with good fairly priced
food from chef-owner, smaller appetites
and gluten-free diets catered for, well kept
ales such as Black Sheep and Thwaites, a
dozen wines by the glass and decent coffee,
friendly efficient service; Weds quiz; children
welcome, no dogs inside, pretty garden by car
park at back, six bedrooms, good breakfast,
open all day. *(John and Sylvia Harrop)*

MORPETH   NZ1986
Tap & Spile (01670) 513894
Manchester Street; NE61 1BH Cosy two-
room pub with up to eight well kept ales
including Everards, Greene King and Timothy
Taylors, Weston's cider, fruit wines and short
choice of good value lunchtime food, friendly
staff, traditional pub furniture and interesting
old photographs, quieter back lounge
(children allowed here) with coal-effect gas
fire, board and other games; background music,
live acoustic music Sun afternoon, sports
TV; dogs welcome in front bar, open all day
Fri-Sun. *(Andy and Louise Ramwell)*

NETHERTON   NT9807
Star (01669) 630238
Off B6341 at Thropton, or A697 via
Whittingham; NE65 7HD Simple
unchanging village local run by charming
long-serving landlady (licence has been in
her family since 1917); large high-ceilinged
room with wall benches and many original
features, friendly regulars, range of bottled
beers, no food, music, children or dogs; only
open evenings two days a week (Fri, Sun,
from 7.30pm) and first Weds of month (quiz
night). *(Freddie and Sarah Banks)*

NEWBROUGH   NY8768
Red Lion (01434) 674226
Stanegate Road; NE47 5AR Former
coaching inn with light airy feel; log fire,
flagstones and half-panelling, old local
photographs and some large paintings, good
sensibly priced food in bar and two dining
areas from well filled baguettes up (more
elaborate evening menu), a couple of well
kept local ales, friendly efficient service,
games room with pool and darts, little shop
selling local art/craftwork; children and dogs
(not at food times) welcome, garden behind
with decking, good walks and on NCN cycle
route 72, six bedrooms, open all day.
(David Appleyard)

NEWCASTLE UPON TYNE NZ2464
★**Bacchus** (0191) 261 1008
High Bridge E, between Pilgrim Street
and Grey Street; NE1 6BX Smart,
spacious and comfortable Sir John Fitzgerald
pub with ocean liner look; two-level interior
with lots of varnished wood, pillars, ship and
shipbuilding photographs, nine very well
kept changing ales (beer festivals), plenty
of bottled imports, farm cider and splendid
range of whiskies, decent coffee too, friendly
helpful staff, no food; background music;
disabled facilities, handy for the Theatre
Royal, open all day and can get very busy.
(Peter Smith and Judith Brown)

NEWCASTLE UPON TYNE NZ2464
Bodega (0191) 221 1552
Westgate Road; NE1 4AG Majestic
Edwardian drinking hall next to Tyne
Theatre; eight real ales and good range
of bottled beers, friendly service, snug
front cubicles, spacious back area with
two marvellous stained-glass cupolas;
background music, big-screen TVs (very busy
on match days), darts, free wi-fi; open all day.
(David Travis)

NEWCASTLE UPON TYNE NZ2563
★**Bridge Hotel** (0191) 232 6400
Castle Square, next to high-level bridge;
NE1 1RQ Spacious 19th-c Sir John
Fitzgerald pub with well divided bar; high-
ceiling, stained-glass windows, replica slatted
snob screens and magnificent fireplace, well
kept Anarchy Blonde Star, Sharps Doom
Bar and seven quickly changing guests, real
cider, bargain lunchtime food, great river
and bridge views from raised back area,
live music upstairs including long-standing
Mon folk club; background music, sports

We say if we know a pub allows dogs.

TV, games machines; flagstoned terrace overlooking part of old town wall, open all day. *(Bob Atkins)*

NEWCASTLE UPON TYNE NZ2563
Bridge Tavern (0191) 261 9966
Under the Tyne Bridge; NE1 3UF
Bustling brewpub under same ownership as the Town Wall; airy interior with exposed brickwork and lots of wood, industrial-style ceiling, view into back microbrewery (joint venture with Wylam), a dozen or so beers including local guests (tasting trays available), generous helpings of well liked often unusual food (all day, till 7pm Fri-Sun) from snacks and sharing boards up, friendly helpful staff; background music; well behaved children and dogs allowed before 7pm, upstairs bar and good roof terrace, open all day (till 1am Fri, Sat).
(Peter Smith and Judith Brown)

NEWCASTLE UPON TYNE NZ2563
Broad Chare (0191) 211 2144
Broad Chare, just off quayside opposite law courts; NE1 3DQ Traditional feel although only recently converted to a pub; popular british-leaning food from bar snacks such as crispy pigs ears and Lindisfarne oysters to hearty main courses, four real ales including a house beer from Wylam (Writer's Block), good choice of bottled beers, wines and whiskies, bare-boards bar and snug, old local photographs, upstairs dining room; background music; children welcome till 7pm (later upstairs), no dogs, next to the Live Theatre, open all day (no food Sun evening). *(Bob Atkins)*

NEWCASTLE UPON TYNE NZ2464
Centurion (0191) 261 6611
Central Station, Neville Street; NE1 5HL Glorious high-ceilinged Victorian décor with tilework and columns in former first-class waiting room, well restored with comfortable leather seats giving club-like feel, half a dozen real ales, good value food till early evening; background music, big-screen sports TV; useful café-deli next door, open all day. *(Susan and John Douglas)*

NEWCASTLE UPON TYNE NZ2464
City Tavern (0191) 232 1308
Northumberland Road; NE1 8JF
Revamped half-timbered city-centre pub on different levels; ten real ales including a couple badged for them, decent wine list and around 60 gins, enjoyable food from reasonably priced varied menu, plenty of vegan and gluten-free choices, friendly staff; children and dogs welcome (menus for both), open (and food) all day, kitchen closes at 7pm Sun. *(Bob Atkins)*

NEWCASTLE UPON TYNE NZ2664
Cluny (0191) 230 4474
Lime Street; NE1 2PQ Bar-café-music venue in interesting 19th-c mill/warehouse

(part of the Head of Steam group); low-priced home-made food including various burgers and hot dogs, Sun brunch, up to seven well kept ales, good selection of other beers, ciders and some exotic rums, efficient friendly service, sofas in comfortable raised area with daily papers and art magazines, back gallery featuring local artists; background music and regular live bands (also in Cluny 2 next door); children (till 7pm) and dogs allowed, picnic-sets out on green, striking setting below Metro bridge, parking nearby can be difficult, open (and food) all day. *(David Travis)*

NEWCASTLE UPON TYNE NZ2365
Cosy Dove (0191) 260 2895
Hunters Road, Spital Tongues; NE2 4NA Revamped pub on city fringe; opened-up interior blending contemporary and traditional features, leather sofas and rugs on wood floor, log fire, good fairly priced food from open kitchen including range of burgers and some clay oven dishes, a beer badged for the pub and up to three guests, good range of wines and gins, friendly welcoming staff; background music, quiz nights and sports TV; a few pavement tables, open all day, no food Sun evening. *(David Travis)*

NEWCASTLE UPON TYNE NZ2563
★Crown Posada (0191) 232 1269
The Side; off Dean Street, between and below the two high central bridges (A6125 and A6127); NE1 3JE City's oldest pub, just a few minutes' stroll from the castle; long narrow room with elaborate coffered ceiling, stained-glass counter screens and fine mirrors with tulip lamps on curly brass mounts (matching the great ceiling candelabra), long green built-in leather wall seat flanked by narrow tables, old photos of Newcastle and plenty of caricatures, Allendale, Hadrian Border, Highland, Titanic and Wylam, may do sandwiches, heating from fat low-level pipes, music from vintage record player; no credit cards; well behaved children in front snug till 6pm, open all day (midnight Fri, Sat) and can get packed at peak times.
(Roger and Donna Huggins, Peter Smith and Judith Brown)

NEWCASTLE UPON TYNE NZ2664
Cumberland Arms (0191) 265 1725
James Place Street; NE6 1LD Unspoilt traditional 19th-c pub with half a dozen well kept mainly local ales along with good range of craft beers and ciders, two annual beer festivals, limited choice of reasonably priced snacky food, friendly obliging staff, bare boards and open fires; events most nights including regular folk sessions, film and quiz evenings; dogs welcome, tables out overlooking Ouseburn Valley, four bedrooms, open all day weekends, from 1pm Mon-Fri. *(Bob Atkins)*

NEWCASTLE UPON TYNE NZ2664
Free Trade (0191) 265 5764
*St Lawrence Road, off Walker Road
(A186); NE6 1AP* Splendidly basic and
unpretentious with outstanding views up
river from big windows, terrace tables
and seats on grass; up to seven real ales,
traditional ciders and plenty of bottled
beers and whiskies, good sandwiches/pasties
and regular pizza nights, warm friendly
atmosphere, original Formica tables and
coal fire, free juke box, steps down to
back room and loos; open all day.
(Roger and Donna Huggins)

NEWCASTLE UPON TYNE NZ2266
Old George (0191) 260 3035
*Cloth Market, down alley past
Pumphreys; NE1 1EZ* Attractive 16th-c
former coaching house in cobbled yard;
painted beams and panelling, comfortable
armchairs by open fire, half a dozen well
kept/priced ales including Bass, plenty
of wines by the glass and cocktails, good
value food including deals, friendly staff;
background music at one end, open mike
Thurs and Sun, DJs Fri and Sat, sports TV,
free wi-fi; children welcome, open all day
(till 2am Fri, Sat). *(David Travis)*

NEWCASTLE UPON TYNE NZ2463
Split Chimp
Arch 7, Westgate Road; NE1 1SA
Two-floor micropub built into a railway arch;
ground-floor bar with cask tables, stools,
pews and leather sofas, six well kept ales,
five craft beers (more in bottles), real cider
and some wines by the glass, snacky food,
upstairs skittle alley; live music; open all
day Fri and Sat, till 8pm Sun, from 3pm
other days. *(Tom Stone)*

NEWCASTLE UPON TYNE NZ2463
Town Wall (0191) 232 3000
*Pink Lane; across from Central Station;
NE1 5HX* In handsome listed building with
spacious bare-boards interior (sister pub
is Bridge Tavern); dark walls, button-back
banquettes and mix of well spaced tables
and chairs, pictures in heavy gilt frames, up
to a dozen ales (one badged for them), good
choice of bottled beers and several wines by
the glass, well priced food including sharing
boards, burgers and pub favourites, basement
overspill/function room; background music,
free wi-fi; well behaved children and dogs
allowed, open all day (till 1am Fri, Sat),
food till 7pm Fri-Sun. *(Peter Smith and
Judith Brown)*

NEWTON-BY-THE-SEA NU2325
★ Joiners Arms (01665) 576112
*High Newton-by-the-Sea, by turning to
Linkhouse; NE66 3EA* Open-plan village
pub-restaurant; flagstoned bar with big front
windows and open fire, wood-clad dining

area behind, good well presented food
from interesting sandwiches (stotties) and
sharing plates up, four local ales, carefully
chosen wines; background music; children
and dogs (in bar) welcome, picnic-sets out
at front and behind, good coastal walks,
five stylish bedrooms, open all day.
(Dr Simon Innes)

NEWTON-ON-THE-MOOR NU1705
Cook & Barker Arms
(01665) 575234 *Village signed from A1
Alnwick–Felton; NE65 9JY* Traditional
stone-built country inn; rustic beamed bar
with partly panelled walls, upholstered wall
benches by scrubbed pine tables, bottles
and bric-a-brac on delft shelf, fire in old
range one end, woodburner the other, four
real ales and several wines by the glass
from extensive list, popular food including
several fish options, weekday set lunch and
early bird deal Weds and Thurs, friendly
efficient staff, separate restaurant with
exposed stonework and raftered ceiling;
background music; children welcome, dogs
in snug and lounge, small outside seating
area, 16 bedrooms, Boxing Day hunt starts
from here, open (and food) all day.
(Darren and Jane Staniforth)

NORTH SHIELDS NZ3668
Salty Sea Dog 07455 107470
Union Quay; NE30 1HJ Quirky little bar
in the Fish Quay district; local ales, craft
beers and great selection of gins and other
spirits, friendly helpful staff; dogs welcome,
some pavement seating, open all day (till
1am Fri, Sat). *(Darren Liddle)*

OTTERBURN NY8992
William de Percy (01830) 520261
Jedburgh Road; NE19 1NR Former
coaching inn with french-inspired shabby-
chic décor; good food from sharing plates
up including range of crêpes, a couple of
real ales, continental beers and decent
choice of wines and cocktails; background
music; children and dogs welcome, lovely
mediterranean-style gardens with palms and
fountain, eight stylish bedrooms, more in
adjoining Petit Chateau (popular venue for
weddings), open (and food) all day.
(Andy and Louise Ramwell)

PIERCEBRIDGE NZ2115
Fox Hole (01325) 374286
B6275 N of village, or off A67; DL2 3SJ
Friendly 19th-c roadside pub with well liked
interesting food from lunchtime sandwiches
and sharing plates up, Theakstons beers,
decent wine choice and extensive range of
spirits, contemporary opened-up interior,
woodburners, dining room with kitchen
view; TV for major sports; children welcome
(under-7s till 7.30pm), dogs in bar, tables on
terrace and small lawn, open all day, food till
4pm Sun. *(Elaine Taylor, Rod Lambert)*

PONTELAND NZ1773
Blackbird (01661) 822684
North Road opposite church; NE20 9UH
Imposing ancient stone pub with opened-up interior; mix of furniture including several high tables and button-back banquettes, wood, slate and tartan-carpeted floors, striking old map of Northumberland and etching of Battle of Otterburn either side of fireplace, larger Tudor stone fireplace in unusual Tunnel Room, good popular food from bar snacks to restauranty dishes, six well kept ales and over 50 gins, friendly service; background music, sports TV, free wi-fi; children and dogs welcome, picnic-sets out at front, more tables on back lawn, open all day, food till 5pm Sun.
(Freddie and Sarah Banks)

RENNINGTON NU2118
★Horseshoes (01665) 577665
B1340; NE66 3RS Comfortable and welcoming little family-run pub with nice local feel (may be horses in car park); a couple of well kept ales including Hadrian Border Farne Island, decent wines by the glass and ample helpings of enjoyable pubby food using local suppliers, friendly efficient service, simple well worn-in bar with flagstones, padded benches and woodburner, carpeted restaurant; darts, free wi-fi; children welcome, picnic-sets out on small front lawn, attractive quiet village near coast, Aug scarecrow competition, closed Mon.
(GSB)

ROCHESTER NY8497
Redesdale Arms (01830) 520668
A68 3 miles W of Otterburn; NE19 1TA Isolated old roadside inn (aka the First & Last) surrounded by unspoilt countryside; enjoyable home-made food including daily specials, vegan and gluten-free diets catered for, Allendale ales, friendly attentive staff; ten bedrooms, open (and food) all day.
(Celia and Robert Lemming)

SEATON SLUICE NZ3477
Kings Arms (0191) 237 0275
West Terrace; NE26 4RD Friendly old pub in pleasant seaside location perched above tidal Seaton Sluice Harbour; good range of real ales and enjoyable pubby food (not Sun evening) including gluten-free choices and blackboard specials, beamed and carpeted bar with old photographs and woodburner at each end, restaurant; children welcome, a few picnic-sets on sunny front grass, more seats in enclosed beer garden behind, open all day. *(Elise and Charles Mackinlay)*

SEDGEFIELD NZ3528
Dun Cow (01740) 620894
Front Street; TS21 3AT Popular 18th-c village inn with low-beamed bar, back tap room and restaurant, extensive choice of enjoyable reasonably priced food including

good Sun roast, four well kept ales such as Black Sheep and Theakstons; children welcome, six comfortable bedrooms, open (and food) all day weekends.
(Amy and Luke Buchanan)

SHINCLIFFE NZ2940
Seven Stars (0191) 384 8454
High Street N (A177 S of Durham); DH1 2NU Comfortable and welcoming 18th-c village inn; good generously served food from pub favourites up including weekday set menu and other deals, three well kept changing ales, coal-effect gas fire in lounge bar, panelled dining room; children welcome in eating areas, dogs in bar, some picnic-sets outside, eight bedrooms, closed Mon, otherwise open all day.
(Dr Simon Innes)

SLALEY NY9757
Rose & Crown (01434) 673996
Church Close; NE47 0AA Welcoming 17th-c pub owned by the village; enjoyable good value pubby food from sandwiches/baguettes up (not Sun evening), local ales such as Allendale, beams and log fires; Sun quiz; children and dogs welcome, garden with long country views, two bedrooms, open all day. *(Patricia Hawkins)*

SLALEY NY9658
Travellers Rest (01434) 673231
B6306 S of Hexham (and N of village); NE46 1TT Attractive stone-built country pub, spaciously opened up, with farmhouse-style décor, beams, flagstones and polished wood floors, huge fireplace, comfortable high-backed settles forming discrete areas, friendly welcoming staff, enjoyable food (not Sun evening, Mon) in bar or quieter dining room, two real ales such as Black Sheep and Caledonian; children and dogs welcome, tables outside and well equipped adventure play area, three good value bedrooms, open all day. *(Andrew Lawson)*

SOUTH SHIELDS NZ3567
Alum Ale House (0191) 427 7245
Ferry Street (B1344); NE33 1JR Welcoming 18th-c bow-windowed pub adjacent to North Shields ferry; open-plan bare-boards bar with fire in old range, a dozen well kept Marstons-related ales; music and quiz nights; no children, seats on front deck overlooking the river, handy for marketplace, open all day.
(Victoria and James Sargeant)

SOUTH SHIELDS NZ3566
Steamboat (0191) 454 0134
Mill Dam/Coronation Street; NE33 1EQ Friendly 19th-c corner pub with nine well kept changing ales; lots of nautical bric-a-brac, bar ceiling covered in flags, raised seating area and separate lounge; near river and marketplace, open all day.
(Victoria and James Sargeant)

STANNINGTON   NZ2179

★ **Ridley Arms** (01670) 789216

Village signed off A1 S of Morpeth;
NE61 6EL Extended Fitzgerald pub
with several separate areas; open fire and
cushioned settles in proper front bar, stools
along counter serving up to seven local ales
such as Alnwick and Hadrian Border, a dozen
wines by the glass and good coffee, decent
choice of enjoyable reasonably priced food,
pleasant helpful staff, several dining areas
with upholstered bucket chairs around dark
tables on bare boards or carpet, cartoons and
portraits on cream, panelled or stripped-
stone walls; background music, Tues quiz,
free wi-fi; children welcome, good disabled
access, picnic-sets out at front and on back
terrace, open (and food) all day, handy for A1.
(Gordon and Margaret Ormondroyd)

STANNINGTON   NZ1881

St Marys Inn (01670) 293293

Turn left in Stannington village and
past the church, follow Green Lane to
St Marys Lane; NE61 6BL Major rework
of gabled Edwardian building with clock
tower (admin block for former asylum);
series of rooms, each with own character,
wood floors throughout, interesting artwork
and several woodburners, well executed
food from bar snacks and pub favourites up,
efficient friendly service, a house beer from
Rigg & Farrow, guest ales and good wine/
whisky choice, decent coffee; children and
dogs (in bar areas) welcome, comfortable
bedrooms, generous breakfast, useful for
A1, open all day from 8am, kitchen closes
6pm Sun. *(Michael Doswell)*

SUNDERLAND   NZ4057

Ivy House (0191) 567 3399

Worcester Terrace; SR2 7AW Friendly
Victorian corner pub off the beaten track;
five well kept changing ales, interesting
bottled beers and good range of spirits,
popular reasonably priced food from open
kitchen including burgers and pizzas;
background and live music, quiz Weds (and
sometimes Sun), sports TV; open (and food)
all day. *(Dr Simon Innes)*

THROPTON   NU0202

Three Wheat Heads (01669) 620262

B6341; NE65 7LR Popular 18th-c village
inn with good generously served food
including Sun carvery, three well kept local
ales and decent choice of wines, busy but
friendly service, open fires (one in fine tall
stone fireplace), glorious far-reaching
country views from dining room's picture
windows; children and dogs (in bar) welcome,
disabled access, garden with play area,

comfortable bedrooms and good breakfast,
handy for Cragside (NT), open (and food)
all day. *(Julie Swift)*

TYNEMOUTH   NZ3669

Hugos (0191) 257 8956

Front Street; NE30 4DZ Refurbished
Sir John Fitzgerald pub with open-plan
split-level interior, four changing ales, decent
choice of wines by the glass and cocktails,
reasonably priced food from shortish menu
including sandwiches; Weds quiz, sports TV;
children welcome, some pavement seating,
open all day, no evening food Fri-Sun.
(David Appleyard)

TYNEMOUTH   NZ3668

Turks Head (0191) 257 6547

Front Street; NE30 4DZ Friendly drinkers'
pub with eight changing ales and three
craft kegs, some food, steps between two
comfortable small bars, ancient stuffed
border collie and accompanying sad story
(pub known locally as the Stuffed Dog);
juke box, sports TVs, darts; open all day.
(Patricia Hawkins)

WARDEN   NY9166

Boatside (01434) 602233

Village signed N of A69; NE46 4SQ
Modernised old stone pub in attractive spot
by Tyne bridge; enjoyable fairly priced food
from varied menu, a couple of local ales and
decent selection of new world wines, good
friendly service; sports TV; children welcome,
small neat enclosed garden, bedrooms in
adjoining cottages (some self-catering), open
(and food) all day. *(Miles Green)*

WARENFORD   NU1429

White Swan (01668) 213453

Off A1 S of Belford; NE70 7HY Friendly
bar with three real ales such as Alnwick,
Firebrick and Greene King, steps down to
cosy restaurant serving good imaginative food
along with more traditional choices, cheerful
efficient service, warm fires; children and
dogs (in bar) welcome, three bedrooms, open
all day. *(Darren and Jane Staniforth, Ian Wilson,*
Gordon and Margaret Ormondroyd)

WARKWORTH   NU2406

Hermitage (01665) 711258

Castle Street; NE65 0UL Rambling former
coaching inn with good choice of home-
made food including Sun carvery, Jennings,
Marstons and guests, decent range of ales,
friendly staff, quaint décor with fire in old
range, small upstairs restaurant; background
music (live Fri), Thurs quiz; children and
dogs welcome, benches and hanging baskets
out at front, attractive setting, bedrooms,
open (and food) all day. *(Andrew Lawson)*

WELDON BRIDGE   NZ1398

★ **Anglers Arms**   (01665) 570271

*B6344, just off A697; village signposted
with Rothbury off A1 N of Morpeth;
NE65 8AX* Traditional coaching inn nicely
located by bridge over River Coquet; two-part
bar with cream walls or oak panelling,
shiny black beams hung with copper pans,
profusion of fishing memorabilia, taxidermy
and a grandfather clock, some low tables
with matching chairs, sofa by coal fire, three
changing ales, around 40 malt whiskies
and decent wines by the glass, well liked
generously served food including Tues curry,
friendly helpful staff; background music,
Thurs quiz; children and dogs (in bar)
welcome, attractive garden with good play
area, fishing rights, comfortable bedrooms,
open (and food) all day. *(Freddie and
Sarah Banks)*

WEST BOLDON   NZ3460

Red Lion   (0191) 536 4197

Redcar Terrace; NE36 0PZ Bow-
windowed, flower-decked pub with cosy
linked areas; open fire in beamed bar, three
real ales such as Black Sheep and Theakstons
from ornate wood counter, separate snug
and conservatory dining room, good choice
of popular well priced food, friendly relaxed
atmosphere; seats out on back decking, open
all day. *(Roger and Donna Huggins)*

WHALTON   NZ1281

Beresford Arms   (01670) 775273

B6524; NE61 3UZ Refurbished pub-
restaurant in attractive village; small bar
area serving three real ales (at least one
from a local brewery) and interesting
range of gins, good variety of well liked
fairly priced food from sandwiches to daily
specials, friendly helpful staff, spacious
carpeted restaurant; converted stables
for events/functions; children and dogs
(in bar) welcome, a few seats out at front,
more in enclosed back garden, comfortable
bedrooms, open all day. *(GSB)*

WHITFIELD   NY7857

Elks Head   (01434) 345282

*Off A686 SW of Haydon Bridge;
NE47 8HD* Extended old stone pub
attractively set in steep wooded valley:
light and spacious, with bar and two dining
areas, good value tasty food, a couple of real
ales and several wines by the glass, friendly
helpful service; children and dogs (in bar)
welcome, picnic-sets in small pretty front
garden by little river, scenic area with good
walks, ten bedrooms (some in adjacent
cottage), open all day in summer.
(Elise and Charles Mackinlay)

WHITLEY BAY   NZ3742

Left Luggage Room

*Metro Station, Northam Road;
NE26 3NR* Quirky micropub in former
station room; high vaulted ceiling and brick
walls left in original rough condition adding
to the character, mismatched wooden
furniture on boarded floor, artwork for sale,
old suitcases and trunks stacked below
bar counter, changing ales, craft beers and
ciders, good range of other drinks including
several whiskies and gins (all listed on
blackboards), no food apart from bar
snacks, friendly knowledgeable staff;
live music some evenings; dogs welcome,
tables out on platform, open all day.
(Martinthehills)

WHORLTON   NZ1014

Fernavilles Rest   (01833) 627341

*High Stakes, N of village green;
DL12 8XD* Old stone pub on pretty village's
green; log-fire bar and well divided half-
panelled restaurant, popular reasonably
priced food catering for special diets, well
kept beers including a house beer from
Mithril, friendly young staff; children,
walkers and dogs welcome, three good value
comfortable bedrooms, near historic narrow
suspension bridge over the Tees and handy
for Bowes Museum, open all day weekends,
closed Mon and till 5pm Tues-Fri, may shut
early if quiet. *(David Appleyard)*

WYLAM   NZ1164

★ **Boathouse**   (01661) 853431

*Station Road, handy for Newcastle–
Carlisle railway; across Tyne from
village; NE41 8HR* Convivial two-room pub
with a dozen real ales, traditional ciders and
good choice of malt whiskies, thai menu and
some snacky food, friendly knowledgeable
staff, light interior with one or two low beams
and woodburner; fortnightly buskers night
(Tues), juke box, sports TV; children and dogs
welcome, seats outside, close to station and
river, open all day (evenings can be very busy).
(Roger and Donna Huggins)

WYLAM   NZ1164

Ship   (01661) 854538

Main Road; NE41 8AQ Genuine warm
welcome at this sizeable open-plan dining
pub; good individual cooking from owner-chef
including Sat steak night and Sun set lunch,
a house beer from Theakstons and well
chosen wine list, happy hour 5-7pm Fri; free
wi-fi, children and dogs welcome, picnic-sets
in beer garden, bedrooms, closed Mon and
lunchtime Tues, otherwise open all day (till
6pm Sun). *(Michael Doswell)*

Nottinghamshire

CAYTHORPE
SK6845 Map 7

Black Horse

(0115) 966 3520

Turn off A6097 0.25 miles SE of roundabout junction with A612, NE of Nottingham; into Gunthorpe Road, then right into Caythorpe Road and keep on; NG14 7ED

Quaintly old-fashioned little pub brewing its own beer, with simple interior and enjoyable homely food; no children, no credit cards

For 300 years the same friendly family have run this simple country local. Little changes, thankfully, and our readers enjoy their visits very much. The homely, uncluttered, carpeted bar has just five tables, along with brocaded wall banquettes and settles, decorative plates on a delft shelf, a few horsebrasses attached to the ceiling joists, and a coal fire. Cheerful regulars might occupy the few bar stools to enjoy the well kept Brewsters Marquis, Castle Rock Harvest Pale and Greene King Abbot on handpump, seven wines by the glass and half a dozen whiskies. Off the front corridor is an inner room, partly panelled with a wall bench running all the way round three unusual, long, copper-topped tables; there are several old local photographs, darts and board games. Down on the left, an end room has just one huge round table. There are seats outside. Their smart new loos will be ready by the time this book is published. The pub is close to the River Trent where there are waterside walks. No children.

🍴 Good value home-cooked food (you'll need to book a table in advance) includes sandwiches, prawn cocktail, mushrooms on toast, three-egg omelettes, lamb chops with creamed potatoes, gammon and eggs, fish in parsley sauce, and puddings such as sticky toffee pudding and treacle sponge with custard. *Benchmark main dish: fresh fish of the day £13.00. Two-course evening meal £19.00.*

Free house ~ Licensee Sharron Andrews ~ Real ale ~ No credit cards ~ Open 12-2.30, 5.30-11; 12-5 Sun; closed Mon except bank holidays ~ Bar food 11.45-1.45, 6-8.30; not Sat evening; 12-5 Sun ~ Dogs allowed in bar ~ Wi-fi *Recommended by Thomas Green, Peter Pilbeam, Anne and Ben Smith, Maddie Purvis, Sally and David Champion, Alfie Bayliss*

CLAYWORTH
SK7288 Map 7

Blacksmiths 🌟 🛏

(01777) 818171 – www.blacksmithsclayworth.com

Town Street; DN22 9AD

Bustling dining pub with stylish décor and imaginative food; comfortable bedrooms

First class food, a genuinely friendly welcome and comfortable, well appointed bedrooms make this pub a winner with our readers. The dining areas have a stylish, contemporary feel that includes cushioned wall seats and high-backed chairs around a mix of tables, dramatic flower arrangements and candles in large glass jars. The bar is furnished with leather chesterfields and armchairs together with upholstered cube-style seats by a woodburning stove, and high stools by the counter where you'll find a beer named for the pub (from Pheasantry) and a guest from perhaps Theakstons or Welbeck Abbey on handpump, and good wines by the glass. Stairs lead up to a private dining area with a balcony overlooking the countryside. A sunny walled garden contains plenty of tables and chairs and a quirky water feature. Dogs are allowed in the bar until 6pm and there's a cottage that they may use for overnight stays with their owners. The Chesterfield Canal circles the village and is popular with bird-watchers, walkers and cyclists.

Excellent food includes watermelon salad with labneh, hazelnut, sesame, pickled shallots and nasturtium pesto, chicken and smoked eel terrine with peas, asparagus and lovage, tomato and onion tart with tomato and chilli jam, herb salad and balsamic dressing, duck with kohlrabi choucroute, tarragon, salted cherry and spring onions, halibut with potato spaghetti, clams, sea vegetables, crispy capers and preserved lemon, pork belly with hash brown, broccoli purée and black garlic mayonnaise, and puddings such as lemon verbena set custard with strawberries and pink pepper meringue and coconut and cardamom arancini with poached rhubarb and sorbet. *Benchmark main dish: lamb rump and rib with spelt, pea and mint risotto £21.50. Two-course evening meal £26.00.*

Free house ~ Real ale ~ Open 12-3, 5.30-11; 12-8 Sun; closed Mon except bank holidays (when they close on Tues instead) ~ Bar food 12-2.30, 6-9 (9.30 Fri, Sat); 12-4.30 Sun ~ Children welcome ~ Wi-fi ~ Bedrooms: £108/£120 *Recommended by Ian Prince, Patricia Hawkins, Peter and Emma Kelly, Geoffrey Sutton, Melanie and David Lawson*

COLSTON BASSETT
SK6933   Map 7

Martins Arms 🌟 🍷 🍺

(01949) 81361 – www.themartinsarms.co.uk

Village signposted off A46 E of Nottingham; School Lane, near market cross in village centre; NG12 3FD

Nottinghamshire Dining Pub of the Year

Smart dining pub with impressive food, good range of drinks including seven real ales and attractive grounds

Most customers in this lovely country pub tend to head to the elegant restaurant to enjoy the top class, imaginatively presented food in civilised surroundings. There's a comfortably relaxed atmosphere, warm log fires in Jacobean fireplaces, fresh flowers and candlelight, and the smart décor includes period fabrics and colours, antique furniture and hunting prints; board games. The main dining room is painted in a warm red with gold silk curtains. Neatly uniformed staff serve a beer named for the pub, Bass, Greene King Ruddles County, Marstons Wainwright, Sharps Doom Bar and Timothy Taylors Landlord on handpump, 22 wines by the glass or carafe (including prosecco, champagne and sweet wines) and a fair choice of whiskies and armagnacs. The lawned garden (with summer croquet and barbecues) backs on to National Trust parkland. As we went to press, we heard that they have now been given planning permission to convert the stable block into two luxury holiday apartments. Do visit the church opposite and Colston Bassett Dairy (just outside the village) which produces and sells its own stilton cheese.

🍴⭐ Creative food includes sandwiches, eggs benedict with poached eggs, toasted muffin and hollandaise, terrine of smoked and poached salmon with citrus and herb salad, roasted pumpkin risotto with amaretti crumble and parmesan, local sausages with pomme purée and red onion gravy, corn-fed venison loin ragoût with potato terrine and salt-baked celeriac, maigret of duck with cherries and potato rösti, hake fillet with garlic beans, chorizo and kale, and puddings such as chocolate and lime pannacotta with roasted pineapple, lime purée and roasted pineapple sorbet and rice pudding mousse with apple purée and malted milk ice-cream. *Benchmark main dish: pheasant curry with confit leg, carrot bhaji and spiced apricot sauce £23.00. Two-course evening meal £23.00.*

Free house ~ Licensees Lynne Strafford Bryan and Salvatore Inguanta ~ Real ale ~ Open 12-3, 6-11; 12-3.30, 6-11 Sat; 12-4, 7-10 Sun ~ Bar food 12-2, 6-9; not Sun evening ~ Restaurant ~ Children welcome ~ Wi-fi *Recommended by Rosie and John Moore, Matt and Hayley Jacob, Patrick and Emma Stephenson, William and Natasha Pace, George and Melody Sanderson*

NEWARK SK7953 Map 7
Prince Rupert 🍷 🍺
(01636) 918121 – www.kneadpubs.co.uk/the-prince-rupert
Stodman Street, off Castle Gate; NG24 1AW

Thoughtfully restored historic pub with fine original features, interestingly furnished small bars, local ales and tasty food

Convivial staff warmly welcome customers to this timber-framed 15th-c pub with its lively atmosphere. The cosy, carefully renovated rooms have a lot of character with some very fine high-backed settles, cushioned wall seats, pubby chairs around polished antique tables, advertising mirrors and old enamelled wall signs, hops, open fires and floors of terracotta tiles, bare floorboards and some carpet. A light and airy conservatory has tricycles hanging from the ceiling, and doors that lead out to the terraced garden. Ales served on handpump from the ornately carved counter include Brains Rev James and Oakham JHB plus a couple of local guests and 22 wines by the glass; background music and TV. The pub is close to the market square in the town centre.

🍴 Good food includes ciabattas, nibbles such as yorkshire pudding with dipping gravy, pigs in blankets with rosemary potatoes and mini baked camembert with chutney plus sharing boards, mozzarella and spinach tortellini with olives, artichokes and arrabiata sauce, burger with toppings and twice-cooked chips, pesto chicken supreme with chorizo and butter bean cassoulet, harissa lamb shoulder with couscous, tzatziki and honey-glazed flatbread, and puddings such as chocolate brownie with ice-cream and banana sticky toffee pudding with caramel sauce. *Benchmark main dish: stone-baked pizzas £10.95. Two-course evening meal £21.00.*

Knead Pubs ~ Managers Sam Johnson and Nikki Booth ~ Real ale ~ Open 11-11 (1am Fri-Sat) ~ Bar food 12-2.30, 5-9; 12-9 Sat; 12-8 Sun ~ Children welcome ~ Dogs welcome ~ Wi-fi *Recommended by David Hunt, Mary Joyce, Max Simons, Michael Butler, Belinda and Neil Garth, Charlotte and William Mason*

'Children welcome' means the pub says it lets children inside without any special restriction. If it allows them in, but to restricted areas such as an eating area or family room, we specify this. Some pubs may impose an evening time limit. We do not mention limits after 9pm as we assume children are home by then.

Also Worth a Visit in Nottinghamshire

Besides the fully inspected pubs, you might like to try these pubs that have been recommended to us and described by readers. Do tell us what you think of them: feedback@goodguides.com

AWSWORTH   SK4844
Gate (0115) 932 9821
Main Street, via A6096 off A610
Nuthall–Eastwood bypass; NG16 2RN
Renovated red-brick Victorian free house near site of once-famous railway viaduct; seven well kept changing beers and some snacky food, bar with woodburner, coal fire in lounge, friendly welcoming atmosphere; occasional live music and comedy nights, skittle alley; dogs welcome, disabled access/loo, back courtyard and roof terrace, open all day. *(Mike Benton)*

BAGTHORPE   SK4751
Dixies Arms (01773) 810505
A608 towards Eastwood off M1 junction 27, right on B600 via Sandhill Road, left into School Road; Lower Bagthorpe; NG16 5HF Friendly unspoilt 18th-c brick local with DH Lawrence connections; beams and tiled floors, well kept Greene King Abbot, Timothy Taylors Landlord and a guest, no food, entrance bar with tiny snug, good fire in small part-panelled parlour's fine fireplace, longer narrow room with toby jugs, darts and dominoes; live music Sat, beer/folk festival June, free wi-fi; children and dogs welcome, picnic-sets out at front, big garden and play area behind, open all day. *(Simon and Jenny Galston)*

BEESTON   SK5236
Crown (0115) 925 4738
Church Street; NG9 1FY Everards pub with 14 well kept ales, real ciders/perry and good choice of other drinks, friendly knowledgeable staff, no hot food but fresh cobs and snacks; front snug and bar with slate and quarry-tiled floors, carpeted parlour, Victorian décor in lounge, beams, panelling and bric-a-brac including an old red telephone box; weekend live music, regular quiz nights and beer festivals; dogs welcome, terrace tables (some under cover), open all day. *(David Hunt)*

BEESTON   SK5336
Star (0115) 854 5320
Middle Street; NG9 1FX Three-room inn with fine range of well kept changing ales and extensive choice of whiskies, friendly knowledgeable staff, good keenly priced pub food along with freshly baked pizzas; live music and quiz nights, separate games room with pool, darts and sports TV; children and dogs welcome, permanent marquee leading through to heated terrace and large grassy garden with play equipment, eight good value bedrooms, open all day. *(David Hunt)*

BEESTON   SK5336
★**Victoria** (0115) 925 4049
Dovecote Lane, backing on to the station; NG9 1JG Red-brick former station hotel attracting good mix of customers; up to 14 real ales (regular beer festivals), two farm ciders, 120 malt whiskies and 30 wines by the glass, good sensibly priced food (order at bar) from varied blackboard menu including plenty for vegetarians, efficient friendly service, three fairly simple unfussy rooms with original long narrow layout (last one for diners only), solid furnishings, bare boards and stripped woodwork, stained-glass windows, some breweriana, open fires; live music and other events including July VicFest, newspapers and board games; children welcome till 8pm, dogs in bar, seats out on covered heated area overlooking platform (trains pass just a few feet away), limited parking, open (and food) all day. *(David Hunt)*

BINGHAM   SK7039
Horse & Plough (01949) 839313
Off A52; Long Acre; NG13 8AF Castle Rock pub in 1818 Methodist chapel; low beams, flagstones and stripped brickwork, comfortable open-plan seating including pews, prints and old brewery memorabilia, their beers and guests (tasters offered), real cider and decent wine choice, enjoyable reasonably priced bar food and popular upstairs grill room with open kitchen, good friendly service; background music; children and dogs welcome, disabled facilities, open all day. *(Jeff Davies)*

BLYTH   SK6287
White Swan (01909) 591222
High Street; S81 8EQ Old whitewashed pub opposite village green, comfortable and well maintained, with beams and exposed brickwork, mix of dining chairs and padded banquettes around assorted tables on flagstones or carpet, Black Sheep, Sharps Doom Bar and Timothy Taylors Landlord, enjoyable good value pubby food including vegetarian/vegan choices and Sun carvery, friendly welcoming staff; TV; children welcome, no dogs inside, tables out in front and in small back garden, open all day, no food Sun evening, Tues. *(John Saville, B and M Kendall)*

BUNNY   SK5829
Rancliffe Arms (0115) 984 4727
Loughborough Road (A60 S of Nottingham); NG11 6QT Substantial old coaching inn with linked dining areas,

enjoyable food including carvery (Mon evening, Weds, Sat and Sun) friendly welcoming staff, chunky country chairs around mixed tables on flagstones or carpet, four well kept Marstons-related beers in comfortable log-fire bar with sofas and armchairs; background music, TV; children welcome, no dogs inside, rattan-style furniture on outside decking, open all day Fri-Sun. *(Gerry and Rosemary Dobson)*

CAR COLSTON   SK7242
Royal Oak (01949) 20247
The Green, off Tenman Lane (off A46 not far from A6097 junction); NG13 8JE
Good well priced traditional food (not Sun evening) in biggish 19th-c pub opposite one of England's largest village greens; well kept Marstons-related ales such as Courage, Bombardier and Wainwright, decent choice of wines by the glass, woodburner in lounge bar with tables set for eating, public bar with unusual barrel-vaulted brick ceiling; skittle alley, free wi-fi; children and dogs welcome, picnic-sets on spacious back lawn, heated smokers' den, camping, open all day.
(John Bryant)

CAUNTON   SK7459
Caunton Beck (01636) 636793
Newark Road; NG23 6AE Reconstructed low-beamed dining pub (on site of 16th-c tavern) made to look old using original timbers and reclaimed oak; scrubbed pine tables and country kitchen chairs, open fire, Oakham JHB and a couple of beers from sister pub's microbrewery (see Bottle & Glass at Harby), over two dozen wines by the glass, generally well liked food from breakfast on, cheerful if not always speedy service; daily newspapers, free wi-fi; children and dogs (in bar) welcome, seats on flowery terrace, handy for A1, open (and food) all day from 8.30am. *(Emily Knight)*

CAYTHORPE   SK6846
Old Volunteer (0115) 966 5822
Caythorpe Road; NG14 7EB Village dining pub with good food, decent wines and four well kept ales, friendly helpful service, upstairs dining room with view over fields; children and dogs (in bar) welcome, seats out at front and on back deck, open (and food) all day, but may close early if quiet. *(Mike Benton)*

CUCKNEY   SK5671
Greendale Oak (01623) 844441
A616, E of A60; NG20 9NQ Updated country pub with good all-day food (till 7pm Sun) from sandwiches and pizzas to chargrilled steaks, eight real ales including

Everards, friendly helpful service, restaurant; background music; children welcome, no dogs inside, sturdy bench seating on front terrace, garden behind, open all day (till 1am Fri, Sat). *(Jeremy)*

EDWINSTOWE   SK6266
Forest Lodge (01623) 824443
Church Street; NG21 9QA Friendly 18th-c inn with enjoyable home-made food in pubby bar or restaurant, good service, five well kept ales including Bombardier and a house beer from Welbeck Abbey, beams and log fire; children welcome, 13 bedrooms, handy for Sherwood Forest. *(Emily Knight)*

EPPERSTONE   SK6548
Cross Keys (0115) 966 9430
Main Street; NG14 6AD Refurbished dining pub with chef-proprietor's good well presented/priced food from regularly changing menu, three real ales including Nottingham and nice wines by the glass, friendly efficient service, woodburner separating lounge bar and restaurant; quiz Sun; children welcome, muddy walkers and dogs in boot room, a few picnic-sets out at front, more in back garden with raised deck, pretty conservation village and surrounding countryside, open (and food) all day, except Sun when kitchen closes at 6pm.
(Gerry and Rosemary Dobson)

FARNDON   SK7652
Boathouse (01636) 676578
Off A46 SW of Newark; keep on towards river – pub off Wyke Lane, just past the Riverside pub; NG24 3SX Big-windowed contemporary bar-restaurant overlooking the Trent, emphasis on food but they do serve a couple of changing ales, good choice of wines and some interesting cocktails; main area with high ceiling trusses supporting bare ducting, simple modern tables and upholstered chairs, shallow step up to second similarly furnished dining area, good variety of food including early bird deal; background and Sun live music, July garden party with live bands, free wi-fi; children welcome, wicker chairs around teak tables on heated terrace, own moorings, open all day, food all day Sun. *(Mike Benton)*

FISKERTON   SK7351
Bromley Arms (01636) 830789
Main Street; NG25 0UL Popular Trentside pub with modernised opened-up interior; fairly compact bar area with upholstered stools and leather armchairs/sofas, two-way fireplace, three well kept Greene King ales and a beer badged for them, decent range of wines by the glass, river-view dining part

---

with upholstered chairs on patterned carpet (some matching wallpaper), enjoyable fairly priced food including weekday set menu till 6pm, friendly helpful service; background music; children welcome, rattan-style furniture on narrow walled terrace, picnic-sets by edge of wharf giving best views, open (and food) all day and can get very busy in summer. *(Paul Walker)*

GRANBY   SK7436
★**Marquis of Granby** (01949) 870621
Off A52 E of Nottingham; Dragon Street; NG13 9PN Friendly 18th-c pub in attractive Vale of Belvoir village; tap for Brewsters with their well kept ales and interesting guests from chunky yew counter, no food, two small comfortable rooms, broad flagstones, some low beams, open fire; children and dogs welcome, open all day weekends, from 4pm Mon-Fri. *(Jeff Davies)*

HARBY   SK8870
Bottle & Glass (01522) 703438
High Street; village signed off A57 W of Lincoln; NG23 7EB 19th-c pub with pair of bay-windowed front bars and restaurant extension; enjoyable food including set menu and blackboard specials, a couple of beers from on-site microbrewery along with a guest such as Black Sheep, good choice of wines, friendly service, open fire and woodburners; shop selling their bottled beers, general provisions and gifts; children welcome, dogs in bar, modern wrought-iron furniture on back terrace, picnic-sets on grass beyond and out at front, open (and food) all day, except Sun when kitchen closes 6pm, breakfast from 10am (9am weekends). *(Jeremy)*

HOCKERTON   SK7156
Spread Eagle (01636) 813322
Caunton Road; A617 Newark–Mansfield; NG25 0PL Refurbished village corner pub; compact interior with linked beamed rooms, a couple of woodburners, smallish bar area serving three real ales and decent choice of wines, generous helpings of good freshly made food from baguettes to daily specials, friendly accommodating staff; children welcome, dogs in one area, beer garden and separate deck, closed Mon, otherwise open (and food) all day, till 8pm (7pm) Sun. *(John Bryant)*

KIMBERLEY   SK4944
★**Nelson & Railway** (0115) 938 2177
Station Road; handy for M1 junction 26 via A610; NG16 2NR Cheery Victorian beamed pub in same family for over four decades, popular and comfortable, with decent inexpensive home-made food from snacks to blackboard specials, well kept Greene King ales and guests, mix of Edwardian-looking furniture, brewery prints (was tap for defunct Hardys & Hansons Brewery) and railway signs, dining extension; juke box, games machine and darts; children and dogs

allowed, disabled access, nice front and back gardens, 11 good value bedrooms, proper breakfast, open all day, food all day Sat, till 6pm Sun. *(Emily Knight)*

KIMBERLEY   SK5044
Stag 07934 043755
Nottingham Road; NG16 2NB Traditional 18th-c local with two cosy rooms, small central counter and corridor; low beams, dark panelling, high-backed settles and some old Shipstones Brewery photographs, up to eight well kept ales including Adnams, Bass, Oakham and Timothy Taylors (beer festival first weekend Aug), no food apart from weekend rolls; some live music, sports TV, table skittles, darts and dominoes, free wi-fi; children and dogs welcome, wheelchair access from behind, front decking and attractive back garden with play area and summer barbecues, open all day Sat and Sun, from 4pm other days. *(Simon and Jenny Galston)*

LANEHAM   SK8176
Ferry Boat (01777) 228350
Main Street, Church Laneham; DN22 0NQ Welcoming early 19th-c country pub in quiet hamlet close to the River Trent; bar with nice log fire and well kept beers such as Pheasantry and Oakham, enjoyable good value food (not Sun evening) including stone-baked pizzas, home-made pies and blackboard specials, steak nights Thurs and Sat, friendly efficient service, restaurant; occasional live music; children and dogs welcome, disabled access, picnic-sets on raised front terrace, open all day weekends, closed Mon and till 4.30pm Tues-Fri. *(Derek and Sylvia Stephenson)*

LAXTON   SK7266
Dovecote (01777) 871586
Off A6075 E of Ollerton; NG22 0NU Red-brick dining pub under hard-working owners; cosy country atmosphere in three traditionally furnished eating areas, popular home-made food from sandwiches and light lunches to daily specials, also a children's menu, three well kept changing ales, proper cider and several wines by the glass, friendly helpful staff; background music, free wi-fi, no dogs inside, disabled access, small front terrace and sloping garden with views towards church, interesting village still using the medieval 'strip farming' system, two bedrooms, open all day Sat, Sun till 9pm (food till 6.30pm); well placed for A1. *(Derek and Sylvia Stephenson)*

LOWDHAM   SK6745
Railway (0115) 966 3222
Longmoor Avenue, near the station; NG14 7DU Welcoming 19th-c village pub with clean modern décor; five real ales such as Castle Rock and Theakstons, 20 wines by the glass and plenty of gins, shortish but varied choice of well liked/presented food

cooked in open kitchen including good value set menu (lunchtime, early evening), friendly helpful staff; children and dogs welcome, chunky picnic-sets outside and play area, more seats on elevated back terrace, open all day, no food Sun evening. *(Jeremy)*

MANSFIELD   SK5363
Railway Inn (01623) 623086
Station Street; best approached by viaduct from near Market Place; NG18 1EF Friendly traditional local; four changing ales, real cider and good low-priced home-made food (till 5pm Sun), two little front rooms leading to main bar, another cosy room at back, laminate flooring throughout; some live music; children and dogs welcome, small courtyard and beer garden, handy for Robin Hood Line station and the newish bus station, open all day. *(David Hunt)*

MAPLEBECK   SK7160
Beehive
Signed down pretty country lanes from A616 Newark–Ollerton and from A617 Newark–Mansfield; NG22 0BS Tiny beamed country tavern in nice spot, unpretentious and welcoming, with cosy front bar and slightly bigger side room, traditional furnishings and open fire, a couple of well kept changing ales, no food; children and dogs welcome, tables on small front terrace and grassy bank running down to stream, play area, may be closed weekday lunchtimes, busy weekends and bank holidays. *(Diana Watt)*

MORTON   SK7251
Full Moon (01636) 830251
Pub and village signed off Bleasby–Fiskerton back road, SE of Southwell; NG25 0UT Attractive old brick pub tucked away in remote hamlet close to the River Trent; modernised pale-beamed bar with two roaring fires, comfortable armchairs, eclectic mix of tables and other simple furnishings, up to five real ales, nine wines by the glass and cocktails, enjoyable sensibly priced food from ciabattas up including good value lunchtime/early evening set menu, afternoon teas, separate carpeted restaurant; background and some live music, board games, free wi-fi; children and dogs (in bar) welcome, picnic-sets out at front, more on peaceful back terrace and sizeable lawn with sturdy play equipment, open all day Fri-Sun, no food Sun evening. *(Chris Stevenson)*

NEWARK   SK8054
Castle Barge (01636) 677320
Town Wharf next to Trent Bridge; NG24 1EU Old grain barge moored near the castle; top deck has enclosed dining area, below is cosy bar, four local beers (cheaper Thurs and Sun evenings), proper cider and cocktails (happy hour 5-8pm), good value straightforward food including

pizzas, friendly service; Weds quiz, free wi-fi; children (not in bar) and dogs welcome, picnic-sets out on wharf, open all day. *(David Hunt)*

NEWARK   SK7953
Just Beer (01636) 312047
Swan & Salmon Yard, off Castle Gate (B6166); NG24 1BG Welcoming one-room micropub tucked down alley; four or five interesting quickly changing beers from brick counter, real cider/perry, limited range of other drinks, bright airy minimalist décor with some brewery memorabilia, half a dozen tables on stone floor, good mix of customers; darts, dominoes and board games; dogs welcome, open all day (from 1pm weekdays). *(Jeremy)*

NORMANTON ON
THE WOLDS   SK6232
Plough (0115) 937 2401
Off A606 5 miles S of Nottingham; NG12 5NN Welcoming ivy-clad pub on edge of village; good food from extensive menu including nice steaks, popular Sun lunch (booking advised) and set deal (Tues-Thurs 5.30-6.30pm), Black Sheep, Timothy Taylors and a guest, friendly uniformed staff, fires in bar and extended restaurant; soft background music; children welcome, large garden with play area and boules, open all day, no food Sun evening. *(Simon and Jenny Galston)*

NOTTINGHAM   SK5739
★ Bell (0115) 947 5241
Angel Row; off Market Square; NG1 6HL Deceptively large pub with late Georgian frontage concealing two much older timber-framed buildings; front Tudor Bar with glass panels protecting patches of 300-year-old wallpaper, larger low-beamed Elizabethan Bar with half-panelled walls and maple parquet flooring, more heavy panelling and a 15th-c crown post in upstairs Belfry; up to a dozen real ales including Greene King and Nottingham from remarkable deep sandstone cellar (can arrange tours), ten wines by the glass, reasonably priced straightforward bar food; background music, TV; children welcome in some parts, pavement tables, open all day (till 12.30am Fri, Sat). *(John Bryant)*

NOTTINGHAM   SK5843
Bread & Bitter (0115) 960 7541
Woodthorpe Drive; NG3 5JL Welcoming pub in former suburban bakery (ovens remain); three bright and airy bare-boards rooms with brewery memorabilia, around a dozen well kept ales including Castle Rock, good range of bottled beers, traditional cider and decent choice of wines, reasonably priced pubby food from cobs to specials, friendly staff; well behaved children and dogs welcome, open (and food) all day, kitchen closes 7pm Sun. *(John Bryant)*

NOTTINGHAM SK5739

Canalhouse (0115) 955 5060

Canal Street; NG1 7EH Converted wharf
building with bridge over indoors canal spur
(complete with narrowboat); lots of bare
brick and varnished wood, huge joists on
steel beams, long bar serving Castle Rock and
three guests, well over 100 bottled beers and
good choice of wines, sensibly priced food
from snacks up including range of burgers;
background music; masses of tables out on
attractive waterside terrace, open all day
(till 1am Fri, Sat), food till 7pm Sun.
(Jess and George Cowley)

NOTTINGHAM SK5739

Cock & Hoop (0115) 948 4414

*High Pavement opposite Galleries of
Justice; NG1 1HF* Pub attached to the
Lace Market Hotel; cosy panelled front bar
with fireside armchairs and characterful
décor, Castle Rock and several local guests,
enjoyable fairly priced food from sandwiches
to good Sun roasts, more room downstairs;
children and dogs welcome, covered outside
seating area, 42 bedrooms (ones by the street
can be noisy at weekends), open (and food)
all day. *(John Bryant)*

NOTTINGHAM SK5739

★ Cross Keys (0115) 941 7898

Byard Lane; NG1 2GJ Victorian city-
centre pub on two levels; lower carpeted
part with leather banquettes, panelling and
chandeliers, upper area with old wooden
tables and chairs and some bucket seats on
bare boards, interesting pictures/prints, well
kept Navigation beers and a couple of guests,
good reasonably priced food from breakfast
on, friendly service, upstairs function/dining
room; sports TV; seats outside, open all day
from 9am. *(Jeremy)*

NOTTINGHAM SK5739

Fellows Morton & Clayton

(0115) 924 1175 *Canal Street (part of
inner ring road); NG1 7EH* Flower-
decked former canal warehouse; up to eight
well kept mainly local ales, four real ciders
and a dozen wines by the glass, enjoyable
food (till 7pm Sun) from snacks and sharing
plates up including range of burgers and
pizzas, friendly staff, softly lit downstairs
bar with alcove seating, wood floors and
lots of exposed brickwork, pictures of old
Nottingham, two raised areas and upstairs
restaurant/function room; background music,
sports TVs, free wi-fi; children and dogs
welcome, tables outside, open all day (till
midnight Fri, Sat). *(John Bryant)*

NOTTINGHAM SK5542

Fox & Crown (0115) 942 2002

*Church Street/Lincoln Street, Old
Basford; NG6 0GA* Range of Shipstones
beers from the Little Star brewery behind
this tucked-away pub, also guest ales,
continentals and good choice of wines,
restaurant area serving reasonably priced
authentic thai food (not Sun); events
including quiz, live music and card nights,
sports TV, games machines, pool and darts;
disabled access/loo, tables on back terrace,
open all day till 1am. *(David Hunt)*

NOTTINGHAM SK5642

Gladstone (0115) 912 9994

Loscoe Road, Carrington; NG5 2AW
Welcoming mid-terrace backstreet local;
half a dozen well kept ales such as Castle
Rock, Fullers, Oakham and Timothy Taylors,
good range of malt whiskies too, comfortable
lounge with collection of books, bar with old
sporting memorabilia and darts; background
music, sports TV, free wi-fi; tables in small
back garden among colourful tubs and
hanging baskets, open all day weekends,
closed weekday lunchtimes. *(David Hunt)*

NOTTINGHAM SK5640

Hand & Heart (0115) 958 2456

Derby Road; NG1 5BA Unexceptional
exterior but unusual inside with bar and
dining areas cut deep into back sandstone;
a house beer from Dancing Duck, Maypole
and guests, two real ciders and good wine
and whisky choice, enjoyable fairly priced
traditional food from sandwiches and snacks
up, friendly helpful service, glassed-in
upstairs room overlooking street; background
music; children welcome till 7pm if eating,
dogs in bar, open all day Fri-Sun, from 4pm
other days. *(John Bryant)*

NOTTINGHAM SK5739

★ Kean's Head (0115) 947 4052

St Marys Gate; NG1 1QA Cheery pub in
attractive Lace Market area; fairly functional
single room with big windows overlooking
the street, simple wooden café furnishings
on wood-strip floor, some exposed brickwork,
red tiling and small fireplace, six real ales
including Castle Rock, ten craft kegs, draught
belgian beers and extensive bottled range,
also 20 wines by the glass, over 60 malt
whiskies and similar number of gins, teas/
coffees, popular fairly traditional food (not
Sun evening), friendly service; background
music, daily papers and free wi-fi; children
welcome till 7pm, church next door worth
a look, open all day. *(Jeremy)*

NOTTINGHAM SK5539

King William IV (0115) 958 9864

*Manvers Street/Eyre Street, Sneinton;
NG2 4PB* Victorian corner local with plenty
of character (aka the King Billy); well kept
Black Iris, Oakham and six guests from
circular bar, also craft beers and real cider,
good fresh cobs and sausage rolls, friendly
staff; irish folk session Thurs, monthly quiz,
silent sports TV, pool upstairs, free wi-fi; dogs
welcome, seats on roof terrace, handy for
cricket, football and rugby grounds, open all
day (from 2pm Mon). *(John Bryant)*

NOTTINGHAM   SK5740

★ Lincolnshire Poacher

(0115) 941 1584 *Mansfield Road; up hill from Victoria Centre; NG1 3FR*
Impressive range of drinks at this popular down-to-earth pub (attracts younger evening crowd), 13 well kept ales including Castle Rock, lots of continental draught/bottled beers, half a dozen ciders and over 70 malt whiskies, shortish choice of reasonably priced uncomplicated food; big simple traditional front bar with wall settles, wooden tables and breweriana, plain but lively room on left and corridor to chatty panelled back snug with newspapers and board games, conservatory overlooking large heated outside area; occasional live music, free wi-fi; children (till 8pm) and dogs welcome, open all day (till midnight Thurs-Sat). *(David Hunt, Jeremy)*

NOTTINGHAM   SK5541

★ Lion (0115) 970 3506

Lower Mosley Street, New Basford; NG7 7FQ Around ten real ales including Bass and Castle Rock from one of the city's deepest cellars (glass viewing panel, can be visited at quiet times), also plenty of craft beers and proper ciders, good well priced burger/hot dog menu (all day weekends); big open-plan room with feel of separate areas, bare bricks and dark oak boards, old brewery pictures and posters, open fires; regular live music including popular Sun lunchtime jazz, Weds quiz; children welcome till 6pm, no dogs, disabled facilities, garden with terrace and smokers' shelter, open all day.
(Diana Watt)

NOTTINGHAM   SK5739

Malt Cross (0115) 941 1048

St James's Street; NG1 6FG Former Victorian music hall with high vaulted glass roof and gallery overlooking bar area; ornate iron pillars, chesterfield sofas and button-back seating booths on bare boards, good selection of drinks including some interesting real ales, decent well priced food from shortish menu, teas/coffees and daily newspapers; regular live music on small stage, Mon quiz; cellars converted into art gallery and workshops, ancient caves (tours available); open all day (till 9pm Sun). *(Mike Benton)*

NOTTINGHAM   SK5739

Newshouse (0115) 952 3061

Canal Street; NG1 7HB Friendly two-room 1950s Castle Rock pub with blue tiled exterior; their ales and four changing guests, belgian and czech imports, decent lunchtime food, mix of bare boards and carpet, local newspaper/radio memorabilia, beer bottles on shelves, darts, table skittles and bar billiards; background music, big-screen sports TV; a few tables out in front, walking distance from both football grounds (busy on match days), open all day.
(Jeremy)

NOTTINGHAM   SK6141

Old Volunteer (0115) 987 2299

Burton Road, Carlton; NG4 3DQ
Imposing 19th-c community pub acting as tap for Flipside; five of their well kept ales and several guests, good range of whiskies, friendly helpful staff, some food including burgers; live music and beer festivals; dogs welcome, picnic-sets on side terrace, open all day. *(John Bryant)*

NOTTINGHAM   SK5739

Olde Salutation (0115) 947 6580

Hounds Gate/Maid Marian Way; NG1 7AA Low beams, flagstones, ochre walls and cosy corners including two small quiet rooms in ancient lower back part, plusher modern front lounge, up to eight real ales and good choice of draught/bottled ciders, quickly served food till 8pm (6pm Sun, not Mon), helpful friendly staff (ask them to show you the haunted caves below the pub); background music, weekend live bands/DJs upstairs; open all day (till 3am Fri, Sat). *(John Bryant)*

NOTTINGHAM   SK5739

★ Olde Trip to Jerusalem

(0115) 947 3171 *Brewhouse Yard; from inner ring road follow 'The North, A6005 Long Eaton' signpost until in Castle Boulevard, then right into Castle Road; pub is on the left; NG1 6AD* Unusual rambling pub seemingly clinging to sandstone rock face, largely 17th-c and a former brewhouse for the hilltop castle; downstairs bar carved into the stone with some rocky alcoves, dark panelling and simple built-in seats, tables on flagstones, Greene King IPA and Hardys & Hansons Olde Trip plus guests (tasting trays available), good value food all day, efficient staff dealing well with busy mix of customers; popular little tourist shop with panelled walls soaring into dark cavernous heights; children welcome, seats and ring the bull in snug courtyard, open all day (till midnight Fri, Sat). *(Jess and George Cowley, John Bryant)*

NOTTINGHAM   SK5640

Organ Grinder (0115) 970 0630

Alfreton Road; NG7 3JE Tap for Blue Monkey with up to nine well kept ales including guests, a couple of ciders and

---

Post Office address codings confusingly give the impression that a few pubs are in Nottinghamshire, when they're really in Derbyshire (which is where we list them).

a perry, good local pork pies, open-plan bare-boards interior with woodburner; sports TV; well behaved dogs welcome, seats out behind, open all day. *(Jeremy)*

NOTTINGHAM SK5739
Pitcher & Piano (0115) 958 6081
High Pavement; NG1 1HN Remarkable lofty-roofed conversion of 19th-c church; popular all-day food including deals, good range of drinks from craft beers to cocktails; some live music; children welcome, outside bar and terrace, open all day (till late Thurs-Sat). *(Jess and George Cowley)*

NOTTINGHAM SK5540
Plough (0115) 970 2615
St Peters Street, Radford; NG7 3EN Friendly 1930s local with own good value Nottingham ales brewed behind, also guest beers and traditional cider; two bars (one carpeted, the other with terrazzo flooring), banquettes, old tables and chairs, bottles on delft shelving, coal fires; Thurs quiz, TV, traditional games including outside skittle alley; dogs welcome, beer garden with covered smokers' area, open all day. *(John Bryant)*

NOTTINGHAM SK5344
Roebuck (0115) 979 3400
St James's Street (pedestrianised) off Old Market Square; NG1 6FH Light airy Wetherspoons conversion of 18th-c red-brick townhouse; high ceilings and some original features, extensive choice of well kept ales (tasting trays available), ciders/perry and good wine choice, their usual reasonably priced food from toasties up, Tues steak night, friendly staff, upper galleried area and enclosed roof terrace; muted TV; children welcome, disabled facilities, open all day from 8am. *(David Hunt)*

NOTTINGHAM SK5838
Trent Navigation (0115) 986 5658
Meadow Lane; NG2 3HS Welcoming tile-fronted Victorian pub close to canal and home to the Navigation Brewery; their beers and guests from half a dozen pumps along with ciders/perries, popular pubby food including daily deals; Sun quiz, sports TVs (pub is next to Notts County FC); children welcome, brewery shop at back, open all day, food all day Thurs-Sun. *(Jeremy)*

NOTTINGHAM SK5739
★Vat & Fiddle (0115) 985 0611
Queensbridge Road; alongside Sheriffs Way (near multi-storey car park); NG2 1NB Open-plan 1930s tap for next-door Castle Rock Brewery; varnished pine tables, bentwood chairs and stools on parquet or terrazzo flooring, some brewery memorabilia and interesting photographs of demolished local pubs, up to 13 real ales, bottled continentals, traditional ciders and over 30 malt whiskies, decent pub food (not Sun evening), modern dining extension, visitors'

centre with own bar; some live music, free wi-fi; children and dogs welcome, picnic-sets out at front by road, open all day (till midnight Fri-Sat). *(Sid Hunt)*

RADCLIFFE ON TRENT SK6439
Horse Chestnut (0115) 933 1994
Main Road; NG12 2BE Smart pub with plenty of Victorian/Edwardian features; well kept Adnams, St Austell, Woodfordes and four guests, craft beers and decent wines by the glass, sensibly priced home-made food (not Sun evening) including some italian choices (good pizzas) and deal nights such as Tues curry and Thurs steak, friendly service, two-level main bar, parquet and mosaic floor, panelling, big mirrors and impressive lamps, handsome leather wall benches and period fireplaces; some live music; children and dogs welcome, disabled access, terrace seating, open all day. *(Simon and Jenny Galston)*

RAMPTON SK7978
Eyre Arms (01777) 248771
Main Street; DN22 0HR Shuttered red-brick village pub with enjoyable good value food from chef-owner including extensive specials menu and weekday lunchtime bargains, well kept changing ales, friendly helpful service, dining area overlooking pleasant garden, locals bar with pool; open all day. *(Emily Knight)*

RUDDINGTON SK5733
Three Crowns (0115) 846 9613
Easthorpe Street; NG11 6LB Open-plan pub known locally as the Top House; four well kept ales and very good indian food in back Three Spices evening restaurant; open all day weekends, closed weekday lunchtimes. *(Diana Watt)*

SCAFTWORTH SK6692
King William (01302) 710292
A631 Bawtry–Everton; DN10 6BL Popular red-brick country pub with friendly relaxed atmosphere; good well presented home-made food (best to book Sun lunch), Theakstons Best, a couple of regional guests and good choice of wines by the glass, bar, snug and two dining rooms with old high-backed settles, plain tables and chairs and log fires; background music; children and dogs welcome, seats on terrace and in big back garden running down to River Idle, swings, open all day, food till 7.30pm Sun. *(Chris Stevenson)*

SELSTON SK4553
★Horse & Jockey (01773) 781012
Handy for M1 junctions 27/28; Church Lane; NG16 6FB Interesting pub on different levels dating from the 17th c; low heavy beams, dark flagstones, individual furnishings and good log fire in cast-iron range, friendly staff, Greene King Abbot and Timothy Taylors Landlord poured from the jug and up to four guests, real cider,

no food, games area with darts and pool; folk night Weds, quiz Sun; dogs welcome, terrace and smokers' shelter, pleasant rolling countryside. (Mike Benton)

SOUTHWELL   SK7054
★ Final Whistle (01636) 814953
Station Road; NG25 0ET Popular railway-themed pub commemorating the long defunct Southwell line; ten well kept ales including Brewsters and Salopian (beer festivals), real ciders/perries, foreign bottled beers and good range of wines, snacky food such as pork pies; traditional opened-up bar with tiled or wood floor, settles and armchairs in quieter carpeted room, corridor drinking area, two open fires, panelling, lots of railway memorabilia and other odds and ends; quiz and live music nights (folk club third Thurs of month); children (till 9pm) and dogs welcome, back garden with wonderful mock-up of 1920s platform complete with track and buffers, on Robin Hood Way and Southwell Trail, open all day. (Liz Stanwell)

SOUTHWELL   SK7053
Hearty Goodfellow (01636) 919176
Church Street (A612); NG25 0HQ Welcoming open-plan mock-Tudor pub; up to eight real ales, traditional ciders and good range of house wines, popular fairly straightforward food (till 7pm Sun) at reasonable prices, also takeaway fish and chips and pop-up fish/seafood restaurant in converted outbuilding, cheerful young staff, lots of polished wood, beams and two brick fireplaces; background and some live music, sports TVs; children and dogs welcome, covered terrace and nice big tree-shaded garden beyond car park, play area, handy for Southwell Workhouse (NT) and the Minster, open all day Fri-Sun. (Liz Stanwell)

STAUNTON IN THE VALE SK8043
Staunton Arms (01400) 281218
High Street, N of church on crossroads; NG13 9PE Attractive early 19th-c brick-built country inn; good well presented food from pub standards to more imaginative modern dishes, also lighter lunchtime choices and brunch from 10am Mon-Sat, Bass, Castle Rock and a guest, good range of wines and other drinks, efficient friendly service, L-shaped beamed bar with bare boards and open fire, steps up to dining area; free wi-fi; children and dogs welcome, rattan-style furniture on front terrace, eight good bedrooms, open (and food) all day. (Michael and Lucy Archer)

TUXFORD   SK7471
Fountain (01777) 872854
Lincoln Road on edge of village near East Coast railway line; NG22 0JQ

Comfortably updated family dining pub with welcoming atmosphere; enjoyable affordably priced food (not Sun evening) from pub favourites, pizzas and grills to daily specials, local ales and ciders such as Welbeck Abbey and Scrumpy Wasp, friendly service; pool, free wi-fi; picnic-sets out in fenced area, open all day Fri-Sun, closed lunchtimes Mon-Thurs. (Emily Knight)

UPTON   SK7354
★ Cross Keys (01636) 813269
Main Street (A612); NG23 5SY 17th-c pub with rambling heavy-beamed bar, log fire in brick fireplace, own Mallard ales (brewed in Maythorne) and good home-made food from lunchtime sandwiches to specials, friendly staff, back extension; live music Sat; seats on decked terrace, handy for the Museum of Timekeeping (British Horological Institute), open all day Fri-Sun, closed lunchtimes Mon and Tues, no food Sun evening. (Simon and Jenny Galston)

WEST BRIDGFORD   SK5838
Larwood & Voce (0115) 981 9960
Fox Road; NG2 6AJ Open-plan dining pub (part of the small Moleface group); enjoyable food in bar and restaurant area including some imaginative choices, afternoon teas, plenty of wines by the glass, cocktail menu and four well kept ales, attentive staff; sports TV; children welcome away from bar, seats out on raised deck with heaters, on edge of the cricket ground and handy for Nottingham Forest FC, open all day, from 10am weekends for breakfast. (David Hunt)

WEST BRIDGFORD   SK5938
Poppy & Pint (0115) 981 9995
Pierrepont Road; NG2 5DX Converted former British Legion Club backing on to bowling green and tennis courts; large bar with raised section and family area, around a dozen real ales including Castle Rock, a couple of ciders and decent food from breakfast on, friendly atmosphere; live music and other events (some in upstairs function room); dogs welcome, open all day from 9.30am (10am Sun). (Jeff Davies)

WEST BRIDGFORD   SK5837
Stratford Haven (0115) 982 5981
Stratford Road, Trent Bridge; NG2 6BA Traditional red-brick Castle Rock pub; bare-boards front bar leading to linked areas including airy skylit back part, a dozen well kept ales, interesting bottled beers, proper ciders and good wine and whisky choice, reasonably priced pubby food including Tues pie and Thurs burger nights, friendly service; Sun quiz, live music and beer events; children (during the day) and dogs welcome, tables outside,

---

We accept no free drinks or meals and inspections are anonymous.

handy for cricket ground and Nottingham Forest FC (busy on match days), open (and food) all day. *(Jeff Davies)*

WEST STOCKWITH SK7994
White Hart (01427) 892672
Main Street; DN10 4EY Small country pub at junction of Chesterfield Canal and River Trent; own good Idle beers from next-door brewery plus guests, enjoyable well priced traditional food (not Sun evening) including blackboard specials and regular evening deals; live music Fri, pool and sports TV; children and dogs welcome, garden overlooking the water, open all day. *(Jeremy)*

WYSALL SK6027
Plough (01509) 880339
Keyworth Road; off A60 at Costock, or A6006 at Wymeswold; NG12 5QQ Attractive 17th-c beamed village local; popular good value lunchtime food from shortish menu, cheerful staff, Bass, Greene King Abbot, Sharps Doom Bar, Timothy Taylors Landlord and three guests, rooms either side of bar with nice mix of furnishings, big log fire; Tues quiz, pool; children welcome, dogs after 2.30pm, french doors to pretty terrace garden, open all day. *(Chris Stevenson)*

Oxfordshire

ASTHALL

 SP2811 Map 4

Maytime 🍴 🛏

(01993) 822068 – www.themaytime.com

Off A40 at W end of Witney bypass, then first left; OX18 4HW

17th-c former coaching inn with individually furnished bar and dining rooms, good food and seats outside; smart bedrooms

The careful renovations done here a few years ago created an inn of style and character, and our readers enjoy their visits here very much. The lofty, character bar has a lively feel, exposed roof trusses, flagstones, leather sofas, cushioned wall seats and stools against the counter where friendly staff serve two quickly changing ales such as Bluestone Bedrock Blonde and Otter Bitter on handpump, 30 good wines by the glass from a fine list, over 100 gins and cocktails; background music and board games. Several white-painted beamed rooms lead off on different levels with cushioned window seats, a mix of tartan upholstered and traditional wooden chairs around tables of varying size on black slates or bare boards, and pictures on painted or stone walls; one room has a glass ceiling. The pub's springer is called Alfie. There are seats outside under parasols on the back terrace and more in the extended garden overlooking the River Windrush; boules. Bedrooms are stylish and well equipped and breakfasts are highly rated. Good walks from the door.

🍴 Imaginative food includes sandwiches, game terrine with plum chutney, beetroot-cured gravadlax with pickled cucumber, orange segments and chive cream cheese, sharing boards, potato and walnut strudel with poached pear, seasonal vegetables and stilton sauce, pie of the day, moroccan-spiced chicken breast with chicken samosa, couscous and apricots, slow-roast pork belly with wholegrain mustard mash, spiced red cabbage and apple sauce, scallops with black pudding, nduja, tempura cauliflower and cauliflower purée and puddings such as baked elderflower cheesecake with ginger ice-cream and rhubarb trifle. *Benchmark main dish: wild boar burger with toppings, onion rings and skinny chips £15.00. Two-course evening meal £22.00.*

Free house ~ Licensee Dominic Wood ~ Real ale ~ Open 11-11 ~ Bar food 12-2.30, 6-9.30; 12-3, 6-9 Sun ~ Restaurant ~ Children welcome but not in bedrooms ~ Dogs allowed in bar ~ Wi-fi ~ Live music 3-5pm alternate Sun in summer ~ Bedrooms: £85/£95 *Recommended by Helene Grygar, Katharine Cowherd, John and Sharon Hancock, William and Sophia Renton, Guy Vowles, M G Hart*

Pubs close to motorway junctions are listed at the back of the book.

BANBURY SP4540 Map 4
Olde Reindeer

(01295) 270972 – www.ye-olde-reinedeer-inn-banbury.co.uk

Parsons Street, off Market Place; OX16 5NA

Rewarding town pub with a friendly welcome, real ales and decent food

No matter how busy this fine old tavern is with shoppers and regulars, you'll be just as warmly welcomed as a visitor. There's plenty of history and the front bar has a pleasing, easy-going atmosphere, heavy 16th-c beams, very broad polished oak floorboards, a magnificent carved overmantel for one of the two roaring log fires and traditional solid furnishings; some interesting breweriana too. It's worth looking at the handsomely proportioned Globe Room used by Oliver Cromwell as his base during the Civil War. Quite a sight, it still has some lovely 17th-c carved dark oak panelling. Attentive staff serve Hook Norton Hooky, Old Hooky, Hooky Mild and a couple of seasonal guest beers on handpump, three craft beers from Hook Norton, 12 wines by the glass, eight gins, fruit wines and several malt whiskies. The little back courtyard has tables and benches under parasols, aunt sally and pretty flowering baskets.

Honest, reasonably priced food includes lunchtime sandwiches and basket meals, baked garlic and rosemary camembert with onion chutney, mushroom and chickpea curry with onion bhaji and poppadums, house salad with toppings such as sea bass, rump steak, chicken or halloumi skewers, ham and eggs, barbecue beef brisket with coleslaw and corn on the cob, pork chop with mustard mash and apple and cider sauce, T-bone steak with onion rings, chips and a choice of sauce, and puddings such as plum and apple crumble with custard and chocolate orange fondant. *Benchmark main dish: venison burger with toppings, coleslaw and chips £14.00. Two-course evening meal £19.00.*

Hook Norton ~ Tenant Anthony Murray ~ Real ale ~ Open 11-11; 11-midnight Fri, Sat; 12-10.30 Sun ~ Bar food 12-3, 6-9; 12-9 Fri, Sat; 12-6 Sun ~ Restaurant ~ Children welcome ~ Dogs welcome ~ Wi-fi ~ Blues/jazz first Sun of month *Recommended by Camilla and Jose Ferrera, Charlie Stevens, Rosie and John Moore, Cliff and Monica Swan, Maria and Henry Lazenby, Edward Edmonton*

BECKLEY SP5611 Map
Abingdon Arms

(01865) 655667 – www.theabingdonarms.co.uk

Signed off B4027; High Street; OX3 9UU

Cheerful village pub with restored bar and dining room, four real ales, popular food and seats in garden with fine views

Saved by the community in 2016, this is a friendly, bustling pub in a lovely unspoilt village. The sympathetically refurbished beamed rooms have a warm welcome for all plus country kitchen chairs around scrubbed tables on bare boards, homely armchairs and button-back wall seats, exposed stone walls and open fires. Fullers London Pride, Shotover Prospect and Trinity and a guest from Vale on handpump, seven wines by the glass, nine gins and six malt whiskies; background music and board games. A pitched-roof dining room leads off with more beams and timbering and half-panelled, turquoise-painted walls. Outside, the big garden is made up of two-tiered, decked terraces looking over the RSPB Otmoor nature reserve – the far-reaching views are superb. Good nearby walks.

🍽 Well regarded food using local produce from a shortish menu includes octopus with white beans, chorizo and slow-roasted tomatoes, charcuterie selection with quince, red wine and pearl barley risotto with wild mushrooms and taleggio, pie of the week, lamb rump with romesco sauce, smoked aubergine and radicchio, duck breast with beetroot, spelt and blackberries, whole roast sole with mussels, garlic, parsley and runner beans, puddings such as apple and cinnamon compote with cream cheese mousse and hazelnut crumble and treacle tart with brown butter pecan ice-cream. *Benchmark main dish: beer-battered fish and chips £14.50. Two-course evening meal £22.00.*

Free house ~ Licensee Aimee Bronock ~ Real ale ~ Open 10-6 Mon; 12-11 Tues-Thurs, Sat; 10-11 Fri; 12-9 Sun; closed Mon evening ~ Bar food 12-2.30, 6-9.30; 12-3, 6-9.30 Fri, Sat; 12-4 Sun ~ Restaurant ~ Children welcome ~ Dogs allowed in bar ~ Wi-fi
Recommended by Helene Grygar, Simon and Mary Todd, Diana and Richard Gibbs, Jim and Sue James, Susan and Callum Slade

BESSELS LEIGH
Greyhound 🍷 🦮
SP4501 Map 4

(01865) 862110 – www.brunningandprice.co.uk/greyhound
A420 Faringdon–Botley; OX13 5PX

Cotswold-stone inn with rambling rooms, a fine range of real ales, lots of wines by the glass and enjoyable food

There's plenty of character and interest in this handsome old place. The knocked-through rooms have individually chosen cushioned dining chairs, leather-topped stools and dark wooden tables grouped on carpeting or rug-covered floorboards and three fireplaces (one housing a woodburning stove). Also, all manner of old photographs and pictures covering the half-panelled walls, books on shelves, glass and stone bottles on windowsills, big gilt mirrors and sizeable pot plants. Wooden bar stools line the counter where efficient, friendly staff serve St Austell Brunning & Price Traditional Bitter and Timothy Taylors Landlord with guests such as Adnams Ghost Ship, Froth Blowers Piffle Snonker, Loose Cannon Abingdon Bridge, Siren Craft Brew Liquid Mistress and XT Three on handpump, 22 wines by the glass, around 70 gins, 30 rums and up to 70 malt whiskies; board games. By the back dining extension there is a white picket fence-enclosed garden with picnic-sets under green parasols; the summer window boxes and hanging baskets are very pretty.

🍽 Interesting food includes sandwiches, beef hash cake with poached egg and wholegrain mustard sauce, potted smoked mackerel with lemon jelly and pickled cucumber and samphire salad, vegetarian cottage pie topped with sweet potato mash, chilli crab linguine with ginger and coriander, burger with toppings, coleslaw and chips, trinidadian chicken curry with deep-fried dumplings and coconut rice, slow-braised ox cheek ragoût with pasta and parmesan, sicilian fish stew, and puddings such as dark chocolate and orange tart with passion-fruit sorbet and crème brûlée. *Benchmark main dish: crispy beef salad with sweet chilli dressing, lotus root crisps and cashews £13.95. Two-course evening meal £21.00.*

Brunning & Price ~ Manager Damien Mann ~ Real ale ~ Open 10am-11pm; 10am-10.30pm Sun ~ Bar food 10-9.30; 10-10 Fri, Sat; 10-9 Sun ~ Children welcome ~ Dogs allowed in bar ~ Wi-fi *Recommended by Neil and Angela Huxter, Cliff and Monica Swan, Simon Day, William Slade, David Longhurst, Julie Swift, Douglas Power*

If we know a featured-entry pub does sandwiches, we always say so – if they're not mentioned, you'll have to assume you can't get one.

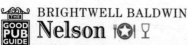

BRIGHTWELL BALDWIN
Nelson 🏴☆ ♟

SU6594   Map 4

(01491) 612497 – www.thenelsonbrightwell.co.uk

Off B480 Chalgrove–Watlington, or B4009 Benson–Watlington; OX49 5NP

Attractive inn with several character bars, real ales, good wines by the glass and enjoyable well regarded food; bedrooms

This is a friendly, relaxed 300-year-old inn, where you'll find a chatty atmosphere and a good mix of customers. The bar has candles and fresh flowers, wine bottles on windowsills, horsebrasses on standing timbers, lots of paintings on white or red walls, wheelback and other dining chairs around assorted dark tables and a big brick inglenook fireplace. One cosy room has cushions on comfortable sofas, little lamps on dark furniture, ornate mirrors and portraits in gilt frames; background music. Rebellion IPA and Zebedee and a changing guest on handpump, 20 wines (including champagne) by the glass, a dozen malt whiskies and winter mulled wine. There are seats and tables on the back terrace and in the willow-draped garden.

 From a seasonal menu, the well regarded food includes tempura king prawns with sweet chilli dipping sauce, pigeon breast with smoked bacon, black pudding and red wine sauce, creamy risotto with leeks, kale and parmesan, smoked haddock on colcannon topped with a poached egg and wholegrain mustard sauce, rack of lamb with rosemary and red wine sauce and dauphinoise potatoes, half roast duck with orange sauce, carrots and greens, steaks with a choice of three sauces, and puddings such as banana crêpe with toffee sauce and ice-cream and crème brûlée. *Benchmark main dish: burger with toppings with coleslaw and skinny fries £14.95. Two-course evening meal £20.00.*

Free house ~ Licensees Roger and Carole Shippey ~ Real ale ~ Open 12-3, 6-11; 12-5 Sun ~ Bar food 12-2.15, 6-10; 12-4 Sun ~ Restaurant ~ Children welcome ~ Dogs allowed in bar ~ Wi-fi ~ Bedrooms: £75/£100 *Recommended by Gerald and Brenda Culliford, Roy Hoing, Max and Steph Warren, Lenny and Ruth Walters, Caroline and Peter Bryant, Trish and Karl Soloman*

BURFORD
Highway ♟ 🛏

SP2512   Map 4

(01993) 823661 – www.thehighwayinn.co.uk

High Street (A361); OX18 4RG

Comfortable old inn with a good choice of wines, well liked bar food and seats outside; bedrooms

The original fireplaces in this 15th-c timber and stone building are lit every day between October and April, but in warmer months head for the high-walled courtyard garden with its painted chairs and picnic-sets under parasols; there are also a few picnic-sets above the pavement at the front. The bars have all sorts of interesting touches to look at but the main feature is the pair of large windows overlooking the bustle of the pretty High Street; each consists of several dozen panes of old float glass and has a long cushioned window seat. There are upholstered tartan, leather or button-back chairs around wooden tables on bare boards, mirrors and old photographs, and candles and fresh flowers. A small corner counter has Hook Norton Hooky and Hooky Gold on handpump, 20 wines (including champagne) by the glass and 13 malt whiskies; background music and board games. Bedrooms are individually decorated in a country house style.

🍴 High quality food includes ham hock and apple terrine with piccalilli, lightly dusted calamari with garlic and paprika mayonnaise, moroccan-spiced butternut squash tagine with flatbread and mint yoghurt, corn-fed chicken supreme with fondant potato, black garlic chicken sausage and tarragon jus, salmon fillet with burnt lemon butter and horseradish-crushed new potatoes, duck breast with cherry brandy sauce and crispy leeks, and puddings such as lemon curd meringue roulade and Baileys pannacotta. *Benchmark main dish: beer-battered fish and chips £13.50. Two-course evening meal £21.00.*

Free house ~ Licensee Scott Williamson ~ Real ale ~ Open 12-11; 12-midnight Sat; 12-10.30 Sun ~ Bar food 12-3, 5.30-9; 12-4, 5.30-9.30 Fri-Sun ~ Restaurant ~ Children welcome ~ Dogs allowed in bar and bedrooms ~ Wi-fi ~ Bedrooms: /£130
Recommended by Celia and Geoff Clay, Ivy and George Goodwill, Geoffrey and Sarah Sutton, Valerie and Colin Sayer, Kate Moran

CHARLBURY
Bull 🌟🍷🛏
SP3519   Map 4

(01608) 810689 – www.bullinn-charlbury.com
Sheep Street; OX7 3RR

Handsome old inn with a civilised but informal atmosphere throughout, imaginative food and seats on terrace; lovely bedrooms

Original features and shabby chic décor have been cleverly mixed together in the bar and dining rooms of this stylishly refurbished 16th-c inn. You'll find exposed stone and grey-painted panelled walls hung with colourful modern artwork, linen-cushioned seats with bright scatter cushions, painted wooden and upholstered dining chairs around simple tables on rugs or wooden floors and both a woodburning stove and an inglenook log fire. Fullers Olivers Island, Hook Norton Hooky and Wye Valley HPA on handpump from a bar made from an apothecary's chest painted peacock blue, plus good wines by the glass and 14 whiskies served by friendly, helpful staff; background music and daily papers. The attractive and sunny back terrace has a vine-covered pergola. Bedrooms are individually styled and comfortable, with four in a converted barn.

Modern british food includes breakfasts for non-residents (8-11am daily), thai-style fishcake with sweet chilli mayonnaise, gin and beetroot-cured salmon with dill crème fraîche, sharing boards, cep mushroom risotto with parmesan, pie of the day, stone bass with artichoke hearts, celeriac croquettes and velouté and pea purée, lamb rump with truffle mash and minted sauce vierge, 21-day aged 10oz feather steak with chimichurri sauce and fries, and puddings such as dark chocolate mousse with chocolate brownie, honeycomb and vanilla ice-cream and mango pannacotta with coconut sorbet, passion-fruit curd and mint syrup. *Benchmark main dish: burger with toppings and chips £15.00. Two-course evening meal £20.00.*

Free house ~ Licensees Charlie and Willow Crossley ~ Real ale ~ Open 8am-11pm; 8am-midnight Sat ~ Bar food 8am-9pm ~ Restaurant ~ Children welcome ~ Dogs allowed in bar and bedrooms ~ Wi-fi ~ Bedrooms: /£99 *Recommended by Rosie and Marcus Heatherley, Jennifer and Nicholas Thompson, Julia and Fiona Barnes, Margo and Derek Stapley, Neil Allen*

CHAZEY HEATH
Packhorse 🍷🍺
SU6979   Map

(0118) 9722140 – www.brunningandprice.co.uk/packhorse
Off A4074 Reading–Wallingford by B4526; RG4 7UG

Attractive pub with interlinked bar and dining areas, a fine choice of drinks, rewarding food and seats outside

Tucked away down a lane in a quiet village, this brick-built pub is a former farmhouse and dates back to the 17th c. The main bar has a raised inglenook fireplace with logs piled to each side and large brass platters above the bressummer beam, cushioned wall seating, antique-style dining chairs and stools around mixed wooden tables, stubby candles and house plants. Other connected rooms are similarly furnished and throughout you'll find rugs, polished bare boards and carpeting, walls hung with prints, old photographs and mirrors, books on shelves and stone and glass bottles. Friendly, well trained staff serve St Austell Brunning & Price Traditional Bitter plus guests such as Glastonbury Session IPA, Loddon Hoppit and West Berkshire Good Old Boy on handpump, good wines by the glass and 104 gins. In front of the pub are picnic-sets among flowering plants and in the back garden wooden chairs and tables sit under giant parasols beside their trademark play tractor.

A wide choice of interesting food includes sandwiches, sesame crab cakes with asian coleslaw and chilli and red pepper dressing, barbecue chicken wings, cheese, potato and onion pie with carrot purée and gravy, warm crispy beef salad with sweet chilli dressing and cashew nuts, cumberland pork sausages with mash, buttered greens and onion gravy, sea bass with stir-fried vegetables, wasabi, rice croquettes and teriyaki sauce, braised lamb shoulder with dauphinoise potatoes, carrot mash and rosemary gravy, and puddings such as crème brûlée and triple chocolate brownie with chocolate sauce. *Benchmark main dish: steak burger with toppings, coleslaw and chips £13.95. Two-course evening meal £21.00.*

Brunning & Price ~ Manager Sarah Livesey ~ Real ale ~ Open 11.30-11; 11.30-10.30 Sun ~ Bar food 12-9; 12-9.30 Fri, Sat ~ Children welcome ~ Dogs allowed in bar ~ Wi-fi
Recommended by Margo and Derek Stapley, George and Melody Sanderson, Charles Welch, Millie and Peter Downing, Andrew Vincent

CHURCH ENSTONE
Crown 🏴

SP3725   Map 4

(01608) 677262 – www.crowninnenstone.co.uk
Mill Lane; from A44 take B4030 turn-off at Enstone; OX7 4NN

Friendly country pub with helpful licensees, enjoyable food and well kept real ales

The food here is particularly good, so to be sure of a table it's best to book one in advance. It's a handsome golden-stone inn and the smart, uncluttered, congenial bar has beams, cushioned window seats and dark farmhouse chairs around long tables on big flagstones, and an open fire; one of the owners is an artist and his work adorns the walls. Stools line the counter where they keep Hook Norton Hooky Bitter, RCH Double Header and Shepherd Neame Spitfire on handpump and 11 wines by the glass; board games. There's also a white-painted beamed dining room with high-backed wooden chairs around sturdy tables on a large, colourful rug or bare boards and an airy, simply furnished conservatory. The front terrace has seats and tables overlooking the quiet lane, and there are more in the sheltered suntrap back garden.

Enjoyable food includes lunchtime sandwiches and smoked salmon eggs benedict with spinach and hollandaise, as well as ham hock terrine with rhubarb chutney, calamari with chermoula and salsa verde, home-made tart of the day, beer-battered fish and chips, pie of the day, chicken supreme with hickory-smoked chickpeas, grilled courgette, charred peppers and lemon and basil dressing, sea bream fillet with baked polenta and red pepper salsa, barnsley lamb chop with mint gremolata and roasting jus, and puddings such as white chocolate marquise with cocoa syrup and pistachio crème brûlée. *Benchmark main dish: roast porchetta with creamy mash, pak choi and honey and mustard cream sauce £15.00. Two-course evening meal £20.00.*

Free house ~ Licensees George and Victoria Irvine ~ Real ale ~ Open 12-3, 6-11; 12-11 Sat; 12-6 Sun ~ Bar food 12-3, 6.30-9; 12-3 Sun; not Sun evening ~ Restaurant ~ Children welcome ~ Dogs allowed in bar ~ Wi-fi ~ Bedrooms: /£120 *Recommended by Helene Grygar, George and Alison Bishop, Patricia and Gordon Tucker, Elizabeth and Andrew Harvey, Mick Allen*

FILKINS

SP2304   Map 4

Five Alls 🍴⭐🛏

(01367) 860875 – www.thefiveallsfilkins.co.uk

Signed off A361 Lechlade–Burford; GL7 3JQ

Thoughtfully refurbished inn with enjoyable food, quite a range of drinks, a friendly welcome and seats outside; bedrooms

Of course, many customers are here to enjoy the impressive food served in the elegant dining room, but there's also a beamed bar liked by locals. This has a cosy area with leather chesterfields grouped around a table by an open fire, an informal dining space with farmhouse chairs and cushioned pews around tables on bare boards and a nice little window seat for two. Stools line the counter where friendly staff serve Brakspears Bitter and Oxford Gold and Marstons Pedigree on handpump, 16 wines by the glass, ten gins and seven malt whiskies. Décor in the dining room includes some large portraits and unusual postage-stamp wallpaper, an attractive mix of chairs and tables on rugs, floorboards and flagstones, plus church candles, fresh flowers and modern artwork on pale painted walls; background music. The back terrace has chunky tables and chairs under parasols and there are a few picnic-sets at the front. Bedrooms are comfortable and attractively refurbished and make a good base for exploring the area. Sister pubs are the Plough at Kelmscott (also in Oxfordshire) and the Bull in Fairford (Gloucestershire). Disabled access.

🍴⭐ Highly thought-of food includes sandwiches, salt and pepper squid with saffron aioli, rare beef salad with truffle oil and parmesan shavings, wild mushroom risotto, tiger prawn and caper linguine with chilli, tomato and basil sauce, steak and mushroom pie, sea bream fillet with pea purée, spinach and mushrooms, 12-hour cooked ox cheek with chestnuts, bacon and mash, lamb kofta with dried fruit, chickpeas, couscous and tzatziki, and puddings such as caramelised lemon tart with raspberry sauce and coffee crème brûlée; they also offer a two- and three-course lunch menu (not Fri-Sun). *Benchmark main dish: moroccan-style lamb shoulder with dried fruit, chickpeas, couscous and harissa £18.50. Two-course evening meal £25.00.*

Free house ~ Licensee Steve Cook ~ Real ale ~ Open 12-11; 12-9 Sun ~ Bar food 12-2.30 (3 Sat), 6-9.30; 12-3 Sun ~ Restaurant ~ Children welcome ~ Dogs allowed in bar ~ Wi-fi ~ Bedrooms: £95/£120 *Recommended by Beverley and Andy Butcher, Liz and Mike Newton, Bernard Stradling, Katharine Cowherd, Tracey and Stephen Groves, Edward May*

GORING

SU5980   Map 2

Miller of Mansfield 🍴⭐♀🛏

(01491) 872829 – www.millerofmansfield.com

High Street; RG8 9AW

First class food and drink in handsome inn with easy-going bars and dining rooms; comfortable bedrooms

This is not a straightforward dining pub (despite the excellent food), but a friendly former coaching inn with an informal, relaxed feel and a carefully chosen range of drinks. Décor in the beamed bars is simple and unfussy with armchairs around open fires or in bay windows, plain wooden tables, bare floorboards, exposed stone and brick walls and a few prints and gilt-edged mirrors. Sharps Cornish Coaster and West Berkshire Good Old Boy on handpump, ten wines by the glass from a thoughtful list and a large choice of gins, rums and malt whiskies; service is courteous and helpful. The dining rooms have antique-style or contemporary dining chairs on more boards; background music. The multi-level terraced garden has solid furniture under parasols among flowering tubs. Bedrooms are individually decorated and well equipped, and breakfasts are good. Woodland walks are a few minutes away.

Cooked by the landlord, the innovative food includes duck liver pâté with pumpkin chutney, mushroom cheesecake with walnuts, pickled mushrooms, confit egg yolk and madeira, jerusalem artichoke gnocchi with apple chutney, sprout hearts, crispy skins and cheese, sea bream with sea beet, crispy potatoes, capers and tartare sauce, duck with a potato cake, cavolo nero and orange and spiced duck sauce, lamb cannon with broad beans, sheeps yoghurt and burnt rosemary, poached cod with crab toast, braised chicory, golden beetroot and crab sauce, and puddings such as glazed and roasted pineapple with golden raisins, pink peppercorn and milk ice-cream and rhubarb and custard with ginger granola, Marmite meringue and rhubarb sorbet; they also offer afternoon tea. *Benchmark main dish: local fallow deer with caramelised cauliflower, dukkah and douglas fir £25.50. Two-course evening meal £30.00.*

Enterprise ~ Lease Mary and Nick Galer ~ Real ale ~ Open 11-11; 11-9 Sun ~ Bar food 12-2, 6-9; 12-2, 5-7 Sun ~ Restaurant ~ Children welcome ~ Dogs allowed in bar and bedrooms ~ Wi-fi ~ Bedrooms: £79/£99 *Recommended by Charles and Maddie Bishop, Ted and Mary Bates, Andrew and Ruth Simmonds, Alexandra and Tim Fledgling, Sarah Roberts, Rona Mackinlay*

KELMSCOTT
SU2499   Map 4

Plough 🍽️⭐🛏️

(01367) 253543 – www.theploughinnkelmscott.com
NW of Faringdon, off B4449 between A417 and A4095; GL7 3HG

Lovely spot for tranquil pub with character bar and dining rooms, attractive furnishings and well regarded food; bedrooms

Pretty little inn with a 17th-c heart and in a charming setting by the upper Thames. The small, traditional, beamed front bar offers a warm welcome from the convivial licensee, and has ancient flagstones and stripped-stone walls along with a woodburning stove, seats against the counter and a village pub atmosphere. A beer named for the pub (from Hook Norton), Black Sheep and Sharps Doom Bar on handpump, good wines by the glass and maybe farm cider. The dining room has elegant wooden or painted dining chairs around all sorts of tables, striped and cushioned wall seats, paintings on exposed stone walls, and rugs on the floor. Outside in the garden are seats and tables under parasols. Bedrooms are attractive, light and comfortable and breakfasts good. The Oxfordshire Cycleway runs close by and the inn is handy for Kelmscott Manor (open Wednesdays and Saturdays April-October). This is sister pub to the Five Alls at Filkins (also in Oxfordshire) and Bull in Fairford (Gloucestershire).

Enjoyable food includes duck liver parfait with cranberry sauce and hazelnut and raisin toast, salad of figs, blue cheese, walnuts and chicory, bubble and squeak with spinach and a fried egg, local sausages with mash and sage and onion gravy, chicken, bacon and leek tart with fries, partridge with thyme roast new potatoes and creamed savoy cabbage, gilt-head bream with crushed new potatoes and lemon caper butter, flat-iron steak with tomatoes, peppercorn sauce and chips, and puddings such as chocolate fondant with mint chocolate ripple ice-cream and apple, raisin and pear crumble with custard. *Benchmark main dish: pie of the day £17.50. Two-course evening meal £22.00.*

Free house ~ Licensee Steve Cook ~ Real ale ~ Open 12-11 (4-8 Mon); closed Mon lunchtime ~ Bar food 12-2.30, 6-9.30; 12-3, 6-10 Sat; 12-3 Sun; not Mon ~ Restaurant ~ Children welcome ~ Dogs allowed in bar ~ Wi-fi ~ Bedrooms: /£110 *Recommended by Dr Simon Barley, R K Phillips, Martine and Lawrence Sanders, Victoria and James Sargeant, Dave Braisted, Nik and Gloria Clarke, Audrey and Paul Summers*

KINGHAM
SP2624 Map 4

Plough 🎖 ♟ 🛏

(01608) 658327 – www.thekinghamplough.co.uk

Village signposted off B4450 E of Bledington; or turn S off A436 at staggered crossroads a mile SW of A44 junction – or take signed Daylesford turn off A436 and keep on; The Green; OX7 6YD

Friendly dining pub combining an informal pub atmosphere with highly regarded food; bedrooms

New owners now run this bustling pub overlooking the village green, and early reports from our readers have been warmly enthusiastic. The little bar has some nice old high-backed settles and cushioned chapel chairs on broad dark boards, candles on stripped tables and country-style prints; at one end is a big log fire, at the other a woodburning stove. A snug one-table area is opposite the servery where they keep Hook Norton Hooky and guests such as Goffs Jouster and Prescott Hill Climb on handpump, ten wines by the glass including three sparkling ones, 14 malt whiskies, several gins and local cider; background music. The fairly spacious and raftered two-part dining room is up a few steps. The bedrooms are comfortable and pretty and the breakfasts are good.

🎖 First class, modern cooking includes gin-cured salmon with apple, radish and buttermilk, beef tartare with egg yolk and lemon, risotto primavera, home-made sausage in a brioche bun with celeriac rémoulade and onion butter, stone bass with clams, fennel and lettuce, rare-breed pork loin with onion, asparagus and pomme mousseline, and puddings such as white chocolate and pistachio with lime and iced pomegranate parfait. *Benchmark main dish: rib-eye steak with peppercorn butter £28.00. Two-course evening meal £27.00.*

Free house ~ Licensee Matt Beamish ~ Real ale ~ Open 11-11 ~ Bar food 12-2.30, 6-9; 11.30-3 Sun ~ Children welcome ~ Dogs allowed in bar and bedrooms ~ Wi-fi ~ Bedrooms: £110/£145 *Recommended by Alun and Jennifer Evans, Neil and Angela Huxter, Bernard Stradling, Liz Bell, Gordon and Margaret Ormondroyd, Peter and Alison Steadman, Geoff and Ann Marston, Celia and Rupert Lemming*

KIRTLINGTON
SP4919 Map 4

Oxford Arms 🎖 ♟

(01869) 350208 – www.oxford-arms.co.uk

Troy Lane, junction with A4095 W of Bicester; OX5 3HA

Civilised and friendly stripped-stone pub with enjoyable food using local produce and good wine choice

The hands-on licensees (Mr Jones also does the cooking) continue to run their appealing pub with great care and attention. The long line of linked rooms is divided by a central stone hearth with a great circular stove, and by the servery itself – where you'll find Black Sheep Holy Grail and Hook Norton Hooky on handpump, an interesting range of 13 wines by the glass, eight malt whiskies, farm cider and organic soft drinks. Past the bar area with its cushioned wall pews, creaky beamed ceiling and age-darkened floor tiles, dining tables on parquet have neat high-backed chairs; beyond that, leather sofas cluster round a log fire at the end. Also, church candles, fresh flowers and plenty of stripped stone. A sheltered back terrace has teak tables under giant parasols with heaters, as well as white metal furniture and picnic-sets on neat gravel. The geranium-filled window boxes are pretty. Dogs must be kept on a lead. No children under 12. Disabled access.

Using local and their own organic seasonal produce, the first class food includes natural smoked haddock and leek tart, baked fig with blue cheese and air-dried ham, truffle and mushroom tortelloni with wild mushroom sauce and aged parmesan, salmon and prawn fishcake with sweet chilli sauce, warm game salad with black pudding and blueberries, pork loin with chorizo and chickpeas, 28-day aged rib-eye steak with mustard and horseradish butter and triple-cooked chips, and puddings such as chocolate and Grand Marnier mousse and plum preserve with vanilla ice-cream. *Benchmark main dish: wild sea bass with lemon oil £19.50. Two-course evening meal £26.00.*

Star Pubs & Bars ~ Lease Bryn Jones ~ Real ale ~ Open 12-2, 6-11; 12-3, 6-11 Sat; 12-4 Sun; closed Sun evening, Weds ~ Bar food 12-2, 6.30-8.30; 12-2.30 Sun ~ Restaurant ~ No children under 12 ~ Dogs welcome ~ Wi-fi *Recommended by John and Lorna Chew, Tim and Mary Thomson, Hunter and Christine Wright, Camilla and Jose Ferrera, Louise and Oliver Redman*

LETCOMBE REGIS

SU3886 Map 2

Greyhound

(01235) 771969 – www.thegreyhoundletcombe.co.uk
Main Street; OX12 9JL

Refurbished pub with original windows and fireplaces, plenty of eating and dining space and seats outside; bedrooms

'First class at everything' says one reader with enthusiasm, and many others agree. This is a lovely red-brick village pub with a genuine welcome and excellent food. The bar is just the place for a drink by the woodburning stove, and simple furnishings include pubby chairs and plush stools around a mix of tables on wide floorboards, with more stools against the counter. As well as four real ales, such as Little Ox Wipeout, Millstone Tiger Rut, North Cotswold Windrush Ale and West Berkshire Good Old Boy on handpump, you'll find 20 wines by the glass and ten gins; background music, TV, darts and board games. The main dining room has lots of prints on pale walls, cushioned wooden dining chairs and settles with scatter cushions around solid tables and rugs on more bare boards; one red-walled room has similar furnishings on quarry tiles. At the back, picnic-sets sit under parasols on a lawn. Bedrooms are light, well equipped and up to date (dogs are allowed in three of them) and make a good base for enjoying the fine surrounding walks; the chalk horse at Uffington is nearby.

As well as lunchtime sandwiches, the highly regarded food includes lunchtime sandwiches, ale-glazed ox cheek with charred onion, pineapple, puffed crispy rice and coriander, potted rabbit with mushroom crumb, apricot purée and pickled turnips, lasagne of leeks, roasted cauliflower and truffled ricotta with spinach velouté, free-range chicken supreme with black garlic butter, celeriac fondant, baby leeks, pickled lemons and roast chicken sauce, roast cod with shallot purée, mussels, clams, sea vegetables and ale broth, cider-braised lamb shoulder with beetroot dauphinoise, salsa verde and lamb sauce, and puddings such as ginger crème caramel with forced rhubarb and date cake with banana, hazelnuts, banana ice-cream and whisky caramel sauce. *Benchmark main dish: beer-battered fish and chips £14.00. Two-course evening meal £23.00.*

Free house ~ Licensee Catriona Galbraith ~ Real ale ~ Open 10am-11pm; 3.30-11 Mon; 10am-11.30pm Sat; 11-10 Sun; closed Mon lunchtime; ten days early/mid Jan ~ Bar food

12-2.30, 6-9 (9.30 Fri, Sat); 12-3.30, 6-9 Sun ~ Children welcome ~ Dogs allowed in bar
and bedrooms ~ Wi-fi ~ Live music some Sun afternoons ~ Bedrooms: $80/$95
*Recommended by Neil and Angela Huxter, Gail and Arthur Roberts, Sophie and James Collier,
Martine and Colin Fresher, Len and Lilly Dowson, Andy and Louise Ramwell, Rosie and
Marcus Heatherley*

 MILTON UNDER WYCHWOOD   SP2618   Map 4
Hare ♀
(01993) 835763 – www.themiltonhare.co.uk
High Street; OX7 6LA

**Renovated inn with linked bar and dining rooms, attractive
contemporary furnishings, real ales, good food and seats
in the garden**

A golden-stone pub with a stylish interior, the rooms here have all manner
of hare paraphernalia including photos, paintings, statues, a large glass
case with stuffed boxing hares, motifs on scatter cushions and so forth.
There's a bar and a couple of little drinking areas warmed by a woodburning
stove, with various dining areas leading off: wooden floors, dark grey-painted
or exposed-stone walls, painted beams, big gilt-edged mirrors and seating
that includes stools, wooden or leather dining chairs, long button-back wall
seats and cushioned settles around tables of every size – each set with a
little glass oil lamp. Splashes of bright colour here and there brighten things
considerably. Stools line the counter, where friendly, well trained staff serve
beers from breweries such as Butcombe, Hook Norton, Otter and Purity on
handpump and good wines by the glass; they have a champagne happy hour
on Fridays (5-6pm). The garden is furnished with tables, benches and
chairs on a terrace and on a lawn.

They specialise in fresh fish and seafood from Cornwall including moules
marinière, smoked mackerel pâté, tartare of sea bass with a soft boiled egg
and red chard and rocket salad and grilled plaice with lemon and chive butter; also
lunchtime sandwiches and chicken caesar salad plus shredded duck with roast figs and
blue cheese, walnut and spinach salad, five-spice spare ribs, mediterranean vegetable
and lentil moussaka, calves liver with bacon, bubble and squeak and red onion sauce,
venison and parsnip pie, and puddings such as treacle tart with clotted cream and white
and dark chocolate mousse. *Benchmark main dish: fish pie topped with cheddar
mash £16.50. Two-course evening meal £23.00.*

Free house ~ Licensees Sue and Rachel Hawkins ~ Real ale ~ Open 12-3, 5-11; 12-11 Sat;
12-10 Sun ~ Bar food 12-2.30, 6-9; 12-9.30 Sat; 12-8 Sun ~ Restaurant ~ No children after
6pm ~ Dogs allowed in bar *Recommended by Richard Tilbrook, Susan Eccleston, John and
Delia Franks, Liz and Martin Eldon, Tim and Sarah Smythe-Brown, Len and Lilly Dowson,
Belinda Stamp*

 MINSTER LOVELL   SP3211   Map 4
Old Swan ◉ ♀ 🛏
(01993) 862512 – www.oldswan.co.uk
Just N of B4047 Witney–Burford; OX29 0RN

**15th-c building with a lovely old bar, real ales, a fine wine list,
excellent food and acres of gardens and grounds; exceptional
bedrooms**

The unchanging and tranquil little bar in this ancient inn is just the place to
head for if a pint and a chat is what you're after. Here, you'll find stools at
the wooden counter, Brakspears Oxford Gold, North Cotswold Windrush Ale

and Wychwood Hobgoblin on handpump, 15 good wines by the glass from a fine list, 13 whiskies and quite a choice of teas and coffees. Leading off are several attractive low-beamed rooms with big log fires in huge fireplaces, comfortable armchairs, sofas, dining chairs and antique tables, rugs on bare boards or ancient flagstones, antiques, prints, lots of horsebrasses, bed-warming pans, swords, hunting horns and even a suit of armour; also, fresh flowers and board games. There are seats and tables under big parasols on the attractive terrace and they have fishing rights to a mile of the River Windrush, as well as tennis courts, boules and croquet. The bedrooms have plenty of character and some are positively luxurious.

Accomplished food includes sandwiches, barbecue garden vegetable and cheese salad, mackerel with grilled asparagus, lovage and cured egg yolk, marjoram dumplings with kale and sunflower pesto and young vegetables, egg spaghetti carbonara with cured pork cheek, lamb neck and shank pie for two to share, salt-aged rib-eye steak with café de paris butter and dripping chips, and puddings such as chocolate and meadowsweet mousse with passion fruit and salted caramel profiteroles with soured cream ice-cream; they also offer full afternoon tea (12-6). *Benchmark main dish: beer-battered pollack with sea herb tartare and triple-cooked chips £15.00. Two-course evening meal £24.00.*

Free house ~ Licensee Oscar Garcia ~ Real ale ~ Open 10am-midnight ~ Bar food 12.30-9 ~ Restaurant ~ Children welcome ~ Dogs allowed in bar ~ Wi-fi ~ Bedrooms: /£145
Recommended by Rosie and Marcus Heatherley, Alison and Tony Livesley, Isobel Mackinlay, Patti and James Davidson, Gail and Frank Hackett, Edward May

NORTHMOOR
Red Lion

SP4202 Map 4

(01865) 300301 – www.theredlionnorthmoor.com
B4449 SE of Stanton Harcourt; OX29 5SX

Community pub in pretty village with cheerful staff, good food and drink, and seats outside

This carefully renovated 15th-c pub is owned by the local community and run by the friendly, helpful team of Ian and Lisa Neale. It has a cosy atmosphere with heavy beams and bare stone walls, built-in wall seats and painted chairs around scrubbed tables on bare boards, books on shelves, and an open fire at one end (with a piano beside it) and a woodburning stove at the other. Up to four real ales on handpump include a beer named for the pub, Brakspears Bitter, Loose Cannon Abingdon Bridge and Two Cocks 1643 Cavalier, plus ten wines by the glass and ten local gins, all served by accommodating young staff. At the front of the pub are a couple of picnic-sets, with more seats in the garden. Disabled access. The Thames Trail is nearby. They hope to have shepherd's huts for hire by the time this *Guide* is published.

The sensibly short choice of tasty food is cooked by the landlord using home-grown produce: sandwiches, pigeon with pancetta, beetroot and onion purée, brown and white crab meat with chicory, carrot, coriander and chilli salad, cannellini bean, butternut squash and tomato topped with pistachio crumble and sweet potato mash, chicken breast with truffled pomme purée and roasted jerusalem artichokes, halibut fillet with cucumber and brown shrimp risotto, local lamb shoulder with fondant potatoes and honey-roast carrots, local steaks with skinny fries and a choice of sauce, and puddings such as chocolate fondant with salt caramel and vanilla pannacotta with poached rhubarb and rhubarb sorbet. *Benchmark main dish: beer-battered cod and chips £13.50. Two-course evening meal £20.00.*

Free house ~ Licensees Ian and Lisa Neale ~ Real ale ~ Open 11-3, 5.30-11; 11-11 Sat; 12-6 Sun; closed Sun evening, Mon ~ Bar food 12-2.30, 6-9.30; 12-3 Sun ~ Restaurant ~ Children welcome ~ Dogs allowed in bar ~ Wi-fi *Recommended by Franklyn Roberts, Darrell Barton, Sam Cole, Charlie and Mark Todd, Martine and Colin Fresher, Garth Lewis, Peter Pilbeam*

OXFORD

SP5106   Map 4

Bear

(01865) 728164 – www.bearoxford.co.uk
Alfred Street/Wheatsheaf Alley; OX1 4EH

Delightful pub with two cosy character rooms, six real ales and well liked bar food

There's always a good mix of customers here and because it's the oldest drinking house in the city (dating from 1242), it has a lot of charm and character. Two small bar rooms are beamed and partly panelled with thousands of vintage ties on the walls, a winter coal fire and a chatty, bustling atmosphere. Friendly, helpful staff serve up to six real ales on handpump from a fine pewter bar counter: Fullers Day Dreamer, ESB, HSB, London Pride and Olivers Island and a changing guest. Staff are friendly and helpful; board games. A large terraced back garden has seats under parasols; summer barbecues.

Bar food includes sandwiches, duck liver pâté with caramelised onion jam, black pudding hash and fried egg, sharing boards, butternut squash and sweet potato tagine with apricot and toasted almond couscous, lamb and mint burger with yoghurt and triple-cooked chips, toulouse sausage, flageolet bean and smoked bacon casserole, blackened salmon with avocado, tomato and tarragon salad, lamb shoulder shepherd's pie with red wine gravy, and puddings such as chocolate brownie with buffalo milk ice-cream and vintage ale sticky toffee pudding with toffee sauce. *Benchmark main dish: beer-battered fish and chips £14.00. Two-course evening meal £19.00.*

Fullers ~ Manager James Vernede ~ Real ale ~ Open 11-11 (midnight Fri, Sat); 11.30-10.30 Sun ~ Bar food 12-4, 5-9; 12-9 Fri, Sat; 12-6 Sun (barbecue 6-9 in summer) ~ Children welcome but no pushchairs inside ~ Dogs welcome ~ Wi-fi *Recommended by Richard Tilbrook, Revd R P Tickle, Nicola and Holly Lyons, Mary and Douglas McDowell, Paddy and Sian O'Leary, Charles Fraser*

OXFORD

SP4907   Map 4

Perch ♀

(01865) 728891 – www.the-perch.co.uk
Binsey Lane, on right after river bridge leaving city on A420; OX2 0NG

Beautifully set inn with riverside gardens, local ales, popular food and friendly service

All are welcomed here, which means at weekends in particular children and dogs are added to the mix; the efficient, helpful staff always cope with cheerful good humour. The heavily beamed bar has a huge, curved red leather chesterfield in front of a woodburning stove, a very high-backed settle, little stools around tables and fine old flagstones. You'll find Hook Norton Hooky and guests such as Prescott Hill Climb and XT Eight on handpump and plenty of wines by the glass. Leading off here are the dining areas with bare floorboards, scatter cushions on built-in wall seats, wheelbacks and other chairs around light tables, a second woodburner with logs piled to the ceiling next to it and a fine brass chandelier. They hold an annual beer and cider festival, outdoor film evenings in summer and a folk festival. A partly covered terrace has seats and tables, there are picnic-sets on the lawn (which runs down to the Thames Path where there are moorings), a summer bar and an attractively furnished marquee. It's said that this might be one of the first places that Lewis Carroll gave public readings of *Alice in Wonderland*.

 Enjoyable food includes sandwiches, pressed ox tongue with red chicory and stilton salad, hot smoked salmon with beetroot and horseradish crème fraîche, sharing boards, cheddar and ale-braised onion tart with wild nettle and almond pesto, free-range chicken with pease pudding and crispy smoked bacon, mussels in cider with leeks and lovage cream, ham hock, pea and mustard pie, beer-battered fish and triple-cooked chips, and puddings such as rhubarb and custard eton mess and queen of puddings. *Benchmark main dish: pot-roasted ox cheeks with braised cabbage £17.95. Two-course evening meal £21.00.*

Free house ~ Licensee Jon Ellse ~ Real ale ~ Open 10.30am-11pm ~ Bar food 12-9.30 ~ Restaurant ~ Children welcome ~ Dogs welcome ~ Wi-fi *Recommended by Angela, Neil and Angela Huxter, David and Charlotte Green, Susan and Callum Slade, Melanie and David Lawson, Beth Aldridge, Samuel and Melissa Turnbull, Patricia and Gordon Tucker*

OXFORD
Punter

SP5005 Map 4

(01865) 248832 – www.thepunteroxford.co.uk
South Street, Osney (off A420 Botley Road via Bridge Street); OX2 0BE

Easy-going atmosphere in bustling pub overlooking the water with plenty of character and enjoyable food

This is actually on Osney Island and has views over the Thames. Run by an enthusiastic landlord and his friendly staff, it's on two levels. The lower part has attractive rugs on flagstones and an open fire, while the upper room has more rugs on bare boards and a single big table surrounded by oil paintings (just right for a private group). Throughout are all manner of nice old dining chairs around an interesting mix of tables, art for sale on whitewashed walls and a rather fine stained-glass window. Greene King Morlands Original and Old Golden Hen and a changing guest beer on handpump from the tiled counter and several wines by the glass; board games. The side terrace has a range of tables and chairs.

 Well regarded food includes potted hogget with mint yoghurt, breaded whitebait with smoked chilli mayonnaise, camembert, roasted leek and chestnut risotto, crayfish, tarragon and wild mushroom linguine, grilled swordfish steak with sicilian stew and sautéed potatoes, marinated venison steak with juniper butter and frites, burger with toppings, mustard mayonnaise and onions, and puddings such as belgian waffle with maple syrup and vanilla ice-cream and rhubarb and apple crumble with cream. *Benchmark main dish: wild boar and lentil pie with celeriac mash £12.00. Two-course evening meal £19.00.*

Greene King ~ Lease Tom Rainey ~ Real ale ~ Open 12-midnight; 12-11.30 Sun ~ Bar food 12-3, 6-10; 12-10 Sat; 12-9 Sun ~ Children welcome ~ Dogs welcome ~ Wi-fi *Recommended by Richard Tilbrook, Diane Abbot, Amanda Shipley, Stephen Funnell, Nick Sharpe, Mark Hamill, Charles Todd*

OXFORD
Rose & Crown

SP5107 Map 4

(01865) 510551 – www.roseandcrownoxford.com
North Parade Avenue; very narrow, so best to park in a nearby street; OX2 6LX

Lively, friendly local with a fine choice of drinks and proper home cooking

For 35 years, the long-serving licensees have given this straightforward-looking pub a great deal of atmosphere and individuality. The front door opens into a passage with a small counter and shelves of reference books for crossword buffs. This leads to two rooms: a cosy one at the front overlooking the street, and a panelled back room housing the main bar and traditional pub furnishings. A good mix of customers of all ages enjoy well kept Adnams Southwold, Hook Norton Old Hooky, Prescott Chequered Flag and Shotover Scholar on handpump, around 35 malt whiskies and 20 wines by the glass (including champagne and sparkling wine). The pleasant walled and heated back courtyard can be covered with a huge awning; at the far end is a ten-seater dining/meeting room. Please note, no dogs or children.

Honest, reasonably priced food includes sandwiches and baguettes, english breakfast, pie and mash with thick gravy, niçoise or greek salads, very good chips with burger, scampi or a choice of pie, salmon fillet with a sweet, smoky sauce, gammon steak with egg and pineapple, sirloin steak with peppercorn sauce or red wine gravy, and puddings such as apple pie and a daily hot pudding. *Benchmark main dish: pint of sausages £13.00. Two-course evening meal £17.00.*

Free house ~ Licensees Andrew, Debbie and Adam Hall ~ Real ale ~ Open 11-11; 11-2.30, 4.30-11 Aug-late Sept ~ Bar food 12-2.15 (3 Sun), 6-9 ~ Wi-fi ~ Live jazz Sun 7-9pm
Recommended by Peter Brix, Toby Jones, Susan Eccleston, Barbara and Thomas Brown, John Harris, Gus Swan, Nick Higgins

SHILTON
SP2608   Map 4
Rose & Crown ⭐
(01993) 842280 – www.shiltonroseandcrown.com
Just off B4020 SE of Burford; OX18 4AB

Simple and appealing small pub with particularly good food, real ales and fine wines

This pretty little place is very much the focus of a lovely village. The chatty, bustling small front bar has an unassuming but civilised feel, low beams and timbers, exposed stone walls, a log fire in a big fireplace and half a dozen or so farmhouse chairs and tables on the red-tiled floor. There are usually a few locals at the planked counter where they serve Butcombe Rare Breed, Hook Norton Hooky Gold and Youngs Bitter on handpump, along with ten wines by the glass, seven malt whiskies and farm cider. A second room, similar but bigger, is used mainly for eating, and has another fireplace. The attractive side garden has picnic-sets.

Cooked by the chef-patron, the rewarding food includes ciabatta sandwiches, chicken liver parfait with red onion marmalade, gravadlax with dill and mustard sauce, aubergine parmigiana, lambs liver and bacon with mash, smoked haddock, salmon and prawn fish pie, pressed lamb shoulder with greens and mash, sirloin steak with garlic butter and chips, and puddings such as spotted dick with custard and pear and almond tart with cream. *Benchmark main dish: steak and mushroom pie £14.00. Two-course evening meal £21.00.*

Free house ~ Licensee Martin Coldicott ~ Real ale ~ Open 11.30-3, 6-10; 11.30-10 Sat; 12-9 Sun; closed Mon Jan-Feb ~ Bar food 12-2 (2.45 weekends and bank holidays), 7-9 (8 Sun) ~ Restaurant ~ Children welcome lunchtime only ~ Dogs allowed in bar ~ Wi-fi *Recommended by Helene Grygar, R K Phillips, Gwendoline and Ralph Mason, Sally and Brian Turner, Selwyn Jones, Amy and Luke Buchanan, Alexander and Trish Gendall, George and Alison Bishop*

The 🍺 symbol shows pubs that keep their beer unusually well, have a particularly good range or brew their own.

SHIPLAKE
SU7779 Map 2

Baskerville 🌟 ♀ 🍺 🛏

(0118) 940 3332 – www.thebaskerville.com

Station Road, Lower Shiplake (off A4155 just S of Henley); RG9 3NY

Emphasis on imaginative food but a proper bar too, interesting sporting memorabilia and a pretty garden; cosy, comfortable bedrooms

We always get warmly enthusiastic reports on all aspects of this family-run inn. As well as a gently civilised atmosphere, the bar has a few beams, leather tub chairs and dining chairs around pine tables on oak floors or patterned carpet, plush red banquettes by the windows and a couple of log fires in brick fireplaces. Flowers and large house plants are dotted about, and the pale walls are hung with a fair amount of signed rugby shirts and rowing memorabilia, oars, pictures and river maps (Henley is a 35-minute walk away via the Thames Path or a four-minute train journey); TV. Bar chairs line the light, modern counter where they keep Loddon Hoppit and a guest plus Rebellion IPA and Smuggler on handpump, 13 wines by the glass from a thoughtfully chosen list, 50 malt whiskies and farm cider, all served by friendly, enthusiastic staff. They support WaterAid by charging 75p for a jug of iced water and at the time of writing have raised £10,500. The separate restaurant plays background music when it's quiet. A pretty garden has a covered barbecue area, teak furniture and picnic-sets under parasols. Bedrooms are well equipped and comfortable and the breakfasts are excellent. Wheelchair access using a ramp; no disabled loos.

 Appetising food includes lunchtime open sandwiches, moules marinière, duck and orange parfait with apricot and orange jam, grilled polenta with aubergine, sweet potato, wild mushrooms, spinach and balsamic dressing, steak, Guinness and mushroom pie, grilled smoked mackerel with black olives, crushed new potatoes and sauce verjus, chicken breast with haggis croquettes, smoked bacon, leek, pearl barley and romanesco sauce, braised lamb shoulder with champ mash, lamb lollipop, silverskin onions and red wine jus, and puddings such as plum frangipane tart with vanilla ice-cream and orange crème brûlée. *Benchmark main dish: 30-day aged beef burger with toppings, fries and worcestershire mayonnaise £15.50. Two-course evening meal £23.00.*

Free house ~ Licensee Kevin Hannah ~ Real ale ~ Open 11-11; 12-10.30 Sun ~ Bar food 12-2.30, 6-9.30; 12-3.30 Sun ~ Restaurant ~ Children welcome but not in restaurant after 7pm Fri, Sat ~ Dogs allowed in bar and bedrooms ~ Wi-fi ~ Bedrooms: $109/$119
Recommended by John Pritchard, Matt and Hayley Jacob, Miranda and Jeff Davidson, Nick and Willow Brown, Simon and Mary Todd

STANFORD IN THE VALE
SU3393 Map 4

Horse & Jockey ♀

(01367) 710302 – www.horseandjockey.org

A417 Faringdon–Wantage; Faringdon Road; SN7 8NN

Bustling, traditional village local with real character, highly regarded and fair value food and well chosen wines; bedrooms

Whether you are dropping into this charming pub for a drink, here to enjoy a good meal or staying overnight, you'll be sure to get a genuinely warm welcome from the convivial licensees. The place is split into two sections: a contemporary dining area and an older part with flagstones, wood flooring, low beams and raftered ceilings. As it's surrounded by racehorse-training country, the walls are hung with big Alfred Munnings racecourse prints, card collections of Grand National winners and other horse and jockey pictures. There are old high-backed settles and leather armchairs, a woodburning stove in a big fireplace and an easy-going atmosphere. A beer named for the pub (from Greene King), Ruddles Best and a changing guest on handpump, carefully chosen wines by the glass, 20 gins and a dozen malt whiskies; background music and board games. As well as tables under a heated courtyard canopy, there's a separate enclosed informal garden. Bedrooms, housed in another building, are quiet and comfortable. Disabled access.

 Quite a choice of popular food includes sandwiches, wild boar and armagnac pâté with spicy tomato and onion chutney, king prawn skewer with sweet chilli and garlic, wild mushroom tagliatelle with a creamy wine and cheese sauce, stone-baked pizzas, breadcrumbed pork fillet with wholegrain mustard mash, brown sugar-glazed pear and cider reduction topped with bacon powder, fish pie, chicken, bacon and avocado salad with crumbled stilton and honey and mustard dressing, steaks with a choice of sauce, onion rings and chips, and puddings such as passion-fruit tart with berry-infused chantilly cream and seasonal crumble with vanilla custard. *Benchmark main dish: beer-battered haddock and chips £12.95. Two-course evening meal £19.00.*

Greene King ~ Lease Charles and Anna Gaunt ~ Real ale ~ Open 11-3, 5-midnight; 11am-midnight Fri, Sat; 12-11 Sun ~ Bar food 12-3, 6.30-9; 12-2.30 Sun ~ Restaurant ~ Children welcome but not in bedrooms ~ Dogs allowed in bar ~ Wi-fi ~ Open mike first Weds of month ~ Bedrooms: £65/£85 *Recommended by R K Phillips, Gwendoline and Ralph Mason, Sally and Brian Turner, Steve Whalley, Ian Phillips, Bob and Melissa Wyatt, Chloe and Tim Hodge, John Harris*

SWINBROOK   SP2812   Map 4

Swan 🏵 ⚘ 🍷 🛌

(01993) 823339 – www.theswanswinbrook.co.uk
Back road a mile N of A40, 2 miles E of Burford; OX18 4DY

Oxfordshire Dining Pub of the Year

Smart old pub with handsome oak garden rooms, antiques-filled bars, local beers and contemporary food; bedrooms

This smartly converted stone barn makes the best of its lovely position by a bridge over the River Windrush. Some of the elegant, comfortable and warm bedrooms are set beside by the water, and the outdoor seats and picnic-sets share the same view. The little bar has simple antique furnishings, settles and benches, an open fire and (in an alcove) a stuffed swan; locals do drop in for a pint and a chat. The inn is owned by the Devonshire Estate, so there are plenty of interesting Mitford family photographs blown up on the walls. A small dining room leads off from the bar to the right of the entrance, and there are also two garden rooms with high-backed beige and green dining chairs around pale wood tables and views across the garden and orchard. Hook Norton Hooky Gold, North Cotswold Windrush Ale and Purity Bunny Hop on handpump, nine wines by the glass, farm ciders and local draught lager; staff are excellent. Background music, board games and TV. The Kings Head in Bledington (Gloucestershire) is run by the same first class licensees.

🏵 Excellent food includes devilled lambs kidneys with crispy shallots, smoked ham hock terrine with piccalilli, grilled halloumi with bulgar wheat, pomegranate, mint, coriander, spring onion and harissa dressing, steak pie with mash and red wine gravy, stone bass fillet with gnocchi, clams, peas, seaweed, samphire and creamy white wine sauce, duck breast with peaches, parma ham, walnuts, raspberries, goats cheese and balsamic dressing, lamb chump with beetroot, wild garlic, fresh horseradish and salsa verde, and puddings such as vanilla cheesecake with poached rhubarb and rhubarb sorbet and apple and cinnamon crumble with cinnamon ice-cream. *Benchmark main dish: local roe deer with fregola, sugar snaps and teriyaki sauce £19.00. Two-course evening meal £23.00.*

Free house ~ Licensees Archie and Nicola Orr-Ewing ~ Real ale ~ Open 11-11 ~ Bar food 12-2, 6.30-9; 12-2.30, 6.30-9.30 Fri, Sat; 12-2.30, 6.30-8.30 Sun ~ Restaurant ~ Children welcome ~ Dogs allowed in bar ~ Wi-fi ~ Bedrooms: /£150 *Recommended by Guy Vowles, Neil and Angela Huxter, William and Sophia Renton, Moira and Jon Weller, Mark Wilson, Bob and Melissa Wyatt, Chloe and Tim Hodge*

TADPOLE BRIDGE
Trout ♀ 🛏
SP3200 Map 4

(01367) 870382 – www.trout-inn.co.uk
Back road Bampton–Buckland, 4 miles NE of Faringdon; SN7 8RF

Busy country inn with waterside gardens, civilised bar and dining rooms and a fine choice of drinks and food; bedrooms

This good-looking 17th-c inn is on the banks of the Thames (there are moorings for six boats and seats and tables by the water), which means it gets pretty busy, especially in warm weather, when you'll need to book a table in advance. The smart bar has exposed stone walls, beams and standing timbers, a woodburning stove with logs neatly piled to one side, leather armchairs and stools, scatter cushions on window seats, a large stuffed trout and bare boards and flagstones. Upholstered stools line the blue-painted counter where helpful staff serve a beer named for the pub (from Ramsbury), Loose Cannon Abingdon Bridge, Purity Pure Gold and Wychwood Hobgoblin Gold on handpump, 15 wines by the glass from a wide-ranging, carefully chosen list, a growing number of gins and 12 malt whiskies; background music and board games. Dining rooms have green-and-brown-checked chairs around a mix of nice wooden tables, fresh flowers and candlelight; the pale wood or blue-painted tongue-and-groove walls are hung with trout and stag prints, oars and mirrors. The six bedrooms (three open on to a small courtyard and four are suitable for dogs) are attractive and comfortable.

Pleasing food includes sandwiches, wild mushroom on toasted polenta with a poached egg, creamed taleggio cheese and truffle, smoked trout crispy scotch egg with leeks, roast celeriac and mixed vegetables with yuzu and kale, burger with toppings, smoked horseradish mayonnaise, coleslaw and triple-cooked chips, pollack with olives, mussels and nduja salami, and puddings such as coconut crème brûlée with passion fruit and pistachio cake with lemon curd, meringue and chocolate ice-cream. *Benchmark main dish: brill with scallops, prawns, samphire and bisque £20.00. Two-course evening meal £25.00.*

Free house ~ Licensee Tom Brady ~ Real ale ~ Open 12-11 ~ Bar food 12-3, 6-10 ~ Restaurant ~ Children welcome ~ Dogs welcome ~ Wi-fi ~ Bedrooms: /£125 *Recommended by Colin McLachlan, Alan and Linda Blackmore, Max Simons*

WOLVERCOTE
Jacobs Inn 🍴 ♀
SP4809 Map 4

(01865) 514333 – www.jacobs-inn.com
Godstow Road; OX2 8PG

Enjoyable pub with enthusiastic staff, simple furnishings, inventive cooking and seats in the garden

We like this pub and are glad that our readers do too, all commenting on the slightly quirky décor and bustling and easy-going atmosphere. The simply furnished bar has leather armchairs and chesterfields, some plain tables and benches, wide floorboards, a small open fire and high chairs at the counter where they keep Brakspears Bitter, Marstons Eagle IPA and Pedigree Amber and Wychwood Hobgoblin on handpump, 13 wines by the glass, a good choice of spirits and lots of teas and coffees; background music. You can eat at plain wooden tables in a grey panelled area with an open fire or in the smarter knocked-through dining room. This has standing timbers in the middle, a fire at each end and shiny, dark wooden chairs and tables on floorboards; there are standard lamps, stags' heads, a reel-to-reel tape recorder, quite a few mirrors and various deli items for sale. Several seating areas outside have good quality tables and chairs under parasols, picnic-sets on decking and deckchairs and more picnic-sets on grass. This is sister pub to the Woodstock Arms in Woodstock.

As well as breakfasts (9-11.45am), the interesting food (using home-reared pigs, free-range eggs and other local produce) includes sandwiches, pigeon breast with pickled wild mushrooms and shallot and orange dressing, potted Morecambe Bay shrimps with anchovy and lemon butter, quinoa, spinach, kale, ginger and chilli burger with pickles and fries, smoked haddock and salmon fishcakes with mustard creamed leeks, flat-iron chicken with café de paris butter, braised pork ribs with barbecue sauce and coleslaw, lamb rump with chorizo mash and red wine and rosemary jus, and puddings such as chocolate brownie with chocolate sauce and strawberry cheesecake with white chocolate shortbread. *Benchmark main dish: ham hock, chicken and mushroom pie £13.50. Two-course evening meal £21.00.*

Marstons ~ Lease Damion Farah and Johnny Pugsley ~ Real ale ~ Open 9am-11pm; 9am-10pm Sun ~ Bar food 9am-10pm ~ Restaurant ~ Children welcome ~ Dogs allowed in bar ~ Wi-fi *Recommended by Richard Tilbrook, Alison and Tony Livesley, Nicola and Holly Lyons, Rosie and John Moore, Colin McLachlan, Elise and Charles Mackinlay, Caroline Prescott, Phoebe Peacock*

WOODSTOCK   SP4416 Map 4

Woodstock Arms

(01993) 811251 – www.woodstockarms.co.uk
Market Street; OX20 1SX

Cheerful pub with bustling bar and dining room, highly regarded food, four real ales, big back courtyard and knowledgeable staff; bedrooms

A lively and pretty town pub, this has enjoyable food and drinks, friendly service and nice surroundings – what more could you want? The bar has a few leather winged chairs, wooden tables and chairs on patterned floor tiles or large rugs, hops on beams, bare stone walls, a log fire beneath a large copper hood and high chairs by the green-painted counter. A beer named for the pub, Greene King IPA and Old Speckled Hen, Timothy Taylors Landlord and a guest from North Cotswold on handpump and good wines by the glass, served by cheerful staff. The hop-strung, dark beamed dining room has chunky tables and dark wooden chairs on parquet flooring, scatter cushions or animal hides on wall seating and a woodburning stove. It's all very easy-going and friendly. The back courtyard has rustic benches and chairs and tables on flagstones, and there are a few seats out in front as well. Bedrooms are comfortable, contemporary and compact. This is sister pub to the Jacobs Inn at Wolvercote.

Food is enjoyable and includes good breakfasts (7.30am-midday weekdays; 8-11.30am Sat; 8-11am Sun) plus lunchtime sandwiches and baguettes, wild mushroom scotch egg with beetroot purée, crispy duck salad with soy and sesame dressing, roasted squash risotto with pumpkin purée and sage pesto, steak burger with toppings, burger sauce and chips, lobster and crayfish spaghetti with tarragon, brandy, clams and shellfish sauce, chicken breast stuffed with mushrooms with madeira cream sauce, and puddings such as rhubarb and custard tart with crème fraîche and salted caramel crème brûlée. *Benchmark main dish: chicken, bacon and mushroom pie £14.50. Two-course evening meal £21.00.*

Greene King ~ Lease Damion Farah and Johnny Pugsley ~ Real ale ~ Open 7.30am-11pm; 8am-11pm Sat; 8am-10.30pm Sun ~ Bar food all day ~ Restaurant ~ Children welcome ~ Dogs allowed in bar ~ Wi-fi ~ Bedrooms: /£100 *Recommended by John Pritchard, Colin McLachlan, Jeremy and Susan Steadman, Archie and Melanie Garnett, Maria and Stephen Braeburn*

WOOTTON   SP4320 Map 4

Killingworth Castle 🏅🎔

(01993) 811401 – www.thekillingworthcastle.com
Glympton Road; B4027 N of Woodstock; OX20 1EJ

Handsome stone pub with own-brews and good wines, pleasing food and pretty back garden; lovely bedrooms

In the bare-boards bar of this striking 17th-c inn, there's a woodburning stove at one end, benches and wall seats around wooden tables and plush-topped stools at the counter. They offer their own-brewed Yubberton Goldie, Yawnie and Yubby ales on handpump and guests from breweries such as North Cotswold, Shepherd Neame and Stroud plus a thoughtful wine list and a good range of gin and whisky – all served by friendly staff. The simply furnished and candlelit dining rooms have built-in wall seats as well as chapel and other chairs around rustic tables on more floorboards, and there's an open log fire. There are seats out in front of the inn, and a back garden with picnic-sets under parasols. Boutique-style bedrooms, some on the ground floor, some on the first, are well equipped and most appealing. This is sister pub to the Ebrington Arms in Ebrington (Gloucestershire).

🏅 Highly regarded food using as much organic produce as possible includes mackerel with cucumber, fennel, chilli and ginger, chicken liver parfait with turnip relish, sag aloo (sweet potato, curried sultanas, spinach, rice flakes and coriander), beef bourguignon, cod with chorizo, kohlrabi, mash and caramelised cauliflower purée, pork belly with crushed celeriac croquette, butternut squash and toffee apple, and puddings such as chocolate fondant with peanut butter ice-cream and lime crème fraîche and bergamot and white chocolate cheesecake with coconut and blueberries; they also offer a two- and three-course set menu (not weekends). *Benchmark main dish: beer-battered fish and chips £15.00. Two-course evening meal £21.00.*

Free house ~ Licensees Claire and Jim Alexander ~ Real ale ~ Open 9am-11pm ~ Bar food 12-2, 6-9; 12-3.30, 6-9.30 Sat; 12-3.30, 6-8.30 Sun ~ Restaurant ~ Children welcome ~ Dogs allowed in bar ~ Wi-fi ~ Bedrooms: /£120 *Recommended by Peter and Alison Steadman, William and Sophia Renton, Scott and Charlotte Havers, Paul Scofield*

Post Office address codings confusingly give the impression that some pubs are in Oxfordshire, when they're really in Berkshire, Buckinghamshire, Gloucestershire or Warwickshire (which is where we list them).

Also Worth a Visit in Oxfordshire

Besides the fully inspected pubs, you might like to try these pubs that have been recommended to us and described by readers. Do tell us what you think of them: feedback@goodguides.com

---

ABINGDON   SU4997

Brewery Tap (01235) 521655

Ock Street; OX14 5BZ Former tap for defunct Morland Brewery; half a dozen well kept ales (beer festivals), proper ciders and good choice of wines, enjoyable well priced food (not Sun evening) from bar snacks to popular Sun roasts, stone floors and panelled walls, two log fires; background and weekend live music, Tues quiz, darts, free wi-fi; children and dogs welcome, enclosed courtyard where aunt sally is played, three bedrooms, open all day (till 1am Fri, Sat). *(Caroline and Peter Bryant)*

ADDERBURY   SP4735

★**Red Lion** (01295) 810269

The Green; off A4260 S of Banbury; OX17 3NG Attractive 17th-c stone coaching inn with good choice of enjoyable well priced food (all day weekends) including deals, Greene King ales and decent range of wines, linked bar rooms with high stripped beams, panelling and stonework, big inglenook log fire, old books and Victorian/Edwardian pictures, more modern restaurant extension; background music, games area; children and dogs welcome, picnic-sets out on roadside terrace, 13 character bedrooms, good breakfast, open (and food) all day. *(Sandra and Nigel Brown)*

ALVESCOT   SP2704

Plough (01993) 842281

B4020 Carterton–Clanfield, SW of Witney; OX18 2PU Popular stone-built village pub with welcoming hands-on landlord; Wadworths ales, decent range of wines and enjoyable food from sandwiches and pub standards up including home-made pies and burgers, some choices available in smaller servings, friendly helpful staff; children and dogs (in bar) welcome, back terrace and garden with play area, open all day (till 10pm Sun-Thurs). *(R K Phillips, Ian Phillips)*

ARDINGTON   SU4388

Boars Head (01235) 835466

Signed off A417 Didcot–Wantage; OX12 8QA Modernised 17th-c timber-framed pub with good value popular food from daily changing menu (more evening choice), friendly attentive staff, well kept ales including Loose Cannon, Fullers London Pride and one badged for them, low beams and log fires; background music (maybe live piano); children and dogs (in one area) welcome, terrace seating, peaceful attractive village. *(Neil and Angela Huxter)*

ASCOTT UNDER WYCHWOOD   SP2918

Swan (01993) 832332

Shipton Road; OX7 6AY This 16th-c coaching inn had just reopened after major refurbishment as we went to press (same owners as the Chequers at Churchill); main drinking area with beams, wide floorboards and inglenook, apple-green walls and low-hung crimson lampshades, carved ecclesiastical counter serving Butcombe, Hook Norton and Stroud, well chosen wines and good interesting food using local produce from bar snacks up, afternoon teas, small relaxed dining area and more formal restaurant with large Cotswold-stone fireplace and papered walls, further room (seats ten) with floor-to-ceiling windows overlooking the large split-level terrace; children, dogs and boots welcome, eight stylish bedrooms (two in outbuilding), good walks (Oxfordshire Way and Wychwood Way run through the village), open (and food) all day. *(Liz Bell)*

ASHBURY   SU2685

Rose & Crown (01793) 710222

B4507/B4000; High Street; SN6 8NA Friendly 16th-c coaching inn with roomy open-plan beamed bar; three well kept Arkells beers and decent range of wines by the glass, enjoyable generously priced food including specials and popular Sun lunch (booking advised), polished woodwork, traditional pictures, chesterfields and pews, a raised section with oak tables and chairs, separate restaurant and games room (table tennis, pool and darts); background and occasional live music, quiz first Weds of month, sports TV; children and dogs welcome, disabled facilities, tables out at front and in back garden, lovely view down pretty village street of thatched cottages, well placed for Ridgeway walks, eight bedrooms, open all day Sat, till 7pm Sun, closed Mon lunchtime. *(R K Phillips, David and Judy Robison)*

ASTON TIRROLD   SU5586

Chequers (01235) 850666

Aka Fat Frog; Fullers Road; village signed off A417 Streatley–Wantage; OX11 9EN Rustic brick-built dining pub (former Sweet Olive) with highly regarded quite restauranty food including tasting menus, also more affordable set lunch and popular Sun roasts, Sharps Doom Bar and a guest such as Hook Norton Hooky, nice wines by the glass, friendly helpful service; monthly quiz; children and dogs (in bar area) welcome, wheelchair access, cottagey garden with play area, closed Sun evening, Mon and lunchtimes Tues, Weds and Sat. *(Margo and Derek Stapley)*

BANBURY   SP4540
Three Pigeons (01295) 275220
Southam Road; OX16 2ED Renovated 17th-c coaching inn (handy for town centre) with several small rooms surrounding bar; beams, flagstones, bare boards and gas woodburners (no logs because of part-thatched roof), good friendly atmosphere, well prepared food (all day weekends) from sandwiches to restaurant dishes, efficient unobtrusive service, a couple of real ales such as Purity and Sharps, decent selection of wines by the glass and over 30 malt whiskies; children welcome, tables under parasols on paved terrace, well equipped up-to-date bedrooms, useful but limited parking, open all day. *(Tony and Wendy Hobden)*

BEGBROKE   SP4713
Royal Sun (01865) 374718
A44 Oxford–Woodstock; OX5 1RZ Welcoming old stone-built pub with modernised bare-boards interior; good choice of enjoyable food from lunchtime sandwiches and pub favourites up, well kept Hook Norton, a guest beer and several wines by the glass, efficient friendly service; may be background music, free wi-fi; children welcome, no dogs inside, tables on terrace and in small garden, open all day Fri and Sat, till 6pm Sun. *(Peter Barratt)*

BICESTER   SP5822
Jacobs Plough (01869) 388101
North Street; OX26 6NB Stone-built village pub with open-plan bar and dining rooms; leather chesterfields by open fire, button-back wall seating, painted and wooden dining chairs around simple tables on bare boards and flagstones, antlers and various stuffed animals, Greene King, Hook Norton and Timothy Taylors, good choice of wines by the glass and wide range of spirits, enjoyable food including popular roasts, grills and weekday set lunch, friendly helpful staff; seats outside in courtyard; comfortable cosy bedrooms, open (and food) all day. *(Paddy and Sian O'Leary)*

BLEWBURY   SU5385
Red Lion (01235) 850403
Nottingham Fee – narrow turning N from A417; OX11 9PQ Attractive red-brick downland village pub dating from the early 17th c; emphasis on owner-chef's highly regarded food from interesting varied menu including set lunch and evening deals, well kept Brakspears and good choice of wines from brick-faced counter, efficient service, dark beams, quarry-tiled floor and big log fire, separate dining area; free wi-fi; children and dogs (in bar) welcome, wheelchair access, peaceful enclosed back garden, three

bedrooms (Mole, Badger and Toad), good breakfast, closed Sun evening and Tues, otherwise open all day. *(Sally Wright)*

BRIGHTWELL   SU5890
Red Lion (01491) 837373
Signed off A4130 2 miles W of Wallingford; OX10 0RT Busy but welcoming 16th-c thatched village pub; four or five well kept ales such as Loddon and West Berkshire, decent wines and enjoyable good value home-made food including popular pies, friendly efficient staff, two-part bar with snug seating by log fire, dining extension to the right; live music Sun, quiz last Mon of the month, free wi-fi; children and dogs welcome, tables out at front and in back garden, open (and food) all day weekends. *(Mike Kavaney, John Pritchard)*

BRITWELL SALOME   SU6793
★ Red Lion (01491) 613140
B4009 Watlington–Benson; OX49 5LG Brick and flint pub-restaurant with modernised bar and dining room in pastel greys; highly regarded food from french chef-patron including set lunch and daily specials, efficient welcoming service, West Berkshire Mr Chubbs, a real cider and good choice of wines; children welcome, seats in courtyard garden, closed Sun evening, Mon and Tues. *(Colin McLachlan)*

BROUGHTON   SP4238
★ Saye & Sele Arms (01295) 263348
B4035 SW of Banbury; OX15 5ED New management for this attractive old stone house, part of the Broughton Estate (castle just five minutes away); sizeable bar with polished flagstones, cushioned window seats and dark wooden furnishings, Sharps Doom Bar, a couple of guest beers and several wines by the glass, good food from sandwiches up including Weds steak night (free pudding), friendly service, two carpeted dining rooms with exposed stone walls, open fires, over 200 ornate water jugs hanging from beams; children welcome, no dogs inside, picnic-sets on terrace, neat lawn with tables under parasols, pergola and smokers' shelter, aunt sally, closed Sun evening. *(Richard Tilbrook)*

BUCKLAND   SU3497
★ Lamb (01367) 870484
Off A420 NE of Faringdon; SN7 8QN Well run 18th-c stone-built dining pub in lovely Estate village; highly praised interesting food cooked by chef-owner, can eat in low-beamed bar with log fire or restaurant, a couple of changing local ales and good choice of wines by the glass, also local gin and vodka, friendly helpful staff; well behaved children and dogs welcome, seats in courtyard and pleasant tree-shaded garden, good walks (close to Thames Path), three comfortable well equipped bedrooms, closed Sun evening, Mon. *(Maddie Purvis)*

BUCKNELL   SP5525

Trigger Pond (01869) 252817

Handy for M40 junction 10; Bicester Road; OX27 7NE Cotswold-stone beamed pub opposite pond; small bar with dining areas either side, inglenook woodburner, conservatory, Wadworths ales and good choice of enjoyable food from sandwiches, pizzas and pub favourites up, helpful cheery staff, lots of humorous signs and notices; children and dogs welcome, tables out on colourful terraces, steps up to back lawn with more picnic-sets, closed Mon, otherwise open all day (till 7pm Sun). *(Philippa Ward)*

BURFORD   SP2512

Angel (01993) 822714

Witney Street; OX18 4SN Long heavy-beamed dining pub in interesting 16th-c building, warmly welcoming with roaring log fire, good popular food from sandwiches and pub favourites up, Hook Norton ales and well chosen wines, TV; children and dogs welcome, large secluded garden, three comfortable bedrooms, open (and food) all day. *(Christine and Tony Garrett)*

BURFORD   SP2412

★**Lamb** (01993) 823155

Village signposted off A40 W of Oxford; Sheep Street (B4425, off A361); OX18 4LR Fine 16th-c stone inn with civilised bustling atmosphere; cosy bar with armchairs on rugs and flagstones in front of log fire, china plates on shelves, Hook Norton Hooky and Wickwar Cotswold Way, extensive wine list (17 by the glass), 26 malt whiskies, traditional beamed lounge has polished floorboards, distinguished old chairs, oak tables and seats built into stone-mullioned windows, good seasonal food, separate restaurant; children welcome, dogs in bar (menu for them), teak furniture on pretty terrace leading down to neatly kept lawns, well appointed bedrooms, open (and food) all day. *(Peter and Jan Humphreys, Richard Tilbrook, Sarah Roberts, Sandra and Michael Smith)*

BURFORD   SP2512

Mermaid (01993) 822193

High Street; OX18 4QF Handsome 16th-c beamed dining pub with flagstones, stripped stone and good log fire, enjoyable food (all day weekends) at sensible prices including gluten-free menu, friendly service, well kept Greene King ales and a guest, bay window seating at front, airy back dining room and upstairs restaurant, afternoon cream teas; background music (live Fri); children and dogs welcome, tables out at front and in courtyard behind, open all day. *(M J Winterton)*

CAULCOTT   SP5024

★**Horse & Groom** (01869) 343257

Lower Heyford Road (B4030); OX25 4ND Pretty 16th-c roadside thatched cottage; L-shaped red-carpeted room with log fire in big inglenook (brassware under its long bressumer), plush-cushioned settles, chairs and stools around a few dark tables at low-ceilinged bar end, Black Sheep and three guests (July beer festival), decent house wines, popular food (booking essential) cooked by french owner-chef, also O'Hagans sausage menu, dining room at far end with jugs hanging on black joists, decorative plates, watercolours and original drawings, small side sun lounge; live music second Sun of month, shove-ha'penny and board games; well behaved over-5s welcome, awkward for disabled customers (some steps and no car park), picnic-sets in nice little front garden, closed Sun evening, Mon. *(Richard Heath)*

CHADLINGTON   SP3222

Tite (01608) 676910

Off A361 S of Chipping Norton; Mill End; OX7 3NY Friendly 17th-c country pub; bar with eating areas either side, beams and stripped stone, pubby furniture including spindleback chairs and settles, flagstones and bare boards, woodburner in large fireplace, well kept Sharps Doom Bar and a couple of guests, Weston's cider and a dozen wines by the glass, enjoyable fairly traditional home-cooked food (not Sun evening), good service; occasional live music, winter quiz nights; well behaved children and dogs welcome, lovely shrub-filled garden with split-level terrace, good walks nearby, open all day. *(Helene Grygar)*

CHALGROVE   SU6397

Red Lion (01865) 890625

High Street (B480 Watlington–Stadhampton); OX44 7SS Attractive beamed village pub owned by local church trust since 1637; good variety of freshly made food (not Sun evening) from sandwiches to blackboard specials, popular pudding evening second Tues of the month, well kept Butcombe, Fullers, Rebellion and two guests, friendly helpful staff, quarry-tiled bar with big open fire, separate carpeted restaurant; children and dogs welcome, nice gardens (front one borders stream), public car park across the road, open all day Sun. *(Jim King)*

CHARLTON-ON-OTMOOR   SP5615

Crown (01865) 331850

Signed off B4027 in Islip; High Street, opposite church; OX5 2UQ Updated 17th-c village local under welcoming new

---

If you stay overnight in an inn or hotel, they are allowed to serve you an alcoholic drink at any hour of the day or night.

family management; relaxed atmosphere in bar and lounge, well kept Brakspears, Timothy Taylors and Vale, around 100 gins, no food; darts; children and dogs welcome, back garden where aunt sally is played, open all day Sat, till 7pm Sun, closed Tues and till 4pm other weekdays. *(Charles Fraser)*

CHARNEY BASSETT   SU3794
Chequers   (01235) 868642
Chapel Lane off Main Street; OX12 0EX
Welcoming 18th-c village-green pub with spacious modernised interior; Marstons-related ales and enjoyable fairly priced food from lunchtime sandwiches/baguettes to steaks (booking advised), log fire; free wi-fi; children and dogs (in bar) welcome, picnic-sets in small garden, three bedrooms. *(Edward May)*

CHECKENDON   SU6684
★Black Horse   (01491) 680418
Village signed off A4074 Reading–Wallingford; RG8 0TE Charmingly old-fashioned country tavern (run by the same family since the 1900s) tucked into woodland away from the main village; relaxing and unchanging series of rooms, back one with West Berkshire and Rebellion tapped from the cask, one with bar counter has tent pegs above the fireplace (they used to be made here), there's also a homely side lounge and another room beyond that, some snacky food such as baguettes and pickled eggs; no credit cards; children allowed but must be well behaved, dogs outside only, seats on verandah and in garden, popular with walkers and cyclists, closed Sun evening in winter and may shut early if quiet. *(Professor James Burke)*

CHIPPING NORTON   SP3127
Blue Boar   (01608) 643108
High Street/Goddards Lane; OX7 5NP
Spacious revamped former coaching inn (first licensed in 1683); four well kept Youngs ales, lots of wines by the glass and good choice of popular sensibly priced food from bar snacks up, friendly helpful staff, woodburner in big stone fireplace, raftered back restaurant and airy flagstoned garden room; background and some live music, Weds quiz, darts, sports TV, free wi-fi; children and dogs welcome, open (and food) all day. *(Patricia Healey)*

CHIPPING NORTON   SP3127
Chequers   (01608) 644717
Goddards Lane; OX7 5NP Bustling town pub with three softly lit beamed rooms; flagstones and wood floors, panelling and exposed stone walls, inglenook log fire, half a dozen mainly Fullers ales, 15 wines by the glass and enjoyable food from shortish menu, friendly staff, airy conservatory restaurant behind; TV, free wi-fi; children and dogs (in bar) welcome, theatre next door, open all day, food all day weekends. *(Monty Green)*

CHISELHAMPTON   SU5998
Coach & Horses   (01865) 890255
B480 Oxford–Watlington, opposite B4015 to Abingdon; OX44 7UX Extended 16th-c coaching inn with two beamed bars, large log fire, well kept Hook Norton and a guest, good choice of popular reasonably priced food (not Sun evening), friendly obliging service, sizeable restaurant with polished oak tables and wall banquettes; background music; children welcome, neat terraced gardens overlooking fields by River Thame, some tables out in front, nine bedrooms in courtyard block, closed 3.30-7pm Sun, otherwise open all day. *(Roy Hoing)*

CHOLSEY   SU5886
Red Lion   (01491) 651295
Cholsey–Wallingford road; OX10 9LG
Old village pub under consortium of three local families; decent choice of enjoyable food (not Sun evening, Mon) including burgers and pizzas, friendly helpful staff, Brakspears, guest ales and good range of gins; children and dogs welcome, picnic-sets out at front behind picket fence, more tables in back garden, open all day weekends, closed Mon lunchtime. *(Jeremy Charnaud)*

CHRISTMAS COMMON   SU7193
Fox & Hounds   (01491) 612599
Off B480/B481; OX49 5HL Old Chilterns pub in lovely countryside; spacious front barn restaurant serving enjoyable home-made food from open kitchen, Brakspears, a guest beer and decent wines in two cosy beamed bar rooms, simply but comfortably furnished with bow windows, red and black floor tiles and big inglenook, snug little back room too; board games; children, walkers and dogs (in bar) welcome, rustic benches and tables out at front, open all day (till 7pm Sun). *(Richard Wilton, R J Herd)*

CHURCH HANBOROUGH   SP4212
Hand & Shears   (01993) 875047
Opposite church; signed off A4095 at Long Hanborough, or off A40 at Eynsham roundabout; OX29 8AB
Village pub with opened-up interior on different levels; L-shaped bare-boards bar, exposed stonework, some rustic half-panelling and a couple of cushioned window seats, sofa by log fire, Bombardier, Youngs Bitter and a guest from stone-faced counter, steps down to spacious part-raftered dining area divided by balustrades, enjoyable fairly pubby food, attentive friendly service; children welcome, closed Sun evening, Mon. *(Val and Malcolm Travers)*

CHURCHILL   SP2824
★Chequers   (01608) 659393
Church Road; B4450 Chipping Norton to Stow-on-the-Wold (and village signed off A361 Chipping Norton–Burford);

OX7 6NJ Well run golden-stone pub in pretty village opposite impressive church; relaxed bare-boards bar with low beams and mix of seating around nice old tables, some exposed stonework and inglenook log fire, stag's head over counter serving ales such as Hook Norton, Otter, Sharps and Wye Valley, real cider, 16 wines by the glass (three champagnes) and a dozen malt whiskies; good modern food plus some pub favourites, large high-raftered back extension with big lantern lights and long button-back leather banquettes, more dining space upstairs; background music, darts, free wi-fi; children and dogs welcome, wheelchair access, flagstoned back terrace, open all day. *(Guy Vowles, Richard Kennell, Liz Bell)*

CLANFIELD SP2802
Clanfield Tavern (01367) 810117
Bampton Road (A4095 S of Witney); OX18 2RG Pleasantly extended 17th-c stone pub (former coaching inn) adjacent to the Plough; opened-up beamed interior keeping feel of separate areas, mostly carpeted with mix of pubby furniture including some old settles (built-in one by log fire), smallish bar with comfortable seating and woodburner in snug flagstoned area, Marstons-related ales and enjoyable food (not Sun evening) cooked by new chef-landlord, friendly if not always speedy service, more contemporary dining conservatory; background music, free wi-fi; children and dogs welcome, picnic-sets on small flower-bordered lawn looking across to village green, open all day. *(R K Phillips, Ian Phillips)*

CLANFIELD SP2802
★Plough (01367) 810222
Bourton Road; OX18 2RB Substantial stone inn with lovely Elizabethan façade, civilised atmosphere and plenty of character; log fires in comfortable beamed lounge bar, various dining areas, good food, particularly fish and seasonal game, well kept Hook Norton Hooky and a guest, over two dozen wines by the glass and more than 300 gins (they have a 'gin pantry' and can organise tasting sessions), friendly attentive service; children and dogs welcome, attractive gardens with teak tables on sunny front terrace, 11 bedrooms, open all day. *(Ian Phillips, R K Phillips)*

CLIFTON SP4931
Duke of Clifton (01869) 226334
B4031 Deddington–Aynho; OX15 0PE Attractive 17th-c thatch and stone pub; low beams and flagstones, log fire in vast fireplace, enjoyable food including good vegetarian choices and daily specials, well

kept Hook Norton and guests, friendly helpful service; children and dogs welcome, nice back garden, five comfortable bedrooms along with on-site camping and a shepherd's hut, closed Mon lunchtime, otherwise open all day (till 9pm Sun). *(Camilla and Jose Ferrera)*

CROWELL SU7499
Shepherds Crook (01844) 355266
B4009, 2 miles from M40 junction 6; OX39 4RR Welcoming old village pub with good varied choice of freshly made food (not Sun evening) including daily specials, up to six real ales, extensive wine list (ten by the glass) and 30 or so whiskies, beamed bar with stripped brick and flagstones, woodburner, high-raftered dining area; monthly live music; children and dogs welcome, tables out on front terrace and small green, enjoyable walks, open all day in summer. *(Mark Morgan)*

CROWMARSH GIFFORD SU6189
Queens Head (01491) 839857
The Street (A4130); OX10 8ER Ancient village pub with four well kept Fullers/Gales beers and good selection of wines, enjoyable food from varied (if fairly compact) menu including blackboard specials, good friendly service, oak-beamed bar and medieval dining hall; Mon quiz, children and dogs welcome, tables in large garden, open all day, food all day Sat, till 7pm Sun. *(John Pritchard)*

CUDDESDON SP5902
Bat & Ball (01865) 874379
S of Wheatley; High Street; OX44 9HJ Old coaching inn with low beams (mostly painted), flagstones and wood floors, exposed stone/brickwork and lots of cricketing memorabilia, three well kept Marstons-related ales, decent wines and cocktails, enjoyable food from ciabattas and panini up, helpful friendly young staff, tables laid for dining throughout (feels more pubby at the front); background music; children and dogs (in bar area) welcome, sunny back terrace, seven bedrooms (some quite small), open all day. *(David Smith)*

CUMNOR SP4503
Bear & Ragged Staff
(01865) 862329 *Signed from A420; Appleton Road; OX2 9QH* Extensive pub-restaurant (Peach group) dating from the 16th c; contemporary décor in linked rooms with wood or flagstone floors, painted beams, exposed stonework and log fires, well liked food (something available all day) including good value weekday set lunch, five real ales, 15 wines by the glass and cocktails, airy garden room; background music, free wi-fi;

We mention bottled beers and spirits only if there is something unusual about them – imported belgian real ales, say, or dozens of malt whiskies; so do please let us know about them in your reports.

children and dogs (in bar) welcome, tables on sunny terrace, nine bedrooms (four in converted cottages), open all day from 7am (7.30am weekends) for breakfast. *(Len and Lilly Dowson)*

CURBRIDGE SP3208
Lord Kitchener (01993) 772613
Lew Road (A4095 towards Bampton); OX29 7PD Modernised and extended roadside pub with wide range of food including gluten-free choices and signature pies, many dishes available in smaller helpings, Greene King Old Speckled Hen and a beer badged for the pub, several wines by the glass, good friendly service; live music Sat; children and dogs welcome, wheelchair access, closed Sun evening, Mon. *(R K Phillips)*

CUXHAM SU6695
Half Moon (01491) 612165
4 miles from M40 junction 6; S on B4009, then right on B480 at Watlington; OX49 5NF 16th-c thatched and beamed pub in sleepy village surrounded by fine countryside; sensibly priced italian-leaning food including popular pizzas, a couple of Rebellion ales, several wines by the glass and good coffee, friendly accommodating staff; free wi-fi; children and dogs welcome, nice garden behind, open (and food) all day. *(Caroline and Peter Bryant)*

DEDDINGTON SP4631
Deddington Arms (01869) 338364
Off A4260 (B4031) Banbury–Oxford; Horse Fair; OX15 0SH Beamed and timbered 16th-c hotel in charming village with lots of antiques shops and good farmers' market (last Sat of month); well liked food in sizeable modernised back dining room or more traditional bar with mullioned windows, flagstones and log fire, four real ales including Butcombe and Hook Norton, plenty of wines by the glass, friendly service; background music, TV for major sports, free wi-fi; children welcome, no dogs inside, 27 comfortable bedrooms (some in modern courtyard annexe), nice local walks, open all day. *(John Evans)*

DENCHWORTH SU3891
Fox (01235) 868258
Off A338 or A417 N of Wantage; Hyde Road; OX12 0DX Comfortable 17th-c thatched and beamed pub in pretty village; good sensibly priced food from extensive menu including Sun carvery (best to book), friendly efficient staff, a couple of changing ales and good choice of reasonably priced wines, plush seats in low-ceilinged connecting areas, two log fires, old prints and paintings, airy dining extension; children and dogs welcome, tables under umbrellas in pleasant sheltered garden with heated terrace, play area and aunt sally. *(Margo and Derek Stapley)*

DORCHESTER-ON-THAMES SU5794
Fleur de Lys (01865) 340502
Just off A4074 Maidenhead–Oxford; High Street; OX10 7HH Traditional 16th-c coaching inn opposite abbey; knocked-through split-level bar/dining area with open fire and woodburner, plain wooden tables and some interesting old photographs of the pub, fairly limited lunchtime food but more evening choice including good restaurant-set menu, two or three changing ales, friendly efficient service; children (away from bar) and dogs welcome, picnic-sets on front terrace, more in back garden with play area and aunt sally, five bedrooms, closed Sun evening, Mon lunchtime (no food Mon evening); still for sale, so could be changes. *(John Pritchard)*

DORCHESTER-ON-THAMES SU5794
George (01865) 340404
Just off A4074 Maidenhead–Oxford; High Street; OX10 7HH Handsome 15th-c timbered hotel in lovely village (both used for TV's *Midsomer Murders*); inglenook log fire in comfortably furnished beamed bar, good choice of enjoyable well presented food from baguettes up, three or four real ales such as Brakspears and Wadworths, cheerful efficient uniformed staff, high-raftered restaurant; background music; children welcome, 17 bedrooms, open all day. *(John Saville)*

DUCKLINGTON SP3507
Bell (01993) 700341
Off A415, a mile SE of Witney; Standlake Road; OX29 7UP Pretty thatched and beamed village local; good value home-made food including OAP lunch deal and Sun carvery, Greene King ales, friendly service, big stripped-stone bar with scrubbed tables on flagstones, log fires and glass-covered well, old local photographs and farm tools, hatch-served public bar and roomy restaurant; background music, sports TV, pool, free wi-fi; children welcome, seats outside and play area, five bedrooms, open all day, no food Sun evening. *(Patti and James Davidson)*

DUNS TEW SP4528
White Horse (01869) 340272
Off A4260 N of Kidlington; OX25 6JS Former 17th-c coaching house set in attractive village; stripped brick and stonework, rugs on flagstones or wood floors, oak timbers and panelling, inglenook woodburners, up to three well kept ales including Greene King, over a dozen wines by the glass and enjoyable food from shortish menu, two dining rooms; children and dogs welcome, disabled access, teak tables on sunny paved terrace, 11 bedrooms in former stables, open all day. *(Sandra and Nigel Brown)*

EAST HAGBOURNE   SU5288

Fleur de Lys (01235) 813247

Main Road; OX11 9LN Welcoming 17th-c
white-rendered village pub; open-plan
timbered bar with log fire, half a dozen well
kept changing ales and enjoyable pubby food
from sandwiches to grills, good Sun lunch;
live music including popular folk night third
Weds of month, quiz second Mon, darts;
children and dogs welcome, tables in back
garden with marquee, open all day Fri-Sun,
no food Sun evening, Mon. *(Franklyn Roberts,
Baz Manning)*

EAST HENDRED   SU4588

★ Eyston Arms (01235) 833320

*Village signposted off A417 E of
Wantage; High Street; OX12 8JY* Popular dining pub with good mix of
customers, relaxed atmosphere and
impressive food including daily specials;
several separate candlelit areas with low
beams, contemporary paintwork and modern
country-style furnishings, flagstones and
inglenook log fire, a few tables kept just for
drinkers, Hook Norton, Timothy Taylors and
Wadworths, ten wines by the glass and decent
range of whiskies and gins; background
music, TV; children and dogs (in bar)
welcome, picnic-sets outside overlooking the
pretty lane, more seats in back courtyard
garden, open all day (till 9pm Sun).
*(R K Phillips, Alistair Forsyth, Neil and Angela
Huxter, Rob Anderson)*

EATON   SP4403

Eight Bells (01865) 862261

*Signed off B4017 SW of Oxford;
OX13 5PR* Popular old low-beamed pub
with welcoming irish landlord and relaxed
local atmosphere; two small knocked-
through bars with open fires and a dining
area, well kept ales including Loose Cannon,
several gins and good authentic thai food,
friendly helpful staff; Tues folk night, darts;
children and dogs welcome, pleasant garden
with aunt sally, nice walks, open all day
weekends, closed Mon and till 5pm Tues-Fri.
(The Rogue)

EPWELL   SP3540

★ Chandlers Arms (01295) 780153

Sibford Road, off B4035; OX15 6LH Warmly welcoming little 17th-c stone pub
with very good freshly made food (booking
advised) from sandwiches and bar meals up,
well kept Fullers London Pride and Hook
Norton, proper coffee, bar with country-style
furniture, two dining areas, good attentive
service; free wi-fi; children welcome, no dogs,
pleasant garden with aunt sally and summer

entertainment, attractive out-of-the-way
village near Macmillan Way long-distance
path, open all day. *(Bernard Stradling)*

EWELME   SU6491

Shepherds Hut (01491) 836636

*Off B4009 about 6 miles SW of M40
junction 6; High Street; OX10 6HQ* Popular extended bay-windowed village pub
with beams, bare boards and woodburner;
good home-made food (not Sun evening)
from baguettes and snacks up including OAP
set menu, four mainly Greene King ales and
good range of wines by the glass, friendly
staff, back dining area; children, walkers
and dogs welcome, terrace picnic-sets
with steps up to lawn and play area, car
park over the road, open all day.
(John Pritchard, David Lamb)

EXLADE STREET   SU6582

★ Highwayman (01491) 682020

*Just off A4074 Reading-Wallingford;
RG8 0UA* Whitewashed brick building
(mainly 17th-c – parts older) with
interesting rambling layout; mix of furniture
and two-way woodburner in beamed bar
rooms, three well kept beers and plenty
of wines by the glass, good freshly cooked
food from landlord-chef including weekday
set lunch, friendly efficient service; airy
conservatory dining room; soft background
music; children and dogs welcome, terrace
and garden with fine views, closed Sun
evening, Mon. *(David Lamb)*

EYNSHAM   SP4209

Evenlode (01865) 882878

Old Witney Road; OX29 4PS Nicely
renovated 1930s stone-built roadhouse;
decent choice of well liked food including
fixed-price menu, five Marstons-related beers
and a dozen wines by the glass, coffee and
afternoon teas, friendly if not always speedy
service; TV, free wi-fi; children and dogs
welcome, wheelchair access, two terraces,
open (and food) all day from 8am (9am
weekends) for breakfast. *(Helene Grygar,
Richard Tilbrook)*

FERNHAM   SU2991

★ Woodman (01367) 820643

*A420 SW of Oxford, then left into B4508
after about 11 miles; village another
6 miles on; SN7 7NX* 17th-c country dining
pub with heavily beamed character main
rooms, candlelit tables and a big open fire,
also some newer areas, up to three changing
ales, several gins/malt whiskies and decent
choice of wines by the glass, good generously
served food from pub standards up including
Tues steak and Weds pie nights, free minibus

---

for eight or more local diners, friendly helpful service; background and some live music; children and dogs welcome, disabled access/loos, seats on small front lawn and heated back terrace, good walks below the downs, open all day Sun till 9pm, closed Mon. *(R K Phillips)*

FINSTOCK   SP3616
★**Plough** (01993) 868333
Just off B4022 N of Witney; High Street; OX7 3BY Thatched and low-beamed village pub with long rambling bar; leather sofas by massive stone inglenook, pictures of local scenes and some historical documents, two or three well kept ales including Adnams, traditional cider, several wines by the glass and decent choice of whiskies, friendly landlord and staff, popular home-made pubby food (best to book) including deals, roomy dining room with candles on stripped-pine tables; soft background music, bar billiards; children and dogs (in bar) welcome, seats in neatly kept garden with aunt sally, woodland and River Evenlode walks, open all day Sat, closed Sun evening, Mon lunchtime. *(Peter Barratt)*

FRINGFORD   SP6028
Butchers Arms (01869) 277363
Off A421 N of Bicester; Main Street; OX27 8EB Welcoming partly thatched creeper-clad local in Flora Thompson's 'Candleford' village; traditional food including good Sun roasts (three sittings, must book), four well kept real ales such as Black Sheep, charming efficient service, unpretentious interior with L-shaped bar and back dining room, good log fire; children and dogs welcome, picnic-sets out at front beside cricket green, open all day. *(Sally Wright)*

FYFIELD   SU4298
★**White Hart** (01865) 390585
Main Road; off A420 8 miles SW of Oxford; OX13 5LW Grand medieval hall with soaring eaves, huge stone-flanked window embrasures and minstrels' gallery, contrasting cosy low-beamed side bar with woodburner in large inglenook, fresh flowers and evening candles, civilised friendly atmosphere and full of history; good imaginative modern food (not Sun evening, best to book) cooked by licensee-chef using home-grown produce, Loose Cannon and a couple of guests, around 12 wines by the glass and several malt whiskies, cocktails too (Fri happy hour 5-6pm); background music; well behaved children welcome, elegant furniture under umbrellas on spacious heated terrace, lovely gardens, good Thames-side walks, open all day weekends, closed Mon. *(S F Parrinder)*

GODSTOW   SP4809
★**Trout** (01865) 510930
Off A40/A44 roundabout via Wolvercote; OX2 8PN Pretty 17th-c Mitchells & Butlers dining pub in lovely riverside location (gets

packed in fine weather); good choice of food from varied menu including vegan choices and weekday set deal till 6pm (booking essential at busy times), four beamed linked rooms with contemporary furnishings, flagstones and bare boards, log fires in three huge hearths, Brakspears, Sharps and a guest, several wines by the glass, cocktails, friendly helpful staff; background music; children and dogs (in bar) welcome, lots of terrace seats under big parasols, footbridge to island (may be closed), abbey ruins opposite, car park fee refunded at bar, open (and food) all day. *(Richard Tilbrook, B and F A Hannam, Peter Soles)*

GORING   SU5980
★**Catherine Wheel** (01491) 872379
Station Road; RG8 9HB Friendly 18th-c village pub with two cosily traditional bar areas, especially the more individual lower room with its dark beams and inglenook log fire; popular home-made food (not Sun evening) from seasonal menu, well kept Brakspears and other Marstons-related ales, Aspall's cider and a dozen wines by the glass, back restaurant, notable doors to lavatories; background and some live music, monthly quiz, TV, free wi-fi; children and dogs welcome, sunny garden with gravel terrace and summer pizza oven, handy for Thames Path, open all day. *(Val and Malcolm Travers)*

GORING   SU5980
John Barleycorn (01491) 872509
Manor Road; RG8 9DP Friendly low-beamed cottagey local with cosy unpretentious lounge bar and adjoining dining room; Brakspears, Ringwood and a guest, seven wines by the glass and popular good value pubby food (not Sun evening) from lunchtime sandwiches up, efficient cheerful service, public bar with log fire and bar billiards; children welcome, enclosed beer garden, short walk to the Thames, three bedrooms, open all day. *(Edward May)*

GREAT TEW   SP3929
★**Falkland Arms** (01608) 683653
The Green; off B4022 about 5 miles E of Chipping Norton; OX7 4DB Part-thatched 16th-c golden-stone pub in lovely village; unspoilt partly panelled bar with high-backed settles, stools and plain tables on flagstones or bare boards, lots of mugs and jugs hanging from beam-and-plank ceiling, interesting breweriana and dim converted oil lamps, shutters for mullioned lattice windows, log fire in fine inglenook, four Wadworths ales and guests, proper cider and good selection of whiskies and gins, snuff for sale, locally sourced freshly made food, friendly service, separate dining room; folk night Sun; children and dogs welcome, tables out at front and under parasols in back garden, six bedrooms and cottage, open all day. *(Helene Grygar)*

HAILEY   SP3414

Bird in Hand (01993) 868321
Whiteoak Green; B4022 Witney–
Charlbury; OX29 9XP Attractive 17th-c
extended stone inn with good food from fairly
pubby menu (highish prices), well kept ales
such as Hook Norton and several wines by the
glass, helpful friendly service, beams, timbers
and stripped stone, comfortable armchairs on
polished boards, large log fire, cosy corners in
carpeted restaurant, lovely Cotswold views;
parasol-shaded terrace tables, 16 bedrooms
in modern block around grass quadrangle,
open all day. *(Helene Grygar)*

HAILEY   SU6485

★ **King William IV** (01491) 681845
The Hailey near Ipsden, off A4074 or
A4130 SE of Wallingford; OX10 6AD
Popular fine old pub in lovely countryside;
beamed bar with good sturdy furniture on
tiles in front of big log fire, three other cosy
seating areas opening off, good freshly made
food (not Sun evening) from baguettes to
specials, Brakspears and guests tapped from
the cask, helpful friendly staff; children and
dogs welcome, terrace and large garden
enjoying peaceful far-reaching views, good
walking (Chiltern Way and Ridgeway),
leave muddy boots in porch, open all day
weekends in summer (closed Sun evening
in winter). *(Colin McLachlan)*

HAMPTON POYLE   SP5015

Bell (01865) 376242
From A34 S, take Kidlington turn and
village signed from roundabout; from
A34 N, take Kidlington turn, then A4260
to roundabout, third turning signed
for Superstore (Bicester Road); village
signed from roundabout; OX5 2QD
Extended old stone-built country inn;
front bar with three snug rooms, lots of big
black and white photoprints, sturdy simple
furnishings, scatter cushions and window
seats, a stove flanked by bookshelves one
end, large fireplace the other, open kitchen
(feature pizza oven) in biggish inner room,
spreading restaurant with plenty of tables
on pale limestone floor, inventive well liked
food including cheaper weekday set menu,
good choice of wines by the glass, ales such
as Hook Norton and Sharps, friendly service
and cheerful buzzy atmosphere; background
music; children and dogs (in bar) welcome,
modern seats on sunny front terrace by
quiet village lane, nine good bedrooms,
open all day. *(John and Claire Masters)*

HANWELL   SP4343

Moon & Sixpence (01295) 730544
Main Street; OX17 1HW Refurbished
stone-built pub in attractive village setting;
good food cooked by owner-chef from pub
favourites up including set menu choices,
comfortable bar and dining areas with view
into kitchen, well kept Bombardier and

Courage, several wines by the glass from
carefully chosen list; children welcome,
disabled access, seats on back terrace, open
till 6pm Sun. *(Paddy & Sian O'Leary)*

HEADINGTON   SP5406

Butchers Arms (01865) 742470
Wilberforce Street; OX3 7AN Welcoming
backstreet local attracting good mix of
customers; bare-boards interior with roaring
fire, well kept Fullers beers and good value
tasty food including ciabattas, pub favourites
and stone-baked pizzas; Sun quiz, occasional
live music, darts, free wi-fi; children and
dogs welcome, disabled access, heated
terrace with smokers' shelter, open all day
Fri-Sun. *(Monty Green)*

HEADINGTON   SP5407

White Hart (01865) 761737
St Andrews Road, Old Town; OX3 9DL
Traditional split-level 18th-c stone pub facing
the church; well kept Everards and changing
guests, real cider, reasonably priced wines
and enjoyable pubby food including range
of pies, friendly staff; children welcome,
delightful sunny back garden (May beer
festival), open and food all day, kitchen
closes 5pm Sun. *(Monty Green)*

HENLEY   SU7682

Angel on the Bridge (01491) 410678
Thames-side, by the bridge; RG9 1BH
17th-c and worth knowing for its prime
Thames-side position (packed during the
regatta); small front bar with log fire,
downstairs back bar and adjacent restaurant,
beams, uneven floors and dim lighting,
Brakspears ales and maybe a guest such
as Ringwood, good choice of wines by the
glass, enjoyable food from sandwiches and
pubby choices up, cheerful efficient service;
tables under parasols on popular waterside
deck with own bar (plastic glasses here),
moorings for two boats, open all day at least
in summer. *(Simon Collett-Jones)*

HENLEY   SU7582

Argyll (01491) 573400
Market Place; RG9 2AA Comfortable
traditional pub with panelled walls, wood
flooring and suit of armour by the bar, well
kept Greene King ales, a house beer called
Midsomer Murders (the pub has featured
in the TV series) and decent wines by the
glass, enjoyable reasonably priced pubby food
from good sandwiches up, efficient friendly
service; background music, TV; nice terrace
garden behind and useful parking, open (and
food) all day. *(Martin Day)*

HIGHMOOR   SU6984

★ **Rising Sun** (01491) 640856
Witheridge Hill, signposted off B481;
OS Sheet 175 map reference 697841;
RG9 5PF Welcoming 17th-c pub in small
Chilterns village; cosy beamed bar with red
and black quarry-tiled floor, comfortable sofa

by inglenook woodburner, Brakspears Bitter and a couple of Marstons-related guests, a dozen wines by the glass, three linked eating areas with rugs and pubby furniture on bare boards, pictures on dark red walls, log fire, well liked food from baguettes up; background music, free wi-fi; children and dogs (in bar) welcome, picnic-sets and white metal tables and chairs in pleasant back garden, good surrounding walks, open all day Fri-Sun, no food Sun evening. *(Gene and Kitty Rankin)*

HOOK NORTON   SP3534
Gate Hangs High (01608) 737387
N towards Sibford, at Banbury–Rollright crossroads; OX15 5DF Tucked-away old stone pub under new management; cosy low-ceilinged bar with attractive inglenook and traditional furniture on bare boards, Hook Norton ales, side dining extension; background music; children and dogs (in bar) welcome, pretty courtyard and country garden, four bedrooms, camping, quite near Rollright Stones (EH), open all day. *(Gail and Frank Hackett)*

ISLIP   SP5214
Red Lion (01865) 375367
High Street (B4027); OX5 2RX Part of small local group including the Jacobs Inn at Wolvercote and Woodstock Arms in Woodstock (see Main Entries for both); spreading bar and dining areas with cushioned wooden chairs, upholstered benches and wall seats around simple tables on bare boards, carpet or flagstones, some leather sofas and armchairs, two woodburners (one in a sizeable inglenook), Black Sheep, Sharps and a guest, good choice of wines by the glass and enjoyable food from pub classics up including set lunch, friendly helpful staff; children welcome, tables and chairs outside in roped-off area, picnic-sets on lawn, open (and food) all day from 9am for breakfast. *(Camilla and Jose Ferrera)*

KIDMORE END   SU6979
New Inn (0118) 972 3115
Chalkhouse Green Road; signed from B481 in Sonning Common; RG4 9AU Extended black and white pub by village church; beams and big log fire, enjoyable freshly made food, well kept Brakspears ales and decent wines by the glass, pleasant restaurant; children welcome, tables in large sheltered garden with pond, six bedrooms, open all day Thurs-Sat, till 8pm Sun, shuts 3-6pm Mon-Weds. *(Mark Morgan)*

KINGHAM   SP2523
Wild Rabbit (01608) 658389
Church Street; OX7 6YA Revamped former 18th-c farmhouse (part of the Daylesford Estate); limestone floors, exposed stone walls and lofty beams, antique country furniture and huge fireplaces, several wines by the glass including champagne, Hook Norton

Hooky, Purity Mad Goose and guests, top notch modern cooking with emphasis on organic produce (not cheap and booking advised), floor-to-ceiling windows in spacious restaurant with kitchen view; children welcome, dogs in bar, paved front terrace with topiary rabbits and elegant furniture under cream parasols, 12 individually designed well appointed bedrooms, also five self-catering cottages nearby, open all day. *(Liz Bell)*

LANGFORD   SP2402
Bell (01367) 860249
Village signposted off A361 N of Lechlade, then pub signed; GL7 3LF 17th-c pub set in charming village; cosy flagstoned bar with Hook Norton Hooky, Sharps Doom Bar and a guest, several wines by the glass from good list, two heavily beamed dining rooms with traditional furniture on more flagstones, log fires, well liked varied choice of food from snacks and wood-fired pizzas up (best to book), pleasant helpful staff; children and dogs welcome, tables out at front and to the side, eight bedrooms, open all day. *(R K Phillips, Liz Bell, Bernard Stradling, Roy Shutz)*

LEWKNOR   SU7197
★Olde Leathern Bottel
(01844) 351482 *Under a mile from M40 junction 6; off B4009 towards Watlington; OX49 5TW* Popular old village pub with two heavy-beamed bars; understated décor and rustic furnishings, woodburners (one in brick inglenook), well kept Brakspears, Marstons Pedigree and a guest, several wines by the glass and tasty pub food including specials, good friendly service, family room separated by standing timbers; dogs welcome, nice garden with lots of picnic-sets under parasols, play area, boules and aunt sally, handy for walks on Chiltern escarpment. *(Gail and Frank Hackett)*

LITTLE MILTON   SP6100
Lamb (01844) 279527
3 miles from M40 junction 7: A329 Thame–Wallingford; OX44 7PU Attractive little 16th-c thatched pub with dark beams, stripped stone and low windows, three interconnecting carpeted rooms on two levels, woodburner, good choice of enjoyable food (not Sun evening) from lunchtime sandwiches/baguettes up, wider evening choice, three well kept ales including Brakspears and decent range of wines, friendly attentive service; background music; children and dogs welcome, tables on paved back terrace and in pretty garden beyond car park, open all day Sun. *(John Pritchard)*

LONG HANBOROUGH   SP4214
★George & Dragon (01993) 881362
A4095 Bladon–Witney; Main Road; OX29 8JX Substantial pub with original two-room bar (17th c or older); low beams,

stripped stone and two woodburners, Wells and Youngs ales and decent range of wines, roomy thatched restaurant extension with comfortably padded dining chairs around sturdy tables, wide choice of good food from sandwiches and snacks up, Thurs pie night, prompt friendly service; background music; children and dogs (in bar) welcome, large back garden with picnic-sets among shrubs, tables beneath canopy on separate sheltered terrace, summer barbecues, open (and food) all day. *(Len and Lilly Dowson)*

LONG WITTENHAM   SU5493
Plough (01865) 407738
High Street; OX14 4QH Welcoming 17th-c two-bar local with low beams, inglenook fires and lots of brass, two or three well kept ales including Butcombe, generous helpings of good reasonably priced food (not Sun evening) from sandwiches and traditional choices to interesting specials, efficient service, dining room, games in public bar; children and dogs welcome, two bedrooms, Thames moorings at bottom of long garden, play area, June music festival, open all day. *(David Lamb)*

MAIDENSGROVE   SU7288
Five Horseshoes (01491) 641282
Off B480 and B481, W of village; RG9 6EX Character 16th-c dining pub set high in the Chilterns; rambling bar with low ceiling and log fire, well liked food from changing menu including seasonal game, friendly service, well kept Brakspears and good choice of wines by the glass, airy conservatory restaurant; regular jazz evenings; children and dogs (in bar) welcome, plenty of tables in suntrap garden with views of rolling countryside, good walks, open all day Sat, closed Sun evening, Mon and Tues. *(Sally Wright)*

MARSH BALDON   SU5699
Seven Stars (01865) 343337
The Baldons signed off A4074 N of Dorchester; OX44 9LP Competently run, community-owned beamed pub on edge of village green; enjoyable food (all day Weds-Sat) including plenty of gluten-free and vegan choices, well kept Fullers London Pride and three mainly local guests, helpful friendly young staff coping well at busy times, modernised bar areas, seats by corner fire, raftered barn restaurant; monthly quiz and occasional live music; children, dogs and muddy boots welcome, seats outside overlooking fields and horses, open all day (till midnight Fri, Sat, 7pm Sun). *(Katharine Cowherd, Mike Kavaney, John Pritchard, Baz Manning)*

MILCOMBE   SP4034
Horse & Groom (01295) 722142
Off A361 SW of Banbury; OX15 4RS Stone-built 17th-c pub at western edge of the village; generous servings of good freshly made food from lunchtime sandwiches up, three changing ales and a dozen wines by the glass, friendly helpful service, inglenook woodburner in appealing low-beamed and flagstoned bar, back restaurant; children and dogs welcome, picnic-sets out in front, four bedrooms, good breakfast, handy for Wigginton Heath waterfowl and animal centre, closed Sun evening. *(Gail and Frank Hackett)*

MURCOTT   SP5815
★ **Nut Tree** (01865) 331253
Off B4027 NE of Oxford, via Islip and Charlton-on-Otmoor; OX5 2RE Despite its Michelin star, this 15th-c beamed and thatched place manages to keep a relaxed pubby atmosphere; first rate imaginative cooking using own produce including home-reared pigs (they also do sandwiches and cheaper bar food), good attentive but not intrusive service from friendly staff, well spaced tables with crisp white cloths, leather chesterfields in bar area, Vale, two guest beers and carefully chosen wines; background music; children and dogs (in bar) welcome, terrace and pretty garden, unusual gargoyles on front wall (modelled loosely on local characters), closed Sun evening and Mon, otherwise open all day. *(Paddy and Sian O'Leary)*

NORTH HINKSEY   SP4905
Fishes (01865) 249796
Off A420 just E of A34 ring road; N Hinksey Lane, then turn left opposite church into cul-de-sac signed to rugby club; OX2 0NA Popular brick and tile Victorian pub (Peach group) set in three acres of wooded grounds; extended open-plan interior with conservatory, good choice of food from sandwiches and deli boards up including weekday set menu till 6pm, well kept Greene King ales and a guest, plenty of wines by the glass and nice selection of gins, friendly helpful staff; children welcome, dogs in bar and snug, tables out at front, on back deck and in streamside garden with summer barbecues and tipi, open (and food) all day from 9.30am for breakfast. *(Val and Malcolm Travers)*

NORTH MORETON   SU5689
Bear at Home (01235) 811311
Off A4130 Didcot–Wallingford; High Street; OX11 9AT Village pub dating from the 16th c run by friendly father and daughter team; traditional bar with country pine furniture and cosy fireside areas, small dining room to the right and larger extension (function room) beyond, lots of beams, carpeted floors, pictures on rough walls, enjoyable sensibly priced food from lunchtime baguettes and pub staples up including daily specials, Weds steak night, Timothy Taylors, a house beer from West Berkshire and a couple of local guests, Weston's cider and a dozen wines by the

glass; children and dogs welcome, nice back garden overlooking cricket pitch (July beer and cricket festival), pretty village, open all day Sat, closed Sun evening. *(John Pritchard)*

OXFORD   SP5106
Chequers (01865) 727463
Off High Street; OX1 4DH Narrow 16th-c pub tucked away in courtyard down small alleyway; several areas on three floors with interesting architectural features, beams, panelling and stained glass, eight or so well kept ales and enjoyable good value Nicholsons menu, afternoon tea; background music; walled garden, open (and food) all day. *(Peter Barratt)*

OXFORD   SP5106
Eagle & Child (01865) 302925
St Giles; OX1 3LU Long narrow Nicholsons pub dating from the 16th c; two charmingly old-fashioned panelled front rooms with Tolkien and C S Lewis connections (the Inklings writers' group used to meet here and referred to it as the Bird & Baby), ales including Brakspears and Hook Norton, enjoyable pubby food in stripped-brick dining extension and conservatory, can get busy but service remains good; children allowed in back till 8pm, open all day. *(Richard Tilbrook, Revd R P Tickle, Tony Scott)*

OXFORD   SP5105
Head of the River (01865) 721600
Folly Bridge; between St Aldates and Christ Church Meadow; OX1 4LB Renovated pub set down by the river; spacious split-level bar with dividing brick arches, rugs on stone or wood-strip floors, open fire, well kept Fullers/Gales beers and good choice of wines by the glass, popular food from sandwiches and pub staples up, helpful friendly service; background music can be loud, daily papers, TV; tables on stepped waterside terrace, boats for hire and nearby walks, 20 comfortable bedrooms, open all day. *(Richard Tilbrook, Tony Scott)*

OXFORD   SP5203
Isis Farmhouse (01865) 243854
Off Donnington Bridge Road; no car access; OX4 4EL Early 19th-c former farmhouse in charming waterside spot (accessible only to walkers/cyclists/boaters); relaxed lived-in interior with two woodburners, three beers from local Shotover and decent wines, sensibly priced food from shortish menu including afternoon teas, friendly if not always speedy service; background and weekend live music including Sun afternoon jazz, folk club second Fri of month; children and dogs welcome, terrace and garden picnic-sets, short walk to Iffley Lock and nearby lavishly decorated early Norman church, open all day till 9pm (11pm Fri, Sat), closed Mon-Thurs in winter. *(Jim King)*

OXFORD   SP5006
Jam Factory (01865) 244613
Hollybush Row; OX1 1HU Bar/restaurant/art gallery in former marmalade factory; good range of ales and craft beers, 15 wines by the glass and cocktails (happy hour 5-7pm Mon-Fri), well liked food including vegetarian/vegan choices and good value two-course lunch, relaxed friendly atmosphere; regular events such as music, poetry and film nights, art workshops and life drawing classes; children welcome, wheelchair access, large outdoor seating area, open all day from 8am breakfast on. *(Richard Tilbrook)*

OXFORD   SP5106
Kings Arms (01865) 242369
Holywell Street/Parks Road; OX1 3SP Relaxed corner pub dating from the early 17th c opposite the New Bodleian Library; popular with locals and students (next-door Wadham College owns it), various cosy rooms up and down steps, lots of panelling and pictures, open fires, well kept Youngs ales and guests, several wines by the glass, enjoyable pubby food from baked potatoes and sandwiches up; free wi-fi; children and dogs welcome, a few pavement tables, open (and food) all day. *(Revd R P Tickle)*

OXFORD   SP5006
Lighthouse (01865) 204060
Park End Street; OX1 1HH Long narrow pub by Pacey's Bridge; modernised nautical-theme interior with wood floors (some steps), padded wall benches and stools at high tables, small front bar with fire in old range, other rooms leading back to restaurant, a couple of Wychwood ales, craft beers and cocktails, decent coffee too and good fairly priced food including tapas, nice staff; french windows to small decked area overhanging Castle Mill Stream, open all day (till 1.30am Fri, Sat). *(Richard Tilbrook)*

OXFORD   SP5006
Old Bookbinders (01865) 553549
Victor Street; OX2 6BT Dark and mellow family-run local tucked away in the Jericho area; friendly and unpretentious, with old fittings and lots of interesting bric-a-brac, Greene King ales and three guests, decent choice of whiskies and other spirits, enjoyable french-leaning food including speciality crêpes and good value lunchtime/early evening set menu; shove-ha'penny and board games, Tues quiz, open mike night Sun; children, dogs and students welcome, some entertaining features such as multiple door handles to the gents', tables out on pavement, open all day, food all day Sun till 7pm. *(Richard Tilbrook, Michael Long)*

OXFORD   SP5105
Royal Blenheim (01865) 242355
Ebbes Street; OX1 1PT Popular corner

pub opened by Queen Victoria during her Golden Jubilee and now jointly owned by Everards, Titanic and White Horse; their well kept beers and guests, good value well presented pub food (till 5pm Sun) including some decent vegetarian/vegan options, friendly chatty staff, single airy room with raised perimeter seating; TV projector for major sports; open all day (till midnight Fri, Sat). *(Jim King)*

OXFORD   SP5106
Turf Tavern (01865) 243235
Bath Place; via St Helens Passage, between Holywell Street and New College Lane; OX1 3SU Interesting characterful pub hidden away behind high walls; small dark-beamed bars with lots of snug areas, up to ten constantly changing ales including Greene King, Weston's and Lilley's ciders, winter mulled wine, popular reasonably priced food from sandwiches up, pleasant helpful service; newspapers and free wi-fi; children and dogs welcome, three walled-in courtyards (one with own bar), open (and food) all day. *(Tony Scott, Tracey and Stephen Groves)*

PISHILL   SU7190
★**Crown** (01491) 638364
B480 Nettlebed–Watlington; RG9 6HH 15th-c inn at heart of the Chilterns; beamed bars with old local photographs, prints and maps, some panelling and nice mix of wooden tables and chairs, well kept Brakspears and Rebellion ales, seven wines by the glass and a dozen malt whiskies, tasty generously served food, good service, knocked-through back area with standing timbers and three log fires; priest hole is thought to be one of the largest in the country; well behaved children welcome, dogs in bar, seats in pretty garden with thatched barn for functions, lots of nearby walks, self-catering cottage, closed Sun evening. *(Monty Green)*

PLAY HATCH   SU7477
Shoulder of Mutton (0118) 947 3908
W of Henley Road (A4155) roundabout; RG4 9QU Dining pub with low-ceilinged log-fire bar and large back conservatory restaurant, good food from landlord-chef including signature mutton dishes, well kept Greene King and a guest such as nearby Loddon, reasonably priced house wines, friendly service; children welcome, picnic-sets in carefully tended walled garden with well, closed Sun evening, Mon (and Tues evening Jan-June). *(John Pritchard)*

ROKE   SU6293
Home Sweet Home (01491) 838249
Off B4009 Benson–Watlington; OX10 6JD Wadworths country dining pub with several linked rooms; two smallish bars, heavy stripped beams, big central log fire and traditional furniture, carpeted room on right leading to restaurant area, good

food including set lunch menu and popular Sun roasts, friendly accommodating staff; background music, Rokefest music/beer festival late May Bank Holiday; children and dogs welcome, seats in attractive low-walled front garden, open all day Sat, till 5pm Sun (food till 3.30pm), closed Mon. *(John Pritchard)*

ROTHERFIELD GREYS   SU7282
★**Maltsters Arms** (01491) 628400
Can be reached off A4155 in Henley, via Greys Road passing Southfields long-stay car park; or follow Greys Court signpost off B481 N of Sonning Common; RG9 4QD Chilterns country pub with black-beamed front bar, comfortable wall banquettes and woodburner, Brakspears and other Marstons-related beers, Aspall's cider and eight wines by the glass, linked lounge and restaurant, good sensibly priced food from fairly pubby menu plus several blackboard specials, friendly service; background music; children and dogs (in bar) welcome, terrace tables under big heated canopy, picnic-sets on grass looking over paddocks and rolling countryside, good walks nearby and handy for Greys Court (NT), open all day Sun. *(Paul Humphreys, Gail Plews)*

ROTHERFIELD PEPPARD   SU7081
Unicorn (01491) 628674
Colmore Lane; RG9 5LX Attractive little country pub under newish management; bustling bare-boards bar with open fire, Brakspears Bitter and a couple of guests, enjoyable food including daily specials and deals, friendly service, separate dining room; Weds quiz and some live music, TV for major sports; children, walkers and dogs welcome, seats in back garden, open all day, no food Sun evening. *(John and Claire Masters)*

SHENINGTON   SP3742
Bell (01295) 670274
Off A422 NW of Banbury; OX15 6NQ Early 18th-c two-room pub in charming quiet village; good popular food cooked by landlord-chef, well kept Hook Norton Hooky, a guest beer and good range of wines by the glass, friendly service, heavy beams, some flagstones, stripped stone and pine panelling, two woodburners; children welcome in eating areas, dogs in bar, picnic-sets out at front, good surrounding walks, open all day Sat, closed Sun evening to Weds lunchtime. *(Mark Morgan)*

SHIPTON-UNDER-WYCHWOOD   SP2717
Shaven Crown (01993) 830500
High Street (A361); OX7 6BA Ancient monastic building with magnificent lofty medieval rafters and imposing double stairway in hotel part's hall, separate beamed bar serving Hook Norton ales and several wines by the glass, good food from

sandwiches and pubby choices up, helpful friendly staff, restaurant; background music; children and dogs (in bar) welcome, peaceful central courtyard, seven bedrooms including one in former chapel with four-poster, closed Sun evening, otherwise open all day. *(Patricia Healey)*

SHIPTON-UNDER-WYCHWOOD   SP2717
Wychwood Inn   (01993) 831185
High Street; OX7 6BA Former coaching inn run by mother and son team; contemporary décor in extended open-plan bar/dining area, more period character in flagstoned public bar with black beams and inglenook, four changing beers, plenty of wines by the glass and enjoyable food from sharing plates to grills, Mon burger night, friendly young staff, private dining room in glassed-in coach entrance; TV for major sporting events; children and dogs welcome, picnic-sets on small terrace, five bedrooms, open all day. *(Professor James Burke)*

SIBFORD GOWER   SP3537
Wykham Arms   (01295) 788808
Signed off B4035 Banbury to Shipston-on-Stour; Temple Mill Road; OX15 5RX Cottagey 17th-c thatched and flagstoned dining pub; good food (not Sun evening) from light dishes up, friendly attentive staff, two well kept changing ales and more than 20 wines by the glass, comfortable open-plan interior with low beams and stripped stone, glass-covered well, inglenook; children and dogs welcome, country views from big garden, lovely manor house opposite and good walks nearby, open all day Sun, closed Mon. *(Charles Fraser)*

SOULDERN   SP5231
Fox   (01869) 345284
Off B4100; Fox Lane; OX27 7JW Early 19th-c pub set in delightful village; open-plan beamed interior with woodburner in two-way fireplace, well kept ales such as Hook Norton, Otter and Timothy Taylors, several wines by the glass and good fairly priced food from shortish menu, friendly attentive service; regular quiz nights, Aug beer festival; terrace and walled garden, aunt sally, four bedrooms, open all day Sat, till 5pm Sun. *(Christine and Tony Garrett)*

SOUTH LEIGH   SP3908
Mason Arms   (01993) 656238
3 miles S of A40 Witney–Eynsham; Station Road; OX29 6XN Pretty 16th-c thatched country inn-restaurant refurbished under present owners; very good food (can be pricey) from short but varied menu, Hook Norton Hooky and a guest, craft beers, cocktails and plenty of wines by the glass, efficient friendly service, individual décor with some quirky touches such as decanter lampshades, neon signs and prison doors to the loos; quiz every other

Weds, some live music; children and dogs allowed, rustic furniture and old olive tree in front courtyard, more seats in garden with shepherd's hut, seven stylish bedrooms (three suites in converted outbuildings), open all day. *(S F Parrinder, Liz Bell)*

SOUTH NEWINGTON   SP4033
Duck on the Pond   (01295) 721166
A361; OX15 4JE Roadside dining pub with small flagstoned bar and linked carpeted eating areas up a step; much enjoyed food from lunchtime baguettes up including some good vegetarian choices and popular Sun lunch, Hook Norton Hooky and a couple of guests, good range of wines and gins, also a driver-friendly drinks list, cheerful pleasant staff, lots of duck-related items, woodburner; children welcome, no dogs inside, spacious grounds with tables on deck and lawn, pond with waterfowl and little River Swere winding down beyond, open all day Sat, till 4pm Sun, closed Mon, Tues. *(Gail and Frank Hackett)*

SPARSHOLT   SU3487
Star   (01235) 751873
Watery Lane; OX12 9PL Modernised 16th-c dining pub with easy-going relaxed atmosphere; good up-to-date food along with more traditional choices and lunchtime set menu, friendly efficient service, dining rooms with pale farmhouse chairs around chunky tables on floorboards or big flagstones, hop-strung beams, open fire, ales such as Hook Norton and Sharps in simply furnished bar; background music, board games; children and dogs welcome, seats in back garden, attractive village – snowdrops fill the churchyard in spring, eight comfortable barn conversion bedrooms, open all day. *(Neil and Angela Huxter)*

STANTON ST JOHN   SP5709
Talk House   07926 249157
Middle Road/Wheatley Road (B4027 just outside village); OX33 1EX Attractive part-thatched dining pub; older part on left with steeply pitched rafters soaring above stripped-stone walls, mix of old dining chairs and big stripped tables, large rugs on flagstones; rest of building converted more recently but in similar style with massive beams, flagstones or stoneware tiles and log fires below low mantelbeams, good food from lunchtime sandwiches up, brunch from 10.15am, Fullers ales and over 20 wines by the glass; children welcome, inner courtyard with teak tables and chairs, a few picnic-sets on side grass, four bedrooms, open all day Fri, Sat, till 9pm Sun, closed Mon. *(Edward May)*

STEEPLE ASTON   SP4725
★ Red Lion   (01869) 340225
Off A4260 12 miles N of Oxford; OX25 4RY Cheerful village pub with neatly kept beamed and partly panelled bar, antique settle and other good furnishings,

well kept Hook Norton ales and decent wines by the glass, enjoyable food from shortish menu including stone-baked pizzas, obliging young staff, back timber-framed dining extension; Mon quiz; well behaved children welcome till 7pm, dogs in bar, suntrap front garden with lovely flowers and shrubs, parking can be tricky, handy for Rousham House and Garden, open all day Sat, till 5.30pm Sun. *(David Lamb)*

STEVENTON   SU4691

North Star

Stocks Lane, The Causeway, central westward turn off B4017; OX13 6SG
Very traditional little village pub through yew tree gateway; tiled entrance corridor, main area with ancient high-backed settles forming booth in front of brick fireplace, three well kept ales from side tap room, hatch service to another room with plain seating, a couple of tables and coal fire, simple lunchtime food, friendly staff; children and dogs welcome, picnic-sets on front grass, aunt sally, open all day weekends, closed weekday lunchtimes. *(Maddie Purvis)*

STOKE LYNE   SP5628

Peyton Arms 07546 066160

From minor road off B4110 N of Bicester fork left into village; OX27 8SD
Beautifully situated and largely unspoilt one-room alehouse run by character landlord (Mick the Hat); very well kept Hook Norton ales from casks behind small corner bar, no food apart from filled rolls, inglenook fire, tiled floor and lots of memorabilia; no children or dogs; pleasant garden, open all day weekends till 7pm, closed Mon, Tues, opens 5pm Weds-Fri. *(Sandra and Nigel Brown)*

STOKE ROW   SU6884

Cherry Tree (01491) 680430

Off B481 at Highmoor; RG9 5QA
Sympathetically modernised 18th-c pub-restaurant (originally three cottages); enjoyable often interesting food from sharing plates to daily specials, Brakspears ales and good range of wines by the glass, helpful friendly staff, small linked rooms mainly set for dining, heavy low beams, stripped boards and flagstones; background music, TV in bar; well behaved children and dogs welcome, lots of tables in attractive garden, nearby walks, four good bedrooms in converted barn, open all day, no food Sun evening. *(Paddy and Sian O'Leary)*

STOKE ROW   SU6884

★Crooked Billet (01491) 681048

Nottwood Lane, off B491 N of Reading – OS Sheet 175 map reference 684844; RG9 5PU Nice place, but more restaurant than pub; charming rustic layout with heavy beams, flagstones, antique pubby furnishings and fine inglenook log fire, crimson Victorian-

---

style dining room, very good interesting food cooked by owner-chef using local and home-grown produce, cheaper set lunches Mon-Fri, helpful friendly staff, Brakspears Oxford Gold tapped from the cask (no counter), good wines, relaxed homely atmosphere; weekly live music often including established artists; children very welcome, big garden by Chilterns beechwoods, open all day, food all day weekends. *(Colin McLachlan)*

STONESFIELD   SP3917

★White Horse (01993) 891063

Village signposted off B4437 Charlbury–Woodstock; Stonesfield Riding; OX29 8EA Attractively upgraded little country pub; bar with stools and country-style chairs around solid tables on bare boards, woodburner in small brick fireplace, ales such as Little Ox and XT, six wines by the glass and well liked food including good Sun lunch, dining room has similar but more elegant furnishings; background music; children and dogs welcome, seats in neat walled garden, more in courtyard, handy for Oxfordshire Way long-distance path and the Roman Villa at North Leigh (EH); closed Sun evening, Mon and lunchtimes Tues-Thurs. *(Gerry and Pam Pollard, Maggie and Matthew Lyons)*

SUNNINGWELL   SP4900

Flowing Well (01865) 735846

Just N of Abingdon; OX13 6RB Timbered pub in former 19th-c rectory; well liked food including british tapas, range of burgers and gluten-free menu, a couple of Greene King ales and a guest, good choice of wines; free wi-fi; children welcome, dogs in bar, large heated raised terrace, more seats in garden with small well, open (and food) all day. *(Sally Wright)*

SUTTON COURTENAY   SU5094

Swan (01235) 847446

The Green; OX14 4AE Red-brick restaurant pub (calls itself a foodhouse and bar) overlooking green; unfussy décor with grey-painted woodwork and white walls, plain modern wooden tables on quarry tiles, log fire, good well presented food including tapas, blackboard specials and Fri evening fish, stools at bar serving a couple of real ales such as Timothy Taylors Landlord, friendly staff; background music; children welcome, picnic-sets out at front and in enclosed back garden with play area, open all day Sat, till 6pm Sun, closed Mon. *(John Pritchard)*

SWERFORD   SP3830

★Boxing Hare (01608) 683212

A361 Banbury–Chipping Norton; OX7 4AP Old stone dining pub with highly regarded food including signature dry-aged steaks, lunchtime set menu (Weds-Fri) and daily specials, friendly attentive service, well kept Hook Norton and Timothy Taylors, good wines by the glass and several whiskies/

gins such as local Cotswold, attractive split-level interior with rugs on bare boards, white-painted beams and log fires; children welcome, lovely country views from neat garden, closed Sun evening to Tues lunchtime. *(M J Winterton, Philippa Ward)*

SWINFORD
SP4308

Talbot (01865) 881348

B4044 just S of Eynsham; OX29 4BT Roomy and comfortable 17th-c beamed pub; well kept Arkells tapped from cooled casks and good choice of wines, enjoyable well priced pubby food from sandwiches and basket meals up including weekday deals, Sun carvery, long attractive flagstoned bar with some stripped stone, cheerful log-effect gas fire; charity quiz second Mon of month; children and dogs welcome, garden with decked area overlooking Wharf Stream, nice walk along lovely stretch of the Thames towpath, moorings quite nearby, 11 bedrooms, open all day. *(Richard Tilbrook)*

THAME
SP7105

Cross Keys (01844) 218202

Park Street/East Street; OX9 3HP Friendly one-bar 19th-c corner local; eight well kept ales including own Thame beers (not always available) and half a dozen ciders, no food apart from scotch eggs and occasional cheese and wine nights but can bring your own; Weds quiz and regular comedy nights; courtyard garden, open all day weekends. *(Charles Fraser)*

THAME
SP7005

James Figg (01844) 260166

Cornmarket; OX9 2BL Friendly coaching inn with four well kept ales such as Hook Norton, Purity and Sharps, Aspall's cider and ten wines by the glass, enjoyable good value food including pizzas and burgers, two-for-one deals Mon-Weds, log fire in brick fireplace with moose's head above, portrait of eponymous James Figg (local 18th-c boxer) and photos of more recent sporting champions, converted stables with own bar for music/functions; gets busier and noisier in the evening; children and dogs welcome, back beer garden, open (and food) all day, kitchen closes 6pm Sun. *(John Saville)*

THAME
SP7006

Thatch (01844) 214340

Lower High Street; OX9 2AA Characterful timbered and thatched 16th-c dining pub (Peach group); enjoyable food from deli boards to daily specials, good value weekday set menu till 6pm, well kept ales, nice wines and some interesting gins, friendly service, cosy bar and appealing collection of little higgledy-piggledy rooms, heavy beams, old quarry tiles, flagstones and double-sided inglenook, smart contemporary furnishings and bold paintwork; children welcome, prettily planted terraced garden with tables

under parasols, open (and food) all day. *(Andrew Chetty)*

THRUPP
SP4815

Boat (01865) 374279

Brown sign to pub off A4260 just N of Kidlington; OX5 1JY Attractive 16th-c stone pub set back from the southern Oxford Canal (moorings); modernised interior with low ceilings, bare boards and some ancient floor tiles, log fires and old coal stove, well priced home-made food including vegetarian options, specials and Sun carvery, three Greene King ales and a guest such as Timothy Taylors, decent wines, dining room with *Inspector Morse* photos (pub featured in the TV series); children and dogs welcome, disabled facilities, plenty of tables in fenced back garden, open (and food) all day weekends, gets busy in summer. *(Terry Davis)*

TOOT BALDON
SP5600

★ Mole (01865) 340001

Between A4074 and B480 SE of Oxford; OX44 9NG Light open-plan restaurant pub; very good if not cheap food (booking advised) including light lunch and weekly changing set menus, friendly attentive service, nice wines by the glass and a couple of well kept ales such as Hook Norton Hooky, leather sofas by bar, neat country furniture or more formal leather dining chairs in linked eating areas including conservatory, stripped 18th-c beams and big open fire; background music; children welcome, no dogs inside, lovely gardens, open all day. *(M A Borthwick)*

UFFINGTON
SU3089

Fox & Hounds (01367) 820680

High Street; SN7 7RP Welcoming beamed village pub; three changing ales and good home-made food from shortish menu including one or two specials, morning coffee and afternoon teas, friendly helpful staff, pubby furniture on quarry tiles or flagstones, woodburner in large stone fireplace, garden room extension with view of White Horse Hill; live music and quiz nights, free wi-fi; children and dogs welcome, picnic-sets outside (maybe summer pizzas Sun), handy for Tom Brown's School Museum, four ground-floor bedrooms, open all day, no food Sun evening, Mon. *(R K Phillips)*

WANTAGE
SU3987

Shoulder of Mutton (01235) 767158

Wallingford Street; OX12 8AX Renovated Victorian corner pub keeping character in bar, lounge and snug, ten well kept regularly changing beers, no food; quiz Mon, open mike Tues; seats in back courtyard, comfortable affordably priced bedrooms, open all day. *(John Phizackerley, Nick Hales)*

WARBOROUGH
SU6093

Six Bells (01865) 858265

The Green S; just E of A329, 4 miles N of Wallingford; OX10 7DN Thatched 16th-c pub opposite village cricket green (both used in filming *Midsomer Murders*); a couple of well kept Brakspears ales and good food (not Sun evening) from sharing boards to interesting specials, friendly staff, low beams and attractive country furnishings in small linked areas off bar, bare boards, stripped stone and big log fire; children and dogs (in bar) welcome, tables out in front and in pleasant orchard garden behind where aunt sally is played, open all day weekends, closed Mon. *(Paul Humphreys, John Pritchard)*

WARDINGTON   SP4946
Hare & Hounds (01295) 750645
A361 Banbury–Daventry; OX17 1SH
Comfortable and welcoming traditional village local, well kept Hook Norton ales and enjoyable home-made food including bargain OAP lunch, low-ceilinged bar leading to dining area, woodburner; quiz nights, darts and dominoes; children and dogs welcome, garden with play area and aunt sally, open all day Fri, Sat, till 8pm Sun. *(Mark Morgan)*

WATLINGTON   SU6994
Fat Fox (01491) 613040
Shireburn Street; OX49 5BU Centrally placed 17th-c inn; beamed bar with bare boards and open fire, four real ales including Brakspears and good choice of wines by the glass, well liked food from changing menu using local produce, friendly helpful staff, separate restaurant; free wi-fi; children and dogs (in bar) welcome, Ridgeway walks, nine bedrooms (seven in converted back barn), good breakfast, handy for M40 (junction 3), open all day. *(Gail and Frank Hackett)*

WESTON-ON-THE-GREEN SP5318
Chequers (01869) 351743
Handy for M40 junction 9, via A34; Northampton Road (B430); OX25 3QH
Extended thatched and beamed village pub with three areas off main bar; well kept Fullers ales, a dozen wines by the glass and decent range of gins from semicircular servery, good fairly priced food including sandwiches and snacks, chargrills and popular Sun carvery, breakfast from 10am, friendly attentive service, mix of traditional furniture on flagstone or parquet floors, some painted panelling; background music, children and dogs welcome, terrace and garden tables, open all day Sat, till 5pm Sun. *(Caroline and Peter Bryant)*

WHITCHURCH   SU6377
Ferry Boat (0118) 984 2161
High Street, near toll bridge; RG8 7DB
Welcoming comfortably updated 18th-c pub; airy bar with log fire and separate restaurant, good choice of home-made food including stone-baked pizzas, real ales such as Black Sheep and Timothy Taylors, several wines by the glass; background music, free wi-fi; well behaved children and dogs (in bar) welcome,

café-style seating in courtyard garden, closed Sun evening, Mon. *(Professor James Burke)*

WHITCHURCH   SU6377
Greyhound (0118) 343 3016
High Street, just over toll bridge from Pangbourne; RG8 7EL Attractive former ferryman's cottage with small knocked-together low-beamed rooms; four real ales including Black Sheep, St Austell and Sharps, good value pubby food, friendly efficient staff; quiz first and third Thurs of month; children and dogs welcome, small sheltered back garden, pretty village on Thames Path, open all day, no food Sun evening, Mon or Tues. *(Maddie Purvis)*

WITNEY   SP3509
Angel (01993) 703238
Market Square; OX28 6AL Unpretentious 17th-c town local with wide choice of enjoyable well priced food from sandwiches up, Marstons-related ales including a house beer from Wychwood and an occasional guest, efficient friendly service even when packed, beams and open fire; background music (live weekends), sports TVs; lovely hanging baskets, back terrace with smokers' shelter, parking nearby can be difficult, open (and food) all day. *(Margo and Derek Stapley)*

WITNEY   SP3509
Fleece (01993) 892270
Church Green; OX28 4AZ Smartly presented town pub (Peach group); wide choice of good often imaginative food from sandwiches and deli boards up, fixed-price menu too (Mon-Fri 12-6pm), Greene King and a couple of guests, decent coffee, friendly helpful service, leather armchairs on wood floors, restaurant; background and occasional live music, daily papers; children and dogs (in bar) welcome, café-style tables out at front overlooking town square, ten comfortable bedrooms, good breakfast, open (and food) all day from 9am. *(R K Phillips, Ian Phillips)*

WITNEY   SP3509
Hollybush (01993) 708073
Corn Street; OX28 6BT Popular modernised 18th-c pub under same ownership as the Horseshoes across the road; front bar with woodburner in big fireplace, settles and window seats, various dining areas off, good food from sandwiches and deli boards up, weekday lunchtime set menu and other offers, three well kept ales including a house beer from Greene King and nice selection of wines, efficient friendly staff; background music, free wi-fi; children and dogs welcome, open (and food) all day. *(Sandra and Nigel Brown)*

WITNEY   SP3510
Horseshoes (01993) 703086
Corn Street, junction with Holloway Road; OX28 6BS Attractive 16th-c stone

pub with good freshly made food (all day weekends) from pub favourites up including gluten-free choices, weekday set lunch and other deals, three changing ales and decent wines by the glass, heavy beams, stripped-stone walls, oak floors and log fires, separate back dining room; children and dogs welcome, a few seats out at front, tables on sunny paved terrace behind, open all day. *(Jim King)*

WOLVERCOTE   SP4909
Plough (01865) 556969
First Turn/Wolvercote Green; OX2 8AH Two connecting buildings with comfortably worn-in pubby rooms; armchairs and Victorian-style carpeted bays in main lounge, a well kept Greene King beer such as Hardys & Hansons and a couple of guests, traditional cider and decent wines by the glass, good value enjoyable usual food in flagstoned stables dining room and library (children allowed here), bargain OAP lunchtime menu, traditional snug, woodburner; dogs welcome in bar, disabled access/facilities, picnic-sets on part-decked terrace looking over rough meadow to canal and woods, open all day Sun. *(Tony and Jill Radnor)*

WOODSTOCK   SP4417
Black Prince (01993) 811530
Manor Road (A44 N); OX20 1XJ Old pub with single low-ceilinged bar; timbers, stripped stone and log fire, suit of armour, good value home-made food (not Sun evening) from sandwiches to specials, well kept St Austell and guests, friendly service; some live music, outside lavatories; children, walkers and dogs welcome, tables in pretty garden by small River Glyme, nearby right of way into Blenheim parkland, open all day. *(Len and Lilly Dowson)*

WOODSTOCK   SP4416
★ Kings Arms (01993) 813636
Market Street/Park Lane (A44); OX20 1SU Bustling town-centre hotel with unfussy bar attracting good mix of customers; appealing variety of old and new furnishings on stripped-wood floor, some black and white photographs and a modern woodburning stove, neat restaurant with high-backed leather chairs around mix of tables on black and white tiles, logs stacked either side of another woodburner, Fullers/Gales beers, a dozen wines by the glass and 35 malt whiskies, good food from

varied menu; background music, free wi-fi; children and dogs (in bar) welcome, café-style pavement tables, 15 bedrooms, open all day from 7am. *(David and Judy Robison, Mike Kavaney)*

WOODSTOCK   SP4416
Star (01993) 811373
Market Place; OX20 1TA Sizeable bustling old inn; airy front part with bare boards and big windows, lower ceilinged area with pale stripped stone and comfortable seats on carpet, back part has a profusion of beams, coal-effect stove and an unusually wide antique settle; enjoyable food from varied menu catering for special diets, well kept ales such as Bombardier, Courage Directors and Eagle IPA, good choice of wines by the glass, friendly helpful staff; background music, Tues quiz; sheltered flagstoned courtyard behind, more seats out in front, four bedrooms, open (and food) all day from 8am. *(Richard Tilbrook)*

WOOLSTONE   SU2987
White Horse (01367) 820726
Off B4507; SN7 7QL Appealing partly thatched black and white pub with prominent gables and latticed windows; stone flooring and two open fires in spacious beamed bar, Arkells ales and enjoyable food from regularly changing menus, wood-fired pizzas (Weds-Sat), friendly service, restaurant; well behaved children and dogs allowed, plenty of seats in front and back gardens, secluded interesting village handy for White Horse and Ridgeway (enjoyable circular walk), six bedrooms, open all day. *(Ian Phillips, Peter Meister)*

WYTHAM   SP4708
White Hart (01865) 244372
Off A34 Oxford ring road; OX2 8QA Renovated 16th-c country dining pub in unspoilt preserved village; several areas with log fires including converted stables, some settles, handsome panelling and uneven flagstones, good food (not Sun evening) from lunchtime sandwiches to blackboard specials, also vegetarian/vegan choices, cosy bar with well kept Wadworths ales and lots of wines by the glass, conservatory; children and dogs welcome, courtyard tables, evening barbecues Fri and Sat (weather permitting), open all day (till 8pm Sun). *(S F Parrinder, Mark Butcher)*

Shropshire

KEY	★ Star Pub	🍴 Top Quality Food	🍺 Great Beer
🍷 Good Wines	£ Bargain Meals	🛏 Good Bedrooms	🍴 Serves Food

BASCHURCH
SJ4221 Map 7

New Inn 🍴 🍺

(01939) 260335 – www.newinnbaschurch.com

Church Road; SY4 2EF

A good mix of customers for bustling village pub with several beers and highly popular food; seats in attractive garden

The appealing food in this handsome whitewashed pub is one of its major strengths, of course, but they also keep five real ales, and the atmosphere is friendly and informal. There are several attractively refurbished interlinked rooms, and the chatty bar at one end has a woodburning stove, a leather sofa and armchairs, traditional wooden chairs and stools around tables on quarry tiles and bare boards, and lots of wall prints. Cheerful staff serve Hobsons Best Bitter, Salopian Shropshire Gold, Stonehouse Station Bitter and Wye Valley Butty Bach on handpump, ten wines by the glass and 20 gins. The two heavily beamed dining rooms have logs piled into brick fireplaces, high-backed leather-seated chairs around more light tables and candles in glass jars and lanterns; the table flowers are pretty. There are seats outside in a well tended garden. Partial disabled access.

🍴 Imaginative food includes sandwiches, gin-cured salmon with compressed cucumber, tonic gel and dill mayonnaise, smoked haddock arancini with wild garlic mayonnaise, stir-fried vegetables on a sizzling skillet with teriyaki and wild basmati rice, chicken breast with smoked bacon, tomato, mushroom and thyme sauce, a pie of the day, indian-spiced cod loin with curried mussels, coconut and coriander, roasted lamb rump with minted lamb bonbon and salsa verde, and puddings such as lavender crème brûlée and cherry and pistachio rolled pavlova with chantilly cream. *Benchmark main dish: steak in ale pie £12.50. Two-course evening meal £20.00.*

Free house ~ Licensees Graham and Clare Jenkins ~ Real ale ~ Open 12-3, 6-11; 12-11 Fri, Sat; 12-7 Sun; closed Mon except bank holidays ~ Bar food 12-3, 6-9; 12-9 Sat; 12-5 Sun ~ Restaurant ~ Children welcome ~ Dogs allowed in bar ~ Wi-fi *Recommended by Charles Welch, Julian Richardson, Colin and Daniel Gibbs, Jacqui and Alan Swan, Caroline and Peter Bryant, Nick Higgins*

BRIDGNORTH
SO7192 Map 4

Old Castle 🍺 £

(01746) 711420 – www.oldcastlebridgnorth.co.uk

West Castle Street; WV16 4AB

Cheerful town pub, relaxed and friendly, with fair value pubby food, well kept ales and good-sized suntrap terrace

It's so popular here that you need to book a table in advance to enjoy the generously served food. There's an open-plan low-beamed bar of proper character with tiles and bare boards, cushioned wall banquettes and settles around cast-iron-framed tables, and bar stools arranged along the counter where the friendly landlord and his helpful staff serve Hobsons Town Crier, Sharps Doom Bar and Wye Valley Butty Bach and HPA on handpump. A back conservatory extension has darts, pool and a games machine; background music and big-screen TV for sports events. A big plus is the sunny back terrace with picnic-sets, lovely hanging baskets, large pots of flowers, shrub borders and decking at the far end that gives an elevated view over the west side of town; children's playthings. Wheelchair access through the front door to the top dining area; bar access through a side passage and door into their glass-roofed courtyard. No disabled loos. Do walk up the street to see the ruined castle – its 20-metre Norman tower tilts at such an extraordinary angle that it makes the Leaning Tower of Pisa look like a model of rectitude.

Reasonably priced traditional food includes sandwiches and baguettes, southern fried chicken dippers with barbecue sauce, devilled whitebait, sweet potato, red pepper and spinach lasagne, creamy fish and prawn pie topped with cheesy mash, cajun chicken burger with onion rings, relish and chips, steak and stilton pie, mixed grill, and puddings. *Benchmark main dish: lamb shank with mash and lamb gravy £11.25. Two-course evening meal £19.00.*

Punch ~ Tenant Bryn Charles Masterman ~ Real ale ~ Open 11.30-11; 11.30-10.30 Sun ~ Bar food 12-3, 6.30-8.30 ~ Children welcome ~ Dogs welcome ~ Wi-fi *Recommended by Dave Braisted, John Harris, David and Leone Lawson, Julian Richardson, Rona Mackinlay, Geoff and Ann Marston*

CARDINGTON
Royal Oak

SO5095   Map 4

(01694) 771266 – www.at-the-oak.com
Village signposted off B4371 Church Stretton–Much Wenlock, pub behind church; also reached via narrow lanes from A49; SY6 7JZ

Heaps of character in well run and friendly rural pub with seasonal bar food and real ales

The county's oldest pub, this place was first licensed in the 15th c. It's in a delightful rural setting where little has changed over the centuries and our readers are as fond of the place as the chatty locals are. The rambling, low-beamed traditional bar has a roaring winter log fire, a cauldron, black kettle and pewter jugs in a vast inglenook fireplace, aged standing timbers from a knocked-through wall, and red and green tapestry seats solidly capped in elm; board games and dominoes (they have two pub teams). Ludlow Best and Sharps Doom Bar with guests such as Purple Moose Elderflower Ale and Three Tuns XXX on handpump, eight wines by the glass, ten gins, several malt whiskies and farm cider. A comfortable dining area has exposed old beams and studwork. This is a glorious spot for walks, such as the one up to the summit of Caer Caradoc, a couple of miles to the west (ask for directions at the pub), and the front courtyard takes full advantage of its beautiful position.

Proper home cooking using local produce from a seasonal menu includes baguettes, venison liver and chilli pâté, chicken dumplings with hoisin dip, wild mushroom broth with udon noodles and asian vegetables, southern-fried chicken with barbecue ribs, corn on the cob, coleslaw and chips, a choice of curry, whole plaice with roast cauliflower and almond beurre noisette, rosemary and garlic lamb rump with red wine, redcurrant and rosemary sauce, steaks with a choice of sauce, and puddings. *Benchmark main dish: fidget pie (gammon cooked with spiced cider and apples) £12.95. Two-course evening meal £18.00.*

Free house ~ Licensees Steve and Eira Oldham ~ Real ale ~ Open 12-2.30, 6-11; 12-11 Sat; 12-9 Sun (12-4 in winter); closed Mon except bank holiday lunchtime ~ Bar food 12-2.30, 6-9 ~ Restaurant ~ Children welcome ~ Dogs allowed in bar ~ Wi-fi *Recommended by M G Hart, Celia and Andrew King, Valerie and Gordon Wauton, Mick Allen, Roger and Anne Newbury*

 CHETWYND ASTON   SJ7517   Map 7

Fox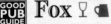

(01952) 815940 – www.brunningandprice.co.uk/fox
Village signposted off A41 and A518 just S of Newport; TF10 9LQ

Civilised dining pub with generous helpings of well liked food and a fine array of drinks served by ever attentive staff

In warm weather, the large garden behind this well run pub is quite lovely, with a sunny terrace, picnic-sets tucked into the shade of mature trees and extensive views across quiet country fields; there's a play tractor and swings for children. Inside, it's large and spreading, but with cosy corners too. The linked rooms (one with a broad arched ceiling) have plenty of tables of varying shapes and sizes and a diversity of comfortable chairs on parquet, polished boards or attractive floor tiles. Masses of prints and photographs line the walls, there are three open fires and big windows and careful lighting contribute to the relaxed atmosphere; board games. Bar stools line the long bar counter where helpful, polite staff keep some 20 wines by the glass, 60 rums, 130 gins, 80 malt whiskies, two farm ciders and Phoenix Brunning & Price Original, Weetwood Cheshire Cat, Woods Shropshire Lad and three quickly changing guests such as Clun Pale Ale, Tatton Blonde and Titanic Cappuccino Stout on handpump. Good disabled access.

A wide choice of highly rated food includes sandwiches, scallops with cauliflower purée, black pudding fritters and apple dressing, sticky chicken wings, chickpea, cauliflower and sweet potato curry with tempura okra, venison and juniper meatballs with pasta and red wine sauce, pork and leek sausages with mash and onion gravy, chicken breast with wild mushroom and chestnut cream sauce and dauphinoise potatoes, sea bass with crab and chive risotto and pea and ham velouté, and puddings such as lemon posset with ginger crumb and honey-roast fig and chocolate brownie with chocolate fudge sauce. *Benchmark main dish: beer-battered fish and chips £13.75. Two-course evening meal £20.00.*

Brunning & Price ~ Manager Samantha Forrest ~ Real ale ~ Open 11-11; 11-10.30 Sun ~ Bar food 12-9.30; 12-10 Fri, Sat; 12-9 Sun ~ Children welcome ~ Dogs allowed in bar ~ Wi-fi *Recommended by Andrew Lawson, Angela and Steve Heard, Trevor and Michele Street, Monty Green, Phoebe Peacock, Tony Smaithe, John and Mary Warner*

 CLUN   SO3080   Map 6

White Horse £

(01588) 418139 – www.whi-clun.co.uk
The Square; SY7 8JA

Bustling local with own-brewed and guest ales and good value traditional food; bedrooms

If you stay in the quiet and comfortable bedrooms here, you can make the best of their own-brewed beers. Served by attentive staff, these include well kept Clun Citadel, Loophole, Pale Ale and Solar, with guests such as Hobsons Best Bitter and Wye Valley Butty Bach on handpump; they also offer five wines by the glass, half a dozen malt whiskies and two farm ciders. The low-beamed front bar is cosy and friendly and warmed in winter by an inglenook woodburning stove; from here, a door leads into a separate little dining room with a rare plank and muntin screen. In the games room at the back you'll find a TV, games machine, darts, pool, juke box and board games. There's also a small garden.

Fairly priced, honest food includes baguettes, mackerel pâté, chilli chicken stir-fry, mushroom stroganoff, pork and cider casserole, chicken korma with rice, liver and bacon with mustard mash, salmon in butter and tarragon sauce, burger with toppings, onion rings and chips, gammon with egg and pineapple, sea bass fillet with tomato and basil sauce, 28-day hung rib-eye steak with a choice of sauce, and puddings. *Benchmark main dish: steak in ale pie £10.25. Two-course evening meal £19.00.*

Own brew ~ Licensee Jack Limond ~ Real ale ~ Open 11-11; 11am-midnight Sat ~ Bar food 12-3, 6-9 ~ Restaurant ~ Children welcome ~ Dogs welcome ~ Wi-fi ~ Open mike night alternate Mon evenings, band most Fri evenings ~ Bedrooms: £55/£75
Recommended by Peter Pilbeam, Daniel King, John and Sharon Hancock, Lance and Sarah Milligan, Trish and Karl Soloman

COALPORT
Woodbridge 🍷 🛏

SJ7002   Map 4

(01952) 882054 – www.brunningandprice.co.uk/woodbridge
Village signposted off A442 1.5 miles S of A4169 Telford roundabout; down in valley, turn left across narrow bridge into Coalport Road, pub immediately left; TF8 7JF

Superb Ironbridge Gorge site for extensive, handsomely reworked pub, an all-round success

Thanks to its interesting food and a wide choice of drinks, our readers visit this attractively placed pub on a regular basis. The spreading series of linked rooms are comfortable and civilised with log fires and Coalport-style stoves, rugs on broad boards as well as tiles or carpet, black beams in the central part and plenty of polished tables and cosy armchair corners. A mass of mainly 18th- and 19th-c prints, often of local scenes, line the walls and are well worth a look. Quick, friendly staff serve Phoenix Brunning & Price Original and guests such as Enville Ale, Gorgeous Beer Blonde, Timothy Taylors Boltmaker and Weetwood Cheshire Cat on handpump, ten wines by the glass, 50 malt whiskies and 30 gins; background music and board games. Named after the original wooden bridge that once connected the pub to the village, the pub is on the bank of the River Severn, with tables and chairs on a big deck looking over the water and picnic-sets on grass.

High quality food includes sandwiches, box camembert with chutney, smoked mackerel terrine with preserved lemon, samphire and cucumber vinaigrette, cauliflower, chickpea and spinach dhal with coriander rice and tomato, onion and coriander salad, cumberland sausages with mash and onion gravy, steak and kidney suet pudding, hake fillet with caper gnocchi, queen scallops, samphire and lemon gel, garlic-roasted chicken breast with arrabiata pasta, mozzarella, olives, parmesan and basil, crispy beef salad with sweet chilli sauce and roasted cashew nuts, and puddings such as dark chocolate and orange tart with passion-fruit sorbet and crème brûlée. *Benchmark main dish: braised lamb shoulder with vegetables and gravy £17.95. Two-course evening meal £22.00.*

Brunning & Price ~ Manager Vrata Krist ~ Real ale ~ Open 11.30-11; 11.30am-midnight Sat; 11.30-10.30 Sun ~ Bar food 12-9.30; 12-10 Fri, Sat; 12-9 Sun ~ Restaurant ~ Children welcome ~ Dogs allowed in bar ~ Wi-fi *Recommended by Michael Sargent, Alfie Bayliss, Dan and Nicki Barton, Susan and John Douglas, Richard and Tessa Ibbot, Max Simons, James and Sylvia Hewitt*

IRONBRIDGE

SJ6703   Map 4

Golden Ball ✏

(01952) 432179 – www.goldenballironbridge.co.uk

Brown sign to pub off Madeley Road (B4373) above village centre – pub behind
Horse & Jockey, car park beyond on left; TF8 7BA

Low-beamed, friendly inn with popular food and drink; bedrooms

Our readers enjoy this partly Elizabethan pub, tucked away in a small hamlet of other ancient buildings. It's a nice place to stay – bedrooms are comfortable and breakfasts are good. The bar has worn floorboards, red-cushioned pews, one or two black beams and a woodburning stove. Black Sheep Monty Python's Holy Grail, Hobsons Town Crier and Wye Valley HPA on handpump, quite a few belgian bottled ales, six wines by the glass, several gins and whiskies and a farm cider; background music, darts and TV. A pretty fairy-lit pergola path leads to the door and a sheltered side courtyard has tables under parasols. You can walk from here down to the River Severn and beyond, but it's rather steep getting back up.

🍴 Tasty food includes lunchtime sandwiches and baguettes, baked camembert with home-made chutney, confit duck leg with orange salad, greek salad with feta cheese, chicken with pineapple, mozzarella and tomato sauce, tuna steak with crushed new potatoes and caper butter, pork belly with celeriac mash, honey-roasted parsnips and cider and sage sauce, sirloin steak with brandy and cracked peppercorn sauce, and puddings such as lemon meringue roulade and banana and walnut sponge with custard. *Benchmark main dish: steak in ale pie £10.95. Two-course evening meal £20.00.*

Enterprise ~ Lease Jessica Janke ~ Real ale ~ Open 12-11; 12-11.30 Sat; 12-10.30 Sun ~ Bar food 12-8.45; 12-7 Sun ~ Restaurant ~ Children welcome ~ Dogs allowed in bar and bedrooms ~ Wi-fi ~ Open mike second Sun of month, live band monthly, quiz every two weeks ~ Bedrooms: £60/£70 *Recommended by Ian Herdman, John and Lorna Chew, Alexandra and Tim Fledgling, Dr and Mrs A K Clarke, Belinda Stamp*

LUDLOW

SO5174   Map 6

Charlton Arms 🍺 ✏

(01584) 872813 – www.thecharltonarms.co.uk

Ludford Bridge, B4361 Overton Road; SY8 1PJ

Fine position for bustling pub with plenty of space for both drinking and dining and extensive terraces looking over the river; bedrooms

It's just a short walk from the town centre to this popular pub, but it's best to arrive early if you want a seat on the balcony overlooking the River Teme and the massive medieval bridge. The character bar has proper pubby tables and chairs on tiled and bricked floors, gluggle jugs along the gantry, a double-sided woodburner, and stools against the hop-hung counter where friendly staff serve Hobsons Best Bitter, Ludlow Gold and Stairway and Wye Valley Butty Bach and HPA on handpump, 15 wines by the glass and a farm cider. The two rooms of the lounge (sharing a two-way woodburning stove) are comfortable and chatty with tub chairs, armchairs and high-backed black leather seats on pale wooden floors. The dining room looks over the fine bridge; background music and board games. Bedrooms are well equipped and cosy and have views of the water.

🍴 Interesting food includes lunchtime sandwiches, fish soup with rouille, gruyère and croutons, duck liver parfait with onion marmalade, wild mushroom and spinach tagliatelle with parmesan, dressed Cromer crab with lemon mayonnaise, burger with toppings, barbecue sauce and skinny fries, chicken ballotine with wild mushrooms and tarragon, fondant potato and watercress velouté, hake fillet with saffron mash and asparagus and mussel broth, rib-eye steak with bone marrow butter and sauce diane, and puddings such as vanilla crème brûlée and chocolate fondant with mint chocolate ice-cream. *Benchmark main dish: gluten-free beer-battered haddock and chips £13.00. Two-course evening meal £21.00.*

Free house ~ Licensee Cedric Bosi ~ Real ale ~ Open 11am-11.30pm; 11am-midnight Sat; 12-10.30 Sun ~ Bar food 12-2.30, 6-8.30 ~ Restaurant ~ Children welcome ~ Dogs allowed in bar and bedrooms ~ Wi-fi ~ Bedrooms: £95/£100 *Recommended by Katherine and Hugh Markham, Alison and Dan Richardson, Alan and Linda Blackmore, Frances and Hamish Porter, M and GR*

LUDLOW
SO5174 Map 4

Church Inn 🍺 🛏

(01584) 874034 – www.thechurchinn.com

Church Street, behind Butter Cross; SY8 1AW

Splendid range of real ales in character town-centre pub; bedrooms

Four comfortable rooms with balconies and church views are now available here, and they also have nine luxury rooms in their nearby Town House. The ground floor of the pub is divided into three appealingly decorated areas, with hops hanging from heavy beams and comfortable banquettes in cosy alcoves; the pulpit and pews come from a local church. A long central area has a fine stone fireplace, a chess table and board games, while, upstairs, the civilised lounge bar has vaulted ceilings and gives good views of St Laurence's church and the surrounding countryside. Friendly staff serve a fine range of real ales that includes Hobsons Best Bitter, Ludlow Boiling Well, Gold and Stairway, Salopian Darwins Origin and a rotating guest on handpump, 12 wines by the glass, 25 gins and a farm cider; background music. There are picnic-sets in the back garden (which they share with the church).

Food is very good and includes lunchtime sandwiches, deep-fried whitebait with aioli, fish and shellfish soup with crème fraîche and croutons, sweet potato and black bean lasagne, chicken and tarragon risotto, burger with toppings, rhubarb ketchup and skinny fries, beer-battered haddock and chips, rare-breed pork chop with savoy cabbage and bacon, 8oz rump steak with onion rings and peppercorn sauce, and puddings such as pear and almond tart with pear sorbet and warm chocolate fondant with toffee apple ice-cream. *Benchmark main dish: pie of the day £11.00. Two-course evening meal £20.00.*

Free house ~ Licensee Matt Tommey ~ Real ale ~ Open 11-11; 11am-midnight Sat; 12-10.30 Sun ~ Bar food 12-3, 6-9 (8.30 Sun) ~ Restaurant ~ Children welcome ~ Dogs allowed in bar ~ Wi-fi ~ Bedrooms: /£120 *Recommended by Susie and Spencer Gray, Adam and Natalie Davis, Christopher May, Shona and Jimmy McDuff, Sam Cole, Dan and Belinda Smallbone, Darrell Barton*

MAESBURY MARSH
SJ3125 Map 6

Navigation

(01691) 672958 – www.thenavigation.co.uk

Follow Maesbury Road off A483 S of Oswestry; by canal bridge; SY10 8JB

Friendly canalside pub with cosy bar and local seasonal produce in a choice of dining areas

There's a proper community feel in this traditional pub overlooking the Montgomery Canal, and all customers are made to feel genuinely welcome. The old-fashioned, quarry-tiled bar on the left has squishy brown leather sofas by an old-style black range, upholstered cask seats around three small tables, and dozens of wrist- and pocket-watches hanging from the beams. A couple of steps lead up beyond a balustrade to a carpeted area, with armchairs and sofas around low tables, and a piano (which does get used); off to the left is a dining area with paintings by local artists. The main beamed dining room, with some stripped stone, is beyond another small bar with a coal-effect gas fire, and an amazing row of cushioned carved choir stalls complete with misericord seats. Joules Slumbering Monk and Stonehouse Cambrian Gold and Station Bitter on handpump, 11 wines by the glass, nine malt whiskies (including one from Wales) and a farm cider (in summer); quiet background music and board games. There are picnic-sets beside the water. The hands-on licensees also run a book exchange and offer a two-pint takeaway service.

Using seasonal, local and free-range produce, the pleasing food includes lunchtime sandwiches, baked camembert with roasted garlic and cranberry sauce, duck rillettes with gherkins and pickled onions, risotto of the day, free-range ham with sautéed potatoes and wholegrain mustard sauce, trio of local sausages with mash, braised red cabbage and gravy, chicken breast wrapped in bacon with sautéed leeks and mushrooms and a choice of sauce, duck with crispy kale and passion fruit, maple syrup and whisky sauce, and puddings such as pear and plum crumble with apple sorbet and crème caramel with dark chocolate mousse. *Benchmark main dish: crispy pork belly with creamed spinach, black pudding mash and apple purée £14.95. Two-course evening meal £21.00.*

Free house ~ Licensees Brent Ellis and Mark Baggett ~ Real ale ~ Open 12-2, 6-11; 12-6 Sun; closed Sun evening, all day Mon, lunchtime Tue; first two weeks Jan ~ Bar food 12-2, 6-8.30; 12-2 Sun ~ Restaurant ~ Children welcome ~ Dogs allowed in bar ~ Wi-fi
Recommended by Gordon and Patricia Gorringe, Catherine and Daniel King, Trish and Karl Soloman, Jill and Hugh Bennett, Sabina and Gerald Grimshaw

NEENTON
SO6387 Map 4
Pheasant ✪◨⌂

(01746) 787955 – www.pheasantatneenton.co.uk
B4364 Bridgnorth–Ludlow; WV16 6RJ

Renovated village inn with a traditionally furnished bar and dining room, local ales and good food; seats in orchard garden

Although this bustling pub is owned and run by the community there's a genuine welcome for visitors as well. The cosy front bar has leather sofas and armchairs by a woodburning stove, rugs on tiles and stools by the counter where friendly, helpful staff serve Enville Ale, Hop & Stagger Simpsons Original, Hobsons Twisted Spire and Wye Valley HPA on handpump, 14 wines by the glass, quite a few gins and farm cider; background music, darts and board games. The airy dining room is in an oak-framed extension at the back with a homely medley of cushioned chairs and wooden tables on bare boards. There are picnic-sets on the lawn and under trees in the orchard and a children's play area; boules. The three simply furnished bedrooms are comfortable, and breakfasts are first class. Disabled access. The village is surrounded by very pretty hilly countryside, so you'll find plenty of good walks to explore.

Highly enjoyable food includes mackerel confit with cucumber tartare and lemon sherbet dressing, 30-hour braised oxtail ravioli with beef broth and goats cheese, butternut squash with red pepper and pea risotto, ricotta, crispy shallots and herb oil, venison haunch with celeriac purée, damson jus, rosemary pesto and fondant potato, interesting evening specials such as wild mushroom risotto with a duck egg yolk, parmesan and truffle oil, pork fillet with black pudding, peaches and mustard, hake fillet with confit chicken wing, wild mushrooms, samphire and chicken butter sauce, and puddings such as orange marmalade gin-soaked savarin with chantilly cream and fresh fruit and black forest cheesecake with chocolate sauce and clotted cream ice-cream. *Benchmark main dish: steak in ale pie £14.95. Two-course evening meal £22.00.*

Free house ~ Licensees Mark Harris and Sarah Cowley ~ Real ale ~ Open 12-3, 6-11; 12-11 Fri, Sat; 12-8 Sun ~ Bar food 12-2.30, 6-9; 12-4 Sun ~ Restaurant ~ Children welcome ~ Dogs allowed in bar and bedrooms ~ Wi-fi ~ Bedrooms: /£90 *Recommended by Alun Jones, Celia and Andrew King, Alexandra and Tim Fledgling*

NORTON
SJ7200 Map 4
Hundred House 🍷 🛏

(01952) 730353 – www.hundredhouse.co.uk
A442 Telford–Bridgnorth; TF11 9EE

Family-run inn with rambling rooms, open fires, a very good choice of drinks and rewarding food; large, comfortable bedrooms

Try to come in summer when you can visit the lovely garden at the back of this well run inn: it boasts old-fashioned roses, herbaceous plants and a big working herb garden (with around 50 varieties). Inside, the rambling bar rooms have a variety of interesting chairs and settles with long colourful patchwork leather cushions around sewing machine tables, beams hung with hops and huge bunches of dried flowers and herbs and pretty fresh flowers. Winter log fires in handsome fireplaces include one with a large Jacobean arch and old black cooking pots. Steps lead up past a little balustrade to a partly panelled eating area, where the stripped brickwork looks older than it does elsewhere. Hobsons Mild, Sadlers Hop Bomb and Peaky Blinder, Three Tuns 1642 Bitter and Woods Shropshire Lass on handpump, 18 wines by the glass, a dozen malt whiskies, a growing choice of gins and a farm cider; background music and TV. Bedrooms feature antique four-posters or half-testers, Victorian-style baths and rain showers, and their trademark velvet-cushioned swing. Disabled access.

Well regarded food includes sandwiches, open ravioli with smoked haddock, creamed leek, carrot and ginger sauce and pickled radish, black pudding, apple and chorizo stack with smoked cheese sauce and crispy onion rings, sweet potato and black bean empanada with grilled courgettes and peppers and spicy lime marinade, chicken breast with mini kiev and smoked bacon and potato terrine, 10oz local sirloin steak with herbed wedges, cream cheese and garlic and chive mushrooms, and puddings such as treacle tart with custard and coconut and raspberry macaroon with raspberry ripple ice-cream. *Benchmark main dish: lamb cutlets with lamb sausage roll, minted crushed peas and rosemary jus £20.00. Two-course evening meal £24.00.*

Free house ~ Licensees Henry, Stuart and David Phillips ~ Real ale ~ Open 8am-11pm; 8am-10pm Sun ~ Bar food 12-2.30, 6-9; 12-8 Sun ~ Restaurant ~ Children welcome ~ Dogs allowed in bar and bedrooms ~ Wi-fi ~ Bedrooms: £75/£85 *Recommended by Peter and Emma Kelly, Chloe and Tim Hodge, Frank and Marcia Pelling, Jill and Hugh Bennett, Charlie May, Alfie Bayliss*

'Children welcome' means the pub says it lets children inside without any special restriction. If it allows them in, but to restricted areas such as an eating area or family room, we specify this. Places with separate restaurants often let children use them, and hotels usually let children into public areas such as lounges. Some pubs impose an evening time limit – let us know if you find one earlier than 9pm.

SHIPLEY
SO8095 Map 4

Inn at Shipley ☪ ◧

(01902) 701639 – www.brunningandprice.co.uk/innatshipley

Bridgnorth Road; A454 W of Wolverhampton; WV6 7EQ

Light and airy country pub – a good all-rounder

A handsome old pub, this has rambling rooms with a chatty, informal atmosphere and several woodburning stoves and log fires that surround the central bar: one in a big inglenook in a cosy, traditionally tiled black-beamed end room and another by a welcoming set of wing and other leather armchairs. All sorts of dining chairs are grouped around a variety of tables on rugs or polished floorboards, attractive pictures are hung frame-to-frame and big windows let in plenty of daylight; church candles, careful spotlighting and chandeliers add atmosphere. The various areas are interconnected but manage to also feel distinct and individual; upstairs is a separate private dining room. Phoenix Brunning & Price Original, Enville Ale and Wye Valley HPA plus three rotating guests such as Hobsons Mild, Rowton Meteorite and Three Tuns Best on handpump, 17 wines by the glass, 80 malt whiskies, 70 gins and two farm ciders; good, neatly dressed staff, background music and board games. There are plenty of sturdy tables outside, some on a sizeable terrace with a side awning, others by weeping willows on the main lawn behind the car park, more on smaller lawns around the building.

 A wide choice of interesting food includes sandwiches, chicken liver pâté with plum and ginger chutney, smoked salmon with fennel yoghurt, pickled vegetable salad and crispy onions, cauliflower, sweet potato and chickpea curry with peshwari rice, naan and mint yoghurt, honey-roast ham and eggs, chicken, ham and leek pie, sea bream with lemon and dill potato cake, poached leeks and watercress velouté, ginger beer-glazed pork belly with black pudding croquette, apple and vanilla ketchup and crackling, and puddings such as hot waffle with boozy cherry compote, roasted plums and cherry bakewell ice-cream and triple chocolate brownie with chocolate sauce and white chocolate ice-cream. *Benchmark main dish: slow-braised lamb shoulder with dauphinoise potatoes and red wine and rosemary jus £17.95. Two-course evening meal £21.00.*

Brunning & Price ~ Manager Oliver Parrish ~ Real ale ~ Open 10.30am-11pm; 10.30-10.30 Sun ~ Bar food 12-9.30; 12-10 Fri, Sat; 12-9 Sun ~ Restaurant ~ Children welcome ~ Dogs allowed in bar ~ Wi-fi *Recommended by Alexandra and Tim Fledgling, David and Leone Lawson, Mark Hamill, Edward Nile, Sandra and Michael Smith, Patricia Healey*

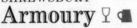

SHREWSBURY
SJ4812 Map 6

Armoury ☪ ◧

(01743) 340525 – www.brunningandprice.co.uk/armoury

Victoria Quay, Victoria Avenue; SY1 1HH

Vibrant atmosphere in interestingly converted riverside warehouse with tempting all-day food

In summer, the massive red-brick frontage of this 18th-c former warehouse looks fetching, with seats and tables under the lovely hanging baskets. Once inside, it's pretty impressive with spacious open-plan rooms and long runs of big arched windows looking across the broad River Severn at the back. But despite its size the pub has a personal feel, helped by the eclectic décor, furniture layout and cheerful bustle. A mix of wood tables and chairs are grouped on stripped-wood floors, the huge brick walls display floor-to-ceiling books or masses of old prints mounted edge-to-edge, and there's a grand stone fireplace at one end. Colonial-style fans whirr away on the ceilings, which are supported by green-painted columns, and small wall-mounted glass cabinets display smokers' pipes. Phoenix Brunning & Price Original, Salopian Oracle and Three Tuns XXX on handpump plus guests from breweries such as Hobsons, Purple Moose, Stonehouse and Woods, 19 wines by the glass, 100 malt whiskies, 84 gins, lots of rums and vodkas, a variety of brandies and a farm cider. The pub doesn't have its own car park, but there are plenty of parking places nearby. Dogs are welcome except after 7pm on Friday and Saturday evenings.

Top quality food includes sandwiches, crispy salt and pepper squid with chilli and mango dip, garlic and rosemary-studded baked camembert with fruit chutney, beetroot, soya and quinoa burger with guacamole, red cabbage slaw and skinny fries, pork and leek sausages with mash and onion gravy, spinach and ricotta-stuffed chicken breast with parmesan and thyme polenta and tomato sauce, sea bass fillets with olive-crushed potato and mediterranean vegetable ragoût, and puddings such as lemon and pomegranate cheesecake with orange sorbet and warm chocolate brownie with chocolate sauce. *Benchmark main dish: steak in ale pie £14.50. Two-course evening meal £21.00.*

Brunning & Price ~ Manager Emily Periam ~ Real ale ~ Open 10am-11pm; 10am-midnight Fri, Sat; 10am-10.30pm Sun ~ Bar food 12-9.30; 12-10 Fri, Sat; 12-9 Sun ~ Children welcome but not Fri, Sat evenings ~ Dogs allowed in bar ~ Wi-fi *Recommended by Christine and Tony Garrett, Ian Duncan, Richard Tilbrook, Julie Swift, Christopher Mannings, Jack and Hilary Burton, Sandra and Nigel Brown*

SHREWSBURY
Lion & Pheasant 🎯 🍷 🛏

SJ4912   Map 6

(01743) 770345 – www.lionandpheasant.co.uk
Follow City Centre signposts across the English Bridge; SY1 1XJ

Shropshire Dining Pub of the Year

Stylish bar and upstairs restaurant in comfortable, neatly updated and well placed inn; bedrooms

This is a lovely town-centre inn with a gently civilised but welcoming atmosphere, excellent food, a fine choice of drinks and highly regarded bedrooms. The décor throughout is most appealing and cleverly combines original 16th-c features with more contemporary touches. The big-windowed bar consists of three linked levels, the lowest of which has armchairs on dark flagstones by a big inglenook; elsewhere, there's a cushioned settee or two, but most of the seats are at sturdy stripped tables on dark floorboards. A few modern paintings, plentiful flowers and church candles brighten up the restrained cream and grey décor, as do the friendly staff and background music. Hobsons Old Prickly, Salopian Shropshire Gold and Wye Valley Butty Bach on handpump, 14 wines by the glass and farm cider. Off quite a warren of corridors, the restaurant is in the older back part of the building with beams and timbering (you can eat from the restaurant menu in the bar too). Outside, there are seats and tables under parasols with olive trees and flowering pots dotted about. A splendid place to stay, the bedrooms are pretty, well equipped and comfortable and breakfasts are good; some rooms offer glimpses of the River Severn below the nearby English Bridge.

Delicious food includes lunchtime sandwiches (until 5pm), chicken and duck liver parfait with red onion jam, brown crab bavarois with white crab, pickled apple, dashi jelly and coriander, sharing boards, chickpea and spinach curry with red pepper and wild rice, local sausages with mash and onion gravy, brill with crispy chicken wings, baby leeks, jerusalem artichoke and chicken jus, duck breast with confit duck and date rillettes, roasted pear, dauphinoise potatoes and port jus, pigeon pithivier with roast onion purée, spinach, carrot, kale and jus, and puddings such as passion-fruit délice with lime and chilli curd and coconut sorbet and coffee pannacotta with dark chocolate ganache, milk ice-cream and caramel. *Benchmark main dish: 21-day aged sirloin steak with mushroom duxelles, parmesan and truffle salad and a choice of sauce £23.00. Two-course evening meal £23.00.*

Free house ~ Licensee Jim Littler ~ Real ale ~ Open 10.30am-11pm; 10.30am-midnight Sat ~ Bar food 12-3, 6-9; 12-9.30 Sat; 12-4, 6-8 Sun ~ Restaurant ~ Children welcome ~ Wi-fi ~ Live music Fri evening ~ Bedrooms: £105/£120 *Recommended by Miranda and Jeff Davidson, Justine and Neil Bonnett, Claire and Nigel Swanning, Simon and Mary Todd, Elodie and Edward Blake*

Also Worth a Visit in Shropshire

Besides the fully inspected pubs, you might like to try these pubs that have been recommended to us and described by readers. Do tell us what you think of them: feedback@goodguides.com

ADMASTON   SJ6313
Pheasant (01952) 251989
Shawbirch Road; TF5 0AD Modernised 19th-c red-brick pub fronting the road; enjoyable generously served home-made food (all day Sat, till 7pm Sun), three or four well kept ales including Salopian and Wye Valley, decent range of wines, helpful service; background music, free wi-fi; children welcome, no dogs during food times, garden with picnic-sets and play area, open all day. *(Patricia Healey)*

BISHOP'S CASTLE   SO3288
★**Castle Hotel** (01588) 638403
Market Square, just off B4385; SY9 5BN Substantial coaching inn at top of lovely market town; clubby little beamed and panelled bar with log fire, larger rooms off and another fire, well kept ales such as Hobsons, Six Bells and Three Tuns, local cider, ten wines by the glass and 30 or so malt whiskies, popular food served by friendly staff, handsome panelled dining room; background music; children and dogs welcome, pretty hanging baskets at front, garden behind with terrace seating and pergolas, good views and surrounding walks, 13 spacious bedrooms, useful big car park, open all day. *(Caroline and Peter Bryant)*

BISHOP'S CASTLE   SO3288
Six Bells (01588) 630144
Church Street; SY9 5AA Friendly unspoilt 17th-c pub brewing its own good beers in back microbrewery (tours available); simple little bar with inglenook woodburner, old local photographs and prints, bigger room with mix of furniture on bare boards and another woodburner, sandwiches only lunchtimes Mon-Sat, good value meals Thurs-Sat evenings, roasts Sun lunchtime; July beer/cider festival; well behaved children and dogs welcome, café in brewery, open all day. *(Mike and Eleanor Anderson)*

BISHOP'S CASTLE   SO3288
★**Three Tuns** (01588) 638797
Salop Street; SY9 5BW Extended old pub adjacent to unique four-storey Victorian brewhouse (a brewery is said to have existed here since 1642); busy chatty atmosphere in public, lounge and snug bars, Three Tuns beers from old-fashioned handpumps (cheaper 5-7pm Fri), a dozen wines by the glass and good variety of tasty food (not Sun evening) from lunchtime sandwiches up, friendly young staff, modernised dining room done out in smart oak and glass; lots going on including fortnightly open mike night (Tues), film club every other Weds and summer beer festival; children and dogs welcome, open all day. *(Mike and Eleanor Anderson)*

BOULDON   SO5485
Tally Ho (01584) 841811
W end of village, set back from road; SY7 9DP Welcoming tucked-away pub owned by group of villagers; good local beers such as Hobsons and Salopian, enjoyable fairly priced food (not Mon) from sandwiches and light meals up, rugs on quarry tiles, woodburner in big stone fireplace, various pictures and memorabilia; darts; children and dogs welcome, country views from nice garden, open all day weekends, closed Mon lunchtime. *(Shona and Jimmy McDuff)*

BRIDGES   SO3996
★**Bridges** (01588) 650260
Pub signed from Pulverbatch–Wentnor road, W of Ratlinghope; SY5 0ST Renovated beamed country pub owned by Three Tuns with their full range in excellent condition; bare-boards bar on the right, large dining room to the left, enjoyable fairly traditional home-made food including daily specials, helpful friendly staff; occasional live music; children and well behaved dogs welcome, tables out by little River Onny (some on raised deck), bedrooms in separate

buildings, also camping and youth hostel nearby, great walking country, open (and food) all day, breakfast from 9.30am. *(Amy and Luke Buchanan)*

BRIDGNORTH   SO6890
★**Down** (01746) 789539
The Down; B4364 Ludlow Road
3 miles S; WV16 6UA Spotless roadside dining pub overlooking rolling countryside; enjoyable good value food (all day weekends) including popular daily carvery, efficient welcoming staff, four well kept ales such as Hobsons and Salopian; background music; children welcome, no dogs, nine comfortable bedrooms, open all day. *(Ian Herdman)*

BRIDGNORTH   SO7193
Golden Lion (01746) 762016
High Street; WV16 4DS Friendly 18th-c coaching inn refurbished by Holdens; five of their ales kept well and good range of gins, no food apart from cobs, separate lounge and public bar; sports TV, free wi-fi; five comfortable individually decorated bedrooms, good breakfast, open all day. *(Tony Smaithe)*

BRIDGNORTH   SO7193
Kings Head (01746) 762141
Whitburn Street; WV16 4QN 16th-c timbered coaching inn with high-raftered back stable bar and restaurant; Hobsons, Wye Valley and a couple of guests, decent choice of wines and good popular food served by friendly helpful staff, log fires, beams and flagstones, pretty leaded windows; children and dogs welcome, courtyard tables, open all day, food all day Sun. *(Tony Smaithe)*

BRIDGNORTH   SO7192
★**Railwaymans Arms** (01746) 760920
Severn Valley Railway station,
Hollybush Road (off A458 towards
Stourbridge); WV16 5DT Chatty old-fashioned waiting room conversion at Severn Valley steam railway terminus, bustling on summer days; old station signs and train nameplates, superb mirror over fireplace, Bathams, Hobsons and plenty of other well kept ales along with a couple of proper ciders, bar snacks such as pork pies (can also bring food from the station café); children and dogs welcome, wheelchair access possible through side door (staff will help), tables out on platform, the train to Kidderminster (station bar there too) has an all-day bar and bookable Sun lunches, open all day. *(Chris and Angela Buckell)*

BRIDGNORTH   SO7192
White Lion (01746) 763962
West Castle Street; WV16 4AB Fairly compact 18th-c two-bar pub with seven well kept ales including own Hop & Stagger brews, traditional cider and reasonably priced bar food such as home-made scotch eggs and butcher-made pies, friendly helpful staff, comfortable carpeted lounge with open fire; regular events including folk club (first Tues of month), storytelling (second Tues) and charity quiz (last Tues); children and dogs welcome, lawned garden with terrace, four good value cosy bedrooms (no breakfast), open all day. *(Tony Smaithe)*

BRIDGNORTH   SO7093
Woodberry (01746) 762950
Victoria Road/Sydney Cottage Drive;
WV16 4LF Welcoming dining inn with good choice of enjoyable locally sourced food, ales such as Battlefield and Hobsons, friendly efficient service; background music, free wi-fi; children welcome, large garden with benches, comfortable bedrooms, good breakfast, closed Sun evening, otherwise open (and food) all day. *(Tony Smaithe)*

BROMFIELD   SO4877
★**Clive** (01584) 856565
A49, 2 miles NW of Ludlow; SY8 2JR Civilised bar-restaurant-hotel named after Clive of India who once lived here; much emphasis on their popular well presented food but also Hobsons and Ludlow ales, several wines by the glass and good bar snacks, friendly helpful service; dining room with light wood tables and chairs on wood-strip floor, door to bar and step down to raftered room with woodburner in huge fireplace; background music, free wi-fi; children welcome, tables under parasols on secluded terrace, garden with fish pond, 15 bedrooms in separate building, Ludlow Food Centre next door, open all day. *(Mike and Mary Carter, Miss B D Picton)*

BUCKNELL   SO3574
★**Baron** (01547) 530549
Chapel Lawn Road; just off B4367
Knighton Road; SY7 0AH Modernised family-owned country inn, friendly and efficiently run, with enjoyable sensibly priced food cooked to order from pub favourites and pizzas up, a couple of well kept ales such as Ludlow and Wye Valley, woodburner in carpeted bar opening into conservatory, pitched-roof dining room with small gallery, old cider press and grindstone, further Stable Bar with pool and TV where dogs allowed; children welcome, peaceful setting with lovely views from big garden, good walks from the door, eight bedrooms including three chalets with hot tubs, open all day Sat, till 6pm Sun, closed lunchtimes Mon-Thurs. *(Emily and Toby Archer)*

BURLTON   SJ4526
Burlton Inn (01939) 270284
A528 Shrewsbury–Ellesmere, near
B4397 junction; SY4 5TB Welcoming attractively updated 18th-c inn; enjoyable pubby food and well kept Robinsons ales (maybe a guest), friendly helpful staff, beams, timbers and log fires, comfortable snug, restaurant with garden room; Sun

quiz; children and dogs (in bar) welcome, disabled access/facilities, teak furniture on pleasant terrace, six comfortable well equipped bedrooms, open all day Sun (food till 7pm). *(Richard and Tessa Ibbot)*

BURWARTON   SO6185
★ **Boyne Arms** (01746) 787214
B4364 Bridgnorth–Ludlow; WV16 6QH
Handsome Georgian coaching inn under welcoming management; good home-made food (not Sun evening, Mon, Tues) including Fri steak night, two Wye Valley ales, Robinson's and Thatcher's ciders, friendly helpful service, separate restaurant and public bar (dogs allowed here); children welcome, play area in pretty garden, open all day weekends, closed Mon lunchtime. *(Paul Scofield)*

CHURCH STRETTON   SO4593
Housmans (01694) 724441
High Street; SY6 6BX Buzzing and welcoming restaurant-bar with good wine, gin and cocktail lists plus two or three well kept ales, nice range of food including tapas-style plates, local artwork on display, some live music; children welcome, open all day Sat, till 9pm Sun, closed Mon lunchtime.
(George Sanderson)

CLAVERLEY   SO8095
Woodman (01746) 710553
B4176/Danford Lane; WV5 7DG Rural 19th-c red-brick dining pub; contemporary beamed interior arranged around central bar, good popular food (must book) using local produce including some from farm opposite, well kept Black Sheep and Enville, lots of wines by the glass and interesting range of gins, efficient service; terrace and garden tables, closed Sun evening, Mon.
(Claire Adams)

CLUN   SO3080
Sun (01588) 640559
High Street; SY7 8JB Beamed and timbered 15th-c pub in peaceful village surrounded by lovely rolling countryside; traditional flagstoned public bar with inglenook woodburner, larger carpeted lounge with fragment of 17th-c wallpaper and set of fine old beer pumps, six well kept Three Tuns beers and good reasonably priced home-made food from varied menu, Tues curry night, friendly helpful staff; children (in lounge), walkers and dogs (in bar) welcome, paved back terrace, three bedrooms (one in converted outbuilding), open all day, no food Sun evening.
(Caroline and Peter Bryant)

CLUNTON   SO3381
Crown (01588) 660265
B4368; SY7 0HU Welcoming community-owned country local; up to four well kept ales including Hobsons and Ludlow, traditional ciders and enjoyable home-made food from shortish menu, log fire in cosy flagstoned bar,

---

carpeted dining room and separate games room with pool and darts; children welcome in restaurant, dogs in bar, a few seats out at front with more in small back garden, open all day Fri-Sun, closed Weds and lunchtimes Mon, Tues and Thurs, kitchen additionally closed Sun evening, Tues. *(Paul Scofield)*

CORFTON   SO4985
Sun (01584) 861239
B4368 Much Wenlock–Craven Arms; SY7 9DF Lived-in and unchanging three-room country local with own good Corvedale ales (including an unfined beer), friendly long-serving landlord often busy in the back brewery, decent affordably priced pubby food from baguettes to steaks, lots of breweriana, basic quarry-tiled public bar with darts, pool and juke box, quieter carpeted lounge, dining room with covered well; children and dogs (in bar) welcome, good wheelchair access throughout and disabled loo, tables on terrace and in large garden with play area.
(Shona and Jimmy McDuff)

ELLERDINE HEATH   SJ6122
Royal Oak (01939) 250300
Hazles Road; TF6 6RL Friendly little country pub known locally as the Tiddly (Wink); half a dozen well kept ales and good value straightforward food (not Mon, Tues), open fires; children and dogs welcome, good-sized garden, open all day. *(Julian and Fiona)*

GOLDSTONE   SJ7128
Wharf (01630) 661226
Off A529 S of Market Drayton, at Hinstock; keep on towards Cheswardine; TF9 2LP Clean and tidy pub by Shropshire Union Canal (Bridge 55); Exmoor Gold, Joules Pale Ale, Sharps Doom Bar and a guest served from central bar, generous helpings of popular pub food (should book), good friendly service, winter fire; children welcome, no dogs inside, plenty of seats out by canal, caravan park, open all day.
(Tony Hobden)

GRINDLEY BROOK   SJ5242
Horse & Jockey (01948) 662723
A41; SY13 4QJ Extended 19th-c roadside pub with enjoyable good value food from varied menu, eight well kept ales including a house beer from Woods named after pub's chocolate labrador Blaze, teas and coffees, friendly helpful service, well divided open-plan interior with mix of furniture on wood or carpeted floors, woodburners and some interesting bits and pieces; sports TV, pool; children, dogs and muddy boots welcome, play area on side lawn, handy for Sandstone Trail and Llangollen Canal, open (and food) all day. *(Ed McKeegan)*

HIGHLEY   SO7483
Ship (01746) 861219
Severnside; WV16 6NU Modernised 18th-c inn set in lovely riverside location; pubby

food including pizzas, steak nights (Tues, Thurs) and Sun carvery, five real ales such as Banks's and Hobsons; children welcome, disabled access and facilities, tables on raised front deck, handy for Severn Way walks (and Severn Valley Railway), fishing rights, bedrooms and nearby camping, open all day. *(Dave Braisted)*

HODNET   SJ6128

★**Bear** (01630) 685214

Drayton Road (A53); TF9 3NH Black and white timbered inn with rambling open-plan main room; heavy 16th-c beams and timbers creating separate areas, wooden tables and chairs on rugs or flagstones, woodburner in large stone fireplace (there are three other woodburners), view into former bear pit through glass floor panel; smaller beamed and quarry-tiled bar with four changing ales, 14 wines by the glass, 20 malt whiskies and around 30 gins, well liked food (not Mon, Tues) served by friendly helpful staff; children and dogs (in bar) welcome, picnic-sets and play area in garden, comfortable well equipped bedrooms, Hodnet Hall Gardens opposite and well placed for Hawkstone Park, open all day Fri and Sat, till 9pm Sun, from 4pm Mon and Tues. *(Amy and Luke Buchanan)*

HOPE   SJ3401

Stables (01743) 891344

Just off A488 3 miles S of Minsterley; SY5 0EP Hidden-away little 17th-c beamed country pub (former drovers' inn), friendly and welcoming, with good home-made food and a couple of well kept ales such as Three Tuns, log fires; dogs welcome, fine views from garden, two bedrooms and shepherd's hut, open all day weekends, closed weekday lunchtimes. *(Paul Scofield)*

HOPTON WAFERS   SO6376

Hopton Crown (01299) 270372

A4117; DY14 0NB Attractive 16th-c inn recently refurbished under same owners as the Admiral Rodney at Berrow Green (Worcestershire) and Baiting House in Upper Sapey (Herefordshire); bar and two dining rooms, black beams, painted panelling and inglenook log fires, good variety of enjoyable food (all day Sun) including vegan options, real ales such as Woods and Wye Valley, cheerful helpful staff; children and dogs welcome, garden with large terrace, duck pond and stream, 12 updated bedrooms (some in new adjoining building) and two self-catering cottages, closed till 4pm Mon and Tues, otherwise open all day. *(George Sanderson)*

KNOCKIN   SJ3322

Bradford Arms (01691) 682358

B4396 NW of Shrewsbury; SY10 8HJ Sizeable neatly kept village local with notable three-faced roof clock; popular good value pubby food (best to book) and well kept

Marstons-related beers, friendly welcoming staff, games rooms; TV, free wi-fi; children and dogs welcome, garden behind by car park, open (and food) all day. *(Sandra and Michael Smith)*

LEEBOTWOOD   SO4798

Pound (01694) 751477

A49 Church Stretton–Shrewsbury; SY6 6ND Thatched cruck-framed building dating from 1458; opened-up, extended and much modernised interior, core keeping hefty beams and woodburner in big fireplace, enjoyable reasonably priced pubby food from sandwiches to daily specials, pie and a pint night Thurs, real ales such as Hobsons and Wye Valley, friendly helpful service; Sun quiz and occasional live music; children and dogs (in bar) welcome, seats on flagstoned terrace, open (and food) all day. *(Emily and Toby Archer)*

LEIGHTON   SJ6105

Kynnersley Arms (01952) 510233

B4380; SY6 6RN New management for this Victorian pub built on remains of an ancient corn mill; coal fire in opened-up bar, woodburner in connecting dining area, stairs to lower level containing mill machinery (there's also a 17th-c blast furnace), up to five well kept mainly local ales such as Salopian and Three Tuns, enjoyable pub food with a twist including pizzas, daily specials and Tues steak night, friendly helpful staff; background music, sports TV, pool, free wi-fi; children and dogs welcome, good walks nearby, open all day, no food Sun evening, light lunchtime menu Mon and Tues. *(Claire Adams)*

LITTLE STRETTON   SO4491

★**Green Dragon** (01694) 722925

Village well signed off A49 S of Church Stretton; Ludlow Road; SY6 6RE Popular village pub at the foot of the Long Mynd; good reasonably priced fairly traditional food (also a vegan menu) in bar or small adjacent dining area (well behaved children allowed here), well kept ales such as Hobsons, Ludlow and Wye Valley, proper cider, friendly helpful staff, cosy beamed interior with warm woodburner, area for muddy paws and boots; tables outside and play area, handy for Carding Mill Valley (NT), open (and food) all day, best to book evenings. *(Don Beattie, Ian Wilson, David and Doreen Beattie)*

LITTLE STRETTON   SO4492

★**Ragleth** (01694) 722711

Village well signed off A49 S of Church Stretton; Ludlow Road; SY6 6RB Characterful 17th-c wisteria-clad dining pub; light and airy bay-windowed front bar with eclectic mix of old tables and chairs, some exposed brick and timber work, huge inglenook in heavily beamed brick and tile-floored public bar, four real ales such as Hobsons, Ludlow, Three Tuns and Wye

Valley, good food including several fish and vegetarian dishes, cheerful attentive service; background music, TV, darts and board games; children welcome, dogs in bar, lovely garden with tulip tree-shaded lawn and play area, thatched and timbered church and fine hill walks nearby, open all day Sun. *(David and Doreen Beattie)*

LITTLE WENLOCK   SJ6507
Huntsman (01952) 503300
Wellington Road; TF6 5BH Welcoming modernised village pub; enjoyable food from sandwiches/snacks and pub standards up, four well kept/priced changing ales and good selection of wines, black beamed bar with stone floor and central log fire, restaurant has high-backed upholstered chairs at light wood tables and woodburner in big fireplace; children and dogs (in bar) welcome, terrace seating, bedrooms and self-catering cottage, handy for Wrekin walks, open (and food) all day, kitchen shuts 7pm Sun. *(Jo Garnett)*

LOPPINGTON   SJ4729
Dickin Arms (01939) 233471
B4397; SY4 5SR Welcoming recently refurbished pub in pretty village; split-level interior with up-to-date country-style décor, beams, flagstones, some painted panelling and big woodburner in two-way brick fireplace, good freshly made food (not Sun evening, Mon) including range of tapas-style starters/snacks, four well kept local ales and good range of other drinks, attentive friendly service; children welcome, dogs and muddy boots in bar, open all day Sat, till 9pm Sun, closed Mon lunchtime. *(Tony Smaithe)*

LUDLOW   SO5174
Blue Boar (01584) 878989
Mill Street; SY8 1BB Recently renovated former coaching inn with lots of linked areas, well kept ales such as Black Sheep, Hobsons and Three Tuns, good choice of wines by the glass and enjoyable well priced home-made food (not Sun evening), friendly staff; live music upstairs, quiz third Thurs of month; children and dogs welcome, back suntrap courtyard, open all day.
(Paul Scofield)

LUDLOW   SO5174
Queens (01584) 879177
Lower Galdeford; SY8 1RU Welcoming and popular 19th-c family-run pub; good reasonably priced food with emphasis on fresh local produce (booking advised, particularly Sun lunchtime), four well kept ales including Hobsons, Ludlow and Wye Valley, helpful friendly service, long narrow oak-floor bar, steps down to dining area with vaulted ceiling; some live music; children welcome (not in bar after 6pm), dogs allowed in one area, modern seating on enclosed deck, courtyard bedrooms, open all day. *(Patricia Healey)*

LUDLOW   SO5174
Rose & Crown (01584) 875726
Off Church Street, behind Buttercross; SY8 1AP Small refurbished Joules pub with 13th-c origins (retains many original features); six well kept ales from well stocked bar, enjoyable good value pubby food using local suppliers, quick friendly service; live jazz and blues nights; children and dogs welcome, approached through passageway with a few courtyard seats at front, pretty location, bedrooms, open all day.
(Stephen Funnell)

LUDLOW   SO5175
Unicorn (01584) 873555
Corve Street, bottom end; SY8 1DU Small half-timbered 17th-c coaching inn; character bare-boards bar with beams and part panelled walls, log fire, well kept ales such as Ludlow and Wye Valley, good wine list and enjoyable food cooked by owner-chefs (more restauranty evening choice), friendly service, back dining room; background music; children and dogs welcome (there are resident cockapoos), terrace among willows by river. *(Roger Yates)*

LUDLOW   SO5174
Wheatsheaf (01584) 872980
Lower Broad Street; SY8 1PQ Traditional 17th-c pub spectacularly built into medieval town gate; good reasonably priced food including daily specials and popular Sun lunch, a couple of Marstons-related ales and a guest, decent range of gins, welcoming helpful staff, dark beams, exposed stonework and open fire; children and dogs welcome, a few seats out in front, five bedrooms, hearty breakfast, open all day, food all day weekends. *(Roy and Gill Payne)*

MAESBURY   SJ3026
Original Ball (01691) 587360
Maesbury Road; SY10 8HB Old renovated brick-built country pub under newish management; hefty beams and woodburner in bar's central fireplace, Marstons Pedigree, Stonehouse Station Bitter and a guest, decent wines, enjoyable fairly traditional food including grills, Thurs steak night, friendly helpful staff; background and some live music, sports TV; children and dogs (in bar) welcome, disabled access, seats outside (some under cover), self-catering apartment on top floor, closed lunchtimes apart from Sun. *(Andrew and Michele Revell)*

MARKET DRAYTON   SJ6734
Red Lion (01630) 652602
Great Hales Street; TF9 1JP Extended 17th-c coaching inn acting as tap for Joules Brewery; back entrance into attractive modern bar with light wood floor and substantial oak timbers, traditional dark-beamed part to the right, updated but keeping original features, with pubby

furniture on flagstones, brewery mirrors and signs, woodburner, more breweriana in dining/function room to left featuring 'Mousey' Thompson carved oak panelling and fireplace; Joules Blonde, Green Monkey, Pale Ale, Slumbering Monk and a couple of seasonal beers (tasting trays available), good selection of wines, fairly standard home-made food including Sun carvery till 4pm; some live music; picnic-sets outside, brewery tours first Weds of month (must pre-book), open (and food) all day. *(Tony Hobden)*

MARTON   SJ2802
★ **Sun** (01938) 561211
B4386 NE of Chirbury; SY21 8JP Welcoming family-run dining pub, clean and neatly kept, with high standard of cooking including seasonal game and good fresh fish, light and airy black-beamed bar with comfortable sofa and traditional furnishings, stove in big stone fireplace, Hobsons Best and several wines by the glass, chunky pale tables and ladder-back chairs in restaurant; children welcome, dogs in bar (but do ask first), front terrace, closed Sun evening to Weds lunchtime.
(Caroline and Peter Bryant)

MUCH WENLOCK   SO6299
Gaskell Arms (01952) 727212
High Street (A458); TF13 6AQ Substantial 17th-c coaching inn with comfortable old-fashioned lounge divided by two-way fireplace, brassware and prints, well kept Wye Valley Butty Bach and a couple of local guests, enjoyable straightforward food served by friendly attentive staff, civilised beamed restaurant and separate locals' bar; background music, free wi-fi; well behaved children allowed, no dogs inside, disabled facilities, spacious walled garden behind with terrace, 14 bedrooms (four in mews building), open all day. *(Shona and Jimmy McDuff)*

MUCH WENLOCK   SO6299
★ **George & Dragon** (01952) 727009
High Street (A458); TF13 6AA Popular and welcoming traditional town pub; quarry-tiled front bar with jugs hanging from beams, antique settles and open fires in two attractive Victorian fireplaces, collection of memorabilia including old brewery advertisements and George and the Dragon pictures, timbered back dining room, Greene King, St Austell and guests, enjoyable well priced food (not Weds or Sun evenings), good friendly service; background and some live music; children and dogs (in bar) welcome, pay-and-display car park behind, open all day Fri–Sun. *(Amy and Luke Buchanan)*

MUNSLOW   SO5287
★ **Crown** (01584) 841205
B4368 Much Wenlock–Craven Arms; SY7 9ET Former courthouse with imposing exterior and pretty back façade showing

Tudor origins; lots of nooks and crannies, split-level lounge bar with old-fashioned mix of furnishings on broad flagstones, bread oven by log fire, another fire in traditional snug, eating area with more beams, flagstones and stripped stone, also upstairs restaurant (weekends only), good food from sandwiches and sharing boards through pub standards to restauranty dishes, popular Sun lunch, steak nights Tues and Weds, ales such as Otter, Three Tuns and Wye Valley, local bottled cider and nice wines, helpful efficient staff, friendly bustling atmosphere; background music; children welcome, level wheelchair access to bar only where dogs allowed, bedrooms, closed Sun evening, Mon.
(Claire Adams)

NEWPORT   SJ7419
New Inn (01952) 812295
Stafford Road; TF10 7LX Modernised and extended Joules pub on crossroads; their beers and a guest from five handpumps, over 50 gins and good uncomplicated food (not Sun evening) served by friendly staff, opened-up interior with some cosy corners, log fire and woodburner; live music Sun, beer and gin festivals; children and dogs welcome, picnic-sets under parasols on terrace and lawn, open all day. *(Tony Smaithe)*

PICKLESCOTT   SO4399
Bottle & Glass (01694) 751252
Off A49 N of Church Stretton; SY6 6NR Remote 17th-c country pub with plenty of character in quarry-tiled bar and lounge/dining areas; low black beams, oak panelling and log fires, assortment of old tables and chairs, good traditional home-made food from baguettes up, well kept ales such as Hobsons and Three Tuns, friendly helpful service; TV; children welcome, dogs in bar, seats out on raised front area, good walks, bedrooms, open till 7pm Sun, closed Mon. *(Andrew and Michele Revell)*

ROWTON   SJ3612
Windmill (01743) 884234
A458; SY5 9EJ Popular and welcoming 18th-c pub in same family for nearly a century; refurbished beamed bar with inglenook and a couple of dining areas off, good interesting food at sensible prices along with pub favourites, three well kept ales such as Hobsons, Salopian and Wye Valley, nice choice of wines; children and dogs (in bar) welcome, lovely country views from garden, open all day Sat, till 8pm Sun.
(Tony and Jill Radnor)

SHAWBURY   SJ5621
Fox & Hounds (01939) 250600
Wytheford Road; SY4 4JG Light and spacious 1960s pub; various opened-up areas including book-lined dining room with woodburner, rugs and assorted dark furniture on wood floors, cream-painted dados and lots of pictures, good fairly priced food from

light lunches and sharing boards to daily specials, Weds pie night, four or five well kept ales such as Greene King and Rowton, good choice of wines, efficient helpful service; free wi-fi; children welcome, picnic-sets on terrace and lawn, open (and food) all day. *(Amy and Luke Buchanan)*

SHIFNAL   SJ74508
White Hart (01952) 461161
High Street; TF11 8BH Nine well kept ales in this chatty 17th-c timbered pub, quaint and old-fashioned with separate bar and lounge, good home-made lunchtime food (not Sun) at reasonable prices, several wines by the glass and a proper cider, friendly welcoming staff; no credit cards; children and dogs (in bar) welcome, couple of steep steps at front door, back terrace and beer garden, open all day. *(Emily and Toby Archer)*

SHREWSBURY   SJ4912
Admiral Benbow (01743) 244423
Swan Hill; SY1 1NF Great choice of regional ales, also ciders and bottled foreign beers, friendly staff; darts, free wi-fi; no children, beer garden behind, closed lunchtimes except Sat.
(Richard and Tessa Ibbot)

SHREWSBURY   SJ4812
Boathouse (01743) 231658
New Street/Quarry Park; leaving centre via Welsh Bridge/A488 turn into Port Hill Road; SY3 8JQ Well positioned by footbridge to Severn park with river views from living bar and terrace tables; pastel blue panelling, painted tables and chairs on bare boards, some beams and timbering, woodburner, well kept ales such as Three Tuns and enjoyable food from sandwiches, sharing plates and pub favourites up, service can be slow; background music, TV; children welcome, no dogs inside, summer bar on decked riverside terrace, open all day.
(Richard Tilbrook)

SHREWSBURY   SJ4812
Bricklayers Arms (01743) 359999
Copthorne Road/Hafren Road; SY3 8NL Spotless 1930s suburban pub (walkable from the town centre) owned by Joules; their well kept beers and generous helpings of popular traditional food including good Sun lunch, cheerful efficient service, bare boards, panelling and open fire, screens and gleaming stained glass, one wall with examples of different bricklaying patterns; children and dogs welcome, picnic-sets out in front, open (and food) all day Fri-Sun, from 4pm other days. *(Claire Adams)*

SHREWSBURY   SO4912
Coach & Horses (01743) 365661
Swan Hill/Cross Hill; SY1 1NF Relaxed beamed corner local off the beaten track; chatty panelled bar, cosy little side room and back dining lounge, well kept Salopian,

Stonehouse and guests, real cider, happy hour 5-7.30pm Mon-Fri, popular freshly made food including Thurs fish night and Sun carvery; background music, quiz first Mon of month, free wi-fi; children allowed in dining room, dogs in bar, open all day. *(Jo Garnett)*

SHREWSBURY   SJ4913
Dolphin (01743) 247005
A49 0.5 miles N of station; SY1 2EZ Traditionally renovated 19th-c pub with friendly welcoming atmosphere; well kept Joules ales and guests, good interesting snacks and other reasonably priced food from short blackboard menu, compact bare-boards interior keeping original gas lighting and open fires; music and quiz nights, darts, free wi-fi; dogs welcome; seats on sunny back deck, open all day Fri-Sun, from 2pm other days. *(Jo Garnett)*

SHREWSBURY   SJ4513
Ego at the Grapes (01743) 369621
Welshpool Road; SY3 5BH After major refurbishment now part of the Ego chain of Italian-themed pub-restaurants; modern central bar with three distinct drinking areas, a couple of real ales, 17 wines by the glass and range of cocktails, popular mostly mediterranean dishes including good value set menu, friendly helpful staff, restaurant occupies the left wing of the pub; children welcome, open (and food) all day.
(George Sanderson)

SHREWSBURY   SJ4912
Golden Cross (01743) 362507
Princess Street; SY1 1LP Attractive town-centre inn first licensed in 1428; lots of old-world character blending with stylish shabby-chic décor, emphasis firmly on their highly praised food from lunchtime snacks up including plenty of vegan and gluten-free choices, good range of wines and a real ale such as Hobsons or Salopian, friendly helpful staff; children welcome, dogs too but do check first, five appealing bedrooms, no food Sun evening, Mon. *(Richard Tilbrook)*

SHREWSBURY   SJ4912
Loggerheads (01743) 362398
Church Street; SY1 1UG Chatty old-fashioned local with panelled back room, flagstones, scrubbed-top tables, high-backed settles and coal fire, three other little rooms with lots of prints, bare boards and more flagstones, quaint linking corridor and hatch service for their seven well kept beers, no food, friendly service; weekly folk session, TV for major sports, traditional games including shove-ha'penny; dogs welcome (in some areas), open all day. *(Jo Garnett)*

SHREWSBURY   SJ4912
Nags Head (01743) 362455
Wyle Cop; SY1 1XB Attractive old two-room pub, small, unpretentious and welcoming, with good range of well kept

ales such as Hobsons, Timothy Taylors and
Wye Valley, no food; TV and juke box; dogs
welcome, garden behind with remains
of ancient timbered building (used as a
smokers' shelter), open all day (till 1am Fri).
(George Sanderson)

SHREWSBURY   SJ4812
Shrewsbury Hotel (01743) 236203
Mardol/Mardol Quay; SY1 1PU Partly
open-plan Wetherspoons (former coaching
inn) opposite the river; seven well kept/
priced ales and their usual good value food,
helpful friendly service; TVs for subtitled
news, free wi-fi; children welcome, tables out
in front, 22 bedrooms (residents' car park),
open all day from 7am. *(James)*

SHREWSBURY   SJ4912
★Three Fishes (01743) 344793
Fish Street; SY1 1UR Timbered and
heavily beamed 16th-c pub in quiet cobbled
street; small tables on flagstones around
three sides of central bar, old pictures, up to
six well kept mainly local beers, good value
wines and enjoyable fairly priced food (not
Sun) from baguettes to blackboard specials,
good friendly service even when busy; Mon
quiz, free wi-fi; dogs welcome, open all day
Fri-Sun. *(Jo Garnett)*

STIPERSTONES   SJ3600
★Stiperstones Inn (01743) 791327
*Village signed off A488 S of Minsterley;
SY5 0LZ* Cosy traditional pub in fine
walking country – some stunning hikes on
the Long Mynd or up dramatic quartzite
ridge of the Stiperstones; small carpeted
lounge with comfortable leatherette
wall banquettes and lots of brassware on
ply-panelled walls, plainer public bar with
darts, TV and fruit machine, open fires,
a couple of real ales such as Six Bells and
Stonehouse, various home-infused gins
such as rose petal and whinberry, good
value bar food usefully served all day,
afternoon teas with freshly baked cakes
and home-made jams, friendly helpful
service; background music; children and
dogs (in bar and garden) welcome, two
comfortable bedrooms, also self-catering
in nearby converted chapel, open all day.
(Sandra and Michael Smith)

STOTTESDON   SO6782
Fighting Cocks (01746) 718270
High Street; DY14 8TZ Welcoming old
half-timbered community pub in unspoilt
countryside; carpeted split-level interior
with low ceilings and log fire, four well kept
mainly local ales, real ciders and decent
gin selection, good reasonably priced
home-made food including range of pies,
more dining space upstairs; regular live
music; children and dogs welcome, garden
with play area and rural views, good walks,
small shop behind, open all day weekends,
closed Mon. *(Don Beattie)*

UPTON MAGNA   SJ5512
Haughmond (01743) 709918
Pelham Road; SY4 4TZ Welcoming 17th-c
village inn; bar with painted beams, oak-
strip flooring/carpet and log fire, a house
beer (Antler) brewed by Marstons and
two local guests from brick servery, good
food in brasserie (shuts Sun evening, Mon)
including tasting menus, village shop/café;
children and dogs (in bar) welcome,
great view to the Wrekin from attractive
back garden, handy for Haughmond Hill
walks and Attingham Park (NT), five
bedrooms named after deer, open all day
weekends, closed Mon lunchtime.
(Emily and Toby Archer)

WELLINGTON   SJ6511
Cock (01952) 244954
*Holyhead Road (B5061 – former A5);
TF1 2DL* Welcoming 18th-c coaching inn
with well kept Joules, four changing guests
(usually from small regional breweries)
and extensive range of draught and bottled
belgian beers, friendly helpful staff, some
food such as pork pies, big fireplace; free
wi-fi; dogs welcome, beer garden with
covered area, bedrooms, closed lunchtime
Mon-Weds, otherwise open all day.
(Patricia Healey)

WELLINGTON   SJ6411
Pheasant (01952) 260683
Market Street; TF1 1DT Town-centre pub
with one long room; seven well kept ales
including Everards Tiger and up to three
from own Rowton brewery, two real ciders
and enjoyable good value lunchtime food
served till 4pm (not Sun), friendly helpful
staff; children and dogs welcome, disabled
access and facilities, beer garden behind,
open all day. *(Patricia Healey)*

WELSHAMPTON   SJ4335
Sun (01948) 710847
A495 Ellesmere–Whitchurch; SY12 0PH
Extended roadside village pub; good choice of
enjoyable reasonably priced food, Stonehouse
Station Bitter and three guests, friendly
helpful service; live music and quiz nights;
children and dogs welcome, tables in fenced
back garden, 15-minute walk to Llangollen/
Shropshire Union Canal, three bedrooms,
open (and food) all day. *(Claire Adams)*

WHITCHURCH   SJ5441
Black Bear (01948) 663800
High Street/Bargates; SY13 1AZ
Black and white building opposite
church (a pub since 1667); half a dozen
well kept interesting beers including
Stonehouse, enjoyable home-made food
from sandwiches up, characterful interior
and good atmosphere; regular live music;
children and dogs (in bar) welcome, beer
garden behind, open all day. *(Andrew and
Michele Revell)*

WHITCHURCH   SJ5441

Old Town Hall Vaults

(01948) 664682 *St Marys Street;*
SY13 1QU Red-brick 19th-c Joules
local (birthplace of composer Sir Edward
German); four of their ales and a guest,
enjoyable good value food from snacks up,
main room divided into distinct areas with
bar in one corner, oak panelling, stained
glass, mirrors and signs, sturdy furniture
including bench seating and cast-iron-framed
tables, log fires, further room with glazed
ceiling; outside listed gents'; dogs welcome,
partly covered yard with barrel tables, open
(and food) all day, apart from Sun when
kitchen shuts at 4pm. *(George Sanderson)*

WHITCHURCH   SJ5345

Willey Moor Lock   (01948) 663274

Tarporley Road; signed off A49 just
under 2 miles N; SY13 4HF Large
opened-up pub in picturesque spot by
Llangollen Canal; low beams, two log fires
and sizeable collection of teapots and toby
jugs, cheerful chatty atmosphere, half a
dozen changing local ales (fewer in winter)
and 30 or so malt whiskies, good value pub
food from sandwiches up; background music,
games machine; children welcome away
from bar, well behaved dogs in some areas,
terrace tables, secure garden with good-sized
play area. *(George Sanderson)*

Somerset
with Bristol

KEY   ★ Star Pub   🍴 Top Quality Food   🍺 Great Beer

🍷 Good Wines   £ Bargain Meals   🛏 Good Bedrooms   🍴 Serves Food

---

ASHCOTT
ST4337   Map 1

Ring O'Bells 🍺

(01458) 210232 – www.ringobells.com

High Street; pub well signed off A39 W of Street; TA7 9PZ

Friendly village pub with homely décor in several bars, separate restaurant, tasty bar food and changing local ales

E xtremely popular locally but with a warm welcome for visitors too, this is a reliably well run pub owned by the same family for many years. The three main bars, on different levels, are all comfortable, with maroon plush-topped stools, cushioned mate's chairs and dark wooden pubby tables on patterned carpet, horsebrasses along the bressumer beam above a large stone fireplace and a growing collection of hand bells; background music and board games. Changing local ales include Bays Topsail and Cheddar Potholer on handpump, nine wines by the glass and local farm cider. There's also a separate restaurant, a skittle alley/function room, and plenty of picnic-sets out on the terrace and in the garden. Disabled access. RSPB Ham Wall nature reserve is nearby.

🍴 Honest food includes sandwiches, fresh grilled sardines, local brie fritters with cranberry sauce, mushroom and butter bean goulash, lasagne, chicken with bacon, barbecue sauce and mozzarella cheese, 10oz gammon steak with free-range egg or pineapple, slow-cooked lamb shank in red wine sauce, lemon sole grilled with lemon and parsley butter, pork chop with honey and wholegrain mustard sauce, and puddings such as sherry trifle and bakewell tart with custard. *Benchmark main dish: pie of the day £12.50. Two-course evening meal £19.00.*

Free house ~ Licensees John and Elaine Foreman and John Sharman ~ Real ale ~ Open 12-3, 7-11; 12-3, 7-10.30 Sun ~ Bar food 12-2, 7-10 ~ Restaurant ~ Children welcome ~ Dogs allowed in bar ~ Wi-fi *Recommended by M G Hart, Marianne White, Camilla and Jose Ferrera, Shona and Jimmy McDuff, Molly and Stewart Lindsay, Patricia and Gordon Tucker*

BABCARY
ST5628   Map 2

Red Lion 🍷 🛏

(01458) 223230 – www.redlionbabcary.co.uk

Off A37 S of Shepton Mallett; 2 miles or so N of roundabout where A37 meets A303 and A372; TA11 7ED

Thatched pub with comfortable rambling rooms, interesting food and local beers and seats outside; bedrooms

There's quite a lot to see near this handsome thatched inn (the Fleet Air Museum at Yeovilton, the Haynes Motor Museum in Sparkford and shopping at Clarks Village in Street), so the comfortable, well equipped bedrooms make a good base. Downstairs, several distinct areas work their way around the bar counter. To the left is a longish room with dark red walls, a squashy leather sofa and two winged armchairs around a low table by a woodburning stove – plus a few well spaced tables and captain's chairs. There are elegant rustic wall-lights, clay pipes in a display cabinet, daily papers, magazines and board games. A more dimly lit public bar with lovely dark flagstones has a high-backed old settle and other more straightforward chairs; table skittles and background music. In the good-sized dining room a large stone lion's head sits on a plinth above a large open fire, and tables and chairs are set on polished boards. Exmoor Ale, Otter Amber and a local rotating guest on handpump, 18 wines by the glass, farm cider and cocktails. The Den, set in a pretty courtyard, has light modern furnishings and doubles as a party, wedding and conference venue. The long informal garden has a play area and plenty of seats. Wheelchair access.

High quality food includes leek bhaji with smoked garlic hummus, pickled carrot and coriander salad, mussels with cider, bacon and leeks, asparagus, pea and feta risotto with crispy shallots, steak burger with toppings and french fries, hake fillet with chilli celeriac and chickpeas, pickled shallots and crispy parsnip, duck with curried lentils, lime, spinach, pomegranate and dukkah, and puddings such as dark chocolate tart with poached rhubarb and sticky toffee pudding with toffee sauce and salted caramel ice-cream. *Benchmark main dish: slow-cooked pork belly with herb gnocchi, watercress pesto and fennel seed crackling £16.50. Two-course evening meal £25.00.*

Free house ~ Licensee Charles Garrard ~ Real ale ~ Open 11-3, 6-11; 11am-midnight Fri-Sun ~ Bar food 12-2.30, 6.30-9; 12-3, 6.30-9.30 weekends ~ Restaurant ~ Children welcome ~ Dogs allowed in bar ~ Wi-fi ~ Bedrooms: £95/£115 *Recommended by Adam Jones, Charlie Stevens, David Fowler, Trevor and Michele Street, Mike and Sarah Abbot, Buster May, Martine and Lawrence Sanders*

BATH
Old Green Tree 🍺

ST7564   Map 2

(01225) 448259
Green Street; BA1 2JZ

Tiny, unspoilt local with up to six real ales and lots of cheerful customers

A favourite with so many, this charming little 18th-c tavern simply doesn't change, and we're all so grateful for that. There's oak panelling and low ceilings of wood and plaster, and just three small rooms. These include a comfortable lounge on the left as you go in – its walls decorated with wartime aircraft pictures (in winter) and local artists' work (in spring and summer) – and a back bar. The big skylight lightens things attractively. Half a dozen beers on handpump might include Green Tree Bitter (named for the pub by Blindmans Brewery) and Butcombe Original with guests such as Pitchfork Ales Pitchfork and Plain Inntrigue; also, seven wines by the glass from a nice little list with helpful tasting notes, 36 malt whiskies and a farm cider. The gents' is basic and down steep steps. No children and no dogs.

Lunchtime-only food includes doorstep sandwiches, soup, pâté, fish and chips, vegetable curry, burger with toppings and chips, and lambs liver with bacon and roast garlic mash. *Benchmark main dish: rare roast beef platter £10.50.*

Free house ~ Licensee Tim Bethune ~ Real ale ~ No credit cards ~ Open 11-11; 12-4.30 Sun; 12-6.30 Sun in winter ~ Bar food 12-3.30; not Mon, Tues or Sun (though they do Sun roasts in winter) *Recommended by Dr and Mrs A K Clarke*

BATH

ST7565 Map 2

Star 🍺

(01225) 425072 – www.abbeyales.co.uk

Vineyards; The Paragon (A4), junction with Guinea Lane; BA1 5NA

Quietly chatty and unchanging old town local, the brewery tap for Abbey Ales

You get a real sense of the past in the four small linked rooms of this unspoilt little place, where there's always a good mix of customers. Many original features include traditional wall benches (one is known as Death Row), panelling, dim lighting and an open fire, and the atmosphere is lively and chatty. Abbey Bellringer and Bass plus guests such as Sharps Sea Fury and Timothy Taylors Landlord tapped from the cask, several wines by the glass, 30 malt whiskies and Cheddar Valley cider; darts, shove-ha'penny, cribbage and board games – and complimentary snuff. As this is just five minutes' walk from the city centre, it can get pretty busy at peak times.

🍴 Food consists of filled rolls.

Star Pubs & Bars ~ Lease Jon Ingall ~ Real ale ~ Open noon-midnight; noon-1am Sat ~ Children welcome ~ Dogs welcome ~ Wi-fi *Recommended by Glen and Patricia Fuller, Alf and Sally Garner, Sabina and Gerald Grimshaw, Chloe and Tim Hodge, Shona and Jimmy McDuff*

BISHOPSWOOD

ST2512 Map 1

Candlelight 🍷 🍺

(01460) 234476 – www.candlelight-inn.co.uk

Off A303/B3170 S of Taunton; TA20 3RS

Neat dining pub with a good choice of drinks, enjoyable food and seats in the garden; handy for A303

This is a pretty 17th-c pub in the Blackdown Hills. The neatly kept interconnected dining rooms have exposed stone walls and pillars, wooden beams, church, farmhouse and antique dining chairs around solid, rustic tables on polished floorboards, open fires and two woodburning stoves. High chairs line the bar counter where you'll find Hanlons Yellow Hammer and Otter Bitter on handpump, 27 wines by the glass and their own distilled Beau Gin. Outside, there are picnic-sets on decking and seats in the neatly landscaped garden and the pub is both dog- and welly-friendly.

🍴 Local produce is used in the interesting food, which includes sandwiches, confit rabbit and wild garlic rillettes with pickled samphire, gin-cured mackerel with carrot and orange and seaweed tartare sauce, tomato and olive fritters with poached cauliflower, wilted spinach, shaved asparagus, pine nuts and nettle verde, honey and balsamic-glazed ham with pineapple and chilli relish and triple-cooked chips, butter-roasted cod with chorizo and cod fritter, asparagus and broad bean salad, crushed jersey royals and chorizo sauce, and puddings such as warm chocolate brownie with coffee gel, peanut, coffee bean and cocoa nib granola with peanut butter ice-cream and vanilla rice pudding with elderflower-poached rhubarb compote with pink peppercorn shortbread and elderflower sorbet. *Benchmark main dish: braised beef short rib with potato and horseradish terrine, watercress purée and treacle jus £19.00. Two-course evening meal £25.00.*

Free house ~ Licensee Mike Rose ~ Real ale ~ Open 12-3, 6-11; 12-11 Sat; 12-7 Sun ~ Bar food 12-2, 7-9; 12-2.30, 6.30-9.30 Fri, Sat; 12-2, 6.30-9 Sun ~ Children welcome ~ Dogs welcome ~ Wi-fi ~ Live jazz last Sun of month *Recommended by Margo and Derek Peters, Julia and Fiona Barnes, Bob and Margaret Holder, Pauline and Mark Evans, Ivy and George Goodwill*

BRISTOL   ST5873   Map 2

Highbury Vaults ☺ £

(0117) 973 3203 – www.highburyvaults.co.uk

St Michaels Hill, Cotham; BS2 8DE

Cheerful town pub with up to eight real ales, good reasonably priced food and friendly atmosphere

Honest food, an excellent choice of real ales and a bustling, convivial atmosphere continue to draw the crowds here. The little front bar, with a corridor beside it, leads through to a series of small rooms: wooden floors, green and cream paintwork and old-fashioned furniture and prints (including plenty of royal family period engravings and lithographs in the front room). A model railway runs on a shelf the full length of the pub, with tunnels through the walls. On handpump and quickly changing, the ales might include Bath Gem, Dorset Jurassic, St Austell Proper Job and Tribute, XT 19 Red Rye IPA and Youngs Bitter and Special; also, six wines by the glass and nine malt whiskies. They offer hot sausage rolls from the oven on Thursday and Friday evenings at 10pm; bar billiards, TV and board games. An attractive back terrace has tables built into a partly covered flowery arbour, and there's disabled access to the main bar (but not to the loos).

Good value food includes toasties, burgers with toppings and sweet potato wedges, vegetable chilli with rice, lasagne, fish or steak in ale pies, chilli con carne, and puddings such as chocolate brownie with chocolate sauce and a choice of ice-cream. *Benchmark main dish: chilli nachos £9.50. Two-course evening meal £16.00.*

Youngs ~ Manager Bradd Francis ~ Real ale ~ Open 12-midnight; 12-11 Sun ~ Bar, food 12-2 (2.30 Sat), 5.30-8.30; 12-4 Sun ~ Children welcome ~ Wi-fi *Recommended by Sally and Colin Allen, Darrell Barton, Camilla and Jose Ferrera, Chris and Angela Buckell, Edward May, Megan and William Stapley*

CHURCHILL   ST4459   Map 1

Crown ☺ £

(01934) 852995 – www.the-crown-inn.co.uk

The Batch; in village, turn off A368 into Skinners Lane at Nelson Arms; BS25 5PP

Unchanging small cottage with friendly customers and staff, super range of real ales and homely lunchtime food

The interior in this smashing little tavern is completely untouched and this is just how the chatty, friendly locals like it. Seven real ales are tapped from the cask, including Bath Gem, Butcombe Bitter, Exmoor Ale, Palmers IPA, St Austell Tribute and a quickly changing guest such as Batch Terriers Bitter; also several wines by the glass and five local ciders. The small and rather local-feeling room on the right, with a stone floor and cross beams, has a big log fire in a large stone fireplace and steps that lead up to another seating area. The left-hand room – with a slate floor, window seats and a log burner – leads through to the Snug. The outside lavatories are basic. As well as garden tables at the front, there are more seats on the back lawn with hill views; the Mendip morris men visit in summer and some of the best walking on the Mendips is nearby. There isn't a pub sign outside, but no one seems to have a problem finding the place.

Traditional, lunchtime-only food includes sandwiches (the rare roast beef is popular), beef casserole, cauliflower cheese, lasagne, and puddings.
Benchmark main dish: rare roast beef sandwich £6.25.

Free house ~ Licensee Brian Clements ~ Real ale ~ No credit cards ~ Open 11-11; 12-10.30
Sun ~ Bar food 12-2.30 ~ Children must be well behaved ~ Dogs allowed in bar ~ Wi-fi
*Recommended by Hugh Roberts, Dr and Mrs A K Clarke, Belinda Stamp, Sophie Ellison,
Patricia Hawkins*

CROSCOMBE   ST5844   Map 2

George 🍴 🛏

(01749) 342306 – www.thegeorgeinn.co.uk
Long Street (A371 Wells–Shepton Mallet); BA5 3QH

**Warmly welcoming, family-run coaching inn with charming canadian
landlord, enjoyable food, good local beers and attractive garden;
bedrooms**

This is an enjoyable and popular place to stay overnight and the
bedrooms are clean and comfortable; good breakfasts too. You'll be
made personally welcome by the licensees in the main bar where there's
stripped stone, dark wooden tables and chairs and more comfortable seats,
a settle by one of the log fires in the inglenook fireplaces and the family's
grandfather clock; a snug area has a woodburning stove. As well as four
farm ciders, they keep George & Dragon and King George the Thirst (named
for the pub from Blindmans) and three guests such as Bath Gem and
Prophecy and Goldmark Liquid Gold on handpump or tapped from the cask,
ten wines by the glass and home-made elderflower cordial. The attractive
dining room has more stripped stone, local artwork and family photographs
on burgundy walls and high-backed cushioned dining chairs around a mix
of tables. The back bar has canadian timber and a pew reclaimed from the
local church, and there's a family room with games and books for children.
There's also darts, a skittle alley, board games, shove-ha'penny and a
canadian wooden table game called crokinole. The pub dogs are called
Tessa and Pixy. An attractive, sizeable garden has seats on a heated and
covered terrace, flower borders, a grassed area, a wood-fired pizza oven
(used on Fridays) and chickens; children's swings.

Highly regarded food includes lunchtime sandwiches, baguettes and omelettes,
smoked haddock and dill fishcakes with anchovy and lemon mayonnaise, chicken
and smoked bacon terrine with apple chutney, cashew nut terrine with sweet potato
mash and red pepper sauce, burger with toppings, onion rings and chips, fillet of
cod with pea and mint mash and prawn and saffron velouté, guinea fowl breast with
bacon and leek rösti, wild mushrooms and madeira jus, and puddings such as a trio of
chocolate brownie with chocolate sauce and Cointreau and chocolate ice-cream and
apple and blackberry crumble with custard. *Benchmark main dish: pie of the day
£13.95. Two-course evening meal £21.00.*

Free house ~ Licensees Peter and Veryan Graham ~ Real ale ~ Open 7.30-3, 6-11; 7.30-3,
5-midnight Fri; 8am-midnight Sat; 8am-11pm Sun ~ Bar food 7.30-2.30, 6-9; 8am-9pm Sat;
8-8 Sun ~ Restaurant ~ Children welcome ~ Dogs allowed in bar ~ Wi-fi ~ Bedrooms: /$80
*Recommended by Freddie and Sarah Banks, Dr Stuart Jenkins, Frances and Hamish Porter,
Amy and Luke Buchanan, Maria and Henry Lazenby*

DULVERTON   SS9127   Map 1

Woods ★ 🍽 ♀

(01398) 324007 – www.woodsdulverton.co.uk
Bank Square; TA22 9BU

**Smartly informal place with exceptional wines, real ales, first rate
food and a good mix of customers**

'This never disappoints' and 'an absolute gem' is how customers describe this particularly well run inn. There's a fantastic mix of both drinkers and diners and the atmosphere is gently civilised yet informally friendly. The pub is on the edge of Exmoor, so there are plenty of good sporting prints on salmon pink walls, antlers and other hunting trophies, stuffed birds and a couple of salmon rods. By the bar counter are bare boards, daily papers, tables partly separated by stable-style timbering and masonry dividers, and (on the right) a carpeted area with a woodburning stove in a big fireplace; maybe unobjectionable background music. The marvellous drinks choice includes Hop Back Crop Circle, Otter Ale and St Austell Cornish Best tapped from the cask, farm cider, many sherries and some unusual spirits – but it's the stunning wine list that draws the most attention. Mr Groves reckons he could put 1,000 different wines up on the bar and will open any of them (with a value of up to £100) for just a glass. He is there every night and will happily chat to tables of restaurant customers about any wines they might be interested in. Big windows look on to the quiet town centre (there are also a couple of metal tables on the pavement) and a small suntrap courtyard at the back has a few picnic-sets.

 The excellent food uses produce from their own farm: sandwiches, seared scallops with rhubarb, vanilla and coriander, duck, pigeon and foie gras terrine with spiced apple jelly, hazelnut cream and toasted brioche, chestnut risotto with truffle oil and parmesan, chicken breast with bubble and squeak, roasted beetroot and wholegrain mustard velouté, plaice fillets with tiger prawns, herb salad and caper and shrimp nut brown butter, confit leg and roast loin of local lamb with fondant potato, confit garlic and salsa verde, and puddings such as vanilla pannacotta with poached rhubarb and stem ginger ice-cream and sticky toffee pudding with toffee sauce and clotted cream ice-cream. *Benchmark main dish: seared steak and bacon salad £13.50. Two-course evening meal £22.00.*

Free house ~ Licensee Patrick Groves ~ Real ale ~ Open 12-3, 6-11; 12-3, 7-11 Sun ~ Bar food 12-2, 6-9.30; 12-2, 7-9 Sun ~ Restaurant ~ Children welcome ~ Dogs welcome ~ Wi-fi
Recommended by Valerie and Gordon Wauton, Alison and Michael Harper, Elisabeth and Bill Humphries, Elodie and Edward Blake, Diana and Richard Gibbs, Maria and Stephen Braeburn

DUNSTER
Luttrell Arms ⭐ 🍷 🛏
(01643) 821555 ~ www.luttrellarms.co.uk
High Street; A396; TA24 6SG

SS9943 Map 1

Somerset Dining Pub of the Year

Character bars and dining areas in lovely hotel, a thoughtful choice of drinks, enjoyable food and seats in courtyard and garden; luxurious bedrooms

A very special place to stay, the opulent bedrooms here have four-posters, antiques and carved fireplaces. This is a civilised and imposing building that's based around a great hall built for the Abbot of Cleeve some 500 years ago; many of the medieval features are lovely. The Old Kitchen Bar retains the workings of the former kitchen with meat hooks on the beamed ceiling and a huge log fire and bread oven. The main bar is popular locally and has swords and guns on the wall above a huge fireplace, cushions on antique chairs, horsebrasses, copper kettles, plates and warming pans, animal furs dotted here and there, a stag's head and an antler chandelier, and various country knick-knacks. Exmoor Ale and Otter Amber on handpump, 25 good wines by the glass, a dozen malt whiskies and three farm ciders; staff are courteous and helpful. There's also the Boot Bar with a lovely panelled wall seat and rugs on quarry tiles, a small snug and a deeply comfortable sitting room with one beautiful panelled wall, a woodburning stove and plenty of armchairs, sofas and window seats; board games. The pretty garden is on several levels with seats on lawns or terraces and haunting castle views; a little galleried courtyard has metalwork chairs and tables.

Delicious food beautifully presented includes sandwiches (until 5.30pm), pressed ham hock terrine with crispy parma ham, confit egg yolk and peas, scotch egg with curry sauce and streaky bacon, charred cauliflower steak with fricassée of seasonal vegetables, black-eyed peas, goats curd, mint and truffle oil, honey-roasted ham and egg, chicken caesar salad, oak smoked salmon linguine with pine nuts, capers, dill and parmesan, pork belly with fennel purée, charred pak choi, artichoke, croquette potatoes and five spice, and puddings such as coconut pannacotta with passion-fruit gel, mango and mango sorbet and chocolate bavarois with orange purée, orange cake and orange cream; they also offer breakfasts (9-10.30am). *Benchmark main dish: beer-battered fish and chips £13.00. Two-course evening meal £21.00.*

Free house ~ Licensee Tim Waldren ~ Real ale ~ Open 8am-11pm; 9am-11pm Sun ~ Bar food 9am-9.30pm ~ Restaurant ~ Children welcome ~ Dogs allowed in bar and bedrooms ~ Wi-fi ~ Bedrooms: /£150 *Recommended by Mr and Mrs D J Nash, Joe and Belinda Smart, Victoria and James Sargeant, Robert Anderson, Simon and Alex Knight, Elizabeth and Peter May, Liz and Martin Eldon*

EXFORD
Crown 🛏

SS8538 Map 1

(01643) 831554 – www.crownhotelexmoor.co.uk
The Green (B3224); TA24 7PP

17th-c coaching inn with character bar, real ales and enjoyable food, and big back garden; bedrooms

Some changes here this year include opening up the big fireplace to house a two-way woodburning stove, which warms both the two-room bar and the lounge, but they've kept the stuffed animal heads and hunting prints, hunting-themed plates and old photographs of the area. Traditional furniture includes cushioned benches and pubby chairs around polished tables on bare boards and there are still stools against the counter where they serve Bath Gem and Exmoor Ale and Gold on handpump, 12 wines by the glass, ten malt whiskies, 20 gins and local farm cider; TV. A wall has also been knocked through into what was the old residents' bar to create an informal lounge. At the front of the building are some tables and chairs with more on a back terrace; a stream threads its way past gently sloping lawns in the three-acre garden. Bedrooms are warm and comfortable and breakfasts are tasty. They're very dog-friendly and can arrange riding, fishing, shooting, hunting, wildlife-watching, cycling and trekking. Disabled access to bar. This is a pretty moorland village.

Pleasing food includes sandwiches, twice-baked cheese soufflé with red onion jam, button mushrooms in creamy garlic and white wine sauce on focaccia, roasted butternut squash risotto with parmesan, chicken breast with leeks and smoked bacon, parmentier potatoes and mushroom sauce, slow-braised lamb shoulder with cauliflower purée, fondant potato and lamb jus, hake with chorizo and spinach in creamy fish velouté, and puddings such as dark chocolate and Baileys mousse with raspberry coulis and sour cherry sorbet and banana and peanut butter bread pudding with crème anglaise. *Benchmark main dish: steak in ale pie £15.25. Two-course evening meal £25.00.*

Free house ~ Licensee Sara Whittaker ~ Real ale ~ Open 12-11; 3.30-11 Mon-Thurs in winter ~ Bar food 12-2.30, 6-9.30; 6-9.30 Mon-Thurs in winter ~ Restaurant ~ Children welcome ~ Dogs welcome ~ Wi-fi ~ Bedrooms: £75/£129 *Recommended by Buster and Helena Hastings, Patricia Healey, S G N Bennett, William and Natasha Pace, Charles Fraser, Ian and Sally Duncan*

FROME
Archangel
ST7747 Map 2

(01373) 456111 – www.archangelfrome.com

King Street; BA11 1BH

Ancient place with contemporary design, several eating and drinking areas, a bustling atmosphere, pleasing food and drink and courtyard seats; bedrooms

Located in a pleasant old town, this has been an inn since 1311. It was last updated a few years ago, and they've managed to blend the ancient and the modern cleverly and effectively. Original beams and walls remain but there are touches of glass, steel, slate and leather throughout. The bar is bustling and convivial with wall banquettes, high tables and chairs dotted here and there, white-painted walls and a strip of blue neon lighting at ground level. Box Steam Golden Bolt, Marstons Wainwright and Ringwood Boondoggle and Fortyniner on handpump, good wines by the glass and a large cocktail list. Stairs lead up to the restaurant with its rather dramatic glass-enclosed mezzanine cube, there are mustard yellow and pale green leather chairs around a mix of tables on big floorboards, high rafters lined with electric candles and a large carved angel on a plinth; background music. A long slate-floored passageway links this main part to a two-roomed snug area with sizeable leather sofas and armchairs and an open fire, and a small, rather cosy dining room. The central courtyard has colourful tables and chairs and a mediterranean feel. Disabled access.

Well regarded food includes sandwiches, pigeon breast with black pudding, parsnip and pickled red cabbage, smoked salmon with roast freekeh, rice wine, cucumber and gooseberry gel, beer-battered fish of the day with chips, sautéed hispi cabbage with wild garlic hummus, globe artichoke, crisp kalettes and roasted lemon purée, chicken breast with confit squash, romanesco sauce and chorizo and red pepper dressing, pork fillet spare rib with salt-baked celeriac, onion and thyme, and puddings such as dark chocolate tart with avocado ice-cream and caramel crémeux and rhubarb and almond custard with rhubarb granita. *Benchmark main dish: rarebit with apple, grape and pickled walnut salad £8.00. Two-course evening meal £20.00.*

Free house ~ Licensee Tom Halloran ~ Real ale ~ Open 11-11; 11am-midnight Sat ~ Bar food 12-2.30, 6-9.30; 12-4.30, 6-9.30 Sat; 12-4.30, 6-9 Sun ~ Restaurant ~ Children welcome ~ Dogs allowed in bar and bedrooms ~ Wi-fi ~ Live music last Sun of month ~ Bedrooms: £80/£95 *Recommended by Ivy and George Goodwill, Sylvia and Phillip Spencer, Jo Garnett, Gus Swan, Harvey Brown, Toby Jones*

HINTON ST GEORGE
Lord Poulett Arms 🔘 ⚐ 🛏
ST4212 Map 1

(01460) 73149 – www.lordpoulettarms.com

Off A30 W of Crewkerne and off Merriott road (declassified – former A356, off B3165) N of Crewkerne; TA17 8SE

Honey-coloured 17th-c stone inn with a thoughtful choice of enjoyable food and drinks and pretty garden; attractive bedrooms

This is a civilised old place with a relaxed, friendly atmosphere and a good mix of customers from both the peaceful village and further afield. Several linked character rooms have exposed stone or painted walls hung with portraits and mirrors, hop-draped beams, rugs on flagstones or bare boards and some lovely antique farmhouse, ladderback and windsor chairs and high-backed settles around fine oak or elm tables. There's also a woodburning stove in an inglenook plus a raised two-way fireplace, candles in brass sticks, a silver tea set, a grandfather clock and fresh flowers. A beer named for the pub, Butcombe Original and Timothy Taylors Landlord on handpump, 14 wines by the glass, home-made cordial, some interesting spirits and local bottled cider; background music, board games and table skittles. Outside, there are elegant metalwork chairs and tables in a mediterranean-style, gravelled area with flowering tubs and a lawn with picnic-sets and wooden furniture; boules. Bedrooms are comfortable and attractive. This is sister pub to the Talbot at Mells (also in Somerset) and the Beckford Arms at Fonthill Gifford (Wiltshire).

Highly regarded food from a seasonal menu includes black pudding scotch egg with home-made brown sauce, twice-baked stilton soufflé with cider cream, pie of the day, baba ganoush with grilled flatbread, tabbouleh and roasted peppers, roasted cod with squid bolognese and cured fennel, local lamb rump with leeks and boulangère potatoes, pigeon with baked radish and truffle bread pudding, rump steak with peppercorn sauce and chips, and puddings such as vanilla cheesecake with blood orange salad, streusel, lemon curd and poppy seed ice-cream and coconut and almond rice pudding with confit lime. *Benchmark main dish: chicken with chorizo, jersey royals and peas £16.50. Two-course evening meal £21.00.*

Free house ~ Licensees Dan Brod and Charlie Luxton ~ Real ale ~ Open 12-11 ~ Bar food 12-2.30, 6-9.15; 12-3, 6-9 Sun ~ Children welcome ~ Dogs welcome ~ Wi-fi ~ Bedrooms: /£95
Recommended by Sally and Brian Turner, Sam Cole, Patricia and Anton Larkham, Monica and Steph Evans, Katherine Matthews, Andrew and Michele Revell

HOLCOMBE

Holcombe Inn 🌟 🛏

ST6649   Map 2

(01761) 232478 – www.holcombeinn.co.uk
Off A367; Stratton Road; BA3 5EB

Charming inn with cosy bars, a wide choice of drinks and good food; lovely bedrooms

Our readers enjoy their visits to this well run, friendly inn, often choosing to stay overnight in the well equipped bedrooms (which have views over peaceful farmland to Downside Abbey school). To the right of the main entrance is a cosy room with sofas around a central table and an open woodburning stove. To the left is the bar: fine old flagstones, window seats and chunky captain's chairs around pine-topped tables, and a carved wooden counter where they serve Bath Gem, Butcombe Original and Otter Ale on handpump, 21 wines and champagne by the glass, 25 malt whiskies, cocktails and a thoughtful choice of local drinks (cider, vodka, sloe gin, various juices); board games and background music. A two-way woodburning stove also warms the dining room, which is partly carpeted and partly flagstoned and has partitioning creating snug seating areas, and a mix of high-backed patterned or leather and brass-studded dining chairs around all sorts of tables; daily newspapers. Just off here is a little sitting area serving specialist teas and coffees. Picnic-sets on a terrace and side lawn make the most of the stunning sunsets. Dogs are welcome everywhere (except the restaurant) and in two of the accommodation lodges by prior arrangement. Disabled access.

Enjoyable food includes grilled quail with onion purée, diced celeriac, caramelised apple and meat juices, salt pork and pistachio terrine with spiced oranges, buckwheat pancakes filled with mushrooms and spinach with béchamel sauce, home-cooked honey-roast ham and eggs, braised local lamb shoulder with peas, bacon, lettuce and mint, venison steak with fondant potato, wild mushrooms and red wine sauce, cod with ratte potatoes, spinach, beetroot and horseradish purée and orange and chardonnay beurre blanc, and puddings such as coffee crème caramel with praline and ginger pudding with marmalade ice-cream. *Benchmark main dish: pie of the day £14.50. Two-course evening meal £23.00.*

Free house ~ Licensee Julie Berry ~ Real ale ~ Open 8am-11pm ~ Bar food 12-2.30, 6-9; 12-9 Sat, Sun ~ Restaurant ~ Children welcome ~ Dogs allowed in bar and bedrooms ~ Wi-fi ~ Bedrooms: £75/£120 *Recommended by Roger and Anne Mallard, Lenny and Ruth Walters, Claire Adams, Ian Herdman, Geoff and Ann Marston, Julie Swift, Barbara and Phil Bowie*

 HUISH EPISCOPI ST4326 Map 1

Rose & Crown 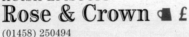 £
(01458) 250494
Off A372 E of Langport; TA10 9QT

17th-c pub with local cider and real ales, tasty food and a friendly welcome from long-serving licensees

Determinedly unpretentious and unspoilt, this thatched inn (known locally as 'Eli's' after the licensees' grandfather) has been run by the same family for 150 years. There's no bar as such, just a central flagstoned still room where drinks are served: Teignworthy Reel Ale and a couple of guests such as Butcombe Rare Breed and Hop Back Crop Circle, local farm cider and Somerset cider brandy. The casual little front parlours, with their unusual pointed arch windows, have family photographs, books, cribbage, dominoes, shove-ha'penny and bagatelle and attract a good mix of both locals and visitors. A much more orthodox big back extension has pool, a games machine and a juke box. There are plenty of seats and tables in the extensive outdoor area and two lawns – one is enclosed and has a children's play area. Pub customers and Brit. members can camp (by arrangement) on the adjoining paddock. There's also a separate skittle alley, a large car park, morris men (in summer) and fine nearby river walks; they hold a Friday evening organic produce co-op in one of their rooms (4.30-7pm) and classic car and motorbike meetings (check the website for details). The Civil War site where the Battle of Langport (1645) occurred is just a short walk away.

Fairly priced, home-made food includes sandwiches, good soups, cottage pie, vegetarian bean chilli, pork, apple and cider cobbler, chicken in tarragon sauce, and puddings such as apple crumble and white chocolate and raspberry bread and butter pudding. *Benchmark main dish: steak in ale pie £9.20. Two-course evening meal £13.70.*

Free house ~ Licensees Maureen Pittard, Stephen Pittard and Patricia O'Malley ~ Real ale ~ Open 11.30-2.30, 5.15-11 (closes 8.30pm Mon Oct-Mar); 11.30-11.30 Fri, Sat; 12-10.30 Sun ~ Bar food 12-2, 5.30-7.30; not Sun or Mon evenings ~ Children welcome ~ Dogs welcome ~ Wi-fi ~ Live folk third Sat of month Sept-May *Recommended by Edward May, Isobel Mackinlay, Valerie and Gordon Wauton, Lorna and Jeff Mason, Emily and Toby Archer, Julie Swift*

 LITTON ST5954 Map 2

Litton 🌟🍴🛏
(01761) 241554 – www.thelitton.co.uk
B3114, NW of Chewton Mendip; BA3 4PW

Attractive stone pub near Bath and Bristol with plenty of drinking and dining space and riverside garden; stylish bedrooms

Extensively refurbished and smartened up, this is a partly 15th-c stone pub that our readers enjoy very much. The various bars and dining areas have seats ranging from hoopback, bentwood, spindleback and modern leather chairs to fur-draped settles and leather armchairs and sofas, tables are scrubbed wood or beer barrels on bare boards and two woodburning stoves keep everything cosy and warm. Walls of exposed stone or contemporary paintwork are hung with mirrors and modern artwork and décor includes boxing gloves, bowler hat or jam jar lights and books on shelves. Friendly staff serve a beer named for the pub from Great Western plus Bristol Beer Factory Independence and Notorious, Cheddar Potholer and Wild Beer Bibble on handpump, plenty of wines by the glass and a fine choice of spirits from a long, polished elm counter; there's also a separate whisky bar with a copper-topped counter. French windows lead out to a sunken courtyard with steps up to a lawned area and a riverside terrace with a fire pit. The individually styled bedrooms are well equipped and up to date and breakfasts are good. There's plenty to do and see nearby, as well as local reservoir walks. Wheelchair access from back entrance and disabled loos.

Appealing modern british food includes pork bhuna scotch egg with pickled radish, roasted scallops with corn purée and spiced succotash, butternut squash and sage risotto with blue cheese, truffle and chives, roasted sea bream with provençale lentils, salsa verde and fennel, orange and dill salad, confit duck leg with chorizo and white bean cassoulet, slow-cooked spiced lamb shoulder with harissa pearl barley, butternut squash and garlic yoghurt, and puddings such as salted caramel brownie with raspberry and white chocolate ripple ice-cream and lemon posset with poached fruits and butter shortbread. *Benchmark main dish: steak and pulled pork burger with spicy cheese, bacon and triple-cooked chips £13.50. Two-course evening meal £20.00.*

Free house ~ Licensee Sally Billington ~ Real ale ~ Open 8am-11pm ~ Bar food 8am-9pm; 8am-10pm Fri, Sat ~ Restaurant ~ Children welcome ~ Dogs welcome ~ Wi-fi ~ Live acoustic music Thurs evening ~ Bedrooms: /£140 *Recommended by Chris and Angela Buckell, Pete and Sarah, Matilda and Gerald Thoms, Elodie and Edward Blake, Diana and Richard Gibbs, Jeremy and Susan Steadman*

LUXBOROUGH
Royal Oak 🛏

SS9837   Map 1

(01984) 641498 – www.theroyaloakinnluxborough.co.uk
Kingsbridge; S of Dunster on minor roads into Brendon Hills; TA23 0SH

Smashing place in wonderful countryside with local beers and ciders and popular food; lovely bedrooms

If you want to enjoy memorable walks and relax afterwards, stay in the warm, comfortable bedrooms here (some are dog-friendly). The compact beamed bar has the most character, a good mix of chatty locals (often with their dogs) and an informal and cheerful feel: ancient flagstones, several rather fine settles, scrubbed kitchen tables and a huge brick fireplace with a warm log fire; a simpler back room has a very old cobbled floor, some quarry tiles and a stone fireplace. A room just off the bar is set for eating, with attractive pine furniture, and there are two dining rooms as well. Cheddar Potholer, Exmoor Ale and a guest from Butcombe on handpump, several wines by the glass and farm cider; they have a record player for customers to use. There are some seats out in the charming back courtyard.

Well regarded food includes lunchtime sandwiches, chicken liver pâté with chutney, beetroot and dill-cured salmon with mustard and dill sauce, aubergine parmigiana, beer-battered cod and chips, lambs liver and crispy bacon with mash, herb-crusted hake with tomato, olive and chorizo tapenade and white wine butter, pork fillet stuffed with apple, black pudding and sage with cider sauce, and puddings such as crème brûlée and upside-down chocolate crumble with vanilla ice-cream. *Benchmark main dish: pie of the day £14.00. Two-course evening meal £20.00.*

Free house ~ Licensee Douglas Yiend ~ Real ale ~ Open 12-11; closed Mon ~ Bar food 12-2, 6.30-9 ~ Restaurant ~ Children welcome ~ Dogs allowed in bar and bedrooms ~ Bedrooms: /£100 *Recommended by Pauline and Mark Evans, Jane Rigby, Sarah Roberts, David Appleyard, Guy Vowles, Belinda Stamp, Harvey Brown, Phoebe Peacock*

MELLS
ST7249 Map 2
Talbot ♀ ⇌
(01373) 812254 – www.talbotinn.com

W of Frome, off A362 or A361; BA11 3PN

Interesting old coaching inn with real ales and good wines, seasonal food and seats in courtyard; lovely bedrooms

In an interestingly preserved feudal village, this is a handsome former coaching inn. There's a relaxed, candlelit bar with various wooden tables and chairs on big quarry tiles, a woodburning stove in a stone fireplace, and stools (popular with locals) against the counter where friendly staff serve a beer named for the pub (from Keystone), Butcombe Original and a guest on handpump, 14 good wines by the glass and a farm cider. Two interconnected dining rooms have brass-studded leather chairs around wooden tables, a log fire with candles in fine clay cups on the mantelpiece above and lots of coaching prints on the walls; quiet background music and board games. Outside, the courtyard has metalwork chairs and tables. Off here, in separate buildings, are the rustic-feeling sitting room with a huge mural and vast glass bottles, and the grill room with a big open fire overlooked by 18th-c portraits. Bedrooms are smart and stylish and breakfasts are good. Do visit the lovely church where the poet Siegfried Sassoon is buried; the walled gardens opposite the inn are very pretty. This is sister pub to the Lord Poulett Arms in Hinton St George (also in this chapter) and the Beckford Arms at Fonthill Gifford (Wiltshire).

 Up-to-date food includes pork and black pudding croquette with charred sprouting broccoli and apple purée, mackerel tartare with pickled lemon, whipped crème fraîche and horseradish, beetroot, quince and red onion tarte tatin with whipped blue cheese, burger with toppings, coleslaw and chips, fennel-cured hake with mussels, samphire, aioli and sourdough crumbs, pork loin with hispi cabbage, creamed pearl barley, bacon and charred shallots, 42-day aged sirloin steak with parsley and truffle butter and chips, and puddings such as chocolate and peanut butter tart with hazelnut praline and vanilla ice-cream and blackberry mousse with baked white chocolate, meringue and raspberry sorbet. *Benchmark main dish: local sirloin steak with peppercorn sauce £24.00. Two-course evening meal £23.00.*

Free house ~ Licensee Matt Greenlees ~ Real ale ~ Open 8am-11pm; 8am-10.30pm Sun ~ Bar food 12-3, 6-9.30 ~ Restaurant ~ Children welcome ~ Dogs welcome ~ Wi-fi ~ Bedrooms: /£120 *Recommended by R L Borthwick, S G N Bennett, Roy Hoing, Sandra and Miles Spencer, Jamie and Lizzie McEwan, Matthew and Elisabeth Reeves, Rupert and Sandy Newton, Alison and Dan Richardson*

MILVERTON
ST1225 Map 1
Globe
(01823) 400534 – www.theglobemilverton.co.uk

Fore Street; TA4 1JX

Handsome old place with good ales, quite a choice of tasty food and seats outside; bedrooms

Family-run and friendly, you'll find a cheerful mix of locals and visitors in the bars here. The opened-up rooms have solid rustic tables surrounded by an attractive mix of wooden or high-backed black leather chairs, artwork on pale-painted walls above a red dado, and a big gilt-edged mirror above a woodburning stove in an ornate fireplace; background music. Bar chairs line the counter where they keep Exeter 'fraidNot, Exmoor Ale and Otter Bitter on handpump, ten wines by the glass and local farm cider. The sheltered outside terrace has raffia-style chairs and tables and cushioned wall seating under parasols. The two bedrooms are comfortable and breakfasts are continental.

Well liked food includes sandwiches, crayfish and prawn ravioli with olive oil and parmesan, grilled goats cheese with pickled beetroot and toasted pine nuts, lentil shepherd's pie with onion gravy, burger with toppings, coleslaw and chips, smoked haddock and pea risotto with crispy greens, confit duck leg with truffle mash and cherry sauce, prawn thai green curry, and puddings such as blackcurrant crème brûlée and sticky toffee pudding with toffee sauce and clotted cream. *Benchmark main dish: slow-roasted, honey-glazed pork belly £18.00. Two-course evening meal £22.00.*

Free house ~ Licensees Mark and Adele Tarry ~ Real ale ~ Open 12-3, 6-11; 12-3 Sun; closed Mon ~ Bar food 12-2, 6.30-9 ~ Restaurant ~ Children welcome ~ Dogs allowed in bar ~ Wi-fi ~ Bedrooms: £65/£70 *Recommended by Alexandra and Tim Fledgling, Belinda and Neil Garth, Neal Griffith*

NORTON ST PHILIP
George
ST7755   Map 2

(01373) 834224 – www.georgeinnnsp.co.uk
A366; BA2 7LH

Wonderful ancient building full of history and interest with well liked food, real ales and decent wines by the glass; character bedrooms

There's a real sense of history here (not surprising, since the building is 700 years old) and so much to look at. The main room, which serves as the bar, has heavy beams, an oak-panelled settle and old church chairs on the narrow wooden floorboards, various illustrations on the walls (as well as an early 18th-c clock) and an open fire with an old iron fireback in the handsome stone fireplace. Wadworth IPA, 6X and Horizon on hand pump and several wines by the glass. As you enter the building from the car park, there's a room on the right with high dark beams, squared dark half-panelling, a broad carved stone fireplace and a big mullioned window. The dining room has a wonderful pitched ceiling with trusses and timbering, a fine tapestry on the walls, a big old stone fireplace, high-backed cushioned dining chairs on floorboards and an oak dresser. Bedrooms are full of character; one has a large queen bed with an oval table reputed to have been used by the Duke of Monmouth, who stayed overnight and was shot through the window before the Battle of Sedgemoor. Some bedrooms, with four-posters, are reached up a Norman stone stair-turret, while others are across the cobbled courtyard in a fine half-timbered upper gallery. Opposite the inn is the 500-year-old Plaine B&B (part of the same business), where the rooms are more contemporary in design. The attractive churchyard around the medieval church has bells that struck Pepys (who passed through on 12 June 1668) as 'mighty tuneable'. The terraced garden has a beautiful view of the church and the village cricket pitch.

Quite a choice of food includes sandwiches, lightly battered fresh squid with chilli sea salt and wasabi mayonnaise, chargrilled aubergine salad with lemon, mint, chickpeas and peas, sharing boards, minted broad bean, pea, asparagus and black garlic risotto with vegan cheese, beer-battered fish of the day with chips, grilled boneless poussin marinated in chilli, lime, ginger and olive oil with polenta chips and rocket and tomato salad, calves liver with crispy bacon, garlic mash and roasted shallot jus, 28-day dry-aged steak with dauphinoise potatoes and a choice of sauce, and puddings such as lemon curd and coconut cheesecake with raspberry coulis and sticky toffee pudding with toffee sauce. *Benchmark main dish: beer-battered fish and chips £14.50. Two-course evening meal £20.00.*

Wadworths ~ Manager Jenny Searle ~ Real ale ~ Open 11-10.30; 12-10 Sun ~ Bar food 12-2.30, 6-9; 12-8 Sun ~ Restaurant ~ Children welcome ~ Dogs allowed in bar and bedrooms ~ Wi-fi ~ Bedrooms: /$90 *Recommended by Lucy and Giles Gibbon, Elise and Charles Mackinlay, Katherine and Hugh Markham, Nicola and Nigel Matthews, R K Phillips, Alec and Susan Hamilton, Dr and Mrs A K Clarke*

PITNEY
ST4527 Map 1

Halfway House 🍺 £

(01458) 252513 – www.thehalfwayhouse.co.uk

Just off B3153 W of Somerton; TA10 9AB

Bustling, friendly local with a fine choice of real ales, local ciders and simple food

Although it's often packed out, there's a really good chatty and easy-going atmosphere here. It's an unpretentious village local with a cheerful mix of customers in three old-fashioned rooms: communal tables, roaring log fires and a homely feel underlined by a profusion of books, maps and newspapers. Tapped from the cask, the ales might include Hop Back Summer Lightning, Oakham Citra, Otter Bright, Plain Inncognito, Saltaire Eureka! and Teignworthy Neap Tide and Reel Ale, alongside four farm ciders, a dozen malt whiskies and several wines by the glass; board games. Tables and chairs are set outside on the lawn.

Simple, fair priced food includes sandwiches, faggots with mash and onion gravy, pork steak with scrumpy sauce and mash, ham and eggs, vegetable tagine, fish casserole, chicken breast wrapped in bacon and stuffed with mozzarella and creamy sun-dried tomato sauce, a pie of the day and chilli beef. *Benchmark main dish: beer-battered fish and chips £10.50. Two-course evening meal £16.00.*

Free house ~ Licensee Mark Phillips ~ Real ale ~ Open 11.30-3, 4-11; 11.30-11 Sat; 12-11 Sun ~ Bar food 12-2.30, 7-9.30; 1-4 Sun ~ Children welcome ~ Dogs welcome ~ Wi-fi *Recommended by Edward May, S G N-Bennett, Julie and Andrew Blanchett, Rob Anderson, Jamie Green, Jeremy Snaithe, Nick Higgins*

PRIDDY
ST5250 Map 2

Queen Victoria £

(01749) 676385 – www.thequeenvicpriddy.co.uk

Village signed off B3135; Pelting Drove; BA5 3BA

Stone-built country pub with a friendly atmosphere, real ales and honest food; seats outside

The various rooms and alcoves in this popular pub have a lot of character and plenty of original features. There's both an open fire in a big grate and a woodburning stove (in a back bar), flagstoned or slate floors, bare stone walls (the smarter dining room is half panelled and half painted), horse tack, farm tools and photos of Queen Victoria. Furniture is traditional: cushioned wall settles, farmhouse and other solid chairs around all manner of wooden tables, a nice old pew beside a screen settle making a cosy alcove, and high chairs next to the bar counter where they serve Butcombe Bitter and Rare Breed and a changing guest on handpump, four farm ciders, seven malt whiskies, nine gins and nine wines by the glass. There are plenty of seats in the front courtyard, with more across the lane where there's also a children's playground; the smokers' shelter is a converted dray wagon. Wheelchair access.

 Food is traditional and fair priced: chicken liver and bacon pâté, crab cakes with sweet chilli dip, pepper, tomato and garlic pasta, steak and mushroom in ale pie, burger with toppings and chips, chicken curry, chilli beef, 28-day aged sirloin steak with onion rings and chips, and puddings such as chocolate fudge cake and treacle sponge and custard. *Benchmark main dish: beer-battered fish and chips £10.95. Two-course evening meal £16.00.*

Butcombe ~ Tenant Mark Walton ~ Real ale ~ Open 12-11; 12-10.30 Sun ~ Bar food 12-3, 6-9; 12-9 Sat; 12-8 Sun ~ Children welcome ~ Dogs welcome ~ Wi-fi ~ Live music monthly in summer *Recommended by M G Hart, Ivy and George Goodwill, Emily and Toby Archer, Jacqui and Alan Swan, Nik and Gloria Clarke*

SOMERTON
White Hart ★ ♀ ⌂
(01458) 272273 ~ www.whitehartsomerton.com
Market Place; TA11 7LX

ST4828   Map 2

Attractive old place with several bars, open fires, spacious dining room and smashing food; bedrooms

Right in the market square of a lovely village, this well run pub is usefully open all day. The main bar has long wall seats with attractive scatter cushions, stools around small tables, large wall mirrors and Bath Gem, Cheddar Potholer, Otter Amber and a local guest on handpump, 22 wines by the glass and local cider; staff are helpful and friendly. A doorway leads to a cosy room with a leather sofa, armchairs, a chest table and an open fire; another snug bar is similarly furnished, while a simpler room has straightforward wooden dining chairs and tables, a little brick fireplace and some stained glass. Throughout there are rugs on parquet flooring (some plain bare boards too), church candles, contemporary paintwork and interesting lighting – look out for the antler chandelier with its pretty hanging lampshades; background music and board games. Outside, the flower-filled terrace has tables and chairs under parasols, with more on grass. Some of the airy, well equipped and comfortable bedrooms overlook the square and church; breakfasts are available to non-residents.

Highly enjoyable food includes grilled cornish mackerel fillet with chermoula, yoghurt, quinoa, radish and dukkah, smoked ham hock terrine with pickles, nasturtiums and malted toast, gnocchi with baked ricotta and romesco sauce, wood-fired pizzas, flat-iron chicken with spicy glaze, slaw and rosemary fries, hake fillet with beetroot and spelt risotto, samphire, pea purée and café de paris butter, slow-roast pork belly with leeks, lentils with red wine vinegar, basil oil and fennel and sea salt crackling, and puddings such as rocky road sundae with toffee sauce and salted caramel and chocolate tart with cherry sorbet. *Benchmark main dish: burger with toppings and chips £13.50. Two-course evening meal £20.00.*

Free house ~ Licensee Abbie Windust ~ Real ale ~ Open 9am-11pm ~ Bar food 9am-9.45pm ~ Restaurant ~ Children welcome ~ Dogs allowed in bar and bedrooms ~.Wi-fi ~ Bedrooms: /$94.50 *Recommended by Edward Mirzoeff, Trevor and Michele Street, Katherine and Hugh Markham, Dan and Nicki Barton, Holly and Tim Waite*

The details at the end of each featured entry start by saying whether the pub is a free house, or if it belongs to a brewery or pub group (which we name).

STANTON WICK
ST6162 Map 2

Carpenters Arms 🏅 ⭐ ♀ 🛏

(01761) 490202 – www.the-carpenters-arms.co.uk

Village signposted off A368, just W of junction with A37 S of Bristol; BS39 4BX

Bustling, friendly dining pub with pleasing food, helpful staff and fine choice of drinks; comfortable bedrooms

Just ten minutes' drive from the Chew Valley, this is an attractive little stone inn on a quiet country lane. It was refurbished in 2019 and the various bars and dining areas have button-back wall banquettes, sofas and armchairs, wooden and leather dining chairs around all sorts of tables, smart curtains, stripped stone walls, two woodburning stoves and a big log fire in an inglenook. Friendly, helpful staff serve Butcombe Original and Sharps Cornish Coaster and Doom Bar on handpump, ten wines by the glass (and some interesting bin ends) and several malt whiskies; TV in the snug. The front terrace has picnic-sets and there are pretty flower beds, hanging baskets and tubs. Bedrooms are quiet and comfortable and breakfasts are recommended. Enjoyable walks in the peaceful surrounding countryside.

Good food includes sandwiches, whole baked camembert with rosemary and honey, sautéed chicken livers with mustard sauce, macaroni cheese with parmesan herb crumb, steak in ale pie, cod and prawn fishcake with beetroot, fennel and watercress salad, herb-crusted lamb rump with sweet potato mash, confit leek and mint jus, thai fish curry, 10oz rib-eye steak with a choice of sauce, and puddings such as rhubarb cheesecake and chocolate and orange torte. *Benchmark main dish: lemon-roasted chicken supreme £17.00. Two-course evening meal £25.00.*

Buccaneer Holdings ~ Manager Simon Pledge ~ Real ale ~ Open 11-11; 12-10.30 Sun ~ Bar food 12-2.30, 6-9.30; 12-9 Sun ~ Restaurant ~ Children welcome ~ Dogs allowed in bar ~ Wi-fi ~ Bedrooms: $80/$120 *Recommended by Trish and Karl Soloman, Dr and Mrs A K Clarke, Michael Doswell, Chris Pocock, Christine and Tony Garrett, Nicholas and Lucy Sage, Darrell Barton*

WATERROW
ST0525 Map 1

Rock 🏅 ⭐ 🛏

(01984) 623293 – www.rockinnwaterrow.co.uk

B3227 Wiveliscombe–Bampton; TA4 2AX

Handsome inn with local ales, interesting food and a nice mix of customers; comfortable bedrooms

Not far from the southern fringes of Exmoor National Park, this striking half-timbered inn cleverly appeals to both diners and those just wanting a drink and a chat, so the atmosphere is informal and easy-going. The bar area has wheelback chairs and cushioned window seats around scrubbed kitchen tables on pale floorboards, sympathetic lighting and a woodburning stove in a stone fireplace. High black leather bar chairs line the copper-topped bar counter where they serve Otter Bitter, St Austell Tribute and a guest beer on handpump, 14 wines by the glass, a dozen malt whiskies and local farm cider; TV, darts and board games. The elegant restaurant is up some steps with pale grey-painted panelled walls, a large wicker stag's head and high-backed wooden chairs around chunky kitchen tables on more pale floorboards; there's also a snug with sofas and leather armchairs. In front of the building is a terrace with seating. Although parking by the inn is limited, there's more on the far side of the main road over the bridge. The bedrooms are tastefully furnished, warm and comfortable.

First class food cooked by the landlord includes soufflé omelette with smoked haddock and cheese, pigeon breast with black pudding on truffle-dressed salad, sweet potato gnocchi with spinach, red onions, pine kernels, grilled artichoke and parmesan, free-range duck with creamed onion purée and dauphinoise potatoes, cannon of lamb with creamed carrot and hispi cabbage and boulangère potatoes, 28-day aged 10oz sirloin steak with café de paris butter, and puddings. *Benchmark main dish: featherblade of beef with black garlic and treacle £17.00. Two-course evening meal £25.00.*

Free house ~ Licensees Daren and Ruth Barclay ~ Real ale ~ Open 12-3, 6-11; 12-3 Sun; closed Sun evening, all day Mon, Tues lunchtime (all day in winter) ~ Bar food 12-3, 6.30-9; 12-2 Sun ~ Restaurant ~ Children welcome ~ Wi-fi ~ Bedrooms: £75/£85
Recommended by Kate and Mark Foskett, Audrey and Andrew Nichols, Gwendoline and Ralph Mason, S G N Bennett, William and Ann Reid, Robin Silverman

WEDMORE
Swan
ST4348   Map 1

(01934) 710337 – www.theswanwedmore.com
Cheddar Road, opposite Church Street; BS28 4EQ

Lively place with a friendly, informal atmosphere, lots of customers, efficient service and tasty food; bedrooms

Usefully open and serving food all day, this is a handsome place at the centre of the village with plenty of customers dropping in and out. The open-plan layout feels even more spacious with plenty of mirrors dotted about, and the main bar has wooden tables and chairs on floorboards, a wall seat with attractive scatter cushions, a woodburning stove, suede stools against the panelled counter and a rustic central table with daily papers; background music. Cheddar Potholer, Otter Bitter and a guest beer on handpump, 21 wines by the glass, local gin and two farm ciders are served by quick, friendly staff. At one end of the room, a step leads down to an area with rugs on huge flagstones, a leather chesterfield, armchairs and brass-studded leather chairs, then down another step to more sofas and armchairs. An airy dining room has attractive high-backed chairs, tables set with candles in glass jars and another woodburner. The terrace and lawn have plenty of seats and tables, and the metal furniture among flowering tubs at the front of the building gives a continental feel. Bedrooms are pretty (some are generously proportioned) and breakfasts are good. Disabled access.

Appealing food includes sandwiches, crab cakes with pickled shallots and celeriac rémoulade, smoked ham hock terrine with apple and gherkin salsa, gnocchi with wild mushroom ragoût, baked ricotta, beetroot and spinach, flat-iron tikka chicken with raita and potato bhaji, butternut dhal, coriander and lime, hake fillet with café de paris butter, polenta and salsify, featherblade of beef with gremolata, potato terrine and parsnip purée, and puddings such as caramel and chocolate tart with cherry sorbet and sticky toffee apple pudding with toffee sauce. *Benchmark main dish: stuffed rare-breed pork belly with lentils, celeriac purée, sea salt and fennel crackling £17.00. Two-course evening meal £23.00.*

Free house ~ Licensee Sofie Baugh ~ Real ale ~ Open 9am-11pm; 9am-10.30pm Sun ~ Bar food 9am-10pm ~ Restaurant ~ Children welcome ~ Dogs allowed in bar and bedrooms ~ Wi-fi ~ Live music Fri evening ~ Bedrooms: /£85 *Recommended by Bob and Melissa Wyatt, S Holder, Sylvia and Phillip Spencer, Millie and Peter Downing, Alison and Michael Harper, Mark Morgan, Hilary and Neil Christopher*

If we don't specify bar meal times for a featured entry, these are normally 12-2 and 7-9; we do show times if they are markedly different.

WRAXALL
ST4971   Map 2

Battleaxes 🛏

(01275) 857473 – www.flatcappers.co.uk

Bristol Road B3130, E of Nailsea; BS48 1LQ

Bustling pub with relaxed dining and drinking areas, helpful staff and good food; big bedrooms with contemporary bathrooms

Starting with breakfasts (from 8-11am), this bustling Victorian pub is popular for its all-day food. The spacious interior is split into separate areas with an easy-going atmosphere throughout: polished floorboards or flagstones, portraits and pictures on walls above painted and panelled dados, mirrors on boldly patterned wallpaper, fresh flowers and house plants, books on windowsills and church candles. The bar has leather-topped stools against the counter where they keep a beer named for the pub (from Three Castles) and a guest such as Bristol Beer Factory Fortitude on handpump, ten wines by the glass and quite a few gins; background music. You'll find long pews with scatter cushions, church chairs and a medley of other wooden dining chairs around chunky tables and groups of leather armchairs. There are picnic-sets outside and some of the spacious bedrooms have country views. Wheelchair access using ramps. The pub is handy for Tyntesfield (National Trust).

 A wide choice of well regarded food includes sandwiches, chicken and tarragon terrine with pickled pears, confit pork belly with a quail egg, apple purée, black pudding, sage crisps, mixed bean and avocado burger with slaw and fries, smoked mackerel niçoise salad with soft boiled egg, green beans, olives, anchovies and herb oil, chicken and ham pie, lamb rump with dauphinoise potatoes, chorizo, asparagus and veal jus, and puddings such as triple chocolate brownie with toffee sauce and apple and rhubarb crumble with crème anglaise. *Benchmark main dish: beer-battered haddock with triple-cooked chips £13.00. Two-course evening meal £20.00.*

Flatcappers ~ Manager Tony De Brito ~ Real ale ~ Open 12-11; 12-10.30 Sun ~ Bar food 12-9; 12-10 Fri, Sat ~ Children welcome ~ Dogs allowed in bar ~ Wi-fi ~ Bedrooms: /£110
Recommended by Celia and Andrew King, Sandra and Neil White, Martine and Colin Fresher, John and Claire Masters, Richard and Tessa Ibbot, Mick Allen

WRINGTON
ST4762   Map 2

Plough

(01934) 862871 – www.theploughatwrington.co.uk

2.5 miles off A370 Bristol–Weston, from bottom of Rhodiate Hill; BS40 5QA

Welcoming pub with bustling bar and two dining rooms, good food, well kept beer and seats outside

With tempting food and a good choice of drinks, this well run, neatly kept pub is handy for both Cheddar Gorge and Bristol Airport. The bar is chatty and convivial with locals perched on stools against the counter where they keep Butcombe Original (the brewery is in the village), St Austell Tribute and Youngs Bitter on handpump and 18 wines by the glass, served by friendly and efficient staff. Two dining rooms (the one at the back has plenty of big windows overlooking the gazebo and garden) have open doorways and throughout you'll find (three) winter fires, slate or wooden floors, beams and standing timbers, plenty of pictures on the planked, red or yellow walls and all manner of high-backed leather, wooden dining or farmhouse chairs around tables of many sizes. Also, fresh flowers, table skittles and a chest containing games. There are picnic-sets at the front and on the back grass; boules. They hold a farmers' market on the second Friday of the month. This is sister pub to the Rattlebone at Sherston (Wiltshire). Disabled access and loos.

From a thoughtful menu, the food includes sandwiches, a choice of tapas, ham hock with terrine with piccalilli and truffled croutons, grilled octopus with pho broth and warm asian salad, tuscan vegetable braised lentils with sicilian dressing, pie of the day, burger with coleslaw and sweet potato fries, sausage and mash with onion gravy and vegetable crisps, confit tuna belly with fennel and new potato lyonnaise and red pepper tapenade, and puddings such as lemon tart with raspberry sorbet and a cake of the day; steak night is Wednesday. *Benchmark main dish: creamy smoked haddock with cheese and spinach topping £14.95. Two-course evening meal £21.00.*

Youngs ~ Tenant Jason Read ~ Real ale ~ Open 12-3, 5-11 Mon, Tues; 12-11 Weds, Thurs, Sun; 12-midnight Fri, Sat ~ Bar food 12-2.30, 6-9.30; 12-4, 7-9 Sun ~ Restaurant ~ Children welcome ~ Dogs welcome ~ Wi-fi *Recommended by Dr A J and Mrs B A Tompsett, Mark Morgan, Katherine Matthews, M G Hart, Chris and Angela Buckell, Edward May, Alfie Bayliss*

Also Worth a Visit in Somerset

Besides the fully inspected pubs, you might like to try these pubs that have been recommended to us and described by readers. Do tell us what you think of them: feedback@goodguides.com

AXBRIDGE   ST4354
Lamb (01934) 732253
The Square; off A371 Cheddar–Winscombe; BS26 2AP Big rambling carpeted pub with heavy 15th-c beams and timbers, stone and roughcast walls, old settles and large stone fireplaces, unusual bar front with bottles set in plaster, Butcombe beers and a guest, well chosen wines and good coffee, enjoyable food (all day weekends) from sandwiches up; board games, table skittles and skittle alley, sports TV, free wi-fi; children and dogs allowed, seats out at front and in small sheltered back garden, medieval King John's Hunting Lodge (NT) opposite, open all day.
(Ben and Jenny Settle)

BACKWELL   ST4969
George (01275) 462770
Farleigh Road; A370 W of Bristol; BS48 3PG Modernised and extended roadside dining pub (former coaching inn); enjoyable food in bar and restaurant from ciabattas to daily specials, also a gluten-free menu, well kept Bath, Butcombe and St Austell, good choice of wines; background music in some areas; children and dogs welcome, gravel terrace and lawn behind, seven bedrooms, open (and food) all day.
(Geoff and Ann Marston)

BARRINGTON   ST3918
Barrington Boar (01460) 259281
Opposite church; TA19 0JB Old stone-built dining pub in pretty village; good variety of well liked food (not Sun evening, Mon, Tues) from lunchtime sandwiches and light meals up, friendly helpful service, Exmoor, St Austell and a beer badged for

them, Thatcher's cider, updated interior with solid furnishings, wood and stone floors, logburners (boar's head above one); children and dogs welcome, picnic-sets out in front and in pleasant beer garden behind, four bedrooms, handy for Barrington Court (NT), open all day Sun till 9pm, closed lunchtimes Mon, Tues. *(Bob and Melissa Wyatt)*

BARROW GURNEY   ST5367
Princes Motto (01275) 474608
B3130, just off A370/A38; BS48 3RY Cosy pub refurbished under friendly australian licensees; four Wadworths ales served from casks behind the bar, Weston's and Thatcher's ciders and nice wines by the glass, good food from lunchtime ciabattas and pub favourites to blackboard specials, also a vegan menu, log fire; children and dogs welcome, pleasant garden with terrace, convenient for Bristol Airport, closed Sun evening and Mon, otherwise open all day.
(Roger and Donna Huggins)

BATCOMBE   ST6839
★**Three Horseshoes** (01749) 850359
Village signposted off A359 Bruton–Frome; BA4 6HE Handsome honey-stone inn with long narrow main room; beams, local pictures, built-in cushioned window seats and nice mix of tables, woodburner one end, open fire the other, Butcombe and guests, local ciders, around a dozen wines by the glass and several malt whiskies, well liked food (best to book, especially weekends), helpful friendly service, attractive stripped-stone dining room; children, walkers and dogs welcome, three simple but pretty bedrooms, lovely church next door, open all day weekends.
(Simon and Alex Knight)

BATH ST7464
Bath Brew House (01225) 805609
James Street West; BA1 2BX Interesting
spaciously converted pub visibly brewing
its own James Street beers (brewery tours
available), also guest ales and craft kegs,
food from open kitchen including spit-roasts,
various events such as comedy nights and
live music in upstairs room with own bar
and sports TV; well behaved children and
dogs allowed in some areas, sizeable split-
level beer garden with covered eating area,
summer barbecues, open (and food) all day.
(Dr and Mrs A K Clarke)

BATH ST7565
Bell (01225) 460426
Walcot Street; BA1 5BW Long narrow
split-level pub owned by the local community;
nine real ales, traditional ciders and some
basic good value food, lots of pump clips and
gig notices, a couple of fires (one gas), bar
billiards, table football and board games;
packed and lively in the evening with regular
live music and DJs; canopied garden, even
has its own laundrette, open all day.
(Dr and Mrs A K Clarke)

BATH ST7465
Chequers (01225) 360017
Rivers Street; BA1 2QA Busy 18th-c
city-centre pub with good interesting food
(can be pricey) along with more standard
choices, Bath Gem, Butcombe Bitter and
several wines by the glass, friendly service,
parquet-floored bar with wedgwood-blue
paintwork and some fine plasterwork,
cushioned wall pews, chapel, farmhouse and
kitchen chairs around mix of flower-topped
tables, coal-effect gas fire, attractive little
candlelit restaurant upstairs with view into
kitchen; children and dogs (in bar) welcome,
pavement picnic-sets under awning, open
all day. *(Jim King, Dr and Mrs A K Clarke)*

BATH ST7564
★Coeur de Lion (01225) 463568
*Northumberland Place, off High Street;
BA1 5AR* Tiny stained-glass-fronted
single-room pub, simple, cosy and friendly,
with candles and log-effect gas fire, well
kept Abbey ales and guests, good well priced
traditional food from snacks and baguettes
up (vegetarian options), Christmas mulled
wine, more room and loos upstairs; may be
background music; tables out in charming
flower-filled flagstoned pedestrian alley, open
all day, food till 6pm. *(Dr and Mrs A K Clarke)*

BATH ST7564
★Crystal Palace (01225) 482666
Abbey Green; BA1 1NW Spacious
two-room Fullers pub; rugs on wood floors
and comfortable mix of seating, panelled
walls and groups of pictures, popular sensibly
priced food from lunchtime sandwiches up,
speedy friendly service, four well kept ales

from plank-faced bar, log fire, garden room
opening on to nice sheltered courtyard;
background music, sports TV, free wi-fi;
children and dogs welcome, handy for Roman
Baths and main shopping areas, open (and
food) all day. *(Dr and Mrs A K Clarke,
Ian Herdman)*

BATH ST7464
Garricks Head (01225) 318368
*St Johns Place/Westgate, beside Theatre
Royal; BA1 1ET* Civilised and relaxed
dining pub with good food including
pre-theatre menu; bar with tall windows,
wheelback and other chairs around wooden
tables on bare boards, candles and a couple
of sizeable brass chandeliers, gas-effect
coal fire with fine silver meat domes on wall
above, four interesting regional ales, real
ciders and decent wines by the glass, proper
cocktails, separate smartly set dining room;
may be soft background jazz; children and
dogs (in bar) welcome, pavement tables,
open all day. *(Dr and Mrs A K Clarke)*

BATH ST7464
Griffin (01225) 420919
Monmouth Street; BA1 2AP Nicely
updated little corner pub now owned by
St Austell; three well kept ales, craft beers
and extensive range of spirits (particularly
gins and tequilas), interesting freshly made
food from small plates menu, good Sun
roasts, friendly staff; children welcome, eight
comfortably refurbished bedrooms, open all
day, no food Sun evening, Mon, Tues.
(Dr and Mrs A K Clarke, Hugh Roberts)

BATH ST7465
Hall & Woodhouse (01225) 469259
Old King Street; BA1 2JW Conversion
of stone-fronted warehouse/auction rooms;
big open-plan interior on two floors, steel
girders and glass, palms and chandeliers,
mix of modern and traditional furniture
including old-fashioned iron-framed tables
with large candles and some simple bench
seating, parquet and slate floors, Badger
ales from full-length servery on the right,
sweeping stairs up to another bar and eating
area (disabled access via lift), roof terrace,
decent choice of food from pub favourites to
specials, helpful chatty staff; gets very busy
with after-work drinkers when standing room
only, open (and food) all day from 9am for
breakfast. *(Dr and Mrs A K Clarke)*

BATH ST7467
★Hare & Hounds (01225) 482682
*Lansdown Road, Lansdown Hill;
BA1 5TJ* Wonderful far-reaching views
over villages and fields from inside and out;
long single bar with easy-going feel, chapel
chairs and cushioned wall settles around
pale wood-topped tables on bare boards,
minimal decoration on pale walls above
blue-grey dado, Bath, Butcombe and a beer
badged for the pub from attractively carved

counter, several wines by the glass, good food from breakfasts on, log fire with bronze hare and hound above, small slate-floored conservatory; background music, free wi-fi; children and dogs welcome, decked terrace, more seats and tables down steps, open all day from 8.30am. *(Dr and Mrs A K Clarke, Tom and Ruth Rees)*

BATH   ST7465
★**Hop Pole** (01225) 446327
Albion Buildings, Upper Bristol Road; BA1 3AR Bustling family-friendly Bath/St Austell pub, their beers and guests kept well, decent wines by the glass and good choice of spirits, popular food from traditional favourites up in bar and former skittle alley restaurant, friendly helpful staff, settles and other pub furniture on bare boards in four linked areas; background music, quiz nights; dogs welcome, wheelchair access to main bar area only, pleasant two-level back courtyard, opposite Royal Victoria Park (great kids' play area), open all day (till 8pm Sun). *(Jim King, Dr and Mrs A K Clarke)*

BATH   ST7565
King William (01225) 428096
Thomas Street/A4 London Road; BA1 5NN Cosy corner dining pub with well cooked food from short daily changing menu, four local ales and good choice of wines by the glass, chunky old tables on bare boards, steep stairs up to restaurant (a little more formal); background music; children and dogs welcome, open all day weekends. *(Dr and Mrs A K Clarke, Jane Jones)*

BATH   ST7465
★**Marlborough** (01225) 423731
35 Marlborough Buildings/Weston Road; BA1 2LY Busy pub centrally placed and usefully open all day from 9am; U-shaped bare-boards bar with flowers on tables, seating ranging from thick button-back wall seats to chapel, kitchen and high-backed dining chairs, a couple of ales such as Butcombe and Box Steam, traditional cider and lots of wines by the glass, well liked food from pub favourites up including some vegan choices, Thurs steak night, cheerful young staff; background music, free wi-fi; children and dogs welcome, suntrap courtyard garden. *(Dr and Mrs A K Clarke)*

BATH   ST7565
Pig & Fiddle (01225) 460868
Saracen Street; BA1 5BR Lively place (particularly weekends) with five well kept ales including Butcombe and fairly simple affordably priced food, friendly staff, bare-boards interior with two big open fires and collection of sporting memorabilia, steps up to bustling servery and tidied dining area, games part (darts and table football); live music and DJ nights, several TVs for sport; picnic-sets on big heated terrace, open all day, food till early evening. *(Dr and Mrs A K Clarke)*

BATH   ST7565
Pulteney Arms (01225) 463923
Daniel Street/Sutton Street; BA2 6ND Cosy, cheerful and largely unspoilt 18th-c pub; Box Steam Piston Broke, Fullers London Pride, Timothy Taylors Landlord and guests, Thatcher's cider, enjoyable freshly made food at sensible prices, traditional furniture on wooden floors, old gas lamps, woodburner and lots of Bath RFC memorabilia; background music, sports TV, darts, Mon quiz; children (until 9pm) and dogs welcome, pavement tables and small back terrace, handy for Sydney Gardens and Holburne Museum, open all day Fri-Sun, no food Sun evening. *(Dr and Mrs A K Clarke)*

BATH   ST7464
Raven (01225) 425045
Queen Street; BA1 1HE Small buoyant 18th-c city-centre free house; two well kept house ales from Blindmans and four guests, craft beers and a changing cider, decent wines by the glass too, limited choice of food including range of pies and sausages, quick friendly service, bare boards, some stripped stone and an open fire, newspapers, quieter upstairs bar; no under-14s or dogs; open (and food) all day. *(Dr and Mrs A K Clarke)*

BATH   ST7364
Royal Oak (01225) 481409
Lower Bristol Road; near Oldfield Park station; BA2 3BW Friendly roadside pub with its own Ralphs beers (named after resident husky) and up to five guests, also bottled beers and range of ciders/perries, no food, two bare-boards bar areas with open fires; regular live music and monthly quiz; dogs welcome, side beer garden, open all day Fri-Sun, from 4pm other days. *(Dr and Mrs A K Clarke)*

BATH   ST7464
Salamander (01225) 428889
John Street; BA1 2JL Busy city local with full range of well kept Bath ales, St Austell Tribute and good choice of wines by the glass, bare boards, black woodwork and ochre walls, popular food from sandwiches up (more choice evenings/weekends), friendly helpful young staff, upstairs restaurant with open kitchen; background music, daily papers; children till 8pm, no dogs, open all day (till 1am Fri, Sat), gets really busy on Bath RFC match days. *(Dr and Mrs A K Clarke, Ian Herdman)*

BATH   ST7564
Sam Weller (01225) 474910
Upper Borough Walls; BA1 1RH Fairly simple little pub with ales such as Abbey, St Austell, Sharps and Timothy Taylors, decent choice of wines by the glass and sensibly priced tasty food from sandwiches up, friendly service, cosy inside with big

window to watch the world go by; light background music; open all day (till 6pm Sun). *(Mike Kavaney, Dr and Mrs A K Clarke)*

BATH   ST7365

Victoria Pub & Kitchen

(01225) 422563 *Upper Bristol Road; BA1 3AT* Opened-up and modernised gastropub opposite Royal Victoria Park (sister to the Duke of Cumberland at Holcombe); bar/kitchen area with a couple of easy chairs and small dining section, two further rooms (one down steps) with mix of furniture including some bench tables and old metal chairs, polished wood floors, pale grey walls and painted panelling, reclaimed floorboards used to clad one part, Butcombe, Sharps and a guest, Thatcher's ciders and good wines, much liked food at fair prices including weekday lunchtime/early evening deal, friendly helpful staff; background music; children and dogs welcome, partial wheelchair access, disabled loo, small decked terrace and raised beer garden, open all day, food all day Fri-Sun. *(Chris and Angela Buckell, Dr and Mrs A K Clarke)*

BATH   ST7564

Volunteer Riflemans Arms

(01225) 425210 *New Bond Street Place; BA1 1BH* Friendly little city-centre pub with leather sofas and a few close-set tables, wartime/military posters, open fire, half a dozen well kept ales including a house beer from Yeovil, a couple of draught ciders and good value tasty lunchtime food, small upstairs dining room and roof terrace; background music; pavement tables, open all day. *(Dr and Mrs A K Clarke, Mike Kavaney)*

BATH   ST7564

★White Hart (01225) 338053

Widcombe Hill; BA2 6AA Bistro-style pub with scrubbed pine tables on bare boards, candles and fresh flowers, good imaginative if not cheap food, well kept Butcombe from traditional panelled counter, proper cider and plenty of wines by the glass, quick friendly service; background and occasional live music outside in summer; children and dogs welcome, pretty beer garden, four bedrooms (some sharing bathroom), open all day (Sun till 5pm). *(Roger and Anne Mallard, Dr and Mrs A K Clarke, Guy Vowles)*

BATHFORD   ST7866

Crown (01225) 852426

Bathford Hill, towards Bradford-on-Avon, by Batheaston roundabout and bridge; BA1 7SL Bistro pub with good french-influnced blackboard food, ales such as Bath and Timothy Taylors, nice wines, friendly service; children and dogs

welcome, tables out in front and in back garden with pétanque, open all day. *(Dr and Mrs A K Clarke)*

BICKNOLLER   ST1139

Bicknoller Inn (01984) 656234

Church Lane; TA4 4EW Welcoming old thatched pub nestling below the Quantocks; traditional flagstoned front bar, side room and large back restaurant with open kitchen, popular food from pub favourites up, Sun carvery (booking advised), friendly helpful service, four well kept Palmers ales and a couple of real ciders, skittle alley, free wi-fi; children and dogs (in bar) welcome, courtyard and nice back garden, boules, attractive village, open all day weekends; changing hands as we went to press. *(Graham Smart)*

BLAGDON HILL   ST2118

Lamb & Flag (01823) 421893

4 miles S of Taunton; TA3 7SL Atmospheric beamed pub with traditional furniture including some slab-topped tables on bare boards or flagstones, woodburner in two-way fireplace, four changing real ales, traditional ciders and decent wines by the glass, good reasonably priced home-made food (not Sun evening) from sandwiches up, helpful friendly service, galleried upstairs area, skittle alley; background and occasional live music; children and dogs welcome, picnic-sets in nice garden with Taunton Vale views, open all day. *(Peter Kirkman)*

BLEADON   ST3457

Queens Arms (01934) 812080

Just off A370 S of Weston; Celtic Way; BS24 0NF Popular 16th-c beamed village pub with enjoyable reasonably priced food from lunchtime baguettes to steaks, Butcombe and other well kept ales, friendly service, stripped-stone back bar with woodburner, winged settles and sturdy tables, flagstoned restaurant; children and dogs welcome, partial wheelchair access, picnic-sets on attractive terrace, open all day, no food Sun evening, Mon. *(Patricia and Anton Larkham)*

BRADFORD-ON-TONE   ST1722

White Horse (01823) 461239

Fairly near M5 junction 26, off A38 towards Taunton; TA4 1HF Popular 17th-c family-run village pub across from the church; ample helpings of enjoyable good value food from fairly pubby menu including blackboard specials and weekday light lunch deal, friendly helpful staff, well kept ales such as Hanlons, Otter and St Austell, bare-boards bar with leather sofas and armchair by woodburner, linked dining areas; background and occasional live music, Mon

---

All *Guide* inspections are anonymous. Anyone claiming to be a *Good Pub Guide* inspector is a fraud. Please let us know.

quiz, skittle alley; children and dogs (in bar) welcome, picnic-sets in nice garden (maybe Percy the peacock), unusual glass pub sign, closed Sun evening, Mon lunchtime. *(Ian Herdman)*

BRISTOL   ST5773
Albion (0117) 973 3522

Boyces Avenue, Clifton; BS8 4AA Popular former 17th-c coaching house tucked away in backstreet courtyard; refurbished interior on two floors (private dining upstairs), enjoyable food from sandwiches and sharing plates up including Mon steak night, well kept Bath and St Austell ales, lots of wines by the glass and good choice of other drinks, cheerful attentive service; background music; children and dogs welcome, tables and heaters out in front, open all day, food till 4pm Sun.
(Chris and Angela Buckell)

BRISTOL   ST5773
Alma (0117) 973 5171

Alma Vale Road, Clifton; BS8 2HY Two-bar pub with west country beers, Aspall's and Thatcher's ciders and several wines by the glass, good range of whiskies too, well liked imaginative food along with more standard choices including pizzas and good Sun roasts, friendly hard-working staff, dark panelled traditionally furnished front bars with wood flooring, more contemporary back room with bright modern wallpaper and local artwork, thriving upstairs theatre (10% food discount for ticket holders); background music (live Sun), comedy nights, easy wheelchair access to ground floor (no disabled loo), small paved terrace behind (closed late evening), open all day.
(Chris and Angela Buckell)

BRISTOL   ST5873
Bank (0117) 930 4691

John Street; BS1 2HR Small proper single-bar pub, centrally placed (but off the beaten track) and popular with office workers; four changing local ales (may include a porter), real ciders and enjoyable well priced food till 4pm including sandwiches, burgers and one or two unusual choices, good Sun lunch too, comfortable bench seats, newspapers, books on shelf above fireplace; background and regular live music, Tues quiz, free wi-fi; children and dogs welcome, wheelchair access, tables under umbrellas in paved courtyard, open all day (till 1am Thurs-Sat).
(Edward May)

BRISTOL   ST5972
Barley Mow (0117) 930 4709

Barton Road; The Dings; BS2 0LF Late 19th-c Bristol Beer Factory pub in old industrial area close to the floating harbour; up to eight well kept changing ales, excellent selection of craft kegs and bottled beers, proper cider and decent choice of wines by the glass, enjoyable good value food (not Sun evening) from short menu catering

for vegetarians, cheerful chatty staff, wood floors, off-white walls and blue half-panelling, cushioned wall seats and pubby furniture, various odds and ends dotted about, open fire in brick fireplace; Tues quiz, free wi-fi; disabled access, open all day (till 10pm Sun).
(Sophie Ellison)

BRISTOL   ST5872
Beer Emporium (0117) 379 0333

King Street opposite the Old Vic; BS1 4EF Unusual staircase down to bar-restaurant in vaulted cellars; long stone-faced counter under stained-glass skylight, 24 regularly changing ales/craft beers (tasters offered) plus over 150 in bottles from around the world, good selection of malt whiskies and other spirits, interesting wine list, coffees and teas, italian food including range of pizzas (vegetarians/vegans catered for), cheerful chatty staff; some live music; wheelchair access via lift, disabled loos, open (and food) all day (till 2am Mon-Sat), can get crowded; beer shop upstairs. *(Chris and Angela Buckell, Dr and Mrs A K Clarke)*

BRISTOL   ST5872
BrewDog (0117) 927 9258

Baldwin Street, opposite church; BS1 1QW Corner bar serving own BrewDog beers and guests from other craft breweries (draught and bottled), tasters offered by knowledgeable young staff, limited but interesting selection of bar snacks and pizzas, starkly modern feel with exposed brick, stainless-steel furniture and granite surfaces, can get noisily busy; wheelchair access, open all day till midnight (1am Thurs-Sat). *(Sophie Ellison)*

BRISTOL   ST5874
Chums (0117) 973 1498

Chandos Road; BS6 6PF Micropub in former corner shop; mismatched furniture on boarded floor, painted half-panelling and lots of local artwork for sale, pine-planked bar serving up to six real ales including Palmers and Wye Valley, real ciders/perries and range of bottled belgian beers, also good quality wines and interesting spirits, some snacky food, friendly chatty atmosphere (mobile phones discouraged); live music Sat and alternating with quiz night Weds; dogs welcome, wheelchair access using ramp (staff will help), disabled loo, open all day Fri-Sun, from 4pm other days.
(Chris and Angela Buckell)

BRISTOL   ST5872
Commercial Rooms (0117) 927 9681

Corn Street; BS1 1HT Spacious colonnaded Wetherspoons (former early 19th-c merchants' club) in good location; main part with lofty stained-glass domed ceiling, large oval portraits of Bristol notables and gas lighting, comfortable quieter back room with ornate balcony, note the unusual wind gauge above horseshoe servery; good changing choice of real ales, local ciders and expanding range of gins, nice chatty bustle (busiest weekend evenings), their usual food and low prices; ladies' with chesterfields and open fire; children welcome, no dogs, side wheelchair access and disabled facilities, open all day from 8am and till late Fri-Sun. *(Roger and Donna Huggins, Dr and Mrs A K Clarke, Chris and Angela Buckell)*

BRISTOL   ST5872
Cornubia (0117) 925 4415
Temple Street opposite fire station;
BS1 6EN Tucked-away 18th-c pub with up to eight real ales including a good locally brewed house beer, also interesting bottled beers, farm ciders and perry, snacky food such as pasties and pork pies, friendly helpful service, walls and ceilings covered in pump clips, union jacks and other patriotic memorabilia, open fire and an aquarium for turtles; weekly quiz; dogs welcome, not suitable for wheelchairs, picnic-sets in secluded front beer garden (summer barbecues and jazz Sun afternoons), boules pitch, closed Sun evening, otherwise open all day. *(Dr and Mrs A K Clarke, Edward May)*

BRISTOL   ST5976
Drapers Arms
Gloucester Road; BS7 8TZ Welcoming one-room micropub in former draper's shop; five well kept local beers tapped from the cask, proper ciders and decent wines by the glass, no food apart from bar snacks; donation to charity box if you use a mobile phone; open from 5pm (midday Sat) till 9.30pm. *(Roger and Donna Huggins)*

BRISTOL   ST5773
Eldon House (0117) 922 1271
Lower Clifton Hill, Clifton; BS8 1BT
Extended terrace-end Clifton pub; mix of wooden tables and chairs on bare boards, circular stone-walled dining area with glazed roof, snug with original stained glass and half-door servery, well kept Bath, guest beers and several wines by the glass, enjoyable food from lunchtime snacks to daily changing evening menu (pop-up kitchens), friendly staff; background and regular live music, other events including Mon quiz, free wi-fi; children welcome till 8pm, dogs in bar, open (and some food) all day. *(Sophie Ellison)*

BRISTOL   ST5876
Gloucester Old Spot
(0117) 924 7693 *Kellaway Avenue;*
BS6 7YQ Popular opened-up and refurbished family-run pub; well kept ales such as Butcombe, Exmoor and Timothy Taylors from horseshoe servery, decent wines and enjoyable reasonably priced food from sandwiches and sharing boards up, friendly prompt service, back bar and large parquet-floored dining lounge opening on to verandah and AstroTurf beer garden; background music, Tues quiz, free wi-fi; children and dogs

welcome, wheelchair access using portable ramp (staff will help, no disabled loos), play area with wendy house, open all day from 9am for breakfast. *(Chris and Angela Buckell)*

BRISTOL   ST5872
Golden Guinea (0117) 987 2034
Guinea Street; BS1 6SX Steps up to cosy backstreet pub with well kept changing ales, interesting craft beers and proper ciders, simple bargain home-made food, friendly staff, pews, wing armchairs and farmhouse tables on bare boards, some flock wallpaper and contemporary street art; live music (including Tues folk night), sports TV; dogs welcome, seats out in front and behind, closed till 4pm Mon-Weds, otherwise open all day from noon (1pm Sun). *(Chris and Angela Buckell)*

BRISTOL   ST5772
Grain Barge (0117) 929 9347
Hotwell Road; BS8 4RU Converted 100-ft barge owned by Bristol Beer Factory, their ales kept well and fair priced food (all day weekends) including good sandwiches, burgers and Sun roasts, steak night Thurs, great harbour views from seats out on top deck, tables and sofas in wood floor bar below, also a 'hold bar' for events and functions; children welcome, open all day. *(Chris and Angela Buckell)*

BRISTOL   ST5873
Green Man (0117) 925 8062
Alfred Place, Kingsdown; BS2 8HD
Cosy local with country pub feel; bare boards and dark woodwork, well kept Dawkins and guests, real cider, several wines by the glass and around 60 gins, food served Weds-Fri evenings only including good burgers, also popular Sun roasts from 12.30pm, friendly staff; background and regular live music, Weds quiz, free wi-fi; children and dogs welcome, wheelchair access with help, open from 4pm Mon-Thurs, 2pm Fri and Sat, midday Sun. *(Edward May)*

BRISTOL   ST5873
Horts City Tavern (0117) 925 2520
Broad Street; BS1 2EJ Imposing 18th-c Youngs pub, their well kept beers along with Bath and St Austell, good fairly priced food (all day Fri-Sun) including sharing boards and burgers, spacious interior with big windows overlooking street, some raised sections and side rooms, old pictures of the city, 26-seat cinema at back (free film Weds evening); background music, sports TVs; tables in cobbled courtyard, open all day and at its busiest lunchtime/early evening. *(Chris and Angela Buckell)*

BRISTOL   ST5977
Inn on the Green (0117) 952 1391
Filton Road (A38), Horfield; BS7 0PA
Busy open-plan pub with up to 12 changing ales, half a dozen ciders and good selection

of whiskies/gins, enjoyable generously served food including daily deals, helpful friendly staff, wood or slate floors, lots of mirrors and old prints, modern pub furniture along with sofas and armchairs, more screened seating in former skittle alley dining area; bar billiards and darts; children and dogs welcome, disabled access/facilities, beer garden with sheltered pool table and summer table tennis, open (and food) all day. *(Jim King)*

BRISTOL ST5774
Jersey Lily (0117) 973 8590
Whiteladies Road; BS8 2SB Compact corner pub with matt-black frontage; well kept Wickwar ales and guests, decent wines and good range of gins, enjoyable reasonably priced food from shortish menu including lunchtime ciabattas, sharing plates and range of burgers, busy but attentive service, painted dados and polished wood floors, some high tables and stools, step up to part with sofas and easy chairs; live acoustic music Thurs, Sun quiz, sports TV, free wi-fi; partial wheelchair access, pavement seats and awning, decked side area through arch, open all day. *(Chris and Angela Buckell)*

BRISTOL ST5874
Kensington Arms (0117) 944 6444
Stanley Road; BS6 6NP Dining pub (aka the Kenny) in centre of Redland; highly regarded food at fair prices from chef-patron including weekday set lunch deal, well kept Bristol Beer Factory ales and guests, Thatcher's cider and plenty of wines by the glass from comprehensive list, happy hour 4.30-6.30pm Mon-Thurs, friendly attentive staff; background music; children and dogs welcome, disabled facilities (no wheelchair access to dining room, but can eat in bar), heated front terrace, open all day. *(Edward May)*

BRISTOL ST5972
Kings Head (0117) 929 2338
Victoria Street; BS1 6DE Welcoming and relaxed little 17th-c pub; traditional bar with big front window and splendid mirrored bar-back, corridor to cosy panelled snug with serving hatch, toby jugs on joists, old-fashioned local prints and photographs, five well kept ales including Fullers, Harveys and Wye Valley, no food; a few pavement tables, open all day. *(Maddie Purvis)*

BRISTOL ST5972
Knights Templar (0117) 930 8710
The Square; BS1 6DG Glass and steel Wetherspoons very handy for Temple Meads station; spacious carpeted room with raised area, great range of beers from well stocked bar, their usual reasonably priced food served from breakfast till late, helpful staff; lots of TVs, free wi-fi; children welcome, disabled access/loos, plenty of outside seating, open all day. *(Giles and Annie Francis)*

BRISTOL ST5276
Lamplighters (0117) 279 3754
End of Station Road, Shirehampton; BS11 9XA Popular 18th-c riverside pub; well kept Bath, St Austell and a guest, Thatcher's ciders, teas and coffees, competitively priced fairly traditional food (not Sun evening) including children's choices, blackboard specials and Tues OAP lunch deal, modern bar furniture on carpet or bare boards, some faux leather sofas and armchairs, pastel walls with darker greeny-blue dados, bold patterned wallpaper here and there, mezzanine dining area and cellar bar (not always open); occasional live music; wheelchair access, disabled loos/baby changing, picnic-sets on paved front terrace, limited parking nearby (beware high spring tides), riverside walks, open all day. *(Chris and Angela Buckell)*

BRISTOL ST5976
Lazy Dog (0117) 924 4809
Ashley Down Road; BS7 9JR Popular local with two bar areas (one upstairs), ales such as Bath, Bristol Beer Factory, Purity and Wye Valley, local ciders, interesting wines and good range of spirits, well liked food from fairly extensive menu including some unusual dishes, helpful chatty staff, charcoal grey interior with wood panelled alcoves, white marble-effect bar counter, leather wall benches, sofas and armchairs on light wood floors, family room with metal furniture (children till 7pm); quiz and comedy nights; dogs welcome, disabled access/loos, seats out at front and in partly decked back garden, open all day. *(John and Mary Warner)*

BRISTOL ST5772
Nova Scotia (0117) 929 7994
Baltic Wharf, Cumberland Basin; BS1 6XJ Welcoming old local on south side of floating harbour with views to Clifton and Avon Gorge; Caledonian ales, a guest beer and Thatcher's ciders, generous helpings of enjoyable pub food (not Sun evening) from doorstep sandwiches to blackboard specials, four linked areas, snob screen, mahogany and mirrors, nautical charts as wallpaper, maritime photographs and some murals, welcoming relaxed atmosphere; Mon folk night; wheelchair access with help through snug's door, no disabled loo, plenty of tables out by water, open all day. *(Chris and Angela Buckell)*

Half pints: by law, a pub should not charge more for half a pint than half the price of a full pint, unless it shows that half-pint price on its price list.

BRISTOL   ST5872
Old Duke (0117) 401 9661
King Street; BS1 4ER Corner pub named
after Duke Ellington and festooned with
jazz posters, good bands nightly and Sun
lunchtime, up to six real ales and a couple
of ciders, simple food, usual pub furnishings;
tables on pedestrianised cobbled street,
open all day (till 1am Fri, Sat), gets packed
evenings. *(Dr and Mrs A K Clarke, Chris and
Angela Buckell)*

BRISTOL   ST5872
Old Fish Market (0117) 921 1515
Baldwin Street; BS1 1QZ Popular
Fullers pub in imposing brick-built former
fish market; well kept ales, craft beers,
a dozen wines by the glass and fine range
of whiskies/gins from handsome wooden
counter, enjoyable food including pizzas
and various chowders, friendly relaxed
atmosphere; background music, Sun live jazz
from 7pm, sports TVs, free wi-fi; children
and dogs welcome, open all day (food all day
weekends). *(Dr and Mrs A K Clarke)*

BRISTOL   ST5772
Orchard 07405 360994
Hanover Place, Spike Island; BS1 6XT
Friendly corner local under newish
management; several well kept stillaged
ales including St Austell and over 20 ciders/
perries, simple lunchtime food such as rolls,
pasties and pork pies, woodburner, piano;
Mon blues jam and Tues jazz; tables out in
front, convenient for SS *Great Britain*, open
all day. *(Chris and Angela Buckell)*

BRISTOL   ST5672
Portcullis (0117) 973 0270
Wellington Terrace; BS8 4LE Compact
pub in Regency terrace close to Clifton
Suspension Bridge; six well kept ales
including three from Dawkins, traditional
cider and good range of wines and spirits,
low-priced pubby food (not Weds, Thurs),
friendly service, flame-effect gas fire, dark
wood and usual pubby furniture, upstairs
room leading to beer garden; occasional
acoustic live music, board games, free wi-fi;
dogs welcome, tricky wheelchair access,
open all day Sat, Sun, closed lunchtimes
Mon-Thurs (also Fri in winter).
(Chris and Angela Buckell)

BRISTOL   ST5772
Pump House (0117) 927 2229
Merchants Road; BS8 4PZ Spacious well
converted dockside building (former 19th-c
pumping station); charcoal-grey brickwork,
tiled floors and high ceilings, good locally

sourced food in bar and smart candlelit
mezzanine restaurant, Butcombe and guests
such as Bristol Beer Factory, decent wines
from comprehensive list and over 400 gins,
good selection of rums and whiskies too,
friendly staff and cheerful atmosphere;
waterside tables, open all day. *(Edward May)*

BRISTOL   ST5872
Riverstation (0117) 914 4434
*The Grove; opposite Hole in the Wall
pub; BS1 4RB* Modern harbourside
bar-restaurant converted some years ago
from a former police building; light and airy
split-level bar/dining area with tiled and
polished wood floors, mix of seating including
sofas and squashy banquettes, good views
from french windows opening on to waterside
terrace, Youngs ales, Orchard Pig cider and
several international bottled beers, good
selection of wines, spirits and cocktails too,
spacious upstairs restaurant with high curved
ceiling and lots of glass, further terraces
overlooking the water, well liked food from
interesting varied menu including weekend
brunch, helpful staff; background music;
limited wheelchair access, open (and food)
all day. *(John and Mary Warner)*

BRISTOL   ST5872
Royal Naval Volunteer
07487 242300 *King Street; BS1 4EF*
17th-c pub in cobbled street, wide range of
draught and bottled british beers, ciders/
perries and a dozen wines by the glass,
friendly knowledgeable staff, good interesting
food in back restaurant; weekend live music,
sports TV; dogs welcome, terrace seating,
open all day. *(Dr and Mrs A K Clarke)*

BRISTOL   ST5972
Seven Stars (0117) 927 2845
Thomas Lane; BS1 6JG Unpretentious
one-room real ale pub near harbour (and
associated with Thomas Clarkson and slave
trade abolition), popular with students
and local office workers; up to eight well
kept changing ales (20 from a featured
county on first Mon-Thurs of the month),
some interesting malts and bourbons, dark
wood and bare boards, old local prints
and photographs, no food – can bring in
takeaways; weekend acoustic music, pool,
games machine; dogs welcome, disabled
access (but narrow alley with uneven cobbles
and cast-iron kerbs), open all day.
(Sophie Ellison)

BRISTOL   ST5872
Small Bar
King Street; BS1 4DZ Bustling real ale/
craft beer pub with over 30 choices including

We mention bottled beers and spirits only if there is something unusual about them
– imported belgian real ales, say, or dozens of malt whiskies; so do please let us know
about them in your reports.

own Left Handed Giant, all served in smaller glasses (up to two-thirds of a pint), good range of bottled beers too, enjoyable food such as burgers and hotdogs along with vegetarian/vegan choices, bare boards and flagstones, roughly exposed brickwork here and there and wood plank walls, some barrel tables and a couple of old fireplaces, upstairs area with armchairs, sofas and shelves of books; background music; open all day (till 1am Fri, Sat). *(Dr and Mrs A K Clarke)*

BRISTOL   ST6375
Snuffy Jacks Ale House
(0117) 965 5158
Fishponds Road; BS16 3TE Micropub in former stationers; up to eight cask-tapped ales, real ciders and some good quality gins from planked servery, friendly knowledgeable staff, mismatching furniture including old church pews on wood-strip floor, vibrant blue walls hung with local artwork, bare pendant lighting; no mobile phones, credit cards or food (maybe bar nibbles Sun); dogs welcome, wheelchair access, open all day Sat, till 4.30pm Sun and from 5pm weekdays.
(Chris and Angela Buckell)

BRISTOL   ST5872
Three Tuns (0117) 329 4310
St Georges Road; BS1 5UR Popular old yellow-painted pub just behind City Hall; seven real ales including local Arbor, four craft kegs and interesting selection of bottled beers, also local ciders and good range of spirits, snacky food along with decent burgers and Sun roasts, prompt service, L-shaped bar with pine tables on bare boards, a couple of small leather sofas in alcoves, open fire in cast-iron fireplace with mirror above; background and live music, other events such as quiz, magic and movie nights; dogs welcome, wheelchair access (no disabled loo), steps down to small covered and heated terrace, near cathedral, open all day (till midnight Thurs-Sat), no food Sun evening, Mon. *(Chris and Angela Buckell)*

BRISTOL   ST5971
Victoria Park (0117) 330 6043
Raymend Road; BS3 4QW Brick-fronted family dining pub in hilly residential part of the city, welcoming and friendly, with large opened-up L-shaped interior, mix of furniture including long refectory tables and old pews on stripped-wood floors, dark-grey walls hung with local artwork, modern pendant lighting, white tiled back bar with folding glass doors to splendid tiered garden (rooftop views over to Dundry Hill), three changing ales, Weston's ciders and good choice of other drinks, popular food from interesting blackboard menu (booking advised weekends), also sandwiches and pizzas; background music, quiz nights and book club; dogs welcome, tricky wheelchair access and no disabled loos, nearby parking at a premium, open all day. *(Chris and Angela Buckell)*

BRISTOL   ST5973
Volunteer (0117) 955 8498
New Street, near Cabot Circus; BS2 9DX Tucked-away local with good choice of changing ales/craft beers, a couple of ciders and decent wines by the glass, pop-up kitchens (vegetarian at time of writing) along with popular Sun roasts, friendly relaxed atmosphere; live music and beer festivals; children and dogs welcome, walled garden behind, open all day from 1pm Sun, 4pm Mon-Weds, noon other days, no food Mon (but can bring your own). *(Edward May)*

BRISTOL   ST5976
Wellington (0117) 951 3022
Gloucester Road, Horfield (A38); BS7 8UR Updated and opened-up 1920s red-brick pub on edge of Horfield Common; well kept Bath and St Austell, craft beers, local cider and good choice of other drinks including range of gins, enjoyable reasonably priced food till 10pm, pleasant efficient service, separate dining area opening on to sunny paved terrace and grassy beer garden; background music, drop-down screens for major sports, pool; children welcome, wheelchair access from back door (or front using ramp), disabled loos, popular boutique bedrooms (best to book early), open all day (from 9am weekends for breakfast). *(Chris and Angela Buckell)*

BRISTOL   ST5872
Wild Beer (0117) 329 4997
Gaol Ferry Steps, Wapping Wharf, behind the M Shed Museum; BS1 5WE Busy bar in new development overlooking the old docks; over 20 craft beers (including Wild Beer) listed on blackboards and served in third, half and two-thirds of a pint glasses (tasters offered), interesting wines and good selection of whiskies/gins, reasonably priced food from snacks up, cheerful helpful staff, flagstones, pale green walls and floor-to-ceiling windows, exposed ducting and a large mural on one wall, a couple of steps up to dining area with open kitchen; background music; children welcome, disabled access/facilities, split-level terrace with deckchairs and picnic-sets, parking nearby difficult, open all day. *(Maddie Purvis)*

BROADWAY   ST3215
Bell (01460) 52343
Broadway Lane; TA19 9RG Welcoming 18th-c stone-built village pub refurbished under current owners; opened-up interior with flagstones and log fires, enjoyable fairly priced food including wood-fired pizzas, Bath and St Austell ales, decent choice of wines and some interesting local gins, friendly attentive service; live band first Sun of month; children and dogs welcome, tables on front walled terrace, open all day from 9am for breakfast. *(Ben and Jenny Settle)*

BURROW BRIDGE   ST3530
King Alfred   (01823) 698379
Main Road, by the bridge; TA7 0RB
Old-fashioned pub with relaxed friendly
atmosphere in flagstoned bar, well kept ales
such as Butcombe and Otter, local ciders and
decent wines by the glass, good generously
served food from pub standards up including
daily specials, comfortable dining room
upstairs with view over River Parrett and
Somerset Levels, roof terrace; live music and
quiz nights; children and dogs welcome, self-
catering cottage, open all day (till 9pm Sun).
(Tessa Barton)

BUTLEIGH   ST5133
Rose & Portcullis   (01458) 850287
Sub Road/Barton Road; BA6 8TQ
Welcoming stone-built country pub with
enjoyable good value home-made food
(not Sun evening), four well kept ales and
good range of local ciders, helpful friendly
staff, bar and airy dining extension; sports
TV, free wi-fi; children and dogs welcome,
tables outside, closed Mon lunchtime in
winter. *(Simon and Alex Knight)*

CASTLE CARY   ST6432
George   (01963) 350761
*Just off A371 Shepton Mallet–Wincanton;
Market Place; BA7 7AH*   Old-fashioned
thatched country-town hotel (former 15th-c
coaching inn); popular front bar with
big inglenook, bistro-bar and restaurant,
enjoyable food from sandwiches up, three
changing real ales and decent wines by
the glass, friendly staff; free wi-fi; children
and dogs welcome, 17 bedrooms (some in
courtyard), open all day. *(Bob and Melissa
Wyatt)*

CATCOTT   ST3939
Crown   (01278) 722288
*Off A39 W of Street; Nidon Lane, via
Brook Lane; TA7 9HQ*   Roomy traditional
old pub just outside the village; welcoming
landlord and staff, enjoyable food including
good Sun carvery (booking advised), real
ales such as Otter and Sharps, decent wines
by the glass, cosy area by log fire; skittle
alley; children and dogs welcome, picnic-
sets and play area out behind, closed Mon
lunchtime. *(Roy Hoing)*

CHARLTON HORETHORNE ST6623
★ Kings Arms   (01963) 220281
B3145 Wincanton–Sherborne; DT9 4NL
Bustling rather smart 19th-c inn; main bar
with assortment of local art (all for sale)
on dark walls, carved wooden dining chairs
and pine pews around mix of tables, slate
floor and logburner, cosy room off with
sofas, dining room and more formal back
restaurant, Butcombe Bitter and a couple
of guests, local cider, 16 wines by the glass
and decent range of whiskies/gins, good
up-to-date food served by efficient friendly
staff; children and dogs (in bar) welcome,
attractive back courtyard with modern
seating under parasols, croquet, comfortable
well equipped bedrooms, good breakfast,
open all day. *(Mrs Zara Elliott, Robert and Diana
Ringstone, Ian Herdman, Mike and Mary Carter)*

CHARLTON MUSGROVE   ST7229
Smithy   (01963) 824899
*B3081, 5 miles SE of Bruton; about
a mile off A303; BA9 8HG*   Restored
18th-c pub under friendly licensees; bar with
stripped stone, heavy beams and inglenook
woodburner, rugs on flagstone/concrete floor,
mismatch of furniture (some tables made
from old cheeseboards), Greene King ales
and guests from plank-fronted servery, well
liked uncomplicated food (not Sun evening),
intimate dining area overlooking garden,
restaurant in former skittle alley; background
and monthly live music, quiz nights, TV for
major sports; children and dogs welcome,
open all day. *(Holly and Tim Waite)*

CHEDDAR   ST4653
White Hart   (01934) 741261
The Bays; BS27 3QN   Welcoming village
local at the bottom of Cheddar Gorge; well
kept beers, traditional cider and enjoyable
competitively priced food from good
ploughman's to Sun carvery, log fire; live
music, quiz third Weds of month, free wi-fi;
children and dogs welcome, picnic-sets out
at front and in back garden with play area,
open (and food) all day. *(Tony Scott)*

CHEW MAGNA   ST5861
★ Pony & Trap   (01275) 332627
*Knowle Hill, New Town; from B3130
in village, follow Bishop Sutton, Bath
signpost; BS40 8TQ*   Michelin-starred
dining pub in nice rural spot near Chew
Valley Lake; excellent food from snacks and
some lunchtime pubby choices through to
beautifully presented expensive restaurant
dishes (must book), professional friendly
service, Butcombe Bitter and a guest,
extensive wine list and good choice of other
drinks including cocktails, front bar with
cushioned wall seats and built-in benches on
parquet, old range in snug area on left, dark
plank panelling and housekeeper's chair in
corner, lovely pasture views from two-level
back dining area with white tables on slate
flagstones; children welcome, dogs in bar,
modern furniture on back terrace, picnic-sets
on grass with chickens in runs below, good
local walks. *(R L Borthwick, Mrs Zara Elliott,
Dr and Mrs A K Clarke)*

CHEWTON MENDIP   ST5953
Waldegrave Arms   (01761) 241384
High Street (A39); BA3 4LL   Friendly
roadside village pub run by the same family
for over 30 years; traditional food from
sandwiches up including Sun roasts, well
kept ales such as Butcombe, Cottage and
Slaters; quiz nights and darts leagues; dogs

welcome in bar, colourful window boxes and hanging baskets, flower-filled garden behind, open (and food) all day Sun. *(Charles Todd)*

CHISELBOROUGH ST4614
Cat Head (01935) 881231
Cat Street; leave A303 on A356 towards Crewkerne; take the third left (at 1.4 miles) signed Chiselborough, then left after 0.2 miles; TA14 6TT Character 15th-c hamstone pub with bar and two dining areas, flagstones, mullioned windows and two permanently lit woodburners (one in fine inglenook), well executed fairly traditional food cooked by landlady, a couple of ales such as Sharps and Butcombe; classical background music; children and dogs (in bar) welcome, picnic-sets in lovely back garden, closed Sun evening, Mon. *(Miranda and Jeff Davidson)*

CLAPTON-IN-GORDANO ST4773
★ Black Horse (01275) 842105
4 miles W of M5 junction 19; A369 towards Portishead, then B3124 towards Clevedon; in North Weston opposite school, turn left signposted Clapton, then in village take second right, may be signed 'Clevedon, Clapton Wick'; BS20 7RH Unpretentious 14th-c pub with plenty of cheerful locals; main room has winged settles and built-in wall benches around narrow tables, flagstone and quarry-tiled floors, big log fire, other rooms including inner snug with barred windows (was the petty sessions gaol), ales such as Bath, Butcombe, Otter and St Austell (some tapped from the cask), three farm ciders and six wines by the glass, honest lunchtime food (not Sun); background music; children in family room only, dogs welcome, wheelchair access but no disabled loos, rustic tables and benches in garden with play area, paths from the pub lead up Naish Hill or to Cadbury Camp (NT), open all day (till 9.30pm Sun); due to change hands as we went to press. *(Roger and Donna Huggins, Chris and Angela Buckell, Donald Allsopp, Anne Taylor)*

COMBE FLOREY ST1531
★ Farmers Arms (01823) 432267
Off A358 Taunton–Williton, just N of main village turn-off; TA4 3HZ Popular 14th-c thatched and beamed pub well restored after severe fire damage; good food from interesting varied menu including Josper grills, five real ales such as Exmoor and Patriot, proper ciders and good range of whiskies and gins, friendly helpful staff; children and dogs welcome, tables out under parasols, maybe wood-fired pizzas in summer, Evelyn Waugh lived in the village, as did his son Auberon, open all day (till 7pm Sun). *(Simon Earp)*

COMBE HAY ST7359
★ Wheatsheaf (01225) 833504
Village signposted off A367 or B3110 S of Bath; BA2 7EG Country dining pub with good imaginative food; sofas on dark flagstones by big fireplace in central part, other informal areas with high-backed dining chairs around chunky modern tables on parquet or coir matting, contemporary artwork and mirrors with colourful ceramic mosaic frames (many for sale), some interesting knick-knacks on windowsills, ales such as Butcombe and Otter, real cider and 16 wines by the glass, good selection of malt whiskies too, efficient friendly service; background music; children and dogs welcome, two-level front garden with fine view over the church and valley; good surrounding walks, spacious comfortable bedrooms, closed Sun evening and Mon (except bank holidays). *(Patricia and Gordon Thompson, Jane Rigby, Dr and Mrs A K Clarke)*

COMPTON DANDO ST6464
Compton Inn (01761) 490321
Court Hill; BS39 4JZ Welcoming stone-built village pub in lovely setting; enjoyable home-made food (not Sun evening), well kept Butcombe, Sharps and a guest, wood-floored bar with dining area at each end (one down a couple of steps), two-way woodburner in stone fireplace; charity quiz first Mon of month, TV; children, walkers and dogs welcome, picnic-sets out in front, garden behind with boules, open all day. *(Charles and Maddie Bishop)*

CONGRESBURY ST4363
Old Inn (01934) 832270
Pauls Causeway, down Broad Street opposite The Cross; BS49 5DH Popular low-beamed and dimly lit 16th-c local; deep-set windows, flagstones and huge fireplaces, one with stove opening to both bar and dining area, mix of old furniture including pews and upholstered benches, leather ceiling straps, good choice of enjoyable reasonably priced pubby food (not Sun evening, Mon), well kept Youngs and a couple of guests tapped from casks, Thatcher's cider and decent wines; children and dogs welcome, tables in back garden with pétanque, open all day. *(Graham Smart)*

CONGRESBURY ST4363
★ Plough (01934) 877402
High Street (B3133); BS49 5JA Popular old-fashioned character local – a pub since the 1800s; half a dozen well kept changing west country ales such as Butcombe, Cheddar and St Austell, ciders from Orchard Pig and Thatcher's, quick friendly service, generous helpings of well cooked food (not

---

We include some hotels with a good bar that offers facilities comparable to those of a pub.

Sun evening) including daily specials, several small interconnecting rooms off flagstoned main bar, mix of old and new furniture, built-in pine wall benches, old prints, photos, farm tools and some morris dancing memorabilia, log fires; Sun quiz; no children inside, dogs welcome, wheelchair access from car park, garden with rustic furniture and boules. *(Graham Smart)*

CORFE   ST2319
White Hart (01823) 421388
B3170 S of Taunton; TA3 7BU Traditional 17th-c village pub; enjoyable sensibly priced pubby food (not Tues) including vegetarian options, curry night last Thurs of the month (booking advised), well kept ales such as Butcombe and Otter, beams, woodburner and open fire; bar billiards, skittle alley; dogs welcome, open all day Sat, closed Tues lunchtime. *(Sophie Ellison)*

CORSTON   ST6764
Wheatsheaf (01225) 874518
A39 towards Marksbury; BA2 9HB
Old mansard-roofed roadside pub improved under welcoming new management; good food from varied menu including popular Sun roasts (must book), well kept Butcombe and Sharps, Thatcher's cider, friendly attentive service, cosy bar with comfortable seating by roaring woodburner, smart restaurant; children and dogs welcome, open all day Fri-Sun, closed Mon. *(Pete and Sarah)*

CORTON DENHAM   ST6322
★ **Queens Arms** (01963) 220317
Village signposted off B3145 N of Sherborne; DT9 4LR Handsome 18th-c inn with bustling high-beamed bar, rugs on flagstones, old pews, barrel seats and a couple of big armchairs in front of open fire, Wild Beer Bibble and guests, local ciders and some unusual bottled beers, 22 wines by the glass including champagne from carefully chosen list, extensive range of malt whiskies and gins, rewarding food from pub classics to restauranty dishes using local suppliers, two separate dining rooms; children and dogs (in bar) welcome, teak tables under parasols on sunny back terrace, comfortable bedrooms with lovely country views, fine nearby walks and Cadbury Castle hill fort is not far away, open all day from 8am, breakfast for non-residents. *(Christopher and Elise Way, Tracey and Stephen Groves, Dan and Belinda Smallbone, Helene Grygar)*

CRANMORE   ST6643
Strode Arms (01749) 880450
West Cranmore; signed with pub off A361 Frome–Shepton Mallet; BA4 4QJ
Pretty stone dining pub (former 15th-c farmhouse) overlooking village duck pond; rambling beamed rooms with log fires in

handsome fireplaces, carpeted or flagstone floors, country furnishings, enjoyable generously served food from snacks up, Wadworths ales and decent wines by the glass, good friendly service; children, walkers and dogs welcome, seats on front terrace, handy for East Somerset Railway (steam trains), open all day weekends. *(John Harris)*

CROSS   ST4254
New Inn (01934) 732455
A38 Bristol–Bridgwater, junction A371; BS26 2EE Steps up to popular old roadside pub with well kept Otter and several interesting guest beers, good choice of enjoyable fairly traditional food from baguettes and baked potatoes up (booking advised), friendly service, more dining space upstairs; children and dogs welcome (resident cocker is called Guinness), views from nice hillside garden with play area, Aug bank holiday mower racing/beer festival, open (and food) all day. *(Tessa Barton, Hugh Roberts)*

CROWCOMBE   ST1336
Carew Arms (01984) 618631
Just off A358 Taunton–Minehead; TA4 4AD Interesting 17th-c beamed country inn attracting good mix of customers; hunting trophies, huge flagstones and good inglenook log fire in small lived-in front bar, up to five well kept ales such as Exmoor, Otter and St Austell, real cider and enjoyable home-made food (not Sun evening in winter), friendly service; children (in dining room), walkers and dogs welcome, tables in good-sized garden, outside skittle alley, six bedrooms, open all day in summer (all day Fri-Sun winter). *(Guy Vowles)*

CURRY RIVEL   ST3925
Firehouse (01458) 887447
Church Street; TA10 0HE Stylishly renovated village pub; light beams, exposed stonework and log fires, cosy bar with tractor-seat stools at counter serving four real ales (always Butcombe), decent wines and cocktails, happy hour 4-6pm, pubby food along with pizzas from feature oven, lunchtime/early evening deal (Mon-Fri), friendly helpful young staff, various dining areas including upstairs raftered room and cellar bar with fine 14th-c vaulted ceiling; live music and quiz nights; children welcome, circular picnic-sets on paved terrace, open all day. *(Geoff and Ann Marston)*

DINNINGTON   ST4013
Dinnington Docks (01460) 52397
NE of village; Fosse Way; TA17 8SX
Large rural local freshened up but unspoilt under welcoming new owners; enjoyable home-made food (some choices available in smaller helpings), well kept Butcombe and

---

guests, farm ciders, friendly attentive staff, memorabilia of former railway and canal dock, log fire; some live music, TV for major sports; children and dogs (theirs is Saffy) welcome, new chunky picnic-sets in large garden behind, good walks, open all day, no evening food Sun or Tues. *(DavidM)*

DITCHEAT ST6236

★**Manor House** (01749) 860276

Signed off A37 and A371 S of Shepton Mallet; BA4 6RB Pretty 17th-c red-brick village inn (sister to the Rockford Inn at Brendon, Devon); enjoyable food from short but varied menu, well kept ales such as Butcombe and Cotleigh, friendly helpful staff, unusual arched doorways linking big flagstoned bar to comfortable lounge and restaurant, open fires; skittle alley; children welcome, tables on back grass, handy for Bath & West Showground, five bedrooms, good breakfast, open all day. *(Ben and Diane Bowie)*

DOULTING ST6444

Poachers Pocket (01749) 880220

Chelynch Road, off A361; BA4 4PY Popular village pub with good reasonably priced wholesome food including Sun roasts in three sizes (must book), well kept Butcombe, Wadworths and a guest, friendly attentive service, country furniture on flagstones or carpet, log fire in stripped-stone end wall, dining conservatory; skittle alley/function room; children and dogs welcome, back garden with nice country views. *(Pete and Sarah)*

DOWLISH WAKE ST3712

New Inn (01460) 52413

Off A3037 S of Ilminster, via Kingstone; TA19 0NZ Comfortable and welcoming dark-beamed village pub; enjoyable home-made food from sandwiches and pub favourites up including Mon steak night, well kept Butcombe and Timothy Taylor, local cider, friendly helpful staff, woodburners in stone inglenooks, pleasant dining room; quiz first Sun of the month; dogs welcome, attractive garden and village, Perry's cider mill and shop nearby, four bedrooms in separate annexe. *(Maddie Purvis)*

DULVERTON SS9127

Bridge Inn (01398) 324130

Bridge Street; TA22 9HJ Welcoming unpretentious little pub next to River Barle; reasonably priced locally sourced food from snacks and sandwiches up, four well kept ales including Exmoor and some unusual imported beers, comfortable sofas, woodburner; children and dogs welcome, two terraces, open all day in summer. *(Edward May)*

DUNSTER SS9843

Stags Head (01643) 821229

West Street (A396); TA24 6SN Friendly accommodating staff in this unassuming

16th-c roadside inn; popular food from sandwiches to blackboard specials, Exmoor, Otter and a guest, beams, timbers and inglenook log fire, steps up to small back dining room; children and dogs (in bar) welcome, long narrow garden behind, four comfortable simple bedrooms, open all day in summer and school holidays, all day weekends at other times. *(Patricia and Anton Larkham)*

EAST HARPTREE ST5453

Castle of Comfort (01761) 221321

B3134, SW on Old Bristol Road; BS40 6DD Former coaching inn set high in the Mendips (last stop before the gallows for some past visitors); hefty timbers and exposed stonework, cushioned settles and other pubby furniture on carpet, log fires, Butcombe, Sharps and a guest, ample helpings of reasonably priced traditional food including good steaks, friendly staff; children and dogs (in bar) welcome, wheelchair access, large garden with raised deck and play area, rewarding walks nearby. *(Peter and Emma Kelly)*

EAST HARPTREE ST5655

Waldegrave Arms (01761) 221429

Church Lane; BS40 6BD Welcoming old beamed pub restored after two-year closure; well kept Butcombe and Sharps, decent wines and plenty of gins, good food from wraps and pub favourites up, rooms arranged around central bar, eclectic mix of furniture on wood or stone floors, log fires; some live music; children and dogs welcome, picnic-sets in attractive sheltered garden with play area, delightful village, open (and food) all day, kitchen closes 6pm Sun. *(Pete and Sarah, M G Hart)*

EAST LAMBROOK ST4218

Rose & Crown (01460) 240433

Silver Street; TA13 5HF Stone-built dining pub (new management) spreading extensively from compact 17th-c core with beams and inglenook woodburner, enjoyable food from shortish menu, Palmers ales and several wines by the glass, friendly service, restaurant extension with glass-covered well, skittle alley; charity quiz third Sun of month; children and dogs (in bar) welcome, disabled access from the side, picnic-sets on neat lawn, opposite East Lambrook Manor Gardens, open all day weekends. *(Bob and Melissa Wyatt)*

EVERCREECH ST6336

Natterjack (01749) 860253

A371 Shepton Mallet–Castle Cary; BA4 6NA Welcoming former Victorian station hotel (line closed 1966); good choice of generously served food at reasonable prices, cheerful helpful service, three changing ales, real cider and nice range of wines, long bar with eating areas off; children and dogs welcome, lots of tables under parasols in big neatly kept garden, nine bedrooms, closed Sun evening. *(Holly and Tim Waite)*

EXFORD   SS8538
★**Exmoor White Horse**
(01643) 831229 *B3224; TA24 7PY*
Popular and welcoming old creeper-clad inn; more or less open-plan bar with good log fire, high-backed antique settle among more conventional seats, scrubbed deal tables, hunting prints and local photographs, Exmoor ales, Thatcher's cider and over 200 malt whiskies, good locally sourced bar and restaurant food including Sun carvery; children and dogs welcome, tables outside by river, pretty village, Land Rover Exmoor safaris, 28 comfortable bedrooms, open (and food) all day. *(Charles Todd)*

FAULKLAND   ST7555
★**Tuckers Grave** (01373) 834230
A366 E of village; BA3 5XF Tiny totally unspoilt place named after Edward Tucker who hanged himself nearby in 1747 and was buried at the pub crossroads; entrance opening into simple tap room with woodburner, casks of Butcombe and Thatcher's Cheddar Valley cider in alcove on left, lunchtime sandwiches on request and occasional evening meals, two high-backed settles facing each other across a single table in right, side room, snug lounge (Rose Room) with Victorian fireplace; monthly live music; shove-ha'penny, skittle alley, outside loos; well behaved children and dogs allowed, lots of tables and chairs on attractive back lawn with good views, summer barbecues, camping, open all day weekends, closed Mon lunchtime. *(Dr and Mrs A K Clarke)*

FRESHFORD   ST7960
★**Inn at Freshford** (01225) 722250
Off A36 or B3108; BA2 7WG Refurbished 16th-c village pub in lovely spot across from River Frome; well kept ales such as Box Steam, craft beers, a couple of local ciders and 24 wines by the glass, interesting whiskies and gins too, popular home-made food from varied menu including selection of small plates and lunchtime sandwiches, friendly efficient young staff; background music; children and dogs welcome, wheelchair access to bar area (steps to dining room), no disabled loo, attractive tiered hillside garden overlooking valley with outside bar and barbecue, good riverside walks, open (and food) all day, till 8pm (6pm) Sun. *(Alistair Holdoway, Chris and Angela Buckell, Ian Herdman, David Eberlin)*

FROME   ST7748
Griffin (01373) 301251
Milk Street; BA11 3DB Under new ownership and some refurbishment; bare-boards bar with etched glass and open fires, long counter serving Frome ales, guest beers and good range of gins, rums and tequilas,

enjoyable food from snacks and sharing plates to burgers, Sun roasts; small garden, open all day Fri and Sat, till 9pm Sun, from 4pm other days. *(Charles Todd)*

FROME   ST7747
Three Swans (01373) 452009
King Street; BA11 1BH Appealing and quirky 17th-c beamed pub; well kept Abbey Bellringer, Butcombe and a local guest, nice wines by the glass, snacky food such as home-made pork pies and scotch eggs, also popular Sun roasts (must book), good friendly service, more space in small upstairs room; children welcome till 7pm, dogs in bar (not after 8pm Fri, Sat), part-covered beer garden, open all day Fri-Sun, closed other days till 4.30pm. *(Charles Todd)*

HALLATROW   ST6357
★**Old Station** (01761) 452228
A39 S of Bristol; BS39 6EN Former 1920s station hotel with extraordinary collection of bric-a-brac including railway memorabilia, musical instruments, postboxes, even half an old Citroën, eclectic mix of furnishings too; Butcombe ales, several wines by the glass and good choice of highly regarded food cooked by landlord-chef, Pullman carriage restaurant, cheerful helpful service; children and dogs (in bar) welcome, café-style furniture on decking, picnic-sets on grass, polytunnel growing own vegetables, five bedrooms in converted outbuilding (no breakfast), open all day Fri-Sun. *(Jim King)*

HARDWAY   ST7234
Bull (01749) 812200
Off B3081 Bruton–Wincanton at brown sign for Stourhead and King Alfred's Tower; Hardway; BA10 0LN Welcoming and relaxed 17th-c country pub under newish management; beams and log fires, good food from fairly pubby blackboard menu (best to book weekends), ales such as Butcombe, maybe winter mulled cider, cheerful helpful service; children and dogs welcome, wheelchair access, picnic-sets in nice garden behind, more seats over the road, closed Sun evening, Mon and Tues. *(Edward Mirzoeff)*

HASELBURY PLUCKNETT   ST4711
★**White Horse** (01460) 78873
North Street; TA18 7RJ Popular open-plan village dining pub; good enterprising food cooked by chef-landlord from bar snacks up including set menu choices, west country ales tapped from the cask, local ciders and ten wines by the glass, friendly efficient service, candlelit tables on flagstones or bare boards, leather sofa by inglenook log fire; children and dogs welcome, pretty back terrace with roses and old well, closed Sun evening, Mon and Tues. *(Alistair Newton)*

HILLFARRANCE   ST1624
Anchor (01823) 461334
Oake; pub signed off Bradford-on-Tone

to Oake road; TA4 1AW Comfortable village pub with dining area off attractive two-part bar; four local ales and good choice of enjoyable fairly priced food including home-made pies and Sun carvery, friendly atmosphere; children welcome, garden with play area, bedrooms, open all day Sun. *(Sophie Ellison)*

HINTON BLEWETT ST5956
★ **Ring o' Bells** (01761) 452239
Signed off A37 in Clutton; BS39 5AN
Charming and welcoming low-beamed stone-built country local opposite village green; old-fashioned bar with solid furniture including pews, log fire, enjoyable home-cooked food catering for vegan and gluten-free diets, obliging service, well kept ales such as Butcombe and Fullers, local cider and good wines by the glass, dining room; children, walkers and dogs welcome, nice view from tables in sheltered front courtyard, open all day Fri and Sat, till 9pm Sun, no food Sun evening. *(M G Hart, Rod and Chris Pring)*

HINTON CHARTERHOUSE ST7758
Rose & Crown (01225) 722153
B3110 about 4 miles S of Bath; BA2 7SN
18th-c village pub refurbished under new management; partly divided carpeted bar with fine panelling, cushioned wall seats and mix of chairs around chunky tables, woodburner in ornate carved stone fireplace (smaller one the other side), well kept Butcombe and Fullers, several wines by glass and enjoyable fairly priced home-made food, long dining room and steps to lower area with unusual beamed ceiling; background music, board games; children and dogs welcome, terraced garden, six comfortable bedrooms, open all day. *(Graham Smart)*

HOLCOMBE ST6648
Duke of Cumberland
(01761) 233731 *Edford Hill; BA3 5HQ*
Modernised riverside pub, sister to the Victoria Pub & Kitchen in Bath; enjoyable fairly priced food including home-made pizzas, Butcombe, Wadsworth and guests, Thatcher's cider, friendly helpful staff, flagstoned bar with easy chairs by log fire, comfortable cosy snug, skittle alley in the dining area; background music, sports TV; children and dogs welcome, small waterside garden, open all day. *(Miranda and Jeff Davidson)*

HORSINGTON ST7023
Half Moon (01963) 370140
Signed off A357 S of Wincanton; BA8 0EF Friendly 17th-c pub with light and airy knocked-through bars; beams, stripped stone and oak floors, inglenook log fires, decent sensibly priced pubby food, up

to five well kept ales including Fullers and Wadworths, decent range of wines and gins, evening restaurant, skittle alley; children and dogs welcome, disabled access, attractive sloping front garden and big back one, good walks nearby, bedrooms in separate buildings behind, closed Sun evening and lunchtimes Mon, Tues and Sat, best to check winter hours. *(Ben and Diane Bowie)*

HORTON ST3214
★ **Five Dials** (01460) 55359
Hanning Road; off A303; TA19 9QH
Smartly updated village pub run by friendly helpful licensees; popular fairly priced food including good steaks and fish dishes, Otter, Sharps Doom Bar and a guest, local ciders and well chosen wines by the glass, restaurant; children and dogs welcome, attractive enclosed terrace garden, six comfortable bedrooms, open all day Fri-Sun, closed Mon. *(Simon and Alex Knight)*

KELSTON ST7067
Old Crown (01225) 423032
Bitton Road; A431 W of Bath; BA1 9AQ
Nicely updated 15th-c pub in same small group as the Inn at Freshford (this chapter) and Cross Guns in Avoncliff (Wiltshire); four small rooms, beams and polished flagstones, carved settles and cask tables, logs burning in ancient open range, also woodburner and coal-effect gas fire, well kept Bass, Butcombe and guest, real cider, enjoyable good value food from shortish menu plus daily specials in bar or restaurant, sandwiches available till 6pm Mon-Fri; children and dogs welcome, wheelchair access with help, picnic-sets under apple trees in sheltered sunny back garden with covered deck, outside bar and barbecue, open (and food) all day, kitchen shuts 7pm Sun. *(Tom and Ruth Rees, Dr and Mrs A K Clarke)*

KEYNSHAM ST6669
★ **Lock-Keeper** (0117) 986 2383
Keynsham Road (A4175 NE of town); BS31 2DD Welcoming riverside pub with relaxed worn-in feel and plenty of character; simple left-hand bar with big painted settle, cushioned wall benches, trophy cabinet and old local photographs, two more little rooms with assorted cushioned dining chairs, more photographs and rustic prints, Youngs ales with guests such as Bath and St Austell, Thatcher's ciders and good range of wines/spirits, popular well priced bar food from lunchtime ciabattas up, cheerful helpful young staff, light modern conservatory (quite different in style); background music; children and dogs (in bar) welcome, disabled access/loos, rattan furniture and giant parasols on big heated deck overlooking water, steps down to picnic-sets on grass,

---

We say if we know a pub has background music.

outside bar/barbecue, pétanque, open
(and food) all day and can get very busy.
*(Dr and Mrs A K Clarke, Pete and Sarah,
Chris and Angela Buckell)*

KILVE ST1442

Hood Arms (01278) 741114

A39 E of Williton; TA5 1EA Welcoming
17th-c village inn; well kept Exmoor,
St Austell and a guest, good reasonably
priced food including popular Sun lunch
(booking advised), friendly helpful service,
warm woodburner in beamed bar, carpeted
restaurant; children and dogs welcome,
ramp for wheelchairs, disabled loo, tables in
back garden, bedrooms, closed Sun evening,
Mon. *(Richard and Penny Gibbs)*

KINGSDON ST5126

★**Kingsdon Inn** (01935) 840543

*At Podimore roundabout on A303,
follow sign to Langport (A372) then
right on B3151; TA11 7LG* Pretty little
thatched cottage; main quarry-tiled bar with
woodburner, built-in cushioned wall seats
and country chairs around scrubbed kitchen
tables, steps up to carpeted, half-panelled
dining area, Butcombe Bitter, Teignworthy
Neap Tide and a guest, local cider and
14 wines by the glass, very good imaginative
food cooked by landlord, second dining area
plus an attractive separate restaurant with
another woodburner; background classical
music, TV; children and dogs (in bar)
welcome, picnic-sets on lawn, herb garden,
handy for the Fleet Air Arm Museum, cosy
bedrooms, closed Sun evening and first week
of Jan. *(David and Sally Cullen, Sandra and
Miles Spencer, Hugh Roberts)*

KNAPP ST3025

Rising Sun (01823) 491027

*Village W of North Curry (pub signed
from here); TA3 6BG* Tucked-away 15th-c
longhouse surrounded by lovely countryside;
handsome beams, flagstones and two
inglenooks with woodburners, Otter Bitter
and Sharps Doom Bar, Bray's cider, good
home-made food (booking advised) including
popular Sun roasts, friendly helpful service;
monthly quiz and some live music, pool;
children and dogs welcome, sunny little front
terrace, open all day Sat, closed Sun evening
and weekday lunchtimes (till 3pm Fri), no
food Mon, Tues. *(Ben and Jenny Settle)*

LANGFORD BUDVILLE ST1122

Martlet (01823) 400262

Off B3187 NW of Wellington; TA21 0QZ
Cosy and comfortable 17th-c village pub;
well kept ales such as Exmoor, Otter and
St Austell, good generously served food
from varied menu cooked by chef-landlord
including Tues curry night and Fri fish,
friendly helpful service, beams, flagstones
and inglenook, steps up to dining room,
conservatory; children welcome, picnic-sets
in courtyard garden, closed Mon. *(Jim King)*

LANGPORT ST4625

★**Devonshire Arms** (01458) 241271

*B3165 Somerton–Martock, off A372 E
of Langport; TA10 9LP* Handsome gabled
inn (former hunting lodge) on village green;
simple flagstoned back bar with high-backed
chairs around dark tables, up to three
west country ales tapped from the cask,
several wines by the glass and local cider
brandy, stylish main room with comfortable
leather sofas and glass-topped log table by
fire, scatter cushions on long wall bench,
church candles, elegant dining room with
wicker chairs and pale wood tables on
broad boards, good interesting food from
lunchtime sandwiches up (local suppliers
listed), efficient friendly service; wheelchair
access from car park, teak furniture out at
front, pretty box-enclosed courtyard behind
with water-ball feature, more seats on raised
terraces, nine comfortable bedrooms,
good breakfast. *(Hugh Roberts)*

LANSDOWN ST7268

Blathwayt Arms (01225) 421995

*Next to Lansdown Golf Club and Bath
Racecourse; BA1 9BT* Hilltop stone pub
with well prepared traditional food (not Sun
evening) including themed nights, ales such
as Butcombe and Otter from dark wood bar,
also Weston's cider, decent wines and good
range of gins, pleasant prompt service, mix
of carpeted, wood and stone flooring, simple
furniture, some raised areas in bar and
conservatory, local photos and a map of the
Battle of Lansdown (Civil War); background
music; children welcome, wheelchair access
to most areas, disabled loo, racecourse view
from garden, play area, open all day. *(Chris
and Angela Buckell, Dr and Mrs A K Clarke)*

LONG ASHTON ST5370

Bird in Hand (01275) 395222

Weston Road; BS41 9LA Painted stone
dining pub (sister to the Pump House in
Bristol); good modern food from seasonal
menu including popular Sun roasts, well
kept Bath Gem, St Austell Tribute and two
guests, Ashton Press cider, nice wines and
some interesting gins, friendly helpful young
staff, spindleback chairs and blue-painted
pine tables on wood floors, collection of old
enamel signs, open fire and woodburner;
children and dogs welcome, side terrace,
parking can be tricky, open all day.
(Maddie Purvis)

LONG ASHTON ST5370

Miners Rest (01275) 393449

Providence Lane; BS41 9DJ Welcoming
three-room country pub, comfortable and
unpretentious, with well kept Butcombe,
Fullers and an occasional guest tapped
from the cask, traditional ciders, generous
helpings of simple inexpensive lunchtime
food, cheerful prompt service, local mining
memorabilia, log fire, darts; no credit cards;

well behaved children and dogs welcome, wheelchair access possible, vine-covered verandah and suntrap terrace, open all day. *(Geoff and Ann Marston)*

LOWER GODNEY ST4742

★**Sheppey Inn** (01458) 831594

Tilleys Drove; BA5 1RZ Although rather unprepossessing from the outside, this quirky fun place is full of character and surprisingly popular for its remote setting; eclectic mix of furniture on bare boards including plastic chairs by chunky wooden tables, cushioned wall benches and some 1950s retro, various stuffed animals, old photographs, modern artwork and assorted kitsch, at least six ciders tapped from the barrel along with local ales and craft beers, imaginative choice of well liked food, some cooked in charcoal oven, friendly staff, black beams and log fire, long dining area with high pitched ceiling; background and regular live music; children and dogs welcome, seats on deck overlooking small River Sheppey, three individually styled bedrooms, open all day weekends. *(Charles Todd)*

LYDFORD ON FOSSE ST5630

Cross Keys (01963) 240473

Just off A37; TA11 7HA Beamed and flagstoned pub with good traditional home-made food including Sun carvery, cheerful service, up to half a dozen well kept ales tapped from the cask such as Downton and Twisted Oak, proper cider and 11 wines by the glass, connecting rooms (main dining area at front), chunky rustic furniture and log fires in substantial old fireplaces; live music, quizzes and other events in function room; children and dogs welcome, disabled access/loos, seats on covered terrace and in sunny garden, six comfortable well equipped bedrooms, camping field, popular with Fosse Way walkers, open all day. *(Simon and Alex Knight)*

MIDDLEZOY ST3732

George (01823) 698215

Off A372 E of Bridgwater; TA7 0NN Steps up to friendly 17th-c beamed village pub; well kept St Austell Tribute and a couple of guests (Easter beer festival), proper ciders and eight wines by the glass, simple home-made lunchtime food, more evening choice including good steaks, attentive welcoming staff, bare stone walls, flagstones and a couple of log fires; quiz, live music and bingo nights, pool, darts, skittle alley; children and dogs welcome, a few tables outside, three bedrooms, open Sun 2-7pm (no food), closed all day Mon, Tues and lunchtimes Weds-Fri. *(Ben and Diane Bowie)*

MIDFORD ST7660

Hope & Anchor (01225) 832296

Bath Road (B3110); BA2 7DD Ivy-covered 17th-c pub near Colliers Way cycling/walking path and close to walks

on the disused Somerset & Dorset railway; neatly kept open-plan interior with civilised bar, heavy-beamed flagstoned restaurant with mix of dark wooden furniture and woodburner, modern back conservatory liked by families, enjoyable good value food including daily specials, up to three real ales, traditional cider and plenty of wines by the glass, courteous staff; dogs welcome in bar, seats on two-tier back terrace, open all day weekends. *(Peter and Emma Kelly)*

MINEHEAD SS9746

★**Old Ship Aground** (01643) 703516

Quay West next to lifeboat station; TA24 5UL Friendly flower-decked Edwardian quayside pub owned by local farming family; Marstons-related ales, Thatcher's cider and good selection of wines and spirits including Exmoor distillery's Northmoor gin, enjoyable food using own meat and other local produce, Sun carvery, cheerful efficient service even when busy, faux black beams decorated with pump clips and nautical ropework, lots of pictures, pubby furniture on carpeted or polished wood floors, window-seat views; live music Fri, juke box in bar, free wi-fi; children and dogs welcome, wheelchair access via side door, disabled loo, picnic-sets out at front overlooking harbour, 12 bedrooms (sea views), open all day. *(Mr and Mrs D J Nash, Chris and Angela Buckell)*

MONKSILVER ST0737

Notley Arms (01984) 656095

B3188; TA4 4JB Bustling pub in lovely village on edge of Exmoor National Park; open-plan bar rooms with log fires and woodburners, cushioned window seats and settles, appealing collection of old dining chairs around mixed wooden tables on slate tiles or flagstones, paintings on cream or panelled walls, flowers and church candles, tractor-seat stools by counter serving Exmoor, St Austell and a guest, proper cider, 30 wines by the glass and 20 malt whiskies, good well presented food from pub classics (with a twist) to inventive restaurant dishes, helpful friendly service; background music; children and dogs welcome, neat garden with plenty of picnic-sets, heated pavilion and clear-running stream at the bottom, attractive comfortable bedrooms in former coach house, good breakfast, open all day from 8am. *(Martin Day, Andrew Low, Paul White, Richard and Penny Gibbs)*

MONTACUTE ST4917

Kings Arms (01935) 822255

Bishopston; TA15 6UU Extended 17th-c stone inn next to church; stripped-stone bar with comfortable seating and log fire, contemporary restaurant, three real ales including Timothy Taylors, nice house wines and well liked food from bar snacks to restaurant dishes, friendly courteous staff; background music; children welcome, pleasant garden behind, 15 bedrooms (most ensuite), handy for Montacute House (NT), open all day. *(Jim King)*

NAILSEA   ST4469
Blue Flame (01275) 856910
Netherton Wood Lane, West End; BS48 4DE Small friendly 19th-c farmers' local with two unchanging lived-in rooms; well kept ales from casks behind bar, traditional ciders and some snacky food such as fresh rolls and pies, coal fire, pub games; outside gents'; sizeable informal garden, limited parking, open all day Thurs-Sun, closed lunchtimes Mon, Tues. *(John and Mary Warner)*

NORTH CURRY   ST3125
Bird in Hand (01823) 490248
Queens Square; off A378 (or A358) E of Taunton; TA3 6LT Friendly village pub with cosy main bar, old pews, settles, benches and yew tables on flagstones, some original beams and timbers, good inglenook log fire, well kept local ales and decent wines by the glass, popular food (not Mon) from varied blackboard menu, restaurant part; background music; children, dogs and muddy boots welcome, closed evenings Sun and Mon. *(Charles and Maddie Bishop)*

ODCOMBE   ST5015
★Masons Arms (01935) 862591
Off A3088 or A30 just W of Yeovil; Lower Odcombe; BA22 8TX Thatched village pub with simple bar, joists and standing timbers, cushioned dining chairs around tables on patterned carpet, a couple of tub chairs and a table in former inglenook fireplace, steps down to dining room with woodburner; own-brewed ales, real cider and 11 wines by the glass, good popular food from varied menu; children and dogs welcome, thatched shelter and picnic-sets in garden, also a vegetable patch, chicken coop and campsite, six well equipped bedrooms, hearty breakfast, open all day Sun. *(Mrs Zara Elliott, Peter Pilbeam, Andy and Louise Ramwell)*

OVER STRATTON   ST4315
Royal Oak (01460) 240906
Off A303 via Ilminster turn at South Petherton roundabout; TA13 5LQ Attractive 17th-c thatched dining pub with linked rooms; oak beams, flagstones and thick stone walls, scrubbed kitchen tables, pews and settles, log-effect gas fire, much enjoyed food cooked by landlord-chef from pub favourites up including daily specials, fair prices, well kept Badger ales and good wines, friendly attentive service; children and dogs (theirs is Alfie) welcome, wheelchair access, back garden with paved

terrace, open (and food) all day weekends, closed Mon evening (although may open in summer). *(Jason Caulkin)*

PORLOCK   SS8846
★Ship (01643) 862507
High Street; TA24 8QD Picturesque old thatched pub with beams, flagstones and big inglenook log fires, popular reasonably priced food from sandwiches up, well kept ales such as Exmoor and Otter, friendly service, back dining room, small locals' front bar with games; children welcome, attractive split-level sunny garden with decking and play area, nearby nature trail to Dunkery Beacon, five bedrooms, open all day; known as the Top Ship to distinguish it from the Ship at Porlock Weir. *(Sophie Ellison)*

PORLOCK WEIR   SS8846
★Ship (01643) 863288
Porlock Hill (A39); TA24 8PB Unpretentious thatched pub in wonderful spot by peaceful harbour – can get packed; long and narrow with dark low beams, flagstones and stripped stone, simple pub furniture, woodburner, west country ales including Exmoor and St Austell, real ciders, a perry and good whisky and soft drinks choice, enjoyable pubby food served promptly by friendly staff, games rooms across small backyard, also a tea room; background and occasional live music, TV; children and dogs welcome, sturdy picnic-sets out at front and side, good coastal walks, three bedrooms, limited free parking but pay-and-display opposite; calls itself the Bottom Ship to avoid confusion with the Ship at Porlock. *(Mr and Mrs D J Nash)*

PORTISHEAD   ST4776
Hall & Woodhouse (01275) 848685
Chandlery Square, Portishead Quays Marina; BS20 7DF Striking contemporary building overlooking marina slipway, unusual steel and glass construction incorporating shipping containers; main entrance with old admiralty charts, bar with floor-to-ceiling windows, exposed utilities and suspended copper-shaded lights, mix of furniture including refectory tables, easy chairs and sofas, bookshelves one end with old radios, ship's telegraph etc, woodburner, Badger ales, local ciders and good selection of wines/spirits from plank-faced servery, enjoyable food from baguettes and sharing plates up, more elaborate menu in upstairs restaurant (lift) with reclaimed wood floors and open kitchen, helpful cheerful staff; children welcome, dogs in bar, disabled access and facilities, covered seating area outside, open all day from 9am for breakfast. *(Chris and Angela Buckell)*

If you report on a pub that's not a featured entry, please tell us any lunchtimes or evenings when it doesn't serve bar food.

PORTISHEAD
ST4576
Windmill (01275) 818483
M5 junction 19; A369 into town, then follow 'Sea Front' sign and into Nore Road; BS20 6JZ Busy dining pub perched on steep hillside with panoramic Severn estuary views; curving glass frontage rising two storeys (adjacent windmill remains untouched), contemporary furnishings, four Fullers ales and a couple of guests, Thatcher's cider and plenty of wines by the glass, decent range of enjoyable food from sandwiches and baked potatoes up (some main courses available in smaller helpings); children welcome, dogs allowed in bar, disabled access/facilities including chairlift, metal furniture on tiered lantern-lit terraces and decking, open (and food) all day.
(Graham Smart)

PRIDDY
ST5450
★ Hunters Lodge (01749) 672275
From Wells on A39 pass hill with TV mast on left, then next left; BA5 3AR Welcoming farmers', walkers' and potholers' pub above Ice Age cavern, unchanging and in same family for generations; well kept local beers tapped from casks behind bar, Thatcher's and Wilkin's ciders, simple cheap home-made food, low beams, flagstones and panelling, log fires in huge fireplaces, caving memorabilia and old lead mining photographs; no mobiles or credit cards; children and dogs in family room, wheelchair access, garden picnic-sets.
(Holly and Tim Waite)

PRISTON
ST6960
Ring o' Bells (01761) 471467
Village SW of Bath; BA2 9EE Unpretentious old stone pub with large knocked-through bar; good reasonably priced traditional food cooked by licensees using nearby farm produce, well kept Butcombe, quick friendly service, flagstones, beams and good open fire; regularly used skittle alley, free wi-fi; children, dogs and muddy boots welcome, benches out at front overlooking little village green (maypole here on May Day), good walks, closed Mon and lunchtimes Tue-Thurs, no food Sun evening.
(Michael Doswell)

RICKFORD
ST4859
Plume of Feathers (01761) 462682
Very sharp turn off A368; BS40 7AH Cottagey 17th-c local in pretty streamside hamlet; enjoyable reasonably priced home-made food including pizzas in bar and dining room, well kept Butcombe, Cheddar and a guest, local cider and good choice of wines, black beams and half-panelling, cast-iron tables, settles and other traditional furniture, log fires; table skittles, shove-ha'penny, darts and pool; well behaved children and dogs welcome, rustic tables on narrow front terrace, garden behind, charity duck race held in July, five bedrooms, open all day.
(Patricia and Anton Larkham)

RIMPTON
ST6021
White Post Inn (01935) 851525
Rimpton Hill, B3148; BA22 8AR Small modern dining pub straddling Dorset border (boundary actually runs through the bar); highly rated imaginative food from chef-owner including reworked pub favourites and tasting menus, local ales and ciders, a dozen wines by the glass and interesting list of spirits including a milk vodka, friendly helpful staff, cosy carpeted bar area with leather sofas and woodburner, fine country views from restaurant and back terrace; children welcome, three ensuite bedrooms, closed Sun evening, Mon and Tues.
(Simon and Alex Knight)

RODE
ST8053
Cross Keys (01373) 830900
High Street; BA11 6NZ Popular pub in former brewery; two bars and restaurant, old well in one part, enjoyable freshly made food (not Sun evening, Mon) including good value Fri steak night, well kept Butcombe and a couple of guests, proper ciders and decent range of gins, good friendly service; monthly comedy night; children and dogs welcome, large enclosed garden and terrace, three bedrooms, open all day weekends, closed Mon lunchtime.
(Guy Vowles)

ROWBERROW
ST4458
Swan (01934) 852371
Off A38 S of A368 junction; BS25 1QL Spacious dining pub (originally three miner's cottages) opposite village pond; modernised interior with beams, exposed stonework and woodburner in big fireplace, some booth seating and animal head wallpaper in one part, good food from ciabattas and pizzas up, Butcombe and a guest, real cider and decent choice of wines by the glass; some live music; children and dogs welcome, good-sized garden over road with play area, open all day.
(Jim King)

SALTFORD
ST6867
Bird in Hand (01225) 873335
High Street; BS31 3EJ Comfortable and friendly with busy L-shaped bar; four well kept ales such as Butcombe and Sharps, good choice of popular fairly priced food (all day weekends) from well filled rolls up, prompt cheerful service, pubby furniture including settles, carpets throughout, back conservatory dining area; beer festival, free wi-fi; wheelchair access at front (not from car park), picnic-sets down towards river, pétanque, handy for Bristol & Bath Railway Path, open all day. *(Dr and Mrs A K Clarke, Roger and Anne Mallard)*

SALTFORD
ST6968
Jolly Sailor (01225) 873002
Off A4 Bath–Keynsham; Mead Lane;

BS31 3ER Worth knowing for its great River Avon setting by lock and weir; good range of food from bar snacks to authentic indian curries, OAP set lunch Mon-Fri, three Wadworths ales, flagstones, low beams and two log fires, conservatory dining room overlooking the water; background and weekend live music, Thurs quiz; children and dogs (in bar) welcome, disabled access/facilities, paved lockside terrace, open (and food) all day. *(Dr and Mrs A K Clarke)*

SANDFORD   ST4159
Railway (01934) 611518
Station Road; BS25 5RA Owned by Thatcher's and extensively modernised; their full range of ciders, real ales such as Butcombe, plenty of wines by the glass and enjoyable food from shortish menu including good value set lunch, pleasant young staff, lofty flagstoned bar with long oak counter, comfortable bare-boards area off with exposed stone walls and open fire, attractive timber-framed dining extension; free wi-fi; children and dogs welcome, outside seating on two levels, open all day. *(M G Hart)*

SHEPTON MONTAGUE   ST6731
★ Montague Inn (01749) 813213
Village signed off A359 Bruton–Castle Cary; BA9 8JW Simply but tastefully furnished dining pub with welcoming licensees, popular for civilised meal or just a drink; stripped-wood tables and kitchen chairs, inglenook log fire, nicely presented often interesting food including range of burgers from shortish menu plus a few specials, three well kept ales such as Bath and Wadworths, real ciders and good wine and whisky choice, helpful well informed young staff, bright spacious restaurant extension behind; children and dogs (in bar) welcome, disabled access, garden and big terrace with teak furniture, maybe Sun jazz in summer, peaceful farmland views, closed Sun evening. *(Edward Mirzoeff)*

SIMONSBATH   SS7739
★ Exmoor Forest Inn (01643) 831341
B3223/B3358; TA24 7SH Welcoming 19th-c inn beautifully placed in remote countryside; split-level bar with circular tables by counter, larger area with cushioned settles, upholstered stools and mate's chairs around mix of tables, hunting trophies, antlers and horse tack, woodburner, generously served good traditional food alongside more imaginative choices including local game, well kept ales such as Clearwater, Exmoor and Otter, Weston's cider, good range of wines and malt whiskies, airy dining room, residents' lounge; children and dogs welcome, seats in front garden, fine walks along River Barle, own trout and salmon fishing, comfortable bedrooms and self-catering cottage, good breakfast, open all day in high season. *(Ian Herdman)*

SOUTH CHERITON   ST6924
White Horse (01963) 370394
A357 Wincanton–Blandford; BA8 0BL Renovated 17th-c roadside country pub under friendly family management; well kept ales, craft beers and decent range of wines by the glass, good locally sourced home-made food (not Sun evening) in bar or restaurant (separate menus), cheerful service; some live music, skittle alley; children and dogs welcome, picnic-sets in small back garden, open all day weekends. *(Edward May)*

SOUTH STOKE   ST7461
Pack Horse (01225) 830300
Off B3110, S edge of Bath; BA2 7DU Historic pub saved from developers by the local community; two sympathetically restored rooms separated by servery, main one with heavy black beam-and-plank ceiling, stone-mullioned windows, quarry-tiled floor and log fire in handsome stone inglenook, room on left with another fire, changing local beers, traditional cider and enjoyable reasonably priced food from sandwiches/snacks and pub favourites up, Tues curry night, good friendly service, two further rooms upstairs; quiz Weds, some live music; children and dogs (downstairs) welcome, picnic-sets in nice garden with lovely valley views, good walks (route sheets available from the bar), limited parking, best to park at top of village and walk down, open all day, no food Sun evening. *(Pete and Sarah, Mike Coupe)*

SPAXTON   ST2336
Lamb (01278) 671350
Barford Road, Four Forks; TA5 1AD Welcoming simply furnished little pub at foot of the Quantocks; open-plan beamed bar with woodburner, well kept beers and enjoyable good value food (not Sun evening) including notable local steaks, pies and blackboard specials (booking advised); quiz last Sun of month; tables on lawn behind, closed all day Mon and lunchtimes apart from Sun. *(Ben and Diane Bowie)*

STANTON DREW   ST5963
Druids Arms (01275) 332230
Off B3130; BS39 4EJ Updated old pub in stone-circle village (there are some standing stones in the garden); linked flagstoned rooms with low black beams, bare stone walls and green dados, cushioned window seats and pubby furniture, candles here and there, open fires, tractor-seat stools by pale wood bar serving Butcombe and Sharps Doom Bar, Thatcher's cider and modest wine list, friendly service, enjoyable often creative food from bar snacks up (not Sun evening), Mon fish and chips, Tues OAP lunch deal; occasional live music, darts, free wi-fi; children and dogs welcome, front wheelchair access using portable ramp, picnic-sets out by lane and in garden backing on to 14th-c

church, maybe summer bouncy castle, open all day. *(Michael Doswell, Dr and Mrs A K Clarke)*

STAPLE FITZPAINE   ST2618

Greyhound (01823) 480227

Off A358 or B3170 S of Taunton; TA3 5SP
Rambling country pub much improved under new family management; good fairly straightforward home-made food at reasonable prices, well kept Badger ales and decent wines by the glass, welcoming helpful staff, traditional interior with flagstones, nice mix of old furniture and log fires; children and dogs welcome, bedrooms, good breakfast, open all day. *(Sara Fulton, Roger Baker)*

STOKE ST GREGORY   ST3527

Rose & Crown (01823) 490296

Woodhill; follow North Curry signpost off A378 by junction with A358 – keep on to Stoke, bearing right in centre, passing church and follow lane for 0.5 miles; TA3 6EW Popular dining pub with good food (best to book) and two or three local ales, friendly helpful staff, more or less open-plan, with stools by curved brick and wood counter, long high-raftered flagstoned dining room and two further beamed eating areas, one with glass-covered well; background music; children welcome, seats on sheltered front terrace, one bedroom, closed Sun evening. *(Bob and Margaret Holder, Paul and Claudia Dickinson)*

STOKE SUB HAMDON   ST4717

Prince of Wales (01935) 822848

Ham Hill; TA14 6RW Traditional stone pub at top of Ham Hill with superb views; local cask-tapped ales, traditional ciders and good food from sandwiches and west country deli boards up, summer pizzas from outside oven, friendly staff; children, dogs and muddy boots welcome, open (and food) all day, breakfast 9-11am. *(Graham Smart)*

TARR   SS8632

★Tarr Farm (01643) 851507

Tarr Steps – narrow road off B3223 N of Dulverton; deep ford if you approach from the W (inn is on E bank); TA22 9PY Fine Exmoor position for this 16th-c inn above River Barle's medieval clapper bridge (lovely walks); compact unpretentious bar rooms with good views, leather chairs around slabby rustic tables, some stall and wall seating, game bird pictures on wood-clad walls, three woodburners, well kept Exmoor ales and several wines by the glass, good food using local produce, residents' end with smart evening restaurant, friendly helpful service, log fire in pleasant lounge with dark leather armchairs and sofas; children and dogs welcome, slate-topped stone tables outside making most of the setting, extensive grounds, good bedrooms (no under-10s) in separate modern building, open all day but may be closed early Feb. *(Peter L Harrison, Andrew Low)*

TAUNTON   ST2525

Hankridge Arms (01823) 444405

Hankridge Way, Deane Gate (near Sainsbury's); just off M5 junction 25 – A358 towards city, then right at roundabout, right at next roundabout; TA1 2LR Interesting well restored Badger dining pub based on 16th-c former farmhouse – quite a contrast to the modern shopping complex surrounding it; different-sized linked areas, beams, timbers and big log fire, food from lunchtime sandwiches through pubby choices up, well kept (if pricey) ales and decent wines by the glass, friendly efficient young staff; background music; dogs welcome, plenty of tables in pleasant outside area, open all day Sat, till 6pm Sun. *(Geoff and Ann Marston)*

TAUNTON   ST2225

Plough (01823) 324404

Station Road; TA1 1PB Popular little pub with three or four changing local ales, racked ciders and seven wines by the glass, simple food including range of pies, bare boards and panelling, candles on tables, cosy nooks and open fire, hidden door to lavatories; background and some live music, weekly quiz; dogs welcome, handy for station, open all day Fri-Sun, closed lunchtimes Mon-Thurs. *(Geoff and Ann Marston)*

TAUNTON   ST2223

Vivary Arms (01823) 272563

Wilton Street; across Vivary Park from centre; TA1 3JR Popular low-beamed 18th-c local (Taunton's oldest pub); good value fresh food from light lunches up in snug plush lounge and small dining room, also takeaway fish and chips, well kept ales including Butcombe and decent wines by the glass, friendly helpful young staff, interesting collection of drink-related items; pool and darts; lovely hanging baskets and flowers out at front, nice little garden behind, open all day. *(Geoff and Ann Marston)*

TIMBERSCOMBE   SS9542

Lion (01643) 841243

Church Street; TA24 7TP Refurbished Exmoor-edge village pub; enjoyable food from shortish well priced menu, OAP lunch deal Thurs, changing local ales and good selection of gins, friendly efficient service; quiz first Weds of month, games area with darts, pool and juke box; children and dogs welcome, closed Mon and lunchtimes Tue, Weds and Fri, no food Sun evening. *(Stuart Norris)*

TINTINHULL   ST5019

★Crown & Victoria (01935) 823341

Farm Street, village signed off A303; BA22 8PZ Handsome golden-stone inn useful for the A303; carpeted bar with farmhouse furniture and big woodburner, high bar chairs at light oak counter serving four well kept ales, good popular food from shortish but varied menu using free range/ local produce including own pork, efficient friendly service, dining room with more pine tables and chairs, former skittle alley also used for eating, end conservatory; well behaved children welcome, dogs in bar, disabled facilities, big garden with play area, five bedrooms, handy for Tintinhull Garden (NT), closed Sun evening. *(Peter and Emma Kelly)*

TRULL   ST2122
Winchester Arms (01823) 284723
Church Road; TA3 7LG Cosy streamside village pub with good value generous food including blackboard specials and popular Sun lunch, curry night first Weds of the month, west country ales and local ciders, friendly helpful service, small dining room; Sun quiz, skittle alley, free wi-fi; dogs welcome, garden with decked area and summer barbecues, six cosy bedrooms. *(Ben and Jenny Settle)*

TUNLEY   ST6959
King William (01761) 470408
B3115 SW of Bath; BA2 0EB Updated family-run 17th-c coaching inn with good fairly priced pub food from baguettes to daily specials (smaller helpings available and plenty of gluten-free choices), some themed nights too, well kept ales such as St Austell, decent wines and good range of gins, friendly efficient staff, bar popular with locals, other room set for dining; courtyard tables, three comfortable bedrooms, open all day Sat, till 6pm Sun, closed Mon. *(John and Mary Warner)*

UPTON   ST0129
Lowtrow Cross Inn (01398) 371220
A3190 E of Upton; TA4 2DB Welcoming old pub under new management; low-beamed bar with bare boards, flagstones and log fire, pine furniture in two carpeted dining areas, one with enormous inglenook, the other doubling as a games room (pool, darts, skittle alley), three well kept ales including Exmoor, proper ciders and over 35 gins, good coffee, popular generously served home-made food; occasional live music; children and dogs welcome, picnic-sets in front garden, lovely surroundings, three bedrooms, camping next door (separately operated), open (and food) all day. *(Holly and Tim Waite)*

VOBSTER   ST7049
Vobster Inn (01373) 812920
Lower Vobster; BA3 5RJ Spacious old stone-built dining pub; enjoyable reasonably priced home-made food (special diets catered for), Butcombe, Ashton Press cider and nice wines by

the glass, three comfortable open-plan areas with antique furniture, plenty of room for just a drink; children and dogs (in bar) welcome, seats on lawn, boules, four bedrooms (also yurts and shepherd's huts), closed Sun evening, Mon and Tues. *(Miranda and Jeff Davidson)*

WASHFORD   ST0440
White Horse (01984) 640415
Abbey Road/Torre Rocks; TA23 0JZ Welcoming and popular old beamed local; three well kept changing ales, proper cider and enjoyable reasonably priced pubby food from baguettes to daily specials, can eat in bar or separate restaurant, log fires; pool; children and dogs welcome, picnic-sets and large smokers' pavilion over road next to trout stream, field with interesting collection of fowl and goats, handy for visits to Exmoor National Park and close to Cleeve Abbey (EH), seven bedrooms (three in newly built timber lodge), open all day. *(Richard and Penny Gibbs)*

WATCHET   ST0743
Pebbles (01984) 634737
Market Street; TA23 0AN Popular, welcoming and relaxed little bar in former shop near Market House Museum and the harbour; extensive range of regional ciders (tasters offered), also cask-tapped ales such as Exmoor and Timothy Taylors, good choice of whiskies, cider brandies and other drinks, friendly helpful staff, no food but can bring your own (plates and cutlery provided, fish and chip shop next door); regular live music (some impromptu) including folk and jazz, sea shanty and poetry evenings, free wi-fi; dogs welcome, no wheelchair access (high front step), open all day. *(Richard and Penny Gibbs)*

WATCHET   ST0643
Star (01984) 631367
Mill Lane (B3191); TA23 0BZ Late 18th-c beamed pub at end of lane just off Watchet harbour; main flagstoned bar with other low-ceilinged side rooms, some exposed stonework and rough wood partitioning, mix of traditional furniture including oak settles, window seats, woodburner in ornate fireplace, good selection of pubby food mostly sourced locally including fresh fish, half a dozen well kept west country ales such as Butcombe, Cotleigh and Exmoor, real cider and some interesting gins and rums, cheerful helpful staff; background music; children and dogs welcome, wheelchair access to main bar, picnic-sets out in front and in sloping beer garden behind, handy for marina and West Somerset Railway. *(Nigel Morton, David Delaney, Chris and Angela Buckell)*

If you stay overnight in an inn or hotel, they are allowed to serve you an alcoholic drink at any hour of the day or night.

WEDMORE ST4347
New Inn (01934) 712099
Combe Batch; BS28 4DU Welcoming
unpretentious village pub popular with
locals and visitors alike; well kept Butcombe
and guests, real cider and big helpings
of enjoyable sensibly priced pubby food,
comfortable dining area; skittle alley, darts,
sports TV and lots of local events including
penny chuffing, conker competitions and
the Turnip Prize (for worst piece of local
artwork); children and dogs welcome, open
all day weekends, closed lunchtimes Mon
and Tues. *(John Harris)*

WELLOW ST7358
Fox & Badger (01225) 832293
Signed off A367 SW of Bath; BA2 8QG
Popular village pub under same owners as
the White Hart at Widcombe Hill (Bath);
opened-up interior with flagstones one end,
bare boards the other, woodburner in massive
hearth, some snug corners, Butcombe and
two guests, real ciders and good range of
well liked food (booking advised weekends),
friendly service; children and dogs welcome,
picnic-sets in covered courtyard, open all
day Fri and Sat, closed Sun evening.
(Edward May, Maddie Purvis)

WELLS ST5546
★ Fountain (01749) 672317
St Thomas Street; BA5 2UU Relaxed
restauranty place with big comfortable bar,
interesting décor and large open fire; good
helpings of popular food here or in upstairs
dining room (booking advised weekends),
ales such as Bath, Butcombe and Fullers,
several wines by the glass, chatty attentive
staff; unobtrusive background music,
newspapers; well behaved children
welcome, no dogs, pretty in summer with
window boxes and shutters, handy for
cathedral and moated Bishop's Palace,
closed Sun evening, Mon lunchtime.
(Mark Kerrigan, R K Phillips)

WEST CHINNOCK ST4613
Muddled Man (01935) 881235
Lower Street; TA18 7PT Friendly
unassuming family-run pub in attractive
rustic village; single bar with three well
kept changing west country ales, real
cider and over 50 malt whiskies, enjoyable
straightforward food using local produce;
skittle alley; children and dogs welcome,
small garden, two bedrooms, open all day
Fri-Sun. *(Pete and Sarah)*

WEST HUNTSPILL ST3145
Crossways (01278) 783756
*A38, between M5 junctions 22 and 23;
TA9 3RA* Rambling 17th-c tile-hung pub
with split-level carpeted areas, beams and log
fires, eight well kept ales including Exmoor,
Otter and Pitchfork (tasting trays available),
good choice of enjoyable generously

served food at reasonable prices (booking
recommended), cheerful efficient staff; TV,
free wi-fi; children welcome and dogs (not
Fri, Sat evenings in dining areas), disabled
access/loo, garden with play area and heated
smokers' shelter, eight bedrooms, open all
day, till 1am Fri, Sat. *(R K Phillips)*

WEST MONKTON ST2628
Monkton (01823) 412414
*Blundells Lane; signed from A3259;
TA2 8NP* Popular village dining pub with
good choice of freshly made food including
some south african dishes (best to book
weekends); bare-boards bar with central
woodburner, snug and separate restaurant,
well kept Exmoor, Otter and Sharps, real
ciders and a dozen wines by the glass,
good service; children and dogs welcome,
wheelchair access from the front, lots of
tables in big garden bounded by stream,
play area. *(R C Hastings)*

WEST PENNARD ST5438
Red Lion (01458) 832941
*A361 E of Glastonbury; Newtown;
BA6 8NH* Traditional 16th-c stone-built
village inn; bar and dining areas off small
flagstoned black-beamed core, enjoyable
home-made food including pub favourites
and popular Sun roasts, vegan and gluten-
free diets catered for, three changing ales
and good selection of gins, also a cider
using apples from own orchard, friendly
attentive staff, inglenook woodburner and
open fires; background and some live music,
skittle alley, pool, free wi-fi; children and
dogs welcome, tables on big forecourt, good
nearby walks, bedrooms in converted side
barn, no food Sun evening or lunchtimes
Mon and Tues. *(Graham Smart)*

WIDCOMBE ST2216
Holman Clavel (01823) 421070
*Culmhead, on ridge road W of B3170,
follow sign for Blagdon; 2 miles S of
Corfe; TA3 7EA* Country local dating
from the 14th c, friendly and relaxed, with
good food from varied blackboard menu
(vegetarian and gluten-free diets catered
for), several real ales including Butcombe
and Otter, own Tricky cider, flagstoned bar
with woodburner in big fireplace, room off
has a long dining table (seats 24); some
live music; children, dogs and muddy boots
welcome, handy for Blackdown Hills, two
comfortable bedrooms, campsite next
door, open all day Fri-Sun, closed Tues.
(Guy Vowles)

WINCANTON ST7028
Nog Inn (01963) 32998
South Street; BA9 9DL Friendly old split-
level town pub; well kept Otter, Sharps and
a couple of guests, continental beers and
real cider, good reasonably priced traditional
food including Sun carvery (not summer),
Tues steak night and Weds pie and pint, bare

boards, carpet and flagstones, pump clips on bar ceiling, log fires; background music, knitting group Mon evening, quiz second Tues of month, darts; well behaved children and dogs welcome, pleasant back garden with heated smokers' shelter, open (and food) all day. *(Ben and Diane Bowie)*

WINFORD   ST5262
Crown (01275) 472388
Crown Hill, off Regil Road; BS40 8AY
Popular old pub set deep in the countryside; linked beamed rooms with mix of pubby furniture including settles on flagstones or quarry tiles, old pictures and photographs on rough walls, copper and brass, leather sofas in front of big open fire, enjoyable generous home-made food (all day Sun) at very reasonable prices, three real ales such as Butcombe and good choice of wines by the glass, friendly landlord and staff; table skittles and skittle alley; children and dogs welcome, wheelchair access with help, tables out in front and in back garden, closed Mon-Weds lunchtime, otherwise open all day. *(John Harris)*

WINSFORD   SS9034
★ **Royal Oak** (01643) 851455
Off A396 about 10 miles S of Dunster; TA24 7JE Prettily placed thatched and beamed Exmoor inn; enjoyable often interesting home-made food (greater evening choice), Exmoor ales, west country ciders and decent wine list, friendly helpful staff, carpeted bar with woodburner in big stone fireplace, large bay window seat looking across to village green and foot and packhorse bridges over River Winn, restaurant and other lounge areas; children and dogs (in bar) welcome, disabled facilities, eight good bedrooms some with four-posters. *(Miranda and Jeff Davidson)*

WITHAM FRIARY   ST7440
★ **Seymour Arms** (01749) 850742
Signed from B3092 S of Frome; BA11 5HF Well worn-in unchanging flagstoned country tavern, in same friendly family since 1952; two simple rooms off 19th-c hatch-service lobby, panelled benches and open fires, well kept Cheddar Potholer and an occasional guest, Rich's local cider tapped from back room, low prices, no food but can bring your own; bar billiards, darts and table skittles; children and dogs welcome, picnic-sets in large garden by main rail line, cricket pitch over the road, open all day. *(Edward Mirzoeff)*

WITHYPOOL   SS8435
Royal Oak (01643) 831506
Village signed off B3233; TA24 7QP
This prettily placed country inn (where R D Blackmore stayed while writing *Lorna Doone*) was about to reopen after major refurbishment as we went to press – reports please.

WOOKEY   ST5245
Burcott (01749) 673874
B3139 W of Wells; BA5 1NJ Beamed roadside pub with two simply furnished old-fashioned front bar rooms; flagstones, some exposed stonework and half-panelling, lantern wall lights, old prints, woodburner, a couple of ales such as Hop Back and a real cider, enjoyable food from snacks up in bar and restaurant, small games room; soft background music; children welcome in restaurant, no dogs inside, front window boxes and tubs, picnic-sets in sizeable garden with Mendip Hills views, four self-catering cottages in converted stables, closed Sun evening, Mon. *(Charles Todd)*

WOOKEY HOLE   ST5347
Wookey Hole Inn (01749) 676677
High Street; BA5 1BP Open-plan family dining pub usefully placed opposite the caves; welcoming and relaxed with unusual contemporary décor, wooden and tiled floors, tables with paper cloths for drawing on (crayons provided), two woodburners, decent food from lunchtime sandwiches and pub favourites to blackboard specials, three changing local ales, several belgian beers, ciders and perry, efficient friendly staff; background music; dogs welcome, pleasant garden with various sculptures, five individually styled bedrooms, open all day apart from Sun evening. *(Tony Scott)*

YARLINGTON   ST6529
Stags Head (01963) 440393
Pound Lane; BA9 8DG Some updating for this old low-ceilinged pub tucked away by the church in tiny village; cosy bar serving well kept ales such as Exmoor, Otter and Wild Beer, traditional ciders, good food from sandwiches and pub favourites to more restauranty choices, efficient friendly service, wood-floored restaurant with big log fire, high-backed chairs and feature cider-press table; background music; well behaved children welcome, dogs in bar, small stream in sheltered back garden, good walks, closed Sun evening. *(John and Mary Warner)*

Staffordshire

BREWOOD
SJ8708 Map 4

Oakley ♀ 🍺

(01902) 859800 ~ www.brunningandprice.co.uk/oakley

Kiddemore Green Road; ST19 9BQ

Substantial, cleverly extended pub with interesting food and drink and seats outside

In fine weather, do make use of the seats and benches among flowering tubs and raised flower beds on the spreading terrace behind the sizeable pub – it also overlooks a lake. Inside, partitioning and metal standing posts split larger areas in the open-plan rooms into cosier drinking and dining spaces and throughout there are the trademark house plants, books on shelves, elegant metal chandeliers and standard lamps, stubby candles and fresh flowers. Seating ranges from groups of leather armchairs to all manner of cushioned wooden dining chairs around character tables on rugs or bare boards, the walls (some half-panelled) are hung with hundreds of prints, and mirrors hang above open fires (some in pretty Victorian fireplaces). From the long counter, friendly, helpful staff serve Phoenix Brunning & Price Original and Wye Valley Butty Bach with guests such as Greene King Escapade and XX Mild, Hobsons Best, Titanic Plum Porter and Weetwood Eastgate on handpump, 16 wines by the glass, 100 whiskies, 120 gins and 80 rums; board games. There's a rack outside for cyclists. Disabled parking and loos.

🍴 Rewarding food includes sandwiches, sticky ginger chicken thigh with asian salad and teryaki dressing, cauliflower fritters with curried mayonnaise, cheese, potato and onion pie with carrot purée and red wine jus, steak in ale pudding, smoked haddock and salmon fishcake with a poached egg and white wine, dill and caper sauce, ham hock carbonara with creamy tarragon sauce, asparagus and edamame beans, sea bass with crab and crayfish risotto, pea velouté and crisp parma ham, and puddings such as hot waffle with a boozy cherry compote and cherry crumble ice-cream and chocolate fudge sundae with salted caramel, cream and chocolate sauce. *Benchmark main dish: katsu chicken curry £14.95. Two-course evening meal £21.00.*

Brunning & Price ~ Manager John Duncan ~ Real ale ~ Open 10am-11pm; 10am-10.30pm Sun ~ Bar food 12-9.30; 12-10 Fri, Sat; 12-9 Sun ~ Restaurant ~ Children welcome ~ Dogs allowed in bar ~ Wi-fi *Recommended by Andrew and Ruth Simmonds, Edward May, Claire Adams, Dr and Mrs A K Clarke, Andrew Vincent, Sophie Ellison, Julian Richardson*

Post Office address codings confusingly give the impression that some pubs are in Staffordshire, when they're really in Cheshire or Derbyshire (which is where we list them).

CAULDON   SK0749   Map 7

Yew Tree ★★ £

(01538) 309876 – www.yewtreeinncauldon.co.uk

Village signposted from A523 and A52 about 8 miles W of Ashbourne; ST10 3EJ

An extraordinary collection of curios in friendly pub with good value food and bargain beer – very eccentric

This remarkable place is quite unique and rather like a museum, filled with fascinating curiosities and antiques. The most impressive pieces are the working polyphons and symphonions which are 19th-c developments of the musical box, some taller than a person, each with quite a repertoire of tunes and elaborate sound-effects. There are also two pairs of Queen Victoria's stockings, an amazing collection of ceramics and pottery including a Grecian urn dating back almost 3,000 years, penny-farthing and boneshaker bicycles and the infamous Acme Dog Carrier. Seats include 18th-c settles, plenty of little wooden tables and a four-person oak church choir seat with carved heads that came from St Mary's church in Stafford. Look out for the array of musical instruments ranging from a one-string violin (phonofiddle) through pianos and a sousaphone to the aptly named serpent. Drinks are very reasonably priced, so it's no wonder the place is popular with locals. Burton Bridge Bitter, Rudgate Ruby Mild and a guest from Dancing Duck on handpump, eight interesting malt whiskies, eight wines by the glass and eight farm ciders; they hold a music and beer festival in July and a vintage vehicle rally in September. Darts and table skittles. There are seats outside the front door and in the cobbled stableyard, they now have a collection of vintage motorcyles and memorabilia, and offer electric hook-ups for motorhomes. The pub is almost hidden by a towering yew tree. Disabled access.

The modest menu includes staffordshire oatcakes, home-baked pies, vegetable or beef chilli, beef stew with mash, and puddings. *Benchmark main dish: steak in ale pie £8.50. Two-course evening meal £12.50.*

Free house ~ Licensee Dan Buckland ~ Real ale ~ Open 12-3, 6-11; 12-midnight Sat; 12-11 Sun ~ Bar food 12-3, 6-8; 12-8 weekends ~ Children welcome away from bar area ~ Dogs welcome ~ Wi-fi *Recommended by Len and Lilly Dowson, Dan and Nicki Barton, Buster May, Charles Todd*

 CHEADLE   SK0342   Map 7

Queens at Freehay ⭐

(01538) 722383 – www.queensatfreehay.co.uk

A mile SE of Cheadle; take Rakeway Road off A522 (via Park Avenue or Mills Road), then after a mile turn into Counslow Road; ST10 1RF

Gently civilised dining pub with three real ales and attractive garden

In warm weather, the appealing and immaculately kept little back garden is a fine place to sit, with picnic-sets among mature shrubs and flowering tubs. It's a friendly pub and although many are here to enjoy the good food, those who want a drink and a chat are made just as welcome. The neat rooms have some cottagey touches that blend in well with the modern refurbishments. The comfortable lounge bar has pale wood tables on stripped-wood floors, small country pictures and curtains with matching cushions. It opens via an arch into a simple light and airy dining area with elegant chairs and tables on tartan carpeting. Helpful and efficient staff serve Marstons Bombardier and Pedigree on handpump and ten wines by the glass. Disabled access.

Interesting food includes duck and pancetta roulade with herb salad and orange gel, mushroom, black pudding and cheddar melt with creamy peppercorn sauce, roasted vegetable enchilada with spiced fajita sauce, chicken caesar burger with toppings, crispy onion rings and chips, gammon and egg with pineapple, lamb rump with redcurrant, red wine and mint jus, slow-braised pork belly with three-mustard croquette and sage and juniper jus, mixed grill, and puddings such as Tia Maria and chocolate cheesecake with cappuccino ice-cream and lime and lemon crème brûlée. *Benchmark main dish: beef in red wine pie £13.95. Two-course evening meal £19.00.*

Free house ~ Licensee Adrian Rock ~ Real ale ~ Open 12-3, 6-11; 12-3.30, 6.30-10.30 Sun ~ Bar food 12-2, 6-9.30; 12-2.30, 6.30-9.30 Sun ~ Restaurant ~ Children welcome ~ Wi-fi
Recommended by Frank and Marcia Pelling, George Sanderson, Alexander and Trish Cutter, Amy and Luke Buchanan, Greta and Gavin Craddock, Martine and Fabio Lockley, Jane and Philip Saunders

ELLASTONE

SK1143   Map 7

Duncombe Arms 🌟 ♀ 🛏

(01335) 324275 – www.duncombearms.co.uk

Main Road; DE6 2GZ

Staffordshire Dining Pub of the Year

Nooks and crannies, a thoughtful choice of drinks, friendly staff and lovely food; seats and tables in large garden; bedrooms

Whatever your mood, you'll find somewhere interesting to sit in this stylishly refurbished village pub. There are beams and bare-brick, exposed-stone and painted walls covered with prints and photos of horses and big bold paintings of pigs, sheep, cows and chickens. Also, open fires and woodburners, large clocks, fresh flowers and stubby candles on mantelpieces, in big glass jars and on the tables. Flooring ranges from carpet to flagstones, bare floorboards and brick. Furnishings are just as eclectic: long leather button-back and cushioned wall seats, armchairs, all manner of wooden or upholstered dining chairs and tables made from mahogany, pine and even driftwood. A beer named for the pub plus Peak Chatsworth Gold and Marstons Pedigree on handpump, 50 wines by the glass from a fine list, 40 gins (and 20 tonics) and 30 malt whiskies; background music. An appealing terrace has wooden or rush seats around tables under parasols, braziers for cooler evenings and a view down over the garden to Worthy Island Wood. The individually designed and well equipped bedrooms are in Walnut House just a few paces from the pub; they also have a self-catering cottage to rent.

🌟 Impressive food includes sandwiches, house-smoked salmon with buttermilk pancake, pickled cucumber and dill, duck liver parfait with burnt orange purée, jerusalem artichoke risotto with cheese beignet, salsify and charred spring onion, honey-glazed ham with poached eggs and skinny fries, roast cod loin with brown shrimps, crushed potatoes and beurre blanc, two-bone rack of lamb with crispy sweetbreads and rosemary jus, and puddings such as vanilla rice pudding with candied orange and puffed wild rice and sticky toffee pudding with salted walnut ice-cream; they also offer a two- and three-course set menu (not Sunday). *Benchmark main dish: dry-aged rib-eye steak with béarnaise sauce and triple-cooked chips £25.00. Two-course evening meal £26.00.*

Free house ~ Licensees Johnny and Laura Greenall ~ Real ale ~ Open 12-11; 12-midnight Sat; 12-10 Sun; closed one week Jan ~ Bar food 12-2.30, 6-9 (10 Fri, Sat); 12-4, 6-9 Sun ~ Restaurant ~ Children welcome ~ Dogs allowed in bar and bedrooms ~ Wi-fi ~ Bedrooms: /£160 *Recommended by Elise and Charles Mackinlay, Brian and Sally Wakeham, Martine and Fabio Lockley, Alison and Dan Richardson, Peter and Alison Steadman*

LONGDON GREEN   SK0813 Map 7

Red Lion ♀ ◗

(01543) 490410 – www.brunningandprice.co.uk/redlion

Hay Lane; WS15 4QF

**Large, well run pub with interesting furnishings, a fine range
of drinks, enjoyable food and spreading garden**

Friendly, courteous staff serve a good range of drinks here. You'll find
Phoenix Brunning & Price Original and guests such as Blythe Bagots
Bitter, Salopian Oracle and Shropshire Gold, Timothy Taylors Boltmaker
and a seasonal ale from Wye Valley on handpump, 20 wines by the glass,
50 malt whiskies, 30 gins and two farm ciders. Although the interior has
been extended and thoughtfully opened up, the bustling bar remains the
heart of the place with spreading rooms and nooks and crannies leading
off. One dining room has skylights, rugs on nice old bricks, house plants
lining the windowsill, an elegant metal chandelier and a miscellany of
cushioned dining chairs around dark wooden tables. Similar furnishings
fill the other rooms, and the walls are covered with old photos, pictures
and prints relating to the local area and big gilt-edged mirrors; background
music and board games. Open fires include a raised central fire pit. In
summer, it's relaxing to sit and watch cricket matches on the village green
opposite this handsome pub; there's also a large garden with seats and
tables on a suntrap terrace, picnic-sets on grass, a gazebo and swings
and a play tractor for children.

Enterprising food includes sandwiches, maple-glazed pork belly with cauliflower
purée, apple and caramelised baby onions, crumbed cod cheeks with pea purée,
crispy pancetta and lemon dressing, asparagus and goats cheese quiche with crème
fraîche potato salad, grilled whole trout with crab and chervil butter and greens, crispy
beef salad with sweet chilli sauce, cashews and lotus root crisps, chicken breast with
roasted peppers, artichokes and chorizo and tomato sauce on pasta, 10oz rib-eye steak
with dijon and tarragon butter and chips, and puddings such as crème brûlée and
triple chocolate brownie with chocolate sauce. *Benchmark main dish: braised lamb
shoulder with dauphinoise potatoes and carrot mash £17.95. Two-course evening
meal £21.00.*

Brunning & Price ~ Manager Paul Drain ~ Real ale ~ Open 10.30am-11pm; 10.30-10.30 Sun
~ Bar food 12-9.30; 12-9 Sun ~ Restaurant ~ Children welcome ~ Dogs allowed in bar ~ Wi-fi
*Recommended by Christine and Tony Garrett, Usha and Terri Patel, Serena and Adam Furber,
Miranda and Jeff Davidson, Tim Buckley*

SALT   SJ9527 Map 7

Holly Bush £

(01889) 508234 – www.hollybushinn.co.uk

Village signposted off A51 S of Stone (and A518 NE of Stafford); ST18 0BX

Delightful medieval pub with all-day food

'This is just what a good local village pub is all about' says a reader who
very much enjoyed his visit; other reports are just as enthusiastic.
From the standing-only serving section, several cosy areas spread out with
high-backed cushioned pews, old tables and more conventional seats. The
oldest part has a heavy-beamed and planked ceiling (some of the beams
are attractively carved), a woodburning stove and a salt cupboard built into
a big inglenook, with other nice old-fashioned touches including copper
utensils, horsebrasses and an ancient pair of riding boots on the mantelpiece.
A modern back extension, with beams, stripped brickwork and a small

coal fire, blends in well. Adnams Southwold, Marstons Pedigree and Sharps Doom Bar on handpump, alongside ten wines by the glass. It's worth arriving early on a sunny day as the back garden is beautifully tended and filled with flowers, and the rustic picnic-sets on a big lawn get quickly snapped up; the window boxes are stunning. They operate a secure locker system for credit cards, which they'll ask to keep if you run a tab.

‖ Pleasing food (the Value Award is for lunchtime choices) includes sandwiches, toasties and baguettes, baked camembert with apricot preserve, duck liver, orange and cognac pâté with ale and apple chutney, a vegetarian choice of the day, burger with beer-battered onion rings, coleslaw and chips, greek-style greek lamb, free-range chicken with smoked bacon, chorizo, salami, barbecue sauce and mozzarella, venison casserole, mixed grill, fish dish of the day, and puddings. *Benchmark main dish: steak in ale pie £12.95. Two-course evening meal £17.00.*

Admiral Taverns ~ Licensee Geoffrey Holland ~ Real ale ~ Open 12-11; 12-11.30 Sat; 12-10.30 Sun ~ Bar food 12-9.30 (9 Sun) ~ Children welcome ~ Wi-fi *Recommended by Belinda Stamp, Martine and Lawrence Sanders, Celia and Geoff Clay, Peter Meister, Trish and Karl Soloman, Chloe and Tim Hodge, Maria and Henry Lazenby*

SWYNNERTON
Fitzherbert Arms ‖◎★ ⸮ 🍺

SJ8535   Map 7

(01782) 796782 – www.fitzherbertarms.co.uk
Off A51 Stone–Nantwich; ST15 0RA

Character rooms with interesting décor, local ales and rewarding food; seats outside with country views

Consistently well run and welcoming, this is a thoughtfully renovated pub with a fine choice of drinks and pleasing food. Once through an impressive glass door, the bar sits to the right with a raised fireplace styled like a furnace along with blacksmith's tools and relics. Down a step to the left is the older part of the pub, with button-back leather armchairs beside a two-way fireplace, rugs on flagstones, hops and some fine old brickwork. Fitzherbert Best (from Weetwood) and Swynnerton Stout (from Staffordshire) on handpump with a couple of guests from breweries within a 35-mile radius such as Merlin, Salopian, Spitting Feathers and Titanic; also, 16 good wines by the glass, 30 fantastic and carefully chosen ports with helpful notes (they hold port tasting evenings – phone for details), a dozen gins and a farm cider from the Apple County Cider Company. Staff are helpful and friendly. The beamed dining room is similarly furnished with a nice mix of old dining chairs and tables, plus window seats with scatter cushions, gilt-edged mirrors, black and white photographs and chandeliers; background music and board games. Do look out for the glass-topped giant bellows and anvil tables, door handles made of historic smithy irons, and candles in old port bottles. Outside, a covered, oak-timbered terrace has contemporary seats around rustic tables, heaters, fairy-lit shrubs in pots and country views; there are more seats in a small hedged garden. There's a circular walk from the pub; dogs are made welcome and greeted with a biscuit and bowl of water. The pub is owned by Tim Bird and Mary McLaughlin of Cheshire Cat Pubs & Bars.

◎★ Creative food includes sandwiches, crispy soft shell crab with coconut and pineapple salsa, chicken liver and port parfait with balsamic onion chutney, sharing boards, sweet potato and smoked cheese pie with roasted red pepper and pomegranate salad, steak burger with toppings, coleslaw and chips, five-spice duck leg with roasted plum and pickled fennel salad, sea bass with mussels and prawns in spiced creamy coconut sauce, local pork chop with wholegrain mustard mash and smoked bacon sauce, and puddings such as chocolate brownie with chocolate sauce and honeycomb ice-cream and sticky toffee pudding with rum and raisin ice-cream. *Benchmark main dish: steak in ale pie £13.95. Two-course evening meal £21.00.*

Free house ~ Licensee James Griffiths ~ Real ale ~ Open 12-11; 12-10.30 Sun ~ Bar food 12-9; 12-9.30 Fri, Sat ~ Children welcome but no under-10s after 7pm ~ Dogs allowed in bar ~ Wi-fi *Recommended by Charlotte and William Mason, Naomi and Andrew Randall, Ian Wilson, Matthew and Elisabeth Reeves, Chloe and Tim Hodge, Mike Benton*

WRINEHILL

SJ7547   Map 7

Hand & Trumpet ♀ ⬫

(01270) 820048 – www.brunningandprice.co.uk/hand

A531 Newcastle–Nantwich; CW3 9BJ

Big attractive dining pub with a good choice of ales and wines by the glass, served by courteous staff

As it's open (and serves food) all day, the atmosphere here is bustling and chatty. The linked open-plan areas work their way around the long, solidly built counter, with a mix of dining chairs and sturdy tables on polished tiles or stripped oak boards with rugs. There are nicely lit prints and mirrors on cream walls between a mainly dark dado, plenty of house plants, open fires and deep red ceilings. Original bow windows and a large skylight keep the place light and airy, and french windows open on to a spacious balustraded deck with teak tables and chairs, and a view down to ducks swimming on a big pond in the sizeable garden. Friendly attentive staff serve Phoenix Brunning & Price Original and Weetwood Eastgate with guests such as Peerless Pale, Salopian Oracle, Timothy Taylors Landlord and Wincle Indian Runner on handpump, as well as 16 wines by the glass, 20 rums, 40 gins, 20 bourbons and about 70 whiskies; board games. Good disabled access and facilities.

Inventive food includes sandwiches, scallops with pea purée and shredded ham hock, chicken liver pâté with carrot and apricot chutney, mushroom bourguignon pie with black truffle mash, spring greens and red wine jus, steak burger with toppings, coleslaw and chips, soy and ginger sea trout with asian noodle salad and sesame dressing, chicken kiev with goats cheese mousse, harissa-spiced lamb rump with tomato and cumin sauce, cauliflower couscous, chickpeas, feta and apricots, and puddings such as hot waffle with glazed bananas and crème brûlée. *Benchmark main dish: crispy beef salad with sweet chilli, lime, lemongrass and cashews £13.95. Two-course evening meal £21.00.*

Brunning & Price ~ Manager Ryan Platt ~ Real ale ~ Open 12-11; 12-10.30 Sun ~ Bar food 12-9.30; 12-9 Sun ~ Children welcome ~ Dogs allowed in bar ~ Wi-fi *Recommended by Sabine and Gerald Grimshaw, Caroline and Peter Bryant, Alexandra and Richard Clay, Mark and Mary Setting, Edward May*

A star symbol after the name of a pub shows exceptional character and appeal. It doesn't mean extra comfort. And it's nothing to do with exceptional food quality, for which there's a separate star-on-a-plate symbol. Even quite a basic pub can win a star, if it's individual enough.

Also Worth a Visit in Staffordshire

Besides the fully inspected pubs, you might like to try these pubs that have been recommended to us and described by readers. Do tell us what you think of them: feedback@goodguides.com

ABBOTS BROMLEY   SK0824
Coach & Horses (01283) 840256
High Street; WS15 3BN Well cared for
18th-c village pub with good choice of
popular home-made food (not Sun evening)
from baguettes and pizzas up, also good
value weekday deals, Marstons Pedigree,
St Austell Tribute and a guest, several wines
by the glass; beamed bar with stone floor and
button-back banquettes, dark wood pubby
furniture in carpeted restaurant, log fire;
children and dogs (in bar) welcome, pleasant
garden with circular picnic-sets, open all
day Sun. *(Sandra Hollies)*

ABBOTS BROMLEY   SK0824
Goats Head (01283) 840254
Market Place; WS15 3BP Welcoming
16th-c black and white village pub under
new management; well kept ales such as
Jennings Cumberland and enjoyable food
from pizzas up, opened-up beamed interior
with oak floors, traditional furnishings and
fire in big inglenook; children and dogs
welcome, tables on deck and sheltered
lawn looking up to church tower, closed
Mon lunchtime, otherwise open all day.
(Sandra Hollies)

ALSAGERS BANK   SJ8048
Gresley Arms (01782) 722469
High Street; ST7 8BQ Popular and
welcoming pub at top of Alsagers Bank with
wonderful far-reaching views from the back;
eight or more interesting ales from smaller
breweries and half a dozen real ciders,
ample helpings of good value pubby food
(not Mon-Weds lunchtimes or Sun evening)
including bargain Thurs steak night (must
book) and eat-for-£1 Mon evening if you buy
a drink, traditional slate-floor bar with beams
and open fire, comfortable lounge, picture-
window dining room taking in the view, and
a lower family room (children's menu – free
main course Tues and Weds evenings); Mon
quiz; walkers and dogs welcome, garden
picnic-sets, Apedale Heritage Centre nearby,
open all day Thurs-Sun, otherwise from 3pm.
(Nick)

ALSTONEFIELD   SK1355
★ **George** (01335) 310205
*Village signed from A515 Ashbourne–
Buxton; DE6 2FX* Simply furnished
family-run pub in pretty village overlooking
small green; chatty bar with low beams and
quarry tiles, old Peak District photographs
and pictures, log fire, Marstons-related ales
and a dozen wines by the glass from copper-
topped counter, really good imaginative

food using some home-grown produce,
friendly efficient service, small snug and
neat candlelit dining room with farmhouse
furniture and woodburner; children welcome,
dogs weekdays only (must book a table if
eating), picnic-sets out at front, more seats in
big sheltered stableyard behind, closed Sun
evening. *(GSB, Maxine Carlier, Brian Dunn)*

ARMITAGE   SK0716
Plum Pudding (01543) 490330
Rugeley Road (A513); WS15 4AZ
Canalside pub and italian restaurant; good
food in bar and dining room including daily
specials, well kept ales such as Bass and
Greene King, friendly helpful staff; children
welcome, no dogs inside, tables on waterside
terrace and narrow canal bank, moorings,
open (and food) all day. *(Christine and
Tony Garrett)*

BARLASTON   SJ8838
Plume of Feathers (01782) 373100
Station Road; ST12 9DH Modernised
village pub owned by actor Neil Morrissey;
well kept ales including a couple named for
them (tasting paddles available), decent
selection of gins and good food at sensible
prices, friendly attentive service, restaurant;
Weds quiz; children and dogs welcome, seats
outside overlooking canal and bowling green
behind, open (and food) all day bar, kitchen
closes 7.30pm Sun. *(Clive and Fran Dutson)*

BIDDULPH   SJ8959
Talbot (01782) 512608
*Grange Road (N, right off A527);
ST8 7RY* Family dining pub in 19th-c stone
building (Vintage Inn); their usual fair value
food from sandwiches and sharing plates up
including weekday set menus, well kept ales
such as Sharps, and decent choice of other
drinks, raised two-way log fire in restaurant
part, some secluded areas; background
music; dogs allowed in tiled bar area, handy
for Biddulph Grange (NT), open (and food)
all day. *(Usha and Terri Patel)*

BLACKBROOK   SJ7638
Swan with Two Necks
(01782) 680343 *Nantwich Road
(A51); ST5 5EH* Refurbished country
pub-restaurant with smart modern décor
in open-plan split-level dining areas, good
well presented food (booking advised) from
sharing boards up, Timothy Taylors Landlord,
three guest ales and plenty of wines by the
glass including champagne; background
music; children welcome, tables in garden
and on parasol-shaded deck, open (and food)
all day. *(Jo and Belinda Smart)*

BREWOOD   SJ8808

Swan (01902) 850330

Market Place; ST19 9BS Former coaching
inn with two low-beamed bars and inglenook
log fire; well kept Wye Valley HPA, Courage
Directors and four guests such as Salopian
and Burton Bridge, good selection of whiskies
and gins, no food; upstairs skittle alley, Sun
quiz; dogs allowed, open all day.
(Tony Hobden)

BURTON UPON TRENT   SK2523

Burton Bridge Inn (01283) 536596

Bridge Street (A50); DE14 1SY Friendly
down-to-earth local with good Burton Bridge
ales from brewery across old-fashioned brick
yard; simple little front area leading into
adjacent bar, plain walls hung with brewery
memorabilia, small beamed and oak-panelled
lounge with coal-effect gas fire, upstairs
skittle alley, no food; children and dogs
welcome, closed lunchtimes apart from Fri
and Sat. *(Colin Gooch)*

BURTON UPON TRENT   SK2423

★Coopers Tavern (01283) 567246

Cross Street; DE14 1EG Traditionally
refurbished 19th-c backstreet local tied to
Joules – was tap for the Bass brewery and
still has some wonderful ephemera including
mirrors and glazed adverts; homely and warm
with coal fire, straightforward front parlour,
back bar doubling as tap room with their
beers, up to half a dozen guests (including
Bass) and good selection of ciders/perries,
cheese boards and pies only but can bring
your own food (or take beer to next-door
curry house); occasional live music; children
(till 8pm) and dogs welcome, small back
garden, open all day Thurs-Sun, from 5pm
other days. *(Dave Braisted)*

CHEDDLETON   SJ9752

Black Lion (01538) 360620

Leek Road, by the church; ST13 7HP
Convivial bustling atmosphere at this
19th-c village local; generous helpings of
good traditional lunchtime food including
popular Sun roasts, Fri night fish and chips,
otherwise just snacks such as local pork
pies in the evening, Bass, Timothy Taylors
Landlord and a couple of guests, Weston's
cider, friendly efficient staff; some live music,
pool and darts; children and dogs welcome,
seats out in front and in fenced back garden,
open all day. *(Brian and Anna Marsden)*

CHEDDLETON   SJ9751

Boat (01538) 360521

*Basford Bridge Lane, off A520;
ST13 7EQ* Cheerful unpretentious
canalside local handy for Churnet Valley
steam railway, flint mill and country park;
long bar with low plank ceiling, well kept
Marstons-related ales and enjoyable honest
food from sandwiches to steaks, dining room
behind; live music; children welcome, dogs in

bar, seats out overlooking Caldon Canal,
open all day, no food Sun evening.
(Dan and Nicki Barton)

CODSALL   SJ8603

Codsall Station (01902) 847061

Chapel Lane/Station Road; WV8 2EH
Converted vintage waiting room and ticket
office of working station, comfortable and
welcoming with well kept Holdens ales and
a couple of guests, good value pubby food
including blackboard specials (just cobs
and pork pies Sun, Mon), lots of railway
memorabilia, open fire, conservatory;
children and dogs welcome, disabled access,
terrace seating, open all day. *(Jane Rigby)*

CONSALL   SK0049

Black Lion (01782) 550294

*Consall Forge, OS Sheet 118 map
reference 000491; best approach from
Nature Park, off A522, using car park
0.5 miles past Nature Centre; ST9 0AJ*
Traditional take-us-as-you-find-us place
tucked away in rustic canalside spot by
restored steam railway station; generous
helpings of enjoyable pub food (just bar
snacks Sun evening-Weds), up to five
well kept ales including Black Hole and
several ciders, flagstones and good coal
fire; background music; children and dogs
welcome, seats out overlooking canal, area
for campers and shop for boaters, good walks,
open all day and can get very busy weekend
lunchtimes. *(Clive and Fran Dutson)*

COPMERE END   SJ8029

Star (01785) 850279

W of Eccleshall; ST21 6EW Friendly 19th-c
two-room country local; well kept Bass,
Bombardier, Titanic Anchor and a couple of
guests, decent choice of reasonably priced
food from sandwiches up (not Sun evening),
open fire and woodburner; occasional live
music; children and dogs welcome, tables
and play area in back garden overlooking
mere, good walks, open all day weekends,
closed Mon. *(Brian and Sally Wakeham)*

DENSTONE   SK0940

Tavern (01889) 590847

College Road; ST14 5HR Welcoming
17th-c stone-built pub with good food (not
Mon) including freshly made pizzas (Fri,
Sat evenings) and Sun carvery, well kept
Marstons ales and good range of wines by
the glass, pleasant service, comfortable
lounge with antiques, dining conservatory;
darts, free wi-fi; children and dogs welcome,
picnic-sets out at front among tubs and
hanging baskets, village farm shop and lovely
church, open all day Fri-Sun, closed Mon
lunchtime. *(Caroline and Peter Bryant)*

DRAYCOTT IN THE MOORS SJ9840

Draycott Arms (01782) 911030

*Junction of Uttoxeter Road and Cheadle
Road; ST11 9RQ* Welcoming modernised

pub with good sensibly priced food including selection of small tapas-style plates, Sharps Doom Bar and a guest, Aspall's cider, friendly attentive service, two-way woodburner separating bar and restaurant; darts; children and dogs (in bar) welcome, garden with covered area, open all day Sat, till 5pm Sun, closed Mon. *(Valerie Davis)*

DUSTON   SP7262
Hopping Hare (01604) 580090
Hopping Hill Gardens; NN5 6PF
Imposing red-brick former manor surrounded by housing; largish bar adjacent to entrance, log fires and lots of different dining areas, well kept Adnams, Black Sheep and a guest, good range of wines by the glass and highly rated attractively presented food, friendly efficient service; children welcome, no dogs inside, seats out on decking, 20 modern bedrooms, open (and food) all day.
(Usha and Terri Patel)

ECCLESHALL   SJ8329
Old Smithy (01785) 850564
Castle Street; ST21 6DF Comfortable pub-restaurant with clean modern décor; good freshly made food from sandwiches and sharing boards up including vegetarian menu, four fairly mainstream ales and good choice of wines and other drinks, friendly efficient staff; children welcome, small outside seating area, open all day, food all day Sat, till 7.30pm Sun. *(Tim Jamieson)*

ECCLESHALL   SJ8329
Royal Oak (01785) 859065
High Street; ST21 6BW Restored beamed coaching inn with colonnaded frontage; well kept Joules ales and enjoyable locally sourced food, friendly chatty staff; live music; children and dogs (in bar) welcome, beer garden, open (and food) all day except Sun when kitchen shuts 4.30pm. *(Christine and Tony Garrett)*

FLASH   SK0267
Travellers Rest/Knights Table
(01298) 236695 *A53 Buxton–Leek; SK17 0SN* Isolated main-road pub, one of the highest in Britain; good reasonably priced traditional food (not Sun evening), four well kept ales and good selection of wines, friendly service, beams, bare stone walls and open fires, medieval knights theme; free wi-fi; children very welcome, no dogs inside, great Peak District views from back terrace, classic car meeting last Thurs of month, bedrooms, closed Mon and Tues, otherwise open all day. *(Stan Lorimer)*

FRADLEY   SK1414
White Swan (01283) 790330
Fradley Junction; DE13 7DN Terrace-row pub (aka the Mucky Duck) in good canalside location at Trent & Mersey and Coventry junction; Everards ales and guests, enjoyable reasonably priced food including pizzas

and popular Sun carvery, cheery traditional public bar with woodburner and open fire, quieter lounge and lower vaulted dining room (former stable); Tues quiz, Thurs folk night, Sun open mike; children and dogs welcome, waterside tables, open all day. *(Jo and Belinda Smart)*

GNOSALL   SJ8220
Boat (01785) 822208
Gnosall Heath, by Shropshire Union Canal Bridge 34; ST20 0DA Popular little canalside pub run by friendly family; comfortable first-floor bar with curved window seat overlooking narrowboats, Marstons-related ales and decent choice of reasonably priced pubby food including vegetarian/vegan choices and Mon evening meal deal, open fire; darts and dominoes; children and dogs welcome, tables out by canal, moorings and nice walks, open all day weekends (no food Sun evening), closed Mon lunchtime. *(Tim Jamieson)*

GNOSALL   SJ8220
George & Dragon 07779 327551
High Street; ST20 0EX Unpretentious welcoming little pub dating from the 18th c; well kept Holdens Golden Glow, Woods Shropshire Lad and three guests, four proper ciders and decent range of other drinks, just snacky food such as cobs and home-made sausage rolls, simple interior with woodburner and some quirky tables made from old farming gear; dogs welcome, open all day weekends, from 4pm weekdays. *(Tony Hobden)*

HANLEY   SJ8847
Coachmakers Arms 07876 144818
Lichfield Street; ST1 3EA Chatty traditional 19th-c local reopened under welcoming new licensees (was under threat of demolition); well kept Bass and a couple of guests, snacky food such as pork pies, four small rooms and drinking corridor (some redecoration), original seating and open fires; darts; dogs welcome, open all day weekends, from 4pm other days (2pm Fri). *(Dan and Nicki Barton)*

HARTSHILL   SJ8645
Jolly Potters (01782) 761717
Hartshill Road (A52); ST4 7NH
Welcoming traditional drinkers' pub with five rooms off central corridor; well kept Bass, Marstons and up to three guests, good selection of gins, no food apart from summer pizzas from outside oven; pool and darts; children and dogs welcome, garden with stage for live music, open from 3pm Mon-Fri (noon Sat, Sun). *(Stan Lorimer)*

HIGH OFFLEY   SJ7725
Anchor (01785) 284569
Off A519 Eccleshall–Newport; towards High Lea, by Shropshire Union Canal Bridge 42; Peggs Lane; ST20 0NG Built

around 1830 to serve the Shropshire Union Canal and little changed in the century or more this family has run it; two small simple front rooms, one with a couple of fine high-backed settles on quarry tiles, Wadworths 6X and Weston's cider, sandwiches on request, owners' sitting room behind bar; outbuilding with semi-open lavatories (swallows may fly through); no children inside, lovely garden with hanging baskets and notable topiary anchor, small shop, moorings (near Bridge 42), caravans/camping, closed Mon-Thurs in winter. *(John)*

HIMLEY   SO8990

★**Crooked House** (01384) 238583
Signed down long lane from B4176 Gornalwood–Himley, OS Sheet 139 map reference 896908; DY3 4DA Extraordinary sight, building thrown wildly out of kilter by mining subsidence, one side 4-ft lower than the other and slopes so weird that things appear to roll up them rather than down; public bar (dogs allowed here) with grandfather clock and hatch serving Banks's and other Marstons-related ales, lounge bar, enjoyable food from chop-house menu including set deal, some local antiques in level extension, conservatory; children welcome in eating areas, large outside terrace, closed Mon, otherwise open all day (till 6pm Sun). *(Jane Rigby)*

HULME END   SK1059

Manifold Inn (01298) 84537
B5054 Warslow–Hartington; SK17 0EX Fairly isolated stone coaching inn near River Manifold; enjoyable traditional home-made food at reasonable prices, four well kept ales such as Cottage, Leatherbritches and Marstons, pleasant friendly staff, log fire in traditional carpeted bar, adjacent restaurant and conservatory; background music, TV; children and dogs (in some parts) welcome, disabled facilities, tables outside, 11 bedrooms (eight in converted barns), self-catering cottage, good walks including Manifold Trail, cycling routes nearby, open (and food) all day. *(Usha and Terri Patel)*

LEEK   SJ9956

Earl Grey (01538) 372570
Ashbourne Road; ST13 5AT Traditional little red-brick corner pub with split-level interior; a house ale brewed by Whim plus several other interesting changing beers (tasters offered), real ciders and decent range of whiskies/gins, friendly knowledgeable staff and good mix of customers, no food; juke box and some live music, quiz nights; dogs welcome, open all day Fri-Sun, from 5pm Mon, 3pm other days. *(Tim Jamieson)*

LEEK   SJ9856

Wilkes Head 07976 592787
St Edward Street; ST13 5DS Friendly no-frills three-room local dating from the early 18th c (still has back coaching stables); Whim ales, interesting guests, real ciders and good choice of whiskies, no food apart from rolls; juke box in back room and regular live music events including festivals organised by musician landlord; children allowed in one room (not really a family pub), dogs on leads (but do ask first), fair disabled access, garden with stage, open from 3pm Mon, Tues and Thurs, otherwise open all day. *(Tim Jamieson)*

LICHFIELD   SK1109

Beerbohm (01543) 898252
Tamworth Street; WS13 6JP Popular continental style café-bar; four real ales including Salopian and a beer badged for them, plenty of international beers (draught and bottled) and good choice of other drinks, friendly knowledgeable staff, cosy bar with comfortable seating and iron-framed tables on wood floor, upstairs lounge, no food but can bring your own (plates and cutlery supplied), tea and coffee; background music, free wi-fi; well behaved dogs welcome, closed Sun and Mon, otherwise open all day. *(John)*

LICHFIELD   SK0705

Boat (01543) 361692
A461; from A5 at Muckley Corner, take A461 signed Walsall; continue over M6 Toll bridge and take next right (Hilton) to return on dual carriageway; WS14 0BU Highly regarded imaginative food including tasting menus (not cheap) at this modernised restaurranty-pub; split-level interior with view into kitchen from skylit entrance, upholstered dining chairs at sturdy tables, woodburner in cosy bar area serving up to three changing ales and several wines by the glass, attentive friendly service; background music; small outside bar in garden with central raised deck, closed Sun evening, Mon and Tues, otherwise open all day. *(Rupert Bursell)*

LICHFIELD   SK1109

Duke of York (01543) 307313
Greenhill/Church Street; WS13 6DY Old beamed pub with split-level front bar, cosy carpeted lounge and converted back stables, inglenook woodburners, Joules ales and guests, simple lunchtime food (not Sun) served by pleasant staff; some live music, Apr beer festival; no children but dogs allowed, terrace picnic-sets behind and own bowling green, open all day. *(John)*

LICHFIELD   SK1109

Horse & Jockey 07912 881914
Sandford Street (cul-de-sac); WS13 6QA Traditional free house with eight very well kept ales including Holdens, Marstons, Timothy Taylors and Wye Valley, some lunchtime food such as pork pies, good friendly service; games room, sports TV; no under-21s, dogs welcome, small garden behind, open all day. *(Dave Skipp, John)*

LITTLE BRIDGEFORD   SJ8727
Mill   (01785) 282710
Worston Lane; near M6 junction 14; turn right off A5013 at Little Bridgeford; ST18 9QA Dining pub in attractive 1814 watermill; decent sensibly priced food including Sun carvery, Greene King ales, good friendly service; Thurs quiz; children and dogs welcome, disabled access, nice grounds with adventure playground and nature trail (lakes, islands etc), open (and food) all day. *(Stan Lorimer)*

LONGDON   SK0814
Swan with Two Necks
(01543) 491570   *Off A51 Lichfield–Rugeley; Brook Lane; WS15 4PN* Welcoming village pub with long low-beamed quarry-tiled bar, two-way woodburner and some leather wall benches, separate wood-floored lounge/restaurant with a couple of open fires, enjoyable fairly pubby food, Marston Pedigree, Sharps Doom Bar and two guests, good range of gins, friendly helpful service; children (away from bar) and dogs (in bar) welcome, garden with play area, open (and food) all day, kitchen shuts 7pm Sun. *(Christine and Tony Garrett)*

MARCHINGTON   SK1330
Dog & Partridge   (01283) 820394
Church Lane; ST14 8LJ Flower-decked 18th-c village pub with various beamed and tile-floored rooms; Bass and three changing guests (beer festivals), good food (not Sun evening) including themed nights and bargain two-course lunch, good value wines, attentive friendly staff, real fires and some interesting bits and pieces; background music (live Sun from 5.30pm), free wi-fi; children and dogs (in bar) welcome, tables under parasols in paved back terrace by car park, open all day weekends. *(Sandra Hollies)*

MEERBROOK   SJ9960
Lazy Trout   (01538) 300385
Centre of village; ST13 8SN Popular country dining pub with good sensibly priced food from regularly changing menu, friendly helpful staff, small bar area serving five well kept ales including Greene King from curved stone counter, good selection of gins too, log fire in comfortable dining lounge on right, another dining room to the left with quarry tiles, pine furniture and old cooking range; juke box; children welcome, dogs and muddy boots in some parts, seats out at front by quiet lane and in appealing garden behind (splendid views to the Roaches and Hen Cloud), good walks, open (and food) all day. *(Clive and Fran Dutson, Malcolm and Pauline Pellatt)*

NEWBOROUGH   SK1325
Red Lion   (01283) 576182
Duffield Lane; DE13 8SH Old pub facing church in quiet village; comfortable bar with open fire, three Marstons-related ales and good choice of other drinks, enjoyable fair priced food from snacks and pub classics up including signature rotisserie chicken, smallish dining room, friendly accommodating staff; children welcome, seats out at front, open all day, kitchen shuts 6pm Sun. *(Phil and Anne Nash)*

ONECOTE   SK0455
★ Jervis Arms   (01538) 304206
B5053; ST13 7RU Cosy whitewashed country dining pub refurbished under present welcoming management; up to five well kept changing ales, proper cider and good range of wines and gins, generous helpings of popular reasonably priced food including good Sun roasts, friendly efficient service, woodburners in all three rooms, beams and some exposed stonework, settles and other country furniture on old quarry tiles or wood floors; occasional live music, darts; children and dogs welcome, streamside (River Hamps) garden with footbridge to car park, closed Mon, otherwise open (and food) all day. *(Clive and Fran Dutson)*

PENKRIDGE   SJ9214
Littleton Arms   (01785) 716300
St Michaels Square/A449 – M6 detour between junctions 12 and 13; ST19 5AL Cheerfully busy dining pub-hotel (former coaching inn) with contemporary open-plan interior; good variety of enjoyable well presented food from sandwiches and sharing boards to popular Sun roasts, six well kept changing ales and appealing choice of wines/gins from island servery, afternoon teas, friendly accommodating staff; background music (live last Fri of the month); children and dogs (in bar area) welcome, terrace seating under parasols, ten bedrooms, open all day (till midnight Fri, Sat), breakfast from 7am Mon-Fri (8am weekends). *(Caroline and Peter Bryant)*

SANDON   SJ9429
Dog & Doublet   (01889) 508331
B5066 just off A51; ST18 0DJ Sizeable Edwardian pub with various linked bar and dining areas, good choice of enjoyable food (special diets catered for) including early evening deal (weekdays 5-6.30pm) and Thurs steak night, well kept ales including Banks's and Titanic, over 20 wines by the glass, cocktails and afternoon teas, friendly staff; background music, sports TV; children and dogs (in bar) welcome, tables on front paved terrace and in central courtyard, 11 bedrooms, open all day. *(Clive and Fran Dutson)*

SEIGHFORD   SJ8725
Hollybush   (01785) 281644
3 miles from M6 junction 14 via A5013/B5405; ST18 9PQ Modernised and extended beamed pub owned by the village; good value locally sourced pubby food (not

Sun evening, Mon) from sandwiches and light choices up, ales including Titanic and Everards; Sun quiz, portable skittle alley; children and dogs welcome, disabled access, beer garden, open all day Fri-Sun. *(Dan and Nicki Barton)*

SHEEN   SK1160
Staffordshire Knot (01298) 84329
Off B5054 at Hulme End; SK17 0ET
Welcoming traditional 17th-c stone-built village pub; nice mix of old furniture on flagstones or red and black tiles, stag's head and hunting prints, two log fires in hefty stone fireplaces, good interesting food cooked by landlady (booking required), a couple of well kept ales from Wincle and reasonably priced wines, friendly helpful staff; children welcome, dogs at owners' discretion, closed Mon, and may shut if quiet. *(John)*

SHENSTONE   SK1004
Plough (01543) 481800
Pinfold Hill, off A5127; WS14 0JN
Village dining pub with clean modern interior; enjoyable food from sandwiches, sharing boards and pizzas up, ales such as Greene King and Holdens, good range of wines and other drinks including cocktails, friendly service; children welcome, dogs in bar, tables out on front terrace, open all day, no food Sun evening. *(Stan Lorimer)*

STAFFORD   SJ9323
Swan (01785) 258142
Greengate Street; ST9 2JA Refurbished 18th-c two-bar coaching inn; well kept changing ales, craft beers, plenty of wines by the glass and wide choice of other drinks including cocktails, good bar and brasserie food, coffee shop, friendly helpful staff; live music Fri in courtyard garden, 31 bedrooms, open (and food) all day. *(Sandra Hollies)*

STANLEY   SJ9352
Travellers Rest (01782) 502580
Off A53 NE of Stoke; ST9 9LX
Comfortable old village pub with large restaurant/bar area; beams and some exposed stonework, pubby tables and chairs on patterned carpet, button-back banquettes, brassware and knick-knacks, well kept Bass, Marstons Pedigree and guests from central servery, wide choice of reasonably priced popular food including deals (booking advised), friendly helpful service; children allowed away from bar, no dogs inside, tables out at front under parasols, self-catering cottages, open all day, food all day weekends. *(Jane Rigby)*

STOKE-ON-TRENT   SJ8649
Bulls Head (01782) 834153
St Johns Square, Burslem; ST6 3AJ

Old-fashioned two-room tap for Titanic with up to ten real ales (including guests) from horseshoe bar, also good selection of belgian beers, ciders and wines; well cared-for interior with varnished tables on wood and carpeted floors, coal fire; bar billiards and table skittles; drinking area outside (may be barbecue if Port Vale are at home), open all day Fri-Sun, closed till 3pm other days. *(Jo and Belinda Smart)*

STOKE-ON-TRENT   SJ8745
Glebe (01782) 860670
35 Glebe Street, by the Civic Centre; ST4 1HG Well restored 19th-c Joules corner pub, their ales, Weston's cider and good reasonably priced wines from central mahogany counter, William Morris leaded windows, bare boards and panelling, some civic portraits and big fireplace with coat of arms above, wholesome bar food (not Sun) and all-day deli counter, friendly staff; children and dogs welcome, quite handy for station, closed Mon evening, otherwise open all day. *(Dr J Barrie Jones)*

STOKE-ON-TRENT   SJ8647
Holy Inadequate 07771 358238
Etruria Old Road; ST1 5PE Drinkers' pub with five well kept ales including Joules Pale and maybe one from on-site microbrewery, craft kegs, german lagers and lots of bottled beers, snacky food such as pies and scotch eggs, friendly staff; dogs welcome, open all day Fri-Sun, from 4pm other days. *(Jo and Belinda Smart)*

STONE   SJ9034
Royal Exchange (01785) 812685
Corner Radford Street (A520) and Northesk Street; ST15 8DA End-of-terrace pub owned by Titanic; their well kept ales and several guests including Everards, snacky lunchtime food (Fri and Sat only), also Mon evening meal deal, friendly helpful staff, three seating areas (steps) and two fires; occasional acoustic music and quiz nights; dogs welcome, open all day (till midnight Fri, Sat). *(Sandra Hollies)*

STOWE   SK0027
Bistro le Coq (01889) 270237
Off A518 Stafford–Uttoxeter; ST18 0LF Bistro-style conversion of old beamed pub opposite village church; well executed french food including good value set menus, split-level restaurant and small bar area serving real ale and seven wines by the glass from french list (mainly smaller producers), friendly efficient service; well behaved children welcome, country views from garden behind, closed Sun evening, Mon. *(Usha and Terri Patel)*

Real ale to us means beer that has matured naturally in its cask – not pressurised or filtered. We name all real ales stocked.

TAMWORTH SK2004
Market Vaults (01827) 66552
*Market Street next to Town Hall;
B79 7LU* Recent refurbishment for this
friendly little pub but keeping traditional
character; front bar and raised back lounge,
dark oak, brasswork, etched and stained
glass, original fireplaces and some interesting
old photographs, well kept Joules ales and
guests, real ciders, bargain lunchtime food;
live music Thurs evening; children (till 6pm)
and dogs welcome, nice garden behind, open
all day. *(Colin Gooch, Dave Braisted)*

TAMWORTH SK2003
Tamworth Tap (01827) 319872
Market Street; B79 7LR Cosy brewpub
in former shop; own Tamworth ales and
guests, real ciders, bottled belgian beers
and 80 gins, good mix of customers and
friendly atmosphere, more room upstairs;
no children, dogs welcome, tables out at
front and in back courtyard with view of
the castle, open all day weekends (till 9pm
Sun), closed Mon, Tues and lunchtimes
Weds-Fri. *(Colin Gooch)*

TRYSULL SO8594
Bell (01902) 892871
Bell Road; WV5 7JB Extended 18th-c red-
brick village pub next to church; cosy bar,
inglenook lounge and large high-ceilinged
back dining area, well kept Bathams,
Holdens and guests, reasonably priced
wines and decent food including Sun roasts;
children and dogs (in bar) welcome, paved
front terrace, no food Sun evening.
(Dan and Nicki Barton)

WATERFALL SK0851
Red Lion (01538) 308279
*From A523 at Waterhouses, take
Waterfall Lane; ST10 3HZ* Welcoming
stone-built pub in quiet Peak village; log
fires in two linked rooms, three well kept
ales and enjoyable traditional food (not Sun
evening); darts; children and dogs welcome,
tables outside with lovely country views,

closed weekday lunchtimes, open all day
weekends. *(Stan Lorimer)*

WETTON SK1055
Royal Oak (01335) 310287
*Village signed off Hulme End–
Alstonefield road, between B5054 and
A515; DE6 2AF* Old stone pub in lovely
NT countryside – a popular stop for walkers;
traditional bar with white ceiling boards
above black beams, quarry tiles and log fire
in stone fireplace, carpeted sun lounge, well
kept ales such as Heritage, Storm and Wincle,
good selection of gins and malt whiskies,
enjoyable fairly priced home-made food
from sandwiches to specials, friendly helpful
staff; children, dogs and muddy boots
welcome, picnic-sets in shaded garden,
camping, closed Tues and Weds, otherwise
open all day (till 6pm Sun), winter hours
may vary. *(Tim Jamieson)*

WHEATON ASTON SJ8512
Hartley Arms (01785) 840232
*Long Street (canalside, Tavern Bridge);
ST19 9NF* Popular roomy pub in pleasant
spot just above Shropshire Union Canal
(Bridge 19); good affordably priced food
from landlord-chef including OAP lunch deal
(Mon-Fri), Thurs grill night and Sun carvery,
well kept Banks's and other Marstons-related
beers, efficient friendly service; children
welcome, no dogs, picnic-sets outside, open
all day. *(Brian and Sally Wakeham)*

WHISTON SJ8914
Swan (01785) 716200
*Whiston Road, W of Penkridge;
ST19 5QH* Large rambling country pub;
beamed bar with quarry-tiled floor and open
fire, real ales such as Hobsons, Holdens
and Wye Valley, proper ciders, extended
tartan-carpeted dining lounge, good choice
of enjoyable reasonably priced food including
range of burgers, friendly staff; TV, pool
and darts children and dogs welcome,
grassy garden with play area, open all day
weekends, closed Mon lunchtime.
(Colin Gooch)

Suffolk

ALDEBURGH   TM4656   Map 5
Cross Keys
(01728) 452637 – www.thecrosskeysaldeburgh.co.uk
Crabbe Street; IP15 5BN

16th-c pub with seats outside near the beach, chatty atmosphere, friendly licensee and local beers; bedrooms

Dating from 1540, this is a traditional pub with a fine seafront position; seats on the sheltered back terrace look across the promenade and shingle to the water. The low-ceilinged interconnecting bars have a cheerful, bustling atmosphere and a warm welcome from the obliging landlord, as well as antique and other pubby furniture, miscellaneous paintings on the walls and log fires in two inglenook fireplaces. Adnams Broadside, Ghost Ship, Southwold and a seasonal guest on handpump, six decent wines by the glass and eight malt whiskies; background music and games machine. The bedrooms are attractively furnished.

🍴 Tasty food includes lunchtime sandwiches, rosemary and garlic-baked camembert, crab salad, asparagus risotto, ham and eggs, home-made fish pie, pork belly with sticky pomegranate glaze and tabbouleh, a fresh fish dish of the day, and puddings such as vanilla crème brûlée with rhubarb compote and mango pannacotta with mango and mint salsa. *Benchmark main dish: steak burger with toppings and chips £13.50. Two-course evening meal £20.00.*

Adnams ~ Manager Emily Portsmouth ~ Real ale ~ Open 11-11 ~ Bar food 12-3, 6-9 ~ Children welcome away from bar ~ Dogs allowed in bar ~ Wi-fi ~ Bedrooms: /£95
Recommended by Sandra Morgan, Tracey and Stephen Groves, Rupert and Sandy Newton, Claire Adams, Alfie Bayliss

BARROW   TL7663   Map 5
Weeping Willow 🎯 🍷 🍺
(01284) 771881 – www.theweepingwillow.co.uk
Off A45 W of Bury; IP29 5AB

Carefully refurbished old village pub with up-to-date colourful furnishings, first class food, kind service and prettily planted garden

The restoration here has been thoughtfully done, blending up-to-date décor with some fine original features. An area through the main door has very high-backed floral as well as purple leather armchairs in front of an open fire, and this leads into the bar with black leather stools against the counter, plush button-back bucket seats and candy-striped wall seats around a few tables on pale wood flooring and blue leather chesterfield sofas. The raftered dining room gives 90-degree views through huge glass windows of the garden and is furnished with colourful upholstered dining chairs, marble-topped tables and a long, high-backed banquette that separates this from a 'chef's table' area by the open kitchen; there's also a private dining room that seats up to 14 people. A small beamed room has blue, purple and pink plush stools and cushioned wall seating. A fine range of drinks includes Adnams Ghost Ship, Timothy Taylors Landlord and Woodfordes Wherry on handpump, good wines by the glass, 21 gins and farm cider; background music. The terrace has seats under parasols and stools by long rustic tables; this spills into the beautifully planted garden with walkways, which in turn extends into a meadow with a safely fenced area for children to run around.

Enterprising food includes chicken and duck liver parfait with fig and apple chutney, crayfish salad with sweet chilli, coriander and citrus labneh, pea, broad bean and asparagus risotto with pine nuts, trio of local sausages with mash, crispy onions and red wine jus, beer-battered pollack with chips, lamb rump with fondant potato, barbecued cabbage and pea and mint purée, 28-day aged rib-eye steak with béarnaise sauce and chips, and puddings such as lemon posset with hazelnut crumb and raspberry sorbet and triple chocolate brownie with muscovado ice-cream. *Benchmark main dish: monkfish and scallop linguine with horseradish crème fraîche £16.90. Two-course evening meal £21.00.*

Chestnut Group ~ Manager Philip Turner ~ Real ale ~ Open 11-11; 12-10 Sun ~ Bar food 12-2.30, 6-9; 12-5 Sun ~ Restaurant ~ Children welcome ~ Dogs allowed in bar ~ Wi-fi
Recommended by Alexandra and Tim Fledgling, Barbara and Phil Bowie, Jamie and Lizzie McEwan, Robert Wivell, Douglas Power, Rona Mackinlay

BRANDESTON
Queen 🛏

TM2460 Map 5

(01728) 685307 – www.thequeenatbrandeston.co.uk
The Street/Low Lane; IP13 7AD

Welcoming country pub with popular food, local ales, simple furnishings and seats in the garden; shepherd's huts

The keen reports from our readers make it clear that the interesting modern food remains the main draw at this attractive brick-built place – but plenty of locals do still drop in for a pint and a chat. The open-plan rooms are simply decorated, with settles, built-in wall seats, grey-painted and cushioned dining chairs around rustic tables on stripped floorboards or quarry tiles, an open fire, a woodburning stove and a few wall prints. Adnams Ghost Ship, Calvors Smooth Hoperator and Earl Soham Brandeston Gold on handpump, 13 wines by the glass, fruit gins and home-made fruit cordials; background music and board games Outside, teak tables and chairs sit among planter boxes on gravel. The two refurbished shepherd's huts and two yurts are comfortable, warm and great fun as accommodation.

Good food includes ciabatta sandwiches, breaded whitebait with tartare sauce, crispy chicken strips with garlic mayonnaise, jamaican bean stew, cumberland sausage ring with pea mash and roasted vegetables, burger with toppings, slaw and chips, beer-battered cod with crushed peas, rib-eye steak with a choice of sauce, and puddings such as custard and caramel-filled dough balls and white chocolate and raspberry parfait. *Benchmark main dish: pie of the day £13.95. Two-course evening meal £19.00.*

Free house ~ Licensee Harriet Aitchison ~ Open 12-3, 6-11; 12-11 Fri, Sat; 12-9 Sun; closed Mon, two weeks Jan ~ Bar food 12-2.30, 6-8.45; 12-9 summer Fri; 12-4 Sun ~ Restaurant ~

Children welcome ~ Dogs welcome ~ Wi-fi ~ Bedrooms: /£95 *Recommended by Jim King, David Appleyard, Justine and Neil Bonnett, Bob and Melissa Wyatt, Neil Allen, Nick Sharpe, Harvey Brown*

BROMESWELL
Unruly Pig

TM3050   Map 5

(01394) 460310 – www.theunrulypig.co.uk
Orford Road, Bromeswell Heath; IP12 2PU

Refurbished dining pub with local ales, creative food, an informal feel, helpful, attentive staff and seats outside

With a friendly and relaxed atmosphere and a wide mix of customers, this bustling pub is a winner. The bar has button-back leather wall seats, black leather dining chairs, simple tables, rugs on floorboards, woodburning stoves and contemporary seats against the counter where charming, courteous staff serve Adnams Southwold on handpump, 60 good wines by the glass, home-made cordials and interesting non-alcoholic drinks for drivers. The various linked dining rooms have beams and standing timbers, modern art and photos of well known pop stars on painted panelling, more up-to-date leather chairs and banquettes and rugs on bare boards; background music. There are seats and tables under cream parasols on the front terrace and they have bicycle racks. The pub is just a few minutes' drive from Sutton Hoo (National Trust).

First class food includes sandwiches, rabbit terrine with carrot, prosciutto and pistachio, crab tartlet with parmesan and herb salad, trio of pork with black pudding, smoked celeriac and apple, cod with braised lentils, pancetta, mussels and turnip, partridge with potato terrine, salsify and leeks, featherblade of beef with truffle mash, jerusalem artichoke and cavolo nero, and puddings such as egg custard tart with orange, rhubarb and pistachio and chocolate fondant with banana, rum and raisins; they also offer a two- and three-course set menu (not after 7pm Friday, not weekends). *Benchmark main dish: burger with roquefort and onion jam £11.25. Two-course evening meal £25.00.*

Punch ~ Lease Brendan Padfield ~ Real ale ~ Open 12-2.30, 6-10.30; 12-11 Sat; 12-10 Sun ~ Bar food 12-2.30, 6-9 (9.30 Fri); 12-3, 5-9.30 Sat; 12-8 Sun ~ Restaurant ~ Children welcome ~ Dogs allowed in bar ~ Wi-fi *Recommended by W K Wood, Alexander and Trish Cutter, Christopher Mannings, William Slade, Brian and Sally Wakeham, Julian Thorpe*

CHELMONDISTON
Butt & Oyster

TM2037   Map 5

(01473) 780764 – www.debeninns.co.uk/buttandoyster
Pin Mill – signposted from B1456 SE of Ipswich; continue to bottom of road; IP9 1JW

Chatty old riverside pub with pleasant views, good food and drink and seats on the terrace

The seating outside this simple former bargemen's pub makes the most of its fine River Orwell position, so it's best to get here early on a warm day. The half-panelled little smoke room is pleasantly worn and unfussy with high-backed and other old-fashioned settles on a tiled floor. There's also a two-level dining room with country kitchen furniture on bare boards, and pictures and boat-related artefacts on the walls above the dado. Adnams Ghost Ship, Southwold and a guest beer tapped from the cask by friendly, efficient staff, several wines by the glass and local cider; board games. Disabled access. The annual Thames Barge Race (end June/early July) is fun. The car park can fill up pretty quickly.

As well as enjoyable fish dishes, food includes sandwiches, duck spring roll with asian slaw, garlic and rosemary-studded baked camembert with truffle honey, sweet potato and butternut squash curry, local sausages and mash with caramelised onion gravy, superfood salad with a choice of toppings, assiette of pork (tenderloin, belly and crispy head) with crackling, mustard mash and apple, moroccan-style lamb tagine with couscous and minted yoghurt, slow-braised beef shortrib with red wine jus, mushrooms and jerusalem artichokes, and puddings. *Benchmark main dish: beer-battered fish and chips £22.95. Two-course evening meal £16.00.*

Deben Inns ~ Lease Steve Lomas ~ Real ale ~ Open 9am-11pm ~ Bar food 9am-9.30pm ~ Restaurant ~ Children welcome ~ Dogs allowed in bar ~ Wi-fi *Recommended by Nicholas and Maddy Trainer, Sophie Ellison, Richard and Penny Gibbs, Charlie May, Peter Brix, Belinda Stamp*

HASKETON
Turks Head 🌟◉ 🍷

TM2450 Map 5

(01394) 610343 – www.theturksheadhasketon.co.uk

Top Road; follow village signs taking B1079 from second Woodbridge roundabout; IP13 6JG

Neatly renovated pub with airy bar, snug and dining room, local ales, imaginative food, attentive service and seats outside

In warm weather, the three pétanque pistes here are put to good use – as are the chairs and tables under large parasols on the terrace and the picnic-sets on the lawn. Inside, the fresh modern décor is light and appealing and there's a genuine welcome for all. The bar has white-painted beams, traditional chairs, stools and cushioned wall seats around tables on big flagstones, a woodburning stove in a large fireplace, books on shelves and high chairs against the pale oak counter. Courteous staff serve Adnams Ghost Ship, Earl Soham Victoria Bitter, Fullers London Pride and a guest such as Captain Barlow (named for them from Greene King) on handpump, over 20 wines by the glass and 22 gins. A similarly furnished snug has a small woodburner (dogs are allowed in here) and the spreading, high-raftered, airy dining room has cushioned chairs and cream upholstered banquettes around dark tables on floorboards, animal sketches and butterfly prints on RAF-blue paintwork and doors out to the terrace; background music and board games.

Enjoyable food includes sandwiches, chorizo-stuffed squid with aioli, oxtail tortellini with beef consommé and horseradish cream, roasted root vegetables with chicory, lotus seed popcorn and gremolata, burger with toppings and chips, sea trout fillet with smashed kohlrabi, grapefruit and turnips, pork chop with charred pineapple, kappa root croquette and mustard relish, 28-day aged steak with dauphinoise potatoes and peppercorn sauce, and puddings such as dark chocolate mousse trifle and confit apple tart with honeycomb and clotted cream; they also offer Saturday brunch (10am-2pm), a two- and three-course weekday lunchtime menu and Friday evening indian specials. *Benchmark main dish: monkfish curry with tiger prawn pakora and fresh coconut rice £22.00. Two-course evening meal £26.00.*

Free house ~ Licensee Jemima Withey ~ Real ale ~ Open 11-11; 11-midnight Sat; 11-8 Sun; 4-8 Mon, Tues Jan-Feb ~ Bar food 12-3, 6-9; 10-3, 6-9 Sat; 12-3 Sun; no food Mon, Tues Jan-Feb ~ Restaurant ~ Children welcome ~ Dogs allowed in bar ~ Wi-fi *Recommended by Freddie and Sarah Banks, Jim and Sue James, Michael and Sarah Lockley, Mary and Nigel Joyce, Patti and James Davidson*

Please tell us if the décor, atmosphere, food or drink at a pub is different from our description. We rely on readers' reports to keep us up to date: feedback@goodguides.com, or (no stamp needed) Freepost THE GOOD PUB GUIDE, Random House Publishing, 20 Vauxhall Bridge Road, London SW1V 2SA.

IPSWICH
Fat Cat 🍺

TM1844 Map 5

(01473) 726524 – www.fatcatipswich.co.uk

Spring Road, opposite junction with Nelson Road (best bet for parking is up there); IP4 5NL

Wonderful choice of changing real ales in a well run town pub; garden

A beer lover's dream and packed with cheerful customers, this well run pub stocks a huge range of up to 18 real ales from around the country on handpump or tapped from the cask. There might be Adnams Southwold, Crouch Vale Brewers Gold and Yakima Gold plus Fullers London Pride, Mighty Oak Oscar Wilde, Oakham Citra, Sharps Doom Bar, Titanic Plum Porter, Woodfordes Wherry and ales from local breweries such as Bishop Nick, Earl Soham, Grain and Green Jack. They also stock quite a few belgian bottled beers, farm cider and seven wines by the glass. The bars have a mix of café chairs and stools, unpadded wall benches and cushioned seats around cast-iron and wooden pub tables, bare floorboards and lots of enamel brewery signs and posters; board games and shove-ha'penny. There's also a spacious back conservatory and several picnic-sets arranged on the terrace and lawn. Very little nearby parking. Well behaved dogs are welcome but they must be kept on a lead.

🍴 They keep a supply of rolls, spicy scotch eggs and sausage rolls made in their small kitchen and are happy for you to bring in takeaway food (not Friday or Saturday).

Free house ~ Licensee John Keatley ~ Real ale ~ No credit cards ~ Open 12-11; 12-midnight Fri; 11am-midnight Sat ~ Bar food all day while it lasts ~ Dogs welcome ~ Wi-fi
Recommended by Geoff and Ann Marston, Alexandra and Richard Clay, Charles Fraser, Paddy and Sian O'Leary, Chloe and Michael Swettenham, Scott and Charlotte Havers

LAXFIELD
Kings Head 🍺 🛏

TM2972 Map 5

(01986) 798395 – www.lowhouselaxfield.com
Gorams Mill Lane, behind church; IP13 8DW

Largely unaltered 500-year-old inn behind the church in a charming rural village; bedrooms

This is a lovely, unspoilt thatched pub (known locally as the Low House) owned for the community by a small group of residents. There's an easy-going, genuinely friendly atmosphere and, unusually, no bar counter. Instead, the helpful staff potter in and out of a cellar tap bar to pour your pints of Adnams plus guests such as Earl Soham Victoria, Green Jack Golden Best, Shortts Blondie and Timothy Taylors Landlord straight from the cask; also, eight wines by the glass, ten malt whiskies and 16 gins. The interesting little chequer-tiled front room is dominated by a booth of high-backed settles next to an open fire topped by an old-fashioned stove, two other rooms have pews, old seats and scrubbed deal tables, and decorations consist of old prints and photographs. Outside, a neatly kept garden has colourful herbaceous borders, an immaculately mown lawn with picnic-sets, and a pavilion for colder evenings. Three attractive, comfortable and well appointed bedrooms are in the converted stables. They hold regular events such as morris and molly dancing, classic car days, speciality food nights, beer festivals, plays in the garden and music and art shows.

🍴 Good, popular food includes sandwiches, ploughman's, smoked salmon pâté, chicken satay with peanut sauce, vegan curry with beans, rice, chickpeas and spicy vegetables, smoked haddock rarebit with sautéed potatoes, sausages with leek, cheese and mustard mash, chicken parmigiana, beef bourguignon with celeriac mash, lamb tagine with tabbouleh, and puddings. *Benchmark main dish: pie of the day £11.95. Two-course evening meal £18.00.*

Adnams ~ Tenant Alastair Clarke ~ Real ale ~ Open 12-11; 12-7 Sun ~ Bar food 12-2 (3 weekends), 6.30-9; not Sun evening ~ Restaurant ~ Children welcome away from Tap Room ~ Dogs welcome ~ Wi-fi ~ Local folk music alternate Thurs afternoons ~ Bedrooms: /£85
Recommended by Dr Peter Crawshaw, James Allsopp, Brian and Sally Wakeham, Andrew and Michele Revell, Rosie and John Moore

PETTISTREE
Greyhound

TM2954   Map 5

(01728) 746451 – www.greyhoundinnpettistree.co.uk
The Street; brown sign to pub off B1438 S of Wickham Market, 0.5 miles N of A12; IP13 0HP

Neatly kept village pub with enjoyable food and drink; seats outside

Our readers enjoy this nice old place very much, and you can be sure of a genuine welcome. It's basically two smallish rooms with open fires, some rather low beams, chunky farmhouse chairs and cushioned settles around dark wooden tables on bare floorboards and candlelight. Earl Soham Victoria Bitter and guests such as Adnams Ghost Ship and Mosaic on handpump, 11 wines by the glass, 15 gins and 20 malt whiskies; it's best to book in advance to be sure of a table. The well kept side garden has picnic-sets under parasols, with more beside the gravelled front car park. The church is next door. Check the website for details of circular walks from the pub.

The landlady cooks the interesting food: pork and pistachio terrine with apple and pear chutney, treacle and whisky-cured sea trout with horseradish cream and pickled cucumber, filo pastry parcel stuffed with vegetables, brie and wild garlic pesto, hake fillet with samphire, crispy capers and red pepper romesco sauce, slow-braised venison shoulder with mini pie, dauphinoise potatoes, mushroom ketchup and redcurrant reduction, rosemary and garlic-marinated hanger steak with chips, and puddings such as lemon posset with blood orange jelly and pistachio brittle and chocolate mousse with hazelnut crumb and cacao nibs. *Benchmark main dish: slow-roasted lamb shoulder £17.00. Two-course evening meal £20.00.*

Free house ~ Licensees Stewart and Louise McKenzie ~ Real ale ~ Open 12-3, 6-11; 12-4 Sun; closed Mon ~ Bar food 12-2.30, 6-9; 12-3 Sun ~ Restaurant ~ Children welcome ~ Dogs allowed in bar ~ Wi-fi *Recommended by Sarah and David Gibbs, Diane Abbot, Neil Allen, Beth Aldridge, Jim King, Miles Green, Donald Allsopp, Caroline Sullivan*

SIBTON
White Horse

TM3570   Map 5

(01728) 660337 – www.sibtonwhitehorseinn.co.uk
Halesworth Road/Hubbards Hill, N of Peasenhall; IP17 2JJ

Particularly well run inn with nicely old-fashioned bar, good mix of customers, real ales and imaginative food; bedrooms

As well as being a proper village pub with a good local following and genuinely friendly, hands-on licensees, this place offers first class food and comfortable bedrooms. The appealing bar has a roaring log fire in a large inglenook fireplace, horsebrasses and tack on the walls, vintage settles and pews, Adnams Southwold, Green Jack Trawlerboys Best Bitter and Woodfordes Nelsons Revenge on handpump, ten wines by the glass and 12 malt whiskies served from an old oak-panelled counter. A viewing panel reveals the working cellar and its ancient floor, and they hold beer and music events during the summer. Steps lead up past an old, partly knocked-through timbered wall into a carpeted gallery, and there's also a smart dining room and a secluded (and popular) dining terrace. The big garden has plenty of seats. The five bedrooms, housed in a separate building next door, are warm, contemporary and well equipped and breakfasts are good. Disabled access but not to the loos.

 Impressive food using home-grown and free-range produce includes sandwiches, roquefort mousse with hazelnut, pear, oatcake and mustard dressing, liquorice-cured salmon, candied beetroot, kohlrabi and fennel salad, crème fraîche and yuzu dressing, wild mushroom steamed pudding, confit garlic mash and mustard sauce, loin of coley with thai green mussel curry, water chestnuts, pak choi and bamboo shoots, local pigeon breast with fondant potato, apple, fruity red cabbage and pickled walnuts, and puddings such as spiced banana cake with bacon and tamarind caramel, chilli yoghurt and cinnamon ice-cream and white chocolate and whisky parfait with spiced macadamia nut crumble and apple sorbet. *Benchmark main dish: beer-battered line-caught cod and chips £13.75. Two-course evening meal £24.00.*

Free house ~ Licensees Neil and Gill Mason ~ Real ale ~ Open 12-3, 6.30-11; 12-3, 6-11 Sat; 12-4, 7-10.30 Sun; closed Mon and lunchtime Tues ~ Bar food 12-2, 6.30-9; 12-2, 7-8.30 Sun ~ Restaurant ~ Well behaved children welcome but no under-6s in evening; no children (of any age) in bedrooms ~ Dogs allowed in bar ~ Wi-fi ~ Bedrooms: £90/£105 *Recommended by Buster and Helena Hastings, Guy Henderson, John Harris, Patrick and Martine Lawson, Maria and Stephen Braeburn, Edward and William Johnston*

SOUTHWOLD
TM5076 Map 5

Crown ♀ 🍺 🛏

(01502) 722275 – www.thecrownsouthwold.co.uk
High Street; IP18 6DP

Graceful old coaching inn with plenty of room for both drinking and dining, local ales, good wines and seats outside; good bedrooms

Of course, the large majority of customers are here for the particularly good food and comfortable bedrooms, but our readers are fond of the informal and chatty back bar. Here you'll find oak panelling, bare floorboards and antique tables and chairs and Adnams Bitter, Broadside and Ghost Ship on handpump, 20 wines by the glass and eight malt whiskies served by friendly staff; background music and board games. The elegant beamed front bar and dining room are light and airy with a curved high-backed settle and other dark varnished settles, kitchen chairs and bar stools, a carefully restored and rather fine carved wooden fireplace; daily papers. There are seats on the sheltered side terrace or outside at the front by the High Street. Bedrooms are well equipped and individually furnished and breakfasts highly rated.

The well regarded food includes mussels in cider with shallots and parsley, chicory, pear, walnut and blue cheese salad, wild mushroom and cheese risotto with truffle oil and parmesan, burger with toppings, pickles and fries, confit duckling with lyonnaise potatoes and macerated plums, roast cod with bacon lardons, cabbage and Adnams beer and butter sauce, chicken breast with artichoke, leeks, salami and balsamic dressing, and puddings such as chocolate tart with blood orange sorbet and marmalade sponge with vanilla custard. *Benchmark main dish: rib-eye steak with dripping chips and béarnaise sauce £25.00. Two-course evening meal £26.00.*

Adnams ~ Manager Nick Attfield ~ Real ale ~ Open 11-11; 12-10.30 Sun ~ Bar food 12-3, 6-9 ~ Children welcome ~ Wi-fi ~ Bedrooms: £135/£185 *Recommended by Frances Parsons, Ted and Mary Bates, Sandra and Michael Smith, Kim Holt, Sam Cole, Jamie and Lizzie McEwan, Alister and Margery Bacon*

SOUTHWOLD
TM4975 Map 5

Harbour Inn ♀ ◉

(01502) 722381 – www.harbourinnsouthwold.co.uk

Blackshore, by the boats; from A1095, turn right at the Kings Head, and keep on past the golf course and water tower; IP18 6TA

Great spot down by the boats with lots of outside tables and interesting interior; popular food with emphasis on local seafood

This is especially enjoyable in warm weather with picnic-sets on the terrace giving views of the boats on the estuary and seats and tables behind the pub overlooking the marshy commons to the town. Inside, the back bar is nicely nautical with dark panelling and built-in wall seats around scrubbed tables, and cheerful staff serve a dozen wines by the glass, along with Adnams Broadside, Ghost Ship, Southwold and a guest beer on handpump. The low ceiling is draped with ensigns, signal flags and pennants, and there's a quaint old stove, rope fancywork, local fishing photographs and even portholes with water bubbling behind them; they have their own weather station for walkers and sailors. The lower front bar, with a tiled floor and panelling, is broadly similar, while the large, elevated dining room has panoramic views of the harbour, lighthouse, brewery and churches beyond the marshes. You can walk from here along the Blyth estuary to Walberswick (where the Bell is under the same good management) via a footbridge and return by the one-man ferry.

 Locally caught fish is the highlight here with choices such as prawn and crayfish cocktail, smoked haddock chowder, fish pie and dover sole, but they also offer pâté of the day with ale chutney, vegetarian calzone pizza, steak in ale pie, slow-cooked lamb shoulder with dauphinoise potatoes, and puddings such as chocolate brownie with salted caramel ice-cream and mixed berry pavlova. *Benchmark main dish: beer-battered fish and chips £13.50. Two-course evening meal £20.00.*

Adnams ~ Tenant Nick Attfield ~ Real ale ~ Open 11-11 ~ Bar food 12-9 ~ Restaurant ~ Children welcome ~ Dogs allowed in bar ~ Folk music first and third Sun of month
Recommended by Celia and Andrew King, Mandy and Gary Redstone, Robert Wivell, Paddy and Sian O'Leary, Paul Farraday, Andrew Vincent

STOKE-BY-NAYLAND
TL9836 Map 5

Crown ★ ⦿ ♀ ⇌

(01206) 262001 – www.crowninn.net

Park Street (B1068); CO6 4SE

● ●
Suffolk Dining Pub of the Year

Smart dining pub with attractive modern furnishings, imaginative food, real ales and a great wine choice; good bedrooms

Our readers praise all aspects of this well run, civilised inn, with many of them returning on a regular basis. The extensive open-plan dining bar is carefully laid out to give several distinct-feeling areas: a sofa and easy chairs on flagstones near the serving counter, a couple of armchairs under heavy beams by the big woodburning stove, one sizeable table tucked nicely into a three-sided built-in seat and a lower side room with more beams and cheerful floral wallpaper. Tables are mostly stripped veterans, with high-backed dining chairs, but there are more modern chunky pine tables at the back; also, contemporary artwork (mostly for sale) and daily papers. Friendly staff serve Adnams Ghost Ship, Crouch Vale Brewers Gold, Woodfordes Wherry and a changing guest such as Humpty Dumpty Broadland Sunrise on handpump and Aspall's cider. Wine is a key feature, with 30 by the glass and hundreds more from the glass-walled 'cellar shop' in one corner – you can buy wine there to take away too. A sheltered flagstoned back terrace has comfortable teak furniture, heaters, big terracotta-coloured parasols and a peaceful view over rolling, lightly wooded countryside. Bedrooms are well equipped and comfortable and breakfasts are first class. This is a pretty village and you'll find many well marked surrounding footpaths. Good disabled access.

🍴 Excellent food includes breakfasts (7.30-10.30am Monday-Saturday; 8-10.30am Sunday) plus pigeon breast with roasted cauliflower purée, shallots and crispy prosciutto, tempura oysters and king prawns with pickled samphire, soy and spring onions, lemon and thyme tagliatelle with goats cheese and sunblush tomatoes, corn-fed chicken and prawn skewer with chilli and lime marinade, garlic butter and french fries, cod fillet with chorizo and crayfish butter and roasted garlic mash, local game pie, local lamb chops with apricot and pine nut couscous and sweet and sour aubergine, and puddings such as chocolate fondant with caramelised apple and fig syrup and lemon tart with raspberry and chantilly cream. *Benchmark main dish: beer-battered haddock and chips £15.50. Two-course evening meal £25.00.*

Free house ~ Licensee Richard Sunderland ~ Real ale ~ Open 11-11; 11-10.30 Sun ~ Bar food 12-2.30, 6-9.30 (10 Fri, Sat); 12-9 Sun ~ Children welcome ~ Dogs allowed in bar ~ Wi-fi ~ Bedrooms: £100/£145 *Recommended by Ted and Mary Bates, Mrs Margo Finlay, Jörg Kasprowski, Charlie and Mark Todd, Belinda and Neil Garth*

WALBERSWICK
Anchor 🏅 ♟ 🛏
TM4974 Map 5

(01502) 722112 – www.atwalberswick.com
The Street (B1387); village signed off A12; IP18 6UA

Friendly, bustling pub with good food and thoughtful choice of drinks; bedrooms and chalets

Drinkers and diners are equally well served here – though many customers have come to enjoy the interesting food. The simply furnished front bar, divided into snug halves by a two-way open fire, has big windows, heavy stripped tables on original oak flooring, sturdy built-in green leather wall seats and nicely framed black and white photographs of fishermen that are displayed on colour-washed panelling; there's a woodburner too, as well as daily papers and board games. Helpful, friendly staff serve Adnams Ghost Ship and Southwold on handpump, 50 bottled beers and around 20 wines by the glass; they hold an oyster and beer festival in August. An extensive dining area stretches back from a small, more modern-feeling lounge. There are plenty of seats in the attractive garden, with an outdoor bar and wood-fired pizza oven serving the flagstoned terraces. Six spacious chalet-style rooms in the garden have views of either the water or beach huts and sand dunes, while from the bedrooms in the main house you can hear the sea just a few hundred metres away; dogs are allowed in some rooms. As well as the coast path, there's a pleasant walk to Southwold.

🍴 Food is excellent and includes breakfasts (8.30-10am) plus pigeon breast with bacon, mushrooms and spinach on toast, scallops with coriander and hazelnut butter, local oysters, butternut squash with turmeric, kale and pearl barley hotpot with herb dumplings, crab with linguine, chilli and garlic, venison burger with red onion marmalade, miso-roasted salmon with kale, soya beans and ginger and chilli dressing, pheasant au vin with spiced red cabbage and mash, and puddings such as chocolate fondant with salted caramel ice-cream and apple crumble with custard. *Benchmark main dish: smoked haddock, salmon and cod fishcake with creamed spinach £15.75. Two-course evening meal £21.00.*

Boudica Inns ~ Lease Mark and Sophie Dorber ~ Real ale ~ Open 8am-11pm ~ Bar food
12-3, 6-9 ~ Restaurant ~ Children welcome ~ Dogs allowed in bar and bedrooms ~ Wi-fi ~
Bedrooms: /£135 *Recommended by Liz and Martin Eldon, Andrew Vincent, Kim Holt, Helena and
Trevor Fraser, Valerie and Colin Sayer, Julie Swift, Kate Moran*

WALBERSWICK
Bell 🍷 🍴 🛏

TM4974 Map 5

(01502) 723109 – www.bellinnwalberswick.co.uk
Just off B1387; IP18 6TN

**Interesting and thriving 16th-c inn with good food and drinks choice,
friendly atmosphere and nice garden; cosy bedrooms**

You'll find a lot of original character in the various rooms in this 600-year-
old pub. The charming, rambling bar has a chatty atmosphere, antique
curved settles, cushioned pews and window seats, scrubbed tables, and two
huge fireplaces. The fine old flooring encompasses sagging ancient bricks,
broad boards, flagstones and black and red tiles. Welcoming staff serve
12 wines by the glass and Adnams Broadside, Ghost Ship, Southwold and
a seasonal guest on handpump; darts. The Barn Café is open during school
holidays for light snacks, cakes, teas and so forth. A large, neatly planted
sheltered garden behind has picnic-sets and the rolling sand dunes are
a stroll away. The summer rowing-boat ferry to Southwold is nearby (there's
also a footbridge a bit further away). Bedrooms, some with sea or harbour
views, are attractively decorated, and breakfasts are good.

 Rewarding food includes sandwiches, potted ham hock with pistachios and
piccalilli, smokies (flaked local smoked haddock in cheese sauce) on toast,
harissa-spiced charred broccoli with toasted almonds, hazelnuts and chickpeas with
roasted onion, pepper, cauliflower couscous and tahini dressing, cumberland sausage
with free-range eggs, crispy beef salad with crushed cashews, water chestnuts, coriander
and thai dressing, chargrilled chicken with dauphinoise potatoes and wild mushroom,
baby onion and pancetta sauce, and puddings such as white chocolate torte with orange
sorbet and passion-fruit coulis and rhubarb curd with lemon and pistachio sponge and
stem ginger ice-cream. *Benchmark main dish: beer-battered cod or plaice and chips
£13.50. Two-course evening meal £20.00.*

Adnams ~ Tenant Nick Attfield ~ Real ale ~ Open 11-11 ~ Bar food 12-2.30, 6-9 ~ Children
welcome ~ Dogs allowed in bar and bedrooms ~ Wi-fi ~ Bedrooms: /£110 *Recommended by
Usha and Terri Patel, Greta and Gavin Craddock, Nik and Gloria Clarke, M and GR, Lee and Jill
Stafford, Margaret McDonald, Sally Harrison*

WALDRINGFIELD
Maybush

TM2844 Map 5

(01473) 736215 – www.debeninns.co.uk/maybush
Off A12 S of Martlesham; The Quay, Cliff Road; IP12 4QL

**Busy pub with tables outside by the riverbank; nautical décor
and a fair choice of drinks and fair value food**

Because of its lovely spot by the River Deben, this family-friendly pub is
open (and serves food) all day. Some of the window tables inside look
over the water and the spacious knocked-through bar is divided into separate
areas by fireplaces or steps. There's a nautical theme, with an elaborate
ship's model in a glass case and a few more models in a light, high-ceilinged
extension, as well as lots of old lanterns, pistols and aerial photographs;
background music and board games. Adnams Ghost Ship and Southwold
and a guest beer on handpump and a fair choice of wines by the glass; board

games. The numerous picnic-sets on a terrace behind the pub overlook the water but do get snapped up quickly in warm weather. Disabled access. River cruises are available nearby, though you have to pre-book. There is a large pay-and-display car park (charges are refunded to pub customers).

🍴 Popular food includes sandwiches, prawn, crayfish and avocado cocktail, crispy pork belly bites with sweet chilli-dressed asian salad, local sausages and mash with cider gravy, lasagne, sea bass fillets with basil pesto, roasted baby vine tomatoes and herb-crushed new potatoes, beef, chorizo and black bean chilli with lime and coriander rice, cajun chicken salad with yoghurt dressing and toasted pitta bread, fresh fish dish of the day, and puddings such as fruit crumble and banoffi pie. *Benchmark main dish: beer-battered fish and chips £11.95. Two-course evening meal £19.00.*

Deben Inns ~ Lease Steve and Louise Lomas ~ Real ale ~ Open 9am-11pm ~ Bar food 9am-9.30pm ~ Restaurant ~ Children welcome ~ Dogs allowed in bar ~ Wi-fi *Recommended by Nik and Gloria Clarke, Dr Martin Owton, Adam Jones, Phoebe Peacock, Alison and Michael Harper, Tony Smaithe, Peter and Emma Kelly*

Also Worth a Visit in Suffolk

Besides the fully inspected pubs, you might like to try these pubs that have been recommended to us and described by readers. Do tell us what you think of them: feedback@goodguides.com

ALDEBURGH TM4656
Mill (01728) 452563
Market Cross Place, opposite Moot Hall; IP15 5BJ Part-timbered, latticed-windowed seafront pub; split-level interior with cosy beamed areas, log fire and some RNLI memorabilia, enjoyable pubby food including good fresh fish and one or two smokehouse dishes, four Adnams ales and decent choice of wines by the glass; background and monthly live music; children (until 9pm) and dogs welcome, handy for the fishermen's huts, open all day. *(Eddie Edwards)*

ALDEBURGH TM4656
White Hart (01728) 453205
High Street; IP15 5AJ Friendly one-room local in former 19th-c reading room; high ceiling, panelled walls and stained-glass windows, scrubbed tables on bare boards, open fire in cast-iron fireplace, Adnams ales and guests, decent wines by the glass, bar snacks, also summer pizzas in back courtyard; occasional live music, free wi-fi; no children inside, dogs welcome, open all day. *(Christopher Manning)*

ALDRINGHAM TM4461
Parrot & Punchbowl (01728) 830221
B1122/B1353 S of Leiston; IP16 4PY Welcoming 17th-c beamed country pub; good fairly priced traditional food catering for special diets, well kept Adnams Southwold and a couple of guests, two-level restaurant; occasional quiz nights; children and dogs (in bar) welcome, nice sheltered garden, also family garden with play area, closed Sun evening. *(Deborah and Duncan Walliams)*

BADINGHAM TM3068
White Horse (01728) 638280
A1120 S of village; IP13 8JR Welcoming low-beamed 15th-c inn; generous helpings of enjoyable reasonably priced food from standards up, Adnams and guests tapped from the cask, real ciders and good range of other drinks, inglenook log fire and a couple of woodburners; children, dogs and muddy boots welcome, disabled access, nice rambling garden with summer pizza oven and neat bowling green, three timbered bedrooms, open all day Sun (food till 6pm). *(John Harris)*

BARHAM TM1251
Sorrel Horse (01473) 830327
Old Norwich Road; IP6 0PG Friendly open-plan beamed and timbered country inn with good log fire in central chimneybreast, well kept ales including Adnams, popular home-made pubby food (all day weekends); free wi-fi; children and dogs welcome, disabled facilities, picnic-sets on side grass with large play area, bedrooms in converted barn, open all day Weds-Sun. *(Mark and Mary Setting)*

BENTLEY TM1138
Case is Altered (01473) 805575
Capel Road; IP9 2DW Friendly community-owned pub in charming village; well kept Adnams Southwold and three local guests, snacky lunchtime food including sandwiches/panini and good ploughman's, full Sun lunch and occasional themed evenings, long main bar with woodburner, smaller bar behind and sizeable dining room with another woodburner; regular events such

as open mike, games and quiz nights, free wi-fi; children and dogs (in bar) welcome, disabled access/loos, nice fenced garden adjoining village playground, closed Mon and Tues. *(Lesley Broadbent)*

BILDESTON   TL9949
★**Crown** (01449) 740510
B1115 SW of Stowmarket; IP7 7EB
Picturesque 15th-c timbered country inn; smart beamed main bar with leather armchairs and inglenook log fire, contemporary artwork in back area, ales such as Adnams and Greene King along with good choice of wines, gins and cocktails, highly praised imaginative food from snacks and reworked pub favourites up including set lunch (Mon-Thurs) and tasting menus, afternoon teas (maybe with a glass of champagne), more formal dining room; children welcome, disabled access and parking, tables laid for eating in appealing central courtyard, more in large beautifully kept garden with decking, 13 bedrooms, open all day. *(David Appleyard)*

BILDESTON   TL9949
Kings Head (01449) 741434
High Street; IP7 7ED Small 16th-c beamed village pub with own good beers (brewery behind – can view by appointment) plus local guests, enjoyable well priced home-made food (Fri evening to Sun lunchtime only), pleasant chatty staff, wood floor bar with inglenook woodburner; music evenings including Weds open mike, quiz last Thurs of month, May beer festival; children and dogs welcome, back garden with terrace and play equipment, open all day weekends, closed Mon, Tues and lunchtimes Weds-Fri. *(David Appleyard)*

BLAXHALL   TM3656
Ship (01728) 688316
Off B1069 S of Snape; can be reached from A12 via Little Glemham; IP12 2DY Popular low-beamed 18th-c pub in charming country setting; enjoyable reasonably priced traditional food in bar or restaurant, well kept Adnams and guests; regular live music including folk sessions and Mon afternoon sing-around; children in eating areas, dogs in bar, eight chalet bedrooms, open all day. *(Graham Smart)*

BLYFORD   TM4276
Queens Head (01502) 478404
B1123 Blythburgh–Halesworth, opposite the church; IP19 9JY Attractive 15th-c thatched pub under newish management; Adnams ales and good freshly made food from varied but not overlong menu, very low beams, some antique settles, huge fireplace; children and dogs welcome, tables out at

front and in big garden to the side, open all day, food all day weekends. *(Steve Bullard)*

BRAMFIELD   TM3973
Queens Head (01986) 784214
The Street; A144 S of Halesworth; IP19 9HT Smartly restored village pub next to interesting church; various rooms with heavy beams, timbering and tiled floors, woodburner in impressive brick fireplace in high-raftered dining room, Adnams and guests, good often imaginative food from sandwiches and deli boards up, special diets catered for, friendly service; children welcome, tiered garden, open (and food) all day. *(Robert Wivell)*

BRENT ELEIGH   TL9348
★**Cock** (01787) 247371
A1141 SE of Lavenham; CO10 9PB Timeless thatched country pub; well kept Adnams and guests, proper cider and enjoyable traditional food cooked by landlady, cosy ochre-walled snug and second small room, antique floor tiles, lovely coal fire, old photographs of village (church well worth a look); darts, shove-ha'penny and toad in the hole; well behaved children and dogs welcome, picnic-sets up on side grass with summer hatch service, one bedroom, open (and food) all day Fri-Sun. *(Mark and Sian Edwards)*

BROCKLEY GREEN   TL7247
Plough (01440) 786789
Hundon Road; CO10 8DT Neat knocked-through bar with beams, timbers and stripped brick, scrubbed tables and open fire, well liked food from lunchtime sandwiches and pub standards up, Tues steak night, three changing ales, good choice of wines by the glass and several malt whiskies/gins, friendly helpful service, restaurant; children and dogs welcome, attractive grounds with peaceful country views, comfortable bedrooms, open all day Sun till 9pm (food till 7pm). *(Lenny and Ruth Walters)*

BROME   TM1376
Oaksmere (01379) 873940
Rectory Road, off B1077; IP23 8AJ Nice old furnishings, glazed-over well and handsome woodburner in 19th-c hotel's beamed and timbered bar, Adnams ales, Aspall's cider and lots of wines by the glass, separate cocktail bar in Victorian-style conservatory, good food from 'Suffolk tapas' and pub favourites up including signature steaks cooked in a wood-fired oven, also weekday set lunch and afternoon teas, airy restaurant; background music; children welcome, splendid 17-acre grounds with kid's play galleon, 14 comfortable bedrooms, open (and some food) all day. *(Dr Martin Owton)*

Virtually all pubs in this book sell wine by the glass. We mention wines
if they are a cut above the average.

BUCKLESHAM   TM2441
Shannon (01473) 659512
Main Road; IP10 0DR Extended and
updated old village pub run by two brothers;
enjoyable food from regularly changing menu
including good Sun roasts, Adnams ales and
decent range of gins, friendly helpful service;
live music, quiz nights, darts and board
games; children and dogs welcome, seats out
at front behind picket fence, open all day
weekends, closed Mon. *(Charlotte Stiff)*

BUNGAY   TM3389
Castle (01986) 892283
Earsham Street; NR35 1AF Pleasantly
informal 16th-c dining inn with good
interesting food from chef-owner including
themed nights; opened-up beamed interior
with restaurant part at front, two open fires,
Cliff Quay Sea Dog, Earl Soham Victoria and
a couple of craft beers, Aspall's cider, nice
choice of wines by the glass and several gins,
afternoon teas, friendly efficient staff, french
windows to pretty courtyard garden shaded
by an indian bean tree; children welcome,
dogs in bar area, four comfortable bedrooms,
closed Sun evening, Mon (also Tues evening
in winter), otherwise open all day. *(Alf and
Sally Garner)*

BUNGAY   TM3491
Green Dragon (01986) 892681
Broad Street; NR35 1EF Unpretentious
1930s corner pub brewing its own good well
priced beers, tapas menu Thurs-Sat 5-9pm,
friendly local atmosphere; occasional live
music; children and dogs welcome, tables
on terrace, open all day (till 9pm Sun).
(Philip Saunders)

BURY ST EDMUNDS   TL8463
Dove (01284) 702787
Hospital Road; IP33 3JU Friendly 19th-c
alehouse with rustic bare-boards bar and
separate parlour, half a dozen well kept/
priced mainly local beers and a couple of
proper ciders; regular folk sessions and
other acoustic music, comedy nights; dogs
welcome, some seats out at front, closed
weekday lunchtimes. *(Christopher Manning)*

BURY ST EDMUNDS   TL8564
★Nutshell (01284) 764867
*The Traverse, central pedestrian link
off Abbeygate Street; IP33 1BJ* Simple
timeless local with tiny interior (can be
a crush at busy times); lots of interest
including vintage bank notes, military and
other badges, a wooden propeller and a
great metal halberd, even a mummified
cat (found walled up here) and companion
rat, short wooden benches along shopfront
windows and a cut-down sewing-machine
table, Greene King ales, no food; background

music, steep narrow stairs up to lavatories;
children (till 7pm) and dogs welcome, open
all day. *(Andy and Rosemary Taylor)*

BURY ST EDMUNDS   TL8564
Old Cannon (01284) 768769
*Cannon Street, just off A134/A1101
roundabout at N end of town; IP33 1JR*
Early Victorian town house brewing its
own beers in the bar (two huge gleaming
stainless-steel vessels and views up to
balustraded malt floor above the counter),
Old Cannon Best, Gunner's Daughter and
seasonal ales, also guests such as Adnams
Southwold and good range of other drinks,
enjoyable pubby food (not Sun evening)
including weekday set lunch and monthly
themed evenings, assortment of old and
new furniture on bare boards; well behaved
children and dogs allowed, comfortable
bedrooms in former brewhouse across
courtyard, open all day. *(Adrian Johnson,
Alison Nicholls)*

BURY ST EDMUNDS   TL8564
One Bull (01284) 848220
Angel Hill; IP33 1UZ Contemporary
pub with own Brewshed beers, local guests
and extensive range of wines by the glass
(some unusual choices), good food (all day
Sat) from sandwiches and sharing boards
up including set lunch (Mon-Sat), friendly
attentive service; free wi-fi; children till 6pm
in bar (8pm restaurant), closed Sun evening,
otherwise open all day and can get very busy.
(D Hillaby)

BURY ST EDMUNDS   TL8563
★Rose & Crown (01284) 755934
Whiting Street; IP33 1NP Cheerful
black-beamed corner local under affable
long-serving licensees; particularly well kept
Greene King ales (including XX Mild) and
guests, simple lunchtime home cooking (not
Sun) at bargain prices, pleasant lounge with
lots of piggy pictures, good games-oriented
public bar, rare separate off-sales hatch;
background radio, no credit cards or under-
14s; pretty back courtyard, open all day
weekdays. *(Julian Richardson)*

BUXHALL   TM9957
★Crown (01449) 736521
*Off B1115 W of Stowmarket; Mill Road;
IP14 3DW* A pub of two halves; steps
down to cosy low-beamed bar on left with
woodburner in brick inglenook, larger
timbered dining area beyond with view of
old windmill, well kept Adnams Broadside,
Earl Soham Victoria and nice choice of
wines by the glass; light airy dining room
to the right with its own bar and another
woodburner, very good if not particularly
cheap food from interesting menu using local
produce, charming service; children and dogs

welcome, plenty of parasol-shaded tables on terrace with views over open country (ignore the pylons), herb garden, closed Sun evening, Mon. *(Mrs J Ekins-Daukes)*

CAVENDISH   TL8046
★**George** (01787) 280248
A1092; The Green; CO10 8BA Restauranty 16th-c inn with contemporary feel in two bow-windowed front areas; beams and timbers, large woodburner in stripped-brick fireplace, well liked food from short but varied menu including lunchtime sandwiches, also good value set deal, Nethergate and plenty of wines by the glass, Aspall's cider, back servery and further eating area, charming helpful staff; background music, daily newspapers; children and well behaved dogs welcome, stylish furniture on sheltered back terrace, tree-shaded garden with lovely village church behind, five bedrooms up rather steep staircase, good breakfast, closed Sun evening, otherwise open all day. *(John Harris)*

CHELSWORTH   TL9848
Peacock (01449) 743952
B1115 Sudbury–Needham Market; IP7 7HU Prettily set 14th-c dining pub in conservation village; cosy beamed bar with exposed brickwork, grandfather clock and inglenook woodburner, ales such as Adnams, Nethergate and Woodfordes, separate timbered dining room, good sensibly priced food from sandwiches/baguettes up including seasonal game, friendly service; occasional music and quiz nights; children and dogs welcome, four bedrooms, picnic-sets in small side garden, open all day Fri, Sat, till 6pm Sun. *(Val and Malcolm Travers)*

CHILLESFORD   TM3852
★**Froize** (01394) 450282
B1084 E of Woodbridge; IP12 3PU More restaurant than pub and only open during mealtimes; very good if not cheap buffet-style food from owner-chef using carefully sourced local produce including seasonal game, nice wines by the glass and well kept Adnams, warmly welcoming service, little deli next to bar; occasional events including folk music; seats on terrace, no dogs inside, closed evenings Sun-Thurs, all day Mon. *(Graham Smart)*

CREETING ST MARY   TM1155
Highwayman (01449) 760369
A140, just N of junction with A14; IP6 8PD Attractively updated 17th-c pub with two bars and pleasant galleried barn extension; welcoming landlord and friendly relaxed atmosphere, popular freshly cooked food from landlady-chef, well kept Greene King IPA and guests, decent wines; unobtrusive background music; children welcome, no dogs inside, tables on gravel terrace and back lawn with pretty pond, closed Sun evening, Mon. *(David Twitchett)*

CRETINGHAM   TM2260
Bell (01728) 685419
The Street; IP13 7BJ Attractive and welcoming old beamed and timbered pub; enjoyable traditional home-made food from sandwiches up, well kept ales such as Adnams and Earl Soham, nice wines by the glass, bare-boards bar, dining tables in tiled second room with woodburner in big fireplace; regular live music; children and dogs (in snug) welcome, garden picnic-sets. *(Freddie and Sarah Banks)*

DUNWICH   TM4770
★**Ship** (01728) 648219
St James Street; IP17 3DT Traditional red-brick pub in coastal village; main bar with benches, pews, captain's chairs and wooden tables on tiled floor, lots of sea prints, woodburner, ales such as Adnams, Calvors, Wolf and Woodfordes from antique handpumps, several wines by the glass and well regarded home-made food including good fish pie, simple conservatory; background music in dining areas; children and dogs (in bar) welcome, terrace and large garden with well spaced picnic-sets, two large anchors and an enormous fig tree, comfortable bedrooms, good hearty breakfasts, handy for RSPB reserve at Minsmere and Dunwich Museum, good walks and lovely coastal scenery, open all day. *(Tracey and Stephen Groves, Dan and Anne Morgan, Chris Stevenson, Kim Holt)*

EARL SOHAM   TM2263
Victoria (01728) 685758
A1120 Yoxford–Stowmarket; IP13 7RL Simple two-bar pub popular with locals; well kept Earl Soham ales (used to be brewed here) and reasonably priced home-cooked food, friendly service, kitchen chairs, pews and scrubbed country tables on bare boards or tiled floors, panelling and open fire; outside gents'; children and dogs welcome, seats out in front and on raised back lawn, well placed for the working windmill at Saxtead (EH). *(Mark and Sian Edwards)*

EASTBRIDGE   TM4566
★**Eels Foot** (01728) 830154
Off B1122 N of Leiston; IP16 4SN Country local bordered by freshwater marshes; split-level bar with light modern furnishings on stripped-wood floors, open fire, Adnams ales including seasonals, traditional cider, 11 wines by the glass and several malt whiskies, popular good value food from sandwiches up, neat back dining room; live folk music Thurs and last Sun of month, darts, board games; children and dogs welcome, tables on terrace and in attractive big back garden, quiet comfortable bedrooms in separate building (one has wheelchair access), certified Caravan Club site, footpath to the sea and

handy for RSPB Minsmere, open (and food) all day Fri-Sun. *(Matt and Hayley Jacob, Patrick and Emma Stephenson)*

EASTON   TM2858
White Horse   (01728) 746456
N of Wickham Market on back road to Earl Soham and Framlingham; IP13 0ED Attractive 16th-c village dining pub refurbished under same owners as the Anchor at Woodbridge; much liked food from pub favourites up, three well kept ales including Adnams and good choice of wines, friendly attentive service; children and dogs welcome, a few tables out at front, more in enclosed back garden with play area, open all day Fri-Sun, closed Mon. *(Val and Malcolm Travers)*

EDWARDSTONE   TL9542
White Horse   (01787) 211211
Mill Green, just E; village signed off A1071 in Boxford; CO10 5PX Unpretentious pub with up to a dozen well kept ales including own Little Earth Project brews, also craft kegs and real ciders, various sized bars with beer mats, rustic prints and photos on the walls, second-hand tables and chairs including an old steamer bench and panelled settle on bare boards, three woodburners, straightforward home-made food; live music, beer/cider festivals and various outdoor events, traditional games such as bar billiards, darts and ring the bull; children and dogs welcome, end terrace with sturdy teak furniture, smokers' shelter, makeshift picnic-sets on grass, two scandinavian-style self-catering chalets plus campsite with shower block, closed lunchtimes Mon and Tues, otherwise open all day, no food Sun evening. *(Julian Richardson)*

EYE   TM1473
Queens Head   (01379) 870153
Cross Street; IP23 7AB Popular three-room beamed pub; Adnams and local guests such as Bullards tapped from the cask (July beer festival), 11 wines by the glass and good fairly priced food (not Sun evening) cooked by landlord including fish specials, friendly accommodating staff, interesting local artwork, woodburner; background music, monthly quiz and karaoke, free wi-fi; children and dogs (on leads, theirs is Franco) welcome, garden with play area, open all day (Sun till 9pm). *(Lenny and Ruth Walters)*

FELIXSTOWE   TM3134
Fludyers Arms   (01394) 691929
Undercliff Road E; IP11 7LU Restored and extended Edwardian pub-hotel on seafront; opened-up bare-boards bar and several dining areas including panelled restaurant, Adnams, Woodfordes and guests,

good food from bar snacks to upmarket restaurant choices, weekday set menu, friendly attentive service; jazz and some other live music; children welcome, sea views from modern heated front terrace, 12 bedrooms (more views) and mews apartment, open (and food) all day. *(Alf and Sally Garner)*

FELIXSTOWE FERRY   TM3237
Ferry Boat   (01394) 284203
Off Ferry Road, on the green; IP11 9RZ Nautical-themed 17th-c pub tucked between golf links and dunes near harbour, martello tower and summer rowing-boat ferry; enjoyable food including range of fish dishes and some vegetarian options, friendly efficient staff, well kept Adnams Southwold, Woodfordes Wherry and a guest, decent coffee, warm log fire; background music; children and dogs welcome, tables out in front, on green opposite and in fenced garden, good coast walks, open all day weekends and busy in summer. *(John Harris)*

FRAMLINGHAM   TM2862
Station Hotel   (01728) 723455
Station Road (B1116 S); IP13 9EE Simple high-ceilinged bar with big windows, scrubbed tables on bare boards, half-panelling and woodburner, well kept Earl Soham ales and good choice of wines, popular freshly cooked food from interesting menu, also wood-fired pizzas Thurs-Sat evenings, friendly relaxed atmosphere, back snug with tiled floor; free wi-fi; children and dogs welcome, picnic-sets in pleasant garden. *(Julian Richardson)*

FRESSINGFIELD   TM2677
★ ## Fox & Goose   (01379) 586247
Church Street; B1116 N of Framlingham; IP21 5PB Relaxed dining pub in beautifully timbered 16th-c former Guildhall next to church; highly regarded food from bar meals served in cosy informal heavy-beamed rooms to upscale fixed-price menus in upstairs restaurant, friendly efficient service, Adnams and a guest tapped from the cask and a dozen wines by the glass; soft background music; children welcome, disabled loos on ground floor, tables out by duck pond, closed Mon. *(Caroline and Steve Archer)*

FRISTON   TM4160
Old Chequers   (01728) 688039
Just off A1094 Aldeburgh–Snape; IP17 1NP Welcoming village pub with modernised L-shaped bar, well kept ales such as Adnams, Greene King and Woodfordes from brick-faced servery, enjoyable home-made food including daily specials, woodburner in brick fireplace; well behaved

---

Ring the bull is an ancient pub game – you try to lob a ring on a piece of string over a hook (occasionally a bull's horn) on a wall or ceiling.

children and dogs welcome (resident scottie is Lucy), sunny back terrace, nice circular walks to Aldeburgh and Snape, open all day Sun till 7pm, closed Mon, Tues. *(Andy and Rosemary Taylor)*

GREAT BRICETT   TM0450
Red Lion (01473) 657863
B1078, E of Bildeston; IP7 7DD Modernised and extended old beamed pub; very good vegetarian and vegan food at competitive prices (nothing for meat eaters), children's menu and takeaways too, real ales such as Greene King, efficient friendly service; dogs welcome in bar, garden with deck and play equipment, closed Sun evening to Weds lunchtime. *(John Harris)*

GREAT GLEMHAM   TM3461
Crown (01728) 663693
Between A12 Wickham Market–Saxmundham and B1119 Saxmundham–Framlingham; IP17 2DA Early 19th-c red-brick village pub; four fireplaces and some nice old suffolk furniture on wood and quarry-tiled floors, mostly local beers from old brass handpumps, good well priced food (not Tues) including pub favourites with a twist, Weds steak night, back coffee lounge with freshly baked cakes, friendly helpful staff; some acoustic music and themed events, quiz third Tues of month, darts, table skittles, free wi-fi; well behaved children and dogs welcome, disabled facilities, cast-iron furniture on back lawn, closed Sun evening to Tues lunchtime, weekend breakfasts from 9am. *(David Appleyard)*

GREAT WRATTING   TL6848
Red Lion (01440) 783237
School Road; CB9 7HA Popular village pub with a couple of ancient whale bones flanking the entrance; log fire in bar and lots of copper and brass, well kept Adnams and generous helpings of enjoyable pubby food, friendly staff, restaurant; children and dogs welcome, big back garden with play equipment, open all day Sat. *(Thomas Green)*

GRUNDISBURGH   TM2250
Dog (01473) 735267
The Green; off A12 via B1079 from Woodbridge bypass; IP13 6TA Friendly pink-washed pub with villagey public bar; log fire, settles and dark wooden carvers around pubby tables on tiles, Adnams, Earl Soham, Woodfordes and a guest, craft beers and good range of other drinks, enjoyable food (all day Sun) including Tues burger, Weds curry and Thurs steak nights, carpeted lounge linking to bare-boards dining room; free wi-fi; children and dogs welcome, picnic-sets out in front by flowering tubs, more seats in wicker-fenced mediterranean-feel back garden, play area, closed Mon, otherwise open all day. *(Alf and Sally Garner)*

HADLEIGH   TM0242
Kings Head (01473) 828855
High Street; IP7 5EF Modernised Georgian-fronted pub (building is actually much older); popular food from breakfast on including some themed nights, lobster week July and Oct, well kept Adnams and guests, Aspall's cider, friendly helpful staff; children and dogs (in some areas) welcome, open all day from 9am (11am Sun), food till 7pm Sun. *(Andy and Rosemary Taylor)*

HARTEST   TL8352
Crown (01284) 830250
B1066 S of Bury St Edmunds; IP29 4DH Old pub by church behind pretty village green; good food (all day Sun) from sandwiches and sharing boards up, popular Weds pie and pint deal, own Brewshed beers plus a couple from Greene King, plenty of wines by the glass, friendly attentive uniformed staff, split-level beamed interior (note the coins left by departing World War I soldiers), good log fire in large fireplace; free wi-fi; children (not in bar after 8pm) and well behaved dogs welcome, tables on big back lawn and in sheltered side courtyard, good play area, open all day. *(Mark and Mary Setting)*

HAUGHLEY   TM0262
Kings Arms (01449) 257120
Off A45/B1113 N of Stowmarket; Old Street; IP14 3NT Extended 16th-c village pub with good food (not Sun evening) cooked by owner-chef including set lunch deal, Greene King beers (Abbot ale was named here by a landlord in 1950), also a guest and decent choice of wines, friendly service, spacious timbered interior with plenty of room for diners, woodburner in big brick fireplace; children and dogs (in bar) welcome, back garden, open all day Fri and Sat, till 6pm Sun, closed Mon, Tues. *(John Harris)*

HAWKEDON   TL7953
Queens Head (01284) 789218
Off A143 at Wickham Street, NE of Haverhill; and off B1066; IP29 4NN Tudor pub in pretty setting looking down broad peaceful green to interesting village church; quarry-tiled bar with dark beams and ochre walls, plenty of pews and chapel chairs around scrubbed tables, elderly armchairs by antique woodburner in huge fireplace, cheerful helpful staff, Adnams, Woodfordes and guests, proper cider/perry and nice choice of wines, good food (not Mon, Tues) using home-reared meat, dining area stretching back with country prints and a couple of tusky boars' heads; occasional live music and wine tastings in evening; picnic-sets out in front, more on back terrace overlooking rolling country, little shop (Fri and Sat mornings) selling their own bacon, pies etc, vintage car meeting first

Sun of month, open all day Fri-Sun, closed lunchtimes Mon-Thurs. *(Val and Malcolm Travers)*

HORRINGER   TL8261
Beehive (01284) 736737
A143; IP29 5SN Brick and flint village pub with cosy series of beamed rooms; ales such as Adnams, Humpty Dumpty, Oakham and Mauldons, enjoyable fair priced food including daily specials; some live music, pool; children and dogs welcome, back terrace and raised lawn, handy for Ickworth (NT), closed Sun evening, Mon and lunchtime Tues. *(Bramley)*

IPSWICH   TM1644
Dove Street (01473) 211270
St Helens Street; IP4 2LA Drinkers' pub with over 20 well kept quickly changing ales including their own brews (regular beer festivals), farm ciders, bottled beers and good selection of whiskies, low priced simple pub food, bare-boards bar, carpeted snug and back conservatory; free wi-fi; children (till 7pm) and dogs welcome, disabled facilities, seats on heated covered terrace, two bedrooms over the road along with the brewery shop, open (and food) all day. *(Thomas Green)*

IPSWICH   TM1645
Greyhound (01473) 252862
Henley Road/Anglesea Road; IP1 3SE Popular 19th-c pub close to picturesque Christchurch Park; cosy front bar with corridor to larger lounge/dining area, five well kept Adnams ales and a couple of guests, good home cooking including bargain weekday lunch and daily specials, quick friendly service; occasional Sun quiz, sports TV, free wi-fi; children welcome, picnic-sets under parasols on back terrace, open (and food) all day weekends. *(Thomas Green)*

IPSWICH   TM1747
Railway Inn (01473) 252337
Westerfield Road close to the station; IP6 9AA Popular split-level roadside pub with reasonably priced food (all day weekends) including daily specials and set menus, three well kept Adnams ales and several wines by the glass; children and dogs (in bar) welcome, four bedrooms, outside tables and colourful hanging baskets, open all day. *(John Harris)*

IPSWICH   TM1744
Woolpack (01473) 215862
Tuddenham Road; IP4 2SH Welcoming traditional red-brick pub dating from the 1600s; Adnams and four other well kept beers, several wines by the glass and popular fairly pubby food at reasonable prices, helpful accommodating service, two bars, snug and

back dining area, corner with piano and board games; live music including jazz last Weds of the month, quiz second Sun; children and dogs welcome, seats on heated front terrace, opposite Christchurch Park, open all day from 10am for breakfast. *(Thomas Green)*

KERSEY   TM0044
Bell (01473) 823229
Signed off A1141 N of Hadleigh; The Street; IP7 6DY Attractive 14th-c black and white pub in notably picturesque village with ford; popular home-made food from well priced fairly traditional menu including good steak and kidney pudding, Adnams and a couple of guests, friendly service, low-beamed carpeted bar with log fire, restaurant; children and dogs welcome, hanging baskets out at front, split-level terrace and garden behind, open all day, food till 7.30pm Sun, kitchen closed Mon evening. *(Tina and David Woods-Taylor)*

KESGRAVE   TM2346
Kesgrave Hall (01473) 333741
Hall Road; IP5 2PU Country hotel with comfortably modern bare-boards bar; Greene King and a couple of guests from granite-topped servery, several wines by the glass and cocktails, popular if pricey food cooked in brasserie's open kitchen (no booking so best to arrive early), afternoon teas, children and dogs welcome, attractive heated terrace with huge retractable awning, sweeping grounds, 23 stylish bedrooms, open (and food) all day. *(Mark and Sian Edwards)*

LAVENHAM   TL9149
★Angel (01787) 247388
Market Place; CO10 9QZ Handsome Tudor building in delightful small town; long bar with inglenook log fire and some fine 16th-c ceiling plasterwork, relaxed feel with chesterfield sofas and armchairs, further dining areas and more heavy beams and panelling, popular food including pub favourites, pizzas and grills, well kept ales Adnams and a guest, Aspall's cider and good range of wines, friendly staff; children and dogs (in bar) welcome, sizeable back garden, eight bedrooms, open all day from 8am for breakfast. *(Tony Scott)*

LAVENHAM   TL9149
Swan (01787) 247477
High Street; CO10 9QA Smart hotel in series of handsome medieval buildings; appealing network of beamed and timbered rooms including tiled-floor inner bar, log fire and memorabilia from its days as a local for US pilots, well kept Adnams and a guest, lots of wines by the glass from extensive list and good range of other drinks, well thought-of innovative food, can eat in bar, informal brasserie or lavishly timbered restaurant,

afternoon teas, efficient friendly young staff; children and dogs welcome, sheltered courtyard garden, 45 bedrooms, open all day. *(Jamie Green)*

LINDSEY TYE TL9846
Lindsey Rose (01449) 741424
Village signposted off A1141 NW of Hadleigh; IP7 6PP Refurbished old village pub; main bar with low beams, standing timbers and open fire, second similarly furnished room and another big fireplace, good fairly priced food from shortish but varied menu plus daily specials, Adnams ales and a guest, friendly helpful staff; occasional live music and quiz nights; children and dogs welcome, a few picnic-sets out on front gravel, more on back lawn with play area, open all day (till 6pm Sun, 9.30pm Mon, Tues). *(Martin Orton)*

LONG MELFORD TL8646
★**Black Lion** (01787) 312356
Church Walk; CO10 9DN Gently civilised hotel opposite village green; open fire and comfortable leather chairs in back bar (liked by locals), stools by counter serving Adnams, Nethergate and 20 well chosen wines by the glass, two dining rooms with portraits and gilt-edged mirrors on green walls, candlelit tables and another log fire, good attractively presented food from shortish menu, afternoon teas, friendly efficient staff, also drawing room and conservatory; background music; children and dogs (in bar) welcome, front terrace and charming walled garden, comfortable well equipped bedrooms, the grand cathedral-like church is also worth a visit, open all day. *(Susie and Spencer Gray, Rosie and Marcus Heatherley)*

MELTON TM2850
Olde Coach & Horses
(01394) 384851 *Melton Road; IP12 1PD*
Modernised beamed former staging inn; good choice of enjoyable fairly priced food from sandwiches, snacks and sharing plates up (special diets catered for), lunchtime meal deal Mon-Sat, ales including Adnams and Woodfordes, decent wines by the glass, good friendly service; free wi-fi; children welcome, dogs in wood-floored area, tables out under parasols among colourful hanging baskets and planters, open (and food) all day from 9am for breakfast. *(Freddie and Sarah Banks)*

MIDDLETON TM4267
★**Bell** (01728) 648286
Off A12 in Yoxford via B1122 towards Leiston; also signposted off B1125 Leiston–Westleton; The Street; IP17 3NN Attractive part-thatched pub once the brewhouse for Leiston Abbey; traditional bar on left with log fire in big hearth, low plank-panelled ceiling, old local photographs, bar stools and pews, Adnams ales tapped from the cask, nine wines by the glass and enjoyable good value food (not Sun evening),

informal two-room dining area on right has black beams, bare boards and mix of painted farmhouse and wheelback chairs around pale-topped wooden tables, further room with large table (just right for a family) by woodburner; children and dogs welcome, picnic-sets under parasols out at front, more in large back garden, pétanque and pretty summer hanging baskets, handy for RSPB Minsmere and coast walks, open all day Sun till 10pm. *(Revd Carol Avery, Cecily and Steven Evans, Dan and Anne Morgan, M J Winterton)*

MOULTON TL6964
★**Packhorse** (01638) 751818
Bridge Street; CB8 8SP Civilised, stylish inn adjacent to delightful 15th-c bridge across the River Kennett; simply furnished split-level bar with wooden tables and chairs on bare boards, some scatter-cushion armchairs and two-way log fire, Adnams Mosaic, Woodfordes Wherry and 20 wines by the glass, good interesting food including weekday set lunch, opened-up dining rooms keeping cosy areas, candlelight and exotic flower arrangements; children and dogs welcome, tables on terrace and lawn, smart up-to-date bedrooms and very good breakfasts, handy for Newmarket races, open all day. *(Caroline and Steve Archer, Max and Steph Warren, Patti and James Davidson)*

NAYLAND TL9734
★**Anchor** (01206) 262313
Court Street; just off A134 – turn-off S of signposted B1087 main village turn; CO6 4JL Friendly pub by River Stour under same ownership as the Angel at Stoke-by-Nayland; bare-boards bar with assorted wooden dining chairs and tables, big gilt mirror on silvery wallpaper one end, another mirror above pretty fireplace the other, five changing ales and several wines by the glass, enjoyable food including some home-smoked dishes and flame grills, pie and pint Tues, steak night Thurs, two other rooms behind and steep stairs up to cosy restaurant; quiz first Mon of month, some live music; children welcome, dogs in bar, terrace tables overlooking the River Stour, open all day, food till 6pm Sun. *(Graham Smart)*

NEWBOURNE TM2743
Fox (01473) 736307
Off A12 at roundabout 1.7 miles N of A14 junction; The Street; IP12 4NY
Pink-washed 16th-c pub decked in summer flowers; low-beamed bar with slabby elm and other dark tables on quarry-tiled floor, stuffed fox in inglenook, comfortable carpeted dining room, Adnams Southwold, guest ales and decent wines by the glass, popular food catering for special diets; background music, free wi-fi; children and dogs (in bar) welcome, wheelchair access, attractive grounds with rose garden and pond, open (and food) all day from 9am for breakfast. *(Andy and Rosemary Taylor)*

NEWTON   TL9140
Saracens Head (01787) 379036
A134 4 miles E Sudbury; CO10 0QJ
Old beamed and timbered roadside pub; good
choice of food including vegetarian options
and generous Sun lunch, Adnams and Greene
King beers, friendly attentive service; bar
billiards; children and dogs welcome, garden
overlooking pond and common/golf course,
closed Mon, otherwise open all day, food till
6pm Sun. *(Giles and Annie Francis)*

ORFORD   TM4249
★ Jolly Sailor (01394) 450243
Quay Street; IP12 2NU Welcoming old pub
under mother and daughter team; several
snug rooms with exposed brickwork, boating
pictures and other nautical memorabilia, four
well kept Adnams beers and popular sensibly
priced food from good lunchtime sandwiches
up, efficient cheerful service, unusual spiral
staircase in corner of flagstoned main bar
by brick inglenook, horsebrasses and local
photographs, two cushioned pews and
long antique stripped-deal table; free wi-fi;
children and dogs welcome, back terrace and
lawn with views over marshes, popular with
walkers and bird-watchers, bedrooms, open
all day weekends. *(Caroline and Steve Archer)*

ORFORD   TM4249
★ Kings Head (01394) 450271
Front Street; IP12 2LW Friendly 13th-c
village inn surrounded by fine walks and
lovely coastline; snug main bar with heavy
low beams, Adnams ales and several wines
by the glass, good home-made food (not Sun
evening) from sandwiches to daily specials
with a focus on fish, popular Sun roast
(must book), dining room has old stripped-
brick walls and rugs on ancient boards,
woodburners; occasional live music and quiz
nights; children and dogs welcome, four
bedrooms, open all day Fri-Sun, closed Mon.
(Christopher Manning)

POLSTEAD   TL9938
Cock (01206) 263150
*Signed off B1068 and A1071 E of
Sudbury, then pub signed; Polstead
Green; CO6 5AL* Beamed and timbered
16th-c village local; bar with woodburner and
country kitchen furniture, three real ales
(usually one from Greene King), good choice
of wines and enjoyable home-made food from
lunchtime baguettes up, afternoon teas, light
and airy barn restaurant; background music;
children, walkers and dogs welcome, disabled
facilities, picnic-sets overlooking small green,
shuts around 8pm Sun, closed Mon and Tues.
(Jamie Green)

RAMSHOLT   TM3041
Ramsholt Arms (01394) 411209
Signed off B1083; Dock Road; IP12 3AB
Lovely isolated spot overlooking River Deben;
modernised open-plan bar with log fire,
enjoyable good value food from lunchtime
sandwiches up, Adnams, a couple of guest
beers and decent choice of wines by the
glass; children and dogs welcome, plenty
of tables outside taking in the view, nice
walks and handy for Sutton Hoo (NT), open
all day Sat, till 7pm Sun, closed evenings
Mon-Fri. *(John Harris)*

REDE   TL8055
★ Plough (01284) 789208
*Village signposted off A143 Bury St
Edmunds–Haverhill; IP29 4BE* Quaint
partly thatched pub at end of quiet green in
tucked-away village; traditional low-beamed
rooms kept spic and span, wheelback chairs
and plush red wall banquettes around dark
pubby tables, solid-fuel stove in a brick
fireplace, three changing ales and several
wines by the glass, well liked food (not Sun
evening) from blackboard menu; background
music, free wi-fi; children welcome till 8pm,
picnic-sets out at front and in sheltered
cottagey garden, closed Mon; licensees still
hoping to retire, so could be changes.
(Mark and Mary Setting)

ROUGHAM   TL9063
Ravenwood Hall (01359) 270345
*Off A14 E of Bury St Edmunds;
IP30 9JA* Country-house hotel set in seven
acres of lovely grounds; two compact bar
rooms, high ceilings, patterned wallpaper
and big heavily draped windows overlooking
sweeping lawn with stately cedar, well
kept Adnams, good choice of wines and
malt whiskies, back area set for eating
with upholstered settles and dining chairs,
sporting prints and log fire, enjoyable food
served by pleasant staff, comfortable lounge
area has horse pictures, a few moulded
beams and early Tudor wall decoration
above big inglenook, separate more formal
restaurant; background music; children and
dogs welcome, teak furniture in garden,
swimming pool and croquet, big enclosures
for geese, pygmy goats and shetland ponies,
14 bedrooms, open all day. *(Caroline and
Steve Archer)*

SHOTTISHAM   TM3244
Sorrel Horse (01394) 411617
Hollesley Road; IP12 3HD Charming
15th-c thatched community-owned local; well
kept Adnams, Woodfordes and guests tapped
from the cask, decent choice of home-made
traditional food, attentive friendly young
staff, good log fire in tiled-floor bar with
games area (bar billiards), woodburner in
attractive dining room; occasional live music,
quiz every other Weds, free wi-fi; children
and dogs welcome, tables out on sloping front
lawn and in small garden behind, open all
day weekends. *(Christopher Manning)*

SNAPE   TM3958
★ Crown (01728) 688324
Bridge Road (B1069); IP17 1SL

Small well laid-out 15th-c beamed pub with brick floors, inglenook log fire and fine double suffolk settle, good reasonably priced food using local ingredients including own meat (reared behind the pub), steak night first Thurs of month, well kept Adnams ales, efficient friendly young staff; folk evening last Thurs of month, darts, free wi-fi; children and dogs welcome, garden, two bedrooms. *(Jamie Green)*

SNAPE TM4058

Golden Key (01728) 688510

Priory Lane; IP17 1SA Welcoming village pub under same management as the nearby Plough & Sail; low-beamed lounge with old-fashioned settle and straightforward tables and chairs on stripped-wood or chequerboard tiled floor, woodburner, small snug and two cosy dining rooms, well kept Adnams ales, local cider and several wines by the glass, good well presented food from sandwiches to daily specials, cheerful efficient young staff; children and dogs welcome, two terraces with pretty hanging baskets and seats under parasols, handy for the Maltings, two refurbished bedrooms, open all day weekends. *(Lenny and Ruth Walters)*

SNAPE TM3957

★ Plough & Sail (01728) 688413

The Maltings, Snape Bridge (B1069 S); IP17 1SR Part of the Maltings complex, this former smugglers' haunt is run by twin brothers (one is the chef); mostly open-plan with good blend of traditional and modern furnishings, the original 17th-c core has country pine tables and chairs on terracotta tiles and open fire, there's a second cosy room with leather chesterfields by woodburner, a simply furnished bar hall and spacious modern dining room with wood-strip floor and pitched ceiling, an additional restaurant is upstairs, Adnams and Greene King ales, several wines by the glass and good up-to-date food along with pub favourites (they do a pre/post-concert set menu); background music, free wi-fi; children and dogs (in bar) welcome, some picnic-sets out at front, more tables on flower-filled terrace, open all day and can get packed. *(Richard Tilbrook, Tracey and Stephen Groves, Kim Holt)*

SOMERLEYTON TM4797

Dukes Head (01502) 730281

Slugs Lane (B1074); NR32 5QR Nicely positioned red-brick pub (part of the Somerleyton Hall Estate); bare-boards bar with country furniture, painted panelling and woodburner in brick fireplace, four local ales, interesting wines and good selection of other drinks, well liked seasonal food from Estate's own farms, friendly attentive staff, dining extension; children and dogs welcome, tables in tree-shaded garden with rural views, a stiff walk up from River Waveney (moorings), open all day, no food Sun evening, Mon, Tues. *(Julian Richardson)*

SOUTH ELMHAM TM3385

St Peters Brewery (01986) 782288

St Peter South Elmham; off B1062 SW of Bungay; NR35 1NQ Beautifully but simply furnished manor dating from the 13th c (much extended in the 16th c); own St Peters beers on draught and in bottles (can arrange brewery tours), they also make their own cider; bar and dining hall with dramatic high ceiling, elaborate woodwork and flagstoned floor, antique tapestries, woodburner in fine fireplace, two further rooms reached up steepish stairs, short choice of food including sandwiches, afternoon teas; children and dogs (in bar) welcome, outside tables overlooking original moat, open 9am-6pm, closed Mon and Tues (winter hours may vary), they also hold weddings and other events, so best to check. *(Thomas Green)*

SOUTHWOLD TM5076

★ Lord Nelson (01502) 722079

East Street, off High Street (A1095); IP18 6EJ Busy local near seafront with partly panelled traditional bar and two small side rooms, coal fire, light wood furniture on tiles, lamps in nice nooks and corners, interesting Nelson memorabilia including attractive nautical prints and fine model of HMS *Victory*, five well kept Adnams ales, several wines by the glass and decent pubby food, good friendly service; board games, free wi-fi; children (away from the bar) and dogs welcome, wheelchair access possible, seats out in front with sidelong view of the sea, sheltered and heated back garden with Adnams brewery in sight, open all day. *(John Wooll, Iceman)*

SOUTHWOLD TM5076

Red Lion (01502) 723227

South Green; IP18 6ET Updated 17th-c beamed pub with big windows looking over green towards the sea; sturdy wall benches and bar stools on wood floor, well kept Adnams including seasonals, back room with mate's chairs, pews and polished dark tables, lots of framed black and white photographs, good range of popular food served by friendly staff, three linked dining rooms; background music (live Sun afternoon); tables out in front (dogs welcome here) and in small sheltered back courtyard, next to the Adnams retail shop, open all day. *(John Wooll)*

SOUTHWOLD TM5076

Sole Bay (01502) 723736

East Green; IP18 6JN Busy single-room pub near Adnams Brewery; their full range kept well and good wine choice, cheerful helpful staff, enjoyable reasonably priced simple food including good fish and chips (no booking), airy contemporary interior with well spaced tables; sports TV; children and dogs welcome, disabled access/loos, picnic-sets outside, moments from sea and lighthouse, open (and food) all day. *(Pat and Tony Martin)*

SOUTHWOLD   TM5076
Swan (01502) 722186
Market Place; IP18 6EG Smartly revamped
Adnams-owned hotel dating from the early
17th c; their full range kept well plus bottled
beers and good choice of wines and spirits,
enjoyable food in back bar or restaurant
(separate menus), afternoon teas in front
lounge; children welcome, no dogs inside,
attractive courtyard garden, 42 bedrooms
(some in separate block), open all day.
(Lesley Broadbent)

STANSFIELD   TL7851
Compasses (01284) 789263
High Street; CO10 8LN Simple little
country pub with good often interesting
locally sourced food cooked by character
landlord (some ingredients from next-door
farm), own-brewed beers and local guests,
beams, bare boards and large woodburner;
monthly quiz and occasional live music;
children, walkers and dogs welcome,
outside tables with lovely rural views,
open from 5pm Thurs to 4pm Sun.
(Caroline and Steve Archer)

STOKE ASH   TM1170
White Horse (01379) 678222
A140/Workhouse Road; IP23 7ET
Sizeable early 17th-c gabled coaching
inn on crossroads; beams and inglenook
fireplaces, generous helpings of enjoyable
reasonably priced pub food, well kept
ales such as Adnams, Greene King and
Woodfordes, Aspall's cider, efficient
friendly service; free wi-fi; children
welcome, bedrooms in modern annexe,
open (and food) all day from 7am (8am
weekends). *(Lenny and Ruth Walters)*

STOKE-BY-NAYLAND   TL9836
★**Angel** (01206) 263245
*B1068 Sudbury–East Bergholt;
CO6 4SA* Elegant 17th-c inn (same owners
as the Anchor at Nayland); lounge with
handsome beams, timbers and stripped
brickwork, leather chesterfields and wing
armchairs around low tables, more formal
room featuring deep glass-covered well,
chatty bar with straightforward furniture on
red tiles, well kept Adnams and Woodfordes,
several wines by the glass and good range
of gins and cocktails, very well liked food
including lunchtime set menu, afternoon
teas (not Sun, booking required), efficient
friendly service; children and dogs (in some
parts) welcome, seats on sheltered terrace,
six individually styled bedrooms, good
breakfast, open all day from 10am.
(Alf and Sally Garner)

STOWUPLAND   TM0759
Crown (01449) 490490
*Church Road (A1120 just E of
Stowmarket); IP14 4BQ* Extended
thatched pub set back from the road behind
white picket fence; refurbished interior
blending traditional and contemporary
features, well liked sensibly priced food from
pub favourites up including good stone-baked
pizzas (visible oven), real ales and a dozen
wines by the glass, friendly efficient service,
bar with log fire, restaurant; children and
dogs welcome, spacious garden, open all day,
just pizzas Sun evening. *(David Appleyard)*

STRATFORD ST MARY   TM0434
Swan (01206) 321244
Lower Street; CO7 6JR Big changes still
planned for this 16th-c coaching inn and best
to check it is open; good choice of drinks
and creative food in two beamed bars and
timbered back restaurant; children and dogs
welcome, seats on terrace and large lawn
across road, some tables under willows
by River Stour, closed Mon and Tues.
(Paul Farraday)

STUTTON   TM1434
Gardeners Arms (01473) 328868
*Manningtree Road, Upper Street
(B1080); IP9 2TG* Cottagey roadside pub
on edge of small village; well kept Adnams
Southwold and guests, good value home-made
food including daily specials, friendly helpful
service, cosy L-shaped bar with log fire, side
dining room and larger area stretching to
the back, lots of bric-a-brac, film posters
and musical instruments; children and
dogs welcome, two-tier back garden with
pond, open all day Sun, closed Mon.
(Graham Smart)

SUDBURY   TL8741
Brewery Tap (01787) 370876
East Street; CO10 2TP Corner tap for
Mauldons brewery; their range and guests
kept well, also belgian fruit beers and good
range of malt whiskies, some snacky food
(can bring your own, cutlery provided);
comedy club first Weds of month, quiz
and live music nights, darts, cribbage and
bar billiards; dogs welcome, open all day.
(Deborah and Duncan Walliams)

SWEFFLING   TM3464
White Horse (01728) 664178
*B1119 Framlingham–Saxmundham;
IP17 2BB* Traditional little two-room
country pub with woodburner in one room,
range in the other, up to three well kept
changing east anglian beers served from tap

Cribbage is a card game using a block of wood with holes for matchsticks or
special pins to score with; regulars in cribbage pubs are usually happy to teach
strangers how to play.

room door, real cider and some interesting local wines and spirits, simple food such as ploughman's and locally made winter pies, friendly service; some live acoustic music, bar billiards, darts and other traditional games; children and dogs welcome, small beer garden with rustic arbour, self-catering cottage and campsite including yurts, closed lunchtimes (apart from Sun) and evenings Tues-Thurs. *(Mark and Mary Setting)*

SWILLAND   TM1852
Moon & Mushroom (01473) 785320
Off B1078; IP6 9LR Popular 16th-c country local serving four changing east anglian beers from racked casks behind long counter, old tables and chairs on quarry tiles, log fire, enjoyable good value home-made food sourced locally; quiz first Weds of month, occasional live music; children and dogs welcome, heated flower-filled terrace, closed Sun evening, Mon. *(Mark and Sian Edwards)*

THORNDON   TM1469
Black Horse (01379) 678523
Off A140 or B1077, S of Eye; The Street; IP23 7JR Welcoming 17th-c village pub with enjoyable fairly traditional food including good lunchtime carvery, three well kept local ales such as Adnams, friendly helpful service, lots of timbering, stripped brick and big fireplaces; well behaved children and dogs (in bar) welcome, tables on lawn, country views behind, open all day Sun till 9pm, closed Tues. *(Jamie Green)*

THORNHAM MAGNA   TM1070
Four Horseshoes (01379) 678777
Off A140 S of Diss; Wickham Road; IP23 8HD Extensive thatched dining pub dating from the 12th c; well divided dimly lit carpeted bar, Greene King ales and good choice of wines and whiskies, enjoyable reasonably priced food with some main courses available in smaller helpings, popular Sun carvery, friendly helpful staff, very low heavy black beams, country pictures and brass, large fireplace and an old illuminated well; background music; children and dogs (in bar) welcome, disabled access, picnic-sets on big sheltered lawn, handy for Thornham Walks and interesting thatched church, seven comfortable bedrooms, open all day. *(Val and Malcolm Travers)*

THORPENESS   TM4759
★**Dolphin** (01728) 454994
Just off B1353; Old Homes Road; village signposted from Aldeburgh; IP16 4FE Extended and neatly kept dining pub in interesting seaside village (all built in the early 1900s); main bar with scandinavian feel, pale wooden tables and assortment of old chairs on broad modern quarry tiles, log fire, well kept Adnams, guest beers and several wines by the glass from good value list, more traditional public bar with pubby furniture on stripped-wood floor,

built-in cushioned wall seats and old local photographs, airy dining room has country kitchen-style furniture and traditional panelling, enjoyable locally sourced food from shortish but interesting menu, friendly service; background music, TV, free wi-fi; children and dogs welcome, spacious garden with boules, three bedrooms, open all day weekends, closed Mon lunchtime in winter. *(Tracey and Stephen Groves)*

THURSTON   TL9165
Fox & Hounds (01359) 232228
Barton Road; IP31 3QT Rather imposing former 19th-c station inn; well kept Adnams Broadside, Greene King IPA and four guests, traditional furnishings in carpeted lounge (back part set for dining), ceiling fans and lots of pump clips, generously served reasonably priced pubby food (not Sun evening) including regular themed nights, friendly service, bare-boards public bar with pool, darts and machines; background and some live music, quiz and bingo nights; children and dogs welcome, picnic-sets on grassed area by car park and on small covered side terrace, pretty village, self-catering apartment, open all day. *(Graham Smart)*

TUDDENHAM   TM1948
★**Fountain** (01473) 785377
The Street; village signed off B1077 N of Ipswich; IP6 9BT Popular dining pub in nice village; several linked café-style rooms with heavy beams and timbering, stripped floors, wooden dining chairs around light tables, open fire, lots of prints (some by cartoonist Giles who spent time here after World War II), wide choice of well cooked food (all day Sun till 7pm) including set menus and blackboard specials, Adnams Southwold and good selection of wines by the glass, decent coffee; background music; no under-10s in bar after 6.30pm, dogs welcome, wicker and metal chairs on covered heated terrace, rows of picnic-style tables under parasols on sizeable lawn. *(Andy and Rosemary Taylor)*

UFFORD   TM2952
★**Crown** (01394) 461030
High Street; IP13 6EL Broad mix of customers at this popular family-run pub-restaurant; good food from interestingly varied menu including lunchtime sandwiches, bar and dining areas with cushioned wooden chairs and leather banquettes around medley of dark tables, shelves of books, open fires in brick fireplaces, stools against counter serving ales such as Adnams and Earl Soham, a dozen good wines by the glass, friendly service; free wi-fi; children and dogs (in bar) welcome, seats out at front, picnic-sets under parasols in back garden with play area, open all day weekends, closed Tues. *(Andrea and Philip Crispin)*

UFFORD   TM2952
White Lion (01394) 460770
Lower Street (off B1438, towards Eyke); IP13 6DW 16th-c village pub near quiet stretch of River Deben; home to the Uffa Brewery with their beers and guests tapped from the cask (Aug beer festival), generous helpings of enjoyable home-made food (own pigs, hens and bees), raised woodburner in large central fireplace, captain's chairs and spindlebacks around simple tables on quarry tiles; shop/deli; nice views from outside tables, summer barbecues and wood-fired pizzas, closed Sun evening, Mon lunchtime. *(Andrea and Philip Crispin)*

WANGFORD   TM4779
Plough (01502) 578239
Barnaby Green; A12 next to service station; NR34 8AY Useful roadside stop with enjoyable reasonably priced home-made food from sandwiches to daily specials, well kept Adnams and decent range of wines, friendly staff; children and dogs welcome, big garden with play area, five courtyard bedrooms and small campsite, handy for Africa Alive wildlife park, open all day, no food Sun evening. *(Freddie and Sarah Banks)*

WENHASTON   TM4274
Star (01502) 478240
Hall Road; IP19 9HF Traditional 19th-c country pub with three small rooms; well kept Adnams Southwold, four guest beers, a proper cider and decent wines by the glass, enjoyable inexpensive home-made food (smaller appetites catered for), friendly helpful staff, old enamel signs and other bits and pieces, open fires, dining room with local artwork (some by the landlady); Sun afternoon live music; children, dogs and muddy boots welcome, sizeable lawn with boules, nice views, camping (must pre-book) open all day Sun (no food then but customers bring their own). *(John Harris)*

WESTLETON   TM4469
Crown (01728) 648777
B1125 Blythburgh–Leiston; IP17 3AD Stylish old coaching inn with chatty informal bar; country furniture on bare boards, lovely log fire in big brick fireplace, Adnams Southwold, Woodfordes Wherry and 26 wines by the glass from thoughtful list, several malt whiskies, also parlour with sofas and woodburner, dining room and modern conservatory, food can be good; background music, board games; children and dogs (in bar) welcome, charming terraced garden, comfortable neatly kept bedrooms (some in converted stables and cottages), open all day. *(Mike Benton, Simon Day, Robert Wivell)*

WESTLETON   TM4469
White Horse (01728) 648222
Darsham Road, off B1125 Blythburgh–Leiston; IP17 3AH Traditional dutch-gabled brick pub with welcoming relaxed atmosphere; enjoyable pubby food including blackboard specials, up to five well kept Adnams ales, friendly attentive service, high-ceilinged bar with central fire, steps down to stone-floored back dining room; Tues quiz, free wi-fi; children and dogs welcome (resident black lab is Sky), picnic-sets in cottagey garden, more out by village duck pond, four bedrooms. *(Thomas Green)*

WHEPSTEAD   TL8258
★ White Horse (01284) 735760
Off B1066 S of Bury; Rede Road; IP29 4SS Welcoming partly 17th-c village pub; dark-beamed bar with woodburner in a low fireplace, stools around pubby tables on tiles, Woodfordes and a guest from copper-topped counter; good food including weekday set lunch, other linked rooms with country kitchen tables and chairs and traditional wall seats; background music; children and dogs welcome (Tilly is the friendly pub dog), tables under parasols on sheltered back terrace, picnic-sets and play area on grass, good surrounding walks, closed Sun evening, Mon (except bank holidays). *(Marianne and Peter Stevens, Marianne and Michael Huggins)*

WINGFIELD   TM2276
De La Pole Arms (01379) 384983
Off B1118 N of Stradbroke; Church Road; IP21 5RA Welcoming 16th-c timbered pub opposite church; enjoyable lunchtime food from sandwiches and deli boards to daily specials, Sun carvery, well kept Adnams, Earl Soham and decent wines by the glass, good friendly service, beams, flagstones and quarry tiles, bar with log fire in big fireplace, raftered restaurant, deli/shop; children and dogs welcome, disabled access, tables under parasols on sunny terrace, closed Mon, otherwise open all day from 11am (till 7pm Sun); kitchen may close for two weeks Feb/Mar and opening times reduce (check website). *(M and GR)*

WOODBRIDGE   TM2748
Anchor
Quay Street; IP12 1BX Popular 18th-c corner pub (sister to the White Horse at Easton); good food from shortish but varied menu, Thurs lunchtime asian street food, well kept Greene King ales and decent wines by the glass, efficient friendly service, two-room bar and beamed back dining area, some nautical touches, log fires including woodburner in big fireplace; children and dogs welcome, seats out at front and on side terrace, open all day. *(Julian Richardson)*

We say if we know a pub allows dogs.

WOODBRIDGE   TM2648

Cherry Tree (01394) 384627

Opposite Notcutts Nursery, off A12;
Cumberland Street; IP12 4AG Opened-up
17th-c pub (bigger than it looks) with
eight well kept ales including Adnams
(beer festivals), good wines by the glass
and generous helpings of tasty reasonably
priced food, friendly service, beams and
two log fires, mix of pine furniture, old local
photographs; Thurs quiz; children and dogs
(in bar) welcome, garden with play area,
three bedrooms in converted barn, good
breakfast (for non-residents too), open
(and food) all day. *(Julian Richardson)*

WOODBRIDGE   TM2748

Crown (01394) 384242

Thoroughfare/Quay Street; IP12 1AD
Stylish 17th-c dining inn; well kept ales
such as Adnams from glass-roofed bar (boat
suspended above counter), lots of wines by
the glass and cocktails, good imaginative
food from light meals up including set menu,
afternoon teas (must book), pleasant young
staff, various eating areas with contemporary
furnishings; occasional live jazz; children and
dogs (in bar) welcome, courtyard tables, ten
well appointed bedrooms, open (and food)
all day. *(Julian Richardson, Thomas Green)*

WOODBRIDGE   TM2749

Old Mariner (01394) 382679

New Street; IP12 1DX Traditional little
side-street local with cosy bustling bar,
well kept Adnams Ghost Ship, Fullers
London Pride and a couple of guests, three
craft beers, no food, friendly welcoming
staff, log fire; children and dogs welcome,
sunny back garden, open all day.
(Julian Richardson)

WOODBRIDGE   TM2749

Olde Bell & Steelyard

(01394) 382933 *New Street, off*
Market Square; IP12 1DZ Ancient
timber-framed pub with plenty of old-
world character (the listed steelyard
still overhangs the street); two smallish
beamed bars and cosy dining room, log
fire, well kept Greene King and guests from
canopied servery, standard home-made
food; traditional games including bar
billiards, sports TV, free wi-fi; children
and dogs welcome, disabled access, pretty
flower-filled back terrace, open all day
Fri-Sun. *(Thomas Green)*

WOOLPIT   TL9762

Swan (01359) 240482

The Street; IP30 9QN Welcoming old
coaching house pleasantly situated in village
square; heavy beams and painted panelling,
mixed tables and chairs on carpet, roaring
log fire at one end, good seasonal food served
by efficient friendly staff, well kept Adnams
from slate-topped counter and lots of wines
by the glass; maybe background music, quiz
last Sun of month; walled garden behind, four
bedrooms in converted stables, closed Sun
evening, Mon. *(Lenny and Ruth Walters)*

Surrey

BUCKLAND   TQ2250 Map 3

Pheasant 🍷 🍺

(01737) 221355 ~ www.brunningandprice.co.uk/pheasant
Reigate Road (A25 W of Reigate); RH3 7BG

Busy roadside pub with a thoughtful range of drinks and food served by friendly staff, character rooms and seats on terrace and lawn

They keep a fine range of drinks in this partly 18th-c, carefully extended pub including St Austell Brunning & Price Traditional Bitter plus guests such as Crafty Brewing Crafty One, Harveys Best, Sambrooks Wandle Ale, Surrey Hills Shere Drop and Timothy Taylors Landlord on handpump, 24 wines by the glass, 60 whiskies and 73 gins. Various open-plan rooms are interconnected and split into cosier areas by timbering and painted standing pillars. A couple of dining rooms at one end, separated by a two-sided open fire, have captain's chairs and cushioned dining chairs around a mix of tables on bare boards or rugs – and throughout there are wall-to-wall prints and pictures, gilt-edged mirrors, house plants, old stone bottles and elegant metal chandeliers. The busy bar has a long high table with equally high chairs, another two-way fireplace with button-back leather armchairs and sofas in front of it and stools against the counter; background music and board games. One of the two other dining rooms has a big open fire pit in the middle. Out on the terrace is another open fire pit surrounded by built-in seats plus solid tables and chairs, while the lawn has plenty of picnic-sets and their usual trademark play tractor for children.

🍴 Up-to-date food includes Saturday breakfast (8-10.45am) as well as smoked fish terrine with beetroot and horseradish crème fraîche, crispy salt and pepper squid, beetroot, carrot and chickpea burger with pak choi and fennel slaw and chips, chicken, ham and leek pie, warm crispy beef salad with sweet chilli dressing and roasted cashews, mint and lime harissa rump of lamb with cumin roasted new potatoes and tzatziki, 10oz rib-eye steak with dijon and tarragon butter, portobello mushrooms and chips, and puddings such as lemon pannacotta with champagne sorbet and dried apricot and walnut granola and crème brûlée. *Benchmark main dish: sea bass with creamed leeks and wholegrain mustard and sauce vierge £16.95. Two-course evening meal £21.00.*

Brunning & Price ~ Manager Bethany Wells ~ Real ale ~ Open 10am-11pm; 9am-11pm Sat; 9am-10.30pm Sun ~ Bar food 12-9; 8am-10pm Sat ~ Restaurant ~ Children welcome ~ Dogs allowed in bar ~ Wi-fi *Recommended by Chantelle and Tony Redman, Sarah and David Gibbs, Dave Chapman, Mike and Sarah Abbot, Patrick and Emma Stephenson, Tony Scott*

CHIDDINGFOLD

SU9635 Map 3

Swan 🏅 🛏

(01428) 684688 – www.theswaninnchiddingfold.com

Petworth Road (A283 S); GU8 4TY

Open-plan, light and airy rooms in well run inn, with local ales, modern food and seats in terraced garden; bedrooms

It's best to arrive early or book a table in advance on Goodwood race days, when this stylishly updated, tile-hung inn gets pretty packed. The bar has an open fire in an inglenook fireplace with leather armchairs in front and antlers above, wooden tables and chairs and cushioned wall seats on pale floorboards and leather-topped stools against the counter where they keep Crafty Brewing Crafty One and Dunsfold Best and a guest on handpump, 19 wines by the glass and a good choice of spirits. Staff are helpful and friendly. A dining room leads off here with modern chairs and chunky tables on more bare floorboards. Outside, a three-tiered terraced garden has plenty of seats and tables. The well equipped and comfortable bedrooms make a good base for exploring the area – there's lots to do and see nearby.

 Food is enjoyable and includes crayfish and avocado salad, grilled asparagus with a crispy duck egg and garlic purée, halloumi burger with toppings, tomato and onion chutney and fries, gammon and eggs with triple-cooked chips, corn-fed chicken breast with tomato and pepper sauce and sautéed potatoes, cod with saffron and dried fruit couscous and samphire, pork chop with spicy sweet potato wedges, tomato salsa and lemon crème fraîche, rib-eye steak with a choice of sauce, and puddings such as apple and rhubarb crumble and white chocolate pannacotta with raspberry coulis. *Benchmark main dish: braised lamb with fondant potato, pea purée and rosemary jus £22.00. Two-course evening meal £23.00.*

Upham ~ Managers Zach and Sinead Leach ~ Real ale ~ Open 7am-11pm; 9am-11pm Sat; 9am-10pm Sun ~ Bar food 12-3, 6-9; 12-3, 6-9.30 Fri, Sat; 12-8 Sun ~ Children welcome ~ Dogs allowed in bar ~ Wi-fi ~ Bedrooms: /£70 *Recommended by Bridget and Peter Gregson, Alison and Dan Richardson, Christopher and Elise Way, Patricia and Anton Larkham, Serena and Adam Furber, Freddie and Sarah Banks*

CHIPSTEAD

TQ2757 Map 3

White Hart ♀

(01737) 554455 – www.brunningandprice.co.uk/whitehartchipstead

Hazelwood Lane; CR5 3QW

Airy open-plan rooms, a thoughtful choice of drinks, rewarding food and friendly staff

There are charming country views all around this well run, popular pub and a good mix of customers of all ages. The raftered dining room to the right has elegant metal chandeliers, rough-plastered walls, an open fire in a brick fireplace and a couple of carved metal standing uprights. Helpful staff serve St Austell Brunning & Price Traditional Bitter plus guests such as Adnams Broadside, Crafty Brewing Dunsfold Best, Surrey Hills Shere Drop and Westerham Summer Perle on handpump, 20 wines by the glass, more than 45 gins and up to 60 malt whiskies; background music and board games. The long room to the left is light and airy, with wall panelling at one end, a woodburning stove and numerous windows overlooking the tables and Lloyd Loom-style seats on the terrace. Throughout there's a fine mix of antique dining chairs and settles around all sorts of tables, rugs on bare boards, hundreds of interesting cartoons, country pictures, cricketing prints and rugby team photographs, large ornate mirrors and, on the windowsills and mantelpieces, old glass and stone bottles, clocks, books and plants.

Well executed food includes sandwiches, baked camembert with candied walnuts and celery salad, satay king prawns with peanuts, fish pie, cauliflower, chickpea and pepper jalfrezi with almond pilaf rice and sweet potato bhaji, confit pork belly with sherry-braised pig cheek, fondant potato and butternut squash purée, braised lamb shoulder with dauphinoise potatoes and gravy, and puddings such as dark chocolate and orange tart with orange sorbet and hot belgian waffle with honeycomb ice-cream and butterscotch sauce. *Benchmark main dish: sea bream with cauliflower, potato and spinach curry £17.95. Two-course evening meal £22.00.*

Brunning & Price ~ Manager Jason Patterson ~ Real ale ~ Open 11.30-11; 11.30-10.30 Sun ~ Bar food 12-9.30; 12-10 Fri, Sat; 12-9 Sun ~ Restaurant ~ Children welcome ~ Dogs allowed in bar ~ Wi-fi *Recommended by Robert and Diana Ringstone, Sally and Colin Allen, Martin and Joanne Sharp, Andrew and Ruth Simmonds, Sandra and Nigel Brown, Christopher Mannings*

 CHOBHAM   SU9761 Map 2

White Hart 🍷 🍺

(01276) 857580 – www.brunningandprice.co.uk/whitehartchobham
High Street; GU24 8AA

Brick-built village pub with cheerful customers and a thoughtful choice of food and drink

The heart of this venerable inn remains the opened-up bar with its bustling atmosphere. This has white-painted beams, standing pillars, rugs on parquet or wide boards, an assortment of dark wooden dining chairs and tables, and armchairs beside two fireplaces; background music and board games. High chairs line the counter where cheerful, well trained staff serve St Austell Brunning & Price Traditional Bitter and guests such as Ascot Starting Gate, Park Brewery Two Storm Ruby, Reunion Minimalist and Tillingbourne Hop Troll on handpump, 20 wines by the glass, 40 gins and over 40 malt whiskies. An L-shaped dining room has a leather wall banquette and leather and brass-studded dining chairs around a mix of tables and numerous old photos and prints on exposed-brick or painted walls. There's also a comfortable dining room with similar furniture, carpeting and a big elegant metal chandelier. The little side garden has seats under parasols.

As well as weekend brunch (9-11am), the wide choice of modern food includes sandwiches, shredded ham, caper and parsley fritter with piccalilli, korean-style chicken wings with kimchi salad, wild mushroom tortelloni with a creamy white sauce, cumberland sausages with mash and onion gravy, confit duck leg with smoked sausage cassoulet, sea bass, crayfish and samphire risotto with roasted fennel and rocket pesto, 10oz rump steak with dijon and tarragon mayonnaise and chips, and puddings such as white chocolate cheesecake with blackcurrant sorbet and bread and butter pudding with apricot sauce. *Benchmark main dish: braised lamb shoulder with dauphinoise potatoes and rosemary gravy £17.95. Two-course evening meal £21.00.*

Brunning & Price ~ Manager Stan Morgan ~ Real ale ~ Open 11-11; 12-10.30 Sun ~ Bar food 12-9; 12-10 Fri; 9-10 Sat; 9-9 Sun ~ Restaurant ~ Children welcome but not in bar area after 5pm ~ Dogs allowed in bar ~ Wi-fi *Recommended by Jo Garnett, Liz and Martin Eldon, William and Sophia Renton, Francis and Mandy Robertson, Mark Hamill*

'Children welcome' means the pub says it lets children inside without any special restriction. If it allows them in, but to restricted areas such as an eating area or family room, we specify this. Some pubs may impose an evening time limit. We do not mention limits after 9pm as we assume children are home by then.

ELSTEAD

SU9044 Map 2

Mill at Elstead

(01252) 703333 – www.millelstead.co.uk

Farnham Road (B3001 just W of village, which is itself between Farnham and Milford); GU8 6LE

Fascinating building with big attractive waterside garden, Fullers beers and well liked food

Rising four storeys, this prettily set and carefully converted watermill above the banked River Wey has picnic-sets dotted about by the water and there's a lovely millpond with swans and weeping willows. Inside, a series of rambling linked bar areas on the spacious ground floor have large windows that make the most of the view; there's an upstairs restaurant too. You'll find brown leather armchairs and antique engravings by a longcase clock, neat modern tables and dining chairs on bare boards, big country tables on broad ceramic tiles, iron pillars, stripped masonry and a log fire in a huge inglenook. Fullers ESB and London Pride and guests from breweries such as Castle Rock and Dark Star on handpump, 22 wines by the glass and several malt whiskies and 30 gins; background music, board games and TV.

Well regarded food includes lunchtime sandwiches, black pudding and leek croquettes with apple ketchup, chicken caesar salad, scampi with triple-cooked chips, salt and pepper squid with nam jim dipping sauce, sharing platters, tagliatelle with roasted squash, blue cheese sauce and crispy spinach, burger with toppings and fries, cod loin with parsley sauce, duck breast with fondant potato, caramelised shallots and red wine jus, lamb rump with green bean and chorizo fricassée and mint sour cream, and puddings such as apple pie with buffalo milk vanilla ice-cream and lemon posset. *Benchmark main dish: beer-battered fresh haddock and triple-cooked chips £13.50. Two-course evening meal £25.00.*

Fullers ~ Manager Rachel Watson ~ Real ale ~ Open 11-11; 11-10.30 Sun ~ Bar food 12-9; 12-8 Sun ~ Restaurant ~ Children welcome ~ Dogs allowed in bar ~ Wi-fi *Recommended by Heather and Richard Jones, Joe and Belinda Smart, William Slade, Peter and Emma Kelly, James Allsopp, Charles Todd*

ENGLEFIELD GREEN

SU9869 Map 2

Bailiwick ♀ ◗

(01784) 477877 – www.brunningandprice.co.uk/bailiwick

Wick Road; TW20 0HN

Fine position by parkland for busy pub, with lots of interest in various bars and dining rooms, well liked food and drink and super staff

Dogs are allowed in the front part of the open-plan bar area, so this is where walkers tend to congregate. Informally friendly, it has cushioned dining chairs around wooden tables on rugs and bare boards, and a pretty Victorian fireplace with a large mirror above. Stools line the counter where knowledgeable, helpful staff serve St Austell Brunning & Price Traditional Bitter plus guests such as Thames Side Mallard Mild, Timothy Taylors Landlord and Twickenham Redhead on handpump, 21 good wines by the glass, 20 rums, 26 vodkas, 48 gins, 96 malt whiskies and farm cider. Steps lead down to a dining area and on again to a bigger room with caramel-coloured leather dining chairs, banquettes and tables of every size. Throughout there are elegant metal chandeliers, prints and black and white photographs, lots of house plants and windowsills full of old stone and glass bottles; background music and board games. A small front terrace has a few seats and tables. Do enjoy the circular walk that starts at the pub and follows the south-east corner of Windsor Great Park – you can see the polo lawns, Virginia Water lake and the vast expanses of landscaped parkland. There's no car park but there are 20 free spaces in the long lay-by on Wick Road; if these are full there's a large pay-on-entry car park alongside.

Enterprising food includes breafasts (9-11am weekends) plus sandwiches, grilled mackerel fillet with celeriac rémoulade and pickled watermelon, spicy barbecued duck wings, sharing boards, mushroom bourguignon, braised pork belly with celeriac purée, bubble and squeak croquette and red wine jus, pork sausages with mash and onion gravy, salmon with wild garlic velouté and herb-crushed potatoes, 10oz rib-eye steak with garlic butter and chips, and puddings such as hot waffle with caramelised banana and banana ice-cream. *Benchmark main dish: chicken, ham hock and leek pie £14.95. Two-course evening meal £21.00.*

Brunning & Price ~ Manager Claudette Thake ~ Real ale ~ Open 10am-11pm; 9am-11pm Sat; 9am-10pm Sun ~ Bar food 12-9 (9.30 Fri, Sat) ~ Children welcome ~ Dogs allowed in bar ~ Wi-fi *Recommended by Alexander and Trish Gendall, Nick and Meriel Cox, Maggie and Matthew Lyons, Martin and Sue Neville, Len and Lilly Dowson, Sam Cole, Mary and Nigel Joyce*

ESHER   TQ1566   Map 3
Marneys
(020) 8398 4444 ~ www.marneys.co.uk
Alma Road (one-way), Weston Green; heading N on A309 from A307 roundabout; after half a mile turn left into Lime Tree Avenue (signposted to All Saints Parish Church), then left at T junction into Chestnut Avenue; KT10 8JN

Country-feeling pub with good value food and attractive garden

Feeling surprisingly rural for the area, it's a real delight to find this cottagey little pub in such a pleasant spot right on the edge of a well wooded common. The chatty low-beamed bar has a good mix of customers, Fullers London Pride, Sharps Doom Bar and Youngs Bitter on handpump, 16 wines by the glass, ten malt whiskies and perhaps horse-racing on the unobtrusive corner TV. To the left, past a little cast-iron woodburning stove, the dining area is furnished with big pine tables, pews, pale country kitchen chairs and cottagey blue-curtained windows; background music. There are seats and wooden tables on the front terrace, which has views over the common, village church and duck pond, and more seats on the decked area in the pleasantly planted sheltered garden. The pub is handy for Hampton Court Palace.

Pleasing food includes baked camembert with roasted garlic and chutney, king prawns with chilli and parsley, pear, walnut and roquefort salad with toasted ciabatta, steak in ale pie, thai-style salmon fishcakes with sweet chilli sauce, cumberland sausages with mustard mash and caramelised onion gravy, and puddings such as hot chocolate brownie and sticky toffee pudding, both with ice-cream. *Benchmark main dish: burger with toppings and chips £10.95. Two-course evening meal £20.00.*

Free house ~ Licensee Thomas Duxberry ~ Real ale ~ Open 11-11; 12-10.30 Sun ~ Bar food 12-2.30, 6-9; 12-3.30 Sun; not Fri-Sun evenings ~ Restaurant ~ Children welcome away from bar ~ Dogs allowed in bar ~ Wi-fi *Recommended by Dan and Nicki Barton, Chloe and Tim Hodge, Margo and Derek Stapley, davidgviner, Heather and Richard Jones, Mike Benton, Richard and Tessa Ibbot*

The star-on-a-plate award, ✪, distinguishes pubs where the food is of exceptional quality. The knife-and-fork symbol just means the pub serves food.

FOREST GREEN

TQ1241 Map 3

Parrot ♀ ◀

(01306) 775790 – www.brunningandprice.co.uk/parrot

B2127 just W of junction with B2126, SW of Dorking; RH5 5RZ

Bustling pub in the Surrey Hills with plenty of space, a thoughtful choice of food and drinks, lots to look at and seats in the garden

With a cheerful pub sign and facing the green and cricket ground, this carefully and attractively refurbished pub is much bigger than it looks from outside. The cosy bar area by the main door has a woodburning stove in an inglenook fireplace (plus a smaller two-way one in another knocked-through wall), leather button-back armchairs, small stools and rugs on flagstones. From the heavy panelled counter, helpful, friendly staff serve St Austell Brunning & Price Traditional Bitter plus guests such as Dark Star American Pale Ale, Hogs Back TEA, Odyssey Nirvana and Surrey Hills Gilt Complex and Shere Drop on handpump, 22 wines by the glass, 73 gins, 63 whiskies and a farm cider; background radio. Lots of beamed, spreading eating areas are separated by open doorways and standing timbers, with a mix of cushioned wooden or leather dining chairs around polished tables on more rugs and floorboards. Throughout there are country prints and photographs on walls above oak dados, large house plants with smaller ones on windowsills, shelves of books and old bottles, elegant metal chandeliers and even an indoor fire pit. One room (which is just right for a private party) is lined with lovely parrot prints. French windows lead to a large terrace where there are plenty of wooden chairs and tables and the lawn is lined with picnic-sets.

 Up-to-date food includes sandwiches, smoked duck breast with blackberry, orange, pistachio and chicory, chicken liver pâté with apricot chutney, sharing platters, aubergine, potato and okra curry with coriander and lime rice, sicilian fish stew with saffron aioli, braised pork belly with champ mash and apple and cider sauce, chicken breast with tarragon, wild mushrooms, bacon and spinach pasta, fillet steak rossini with mushrooms, potatoes and cep sauce, and puddings such as crème brûlée and sticky toffee pudding with toffee sauce and vanilla ice-cream. *Benchmark main dish: beer-battered fish and chips £13.75. Two-course evening meal £21.00.*

Brunning & Price ~ Licensee Duncan Moore ~ Real ale ~ Open 11-11; 12-10.30 Sun ~ Bar food 12-9.30; 12-9 Sun ~ Restaurant ~ Children welcome ~ Dogs allowed in bar ~ Wi-fi
Recommended by Tony Scott, Julia and Fiona Barnes, Mike Benton, Jane and Philip Saunders, Julie Braeburn, David Longhurst, Peter Barratt

MICKLEHAM

TQ1753 Map 3

Running Horses ⭐ ♀ 🛏

(01372) 372279 – www.therunninghorses.co.uk

Old London Road (B2209); RH5 6DU

Surrey Dining Pub of the Year

Country pub with plenty of customers in bar and dining rooms, enjoyable food and drink and seats on big front terrace; bedrooms

The tempting food continues to draw plenty of customers into this well run and popular pub. The stylish and spacious bar has cushioned wall settles and other dining chairs around straightforward tables on parquet flooring, racing cartoons and Hogarth prints on the walls, lots of race tickets hanging from a beam and a log fire in an inglenook fireplace; some wood-panelled booths have red leather banquettes. Stools line the counter where friendly, helpful staff serve Brakspears Bitter and Oxford Gold, Fullers London Pride and a monthly guest beer on handpump and around 20 wines by the glass; background music. The panelled restaurant is an attractive mix of upholstered and wooden dining chairs around a medley of tables on tartan carpet. Picnic-sets on the front terrace with its lovely flowering tubs and hanging baskets take in a peaceful view of the old church with its strange stubby steeple, just across the quiet lane. Bedrooms are comfortable and pretty and breakfasts are good.

The very good food includes breakfasts for non-residents (8-10am) plus lunchtime sandwiches (with a choice of a mug of soup or triple-cooked chips), goats cheese and red pepper ravioli, rocket and lemon pesto and pine nuts, chicken kiev ballotine with parmentier potatoes and tomato and thyme dressing, smoked haddock, chive and sweet potato fishcakes with french-style peas and hollandaise, local lamb rump with beetroot, spinach, shallot purée and port sauce, and puddings such as treacle tart with raspberry compote and milk ice-cream and vanilla crème brûlée with poached peaches. *Benchmark main dish: parma ham-wrapped monkfish with courgettes, broad beans and shallot and chive vinaigrette £17.95. Two-course evening meal £21.00.*

Brakspears ~ Manager Kat Griffiths ~ Real ale ~ Open 11-11; 11-10.30 Sun ~ Bar food 12-3, 6-9; 12-10 Sat; 12-8 Sun ~ Restaurant ~ Children welcome ~ Dogs allowed in bar ~ Wi-fi ~ Bedrooms: /£125 *Recommended by Professor James Burke, Jennifer and Nicholas Thompson, Reg Robertson, Sophie Ellison, Jim King, Carol and Barry Craddock*

MILFORD
Refectory ♀ ◀

SU9542   Map 2

(01483) 413820 – www.brunningandprice.co.uk/refectory
Portsmouth Road; GU8 5HJ

Beamed and timbered rooms of much character, six real ales and other thoughtful drinks and well liked food

Friendly, courteous staff create an easy-going atmosphere in this beautifully restored pub that our readers enjoy very much. The L-shaped, mainly open-plan rooms are spacious and interesting with exposed-stone walls, stalling and standing timbers creating separate seating areas, strikingly heavy beams and a couple of big log fires in fine stone fireplaces. A two-tiered and balconied part at one end has a wall covered with huge brass platters; elsewhere there are nice old photographs and a variety of paintings. Dining chairs and dark wooden tables are grouped on wooden, quarry-tiled or carpeted floors, and there are bookshelves, big pot plants, stone bottles on windowsills and fresh flowers. High wooden bar stools line the long counter where they serve Phoenix Brunning & Price Traditional Bitter, Crafty Brewing Dunsfold Best and Dark Star Hophead with three quickly changing guests on handpump, a dozen wines by the glass, 67 gins and around 80 malt whiskies. The back courtyard (adjacent to the characterful pigeonry) has teak tables and chairs. Wheelchair facilities and disabled parking.

Appetising food includes sandwiches, tandoori king prawns, beetroot-cured salmon with orange and beetroot salad and horseradish cream, butternut squash and sage risotto with salsa verde, beer-battered cod and chips, steak in ale pie with english mustard mash and beer gravy, sticky pork belly with watermelon, pineapple and pickled ginger and chilli dressing, sea bream with lemon and dill potato cake, poached leeks and watercress velouté, and puddings such as dark chocolate and orange tart with passion-fruit sorbet and apple and mixed berry crumble with vanilla custard. *Benchmark main dish: fish pie £14.45. Two-course evening meal £21.00.*

Brunning & Price ~ Manager Michael Collins ~ Real ale ~ Open 10.30am-11pm; 12-10.30 Sun ~ Bar food 12-9; 12-9.30 Fri, Sat ~ Restaurant ~ Children welcome ~ Dogs allowed in bar ~ Wi-fi *Recommended by Brian and Susan Wylie, Jeff Davies, Edward May, R and M Thomas, Miss A E Dare, Christopher and Elise Way, Tony Scott*

 NORWOOD HILL   TQ2342   Map 3

Fox Revived ♀ ◖

(01293) 229270 – www.brunningandprice.co.uk/foxrevived
Leigh–Charlwood back road; RH6 0ET

Extended, well run pub with attractive, interesting bar and dining areas, super staff, interesting food and a fine range of drinks; seats outside

Not far from Gatwick Airport, yet comfortably tucked away in remote countryside, this place has seats and tables on a stone terrace that look over the hills beyond, and a five-mile walk that starts straight from the door. The various open-plan dining areas and nooks are divided up by balustrading and standing timbers, creating cosier and more private spaces. Button-back armchairs and stools sit by open fires, antique-style and high-backed leather dining chairs are grouped around tables of varying size on rugs and bare boards and the walls are hung with photos, prints and gilt-edged mirrors; also, big house plants, lots of books on shelves and elegant metal chandeliers. Courteous, helpful staff serve St Austell Brunning & Price Traditional Bitter and Surrey Hills Shere Drop plus guests such as Adnams Ghost Ship, Gun Scaramanga, Long Man Old Man and Timothy Taylors Boltmaker on handpump, 18 wines by the glass, 17 rums, 60 gins, 40 whiskies and farm cider; background music and board games.

High quality food includes sandwiches, braised pig cheek with celeriac purée and sage crackling, smoked salmon with orange and beetroot salad and horseradish cream, moroccan vegetable and chickpea pie with mediterranean vegetables and tomato jus, grilled sea bass with wild mushroom tortellini, cherry tomato sauce and braised fennel, pork and leek sausages with mash and onion gravy, salmon, smoked haddock and prawn pie with french-style peas, braised shoulder of lamb with dauphinoise potatoes, carrot mash and rosemary gravy, and puddings such as hot waffle with boozy cherries and vanilla ice-cream and orange chocolate mousse with Cointreau cream. *Benchmark main dish: beer-battered fish and chips £13.95. Two-course evening meal £22.00.*

Brunning & Price ~ Manager Alastair Craig ~ Real ale ~ Open 10.30am-11pm; 10.30-10.30 Sun ~ Bar food 12-9.30; 12-10 Fri, Sat ~ Restaurant ~ Children welcome ~ Dogs allowed in bar ~ Wi-fi *Recommended by Belinda Stamp, Dave Chapman, Anne Taylor, Tony Scott, Andrew Vincent, Pauline and Mark Evans, Mike and Sarah Abbot*

 OXTED   TQ3951   Map 3

Haycutter ♀ ◖

(01883) 776955 – www.brunningandprice.co.uk/haycutter
Tanhouse Road, Broadham Green; off High Street opposite Old Bell; RH8 9PE

Plenty of chatty dining rooms and bars, lots to look at, attentive staff serving a fine choice of drinks and food and seats outside

Entering from the terrace, you'll find a large main bar in this much extended character pub that's split up into different, snugger areas by metal uprights. There are all sorts of dining chairs around wooden tables on parquet flooring or large rugs, some high tables with equally high stools in one corner, masses of photos and pictures on pale grey-green walls, house plants and bookshelves and a long counter stretching along a back wall.

Here, friendly young staff serve St Austell Brunning & Price Traditional Bitter plus Adnams Broadside, Harveys Best, Surrey Hills Shere Drop, Timothy Taylors Landlord, Wantsum Montgomery and Westerham Hay Today on handpump, 19 wines by the glass, 58 gins and 78 whiskies. A quarry-tiled walkway leads down towards the original building with a couple of small rooms leading off to each side with similar furnishings and décor, and there's also a massive circular table surrounded by a dozen chairs plus a private dining room. Outside, a large paved area with raised flower beds has good quality tables and chairs under big parasols and there are picnic-sets on lawns. Dogs are welcomed with a bowl of water and a biscuit.

Interesting food includes sandwiches, lamb koftas with fattoush salad, tzatziki and chilli sauce, scallops with honey-roast shallots, smoked bacon and apple, moroccan vegetable and chickpea pie with charred courgettes, baby peppers and toasted almonds, steak burger with toppings, coleslaw and chips, thai green chicken laksa with buckwheat noodles, pak choi and thai basil, duo of lamb (roasted rump and mini pie) with glazed shallots, smoked haddock crumble with leek, clams, prawns and tarragon cream, and puddings such as crème brûlée and sticky toffee pudding with toffee sauce. *Benchmark main dish: chicken, ham hock and leek pie £13.95. Two-course evening meal £21.00.*

Brunning & Price ~ Manager Chris Little ~ Real ale ~ Open 11.30-11; 12-10.30 Sun ~ Bar food 12-9.30; 12-10 Fri, Sat ~ Restaurant ~ Children welcome away from front area ~ Dogs welcome ~ Wi-fi *Recommended by Amy Ledbetter, William Pace, Camilla and Jose Ferrera, Peter and Alison Steadman, Professor James Burke, Mark Morgan, Andrew Stone*

RIPLEY
Anchor 🏆 ♟ TQ0556 Map 2
(01483) 211866 – www.ripleyanchor.co.uk
High Street; GU23 6AE

Stylish dining pub with first class food, real ales, friendly service and sunny courtyard

A former almshouse and dating back to the 16th c, this is gently civilised but convivial and easy-going. Several low-ceilinged, interlinked rooms have heavy beams, slate floors and open fires and are decorated in a stylish, simple way that's immediately inviting. There are church chairs around polished tables in the bar, comfortable seating in the dining areas, contemporary paintwork or exposed-brick walls, and elegant flower arrangements; background music. Dorking DB One and guests such as Exeter Avocet and Tillingbourne Falls Gold on handpump, 20 good wines by the glass, 16 gins (some local) and nine malt whiskies; background music. Outside, a sunny, decked back courtyard has cushioned wicker chairs and sofas.

Imaginative food includes black pudding scotch egg with puffed pork skin and apple sauce, grilled mackerel escabeche with garlic and saffron mayonnaise, tarragon gnocchi with curried cauliflower and gouda sauce, burger with toppings and red onion marmalade, slow-cooked duck leg with chicory and parsley mash, cod with carrot purée, mussels and coconut sauce, and puddings such as chocolate parfait with walnut praline, apricot sorbet and basil and sticky beer cake with spiced apple ice-cream. *Benchmark main dish: guinea fowl with charred cabbage and sarladaises potatoes £24.00. Two-course evening meal £28.00.*

Free house ~ Licensee Michael Wall-Palmer ~ Real ale ~ Open 12-3, 5.30-11; 12-11 Sat; closed Mon ~ Bar food 12-2.30, 6-9; 12-4, 6-8 Sun ~ Restaurant ~ Children welcome ~ Wi-fi *Recommended by Mary and Douglas McDowell, Andrew Wall, Ian Wilson, John Evans, Dan and Anne Morgan, Gordon and Patricia Gorringe, Christopher and Elise Way*

SHAMLEY GREEN
TQ0343 Map 3

Red Lion

(01483) 892202 – www.redlionshamleygreen.com

The Green; GU5 0UB

Pleasant dining pub with popular food and attractive gardens

This is a friendly pub with a good, cheerful mixture of both diners and drinkers. The two interconnected bars are fairly traditional with a range of new and old wooden tables, chairs and cushioned settles on bare boards and red carpet, stripped standing timbers, fresh white walls, deep red ceilings and open fires. Harveys Best, Hogs Back TEA and Sharps Doom Bar on handpump, 11 wines by the glass and several gins and malt whiskies; background music. At the front of the pub there are plenty of hand-made rustic tables and benches looking over the village green and cricket pitch; it's more secluded at the back, where you'll find more seats on a heated, covered terrace and grassed dining areas.

From a well judged menu, the good quality food includes lunchtime baguettes, tea-smoked duck with chargrilled asparagus and parmesan, prawn cocktail, goats cheese, walnut and caramelised onion filo parcel with tomato and red pepper chutney and dressed salad, honey-roast ham and eggs, moules frites, beef curry, beer-battered haddock and chips, calves liver with onions, pancetta and sautéed potatoes, veal escalope with creamy mushroom sauce, and puddings such as peach and apricot crumble with custard and ginger pudding with ginger wine and brandy sauce. *Benchmark main dish: pie of the day £13.95. Two-course evening meal £20.00.*

Punch ~ Lease Debbie Ersser ~ Real ale ~ Open 11.30-11; 12-10 (12-8 in winter) Sun ~ Bar food 12-2.30 (3 Sat), 6.30-9.30; 12-3, 6-8 Sun; no food Sun evening in winter ~ Restaurant ~ Children welcome ~ Dogs allowed in bar ~ Wi-fi *Recommended by Gerry and Pam Pollard, Margaret McDonald, Rosie and John Moore, Pauline and Mark Evans, Ian Wilson, Belinda Stamp, Susan and Callum Slade*

SUNBURY
TQ1068 Map 3

Flower Pot ⚓

(01932) 780741 – www.theflowerpotsunbury.co.uk

1.6 miles from M3 junction 1; follow Lower Sunbury sign from exit roundabout, then at Thames Street turn right; pub on next corner, with Green Street; TW16 6AA

Handsome place with an appealing, contemporary bar and dining room, real ales and all-day food; bedrooms

With elegant wrought-iron balconies and an attractive façade, this is a former coaching inn with a villagey feel and nearby waterside walks. The airy bar has leather tub chairs around copper-topped tables, high chairs upholstered in brown and beige tartan around equally high tables in pale wood, attractive flagstones, contemporary paintwork and stools against the counter; there's also a couple of comfortably plush burgundy armchairs. The bar leads into a dining area with pale blue-painted and dark wooden cushioned dining chairs around an assortment of partly painted tables on bare boards, artwork on papered walls and a large gilt-edged mirror over an open fireplace; candles in glass jars, fresh flowers, background music and newspapers. Brakspears Bitter, Ringwood Boondoggle and Youngs Special on handpump and 15 wines by the glass. A side terrace has wood and metal tables and chairs and the summer hanging baskets are pretty. Bedrooms are smart and comfortable.

Highly thought-of food includes breakfasts (7-11am; 8-11am weekends) plus garlic and rosemary-studded baked camembert with seasonal chutney, salmon and prawn fishcakes with tartare sauce, falafel burger with sweet potato fries, pizzas, chicken and avocado salad with croutons and honey mustard dressing, beer-battered fish and chips, duck confit with dauphinoise potatoes and orange sauce, 28-day aged local rib-eye steak with a choice of sauce, and puddings such as cherry and chocolate cheesecake and seasonal crumble with custard. *Benchmark main dish: slow-cooked baby back ribs in barbecue sauce with coleslaw and chips £13.50. Two-course evening meal £21.00.*

Authentic Inns ~ Tenant Simon Bailey ~ Real ale ~ Open 7am-11pm; 8am-11pm Sat, Sun ~ Bar food 12-3, 6-9; 12-9 Sat ~ Restaurant ~ Children welcome ~ Dogs allowed in bar ~ Wi-fi ~ Bedrooms: /£99 *Recommended by Diana and Bertie Farr, Mary and Douglas McDowell, Kerry and Guy Trooper, Sabina and Gerald Grimshaw, Tom Stone, Margaret McDonald*

WALTON ON THE HILL   TQ2255   Map 3
Blue Ball

(01737) 819003 – www.theblueball.co.uk

Not far from M25 junction 8; Deans Lane, off B2220 by pond; KT20 7UE

Popular pub with spreading drinking and dining areas, helpful staff, well liked food and drink and lots of outside seating

On a sunny day, you'll be hard-pushed to bag one of the seats and tables on the terrace behind this sizeable pub, unless you arrive early; there's also a fire pit under a gazebo and you can hire cabanas for a private group (these need booking in advance). The entrance bar has a chatty atmosphere, colourful leather-topped stools at the counter plus rugs on bare boards, house plants on windowsills, all manner of old pictures and photographs on the walls, antique-style cushioned, farmhouse and high-backed kitchen chairs around tables of every size, and a large wine cage. There's a beer named for the pub plus Fullers London Pride, Timothy Taylors Landlord and Wadworths 6X on handpump and good wines by the glass. Leading back from here, several dining rooms have multicoloured button-back leather banquettes, similar chairs and tables on more rugs and wooden floors, bookshelves, gilt-edged mirrors and a big central conical open fire; background music.

Interesting food includes sandwiches (until 5pm), jackfruit spring rolls with japanese salad and hoisin and peanut butter dipping sauce, chicken liver parfait with red onion jam, free-range three-egg omelette with a choice of filling, smoked salmon and haddock fishcake with tomato and onion salad and dill mayonnaise, corned-beef hash with bubble and squeak and local free-range eggs, a pie and a roast of the day, 21-day aged fillet steak with a choice of sauce and triple-cooked chips, and puddings such as bakewell tart with vanilla ice-cream and sticky toffee pudding with toffee sauce. *Benchmark main dish: chicken katsu curry £13.45. Two-course evening meal £21.00.*

Whiting & Hammond ~ Manager Gareth Nixon ~ Real ale ~ Open 10am-11pm; 9am-11pm Sat; 9am-10.30pm Sun ~ Bar food 12-9.30; 9am-9.30pm Sat; 9-9 Sun ~ Restaurant ~ Children welcome ~ Dogs allowed in bar ~ Wi-fi *Recommended by Maggie and Matthew Lyons, Charles Fraser, Gene and Kitty Rankin, Kitty and Stuart Flint, Martine and Derek Cotton, Edward May, Alfie Bayliss*

WEST END   SU9461   Map 2
The Inn West End ⌂

(01276) 858652 – www.the-inn.co.uk

Just under 2.5 miles from M3 junction 3; A322 S, on right; GU24 9PW

Plenty of dining and drinking space in carefully refurbished rooms, highly regarded food and drink and seats in the garden; bedrooms

New people at the helm here have made quite a few changes. The bar has white-painted beams, a mix of nice old traditional chairs around dark, rustic tables on bare boards, parquet and carpet, and a few high chairs around equally high tables and stools against the blue-painted counter where friendly staff serve Fullers London Pride and Thurstons Horsell Gold on handpump, several wines by the glass and around a dozen gins (with some interesting gin cocktails). There's also a restaurant. The pretty terrace has new rattan-style chairs and the courtyard has plenty of picnic-sets. Bedrooms are comfortable and breakfasts are good.

As well as breakfasts (7-11am weekdays; 8-11am Sat; 8-10.30am Sun), a good choice of interesting food includes salt and pepper squid with lime mayonnaise, spiced lamb koftas with mint yoghurt and flatbread, roasted vegetable and butter bean pie with olive oil mash and tomato and herb sauce, lunchtime home-cooked ham with a wholegrain mustard crust and eggs, thai-spiced steak salad with coriander, mint and thai basil dressing, hake with wilted spinach, cannellini bean, tomato and chorizo stew and parsley and garlic aïoli, chicken, leek and ham pie, steak burger with toppings, coleslaw and skin-on fries, confit duck with peppercorn sauce and pommes anna, and puddings such as black forest chocolate cheesecake with hot chocolate sauce and lemon, blueberry and raspberry pavlova with lemon curd and ice-cream. *Benchmark main dish: calves liver and bacon with colcannon mash and onion gravy £15.95. Two-course evening meal £22.00.*

Free house ~ Licensee Mirela Lepadatu ~ Real ale ~ Open 7am-11pm; 8am-11pm Sat; 8am-10.30pm Sun ~ Bar food 12-9.30 (9 Sun) ~ Restaurant ~ Children welcome ~ Wi-fi ~ Bedrooms: /£95 *Recommended by Peter and Alison Steadman, Alison and Dan Richardson, Derek Stafford, Louise and Simon Peters, Jill and Dick Archer, Edward Mirzoeff*

Also Worth a Visit in Surrey

Besides the fully inspected pubs, you might like to try these pubs that have been recommended to us and described by readers. Do tell us what you think of them: feedback@goodguides.com

ABINGER COMMON   TQ1146
Abinger Hatch (01306) 730737
Off A25 W of Dorking, towards Abinger Hammer; RH5 6HZ Dining pub dating from the 17th c in beautiful woodland spot; spacious split-level interior with heavy beams and log fires, enjoyable well cooked food from toasted bagels and sharing plates to blackboard specials, friendly if not always speedy service, Ringwood Razorback and three guests, decent wine; children and dogs welcome, some disabled access, picnic-sets in side garden, near pretty church and pond, open (and food) all day. *(Tom and Ruth Rees)*

ALBURY   TQ0447
Drummond Arms (01483) 202039
Off A248 SE of Guildford; The Street; GU5 9AG Modernised 19th-c pub in pretty village; four real ales such as Adnams, Courage and Hogs Back, good choice of wines and enjoyable food from sandwiches and sharing plates up, opened-up bar with leather chesterfields and log fire, parquet-floored dining room, conservatory; children welcome, pretty back garden by little River Tillingbourne, summer barbecues and hog roasts, pleasant walks nearby, 11 bedrooms, open all day, food all day Sun. *(Alison and Dan Richardson)*

ALBURY HEATH   TQ0646
William IV (01483) 202685
Little London, off A25 Guildford–Dorking; OS Sheet 187 map reference 065468; GU5 9DG Refurbished 16th-c pub doing well under welcoming new owners; rustic low-beamed bar with flagstones and inglenook log fire, well kept ales such as Surrey Hills, a dozen wines by the glass and some interesting gins (including a non-alcoholic one), good freshly made food served by friendly accommodating staff, restaurant area up steps; children and dogs (in bar) welcome, picnic-sets in small front garden behind picket fence, good walks, open all day (till 9pm Sun), no evening food Sun-Tues. *(Geoff and Ann Marston)*

ALFOLD   TQ0435
Alfold Barn (01403) 752288
Horsham Road, A281; GU6 8JE Beautifully preserved 16th-c building with bar and restaurant; very good locally sourced home-made food from daily changing menu

with some emphasis on fish/seafood (Sun booking esential), friendly attentive service, a beer or two from nearby breweries, black beams and rafters, mixed furniture on flagstones or carpet, log fires; children welcome, dogs in garden only, closed Sun evening, Mon, Tues. *(Tony and Wendy Hobden)*

ALFOLD TQ0334
Three Compasses (01483) 275729
Dunsfold Road; GU6 8HY Welcoming 450-year-old pub with good fairly priced food (not Sun evening, Mon) in bar and restaurant areas, three well kept ales such as Otter, big log fire; children and dogs welcome, large garden, on back lane to former Dunsfold Aerodrome (now Dunsfold Park with little museum), Wey & Arun Canal nearby, open all day (till 9pm Sun). *(Liz and Martin Eldon)*

BATTS CORNER SU8140
Bluebell (01252) 792801
Batts Corner; GU10 4EX Busy tucked-away country pub with linked stone-floor rooms, light fresh décor and mix of furniture including sofas by big log fire, well kept ales such as Frensham, Langham and Triple fff, good home-made food from sandwiches to popular Sun lunch (must book), also weekday set lunch deal, helpful friendly staff; children, walkers and dogs welcome, attractive spacious garden with rolling views, summer barbecues and good play area, handy for Alice Holt Forest, open all day Sat, till 8pm Sun. *(Mike Benton)*

BLETCHINGLEY TQ3250
Bletchingley Arms (01883) 740142
High Street (A25); RH1 4PE Spacious modernised Barons group pub with plenty of opened-up areas (some steps) including beamed part with flagstones and woodburner, good choice of well prepared sensibly priced food from snacks up, three real ales, plenty of wines by the glass and interesting range of gins, friendly staff; background music (live last Fri of month), newspapers, sports TV; children and dogs (in bar) welcome, outside seating areas with own bar, beach huts and good play area, open all day. *(Ian Wilson)*

BLETCHINGLEY TQ3250
Red Lion (01883) 743342
Castle Street (A25), Redhill side; RH1 4NU Modernised and well looked-after beamed village dining pub, decent range of good home-made food including gluten-free and vegan menus, well kept Greene King ales and a dozen wines by the glass, friendly staff; quiz and live music nights; children welcome, heated part-covered terrace, secret garden, open (and food) all day. *(Dave Chapman)*

BRAMLEY TQ0044
★**Jolly Farmer** (01483) 893355
High Street; GU5 0HB Family-run village pub with traditional beamed interior packed with collections of plates and old bottles,

enamel signs, sewing machines, antique tools and so forth, timbered semi-partitions and open fire, Crafty Brewing, Greene King and up to six guests, a couple of summer ciders and over a dozen wines by the glass, generous helpings of fairly traditional food including good Sun carvery (worth booking); background music, quiz every other Weds, board games, free wi-fi; children and dogs (in bar) welcome, tables out by car park, walks up St Martha's Hill and handy for Winkworth Arboretum (NT), bedrooms, open all day. *(Sarah and John Webb)*

BROCKHAM TQ1949
Inn on the Green (01737) 845101
Brockham Green; RH3 7JS Restaurany pub facing village green (part of the small Grumpy Mole group); good food from traditional choices up including cook-your-own steaks on a hot stone, helpful friendly service, well kept Fullers London Pride and Surrey Hills Shere Drop, several wines by the glass, afternoon teas, conservatory; children welcome, picnic-sets out at front, garden behind, open all day, food all day weekends. *(Christopher and Elise Way)*

BROCKHAM TQ1949
Royal Oak (01737) 843241
Brockham Green; RH3 7JS Nice spot on charming village green below the North Downs; bare-boards bar and airy dining area, three or four well kept ales such as Fullers and Sharps, enjoyable home-made food from burgers and pub favourites up, log fires; quiz and live music nights; children and dogs welcome, tables out in front looking across to fine church, more seats in back garden, handy for Greensand Way, open all day. *(Colin Swift)*

BROOK SU9238
Dog & Pheasant (01428) 682763
Haslemere Road (A286); GU8 5UJ Popular pub looking across busy road to cricket green; long beamed bar divided by standing timbers, cushioned wall settles, open fire in brick fireplace, four well kept ales such as Sharps from linenfold counter, plenty of wines by the glass and decent range of gins, dining area on right, further room to left with big inglenook, generally well liked food including a pie of the day and Weds grill night; children and dogs welcome, picnic-sets on back deck and grass, play equipment, open all day, food till 4pm Sun. *(George Todd)*

BURROWHILL SU9763
Four Horseshoes (01276) 856257
B383 N of Chobham; GU24 8QP Busy pub attractively set by village green; updated interior with beams and log fires, up to four well kept ales including Fullers London Pride and a Caledonian house beer (Shoes), popular interesting food from sandwiches and sharing boards up (best to book weekends, kitchen shuts 4.30pm Sun),

cheerful helpful staff, dining extension; children, dogs and muddy boots welcome, tables out at front (some under ancient yew), also back terrace and garden with picnic-sets and deck chairs, open all day (till 7pm Sun). *(Ian Phillips)*

CARSHALTON TQ2764
Hope (020) 8240 1255
West Street; SM5 2PR Chatty community-owned mock-Tudor local; Downton, Windsor & Eton and five guests, also craft kegs, real cider/perry and over 50 bottled beers, generous low-priced pubby food (limited evening choice); 1950s-feel U-shaped bar with open fire, lots of pump clips, larger back room with bar billiards; live acoustic music second Weds of month, regular beer and cider festivals, board games; no under-14s, dogs welcome, disabled access/loos, garden, open all day. *(Gerry and Pam Pollard)*

CATERHAM TQ3254
Harrow (01883) 343260
Stanstead Road, Whitehill; CR3 6AJ Simple 16th-c beamed pub high up in open country by North Downs Way; L-shaped bare-boards bar and carpeted back dining area, several real ales (sometimes tapped from the cask) such as Fullers and Ringwood, well liked food including daily specials, friendly staff and good local atmosphere; children and dogs welcome, garden picnic-sets, popular with walkers and cyclists, open all day, no food Sun evening. *(Colin Swift)*

CHARLESHILL SU8844
Donkey (01252) 702124
B3001 Milford–Farnham near Tilford; coming from Elstead, turn left as soon as you see pub sign; GU10 2AU Old-fashioned beamed dining pub with enjoyable home-made food including weekday deals, up to three well kept changing ales and good choice of wines by the glass, prompt friendly service, conservatory restaurant; children and dogs welcome, attractive garden with paddock for much loved donkeys Pip and Dusty, good walks, open all day weekends. *(Liz and Martin Eldon)*

CHARLTON TQ0868
Harrow (01932) 783122
Charlton Road, Ashford Common; off B376 Laleham–Shepperton; TW17 0RJ Pretty little thatched pub thought to date from 1130; simple beamed and carpeted interior with inglenook, Greene King ales and well priced food from pubby choices to good authentic indian dishes (takeaways available), side dining extension, some signed celebrity photos (Shepperton film studios nearby); sports TV, free wi-fi; picnic-sets in flower-filled front area, more

seats in bigger back garden, small car park across busy road, open all day. *(Susan and John Douglas)*

CHARLWOOD TQ2441
Half Moon (01293) 863414
The Street; RH6 0DS Old pub next to churchyard in attractive village; spacious L-shaped bar (front part open to original upstairs windows), well kept Sharps Doom Bar, St Austell Tribute and a guest, enjoyable sensibly priced traditional food from sandwiches up, friendly service, back dining room, occasional live music; children and dogs (in bar) welcome, picnic-sets in nice courtyard area, handy for Gatwick Airport, food all day weekends. *(Tony Scott)*

CHERTSEY TQ0466
Olde Swan (01932) 562129
Windsor Street; KT16 8AY Former coaching house run by McLean Inns; generous helpings of popular reasonably priced food including pizzas, burgers and good Sun lunch, four well kept ales such as Marstons Wainwright and Sharps Doom Bar from well stocked bar, friendly efficient young staff, opened-up split-level interior with rugs on bare boards, candles on tables, comfortable seating and lots of pictures, mirrors and other bits and pieces; weekend live music; children and dogs welcome, attractive outside area, seven bedrooms, open all day, food till 6pm Sun. *(Hunter and Christine Wright)*

CHIDDINGFOLD SU9635
★ Crown (01428) 682255
The Green (A283); GU8 4TX Lovely 700-year-old timbered building with strong sense of history; bar and linked dining rooms with massive beams (some over 2-ft thick), oak panelling, moulded plasterwork and fine stained-glass windows, magnificently carved fireplace, some nice antique tables along with cushioned wall seats, mate's and other pubby chairs, lots of portraits, simple split-level back public bar with open fire, up to five changing ales including Hogs Back and Ringwood and several wines by the glass, enjoyable often interesting food (all day Fri-Sun); quiz first Thurs of month; children welcome, dogs in some areas, seats out looking across village green to interesting church, more tables in sheltered central courtyard, character creaky bedrooms, open all day Fri-Sun. *(George Todd)*

CHILWORTH TQ0347
Percy Arms (01483) 561765
Dorking Road; GU4 8NP Extended stylishly decorated pub with two bustling bars; smaller one has logs neatly piled above woodburner, a long slate-topped table and

---

We checked prices with the pubs as we went to press in summer 2019. They should hold until around spring 2020.

L-shaped settle, flagstoned main room with tartan-cushioned chairs against counter serving Greene King ales (one named for the pub), a guest beer and 16 wines by the glass, interesting food including some south african specialities and good value set lunch (Mon-Fri), courteous efficient service, restaurant rooms to left of entrance with upholstered tub and high-backed chairs on bare boards or rugs, further dining rooms down steps; TV, free wi-fi; children and dogs (in bar areas) welcome, two-part garden connected by bridge over little stream, play equipment, five comfortable bedrooms, open all day, food all day weekends. *(Elise and Charles Mackinlay)*

CHIPSTEAD
Well House (01737) 830640   TQ2555

Chipstead signed with Mugswell off A217, N of M25 junction 8; CR5 3SQ Originally three 16th-c cottages (converted from tea rooms to pub in 1955); log fires in all three rooms, low beams and rustic décor, bric-a-brac and pewter tankards hanging from ceiling, well kept Fullers, Surrey Hills and a local guest, food from ciabattas up, friendly staff, small dining conservatory, resident ghost (Harry the Monk); Tues quiz, occasional live music, free wi-fi; children and dogs allowed (in bars, they have cats), large pleasing hillside garden with ancient well (mentioned in the Domesday Book), delightful country setting, open all day. *(Tony Scott, Dave Chapman)*

CHURT
Crossways (01428) 714323   SU8538

Corner of A287 and Hale House Lane; GU10 2JE Friendly down-to-earth local attracting good mix of customers; quarry-tiled public bar with small brick fireplace, saloon with wood floor, panelling and banquettes, good beer range (some served direct from the cellar) and three or four real ciders, enjoyable well priced pub lunches (not Sun) including locally made pies, evening food Weds only, cheerful staff; darts, TV; no under-10s inside, dogs welcome, open all day Fri, Sat. *(Gerry and Pam Pollard)*

CLAYGATE
Foley (01372) 462021   TQ1563

Hare Lane; KT10 ORZ Restored 19th-c Youngs inn; pubby part at front with wooden tables and chairs on bare boards, comfortable seats by Victorian fireplace, lots of interconnected sitting and dining areas leading off, their well kept ales, plenty of wines by the glass and interesting range of spirits, good choice of coffees and teas too, enjoyable food from open kitchen; background music, sports TV, daily papers and free wi-fi; children and dogs (in bar) welcome, seats on two-level part-covered terrace, 17 modern bedrooms, open (and food) all day including breakfast from 8am. *(Gail and Frank Hackett)*

CLAYGATE
Hare & Hounds (01372) 465149   TQ1563

The Green; KT10 OJL Renovated 19th-c flower-decked village pub; good sensibly priced french food along with some pub favourites in bar or smaller restaurant, nice wines and well kept changing ales including local Brightwater, friendly caring service; regular live music, occasional Sun quiz, free wi-fi; children and dogs welcome, disabled access/loo, tables on attractive front terrace and in small back garden with play area, open (and food) all day, kitchen closes 7pm Sun and Mon afternoon. *(Colin Swift)*

CLAYGATE
Platform 3 (01372) 462334   TQ1563

The Parade, next to Claygate station; KT10 OPB Tiny pub in converted taxi office acting as tap for the Brightwater brewery, a couple of their beers and often a guest, Claygate cider and good range of wines and soft drinks, no food apart from crisps and nuts; outside seating (there's no room inside), closed Mon-Weds, otherwise open 3-9pm, but weather/season dependent (best to check website/Twitter). *(Sean, Colin Swift)*

COBHAM
Plough (01932) 589790   TQ1059

3.2 miles from M25 junction 10; right off A3 on A245; in Cobham, right into Downside Bridge Road; Plough Lane; KT11 3LT Smartly updated beamed village pub, part of the small Rarebreed group (see Shurlock Inn, Shurlock Row, Berkshire); much liked food cooked in open kitchen from bar snacks to grills, real ales including a Caledonian house beer and St Austell Tribute, good wine list, interesting gins and cocktails, friendly helpful service, roaring log fire; background and live music; children and dogs (in more informal area) welcome, some outside seating, open (and food) all day, kitchen closes 6pm Sun. *(Ian Phillips)*

COBHAM
Running Mare (01932) 862007   TQ1159

Tilt Road; KT11 3EZ Attractive old flower-decked pub overlooking green (can get very busy); well kept Fullers ales, guest beers and over a dozen wines by the glass, good food from varied menu including popular Sun lunch, efficient friendly service, two timbered bars and restaurant; children and dogs welcome, a few tables out at front and on rose-covered back terrace, open all day, no food Sun evening. *(Mike Benton)*

COLDHARBOUR
Plough (01306) 711793   TQ1544

Village signposted in the network of small roads around Leith Hill; RH5 6HD Former 17th-c beamed coaching house under welcoming licensees – also incorporates the village shop; own-brew Leith Hill beers and guests, proper cider and a dozen wines by the glass, good popular food (not Sun evening) in bar or restaurant; background music, TV, free wi-fi, events in barn room such as live music, food fairs, bridge nights and french lessons; children, walkers and dogs welcome, seats out at front and on back terrace overlooking fields, six comfortable bedrooms, open all day (till 9pm Sun). *(Jeff Davies)*

COMPTON   SU9646
★ **Withies** (01483) 421158
Withies Lane; pub signed from B3000; GU3 1JA Gently old-fashioned and civilised 16th-c pub on edge of Loseley Park; atmospheric low-beamed carpeted bar, some 17th-c carved panels between windows, splendid art nouveau settle among old sewing-machine tables, log fire in massive inglenook, well kept Adnams, Greene King, Hogs Back and Sharps, highly regarded food (restaurant choices can be pricey and they add a service charge), efficient staff in bow ties; children welcome, no dogs inside, seats on terrace, under apple trees and creeper-hung arbour, flower-edged neat front lawn, handy for Watts Gallery, closed Sun evening. *(Helen and Brian Edgeley, Nick Hales, Susan and John Douglas)*

CRANLEIGH   TQ0739
Park Hatch (01483) 274374
Bookhurst Road, Parkmead Estate – towards Shere; GU6 7DN Modernised 17th-c brick and tile-hung dining pub; low beams, flagstones and big inglenook with woodburner, good food cooked by owner-chef including set lunch menu and themed nights, up to five well kept changing beers, friendly service, new oak-framed dining extension; children and dogs (in some parts) welcome, garden tables under parasols, closed Mon lunchtime, otherwise open all day, weekend breakfasts from 10am. *(Jim and Sue James)*

CRANLEIGH   TQ0539
Richard Onslow (01483) 274922
High Street; GU6 8AU Busy Peach group pub with cheerful small bar, leather tub chairs and built-in sofa, slate-floored drinking area, ales including Greene King and Surrey Hills, a proper cider and ten wines by the glass, generally well liked food from deli boards up including weekday set menu, two dining rooms (open fires) and sizeable restaurant with pale tables on wood floor, modern flowery wallpaper and big windows overlooking the street; background music, board games, free wi-fi; children and dogs (in bar) welcome, seats out at front and in terraced back garden, ten well equipped bedrooms, open (and food) all day from 7am (8am weekends) for breakfast. *(George Todd)*

DORKING   TQ1649
Cricketers (01306) 889938
South Street; RH4 2JU Chatty and relaxed little Fullers local with up to five well kept ales and simple weekday lunchtime food, friendly service, some cricketing memorabilia on stripped-brick walls; events including monthly quiz, beer festivals, Scalextric championship and onion-growing competition, darts, sports TV and free wi-fi; children allowed until early evening, nice split-level suntrap back terrace, open all day. *(Gail and Frank Hackett)*

DORKING   TQ1649
Kings Arms (01306) 883361
West Street; RH4 1BU Rambling 15th-c pub (originally three cottages) in antiques area; cosy split-level interior with low black beams and timbers, some old panelling and leaded windows, mix of furniture on bare boards, brick or tiled floors, Shepherd Neame ales and an occasional guest, decent choice of fair value food from sandwiches and wraps up, friendly service; background music (live Fri, Sat), quiz Mon, sports TVs, fruit machine; children welcome, tables in two courtyards behind, open all day, food all day Sat, till 5pm Sun. *(Tony Scott, Tony and Wendy Hobden)*

DORKING   TQ1649
Old House at Home (01306) 889664
West Street; RH4 1BY Bustling old Youngs pub with opened-up beamed interior; good food from bar snacks up (not Sun evening, Mon, Tues), friendly staff; dogs welcome, back terrace with heated beach huts, closed Mon lunchtime, otherwise open all day (till 8pm Sun). *(Mike Benton)*

DORMANSLAND   TQ4042
Old House at Home (01342) 836828
West Street; RH7 6QP Friendly 19th-c village pub; beamed bar with traditional furniture on parquet floor, two-way woodburner, Shepherd Neame ales and several wines by the glass from unusual barrel-fronted counter, good well priced traditional food (not Sun evening, Mon, Tues), restaurant with wood and stone floor, darts and TV in snug; some live music, free wi-fi; children and dogs (in bar) welcome, tables out in front, open all day Thurs-Sun. *(Helena and Trevor Fraser)*

DORMANSLAND   TQ4042
Plough (01342) 832933
Plough Road, off B2028 NE; RH7 6PS Friendly traditional old pub in quiet village; well kept Fullers, Harveys and Sharps, Weston's cider and decent wines, good

---

Anyone claiming to arrange, or prevent, inclusion of a pub in the *Guide* is a fraud. Pubs are included only if recommended by readers and if our own anonymous inspection confirms that they are suitable.

choice of enjoyable lunchtime bar food including specials and popular Sun roasts, thai restaurant (Mon evening-Sat), log fires and other original features; charity quiz nights and some live music; children and dogs welcome, disabled facilities, good-sized garden, open all day, no food Sun evening. *(Tony Scott)*

DUNSFOLD
TQ0036
Sun (01483) 200242
Off B2130 S of Godalming; GU8 4LE
Old brick pub with four rooms (brighter at the front), beams and some exposed brickwork, scrubbed pine furniture, two massive log fires, five real ales such as Greene King, Sharps and Tillingbourne, decent wines and enjoyable reasonably priced home-made food including curry evening (second Sat of month) and popular Sun lunch (best to book), good friendly service; quiz night Sun, darts; children and dogs welcome, seats on terrace and common opposite, good walks, open all day, no food Sun evening. *(Tony and Wendy Hobden)*

EASHING
SU9543
★**Stag on the River** (01483) 421568
Lower Eashing, just off A3 southbound; GU7 2QG Gently upmarket riverside inn with Georgian façade concealing much older interior; attractively opened-up rooms including charming old-fashioned locals' bar with armchairs on red and black quarry tiles, log fire in cosy snug beyond, Hogs Back TEA, one or two Marstons-related ales and a Red Mist house beer from Tilford, Hazy Hog cider, plenty of emphasis on food with several linked dining areas including river room up a couple of steps, attentive courteous staff; children welcome, dogs in bar, extensive terrace with rattan and wood furniture under parasols (some by weir), picnic-sets on grass, seven bedrooms, open all day, food all day weekends. *(George Todd)*

EAST CLANDON
TQ0551
★**Queens Head** (01483) 222332
Just off A246 Guildford–Leatherhead; The Street; GU4 7RY Busy attractively updated dining pub in same small group as Duke of Cambridge at Tilford, Stag at Eashing and Wheatsheaf in Farnham; well liked food (best to book) from light dishes to good daily specials, set lunch deal (Mon-Thurs), Red Mist house beer along with Surrey Hills and a couple of guests from fine elm-topped counter, also Hazy Hog cider and nice wines by the glass, efficient friendly service, comfortable linked rooms, woodburner in big inglenook; daily newspapers and free wi-fi, silent TV in bar; children welcome, tables

out in front and on side terrace, handy for Hatchlands Park (NT), open (and food) all day Fri and Sat, shuts 9pm (8pm) Sun. *(John Evans, Ian Phillips, Tom and Ruth Rees)*

EFFINGHAM
TQ1153
Plough (01372) 458121
Orestan Lane; KT24 5SW Youngs pub with their well kept ales and a guest, plenty of wines by the glass and good home-made food including Tues pie day, open interior around central bar, grey-painted beams, delft shelving and half panelling, wood floors, two coal-effect gas fires; children and dogs welcome (pub dog is Ruby), disabled access/parking, plenty of tables on forecourt and in pretty garden among fruit trees, handy for Polesden Lacey (NT), open all day Fri and Sat, closed Sun evening. *(Katharine Cowherd)*

ELSTEAD
SU9043
Woolpack (01252) 703106
B3001 Milford–Farnham; GU8 6HD Comfortably modernised tile-hung dining pub run by italian family; enjoyable home-cooked food including stone-baked pizzas and weekly themed nights, cask-tapped ales and decent wines by the glass, friendly efficient service, long main bar, restaurant, open fires; children welcome, garden with picnic-sets, open all day Sun. *(Alison and Dan Richardson)*

ESHER
TQ1364
Wheatsheaf (01372) 464014
The Green; KT10 8AG Early 19th-c dining pub with neat opened-up bar area; light wood flooring, a mix of furniture including sofas and easy chairs, lots of colourful artwork and a couple of Victorian fireplaces, four well kept beers including Surrey Hills and plenty of wines by the glass, good food from upscale bar snacks, sharing plates and traditional favourites to more enterprising restauranty dishes, friendly staff, high-ceilinged back dining extension with small outside eating area; background music, sports TV, daily newspapers and free wi-fi; well behaved children till 7.30pm, dogs in bar, teak tables under parasols on front paved terrace looking across to green, open (and food) all day. *(Mike Benton)*

FARNHAM
SU8545
Spotted Cow (01252) 726541
Bourne Grove, Lower Bourne (towards Tilford); GU10 3QT Welcoming red-brick dining pub on edge of town in nice wooded setting (good walks nearby); highly regarded food from pub favourites and sharing boards up (booking advised), three changing ales

---

A star symbol before the name of a pub shows exceptional character and appeal.
It doesn't mean extra comfort. Even quite a basic pub can win a star,
if it's individual enough.

and decent range of wines, friendly helpful staff; children and dogs welcome, big garden, open all day weekends (food till 7.30pm Sun). *(George Todd)*

FETCHAM TQ1456
Bell (01372) 372624
Bell Lane; KT22 9ND Attractively modernised Youngs dining pub; their ales, guest beers and over 30 wines by the glass, good choice of other drinks including cocktails, well liked food from varied menu in bar or restaurant, friendly helpful staff; Mon quiz, live music and other events; children and dogs welcome, tables out on gravel terrace, weekend burger shack, open (and food) all day. *(Martin Cooke)*

FICKLESHOLE TQ3960
White Bear (01959) 573166
Featherbed Lane/Fairchildes Lane; off A2022 just S of A212 roundabout; CR6 9PH Long 16th-c country dining pub with lots of small rooms; beams, flagstones and open fires, tasty food from home-made classics up (order at the bar), four real ales including Brakspears; children and well behaved dogs welcome, picnic-sets and stone bear on front terrace, sizeable back garden with pond and summer weekend 'burger shack', open all day, food till 7.30pm Sun. *(Jim and Sue James)*

FRIDAY STREET TQ1245
Stephan Langton (01306) 730775
Off B2126; RH5 6JR Refurbished 1930s pub prettily placed in tucked-away hamlet; good imaginative food from sandwiches up (all day Sat, till 4pm Sun), well kept local Tillingbourne beers and guests, nice wines and fine gin selection, afternoon teas (must book), efficient friendly service; children and dogs (in bar and snug) welcome, wooded setting with pond, good nearby walks, closed Mon (except bank holidays), otherwise open all day (till 7pm Sun). *(Glen Locke)*

GODALMING SU9643
Star (01483) 417717
Church Street; GU7 1EL Friendly 17th-c local in pedestrianised cobbled street; cosy low-beamed and panelled L-shaped bar, up to 15 well kept ales (some tapped from the cask) and extensive range of ciders/perries, enjoyable food including range of burgers (only bar snacks in the evening), more modern back room; Sun quiz, Mon folk session from 9pm, regular beer/cider festivals; heated terrace behind, open all day. *(Dave Chapman)*

GRAYSWOOD SU9134
Wheatsheaf (01428) 644440
Grayswood Road (A286 NE of Haslemere); GU27 2DE Welcoming family-run dining pub with light airy décor; enjoyable freshly made food in bar or restaurant, good range of well kept beers, friendly helpful staff; occasional live music, quiz first Tues of month, free wi-fi; children and dogs welcome, disabled access, front verandah and side terrace, six bedrooms in extension, good breakfast, open all day Sun till 7pm. *(Gerry and Pam Pollard)*

GUILDFORD SU9950
Stoke (01483) 504296
Stoke Road; GU1 4JN Popular Greene King pub with good choice of drinks and enjoyable reasonably priced food including burgers, fajitas and stone-baked pizzas, plenty of deals, friendly helpful service; quiz nights, sports TV, pool; children and dogs welcome, disabled facilities, seats on side terrace, refundable car parking fee, open (and food) all day. *(Adam Bellinger, Tony Scott)*

GUILDFORD SU9949
White House (01483) 302006
High Street; GU2 4AJ Modernised Fullers pub in pretty waterside setting; their ales and good range of wines, fair-priced food from small plates up, sizeable bar with conservatory, upstairs rooms and roof terrace; children welcome, a few picnic-sets out by River Wey, open (and food) all day. *(Mike Benton)*

HASCOMBE TQ0039
White Horse (01483) 208258
B2130 S of Godalming; GU8 4JA Spacious renovated pub with 16th-c origins; four well kept ales including Otter, decent wines by the glass and good food from traditional choices up, friendly efficient staff, scrubbed tables and pews in beamed bar, some old black and white photographs and farming memorabilia, various other linked rooms including smart pitched ceiling restaurant (separate more upmarket menu); children and dogs welcome in some parts, small front terrace and attractive back garden, pretty village with duck pond, good walks and handy for Winkworth Arboretum (NT), open all day. *(Colin Swift)*

HEADLEY TQ2054
Cock (01372) 377258
Church Lane; KT18 6LE Relaxed opened-up country pub in same group as the Queens Head at East Clandon and the Duke of Cambridge at Tilford; light modern interior (parts date from the 18th c) with open fires and comfortable seating, enjoyable food (all day weekends) from lunchtime sandwiches and sharing plates. up, set lunch Mon-Thurs, a house beer (Red Mist) and a couple of guests, plenty of wines by the glass from interesting list and some local gins; free wi-fi; children and dogs (in one area) welcome, disabled access using lift from upper car park, terrace picnic-sets under parasols, attractive setting and good woodland walks, open all day. *(Geoff and Ann Marston)*

HORSELL   SU9959
★ **Red Lion** (01483) 768497
High Street; GU21 4SS Spacious popular
pub with airy split-level bar, comfortable
sofas and easy chairs on wood flooring,
clusters of pictures on cream-painted walls,
Fullers London Pride and a couple of guests
from long wooden servery, a dozen wines by
the glass and good range of other drinks, well
liked bistro-style food served by friendly staff,
back dining rooms; newspapers and free
wi-fi; children allowed till 8pm, attractive
tree-sheltered terrace, steps up to garden
with picnic-sets and shelter, good local walks,
open (and food) all day. *(Jim and Sue James)*

HORSELL COMMON   TQ0160
Sands at Bleak House
(01483) 756988 *Chertsey Road, The
Anthonys; A320 Woking–Ottershaw;
GU21 5NL* Smart contemporary pub-
restaurant on edge of Horsell Common;
grey sandstone floor (and bar front), brown
leather sofas and cushioned stools, two
dining rooms with dark wood furniture,
woodburners, good well presented food (can
be pricey), Hogs Back and Sharps, friendly
attentive uniformed staff; background music,
TV, free wi-fi; children welcome, dogs in
courtyard only, good shortish walk to sandpits
that inspired H G Wells's *The War of the
Worlds*, seven bedrooms, open all day (till
6pm Sun). *(Charlie)*

LALEHAM   TQ0568
★ **Three Horseshoes** (01784) 455014
Shepperton Road (B376); TW18 1SE
Bustling dining pub near pleasant stretch
of the Thames with several interconnecting
rooms; bar with white walls and contrasting
deep blue woodwork, easy-going mix
of tables and chairs on bare boards,
woodburner fronted by armchairs and
squashy sofa, well kept Fullers/Gales
beers and plenty of wines by the glass,
highly regarded food (booking advised)
from sandwiches and sharing plates up,
efficient friendly young staff, dining areas
with assorted tables and chairs, pictures
and mirrors on grey walls; soft background
music, free wi-fi; children welcome till 8pm,
attractive flagstoned terrace, picnic-sets on
grass, open (and food) all day. *(Simon Collett-
Jones, Hunter and Christine Wright)*

LEIGH   TQ2147
★ **Seven Stars** (01306) 611254
*Dawes Green, south of A25 Dorking–
Reigate; RH2 8NP* Attractive tile-hung
country dining pub; comfortable beamed and
flagstoned bar with traditional furnishings
and inglenook, Fullers, Harveys, Sharps
and Youngs from glowing copper counter,
several wines by the glass and enjoyable
sensibly priced food, plainer public bar and
sympathetic restaurant extension where
children allowed; dogs welcome in bar areas,

plenty of outside seating, open all day, food
all day Sat, till 6pm Sun. *(Dave Chapman)*

LIMPSFIELD   TQ4053
Bull (01883) 713469
High Street; RH8 0DR Old red-brick
village pub recently bought and refurbished
by the local community; stylish décor with
modern artwork, mirrors etc on deep blue
walls, banquettes and other comfortable
seating on wood-strip floors, nice open
fire, good often imaginative food (not Sun
evening) from sharing boards up including
set menu, three changing ales, craft beers
and well chosen wines from marble-topped
counter; children and dogs (in bar) welcome,
tables out on back deck under heated
parasols, closed Mon, otherwise open all
day (till 8pm Sun). *(George Todd)*

MARTYRS GREEN   TQ0857
Black Swan (01932) 862364
*Handy for M25 junction 10; off A3
S-bound, but return N of junction;
KT11 1NG* Spacious country dining pub
with contemporary décor (utterly changed
from its days as the 'Slaughtered Lamb' in
the movie *An American Werewolf in London*);
good freshly made food from sandwiches and
pub favourites up, fine choice of wines and
champagnes, real ales such as Greene King
IPA, Surrey Hills Shere Drop and Timothy
Taylors Landlord, friendly efficient service,
log fire and underfloor heating; background
music; children and dogs (in bar) welcome,
plenty of outside tables, summer barbecues,
open (and food) all day. *(Smith Paul)*

MICKLEHAM   TQ1753
King William IV (01372) 372590
*Just off A24 Leatherhead–Dorking;
Byttom Hill; RH5 6EL* Steps up to small
pub tucked away from the main road; well
kept Hogs Back TEA, Surrey Hills Shere Drop
and a guest, enjoyable food from lunchtime
sandwiches to blackboard specials, friendly
attentive service, pleasant outlook from
cosy plank-panelled front bar, carpeted
dining area with grandfather clock and log
fire; background music, live summer jazz
outside (Sun 4.30-7.30pm); children and dogs
welcome, plenty of tables in pretty terraced
garden (some in open-sided timber shelters),
lovely valley views, open (and food) all day.
(Colin Swift)

MOGADOR   TQ2453
Sportsman (01737) 246655
*From M25 up A217 past second
roundabout, then Mogador signed;
KT20 7ES* Modernised and extended
low-ceilinged pub on edge of Walton Heath
(originally a 16th-c royal hunting lodge);
well kept ales including Sharps and Youngs,
good food from interesting varied menu,
restaurant with raised section; free wi-fi;
children welcome (no pushchairs), dogs in
bar, seats out on common, front verandah

and back lawn, popular with walkers and riders, open (and food) all day. *(Mary and Douglas McDowell)*

OCKLEY   TQ1337
Punchbowl (01306) 627249
Oakwood Hill, signed off A29 S; RH5 5PU Attractive 16th-c tile-hung country pub with slabby Horsham stone roof; enjoyable good value pubby food, Fullers HSB, London Pride and a couple of guests, central bar with flagstones and low beams, inglenook log fire decorated with horsebrasses, carpeted restaurant on the left, second bar to the right; quiz first Weds of month; children and dogs welcome, picnic-sets in pretty garden, quiet spot with good walks including Sussex Border Path, open all day. *(Helena and Trevor Fraser)*

OUTWOOD   TQ3246
★ **Bell** (01342) 842989
Outwood Common, just E of village; off A23 S of Redhill; RH1 5PN Attractive 17th-c extended dining pub; smartly rustic beamed bar with oak and elm furniture (some Jacobean in style), soft lighting, low beams and vast stone inglenook, Fullers London Pride, ESB and a guest, 20 wines by the glass and wide range of spirits, popular food from pub standards to good fresh fish (best to book, especially evenings when drinking-only space limited); background music, free wi-fi; children and dogs (in bar) welcome, disabled access, well maintained garden looking out past pine trees to rolling fields, open all day, food all day weekends. *(Tony Scott)*

OUTWOOD   TQ3146
Dog & Duck (01342) 844552
Prince of Wales Road; turn off A23 at station sign in Salfords, S of Redhill – OS Sheet 187 map reference 312460; RH1 5QU Relaxed beamed country pub with enjoyable fairly priced home-made food in bar or large two-part restaurant, four well kept Badger ales and good range of wines, friendly helpful service; children and dogs (in bar) welcome, sizeable garden with raised deck, fenced duck pond and play area (also circuit for motorised kids' jeeps), open all day (till 9pm Sun). *(Liz and Martin Eldon)*

OXTED   TQ4048
Grumpy Mole (01883) 722207
Caterfield Lane, Staffhurst Wood, S of town; RH8 0RR Popular and welcoming country pub refurbished a couple of years ago; Greene King ales (including one badged for them), a guest beer and lots of wines by the glass, good food from sandwiches and pub staples up, afternoon teas, friendly obliging service, well divided bar and dining areas, open fire; children and dogs welcome, rattan-style furniture on paved terrace, picnic-sets on lawn, lovely views across fields, open all day. *(Charlie)*

PUTTENHAM   SU9347
Good Intent (01483) 810387
Signed off B3000 just S of A31 junction; The Street/Seale Lane; GU3 1AR Convivial beamed village local with big log fire in cosy front bar, alcove seating, some old farming tools and photographs of the pub, Timothy Taylors, Hogs Back and guests, reasonably priced traditional food (not Sun evening, Mon) from sandwiches up, parquet-floored dining area; darts, free wi-fi; well behaved children and dogs welcome, small sunny garden, good walks, open all day weekends. *(Jeff Davies)*

REDHILL   TQ2749
Plough (01737) 766686
Church Road, St Johns; RH1 6QE Popular early 17th-c pub with warm friendly local atmosphere; lots of bits and pieces to look at including copper and brass hanging from beamed ceiling, nice open fire, Fullers London Pride and three guests, enjoyable sensibly priced blackboard food (not Sun evening), good helpful service; Weds quiz; no under-10s inside, dogs welcome, back garden with covered area (barbecues and spit roasts), open all day. *(Gail and Frank Hackett)*

REIGATE   TQ2349
Black Horse (01737) 230010
West Street (A25); RH2 9JZ Popular and welcoming White Brasserie pub; emphasis on their highly regarded food including some pub favourites and set menu (Mon-Sat till 6.30pm), engaging professional service, well kept ales such as Harveys, Sharps and Timothy Taylors, over 20 wines by the glass and good selection of other drinks, modern flagstoned bar area and good-sized dining extension; children and dogs welcome, disabled access, tables on paved terrace and lawn, nice spot by heathland, open (and food) all day. *(Martin Day)*

REIGATE HEATH   TQ2349
★ **Skimmington Castle** (01737) 243100
Off A25 Reigate–Dorking via Flanchford Road and Bonny's Road; RH2 8RL Nicely located small country pub with emphasis on good home-made food from baguettes up (can get very busy and best to book), well kept Harveys, St Austell and a couple of guests, a dozen wines by the glass, friendly efficient service, snug beamed and panelled rooms, log fires; children, dogs and muddy boots welcome, seats out on three sides (some heaters), open all day, food till 7.30pm Sun (9pm summer). *(Dave Chapman, Tony Scott)*

RIPLEY   TQ0456
Seven Stars (01483) 225128
Newark Lane (B367); GU23 6DL Neat 1930s pub with various snug areas; enjoyable food from varied menu, real ales such as Greene King, Fullers, Sharps and Shepherd

Neame, good wines and coffee, red patterned carpet, gleaming brasses and open fire; quiet background music; picnic-sets and heated wooden booths in well tended garden, river and canalside walks, closed Sun evening. *(Tony and Jill Radnor)*

ROWLEDGE SU8243
Hare & Hounds (01252) 792287
The Square; GU10 4AA Popular village pub with friendly welcoming atmosphere; good honest home cooking and four well kept ales including Greene King Ruddles County, smallish eating area; children and dogs welcome, garden with tables on terrace and play area, open all day, no food Sun evening. *(Tony and Jill Radnor)*

SEND TQ0156
New Inn (01483) 762736
Send Road, Cartbridge; GU23 7EN Traditional old beamed pub by River Wey Navigation; long bar and dining room, log fires, ales such as Adnams, Fullers, Hogs Back and Sharps, good choice of generously served food (all day weekends) from ciabattas to blackboard specials, friendly helpful service; quiz first Weds of month; children and dogs welcome, large waterside garden with moorings, open all day and can get very busy in summer. *(John Pritchard)*

SHACKLEFORD SU9345
Cyder House (01483) 810360
Peper Harow Lane; GU8 6AN Refurbished 1920s village pub in pleasant leafy setting; Badger ales, proper ciders/perry and nice selection of wines by the glass, good home-made food from lunchtime sandwiches and baked potatoes up, popular burger night Mon, airy linked areas around central servery, wood floors, log fire; quiz every other Mon, free wi-fi; children and dogs welcome, back terrace with steps up to play area, good walks, open all day (till 7pm Sun). *(Jim and Sue James)*

SHALFORD TQ0047
Queen Victoria (01483) 566959
Station Row; GU4 8BY Tile-hung, bay-windowed local with compact modernised interior around central bar, enjoyable reasonably priced food (not Sun evening, Mon) from lunchtime sandwiches up, smaller appetites catered for, well kept Otter and guests such as St Austell and Sharps, woodburner; quiz first and third Thurs of month, some live music, sports TV; well behaved children and dogs welcome, seats out at front and on back terrace, open all day. *(Tony Hobden)*

SHALFORD TQ0047
Seahorse (01483) 514351
A281 S of Guildford; The Street; GU4 8BU Gently upmarket Mitchells & Butlers dining pub with contemporary décor and comfortable relaxed atmosphere; wide range of food including vegan choices and set menu (from 6pm Tues, Weds), three well kept ales such as Hogs Back TEA and Sharps Doom Bar, good choice of wines and other drinks, cheerful young staff; children welcome, big garden with heated terraces, handy for Shalford Mill (NT), open (and food) all day. *(Richard Tilbrook)*

SHAMLEY GREEN TQ0343
Bricklayers Arms (01483) 898377
Guildford Road, S of the green; GU5 0UA Red-brick village pub with five well kept ales such as Harveys, Sharps and Surrey Hills, enjoyable pubby food (not Sun evening) including themed evenings, U-shaped layout (a couple of steps) with bare boards, carpets and flagstones, exposed brickwork and stripped wood, old local photographs, sofas by woodburner; quiz nights, pool, darts and TV; children and dogs welcome, a couple of picnic-sets out in front, more seats behind, open all day. *(Alison and Dan Richardson)*

SHEPPERTON TQ0866
Red Lion (01932) 244526
Russell Road; TW17 9HX In nice position across from Thames; bistro-style renovation (oldest part a pub since the 18th c), good well presented food from varied regularly changing menu (can be pricey), Sat brunch and popular Sun lunch, Fullers London Pride and local Thames Side White Swan from well stocked bar, afternoon teas, friendly staff; children and dogs welcome, modern furniture on fenced front terrace, more seats over road on riverside deck, open all day. *(Jeff Davies)*

SHERE TQ0747
White Horse (01483) 202518
Shere Lane; signed off A25 3 miles E of Guildford; GU5 9HS Splendid Chef & Brewer with several rooms off small bar; uneven floors, massive beams and timbers, Tudor stonework, oak wall seats and two log fires (one in huge inglenook), interesting range of enjoyable food including deals, Greene King IPA and a couple of guests, Weston's cider and plenty of wines by the glass, good, friendly service; children and dogs (in bar) welcome, seats out at front and in big garden behind, beautiful Tudor-set village, open (and food) all day. *(Tony Scott)*

STAINES TQ0371
Bells (01784) 454240
Church Street; TW18 4ZB Comfortable and sociable Youngs pub in old part of town by St Mary's church; their well kept ales and a guest, decent choice of wines and good food (not Sun evening) from pub standards up, attentive friendly service, central fireplace; sports TV; dogs allowed in bar, disabled access, tables in nice back garden with heated terrace, limited roadside parking, open all day. *(Mike Benton)*

STOKE D'ABERNON TQ1259

★**Old Plough** (01932) 862244

Station Road, off A245; KT11 3BN
Popular attractively updated 300-year-old
pub; good freshly made food including daily
specials, Fullers beers, a couple of guests
and plenty of wines by the glass, competent
friendly staff, restaurant with various knick-
knacks; newspapers and free wi-fi; children
(not in bar after 7pm) and dogs welcome,
seats out under pergola and in pretty garden,
open (and food) all day. *(George Todd)*

TADWORTH TQ2355

★**Dukes Head** (01737) 812173

*Dorking Road (B2032 opposite common
and woods); KT20 5SL* Welcoming 19th-c
pub, roomy and comfortably modernised,
with popular generously served food from
varied menu (booking advised), five well
kept ales including Fullers, Youngs and a
Morlands house beer (KT20), Aspall's cider,
good choice of wines by the glass, helpful
friendly staff, three dining areas and two big
inglenook log fires; background music, Weds
quiz; children welcome (no highchairs),
dogs in some areas, lots of hanging baskets
and plenty of tables in well tended terraced
garden, open (and food) all day, till 8pm
(6.30pm) Sun. *(Helena and Trevor Fraser)* .

THAMES DITTON TQ1667

Red Lion (020) 8398 8662

High Street; KT7 0SF Refurbished under
welcoming new management; enjoyable
freshly made food from traditional favourites
up including range of sharing dishes, a
beer named for the pub and a guest such as
Twickenham, plenty of wines by the glass,
cocktails, servery made from reclaimed
doors, colander lampshades overhead, mix
of seating on bare boards, open fires, back
dining conservatory with smart high-backed
chairs on grey tartan carpet; some live
music; children welcome, enclosed split-level
terrace, open (and food) all day. *(Gail and
Frank Hackett)*

THURSLEY SU9039

Three Horseshoes (01252) 703268

*Dye House Road, just off A3 SW of
Godalming; GU8 6QD* Pretty tile-hung
pub owned by village consortium; convivial
beamed front bar with log fire, ales such
as Hogs Back TEA and several wines by the
glass, good food (not Sun evening) from
pubby choice up, friendly helpful staff,
restaurant and small shop; children, walkers
and dogs welcome, attractive two-acre
garden with nice views over common and
Saxon church, play fort, open all day, till
9pm Sun. *(Tony and Jill Radnor)*

TILFORD SU8742

Duke of Cambridge (01252) 792236

Tilford Road; GU10 2DD Refurbished
dining pub in same small group as the

Queens Head at East Clandon, Stag at
Eashing and Wheatsheaf at Farnham; nice
food from varied menu including gluten-free
and children's choices, good selection of
wines and gins (some local), well kept ales
such as Hogs Back and Surrey Hills along
with a Tilford craft beer (brewed on-site),
helpful service; May charity music festival;
children and dogs welcome, terrace and
garden with outside bar/grill, good play area,
open all day, food all day Sun. *(John and
Bernadette Elliott, Patric Curwen)*

VIRGINIA WATER SU9968

Rose & Olive Branch

(01344) 843713 *Callow Hill; GU25 4LH*
Cosy unpretentious red-brick pub with good
choice of nicely presented food including
speciality pies and several vegetarian and
gluten-free options, two Greene King ales
and a guest, decent wines, friendly busy
staff; background music; children and dogs
welcome, tables on front terrace and in
garden behind, good walks, open (and food)
all day weekends. *(Nick and Meriel Cox)*

WALLISWOOD TQ1138

Scarlett Arms (01306) 627243

*Signed from Ewhurst–Rowhook back
road, or off A29 S of Ockley; RH5 5RD*
Cottagey 16th-c village pub; low beams,
two log fires (one in big inglenook) and
simple furniture on flagstones, well kept
Badger ales and enjoyable reasonably priced
food (not Sun evening), friendly prompt
service, various smaller rooms off main bar;
background music, darts; children and dogs
welcome, tables out at front and in garden
under parasols, play area, good walks, closed
Mon lunchtime, otherwise open all day.
(Geoff and Ann Marston)

WARLINGHAM TQ3955

Botley Hill Farmhouse

(01959) 577154 *S on Limpsfield Road
(B269); CR6 9QH* 16th-c country pub
set high on the North Downs; low-ceilinged
linked rooms up and down steps, fresh
flowers and candles, popular locally sourced
food from sandwiches and pub standards
up (till 7pm Sun, booking advised), own
Titsey beers from on-site microbrewery
plus a couple of guests such as Pilgrim and
Westerham tapped from the cask (tasters
offered), a dozen wines by the glass, good
friendly service, big log fire in one room, tea
room selling local produce; children and dogs
welcome, disabled access, terrace and garden
with far-reaching rural views, good local
walks, open all day, Sun breakfast from 9am.
(Jim and Sue James)

WEST CLANDON TQ0451

★**Bulls Head** (01483) 222444

A247 SE of Woking; GU4 7ST
Comfortably old-fashioned village pub based
around 1540s timbered hall-house; enjoyable
good value pubby food (not Sun evening)

including proper home-made pies, friendly helpful staff, Youngs ales and guests, small lantern-lit beamed front bar with open fire, some stripped brickwork, old local prints and bric-a-brac, simple raised back inglenook dining area, games room (darts and pool); children and dogs welcome, disabled access from car park, play area in neat little garden, nice walks, open all day Sun. *(Liz and Martin Eldon)*

WEST CLANDON   TQ0452

Onslow Arms (01483) 222447

A247 SE of Woking; GU4 7TE Busy modernised pub with heavily beamed rambling rooms leading away from central bar; wooden dining chairs and tables on wide floorboards, painted panelling, all sorts of copper implements, hunting horns and pictures, leather chesterfields in front of open fire, four real ales including Surrey Hills and a beer named for the pub, 20 wines by the glass, good popular food from lunchtime sandwiches, sharing boards and traditional choices up; live music first Weds of month, TV, daily papers and free wi-fi; children (till early evening) and dogs (in bar) welcome, pretty courtyard garden with tables under parasols, open (and food) all day. *(Kirsty, Mrs P Sumner, Christopher and Elise Way)*

WEST HORSLEY   TQ0853

Barley Mow (01483) 282693

Off A246 Leatherhead–Guildford at Bell & Colvill garage roundabout; The Street; KT24 6HR Welcoming beamed village pub with well kept ales such as Fullers and Surrey Hills, decent wines and good thai food (not Sun) along with more conventional lunchtime menu, log fires, barn function room; background music; children and dogs (in bar) welcome, spacious garden, open all day. *(Mary and Douglas McDowell)*

WEST HORSLEY   TQ0752

King William IV (01483) 282318

The Street; KT24 6BG Comfortable and welcoming early 19th-c village pub; low entrance door to front and side bars, beams, flagstones and log fire, back conservatory restaurant, good variety of food (not Sun evening) including gluten-free menu, five real ales such as Courage and Surrey Hills; background and occasional live music, quiz nights, free wi-fi; children and dogs welcome, disabled access, small sunny garden with deck and play area, good for walkers, open all day. *(Colin Swift)*

WEYBRIDGE   TQ0765

Old Crown (01932) 842844

Thames Street; KT13 8LP Comfortably old-fashioned three-bar pub dating from the 17th c; good value traditional food

(not Sun-Tues evenings) from sandwiches to fresh fish, Courage, Youngs and a guest kept well, good choice of wines by the glass, friendly efficient service, family lounge and conservatory; dogs welcome, secluded terrace, steps down to suntrap garden overlooking Wey/Thames confluence, mooring for small boats, open all day. *(Charlie)*

WEYBRIDGE   TQ0664

Queens Head (01932) 839820

Bridge Road; KT13 8XS 18th-c pub owned by Raymond Blanc's White Brasserie Company; good food from open kitchen including well priced lunchtime/early evening set menu (not Sun), also a proper bar serving real ales and plenty of wines by the glass, friendly staff; soft background music, newspapers; children welcome, tables out on small front terrace, open (and food) all day. *(Charlie, George Todd)*

WINDLESHAM   SU9264

Bee (01276) 479244

School Road; GU20 6PD Cosy village pub with good food from sandwiches and traditional favourites up including steaks cooked on a hot stone, four well kept ales and decent wines by the glass, friendly accommodating staff, bar area with painted panelling and open fire in small brick fireplace, back dining room; TV; children and dogs (in bar) welcome, picnic-sets on small front terrace and in garden behind with play area, open all day, no food Sun evening. *(Dr Martin Owton)*

WITLEY   SU9439

White Hart (01428) 683695

Petworth Road; GU8 5PH Picture-book beamed Tudor pub; well kept St Austell Tribute, Youngs Bitter and a guest, craft beers, plenty of wines by the glass and extensive range of whiskies, popular food including signature home-smoked/chargrilled dishes, friendly accommodating staff, bar, restaurant and cosy panelled snug with inglenook (where George Eliot used to drink); children and dogs welcome, seats on cobbled terrace and in garden, nice walks nearby, open (and food) all day, till 6pm (4pm) Sun. *(Jestyn Phillips)*

WONERSH   TQ0145

Grantley Arms (01483) 893351

The Street; GU5 0PE Popular 16th-c village pub; opened-up beamed and timbered bar with mix of new and old furniture on light wood floor, a couple of steps up to long pitched-roof dining area, four real ales and interesting wine list, good well presented food from lunchtime sandwiches up, former bakery for private dining, friendly accommodating young staff; occasional live music and quiz nights, daily newspapers,

---

It's very helpful if you let us know up-to-date food prices when you report on pubs.

free wi-fi; children welcome till 7.30pm, dogs in bar, wheelchair access using ramp, attractive paved terrace, open (and food) all day. *(Hunter and Christine Wright, Adam Bellinger)*

WOOD STREET SU9550
Royal Oak (01483) 235137
Oak Hill; GU3 3DA 1920s red-brick village local; up to six well kept ales and good value traditional home-made food (not Sun evening, Mon), friendly staff; music and quiz nights, free wi-fi; children and dogs welcome, decent sized back garden with play area, open all day Fri-Sun, closed Mon lunchtime. *(Jim and Sue James)*

WORPLESDON SU9854
Jolly Farmer (01483) 235897
Burdenshott Road, off A320 Guildford–Woking, not in village; GU3 3RN Old Fullers pub in pleasant country setting; their well kept ales in beamed and flagstoned bar with small log fire, enjoyable fairly traditional food from lunchtime sandwiches up, bare-boards dining extension under pitched roof; background music, free wi-fi; children welcome and dogs (theirs is called Tyson), garden with parasol-shaded tables and pergola, open all day (till 9pm Sun). *(Gail and Frank Hackett)*

WRECCLESHAM SU8344
Bat & Ball (01252) 792108
Bat & Ball Lane, South Farnham; approach from Sandrock Hill and Upper Bourne Lane, then narrow steep lane to pub; GU10 4SA Fairly traditional pub tucked away in hidden valley; enjoyable food (all day weekends) from interestingly varied menu, special diets catered for, six well kept local ales and plenty of wines by the glass; live music including open mike last Thurs of month and June beer/music festival, charity quiz Tues, free wi-fi; children and dogs welcome, disabled facilities, attractive terrace with vine arbour, more tables and substantial play fort in garden, open all day and can get very busy in summer. *(Tony and Jill Radnor)*

WRECCLESHAM SU8244
Royal Oak (01252) 728319
The Street; GU10 4QS Buoyant 17th-c black-beamed village local; enjoyable good value home-made food (smaller helpings available for some main courses), steak night Weds, burgers Thurs, three well kept Greene King ales, friendly helpful staff, log fire; Sun quiz, sports TV, darts; children and dogs welcome, large garden with play area, open all day. *(Tony and Jill Radnor)*

Sussex

KEY ★ Star Pub 🍽 Top Quality Food 🍺 Great Beer
🍷 Good Wines £ Bargain Meals 🛏 Good Bedrooms 🍴 Serves Food

ALFRISTON
George 🍷
(01323) 870319 ~ www.thegeorge-alfriston.com

High Street; BN26 5SY

TQ5203 Map 3

Venerable 14th-c timbered inn with comfortable, heavily beamed bars, good wines and several real ales; bedrooms

If you want a walk before lunch you have two long-distance paths (the South Downs Way and Vanguard Way) to choose from, and the quietly beautiful Cuckmere Haven is nearby. There's a great deal of character here and the long bar, dominated by a huge stone inglenook fireplace with a winter log fire (or summer flower arrangement), has massive hop-hung low beams, settles and chairs around sturdy stripped tables, soft lighting and lots of copper and brass. Greene King Abbot and Old Speckled Hen, Dark Star Hophead and a guest beer on handpump, 16 wines by the glass (including champagne and a pudding wine) and 25 gins served by friendly staff; background music and board games. The lounge has comfortable sofas, standing timbers and rugs on the wooden floor, and the restaurant is cosy and candlelit. There are seats in the spacious flint-walled garden, and the beamed bedrooms are comfortable. There's no car park but you can park a couple of minutes away. This is a lovely village.

🍴 Quite a choice of all-day food includes sandwiches, ham hock terrine with apple chutney, garlic and rosemary-studded camembert with toasted ciabatta, sharing boards, vegetarian burger with hummus and sweet chilli sauce, confit duck leg with creamy bacon, lentils and honey, chicken, leek and mushroom pie, pork belly with bubble and squeak and red cabbage, hake fillet with prawn and white wine sauce, and puddings such as crème brûlée and crumble of the day with custard. *Benchmark main dish: lamb shank with dauphinoise potatoes and red wine and mint sauce £17.50. Two-course evening meal £22.00.*

Greene King ~ Lease Roland and Cate Couch ~ Real ale ~ Open 11-11; 12-11 Sat, Sun ~ Bar food 12-9 ~ Restaurant ~ Children welcome ~ Dogs welcome ~ Wi-fi ~ Bedrooms: £75/£110
Recommended by Chantelle and Tony Redman, Kerry and Guy Trooper, Tina and Steven Hobden, Adam and Betty Lawrence, Tony Scott

---

Please keep sending us reports. We rely on readers for news of new discoveries, and particularly for news of changes – however slight – at the fully described pubs: feedback@goodguides.com, or (no stamp needed) Freepost THE GOOD PUB GUIDE, Random House Publishing, 20 Vauxhall Bridge Road, London SW1V 2SA.

BOLNEY   TQ2623   Map 2

Bolney Stage 🍷 🍺

(01444) 881200 – www.brunningandprice.co.uk/bolneystage

London Road, off old A23 just N of A272; RH17 5RL

Historic pub of much character with plenty of drinking and dining space, lots to look at, a wide choice of drinks and interesting food and seats outside

Handy for the Bluebell Railway and Sheffield Park (National Trust), this sizeable 16th-c black and white pub has been gently refurbished by Brunning & Price. The bar and dining rooms are interconnected by open doorways and standing timbers to create separate areas that share the same bustling, friendly and informal atmosphere: heavy beams, assorted flooring including polished flagstones, old brickwork, bare boards and carpet (often topped with rugs), a two-way open log fire, and wooden stools against a rustic bar counter. Throughout there are handsome antique chairs, some cushioned and some leather, a medley of solid tables, lots of prints, portraits and mirrors on pale contemporary paintwork, elegant metal chandeliers and numerous house plants. St Austell Brunning & Price Traditional Bitter, Harveys Old Ale, Long Man Best Bitter, Timothy Taylors Landlord on handpump, 16 wines by the glass and 38 gins. Staff are efficient and cheerful; background music. There are seats and tables on terraces and under a gazebo, a fire pit and picnic-sets on a lawn; also, a play tractor and an equipped play area for children.

Good, up-to-date food includes sandwiches, tandoori king prawns, garlic and rosemary-studded camembert with walnut and apple salad, aubergine, potato and okra curry with coconut rice, moroccan lamb salad with feta, couscous and red pepper coulis, chicken breast with truffle arancini, wild mushrooms, celeriac cream and madeira sauce, smoked haddock, cod, king prawn, mussel and bacon chowder with sweetcorn dumplings, venison rump with dauphinoise potates and blackberry jus, and puddings such as rhubarb and ginger trifle and triple chocolate brownie with chocolate sauce. *Benchmark main dish: salmon, smoked haddock and prawn pie with french-style peas £14.95. Two-course evening meal £21.00.*

Brunning & Price ~ Manager Mark Lavis ~ Real ale ~ Open 11-11; 11-10.30 Sun ~ Bar food 12-9; 12-9.30 Fri, Sat ~ Restaurant ~ Children welcome ~ Dogs allowed in bar ~ Wi-fi
Recommended by Jenny and Michael Clarke, Mrs P R Sykes, Tony Scott, Louise and Anton Parsons, Margaret McDonald, Sally and Lance Oldham

CHARLTON   SU8812   Map 2

Fox Goes Free 🍷

(01243) 811461 – www.thefoxgoesfree.com

Village signposted off A286 Chichester–Midhurst in Singleton, also from Chichester–Petworth via East Dean; PO18 0HU

400-year-old pub with beamed bars, popular food and drink and big garden; bedrooms

Race-goers (Goodwood is nearby) and walkers enjoy this bustling little pub but it might be wise to book a table in advance. The bar, the first of several cosy separate rooms, has old irish settles, tables and chapel chairs and an open fire. Standing timbers divide up a larger beamed bar with a huge brick fireplace and old local photographs on the walls. A dining area overlooks the garden. A family extension is cleverly converted from horse boxes and the stables where the 1926 Goodwood winner was once housed; board games and background music. They keep a beer named for the pub (from Arundel) and guests such as Fownes Smokestack Lightning and Greene King Scrum Down on handpump, 15 wines by the glass, quite a few gins and Addlestone's cider. An attractive back garden has picnic-sets under apple trees and the South Downs as a backdrop, and there are rustic benches and tables on the gravelled front terrace too. The charming, country-style bedrooms are comfortable and breakfasts well thought-of. Disabled ramps available. You can walk up to Levin Down nature reserve, or stroll around the Iron Age hill fort on the Trundle with huge views to the Isle of Wight; the Weald & Downland Living Museum and West Dean Gardens are nearby too.

A wide choice of food includes lunchtime sandwiches (not Sunday), garlic and rosemary-studded baked camembert with red onion marmalade, moules marinière, vegetarian risotto of the day, pork and leek sausages with mash and red wine and mushroom sauce, salt marsh beef or garlic and herb-marinated chicken burgers with toppings, harissa mayonnaise and chips, slow-cooked pork belly with wholegrain mustard mash and apple cider sauce, and puddings such as lemon posset with lychee and pomegranate coulis and red velvet brownie with ice-cream. *Benchmark main dish: fish pie £14.50. Two-course evening meal £22.00.*

Free house ~ Licensee David Coxon ~ Real ale ~ Open 11-11; 11am-midnight Sat; 12-11 Sun ~ Bar food 12-5, 6.15-9.30; 12-10 Sat; 12-5, 6.15-9.30 Sun ~ Restaurant ~ Children welcome ~ Dogs allowed in bar ~ Wi-fi ~ Bedrooms: £80/£109 *Recommended by Susie and Spencer Gray, Simon Collett-Jones, Tim and Sue Mulligan, Tina and Steven Hobden, Martin Day, Ben and Diane Bowie, Kate Moran*

CHILGROVE

White Horse 🏵️ ♈ 🛏️

SU8214 Map 2

(01243) 519444 – www.thewhitehorse.co.uk

B2141 Petersfield–Chichester; PO18 9HX

Handsome coaching inn with a thoughtful choice of drinks, first class food and plenty of outside seating; bedrooms

Set in a lovely downland valley, this whitewashed inn is a gently civilised place for a drink or a meal. The bar area has a relaxed atmosphere, leather armchairs in front of a woodburning stove and daily papers on the light oak counter where friendly staff serve Tipsy Horse (named for the pub from Ringwood) plus Dark Star Hophead and Marstons 61 Deep on handpump and 18 good wines by the glass. Just off here, a room with leather button-back wall seats and mate's and other dark wooden dining chairs has all sorts of country knick-knacks: stuffed animals, china plates, riding boots, flower paintings, dog drawings, stone bottles and books on shelves. The dining room to the other side of the bar has a huge painting of a galloping white horse, a long suede wall banquette, high-backed settles creating stalls, elegant chairs, lots of mirrors and big metal chandeliers. Throughout, there are fat candles in lanterns, flagstones and coir carpet, beams and timbering, and animal skin throws; background music and board games. A two-level terrace has dark grey rattan-style seats around glass-topped tables under parasols among pretty flowering tubs; an area up steps has rustic benches and tables and there are picnic-sets on grass at the front. Each of the comfortable, contemporary and light bedrooms has a little private courtyard (two have a hot tub). Good surrounding walks.

Interesting food includes sandwiches, confit smoked trout, avocado and pumpkin seed salad, sautéed foie gras with blood orange and red wine jus, twice-baked cheese and walnut soufflé, burger with toppings, red cabbage slaw and fries, crispy confit pork belly with pickled pineapple salad, lamb rump with sweet potato dauphinoise and rosemary and olive jus, grilled lemon sole with gremolata and jersey royals, local rib-eye steak with onion rings and chips, and puddings such as After Eight cheesecake with chocolate ice-cream and rum pannacotta with plum compote. *Benchmark main dish: pie of the day £16.95. Two-course evening meal £23.00.*

Free house ~ Licensee Richard Miller ~ Real ale ~ Open 12-11 ~ Bar food 12-3, 6-9; 12-9.30 Sat; 12-8 Sun ~ Restaurant ~ Children welcome ~ Dogs allowed in bar and bedrooms ~ Wi-fi ~ Live jazz 2-4pm Sunday ~ Bedrooms: /£120 *Recommended by Katherine Matthews, Celia and Geoff Clay, Miss A E Dare, Tracey and Stephen Groves, Peter L Harrison, Mary and Douglas McDowell, Andrea and Philip Crispin*

COPTHORNE
Old House ♟ 🛏

TQ3240 Map 3

(01342) 718529 ~ www.theoldhouseinn.co.uk
B2037 NE of village; RH10 3JB

Charming old pub with plenty of character, real ales, enjoyable food and attentive staff; attractive bedrooms

If you're heading to or from Gatwick Airport, you might find the smartly comfortable bedrooms in a converted barn here rather useful. It's a higgledy-piggledy timbered building and you'll feel immediately welcomed on walking into the little entrance bar. There's a brown leather chesterfield sofa, armchairs and carved wooden chairs around all sorts of tables, a big sisal mat on flagstones, a decorative fireplace and nightlights. Courage Best, Ringwood Razorback and a guest beer on handpump, several good wines by the glass and a couple of huge glass flagons holding Sipsmith vodka and gin; staff are friendly and helpful. The nooks and crannies in the interconnected rooms leading off here are just as cosy. Off to the left is a charming small room with a woodburning stove in an inglenook fireplace and two leather armchairs in front, white-painted beams in a low ceiling (this is the oldest part, dating from the 16th c), cushioned settles and pre-war-style cushioned dining chairs around varying tables. A teeny back room, like something you'd find on an old galleon, has button-back wall seating up to the roof, a few chairs and heavy ropework. Dining rooms are beamed (some painted) and timbered with parquet, quarry tiles or sisal flooring, high-backed leather and other dining chairs, more wall seating and fresh flowers and candles; background music and board games. The terraced garden has heavy rustic tables and benches and a children's play area.

Rewarding food includes sausage and black pudding scotch egg with caramelised apple purée, smoked mackerel pâté with horseradish mayonnaise, red lentil and aubergine dhal with poppadoms and basmati rice, a pie of the day, corn-fed chicken breast with dauphinoise potatoes, wild mushrooms and pink peppercorn sauce, venison haunch with fondant potato, romanesco, parsnip purée and red wine jus, and puddings such as warm chocolate brownie with salted caramel ice-cream and Baileys panettone bread and butter pudding with crème anglaise; they also offer afternoon tea (1.30-5.30pm; bookings only). *Benchmark main dish: sea bream fillets with fennel, rösti potato and caviar cream sauce £18.00. Two-course evening meal £21.00.*

Free house ~ Licensee Robbie Higgs ~ Real ale ~ Open 11-11; 12-10.30 Sun ~ Bar food 12-3, 6-9 (9.30 Fri, Sat); 12-4, 6-8 Sun ~ Restaurant ~ Children welcome ~ Dogs welcome ~ Wi-fi ~ Bedrooms: /£110 *Recommended by Andrew and Michele Revell, R and M Thomas, Jonny and Andrew Haughton, Andrea and Laurie Grist, Jane and Philip Saunders, Jill and Dick Archer, Frank and Marcia Pelling*

If we know a featured-entry pub does sandwiches, we always say so – if they're not mentioned, you'll have to assume you can't get one.

DANEHILL

TQ4128   Map 3

Coach & Horses 🍴⭐ 🍷

(01825) 740369 – www.coachandhorses.co

Off A275, via School Lane towards Chelwood Common; RH17 7JF

Well run dining pub with bustling bars, a welcoming landlord, very good food and ales and sizeable garden

The highly regarded food draws in plenty of customers, but this pub also has a fine setting on the fringes of Ashdown Forest. The large garden is rather special too, with an adults-only terrace beneath a huge maple, picnic-sets and a children's play area on lawns and views of the South Downs. The little bar to the right has half-panelled walls, simple furniture on polished floorboards, a woodburner in a brick fireplace and a big hatch to the bar counter: Harveys Best and Long Man Best Bitter on handpump, local Black Pig farmhouse cider and eight wines by the glass including prosecco and Bluebell sparkling wine from Sussex. A couple of steps lead down to a half-panelled area with a mix of dining chairs around characterful wooden tables (set with flowers and candles) on a fine brick floor, and changing artwork on the walls. Down another step is a dining area with stone walls, beams, flagstones and a woodburning stove.

🍴⭐ Top rated food includes sandwiches, crispy duck egg with butternut squash velouté and coriander oil, citrus-cured local scallops with pickled kohlrabi, vegetable hash with wilted spinach, poached egg and curried pumpkin velouté, local pork and herb sausages with mash and caramelised onions, sea bass with champ potato, fennel slaw and nduja butter, venison stew with braised red cabbage, tabbouleh and mint yoghurt, mackerel pasty with ratte potato salad and pickled fennel and cucumber, and puddings such as peanut butter pannacotta with frosted black sesame seeds and mango lime sorbet and apple and pear crumble with salted caramel ice-cream. *Benchmark main dish: calves liver and bacon with mash £15.00. Two-course evening meal £22.00.*

Free house ~ Licensee Ian Philpots ~ Real ale ~ Open 12-3, 5.30-11; 12-11 Sat; 12-10.30 Sun ~ Bar food 12-2, 6.30-9 (9.30 Fri); 12-2.30, 6.30-9.30 Sat; 12-3 Sun ~ Restaurant ~ Children welcome ~ Dogs allowed in bar ~ Wi-fi *Recommended by Robert and Diana Ringstone, Kate and Mark Foskett, Abigail Slater, Bridget and Peter Gregson, Rupert and Sandy Newton, Sally Harrison*

DIAL POST

TQ1519   Map 3

Crown 🍴⭐

(01403) 710902 – www.crown-inn-dialpost.co.uk

Worthing Road (off A24 S of Horsham); RH13 8NH

Tile-hung village pub with interesting food and a good mix of customers; bedrooms

Although many are here for the good, up-to-date food, there are always lots of chatty drinkers too. The bustling, beamed bar has a couple of standing timbers, brown squashy sofas, pine tables and chairs on the stone floor and a small woodburning stove in a brick fireplace. Greyhound Good Ordinary Bitter, Hammerpot Mosaic Pale and Long Man Best Bitter on handpump are served from the attractive herringbone brick counter, alongside a local cider, ten wines by the glass plus prosecco, champagne, interesting soft drinks and farm cider. To the right of the bar, the restaurant (with more beams) has an ornamental woodburner in a brick fireplace, a few photographs, chunky pine tables and chairs, a couple of cushioned pews and a shelf of books; steps lead down to an additional dining room;

background music and board games. The pub dog is called Chops. A new, straightforwardly furnished dining conservatory, facing the village green, is light and airy, and there are picnic-sets in the back garden.

The quickly changing menu, using the best local, seasonal produce, includes lunchtime sandwiches, crispy whitebait with curried mayonnaise, potted crayfish with fennel, cucumber and dill salad, macaroni and cheese fritter with goats cheese and tomato fondue, steak burger with toppings, coleslaw and chips, king scallops with crispy potatoes and café de paris butter, beer-battered haddock and chips, local venison loin with honey-roasted root vegetables, fondant potato and game jus, and puddings such as chocolate sponge with chocolate sauce and vanilla ice-cream and rhubarb crumble with custard. *Benchmark main dish: pie of the day £12.50. Two-course evening meal £20.00.*

Free house ~ Licensees James and Penny Middleton-Burn ~ Real ale ~ Open 12-3, 6-11; 12-4 Sun; closed Sun evening ~ Bar food 12-2, 6-9; 12-2, 6-9.30 Fri, Sat; 12-2.30 Sun ~ Restaurant ~ Children welcome unti 7pm unless dining ~ Dogs welcome ~ Wi-fi ~ Bedrooms: £51/£69 *Recommended by Elisabeth and Bill Humphries, Barbara and Phil Bowie, R and M Thomas, Martin Bailey, Martine and Derek Cotton, Tony Scott*

DUNCTON
Cricketers

SU9517   Map 3

(01798) 342473 – www.thecricketersduncton.co.uk
Set back from A285; GU28 0LB

Charming old coaching inn with real ales, popular food and suntrap back garden

If there's an event at nearby Goodwood, why not make a weekend of it and stay in the smart bedrooms in a converted barn; they're well equipped and comfortable and breakfasts are highly rated. The traditional bar has a display of cricketing memorabilia, a few standing timbers, simple seating and an open woodburning stove in an inglenook fireplace. Steps lead down to a dining room with farmhouse chairs around wooden tables. Flowerpots Bitter, Triple fff Moondance and a couple of guest beers on handpump, nine wines by the glass and three farm ciders; board games. There are picnic-sets out in front beneath the flowering window boxes and more on decked areas and under parasols on grass in the picturesque back garden. The pub got its present name from its 19th-c owner John Wisden, the cricketer who published the famous *Wisden Cricketers' Almanack*.

Well presented food includes lunchtime sandwiches, crab, prawn and leek gratin, oriental duck pancakes, mushroom, spinach and red onion pie, chicken caesar salad, haddock, prawn and crayfish fishcake, ham and eggs, lamb rump with dauphinoise potatoes and red wine and redcurrant sauce, katsu chicken curry, a trio of sausages with mash and onion gravy, 28-day aged sirloin steak with onion rings and chips, and puddings. *Benchmark main dish: steak and mushroom in ale pie £12.95. Two-course evening meal £19.00.*

Free house ~ Licensee Martin Boult ~ Real ale ~ Open 11-11; 12-10.30 Sun ~ Bar food 12-2.30, 6-9; 12-9 weekends; cream teas 2.30-6 ~ Children welcome ~ Dogs welcome ~ Wi-fi ~ Bedrooms: /£95 *Recommended by Chris and Sophie Baxter, Alexander and Trish Cutter, Richard and Tessa Ibbot, Charles Fraser*

Bedroom prices are for high summer. Even then you may get reductions for more than one night, or (outside tourist areas) weekends. Winter special rates are common, and many inns reduce bedroom prices if you have a full evening meal.

EARTHAM   SU9309 Map 2

George ♀ ◀

(01243) 814340 – www.thegeorgeeartham.com

Signed off A285 Chichester–Petworth, from Fontwell off A27, from Slindon off A29;
PO18 0LT

**170-year-old pub in tucked-away village with country furnishings
and contemporary touches, local ales and enjoyable food**

If you want to work up an appetite before a visit to this well run, friendly
place, there are some lovely walks and cycle routes in the surrounding
rolling South Downs. The light and prettily decorated bar has dining
chairs around wood-topped tables on parquet flooring, sofas, armchairs,
a dresser with country knick-knacks, paintings on cream-painted walls
above a grey-planked dado and stone bottles and books. The charming,
heavily beamed restaurant has high-backed grey tartan chairs and pale
settles on more floorboards, books on shelves and a huge metal wall clock;
background music and board games. In cold weather, three open fires keep
the pub warm. A beer named for the pub (from Otter) and guests from local
breweries such as Arundel, Goldmark, Gun, Hepworth and Langham on
handpump plus 40 craft beers, 13 wines by the glass, up to 40 gins, 20 malt
whiskies and farm cider. The large garden has picnic-sets on grass and seats
and tables under a gazebo. Easy disabled access.

Imaginative food includes sandwiches, spiced baby beetroot with goats cheese,
syrup-roasted radishes, carrot noodles, roasted pine nuts and lemon dressing,
chicken liver pâté with port and brandy and pear and apricot chutney, jackfruit and
chickpea curry with spring onion and pomegranate, a pie of the day, pork belly with
bubble and squeak, apple sauce, caper and sage butter and a duck egg, haddock fillet
with charred baby gem lettuce, silverskin onions, bacon, peas, broad beans and white
wine sauce, and puddings such as warm chocolate brownie with chocolate sauce and
ice-cream and fruit crumble of the day with custard. *Benchmark main dish:
beer-battered fish and chips £12.95. Two-course evening meal £19.00.*

Free house ~ Licensees James and Anita Thompson ~ Real ale ~ Open 11.30-11; 12-6 Sun;
closed Mon ~ Bar food 12-3, 6-9 (9.30 Fri, Sat); 12-4 Sun ~ Restaurant ~ Children welcome
~ Dogs welcome ~ Wi-fi *Recommended by Adam and Natalie Davis, Simon Collett-Jones, Colin
and Daniel Gibbs, Beverley and Andy Butcher, William and Natasha Pace, Isobel and Anthony
Mackinley, Cliff and Monica Swan*

EAST LAVANT   SU8608 Map 2

Royal Oak ◉ ♀ 🛏

(01243) 527434 – www.royaloakeastlavant.co.uk

Pook Lane, off A286; PO18 0AX

**Bustling dining pub with interesting food, a thoughtful wine list
and seats outside; stylish bedrooms**

There's a proper drinking area to the left of the door of this pretty
little white house. This has an open fire, a high, button-back wall seat
and wooden chairs around a few tables on stripped wooden boards and
stools against the brick counter where helpful, friendly staff keep Long
Man Copper Hop, Marstons Pedigree and a guest beer on handpump,
11 wines by the glass and a growing number of gins and malt whiskies;
background music, board games. The open-plan dining areas to the right
have crooked beams and are furnished with upholstered armchairs, red
button-back banquettes and cushioned wooden chairs around rustic tables
on a fine old brick floor; also, hunting scenes and mirrors on the walls and

a woodburning stove in one fireplace with a large lamp in another. An end room with green or black banquettes on floor tiles has a large wooden propeller from a World War I french fighter plane on a flint wall. There's a flagstoned front terrace with seats and tables underneath parasols and more seats on a stepped side terrace. The bedrooms are charming and up to date, and you can walk up a couple of steps to fields with a view of the church to the left. The car park is across the lane, where they also have a couple of self-catering cottages. Disabled access.

 The standard of food is high here: lunchtime sandwiches, pork and pistachio terrine with pickled beetroot, kiln-smoked salmon with pickled cucumber and horseradish crème fraîche, assiette of cauliflower with herbs and nut butter, beer-battered fish with triple-cooked chips, duck breast with crispy leg, blood orange and potato confit, lamb shoulder with smoked almond crust and kale and celeriac dauphinoise, 30-day aged steak with rösti chips and a choice of sauce, and puddings such as dark chocolate torte with blackcurrants and coconut and almond dumplings with rhubarb soup. *Benchmark main dish: burger with toppings and chips £15.50. Two-course evening meal £21.00.*

Free house ~ Licensee Szilard Szucs ~ Real ale ~ Open 10am-11pm ~ Bar food 12-2.30, 6-9; 12-3, 6.30-8.30 Sun ~ Restaurant ~ Children welcome ~ Dogs allowed in bar ~ Wi-fi ~ Bedrooms: $85/$120 *Recommended by Andrea and Laurie Grist, Jonny and Andrew Haughton, Dan and Anne Morgan, Charles and Cynthia Todd, Julia and Martin Swift*

ERIDGE GREEN
Nevill Crest & Gun ♀ 🍺

TQ5535 Map 3

(01892) 864209 – www.brunningandprice.co.uk/nevillcrestandgun
A26 Tunbridge Wells–Crowborough; TN3 9JR

Handsome old building with lots of character, plenty to look at, six real ales and enjoyable modern food

The clever renovations here have been done with great care and the original features of a 500-year-old farmhouse blend in well with modern touches and furnishings. The whole building has been opened up and extended with standing timbers and doorways keeping some sense of separate rooms. Throughout there are heavy beams (some carved), panelling, rugs on wooden floors and woodburning stoves and open fires in three fireplaces (the linenfold carved bressumer above one is worth seeking out). Also, all manner of individual dining chairs around dark wood or copper-topped tables, lots of pictures, maps and photographs relating to the local area, and windowsills crammed with toby jugs, stone and glass bottles and plants. St Austell Brunning & Price Traditional Bitter plus Harveys Best, Long Man Long Blonde and Old Man, Sambrooks Pumphouse Pale Ale and three quickly changing guests on handpump, 17 wines by the glass, 150 gins and 40 malt whiskies; board games and background music. At the front are some picnic-sets and on a back terrace – beside the airy, raftered dining extension – are plenty of good quality wooden tables and chairs.

An extensive choice of enterprising food includes sandwiches, seared mackerel fillet with beetroot relish, barbecue chicken wings, cauliflower, chickpea and sweet potato jalfrezi and almond pilaf rice, pork and leek sausages with mash and onion gravy, cod fillet with baby beetroot, asparagus and jersey royal potato salad with horseradish and lemon yoghurt, braised lamb shoulder with dauphinoise potatoes, carrot and swede mash and rosemary gravy, and puddings such as triple chocolate brownie with chocolate sauce and vanilla ice-cream and coconut pannacotta with exotic fruit salad and mango sorbet. *Benchmark main dish: crispy beef salad with sweet chilli sauce and cashews £13.95. Two-course evening meal £20.00.*

Brunning & Price ~ Manager Tom McGloin ~ Real ale ~ Open 11.30-11; 12-10.30 Sun ~
Bar food 12-9.30; 12-10 Fri, Sat; 12-9 Sun ~ Children welcome ~ Dogs allowed in bar ~ Wi-fi
*Recommended by Paddy and Sian O'Leary, Nicola and Stuart Parsons, R and M Thomas, Belinda
Stamp, Rosie and John Moore, Elise and Charles Mackinlay, PL*

EWHURST GREEN   TQ7924   Map 3
White Dog 🏮
(01580) 830264 – www.thewhitedogewhurst.co.uk
*Turn off A21 to Bodiam at S end of Hurst Green, cross B2244, pass Bodiam Castle,
cross river then bear left uphill at Ewhurst Green sign; TN32 5TD*

**Welcoming village pub with a nice little bar, several real ales
and popular food; bedrooms**

This is a particularly well run 17th-c inn with local ales and well thought-of
food, with a daughter and father team at the helm. The bustling bar has a
roaring log fire in an inglenook fireplace, beams, wood panelling and a mix of
chairs and tables on old brick or flagstoned floors. They keep a beer named
for the pub (from Hardys & Hansons), Harveys Best, Rother Valley Level
Best and a guest from Tonbridge on handpump and 20 wines by the glass.
A dining room has sturdy wooden tables and chairs on more flagstones,
while the games room (which opens on to the front terrace) has darts, board
games and pool; background music. There can be few pubs with a view as
stunning as the one over Bodiam Castle (National Trust) from the seats and
tables in the back garden here, and one of the light and airy bedrooms shares
this view; they also have tipis for hire. Disabled access.

 From a well judged menu, the appetising food includes sandwiches, crispy ham
hock bonbons with creamy grain mustard sauce, bouillabaisse with rouille,
asparagus and samphire risotto, grilled mackerel fillets with chilli jam on wild garlic
mash, roasted guinea fowl breast with wilted spinach and tarragon cream sauce, glazed
rack of local lamb with port wine jus and wild garlic mash, 28-day aged local 10oz rib-eye
steak with béarnaise sauce and french fries, and puddings such as crème brûlée of the
day and vanilla sponge topped with plum and apple compote with custard. *Benchmark
main dish: crayfish and crab linguine with chilli, coriander and cheese £13.50.
Two-course evening meal £21.00.*

Free house ~ Licensees Harriet Bull and Dale Skinner ~ Real ale ~ Open 12-11 ~ Bar food
12-2, 6-9; 12-2.30, 6-9.30 Fri-Sun ~ Restaurant ~ Children welcome ~ Dogs allowed in bar
and bedrooms ~ Wi-fi ~ Bedrooms: /£95 *Recommended by Mandy and Gary Redstone, Gene and
Kitty Rankin, Marianne and Michael Huggins, Darrell Barton, Martin Day, David Jackman*

FLETCHING   TQ4223   Map 3
Griffin 🏮 ♟ 🛏
(01825) 722890 – www.thegriffininn.co.uk
Village signposted off A272 W of Uckfield; TN22 3SS

**Busy, gently upmarket inn with a fine wine list, real ales, bistro-style
bar food and a big garden; pretty bedrooms**

This place is very much the focal point of a handsome village – it shows
in the bustling atmosphere in the chatty bar and the cheerful mix of
customers. There's a civilised feel throughout and the beamed and quaintly
panelled bar rooms have blazing log fires, old photographs and hunting
prints, straightforward close-set furniture including some captain's chairs,
and china on a delft shelf. A small bare-boarded serving area is off to one
side and there's another cosy bar with sofas and a TV; background music.
The place gets pretty packed at weekends. Harveys Best, Long Man American

Pale Ale and a couple of guests from Cellar Head and Pig & Porter on handpump, plus 20 wines by the glass from a good list (including champagne, prosecco and sweet wine); they hold a monthly wine club with supper (on Thursday evenings). At the garden entrance there's an outside bar and wood oven, tables and chairs under parasols and a stunning view over Sheffield Park (National Trust); there are more seats on a sandstone terrace. The bright and pretty bedrooms are comfortable and breakfasts good. There are ramps for wheelchairs.

First class food includes crab and chive tortellini with lobster bisque and chargrilled king prawn, crispy guinea fowl salad with mango, pineapple, mint and chilli and lime salsa, oyster and chestnut mushroom risotto with parmesan, confit pork belly with lyonnaise potatoes and wholegrain mustard sauce, sea bream fillet with champ mash and beurre blanc, 28-day rib-eye steak with chilli and garlic butter and skinny fries, and puddings such as blackberry, apple and rhubarb crumble with vanilla crème anglaise and vanilla pannacotta with espresso syrup and raspberry and chocolate crumb. *Benchmark main dish: beer-battered cod and chips with pea purée £14.50. Two-course evening meal £22.00.*

Free house ~ Licensees James Pullan and Samantha Barlow ~ Real ale ~ Open 12-midnight; 12-11 Sun ~ Bar food 12-2.30 (3 Sat), 7-9.30; 12-3, 7-9 Sun ~ Restaurant ~ Children welcome ~ Dogs allowed in bar and bedrooms ~ Wi-fi ~ Bedrooms: £80/£110
Recommended by Amanda Shipley, Richard Cole, John Preddy, Peter Meister, Carol and Barry Craddock, Sam Cole, Miss B D Picton, Tony Scott

FRIDAY STREET
TV6203   Map 3
Farm at Friday Street ♀ 🍺
(01323) 766049 – www.farmfridaystreet.com
B2104, Langney; BN23 8AP

Handsome old place with lots to look at, efficient staff serving popular food and drink and seats outside

A much extended former farmhouse, this is a well run place with plenty of atmosphere. The open-plan rooms are split by brick pillars into cosier areas with sofas, stools and all manner of wooden dining chairs and tables on bare boards, creamy coloured flagstones, coir or carpet. Throughout, there are open fires, big house plants, stubby church candles, frame-to-frame prints and pictures and farming implements; the atmosphere is easy-going and friendly. Long Man Best Bitter, Timothy Taylors Landlord and a guest such as Long Man Long Blonde on handpump and 14 wines by the glass; background music. Events (check the website) include a summer beer festival. The dining room is on two levels with timbered walls, glass partitions, a raised conical roof and an open kitchen. The front lawn has plenty of picnic-sets.

As well as weekend breakfasts (9-11am), the good, seasonal food includes deep-fried smoked beef croquettes with barbecue sauce, salmon and cod fishcakes with sweet chilli sauce, chickpea, mushroom and lentil burger with toppings and skinny fries, beef stroganoff with flatbread, prawn curry, local leek and pork sausages with mash and gravy, moules frites, coq au vin, 28-day aged sirloin steak with triple-cooked chips and a choice of sauce, and puddings such as banoffi pie with coffee ice-cream and treacle tart with clotted cream. *Benchmark main dish: corned beef hash with bubble and squeak, baked beans and a fried egg £13.95. Two-course evening meal £21.00.*

Whiting & Hammond ~ Manager Emma Paine ~ Real ale ~ Open 11-11; 9am-11pm Sat, Sun ~ Bar food 12-9; 12-9.30 Sat ~ Restaurant ~ Children welcome ~ Dogs allowed in bar ~ Wi-fi
Recommended by Greta and Gavin Craddock, Chloe and Tim Hodge, Richard Cole, Sally and Brian Turner, Anna and Mark Evans, Philip Chesington, Sally and Colin Allen

GORING-BY-SEA

TQ0904   Map 2

Highdown 🍷 🍺 🛏

(01903) 924 670 – www.brunningandprice.co.uk/highdown

Littlehampton Road; BN12 6FB

Handsome pub in a fine spot with interconnected rooms, lots to look at, seats outside and a tea room; bedrooms

An interesting new addition for Brunning & Price, this is both pub and tea room – and is only the second place belonging to the group to offer bedrooms. A substantial former family home, the pub part is made up of several open-plan rooms, each with their own character and with plenty of space for both drinking and eating. There are long cushioned wall settles, turn-of-the-century-style dining chairs, chunky or high-backed leather seats around solid dark polished tables, rugs on bare floorboards, parquet, black and white floor tiles and carpet, and lots of prints and photos on flint or painted walls. One smallish room is panelled with handsome portraits and another has books on shelves. Throughout you'll find house plants of every size, table and standard lamps, elegant metal chandeliers, fresh flowers and candles, open fires in stone fireplaces and, in the hall, a two-way fireplace fronted by a couple of armchairs. There's an easy-going atmosphere helped along by friendly, efficient staff and a fine choice of drinks that includes St Austell Brunning & Price Traditional Bitter, Harveys Best and guests such as Gun Scaramanga Extra Pale and Langham Hip Hop on handpump, 20 wines by the glass, 84 gins and 51 whiskies; background music and board games. Outside at the front of the building is a terrace with teak tables and chairs under parasols and picnic-sets on a lawn. The tea room is separate and set further back: simple tables and chairs on parquet flooring, flint walls, heavy beams, a dresser lined with teas, a glass counter filled with cakes and its own terrace with tables and chairs. Bedrooms are well appointed, comfortable and contemporary. Next to the pub are Highdown Gardens, created out of an old chalk pit and particularly lovely in spring. You can walk straight from the pub on to the South Downs for far-reaching views and the sea is just four minutes' drive away.

Good contemporary food includes sandwiches, crispy baby squid with mango and chilli sauce, garlic and rosemary-studded camembert with walnut and apple salad, beetroot, quinoa and soya bean burger with red cabbage slaw and fries, cauliflower, chickpea and pepper jalfrezi with almond pilaf rice and sweet potato bhaji, chicken, ham and leek pie, king prawn linguine with garlic and chilli, beef bourguignon with mustard mash, confit belly of pork with sherry-braised pig cheek, fondant potato and butternut squash purée, and puddings such as toasted waffle with glazed pineapple, passion-fruit sauce and coconut ice-cream and triple chocolate brownie with chocolate sauce. *Benchmark main dish: beer-battered fish and chips £13.95. Two-course evening meal £19.50.*

Brunning & Price ~ Manager Tom Foster ~ Real ale ~ Open 11-11 ~ Bar food 12-9.30; 12-10 Fri, Sat; 12-9 Sun ~ Restaurant ~ Children welcome ~ Dogs allowed in bar and bedrooms ~ Wi-fi ~ Bedrooms: /£85 *Recommended by Simon and Mary Todd, Diana and Richard Gibbs, Simon and Alex Knight, Sandra King, Rosie and John Moore*

HASTINGS

TQ8109   Map 3

Crown ⭐ 🍷 🍺

(01424) 465100 – www.thecrownhastings.co.uk

All Saints Street, Old Town; TN34 3BN

Informal and friendly corner pub with high quality food, local ales and simple furnishings

This is a smashing little pub and, once found, our readers come back on a regular basis. It's just back from the seafront in the Old Town, and the simply furnished bar has bare boards, plain chairs around tables inlaid with games and set with posies of flowers, a log fire and plenty of windows to keep everything light (despite the dark paintwork). A snug has leather armchairs in front of another open fire, a couple of tables, and books and house plants on a windowsill and mantelpiece; background music and board games. Stools line the counter where they keep four changing ales from breweries such as Holler Boys, Old Dairy, Romney Marsh and Three Legs on handpump, 14 good wines by the glass, 15 gins, 15 whiskies and local cider; service is friendly and helpful. There's a dining area at one end of the bar with scatter cushions on wall seats, mismatched chairs and some large tables. Local art (for sale) hangs on the walls and one window is hung with aprons and lined with shelves of local pottery, greetings cards and hand-made purses; daily papers and background music. Dogs and children receive a genuinely warm welcome. There are a few picnic-sets outside at the front.

 Inventive food (they bake their own sourdough bread and churn their own butter) includes weekend brunch (11am-2pm), roast quail with bacon and mushrooms on toast, tempura cuttlefish with pickled onion and marie rose sauce, wild garlic gnocchi with cheesy duchess potatoes, hazelnut pesto, asparagus and wild garlic mayonnaise, baked jerusalem artichoke with artichoke rösti, swede and mustard purée and hazelnut granola, smoked haddock fillet and polenta fishcake with bacon and creamed cabbage, local lamb cutlet with meatballs, orzotto and pea and mint fritter, and puddings such as rhubarb and oat milk custard tart with rhubarb and local gin sorbet and fig and apple pudding with stout butterscotch and honeycomb ice-cream. *Benchmark main dish: local fish finger sandwich £7.50. Two-course evening meal £23.00.*

Free house ~ Licensees Tess and Andrew Swan ~ Real ale ~ Open 11-11; 11-10.30 Sun ~ Bar food 12-5, 6-9.30; 11-5, 6-9.30 weekends ~ Children welcome ~ Dogs welcome ~ Wi-fi
Recommended by Julie and Andrew Blanchett, Angela and Steve Heard, Adam and Natalie Davis, George and Alison Bishop, Tony Scott, Monty Green

HORSHAM
TQ1730   Map 3

Black Jug ♀ ◖
(01403) 253526 – www.brunningandprice.co.uk/blackjug
North Street; RH12 1RJ

Busy town pub with wide choice of drinks, attentive staff and rewarding food

To keep the mixed crowd of office workers, theatre-goers and couples happy, efficient, friendly staff offer a fine choice of drinks: Harveys Best and Wychwood Hobgoblin Gold with guests such as Jennings Cumberland, Pilgrim Surrey and Theakstons Black Bull on handpump, 16 wines by the glass, 150 malt whiskies, 50 gins, 30 rums, 30 bourbons and farm cider – and tasty, brasserie-style food. The single, large, early 20th-c room has a long central bar, a nice collection of sizeable dark wood tables and comfortable chairs on a stripped-wood floor, bookcases and interesting old prints and photographs above a dark wood-panelled dado on cream walls; background music and board games. A spacious, bright conservatory has similar furniture and lots of hanging baskets, while the pretty, flower-filled back terrace has plenty of garden furniture. Parking is in the council car park next door, as the small one by the pub is for staff and deliveries only.

Good, modern food includes sandwiches, crab with carrot and coriander salad and sea salt flatbread, watermelon with aged feta, pistachio and mint salad and honey dressing, cauliflower, chickpea and pepper jalfrezi with vegetable bhaji, steak burger with toppings, coleslaw and chips, sea trout with mussels, brown butter mayonnaise and crispy fennel, chicken caesar salad with a poached egg, and puddings such as hot waffle with boozy cherries, chocolate sauce and white chocolate chip ice-cream and lemon cake with strawberry sorbet. *Benchmark main dish: braised lamb shoulder with dauphinoise potatoes, carrot and swede mash and rosemary gravy £17.95. Two-course evening meal £21.00.*

Brunning & Price ~ Tenant Kelly Woodall ~ Real ale ~ Open 11.30am-11pm; 12-10.30 Sun ~ Bar food 12-10 (9.30 Sun) ~ Children welcome till 7pm ~ Dogs allowed in bar ~ Wi-fi *Recommended by Gail and Arthur Roberts, Sarah and David Gibbs, Graeme and Sally Mendham, Bob and Melissa Wyatt, Tony Scott, Edward May, Phoebe Peacock*

LODSWORTH
SU9223 Map 2

Hollist Arms

(01798) 861310 – www.thehollistarms.com
Off A272 Midhurst–Petworth; GU28 9BZ

Country pub with a relaxed, friendly atmosphere, traditional décor and furnishings, enjoyable food and drink and seats outside

A bustling 18th-c pub, this is in an attractive spot by the village green. The small snug on the right has an open fire, while the left-hand bar has a cushioned window seat, a couple of armchairs and a bench around a table, bare boards and stools at the counter where helpful staff serve Dark Star Hophead, Hogs Back TEA, Langham Hip Hop and a couple of guest ales on handpump, 14 wines by the glass including champagne and ten local gins. An open doorway leads through to the L-shaped dining room with lots of photos on the walls, farmhouse and wheelback chairs and painted settles around all sorts of tables on more bare boards, a semi-circular cushioned seat in a bay window, a piano and a log fire in a brick inglenook; pretty country flowers and candles. Steps lead up to a cottagey back garden with picnic-sets on a terrace and on grass; there are a few seats out in front too. Disabled access. Enjoyable nearby walks.

Local produce is used for the tasty food: lunchtime sandwiches and smoked haddock, spinach and duck egg bake, devilled crab salad with avocado, spring onion, chilli and spinach, lamb kofta kebabs with carrot, cumin, cucumber and yoghurt, sweet potato and white bean chilli with coriander and guacamole, beer-battered hake and chips, burger with toppings and chips, teriyaki-marinated salmon with radish, carrot and soba noodle salad, confit duck leg with celeriac and potato dauphinoise and duck sauce, 10oz sirloin steak with chips and peppercorn sauce, and puddings. *Benchmark main dish: pie of the day £14.50. Two-course evening meal £21.50.*

Free house ~ Licensees Amy Whitmore and Henry Coghlan ~ Real ale ~ Open 12-3.30, 5-11; 12-12 Sat; 12-10 Sun ~ Bar food 12-2.30, 6.30-9; 12-4 Sun ~ Children welcome ~ Dogs welcome *Recommended by Stephen Saunders, Elodie and Edward Blake, Maria and Stephen Braeburn, Archie and Melanie Garnett, Anne and Ben Smith*

LOWER BEEDING
TQ2225 Map 3

Crabtree 🌟 ♟

(01403) 892666 – www.crabtreesussex.co.uk
Brighton Road; RH13 6PT

Airy bar and cosy dining rooms in bustling pub with excellent food, helpful service and pretty garden

B ehind the Victorian façade of this family-run pub are Tudor beams and a huge inglenook dated 1537. The airy, simply furnished front bar has a green leather chesterfield, plush stools around just three tables on parquet flooring, a warming woodburning stove, fresh flowers and nightlights and maybe background jazz. Badger Best and a seasonal guest on handpump, 15 wines (some organic) by the glass, ten malt whiskies and local cider; board games. A garden room leads off with wicker chairs, leather wall banquettes and a dresser full of home-made jellies and chutney. Several dining rooms towards the back are interlinked and cosy, with beams, brick floors, high-backed dining chairs around wooden-topped painted tables and country paintings (which are for sale); a small room to the right of the entrance is similarly furnished. In warm weather, head for the lovely landscaped garden with its picnic-sets, wendy house and fine country views. Disabled access. The pub is handy for Nymans (National Trust).

Creative food includes crab roulade with cured melon and cucumber textures, chicken and ham hock terrine with tarragon mayonnaise and honey and mustard-dressed leaves, asparagus and lemon risotto with crispy egg and cheese, burger with toppings and chips, cider-battered fish and chips with malt vinegar gel, stuffed corn-fed chicken breast with wild mushrooms, puy lentil and tarragon cassoulet, spring onion and mushroom sauce, lamb rump with crushed new potatoes, peas, wild garlic and red wine jus, and puddings such as spiced pear parfait with mulled cider jelly, ginger bread and clotted cream and sticky toffee pudding with toffee popcorn, caramel sauce and vanilla ice-cream; they also offer a two- and three-course weekday menu (12-3pm, 6-7pm). *Benchmark main dish: sea bream with chorizo and clam butter £16.00. Two-course evening meal £25.00.*

Badger ~ Tenant Simon Hope ~ Real ale ~ Open 11am-midnight; 11am-1am Sat; 11am-10pm Sun ~ Bar food 12-9.30; 12-6 Sun ~ Restaurant ~ Children welcome ~ Dogs allowed in bar ~ Wi-fi *Recommended by David and Leone Lawson, David and Charlotte Green, Martin Day, Jill and Dick Archer, Alison and Michael Harper, David Jackman, Miles Green*

LURGASHALL
Noahs Ark 🍴

SU9327 Map 2

(01428) 707346 – www.noahsarkinn.co.uk
Off A283 N of Petworth; GU28 9ET

Busy old pub in nice spot with neatly kept bar and dining rooms, real ales and pleasing food using local produce

A pint of ale and a cricket game on the pitch opposite this friendly old pub is as English as you can get. There's always a good, cheerful crowd in the simple, traditional bar and the atmosphere is buoyant and easy-going. There are beams, a mix of wooden chairs and tables, parquet flooring and an inglenook fireplace plus Greene King IPA, St Austell Tribute and a guest ale on handpump, 24 wines by the glass, a cocktail of the month and a fine bloody mary. Open to the top of the rafters, the dining room is spacious and airy with church candles and fresh flowers on light wood tables, and a couple of comfortable sofas facing each other in front of an open woodburning stove; background music and board games. The border terrier is called Gillie and visiting dogs may get a dog biscuit. There are tables in a large side garden. Wheelchair ramp but no disabled loo.

Well liked food includes smoked duck breast with celeriac rémoulade and caramelised hazelnuts, crab mayonnaise with avocado, burger with toppings, slaw and chips, beer-battered hake and chips, slow-roasted pork belly with parsley mash and cider jus, sea bass fillet with boulangère potatoes and salsa verde, rib-eye steak with peppercorn sauce and chips, and puddings such as spotted dick with custard and chocolate mousse and peanut brittle. *Benchmark main dish: creamy leek and walnut risotto with cambozola £14.00. Two-course evening meal £22.00.*

Greene King ~ Lease Henry Coghlan and Amy Whitmore ~ Real ale ~ Open 11-11.30;
12-10 Sun; 12-8 Sun in winter ~ Bar food 12-2.30, 7-9.30; 12-3.15 Sun ~ Restaurant ~
Children welcome ~ Dogs allowed in bar ~ Wi-fi *Recommended by Jennifer and Nicholas
Thompson, Liz and Mike Newton, Miss A E Dare, Chantelle and Tony Redman, Gary and Marie
Miller, Nick Sharpe*

 MARK CROSS   TQ5831 Map 3

Mark Cross Inn ♀

(01892) 852423 – www.themarkcross.co.uk
A267 N of Mayfield; TN6 3NP

**Sizeable pub with interconnected rooms, real ales and popular food,
and good views from seats in the garden**

The far-reaching views behind this spreading pub can be enjoyed from
benches and tables on the terrace and from picnic-sets on the lawn – it's
best to get here early on a sunny day. There's also a children's play fort. The
bar and dining rooms are on several linked levels but kept cosy with church
candles and open fires, shelves lined with books and stone bottles, gilt-edged
mirrors, big clocks and large house plants. There's all manner of seating from
farmhouse, mate's and cushioned dining chairs to settles and stools grouped
around dark shiny tables on rugs and bare boards, and the walls are lined
almost frame-to-frame with photographs, prints, paintings and old newspaper
cuttings. Helpful staff serve Fullers London Pride, Long Man Best Bitter and
guests from breweries such as Timothy Taylor and Westerham on handpump
and good wines by the glass; background music.

Pleasing food includes sandwiches, jackfruit spring rolls with hoisin and peanut
butter sauce, parsley and garlic butter field mushrooms with crusty bread, creamy
minted pea and parmesan risotto, corned beef hash with bubble and squeak and a fried
egg, moules frites, a pie of the day, confit duck leg with dauphinoise potatoes and cherry
sauce, 28-day aged sirloin steak with triple-cooked chips and a choice of sauce, and
puddings such as warm chocolate brownie with chocolate sauce and banoffi pie with
caramel sauce and coffee ice-cream. *Benchmark main dish: beer-battered fish and
chips £15.95. Two-course evening meal £22.00.*

Whiting & Hammond ~ Real ale ~ Open 9am-11pm; 9am-midnight Fri, Sat; 9am-10.30pm
Sun ~ Bar food 12-9.30 (9 Sun) ~ Restaurant ~ Children welcome ~ Dogs allowed in bar ~
Wi-fi *Recommended by Jo Garnett, Rob Anderson, Valerie and Gordon Wauton, Kitty and Stuart
Flint, Peter Pilbeam, Gene and Kitty Rankin, Belinda Stamp*

 OVING   SU9005 Map 2

Gribble Inn ◀

(01243) 786893 – www.gribbleinn.co.uk
Between A27 and A259 E of Chichester; PO20 2BP

**Own-brewed beers in bustling village pub with popular bar food
and pretty garden**

'A little gem' is how several readers describe this 16th-c thatched pub.
One of the main draws, of course, are their own-brewed beers. On
handpump, these might include Fuzzy Duck, Gribble Ale, Lazy Buzzard, Pig's
Ear, Reg's Tipple and seasonal ales; they also have 16 wines by the glass,
40 gins, 20 malt whiskies, 30 vodkas and unusual rums. The chatty bar
features a lot of heavy beams and timbering while the other various linked
rooms have a cottagey feel with sofas by two roaring log fires; board games.
The barn houses a venue for parties. There are seats outside in a covered area
and more chairs and tables in the pretty garden with its apple and pear trees.

¶¶ Tasty food includes home-smoked local pheasant, goose rillettes, pheasant and bacon nugget and red pepper pesto, seared queen scallop and chorizo risotto with basil oil, sharing platters, root vegetable tagine with lemon, chilli and coriander and cauliflower couscous, pork and herb sausages with bubble and squeak and onion gravy, slow-braised oxtail with grain mustard mash and parsnip purée, beer-battered haddock and chips, 10oz rib-eye steak with chips and a choice of sauce, and puddings such as white chocolate and vanilla rice pudding with sloe gin berry compote and layers of chocolate sponge, chocolate mousse and chocolate granache. *Benchmark main dish: slow-roasted pork belly £15.00. Two-course evening meal £22.00.*

Free house ~ Licensees Simon Wood and Nicola Tester ~ Real ale ~ Open 11-11; 11-midnight Sat; 12-10 Sun ~ Bar food 12-9; 12-4 Sun ~ Restaurant ~ Children welcome ~ Dogs allowed in bar ~ Wi-fi *Recommended by Kitty and Stuart Flint, John Beeken, Naomi and Andrew Randall, Mandy and Gary Redstone, Anna and Mark Evans, Philip Chesington*

PETWORTH
Angel 🎖️ ⏲️ 🛏️

SU9721   Map 2

(01798) 342153 – www.angelinnpetworth.co.uk
Angel Street; GU28 0BG

Medieval building with 18th-c façade, chatty atmosphere in beamed bars, friendly service and good, interesting food; bedrooms

This is a perfect place for lunch after exploring this pretty market town, with highly rated food and drink and a convivial atmosphere. The interconnected rooms have the feel of a country inn and retain many of their original features. The front bar has beams, a log fire in an inglenook fireplace and an appealing variety of old wooden and cushioned dining chairs and tables on wide floorboards. It leads through to the main room with high chairs by the counter where they keep a beer named for the pub (from Langham), Arundel Sussex Gold and Greyhound Blonde Bird on handpump, 22 wines by the glass from an extensive list and ten gins; board games. Staff are courteous and helpful. There are also high-backed brown leather and antique chairs and tables on pale wooden flooring, the odd milk churn and french windows to a three-level terrace garden. A cosy and popular back bar is similarly furnished, with a second log fire. Bedrooms (named after trees) are warm and comfortable and breakfasts good – some rooms are in the inn and some in a Georgian town house next door which has a walled courtyard garden.

🎖️ Appetising food includes crispy lamb belly fritters with anchovy mayonnaise, pigeon with black pudding, endive and balsamic dressing, fennel, asparagus and broad bean risotto with parmesan, burgers with toppings and french fries, chicken, ham and tarragon pie, duck breast with braised chicory, dauphinoise potatoes and red wine jus, smoked haddock and salmon fishcake with a poached egg and chive and vermouth velouté, rib-eye steak with wild garlic pesto and triple-cooked chips, and puddings such as glazed lemon tart with raspberry sorbet and rhubarb trifle. *Benchmark main dish: beer-battered fish and chips £14.50. Two-course evening meal £22.00.*

Free house ~ Licensee Philippe Diez ~ Real ale ~ Open 10.30am-11pm; 11.30-10.30 Sun ~ Bar food 12-2.30, 6.30-9; 12-4.30 Sun ~ Children welcome ~ Dogs welcome ~ Wi-fi ~ Bedrooms: £100/£160 *Recommended by Belinda and Neil Garth, Simon Collett-Jones, Robin and Anne Triggs, Rupert and Sandy Newton, Tony and Wendy Hobden, Darren Jones*

'Children welcome' means the pub says it lets children inside without any special restriction. If it allows them in, but to restricted areas such as an eating area or family room, we specify this. Some pubs may impose an evening time limit. We do not mention limits after 9pm as we assume children are home by then.

PETWORTH
SU9921 Map 2

Welldiggers Arms 🛏

(01798) 344288 – www.thewelldiggersarms.co.uk

Low Heath; A283 E; GU28 0HG

Bustling inn with character bar and airy dining room, four real ales and good wines, helpful service and seats on terrace; bedrooms

There's a gently civilised but friendly atmosphere here, with most customers aiming to enjoy the high quality food. The bar has a woodburning stove with long wooden slab tables to either side (each set with candles in brass holders and a plant) and there are wall banquettes and settles with scatter cushions, wheelback chairs, white-painted beams and stools against the counter where cheerful, attentive staff serve Banks's Amber Ale and Langham Best and Halfway to Heaven on handpump and good wines by the glass; background music. An end room is just right for a small group with a wooden settle and chunky chairs around a single table, and horse and hunting pictures. The big, airy dining room at the back has spreading country views from large picture windows, wall settles and more wheelbacks and country kitchen chairs with pretty cushions around tables of all sizes on flagstones, and a busy open kitchen. Through french windows is the terrace, largely enclosed by a marquee and with teak tables and chairs. The cottagey-style bedrooms (either in the pub or in a separate annexe and all with views) are attractive and comfortable.

Interesting food includes oak-smoked trout with pickled beetroot and dill mayonnaise, pheasant and chicken hash with house sauce, bacon crumb and a fried egg, chestnut mushroom and cauliflower spätzle, fondue sauce and vegetarian parmesan, burger with toppings, home-made ketchup and fries, hake fillet with celeriac rémoulade, fondant potato, roasted beetroot and parsley dressing, slow-braised ox cheeks with date and apple glaze, creamy mash and horseradish, and puddings such as treacle tart with ginger ice-cream and hot chocolate pudding with chocolate sauce and salted caramel ice-cream. *Benchmark main dish: beer-battered fish and chips £15.75. Two-course evening meal £24.00.*

Free house ~ Licensee Stephen Bone ~ Real ale ~ Open 11-11; 11-10.30 Sun ~ Bar food 12-2, 6.30-9; 12-3, 6.30-8.30 Sun ~ Restaurant ~ Children welcome ~ Dogs allowed in bar and bedrooms ~ Wi-fi ~ Bedrooms: /£100 *Recommended by Sandra and Miles Spencer, Belinda and Neil Garth, Richard Tilbrook, Tina and Steven Hobden, Ruth and Peter Bacon, Darren and Clare Jones*

RINGMER
TQ4313 Map 3

Cock 🍺 £

(01273) 812040 – www.cockpub.co.uk

Uckfield Road – blocked-off section of road off A26 N of village turn-off; BN8 5RX

Country pub with a wide choice of popular bar food, real ales in character bar, and plenty of seats in the garden

'Always excellent' and 'consistently top notch' are comments from readers who've enjoyed this well run 16th-c coaching inn on many occasions over the years. You'll find a warm welcome from the convivial licensees and the unspoilt bar has traditional pubby furniture on flagstones, heavy beams, a log fire in an inglenook fireplace, Harveys Best and a couple of guests from local breweries such as Downlands, Gun, Hammerpot and Holler Boys on handpump, ten wines by the glass, 12 gins and a dozen malt whiskies. There are also three dining areas; background music. Outside, on terraces and in the garden, are lots of picnic-sets with views across open fields to the South Downs. The owners' dogs are called Bailey and Tally, and visiting canines are offered a bowl of water and a chew. This is sister pub to the Highlands at Uckfield.

Rewarding food includes lunchtime sandwiches, prawn and avocado cocktail, deep-fried camembert with cranberry sauce, halloumi and vegetable wellington with tomato sauce, venison sausages with mustard mash and gravy, gammon with egg and pineapple, chicken curry, lambs liver and bacon with mash and onion gravy, pork fillet with cream and dijon mustard sauce and new potatoes, salmon fillet with creamy watercress sauce and sautéed potatoes, and puddings such as banoffi pie with salted caramel ice-cream and fruit crumble with custard. *Benchmark main dish: steak in ale pie £12.50. Two-course evening meal £19.00.*

Free house ~ Licensees Ian, Val, Nick and Matt Ridley ~ Real ale ~ Open 11-3, 6-11.30; 11-9.30 Sun ~ Bar food 12-2.15 (2.30 Sat), 6-9.30; 12-8.30 Sun ~ Restaurant ~ Well behaved children welcome but no toddlers ~ Dogs allowed in bar ~ Wi-fi *Recommended by James and Sylvia Hewitt, Martine and Fabio Lockley, Liz and Martin Eldon, Katherine Matthews, Ted and Mary Bates, John Beeken, Tony and Wendy Hobden*

ROBERTSBRIDGE
George 🛏
TQ7323   Map 3

(01580) 880315 – www.thegeorgerobertsbridge.co.uk
High Street; TN32 5AW

Handsome inn with pleasing food and ales and seats in courtyard garden; bedrooms

A former coaching inn with friendly, hands-on licensees, this is right in the middle of a bustling village. The right-hand bar area has a log fire in a brick inglenook with a leather sofa and a couple of armchairs in front – just the place for a quiet pint and a chat – plus high bar stools by the counter where they serve Cellar Head Single Hop Pale, Dark Star Hophead and Harveys Best on handpump, good wines by the glass and a farm cider. The dining area is opposite with elegant high-backed tartan or leather chairs around a mix of tables (each with fresh flowers and a tea-light) on stripped floorboards and more tea-lights in a small fireplace; background music. The back terrace has plenty of seats and tables. Bedrooms are comfortable and the breakfasts well regarded.

Food is good and includes lunchtime sandwiches and baguettes, pork terrine with roasted apples, potted shrimps on toast, sharing boards, breaded halloumi burger with toppings, sweet chilli sauce and sweet potato fries, home-cooked ham and free-range eggs, local 8oz rib-eye steak with pink peppercorn sauce and chips, daily specials, and puddings such as cherry almond pudding with creamy cherry liqueur sauce and vanilla ice-cream and a chocolate pudding of the day. *Benchmark main dish: beer-battered fish and chips £12.50. Two-course evening meal £20.50.*

Free house ~ Licensees John and Jane Turner ~ Real ale ~ Open 12-11; 12-9 Sun; closed Mon ~ Bar food 12-9; 12-7 Sun ~ Children welcome but must be accompanied by an adult at all times ~ Dogs allowed in bar ~ Wi-fi *Recommended by Heather and Richard Jones, Sheila and Sam Thorpe, Kate and Mark Foskett, James and Sylvia Hewitt, Audrey and Paul Summers*

SALEHURST
Salehurst Halt 🍽 £
TQ7424   Map 3

(01580) 880620 – www.salehursthalt.co.uk
Village signposted from Robertsbridge bypass on A21 Tunbridge Wells–Battle; Church Lane; TN32 5PH

Well run country local in quiet hamlet with easy-going atmosphere, real ales, well liked bar food and seats in pretty back garden

To find this chatty and friendly little pub, just head for the attractive 14th-c church. To the right of the door is a small bare-boards area with a few tables and chairs, a woodburning stove and shelves of books. The main bar has hops on beams, farmhouse and wheelback chairs, settles with scatter cushions and scrubbed tables on floorboards; background music and board games. Harveys Best and guests from breweries such as Cellar Head, Dark Star, Long Man and Old Dairy on handpump, farm cider, several malt whiskies and eight wines by the glass. There's also an upstairs private dining room for hire. The charming, cottagey back garden has views over the Rother Valley and there's a terrace with metal chairs and tiled tables under a vine-covered arbour; outdoor table tennis.

As well as the popular pizzas from the wood-fired oven (Wednesday evenings in summer), the tasty food includes lunchtime sandwiches, salt fish fritters with aioli, mixed meze plate, falafel with middle eastern vegetarian toppings, piri-piri spatchcocked poussin, goat curry with rice, burgers with toppings and chips, flat-iron steak with trimmings, and puddings such as salted caramel torte with ice-cream and cherry bakewell tart with cream. *Benchmark main dish: home-made fishcakes £11.00. Two-course evening meal £19.00.*

Free house ~ Licensee Andrew Augarde ~ Real ale ~ Open 12-11; 12-10.30 Sun; closed Mon except bank holidays ~ Bar food 12-2.30, 6-9; 12-3 Sun ~ Children welcome ~ Dogs welcome ~ Wi-fi *Recommended by Peter Meister, Adam and Betty Lawrence, Chris and Sophie Baxter, Audrey and Paul Summers, Martine and Fabio Lockley, Sophia and Hamish Greenfield*

TICEHURST
Bell ♀ ⌂

TQ6830   Map 3

(01580) 200300 – www.thebellinticehurst.com
High Street; TN5 7AS

Carefully restored inn with beamed rooms, real ales and good wines by the glass, popular food and seats in pretty courtyard garden; bedrooms

There's a lot of history and character here, especially in the heavily beamed main bar: you'll find quirky decorations such as a squirrel in a rocking chair, cushioned wooden dining chairs around nice wooden tables on bare boards, an inglenook fireplace and stools by the counter where they serve Brumaison Beulter, Cellar Head Single Hop Pale and Harveys Best on handpump, ten wines by the glass, local gin and a dozen malt whiskies. The dining room continues on from the bar and is similarly furnished, with the addition of cushioned wall settles and an eclectic choice of paintings on the red walls; background music. A separate snug has comfortable sofas grouped around a low table in front of another open fire, interesting wallpaper, a large globe, an ancient typewriter and various books and pieces of china. What was the carriage room holds a long sunken table with benches on either side (perfect for an informal party) and there's an upstairs function room too. At the back is a courtyard garden with seats and tables and built-in cushioned seating up steps on a raised area. The bedrooms in the coaching inn are comfortable and very individually decorated, while the separate lodges each have their own little garden built around a fire pit.

Championing local produce, the well regarded food includes black pudding scotch egg with avocado and piquillo pepper, chicory, serrano ham, salmorego (a spanish tomato and bread purée) and quail egg, vegetable chaufa (a peruvian fried rice dish) with mushrooms, peanuts and a poached egg, beer-battered fish and chips, pork collar with cauliflower, onions and pedro ximénez prunes, tiger prawns with chilli and garlic, rib-eye steak with chimichurri and frites, and puddings such as cheesecake with rhubarb and popcorn and devil's chocolate cake. *Benchmark main dish: steak burger with toppings and frites £14.00. Two-course evening meal £23.00.*

Free house ~ Licensee Howard Canning ~ Real ale ~ Open 7am-midnight ~ Bar food 12-3, 6-9 (8.30 Sun) ~ Restaurant ~ Children welcome ~ Dogs allowed in bar and bedrooms ~ Wi-fi ~ Bedrooms: /£95 *Recommended by Barbara and Phil Bowie, Belinda Stamp, Edward Nile, Elise and Charles Mackinlay, Nick Sharpe, Sylvia and Phillip Spencer, Nicholas and Maddy Trainer*

TILLINGTON
SU9621 Map 2
Horse Guards
(01798) 342332 – www.thehorseguardsinn.co.uk
Off A272 Midhurst–Petworth; GU28 9AF

Sussex Dining Pub of the Year

300-year-old inn with beams, panelling and open fires in rambling rooms, excellent food and charming garden; cottagey bedrooms

Particularly well run and highly enjoyable, this 18th-c inn remains on top form. The neatly kept, beamed front bar has a gently civilised atmosphere, country furniture on bare boards, a chesterfield in one corner and a fine view beyond the village to the Rother Valley from a seat in the big panelled bow window. High bar chairs line the counter where friendly, efficient staff serve 360 Degrees Best and Firebird Two Horses on handpump, 17 wines by the glass, home-made liqueurs and cordials and local farm juices. Other rambling beamed rooms have similar furniture on brick floors, rugs and original panelling and there are fresh flowers throughout; background music and board games. When the weather is fine the leafy, sheltered garden has picnic-sets, day beds, deckchairs and even a hammock, and there's also a charming terrace. Cosy country bedrooms are comfortable and breakfasts are good. Constable and Turner both painted the medieval church with its unusual spire; Petworth mansion and park (National Trust) is nearby.

 The first class food (using some home-grown and foraged produce) includes sandwiches, black treacle and whisky-cured salmon with mediterranean couscous, pork rillette and game terrine with pickles, wild mushroom gnocchi with blue cheese, mushroom velouté and truffle oil crumbs, confit pork belly with roast celeriac and black pudding, local chalk stream trout with crab beignet, black olive tapenade and ratte potatoes, organic 35-day aged, rare-breed flat-iron steak with a choice of sauce, and puddings such as red velvet ice-cream sandwich with raspberry coulis and buttermilk pudding with poached rhubarb and ginger nut crumb. *Benchmark main dish: venison haunch with coriander couscous, moroccan-spiced pigeon pastilla and date and cinnamon gravy £21.50. Two-course evening meal £26.00.*

Enterprise ~ Lease Sam Beard and Michaela Hofirkova ~ Real ale ~ Open 12-midnight ~ Bar food 12-2.30, 6.30-9 (9.30 Fri); 12-3, 6-9.30 Sat; 12-3.30 Sun ~ Children welcome ~ Dogs welcome ~ Wi-fi ~ Bedrooms: £90/£110 *Recommended by Miss A E Dare, Richard Tilbrook, Alison and Tony Livesley, Rosie and John Moore, Tracey and Stephen Groves, David and Charlotte Emslie, Matilda and Gerald Thoms*

UCKFIELD
TQ4720 Map 3
Highlands
(01825) 762989 – www.highlandsinn.co.uk
Eastbourne Road/Lewes Road; TN22 5SP

Busy, well run pub with plenty of space, real ales and well thought-of food; seats outside

Our favourite spot in this large, spreading pub is around the bar counter: tartan-covered benches, high leather chairs around equally high tables and armchairs, and Harveys Best and two quickly changing local guests on handpump, nine wines by the glass, a dozen malt whiskies and a cocktail menu. Service from friendly, helpful young staff is good. The restaurant on the right is split into two by a dividing wall featuring bookcase wallpaper, and has painted rafters in high ceilings, big glass lamps and walls decorated with local photographs and animal pictures. Also, all manner of cushioned dining and painted farmhouse chairs, long chesterfield sofas, upholstered banquettes and scatter cushions on settles around wooden tables on the part-carpeted, part-wooden and part-ceramic flooring; background music. An end bar, liked by locals, has a games area and an open fire. At the front of the building is a two-level terrace – the sunny top half is used for dining while the lower decked area has sofas and more tables and chairs. This is sister pub to the Cock at Ringmer. Disabled access.

🍴 A wide choice of popular food includes sandwiches, baked camembert with garlic, honey and rosemary, smoked salmon, prawn and avocado cocktail, sweet potato, spinach, cauliflower and chickpea curry, pork and herb sausages with mash and onion gravy, salmon fillet with honey, orange, redcurrant, ginger and soy glaze, slow-cooked lamb shank with sweet potato and garlic mash, braised red cabbage and balsamic gravy, and puddings such as ginger and treacle tart with custard and crumble of the day. *Benchmark main dish: burgers with toppings, coleslaw and fries £11.50. Two-course evening meal £21.00.*

Ridley Inns ~ Managers Ian, Val, Nick and Matt Ridley ~ Real ale ~ Open 11-11; 11am-midnight Fri, Sat; 11-10.30 Sun ~ Bar food 12-2.30, 6-9.30; 12-9.30 Sat; 12-7.30 Sun ~ Restaurant ~ Children welcome ~ Dogs allowed in bar ~ Wi-fi *Recommended by Andrea and Philip Crispin, Charlie Stevens, Peter Brix, John and Delia Franks, Gus Swan, Matthew and Elisabeth Reeves, Audrey and Paul Summers*

WARNINGLID
TQ2425   Map 3

Half Moon ♀

(01444) 461227 – www.thehalfmoonwarninglid.co.uk
B2115 off A23 S of Handcross or off B2110 Handcross–Lower Beeding; RH17 5TR

Simply furnished pub with real ales, rewarding food, lots of wines by the glass and seats in sizeable garden; bedrooms

Many customers come to this bustling 18th-c inn for a good meal, but the lively locals' bar is full of cheerful drinkers and the atmosphere is properly pubby. There's straightforward wooden furniture on bare boards and a small Victorian fireplace, and helpful staff serve Greene King Old Speckled Hen, Harveys Best and a guest from Wimbledon on handpump, around 18 wines by the glass, several malt whiskies and a farm cider; a room just off here has oak beams and flagstones. A couple of steps lead down to the dining areas, which have a mix of wooden chairs, cushioned wall settles and nice old tables on floorboards, plank panelling and bare brick, and old village photographs; there's also another open fire and a glass-covered well. A sizeable sheltered garden has picnic-sets on a lawn and a stunning avenue of trees with uplighters that glow at night. Bedrooms are contemporary and comfortable and breakfasts highly rated.

🍴 Highly popular food includes goats cheese pannacotta with fig jelly and walnut and honey dressing, wild halibut in fragrant thai broth with pak choi and spring onions, sunblush tomato, lemon and pea risotto with halloumi and chermoula dressing, beer-battered cod and fries, moroccan-style lamb burger with mint yoghurt and sweet chilli sauce, barbary duck breast with Marmite, glazed liver and celeriac rösti, roast venison haunch with braised shoulder, faggot, parsnip purée and port and redcurrant jus, and puddings such as crème brûlée with a changing salsa and Grand Marnier marquise. *Benchmark main dish: calves liver and bacon with creamed potatoes and onion gravy £16.00. Two-course evening meal £22.00.*

Free house ~ Licensee James Amico ~ Real ale ~ Open 11.30-3, 5.30-11; 12-7 Sun; closed Mon ~ Bar food 12-2, 6-9.30; 12-3 Sun ~ Restaurant ~ Children welcome ~ Dogs allowed in bar ~ Wi-fi ~ Bedrooms: /£95 *Recommended by Belinda Stamp, Margo and Derek Peters, Serena and Adam Furber, Alexandra and Richard Clay, Miss B D Picton, Nicholas and Lucy Sage, Charlotte and William Mason, Sally and Colin Allen*

WEST HOATHLY

Cat 🏠⭐ ⏻ 🛏

TQ3632   Map 3

(01342) 810369 – www.catinn.co.uk

Village signposted from A22 and B2028 S of East Grinstead; North Lane; RH19 4PP

16th-c inn with old-fashioned bar, airy dining rooms, local real ales, tempting food and seats outside; charming bedrooms

This is a smashing little all-rounder – as reflected by the warm reports we receive. You'll get a genuine welcome from the hands-on licensees and the lovely old bar has beams, pubby tables and chairs on an old wooden floor, and a fine log fire in an inglenook fireplace. Harveys Best and Old Ale and guests such as Bedlam Hibernation, Firebird Parody Session IPA and Larkins Traditional on handpump, as well as two local farm ciders, local apple juice, over 20 wines by the glass or carafe (plus six locally made sparkling wines) from a carefully chosen list, and a growing list of non-alcoholic choices. Look out for the glass cover over the 75-ft deep well. Light, airy dining rooms have a nice mix of wooden dining chairs and tables on pale wood-strip flooring, and throughout there are hops, china platters, brass and copper ornaments and a gently upmarket atmosphere. Glass doors from a contemporary-style garden room open on to a terrace with teak furniture. The cocker spaniel is called Harvey. Bedrooms are comfortable and well equipped and breakfasts are particularly good. Disabled access. Parking is limited but there is a public car park 300 metres away. Steam train enthusiasts can visit the Bluebell Railway, and the Priest House in the village is a fascinating museum in a cottage endowed with an extraordinary array of ancient anti-witch symbols.

🍽️ Local, seasonal produce is at the heart of the first class food: sandwiches, pork croquette with apple, goats cheese and walnut salad, harissa and dill mussels with beer bread, sesame-glazed tofu with purple sprouting broccoli, spring onions and cashew nuts, chargrilled chicken caesar salad, roast cod with sausage and butter bean cassoulet, peppered venison haunch with braised red cabbage and red wine sauce, 12-hour pork belly with pear compote and creamed potatoes, and puddings such as spiced ginger cake with salted caramel sauce and vanilla ice-cream and chocolate délice with almond brittle and raspberry sorbet. *Benchmark main dish: steak and mushroom in ale pie £14.75. Two-course evening meal £21.00.*

Free house ~ Licensee Andrew Russell ~ Real ale ~ Open 12-11; 12-10 Sun ~ Bar food 12-2, 6-9; 12-2.30, 6-9.30 Fri, Sat; 12-2.30, 6-8.30 Sun ~ Children over 7 welcome ~ Dogs allowed in bar and bedrooms ~ Wi-fi ~ Bedrooms: £105/£130 *Recommended by Robert and Diana Ringstone, Sylvia and Phillip Spencer, Nicholas and Maddy Trainer, Tony Scott, Frances and Hamish Porter, Louise and Oliver Redman, Fiona and Jack Henderson*

Anyone claiming to arrange, or prevent, inclusion of a pub in the *Guide* is a fraud. Pubs are included only if recommended by readers and if our own anonymous inspection confirms that they are suitable.

WITHYHAM
TQ4935 Map 3

Dorset Arms ♀ ⇔

(01892) 770278 – www.dorset-arms.co.uk

B2110; TN7 4BD

Friendly, bustling inn with beamed rooms, real ales and good wines, interesting food and seats in garden; bedrooms

Behind the tall white Georgian façade is a building dating back to 1556. It's part of the Buckhurst Estate and named after the Earls and Dukes of Dorset. A friendly and informal beamed bar is to the left of the front door, with fender seats around an open fire, scatter cushions on a built-in wall seat, a couple of armchairs, a few simple seats and tables, and darts. Harveys Best and a couple of guests from breweries such as Larkins and Long Man on handpump, good wines by the glass and a growing collection of gins, served by friendly, courteous staff. The dining room has a cottagey feel with pretty curtains, bookshelves to either side of a small fireplace, horse pictures and paintings, rosettes and pieces of china, a long red leather wall seat and wheelback and farmhouse chairs around white tables; board games. A small room leads off with high-backed red leather chairs around light tables, a large ornate gilt-edged mirror, antlers and a chandelier; a lower room with contemporary seats and tables has a retractable roof. Outside there are seats on the front terrace and picnic-sets on grass, and steep steps lead up to a lawned garden with more picnic-sets. Bedrooms are attractively decorated and comfortable.

Enjoyable food includes sandwiches, ham hock terrine with piccalilli, prawn cocktail, olive, spinach, feta and tomato pappardelle, plaice goujons with tartare sauce and frites, duck breast with spring onion rösti, asparagus and honey and five-spice dressing, sea bass with lemon-crushed new potatoes and salsa verde, barnsley chop with anchovy butter, côte de beouf (for two to share) with watercress salad, frites and béarnaise sauce, and puddings such as lemon posset and chocolate and hazelnut brownie with hot fudge sauce and vanilla ice-cream. *Benchmark main dish: venison steak with blue cheese, mash and spinach £20.00. Two-course evening meal £22.00.*

Free house ~ Licensee Simon Brazier ~ Real ale ~ Open 12-11; 12-10 Sun ~ Bar food 12-2.30, 6-9; 12-8 Sat; 12-8 Sun ~ Restaurant ~ Children welcome ~ Dogs allowed in bar and bedrooms ~ Wi-fi ~ Bedrooms: £80/£115 *Recommended by Tim and Sue Mulligan, Victoria and Len Meadows, Richard and Penny Gibbs, Mike and Sarah Abbot, Paul Faraday, Miranda and Jeff Davidson*

Also Worth a Visit in Sussex

Besides the fully inspected pubs, you might like to try these pubs that have been recommended to us and described by readers. Do tell us what you think of them: feedback@goodguides.com

ALBOURNE TQ2514
Ginger Fox (01273) 857888
Take B2117 W from A23; pub at junction with A281; BN6 9EA Thatched country dining pub with simple rustic interior; highly regarded modern cooking, not cheap but they also do a good value two-course weekday lunch and popular Sun roasts (booking recommended), small bar area serving local ales such as Bedlam, Dark Star and Long Man, plenty of wines by the glass from good list, friendly professional service; children welcome, attractive garden with downs views, play area, open all day. *(Paddy and Sian O'Leary)*

ALFOLD BARS TQ0333
Sir Roger Tichborne
(01403) 751873 *B2133 N of Loxwood; RH14 0QS* Renovated and extended beamed country pub keeping original nooks and crannies; five well kept ales such as Dark Star, Hammerpot and Youngs from brick-

faced servery, popular well presented food (all day Fri-Sun) from varied menu including weekday set lunch, some themed evenings, friendly attentive service, flagstones and inglenook log fire, pitched-roof restaurant with french windows to garden; children and dogs (in bar) welcome, back terrace and large sloping lawn with lovely rural views, play area, good walks, open all day. *(Tony and Wendy Hobden, Tony Scott)*

ALFRISTON   TQ5203
★**Star** (01323) 870495
High Street; BN26 5TA Handsome 13th-c timbered inn decorated with fine medieval carvings, the striking red lion on the corner (known as Old Bill) was probably the figurehead from a wrecked dutch ship; heavy dark beams in character front bar, cushioned settles, stools and captain's chairs around pubby tables on bare boards, log fire in Tudor fireplace, tankards over counter serving Dark Star, Long Man and ten wines by the glass, steps down to big two-level bar (one level has lovely herringbone brick floor), rustic tables, chapel chairs, open fire and woodburner, further room with book wallpaper, plush burgundy armchairs/sofas and another woodburner, good locally sourced food served by friendly young staff; regular music evenings, TV; children and dogs welcome, comfortable contemporary bedrooms, open all day, food all day Fri-Sun. *(Richard Cole)*

AMBERLEY   SO0313
Black Horse (01798) 831183
Off B2139; BN18 9NL Pretty village pub reopened after extensive refurbishment; character main bar, garden room and restaurant with view into kitchen, log fires, highly thought-of food from interesting fairly short menu (booking advised), three real ales and well chosen wines, friendly attentive service; children welcome, attractive garden with downs view, seven bedrooms, parking can be difficult, open all day. *(Maggie and Matthew Lyons)*

AMBERLEY   TQ0211
Bridge (01798) 831619
Houghton Bridge, off B2139; BN18 9LR Comfortable open-plan dining pub with good mix of locals and visitors; pleasant bar and two-room dining area, candles on tables, log fire, wide range of popular reasonably priced food from good sandwiches up, well kept Harveys and two guests, cheerful efficient young staff; children and dogs welcome, seats out in front, more tables in enclosed side garden, handy for the station, open all day. *(Maggie and Matthew Lyons)*

AMBERLEY   TQ0313
Sportsman (01798) 831787
Crossgates; Rackham Road, off B2139; BN18 9NR Popular 17th-c tile-hung pub with three rooms around central bar; well kept local ales such as Ballards, Goldmark,

Hammerpot, Harveys and Listers, good value home-cooked food from sandwiches up, friendly staff, great views over Amberley Wildbrooks nature reserve from back conservatory (binoculars provided) and decked terrace; children and dogs welcome, pretty little front garden, good walks, five bedrooms (three taking in the view), open all day Sat, till 6pm Sun. *(Tony and Wendy Hobden, Tony Scott)*

ANGMERING   TQ0604
Lamb (01903) 774300
The Square; BN16 4EQ Updated 18th-c village coaching inn; popular food from varied menu including good value two-course lunch, ales such as Fullers and Listers from light wood servery, good choice of wines by the glass, helpful friendly service, painted half-panelling and wood-strip floors, inglenook log fire in bar, raised woodburner in restaurant; children and dogs welcome, terrace seating, eight modernised bedrooms, open all day. *(Chantelle and Tony Redman)*

ARDINGLY   TQ3430
Gardeners Arms (01444) 892328
B2028 2 miles N; RH17 6TJ Cosy and relaxed 17th-c pub opposite South of England showground; enjoyable food (all day Sun) from sandwiches and pub favourites up, Badger ales, pleasant efficient service, linked rooms with standing timbers and inglenooks, scrubbed pine furniture on flagstones and broad boards, old local photographs, mural in back part, children and dogs welcome, disabled facilities, pretty terrace and side garden, well placed for Borde Hill Garden and Wakehurst (NT), open all day. *(Victoria and Stuart Parsons)*

ARLINGTON   TQ5507
Old Oak (01323) 482072
Caneheath; off A22 or A27 NW of Polegate; BN26 6SJ 17th-c former almshouse with L-shaped bar, beams, log fires and comfortable seating, well kept Harveys and Long Man, enjoyable traditional food from sandwiches to specials, afternoon teas; background music, old sussex coin game toad in the hole played here; children and dogs welcome, circular picnic-sets out in front and in garden with play area, walks in nearby Abbots Wood, open all day (food all day weekends). *(Peter Barratt)*

ARLINGTON   TQ5407
Yew Tree (01323) 870590
Off A22 near Hailsham, or A27 W of Polegate; BN26 6RX Neatly cared-for Victorian village pub under long-serving licensees; generous helpings of good home-made food (booking advised), well kept Harveys and Long Man, decent wines, prompt friendly service, log fires, hop-covered beams and old local photographs, darts in thriving bare-boards bar, bigger plush dining lounge and comfortable conservatory; children and

dogs (in one area) welcome, big garden with play area, good local walks, open (and food) all day Sun. *(Tony Scott)*

ARUNDEL　　　　　　　　　TQ0208
Black Rabbit　(01903) 882638
Mill Road, Offham; keep on and don't give up; BN18 9PB Riverside pub in lovely spot near wildfowl reserve, popular with families and can get very busy; long bar with eating areas at either end, good choice of reasonably priced food from sandwiches and sharing boards up, well kept Badger ales and decent wines by the glass, friendly service, various bits and pieces including stuffed fish, fishing rods and a rowing boat used in filming *Harry Potter and the Philosopher's Stone*, log fires; dogs welcome, covered tables and pretty hanging baskets out at front, extensive terrace across road overlooking River Arun, good walks, open (and food) all day. *(Ian Phillips, Darren and Clare Jones, Sheila Topham)*

ARUNDEL　　　　　　　　　TQ0107
Swan　(01903) 882314
High Street; BN18 9AG Georgian inn's comfortably relaxed L-shaped bar, well kept Fullers/Gales beers and occasional guests, popular fairly priced food including set lunch and other deals, friendly efficient young staff, wood flooring, sporting memorabilia and old photographs, local artwork for sale, open fire, connecting restaurant; children and dogs (in bar) welcome, 14 bedrooms, no car park (pay-and-display opposite), open all day, breakfast for non-residents. *(Ann and Colin Hunt)*

ASHURST　　　　　　　　　　TQ1816
Fountain　(01403) 710219
B2135 S of Partridge Green; BN44 3AP Attractive 16th-c pub with plenty of character; rustic tap room on right with log fire in brick inglenook, country dining chairs around polished tables on flagstones, opened-up snug has heavy beams and another inglenook, Harveys Best, guest beers and plenty of wines by the glass, well liked home-cooked food including blackboard specials, skittle alley/function room; children and dogs welcome, seats on front brick terrace, pretty garden with orchard and duck pond, open (and food) all day, kitchen shuts 4pm Sun. *(Tony and Wendy Hobden, Tony Scott)*

BALLS CROSS　　　　　　　SU9826
★Stag　(01403) 820241
Village signed off A283 at N edge of Petworth; GU28 9JP Cheery unspoilt 17th-c country pub under welcoming new management; cosy flagstoned bar with log fire in huge inglenook, a few seats and bar stools, Badger beers, Weston's Old Rosie cider and several wines by the glass, second tiny room and appealing bare-boards cottagey restaurant, fishing rods, horse tack, country knick-knacks and old photographs, good fairly pubby food (not Mon or Sun evenings);

darts and board games in separate room, outside loos; children and dogs welcome, seats out in front and in pretty back garden, classic car meeting last Weds of month, open all day Sat, till 9pm Sun. *(Douglas Power)*

BARCOMBE CROSS　　　　　TQ4212
Royal Oak　(01273) 400418
Off A275 N of Lewes; BN8 5BA Village pub with good mix of locals and visitors, well kept Harveys ales, reasonably priced wines and 20 malt whiskies, generously served food from bar snacks up (kitchen closes Sun evening-Weds, pizza van Mon evening), long bar with restaurant attached, beams, bare boards and open fire; skittle alley; children and dogs welcome, a few tables out in front and in small tree-shaded garden, open all day. *(John Beeken)*

BARNS GREEN　　　　　　　TQ1227
Queens Head　(01403) 730436
Chapel Road; RH13 0PS Welcoming traditional tile-hung village pub; generous helpings of popular home-made food including daily specials, five well kept ales such as Fullers, Harveys and local Hepworths, good range of wines by the glass; acoustic music first Weds of the month, quiz second Tues, classic car event Aug; children and dogs welcome, tables out at front and in back garden with play area, open all day, no food Sun evening. *(Brian and Sally Wakeham)*

BERWICK　　　　　　　　　　TQ5206
Berwick Inn　(01323) 870018
By station; BN26 6SZ Roomy beamed and carpeted pub with large lounge/eating area, downstairs restaurant and upstairs coffee shop (open from 7.30am), copperware and railway pictures, log fires, well kept ales such as Harveys, good choice of wines by the glass and popular enterprising food from shortish menu including some pub classics; children welcome, large garden behind, good walking/cycling, handy for Drusillas Park zoo, open all day (till 9pm Sun). *(John Beeken)*

BERWICK　　　　　　　　　　TQ5105
★Cricketers Arms　(01323) 870469
Lower Road, S of A27; BN26 6SP Charming brick and flint local with three small unpretentious bars, huge supporting beam in each low ceiling, simple country furnishings on quarry tiles, cricketing pictures and bats, two log fires, friendly staff, four Harveys ales tapped from the cask, over a dozen wines by the glass and decent range of gins, well cooked uncomplicated food at reasonable prices; old sussex coin game toad in the hole; children (in family room) and dogs welcome, delightful cottagey front garden with picnic-sets among small brick paths, more seats behind, Bloomsbury Group wall paintings in nearby church and handy for Charleston, good South Downs walks, open (and food) all day Sat, shuts 7pm Sun and may close Mon evening in winter. *(Alan Cowell, Tony Scott)*

BILLINGSHURST   TQ0830
Blue Ship   (01403) 822709
The Haven; hamlet signposted off A29 just N of junction with A264, then follow signpost left towards Garlands and Okehurst; RH14 9BS Unspoilt pub in quiet country spot; beamed front bar with wall benches and scrubbed tables on brick floor, inglenook woodburner, cask-tapped Badger ales served from hatch, good home-made food from pub favourites up, two small carpeted back rooms; bar billiards, darts, shove-ha'penny, cribbage and dominoes; children and dogs welcome, tables out at front and in side garden with play area, camping, closed Sun evening, Mon. *(Ruth May)*

BILLINGSHURST   TQ0725
Limeburners   (01403) 782311
Lordings Road, Newbridge (B2133/A272 W); RH14 9JA Friendly characterful local in converted row of cottages; three Fullers ales and generous helpings of enjoyable reasonably priced pubby food from snacks up, part-carpeted bar with horsebrasses on dark beams and inglenook at each end, chatty atmosphere; live music and quiz nights, bar billiards, TV; children and dogs welcome, picnic-sets in nice front garden with play area, campsite behind. *(Tony and Wendy Hobden)*

BILLINGSHURST   TQ0825
Olde Six Bells   (01403) 782124
High Street (A29); RH14 9QS Picturesque partly 14th-c timbered pub; updated interior with large bar and split-level restaurant, flagstone and wood floors, inglenook log fire, four well kept Badger ales and a guest, enjoyable reasonably priced pubby food (not Sun evening) from baguettes and baked potatoes up; occasional live music, games room, free wi-fi; children and dogs welcome, roadside garden and terrace, open all day. *(Ruth May)*

BINSTED   SU9806
Black Horse   (01243) 553325
Binsted Lane; about 2 miles W of Arundel, turn S off A27 towards Binsted; BN18 0LP Modernised 17th-c dining pub with good varied choice of food from sandwiches up, ales such as Harveys and local Listers, wood-floored bar and separate dining room; regular live music; children and dogs welcome, plenty of outside seating on terrace with covered well, lawn and in open-fronted cart lodge, valley views over golf course, closed Sun evening, Mon. *(Tony and Wendy Hobden)*

BLACKBOYS   TQ5220
★ Blackboys Inn   (01825) 890283
B2192, S edge of village; TN22 5LG Old weatherboarded inn set back from the road; main bar to the right with beams, timbers, dark wooden furniture and log fire, locals' bar to left with lots of bric-a-brac, Harveys ales including seasonals, several wines by the glass and wide choice of enjoyable food (all day Sat, till 6pm Sun), panelled dining areas; background and some live music including open mike nights; children and dogs (in bar) welcome, sizeable garden with seats under trees, on terrace and under cover by duck pond, good walks (Vanguard Way passes the pub, Wealdway close by), eight bedrooms in converted stables, open all day. *(Andrew Stone)*

BODIAM   TQ7825
Castle Inn   (01580) 830330
Village signed from B2244; opposite Bodiam Castle; TN32 5UB Bustling country pub very handy for Bodiam Castle (NT); Shepherd Neame ales and a couple of guests, good choice of wines, popular reasonably priced food from sandwiches up, friendly helpful service, plain tables and chairs in snug bar with log fire, back restaurant; occasional live music; picnic-sets on big sheltered terrace, open all day, food all day weekends. *(Charles Welch)*

BOGNOR REGIS   SZ9201
Royal Oak   (01243) 821002
A259 Chichester Road, North Bersted; PO21 5JF Old-fashioned two-bar beamed local (aka the Pink Pub); well kept Shepherd Neame Spitfire and guest such as Wadworths, shortish choice of popular reasonably priced food till 6.30pm (2.30pm Sun), friendly service; Thurs quiz and occasional live music, darts, bar billiards and sports TV, free wi-fi; children and dogs welcome, open all day. *(Harvey Brown)*

BOLNEY   TQ2622
Eight Bells   (01444) 881396
The Street; RH17 5QW Popular and welcoming family-run village pub; wide choice of good sensibly priced food from bar snacks up, breakfasts (7.30-11am Mon-Sat), OAP lunch (Mon-Weds), efficient friendly young staff, well kept Harveys, a couple of guests and decent range of wines, brick-floored bar with eight handbells suspended above servery, second flagstoned bar and timbered dining extension, open fires; bar billiards, pool and darts, sports TV; children and dogs welcome, disabled facilities, tables out on deck under huge canopy, outside bar and play area, various events including Easter Mon pram race, three bedrooms in separate beamed cottage, open all day (till 1am Fri, Sat), no food Sun evening (or Mon in Jan). *(Gavin Dunbar, Tony Scott)*

BOSHAM   SU8003
★ Anchor Bleu   (01243) 573956
High Street; PO18 8LS Waterside inn overlooking Chichester Harbour; two simple bars with low ochre ceilings, worn flagstones and exposed timbered brickwork, lots of

nautical bric-a-brac, robust furniture (some tables close together), up to six real ales and popular sensibly priced bar food, efficient friendly staff (they may ask for a credit card if you run a tab), upstairs dining room; children and dogs welcome, seats on front terrace and raised back one (access through massive wheel-operated bulkhead door), lovely views over sheltered inlet, can park by water but note tide times, church up lane depicted in Bayeux Tapestry, village and shore worth exploring, open all day and can get very crowded. *(Miss A E Dare)*

BOSHAM SU8105
White Swan (01243) 696465
A259 roundabout; Station Road; PO18 8NG Spic and span 18th-c dining pub with sensibly priced blackboard food including daily specials, three well kept ales such as Dark Star, Hop Back and Upham, cheerful helpful service, good-sized flagstone bar, restaurant behind with old bread oven, darts in snug; fortnightly quiz Weds, sports TV; children and dogs welcome in certain areas, open all day, no food Sun evening. *(Ann and Colin Hunt, Tony and Wendy Hobden)*

BRIGHTON TQ3104
★**Basketmakers Arms**
(01273) 689006 *Gloucester Road – the E end, near Cheltenham Place; off Marlborough Place (A23) via Gloucester Street; BN1 4AD* Cheerful bustling backstreet local run by long-serving landlord; Fullers beers and guests from eight handpumps, decent wines by the glass and over 100 malt whiskies (good range of other spirits too), well liked reasonably priced food, two small low-ceilinged rooms, lots of interesting old tins, enamel signs, photographs and posters; background music; children (till 8pm) and dogs welcome, disabled access, a few pavement tables, open (and food) all day, shuts midnight Fri, Sat. *(Katherine Matthews)*

BRIGHTON TQ3004
Brighton Beer Dispensary
(01273) 710624 *Dean Street; BN1 3EG* Popular little terraced pub owned by Southey, their ales and guests, craft beers and an extensive bottled range, hand-pulled ciders too, friendly knowledgeable staff, food provided by pop-up kitchens, small back conservatory; quiz nights; open all day and can get packed. *(Miles Green)*

BRIGHTON TQ3203
Bristol Bar (01273) 605687
Paston Place; BN2 1HA Kemptown pub overlooking the sea; well kept Harveys and plenty of wines by the glass, enjoyable fairly priced bistro-style food from open kitchen, friendly staff; children (at lunchtime) and dogs welcome, wheelchair access, open all day. *(Miles Green)*

BRIGHTON TQ3104
Colonnade (01273) 328728
New Road, off North Street; by Theatre Royal; BN1 1UF Small richly restored theatre bar with ornate frontage – note Willie the 19th-c automaton in small bay window; shining brass and mahogany, plush banquettes, velvet swags and gleaming mirrors, interesting pre-war playbills and signed theatrical photographs, three well kept ales including Fullers London Pride, good range of wines and interesting gins; downstairs loos; pavement seats overlooking Pavilion gardens, open all day. *(Miles Green)*

BRIGHTON TQ3004
Craft Beer Company
(01273) 723736 *Upper North Street; BN1 3FG* Busy corner pub with fine selection of interesting draught and bottled beers served by friendly knowledgeable staff, enjoyable food (not Mon) limited to burgers and Sun roasts, simple L-shaped bar with raised back section; sports TV; closed Mon lunchtime, otherwise open all day (till 1am Fri, Sat). *(Andrew Stone)*

BRIGHTON TQ3004
Evening Star (01273) 328931
Surrey Street; BN1 3PB Chatty drinkers' pub attracting good mix of customers; simple pale wood furniture on bare boards, up to four well kept Dark Star ales (originally brewed here) and lots of changing guests, continental beers (in bottles too) and traditional ciders/perries, bar snacks, friendly staff coping well at busy times; background and some live music, free wi-fi; pavement tables, open all day and handy for the station. *(Miles Green)*

BRIGHTON TQ3203
Ginger Dog (01273) 620990
College Place, Kemptown; BN2 1HN Restauranty Kemptown pub in same small group as the Ginger Pig (Hove) and Ginger Fox (Albourne); well regarded modern food from changing menu (not especially cheap), good wines, cocktails and local beers, well informed friendly service, fairly traditional bare-boards interior; children and dogs (in bar) welcome, open all day. *(Andrew Stone, Miles Green)*

BRIGHTON TQ2804
★**Ginger Pig** (01273) 736123
Hove Street; BN3 2TR Bustling place just a short walk from the beach; informal bare-boards bar area with plush stools and simple wooden dining chairs around mixed tables, armchairs and sofas here and there, Harveys Best and a guest, nice wines by the glass and interesting local spirits and soft drinks, raised restaurant part with long button-back wall seating and more wooden tables and chairs, enterprising modern food (highish prices) served by friendly attentive staff;

background music; children welcome, 11 stylish ensuite bedrooms, open all day. *(Miles Green)*

BRIGHTON TQ3103
Hand in Hand (01273) 699595
Upper St James Street, Kemptown; BN2 1JN It may be Brighton's smallest pub, but the canary yellow exterior makes it hard to miss; own-brewed beers along with a local guest, plenty of bottled beers and real cider, dimly lit bar with a few tables and benches, tie collection and lots of newspaper cuttings on the walls, photographs including Victorian nudes on the ceiling, some snacky food, cheerful service and colourful mix of customers; interesting background music (live jazz Sun), veteran fruit machine; dogs welcome, open all day and can get crowded. *(Andrew Stone)*

BRIGHTON TQ3004
Lion & Lobster (01273) 327299
Sillwood Street; BN1 2PS Red-painted backstreet pub spread over three floors (three bars and restaurant); softly lit interior with lots of pictures, well kept ales such as Dark Star and Harveys, extensive choice of well presented enterprising food (booking advised) including daily specials and a late-night menu, friendly efficient young staff; regular jazz evenings, Mon quiz, sports TV; large terrace on two levels (can get very busy in summer), open (and food) all day, till 2am Fri and Sat. *(Tony Scott)*

BRIGHTON TQ3309
Stanmer House (01273) 680400
Stanmer Park; BN1 9QA Whiting & Hammond pub-restaurant in 18th-c parkland mansion; three impressive front rooms with button-back leather chesterfields on bare boards or marble, ornate fireplaces, gilt-edged mirrors and chandeliers, stone lions/metal sculptures in wall recesses, old local photographs and shelves of books, well kept Park Life (brewed for them by Turners), guest ales and 16 wines by the glass, enjoyable interesting food, popular afternoon teas, dining rooms (to left) with Victorian and Edwardian-style chairs around heavy dark tables, big portraits, church candles and opulent flower arrangements; children and dogs (in some parts) welcome, rustic furniture on terrace and around garden's pond, contemporary seats on front flagstones, open (and some food) all day from 10am. *(R and M Thomas)*

BROWNBREAD STREET TQ6714
Ash Tree (01424) 892104
Off A271 (was B2204) W of Battle; first northward road W of Ashburnham Place, then first fork left, then bear right into Brownbread Street; TN33 9NX Tranquil 17th-c country local tucked away in isolated hamlet; enjoyable affordably priced home-made food including specials, good choice

of wines and well kept ales such as Harveys Best, cheerful service, cosy beamed bars with nice old settles and chairs, stripped brickwork, interesting dining areas with timbered dividers, good inglenook log fire; children (in eating area) and dogs welcome, pretty garden, closed Sun and Mon evenings, otherwise open all day. *(J H Bell)*

BURPHAM TQ0308
★George (01903) 883131
Off A27 near Warningcamp; BN18 9RR Community-owned cottagey pub with attractively updated beamed interior; sofas by woodburner in bar, ales such as Arundel, Greyhound and Hammerpot, 21 wines by the glass and good choice of popular food, interconnected eating areas with farmhouse and other dining chairs around wooden tables on bare board, friendly helpful service; background music, darts and board games; children and dogs welcome, picnic-sets out at front under parasols, short walk away are splendid views down to Arundel Castle and the river, open all day weekends (closed Sun evening and Mon in winter). *(Ruth and Peter Bacon, Jocelyn and Helen Dalby, Victoria and Len Meadows)*

BURWASH TQ6724
Rose & Crown (01435) 882600
Inn sign on A265; TN19 7ER Old tile-hung local tucked down lane (parking can be tricky) in pretty village; well kept Harveys ales, decent wines and enjoyable fairly priced food (not Sun or Mon evenings), friendly french landlady and staff, very low beamed ceilings, pubby furniture on patterned carpet, inglenook log fire, restaurant to the left with another inglenook, glass-covered well just inside front door; monthly live music; children and dogs welcome, small side garden and pleasant back terrace, four bedrooms, handy for Batemans (NT), open all day (till 9pm Sun). *(Martin Day, Martin Bradley, Christopher Warren)*

BURWASH WEALD TQ6523
Wheel (01435) 882299
A265 Burwash–Heathfield; TN19 7LA Steps up to recently refurbished village pub; opened up bar area with beams, bare boards and inglenook log fire, mix of old tables and chairs, candles in bottles and some interesting old local photographs, well kept Harveys, a guest beer and well chosen wines, good sensibly priced food from sharing plates up, friendly helpful service, a couple of separate dining areas; background music; children and dogs (in bar) welcome, seats out in front and in tree-shaded back garden, open all day. *(Brian and Sally Wakeham)*

BURY TQ0013
Squire & Horse (01798) 831343
Bury Common; A29 Fontwell–Pulborough; RH20 1NS 16th-c roadside dining pub with very good attractively

presented food from australian chef, well kept Harveys, a guest ale and good choice of wines, several partly divided beamed areas, plush wall seats, hunting prints and ornaments, log fire; children welcome, no dogs inside, pleasant garden and pretty terrace (some road noise), open (and food) all day Sun. *(Ruth May)*

BYWORTH   SU9821
★ **Black Horse** (01798) 342424
Off A283; GU28 0HL Popular chatty country pub with smart simply furnished bar, pews and scrubbed tables on bare boards, pictures and old photographs, open fire, four real ales including Flowerpots and Fullers, Cornish Orchards cider, enjoyable food (not Sun evening) from light lunchtime dishes up, back restaurant with nooks and crannies and old range, spiral staircase to heavily beamed function/dining room, games area (pool and darts); occasional live music and other events; children welcome, dogs in bar, attractive garden with tables on steep grassy terraces, lovely downs views, one bedroom in converted stable, open all day. *(Tony Scott)*

CATSFIELD   TQ7213
White Hart (01424) 892650
B2204, off A269; The Green; TN33 9DJ Friendly weatherboarded and beamed village pub; well kept Harveys and Sharps, good range of malt whiskies and enjoyable reasonably priced traditional food including Mon curry night, warm log fire, raftered dining room with pubby furniture and woodburner; quiz first Tues of month, some live music; children, walkers and dogs welcome, fenced garden, two bedrooms, open all day, no food Sun evening.
(Gene and Kitty Rankin)

CHAILEY   TQ3919
Five Bells (01825) 722259
A275, 9 miles N of Lewes; BN8 4DA Attractive old roadside pub with good food (not Sun evening, Mon) cooked by landlord-chef from bar snacks and pub favourites up, some themed evenings, four well kept ales including Harveys and decent choice of wines, friendly staff, different rooms and alcoves leading from low-beamed central bar, older-style furniture on bare boards or quarry tiles, inglenook log fire; board games; children and dogs welcome, pretty garden front and side, open all day (till 8pm Sun and Mon). *(Peter Meister)*

CHICHESTER   SU8605
Chichester Inn (01243) 783185
West Street; PO19 1RP Georgian pub with half a dozen local ales such as Dark Star, Harveys and Langham, good value pubby food from snacks up, smallish front lounge with plain wooden tables and chairs, sofas by open fire, larger back public bar; live music and other events such as comedy nights and beer festivals, sports TV, pool; courtyard garden

with smokers' shelter, four bedrooms, open all day. *(Douglas Power)*

CHICHESTER   SU8504
Crate & Apple (01243) 539336
Westgate; PO19 3EU Refurbished dining pub with enjoyable food from shortish but varied menu, local ales such as Harveys and Long Man, good range of wines by the glass, cocktails, friendly helpful service, modern décor with simple tables and chairs on wood or stone floors, painted dados, leather sofas by woodburner; quiz nights; children welcome, sunny front terrace with umbrellas, more seats behind, open all day from 10am. *(Ann and Colin Hunt)*

CHICHESTER   SU8604
Eastgate (01243) 774877
The Hornet (A286); PO19 7JG Welcoming town pub with light airy interior extending back; Fullers/Gales beers and a guest, well cooked affordably priced food (not Sat, Sun evenings), cheerful prompt service, pubby furniture on bare boards or patterned carpet, woodburner; background and weekend live music, pool, darts and sports TV; dogs welcome, small heated back terrace, open all day. *(Douglas Power)*

CHICHESTER   SU8605
George & Dragon (01243) 785660
North Street; PO19 1NQ Bustling L-shaped bar with comfortable leather sofas on bare boards, open fire, Dark Star Hophead, Sharps Doom Bar, Timothy Taylors Landlord and a guest, Weston's cider, reasonably priced food from ciabattas up including some smokehouse dishes and daily specials, friendly service, conservatory restaurant; children welcome, decked back terrace with café-style tables and chairs, ten bedrooms in converted stables, open (and food) all day, except Sun when kitchen closes at 4pm. *(Tony and Wendy Hobden)*

CHICHESTER   SU8605
Park Tavern (01243) 785057
Priory Road; PO19 1NS Popular pub in pleasant spot opposite Priory Park; good choice of Fullers/Gales beers and enjoyable reasonably priced pubby food (not Sun or Mon evenings), smallish front bar, extensive back eating area; live music and quiz nights; children and dogs welcome, open all day.
(Douglas Power)

CHIDDINGLY   TQ5414
★ **Six Bells** (01825) 872227
Village signed off A22 Uckfield–Hailsham; BN8 6HE Lively unpretentious village local run well by hard-working hands-on landlord; small linked bars with interesting bric-a-brac, local pictures and posters, old furniture, cushioned window seats and log fires, family extension giving much needed extra space, well kept Courage, Harveys and a guest, decent wines by the

glass and a proper cider, enjoyable low-priced food; regular live music including blues/folk night every other Tues, free wi-fi; dogs welcome in bar, seats out at back by big raised goldfish pond, boules, monthly vintage and kit-car meetings, church opposite with interesting Jefferay Monument, open all day. *(Gene and Kitty Rankin)*

CHIDHAM   SU7804

★**Old House at Home**   (01243) 572477

Off A259 at Barleycorn pub in Nutbourne; Cot Lane; PO18 8SU Neat 18th-c red-brick pub in remote unspoilt farm hamlet; good choice of popular food from open sandwiches to fish specials, lunchtime set menu, several wines by the glass and at least four real ales including a Langham house beer, friendly service, low beams and timbering, log fire; children allowed in eating areas, tables on front terrace and in attractive back garden, Chichester Harbour walks nearby, open all day. *(J A Snell)*

CHILGROVE   SU8116

Royal Oak   (01243) 535257

Off B2141 Petersfield–Chichester, signed Hooksway; PO18 9JZ Unchanging little country pub run by same licensees for three decades; two simple cosy bars with huge log fires, country kitchen furniture and cottagey knick-knacks, Bowman Wallops Wood, Exmoor Beast, Fullers HSB and a guest, good honest food at reasonable prices, homely dining room with woodburner, plainer family room; background and occasional live music, cribbage, dominoes and shut the box, free wi-fi; dogs welcome in bars, picnic-sets under parasols in pretty garden, handy for South Downs Way walkers, closed Mon (except bank holidays) and evenings apart from Fri and Sat. *(David Hastings)*

COCKING CAUSEWAY   SU8819

Greyhound   (01730) 814425

A286 Cocking–Midhurst; GU29 9QH Pretty 18th-c tile-hung pub set back from the road; four well kept changing ales and popular good value home-made food including daily specials (booking advised), friendly helpful staff, open-plan but cosy beamed and panelled bar with alcoves, log fire, pine furniture in modern back dining conservatory; monthly quiz; children and dogs welcome, grassed area at front with picnic-sets, sizeable garden and play area behind, open all day, food all day Sun. *(Tony and Wendy Hobden, John Beeken)*

COLEMANS HATCH   TQ4533

★**Hatch**   (01342) 822363

Signed off B2026, or off B2110 opposite church; TN7 4EJ Quaint and appealing little weatherboarded pub dating from 1430 on the edge of Ashdown Forest; big log fire in quickly filling beamed bar, small back dining room with another fire, popular freshly made

food (not Sun evening) from wide-ranging menu, well kept Harveys, Larkins and one or two guests, friendly staff and good mix of customers including families and dogs; picnic-sets on front terrace and in beautifully kept big garden, not much parking so get there early, open all day weekends. *(Nick Sharpe)*

COOLHAM   TQ1423

★**George & Dragon**   (01403) 741320

Dragons Green, Dragons Lane; pub signed off A272; RH13 8GE Tile-hung cottage surrounded by fine countryside; cosy bar with massive unusually low beams (date cut into one is either 1577 or 1677), heavily timbered walls, traditional furniture and log fire in big inglenook, Chapeau Rouleur, Harveys Best and Skinners Betty Stogs, decent wines by the glass and enjoyable food (not evenings Sun, Mon or Tues), dining room with pale farmhouse chairs around rustic tables on wood floor, quiz nights; children and dogs (in bar) welcome, pretty garden, two attractive double bedrooms in converted cottage-style stable, open all day Fri-Sun. *(Susan Eccleston)*

COUSLEY WOOD   TQ6533

Old Vine   (01892) 782271

B2100 Wadhurst–Lamberhurst; TN5 6ER Newish owners for this 16th-c weatherboarded dining pub; linked rooms with heavy beams and open timbering, inglenook log fire, ales such as Harveys and Timothy Taylors, several wines by the glass and interesting latin american food cooked by ecuadorian chef-landlord; children and dogs welcome, picnic-sets on front terrace, closed Sun evening, Mon, otherwise open (and food) all day. *(Kerry and Guy Trooper)*

COWFOLD   TQ2122

Hare & Hounds   (01403) 865354

Henfield Road (A281 S); RH13 8DR Small friendly village pub with popular good value pubby food and a couple of well kept ales including Harveys, beamed and flagstoned bar with log fire, little room off to the right, dining room to the left; children and dogs welcome, a couple of picnic-sets out in front, more seating on back terrace, open all day Fri-Sun, no food Sun evening. *(Andrew Stone)*

CRAWLEY   TQ2636

Brewery Shades   (01293) 514255

High Street; RH10 1BA Popular old tile-hung pub in town centre; ten well kept beers, several ciders and good choice of other drinks, enjoyable all-day pubby food from sandwiches up including range of 'sizzling' dishes, friendly helpful young staff, rambling interior on different levels; silent sports TV; children welcome, seats outside in pedestrianised area, open all day till 12.30am (1.30am Fri, Sat). *(Tony Hobden, Tony Scott)*

CROWBOROUGH   TQ5332
Boars Head (01892) 331070
*Boars Head; pub signed from
A26; TN6 3GR* Old tile-hung pub doing
well under new management; linked rooms
including low-beamed bar and bright
modern dining conservatory, log fires in big
stone fireplaces, good choice of enjoyable
food including daily specials, Harveys and
local guests such as Larkins and Long Man,
friendly efficient service; children and dogs
welcome, garden next to farm, open all day
(till 7pm Sun). *(Nigel and Jean Eames)*

CUCKFIELD   TQ3025
Rose & Crown (01444) 414217
London Road; RH17 5BS Former 17th-c
coaching inn run by father and son team;
good if not particularly cheap food from
regularly changing menus (not Sun evening),
early evening discount before 7pm, well kept
Harveys and a guest, local Hepworth lager
and good choice of wines/gins; children and
dogs welcome, tables out in front and in nice
garden behind, open all day (till 9pm Sun),
weekend brunch from 9am. *(David and Leone
Lawson)*

DALLINGTON   TQ6619
Swan (01424) 838242
Woods Corner; B2096 E; TN21 9LB
Old tile-hung roadside local with cheerful
chatty atmosphere; well kept Harveys and
a guest, decent wines by the glass and good
blackboard food including deals, efficient
friendly service, bare-boards bar divided
by standing timbers, old enamel signs (on
walls and floor), mixed furniture including
cushioned settle and high-backed pew,
candles in bottles, swan ornaments, big
woodburner, simple back restaurant with
far-reaching views to the coast; occasional
background music, board games; children
and dogs welcome, steps down to loos and
garden, may close early if quiet. *(Miles Green)*

DELL QUAY   SU8302
Crown & Anchor (01243) 781712
*Off A286 S of Chichester – look out
for small sign; PO20 7EE* 19th/20th-c
beamed pub in splendid spot overlooking
Chichester Harbour – best at high tide
and quiet times (can get packed on sunny
days and parking difficult); comfortable
bow-windowed lounge and panelled public
bar, two log fires, well kept Youngs Best and
a couple of guests, plenty of wines by the
glass, enjoyable freshly made food including
fresh fish/seafood, friendly efficient young
staff; children and dogs welcome, views from
large waterside terrace with Crab & Burger
Shack, nice walks, open all day, food all day
weekends. *(John Beeken)*

DONNINGTON   SU8501
Blacksmiths (01243) 785578
B2201 S of Chichester; PO20 7PR
Neatly kept little roadside pub; bar with
pale wooden wall seats, plush-topped
stools and metal-legged tables on wide
floorboards, open fire, high wicker chairs
against counter serving a couple of
changing ales from Arundel or Langham,
ten wines by the glass, popular food from
sandwiches up, two dining rooms, one with
another fire; maybe live music Sun evening
in summer, free wi-fi; children and dogs (in
bar) welcome, teak tables under parasols on
terrace enclosed by glass panels, fire pit and
country views, attractive comfortable
bedrooms, open all day (till 6pm Sun).
(Alan and Alice Morgan)

DURRINGTON   TQ1104
Park View (01903) 521397
Salvington Road; BN13 2JR Recently
refurbished former Lamb opposite recreation
ground; three well kept ales and good
fairly traditional food at fair prices from
sandwiches/wraps up, friendly helpful staff;
some live music and other events, sports TV,
pool; children and dogs welcome, large sunny
beer garden behind, open all day, no food Sun
night, Mon. *(Ruth May)*

EAST ASHLING   SU8207
Horse & Groom (01243) 575339
B2178; PO18 9AX Busy unpretentious
country pub run by long-serving landlord;
five well kept ales including Dark Star, Hop
Back and Youngs, decent choice of wines
by the glass and sensibly priced tasty food
from open sandwiches and baguettes up,
unchanging front drinkers' bar with old pale
flagstones and inglenook range, scrubbed
trestle tables in carpeted area, airy extension
with solid country kitchen furniture;
children and dogs allowed in some parts,
garden picnic-sets under umbrellas, 11 neat
bedrooms (some in barn conversion), open
all day (closes 6pm Sun evening).
(Ann and Colin Hunt)

EAST CHILTINGTON   TQ3715
Jolly Sportsman (01273) 890400
*2 miles N of B2116; Chapel Lane – follow
sign to 13th-c church; BN7 3BA* Civilised
place with impressive modern cooking from
landlord-chef including set lunch Tues-Sat
and Fri fish night; small character log-fire
bar for drinkers, local ales such as Harveys,
excellent range of malt whiskies, cognacs
and Armagnacs and very good wine list,
smart but cosy restaurant with contemporary
light wood furniture and modern landscapes,
garden room; free wi-fi; children and dogs
(in bar) welcome, rustic tables under trees

If you report on a pub that's not a featured entry, please tell us any lunchtimes
or evenings when it doesn't serve bar food.

in front garden, more seats on big back lawn with views towards the South Downs, closed Sun evening, Mon. *(Miles Green)*

EAST DEAN SU9012
Star & Garter (01243) 811318
Village signed with Charlton off A286 in Singleton; also signed off A285; PO18 0JG Brick and flint pub in peaceful village setting; pleasant bar and restaurant with exposed brickwork, panelling and oak floors, furnishings from sturdy stripped tables and country kitchen chairs through chunky modern to antique carved settles, well kept Sharps Doom Bar, a couple of guest ales and several wines by the glass, good food including local fish/seafood and some themed evenings, friendly service; background music, quiz nights, free wi-fi; children and dogs (in bar) welcome, teak furniture on heated terrace, steps down to walled lawn with picnic-sets, near South Downs Way, bedrooms, open all day, food till 6pm Sun. *(Katherine Matthews)*

EAST DEAN TV5597
★ **Tiger** (01323) 423209
Off A259 Eastbourne–Seaford; BN20 0DA Attractive old pub overlooking delightful cottage-lined sloping green; small beamed bar with window seat, long cushioned wall bench and other rustic tables and chairs, walls hung with fish prints and a stuffed tiger's head, open woodburner, five real ales such as Harveys, Long Man and St Austell, proper cider, nine wines by the glass and local gin, step down to another little room with fine high-backed curved settle, separate dining room serving enjoyable fairly traditional food; children and dogs (in bar) welcome, seats on flower-filled terrace (can also sit on the green), comfortable bedrooms, walks to the coast and along Seven Sisters clifftops, open all day. *(Martin Day, Peter Meister, Tony Scott)*

EAST HOATHLY TQ5216
Kings Head (01825) 840238
High Street/Mill Lane; BN8 6DR Creeper-clad 17th-c pub on crossroads (was the village school); long open-plan room with wood floor, brick walls and log fire, pubby furniture including upholstered settles, own 1648 ales (brewed next door) plus Harveys Best, enjoyable reasonably priced traditional food; occasional quiz nights, TV, free wi-fi; children and dogs welcome, steps up to walled back garden, open all day. *(Charles Welch)*

EASTBOURNE TV6098
Bibendum (01323) 735363
Grange Road/South Street opposite Town Hall; BN21 4EU Roomy 19th-c corner pub with wine bar feel; well kept ales such as Harveys and Long Man, several wines by the glass and interesting selection of gins, enjoyable varied choice of food from snacks

up, friendly helpful staff, restaurant serving tasty pubby food; quiz first Sun and third Tues of month; seats out in front under awning, open all day, food till 6pm Sun. *(Miles Green)*

EASTBOURNE TV5999
Lamb (01323) 720545
High Street; BN21 1HH Ancient inn arranged around central servery; lounge bar with sturdy beams and substantial stone fireplace, latticed bow windows and antique furnishings, steps down to half-panelled bare-boards dining area with mix of old tables and chairs and another big fireplace, well kept Harveys ales, good choice of wines and enjoyable home-made food at fair prices, friendly efficient service, internal glass-covered well and historic cellars; upstairs live music including folk club, also quiz and comedy nights, TV and darts in public bar; children and dogs welcome, by 12th-c church away from seafront, five bedrooms, open all day. *(Tony Scott)*

EASTBOURNE TV6199
Marine (01323) 720464
Seaside Road (A259); BN22 7NE Comfortable spacious pub under long-serving licensees (well known for its extravagant Christmas decorations); panelled and carpeted bar, steps down to lounge with sofas, tub chairs and log fire, three well kept ales, good choice of wines and around 45 whiskies/brandies, generous helpings of good freshly made food including up to a dozen daily specials, back conservatory; children welcome, terrace and covered smokers' area, near the seafront, open (and food) all day Sun. *(Alan Johnson)*

EASTBOURNE TV6097
Pilot (01323) 723440
Holywell Road, Meads; just off front below approach from Beachy Head; BN20 7RW Busy corner inn with good fairly priced home-cooked food from lunchtime sandwiches up, well kept ales such as Harveys and Sharps, good selection of wines by the glass, friendly staff; free wi-fi; children welcome, dogs in bar, seats out front and in nice split-level beer garden behind, walks up to Beachy Head, four bedrooms, open all day, till 8pm Sun. *(Celia and Geoff Clay)*

EASTERGATE SU9405
Wilkes Head (01243) 543380
Just off A29 Fontwell–Bognor; Church Lane; PO20 3UT Small friendly red-brick local with two traditional bars and back dining extension; beams, flagstones and inglenook log fire, enjoyable reasonably priced blackboard food from sandwiches up, Adnams Southwold, several guest ales and proper cider; occasional live music, beer festivals, darts; children welcome, tables in big garden with play area, open all day. *(Harvey Brown)*

ELSTED
SU8320

Elsted Inn (01730) 813662
Elsted Marsh; GU29 0JT Attractive and welcoming Victorian country pub; good interesting food from shortish regularly changing menu using local produce, three or four well kept ales and plenty of wines by the glass, friendly accommodating service, two log fires, nice country furniture on bare boards, old Goodwood racing photos (horses and cars), dining area at back; folk night first Sun of the month, classic car meeting second Weds; children and dogs (in bar) welcome, downs-view garden with large part-covered terrace, four comfortable bedrooms, closed Mon lunchtime, otherwise open all day, restaurant closed Sun evening and Mon, but some snacky food available. *(Charles Welch)*

ELSTED
SU8119

★ Three Horseshoes (01730) 825746
Village signed from B2141 Chichester–Petersfield; from A272 about 2 miles W of Midhurst, turn left heading W; GU29 0JY Good mix of customers and a congenial bustle at this pretty white-painted old pub; beamed rooms, log fires and candlelight, ancient flooring, antique furnishings and interesting prints/photographs, up to five real ales tapped from the cask such as Bowman, Flowerpots, Langham and Youngs, summer cider, highly rated food from extensive blackboard menu, good friendly service; children allowed, dogs in bar, two delightful connecting gardens with plenty of seats, lovely roses and fine South Downs views, maybe wandering chickens, good surrounding walks.
(Tony and Jill Radnor, Christopher and Elise Way, John Evans, Hugh Duncan)

ERIDGE STATION
TQ5434

★ Huntsman (01892) 864258
Signed off A26 S of Eridge Green; TN3 9LE 19th-c brick and tile country local; two cosy opened-up rooms with painted half-panelling and lots of old photographs and prints, mix of furniture on bare boards including scrubbed pine, sofa in front of log fire, three well kept Badger ales and several wines by the glass, good home-made food (not Sun evening) from baguettes up, friendly helpful service, downstairs function/overflow room; children and dogs welcome, tables on fenced front terrace, picnic-sets in garden set down behind, next to Eridge station with lots of cars parked on the road (pub has its own parking), closed Mon, otherwise open all day. *(Nick Sharpe)*

FALMER
TQ3508

Swan (01273) 681842
Middle Street (just off A27 bypass); BN1 9PD Long thin building with seating areas either side of small central bar, Palmers and four local guests, straightforward sensibly priced lunchtime food (evenings Thurs and Fri), barn function room; some live music, sports TV, free wi-fi; dogs welcome, seats on little terrace, near Sussex University (student discounts), closed Mon, otherwise open all day, busy on Albion match days. *(Harvey Brown)*

FERNHURST
SU9028

Red Lion (01428) 643112
The Green, off A286 via Church Lane; GU27 3HY Friendly 16th-c wisteria-clad pub tucked quietly away on edge of green; heavy beams and timbers, inglenook woodburner and attractive furnishings, good food (not Sun evening) from sandwiches/snacks up, well kept Fullers/Gales beers and a guest, decent wines, restaurant; children and dogs welcome, seats out in front and in back garden with well, walks from the door, open all day. *(Angela and Steve Heard)*

FERRING
TQ0903

Henty Arms (01903) 241254
Ferring Lane; BN12 6QY Popular 19th-c local with five well kept changing ales and a real cider, generous helpings of well priced food (can get busy so best to book), breakfast 9am-midday Tues-Sat, friendly staff, opened-up lounge/dining area, log fire, separate bar with TV and games including bar billiards; children and dogs welcome, garden tables, play area, open (and food) all day. *(Tony and Wendy Hobden)*

FINDON
TQ1208

Gun (01903) 872 235
High Street; BN14 0TA Welcoming low-beamed pub with opened-up bar area and restaurant; very good food (not Sun evening) including burger night (Mon), french night (Tues) and popular Sun lunch, four well kept Marstons-related beers, friendly chatty staff, log fire; free wi-fi; children and dogs (in bar) welcome, sheltered garden, pretty village below Cissbury Ring (NT), open all day. *(David and Leone Lawson)*

FIRLE
TQ4607

★ Ram (01273) 858222
Village signed off A27 Lewes–Polegate; BN8 6NS Bustling 500-year-old village pub tucked away beneath the South Downs and popular with walkers; main bar with log fire, captain's and mate's chairs around dark pubby tables on bare boards or quarry tiles, gilt-edged paintings on dark brown walls, Harveys Best, guest ales and 21 wines by the glass, second cosy bar with another fire, built-in cushioned wall seats and more dark furniture on parquet flooring, throughout are ceramic rams' heads, black and white local photos and candles in hurricane jars, back dining room is up steps and overlooks the flint-walled garden, good food using produce from Firle Estate, friendly helpful service; live folk night first Mon of month, darts and toad in the hole, daily papers, free wi-fi; children (away from bar) and dogs welcome,

picnic-sets under parasols on front terrace, comfortable bedrooms, good breakfast, open (and food) all day from 9am. *(PL, Matthew and Elisabeth Reeves, Martin Day, Tony Scott)*

FISHBOURNE SU8304
Bulls Head (01243) 839895
Fishbourne Road (A259 Chichester–Emsworth); PO19 3JP Former 17th-c farmhouse with traditional interior; copper pans on black beams, some exposed brickwork and panelling, paintings of local scenes, good log fire, four well kept Fullers/Gales beers from wood-faced bar, good choice of enjoyable reasonably priced food from lunchtime baguettes up, friendly efficient service, intimate dining room; background music; children and dogs (in bar) welcome, tables on small covered deck, four bedrooms in former skittle alley, interesting harbour walks and handy for Fishbourne Roman Palace, open all day weekends. *(John Beeken)*

FITTLEWORTH TQ0118
Swan (01798) 865154
Lower Street (B2138, off A283 W of Pulborough); RH20 1EN Pretty tile-hung dining inn; beamed main bar with mix of furniture including windsor chairs, high-backed stools and banquettes on wood flooring, wall of pictures and old pub sign one end, big inglenook log fire the other, ales such as Harveys and Langham, several wines by the glass and traditional cider, good food from pubby choices up in bar and separate panelled restaurant, efficient friendly staff; background music, free wi-fi; children and dogs (in bar) welcome, plenty of tables on big back lawn, good walks nearby, 16 well priced comfortable bedrooms, open all day. *(Brian and Sally Wakeham)*

FRANT TQ5835
Abergavenny Arms (01892) 750233
A267 S of Tunbridge Wells; TN3 9DB Attractively updated beamed dining pub; good freshly cooked food from varied menu including themed evenings, six well kept local ales such as Harveys, Larkins, Long Man and Tonbridge (maybe bank holiday beer festivals), good choice of wines by the glass and several interesting gins, friendly efficient staff, leather sofas by large woodburner in brick inglenook, three separate dining areas; background music, daily papers; children and dogs welcome, terrace seating on different levels, front part looking over road to Eridge Park (good walks), open (and food) all day. *(Martin Day)*

FULKING TQ2411
Shepherd & Dog (01273) 857382
Off A281 N of Brighton, via Poynings; BN5 9LU 17th-c bay-windowed pub in beautiful spot below the South Downs; low beams, panelling and inglenook, fine range of real ales and craft beers including Downlands (brewed a couple of miles

away), also bottled beers, ciders and plenty of wines by the glass, enjoyable food from light lunches up, friendly young staff; free wi-fi; children and dogs welcome, terrace and pretty streamside garden with own bar (summer barbecues), straightforward climb to Devil's Dyke, open all day (till 8pm Sun). *(David Smith)*

FUNTINGTON SU7908
Fox & Hounds (01243) 575246
Common Road (B2146); PO18 9LL Bustling old bay-windowed pub with updated beamed rooms; enjoyable food from sandwiches and snacks to daily specials, popular Sun carvery, well kept Timothy Taylors Landlord and guests, lots of wines by the glass and good coffee, friendly service, comfortable spacious dining extension; some live music and quiz nights, free wi-fi; children and dogs (in bar) welcome, tables out in front and in walled back garden, open (and food) all day. *(Katherine Matthews)*

GRAFFHAM SU9217
White Horse (01798) 867331
On road signed to Heyshott/Midhurst at W end of village; GU28 0NT Large refurbished dining inn; highly rated restauranty food along with some more traditional choices, Sharps Doom Bar, local guests and plenty of wines by the glass, welcoming attentive service, bar/dining room and conservatory restaurant with South Downs views; children and dogs welcome, big back garden and terrace (maybe summer jazz), good local walks, six well appointed bedrooms in two courtyard blocks, open all day Sat, till 6pm Sun, closed Mon. *(Tony and Wendy Hobden)*

GUN HILL TQ5614
Gun (01825) 872361
Off A22 NW of Hailsham, or off A267; TN21 0JU Big 15th-c country dining pub (part of the small Elite group) with enjoyable bistro-style food from sharing boards and pizzas up; large central bar with nice old brick floor, stools against counter, Aga in corner, small grey-panelled room off with rugs on bare boards, animal skins on cushioned wall benches and mix of scrubbed and dark tables, logs piled into tall fireplace, well kept ales such as Harveys and Timothy Taylors, decent wines by the glass, cocktails (happy hour 4-6pm Mon-Fri), close-set tables in two-room cottagey restaurant, beams and open fires, old bottles and glasses along gantry, gun prints and country pictures; background music; children welcome, picnic-sets in garden and on lantern-lit front terrace, Wealdway walks, open (and food) all day. *(John Preddy)*

HALNAKER SU9008
★ Anglesey Arms (01243) 773474
A285 Chichester–Petworth; PO18 0NQ Georgian pub belonging to the Goodwood

Estate and very much a village local; bare boards, settles and other country furniture, log fire, four well kept ales such as Harveys and Youngs, decent wines, good food from varied if not particularly cheap menu including local organic produce and Selsey fish, friendly accommodating service, simple L-shaped dining room (children allowed) with woodburners, stripped pine and some flagstones; traditional games, occasional live music; dogs welcome in bar, tables in big tree-lined garden, good nearby walks, open all day Fri and Sat, till 7pm Sun. *(Simon Collett-Jones)*

HANDCROSS   TQ2629
Red Lion (01444) 400292
High Street; RH17 6BP Extensive stylishly renovated dining pub; beamed bar with wood and polished stone floor, armchairs and long thickly cushioned banquette facing circular copper-topped tables, Harveys and Sharps, plenty of wines by the glass and good range of other drinks including cocktails, side area has some ancient recycled timbers and stripped tables on nice oak boards, another part with lower white-painted plank ceiling, rather more contemporary furnishings and big two-way fireplace, good choice of popular well presented food from sandwiches, sharing plates and pizzas up, also a vegan menu, friendly service; background music; children and dogs (in bar) welcome, well placed for Nymans (NT), open all day. *(Celia and Geoff Clay)*

HANDCROSS   TQ2529
Royal Oak (01444) 401406
Horsham Road (B2110), W of A23; RH17 6DJ Traditional tile-hung village pub under friendly canadian landlady; well kept Harveys and a couple of guests, Weston's cider, decent wines and nice coffee, good well presented food cooked to order including some canadian recipes such as barbecue ribs, happy hour 3-5pm weekdays; fortnightly quiz Tues, bar billiards and darts, daily newspapers, free wi-fi; children and dogs welcome, seats out at front and on small terrace overlooking fields and woods, handy for Nymans (NT), open all day. *(Ian Phillips, Tony Scott)*

HARTFIELD   TQ4634
Gallipot (01892) 770008
B2110 towards Forest Row; TN7 4AJ Traditional stone and weatherboarded country pub; long narrow beamed interior with central bar and fire at one end, good home-made food from pub classics up (not many tables so best to book), three well kept local beers such as Harveys and Larkins, friendly helpful staff; some live music; children and dogs welcome, pleasant sloping

garden behind with good views, handy for Pooh Bear country, open all day. *(Susan Eccleston)*

HASSOCKS   TQ3115
Thatched Inn (01273) 842946
Ockley Lane/Grand Avenue; BN6 8DH Popular 1950s thatched pub among modern bungalows; good choice of enjoyable reasonably priced food in bar and extended restaurant, well kept Brakspears, Harveys and a guest, several wines by the glass, welcoming efficient young staff; local artwork for sale, pool, darts and fruit machine; children and dogs welcome, back garden, lovely views towards the South Downs. *(Tony and Wendy Hobden, John Beeken)*

HASTINGS   TQ8109
Dolphin (01424) 431197
Rock-a-Nore, off A259 at seafront; TN34 3DW Friendly tile-hung pub facing the fishermen's huts; compact carpeted interior with masses of fishing/maritime paraphernalia, enjoyable food including fresh local fish and tapas nights, well kept Dark Star, Harveys, Youngs and guests plus craft beers; background and regular live music, quiz Thurs; children (till 7pm) and dogs welcome, raised front terrace, open all day, no food weekend evenings. *(Charles Welch)*

HASTINGS   TQ8209
First In Last Out (01424) 425079
High Street, Old Town; TN34 3EY Congenial pub serving its own FILO beers (brewed close by) and a guest ale, good fairly priced food including some interesting vegetarian/vegan choices, evening tapas (Mon) and indian thali (Thurs), friendly helpful staff, open-plan carpeted bar with 1970s Artex walls, dark wood booths and feature central raised log fire, lighter back dining room; regular live music, quiz first Sun of month; open all day, no food Sun evening, Mon lunchtime. *(Erik Wilkinson)*

HASTINGS   TQ8110
Imperial
Queens Road; TN34 1RL Popular Victorian corner pub (same owners as the Lamb at Wartling) visibly brewing its own craft beers, also several other keg beers (tasters offered), proper ciders and range of spirits, good wood-fired pizzas including vegan; some live music; dogs welcome, closed till 4pm Mon and Tues, otherwise open all day (till midnight Fri, Sat). *(Charles Welch)*

HEATHFIELD   TQ5920
★ Star (01435) 863570
Church Street, Old Heathfield, off A265/ B2096 E; TN21 9AH Nice old country pub next to church; ancient heavy beams,

---

If you stay overnight in an inn or hotel, they are allowed to serve you an alcoholic drink at any hour of the day or night.

built-in wall settles, window seats, panelling and inglenook log fire, doorway to similarly decorated room set up more for eating, upstairs dining room with striking barrel-vaulted ceiling, Harveys Best and guests, 11 wines by the glass and well liked food; background music, free wi-fi; children and dogs welcome, seats in pretty garden with views of rolling pasture dotted with sheep and lined with oak trees, open all day. *(Kerry and Guy Trooper)*

HENFIELD
TQ2115
George (01273) 492296
High Street; BN5 9DB Former coaching inn dating from the 16th c; easy chairs and stools in central bar area, Harveys, Timothy Taylors and good wines by glass, room to the left with open fire and portraits on green panelled walls, dining room to the right with heavy beams and inglenook, decent food including Weds thai night and weekend breakfasts, friendly landlord and helpful young staff; background music (live first Fri of month); children and dogs (in bar) welcome, disabled access/loo, seats in back courtyard, eight bedrooms, open all day (till 8pm Sun). *(David and Leone Lawson)*

HENLEY
SU8925
★Duke of Cumberland Arms
(01428) 652280 *Down steep narrow lanes off A286 S of Fernhurst; GU27 3HQ* Pretty country cottage with two small low-ceilinged rooms; big scrubbed oak tables on brick or flagstoned floors, rustic decorations and open fire, Harveys and a couple of guests tapped from the cask, several wines by the glass and much enjoyed food (not Sun or Mon evenings), more modern dining extension with sofas in front of woodburner; background music, board games, free wi-fi; well behaved children and dogs (in bar) welcome, seats and picnic-sets on decking and in big tiered garden with trout ponds, beautiful views, open all day. *(Miss A E Dare, Christopher and Elise Way, David Jackman)*

HERMITAGE
SU7505
★Sussex Brewery (01243) 371533
A259 just W of Emsworth; PO10 8AU Bustling little 18th-c pub on the West Sussex/Hampshire border; small bare-boards bar with good fire in brick inglenook, simple furniture, flagstoned snug, well kept Youngs ales and guests, ten wines by the glass and popular hearty food including speciality sausages (even vegetarian ones), small upstairs restaurant; children and dogs welcome, picnic-sets in back courtyard, open all day (food all day Sun till 7.30pm). *(Ann and Colin Hunt)*

HIGH HURSTWOOD
TQ4925
★Hurstwood (01825) 732257
Hurstwood Road off A272; TN22 4AH Although the main draw to this small country

pub is their excellent inventive food (must book), they still attract some loyal local drinkers; open-plan U-shaped interior with beams and bare boards, high spindleback chairs against counter serving Harveys and Sharps, good wines by the glass and cocktails, friendly attentive young staff, area by tiled Victorian fireplace with sofas and armchairs, dining tables set with red gingham napkins, little plants and church candles, hunting prints and other artwork above painted dado, various lamps/lanterns and a piano (which does get played); children and dogs (in bar area) welcome, french windows to deck with lawn beyond, open all day (till 6pm Sun). *(Victoria and Stuart Parsons)*

HOOE
TQ6910
Red Lion (01424) 892371
Denbigh Road; off B2095; TN33 9EW Attractive old local behind screen of pollarded lime trees – originally a farmhouse but a pub since the 17th c; plenty of original features including hop-strung beams, flagstones and two big inglenooks, generous helpings of popular home-cooked food (worth booking), well kept Harveys, a guest and plenty of continental beers, good friendly service, main bar and back snug, overflow function room and further eating space upstairs; children and dogs welcome, wheelchair access, seats out at front and in garden behind, closed Mon evening, otherwise open all day. *(Peter Meister)*

HOUGHTON
TQ0111
★George & Dragon (01798) 831559
B2139 W of Storrington; BN18 9LW Brick and flint pub (former coaching house) with 13th-c beams and timbers in attractive bar rambling up and down steps, note the elephant photograph above the fireplace, lovely Arun Valley views from back extension, good fairly priced pubby food including popular Sun lunch (booking advised), Marstons-related ales and decent wines by the glass, friendly helpful service; background music; children and dogs welcome, tables on decked terrace with views (they may ask for a credit card if you eat out here), charming sloping garden, good walks, open all day Fri and Sat, till 9pm Sun. *(Darren and Clare Jones, Tony Scott)*

HUNSTON
SU8601
Spotted Cow (01243) 786718
B2145 S of Chichester; PO20 1PD Modernised slate-faced village pub with beams, flagstones and big log fires; good choice of food (not Sun evening) including specials, Fullers/Gales beers, friendly helpful staff, small front bar, roomier side lounge with armchairs, sofas and low tables, airy high-ceilinged restaurant; maybe background music, darts; children (if eating) and dogs welcome, good disabled access, enclosed garden with play equipment, handy for towpath walkers, open all day. *(R and M Thomas)*

HURSTPIERPOINT   TQ2816
New Inn   (01273) 834608
High Street; BN6 9RQ Popular 16th-c
beamed village pub; Harveys and a couple of
guests, good wines by the glass and enjoyable
food from pub favourites up, seafood specials
(Fri, Sat), themed evenings and summer
wood-fired pizzas, friendly staff, linked
areas including oak-panelled back bar with
log fire and more formal restaurant; quiz
nights, sports TV; children and dogs welcome,
enclosed garden with terrace and play
area, open all day, no food Sun evening.
(Tony Scott)

ICKLESHAM   TQ8716
★Queens Head   (01424) 814552
Off A259 Rye–Hastings; TN36 4BL
Friendly well run country pub, popular locally
(and at weekends with cyclists and walkers);
open-plan areas around big counter, high
timbered walls and vaulted roof, old beer
bottles on shelves, farming implements,
a grandfather clock behind the bar and
a bike over it, pubby furniture on patterned
carpet, other areas with inglenooks and
a separate back room, six well kept ales
including Greene King, Hardys & Hansons
and Harveys, local cider, several wines by
the glass and good choice of generous fairly
priced food; background music (live 4-6pm
Sun), occasional pub quiz; well behaved
children (till 8.30pm) and dogs welcome,
picnic-sets, boules and play area in peaceful
garden, fine Brede Valley views, you can walk
to Winchelsea from here, open (and food)
all day. *(Mike and Eleanor Anderson, Tony
Scott, Richard and Penny Gibbs)*

ICKLESHAM   TQ8716
★Robin Hood   (01424) 814277
Main Road; TN36 4BD Friendly family-run
beamed pub with buoyant local atmosphere;
good value unpretentious home-made food
(all day Sun) including blackboard specials,
Mon steak night and Weds curry, well kept
Greene King IPA, up to six guests and three
proper ciders, hops overhead and lots of
copper bric-a-brac, log fire, games part with
pool, back dining conservatory; free wi-fi;
children and dogs (in bar) welcome, play
area and boules in big garden, lovely views
of Brede valley, open all day Fri-Sun.
(Tony Scott)

ISFIELD   TQ4417
Laughing Fish   (01825) 750349
Station Road; TN22 5XB Bustling
opened-up Victorian local with affable
landlord and cheerful efficient staff;
enjoyable good value home-cooked food
(not Sun evening) including daily specials
and themed nights, well kept Greene King
ales and local guests, open fire; bar billiards
and other traditional games, various events
including entertaining beer race Easter Mon;
children and dogs welcome, disabled access,

small pleasantly shaded walled garden with
enclosed play area, field for camping, right
by Lavender Line railway (pub was station
hotel), post office facilities Thurs morning,
open all day. *(Angela and Steve Heard)*

JEVINGTON   TQ5601
Eight Bells   (01323) 484442
*Jevington Road, N of East Dean;
BN26 5QB* Friendly village pub in good
walking country; simple furnishings,
heavy beams, panelling, parquet floor and
inglenook, popular home-made food from
sandwiches and good ploughman's up, well
kept ales including Harveys; background
music (live Mon), Tues quiz; children and
dogs welcome, front terrace and secluded
downs-view garden, adjacent cricket field,
open all day. *(Gene and Kitty Rankin,
Mrs J Ekins-Daukes)*

KINGSTON   TQ3908
Juggs   (01273) 472523
*Village signed off A27 by roundabout
W of Lewes; BN7 3NT* Tile-hung village
pub with very low front door and heavy 15th-c
beams, lots of neatly stripped masonry, sturdy
wooden furniture on bare boards and stone
slabs, log fires, smaller eating areas including
a family room, food from sandwiches and pub
standards up, Harveys and Shepherd Neame
ales, good wines and coffee; background
music, quiz nights; children and dogs
welcome, disabled access/facilities, lots of
outside tables including covered area with
heaters, tubs and hanging baskets, play area,
nice South Downs walks, open (and food)
all day. *(Katherine Matthews)*

KIRDFORD   TQ0126
★Half Moon   (01403) 820223
*Opposite church, off A272 Petworth–
Billingshurst; RH14 0LT* Attractive old
tile-hung village pub owned by celebrity
model Jodie Kidd; beamed bar on right with
cushioned window seat, barrel stools and
armchairs by woodburner, some nice old
photos and hunting wallpaper, a couple of
local ales and plenty of wines by the glass
from blue-painted counter, two restaurant
rooms with rustic planked wall seats,
painted or wooden chairs around simple
tables and fine inglenook fireplace, good
interesting food (not Sun evening) including
weekday set lunch and tasting menus,
friendly staff, background music; tables on
terrace and lawn, kitchen garden to one side
overlooked by church tower, closed Mon and
Tues, otherwise open all day (till 8.30pm Sun).
(Maggie and Matthew Lyons)

LEWES   TQ4110
Black Horse   (01273) 473653
Western Road; BN7 1RS Bow-windowed
pub with knocked-through bar keeping
traditional feel, two log fires, wood floor,
panelling and lots of old pictures, seven well
kept ales including Greene King, interesting

gins, enjoyable home-made food, friendly service; occasional live music and quiz nights, sports TV, bar billiards and toad in the hole; children welcome, beer garden, open all day. *(Tony Scott)*

LEWES TQ4210
Gardeners Arms (01273) 474808
Cliffe High Street; BN7 2AN
Unpretentious little bare-boards local opposite Harveys brewery shop; lots of beer mats on gantry, homely stools, built-in wall seats and plain scrubbed tables around three narrow sides of bar, photos of Lewes bonfire night, well kept Harveys and five interesting guests, real ciders, some lunchtime food such as sandwiches, pasties and pies; background music, TV, darts; no children, dogs welcome; open all day. *(Miles Green)*

LEWES TQ4210
★**John Harvey** (01273) 479880
Bear Yard, just off Cliffe High Street; BN7 2AN Bustling tap for nearby Harveys brewery, four of their beers including seasonals kept in top condition (some poured from the cask), small choice of enjoyable well priced traditional food including good Sun roasts, friendly efficient young staff, beamed and flagstoned bar with woodburner, huge vat halved to make two snug seating areas, lighter room on left and upstairs restaurant/function room; live music first Sun of the month; children welcome in restaurant, dogs in bar, a few tables outside, open all day, no food Sun evening. *(Ann and Colin Hunt)*

LEWES TQ4110
★**Lewes Arms** (01273) 473152
Castle Ditch Lane/Mount Place – tucked behind castle ruins; BN7 1YH Cheerful unpretentious little corner local; well kept Fullers/Gales beers and guests such as Harveys Best, around 30 malt whiskies and plenty of wines by the glass, generous helpings of enjoyable reasonably priced food including good Sun roasts; tiny front bar on right with stools along curved counter and bench window seats, two other simple rooms hung with photographs and information about the famous Lewes bonfire night; folk evenings, quiz nights and more obscure events such as pea throwing and dwyle flunking; children (away from front bar) and dogs welcome, picnic-sets on attractive split-level back terrace, open all day (till midnight Fri, Sat). *(Tony Scott, Colin McLachlan)*

LEWES TQ4110
Pelham Arms (01273) 476149
At top of High Street; BN7 1XL Popular 17th-c beamed pub with characterful rambling interior; well presented food (not Mon, booking advised) including some interesting vegetarian choices and meat/fish from on-site smokehouse, friendly efficient service, own Abyss beers and guests; children

and dogs (in bar) welcome, small courtyard garden, closed Mon lunchtime, otherwise open all day. *(Alan Johnson)*

LEWES TQ4110
Rights of Man (01273) 486894
High Street; BN7 1YE Harveys pub close to the Crown Court; five of their well kept ales and enjoyable food including tapas, Victorian-style décor with a series of booths, another bar at the back and roof terrace; background music, free wi-fi; open all day, food till 6pm Sun. *(Miles Green)*

LEWES TQ4210
★**Snowdrop** (01273) 471018
South Street; BN7 2BU Welcoming pub tucked below the chalk cliffs; narrowboat theme with brightly painted servery and colourful jugs, kettles, lanterns etc hanging from curved planked ceiling, wide mix of simple furniture on parquet floor, old sewing machines and huge stone jars, rather bohemian atmosphere; well kept local ales such as Bedlam, Gun and Harveys, a couple of ciders and enjoyable reasonably priced food from interestingly varied menu (some good vegetarian options), nice coffee, cheerful efficient staff (may ask for a card if running a tab), more tables in upstairs room (spiral stairs) with bar billiards and darts; background and frequent live music including Mon jazz; dogs very welcome (menu for them), outside seating on both sides, pretty hanging baskets, open (and food) all day, kitchen shuts 6pm Sun. *(John Beeken)*

LICKFOLD SU9226
★**Lickfold Inn** (01789) 532535
NE of Midhurst, between A286 and A283; GU28 9EY Tucked-away Tudor inn with impressive food in bars and upstairs restaurant; two easy-going downstairs rooms with heavy Tudor beams, chapel chairs, Georgian settles and nice old tables on fine herringbone brick floor, comfortable sofas by woodburner, three well kept ales such as Langham, a dozen wines by the glass and a good choice of gins, rums and whiskies, restaurant with upholstered chairs and dark polished tables on bare boards, more heavy beams and second woodburner; live music first Sun of month; children and dogs (in bar) welcome, plenty of seating on terrace and in garden on several levels, closed Mon and Tues, otherwise open all day (till 7pm Sun), shuts for ten days in Jan. *(Celia and Rupert Lemming, Miss A E Dare, Christopher and Elise Way)*

LINDFIELD TQ3425
Bent Arms (01444) 483146
High Street; RH16 2HP Surprisingly spacious 16th-c village coaching inn with low beams, timbers and some stained glass, most tables set for their popular affordably priced food including lunchtime sandwiches and ploughman's using own bread and daily

changing set menu, three well kept Badger ales, friendly service; children welcome, sizeable back garden with covered area, eight bedrooms and cottage, open all day, no food Sun evening. *(Mrs P R Sykes)*

LITLINGTON TQ5201

Plough & Harrow (01323) 870632

Between A27 Lewes–Polegate and A259 E of Seaford; BN26 5RE Neatly extended 17th-c brick and flint village pub; large beamed and wood-floored bar with smaller rooms off, candles on tables, brewery mirrors and old farming implements on the walls, snug with inglenook, half a dozen well kept ales including at least three from nearby Long Man, decent wines by the glass and good food from pub staples up, friendly efficient service; quiz second Weds of month, some live music, Aug beer festival; children and dogs welcome, pretty back garden, good walks (on South Downs Way), open all day. *(Sue Parry-Davies, John Beeken, Tony Scott)*

LITTLEHAMPTON TQ0202

★ **Arun View** (01903) 722335

Wharf Road; W towards Chichester; BN17 5DD In lovely harbour spot with busy waterway directly below windows; popular good value food (all day Sun) from sandwiches/ciabattas to good fresh fish, well kept Fullers, guest beers and several wines by the glass, cheerful helpful staff, flagstoned and panelled back bar with banquettes and dark wood tables, large dining conservatory; background music, TVs, pool; children and dogs welcome, disabled facilities, flower-filled terrace, interesting waterside walkway to coast, four bedrooms, open all day. *(Tony Scott)*

LITTLEHAMPTON TQ0202

Steam Packet (01903) 715994

River Road; BN17 5BZ 19th-c corner pub just across from the Arun View; open-plan interior providing several separate seating areas, well kept ales such as Bedlam, Downlands, Fallen Acorn and Langham, enjoyable reasonably priced food including daily specials and Weds tapas night; regular live jazz; seats out in small area facing river, raised back garden, three bedrooms, closed Mon and lunchtime Tues, no food Sun evening. *(Tony and Wendy Hobden, Ray Hagger, Tony Scott)*

LITTLEWORTH TQ1921

Windmill (01403) 710308

Pub signed off B2135; village signed off A272 southbound, W of Cowfold; RH13 8EJ Brick and tile inn dating from the 17th c; two beamed and flagstoned bars, one with inglenook log fire, woodburner in the other, lots of old farming tools and so forth on walls and ceiling, enjoyable home-made food (all day weekends) from sandwiches and pub standards up, summer wood-fired pizzas, well kept Harveys ales and a couple of guests, restaurant; quiz second

Mon of month, occasional live music, bar billiards, darts, TV and free wi-fi; children and dogs welcome, picnic-sets in peaceful garden overlooking fields, bedrooms, open all day. *(Ruth May)*

LODSWORTH SU9321

Halfway Bridge Inn (01798) 861281

Just before village, on A272 Midhurst–Petworth; GU28 9BP Restauranty 17th-c coaching inn with characterful linked rooms; beams, wooden floors and log fires (one in polished kitchen range), good if not especially cheap food from interesting menu (also pub favourites and set lunch), ales such as Arundel, Langham and Sharps, wide range of wines by the glass, pleasant helpful staff; background music, newspapers and free wi-fi; children and dogs (in bar) welcome, small back terrace, six bedrooms in former stables, open all day, food all day weekends. *(Julian Richardson)*

LYMINSTER TQ0204

Six Bells (01903) 713639

Lyminster Road (A284), Wick; BN17 7PS Unassuming 18th-c flint pub with opened-up bar and separate dining room; well kept Fullers London Pride and a guest, decent house wines and enjoyable sensibly priced food, friendly attentive staff, low black beams, wood floor and big inglenook with horsebrasses on bressumer, pubby furnishings; background music, free wi-fi; children and dogs (in one area) welcome, terrace and garden seating. *(Tony and Wendy Hobden)*

MAREHILL TQ0618

White Horse (01798) 872189

Mare Hill Road (A283 E of Pulborough); RH20 2DY White-painted roadside country pub dating from the 15th c; several linked areas with beams, timbers and log fires, good reasonably priced food including daily specials, well kept Fullers/Gales beers and a guest such as Dark Star, several wines by the glass, friendly attentive staff, nice views from restaurant; some live music; children and dogs welcome, attractive garden behind, handy for RSPB Pulborough Brooks reserve, open all day. *(John Beeken)*

MAYFIELD TQ5826

Middle House (01435) 872146

High Street; TN20 6AB Handsome 16th-c timbered inn (Grade I listed); L-shaped beamed bar with massive fireplace, several well kept ales including Harveys, local cider and decent wines, quiet lounge area with leather chesterfields around log fire in ornate carved fireplace, good choice of enjoyable food, friendly staff coping well at busy times, attractive panelled restaurant with modern glass extension; background music; children welcome, no dogs inside, lovely country views from terraced back garden, bedrooms, open (and food) all day weekends. *(Tony Scott)*

MAYFIELD TQ5927
Rose & Crown (01435) 872200
Fletching Street; TN20 6TE
New management for this pretty 16th-c
weatherboarded pub set down lane from
village centre; two cosy front rooms with
coins stuck to low ceiling boards, bench seats
built into partly panelled walls and simple
furniture on floorboards, inglenook log fire,
Harveys, a guest beer and several wines
by the glass, food and service can be good,
further small room behind servery and larger
carpeted one down steps; children welcome,
dogs in bar, raised front terrace and decked
back garden, two bedrooms, open all day,
food till 4pm Sun. *(Charles Welch)*

MID LAVANT SU8508
Earl of March (01243) 533993
A286 Lavant Road; PO18 0BQ Updated
and extended with emphasis on eating, but
seats for drinkers in flagstoned log-fire bar,
well kept Harveys, Timothy Taylors and
a guest, nice wines by the glass including
champagne and english fizz, good well
presented restaurant-style food (not
cheap) along with some pub favourites
and lunchtime sandwiches, pleasant staff;
free wi-fi; children and dogs welcome, super
location and local walks, view to Goodwood
from neatly kept garden, open all day.
(Miss A E Dare, Tracey and Stephen Groves)

MILLAND SU8328
Rising Sun (01428) 741347
*Iping Road junction with main road
through village; GU30 7NA* Busy 20th-c
red-brick Fullers pub; their ales and a guest
such as Dark Star, varied choice of fresh
well presented food from sharing boards
and pub favourites up, also two-course lunch
deal, friendly helpful staff, three linked
rooms including cheery log-fire bar and
bare-boards restaurant; live music first Fri of
month, occasional quiz and curry night, free
wi-fi; children and dogs welcome, extensive
lawns attractively divided by tall yew hedge,
canopied heated terrace and smokers'
gazebo, good walking area, open all day
(Fri-Sun). *(David and Leone Lawson)*

MILTON STREET TQ5304
Sussex Ox (01323) 870840
*Off A27 just under a mile E of Alfriston
roundabout; BN26 5RL* Extended country
pub (originally a 1900s slaughterhouse)
with magnificent downs views; bar area
with a couple of high tables and chairs on
bare boards, old local photographs, three
well kept local ales such as Long Man and
good choice of wines by the glass, lower
brick-floored room with farmhouse furniture
and woodburner, similarly furnished dining
room (children allowed here), further front
eating area with high-backed rush-seated
chairs, food can be good from traditional
choices up (meat from own organic farm),

friendly service; dogs welcome in bar,
teak seating on raised back deck taking in
the view, picnic-sets in garden below and
more under parasols at front, open all day
weekends. *(John Beeken, Tony Scott)*

NETHERFIELD TQ7118
Netherfield Arms (01424) 838282
*Just off B2096 Heathfield–Battle;
TN33 9QD* Welcoming low-ceilinged
18th-c country dining pub; wide choice of
enjoyable food including good specials and
vegetarian/vegan dishes, friendly attentive
service, decent wines and well kept ales
such as Long Man, inglenook log fire, cosy
restaurant; picnic-sets in lovely back garden,
far-reaching views from front, closed Sun
evening, Mon. *(Andrew Stone)*

NETHERFIELD TQ7118
White Hart (01424) 838382
Darwell Hill, B2096; TN33 9QH
Weatherboarded country pub with busy
little front bar, cushions on built-in wall
seats, log fire at one end, hops and country
prints, stools by counter serving well kept
Harveys and Sharps, lounge area with sofas
and scatter cushions, huge stag's head
and bookshelves, tasty food including OAP
weekday lunch deal, friendly helpful staff,
dining room has rush-seated chairs around
dark tables on coir, some half-panelling and
woodburner; children and dogs welcome,
rattan chairs around tables out on gravel
terrace, fine far-reaching views, closed Sun
evening, Mon. *(Andrew Stone)*

NEWHAVEN TQ4500
Hope (01273) 515389
*Follow West Beach signs from A259
westbound; BN9 9DN* Big-windowed
pub overlooking busy harbour entrance;
long nautical-themed bar with raised area,
comfy sofas and open fires, well kept ales
such as Dark Star and Harveys, upstairs
dining conservatory and breezy balcony with
even better view towards Seaford Head,
good choice of generous well priced food,
friendly staff; regular live music, Weds quiz;
children and dogs welcome, tables on grassed
waterside area, open all day, food all day Sat,
till 7pm Sun. *(Tony Scott)*

NUTBOURNE TQ0718
Rising Sun (01798) 812191
*Off A283 E of Pulborough; The Street;
RH20 2HE* Unspoilt creeper-clad village
pub dating partly from the 16th c (same
owner for 38 years); front bar with beams,
exposed brickwork and woodburner,
scrubbed tables on bare boards, some 1920s
fashion and dance posters, Fullers London
Pride and three guests, enjoyable pubby food
from lunchtime sandwiches up including
daily specials, friendly service, second bar
leading through to quarry-tiled restaurant,
cosy back family room; background music
(live last Tues of month); dogs welcome,

terrace with small pond and smokers' shelter, archway through to lawned area, closed Sun evening. *(Tony Scott, Tony and Wendy Hobden)*

NUTHURST   TQ1926
Black Horse   (01403) 891272
Off A281 SE of Horsham; RH13 6LH
Welcoming 17th-c country pub with plenty of character in its several small rooms; low black beams, flagstones/bare boards and inglenook log fire, enjoyable good value pubby food served by friendly attentive staff, four real ales including Harveys; popular charity quiz Weds; children and dogs welcome, pretty streamside back garden, more seats on front terrace, open all day weekends. *(Ruth May)*

OFFHAM   TQ3912
Blacksmiths Arms   (01273) 472971
A275 N of Lewes; BN7 3QD Popular open-plan dining pub in rural village; good food including some jamaican choices, well kept ales such as Harveys and Long Man, efficient friendly service, clean updated interior with a couple of woodburners, one in huge end inglenook; children and dogs welcome, french windows to terrace, four bedrooms (steep stairs) open all day (till 8pm Sun). *(Paddy and Sian O'Leary)*

PARTRIDGE GREEN   TQ1819
★ Green Man   (01403) 710250
Off A24 just under a mile S of A272 junction – take B2135 at West Grinstead signpost; pub at Jolesfield, N of Partridge Green; RH13 8JT Relaxed gently upmarket dining pub with popular enterprising food cooked by chef-landlord, ales such as Sharps and well chosen wines by the glass including champagne, good friendly service; unassuming front area by counter with bentwood bar seats, stools and library chairs around one or two low tables, old curved high-back settle, main eating area widening into back part with pretty enamelled stove, pitched ceiling area on left, more self-contained room on right; children and dogs (in bar) welcome, cast-iron seats and picnic-sets under parasols in neat back garden, closed Sun evening, Mon. *(Sarah and David Gibbs)*

PARTRIDGE GREEN   TQ1819
Partridge   (01403) 710391
Church Road/High Street; RH13 8JS
Spacious 19th-c roadside village pub (former station hotel) run by father and daughter team; three Dark Star ales and a couple of guests, enjoyable sensibly priced home-made food (not Sun or Mon evenings) from sandwiches and sharing plates up including deals, some main courses available in smaller helpings, friendly relaxed atmosphere; sports TV, free wi-fi; children and dogs welcome, lawned garden with large terrace and play equipment, open all day.
(Chantelle and Tony Redman)

PATCHING   TQ0705
Fox   (01903) 871299
Arundel Road; signed off A27 eastbound just W of Worthing; BN13 3UJ Neatly kept pub with generously served food including popular Sun roasts (best to book), quick friendly service even at busy times, two or three well kept local ales including Harveys, large dining area off roomy panelled bar, dark pubby furniture on patterned carpet, hunting pictures; quiet background music; children and dogs welcome, disabled access, colourful hanging baskets and good-sized tree-shaded garden with well laid-out seating, heaters and play area, open all day Sun till 9pm.
(Peter Barratt)

PATCHING   TQ0805
Worlds End   (01903) 871346
Former A27 Worthing–Arundel, off A280 roundabout; BN13 3UQ Long roomy pub next to Patching Pond; good range of food from sandwiches and snacks up (smaller helpings available for some main courses), well kept Badger beers and lots of wines by the glass, efficient friendly service, opened-up beamed interior including large raftered barn-style dining room; children and dogs welcome, good-sized garden behind with paved terrace and play area, open (and food) all day, kitchen closes 8pm Sun. *(Tony and Wendy Hobden)*

PEASMARSH   TQ8822
Horse & Cart   (01797) 230034
School Lane; TN31 6UW Updated village pub with welcoming atmosphere; light beams and wood floors, red leather sofa and armchair by open fire, back restaurant separated by gas woodburner in two-way brick fireplace, good mix of seating from pews to banquettes, beer badged for the pub from Romney Marsh along with local Three Legs, extensive wine list (several by the glass), good food from pub stables up, also takeaway pizzas and weekend breakfast from 8.30am, friendly helpful service; games including shove-ha'penny; children and dogs welcome, a couple of tables out at front with more on back terrace and lawn, outside bar and pétanque, four bedrooms, closed Sun evening and Mon lunchtime, otherwise open all day. *(Peter Meister)*

PETT   TQ8713
Royal Oak   (01424) 812515
Pett Road; TN35 4HG Friendly brick and weatherboarded village pub; roomy main bar with big open fire, well kept Harveys and a couple of changing guests (happy hour 4-6pm Mon-Thurs), popular home-made food including several fish dishes, two dining areas, efficient helpful service; occasional live music and quiz nights, traditional games; dogs welcome, small garden behind, open all day, no food Sun evening. *(Nick Sharpe)*

PETT TQ8613
Two Sawyers (01424) 812255
Pett Road, off A259; TN35 4HB
Meandering low-beamed rooms including
bare-boards bar with stripped tables,
tiny snug and restaurant down sloping
passageway, open fires, well kept Ringwood,
Sharps and guests, local cider/perry and
wide range of wines, popular good value
home-made food, friendly helpful service;
background and some live music; children in
restaurant and dogs in bar welcome, suntrap
front courtyard, back garden with shady trees
and well spaced tables, four bedrooms, open
all day. *(Nick Sharpe)*

PETWORTH SU9719
Badgers (01798) 342651
*Station Road (A285 1.5 miles S);
GU28 0JF* Restauranty dining pub with
good up-to-date food from snacks and sharing
plates up including fresh fish and seasonal
game, can eat in bar areas or restaurant,
friendly accommodating staff, a couple
of changing ales and well chosen wines,
cosy fireside area with sofas; free wi-fi;
over-5s allowed in bar's eating area, stylish
tables and seats on terrace by water lily
pool, summer hog/lamb roasts, three well
appointed bedrooms, good breakfast, open
all day. *(Julian Richardson)*

PETWORTH SU9721
Star (01798) 368114
Market Square; GU28 0AH Opened-up
and refurbished old pub with well kept
Fullers/Gales beers, decent wines and
enjoyable food including pie and mash menu,
friendly helpful service, log fire, free wi-fi;
children and dogs (in bar) welcome, a few
seats on terrace overlooking market square,
open all day. *(Julian Richardson)*

PETWORTH SU9722
Stonemasons (01798) 342510
North Street; GU28 9NL Attractive 17th-c
low-beamed inn; enjoyable freshly made food
from sandwiches up including blackboard
specials, Skinners Betty Stogs and guests,
helpful friendly staff, opened-up modernised
areas in former adjoining cottages, inglenook
log fires; TV; children and dogs welcome,
picnic-sets in sheltered back garden, five
bedrooms, opposite Petworth House (NT) so
can get busy, open (and food) all day, kitchen
shuts 5.30pm Sun. *(Ann and Colin Hunt)*

PLUMPTON TQ3613
Half Moon (01273) 890253
Ditchling Road (B2116); BN7 3AF
Enlarged beamed and timbered roadside
dining pub; good food from pub favourites up,

local ales and plenty of wines by the glass,
log fire with unusual flint chimneybreast;
background music; children and dogs (in
bar) welcome, tables in wisteria-clad front
courtyard and on back terrace, big downs-
view garden, good walks, open all day (till
6pm Sun). *(Angela and Steve Heard)*

POYNINGS TQ2611
Royal Oak (01273) 857389
The Street; BN45 7AQ Welcoming
traditional 19th-c pub in rural setting; large
beamed bar with smaller more intimate areas
up steps, well kept Harveys and a guest from
three-sided servery, enjoyable reasonably
priced home-cooked food, friendly efficient
service, traditional furnishing, hanging hops
and old photographs, paintings for sale,
woodburner; children and dogs welcome, big
garden with country/downs views, play area
and barbecue, good walks, open (and food)
all day. *(Patric Curwen, John Beeken, Gail Plews)*

RINGMER TQ4512
Green Man (01273) 812422
Lewes Road; BN8 5NA Welcoming 1930s
roadside pub with busy mix of locals and
visitors; six real ales from brick-faced
counter including Greene King, wide range
of generous good value food, efficient
friendly service, long bar with log fire, large
restaurant and conservatory; children and
dogs welcome, terrace tables, more on lawn
under trees, play area, open (and food)
all day. *(Kerry and Guy Trooper)*

RODMELL TQ4105
Abergavenny Arms (01273) 472416
Back road Lewes–Newhaven; BN7 3EZ
Welcoming beamed and raftered ex-barn;
large open-plan bar with wood and tiled
floors, several recesses and log fire in
big fireplace, good selection of enjoyable
home-made food (not Sun evening) from
daily changing menu, steak night Thurs, well
kept Harveys and one or more local guests,
upstairs eating area, games room; occasional
live music, free wi-fi; children welcome,
large two-level back terrace with painted
picnic-sets, convenient for Virginia Woolf's
Monk's House (NT) and South Downs Way,
open all day. *(John Beeken)*

ROWHOOK TQ1234
★Chequers (01403) 790480
Off A29 NW of Horsham; RH12 3PY
Attractive 15th-c country pub; beamed
and flagstoned front bar with portraits and
inglenook log fire, step up to low-ceilinged
lounge, well kept Harveys and guests, decent
wines by the glass and good food from chef-
landlord using local ingredients including
home-grown vegetables, efficient service

Virtually all pubs in this book sell wine by the glass. We mention wines
if they are a cut above the average.

from friendly chatty young staff, separate restaurant; background music; children and dogs welcome, tables out on front terraces and in pretty garden behind, good play area, closed Sun evening. *(Christopher and Elise Way)*

RUSPER   TQ2037
Star (01293) 871264
Off A264 S of Crawley; RH12 4RA
Several linked rooms in this cosy 15th-c beamed coaching inn; well kept ales such as Fullers, Greene King and Ringwood, decent food (all day Sun) from sandwiches and light meals up including some greek and vegan dishes, wood floors, old tools on walls, fine brick inglenook; children and dogs welcome, small back terrace, open all day.
(Douglas Power)

RYE   TQ9220
★**George** (01797) 222114
High Street; TN31 7JT Sizeable hotel with popular beamed bar; mix of furniture including settles on bare boards, log fire, local ales such as Dark Star, Harveys and Old Dairy, continental beers on tap too, friendly helpful service from neat young staff, interesting bistro-style food and good selection of wines including local vineyards such as Chapel Down, large spreading restaurant to right of main door; maybe background jazz; children and dogs welcome, seats on pleasant back terrace, attractive bedrooms, open all day. *(Mike Buckingham)*

RYE   TQ9220
★**Globe** (01797) 225220
Military Road; TN31 7NX Small weatherboarded pub under same owners as the Woolpack at Warehorne (Kent); quirky touches such as corrugated iron-clad walls, hanging lobster-pot lights and eclectic range of furniture from school chairs to a table made from part of an old fishing boat, even hay bale seats in one part, fresh flowers, candles and paraffin lamps, two log fires, good locally sourced food from open kitchen with wood-fired oven, interesting local ales and ciders (no bar counter), also some wines from nearby Chapel Down, shelves of home-made preserves for sale, quick cheerful service; unisex loos; children and dogs welcome, seats on side decking, Sat market, open all day. *(Celia and Geoff Clay)*

RYE   TQ9220
★**Mermaid** (01797) 223065
Mermaid Street; TN31 7EY Fine old timbered inn on famous cobbled street (cellars date from 12th c, although pub was rebuilt in 1420); civilised antiques-filled bar, Victorian gothick carved chairs, older but plainer oak seats and huge working inglenook with massive bressumer (ask about the priest hole and secret passages), Harveys, Sharps and a guest, good selection of wines, gins and malt whiskies, enjoyable bar food (not Sat evening) or more elaborate

and expensive restaurant choices, efficient friendly service, reputedly haunted by five ghosts; background music; children welcome, seats on small back terrace, bedrooms (most with four-posters), good breakfast, open all day. *(Martin Cooke)*

RYE   TQ9120
★**Standard** (01797) 225231
The Mint, High Street; TN31 7EN
Ancient pub sympathetically opened up and renovated; moulded beams, exposed brickwork and panelling, brown leather and farmhouse chairs at rustic tables on quarry tiles, candles and log fires (stag's head above one), four well kept ales including local Three Legs, good fairly priced food using local ingredients (fish from the harbour), nice wines and decent coffee, friendly accommodating staff; outside gents'; well behaved children and dogs welcome, picnic sets on small back terrace, five well appointed character bedrooms (more in their nearby café/bakery), open all day.
(Mike and Eleanor Anderson, Paul and Karen Cornock, Tony Scott)

RYE   TQ9220
Waterworks Micropub
07974 941393 *Tower Street/Rope Walk; TN31 7AT* Micropub in interesting old building (former waterworks); friendly hard-working landlord serving eight well kept local beers and three or four real ciders (all marked-up on blackboard), also wines by the glass and some snacky food, furniture and other bits and pieces for sale; dogs welcome, open all day weekends, otherwise from 2pm, handy for the station. *(Mike and Eleanor Anderson, Peter Meister)*

RYE   TQ9220
★**Ypres Castle** (01797) 223248
Gun Garden; steps up from A259, or down past Ypres Tower; TN31 7HH
Traditional tucked-away 17th-c pub; main bar with wall banquettes, assorted tables and chairs on bare boards and open fire, half a dozen well kept local beers and a couple of proper ciders, good reasonably priced food from pub favourites up, two dining rooms, friendly relaxed atmosphere; background music (live 5-7pm Sun); children and dogs welcome, lovely views from sheltered garden down over River Rother, open all day.
(Alexandra and Richard Clay, Richard Cole, Mike and Eleanor Anderson, Richard Tilbrook, D W Stokes, Tony Scott)

RYE HARBOUR   TQ9419
Inkerman Arms (01797) 222464
Rye Harbour Road; TN31 7TQ Friendly 19th-c end-of-terrace pub near nature reserve; enjoyable food including good fish and chips, well kept ales; children and dogs welcome, picnic-sets on sheltered back terrace with pond, open all day.
(Charles Welch)

RYE HARBOUR TQ9419
William the Conqueror
(01797) 223315 *Opposite lifeboat station, bottom of Harbour Road; TN31 7TU* Welcoming refurbished harbourside pub (sister to the Royal Oak in Whatlington); three well kept Shepherd Neame ales and decent choice of wines by the glass, good reasonably priced food including local fish and some greek dishes, friendly helpful staff, three main areas (ramp down to lower dining part), nautical-themed décor with framed charts and old local pictures, some wooden booth seating and cushioned benches on bare boards, log fires; background and occasional live music, free wi-fi; children and dogs welcome, picnic-sets out in front, open all day (till 10pm Mon-Thurs, 6pm Sun). *(Peter Meister, Richard and Penny Gibbs)*

SEDLESCOMBE TQ7817
Queens Head (01424) 870228
The Green; TN33 0QA Attractive old tile-hung village green pub (watch out for the wandering geese); beamed central bar with armchairs on bare boards, some window seats and a huge cartwheel, Harveys, Sharps Doom Bar and a guest such as Old Dairy, decent choice of wines by the glass, dining areas either side with open fires (one in large inglenook), good popular food from shortish menu (also blackboard specials), helpful friendly staff; maybe quiet background music; children and dogs welcome, picnic-sets in spacious side garden, open all day, food till 6.30pm Sun. *(John Davies)*

SHORTBRIDGE TQ4521
Peacock (01825) 762463
Piltdown; OS Sheet 198 map reference 450215; TN22 3XA Old black and white country dining pub, civilised and welcoming, with dark beams, timbers and big inglenook, some nice old furniture on parquet floors, good food from ciabattas up, two or three well kept ales and decent wines by the glass, friendly attentive staff, restaurant; children and dogs welcome, tables out at front and in back garden, bedrooms, open all day Fri-Sun. *(Tony Scott)*

SIDLESHAM SZ8697
⋆ **Crab & Lobster** (01243) 641233
Mill Lane; off B2145 S of Chichester; PO20 7NB Restaurant-with-rooms rather than pub but does have a small flagstoned bar serving real ales, plenty of wines by the glass (including champagne) and light meals; stylish upmarket restaurant with good imaginative (and pricey) food including excellent local fish, competent friendly young staff; background music; children welcome, tables on back terrace overlooking marshes,

smart bedrooms and self-catering cottage, open all day (food all day weekends). *(Guy Vowles, Philippa Ward)*

SINGLETON SU8713
Partridge (01243) 811251
Just off A286 Midhurst–Chichester; PO18 0EY Pretty 16th-c pub in attractive village setting; all sorts of light and dark wood tables and dining chairs on polished wood floors, flagstones or carpet, some country knick-knacks, open fires and woodburner, three well kept changing ales, several wines by the glass and enjoyable food (all day Sat, till 6.30pm Sun) from sandwiches up, cream teas (must book), friendly welcoming service; background and live music, monthly quiz, free wi-fi; children and dogs welcome, plenty of seats under parasols on terrace and in walled garden, play area, well placed for Weald & Downland Living Museum, open all day. *(Simon Collett-Jones)*

SLINDON SU9708
Spur (01243) 814216
Slindon Common; A29 towards Bognor; BN18 0NE Roomy 17th-c pub with well kept ales such as Courage Directors and Sharps Doom Bar, good choice of popular sensibly priced food from bar snacks up, friendly staff, pine tables and two big log fires, large panelled restaurant, games room with darts and pool, also a skittle alley; quiz fourth Weds of month, some live music; children and dogs (in bar) welcome, pretty garden (some traffic noise), good local walks, open all day Sun. *(Tony and Wendy Hobden)*

SMALL DOLE TQ2112
Fox (01273) 491196
Henfield Road; BN5 9XE Busy roadside village pub with good choice of well liked/priced home-made food including popular weekday set menu, quick friendly service, well kept Harveys and one or two guests, cosy dining areas off long panelled bar, dark pubby furniture on wood or carpeted floors, pictures of plants, fish and hunting scenes; quiet background music; children and dogs welcome, disabled access, seats out at front and in tree-shaded garden with play area, open (and food) all day Sun. *(Tony and Wendy Hobden, John Beeken)*

SOUTH HARTING SU7819
⋆ **White Hart** (01730) 825124
B2146 SE of Petersfield; GU31 5QB Sympathetically renovated 16th-c village inn; bars and dining area with beams and standing timbers, a couple of woodburners and open fire, nice mix of furniture on bare boards or flagstones, candles and fresh flowers, up to four well kept changing ales, 17 wines by the glass (from Berry Brothers

---

If you know a pub is ever open all day, please tell us.

of London) and a dozen malt whiskies, good food including lunchtime set menu, pleasant service; live music and quiz nights; children and dogs (in bar) welcome, terrace and garden tables, handy for Uppark (NT), comfortable character bedrooms, open all day, breakfast for non-residents. *(Simon Collett-Jones)*

SOUTHWATER   TQ1528
Bax Castle (01403) 730369
Two Mile Ash, a mile or so NW; RH13 0LA Early 19th-c country pub with well liked/priced home-made food including burgers, wood-fired pizzas and Sun carvery, two or three well kept Ringwood ales, friendly staff, sofas next to big log fire, barn restaurant; background music; children and dogs welcome, pleasant garden with play area, near Downs Link path on former railway track, shuts 7pm Sun, otherwise open (and food) all day. *(Tony and Wendy Hobden)*

STAPLEFIELD   TQ2728
Jolly Tanners (01444) 400335
Handcross Road, just off A23; RH17 6EF Split-level local by cricket green, welcoming landlord and pub dogs, two good log fires, padded settles and lots of china, brasses and old photographs, Harveys and guests (beer festivals), real cider, enjoyable pubby food including burgers, 'sizzling' dishes and blackboard specials, friendly chatty atmosphere; background music (live Tues and Sat), Thurs quiz, darts; children and dogs welcome, attractive suntrap garden, quite handy for Nymans (NT), open all day, food till 5.30pm Sun. *(Tony Scott)*

STAPLEFIELD   TQ2728
Victory (01444) 400463
Warninglid Road; RH17 6EU Pretty little shuttered dining pub overlooking cricket green (and London to Brighton veteran car run, first Sun in Nov); friendly welcoming staff, good choice of popular home-made food (all day Sat, till 7pm Sun) with smaller helpings for children, well kept Harveys Best and a guest, local cider and decent wines from zinc-topped counter, beams and woodburner; dogs welcome in bar, spacious tree-shaded garden with play area, closed Mon, otherwise open all day. *(Tony and Wendy Hobden)*

STEDHAM   SU8522
Hamilton Arms (01730) 812555
School Lane (off A272); GU29 0NZ Village local run by friendly thai family; standard pub food as well as popular thai bar snacks and restaurant dishes (you can buy ingredients in their little shop), reasonably priced wines and four or more well kept ales; background and occasional live music; pretty hanging baskets on front terrace overlooking small green, nearby walks, open all day Thurs-Sun, closed Mon. *(Richard Wilton)*

STOPHAM   TQ0318
White Hart (01798) 874903
Off A283 E of village, W of Pulborough; RH20 1DS Fine old beamed pub by medieval River Arun bridge; well kept Harveys, Sharps and a guest, generally well liked food from sandwiches, sharing plates and stone-baked pizzas up; some live music; children and dogs (in bar) welcome, waterside tables, open all day, no food Sun evening. *(Ruth May)*

STOUGHTON   SU8011
Hare & Hounds (023) 9263 1433
Signed off B2146 Petersfield–Emsworth; PO18 9JQ Brick and flint country pub with good reasonably priced home-cooked food from baguettes up, several well kept ales such as Dark Star, Long Man and Otter, Weston's cider and good choice of wines by the glass, cheerful service, flagstones and big open fires, locals' bar with darts; quiz nights; children (in eating areas) and dogs welcome, tables on pretty front terrace and grass behind, lovely setting near Saxon church, good walks, open all day. *(Tony and Jill Radnor)*

SUTTON   SU9715
White Horse (01798) 869191
The Street; RH20 1PS Recently reopened/refurbished 18th-c village inn; wood-floored bar with open brick fireplace at each end, wooden chairs around well spaced tables, also banquette seating, three well kept local ales and nice wines by the glass, good food (not especially cheap) from lunchtime sandwiches and a few pub favourites up, friendly efficient service, restaurant area; children and dogs welcome, some seats out at front, more on back terrace, good surrounding walks and handy for Bignor Roman Villa, comfortable well appointed bedrooms, open all day, food till 7pm Sun. *(Martin Day)*

THAKEHAM   TQ1017
White Lion (01798) 813141
Off B2139 N of Storrington; The Street; RH20 3EP Steps up to 16th-c pub in pretty village; heavy beams, panelling, bare boards and traditional furnishings, four changing ales including Fullers and Harveys, decent wines by the glass and well liked food (not Sun evening) including good selection of blackboard specials, efficient service, pleasant dining room with inglenook; children and dogs welcome, sunny terrace and small enclosed lawn, open all day. *(Katherine Matthews)*

TICEHURST   TQ6831
★ **Bull** (01580) 200586
Three Leg Cross; off B2099 towards Wadhurst; TN5 7HH Attractive 14th-c country pub popular with good mix of customers; big log fires in two heavy-beamed

old-fashioned bars, well kept Harveys and a couple of guests, contemporary furnishings in light airy dining extension, friendly service; children and dogs welcome, charming front garden (busy in summer), bigger back one with play area, good PYO fruit farm nearby, four bedrooms, open all day. *(P Beardsell)*

TURNERS HILL   TQ3435
★ **Red Lion** (01342) 715416
Lion Lane, just off B2028; RH10 4NU
Welcoming traditional country local; snug parquet-floored bar with plush wall benches and small open fire, steps up to carpeted dining area with inglenook log fire, cushioned pews and settles, old photos and brewery memorabilia, well kept Harveys ales and good home-made food (lunchtime only – must book Sun); occasional live music including open mike nights, fortnightly quiz Weds; children (away from bar) and dogs welcome, picnic-sets on side grass overlooking village, open all day weekends, no food Thurs apart from rolls. *(Tony Scott, David Chubb)*

UDIMORE   TQ8818
Plough (01797) 223381
Cock Marling (B2089 W of Rye); TN31 6AL Traditionally updated and extended 17th-c roadside pub; enjoyable freshly made food including tapas and good steaks, well kept Harveys, Long Man and Three Legs, decent choice of wines by the glass, happy hour 5.30-7pm Fri, friendly welcoming staff, U-shaped bar with wood and quarry-tiled floors, two woodburners; occasional live music; children and dogs welcome, tables on good-sized sunny back terrace, Brede Valley views, self-catering apartment, open (and food) all day Fri, Sat, till 6pm (3pm) Sun. *(Mike and Eleanor Anderson)*

UPPER DICKER   TQ5409
Plough (01323) 844859
Coldharbour Road; BN27 3QJ Extended 17th-c pub with small central beamed bar, seats by inglenook, two restaurant areas off to the left and step up to larger dining bar on right with raised section, well kept Harveys and Shepherd Neame, enjoyable food from pubby choices up, friendly young staff; background and occasional live music, free wi-fi; children and dogs welcome, spacious garden with play area, open all day. *(Nigel and Jean Eames)*

WALBERTON   SU9705
Holly Tree (01243) 553110
The Street; BN18 0PH Quirky grey-painted Victorian pub under new management; enjoyable food (not Sun evening) including

Weds steak and Thurs curry nights, changing ales and decent wines (weekday happy hour 4-6pm), friendly young staff; Tues quiz, some live music and other events, big-screen sports TV; children and dogs welcome, café-style furniture and planters on front terrace, open all day. *(Susan Eccleston)*

WALDERTON   SU7910
Barley Mow (023) 9263 1321
Stoughton Road, just off B2146 Chichester–Petersfield; PO18 9ED
Popular red-brick country pub with well liked food including Weds curry night, Thurs steaks and Sun carvery, five real ales such as Dark Star, Harveys and Ringwood, a dozen wines by the glass, friendly welcoming staff, two log fires in U-shaped bar with roomy dining areas; skittle alley; children and dogs welcome, big streamside back garden, good walks (Kingley Vale nearby) and handy for Stansted Park, open all day Sat, till 6pm Sun. *(Tony and Jill Radnor)*

WALDRON   TQ5419
★ **Star** (01435) 812495
Blackboys–Horam side road; TN21 0RA Pretty pub in quiet village across from the church; beamed main bar with settle next to good log fire in brick inglenook, wheelbacks around pubby tables on old quarry tiles, several built-in cushioned wall and window seats, old local pictures and photographs, high stools by central counter serving well kept Harveys, Sharps and a guest, maybe own apple juice, good food (not Sun evening) including bar snacks, pubby dishes and specials, dining areas with painted chairs around pine-topped tables on parquet or bare boards, bookshelf wallpaper, chatty local atmosphere and friendly staff; Mon quiz, live music and comedy nights; picnic-sets in pleasant back garden, small café and shop next door.
(David and Leone Lawson)

WARBLETON   TQ6018
★ **Black Duck** (01435) 830636
S of B2096 SE of Heathfield; TN21 9BD Small renovated tile-hung pub tucked down from church; L-shaped main room with pale oak flooring, cushioned leather sofas in front of inglenook log fire, beams and walls hung with horsebrasses, tankards, musical instruments, farm tools, even an old typewriter, high-backed dining chairs around mix of tables, good fairly pubby food including daily specials, bar area up a step with stools along counter, Harveys and a guest, nice wines by the glass, cabinet

---

Half pints: by law, a pub should not charge more for half a pint than half the price of a full pint, unless it shows that half-pint price on its price list.

of books and board games; background and occasional live music; children and dogs welcome (pub dog is Dusty), picnic-sets in back garden with sweeping valley views, more on front grass, open all day Fri and Sat, closed Mon. *(Gordon Bradley)*

WARNHAM   TQ1533
Greets (01403) 265047
Friday Street; RH12 3QY Welcoming 15th-c beamed pub with appealing simple décor; stripped pine tables on uneven flagstones, inglenook log fire, lots of nooks and corners, well kept Harveys and a dozen wines by the glass, good choice of fairly traditional food at sensible prices, friendly helpful staff, convivial locals' side bar with leather ceiling straps; children welcome, lawned garden with tables, open (and food) all day weekends.
(Mike and Marion Higgins, Tony Scott)

WARNHAM   TQ1533
Sussex Oak (01403) 265028
Just off A24 Horsham–Dorking; Church Street; RH12 3QW Cheerfully busy country pub with heavy beams and timbers, mix of flagstones, tiles, wood and carpeting, big inglenook log fire, well kept Fullers, Harveys and guests from carved servery, real cider and plenty of wines by the glass, enjoyable fairly traditional food (smaller helpings available); background music, Thurs quiz, darts, free wi-fi; children and dogs welcome, disabled facilities/parking, picnic-sets in large tree-shaded garden, good local walks, open all day, food all day weekends.
(Tony and Wendy Hobden)

WARTLING   TQ6509
★ **Lamb** (01323) 832116
Village signed with Herstmonceux Castle off A271 Herstmonceux–Battle; BN27 1RY Popular family-owned country pub; small entrance bar with open fireplace, Harveys Best and a couple of local guests, several wines by the glass from good list, two-level beamed and timbered dining room to the left with inglenook woodburner, bigger back bar and restaurant, well liked food including blackboard specials, friendly service; children and dogs welcome, steps up to garden with chunky seats, five bedrooms, closed Sun evening, otherwise open all day.
(Bob)

WEST ASHLING   SU8007
Richmond Arms (01243) 572046
Just off B2146; Mill Road; PO18 8EA Village dining pub in pretty setting near big millpond with ducks and geese; highly regarded imaginative food (quite pricey, best to book) from bar snacks up, also wood-fired pizzas cooked in a vintage van (Fri, Sat

evenings), well kept Harveys ales and good wines by the glass, competent friendly staff; children welcome, two nice bedrooms, closed Sun evening, Mon and Tues. *(Tracey and Stephen Groves)*

WEST HOATHLY   TQ3632
Fox (01342) 810644
Hammingden Lane/North Lane, towards Sharpthorne; RH19 4QG Welcoming corner pub with good food (not Sun evening) cooked by landlord-chef, Harveys Best Bitter and a guest such as St Austell Tribute, decent wines and lots of gins, friendly accommodating service, slightly quirky décor with curtain pelmets made from old pallets, bottle lampshades and floor-to-ceiling column of books in the bar, cosy log fires; some live music and quiz nights; children and dogs welcome, pavement tables under parasols, closed Mon, otherwise open all day (till 9pm Sun). *(Richard and Penny Gibbs)*

WEST MARDEN   SU7713
Victoria (023) 9263 1330
B2146 2 miles S of Uppark; PO18 9EN Friendly village pub popular with downland walkers; good traditional food (not Sun evening) in beamed bar and small back restaurant, well kept changing ales (beer, cider and gin festivals), log fire; occasional live music; children and dogs welcome, attractive garden, open all day Sat, till 9pm Sun, closed Mon (except bank holidays). *(Tony and Jill Radnor)*

WEST WITTERING   SZ8099
Lamb (01243) 511105
Chichester Road; B2179/A286 towards Birdham; PO20 8QA Modernised 18th-c tile-hung country pub; three Badger ales and enjoyable home-cooked food including popular Sun roasts (booking advised), bar with painted beams and timbers, assorted furniture on parquet including kitchen chairs and scrubbed pine tables, woodburner in brick fireplace, two bare-boards dining rooms, some interesting artwork; background music; children and dogs welcome, tables out at front and in small sheltered back garden with pizza oven and play area, open all day, food all day Sun till 8pm. *(Charles Welch)*

WESTFIELD   TQ8115
New Inn (01424) 752800
Main Road; TN35 4QE Popular village pub with light open-plan interior, pubby furniture including wheelback and captain's chairs on pale wood floors, sparsely decorated white walls, conservatory, four or five mainly local ales including a house beer from Long Man, enjoyable reasonably priced home-made food from weekly changing menu (till 7pm Sun,

---

There are report forms at the back of the book.

not Mon evening), cheerful helpful staff; free wi-fi; children and dogs welcome, disabled access, seats out on gravel terrace, open all day. *(Angela and Steve Heard)*

WHATLINGTON TQ7619
Royal Oak (01424) 870492
A21 N of village; TN33 0NJ Welcoming 15th-c weatherboarded pub set down from the road (sister to the William the Conqueror in Rye Harbour); cosy split-level interior with series of linked rooms, black beams and log fires (one in brick inglenook), deep well in another part, good reasonably priced food including steak cooked on a hot stone Fri evening and popular greek meze night Sat (landlady-chef is cypriot), well kept Long Man and Shepherd Neame, decent wines by the glass, friendly helpful service; background music, Thurs quiz; children and dogs welcome, play area inside and in back garden, boules pitch, open (and food) all day Sat, till 6pm (4pm) Sun, closed Mon. *(Celia and Geoff Clay)*

WILMINGTON TQ5404
Giants Rest (01323) 870207
Just off A27; BN26 5SQ Popular early 20th-c country pub; long wood-floored bar with adjacent open areas, simple furniture, rural pictures and log fire, Long Man and a couple of local guests, South Downs cider (made in the village), enjoyable pubby food including good home-made pies, friendly service; wooden puzzles and games; children and dogs welcome, picnic-sets on front grass, surrounded by South Downs walks and village famous for chalk-carved Long Man, two bedrooms, open (and food) all day, kitchen may shut early Sun evening if quiet. *(Richard Kennell, Mrs J Ekins-Daukes, John Beeken)*

WINEHAM TQ2320
★ Royal Oak (01444) 881252
Village signposted from A272 and B2116; BN5 9AY Splendidly old-fashioned local with log fire in big inglenook, jugs and ancient corkscrews on very low beams, collection of cigarette boxes and old bottles, various stuffed animals including a stoat and crocodile, Harveys Best and guests tapped from stillroom casks, enjoyable home-cooked food (not Sun evening), more bric-a-brac and old local photographs in back parlour with views of quiet countryside; occasional folk music and morris men; children away from bar and dogs welcome, picnic-sets out at front, closed evenings 25 and 26 Dec, 1 Jan. *(Tony Scott)*

WISBOROUGH GREEN TQ0626
Bat & Ball (01403) 700199
Newpound Lane; RH14 0EH Refurbished 18th-c red-brick Badger dining pub set in six-acre grounds; their ales and 20 wines by the glass including champagne from counter faced in wine boxes, short but varied choice of well liked food, afternoon teas, connecting beamed rooms with cosy corners and plenty of rustic charm including high-raftered restaurant, quiz nights; children and dogs (in bar) welcome, pretty front garden with pond, camping and shepherd's huts, handy for Fishers Farm Park, open all day (till 8pm Sun). *(Kerry and Guy Trooper)*

WISBOROUGH GREEN TQ0526
Cricketers Arms (01403) 700369
Loxwood Road, just off A272 Billingshurst–Petworth; RH14 0DG Attractive old pub on edge of village green; well kept ales such as Harveys, St Austell and Sharps, good choice of fairly priced food (not Mon evening) including specials and deals, gluten-free diets catered for, cheerful welcoming staff, open-plan with two big woodburners and pleasing mix of country furniture on parquet flooring, stripped-brick dining area on left; Fri live music; children and dogs welcome, tables out in front, annual lawn mower race on the green, open all day. *(Tony and Wendy Hobden, Tony Scott)*

WIVELSFIELD GREEN TQ3519
Cock (01444) 471668
North Common Road; RH17 7RH Pleasant red-brick village pub; good choice of enjoyable reasonably priced food including themed nights, Harveys and guests, helpful friendly staff, two bars and restaurant, log fire; monthly quiz night, darts, bar billiards, pool and sports TV; children, walkers and dogs welcome, seats out at front and in back garden, open all day, food all day Fri and Sat, till 8pm Sun. *(Miles Green)*

WOODMANCOTE SU7707
Woodmancote (01243) 371019
The one near Emsworth; Woodmancote Lane; PO10 8RD Village pub with unusual contemporary décor – plenty of quirky touches; good popular food (best to book) from sandwiches and sharing boards up, Weds steak night, three real ales including one badged for them and several wines by the glass, happy hour 4-6pm Mon-Sat, friendly staff, restaurant; acoustic music Sun afternoon, quiz every other Tues; children and dogs (in bar) welcome, seats out under cover, open (and food) all day from 9.30am for breakfast, kitchen shuts 7pm Sun. *(Ann and Colin Hunt)*

WORTHING TQ1502
Corner House (01903) 216463
High Street; BN11 1DJ Refurbished and extended pub with bright modern interior; comfortable seating including some sofas around three sides of central bar, four real ales, craft beers and good range of wines marked up on blackboard, enjoyable reasonably priced food (they may ask for a credit card if you run a tab); quiz Mon; children and dogs welcome, paved and

heated back terrace, open all day, no food Sun evening. *(Tony and Wendy Hobden)*

WORTHING TQ1402

Egremont (01903) 600064

Brighton Road; BN11 3ED Restored 19th-c pub near seafront; up to six real ales including Harveys and a couple from Hand badged for them, extensive range of interesting gins and enjoyable reasonably priced pubby food from ciabattas and sharing plates up, some lunchtime choices available in smaller helpings, friendly helpful staff, split-level mainly bare-boards interior arranged around central bar, one part laid for dining, mix of furniture including button-back banquettes, stools, sofas and some high tables, original Kemptown Brewery stained glass, old enamel signs and other interesting bits and pieces; quiz and live music nights, TV for major sports; children and dogs

welcome, pavement picnic-sets, open all day. *(Tony and Wendy Hobden)*

WORTHING TQ1502

Selden Arms (01903) 234854

Lyndhurst Road, between Waitrose and hospital; BN11 2DB Friendly unchanging 19th-c backstreet local opposite the gasworks; welcoming long-serving licensees, six well kept changing ales, craft kegs and extensive range of bottled belgian beers (Jan beer festival), bargain lunchtime food (not Sun) including doorstep sandwiches and various pies, regular curry nights, seafood Fri, comfortably worn interior with photographs of old Worthing pubs, pump clips on ceiling, log fire; occasional live music and quiz nights, darts; dogs welcome, open all day. *(Tony and Wendy Hobden, Tony Scott)*

Warwickshire

with Birmingham and West Midlands

KEY

★ Star Pub   🔘 Top Quality Food   🍺 Great Beer

♈ Good Wines   £ Bargain Meals   🛏 Good Bedrooms   🍴 Serves Food

---

ARMSCOTE

SP2444   Map 4

Fuzzy Duck 🔘 ♈ 🛏

(01608) 682635 – www.fuzzyduckarmscote.com

Off A3400 Stratford–Shipston; CV37 8DD

**Interestingly refurbished former coaching inn with real ales, a good
wine list, inventive food and seats outside; bedrooms**

A stylishly reworked 18th-c inn that's handy for Stratford-upon-Avon
and surrounded by Cotswold countryside, this is a lovely place to stay
and the bedrooms (each named after a species of duck) are extremely
comfortable and well equipped; first class breakfasts too. The bustling bar
has an open fire, high chunky leather chairs around equally high metal tables
on flagstones, with more leather chairs against the counter where they
serve Purity Mad Goose and a weekly guest such as Church Farm IPA on
handpump, a dozen wines by the glass, 12 malt whiskies and a farm cider;
a wall of glass-faced boxes holds bottles of spirits belonging to regular
customers. Three interconnected dining rooms have a mix of dark wooden
tables surrounded by leather and other elegant chairs on pale floorboards,
a sofa here and there and a two-way woodburning stove in an open fireplace.
Throughout, cartoons and arty photographs hang on pale or dark grey walls
and flowers are arranged in big vases; background music and board games.
At the back, another dining room (also used for private parties) leads to
a decked terrace with basket-weave armchairs, cushioned sofas and small
modern metal chairs and tables under large parasols; there's also a small
lawn with fruit trees.

🔘 Tempting food includes crab tart with avocado purée, grapes, radish and green
apple, shredded duck spring roll with vietnamese-style vegetable and cashew
salad, moroccan-spiced roasted cauliflower with chickpeas, couscous, apricots, yoghurt
and coriander, beer-battered cod and chips, chipotle-spiced confit duck with soft corn
tortillas, sweet potato salad and pineapple salsa, 10oz rib-eye steak with duck fat chips
and parsley hollandaise, and puddings such as lemongrass crème brûlée with stem
ginger shortbread and coconut and lime sorbet and poached rhubarb and vanilla pastry
cream tart. *Benchmark main dish: rare-breed lamb rump and panko-crumbed breast,
peas, beans and mint and white wine jus £23.00. Two-course evening meal £26.00.*

Free house ~ Licensee Laurent Toma ~ Real ale ~ Open 10am-11pm; 11-5 Sun; closed Sun
evening, Mon ~ Bar food 12-3, 6-9; 12-4 Sun ~ Restaurant ~ Children welcome ~ Dogs
welcome ~ Wi-fi ~ Bedrooms: /£140 *Recommended by Ian Herdman, Dave Braisted, Susan and
John Douglas, Martin and Sue Neville, John and Abigail Prescott, Camilla and Jose Ferrera*

ARROW
SP0856 Map 4

Arrow Mill ♀ 🍺 🛏

(01789) 333790 – www.brunningandprice.co.uk/arrowmill

Opposite gates of Ragley Hall; B49 5NL

Splendid former mill, carefully extended with airy drinking and dining rooms, a large selection of drinks, rewarding food and sunny terrace; good bedrooms

As this is in a lovely setting, overlooks the grounds of Ragley Hall and is close to Stratford-upon-Avon and the Roman town of Alcester, why not make the most of the spacious, comfortable and up-to-date bedrooms here and use them as a base for exploring? This is a beautifully and thoughtfully transformed old mill and it's certainly worth looking around before you decide where to sit. The original mill workings are on show, along with high raftered ceilings, heavy beams and timbers, fine brickwork and open fires – and some windows look out over the mill pond where you'll see their family of swans. The rooms and corridors are furnished with antique-style dining chairs, colourful leather armchairs, cushioned settles and stools, all manner of wooden tables on polished floorboards, parquet and rugs, plus elegant metal chandeliers, hundreds of prints and photographs, shelves of books and big house plants; one area is rather like a private sitting room and is much coveted by customers. Quick, friendly staff serve Phoenix Brunning & Price Original plus Hook Norton Hook, Pershore Man in a Hat, Purity Mad Goose, Wadworths Horizon and Wye Valley Butty Bach on handpump, over 110 gins and 18 wines by the glass from the panelled counter. A carefully planted terrace has wooden chairs and tables under green parasols, and the River Arrow runs the length of the garden.

 Brasserie-style food includes sandwiches, teriyaki king prawns with tamari and ginger dressing, crispy lamb and feta salad with mint and broad beans, mushroom bourguignon pie with red wine jus, salmon and smoked haddock fishcake with a poached egg, cumberland sausages with mash and onion gravy, harissa-spiced lamb rump with tomato and cumin sauce, couscous and marinated apricots, crispy beef salad with sweet chilli sauce and roasted cashews, thai red fish curry with mussels and prawns and coconut rice, and puddings such as dark chocolate and orange tart with orange sorbet and crème brûlée. *Benchmark main dish: braised lamb shoulder with carrot mash and rosemary gravy £17.95. Two-course evening meal £21.00.*

Brunning & Price ~ Manager Peter Palfi ~ Real ale ~ Open 8am-11pm; 8am-10.30pm Sun ~ Bar food 12-10; 12-9.30 Sun ~ Restaurant ~ Children welcome ~ Dogs allowed in bar ~ Wi-fi ~ Bedrooms: /£95 *Recommended by James and Sylvia Hewitt, Emily and Toby Archer, Ruby and Simon Swettenham, Bob and Melissa Wyatt, Charles Fraser*

BARSTON
SP1978 Map 4

Malt Shovel ⭐ ♀

(01675) 443223 – www.themaltshovelatbarston.com

3 miles from M42 junction 5; A4141 towards Knowle, then first left into Jacobean Lane/Barston Lane; B92 0JP

Well run country dining pub full of happy customers, with an attractive layout, good service and seats in sheltered garden

Plenty of happy customers fill the bar and dining rooms here and, of course, you'll be made just as welcome if you're only here for a chat and a drink – though it would be a great shame to miss out on the first class food. The light and airy bar rambles extensively around the zinc-topped central counter, with big terracotta floor tiles neatly offset by dark grouting, and cream, tan and blue paintwork. Bombardier and Sharps Atlantic and Doom Bar on handpump, 18 wines by the glass and 17 malt whiskies; service is exemplary. Furnishings are comfortable, with informal dining chairs and scatter-cushioned pews around stripped-top tables of varying types and sizes, there are cheerful fruit and vegetable paintings on the walls, and french café-style shutters. The barn restaurant to the side is partially panelled with distressed dark grey paintwork that is topped with rows of pewter plates; background music. The sheltered back garden has a weeping willow and picnic-sets, and the terrace and verandah are furnished with cushioned teak seats and tables.

Enticing food includes seared scallops with honey and pumpkin tortellini and black pudding crumb, mandarin-marinated tuna tartare with duck yolk and wasabi, pea and shallot pasta with prosecco cream and cantucci crumb, cod with chestnut and rosemary crumble, spring onion crushed potatoes, asparagus, bacon and béarnaise, slow-roast char sui pork belly with chicken wonton, pak choi and a fried duck egg, calves liver with bacon, creamed mash and onion gravy, 28-day aged rare-breed rump steak with creamy peppercorn sauce and chips, and puddings such as pineapple and muscovado baked alaska with coconut crumble and white chocolate brioche bread and butter pudding with spiced rum custard. *Benchmark main dish: salmon fishcake with spinach, a poached egg and hollandaise £14.95. Two-course evening meal £22.00.*

Free house ~ Licensee Helen Somerfield ~ Real ale ~ Open 12-midnight; 12-7 Sun ~ Bar food 12-2.30, 6-9.30; 12-5 Sun ~ Restaurant ~ Children welcome ~ Dogs allowed in bar
Recommended by Alison and Graeme Spicer, Ian Herdman, John and Claire Masters, Julia and Fiona Barnes, Susan and John Douglas, Louise and Simon Peters, Sandra and Miles Spencer, Samuel and Melissa Turnbull

BIRMINGHAM
Old Joint Stock 🍺 £

SP0686   Map 4

(0121) 200 1892 – www.oldjointstocktheatre.co.uk
Temple Row West; B2 5NY

Big bustling Fullers pie-and-ale pub with impressive Victorian façade and interior, and a small back terrace; own theatre

Even when this particularly well run place is packed out (which it usually is), staff remain efficient and friendly. It's all impressively flamboyant: chandeliers hang from the soaring pink and gilt ceiling, gently illuminated busts line the top of the ornately plastered walls and there's a splendid cupola above the centre of the room. Photographs of the historic building's past line the walls; there's also a big dining balcony reached up a grand sweeping staircase. You'll find Fullers ESB, HSB, London Pride, Olivers Island and a guest or two on handpump, 17 wines by the glass and 36 gins; background music. The small and colourful back terrace has nicely quirky seats and tables and heaters. Most nights there's something on in the purpose-built, first-floor theatre and you can book a two-course pre-theatre meal in advance. Birmingham Cathedral is opposite.

Popular food includes breakfasts (9-11.30am) plus sandwiches, crispy squid with coriander and chilli jam, vietnamese spicy chicken wings, black bean burger with vegan coleslaw and chips, ham, pork pie and cheddar with piccalilli, apple and breads, ham and eggs, beer-battered haddock with triple-cooked chips, chicken madras curry, slow-cooked shoulder of local lamb with apricot, red wine and mint gravy, and puddings such as chocolate brownie with buffalo milk ice-cream and apple pie with crème anglaise. *Benchmark main dish: pie of the day £14.00. Two-course evening meal £19.00.*

Fullers ~ Manager Paul Bancroft ~ Real ale ~ Open 9am-11pm; 9-6 Sun; closed Sun evening ~ Bar food 9am-10pm; 9-4 Sun ~ Restaurant ~ Children allowed until 6pm ~ Wi-fi ~ Regular live entertainment in theatre (check website) *Recommended by Colin Gooch, Susan and John Douglas, Alan Johnson, Sandra and Neil White, Martine and Derek Cotton, Dr and Mrs A K Clarke*

BIRMINGHAM

SP0585   Map 4

Physician ♀ 🍺

(0121) 272 5900 – www.brunningandprice.co.uk/physician

Harborne Road, Edgbaston; pay-and-display parking in Highfield Road behind pub; B15 3DH

Substantial, extended pub with plenty of drinking and dining space, super drinks, interesting food and friendly atmosphere; seats outside

Friendly, well trained staff serve a fantastic range of drinks here: Phoenix Brunning & Price Original plus Fixed Wheel Through & Off, Green Duck Madness, St Austell Tribute, Timothy Taylors Boldmaker and Wye Valley HPA on handpump, over 20 wines by the glass, 100 gins, 50 rums, 80 malt whiskies and farm cider. There's a lot of historical grandeur and the high ceilings and big sash windows have been used to great effect. The interlinked areas of all shape and size have leather armchairs in front of open fires, a medley of cushioned wooden dining chairs and mate's chairs around polished solid tables on bare boards, rugs or carpet, lots of old prints on pale-painted walls, large gilt-edged mirrors and big house plants, stone bottles and books on shelves and lighting that ranges from table lamps to elegant metal chandeliers; background music. Terraces have good quality wooden seats and tables under green parasols among flowering tubs and flower beds. The building once housed the Sampson Gamgee Library for the History of Medicine. Disabled access.

 Rewarding food includes sandwiches, deep-fried brie with pickled cranberries and candied pecans, shredded ham, caper and parsley fritter with piccalilli, sharing boards, goan vegetable curry with sticky rice and chapatis, steak in ale pudding, sea bass fillets with butter bean, chickpea and chorizo cassoulet, pork rib-eye with roasted shallots, blue cheese potato gratin and apple and sage jus, chicken breast with truffle arancini, wild mushrooms, celeriac cream and madeira sauce, sirloin steak with tarragon and dijon butter and chips, and puddings such as triple chocolate brownie with chocolate sauce and apple and raspberry crumble with custard. *Benchmark main dish: braised lamb shoulder with dauphinoise potatoes, carrot mash and rosemary gravy £17.95. Two-course evening meal £24.00.*

Brunning & Price ~ Manager Lisa Rogers ~ Real ale ~ Open 10am-11pm; 10am-10.30pm Sun ~ Bar food 12-10 (9 Sun) ~ Children welcome ~ Dogs allowed in bar ~ Wi-fi *Recommended by Chris and Sophie Baxter, Mandy and Gary Redstone, Audrey and Paul Summers, Peter and Emma Kelly, Freddie and Sarah Banks, Nick Sharpe, Gus Swan*

HAMPTON-IN-ARDEN

SP2080   Map 4

White Lion 🍺

(01675) 442833 – www.thewhitelioninn.com

High Street; handy for M42 junction 6; B92 0AA

Popular village local with a good choice of ales; bedrooms

A former farmhouse and in an attractive village, this bustling pub offers a fine choice of real ales on handpump: Banks's Mild, Hobsons Best, M&B Brew XI, St Austell Proper Job, Skinners Betty Stogs and Wye Valley HPA plus 12 wines by the glass and two farm ciders. The carpeted bar is nice and relaxed, with a mix of furniture tidily laid out, neatly curtained small windows, low-beamed ceilings and some local memorabilia on the cream-painted walls; background music, TV and board games. The modern dining areas are fresh and airy with farmhouse, wheelback and cane chairs around a mix of tables on stripped floorboards. Bedrooms are quiet and comfortable. The church opposite is mentioned in the Domesday Book.

Traditional food (it may be more limited at lunchtime, best to check) includes lunchtime sandwiches, croque madame and monsieur, omelettes, steak burger with coleslaw and chips, rump steak and Sunday lunch. *Benchmark main dish: beer-battered cod and chips £12.00. Two-course evening meal £20.00.*

Free house ~ Licensee Chris Roach ~ Real ale ~ Open 12-11; 12-midnight Sat; 12-10.30 Sun ~ Bar food 12-2.30, 6-9; 12-4 Sun ~ Restaurant ~ Children welcome ~ Dogs welcome ~ Wi-fi ~ Monthly quiz and live music ~ Bedrooms: £90/£110 *Recommended by Andrew Wall, Gerry and Pam Pollard, Charlie Stevens, Moira and Jon Weller, Rupert and Sandy Newton, Max Simons, Sally Harrison*

HUNNINGHAM
Red Lion ♀
SP3768 Map 4

(01926) 632715 – www.redlionhunningham.co.uk
Village signposted off B4453 Leamington–Rugby just E of Weston, and off B4455 Fosse Way 2.5 miles SW of A423 junction; CV33 9DY

Friendly pub with a good range of drinks and well liked food

Popular food and an appealing, open-plan interior draw plenty of customers to this gently civilised place. Cleverly divided up, the rooms have pews with scatter cushions, an assortment of antique dining chairs and stools around nice polished tables on bare boards (with a few big rugs here and there) and contemporary paintwork. A cosy room has tub armchairs around an open coal fire. They keep a beer named for the pub, Gun Dog Jacks Spaniels, Purity Pure UBU, Stratford Upon Avon Stratford Mosaic and Wye Valley HPA on handpump and 17 wines by the glass; background music. Picnic-sets in the garden are much prized as they look across to the arched 14th-c bridge over the River Leam. There's a basket of rugs for customers to take outside and more picnic-sets are set out at the front.

Rewarding food includes sandwiches, smoked chicken and wild mushroom terrine with spiced poached pear compote, scallops of the day, sharing boards, falafel burger with sweet chilli sauce and chips, Josper-oven tuna with vegetable stir-fry, carrot and ginger purée and soy dressing, guinea fowl with sweet potato mash and madeira and raisin jus, 28-day aged 10oz sirloin with a choice of sauce, and puddings such as apple and black cherry crumble with custard and banana tarte tatin with honey and ginger ice-cream and popcorn toffee sauce. *Benchmark main dish: cassoulet £15.00. Two-course evening meal £23.00.*

Free house ~ Licensee Richard Merand ~ Real ale ~ Open 11-11; 11-10.30 Sun ~ Bar food 12-9; 12-7.30 ~ Restaurant ~ Children welcome ~ Dogs allowed in bar ~ Wi-fi *Recommended by Belinda and Neil Garth, Buster May, Jane Rigby, John and Claire Masters, Nik and Gloria Clarke, Christine and Tony Garrett*

ILMINGTON
Howard Arms ⭑♀🛏
SP2143 Map 4

(01608) 682226 – www.howardarms.com
Village signed with Wimpstone off A3400 S of Stratford; CV36 4LT

Lovely mellow-toned interior, lots to look at and tasty food and drink; bedrooms

This golden-stone inn has various beamed and flagstoned rooms with a pleasing mix of furniture ranging from pews and rustic stools to leather dining chairs around all sorts of tables, rugs on bare boards, shelves of books, candles and a log fire in a big inglenook. Hook Norton Hooky, Purity Mad Goose, Timothy Taylors Landlord and Wye Valley HPA on handpump, 14 wines by the glass, a fair choice of whiskies and brandies, and local cider; background music and board games. In warm weather, the big back garden has seats under parasols and a colourful herbaceous border. Bedrooms are well equipped and comfortable and the breakfasts highly regarded. There are good walks on the nearby hills.

Pleasing food includes sandwiches, spiced lamb kofta kebab with red pepper salsa and tzatziki, stilton bonbon with grilled pear, pine nuts and port wine dressing, sharing boards, wild mushroom, spinach and tomato stack with lemon and parsley polenta and chickpea and pepper stew, honey-glazed ham with duck eggs and piccalilli, stone bass fillet with clam and mussel chowder, chicken breast with jerusalem artichokes, sweet potato purée and mushrooms, twice-cooked pork belly with dauphinoise potatoes, creamed cabbage and bacon and jus, and puddings such as chocolate mousse and banoffi cheesecake with chocolate ice-cream. *Benchmark main dish: calves liver with mash and smoked bacon gravy £15.50. Two-course evening meal £22.00.*

Free house ~ Licensee Pawel Sobiszek ~ Real ale ~ Open 11-11; 11-10.30 Sun ~ Bar food 12-2.30, 6-9; 12-7.30 Sun ~ Restaurant ~ Children welcome ~ Dogs allowed in bar ~ Wi-fi ~ Bedrooms: /£140 *Recommended by Chantelle and Tony Redman, Ian Herdman, Matt and Hayley Jacob, Emma Scofield, Alison and Michael Harper, Rob Anderson*

LEAMINGTON SPA
Drawing Board ♀ ◗

SP3265 Map 4

(01926) 330636 – www.thedrawingboard.pub
Newbold Street; CV32 4HN

Town-centre pub with interesting, quirky décor, a thoughtful choice of food and drinks; good fun

Set out over two floors with some intriguing design features and a cheery bustling atmosphere, this place also has a hard-working, hands-on landlord and plenty of chatty customers. There are rugs on bare boards, flagstones, leather sofas and chesterfields, mismatched dining chairs and rustic tables interspersed with contemporary furniture, large house plants, antlers, several woodburning stoves and even a bike. But it's the framed vintage comic books on the grey walls and shelves of old-fashioned boys' and girls' annuals that are really worth looking at, along with some pop art and neon lighting. Cloudwater Bitter, Northern Monk Eternal Session IPA, Old Pie Factory Elephant Wash and Purity Bunny Hop on handpump, several craft ales, 18 wines by the glass, 80 malt whiskies, 30 gins, 26 bourbons, 120 rums and farm cider, all served by friendly, young staff. Also, background music, TV, a retro arcade games machine and board games. Disabled access.

Creative food includes lunchtime sandwiches, a choice of tapas, courgette, basil, feta and sunblush tomato risotto, honey-braised ham and poached eggs, korean barbecue beef short rib with kimchi, cauliflower rice and white bean hummus, roast salmon fillet with mussel and clam chowder and root vegetable dauphinoise, a pie of the day, tempura sea bass with butternut squash and thai dressing, and puddings such as baked banana cheesecake with spiced rum sauce and warm chocolate praline brownie with vanilla ice-cream. *Benchmark main dish: steak burger with marrow mustard butter, toppings and fries £12.95. Two-course evening meal £21.00.*

Free house ~ Licensee Sam Cornwall Jones ~ Real ale ~ Open 11-11; 12-10.30 Sun ~
Bar food 12-3, 5.30-9.30; 12-9.30 Sat; 12-6 Sun ~ Restaurant ~ Children welcome ~
Dogs welcome ~ Wi-fi *Recommended by Chris and Sophie Baxter, Charlie and Mark Todd,
Bridget and Peter Gregson, Philip J Alderton, Alf and Sally Garner, Belinda Stamp*

LONG COMPTON
SP2832 Map 4
Red Lion ⭐ 🛏
(01608) 684221 – www.redlion-longcompton.co.uk
A3400 S of Shipston-on-Stour; CV36 5JS

**Traditional character and contemporary touches in comfortably
furnished coaching inn; bedrooms**

A lovely old coaching inn that our readers enjoy greatly, this has a roomy,
charmingly furnished lounge bar with beams and some exposed stone
and nice rambling corners with cushioned settles among pleasantly assorted
and comfortable seats and leather armchairs; there are tables on flagstones
and carpets, animal prints on warm paintwork and both an open fire and
a woodburning stove. Friendly, attentive staff serve Brains Rev James, Hook
Norton Hooky and Purity Mad Goose on handpump, a dozen wines by the
glass, and summer farm cider. The chocolate labrador is called Cocoa. The
simple public bar has darts, pool, a juke box and a TV; background music.
There are tables out in the large back garden, with a play area. Bedrooms are
spotlessly kept and quiet and breakfasts are particularly good.

 Quite a choice of rewarding food includes sandwiches, baked avocado with
stilton and crispy bacon, oat-crusted goats cheese with poached pear and walnut
and wild rocket salad, spiced butternut squash, spinach and red onion filo parcel with
curried cream sauce, pancetta-wrapped chicken breast with sweet potato purée, wild
mushrooms and red wine jus, sea bass with tomato provençale and salsa verde, slow-
braised lamb shank with cannellini beans, tomatoes, garlic and rosemary, and puddings
such as lemon pannacotta with raspberry compote and spotted dick pudding with apples
and custard. *Benchmark main dish: steak in ale pie £16.00. Two-course evening
meal £21.00.*

Cropthorne Inns ~ Manager Lisa Phipps ~ Real ale ~ Open 10am-11pm ~ Bar food 12-2.30,
6-9; 12-9.30 Fri, Sat; 12-9 Sun ~ Restaurant ~ Children welcome ~ Dogs welcome ~ Wi-fi ~
Bedrooms: £65/£100 *Recommended by Michael Doswell, Steve Whalley, Trevor Crowther,
Paul Faraday, Sarah Roberts, Guy Vowles, John Harris, Anne and Ben Smith*

SHIPSTON-ON-STOUR
SP2540 Map 4
Black Horse 🍺
(01608) 238489 – www.blackhorseshipston.co.uk
Station Road (off A3400); CV36 4BT

**16th-c pub with simple country furnishings, well kept ales,
an extensive choice of thai food and seats outside**

Once found, our readers tend to come back to this very pretty old stone
tavern on a regular basis. From a central entrance passage, low-beamed,
character bars lead off with some fine old flagstones and floor tiles and two
open fires (one in an inglenook). There are also wheelbacks, stools, rustic
seats and tables and built-in wall benches, half-panelled or exposed-stone
walls, and plenty of copper kettles, pans and bedwarmers, horse tack and
toby jugs. Friendly staff serve Prescott Hill Climb, Wychwood Dirty Tackle
and Wye Valley Butty Bach on handpump, eight wines by the glass, 18 gins
and ten malt whiskies; background music, TV, darts and board games. The
little dining room has pale wooden tables and chairs on bare boards. There

are a couple of benches on the front cobbles, contemporary seats and tables on a partly covered, raised decked area at the back and picnic-sets on grass; in summer, the flowering baskets and tubs are lovely. Disabled access.

The popular food is thai: tom yum soups, steamed dumplings, chicken satay, spicy salads such as seafood, lots of curries, chicken, duck and pork in tamarind, sweet soy and plum sauces, vegan and vegetarian stir-fries and a large choice of dishes with noodles and rice. *Benchmark main dish: thai green curry £8.99. Two-course evening meal £18.00.*

Free house ~ Licensee Gabe Saunders ~ Real ale ~ Open 12-11; 6-11 Mon ~ Bar food 12-2, 6-10; not Mon ~ Restaurant ~ Children welcome ~ Dogs allowed in bar ~ Wi-fi
Recommended by Mark Hamill, Graham Smart

SHIPSTON-ON-STOUR   SP2540   Map 4

George ♈ ⇌

(01608) 661453 – www.thegeorgeshipston.co.uk
High Street; CV36 4AJ

Handsome inn with opened-up bars and dining areas, rewarding food and drink and seats in courtyard; bedrooms

This Georgian town-centre hotel is open and offers food all day, so customers drop in and out on a regular basis. The opened-up, spacious interior has several updated areas linked by timbering and bare-stone or brick walls. The bar has high stools and chairs around equally high tables, cushioned wall seating and all sorts of armchairs and sofas. There are colourful rugs on wooden floors, wall prints, mirrors, modern ceiling lights and the atmosphere is friendly and easy-going. High-backed upholstered or wooden chairs around a medley of tables fill the various dining areas and fireplaces house two woodburning stoves. Friendly, helpful staff keep Brakspears Bitter and Oxford Gold and a guest from North Cotswold on handpump, 17 wines by the glass, ten gins and proper cocktails. The courtyard is furnished with quality tables and chairs with bright orange cushions under parasols. Bedrooms are contemporary and comfortable and breakfasts are highly regarded.

A fine choice of food includes breakfasts for non-residents (8-11am) plus chicken wings in barbecue sauce, garlic and rosemary-studded camembert with damson conserve, sharing boards, sweet potato gnocchi with spinach, balsamic onions and pesto, beer-fed beef burger with toppings and skin-on fries, smoked haddock and chive fishcakes with french-style peas and hollandaise, rare-breed pork rib-eye with garlic broad beans, sautéed potatoes and chimichurri, chicken milanese with parmesan and balsamic dressing, and puddings such as choux buns with crème patisserie filling and belgian chocolate fudge sauce and warm treacle tart with raspberry compote and milk ice-cream. *Benchmark main dish: king prawn and chorizo linguine with garlic and chilli £16.50. Two-course evening meal £22.00.*

Brakspears ~ Manager Matthew Hiscoe ~ Real ale ~ Open 8am-11pm; 8am-midnight Sat; 8am-10pm Sun ~ Bar food 11-9.30; lighter meals in afternoon ~ Restaurant ~ Children welcome ~ Dogs allowed in bar and bedrooms ~ Wi-fi ~ Live 'rock & rum' night last Fri evening of month ~ Bedrooms: /£120 *Recommended by Martin and Joanne Sharp, Charle and Maddie Bishop, Angela and Steve Heard, Monty Green, Nicola and Holly Lyons, Sally and Lance Oldham*

Real ale may be served from handpumps, electric pumps (not just the on-off switches used for keg beer) or – common in Scotland – tall taps called founts (pronounced 'fonts') where a separate pump pushes the beer up under air pressure.

WARMINGTON

SP4147   Map 4

Falcon ♀ ◼

(01295) 692120 – www.brunningandprice.co.uk/falcon

B4100 towards Shotteswell; OX17 1JJ

Carefully extended roadside pub with spreading bar and dining rooms, a fine choice of drinks and food, and seats outside

Originally, this beautifully restored golden-stone inn was built to take advantage of what was a busy turnpike road. The beamed interconnected bar and dining areas have a lot of character, with cushioned Edwardian-style chairs and leather armchairs grouped around a wide mix of tables on rugs and pale floorboards – and the main dining room has a central fire pit. Also, prints and photos covering pale-painted walls, books on shelves, mirrors over several open fires, elegant metal chandeliers, house plants and stone bottles. Friendly young staff serve St Austell Brunning & Price Traditional Bitter and guests from breweries such as Church Farm, Hook Norton, North Cotswold, Timothy Taylors and Warwickshire on handpump, 18 wines by the glass, 120 gins and numerous malt whiskies; background music and board games. The garden has good quality seats and tables under a gazebo.

 Brasserie-style food includes sandwiches, chicken liver parfait with carrot chutney, wild mushrooms on toast with truffle oil, thai green sweet potato and aubergine curry with tempura okra, smoked haddock fishcake with poached egg and white wine and caper sauce, warm crispy beef salad with sweet chilli dressing and toasted cashews, chicken, ham and leek pie with tarragon sauce, lamb rump with gremolata potatoes, roast tomato, basil, rocket, olive and feta salad, 10oz rump steak with dijon and tarragon butter and chips, and puddings such as triple chocolate brownie with chocolate sauce and hot waffle with toffee sauce, caramelised banana and honeycomb ice-cream. *Benchmark main dish: steak burger with toppings, coleslaw and chips £13.95. Two-course evening meal £22.00.*

Brunning & Price ~ Manager Stuart Groves ~ Real ale ~ Open 10am-11pm; 10am-10.30pm Sun ~ Bar food 12-9.30; 12-10 Fri, Sat; 12-9 Sun ~ Restaurant ~ Children welcome ~ Dogs allowed in bar ~ Wi-fi *Recommended by Peter and Caroline Waites, Dr and Mrs H J Field, Charles Todd, William Slade, James Allsopp, Brian and Sally Wakeham, Geoff and Ann Marston*

WARWICK

SP2864   Map 4

Rose & Crown ⇐

(01926) 411117 – www.roseandcrownwarwick.co.uk

Market Place; CV34 4SH

Busy town pub with customers popping in and out all day, wide choice of drinks and food, helpful staff and seats outside; bedrooms

Open and serving food all day from breakfasts at 7am, this town-centre inn is full of cheerful customers. The sizeable, open-plan bar has big windows overlooking the street, wooden flooring, seating that ranges from sofas with big colourful cushions to benches and leather or cushioned wall seats, all sorts of wall prints, and a winter open fire. Friendly, efficient staff serve Greene King Old Golden Hen and guests from breweries such as Church Farm and Purity on handpump, 15 wines by the glass including champagne, several gins and a cocktail list; background music. At the back is a dining room with upholstered chairs and stools around wooden tables and celebrity photos and mirrors on pale-painted walls. There are tables and chairs out on the wide pavement at the front. Bedrooms are light, airy and comfortable. Disabled access to bars (but not bedrooms).

🍴 Popular food includes sandwiches, garlic and rosemary-studded camembert, ham hock terrine with piccalilli, wild mushroom and pea tart with truffle hollandaise, steak burger with relish and chips, slow-cooked sea bass with fennel purée, samphire and butter sauce, korean-glazed pork with kimchi slaw and crispy noodles, free-range chicken milanese with garlic and sage butter and skinny fries, and puddings such as treacle tart with clotted cream and black cherry cheesecake; they also offer a two- and three-course set menu (12-6, not Sunday). *Benchmark main dish: chicken and ham pie £14.75. Two-course evening meal £21.00.*

Peach Pub Company ~ Manager Katie Middleton ~ Real ale ~ Open 7am-11pm (12.30am Fri); 8am-12.30am Sat; 8am-10.30pm Sun ~ Bar food 7am-9pm (10pm Fri); 8am-10pm Sat; 8-8 Sun ~ Restaurant ~ Children welcome ~ Dogs allowed in bar and bedrooms ~ Wi-fi ~ Bedrooms: /£100 *Recommended by Ian Herdman, Stuart and Natalie Granville, Charlotte and William Mason, Patricia and Gordon Tucker, Mandy and Gary Redstone*

WELFORD-ON-AVON
SP1452 Map 4

Bell 🏠 🍷 🍽

(01789) 750353 ~ www.thebellwelford.co.uk

Off B439 W of Stratford; High Street; CV37 8EB

Warwickshire Dining Pub of the Year

Enjoyably civilised pub with appealing ancient interior, good carefully sourced food, a great range of drinks and an attractive garden with table service

All aspects of this particularly well run pub are highly and consistently praised by our readers, and the professional, hands-on licensees work very hard to achieve this. The attractive interior has plenty of signs of the building's venerable age, and is divided into five comfortable areas, each with its own character. These range from the cosy terracotta-painted bar to a light and airy gallery room with antique wood panelling, solid oak floor and contemporary Lloyd Loom chairs. Flagstone floors, stripped or well polished antique or period-style furniture and three good fires (one in an inglenook) add warmth and cosiness. You'll find Greene King Old Speckled Hen, Hobsons Best, Purity Pure Gold and Pure UBU and Woods Shropshire Lad on handpump and 15 wines (including prosecco, champagne and sweet wine) by the glass; background music. In summer, the virginia creeper-covered exterior is festooned with colourful hanging baskets. The lovely garden has solid teak furniture, a vine-covered terrace, water features and gentle lighting. Disabled access.

⭐ Appealing food using local, seasonal produce includes sandwiches, devilled crab on toast, baked avocado with blue cheese and crispy pancetta, roasted red pepper, brie and cheddar quiche, parmesan-breaded and butterflied chicken breast with chorizo jam, coleslaw and chips, local pork and smoked bacon sausages with mash and cider, leek and tomato gravy, gammon with pineapple or free-range eggs, chunky beef chilli with sour cream and tortilla crisps, black bream fillets on lemon and rosemary-roasted mediterranean vegetables, sirloin steak with a choice of sauce and chips, and puddings such as chocolate torte with chocolate ice-cream and sticky toffee pudding with vanilla ice-cream; they hold a curry night on Fridays. *Benchmark main dish: steak pie £14.95. Two-course evening meal £22.00.*

Free house ~ Licensees Colin and Teresa Ombler ~ Real ale ~ Open 11.30-3, 6-11; 11.30-midnight Sat; 11.45-10.30 Sun ~ Bar food 11.30-2.30, 6-9.30 (10 Fri); 11.30-10 Sat; 11.45-9.30 Sun ~ Children welcome ~ Wi-fi *Recommended by R and P Irani, Phil and Helen Holt, T M Parsons, P Gwilliam, Ian and Liz Lowe, John and Sharon Hancock, Frank and Anne Busby, Mr and Mrs Ted Hollingworth, Melissa Long, Sylvia Hancock, Roy and Lyn Dempster, Ian Herdman, Carole May, Emma Lee, Mrs Angela Henstridge, Peter Northover and Sheila Ward, Lynda Cooper*

Also Worth a Visit in Warwickshire

Besides the fully inspected pubs, you might like to try these pubs that have been recommended to us and described by readers. Do tell us what you think of them: feedback@goodguides.com

ALCESTER SP0857
Turks Head (01789) 765948
High Street, across from church; B49 5AD Updated old town pub with good friendly atmosphere; small front room and another off corridor, well kept Wye Valley and three guests, craft and continental beers, local cider and decent choice of wines and whiskies, enjoyable food from sharing plates and pizzas up including good fish and chips, Sat brunch from 10am; free wi-fi; children and dogs welcome, tables out in walled garden behind, open all day, no food Sun evening. *(Sandra King)*

ALDERMINSTER SP2348
★ Bell (01789) 450414
A3400 Oxford–Stratford; CV37 8NY Civilised Georgian coaching inn blending contemporary styling with low beams and other original features; the bustling bar has mix of traditional wooden tables and chairs, upholstered sofas and armchairs in front of open fires, blue-painted counter serving North Cotswold, Purity and a house beer (Alscot Ale), a dozen wines by the glass and cocktails, highly regarded interesting food in stylish two-floor restaurant, upper part with balcony and lovely views across Stour Valley; background music, daily papers; children and dogs (in bar) welcome, appealing courtyard and gardens looking over water meadows, individually decorated boutique bedrooms, open all day from 9am.
(Mitchell Cregor, Julie and Andrew Blanchett, Victoria and James Sargeant, Ian Herdman, John and Sharon Hancock)

ALDRIDGE SK0500
Turtles Head (01922) 325635
Croft Parade; off High Street; WS9 8LY Friendly micropub in row of 1960s shops; simple drinking area with leather sofa and some tub chairs on light wood floor, four well kept/priced ales, proper ciders and decent choice of other drinks, snacky food such as rolls and pork pies, very popular with locals; closed Mon, otherwise open all day (till 9pm Sun). *(Bridget and Peter Gregson)*

ALVESTON SP2356
Ferry (01789) 269883
Ferry Lane; end of village, off B4086 Stratford–Wellesbourne; CV37 7QX Comfortable beamed dining pub with enjoyable food and well kept ales such as Black Sheep and Wye Valley, friendly staff; occasional live music and quiz nights; children and dogs welcome, nice spot with seats out at front (some on

raised deck), open all day Sat, closed Sun evening, Mon. *(Jeremy Snaithe)*

ARDENS GRAFTON SP1153
Golden Cross (01789) 772420
Off A46 or B439 W of Stratford, corner of Wixford Road/Grafton Lane; B50 4LG Modernised 18th-c stone pub; beamed bar with dark flagstones, mix of furniture including chapel chairs and pews around kitchen tables, woodburner in big old fireplace, ales such as Bombardier, eight wines by the glass and tasty uncomplicated home-made food including deals and themed nights, friendly helpful service, attractive lounge with unusual coffered ceiling, big mullioned bay window and log fire; background music, free wi-fi; children and dogs (in bar) welcome, wheelchair access, back garden with sturdy rustic furniture on terrace and picnic-sets on lawn, nice views, open (and food) all day. *(Laura Reid)*

ASTON CANTLOW SP1360
Kings Head (01789) 488242
Village signed off A3400 NW of Stratford; B95 6HY Black and white Tudor pub with low-beamed bar on right, old settles on flagstones and woodburner in big inglenook, quarry-tiled main room with window seats and large country tables, ales such as Greene King and Purity, real cider and several wines by the glass, enjoyable food from sandwiches and pub favourites up, friendly efficient service; background music, free wi-fi; children welcome, dogs in bar, garden with picnic-sets and big chestnut tree, open (and food) all day. *(Clive and Fran Dutson)*

BARSTON SP2078
★ Bulls Head (01675) 442830
From M42 junction 5, A4141 towards Warwick, first left, then signed down Barston Lane; B92 0JU Unassuming and unspoilt partly Tudor village pub; well kept ales such as Adnams, Exmoor, Purity and Sharps, popular traditional home-made food (not Sun evening) from sandwiches to specials, cheerful helpful staff, log fires, comfortable lounge with pictures and plates, oak-beamed bar and separate dining room; monthly quiz; children and dogs allowed, good-sized secluded garden, open all day Fri-Sun. *(Fred Peterson)*

BINLEY WOODS SP3977
Roseycombe (024) 7654 1022
Rugby Road; CV3 2AY Warm and friendly 1930s pub with wide choice of bargain home-made food (not Mon evening, Sun), Bass, Fullers London Pride and Greene

King IPA; Weds quiz, some live music; children welcome, big garden, open all day Fri-Sun. *(Alan Johnson)*

BIRMINGHAM   SP0788

★ **Bartons Arms** (0121) 333 5988
High Street, Aston (A34); B6 4UP
Magnificent listed Edwardian landmark standing alone among busy roads and modern development; impressive richly decorated linked rooms from the palatial to the snug, original tilework murals, stained glass and mahogany, decorative fireplaces, sweeping stairs to handsome upstairs rooms, well kept Oakham ales and interesting bottled beers from ornate island bar with snob screens, reasonably priced thai food (vegan options available) good friendly service; occasional live music; open all day. *(Charles Welch)*

BIRMINGHAM   SP0686

Brasshouse (0121) 633 3383
Broad Street; B1 2HP Spacious bank conversion with enjoyable good value food from tapas, burgers and pizzas up, various deals, well kept Marstons-related ales and guests, good range of other drinks including craft beers and cocktails, efficient friendly service; TV and games machines; children welcome in dining area till 6pm, seats out overlooking canal, handy for National Sea Life Centre, International Convention Centre and Symphony Hall, open all day from 8am (till 2am Fri, Sat). *(Dr and Mrs A K Clarke)*

BIRMINGHAM   SP0688

Lord Clifden (0121) 523 7515
Great Hampton Street (Jewellery Quarter); B18 6AA Fairly traditional pub with some contemporary touches; leather banquettes and padded stools around dimpled copper-top tables, interesting collection of urban street art including Banksy prints, bustling atmosphere, wide choice of good value generous food from sandwiches and burgers to daily specials, Wye Valley and guests plus draught continentals, prompt friendly service; darts in front bare-boards section, sports TVs (outside too), Thurs quiz and weekend DJs; children over 10 welcome for lunch, otherwise over-21s only, plenty of seats in enclosed part-covered beer garden with table tennis and table football, open all day (till late Fri, Sat). *(Dr and Mrs A K Clarke)*

BIRMINGHAM   SP0786

Old Contemptibles (0121) 200 3310
Edmund Street; B3 2HB Spacious Edwardian corner pub (Nicholsons) with lofty ceiling and lots of woodwork, good choice of real ales and enjoyable well priced food, friendly efficient young staff; upstairs loos; no children, handy central location and popular at lunchtime with office workers, open all day (till 6pm Sun). *(Alan Johnson, Dr and Mrs A K Clarke)*

BIRMINGHAM   SP0784

Old Moseley Arms (0121) 440 1954
Tindal Street; B12 9QU Tucked-away red-brick Victorian pub; five well kept ales such as Church End, Enville and Wye Valley (regular festivals), nice selection of gins and good value authentic indian food (evenings and all day Sun); sports TVs, darts; outside seating area, handy for Edgbaston cricket ground, open all day. *(Charles Welch)*

BIRMINGHAM   SP0686

Pint Shop (0121) 236 9039
Bennetts Hill; B2 5SN Newly opened sister to the Pint Shop in Cambridge (see Main Entries); stylish refurbishment with bustling bar and upstairs restaurant, half a dozen real ales and 21 craft beers (listed on blackboard), also good choice of wines and around 100 gins, enjoyable food from open kitchen including burgers, pies, kebabs and some vegan choices, friendly knowledgeable staff; background music, sports TV; dogs welcome in bar, open (and food) all day. *(Charles Welch)*

BIRMINGHAM   SP0384

Plough (0121) 427 3678
High Street, Harborne; B17 9NT Popular place with spacious modern interior (one or two steps); enjoyable food including stone-baked pizzas and chargrilled burgers, regular offers, well kept ales such as Purity and Wye Valley, plenty of wines by the glass and 50 or so whiskies, good coffee, friendly staff; background music, TVs and various events such as wine/gin tastings; well behaved children welcome, paved garden with covered area, open (and food) all day from 8am (9am weekends) for breakfast. *(Charles Welch)*

BIRMINGHAM   SP0686

Post Office Vaults (0121) 643 7354
New Street/Pinfold Street; B2 4BA
Two entrances to this simple downstairs bar serving a dozen interesting ciders/perries, eight real ales including a house beer from Kinver (First Class Stamp) and over 350 international bottled beers, friendly knowledgeable staff, no food but can bring your own (plates and cutlery provided); bar billiards; handy for New Street station, open all day. *(Dr and Mrs A K Clarke)*

BIRMINGHAM   SP0686

Purecraft Bar & Kitchen
(0121) 237 5666 *Waterloo Street; B2 5TJ*
Industrial-chic bar with excellent range of cask and craft beers including several from Purity, interesting bottled range too along with Dunkerton's cider and a dozen wines by the glass, open kitchen serving good food all day (not Sun evening) from sandwiches and deli boards up (food/beer pairings), friendly attentive service; children welcome, open all day. *(Dr and Mrs A K Clarke)*

BIRMINGHAM   SP0687
Rose Villa   (0121) 236 7910
By clocktower in Jewellery Quarter (Warstone Lane/Vyse Street); B18 6JW Well preserved 1920s red-brick pub (Grade II listed); front saloon with impressive stained-glass windows leading through to splendid little skylit bar with floor-to-ceiling green tiles and massive tiled arch over fireplace, quirky touches here and there such as antler chandeliers and a red phone box, four or five well kept ales including Sharps Doom Bar, craft beers and over 100 vodkas, reasonably priced food from american diner menu, also themed nights and deals; live music and DJs Fri, Sat night when can get very busy; children and dogs welcome, open all day, weekend brunch from 11am.
(Dr and Mrs A K Clarke)

BIRMINGHAM   SP0686
Tap & Spile   (0121) 632 5602
Gas Street; B1 2JT Refurbished canalside pub on three floors; main bar/restaurant downstairs opening on to the towpath, three real ales such as Theakstons Old Peculier, Timothy Taylors Landlord and Wychwood Hobgoblin, decent range of wines and enjoyable good value food including grills and pizzas, another bar upstairs (open till 4am) and new cocktail lounge on top floor; children and dogs welcome, picnic-sets out by Gas Street canal basin, open all day.
(Dr and Mrs A K Clarke)

BIRMINGHAM   SP0686
★Wellington   (0121) 200 3115
Bennetts Hill; B2 5SN Traditionally renovated high-ceilinged pub with 17 well kept interesting ales (listed on TV screens) including three from Black Country, real ciders, bottled beers and good range of gins/ whiskies, they also have a vegan drinks menu and sell snuff, experienced landlord and friendly staff, no food but plates and cutlery provided if you bring your own, more room and roof terrace upstairs; regular beer festivals and quiz nights, folk evening third Tues of month, darts; open all day and can get very busy. *(Dr and Mrs A K Clarke, Alan Johnson)*

BRIERLEY HILL   SO9286
★Vine   (01384) 78293
B4172 between A461 and (nearer) A4100; immediately after the turn into Delph Road; DY5 2TN Popular black country pub (aka the Bull & Bladder) offering a true taste of the West Midlands; down-to-earth welcome and friendly chatty locals in meandering series of rooms, each different in character, traditional front bar with wall benches, comfortable extended snug has solidly built red plush seats and there's a tartan-decorated back bar, well kept/priced Bathams from next-door brewery, a couple of simple low-priced lunchtime dishes, cobs and snacks the rest of the day; quiz nights, TV, games machine, darts and dominoes; children and dogs welcome, tables in backyard, open all day. *(Andrew Wall)*

BROOM   SP0853
★Broom Tavern   (01789) 778199
High Street; off B439 in Bidford; B50 4HL Spacious 16th-c brick and timber village pub, relaxed and welcoming, with good interesting food from chef-owners including weekly themed specials and excellent Sun roasts, four well kept ales such as North Cotswold, Purity, Sharps and Wye Valley, well chosen wine list with several by the glass, good attentive (but not intrusive) service, main room divided into two parts, one with cottage-style tables and chairs, the other with oak furniture, black beams and log fire, also a snug perfect for a group of diners; Mon quiz; children welcome, dogs in lower bar area, tables out on grass either side, handy for Ragley Hall, open all day, no food Sun evening. *(Dave Braisted)*

CHERINGTON   SP2836
Cherington Arms   (01608) 685183
Off A3400; CV36 5HS 17th-c stone-built village pub; popular food (not Mon) from french landlord-chef including open sandwiches, pub favourites, blackboard specials and Sun carvery, well kept Hook Norton and a guest, welcoming efficient staff, beamed bar with log fire, separate dining room; regular live music; children and dogs welcome, tables on terrace and in big garden bordering River Stour, good nearby walks, open all day Fri and Sat, till 6pm Sun, closed Mon lunchtime. *(Guy Vowles)*

CLAVERDON   SP2064
★Red Lion   (01926) 842291
Station Road; B4095 towards Warwick; CV35 8PE Upmarket beamed Tudor dining pub with highly regarded food from sharing plates up including some mediterranean and middle eastern influences, well kept Hook Norton and several wines by the glass, friendly efficient staff, log fires in linked rooms, back area with country views over heated terrace and gardens; children welcome, no dogs inside, open all day Sat, closed Sun evening. *(Phil and Helen Holt)*

COVENTRY   SP3279
Old Windmill   (024) 7625 1717
Spon Street; CV1 3BA Friendly 15th-c pub with lots of tiny rooms (known locally as Ma

---

A star symbol before the name of a pub shows exceptional character and appeal. It doesn't mean extra comfort. Even quite a basic pub can win a star, if it's individual enough.

Brown's); exposed beams in uneven ceilings, inglenook woodburner, seven well kept ales including Theakstons and Timothy Taylors, good local pork pies; juke box and occasional live music, sports TV, darts; closed Mon lunchtime, otherwise open all day (till 1am Fri, Sat), busy at weekends. *(Alan Johnson)*

COVENTRY   SP3379
Slug & Lettuce (024) 7622 2727
Bayley Lane; CV1 5RN Former courtroom in the cathedral quarter preserving judge's bench, witness box, dock and public gallery, also steps down to cells (now a dining area); three changing ales, decent choice of wines and cocktails, fairly extensive good value menu from sandwiches and sharing boards up, welcoming hard-working young staff; DJs Fri and Sat night, TVs, free wi-fi; children welcome, disabled loo, open (and food) all day from 10am for breakfast, shuts 2am Fri, 3am Sat. *(Dave Braisted, Alan Johnson)*

COVENTRY   SP3379
Town Wall (024) 7622 0963
Bond Street, among car parks behind Belgrade Theatre; CV1 4AH Busy 19th-c city-centre local surviving among new-builds; half a dozen or more well kept ales including Adnams, Bass, Caledonian and Theakstons, Weston's cider, enjoyable good value pub food (not Sun evening, Mon) from lunchtime sandwiches up, unspoilt basic front bar and tiny snug, etched windows, bigger back lounge with actor/playwright photographs and pictures of old Coventry, open fires; big-screen sports TV, juke box; no children, closed Mon lunchtime, otherwise open all day. *(Alan Johnson)*

EARLSWOOD   SP1274
Blue Bell Cider House
(01564) 702328 *Warings Green Road, not far from M42 junction 4; B94 6BP* Welcoming 19th-c red-brick pub by Stratford Canal; roomy lounge, cosy bar and conservatory, good value generous food including OAP weekday lunch and popular Sun carvery, own-brew organic beers plus guests, traditional ciders, friendly helpful staff; open mike nights and Weds quiz; children and dogs welcome, plenty of outside seating, moorings, open all day. *(Geoff and Ann Marston)*

EASENHALL   SP4679
Golden Lion (01788) 833577
Main Street; CV23 0JA Bar in 16th-c part of busy hotel; white-painted beams, half-panelling and log fire, some original wattle and daub and fine 17th-c carved bench depicting the 12 apostles, a couple of real ales and good food including cook your own meat on a hot rock and Sun carvery, prompt friendly service, more formal restaurant; background music; children and small dogs welcome, disabled access/loos, tables on side terrace and spacious lawn, 17 well

equipped bedrooms (some with four-posters), attractive village, open (and food) all day. *(Laura Reid)*

EDGE HILL   SP3747
★ **Castle** (01295) 670255
Off A422; OX15 6DJ Crenellated octagonal tower built in 1742 as gothic folly (marks where Charles I raised his standard at the Battle of Edgehill); major renovation creating bar and four dining areas, plenty of original features including arched windows and doorways, beams and stone fireplaces, fantastic views (some floor-to-ceiling windows), good food (not Sun evening), also deli bar for sandwiches, coffee and afternoon teas (must book), well kept Hook Norton ales, friendly helpful young staff; downstairs lavatories; children welcome, seats in lovely big garden with more outstanding views, beautiful Compton Wynyates nearby, four bedrooms, parking can be tricky at busy times, open all day Sat, till 7pm Sun. *(Dr and Mrs H J Field, Susan and John Douglas)*

ETTINGTON   SP2748
Chequers (01789) 740387
Banbury Road (A422); CV37 7SR Newly refurbished 18th-c dining pub; good fair priced food from sharing plates and pub favourites up, three real ales including a beer badged for them, a dozen wines by the glass and some interesting gins and coctkails, efficient friendly service, modern décor in bar and restaurant areas, upholstered chairs around pale wooden tables on wood-strip flooring, lots of pictures and some bold floral wallpaper; children welcome, no dogs inside, attractive back garden, open all day Sat, till 6pm Sun, closed Mon. *(Sandra King)*

FARNBOROUGH   SP4349
Kitchen (01295) 690615
Off A423 N of Banbury; OX17 1DZ Golden-stone dining pub in NT village; bar with painted beams, wood floor and cushioned window seats, red woodburner in big fireplace, saddle- and tractor-seat stools at blue-panelled counter serving Purity ales and nice wines by the glass, good seasonal food from interesting if not especially cheap menu, some produce from own kitchen garden, two-room dining area, friendly helpful staff; background music, free wi-fi; children and dogs (in bar) welcome, neat sloping garden with blue picnic-sets and pizza oven, local walks, open all day weekends, closed Tues, Weds and lunchtime Thurs. *(Mandy and Gary Redstone)*

FENNY COMPTON   SP4152
Merrie Lion (01295) 771134
Brook Street; CV47 2YH Early 18th-c beamed village pub with three well kept beers (including one badged for them), decent range of wines and good freshly made food from pubby choices up, friendly welcoming atmosphere; fortnightly Weds

quiz and other events; dogs welcome, tables outside, handy for Burton Dassett Hills Country Park, open all day. *(Andrew Wall)*

FILLONGLEY   SP2787
Cottage (01676) 540599
Black Hall Lane; CV7 8EG Popular country dining pub on village outskirts; good value food including vegetarian menu, OAP lunch and early evening deal, beers such as Bass, St Austell and Timothy Taylors, friendly service; back terrace and lawn overlooking fields, closes 6pm Sun evening. *(Fred Peterson)*

FIVE WAYS   SP2270
⋆Case Is Altered (01926) 484206
Follow Rowington signs at junction roundabout off A4177/A4141 N of Warwick, then right into Case Lane; CV35 7JD Convivial unspoilt old cottage licensed for over three centuries; well kept ales including Old Pie Factory and Wye Valley served by friendly long-serving landlady, no food (can bring your own sandwiches), simple small main bar with fine old poster of Lucas Blackwell & Arkwright Brewery (now flats), clock with hours spelling out Thornleys Ale (another defunct brewery), and just a few sturdy old-fashioned tables and a couple of stout leather-covered settles facing each other over spotless tiles, roaring log fire, modest little back room with old bar billiards table (takes sixpences); no children, dogs or mobile phones; full disabled access, stone table on little brick courtyard. *(Clive and Fran Dutson)*

FLECKNOE   SP5163
Old Olive Bush (01788) 891134
Off A425 W of Daventry; CV23 8AT Unspoilt chatty little Edwardian pub in quiet photogenic village; enjoyable traditional food cooked by landlady (Weds-Sat evenings, Sun lunchtime), well kept changing ales and decent wines, open fire in bar with stripped-wood floor, steps up to games room (table skittles), small dining room with etched windows and another fire; Thurs quiz, summer beer festival; children welcome, pretty garden, closed Sun evening, Mon and lunchtimes Tues-Fri. *(Jeremy Snaithe)*

FRANKTON   SP4270
Friendly (01926) 632430
Just over a mile S of B4453 Leamington Spa–Rugby; Main Street; CV23 9NY Popular 16th-c village pub living up to its name; four well kept ales including Greene King IPA and good reasonably priced traditional food (not Sun evening, Mon), two low-ceilinged rooms, open fire; dogs welcome, open all day weekends, closed Mon lunchtime. *(Melanie and David Lawson)*

GAYDON   SP3654
Malt Shovel (01926) 641221
Under a mile from M40 junction 12; B4451 into village, then over roundabout and across B4100; Church Road; CV35 0ET Welcoming new licensees for this bustling village pub; varnished mahogany floorboards and some carpeting linking entrance to bar, main area with high-pitched ceiling, milk churns and earthenware in loft above servery, woodburner and a vocal cockatoo, steps up to space with comfortable sofas and big stained-glass window, dining room, three well kept changing ales and enjoyable food served by friendly staff; background music, TV; children and dogs (in bar) welcome, open (and food) all day, kitchen shuts 6pm Sun. *(John Evans, Rob Anderson, Alistair Forsyth)*

HALESOWEN   SO9683
Waggon & Horses (0121) 585 9699
Stourbridge Road; B63 3TU Popular refurbished and extended 19th-c red-brick corner pub; Black Country ales along with plenty of interesting guests (tasting trays available) and four real ciders, friendly knowledgeable staff, snacky food such as cobs and pork pies, sloping floor in narrow main bar, open fire; dogs welcome in some parts, open all day. *(Peter and Caroline Waites)*

HAMPTON LUCY   SP2557
Boars Head (01789) 840533
Church Street, E of Stratford; CV35 8BE Welcoming two-room village pub with five changing ales, reasonably priced wines and enjoyable good value pubby food (all day Sat, not Sun evening), friendly helpful staff, updated interior with beams and log fires; darts, children welcome, seats in enclosed back courtyard, near lovely church and well placed for Charlecote Park (NT) and M40, open all day. *(Paul Humphreys)*

HARBOROUGH MAGNA   SP4779
Old Lion (01788) 833238
3 miles from M6 junction 1; B4112 Pailton Road; CV23 0HQ Stylishly modernised village pub; good food from pub favourites and pizzas to steaks, friendly attentive staff, well kept ales, nice choice of wines and over 70 gins; some live music; children and dogs (in bar) welcome, terrace seating, open all day Sat, till 4.30pm Sun. *(Fred Peterson)*

HATTON   SP2367
⋆Falcon (01926) 484281
Birmingham Road, Haseley (A4177, not far from M40 junction 15); CV35 7HA Modernised dining pub with rooms around island bar, lots of stripped brickwork and low

beams, tiled and oak-planked floors, good moderately priced food from sandwiches, sharing boards and pub favourites up, lunchtime/early evening deal Mon-Fri, friendly service, nice choice of wines by the glass and well kept ales such as Marstons, barn-style back restaurant; children and dogs (in bar) welcome, disabled facilities, garden with heated covered terrace, bedrooms in adjacent building, open (and food) all day. *(Belinda and Neil Garth)*

HATTON   SP2467

Hatton Arms   (01926) 492427

A4177, by Grand Union Canal; CV35 7JJ Former 18th-c coaching inn (part of the Hatton Estate) above flight of 21 locks known as 'Stairway to Heaven', views from sunny balcony and huge garden; spacious modernised interior with linked rooms, some beams and log fire, good popular food using Estate produce including sandwiches, pub favourites and one or two unusual dishes, also vegan and gluten-free menus, real ales such as Hook Norton, Purity and Wye Valley, ten wines by the glass, efficient friendly service; children welcome, good walks nearby, moorings, open (and food) all day, kitchen closes 7.30pm Sun. *(Ian Herdman)*

HENLEY-IN-ARDEN   SP1566

Bluebell   (01564) 793049

High Street (A3400, off M40 junction 16); B95 5AT Impressive timber-framed dining pub with fine coach entrance; rambling old beamed and flagstoned interior with contemporary furnishings creating stylish but relaxed atmosphere, big fireplace, well kept ales such as Purity, Sharps and Wye Valley, a dozen wines by the glass and good variety of enjoyable food cooked by chef-owner, friendly staff, coffee and afternoon teas; background music; children welcome if eating, dogs allowed in one part, tables out at front and on narrow back terrace, open till 9pm Sun (no evening food), closed Mon, otherwise open all day. *(Charles Welch)*

KENILWORTH   SP2872

Clarendon Arms   (01926) 852017

Castle Hill; CV8 1NB Busy pub opposite castle and under same ownership as next-door Harringtons restaurant; several rooms off long bare-boards bar, up to five well kept ales and tasty reasonably priced pub food including range of burgers, cheerful staff, largish peaceful upstairs dining room; children and dogs (in bar) welcome, metal tables on small raised terrace, daytime car park fee deducted from food bill, open (and food) all day weekends. *(Laura Reid)*

KENILWORTH   SP2872

Cross   (01926) 853840

New Street; CV8 2EZ Smart 19th-c Michelin-starred restaurant-pub; first class skilfully cooked food (not cheap) including

tasting menus and set lunch (Tues-Sun), lots of wines by the glass from impressive list, fine range of spirits and a couple of real ales such as Bombardier, friendly well informed staff, open-plan split-level interior with view into kitchen, front bar for drinkers; children welcome (menu for them), terrace and small garden, closed Mon, no food Sun evening. *(Paul Westwood)*

KENILWORTH   SP2872

Old Bakery   (01926) 864111

High Street, off A452; CV8 1LZ Small hotel's cosy two-room bar (popular with older customers); four well kept ales including Wye Valley HPA and good choice of wines, whiskies and gins, food Mon evening only (till 7.30pm); disabled access from behind, 14 comfortable bedrooms, good english breakfast, opens from 5.30pm (5pm Fri-Sun) and can get very busy. *(Laura Reid)*

KENILWORTH   SP2872

★**Virgins & Castle**   (01926) 853737

High Street; CV8 1LY Small snugs by entrance corridor and maze of intimate rooms off inner servery; flagstones, heavy beams and lots of woodwork, coal fire, four well kept Everards ales and guests, good reasonably priced food, friendly service, games bar upstairs; children allowed in eating areas, dogs in some parts, disabled facilities, tables in sheltered garden, parking close can be tricky, open all day, no food Sun evening. *(Laura Reid)*

LADBROKE   SP4158

Bell   (01926) 811224

Signed off A423 S of Southam; CV47 2BY New owners for this beamed country pub set back from the road; smallish bar with tub chairs by log fire, snug off with library wallpaper and another fire in little brick fireplace, three well kept ales and plenty of wines by the glass, very good food from pub favourites and grills up, also gluten-free choices and weekday set menu, airy restaurant with light oak flooring, friendly young staff; background music, free wi-fi; children and dogs (in bar) welcome, a few picnic-sets out in front and on side grass, pleasant surroundings, closed Sun evening, Mon and Tues. *(Bridget and Peter Gregson)*

LAPWORTH   SP1871

★**Boot**   (01564) 782464

Old Warwick Road; B4439 Hockley Heath–Warwick – 2.8 miles from M40 junction 1, but from southbound carriageway only, and return only to northbound; B94 6JU Popular upmarket dining pub near Stratford Canal; good range of food from enterprising menu including weekday fixed-price lunch (Mon-Thurs), efficient cheerful young staff, well kept Purity and Sharps, upscale wine list with over 20 by the glass, stripped beams and dark panelling, big antique hunting prints, cushioned pews and bucket chairs on ancient quarry tiles and bare boards, warm fire, charming low-raftered upstairs dining room; background music; children and dogs welcome, tables on side terrace (some under extendable canopy), more seating on grass beyond with tipi, nice walks, open all day, food till 7.30pm Sun. *(Phil and Helen Holt, Ian Herdman, Dave Braisted)*

LAPWORTH
SP1970
Navigation (01564) 783337
Old Warwick Road (B4439 SE); B94 6NA Modernised beamed pub by the Grand Union Canal; slate-floor bar with woodburner, bare-boards snug and restaurant, well kept Purity, Timothy Taylors, Wadworths and a guest, unusually Guinness also on handpump, decent wines and enjoyable reasonably priced food from sandwiches and other bar choices up, good Sun roasts; children welcome, dogs in bar, covered terrace and waterside garden, moorings, handy for Packwood House and Baddesley Clinton (both NT), open all day, food all day weekends including breakfast from 10am. *(Peter and Caroline Waites)*

LEAMINGTON SPA
SP3165
Cricketers Arms (01926) 881293
Archery Road; CV31 3PT Friendly town local opposite bowling greens; enjoyable fairly priced food using meat from good local butcher including popular Sun roasts (till 6pm), well kept ales such as Timothy Taylors from central bar, Weston's cider, some panelling and cricketing memorabilia, comfortable banquettes, open fires; fortnightly quiz Mon, poker night Weds, occasional live music, sports TV, darts, free wi-fi; children and dogs welcome, heated back terrace, open all day. *(Fred Peterson)*

LEAMINGTON SPA
SP3166
★ Star & Garter (01926) 359960
Warwick Street; CV32 5LL Bustling open-plan town-centre pub (Peach group); bare-boards bar with upholstered wall seats, blue leather banquettes, red leather armchairs and small wooden stools around mix of tables, four real ales such as Greene King and Purity, lots of wines by the glass and good selection of gins/cocktails, enjoyable food from sandwiches/snacks up including meal deals Mon-Weds, open-kitchen dining area with booths down one side, steps up to second bar, friendly helpful staff; background music, free wi-fi; children and dogs welcome, open all day, breakfast from 9am Fri-Sun. *(Fred Peterson)*

LEEK WOOTTON
SP2868
Anchor (01926) 853355
Warwick Road; CV35 7QX Pub-restaurant with popular fairly pubby food including range of burgers and daily specials, well kept ales such as Bass, Hook Norton and Purity,

good selection of wines and soft drinks, friendly service; background music, free wi-fi; children welcome, long garden behind with play area, open all day Fri-Sun. *(Alan Johnson)*

LIGHTHORNE
SP3455
Antelope (01926) 651188
Old School Lane, Bishops Hill; a mile SW of B4100 N of Banbury; CV35 0AU Attractive early 18th-c stone-built pub in pretty village setting; two neatly kept comfortable bars and separate dining area, beams, flagstones, exposed stonework and big open fire, well kept Greene King IPA, Sharps Doom Bar and a couple of guests, enjoyable food from sandwiches up including a vegan menu, Weds burger night, friendly efficient service; children and dogs welcome, picnic-sets out by well and on small grassy area, open (and food) all day Fri-Sun. *(Gerald and Brenda Culliford)*

LITTLE COMPTON
SP2530
★ Red Lion (01608) 674397
Off A44 Moreton-in-Marsh to Chipping Norton; GL56 0RT Low-beamed 16th-c Cotswold-stone inn; well liked food (not Sun evening, Mon) cooked by landlord-chef from fairly traditional menu, Donnington ales and good choice of wines by the glass, friendly helpful service, snug alcoves, inglenook woodburner; darts and pool in public bar; some live music, Weds bingo; well behaved children and dogs (in bar) welcome, white-painted metal furniture in pretty garden, comfortable bedrooms, open all day Fri and Sat, till 6pm Sun, closed Mon lunchtime. *(Sandra King)*

LONG ITCHINGTON
SP4164
Two Boats (01926) 812640
A423 N of Southam, by Grand Union Canal; CV47 9QZ Traditional brick-built pub with lovely canal views from window seats in long picture-filled main room, enjoyable generously served food from good value pubby menu, four well kept ales including Bombardier and Youngs, friendly helpful staff; TV and darts in side bar; children and dogs welcome, waterfront terrace and moorings, open all day, no food Sun evening. *(Geoff and Ann Marston)*

LONGFORD
SP3684
Greyhound (024) 7636 3046
Sutton Stop, off Black Horse Road/ Grange Road; junction of Coventry and North Oxford canals; CV6 6DF Cosy 19th-c canalside pub with plenty of character; up to five well kept ales and good range of enjoyable food including home-made pies, friendly helpful staff, woodburner and two-way coal fire, unusual tiny snug; occasional live music; children and dogs (in bar) welcome, tables on attractive waterside terrace, nice spot (if you ignore the pylons), open all day. *(Andrew Wall)*

LOWER BRAILES SP3139
George (01608) 685788
B4035 Shipston–Banbury; OX15 5HN
Handsome 14th-c pub under newish
ownership; roomy front bar with dark oak
tables on flagstones and inglenook log fire,
beamed and panelled back bar, separate
restaurant, well kept Hook Norton ales and
very enjoyable food cooked by chef-patron
including good Sun roasts, efficient helpful
service; sizeable sheltered back garden with
terrace, also a few tables out at front, lovely
village and interesting church, good nearby
walks, comfortable bedrooms. *(Sally Harrison,
Clive and Fran Dutson)*

LOWSONFORD SP1868
Fleur de Lys (01564) 782431
*Off B4439 Hockley Heath–Warwick;
Lapworth Street; B95 5HJ* Prettily placed
old pub by Stratford Canal; linked beamed
rooms of varying sizes, log fires, enjoyable
fairly priced food including range of pies and
gluten-free menu, Greene King Abbot, IPA and
a couple of guests, plenty of wines by the glass,
cocktails, friendly helpful service; children and
dogs (in lower bar) welcome, large waterside
garden with play area, open (and food) all day,
till 9pm (7pm) Sun. *(Neil Hawkswood)*

LYE SO9284
★ Windsor Castle (01384) 897809
*Stourbridge Road (corner A458/A4036;
car park in Pedmore Road just above
traffic lights – don't be tempted to use the
next-door restaurant's parking!);
DY9 7DG* Interesting range of well kept
beers from impressive row of handpumps
including own Sadlers ales (brewery tours
available); central flagstoned part with
bar stools by counter and window shelf
overlooking road, several other rooms
including 1920s-inspired gin bar, enjoyable
home-cooked food (not Sun evening), burger
night Tues, friendly service; free wi-fi;
children and dogs (in bar) welcome, disabled
facilities, terrace and verandah seating, four
bedrooms, handy for Lye station, open all day
(from 9am Sat for breakfast). *(Melanie and
David Lawson)*

NAPTON SP4560
Folly (01926) 815185
*Off A425 towards Priors Hardwick;
Folly Lane, by locks; CV47 8NZ* Beamed
red-brick pub in lovely spot on Oxford
Canal by Napton Locks and Folly Bridge
(113); three bars on different levels, mix
of furnishings and two big fireplaces (one
with woodburner), lots of interesting bric-
a-brac, pictures and old photographs, good
straightforward home-made food (not Sun

evening), well kept ales including Hook
Norton; sports TV, free-wi-fi; children and
dogs welcome, open all day. *(Charles Welch)*

NETHER WHITACRE SP2292
Gate (01675) 481292
Gate Lane; B46 2DS Welcoming traditional
community pub; good home-cooked food
including themed evenings, seven well kept
Marstons-related ales, log-fire bar, lounge
and dining conservatory; games room with
pool and darts; occasional quiz nights;
children and dogs (in bar) welcome, garden
picnic-sets and play area, open all day, food
all day weekends (till 7pm Sun). *(Sampson)*

NETHERTON SO9488
★ Old Swan (01384) 253075
*Halesowen Road (A459 just S of centre);
DY2 9PY* Victorian tavern full of traditional
character and known locally as Ma
Pardoe's after former long-serving landlady;
wonderfully unspoilt front bar with big swan
centrepiece in patterned enamel ceiling,
engraved mirrors, traditional furnishings and
old-fashioned cylinder stove, other rooms
including cosy back snug and more modern
lounge, own well priced ales and enjoyable
good value bar food, upstairs restaurant
(Sun lunchtime only); no under-16s, dogs
allowed in bar, open (and food) all day.
(Jeremy Snaithe)

NORTON LINDSEY SP2263
New Inn (01926) 258411
Main Street; CV35 8JA Popular village
pub owned by the local community; enjoyable
reasonably priced food (not Sun evening,
Mon) including blackboard specials and
OAP weekday lunch deal, booking advised,
well kept ales such as Greene King, Purity
and Windmill, good range of gins, friendly
accommodating staff; monthly quiz; children
and dogs welcome, back garden, closed
Mon lunchtime, otherwise open all day.
(Mark Tomlinson, Clive and Fran Dutson)

OFFCHURCH SP3665
★ Stag (01926) 425801
*N of Welsh Road, off A425 at Radford
Semele; CV33 9AQ* Popular 16th-c
thatched and beamed village dining
pub; oak-floored bar with log fires, ales
such as Purity and Wye Valley, a dozen
wines by the glass and good food from
interesting menu including excellent
steaks, friendly efficient young staff, more
formal cosy restaurant areas with bold
wallpaper, striking fabrics, animal heads
and big mirrors; children and dogs (in bar)
welcome, nice garden with rattan-style
furniture on terrace, open all day.
(Dr Matt Burleigh, Clive and Fran Dutson)

We include some hotels with a good bar that offers facilities comparable
to those of a pub.

OLD HILL   SO9686
Waterfall (0121) 559 9198
Waterfall Lane; B64 6RG Unpretentious
two-room local with tankards and jugs
hanging from boarded ceiling, well kept
Holdens and guests, good straightforward
low-priced food, friendly atmosphere; dogs
welcome, seats on small raised front area
and in back garden, open all day. *(Mandy and
Gary Redstone)*

OXHILL   SP3149
★Peacock (01295) 688060
Off A422 Stratford–Banbury; CV35 0QU
Popular stone-built pub in pretty village; good
varied menu including blackboard specials
(no food Sun evening), friendly attentive
staff, four changing ales and good selection of
wines by the glass, cosy beamed bar with big
solid tables and woodburner, half-panelled
bare-boards dining room; background music;
children and dogs (in bar) welcome, nice
back garden, closed Mon, otherwise open
all day. *(Dr and Mrs H J Field)*

RATLEY   SP3847
Rose & Crown (01295) 678148
Off A422 NW of Banbury; OX15 6DS
Ancient golden-stone pub, charming and
cosy, with five well kept ales such as St
Austell Tribute and Wye Valley Butty Bach,
blackboard list of wines, enjoyable good value
food (not Sun evening, Mon) including daily
specials, friendly efficient staff, carpeted
black-beamed bar with woodburner each
end, traditional furniture and window seats,
cosy snug; background music, darts; children,
walkers and dogs welcome, tables on sunny
split-level terrace, aunt sally, near lovely
church in sleepy village, handy for Upton
House (NT), open all day Fri-Sun, closed
Mon lunchtime. *(Franklyn Roberts, Clive
and Fran Dutson)*

ROWINGTON   SP1969
Tom o' the Wood (01564) 782252
*Off B4439 N of Rowington, following
Lowsonford sign; Finwood Road;
CV35 7DH* Spaciously modernised and
extended canalside pub; good home-cooked
food (not Sun evening) from sharing
baskets and stone-baked pizzas up, themed
evenings including Thurs pie night, well
kept Greene King IPA and guests, Weston's
Rosie's Pig cider, friendly staff, conservatory;
live music, free wi-fi; children and dogs
(not in restaurant) welcome, tables on
terrace and side lawn, open all day (till
8pm Sun). *(Charles Welch)*

RUGBY   SP5075
Merchants (01788) 571119
Little Church Street; CV21 3AN Open-
plan pub tucked away near main shopping
area, cheerfully busy, with nine well kept ales
including Nethergate, Oakham and Purity,
real ciders and huge selection of belgian and
other bottled imports, regular beer/cider/
gin festivals, low-priced lunchtime food
including range of burgers, quite dark inside
with beams, bare boards and flagstones, lots
of pump clips and interesting breweriana;
background music (live Tues), quiz last Mon
of month, sports TVs; open all day, till 1am
Fri, Sat. *(Steve Hall)*

RUGBY   SP5075
Seven Stars (01788) 535478
Albert Square; CV21 2SH Traditional
19th-c red-brick local with 11 well kept
ales such as Everards, Grainstore, Gun Dog
and Oakham, friendly landlord and staff,
main bar, lounge, snug and conservatory,
rugby memorabilia, snacky food including
home-made scotch eggs, pie and pint night
Weds; sports TV, darts and board games;
children (till 7pm) and dogs welcome, café-
style seating in part-covered courtyard with
murals, closed Mon lunchtime, otherwise
open all day. *(Steve Hall)*

RUSHALL   SK03001
Manor Arms 07428 521730
Park Road, off A461; WS4 1LG
Interesting low-beamed 18th-c pub (on
much older foundations) by Rushall Canal;
three rooms in contrasting styles, one with
big inglenook, well kept Banks's ales from
pumps fixed to the wall (there's no counter),
simple snacky food, friendly staff; no card
payments; children, walkers and dogs
welcome, waterside garden with moorings,
next to Park Lime Pits nature reserve, open
all day. *(Belinda and Neil Garth)*

SEDGLEY   SO9293
★Beacon (01902) 883380
*Bilston Street; A463, off A4123
Wolverhampton–Dudley; DY3 1JE*
Plain old brick pub with own good Sarah
Hughes ales from traditional Victorian
tower brewery behind; cheery locals in
simple quarry-tiled drinking corridor,
little snug on left with wall settles,
imposing green-tiled marble fireplace
and glazed serving hatch, blackened
range in sparse tap room on right, also
a dark-panelled lounge with sturdy red
leather wall settles and dramatic sea
prints, plant-filled conservatory (no
seats), little food apart from cobs; no
credit cards or dogs; children allowed
in some parts including garden with
play area. *(Laura Reid)*

SHIPSTON-ON-STOUR   SP2540
Horseshoe (01608) 662190
Church Street; CV36 4AP Popular 17th-c
timbered local (former coaching inn)
refurbished under present management;
two-room carpeted bar with cushioned wall
seats, scrubbed tables and open fire, Purity,
Sharps and Wye Valley, Weston's Old Rosie
cider, enjoyable traditional food including
Sun carvery, can eat in bar or end dining

room; children and dogs welcome, café style tables and chairs on back terrace, open all day Fri-Sun, closed Mon. *(Carla Lambourne)*

SHUSTOKE
SP2290
★ **Griffin** (01675) 481205
Church End, a mile E of village; 5 miles from M6 junction 4; A446 towards Tamworth, then right on to B4114 straight through Coleshill; B46 2LB
Unpretentious country local with ten well kept changing ales including own Freestyle (brewed in next-door barn), farm cider and country wines, standard lunchtime bar food (not Sun); cheery low-beamed L-shaped bar with log fires in two stone fireplaces (one a big inglenook), fairly simple décor, some elm-topped sewing trestles and a nice old-fashioned settle, conservatory (children allowed here); dogs welcome, picnic-sets on back grass with far views of Birmingham, large terrace, play area and summer marquee (live music, beer/cider festivals), camping field, open all day Fri-Sun.
(Geoff and Ann Marston)

SHUSTOKE
SP2290
Plough (01675) 481557
B4114 Nuneaton–Coleshill; B46 2AN
Old-fashioned feel with rooms arranged around central bar; well kept Bass and four guests, good choice of fairly straightforward food from sandwiches and baked potatoes up, some themed food nights, friendly helpful staff, separate dining room, black beams, open fire and gleaming brassware; regular quiz nights (usually Mon), pool and darts, fruit machine, free wi-fi; children and dogs welcome, disabled facilities, seats out at back, open all day. *(Melanie and David Lawson)*

STOCKTON
SP4365
Boat (01926) 812657
A426 Southam–Rugby; CV23 8HQ
Fairly traditionally updated canalside pub with open-plan split-level interior (raised part mainly for dining); dark wood furniture on pale stone or stripped boards, woodburner in brick fireplace, brewery mirrors and advertising signs, bottles and jugs on delft shelf, a house beer from Nethergate, three guest ales and several craft beers, popular reasonably priced pubby food (not Sun evening), friendly staff; children and dogs (in bar) welcome, waterside picnic-sets under pergola, garden behind with play area, moorings, open all day (till 8pm Sun).
(Jeremy Snaithe)

STOCKTON
SP4363
Crown (01926) 812255
High Street; CV47 8JZ Friendly village pub with generous helpings of popular

straightforward food and four well kept ales including Marstons Pedigree, restaurant in ancient barn, log fires; children and dogs welcome, garden with play area, open all day, no food Sun evening or lunchtimes Mon-Thurs.
(Chris and Sophie Baxter)

STOURBRIDGE
SO9084
Duke William (01384) 440202
Coventry Street; DY8 1EP Popular and friendly Edwardian corner pub in semi-pedestrianised area; own Craddocks beers from on-site microbrewery (tours available) plus guests and draught/bottled imports, good pie, mash and peas menu, traditional old black country feel with long corridor, open fire in bar and cosy snug; regular events including music, quiz and film nights (some in upstairs function room); no children, beer garden behind, open all day.
(Douglas Power)

STOURBRIDGE
SO8983
Plough & Harrow (01384) 397218
Worcester Street; DY8 1AX Friendly little end-of-terrace bay-windowed local (sister to the nearby Duke William); well kept Craddocks ales and several guests, snacky food (nothing hot), cosy horseshoe bar with log fires and piano; live music and quiz nights; dogs welcome, no children inside, partly covered beer garden with woodburner, close to Mary Stevens Park, open all day.
(Douglas Power)

STRATFORD-UPON-AVON
SP2054
Dirty Duck (01789) 297312
Waterside; CV37 6BA Bustling 16th-c Greene King pub near the Memorial Theatre (popular with actors after performances); their well kept ales, good choice of wines and enjoyable fairly priced food including deals (allow plenty of time for a pre-theatre meal), wood floors and panelling, lots of signed RSC photographs, open fire, modern conservatory restaurant (best to book weekends); children allowed in dining areas, dogs in bar, attractive small terrace looking over riverside public gardens which act as an overflow area in summer, open (and food) all day.
(Richard Tilbrook)

STRATFORD-UPON-AVON
SP2054
Garrick (01789) 292186
High Street; CV37 6AU Ancient pub with fine timbered frontage, heavy beams in irregularly shaped rooms, simple furnishings on bare boards or flagstones, well kept Greene King ales and decent wines by the glass, fairly priced food from sandwiches and light dishes up, small back dining area; background music, TV, games machine; children welcome, open (and food) all day.
(Tony Selinger, Alan Johnson)

We say if we know a pub has background music.

STRATFORD-UPON-AVON SP1955
Old Thatch (01789) 295216
Rother Street/Greenhill Street; CV37 6LE
Cosy and welcoming 15th-c thatched pub on corner of market square; well kept Fullers ales, nice wines and popular fairly priced food including Sun carvery, rustic décor, beams, slate or wood floors, sofas and log fire, back dining area; children and dogs welcome, covered tables outside, open all day.
(Alan Johnson)

STRATFORD-UPON-AVON SP2055
One Elm (01789) 404919
Guild Street; CV37 6QZ Modernised Peach group pub on two floors; well liked food from sandwiches and pub standards up (smaller helpings for children), Church Farm, Purity and guests, plenty of wines by the glass and good range of gins and cocktails, friendly efficient service; dogs welcome, seats out at front and in attractive paved courtyard behind, open (and food) all day. *(Laura Reid)*

STRATFORD-UPON-AVON SP1955
White Swan (01789) 297022
Rother Street; CV37 6NH Extensively renovated historic hotel (dates from 1450) with warren of connecting heavily beamed areas around central bar (one or two steps), good mix of seating including leather armchairs/sofas and antique settles, Shakespearean themed pictures and prints, oak-panelled dining room with two fine carved fireplaces and 16th-c wall painting of Tobias and the Angel, five Fullers/Gales beers, several wines by the glass and good choice of food to suit all tastes and occasions, quick friendly service; background music, daily newspapers, free wi-fi; children welcome, seats out at front overlooking market square and to the side, character bedrooms, open (and food) all day.
(Alan Johnson, Susan and John Douglas)

STRATFORD-UPON-AVON SP1954
Windmill (01789) 297687
Church Street; CV37 6HB Near the striking Guild Chapel, this pub was first licensed in 1600 (there's a list of landlords back to 1720); updated interior with low beams and standing timbers, big fireplaces and wood and carpeted floors, Greene King, Purity and guests, good choice of enjoyable fairly priced food including range of burgers, various deals, friendly efficient staff; background music, sports TV, games machine, free wi-fi; children welcome, courtyard tables, open (and food) all day.
(Laura Reid)

STRETTON-ON-FOSSE SP2238
★ Plough (01608) 661053
Just off A429; GL56 9QX Popular and welcoming little 17th-c village local; central servery separating small bar and snug dining

area, well kept Sharps, Timothy Taylors and guests, good home-cooked food (not Sun evening) including blackboard specials, low oak beams, stripped-brick/stone walls and some flagstones, inglenook log fire; dominoes and cribbage, free wi-fi; children welcome, no dogs, a few tables outside, open all day Fri-Sun, closed Mon. *(Charles Welch)*

SUTTON COLDFIELD SP1195
Brewhouse & Kitchen
(0121) 796 6838 *Birmingham Road; B72 1QD* Mock-Tudor pub with own microbrewery (tours available), eight real ales (mainly theirs) plus good range of craft kegs and bottled beers, around a dozen wines by the glass and enjoyable reasonably priced food from snacks, burgers and ribs up (menu suggests beer pairings), friendly helpful staff, spacious modern interior with plenty of different seating areas including boothed dining part; children welcome, open (and food) all day. *(Bridget and Peter Gregson)*

TANWORTH-IN-ARDEN SP1071
Warwickshire Lad (01564) 742346
Broad Lane/Wood End Lane, Wood End; B94 5DP Beamed country pub with good choice of enjoyable food cooked by landlord-chef, well kept ales such as St Austell, Sharps, Silhill and Wye Valley, friendly service; children and dogs welcome, popular with walkers (bridleway opposite), seats outside, open all day, food all day Fri and Sat, till 7pm Sun, handy for M42 (junction 3). *(Chris and Sophie Baxter)*

TEMPLE GRAFTON SP1355
Blue Boar (01789) 750010
1 mile E, towards Binton; off A422 W of Stratford; B49 6NR Welcoming stone-built dining inn with good food from sandwiches and sharing plates up, well kept Banks's, Wychwood and a couple of guests, afternoon teas, beams, stripped stonework and log fires, glass-covered walls with goldfish, smarter dining room up a couple of steps; occasional live music, sports TV, free wi-fi; children and dogs welcome, picnic-sets outside, bedrooms. *(Jeremy Snaithe)*

TIDDINGTON SP2255
Crown (01789) 297010
Main Street; CV37 7AZ Family-friendly pub with good well priced food (smaller helpings available) and four well kept ales including Sharps Doom Bar, friendly staff, darts, pool and TV in side bar; monthly quiz night; dogs welcome, garden with play area, open all day Fri-Sun, no food Sun evening. *(Geoff and Ann Marston)*

TIPTON SO9492
Pie Factory (0121) 557 1402
Hurst Lane, Dudley Road towards Wednesbury; A457/A4037; DY4 9AB Eccentric décor and quirky food – mixed

grill served on a shovel, and you're awarded a certificate if you finish their massive Desperate Dan Cow Pie, other good value food including Sun lunchtime carvery, meal deals Mon-Weds, well kept Lump Hammer house beers (brewed by Enville) and guests; background and weekend live music, TV; children welcome, open (and food) all day. *(Charlie)*

UFTON   SP3762
White Hart (01926) 612976
Just off A425 Southam–Leamington; CV33 9PJ Friendly old pub in elevated roadside position next to church; modernised beamed bar with log fire, high-backed leather chairs and some booth seating, stripped-stone walls, a few steps here and there, well kept ales such as Greene King, St Austell and Slaughterhouse, several wines by the glass and enjoyable good value food, efficient service; children and dogs welcome, picnic-sets in hilltop garden with panoramic views, closed Sun evening, otherwise open (and food) all day. *(Douglas Power)*

UPPER BRAILES   SP3039
Gate (01608) 685212
B4035 Shipston-on-Stour to Banbury; OX15 5AX Traditional low-beamed village local; well kept Hook Norton and a guest, Weston's cider and enjoyable reasonably priced food from shortish menu, efficient friendly service, coal fire; TV and darts; children welcome, play area and aunt sally in extensive back garden, pretty hillside spot with lovely walks, two comfortable bedrooms, good breakfast, closed weekday lunchtimes, no food Sun evening, Mon. *(Mandy and Gary Redstone)*

UPPER GORNAL   SO9292
★Britannia (01902) 883253
Kent Street (A459); DY3 1UX Popular old-fashioned 19th-c local with friendly chatty atmosphere (known locally as Sally's after former landlady); coal fires in front bar and time-trapped little back room with its wonderful wall-mounted handpumps, particularly well kept/priced Bathams, some bar snacks including good local pork pies; occasional live music, sports TV; dogs welcome, flower-filled back courtyard, open all day. *(Andrew Wall)*

WALSALL   SP0198
Black Country Arms
(01922) 640588 *High Street; WS1 1QW* Imposing building dating from the 17th c with pillared frontage and big Georgian-style windows; refurbished high-ceilinged bar on different levels including mezzanine, Black Country ales and many guests from traditional wooden servery, also craft beers and real ciders, enjoyable home-made pubby food at bargain prices, good friendly service; background and live music, quiz nights,

sports TV; dogs welcome, small side terrace, open all day (till midnight Fri, Sat), no food Mon or evenings Tues, Sun. *(Belinda and Neil Garth)*

WHATCOTE   SP2944
★Royal Oak (01295) 688100
Upper Farm Barn; centre of village; CV36 5EF Beautifully restored golden-stone inn; much emphasis on their first class food but locals do gather around the bar for well kept ales such as Anarchy and Clouded Minds and good wines by the glass; beams, timbering, flagstones and polished floorboards, leather chesterfield in front of inglenook log fire, farmhouse and wheelback chairs around mix of tables, cushioned window seats and some stall-type areas with modern oak settles, restaurant in conservatory-style room; seats outside, open all day Sat, till 4pm Sun, closed Mon, Tues and lunchtimes Weds-Thurs. *(Bernard Stradling)*

WHICHFORD   SP3134
Norman Knight (01608) 684621
Ascott Road, opposite village green; CV36 5PE Sympathetically extended beamed and flagstoned pub; four well kept ales such as Goffs and Prescott, a couple of proper ciders and good food (not Sun evening, Mon) using local produce (organic meat from the family farm, helpful friendly service; quiz last Mon of month, occasional live music; children and dogs welcome, picnic-sets on front lawn facing lovely village green, aunt sally, four glamping pods and a shepherd's hut, nice walks, open all day Fri, Sat, till 6pm Sun, closed Mon lunchtime. *(Clive and Fran Dutson, Guy Vowles)*

WILLEY   SP4885
Barn (01788) 833810
Coalpit Lane; CV23 0SL Family-run pub-restaurant in converted barn; own O'Neills beers (view into the brewery) plus a guest, decent range of wines and gins, enjoyable reasonably priced food from sandwiches and sharing boards to burgers and grills, Sun carvery till 6pm, friendly helpful service, more room in upstairs galleried area; occasional live music, beer/gin festivals; children and dogs welcome, terrace with country views, open all day, food all day Fri, Sat. *(Andrew Wall)*

WILLEY   SP4984
Sarah Mansfield (01455) 324596
Just off A5, N of A427 junction; Main Street; CV23 0SH Comfortable 17th-c beamed village pub under new management; enjoyable well priced pubby food from sandwiches and baked potatoes up, friendly efficient, staff, well kept Black Sheep, Greene King and Sharps from stone-faced servery, open fire; free wi-fi; children welcome, a few tables outside, closed Sun evening, Mon. *(Clive and Fran Dutson)*

WILLOUGHBY   SP5267
Rose   (01788) 891180

Just off A45 E of Dunchurch; Main Street; CV23 8BH Neatly decorated old thatched dining pub; low beam and plank ceiling, wood or tiled floors, some panelling and inglenook woodburner, good range of popular food cooked by chef-landlord including monthly tapas night, well kept ales and reasonably priced house wines, friendly attentive young staff; children and dogs welcome, disabled facilities, seating in side garden with gate to local park and play area, closed Sun evening, Mon. *(Peter and Caroline Waites)*

WOLVERHAMPTON   SO9298
★ Great Western   (01902) 351090

Corn Hill/Sun Street, behind railway station; WV10 0DG Cheerful pub hidden away in cobbled lane down from mainline station; Holdens and guests kept well, real cider and bargain lunchtime food (not weekends), helpful friendly staff, traditional front bar, other rooms including neat conservatory, open fires and interesting railway memorabilia; TV; children and dogs welcome, maybe summer barbecues in yard, open all day and busy with Wolves fans on match days. *(Alan C Curran)*

WOLVERHAMPTON   SJ8901
Hail to the Ale   07846 562910

Pendeford Avenue/Blackburn Avenue; WV6 9JN One-room micropub in converted shop, four well kept/priced beers including Morton and several real ciders, simple food such as pork pies and sausage rolls, warm friendly atmosphere; dogs welcome, seats outside, closed Mon-Weds, otherwise open all day (till 5pm Sun). *(Philip Farmer)*

WOOTTON WAWEN   SP1563
Bulls Head   (01564) 795803

Stratford Road, just off A3400; B95 6BD Attractive black and white dining pub; Elizabethan beams and timbers, stone and quarry-tiled floors, log fires, decent choice of enjoyable fairly priced food from sandwiches up, deals for two on some main courses, Marstons, Ringwood and a guest, friendly staff; children welcome, dogs in bar, outside tables front and back, handy for one of England's finest churches and Stratford Canal walks, open all day (till 8pm Sun). *(Dave Braisted)*

Wiltshire

ALDBOURNE

SU2675 Map 2

Blue Boar ▣ £

(01672) 540237 – www.theblueboarpub.co.uk

The Green (off B4192 in centre); SN8 2EN

Simple pubby furnishings in bar, cosy restaurant, decent food and seats outside

The heavily beamed bar here has a relaxed, chatty atmosphere helped along by cheerful staff and plenty of regulars. You'll find built-in wooden window seats, tall farmhouse and other red-cushioned pubby chairs on flagstones or bare boards, a woodburning stove in an inglenook fireplace with a stuffed boar's head and large clock above it, and horsebrasses on the bressumer beam; a noticeboard has news of beer festivals and live music events. Wadworths IPA, 6X and a guest beer such as Bath Gem on handpump, eight wines by the glass, 17 malt whiskies and a farm cider. The back restaurant is beamed and cottagey with standing timbers, dark wooden chairs and tables on floorboards and rugs, and plates on a dresser. Picnic-sets at the front make the most of the charming location by the pretty village green, and the summer window boxes are lovely.

Remarkably fair value, honest food includes lunchtime sandwiches, deep-fried whitebait with tartare sauce, smoked mackerel pâté, pumpkin and parmesan ravioli with green pesto, home-cooked ham and eggs, lambs liver and bacon, beer-battered cod and chips, butterflied chicken breast with white wine and tarragon sauce, salmon fillet with lemon and parsley butter, 10oz local sirloin steak with red wine sauce, and puddings such as Baileys and dark chocolate cheesecake and lemon tart with whipped cream. *Benchmark main dish: steak and kidney pie £9.50. Two-course evening meal £18.00.*

Wadworths ~ Tenants Michael and Joanne Hehir ~ Real ale ~ Open 11.30-3, 5.30-11.30; 11.30am-midnight Fri, Sat; 12-11 Sun ~ Bar food 12-2 (2.30 Fri, Sat), 6.30-9; 12-3 Sun ~ Restaurant ~ Children welcome ~ Dogs allowed in bar ~ Wi-fi ~ Live music Sun (4-6pm)
Recommended by Andrew Vincent, Simon Day, Dan and Anne Morgan, Celia and Andrew King, Julian Richardson, Katherine Matthews, William and Natasha Pace

BRADFORD-ON-AVON

ST8261 Map 2

Bunch of Grapes ▣ ♀

(01225) 938088 – www.thebunchofgrapes.com

Silver Street; BA15 1JY

Stylish pub-cum-bar, carefully refurbished, with enjoyable food and drink and friendly mix of customers

This handsome place has been extensively and attractively renovated by new owners. The appealing décor, with large windows overlooking the wide town street, has been done with style. The main bar has cushioned wall seats and mate's chairs on bare boards, stools against a high shelf and the bar counter, where friendly staff serve real ales such as Butcombe Original and a guest from Brotherhood or Otter on handpump and good wines by the glass. The upstairs dining rooms have big plant prints on pale-painted walls, elegant chairs around traditional tables on more floorboards and fresh flowers and candles; background music.

The beautifully presented food includes salt and pepper squid with garlic mayonnaise, chilli and lime, lamb shoulder with mint yoghurt, radishes and pickled cucumber, cauliflower risotto with truffle, trompette mushrooms, hazelnuts and pickled golden raisins, flat-iron steak with shallot and caper salad and skinny fries, chicken breast with mini pie, leeks, morels and choi sum, venison haunch and faggot with beetroot, chicory and mash, cod with crab bisque, clams, grapes and samphire, and puddings such as dulce de leche pannacotta with rhubarb and milk crisps and sticky toffee pudding with toffee sauce; they also offer a two- and three-course weekday lunch menu. *Benchmark main dish: venison burger with toppings and french fries £13.95. Two-course evening meal £21.00.*

Free house ~ Real ale ~ Open 11-3, 6-11; 11-11 Fri, Sat; 11-6 Sun ~ Bar food 12-2.30, 6-9; 12-3 Sun ~ Children welcome ~ Dogs allowed in bar ~ Wi-fi *Recommended by Jill and Hugh Bennett, Peter and Emma Kelly, Neil Allen, Paddy and Sian O'Leary, Professor James Burke, Rupert and Sandy Newton*

BRADFORD-ON-AVON
Castle

ST8261   Map 2

(01225) 865657 – www.flatcappers.co.uk
Mount Pleasant, by junction with A363, N edge of town; extremely limited pub parking but spaces in nearby streets; BA15 1SJ

Substantial stone inn with local ales, popular food, plenty of character and fine views; bedrooms

Before becoming a pub in 1834, this was once a toll house, and it retains a lot of individual character. The unspoilt bar has a good log fire, a wide range of seats (church chairs, leather armchairs, cushioned wall seating, brass-studded leather dining chairs) around chunky pine tables on dark flagstones, church candles and fringed lamps; daily papers, background music and board games. A bare-boards snug on the right is similar in style. Cheerful staff serve a couple of beers named for the pub (from Three Castles), Kettlesmith Fogline, Twisted WTF and a changing guest on handpump and several wines by the glass; they hold a beer and music festival twice a year. Seats outside at the front offer sweeping town views, while in the back garden you look across lovely countryside. The boldly decorated bedrooms are comfortable and have spacious bathrooms. There's wheelchair access at the back.

As well as breakfasts (8.30am-midday), the well regarded food includes weekday sandwiches (until 5pm), roast asparagus with mushroom mayonnaise and prosciutto, smoked salmon with poppy seeds, crème fraîche, avocado, fennel and seaweed crisp, bean burger with slaw and fries, lamb rump with dauphinoise potatoes, chorizo and veal jus, hake fillet with sun-dried tomato and olive risotto and pesto, braised beef with herb mash, horseradish and beef jus, sirloin steak with triple-cooked chips and café de paris butter, and puddings such as local honey pannacotta with cardamom and honeycomb and apple and rhubarb crumble with custard. *Benchmark main dish: chicken, ham and leek pie £14.00. Two-course evening meal £21.00.*

Free house ~ Licensee Georgia Alexander ~ Real ale ~ Open 8.30am-11pm; 8.30am-10.30pm Sun ~ Bar food 8.30am-10pm (9.30pm Sun) ~ Children welcome ~ Dogs welcome ~ Wi-fi ~ Bedrooms: /£110 *Recommended by Dr and Mrs A K Clarke, Jonny and Andrew Haughton, Alister and Margery Bacon, Darrell Barton, Maggie and Stevan Hollis*

 BRADFORD-ON-AVON   ST8260   Map 2
Timbrells Yard ♀ 🍺 🛏
(01225) 869492 – www.timbrellsyard.com
St Margarets Street; BA15 1DE

Town-centre pub next to the river, with interesting décor, a thoughtful choice of drinks and food and cheerful staff; bedrooms

The décor here is certainly not traditional and cleverly blends original features with quirky, contemporary décor and furnishings; it's fun and our readers enjoy their visits very much. The bar, with its pleasantly chatty atmosphere, has stripped floorboards, walls of exposed stone, planking and grey paintwork, upholstered and modern dining chairs, scatter-cushioned wall seats, cubed or leather-topped stools, wooden tables of every size and shape, mirrors, hanging lamps, a group of sofas and armchairs and both a woodburning stove and an open fire. From the tiled counter, friendly, efficient staff serve Box Steam Tunnel Vision, Kettlesmith Faultline and Otter Bitter on handpump, 22 wines by the glass, local cider and perry and cocktails. The light and airy restaurant is similarly furnished, and the sunny front terrace has seats and tables. The stylish, up-to-date bedrooms (some with mezzanines) are deeply comfortable and well equipped.

As well as breakfasts (7.30-11am) and all-day cakes and coffee, the good food includes lunchtime ciabattas, crab cakes with harissa, citrus and coriander slaw, smoked ham hock terrine with pickles, sharing platters, gnocchi with ricotta, spinach, pine nuts and romesco sauce, grilled tikka chicken salad with quinoa, raita and spiced pumpkin seeds, hake fillet with café de paris butter, beetroot and spelt risotto, samphire and pea purée, slow-roast rare-breed pork belly with fennel and sea salt crackling, lentils with red wine vinegar and basil oil, and puddings such as elderflower and yoghurt pannacotta with honey and almond crumble and rocky road sundae with toffee sauce. *Benchmark main dish: dry-aged rump steak with a choice of sauce and chips £20.00. Two-course evening meal £22.00.*

Free house ~ Licensee Gemma Bates ~ Real ale ~ Open 7.30am-11pm; 8am-10.30pm Sun ~ Bar food 12-3, 6-9.45 Mon; 12-9.45 Tues-Sat; 12-9 Sun ~ Restaurant ~ Children welcome ~ Dogs allowed in bar and bedrooms ~ Wi-fi ~ Bedrooms: /£110 *Recommended by Chris and Sophie Baxter, Alexander and Trish Gendall, Ben and Jenny Settle, Dr and Mrs A K Clarke, Ruth and Peter Bacon, Edward May*

 CHILTON FOLIAT   SU3270   Map 2
Wheatsheaf ⭐♀
(01488) 680936 – www.thewheatsheafchiltonfoliat.co.uk
B4192; RG17 0TE

Lots going on in bustling old pub with a good mix of customers, simple furnishings, local ales and smashing food

The landlord cooks the enterprising food in this delightful 17th-c thatched pub (he was a *MasterChef* semi-finalist), his wife oversees front of house and their hands-on approach and friendly welcome draw in customers from far and wide. The carefully restored, character rooms include a beamed bar and dining room furnished with wheelbacks and mate's chairs, built-in settles and bow-window seats around dark tables on patterned carpets, artwork on the walls (some painted by the landlord), a piano and woodburning stoves. Local ales include one named for the pub (from Butts) plus Brunswick The Usual and Ramsbury Gold on handpump, 15 organic wines by the glass, home-made liqueurs, organic soft drinks and farm cider; darts, board games and background music. You'll find plenty going on here including live music events, a regular pub quiz (every third Tuesday), cookery classes and an upstairs shop selling vintage furniture, clothes and shoes. Eco-friendly values are important, as is the use of seasonal, local produce, free-range, organic or wild meat and responsibly sourced fish. There are a few picnic-sets at the front. Disabled access.

 Using his father's rare-breed pigs, sheep and chickens and other local produce and describing his cooking as 'upmarket peasant food', the landlord offers a variety of tapas-style nibbles such as crispy calves liver with onions and pickled carrot, a plate of bresaola and moules marinière plus asparagus risotto with spelt, fennel tops, feta and cream, fish pie with smoked haddock, leeks and capers, persian-style chicken with pomegranate, walnuts, molasses, rice, chilli and salsa, john dory with mussels, samphire and jersey royals, and puddings such as polenta and almond cake with clementine marmalade and crème fraîche and rhubarb frangipane with rhubarb sorbet. *Benchmark main dish: wood-fired organic pizzas £15.00. Two-course evening meal £20.00.*

Free house ~ Licensees Ollie and Lauren ~ Real ale ~ Open 12-3, 5.30-11.30; 12-11.30 Fri, Sat; 12-9.30 Sun ~ Bar food 12-2.15, 6-9.15 ~ Restaurant ~ Children welcome ~ Dogs welcome ~ Wi-fi ~ Live music (check website) *Recommended by Michael Doswell, Charlotte and William Mason, Sophie and James Collier, Selwyn Jones, William and Natasha Pace, Ben and Diane Bowie, Charles and Cynthia Todd*

COMPTON BASSETT

SU0372   Map 2

White Horse

(01249) 813118 – www.whitehorse-comptonbassett.co.uk
At N end of village; SN11 8RG

Bustling pub with three ales, good wines by the glass, interesting food and seats in big garden; pretty bedrooms

With creative food, comfortable bedrooms and a genuine welcome, this pub gets top marks all round from our readers. The friendly, bustling bar has cushioned window and wall seats and settles, chunky wood and leather dining chairs around assorted tables on parquet flooring, a woodburning stove, and bar stools against the counter where they keep Box Steam Tunnel Vision, Ramsbury Gold and Three Daggers Blonde on handpump, 15 wines by the glass, 13 malt whiskies, a cocktail list, a good range of spirits and farm cider. The dining room has dark red walls and tiles at one end and bare floorboards and pale paintwork at the other; throughout there are beams and joists and miscellaneous antique tables and chairs. Also, there's another woodburning stove, and background music and board games. The large, neatly kept garden has picnic-sets and other seats, while the paddock is home to pigs and geese. Bedrooms (in a separate building overlooking the grounds) are attractive and well equipped and breakfasts are good. There are lovely surrounding walks.

 First class food (they make everything in-house and use local, seasonal produce) includes whitebait with tartare sauce, crispy pork belly with black pudding and caramelised apple purée, butternut squash risotto with toasted pumpkin seeds, a pie of the day, breaded monkfish with fries and aioli, free-range chicken breast with truffle mash and wild mushroom sauce, skate wing with sea vegetables and caper butter, rare-breed sirloin steak with a choice of sauce and triple-cooked chips, and puddings such as passion-fruit crème brûlée with pineapple sorbet and sticky toffee pudding with toffee sauce and clotted cream; they also offer a two- and three-course weekday set menu. *Benchmark main dish: duck breast with rosemary potatoes, savoy cabbage, bacon lardons and game jus £19.50. Two-course evening meal £22.00.*

Free house ~ Licensee Kristian Goodwin ~ Real ale ~ Open 12-11; 12-9 Sun ~ Bar food 12-3, 6-9 ~ Restaurant ~ Children welcome ~ Dogs allowed in bar ~ Wi-fi ~ Bedrooms: £75/£85
Recommended by Karl and Frieda Bujeya, Basil and Joyce Rampley, Victoria and Len Meadows, Michael Doswell, Valerie and Colin Sayer, Penny and David Shepherd

CRICKLADE
SU1093   Map 4
Red Lion 🍺 🛏

(01793) 750776 – www.theredlioncricklade.co.uk
Off A419 Swindon–Cirencester; High Street; SN6 6DD

16th-c inn with well liked food in two dining rooms, ten real ales, friendly, relaxed atmosphere and big garden; bedrooms

From their on-site Hop Kettle microbrewery, the landlord and his cheerful staff offer Hop Kettle C.O.B., Element and North Wall and up to seven quickly changing guests. They also keep 60 bottled beers, six farm ciders, 12 wines by the glass, ten malt whiskies and 15 gins (gin hour is 5.30-6.30pm). The traditional bar has stools by the nice old counter, wheelbacks and other chairs around dark wooden tables on red patterned carpet, an open fire and all sorts of bric-a-brac on the stone walls including stuffed fish, animal heads and old street signs. You can eat here or in the slightly more formal dining room, furnished with pale wooden farmhouse chairs and tables, beige carpeting and a woodburning stove in a brick fireplace. There are plenty of picnic-sets in the big back garden. The five bedrooms are comfortable and breakfasts good. You can walk along the nearby Thames Path or around the historic, pretty town.

🍴 Good, popular food includes lunchtime sandwiches and toasties (not Sunday), curried crab and prawns on toasted home-made fennel bread with fennel and apple dressing, ham hock terrine with fig and pear chutney, sharing boards, cheddar, leek, spring onion and courgette 'speltotto' (pearled spelt), home-cooked ham with free-range eggs, mackerel with bacon, kale, potato cake and tomato and horseradish salsa, slow-braised leg and shoulder of lamb with herbed potato rösti, pea purée, salt-baked celeriac and bacon and red wine sauce, and puddings such as dark chocolate fondant with salted almond brittle and cookie dough ice-cream and orange pannacotta with orange gel and orange and chocolate mousse-filled tuille. *Benchmark main dish: steak in ale pie £14.00. Two-course evening meal £21.00.*

Free house ~ Licensee Tom Gee ~ Real ale ~ Open 12-11; 12-midnight Sat; 12-10.30 Sun ~ Bar food 12-2.30, 6.30-9; 12-2.30, 6.30-9.30 Fri, Sat; 12-3, 6.30-9 Sun ~ Restaurant ~ Children welcome ~ Dogs welcome ~ Wi-fi ~ Bedrooms: /£90 *Recommended by Catherine and Daniel King, John and Lorna Chew, Alison and Michael Harper, Jo Garnett, Phoebe Peacock, Peter Brix*

CRUDWELL
ST9592   Map 4
Potting Shed 🌟 🍷 🍺

(01666) 577833 – www.thepottingshedpub.com
A429 N of Malmesbury; The Street; SN16 9EW

Friendly dining pub with low-beamed rooms, an interesting range of drinks and food, and seats in the big garden

You'll find a friendly welcome and creative cooking here and the relaxed, civilised atmosphere rounds things off nicely. Low-beamed rooms ramble around the bar with its bare stone walls, open fires and woodburning stoves (one in a big worn stone fireplace), mixed plain tables and chairs on pale flagstones, armchairs and a sofa in one corner and daily papers. Four steps lead up into a high-raftered area with wood flooring, and there's another separate, smaller room that's ideal for a lunch or dinner party. Also, lots of dog and country prints and more modern pictures, fresh flowers, candles and some quirky, rustic decorations such as a garden-fork door handle, garden-spade beer pumps and so forth. Butcombe Gold and Original, Flying Monk Elmers, Oakham Citra, Prescott Hill Climb and Ramsbury Bitter on handpump, as well as carefully chosen wines and champagne by the glass, home-made seasonal cocktails and local fruit liqueurs; background music and board games and dogs may get treats. There are teak seats around cask tables among the weeping willows, as well as a boules piste. Sister business the Rectory Hotel is a stone's throw away. Wheelchair access to the front door from the car park, and disabled loos.

 Imaginative food includes pork and pistachio terrine with brandy and prune jam, potted shrimps with sourdough toast, vegetable risotto with pecorino, rare-breed pork sausages with mash and onion gravy, fish stew with saffron potatoes, rouille and croutons, confit duck leg with split green lentils and pancetta, pork chop with nduja, sautéed potatoes, roasted fennel and salsa verde, chicken kiev with mash and green beans, local rib-eye steak with a choice of sauce and french fries, and puddings such as warm treacle tart with clotted cream and sticky toffee pudding with salted caramel sauce. *Benchmark main dish: beer-battered fish and chips £13.50. Two-course evening meal £21.00.*

Enterprise ~ Lease Alex Payne ~ Real ale ~ Open 11-11; 11-midnight Fri, Sat ~ Bar food 12-2.30, 6-9.30; 12-2.30, 6.30-9.30 Fri-Sun ~ Restaurant ~ Children welcome ~ Dogs welcome ~ Wi-fi *Recommended by Chris and Angela Buckell, Mr and Mrs P R Thomas, Charles Fraser, Patricia Hawkins, Sophie Ellison, Millie and Peter Downing*

EAST CHISENBURY

SU1352 Map 2

Red Lion 🌟 ♀ 🛏

(01980) 671124 – www.redlionfreehouse.com
At S end of village; SN9 6AQ

Wiltshire Dining Pub of the Year

Country inn in peaceful village run by hard-working chef-owners, contemporary décor, an informal atmosphere and excellent food; fine bedrooms

Just across the road from the main pub is their boutique guesthouse, Troutbeck. The very well equipped and extremely comfortable bedrooms have private decks just a few metres from the River Avon and breakfasts are delicious; the bloody marys and bucks fizz are complimentary. Of course, it's the superb food cooked by Mr and Mrs Manning (both are top chefs) that draws customers from far and wide, but this is also a proper pub where locals congregate at high chairs by the bar for a pint and a chat. You'll find Ramsbury Blindside and Stonehenge Spire Ale on handpump, 24 wines by the glass, home-made cordial, quite a range of gins and a dozen malt whiskies. One long room is split into different areas by brick and green-planked uprights. A big woodburner sits in a brick inglenook fireplace at one end; at the other is a comfortable black leather sofa and armchairs, and in between are high-backed and farmhouse wooden dining chairs around various tables on bare boards or stone tiles, with pretty flowers and church candles dotted about. There's an additional dining area too and an upstairs private dining room; background music. Outside, the terrace and grassed area above it have picnic-sets and tables and chairs. They make their own dog treats and can organise a packed lunch for walkers.

 Faultless food using their own produce and home-reared pigs and chickens includes lunchtime sandwiches, scallop ceviche with burnt apple, jalepenos and dill, mussel tagliatelle with saffron, Pernod and chives, wild mushroom pithivier with chestnuts, truffle nage and crispy parmesan, herb-roasted guinea fowl with potato millefeuille, charred leeks and madeira velouté, turbot with saffron-braised potatoes, fennel, brown shrimps and sauce bourride, and puddings such as new york cheesecake with bay, rhubarb and iced Hendrick's and tonic and bitter chocolate tart with banana compote, coffee cream and hazelnut praline. *Benchmark main dish: local venison with medjool date and juniper poivrade £27.00. Two-course evening meal £37.00.*

Free house ~ Licensees Britt and Guy Manning ~ Real ale ~ Open 11-11; 11-4 Sun; closed Sun evening, Mon, Tues ~ Bar food 12-2.30, 6-8.30; 12-2 Sun ~ Children welcome ~ Dogs welcome ~ Wi-fi ~ Bedrooms: /$155 *Recommended by Barbara and Phil Bowie, Mary and Nigel Joyce, Anne and Simon Taylor, Luke Morgan, Charlie Parker, Sandra and Nigel Brown*

EAST KNOYLE   ST8731 Map 2
Fox & Hounds ♀
(01747) 830573 – www.foxandhounds-eastknoyle.co.uk
Village signposted off A350 S of A303; The Green (named on some road atlases), a mile NW at OS Sheet 183 map reference 872313; or follow signpost off B3089, about 0.5 miles E of A303 junction near Little Chef; SP3 6BN

Pretty village pub with splendid views, welcoming service, good beers and popular, enjoyable food

This is a lovely rural spot with nearby woods for walking in, the Wiltshire Cycleway passing close by and remarkable views over Blackmore Vale from picnic-sets in front of this part-thatched old place dating from the 15th c. Inside, three linked areas (on different levels around the central horseshoe-shaped server) have woodburning stoves, plentiful oak woodwork and flagstones, comfortably padded dining chairs around big scrubbed tables, and a couple of leather sofas; the furnishings are all very individual and uncluttered. There's also a small light-painted conservatory restaurant. Butcombe Bitter, Hop Back Summer Lightning, Plain Sheep Dip and Triple fff Moondance on handpump, a dozen wines by the glass and Thatcher's farm cider; board games and skittle alley.

As well as lunchtime ploughman's (not Sunday), the appealing food includes deep-fried rosemary and garlic-crusted brie wedges with cranberry sauce, japanese-style battered king prawns with sweet chilli dipping sauce, spinach and ricotta cannelloni, chicken caesar salad, lasagne, pizzas, bacon-wrapped chicken breast with pesto cream sauce and rösti potatoes, slow-braised pork belly with cider and apple sauce, smoked haddock, cod and salmon pie topped with potato, and puddings such as lemon posset and warm pear and almond tart with vanilla ice-cream. *Benchmark main dish: battered cod and chips £12.50. Two-course evening meal £19.00.*

Free house ~ Licensee Murray Seator ~ Real ale ~ Open 11.30-3, 5-11 ~ Bar food 12-2.15, 6.30-9; 12-2, 6.30-8.30 Sun ~ Children welcome ~ Dogs welcome ~ Wi-fi *Recommended by Sally and Colin Allen, Edward Mirzoeff, Helen and Brian Edgeley, Patti and James Davidson, Alexandra and Richard Clay, Freddie and Sarah Banks*

Bedroom prices are for high summer. Even then you may get reductions for more than one night, or (outside tourist areas) weekends. Winter special rates are common, and many inns reduce bedroom prices if you have a full evening meal.

EDINGTON

ST9353 Map 2

Three Daggers 🍺

(01380) 830940 – www.threedaggers.co.uk

Westbury Road (B3098); BA13 4PG

Bustling village pub with open fires, beams and candlelight, helpful staff, enjoyable food and own-brew beers; bedrooms

This bustling pub brews its own Three Daggers beers in the farm shop building opposite – served on handpump, these include Ale, Black, Blonde and Edge, and they also keep 14 wines by the glass, ten malt whiskies and a couple of farm ciders. The open-plan layout of the beamed bars is appealing: leather sofas and armchairs at one end in front of a woodburning stove plus kitchen and chapel chairs and built-in planked wall seats with scatter cushions, leather-topped stools against the counter, and a cosy nook with just one table. A two-way fireplace opens into the candlelit restaurant, which has similar tables and chairs on a dark slate floor. Stairs lead up to another dining room with beams in a high roof and some unusual large wooden chandeliers; background music, darts and board games. An airy conservatory has tea-lights or church candles on scrubbed kitchen tables and wooden dining chairs. Just beyond this are picnic-sets on grass plus a fenced-off, well equipped children's play area. The bedrooms (some in the pub, some in a separate house) are pretty; the luxury ones have access to a spa. The farm shop is well worth a visit.

 Interesting food includes beetroot, goats curd, pickled pear and walnut salad, cod fishcake with poached egg, kale and hollandaise, chickpea and couscous burger with mustard mayonnaise and fries, collar of ham and eggs, whole mackerel with vegetable escabeche and rhubarb purée, duo of lamb (loin and croquette) with wild garlic pesto and jus, local pork belly with caramelised onions and apple mustard sauce, and puddings such as hay and honey pannacotta and sticky toffee pudding with Weetabix ice-cream. *Benchmark main dish: flat-iron steak with béarnaise sauce and triple-cooked chips £24.00. Two-course evening meal £21.00.*

Free house ~ Licensee Richard Smith ~ Real ale ~ Open 10am-11pm; 10am-10.30pm Sun ~ Bar food 12-2.30, 6-9; 12-8 Sun ~ Restaurant ~ Children welcome ~ Dogs allowed in bar and bedrooms ~ Wi-fi ~ Bedrooms: /£99 *Recommended by Revd R P Tickle, Dr and Mrs A K Clarke, Martine and Fabio Lockley, Brian and Sally Wakeham, Edward May, Phoebe Peacock*

FONTHILL GIFFORD

ST9231 Map 2

Beckford Arms ⭐🍽️ ♀ 🛏️

(01747) 870385 – www.beckfordarms.com

Hindon Lane; from Fonthill Bishop, bear left after tea rooms through Estate gate; from Hindon follow High Street signed for Tisbury; SP3 6PX

Handsome 18th-c inn with character bar and restaurant, unfailingly good food, thoughtful choice of drinks and an easy-going atmosphere; comfortable bedrooms

Glorious countryside surrounds this golden-stone Georgian coaching inn and the well equipped and comfortable bedrooms make a good base for exploring the area; breakfasts are good and generous. There are two self-catering lodges too. The atmosphere is gently civilised but informal and friendly, and the main bar has various wooden dining chairs and tables on parquet flooring, a huge fireplace and bar stools beside the counter where they keep an interesting range of drinks. This includes Butcombe Bitter, Keystone Phoenix (named for them) and Timothy Taylors Landlord on handpump, 15 wines by the glass, 20 malt whiskies, farm cider, winter mulled wine and cider, and cocktails such as a bellini using locally produced peach liqueur and a bloody mary using home-grown horseradish. The cosy sitting room is stylish with comfortable sofas facing one another across a low table with newspapers, an appealing built-in window seat among other chairs and tables, and an open fire in a stone fireplace with candles in brass candlesticks and fresh flowers on the mantelpiece. Also, a separate restaurant and private dining room. The mature rambling garden has seats on a brick terrace, hammocks under trees, games for children, a dog bath and boules. This is sister pub to the Lord Poulett Arms at Hinton St George and the Talbot in Mells (both in Somerset).

As well as breakfasts (8-9.30am), the enjoyable food includes chicken liver parfait with pear and saffron compote, chalk-stream trout ceviche with pickled beetroot and dill mayonnaise, chickpea, cumin and walnut salad with pickled red cabbage, apple and umami dressing, burger with toppings, pickled cucumber, chilli slaw and chips, fisherman's board, charred pork chop with fennel and chicory salad, cider-poached apples and black pudding, hake with quinoa, samphire, roasted red peppers, avocado purée and herring roe, 28-day aged rump steak with garlic butter, and puddings such as apple cheesecake with baked white chocolate and apple sorbet and dark chocolate and peanut tart with crème fraîche sorbet. *Benchmark main dish: cider-battered fish and chips £14.50. Two-course evening meal £21.00.*

Free house ~ Licensees Dan Brod and Charlie Luxton ~ Real ale ~ Open 8am-11pm ~ Bar food 12-3, 6-9.30 (9 Sun) ~ Children welcome ~ Dogs welcome ~ Wi-fi ~ Bedrooms: /£95
Recommended by Frances and Hamish Porter, Ian Herdman, David and Sally Cullen, John and Hilary Murphy, Jo Kavaney, Sandra and Michael Smith, Rosie and John Moore

GREAT BEDWYN
Three Tuns ⭐ ☆

SU2764   Map 2

(01672) 870280 – www.tunsfreehouse.com
Village signposted off A338 S of Hungerford, or off A4 W of Hungerford via Little Bedwyn; High Street; SN8 3NU

Friendly village pub with first class food and local ales; seats outside

Run with enthusiasm and care by the hands-on licensees and receiving consistently high praise from our readers, this well run village pub is a winner. The beamed front bar is traditional and simply furnished with pubby stools and chairs on bare floorboards, and has an open fire, artwork by local artists on the walls and plenty of original features. They keep local ales and a guest such as Betteridges Jenny Wren, Butcombe Original and Otter Bitter on handpump plus 12 wines by the glass, several malt whiskies, gins, vodkas and a couple of farm ciders. French doors in the back dining room lead into the garden where there are tables and chairs, an outdoor grill and boules. The Kennet & Avon Canal runs through the village and the pub is on the edge of Savernake Forest, which has lovely walks and cycle routes. It's also convenient for the station.

The marvellous food is cooked by the chef-patron who makes everything in-house: scorched mackerel fillet with cucumber kimchi, rocket and coriander oil, vegetable, hazelnut and rocket ragoût with pasta and croutons, burger with toppings and chips, home-cooked local ham and eggs, guinea fowl with fregola, chorizo, tomato, spinach and gremolata, roasted hake with clam croquette and spring greens, confit chicken leg with smoked bacon and french-style peas and aioli, and puddings such as chocolate cheesecake with griottine cherries, pistachio brittle and cherry sorbet and fruit and nut chocolate 'salami'. *Benchmark main dish: bavette steak with tarragon butter and chips £19.00. Two-course evening meal £21.00.*

Free house ~ Licensees James and Ashley Wilsey ~ Real ale ~ Open 10-3, 6-11; 10am-11pm
Fri, Sat; 12-6 Sun; closed Sun evening, Mon ~ Bar food 12-2.30, 6.30-9.30 ~ Restaurant ~
Children welcome until 8pm ~ Dogs welcome ~ Wi-fi *Recommended by Daphne and Robert
Staples, Belinda Stamp, Miss B D Picton, Trevor and Michele Street, Sandra Hollies, Maddie Purvis*

 GRITTLETON   ST8680   Map 2
Neeld Arms 🍺 🛏

(01249) 782470 – www.neeldarms.co.uk
*From M4 junction 17, follow A429 to Cirencester and immediately left, signed Stanton
St Quintin and Grittleton; SN14 6AP*

**17th-c village pub with a good mix of customers, popular food
and drink and friendly staff; bedrooms**

This place is very much the centre of village life with a cheerful, gently
civilised atmosphere and a welcome for all. The open-plan rooms have
Cotswold-stone walls, contemporary colours on wood panelling and a
pleasant mix of seating ranging from bar stools and traditional settles to
window seats and pale wooden dining chairs around an assortment of tables
– each set with fresh flowers. The little brick fireplace houses a woodburning
stove and there's an inglenook fireplace on the right. Flying Monk Habit,
Moles Best, St Austell Tribute, Wadworths 6X and a guest beer on handpump
and decent wines are served from the blue-painted panelled and oak-
topped bar counter. The back dining area has another inglenook with a big
woodburning stove and white-painted chairs and settles around solid tables;
even back here, you still feel thoroughly part of the action. Bedrooms are
attractive, neatly kept and comfortable. An outdoor terrace has a pergola and
a few tables behind a low roadside wall at the front.

Well regarded food includes chicken liver, port and brandy pâté with onion
marmalade, home-made potted prawns with toast, wild mushroom tagliatelle,
smoked haddock and spring onion fishcake with beetroot and horseradish dressing,
toulouse sausages with mash and onion gravy, lamb rump on potato and bacon rösti
with port sauce, chicken wrapped in bacon with mozzarella and barbecue sauce, local
venison steak with garlic, tomato and chilli sauce, and puddings such as warm treacle
tart with custard and fruit crumble of the day. *Benchmark main dish: pie of the day
£11.00. Two-course evening meal £20.50.*

Free house ~ Licensees Charlie and Boo West ~ Real ale ~ Open 12-3, 5.30-11.30;
12-midnight Sat; 12-11 Sun ~ Bar food 12-2, 6.30-9.30; 12-2.30, 7-9 Sun ~ Restaurant ~
Children welcome ~ Dogs welcome ~ Wi-fi ~ Bedrooms: $65/$80 *Recommended by Charlotte
and William Mason, Roger and Anne Mallard, Patricia and Gordon Thompson, Sophie Ellison,
Ian Herdman, Alison and Tony Livesley, Holly and Tim Waite*

 HORNINGSHAM   ST8041   Map 2
Bath Arms 🛏

(01985) 844308 – www.batharms.co.uk
By tradesmen's entrance to Longleat House; BA12 7LY

**Bustling pub with plenty of space, rustic furnishings, interesting food
and real ales; bedrooms**

A handsome old stone-built inn with a country atmosphere, this has several
linked bar and dining rooms. One simple end room has an open fire
and cushioned pews, wall seats and dining chairs around big tables on wide
floorboards. This leads into a smaller dining room and on into the main bar,
where there's another open fire, rustic tables and chairs and a long cushioned
settle on rugs and bare boards, candles in large wooden candlesticks and

paintings of fancy-plumaged birds. Butcombe Original, Three Daggers Blonde and a changing guest ale on handpump, Orchard Pig cider and a good choice of wines and other drinks; background music, board games, juke box and skittle alley. The restaurant is similarly furnished, with chandeliers and a big painting of a sultan. The bedrooms are light, airy and comfortable. A back garden has a two-level terrace with circular picnic-sets and there are more at the front and on gravel under pollarded trees; views overlook woods to the Avon Valley. Wheelchair access to bars is via a side door; disabled loos.

Quite a choice of food includes oak-smoked bacon, bubble and squeak with a poached egg and hollandaise, rabbit rillettes with gooseberry chutney, herb salad and home-made spinach crouton, spinach, artichoke and wild mushroom risotto, corn-fed chicken ballotine with sautéed spinach, roasted hemp seeds, hickory smoked mash and madeira jus, halibut with white beetroot purée and wild mushroom and leek fricassée, lamb rump with creamed leeks, carrot and cabbage parcel, pickled grapes, red quinoa cake and red wine jus, rare-breed steak with a choice of sauce and triple-cooked chips, and puddings such as passion-fruit tart with stem ginger ice-cream and chocolate brownie. *Benchmark main dish: burger with toppings and chips £13.95. Two-course evening meal £20.00.*

Free house ~ Licensee Des Jones ~ Real ale ~ Open 10am-11pm; 10am-10.30pm Sun ~ Bar food 12-2.45, 6-8.45 ~ Restaurant ~ Children welcome ~ Dogs welcome ~ Wi-fi ~ Bedrooms: /£145 *Recommended by Elise and Charles Mackinlay, Jennifer and Nicholas Thompson, Chris and Angela Buckell, David and Charlotte Green, David and Leone Lawson*

LOWER CHUTE

Hatchet 🍺 🛏

SU3153 Map 2

(01264) 730229 – www.thehatchetinn.com

The Chutes well signposted via Appleshaw off A342, 2.5 miles W of Andover; SP11 9DX

Neatly kept 13th-c thatched inn with a friendly welcome for all, real ales and enjoyable food; comfortable bedrooms

Despite the remote setting, plenty of customers find their way to this charming country cottage. The beamed bar has a splendid 16th-c fireback in a substantial fireplace (and a roaring winter log fire), various comfortable seats around oak tables and a peaceful local feel; there's also an extensive restaurant. The convivial landlord serves Timothy Taylors Landlord and a couple of guests such as Hatchet (named for the pub from Greene King) and Otter Bitter on handpump, eight wines by the glass, 20 malt whiskies and several farm ciders; background music and board games. There are seats out on a terrace and the side grass, and a safe play area for children. The snug bedrooms make this a fine place to stay (dogs are welcome in a couple of rooms) and breakfasts are hearty.

Tasty food includes lunchtime baguettes and toasties, tempura prawns with sweet chilli sauce, farmhouse pâté with apricot chutney, mushroom and red pepper stroganoff with rice, ham and eggs, beef bourguignon, calves liver and bacon with mash and onion gravy, chicken tikka masala with mango chutney, lamb shank with mint sauce and mash, salmon supreme with tarragon and hollandaise sauce, and puddings such as rhubarb crumble and custard and chocolate and coconut tart with cream. *Benchmark main dish: steak in ale pie £11.95. Two-course evening meal £20.00.*

Free house ~ Licensee Jeremy McKay ~ Real ale ~ Open 11.30-3, 6-11; 11.30-11 Sat; 12-4, 7-10.30 Sun ~ Bar food 12-2.15, 6-9.30; 12-3, 7-9 Sun ~ Restaurant ~ Children welcome ~ Dogs allowed in bar and bedrooms ~ Wi-fi ~ Open mike night first Fri of month ~ Bedrooms: £75/£85 *Recommended by Christopher Mannings, Mark Morgan, Julia and Fiona Barnes, Mary and Douglas McDowell, Lee and Jill Stafford, Sally and Lance Oldham*

MARSTON MEYSEY
Old Spotted Cow

SU1297 Map 4

(01285) 810264 – www.theoldspottedcow.co.uk

Off A419 Swindon–Cirencester; SN6 6LQ

An easy-going atmosphere in cottagey bar rooms, friendly young staff, lots to look at, well kept ales and enjoyable food; bedrooms

You'll see numerous cows of all sorts around the bars here and some of them actually are spotted: paintings, drawings, postcards, all manner and colour of china objects and embroidery and toy ones too. It's a charming little pub and the main bar has high-backed cushioned dining chairs around chunky pine tables on wooden floorboards or parquet, an open fire at each end of the room (with comfortable sofas in front of one), fresh flowers, candles in brass candlesticks, and beer mats and banknotes pinned to beams. Bath Gem, Moles Best and Skinners Betty Stogs on handpump, ten wines by the glass, summer farm cider and quite a few gins and malt whiskies; board games. A cottagey dining room leads off here with similar tables and chairs, a couple of long pews and a big bookshelf. There are seats and picnic-sets on the front grass and a children's play area beyond a big willow tree. A classic car show is held here on the late May Bank Holiday with live music and local beers.

 Highly regarded food, cooked by the landlady, includes sandwiches, tapas such as patatas fritas, boquerones, manchego cheese with olive oil and membrillo and ibérico acorn-fed salami with mini breadsticks plus macaroni cheese with bacon and mushroom and garlic bread, burger with mustard mayonnaise, chilli jam and chips, chilli and crab linguine, fillet of bream with crushed potatoes, garlic and black olive tapenade, rib-eye steak with a choice of sauce, and puddings. *Benchmark main dish: bubble and squeak with grilled back bacon, mustard cream sauce and poached egg £9.00. Two-course evening meal £20.00.*

Free house ~ Licensee Anna Langley-Poole ~ Real ale ~ Open 11-11; 11-6.30 Sun; closed Mon ~ Bar food 12-2, 7-9; 12-3 Sun ~ Restaurant ~ Children welcome but must be over 8 in bar ~ Dogs allowed in bar ~ Wi-fi ~ Bedrooms: /£80 *Recommended by Patricia and Gordon Thompson, Katherine and Hugh Markham, Jeff Davies, Glen and Patricia Fuller, Alexandra and Richard Clay*

NEWTON TONY
Malet Arms

SU2140 Map 2

(01980) 629279 – www.maletarms.co.uk

Village signposted off A338 Swindon–Salisbury; SP4 0HF

Smashing village pub with no pretensions, a good choice of local beers and highly regarded food

'It's always such a pleasure to come here' says one reader with enthusiasm – and so many others agree with him. There's genuine unspoilt character, and that, mixed with the warmth of the welcome and a good, chatty bunch of locals, makes the place rather special. Low-beamed interconnecting and homely rooms have all sorts of tables of differing sizes with high-winged wall settles, carved pews, chapel and carver chairs, and lots of pictures of local scenes and from imperial days. The main front windows are said to be made from the stern of a ship, and there's a log and coal fire in a huge fireplace. The snug is noteworthy for its fantastic collection of photographs and prints celebrating the local aviation history of Boscombe Down, alongside archive photographs of Stonehenge festivals of the 1970s and '80s. At the back is a homely, red-painted dining room. Four real ales on handpump come from breweries such as Butcombe, Fullers, Hop Back, Itchen Valley, Palmers, Plain, Ramsbury, Stonehenge and Triple fff and they also keep over 30 malt whiskies, ten wines by the glass and farm cider; board games. There are seats on the small front terrace with more on grass and in the back garden. The road leading to the pub goes through a ford, and it may be best to use an alternative route in winter when the water can be quite deep. There's an all-weather cricket pitch on the village green.

Country cooking uses game from local shoots (some bagged by the landlord), lamb raised in the surrounding fields and free-range local pork, and includes venison carpaccio with truffle oil and parmesan, chicken liver pâté with onion marmalade, vegetarian cottage pie, local sausages with mash and onion gravy, daily fish dishes (with fresh produce from Torbay), lamb shoulder with minted pea purée and mash, crispy pork belly with sage and onion mash and scrumpy gravy, and puddings such as treacle tart and rocky road chocolate crunch. *Benchmark main dish: burger with toppings and chips £10.95. Two-course evening meal £19.00.*

Free house ~ Licensees Noel and Annie Cardew ~ Real ale ~ Open 12-3, 6-11; 12-3, 6-10 Sun; closed Sun evening in winter ~ Bar food 12-2.15, 6.30-9.15; 12-2.15 Sun ~ Restaurant ~ Children allowed only in restaurant or snug ~ Dogs allowed in bar *Recommended by Roger and Donna Huggins, Ian Herdman, Edward Mirzoeff, Gordon and Patricia Gorringe, Ruth and Peter Bacon, Rosemary Mussen, Christopher and Elise Way*

RAMSBURY
Bell 🍽️⭐ 🛏️

SU2771   Map 2

(01672) 520230 – www.thebellramsbury.com
Off B4192 NW of Hungerford, or A4 W; SN8 2PE

300-year-old coaching inn with a civilised feel, character bar and dining rooms, and a thoughtful choice of both drinks and food; spotless bedrooms

The heavy beams and timbering in this lovely old pub blend effortlessly with the contemporary paintwork and furnishings, and the atmosphere throughout is gently civilised and informal. The two rooms of the chatty bar have tartan-cushioned wall seats and pale wooden dining chairs around assorted tables, country and wildlife paintings, interesting stained-glass windows and a woodburning stove. Neat, efficient staff serve Ramsbury Farmers Best, Gold and Flint Knapper and a changing guest on handpump, a dozen wines by the glass, 20 malt whiskies and their own-distilled gin and vodka. A cosy room between the bar and restaurant has armchairs and sofas before an open fire, a table of magazines and papers, a couple of portraits, stuffed birds on shelves and patterned wallpaper. Smart and relaxed, the restaurant is similarly furnished to the bar with white-clothed tables on bare boards or rugs, oil paintings and winter-scene photographs on beige walls; fresh flowers decorate each table. A nice surprise is the charming back café with white-painted farmhouse, tub and wicker chairs on floorboards, where they offer toasties, buns, cakes and so forth. The garden has picnic-sets on a lower terrace and raised lawn, with more on a little terrace towards the front. Bedrooms are well equipped and restful and named after game birds or fish.

Tempting food includes crispy quail eggs with pancetta, potato and apple, blowtorched mackerel with beetroot and horseradish, cream cheese and tarragon risotto with smoked almonds, burger with toppings, mustard mayonnaise and fries, gilt-head bream with local asparagus, baby gem and tarragon sauce, dry-aged sirloin of beef with cheek, bone marrow, king oyster and local asparagus, turbot with crab tortellini, thai purée and pak choi, and puddings such as rhubarb and custard-baked alaska with crumble and honeycomb iced parfait with elderflowers and strawberries. *Benchmark main dish: himalayan salt dry-aged lamb rump with crispy shoulder, morels and lyonnaise potatoes £25.00. Two-course evening meal £25.00.*

Free house ~ Licensee Alistair Ewing ~ Real ale ~ Open 12-10.45; 12-11.45 Sat; 12-10 Sun ~ Bar food 12-2.30, 6-9; 12-3, 6-8 Sun ~ Restaurant ~ Children welcome ~ Dogs allowed in bar and bedrooms ~ Wi-fi ~ Bedrooms: /£130 *Recommended by Sam Cole, Darrell Barton, Nicola and Nigel Matthews, Michael and Sarah Lockley, Caroline Sullivan, Hilary and Neil Christopher*

 ROWDE   ST9762   Map 2
George & Dragon
(01380) 723053 – www.thegeorgeanddragonrowde.co.uk
A342 Devizes–Chippenham; SN10 2PN

Gently upmarket inn with good food, west country ales and a relaxed atmosphere; bedrooms

After enjoying a walk along the nearby Kennet & Avon Canal, why not come to this 16th-c former coaching inn for an excellent meal. The two low-ceilinged character rooms have beams, large open fireplaces, wooden dining chairs (both straightforward and rather elegant) and wall seats with scatter cushions around candlelit tables, antique rugs and walls hung with old pictures and portraits; the atmosphere is pleasantly chatty. From the rustic bar counter, friendly staff serve Butcombe Bitter and guests from breweries such as Prescott and Kennet & Avon on handpump and several wines by the glass. There are tables and chairs in the pretty garden. Bedrooms are individually furnished and well equipped and breakfasts are well regarded.

The first class daily fresh fish from Cornwall is the highlight here: crispy salt cod fritters with garlic aioli, salmon tartare with avocado, lime and chilli on toasted rye bread, hake with prawn and whisky chowder and rainbow chard and cod fillet with heritage tomato-stuffed peppers and olive sauce. They also offer twice-baked cheese soufflé with parmesan cream, asparagus, pea and parmesan risotto with pesto oil, slow-roasted pork belly with borlotti beans and salsa verde, and puddings such as lemon posset with grapefruit mint salad and chocolate espresso roulade with jersey cream. *Benchmark main dish: crispy crumbed dover sole with chips and hollandaise sauce £27.00. Two-course evening meal £26.00.*

Free house ~ Licensee Christopher Day ~ Real ale ~ Open 12-3, 6-11; 12-4, 6-11 Sat; 12-4 Sun; closed Sun evening ~ Bar food 12-3 (4 Sat), 6-10; 12-4 Sun ~ Restaurant ~ Children welcome ~ Dogs allowed in bar and bedrooms ~ Wi-fi ~ Bedrooms: £75/£95 *Recommended by Susie and Spencer Gray, Barry Collett, Ian Malone, Douglas Power, Peter Barratt, Jack and Hilary Burton, Melanie and David Lawson*

SHERSTON   ST8585   Map 2
Rattlebone
(01666) 840871 – www.therattlebone.co.uk
Church Street; B4040 Malmesbury–Chipping Sodbury; SN16 0LR

17th-c village pub with rambling rooms, real ales and good bar food using local and free-range produce; friendly staff

There's a great deal of character here, as well as highly popular food and a good bustling atmosphere, drawing in customers from far and wide. The rambling, softly lit rooms have beams, standing timbers and flagstones, pews, settles and country kitchen chairs around an assortment of tables, and armchairs and sofas by roaring fires. Flying Monk Elmers, St Austell Tribute and Timothy Taylors Landlord on handpump, 20 wines by the glass from a thoughtful list, local cider and home-made lemonade; background music, darts, board games, TV and games machine. Outside is a skittle alley and three boules pitches, often in use by one of the many pub teams; a boules festival is held in July, as well as mangold hurling (similar to boules, but using cattle-feed turnips) and other events. The two pretty gardens include an extended terrace where they hold barbecues and spit roasts. Bedrooms should be ready by the time this *Guide* is published. Wheelchair access.

Tempting food includes lunchtime sandwiches, seafood terrine with lime jelly and potato salad, battered courgette with wasabi mayonnaise and sweetcorn pannacotta, sharing platters, chickpea and sweet potato coconut curry with cauliflower rice, coq au vin with creamy mash, crispy coated mackerel fillets with rhubarb compote and green salad, a pie of the day, duck breast with mango purée, pak choi and spring onion mash, haddock fillet with spicy butter and prawns, and puddings such as peanut butter and white chocolate cheesecake with salted caramel sauce and strawberry trifle; gourmet burger night is Monday and steak night is Wednesday. *Benchmark main dish: pork T-bone steak with goats cheese, pesto and roasted cherry tomatoes £14.25. Two-course evening meal £21.00.*

Youngs ~ Tenant Jason Read ~ Real ale ~ Open 12-3, 5-11; 12-midnight Fri, Sat; 12-11 Sun ~ Bar food 12-2.30, 6-9.30; 12-5 Sun ~ Restaurant ~ Children welcome ~ Dogs allowed in bar ~ Wi-fi *Recommended by Helene Grygar, Lorna and Jeff Mason, Andrea and Laurie Grist, John and Mary Warner, Alfie Bayliss, Alison and Michael Harper, Nick Sharpe*

SOUTH WRAXALL
Longs Arms

ST8364 Map 2

(01225) 864450 – www.thelongsarms.com

Upper S Wraxall, off B3109 N of Bradford-on-Avon; BA15 2SB

Friendly owners for well run and handsome old stone inn with plenty of character, real ales and first class food

Excellent, inventive food is always a huge draw, but when it's also cooked by the convivial landlord, that's the proverbial cherry on the cake. There was some refurbishment in 2019, but the bar still has windsor and other pubby chairs around wooden tables on flagstones, a fireplace with a woodburning stove and high chairs by the counter where they keep Exmoor Gold, Gritchie English Lore and Palmers IPA on handpump, 16 wines and prosecco and champagne by the glass, 24 gins and farm cider. Another room has cushioned and other dining chairs, a nice old settle and a wall banquette around a mix of tables on carpeting, fresh flowers and prints and paintings; background music. There are tables and chairs in the pretty walled back garden, which also has raised beds and a greenhouse for growing their salad leaves and herbs.

Imaginative food includes nibbles such as crab and sesame spring rolls with peanut and chilli pickle and venison scotch egg plus citrus-cured monkfish with smoked almonds, ginger, sesame and yoghurt, chicken liver parfait with rowan jelly and hazelnuts, oyster mushrooms with curry sauce and sautéed potatoes, steamed lamb and mint suet pudding with buttermilk mash, maple-cured ham with crackling and eggs, halibut with potato terrine, samphire, crab sauce and sea kale, duck breast with confit potatoes, red cabbage and caramelised walnuts, and puddings such as caramelised lemon tart with raspberries and mint and salted caramel fondant with biscuit ice-cream. *Benchmark main dish: pork belly with black pudding, truffle mash and crackling £21.00. Two-course evening meal £23.00.*

Free house ~ Licensees Rob and Liz Allcock ~ Real ale ~ Open 12-3.30, 6-11.30; 12-5 Sun; closed Sun evening, Mon, Tues; three weeks Jan, two weeks Sept ~ Bar food 12-2.30, 6-9.30;

12-3 Sun ~ Children welcome ~ Dogs welcome ~ Wi-fi *Recommended by Monica and Steph Evans, GSB, Michael Doswell, Angela and Steve Heard, Julie and Andrew Blanchett, Sarah Roberts, Joe and Belinda Smart*

 SWALLOWCLIFFE ST9627 Map 2
Royal Oak
(01747) 870211 – www.royaloakswallowcliffe.com
Signed just off A30 Wilton–Shaftesbury; Common Lane; SP3 5PA

Thoughtfully restored inn with attractive décor, a well stocked bar, good seasonal food and seats in garden; bedrooms

This is a pretty, part-thatched pub, carefully and stylishly refurbished by a group of villagers after a long closure. There's a gently civilised atmosphere plus contemporary and locally made pale oak chairs, benches and tables on flagstones, light paintwork and chesterfield sofas facing each other in front of the inglenook fireplace. A row of stools line the planked counter where helpful staff serve a beer named for the pub (from Butcombe) plus guests from Box Steam and Flying Monk on handpump, 14 wines by the glass, ten gins, local cider and perry and a good choice of teas and coffee; board games. The conservatory dining room, beautifully beamed and timbered, is similarly furnished to the bar, with logs piled tightly into fireplaces and wall-to-wall windows. Doors open from here on to the terrace and garden, where there are rustic tables surrounded by chairs and benches. The six bedrooms are spotlessly clean, extremely comfortable and up to date; breakfasts are first class. There are plenty of surrounding walks and places to visit, such as Old Wardour Castle (English Heritage).

Enjoyable food includes sandwiches, lamb fritter with goats curd, charred shallots and salsa verde, crisp ricotta dumplings with chilli and almonds, spiced cauliflower steak with almond butter, pomegranate and cauliflower dressing, home-cooked ham and eggs, cod with mussels, charred leeks, apple and cider sauce, duck breast with crispy leg, celeriac and griottine cherry jus, rib-eye steak with garlic butter and chips, and puddings such as coconut pannacotta with pineapple and chilli salsa and pineapple sorbet and orange rice pudding with pistachios and rhubarb. *Benchmark main dish: slow-cooked pork belly with mustard mash and roasting juices £17.00. Two-course evening meal £26.00.*

Free house ~ Licensee Steve Radford ~ Real ale ~ Open 11am-11.30pm ~ Bar food 12-2.30, 6-9 (8.45 Sun) ~ Restaurant ~ Children welcome ~ Dogs allowed in bar and bedrooms ~ Wi-fi ~ Bedrooms: /£100 *Recommended by Sally and Lance Oldham, Michael and Sarah Lockley, Rupert and Sandy Newton, Michael Doswell, Glen and Patricia Fuller, David and Judy Robison*

SWINDON SU1384 Map 2
Weighbridge Brewhouse
(01793) 881500 – www.weighbridgebrewhouse.co.uk
Penzance Drive; SN5 7JL

Stunning building with stylish modern décor, own microbrewery ales, imaginative food and friendly, well trained staff

As we went to press, this stylish place was being refurbished. The bar area will have a striking, illuminated tree at its centre, station clocks on the walls (this was once a weighing station for trains) and upholstered, teal-coloured stools lining the bar. As well as their own-brewed Brinkworth Village, Pooleys Golden and guest ale from the new chrome handpumps, friendly staff serve wines by the glass from a carefully chosen list and cocktails. Smartly modern and open-plan, the dining room has a steel-tensioned high-raftered roof (the big central skylight adds even more light), attractive high-backed orange or teal chairs and long wall banquettes and bare brick walls hung with black and white pictures showcasing the building and the town's railway heritage. There are some seats on the outside terrace.

First class food includes sandwiches, tea-smoked pigeon with lovage emulsion, gooseberries and hazelnuts, crab and crayfish cocktail with avocado and marie rose sauce, vegetable goan curry, burger with toppings, carrot and kohlrabi slaw and fries, calves liver with smoked bacon, olive oil mash and onion jus, mixed seafood linguine, grilled chicken and halloumi salad, duck breast with dauphinoise potatoes, pea and bean fricassée and griottine cherry sauce, slow-cooked pork belly marinated in soy, honey and ginger with asian-style sweet and sour noodles, dry-aged steaks with a choice of sauce and triple-cooked chips, and puddings. *Benchmark main dish: fillet steak with wild mushroom sauce and truffle and parmesan fries £35.00. Two-course evening meal £30.00.*

Upham ~ Real ale ~ Open 12-11; 12-10 Sun ~ Restaurant ~ Children welcome ~ Dogs allowed in bar ~ Wi-fi ~ Regular live music (check website) *Recommended by Julie and Andrew Blanchett, Mike and Sarah Abbot, Geoffrey and Sarah Sutton, Jack and Hilary Burton, Belinda Stamp*

TOLLARD ROYAL
King John 🌟 ⛺
(01725) 516207 – www.kingjohninn.co.uk

ST9317   Map 2

B3081 Shaftesbury–Sixpenny Handley; SP5 5PS

Pleasing contemporary furnishings in carefully opened-up pub, courteous, helpful service, good drinks and excellent food; pretty bedrooms

Our readers enjoy their visits to this friendly, civilised pub very much. The open-plan L-shaped bar has a log fire, nice little touches such as a pot of herbs and tiny metal buckets of salt and pepper on scrubbed kitchen tables, a screen made up of the sides of wine boxes, and candles in big glass jars. An attractive mix of seats takes in spindlebacks, captain's and chapel chairs (some built into the bay windows) plus the odd cushioned settle, and there are big terracotta floor tiles, lantern-style wall lights, hound, hunting and other photographs, and prints of early 19th-c scientists. A beer named for the pub (from Marstons), Gritchie English Lore and Waylands Sixpenny 6d Gold on handpump and wines from a good list. A second log fire has fender seats on each side and leather chesterfields in front, and there's also a stuffed heron and grouse; daily papers and background music. Outside at the front are seats and tables beneath parasols, with more up steps in the raised garden where there's also an outdoor kitchen pavilion. Bedrooms are comfortable and pretty.

Impressive food includes sandwiches, cured mackerel with smoked cods roe, radish and apple, pickled baby vegetables with smoked tofu and wild garlic, twice-baked cheddar cheese soufflé with fries, whole lemon sole with clams, capers and samphire, slow-cooked pig cheeks with vegetable broth, beer-battered fish and chips, local sirloin steak with béarnaise sauce and fries, and puddings such as frangipane tart with cinnamon-poached pear and amaretto ice-cream and apple doughnuts with toffee sauce and bay leaf ice-cream. *Benchmark main dish: burger with toppings and chips £15.50. Two-course evening meal £26.00.*

Free house ~ Licensee Monika Kulicka ~ Real ale ~ Open 11-11; 11-10.30 Sun ~ Bar food 12-2.30, 6-9; 12-4, 6-8.30 Sun ~ Restaurant ~ Children welcome ~ Dogs welcome ~ Wi-fi ~ Bedrooms: /£110 *Recommended by Sam Cole, Mr and Mrs P R Thomas, Tim and Sue Mulligan, Naomi and Andrew Randall, Anne and Ben Smith, Isobel Mackinlay, Alison and Michael Harper*

Also Worth a Visit in Wiltshire

Besides the fully inspected pubs, you might like to try these pubs that have been recommended to us and described by readers. Do tell us what you think of them: feedback@goodguides.com

ALVEDISTON   ST9723
Crown (01722) 780203
Off A30 W of Salisbury; SP5 5JY
Welcoming 15th-c thatched inn reopened in 2018 after long closure; three very low-beamed, partly panelled rooms, two inglenooks, good fairly priced traditional food including signature steak and kidney pudding, four well kept local ales; darts and board games; children, walkers and dogs welcome, pretty views from attractive garden with terrace, good walks nearby, three comfortable bedrooms, generous breakfast.
(Simon and Alex Knight)

BADBURY   SU1980
Plough (01793) 740342
A346 (Marlborough Road) just S of M4 junction 15; SN4 0EP Busy recently refurbished country pub; wide choice of fairly priced food (all day weekends) including daily specials, well kept Arkells beers, decent wines and good range of gins, friendly service, spacious tartan-carpeted bar with log fire, light airy dining room; background music; children and dogs welcome, far-reaching views from tree-shaded garden, open all day, breakfast from 10am Mon-Sat, useful M4 stop. *(Martin Ellis)*

BARFORD ST MARTIN   SU0531
Barford Inn (01722) 742242
B3089 W of Salisbury (Grovely Road), just off A30; SP3 4AB Welcoming 16th-c coaching inn; dark panelled front bar with big log fire, well kept Badger ales and decent wines by the glass, other connecting rooms including beamed bare-brick restaurant, wide choice of popular reasonably priced food (not Sun evening), prompt friendly service; children and dogs welcome, wheelchair access (not to bar), disabled loo, tables on terrace and in back garden, four annexe bedrooms, good walks, open all day.
(Frances and Hamish Porter)

BECKHAMPTON   SU0868
Waggon & Horses (01672) 539418
A4 Marlborough–Calne; SN8 1QJ Handsome stone and thatch former coaching inn; decent choice of enjoyable fairly priced food (not Sun evening) including gluten-free options in open-plan beamed bar or separate dining area, well kept Wadworths ales, friendly service; background music; children and dogs welcome, pleasant raised garden with play area, handy for Avebury (NT), open all day.
(Thomas Green)

BERWICK ST JAMES   SU0739
★**Boot** (01722) 790243
High Street (B3083); SP3 4TN Welcoming 18th-c flint and stone pub not far from Stonehenge; good locally sourced food (not Sun evening, Mon) from daily changing blackboard menu cooked by landlord-chef, friendly efficient staff, well kept Wadworths ales and a guest, huge log fire in inglenook at one end, sporting prints over brick fireplace the other, small back dining room with collection of celebrity boots; children and dogs welcome, sheltered side lawn, open 6-8pm Mon (12-3pm bank holidays), otherwise regular hours. *(Michael Sargent)*

BERWICK ST JOHN   ST9422
★**Talbot** (01747) 828222
Village signed from A30 E of Shaftesbury; SP7 0HA Unspoilt 17th-c pub in attractive village; simple furnishings and big inglenook in heavily beamed bar, Ringwood Best, Wadworths 6X and a guest, several wines by the glass, reasonable choice of popular home-made food including some vegetarian options, friendly service, restaurant; darts, free wi-fi; children and dogs (pub has its own) welcome, seats outside, good local walks, closed Sun evening, Mon. *(David and Judy Robison, James Golob)*

BIDDESTONE   ST8673
White Horse (01249) 713350
The Green; SN14 7DG Prettily placed 16th-c three-room local near the village duck pond; a couple of well kept ales, plenty of wines by the glass and enjoyable good value food (not Sun evening) from snacks up, friendly staff; children and dogs welcome, tables out at front and in back garden with clematis-covered pergola and play area, open all day Sun, closed Mon. *(Michael Doswell, Dr and Mrs A K Clarke)*

BISHOPSTONE   SU2483
Royal Oak (01793) 790481
Cues Lane; near Swindon; at first exit roundabout from A419 N of M4 junction 15, follow sign for Wanborough then

---

We mention bottled beers and spirits only if there is something unusual about them – imported belgian real ales, say, or dozens of malt whiskies; so do please let us know about them in your reports.

*Bishopstone, at small sign on telegraph
pole turn left; SN6 8PP* Informal dining
pub run by local farmers in pretty village
below Ridgeway and White Horse; well liked
seasonal food from daily changing menu
including properly hung home-reared steaks,
Arkells beers, organic wines, and good choice
of whiskies and gins; mainly scrubbed-wood
furnishings on bare boards or parquet,
log fire on left and little maze of pews,
refurbished upstairs dining area (same level
as garden) with own bar and good disabled
access/loos; children and dogs welcome,
modern furniture on front deck, picnic-sets
on grass and among trees, 12 bedrooms in
separate building, open all day Sun.
(Eddie King)

BOX   ST8168
Northey Arms (01225) 742333
A4, Bath side; SN13 8AE 19th-c stone-
built dining pub; good food from snacks
up including daily specials (fresh fish),
children's menu and Tues steak night, up to
four real ales and 18 wines by the glass from
well stocked bar (Fri happy hour 4-6.30pm),
friendly young staff, fresh contemporary
décor with chunky modern tables and high-
backed rattan chairs, open fire; background
music; tables and play area in garden behind,
ten well appointed bedrooms, open (and
food) all day from 8am for breakfast.
(Dr and Mrs A K Clarke)

BOX   ST8369
Quarrymans Arms (01225) 743569
*Pub signed from A4 at Box Hill in both
directions; SN13 8HN* Former local for
Bath-stone miners with related photographs
and memorabilia; well kept Butcombe and
guests, generally well liked food (all day
Fri-Sun) including daily specials, friendly
staff; children, walkers and dogs welcome,
picnic-sets on terrace with sweeping views,
four bedrooms, open all day.
(Dr and Mrs A K Clarke)

BRADFORD-ON-AVON   ST8060
Cross Guns (01225) 862335
*Avoncliff, 2 miles W of Bradford-on-Avon
on Turleigh road, turn left for Avoncliff;
park at dead end and walk across the
bridge; BA15 2HB* Popular 16th-c pub with
steeply terraced areas above the bridges,
aqueduct and river; bare boards, stripped
stone and inglenook log fire in opened-up
low-beamed interior, four changing ales, local
ciders and extensive range of spirits (over
100 gins), enjoyable food including 'bunny
chow' (south african curry in hollowed-out
bread), friendly helpful service, summer
deli with home-made quiches, wraps, cakes
etc; maybe sea shanties Tues evening, beer
festivals Mar and Oct; children and dogs
welcome, wheelchair access but no disabled
loo, canal moorings nearby, open (and food)
all day, till 8pm (7pm) Sun. *(Chris and
Sophie Baxter)*

BRADFORD-ON-AVON   ST8261
Dandy Lion (01225) 863433
Market Street; BA15 1LL Comfortably
modernised 18th-c pub; bar with stripped-
wood floor and painted panelling, steps up to
snug, more room in carpeted upstairs dining
room, Wadworths ales, over a dozen wines by
glass and good reasonably priced home-made
food from fairly pubby menu, friendly service;
background music, board games, free wi-fi;
children and dogs welcome, open (and food)
all day. *(David and Stella Martin)*

BRADFORD-ON-AVON   ST8161
Dog & Fox (01225) 862137
Ashley Road; BA15 1RT Welcoming
unpretentious two-room local on country
outskirts; beams and painted half-panelling,
well kept ales such as Butcombe, Courage
and Timothy Taylors, four ciders and
enjoyable affordably priced pub food, right-
hand part with little serving hatch and comfy
seating by woodburner, carpeted dining area
behind, small bare-boards bar to the left with
darts; children and dogs welcome, picnic-sets
and play area in lawned garden, open all day
Sat, Sun. *(Dr and Mrs A K Clarke)*

BRADFORD-ON-AVON   ST8261
★**George** (01225) 865650
Woolley Street; BA15 1AQ Neatly updated
18th-c stone dining pub with highly regarded
food including good value set menus and
themed evenings (last Thurs of month –
booking advised), also weekend breakfast
(from 9.30am) and afternoon teas (Fri-Sun),
efficient friendly service, a house beer from
Butcombe and a couple of guests, good
choice of wines and whiskies; two smallish
rooms either side of entrance (one with
open kitchen), mix of tables and chairs on
wood floors, pictures for sale, cosy back
lounge bar with sofas and wing chairs by log
fire; children and dogs welcome, attractive
split-level back garden, two self-catering
apartments, open all day Fri and Sat, till
6pm Sun. *(Michael Doswell)*

BRADFORD-ON-AVON   ST8261
Stumble Inn (01225) 862115
Market Street; BA15 1LL Friendly
two-room micropub; four changing ales
(two tapped from the cask), craft beers
and decent range of wines, no food;
settles and pews, old enamel signs and big
fireplace; board games, closed Sun, Mon and
lunchtimes apart from Sat. *(Sue Ormsby)*

BRINKWORTH   SU0184
Three Crowns (01666) 510366
*The Street; B4042 Wootton Bassett–
Malmesbury; SN15 5AF* Old stone pub
under newish ownership; beamed bar with
cushioned wall settles and sturdy mate's
chairs around tables on patterned carpet,
fireplace at each end, Butcombe Original and
a couple of guests, Thatcher's and Weston's

ciders, 15 wines by the glass, flagstoned conservatory restaurant and other spreading dining areas with shelves of bottles and a giant pair of bellows, good food from pub staples up including daily specials and weekend breakfasts, small shop; children welcome, dogs in bar (menu for them), tables under parasols on terrace, more seats in garden, open all day, no food Sun evening. *(Catherine and Daniel King)*

BROKENBOROUGH   ST9189
★**Horse Guards** (01666) 822302
Signed from Malmesbury on Tetbury road; SN16 0HZ Well run 18th-c village dining pub with fresh modern décor; beams and some bare stone walls in cosy bar, large two-way woodburner, lower back part mainly for their good home-made food using local ingredients including seasonal game, well kept Uley and a guest, interesting wines from shortish list (most available by the glass), welcoming owners and friendly staff; children and dogs allowed, two comfortable bedrooms, closed Mon lunchtime. *(Sam Cole)*

BROMHAM   ST9665
★**Greyhound** (01380) 850241
Off A342; High Street; SN15 2HA Popular and welcoming old dining pub (same owners as George in Sandy Lane); bar with white-painted beams and light modern décor, snug area to the right, dining part to the left, wood and tartan-carpeted floors, woodburner, back restaurant with walk-across well, good reasonably priced food cooked by landlord-chef including weekday lunch deal, efficient friendly service, well kept Wadworths ales and wide choice of wines, upstairs skittle alley/overflow restaurant; background music; children welcome, dogs in bar, circular picnic-sets in big enclosed garden with play equipment, ample parking in square opposite, closed Sun evening, Mon, otherwise open all day. *(Barry Collett, Michael Doswell)*

BULKINGTON   ST9458
Well (01380) 828287
High Street; SN10 1SJ Popular dining pub with modernised open-plan interior; good food from sandwiches and traditional favourites up, efficient friendly service, four real ales including Butcombe, Sharps and Timothy Taylors, well priced wines; background music, free wi-fi; children and dogs (in bar) welcome, wheelchair access, closed Mon. *(Darrell Barton)*

CASTLE COMBE   ST8477
Castle Inn (01249) 783030
Off A420; SN14 7HN Handsome old pub in remarkably preserved Cotswold village; beamed bar with big stone fireplace, padded

bar stools and fine old settle, some vintage french posters, ales such as Castle Combe and St Austell from oak servery, 18 wines by the glass including champagne, well liked traditional food served by friendly attentive staff, two snug lounges, formal dining rooms and big upstairs conservatory opening on to charming little terrace; children and dogs (in bar) welcome, tables out at front looking down idyllic main street, fascinating medieval church clock, 12 bedrooms, car park shared with next-door hotel, open all day from 9.30am (food from midday). *(Tony Scott)*

CASTLE COMBE   ST8379
Salutation (01249) 782083
The Gibb; B4039 Acton Turville–Chippenham, near Nettleton; SN14 7LH Friendly old pub with traditional L-shaped bar, beams, stripped stone and woodburner in handsome fireplace, well kept Fortitude and a guest such as Flying Monk, good locally sourced food from regularly changing menu including bargain two-course weekday lunch, lofty thatched and timbered barn restaurant; children and dogs welcome, nice garden, open all day. *(Michael Doswell)*

CHICKSGROVE   ST9729
★**Compasses** (01722) 714318
From A30 5.5 miles W of B3089 junction, take lane on N side signposted 'Sutton Mandeville, Sutton Row', then first left fork (small signs point the way to the pub in Lower Chicksgrove; look out for the car park); can also be reached off B3089 W of Dinton, passing the glorious spire of Teffont Evias church; SP3 6NB Popular 14th-c thatched inn with unchanging character bar; old bottles and jugs hanging from beams above the roughly timbered counter, farm tools and traps on stripped-stone walls, high-backed settles forming snug booths, flagstones and log fire, ales such as Butcombe, Keystone and Three Daggers, real cider and a dozen wines by the glass, good sensibly priced food (not Sun evening) from interesting menu; children and dogs welcome, quiet garden behind with terraces and courtyard, good surrounding walks, comfortable bedrooms and self-catering cottage, open all day in summer. *(Helene Grygar, Harriet, David Hastings)*

CHILMARK   ST9732
Black Dog (01722) 716344
B3089 Salisbury–Hindon; SP3 5AH Cosy and welcoming 15th-c beamed village pub; several linked areas, cushioned window seats, inglenook woodburner and interesting photographs from around the world, good

---

If you stay overnight in an inn or hotel, they are allowed to serve you an alcoholic drink at any hour of the day or night.

food with emphasis on fish/seafood, three well kept Wadworths ales, friendly attentive service; children and dogs (in bar) welcome, disabled access, good-sized garden fenced from the road, open (and some food) all day, breakfast from 9am Sun. *(Gene and Kitty Rankin, Mike Miller)*

CHIPPENHAM ST9173
Old Road Tavern (01249) 247080
Old Road, by N side of station; SN15 1JA Friendly old-fashioned 19th-c town pub; public bar and two-part lounge, half a dozen well kept ales including Bath, Otter and Wye Valley, straightforward lunchtime food Thurs-Sat; live music and comedy nights in side barn, pool; nice secluded back garden, handy for station, open all day. *(Dr and Mrs A K Clarke)*

CHOLDERTON SU2242
Crown (01980) 629247
A338 Tidworth–Salisbury roundabout, just off A303; SP4 0DW Thatched low-beamed cottage with nicely informal eating areas in L-shaped bar; a couple of well kept changing ales, ciders such as Aspall's and Broadoak and good food cooked to order by landlord-chef, separate restaurant; quiz first Weds of month, occasional live music, beer/cider festival Sept; children and dogs welcome, picnic-sets out at front and in garden with play area, open (and food) all day Sun. *(Ian Duncan)*

CHRISTIAN MALFORD ST9678
Rising Sun (01249) 721571
Station Road; SN15 4BL Refurbished community-run village pub dating from the early 19th-c; small beamed bar with wood floor, leather sofas by log fire, three well kept seasonally changing ales, ciders such as Black Rat, carpeted restaurant with high-backed dining chairs around modern wooden tables, enjoyable well presented food (not Sun evening, all Mon, Tues lunchtime), good friendly service; children and dogs (in bar) welcome, disabled loo, a few picnic-sets out at front, play area and boules in back garden, open all day weekends, closed Mon and Tues lunchtimes. *(Charlotte and William Mason)*

COLLINGBOURNE DUCIS SU2453
Tipple Inn (01264) 850050
High Street; SN8 3EQ Comfortable 18th-c village pub well cared for by friendly landlord; three changing ales and fairly standard home-cooked food (not Sun or Mon evenings) from good baguettes up, woodburners in bar and smallish restaurant with light wood furniture and some vibrant artwork; quiz and live music nights, sports TV, pool, darts and free wi-fi; children, walkers and dogs welcome, small roadside terrace with pretty hanging baskets, grassy garden behind beyond car park, one bedroom, closed Tues. *(Adam Jones)*

CORSHAM ST8770
Flemish Weaver (01249) 701929
High Street; SN13 0EZ Town pub in attractive 17th-c building revamped in quirky style with all kinds of bits and pieces; good food (not Sun evening) and four well kept ales including a Wadworths house beer, friendly enthusiastic young staff; some live music; children and dogs welcome, tables in intriguing back courtyard, open all day. *(Dr and Mrs A K Clarke)*

CORSHAM ST8670
★Methuen Arms (01249) 717060
High Street; SN13 0HB Butcombe-owned Georgian inn under new management; bare-boards front bar with stools, built-in cushioned wall seats and a settle around mix of tables, woodburner, their ales and a couple of guests, 21 wines by the glass and decent range of malt whiskies/gins, good food from breakfast and light lunches up (can be pricey) in bar's dining room or parquet-floored restaurant; afternoon teas; background music; children and dogs (in bar) welcome, pretty garden with parasol-shaded tables, smart comfortable bedrooms, open all day. *(Jacqui and Alan Swan, Mr and Mrs P R Thomas, Colin McLachlan, Dr and Mrs A K Clarke, Valerie and Gordon Wauton)*

CORTON ST9340
★Dove (01985) 850109
Off A36 at Upton Lovell, SE of Warminster; BA12 0SZ Modernised and extended brick pub on edge of small Wylye Valley village not far from the A303; popular well prepared food from sandwiches and pub favourites to more enterprising dishes including generous fish boards, well kept Otter, Wadworths and local guests, Thatcher's cider and nice wines by the glass from comprehensive list, chatty helpful staff, opened-up rooms with flagstones and light oak boards, pale green dados and lots of animal pictures/figurines, flowers on good quality dining tables, log fires, sunny conservatory; children and dogs welcome, wheelchair access/loos, grassy beer garden sheltered by thatched cob wall, five good stable-block bedrooms and self-catering cottage, open all day and can get very busy. *(Chris and Angela Buckell, Edward Mirzoeff)*

DEVIZES SU0061
Black Swan (01380) 727777
Market Place; SN10 1JQ Traditional 18th-c coaching inn with plenty of atmosphere; quirky bare-boards interior filled with antiques and interesting bits and pieces (lots for sale), candles and open fire, Wadworths ales and a guest, sensibly priced food (not Sun evening) from fairly pubby menu, friendly service; quiz Thurs; children and dogs welcome, nice courtyard garden with own bar (weekend live music and DJs), 12 bedrooms, open all day. *(Ann and Colin Hunt)*

DEVIZES SU0061
British Lion (01380) 720665
A361 Swindon roundabout; SN10 1LQ
Chatty little drinkers' pub with four well kept
quickly changing ales and a proper cider,
bare-boards bar with brewery mirrors and gas
fire, back part with pool and darts, no food;
free wi-fi; garden behind, open all day.
(Sandra and Nigel Brown)

DEVIZES SU0061
Three Crowns (01380) 722331
Maryport Street; SN10 1AG Popular
town-centre pub with good food and well
kept range of Wadworths ales, cider from
a couple of barrels behind the bar, efficient
helpful staff; some live music; children and
dogs welcome, lovely sunny courtyard garden,
open all day. *(Richard Tilbrook)*

DONHEAD ST ANDREW ST9124
★ Forester (01747) 828038
*Village signposted off A30 E of
Shaftesbury, just E of Ludwell; Lower
Street; SP7 9EE* Attractive 14th-c thatched
restaurant-pub in charming village; nice
relaxed bar with stripped tables on wood
floors and inglenook log fire, sofa and
magazines in alcove, Butcombe Bitter, a
guest beer and good selection of wines by the
glass including champagne, highly regarded
food (some emphasis on fresh fish/seafood),
also lunchtime sandwiches, efficient friendly
service, comfortable restaurant with well
spaced country kitchen tables, second cosier
dining room; children and dogs welcome,
rural views from spacious terrace, can walk
up White Sheet Hill and past the old and 'new'
Wardour castles, closed Sun evening, Mon.
(John and Hilary Murphy, Andrew Low)

DOWNTON SU1721
Wooden Spoon (01725) 511899
*High Street (A338 S of Salisbury);
SP5 3PG* Popular 18th-c red-brick pub with
two bars; well kept ales and good reasonably
priced food from blackboard menus, friendly
efficient service, open fire, extensive
banknote collection; children and dogs
welcome, appealing garden behind, closes
9pm Sun. *(Valerie Sayer)*

EBBESBOURNE WAKE ST9924
★ Horseshoe (01722) 780474
*On A354 S of Salisbury, right at
signpost at Coombe Bissett; village
about 8 miles further; SP5 5JF* Popular
unspoilt village pub under welcoming long-
serving licensees; Bowman, Gritchie, Otter
and guests tapped from chilled casks, real
cider, generous helpings of good traditional
home-cooked food served by friendly staff,
neatly kept and comfortable character bar
with collection of farm tools and bric-a-brac
on beams, small restaurant and conservatory;
children welcome away from bar, dogs at
landlord's discretion, seats in pretty little

garden with views over Ebble Valley, play
area, chickens and goat in paddock, good
nearby walks, one bedroom, closed Sun
evening, Mon. *(David and Judy Robison)*

ENFORD SU14351
★ Swan (01980) 670338
Long Street, off A345; SN9 6DD
Attractive and welcoming thatched village
pub; opened-up beamed interior with log fire
in large fireplace, five well kept changing
ales and good locally sourced home-made
food from lunchtime sandwiches and
snacks up, prompt friendly service; darts
and board games, beer/music festival Aug
Bank Holiday; children, walkers and dogs
welcome, seats out on small front terrace and
in big landscaped back garden, gallows-style
inn sign spanning the road, open all day
weekends, closed Mon lunchtime.
(Michael Doswell)

FORD ST8474
White Hart (01249) 782213
*Off A420 Chippenham–Bristol;
SN14 8RP* Handsome 16th-c Marstons-
managed country inn; beamed bars with bare
boards or quarry tiles, dining and tub chairs,
cushioned wall seats and button-back sofas,
lots of prints on bold paintwork, open fire and
woodburner, three real ales including Bath
Gem and a beer badged for the pub, good
range of other drinks (20 wines by the glass),
much liked food from sandwiches/baguettes
to signature steaks cooked in charcoal oven,
friendly efficient staff; free wi-fi; children and
dogs (in bar) welcome, front courtyard and
terrace, trout stream by small stone bridge,
comfortable modern bedrooms, open (and
food) all day. *(Mr and Mrs D J Nash, Dr and Mrs
A K Clarke, Richard and Judy Winn)*

FOXHAM ST9777
Foxham Inn (01249) 740665
NE of Chippenham; SN15 4NQ Small
tucked-away country dining pub with
simple traditional décor: enterprising food
strong on local produce along with more
straightforward bar meals and themed
nights, well kept ales such as St Austell
Tribute, nice choice of wines by the glass and
good coffee, woodburner, more contemporary
conservatory-style restaurant with kitchen
view, own bread, chutneys, jams etc for sale;
children and dogs welcome, disabled access
and facilities, terrace with pergola, extensive
views from front, two comfortable bedrooms,
closed Mon. *(Michael Doswell)*

FROXFIELD SU2968
Pelican (01488) 682479
Off A4, Bath Road; SN8 3JY Modernised
and extended 17th-c coaching inn; enjoyable
home-made food from sandwiches and
panini up, helpful friendly young staff, local
ales such as Wickwar, comfortable relaxed
atmosphere; children and dogs welcome,
pleasant streamside garden with terrace

and duck pond, Kennet & Avon Canal walks (bridge 90), eight bedrooms, open all day, no food Sun evening. *(Penny and Peter Keevil)*

GASTARD   ST8868
Harp & Crown (01249) 715697
Velley Hill; SN13 9PU Spacious stone-built village pub; well kept Wickwar ales and a guest such as Moles, enjoyable sensibly priced food from shortish traditional menu, friendly staff, bar with two-way fireplace into snug, flagstoned dining conservatory; area for darts; children and dogs welcome, picnic-sets out at front on wide pavement and in back garden, open all day weekends, closed Mon lunchtime. *(Edward May)*

GREAT DURNFORD   SU1337
Black Horse (01722) 782270
Follow Woodfords sign from A345 High Post traffic lights; SP4 6AY Popular 17th-c red-brick country pub with under welcoming licensees; four cosy unpretentious rooms with lots of quirky bits and pieces, large inglenook woodburner in one, well kept ales including Ringwood Razorback, real cider and generous helpings of good straightforward home-made food; darts, table skittles; children and dogs welcome, large informal garden with play area, closed Sun evening, Mon. *(Francis and Mandy Robertson)*

HAMPTWORTH   SU2419
Cuckoo (01794) 390302
Hamptworth Road; SP5 2DU Welcoming 17th-c thatched New Forest pub owned by the Hamptworth Estate; peaceful and unspoilt, with friendly mix of customers from farmers to families in four compact rooms around tiny servery, up to nine real ales such as Hop Back and Palmers tapped from the cask, real ciders/perry, simple lunchtime food including sandwiches, ploughman's, pasties and pies, fish and chip van Fri evening, basic wooden furniture (some tables made using Estate trees), open fire and woodburner; shove-ha'penny, shut the box and other traditional games, acoustic live music Sun afternoon; children (till 9pm) and dogs welcome, big garden with view of golf course, two pétanque pitches, open all day. *(Paul Scofield)*

HANNINGTON   SU1793
Jolly Tar (01793) 762245
Off B4019 W of Highworth; Queens Road; SN6 7RP Old painted stone pub in pretty village; beamed bar with big log fire, steps up to flagstoned and stripped-stone dining area, good reasonably priced home-made food including popular Sun lunch (should book), well kept Arkells ales, friendly helpful service; free wi-fi; children and dogs (in bar) welcome, picnic-sets on front terrace and in big garden with play area, four comfortable bedrooms, good breakfast, closed Mon lunchtime, no food Sun evening. *(Susie and Spencer Gray)*

HEDDINGTON   ST9966
Ivy (01380) 859652
Off A3102 S of Calne; SN11 0PL Picturesque thatched village local dating from the 15th c; L-shaped bar with heavy low beams, timbered walls and inglenook log fire, traditional furniture on parquet floor, Wadworths ales tapped from the cask, good wine choice and enjoyable well priced food (just Sun lunchtime and Fri, Sat evenings), back dining room; darts; children and dogs welcome, wheelchair access (no disabled loo), picnic-sets out at front and in small side garden, open all day Fri and Sat, till 9pm Sun, closed Mon and lunchtimes Tues-Thurs. *(Mrs Zara Elliott)*

HINDON   ST9132
Lamb (01747) 820573
B3089 Wilton–Mere; SP3 6DP Attractive old hotel with roomy log-fire bar; two flagstoned lower sections with long polished table, high-backed pews and settles, steps up to third, bigger area, well kept Youngs and a guest, several wines by the glass and good selection of malt whiskies, cocktails and cuban cigars, enjoyable bar and restaurant food, friendly service, can get very busy; children and dogs welcome, tables on roadside terrace and in garden across the road, 18 bedrooms, open all day from 7.30am (8am weekends) for breakfast. *(Gene and Kitty Rankin, Roger and Donna Huggins)*

HOLT   ST8561
Toll Gate (01225) 782326
Ham Green; B3107 W of Melksham; BA14 6PX Friendly 16th-c stone pub; character bar with mix of tables and chairs on pale floorboards, woodburner, well kept ales from Box Steam (brewed in the village), Butcombe and Sharps, three real ciders, 18 wines by the glass (good list) and some interesting gins, dining room with second woodburner; steps up to high-raftered former chapel restaurant, imaginative well presented food along with pub favourites; background music (live Fri evenings July, Aug); board games; children welcome, wheelchair access to main bar area (no disabled loos), seats on sunny back terrace, boules, bedrooms (some in old farm shop) and holiday cottage, handy for Courts Gardens (NT), closed Sun evening, otherwise open all day from 8am (8.30am weekends). *(Martin and Sue Neville, Michael Doswell, Chris and Angela Buckell, Gene and Kitty Rankin, Ian Herdman, Dr and Mrs A K Clarke)*

KILMINGTON   ST7835
Red Lion (01985) 844263
B3092 Mere–Frome, 2.5 miles S of Maiden Bradley; 3 miles from A303 Mere turn-off; BA12 6RP NT-owned country pub with low-beamed flagstoned bar, cushioned wall and window seats, curved high-backed settle, woodburner in big

fireplace at either end, well kept ales such as Butcombe and Wessex, traditional ciders and enjoyable home-made food including lunchtime sandwiches, newer big-windowed back dining area where children allowed; dogs welcome in bar, attractive big garden with fine views, White Sheet Hill (hang-gliding) and Stourhead gardens (NT) nearby, open till 6pm Sun, 8pm Mon-Weds, 9pm other days, evening food Thurs-Sat.
(Edward Mirzoeff)

KINGTON ST MICHAEL   ST9077
Jolly Huntsman   (01249) 750305
Handy for M4 junction 17; SN14 6JB
Roomy 18th-c stone-built pub; Moles and a couple of guests, proper cider and good home-made food from pub standards up, friendly service, carpeted interior with scrubbed tables, comfortable sofas and good log fire; children and dogs (in bar) welcome, bedrooms in separate block. *(Sam Cole)*

LACOCK   ST9268
Bell   (01249) 730308
E of village; SN15 2PJ Extended cottagey pub with warm welcome; local ales including a house beer from Great Western (beer festivals), traditional ciders, well chosen/priced wines and good selection of malt whiskies and gins, enjoyable generously served food from lunchtime platters, pub favourites and grills up, friendly efficient young staff, linked rooms off bar including more formal restaurant and bright airy conservatory; children and dogs (in bar) welcome, disabled access (not to conservatory) from car park, well tended garden with play area and smokers' shelter (the Coughing Shed), long views across Avon Valley, open (and food) all day weekends.
(Dr and Mrs A K Clarke, Chris and Angela Buckell)

LACOCK   ST9168
George   (01249) 730263
West Street; village signed off A350 S of Chippenham; SN15 2LH Rambling old inn at centre of busy NT tourist village; low-beamed bar with upright timbers creating cosy corners, some flagstones and stone-mullioned windows, dog treadwheel in outer breast of central fireplace, lots of pictures including photos of *Cranford* and *Harry Potter* being filmed in the village, six mainly Wadworths beers and Weston's cider, lots of wines by the glass, popular sensibly priced food from sandwiches up, friendly staff; background music; children and dogs welcome, tricky wheelchair access, nice courtyard with pillory and old well, picnic-sets on grass, open all day summer.
(Dr and Mrs A K Clarke, Ann and Colin Hunt)

LACOCK   ST9168
Red Lion   (01249) 730456
High Street; SN15 2LQ Popular NT-owned Georgian inn; sizeable opened-up interior with log fire in big stone fireplace, bare boards and flagstones, roughly carved screens here and there and some cosy alcoves, well kept Wadworths ales, Thatcher's and Weston's ciders, enjoyable food from sandwiches and sharing plates up, friendly efficient service; background music, free wi-fi; children and dogs welcome, wheelchair access to main bar area only, picnic-sets out on gravel, four modern bedrooms, open (and food) all day.
(Dr and Mrs A K Clarke, Reg Robertson)

LACOCK   ST9367
Rising Sun   (01249) 730363
Bewley Common, Bowden Hill – out towards Sandy Lane, up hill past abbey; OS Sheet 173 map reference 935679; SN15 2PP Old stone pub with three knocked-together simply furnished rooms; beams and log fires, Moles, Wickwar and a guest, several proper ciders and fairly traditional food including daily specials, friendly attentive service; background and some live music, free wi-fi; well behaved children and dogs (in bar) welcome, no wheelchair access, wonderful views across Avon Valley from conservatory and two-level terrace, outside bar, open all day in summer (all day Fri and Sat, till 6pm Sun in winter). *(Dr and Mrs A K Clarke)*

LEA   ST9586
Rose & Crown   (01666) 822053
The Street; SN16 9PA Creeper-clad Victorian stone pub next to the village church; enjoyable good value food from sandwiches up, Arkells and guests kept well, over 20 gins, friendly efficient service, compact interconnecting rooms with mix of furnishings, log fires including two-way woodburner; daily newspapers, free wi-fi; children and dogs welcome, picnic-sets out at front and in large well maintained garden with paved terrace and play area, closed Mon, otherwise open (and food) all day, kitchen shuts 5pm Sun. *(Michael Doswell)*

LITTLE SOMERFORD   ST9784
Somerford Arms   (01666) 826535
Signed off B4042 Malmesbury–Brinkworth; SN15 5JP Modernised village pub with opened-up interior; stone flooring, painted half-panelling and two-way woodburner, enjoyable food cooked by father and son team from pub classics up, three well kept changing ales and over a dozen wines by the glass, friendly helpful service; children and dogs welcome, open till 5pm Sun, closed Mon. *(Martin and Sue Neville)*

LOCKERIDGE   SU1467
Who'd A Thought It   (01672) 861255
Signed off A4 Marlborough–Calne, just W of Fyfield; SN8 4EL Attractively revamped village pub-restaurant (sister to the Outside Chance at Manton); popular food from interestingly varied menu, well kept Wadworths beers and decent wines including champagne by the glass, friendly service;

children and dogs welcome, pleasant back garden with play area, lovely bluebell walks nearby in spring, open all day Thurs-Sat, no food Sun evening. *(Dave Snowden)*

LONGBRIDGE DEVERILL ST8640
George (01985) 840396
A350/B3095; BA12 7DG Popular updated and extended roadside inn owned by Upham; well kept ales and generous helpings of enjoyable freshly made food including Sun carvery, friendly helpful service, conservatory; quiz nights; children and dogs (in bar) welcome, big riverside garden with play area, 12 bedrooms, handy for Longleat, open all day, breakfast for non-residents from 8am Mon-Sat. *(Edward Mirzoeff)*

LOWER WOODFORD SU1235
Wheatsheaf (01722) 782203
Signed off A360 just N of Salisbury; SP4 6NQ Updated and extended 18th-c dining pub with airy open feel; decent choice of fairly priced food from sandwiches and sharing boards up, well kept Badger ales, good wines and coffee, beams, panelling and exposed brickwork, mix of old furniture, log fire and woodburner; background music, free wi-fi; well behaved children welcome in restaurant, muddy boots and dogs in bar, disabled loo and parking, fenced tree-lined garden with play area, pretty setting, open (and food) all day. *(I D Barnett)*

LUCKINGTON ST8384
Old Royal Ship (01666) 840222
Off B4040 SW of Malmesbury; SN14 6PA Friendly pub by village green; one long bar divided into three areas, ales such as Sharps and Wadworths from central servery, also traditional cider and several wines by the glass, good range of food including some vegetarian options, neat tables, spindleback chairs and cushioned settles on dark boards, stripped masonry and small open fire; background music, skittle alley; children welcome, plenty of seats in garden (beyond car park) with boules and play area, Badminton House close by, open all day weekends. *(Rupert and Sandy Newton)*

MANTON SU1768
★**Outside Chance** (01672) 512352
Village (and pub) signposted off A4 just W of Marlborough; High Street; SN8 4HW Popular country pub with three small linked rooms (sister to the Who'd A Thought It in Lockeridge); hop-strung beams, flagstones or bare boards, plain pub furnishings such as chapel chairs and a long-cushioned pew, one room has more cosseted feel with banquette seating, décor (as name suggests) celebrates unlikely racing winners such as 100-1 shot Mr Spooner's Only Dreams, log fire in big main fireplace, wide choice of enjoyable food, Wadworths ales and eight wines by the glass; background music, board games; children and dogs welcome,

suntrap side terrace with contemporary tables, more rustic furniture under ash trees in good-sized garden, private access to local playing fields and play area, open all day weekends. *(Freddie and Sarah Banks)*

MARDEN SU0857
★**Millstream** (01380) 848490
Village signposted off A342 SE of Devizes; SN10 3RH Rather smart red-brick dining pub in leafy setting at top end of this attractive village; highly regarded food cooked by landlady-chef including fish/seafood specials and good value Sun lunch (best to book), well kept Wadworths ales, friendly efficient young staff, appealing layout of linked cosy areas, beams and log fires, red-cushioned dark pews and small padded dining chairs around sturdy oak and other good tables, comfy sofas in one part; free wi-fi; children and dogs welcome (resident pointers are Sophie and Francesca), disabled access/loos, neat terrace by entrance and big lawned garden down to tree-lined stream, 12th-c church worth a visit, closed Sun and Mon evenings. *(Michael Doswell)*

MARKET LAVINGTON SU0154
Green Dragon (01380) 813235
High Street; SN10 4AG Rambling early 17th-c red-brick pub; four well kept Wadworths ales, good value wines and enjoyable reasonably priced food from sandwiches and baked potatoes up, friendly welcoming staff; collection of vintage radios, darts, free wi-fi; children and dogs welcome, wheelchair access, large back garden with shelter, six bedrooms (four in converted outbuildings), hearty breakfast, open all day. *(Revd R P Tickle)*

MARLBOROUGH SU1869
Lamb (01672) 512668
The Parade; SN8 1NE Bustling town local attracting good mix of customers; cheerful lived-in main bar with wall banquettes and wheelback chairs around wooden tables on parquet flooring, Cecil Aldin prints on red walls, two-way woodburner, good home-made food lunchtimes and Fri evening, Wadworths ales tapped from the cask, ten wines by the glass and 15 malt whiskies, friendly staff; juke box (live music Sat), games machine, TV and darts; tables in pleasant courtyard, pretty summer window boxes, seven bedrooms, open all day. *(Graham Wheeler, Dave Snowden, Brian and Margaret Merritt)*

MONKTON FARLEIGH ST8065
Kings Arms (01225) 859761
Signed off A363 Bradford–Bath; BA15 2QH Imposing 17th-c stone pub in lovely village; beamed bar with wood-strip floor and inglenook, zinc-topped counter serving three real ales and a traditional cider, enjoyable food from varied menu, parquet-floored restaurant; Sun quiz and occasional live music; children and dogs welcome, seats

in front courtyard, more in two-tier back garden with country views, bedrooms, open (and food) all day. *(Thomas Green)*

NESTON — ST8668
Neston Country Inn (01225) 811694
Church Rise, Pool Green; SN13 9SN
Welcoming unpretentious early 19th-c inn; good reasonably priced food cooked by landlord including some south african influences and themed nights, well kept Fullers London Pride and a couple of local guests, friendly helpful staff; quiz last Thurs of month, darts; children and dogs welcome, picnic-sets in back garden with gate to village playing field, four bedrooms, open all day Sat, till 9pm Sun, closed Mon lunchtime (Tues lunchtime after bank holiday).
(Mr and Mrs P R Thomas)

NETHERHAMPTON — SU1129
★ Victoria & Albert (01722) 743174
Just off A3094 W of Salisbury; SP2 8PU
Cosy black-beamed bar in simple 16th-c thatched cottage; old-fashioned cushioned wall settles on ancient floor tiles, log fire, three well kept changing ales, proper cider and decent wines, welcoming helpful staff, popular home-made food from sandwiches up at sensible prices, restaurant; children and dogs welcome, hatch service for sizeable terrace and garden behind, convenient for Wilton House and Nadder Valley walks, closed Sun evening. *(Simon and Alex Knight)*

NOMANSLAND — SU2517
Lamb (01794) 390246
Signed off B3078 and B3079, Forest Road; SP5 2BP Lovely New Forest village-green setting (the county border runs through the pub); family run and popular with locals, decent choice of enjoyable home-made food from lunchtime baguettes up, popular Sun roasts, four changing ales and sensibly priced wine list, friendly staff, log fire in traditional carpeted bar, small dining room, lots of bits and pieces to look at, games room with pool; TV; children and dogs welcome, tables on front terrace, green (with grazing ponies) and in colourful back garden, open all day Fri-Sun. *(Ann and Colin Hunt, David and Judy Robison, Tony Scott)*

NORTON — ST8884
Vine Tree (01666) 837654
4 miles from M4 junction 17; A429 towards Malmesbury, then left at Hullavington, Sherston signpost, then follow Norton signposts; in village turn right at Foxley signpost, which takes you into Honey Lane; SN16 0JP Civilised dining pub with three neat small rooms; beams, old settles and unvarnished wooden tables on flagstones, sporting prints and church candles, large fireplace in central bar, ales such as Butcombe and local Flying Monk, 30 wines by the glass from extensive list and over 60 gins, well liked

food from sharing boards up, restaurant with woodburner; children and dogs welcome, hitching rail for horses, picnic-sets and play area in two-acre garden, suntrap terrace, closed Sun evening. *(Dr and Mrs A K Clarke)*

OGBOURNE ST ANDREW — SU1871
Silks on the Downs (01672) 841229
A345 N of Marlborough; SN8 1RZ
Popular restauranty pub with horse-racing theme; highly regarded food (best to book) from shortish but varied menu, Ramsbury Gold and a guest, proper cider and decent wines by the glass, helpful friendly service, stylish décor with mix of dining tables on polished wood floors, some good prints and photographs as well as framed racing silks; well behaved children allowed, no dogs inside, small decked area and garden, closed Sun evening. *(Michael Sargent)*

PEWSEY — SU1561
Waterfront (01672) 564020
Pewsey Wharf (A345 just N); SN9 5NU
Bar-bistro in converted wharf building next to canal; ample helpings of good reasonably priced food including daily specials, three well kept changing ales tapped from the cask in upstairs bar (can eat here too), good quality wines, efficient friendly staff; children and dogs (not downstairs) welcome, waterside picnic-sets, nice walks, parking fee to the Kennet & Avon Canal Trust, open all day Fri-Sun. *(Peter Meister)*

PITTON — SU2131
Silver Plough (01722) 712266
Village signed from A30 E of Salisbury (follow brown signs); SP5 1DU Former 18th-c farmhouse; front bar with pewter and china tankards, copper kettles and toby jugs hanging from black beams, cushioned antique settles around rustic pine tables, counter made from carved Elizabethan overmantel serving Badger ales and good range of wines by the glass, enjoyable food from pub standards up, back locals' bar, a couple of woodburners, skittle alley, some live music; children and dogs welcome, south-facing lawn with tables under parasols, more seats on heated terrace, two bedrooms, good nearby walks including Clarendon Way, closed Sun evening, Mon lunchtime. *(Edward Mirzoeff)*

POULSHOT — ST9760
Raven (01380) 828271
Off A361; SN10 1RW New management for this attractive half-timbered pub opposite village green; two black-beamed carpeted rooms with cushioned wall benches and other pubby furniture, open fire, Wadworths IPA, 6X and several wines by the glass, enjoyable well priced pub food including OAP weekday lunch offer, friendly helpful service; quiz nights; children and dogs (in bar) welcome, walled back garden, open all day Sun till 9pm. *(Mr and Mrs P R Thomas)*

REDLYNCH
SU2021
Kings Head (01725) 510420
Off A338 via B3080; The Row; SP5 2JT
Early 18th-c pub on edge of New Forest;
three or four well kept ales such as Hop
Back and Ringwood, decent house wines and
coffee, good value home-made food from pub
favourites up, beamed and flagstoned main
bar with woodburner in large brick fireplace,
small conservatory; free wi-fi; children, dogs
and muddy boots welcome, picnic-sets out in
front and in side garden, Pepperbox Hill (NT)
walks nearby, open (and food) all day Sun,
closed Mon lunchtime. *(Ian Duncan, Susie and
Spencer Gray)*

SALISBURY
SU1429
★ Haunch of Venison (01722) 411313
*Minster Street, opposite Market Cross;
SP1 1TB* Ancient jettied pub with small
downstairs rooms dating from 1320, massive
beams, stout oak benches built into timbered
walls, log fires, tiny snug (the Horsebox) with
pewter counter and rare set of antique taps
for gravity-fed spirits, well kept Hop Back,
guest beers and extensive range of malt
whiskies, enjoyable food including various
venison dishes, friendly staff, steep stairs
to restaurant, halfway up is panelled room
with splendid fireplace and (behind glass)
the mummified hand of an 18th-c card sharp;
children and dogs (in bars) welcome, open
(and food) all day. *(Ann and Colin Hunt,
Richard Tilbrook, Tony Scott)*

SALISBURY
SU1429 `
New Inn (01722) 326662
New Street; SP1 2PH Much-extended old
building with massive beams and timbers;
good choice of enjoyable fair priced food
from pub staples up, three well kept Badger
ales and decent house wines, flagstones,
bare boards and carpet, quiet cosy alcoves,
inglenook woodburner; children welcome,
pretty walled garden with striking view of
nearby cathedral spire, three bedrooms,
open all day. *(Richard Tilbrook, Tony and
Wendy Hobden)*

SALISBURY
SU1430
Wyndham Arms (01722) 331026
Estcourt Road; SP1 3AS Friendly red-
brick corner local with full Hop Back range
(brewery was originally based here), also
a guest ale, bottled beers and country wines,
no food, small front and side rooms, longer
main bar; Thurs quiz, darts and board games;
children and dogs welcome, open all day
Thurs-Sun, from 4.30pm other days.
(Edward May)

SANDY LANE
ST9668
George (01380) 850403
A342 Devizes–Chippenham; SN15 2PX
Handsome 18th-c stone pub now under
same owners as the Greyhound at Bromham;
long simply furnished bar with wood floor,
light blue dado and log fire, Wadworths ales
and enjoyable pubby food including daily
carvery, airy back dining room with large
woodburner, timber-framed conservatory;
children welcome, tables on terrace and
lawn, charming thatched village, Bowood
Estate walks, closed Mon, otherwise open
(and food) all day, till 7pm (6pm) Sun.
(Toby Jones)

SEEND
ST9361
Barge (01380) 828230
*Seend Cleeve; signed off A361 Devizes–
Trowbridge; SN12 6QB* Busy waterside
pub with plenty of seats in garden making
most of boating activity on Kennet & Avon
Canal (moorings); rambling interior with
log fires, some unusual seating in bar such
as painted milk churns, Wadworths ales and
extensive range of wines by the glass, decent
choice of enjoyable well priced food including
summer barbecues, efficient service;
background music, free wi-fi; children and
dogs welcome, open all day. *(Frances and
Hamish Porter)*

SEMINGTON
ST9259
Lamb (01380) 870263
*The Strand; A361 Devizes–
Trowbridge; BA14 6LL* Modernised
dining pub with various eating areas
including bar with wood-strip floor and
log fire, enjoyable food (not Sun evening)
from pub favourites to specials, tapas
only Mon and Tues, well kept Box Steam
Tunnel Vision, friendly staff; background
music; children and dogs welcome,
pleasant garden with views to the Bowood
Estate, play area, two self-catering cottages.
(Chris and Sophie Baxter)

SEMINGTON
ST8960
Somerset Arms (01380) 870067
*Off A350 bypass 2 miles S of Melksham;
BA14 6JR* 16th-c coaching inn with long
heavy-beamed bar and restaurant, four well
kept local ales, real ciders and enjoyable
pubby food (not Sun evening) from baguettes
up including plenty of gluten-free choices,
friendly young staff; children and dogs
welcome, picnic-sets in small garden behind,
three bedrooms, short walk from Kennet
& Avon Canal, open all day, breakfast
from 9am. *(Edward Mirzoeff)*

SHALBOURNE
SU3162
Plough (01672) 870295
Off A338; SN8 3QF Traditional low-
beamed pub by small village green; good
variety of enjoyable fairly priced food cooked
by landlord including some vegetarian
options, Butcombe and Wadworths ales,
friendly landlady and staff, open fire in
neat bar, separate carpeted restaurant with
central woodburner; free wi-fi; children and
dogs welcome, disabled access, play area
in small garden, closed Mon, no food
Sun evening. *(Darrell Barton)*

SHERSTON   ST8586

Carpenters Arms (01666) 840665

Easton Town (B4040); SN16 0NT
Friendly whitewashed roadside pub; ales
such as Butcombe, Flying Monk and Sharps,
Thatcher's ciders and decent reasonably
priced wines, enjoyable food including
weekday OAP lunch, Weds burger night and
Sat steak/wine deal, small interconnecting
rooms with low beams, stripped-stone or
grey-painted walls, light-wood flooring,
log fires, modern dining conservatory;
background music, pool; children and dogs
welcome, disabled access/loos, grassy garden
with play area, open all day. *(Chris and
Angela Buckell)*

STEEPLE ASHTON   ST9056

Longs Arms (01380) 870245

High Street; BA14 6EU Attractively
presented 17th-c stone coaching inn with
friendly local atmosphere; Sharps and
Wadworths ales kept well, plenty of wines
by the glass and very good locally sourced
food from lunchtime sandwiches/ciabattas
and home-made pizzas up, bar with lots of
pictures and old photos, adjacent dining part,
woodburner; free wi-fi; children and dogs
welcome, play area and boules in big garden,
self-catering cottage, delightful village with
fine church, open all day weekends if busy.
(Rupert and Sandy Newton)

STOURTON   ST7733

Spread Eagle (01747) 840587

*Church Lawn; follow Stourhead brown
signs off B3092, N of junction with A303
W of Mere; BA12 6QE* Busy NT-owned
Georgian inn at entrance to Stourhead
Estate; spacious interior with antique settles,
solid tables and chairs, sporting prints and
handsome fireplaces, well kept Butcombe,
Wessex and interesting wines by the glass
in flagstoned bar, fairly compact but varied
menu, cream teas; background music;
children and dogs (in some parts) welcome,
wheelchair access (step down to dining
areas), smart back courtyard with circular
picnic-sets, five bedrooms (guests can
wander freely around famous gardens outside
normal hours, picnic hampers available),
open all day. *(Edward Mirzoeff)*

SUTTON VENY   ST8941

Woolpack (01985) 840834

High Street; BA12 7AW Small well run
1920s village local with friendly chatty
atmosphere; good food including some
inventive dishes cooked by landlord-chef
from blackboard menu (best to book), home-
made chutneys, pickles etc for sale, a couple
of Butcombe ales, sensibly priced wines by

the glass and good selection of malt whiskies,
efficient amiable service, modernised interior
with compact side dining area screened from
bare-boards bar, woodburner; background
music; dogs welcome, closed Sun evening,
Mon lunchtime, no food Mon. *(Mrs Zara
Elliott, Edward Mirzoeff)*

TISBURY   ST9429

Boot (01747) 870363

High Street; SP3 6PS Unpretentious
ancient village local under welcoming
long-serving licensee; three well kept
changing ales tapped from the cask, cider/
perry, enjoyable reasonably priced pubby
food including range of pizzas, open fire; dogs
welcome, tables in good-sized back garden,
closed Sun evening and lunchtimes Mon, Tues.
(Gene and Kitty Rankin)

UPAVON   SU1355

Ship (01980) 630313

High Street; SN9 6EA Large thatched pub
with good choice of enjoyable home-made
food including wood-fired pizzas (Thurs-
Sat evenings) and Weds steak night, well
kept changing ales such as Butcombe and
Wadworths, a couple of traditional ciders and
decent range of wines and whiskies, some
interesting nautical memorabilia; occasional
live music; dogs and muddy boots welcome,
picnic-sets in front and on small side terrace,
parking can be tricky, open all day.
(Toby Jones)

UPTON LOVELL   ST9441

Prince Leopold (01985) 850460

*Up Street, village signed from A36;
BA12 0JP* Prettily tucked-away Victorian
country pub; simply furnished bar with
light wood floor, ales such as Butcombe
and plenty of wines by the glass from hand-
crafted elm counter, cosy snug leading
off with shelves either side of open fire
and comfortable sofas, two other linked
rooms and airy back restaurant overlooking
River Wylye (as do some balcony tables),
well liked food from sandwiches and pub
favourites up, friendly service; children
and dogs welcome, outside bar in pretty
waterside garden, bedrooms, open all
day Sat, till 8pm Sun, closed Mon.
(Sandra and Nigel Brown)

UPTON SCUDAMORE   ST8647

Angel (01985) 213225

Off A350 N of Warminster; BA12 0AG
Updated 16th-c dining inn well placed for
Longleat; farmhouse tables and chairs and
leather sofas by fire in bare-boards bar,
Sharps Doom Bar, good wines by the glass
and well liked italian food including good
value weekday set lunch, friendly helpful

Virtually all pubs in this book sell wine by the glass. We mention wines
if they are a cut above the average.

service steps up to two dining rooms; children and dogs welcome, tables on back garden, six well equipped comfortable bedrooms, open all day weekends. *(Edward Mirzoeff)*

URCHFONT   SU0357
Lamb (01380) 848848
The Green; SN10 4QU Welcoming part-thatched village local; well kept Wadworths ales and enjoyable good value pubby food from baguettes to blackboard specials, simply furnished with carpeted bar and another adjoining room; skittle alley, darts; free wi-fi; children and dogs welcome, picnic-sets in grassy side garden, pétanque, smokers' shelter, open all day Sun (food till 6pm), closed Mon lunchtime. *(Michael Doswell)*

WARMINSTER   ST8745
Organ (01985) 211777
High Street; BA12 9AQ Former 18th-c inn (reopened 2006 after 93 years as a shop); front bar, games room and skittle alley, welcoming owners and chatty regulars, three well kept regional ales including one badged for them (Sept beer festival), real ciders/perries, no food apart from bar snacks but can bring your own; local artwork in upstairs gallery; quiz nights and occasional live music; no under-21s, dogs welcome, seats in sunny rear courtyard, open all day Sat, from 4pm other days. *(Adam Jones)*

WARMINSTER   ST8745
★ Weymouth Arms (01985) 216995
Emwell Street; BA12 8JA Charming backstreet pub with snug panelled entrance bar, log fire in fine stone fireplace, ancient books on mantelpiece, leather tub chairs around walnut and satinwood table, more seats against the walls, Butcombe, Wadworths 6X and half a dozen wines by the glass, second heavily panelled room with wide floorboards and smaller fireplace, candles in brass sticks, split-level dining room stretching back to open kitchen serving good food from pub favourites up, friendly helpful service; children and dogs (in bar) welcome, seats in flower-filled back courtyard, six comfortable well equipped bedrooms, closed Mon and lunchtimes Tues-Thurs, no evening food Sun. *(Catherine and Daniel King)*

WEST OVERTON   SU1368
Bell (01672) 861099
A4 Marlborough–Calne; SN8 1QD Early 19th-c roadside coaching inn; highly praised imaginative cooking from owner-chef using fresh local ingredients, also lunchtime sandwiches and some pubby choices, well kept local beers including one named for the pub, good wines, attentive friendly service

from uniformed staff, bar with woodburner (dogs allowed here), spacious restaurant beyond; background music; disabled access, nice secluded back garden with terrace and summer bar, country views, good walks nearby, closed Sun evening, Mon. *(Ian Herdman)*

WESTBROOK   ST9565
Westbrook Inn (01380) 850418
A3102 about 4 miles E of Melksham; SN15 2EE Comfortably updated pub in small village; good home-cooked food from varied menu including stone-baked pizzas, Bath ales and a guest, plenty of wines by the glass, hands-on licensees and friendly well trained staff; Tues quiz; good-sized garden with decked terrace and play area, open (and food) all day. *(Mr and Mrs P R Thomas, Peter Webb)*

WESTWOOD   ST8159
★ New Inn (01225) 863123
Off B3109 S of Bradford-on-Avon; BA15 2AE Traditional 18th-c country pub with linked rooms; beams, stripped stonework and log fires, scrubbed tables on slate floor, lots of pictures, highly rated good value food cooked by chef-owner from pub staples to more imaginative choices, a couple of well kept Wadworths ales and a guest such as Moles, good service and cheerful buzzy atmosphere; children and dogs welcome, sturdy furniture and gazebo in paved back garden, pretty village with good surrounding walks, Westwood Manor (NT) in road opposite, closed Sun evening. *(Mike Fountain)*

WHITLEY   ST8866
Pear Tree (01225) 704966
Off B3353 S of Corsham; SN12 8QX Attractive beamed dining pub (former 17th-c farmhouse) with plenty of contemporary/rustic charm in front bar, restaurant and airy garden room, good food from varied if not particularly cheap menu, three regional ales including Bath Gem, interesting wine list (many by the glass) and good range of other drinks, friendly attentive service; comedy nights; children welcome, terrace and pretty garden, eight well equipped bedrooms (four in converted barn), open all day from 7.30am (8.30am Sun) for breakfast. *(Dr and Mrs A K Clarke)*

WILCOT   SU1461
Golden Swan (01672) 562289
Signed off A345 N of Pewsey, and in Pewsey itself; SN9 5NN Steeply thatched country pub near Kennet & Avon Canal, friendly and welcoming, with well kept Wadworths ales and popular good value food cooked by landlady, small bar with log fire, snug and dining room, also games room (pool

---

It's very helpful if you let us know up-to-date food prices when you report on pubs.

and darts); quiz first Sun of month; children and dogs welcome, metal furniture on front grass, more tables and wandering chickens behind, field for camping, three good value bedrooms (not ensuite), open all day weekends. *(Peter Meister)*

WILTON SU2661

★**Swan** (01672) 870274

The village S of Great Bedwyn; SN8 3SS
Popular light and airy 1930s pub; good well presented food (not Sun evening) from sharing boards and basket meals to daily specials, two Ramsbury ales and up to three local cask-tapped guests, real ciders and good value wines from extensive list, friendly efficient staff, stripped pine tables, high-backed settles and pews on bare boards, woodburner; children and dogs welcome, disabled access, picnic-sets in front garden, picturesque village with windmill, open all day weekends. *(Sam Cole)*

WINGFIELD ST8256

Poplars (01225) 752426

B3109 S of Bradford-on-Avon (Shop Lane); BA14 9LN Appealing country pub with warm friendly atmosphere, beams and log fires, enjoyable sensibly priced food from pub staples to interesting specials, Wadworths ales (including seasonal) and Weston's cider, airy family dining extension; quiz first Sun of month; nice garden and own cricket pitch. *(Darrell Barton)*

WINSLEY ST7960

★**Seven Stars** (01225) 722204

Off B3108 bypass W of Bradford-on-Avon; BA15 2LQ Handsome bustling village inn with low-beamed linked areas, pastel paintwork and stripped-stone walls, farmhouse chairs around candlelit tables on flagstones or carpet, woodburner, good food from pub favourites up including highly rated Sun roasts, friendly attentive service, well kept Palmers IPA and west country guests, proper cider; background and live music, winter quiz; children and dogs (in bar) welcome, wheelchair access using ramp giving access to most areas, disabled loo, tables on terrace and neat grassy area, bowling green opposite, open (and food) all day Fri-Sun. *(Dr Matt Burleigh, Pete and Sarah, Chris and Angela Buckell)*

Worcestershire

BAUGHTON   SO8742   Map 4

Jockey ⭐ ☟

(01684) 592153 – www.thejockeyinn.co.uk

4 miles from M50 junction 1; A38 northwards, then right on to A4104 Upton–Pershore; WR8 9DQ

Elegantly redesigned pub with a fine choice of drinks, rewarding food, courteous staff and seats outside

After a visit to nearby Croome (National Trust), why not come to this carefully extended and stylishly refurbished pub for lunch. The contemporary open-plan areas work well together and the smart dining rooms have high-backed upholstered chairs, long button-back wall seats, a mix of pale-topped tables and bare floorboards with décor that takes in an unusual woven-wicker wall, deer antler chandeliers, oil portraits, horse-racing photographs, bookshelves, stubby candles in glass lanterns and old jockey saddles. Stools on flagstones line the counter in the beamed bar, where friendly, attentive staff serve Butcombe Rare Breed, Sharps Doom Bar and Wye Valley Butty Bach and HPA on handpump, and 29 wines by the glass (including champagne and sweet wines) from the large glass walk-in wine cellar on display behind the bar; also, cocktails and 21 gins. Big leather armchairs, sofas and pouffes are grouped together and there's an open fire and a neat, ceiling-high stack of logs beside a two-way woodburning stove; background music. Outside, the attractive paved courtyard is furnished with glass-topped tables, dark wicker chairs and large heated parasols surrounded by bamboo and wild herbs in planters.

Highly enjoyable food includes baguettes, goats cheese bonbons with sun-dried tomato and red pepper chutney and smoked duck salad with burnt coconut, orange, watercress and cashew nuts, sharing boards, porcini mushroom ravioli with wild mushrooms, white truffle cream and parmesan, stone-baked pizzas, burger with toppings, coleslaw and chips, dill and lemon-marinated salmon with asparagus, leeks and lemon beurre blanc, roast breast of guinea fowl with black truffle gnocchi, baby leeks, chestnut mushrooms and chive cream, 10oz rib-eye steak with a choice of sauce and triple-cooked chips, and puddings such as chocolate and banana strudel with chocolate sauce and banana fudge ice-cream and strawberry and white chocolate cheesecake with strawberry compote; they also offer a two- and three-course lunch menu. *Benchmark main dish: rack of lamb with provençale vegetables, olive tapenade, creamed basil and parmesan potatoes £19.50. Two-course evening meal £22.00.*

Free house ~ Licensee Rebekah Seddon-Wickens ~ Real ale ~ Open 11.30am-11pm; 11.30-11.30 Sat; 12-6 Sun; closed Mon except bank holidays ~ Bar food 12-9; 12-9.30 Fri, Sat;

12-4 Sun ~ Restaurant ~ Children welcome ~ Dogs allowed in bar ~ Wi-fi *Recommended by Mike and Mary Carter, Bernard Stradling, Dr and Mrs A K Clarke, Neal Griffith, John and Abigail Prescott, Amanda Shipley*

BRANSFORD
Bear & Ragged Staff ♀

SO8052 Map 4

(01886) 833399 – www.bearatbransford.co.uk
Off A4103 SW of Worcester; Station Road; WR6 5JH

Well run dining pub in Teme Valley hamlet with pleasant places to sit both inside and out, and popular food and drink

This is a civilised dining pub, but it also has a relaxed and friendly bar. Here, helpful staff serve Hobsons Twisted Spire and a guest from Wye Valley on handpump, ten wines by the glass, several malt whiskies and quite a few brandies and liqueurs. The restaurant is more formal, with upholstered dining chairs, proper tablecloths and linen napkins. These interconnecting rooms give fine views of attractive rolling country (as do the pretty garden and terrace). In winter, there's a warming open fire; background music, board games and a pub cat called Princess. Good disabled access and facilities.

The highly regarded food, using some home-grown produce, includes lunchtime sandwiches (not Sunday), baked camembert with red onion marmalade, panko-breaded squid rings with aioli, creamy wild mushroom and tarragon tagliatelle, a curry and a pie of the day, chicken wrapped in parma ham with dauphinoise potatoes and carrot purée, rump steak with a choice of sauce and triple-cooked chips, and puddings such as dark chocolate brownie and chantilly cream-filled profiteroles with chocolate sauce and sticky toffee pudding with butterscotch sauce. They also offer a two- and three-course set lunch (not Sunday). *Benchmark main dish: beer-battered fish and chips £12.95. Two-course evening meal £20.00.*

Free house ~ Licensee Lynda Williams ~ Real ale ~ Open 12-2.30, 6-11; 12-4 Sun; closed Sun evening; first week Jan ~ Bar food 12-2, 6-9 ~ Restaurant ~ Children welcome ~ Dogs allowed in bar ~ Wi-fi *Recommended by Jamie and Lizzie McEwan, Gary and Marie Miller, Jonny and Andrew Haughton, Amy Ledbetter, Amy and Luke Buchanan, Paddy and Sian O'Leary, Bob and Melissa Wyatt*

BRETFORTON
Fleece ★ 🍺 £

SP0943 Map 4

(01386) 831173 – www.thefleeceinn.co.uk
B4035 E of Evesham: turn S off this road into village; pub is in central square by church; there's a sizeable car park at one side of the church; WR11 7JE

Marvellously unspoilt medieval pub owned by the National Trust; bedrooms

For 500 years, this lovely former farm was owned by the same family and many of the furnishings are original heirlooms; it was bequeathed to the National Trust in 1977. The fine country rooms include a great oak dresser holding a priceless 48-piece set of Stuart pewter, two grandfather clocks, ancient kitchen chairs, curved high-backed settles, a rocking chair and a rack of heavy pointed iron shafts, probably for spit roasting in one of the huge inglenook fireplaces; two other log fires. As well as massive beams and exposed timbers, there are worn and crazed flagstones (scored with marks to keep out demons) and plenty of oddities such as a great cheese press and set of cheese moulds and a rare dough-proving table; a leaflet details the more bizarre items. Uley Pigs Ear and Wye Valley Bitter with guests such as North Cotswold Moreton Mild and Purity Mad Goose on handpump, nine wines by the glass, a similar number of malt whiskies and four farm ciders; board games. The lawn, with fruit trees around a beautifully restored thatched and timbered barn, is a lovely place to sit, and there are more picnic-sets and a stone pump-trough in the front courtyard. There's always something going on here, from an annual asparagus festival to folk music sessions, morris dancing and vintage car gatherings – check their website for details.

Food includes lunchtime sandwiches, confit chicken and asparagus terrine with peanut hummus, macaroni cheese with truffle oil, braised faggots with mash and gravy, corned beef, chorizo and onion hash with cheese and fried egg, beer-battered fish and chips, pork fillet wrapped in bacon with sage and onion mash and apricot jus, 28-day aged rib-eye steak with house butter and chips, and puddings such as raspberry and lime eton mess and coconut rice pudding and mango compote. *Benchmark main dish: steak in ale pie £13.00. Two-course evening meal £19.00.*

Free house ~ Licensee Nigel Smith ~ Real ale ~ Open 10.30am-11pm ~ Bar food 12-2.30, 6.30-9; 12-8 Sun ~ Children welcome ~ Dogs welcome ~ Wi-fi ~ Bedrooms: /£97.50
Recommended by John Saville, Beth Aldridge, John and Abigail Prescott, Nigel and Sue Foster, Caroline and Oliver Sterling, Mark and Mary Setting, Dave Braisted

BROADWAY
Crown & Trumpet 🍺 £

SP0937 Map 4

(01386) 853202 – www.crownandtrumpet.co.uk
Church Street; WR12 7AE

Honest local with good real ales and decent food; bedrooms

In a handsome, much-visited town this is an unassuming, old-fashioned golden-stone pub with plenty of cheerful customers. The beamed and timbered bar has a bustling, easy-going atmosphere, antique high-backed dark settles, large solid tables and a blazing log fire. You'll find a beer named for the pub (from Stanway) plus North Cotswold Shagweaver, Stroud Tom Long and Timothy Taylors Landlord on handpump alongside 11 wines by the glass, ten malt whiskies and farm ciders. There's an assortment of pub games including darts, Jenga, shut the box, dominoes and ring the bull; TV and background music. The hardwood chairs and tables outside are arranged among flowers on a slightly raised front terrace and much used by walkers. Disabled access.

Remarkable value food includes lunchtime paninis, deep-fried brie with cranberry sauce, devilled whitebait, omelettes, cheese and asparagus flan, duck and apricot sausages with mash and plum gravy, local faggots and chips, haddock, cod and salmon pie, gammon and egg, chicken breast with chorizo, parsnips and sautéed potatoes, sirloin steak with a choice of sauce and chips, and puddings such as spotted dick and treacle tart, both with custard; they also offer a pie and pudding deal. *Benchmark main dish: meat pies £9.95. Two-course evening meal £12.95.*

Laurel (Enterprise) ~ Lease Andrew Scott ~ Real ale ~ Open 11-11; 11am-11.30pm Fri, Sat ~ Bar food 12-2.30, 5.45-9.30; 12-9.30 Fri-Sun ~ Children welcome ~ Dogs allowed in bar ~ Wi-fi ~ Live music Thurs-Sat evenings ~ Bedrooms: £68/£78 *Recommended by Naomi and Andrew Randall, Stuart and Natalie Granville, Charlie Stevens, Moira and Jon Weller, Dave Braisted, Gordon and Margaret Ormondroyd*

Please keep sending us reports. We rely on readers for news of new discoveries, and particularly for news of changes – however slight – at the fully described pubs: feedback@goodguides.com, or (no stamp needed) Freepost THE GOOD PUB GUIDE, Random House Publishing, 20 Vauxhall Bridge Road, London SW1V 2SA.

CHILDSWICKHAM

SP0738 Map 4

Childswickham Inn

(01386) 852461 – www.childswickhaminn.co.uk

Off A44 NW of Broadway; WR12 7HP

Bustling dining pub with highly regarded food, good drinks choice, attentive staff and seats in neat garden

Many customers are here to enjoy the particularly good food, but there's also a proper chatty bar with friendly regulars (often with their dogs). Also, leather sofas and armchairs and attentive staff serving Bombardier, Fullers London Pride and Sharps Atlantic on handpump, 14 wines by the glass (with Friday evening deals on champagne and prosecco), malt whiskies, a growing collection of gins and farm cider; background music. The two dining areas, one with high-backed dark leather chairs on terracotta tiles, the other with country kitchen chairs on bare floorboards, are best booked in advance. Both have contemporary artwork on part-timbered walls painted cream or pale violet plus an open fire and a woodburning stove. Folding doors from the conservatory lead out into a neat garden where there's a decked area with rush-seated chairs and tables; there are lovely surrounding walks. Disabled facilities.

Rewarding food includes sandwiches, ham hock and pineapple terrine with pulled barbecue pork bonbon, peach glaze and pancetta crisp, confit duck leg on toulouse sausage and mixed bean cassoulet with port reduction, roast sweet potato filled with ratatouille and topped with halloumi marinated in harissa and rose petal spice with basil oil, ham and free-range eggs, pork and leek sausages with mash and onion gravy, herb-crusted cod loin topped with crab and olive tapenade, with chorizo, pepper and caper potato hash and thyme and tomato coulis, lamb shank rogan josh with curried spring onion mash and cumin-spiced spinach and cauliflower pakora, and puddings such as dark chocolate and caramel torte with hazelnut and toffee crunch crumble and salted caramel ice-cream and citrus tart with passion-fruit sauce and blood orange sorbet. *Benchmark main dish: pie of the day £13.50. Two-course evening meal £20.00.*

Star Pubs & Bars ~ Lease Carol Marshall ~ Real ale ~ Open 12-11 ~ Bar food 12-2, 6-9; 12-6 Sun ~ Restaurant not Sun evening or Mon lunch ~ Children welcome ~ Dogs allowed in bar ~ Wi-fi ~ Live music monthly (check website) *Recommended by Mike and Mary Carter, Miranda and Jeff Davidson, Sylvia and Phillip Spencer, Dr A J and Mrs B A Tompsett, Mary and Douglas McDowell*

CLENT

SO9279 Map 4

Fountain ￼ ￼

(01562) 883286 – www.thefountainatclent.co.uk

Adams Hill/Odnall Lane; off A491 at Holy Cross/Clent exit roundabout, via Violet Lane, then right at T junction; DY9 9PU

Restauranty pub often packed to overflowing, with imaginative dishes and good choice of drinks

Tucked away in the Clent Hills, this is a neatly kept, welcoming pub offering a wide choice of good, popular food. The long pattern-carpeted dining bar (consisting of three knocked-together areas) is fairly traditional, with teak chairs and pedestal tables and some comfortably cushioned brocaded wall seats. There are nicely framed local photographs on the rag-rolled pinkish walls above a dark panelled dado, pretty wall lights and candles on the tables (flowers in summer). The changing real ales on handpump include Brakspears Oxford Gold and Marstons EPA and Wainwright, and most of their wines are available by the glass; also farm cider, speciality teas and good coffees. Background music and skittle alley. There are tables outside on a decked area. Disabled access.

 Particularly good food includes sandwiches, tiger prawns in garlic butter, chicken liver parfait with onion marmalade, pumpkin seed and chestnut roast with parmentier vegetables, salmon fillet on egg noodles with sweet thai chilli sauce and courgette ribbons, corn-fed chicken breast stuffed with sage and onion mousse with red wine sauce, half roast duck with orange and star anise reduction and caramelised orange, mixed grilled fish with seaweed butter, chargrilled steaks with a choice of sauce, and puddings such as chocolate délice and sticky date pudding with toffee sauce and vanilla ice-cream; they also offer a two- and three-course menu (Monday-Saturday lunchtimes and Monday-Thursday evenings 6pm and 6.30pm). *Benchmark main dish: lamb pot roast £19.95. Two-course evening meal £26.00.*

Marstons ~ Lease Richard and Jacque Macey ~ Real ale ~ Open 11-11; 12-10 Sun ~ Bar food 12-2, 6-9 (9.30 Fri, Sat); 12-6 Sun ~ Children welcome ~ Wi-fi *Recommended by Sarah and David Gibbs, Dr and Mrs H J Field, Jim King, Peter Brix, Diana and Richard Gibbs, Elodie and Edward Blake, Phoebe Peacock*

CUTNALL GREEN   SO8868 Map 4

Chequers

(01299) 851292 – www.chequerscutnallgreen.co.uk
Kidderminster Road; WR9 0PJ

Bustling roadside pub with plenty of drinking and dining space in interesting rooms, and rewarding food

As ever, we get plenty of enthusiastic reports from our readers about this well run, popular pub. It was built on the site of an old coaching inn and is a clever mix of ancient and modern. There are red-painted walls between beams and timbering, broad floorboards and weathered quarry tiles, and warm winter fires. Also, leather sofas and tub chairs, high-backed purple and red or ladder-back dining chairs around all sorts of tables, plenty of mirrors giving the impression of even more space, brass plates and mugs, candles and fresh flowers. They serve Green Duck Blonde, Sharps Doom Bar and Wye Valley HPA on handpump and 14 wines by the glass. One elegant but cosy room, known as the Players Lounge, has photographs of the landlord Mr Narbett, who is a former chef for the England football team. The pretty garden has three 'beach huts' to hire, chairs with barrel tables and sofas as well as heaters and parasols. Disabled access.

As well as weekend breakfasts (9-11am), the rewarding food includes sandwiches, spicy shrimp tacos with mango and pickled cabbage salad, rosemary and garlic box-baked camembert with red onion confit, sweet potato and coconut curry with turmeric and cashew nut rice, a pie of the day, ham and free-range eggs, stone-baked pizzas, cajun buttermilk chicken burger with sweet potato fries and chipotle chilli mayonnaise, beer-battered cod and chips, chargrilled sirloin steak with oven-fried tomatoes and chips, and puddings such as espresso affogato with vanilla ice-cream and raspberry and white chocolate crème brûlée. *Benchmark main dish: slow-cooked moroccan-style lamb shoulder £17.50. Two-course evening meal £24.00.*

Free house ~ Licensees Roger and Jo Narbett ~ Real ale ~ Open 12-11; 12-10.30 Sun ~ Bar food 12-2, 6-8.30 (9 Sat); 12-2.30, 6-8 Sun ~ Restaurant ~ Children welcome ~ Dogs allowed in bar ~ Wi-fi *Recommended by Camilla and Jose Ferrera, Liz and Mike Newton, Graham Lovis, Gail and Frank Hackett, John and Abigail Prescott, Dr and Mrs A K Clarke*

Real ale to us means beer that has matured naturally in its cask – not pressurised or filtered. We name all real ales stocked.

ELDERSFIELD

SO8131 Map 4

Butchers Arms ⭐ 🛏

(01452) 840381 – www.thebutchersarms.net

Pub and village signposted from B4211; Lime Street (coming from A417, fourth road on left), OS Sheet 150 map reference 815314; village also signposted from B4208 N of Staunton; GL19 4NX

16th-c pub with an unspoilt interior, local ales and carefully chosen wines, excellent food and seats in garden

The first class food draws many customers into this pretty cottage, but there's also a strong drinks trade with chatty locals gathered around the bar counter. Both the bar and the dining room are kept stylishly simple, with black beams, knocked-through walls and standing timbers, cream paintwork, plain but individual wooden chairs, pews and some high-backed settles on bare boards or tiles and rustic tables. Also, two woodburning stoves, hop bines and wall prints. High chairs line the counter where friendly staff serve Wye Valley Butty Bach and Golden Ale tapped from the cask, 11 good wines by the glass including sparkling and pudding choices and farm cider. The good-sized garden has seats on lawns and looks out on to pasture; quoits. Disabled access.

Creative food cooked by the landlord includes gin and citrus-cured salmon with beetroot, horseradish, pickled kohlrabi and dill oil, salt cod scotch egg with chorizo and romesco sauce, line-caught cod with mussels, saffron sauce and mash, lamb faggot and cutlet with pearl barley, squash, dukkah, pomegranate and coriander, fillet steak with cep purée, fondant potato, spinach and armagnac jus, and puddings such as chocolate ganache with mascarpone, pistachios and honeycomb and buttermilk pannacotta with poached rhubarb and cinnamon madeleines. *Benchmark main dish: venison loin and croquette with celeriac purée and griottine cherries £24.50. Two-course evening meal £30.00.*

Free house ~ Licensee Mark Block ~ Real ale ~ Open 7-11; 12-3, 7-11 Fri, Sat; 12-3 Sun; closed all Mon; Tues-Thurs lunchtimes; Sun evening; last two weeks Aug, two weeks over Christmas ~ Bar food 7-8.30pm Tues-Sat; 12-2 Fri-Sun ~ Restaurant ~ Children allowed if over 10 ~ Dogs allowed in bar ~ Wi-fi *Recommended by Dan and Belinda Smallbone, Alister and Margery Bacon, Robin and Anne Triggs, Len and Lilly Dowson, Katherine and Hugh Markham, Amanda Shipley, Muriel and Spencer Harrop*

KNIGHTWICK

SO7355 Map 4

Talbot ⭐ 🍷 🍺 🛏

(01886) 821235 – www.the-talbot.co.uk

Knightsford Bridge; B4197 just off A44 Worcester–Bromyard; WR6 5PH

Worcestershire Dining Pub of the Year

Interesting old coaching inn with good own-brewed beer, highly regarded food and riverside garden; bedrooms

A rambling country hotel, this fine old place appeals to a wide mix of customers due to its accomplished food and own brews. From their own Teme Valley microbrewery (using locally grown hops) they produce Talbot Blonde, That, This, T'Other and a seasonal ale on handpump and hold regular beer festivals; also, a dozen wines by the glass and 16 malt whiskies. The heavily beamed and extended lounge bar is traditionally furnished with a variety of seats from small carved or leatherette armchairs to winged settles by the windows, and there's both a warm log fire and a vast stove in a big central stone hearth. The bar opens into a light and airy garden room. The back public bar has pool on a raised side area, a TV, darts, a juke box and cribbage; in contrast, the dining room is a stylish and sedate place for a quiet meal. In warm weather, it's lovely to sit at tables on the lawn beside the River Teme (it's across the lane from the inn, but they serve out here too) or you can use the old-fashioned seats at the front. Clean, warm bedrooms have a small decanter of their own damson gin and biscuits. A farmers' market takes place here on the second Sunday of the month. Wheelchair access and loo.

The first class, imaginative food – including breakfasts from 8am – uses some home-grown produce (they also make their own preserves, bread, raised pies and black pudding): fresh haddock fishcakes with garlic mayonnaise, rabbit and pork terrine wrapped in bacon with lime and chilli jam, creamy beetroot risotto with parmesan, ham hock and wild goose blanquette with sautéed mushrooms, mutton tagine with orange, star anise, cinnamon and herbs with vegetable couscous, slow-cooked jugged deer with roasted pears, fish platter with celeriac and red onion coleslaw, pork cassoulet topped with garlic breadcrumbs, and puddings such as blackcurrant pannacotta and chocolate and cashew nut brownie. *Benchmark main dish: chicken and leek pie £14.00. Two-course evening meal £21.00.*

Own brew ~ Licensee Annie Clift ~ Real ale ~ Open 8am-11pm ~ Bar food 8am-9pm ~ Restaurant ~ Children welcome ~ Dogs welcome ~ Wi-fi ~ Live jazz every other Tues ~ Bedrooms: £65/£110 *Recommended by Nicola and Stuart Parsons, Lenny and Ruth Walters, Peter Harrison, Steve Whalley, Gordon and Margaret Ormondroyd, P Beardsell, Dr and Mrs H J Field*

MALVERN
Nags Head ◧

SO7845   Map 4

(01684) 574373 – www.nagsheadmalvern.co.uk
Bottom end of Bank Street, steep turn down off A449; WR14 2JG

Delightfully eclectic layout and décor, a remarkable choice of ales, tasty lunchtime bar food and warmly welcoming atmosphere

With 15 real ales to choose from here, it's always going to attract an enthusiastic crowd keen to try the offerings served by knowledgeable, friendly staff. On handpump, there might be Arbor Citra, Aurora Mosaic, Banks's Bitter, Bathams Best Bitter, Cloudwater A.W18 Mild, Hobsons Twisted Spire, Ilkley Mary Jane, Otter Ale and Bitter, Ringwood Boondoggle and Fortyniner, VOG Lady Liberty, Woods Shropshire Lad and Wylam Galatia. Also, two farm ciders, 30 malt whiskies, 30 gins, ten bottled craft ales/lagers and ten wines by the glass including pudding ones. A series of snug, individually decorated rooms, separated by a couple of steps and with two open fires, have leather armchairs, pews sometimes arranged as booths and a mix of tables (including sturdy ones stained different colours). There are bare boards here, flagstones there, carpet elsewhere, plenty of interesting pictures and homely touches such as house plants, shelves of well thumbed books and daily papers; board games. The front terrace and garden have picnic-sets, benches and rustic tables as well as parasols and heaters.

Much liked lunchtime food includes sandwiches, coconut dhal dumplings with sri lankan sauce, smoked trout with a boiled egg and keta, caper and shallot dressing, omelettes, guacamole and mango salad with black beans and ginger and lime dressing and beef and mushroom in ale pie, with evening meals (served in the barn extension dining room only) such as burger with toppings, spicy coleslaw and chips, lamb osso bucco with creamy parmesan polenta and gremolata, rosemary and pink peppercorn pork tenderloin with sautéed red chard and bacon, pesto-crusted cod loin with puy lentils, dried tomatoes and lime vinaigrette, and puddings. *Benchmark main dish: beer-battered cod and chips £13.50. Two-course evening meal £20.00.*

Free house ~ Licensee Alex Whistance ~ Real ale ~ Open 11am-11.15pm; 11am-11.30pm Fri, Sat; 12-11 Sun ~ Bar food 12-2.30, 6.30-8.30; 12-2.30, 7-8.30 Sun ~ Restaurant ~ Children welcome ~ Dogs welcome ~ Wi-fi *Recommended by Patti and James Davidson, Lee and Jill Stafford, Clive and Fran Dutson, Andrew Lawson, Guy Henderson, Guy Vowles, Edward May, Miles Green*

NEWLAND

SO7948   Map 4

Swan

(01886) 832224 – www.theswaninnmalvern.co.uk
Worcester Road (set well back from A449 just NW of Malvern); WR13 5AY

Popular, interesting pub with well kept real ales and seats in the large garden

The garden here is as individual as the pub, with a cluster of huge casks topped with flowers, a piano doing flower-tub duty and a set of stocks on the pretty front terrace. Inside this bustling, creeper-clad pub there's a dimly lit, dark-beamed bar that's quite traditional with a forest canopy of hops, whisky-water jugs, beakers and tankards. Several of the comfortable and clearly individually chosen seats are worth a close look for their carving, and the wall tapestries are interesting. On the right is a broadly similar red-carpeted dining room and beyond it, in complete contrast, an ultra-modern glass garden room. From the carved bar counter, friendly staff offer up to eight real ales on handpump including a beer named for the pub, Marstons Wainwright, Purity Mad Goose, Ringwood Fortyniner and St Austell Tribute plus quickly changing guest ales; also, several wines by the glass, malt whiskies and four farm ciders; board games.

Pleasing food includes lunchtime sandwiches, chicken and lime skewers with spicy bean and coriander salad, pressed ham hock terrine with pickles, open tart of goats cheese, roasted peppers and oregano with sweet potato wedges, chilli con carne, lamb, root vegetable and rosemary casserole with dumplings, pork fillet schnitzel with chips, sea bream fillets with leek and potato latkes, crispy pancetta and caper sauce, chicken curry with flatbread and pickles, and puddings. *Benchmark main dish: steak in ale pie £14.90. Two-course evening meal £20.00.*

Free house ~ Licensee Duncan Ironmonger ~ Real ale ~ Open 12-11.30 ~ Bar food 12-2.30, 6.30-9 ~ Restaurant ~ Children welcome ~ Dogs welcome ~ Wi-fi *Recommended by Alister and Margery Bacon, Chantelle and Tony Redman, Gail and Arthur Roberts, Diane Abbot, Chris Stevenson, Jack Trussler*

TENBURY WELLS

SO6468   Map 4

Talbot

(01584) 781941 – www.talbotinn-newnhambridge.co.uk
Newnham Bridge; A456; WR15 8JF

Carefully refurbished coaching inn with character bar and dining rooms and popular food; bedrooms

The thoughtfully decorated and well equipped bedrooms here (breakfasts are good too) make a perfect base for exploring the lovely surrounding Teme Valley countryside. Staff are helpful and welcoming, the atmosphere is relaxed and gently civilised and you'll find nice old red and black and original quarry tiles, bare floorboards, open fires, hops and candlelight; the bar and dining rooms are quite different in style. There's an assortment of dark pubby, high-backed painted wooden and comfortably upholstered dining chairs around a variety of tables, leather tub chairs and sofas, bookshelves, old photographs of the local area, table lights and standard lamps, and some elegant antiques. It gets pretty busy at the weekend, when you'll need to book a table in advance. Hobsons Best, Wye Valley HPA and a weekend guest on handpump, local cider and good wines by the glass; background music, TV and board games.

 Well regarded food includes includes lunchtime sandwiches, ham hock terrine, beetroot carpaccio, linguine with courgette, lemon and chilli, sausage and mash with carrot purée and onion gravy, ham and free-range eggs, burger with toppings, caramelised onion chutney and chips, curried chicken kiev with bombay potatoes, pork belly with wholegrain mustard mash and cider jus, plaice poached in red wine with salt-baked carrots and slow-roasted onions, steak au poivre with chips, and puddings such as treacle tart and rapsberry cheesecake. *Benchmark main dish: luxury fish pie £16.00. Two-course evening meal £22.00.*

Free house ~ Licensee Liane Phillips ~ Real ale ~ Open 12-11 (midnight Sat); 12-10 Sun ~ Bar food 12-2.30, 6-9; 12-4 Sun ~ Restaurant ~ Children welcome ~ Dogs allowed in bar and bedrooms ~ Wi-fi ~ Bedrooms: $80/$90 *Recommended by Kerry and Guy Trooper, Graham Smart, Isobel Mackinlay, Susan Eccleston, Sandra and Miles Spencer, Diana and Bertie Farr*

WELLAND
Inn at Welland ⭐ 🍷
SO8039   Map 4

(01684) 592317 – www.theinnatwelland.co.uk
Just off A4104 W of Upton upon Severn, signed for Hook Bank; WR13 6LN

Stylish contemporary country dining bar with good food and wines and nice tables outside

The neatly dressed, efficient staff here serve a fantastic choice of wines by the glass – 43, including champagne, sparkling and an unusually wide range of pudding wines; also, Ledbury Gold and Wye Valley Butty Bach on handpump, mocktails, cocktails and quite a few gins. The rooms have a chatty, easy-going atmosphere, grey paintwork, a few carefully chosen modern prints and attractive seat fabrics, with beige flagstones in the central area, wood flooring to the sides and a woodburning stove at one end. The good-sized tidy garden, offering tranquil views of the Malvern Hills, has tables with comfortable teak or wicker chairs on a biggish sheltered deck or on individual separate terraces set into lawn. Disabled access. The pub is handy for the Three Counties Showground.

Excellent food includes king scallops, confit chicken with smoked pancetta and burnt apple and vanilla, local venison and pistachio terrine with cumberland sauce, sharing boards, tartare of butternut squash with white truffle and squash purée and pearl barley risotto, omelette arnold bennett, burger with toppings and triple-cooked chips, crab ravioli with shellfish bisque, wild rock bass with samphire and crayfish beurre blanc, herb-crusted rack of lamb with fondant potatoes, ratatouille with feta cheese crumb and lamb jus, venison wellington with dauphinoise potatoes, 28-day aged local rib-eye steak with thyme and garlic mushrooms and confit vine cherry tomatoes, and puddings such as dark chocolate pave with morello cherries and poached pineapple with miso ice-cream, coconut and coriander. *Benchmark main dish: slow-cooked pork belly £18.90. Two-course evening meal £30.00.*

Free house ~ Licensees David and Gillian Pinchbeck ~ Real ale ~ Open 12-3, 5.30-11; 12-3, 5.30-11 Sat; 12-4 Sun; closed Sun evening, Mon; one week Jan ~ Bar food 12-2.30, 6-9.30; 12-2.30 Sun ~ Restaurant ~ Children welcome ~ Wi-fi *Recommended by Louise and Anton Parsons, Andy and Louise Ramwell, Val and Malcolm Travers, Phil and Helen Holt, Cecily and Steven Evans, Bernard Stradling, Neal Griffith*

Pubs close to motorway junctions are listed at the back of the book.

Also Worth a Visit in Worcestershire

Besides the fully inspected pubs, you might like to try these pubs that have been recommended to us and described by readers. Do tell us what you think of them: feedback@goodguides.com

ABBERLEY   SO7567
Manor Arms (01299) 890300
Netherton Lane; WR6 6BN Modernised
country inn tucked away in quiet village
backwater opposite fine Norman church;
changing local ales and ciders, 20 wines by
the glass and highly praised well presented
food from seasonal menu including snacks
and pub favourites, afternoon tea, helpful
friendly service; children and dogs welcome,
two-level deck with lovely valley views, good
walks (on Worcestershire Way), six bedrooms,
open all day. *(Jack Prest)*

ALVECHURCH   SP0172
Weighbridge (0121) 445 5111
Scarfield Wharf; B48 7SQ Little red-
brick pub (former weighbridge office) by
Worcester & Birmingham Canal marina;
bar and a couple of other small rooms,
half a dozen well kept ales including
Kinver Bargee Bitter and Weatheroak
Tillermans Tipple (beer festivals), simple
low-priced pubby food (not Tues, Weds);
tables outside. *(Jamie and Lizzie-McEwan)*

ASHTON UNDER HILL   SO9938
Star (01386) 881325
Elmley Road; WR11 7SN Smallish pub
perched above road in quiet village at foot
of Bredon Hill; linked beamed rooms around
bar, one with flagstones and log fire, steps up
to pitch-roofed dining room with woodburner,
well liked food including evening deals Tues
and Weds, real ales such as Black Sheep
and Greene King, friendly welcoming staff;
background music, TV and games machine;
children and dogs welcome, picnic-sets in
pleasant garden, good walks (Wyche Way
passes nearby), open all day, no food Sun or
Mon evenings. *(Philip O'Connor, Guy Vowles)*

BELBROUGHTON   SO9277
Olde Horse Shoe (01562) 730460
High Street; DY9 9ST Popular old beamed
corner pub under new management; smallish
stone-floored bar and separate restaurant;
real ales such as St Austell and Wye Valley,
well liked food (not Sun evening, Mon),
friendly service, open fires; children and
dogs welcome, big back garden, closed Mon
lunchtime, otherwise open all day.
(Chris Stevenson)

BERROW   SO7835
Duke of York (01684) 833449
Junction A438/B4208; WR13 6JQ
Bustling old country pub with two linked
carpeted rooms, beams, nooks and crannies
and log fire, enjoyable generously served
food including good seafood platter and
OAP lunch deal, ales such as Otter, Sharps
and Wye Valley, friendly service, restaurant;
children and dogs welcome, large garden
behind, handy for Malvern Hills. *(Simon H)*

BERROW GREEN   SO7458
Admiral Rodney (01905) 886181
B4197, off A44 W of Worcester; WR6 6PL
Refurbished 17th-c beamed inn now under
same ownership as the Baiting House at
Upper Sapey (see Herefordshire); two bars,
snug and former stable block restaurant,
good varied menu from sandwiches and light
lunches up including daily specials, local ales
and ciders, well chosen wines by the glass
and over 20 gins, friendly helpful service;
pool and sports TV in separate function
room; children welcome, dogs in bar, tables
on front and back terraces, pretty views and
good walks, six well appointed comfortable
bedrooms, closed lunchtimes Mon and Tues,
otherwise open all day, no food Sun evening.
(Brian and Susan Wylie)

BEWDLEY   SO7775
Hop Pole (01299) 401295
Hop Pole Lane; DY12 2QH Modernised
19th-c pub with good choice of popular food
(booking advised) from pub favourites up
including set menus and themed nights,
three well kept Marstons-related ales and
several wines by the glass, country-chic
décor, cast-iron range in dining area; regular
live music and other events, free wi-fi;
children and dogs (in bar) welcome, seats on
raised front terrace, vegetable garden to the
side, back play area, open all day. *(Shaun)*

BEWDLEY   SO7875
Mug House (01299) 402543
Severn Side North; DY12 2EE 18th-c
bay-windowed pub in charming spot by
River Severn; good food from traditional
choices up including set menus, can eat in
bar or more upmarket evening restaurant
with lobster tank, six well kept ales such as
Bewdley, Purity, Timothy Taylors and Wye
Valley (May beer festival), log fire; children
(daytime only) and dogs welcome, disabled
access, glass-covered terrace behind, seven
river-view bedrooms, open all day, no food
Sun evening. *(Simon H)*

BIRLINGHAM   SO9343
Swan (01386) 750485
*Church Street; off A4104 S of Pershore,
via B4080 Eckington Road, turn off
at sign to Birlingham with integral
'The Swan Inn' brown sign (not the
'Birlingham (village only)' road), then*

left; WR10 3AQ Pretty family-run thatched and timbered cottage; updated beamed quarry-tiled bar with woodburner in big stone fireplace, well kept ales such as Purity, real cider and good food from reasonably priced varied menu including fresh fish specials, friendly efficient service, dining conservatory; nice back garden, convenient for River Avon walks, open all day Sun till 7pm, closed Mon except bank holidays. *(Dr and Mrs H J Field, Guy Vowles)*

BREDON   SO9236
Fox & Hounds (01684) 772377
4.5 miles from M5 junction 9; A438 to Northway, left at B4079, in Bredon follow sign to church; GL20 7LA Cottagey 16th-c thatched pub with open-plan carpeted bar; low beams, stone pillars and stripped timbers, central woodburner, upholstered settles and variety of wheelback, tub and kitchen chairs around mahogany and cast-iron-framed tables, smaller side bar, ales such as Banks's, Butcombe and Wye Valley, decent wines by the glass and enjoyable food; background and some live music; children welcome, dogs in bar, outside picnic-sets and pretty hanging baskets, closed Mon. *(Louise and Anton Parsons)*

BROADWAS-ON-TEME   SO7555
Royal Oak (01886) 821353
A44; WR6 5NE Red-brick roadside pub with various areas including lofty dining hall; popular good value daily carvery and other enjoyable food, well kept ales such as Courage, Bombardier and Ringwood, decent wines by the glass, friendly helpful service; free wi-fi; children welcome, no dogs inside, disabled access from the back, garden with play area, open (and food) all day. *(Tim Allinson)*

BROADWAY   SP0937
Swan (01386) 852278
The Green (B4362); WR12 7AA Sizeable old Mitchells & Butlers dining pub with contemporary décor in several linked areas; popular sensibly priced food including fixed-price menu (till 6pm Mon-Fri), three well kept ales such as Sharps Doom Bar, plenty of wines by the glass and good range of cocktails, polite friendly young staff; children welcome, tables under parasols on small front terrace looking over road to village green, open all day. *(Sarah and David Gibbs)*

CALLOW END   SO8349
Blue Bell (01905) 830261
Upton Road; WR2 4TY Popular Marstons local with two bars and dining area; their well kept ales and wide variety of reasonably priced food including lots of specials (some good vegetarian choices), friendly welcoming staff, open fire; quiz last Thurs of the month, sports TV, pool and darts; children allowed, dogs in garden only, open all day weekends. *(Dr and Mrs H J Field)*

CALLOW END   SO8349
Old Bush (01905) 830792
Off Upton Road (B4424); WR2 4TE Friendly black and white village local; well kept ales such as Butcombe and Hobsons and enjoyable home-cooked food, cosy small areas around central bar, beams, woodburner and various memorabilia, separate dining room; live music including Aug blues festival; children and dogs welcome, nice garden with play area, camping, open all day Fri-Sun. *(Dave Braisted)*

CALLOW HILL   SP0164
Brook Inn (01527) 543209
Elcocks Brook, off B4504; B97 5UD Modernised country dining pub with well liked locally sourced food from lunchtime sandwiches up (not Sun evening, Mon), Marstons-related ales, friendly staff; tables out at front and in pleasant back beer garden, open all day. *(Jack Prest)*

CAUNSALL   SO8480
Anchor (01562) 850254
Caunsall Road, off A449; DY11 5YL Traditional unchanging two-room pub (in same family since 1927), popular and welcoming, with five well kept ales such as Hobsons, Three Tuns and Wye Valley, traditional ciders and good value generously filled cobs, friendly efficient service; children and dogs welcome, large outside seating area behind, near Staffordshire & Worcestershire Canal. *(Brian and Susan Wylie)*

CHADDESLEY CORBETT   SO8973
Swan (01562) 777302
Off A448 Bromsgrove–Kidderminster; DY10 4SD Popular old local with friendly buoyant atmosphere; well kept Bathams and enjoyable good value pubby food from sandwiches and pizzas up, various rooms including high-raftered lounge bar; Thurs jazz and other live music, TV, games machine; children and dogs welcome, picnic-sets in big lawned garden with play area and country views, Aug classic car show, handy for Harvington Hall, open all day, food all day Sat. *(Louise and Anton Parsons)*

CLAINES   SO8558
Mug House (01905) 456649
Claines Lane, off A449 3 miles W of M5 junction 3; WR3 7RN Fine views from this ancient country tavern in unique churchyard setting by fields below the Malvern Hills; several small rooms around central bar, low doorways and heavy oak beams, well kept Banks's and other Marstons-related ales, simple lunchtime pub food; no credit cards,

---

There are report forms at the back of the book.

outside loos; children (away from servery) and dogs welcome, open all day weekends. *(Chris Stevenson)*

CROPTHORNE SO9944
Bell (01386) 861860
Main Road (B4084); WR10 3NE Isolated rather stark-looking roadside pub with contrasting brightly modernised interior; painted beams, bare boards and colourful carpet in L-shaped bar, well divided seating areas (one down a couple of steps), log fire, small back conservatory, emphasis on dining with popular freshly made food from good ploughman's up, children's choices, three changing ales, welcoming efficient service; background and occasional live music; open all day Sat, till 8pm Sun, closed Mon, Tues. *(Alister and Margery Bacon)*

CROWLE SO9256
Chequers (01905) 381772
Crowle Green, not far from M5 junction 6; WR7 4AA Busy beamed dining pub (sister to the Forest at Feckenham); good food (some quite pricey) from sandwiches and one or two pubby choices up, well kept ales such as St Austell and Wye Valley, lots of wines by the glass and good range of other drinks, friendly attentive staff; children and dogs (in bar) welcome, open all day. *(Shaun)*

DEFFORD SO9042
★ Monkey House (01386) 750234
A4104, after passing Oak pub on right, it's the last of a small group of cottages; WR8 9BW Tiny black and white thatched cider house, a wonderful time warp and in the same family for over 150 years; ciders and a perry tapped from barrels into pottery mugs and served by landlady from hatch, no other drinks or food (can bring your own); children welcome, no dogs, garden with caravans, sheds and small spartan outbuilding with a couple of plain tables, settle and fireplace, only open lunchtimes Fri, Sun and evenings Weds, Sat. *(Jack Prest)*

DEFFORD SO9042
Oak (01386) 750327
Woodmancote (A4104); WR8 9BW Modernised 17th-c beamed country pub with two front bars and back restaurant; well kept ales such as Sharps and Wye Valley, Thatcher's cider, good fairly priced food (all day Sat, till 3pm Sun); occasional live music; children and dogs (in bar) welcome, vine-covered front pergola, garden with orchard and chickens, open all day. *(Jack Prest)*

DODFORD SO9372
Dodford Inn (01527) 835825
Whinfield Road; B61 9BG Refurbished mid 19th-c red-brick country pub tucked away in six-acre grounds; up to four well kept ales including Wye Valley, good home-made food (all day Sat, not Sun evening) from sandwiches up, friendly welcoming staff;

children allowed, no dogs inside, pleasing views over wooded valley from terrace tables, good walks, open all day, till 8pm Sun. *(Mrs B H Adams)*

DROITWICH SO8963
Gardeners Arms (01905) 772936
Vines Lane; WR9 8LU Individual place on the edge of town; cosy traditional bar to the right serving four changing ales, bistro-style restaurant to the left with red gingham tablecloths and lots of pictures (mostly for sale), well priced food from varied menu including range of good local sausages, pizzas and pies; regular live music and quiz nights, also themed food evenings, whisky tastings and a cigar club; children and dogs welcome, outside seating areas on different levels below railway embankment with quirky mix of furniture, play area, camping, close to Droitwich Canal, open (and food) all day. *(Chris Stevenson)*

DROITWICH SO9063
Hop Pole (01905) 770155
Friar Street; WR9 8ED Heavy-beamed 18th-c local with panelled rooms on different levels; well kept Wye Valley beers and a couple of guests, generous helpings of bargain lunchtime food including sandwiches, friendly staff and regulars; dominoes, darts and pool, occasional live music; children and dogs welcome, partly canopied back garden, open all day. *(Dave Braisted)*

DUNLEY SO7969
Dog (01299) 822833
A451 S of Stourport; DY13 0UE Attractive creeper-clad roadside pub and restaurant; good choice of enjoyable reasonably priced food from light meals up, well kept Wye Valley and guests, friendly staff; free wi-fi; children and dogs welcome, garden with play area and bowling green, three bedrooms, bar open all day weekends (from 5pm other days), restaurant open for lunch and dinner apart from Sun evening. *(Brian and Susan Wylie)*

ECKINGTON SO9241
Bell (01386) 750033
Church Street (B4080); WR10 3AN Modernised village dining pub with much liked food (special diets catered for) including good value three-course lunch, you can also cook your own on a hot stone, two well kept ales, efficient friendly service; quiz first Sun of month; children and dogs (in Farmers Bar) welcome, enclosed back garden, on Wyche Way long-distance path, four bedrooms, open (and food) all day weekends. *(Guy Vowles)*

ELMLEY CASTLE SO9841
Queen Elizabeth (01386) 710251
Signed off A44 and A435, not far from Evesham; Main Street; WR10 3HS

Modernised old community-owned pub; central bar with wood floor and small brick fireplace, well kept Purity, Wye Valley and a couple of guests, steps down to beamed and flagstoned snug with inglenook log fire, two dining rooms, enjoyable reasonably priced food (not Sun evening, Mon) including themed nights, good friendly service; children and dogs welcome, tables out in courtyard, closed Mon lunchtime, otherwise open all day (till 8pm Sun). *(Don Humphries)*

EVESHAM   SP0344
Old Red Horse (01386) 442784
Vine Street; WR11 4RE Attractive 15th-c black and white coaching inn; two bars with beams, bare boards and open fires, three real ales, traditional ciders and enjoyable reasonably priced pub food, lunchtime meal deal (Mon-Sat), steak nights (Tues, Weds), good cheerful service; TV, darts and machines, free wi-fi; children and dogs welcome, nice covered inner courtyard with small pond, five bedrooms, open all day, no evening food weekends. *(Dr J Barrie Jones)*

FECKENHAM   SP0061
Forest (01527) 894422
B4090 Droitwich–Alcester; B96 6JE Contemporary décor and good interesting food at this village dining pub (sister to the Chequers at Crowle), well kept Hook Norton and a guest, efficient friendly service, oak-floored bar with light-wood stools at high tables and some other more comfortable seating, panels of bookshelf wallpaper dotted about, woodburner, adjoining restaurant with upholstered booth seats, conservatory; children and dogs welcome, disabled access/loos, rattan furniture on block-paved terrace with big outdoor fireplace, more tables on raised lawn, closed Mon and Tues, otherwise open all day, food till 6pm Sun. *(Mike and Mary Carter)*

FLADBURY   SO9946
Chequers (01386) 861854
Chequers Lane; WR10 2PZ This old village pub was about to reopen under new owners as we went to press; reports please.

FLYFORD FLAVELL   SO9754
Boot (01386) 462658
Off A422 Worcester–Alcester; Radford Road; WR7 4BS Popular food including two-course lunch deal, cook your own steak on a hot stone and blackboard specials, Fullers London Pride and Sharps Doom Bar, good friendly service, log fires in ancient heavily beamed and timbered core, modern conservatory, games room with pool and TV; background music; children, walkers and

dogs (in bar) welcome, tables on split-level terrace and small lawned area, five bedrooms, open all day. *(Dr and Mrs H J Field)*

GRIMLEY   SO8359
Camp House (01905) 640288
A443 5 miles N from Worcester, right to Grimley, right at village T junction; WR2 6LX Simple unpretentious old pub (in same family since 1939) tucked away in appealing Severn-side setting (prone to flooding); well kept Bathams and guests, proper ciders and decent home-made pubby food (no credit cards), rambling interior with open fires, friendly relaxed atmosphere; some live music, darts; children and well behaved dogs welcome, attractive lawns (maybe wandering peacocks), own landing stage and small campsite, open all day. *(Nigel and Sue Foster)*

HADLEY   SO8662
Bowling Green (01905) 620294
Hadley Heath; off A4133 Droitwich–Ombersley; WR9 0AR Popular refurbished 16th-c inn with beams and big log fire, well kept Wadworths ales and decent wines by the glass, good food (all day Sun) from sandwiches and deli boards up, comfortable back lounge and restaurant; children welcome, tables out overlooking own bowling green (UK's oldest), comfortable bedrooms, nice walks (footpath starts from car park), open all day. *(Louise and Anton Parsons)*

HANBURY   SO9662
Vernon (01527) 821236
Droitwich Road (B4090); B60 4DB Former 18th-c coaching inn with contemporary interior; much emphasis on dining, but they also serve up to four real ales including Mad Goose and a dozen wines by the glass in beamed bar, nice food from sharing plates, pub favourites and flatbread pizzas up, good value OAP set lunch too, friendly efficient service, restaurant with kitchen view; children and dogs welcome, modern terrace seating, five boutique-style bedrooms, open all day. *(Nigel and Sue Foster)*

HANLEY CASTLE   SO8342
★ Three Kings (01684) 592686
Church End, off B4211 N of Upton upon Severn; WR8 0BL Timeless, hospitable and by no means smart – in same family since 1911 and a favourite with those who put unspoilt character and individuality first; cheerful, homely tiled-floor tap room separated from entrance corridor by monumental built-in settle, equally vast inglenook fireplace, room on left with darts and board games, separate entrance to

---

Post Office address codings confusingly give the impression that some pubs are in Worcestershire, when they're really in Gloucestershire, Herefordshire, Shropshire or Warwickshire (which is where we list them).

timbered lounge with second inglenook and blacked kitchen range, leatherette armchairs, spindleback chairs and antique winged settle, well kept Butcombe, Hobsons and three guests, Weston's cider and around 75 malt whiskies, simple snacks including good sandwiches; live music; children and dogs welcome, wood and iron seats on front terrace looking across to old cedar shading tiny green, on Wyche Way long-distance path. *(Dave Braisted, Paul Desborough)*

HANLEY SWAN   SO8142
⭐ **Swan**   (01684) 311870
B4209 Malvern–Upton; WR8 0EA
Contemporary/rustic décor and furnishings blending well with old low beams (some painted), bare boards and log fire, extended back part set for their good well presented food (all day Sat, not Sun evening) from sandwiches/baguettes and pub favourites to more restaurant dishes (booking advised), friendly helpful staff, ales such as Hobsons, Lakehouse and Wye Valley, seven wines by the glass, oak-framed conservatory; children and dogs welcome, disabled access/loos, seats out on paved terrace and grass, nice spot facing green and big duck pond, five comfortable good value bedrooms, open all day, weekend breakfast from 8am. *(Chris Stevenson)*

HIMBLETON   SO9458
Galton Arms   (01905) 391672
Harrow Lane; WR9 7LQ Friendly old black and white bay-windowed country pub; good food (not Sun evening, Mon) including daily specials in split-level beamed bar or restaurant, well kept ales such as Banks's, Bathams and Wye Valley, woodburner; sports TV; children and dogs welcome, picnic-sets in small part-paved garden, local walks, open all day Sun, closed Mon lunchtime. *(Shaun)*

HOLT HEATH   SO8063
Red Lion   (01905) 620600
Witley Road (A443/A4133); WR6 6LX
Modernised dining pub specialising in good value caribbean food, also traditional meals including early bird deal till 6pm; bar with white-painted beams, high-backed dining chairs around cheerfully clothed tables and some colourful artwork, three real ales and several rums, good friendly service, raftered restaurant; pool, sports TV, fruit machine; picnic-sets in lawned garden with decked area, open all day weekends, closed Mon and lunchtimes Tues-Fri. *(Dave Braisted)*

HOLY CROSS   SO9278
Bell & Cross   (01562) 730319
2 miles from M5 junction 3: A491 towards Stourbridge, then follow Clent signpost off on left; DY9 9QL Reopened and refurbished early 19th-c village pub; good food from snacks and lighter meals up, four real ales including Enville, Timothy Taylors and Wye Valley, decent wines by the

glass, friendly helpful staff, several small rooms off central corridor including bar with open fire; children and dogs (in some areas) welcome, picnic-sets in nice good-sized garden, open all day Fri-Sun, no food Sun evening. *(Simon H)*

KEMERTON   SO9437
Crown   (01386) 725020
Back Road Bredon–Beckford; GL20 7HP
Small 18th-c pub in pretty village; hospitable landlord and cheerful staff, good freshly made food (not Sun evening) from sandwiches up including sharing dishes and daily specials, ales such as Wye Valley, local cider, flagstoned bar with log fire, separate restaurant; children and dogs welcome, roadside tables and peaceful courtyard garden behind, good walks over Bredon Hill, four pleasant bedrooms, closed Mon lunchtime, otherwise open all day. *(Brian and Susan Wylie)*

KIDDERMINSTER   SO8376
King & Castle   (01562) 747505
Severn Valley Railway station, Comberton Hill; DY10 1QX Neatly recreated Edwardian refreshment room in Severn Valley Railway terminus – steam trains outside and railway memorabilia and photographs inside; eight real ales including Bathams, Bewdley and Hobsons, three traditional ciders, cobs at the bar or reasonably priced straightforward food in adjacent dining room; children welcome, little railway museum close by, open all day and busy bank holidays/railway gala days, open (and food) all day. *(Jamie and Lizzie McEwan)*

LONGDON   SO8434
Hunters Inn   (01684) 833388
B4211 S, towards Tewkesbury; GL20 6AR Beamed and timbered country pub with flagstone floors, stripped brickwork and log fires, enjoyable locally sourced food including popular Sun carvery, real ales such as Donnington and Otter, local ciders and decent wines by the glass, friendly service, raftered dining area with linen-clothed tables, good views; some live music and quiz nights, darts; children welcome, extensive well tended garden, campsite, open all day weekends, closed Mon and lunchtime Tues. *(Tim Allinson)*

LOWER BROADHEATH   SO8056
Dewdrop   (01905) 640012
Bell Lane; WR2 6RR Popular dining pub with contemporary interior; much enjoyed food from sandwiches and snacks up including some pub favourites, ales such as Bathams and Woods, real ciders and a dozen wines by the glass, afternoon teas, friendly attentive service; children welcome, dogs in bar and part of restaurant, rattan-style tables and chairs out at front, nine bedrooms in separate buildings, handy for the Firs (NT)

– Elgar's birthplace, open all day, food all day weekends, breakfast from 7am (8am Sat, Sun). *(Theocsbrian, Dave Braisted, Paul Walker)*

LULSLEY   SO7354
Fox & Hounds (01886) 821228
Signed a mile off A44 Worcester–Bromyard; WR6 5QT Friendly tucked-away country pub with well kept Wye Valley Butty Bach and guests, local cider and good choice of whiskies and gins, enjoyable sensibly priced food (all day Sat, not Sun evening) from sandwiches and pub staples up, parquet-floored bar with open fire, dining area and sizeable conservatory; children and dogs welcome, tables in side garden, separate enclosed play area, nice walks (near Worcestershire Way), closed lunchtimes Mon and Tues, otherwise open all day. *(Dr and Mrs H J Field)*

MALVERN   SO7746
Foley Arms (01684) 580350
Worcester Road; WR14 4QS Substantial Georgian hotel (former coaching inn) owned by Wetherspoons, friendly staff and usual good value, splendid views from main bar, sunny terrace and back bedrooms; free wi-fi; children welcome, open all day from 7am. *(Dr J Barrie Jones)*

MALVERN   SO7640
Malvern Hills Hotel (01684) 540690
Opposite British Camp car park, Wynds Point; junction A449/B4232 S; WR13 6DW Big comfortable lounge bar with oak panelling and woodburner, three well kept Wye Valley ales and a guest (two in summer), quite a few malt whiskies, enjoyable food here or in two more modern restaurants (one with lovely country views), good friendly service; background music; children (till 4pm) and dogs (in bar) welcome, terrace seating under parasols, cosy bedrooms, open (and food) all day. *(John Evans, Clive and Fran Dutson)*

MALVERN   SO7746
Red Lion (01684) 564787
St Anns Road; WR14 4RG Tucked up a narrow lane near town centre; enjoyable food (all day Sat) from sandwiches and baguettes up, also very good adjacent thai restaurant (evenings Tues-Sat), well kept Marstons-related ales such as Ringwood, cheerful prompt service, modern décor with stripped pine, bare boards, flagstones and pastel colours; background music, darts; attractive partly covered front terrace, well placed for hill walks, open (and food) all day Sat, closed Sun-Fri lunchtimes. *(Jack Prest)*

MALVERN   SO7643
Wyche (01684) 575396
Wyche Road; WR14 4EQ Comfortable busy pub near top of Malvern Hills, splendid views and popular with walkers; Wye Valley and guests, decent range of affordable pubby

food from sandwiches up including themed nights, good service; pool and games machine in one bar; children and dogs welcome, four bedrooms plus self-catering apartments, open all day. *(Jack Prest)*

OMBERSLEY   SO8463
Cross Keys (01905) 620588
Just off A449; Main Road (A4133, Kidderminster end); WR9 0DS Refurbished 19th-c country pub; carpeted bar with fire, archways opening into several separate areas, beams, banquettes and brassware, Timothy Taylors Landlord and Wye Valley HPA, well liked food from sandwiches to daily specials, friendly helpful service, dining conservatory; background music; children and dogs welcome, terrace seating, open all day Sun (food till 7pm), closed Mon lunchtime. *(Dave Braisted)*

OMBERSLEY   SO8463
★ **Kings Arms** (01905) 620142
Main Road (A4133); WR9 0EW Imposing beamed and timbered Tudor pub; low-ceilinged brick-floored bar with built-in panelled wall seat and woodburner in large fireplace, three dining areas, steps down to one, another with Charles II coat of arms decorating the ceiling, good food and service, well kept Marstons-related ales; background music; children and dogs welcome, seats on tree-sheltered courtyard, colourful hanging baskets and tubs, open all day Fri-Sun. *(David and Stella Martin)*

PENSAX   SO7368
★ **Bell** (01299) 896677
B4202 Abberley–Clows Top, Snead Common part of village; WR6 6AE Mock-Tudor roadside pub with good local atmosphere, seven well kept ales including Exmoor and Hobsons, real cider/perry and popular good value pub food (not Sun evening) from sandwiches up, L-shaped main bar with traditional décor, cushioned pews and pubby tables on bare boards, vintage beer ads and wartime front pages, two open fires and woodburner, dining room with french windows opening on to deck; children and dogs (in bar) welcome, garden with country views, closed Mon lunchtime. *(Dave Braisted)*

PEOPLETON   SO9350
Crown (01905) 840222
Village and pub signed off A44 at Allens Hill; WR10 2EE Cosy village pub with friendly mix of drinkers and diners; beamed bar with big inglenook and well laid-out eating area, good food (must book) from sandwiches and pub favourites up including OAP deals and regular themed evenings, ales such as Fullers, Sharps and Wye Valley, nice wines by the glass, pleasant efficient service; children allowed till 9pm, dogs in bar, flower-filled back garden, open all day. *(Chris Stevenson)*

PERSHORE — SO9445
Pickled Plum (01386) 556645
High Street; WR10 1EQ Modernised old pub with good range of well kept ales and ciders, enjoyable generously served food at fair prices including lunchtime/early evening two-course deal and blackboard specials, quick friendly service, beams and log fires; Sun quiz, acoustic music session first Mon of month; children and dogs welcome, open all day, no food Sun evening. *(Denis and Margaret Kilner)*

SEVERN STOKE — SO8544
Rose & Crown (01905) 371249
A38 S of Worcester; WR8 9JQ Attractive 16th-c black and white pub, gently refurbished under present owners; low beams, good fire and various knick-knacks in character bar, some cushioned wall seats and high-backed settles among more modern pub furniture, quarry-tiled or carpeted floors, well kept Marstons-related ales, Weston's cider and decent choice of enjoyable sensibly priced food from sharing plates up, good friendly service, carpeted back restaurant; children (away from bar) and dogs welcome, tricky wheelchair access but possible with help, picnic-sets in big garden with play area, Malvern Hills views and good walks, open all day in summer. *(Chris and Angela Buckell)*

SHATTERFORD — SO7981
Bellmans Cross (01299) 861322
Bridgnorth Road (A442); DY12 1RN Welcoming 19th-c mock-Tudor dining pub; good well presented food cooked by french chef-landlord including weekday themed evenings, restaurant with kitchen view, Enville and a couple of guests from neat timber-effect bar, good choice of wines, teas and coffees; children welcome, picnic-sets outside, handy for Severn Woods walks, open all day weekends, no food Sun evening. *(Alister and Margery Bacon)*

STOKE POUND — SO9667
Queens Head (01527) 557007
Sugarbrook Lane, by Bridge 48, Worcester & Birmingham Canal; B60 3AU Smartly modernised by the small Lovely Pubs group; fairly large bar with comfortable seating area, dedicated dining part beyond, good choice of food including sharing plates, wood-fired pizzas and charcoal spit-roasts, early evening discount (Mon-Fri) and two-for-one pizzas (Mon-Thurs), well kept ales such as Sharps

and Wye Valley, large selection of wines from glass-fronted store, helpful pleasant staff; live music Thurs; children welcome, waterside garden with tipi, moorings, good walk up the 30 locks of Tardebigge Steps, quite handy for Avoncroft Museum, open (and food) all day. *(Brian and Susan Wylie)*

STOKE WORKS — SO9365
Boat & Railway (01527) 575597
Shaw Lane, by Bridge 42 of Worcester & Birmingham Canal; B60 4EQ Neat and tidy canalside pub; enjoyable good value home-cooked food including deals, Marstons-related ales, friendly helpful staff, large separate dining area overlooking the water; children (till 9pm) and dogs (in bar) welcome, narrow covered terrace, moorings, open (and food) all day, kitchen shuts 6pm Sun. *(Dave Braisted)*

STOKE WORKS — SO9365
Bowling Green (01527) 861291
A mile from M5 junction 5, via Stoke Lane; handy for Worcester & Birmingham Canal; B60 4BH Friendly comfortable pub with enjoyable straightforward food at bargain prices (particularly good faggots), well kept Banks's ales and a Marstons guest, wall chart showing cost of a pint over the years; children welcome, big garden with play area and well tended bowling green, camping, open all day, no food Sun. *(Dave Braisted)*

TENBURY WELLS — SO5966
Fountain (01584) 810701
Oldwood, A4112 S; WR15 8TB Timbered 17th-c roadside pub with big black-beamed bar, good choice of well prepared/priced pubby food, ales from Hobsons and sometimes Wye Valley, friendly helpful service; children and dogs welcome, a few picnic-sets out at front, more in lawned garden with play equipment, ten bedrooms (separate block), open all day, food all day Sat. *(Theocsbrian)*

TENBURY WELLS — SO5968
Pembroke House (01584) 810301
Cross Street; WR15 8EQ Striking timbered building (oldest in town) with pubby beamed bar and two dining rooms, good popular food (not Sun evening, Tues, best to book) including themed nights, friendly efficient staff, Hobsons Best and a guest, woodburner, games area with pool, darts and TV; background and some live music; children welcome, no dogs inside, smokers' shelter and pleasant garden, open all day. *(Louise and Anton Parsons)*

A star symbol before the name of a pub shows exceptional character and appeal. It doesn't mean extra comfort. Even quite a basic pub can win a star, if it's individual enough.

TIBBERTON   SO9057
Bridge Inn (01905) 345144
Plough Road; WR9 7NQ Welcoming
refurbished pub next to Worcester &
Birmingham Canal (Bridge 25); two
comfortable dining sections with central
fireplace, separate bar, enjoyable reasonably
priced pubby food including stone-baked
pizzas, three well kept changing ales (often
Wadworths 6X), good attentive service;
children and dogs welcome, picnic-sets by
water and in secure front garden, moorings,
open all day (till 9pm Sun and Mon).
(David Dore)

UPHAMPTON   SO8464
Fruiterers Arms (01905) 620305
Off A449 N of Ombersley; WR9 0JW
Friendly country local (looks like a private
house, and has been in the same family
since the mid 19th c); well kept Wye Valley
and a couple of local guests, farm cider/
perry, simple rustic Jacobean panelled bar
and lounge with comfortable armchairs,
beams and log fire, lots of photographs and
memorabilia, snacky food such as rolls and
pork pies; Tues quiz; children allowed till
9pm, dogs in one area, back terrace and
some seats out in front, open all day (from
1pm Tues). *(Shaun)*

WEST MALVERN   SO7645
Brewers Arms (01684) 561989
The Dingle, signed off B4232; WR14 4BQ
Attractive little two-bar beamed country
local down steep path; well kept Malvern
Hills, Wye Valley and up to five guests at busy
times, good value pubby food, airy dining
room; live music Fri, free wi-fi; children,
walkers and dogs welcome, glorious view
from small garden, open all day. *(Jack Prest)*

WILLERSEY   SP1039
New Inn (01386) 853226
Main Street; WR12 7PJ Friendly old stone-
built local in lovely village; generous helpings
of good value pub food (not Sun evening)
from sandwiches up, well kept Donnington
ales, flagstoned bar with raised quarry-tiled
end section, some black beams, games room
(pool and darts) and separate skittle alley;
background music, TV; rattan-style tables and
chairs outside, good local walks, open all day.
(Brian and Susan Wylie)

WORCESTER   SO8554
Cardinals Hat (01905) 724006
*Friar Street; just off A44 near cathedral;
WR1 2NA* Dating from the 14th c with three
small character rooms (one with fine oak
panelling); five changing ales, real ciders
and plenty of bottled beers, friendly well
informed staff, good bar snacks and cheese/
meat platters; free wi-fi; children welcome,
pleasant little brick-paved terrace behind,
four good bedrooms (continental breakfast),
closed Mon lunchtime, otherwise open
all day. *(Tim Allinson)*

WORCESTER   SO8455
Dragon (01905) 25845
The Tything (A38); WR1 1JT Refurbished
Georgian alehouse run by friendly landlady;
L-shaped carpeted bar with woodburner, six
well kept Church End ales and a couple of
guests, traditional cider and seven wines by
the glass, snacky food such as pork pies and
sausage rolls, more room (and loos) upstairs;
no children inside, dogs welcome, partly
covered back terrace, open all day Fri-Sun,
from 4pm other days. *(Tim Allinson)*

WORCESTER   SO8454
Farriers Arms (01905) 27569
Fish Street; WR1 2HN Welcoming and
relaxed old timbered pub off the High Street;
compact interior with bar and dining areas
wrapping around central bar, enjoyable
inexpensive lunchtime food (evening food
Thurs and Fri only), well kept ales such as
Bombardier and St Austell Tribute, decent
house wines, good cheerful service; pool,
darts, TV and machines; children welcome
away from bar until 7pm, beer garden, well
placed for cathedral, open all day and gets
busy lunchtimes. *(Mrs J Ekins-Daukes)*

WORCESTER   SO8554
King Charles II (01905) 726100
New Street; WR1 2DP Small jettied
Tudor building; heavy beams, fine panelling
and woodburners in carved fireplaces,
settles and pews on bare boards, up to
eight well kept ales from Craddocks and
associated Bridgnorth and Two Thirsty
Brewers, traditional ciders, enjoyable range
of Pieminister pies served with peas and
different types of mash (limited range of
other food), friendly helpful staff (ask them
about the skeleton under the floor), more
seating upstairs; quiz night Tues; open all day
(food all day weekends). *(Tim Allinson)*

WORCESTER   SO8455
Ounce (01905) 330460
*The Tything (A38); some nearby
parking; WR1 1JL* Refurbished under
present owners; long narrow series of small
linked areas, dark flagstones and broad
floorboards, stripped or cast-iron-framed
tables, open fires, also an upstairs room,
Sharps Doom Bar and a couple of Wye Valley
beers, a dozen wines by the glass, cocktails,
good food with emphasis on steaks (order
by weight – from £1 per ounce on Tues and
Weds), friendly helpful staff; background
music, live Sat; children and dogs (in bar)

If you know a pub is ever open all day, please tell us.

welcome, sunny flagstoned back courtyard, closed Mon, otherwise open all day (till 7pm Sun). *(Tim Allinson, Shaun)*

WORCESTER   SO8555
Plough (01905) 21381
Fish Street; WR1 2HN Traditional corner pub with two simple rooms off entrance lobby; six well kept interesting beers including Hobsons and Malvern Hills, local cider/perry and good whisky choice, straightforward meals Fri-Sun lunchtimes only; outside loos and small back terrace with cathedral view, open all day. *(Shaun)*

WYRE PIDDLE   SO9647
Anchor (01386) 244590
Off A4538 NW of Evesham; WR10 2JB Great position by River Avon with moorings, decking on three levels, floodlit lawn and view from airy back dining room; good food from sharing plates and pub favourites up including wood-fired pizzas and set lunch deal Tues-Sat, swift friendly service, beers such as Greene King, local Pershore and Wye Valley; children and dogs welcome, kitchen closed Sun evenings, otherwise open (and food) all day. *(Richard Tilbrook)*

Yorkshire

KEY ★ Star Pub | Top Quality Food ▮ Great Beer
♀ Good Wines £ Bargain Meals 🛏 Good Bedrooms ❙❙ Serves Food

BECK HOLE

NZ8202 Map 10

Birch Hall

(01947) 896245 – www.beckhole.info/bhi.htm

Off A169 SW of Whitby, from top of Sleights Moor; YO22 5LE

Extraordinary place in lovely valley with friendly landlady, real ales and simple snacks

Set in a beautiful steep valley village by a bridge over a river and close to Thomason Foss waterfall, this remains an unchanging, tiny pub-cum-village shop; many customers are walkers with their dogs. The two simple rooms have built-in cushioned wall seats, wooden tables (one embedded with 136 pennies), flagstones or composition flooring, unusual items such as a tube of toothpaste priced 1/-3d, and a model train running around a head-height shelf. Black Sheep, North Yorkshire Beckwatter and a guest such as Beer Monkey Blonde on handpump, several malt whiskies and wines by the glass. The shop sells postcards, sweets and ice-creams. There are benches outside in a streamside garden and one of the wonderful nearby walks is along a disused railway. They have a self-catering cottage for hire.

❙❙ Bar snacks only, such as local pork pie, butties, scones and their famous beer cake.

Free house ~ Licensee Glenys Crampton ~ Real ale ~ No credit cards ~ Open 11-11; 11-3, 7.30-11 Weds-Sun in winter ~ Bar food available during opening hours ~ Children in small family room ~ Dogs welcome *Recommended by Sally and Colin Allen, Alexander and Trish Gendall, Nick Sharpe, Toby Jones, Scott and Charlotte Havers, Emily and Toby Archer*

BLAKEY RIDGE

SE6799 Map 10

Lion ▮ 🛏

(01751) 417320 – www.lionblakey.co.uk

From A171 Guisborough–Whitby follow 'Castleton, Hutton-le-Hole' signposts; from A170 Kirkby Moorside–Pickering follow 'Keldholm, Hutton-le-Hole, Castleton' signposts; OS Sheet 100 map reference 679996; YO62 7LQ

Extended pub in fine scenery and open all day; popular food; bedrooms

Said to be the fourth-highest pub in England, this place boasts spectacular moorland views and our readers make the most of the numerous surrounding hikes by staying in the comfortable bedrooms and enjoying the first class breakfasts. The low-beamed rambling bars have open fires, a few big high-backed rustic settles around cast-iron-framed tables, lots of small dining chairs, a nice leather sofa and stone walls hung with old engravings and photographs of the pub under snow (it can easily get cut off in winter – 40 days is the record so far). The fine choice of beers on handpump might include Black Sheep Best, Cropton Yorkshire Moors, Marstons Wainwright and Theakstons Best, Old Peculier and XB and Timothy Taylors Boltmaker, as well as 13 wines by the glass and several malt whiskies; background music and games machine.

Generous helpings of hearty food includes lunchtime sandwiches, mussels in creamy white wine sauce, deep-fried brie with cranberry sauce, mediterranean vegetable risotto, minted lamb pie, local game sausages with yorkshire pudding, mash and onion gravy, beef curry, chicken tikka masala, ham with egg or pineapple, duck breast in orange sauce, salmon steak in creamy white wine and prawn sauce, sirloin steak with a choice of sauce, and puddings such as toffee crunch pie and warm sticky ginger and lemon cake. *Benchmark main dish: steak and mushroom pie £13.50. Two-course evening meal £18.00.*

Free house ~ Licensees Barry, Diana, Paul and David Crossland ~ Real ale ~ Open 10am-11pm; 10am-midnight Fri, Sat ~ Bar food 12-10 ~ Restaurant ~ Children welcome ~ Dogs allowed in bar ~ Wi-fi ~ Bedrooms: $42.50/$88 *Recommended by Martin and Joanne Sharp, Mike and Sarah Abbot, Camilla and Jose Ferrera, Alf and Sally Garner, WAH, John and Mary Warner, Gus Swan, Caroline Prescott*

BRADFIELD
Strines Inn £ 🛏
SK2290 Map 7

(0114) 285 1247 – www.thestrinesinn.co.uk

Pub signed from A57 (first left, E of junction with A6013, Ladybower Reservoir), follow moorland road for 1.5 miles; with a map can also be reached more circuitously from Strines signpost on A616 at head of Underbank Reservoir, W of Stocksbridge; S6 6JE

Bustling inn in stunning scenery with hearty food and plenty of customers; bedrooms

We've had lots of positive reports this year from our readers, who enjoy staying here. The bedrooms have four-poster beds and a dining table (they serve breakfast in your room) and the front one overlooks Strines Reservoir. The main bar has black beams liberally decked with copper kettles and so forth, a coal fire in a rather grand stone fireplace, quite a menagerie of stuffed animals, and homely red plush-cushioned traditional wooden wall benches and small chairs; background music. Two other rooms, to the right and left, are similarly furnished. Acorn Yorkshire Pride, Jennings Cocker Hoop, Marstons Pedigree and a guest from Loxley on handpump, nine wines by the glass and eight malt whiskies. There are plenty of picnic-sets outside, as well as swings, a play area and peacocks and geese. Disabled access. The building originated as a 13th-c manor house, although most of it dates from the 16th c. Its isolated position on the edge of the Peak District National Park means excellent surrounding walks.

Tasty, honest food includes sandwiches, garlic mushrooms on toast, giant yorkshire pudding with onion gravy, macaroni cheese, burger with salad and chips, chilli con carne, cajun chicken with chips, gammon with egg or pineapple, mixed grill, 10oz rump steak with a choice of sauce, and puddings such as chocolate fudge cake and treacle sponge with custard. *Benchmark main dish: steak in ale pie £10.40. Two-course evening meal £16.00.*

Free house ~ Licensee Bruce Howarth ~ Real ale ~ Open 10.30am-11pm ~ Bar food 12-9; 12-2.30, 5.30-8.30 weekdays in winter ~ Children welcome ~ Dogs welcome ~ Bedrooms: $75/$95 *Recommended by Susan and Tim Boyle, Diana and Bertie Farr, Graham Smart, Jamie and Lizzie McEwan, Charlie and Mark Todd, Charlotte and William Mason*

BROUGHTON

SD9450 Map 7

Bull 🍺 ⏷

(01756) 792065 – www.brunningandprice.co.uk/bull

A59; BD23 3AE

Stone pub with interconnected bar and dining areas, a fine choice of drinks, interesting food and seats outside

Recently taken over by Brunning & Price, this is a handsome place with spreading, refurbished rooms. There are rugs on flagstones, open log fires, plenty of prints and cartoons on the walls, a mix of wooden or high-backed leather dining chairs, button-back armchairs and cushioned wooden settles and wall seats and polished tables. Also, elegant metal chandeliers, mirrors, house plants and a bustling, friendly atmosphere. Helpful, efficient staff keep Phoenix Brunning & Price Original, Dark Horse Hatton Pale Ale, Lancaster Blonde, Listers Best Bitter and Timothy Taylors Boltmaker and Landlord on handpump, 18 wines by the glass, 29 gins and 37 whiskies; board games. In warm weather you can sit at rattan-style chairs and tables on the attractive terrace in front of the building. Disabled access. There's a lot to do and see nearby, including exploring Broughton Hall Estate's 3,000 acres of beautiful countryside and parkland.

Brasserie-style food includes sandwiches, five-spice duck leg with spring onion, cucumber, hoisin sauce and pancakes, scallops with pea purée and ham hock fritters, cauliflower, chickpea and pepper curry with sticky almond pilaf rice and sweet potato bhaji, sausages with mash and onion gravy, steak in ale pie, sea trout with chorizo, fennel croquettes and bouillabaisse sauce, crispy beef salad with sweet chilli sauce and cashews, venison haunch with dauphinoise potatoes and blackberry jus, and puddings such as apple tarte tatin with calvados sauce anglaise and hot waffle with caramelised banana and honeycomb ice-cream. *Benchmark main dish: braised lamb shoulder with dauphinoise potatoes and rosemary gravy £17.45. Two-course evening meal £21.00.*

Brunning & Price ~ Manager Steve Larkin ~ Real ale ~ Open 10am-11pm; 10am-10.30pm Sun ~ Bar food 12-9; 12-9.30 Fri, Sat; 12-9 Sun ~ Restaurant ~ Children welcome ~ Dogs allowed in bar ~ Wi-fi *Recommended by Chloe and Michael Swettenham, Pat and Tony Martin, John and Sylvia Harrop, Giles and Suzie Nunn, Gwendoline and Ralph Mason*

CONSTABLE BURTON

SE1690 Map 10

Wyvill Arms ✪ ⏷ 🍺 🛏

(01677) 450581 – www.thewyvillarms.co.uk

A684 E of Leyburn; DL8 5LH

Well run, friendly dining pub with interesting food, a dozen wines by the glass, real ales and efficient helpful service; bedrooms

'Delightful in every way' is how one reader describes this stylish former farmhouse, and many others agree. The small bar area has a finely worked plaster ceiling with the Wyvill family's coat of arms, a mix of seating and an elaborate stone fireplace with a warm winter fire. The second bar has been refurbished but has kept the model train on a railway track running around the room. A reception area includes a huge leather sofa that can seat up to eight people, another carved stone fireplace and an old leaded stained-glass church window partition. Both rooms are hung with pictures of local scenes. Theakstons Best, Wensleydale Coverdale Gamekeeper and a guest beer on handpump, plus nine wines by the glass and nine malt whiskies; chess, backgammon and dominoes. There are several large wooden benches under sizeable white parasols for outdoor dining and picnic-sets by a well.

The comfortable bedrooms make a lovely base for exploring the area and breakfasts are generous. Constable Burton Hall is opposite.

 The best local, seasonal produce is used in the highly enjoyable food, which includes duck liver and orange pâté with home-made rustic toast, smoked haddock, cod and salmon fishcake with poached egg and hollandaise, egyptian-style vegetarian stew topped with mozzarella, pork fillet, belly and cheek with black pudding and cider sauce on coarse grain mustard mash, scallops with greek-style salad, lamb shank on mash with minted mushy peas and jus, half a crispy roast duck with black cherry sauce, beef bourguignon, 28-day aged sirloin steak with a choice of five sauces, and puddings. *Benchmark main dish: lighly curried monkfish on samphire with king prawn and moules marinière sauce £19.95. Two-course evening meal £21.00.*

Free house ~ Licensee Nigel Stevens ~ Real ale ~ Open 11-3, 5.30-11; 11-3, 6-10 Sun; closed Mon, lunchtime Tues ~ Bar food 12-2.15, 5.30-9 ~ Restaurant ~ Children welcome until 8.30 ~ Dogs allowed in bar ~ Wi-fi ~ Bedrooms: £75/£110 *Recommended by Christine and Tony Garrett, Frances and Hamish Porter, Richard Cole, S Holder, Paul Faraday, Joe and Belinda Smart, Susan and John Douglas, Dave Braisted*

CRAYKE
Durham Ox 🍴 ♟ 🛏

SE5670 Map 7

(01347) 821506 – www.thedurhamox.com

Off B1363 at Brandsby, towards Easingwold; West Way; YO61 4TE

Convivial inn with interesting décor in old-fashioned rooms, fine drinks and smashing food; comfortable bedrooms

You'll find plenty of contented customers at this well run all-rounder. It's a civilised and friendly place and the old-fashioned lounge bar has venerable tables, antique seats and settles on flagstones and pictures and photographs on dark red walls; also, interesting satirical carvings in the panelling (Victorian copies of medieval pew ends), polished copper and brass and an enormous inglenook fireplace. In the bottom bar is a framed illustrated account of local history (some of it gruesome) dating from the 12th c, and a large framed print of the famous Durham Ox, which weighed 171 stone. The Burns Bar has a woodburning stove, exposed brickwork and large french windows that open on to a balcony. Black Sheep Bitter, Timothy Taylors Boltmaker and York Guzzler on handpump, 20 wines by the glass, a dozen malt whiskies and interesting spirits including one made locally and named for them; background music and board games. In warm weather you can make the most of the seats in the courtyard garden, the bottom of which offers views on three sides over the Vale of York; on the fourth is a charming view to the medieval church on the hill – supposedly the very hill up which the Grand Old Duke of York marched his men. Bedrooms, in the main building or in renovated farm cottages (dogs allowed here), are well equipped and spacious, and breakfasts are very good. The nearby A19 leads straight to a park & ride for York city centre.

 First class food includes lunchtime sandwiches, dill-cured hot smoked salmon with horseradish crème fraîche and pickled beetroot, sticky spicy pork belly with chilli, honey and sesame dressing on asian salad, caramelised shallot tarte tatin with roasted vegetable cassoulet, beef in ale pie with a horseradish and suet scone dumpling, roast duck with dauphinoise potatoes and orange sauce, slow-cooked confit lamb shoulder with mash and roasted garlic, rosemary and red wine sauce, seafood sharing platter, and puddings such as salted caramel and chocolate bomb with salted caramel ice-cream and hot caramel sauce and crêpes suzette with orange and Grand Marnier flambé and vanilla ice-cream; they also offer an early bird menu (5.30-6.45pm; not Saturday). *Benchmark main dish: hake fillet with brown shrimp and caper butter £19.00. Two-course evening meal £25.00.*

Free house ~ Licensee Michael Ibbotson ~ Real ale ~ Open 12-10.30; 12-midnight Thurs-Sat ~ Bar food 12-2.30, 5.30-9 (9.30 Thurs-Sat); 12-4, 5.30-8.30 Sun ~ Restaurant ~ Children welcome ~ Dogs allowed in bar and bedrooms ~ Wi-fi ~ Bedrooms: £100/£120 *Recommended by Naomi and Andrew Randall, Alister and Margery Bacon, Jamie and Lizzie McEwan, Dr Peter Crawshaw, Peter Pilbeam, Freddie and Sarah Banks, Richard Cole, Martine and Fabio Lockley*

 EAST WITTON   SE1486 Map 10

Blue Lion ⭐ ☆ 🍷 🛏

(01969) 624273 – www.thebluelion.co.uk

A6108 Leyburn–Ripon; DL8 4SN

Civilised dining pub with a proper bar, real ales, highly enjoyable food and courteous service; comfortable bedrooms

A perfect base for exploring the fine surroundings of the Yorkshire Dales National Park, this delightful Georgian coaching inn is run by long-serving owners who welcome damp dog walkers just as warmly as those out for a special meal. The big squarish bar is civilised but informal with soft lighting, high-backed antique settles and old windsor chairs on turkish rugs and flagstones, ham hooks in the high ceiling decorated with dried wheat, teazles and so forth, a delft shelf full of bric-a-brac, plus several prints, sporting caricatures and other pictures; daily papers. Black Sheep Best and Holy Grail and Theakstons Best on handpump, an impressive wine list including 16 (plus champagne) by the glass and 20 malt whiskies. The candlelit, high-ceilinged and elegant dining room has another open fire. Picnic-sets on the gravel outside look beyond the stone houses on the far side of the village green to Witton Fell, and there's a large, attractive back garden. The comfortable bedrooms have pretty country furnishings; some are in the main house, others in converted stables across the courtyard (these are dog-friendly).

🍴⭐ Imaginative food includes sandwiches, seared king scallops with roast cauliflower purée, confit apple and apple salad, beef fillet carpaccio with pomegranate compote, parmesan and beer bread croutons with truffle emulsion, potato and thyme rösti with mushroom, garlic and leek fricassée, ox cheek and real ale suet pudding with maple-glazed parsnips and colcannon potato, plaice meunière with caper beurre noisette and roasted new potatoes, sage and lemon-stuffed porchetta with croquette potatoes, rhubarb compote and cider velouté, chicken with roast jerusalem artichokes, truffle and chestnut mushroom tortellini and hazelnut velouté, and puddings such as confit fig with mascarpone, chocolate sorbet, fresh honeycomb and hazelnuts and Valrhona chocolate fondant with sweet date purée and walnut ice-cream. *Benchmark main dish: smoked haddock with mushroom and leek cream, a soft poached egg and gruyère glaze £19.50. Two-course evening meal £30.00.*

Free house ~ Licensee Paul Klein ~ Real ale ~ Open 11-11 ~ Bar food 12-2, 7-9.15; 12-6, 7-9.15 Sun ~ Restaurant ~ Children welcome ~ Dogs allowed in bar and bedrooms ~ Wi-fi ~ Bedrooms: /£99 *Recommended by Alexandra and Richard Clay, Serena and Adam Furber, Janet and Peter Race, David and Charlotte Emslie, Jeremy and Susan Steadman*

 ELSLACK   SD9249 Map 7

Tempest Arms 🍴⭐ 🍷 🍺 🛏

(01282) 842450 – www.tempestarms.co.uk

Just off A56 Earby–Skipton; BD23 3AY

Busy inn with three log fires in stylish rooms, four real ales, good wines and well regarded food; bedrooms

Even when this stylish 18th-c stone inn is at its busiest, you'll be keenly welcomed as a valued customer and made to feel special. Attracting a good mix of customers, the bar and surrounding dining areas have lots of character: cushioned armchairs, built-in wall seats with comfortable cushions, stools, plenty of tables and three log fires (one greets you at the entrance and divides the bar and restaurant). Also, quite a bit of exposed stonework, amusing prints on cream walls, real ales such as Dark Horse Hetton Pale Ale, Saltaire Blonde, Timothy Taylors Landlord and a guest on handpump, 12 wines by the glass, 30 malt whiskies and 50 gins; background music and board games. Tables outside are largely screened from the road by a raised bank. The 21 bedrooms are comfortable and well equipped and make a perfect base for exploring the beautiful area; the surrounding walks are lovely. Disabled access.

Highly thought-of food includes sandwiches, partridge breast wrapped in serrano ham with wild mushroom jus, beer-soaked mushrooms in creamy sauce with melting stilton top, sharing platters, cheese and onion pie with bubble and squeak mash and asparagus sauce, lasagne, cumberland sausage with mash and onion gravy, sea bass with tomato and chilli salsa and sautéed potatoes, slow-cooked lamb shank with creamy mash and minted gravy, chicken escalopes with rösti potatoes and french-style peas, goan tiger prawn curry with pineapple chutney, and puddings such as crème brûlée and sherry trifle. *Benchmark main dish: steak in ale pudding £14.95. Two-course evening meal £22.00.*

Individual Inns ~ Managers Martin and Veronica Clarkson ~ Real ale ~ Open 10am-11pm; 12-10.30 Sun ~ Bar food 12-2.30, 6-9; 12-7.30 Sun ~ Restaurant ~ Children welcome ~ Dogs allowed in bar and bedrooms ~ Wi-fi ~ Bedrooms: $80/$105 *Recommended by Robert and Diana Ringstone, Steve Whalley, Philip J Alderton, John and Sylvia Harrop, David Heath, Richard Cole, Justine and Neil Bonnett, Nigel and Alison Orchard, Neil Griffin*

FELIXKIRK
SE4684   Map 10

Carpenters Arms

(01845) 537369 – www.thecarpentersarmsfelixkirk.com
Village signed off A170 E of Thirsk; YO7 2DP

Stylishly furnished village pub with spacious rooms, real ales and highly regarded food; lodge-style bedrooms

After enjoying one of the many local walks, the well equipped, up-to-date bedrooms here offer not just a drying wardrobe for wet days but a log-effect gas fire too – and dogs are welcome. The opened-up bars are spacious and relaxed with dark beams and joists, candlelight and fresh flowers, a mix of chairs and tables on big flagstones or carpet, and stools against the panelled counter where they keep Black Sheep Best, York Guzzler and a changing guest ale on handpump, around 20 wines by the glass, 18 malt whiskies, quite a few gins and farm cider. A snug seating area has tartan armchairs in front of a double-sided woodburning stove. In the red-walled dining room you'll find antique and country kitchen chairs around scrubbed tables, and the walls throughout are hung with traditional prints, local pictures and maps; background music. On a raised decked terrace, plenty of seats and tables overlook the landscaped garden, with picnic-sets at the front. This is part of the Provenance Inns & Hotels group.

Appetising food includes lunchtime sandwiches, wild mushroom and chestnuts on toasted sourdough, prawn cocktail, sharing boards, butternut squash and sage ravioli, Whitby scampi with home-made tartare sauce, coriander and lime-griddled chicken with sweet potato fries and yoghurt dip, calves liver and pancetta with glazed onion gravy, and puddings such as berry crumble with vanilla custard and lemon and mascarpone cheesecake with scorched meringue; they also offer an early bird menu (5.30-6.45pm) and breakfasts (8-10am). *Benchmark main dish: steak in ale pie £14.95. Two-course evening meal £22.00.*

Free house ~ General manager Paulo Pinto ~ Real ale ~ Open 8am-11pm ~ Bar food 12-2.30, 5.30-9.30; 12-4, 5.30-8.30 Sun ~ Restaurant ~ Children welcome ~ Dogs allowed in bar and bedrooms ~ Wi-fi ~ Bedrooms: /£120 *Recommended by Janet and Peter Race, Charlie and Mark Todd, Michael and Sarah Lockley, Tom and Lorna Harding, Celia and Rupert Lemming*

GRANTLEY
SE2369 Map 7

Grantley Bar & Restaurant ★♥ ♀

(01765) 620227 – www.grantleyarms.com
Village signposted off B6265 W of Ripon; HG4 3PJ

Relaxed and interesting dining pub with good food

The hospitable, hands-on licensees here offer both regulars and visitors a genuinely warm welcome. There's an easy-going atmosphere in the front bar, which has beams, a huge fireplace built of massive stone blocks and housing a woodburning stove, traditional furnishings such as comfortable dining chairs and polished tables set with evening tea-lights and some of the landlady's own paintings of ponies and dogs. The back dining room has crisp linen tablecloths, decorative plates and more paintings, mainly landscapes. Theakstons Best and a guest ale on handpump, nine wines by the glass, eight malt whiskies, a local farm cider and attentive friendly service. Teak tables and chairs on the flagstoned front terrace have a pleasant outlook. After visiting nearby Fountains Abbey and Studley Royal Water Garden (National Trust), this is a top choice for lunch.

Highly enjoyable food includes lunchtime sandwiches and omelettes, black pudding scotch egg with mustard mayonnaise, chicken liver parfait with plum chutney, butternut squash and feta cheese tart, lager-battered haddock and chips, confit rare-breed pork belly with apple purée, crackling and red wine sauce, sausage meat wrapped in bacon and black pudding with mash and cumberland and green peppercorn sauce, fresh fish dish of the day, and puddings such as a trio of chocolate terrine and pear and ginger sponge pudding with custard; they also offer a two- and three-course set lunch (not Sunday). *Benchmark main dish: pie of the week £12.95. Two-course evening meal £21.00.*

Free house ~ Licensees Valerie Sails and Eric Broadwith ~ Real ale ~ Open 12-3, 5.30-10.30; 12-3, 5.30-11 Fri, Sat; 12-10.30 Sun; closed Mon except bank holidays, Tues ~ Bar food 12-2, 5.30-9 (9.30 Sat); 12-3.30, 5.30-8 Sun ~ Restaurant ~ Well behaved children welcome ~ Wi-fi
Recommended by Trish and Karl Soloman, Charles Todd, David Appleyard, Mark Morgan, Margaret McDonald, William and Natasha Pace

GRINTON
SE0498 Map 10

Bridge Inn ◀

(01748) 884224 – www.bridgeinn-grinton.co.uk
B6270 W of Richmond; DL11 6HH

Bustling pub with traditional, comfortable bars, log fires, real ales, malt whiskies and tasty bar food; neat bedrooms

This is a godsend for thirsty walkers and cyclists (the pub is in the centre of the Yorkshire Dales National Park) and you can be sure of a hearty welcome from the friendly landlord. There's a relaxing, comfortable atmosphere, bow-window seats and a pair of stripped traditional settles among more usual pub seats (all well cushioned), a good log fire and Jennings Cumberland, Marstons 61 Deep and Wainwright and Yorkshire Dales Butter Tubs on handpump; also, eight wines by the glass, 20 malt whiskies, ten gins and farm cider. On the right, a few steps lead down to a room with darts and ring the bull. On the left, past leather armchairs and a sofa next to a second log fire (and a glass chess set), is an extensive two-part dining room with décor in cream and shades of brown, and a modicum of fishing memorabilia. The bedrooms are neat, simple and comfortable, and breakfasts good. There are picnic-sets outside and the lovely church opposite is known as the Cathedral of the Dales.

Tasty food includes lunchtime sandwiches, their own gin-cured salmon with beetroot salad, black pudding scotch egg with mustard dressing, vegetable moussaka, burger with toppings, onion rings and chips, chicken breast stuffed with local cheese and wrapped in bacon with cranberry and red wine sauce, mexican nachos, Whitby scampi with chips, lamb shank in rosemary and red wine with spring onion mash and braised red cabbage, monkfish on dried tomato polenta with yellow and red pepper coulis, and puddings such as peanut butter brownie with salted caramel ice-cream and peanut brittle and toffee apple cheesecake. *Benchmark main dish: steak in ale pie £12.50. Two-course evening meal £18.00.*

Jennings (Marstons) ~ Lease Andrew Atkin ~ Real ale ~ Open 12-11 ~ Bar food 12-2.30, 6-9 (8 Tues); 12-3, 6-9 Sat; 12-3, 6-8 Sun ~ Restaurant ~ Children welcome ~ Dogs allowed in bar and bedrooms ~ Wi-fi ~ Live folk music Thurs evening ~ Bedrooms: £51/£82
Recommended by Sabine and Gerald Grimshaw, Margaret McDonald, Liz and Mike Newton, Trevor and Michele Street, Ivy and George Goodwill, James and Sylvia Hewitt, John and Claire Masters

HALIFAX
SE1027 Map 7
Shibden Mill ⭐ ♀ 🍺 🛏
(01422) 365840 – www.shibdenmillinn.com
Off A58 into Kell Lane at Stump Cross Inn, near A6036 junction; keep on, pub signposted from Kell Lane on left; HX3 7UL

Yorkshire Dining Pub of the Year

Interesting 300-year-old pub with a spreading bar, four real ales and inventive, top class bar food; luxury bedrooms

The creative food here draws in customers from far and wide, but for those just wanting a drink and a chat they've a thoughtful choice of drinks on offer too. A restored 17th-c mill, it has plenty of character and the rambling bar is full of nooks and crannies. Some cosy side areas have banquettes heaped with cushions and rugs, well spaced attractive old tables and chairs, and candles in elegant iron holders giving a feeling of real intimacy; also, old hunting prints, country landscapes and a couple of big log fires. A beer named for them (from Moorhouses) plus Black Sheep Best, Little Valley Withens Pale Ale and a changing guest on handpump, 27 wines by the glass from a wide list, 22 malt whiskies and 20 gins. There's also an upstairs restaurant; background music. Outside on the pleasant heated terrace are plenty of seats and tables, including a charming 'tea shed' and the building is prettily floodlit at night. To make the most of the lovely surrounding countryside, our readers regularly stay in the stylish and well equipped bedrooms; breakfasts are good and hearty.

Highly accomplished food includes lunchtime sandwiches, sea trout millefeuille with trout rillettes, treacle-cured trout, avocado mousse, cucumber and dill gazpacho, pigeon rossini with breast, parfait, hazelnuts, pickled apple, pedro ximénez cream and liquorice root, vegetable and goats cheese risotto with charred baby leek, hazelnuts and wild garlic velouté, burger with toppings, beetroot slaw and skinny fries, lamb rump with belly nugget, potato terrine, lamb fat curds, broad beans, pickled white asparagus and lettuce velouté, hake loin with white crab, asparagus, pickled radish, bottarga and riesling and sorrel sauce, pork belly with crispy pig head, langoustine, baby turnips, pork fat potatoes, toasted almonds and sherry sauce, and puddings such as chocolate and cherry iced parfait with chocolate and kirsch mousse, frangipane and candied almonds and yoghurt pannacotta with strawberry consommé, poached strawberries, pink peppercorn meringue and basil sorbet; they also offer afternoon tea and a seven-course taster menu. *Benchmark main dish: glazed ox cheek with crispy tongue, champ mash, smoked pancetta and chestnut mushrooms £18.00. Two-course evening meal £26.00.*

Free house ~ Licensee Glen Pearson ~ Real ale ~ Open 12-11; 12-10.30 Sun ~ Bar food 12-2 (2.30 Fri), 5.30-9; 12-2.30, 6-9.30 Sat; 12-7.30 Sun ~ Restaurant ~ Children welcome ~ Dogs allowed in bar ~ Wi-fi ~ Bedrooms: £115/£140 *Recommended by Celia and Geoff Clay, Mr and Mrs P R Thomas, Steve Whalley, Helene Grygar, Bob and Melissa Wyatt, Richard Kennell, Matilda and Gerald Thoms, Sally Harrison, Freddie and Sarah Banks*

HELPERBY
Oak Tree 🌟 ⛾ 🛏

SE4370 Map 7

(01423) 789189 – www.theoaktreehelperby.com
Raskelf Road; YO61 2PH

Attractive pub with real ales in friendly bar, fine food in cosy dining rooms and seats on terrace; comfortable bedrooms

A cheerful crowd of customers can be found in this handsome old inn, keen to make the most of the good food and drink. The informal bar has a mix of wooden tables on old quarry tiles, flagstones and oak floorboards, prints and paintings on bold red walls and open fires; background music. Stools line the counter where they keep Black Sheep Best, Theakstons Best, Rudgate York Guzzler and a guest beer on handpump, ten wines by the glass, nine malt whiskies and gin, and farm cider. The main dining room has a large woodburner in a huge brick fireplace, high-backed burgundy chairs around nice old tables on oak flooring, ornate mirrors and some striking artwork on exposed brick walls. French windows lead out to the terrace where there are plenty of seats and tables for summer dining. Upstairs, a private dining room has a two-way woodburner, a sitting room and doors leading to a terrace. The modern bedrooms are comfortable and well equipped. Disabled access. This belongs to the Provenance Inns & Hotels group.

As well as breakfasts (8-11am), the highly regarded food includes lunchtime sandwiches, confit pheasant spring roll with spiced chutney, wild mushroom gnocchi with blue cheese and thyme, sharing boards, spiced squash curry with carrot and cardamom pilaf, chicken in a creamy tarragon sauce with herbed roast potatoes, braised beef in red wine jus, cod loin wrapped in parma ham with lemon and thyme butter, and puddings such as cherry and chocolate marquise and affogato (vanilla bean ice-cream, hot espresso and biscotti); they also offer an early bird menu (5.30-6.45pm). *Benchmark main dish: steak in ale pie £14.95. Two-course evening meal £22.00.*

Free house ~ General manager Elizabeth Richards ~ Real ale ~ Open 8am-11pm ~ Bar food 12-2.30, 5.30-9.30; 12-4, 5.30-8 Sun ~ Restaurant ~ Children welcome ~ Dogs allowed in bar and bedrooms ~ Wi-fi ~ Bedrooms: /£100 *Recommended by George and Alison Bishop, Louise and Simon Peters, Dan and Belinda Smallbone, Nick and Meriel Cox, Julian Richardson, Dave Goodwin, Penny and David Shepherd, Sophia and Hamish Greenfield*

ILKLEY

SE1347 Map 7

Wheatley Arms ♀ 🍺 🛏

(01943) 816496 – www.wheatleyarms.co.uk

Wheatley Lane, Ben Rhydding; LS29 8PP

Smart inn with a cosy bar, restful dining rooms, professional service and good food and drink; comfortable bedrooms

This substantial stone inn is always deservedly busy, particularly at lunchtime with walkers as it's close to Ilkley Moor. The interconnected dining rooms have all manner of nice antique and upholstered chairs and stools and prettily cushioned wooden or rush-seated settles around assorted tables, rugs on bare boards, some bold wallpaper, various prints and two log fires; our readers like the smart garden room. One half of the locals' bar has tub armchairs and other comfortable seats, the other has tartan-cushioned wall seats and mate's chairs, with classic wooden stools against the counter where they keep BAD Love Over Gold, Dark Horse Craven Bitter, Ilkley Mary Jane and a changing guest on handpump. Also, 23 wines by the glass (including prosecco and champagne), a dozen malt whiskies and a farm cider; background music, board games and TV. There are seats and tables on the terrace. Individually decorated, the dozen well equipped and comfortable bedrooms are much used by those exploring the area; some have a private roof terrace.

 Consistently good food includes breakfasts (8-11am) plus sandwiches (until 5.30pm), spiced falafel with broccoli fritters, smashed avocado and sweet chilli ketchup, steak and mushroom in ale pie, lambs liver and bacon with mash and onion gravy, burger with toppings, coleslaw and fries, free-range chicken breast with dauphinoise potatoes and truffled wild mushroom sauce, seared hake with creamed leeks, 10oz rib-eye steak with peppercorn sauce and chips, and puddings such as raspberry cheesecake and warm treacle tart. *Benchmark main dish: beer-battered fish and chips £13.00. Two-course evening meal £21.00.*

Individual Inns ~ Licensee Jonathan Brown ~ Real ale ~ Open 7am-11pm; 8am-midnight Fri, Sat; 8am-10.30pm Sun ~ Bar food 12-2, 5.30-9; 12-7.30 Sun ~ Restaurant ~ Children welcome ~ Dogs allowed in bar and bedrooms ~ Wi-fi ~ Live jazz first Sun lunchtime of month ~ Bedrooms: $80/$90 *Recommended by Dan and Nicki Barton, Martine and Fabio Lockley, Nicola and Holly Lyons, Amy and Luke Buchanan, Bob and Melissa Wyatt, Cliff and Monica Swan*

KIRKBY FLEETHAM

SE2894 Map 10

Black Horse ♀ 🍺 🛏

(01609) 749010 – www.blackhorseinnkirkbyfleetham.com

Village signposted off A1 S of Catterick; Lumley Lane; DL7 0SH

Attractively reworked country inn with well liked food, good drinks choice and cheerful atmosphere; comfortable bedrooms

There's plenty of stylish character here and the long, softly lit beamed bar on the right has flagstones, cushioned wall seats, some little settles and high-backed dining chairs by the log fire at one end, Black Sheep Best, Ossett Yorkshire Blonde and Timothy Taylors Boltmaker on handpump and 11 wines by the glass. The cosy snug has darts. A dining room towards the back is light and open, with big bow windows on either side and a casual contemporary look thanks to loose-covered dining chairs or pastel garden settles with scatter cushions around tables painted pale green; background pop music. The neat sheltered back lawn and flagstoned side terrace have teak seats and tables and there are picnic-sets at the front; quoits.

Bedrooms are attractive and comfortable with plenty of antique charm and breakfasts are good.

🍴 Pleasing food includes blue cheese crème brûlée with honeycomb, red chicory and pressed pear salad, baked queenie scallops with leek, cheddar and gruyère gratin, cheese and spinach wellington with home-dried tomatoes and sweet potatoes, crispy pork belly with braised pig cheek, turnips, quince and fondant potato, charred duck breast with spring onions, kumquat, confit potatoes and caramelised orange sauce, 28-day aged sirloin steak with triple-cooked chips and café de paris butter, and puddings such as Baileys cheesecake with crushed Maltesers and strawberry textures and chocolate nemesis. *Benchmark main dish: fish pie £15.95. Two-course evening meal £21.00.*

Free house ~ Licensee Steven Barker ~ Real ale ~ Open 12-11 ~ Bar food 12-2.30, 5-9; 12-8 Sun ~ Restaurant ~ Children welcome ~ Dogs allowed in bar and bedrooms ~ Wi-fi ~ Bedrooms: /$110 *Recommended by Chantelle and Tony Redman, Karl and Frieda Bujeya, Andrea and Philip Crispin, Alexandra and Tim Fledgling, Giles and Suzie Nunn, Nigel and Alison Orchard*

LEDSHAM
SE4529 Map 7

Chequers ⭐🍴♟

(01977) 683135 – www.thechequersinn.com

1.5 miles from A1(M) junction 42: follow Leeds signs, then Ledsham signposted; Claypit Lane; LS25 5LP

Friendly pub with hands-on landlord, log fires in several beamed rooms, real ales and interesting food; pretty back terrace

If you're leaving the A1 for a lunchtime visit to this well run and neatly kept pub, it's best to book a table in advance. The several small, individually decorated rooms have plenty of character, with low beams, log fires, lots of cosy alcoves, toby jugs and all sorts of knick-knacks on the walls and ceilings (cricket fans will be interested to see a large photo in one room of four yorkshire heroes). From the little old-fashioned, panelled-in central servery they offer Brown Cow Sessions Pale Ale, Leeds Best, Theakstons Best, Timothy Taylors Landlord and a guest beer on handpump and eight wines by the glass. The lovely sheltered two-level terrace at the back has lots of tables among roses, and the hanging baskets and flowers are very pretty. RSPB Fairburn Ings reserve is not far and the ancient village church is worth a visit.

🍴 Enjoyable food includes sandwiches, king scallops with roasted cauliflower purée, bacon crumb and curry oil, smoked duck with candied pumpkin seeds, coriander and house dressing, tomato risotto with buffalo mozzarella and parsley pesto, sausages with mash and onion gravy, roasted cod loin with french-style peas and glazed mussels, calves liver with caramelised onion mash, bacon and gravy, local pheasant breast with prosciutto, apricots, carrots and swede purée and honey and soy glaze, and puddings such as strawberry trifle and Baileys double chocolate cheesecake. *Benchmark main dish: steak and mushroom pie £13.45. Two-course evening meal £20.00.*

Free house ~ Licensee Amanda Wraith ~ Real ale ~ Open 11-11; 12-6 Sun; closed Sun evening ~ Bar food 12-9; 12-5 Sun ~ Restaurant ~ Children welcome ~ Dogs allowed in bar ~ Wi-fi *Recommended by Ian Wilson, Roger and Donna Huggins, Tony and Caroline Elwood, Dave Braisted, Caroline and Peter Bryant, Neil Allen*

LEVISHAM

SE8390   Map 10

Horseshoe

(01751) 460240 – www.horseshoelevisham.co.uk

Off A169 N of Pickering; YO18 7NL

Friendly village pub with super food, neat rooms, real ales and seats on the village green; bedrooms

At the top of a lovely unspoilt village you'll find this bustling, well run pub. The lively bars have beams, blue banquettes, wheelback and captain's chairs around a variety of tables on polished wooden floors, vibrant landscapes by a local artist on the walls and a log fire in the stone fireplace; an adjoining snug has a woodburning stove, comfortable leather sofas and old photographs of the pub and the village. Served by the courteous staff are Black Sheep Best and guests such as Cropton Yorkshire Moors and Timothy Taylors Golden Best on handpump, 14 wines by the glass and more than a dozen malt whiskies. There are seats on the attractive green, with more in the back garden. The clean, comfortable bedrooms make a good base for exploring the North York Moors National Park; breakfasts are hearty. The historic church is worth a visit. This is sister pub to the Fox & Rabbit in Lockton.

 Super food cooked by one of the landlords includes sandwiches, crab and smoked salmon terrine with melba toast, herb-crusted goats cheese with tomato chutney, butternut squash, leek and pine nut risotto with parmesan, sausages and mash with onion gravy, chicken wrapped in bacon on creamed leeks, steak in ale pie, gammon with egg and pineapple, braised lamb shank with rosemary mash and mint gravy, sea bass with sautéed new potatoes, peppers, onions and spinach, pork stroganoff with rice, sirloin steak with peppercorn sauce and chips, and puddings such as lime cheesecake and chocolate truffle torte. *Benchmark main dish: slow-roasted pork belly £14.95. Two-course evening meal £20.00.*

Free house ~ Licensees Toby and Charles Wood ~ Real ale ~ Open 11-10; 11-11 Sat; closed Mon, Tues ~ Bar food 12-2, 6-8.30 ~ Children welcome ~ Dogs allowed in bar ~ Wi-fi ~ Bedrooms: /£90 *Recommended by Stuart and Natalie Granville, Alex Macdonald, Dr K Nesbitt, Martin Day, Monica and Steph Evans, Geoff and Ann Marston, Nigel and Alison Orchard, WAH, John Robinson*

LEYBURN

SE1190   Map 10

Sandpiper

(01969) 622206 – www.sandpiperinn.co.uk

Just off Market Place; DL8 5AT

Appealing food plus a drinkers' bar in pretty inn, with an impressive choice of whisky; bedrooms

The cosy little bar in this 17th-c stone cottage is popular locally, which gives it a chatty, friendly feel. There are a couple of black beams in the low ceiling, a log fire and wooden or cushioned built-in wall seats around a few tables. The back snug, up three steps, features lovely dales photographs – get here early if you want a seat. Beside the linenfold panelled bar counter are photographs and a woodburning stove in a stone fireplace; to the left is the attractive restaurant with dark wooden tables and chairs on bare boards and fresh flowers. Black Sheep Best and a couple of guests from the Wensleydale brewery on handpump, 100 malt whiskies, good wines by the glass and a growing number of gins; background music. In good weather, you can enjoy a drink on the front terrace among the pretty hanging baskets and flowering climbers. Bedrooms are comfortable and well equipped.

🍽️⭐ Good, popular food cooked by the chef-patron includes sandwiches, panko-breaded black pudding with poached egg, crispy smoked bacon and tomato chutney, twice-baked cheddar soufflé with roasted butternut squash, pear and rocket, millefeuille of roasted vegetables and wild garlic, grilled rib burger with toppings and chips, braised beef with garlic mushrooms, carrots and mash, lemon-roasted chicken breast on leek and porcini mushroom risotto with parmesan, cod with potato gnocchi, wilted greens and caviar sauce, fillet steak with pink peppercorn butter and chips, and puddings such as vanilla crème brûlée and rhubarb and almond tart with ice-cream. *Benchmark main dish: chump of lamb with dauphinoise potatoes and elderberry and mint sauce £18.26. Two-course evening meal £25.00.*

Free house ~ Licensees Jonathan and Janine Harrison ~ Real ale ~ Open 12-2.30, 6-11; 12-2.30, 6-10.30 Sun; closed Mon (all year), Tues (in winter), two weeks Jan ~ Bar food 12-2.30, 6-8.30 (8 Sun) ~ Restaurant ~ Children welcome ~ Dogs allowed in bar and bedrooms ~ Wi-fi ~ Bedrooms: £90/£100 *Recommended by Caroline and Steve Archer, Dan and Belinda Smallbone, Michael Butler, Sylvia and Phillip Spencer*

LINTON IN CRAVEN   SD9962   Map 7
Fountaine 🍺

(01756) 752210 – www.fountaineinnatlinton.co.uk
Off B6265 Skipton–Grassington; BD23 5HJ

Neatly kept pub with attractive furnishings, open fires, five real ales and popular food; bedrooms

It's worth wandering around this pretty hamlet before a visit here. The bars have beams and white-painted joists in low ceilings, log fires (one in a beautifully carved heavy wooden fireplace), attractive built-in cushioned wall benches and stools around a mix of copper-topped tables, little wall lamps and quite a few prints on the pale walls. Dark Horse Hetton Pale Ale, John Smiths Bitter, Marstons Wainwright, Tetleys Cask and Timothy Taylors Golden Best on handpump, 20 wines by the glass, ten gins and a dozen malt whiskies served by efficient staff; background music and ring the bull. The terrace, looking across the road to the duck pond, has teak benches and tables under green parasols, and the hanging baskets are most attractive. The five well equipped bedrooms are in a converted barn behind the pub. Fine nearby walks.

🍴 From a thoughtful menu there might be sandwiches, chicken liver pâté with ale chutney, house-cured salmon with beetroot pannacotta, goats cheese and lemon oil, mushroom, cranberry and brie wellington with creamy herb sauce, cumberland sausage ring on bacon and cabbage with mash and gravy, gammon and egg, mixed fish stew in tomato sauce, slow-roast beef brisket in ale with mash and yorkshire pudding, half roast duck with ginger, spring onion and honey sauce, and puddings such as bakewell tart with ice-cream and chocolate fudge brownie. *Benchmark main dish: lamb rump with roast vegetables, couscous and harissa jus £16.00. Two-course evening meal £21.00.*

Individual Inns ~ Manager Christopher Gregson ~ Real ale ~ Open 11-11; 12-10.30 Sun ~ Bar food 12-9 ~ Restaurant ~ Children welcome ~ Dogs allowed in bar and bedrooms ~ Wi-fi ~ Bedrooms: £75/£89 *Recommended by Steve Whalley, Peter Smith and Judith Brown, B and M Kendall, Gus Swan, Michael Butler*

'Children welcome' means the pub says it lets children inside without any special restriction. If it allows them in, but to restricted areas such as an eating area or family room, we specify this. Places with separate restaurants often let children use them, and hotels usually let children into public areas such as lounges. Some pubs impose an evening time limit – let us know if you find one earlier than 9pm.

LOCKTON   SE8488   Map 10
Fox & Rabbit

(01751) 460213 – www.foxandrabbit.co.uk

A169 N of Pickering; YO18 7NQ

Nice little pub pub with fine views, a friendly atmosphere, real ales and highly regarded food

As ever, standards remain high here and the two brothers in charge keep everything running smoothly. The interconnected rooms have beams, panelling and some exposed stonework, wall settles and banquettes, dark pubby chairs and tables on tartan carpet, a log fire and an inviting atmosphere; fresh flowers, brasses, china plates, prints and old local photographs too. The locals' bar is busy and cheerful and there are panoramic views from the comfortable restaurant – it's worth arriving early to bag a window seat. Black Sheep Best, Cropton Yorkshire Moors, Marstons Wainwright and Timothy Taylors Golden Best on handpump, seven wines by the glass, 12 malt whiskies and home-made elderflower cordial; background music and pool. Outside are seats under parasols and some picnic-sets. The inn is in the North York Moors National Park, so there are plenty of surrounding walks. They have a caravan site. This is sister pub to the Horseshoe in Levisham.

 Rewarding food includes sandwiches, prawn cocktail, deep-fried brie with red pepper and ginger chutney, gnocchi with wild mushrooms, samphire and herb sauce, pot-roasted lamb shank with yorkshire pudding, chicken wrapped in bacon with dauphinoise potatoes and red wine and thyme jus, venison burger with toppings, onion marmalade and chips, five-spice duck breast with honey-glazed parsnips and redcurrant and cranberry sauce, pheasant breast with fondant potato, sautéed cabbage and madeira sauce, and puddings such as lemon tart and crème brûlée. *Benchmark main dish: Whitby fresh fish and chips £13.95. Two-course evening meal £20.00.*

Free house ~ Licensees Toby and Charles Wood ~ Real ale ~ Open 11-11; 11-10 Sun ~ Bar food 12-2, 5-8.30; light snacks 2-4pm ~ Restaurant ~ Children welcome ~ Dogs allowed in bar ~ Wi-fi *Recommended by Joe and Belinda Smart, Mark Hamill, Rosie and John Moore, Millie and Peter Downing, Martin Day, Brian and Susan Wylie, Jeff Davies, Peter and Emma Kelly*

MALHAM   SD9062   Map 7
Lister Arms ♀ ◖ ⊨

(01729) 830444 – www.listerarms.co.uk

Off A65 NW of Skipton; BD23 4DB

Friendly inn in fine countryside with cosy bars and dining room, enjoyable food and seats outside; comfortable bedrooms

Mr Dunn runs his handsome inn very well – it's popular locally and with visitors, and there are views over the Yorkshire Dales National Park. One bar has a medley of cushioned dining chairs and leather or upholstered armchairs around antique wooden tables on slate flooring, with a big deer's head above the inglenook fireplace. A second bar has a small brick fireplace with logs piled to each side, rustic slab tables, cushioned wheelback chairs and comfortable wall seats. Thwaites Lancaster Bomber, Nutty Black and Original Bitter on handpump plus three rotating local guests, 20 wines by the glass and Weston's farm cider. A woodburning stove stands in the fireplace of the airy dining room where there are swagged curtains and smartly upholstered high-backed and pale wooden farmhouse chairs around rustic tables on bare floorboards. The flagstoned and gravelled courtyard has seats and benches around tables under parasols – some overlook the small green at the front. With good, hearty breakfasts and attractive, warm and comfortable bedrooms (some in the pub, others in the next-door cottage and more in the barn conversion), our readers regularly stay here.

🍴 Highly rated food includes breakfasts (8-10am) plus sandwiches, warm goats cheese en croûte with sticky red onion marmalade, confit duck spring rolls with spring onions and hoisin sauce, sharing platters, wild mushroom tagliatelle with tarragon and parmesan, honey and mustard-glazed home-cooked ham and free-range eggs, cajun chicken breast with coleslaw and fries, slow-cooked, honey-glazed lamb breast with madeira jus and roast baby potatoes, monkfish wrapped in parma ham with pea and parmesan risotto, and puddings. *Benchmark main dish: steak in ale pie £13.50. Two-course evening meal £20.00.*

Thwaites ~ Manager Darren Dunn ~ Real ale ~ Open 8am-11pm; 8am-10.30pm Sun ~ Bar food 12-9.30 (9 in winter) ~ Restaurant ~ Children welcome ~ Dogs allowed in bar and bedrooms ~ Wi-fi ~ Bedrooms: /£110 *Recommended by Gary and Marie Miller, Celia Caulkin, Peter Smith and Judith Brown, Philip and Susan Robertshaw, Victoria and James Sargeant, Jim King*

MARTON-CUM-GRAFTON
SE4263 Map 7

Punch Bowl 🏵 ♖

(01423) 322519 – www.thepunchbowlmartoncumgrafton.com
Signed off A1 3 miles N of A59; YO51 9QY

Old pub with character bar and dining rooms, real ales, interesting food and seats on terrace

After a wander around the lovely village, come here for lunch. There are lots of original features to look for and the main bar is beamed and timbered with a built-in window seat at one end, lots of red leather-topped stools, and cushioned settles and church chairs around pubby tables on flagstones or bare floorboards. Black Sheep Best, York Guzzler and a guest beer on handpump, 24 wines by the glass and a good number of malt whiskies and gins; background music. Open doorways lead to five separate dining areas, each with an open fire, heavy beams and an attractive mix of cushioned wall seats and wooden or high-backed red-leather dining chairs around antique tables on oak floors; the red walls are covered with photographs of vintage car races and racing drivers, sporting-themed cartoons and old photographs of the pub and village. Up a spiral staircase is a coffee loft and a private dining room. There are seats and tables in the back courtyard where they hold summer barbecues. This is part of the Provenance Inns & Hotels group.

🍴 Top quality food includes lunchtime sandwiches, terrine of confit duck with glazed fig and orange salad, beetroot-cured salmon with grated horseradish, sharing boards, sage and chestnut gnocchi with truffle butter, burger with toppings and chips, chicken breast with bubble and squeak, pearl shallots and pancetta and red wine sauce, beef hotpot, fish pie, and puddings such as gingerbread crème brûlée and cherry and chocolate marquise; they also offer an early bird menu (5.30-7pm) and steak night is Wednesday (from 5.30pm). *Benchmark main dish: steak in ale pie £14.95. Two-course evening meal £22.00.*

Free house ~ General manager Ciaran Byrne ~ Real ale ~ Open 12-3, 5-11; 12-11 Fri, Sat; 12-10.30 Sun ~ Bar food 12-2.30, 5.30-9.30; 12-8 Sun ~ Children welcome ~ Dogs allowed in bar ~ Wi-fi *Recommended by Alison and Tony Livesley, Jacob Matt, Tracey and Stephen Groves, Kate and Mark Foskett, Colin and Daniel Gibbs, Jill and Dick Archer, Graeme and Sally Mendham, Dave Braisted*

MASHAM SE2281 Map 10

Black Sheep Brewery 🍺

(01765) 680100 – www.blacksheepbrewery.co.uk

Brewery signed off Leyburn Road (A6108); HG4 4EN

Lively place with friendly staff, unusual décor in big warehouse room, well kept beers and popular food

If you're keen to try their own-brew ales, then head for the bar in the huge upper warehouse. Here they keep Black Sheep Ale, Best, Golden Sheep and Riggwelter plus a couple of other changing Black Sheep beers such as BAA BAA, Special and Twilighter on handpump, several wines by the glass and a fair choice of soft drinks. The rest of the place is more like a bistro than a pub – the contemporary furnishings are light and attractive with high wooden chairs around equally high tables on stripped floorboards and a good deal of bare woodwork, with cream-painted rough stonework and green-painted steel girders and pillars; background music, TV and friendly service. The guided tours of the sizeable brewery are popular and a glass wall lets you see into the brewing exhibition centre; a shop sells beers and beer-related items from pub games and T-shirts to pottery and fudge. There are picnic-sets out on the grass.

Good quality food includes beer-battered king prawns with sweet chilli sauce, ham hock terrine with quail egg and pineapple chutney, vegetarian cannelloni, sausages with mash and onion gravy, beer-battered haddock and chips, duck breast with confit leg croquette, braised red cabbage and red wine jus, lamb burger with toppings, herby chips and yoghurt, 10oz sirloin steak with a choice of sauce and fries, and puddings such as apple pie and vanilla ice-cream and chocolate brownie with chocolate sauce. *Benchmark main dish: steak in ale pie £12.95. Two-course evening meal £20.00.*

Free house ~ Licensee Jake Humberstone ~ Real ale ~ Open 10am-5pm Sun-Tues, 10am-11pm Weds-Sat ~ Bar food 12-2.30, 6-9 Weds-Sat; 12-4 Sun; no food Mon or Tues evenings ~ Restaurant ~ Children welcome ~ Dogs allowed in bar ~ Wi-fi *Recommended by Barbara and Phil Bowie, Stuart and Natalie Granville, M and GR, Paul Walker, Jo Garnett, Alison and Michael Harper, Peter Brix*

 MINSKIP SE3965 Map 7

Wild Swan 🏅 ⚪ ♀

(01423) 326334 – www.wildswan.pub

Main Street; YO51 9JF

Renovated country pub with stylish but relaxed bar and restaurant, well kept ales, excellent food and seats in charming garden

As you'd expect from our former Licensees of the Year, this is a special pub that's getting high praise from our readers. The heavily beamed bar is just the place for a cosy pint and a chat and has traditional dark wooden chairs, cushioned settles and stools on rugs or bare boards and a couple of armchairs by the two-way open fire; this opens up into an informal dining area with farmhouse chairs around scrubbed kitchen tables, pewter tankards on a delft shelf and a big stag's head; background music. Friendly, helpful staff serve Black Sheep Best, Timothy Taylors Boltmaker and Landlord on handpump, ten wines by the glass and ten local gins. The plusher, carpeted restaurant is furnished with high-backed, tartan-upholstered dining chairs around more stripped farmhouse tables (each set with a church candle and flowers), sage-green walls hung with mirrors, decorative wicker-work and oil paintings, and there's an open kitchen; this shares the open fire with the bar.

The flower-filled garden has plenty of seating. They have plans to open studio bedrooms in a converted barn. Disabled access and loos.

 Food is first class and cooked by the chef-owner: sandwiches, fresh seafood feuilletée, twice-baked cheddar soufflé with tomato chutney, roasted mediterranean vegetables with guacamole and pesto croutes, thai red chicken curry with bang bang cauliflower, steak burger with toppings, aioli and skinny fries, slow-roasted lamb with parma ham, aubergine, red onions, courgettes and rosemary and caper sauce, rib-eye steak with pepper sauce and onion rings, and puddings such as lemon possett laced with gin and brioche bread and butter pudding with Cointreau double cream. *Benchmark main dish: fish pie £14.95. Two-course evening meal £22.00.*

Free house ~ Licensee Karl Mainey ~ Real ale ~ Open 12-11; 12-9 Sun ~ Bar food 12-2.15, 5-9.15; 12-7 Sun ~ Restaurant ~ Children welcome ~ Dogs allowed in bar ~ Wi-fi
Recommended by Les and Sandra Brown, Lorna and Jack Musgrave, David and Leone Lawson, Susan and Callum Slade, R L Borthwick, Gordon and Margaret Ormondroyd

MOULTON   NZ2303   Map 10
Black Bull

(01325) 377556 – www.theblackbullmoulton.com
Just E of A1, a mile E of Scotch Corner; DL10 6QJ

Character pub with a traditional bar, a large open restaurant, high quality food and courteous efficient service; bedrooms

You'll find both imaginative meals and a fine range of drinks here: Black Sheep Best, York Guzzler and a guest beer on handpump, 24 wines by the glass, cocktails and mocktails and over 20 malt whiskies. The bar has a convivial atmosphere, some original panelling and leather wall seating topped with scatter cushions. There's also a dining area with cushioned wooden chairs around a mix of tables on pale flagstones, a couple of leather armchairs in front of a woodburner in a brick fireplace, and horse tack, stone bottles, wooden pails and copper items on windowsills. The dining extension has high windows, attractive brown-orange high-backed dining chairs or cushioned settles on wooden flooring and a rather nice wire bull; background music. Doors from here lead out to a neat terrace with modern seats and tables set among pots of rosemary or tall bay trees. This is part of the Provenance Inns & Hotels group.

Food is excellent and includes lunchtime sandwiches, twice-baked cheese soufflé with celeriac and poached pear salad, king scallops with brown shrimp butter, sharing boards, sage and chestnut gnocchi with truffle butter, baby dover sole meunière, venison loin and braised shoulder crumble with smoked potatoes, moules frites, chicken breast with leek, mushroom and chestnut purée, and puddings such as roast apple cheesecake with calvados ice-cream and fig and mascarpone arctic roll with glazed meringue and pistachios; they also offer an early bird menu (5.30-6.45pm). *Benchmark main dish: luxury fish pie £16.95. Two-course evening meal £22.50.*

Free house ~ General manager Jill Loughborough ~ Real ale ~ Open 12-3, 5-11; 12-11 Fri, Sat; 12-8 Sun ~ Bar food 12-2.30, 5.30-9.30; 12-3, 5.30-8.30 Sun ~ Restaurant evening ~ Children welcome ~ Dogs allowed in bar ~ Wi-fi *Recommended by Richard and Tessa Ibbot, Professor James Burke, Julia and Fiona Barnes, Victoria and Len Meadows, Ian Wilson, Alister and Margery Bacon, Dan and Belinda Smallbone*

RIPPONDEN
SE0419 Map 7

Old Bridge 🍷 🍺

(01422) 822595 – www.theoldbridgeinn.co.uk

From A58, best approach is Elland Road (opposite the Golden Lion), park opposite the church in pub's car park and walk back over ancient hump-back bridge; HX6 4DF

Pleasant old pub run by a long-serving family with relaxed communicating rooms and well-liked food

This ancient pub is a real institution and is now run by the fourth generation of the same welcoming family. The three communicating rooms, each on a slightly different level, have oak settles built into window recesses in the thick stone walls, antique oak tables, rush-seated chairs and comfortably cushioned free-standing settles, a few well chosen pictures and prints on the panelled or painted walls and a big woodburning stove. Timothy Taylors Best, Golden Best, Landlord and Ram Tam, a couple of guests such as Phoenix Arizona and Vocation Bread & Butter on handpump, quite a few foreign bottled beers, 15 wines by the glass, 20 gins, 30 malt whiskies and farm cider; quick, efficient service. Seats in the garden overlook the little River Ryburn. Disabled access but no loos. There's no traditional pub sign outside so to find it, head for the church next door; do note the beautiful medieval packhorse bridge.

 The ever-popular weekday lunchtime cold meat and salad buffet has been running since 1963 (they also offer soup and sandwiches at lunch). Evening and weekend choices include beer-battered mushrooms with blue cheese dip, prawns in tomato, chilli and coriander on toasted bruschetta, mushroom and goats cheese burger with toppings and chips, pie of the day, roasted lamb shank with creamy mash and redcurrant mint jus, chicken kiev with beef-dripping chips, sea bass with chorizo croquettes and tarragon and shrimp sauce, 10oz local sirloin steak with a choice of sauce, and puddings such as ginger sponge with ginger sauce and crumble of the day. *Benchmark main dish: smoked haddock and spinach pancakes £12.00. Two-course evening meal £19.00.*

Free house ~ Licensees Tim and Lindsay Eaton Walker ~ Real ale ~ Open 12-3, 5-11; 12-11 Fri, Sat; 12-10.30 Sun ~ Bar food 12-2, 5-9; 12-2, 5-9.30 Fri, Sat; 12-4 Sun ~ Children allowed until 8pm but must be seated away from bar ~ Wi-fi *Recommended by Jill and Dick Archer, Maria and Henry Lazenby, Graeme and Sally Mendham, Buster and Helena Hastings, Jim and Sue James, Richard Kennell*

SANCTON
SE9039 Map 7

Star 🎖️ 🍷 🍺

(01430) 827269 – www.thestaratsancton.co.uk

King Street (A1034 S of Market Weighton); YO43 4QP

Bustling bar and more formal dining rooms with accomplished food, and a friendly, easy-going atmosphere

A friendly, hands-on landlady and first class food cooked by the landlord are both aspects that receive high praise from our readers. The bar has a woodburning stove, traditional red plush stools around a mix of tables, a cheerful atmosphere and ales from breweries such as Black Sheep, Broughs, Great Newsome, Old Mill and Wold Top on handpump from the brick counter, plus 19 wines by the glass or carafe including prosecco and champagne, 20 gins and over 20 malt whiskies. The more formal (though still relaxed) dining rooms have comfortable high-backed dining chairs around wooden tables on carpeting; background music. At the back are picnic-sets. The pub is at the foot of the Yorkshire Wolds Railway, and at lunchtime in particular there's a good mix of locals, walkers and cyclists. Disabled access.

A wide choice of food includes pub favourites plus top notch modern choices: yorkshire pudding with braised oxtail, caramelised onions and red wine jus, roast breast of quail with smoked garlic pearl barley, poached salsify and crispy cavolo nero, smoked tarragon gnocchi with sautéed wild mushrooms, soya beans and truffled mushroom purée, cumberland sausages with colcannon, bacon and shallot ale gravy, brill and monkfish cheek, sauté potato and samphire with warm tartare sauce, gribiche and dill oil, roast duck with thyme and honey plums, red cabbage purée, glazed turnip and duck jus, 60-day salt-aged 14oz tomahawk steak with béarnaise sauce and chips, and puddings such as key lime pie with toasted coconut and lime syrup and white chocolate and cardamom cheesecake, turkish delight and tonka bean ice-cream. *Benchmark main dish: steak in ale pie £14.95. Two-course evening meal £20.00.*

Free house ~ Licensees Ben and Lindsey Cox ~ Real ale ~ Open 12-3, 6-11.30; 12-11.30 Sun; closed Mon; first week Jan ~ Bar food 12-2, 6-9.30; 12-3, 6-8 Sun ~ Restaurant ~ Children welcome *Recommended by Alison and Graeme Spicer, Monica and Steph Evans, Adam Jones, Val and Malcolm Travers, Mark and Sian Edwards*

SOUTH STAINLEY   SE3163   Map 7

Inn at South Stainley

(01423) 779060 – www.innatstainley.co.uk
Ripon Road; HG3 3ND

Attractively renovated pub with bar and dining rooms, local ales, interesting food and seats in garden

There's plenty of space for both drinking and eating in the interlinked rooms here, but most customers visit to enjoy the excellent food. The bar has button-back and tartan-upholstered dining chairs and wooden settles around a medley of tables on floorboards and high chairs lining the bar counter where friendly, helpful staff serve Black Sheep Best, Ilkley Mary Jane, Marstons Wainwright and Roosters YPA on handpump, good wines by the glass and a growing number of gins and malt whiskies; background music. A two-way woodburning stove separates the bar from the dining rooms which have curved banquettes, long leather wall seats and dark wooden chairs on more bare boards and prints on painted, planked walls. A covered terrace outside has seats and tables under large parasols and there are more seats in the sizeable mature garden. Bedrooms are modern, airy and comfortable and breakfasts are hearty. This is part of the Seafood Pub Company.

First class food includes sandwiches, devilled crab, salmon and shrimp with sea salt croutes, smoked haddock with poached egg, crushed potatoes and grain mustard, fish sharing platter, potato gnocchi with cherry vine tomatoes, smoked almonds, peas and blue cheese sauce, pizzas, persian-spiced chicken with jewelled rice, rose petal harissa, almonds and yoghurt, goat curry with king prawns and grilled flatbread, plaice fillet with mussels, chargrilled asparagus and garlic butter, 28-day aged rib-eye steak with a choice of sauce, and puddings such as gin and raspberry trifle with mint and chocolate crumb and steamed syrup pudding with custard. *Benchmark main dish: chicken, ham hock and leek pie £14.95. Two-course evening meal £21.00.*

Free house ~ Licensee Christopher Ashby ~ Real ale ~ Open 12-10; 12-11 Sat; 12-9.30 Sun ~ Bar food 12-9 (8 Sun) ~ Restaurant ~ Children welcome ~ Dogs allowed in bar and bedrooms ~ Wi-fi ~ Bedrooms: /£80 *Recommended by John Harris, David and Charlotte Green, Andrew and Michele Revell, Scott and Charlotte Havers, Jill and Hugh Bennett*

If we know a featured-entry pub does sandwiches, we always say so – if they're not mentioned, you'll have to assume you can't get one.

THORNTON WATLASS

SE2385 Map 10

Buck 🍺 🛏

(01677) 422461 – www.buckwatlass.co.uk

Village signposted off B6268 Bedale–Masham; HG4 4AH

Honest village pub with up to five real ales, a traditional bar and function room, well liked food and popular Sunday jazz; bedrooms

The hub of the village and with a bustling atmosphere, this friendly place is part of a row of low stone cottages and opposite the green. The pleasantly traditional bar on the right has upholstered wall settles on carpet, a fine mahogany bar counter, local artwork on the walls and a brick fireplace; background music, darts and board games. A snug area overlooks the garden and has a woodburning stove. The Long Room with views of the cricket green has photos and trophies from Thornton Watlass cricket teams past and present, and is the venue for the Sunday afternoon jazz sessions. Black Sheep Best, Hop Studio Bitter, Theakstons Best and Wensleydale Falconer on handpump, eight wines by the glass and eight malt whiskies. The sheltered garden has a well equipped children's play area. Bedrooms are well appointed and comfortable and breakfasts good. Wheelchair access with ramp.

 Tasty food includes sandwiches, ham hock and pistachio terrine, chicken livers with toasted sourdough, vegan chilli with rice, lasagne, chicken korma, salmon en croute, beef bourguignon, duck breast with chinese-spiced sauce, chicken breast in creamy white wine and mushroom sauce, sea bass with lemon and dill butter, 10oz rib-eye steak with trimmings and chips, and puddings. *Benchmark main dish: steak in ale pie £12.95. Two-course evening meal £20.00.*

Free house ~ Licensees Victoria and Tony Jowett ~ Real ale ~ Open 12-11; 12-10.30 Sun ~ Bar food 12-2, 6-9; 12-3, 6-8.30 Sun ~ Restaurant ~ Children welcome ~ Dogs allowed in bar and bedrooms ~ Wi-fi ~ Live trad jazz Sun lunchtime monthly (phone to check) ~ Bedrooms: £65/£95 *Recommended by Peter and Caroline Waites, Martine and Fabio Lockley, Martin and Joanne Sharp, Mark Morgan, Andrew Vincent, S Holder*

WELBURN

SE7168 Map 7

Crown & Cushion 🍷 🍺

(01653) 618777 – www.thecrownandcushionwelburn.com

Off A64; YO60 7DZ

Plenty of dining and drinking space in well run inn with real ales and good food – and seats outside

Plenty of bird-watchers and walkers (and those visiting Castle Howard) make this handsome place a popular spot for lunch. Carefully and attractively refurbished, the little tap room has rustic tables and chairs on wide floorboards, high stools around an equally high central table, beams and timbering, Black Sheep Best, York Guzzler and a guest beer on handpump, a good choice of malt whiskies and gins, 24 wines by the glass and farm cider. The other interconnecting rooms are for dining and on different levels: smart high-backed chairs mix with wooden ones and an assortment of cushioned settles and wall seats around various tables on flagstones or red and black floor tiles. There are open fires and a woodburning stove, old prints of the pub and local scenes on painted or exposed-stone walls and lots of horsebrasses, copper pans and kettles and old stone bottles; background music. Contemporary tables and chairs on the outdoor terrace and picnic-sets below, with long-reaching views across to the Howardian Hills, are quickly snapped up in warm weather. This is part of the Provenance Inns & Hotels group.

 Reliably good food includes lunchtime sandwiches, chicken liver parfait with spiced apple chutney, queenie scallops with butter and garlic butter, sharing boards, wild mushroom risotto, cumberland sausages with mash and gravy, chicken breast with tarragon sauce and sautéed potatoes, swordfish steak with pesto cream, and puddings such as bakewell tart with white chocolate ice-cream and sticky toffee pudding with cinder toffee ice-cream; they also offer an early bird menu (5.30-6.45pm) and Wednesday is steak night (from 5.30pm). *Benchmark main dish: steak in ale pie £14.95. Two-course evening meal £22.00.*

Free house ~ General manager Rachik Essouayah ~ Real ale ~ Open 12-3, 5-11; 12-11 Fri-Sun ~ Bar food 12-2.30, 5.30-9.30; 12-8 Sun ~ Restaurant ~ Children welcome ~ Dogs allowed in bar ~ Wi-fi *Recommended by Jane and Philip Saunders, Caroline and Steve Archer, Elise and Charles Mackinlay, Dan and Belinda Smallbone, Dr and Mrs J D Abell, David and Charlotte Green, Helena and Trevor Fraser*

WIDDOP
SD9531   Map 7
Pack Horse 🍺 £
(01422) 842803 – www.thepackhorseinn.pub
The Ridge; from A646 on W side of Hebden Bridge, turn off at Heptonstall signpost (as it's a sharp turn, coming out of Hebden Bridge the road signs direct you around a turning circle), then follow Slack and Widdop signposts; can also be reached from Nelson and Colne, on high, pretty road; OS Sheet 103 map reference 952317; HX7 7AT

Friendly, family-run pub up on the moors with tasty food, four real ales and plenty of malt whiskies

After a wet moorland walk, this isolated, traditional pub is a perfect refuge; it's on the Pennine Way and Pennine Bridleway. The snug bar has winter fires, window seats cut into the partly panelled stripped-stone walls (from where you can take in the beautiful views), sturdy furnishings and horsey mementoes. Black Sheep Best and Marstons Wainwright plus a couple of changing guests on handpump, over 100 single malt whiskies plus some irish ones, and 14 wines by the glass. There are seats outside in the cobblestoned beer garden and pretty summer hanging baskets.

 Honest, fair priced food includes sandwiches, smoked salmon and horseradish pâté, garlic mushroom with cheese on crusty bread, mushroom, paneer and spinach rogan josh with garlic naan, cottage hotpot, gammon and eggs, giant yorkshire pudding filled with sausages and gravy, liver and bacon with mash and gravy, slow-cooked rack of lamb on creamy mash with garlic, rosemary and red wine gravy, pheasant in cider with pancetta and mushrooms, and puddings such as jam roly-poly and yorkshire parkin with custard. *Benchmark main dish: steak in Guinness pie £10.95. Two-course evening meal £18.00.*

Free house ~ Licensee Sara Hollinrake ~ Real ale ~ Open 12-3, 5.30-10; 12-10 Sat, Sun; closed Mon all day, Tues lunchtime; in winter Tues all day, Weds and Thurs lunchtimes ~ Bar food 12-2, 6.30-9; 12-7 Sun ~ Children welcome ~ Dogs welcome *Recommended by Professor James Burke, John Harris, Alison and Michael Harper, Toby Jones, Gus Swan, Rob Anderson*

YORK
SE5951   Map 7
Judges Lodging 🍷 🛏
(01904) 639312 – www.judgeslodgingyork.co.uk
Lendal; YO1 8AQ

Lovely place with a character cellar bar, several dining rooms, well liked food and outside seating; stylish bedrooms

The contemporary décor in this traditional Georgian townhouse is both interesting and attractive. The bar is in the cellar (and open for drinks and food all day) with fine vaulted ceilings, upholstered dining chairs and sofas on big flagstones, Marstons Lancaster Bomber and Wainwright, Spitting Feathers Empire IPA, Thwaites Original, Timothy Taylors Landlord and Treboom Yorkshire Sparkle on handpump and good wines by the glass; this leads through a dining room to a bright and airy garden room, both of which have green-painted farmhouse chairs around blond wooden tables on pale floorboards. On the first floor is what they call the Medicine Cabinet – a reception room for both the dining rooms and hotel – with quirky men's trouser-leg stools by the bar counter, a couple of grey button-back leather armchairs on either side of the fireplace and plaster judges' heads on Farrow & Ball paintwork. Leading off here, the two restaurants have leather chesterfields and more upholstered chairs around a mix of tables on bare boards, painted panelling, tall window shutters, chandeliers, gilt-edged mirrors and some unusual wire sculptures – it's all very smart and civilised. There are modern seats and tables between lavender pots at the front of the building, white metal furniture beside the garden room and traditional wooden chairs, tables and picnic-sets in the back courtyard. If you stay in the top bedroom (all of them are comfortable, up to date and well equipped) there are York Minster views across the rooftops.

As well as sandwiches (until 5pm) the high quality food includes chicken mousseline with parma ham, chicory and charred pink grapefruit salad, pork and black pudding scotch egg with cider jus, asparagus and tenderstem broccoli risotto with blue cheese crumb, chicken and leek pie with savoy cabbage and bacon, moules frites, burger with toppings, home-made chutney and skinny fries, lamb chump with minted pea purée, fondant potato and blackcurrant jus, 10oz rib-eye steak with a choice of sauce and chips, and puddings. *Benchmark main dish: beer-battered fish and chips £14.00. Two-course evening meal £21.00.*

Thwaites ~ Lease Nik Haywood ~ Real ale ~ Open 8am-11; 8am-10.30 Sun ~ Bar food 12-10 ~ Restaurant ~ Children welcome ~ Dogs allowed in bar ~ Wi-fi ~ Bedrooms: /£125
Recommended by Julian Thorpe, Alice Wright, Paul Baxter, Peter Smith and Judith Brown, Patricia Healey, Monty Green, Liz and Martin Eldon, Richard Tilbrook, Michael Butler

YORK   SE5951   Map 7

Maltings 🍺 £

(01904) 655387 – www.maltings.co.uk
Tanners Moat/Wellington Row, below Lendal Bridge; YO1 6HU

Bustling, friendly city pub with cheerful landlord, interesting real ales and other drinks plus good value standard food

There's a fine range of interesting drinks kept by the convivial, hard-working landlord here, including Black Sheep Best, Roosters YPA, Treboom Yorkshire Sparkle, Titanic Stout and York Guzzler on handpump with four quickly rotating guests, six continental beers on tap, four craft beers, lots of bottled beers, six farm ciders, 15 country wines and 25 whiskies from all over the world. The atmosphere is bustling and friendly and the tricksy décor is strong on salvaged, somewhat quirky junk: old doors for the bar front and much of the ceiling, a marvellous collection of railway signs and amusing notices, an old chocolate dispensing machine, cigarette and tobacco advertisements alongside cough and chest remedies, what looks like a suburban front door for the entrance to the ladies', partly stripped orange brick walls and even a lavatory pan in one corner; games machine. The day's papers are framed in the gents'. The pub is very handy for the National

Railway Museum and the station; nearby parking is difficult. Please note that dogs are allowed only after food service has finished.

🍴 Incredible value food includes sandwiches and toasties, baked potatoes with lots of fillings, mushroom and spinach lasagne, ham and egg, sausage and beans, beef in ale pie, chilli tacos and roast chicken and chips. *Benchmark main dish: chilli chips £5.45.*

Free house ~ Licensee Shaun Collinge ~ Real ale ~ No credit cards ~ Open 11am-11.30pm; 12-10.30 Sun ~ Bar food 12-2 weekdays; 12-4 weekends ~ Children allowed only during meal times ~ Wi-fi ~ Live music Mon and Tues evenings *Recommended by Rob Anderson, Professor James Burke, Andrew and Ruth Simmonds, Graham Smart, Mark Hamill, Dr J Barrie Jones, Caroline and Peter Bryant*

Also Worth a Visit in Yorkshire

Besides the fully inspected pubs, you might like to try these pubs that have been recommended to us and described by readers. Do tell us what you think of them: feedback@goodguides.com

ADDINGHAM SE0749
Fleece (01943) 830397
Main Street (B6160, off A65); LS29 0LY
Old village pub attractively renovated by the Seafood Pub Company; good food from well balanced menu (special diets catered for) including fresh fish/seafood, four real ales such as Black Sheep and Ilkley, comprehensive wine list with plenty by the glass, friendly helpful staff, low ceilings, flagstone and wood floors, log fires, upstairs gin and champagne bar (mainly for functions); children and dogs (in some areas) welcome, wheelchair access using ramp, seats under parasols on front terrace, open (and food) all day. *(Michael Butler)*

ADDINGHAM SE0749
Swan (01943) 430003
Main Street; LS29 0NS Popular local with linked rooms around central servery; flagstones and log fires (one in fine old range), six well kept changing ales and good food from sandwiches/baguettes to daily specials, Tues fish and chips, Fri steak night, friendly helpful service (may be a wait at busy times); live bands Sat, quiz nights; children and dogs welcome, tables out by pavement, open all day, food all day Sun till 7pm. *(Tina and David Woods-Taylor)*

AINDERBY STEEPLE SE3392
Wellington Heifer (01609) 775718
A684, 3 miles from A1; opposite church; DL7 9PU Modernised late 18th-c pub with four connecting rooms (some steps); flagstone and carpeted floors, comfortable scatter-cushion bench seating and sturdy tables, log fires, good range of beers and wines from carved counter, enjoyable food including good value lunchtime/early evening

set menu, restaurant at end of corridor; quiz nights; children welcome, three well appointed bedrooms, open all day Sun (food till 7pm). *(Sarah and David Gibbs)*

AINTHORPE NZ7007
Fox & Hounds (01287) 660218
Brook Lane; YO21 2LD Traditional 16th-c pub in tranquil moorland setting with grazing sheep and wonderful views; comfortable beamed bar with open fire in unusual stone fireplace, well kept changing ales and good choice of wines by the glass, generous fairly priced food including daily specials, friendly staff, restaurant, games room; free wi-fi; dogs welcome (great walks from the door), seven bedrooms and attached self-catering cottage, open all day. *(Helena and Trevor Fraser)*

AISLABY SE8508
Forge (01947) 811522
Main Road, off A171 W of Whitby; YO21 1SW Mellow-stone village pub with opened-up interior, light wood floor, upholstered wall benches and woodburner in brick fireplace, well kept ales such as Black Sheep from small central servery, good home-made food at sensible prices including popular Sun roasts served till 7pm, friendly accommodating staff; Tues quiz; children and dogs welcome, six bedrooms. *(Robert and Diana Ringstone)*

ALDBOROUGH SE4166
Ship (01423) 322749
Off B6265 just S of Boroughbridge, close to A1; YO51 9ER Attractive 14th-c beamed village dining pub adjacent to medieval church; good food from sandwiches and pub standards up including early bird deal, cheerful helpful service, well kept Black

---

We say if we know a pub allows dogs.

Sheep and Theakstons, extensive affordably priced wine list, some old-fashioned seats around cast-iron-framed tables, lots of copper and brass, inglenook fire, candlelit back restaurant; children and dogs welcome, a few picnic-sets outside, well placed for Roman remains and museum, open all day Fri–Sun, food till 6pm Sun, kitchen closed Mon (except bank holidays). *(Lionel Smith)*

ALLERSTON   SE8783
Cayley Arms (01723) 859904
A170 Pickering–Scarborough; YO18 7PJ
Refurbished under present owners; long knocked-through bar with light wood and stone floor, two woodburners, upholstered captain's chairs, leather cushioned wall benches and some comfortable button-back armchairs, antlers on bare stone walls, Theakstons, Wold Top and a guest, generous helpings of good freshly made food in bar or restaurant, friendly helpful service; well behaved children and dogs welcome, picnic-sets at front and in back garden by brook, six well appointed bedrooms, open all day in summer, check website for other times. *(Sara Fulton, Roger Baker)*

APPLETON-LE-MOORS   SE7388
★ Moors (01751) 417435
N of A170, just under 1.5 miles E of Kirkby Moorside; YO62 6TF Traditional 17th-c stone-built village pub; beamed bar with built-in high-backed settle next to old kitchen fireplace, plenty of other seating, three changing regional ales and wide range of malt whiskies and gins, good sensibly priced food from sandwiches/ciabattas and pub favourites up including daily specials, dining room with leather chairs at polished tables, friendly helpful staff; background and occasional live music; children and dogs welcome, tables in lovely walled garden, country views and walks to Rosedale Abbey and Hartoft End, eight good bedrooms, open all day. *(Joe and Belinda Smart)*

APPLETREEWICK   SE0560
★ Craven Arms (01756) 720270
Off B6160 Burnsall–Bolton Abbey; BD23 6DA Character creeper-clad 16th-c beamed pub; cushioned settles and rugs on flagstones, open fires (one in old range), gas lighting and lots of interesting pictures and bric-a-brac, up to eight well kept ales including cask-tapped Theakstons Old Peculier and a house beer from Dark Horse, real cider and several wines by the glass, enjoyable home-made food from hot or cold sandwiches up, friendly helpful service, small dining room and splendid thatched and raftered cruck barn with gallery; free wi-fi; children, dogs and muddy boots welcome (plenty of surrounding walks), wheelchair access, nice country views from front picnic-sets, more seats in back garden, shepherd's hut accommodation, open (and food) all day. *(Lindy Andrews)*

ARNCLIFFE   SD9371
★ Falcon (01756) 770205
Off B6160 N of Grassington; BD23 5QE Basic no-frills tavern in lovely setting on village green; coal fire in small bar with vintage furnishings, well kept Timothy Taylors Boltmaker and a guest either from handpump or poured from stoneware jugs in central hatch-style servery, enjoyable traditional food from sandwiches up, attractive watercolours, sepia photographs and humorous sporting prints, back sun-room overlooking pleasant garden; quiz first Fri of month; children (till 9pm) and dogs welcome, four miles of trout fishing (permits available from the pub), walks in lovely surrounding countryside, six bedrooms (two with own bathroom), open all day in summer, all day Fri–Sun winter, food till 5pm Sun. *(B and M Kendall, Helene Grygar)*

ASKRIGG   SD9491
Crown (01969) 650387
Main Street; DL8 3HQ Friendly open-plan local in James Herriot village; three areas off main bar, open fires (one in old-fashioned range), enjoyable simple pub food at reasonable prices, well kept ales such as Black Sheep and Yorkshire Dales; children, walkers and dogs welcome, tables outside, nearby self-catering barn conversion, open all day. *(Tracey and Stephen Groves)*

ASKRIGG   SD9491
Kings Arms (01969) 650113
Signed from A684 Leyburn–Sedbergh in Bainbridge; DL8 3HQ Popular 18th-c coaching inn freshened up under present friendly management; high-ceilinged main bar with flagstones, traditional furnishings and good log fire, a couple of well kept house beers from nearby Yorkshire Dales plus Black Sheep, Theakstons and a guest, several wines by the glass, enjoyable reasonably priced food including some evening offers, more modern carpeted restaurant with inglenook, games room in former barrel-vaulted beer cellar; background music, sports TV; children and dogs (in bar) welcome, side courtyard, bedrooms run separately as part of Holiday Property Bond complex behind, open (and food) all day. *(John Beeken, Tracey and Stephen Groves)*

AUSTWICK   SD7668
★ Game Cock (01524) 251226
Just off A65 Settle–Kirkby Lonsdale; LA2 8BB Quaint civilised place in pretty spot below Three Peaks; friendly beamed back bar with bare boards and good log fire, well kept Thwaites ales and a guest, winter mulled wine and decent coffee, cheerful efficient staff, plenty of emphasis on french chef-owner's good fairly priced food including blackboard specials and themed nights, two restaurant areas and small conservatory-style extension; children, walkers, cyclists

and dogs welcome, tables out at front and in back garden, five bedrooms, closed Mon till 3pm, otherwise open (and food) all day. *(Tracey and Stephen Groves, Philip and Susan Robertshaw)*

AYSGARTH   SE0188
Aysgarth Falls (01969) 663775
A684; DL8 3SR Creeper-clad moorland hotel with good food and welcoming accommodating service; well kept ales such as Black Sheep, Theakstons and Wensleydale in log-fire bar where dogs allowed, comfortable eating areas, some interesting ancient masonry at the back recalling its days as a pilgrims' inn; great scenery near broad waterfalls, 13 bedrooms, camping (adults only), open all day. *(Revd R P Tickle)*

AYSGARTH   SE0088
George & Dragon (01969) 663358
Just off A684; DL8 3AD 17th-c posting inn with enjoyable home-made food from sandwiches up, two big dining areas and small beamed and panelled bar with log fire, well kept ales including Black Sheep, Theakstons and a house beer from Yorkshire Dales, good choice of wines by the glass; may be background music, free wi-fi; children and dogs (in bar) welcome, nice paved garden, lovely scenery and walks, handy for Aysgarth Falls, bedrooms, open all day. *(Monica and Steph Evans)*

BAILDON   SE1538
Junction (01274) 582009
Baildon Road; BD17 6AB Friendly wedge-shaped local with three traditional linked rooms; half a dozen well kept ales including own Junction brews (July festival), games part with pool; live music Sun evening, quiz nights Tues and Thurs, sports TV; open all day. *(Sally and Colin Allen)*

BARDSEY   SE3642
Bingley Arms (01937) 572462
Church Lane; LS17 9DR Ancient pub with spacious lounge divided into separate areas, substantial beams and huge fireplace (priest holes in the chimney), well kept Black Sheep, Timothy Taylors, Tetleys and a beer named for them (Bingley 953), good range of home-cooked food, afternoon teas, friendly staff, smaller public bar, upstairs raftered restaurant; children welcome, attractive terraced garden behind, lovely Saxon church nearby, open all day. *(Michael Butler)*

BARKISLAND   SE0419
★Fleece (01422) 820687
B6113 towards Ripponden; HX4 0DJ Large well renovated and extended 18th-c beamed moorland dining pub; good popular food including weekday set menu, Timothy Taylors Boltmaker, a guest beer and plenty of wines by the glass, efficient friendly uniformed staff; background music; children welcome, no dogs, front disabled access,

lovely Pennine views from first-floor terrace and garden, summer barbecues, seven bedrooms, useful for M62, open all day from 8am for breakfast, food till 7pm Sun. *(John and Eleanor Holdsworth)*

BARNSLEY   SE3400
Cock (01226) 744227
Pilley Hill, Birdwell; S70 5UD Welcoming village local set down from the road; reasonably priced home-made food (not Sun evening, Mon) and several well kept ales including Tetleys, cheerful helpful staff, main bar with beams, stone floor and open fire, lounge and back dining room; children and dogs welcome, open all day (from 4pm Mon). *(Andrea and Philip Crispin)*

BARNSLEY   SE3203
Strafford Arms (01226) 287488
Near Northern College, about 2.5 miles NW of M1 junction 36; S75 3EW Pretty stone-built village pub (Fine & Country Inns) with opened-up contemporary interior; well liked food from lunchtime sandwiches and platters to Josper grills, ales such as Bradfield and Timothy Taylors, good range of wines and cocktails, friendly service, log fires including one in big yorkshire range; Tues quiz, free wi-fi; children welcome, no dogs inside, garden with play area, on Trans Pennine Trail and by entrance to Wentworth Castle, open (and food) all day. *(Peter Watts)*

BEDALE   SE2688
Old Black Swan (01677) 422973
Market Place; DL8 1ED Popular old pub with attractive bay-windowed frontage; well kept ales including Theakstons and generous helpings of good value food, friendly efficient staff, log fire; darts, pool, sports TV; children and dogs welcome, disabled facilities, small covered back terrace, Tues market, open (and food) all day. *(Mick Allen)*

BEVERLEY   TA0339
★White Horse (01482) 861973
Hengate, off North Bar; HU17 8BN Timeless place known locally as Nellie's; carefully preserved Victorian interior with basic little rooms huddled around central bar, brown leatherette seats (high-backed settles in one snug) and plain chairs/benches on bare boards, antique cartoons and sentimental engravings, gas lighting including chandelier, coal fires, bargain Sam Smiths beers and guests, friendly staff, more space upstairs; charity quiz Tues, games room; children (till 7pm) and dogs welcome, courtyard picnic-sets, open all day. *(Richard Tilbrook)*

BEVERLEY   TA0239
Woolpack (01482) 867095
Westwood Road, W of centre; HU17 8EN Nice little pub (under new management again) at end of 19th-c row of terrace cottages; five Marstons-related beers and

around 20 gins, enjoyable traditional food, friendly service, open fires and simple furnishings, brasses, knick-knacks and prints, cosy snug where dogs allowed; children welcome, benches out at front, small seating area behind, closed Mon, otherwise open all day (may shut early if quiet). *(John Saville)*

BINGLEY SE1039
Brown Cow (01274) 564345
B6429 just W of junction with A650; BD16 2QX Open-plan pub in nice riverside spot; Timothy Taylors range and good choice of enjoyable generously served food, friendly staff; live music and quiz nights; children and dogs welcome, tables out on sheltered terrace, open all day. *(Beth Aldridge)*

BIRSTALL SE2126
Black Bull (01274) 973203
Kirkgate, off A652; head down hill towards church; WF17 9HE Refurbished old stone pub opposite part-Saxon church; long row of small linked rooms, low beams, painted panelling and log fire, real ales such as Black Sheep, Saltaire and York, proper cider and decent range of gins, low-priced food including burgers and pizzas, upstairs former courtroom used for functions; children and dogs welcome, picnic-sets on gravel terrace, open all day, food Weds-Sat evenings and Sun lunchtime. *(Michael Butler)*

BIRSTWITH SE2459
★Station Hotel (01423) 770254
Off B6165 W of Ripley; HG3 3AG Welcoming immaculately kept stone-built dales pub; bar, log-fire restaurant and garden room, very good home-made food from pub staples up including set deal (Mon-Sat till 6pm) and Thurs steak night, four local ales such as Black Sheep and Copper Dragon and 14 wines by the glass, friendly efficient staff; Mon quiz and monthly open mike night; children and dogs (in bar) welcome, attractive back garden with smokers' shelter, picturesque valley, six bedrooms, open (and food) all day. *(Margaret and Peter Staples, M G Hart)*

BISHOPTHORPE SE5947
Woodman (01904) 706507
Village signed just off A64 York S bypass; Main Street; YO23 2RB Welcoming open-plan pub with good range of enjoyable food cooked by landlord-chef, four regional ales and decent choice of wines by the glass, friendly efficient service, woodburner; background music; children and dogs welcome, seats out in front and in large back garden with play equipment, well placed for York Racecourse, open all day, food all day weekends (till 6pm Sun). *(Charlotte and William Mason)*

BOLTON ABBEY SE0754
Devonshire Arms (01756) 710441
B6160; BD23 6AJ Elegant and comfortable 18th-c hotel in wonderful position on edge of Bolton Abbey Estate; good if not cheap food from light meals up in bright modern brasserie-bar, contemporary paintings (some for sale) on roughcast walls, colourful armchairs around cast-iron-framed tables on pale wood floor, up to four well kept ales and good wines by the glass, afternoon teas, more formal restaurant; tables in spacious courtyard with extensive views, Estate and Strid river-valley walks, bedrooms in old and new wings, open all day. *(Gary and Marie Miller)*

BRADFIELD SK2692
Old Horns (0114) 285 1207
High Bradfield; S6 6LG Old Thwaites pub in hill village with stunning views; good hearty food including bargain themed days and Sun carvery, can eat in part-flagstoned bar or carpeted pitch-roofed dining room, half a dozen well kept beers, friendly helpful staff; background music, Tues quiz, TV; children welcome, raised terrace taking in the view, picnic-sets and play area in garden, next to interesting 14th-c church, good walks, open (and food) all day, kitchen shuts 7pm Sun. *(Martin Day)*

BRADFORD SE1533
Fighting Cock (01274) 726907
Preston Street (off B6145); BD7 1JE Traditional bare-boards alehouse by industrial estate; a dozen well kept changing ales, foreign draught/bottled beers and real ciders, friendly staff and lively atmosphere, all-day sandwiches plus good simple lunchtime hot dishes (not Sun), coal fires; dogs welcome, fenced-in garden opposite (beer festivals), open all day. *(Caroline Sullivan)*

BRADFORD SE1533
New Beehive (01274) 721784
Westgate; BD1 3AA Robustly old-fashioned five-room Edwardian inn; plenty of period features including gas lighting, big mirrors, interesting paintings and coal fires, changing ales (mostly from smaller brewers) along with continental bottled beers, welcoming staff and friendly atmosphere (busy on BCFC match days), weekend live music in cellar bar; pool and bar billiards; children (until 8pm) and dogs welcome, back courtyard, 17 simple bedrooms, open all day from around 2pm Fri, Sat, otherwise open from 6pm. *(Caroline Sullivan)*

BRADFORD SE1633
Sparrow Bier Café (01274) 270772
North Parade; BD1 3HZ Bare-boards bar owned by Kirkstall; their ales and guests along with good range of craft kegs and bottled beers, friendly knowledgeable staff, snacky food, more tables in cellar bar; background and live music; open all day (till midnight Thurs-Sat). *(Mick Allen)*

BRAMHAM   SE4242

Swan (01937) 843570

Just off A1 2 miles N of A64; LS23 6QA
Unspoilt and unchanging little local up
steep hill from village square (aka the Top
Pub); friendly atmosphere and good mix
of customers, well kept ales such as Black
Sheep and Leeds, no food, two coal fires;
open all day Sat, from 4pm weekdays.
(Les and Sandra Brown)

BRANTINGHAM   SE9329

Triton (01482) 667261

Ellerker Road; HU15 1QE Spacious
comfortably refurbished and extended old
stone pub; good choice of enjoyable home-
made food in bar and restaurant, three
local ales, prompt friendly service; children,
walkers and dogs welcome, tables out at front
and in sheltered back garden, open all day
weekends (food all day Sat, till 6pm Sun),
closed Mon. *(Margaret McDonald)*

BREARTON   SE3260

Malt Shovel (01423) 862929

*Village signposted off A61 N of
Harrogate; HG3 3BX* Cosy 16th-c
dining pub under newish management;
heavily beamed rooms with two open fires
and woodburner, attractive mix of tables
and chairs on wood or slate floors, some
partitioning separating several eating areas,
good food from lunchtime sandwiches and
pub favourites up, Rudgate, Theakstons and
plenty of wines by the glass from linenfold
oak counter, airy conservatory; children
welcome, no dogs inside, tables under
parasols in garden, pretty hanging baskets,
circular walks from the door, closed Sun
evening, Mon. *(Michael Doswell)*

BRIDGE HEWICK   SE3370

Black-a-moor (01765) 603511

*Boroughbridge Road (B6265 E of
Ripon); HG4 5AA* Roomy family-run dining
pub with good choice of popular home-
cooked food including set menu, well kept
local beers and decent wines, friendly young
staff, sofas and woodburner in bar area; free
wi-fi; children welcome, dogs in snug, five
comfortable bedrooms, open all day, food all
day Tues-Sat, kitchen closed Sun evening,
Mon lunchtime. *(Stuart and Natalie Granville)*

BURN   SE5928

Wheatsheaf (01757) 270614

*Main Road (A19 Selby–Doncaster);
YO8 8LJ* Busy but welcoming 19th-c
roadside pub; comfortable seats in partly
divided open-plan bar with log fire, lots
to look at including air force wartime
memorabilia, gleaming copper kettles,
polished buffalo horns and cases of model
vans and lorries, half a dozen well kept ales,
20 malt whiskies and straightforward good
value food; background and live music, Sun
quiz, games machine, TV; children and dogs

welcome, picnic-sets on terrace in small back
garden, open all day, no evening food Sun,
Mon or Tues. *(Douglas Power)*

BURNISTON   TA0193

Three Jolly Sailors (01723) 871445

*A171 N of Scarborough; High Street;
YO13 0HJ* Comfortable and welcoming
village pub with wide range of enjoyable
reasonably priced food from sandwiches
up, OAP and children's menus, ales such
as Timothy Taylors Landlord, main bar,
restaurant and conservatory, open fires; dogs
welcome, tables under parasols in small side
garden, handy for Cleveland Way and coastal
walks, open (and food) all day. *(Kerry and
Guy Trooper)*

BURYTHORPE   SE7964

★Bay Horse (01653) 658302

*Off A64 8.5 miles NE of York ring road,
via Kirkham and Westow; 5 miles S of
Malton, by Welham Road; YO17 9LJ*
Welcoming old stone pub with plenty of
authentic character; cosy linked rooms
with warming fires, old brick and flagstone
floors, traditional furniture with candles on
tables, lots of bits and pieces on walls and
hanging from beams, eight well kept ales
including All Hallows (brewed at sister pub
the Goodmanham Arms at Goodmanham),
real ciders and generous helpings of good
reasonably priced lunchtime food including
some italian dishes, evening meals till
7.30pm just Tues (steak night) and Fri
(sharing platter or stew), friendly caring
service; children and dogs welcome, flat
disabled access from car park, nice wolds-
edge village with fine surrounding walks,
open all day. *(Liz and Mike Newton)*

CARLTON   SE0684

Foresters Arms (01969) 640272

Off A684 W of Leyburn; DL8 4BB
Old stone pub owned by local co-operative;
bar with dark low beams, flagstones and
log fire, four well kept yorkshire ales and
popular affordably priced food including
evening pizzas, carpeted restaurant; events
including fortnightly quiz; children and dogs
welcome, disabled access/loos, a few picnic-
sets out at front, pretty village in heart of
Yorkshire Dales National Park, lovely views,
three bedrooms, closed lunchtimes Mon
and Tues, no food Sun evening. *(Sally and
Colin Allen)*

CARLTON HUSTHWAITE   SE4976

Carlton Inn (01845) 501265

Butt Lane; YO7 2BW Cosy modernised
beamed dining pub; good fairly priced food
cooked by landlady including daily specials
and early bird menu, friendly helpful service,
John Smiths and Theakstons, local cider,
mix of country furniture including some old
settles, open fire; children welcome, dogs in
back bar area, garden picnic-sets, open all
day Sun, closed Mon. *(Sarah and David Gibbs)*

CARPERBY
SE0089

Wheatsheaf (01969) 663216

A mile NW of Aysgarth; DL8 4DF Friendly early 19th-c inn set in quiet dales village and popular with walkers; cosy traditional bar with warming fire, three or four well kept ales such as Black Sheep, Jennings and Theakstons, enjoyable good value home-cooked food, lounge and dining room; children and dogs welcome, 13 comfortable bedrooms (James Herriot had his honeymoon here in 1941), good breakfast, lovely walks including to Aysgarth Falls, open all day. *(Peter Smith and Judith Brown)*

CARTHORPE
SE3083

★ Fox & Hounds (01845) 567433

Village signed from A1 N of Ripon, via B6285; DL8 2LG Popular neatly kept pub run by same family since 1983 and emphasis on their very good well presented food; attractive high-raftered restaurant with lots of farm and smithy tools, ales such as Timothy Taylors and Theakstons in L-shaped bar with two log fires, plush seating, plates on stripped beams and evocative Victorian photographs of Whitby, some theatrical memorabilia in corridors, good friendly service; background classical music; children welcome, handy for A1, closed Mon and maybe first week Jan. *(Janet and Peter Race)*

CATTAL
SE4455

Victoria (01423) 330249

Station Road; YO26 8EB Bustling Victorian-themed dining pub with extensive choice of good attractively presented food, charming attentive service, well kept ales including one from local Rudgate named for the landlord, good value wines; children welcome, picnic-sets in gravelled back garden, open (and food) all day Sun, from 4pm Tues-Sat, shut Mon, convenient for the station. *(Les and Sandra Brown)*

CHAPEL-LE-DALE
SD7477

★ Old Hill Inn (01524) 241256

B5655 Ingleton–Hawes, 3 miles N of Ingleton; LA6 3AR Welcoming former farmhouse with fantastic views to Ingleborough and Whernside; clean rustic interior, beams, log fires and bare-stone recesses, straightforward furniture on stripped-wood floors, pictures and some interesting local artefacts, Black Sheep, Dent and a guest, good wholesome food including lovely puddings (look out for the landlord's sugar sculptures), separate dining room and sun lounge, relaxed chatty atmosphere; children welcome, dogs in bar, wonderful remote surrounding walks, two bedrooms and space for five caravans, open all day Sat, closed Mon. *(Robert and Diana Ringstone)*

CLAPHAM
SD7469

New Inn (01524) 251203

Off A65 N of Settle; LA2 8HH Nicely renovated 18th-c inn facing the river in this famously pretty village; good food in bar or bistro from lunchtime sandwiches and snacks up, local ales including one named for them, friendly staff, attractive grey colour scheme, stone floors and three open fires; children and dogs welcome, tables out overlooking the water and on back terrace, walk to Ingleborough Cave or more adventurous hikes, 19 neat bedrooms and upmarket bunkhouse, open all day. *(Philip and Susan Robertshaw)*

CLIFTON
SE1622

Black Horse (01484) 713862

Westgate/Coalpit Lane; signed off Brighouse Road from M62 junction 25; HD6 4HJ Friendly 17th-c inn-restaurant at the heart of this pleasant village; good interesting food (can be pricey) in front dining rooms, also some pubby dishes and set menu choices, efficient uniformed staff, open fire in back bar with beam-and-plank ceiling, well kept ales such as Timothy Taylors, good range of wines; children and dogs (in bar) welcome, nice courtyard, 22 comfortable bedrooms, open all day, food all day weekends. *(Barbara and Phil Bowie)*

CLOUGHTON
SE9798

Falcon (01723) 870717

Pub signed just off A171 out towards Whitby; YO13 0DY Large 19th-c country pub set in five-acre grounds; well divided opened-up interior including log-fire lounge and dining conservatory, enjoyable pubby food from sandwiches to daily specials, beers such as Theakstons and good choice of wines, friendly staff, distant sea view from end windows; background music; children welcome, picnic-sets in neat walled garden, good walks (leave muddy boots by the door), eight bedrooms and glamping pods, closed Mon and Tues in winter. *(WAH)*

CLOUGHTON NEWLANDS
TA0195

Bryherstones (01723) 870744

Newlands Road, off A171 in Cloughton; YO13 0AR Popular traditional stone pub; several interconnecting rooms including dining room up on right and flagstoned stable-theme bar on left, good fair priced food using local produce including dry-aged steaks, Timothy Taylors and guests, friendly efficient service, games room (pool and darts); children and dogs welcome, picnic-sets and play area in sheltered back garden, open all day Sun, closed lunchtimes Mon-Weds. *(Helena and Trevor Fraser)*

COLEY
SE1226

Brown Horse (01422) 202112

Lane Ends, Denholme Gate Road (A644 Brighouse–Keighley, a mile N of Hipperholme); HX3 7SD Popular roadside pub with good reasonably priced home-made food (all day Fri, Sat, not Sun evening), well kept Brakspears, Saltaire, Timothy Taylors

Landlord and a guest, cheerful attentive staff, open fires, small back conservatory overlooking beer garden; children welcome, no dogs inside, open all day. *(John and Eleanor Holdsworth)*

COLTON   SE5444
★**Old Sun** (01904) 744261
Off A64 York–Tadcaster; LS24 8EP
Whitewashed 18th-c pub in pretty village; simply furnished bar with stools and small tables on bare boards, built-in window seats, Black Sheep and guests, 13 wines by the glass and good food cooked by landlord-chef, dining areas with solid wood and tartan-upholstered chairs around polished tables, exposed brickwork and log fires; background music; children and dogs welcome, seats on sunny front terrace and in rambling garden, log cabin-style outside bar with pizza oven, country views, accommodation in converted outbuilding, open (and food) all day Fri-Sun, closed Mon and lunchtime Tues; up for sale as we went to press.
(Amy and Luke Buchanan, John and Delia Franks, Simon Sharpe)

CONEYTHORPE   SE3958
★**Tiger** (01423) 863632
2.3 miles from A1(M) junction 47; A59 towards York, then village signposted (and brown sign to Tiger Inn); bear left at brown sign in Flaxby; HG5 0RY
Spreading red-carpeted bar with hundreds of pewter tankards hanging from painted joists, padded wall seats, pews and settles around sturdy scrubbed tables, old prints, china figurines in one arched alcove, open fire, more formal back dining area, good sensibly priced food from pub favourites up including set deals, June lobster festival, well kept Black Sheep Bitter, Timothy Taylors Landlord and extensive range of wines, friendly helpful staff; background music; children welcome, picnic-sets on front gravel terrace and on small green opposite, open (and food) all day.
(Les and Sandra Brown)

COXWOLD   SE5377
Fauconberg Arms (01347) 868214
Off A170 Thirsk–Helmsley, via Kilburn or Wass; easily found off A19 too; YO61 4AD
Early 17th-c village pub under newish ownership; heavily beamed flagstoned bar, log fires in both linked areas (one in broad inglenook), some attractive oak chairs made by local craftsmen alongside more usual pub furnishings, old local photographs and copper implements, well kept beers such as Isaac Poad and Theakstons, good fairly traditional food at sensible prices, friendly service, elegant dining room; children welcome, dogs in bar, views from terrace over fields to Byland Abbey (EH), picnic-sets on

front cobbles, eight comfortable bedrooms, open all day. *(Kerry and Guy Trooper)*

CRATHORNE   NZ4407
Crathorne Arms (01642) 961402
Centre of village; TS15 0BA Village dining pub with good food (can be pricey) from sandwiches up including set menu choices, yorkshire beers such as Timothy Taylors and well chosen wines, friendly obliging staff, atmospheric linked rooms with lots of mirrors and pictures, log fires; sunny back courtyard, open all day (till 6pm Sun). *(Michael Doswell)*

CRAY   SD9479
★**White Lion** (01756) 760262
B6160 N of Kettlewell; BD23 5JB Former drovers' inn set in lovely countryside high up on Buckden Pike; flagstoned bar with button-back leather chesterfields and armchairs in front of woodburner, cushioned window seat and shelves of books, simple little back room (good for wet dogs), Black Sheep Best, Wharfedale Blonde and a guest, eight wines by the glass and good food from short but varied menu, attractive dining room with open fire; background music; children welcome, picnic-sets above the quiet steep lane or can sit on flat limestone slabs in the shallow stream opposite, comfortable bedrooms (some in converted barn), open all day; for sale as we went to press, so may be changes. *(Simon and Sue Lamb, Glen and Patricia Fuller)*

CROPTON   SE7588
New Inn (01751) 417330
Village signposted off A170 W of Pickering; YO18 8HH Modernised village pub with own Great Yorkshire beers and guests (can tour brewery Tues-Sat lunchtime for $7.50 – includes a pint); bar with plush seating, panelling and small fire, restaurant and downstairs conservatory, enjoyable fairly straightforward food from sandwiches up, friendly staff; background music, TV, games machine, darts and pool; well behaved children and dogs (in bar) welcome, garden picnic-sets, bedrooms and self-catering cottage, open all day. *(Nick and Meriel Cox)*

DACRE BANKS   SE1961
★**Royal Oak** (01423) 780200
B6451 S of Pateley Bridge; HG3 4EN Popular 18th-c stone pub with lovely Nidderdale views from the back; good traditional food (not Sun or Mon evenings) along with daily specials and some seafood events, attentive friendly staff, half a dozen well kept changing ales and good choice of wines and gins, beams and panelling, log-fire dining room, games room with darts, dominoes and pool; background music, TV,

---

If we know a pub has an outdoor play area for children, we mention it.

free wi-fi; children welcome in eating areas, no dogs, seats on front terrace and in back garden, three bedrooms, big breakfast, open all day. *(Gary and Marie Miller)*

DANBY   NZ7008
Duke of Wellington (01287) 660351
West Lane; YO21 2LY 18th-c creeper-clad inn overlooking village green; well kept ales such as Daleside, and enjoyable evening food from shortish menu; children and dogs (in main bar) welcome, clean tidy bedrooms, closed Mon lunchtime, open all day Fri-Sun. *(George and Alison Bishop)*

DARLEY   SE1961
Wellington Inn (01423) 780362
B6451; Darley Head; HG3 2QQ Extended roadside stone inn with fine Nidderdale views; beams and big open fire in bar, modern restaurant with light wood floor and small conservatory, enjoyable freshly made food from sandwiches up, Sun set lunch, well kept Black Sheep, Timothy Taylors and Tetleys, helpful friendly staff; children and dogs (in bar) welcome, seats on large grassed area, 12 bedrooms, good breakfast, open all day. *(M G Hart)*

DEWSBURY   SE2622
Huntsman (01924) 275700
Walker Cottages, Chidswell Lane, Shaw Cross – pub signed; WF12 7SW Cosy low-beamed converted cottages alongside urban-fringe farm; original features including an old range in the snug, agricultural bric-a-brac, brassware, plates and bottles on delft shelving, blazing woodburner, small front extension, Timothy Taylors and up to three local guests, well priced traditional home-made food (Thurs-Sat, till 4pm Sun), friendly staff and nice relaxed atmosphere; children welcome, no dogs inside, picnic-sets in side paddock, open all day Fri-Sun, closed Mon and lunchtimes Tues, Weds (also till 4pm Sat in winter). *(Michael Butler)*

DEWSBURY   SE2421
West Riding Licensed Refreshment Rooms (01924) 459193
Station (Platform 2), Wellington Road; WF13 1HF Three-room early Victorian station bar under same owners as the Sportsman in Huddersfield; nine well kept changing ales, foreign bottled beers and farm ciders, good value pizzas, lots of railway memorabilia and pictures, coal fire; juke box and live music; children till 7pm in two end rooms, disabled access, on Transpennine Real Ale Trail, open all day. *(Douglas Power)*

DOWNHOLME   SE1197
★ Bolton Arms (01748) 823716
Village signposted just off A6108 Leyburn–Richmond; DL11 6AE Stone-built pub with wonderful Swaledale views from garden and dining conservatory; simply furnished carpeted bar down a few steps

with two smallish linked areas, plush wall banquettes, collection of gleaming brass and few small country pictures, log fire in neat fireplace, ales such as Timothy Taylors and Wensleydale, ten wines by the glass and eight malt whiskies, good food from lunchtime baguettes up; background music, free wi-fi; children welcome, no dogs inside, two bedrooms sharing a bathroom, closed Tues lunchtime. *(Tracey and Stephen Groves)*

EASINGWOLD   SE5270
George (01347) 821698
Market Place; YO61 3AD Neat market town hotel (former 18th-c coaching inn) with slightly old-fashioned feel; well kept Black Sheep, Timothy Taylors and a guest, good food in bar and restaurant from sandwiches/panini to daily specials, smaller appetites catered for, helpful cheerful service; soft background music, free wi-fi; children welcome, no dogs, disabled access, pleasant bedrooms and good breakfast, open all day. *(Lindy Andrews)*

EAST MARTON   SD9050
Cross Keys (01282) 844326
A59 Gisburn–Skipton; BD23 3LP Spacious 17th-c pub behind small green looking down on Leeds & Liverpool Canal; black beams, bare boards and woodburner in big stone fireplace, enjoyable generously served food from sandwiches and baked potatoes up, well kept ales such as Copper Dragon, Kirby Lonsdale and Timothy Taylors, friendly service, further dining area down steps; background music; children, walkers and dogs welcome, picnic-sets on front deck, near Pennine Way, open all day, food all day weekends. *(Mike and Sarah Abbot)*

EAST MORTON   SE0941
Busfeild Arms (01274) 563169
Main Road; BD20 5SP Attractive 19th-c stone-built village pub (originally a school); traditionally furnished beamed and flagstoned bar with woodburner, Saltaire, Timothy Taylors, Tetleys and a guest, popular fairly priced food from sandwiches up, steak night Mon, efficient cheerful service, restaurant; Thurs quiz, live music Sat, sports TV, free wi-fi; children welcome, picnic-sets on front terrace, three bedrooms, open all day, food till 5.45pm Sun. *(John and Eleanor Holdsworth)*

EAST WITTON   SE1487
★ Cover Bridge Inn (01969) 623250
A6108 out towards Middleham; DL8 4SQ Cosy and welcoming 16th-c flagstoned country local; good choice of well kept yorkshire-brewed ales and enjoyable generously served pub food at sensible prices, small restaurant, roaring fires; children and dogs welcome, riverside garden with play area, three bedrooms, open all day. *(Joe and Belinda Smart)*

EBBERSTON SE8983
Grapes (01723) 859273
High Street (A170); YO13 9PA
Modernised old roadside pub under new
welcoming management; plenty of emphasis
on their good popular food, Tetleys,
Theakstons and a summer guest, decent
wines, friendly helpful service; children
and dogs (in bar) welcome, closed Mon and
lunchtime Tues. *(Charlotte and William Mason)*

EGTON NZ8006
★Wheatsheaf (01947) 895271
Village centre; YO21 1TZ 19th-c village
pub of real character; interesting pictures
and collectables in small bare-boards bar
with fire in old range, very good generously
served food including daily specials, friendly
service, Black Sheep, Timothy Taylors
Landlord and a summer guest, several
wines by the glass, restaurant; children and
dogs (in bar) welcome, four bedrooms and
adjacent cottage, open all day weekends (no
food Sun evening), closed Mon. *(Louise and
Simon Peters)*

EGTON BRIDGE NZ8005
Horseshoe (01947) 895245
*Village signed off A171 W of Whitby;
YO21 1XE* Attractively placed 18th-c stone
inn; open fires and woodburners, high-
backed built-in winged settles, wall seats
and spindleback chairs, various odds and
ends including a large stuffed trout (caught
nearby in 1913), Theakstons Best and three
guests, popular food using their own eggs
and vegetables and locally sourced meat;
background and some live music, free wi-fi;
children welcome, dogs in side bar during
mealtimes, seats on quiet terrace in nice
mature garden by small River Esk, good walks
(on Coast to Coast path), six bedrooms, open
all day, food all day Sun till 7pm. *(Monica and
Steph Evans)*

EGTON BRIDGE NZ8005
★Postgate (01947) 895241
*Village signed off A171 W of Whitby;
YO21 1UX* Moorland village pub next to
railway station; good imaginative food at
fair prices including fresh local fish (lots of
blackboard menus), well kept Black Sheep
and a guest, friendly helpful staff, traditional
quarry-tiled bar with beams, panelled dado
and coal fire in antique range, elegant
restaurant; children and dogs welcome,
walled front garden with picnic-sets either
side of brick path, three comfy bedrooms.
(Monica and Steph Evans)

EMBSAY SE0053
Elm Tree (01756) 790717
Elm Tree Square; BD23 6RB Popular
open-plan beamed village pub; hearty
helpings of good value food including
blackboard specials, Thurs pie night,
four well kept ales such as Tetleys and
Timothy Taylors, cheerful young staff;
comfortable bedrooms, handy for Embsay
& Bolton Abbey Steam Railway, open all
day weekends. *(Patricia Healey)*

FACEBY NZ4903
Sutton Arms (01642) 700382
Mill Lane/Bank Lane; TS9 7BW
Welcoming village dining pub at foot of
Cleveland Hills, clean, comfortable and cosy,
with low beamed central bar flanked by
eating areas, highly regarded freshly made
food (best to book) from pub favourites to
more restaurant choices including excellent
steaks, well kept ales and good selection
of wines, friendly attentive service; tables
on tiered front deck, simply furnished but
well appointed bedrooms, good hearty
breakfast, closed Sun evening, Mon, Tues
and lunchtimes apart from Sun. *(Mark and
Sian Edwards)*

FEARBY SE1980
Black Swan (01765) 689477
Keld Bank; HG4 4NF Refurbished and
extended country pub; beamed bar with
dining area to the right, woodburner in pale
stone fireplace, Black Sheep, Theakstons and
a couple of regional summer guests, several
wines by the glass and good food from varied
menu including daily specials (seafood and
game festivals), friendly helpful service,
lovely valley views from back restaurant
(more rustic in style); children welcome till
7pm, dogs in bar, 14 modern bedrooms (12
in annexe), camping, open all day summer
(from 3pm weekdays, all day weekends
in winter). *(M and GR)*

FERRENSBY SE3660
★General Tarleton (01423) 340284
A655 N of Knaresborough; HG5 0PZ
Carefully renovated 18th-c coaching inn,
more restaurant-with-rooms than pub,
but there's an informal bar with sofas and
woodburner serving well kept Black Sheep,
Timothy Taylors Landlord and a dozen wines
by the glass; other open-plan rooms with low
beams, exposed stonework and brick pillars
creating alcoves, dark leather high-backed
dining chairs around wooden tables; first
class modern cooking from owner-chef along
with more traditional food and children's
menu, friendly well trained staff; seats in
covered courtyard and tree-lined garden,
pretty country views, 13 stylish bedrooms,
good breakfast. *(Janet and Peter Race, WAH,
Paul Walker)*

FILEY TA1180
Bonhommes (01723) 515325
The Crescent; YO14 9JH Friendly old-
fashioned bar with up to five well kept ales
and four ciders, good value food (not Sun
evening, Mon) including home-made pizzas;
live music, karaoke, bingo and quiz nights;
children and dogs welcome, open all day.
(Liz and Mike Newton)

FINGHALL
SE1889

★**Queens Head** (01677) 450259

Off A684 E of Leyburn; DL8 5ND
Welcoming dining pub dating from the 1700s;
log fire either end of low-beamed carpeted
bar divided by stone archway, settles making
stalls around big tables, four real ales such
as Theakstons and Wensleydale, good food
(not lunchtimes Mon-Weds) from traditional
favourites up including set deal, Tues tapas
and Fri fresh fish, efficient service, extended
dining room with fine country views; children
welcome, no dogs inside, disabled access/
facilities, back garden with decking (same
view), three bedrooms. *(Peter Smith and
Judith Brown)*

GARGRAVE
SD9253

Masons Arms (01756) 749304

*Church Street/Marton Road (off A65
NW of Skipton); BD23 3NL* Traditional
beamed pub with welcoming local
atmosphere; opened-up interior divided into
bar, lounge and restaurant, log fire, ample
helpings of enjoyable home-made food at very
fair prices, well kept ales such as Timothy
Taylors and Tetleys from ornate counter,
efficient staff; live acoustic music first Fri of
month in winter, quiz nights, darts; children
and dogs welcome, tables out behind
overlooking own bowling green, charming
village on Pennine Way and not far from
Leeds & Liverpool Canal, six barn conversion
bedrooms, open (and food) all day. *(Mike and
Sarah Abbot)*

GIGGLESWICK
SD8164

Harts Head (01729) 822086

Belle Hill; BD24 0BA Refurbished 18th-c
village inn under same owners as the Plough
at Lupton (see Cumbria Main Entries); bar/
lounge and restaurant, up to half a dozen
well kept ales including Tetleys and good
food from varied menu, friendly helpful staff;
occasional live music; children and dogs (in
bar) welcome, picnic-sets out on sloping
lawn, bedrooms, open (and food) all day.
(Caroline Sullivan)

GILLAMOOR
SE6890

★**Royal Oak** (01751) 431414

Off A170 in Kirkbymoorside; YO62 7HX
18th-c stone-built dining pub in attractive
village; good food at sensible prices including
vegetarian options, daily specials and
two-course deal, ales such as Black Sheep and Copper Dragon, reasonably
priced wines, roomy bar with heavy dark
beams, log fires in two tall stone fireplaces
(one with old kitchen range), overspill dining
room where dogs allowed; children welcome,
eight comfortable modern bedrooms, good

breakfast, handy for Bransdale Moor walks,
open all day. *(Mick Allen)*

GILLING EAST
SE6176

★**Fairfax Arms** (01439) 788212

*Main Street (B1363, off A170 via
Oswaldkirk); YO62 4JH* Welcoming
smartly presented pub in nice village;
beamed bar with woodburner, Black Sheep,
Tetleys and a couple of local guests from
handsome oak counter, interesting wines by
the glass, two-part carpeted dining room,
good modern food (can be pricey) along
with sandwiches and pub favourites, neat
attentive staff, orangery and outside seating
area by floodlit roadside stream; well placed
for Howardian Hills and North York Moors,
comfortable up-to-date bedrooms, good
breakfast, open all day, food till 7pm Sun.
(Sally and Colin Allen)

GILLING WEST
NZ1805

White Swan (01748) 825122

*High Street (B6274 just N of Richmond);
DL10 5JG* Welcoming 17th-c village inn
with open-plan bar and dining room, modern
décor and log fires, well kept ales including
a Mithril house beer and good range of other
drinks, much enjoyed food from interesting
street-food starters to speciality burgers
and dry-aged steaks, friendly staff; games
room; children and dogs welcome, tables
in courtyard, bedrooms, closed lunchtimes
Tues and Weds, otherwise open all day.
(Margaret McDonald)

GOATHLAND
NZ8200

Mallyan Spout Hotel

(01947) 896486 *Opposite church;
YO22 5AN* Late 19th-c creeper-clad stone
hotel; two bars and three spacious lounges,
open fires, popular fairly priced food from
pub favourites up, Black Sheep and a guest
such as Timothy Taylors, good choice of
wines and malt whiskies, afternoon teas,
friendly helpful staff, smart restaurant
(separate menu); well behaved children
welcome, dogs in one bar, lovely gardens
and views, handy for namesake waterfall,
20 comfortable bedrooms, good breakfast,
open all day. *(George and Alison Bishop)*

GOODMANHAM
SE8943

Goodmanham Arms (01430) 873849

Main Street; YO43 3JA Unpretentious
little red-brick country pub (not to everyone's
taste) with three traditional linked areas;
beam-and-plank ceilings, some red and black
floor tiles, mix of new and old furniture and
plenty of interesting odds and ends, even a
Harley-Davidson, seven real ales including
three from on-site All Hallows microbrewery,
unfussy food from italian owner (no starters),

Half pints: by law, a pub should not charge more for half a pint than half the price
of a full pint, unless it shows that half-pint price on its price list.

maybe a winter casserole cooked over the open fire, evening meals 5-7pm Mon and Fri only; folk night first Thurs of month, jazz/blues third Thurs, quiz every other Weds; children welcome, no dogs during food times, good walks (on Wolds Way), open all day. *(Dan and Belinda Smallbone)*

GRANGE MOOR   SE2215
Kaye Arms (01924) 840228
Wakefield Road (A642); WF4 4BG Modernised and opened-up roadside dining pub divided into three distinct areas (small area for drinkers); popular good value food including meal deal for two (not Sat evening, Sun), well kept Black Sheep and plenty of wines by the glass, efficient friendly service; children welcome, some seats out at front, handy for National Coal Mining Museum, open all day weekends, food till 7pm Sun. *(Michael Butler)*

GRASSINGTON   SE0064
Foresters Arms (01756) 752349
Main Street; BD23 5AA Comfortable opened-up coaching inn with friendly bustling atmosphere; six well kept regional ales such as Black Sheep and Tetleys, good hearty food (smaller appetites also catered for) including range of pizzas delivered by dumb waiter from upstairs kitchen, efficient cheerful service, log fires; popular Mon quiz, sports TV, darts and pool; children, walkers and dogs welcome, a few tables out at front, seven affordable bedrooms, good breakfast, open all day, food all day weekends. *(M J Winterton)*

GREAT AYTON   NZ5610
Royal Oak (01642) 722361
Off A173 – follow village signs; High Green; TS9 6BW Popular early 18th-c village inn with good fairly priced food including blackboard specials, meal deals and themed nights, four well kept ales such as Timothy Taylors and Theakstons, bar with log fire, beam-and-plank ceiling and bulgy old partly panelled stone walls, traditional furnishings including antique settles, pleasant views of elegant green from bay windows, two linked dining rooms; children welcome, dogs in bar, comfortable bedrooms, handy for Cleveland Way, open (and food) all day. *(Lindy Andrews)*

GREAT BROUGHTON   NZ5405
Bay Horse (01642) 712319
High Street; TS9 7HA Large creeper-clad dining pub in attractive village; wide choice of food including blackboard specials and good value set lunch, friendly attentive service, real ales such as Camerons and Jennings, restaurant; children welcome (under-5s till 8pm), seats outside, open (and food) all day Sat. *(Luke Morgan)*

GREAT HABTON   SE7576
★Grapes (01653) 669166
Corner of Habton Lane and Kirby Misperton Lane; YO17 6TU Popular and genuinely welcoming beamed dining pub in small village, homely and cosy, with highly praised cooking including fresh local fish and game (booking advised), Marstons-related ales, good service, open fire, small public bar with darts and TV; background music; a few roadside picnic-sets, nice walks, open all day Sun, closed Mon and weekday lunchtimes. *(Sarah and David Gibbs)*

HALIFAX   SE0925
Mill Bar & Kitchen (01422) 647494
Dean Clough; HX3 5AX Bar in former carpet mill; good choice of craft beers, wines and cocktails, enjoyable food from italian leaning menu including good pizzas, friendly efficient service; background music; handy for Northern Broadsides theatre, open all day Fri-Sat and until 8pm Sun. *(Mick Allen)*

HALIFAX   SE0924
Three Pigeons (01422) 347001
Sun Fold, South Parade; off Church Street; HX1 2LX Carefully restored 1930s five-room pub (Grade II listed); original flooring, panelling and tiled fireplaces, art deco fittings, ceiling painting in octagonal main area, range of Ossett beers and guests including related Fernandes and Rat, friendly chatty staff; children and dogs welcome, tables outside, handy for Eureka! Museum and Shay Stadium (pub very busy on match days), open all day Fri-Sun, otherwise from 4pm. *(Mick Allen)*

HARDRAW   SD8691
Green Dragon (01969) 667392
Village signed off A684; DL8 3LZ Traditional dales pub dating from 13th c and full of character; stripped stonework, antique settles and other old furniture on flagstones, lots of pictures and bric-a-brac, low-beamed snug with fire in original range, another in big main bar, five well kept ales including Timothy Taylors, Theakstons and Yorkshire Dales, enjoyable pubby food, small restaurant; children and dogs (in bar) welcome, tables in attractive courtyard, bedrooms, bunkhouse and self-catering, next to Hardraw Force (England's highest single-drop waterfall), open all day weekends. *(D J and P M Taylor)*

HAROME   SE6482
★Star (01439) 770397
High Street; village signed S of A170, E of Helmsley; YO62 5JE Pretty 14th-c thatched pub-restaurant; bar with bowed beam-and-plank ceiling, plenty of bric-a-brac and interesting furniture including Robert

---

We accept no free drinks or meals and inspections are anonymous.

'Mouseman' Thompson pieces, well polished tiled kitchen range, log fire, three changing ales and plenty of wines by the glass, smart restaurant for chef-owner's highly regarded inventive cooking (not cheap), also snacks in cocktail bar and a coffee loft in the eaves, well trained helpful staff; background music; children welcome, seats on sheltered front terrace, more in garden, nine individual bedrooms in building across road, very good breakfast, open all day Sun (and Sat in summer), no food Sun evening, Mon lunchtime. *(Lionel Smith)*

HARPHAM   TA0961
St Quintin Arms (01262) 490329
Main Street; YO25 4QY Comfortable old village inn with enjoyable reasonably priced home-made food (not Sun evening) including specials, well kept Theakstons and Wold Top, efficient friendly service, bar and small dining room; sports TV, daily papers; children welcome, no dogs inside, sheltered garden with pond, on National Cycle Route 1, four bedrooms, open all day Sun, closed lunchtimes Mon and Tues. *(Gary and Marie Miller)*

HARROGATE   SE3155
Coach & Horses (01423) 561802
West Park; HG1 1BJ Friendly bustling pub with up to eight good yorkshire-brewed ales, 80 malt whiskies and over 40 gins, good range of wines too, enjoyable reasonably priced lunchtime food plus some themed evenings, comfortable interior arranged around central bar with booths and other cosy areas; regular Fri charity raffle, Sun quiz; no children or dogs, open all day. *(Sophie and John Moor)*

HARROGATE   SE3157
Gardeners Arms (01423) 506051
Bilton Lane (off A59 either in Bilton itself or on outskirts towards Harrogate – via Bilton Hall Drive); HG1 4DH Stone-built 17th-c house converted into down-to-earth local; tiny bar and three small rooms, flagstone floors, panelling and old prints, roaring fire in big stone fireplace with tree-stump seat either side, cheap Sam Smiths OBB, no food; children and dogs welcome, picnic-sets out at front and in surrounding streamside garden, lovely peaceful setting near Nidd Gorge, open all day. *(Denise Courtney)*

HARROGATE   SE2955
★**Hales** (01423) 725570
Crescent Road; HG1 2RS Classic Victorian décor in 18th-c gas-lit local close to the Pump Rooms; leather seats in alcoves, lots of pictures and stuffed birds, comfortable saloon and tiny snug, half a dozen ales including a house beer from Daleside, simple good value lunchtime food (not Mon), friendly helpful staff; weekly live music; children welcome till 6pm, no dogs during food service, open all day (till

1am Thurs-Sat) and can get lively weekend evenings. *(Alan and Alice Morgan)*

HARROGATE   SE2955
Old Bell (01423) 507930
Royal Parade; HG1 2SZ Market Town Tavern with eight real ales, several craft beers and good selection of wines and gins, friendly helpful staff, fairly traditional food from sandwiches up, mix of furniture including iron-framed tables and leather tub chairs on wood floors, Anaglypta dado, servery made from an old mahogany dresser, some vintage sweet shop ads, further seating upstairs; children (if eating) and dogs welcome, open (and food) all day. *(Mike Benton)*

HAWES   SD8789
White Hart (01969) 667214
Main Street; DL8 3QL Welcoming 16th-c coaching inn on cobbled street; emphasis on good fairly priced food, but also at least four well kept regional ales, friendly fast service, interesting panelled bar with fire in antique range, daily papers, restaurant; children and dogs welcome, five bedrooms, open all day. *(Tracey and Stephen Groves)*

HEADINGLEY   SE2736
Arcadia (0113) 274 5599
Arndale Centre; LS6 2UE Glass-fronted Market Town Tavern in former bank; eight changing regional ales, a couple of craft kegs and over 100 bottled beers, good range of wines too, friendly knowledgeable staff, snacky food including good local cheese, stairs to mezzanine; no children, dogs welcome, handy for cricket ground; open all day. *(Peter Smith and Judith Brown)*

HEATH   SE3520
Kings Arms (01924) 377527
Village signposted from A655 Wakefield– Normanton – or, more directly, turn off to the left opposite Horse & Groom; WF1 5SL Popular old-fashioned gas-lit pub of genuine character; fire in black range (long row of smoothing irons on the mantelpiece), plain elm stools, built-in oak settles and dark panelling, well kept Ossett beers (one named for the pub) and guests, standard food (all day Fri and Sat, till 7pm Sun), more comfortable extension preserving original style, two other small flagstoned rooms and a conservatory; summer folk events, Tues quiz, free wi-fi; children and dogs (in bar) welcome, benches out at front facing village green (surrounded by fine 19th-c stone merchants' houses), picnic-sets on side lawn and in nice walled garden, usually open all day (may shut early if quiet). *(Michael Butler)*

HEBDEN   SE0263
Clarendon (01756) 752446
B6265; BD23 5DE Well cared-for modernised 18th-c inn surrounded by

wonderful moorland walking country; bar, snug and restaurant, open fire, well kept ales such as Black Sheep, Timothy Taylors and Wensleydale, good range of enjoyable food (till 7pm Sun) from pubby choices up including local game and blackboard specials, cheerful relaxed atmosphere; Sun quiz; children and dogs (in bar) welcome, farm shop, five bedrooms, open all day weekends. *(B and M Kendall, John Hunter Wright)*

HEBDEN BRIDGE   SD9922
Hinchcliffe Arms   (01422) 883256
Off B6138; HX7 5TA Tucked-away stone-built pub in great walking country on the Calderdale Way and near Stoodley Pike; open-plan bar to the left, restaurant on right, well kept Lees and a couple of locals guests, very good food from daily changing menu cooked by chef-owner, friendly staff; children, dogs (in bar) and walkers welcome, a few seats out at front, picturesque setting close to stream and Victorian church, open (and food) all day, Sun till 10pm (6pm). *(Jim and Sue James)*

HEBDEN BRIDGE   SD9927
Old Gate   (01422) 843993
Oldgate; HX7 8JP Popular bar-restaurant with wide choice of good food served from 10am breakfast on, nine well kept ales, plenty of bottled beers and good range of wines by the glass including champagne, helpful friendly service, newly refurbished upstairs restaurant; children welcome, tables outside, open (and food) all day. *(Laura Reid)*

HEBDEN BRIDGE   SD9827
Stubbing Wharf   (01422) 844107
About a mile W; HX7 6LU Friendly well presented pub in good spot sandwiched between the Rochdale Canal and River Calder; popular good value food from sandwiches and light meals up, weekday two-course deal till 7pm, four regional ales such as Acorn, Kelham Island and Rudgate kept well, proper ciders, cheerful hard-working young staff; Thurs quiz; well behaved children and dogs welcome, adjacent moorings, open (and food) all day. *(Steve Whalley)*

HELMSLEY   SE6183
Feathers   (01439) 770275
Market Place; YO62 5BH Substantial old stone inn overlooking the market square; enjoyable food (all day Sat) from sandwiches and pub favourites up, well kept Black Sheep, Tetleys and a local guest, afternoon teas, good friendly service, several rooms with comfortable seats, walnut and oak tables (some by Robert 'Mouseman' Thompson, as is the bar counter), flagstones or tartan carpet, heavy medieval beams and huge inglenook; children and dogs (in bar) welcome, terrace tables, 22 bedrooms, open all day. *(Douglas Power)*

HELWITH BRIDGE   SD8169
Helwith Bridge Inn   (01729) 860220
Off B6479 N of Stainforth; BD24 0EH Friendly unpretentious village local popular with walkers; five well kept ales in flagstoned bar, enjoyable reasonably priced pub food including Thurs steak night, friendly if not always speedy service, dining room with light wood furniture on bare boards; free wi-fi; children and dogs welcome, camping and bunkhouse, next to River Ribble and Settle–Carlisle railway, open all day, food all day weekends. *(Mick Allen)*

HETTON   SD9658
★**Angel**   (01756) 730263
Off B6265 Skipton–Grassington; BD23 6LT New owners for this creeper-clad inn surrounded by glorious countryside; panelled and beamed main room with farmhouse and wheelback chairs around wooden tables, standing timbers and working Victorian range set in big stone fireplace, ales such as Black Sheep and local Dark Horse, good wine list, highly praised imaginative food (not cheap) cooked by chef-proprietor including tasting menus, friendly professional service, two smart restaurant rooms; children and dogs (in bar) welcome, seats on front terrace under retractable awnings, nine individually styled bedrooms in converted barn or more modern Sycamore Bank opposite, closed Tues and Weds.
(W K Wood, Len and Lilly Dowson, Beverley and Andy Butcher)

HIGH HOYLAND   SE2710
Cherry Tree   (01226) 382541
Bank End Lane; 3 miles W of M1 junction 38; S75 4BE Split-level whitewashed village pub; five well kept ales including Acorn Barnsley Bitter, Black Sheep Bitter and Bradfield Farmers Blonde, good range of enjoyable generously served food (not Sun evening), competitive prices and friendly young staff, beams and open fire, dining areas each end of bar and separate small restaurant; background music; children, walkers and dogs welcome, front roadside picnic-sets with lovely views over Cannon Hall Country Park, open all day. *(George and Alison Bishop)*

HOLMFIRTH   SD1408
Nook   (01484) 682373
Victoria Square/South Lane; HD9 2DN Friendly tucked-away 18th-c local run by same family for two generations; own-brew beers, guest ales and low-priced food with emphasis on burgers, no-frills bar areas with flagstones and quarry tiles, big open fire; juke box, pool; heated streamside terrace, bedrooms, open all day, kitchen from 4pm Mon-Thurs; they also have the refurbished Nook Tap House bar-restaurant next door. *(Kerry and Guy Trooper)*

HOPPERTON   SE4256

Masons (01423) 330442

Hopperton Street; HG5 8NX Village dining
pub with popular food from standards up,
a couple of real ales and excellent choice of
gins, friendly helpful staff, snug pubby bar
and extended restaurant with high-backed
leather chairs around mix of tables on tiled
floor, open fires; background music, free wi-fi;
children and dogs (in bar) welcome, closed
Mon and Tues, no food Sun evening.
(Patricia Healey)

HORBURY   SE2918

Boons (01924) 277267

Queen Street; WF4 6LP Comfortably
unpretentious part-flagstoned local, chatty
and relaxed, with Timothy Taylors Landlord
and seven quickly changing guests, pleasant
young staff, no food or children, rugby league
memorabilia, warm fire, back tap room with
pool, sports TV and fruit machine; courtyard
tables, open all day. *(Michael Butler)*

HORBURY   SE2918

Cherry Tree (01924) 262916

Church Street; WF4 6LT Victorian pub
recently reopened after several years' closure;
own good Horbury ales from attached
microbrewery plus guests, decent wines by
the glass and well liked food including range
of pizzas and pasta dishes, smart modern
décor with mix of seating on wood floors
including upholstered stools and banquettes,
some beams, exposed brickwork and painted
dados, two logburners; background music,
TV; interesting 18th-c church opposite, open
(and food) all day, apart from Sun when
kitchen shuts at 4pm. *(Michael Butler)*

HORBURY   SE2918

Cricketers (01924) 267032

Cluntergate; WF4 5AG Welcoming late
19th-c red-brick drinkers' pub; Bosuns
Blonde, Timothy Taylors Landlord and six
guests, also craft beers, real cider and good
selection of spirits, no food; open mike
nights, beer festivals and tap takeovers; dogs
welcome, open all day Fri-Sun, from 4pm
other days. *(Sally and Colin Allen)*

HORSFORTH   SE2438

Town Street Tavern (0113) 281 9996

Town Street; LS18 4RJ Market Town
Tavern with eight well kept ales and lots
of draught/bottled continental beers, good
food in small bar or upstairs restaurant,
friendly helpful service; children and dogs
(downstairs) welcome, small terrace,
open all day, food all day Fri, Sat, till
6pm Sun. *(Mark and Sian Edwards)*

HUBBERHOLME   SD9278

★ George (01756) 760223

Dubbs Lane; BD23 5JE Ancient little
dales inn, beautifully placed and run by
warmly welcoming licensees; heavy beams,

flagstones and stripped stone, enjoyable fairly
priced home-made food (booking advised)
from lunchtime sandwiches (not Sun) up,
Mon pie night, well kept Black Sheep and
three guests, open fire, perpetual candle on
bar; outside lavatories; children allowed in
dining area, well-behaved dogs in bar (pub
jack russell is George), terrace seating,
River Wharfe fishing rights, six comfortable
clean bedrooms (three in annexe), good
breakfast, closed Mon lunchtime and Tues,
otherwise open all day (best to check
winter hours). *(Hunter and Christine Wright)*

HUDDERSFIELD   SE1416

Grove (01484) 430113

Spring Grove Street; HD1 4BP Friendly
two-bar pub with huge selection of bottled
beers (some gluten-free), 18 well kept/
priced ales and 15 craft kegs, also an
impressive range of whiskies and other
spirits, knowledgeable staff, no food apart
from interesting bar snacks, eclectic
collection of artwork and taxidermy; live jazz
and folk sessions; children (till 8pm) and
dogs welcome, back terrace, open 12-11pm
Fri-Sun, from 2pm other days. *(Mike and
Sarah Abbot)*

HUDDERSFIELD   SE1416

Rat & Ratchet (01484) 542400

Chapel Hill; HD1 3EB Popular split-level
pub with own-brew beers and plenty of guests
including Ossett, good range of ciders/perries
too, pork pies and sausage rolls, friendly
staff; quiz nights and live music; open all day
Fri-Sun, from 3pm other days. *(Mike Benton)*

HUDDERSFIELD   SE1417

Sportsman (01484) 421929

St Johns Road; HD1 5AY Same owners
as the West Riding Licensed Refreshment
Rooms at Dewsbury; restored 1930s interior
with lounge and two cosy side rooms, eight
real ales and plenty of craft beers, friendly
knowledgeable staff, pie menu served
Fri-Sun; live music; dogs welcome, handy
for station, open all day (till midnight
Fri, Sat). *(Mike Benton)*

HUDDERSFIELD   SE1415

Star (01484) 545443

Albert Street, Lockwood; HD1 3PJ
Friendly unpretentious local with excellent
range of competitively priced ales kept well
by enthusiastic landlady, continental beers
and real cider too, beer festivals in back
marquee, open fire; open all day weekends,
closed Mon and lunchtimes Tues-Fri.
(Mike Benton)

HUDSWELL   NZ1400

George & Dragon (01748) 518373

Hudswell Lane; DL11 6BL Community-
owned village pub, popular and welcoming,
with enjoyable good value food from shortish
menu including speciality home-made pies,
five well kept local ales, various craft kegs

and extensive range of whiskies; small shop and library, monthly live music/quiz nights, free wi-fi; children and dogs welcome, panoramic Swaledale views from back terrace, open all day weekends, no food Sun evening. *(Luke Morgan)*

HULL   TA0928

Chilli Devils   (01482) 961666
Manor Street; HU1 1YP Friendly one-room micropub (opened 2017); four well kept regularly changing ales, craft beers and real cider, short good value chilli-based menu including a vegan option, also Sun roasts; background and live music; open all day Fri-Sun, from 4pm other days. *(Laura Reid)*

HULL   TA1028

★ Olde White Harte   (01482) 326363
Passage off Silver Street; HU1 1JG Dating from the 16th c with Civil War history; carved heavy beams, attractive stained glass, oak panelling and two big inglenooks with frieze of delft tiles, well kept Caledonian, Theakstons and guests from copper-topped counter, 80 or so malt whiskies; old skull (found here in the 19th c and displayed in a Perspex case); children welcome, dogs in bar, heated courtyard, open all day. *(Laura Reid)*

HUNMANBY   TA1077

Piebald   (01723) 447577
Sands Lane; E of level crossing; YO14 0LT Comfortably renovated pub with well stocked bar and separate dining room, popular generously served food featuring more than 50 different pies, up to five real ales including a house beer from Greene King, friendly helpful staff; children and dogs welcome, picnic-sets on side terrace and lawn bordering railway line, camping, open (and food) all day. *(Patricia Healey)*

HUTTON-LE-HOLE   SE7089

Crown   (01751) 417343
The Green; YO62 6UA Friendly village local overlooking pretty green with wandering sheep in classic coach-trip country; Black Sheep, Tetleys and a guest, decent wines by the glass and enjoyable home-made pubby food (till 6pm Sun), cheerful efficient service, opened-up bar with varnished woodwork, dining area; quiz first Sun of month; children and clean dogs welcome, Ryedale Folk Museum next door and handy for Farndale walks, newly built bedrooms, also small site for caravans, open all day (but may close Mon and Tues in winter). *(Nick and Meriel Cox)*

ILKLEY   SE1147

Bar t'at   (01943) 608888
Cunliffe Road; LS29 9DZ Extended Market Town Tavern with eight well kept mainly local ales and good wine and bottled beer choice, enjoyable well priced pubby food from sandwiches and snacks up, friendly

service, candlelit cellar dining area; upstairs loos; children and dogs welcome, back terrace with heated canopy, open (and food) all day, kitchen closes 6pm Sun. *(Gary and Marie Miller)*

ILKLEY   SE1147

Flying Duck   (01943) 609587
Church Street; LS29 9DS Old stone pub with nine well kept beers including own Wharfedale ales brewed in barn behind, tasters offered by friendly knowledgeable staff, shortish choice of enjoyable good value food including selection of light dishes (perfect for sharing), beamed and flagstoned bar with woodburner in large stone fireplace; children and dogs welcome, first-floor terrace, open all day (till late Fri, Sat), no evening food Fri-Sun, kitchen shut Mon (except school and bank holidays). *(Michael Butler)*

KEIGHLEY   SE0641

Boltmakers Arms   (01535) 661936
East Parade; BD21 5HX Small split-level character local, friendly and bustling, with full Timothy Taylors range and a guest kept well, traditional cider and several malt whiskies, lots to look at including brewing pictures and celebrity photos, coal fire; Tues quiz, Weds live music, sports TV; small beer garden, short walk from Keighley & Worth Valley Railway, open all day. *(Stuart and Natalie Granville)*

KETTLESING   SE2257

★ Queens Head   (01423) 770263
Village signposted off A59 W of Harrogate; HG3 2LB Popular stone-built village pub with very good well priced traditional food; L-shaped carpeted main bar, lots of close-set cushioned dining chairs and tables, open fires, little heraldic shields on the walls along with 19th-c song sheet covers and lithographs of Queen Victoria, delft shelf of blue and white china, smaller bar on left with built-in red banquettes and cricketing prints, life-size portrait of Elizabeth I in lobby, well kept Black Sheep, Roosters and Theakstons, efficient friendly service; background music, free wi-fi; children welcome, seats in neatly kept sunny back garden, benches in front by lane, eight bedrooms, open all day Sun. *(Helene Grygar, M G Hart)*

KETTLEWELL   SD9672

Blue Bell   (01756) 760230
Middle Lane; BD23 5QX Roomy knocked-through former coaching inn, popular and welcoming, with well kept Theakstons, Wharfedale and plenty of guest beers, generous helpings of enjoyable pubby food, friendly helpful service, low beams and simple furnishings, old country photographs, woodburner; Sun quiz, TV, free wi-fi; children, walkers and dogs welcome, shaded picnic-sets on cobbles facing bridge over River

Wharfe, seven annexe bedrooms, open (and food) all day. *(Edward Mirzoeff)*

KETTLEWELL SD9772
★ Kings Head (01756) 761600
The Green; BD23 5RD Welcoming old pub tucked away near church; flagstoned main bar with log fire in big arched inglenook, three well kept local ales and well chosen wines, very good affordably priced food (all day Sun till 7pm) cooked by chef-landlord from pub favourites to imaginative restaurant dishes, efficient friendly service; children allowed, no dogs inside, six comfortable bedrooms (some quite small) named after kings, attractive dales village with good surrounding walks, closed Mon (Oct-end Mar), otherwise open all day. *(Martin Day, Edward Mirzoeff, B and M Kendall, Martin and Anne Muers)*

KETTLEWELL SD9672
Racehorses (01756) 760233
B6160 N of Skipton; BD23 5QZ Comfortable and friendly two-bar pub next to River Wharf (across from the Blue Bell); tasty sensibly priced home-made food and three well kept Timothy Taylors ales, log fires, separate dining areas; children and dogs (in some parts) welcome, front and back terrace seating, pretty village well placed for Wharfedale walks, parking can be tricky, 13 good bedrooms, open all day. *(Martin Day)*

KILBURN SE5179
Forresters Arms (01347) 868386
Between A170 and A19 SW of Thirsk; YO61 4AH Beamed village inn next to the Robert 'Mouseman' Thompson furniture workshops (early examples of his work in both bars); roaring fires, well kept local ales and good choice of home-made food, restaurant; background music; children welcome, dogs in some areas, suntrap seats out in front, smokers' shelter behind, ten bedrooms, open all day from 8am. *(Michael Butler)*

KILDWICK SE0145
White Lion (01535) 632265
Priest Bank Road, next to church; off A629 Keighley–Skipton; BD20 9BH New owners and refurbishment for this two-bar stone pub; well kept ales such as Timothy Taylors and enjoyable food; Aire Valley views from sunny garden, attractive village with good surrounding walks, near Leeds & Liverpool Canal, bedrooms, open all day. *(D W Stokes)*

KIRKBY MALHAM SD8960
Victoria (01729) 830499
South end of village; BD23 4BS Mid 19th-c flower-decked pub with sundial above entrance; flagstoned bar with open fire, snug and separate restaurant, well kept Dark Horse and a guest, good wine choice and enjoyable freshly cooked food, friendly

service; children, muddy boots and dogs welcome, picnic-sets out at front, lovely village with interesting church, good walks (close to Pennine Way), four bedrooms, open all day Fri-Sun, closed Mon and till 4pm Tues-Thurs. *(Philip and Susan Robertshaw)*

KIRKBYMOORSIDE SE6986
George & Dragon (01751) 433334
Market Place; YO62 6AA Friendly 17th-c coaching inn; front bar with beams, stripped wood floor and log fire, well kept changing ales and several malt whiskies/gins, decent choice of enjoyable generously served food including range of burgers, good service, more formal restaurant; background music; children welcome, front and back terraces, 20 bedrooms, Weds market, open all day. *(Margaret McDonald)*

KNAYTON SE4388
Dog & Gun (01845) 537368
Moor Road, off A19; YO7 4AZ Well cared-for family-run pub, cosy and comfortable, with roaring fire at one end, tables laid for their popular traditional home-made food (till 6pm Sun, not Mon, Tues, best to book) including blackboard specials and deals, ales such as Black Sheep and Copper Dragon, good friendly service; late summer charity music festival; children and dogs welcome (menus for both), heated outside seating area, open all day weekends, closed Mon and lunchtimes Tues-Fri. *(Mike Benton)*

LANGTHWAITE NY0002
★ Charles Bathurst 0333 7000779
Arkengarthdale, a mile N towards Tan Hill; DL11 6EN Busy 18th-c country inn (sister to the Punch Bowl at Low Row); strong emphasis on dining and bedrooms, but pubby feel in long bar with scrubbed pine tables and country chairs on stripped floors, snug alcoves, open fire, Black Sheep, Theakstons and a local guest, several wines by the glass and good choice of popular interesting food, cheerful helpful staff, dining room with Robert 'Mousey' Thompson furniture and views of Scar House, several other eating areas; background music, TV, pool and darts; children welcome, dogs in bar, lovely walks from the door and views over village and Arkengarthdale, 19 smart bedrooms (best not above dining room), open all day; worth checking there are no corporate events/weddings before you visit. *(Laura Reid)*

LANGTHWAITE NZ0002
★ Red Lion (01748) 884218
Just off Arkengarthdale Road, Reeth–Brough; DL11 6RE Proper pub dating from 17th c in charming dales village with ancient bridge; long-serving character landlady and homely old-fashioned atmosphere, lunchtime sandwiches, pasties and sausage rolls, a couple of well kept Black Sheep ales, Thatcher's cider, country wines, tea

and coffee, well behaved children allowed lunchtime in low-ceilinged side snug, newspapers and postcards; the ladies' is a genuine bathroom; no dogs inside, a few picnic-sets out at front, good walks including circular ones from the pub – maps and guides for sale. *(Alan and Alice Morgan)*

LASTINGHAM   SE7290
★**Blacksmiths Arms** (01751) 417247
Off A170 W of Pickering; YO62 6TL
17th-c pub in charming village opposite beautiful Saxon church; small bar with log fire in open range, tankards hanging from beams, traditional furnishings, well kept Theakstons and other regional ales, several wines by the glass and good sensibly priced home-made food (not Sun evening) including vegetarian and gluten-free choices, prompt friendly service, two dining rooms; background music, darts and board games; children welcome, no dogs inside, seats out at front and in back beer garden, three bedrooms, open all day. *(Nick and Meriel Cox)*

LEALHOLM   NZ7607
★**Board** (01947) 897279
Off A171 W of Whitby; YO21 2AJ 18th-c pub in wonderful moorland village spot by wide pool of River Esk; homely bare-boards bar on right with squashy old sofa and armchairs by big black stove, three well kept changing ales, five ciders and dozens of whiskies, good seasonal food using meat from own farm and other local produce, friendly helpful landlady; children, dogs and muddy boots welcome, secluded waterside garden with decking, bedrooms (good breakfast) and self-catering cottage, open all day. *(Peter and Emma Kelly)*

LEAVENING   SE7863
Jolly Farmers (01653) 658276
Main Street; YO17 9SA Friendly bustling village local with up to five regional ales and popular good value pub food (not Mon, Tues), front bar with eating area behind, separate dining room; some live music; children and dogs welcome, open all day weekends, closed weekday lunchtimes. *(Louise and Simon Peters)*

LEEDS   SE3131
Garden Gate (0113) 345 1234
Whitfield Place, Hunslet; LS10 2QB Impressive Edwardian pub (Grade II* listed) owned by Leeds Brewery; their well kept ales from rare curved ceramic counter, a wealth of other fine period features in rooms off central drinking corridor including intricate glass and woodwork, art nouveau tiling, moulded ceilings and mosaic floors; some live music; dogs welcome, tables out in front, open all day. *(Monica and Steph Evans)*

LEEDS   SE2932
★**Grove** (0113) 243 9254
Back Row, Holbeck; LS11 5PL Unspoilt 1930s-feel local overshadowed by towering office blocks; tables and stools in main bar with marble floor, panelling and original fireplace, large back room and snug off drinking corridor, eight well kept regional ales including Daleside Blonde, Weston's cider, lunchtime food (not Sat, Sun), friendly staff; regular live music including Fri folk club; dogs welcome, open all day. *(Lindy Andrews)*

LEEDS   SE3033
Kirkstall Bridge (0113) 278 4044
Bridge Road, Headingley–Kirkstall; LS5 3BW Welcoming traditionally renovated pub by bridge over River Aire; main bare-boards bar with lots of brewerania and other rescued items from closed pubs, well kept Kirkstall beers and several guests, generous helpings of reasonably priced food from deli boards and pizzas up, downstairs flagstoned bar (dogs welcome here) leading out to riverside garden; Weds quiz, some live music, free wi-fi; handy for Kirkstall Abbey, open (and food) all day, kitchen closes 5pm Sun. *(Lindy Andrews)*

LEEDS   SE2932
Midnight Bell (0113) 244 5044
Water Lane, Holbeck; LS11 5QN Leeds Brewery pub on two floors in Holbeck Urban Village; their ales and guests kept well, enjoyable home-made food, friendly staff, light contemporary décor mixing with original beams and stripped brickwork; children and dogs welcome, courtyard beer garden, open (and food) all day, kitchen shuts 7pm Sun. *(Nick T)*

LEEDS   SE3033
Scarbrough (0113) 243 4590
Bishopgate Street, opposite station; LS1 5DY Nicholsons pub with ornate tiled façade; eight well kept changing ales served by friendly helpful staff, enjoyable food including speciality pies and breakfasts; sports TV; open all day and busy lunchtime, early evening. *(Peter Smith and Judith Brown)*

LEEDS   SE3033
★**Whitelocks** (0113) 245 3950
Turks Head Yard, off Briggate; LS1 6HB Classic Victorian pub full of character (if a little worn around the edges); long narrow bar with fine tiled counter, grand mirrors, mahogany and glass screens, heavy copper-topped tables and red leather seating, coal fire, a dozen well kept ales and enjoyable food; children welcome, tables in narrow courtyard, open (and food) all day, can get crowded at lunchtime. *(Nick T)*

LINTHWAITE   SE1014
★**Sair** (01484) 842370
Lane Top, Hoyle Ing, off A62; HD7 5SG Old-fashioned four-room pub brewing its own good value Linfit beers; pews and chairs on rough flagstones or wood floors, log-burning ranges, dominoes, cribbage and shove-ha'penny, piano and vintage rock juke box;

no food or credit cards; dogs welcome, plenty of tables out in front with fine Colne Valley views, restored Huddersfield Narrow Canal nearby, open all day Fri-Sun, otherwise from 3pm. *(Charlotte and William Mason)*

LINTON SE3846

Windmill (01937) 582209

Off A661 W of Wetherby; LS22 4HT
Character 16th-c inn on different levels, dark beams and stripped stone, antique settles around copper-topped tables on carpeted floors, three log fires; enjoyable food from traditional dishes up including a gluten-free menu, pie night Weds, steak night Thurs, ales such as Theakstons Best and several wines by the glass, friendly young staff, restaurant and airy conservatory; background music, Thurs quiz; children and dogs (in bar) welcome, sunny back terrace and sheltered garden with pear tree (raised from seed brought back from the Napoleonic Wars), two annexe bedrooms, open all day weekends, food all day Sat, till 6pm Sun.
(Peter and Emma Kelly)

LITTON SD9074

Queens Arms (01756) 770096

Off B6160 N of Grassington; BD23 5QJ
Beautifully placed 17th-c whitewashed stone pub under new management; main bar with slate floor and beam-and-plank ceiling, old photographs on rough stone walls, coal fire, plainer carpeted dining room with woodburner, four real ales (maybe one from on-site microbrewery), good freshly made food including range of pies, friendly efficient staff; children and dogs welcome, plenty of seats in two-tier garden, country views and good surrounding walks, four bedrooms, open all day, food till 6pm Sun, (closed lunchtimes Mon, Tues in winter). *(Christopher Acomb)*

LOFTHOUSE SE1073

Crown (01423) 755206

Pub signed from main road; Nidderdale; HG3 5RZ Prettily placed dales inn, friendly and relaxed, with hearty simple food from sandwiches up, well kept Black Sheep and Theakstons, small public bar, comfortable dining extension where children allowed, open fire; outside gents'; dogs welcome, attractive garden and good walks from the door, bedrooms. *(Caroline Sullivan)*

LOW BRADFIELD SK2691

Plough (0114) 285 1280

Village signposted off B6077 and B6076 NW of Sheffield; New Road; S6 6HW
Comfortably modernised old pub ideally placed for some of South Yorkshire's finest scenery; L-shaped bar with stone walls, button-back banquettes and captain's chairs, log fire in big arched fireplace, well kept Bradfield ales and guests, good value food from sandwiches and baked potatoes up; background music, Weds quiz, sports TV and free wi-fi; children and dogs welcome,

seats on back verandah, terrace and lawn, Damflask and Agden Reservoirs close by, open (and food) all day, kitchen shuts 7pm Sun. *(Lionel Smith)*

LOW CATTON SE7053

Gold Cup (01759) 371354

Village signposted with High Catton off A166 in Stamford Bridge or A1079 at Kexby Bridge; YO41 1EA Bustling village pub under long-serving owners; cheerful neatly kept bar, plenty of smart tables and chairs on stripped-wood floors, open fire at one end, John Smiths and Theakstons kept well, enjoyable fairly priced home-cooked food (smaller appetites catered for), spacious restaurant with pleasant views over surrounding fields; background music, pool, free wi-fi; children and dogs (in bar) welcome, pleasant garden, paddock with ponies, pub also has fishing rights on adjacent River Derwent, open (and food) all day weekends, closed Mon lunchtime.
(John Saville, Mark and Sian Edwards)

LOW ROW SD9898

Punch Bowl 0333 7000 779

B6270 Reeth–Muker; DL11 6PF 17th-c country inn under same ownership as the Charles Bathurst at Langthwaite; long bare-boards bar with peaceful view over Swaledale, stripped kitchen tables and a variety of seats including armchairs and sofa by woodburner, enjoyable food (menu on huge mirror), well kept Black Sheep ales, a guest beer and nice wines by the glass, friendly staff, separate dining room similar in style; children and dogs (in bar) welcome, wide views from terrace above road, 11 comfortable bedrooms, good breakfast, open all day. *(Tara Brister)*

LUND SE9748

★**Wellington** (01377) 217294

Off B1248 SW of Driffield; YO25 9TE
Smart busy pub with cosy Farmers' Bar overlooking village green; beams, nicely polished wooden banquettes and square tables, log fire in quirky fireplace, plainer side room with flagstones and wine-theme décor, Yorkstone walkway to further room displaying village's Britain in Bloom awards, well kept ales including Timothy Taylors and Theakstons, good wine list and 25 malt whiskies, highly rated well presented food (not Sun evening, Mon, and not cheap) in restaurant or bistro dining area, friendly efficient staff; background music, TV; children welcome, dogs in some areas (but do ask first), disabled access/loo, picnic-tables in pretty back courtyard, open all day Sun, closed Mon lunchtime. *(Derek Stafford)*

MALTBY NZ4613

Chadwicks (01642) 590300

High Lane; TS8 0BG Beamed 19th-c pub-restaurant; first rate food including some cheaper lunchtime/early evening pub favourites, set menus and Weds steak and wine night, good helpful service, a changing local ale, several gins and cocktails; wine tasting evenings, quiz nights; wheelchair access, seats on front terrace, closed Mon lunchtime, otherwise open all day, no food Sun evening, Mon. *(Beth Aldridge)*

MANFIELD NZ2213
Crown (01325) 374243
Vicars Lane; DL2 2RF Unpretentious two-bar village local, friendly and welcoming, with seven interesting ales including Bass and Village Brewer, proper ciders and enjoyable home-made food, open fires, games room with pool and darts; some live music; children and dogs welcome, picnic-sets and caravan in part-lawned garden, good walks nearby, open all day weekends, from 4pm other days. *(Louise and Simon Peters)*

MARSDEN SE0411
Riverhead Brewery Tap
(01484) 841270 *Peel Street, next to Co-op; just off A62 Huddersfield–Oldham; HD7 6BR* Owned by Ossett with up to ten well kept ales including Riverhead range (microbrewery visible from bare-boards bar); friendly bustling atmosphere, airy upstairs beamed restaurant with stripped tables (moors view from some) and open kitchen, good choice of enjoyable food (till 7pm Sun, just sandwiches Mon and Tues); background and occasional live music, Tues quiz; children and dogs welcome, a few tables out by river, open all day. *(Gary and Marie Miller)*

MASHAM SE2281
White Bear (01765) 689319
Wellgarth, Crosshills; signed off A6108 opposite turn into town; HG4 4EN Comfortably updated beamed inn; small public bar with full Theakstons range kept well and several wines by the glass, welcoming coal fire in larger lounge, decent choice of food, from sandwiches/baguettes up, afternoon teas, friendly efficient staff, restaurant extension; background music; children and dogs (in bar) welcome, terrace tables, 14 bedrooms, open all day. *(Liz and Mike Newton)*

MAUNBY SE3586
Buck (01845) 587777
Off A167 S of Northallerton; YO7 4HD Brick-built dining pub in quiet out-of-the-way village by River Swale; Theakstons and a couple of guests, eight wines by the glass and good food from lunchtime sandwiches and traditional choices up (shortish menu), friendly helpful service, carpeted beamed bar with comfy leather sofa and inglenook fire, more contemporary restaurant and conservatory with one huge table; children welcome, dogs in bar, closed Sun evening, Mon and Tues. *(Mike and Sarah Abbot)*

MIDDLESMOOR SE0974
Crown (01423) 755204
Top of Nidderdale Road from Pateley Bridge; HG3 5ST Remote unpretentious family-run inn with beautiful view over stone-built hamlet high in upper Nidderdale; warmly welcoming character landlord and good local atmosphere, well kept Black Sheep and guests, several whiskies and simple wholesome food, blazing fires in cosy spotless rooms, old photographs and bric-a-brac, homely dining room; children and dogs welcome, small garden, seven good value bedrooms, self-catering cottage and camping, open all day weekends. *(Luke Morgan)*

MIDDLETON TYAS NZ2205
Shoulder of Mutton (01325) 377271
Just E of A1 Scotch Corner roundabout; DL10 6QX Welcoming old pub with three softly lit low-ceilinged rooms on different levels, good freshly made food from sandwiches, sharing boards and pub classics up, Thurs steak night, Black Sheep Bitter and a couple of guests, decent range of wines, whiskies and gins, friendly helpful service; quiz last Weds of month; children and dogs (in bar) welcome, a useful A1/A66 stop, open (and food) all day Sun. *(Sarah and David Gibbs)*

MILLINGTON SE8351
Gait (01759) 302045
Main Street; YO42 1TX Friendly 16th-c beamed local; five well kept regional ales (summer beer festival) and enjoyable straightforward home-made food, nice mix of old and newer furnishings, large map of Yorkshire on the ceiling, big inglenook log fire; fortnightly quiz Weds; children and dogs welcome, garden picnic-sets, appealing village in good wolds walking country, two holiday cottages next door, closed Mon and lunchtimes Tues-Thurs. *(Robert and Diana Ringstone)*

MIRFIELD SE2017
Hare & Hounds (01924) 493814
Liley Lane (B6118 2 miles S); WF14 8EE Popular Vintage Inn with attractive open-plan interior divided into several distinct areas (some steps), their usual good choice of reasonably priced food including weekday fixed-price menus, well kept Black Sheep, Sharps and a guest, cheerful helpful staff, log fire; children welcome, tables outside with good Pennine views, open (and food) all day. *(Michael Butler)*

MOORSHOLM NZ6912
Jolly Sailor (01287) 660270
A171 nearly a mile E; TS12 3LN Remotely placed dining pub set down from the main road; good variety of enjoyable food served by friendly staff, well kept

Black Sheep and a guest, long beamed and stripped-stone bar, separate restaurant; children and dogs welcome, outside tables with moorland views, play area, open all day. *(Sally and Colin Allen)*

MUKER SD9097

★**Farmers Arms** (01748) 886297

B6270 W of Reeth; DL11 6QG Small down-to-earth pub in beautiful valley village popular with walkers and other visitors (can get very busy); warmly welcoming, with four or five well kept ales such as Theakstons, Wensleydale and Yorkshire Dales, good choice of wines by the glass, teas and coffees, enjoyable good value home-made food (delivered by dumb waiter from upstairs kitchen), friendly helpful service, clean interior with warm fire, simple modern pine furniture, flagstones and panelling; darts and dominoes; children, dogs and muddy boots welcome, hill views from terrace tables, self-catering apartment opposite, open all day. *(Roy and Gill Payne)*

NEWTON-ON-OUSE SE5160

★**Dawnay Arms** (01347) 848345

Off A19 N of York; YO30 2BR 18th-c pub with two bars and airy river-view dining room; low beams and stripped masonry, chunky pine tables and old pews on bare boards or flagstones, fishing memorabilia, open fire and inglenook woodburner, highly regarded original food, also good lunchtime sandwiches (home-baked bread), set menu and interesting vegetarian choices, ales such as Tetleys and Timothy Taylors, good range of wines by the glass, friendly efficient service; children welcome, terrace tables, lawn running down to Ouse moorings, handy for Beningbrough Hall (NT), closed Sun evening, Mon (except bank holidays) and winter Tues. *(Laura Reid)*

NORTH DALTON SE9352

Star (01377) 217688

B1246 Pocklington–Driffield; YO25 9UX Picturesque 18th-c red-brick pub next to village pond; open fire in pubby bar with three changing ales, two ciders and good range of gins, separate restaurant serving much enjoyed interesting food (not Sun evening, Mon, Tues); open mike night first Tues of month, sports TV; children and dogs welcome, open all day weekends, from 4pm weekdays. *(Douglas Power)*

NORTH RIGTON SE2749

Square & Compass (01423) 733031

Hall Green Lane/Rigton Hill; LS17 0DJ Much extended stone building with smart modern interior; beamed bar serving four well kept ales including Leeds Pale and Theakstons Best, good range of bottled beers and plenty of wines by the glass, well liked food from sandwiches, sharing boards and pizzas up, friendly efficient service by aproned staff, restaurant; children and

dogs (in bar) welcome, tables out on tiered terrace, peaceful village, open (and food) all day. *(Michael Butler, GSB)*

NUN MONKTON SE5057

★**Alice Hawthorn** (01423) 330303

Off A59 York–Harrogate; The Green; YO26 8EW Attractively renovated village pub next to one of Yorkshire's oldest working greens (cattle roam quite freely); cosy bar with comfortable seats and open fire, Black Sheep Best, Timothy Taylors Landlord and Yorkshire Heart Hearty Bitter (brewed in the village), a dozen wines by the glass, good imaginative food (not Sun evening, can be pricey) using local ingredients including some from own kitchen garden, elegant dining rooms divided by two-way open fire, snug (the oldest part of the building) leads off here with another log fire; children and dogs (in bar) welcome, plenty of tables outside, closed Mon and Tues, otherwise open all day (till 8pm Sun). *(Janet and Peter Race, Brian and Margaret Merritt, Francis and Mandy Robertson)*

OLDFIELD SE0138

Grouse (01535) 643073

Harehills; 2 miles towards Colne; BD22 0RX Comfortable old pub in undisturbed moorland hamlet; well kept Timothy Taylors ales and enjoyable food from light lunches to good steaks and daily specials, weekday deals, friendly attentive service; children and dogs (in snug) welcome, picnic-sets on terrace with lovely Pennine views, open (and food) all day. *(Jim and Sue James)*

OSMOTHERLEY SE4597

Golden Lion (01609) 883526

The Green, West End; off A19 N of Thirsk; DL6 3AA Welcoming bustling atmosphere in this attractive 18th-c inn; roomy beamed bar with cushioned wall seats, pews and dining chairs around pubby tables, mirrors on white walls, woodburner, Timothy Taylors Landlord and guests, a dozen wines by the glass and some 50 malt whiskies, good popular food from traditional choices up, two dining rooms; background music; children and dogs (in bar) welcome, benches out at front overlooking village green, more seats on back terrace, popular with walkers (on Cleveland Way and the 40-mile Lyke Wake Walk starts here), seven modern bedrooms, closed Mon and Tues lunchtimes. *(Millie and Peter Downing)*

OSMOTHERLEY SE4597

Three Tuns (01609) 883301

South End, off A19 N of Thirsk; DL6 3BN Small stylish pub-restaurant with décor inspired by Charles Rennie Mackintosh; very good freshly made food in bistro setting with pale oak furniture and panelling, friendly efficient service, flagstoned bar with built-in cushioned wall benches, stripped-pine tables and stone fireplace, well kept ales such as Timothy Taylors, good friendly service; children welcome, dogs in bar, seats out at front and in charming terrace garden, good nearby walks, comfortable bedrooms, closed Mon and Tues. *(Dan and Belinda Smallbone)*

OSSETT SE2719

★**Brewers Pride** (01924) 273865

Low Mill Road/Healey Lane (long cul-de-sac by railway sidings, off B6128); WF5 8ND Friendly traditional local with well kept Ossett, Rudgate and several guests, cosy front rooms and flagstoned bar, brewery memorabilia, open fires, good well priced food (not Sun evening) including Tues evening tapas, more upmarket weekend menu in upstairs Millers Restaurant; quiz and pie night Mon, live music first Sun of the month; well behaved children and dogs welcome, big back garden, near Calder & Hebble Navigation, open all day. *(Michael Butler)*

OSSETT SE2820

Old Vic (01924) 273516

Manor Road, just off Horbury Road; WF5 0AU Friendly four-room roadside pub; well kept Ossett ales and guests from seven pumps, competitively priced home-cooked food (not Sun evening, Mon), traditional décor with old local photographs, shelves of bottles and antique range; Tues quiz and some live music, pool, darts and sports TV; children and dogs welcome, open all day Fri-Sun, from 4pm other days. *(Michael Butler)*

OSSETT SE2719

Tap (01924) 272215

The Green; WF5 8JS Cosy tap for Ossett Brewery; simple traditional décor with flagstones, bare boards and woodburner, mix of seating including upholstered banquettes and padded stools, photos of other Ossett pubs, their well kept ales and guests plus competitively priced wines by the glass, friendly relaxed atmosphere; dogs on the lead welcome, small car park (other nearby parking can be difficult), open all day Thurs-Sun, from 3pm other days. *(Michael Butler)*

OTLEY SE2045

Old Cock (01943) 464424

Crossgate; LS21 1AA Traditional two-room drinkers' pub with nine mostly local ales and a couple of ciders, also foreign beers and some gluten-free choices, no cooked food but good pork pies and sandwiches, more room upstairs; no under-18s, dogs welcome, open all day. *(Mick Allen)*

OTLEY SE2047

★**Roebuck** (01943) 463063

Roebuck Terrace; LS21 2EY Smartly modernised 18th-c beamed pub; good food from sandwiches and sharing plates up including range of hearty pies, Black Sheep and five changing local beers, plenty of wines by the glass, friendly efficient service, log fire and woodburner, raftered restaurant with mix of old furniture including pews on wood floor; children and dogs (in bar) welcome, wheelchair access, tables out on terrace and small lawn, open all day (closed Mon in winter), food till 7pm Sun. *(John and Eleanor Holdsworth)*

OXENHOPE SE0335

Bay Horse (01535) 642921

Upper Town; BD22 9LN Bustling community pub run by friendly licensees, half a dozen well kept local ales, no food; live music Wed and Thurs, open mike last Sat of month, free wi-fi; children, walkers and dogs welcome, seats outside, open all day Sat and Sun, closed weekday lunchtimes. *(Joe and Belinda Smart)*

OXENHOPE SE0434

Dog & Gun (01535) 643159

Off B6141 towards Denholme; BD22 9SN Spacious beautifully placed 17th-c moorland pub, smartly extended and comfortable, with wide choice of enjoyable generously served food from sandwiches to daily specials, cheerful staff, Timothy Taylors range and good selection of malt whiskies, beamery, copper, brasses, plates and jugs, big log fire each end, padded settles and stools, glass-covered well in one dining area, wonderful views; bedrooms in adjoining hotel, open all day weekends (food all day Sun). *(Peter and Emma Kelly)*

PICKERING SE7983

Black Swan (01751) 798209

Birdgate; YO18 7AL Renovated 18th-c coaching inn with own Great British Breworks beers from on-site brewery, also plenty of guests, real ciders and good choice of wines/gins, enjoyable home-made food from pizzas up, friendly staff, beamed bar with log fire, restaurant and separate cocktail bar; background music, free wi-fi; children and dogs welcome, bedrooms, open all day. *(Monica and Steph Evans)*

PICKERING SE7984

White Swan (01751) 472288

Market Place, just off A170; YO18 7AA Civilised and welcoming 16th-c coaching inn run by same family for 37 years; cosy properly pubby bar, sofas and a few tables, panelling and log fire, Black Sheep, Timothy Taylors Landlord and a dozen wines by the glass, second bare-boards room with big bow window and handsome art nouveau iron fireplace, good food (everything made in-house, even ketchup), flagstoned restaurant and next-door deli, efficient friendly staff, residents' lounge in converted beamed barn; children and dogs (in bar) welcome, bedrooms, open all day from 7.30am. *(Michael Butler)*

POOL   SE2445
★**White Hart** (0113) 203 7862
*Just off A658 S of Harrogate, A659 E
of Otley; LS21 1LH* Popular light and
airy Mitchells & Butlers dining pub (bigger
inside than it looks); good food from sharing
plates and pizzas to more restauranty
dishes, also fixed-price menu, friendly
young staff, 25 wines by the glass including
champagne, cocktails and three well kept
ales, stylishly simple bistro eating areas,
armchairs and sofas on bar's flagstones
and bare boards, welcoming log fires and
relaxing atmosphere; background music;
children and dogs welcome, plenty of
tables outside, open (and food) all day.
(George and Alison Bishop)

PUDSEY   SE2037
Thornhill (0113) 256 5492
Town Gate – Blackett Street; LS28 5NF
Updated 17th-c roadside pub with wide range
of enjoyable food from meze sharing plates,
mexican choices, burgers and hot dogs up,
real ales such as Theakstons and plenty of
wines by the glass, friendly efficient staff;
quiz Tues and Thurs, free wi-fi; children and
dogs welcome, seats outside, open (and food)
all day. *(John and Eleanor Holdsworth)*

REDMIRE   SE0491
Bolton Arms (01969) 624336
Hargill Lane; DL8 4EA Welcoming village
dining pub (former 17th-c farmhouse);
enjoyable fairly traditional food at reasonable
prices, well kept Black Sheep and guests,
efficient friendly service, woodburner in
comfortable carpeted bar, attractive dining
room; free wi-fi; children and dogs welcome,
disabled facilities, picnic-sets in small
part-paved garden, good walks and handy
for Wensleydale Railway and Bolton Castle,
five bedrooms (two with views from shared
balcony, others in converted outbuilding),
open all day. *(Barbara and Phil Bowie)*

REETH   SE0399
Black Bull (01748) 884213
*B6270; W side of village green;
DL11 6SZ* Popular 17th-c village inn
overlooking broad sloping green; Black
Sheep and Theakstons ale, enjoyable
reasonably priced food including good Sun
carvery, friendly helpful staff, traditional
dark beamed and flagstoned L-shaped front
bar, open fires, lovely dales views from
dining room; juke box and some live music,
pool and darts; children and dogs (in bar)
welcome, tables out at front, bedrooms
(also with views), open all day. *(Roy and
Gill Payne)*

REETH   SE0499
Buck (01748) 884210
*Arkengarthdale Road/Silver Street;
DL11 6SW* Friendly 18th-c coaching inn
adjacent to the village green; part-carpeted
beamed bar with open fire, well kept ales
such as Black Sheep and Timothy Taylor,
steps up to dining area serving enjoyable
fairly pubby food; some live music, July
beer festival, free wi-fi; children welcome,
dogs in bar (theirs is Marley), a few tables
out in front, hidden walled garden with
play equipment, good walking country,
ten comfortable bedrooms, open all day.
(Denis and Margaret Kilner)

RIPLEY   SE2860
Boars Head (01423) 771888
Off A61 Harrogate–Ripon; HG3 3AY
Informal and relaxed old hotel belonging
to the Ripley Castle Estate; long bar-bistro
with nice mix of dining chairs and tables,
walls hung with golf clubs, cricket bats, some
jolly cricketing/hunting drawings, a boar's
head and interesting religious carving, local
ales, 20 wines by the glass and several malt
whiskies, good food using Estate produce,
afternoon teas, separate restaurant; children
welcome, dogs in bar and bedrooms, pleasant
little garden, open all day, food all day Sun.
(Sarah and David Gibbs)

RIPON   SE3171
One-Eyed Rat (01765) 607704
Allhallowgate; HG4 1LQ Small friendly
drinkers' pub with seven well kept changing
ales, draught continentals and traditional
cider; roaring fire in long narrow bare-boards
bar, back carpeted area with piano and TV
projector for sports, no food; some live music,
quiz nights and a couple of beer festivals;
dogs welcome, outside seating area, open all
day Fri-Sun, from 5pm other days. *(Liz and
Mike Newton)*

RIPON   SE3171
Royal Oak (01765) 602284
Kirkgate; HG4 1PB Centrally placed
18th-c coaching inn on pedestrianised street;
smart modern décor, Timothy Taylors ales
and guests kept well, nice choice of wines
and good food from pub staples to more
enterprising restauranty dishes, friendly
efficient service, split-level dining area;
background music; children and dogs (in
bar) welcome, seats in courtyard with
retractable awning, eight bedrooms, open
(and food) all day. *(Mike Newton)*

RISHWORTH   SE0316
Booth Wood (01422) 825600
Oldham Road (A672); HX6 4QU
Welcoming beamed and flagstoned country
dining pub; good range of enjoyable food
including bargain classics/retro menu served
lunchtimes Mon-Sat and till 7pm weekdays,
well kept Bradfield Farmers Blonde, Holts
Bitter and up to three guests, friendly staff,
some leather sofas and wing-back chairs, two
blazing woodburners; folk nights and other
live music; children welcome, open (and
food) all day weekends. *(Andrea and
Philip Crispin)*

ROBIN HOOD'S BAY NZ9504
Bay Hotel (01947) 880278
The Dock, Bay Town; YO22 4SJ Old
village inn perched on edge of the bay with
fine sea views from cosy picture-window
upstairs bar (Wainwright bar downstairs
open too if busy), four real ales including
Theakstons, reasonably priced home-made
food in bar and separate dining area from
sandwiches to blackboard specials, log fires;
background music, TV; children and dogs
welcome, popular with walkers (at end of
the 191-mile Coast to Coast path), lots of
tables outside, bedrooms, steep road down
and no parking at bottom, open (and food)
all day. *(WAH)*

ROBIN HOOD'S BAY NZ9505
★**Laurel** (01947) 880400
*Bay Bank; village signed off A171 S of
Whitby; YO22 4SE* Charming little pub
at bottom of row of fishermen's cottages
in especially pretty and unspoilt village;
beamed main bar with open fire, old local
photographs, Victorian prints and brasses,
Adnams and Theakstons ales, no food or
credit cards; background music, darts and
board games; children in snug bar only,
dogs welcome, open all day in summer.
(R J Herd, WAH)

ROBIN HOOD'S BAY NZ9505
Victoria (01947) 880205
Station Road; YO22 4RL Clifftop
Victorian hotel with great bay views; good
choice of local beers from curved counter in
traditional carpeted bar, enjoyable freshly
made food here or in restaurant (separate
evening menu) including bargain weekday
meal deal for two till 6pm, also a coffee
shop/tea room, friendly service; children and
dogs welcome, useful car park, play area and
picnic-sets in big garden overlooking sea
and village, comfortable bedrooms (some
with panoramic views), good breakfast,
open (and food) all day. *(Darren and Jane
Staniforth, Martin Day; R J Herd)*

SANDAL SE3418
Star (01924) 229674
Standbridge Lane; WF2 7DY Friendly
buzzy atmosphere at this comfortable 19th-c
local; well kept ales including own good
Morton Collins microbrews (not always
available), simple well priced lunchtime food
(evening sharing plates); Tues quiz and some
live music; children and dogs welcome, a few
seats out at front, more in back garden with
decked area, open all day. *(Michael Butler,
Alistair Maiden)*

SANDHUTTON SE3882
★**Kings Arms** (01845) 587887
*A167, a mile N of A61 Thirsk–Ripon;
YO7 4RW* Bustling village inn run by father
and son with focus on enjoyable food; easy-

going bar with modern ladder-back chairs
around light pine tables, old photographs of
the pub and unusual circular woodburner
in one corner, ales such as Black Sheep
and Village Brewer, 11 wines by the glass,
efficient friendly service, two similar
furnished dining rooms; background music,
TV, darts and board games; children and
dogs (in bar) welcome, beer garden and secure
bike storage, bedrooms, open all day (can
get packed on Thirsk race days), no food
Sun evening. *(Maggie and Matthew Lyons,
Gail and Frank Hackett)*

SAWLEY SE2467
Sawley Arms (01765) 620642
*Village signposted off B6265 W of Ripon;
HG4 3EQ* Popular village dining pub
with good variety of well liked food from
sandwiches and hot ciabattas up, Timothy
Taylors and Theakstons beers, a dozen
wines by the glass, welcoming helpful staff,
comfortable modernised interior with log fire
and conservatory; quiz first Sun of month;
children welcome, seats on terrace and in
attractive garden, close to Fountains Abbey
(NT), four bedrooms, open (and food) all
day, breakfast from 7.45am. *(Sophie and
John Moor)*

SCARBOROUGH TA0588
Golden Ball (01723) 353899
Sandside, opposite harbour; YO11 1PG
Tall mock-Tudor seafront pub with good
harbour and bay views from highly prized
window seats (busy in summer), panelled
bar with good mix of visitors and locals, some
nautical memorabilia and open fire, well
kept low-priced Sam Smiths; family lounge
upstairs, tables out in yard, open all day.
(Mike Benton)

SCARBOROUGH TA0388
Stumble Inn 07837 716774
Westborough; YO11 1TS Simple one-room
micropub with friendly chatty atmosphere;
half a dozen well kept changing ales
and extensive range of ciders/perries,
knowledgeable landlord happy to offer
tasters, walls and ceiling adorned with
hundreds of pump clips; no food or under-
18s, dogs welcome; café-style tables out
on pavement, open all day and handy for
the station. *(Malcolm Carson)*

SCORTON NZ2500
Farmers Arms (01748) 812533
Northside; DL10 6DW Comfortably
modernised little pub in terrace of old
cottages overlooking green; well kept Sharps
Doom Bar and guests, decent wines and good
freshly made food including popular Sun
lunch, friendly accommodating staff, bar with
open fire, darts and dominoes, restaurant;
background music, fortnightly quiz; children
and dogs welcome, open all day weekends,
closed Mon lunchtime. *(Neil Griffin)*

SCORTON   NZ2400
Heifer (01748) 811357
B1263; High Row; DL10 6DH Welcoming
beamed pub facing village green; comfortably
updated bar and back restaurant, good food
from varied menu including sandwiches
and vegetarian choices, Fri steak night
and other evening deals, well kept local
beers and decent range of wines and gins,
friendly helpful service; children and dogs
(in bar) welcome, closed Mon, Tues and
for a week in Jan, May, Aug and Nov
(check website). *(Michael Doswell)*

SCOTTON   SE3259
Guy Fawkes Arms (01423) 868400
Main Street; HG5 9HU Welcoming pub
(new owners) in village where Guy Fawkes
lived; very popular food (booking advised)
including good value set lunch, well kept
Black Sheep and three local guests; children
and dogs (in bar) welcome, open from 4pm
Mon and Tues (no food those days), otherwise
open all day, kitchen closes 7pm Sun.
(Brian and Anna Marsden)

SETTLE   SD8163
Golden Lion (01729) 823459
*B6480 (main road through town), off
A65 bypass; BD24 9DU* Market town inn
with grand staircase sweeping down into
baronial-style high-beamed bar, lovely log
fire, second bar with bare boards and dark
half-panelling, lots of old local photographs
and another fire, well kept Thwaites, guest
ales and decent wines by the glass, good
value food from deli boards to specials,
helpful friendly staff, refurbished restaurant;
children and dogs welcome, courtyard tables,
14 bedrooms, open (and food) all day.
(Liz and Mike Newton)

SETTLE   SD8263
Talbot Arms (01729) 823924
High Street; BD24 9EX Friendly place
with six well kept ales including Theakstons
and local brews such as Settle and Three
Peaks, reasonably priced traditional food
from sandwiches up including some evening
deals, pubby furniture on carpet, woodburner
in impressive stone fireplace, parquet-floored
games area with pool and darts; live music,
quiz first Mon of the month; children and
dogs welcome, picnic-sets in two-level back
garden, open (and food) all day. *(Brian and
Anna Marsden)*

SHEFFIELD   SK3487
Bath (0114) 249 5151
*Victoria Street, off Glossop Road;
S3 7QL* Victorian corner pub with well
restored 1930s interior; two rooms and a
drinking corridor, black and white floor tiles,
traditional wall benches and some leaded
light partitions, well kept Thornbridge and
guests, simple snacky food including hot
roast pork sandwiches Fri and Sat, friendly

staff; live jazz/blues/folk Weds, quiz Thurs;
closed Sun and bank holiday Mon, otherwise
open all day. *(Richard Tingle, Martin Day)*

SHEFFIELD   SK3687
Fat Cat (0114) 249 4801
Alma Street; S3 8SA Cheerfully busy little
Victorian pub with a dozen interesting beers
on handpump including next-door Kelham
Island, also draught/bottled continentals
and traditional cider, friendly knowledgeable
staff, straightforward bargain food (not Sun
evening) catering for vegetarians/vegans;
Mon quiz; seats in back courtyard, open
all day. *(Richard Tingle)*

SHEFFIELD   SK3588
Harlequin 0779 4156916
Nursery Street; S3 8GG Welcoming
open-plan corner pub owned by nearby Exit
33, their well kept ales and great selection
of changing guests (beer festivals), also
bottled imports and real ciders/perries,
straightforward cheap food including Sun
roasts (no credit cards); weekend live music,
jazz night second Thurs of month, quiz Weds;
no under-18s after 3pm, dogs welcome,
outside seating, open all day. *(Sally and
Colin Allen)*

SHEFFIELD   SK4086
Kelham Island Tavern
(0114) 272 2482 *Kelham Island;
S3 8RY* Busy little pub under newish
ownership; a dozen interesting ales and
good range of other draft and bottled beers,
two rooms with simple pubby furnishings,
decent lunchtime food; Mon quiz, folk night
every other Sun, children till 9pm and dogs
welcome, flower-filled back courtyard garden,
open all day. *(WAH)*

SHEFFIELD   SK3290
★ New Barrack (0114) 232 4225
Penistone Road, Hillsborough; S6 2GA
Friendly buoyant pub with nine real ales
including Castle Rock, lots of bottled
belgian beers and good value traditional
food; comfortable front lounge with log fire
and upholstered seats on old pine floors,
another fire in tap room, function room
(own bar); live music and comedy nights,
pool, darts, sports TV; children (till 9pm)
and dogs welcome, attractive little walled
garden, parking nearby can be difficult,
closed lunchtimes Mon-Fri, open all day
weekends. *(Sally and Colin Allen)*

SHEFFIELD   SK3186
Ranmoor (0114) 230 1325
*Fulwood Road (across from church);
S10 3GD* Comfortable and welcoming
19th-c local; open-plan interior with etched
bay windows, big mirrors and period
fireplaces, four well kept ales including
Abbeydale and Bradfield, enjoyable food;
two outside seating areas, open all day.
(Laura Reid)

SHEFFIELD SK3487
Red Deer (0114) 272 2890
Pitt Street; S1 4DD Friendly traditional backstreet pub among university buildings; bigger inside than it looks with eight well kept ales and a real cider from central bar, good value food (all day weekends) from sandwiches and snacks up catering for vegetarians/vegans; Tues quiz, live music, board games; tables outside, open all day (till 1am Fri, Sat). *(Richard Tingle)*

SHEFFIELD SK3185
Rising Sun (0114) 230 3855
Fulwood Road; S10 3QA Extended community pub with a dozen ales (several from Abbeydale) and good selection of craft beers, tasty fairly priced food, friendly service; background music, quiz Weds and Sun; children and dogs welcome, a few tables out in front, more on back terrace, open all day. *(Laura Reid)*

SHEFFIELD SK3586
Sheffield Tap (0114) 273 7558
Station, platform 1B; S1 2BP Busy station bar in restored Edwardian refreshment room, popular for its extensive range of international beers on draught and in bottles, also own Tapped ales from visible microbrewery and plenty of guests including Thornbridge, knowledgeable helpful staff, snacky food, spacious tiled interior with vaulted ceiling; open all day. *(Nick T)*

SHEFFIELD SK3687
Wellington (0114) 249 2295
Henry Street; by Shalesmoor tram stop; S3 7EQ Traditional little 19th-c corner pub; well kept Neepsend ales and guests from seven handpumps, friendly staff, coal fire in lounge, some photographs of old Sheffield; tables out behind, open all day Fri-Sun, from 3pm Mon-Thurs. *(Nick T)*

SHEFFIELD SK3584
White Lion (0114) 255 1500
London Road; S2 4HT Terrace-row pub dating from the late 18th c with various small lounges and snugs off central corridor, 12 well kept changing ales (marked on blackboard) and good selection of whiskies, friendly relaxed atmosphere; regular live music in back room, Weds quiz; open all day from 4pm (midday Sat, 2pm Sun). *(Nick T)*

SHELLEY SE2112
★**Three Acres** (01484) 602606
Roydhouse (not signed); from B6116 towards Skelmanthorpe, turn left in Shelley (signposted Flockton, Elmley, Elmley Moor), go up lane for 2 miles towards radio mast; HD8 8LR Civilised former coaching inn with emphasis on hotel and dining side; beamed lounge bar with bare boards and open fire, tankards above counter serving well kept ales such as Timothy

Taylors, Tetleys and Yorkshire, 40 malt whiskies and up to 17 wines by the glass from serious list, several formal dining rooms, wide choice of good if expensive food from lunchtime sandwiches up, competent friendly staff; conferences, weddings and other events; children welcome, fine moorland setting and lovely views, smart well equipped bedrooms. *(Louise and Simon Peters)*

SHERIFF HUTTON SE6566
Highwayman (01347) 878328
The Square; YO60 6QZ Friendly family-run pub with hearty helpings of good value home-made food (not Sun evening, Mon) from sandwiches and baguettes up, a house beer from Belhaven (Stand & Deliver) and Theakstons Best and a guest kept well, beamed interior with bar, restaurant and games room (pool and darts); Thurs quiz, TV; children and dogs welcome, picnic-sets in big garden, pretty village with castle ruins and 12th-c church, open all day weekends, closed Mon lunchtime. *(Pat and Tony Martin)*

SHIPLEY SE1437
Fannys Ale House (01274) 591419
Saltaire Road; BD18 3JN Extended bare-boards alehouse on two floors, cosy and friendly, with eight well kept beers including Timothy Taylors, bottled imports and traditional ciders, gas lighting, brewery memorabilia, log fire and woodburner; free wi-fi; dogs welcome, handy for Salts Mill, closed Mon lunchtime, otherwise open all day and can get crowded weekend evenings. *(Charlotte and William Mason)*

SHIPLEY SE1337
Salt Bar & Kitchen (01274) 582111
Bingley Road; BD18 4DH Cavernous glass-fronted tramshed conversion (former Hop) on edge of Saltaire World Heritage Site; high pitched ceilings with some rather grand chandeliers, raised seating areas and stairs up to gallery, well kept Ossett ales along with own brews from central curved counter, good choice of enjoyable food including sandwiches, sharing boards and wood-fired pizzas, friendly helpful service; live music and quiz nights; no under-18s after 8pm, dogs allowed in tap room, picnic-sets out at front among the old tram tracks, open all day, food all day Fri, Sat and till 7pm Sun. *(Liz and Mike Newton)*

SICKLINGHALL SE3648
Scotts Arms (01937) 582100
Main Street; LS22 4BD Popular 17th-c roadside village pub; enjoyable generously served food (all day weekends) including blackboard specials, rambling interior with interesting nooks and crannies, low beams, old timbers and log fires (one in lovely fireplace), four well kept mainstream ales, good wine range, friendly efficient staff; free wi-fi; children and dogs welcome, wheelchair access from behind, disabled loos, big garden

with teak furniture on paved terrace, open all day. *(Malcolm and Pauline Pellatt)*

SINNINGTON   SE7485
★Fox & Hounds (01751) 431577
Off A170 W of Pickering; YO62 6SQ New management for this popular 18th-c coaching house in pretty village; carpeted beamed bar with two-way woodburner, comfortable seating, various pictures and old artefacts, well kept ales such as Abbeydale, Black Sheep and Marstons Wainwright, several wines by the glass, good attractively presented food including a light early evening menu (Mon-Fri), friendly helpful service, lounge and smart restaurant; children and dogs (in bar) welcome, picnic-sets out at front and in garden, ten comfy bedrooms. *(Michael Butler, Janet and Peter Race)*

SKIPTON   SD9851
Beer Engine 07834 456134
Albert Street; BD23 1JD Popular micropub with interesting range of changing ales, bottled imports and real ciders, good choice of wines by the glass too, friendly knowledgeable staff; occasional live music; children and dogs welcome, closed Mon and Tues, otherwise open all day. *(Christopher H)*

SKIPTON   SD9851
Narrow Boat (01756) 797922
Victoria Street; pub signed down alley off Coach Street; BD23 1JE Popular pub down cobbled alley; eight real ales including Ilkley, Okells and Timothy Taylors, also fruit and wheat beers, traditional cider/perry, dining chairs, pews and stools around wooden tables on bare boards, upstairs galleried area with interesting canal mural, generous helpings of enjoyable food at fair prices; background music, folk night Mon, quiz Weds; children (if eating) and dogs welcome, picnic-sets under front colonnade, Leeds & Liverpool Canal nearby, open all day, food all day Sat, till 6pm Sun. *(Kerry and Guy Trooper)*

SKIPTON   SD9851
Woolly Sheep (01756) 700966
Sheep Street; BD23 1HY Bustling narrow pub just off the High Street; full Timothy Taylors range kept well, several wines by the glass and good choice of gins, whiskies and cocktails, friendly service; two beamed bars off flagstoned passage, exposed brickwork, coal fire in stone fireplace, split-level dining area at the back serving enjoyable fairly priced food from pub standards up; children welcome, wheelchair access with help, part-covered terrace and outside bar, 12 bedrooms, good breakfast, open (and food) all day, shuts 1am Fri, Sat. *(Tony Scott)*

SLEDMERE   SE9364
★Triton (01377) 236078
B1252/B1253 junction, NW of Great Driffield; YO25 3XQ Handsome 18th-c inn by Sledmere House; open-plan bar with

old-fashioned atmosphere, dark wooden furniture on patterned carpet, 15 clocks ranging from grandfather to cuckoo, lots of willow pattern plates, paintings and pictures, suit of armour in one part, open fire, Greene King, Timothy Taylors, Tetleys and Wold Top, some 50 gins, big helpings of popular freshly cooked food (only take bookings in separate restaurant), friendly helpful staff; children welcome till 8pm, no dogs, wheelchair access to bar and restaurant, five good bedrooms, generous breakfast, open all day Sun till 9pm (food till 6.30pm), closed Mon. *(Michael Butler, Dr and Mrs J D Abell)*

SLINGSBY   SE6975
Grapes (01653) 628076
Off B1257 Malton–Hovingham; Railway Street; YO62 4AL Busy 18th-c village pub with good sensibly priced food from traditional menu (not Sun evening), well kept Timothy Taylors, Theakstons and guests, cheerful staff, bare boards, flagstones and painted beams, nice mix of old furniture and some interesting bits and pieces including a tusky boar's head above one of the woodburners, games area with bar billiards; children and dogs (in bar and snug) welcome, tables and pizza oven in covered area behind, open all day Fri-Sun, closed Mon. *(Michael Heuck)*

SNAITH   SE6422
Brewers Arms (01405) 862404
Pontefract Road; DN14 9JS Refurbished open-plan Georgian inn; local Old Mill ales and decent home-made food from sandwiches and panini up, friendly helpful staff; children welcome in eating areas, attractive well appointed bedrooms, open all day. *(Jim and Sue James)*

SNAPE   SE2684
★Castle Arms (01677) 470270
Off B6268 Masham–Bedale; DL8 2TB Welcoming pub in pretty village; flagstoned bar with straightforward pubby furniture, horsebrasses on beams and open fire, Marstons-related ales and enjoyable food from sandwiches up, attentive service, dining room (also flagstoned) with dark tables and chairs and another fire; children and dogs (in bar and tap room) welcome, picnic-sets out at front and in courtyard, fine walks in Yorkshire Dales and on North York Moors, nine good bedrooms in converted barn; open all day Sat, closed Mon lunchtime. *(Michael Butler)*

SOUTH DALTON   SE9645
★Pipe & Glass (01430) 810246
West End; brown sign to pub off B1248 NW of Beverley; HU17 7PN Attractive tucked-away village pub with main emphasis on landlord-chef's excellent Michelin-starred food; beamed and bow-windowed bar, copper pans hanging above woodburner in sizeable fireplace, cushioned window seats and high-

backed wooden dining chairs around mix of tables, Black Sheep, a house beer (Two Chefs) from Great Yorkshire and a couple of guests, 15 wines by the glass and some 40 malt whiskies, friendly staff, contemporary area beyond with leather chesterfields and another woodburner leading to airy restaurant overlooking parkland; background music, free wi-fi; children welcome, tables on lawn and front terrace, stylish bedrooms including three luxury suites, charming village with 62-metre church spire, closed Mon, otherwise open (and some food) all day, kitchen closes 4pm Sun. *(Margaret McDonald)*

SOUTH KILVINGTON   SE4284
Old Oak Tree (01845) 523276
Stockton Road (A61); YO7 2NL Spacious low-ceilinged pub with three linked rooms and long back conservatory; ample choice of good honest food from sandwiches up including lunchtime/early evening two-course deal, three well kept beers, friendly staff; children welcome, tables on terrace with steps down to sloping lawn, five bedrooms, open (and food) all day Sun. *(Luke Morgan)*

SOWERBY BRIDGE   SE0623
Hogs Head (01422) 836585
Stanley Street; HX6 2AH Brewpub in former 18th-c maltings; one large room with heavy beams, bare boards and big woodburner, brewery visible behind glass, five of their good beers and guests from well stocked bar, no food; dogs welcome, open all day weekends, from 3pm Mon-Fri. *(Caroline Sullivan)*

STANBURY   SE0037
Old Silent (01535) 647437
Hob Lane; BD22 0HW Old moorland dining inn under new management (some refurbishment); enjoyable good value food (all day weekends) and three real ales such as Timothy Taylors Golden Best, linked rooms with beams, flagstones, mullioned windows and open fires, restaurant and conservatory; children and dogs welcome, eight bedrooms, open all day. *(Andrea and Philip Crispin)*

STAVELEY   SE3662
Royal Oak (01423) 340267
Signed off A6055 Knaresborough–Boroughbridge; HG5 9LD Popular pub in village conservation area under friendly management; beams, panelling and open fires, broad bay windows overlooking small front garden, well kept Black Sheep, Timothy Taylors and two local guests, several wines by the glass, good fairly priced food in bar and restaurant; children and dogs welcome, open all day, food till 7pm Sun. *(Dan and Belinda Smallbone)*

STILLINGTON   SE5867
Bay Tree (01347) 811394
Main Street; leave York on outer ring road (A1237) to Scarborough, first exit
on left signposted B1363 to Helmsley; YO61 1JU* Cottagey pub-restaurant in pretty village's main street; modern bar areas with comfortable cushioned wall seats and kitchen chairs around mix of tables, central gas-effect coal fire, real ales such as Black Sheep, several wines by the glass and extensive range of gins, good interesting food from chef-owner along with some pub favourites and lunchtime sandwiches, steps up to cosy dining area, larger conservatory-style restaurant behind; background music; children and dogs (in bar) welcome, seats in garden and a couple of picnic-sets at front, closed Sun evening to Weds lunchtime. *(Stuart and Natalie Granville)*

STOKESLEY   NZ5208
White Swan (01642) 710263
West End; TS9 5BL Good Captain Cook ales brewed at this attractive 18th-c flower-decked local; L-shaped bar with three relaxing seating areas, log fire, assorted memorabilia and nice bar counter with carved panels; Weds quiz, regular live music and beer festivals, darts and sports TV; no children, dogs welcome, open all day. *(Laura Reid)*

SUTTON UPON DERWENT SE7047
★ St Vincent Arms (01904) 608349
Main Street (B1228 SE of York); YO41 4BN Busy pub with seven well kept ales including Fullers, lots of wines by the glass and good popular food from lunchtime sandwiches/ciabattas to blackboard specials, friendly efficient service; parlour-style front bar with panelling, traditional high-backed settles, windsor chairs and cushioned bow-window seat, gas-effect coal fire, another lounge and separate dining room; children and dogs (in bar) welcome, garden tables, handy for Yorkshire Air Museum. *(Peter and Anne Hollindale)*

SUTTON-UNDER-WHITESTONECLIFFE   SE4983
Whitestonecliffe Inn
(01845) 597271 *A170 E of Thirsk; YO7 2PR* Well located 18th-c beamed roadside pub; enjoyable reasonably priced food from fairly traditional menu including some gluten-free and vegan choices, blackboard specials and themed nights, well kept Tetleys, Theakstons and a guest, friendly staff, log fire and some exposed stonework in bar, separate restaurant, games room with pool and darts; children and dogs welcome, six self-catering cottages with rural views, open all day weekends, closed weekday lunchtimes. *(Nick T)*

TAN HILL   NY8906
Tan Hill Inn (01833) 533007
Arkengarthdale Road, Reeth–Brough, at junction Keld/West Stonesdale Road; DL11 6ED Basic old pub (Britain's highest) in wonderful bleak setting on Pennine Way

and often snowbound; full of bric-a-brac and interesting photographs, simple sturdy furniture on flagstones and an ever-burning log fire with prized stone side seats, five well kept ales including one badged for them from Dent, good cheap pubby food, family room; live music Thurs-Sat evenings; children and dogs welcome, bedrooms, bunk rooms and camping, wandering ducks and chickens, Swaledale sheep show here last Thurs in May, open (and some food) all day, can get very crowded. *(Mike Benton)*

THIRSK   SE4282
Golden Fleece (01845) 523108
Market Place; YO7 1LL Refurbished old brick coaching inn; good food from snacks and sharing plates up including pub favourites and stone-baked pizzas, afternoon teas, friendly helpful service, ales such as Black Sheep and Copper Dragon, craft beers and over 20 wines by the glass, good range of gins too, clean contemporary décor in bar and separate dining rooms, view across marketplace from bay windows; children and dogs (in some areas) welcome, part-covered back courtyard, 26 bedrooms, open (and food) all day. *(Louise and Simon Peters)*

THIXENDALE   SE8461
Cross Keys (01377) 288272
Off A166 3 miles N of Fridaythorpe; YO17 9TG Unspoilt country pub in deep valley below the rolling wolds – popular with walkers; cosy and relaxed L-shaped bar with fitted wall seats, well kept Tetleys and a couple of guests, generous uncomplicated blackboard food; no under-14s or dogs inside, views from big back garden, handy for Wharram Percy earthworks, comfortable bedrooms in converted stables, good breakfast, closed Mon-Thurs lunchtimes (unless pre-booked by walking group). *(Gary and Marie Miller)*

THOLTHORPE   SE4766
New Inn (01347) 838329
Flawith Road; YO61 1SL Updated beamed village-green pub with log-fire bar and candlelit restaurant; good food (allergies catered for) from sandwiches and wood-fired pizzas up including popular Sun lunch, Fri evening fish and chips deal, John Smiths and a local guest, friendly helpful staff; small shop; children welcome, closed Mon and lunchtime Tues. *(Sarah and David Gibbs)*

THORNTON   SE0933
Ring o' Bells (01274) 832296
Hill Top Road, W of village, and N of B6145; BD13 3QL Modernised roadside dining pub in hilltop position with long views towards Shipley and Bingley; series of linked rooms including conservatory-like area, black beams and painted stone walls, banquettes and other pubby furniture on carpet or flagstones, highly rated food from pub favourites up including vegetarian/

vegan choices and good value set menu, beers such as Timothy Taylors Landlord from well stocked bar, friendly efficient service; children and dogs welcome, closed Mon otherwise open (and food) all day, kitchen shuts 6.30pm Sun. *(Gordon and Margaret Ormondroyd)*

THORNTON   SE0832
White Horse (01274) 834268
Well Heads; BD13 3SJ Deceptively large country pub popular for its wide choice of good food including early bird menu (till 6.30pm Mon-Thurs), five well kept Timothy Taylors ales, pleasant helpful staff, four separate areas, two with log fires, busy bustling atmosphere; children welcome, upstairs lavatories (disabled ones on ground level), also disabled parking, open all day, food all day weekends (till 7.45pm Sun). *(John and Eleanor Holdsworth)*

THORNTON DALE   SE8383
New Inn (01751) 474226
The Square; YO18 7LF Friendly early 18th-c beamed coaching inn (packed weekend evenings); three well kept ales and good fairly traditional food cooked by landlord including evening specials and deals; children and dogs (in bar) welcome, courtyard tables, six bedrooms and self-catering cottage, pretty village on edge of Dalby Forest, open all day, food all day Sun. *(Jim and Sue James)*

THORNTON IN
LONSDALE   SD6873
Marton Arms (015242) 42204
Off A65 just NW of Ingleton; LA6 3PB Refurbished old pub opposite 13th-c church where Arthur Conan Doyle was married; half a dozen real ales and around 60 gins, generous helpings of enjoyable food from sandwiches, snacks and pub favourites up, friendly staff, opened-up interior keeping beams and some exposed stonework, built-in settles and mix of wooden tables and chairs on polished wood floor, logburner; background and some live music, Tues quiz, free wi-fi; children and dogs welcome, picnic-sets on front terrace and back lawn, great walking country, 11 comfy bedrooms, open all day, food all day Fri-Sun. *(John and Sylvia Harrop)*

THORNTON-LE-CLAY   SE6865
White Swan (01653) 618286
Off A64 SW of Malton, via Foston; Low Street; YO60 7TG Updated 19th-c family-run village pub; well kept local ales, nice wines by the glass and enjoyable reasonably priced home-made food including daily specials and themed evenings, friendly helpful young staff; live music and quiz nights; children welcome, large garden, attractive countryside nearby and Castle Howard, open all day Sun, closed Mon, Tues. *(Caroline Sullivan)*

THRINTOFT SE3293
New Inn (01609) 771961
Thrintoft Moor Lane, off Bramper Lane;
DL7 0PN Friendly 18th-c village local with
good variety of generously served home-made
food including popular Sun lunch, well kept
Black Sheep, Theakstons and a couple of
guests, restaurant, open fire and woodburner;
occasional quiz nights, free wi-fi; children
and dogs (in bar) welcome, disabled access,
front garden with two quoits pitches, closed
Mon lunchtime. *(Margaret McDonald)*

TIMBLE SE1852
★ Timble Inn (01943) 880530
Off Otley–Blubberhouses moors road;
LS21 2NN Smartly restored 18th-c dining
inn tucked away in quiet farmland hamlet;
good food from pub favourites up including
well aged Nidderdale beef (booking advised,
can be pricey), ales such as Copper Dragon,
Ilkley and Theakstons; children welcome, no
dogs at food times, good walks from the door,
nine well appointed bedrooms, closed Mon
and evening Tues. *(Monica and Steph Evans)*

TONG SE2230
Greyhound (0113) 285 2427
Tong Lane; BD4 0RR Traditional low-
beamed and flagstoned local by village
cricket field; generous helpings of enjoyable
good value food, can eat in bar or cosy dining
room, well kept regional ales and several
wines by the glass, efficient friendly service;
tables outside, open all day. *(George and
Alison Bishop)*

TOPCLIFFE SE4076
Angel (01845) 578000
*Off A1, take A168 to Thirsk, after 3 miles
follow signs for Topcliffe; Long Street;
YO7 3RW* Part of the West Park Inns group;
softly lit bare-boards bar with log fire, four
mainly local ales and good choice of wines
by the glass (happy hour Mon-Sat 4-6pm),
enjoyable food in carpeted grill restaurant
including lunchtime/early evening deal,
cheerful helpful service; background music,
comedy night (usually first Tues of month);
children welcome, nice garden, 16 bedrooms,
open all day (food all day Sun till 8pm).
(Nick T)

TOWTON SE4839
Rockingham Arms (01937) 530948
A162 Tadcaster–Ferrybridge; LS24 9PB
Comfortable 18th-c roadside village pub
with good home-made food from lunchtime
baguettes up, efficient friendly service,
ales such as Black Sheep and Theakstons,
back conservatory overlooking garden;

children and dogs welcome, handy for
Towton Battlefield, open all day, no food
Sun evening. *(Joe and Belinda Smart)*

ULLESKELF SE5140
Ulleskelf Arms (01937) 835515
Church Fenton Lane; LS24 9DS
Refurbished village pub with good home-
made food (till 6pm Sun evening, not Tues)
including daily specials and Mon pie night,
four well kept ales such as Timothy Taylors
Boltmaker, open-plan interior with mix of
old and new furniture on laminate flooring;
background music; children, walkers and
dogs welcome (resident lurcher is Dexter),
beer garden behind, open all day Sun,
closed lunchtimes Mon and Tues.
(Jim and Sue James)

WAKEFIELD SE3417
Castle (01924) 256981
Barnsley Road, Sandal; WF2 6AS
Popular roadside dining pub with good
affordably priced food including set menu
(till 6pm Mon-Sat), four well kept changing
ales, friendly staff and pleasant relaxed
atmosphere; unobtrusive background music;
children welcome, dogs in bar, rattan-style
furniture on paved back terrace overlooking
bowling green, open (and food) all day.
(Mike Benton)

WAKEFIELD SE3320
Fernandes Brewery Tap
(01924) 386348 *Avison Yard, Kirkgate;*
WF1 1UA Owned by Ossett but still brewing
Fernandes ales in the cellar, also interesting
guest beers, bottled imports and traditional
ciders; ground-floor bar with flagstones, bare
brick and panelling, downstairs Bier Keller
(evenings Fri and Sat) and original raftered
top-floor bar with some unusual breweriana;
quiz night Weds, afternoon folk session first
Sun of month; no children, dogs welcome,
open all day Fri-Sun, from 4pm other days.
(Mike Benton)

WAKEFIELD SE3220
Harrys Bar (01924) 373773
Westgate; WF1 1EL Cheery little one-room
local with good selection of real ales and
bottled beers, stripped-brick walls, open fire;
live music Mon and Weds, free wi-fi; small
back garden, open all day Sun, from 5pm
Mon-Thurs, 4pm Fri-Sat. *(Mike Benton, Nick T)*

WALTON SE4447
Fox & Hounds (01937) 842192
*Hall Park Road, off back road Wetherby–
Tadcaster; LS23 7DQ* Popular dining
pub with good reasonably priced food from
sandwiches to specials (should book Sun

A star symbol before the name of a pub shows exceptional character and appeal.
It doesn't mean extra comfort. Even quite a basic pub can win a star,
if it's individual enough.

lunch), early evening set menu Tues-Sat, well kept ales such as Black Sheep and Timothy Taylors, friendly thriving atmosphere; children welcome, handy A1 stop, closed Mon.
(Les and Sandra Brown)

WALTON   SE3517
New Inn (01924) 255447
Shay Lane; WF2 6LA Open-plan village pub with friendly uniformed staff and buoyant atmosphere; seven well kept mainly local ales such as Jolly Boys, decent wines by the glass and some premium gins, extensive choice of good reasonably priced food from sandwiches and sharing plates up, afternoon teas, stylish dining area in building behind with own terrace; quiz nights Sun and Mon; children welcome, dogs in bar, seats out in front and in lawned garden, open (and food) all day. *(Michael Butler)*

WARLEY TOWN   SE0524
Maypole (01422) 835861
Signed off A646 just W of Halifax; HX2 7RZ Popular and welcoming village dining pub; generous helpings of good reasonably priced food from fairly traditional menu including lunchtime/early evening set deal (Tues-Fri), well kept ales such as Black Sheep, efficient friendly young staff, comfortable open-plan interior with two-way woodburner; children welcome, open all day Fri-Sun, closed Mon lunchtime, food till 7.30pm Sun. *(Celia Caulkin)*

WASS   SE5579
Stapylton Arms (01347) 868280
Back road W of Ampleforth; or follow brown sign for Byland Abbey off A170 Thirsk–Helmsley; YO61 4BE Whitewashed village pub with two bustling bars, beams, flagstones and log fires, a couple of ales such as Helmsley and Theakstons, nine wines by the glass from extensive list, restaurant in 18th-c granary serving generous helpings of good freshly made food from lunchtime sandwiches to daily specials, friendly attentive staff; children welcome, no dogs, pretty village and surrounding countryside, near ruins of Byland Abbey (EH), three comfortable well equipped bedrooms. *(Dr Peter Crawshaw)*

WATH-IN-NIDDERDALE   SE1467
★**Sportsmans Arms** (01423) 711306
Nidderdale road off B6265 in Pateley Bridge; village and pub signposted over hump-back bridge, on right after a couple of miles; HG3 5PP Civilised and beautifully located restaurant with rooms run by long-serving owners; although most emphasis on the excellent food and bedrooms, it does have a proper welcoming bar with open fire, well kept Black Sheep and Timothy Taylors, Thatcher's cider, lots of wines by the glass (extensive list) and 40 or so malt whiskies, also a highly rated ploughman's and other bar food, helpful

hospitable staff, elegant dining room; background music; children welcome, dogs in bar, benches and tables outside, pretty garden with croquet, own fishing rights on River Nidd. *(Margaret and Peter Staples)*

WEAVERTHORPE   SE9670
Blue Bell (01944) 738204
Village signed off A64 Malton–Scarborough at Sherburn; Main Road; YO17 8EX Upscale country dining pub, quite ornate in parts, with good attractively presented food and fine choice of wines (many by the glass including champagne), well kept Tetleys and Timothy Taylors, cosy cheerful bar with open fire and unusual collection of bottles and packaging, intimate back restaurant, friendly attentive staff; 12 bedrooms (six in annexe), interesting village, closed Sun evening, Mon and Tues lunchtime. *(Michael Butler)*

WEAVERTHORPE   SE9771
Star (01944) 738346
Village signed off A64 Malton–Scarborough at Sherburn; YO17 8EY Modernised village pub with enjoyable fairly priced food including stone-baked pizzas and good Tues curry night, a couple of well kept Wold Top ales, friendly service, pleasant bar with woodburner and small area for darts, restaurant; children and dogs welcome, picnic-sets on front grass by little stream, five updated bedrooms, closed Mon and lunchtimes (apart from Sun). *(Michael Butler)*

WENSLEY   SE0989
Three Horseshoes (01969) 622327
A684; DL8 4HJ Old whitewashed roadside pub with neat beamed and flagstoned bar; five well kept ales including Theakstons and Wensleydale, enjoyable straightforward food at reasonable prices from sandwiches up, just pizzas and kebabs Mon evening, friendly helpful service, woodburner and open fire; children and dogs welcome, lovely Wensleydale views from paved terrace, popular with walkers, open all day.
(Richard Marshall)

WEST TANFIELD   SE2678
Bruce Arms (01677) 470325
Main Street (A6108 N of Ripon); HG4 5JJ Smart dining pub (18th-c coaching inn) under same ownership as the nearby Bull; good restaurant-style food served by friendly attentive staff, steak nights Wed and Thurs, well kept Theakstons and good range of wines, gins and malt whiskies; terrace tables, three comfortable bedrooms, good breakfast, closed Mon, Tues and Weds lunchtime. *(Sarah and David Gibbs)*

WEST TANFIELD   SE2678
Bull (01677) 470678
Church Street (A6108 N of Ripon); HG4 5JQ Busy pub in picturesque riverside setting; simple décor in flagstoned bar and

slightly raised dining area, popular fairly standard food (all day Sat, till 7pm Sun), well kept Black Sheep and Theakstons; background and live music once or twice a month (Sun), free wi-fi; children (away from bar) and dogs welcome, tables on terraces in attractive garden sloping steeply to River Ure and its old bridge, five bedrooms, open all day weekends. *(Michael Butler)*

WEST WITTON   SE0688
Fox & Hounds (01969) 623650
Main Street (A684); DL8 4LP
Welcoming traditional 17th-c local; central coal fire dividing bar from games area (darts and juke box), bottles on delft shelving, well kept Black Sheep, Theakstons, Yorkshire Dales and guests, Weston's cider, enjoyable reasonably priced pubby food from sandwiches and baked potatoes up, dining room with inglenook; children and dogs welcome, open all day weekends. *(keithash)*

WEST WITTON   SE0588
★**Wensleydale Heifer** (01969) 622322
A684 W of Leyburn; DL8 4LS Stylish restaurant-with-rooms rather than pub, but can pop in for a drink; excellent food with emphasis on fish/seafood and grills (not cheap and best to book), also lunchtime/early evening set menu, sandwiches and snacks, good wines, cosy dining bar with Black Sheep and a house beer brewed by Yorkshire Dales, much bigger and more formal restaurant, attentive helpful service; children welcome, dogs in some areas, 13 good bedrooms (back ones quietest), generous breakfast, open all day. *(Joe and Belinda Smart)*

WESTOW   SE7565
Blacksmiths Arms (01653) 619606
Off A64 York–Malton; Main Street; YO60 7NE Updated 18th-c family-run pub; attractive beamed bar with woodburner in brick inglenook, good food from lunchtime sandwiches up including signature steaks and blackboard specials, well kept beers such as Tetleys, friendly helpful service, restaurant; children welcome, no dogs inside, picnic-sets on side terrace, holiday cottage behind, closed Mon, otherwise open all day. *(Michael Heuck, Peter and Anne Hollindale)*

WHITBY   NZ8911
Abbey Wharf (01947) 600306
Market Place; YO22 4DD Steps up to airy modern bar-restaurant (former Burberry factory) with lots of glass and exposed timberwork; good selection of beers from well stocked tile-fronted bar, enjoyable food including signature fish/seafood (takeaway fish and chips available) and chargrills (they add a service charge), friendly staff, mezzanine floor with own bar; maybe weekend live bands; children and dogs welcome, small terrace overlooking harbour, open (and food) all day. *(Darren and Jane Staniforth)*

WHITBY   NZ9011
Black Horse (01947) 602906
Church Street; YO22 4BH Small traditional two-room pub, much older than its Victorian frontage, and previously a funeral parlour and brothel; friendly and down to earth with five changing ales, continental beers and a proper cider, range of yorkshire tapas, tins of snuff for sale; dogs welcome, four cosy bedrooms, open all day. *(Andrea and Philip Crispin)*

WHITBY   NZ9011
Duke of York (01947) 600324
Church Street, Harbour East Side; YO22 4DE Busy pub in fine harbourside position, great views and handy for the famous 199 steps leading up to the abbey; comfortable beamed lounge bar with fishing memorabilia, well kept ales such as Black Sheep, Greene King and Ossett, decent wines and several malt whiskies, enjoyable straightforward bar food at reasonable prices; background music, TV, games machine, free wi-fi; children welcome, bedrooms overlooking water, no nearby parking, open (and food) all day. *(Peter and Emma Kelly)*

WHITBY   NZ8911
Station Inn (01947) 603937
New Quay Road; YO21 1DH Welcoming red-brick three-room drinkers' pub across from the station and harbour; eight well kept ales including Ossett, Timothy Taylors and Whitby, craft beers, Weston's cider and good wines by the glass, friendly mix of customers; background and regular live music, quiz Thurs, traditional games; dogs welcome, three bedrooms, open all day. *(Tracky Cropper)*

WHITBY   NZ9011
White Horse & Griffin
(01947) 604857 *Church Street; YO22 4BH* Historic 17th-c coaching inn; tall narrow front bar with bare boards and a couple of large chandeliers, ales such as Black Sheep and Timothy Taylors, good wines and over 30 gins, steps down to low-beamed bistro-style dining area with flagstones and log fire, well liked interesting food served by attentive staff; children and dogs welcome, close to the 199 steps up to the abbey, ten bedrooms, open all day. *(John Robinson)*

WIGHILL   SE4746
White Swan (01937) 832217
Main Street; LS24 8BQ Fairly modern village pub with two cosy front rooms and larger side extension; three well kept ales such as Sharps, Timothy Taylors and Theakstons, good food from pub classics up including monthly themed night, friendly helpful staff; children welcome, dogs in bar and snug, wheelchair access with help (steps

down to loos), picnic-sets on side lawn, closed Mon, otherwise open all day, food till 6pm Sun. *(Alan and Alice Morgan)*

WINTERSETT SE3815
Anglers Retreat (01924) 862370
Ferry Top Lane; WF4 2EB Unpretentious rural local by Anglers Country Park and popular with walkers, birders and fishermen; small lounge and tiny flagstoned bar, three well kept ales including Acorn, no food, hospitable landlord and friendly cheerful atmosphere; pleasant side garden; children and dogs (not in garden) welcome, open all day Sat, until 5pm Sun, closed Tues. *(Michael Butler)*

WITHERNWICK TA1940
Falcon (01964) 527925
Main Street; HU11 4TA Welcoming 18th-c beamed corner pub; popular good value food from traditional menu, well kept Tetleys and a guest; children allowed, a few seats outside, closed Mon and lunchtimes apart from Sun, no food Tues. *(Monica and Steph Evans)*

WOMBLETON SE6683
Plough (01751) 431356
Main Street; YO62 7RW Welcoming 15th-c village local with good fairly priced home-made food (not Mon, Tues) including blackboard specials, efficient helpful service, ales such as Black Sheep, John Smiths, Tetleys and Theakstons, bar area and restaurant; quiz last Sun of month; tables outside, open all day Fri-Sun, closed lunchtimes Mon and Tues. *(Dan and Belinda Smallbone)*

WORTLEY SK3099
Wortley Arms (0114) 288 8749
A629 N of Sheffield; S35 7DB 18th-c stone-built coaching adjacent to the church; several comfortably furnished rooms; beams, panelling and large inglenook, enjoyable food (all day Sat) including decent vegetarian options, three well kept ales and good range of gins; occasional live music and quiz nights; children welcome, and dogs in bar, nice village about ten minutes from M1, open all day (till 8pm Sun). *(Laura Reid)*

YORK SE6051
Black Swan (01904) 679131
Peaseholme Green (inner ring road); YO1 7PR Striking black and white Tudor building; compact panelled front bar, central hall with crooked floor and fine period staircase, vast inglenook in black-beamed back bar, good choice of real ales, decent wines and generous helpings of reasonably priced pubby food from sandwiches up; background music, Thurs folk club; children welcome, useful car park behind,

bedrooms, open all day, no food weekend evenings. *(Mike and Sarah Abbot, Lionel Smith)*

YORK SE6051
★ Blue Bell (01904) 654904
Fossgate; YO1 9TF Delightfully old-fashioned little Edwardian pub, very friendly and chatty, with well kept Bradfield Farmers Blonde, Rudgate Ruby Mild, Timothy Taylors Landlord and guests, some snacky food including good pork pies, tiny tiled-floor front bar with roaring fire, panelled ceiling and stained glass, corridor to small hatch-served back room, lamps and candles, pub games; soft background music; no children, dogs welcome, open all day (but maybe just for locals on busy nights due to its size). *(Peter and Anne Hollindale)*

YORK SE5951
★ Brigantes (01904) 675355
Micklegate; YO1 6JX Bar-bistro (Market Town Tavern) with shop-style frontage; wooden tables and chairs on bare boards, blue-painted half-panelling and screens forming booths, ten well kept mainly local ales (York Brewery is in street behind), plenty of bottled beers, decent wines and coffee, good food from fairly priced varied menu, cheerful service, upstairs function room; children and dogs welcome, open (and food) all day. *(Barry Collett)*

YORK SE6051
Golden Ball (01904) 652211
Cromwell Road/Victor Street; YO1 6DU Friendly co-operative-owned Edwardian corner pub with four well preserved rooms; up to seven well kept ales, no food apart from bar snacks, bar billiards, cards and dominoes; Sun folk night and other live music, quiz Tues, TV; lovely small walled garden, open all day weekends, closed weekday lunchtimes. *(Lionel Smith)*

YORK SE6051
Golden Fleece (01904) 625171
Pavement; YO1 9UP Popular little city-centre pub with four well kept ales including Theakstons Old Peculier and enjoyable good value pubby food; long corridor from bar to comfortable back dining room (sloping floors – it dates from 1503), interesting décor and lots of ghost stories; background music and occasional folk evenings, sports TV; children allowed if eating, no dogs, four bedrooms (two with four-posters), open all day. *(Lionel Smith)*

YORK SE6052
Guy Fawkes (01904) 623716
High Petergate; YO1 7HP Splendid spot next to the Minster (claims to be the birthplace of Guy Fawkes); dark panelled

---

Real ale to us means beer that has matured naturally in its cask – not pressurised or filtered. We name all real ales stocked.

interior with small bar to the left, larger room to the right with roaring fire and atmospheric back restaurant lit by candles and gas wall-lights, half a dozen real ales such as Black Sheep, Copper Dragon, Timothy Taylors and York, enjoyable food from pub favourites up including weekday set menu (till 6pm), good helpful service; courtyard tables, 13 bedrooms, open (and food) all day; changing hands as we went to press so could be changes. *(Peter Smith and Judith Brown, Michael Butler)*

YORK   SE6052
House of Trembling Madness   (01904) 640009
Stonegate; YO1 8AS Unusual place above own off-licence; impressive high-raftered medieval room with collection of stuffed animal heads from moles to lions, eclectic mix of furniture including cask seats and pews on bare boards, lovely old brick fireplace, cask and craft beers from pulpit servery, also huge selection of bottled beers (all available to buy downstairs), good knowledgeable staff, reasonably priced hearty food including various platters; two self-catering apartments in ancient courtyard behind, open (and food) all day. *(Lionel Smith)*

YORK   SE6052
Lamb & Lion   (01904) 612078
High Petergate; YO1 7EH Appealing Georgian inn next to Bootham Bar; five well kept local ales and nice wines by the glass, good food from sandwiches and pub favourites to more restaurant choices, friendly helpful staff, bare-boards bar and series of compact rooms off narrow corridors; steep steps up to attractive paved garden below city wall and looking up to the Minster, bedrooms, open all day. *(Nick T)*

YORK   SE6051
Phoenix   (01904) 656401
George Street; YO1 9PT Friendly little pub next to the city walls; proper front public bar and comfortable back horseshoe-shaped lounge, five well kept ales from yorkshire brewers, decent wines and simple food; live jazz Mon, Weds, Fri and Sun, bar billiards; beer garden, handy for Barbican, open all day. *(Lionel Smith)*

YORK   SE6051
Pivni   (01904) 635464
Patrick Pool; YO1 8BB Old black and white pub close to the Shambles with small narrow bar; extensive range of foreign draught and bottled beers (some unusual choices), also good selection of local ales, friendly knowledgeable staff, some snacky food and good coffee, more seats upstairs; Mon quiz, juke box and occasional live music; dogs welcome, open all day. *(Alan and Alice Morgan)*

YORK   SE6051
Punch Bowl   (01904) 655147
Stonegate; YO1 8AN Bustling 17th-c black and white-fronted pub with good choice of well kept ales, decent wines and sensibly priced Nicholsons menu, efficient friendly service, small panelled rooms off corridor, dining room at back with fireplace; background music; a couple of tables out by pavement, open (and food) all day. *(Alan and Alice Morgan)*

YORK   SE6052
Snickleway   (01904) 656138
Goodramgate; YO1 7LS Interesting little open-plan pub behind big shopfront window; lots of antiques, copper and brass, cosy fires, six well kept ales, some lunchtime food (not Sun) including good sandwiches, friendly service, stories of various ghosts including Mrs Tulliver and her cat; live music; open all day. *(Nick T)*

YORK   SE6052
Star Inn the City   (01904) 619208
Museum Street; YO1 7DR Restaurary place (sister to the Star at Harome) in wonderful central riverside setting – a former 19th-c pumping station with modern glass extension; good but not cheap food, beers including a house ale (Two Chefs) from Great Yorkshire and Pilsner Urquell dispensed from two large copper tanks, good range of wines by the glass and cocktails, afternoon teas, friendly service; open all day from 9.30am for breakfast. *(Lionel Smith)*

YORK   SE6051
Swan   (01904) 634968
Bishopgate Street, Clementhorpe; YO23 1JH Unspoilt 1930s pub (Grade II listed) near the city walls; two small rooms either side of lobby bar, several changing ales and ciders, friendly knowledgeable staff; pleasant walled garden, open all day Fri-Sun, from 4pm Mon-Wed, 3pm Thurs. *(Mike Benton)*

YORK   SE6052
Three Legged Mare   (01904) 638246
High Petergate, close to the Minster; YO1 7EN Compact drinkers' pub (aka the Wonkey Donkey) with well kept York Brewery ales, several guest beers (including craft) and some 20 boxed ciders, friendly helpful staff, no food; regular live music including folk and open mike nights, Mon quiz, board games; children (till 7pm) and dogs welcome, disabled loo (others down spiral stairs), back terrace, open all day till midnight (11pm Sun). *(Lionel Smith)*

YORK   SE6051
Walmgate Ale House
(01904) 629222 *Walmgate; YO1 9TX* 17th-c city-centre pub on three levels; ground-floor bar with half a dozen yorkshire

ales and good range of wines, snacks including sausage rolls and local cheeses, upstairs bistro with wide choice of enjoyable food including set menu choices and weekend brunch (from 9.30am), further loft dining area, good friendly service; children welcome, closed Mon, Tues lunchtime otherwise open (and food) all day. *(Martin Cooke)*

YORK   SE5951

Whippet (01904) 500660

Opposite Park Inn Hotel, North Street; YO1 6JD In street set back from the river; good popular food including signature dry-aged steaks, small bar area with four well kept ales from yorkshire brewers, lots of wines by the glass, interesting cocktails and excellent range of gins, friendly well informed staff; no children, open all day. *(Nick T)*

YORK   SE5951

York Tap (01904) 659009

Station, Station Road; YO24 1AB Restored Edwardian bar at York station; high ceiling with feature stained-glass cupolas, columns and iron fretwork, bentwood chairs and stools on terrazzo floor, button-back banquettes, period fireplaces, great selection of real ales from circular counter with brass footrail, also bottled beers listed on blackboard, good pork pies; seats out by platform, open all day. *(Phil Lewis)*

London

 CENTRAL LONDON   Map 13

Admiral Codrington 🍷

(020) 7581 0005 – www.theadmiralcodrington.co.uk

Mossop Street; South Kensington tube; SW3 2LY

Long-standing Chelsea landmark with easy-going bar and pretty restaurant, popular food and seats outside

Tucked away down a small street in Chelsea, this is a well run, bustling place with a civilised but informal atmosphere. A central dark-panelled bar has high red chairs beside the counter with more around equally high tables on either side of the log-effect gas fire, button-back wall banquettes with cream and red patterned seats, little stools and plain wooden chairs around a medley of tables on black-painted floorboards, patterned wallpaper above a dado and a shelf with daily papers. There are ornate flower arrangements, a big portrait above the fire, several naval prints and quiet background music. Helpful staff serve Bombardier, Shepherd Neame Whitstable Bay and a guest ale on handpump, good wines by the glass and a thoughtful range of spirits. The light and airy restaurant area is a total contrast: high-backed pretty wall seats and plush dining chairs around light tables, an open kitchen, fish prints on pale blue paintwork, a second fireplace and an impressive skylight. A back garden is provided with chunky benches and tables under a summer awning.

🍴 Enjoyable food includes tuna tartare with avocado, chilli, sesame and coriander, ham hock terrine with wholegrain mustard and piccalilli, sharing boards, potato gnocchi with wild herb pesto and cheese, hot and spicy chicken burger with asian slaw, sour cream and skinny fries, lamb rump with minted yoghurt, spring onion peas, fish casserole with aioli, rump steak with skin-on fries and bloody mary butter, and puddings such as affogato and sticky toffee pudding with vanilla ice-cream. *Benchmark main dish: beer-battered fish and chips £15.50. Two-course evening meal £25.00.*

Free house ~ Licensee Raphael Nebot ~ Real ale ~ Open 11.30-11; 11.30am-1am Fri, Sat; 12-10.30 Sun ~ Bar food 12-10; 12-9 Sun ~ Restaurant ~ Children welcome ~ Dogs allowed in bar ~ Wi-fi *Recommended by Alister and Margery Bacon, Ian Duncan, Dr and Mrs A K Clarke, David Jackman, Chloe and Michael Swettenham, Sabina and Gerald Grimshaw*

CENTRAL LONDON

Map 13

Alfred Tennyson 🎯 ⭐ 🍷

(020) 7730 6074 – www.thealfredtennyson.co.uk

Motcomb Street; Knightsbridge tube; SW1X 8LA

Bustling and civilised with good drinks choice, rewarding food and friendly, helpful service

There's plenty of space over the four floors here, for both drinking and dining. There are high stools around equally high shelf tables for chatting, cushioned wooden settles around dark tables on parquet flooring for dining and eclectic décor that encompasses Edward Lear illustrations and antique books on windowsills. Stools line the counter where friendly, helpful staff serve Hammerton N1 and Sharps Doom Bar on handpump, 20 malt whiskies, cocktails and 32 wines by the glass. The upstairs restaurant has plush upholstered chairs and wooden tables on more parquet, large house plants and a huge mirror above an open fire. Above that is a loft room that's used for drinks parties. Outside on the front pavement are tables and chairs beneath a striped awning; there's disabled access to the bar but no disabled loos.

 As well as breakfasts (from 8am weekdays, 9am weekends), the enjoyable food includes cured trout with baby beetroots, crème fraîche and elderflower, beef tartare with mustard mayonnaise, stuffed courgette flowers with aubergine and tomato ragoût and thyme dressing, beef and Guinness pie, salt marsh lamb with nettle gnocchi, goats curd, onion relish and almonds, sea bream with white beans, spinach and crayfish dressing, roast chicken with peas, baby gem, mushrooms and baby onions, and puddings such as bramley apple pie with pecans, salted caramel and vanilla ice-cream and dark chocolate pannacotta with malt and barley ice-cream and puffed rice; they also offer a two- and three-course set menu. *Benchmark main dish: beer-battered cod and chips £16.00. Two-course evening meal £25.00.*

Cubitt House ~ Manager Tony Gualtieri ~ Real ale ~ Open 8am-11pm; 9am-11.30pm Fri, Sat; 9am-10.30pm Sun ~ Bar food 8am-10pm Mon-Thurs; 9am-10.30pm Fri, Sat; 9am-9.30am Sun ~ Children welcome ~ Dogs allowed in bar ~ Wi-fi *Recommended by Sam Cole, Stuart and Natalie Granville, Elisabeth and Bill Humphries, Jill and Dick Archer, Ian Herdman, Bridget and Peter Gregson*

CENTRAL LONDON

Map 13

Black Friar 🍺

(020) 7236 5474 – www.nicholsonspubs.co.uk

Queen Victoria Street; Mansion House or Temple tube, Blackfriars rail; EC4V 4EG

Remarkable art nouveau décor, a fine choice of ales, friendly atmosphere and popular all-day food

This is a very special architectural gem that includes some of the best Edwardian bronze and marble art nouveau work to be found anywhere. The inner back room has big bas-relief friezes of jolly monks set into richly coloured florentine marble walls, an opulent marble-pillared inglenook fireplace, a low vaulted mosaic ceiling, gleaming mirrors, seats built into rich golden marble recesses and tongue-in-cheek verbal embellishments such as Silence is Golden and Finery is Foolish. The other large room has a fireplace and plenty of seats and tables. Staff are helpful, efficient and friendly (despite the crowds) and serve a fantastic range of around ten real ales including their core three – Fullers London Pride, Nicholsons Pale Ale (named for the pub from St Austell) and Sharps Doom Bar – on handpump with seven guests from breweries such as Purity, Roosters, Sambrooks, Thornbridge, Titanic and so forth, and several wines by the glass. Background music. In warmer weather, people spill out on to the expansive forecourt, near the approach to Blackfriars Bridge.

🍴 Well thought-of food includes breakfasts and sandwiches plus a cured meat and cheese platter, roasted red pepper tarte tatin with balsamic sherry dressing, smoked haddock and kedgeree fishcakes with lemon aioli, macaroni cheese, burger with toppings, barbecue salsa and skin-on chips, toad in the hole with balsamic onion gravy, chicken topped with smoked back bacon, cheese and barbecue sauce, 10oz rib-eye steak with garlic butter, onion rings and chips, and puddings such as chocolate brownie with vanilla ice-cream and sticky toffee pudding with custard. *Benchmark main dish: pie of the day £13.50. Two-course evening meal £20.00.*

Nicholsons ~ Manager John McKeone ~ Real ale ~ Open 10am-11pm; 9am-11pm Sat; 12-10.30 Sun ~ Bar food 10-10; 9am-10pm Sat; 12-9.30 Sun ~ Children welcome ~ Dogs allowed in bar ~ Wi-fi *Recommended by Darrell Barton, Diana and Bertie Farr, Philip J Alderton, Cliff and Monica Swan, Alan and Linda Blackmore, Tony Scott, Edward May*

CENTRAL LONDON   Map 13

Coach Makers Arms 🍽️⭐ 🍷

(020) 7224 4022 – www.thecoachmakersarms.co.uk
Marylebone Lane; Bond Street tube; W1U 2PY

Restored three-level pub in Marylebone with plenty of room for both eating and drinking, imaginative food and a thoughtful choice of wines and spirits

This carefully restored pub covers several floors, but it's the bustling ground-floor bar that is the heart of the place. This has button-back banquette wall seats, high chairs around equally high tables, striking ceiling lights and friendly staff who serve Hammerton N1 and Sharps Doom Bar on handpump, over 30 wines by the glass and 20 malt whiskies; background music and TV. In the basement, the cosy cocktail bar has beams and panelled walls, red or green plush seats and wall banquettes by simple tables, some modern art and drinks that include a seasonally changing cocktail menu. On the first floor is the bright and airy dining room with a restful atmosphere, leather or elegant wooden chairs around a medley of tables on dark floorboards, oil portraits and old photographs on the walls and stained-glass windows overlooking the Marylebone streets below. There is disabled access to the bar but not to the loos.

⭐ Particularly good food includes mackerel with avocado, gooseberry relish and oyster mayonnaise, pork croquette with green apple sauce, stuffed courgette flower with summer squash, pistachios and pickled cherries, dry-aged burger with smoked cheddar and fries, hake with white beans, fennel, spinach and lemon pickle, chicken kiev with jersey royals, broad beans, garlic and thyme jus, spiced lamb rump with aubergine and tomato ragoût, feta and thyme jus, and puddings such as dark chocolate and salted caramel tart with malt and barley ice-cream and pineapple carpaccio with buttermilk pudding and mint meringue; they also offer two- and three-course set menus. *Benchmark main dish: pie of the day £15.00. Two-course evening meal £26.00.*

Cubitt House ~ Manager Tony Gualtieri ~ Real ale ~ Open 10am-11pm; 10am-midnight Fri, Sat; 10am-10.30pm Sun ~ Bar food 12-10; 12-10.30 Fri, Sat; 12-9.30 Sun ~ Restaurant ~ Children welcome ~ Dogs allowed in bar ~ Wi-fi *Recommended by Georgia Egner, Lucy Spencer-Davidson, Lucia Halliwell, Elizabeth and Giles Hancock, Liz and Martin Eldon, Jeremy Snaithe*

We say if we know a pub has background music.

CENTRAL LONDON

Cross Keys ♀

Map 12

(020) 7351 0686 – www.thecrosskeyschelsea.co.uk

Lawrence Street; Sloane Square tube (some distance away); SW3 5NB

Popular pub with a friendly bar, airy back restaurant, real ales and modern bar food

There's always a chatty crowd filling this gently civilised pub, for both the up-to-date food and good choice of drinks. The central counter has bar areas to each side with simple furnishings: distressed panelled walls, some exposed brickwork, a couple of open fires, framed tobacco postcards and display cases of butterflies, mirrors, tankards on a rack, industrial-style ceiling lights, and a mix of cushioned wooden dining chairs and wheelbacks around scrubbed tables on bare boards and stools against the counter. Here, friendly staff serve Brakspears Bitter, Sambrooks Junction Ale and Trumans Zephyr on handpump, eight wines by the glass and 18 whiskies; background music. At the back, the airy conservatory-style dining room has button-back wall seating and similar chairs and tables.

 Rewarding food includes crispy lamb shoulder with chilli jam and stilton and watercress salad, seared tuna with watermelon, feta, wasabi, avocado purée and pickled cucumber, tagliatelle with morels, asparagus, shallot cream and poached egg, rare-breed burger with toppings and chips, hake with seaweed and ricotta dumplings, braised leeks and garlic velouté, duck breast with confit leg pastilla, fondant potato, savoy cabbage and chicory, halibut with braised baby gem, peas, pancetta and brown shrimps, and puddings such as spiced carrot cake with blood orange sorbet and peanut and chocolate stack with praline foam and vanilla ice-cream. *Benchmark main dish: chicken breast with wild mushrooms and pancetta £18.00. Two-course evening meal £25.00.*

Free house ~ Licensee James Hardesly ~ Real ale ~ Open 12-11; 12-midnight Fri, Sat; 12-10.30 Sun ~ Bar food 12-3, 6-10; 12-4, 6-10 Sat; 12-9 Sun ~ Restaurant ~ Children welcome but must leave bar area by 7pm ~ Dogs welcome ~ Wi-fi *Recommended by Dan and Belinda Smallbone, Sandra and Miles Spencer, James and Sylvia Hewitt, Sarah Kennewell, Shalaine Duffy*

CENTRAL LONDON

Grazing Goat ✪ ♀ ⇐

Map 13

(020) 7724 7243 – www.thegrazinggoat.co.uk

New Quebec Street; Marble Arch tube; W1H 7RQ

A good mixed crowd of customers, restful décor, a thoughtful choice of drinks and good interesting food; bedrooms

If you want to escape the hustle and bustle of Oxford Street and Marble Arch, head for this stylish place. The bar has a big gilt-edged mirror above an open fire and plenty of spreading dining space with white cushioned and beige dining chairs around pale tables on bare boards, sage green or oak-panelled walls, ceiling lamps and lanterns and some goat memorabilia dotted about. Efficient, friendly staff serve Hammerton N1 and Sharps Doom Bar on handpump, over 30 wines by the glass, 17 malt whiskies and cocktails. The upstairs restaurant is more formal with wood-panelled walls and large sash windows. Glass doors open on to the street where there are a few wooden-slatted chairs and tables. The eight bedrooms are modern and well equipped, with good bathrooms. Disabled access to the bar but not to the loos.

As well as breakfasts (from 7.30am), the interesting food includes lamb croquette with mint sauce, mussels in Guinness sauce, white asparagus with stuffed artichoke, smoked almond crumble and nasturtiums, beer-battered cod and chips, roast chicken with purple sprouting broccoli, wild garlic and hazelnuts, slow-cooked venison shoulder with peppered loin, carrots and goats curd, dry-aged sirloin steak with green peppercorn sauce and fries, and puddings such as dark chocolate and salted caramel tart with malt and barley ice-cream and carrot cake with whipped cream cheese and pineapple sorbet; they also offer a two- and three-course set menu. *Benchmark main dish: beer-battered cod and chips £16.00. Two-course evening meal £26.00.*

Cubitt House ~ Lease Tony Gualtieri ~ Real ale ~ Open 7.30am-11pm; 7.30am-11pm Sat; 7.30am-10.30pm Sun ~ Bar food 7.30am-10pm; 7.30am-10.30pm Fri, Sat; 7.30am-9.30pm Sun ~ Restaurant ~ Children welcome ~ Dogs allowed in bar ~ Wi-fi ~ Bedrooms: /£210
Recommended by Heather and Richard Jones, Dr and Mrs A K Clarke, Andrew Lawson, Victoria and James Sargeant, Peter Pilbeam, Harvey Brown

CENTRAL LONDON   Map 13

Harp

(020) 7836 0291 ~ www.harpcoventgarden.com
47 Chandos Place; Leicester Square tube, Charing Cross tube/rail; WC2N 4HS

Ten real ales and lots of ciders and perries in bustling narrow pub

This busy little local is a gem – and a favourite with so many. The main draw, of course, is the choice of ten particularly well kept real ales on handpump: these change quickly but always include Harveys Best, Dark Star American Pale Ale and Hophead and Fullers London Pride, with guests sourced from all over the country. Also, around six farm ciders, a perry and quite a few malt whiskies. The pub pretty much consists of one long narrow, very traditional bar, with lots of high bar stools along the wall counter and around elbow tables, big mirrors on the red walls, some lovely stained glass and loads of interesting, quirkily executed celebrity portraits. If you're lucky, you may be able to snare one of the prized seats by the front windows. A little room upstairs is much quieter, with comfortable furniture and a window overlooking the road below. At any time of day, the pub is always packed; at peak times, customers are happy to spill out on to the pavement or the back alley. The hanging baskets are wonderful in summer.

 Food – served at lunchtime only – consists of sandwiches, sausage rolls and pork pies. *Benchmark main dish: sausages £4.50.*

Free house ~ Licensee Paul Sims ~ Real ale ~ Open 10.30am-11.30pm; 10.30am-midnight Fri, Sat; 12-10.30 Sun ~ Bar food 12-2 ~ Wi-fi *Recommended by Miles Green, Nigel and Jean Eames, Charlotte Smyrk, Lucia Halliwell, Revd R P Tickle*

CENTRAL LONDON   Map 13

Lamb & Flag £

(020) 7497 9504 ~ www.lambandflagcoventgarden.co.uk
Rose Street, off Garrick Street; Covent Garden or Leicester Square tube; WC2E 9EB

Historic yet unpretentious, full of character and atmosphere, with six real ales and pubby food

Thankfully, nothing changes at this characterful old tavern, which is always packed out. The more spartan front room leads into a cosy, atmospheric, low-ceilinged back bar with high-backed black settles and an open fire. Fullers ESB, London Pride, Olivers Island and Seafarers plus guests such as Anstey Ale Daydreamer, Dark Star Hophead and St Austell Tribute on handpump, as well as 12 wines by the glass and 12 malt whiskies. The upstairs Dryden Room is often less crowded and has more seats (though fewer beers). There's a lively and well documented history: poet John Dryden was nearly beaten to death by hired thugs outside, and Charles

Dickens made fun of the Middle Temple lawyers who frequented it when he was working in nearby Catherine Street.

 Popular food includes nibbles such as salt and pepper squid with smoked paprika aioli, truffled mac and cheese croquettes and meatballs in spicy tomato sauce, lamb and pine nut kofta with tzatziki, spiced green lentil curry with cauliflower, spinach and wild rice, pork, ale and wholegrain mustard sausages with mash and onion gravy, chicken and bacon caesar salad with anchovies, garlic croutons and parmesan, steak in ale pie, tea and hop-smoked haddock and salmon fishcakes with sauce gribiche, steak in ale pie, rump steak with béarnaise sauce and chips, and puddings. *Benchmark main dish: beer-battered fish and chips £14.00. Two-course evening meal £19.00.*

Fullers ~ Manager Patrick Linn ~ Real ale ~ Open 11-11; 12-10.30 Sun ~ Bar food 12-10; 12-9 Sun ~ Restaurant ~ Children in upstairs dining room only ~ Dogs allowed in bar ~ Wi-fi
Recommended by Max Simons, Peter Brix, Philip J Alderton, Georgia Egner, Lyn and Freddie Roberts, Martin Holvey, Richard and Penny Gibbs

CENTRAL LONDON   Map 13

Old Bank of England ♀ ◖

(020) 7430 2255 – www.oldbankofengland.co.uk
Fleet Street; Chancery Lane or Temple tube, Blackfriars tube/rail; EC4A 2LT

Dramatically converted former bank building, with gleaming chandeliers in impressive soaring bar, well kept beers and tasty food

Once a subsidiary branch of the Bank of England, this has a quite astounding interior. It's a Grade I-listed Italianate building and the splendid spacious bar has three gleaming chandeliers hanging from an exquisitely plastered ceiling that soars above an unusually tall island bar counter crowned with a clock. The end wall has huge paintings and murals that look like 18th-c depictions of Justice, but, in fact, feature members of the Fuller, Smith and Turner families, who set up the famous London brewery. There are well polished dark wooden furnishings, luxurious curtains swagging massive windows, plenty of framed prints and, despite the grandeur, some surprisingly cosy corners, with screens between tables creating an unexpectedly intimate feel. The quieter galleried section upstairs offers a bird's-eye view of the action; some smaller rooms (used mainly for functions) open off. McMullen AK, Country Bitter and IPA on handpump alongside Rivertown, a good choice of malt whiskies and a dozen wines by the glass. At lunchtime, the background music is generally classical or easy listening; it's louder and livelier in the evenings. There's also a garden with seats (one of the few pubs in the area to have one).

 Pies have a long if rather dubious pedigree in this area: it was in the vaults and tunnels below the Old Bank and the surrounding buildings that Sweeney Todd butchered the clients destined to provide the fillings at his mistress Mrs Lovett's nearby pie shop. The popular food here does indeed include pies, and also sandwiches, cauliflower and red pepper curry, rare-breed sausages and mash with caramelised onion and red wine gravy, honey-roast ham and free-range eggs, burger with toppings and triple-cooked chips, chicken topped with smoked bacon, cheese and barbecue sauce, beer-battered cod and chips, and puddings such as chocolate brownie with hot chocolate sauce and apple and cinnamon crumble with custard. *Benchmark main dish: pie of the day £14.25. Two-course evening meal £18.00.*

McMullens ~ Manager Stuart Elseui ~ Real ale ~ Open 11-11; 12-9 Sat; closed Sun ~ Bar food 12-10; 12-8 Sat ~ Children welcome ~ Dogs allowed in bar ~ Wi-fi *Recommended by Nik and Gloria Clarke, Philip J Alderton, Louise and Anton Parsons, Kerry and Guy Trooper, Tony Scott, Charles and Cynthia Todd, Julie Braeburn*

CENTRAL LONDON

Map 13

Olde Mitre ▦ £

(020) 7405 4751 – www.yeoldemitreholborn.co.uk

Ely Place; the easiest way to find it is from the narrow passageway beside 8 Hatton Garden; Chancery Lane tube, Farringdon tube/rail; EC1N 6SJ

Unspoilt old pub with a lovely atmosphere, unusual guest beers and bargain toasted sandwiches

There's been some sort of tavern here since 1546, although the current building dates from 1782. Quite unspoilt and tucked away, it's a real refuge from the modern city nearby. The cosy small rooms have lots of dark panelling as well as antique settles and (particularly in the popular back room where there are more seats) old local pictures and so forth. It gets good-naturedly packed with the City suited-and-booted between 12.30pm and 2.15pm, filling up again in the early evening, but in the early afternoons and by around 8pm it's a good deal more tranquil. An upstairs room, mainly used for functions, may double as an overflow area at peak periods. Fullers London Pride, Olivers Island and Seafarers with regular guests such as Adnams Broadside and Caledonian Deuchars IPA on handpump plus another couple of guests; they hold three beer festivals a year; eight farm ciders and several wines by the glass. No music, TV or machines – the only games here are cribbage and dominoes. There's some space for outside drinking by the pot plants and jasmine in the narrow yard between the pub and St Etheldreda's church (which is worth a look). Note the pub doesn't open on weekends or bank holidays. The best approach is from Hatton Garden, walking up the right-hand side away from Chancery Lane; an easily missed sign on a lamp-post points the way down a narrow alley. No children.

 Bar snacks, served all day, are limited to scotch eggs, pork pies, sausage rolls and really good value toasties.

Fullers ~ Manager Judith Norman ~ Real ale ~ Open 11-11; closed weekends and bank holidays ~ Bar food 11-10 ~ Wi-fi *Recommended by Margaret McDonald, Adam Jones, Max and Steph Warren, Alison and Michael Harper, Tony Scott, Patricia and Anton Larkham, Beth Aldridge*

CENTRAL LONDON

Map 13

Orange ⭐ ♟ 🛏

(020) 7881 9844 – www.theorange.co.uk

Pimlico Road; Sloane Square tube; SW1W 8NE

Carefully restored pub with simply decorated rooms, thoughtful choice of drinks and up-to-date food; bedrooms

This restored Georgian inn is a comfortable place to stay in well equipped bedrooms – and the breakfasts are first class. At the heart of the place is the ground-floor bar with a lively, chatty and easy-going atmosphere. There are high ceilings, wooden dining chairs around pale tables on bare boards, an open fire at one end and a big carved counter where friendly staff keep Hammerton N1 and Sharps Doom Bar on handpump, over 30 wines by the glass, 17 malt whiskies, a cocktail list and home-made syrups. The dining room to the right, usually packed with cheerful customers, is decorated with prints, glass bottles and soda siphons, big house plants and a few rustic knick-knacks. Upstairs, the linked restaurant rooms are similarly furnished with old french travel posters and circus prints on cream walls, more open fireplaces, big glass ceiling lights, chandeliers and quiet background music. There's disabled access to the bar but not to the loos.

As well as breakfast (from 8am), the good, modern food includes whisky-cured beef with artichokes, watercress mayonnaise and pecorino, charred mackerel with cucumber, fennel and lemon pickle, celeriac, mushroom, spinach and pine nut wellington with truffle dressing, wood-fired pizzas, monkfish with candied aubergine, sea herbs and gooseberry relish, peppered loin and slow-cooked shoulder of venison with nettle gnocchi and dried plum jus, grass-fed rib-eye steak with green peppercorn sauce, and puddings; they also offer two- and three-course set menus. *Benchmark main dish: hake with slow-roasted tomatoes and pea and clam sauce £19.50. Two-course evening meal £28.00.*

Cubitt House ~ Manager Tony Gualtieri ~ Real ale ~ Open 8am-11pm; 8am-midnight Fri, Sat; 8am-10.30pm Sun ~ Bar food 8am-10pm; 8am-10.30pm Fri, Sat; 8am-9.30pm Sun ~ Restaurant ~ Children welcome ~ Dogs allowed in bar ~ Wi-fi ~ Bedrooms: /£205
Recommended by Daisy Rutledge, Megan and Hallam Cunningham, R Gollin, Nicola and Stuart Parsons, Peter and Alison Steadman, Mark and Mary Setting

CENTRAL LONDON
Punchbowl ♀

Map 13

(020) 7493 6841 – www.punchbowllondon.com
Farm Street; Green Park tube; W1J 5RP

Bustling, rather civilised pub with good wines and ales, enjoyable food and helpful service

Perhaps the nicest part of this lively, tucked-away pub is at the back where several panelled booths have suede bench seating, animal-picture scatter cushions, some etched glasswork and oil lights on tables. Elegant spoked chairs are grouped around dark tables on worn floorboards, a couple of long elbow shelves are lined with high chairs and one fireplace has a coal fire while the other is piled with logs. At the front it's simpler, with cushioned bench seating and pubby tables and chairs on floor tiles. All sorts of artwork from cartoons to oil paintings line the walls and the ceiling has interesting old hand-drawn street maps; background music. Caledonian Deuchars IPA, a beer named for the pub (also from Caledonian) and Marstons 61 Deep on handpump, good wines by the glass and professional, friendly service. The smart dining room upstairs has plush furnishings, large artworks and a huge gilt mirror above a fireplace; there are private dining facilities too.

Rewarding food includes lunchtime sandwiches, hot smoked salmon with shaved cucumber, jersey royals and horseradish crème fraîche, smoked chicken terrine with broad beans and pickled walnuts, sharing platters, slow-roasted aubergines on quinoa with chermoula sauce, pomegranate and radish salad and lime dressing, cumberland sausages with mash and caramelised onion and thyme gravy, crab linguine with spring onion, coriander and soy broth, salt marsh lamb rump with belly croquette and pea and mint purée, and puddings such as chocolate brownie with banana ice-cream and pear and elderberry crumble with custard. *Benchmark main dish: beer-battered fish and chips £16.00. Two-course evening meal £25.00.*

Free house ~ Licensee Andres Cabrera ~ Real ale ~ Open 11.30-11; 11.30-10 Sun ~ Bar food 12-10; 12-10.30 Fri, Sat; 12-9 Sun ~ Restaurant ~ Children welcome if seated and dining ~ Dogs allowed in bar ~ Wi-fi *Recommended by Maggie and Stevan Hollis, Samuel and Melissa Turnbull, Isobel Mackinlay, Belinda Stamp, Dr and Mrs A K Clarke*

CENTRAL LONDON
Seven Stars 🍺

Map 13

(020) 7242 8521 – www.thesevenstars1602.co.uk

Carey Street; Temple, Chancery Lane or Holborn tube; WC2A 2JB

Fine pub dating from 1602 with cheerful staff, an interesting mix of customers and a good choice of drinks and food

A favourite haunt of lawyers, Church of England music directors and choir singers, this Grade II-listed pub faces the back of the law courts. Numerous caricatures of barristers and judges line the red-painted walls of the two main rooms and there are posters of legal-themed british films, big ceiling fans and checked tablecloths that add a quirky, almost continental touch. A third area, in what was formerly a legal wig shop next door, still retains its original frontage, with a neat display of wigs in the window. It's worth arriving early as they don't take bookings and tables get snapped up quickly. Adnams Ghost Ship, Black Sheep, Harveys Best, Sambrooks Wandle Ale, Sharps Doom Bar and Whitstable Native Bitter on handpump and six wines by the glass (they import wine from France); they do a particularly good dry martini. On busy evenings, customers overflow on to the quiet road in front; things generally quieten down after 8pm and there can be a nice, sleepy atmosphere some afternoons. The steep Elizabethan stairs up to the loos are covered with English Heritage-approved wrought oak and have two brass handrails. The pub cat wears a ruff. No children.

 Cooked according to the landlady's fancy, the good, interesting food includes chicken liver pâté, black bean and sweetcorn soup, rabbit and chicken pie, merguez sausages with pilau rice, chicken croquettes with mint and tarragon, spiced lamb filo parcels and linguine with prawns and squid or cream and parmesan. *Benchmark main dish: pork and porcini meatballs in broth £11.50. Two-course evening meal £20.00.*

Free house ~ Licensee Roxy Beaujolais ~ Real ale ~ Open 11-11; 12-11 Sat; 12-10 Sun ~ Bar food 12-9.30; 1-9 weekends ~ Wi-fi *Recommended by Philip J Alderton, Elise and Charles Mackinlay, Lucia Halliwell, Angela and Martin Kendall*

CENTRAL LONDON
Star 🍺

Map 13

(020) 7235 3019 – www.star-tavern-belgravia.co.uk

Belgrave Mews West, behind the German Embassy, off Belgrave Square; Hyde Park Corner or Knightsbridge tube; SW1X 8HT

Busy local with restful bar, upstairs dining room, Fullers ales, well liked bar food and colourful hanging baskets

Outside peak times, there's a peaceful, local feel to this hidden-away pub in its cobbled mews. The small bar is pleasant, with sash windows, a wooden floor, stools by the counter, an open winter fire and Fullers ESB, London Pride and Olivers Island plus a couple of guest beers on handpump, nine wines by the glass and a few malt whiskies. An arch leads to the main seating area with well polished tables and chairs and good lighting; there's also an upstairs dining room. In summer, the front of the building is covered with an astonishing array of hanging baskets and flowering tubs. It's said that this is where the Great Train Robbery was planned.

Popular food includes nibbles such as sandwiches, pork pie and piccalilli, harissa prawn skewers, black pudding scotch egg, sharing platters, butternut squash and feta cheese wellington, burger with toppings and chips, a pie of the day, sirloin steak with peppercorn sauce and triple-cooked chips, and puddings such as rice pudding with fruit compote and apple pie with crème anglaise. *Benchmark main dish: beer-battered fish and chips £13.50. Two-course evening meal £20.00.*

Fullers ~ Manager Ollie Coulombeau ~ Real ale ~ Open 11-11; 12-11 Sat; 12-10.30 Sun ~ Bar food 12-3, 5-10 weekdays; 12-10 Sat; 12-4, 5-10 Sun ~ Restaurant ~ Children welcome ~ Dogs welcome ~ Wi-fi *Recommended by Phoebe Peacock, Caroline Prescott, Susan and John Douglas, Shalaine Duffy, Megan and Hallam Cunningham, Christine and Tony Garrett*

CENTRAL LONDON
Thomas Cubitt 🏵 ⛾

Map 13

(020) 7730 6060 – www.thethomascubitt.co.uk
Elizabeth Street; Sloane Square tube, Victoria tube/rail; SW1W 9PA

Belgravia pub with a civilised and friendly atmosphere and enjoyable food and drink

This is a stylish and busy place in well heeled Elizabeth Street, right at the heart of Belgravia. The ground-floor bar has miscellaneous Edwardian-style dining chairs around wooden tables on stripped parquet flooring, and architectural prints and antlers on panelled or painted walls; open fires and lovely flower arrangements. Attentive staff serve Hammerton N1 and Sharps Doom Bar on handpump, over 30 wines by the glass, 17 malt whiskies, home-made syrups and cocktails. The more formal dining room upstairs has smart upholstered wooden chairs around white-clothed tables, candles in wall holders, a few prints, house plants and window blinds; background music and TV. In warm weather, the floor-to-ceiling glass doors are pulled back to the street where there are cordoned-off tables and chairs on the pavement. Disabled access to the bar but not to the loos.

🏵 Interesting food includes stuffed courgette flower with almonds and nasturtiums, chilli salt squid with smoked chilli and lime, nettle gnocchi with peas, broad beans, baby gem and pickled lemon, rare-breed pork sausage with mash and onion gravy, roast chicken with pancetta, pea, baby gem and baby onions, trout with courgettes, pickled lemon and hazelnut gremolata, venison with jersey royals, wild garlic and jus, hake with fennel, samphire and smoked anchovy butter sauce, beef fillet with malt-glazed brisket, mushrooms and chard, and puddings such as coconut pannacotta with pineapple carpaccio and lemon sorbet and dark chocolate mousse with malt and barley ice-cream and puffed rice; they also offer a two- and three-course lunch menu. *Benchmark main dish: dry-aged burger with fries £17.00. Two-course evening meal £26.00.*

Cubitt House ~ Manager Tony Gualtieri ~ Real ale ~ Open 10am-11pm; 10am-10.30pm Sun ~ Bar food 12-10; 12-10.30 Fri, Sat; 12-9.30 Sun ~ Restaurant ~ Children welcome ~ Dogs allowed in bar ~ Wi-fi *Recommended by Barbara and Phil Bowie, Dave Braisted, Nigel and Sue Foster, Dr and Mrs A K Clarke, Charles Welch, Sophie Ellison, Katherine Matthews, Carol and Barry Craddock, Tim and Sarah Smythe-Brown*

NORTH LONDON
Holly Bush ⛾ 🍺

Map 12

(020) 7435 2892 – www.hollybushhampstead.co.uk
Holly Mount; Hampstead tube; NW3 6SG

Unique village local, with good food and drinks and lovely unspoilt feel

Originally a stable block, this place is hidden away among some of Hampstead's most villagey streets. The old-fashioned front bar has a dark sagging ceiling, brown and cream panelled walls (decorated with old advertisements and a few hanging plates), open fires, bare boards and secretive bays formed by partly glazed partitions. The slightly more intimate back room, named after the painter George Romney, has an embossed red ceiling, panelled and etched glass alcoves, and ochre-painted brick walls covered with small prints; lots of board and card games. Fullers ESB, London Pride and Olivers Island plus a guest or two such as Adnams Ghost Ship and Liberation Ale on handpump, as well as 15 malt whiskies and 14 wines by the glass from a good wine list. The upstairs dining room has table service at the weekend, as does the rest of the pub on Sundays. There are benches on the pavement outside. There's disabled access to the ground-floor rooms.

Well regarded food includes wild boar, tarragon and mustard scotch duck egg with HP sauce, garlic prawns, chorizo and paprika oil, burger with toppings and fries, mashed avocado with charred tomato, kale, slow-poached egg and feta, beer-battered haddock and chips, lamb rump with mash, peas, broad beans, lamb jus and salsa verde, griddled octopus with black olive mayonnaise, heritage tomato tartare and sweet potato fries, dry-aged fillet steak with béarnaise sauce and chips, and puddings such as Valrhona chocolate mousse with cherry parfait and sticky toffee pudding with toffee sauce and pecan ice-cream. *Benchmark main dish: pie of the day £15.00. Two-course evening meal £22.00.*

Fullers ~ Manager Mariya Ivanova ~ Real ale ~ Open 12-11; 11-11 Sat; 11.30-10.30 Sun ~ Bar food 12-3.30, 6-10; 12-4.30, 6-10; 12-8 Sun ~ Restaurant ~ Children welcome ~ Dogs welcome ~ Wi-fi *Recommended by Mark Morgan, Philip Chesington, Ben Lees, Ben and Diane Bowie, Peter Barratt, Jack and Hilary Burton*

NORTH LONDON
Lighterman ⭐🍴♟

Map 13

(020) 3846 3400 – www.thelighterman.co.uk
Granary Square, Regent's Canal; King's Cross/St Pancras tube/rail; N1C 4BH

London Dining Pub of the Year

Spacious contemporary place with up-to-date décor and furnishings, a wide range of drinks, interesting all-day food and good, fast service

Ultra-modern and stylish, this is a bar-restaurant on three floors in the redeveloped plaza behind King's Cross station with views across the fountains in Granary Square to Regent's Canal. The ground-floor terrace and the wrap-around decking on the first floor have plenty of seats, benches and tables to make the most of this vista. Floor-to-ceiling windows and big folding doors in the open-plan bars keep it all very light and airy, while the minimalist, industrial-style décor takes in contemporary chairs, wall seats and tables on wood-strip floors. High chairs line the counters where efficient, friendly staff serve 360° American Pale Ale, Five Points Pale and a guest beer on handpump, 22 wines by the glass and seasonal cocktails; background music.

Interesting, attractively presented food includes flatbreads with toppings, crayfish and crab cocktail with apple, pea shoots and bloody mary sauce, potted ham hock with pickled vegetables and melba toast, sharing boards, roast sweet potato with toasted hazelnuts, rocket and pomegranate, chicken caesar salad, herb-crusted cod fillet with vegetable broth and samphire, wood-fired grilled lamb cutlets with pickled morels, grilled spring onions and roasted garlic, yellowfin tuna steak with broad beans and pea salsa, 28-day aged grass-fed rare-breed sirloin steak with a choice of sauce, and puddings such as dark chocolate mousse with pistachios and raspberries and passion-fruit cheesecake with mixed berries. *Benchmark main dish: 45-day aged rare-breed burger with toppings and fries £16.50. Two-course evening meal £27.00.*

Open House London ~ Manager Brett Murray ~ Real ale ~ Open 9am-11.30pm; 9am-midnight, Fri, Sat; 9am-10.30pm Sun ~ Bar food 9am-10.30pm; 9am-11pm Fri, Sat; 9am-9.30 Sun ~ Restaurant ~ Children welcome ~ Dogs allowed in bar ~ Wi-fi *Recommended by Brian Glozier, Maggie and Stevan Hollis, Adam and Natalie Davis, Robert and Diana Ringstone, Trevor and Michele Street, Megan and William Stapley, Edward May*

NORTH LONDON

Map 13

Princess of Wales

(020) 7722 0354 – www.lovetheprincess.com

Fitzroy Road/Chalcot Road; Chalk Farm tube via Regents Park Road and footbridge; NW1 8LL

Friendly place with three different seating areas, enjoyable food, wide choice of drinks and funky garden

Spread over three floors, this bustling pub usefully offers some kind of food all day at weekends. The main bar, at ground level, is open-plan and light with big windows looking out to the street, wooden tables and chairs on bare boards and plenty of high chairs against the counter: Sambrooks Wandle and a beer named for the pub (also from Sambrooks) plus a changing guest ale on handpump, 16 wines by the glass, 11 malt whiskies and good cocktails. Upstairs, the smarter dining room has beige- and white-painted chairs, leather sofas and stools around wooden tables on more bare boards, big gilt-edged mirrors and chandeliers; two TVs. The Garden Room downstairs has a bar, three connected areas and access to the suntrap garden with its Bansky-style mural, framed wall mirrors and picnic-sets (some painted pink and purple) under parasols.

Pleasing food includes lunchtime sandwiches (not weekends), salt fish croquettes with tartare sauce, chicken wings with blue cheese dip, lentil burger with rhubarb chutney, pizzas, thai beef salad, seafood linguine, half roast chicken with coleslaw and fries, pie of the day, fishcake with spinach, peas and poached egg, rib-eye steak with café de paris butter, and puddings such as bakewell tart with clotted cream and banoffi pie. *Benchmark main dish: burger with toppings and chips £12.95. Two-course evening meal £21.00.*

Free house ~ Licensee Lawrence Santi ~ Real ale ~ Open 11am-midnight; 10am-midnight Sat; 10am-11.30pm Sun ~ Bar food 12-3, 6-10; 10am-10.30pm weekends ~ Restaurant ~ Children welcome ~ Dogs allowed in bar ~ Wi-fi *Recommended by Alf and Sally Garner, Glen and Patricia Fuller, Ben Lees, Lucy Spencer-Davidson, Neil Allen, Caroline Prescott, Charles Fraser*

SOUTH LONDON

Map 12

Fox & Grapes 🏮⭐ ☆

(020) 8619 1300 – www.foxandgrapeswimbledon.co.uk

Camp Road; Wimbledon rail; SW19 4UN

Wide mix of customers for very popular pub with enjoyable food and drink; bedrooms

This 18th-c pub is ideally placed on the edge of Wimbledon Common and is extremely popular with walkers at lunchtime. There's always a good mix of both drinkers and diners, and the efficient, friendly staff manage to keep things running smoothly, even at peak times. The spacious main bar, with a step between its two halves, has high ceilings with unusual chandeliers, all sorts of wooden and leather dining chairs around scrubbed or painted tables on stripped boards or parquet flooring, and built-in wall seats and settles with pretty scatter cushions. Purity Mad Goose, Wimbledon Common PA and a changing guest on handpump, 13 wines by the glass (plus two sparkling ones) and a few malt whiskies; background music. The bedrooms are light, airy and pretty. Parking is now pay-and-display. This is sister pub to the Malt House in Fulham (West London) and the Victoria in East Sheen (South London) and is part of the Jolly Fine Pub Group.

 As well as breakfasts (8.30-11am), the pleasing food includes sandwiches, roasted quail with crispy polenta, shimeji mushrooms and red wine jus, salmon and haddock fishcake with lemon gel and soft herbs, semolina gnocchi with beetroot purée and wild mushrooms, chicken scaloppine with couscous, grilled peppers, courgettes and basil, monkfish, mussel, prawn, calamari and octopus stew with garlic toast, confit duck leg with puy lentils, mushrooms, button onions and bacon, slow-cooked rare-breed pork belly with sun-dried tomatoes and gremolata, and puddings such as warm chocolate brownie with salted caramel ice-cream and crème brûlée; steak night is Tuesday. *Benchmark main dish: lamb shoulder with stuffed courgette flower, stuffed calamari, anchovies and sun-dried tomato purée £28.00. Two-course evening meal £25.00.*

Enterprise ~ Manager Daniel Britz ~ Real ale ~ Open 12-11; 12-10 Sun ~ Bar food 8-3, 6-9.30; 12-4, 6-9.30 Sat; 12-8 ~ Restaurant ~ Children welcome ~ Dogs allowed in bar ~ Wi-fi ~ Bedrooms: /£125 *Recommended by Nick Higgins, Daniel King, Julian Thorpe, Moira and Jon Weller, Susan and John Douglas, Belinda Stamp, Edward May*

SOUTH LONDON   Map 12

Rose & Crown 🍷 🍺

(01689) 869029 – www.the-roseandcrown.co.uk
Farnborough Way (A21); Chelsfield rail (some distance away); BR6 6BT

Sizeable pub on the edge of London with large back garden, character bars, a wide choice of food and drink and cheerful service

The large garden behind this renovated pub is quite a surprise – it has colourful beach huts and cabanas, chairs and tables on a terrace, picnic-sets on grass and a sizeable children's play area. Inside, the open-plan, interconnected rooms (there are alcoves and smaller, cosier areas too) are interestingly furnished. There's every shape and size of Edwardian-style dining chairs, leather tub seats, upholstered stools and coloured button-back banquettes grouped around polished tables on rugs, bare boards or black and white tiles, and the walls are hung with frame-to-frame prints and pictures; also, house plants, church candles, lots of mirrors, hundreds of books on shelves and three log fires (one is a woodburner). Friendly, efficient young staff serve a beer named for the pub (from Marstons), Dorking Washington Gold, Timothy Taylors Landlord and Youngs Bitter and Special on handpump, and 16 wines by the glass.

As well as weekend breakfasts (9-11am), the enjoyable food includes sandwiches (until 5pm), salt and pepper calamari with sweet chilli dipping sauce, chicken liver parfait with red onion jam, vegan burger with toppings and skinny fries, salmon and cod fishcake with tomato and onion salad and dill mayonnaise, gammon and free-range eggs, chicken curry, fresh fish dish of the day, slow-cooked pulled pork with onion rings, coleslaw and chips, 28-day aged sirloin steak with a choice of sauce, and puddings such as pineapple upside-down cake with mango sorbet and sticky toffee pudding with toffee sauce. *Benchmark main dish: beer-battered fish and chips £12.95. Two-course evening meal £20.00.*

Whiting & Hammond ~ Manager Andrew Roberts ~ Real ale ~ Open 11-11; 9am-11pm Sat; 9am-10.30pm Sun ~ Bar food 12-9.30 (9 Sun) ~ Restaurant ~ Children welcome ~ Dogs allowed in bar ~ Wi-fi *Recommended by B and M Kendall, Philip Chesington, Mike Buckingham, Matt and Hayley Jacob, Buster May, Sarah Roberts, Victoria and James Sargeant*

SOUTH LONDON

Victoria 🍴⭐ ♟ 🛏

Map 12

(020) 8876 4238 – www.victoriasheen.co.uk

West Temple Sheen; Mortlake rail; SW14 7RT

Bustling pub serving all-day food and drink, with open fires in winter and a leafy garden in summer; comfortable bedrooms

Just a five-minute walk from Richmond Park, this buzzing but informal pub serves customers all day. The bar rooms have button-back leather sofas and simple chairs and tables on bare floorboards, candles in lanterns, decorative bright pink or stag's head wallpaper, and stools against the blue-painted counter where friendly young staff serve Timothy Taylors Boltmaker, Wimbledon Common Pale Ale and a changing guest on handpump, 14 good wines by the glass, and winter mulled wine. There's also a room with chandeliers and another stag's head. Background music and board games. A conservatory-style dining room has comfortable, contemporary orange leather chairs around tables of varying sizes on pale floorboards, and doors that lead into the leafy walled (and heated) garden where good quality seats and tables sit under parasols and there's a children's play area. The old stables have been converted into comfortable, contemporary bedrooms and breakfasts are good. Disabled access but no disabled loos. This is sister pub to the Fox & Grapes in Wimbledon (South London) and the Malt House in Fulham (West London) and is part of the Jolly Fine Pub Group.

 Good, interesting food includes lunchtime sandwiches, crispy squid with wasabi and lime mayonnaise, whipped truffled goats cheese with almonds, radish and honeycomb, butternut squash, roasted pepper and apricot tagine with couscous and smashed avocado, a pie of the day, moroccan-spiced lamb burger with tomato chilli jam, tzatziki and chips, sea bass fillets with crispy potatoes, tomato, caper and crushed olive dressing, rare-breed pork belly with black pudding stuffing, creamy mash, red onion jam and mustard jus, and puddings such as lemon and lime cheesecake with blackcurrant sorbet and chocolate fudge cake with honeycomb and chocolate ice-cream; steak night is Tuesday. *Benchmark main dish: roast beef £18.00. Two-course evening meal £23.00.*

Enterprise ~ Lease Jake Smith ~ Real ale ~ Open 8am-11pm; 8am-midnight Sat; 12-8 Sun ~ Bar food 8am-10pm; 12-8 Sun ~ Restaurant ~ Children welcome ~ Dogs allowed in bar ~ Wi-fi ~ Quiz Thurs evening ~ Bedrooms: /£135 *Recommended by Jamie Dorman, Charlie Stevens, Mark and Mary Setting, Geoff and Ann Marston, Dan and Belinda Smallbone, Gary and Marie Miller*

WEST LONDON

Bell

Map 12

(020) 8941 9799 – www.thebellinnhampton.co.uk

Thames Street, Hampton; Hampton rail; TW12 2EA

Bustling pub by the Thames with seats outside, real ales, a good choice of food and friendly service

In warm weather, head for the garden of this friendly riverside pub, where you'll find plenty of contemporary chairs and tables plus wooden booth seating, heaters, lighting and barbecues. Inside, a wide mix of customers create a good vibrant atmosphere in the interconnected rooms. Furnishings include wooden dining and tub chairs around copper-topped or chunky wooden tables, comfortably upholstered wall seats with scatter cushions, mirrors, old photographs and lots of church candles. From the long panelled bar counter, helpful staff serve Sharps Doom Bar, Park Brewery Gallows Gold and Timothy Taylors Landlord on handpump, 18 wines by the glass, ten gins and cocktails. Background music.

 Pleasing food includes sandwiches, wild boar liver, rum and ginger pâté, haddock and smoked pancetta fishcake with poached duck egg and béarnaise, spiced quinoa salad with borlotti and kidney beans, peppers and avocado, stone-baked pizzas, steak in ale pie with mustard mash, coq au vin with savoy cabbage, slow-roast pork belly with crackling, roast parsnips and cider gravy, beer-battered haddock and chips, 12oz dry-aged, bone-in rib-eye steak with a choice of sauce and chips, and puddings such as Baileys and mascarpone cheesecake with raspberry brûlée and dark chocolate brownie with vanilla bean cream. *Benchmark main dish: burger with toppings, coleslaw and chips £12.95. Two-course evening meal £21.00.*

Authentic Inns ~ Lease Simon Bailey ~ Real ale ~ Open 11am-midnight; 12-11 Sun ~ Bar food 12-3, 5-10; 12-10 Sat; 12-9 Sun ~ Restaurant ~ Children welcome ~ Dogs allowed in bar ~ Wi-fi ~ Quiz Sun evening, music and comedy evenings monthly (see website)
Recommended by Martin and Sue Neville, Fiona and Jack Henderson, Tony Scott, Alan and Alice Morgan, Rosie and John Moore, Liz and Martin Eldon

WEST LONDON   Map 12
Brown Cow ♀
(020) 7384 9559 – www.thebrowncowpub.co.uk
Fulham Road; Parsons Green tube; SW6 5SA

Busy pub with food and drinks served all day by cheerful staff

This efficiently run dining pub is open (and serves food) all day, so there are always plenty of customers popping in and out. The open-plan bar is furnished and decorated in a minimalist style with wooden and cushioned dining chairs and leather-topped stools around rustic tables on bare boards, button-back wall banquettes, prints on pale painted walls, a few suitcases on racks, house plants and industrial-style ceiling lamps. From a small bar counter lined with stools, friendly staff serve Shepherd Neame Whitstable Bay and Wychwood Hobgoblin on handpump, good wines by the glass and a growing collection of gins; background music and TV. There are a couple of tables outside on a side road.

 As well as offering weekend brunches, the enjoyable food includes chicken liver parfait with berry chutney, mussels with garlic and white wine, baby pumpkin, spinach, chestnuts and wild mushrooms, hake with boulangère potatoes, mussels and tarragon velouté, pork belly with truffled mash, kale and wholegrain mustard gravy, confit barbary duck leg with crispy kale, wild rice and pancetta, chargrilled flat-iron steak with sautéed mushrooms, a fried egg and triple-cooked chips, and puddings such as caramel affogato and chocolate brownie with butterscotch sauce. *Benchmark main dish: 28-day dry-aged rib-eye steak £25.00. Two-course evening meal £28.00.*

Free house ~ Licensee Conrad Allard ~ Real ale ~ Open 10am-midnight; 10am-10.30pm Sun ~ Bar food 10-11; 10-9 Sun ~ Restaurant ~ Children welcome ~ Dogs welcome ~ Wi-fi
Recommended by Gail and Arthur Roberts, Sally and Colin Allen, Julia and Fiona Barnes, Rosie and Marcus Heatherley, Mary and Douglas McDowell

WEST LONDON   Map 12
Colton Arms
(020) 3757 8050 – www.thecoltonarms.co.uk
Greyhound Road; Barons Court tube; W14 9SD

Extended pub with attractive bar and dining rooms, interesting décor, well liked food and seats outside

Handy for the nearby tennis courts of the renowned Queen's Club, this is a cosy pub with good food. The small front Dot's Bar (named after the long-serving former landlady) has painted panelling, wooden stools and chairs and simple tables on bare floorboards, an open fire and friendly staff serving Purity Pure Gold and Timothy Taylors Landlord on handpump and good wines by the glass. The extended sky-lit back dining room has striped and floral upholstered wall seating, all sorts of wooden or leather chairs and tables on floor tiles and some quirky touches such as brightly coloured artificial birds in cages, taxidermy, an eclectic range of artwork and portraits, ornamental old cash registers and sawn-off antique tennis rackets acting as coat racks; background music. Glass doors lead into the terraced garden which is marked out and painted like a tennis court. Street parking is free at weekends and after 5pm on weekdays.

Rewarding food includes Brixham crab with avocado, frisée, endive and white truffle oil, duck liver and foie gras parfait with red onion marmalade, pea, broad bean and goats curd ravioli with asparagus and mint oil, free-range chicken with parsley mash, grilled spring onions and smoked chicken broth, sea trout with mussel beurre blanc, rare-breed pork belly with stir-fried vegetables, caramel soy and crackling, and puddings such as blueberry brûlée and elderflower sponge with elderflower crème fraîche; they also offer pre-booked afternoon tea (3-6pm; not Sunday). *Benchmark main dish: wagyu burger and chips £19.00. Two-course evening meal £22.00.*

Hippo Inns ~ Licensees Rupert and Jo Clevely ~ Real ale ~ Open 12-11; 10am-midnight Sat; 12-10.30 Sun ~ Bar food 12-3, 6-10; 10-10 Sat; 12-9 Sun ~ Restaurant ~ Children welcome ~ Dogs allowed in bar ~ Wi-fi *Recommended by Susan and John Douglas, William and Tasha Fraser, Elizabeth and Giles Hancock, Archie and Melanie Garnett, Diana and Richard Gibbs, Patrick and Martine Lawson*

WEST LONDON
Dove ♀ ☕

Map 12

(020) 8748 9474 ~ www.dovehammersmith.co.uk
Upper Mall; Ravenscourt Park tube; W6 9TA

Character pub with a lovely riverside terrace, cosily traditional front bar and an interesting history

The front snug in this very popular, old-fashioned riverside place is in the *Guinness World Records* as being the smallest bar room – a mere 1.3 metres by 2.4 metres. The main bar is cosy, traditional and unchanging, with black panelling and red leatherette cushioned built-in wall settles and stools around assorted tables. It leads to a bigger, similarly furnished back room that's more geared to eating, which in turn leads to a conservatory. Fullers ESB, London Pride and a couple of guests such as Olivers Island and Seafarers on handpump and 19 wines by the glass including champagne and sparkling wine. Head down steps at the back to reach the verandah with its highly prized tables looking over a low river wall to the Thames Reach just above Hammersmith Bridge; a tiny exclusive area, reached up a spiral staircase, is a prime spot for watching rowers on the water. The pub has played host to many writers, actors and artists over the years (there's a fascinating framed list on a wall); it's said to be where 'Rule Britannia' was composed and was a favourite with Turner, who painted the view of the Thames from here, and with Graham Greene. The street itself is associated with the foundation of the arts and crafts movement – William Morris's Kelmscott House (open certain afternoons) is nearby.

Pleasing food includes sandwiches, gin-cured mackerel with gooseberry chutney and celeriac rémoulade, chicken and black pudding terrine with piccalilli, sweet potato and manchego hash with a baked egg and smoked chilli romesco sauce, beer-battered haddock and chips, burger with toppings and triple-cooked chips, rack of lamb with pine nut pesto crust with anchovy and caper butter, corn-fed chicken with sautéed potatoes and bacon, and puddings such as rhubarb crème brûlée and chocolate brownie with peanut brittle, salted caramel and buffalo milk ice-cream. *Benchmark main dish: shepherd's pie £14.00. Two-course evening meal £20.50.*

Fullers ~ Manager Sonia Labatut ~ Real ale ~ Open 11-11; 12-10.30 Sun ~ Bar food 12-10; 12-9 Sun ~ Children welcome ~ Dogs welcome ~ Wi-fi *Recommended by Chantelle and Tony Redman, Belinda and Neil Garth, Gary and Marie Miller, Dave Chapman, B and M Kendall, Nicholas and Maddy Trainer*

WEST LONDON Map 12
Malt House ♀ 🛏

(020) 7084 6888 ~ www.malthousefulham.co.uk
Vanston Place; Fulham Broadway tube; SW6 1AY

Creative food and good drinks choice in refurbished Georgian pub, stylish bar and dining areas and hidden-away garden; bedrooms

Dating from 1729, this large refurbished corner pub has a good, bustling atmosphere in its U-shaped bar. There are big windows, high ceilings, wooden or tiled floors, green leather button-back wall seating and dark wooden dining chairs around pale-topped tables and groups of sofas and armchairs dotted here and there. Planked walls are hung with watercolours, there's a lot of cream paintwork throughout and some bookshelf wallpaper. Contemporary high chairs line the counter where helpful staff serve Brakspears Bitter and Oxford Gold and Ringwood Boondoggle on handpump, 16 wines by the glass, 16 malt whiskies and 40 gins; background music, TV and board games. The small paved back garden has pretty hanging baskets and bunting, candles in lanterns, cheerful scatter cushions and wooden tables and chairs. Bedrooms are comfortable and light and airy. This is sister pub to the Fox & Grapes in Wimbledon and Victoria in East Sheen (both in South London) and is part of the Jolly Fine Pub Group.

As well as breakfasts (8-11am), the enjoyable food includes sandwiches, beetroot carpaccio with feta cheese and pine nut salad, crispy pork belly with apple purée and fresh horseradish, gnocchi with wild mushrooms, cavolo nero and cheese sauce, corn-fed chicken with dauphinoise potatoes and mustard cream sauce, burger with toppings, pickles and chips, brazilian fish stew with monkfish, mussels and king prawns, lamb rump with crushed leek and sweet potato mash and rosemary jus, and puddings such as red velvet brownie with chocolate ice-cream and sticky toffee pudding with toffee sauce and salted caramel ice-cream. *Benchmark main dish: beer-battered fish and chips £14.00. Two-course evening meal £20.00.*

Brakspears ~ Lease Scott Johnson ~ Real ale ~ Open 8am-11pm; 8am-midnight Sat; 8am-10.30pm Sun ~ Bar food 12-3, 6-10; 12-10 Weds-Sun ~ Restaurant ~ Children welcome ~ Dogs allowed in bar ~ Wi-fi ~ Live music Thurs evening ~ Bedrooms: /£150
Recommended by Belinda Stamp, Elise and Charles Mackinlay, Robert and Diana Ringstone, Sandra and Miles Spencer, George and Alison Bishop

WEST LONDON Map 12
Mute Swan ♀ 🍴

(020) 8941 5959 ~ www.brunningandprice.co.uk/muteswan
Palace Gate, Hampton Court Road; Hampton Court rail; KT8 9BN

Handsome pub close to the Thames with sunny seats outside, relaxed bar, upstairs dining room and imaginative food and drinks choice

Just yards from the River Thames (though there's no view), this remains a friendly, busy and well run pub. The light and airy bar has four big leather armchairs grouped around a low table, while the rest of the room has brown leather wall seats, high-backed Edwardian-style cushioned dining chairs around dark tables and rugs on bare boards. The walls are covered in interesting photographs, maps, prints and posters and there are sizeable house plants, glass and stone bottles on the windowsills and a woodburning stove; the atmosphere is informal and relaxed. St Austell Brunning & Price Traditional Bitter plus guests from breweries such as Adnams, Hogs Back, Loddon, Park Brewery, Twickenham, Windsor & Eton and XT on handpump, a carefully chosen wine list with 30 by the glass, 70 gins, 90 malt whiskies and farm cider; staff are efficient and helpful. A metal spiral staircase – presided over by an elegant metal chandelier – leads up to the dining area where there are brass-studded caramel leather chairs around well spaced tables on bare boards or carpeting, and numerous photos and prints. The tables and chairs on the front terrace get snapped up quickly and the pub is opposite the gates to Hampton Court Palace. There are a few parking spaces in front, but you'll probably have to park elsewhere.

Well regarded food includes sandwiches, scallops with arancini and gazpacho dressing, sticky chinese chicken wings, beetroot and quinoa burger with spiced guacamole and fries, honey-roast ham with free-range eggs, chicken, ham and leek pie, pork and leek sausages with mash and onion gravy, sri lankan seafood curry with yellow crab rice and bisque sauce, lamb rump with vegetable risotto and wild garlic and hazelnut pesto, 10oz rib-eye steak with dijon and tarragon butter and chips, and puddings such as hot waffle with caramelised banana, toffee sauce and salted caramel ice-cream and rhubarb cheesecake with orange sorbet, grenadine poached rhubarb and ginger syrup. *Benchmark main dish: beer-battered fish and chips £13.95. Two-course evening meal £20.00.*

Brunning & Price ~ Manager Alessio Porti ~ Real ale ~ Open 11-11; 11am-midnight Fri, Sat; 11-10.30 Sun ~ Bar food 12-9.30 ~ Restaurant ~ Children welcome in upstairs restaurant only ~ Dogs allowed in bar ~ Wi-fi *Recommended by Miranda and Jeff Davidson, Andrew and Michele Revell, Charlotte Smyrk, Tony Scott, Barbara and Phil Bowie, Gail and Arthur Roberts, Charlotte and William Mason*

WEST LONDON
Map 3
Old Orchard ♀ ▨

(01895) 822631 – www.brunningandprice.co.uk/oldorchard
Off Park Lane, Harefield; Denham rail (some distance away); UB9 6HJ

Wonderful views from the front garden, a good choice of drinks and interesting brasserie-style food

Tables on the front terrace and in the garden provide stunning views down to the narrowboats on the canal way below and across to the lakes that are part of the conservation area known as the Colne Valley Regional Park – it's a haven for wildlife. Inside, the open-plan rooms have an attractive mix of cushioned dining chairs around all sizes and shapes of dark wooden tables, lots of prints, maps and pictures covering the walls, books on shelves, old glass bottles on windowsills and rugs on wood or parquet flooring. One room is hung with a large rug and some tapestries. There are daily papers to read, two cosy coal fires, big pot plants and fresh flowers. Half a dozen real ales on handpump served by friendly, efficient staff include St Austell Brunning & Price Traditional Bitter, Mighty Oak Oscar Wilde, Nene Valley Manhattan Project, Redemption Trinity, Tring Side Pocket for a Toad and XT Hop Kitty; also, 20 wines by the glass, 80 gins, 140 malt whiskies and farm cider.

🍴 Interesting food includes sandwiches, sea bass and seared scallop with pancetta, peas and cauliflower, chicken liver parfait with chutney, sharing plates such as baked garlic and rosemary camembert with apple and candied walnut salad, chicken, ham and leek pie, tempura king prawns with chilli turmeric rice, mint yoghurt, pepper and onion seed salsa, crispy pork belly with rice noodle salad, toasted peanuts and charred pak choi, sea bass with crispy cauliflower, okra and coconut curry, 10oz rump steak with horseradish butter and chips, and puddings such as dark chocolate and orange tart with mango sorbet and crème brûlée. *Benchmark main dish: braised lamb shoulder with dauphinoise potatoes and rosemary gravy £18.95. Two-course evening meal £23.00.*

Brunning & Price ~ Manager Alisha Craigwell ~ Real ale ~ Open 11.30-11; 12-10.30 Sun ~ Bar food 12-9.30; 12-10 Fri, Sat; 12-9 Sun ~ Children welcome ~ Dogs welcome ~ Wi-fi
Recommended by Trevor and Michele Street, Buster and Helena Hastings, Holly and Tim Waite, Colin and Daniel Gibbs, Susan and John Douglas

WEST LONDON   Map 12
Sands End ⭐ 🍴 ♟

(020) 7731 7823 – www.thesandsend.co.uk
Stephendale Road; Imperial Wharf rail; SW6 2PR

Simply furnished, bustling pub in a quiet street with interesting food and a thoughtful range of drinks; seats outside

Busy and friendly with lots of young locals and visitors, this Fulham dining pub has an informal but gently civilised atmosphere. The open-plan bar features a mix of wooden dining chairs, the odd settle and cushioned wall seat and scrubbed pine, painted or polished wooden tables on bare boards; the dining area is quieter and more spacious; background music. From the solid, central counter, efficient staff serve Otter Bitter, Sambrooks Wandle and a couple of changing guest ales on handpump and good wines by the glass. Upstairs is a private dining room. Outside, there are seats and tables at the front on the quiet residential street. Disabled access.

🍴⭐ Imaginative food includes roasted quail with parma ham and oranges, scallops with minted pea purée and balsamic reduction, potato gnocchi with broccoli and stilton sauce with toasted walnuts, black bream fillet with crushed new potatoes, carrot ribbons and salsa verde, crispy duck leg with pea, bacon and gem lettuce and tarragon jus, thyme-roasted poussin with spicy potato wedges, caramelised lemon and aioli, flat-iron steak with a choice of sauce, and puddings such as pear and pistachio tart with vanilla ice-cream and chocolate and salted caramel brownie with sour cherry compote. *Benchmark main dish: half corn-fed chicken with a choice of sauce and fries £17.50. Two-course evening meal £22.00.*

Free house ~ Licensee Susan Carrol ~ Real ale ~ Open 12-midnight; 10am-midnight Sat; 10am-10.30pm Sun ~ Bar food 12-4, 6-10; 10-4, 6-10 Sat; 10-8 Sun ~ Restaurant ~ Children allowed but no high chairs ~ Dogs allowed in bar *Recommended by John and Claire Masters, Patricia and Anton Larkham, Lucy and Giles Gibbon, Nicola and Holly Lyons, Edward May, Harvey Brown*

'Children welcome' means the pub says it lets children inside without any special restriction. If it allows them in, but to restricted areas such as an eating area or family room, we specify this. Places with separate restaurants often let children use them, and hotels usually let children into public areas such as lounges. Some pubs impose an evening time limit – let us know if you find one earlier than 9pm.

Also Worth a Visit in London

Besides the fully inspected pubs, you might like to try these pubs that have been recommended to us and described by readers. Do tell us what you think of them: feedback@goodguides.com

CENTRAL LONDON

EC1

Bishops Finger (020) 7248 2341
West Smithfield; EC1A 9JR Welcoming little pub close to Smithfield Market; Shepherd Neame ales (including seasonals) and enjoyable pubby food from bar snacks and sharing boards up, can eat in bar or upstairs room; children welcome, seats out in front, closed weekends and bank holidays, otherwise open all day and can get crowded, no food Fri evening. *(Jim Stevens)*

Butchers Hook & Cleaver
(020) 7600 9181 *West Smithfield; EC1A 9DY* Fullers conversion of bank and adjoining butcher's shop; their full range kept well and enjoyable pubby food including various pies, helpful efficient service, spiral stairs to mezzonine; background music, free wi-fi; children welcome, closed weekends, otherwise open (and food) all day, popular with after-work drinkers, when it gets busy. *(Gail and Arthur Roberts)*

Coach (020) 3954 1595
Ray Street; EC1R 3DJ Smartly revamped Clerkenwell dining pub with very good french-inspired cooking from chef-owner; traditional oak-panelled front bar serving Adnams, Timothy Taylors and well chosen wines by the glass, airy pitched-roof back dining room with floor-to-ceiling glass overlooking small courtyard garden, more dining space upstairs; occasional quiz; open all day, kitchen closes 4pm Sun. *(Caroline Warwick)*

Craft Beer Company
(020) 7404 7049 *Leather Lane; EC1N 7TR* Corner drinkers' pub with excellent selection of real ales and craft beers plus an extensive bottled range, good choice of wines and spirits too, stools by high tables on bare boards, big chandelier hanging from mirrored ceiling, food limited to snacks, more room upstairs; closed Sun, otherwise open all day and can get very busy. *(Maggie and Stevan Hollis)*

Dovetail (020) 7490 7321
Jerusalem Passage; EC1V 4JP Fairly small and can get very busy with drinkers spilling into alleyway, specialises in draught/bottled belgian beers and serves popular food including some belgian and vegetarian/vegan dishes, efficient staff coping well at peak times; events such as beer tasting, acoustic music and quiz nights; closed Sun, otherwise open all day. *(Sophie and John Moor)*

Fox & Anchor (020) 7250 1300
Charterhouse Street, by Smithfield Market; EC1M 6AA Beautifully restored late Victorian pub/boutique hotel with fine art nouveau façade; long slender bar with unusual pewter-topped counter, lots of mahogany, green leather and etched glass, small back snugs, Youngs ales and guests, enjoyable food from good breakfast onwards, friendly efficient staff; six individual well appointed bedrooms, open all day from 7am (8.30am Sat, 11am Sun). *(Robert and Diana Ringstone)*

Gunmakers (020) 7278 1022
Eyre Street Hill; EC1R 5ET Small Victorian pub with renovated split-level bar; bare boards and modern artwork, a couple of changing ales and enjoyable food with some emphasis on burgers, more room upstairs including (at the top) a hairdressers/barbers offering cocktails; background music; back garden, open all day weekdays, closed weekends. *(Darrell Barton)*

★**Hand & Shears** (020) 7600 0257
Middle Street; EC1A 7JA Traditional unspoilt Smithfield corner pub; three rooms and small snug arranged around central servery, up to six changing ales served by friendly staff, bare boards, panelling and a couple of gas fires, interesting prints and vintage photographs; closed weekends, otherwise open all day (busy lunchtime/early evening). *(Julie Swift)*

★**Jerusalem Tavern** (020) 7490 4281
Britton Street; EC1M 5UQ Atmospheric re-creation of a dark 18th-c tavern (1720 merchant's house with shopfront added 1810); tiny dimly lit bar with simple wood furnishings on bare boards, some remarkable old wall tiles, coal fires and candlelight, stairs to a precarious-feeling (though perfectly secure) balcony, plainer back room, St Peters beers tapped from the cask and in bottles, short choice of lunchtime food including sandwiches, friendly attentive young staff; no children but dogs welcome, seats out on pavement (plastic glasses), open all day weekdays, closed weekends, bank holidays and 24 Dec-2 Jan; can get very crowded at peak times. *(Giles and Annie Francis)*

Ninth Ward (020) 7833 2949
Farringdon Road; EC1R 3BN American-themed bar/grill (has sister restaurant in New York) with unusual New Orleans-inspired interior (quite dark), tasty food such as burgers and fried chicken, good range of craft and bottled beers, cocktails, friendly staff; background music; closed Sat lunchtime and Sun, otherwise open all day till late. *(Peter and Emma Kelly)*

Old Fountain (020) 7253 2970
Baldwin Street; EC1V 9NU Popular traditional old pub in same family since 1964; long bar serving two rooms, excellent range of real ales and craft beers chalked on blackboard (some brewed in the cellar), friendly knowledgeable staff, enjoyable good value food from open kitchen, main carpeted part with wooden tables and chairs and padded stools; function room for live music, darts; nice roof terrace; open (and food) all day. *(Rona Mackinlay)*

Old Red Cow (020) 7600 6240
Long Lane; EC1A 9EJ Cheerful little pub close to the Barbican and within sight of Smithfield Market; fine changing selection of cask, craft and bottled beers, tasters offered by friendly knowledgeable staff, decent range of wines and well liked food from pizzas to popular Sun roasts, modernised interior with larger room upstairs; open (and food) all day and popular with after-work drinkers. *(Patricia and Gordon Tucker)*

Viaduct (020) 7600 1863
Newgate Street; EC1A 7AA Opposite Old Bailey on site of Newgate Prison (a couple of cells survive below), big copper lanterns outside, fine ornate high-ceilinged Victorian interior with three or four snug areas, Fullers ales and good selection of gins from horseshoe bar, snacky food such as sausage rolls and toasties; gets busy with after-work drinkers; open all day weekdays, closed weekends. *(James Butcher)*

EC2
Hamilton Hall (020) 7247 3579
Bishopsgate; also entrance from Liverpool Street station; EC2M 7PY Showpiece Wetherspoons with flamboyant Victorian baroque décor mixing with contemporary bar counter and modern furniture; lots of real ales, decent wines and their usual food and competitive pricing, friendly staff coping well at busy times, good-sized comfortable mezzanine; silenced machines, free wi-fi, screens showing train times; good disabled access, café-style tables and chairs out in front, open all day from 7am, can get very crowded after work. *(Ted Wright)*

Lord Aberconway (020) 7929 1743
Old Broad Street; EC2M 1QT Victorian feel with high moulded ceiling, dark panelling, some red leather bench seating and drinking booths, six well kept ales and reasonably priced Nicholsons menu, dining gallery; handy for Liverpool Street station, gets busy with after-work drinkers, open all day (till 6pm Sun). *(Chaz)*

EC3
★**Counting House** (020) 7283 7123
Cornhill; EC3V 3PD Spacious bank conversion retaining original Victorian character; grand ceiling with impressive glass dome, chandeliers, rich polished mahogany and mosaics, stairs up to galleried seating area, well kept Fullers beers from island bar with four-sided clock, enjoyable food including range of pies, efficient friendly service; wheelchair access, 15 bedrooms, shuts 5pm Sun, otherwise open (and food) all day. *(Louise and Simon Peters)*

East India Arms (020) 7265 5121
Fenchurch Street; EC3M 4BR Standing-room 19th-c corner pub popular with City workers; small single room with wood floor, half-panelling, old local photographs and brewery mirrors, well kept Shepherd Neame ales served by efficient staff; tables outside, closed weekends, otherwise open all day. *(James Butcher)*

Hoop & Grapes (020) 7481 4583
Aldgate High Street; EC3N 1AL Originally 17th-c (dismantled and rebuilt 1983) and much bigger inside than it looks; long partitioned bare-boards bar with beams, timbers, exposed brickwork and panelling, mix of seating including some button-back wall benches, eight real ales and standard Nicholsons menu (popular lunchtime), friendly efficient service; muted sports TV; a few seats in front, open (and food) all day. *(Tony Scott)*

Jamaica Wine House
(020) 7929 6972 *St Michael Alley, Cornhill; EC3V 9DS* 19th-c red-stone pub (site of London's first coffee house) in warren of small alleys; traditional Victorian décor with ornate coffered ceiling, oak-panelled booths and bare boards, Shepherd Neame ales and wide choice of wines, friendly helpful service, food in bar or downstairs dining room; busiest lunchtime/early evening, closed weekends. *(Tony Scott)*

Lamb (020) 7626 2454
Leadenhall Market; EC3V 1LR Stand-up bar with friendly staff coping admirably with hordes of after-work drinkers; Youngs ales and good choice of wines, dark panelling, engraved glass and plenty of ledges and shelves, corner servery for lunchtime food, spiral stairs up to small carpeted gallery overlooking market's central crossing, separate stairs to nice bright dining room (separate menu), also basement bar with

shiny wall tiles; tables out under splendid Victorian market roof – crowds here in warmer months, closed Sun, otherwise open (and food) all day. *(Samuel and Melissa Turnbull)*

Ship (020) 7929 3903

Talbot Court, off Eastcheap; EC3V 0BP Interesting Nicholsons pub tucked down alleyway; busy bare-boards bar with soft lighting and ornate décor, candles in galleried dining area, friendly efficient staff, several well kept ales including their St Austell house beer, well liked good value food; closed Sun, otherwise open all day, till 6pm Sat. *(Chaz)*

Ship (020) 7702 4422

Hart Street; EC3R 7NB Tiny one-room 19th-c City pub with ornate flower-decked façade; well kept Caledonian and a couple of guests, craft beers and eight wines by the glass, lunchtime food including selection of bar snacks and signature burgers, meal/drink deals, friendly staff, limited seating and can get packed, upstairs dining room; spiral stairs down to lavatories; closed weekends, otherwise open all day. *(Jamie Green)*

Swan (020) 7929 6550

Ship Tavern Passage, off Gracechurch Street; EC3V 1LY Traditional Fullers pub with bustling narrow flagstoned bar; their well kept ales and lunchtime sandwiches/ burgers, friendly efficient service, neatly kept Victorian panelled décor, low lighting, larger more ordinary carpeted bar upstairs; silent TV; covered alley used by smokers, open all day Mon-Fri, closed weekends. *(Charlie and Mark Todd)*

EC4

Cockpit (020) 7248 7315

St Andrews Hill/Ireland Place, off Queen Victoria Street; EC4V 5BY Plenty of atmosphere in this little corner pub near St Paul's Cathedral; as name suggests, a former cockfighting venue with surviving spectators' gallery; good selection of beers such as Adnams, St Austell and Shepherd Neame, lunchtime food; open all day. *(Barbara and Phil Bowie)*

Old Bell (020) 7583 0216

Fleet Street, near Ludgate Circus; EC4Y 1DH Dimly lit 17th-c tavern backing on to St Bride's Church; stained-glass bow window, heavy black beams, bare boards and flagstones, half a dozen or more well kept changing beers from island servery (tasting trays available), usual Nicholsons food, friendly helpful young staff, various

seating nooks with brass-topped tables, coal fire; background music; covered and heated outside area, open all day. *(Jeff Davies)*

★ Olde Cheshire Cheese

(020) 7353 6170 *Wine Office Court, off 145 Fleet Street; EC4A 2BU* Best to visit this 17th-c former chophouse outside peak times as it can be packed (early evening especially); soaked in history with warren of old-fashioned unpretentious rooms, high beams, bare boards and old built-in black benches, Victorian paintings on dark brown walls, big open fires, tiny snug and steep stone steps down to unexpected series of cosy areas and secluded alcoves, Sam Smiths beers, all-day pubby food; look out for Polly the parrot (now stuffed) who entertained distinguished guests for over 40 years; children allowed in eating area lunchtime only, closed Sun evening. *(Sally and Colin Allen)*

Olde Watling (020) 7248 8935

Watling Street; EC4M 9BR Heavy-beamed and timbered post-blitz replica of pub built by Wren in 1668; interesting choice of well kept beers, standard Nicholsons menu, good friendly service, quieter back bar and upstairs dining room; open all day. *(B and M Kendall)*

Three Cranes (020) 3455 7437

Garlick Hill opposite Mansion House tube; EC4V 2BA Revamped City pub under same ownership as the Coach (EC1) and Hero of Maida (W9); blue panelled bar with beers such as Beavertown, Portobello and Timothy Taylors, good range of wines and other drinks, snacky food including sharing boards, full meals in upstairs grill room, good friendly service; open all day weekdays, closed weekends. *(Jim Stevens)*

SW1

Antelope (020) 7824 8512

Eaton Terrace; SW1W 8EZ Pretty little flower-decked local in Belgravia; traditional interior with bare boards, panelling and etched windows, mix of old and new furniture, interesting prints and gas-effect coal fire in tiled Victorian fireplace, well kept Fullers ales from central counter, upstairs dining room serving decent pubby food (all day weekends) including popular Sun roasts; TVs, free wi-fi, daily papers; children (if eating) and dogs welcome, open all day and can get crowded in the evening. *(Maggie and Stevan Hollis)*

Buckingham Arms (020) 7222 3386

Petty France; SW1H 9EU Welcoming and relaxed early 19th-c bow-windowed

---

If you report on a pub that's not a featured entry, please tell us any lunchtimes or evenings when it doesn't serve bar food.

local; Youngs ales and a guest from long curved bar, good range of wines by the glass and well liked pubby food from back open kitchen, elegant mirrors and dark woodwork, stained-glass screens, stools at modern high tables, some armchairs and upholstered banquettes, unusual side corridor with elbow ledge for drinkers; background music, TV; dogs welcome, well placed for Buckingham Palace, Westminster Abbey and St James's Park, open all day, till 5pm Sun. *(Dr and Mrs A K Clarke)*

Cask & Glass (020) 7834 7630
Palace Street; SW1E 5HN Snug traditional one-room pub with friendly atmosphere; black panelling, button-back wall benches and old prints, good range of Shepherd Neame ales, lunchtime toasties; quiet corner TV, free wi-fi; a few tables outside under awning, handy for Queen's Gallery, open all day, till 8pm Sat, closed Sun. *(James Butcher)*

Cask Pub & Kitchen
(020) 7630 7225 *Charlwood Street/ Tachbrook Street; SW1V 2EE* Spacious simply furnished modern bar; excellent choice of draught beers with over 500 more in bottles, decent range of wines too, friendly knowledgeable staff, good burgers, bar snacks and Sun roasts, chatty atmosphere – can get packed and noisy in the evening; Sun live music, regular beer-related events such as Meet the Brewer; downstairs gents'; some outside tables and chairs, open all day, food all day weekends. *(Tony Scott)*

Clarence (020) 7930 4808
Whitehall; SW1A 2HP Popular beamed corner pub (Geronimo Inn) with cheerful quirky décor; Youngs and guests such as Twickenham, decent wines by the glass and good food from snacks up, quick friendly service, well spaced tables and varied seating including tub chairs and banquettes, upstairs dining area; children welcome till 4pm (9pm upstairs), pavement tables, open (and food) all day. *(Dr and Mrs A K Clarke, Dave Braisted)*

★**Fox & Hounds** (020) 7730 6367
Passmore Street/Graham Terrace; SW1W 8HR Small flower-decked pub in backstreets below Sloane Square; well kept Youngs ales and interesting guests, warm red décor with lots of old pictures, prints and photographs, wall benches and leather chesterfields, coal-effect gas fire, back room with skylight; open (and snacky food) all day, can get crowded early evening. *(Richard and Penny Gibbs)*

★**Grenadier** (020) 7235 3074
Wilton Row; the turning off Wilton Crescent looks prohibitive, but the barrier and watchman are there to keep out cars; SW1X 7NR Steps up to cosy old mews pub with lots of character and military history, but not much space (packed 5-7pm); simple unfussy panelled bar, stools and wooden benches on bare boards, Greene King ales and guests from rare pewter-topped counter, famous bloody marys, well liked food (can be pricey) from bar snacks up including signature beef wellington, intimate back restaurant; children over 8 and dogs allowed, hanging baskets, sentry box and single table outside, open (and food) all day. *(Patricia and Gordon Tucker)*

Grosvenor (020) 7821 8786
Grosvenor Road; SW1V 3LA Traditional pub across from river (no views), chatty and relaxed, with three well kept ales including Sharps and nice selection of wines, enjoyable reasonably priced pubby food including good Sun roasts, friendly staff; pool, darts and TV; some tables out by road, secluded beer garden behind, open (and food) all day. *(Rona Mackinlay)*

Jugged Hare (020) 7828 1543
Vauxhall Bridge Road/Rochester Row; SW1V 1DX Popular Fullers pub in former colonnaded bank; iron pillars, dark woodwork and large chandelier, old photographs of London, smaller back panelled dining room, stairs up to gallery, four well kept ales and straightforward reasonably priced food including range of pies, good friendly service; background music, TVs, silent fruit machine; open all day. *(Nigel and Sue Foster)*

★**Lord Moon of the Mall**
(020) 7839 7701 *Whitehall; SW1A 2DY* Popular Wetherspoons bank conversion; elegant main room with big arched windows looking over Whitehall, old prints and a large portrait of Tim Martin (the chain's founder); through an arch the style is more recognisably Wetherspoons with neatly tiled areas and bookshelves opposite long servery, ten real ales and their good value food (from breakfasts up); children (if eating) and dogs welcome, open all day from 8am (till midnight Fri, Sat). *(Dr and Mrs A K Clarke)*

Morpeth Arms (020) 7834 6442
Millbank; SW1P 4RW Victorian pub facing the Thames with view over to MI6 headquarters from upstairs Spy Room; etched and cut glass, lots of mirrors, paintings, prints and old photographs (some of british spies), well kept Youngs ales and guests, decent choice of wines and fair value pubby food, welcoming efficient staff; built on site of Milbank Prison and cells remain below; seats outside (and a lot of traffic), handy for Tate Britain and Thames Path walkers, open (and food) all day, can get very crowded weekday evenings. *(Nigel and Sue Foster)*

Nags Head (020) 7235 1135
Kinnerton Street; SW1X 8ED
Unspoilt and unchanging little mews pub with no-nonsense plain-talking landlord; low-ceilinged panelled front room with

unusual sunken counter, log-effect gas fire in old range, narrow passage down to even smaller bar, well kept Adnams from 19th-c handpumps, uncomplicated food, theatrical mementoes and other interesting memorabilia including a what-the-butler-saw machine and one-armed bandit; no mobiles, individual background music; well behaved children and dogs allowed, a few seats outside, open (and food) all day. *(Jim Stevens)*

Red Lion (020) 7930 5826

Parliament Street; SW1A 2NH Victorian pub by Houses of Parliament used by Foreign Office staff and MPs; divided bare-boards bar with showy chandeliers suspended from fine moulded ceiling, parliamentary cartoons and prints, Fullers/Gales beers and decent wines from long counter, good range of food including popular fish and chips, efficient staff, also clubby cellar bar and upstairs panelled dining room; free wi-fi; children welcome, outside bench seating, open all day (till 9pm Sun). *(Dr and Mrs A K Clarke)*

Red Lion (020) 7930 4141

Crown Passage, behind St James's Street; SW1Y 6PP Cheerful traditional little pub tucked down narrow passage near St James's Palace; dark panelling and leaded lights, upholstered settles and stools on patterned carpet, lots of prints, decorative plates and horsebrasses, well kept Adnams, St Austell and decent range of malt whiskies, friendly service, lunchtime sandwiches (no hot food), narrow overflow room upstairs; sports TV; colourful hanging baskets, closed Sun, otherwise open all day. *(Dr and Mrs A K Clarke, Tony Scott)*

★ Red Lion (020) 7321 0782

Duke of York Street; SW1Y 6JP Pretty little flower-decked Victorian pub, remarkably preserved and packed with customers often spilling out on to the pavement; series of small rooms with profusion of polished mahogany, gleaming mirrors, cut/etched windows and chandeliers, striking ornamental plaster ceiling, Fullers/Gales beers and traditional lunchtime food; no children; dogs welcome, closed Sun and bank holidays, otherwise open all day. *(Revd R P Tickle)*

Speaker (020) 7222 1749

Great Peter Street; SW1P 2HA Bustling chatty atmosphere in this unpretentious smallish corner pub (can get packed at peak times); well kept Timothy Taylors and guests, bottled beers and lots of whiskies, short choice of enjoyable simple food, friendly staff, panelling, political cartoons and prints, notes here and there on etiquette; no mobile phones, background music or children; open (and food) all day Mon-Fri, closed weekends. *(Tony Scott)*

St Stephens Tavern (020) 7925 2286

Parliament Street; SW1A 2JR Victorian pub opposite Houses of Parliament and Big Ben (so quite touristy); brass chandeliers hanging from lofty ceilings, tall windows with etched glass and swagged curtains, gleaming mahogany, division bell for MPs and lots of parliamentary memorabilia, also charming upper gallery bar (may be reserved for functions), four well kept Badger ales from handsome counter with pedestal lamps, fairly priced traditional food including burgers and pies; open (and food) all day. *(Dr and Mrs A K Clarke)*

White Swan (020) 7828 2000

Vauxhall Bridge Road; SW1V 2SA Roomy split-level corner pub spruced up by McMullens; their ales and guests, decent wines by the glass and enjoyable sensibly priced pubby food, friendly staff; background music, sports TV; handy for Tate Britain, open (and food) all day and can get very busy at peak times. *(Dr and Mrs J D Abell)*

Windsor Castle (020) 7834 7260

Francis Street; SW1P 1DN Traditionally restored 19th-c pub directly behind Westminster Cathedral (was the Cardinal); new etched glass and rebuilt screened snugs matching the original architect's drawings, fine Victorian moulded ceiling, open fires, well kept/priced Sam Smiths beers and enjoyable good value food (not Sun) such as fish and chips and steak and kidney pudding, parquet-floored back dining lounge with half-panelled and papered walls, another bar upstairs (not always open); no children, open all day. *(Dr and Mrs A K Clarke)*

SW3

Coopers Arms (020) 7376 3120

Flood Street; SW3 5TB Refurbished 19th-c pub, a useful bolthole for King's Road shoppers (so can get very busy); comfortable bar with good mix of tables and chairs on stripped boards, large moose head on one wall, open fire, well kept Youngs ales, guest beers and good selection of other drinks including over 20 wines by the glass and cocktails, decent food from fairly pubby menu; Tues quiz, projector for major sports, board games; well behaved children till 7pm, dogs allowed in bar, courtyard garden, open (and food) all day. *(Robert and Diana Ringstone)*

Hour Glass (020) 7581 2497

Brompton Road; SW3 2DY Compact wood-floored bar with open brick fireplace, leather banquette at each end, stools along drinking shelf overlooking street, Harviestoun ales, well chosen wines and good whisky/gin range, snacky food including sharing boards, panelled upstairs dining room, friendly helpful service; handy for V&A and other nearby museums, open all day (till 9.30pm Sun), no food Sun evening to Tues lunchtime. *(Barbara and Phil Bowie)*

Surprise (020) 7351 6954
Christchurch Terrace; SW3 4AJ Late
Victorian Chelsea pub (Geronimo Inn)
popular with well heeled locals; Sharps,
Youngs and a house beer (HMS Surprise)
from light wood servery, champagne and
plenty of other wines by the glass, interesting
food (all day weekends) including british
tapas-style canapé boards, friendly service,
soft grey décor and comfortable furnishings
with floral sofas and armchairs on sturdy
floorboards, stained-glass partitioning,
a model ship or two, upstairs dining room,
daily papers; benches out in front under
awning, open all day. *(Chaz)*

W1

★**Argyll Arms** (020) 7734 6117
Argyll Street; W1F 7TP Popular and
individual Nicholsons pub with three
interesting little front cubicle rooms
(essentially unchanged since 1860s); wooden
partitions and impressive frosted and
engraved glass, mirrored corridor to spacious
back room, eight real ales from well stocked
bar and good sensibly priced food, upstairs
dining room overlooking pedestrianised
street; background music, fruit machine;
children welcome till 8pm, pavement tables,
handy for the Palladium, open (and food)
all day. *(B and M Kendall, Tony Scott)*

Audley (020) 7499 1843
Mount Street; W1K 2RX Classic late
Victorian Mayfair pub; opulent red plush,
mahogany panelling and cut glass, clock in
extravagantly carved bracket and chandeliers
hanging from ornately corniced ceiling, long
polished bar serving Greene King ales and
guests, good choice of pub food (reasonably
priced for the area), upstairs panelled dining
room, cellar wine bar; quiet background
music, TV, pool, free wi-fi; children till 6pm,
pavement tables, open (and food) all day.
(Tony Scott)

Clachan (020) 7494 0834
Kingly Street; W1B 5QH Nicholsons
corner pub behind Liberty (and once owned
by them): ornate plaster ceiling supported by
fluted pillars, comfortable screened leather
banquettes, smaller drinking alcove up three
or four steps, fine selection of real ales from
handsome mahogany counter, affordably
priced meals in upstairs dining room; open
(and food) all day, can get very crowded.
(Sandra and Miles Spencer)

Crown & Two Chairmen
(020) 7437 8192 *Bateman Street/Dean
Street; W1D 3SB* Popular Soho corner pub;
large main room with smaller area off to the
right, different height tables on bare boards,
four real ales along with good range of craft
beers, enjoyable food (shortish menu) from

sharing boards up including Sun roasts,
upstairs dining room, good mix of customers
(busy with after-work drinkers); open (and
food) all day. *(Maggie and Stevan Hollis)*

★**Dog & Duck** (020) 7494 0697
Bateman Street/Frith Street; W1D 3AJ
Bags of character in this tiny Soho pub – best
enjoyed in the afternoon when not so packed;
unusual old tiles and mosaics (the dog with
tongue hanging out in hot pursuit of a duck is
notable), heavy old advertising mirrors and
open fire, seven real ales including St Austell
and Sharps from unusual little counter and
quite a few wines by the glass, enjoyable
well priced food (Nicholsons menu) in
cosy upstairs dining room where children
welcome; background music; dogs allowed
in bar, open (and food) all day with drinkers
often spilling on to the pavement. *(Richard
and Penny Gibbs)*

Flying Horse (020) 7636 8324
*Oxford Street, near junction with
Tottenham Court Road; W1D 1AN* Ornate
late Victorian pub with long narrow bar;
old tiling, mirrors, mahogany fittings and so
forth, also three notable murals behind glass
of voluptuous nymphs, leather button-back
banquettes and other furniture on bare
boards, up to eight real ales and over 20 gins,
friendly service, another bar downstairs;
background music, free wi-fi; children
welcome until 9pm, can get very busy at
lunchtime, open all day. *(Archie Lee)*

French House (020) 7437 2477
Dean Street; W1D 5BG Small character
Soho pub with impressive range of wines,
bottled beers and other unusual drinks, some
draught beers but no real ales or pint glasses,
lively chatty atmosphere (mainly standing
room), theatre memorabilia, good if not
cheap modern food from short daily changing
menu (lunchtimes Mon-Fri, evening Tues-
Thurs) in bar or upstairs restaurant (must
book), attentive friendly staff; no music or
mobile phones; can get very busy evenings
with customers spilling on to the street, open
all day. *(Dave Webster)*

Grapes (020) 7493 4216
Shepherd Market; W1J 7QQ Genuinely
old-fashioned corner pub with dimly lit bar;
stuffed birds and fish in display cases, some
old guns, red button-back banquettes, wood
floors and coal fire, snug back alcove, six
real ales including Fullers, Sharps and a
house beer from Brains, good choice of thai
food (some english dishes too) in upstairs
restauarant, lots of customers (especially
lunchtime/early evening) spilling on to the
square in good weather; children till 6pm
weekdays (anytime weekends), open all day.
(Richard Tilbrook, Dr and Mrs A K Clarke)

There are report forms at the back of the book.

★**Guinea** (020) 7409 1728
Bruton Place; W1J 6NL Lovely hanging
baskets and chatty customers outside this
tiny 17th-c Mayfair mews pub, standing room
only at peak times, a few cushioned wooden
seats and tables on bare boards, side elbow
shelf and snug back area, old-fashioned
prints, planked ceiling, Youngs and a couple
of guests from striking counter, good range of
wines and whiskies, shortish choice of food
(not Sat lunchtime, Sun evening) including
sandwiches and famous steak and kidney
pie, also smart (and expensive) Guinea Grill
restaurant; no children; open all day (till
6pm Sun). *(Dr and Mrs A K Clarke)*

Prince Regent (020) 7486 7395
Marylebone High Street; W1U 5JN
Victorian corner pub in Marylebone village;
spacious bare-boards bar mixing original
features with modern chic, four changing
ales, craft beers such as Camden, good range
of wines and cocktails, enjoyable food from
pub standards up; children welcome, open
(and food) all day. *(Tracey and Stephen Groves)*

Running Horse (020) 7493 1275
Davies Street/Davies Mews; W1K 5JE
Stylish 18th-c Mayfair pub with open-plan
bare-boards bar; appealing collection of
dining chairs and cushioned settles around
mix of tables, tartan armchairs in front of
green-tiled fireplace, horse-racing prints on
plain or navy-painted panelling, ales such as
Rebellion, lots of wines by the glass and good
food from bar snacks up, prices on the high
side, upstairs cocktail bar with button-back
club chairs, brass chandeliers and more
horsey prints; background music, projector
showing live televised racing, free wi-fi;
children and dogs welcome, contemporary
wicker seats and tables out on the pavement,
open all day (till 8pm Sun). *(Rona Mackinlay)*

Three Tuns (020) 7408 0330
Portman Mews S; W1H 6HP Large bare-
boards front bar and sizeable lounge/dining
area with beams and nooks and crannies,
Greene King ales and guests, generous
helpings of enjoyable reasonably priced
pub food, good friendly staff and buoyant
atmosphere; regular quiz; open (and food)
all day. *(Darrell Barton)*

W2

Leinster Arms (020) 7402 4670
Leinster Terrace; W2 3EU Small
traditional flower-decked pub close to Hyde
Park, friendly and busy, with Fullers London
Pride, three guest beers and well liked pubby
food at sensible prices; sports TV, free wi-fi;
children and dogs welcome, a few pavement
tables, open (and food) all day. *(Millie and
Peter Dowling)*

Mad Bishop & Bear
(020) 7402 2441 *Paddington station;
W2 1HB* Fullers pub up escalator from

concourse; their beers kept well and good
choice of wines, reasonably priced standard
food quickly served including breakfast from
7.30am (10am Sun); airy interior with ornate
plasterwork and mirrored columns, high
tables and chairs on light wood or tiled floors,
raised carpeted dining area with some booth
seating; background music, games machines
and TVs (including train times); tables out at
front, open all day till 11pm (10.30pm Sun).
(Dr and Mrs A K Clarke)

★**Victoria** (020) 7724 1191
Strathearn Place; W2 2NH Well run
and restored bare-boards pub with lots
of Victorian pictures and memorabilia,
cast-iron fireplaces, gilded mirrors and
mahogany panelling, brass mock-gas lamps
above attractive horseshoe bar serving
Fullers ales, guest beers and several wines
by the glass, popular reasonably priced food
from sandwiches and snacks up, friendly
service and chatty relaxed atmosphere;
upstairs has small library/snug and replica
of Gaiety Theatre bar (mostly for private
functions); quiet background music, TV;
children and dogs welcome, pavement
tables and pretty hanging baskets, open
(and food) all day. *(Dr and Mrs A K Clarke,
Ian Herdman)*

WC1

Bountiful Cow (020) 7404 0200
Eagle Street; WC1R 4AP Popular for its
excellent burgers and steaks; informal bar
with booth seating and raised area by the
windows, chrome stools against counter
serving ales such as Adnams and several
wines by the glass, smallish upper room and
larger downstairs dining room; background
music, jazz nights, free wi-fi; children
welcome, closed Sun, otherwise open all day.
(Tim and Sarah Smythe-Brown)

Calthorpe Arms (020) 7278 4732
Grays Inn Road; WC1X 8JR Friendly
early Victorian corner local; well kept Youngs
ales and guests such as Sambrooks and
Twickenham, short choice of enjoyable low-
priced food including Sun roasts, carpeted
bar with plush wall seats, upstairs overspill
dining/function room; Sat folk music and
regular film and quiz evenings, sports TV;
dogs welcome, pavement tables, open all day,
no food Sun evening. *(Jim Stevens)*

★**Cittie of Yorke** (020) 7242 7670
High Holborn; WC1V 6BN Splendid
back bar rather like a baronial hall with
extraordinary extended counter, 1,000-
gallon wine vats resting above gantry,
bulbous lights hanging from soaring raftered
roof, intimate ornately carved booths
and unusual triangular fireplace, smaller
comfortable panelled room with lots of little
prints of York, cheap Sam Smiths beers and
reasonably priced bar food, popular with
students, lawyers and City types but plenty

of space to absorb the crowds; children welcome, closed Sun, otherwise open all day. *(Eddie Edwards, Tony Scott)*

Harrison (020) 7278 3966
Harrison Street; WC1H 8JF Tucked-away 1930s red-brick corner pub; modernised bar with simple mix of tables and chairs on bare boards, sofas by woodburner, three real ales such as Sharps Doom Bar and enjoyable food from snacks up (plenty for vegetarians), good friendly service; nightly live music (mainly folk) in basement; pavement picnic-sets, four bedrooms, open all day, kitchen shuts 4-5pm weekdays. *(Julie Swift)*

Lady Ottoline (020) 7831 0008
Northington Street; WC1N 2JF Sympathetically refurbished 19th-c Bloomsbury pub; original fitted benches together with modern high tables and stools on bare boards, woodburner, various artworks including portrait of Lady Ottoline Morrell who had associations with the Bloomsbury Set, enjoyable up-to-date food from short menu (not particularly cheap), four changing ales, over 40 gins and plenty of wines by the glass, attentive friendly service, upstairs dining rooms; background music, TV; children (till 6pm) and dogs allowed, open all day (till 5pm Sun). *(Louise and Simon Peters)*

★Lamb (020) 7405 0713
Lambs Conduit Street; WC1N 3LZ Authentic 19th-c Bloomsbury pub with green-tiled frontage; bank of cut-glass swivelling snob screens around U-shaped counter, sepia photographs of 1890s actresses on ochre-panelled walls, traditional cast-iron-framed tables and button-back wall benches on stripped boards, snug little back room, Youngs ales and guests kept well, good choice of wines and malt whiskies, decent food from sandwiches, sharing boards and pub favourites up, helpful efficient service, function room upstairs; Sun quiz; children welcome till 5pm, seats in small paved courtyard behind, Foundling Museum nearby, open all day (till midnight Thurs-Sat) and can get very busy. *(M G Hart)*

Museum Tavern (020) 7242 8987
Museum Street/Great Russell Street; WC1B 3BA Ornate high-ceilinged Victorian pub opposite British Museum; half a dozen well kept ales and several wines by the glass, standard Taylor Walker menu, friendly helpful staff; one or two tables out on pavement under gas lamps, open (and food) all day and busy lunchtime/early evening. *(Patricia and Gordon Tucker)*

★Princess Louise (020) 7405 8816
High Holborn; WC1V 7EP Splendid Victorian gin palace with extravagant décor – even the gents' has its own preservation order; gloriously opulent main bar with wood and glass partitions, fine etched and gilt mirrors, brightly coloured and fruit-shaped tiles, slender Portland stone columns soaring towards the lofty and deeply moulded plaster ceiling, open fire, good value Sam Smiths beers from long counter, competitively priced pubby food (not Fri evening or weekends) in quieter upstairs room; no children, open all day (till 6.45pm Sun) and gets crowded early weekday evenings. *(Maggie)*

Queens Head (020) 7713 5772
Acton Street; WC1X 9NB Small Victorian terraced pub attracting good mix of customers; wide ever-changing range of UK and European draught beers (plenty more in bottles), real ciders and extensive whisky choice, friendly knowledgeable staff, food such as pork pies and meat/cheese boards, traditional interior with wood floors, several large mirrors and skylit back part; piano, live jazz last Thurs of month; open all day. *(Mark Holmes)*

Queens Larder (020) 7837 5627
Queen Square; WC1N 3AR Cosy little Bloomsbury corner pub also known as the Queen Charlotte (it's where she stored food for her mad husband George III, who was being cared for nearby); character bare-boards bar with cast-iron tables, wall benches and stools around U-shaped counter, theatre posters on dark panelled walls, Greene King ales and a well kept guest such as Redemption Hopspur, decent lunchtime pubby food delivered by dumb waiter from upstairs kitchen, friendly service; background music; dogs welcome, pavement picnic-sets, open all day. *(Brian and Anna Marsden, Dr and Mrs A K Clarke)*

Skinners Arms (020) 7837 5621
Judd Street; WC1H 9NT Richly decorated, with glorious woodwork, marble pillars, high ceilings and ornate windows, lots of London prints on busy wallpaper, interesting layout including comfortable back seating area, coal fire, Greene King and guests from attractive long bar, enjoyable home-made food; unobtrusive background music and muted TV; pavement picnic-sets, handy for British Library, closed Sun, otherwise open all day. *(John E, Anthony Barnes, Dr and Mrs A K Clarke)*

Union Tavern (020) 7278 0111
Lloyd Baker Street; WC1X 9AA Bare-boards Victorian corner pub with attractive period décor; much enjoyed food from varied menu including very good value lunchtime/early evening set deals, friendly helpful service, beers such as Beavertown, Curious, Sambrooks and Trumans, lots of wines by the glass and some premium gins; background music; children and dogs welcome, open all day, food most of the day too, weekend brunch from 10.30am. *(Chaz)*

WC2

Admiralty (020) 7930 0066

Trafalgar Square; WC2N 5DS Handsome
naval-theme pub by Trafalgar Square;
button-back leather seating booths by big
windows, high stools and elbow tables,
grand chandeliers and lots of interesting
prints, flagstaff with white ensigns and union
jacks, Fullers/Gales beers from traditional
counter, grand steps up to mezzanine, also
atmospheric vaulted cellar bar, standard pub
food including speciality pies, efficient staff;
children welcome, a few pavement tables,
open all day from 9am (10am Sun). *(Dr and
Mrs A K Clarke, Steve Haworth)*

Bear & Staff (020) 7321 0814

Bear Street; WC2H 7AX Traditional
Nicholsons corner pub with half a dozen well
kept changing ales and pretty standard food
(including deals) from sandwiches and pies
up, friendly staff, upstairs dining room named
after Charlie Chaplin who was a customer;
open (and food) all day. *(James Butcher)*

Chandos (020) 7836 1401

St Martins Lane; WC2N 4ER Busy
bare-boards bar with snug cubicles and
plenty of standing room (can get packed
early evening), lots of theatre memorabilia
on stairs up to more comfortable split-level
lounge with opera photographs (the Coliseum
is almost next door), low wooden tables,
panelling, leather sofas and stained-glass
windows, well kept/priced Sam Smiths beers
and decent good value pub food; background
music and games machines; children upstairs
till 6pm, note the automaton on the roof
(working 10am-2pm, 4-9pm), open all day
from 9am (for breakfast). *(Nigel and
Jean Eames)*

Coal Hole (020) 7379 9883

Strand; WC2R 0DW Well preserved
Edwardian pub adjacent to the Savoy;
original leaded windows, classical wall
reliefs and high baronial-style ceiling, nine
changing ales from central servery, standard
Nicholsons menu, galleried area at back and
wine bar downstairs; sports TV; open all day
and can get very busy. *(Tony Scott)*

Cross Keys (020) 7836 5185

Endell Street/Betterton Street; WC2H 9EB
Flower-decked Covent Garden pub with
fascinating interior; masses of photographs,
pictures and posters including Beatles
memorabilia, all kinds of brassware and
bric-a-brac from gigantic fish to musical
instruments, well kept Brodies ales, guest
beers and decent wines by the glass, good
lunchtime sandwiches and a few bargain hot
dishes including generous Sun roast; fruit
machine, gents' downstairs; cobbled area out
at front with tubs of flowers, open all day.
(Dave Webster)

Edgar Wallace (020) 7353 3120

Essex Street; WC2R 3JE Spacious
open-plan pub dating from the 18th c; eight
well kept ales and enjoyable good value
traditional food from sandwiches up, friendly
efficient service, half-panelled walls and red
ceilings covered in beer mats, interesting
Edgar Wallace memorabilia and lots of old
cigarette adverts and other signs, upstairs
dining room; a few high tables in side
alleyway, closed weekends, otherwise open
all day. *(Jim Stevens)*

George (020) 7353 9638

Strand; WC2R 1AP Timbered pub near the
law courts with long narrow bare-boards bar,
plenty of real ales and a dozen wines by the
glass, lunchtime food from sandwiches up,
also upstairs Pig and Goose bar-restaurant;
open all day. *(Margaret McDonald)*

Knights Templar (020) 7831 2660

Chancery Lane; WC2A 1DT Good well
managed Wetherspoons in big-windowed
former bank; marble pillars, handsome
fittings and plasterwork, bustling atmosphere
on two levels, ever-changing range of well
kept/priced ales, good wine choice and
enjoyable bargain food, friendly efficient
service no matter how busy; free wi-fi; open
all day Mon-Fri, till 6.30pm Sat, closed Sun.
(Ian Herdman)

Mr Foggs Tavern (020) 7581 3992

St Martins Lane; WC2N 4EA Themed
around Jules Verne's Phileas Fogg; small
Victorian-style bar with appropriate pictures
and stuffed animals on panelled walls,
masses of bric-a-brac hanging from ceiling
including model boats, bird cages, brass
instruments, even an old pram, craft beers
and over a dozen wines by the glass from
metal-topped servery, friendly staff in period
dress, enjoyable food including bar snacks,
sharing plates and range of pies, atmospheric
upstairs re-creation of 19th-c salon/gin
parlour, swagged curtains, chinese wallpaper
and chaise longues, extensive selection of
gins and cocktails; open all day, upstairs from
4pm (7pm weekends). *(Julie Swift)*

Nell Gwynne (020) 7240 5579

Bull Inn Court, off Strand; WC2R 0NP
Narrow dimly lit old pub tucked down
alleyway; character bare-boards interior
with lots of pictures (some of Nell Gwynne)
on papered walls, a few tables but mainly
standing room and drinkers spill outside
at busy times, St Austell Tribute and three
guests, some interesting bottled beers and
extensive range of spirits; good juke box, TV,
darts; open all day. *(Tony Scott)*

Porterhouse (020) 7379 7917

Maiden Lane; WC2E 7NA London outpost
of Dublin's Porterhouse brewery, their
interesting beers along with guests and lots
of bottled imports, good choice of wines by

the glass and irish whiskeys, decent pubby food including pizzas; three-level labyrinth of stairs (lifts for disabled), galleries, gleaming copper ducting and piping, prominent open-work clock hanging from the ceiling and neatly cased bottled beer displays dotted about; background and live music, sports TVs (even in the gents'); tables on front terrace, open all day and can get packed evenings. *(Samuel and Melissa Turnbull)*

Salisbury (020) 7836 5863

St Martins Lane; WC2N 4AP Gleaming Victorian pub in the heart of the West End; a wealth of cut-glass and mahogany, wonderfully ornate bronze light fittings and etched mirrors, some interesting photographs including Dylan Thomas enjoying a drink here in 1941, well kept ales and usual Taylor Walker menu from sharing platters up, cheerful staff; steep stairs down to lavatories; children allowed till 5pm, seats in pedestrianised side alley, open (and food) all day. *(Charlie and Mark Todd)*

Ship (020) 7405 1992

Gate Street; WC2A 3HP Tucked-away Holborn pub with dimly lit bare-boards bar; leaded lights, panelling and plaster-relief ceiling, some booth seating, open fire, six real ales including a Caledonian house beer, good variety of gins and enjoyable bar food, upstairs candlelit restaurant (good separate menu), friendly service; background music, live jazz Sun 4.30-7pm; open (and food) all day. *(Archie Lee)*

★ Ship & Shovell (020) 7839 1311

Craven Passage, off Craven Street; WC2N 5PH Unusually split between two facing buildings, one side brightly lit with dark wood, etched mirrors and interesting mainly naval pictures, some stall seating and open fire, other smaller side (across 'Underneath the Arches' alley) has a cosily partitioned bar; well kept Badger ales, a guest beer and reasonably priced pubby lunchtime food from baguettes up, good friendly service; closed Sun, otherwise open all day. *(Darrel Barton)*

Temple Brew House

(020) 7936 2536 *Essex Street; WC2R 3JF* Popular basement bar with fine range of beers including some from on-site microbrewery, lots of wines by the glass and well liked food from sandwiches, small plates and burgers up (own smokehouse), friendly service from enthusiastic knowledgeable young staff; no under-18s, open (and food) all day. *(Patricia and Gordon Tucker)*

Wellington (020) 7836 2789

Strand/Wellington Street; WC2R 0HS Traditional corner pub next to the Lyceum theatre; long narrow split-level bar with moulded ceiling and ornate mahogany servery, ten real ales including Adnams,

Fullers and Sharps, craft beers and several wines by the glass, usual Nicholsons menu, friendly staff, upstairs restaurant; sports TV; tables outside, open (and food) all day. *(Jamie Green)*

EAST LONDON

E1

Princess of Prussia (020) 7702 0723

Prescot Street; E1 8AZ Atmospheric pub keeping original Burton Brewery signage at front and a couple of large Victorian lanterns; cosy interior with lots of pictures and bits and pieces on shelves, open fire, four well kept Shepherd Neame ales and enjoyable pubby food (all day Sat), relaxed chatty atmosphere; nice terrace garden behind, closed Sun, otherwise open all day. *(Sophie and John Moor)*

★ Prospect of Whitby (020) 3603 4041

Wapping Wall; E1W 3SH Claims to be oldest pub on the Thames dating from 1520 (although largely rebuilt after much later fire), was known as the Devil's Tavern and has a colourful history (Pepys and Dickens used it regularly and Turner came for weeks at a time to study the river views) – tourists love it; L-shaped bare-boards bar with plenty of beams, flagstones and panelling, five changing ales served from fine pewter counter, good choice of wines by the glass, bar food and more formal restaurant upstairs, hard-working staff; children welcome (only if eating after 5.30pm), no dogs inside, unbeatable river views towards Docklands from tables on waterfront courtyard, open all day. *(Gail and Arthur Roberts)*

Town of Ramsgate (020) 7481 8000

Wapping High Street; E1W 2PN Interesting old-London Thames-side setting; long narrow dimly lit bar with squared oak panelling, Fullers, Harveys, Youngs and a guest, good choice of traditional food including daily specials and deals, friendly helpful service; background music, Mon quiz; children (till 8pm) and dogs welcome, restricted river view from small back terrace, open (and food) all day. *(Sandra and Miles Spencer)*

Williams (020) 7247 5163

Artillery Lane; E1 7LS Busy Spitalfields pub with 14 real ales (predominantly from smaller London brewers), craft beers and proper ciders, decent choice of well liked food from snacks up, comfortable seating areas, photographs of old London breweries on stripped-brick walls; background and some live music, sports TV, darts; open (and food) all day. *(Jim Stevens)*

E2

Sun (020) 7739 4097

Bethnal Green Road; E2 0AN Updated 19th-c bar with good choice of local craft beers and other drinks including cocktails, irish whiskeys and poitin, friendly helpful service, bare boards, exposed brickwork and some leather banquettes, padded stools around copper-topped counter with lanterns above, food limited to bar snacks and cheese/meat boards; open all day (till 2am Thurs-Sat). *(Ted Wright)*

E3
Palm Tree (020) 8980 2918
Grove Road; E3 5BH Lone survivor of blitzed East End terrace tucked away in Mile End Park by Regent's Canal; two Edwardian bars around oval server, old-fashioned and unchanging under long-serving licensees, a couple of well kept ales, lunchtime sandwiches, good local atmosphere with popular weekend live music; no credit cards; open all day (till late Sat).
(Sally and Colin Allen)

E7
Forest Tavern (020) 8503 0868
Forest Lane across from Forest Gate station; E7 9BB Part of the Antic group, relaxed and unsmart, with six real ales including house Volden, craft beers and enjoyable food from pub favourites up (shortish menu), friendly staff; live music and DJ nights, Tues quiz, games including table football; children and dogs welcome, seats out on decking, open all day Fri-Sun, from 4pm other days. *(Charlie and Mark Todd)*

E11
Red Lion (020) 8988 2929
High Road Leytonstone; E11 3AA Large 19th-c corner pub (Antic group) with plenty of quirky character; high-ceilinged open-plan interior with lots of pictures, mirrors, books and general bric-a-brac, ten changing ales, craft kegs and real ciders, enjoyable interesting food along with some pub staples, bar billiards and table football; weekend music, Mon quiz and occasional comedy nights; children and dogs welcome, picnic-sets out at front and in good-sized back garden, open all day. *(Dave Webster)*

E13
Black Lion (020) 8472 2351
High Street, Plaistow; E13 0AD Beamed 18th-c coaching inn surviving among 20th-c development; up to four real ales including Mighty Oak and enjoyable well priced pubby food, friendly staff; sports TVs; picnic-sets in spacious garden, open all day, no food weekends except on West Ham match days.
(Laura Reid)

E14
★Grapes (020) 7987 4396
Narrow Street, Limehouse; E14 8BP Relatively unchanged since Dickens used it as a model for his Six Jolly Fellowship Porters in *Our Mutual Friend*; a proper traditional tavern with friendly atmosphere and good

mix of customers; partly panelled bar with prints of actors, old local maps and pictures of the pub itself, elaborately etched windows, plates along a shelf, larger back area leading to small deck looking over the river towards Canary Wharf; Adnams, Black Sheep, Timothy Taylors and two guests, good value tasty bar food, upstairs evening restaurant (Mon-Sat) with more fine views; Mon quiz; no under-18s, dogs welcome in bar, open all day, food all day Sat, till 3.30pm Sun. *(Mike Buckingham)*

Gun (020) 7515 5222
Coldharbour; E14 9NS Welcoming dining pub with great views from riverside terrace of the O2 arena; smart front restaurant and partitioned bar, second flagstoned bar behind with antique guns and log fire, cosy dining room next-door, Fullers beers, guest ales and several wines by the glass, good modern food (not cheap); background music; children welcome till 8pm, open all day. *(Katiej)*

NORTH LONDON

HA3
★Hare (020) 8954 4949
Brookshill/Old Redding; HA3 6SD Carefully renovated old pub with attractive contemporary décor in bar and linked dining rooms; long counter serving Sharps Doom Bar, Timothy Taylors Landlord and several wines by the glass, also extensive range of gins and cocktails, good interesting food including set menu till 6.30pm (not Sun), stylish brasserie with rugs on bare boards and woodburner, two other dining areas, one perfect for a small group, church candles and modern artwork throughout; children and dogs (in bar) welcome, some picnic-sets out at front, more seats in back garden with gazebo, open (and food) all day. *(Jeff Davies)*

N1
Camden Head (020) 7359 0851
Camden Walk; N1 8DY Comfortably preserved Victorian pub in pedestrianised street; lots of fine etched glass and mahogany panelling, unusual clock suspended from ceiling, button-back leather wall seats and a few small booths, half a dozen well kept changing ales including Greene King from oval servery, fairly priced pubby food (order at the bar); free nightly comedy club upstairs; children welcome till 7pm, no dogs, chunky picnic-sets on front terrace, open (and food) all day. *(Peter and Emma Kelly)*

Craft Beer Company
(020) 7278 0318 *White Lion Street; N1 9PP* Flower-decked Victorian pub attracting good mix of customers; extensive choice of interesting draught/bottled beers along with good range of other drinks, cosy and softly lit with dark green walls and wood-strip or red carpeted floors, high tables in main bar, low ones in adjacent areas, burger

menu (all day weekends); occasional live acoustic music; small side garden, open all day Fri-Sun, from 4pm other days. *(Pam Thomas)*

Drapers Arms (020) 7619 0348
W end of Barnsbury Street; N1 1ER
Simply furnished Georgian townhouse in residential Islington; busy U-shaped bar with dark wooden tables and wheelback chairs on bare boards, gilt mirrors over fireplaces, sofa and some comfortable chairs in one part, bright green counter serving Harveys, Sambrooks and Trumans, british draught lagers and over 20 wines by the glass, enjoyable food from shortish but varied menu, stylish upstairs dining room with striking chequerboard-painted floor; background music, free wi-fi; children welcome (must be seated and eating after 6pm), dogs allowed in bar, nice paved back terrace with zinc-topped tables under large parasols, open all day. *(Mrs Margo Finlay, Jörg Kasprowski)*

Earl of Essex (020) 7424 5828
Danbury Street; N1 8LE One-room pub with great choice of beers on draught (listed on boards) and in bottles, decent range of other drinks too, varied menu from small plates up including suggested beer pairings, friendly knowledgeable staff; tables in back walled garden, open (and food) all day. *(Martin Holvey)*

Hemingford Arms (020) 7607 3303
Hemingford Road; N1 1DF 19th-c ivy-clad pub filled with bric-a-brac; good choice of real ales from central servery, thai evening food plus Sunday roasts, open fire, upstairs bar/function room; live music including Mon bluegrass, quiz nights, sports TV, machines; picnic-sets outside, open all day. *(Maggie and Stevan Hollis)*

Islington Townhouse
(020) 3637 6424 *Liverpool Road; N1 0RW* Corner pub owned by Hippo Inns; stylish modern décor over three floors, good selection of beers and other drinks including cocktails and over 20 wines by the glass, good sensibly priced food from assorted small plates up, Sat brunch, friendly engaging staff; background music; children welcome, open (and food) all day. *(Dave Webster)*

★ Parcel Yard (020) 7713 7258
King's Cross station, N end of new concourse, up stairs (or lift); N1C 4AH Impressive restoration of listed Victorian parcel sorting office; lots of interesting bare-boards rooms off corridors around airy central atrium, pleasing old-fashioned feel with exposed pipework and ducting adding to the effect, back bar serving full range of well kept Fullers beers plus guests from long modern counter, plenty of wines by the glass, similar upstairs area with old and new furniture including comfortable sofas, railway memorabilia and some nice touches like Victorian-envelope wallpaper, food from bar snacks up, breakfast till 11.45am; power points to recharge phones/laptops, screens for train times, platform views; seats out at front, open all day from 8am (9am Sun). *(Tom and Ruth Rees)*

Wenlock Arms (020) 7608 3406
Wenlock Road; N1 7TA Friendly old-fashioned corner local with excellent choice of real ales, craft beers and ciders from central servery, plenty of foreign bottled beers too, simple food such as toasties, alcove seating and coal fires; darts, free wi-fi; children (until 8pm) and dogs welcome, open all day. *(Sandra and Miles Spencer)*

N4

Faltering Fullback (020) 7272 5834
Perth Road/Ennis Road; N4 3HB Friendly ivy-covered corner local with two softly lit bars, lots of bric-a-brac, Fullers London Pride and a couple of guests, good value evening thai food in back room; background and live music, Mon quiz, sports TVs, pool; nice outside area on different levels, open all day. *(Tony Scott, Giles and Annie Francis)*

N6

Flask (020) 8348 7346
Highgate West Hill; N6 6BU Traditional Georgian pub with intriguing up-and-down layout; Fullers beers and a guest from unusual sash-windowed bar hatch in snug lower area, log fires, good variety of food from sandwiches and snacks up including popular Sun roasts, barrel-vaulted flagstoned dining part; children and dogs welcome, picnic-sets out in front courtyard, handy for strolls around Highgate village or Hampstead Heath, open all day, food till 7pm Sun. *(Margaret McDonald)*

Red Lion & Sun (020) 8340 1780
North Road (B519); N6 4BE 1920s Highgate Village dining pub with good variety of well liked food (can be pricey) including some decent vegetarian choices, they also do takeaway fish and chips, three real ales such as Brains Rev James, Caledonian Deuchars IPA and Timothy Taylors, lots of wines by the glass (good list) and extensive range of whiskies, cheerful helpful service; well behaved children and dogs welcome, tables on leafy front terrace and in smaller back courtyard, open (and food) all day. *(Tony Scott)*

N16

Railway Tavern (020) 3092 3344
St Jude Street/King Henrys Walk; N16 8JT 19th-c bow-fronted single-bar pub; half a dozen well kept ales along with craft kegs and bottled beers, good authentic thai food (roasts on Sun), reasonable prices and

friendly relaxed atmosphere, some railway memorabilia; acoustic live music; children and dogs welcome, open all day weekends, from 4pm other days. *(Julie Swift)*

NW1

★Chapel (020) 7723 2337

Chapel Street; NW1 5DP Corner dining pub attracting equal share of drinkers (busy and noisy in the evening); spacious rooms dominated by open kitchen, smart but simple furnishings, sofas at lounge end next to big fireplace, a couple of Greene King ales and good choice of wines by the glass, coffees and teas, decent food from weekly changing menu, friendly service; children and dogs welcome, picnic-sets in sizeable back garden, more seats on decking under heated parasols, open all day. *(Pam Thomas)*

Constitution (020) 7380 0767

St Pancras Way; NW1 0QT Traditional standalone 19th-c pub close to Camden Lock and a quieter alternative to the busy market area; four local beers and good selection of wines by the glass, pubby lunchtime food Mon-Fri, friendly staff and pleasant atmosphere; pool, darts and juke box, cellar bar for live music; children (till 9pm) and dogs welcome, barbecues in lovely sunny garden overlooking canal, open all day. *(Ted Wright)*

★Doric Arch (020) 7388 2221

Eversholt Street; NW1 2DN Virtually part of Euston station (up stairs from the bus terminus) and a welcome retreat from the busy concourse; well kept Fullers ales, guest beers and enjoyable well priced pubby food from snacks and sharing plates to specials, friendly efficient service, compact bare-boards bar with railway memorabilia and pretty Victorian fireplace, some button-back bench seating and a cosy boothed alcove, steps to raised back dining area; background music, TVs (including train times); open (and food) all day. *(Dr and Mrs A K Clarke)*

Euston Tap (020) 3137 8837

Euston Road; NW1 2EF Two small 19th-c neoclassical lodges in front of Euston station; around ten quickly changing real ales, along with craft kegs, proper ciders and range of bottled beers, knowledgeable staff, limited seating but more space and lavatories up spiral stairs; outside tables, open all day. *(Dr and Mrs A K Clarke)*

Metropolitan (020) 7486 3489

Baker Street station, Marylebone Road; NW1 5LA Flight of steps up to this spacious Wetherspoons in impressively ornate pillared hall (designed by Metropolitan Railway architect Charles W Clarke), lots of tables on one side, very long bar the other, ten or more real ales, good coffee and their usual food; free wi-fi; family area, open all day from 8am (10am Sun). *(Dr and Mrs A K Clarke, Tony Hobden)*

Somers Town Coffee House (020) 7387 7377

Chalton Street (tucked away between Euston and St Pancras stations); NW1 1HS Despite its name (there was a coffee house here in the 18th c) this is a busy pub with fine range of well kept ales including Youngs and decent choice of enjoyable food (gluten-free and vegan diets catered for), spacious interior with main bar on the ground floor, basement cocktail bar (from 5pm) and upstairs private dining rooms; background music; children and dogs welcome, outside tables front and back, open all day from 8am (10am weekends) for breakfast. *(David Hunt, Anthony Barnes)*

Tapping the Admiral (020) 7267 6118

Castle Road; NW1 8SU Friendly local with fine range of well kept ales mainly from London brewers, fairly priced home-made food including range of pies; quiz nights and live music, free wi-fi; children welcome till 7pm, heated beer garden, open all day. *(Rona Mackinlay)*

NW3

★Flask (020) 7435 4580

Flask Walk; NW3 1HE Bustling local with two traditional front bars divided by unique Victorian screen, smart banquettes, panelling and lots of little prints, attractive fireplace, Youngs ales and a guest, plenty of wines by the glass and maybe winter mulled wine, popular fairly pubby food from sharing plates up, good friendly service, dining conservatory; background music, TV; children (till 8pm) and dogs welcome, seats and tables in alley, open (and food) all day. *(Chaz)*

Spaniards Inn (020) 8731 8406

Spaniards Lane; NW3 7JJ Busy 16th-c pub next to Hampstead Heath; attractive and characterful low-ceilinged rooms with oak panelling, antique winged settles, snug alcoves and open fires, up to five real ales, several craft beers and 18 wines by glass, decent food from sandwiches and sharing boards up, dining room upstairs; free wi-fi; charming garden with own bar (arrive early weekends as popular with dog walkers and families), car park also fills quickly and parking nearby difficult, open (and food) all day. *(Barbara and Phil Bowie)*

Washington (020) 7722 8842

Englands Lane; NW3 4UE Victorian corner pub with plenty of original features; high moulded ceiling, ornate woodwork, etched glass and mirrors, mixed furniture on wood flooring including padded benches and button-back banquettes, stools around central counter serving five real ales, several craft beers and around 25 wines by the glass, enjoyable fairly traditional food at fair prices, friendly relaxed atmosphere; soft background music, Tues quiz and maybe other events held in cellar bar; children and well behaved dogs allowed, open (and food) all day. *(Nina Reynolds)*

NW5
Southampton Arms   07375 755539

Highgate Road; NW5 1LE   Popular simply furnished drinkers' pub; one long room with big front window, wall seats and stools around tables on bare boards, open fire, up to ten changing beers and good range of ciders, some straightforward food, no credit cards; live piano some evenings, Mon quiz; small garden at back, handy for Hampstead Heath, open all day. *(Tony Scott)*

NW10
William IV   (020) 8969 5955

Harrow Road; NW10 5JX   Newly reopened/refurbished 19th-c corner pub in Kensal Green; four separate areas including main bar and dining room keeping original features, wood floors and painted panelling, good fairly pubby food from short reasonably priced menu, beers such as Marstons Wainwright and Youngs from marble-topped servery, friendly staff; children welcome, spacious garden with summer house, 15 bedrooms, open all day from 10am for brunch. *(Patricia and Gordon Tucker)*

SOUTH LONDON

SE1
Dean Swift   (020) 7357 0748

Gainsford Street; SE1 2NE   Comfortably updated corner pub tucked away behind Tower Bridge; well kept cask ales, lots of craft beers and several wines by the glass, friendly well informed staff, good food from bar snacks to Sun roasts, upstairs restaurant; sports TV; open (and food) all day. *(Gail and Arthur Roberts)*

Fire Station   (020) 3727 5938

Waterloo Road; SE1 8SB   Unusual fire station conversion, busy and noisy, with two big knocked-through rooms, burger and pizza menu, craft beers such as Beavertown, Camden and Sambrooks, 11 wines by the glass and cocktails, friendly staff; background music; children welcome, a few tables out in front, handy for Old Vic theatre and Waterloo station, open (and food) all day from 7am (9am weekends) for breakfast. *(Dr and Mrs A K Clarke)*

Founders Arms   (020) 7928 1899

Hopton Street; SE1 9JH   Modern glass-walled building in superb location – outstanding terrace views along Thames and handy for South Bank attractions; plenty of customers including tourists, theatre- and gallery-goers spilling on to pavement and river walls, Youngs Bitter and a guest, craft beers such as Beavertown and Camden, lots of wines by the glass, food served all day, tea and coffee from separate servery; background music; children welcome (till 8pm) away from bar, dogs allowed on terrace, open till midnight Fri, Sat. *(Jim Rawlings)*

★**George**   (020) 7407 2056

Off 77 Borough High Street; SE1 1NH   Tucked-away 16th-c coaching inn mentioned in *Little Dorrit*, owned by the National Trust and beautifully preserved; lots of tables in bustling cobbled courtyard with views of the tiered exterior galleries, series of no-frills ground-floor rooms with black beams, square-latticed windows and some panelling, plain oak or elm tables on bare boards, old-fashioned built-in settles, dimpled glass lanterns and a 1797 Act of Parliament clock, impressive central staircase up to a series of dining rooms and balcony, well kept Greene King ales and a beer badged for the pub, traditional food from sandwiches up; children welcome away from bar, open (and food) all day. *(Dr and Mrs A K Clarke)*

★**Kings Arms**   (020) 7207 0784

Roupell Street; SE1 8TB   Proper corner local tucked away amid terrace houses, bustling and friendly, with curved servery dividing traditional bar and lounge, bare boards, open fire and various bits and pieces including old black and white photographs, decorative china and some local road signs, nine well kept changing beers and good choice of wines and malt whiskies, enjoyable reasonably priced food from thai dishes to Sun roasts, welcoming helpful staff, big back extension with conservatory/courtyard dining area; background music; children till 7pm, open all day. *(Tony Scott)*

★**Market Porter**   (020) 7407 2495

Stoney Street; SE1 9AA   Properly pubby, no-frills place opening at 6am weekdays for workers at neighbouring Borough Market; up to ten unusual real ales (over 60 guests a week) often from far-flung brewers

---

A star symbol before the name of a pub shows exceptional character and appeal. It doesn't mean extra comfort. Even quite a basic pub can win a star, if it's individual enough.

and served in top condition, particularly helpful friendly service, bare boards and open fire, barrels balancing on beams, simple furnishings, food in bar or upstairs lunchtime restaurant with view over market; background music; children allowed weekends till 7pm, dogs welcome, gets very busy with drinkers spilling on to the street, open all day. *(Dr and Mrs A K Clarke, Mike Buckingham)*

Rake (020) 7407 0557

Winchester Walk; SE1 9AG Tiny discreetly modern Borough Market bar with amazing bottled beer range in wall-wide cooler, also half a dozen continental lagers on tap and four real ales, light snacks available or you can bring your own food from the market, good friendly service; fair-sized covered and heated outside area. *(Jim Rawlings)*

Sheaf (020) 7407 9934

Southwark Street; SE1 1TY In cellars beneath the Hop Exchange (easy to miss); brick vaulted ceilings and iron pillars, button-back benches, sofas and some high tables, lots of framed black and white photographs of former regulars, ten real ales and good value pubby food; sports TVs; open all day. *(B and M Kendall)*

Wheatsheaf (020) 7940 3880

Stoney Street; opposite Borough Market main entrance; SE1 9AA Updated Youngs pub directly below new railway bridge; their well kept ales with guests such as Camden Town and Meantime, good choice of wines by the glass and decent food from sandwiches and snacks up, cheerful busy atmosphere; live music; heated outside area with campervan acting as servery, open (and food) all day from 9am (10am Sun, noon Mon). *(Dr and Mrs A K Clarke)*

White Hart (020) 7928 9190

Cornwall Road/Whittlesey Street; SE1 8TJ Backstreet corner pub near Waterloo station with friendly community bustle; interesting range of cask and craft beers, lots more in bottles and good selection of other drinks, sensibly priced up-to-date blackboard food along with pub standards, comfortable sofas on stripped boards, fresh flowers on tables; background music, free wi-fi; disabled facilities, open all day. *(Tony and Jill Radnor)*

SE5

★Crooked Well (020) 7252 7798

Grove Lane; SE5 8SY Popular early 19th-c restaurant pub in heart of Camberwell; button-back sofas, wall seats and variety of wooden dining chairs and tables on bare boards, good food including vegan set menu and other deals, craft beers, a couple of real ales and plenty of wines by the glass, cocktails, happy hour 5-7pm (daily) and

10-11pm (Thurs-Sat), welcoming helpful staff, private dining/function rooms upstairs; children welcome, pavement picnic-sets, open all day weekends, closed lunchtime Mon-Weds. *(Jim Rawlings)*

SE8

Dog & Bell (020) 8692 5664

Prince Street; SE8 3JD Friendly old-fashioned Deptford local tucked away near the river (on the Thames Path); wood benches around bright cheerfully decorated L-shaped bar, open fire, up to half a dozen well kept ales including Fullers, bottled belgian beers and reasonably priced pub food, prompt friendly service, dining room; live folk music, bar billiards, TV; tables out in courtyard, open all day. *(Dave Webster)*

SE9

Park Tavern (020) 8850 3216

Passey Place; SE9 5DA Traditional Victorian corner pub off Eltham High Street; eight well kept changing ales and 14 wines by the glass, log fire, friendly easy-going atmosphere, pizzas and pub snacks served lunchtime; background music; pleasant little garden behind, open all day. *(Maggie and Stevan Hollis)*

SE10

★Greenwich Union (020) 8692 6258

Royal Hill; SE10 8RT More like a bar than pub with full Meantime craft range, over 150 bottled beers, unusual spirits and interesting choice of teas and coffees, enjoyable food from sharing plates and traditional favourites up, friendly prompt service; long narrow stone-flagged room with simple front area, wooden furniture, stove and daily papers, comfortable part with sofas and cushioned pews, booth seating in end conservatory; free wi-fi; well behaved children and dogs welcome, paved terrace with teak furniture and old-fashioned lamp posts, open (and food) all day, kitchen shuts 6pm Sun. *(Rupert Watson)*

★Guildford Arms (020) 8691 6293

Guildford Grove/Devonshire Drive; SE10 8JY This civilised bow-fronted Georgian dining pub was closed for major refurbishment as we went to press – news/reports please.

Pilot (020) 8858 5910

River Way, Blackwall Lane; SE10 0BE Early 19th-c pub surviving amid O2 development; opened-up interior on three levels with roof terrace overlooking park, well kept Fullers/Gales beers, good choice of food (all day Fri, Sat, till 6pm Sun) from pubby choices and charcoal grills to daily specials; background music, newspapers and free wi-fi; dogs welcome, picnic-sets in front, more seating in enclosed back garden, ten well equipped boutique bedrooms, open all day. *(Robert and Diana Ringstone)*

Prince of Greenwich

(020) 8692 6089 *Royal Hill; SE10 8RT*
Victorian pub under warmly welcoming
Sicilian owners; good italian food from
freshly made pizzas up, Fullers London Pride,
Sharps Doom Bar and nice wines by the
glass, quirky décor and unusual furnishings,
lots of black and white jazz photos/posters
(regular live jazz); maybe italian film night
Thurs; children and well behaved dogs
welcome, closed Mon, open from 4pm Tues-
Fri, 12.30pm weekends. *(David Northrop)*

SE11

Prince of Wales   (020) 7735 9916

Cleaver Square; SE11 4EA Comfortably
traditional little Edwardian pub in smart
quiet Georgian square near the Oval; well
kept Shepherd Neame ales and simple pub
food from sandwiches up, warm friendly
atmosphere; pavement seats, boules available
to play in the gravel square, open all day.
(Samuel and Melissa Tucker)

SE12

Lord Northbrook   (020) 8318 1127

Burnt Ash Road; SE12 8PU Opened-up
bare-boards Victorian corner pub; good mix
of seating including a couple of chesterfields
by Victorian fireplace, contemporary
paintwork and lots of pictures, well kept
Fullers/Gales beers, decent food from
shortish menu (all day weekends), friendly
staff, conservatory; children and dogs
welcome, paved split-level back garden; open
all day. *(Charlie and Mark Todd)*

SE14

Ale Bar   (020) 8694 1888

New Cross Road; SE14 6TA Friendly
little three-room pub in basement of the
London Theatre; four changing ales (mainly
kentish) served from polypins, craft beers
and decent selection of gins, quirky interior
with aeroplane seats, working model railway
and theatre memorabilia; Weds quiz, dogs
welcome (beer and treats for them), closed
Sun-Tues, otherwise open from 6pm (4pm Sat).
(Pam Thomas)

SE15

Ivy House   (020) 7277 8233

Stuart Road; SE15 3BE Co-operative
owned pub with eight local ales and good
range of craft beers and ciders, well priced
food (not lunchtimes Mon, Tues) including
burgers, old-fashioned panelled interior,
stage in back room for live music, comedy
and theatre nights; children (till 8pm) and
dogs welcome, rack for cyclists, open all day.
(Archie Lee)

Old Nuns Head   (020) 7639 4007

Nunhead Green; SE15 3QQ Popular
open-plan 1930s brick and timber pub
on edge of small green; half a dozen
interesting changing beers and enjoyable
food provided by pop-up kitchens including

burgers and street food, just roasts on Sun,
cheerful efficient staff; music and comedy
nights; children (till 8.30pm) and dogs
welcome, back garden and a few seats
out in front, handy for fascinating gothic
Nunhead Cemetery, open all day (till 1am
Fri, Sat), food from 6pm weekdays, midday
weekends. *(Millie and Peter Dowling)*

SE16

★Mayflower   (020) 7237 4088

Rotherhithe Street; SE16 4NF Cosy old
riverside pub in unusual street with lovely
early 18th-c church; generous food including
more upmarket daily specials, well kept
Greene King Abbot and four guests, good
value wines and decent coffee, friendly young
staff, black beams, panelling, high-backed
settle and coal fires, nautical bric-a-brac,
great Thames views from upstairs candlelit
evening restaurant; background music,
Tues quiz; children and dogs (in bar area)
welcome, fun jetty/terrace over water
(barbecues), handy for Brunel Museum,
open (and food) all day. *(Richard Tilbrook,
Mike Buckingham)*

SE20

Goldsmiths Arms   (020) 8659 1242

Croydon Road, Penge; SE20 7TJ Popular
and welcoming 19th-c pub just off the high
street; bare-boards front bar with high ceiling
and open fire, large room beyond mainly for
dining, Purity Mad Goose, guest beers and
11 wines by the glass, enjoyable good value
food from shortish menu (order at the bar),
friendly efficient young staff; background
and weekend live music, Tues quiz; children
(till 8pm) and dogs welcome, picnic-sets
out at front and in back garden, open all day
Fri-Sun, from 4pm other days, kitchen shuts
7pm Sun. *(John Wooll)*

SW4

Abbeville   (020) 8675 2201

Abbeville Road; SW4 9JW Popular dining
pub in same small group as the Latchmere in
Battersea; split-level interior including small
mezzanine, bare boards, half-panelling and
open fire, mix of old furniture, vintage prints
and a stag's head, good food from short but
varied menu, beers such as Meantime and
Timothy Taylors, plenty of wines by the glass,
cocktails, efficient friendly service; children
and dogs welcome, pavement tables, open all
day, food all day weekends. *(Jeremy Brodie)*

Clapham Tap   (020) 7498 9633

Clapham Manor Street; SW4 6ED
Friendly little end-of-terrace pub with
U-shaped bare-boards bar, six well kept ales
including Sambrooks, 16 craft beers and good
range of gins and other spirits, enjoyable
pubby food at reasonable prices; TVs, board
games; seats out at front and in back garden
with artificial grass, table tennis and other
games, open all day weekends, from 4pm
weekdays. *(Barry Manning)*

Windmill (020) 8673 4578
Clapham Common South Side; SW4 9DE
Substantial bustling pub by the common;
contemporary front bar with quite a few
original Victorian features, pillared dining
room leading through to conservatory-style
eating area, popular varied choice of food,
Youngs ales and decent wines by the glass;
background music (live Sat), quiz Sun;
children welcome, tables under umbrellas
along front, more seats in side garden with
'burger shack', good bedrooms, open (and
food) all day. *(Jim Stevens)*

SW11
Eagle Ale House (020) 7228 2328
Chatham Road; SW11 6HG Welcoming
unpretentious backstreet local; up to seven
well kept/priced ales such as Harveys,
Pilgrim and Surrey Hills, L-shaped carpeted
bar with simple pubby furniture, shelves of
books either side of Victorian fireplace; some
live music, big-screen sports TV; children
and dogs welcome, back terrace with heated
marquee, open all day weekends, from 4pm
Mon-Thurs, 3pm Fri. *(Chaz)*

Fox & Hounds (020) 7924 5483
Latchmere Road; SW11 2JU Victorian
pub with good italian-influenced food (all
day Sun, not Mon-Thurs lunchtimes), four
real ales including St Austell and several
wines by glass, spacious straightforward
bar with big windows overlooking street,
mismatched tables and chairs on bare
boards, central servery and open kitchen
behind; background music; children and
dogs welcome, terrace picnic-sets, open
all day Fri-Sun, closed Mon lunchtime.
(Louise and Simon Peters)

Latchmere (020) 7223 3549
Battersea Park Road; SW11 3BW Popular
Battersea corner pub with award-winning
theatre upstairs; open-plan bare-boards
interior, Edwardian-style dining chairs, two-
sided banquettes and red leather wall seats
around wooden tables, sofas either side of log
fire, big mirrors, model yachts, animal prints
and posters, stools by counter serving St
Austell, Sharps and Timothy Taylors, 19 wines
by the glass and cocktails, enjoyable food
including pre-theatre set menu; children (till
7pm) and dogs welcome, heated terrace with
booths down one side and plenty of other
seating, open all day, food all day Sun.
(Sally and Colin Allen)

Westbridge (020) 7228 6482
Battersea Bridge Road; SW11 3AG Draft
House pub with interesting ever-changing
choice of real ales, craft beers and ciders
served by friendly knowledgeable staff,
tasting trays available, good reasonably
priced food from open kitchen, can eat in
bar or restaurant; background music (often
blues/jazz), sports TV; small garden, open
(and food) all day. *(Peter and Emma Kelly)*

Woodman (020) 7228 2968
Battersea High Street; SW11 3HX Busy
village-feel pub tucked behind cobbled
Battersea Square; enjoyable food from
sharing boards up, Badger ales, Weston's
Stowford Press cider and a dozen wines
by the glass, good friendly service; TV for
major sports; children and dogs welcome,
largely covered back garden with heaters
and wood-fired pizza oven, open (and food)
all day. *(Richard and Penny Gibbs)*

SW12
★**Nightingale** (020) 8673 1637
Nightingale Lane; SW12 8NX Early
Victorian local, cosy and civilised, with
small front bar opening into larger back
area and attractive family conservatory, well
kept Youngs and guests, decent wines and
enjoyable sensibly priced bar food, friendly
service, open fire; dogs welcome, nice
secluded back beer garden with summer
barbecues, open all day. *(Laura Reid)*

SW13
Bulls Head (020) 8876 5241
Lonsdale Road; SW13 9PY Imposing
Victorian riverside pub famous for its live
jazz in back music room (nightly and Sun
afternoon); comfortable open-plan areas
brightened up in Geronimo Inns usual
colourful, modern style, three real ales
including Sharps and Youngs from central
servery, upstairs balconied restaurant;
children welcome, open (and food)
all day. *(Edward Mirzoeff)*

Coach & Horses (020) 8876 2695
Barnes High Street; SW13 9LW
Cosy long-established Youngs local (some
refurbishment); their well kept beers and
a guest, decent fairly priced food from
sandwiches and snacks up including range of
burgers and maybe a winter après ski menu,
friendly staff; sports TV; children and dogs
welcome, long spacious back garden with
artificial grass and open-sided huts, open
(and food) all day. *(Edward Mirzoeff)*

Red Lion (020) 8748 2984
Castelnau; SW13 9RU Roomy and
comfortably refurbished 19th-c Fullers pub;
their well kept ales and good range of wines
from central counter, friendly staff, varied
choice of popular attractively presented
food including blackboard specials, lofty
back dining part has most character with
big arched windows, impressive Victorian
woodwork and domed stained-glass ceiling
light, also front snug with gas-effect coal fire;
TV, free wi-fi; children and dogs welcome,
disabled access/loo, spacious garden to the
back and side, open (and food) all day.
(Edward Mirzoeff)

Watermans Arms (020) 8878 8800
*Lonsdale Road, next to the Bulls Head;
SW13 9PY* Recently opened riverside

pub (same owners as the Sussex Arms in Twickenham); extensive range of real ales and craft beers, plenty of wines by the glass and enjoyable good value food such as burgers, ribs and pizzas, more room and river-view balcony upstairs; background music; open all day. *(Edward Mirzoeff)*

White Hart (020) 8876 5177
The Terrace; SW13 0NR Imposing 19th-c Barnes pub with fine Thames views; well kept ales including Bombardier and Youngs along with craft beers such as Camden Town and Meantime from island servery, good selection of wines by the glass, popular food in bar or upstairs restaurant with open kitchen and river-view balcony, friendly attentive staff; more seats and tables on side terrace and alongside the towpath, open (and food) all day. *(Darrell Barton)*

SW14

Plough (020) 8876 7833
Christchurch Road; SW14 7AF Attractive 18th-c pub tucked away in East Sheen near Richmond Park; fairly traditional bare-boards interior with pews and plush banquettes, well kept ales including Fullers London Pride and 20 wines by the glass from oak counter, generous helpings of popular home-made food, friendly staff; children and dogs welcome, tables under parasols on nice front terrace, open all day (till midnight Fri, Sat), food all day Sun. *(Edward Mirzoeff)*

SW15

Bricklayers Arms (020) 8246 5545
Down cul-de-sac off Lower Richmond Road near Putney Bridge; SW15 1DD Tucked-away little 19th-c Putney local; well kept changing ales, proper cider/perry and good selection of english wines, efficient friendly staff, long L-shaped room with pitched-roof section, pine tables on bare boards, lots of pictures on painted panelling, log fire; background music, sports TV; open all day. *(Gail and Arthur Roberts)*

Half Moon (020) 8780 9383
Lower Richmond Road; SW15 1EU Good long-standing music venue; Youngs and a couple of guests from elegant curved bar, food from burgers and hot dogs to more elaborate choices and a brunch menu; nightly live music/comedy nights; open (and food) all day. *(Sandra and Miles Spencer)*

Jolly Gardeners (020) 8789 2539
Lacy Road; SW15 1NT Slightly quirky bare-boards pub in residential Putney; gardening theme with trowels and watering cans on the walls, bucket lampshades, a reclining gnome and row of colourful heated sheds in the back garden; four changing ales and several other draught beers, good selection of wines, enjoyable varied choice of food from sandwiches and sharing boards up; quiz nights, sports TV, newspapers and free

wi-fi; tables on front fairy-lit terrace, open (and food) all day. *(James Butcher)*

SW16

Earl Ferrers (020) 8835 8333
Ellora Road; SW16 6JF Streatham corner pub with opened-up bare-boards interior; Sambrooks and several other well kept ales (tasters offered), enjoyable home-made food including popular Sun roasts, good friendly service; live music, DJs and quiz nights, pool and darts; children welcome, tables out at front and in beer garden, open all day weekends from 1pm, closed Mon and till 5pm Tues-Fri. *(Peter and Emma Kelly)*

Railway (020) 8769 9448
Greyhound Lane; SW16 5SD Busy Streatham corner local with two big rooms (back one for families); rotating ales from London brewers such as Belleville, Redemption and Sambrooks, good range of bottled beers and decent wines by the glass, enjoyable freshly made food (all day weekend), tea room serving pastries from 9am, brunch from 10am, friendly staff, events including comedy nights; walled back garden, open all day (till 1am Fri, Sat). *(Charlie and Mark Todd)*

SW18

Alma (020) 8870 2537
York Road, opposite Wandsworth Town station; SW18 1TF Corner Victorian pub-hotel with well kept Youngs ales and good choice of wines from island bar, sofas and informal mix of tables and chairs on wood floor, mosaic plaques and painted mirrors, wide range of good food from bar snacks up, back restaurant, friendly helpful staff; 23 bedrooms, open (and food) all day from 7am (8am weekends). *(Jim Stevens)*

Cats Back (020) 8617 3448
Point Pleasant; SW18 1NN Traditionally refurbished 19th-c Harveys corner pub; four of their ales along with bottled beers, enjoyable food from sandwiches to Sun roasts, friendly staff; upstairs events including live music, life drawing, film and comedy nights; partially covered beer garden with heaters, open all day. *(Tim and Sarah Smythe-Brown)*

Jolly Gardeners (020) 8870 8417
Garrett Lane; SW18 4EA Bustling easy-going Victorian corner pub; L-shaped front bar; high-backed dining chairs around straightforward tables on pale floorboards, stools at high tables and at counter serving By the Horns, Sambrooks and a dozen wines by the glass, good modern food (not Sun evening), dining area with open fire, friendly chatty staff, simply furnished conservatory opening onto courtyard garden with heaters, summer barbecues; children and dogs (in bar) welcome, open all day, till 8pm Sun. *(Pam Thomas)*

SW19

Alexandra (020) 8947 7691

Wimbledon Hill Road; SW19 7NE Busy 19th-c Youngs pub with their well kept beers and guests from central servery, decent wine choice and enjoyable food from sandwiches and sharing boards to good Sun roasts, friendly attentive service, linked rooms with comfortable fairly traditional décor, more contemporary upstairs bar (burger menu); sports TVs; tables out in mews and on attractive popular roof terrace, open (and food) all day. *(Darrell Barton)*

Crooked Billet (020) 8946 4942

Wimbledon Common; SW19 4RQ Busy 18th-c pub popular for its position by Wimbledon Common (almost next door to the Hand in Hand); Youngs ales and guests, good choice of wines and generally well liked up-to-date food in open-plan bar or dining room, mix of wooden dining chairs, high-backed settles and scrubbed pine tables on oak boards, some interesting old prints, winter fire; Tues quiz, board games; children till 6pm in bar (later in restaurant), dogs welcome, plastic glasses for outside, open (and food) all day. *(Barbara and Phil Bowie)*

Hand in Hand (020) 8946 5720

Crooked Billet; SW19 4RQ Recently refurbished Youngs local on edge of Wimbledon Common; their ales and guests kept well, over 30 wines by the glass and good food from sharing plates and pub standards up, friendly helpful service, opened-up interior keeping cosy corners and original character, log fire; children and dogs welcome, front part-covered courtyard, benches out by common, open (and food) all day. *(Jim Rawlings)*

Sultan (020) 8544 9323

Norman Road; SW19 1BN Friendly 1950s red-brick drinkers' pub owned by Hop Back and hidden in a tangle of suburban roads; their well kept/priced ales, a guest beer and real ciders, snacky food such as pork pies and toasties, scrubbed pine tables on patterned carpet, darts in public bar, small conservatory leading to walled beer garden (maybe summer barbecues); fortnightly quiz Tues, some live music; dogs welcome, open all day Thurs-Sun, from 3pm other days. *(James Butcher)*

Woodman (020) 8286 4158

Durnsford Road; SW19 8DR Revamped late Victorian pub behind railings; airy industrial-chic interior with bare boards and exposed brickwork, pendant lighting and fashionable metal chairs at small pale-wood tables, a couple of real ales and good range of interesting craft beers from planked servery, well liked food (shortish menu), friendly attentive young staff; weekly live music; children welcome, open all day. *(Susan and John Douglas)*

WEST LONDON

SW6

★Atlas (020) 7385 9129

Seagrave Road; SW6 1RX Busy ivy-clad pub with long simple bar; panelling and dark wall benches, mix of old tables and chairs on bare boards, brick fireplaces, good if pricey italian-influenced food (all day Sun), four well kept ales, lots of wines by the glass and decent coffee, friendly service; background music, summer quiz Tues; children (till 7pm) and dogs welcome, attractively planted side terrace with arbours, open all day. *(Maggie and Stevan Hollis)*

Eight Bells (020) 7736 6307

Fulham High Street/Ranelagh Gardens; SW6 3JS Friendly traditional local tucked away near Putney Bridge; Fullers London Pride, Sharps Doom Bar and a guest, good value standard pub menu (all day Sun); sports TV; dogs welcome, seats outside under awning, close to Bishop's Park, open all day and busy with away supporters on Fulham match days. *(Sandra and Miles Spencer)*

Harwood Arms (020) 7386 1847

Walham Grove; SW6 1QP Popular Fulham restaurant-pub with top notch Michelin-starred food from fixed-price menus (not cheap), extensive wine list and a couple of well kept ales such as West Berkshire Good Old Boy, opened-up informal bare-boards interior with all tables set for dining, stools at bar for drinkers; credit card required for booking (charge for late cancellations or no show); closed Mon lunchtime. *(Susan and John Douglas)*

White Horse (020) 7736 2115

Parsons Green; SW6 4UL Busy pub with modernised U-shaped bar; leather chesterfields and wooden tables on flagstone or wood floors, huge windows with slatted wooden blinds, winter fires (one in an elegant marble fireplace), Harveys Best and seven constantly changing guests, fantastic choice of foreign bottled beers, 20 wines by the glass and several malt whiskies, good up-to-date food, upstairs dining room (own bar) keeping Victorian character; children and dogs welcome, lots of tables on front terrace overlooking Parsons Green, open all day. *(Mike Buckingham, Tony Scott, Susan and John Douglas)*

SW7

★Anglesea Arms (020) 7373 7960

Selwood Terrace; SW7 3QG Very busy 19th-c South Kensington pub, well run and friendly, with mix of old tables and chairs on wood-strip floor, panelling and heavy portraits, large brass chandeliers hanging from dark ceiling, several booths at one end with partly glazed screens, Greene King Abbott, IPA and four guests, over 20 wines by the glass and good range of malt whiskies, well liked food from sharing plates up, steps down to dining room; children welcome, dogs in bar, picnic-sets on raised front terrace, open all day. *(Chaz)*

Hereford Arms (020) 7370 4988

Gloucester Road, opposite Hereford Square; SW7 4TE Traditional Fullers pub with opened-up bar; wooden furniture including some high tables on bare boards, chequered tiles around carved U-shaped counter serving their ales and a couple of guests, good food from bar snacks to blackboard specials, friendly staff; free wi-fi; children welcome, disabled access, small outside drinking area, open (and food) all day. *(Ted Wright)*

Queens Arms (020) 7823 9293

Queens Gate Mews; SW7 5QL Popular Victorian corner pub with open-plan bare-boards bar; generous helpings of enjoyable good value home-made food, decent wines by the glass and good selection of beers including Fullers and Sharps, friendly helpful service; discreet background music and TV; children welcome, disabled facilities, handy for Royal Albert Hall, open all day. *(Ted Wright)*

W4

★Bell & Crown (020) 8994 4164

Strand on the Green; W4 3PF Fullers local with great Thames views from back bar and conservatory; good interesting food along with pub classics, efficient friendly service, panelling and log fire, lots of atmosphere and can get very busy weekends; children and dogs welcome, terrace and towpath seating, good riverside walks, open (and food) all day. *(Julie Swift)*

Bollo House (020) 8994 6037

Bollo Lane; W4 5LR Spacious 19th-c corner pub in residential Chiswick; four changing local ales and plenty of wines by the glass, cocktails (early bird deal Thurs), good variety of enjoyable food (service charge added), friendly relaxed atmosphere; background and occasional live music, Tues quiz; children and dogs welcome, tables out at front behind wooden planters, open all day, food all day weekends. *(Dr Martin Owton)*

Bulls Head (020) 8994 1204

Strand on the Green; W4 3PQ Cleanly updated old Thames-side pub (said to have served as Cromwell's HQ during the Civil War); seats by windows overlooking the water in beamed rooms (most tables set for dining), steps up and down, Greene King IPA and London Glory along with four guests, several wines by the glass and enjoyable food from pub favourites up, friendly efficient staff; background music; children and dogs (in bar) welcome, seats out by river, pretty hanging baskets, open (and food) all day. *(Peter and Emma Kelly)*

City Barge (020) 8994 2148

Strand on the Green; W4 3PH Attractively furnished old riverside pub; light modern split-level interior keeping a few original features such as Victorian panelling and open fires, good choice of ales/craft beers and wines by the glass (prosecco on tap), interesting food from open kitchen including good fish choice; background music; children and dogs welcome, waterside picnic-sets facing Oliver's Island, deckchairs on grass and more formal terrace, open (and food) all day. *(Rona Mackinlay)*

★Duke of Sussex (020) 8742 8801

South Parade; W4 5LF Attractive Victorian local with unexpectedly large back garden, tables under parasols, nicely laid-out plants and carefully positioned lighting and heaters; simply furnished bar with some original etched glass, chapel and farmhouse chairs around scrubbed pine or dark wood tables, huge windows overlooking Acton Green, horseshoe counter serving ales such as Reunion, Sambrooks, Twickenham and Wimbledon, 30 wines by the glass and 15 malt whiskies, interesting food including tapas, dining room with six-seater booths, chandeliers and splendid skylight framed by colourfully painted cherubs; children and dogs (in bar) welcome, open (and food) all day. *(Alexandra and Richard Clay, Peter Pilbeam)*

Roebuck (020) 8995 4392

Chiswick High Road; W4 1PU Popular Victorian dining pub with bare boards and high ceilings; front bar and roomy back dining area opening on to delightful paved garden, enjoyable well presented food (daily changing menu) from open kitchen, four real ales and good choice of wines by the glass; children and dogs welcome, open all day, food all day weekends. *(James Butcher)*

Swan (020) 8994 8262

Evershed Walk, Acton Lane; W4 5HH Cosy 19th-c local with good mix of customers and convivial atmosphere; well liked italian-influenced food along with more pubby choices, friendly helpful staff, a dozen or so wines by the glass, ales such as St Austell Tribute and decent selection of craft beers, two bars with wood floors and panelling, leather chesterfields by open fire; dogs very welcome, children till 7.30pm, picnic-sets on good spacious terrace, open all day weekends, from 5pm other days. *(Sally and Colin Allen)*

W5

Ealing Park Tavern (020) 8758 1879

South Ealing Road; W5 4RL Sizeable 19th-c bow-windowed corner pub; bare-boards bar with pendant lighting and some exposed brickwork, animal heads including a couple of large moose behind the counter, armchairs by log fire, Sambrooks and maybe a guest, craft beers such as Long Arm and wide range of wines by the glass, good attractively presented food prepared in open kitchen from lunchtime sandwiches and pub favourites up, weekday set deal (12-7pm), oak-panelled dining room with high beamed ceiling, antlers above another open fire; Weds quiz/curry night, Thurs live music, sports TV; children and dogs welcome, cheerfully painted booths in AstroTurfed garden, open all day, food all day weekends. *(Charlie and Mark Todd)*

W6

★ **Anglesea Arms** (020) 8749 1291
Wingate Road; W6 0UR Bustling Victorian corner gastropub; bare-boards panelled bar with open fire, four changing ales and 14 wines by the glass, very good food from short but interesting blackboard menu (not cheap), close-set tables in sky-lit bare-brick dining room, local artwork on display; children and dogs welcome, tables out by quiet street, open all day Fri-Sun, closed Mon-Thurs lunchtimes, food all day Sun. *(Sam Pullin)*

Blue Anchor (020) 3951 0580
Lower Mall; W6 9DJ Right on the Thames, a short walk from Hammersmith Bridge; two traditional linked areas with oak floors and panelling, four real ales including a house beer brewed by Nelsons, enjoyable food from light meals up, nice upstairs river-view dining room with balcony; quiz night Weds, TV; disabled facilities, waterside pavement tables, open (and food) all day. *(Dave Webster)*

Carpenters Arms (020) 8741 8386
Black Lion Lane; W6 9BG Relaxed little corner dining pub in residential Hammersmith; highly regarded imaginative food including good value set lunch, fine too for just a drink with plenty of wines by the glass, cocktails and a well kept beer such as Adnams, friendly staff and good mix of customers, simple bare-boards interior with open fire; dogs welcome, attractive garden, closed Mon lunchtime, otherwise open all day. *(Duncan Milligan)*

Hampshire Hog (020) 8748 3391
King Street; W6 9JT Spacious Hammersmith pub with light airy interior; plenty of emphasis on food from interesting if not extensive menu, good choice of wines including 50cl carafes, cocktails, ales such as Adnams and Fullers, prices can be high; background music; nice big garden with some seats under cover, closed Sun evening, otherwise open all day from 8am (10am weekends) for breakfast/brunch. *(Sally and Colin Allen)*

Latymers (020) 8748 3446
Hammersmith Road; W6 7JP 1990s corner pub with modern bistro-feel bar, wood floor and padded wall benches, feature mirrored ceiling, well kept Fullers ales from blue-painted counter, back restaurant serving good fairly priced thai food, friendly efficient staff; background music, TV, free wi-fi; children and dogs welcome, seating out on pavement, open all day. *(Susan and John Douglas)*

Pear Tree (020) 7381 1787
Margravine Road; W6 8HJ Arts and crafts building (plenty of original features) tucked away behind Charing Cross Hospital; cosy softly lit interior with heavy drapes and open fires, cushions on well worn seating, fresh flowers, candles and crisp white evening tablecloths, good pubby food from bar snacks up, well kept mainstream ales and good range of wines by the glass, efficient service; background music; dogs welcome, seats in small garden, bedrooms, open all day (from 3pm Mon). *(Louise and Simon Peters)*

Queens Head (020) 7603 3174
Brook Green; W6 7BL Spacious Fullers pub dating from the early 19th c; cosy linked areas with beams and open fire, good menu from lunchtime sandwiches and bar snacks up, four well kept ales, craft beers and nice wines by the glass; children and dogs welcome, big garden behind, open (and food) all day. *(James Butcher)*

Thatched House (020) 8741 6282
Dalling Road; W6 0ET New management for this spacious corner pub (Youngs' first); open-plan interior with their ales and guests from large grey-painted servery, rugs on bare boards, candles on mix of wooden tables, open fire, good food with some emphasis on fish, friendly staff, back conservatory with raised log-effect gas fire; paved terrace, open (and food) all day. *(Simon King)*

W7

Fox (020) 8567 4021
Green Lane; W7 2PJ Welcoming 19th-c open-plan local in quiet cul-de-sac near Grand Union Canal; several real ales including Fullers, St Austell and Timothy Taylors, craft beers and decent wines by the glass, popular well priced food (booking advised especially Sun lunch), good friendly service, panelling and stained glass, farm tools hanging from ceiling; quiz Thurs; children and dogs welcome, food/craft market last Sat of month, towpath walks, open all day. *(Darrell Barton)*

W8

Britannia (020) 7937 6905
Allen Street, off Kensington High Street; W8 6UX Smartly presented Youngs pub with spacious front bar; pastel walls contrasting dark panelling, patterned rugs on bare boards, banquettes, leather tub chairs and sofas, steps down to back area with wall-sized photoprint of the demolished Britannia Brewery, dining conservatory

beyond, good freshly prepared food including pub staples, spiral staircase up to overflow/function room; background and occasional live music, sports TV; children welcome, wheelchair access (side passage to back part), open (and food) all day. *(Pam Thomas)*

★**Churchill Arms** (020) 7727 4242
Kensington Church Street; W8 7LN Bustling historic pub crammed with bric-a-brac: countless lamps, miners' lights, horse tack, bedpans and brasses hanging from ceiling, prints of american presidents and lots of Churchill memorabilia, a couple of interesting carved figures and statuettes behind central counter, well kept Fullers ales, 18 wines by the glass and good value thai food, spacious rather smart plant-filled dining conservatory; free wi-fi; children and dogs welcome, some chrome tables and chairs outside, stunning display of window boxes and hanging baskets, open (and food) all day. *(Dave Webster)*

Princess Victoria (020) 7937 4534
Earls Court Road; W8 6EB Popular modern open-plan bar run by spanish landlady; upholstered wall benches and light wood tables on bare boards, cushioned stools along servery, good choice of wines and cocktails (happy Hour Mon-Fri 5-7pm), well liked food in upstairs dining room including tapas; live music/DJs some weekends; wooden tables out at front, open all day. *(Patricia and Gordon Tucker)*

Scarsdale (020) 7937 1811
Edwardes Square; W8 6HE Popular easy-going Georgian pub in leafy Kensington square; scrubbed pine tables, simple cushioned dining chairs, pews and built-in wall seats on bare boards, oil paintings in fancy gilt frames, etched windows with swagged curtains and some stained-glass screens, coal-effect gas fires, well kept Fullers ales and a guest, 16 wines by the glass and a dozen malt whiskies, enjoyable fairly pubby food from lunchtime sandwiches up; free wi-fi; children (in dining area) and dogs welcome, seats and tables under parasols on pretty front terrace, open (and food) all day. *(Louise and Simon Peters)*

Uxbridge Arms (020) 7792 1362
Uxbridge Street; W8 7TQ Welcoming backstreet local with three traditional linked areas; well kept Caledonian Deuchars IPA (rebadged for the pub), Fullers London Pride, St Austell Tribute and a guest, good choice of wines and other drinks including cocktails, friendly helpful service, various meat and cheese platters, china, prints and old photographs; Sun quiz, some live music,

sports TV; children and dogs welcome, a few seats out at front, open all day. *(Brian and Anna Marsden)*

★**Windsor Castle** (020) 7243 8797
Campden Hill Road; W8 7AR Unspoilt pub of much character; lots of dark oak furnishings, sturdy high-backed built-in elm benches, soft lighting and a coal-effect fire, three of the tiny rooms have their own street entrance, but it's more fun trying to navigate the minuscule doors between them, eight well kept ales including Marstons, St Austell, Sharps and Timothy Taylors, traditional ciders, decent house wines and several malt whiskies, good popular food in panelled back dining room; children (if eating) and dogs welcome, nice garden on several levels with high walls giving secluded feel, open (and food) all day. *(Philip J Alderton, Sarah Kennewell, Justine and Neil Bonnett, Tony Scott, Michael Butler)*

W9

Hero of Maida (020) 3960 9109
Shirland Road; W9 2JD Victorian corner pub under same owners as the Coach (EC1) and Three Cranes (EC4); nicely refurbished interior keeping original features, high-ceilinged bare-boards bar with long blue-leather wall bench and other seats, lots of pictures, zinc-topped counter serving beers such as Adnams, Sambrooks and Timothy Taylors, carefully chosen wines by the glass and good range of other drinks, generally well liked food from anglo-french menu, upstairs dining room; courtyard garden, open all day. *(Caroline Warwick)*

Prince Alfred (020) 7286 3287
Formosa Street; W9 1EE Well preserved ornate Victorian corner pub in Maida Vale with wonderful etched-glass frontage; five separate bar areas (lots of mahogany) arranged around central servery, snob screens and duck-through doors, Youngs ales, guest beers and good choice of wines by the glass, enjoyable food from sharing plates up in airy modern dining room with large central skylight, cellar function rooms; background music, quiz Mon; children and dogs welcome, open (and food) all day, Sat brunch from 10am. *(Martin Day, Marion Watts)*

Warwick Castle (020) 7266 0921
Warwick Place; W9 2PX Popular character pub in narrow street near Little Venice; comfortable Victorian-feel rooms including snug with open fire, good variety of food (all day Fri-Sun) from snacks and pub standards up, Greene King IPA and guests; quiz nights; children and dogs welcome, flower-decked frontage and some pavement tables, open all day. *(Marion Watts)*

We accept no free drinks or meals and inspections are anonymous.

W12

Oak (020) 8741 7700

Goldhawk Road; W12 8EU Large refurbished Victorian pub serving interesting mediterranean-influenced food including speciality wood-fired pizzas, good range of beers and wine, friendly staff; open all day weekends, from 6pm other days. *(Margaret McDonald)*

Princess Victoria (020) 8749 4466

Uxbridge Road; W12 9DH Imposing former gin palace with rather grand parquet-floored bar; groups of old prints on off-white walls, blue-painted panelling, comfortable leather wall seats and small 19th-c fireplace, ales such as Sambrooks and Timothy Taylors from handsome marble-topped horseshoe counter, around 130 gins, cocktails and plenty of wines by the glass, food from snacks and pizzas up including weekday set lunch, friendly service, big dining room; Sun quiz, TV for major sports; children (till 8pm) and dogs (in bar) welcome, tables under large parasols on front cobbled terrace, also pretty back courtyard with white wrought-iron furniture, open all day. *(Jamie Green)*

W13

Duke of Kent (020) 8991 7820

Scotch Common; W13 8DL Large Ealing pub built in 1929 (Grade II listed) with warren of interesting linked areas; mix of old and new furniture on wood floors, panelling and coal fires, several Fullers ales and guests, good food from pub standards up, friendly helpful staff, free super-fast wi-fi; children and dogs welcome, steps down to big garden with part-covered terrace, rows of tables and chairs on artificial grass, seating huts and play area, also an outside bar/barbecue, open (and food) all day. *(Revd R P Tickle)*

W14

Crown & Sceptre (020) 7603 2007

Holland Road; W14 8BA Civilised Victorian corner pub with light airy interior; sofas, antique-style dining chairs and leather cube stools around wooden tables, rugs on bare boards, gas fire, Caledonian Golden XPA, Courage Directors and a guest, plenty of wines by the glass and extensive range of whiskies and gins, enjoyable food from reasonably compact but varied menu, friendly service, cosy cellar bar with banquettes, candles in bottles and big prints on rough wood walls; background music, TV, board games; children and dogs (in bar) welcome, pavement tables, comfortable boutique bedrooms, handy for Olympia, open all day from 7.30am. *(Millie and Peter Downing)*

★ **Havelock Tavern** (020) 7603 5374

Masbro Road; W14 0LS Busy 19th-c corner dining pub with blue-tiled frontage on Brook Green; light airy L-shaped bar with plain unfussy décor, second smaller room behind, Sambrooks Wandle, Sharps Doom Bar and guests, wide choice of interesting wines by the glass and good often imaginative food from short changing menu, friendly efficient service; free wi-fi; children and dogs welcome, picnic-sets on small paved terrace, open all day. *(Michael Robinson)*

OUTER LONDON

BARNET EN5

Black Horse (020) 8449 2230

Wood Street/Union Street; EN5 4HY Attractively updated 19th-c pub with eight real ales including own Barnet beers from back microbrewery, good range of food (all day weekends); children (till 7.30pm) and dogs welcome, terrace seating, open all day. *(Charlie and Mark Todd)*

Gate (020) 8449 7292

Barnet Road (A411, near Hendon Wood Lane); EN5 3LA Comfortably opened-up with country pub feel; beams and log fires, ample helpings of enjoyable popular food, well kept ales such as Greene King and Sharps, friendly service and atmosphere; children welcome, tables on sunny terrace, open (and food) all day. *(James Butcher)*

Olde Mitre (020) 8449 6582

High Street; EN5 5SJ Small early 17th-c local (remains of a famous coaching inn); bay windows in low-beamed panelled front bar, back area on two slightly different levels, some bare boards and lots of dark wood, open fires, good choice of well kept ales including Adnams Southwold, Caledonian Deuchars IPA and Timothy Taylors Landlord, craft beers and decent wines, enjoyable pubby food, friendly service; Sun live music, sports TV; children and dogs welcome, nice heated courtyard garden behind, open all day (till 1am Fri, Sat). *(Dr and Mrs A K Clarke, Gavin Conway, Tony Scott)*

BECKENHAM BR3

George (020) 8663 3468

High Street; BR3 1AG Recently refurbished weatherboarded pub with modern U-shaped interior; four real ales, craft beers and decent range of other drinks including cocktails, good choice of enjoyable reasonably priced food from snacks up, efficient friendly staff; background music, sports TV and machines; children till 7pm, no under-21s Fri and Sat nights, nice terrace garden to the side with huts and heaters, open all day. *(Pam Thomas)*

BEXLEYHEATH DA6

Robin Hood & Little John

(020) 8303 1128 *Lion Road; DA6 8PF* Small 19th-c family-run local in residential area, welcoming and spotless, with eight

well kept ales such as Adnams, Bexley, Fullers and Harveys, popular bargain pubby lunchtime food (not Sun); over-21s only, seats out at front and in back garden. *(Sally Martin)*

BRENTFORD TW8
Black Dog (020) 8568 5688
Albany Road; TW8 0NF Popular late Victorian bare-boards corner pub; excellent choice of ales and craft beers (maybe one from their microbrewery), also five real ciders and carefully chosen wines, interesting varied menu including some good vegetarian/vegan choices, friendly knowledgeable staff; background music from vintage vinyl; attractive sunny beer garden, open all day, food all day weekends (booking advised). *(Paul Wheeler)*

Express (020) 8560 8484
Kew Bridge Road; TW8 0EW Two-bar Victorian pub on busy road north of Kew Bridge; traditional high ceilings, button-back banquettes and other pubby furniture on wood floors, lots of pictures and big mirrors, original fireplaces, ten real ales, including Bass and Harveys, several craft beers, proper ciders and good range of other drinks, enjoyable fairly priced food, friendly helpful staff; background music from vinyl collection; big split-level back garden with heaters and artificial grass, open (and food) all day. *(Tony Scott, Alex Macdonald)*

BROMLEY BR1
Red Lion (020) 8460 2691
North Road; BR1 3LG Chatty backstreet local in conservation area; traditional dimly lit interior with wood floor, tiling, green velvet drapes and shelves of books, well kept Greene King, Harveys and guests, lunchtime food, good friendly service; tables out in front, open all day. *(Ted Wright)*

BROMLEY BR2
Two Doves (020) 8462 1627
Oakley Road (A233); BR2 8HD Popular Victorian local, comfortable and unpretentious, with cheerful staff and regulars, well kept Youngs and guests, snacky lunchtime food such as rolls and baked potatoes, modern dusk conservatory and lovely garden; sports TV; open all day Fri-Sun. *(Michael Wong)*

CHELSFIELD BR6
Five Bells (01689) 821044
Church Road; just off A224 Orpington bypass; BR6 7RE Chatty 17th-c white weatherboarded village local; two separate bars and dining area, inglenook fireplace, well kept Courage, Harveys and a couple

of guests, reasonably priced food from lunchtime sandwiches up, evening meals Thurs-Sat only, Sun breakfast 9-11am; live music including jazz and open mike nights, quiz Tues, sports TV; children welcome, picnic-sets among flowers out in front, open all day. *(Mike Buckingham)*

CHISLEHURST BR7
Bulls Head (020) 8467 1727
Royal Parade; BR7 6NR Handsome refurbished pub-hotel (18th-c coaching inn); Youngs ales and lots of wines by the glass, good food from sandwiches and sharing boards up, afternoon teas, two bars and roomy restaurant; children welcome, plenty of tables in back garden, 15 bedrooms, open (and food) all day. *(Dave Webster)*

Crown (020) 8467 7326
School Road; BR7 5PQ Imposing Victorian pub overlooking common; simple attractive interior with flagstoned bar and several dining areas, well kept Shepherd Neame ales and good quality food from sandwiches and traditional choices up, friendly helpful service; events including open mike night first Tues of month; children welcome, terrace tables, pétanque, seven bedrooms, open all day. *(Mike Buckingham)*

CROYDON CR0
Claret & Ale (020) 8656 7452
5 Bingham Corner, Lower Addiscombe Road; CR0 7AA Friendly one-room drinkers' pub; half a dozen good changing ales including Palmers marked up on blackboard, real ciders and decent choice of other drinks, dark pubby furniture on woodstrip or red-carpeted floor, coarse plasterwork and faux black beams; some live music, sports TV; dogs welcome, handy for Addiscombe tram stop, open all day. *(Tony Scott)*

EASTCOTE HA5
Case is Altered (020) 8866 0476
High Road/Southill Lane; HA5 2EW Attractive 17th-c pub in quiet setting adjacent to cricket ground; main bar, flagstoned snug and barn seating/dining area, Rebellion, Oakham, West Berkshire and a couple of guests, draught and bottled craft beers, lots of wines by the glass (can be pricey) and good range of other drinks, enjoyable food from sandwiches and snacks to charcoal grills from open kitchen, friendly staff; background music, weekly quiz, free wi-fi; children and dogs welcome, nice front garden with outside bar (very popular in fine weather), handy for Eastcote House Gardens, open (and food) all day, kitchen shuts 6pm Sun. *(Jasmine)*

Half pints: by law, a pub should not charge more for half a pint than half the price of a full pint, unless it shows that half-pint price on its price list.

GREENFORD UB6

Black Horse (020) 8578 1384

Oldfield Lane; car park is accessed by automatic gate to S side of pub, staff provide exit code; UB6 0AS Spacious pub on two levels by Grand Union Canal; well kept Fullers ales, a dozen wines by the glass and decent choice of enjoyable reasonably priced food from sandwiches and snacks up, efficient friendly service; weekend live music, sports TV, darts and machines; children and dogs welcome, balcony tables overlooking canal and big garden fenced from towpath, open all day, food all day Fri-Sun; note that the car barrier opens automatically but an exit code from the bar is required to leave. *(Tim Charles, Susan and John Douglas)*

HAMPTON TW12

Jolly Coopers (020) 8979 3384

High Street; TW12 2SJ Friendly end-of-terrace Georgian local; four or five well kept ales and good choice of wines, well liked freshly cooked food (all day Sat) in back restaurant extension including good evening tapas and Sun lunch till 5pm; pretty terrace with climbing plants and summer barbecues, open all day. *(Pam Thomas)*

HARROW HA1

Castle (020) 8422 3155

West Street; HA1 3EF Edwardian Fullers pub in picturesque part (steps up from street); their well kept ales and guests, decent food from lunchtime sandwiches up including Thurs pie and craft beer night, several rooms around central servery, rugs on bare boards, lots of panelling, open fires, collection of clocks in cheery front bar, more sedate back lounge; children and dogs welcome, nice garden behind with rattan furniture, open (and food) all day, Sat brunch from 10.30am. *(Will Nicholson)*

ISLEWORTH TW7

London Apprentice (020) 8560 1915

Church Street; TW7 6BG Large Thames-side Taylor Walker pub; reasonably priced food from sandwiches up, well kept ales including Greene King and good wine choice, log fire, pleasant service, upstairs river-view restaurant; quiz nights; children and dogs welcome, attractive waterside terrace with tables under parasols, open (and food) all day. *(Sam Thwaites)*

KINGSTON KT2

Boaters (020) 8541 4672

Canbury Gardens (park in Lower Ham Road if you can); KT2 5AU Family-friendly pub by the Thames in small park; good selection of ales/craft beers, decent wines and varied choice of enjoyable food from changing menu, friendly staff coping well at busy times, comfortable banquettes in split-level wood-floored bar; Sun evening jazz, quiz nights; riverside terrace and balcony, parking nearby can be tricky, open (and food) all day. *(David and Sally Frost)*

Canbury Arms (020) 8255 9129

Canbury Park Road; KT2 6LQ Popular open-plan Victorian pub attractively revamped under new owners; comfortable seating including a button-back banquette in bare-boards bar with open fire and lots of modern artwork, stools by blue-painted counter serving four real ales such as Harveys and Park (brewed nearby), plenty of wines by the glass/carafe and cocktails, good food from sharing plates and pub favourites up, friendly helpful staff, airy restaurant extension with sklights and big windows; newspapers, TV for major sports, free wi-fi; children (till 7.30pm) and dogs (in bar) welcome, picnic-sets and rattan furniture on terrace around three sides behind metal railings, open (and food) all day. *(Sam Thwaites)*

Queens Head (020) 8546 9162

Richmond Road/Windsor Road; KT2 5HA Large refurbished red-brick Fullers pub; modern interior arranged around traditional wooden servery (rescued from another London pub), four real ales and good variety of enjoyable food from snacks up including some themed nights, helpful young staff; background music, free wi-fi; children welcome, part-covered front deck, paved back terrace with wooden planters, cabins and play area, ten bedrooms, open (and food) all day. *(David and Sally Frost)*

ORPINGTON BR6

★ Bo-Peep (01959) 534457

Hewitts Road, Chelsfield; 1.7 miles from M25 junction 4; BR6 7QL Popular country-feel dining pub; old low beams and enormous inglenook in carpeted bar, two cosy candlelit dining rooms, airy side room overlooking lane and fields, well kept Sharps, Westerham and an Adnams house beer, good helpings of enjoyable food (all day Sat, not Sun evening) from traditional choices up, weekday afternoon teas, cheerful helpful staff; background music; children and dogs (in bar) welcome, picnic-sets on big brick terrace, open all day and a useful M25 stop. *(Alan Cowell)*

OSTERLEY TW7

Hare & Hounds (020) 8560 5438

Windmill Lane (B454, off A4 signed for Greenford); TW7 5PR Busy Edwardian pub in nice setting opposite Osterley Park and House (NT); spacious interior with connecting rooms including pitched-ceiling back dining extension, Fullers/Gales beers, decent wines and popular food from sandwiches and small plates up, friendly staff; children and dogs welcome, disabled facilities, picnic-sets out at front on artificial grass, big garden behind with glass-covered eating area with woodburner, summer barbecues, play area and tipi, open (and food) all day. *(Susan and John Douglas)*

RICHMOND UPON THAMES TW9

Mitre (020) 8940 1336

Just off the Upper Richmond Road; TW9 1UY Refurbished Victorian local with ten changing ales and four draught ciders/perries (tasters offered), wood-fired pizzas, friendly staff and pub dog (others welcome), bare boards, leaded windows and woodburner; music nights; children allowed, seats on small front terrace, open all day weekends, from 3pm other days.
(Dave Webster)

Princes Head (020) 8940 1572

The Green; TW9 1LX Spacious open-plan pub overlooking cricket green; low-ceilinged panelled areas off island servery, well kept Fullers ales and popular sensibly priced pub food from sandwiches up, coal-effect fire; background music, TV and daily papers; children allowed in certain areas, circular picnic-sets outside, handy for Richmond Theatre, open (and food) all day. *(Robert and Diana Ringstone)*

White Cross (020) 8940 6844

Water Lane; TW9 1TH Lovely garden with terrific Thames outlook, seats on paved area, outside bar and boats to Kingston and Hampton Court; two chatty main rooms with local prints and photographs, three log fires (one unusually below a window), well kept Youngs and guests from old-fashioned island servery, a dozen wines by the glass and enjoyable fairly pubby food from 10am brunch on, also bright and airy upstairs room (where under-18s allowed) with pretty cast-iron balcony for splendid river view; background music, TV; dogs welcome, tides can reach the pub entrance (wellies provided), open (and food) all day.
(Dave Chapman)

White Swan (020) 8940 0959

Old Palace Lane; TW9 1PG Civilised little 18th-c pub with rustic dark-beamed bar, well kept Harveys, Otter, St Austell and Sharps, generally well liked food including lunchtime sandwiches, coal-effect fires, back dining conservatory and upstairs restaurant; soft background music; children (till 6.30pm) and dogs welcome, some seats on narrow paved area at front, more in pretty walled back terrace below railway, open all day.
(Jim Stevens)

RICHMOND UPON THAMES TW10

New Inn (020) 8940 9444

Petersham Road (A307, Ham Common); TW10 7DB Attractive Georgian pub in good spot on Ham Common; unashamedly old-fashioned inside with very traditional

décor, two open fires and a woodburner, well kept ales such as Adnams Broadside, Fullers London Pride and Youngs Bitter, decent pubby food including daily specials, friendly staff and good chatty atmosphere; children and dogs welcome, disabled facilities, picnic-sets out at front and in back courtyard, well placed for Ham House (NT), open all day.
(Susan and John Douglas)

ROMFORD RM1

Golden Lion (01708) 740081

High Street; RM1 1HR Busy former coaching inn – dates from the 15th c and is one of the town's oldest buildings; enjoyable good value food from sandwiches, sharing plates and pub favourites up, Greene King ales, guest beers and decent range of other drinks, spacious beamed interior, more room upstairs; weekend live music, sports TVs (even in the garden), free wi-fi; children welcome, open (and food) all day.
(Robert Lester)

ROMFORD RM2

Ship (01708) 741571

Main Road; RM2 5EL Friendly black and white pub built in 1762; low beams, panelling and woodburner in fine brick fireplace, Greene King, Sharps, Timothy Taylors and guests, enjoyable good value food (not weekend evenings) from sandwiches and sharing boards up; quiz Thurs, live music Sat; children and dogs welcome, picnic-sets in back garden under parasols, open all day.
(Robert Lester)

SURBITON KT6

Antelope (020) 8399 5565

Maple Road; KT6 4AW Double-fronted Victorian pub with excellent choice of cask and craft beers including own Big Smoke unfined range from on-site microbrewery, several ciders too, friendly knowledgeable staff, split-level bare-boards interior with comfortable mix of seating, grey-painted and tiled walls adorned with pump clips, open fire, tasty food including range of burgers; background music from vinyl collection, board games; dogs welcome, paved back terrace, open (and food) all day.
(Jim Rawlings)

TEDDINGTON TW11

Kings Head (020) 3166 2900

High Street; TW11 8HG White Brasserie pub with comfortably updated front bar, easy chairs and button-back wall benches on bare boards, woodburner, a couple of snug rooms off, well kept changing ales, over 20 wines by the glass and good range of other drinks including cocktails, back dining part with similar décor and open kitchen, wide variety of enjoyable food from bar snacks up, good value set menu till 6.30pm (not Sun),

---

We say if we know a pub allows dogs.

courteous helpful staff; background music; children and dogs welcome, seats out at front and on enclosed back terrace, open (and food) all day. *(Mark Smith)*

TWICKENHAM TW1

★**Crown** (020) 8892 5896

Richmond Road, St Margarets; TW1 2NH Popular Georgian pub with several large dining areas including splendid Victorian back hall, good food from sandwiches and sharing plates to restauranty choices, also well kept ales, nice wines by the glass and good coffee, friendly efficient staff, open fire; newspapers and free wi-fi; children till 7pm and dogs (in bar) welcome, sunny plant-filled courtyard garden, open (and food) all day. *(Michael Massey)*

White Swan (020) 8892 2166

Riverside; TW1 3DN 17th-c Thames-side pub up steep anti-flood steps; L-shaped bar with bare boards and cosy log fire, river views from prized bay window, five real ales including Twickenham and enjoyable fairly priced food (all day Sat, till 6pm Sun), friendly local atmosphere; some acoustic live music, board games; children and dogs welcome, tranquil setting opposite Eel Pie Island with well used balcony and waterside terrace, open all day. *(Michael Massey)*

TWICKENHAM TW2

Sussex Arms (020) 8894 7468

Staines Road; TW2 5BG Traditional bare-boards pub with 18 handpumps plus ciders/perries from long counter, plenty in bottles too, simple food including good home-made pies, pizzas and burgers, friendly staff and welcoming atmosphere, walls and ceilings covered in beer mats and pump clips, open fire; some live acoustic music; large back garden with boules, open all day. *(Susan and John Douglas, Revd R P Tickle)*

Scotland

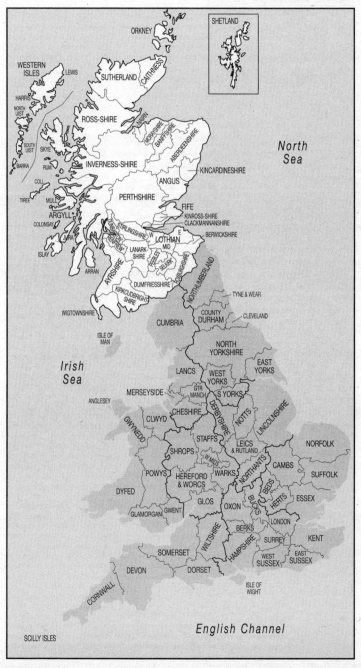

SHETLAND

ORKNEY

WESTERN
ISLES
LEWIS

HARRIS

NORTH
UIST

SOUTH
UIST
SKYE

BARRA
RUM

COLL

TIREE
MULL

ARGYLL

COLONSAY

JURA

ISLAY

ARRAN

SUTHERLAND
CAITHNESS

ROSS-SHIRE

NAIRN

MORAYSHIRE
BANFFSHIRE

ABERDEENSHIRE

INVERNESS-SHIRE

KINCARDINESHIRE

ANGUS

PERTHSHIRE

FIFE

KINROSS-SHIRE
CLACKMANNANSHIRE

STIRLINGSHIRE
W
LOTHIAN
E
MID

DUNBARTON
RENFREW
LANARK-
SHIRE

PEEBLES

BERWICKSHIRE

SELKIRK

ROXBURGHSHIRE

AYRSHIRE

DUMFRIESSHIRE

KIRKCUDBRIGHT-
SHIRE

WIGTOWNSHIRE

North
Sea

NORTHUMBERLAND

TYNE & WEAR

COUNTY
DURHAM

CLEVELAND

CUMBRIA

ISLE OF
MAN

Irish
Sea

NORTH
YORKSHIRE

LANCS

WEST
YORKS

EAST
YORKS

MERSEYSIDE

ANGLESEY

GTR
MANCH

S YORKS

CLWYD

CHESHIRE

DERBYSHIRE

NOTTS

LINCOLNSHIRE

GWYNEDD

STAFFS

LEICS
& RUTLAND

NORFOLK

SHROPS

W MIDS

POWYS

HEREFORD
& WORCS

WARKS

NORTHANTS

CAMBS

SUFFOLK

DYFED

GLOS

OXON

BEDS

HERTS

ESSEX

GLAMORGAN

GWENT

BUCKS

LONDON

BERKS

WILTSHIRE

HAMPSHIRE

SURREY

KENT

SOMERSET

DORSET

WEST
SUSSEX

EAST
SUSSEX

DEVON

ISLE OF
WIGHT

CORNWALL

English Channel

SCILLY ISLES

KEY	★ Star Pub	🌟 Top Quality Food	🍺 Great Beer
🍷 Good Wines	£ Bargain Meals	🛏 Good Bedrooms	🍴 Serves Food

APPLECROSS

NG7144 Map 11

Applecross Inn ★ 🛏

(01520) 744262 – www.applecrossinn.co.uk

Off A896 S of Shieldaig; IV54 8LR

Isolated pub on famously scenic route on west coast, with particularly friendly welcome, real ales and good seafood; bedrooms

Even though getting to this remote little gem is quite an experience, it's always packed with customers from all over the world and the atmosphere remains lively and genuinely friendly. The exhilarating west coast drive to reach the inn is over the Bealach na Bà (Pass of the Cattle) and is one of the highest in Britain; do not attempt it in bad weather. The alternative route, along the single-track lane winding around the coast from just south of Shieldaig, has equally glorious sea loch (and then sea) views nearly all the way. The no-nonsense bar has a woodburning stove, exposed-stone walls, upholstered pine furnishings and a stone floor. There's Applecross Inner Sound and Sanctuary on handpump, over 50 malt whiskies, 25 gins, ten rums and a good, varied wine list (all are available by the glass); background music and board games. Tables in the shoreside garden enjoy magnificent views and there's an outdoor eating area for summer use and an artisan food truck selling fish and chips and local ice-cream. If you wish to stay here in one of the seven bedrooms, you'll have to book months ahead. Some disabled facilities.

🍴 Most people opt for the first class fresh local fish and seafood, which includes squat lobsters, creel-caught prawns, oysters, hand-dived scallops, fresh haddock, langoustines, a seafood platter and dressed crab with smoked salmon, but they also offer sandwiches, local haggis flambéed in Drambuie topped with cream, pigeon breast with crispy bacon and pine nuts, lentil and bean chilli with rice, gammon and egg, thai green chicken curry, sirloin steak with pepper sauce and chips, and puddings such as seasonal fruit crumble with custard and raspberry cranachan with almond praline. *Benchmark main dish: local prawns £22.00. Two-course evening meal £25.00.*

Free house ~ Licensee Judith Fish ~ Real ale ~ Open 11am-11.30pm (midnight Sat); 11am-midnight Sat; 12.30-11 Sun ~ Bar food 12-9 ~ Restaurant ~ Children welcome ~ Dogs allowed in bar and bedrooms ~ Wi-fi ~ Bedrooms: £90/£140 *Recommended by Neil and Angela Huxter, Mandy and Gary Redstone, Murray and Peggy Lindsay, Belinda Stamp, Peter Pilbeam, Julia and Martin Swift*

EDINBURGH

NT2574 Map 11

Bow Bar 🍺

(0131) 226 7667

West Bow; EH1 2HH

Cosy, enjoyably unpretentious pub with an excellent choice of well kept beers

Strong on traditional values, this is an honest pub and a bastion of simple stand-up drinking. The interior is warmly welcoming and customers are here to enjoy the splendid range of drinks served by knowledgeable staff.

From the rectangular bar with its impressive carved mahogany gantry, eight well kept real ales are dispensed from the tall 1920s founts on the counter; these include regulars such as Fallen Odyssey, Tempest Armadillo and Stewart 80/- and five quickly changing guests from breweries such as Black Isle, Campervan, Cromarty, Cross Borders, Swannay and Wild Beer; they hold regular beer festivals. Also on offer are some 400 malts, including five 'malts of the moment', a good choice of rums, 60 international bottled beers and 20 scottish gins. The walls are covered with a fine collection of enamel advertising signs and handsome antique brewery mirrors, and there are sturdy leatherette wall seats and café-style bar seats around heavy narrow tables on the wooden floor. No children allowed.

Lunchtime-only food is limited to pies. *Benchmark main dish: meat pie £4.50.*

Free house ~ Licensee Mike Smith ~ Real ale ~ Open 12-midnight; 12.30-11.30 Sun ~ Bar food 12-4; 12.30-4 Sun ~ Dogs welcome ~ Wi-fi *Recommended by Sarah and David Gibbs, Nicola and Holly Lyons, Jane Rigby, Frances Parsons*

EDINBURGH
Guildford Arms ◀ £

NT2574 Map 11

(0131) 556 4312 – www.guildfordarms.com
West Register Street; EH2 2AA

Busy and friendly with spectacular Victorian décor, a marvellous range of real ales and good food

Our readers always enjoy their visits here, partly for the splendid Victorian décor but also for the ten well kept real ales. It's opulently excessive, with ornate painted plasterwork on the lofty ceiling, dark mahogany fittings, heavy swagged velvet curtains and a busy patterned carpet. Tables and stools are lined up along towering arched windows opposite the bar, where knowledgeable, efficient staff serve quickly changing beers such as Bombardier, Fyne Ales Jarl, Loch Lomond Southern Summit, Orkney Dark Island, Stewart Pentland IPA and Swannay Orkney IPA. Also, ten wines by the glass, 50 malt whiskies, a dozen rums and a dozen gins; TV and background music. The snug upstairs gallery restaurant, with contrasting modern décor, gives a fine dress-circle view of the main bar.

Tasty food includes lunchtime ciabattas and burgers plus fish chowder, pâté of the day, vegetable wellington, moules frites, sausages of the day with mash and onion gravy, steak in ale pie, chicken stuffed with haggis wrapped in smoked bacon with pepper sauce, venison haunch with port and raspberry sauce, salmon fillet with hollandaise, chargrilled 21-day aged rib-eye steak with mushroom and blue cheese sauce and chips, and puddings. *Benchmark main dish: breaded haddock and chips £12.95. Two-course evening meal £20.00.*

Stewart ~ Lease Steve Jackson ~ Real ale ~ Open 11-11; 11am-midnight Thurs- Sat ~ Bar food 12-2.30, 5.30-9.30; 12-10 Fri, Sat; snacks throughout afternoon except Fri, Sat ~ Restaurant 12 (12.30 Sun)-2.30, 6-9.30; 12-2.30, 6-10 Fri, Sat ~ Children welcome in upstairs gallery if dining and over 5 ~ Dogs allowed in bar ~ Wi-fi ~ Live music during Edinburgh Festival *Recommended by Charles Fraser, Rob Anderson, Len and Lilly Dowson, Louise and Anton Parsons, Susan and John Douglas, Barry Collett*

Real ale may be served from handpumps, electric pumps (not just the on-off switches used for keg beer) or – common in Scotland – tall taps called founts (pronounced 'fonts') where a separate pump pushes the beer up under air pressure.

EDINBURGH
Kays Bar 🍺 £

NT2574   Map 11

(0131) 225 1858 – www.kaysbar.co.uk

Jamaica Street West; off India Street; EH3 6HF

Cosy, enjoyably chatty backstreet pub with good value lunchtime food and an excellent choice of well kept beers

A marvellous choice of drinks here includes around seven real ales on handpump with four constants – maybe Caledonian Deuchars IPA, Fyne Ales Jarl, Theakstons Best and Timothy Taylors Landlord – plus more than 50 malt whiskies aged from eight to 50 years old, 20 gins and half a dozen wines by the glass. A friendly little backstreet pub, it's surprisingly untouristy and décor is simple with big casks and vats arranged along the walls, old wine and spirits merchants' notices and gas-type lamps. Also, long, curving, well worn, red plush wall banquettes and stools around cast-iron tables on red carpet, and red pillars supporting a red ceiling. A quiet panelled back room (a bit like a library) leads off, with a narrow, plank-panelled pitched ceiling and a collection of books ranging from dictionaries to ancient steam-train books for boys; a lovely coal fire in winter and board games. In days past, the pub was owned by John Kay, a whisky and wine merchant: wine barrels were hoisted up to the first floor and dispensed through pipes attached to nipples that are still visible around the ceiling light rose. Dogs are allowed before midday and after 2.30pm.

Good value lunchtime-only food includes stovies, pâté with toast, haggis, neeps and tatties, warm brie or prawn salads, beef or chicken curries, chilli con carne, steak pie, and puddings such as chocolate fudge cake. *Benchmark main dish: mince and tatties £5.50.*

Free house ~ Licensee Fraser Gillespie ~ Real ale ~ Open 11am-midnight; 11am-1am Fri, Sat; 12.30-11 Sun ~ Bar food 12-2.30; not Sun ~ Dogs allowed in bar ~ Wi-fi *Recommended by Molly and Stewart Lindsay, William and Tasha Fraser, Murray and Peggy Lindsay*

GLASGOW
Babbity Bowster 🍷

NS5965   Map 11

(0141) 552 5055 – www.babbitybowster.com

Blackfriars Street; G1 1PE

A lively mix of traditional and modern with a continental feel too; bedrooms

This 18th-c former tobacco merchant's house remains very much a Glasgow institution with a thoroughly convivial atmosphere and a good mix of customers. The simply decorated, light-filled interior has fine tall windows, plush stools and cushioned ladder-back chairs around a mix of dark tables on bare boards, some wall bench seating, open fires and attractive plant prints on light paintwork. The bar opens on to a pleasant terrace with picnic-sets under parasols and there's another back terrace too. High chairs line the counter where they keep Caledonian Deuchars IPA, Fyne Ales Jarl and a changing guest on air-pressure tall founts, and a remarkably impressive collection of wines and malt whiskies; good tea and coffee too. They hold traditional live music sessions from 3pm on Wednesdays and Saturdays; boules. Bedrooms are simple and cosy, and the room rate includes tea or coffee with toast and home-made preserves.

Good, popular food includes cullen skink, moules marinière, vegetarian moussaka, haggis, neeps and tatties, stovies, duck breast with orange and star anise sauce, a fresh fish dish of the day, roasted herb-crusted rack of lamb with dijon mustard and white wine jus, braised ox cheeks with port wine sauce, saddle of highland deer coated in oatmeal with black pepper whisky sauce, and puddings such as a seasonal fruit tart with crème anglaise and sticky parkin pudding with hot spicy syrup. *Benchmark main dish: pie of the day £12.50. Two-course evening meal £19.00.*

Free house ~ Licensee Fraser Laurie ~ Real ale ~ Open 11am-midnight; 12.30-midnight Sun ~ Bar food 12-10 ~ Restaurant ~ Children welcome if eating ~ Wi-fi ~ Live traditional music Weds afternoon, Sat early evening ~ Bedrooms: £55/£70 *Recommended by Barry and Daphne Gregson, John Herbert, Elliott Kemp, Maggie and Stevan Hollis, Patricia and Gordon Tucker, Gail and Arthur Roberts*

GLASGOW
NS5965 Map 11

Bon Accord 🍺 £

(0141) 248 4427 – www.bonaccordweb.co.uk
North Street; G3 7DA

Remarkable choice of drinks, a good welcome and bargain food

As well as 500 malt whiskies, the splendid drinks choice in this bustling tavern includes real ales sourced from breweries all around Britain and served from swan-necked handpumps, including Caledonian Deuchars IPA and nine daily changing guests, continental bottled beers, a farm cider and, in a remarkable display behind the counter, 50 gins, 20 rums and lots of vodkas. The several linked traditional bars are warmly understated with cream or terracotta walls, a mix of chairs and tables, a leather sofa and plenty of bar stools on polished bare boards or carpeting; TV, background music and board games. There are circular picnic-sets on a small terrace, and modern tables and chairs set out in front. Disabled access.

🍴 Exceptionally good value food includes baguettes, peppered mushrooms with garlic bread, giant yorkshire pudding filled with sausages and onion gravy, chilli con carne, all-day breakfast, cajun chicken or burger with french fries, gammon and egg, and puddings such as clootie dumpling or apple pie with custard. *Benchmark main dish: fish and chips £6.95. Two-course evening meal £9.50.*

Free house ~ Licensee Paul McDonagh ~ Real ale ~ Open 11am-midnight; 11am-midnight Sat; 12.30-11 Sun ~ Bar food 11-7.45; 12.30-7.45 Sun ~ Children welcome until 8pm ~ Wi-fi *Recommended by Edward and William Johnston, Sophia and Hamish Greenfield*

GLENELG
NG8119 Map 11

Glenelg Inn 🛏️

(01599) 522273 – www.glenelg-inn.com
Unmarked road from Shiel Bridge (A87) towards Skye; IV40 8JR

Outstanding Skye views from charming inn reached by a dramatic drive, with an enjoyably pubby bar and good fresh local food

On a sunny day, head to the tables in the beautifully kept garden of this charming inn for lovely views across the water to Skye; some of the bedrooms have the same views. Feeling a bit like a mountain cabin (and still decidedly pubby given the smartness of the rest of the place), the unpretentious carpeted bar has a big fireplace, simple tables and chairs, black and white photographs on some walls, winter pool and maybe background music; you can be sure of a warm welcome from both locals and staff. Caledonian Deuchars IPA plus beers from the recently opened Dun brewery (in the village) on handpump. The inn is memorably reached by a single-track road climbing dramatically past heather-blanketed slopes and mountains with spectacular views to the lochs below; nearby walks are lovely. In summer there's a little car ferry across to Skye.

Rewarding food includes open sandwiches, charcuterie board, smoked mackerel pâté with toast, wild mushroom gnocchi with creamy pesto sauce, spinach and parmesan, beer-battered haddock and chips, venison burger with mustard mayonnaise and chips, fresh pasta with squat lobsters, pork belly stuffed with apricots and pistachios, duck breast with herbed beans, hand-dived scallops with samphire and lemon, and puddings such as peanut butter brownie with honey, cashews and crème fraîche and cranberry-poached pear with elderflower sorbet and bramble coulis. *Benchmark main dish: local langoustine in paprika and garlic butter £18.95. Two-course evening meal £20.00.*

Free house ~ Licensee Sheila Crondie ~ Real ale ~ Open 11-11 (12.30am Sat); 12.30-11 Sun; closed first week Nov-28 Dec; 5 Jan-Mar ~ Bar food 12.30-2.30, 6.30-9 ~ Restaurant ~ Children welcome ~ Dogs welcome ~ Wi-fi ~ Bedrooms: /$120 *Recommended by David Todd, Elliott Kemp, Sarah Roberts, William and Tasha Fraser, Nicholas and Lucy Sage, Maggie and Stevan Hollis, Mandy and Gary Redstone*

GULLANE

NT4882 Map 11

Bonnie Badger

(01620) 621111 ~ www.bonniebadger.com

Main Street; A198; EH31 2AB

Renovated inn with stylish décor, good choice of drinks, exceptional food and seats in terraced garden; well equipped bedrooms

Just a stroll from the beach and close to Muirfield golf course, this highly acclaimed inn – owned by the Michelin-starred chef Tom Kitchin – has been refurbished in an interesting scandinavian-scottish style. Food is obviously king here, but there's a warm welcome for those who just want a drink and a chat. The bar has high chairs against the counter, upholstered chairs around pubby tables on bare boards, and Belhaven 80/-, Campervan Leith Juice and a guest ale on handpump, 28 wines by the glass and 70 malt whiskies served by knowledgeable, friendly staff; pool table, board games, TV and background music. The main focus is on the dining room (originally the stables) which has a high-raftered ceiling, original sandstone walls, a large open fireplace, panelling and seating that ranges from button-back wall banquettes to cushioned dark wooden dining chairs around pale-topped tables. There's also a lounge with stylish, contemporary armchairs and sofas on more pale floorboards. Outside on a two-level terrace are plenty of seats and tables on gravel, a gazebo and an enclosed brazier. The comfortable, modern bedrooms are either in the main building or in two garden cottages across the courtyard. Good wheelchair access.

Excellent food following the nose-to-tail approach uses the best local, seasonal produce and gives a modern twist to pub classics: roe deer terrine with apricot chutney, cullen skink, vegetable and pearl barley risotto, lamb faggot with peas, broad beans and asparagus, home-made beef sausages, mash and onion gravy, monkfish wrapped in pancetta with coco beans and basil butter, crispy pork belly with braised pork cheek and ratatouille, and puddings such as treacle tart with clotted cream and chocolate and walnut brownie. They also offer a three-course set lunch. *Benchmark main dish: steak pie with bone marrow £16.50. Two-course evening meal £27.00.*

Free house ~ Licensee Tom Kitchin ~ Real ale ~ Open 11-11; 11am-1am Thurs-Sat; 12-midnight Sun ~ Bar food 12-2, 5-9; 12-10 Sun ~ Restaurant ~ Children welcome ~ Dogs welcome ~ Wi-fi ~ Bedrooms: /$195 *Recommended by Adam and Natalie Davis, Sandra and Miles Spencer, Samuel and Melissa Turnbull, Barbara and Phil Bowie, Alister and Margery Bacon*

If we know a pub has an outdoor play area for children, we mention it.

ISLE OF WHITHORN

NX4736 Map 9

Steam Packet ♀ 🛏

(01988) 500334 – www.thesteampacketinn.biz

Harbour Row; DG8 8LL

Waterside views from friendly inn with up to eight real ales and tasty food; bedrooms

The large picture windows here overlook the bustle of yachts and inshore fishing boats – this family-run inn is right on the quayside in a pretty fishing village – and if you stay over, some of the bedrooms have the same view. The comfortable low-ceilinged bar is split into two: on the right, plush button-back banquettes and boat pictures, and on the left, stools around cast-iron-framed tables on big stone tiles, and a woodburning stove in the bare stone wall; TV, board games and pool. They brew their own ales here at the Five Kingdoms Brewery and also keep Belhaven IPA, Fyne Ales Highlander, Greene King Old Speckled Hen and guests from other breweries such as Kelburn and Orkney on handpump, plus 12 gins, 23 malt whiskies, nine wines by the glass and a couple of farm ciders. There's a lower beamed dining room with high-backed dining chairs around square tables on wooden flooring plus another woodburner, a small eating area off the lounge bar, and an airy conservatory leading into the garden. Wheelchair access but no disabled loos. You can walk from here up to the remains of St Ninian's kirk, which is located on a headland behind the village.

 Pleasing food includes chicken liver pâté, vegetable curry, burger with toppings, onion rings and chips, seafood platter, sirloin steak with a choice of sauce, and puddings such as Drambuie crème brûlée and apple and blueberry crumble. *Benchmark main dish: beer-battered fish and chips £11.95. Two-course evening meal £20.00.*

Free house ~ Licensee Alastair Scoular ~ Real ale ~ Open 11-11; 11am-midnight Fri, Sat; 12-midnight Sun ~ Bar food 12-2, 6.30-9; 12-9 Fri-Sun ~ Restaurant ~ Children welcome except in public bar ~ Dogs allowed in bar and bedrooms ~ Wi-fi ~ Monthly events ~ Bedrooms: /£80 *Recommended by Paddy and Sian O'Leary, Philip J Alderton, Victoria and Len Meadows, Tim and Sue Mulligan, Mike and Mary Carter, Tony Smaithe*

KILCHRENAN

NN0323 Map 11

Kilchrenan Inn 🛏

(01866) 833000 – www.kilchrenaninn.co.uk

B845, by road to Ardanaiseig; PA35 1HD

Close to the banks of Loch Awe with good food, scottish drinks, friendly owners and seats outside; bedrooms

To reach this refurbished 18th-c former trading post there's a lovely drive along Loch Awe and then on to Ardanaiseig Gardens. The stylish modern décor in the bar includes high chairs against the counter where they keep Fyne Ales Easy Trail and Jarl on handpump, eight wines by the glass, scottish gins and several malt whiskies, tartan-upholstered stools and wall seats around simple tables on bare floorboards and a woodburning stove. The atmosphere throughout is relaxed and friendly. A dining room leads off and is similarly furnished, with up-to-date lighting and local artwork on planked walls. Outside in front of the inn are benches and tables with picnic-sets arranged on the grass opposite. Three character, contemporary bedrooms are warm and comfortable; one of them is suitable for families, with a bunk bed. Breakfasts are highly rated.

🍴 Enjoyable food includes scotch egg with celeriac rémoulade and herb oil, smoked fish board with toasted sourdough, vegetable burger with roasted root vegetables and fries, chicken, tarragon and ham pie, beer-battered haddock and fries, asparagus, lemon and mint risotto, and puddings such as brown bread and whisky ice-cream and rhubarb fool. *Benchmark main dish: roast rack of lamb with bacon, peas, baby new potatoes and jus £15.50. Two-course evening meal £21.00.*

Free house ~ Licensees Phil Carr and Pip Pedley ~ Real ale ~ Open 12-11; 12-midnight Sat; 12-11 Sun (phone for winter closing time) ~ Bar food 12-3, 6-9; 12-7 Sun ~ Restaurant ~ Children welcome ~ Dogs allowed in bar and bedrooms ~ Wi-fi ~ Bedrooms: /£110
Recommended by Scott and Charlotte Havers, Nicholas and Lucy Sage, Maggie and Stevan Hollis, Philip Chesington, James Allsopp, Peter and Emma Kelly

MEIKLEOUR
Meikleour Arms 🍷 🛏

NO1539   Map 11

(01250) 883206 – www.meikleourarms.co.uk
A984 W of Coupar Angus; PH2 6EB

Beautifully furnished inn with genuinely welcoming, helpful staff and interesting food; lovely bedrooms

Three of the stylish and elegant bedrooms in this charming 19th-c inn have four-poster beds and the downstairs rooms have wooden flooring and are dog-friendly. It's part of the Meikleour Estate, and there's a lot to see and do nearby, including one of the best salmon beats in Scotland. The bar area has high chairs by the counter, painted chairs and sage green tweed banquettes by pale oak tables on flagstones, tree-pattern wallpapered or stone walls and a two-way woodburning stove; darts, board games and background music. Caledonian Deuchars IPA, Strathbraan Head East and a beer named for the pub on handpump, a carefully and thoughtfully chosen wine list with 12 wines by the glass and a wine of the month, 20 gins and 50 malt whiskies. The main dining room is built in the style of a barn with high rafters in an apex ceiling, old family portraits and fly fishing touches on leaf- and gold key-pattern wallpapered or stone walls, and high-backed carved wooden dining chairs and wall seating around rustic tables on more flagstones. There's also a private dining room, a country-style sitting room for residents and a drying room and tackle area for anglers. Seats in the garden and on a small colonnaded verandah (with more on a sloping lawn) have distant highland views. Disabled access. Do visit the spectacular beech hedge just 600 metres away which was planted over 250 years ago – it's the tallest in the world.

🍴 Using produce from the Estate (including venison) and some from their walled garden, their own eggs and local meat and game, the good, beautifully presented food includes sandwiches, moules marinière, twice-baked smoked cheddar soufflé with creamed leeks, beetroot, chickpea and spiced bean burger with chips, steak in ale pie, kedgeree with smoked haddock, cod and quail eggs, cod fillet in lemon and olive oil with vegetable slaw, chicken supreme with root vegetables and pearl barley broth, duo of venison, 28-day aged rump steak with a choice of sauce and chips, and puddings such as dark chocolate fondant with orange and almond praline chantilly and poached spiced pear and vanilla rice pudding. *Benchmark main dish: beer-battered fresh cod and chips £13.95. Two-course evening meal £20.00.*

Free house ~ Licensees Sam and Claire Mercer Naime ~ Real ale ~ Open 11am-midnight ~ Bar food 11-9 ~ Restaurant ~ Children welcome ~ Dogs welcome ~ Wi-fi ~ Bedrooms: /£125
Recommended by Patricia and Gordon Tucker, Jamie and Lizzie McEwan, Neil and Angela Huxter, Jeremy Snow, Anne Taylor, R L Borthwick

---

It's very helpful if you let us know up-to-date food prices when you report on pubs.

MELROSE
NT5433 Map 9

Burts Hotel 🌟 ⬤ 💲 🛏
(01896) 822285 – www.burtshotel.co.uk

B6374, Market Square; TD6 9PL

Scotland Dining Pub of the Year

Comfortable town-centre hotel with imaginative food and a fine array of malt whiskies; bedrooms

With the abbey ruins just a few steps away and at the heart of an attractive border town, there's plenty to do near this family-run place; the bedrooms, though quite small, are immaculate and comfortably decorated and make a lovely base for exploring. Neat public areas are maintained with attention to detail and the welcoming red-carpeted bar has a woodburning stove, tidy pub tables between cushioned wall seats and windsor armchairs, scottish prints on pale green walls and a long dark wood counter serving Lowland Dryfe Ale and Lockerbie and Timothy Taylors Landlord on handpump, 12 wines by the glass from a good wine list, a farm cider and around 80 malt whiskies. The elegant restaurant with its swagged curtains, dark blue wallpaper and tables laid with white linen offers a smarter dining experience; background music. In summer you can sit out in the pleasant well tended garden.

 Using the best local, seasonal produce, the excellent, interesting food includes pheasant breast wrapped in smoked bacon with black pudding croquette and pancetta jus, lobster ravioli with shellfish bisque and creamed leeks, millefeuille of grilled aubergine and ratatouille, sunblush tomato and red pepper compote, goats cheese bonbon and basil pesto, stone bass fillet with white bean and smoked pancetta cassoulet, baby spinach and crayfish and caper butter, chicken supreme stuffed with chorizo mousse, with paprika and parmesan polenta cake, red pepper purée, chargrilled courgette and chicken café au lait, slow-braised pulled lamb shoulder, shank and rump with pearl barley risotto, dauphinoise potatoes, bean and tomato salsa and rosemary jus, and puddings such as lemon and almond tart with berry purée and roasted plum sorbet and white chocolate pannacotta with raspberry jelly, vanilla mascarpone, shortbread crumb and raspberry sorbet. *Benchmark main dish: smoked haddock risotto with spring onions and poached egg £13.50. Two-course evening meal £25.00.*

Free house ~ Licensees Nick and Trish Henderson ~ Real ale ~ Open 11-2.30, 5-11; 12-2.30, 6-11 Sun ~ Bar food 12-2, 6-9 ~ Restaurant ~ Children welcome ~ Dogs allowed in bar and bedrooms ~ Wi-fi ~ Bedrooms: £79/£148 *Recommended by Barbara and Phil Bowie, Dan and Belinda Smallbone, John Stephenson, Mike and Sarah Abbot, Justine and Neil Bonnett, Charles and Cynthia Todd*

PLOCKTON
NG8033 Map 11

Plockton Hotel ★ ⬤ 🛏
(01599) 544274 – www.plocktonhotel.com

Village signposted from A87 near Kyle of Lochalsh; IV52 8TN

Well run small hotel with wonderful views, very good food with emphasis on local seafood and real ales; bedrooms

This neat little hotel is in the centre of a lovely Scottish National Trust village and part of a long, low terrace of stone-built houses. Tables in the front garden look out past the village's trademark palm trees to a shore lined with colourful flowering shrubs and across the sheltered anchorage to rugged mountains. Inside, the welcoming, comfortably furnished lounge bar has window seats with views of the harbour boats, as well as antique dark red leather seating around neat Regency-style tables on a tartan carpet, and three model ships set into the woodwork and partly panelled stone walls. The separate public bar has pool, board games, TV, a juke box and background music. Glen Spean Red Revival, Isle of Skye Red and Orkney Raven on handpump, 20 malt whiskies, nine wines by the glass and ten scottish gins. Half the comfortable bedrooms have extraordinary water views, while the others, some with balconies, look over the hillside garden; breakfasts are good. Disabled access to one bedroom. There's a hotel nearby called the Plockton Inn, so don't get the two confused.

Fresh fish and shellfish play a big part here with dishes including garlic crab claws, queen scallops and smoked bacon with garlic, sole and salmon parcels with prawn thermidor sauce and sea bass with roasted butternut squash risotto; they also offer sandwiches, haggis and whisky starter, vegetarian dish of the day, chicken breast stuffed with smoked ham and cheese with a sun-dried tomato, garlic and cream sauce, venison with cumberland sauce, and puddings. *Benchmark main dish: langoustine platter £24.00. Two-course evening meal £21.00.*

Free house ~ Licensee Alan Pearson ~ Real ale ~ Open 11am-midnight; closed first two weeks Jan ~ Bar food 12-2.15, 6-9 ~ Restaurant ~ Children welcome ~ Dogs allowed in bar ~ Wi-fi ~ Live traditional music Weds May-Oct in back bar ~ Bedrooms: /£150 *Recommended by Philip Chesington, Amy and Luke Buchanan, Sophia and Hamish Greenfield, Patricia and Anton Larkham, Patti and James Davidson*

RATHO
Bridge 🏅○️ 🍷 🍺
NT1470 Map 11

(0131) 333 1320 – www.bridgeinn.com
Baird Road; EH28 8RA

Canalside inn with cosy bar and airy restaurant, a thoughtful choice of drinks and enjoyable food; attractive bedrooms

Very much the heart of the village and with a good mix of customers, this bustling inn is right by the Union Canal; seats on the terrace overlook the water and are quickly snapped up in warm weather. The cosy bar has an open fire with leather armchairs to either side and a larger area with a two-way fireplace and upholstered tub and cushioned wooden chairs on pale boards around a mix of tables; a contemporary and elegant dining room leads off. Belhaven 80/-, Broughton Greenmantle and a guest from Black Isle on handpump, 36 wines by the glass and 50 malt whiskies. The main restaurant is light and airy with up-to-date pale oak settles, antique-style chairs and big windows overlooking the canal. The individually decorated and well equipped bedrooms also have fine views and breakfasts are lovely.

As well as breakfasts (9-11am), the interesting food (using home-grown produce, their own pork and free-range eggs from their own chickens and ducks) includes sandwiches, crispy haggis with confit potato and turnip velouté, smoked and cured salmon with compressed cucumber, watermelon and crème fraîche, sharing platters, chickpea curry in herb-infused pancakes with lime and yoghurt, sausages and mash with sticky onions and black pudding, seared sea trout fillet with smoked trout risotto, honey-glazed duck breast with pak choi, butter-roasted courgettes and tomato couscous, a duo of venison with smoked king oyster mushrooms and celeriac purée, and puddings such as rose petal-poached pear, frangipane and blackberry textures and lemon and gingernut cheesecake with lemon curd ice-cream. *Benchmark main dish: pie of the day £15.50. Two-course evening meal £22.50.*

Free house ~ Licensees Graham and Rachel Bucknall ~ Real ale ~ Open 9am-11pm; 9am-midnight Fri, Sat ~ Bar food 12-3.45, 5-9; 12-3.45, 5-7.45 ~ Restaurant ~ Dogs allowed in bar ~ Wi-fi ~ Bedrooms: /£140 *Recommended by Victoria and James Sargeant, Angela and Steve Heard, Martin and Joanne Sharp, Jim and Sue James, Richard Kennell, Edward May*

SHIELDAIG

NG8153 Map 11

Tigh an Eilean Hotel 🛏

(01520) 755251 – www.tighaneilean.co.uk

Village signposted just off A896 Lochcarron–Gairloch; IV54 8XN

Wonderfully set hotel with separate contemporary bar, real ales and enjoyable food; tranquil bedrooms

For wildlife lovers, this charming place makes a fine base for spotting otters, sea eagles, seals and even the rare pine marten; the view over forested Shieldaig Island to Loch Torridon and then out to the sea beyond is stunning. Separate from the hotel, the bright, attractive bar is on two storeys with an open staircase; dining is on the first floor and a decked balcony has a magnificent water and village view. The place is gently contemporary and nicely relaxed with timbered floors, timber-boarded walls, shiny bolts through exposed timber roof beams and an open kitchen. A couple of changing ales such as Strathcarron Golden Cow and Red Cow on handpump and up to a dozen wines by the glass; background music, TV, darts, pool and board games. Tables outside in a sheltered little courtyard are well placed to enjoy the gorgeous position. To preserve the peace and quiet, the comfortable bedrooms have no TVs and no telephones, though each has its own sitting area; good, ample breakfasts.

As well as shellfish straight from the jetty, the reliably good food includes lunchtime sandwiches, moules marinière, hand-dived scallops with black pudding and cauliflower purée, grilled goats cheese with rosemary and tomato salsa, pizzas from their wood-fired oven, battered fresh haddock and chips, haggis, neeps and tatties, seafood stew, burger with coleslaw and chips, venison casserole with dumplings, fishcakes with cucumber rémoulade, and puddings such as milk chocolate tart with white chocolate sauce and blood orange sorbet and sticky toffee and date pudding with vanilla ice-cream. *Benchmark main dish: seafood platter £18.00. Two-course evening meal £20.00.*

Free house ~ Licensee Cathryn Field ~ Real ale ~ Open 11-11; 11am-midnight Sat; 10am-11pm Sun ~ Bar food 12-2.30, 6.30-9 (8.30 in winter) ~ Restaurant ~ Children welcome ~ Dogs allowed in bar and bedrooms ~ Wi-fi ~ Traditional live folk music Fri or Sat in summer ~ Bedrooms: /£150 *Recommended by Robert and Diana Ringstone, Daisy Rutledge, William and Tasha Fraser, Adam and Natalie Davis, Diana and Bertie Farr*

SLIGACHAN

NG4930 Map 11

Sligachan Hotel 🍺 🛏

(01478) 650204 – www.sligachan.co.uk

A87 Broadford–Portree, junction with A863; IV47 8SW

Spectacularly set mountain hotel with walkers' bar and plusher side, all-day food and impressive range of whiskies

The huge, modern, pine-clad main bar in this stunningly set hotel on the Isle of Skye falls somewhere between a basic climbers' bar and the plusher, more sedate hotel side. It's spaciously open to the ceiling rafters and has geometrically laid-out dark tables and chairs on neat carpets; pool, TV and board games. As well as their own Cuillin Eagle, Old Bridge and Pinnacle, they keep a guest on handpump plus an incredible display of over 400 malt whiskies at one end of the counter. It can get quite lively in here some nights, but there's a more sedate lounge bar with leather bucket armchairs on plush carpets and a coal fire; background highland and islands music. The separate restaurant is in the hotel itself. The interesting little museum, well worth a visit, charts the history of the hotel and its famous climbers, with photographs and climbing and angling records. There are tables out in the garden and a big play area for children, which can be seen from the bar. The bedrooms are comfortable, bright and modern, and they also offer self-catering and have a campsite with caravan hook-ups. Some of the most testing walks in Britain are right on the doorstep.

Some sort of food is on offer all day: cullen skink, local scallops with root purée, bacon crumb and basil oil, baked gnocchi gratin with wild mushrooms, rich tomato sauce, buffalo mozzarella and omega seeds, seafood platter, haggis, neeps and tatties with Talisker whisky sauce and parma ham crisp, thai green chicken curry, battered haddock and chips, venison casserole, and puddings such as baked vanilla cheesecake with berry compote and pistachio salt and sticky toffee pudding with butterscotch sauce. *Benchmark main dish: beer-battered haddock and chips £13.50. Two-course evening meal £20.00.*

Own brew ~ Real ale ~ Open 9am-12.30am; 12-9 in winter; closed early Jan-end Feb ~ Bar food 11-9 ~ Restaurant ~ Children welcome ~ Dogs welcome ~ Wi-fi ~ Live ceilidh Sat evenings ~ Bedrooms: £90/£140 *Recommended by Matthew and Elisabeth Reeves, Harry and Megan Evans, Ben Lees, Julia and Martin Swift, Peter Barratt, Brian and Sally Wakeham, William Slade*

STEIN
Stein Inn 🛏

NG2656 Map 11

(01470) 592362 – www.stein-inn.co.uk
End of B886 N of Dunvegan in Waternish, off A850 Dunvegan–Portree; OS Sheet 23 map reference 263564; IV55 8GA

Skye's oldest inn with good, simple food and lots of whiskies; a rewarding place to stay

This is an inn of great character in a tiny waterside hamlet with classic hebridean views across Loch Dunvegan; benches in front make the most of this. The unpretentious original public bar makes a particularly inviting retreat from the elements, with sturdy country furnishings, flagstones, a beam-and-plank ceiling, partly panelled stripped-stone walls and a warming double-sided stove between the two rooms. Caledonian Deuchars IPA and a couple of local guests such as Isle of Skye Blonde and Orkney Dark Island on handpump, ten wines by the glass, 130 malt whiskies and 18 gins. Good service from smartly uniformed staff. Pool, darts, board games, dominoes and cribbage in the games area, and maybe background music. There's a lively indoor play area for children and showers for yachtsmen. Warm bedrooms overlook the water and they also offer self-catering properties. Dogs are welcome in the inn but not during evening food service.

Good, wholesome food uses local fish, lamb, highland beef and wild venison: sandwiches (the crab is popular), black pudding with whisky and mustard dressing, peat-smoked local salmon, vegetarian, chicken or beef burger with toppings and fries, fresh local langoustines, venison casserole with chocolate, duck breast in garlic, cider and cream, salmon fillet with a cajun crust, slow-cooked lamb shank with mint gravy, and puddings such as lemon cheesecake and fruit crumbles. *Benchmark main dish: beer-battered haddock £12.00. Two-course evening meal £19.00.*

Free house ~ Licensees Angus and Teresa McGhie ~ Real ale ~ Open 11am-midnight; 12-11 Sun; 12-11 (midnight Sat) in winter; closed winter Mon ~ Bar food 12-3, 6-9; 12.30-3, 6-9 Sun ~ Children welcome ~ Dogs allowed in bar and bedrooms ~ Wi-fi ~ Bedrooms: £57/£85 *Recommended by Molly and Stewart Lindsay, Stuart and Natalie Granville, Nicholas and Lucy Sage, Maggie and Stevan Hollis, Philip Chesington*

We say if we know a pub allows dogs.

SWINTON

NT8347 Map 10

Wheatsheaf ⭐ ♀ 🛏

(01890) 860257 – www.wheatsheaf-swinton.co.uk

A6112 N of Coldstream; TD11 3JJ

Civilised place with small bar for drinkers, comfortable lounges, top quality food and drinks and professional service; appealing bedrooms

Of course, many customers are here to enjoy the particularly good food served by attentive, friendly staff, but there's also a little bar and informal lounges. Here they keep Belhaven IPA and a changing guest on handpump alongside 30 malt whiskies and 18 wines by the glass. There are comfortable plush armchairs, several nice old oak settles with cushions, a little open fire, sporting prints and china plates on the bottle-green walls in the bar and small agricultural prints and a fishing-theme décor on the painted or bare-stone walls in the lounges. The dining room and front conservatory with its vaulted pine ceiling are carpeted, with high-backed slate-grey chairs around pale wood tables set with fresh flowers, while the more formal restaurant has black leather high-backed dining chairs around cloth-covered tables; background music. To make the best of the surrounding rolling countryside, why not stay in the well equipped and comfortable bedrooms; breakfasts are good and hearty. This is a pretty village just a few miles from the River Tweed.

As well as some traditional dishes, the creative food includes seared scallops with black pudding, samphire and citrus butter, pigeon breast with parsnip purée and baby courgettes, vegetable moussaka, chicken breast with tarragon cream, roast venison loin with fondant potato, braised red cabbage, mushrooms and pancetta jus, duck breast with colcannon potatoes and raspberry jus, and puddings such as kiwi parfait with honey and ginger jelly, chocolate ice-cream, green tea genoise and vanilla crème anglais and vanilla rice pudding with home-made shortbread. *Benchmark main dish: sea bass with pineapple and red pepper salsa, spinach, saffron potatoes and lemon and chilli dressing £16.95. Two-course evening meal £22.00.*

Free house ~ Licensee Michael Lawrence ~ Real ale ~ Open 11-11; 11-midnight Fri, Sat ~ Bar food 12-2, 6 (5.30 Thurs, Fri)-9 ~ Restaurant ~ Children welcome ~ Dogs allowed in bar and bedrooms ~ Wi-fi ~ Bedrooms: /£137 *Recommended by Rosie and Marcus Heatherley, Kerry and Guy Trooper, Mary and Douglas Kirkwood, Elliott Kemp, Peter and Emma Kelly, Edward May*

THORNHILL

NS6699 Map 11

Lion & Unicorn

(01786) 850204 – www.lion-unicorn.co.uk

Main Street (A873); FK8 3PJ

Busy, family-run pub with emphasis on its home-made food; friendly staff and bedrooms

Our readers enjoy the friendly atmosphere and the warming fires at this attractive, partly 17th-c pub; one of the three log fires is in an original fireplace with a high brazier almost big enough to drive a car into. The pubby character back bar has some exposed stone walls, wooden flooring and stools lined along the counter where they keep a beer named for the pub (from Belhaven), Belhaven 80/- and a changing guest on handpump and several wines by the glass. This opens to a games room with a pool table, juke box, fruit machine, darts, TV and board games. The more restauranty-feeling beamed and carpeted front room is traditionally furnished and set for dining; background music. Outside there are benches in a gravelled garden and a lawn with a play area.

🍴 Food is good and includes sandwiches, moules marinière, garlic and rosemary-studded baked baby camembert with red onion marmalade, leek, field mushroom and parsnip crumble, lasagne, steak burger topped with cheese and bacon, chicken topped with haggis and wrapped in bacon with a whisky cream sauce, 10oz local rib-eye steak with beer-battered onion rings, and puddings such as sticky toffee pudding and assorted ice-creams. *Benchmark main dish: beer-battered fish and chips £10.25. Two-course evening meal £18.00.*

Free house ~ Licensee Fiona Stevenson ~ Real ale ~ Open 12-11; 12-midnight Fri, Sat ~ Bar food 12-9 ~ Restaurant ~ Children welcome ~ Dogs allowed in bar ~ Wi-fi ~ Bedrooms: /£85
Recommended by Patricia Healey, Frances Parsons, Charles and Maddie Bishop, Charles Todd, Miranda and Jeff Davidson, Diana Dobson

Also Worth a Visit in Scotland

Besides the fully inspected pubs, you might like to try these pubs that have been recommended to us and described by readers. Do tell us what you think of them: feedback@goodguides.com

ABERDEENSHIRE

ABERDEEN
NJ9305
Grill (01224) 573530
Union Street; AB11 6BA Don't be put off by the exterior of this 19th-c granite building – the remodelled 1920s interior is well worth a look; long wood-floored bar with fine moulded ceiling, mahogany panelling and original button-back leather wall benches, ornate servery with glazed cabinets housing some of their 600 whiskies (a few from the 1930s, and 60 from outside Scotland), five well kept ales including Harviestoun Bitter & Twisted, basic snacks; no children or dogs; open all day. *(Charlotte and William Mason)*

ABERDEEN
NJ9406
★**Prince of Wales** (01224) 640597
St Nicholas Lane; AB10 1HF Individual and convivial old tavern with eight changing ales from very long counter; painted floorboards, flagstones or carpet, pews and screened booths, original tiled spittoon running length of bar, bargain hearty food; live acoustic music Sun evening, quiz Weds, games machines; children over 5 welcome if eating, open (and food) all day from 10am. *(Edward May)*

ABOYNE
NO5298
Boat (01339) 886137 *Charlestown Road (B968, just off A93); AB34 5EL* Country inn with fine views across River Dee; bare-boards dining bar with contemporary paintwork, scatter cushions on built-in wall seats and woodburner in stone fireplace, model train chugging its way around just below ceiling height, good food from 7.30am breakfast on, three well kept changing ales, decent wines and some 30 malt whiskies, piano and another woodburner in back public bar, additional dining/function room upstairs; background music; children and dogs welcome, eight comfortable well equipped bedrooms, open all day. *(Patricia and Gordon Tucker)*

BALMEDIE
NJ9619
Cock & Bull (01358) 743249
A90 N of Balmedie; AB23 8XY Friendly atmosphere and interesting décor in this country dining pub; good locally sourced food from sandwiches to daily specials, breakfast from 10am and afternoon teas (must book), beamed lounge bar with log fire, restaurant and conservatory; children welcome, dogs in bar (menu for them), picnic-sets out at front with distant sea view, enclosed play area, bedrooms in converted cottage, open (and food) all day. *(Edward May)*

BRAEMAR
NO1591
★**Fife Arms** (01339) 720200
Mar Road; AB35 5YN Large stunningly restored Victorian hotel packed with sumptuous furnishings, modern artwork and many quirky features; welcoming bare-boards bar with lots of pictures and taxidermy including a flying stag suspended over the counter, a couple of local beers such as Cairngorm and over 180 malt whiskies, well liked/priced food from short but varied menu, plenty of other areas (all worth seeing) including separate evening restaurant and cocktail bar, good service from uniformed staff; children and dogs welcome, gardens overlooking River Clune, 46 individually themed bedrooms, open all day, food all day weekends. *(Mike Benton)*

OLDMELDRUM
NJ8127
Redgarth (01651) 872353
Kirk Brae, off A957; AB51 0DJ Good-sized comfortable lounge with traditional décor; two or three well kept ales and interesting range of malt whiskies (village has its own distillery), popular reasonably priced food, friendly attentive service,

restaurant; children welcome, lovely views to Bennachie, six bedrooms, open (and food) all day Sun. *(Charlotte and William Mason)*

PENNAN NJ8465
Pennan Inn (01346) 561201

Just off B9031 Banff–Fraserburgh; AB43 6JB Whitewashed building in long row of old fishermen's cottages, wonderful spot right by the sea (scenes from *Local Hero* filmed here); small bar with simple furniture and exposed stone walls, modern décor in separate restaurant, enjoyable sensibly priced food from shortish menu, at least one real ale; five bedrooms, at foot of steep winding road and parking along front limited, closed Mon, Tues and lunchtimes other days. *(Edward May)*

ANGUS

BROUGHTY FERRY NO4630
★**Fishermans Tavern** (01382) 775941

Fort Street; turning off shore road; DD5 2AD Once a row of fishermen's cottages, this friendly pub is just steps from the beach; up to eight well kept changing ales (summer beer festival) and good range of malt whiskies, comfortable lounge with coal fire, small snug and back dining area with another fire, popular fair priced pubby food from sandwiches up; sports TV; children and dogs welcome, disabled facilities, tables on front pavement, more in secluded little walled garden, 14 bedrooms, open (and food) all day. *(Molly and Stewart Lindsay)*

BROUGHTY FERRY NO4630
Ship (01382) 779176

Fisher Street; DD5 1EF Waterfront pub with fine views over the Tay; dark nautical-feel plank panelling with brass fittings, red leather button-back banquettes and ornate plaster ceiling, woodburner and some old local photographs, beers such as Caledonian, McEwans and Timothy Taylors from impressive mahogany counter, enjoyable fairly priced food from bar snacks up including good fish and chips, upstairs restaurant, friendly accommodating service; open all day. *(Susan and John Douglas)*

CLOVA NO3273
Glen Clova Hotel (01575) 550350

B955 NW of Wheen; DD8 4QS Tucked-away 19th-c hotel's unpretentious climbers' bar; flagstones, bench seats and stone fireplace with woodburner, bric-a-brac and old photographs, a couple of well kept changing beers, 18 malts and plenty of wines by the glass, good food (same menu as their restaurant) using home-reared beef and lamb and venison from surrounding hills, friendly staff; children and dogs welcome, ten bedrooms, eight garden lodges and bunkhouse, glorious walks nearby, open all day. *(Nick Higgins)*

MEMUS NO4259
★**Drovers** (01307) 860322

N of Sheilhill; DD8 3TY Refurbished country pub-restaurant; very good attractively presented food from interesting menu, also more standard bar meals and a vegan menu, friendly professional service, well kept Timothy Taylors Landlord and good selection of wines and whiskies, fairly traditional bar with fire in old range, more modern dining areas; children and dogs welcome, peaceful country views from pretty orchard garden, play area, open (and food) all day. *(Susan and John Douglas)*

ARGYLL

ARDFERN NM8004
Galley of Lorne (01852) 500284

B8002; village and inn signposted off A816 Lochgilphead–Oban; PA31 8QN Family-run 17th-c drovers' inn on edge of Loch Craignish; cosy beamed and flagstoned bar with warming log fire, black panelling and unfussy assortment of furniture including settles, up to four real ales and 50 whiskies, good choice of food from lunchtime sandwiches up, lounge bar with woodburner and spacious picture-window restaurant; background music, small pool room, darts, games machine, sports TV; children and dogs welcome, good sea and loch views from sheltered terrace and deck, seven bedrooms in extension, open all day summer. *(Molly and Stewart Lindsay)*

BRIDGE OF ORCHY NN2939
★**Bridge of Orchy Hotel**
(01838) 400208 *A82 Tyndrum–Glencoe; PA36 4AB* Spectacular spot on West Highland Way; very welcoming with good food in bar, lounge and smarter restaurant, decent choice of well kept ales, house wines and malt whiskies, open fires and interesting mountain photographs; free wi-fi; dogs welcome; good bedrooms, more in airy riverside annexe, open (and food) all day. *(Alison and Michael Harper)*

CAIRNDOW NN1811
★**Cairndow Stagecoach Inn**
(01499) 600286 *Village and pub signed off A83; PA26 8BN* 17th-c coaching inn in wonderful position on edge of Loch Fyne; good sensibly priced food including local venison and fresh fish, ales from nearby Fyne and more than 40 malt whiskies (including a whisky of the month), friendly accommodating staff; children and dogs welcome, lovely peaceful lochside garden, comfortable bedrooms, some in modern annexe with balconies overlooking the water, good breakfast, open (and food) all day. *(Gary Hooper)*

CONNEL   NM9034
Oyster (01631) 710666
A85, W of Connel Bridge; PA37 1PJ
18th-c inn opposite former ferry slipway –
lovely view across the water (especially at
sunset); decent-sized bar (the Glue Pot)
with friendly highland atmosphere, log fire
in stone fireplace, Caledonian Deuchars IPA,
good range of wines, gins and malt whiskies,
enjoyable all-day food from pubby choices to
local seafood, afternoon high teas from 4pm,
friendly attentive service; sports TV; modern
hotel part with 11 bedrooms and separate
evening restaurant (closed winter). *(David
Longhurst)*

GLENCOE   NN1058
★Clachaig (01855) 811252
*Old Glencoe Road, behind NTS Visitor
Centre; PH49 4HX* 18th-c climbers' and
walkers' inn surrounded by the scenic
grandeur of Glencoe; Boots Bar with 14
scottish ales, some 365 malts and interesting
range of artisan gins, vodkas and rums from
across Scotland, slate-floored snug with
whisky barrel-panelled walls and open fire,
lounge (children allowed here) has mix of
tables and booths, photos signed by famous
climbers and local artwork, hearty food;
background and live music, pool, free wi-fi;
dogs welcome, 23 comfortable bedrooms in
adjoining hotel plus self-catering cottages,
open (and food) all day. *(Stuart and
Natalie Granville)*

INVERARAY   NN0908
★George (01499) 302111
Main Street East; PA32 8TT Georgian
hotel at hub of this appealing small town;
pubby bar with exposed joists, bare stone
walls, old tiles and big flagstones, antique
settles, carved wooden benches and
cushioned stone slabs along the walls, four
log/peat fires, a couple of real ales and
over 100 malt whiskies, good food in bar or
smarter restaurant, conservatory; children
and dogs welcome, plenty of seats on well
laid-out terraces, 17 bedrooms, Inveraray
Castle and walks close by, open (and food)
all day, can get packed in high season. *(Mike
Benton)*

OBAN   NM8530
Cuan Mor (01631) 565078
George Street; PA34 5SD Contemporary
quayside bar-restaurant with over 100 malts,
a couple of changing beers and wide variety
of enjoyable food including local fish/seafood,
friendly service; children welcome, some
seats outside, open (and food) all day.
(Chelsea Hoffman)

OBAN   NM8529
Lorne (01631) 570020
Stevenson Street; PA34 5NA Traditional
Victorian pub tucked away behind the
seafront; a well kept changing ale and good
selection of whiskies and gins from island
servery with ornate brasswork, reasonably
priced food including burgers and fish/
seafood, good service; weekend live music
and DJs, Weds quiz, TVs; children and dogs
welcome, café-style tables and chairs in
sheltered beer garden, open (and food)
all day. *(Charlotte and William Mason)*

OBAN   NM8530
★Oban Inn (01631) 562484
*Stafford Street, near North Pier;
PA5 5NJ* Popular 18th-c pub with spotless
beamed and slate-floored bar, well kept ales
such as Fyne and good selection of malt
whiskies including Oban, partly panelled
upstairs dining bar with button-back
banquettes around cast-iron-framed tables,
coffered woodwork ceiling and little stained-
glass false windows, good value hearty food
served by friendly staff; background and
regular live music; dogs welcome, harbour
view from new walled terrace, open (and
food) all day. *(Susan and John Douglas)*

OTTER FERRY   NR9384
Oystercatcher (01700) 821229
B8000, by the water; PA21 2DH Old pub-
restaurant in outstanding spot overlooking
Loch Fyne; good food using local fish and
shellfish, well kept ales including Fyne from
pine-clad bar, decent wine list, friendly staff;
dogs welcome in bar; lots of tables out on spit,
free moorings, open all day (closed Tues, Weds).
(Edward May)

PORT APPIN   NM9045
Pierhouse (01631) 730302
*In Appin, turn right at the Port Appin/
Lismore Ferry sign; PA38 4DE* Beautiful
location with views over Loch Linnhe to
Lismore and beyond; smallish bar with good
range of wines and beers, 100 malt whiskies
and 40 gins (many scottish), excellent fish/
seafood and other much liked food, picture-
window restaurant enjoying the fine view,
helpful friendly staff; children welcome,
comfortable bedrooms, moorings for visiting
yachts, open all day. *(Edward May)*

TARBERT   NR8365
West Loch Hotel (01880) 820283
A83, a mile S; PA29 6YF Friendly 18th-c
inn overlooking sea loch; comfortably
modernised with exposed stone walls, pale-
wood tables and dark high-backed dining
chairs, relaxing lounges with fine views and
warming fires, enjoyable food using local
produce, good selection of whiskies and gins
but no real ales, helpful cheerful service;
children and dogs welcome, bedrooms
(some with loch view), well placed for
ferry terminal. *(Brian and Sally Wakeham)*

TAYVALLICH   NR7487
Tayvallich Inn (01546) 870282
B8025; PA31 8PL Small single-storey
bar-restaurant by Loch Sween specialising

in good local seafood; pale pine furnishings on quarry tiles, local nautical charts, good range of whiskies and three well kept beers such as Fyne and Orkney, friendly atmosphere; background music (live first Fri of month); children and dogs welcome, a few rustic picnic-sets on front deck with lovely views over yacht anchorage, open all day in summer (open all day weekends, closed Mon in winter). *(Brian and Anna Marsden)*

AYRSHIRE

SORN   NS5526
Sorn Inn (01290) 551305
Village signed from Mauchline (A76); Main Street; KA5 6HU Restaurant pub in tiny conservation village; highly regarded imaginative food from brasserie dishes up in two restaurant areas, also smallish bar serving an Orkney ale, friendly staff; children and dogs (not in restaurant) welcome, four comfortable well appointed bedrooms, open (and food) all day weekends, closed Mon. *(Sam Cole)*

SYMINGTON   NS3831
Wheatsheaf (01563) 830307
Just off A77 Ayr–Kilmarnock; Main Street; KA1 5QB Single-storey former 18th-c posting inn, charming and cosy, with good food (must book weekends) including lunchtime/early evening set menu, efficient friendly service, log fire; children welcome, circular picnic-sets outside, quiet pretty village, open (and food) all day.
(Philip Chesington)

BERWICKSHIRE

ALLANTON   NT8654
★**Allanton Inn** (01890) 818260
B6347 S of Chirnside; TD11 3JZ Well run 18th-c stone-built village inn with attractive open-plan interior; very good fairly priced food with emphasis on fresh fish/seafood from daily changing menu, a couple of well kept ales such as Born in the Borders, good wine list and speciality gins, friendly efficient service, cosy bare boards bar with scatter cushions on bench seats, immaculate dining areas, log fire; background music; children welcome, no dogs inside, picnic-sets in sheltered garden behind, nice views, comfortable bedrooms, open all day. *(Rosie)*

AUCHENCROW   NT8560
Craw (01890) 761253
B6438 NE of Duns; pub signed off A1; TD14 5LS Delightful little 18th-c pub in row of cream-washed cottages, friendly and welcoming, with enjoyable well presented food, changing ales from smaller brewers and good wine list, pictures on panelled walls, woodburner, more formal back restaurant; children welcome, tables out on village green and on decking behind, three bedrooms and self-catering annexe, open all day weekends. *(Alison and Michael Harper)*

LAUDER   NT5347
Black Bull (01578) 722208
Market Place; TD2 6SR Comfortable white-painted 18th-c inn festooned with cheerful window boxes and hanging baskets; cosy rustic-feel bar with country scenes on panelled walls, quieter room off and restaurant, well kept Campbells Gunner and a guest, good priced food using local seasonal produce, friendly helpful service; background music, sports TV, free wi-fi; children and dogs (in bar) welcome, ten bedrooms, open all day, food all day weekends. *(Mrs Lynda Kellman)*

BORDERS

AYTON   NT9261
Hemelvaart Bier Café 07968 359917
High Street; TD14 5QL Welcoming village bar with plenty of community spirit; two real ales, six craft kegs and extensive range of bottled beers, interesting collection of gins too, friendly knowledgeable staff, enjoyable good value food including range of burgers and locally made pies, themed nights, also good coffee and home-made cakes; regular live music, comedy evenings and other events; children and dogs welcome, open from 5pm Mon, closed Tues and Weds, otherwise open all day (from 1pm Sun). *(Nick Higgins)*

DUMFRIESSHIRE

LOCKERBIE   NY1382
Townhead (01576) 204627
Townhead Street; DG11 2AG Modernised inn with good well presented food including OAP set lunch deal, can eat in bar or restaurant and they cater for special diets, no real ales (Belhaven Best), friendly helpful service; sports TV; children and dogs (in one area) welcome, comfortable well equipped bedrooms, closed Mon lunchtime, otherwise open all day. *(David Holmes)*

BARGRENNAN   NX3576
House O' Hill (01671) 840243
Off A714, road opposite church; DG8 6RN Small pub on edge of Galloway Forest; decent fair priced food from varied menu including daily specials, a couple of real ales and decent wine list, afternoon teas,

---

If you know a pub is ever open all day, please tell us.

friendly helpful staff; children and dogs (in bar) welcome, two comfortable bedrooms and self-catering cottage, open all day. *(Stuart and Natalie Granville)*

BEATTOCK   NT0702
Old Stables (01683) 300134
Smith Way; 0.25 miles from M74 junction 15; DG10 9QX Turreted 19th-c pub at edge of the village; Belhaven beers and bargain home-cooked food, friendly staff, bar and second railway-themed room with memorabilia from the old Beattock line (famous for its steep gradients); live music, big-screen TVs, pool and darts; children and dogs welcome, covered outside seating area, bedrooms and parking for campervans, open all day. *(Alison and Michael Harper)*

DUMFRIES   NX9776
⋆**Cavens Arms** (01387) 252896
Buccleuch Street; DG1 2AH Good generously served home-made food from pubby choices up, eight well kept interesting ales and wide range of other drinks including fine choice of malts, friendly attentive service, civilised front part with lots of wood, drinkers' area at back with bar stools, banquettes and traditional cast-iron tables, more recently added lounge/restaurant; discreet TV; no children or dogs, disabled facilities, small terrace behind, kitchen shut Mon, otherwise open (and food) all day, can get very busy. *(Sally Jamieson)*

DUMFRIES   NX9775
Globe (01387) 252335
High Street; DG1 2JA This town pub with strong Burns connections was closed for refurbishment as we went to press; has had dark-panelled 17th-century snug and little museum-like room beyond; main part is more modern in feel; ales such as Caledonian and Sulwath, plenty of whiskies and good value pubby food, friendly service; children welcome in eating areas, terrace seating, open all day. *(David Longhurst)*

DUNBARTONSHIRE

ARROCHAR   NN2903
Village Inn (01301) 702279
A814, just off A83 W of Loch Lomond; G83 7AX Friendly 19th-c lochside inn with five well kept changing ales and good range of other drinks, wide choice of popular food (special diets catered for) including evening set menu, heavy beams, bare boards, panelling and roaring fire, steps down to unpretentious bar; background music, sports TV; children (in eating areas) and dogs welcome, tables out on deck and lawn with

lovely loch and hill views, neat comfortable bedrooms (more spacious ones in converted barn), open all day. *(Sam Cole)*

LUSS   NS3498
Inn on Loch Lomond
(01436) 860678
A82, about 3 miles N; G83 8PD Large open-plan inn across the road from Loch Lomond; decent choice of enjoyable food including local fish in bar and restaurant (takeaway menu as well), well kept beers, some 30 wines by the glass and good range of whiskies, friendly helpful staff; children welcome, private jetty and boat trips, bedrooms including eight in water-edge lodge, open (and food) all day. *(Charlotte and William Mason)*

EAST LOTHIAN

GULLANE   NT4882
⋆**Old Clubhouse** (01620) 842008
East Links Road; EH31 2AF Single-storey building in nice position overlooking Gullane Links; cosy bar and more formal dining room, seating from wooden dining chairs and banquettes to big squashy leather armchairs and sofas, Victorian pictures and cartoons, stuffed birds, sheet music covers and other memorabilia, open fires, enjoyable home-made food from ciabattas up, Caledonian Deuchars IPA, Timothy Taylors Landlord and a couple of guests, nice house wines, friendly helpful service; under-10s till 8pm, dogs welcome in bar, plenty of seats out at front, open (and food) all day. *(Terry Grant)*

FIFE

CULROSS   NS9885
Red Lion (01383) 880225
Low Causeway; KY12 8HN Friendly old pub in pretty NTS village; wide choice of fair value food, a beer from Inveralmond and several wines by the glass, beams and amazing painted ceilings; seats outside, open (and food) all day. *(Mike Benton)*

CUPAR   NO3714
Boudingait (01334) 654681
Bonnygate; KY15 4BU Bustling bar with captain's and cushion-seated chairs around dark tables on wood flooring, open fire, high chairs against counter serving a couple of changing ales, good choice of well liked traditional food at reasonable prices, afternoon teas, friendly helpful staff; regular live music including folk nights, quiz Weds; children welcome, open (and food) all day. *(Jane Rigby)*

We include some hotels with a good bar that offers facilities comparable to those of a pub.

ELIE   NO4999

Ship (01333) 330246

The Toft, off A917 (High Street) towards harbour; KY9 1DT Attractively updated and in great position for enjoying a drink overlooking the sandy bay; bar and two restaurants (one upstairs), good seasonal food, friendly service; children and dogs welcome, terrace with own bar looking out to stone granary and pier, maybe beach cricket, six boutique-style bedrooms, open all day. *(Jane Rigby)*

INVERNESS-SHIRE

ARDGOUR   NN0163

Inn at Ardgour (01855) 841225

From A82 follow signs for Strontian A861 and take Corran Ferry across loch to the inn; note that ferry does not sail over Christmas period; PH33 7AA Traditional fairly remote roadside inn by Corran Ferry slipway with fine Loch Linnhe views; enjoyable food and decent beer and whisky choice, friendly accommodating staff, restaurant; children and well behaved dogs welcome, a few tables outside, bedrooms, open all day in season (from 4pm winter). *(Mandy and Gary Redstone)*

AVIEMORE   NH8612

Cairngorm (01479) 810233

Grampian Road (A9); PH22 1PE Large flagstoned bar in traditional turreted hotel, lively and friendly, with Cairngorm ales and good choice of other drinks, well priced food from wide-ranging menu using local produce, prompt helpful service, tartan-walled and carpeted restaurant; daily live music (not Tues when there's a quiz), sports TV; children welcome, comfortable smart bedrooms (some with stunning views), open (and food) all day. *(Sarah and David Gibbs)*

CARRBRIDGE   NH9022

Cairn (01479) 841212

Main Road; PH23 3AS Welcoming traditionally furnished hotel bar; three well kept ales such as local Cairngorm and good range of whiskies including Tomintoul served from the barrel, popular home-cooked food, old local pictures, warm coal fire, separate more formal dining room; pool and sports TV; children and dogs welcome, seats and tables out in front, seven comfortable bedrooms, open all day. *(Martin Cooke)*

DORES   NH5934

★**Dores** (01463) 751203

B852 SW of Inverness; IV2 6TR Traditional country pub with low ceilings and exposed stonework in delightful spot on the shore of Loch Ness; small attractive bar on right with two or three well kept changing scottish ales and several whiskies, two-part dining area to the left serving good food from pub favourites up, friendly staff; children and dogs welcome, sheltered front garden, lots of picnic-sets out behind taking in the spectacular view, open (and food) all day, closed Mon in winter. *(Terry Grant)*

FORT WILLIAM   NN1274

Ben Nevis Inn (01397) 701227

N off A82: Achintee; PH33 6TE Roomy converted stone barn in stunning spot by footpath to Ben Nevis; good mainly straightforward food (lots of walkers so best to book), ales such as Cairngorm and Isle of Skye, prompt cheery service, bare-boards dining area with steps up to bar; live music (Tues in summer, maybe first and third Thurs in winter); children welcome, no dogs, seats out at front and back, bunkhouse below, open all day Apr-Oct, otherwise closed Mon-Weds. *(Edward May)*

GLENFINNAN   NM9080

Glenfinnan House (01397) 722235

Take A830 off A32 to Glenfinnan, turn left after Glenfinnan Monument Visitors Centre; PH37 4LT Beautifully placed 18th-c hotel by Loch Shiel; traditional bar with well kept ales and over 50 whiskies, good food including fish/seafood and local venison, restaurant; lawns down to the water, comfortable bedrooms, may close in winter. *(Alison and Michael Harper)*

GLENUIG   NM6576

Glenuig Inn (01687) 470219

A861 SW of Lochailort, off A830 Fort William–Mallaig; PH38 4NG Friendly bar set on picturesque bay; enjoyable locally sourced food including some from next-door smokery, well kept Cairngorm ales and a scottish cider on tap, lots of bottled beers and good range of whiskies, dining room with woodburner; dogs welcome, bedrooms in adjoining block, also bunkhouse popular with walkers and divers, moorings for visiting yachts, open (and food) all day. *(Andrew Chetty)*

INVERMORISTON   NH4216

Glenmoriston Arms (01320) 351206

A82/A887; IV63 7YA Small civilised hotel dating in part from 1740 when it was a drovers' inn; bare-boards bar with stone fireplace and big old stag's head, a well kept beer such as Orkney and around 80 malt whiskies, good food here from lunchtime sandwiches up or in neatly laid-out restaurant with antique rifles, friendly staff; children and dogs (in bar) welcome, picnic-sets out at front, 11 bedrooms (three in converted outbuilding), handy for Loch Ness, open all day, from 5pm Nov-Apr. *(Philip J Alderton)*

INVERNESS   NH6645

Black Isle (01463) 229920

Church Street; IV1 1EN Buzzy corner bar

owned by Black Isle brewery, over 20 draught beers (listed on screens) plus extensive bottled range from slabby wood counter, long rustic tables, benches and mix of wooden chairs on bare boards, full-length windows at front, some colourful murals and high ceiling with exposed ducting, good wood-fired pizzas, friendly knowledgeable staff; barrel tables and seats made from pallets on part-covered terrace, hostel-style bedrooms (private and shared), open (and food) all day. *(Philip Chesington)*

INVERNESS   NH6644
Castle Tavern (01463) 718178
View Place, top of Castle Street; IV2 4SA
Welcoming little stone-built pub with river and castle views; half a dozen mainly scottish ales and fine whisky choice, good reasonably priced traditional food, informal upstairs restaurant; silent sports TV; children welcome, tables on heated front terrace, open all day. *(Martin Cooper)*

INVERNESS   NH6645
Number 27 (01463) 241999
Castle Street; IV2 3DU Busy pub opposite the castle, friendly and welcoming, with plenty of draught and bottled beers and good choice of well liked/priced food including Mon steak night, restaurant at back; children welcome, open (and food) all day. *(Edward May)*

INVERNESS   NH6645
Phoenix Ale House (01463) 240300
Academy Street; IV1 1LX Popular 1890s bare-boards bar with fine oval servery, up to ten real ales and enjoyable reasonably priced food, neatly furnished adjoining dining room; sports TV; open (and food) all day. *(Edward May)*

MALLAIG   NM6796
Steam (01687) 462002
Davies Brae; PH41 4PU Popular Victorian inn with good food including freshly landed fish/seafood (takeaway menu too), efficient friendly service, bar with open fire, split-level bare-boards restaurant; some live music; children and dogs welcome (resident great dane), tables in back beer garden, five simple but comfortable bedrooms (no breakfast), open all day. *(Jamie and Lizzie McEwan)*

WHITEBRIDGE   NH4815
Whitebridge (01456) 486226
B862 SW of village; IV2 6UN Old-style hunting, shooting and fishing hotel set in the foothills of the Monadhliath Mountains, popular and cheerful, with good traditional food (not Mon lunchtime), well kept ales such as Cairngorm, Cromarty and Loch Ness and around 50 malts, two bars with woodburners, separate restaurant; well behaved dogs welcome, 12 bedrooms, open all day in summer, all day weekends winter. *(Mike Benton)*

KINCARDINESHIRE

FETTERCAIRN   NO6573
Ramsay Arms (01561) 340334
Burnside Road; AB30 1XX Hotel with tartan-carpeted bar and smart oak-panelled restaurant; well kept ales and a dozen malts including the local Fettercairn, enjoyable fairly traditional food, friendly service; children welcome, picnic-sets in garden, attractive village (liked by Queen Victoria who stayed at the hotel), 12 bedrooms, good breakfast. *(Sam Cole)*

STONEHAVEN   NO8595
Lairhillock (01569) 730001
Netherley; 6 miles N of Stonehaven, 6 miles S of Aberdeen, take Durris turn off from the A90; AB39 3QS Extended 200-year-old family-run inn; beamed bar with dark woodwork, panelled wall benches and mix of old seats, lots of brass and copper, nice open fire, Timothy Taylors Landlord and a guest, several wines by the glass and good range of malt whiskies, generally well liked food from lunchtime baguettes up, spacious lounge with unusual central fire, panoramic views from back conservatory; children and dogs (in bar) welcome, open all day; for sale, so may be changes. *(Terry Grant)*

STONEHAVEN   NO8785
Ship (01569) 762617
Shore Head; AB39 2JY Whitewashed 18th-c waterside inn with bustling local atmosphere; good selection of changing beers and over 100 whiskies, well liked food in bar or modern restaurant, friendly staff; sports TV; children (till 8pm) and dogs welcome, disabled access/loos, tables out overlooking pretty harbour, 11 bedrooms (many with sea views), open all day, food all day weekends. *(Gary Bishop)*

KIRKCUDBRIGHTSHIRE

CASTLE DOUGLAS   NX7662
Sulwath Brewery (01556) 504525
King Street; DG7 1DT Friendly bar attached to this small brewery (tours available); six of their ales in top condition along with bottled beers, limited food such as pies, stools and barrel tables, off-sales and souvenirs; dogs welcome, disabled access, open 10am-6pm Mon-Sat. *(Colin Evans)*

DALRY   NX6281
Clachan (01644) 430241
A713 Castle Douglas–Ayr; DG7 3UW Cheerful traditional inn with plenty of character; beams, dark woodwork and open fires, some large stuffed fish in display cases and other interesting bits and pieces, two well kept changing ales and good selection of other drinks, popular affordably priced

food from lunchtime sandwiches and pub favourites up, friendly efficient service, woodburner in timbered restaurant with pitched ceiling; TV, fruit machine; children and dogs welcome, on Southern Upland Way, bedrooms, open all day. *(Nick Higgins)*

GATEHOUSE OF FLEET NX6056
Masonic Arms (01557) 814335
Ann Street; off B727; DG7 2HU Spacious 18th-c dining pub; comfortable two-room pubby bar with traditional seating, pictures on timbered walls and stuffed fish above brick fireplace, Caledonian Deuchars IPA, Sulwath Galloway Gold and good choice of malt whiskies, enjoyable freshly made food from lunchtime sandwiches up, restaurant and new sun room; background music (live Thurs), quiz Fri, pool, free wi-fi; children and dogs (in bar) welcome, picnic-sets under parasols in neatly kept sheltered garden, more seats in front, open all day (although may shut Mon, Tues in winter), food all day weekends. *(Michael and Sheila Hawkins)*

HAUGH OF URR NX8066
Laurie Arms (01556) 660246
B794 N of Dalbeattie; Main Street; DG7 3YA Welcoming 19th-c village pub with good local atmosphere; traditional furnishings and log fire in split-level carpeted bar, well kept changing ales, decent wines by the glass and enjoyable reasonably priced home-made food including good steaks, friendly service, restaurant, games room with darts and pool; quiz first Fri of month; children welcome, dogs in bar, tables out at front and on sheltered terrace behind, open (and food) all day weekends. *(Charlie)*

KIRKCUDBRIGHT NX6850
Selkirk Arms (01557) 330402
High Street; DG6 4JG Comfortable well run 18th-c hotel in pleasant spot by mouth of the Dee; tartan-carpeted lounge with open fire, up to three real ales including a house beer from local Sulwath, 20 malt whiskies and 15 gins, enjoyable food cooked to order in bistro and evening restaurant from pub standards up, afternoon teas (must book), friendly helpful service; background music; children and dogs (not in main eating areas) welcome, tables under parasols in neat garden with 15th-c font, 16 well appointed bedrooms, open all day. *(Michael and Sheila Hawkins, Philip J Alderton)*

LANARKSHIRE

BALMAHA NS4290
Oak Tree (01360) 870357
B837; G63 0JQ Family-run slate-clad inn on Loch Lomond's quiet side; beams, timbers and panelling, pubby bar with lots of old photographs, farm tools, stuffed animals and collection of grandfather clocks, log fire, good choice of enjoyable food from sandwiches

and snacks up (no bookings), scottish beers and over 50 whiskies, coffee shop and ice-cream parlour, village shop; children welcome, no dogs inside, plenty of tables out around ancient oak tree, popular with West Highland Way walkers, attractive bedrooms, cottages and bunkhouses. *(Alison and Michael Harper)*

BIGGAR NT0437
Crown (01899) 220116
High Street (A702); ML12 6DL Friendly old pub with good choice of enjoyable food from tapas-style plates and pizzas up, meal deals and good value Sun carvery, two well kept changing ales (annual beer festival – see website), open fire in beamed front bar, panelled lounge with old local pictures, restaurant; live music every other Fri; children welcome, open (and food) all day. *(Jane Rigby)*

FINTRY NS6186
Fintry (01360) 860224
Main Street; G63 0XA Community-owned 18th-c village pub with friendly relaxed atmosphere; beers from on-site microbrewery and enjoyable fairly priced home-made food, modernised interior with beams and two-way woodburner; ceilidh first Sat of month, quiz last Mon; children welcome, dogs in pool room, suntrap back garden, open (and food) all day. *(Sam Cole)*

GLASGOW NS5767
Belle (0141) 339 2299
Great Western Road; G12 8HX Busy pub with wide mix of customers; leather-topped stools, modern and traditional chairs around all sorts of tables on polished wood floor, stags' heads and unusual mirrors on painted or exposed stone walls, open fire, american craft beers and european lagers; dogs very welcome, tables out on pavement and in tiny leafy back garden, open all day. *(Tim Stewart)*

GLASGOW NS5865
Drum & Monkey (0141) 221 6636
St Vincent Street; G2 5TF Busy Nicholsons bank conversion; lots of carved mahogany, granite pillars and ornate ceiling, island bar serving half a dozen real ales, over 20 gins and decent range of wines, good value food, quieter back area; children allowed till 8pm, open (and food) all day. *(Chelsea Hoffman)*

GLASGOW NS5865
Pot Still (0141) 333 0980
Hope Street; G2 2TH Comfortable and welcoming little pub with over 700 malt whiskies including good value whisky of the month; traditional bare-boards interior with raised back part, button-back leather bench seats, dark panelling, etched and stained glass, columns up to ornately corniced ceiling, four changing ales and interesting bottled beers from nice old-fashioned servery, friendly knowledgeable staff, food limited to

range of good value pies; silent fruit machine; open all day and can get really busy. *(Chelsea Hoffman)*

GLASGOW NS5466

St Louis (0141) 339 1742

Dumbarton Road, by the roundabout; G11 6RD Relaxed bar-café with simple but stylish décor; Williams Bros beers and enjoyable reasonably priced food including sandwiches and range of burgers, friendly staff; live music Sat, quiz Tues, monthly poetry night; dogs welcome, open (and food) all day from 9am (10am weekends). *(Tim Stewart)*

GLASGOW NS5865

State (0141) 332 2159

Holland Street; G2 4NG High-ceilinged bar with marble pillars and lots of carved wood including handsome island servery, half a dozen or so well kept changing ales, food from bargain lunchtime meals up, some areas set for dining, good atmosphere and friendly staff, armchairs among other comfortable seats, coal-effect fire in big fireplace, old prints and theatrical posters; background music (live Tues), comedy night Sat, silent sports TVs, games machine; open all day, no food weekends. *(Tim Stewart)*

GLASGOW NS5666

Tennents (0141) 339 7203

Byres Road; G12 8TN Big busy high-ceilinged Victorian corner pub near the university; ornate plasterwork, panelling and paintings, traditional tables and chairs, stools and wall seating, a dozen well kept ales, craft beers and keenly priced wines from well stocked bar, wide range of good value food including deals, breakfast till midday; basement bar for weekend DJs, sports TVs; children and dogs welcome, open all day from 10am. *(Eddie Gallacher)*

GLASGOW NS5666

Three Judges (0141) 337 3055

Dumbarton Road, opposite Byres Road; G11 6PR Traditional corner bar with eight quickly changing ales from small breweries far and wide (they get through several hundred a year), friendly staff will offer tasters; live afternoon jazz last Sun of month, occasional quiz nights, TV; dogs welcome, open all day. *(Same Cole)*

MIDLOTHIAN

DALKEITH NR3264

Sun (0131) 663 2456

A7 S; EH22 4TR Modernised former coaching inn surrounded by five acres of wooded grounds – new owners taking over as we went to press; bar with stripped-stone walls, wood floors and open fireplaces, built-in cushioned settles and good mix of other furniture, has served a couple of ales

such as Inveralmond and Stewart, good wines by the glass and well liked food; children welcome, disabled access to restaurant only, covered courtyard overlooking the garden and decked area with view of River Esk, comfortable bedrooms, open all day. *(Dave Braisted)*

EDINBURGH NT2574

★Abbotsford (0131) 225 5276

Rose Street; E end, beside South St David Street; EH2 2PR Busy city-centre pub attracting wide mix of customers; long wooden tables and leatherette benches, high panelled walls and handsome green and gold moulded ceiling, hefty Victorian island bar serving beers such as Atlas, Caledonian, Fyne, Harviestoun, Orkney and Stewart, also selection of bottled american beers and around 70 malt whiskies, traditional food (all day Fri, Sat) along with some interesting specials, smarter upstairs restaurant (crisp linen tablecloths) where children over 5 allowed , some outside seating; open all day (till midnight Sat). *(Katherine Matthews, Susan and John Douglas)*

EDINBURGH NT2574

★Café Royal (0131) 556 1884

West Register Street; EH2 2AA Wonderful Victorian baroque interior – floors and stairway laid with marble, chandeliers hanging from magnificent plasterwork ceilings, superb series of Doulton tilework portraits of historical innovators (Watt, Faraday, Stephenson, Caxton, Benjamin Franklin and Robert Peel), substantial island bar serving well kept Greene King IPA, Belhaven 80/-, Stewart Edinburgh Gold and four guests, several wines by the glass and 40 malts, very well liked food with emphasis on fresh seafood, good friendly service, the restaurant's stained glass is also worth a look (children welcome here); background music; open all day (till 1am Fri, Sat), can get very busy. *(Barry Collett)*

EDINBURGH NT2574

Cloisters (0131) 221 9997

Brougham Street; EH3 9JH Friendly and interesting ex-parsonage alehouse with great range of changing beers (cask and keg), some 70 malt whiskies and several wines by the glass, good value food (all day Sat, not Mon), pews and bar gantry recycled from redundant church, bare boards and lots of brewery mirrors; lavatories down spiral stairs; no children, dogs welcome, open all day (till 1am Fri, Sat). *(Paul Baxter)*

EDINBURGH NT2573

Deacon Brodies (0131) 225 6531

Lawnmarket; EH1 2NT Atmospheric corner pub commemorating the notorious town councillor thief who was eventually hanged on the scaffold he'd designed; very busy bar with wonderfully ornate high ceiling, seven well kept ales and decent

selection of whiskies from long counter,
reasonably priced Nicholsons menu in
upstairs dining lounge where children
allowed, friendly hard-working staff;
background music, TV; open (and food) all
day. *(Ian Herdman, Tony Scott)*

EDINBURGH NT2573
Doric (0131) 225 1084
Market Street; EH1 1DE Welcoming 17th-c
pub-restaurant with plenty of atmosphere;
simple furnishings in small bar with wood
floor and lots of pictures, four cask ales
and good range of bottled beers, around 50
single malts, friendly young staff, interesting
modern food (must book) in upstairs wine
bar (children welcome) and bistro; live folk
Fri and Sat evenings; handy for Waverley
station, open all day. *(Nick Higgins)*

EDINBURGH NT2573
Ensign Ewart (0131) 225 7440
*Lawnmarket, Royal Mile; last pub on
right before castle; EH1 2PE* Dimly lit
olde-worlde pub handy for the castle (so gets
busy); dark beams and bare boards, assorted
pubby furniture including a barrel table,
flintlock pistols and swords, big painting of
Ewart capturing french banner at Waterloo,
four well kept scottish ales and extensive
range of whiskies, straightforward bar
food; background and traditional live music
(nightly), TV, keypad entry to lavatories; open
all day (till 1am Fri, Sat). *(Colin McLachlan,
Ian Herdman)*

EDINBURGH NT2472
Fountain (0131) 229 1899
Dundee Street; EH11 1AX Nicely updated
pub with open-plan split-level interior; four
or five draught beers from long well stocked
bar, fairly priced food including brunch, good
friendly service; children and dogs welcome,
open (and food) all day. *(Martin Day)*

EDINBURGH NT2573
★ Halfway House (0131) 225 7101
*Fleshmarket Close (steps between
Cockburn Street and Market Street,
opposite Waverley station); EH1
1BX* Tiny one-room character pub off steep
steps; part carpeted, part tiled, with a few
small tables and high-backed settles, lots of
prints (some golf and railway themes), four
well kept scottish ales and good range of malt
whiskies, short choice of decent low-priced
food, friendly staff; dogs welcome, open (and
food) all day. *(Ian Herdman)*

EDINBURGH NT2473
Hanging Bat (0131) 229 0759
Lothian Road; EH3 9AB Modern bar on
three levels with own microbrewery, six real
ales, craft kegs and plenty of bottled beers,
food such as ribs and hot dogs; children
till 8pm, open (and food) all day.
(David Longhurst)

EDINBURGH NT2573
Inn on the Mile (0131) 556 9940
High Street; EH1 1LL Centrally placed
pub-restaurant-boutique hotel in former
bank; long high-ceilinged bar with booth
seating, good selection of drinks including
cocktails, well priced pubby food, friendly
efficient service; live music, projector for
major sports, free wi-fi; children welcome,
a few seats outside, nine bedrooms, open
all day from 8am (till 1am Fri, Sat when can
be lively). *(Sam Cole)*

EDINBURGH NT2573
Jolly Judge (0131) 225 2669
*James Court, by 495 Lawnmarket; EH1
2PB* Small comfortable basement bar with
interesting fruit and flower-painted wooden
ceiling, welcoming relaxed atmosphere,
three changing ales and good range of malts,
lunchtime bar meals, log fire; quiz night Mon;
no children, open all day. *(Tony Scott)*

EDINBURGH NT1968
Kinleith Mill (0131) 453 3214
Lanark Road (A70); EH14 5EN Old pub
with contemporary bar; three well kept ales,
11 wines by the glass and 19 gins, enjoyable
food from sandwiches and wraps up, friendly
staff; sports TV, darts; children and dogs
welcome, suntrap back garden, open (and
food) all day. *(Charlie)*

EDINBURGH NT2573
Sandy Bells (0131) 225 1156
Forrest Road; EH1 2QH Small
unpretentious place popular for its nightly
folk music; up to eight scottish ales and wide
choice of whiskies, simple snacky food, good
mix of customers and friendly atmosphere;
open all day. *(Nick Higgins)*

EDINBURGH NT2374
Scran & Scallie (0131) 332 6281
Comely Bank Road; EH4 1DT Well
thought-of dining pub with very good
traditional food including weekday set lunch
and weekend breakfasts (8.30-11am); bar has
blue button-back wall seats, leather-topped
stools and blue-painted chairs on bare
boards, well kept scottish ales, impressive
collection of whiskies and house cocktails,
sizeable dining area with painted brick walls,
contemporary wallpaper and woodburner,
helpful friendly service; TV; children and
dogs welcome, open all day. *(Belinda and
Neil Garth)*

EDINBURGH NT2872
Sheep Heid (0131) 661 7974
The Causeway, Duddingston; EH15 3QA
Comfortably updated former coaching house
in lovely spot near King Arthur's Seat, long
history (dates from the 14th c) and some
famous guests such as Mary, Queen of Scots;
emphasis on dining but there is a cosy bar
with fine rounded counter serving three well

kept beers, enjoyable food from pizzas and burgers to more restaurauty choices, also good value weekday set menu (12-6pm) and children's meals, friendly young staff, skittle alley; courtyard tables, open (and food) all day. *(Tim Stewart)*

EDINBURGH   NT2574

★**Starbank** (0131) 552 4141
Laverockbank Road, off Starbank Road, just off A901 Granton–Leith; EH5 3BZ Cheerful pub in a fine spot with terrific views over the Firth of Forth; long airy bareboards bar with leather bench and tub seats, up to eight well kept ales and good choice of malt whiskies, interesting food from sharing plates up in conservatory restaurant; live music and quiz nights, sports TV; children (till 9pm if eating) and dogs welcome, sheltered back terrace, parking on adjacent hilly street, open all day. *(Sam Cole)*

EDINBURGH   NT2574

Stockbridge Tap (0131) 343 3000
Raeburn Place, Stockbridge; EH4 1HN Welcoming corner pub with traditional L-shaped interior, seven interesting beers and good reasonably priced food (not Mon or Tues); no children, dogs welcome, open all day. *(Nick Higgins)*

EDINBURGH   NT2676

Teuchters Landing (0131) 554 7427
Great Junction Street, Leith; EH6 6LU Interesting waterside pub in former ferry waiting room; great choice of whiskies and wines (listed on blackboard), half a dozen well kept ales such as Caledonian, Fyne, Inveralmond and Timothy Taylors, plus several craft beers, generous helpings of popular food (best to book, especially in summer for conservatory or floating terrace), friendly staff; TV for rugby; children and dogs welcome, open (and food) all day. *(Nick Higgins)*

MORAYSHIRE

FINDHORN   NJ0464

Crown & Anchor (01309) 690243
Off A96; IV36 3YF Nice village setting adjacent to small sheltered harbour; enjoyable food including good fresh fish/seafood specials, a couple of real ales, over 50 gins and plenty of whiskies, woodburner in cosy bar; sports TV; children allowed in conservatory and restaurant till 8pm, outside seating and smokers' shelter (the Smokooterie), seven bedrooms, sand dune walks and good boating in Findhorn Bay, open all day. *(John Evans)*

NAIRNSHIRE

CAWDOR   NH8449

Cawdor Tavern (01667) 404777
Pub signed from B9090; IV12 5XP Busy dining pub in lovely conservation village near the castle; well kept Orkney ales, nine wines by the glass (comprehensive list) and good range of malt whiskies, freshly cooked food from traditional choices up, friendly staff, oak-panelled lounge with log fire, pool in public bar, restaurant; children welcome, dogs in bar, seats on front terrace, open (and food) all day in summer. *(John Evans)*

PEEBLESSHIRE

INNERLEITHEN   NT3336

★**Traquair Arms** (01896) 830229
B709, just off A72 Peebles–Galashiels; follow signs for Traquair House; EH44 6PD Old stone inn at heart of this pretty borders village; one of the few places serving Traquair ale (produced in original oak vessels in 18th-c brewhouse at nearby Traquair House), also Tempest Cascadian and Timothy Taylors Landlord, over 40 malt whiskies, enjoyable traditional food (all day weekends); main bar with warm open fire, another in relaxed bistro-style restaurant, good mix of customers; background music; children welcome, dogs in bar, seats out at front and in attractive bar garden, 16 bedrooms and two self-catering cottages, open all day. *(Andy Reiss)*

PERTHSHIRE

BANKFOOT   NO0635

Bankfoot (01738) 787243
Main Street; PH1 4AB Traditional coaching inn dating from 1760; two bars and restaurant, well kept local ales and enjoyable food cooked by landlady, friendly helpful staff, open fires; live folk/acoustic night Weds; children and dogs welcome, comfortable bedrooms, open all day weekends, closed Mon lunchtime and all day Tues (food for residents only those days), check website for winter hours. *(Clare Rigby)*

BLAIR ATHOLL   NN8765

★**Atholl Arms** (01796) 481205
B8079; PH18 5SG Sizeable stone hotel with nice old-fashioned scottish feel; traditional beamed Bothy bar serving four local Moulin ales and good well priced food, quick friendly service, cosy lounges and grand dining room with suit of armour

Half pints: by law, a pub should not charge more for half a pint than half the price of a full pint, unless it shows that half-pint price on its price list.

and stag's head; 31 good value bedrooms, self-catering cottages, lovely setting near the castle, open (and food) all day. *(Fergus Lyle)*

BRIG O' TURK NN5306
Byre (01877) 376292
A821 Callander–Trossachs, just outside village; FK17 8HT Refurbished and beautifully placed byre conversion; slate-floored log-fire bar and roomier high-raftered restaurant, good popular food including local game and fish, a couple of changing scottish ales and nice wines, friendly helpful staff; background music; children welcome, outside tables and boules piste, lovely walks, bike hire available (pre-book), open all day. *(Jim Harper)*

CALLANDER NN6208
Old Rectory (01877) 339215
Leny Road (A84); FK17 8AL Friendly 19th-c stone inn away from the town centre; cosy little bar with fine range of whiskies, well liked reasonably priced food in small adjoining restaurant including good Sun roasts, pleasant helpful staff; live folk music Weds and Sat, quiz second Tues of month, free wi-fi; children and dogs welcome, four bedrooms, handy for Trossachs National Park, open all day. *(John Evans)*

DUNBLANE NN7801
Tappit Hen (01786) 825226
Kirk Street; FK15 0AL Small welcoming drinkers' pub across close from cathedral; five changing ales and good range of malt whiskies, friendly busy atmosphere; sports TV, fruit machine; dogs welcome, open all day (till late Fri, Sat). *(Les and Sandra Brown)*

DUNKELD NO0243
Atholl Arms (01350) 727219
Atholl Street (A923); PH8 0AQ Sizeable 19th-c hotel with smallish bar and lounge, open fires, well kept ales such as Inveralmond, enjoyable food including burgers, pizzas and some vegan choices, attentive, warmly friendly service, restaurant; children and dogs welcome, garden across road running down to the River Tay, pavilion serving teas, coffees and cakes, 17 bedrooms (some with river views), open (and food) all day. *(Fergus Lyle)*

DUNNING NO0114
Kirkstyle (01764) 684248
B9141, off A9 S of Perth; Kirkstyle Square; PH2 0RR Character 18th-c streamside pub with log fire in snug bar, up to three real ales including one badged for them (Risky Kelt) and good choice of whiskies, enjoyable fairly priced home-made food, attentive friendly service, split-level stripped-stone restaurant behind; background and live traditional music (usually last Sun of month); children and dogs welcome, closed Mon lunchtime, otherwise open all day. *(Charlotte and William Mason)*

INCHTURE NO2828
Inchture Hotel (01828) 686298
Just off A90 Perth–Dundee; PH14 9RN Small creeper-clad 19th-c hotel in conservation village; updated lounge bar in fashionable greys with some exposed stonework and open fire, enjoyable well priced food here or in spacious conservatory restaurant, also bar snacks (try the haggis flavour crisps made in the village), craft kegs, local Abernyte bottled beers and good choice of wines by the glass, decent coffee, friendly efficient service, separate public bar; children welcome, eight good value bedrooms and self-catering cottage. *(Susan and John Douglas)*

KENMORE NN7745
Kenmore Hotel (01887) 830205
A827 W of Aberfeldy; PH15 2NU Hotel dating from the 16th c in pretty Loch Tay village; comfortable traditional front lounge with warm log fire (there's a poem pencilled by Burns himself on the chimney breast), dozens of malts helpfully arranged alphabetically, friendly attentive staff, modern restaurant with balcony; also back bar and terrace overlooking River Tay with enjoyable food from lunchtime soup and sandwiches to grills, Inveralmond Ossian and decent wines by the glass; pool and winter darts, juke box, TV, fruit machine; children and dogs welcome, 40 bedrooms plus lodges, open all day. *(Susan and John Douglas)*

KILMAHOG NN6008
★ Lade (01877) 330152
A84 just NW of Callander, by A821 junction; FK17 8HD Lively place with plenty of character in several cosy beamed areas; panelling and stripped stone, highland prints and local artwork, good home-made food from bar snacks up (booking advised), own-brewed ales and around 40 malt whiskies, big-windowed restaurant, friendly staff, shop selling extensive range of scottish bottled beers; background and traditional live music (weekends); children and dogs welcome, disabled access/loo, terrace and pleasant garden with fish ponds, open all day (till 1am Fri, Sat, but may close early in winter if quiet). *(Nick Higgins)*

KIRKTON OF GLENISLA NO2160
Glenisla Hotel (01575) 582223
B951 N of Kirriemuir and Alyth; PH11 8PH Refurbished 17th-c coaching inn; high-ceilinged bar with woodburner, beamed lounge with another fire leading through to restaurant, two well kept changing scottish ales, eight wines by the glass and good selection of whiskies and gins, popular freshly made food from traditional choices up, good friendly service; children and dogs (not in restaurant) welcome, garden with gravel terrace, ten well appointed bedrooms, good walks from the door (on circular Cateran

Trail), open all day, kitchen shuts 5-6pm. *(Stuart and Natalie Granville)*

PERTH   NO1223

Greyfriars (01738) 633036

South Street; PH2 8PG Small comfortable local in old part of town; a couple of well kept changing ales and good collection of whiskies and gins, enjoyable lunchtime food (not Sun) in bar or little upstairs dining room, friendly welcoming staff; live music; open all day. *(Tony Scott)*

PITLOCHRY   NN9163

★Killiecrankie Hotel (01796) 473220

Killiecrankie, off A9 N; PH16 5LG Comfortable splendidly placed country hotel with attractive panelled bar and airy conservatory, well kept ales, more than 55 malt whiskies and well chosen wines, good imaginative food in bar or more formal evening restaurant, friendly efficient service; children in eating areas, dogs welcome, four acres of peaceful grounds with dramatic views, handy for Blair Castle, ten bedrooms. *(Brian and Sally Wakeham)*

PITLOCHRY   NN9459

★Moulin (01796) 472196

Kirkmichael Road, Moulin; A924 NE of Pitlochry centre; PH16 5EW Attractive much extended inn brewing its own good beers in stables across the street, decent wines by the glass too and around 45 malt whiskies, cheerfully busy down-to-earth bar in oldest part with traditional character, smaller bare-boards room and bigger carpeted area with booths divided by stained-glass country scenes, popular quickly served food, separate restaurant; bar billiards and 1960s one-arm bandit; children and dogs (in bar) welcome, picnic-sets on gravel at front looking across to village kirk, good nearby walks, 15 well appointed comfortable bedrooms and two self-catering cottages, open all day. *(Philip J Alderton, Barry Collett, Adrian Buckland)*

PITLOCHRY   NN9358

Old Mill (01796) 474020

Mill Lane; PH16 5BH Welcoming family-run inn (former 19th-c watermill) with enjoyable food from sandwiches and sharing plates up, four real ales including Strathbraan, traditional cider and good wine and whisky choice, quick friendly service; weekend live music, free wi-fi; courtyard tables by Moulin Burn, comfortable well equipped bedrooms, open all day. *(Sarah and David Gibbs)*

WEEM   NN8449

★Ailean Chraggan (01887) 820346

B846; PH15 2LD There's plenty to do and see close to this little hotel; chatty bar with good mix of customers, local Strathbraan ales and around 100 malt whiskies, popular locally sourced food including Sun carvery,

efficient friendly service, adjoining neatly old-fashioned dining room and a comfortable carpeted modern lounge; quiz and live music nights; children and dogs (in bar) welcome, covered terrace and garden behind, views stretching beyond the Tay to Ben Lawers (the highest peak in this part of Scotland), four spacious bedrooms, open all day Thur-Sun, from 5pm other days. *(Dave Braisted)*

ROSS-SHIRE

BADACHRO   NG7873

★Badachro Inn (01445) 741255

2.5 miles S of Gairloch village turn off A832 on to B8056, then after another 3.25 miles turn right in Badachro to the quay and inn; IV21 2AA Superbly positioned by Loch Gairloch with terrific views from decking down to water's edge, popular (especially summer) with mix of sailing visitors (free moorings) and chatty locals; welcoming bar with interesting photographs, An Teallach, Caledonian and a guest ale, some 50 malt whiskies and eight wines by the glass, quieter eating area with big log fire, dining conservatory overlooking bay, fairly priced food including locally smoked fish and seafood; background music, free wi-fi; children and dogs welcome, one bedroom, open all day. *(Gary Hooper)*

DORNIE   NG8826

Dornie Hotel (01599) 555205

Francis Street; IV40 8DT Friendly hotel with lovely views over Loch Long; lively bar with Isle of Skye Cuillin Beast and good value traditional food, pleasant restaurant specialising in good local fish/seafood; children and dogs welcome, 11 bedrooms (book early), very handy for Eilean Donan Castle, open all day. *(Dave Braisted)*

GAIRLOCH   NG8075

Old Inn (01445) 712006

Just off A832/B8021; IV21 2BD Quietly positioned old drovers' inn by stream; own-brew beers and guests, decent wines by the glass and some 20 malt whiskies, enjoyable food (not Sun evening) including local fish and game, relaxed locals' bar with traditional décor and woodburner, bistro/restaurant; background music (live Fri in summer), TV; children and dogs welcome, picnic-sets out by trees, bedrooms, open all day. *(Colin McLachlan)*

PLOCKTON   NG8033

★Plockton Inn (01599) 544222

Innes Street; not connected to Plockton Hotel (see Main Entries); IV52 8TW Close to the harbour in this lovely village, and with a congenial bustling atmosphere even in winter; good fairly priced food with emphasis on local fish/seafood (some from own smokery), friendly efficient service, well kept changing beers and good range of malts, lively public bar with traditional music Thurs (also Tues in summer); children welcome, seats out on decking, 14 bedrooms (seven in annexe over road), good breakfast, open all day. *(Mandy and Gary Redstone)*

SHIEL BRIDGE   NG9319
Kintail Lodge (01599) 511275
A87, N of Shiel Bridge; IV40 8HL Large bar adjoining hotel nestled down by Loch Duich, convivial bustle in season, Isle of Skye Red and plenty of malt whiskies, good food here and in restaurant/conservatory (weekends only during winter) with magnificent view to Skye, friendly efficient service; children and dogs welcome, 12 comfortable bedrooms, bunkhouse and moorings for visiting yachts, good breakfast, open all day from Easter, ring for out-of-season hours. *(Edward May)*

ULLAPOOL   NH1293
★Ceilidh Place (01854) 612103
West Argyle Street; IV26 2TY More arty café-bar than pub with gallery, bookshop and coffee shop; conservatory-style main area with mix of dining chairs around dark wood tables, cosy bar and other rooms filled with armchairs, sofas and scatter-cushioned wall seats, rugs on floors, woodburner, a beer from An Teallach, lots of wines by the glass and around 75 malt whiskies, tasty food (something available all day); regular jazz, folk and classical music, art exhibitions; children welcome but must leave bar by 7pm, tables on front terrace looking over houses to distant hills beyond natural harbour, comfortable bedrooms, open all day. *(Philip Chesington)*

ULLAPOOL   NH1294
Morefield Motel (01854) 612161
A835 N edge of town; IV26 2TQ Modern family-run place, clean and bright, with cheerful L-shaped lounge bar, good food including local fish/seafood, well kept changing ales, decent wines and over 50 malt whiskies, large conservatory; background music, pool and darts; children welcome, terrace tables, ten bedrooms, bike lock-up, open all day. *(Philip Chesington)*

ROXBURGHSHIRE

ANCRUM   NT6224
Cross Keys (01835) 830242
Off A68 Jedburgh–Edinburgh; TD8 6XH Early 19th-c terrace-row pub overlooking village green; chatty bar with good mix of customers and a dog or two by the open fire, minimal décor and simple furnishings, stools against counter serving Born in the Borders Foxy Blonde and Gold Dust, several wines by the glass and quite a few whiskies, well regarded often interesting food in second side bar or dining room with open kitchen; children and dogs welcome,

seats out at front and in back garden with gate leading down to Ale Water, open all day weekends (till 1am Sat) from 5pm weekdays. *(Mary and Douglas Kirkwood, Richard Kennell)*

KELSO   NT7234
★Cobbles (01573) 223548
Bowmont Street; TD5 7JH Small comfortably updated 19th-c dining pub just off the main square; friendly and well run with good range of food from pub standards to more enterprising dishes, local Tempest beers and decent range of wines/malt whiskies, pubby furniture and open fire in bar, elegantly furnished restaurant with overspill room upstairs; folk music Fri evening; children welcome, disabled facilities, open all day (till late Fri, Sat). *(Brian and Sally Wakeham)*

KIRK YETHOLM   NT8328
★Border (01573) 420237
Village signposted off B6352/B6401 crossroads, SE of Kelso; TD5 8PQ Popular village inn facing green; welcoming traditional locals' bar with beams, flagstones and log fire, snug side rooms, two or three real ales, decent wines by the glass and numerous whiskies, good home-made food from extensive menu (all day Sun), friendly service, spacious dining room, lounge with another fire and neat conservatory; background music; children and dogs (in bar) welcome, sheltered back terrace, five well appointed comfortable bedrooms plus new self-catering cottage, good breakfast, at end of Pennine Way and start of Scottish National Trail, open all day. *(Sara Fulton, Roger Baker)*

ST BOSWELLS   NT5930
Buccleuch Arms (01835) 822243
A68 just S of Newtown St Boswells; TD6 0EW Civilised 19th-c sandstone hotel opposite village green; updated bar, comfortable lounge and bistro, good popular food from bar snacks up, charming service, two or three local ales, open fires; children and dogs welcome, tables in attractive garden behind (plants for sale), 19 bedrooms, open (and some food) all day. *(Susan and John Douglas, Martin Day)*

SELKIRKSHIRE

MOUNTBENGER   NT3324
Gordon Arms (01750) 82261
A708/B709; TD7 5LE Nice old inn – an oasis in these empty moorlands; a couple of real ales and enjoyable reasonably priced pubby food cooked by landlord; acoustic music every third Sun of month from 3pm (there's a recording studio on site), free wi-fi; children and dogs welcome, comfortable bedrooms, good walking country, open (and food) all day. *(Jamie and Lizzie McEwan)*

STIRLINGSHIRE

KIPPEN NS6594
★**Cross Keys** (01786) 870293
Main Street; village signposted off A811 W of Stirling; FK8 3DN Cosy and gently civilised 18th-c inn; log fires in two bars, exposed stonework, bare boards or carpeting, built-in wall seating, wooden dining chairs and stools against counter serving a couple of Fallen ales (one brewed for the pub), a guest beer, 20 malt whiskies and a dozen wines by the glass, very good food (all day weekends), including lighter lunch menu, friendly staff; background music, occasional folk nights, free wi-fi; children (till 9pm) and dogs welcome, tables in garden looking across to the Ochil Hills, play area, three comfortable bedrooms, generous breakfast, open all day Fri-Sun. *(Mollie and Stewart Lindsay)*

STRATHCLYDE

CAIRNDOW NN1810
Stagecoach (01499) 600286
Just off and signed from A83; PA26 8BN Old inn run by same family for over 50 years in lovely setting overlooking Loch Fyne; good local fish and seasonal produce in bar and restaurant, Fyne ales and plenty of whiskies, efficient friendly service; live music and quiz nights; children welcome, garden picnic-sets, bedrooms (some in separate building with balconies), open (and food) all day. *(Gary Hooper)*

SUTHERLAND

KYLESKU NC2333
★**Kylesku Hotel** (01971) 502231
A894, S side of former ferry crossing; IV27 4HW Remote but surprisingly busy hotel on shores of Loch Glendhu; bar with glorious mountain and loch view, well kept ales such as An Teallach, nice wines by the glass and numerous malt whiskies, wonderfully fresh seafood along with other good locally sourced food (booking advised), friendly accommodating staff, restaurant extension; children and dogs welcome, tables outside taking in the view (seals and red-throated divers often in sight), good boat trips from hotel slipway, comfortable bedrooms, closed during winter. *(Neil and Angela Huxter)*

LAIRG NC5224
★**Crask Inn** (01549) 411241
A836 13 miles N towards Altnaharra; IV27 4AB Remote whitewashed inn on single-track road through peaceful moorland, homely and welcoming, with basic but comfortable bar, large stove, interesting books and harmonium, a couple of Black

Isle ales (more in bottles), good simple food from toasties to three-course evening meals cooked by landlord including own lamb, friendly helpful staff, separate dining room; church service third Thurs of month (pub is church-owned); children and dogs welcome, four bedrooms, camping (no facilities), closed till 1pm Tues, otherwise open all day. *(Alison and Michael Harper)*

WEST LOTHIAN

BO'NESS NS9981
Corbie (01506) 825307
A904 Corbiehall; EH51 0AS Neatly furnished pub with up to six well kept local ales including one from adjacent Kinneil brewery, 70 malt whiskies (tasting evenings), 80 gins and quite a choice of enjoyable food at fair prices, friendly staff; children welcome, garden with play area, open (and food) all day. *(Mike Benton)*

LINLITHGOW NS0077
★**Four Marys** (01506) 842171
High Street; 2 miles from M9 junction 3 (and little further from junction 4) – town signposted; EH49 7ED Named after Mary, Queen of Scots' four ladies-in-waiting and filled with mementoes of the ill-fated queen – pictures and written records, pieces of bed curtain and clothing, even a facsimile of her death-mask; L-shaped room with traditional and more modern seating on wood-block floor, mainly stripped-stone walls (some remarkable masonry in the inner area), elaborate Victorian dresser serving as part of the bar, seven well kept ales (taster glasses available, beer festivals), 70 malt whiskies and 45 gins, enjoyable reasonably priced food, friendly staff, tartan-carpeted dining area where children allowed till 8pm; enclosed terrace, open (and food) all day. *(Sarah and David Gibbs)*

WIGTOWNSHIRE

BLADNOCH NX4254
Bladnoch Inn (01988) 402200
Corner of A714 and B7005; DG8 9AB Roadside pub across from Bladnoch distillery (tours) in nice riverside setting; cheerful neat bar with eating area, separate restaurant, tasty pubby food from sandwiches up including Fri fish specials, Sat curry and Sun carvery, a couple of changing real ales, friendly obliging service; background music; children and dogs welcome, four good value bedrooms, open all day, from 4pm Mon. *(Dan Peters)*

PORTPATRICK NW9954
Crown (01776) 810261
North Crescent; DG9 8SX Popular seafront hotel in delightful harbourside village; enjoyable reasonably priced food

including notable seafood and local game, efficient friendly service, two changing ales such as local Portpatrick, several dozen malts and decent wines by the glass, warm fire in rambling traditional bar with cosy corners, sewing-machine tables, old photographs and posters, attractively decorated early 20th-c dining room opening through conservatory into sheltered back garden; background music, TV; children and dogs welcome, tables out in front, 12 bedrooms, open (and food) all day. *(Mike and Mary Carter)*

STRANRAER   NX0660
Grapes   (01776) 703386
Bridge Street; DG9 7HY Popular and welcoming 19th-c local; simple and old-fashioned, with a couple of well kept ales and over 60 malts, live music in bar or upstairs room including bluegrass Fri lunchtime; children and dogs welcome, courtyard seating, open all day. *(Dan Peters)*

Scottish Islands

ARRAN

BRODICK   NS0137
Wineport   (01770) 302101
Signed off A841 at visitor centre; KA27 8DE Friendly pink-painted pub-bistro near Brodick Castle (NTS); well kept Arran Blonde (brewery next door) and a guest, decent food from blackboard menu catering for special diets, kitchen open all day in summer (11-5pm out of season), modernised interior with open fire; children and dogs welcome, plenty of picnic-sets on front lawn. *(Brian and Anna Marsden)*

CATACOL   NR9049
Catacol Bay   (01770) 830231
A841; KA27 8HN Unpretentious hotel rather than pub run by same family for 40 years; wonderful setting just yards from the sea looking across to Kintyre; simple bar with log fire, Timothy Taylors Landlord and a guest, all-day food (Sunday buffet until 4pm) and hearty breakfasts; pool, TV; tables outside and children's play area, six simple bedrooms with washbasins (ones at front have the view), own mooring, open all day in summer. *(Tony Scott)*

LAMLASH   NS0231
Pier Head Tavern   (01770) 600418
A841; KA27 8JN Refurbished bayside pub with opened-up bar; enjoyable traditional food along with fresh seafood and some vegetarian choices, three real ales such as Arran and William Bros, good selection of malt whiskies and growing range of gins, efficient friendly service; live music Sat evening and Sun afternoon; roof terrace with views across Lamlash Bay to the Holy Isle, open all day. *(Bob Ott)*

BARRA

CASTLEBAY   NL6698
Castlebay Hotel   (01871) 810223
By aeroplane from Glasgow or ferry from Oban; HS9 5XD Comfortable cheerful bar next to the hotel; popular food from sandwiches up, keg and bottled beers, also two-level lounge/restaurant with great harbour view, pleasant young staff; live music and comedy nights; decent bedrooms. *(Nick Higgins)*

BUTE

ROTHESAY   NS0864
Black Bull   (01700) 502366
W Princes Street; PA20 9AF Traditional comfortably furnished two-bar pub; three well kept changing ales and generous helpings of enjoyable reasonably priced food, good friendly service; weekend live music, TV, pool; children welcome till 8pm, no dogs, opposite pier with its wonderfully restored Victorian gents', open all day and may serve food all day in summer, otherwise kitchen closed Mon, Tues and Weds evening. *(Tony Scott)*

COLONSAY

SCALASAIG   NR3893
★ Colonsay   (01951) 200316
W on B8086; PA61 7YP Stylish extended 18th-c hotel, a haven for ramblers, cyclists and birders; chatty bar is hub of the island and full of locals and visitors, comfortable sofas and armchairs on painted boards, pastel walls hung with interesting old islander pictures, log fires, Colonsay IPA, several wines by the glass and interesting selection of whiskies, relaxed informal restaurant overlooking the harbour, good food using home-grown produce (own oyster farm) including pre-ferry two-course offer (from 5.30pm; not Tues, Weds or Sat), friendly efficient service; children and dogs (in bar) welcome, nice views from garden, nine comfortable pretty bedrooms, backpackers' lodge and holiday cottages, closed Nov-Mar except Christmas and New Year, otherwise open all day (till 1am Sat). *(Alison and Michael Harper)*

CUMBRAE

MILLPORT   NS1554
Frasers   (01475) 530518
Cardiff Street; KA28 0AS Small cheerful pub set just back from the harbour; bar with old paddle-steamer pictures and woodburner, back vaulted dining room, a couple of changing beers and enjoyable

really good value pubby food, friendly staff; children welcome till 8pm, no dogs, tables in yard behind, open all day. *(Mike Benton)*

HARRIS

TARBERT   NB1500
★ **Harris Hotel** (01859) 502154
Scott Road; HS3 3DL Large hotel in same family for over a century; small welcoming panelled bar with Hebridean brewed ales and fine selection of malt whiskies including some rarities, interesting food using local game and seafood, morning coffee and afternoon teas, they can also provide packed lunches, friendly accommodating staff, smart (but relaxed) airy restaurant; 23 comfortable sea-view bedrooms (some up narrow stairs). *(Sam Cole)*

ISLAY

BOWMORE   NR3159
★ **Harbour Inn** (01496) 810330
The Square; PA43 7JR Attractively updated old whitewashed inn opposite the distillery; lovely harbour/loch views from dining room and conservatory, good fish/seafood and other locally sourced food, nice wines and plenty of Islay malts including some rarities, Belhaven keg beer, traditional snug bar with unusual barrel counter, friendly helpful staff; children and dogs (in bar) welcome, seven bedrooms. *(Jamie and Lizzie McEwan)*

PORT ASKAIG   NR4369
Port Askaig (01496) 840245
A846, by port; PA46 7RD Family-run inn on Sound of Islay shore overlooking ferry pier; snug, tartan-carpeted bar with good range of malt whiskies and local bottled ales, popular food using some home-grown produce, neat sea-view restaurant and traditional first-floor residents' lounge; regular live music; dogs welcome in bar, plenty of picnic-sets on waterside grass, 11 neat bedrooms and self-catering annexe, open (and food) all day. *(Jamie and Lizzie McEwan)*

PORT CHARLOTTE   NR2558
★ **Port Charlotte Hotel** (01496) 850360
Main Street; PA48 7TU Most beautiful of Islay's Georgian villages and in lovely position with sweeping views over Loch Indaal; exceptional collection of some 150 Islay malts including rarities, two changing local ales and decent wines by the glass, good food using local meat, game and seafood (packed lunches on request), civilised bare-boards pubby bar with padded wall seats, open fire and modern artwork, second comfortable back bar, neatly kept restaurant and roomy conservatory (overlooking beach); regular

traditional live music; children welcome, garden tables, ten attractive bedrooms (most with sea view), open all day till 1am. *(Brian and Sally Wakeham)*

PORTNAHAVEN   NN1652
An Tighe Seinnse (01496) 860224
Queen Street; PA47 7SJ Friendly little end-of-terrace harbourside pub tucked away in this remote attractive fishing village; cosy bar with room off, open fire, good fair priced food including local seafood, Belhaven keg beer and bottled Islay ales, good choice of malts; sports TV and occasional live music; can get crowded, open all day. *(Brian and Sally Wakeham)*

JURA

CRAIGHOUSE   NR5266
Jura Hotel (01496) 820243
A846, opposite distillery; PA60 7XU Family-run and in superb setting with views over the Small Isles to the mainland; bar, two lounges and restaurant, good food using local fish, seafood and game (breakfasts for non-residents if capacity allows), warm friendly service; garden down to water's edge, 17 bedrooms (mainly ensuite and most with sea view), camping. *(Edward May)*

MULL

DERVAIG   NM4251
★ **Bellachroy** (01688) 400314
B8073; PA75 6QW Island's oldest inn dating from 1608; pub and restaurant food including local fish/seafood, afternoon teas and packed lunches, ales such as Isle of Mull and good choice of whiskies and wines, traditional bar with darts, attractive dining area, comfortable residents' lounge with games and TV; occasional live music and quiz nights; children and dogs welcome, covered outside area plus plenty of picnic-sets, nice spot in sleepy lochside village, seven comfortable bedrooms, open all year. *(Gary Hooper)*

FIONNPHORT   NM3023
Keel Row (01681) 700458
A849; PA66 6BL Simply furnished bare-boards bar with exposed stone walls and woodburner, Caledonian Deuchars IPA and several whiskies, generous helpings of tasty pub food, friendly helpful staff, sea views over to Iona from dining room's big windows; TV, darts; children welcome, handy for ferry, open all day. *(David Eberlin)*

TOBERMORY   NM5055
Mishnish (01688) 302500
Main Street – the yellow building; PA75 6NU Popular lively place right on the bay; dimly lit two-room bar with cask tables, old photographs and nautical/fishing

bric-a-brac, woodburner, little snugs, well kept Belhaven and Isle of Mull, enjoyable bar food, can also eat in next-door Mishdish or italian restaurant upstairs; background and live music, pool; beer garden behind, 12 attractive bedrooms (some with sea view), good breakfast, open all day till late. *(Andrew Caleya-Chetty)*

ORKNEY

DOUNBY   HY3001
Merkister (01856) 771366
Russland Road, by Harray Loch; KW17 2LF Fishing hotel in great location on the loch shore; bar dominated by prize catches, good food here and in evening restaurant including hand-dived scallops and local aberdeen angus steaks, helpful friendly service; 16 bedrooms, open all day. *(David Longhurst)*

ST MARY'S   HY4700
Commodore (01856) 781788
A961; KW17 2RU Modern single-storey building with stunning views over Scapa Flow; bar with well kept Orkney beers, pool and darts, good food using local produce in contemporary restaurant; only open Fri, Sat from 6pm. *(David Longhurst)*

WESTRAY   HY4348
Pierowall Hotel (01857) 677472
Centre of Pierowall village, B9066; KW17 2BZ Comfortable pub-hotel with enjoyable home-cooked food from sandwiches and snacks to good fresh fish (takeaways available until 7.30pm; no food Tues evening except for residents); bottled Orkney beers and plenty of malts, lounge bar with warming stove, public bar and separate restaurant; six bedrooms (four ensuite) with bay or hill views; tables out on front grass, convenient for ferry. *(Mrs Gray)*

SKYE

ARDVASAR   NG6303
Inn at Aird a' Bhasair
(01471) 844223 *A851 at S of island, near Armadale pier; IV45 8RS* Wonderful sea and mountain views from this peacefully placed early 19th-c white stone inn (former Ardvasar Hotel); newish owners and some recent redecoration, much liked food using local fish and meat, good selection of whiskies, a craft keg such as Drygate Gladeye and bottled beers from Isle of Skye, friendly helpful staff, two bars, restaurant and games room; background music, TV; children welcome in eating areas, dogs in one bar, tables outside, lovely walks, ten comfortable bedrooms (front ones overlook the sound), open all day. *(Sarah and David Gibbs)*

CARBOST   NG3731
★ Old Inn (01478) 640205
B8009; IV47 8SR Unpretentious waterside pub with stunning views and well positioned for walkers and climbers; simply furnished chatty bar with exposed stone walls, bare-boards or tiled floors, open fire, Cuillin ales and a guest, traditional cider and quite a few malt whiskies, tasty fairly priced food using local fish/shellfish and highland meat; background and regular live music, darts, pool; children and dogs welcome, picnic-sets on waterside terrace, bedrooms and family chalet also enjoying the views, Talisker distillery nearby, closed afternoons in winter, otherwise open (and food) all day, breakfast 7.45-9.30am. *(Edward May)*

EDINBAINE   NG3451
Edinbaine (01470) 582414
Just off A850, signed for Meadhan a Bhaile; IV51 9PW Friendly former farmhouse with simply furnished bar, light wood flooring and woodburner in stone fireplace, well kept Isle of Skye beers, airy carpeted dining room serving good attractively presented food including local fish/seafood, friendly staff; live traditional music (Sun); children and dogs welcome, six bedrooms, open all day (but best to check winter hours). *(Jane Rigby)*

ISLE ORNSAY   NG7012
★ Eilean Iarmain (01471) 833332
Off A851 Broadford–Armadale; IV43 8QR Smartly old-fashioned 19th-c hotel in beautiful location looking over the Sound of Sleat; cosy traditional bar with panelling and open fire, well kept Isle of Skye and good choice of vatted (blended) malt whiskies including their own Gaelic Whisky Collection, good food here or in charming sea-view restaurant, friendly efficient service; traditional background and live music; children welcome, outside tables with spectacular views, 16 comfortable bedrooms, open all day. *(Jane Rigby)*

SOUTH UIST

LOCH CARNAN   NF8144
Orasay Inn (01870) 610298
Signed off A865 S of Creagorry; HS8 5PD Wonderful remote spot overlooking the sea (lovely sunsets); good local food including fish/seafood and beef from own herd, can eat in modern lounge or conservatory-style restaurant, friendly service; pleasant simply furnished public bar; seats outside on raised decked area, compact comfortable bedrooms (two with terraces), open all day in summer. *(Fiona Scott)*

WALES

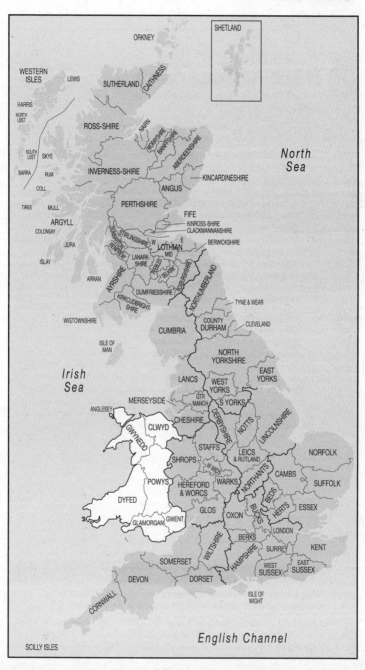

SHETLAND

ORKNEY

WESTERN
ISLES

LEWIS

SUTHERLAND

CAITHNESS

HARRIS

NORTH
UIST

ROSS-SHIRE

NAIRN

MORAYSHIRE

BANFFSHIRE

ABERDEENSHIRE

*North
Sea*

SOUTH
UIST

SKYE

BARRA

RUM

INVERNESS-SHIRE

KINCARDINESHIRE

COLL

ANGUS

TIREE

MULL

PERTHSHIRE

FIFE

ARGYLL

COLONSAY

KINROSS-SHIRE

CLACKMANNANSHIRE

STIRLINGSHIRE

W

E

BERWICKSHIRE

JURA

DUNBARTON

LOTHAN

RENFREW

LANARK
SHIRE

MID

ISLAY

PEEBLES

SELKIRK

ARRAN

AYRSHIRE

ROXBURGHSHIRE

DUMFRIESSHIRE

NORTHUMBERLAND

KIRKCUDBRIGHT-
SHIRE

TYNE & WEAR

WIGTOWNSHIRE

COUNTY
DURHAM

CLEVELAND

*Irish
Sea*

ISLE OF
MAN

CUMBRIA

NORTH
YORKSHIRE

LANCS

WEST
YORKS

EAST
YORKS

MERSEYSIDE

GTR
MANCH.

S YORKS

ANGLESEY

CHESHIRE

DERBYSHIRE

NOTTS

LINCOLNSHIRE

GWYNEDD

CLWYD

STAFFS

SHROPS

LEICS
& RUTLAND

NORFOLK

POWYS

W.MIDS

WARKS

NORTHANTS

CAMBS

SUFFOLK

HEREFORD
& WORCS

BEDS

DYFED

GLOS

OXON

BUCKS

HERTS

ESSEX

GLAMORGAN

GWENT

LONDON

WILTSHIRE

BERKS

SURREY

KENT

HAMPSHIRE

SOMERSET

WEST
SUSSEX

EAST
SUSSEX

DEVON

DORSET

ISLE OF
WIGHT

CORNWALL

English Channel

SCILLY ISLES

KEY   ★ Star Pub   🌟 Top Quality Food   🍺 Great Beer
🍷 Good Wines   £ Bargain Meals   🛏 Good Bedrooms   🍴 Serves Food

---

ABERTHIN   ST0075 Map 6
Hare & Hounds 🌟 🍷
(01446) 774892 – www.hareandhoundsaberthin.com
NE of Cowbridge; CF71 7HB

**First class food in easy-going country pub, interesting drinks,
helpful courteous service and seats in garden**

This is no straightforward dining pub (though the food cooked by the
chef-landlord is excellent) but a place where locals drop in for a pint
and a chat in friendly, relaxed surroundings – just as they have done for 300
years. The simply furnished rooms have whitewashed walls, mate's chairs
and wheelbacks around wooden tables on bare boards, posies of flowers
in vases, a dresser with home-made preserves, a woodburning stove in an
inglenook fireplace, bookshelves with cookbooks and an open kitchen.
Brains Hancocks HB, Cotleigh Long Eared Owl, Muirhouse Pirates Gold and
Wye Valley HPA on handpump, 24 wines by the glass from a thoughtfully
chosen list, local cider, home-made seasonal drinks such as damson gin, sloe
gin and cherry brandy; background music (restaurant only) and darts. The
hanging baskets at the front of the building are pretty and there are benches
and picnic-sets in the garden. Disabled access.

🌟 Everything is made from scratch (including their own butter and sourdough
bread) using home-grown and other local produce for the accomplished seasonal
food: crispy pig cheek with chicory, mustard and pickled apple, braised squid with
fennel and green sauce, wild mushroom, chestnut and truffle risotto, skate wing with
shrimp, salsify, cockles and brown butter, venison haunch with dauphinoise potatoes
and red cabbage, confit pork belly with salt-baked celeriac and smoked carrot,
marinated hanger steak with red onion, celeriac and spinach, and puddings such as
rhubarb and almond tart with salted caramel and vanilla ice-cream and plum soufflé;
they also offer a two- and three-course set weekday lunch. *Benchmark main dish: local
lamb with mint sauce £17.00. Two-course evening meal £22.00.*

Free house ~ Licensee Tom Watts-Jones ~ Real ale ~ Open 2.30-9 Mon, Tues; 12-11 Weds,
Thurs; 12-midnight Fri, Sat; 12-10 Sun ~ Bar food 12-2.30, 6-9; 12-4 Sun ~ Restaurant ~
Children welcome but must leave bar by 7.30pm ~ Dogs allowed in bar ~ Wi-fi
Recommended by Alister and Margery Bacon, Naomi and Andrew Randall

---

BEAUMARIS   SH6076 Map 6
Bull 🌟 🍷 🛏
(01248) 810329 – www.bullsheadinn.co.uk
Castle Street; LL58 8AP

Wales Dining Pub of the Year

**Interesting historic inn with a rambling bar, stylish brasserie
and restaurant; quite a choice of well equipped bedrooms**

At the heart of this pretty town and near the castle, this 15th-c inn is a first
class all-rounder. You'll find a wide mix of customers in the charming
beamed bar which has a fine log fire and reminders of the town's past such as

a rare 17th-c brass water clock, a bloodthirsty array of cutlasses and even an oak ducking stool tucked in the snug alcove. Previous visitors have included Samuel Johnson and Charles Dickens. Seats range from comfortable low settles and leather-cushioned window seats, there are lots of copper and china jugs and courteous staff serve Bass, Brains Hancocks HB and guests such as Conwy San Francisco and Sharps Doom Bar on handpump, 18 wines by the glass (and 120 by the bottle) and around 28 gins with interesting tonics; board games. A stylish brasserie (called Coach) serves an informal menu in relaxed surroundings and you can also dine outside in the adjacent courtyard. The five bedrooms are named after characters in Dickens' novels and are very well equipped; some are traditional, others more contemporary in style. They also have bedrooms in the 17th-c Townhouse, an adjacent property with disabled access.

Making the most of their surroundings by using local meat and fish, the beautifully presented food includes lunchtime sandwiches, gin-cured sea trout with pickled cucumber and pea purée, braised beef cheek with horseradish and crispy pastry, crispy asian vegetables with tofu, ginger and lemongrass thai broth, beef and bacon burger with toppings, chipotle mayonnaise and chips, herb-crusted halibut with orange whisky butter sauce, mussels and parmentier potatoes, lamb rump with thyme crumb, jerusalem artichokes, baby carrots and lamb jus, steak frites with peppercorn sauce, and puddings such as dark chocolate délice with orange gel and coffee granita and rhubarb and vanilla custard trifle. *Benchmark main dish: local beer-battered cod and chips £16.00. Two-course evening meal £22.00.*

Free house ~ Licensees Kate and David Robertson ~ Real ale ~ Open 11-11; 11-10.30 Sun ~ Bar food 12-2, 6-9; 12-9 weekends ~ Restaurant ~ Children welcome ~ Dogs allowed in bar ~ Wi-fi ~ Bedrooms: £105/£115 *Recommended by Elizabeth and Andrew Harvey, Holly and Tim Waite, Daisy and Jonathan Spicer, Elizabeth and Peter May, Pauline and Mark Evans, Jamie Green*

BODFARI
Dinorben Arms ♀ ◖

SJ0970   Map 6

(01745) 775090 – www.brunningandprice.co.uk/dinorbenarms
Off A541, near church; LL16 4DA

Carefully extended village pub with interesting furnishings in open-plan bars, a fine choice of drinks and rewarding food

In the shadow of the church at the heart of this small village you'll find a carefully renovated pub of character. The large open-plan bar has several cosier areas leading off, the oldest of which is heavily beamed and has antique settles, stone bottles on a delft shelf and a woodburning stove. There's a glassed-over well in one corner, a curved central counter, leather armchairs grouped around one open fire (there are others), all manner of wooden dining chairs around tables on rugs or bare boards, elegant metal chandeliers, hundreds of prints on pale-painted or exposed-stone walls, large house plants and sizeable gilt-edged mirrors. Brunning & Price Phoenix Original, Facers North Star Porter and Timothy Taylors Boltmaker plus quickly changing guests from breweries such as Castle Rock, Hafod, Purple Moose and Spitting Feathers on handpump, lots of wines by the glass and a good choice of spirits. Far-reaching views can be enjoyed from a spacious partly covered terrace with qood quality seats and tables and from a high tower; there are plenty of picnic-sets on grass too.

Highly regarded food includes sandwiches, garlic and chilli prawns, smoked ham hock and caper croquettes with piccalilli, thai green vegetable curry with coconut rice and tempura courgette, steak burger with toppings, coleslaw and chips, baked hake with parma ham, butter bean and spinach cassoulet, marinated chicken with orange and chilli glaze, tzatziki salad and carrot and apricot couscous, glazed pork belly with wholegrain mustard mash, apple purée and cider sauce, and puddings such as hot waffle with caramelised banana and banoffi ice-cream. *Benchmark main dish: braised lamb shoulder with minted crushed potatoes and rosemary gravy £17.95. Two-course evening meal £21.00.*

Brunning & Price ~ Licensee John Unsworth ~ Real ale ~ Open 11-11; 12-10.30 Sun ~ Bar food 12-9.30; 12-10 Fri, Sat; 12-9 Sun ~ Restaurant ~ Children welcome ~ Dogs allowed in bar ~ Wi-fi *Recommended by Richard and Tessa Ibbot, Maggie and Stevan Hollis, Chloe and Michael Swettenham, Donald Allsopp, Andrew and Michele Revell*

 COLWYN BAY   SH8478 Map 6

Pen-y-Bryn ♀ ◖

(01492) 533360 – www.brunningandprice.co.uk/penybryn

B5113 Llanwrst Road, on southern outskirts; when you see the pub, turn off into Wentworth Avenue for the car park; LL29 6DD

Spacious, open-plan, one-storey building overlooking the bay with all-day brasserie-style food, a good range of drinks and obliging staff

The views alone are reason enough for seeking out this efficiently run pub, and it's much more special than its bungalow exterior suggests. Extending around the three long sides of the bar counter, you'll find welcoming open fires, oriental rugs on pale stripped boards, a mix of seating and well spaced tables, shelves of books, a profusion of pictures, big pot plants, careful lighting and dark green old-fashioned school radiators. A fine choice of drinks served by knowledgeable young staff includes Phoenix Brunning & Price Original, Purple Moose Snowdonia Ale and Timothy Taylors Boltmaker plus three quickly changing guests such as Castle Rock Elsie Mo, Jennings Cumberland and Purple Moose Elderflower Ale on handpump, well chosen, good value wines (including 16 by the glass) and 40 malt whiskies; board games and background music. The big windows at the back look over seats and tables on the terraces and in the sizeable garden and then out to the sea and the Great Orme. In summer, the award-winning flowering tubs and hanging baskets are lovely.

Tempting food includes sandwiches, barbecue chicken wings, prawn cocktail, moroccan-spiced vegetable and chickpea pie, pork and leek sausages with mash and onion gravy, salt beef hash cake with home-made baked beans and fried egg, five-spice pork belly with plum sauce, sticky coconut rice and stir-fried vegetables, steak in ale pie, sicilian fish stew with saffron aioli, braised lamb shoulder with minted crushed potatoes and rosemary gravy, and puddings such as raspberry bakewell tart with fruit compote and sticky toffee pudding with toffee sauce and vanilla ice-cream. *Benchmark main dish: beer-battered cod and chips £13.95. Two-course evening meal £21.00.*

Brunning & Price ~ Manager Andrew Grant ~ Real ale ~ Open 11-11; 11-10.30 Sun ~ Bar food 12-9.30; 12-9 Sun ~ Children welcome ~ Dogs allowed in bar ~ Wi-fi *Recommended by Fiona and Jack Henderson, Mike Kavaney, Joe and Belinda Smart, Andrew Wall, Max Simons, Lenny and Ruth Walters*

 CRICKHOWELL   SO2118 Map 6

Bear ★ ♀ ⇌

(01873) 810408 – www.bearhotel.co.uk

Brecon Road; A40; NP8 1BW

Convivial and interesting inn with a splendid, old-fashioned bar area warmed by a log fire and rewarding food and drink; comfortable bedrooms

Guests have been coming here for 500 years and the long-serving family in charge continue to offer a warm and genuine welcome to all. The bustling bar has a wide mix of customers, heavy beams, little plush-seated bentwood armchairs and handsome old cushioned settles, fresh flowers on tables, and a window seat that looks down on the market square. Next to the great roaring log fire are a big sofa and leather easy chairs on oak parquet flooring with rugs and antiques including lots of pewter mugs and brassware, a longcase clock and interesting prints. Brains Rev James, Caledonian Deuchars IPA, Grey Trees Afghan Pale and Wadworths 6X on handpump, alongside 35 malt whiskies, 30 gins, local ciders, vintage and late-bottled ports and unusual wines (with 11 by the glass). Reception rooms are comfortably furnished, and there are tables and chairs in the small flower-filled garden. This is a particularly appealing place to stay with quite a choice of bedrooms: the older ones in the main building have antiques, others are in a country style and the luxury ones have hot tubs and four-poster beds. Breakfasts are excellent. Disabled loos.

Using organic local produce and artisan makers, the enjoyable food includes sandwiches, game terrine with real ale chutney, chicken satay skewers with peanut sauce and crostini, aubergine and tomato parmigiana with vegetarian parmesan, burger with toppings and chips, indian chicken curry with fragrant rice, cumberland sausage ring with mash, shoestring onions and gravy, seafood linguine, local 30-day aged rib-eye steak with a choice of sauce, and puddings such as pannettone bread and butter pudding with rum, bananas and brown bread ice-cream and vanilla bean crème brûlée. *Benchmark main dish: braised lamb shank with spring onion mash and braising juices £17.50. Two-course evening meal £21.00.*

Free house ~ Licensee Stephen Hindmarsh ~ Real ale ~ Open 11-11; 12-11 Sun ~ Bar food 12-10; 12-9.30 Sun ~ Restaurant ~ Children welcome ~ Dogs allowed in bar and bedrooms ~ Wi-fi ~ Bedrooms: £124/£177 *Recommended by Lorna and Jack Mulgrave, Miranda and Jeff Davidson, B and M Kendall, Mike and Mary Carter, Sheila and Sam Thorpe, Martine and Derek Cotton*

DALE
Griffin

SM8105   Map 6

(01646) 636227 – www.griffininndale.co.uk
B4327, by sea on one-way system; SA62 3RB

Friendly waterside pub with fresh fish and shellfish, local ales and an airy extension with lovely views

The convivial licensees have created a warm, cosy atmosphere here, helped along by beams, wood panelling, traditional red quarry tiles and open fires. Brains Rev James, Cwrw Iâl Hâf Gwyn and Harbwr Tenby Red Ale on handpump, six wines by the glass, local cider and malt whiskies – including a welsh one; background music. There's also a modern, glass-fronted extension with its own stand-alone stove, and the big windows and doors take in the wonderful view of the coastline. The pub is right by the water with a pontoon and a seawall, and seats on the rooftop terrace (you can eat up here too) make the most of the lovely view of Milford Haven waterway. There are fine coastal walks to either side. Disabled access and they have a key for a disabled loo next to the pub.

As well as fresh fish and shellfish straight from local fishermen on the pontoon and using the best local produce, the enjoyable food includes smoked mackerel pâté, goats cheese on toasted brioche with red onion marmalade and beetroot purée, vegetable lasagne, gammon steak with mash and parsley sauce, beer-battered cod and chips, chicken and leek pie, spicy prawn and mango curry, daily seasonal specials, and puddings such as chocolate brownie with ice-cream and lime and lemon cheesecake. *Benchmark main dish: hake steak with chorizo and yellow pepper sauce £22.95. Two-course evening meal £22.00.*

Free house ~ Licensees Sian Mathias and Simon Vickers ~ Real ale ~ Open 12-11; closed Oct-Christmas; mid Jan-Feb half term – check website in winter ~ Bar food 12-2.30, 6-8.30 ~ Restaurant ~ Children welcome ~ Wi-fi *Recommended by Ted and Mary Bates, Roy and Gill Payne, Bernard Stradling, Caroline Sullivan, Jim King, William and Natasha Pace, Carol and Barry Craddock*

EAST ABERTHAW
ST0366 Map 6
Blue Anchor 🍺 £
(01446) 750329 – www.blueanchoraberthaw.com
Village signed off B4265; CF62 3DD

Thatched character pub with a cosy range of small rooms, making a memorable spot for a drink

The snug, low-beamed little rooms here date back over 600 years, making it one of the oldest pubs in Wales. These lead off the central servery, with tiny doorways, open fires (including one in an inglenook with antique oak seats built into the stripped stonework) and other seats and tables worked into a series of small, chatty alcoves. The more open front bar still has an ancient lime-ash floor and keeps Brains Bitter, Theakstons Old Peculier, Wadworths 6X, Wye Valley HPA and a guest beer on handpump, as well as farm cider, ten malt whiskies and eight wines by the glass. Outside, rustic seats shelter peacefully among tubs and troughs of flowers, with stone tables on a terrace. The pub can get very full in the evenings and on summer weekends. A path from here leads to the shingle flats of the estuary.

Tasty food includes baguettes, home-cured whisky and treacle salmon with pepper chutney, spiced salt beef with dijon mustard and pickled onions, roasted butternut squash gnocchi in creamy sauce with sage, pine nuts and parmesan, steak and kidney pie, thai green chicken curry, venison haunch with beetroot tarte tatin, hake with chorizo mash, red pepper pesto and samphire, 10oz gammon with fresh pineapple and egg, honey-glazed, slow-cooked pork belly with pak choi and spiced rice, and puddings such as coffee crème brûlée and vanilla pannacotta with roasted pineapple and tarragon. *Benchmark main dish: monkfish and king prawn curry £12.50. Two-course evening meal £20.00.*

Free house ~ Licensee Jeremy Coleman ~ Real ale ~ Open 11-11; 12-10.30 Sun ~ Bar food 12-2, 6-9; 12-3 Sun ~ Restaurant ~ Children welcome ~ Dogs allowed in bar ~ Wi-fi *Recommended by Sandra and Miles Spencer, Monty Green, Alfie Bayliss, Katherine and Hugh Markham, Maggie and Matthew Lyons, Alison and Dan Richardson, William and Sophia Renton*

FELINFACH
SO0933 Map 6
Griffin 🍴⭐🍷🍺🛏
(01874) 620111 – www.eatdrinksleep.ltd.uk
A470 NE of Brecon; LD3 0UB

Highly regarded dining pub with exceptional food, a fine range of drinks and upbeat rustic décor; inviting bedrooms

Our readers greatly enjoy their visits to this particularly well run and gently civilised inn. The back bar is quite pubby in an up-to-date way, with four leather sofas around a low table on pitted quarry tiles by a high slate hearth with a log fire. Behind them are mixed stripped seats around scrubbed kitchen tables on bare boards, and a bright blue and ochre colour scheme with some modern prints; background music, board games and plenty of books. Friendly, efficient staff serve interesting drinks, many from smaller independent suppliers, including well chosen wines (18 by the glass and carafe and they have a wine shop), welsh spirits, cocktails, local bottled cider, locally sourced apple juice, non-alcoholic cocktails made with produce from their garden, unusual continental and local bottled beers and a range of sherries. Grey Trees Caradog, Montys Pale Ale and Wye Valley Butty Bach are served on handpump. The two smallish front dining rooms that link to the back bar are attractive. On the left: mixed dining chairs around mainly stripped tables on flagstones and white-painted rough stone walls, with a cream-coloured Aga in a big stripped-stone embrasure. On the right: similar furniture on bare boards, big modern prints on terracotta walls and smart dark curtains. Dogs may sit with their owners at certain tables while dining. There are seats and tables outside on grass. The seven bedrooms are comfortable and tastefully decorated and the hearty breakfasts are nicely informal (you make your own toast and help yourself to home-made marmalade and jam). Good wheelchair access.

 Seriously good food using home-grown and other local produce includes smoked duck with feta and pickled berries, oak-smoked salmon fishcake with aioli, gnocchi with peas, girolles and spring onions, beef bourguignon, lamb breast with white bean mash, salsa verde and sweetbreads, duck breast with sweet potato and beetroot, sea trout with fregola and little gem, and puddings such as coconut and cardamom rice pudding with lime and mango and dark chocolate mousse with caramel and pecans; they also offer a two- and three-course menu. *Benchmark main dish: hanger steak with ale-braised shallots, fondant potato, beans and jus £23.50. Two-course evening meal £23.00.*

Free house ~ Licensees Charles and Edmund Inkin and Julie Bell ~ Real ale ~ Open 11-11 ~ Bar food 12-2.30, 6-9; 12-2.30, 6-9.30 Fri, Sat ~ Restaurant ~ Children welcome ~ Dogs allowed in bar and bedrooms ~ Wi-fi ~ Bedrooms: /£140 *Recommended by Ian Herdman, Megan and Wliam Revell, Ian and Rose Lock, M and GR, Holly and Tim Waite, Patricia and Anton Larkham, James and Becky Plath*

GRESFORD
Pant-yr-Ochain ♀ ◀

SJ3453 Map 6

(01978) 853525 – www.brunningandprice.co.uk/pantyrochain
Off A483 on N edge of Wrexham: at roundabout take A5156 (A534) towards Nantwich, then first left towards the Flash; LL12 8TY

Popular dining pub with good all-day food, a wide range of drinks and lovely lakeside garden

Reached down a long drive, this place feels more like a country house than a pub – and the 16th-c inglenook fireplace merely adds to the atmosphere. Light and airy, the rooms are stylishly decorated with a wide range of interesting prints and bric-a-brac, and a good mix of individually chosen furnishings, including comfortable seats for relaxing as well as more upright ones for eating. One area is set out as a library with floor-to-ceiling bookshelves, while the popular dining conservatory overlooks the pretty garden; board games. An impressive line-up of drinks served by well trained staff includes Phoenix Brunning & Price Original and guests such as Big Hand Seren, Brimstage Trappers Hat Bitter, Hawkshead Windermere Pale, Purple Moose Snowdonia Ale, Timothy Taylors Landlord and Weetwood Eastgate on handpump, a farm cider, 20 wines by the glass, around 80 malt whiskies, 50 gins and 30 rums. The seats on the front terrace and the picnic-sets on the lawn in the flower-filled grounds (many are beside the small lake) are quickly snapped up in warm weather. Good disabled access.

Good modern food includes sandwiches, sticky honey pork belly and toasted peanuts, smoked salmon with gin, cucumber, shaved fennel and radish, beetroot, quinoa and soya bean burger with red cabbage slaw and fries, honey-roast ham and eggs, jerk chicken supreme with rice and peas and sweetcorn, pineapple and chilli salsa, roasted trout salad with asparagus, edamame beans, new potatoes and lemon herb crème fraîche, lamb, roasted parsnip and rosemary pie with mash and greens, duck breast with fondant potato, baby vegetables, beetroot purée and blackberry jus, and puddings such as crème brûlée and triple chocolate brownie with chocolate sauce. *Benchmark main dish: beer-battered fish and chips £13.75. Two-course evening meal £20.00.*

Brunning & Price ~ Licensee James Meakin ~ Real ale ~ Open 11-11; Sat; 12-10.30 Sun ~ Bar food 12-9.30; 12-9 Sun ~ Children welcome ~ Dogs allowed in bar ~ Wi-fi *Recommended by Trish and Karl Soloman, Georgia Egner, Lenny and Ruth Walters, Claire and Nigel Swanning, Patrick and Martine Lawson, Elodie and Edward Blake*

LITTLE HAVEN
Swan 🍺 🍴

SM8512   Map 6

(01437) 781880 – www.theswanlittlehaven.co.uk
Point Road; SA62 3UL

Charming village pub with sea views from both inside and outdoor terrace, and popular food and ales

As this quaint little place is right on the Pembrokeshire Coast Path, quite a few of the customers at lunchtime are walkers. The traditional oak-floored bar has a mix of furniture including cask tables, a couple of leather armchairs by an open fire at one end, and a woodburning stove at the other, while the snug has a large table suitable for around ten diners. From the heavily panelled counter, helpful staff serve Brains Rev James and Sharps Doom Bar with guests such as Bluestone Rockhopper and Harbwr Tenby North Star on handpump and ten wines by the glass. There's a blue-painted dining room and a more contemporary upstairs restaurant. Expansive views across a broad and sandy, hill-sheltered cove to the sea can be enjoyed from seats in the bay window and from a heated terrace where there are rattan-style chairs and tables. This is one of the prettiest coastal villages in west Wales.

Well regarded food includes smoked duck salad with asian coleslaw, pak choi and hoisin, crispy cockles and seaweed with chilli salt and vinegar, sharing antipasti plate, courgette flower linguine with tomato, purple radish and chickweed oil, beer-battered cod and chips, burger with black pudding, Guinness-caramelised onions and chips, crab and mixed seafood chowder, local sirloin steak with a choice of sauce and chips, and puddings. *Benchmark main dish: pressed local pork belly with celeriac mash, caramelised cabbage and bitter toffee sauce £22.00. Two-course evening meal £22.00.*

Free house ~ Licensees Matt and Helen John ~ Real ale ~ No credit cards ~ Open 12-midnight; 12pm-1am Fri, Sat ~ Bar food 12-4, 6-8.30 ~ Restaurant Thurs-Sat evenings, also Weds evening in summer ~ Children welcome ~ Dogs allowed in bar ~ Wi-fi *Recommended by Nik and Gloria Clarke, Alison and Graeme Spicer, William and Sophia Renton, Mark Holmes, Simon Rowntree, David and Leone Lawson, John Ellis*

'Children welcome' means the pub says it lets children inside without any special restriction. If it allows them in, but to restricted areas such as an eating area or family room, we specify this. Some pubs may impose an evening time limit. We do not mention limits after 9pm as we assume children are home by then.

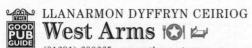

LLANARMON DYFFRYN CEIRIOG

SJ1532   Map 6

West Arms 🏠⭐ 🛏️

(01691) 600665 – www.thewestarms.com

End of B4500 W of Chirk; LL20 7LD

Idyllic location for 16th-c inn with reliably good food and picturesque gardens; comfortable bedrooms

This friendly, recently updated former drovers' inn has been welcoming guests since 1570. There's a comfortable back bar with antique settles, armchairs and a friendly, informal atmosphere, and a front lounge with an inglenook fireplace and original flagstones. Five log fires keep everything warm in winter. Three quickly changing ales from Big Hand plus Timothy Taylors Landlord on handpump, 14 wines by the glass, 20 malt whiskies and 42 gins; background music. The restaurant is slightly more formal but still has a relaxed, traditional feel. In warm weather you can sit in the garden against a backdrop of the Ceiriog Valley and the Brwyn mountains, and the pub makes a good base for exploring the area on foot, bike, car or horse. The bedrooms, some with valley views, are comfortable and well appointed and the breakfasts are highly regarded.

 Food is good, seasonal and uses some home-grown produce, local game, meat and trout: sandwiches, pork and chorizo samosas with apple and pepper relish, native oyster and monkfish fritters with pea purée and spicy aioli, parsnip and chestnut dhal with home-made naan bread and rhubarb chutney, shepherd's pie with chestnut and bacon, pheasant breast with honey-glazed carrots and pomme anna, smoked haddock fishcakes with spinach, poached eggs and hollandaise, rib-eye steak with a choice of sauce and beef dripping chips, and puddings such as chocolate brownie with almond and white chocolate sauce and warm banana bread with toffee sauce and vanilla ice-cream. *Benchmark main dish: local honey-glazed lamb chump with dauphinoise potatoes, parsnip purée and jus £20.00. Two-course evening meal £26.00.*

Free house ~ Licensees Nicky and Mark Williamson ~ Real ale ~ Open 11.30-midnight ~ Bar food 12-2.30, 6.30-9 ~ Restaurant ~ Children welcome ~ Dogs welcome ~ Wi-fi ~ Bedrooms: /$115 *Recommended by Dave Snowden, Maria and Stephen Braeburn, Archie and Melanie Garnett, Nick and Willow Brown, Jeremy and Susan Steadman, Jamie and Lizzie McEwan*

LLANBERIS

SH6655   Map 6

Pen-y-Gwryd 🛏️

(01286) 870211 – www.pyg.co.uk

Nant Gwynant; at junction of A498 and A4086, ie across mountains from Llanberis – OS Sheet 115 map reference 660558; LL55 4NT

Atmospheric and unchanged mountaineers' haunt in the wilds of Snowdonia; bedrooms

The same family have run this much loved Snowdonia institution since 1947. There are views across a striking mountain landscape and the place is packed with items left by the climbing fraternity over the years. You can still make out the fading signatures scrawled on the ceiling by the 1953 Everest team who used this as a training base; on display is the very rope that connected Hillary and Tenzing on top of the mountain. One snug little room in the homely slate-floored log cabin bar has built-in wall benches and sturdy country chairs; from here you can look out to precipitous Moel Siabod beyond the lake opposite. A smaller room has a worthy collection of illustrious boots from famous climbs, while a cosy panelled smoke room has more fascinating climbing mementoes and equipment; darts, pool, board games, bar billiards and table tennis. Purple Moose Glaslyn and Madogs are on handpump and they have several malts. Staying in the comfortable but basic bedrooms can be quite an experience, and there's an excellent traditional breakfast (served 8.30-9am, though they may serve earlier). The inn has its own chapel (built for the millennium and dedicated by the Archbishop of Wales), sauna and outdoor natural pool.

A short choice of simple, good-value lunchtime food includes rolls, ploughman's, pies, salads and quiche of the day as well as daily specials such as roast beef or lamb. The hearty three- or five-course set meal in the evening restaurant is signalled by a gong at 7.30pm (if you're late, you'll miss it): maybe warm goats cheese and parma ham salad, smoked mackerel mousse, beef in ale pie, salmon fillet with hollandaise, peppered tenderloin of pork with wild mushroom and tomato risotto, cod in a leek, onion and butter sauce, and puddings such as sticky toffee pudding with toffee sauce and strawberry and vanilla cheesecake. *Benchmark main dish: roast leg of local lamb £10.00. Two-course evening meal £27.00.*

Free house ~ Licensee Nicholas Pullee ~ Real ale ~ Open 11-11; closed weekdays in Dec, all Jan and Feb ~ Bar food 12-2; evening meal 7.30pm ~ Restaurant evening ~ Children welcome ~ Dogs welcome ~ Wi-fi ~ Bedrooms: /£95 *Recommended by Anna and Mark Evans, John Herbert, William and Tasha Fraser, Professor James Burke, David and Charlotte Emslie, Elodie and Edward Blake*

LLANDUDNO JUNCTION
SH8180 Map 6
Queens Head ★ ♀

(01492) 546570 – www.queensheadglanwydden.co.uk

Glanwydden; heading towards Llandudno on B5115 from Colwyn Bay, turn left into Llanrhos Road at roundabout as you enter the Penrhyn Bay speed limit; Glanwydden is signed as the first left turn; LL31 9JP

Consistently good food served all day at comfortably modern dining pub

Food remains king here, so don't be put off by the unassuming whitewashed exterior; it's best to book a table in advance. The spacious yet intimate lounge bar is a mix of beams, rustic wooden tables and chairs, an open woodburning stove and fresh flowers. The little snug bar keeps Conwy Clogwyn Gold and Timothy Taylors Landlord on handpump, over 15 decent wines by the glass, several malt whiskies and good coffee; background music. There's a pleasing mix of seats and tables under parasols outside. You're within easy reach of northern Snowdonia from here.

Using the best local, seasonal produce, the particularly good food includes ciabattas, citrus-cured scottish salmon with horseradish rémoulade, soft quail egg and heirloom tomatoes, duck liver and orange gin parfait with redcurrant and fig chutney, chickpea, spinach, apricot and sweet potato tagine with pomegranate and sultana couscous, cassoulet of confit duck leg, slow-roasted pork belly, toulouse sausage and haricot beans, grilled tiger prawns, monkfish, mussels, sea bass and cod cheeks with lemon, courgette and broad bean couscous and saffron and dill yoghurt, chicken supreme stuffed with mushroom and sage mousse with truffled roast potatoes and madeira sauce, and puddings. *Benchmark main dish: steak and mushroom pie £13.50. Two-course evening meal £21.00.*

Stange & Co Pub Group ~ Lease Dan McLennan ~ Real ale ~ Open 12-11 ~ Bar food 12-9 ~ Restaurant ~ Children welcome ~ Wi-fi *Recommended by Mike and Mary Carter, Harry and Megan Evans, Daisy and Jonathan Spicer, Millie and Peter Downing, Sandra and Miles Spencer, Charlotte and William Mason*

Pubs close to motorway junctions are listed at the back of the book.

LLANELIAN-YN-RHOS
White Lion

SH8676 Map 6

(01492) 515807 – www.whitelioninn.co.uk

Signed off A5830 (shown as B5383 on some maps) and B5381, S of Colwyn Bay; LL29 8YA

Bustling local with bar and spacious dining areas, tasty food, real ales and helpful staff

There's been some sort of building here for 1,200 years, though the present one is only a few centuries old. It's a picturesque old village pub tucked away at a crossing of narrow lanes in quiet hilly countryside above Colwyn Bay. There are two distinct parts linked by a broad flight of steps, and each has its own cheery personality. Up at the top is a very spacious and neat dining area, while at the other end is a traditional old bar with antique high-backed settles fitting snugly around a big fireplace, and flagstones by the counter. Marstons Saddle Tank, VOG South Island and Youngs London Gold on handpump, 15 wines by the glass, farm cider, several gins including welsh ones and ten malt whiskies are served by helpful staff. Off to the left is another dining room with jugs hanging from beams and teapots above the windows; background music and board games. An attractive courtyard (also used for parking) has tables and chairs, and the church is next door.

Popular food includes lunchtime sandwiches and hot baguettes plus deep-fried breaded goats cheese with red onion chutney, spanish-style piri-piri garlic prawns, chickpea and sweet potato coconut curry, gammon with egg and pineapple, beer-battered hake and chips, a pie of the day, local braised lamb shoulder with roasted honey-glazed root vegetables and gravy, slow-cooked beef in Guinness with mash, chicken topped with cheese, bacon and mushrooms in cider, rosemary and sage sauce, and puddings. *Benchmark main dish: roast beef with yorkshire pudding £11.95. Two-course evening meal £20.00.*

Free house ~ Licensee Simon Cole ~ Real ale ~ Open 11.30-3.30, 6-11; 11.30-3.30, 5-11 Sat; 12-10.30 Sun; closed Mon except school and bank holidays ~ Bar food 12-2, 6-9; 12-2, 5-9 Fri, Sat; 12-8.30 Sun ~ Restaurant ~ Children welcome ~ Wi-fi ~ Live jazz Tues; acoustic music Weds; quiz Thurs; welsh singing fourth Sat of month; singalong first Sun of month
Recommended by Darrell Barton, Patricia and Gordon Tucker, Louise and Anton Parsons, Alison and Michael Harper, Jill and Dick Archer, David Longhurst

LLANGOLLEN
Corn Mill ♀ ◀

SJ2142 Map 6

(01978) 869555 – www.brunningandprice.co.uk/cornmill

Dee Lane, very narrow lane off Castle Street (A539) just S of bridge; nearby parking can be tricky, may be best to use public car park on Parade Street/East Street and walk; LL20 8PN

Fascinating riverside building with fine views, personable young staff, super food all day and good beers

The interestingly fitted-out interior of this cleverly restored watermill has a striking open stairway with gleaming timber and tensioned steel rails, pale pine flooring on stout beams, and mainly stripped-stone walls. Quite a lot of the old machinery is still in place, including the huge waterwheel (often turning) and there are good-sized dining tables, big rugs, thoughtfully chosen pictures (many to do with water) and several pot plants. One of the two serving bars, away from the water, has a much more local feel with regulars sitting on bar stools, pews on dark slate flagstones and daily papers. Phoenix Brunning & Price Original and Facers DHB on handpump with guests such as Facers North Star Porter, Hawkshead Windermere Pale and Moorhouses Pendle Witches Brew, 20 wines by the glass, 50 malt whiskies and farm cider. Seats on a raised deck in front of the pub overlook the rushing mill race and rapids below; you can also watch steam trains arriving and leaving the station on the opposite riverbank.

🍴 Food is interesting and includes sandwiches, smoked salmon with spiced avocado purée, shaved fennel and radish, sticky chinese chicken wings, baked garlic and rosemary-studded camembert with walnut and apple salad, wild mushroom tortellini with spinach and leek purée, roast artichokes and mushroom glaze, steak in ale pie, chicken with puttanesca sauce on pasta with parmesan, confit pork belly with sherry-braised pig cheeks, fondant potato and butternut squash purée, vietnamese king prawn and rice noodle salad with toasted peanuts, coriander, chilli and lime dressing, and puddings such as crème brûlée and dark chocolate and orange tart with passion-fruit sorbet. *Benchmark main dish: braised lamb shoulder with crushed minted new potatoes and rosemary gravy £17.95. Two-course evening meal £21.00.*

Brunning & Price ~ Manager Andrew Barker ~ Real ale ~ Open 11-11; 11-10.30 Sun ~ Bar food 12-9.30; 12-9 Sun ~ Restaurant ~ Children welcome ~ Dogs allowed in bar ~ Wi-fi
Recommended by Andrew and Ruth Simmonds, Mark Hamill, Mike and Mary Carter, Colin and Daniel Gibbs, Sally Harrison, Peter Meister, Anna and Mark Evans

LLANMADOC
SS4493   Map 6

Britannia

(01792) 386624 – www.britanniagower.com
The Gower, near Whiteford Burrows (NT); SA3 1DB

Fine views from seats behind this popular pub with more in the large garden, well liked food and ales

As this 18th-c dining pub is on the north coast of the Gower peninsula, there are lovely nearby walks; come here for refreshment afterwards. The refurbished beamed bar has a woodburning stove and plenty of space to enjoy a pint of Gower Gold, Sharps Doom Bar and Wye Valley HPA on handpump and several wines by the glass served by friendly staff; background music, darts, TV and board games. The beamed restaurant has attractive modern wooden tables and chairs on a striped carpet, paintings on exposed-stone walls and another woodburning stove. Picnic-sets on the raised decked area at the back have marvellous views over the Loughor estuary and do get snapped up quickly; there are also tables out in front and in the big garden. They have a rabbit hutch and an aviary with budgies, cockatiels, quail and a parrot.

🍴 Food is good and includes lunchtime baguettes, smoked confit duck pot with fig and date chutney, mussels in white wine, garlic, chilli and confit tomato broth, thai vegetable curry with sticky rice, spare ribs with barbecue sauce and fries, steak in ale pie, beer-battered hake and chips, slow-roasted poussin with pomme purée, fricassée of savoy cabbage, wild mushrooms and port jus, sea bream fillet with crushed potatoes and saffron and mussel curry cream, and puddings such as pistachio and polenta cake with apple and cinnamon doughnut, pistachio biscuit and fresh apple sorbet and chocolate fondant with Merlyn Welsh Cream liqueur ice-cream. *Benchmark main dish: local salt marsh lamb shank with mixed bean and roast vegetable casserole £19.00. Two-course evening meal £21.00.*

Enterprise ~ Tenants Martin and Lindsey Davies ~ Real ale ~ Open 12-11 ~ Bar food 12-3.30, 6-9; 12-9 weekends ~ Restaurant ~ Children welcome ~ Dogs allowed in bar ~ Wi-fi
Recommended by Trevor and Michele Street, Rosie and John Moore, I D Barnett, Hugh Roberts, Archie and Melanie Garnett, Philip Chesington, Fiona and Jack Henderson

MOLD   SJ2465 Map 6

Glasfryn 🍷 🍺

(01352) 750500 – www.brunningandprice.co.uk/glasfryn

N of the centre on Raikes Lane (parallel to the A5119), just past the well signposted Theatr Clwyd; CH7 6LR

Busy bistro-style pub with inventive all-day food, nice décor and wide choice of drinks

A former judges' residence and farm, this cheerful pub has an open-plan interior with a lively atmosphere and wide mix of customers. It's cleverly laid out to create plenty of nice quiet corners with a mix of informal, attractive country furnishings: rugs on bare boards, shelves of books, house plants, a warming fire and plenty of close-hung homely pictures. Phoenix Black Bee and Brunning & Price Original, Buzzard Chinook, Conwy Scrum Down, Facers North Star Porter, Hobsons Best, Muirhouse Pirates Gold, Purple Moose Snowdonia Ale and Timothy Taylors Boltmaker on handpump, 22 wines by the glass, 40 gins, 25 rums and 60 malt whiskies; background music. On warm days, the wooden tables on the large front terrace are a restful place to sit, providing sweeping views of the Clwydian Hills. Disabled access. Theatre Clwyd is just over the road.

 Highly regarded food includes sandwiches, duck hash cake with chicory salad, fried egg and beetroot ketchup, crispy sea bass with chorizo sausage fritters and citrus crème fraîche, butter bean, sweet potato and smoky tomato stew with rosemary dumplings, steak in ale pudding, smoked haddock and salmon fishcakes with tomato and spring onion salad, pork rib-eye with roasted shallots, blue cheese potato gratin and apple and sage jus, slow-cooked beef ragoût with pasta, sunblush tomatoes, wild mushrooms and parmesan, and puddings such as lemon posset with blackcurrant sorbet and hot waffle with caramelised banana and toffee sauce. *Benchmark main dish: beer-battered cod and chips £13.75. Two-course evening meal £21.00.*

Brunning & Price ~ Manager Graham Arathoon ~ Real ale ~ Open 10.30-11; 11.30-10.30 Sun ~ Bar food 12-9.30; 12-9 Sun ~ Children welcome ~ Dogs allowed in bar ~ Wi-fi
Recommended by Molly and Stewart Lindsay, Chantelle and Tony Redman, Elliott Kemp, Daisy Rutledge, Edward and William Johnston, Jim and Sue James, Simon and Alex Knight

NEWPORT   SN0539 Map 6

Golden Lion 🛏

(01239) 820321 – www.goldenlionpembrokeshire.co.uk

East Street (A487); SA42 0SY

Attractive, friendly local with tasty food and pleasant staff; well appointed bedrooms

G ood food and a genuinely friendly welcome from helpful staff continue to draw in a good mix of customers to this popular inn. The genuinely pubby bar has Sharps Doom Bar and a couple of guest ales from the nearby Bluestone Brewery on handpump, several malt whiskies, wines by the glass and Gwynt y Ddraig cider; background music, TV, pool, juke box, darts and games machine. There's also a cosy series of beamed rooms with distinctive old settles and the dining room has elegant blond oak furniture, whitewashed walls and potted plants. You can sit outside at the front and in a side garden. This coastal village makes a good base for exploring northern Pembrokeshire and the bedrooms are comfortable and fair value. Good disabled access and facilities.

🍴 A fine choice of good food includes lunchtime sandwiches, home-made scotch egg with piccalilli gel, smoked mackerel pâté with apple and ale chutney, thai green vegetable curry with pilau rice, burger with toppings, mustard mayonnaise and fries, a pie of the day, lemon, garlic and chilli chicken with a choice of potatoes, lamb chops with rosemary and mint sauce and seasonal vegetables, rib-eye steak with a choice of sauce and chips, daily specials, and puddings such as dark chocolate and peanut butter brownie with vanilla pod ice-cream and lemon tart with berry compote and chantilly cream. *Benchmark main dish: tempura-battered coriander and chilli haddock fillet with sweet chilli dip £16.20. Two-course evening meal £21.00.*

Free house ~ Licensee Daron Paish ~ Real ale ~ Open midday-2am ~ Bar food 12-2.30, 6.30-9 ~ Restaurant ~ Children welcome ~ Dogs allowed in bar ~ Wi-fi ~ Bedrooms: $80/$100 *Recommended by Colin and Daniel Gibbs, Peter Brix, Frank Price, Frances Parsons, Matt and Hayley Jacob, Ian and Rose Lock, Gary and Marie Miller, Maggie and Stevan Hollis*

OLD RADNOR

Harp 🎖️📧🛏️

SO2459 Map 6

(01544) 350655 – www.harpinnradnor.co.uk

Village signposted off A44 Kington–New Radnor in Walton; LD8 2RH

Lovely inn in beautiful spot, with cottagey bar, tasty food and well kept ales; comfortable bedrooms

Friendly, hands-on licensees run this charming old hilltop pub, set in perfect walking country and overlooking the heights of Radnor Forest. We get nothing but warm praise from our readers on all aspects of the place. The public bar has a great deal of character, high-backed settles, an antique reader's chair and other venerable chairs around a log fire; board games, cribbage, darts and quoits. The snug slate-floored bar contains a handsome curved antique settle, a log fire in a fine inglenook and lots of local books, maps and guides for residents; a quieter dining area off to the right extends into another dining room with a woodburning stove. Ludlow Gold and Skinners Betty Stogs on handpump, as well as five wines and prosecco by the glass, local cider and local gins, vodkas and whiskies. Tables outside make the most of the glorious view. The spic and span bedrooms are highly sought after and share the same lovely views; good breakfasts too. Do visit the impressive village church and look for its early organ case (Britain's oldest), fine rood screen and ancient font.

🍴 As well as lunchtime sandwiches (Friday and Saturday lunchtimes only), the well liked food includes duck and spring onion terrine with hoisin sauce, cucumber salad, sesame and five-spice dressing and chinese pancakes, smoked haddock and leek fishcake with spinach and hollandaise, wild mushroom, garlic, spinach and smoked cheddar linguine with pecorino shavings, lamb and mint burger with whipped feta cheese, pickled red cabbage, baby spinach and sweet potato fries, whole grilled plaice with sautéed potatoes, fennel and cherry tomatoes and herb butter, and puddings such as dark chocolate and pecan nut brownie with tayberry sorbet and berry coulis and brandied raspberry and mascarpone creme brûlée with lemon shortbread. *Benchmark main dish: local rump steak and chips £19.00. Two-course evening meal £20.00.*

Free house ~ Licensees Chris and Angela Ireland ~ Real ale ~ Open 6-11 Weds, Thurs; 12-3, 6-11 Fri, Sat; 12-3, 6-10.30 Sun; closed Mon except bank holidays, Tues ~ Bar food 6-9 Weds, Thurs; 12-2, 6-9 Fri, Sat; 12-2.30 Sun ~ Children welcome ~ Dogs allowed in bar and bedrooms ~ Wi-fi ~ Bedrooms: /£105 *Recommended by Professor James Burke, Peter and Emma Kelly, Belinda and Neil Garth, Maria and Stephen Braeburn, Matilda and Gerald Thoms, Andrew and Nicky Churcher*

There are report forms at the back of the book.

OVERTON BRIDGE   SJ3542 Map 6

Cross Foxes ♀ ◖

(01978) 780380 – www.brunningandprice.co.uk/crossfoxes

A539 W of Overton, near Erbistock; LL13 0DR

Terrific river views, contemporary food and an extensive range of drinks in bustling, well run pub

In a splendid spot, this substantial 18th-c coaching inn has seats on a raised terrace overlooking the River Dee below and picnic-sets on a lawn that are even closer to the water; there's also a swing and tractor for children. The ancient low-beamed bar has a red tiled floor, dark timbers, a log fire in a big inglenook and built-in old pews, and several dining areas are furnished with turkey rugs, big pot plants and frame-to-frame wall pictures; large windows in the airy dining conservatory also look over the river. Board games and newspapers. A fine range of drinks includes 40 malt whiskies, 30 armagnacs, 45 gins and lots of wines by the glass – plus Brakspears Bitter, Jennings Cumberland, Marstons EPA and Ringwood Boondoggle on handpump and a farm cider. Service is friendly and efficient.

Brasserie-style food includes sandwiches, bourbon-glazed pork belly with red slaw, sweetcorn and watermelon, garlic and rosemary-baked camembert with walnut and apple salad, malaysian vegetable curry with coconut rice and tempura corn, smoked haddock and salmon with tomato and spring onion salad, local sausages with mash and onion gravy, chicken, ham and leek pie, lemon curd-glazed duck breast with orange and carrot purée, dauphinoise potatoes and blackberry jus, soy-marinated salmon and king prawns with rocket and pickled ginger salad and wasabi crème fraîche, and puddings such as crème brûlée and triple chocolate brownie with chocolate sauce and ice-cream. *Benchmark main dish: crispy beef salad with cashews, peppers and sweet chilli dressing £13.95. Two-course evening meal £21.00.*

Brunning & Price ~ Real ale ~ Open 11-11; 12-10.30 Sun ~ Bar food 12-9; 12-9.30 Fri, Sat ~ Children welcome ~ Dogs allowed in bar ~ Wi-fi *Recommended by Samuel and Melissa Turnbull, Nicholas and Lucy Sage, Edward Nile, John and Delia Franks, Simon and Alex Knight, Mike Benton, Jack Trussler, Susan and Callum Slade*

PANTYGELLI   SO3017 Map 6

Crown ⬢ ♀ ◖

(01873) 853314 – www.thecrownatpantygelli.com

Old Hereford Road N of Abergavenny; off A40 by war memorial via Pen Y Pound, passing leisure centre; Pantygelli also signposted from A465; NP7 7HR

Country pub in fine scenery, attractive inside and out, with good food and drinks

On the flower-filled terrace in front of this friendly, well run pub you look up from the lush valley to the hills, and there's also a smaller back terrace surrounded by lavender. The dark flagstoned bar, with sturdy timber props and beams, has a woodburning stove in a stone fireplace, a piano at the back with darts opposite, Bass, Hereford HLA, Rhymney Best and a seasonal guest from Tomos Watkin on handpump from the slate-topped counter, nine good wines by the glass and local organic apple juice and cider. On the left are four smallish, linked, carpeted dining rooms, the front pair separated by a massive stone chimneybreast; thoughtfully chosen individual furnishings and lots of attractive prints by local artists make it all thoroughly civilised. Background music, darts and board games.

 A wide choice of rewarding food includes lunchtime baguettes, grilled grey mullet with bombay potatoes and mango, ham hock hash with a fried egg, spinach and ricotta ravioli in plum tomato sauce, local venison sausages and mash with red onion gravy, braised lamb shoulder with fondant potato and braising sauce, chicken and mango curry, creamy seafood risotto, rolled pork belly with spicy tomato, chorizo and butter bean stew, and puddings such as banana pancake with butterscotch sauce and toffee ice-cream and whisky chocolate pot with praline. *Benchmark main dish: chicken breast with flat mushroom topped with leek and blue cheese, potato rösti and red wine jus £15.00. Two-course evening meal £24.00.*

Free house ~ Licensees Steve and Cherrie Chadwick ~ Real ale ~ Open 12-2.30, 6-11; 12-3, 6-11 Sat; 12-3, 6-10.30 Sun; closed Mon lunchtime ~ Bar food 12-2, 7-9; not Sun evening or Mon ~ Restaurant ~ Children welcome ~ Dogs allowed in bar ~ Wi-fi *Recommended by Liz and Martin Eldon, Greta and Gavin Craddock, Chloe and Tim Hodge, Amy and Luke Buchanan, Martine and Fabio Lockley*

PENNAL
Riverside

SH6900   Map 6

(01654) 791285 – www.riversidehotel-pennal.co.uk
A493; opposite church; SY20 9DW

Carefully refurbished pub with tasty food and local beers, and efficient young staff; bedrooms

The pleasing food is at the top of the agenda here, of course, but there's a thoughtful range of drinks too. The neatly furnished rooms have green and white walls, slate tiles on the floor, a woodburning stove, modern light wood dining furniture and some funky fabrics. High-backed stools are lined up along the stone-fronted counter where they serve Purple Moose Glaslyn, Salopian Golden Thread and Wye Valley Butty Bach on handpump, 30 malt whiskies, 45 gins, 12 wines by the glass and farm cider. There are seats and tables in the garden. As the pub is just inside the southern boundary of Snowdonia National Park, there are plenty of fine surrounding walks. They also run a Georgian guesthouse with five bedrooms in the pretty village. Disabled access to restaurant (no disabled loos).

Enjoyable food includes lunchtime baguettes, sharing platters, smoked salmon with spiced avocado purée, sweet potato ribbon with hazelnut and apple salad and honey dressing, mushroom, hazelnut and brie wellington with red cabbage and sautéed potatoes, steak burger with toppings, chilli relish and skinny fries, spiced mediterranean fish stew with king prawns and chorizo, chicken breast with spring green vegetable risotto and basil dressing, teriyaki salmon on noodle salad, and puddings. *Benchmark main dish: leg of lamb steak with braised red cabbage, dauphinoise potatoes and red wine jus £21.00. Two-course evening meal £21.00.*

Free house ~ Licensees Glyn and Corina Davies ~ Real ale ~ Open 12-3, 6-11.30; 12-11.30 Sat, Sun; closed Mon and Tues Nov-Mar, two weeks mid Jan ~ Bar food 12-2 (2.30 Sun), 6-9; no food Mon except school holidays ~ Restaurant ~ Children welcome ~ Dogs allowed in bar and bedrooms ~ Wi-fi ~ Bedrooms: /$80 *Recommended by Mike and Mary Carter, Shalaine Duffy, Mary and Douglas Kirkwood, Sally and Colin Allen, Catherine and Daniel King, Diana and Bertie Farr*

PONTYPRIDD
Bunch of Grapes

ST0790   Map 6

(01443) 402934 – www.bunchofgrapes.org.uk
Off A4054; Ynysangharad Road; CF37 4DA

Unpretentious, bustling gastropub with first class inventive food and fine drinks choice

Our readers are quick to heap praise on this very well run 18th-c pub: it's a first class all-rounder. A fantastic range of drinks, served by knowledgeable, friendly staff, includes Bristol Beer Factory Pale Blue Dot, Grey Trees Diggers Gold, North Riding Mocha Porter, Oakham Citra on handpump, five local craft keg beers, local ciders and perries, nine wines by the glass and up to 20 small batch gins. The cosy bar has an informal, relaxed atmosphere, comfortable leather sofas, wooden chairs and tables, a roaring log fire, newspapers to read and background music. There's also a restaurant with elegant high-backed wooden dining chairs around a mix of tables and black and white local photo-prints taken by the landlord (an ex-professional photographer). A suntrap decked area has seats and tables. Disabled access.

Excellent food using the best local, seasonal produce includes lunchtime sandwiches, cockles with leeks, laverbread and pancetta on fried bread with charred lemon, devilled lamb kidneys and shredded heart on toast, beetroot risotto with goats cheese, thyme and roasted garlic mousse and roasted beetroot, steak and mushroom in ale pie, boiled ham with poached free-range eggs, sea trout fillet with crushed potatoes, chilli, crayfish and kale broth, slow-cooked pork belly with black pudding potato cake and red wine and mustard jus, and puddings such as milk chocolate cheesecake with cocoa syrup and strawberry sorbet and vanilla pannacotta with plums and figs marinated in mulled wine with cinnamon ice-cream. *Benchmark main dish: slow-braised ox cheek with potato and celeriac terrine, oyster fritter and cavolo nero £15.50. Two-course evening meal £22.00.*

Free house ~ Licensee Nick Otley ~ Real ale ~ Open 11am-11.30pm; 11.45am-11pm Sun ~ Bar food 12-3, 6-9; 12-9 Fri, Sat; 12-3.30 Sun ~ Restaurant ~ Children welcome ~ Dogs allowed in bar ~ Wi-fi *Recommended by Kerry and Guy Trooper, Philip J Alderton, Peter and Alison Steadman, Alison and Michael Harper, Alfie Bayliss, Harvey Brown*

PUMSAINT
Dolaucothi Arms 🛏
SN6540 Map 6

(01558) 650237 – www.thedolaucothiarms.co.uk
A482 Lampeter–Llandovery; SA19 8UW

Enjoyable inn with simply furnished bar and dining room, local beers and riverside garden; bedrooms

Part of the Dolaucothi Estate and owned by the National Trust, this is a former drovers' inn dating back to the 16th c. The chatty bar has three comfortable armchairs and a sofa, red and black floor tiles and a welcoming woodburning stove. There are stone and glass bottles on the mantelpiece, local artwork on the walls and books of local and historic interest; darts in both bars and a children's corner with colouring books and board games; background music. Evan Evans Cwrw and Warrior and Gower Gold on handpump, several wines by the glass, local farm cider and a range of malt whiskies and gins. The terracotta-painted dining room has another woodburning stove, traditional local furniture to include nice dining room chairs and tables on flagstones, and walls that are hung with local maps and old photos of the pub, the village and the Estate. Picnic-sets in a neat garden overlook the Cothi River where the pub has four miles of fishing rights. This is a warm and cosy place to stay, with simply furnished bedrooms (one is dog-friendly) complete with a half decanter of port and shortcake biscuits.

Using garden herbs and local produce, the reliably tasty food includes sandwiches, chicken liver and Cointreau pâté, bruschetta with a choice of toppings, pizzas, field mushroom, nut and goats cheese burger with coleslaw and chips, pasta with toppings such as meat ragoût or king prawns in spicy tomato sauce, moussaka, ham, eggs and chips, salmon fillet with prawn thermidor sauce, slow-braised beef with chorizo, tomatoes and olives in red wine sauce, and puddings such as stuffed amaretto peaches and whisky and marmalade bread and butter pudding. *Benchmark main dish: huevos rancheros £8.95. Two-course evening meal £19.00.*

Free house ~ Licensees Karen Charles and Clare Perry ~ Real ale ~ Open 12-11; 12-8 Sun; 4-11 Tues in winter; closed Mon ~ Bar food 12-3, 6-9 ~ Restaurant ~ Children welcome ~ Dogs allowed in bar ~ Wi-fi ~ Bedrooms: /$80 *Recommended by Christine and Tony Garrett, Sara Fulton, Roger Baker, Buster and Helena Hastings, Ted and Mary Bates, Nick and Willow Brown, Alister and Margery Bacon, Sam Cole*

RAGLAN
SO3609 Map 6
Clytha Arms 🌟 ♈ 🍺 🛏

(01873) 840206 – www.clytha-arms.com

Clytha, off Abergavenny road – former A40, now declassified; 3 miles W of Raglan; NP7 9BW

Fine setting in spacious grounds, a relaxing spot for enjoying good food and impressive range of drinks; comfortable bedrooms

This fine old country inn stands in its own extensive and well cared-for grounds on the edge of Clytha Park – a mass of colour in spring; long heated verandahs and diamond-paned windows take in the garden views. Inside, there's a chatty, easy-going atmosphere and a wide array of customers, and the bar and lounge are comfortable, light and airy, with a good mix of nice old furniture, pine settles, window seats with big cushions, scrubbed wooden floors and open log fires; the contemporary restaurant is linen-set. A notable array of drinks includes Felinfoel Double Dragon Export, Harbwr Tenby North Star, Untapped Monnow and Whoosh (from a little brewery just down the road) and Uley Bitter on handpump, an extensive wine list with 13 by the glass, 20 malt whiskies and various continental beers; they hold a cider and beer festival over the late May Bank Holiday weekend. You will also find darts, bar skittles, boules, board games and a large-screen TV for rugby matches. Bedrooms are comfortable and the welsh breakfasts good. Dogs are welcome and the pub has its own labrador and collie. The riverside path by the Usk is just a short stroll away.

Reliably high quality food includes a choice of tapas such as catalan tomato bread with anchovies, cockles and laverbread, and meatballs with chorizo and peppers, plus beetroot and gin-cured salmon with seaweed salad and potato cake, caribbean fruit curry, pork and wild mushroom faggots with black pudding mash, a pie of the day, pomegranate-glazed beef short ribs with celeriac and mustard mash, chicken with sweetcorn fritters and avocado salad, wild boar and duck cassoulet, a fresh fish dish of the day, and puddings such as lemon, lime and earl grey cheesecake and treacle pudding and custard. *Benchmark main dish: rabbit in cider with bacon dumpling £17.50. Two-course evening meal £24.00.*

Free house ~ Licensees Andrew and Beverley Canning ~ Real ale ~ Open 12-3, 6-11; 12-11 Fri, Sat; 12-9 Sun; closed Mon lunchtime ~ Bar food 12.30-2.15, 7-9.30; 12.30-3.30 Sun ~ Restaurant ~ Children welcome ~ Dogs allowed in bar and bedrooms ~ Wi-fi ~ Bedrooms: £70/£90 *Recommended by Ian Herdman, Katherine Matthews, John and Hilary Murphy, Maria and Stephen Braeburn, Andrew and Nicky Churcher, David and Charlotte Emslie*

ST GEORGE
SH9775 Map 6
Kinmel Arms 🌟 🛏

(01745) 832207 – www.thekinmelarms.co.uk

Off A547 or B5381 SE of Abergele; LL22 9BP

Bustling inn with a good choice of drinks, popular food and lovely position; bedrooms

There's a great deal to see and do around this 17th-c sandstone inn, so it makes sense to stay in one of the comfortable, contemporary suites here, each with their own decked area. The bar has sofas on either side of a woodburning stove, a mix of traditional chairs and tables on the wooden floor and seats against the counter where they keep Brains Rev James, St Austell Tribute and Weetwood Cheshire Cat on handpump, 18 wines by the glass, 23 malt whiskies and farm cider. The restaurant, with rattan chairs around marble-topped tables, has big house plants and evening candles and twinkling lights; background music. The new owners have kept the tea room with its silver teapots and pretty bone-china cups, and afternoon teas are still served (1-6pm Monday-Saturday) but must be booked in advance. There are plenty of picnic-sets for warm weather and the surrounding countryside is stunning, with good walks right from the front door. Disabled access.

Interesting food includes sandwiches, pork belly with apple purée, pickled apple, tenderstem broccoli, crackling and jus, mushroom parfait with shiitake jelly and tarragon butter, creamy butternut squash risotto, mussels in thai curry sauce, corn-fed chicken three-ways with french-style peas, rolled oats and chicken cream, plaice with shrimp and caper butter and caviar beurre blanc, local rib-eye steak with a choice of sauce, and puddings such as salted cumin chocolate tart with yoghurt ice-cream and lemon soufflé with Hobnob crumble and raspberry sorbet. *Benchmark main dish: pie of the day £12.00. Two-course evening meal £19.00.*

Free house ~ Licensee Adam Williams ~ Real ale ~ Open 11am-11.30 pm ~ Bar food 12-9.30; 12-8 Sun ~ Restaurant ~ Children welcome ~ Dogs allowed in bar ~ Wi-fi ~ Live music Fri, Sat evenings ~ Bedrooms: /£135 *Recommended by Julie and Andrew Blanchett, John and Delia Franks, Neil Griffin*

STACKPOLE

Stackpole Inn 🌟 ⊨

SR9896 Map 6

(01646) 672324 – www.stackpoleinn.co.uk
Village signed off B4319 S of Pembroke; SA71 5DF

Busy pub, a good base for the area, with enjoyable food and friendly service; comfortable bedrooms

You can walk along the Pembrokeshire Coast Path or on two stunning nearby beaches and then come here for lunch. It's a well run and friendly place and although there's an area around the bar with pine tables and chairs, most of the L-shaped pub, on four different levels, is given over to diners, with neat light oak furnishings, ash beams and low ceilings to match; background music and board games. Brains Rev James, Felinfoel Double Dragon and guests such as Brains Ale Wyn and Harbwr Tenby MV Enterprise on handpump, 16 wines by the glass, 15 malt whiskies and two farm ciders. Attractive gardens feature colourful flower beds and mature trees and there are plenty of picnic-sets at the front. The four bedrooms are spotless and very comfortable and breakfasts are very good.

As well as daily fresh fish dishes (with a choice of sauce and double-cooked chips), the rewarding food includes sandwiches, smoked salmon with beetroot purée and pickled fennel, confit duck rillettes with hoisin sauce, five-bean chilli with steamed rice, sour cream and japalenos, cawl (traditional lamb broth with potato, swede and carrots), chicken, roasted onion and mushroom tagliatelle in creamy madeira sauce, lamb loin with minted peas, tzatziki, pearl couscous, butternut squash and lamb shoulder croquettes, and puddings such as chai pannacotta with spiced dates and pink peppercorn shortbread and sticky toffee pudding with toffee sauce and vanilla ice-cream. *Benchmark main dish: dry-aged local steaks £23.00. Two-course evening meal £21.00.*

Free house ~ Licensees Gary and Becky Evans ~ Real ale ~ Open 12-11; 12-3, 6-11; 12-4 Sun in winter ~ Bar food 12-9; 12-2.30, 6-9 Sun; 12-2.15, 6.30-9 and 12-2.30 Sun in winter ~ Restaurant ~ Children welcome ~ Dogs allowed in bar ~ Wi-fi ~ Bedrooms: /£120
Recommended by Alexander and Trish Gendall, Stephen Funnell, Guy Vowles, Ian Wilson, Ralph Darell-Seal, Edward May, Phoebe Peacock

USK
SO3700 Map 6

Nags Head ♀

(01291) 672820 – www.nagsheadusk.co.uk
The Square; NP15 1BH

Traditional in style with a hearty welcome and good food and drinks

A reliable favourite with many of our readers, this is a handsome old coaching inn owned and run for more than half a century by the genuinely welcoming Key family. The traditional main bar is cosy and friendly with well polished tables and chairs packed under its beams (some of these have farming tools, lanterns or horsebrasses and harness attached), as well as leatherette wall benches, and various sets of sporting prints and local pictures; look out for the original deeds to the pub. Tucked away at the front is an intimate little corner, while on the other side of the room a passageway leads to a dining area. Brains Rev James and SA and Sharps Doom Bar on handpump and a dozen wines by the glass. There are seats outside at the front under fantastic hanging baskets overlooking the town square. Disabled access. The church is well worth a look. The pub has no parking, and nearby street parking can be limited.

Honest food using local meat and seasonal game includes sandwiches, prawn cocktail, country pâté with toast, lentil and vegetable cottage pie, rare-breed local sausages with mash and onion gravy, steak pie, crispy half duck in orange and Cointreau sauce, local pheasant (available November to February) with port wine sauce, half a chicken with mushrooms, tomatoes and onions in red wine sauce, sirloin steak with peppercorn sauce, and puddings such as treacle and walnut tart and sticky toffee pudding with toffee sauce. *Benchmark main dish: rabbit pie £10.75. Two-course evening meal £18.00.*

Free house ~ Licensee Key family ~ Real ale ~ Open 10-3, 5-11 ~ Bar food 11.30-2, 5.30-9 ~ Restaurant ~ Children welcome ~ Dogs welcome ~ Wi-fi *Recommended by Diana and Bertie Farr, Louise and Simon Peters, Amanda Shipley, Alison and Graeme Spicer, Frank Price, Sarah Roberts, Rosie and John Moore*

Also Worth a Visit in Wales

Besides the fully inspected pubs, you might like to try these pubs that have been recommended to us and described by readers. Do tell us what you think of them: feedback@goodguides.com

ANGLESEY

ABERFFRAW
SH3568
Crown (01407) 840222
Bodorgan Square; LL63 5BX Village-square pub with two well kept changing ales, over 40 gins and enjoyable home-made food including daily specials, quick friendly service; sports TV; well behaved children and dogs welcome, suntrap beer garden behind with sturdy furniture and views towards the dunes, open all day, food all day Sat, till 6pm Sun (winter hours may vary). *(Brian and Anna Marsden)*

MENAI BRIDGE
SH5773
Gazelle (01248) 713364
Glyngarth; A545, halfway towards Beaumaris; LL59 5PD Hotel and restaurant rather than pub in outstanding waterside position looking across to Snowdonia; main bar with smaller rooms off, up to three Robinsons ales kept

well and good choice of wines and gins, enjoyable pubby food from sandwiches and baked potatoes up; children and dogs (in bar) welcome, steep garden behind (and walk down from car park), eight bedrooms and separate annexe, slipway and mooring for visiting boats, open all day weekends. *(Chantelle and Tony Redman)*

MENAI BRIDGE   SH5572
Liverpool Arms (01248) 712453
St Georges Road/Water Street; LL59 5EY
Refurbished pub close to the quay and not far from the famous suspension bridge; three real ales such as Facers and Purple Moose, enjoyable home-made food including daily specials and Mon steak night, quick friendly service; quiz Weds and Sun; children welcome, part-covered terrace, open (and food) all day Fri-Sun. *(Chantelle and Tony Redman)*

MOELFRE   SH5186
Kinmel Arms (01248) 410231
Moelfre Bay; LL72 8LL Popular sea-view pub with nautical-theme interior, four Robinsons ales and generous helpings of enjoyable traditional food from sandwiches up, friendly service; dogs welcome, picnic-sets on paved front terrace, open all day. *(Mike Benton)*

PENTRAETH   SH5278
Panton Arms (01248) 450959
The Square; LL75 8AZ Welcoming 18th-c roadside pub with spacious cleanly presented interior; enjoyable good value food and three well kept ales such as Purple Moose; free wi-fi; children and dogs (in bar) welcome, good-sized back garden with play area, open all day in summer, food all day weekends. *(John and Louise Gittins)*

RED WHARF BAY   SH5281
Ship (01248) 852568
Village signed off A5025 N of Pentraeth; LL75 8RJ Whitewashed 18th-c pub right on Anglesey's east coast – fantastic views of miles of tidal sands; big old-fashioned rooms either side of servery, nautical bric-a-brac, long varnished wall pews, cast-iron-framed tables and open fires, three well kept ales, 50 malt whiskies and decent choice of wines, enjoyable food (may ask for a card if you run a tab); background music; children welcome in room on left, dogs in bar, limited disabled access, numerous outside tables, open all day. *(Paul Humphreys)*

RHOSCOLYN   SH2675
★ ## White Eagle (01407) 860267
Off B4545 S of Holyhead; LL65 2NJ Remote place rebuilt almost from scratch on site of an old pub; airy modern feel in neatly kept rooms, relaxed atmosphere and nice winter fire, Conwy, Weetwood and guests from smart oak counter, several wines by the glass, extensive choice of good locally sourced interesting food, friendly helpful

service, restaurant; children welcome, dogs in bar, terrific sea views from decking and garden, lane down to beach, open (and food) all day. *(Dave Snowden)*

RHOSNEIGR   SH3272
Oystercatcher (01407) 812829
A4080; LL64 5JP Modern glass-fronted Huf Haus set in dunes close to the sea, not really a pub (created as a restaurant/chefs' academy); great views from upstairs restaurant and bar with wide range of much enjoyed interesting food, well kept ales from breweries such as Conwy, Great Orme and Weetwood, decent choice of wines by the glass, ground-floor coffee/wine bar serving lighter meals till 6pm; children, walkers and dogs welcome, upper terrace with rattan sofas and colourful beach huts, full wheelchair access, open all day. *(Brian and Anna Marsden)*

CLWYD

CAERWYS   SJ1373
Piccadilly (01352) 720284
North Street; CH7 5AW Pleasantly modernised pub-restaurant under newish management; high-ceilinged bare-boards bar with raised central woodburner, dining room across corridor and spacious slate-floor restaurant behind with banquettes and light wood furniture, stairs up to further eating area, ample helpings of good fairly priced food, up to four real ales such as Big Hand and Sadlers, efficient friendly service; background and weekend live music; children welcome, partly covered side beer garden, open (and food) all day, till 9.30pm Sun. *(Diana and Bertie Farr)*

CARROG   SJ1143
Grouse (01490) 430272
B5436, signed off A5 Llangollen–Corwen; LL21 9AT Welcoming little pub with superb views over River Dee and beyond from bay window and covered terrace; well kept Lees ales and enjoyable reasonably priced food from sandwiches up, vegetarian/vegan and gluten-free diets catered for, friendly helpful staff, small bar with dining area to the side; background music; children, walkers and dogs welcome, handy for Llangollen steam railway; open (and food) all day. *(Peter Meister)*

COLWYN BAY   SH8579
Toad (01492) 532726
Promenade; LL28 4BU Steps up to seafront pub overlooking the prom and beach; enjoyable varied choice of food including fixed-price menu, good wine list and real ales such as Jennings, friendly efficient service; children welcome, tables on front terrace, open all day Sun till 8pm. *(Paul Humphreys, Neil Griffin)*

GRAIG FECHAN SJ1454
Three Pigeons (01824) 703178
Signed off B5429 S of Ruthin; LL15 2EU
Extended largely 18th-c beamed pub with
good choice of enjoyable sensibly priced
food (all day weekends) from sandwiches
and light dishes up, OAP lunch deal Weds,
four quickly changing ales, local cider and
plenty of wines by the glass, friendly service,
various nooks and corners, interesting mix
of furniture and some old signs on the walls,
great country views from restaurant; children
and dogs (in bar) welcome, big garden with
terrace and same views, good walks, two
self-catering apartments, camping, open
all day Sat, till 9.30pm Sun, closed Mon and
lunchtime Tues (all day Tues in Jan).
(Darrell Barton)

HAWARDEN SJ3266
★Glynne Arms (01244) 569988
Glynne Way; CH5 3NS Golden-stone
Georgian pub with friendly easy-going
atmosphere; interconnecting character
rooms with bare boards or parquet, a few
bright rugs, mix of furniture including dark
pubby chairs and built-in leather wall seats,
mirrors, antlers and some interesting framed
posters, three open fires, enjoyable food
from snacks to steaks using local produce
(they also own the nearby Hawarden Estate
farm shop), well kept ales such as Big Hand,
Facers, Mobberley and Sandstone, eight
wines by the glass; background music, TV,
board games; children and dogs (in bar)
welcome, picnic-sets in back courtyard, open
(and food) all day. *(Heather and Richard Jones,
Michael Butler)*

LLANARMON DYFFRYN CEIRIOG SJ1532
★Hand (01691) 600666
B4500 from Chirk; LL20 7LD Peaceful
former farmhouse at heart of Upper Ceiriog
valley set against backdrop of the Berwyn
Mountains; low-beamed bar with inglenook
log fire, sturdy tables and a mix of seating
including settles, wheelbacks and mate's
chairs on carpet, old prints on the walls,
real ales such as Stonehouse and Weetwood,
seven wines by the glass and 20 malt
whiskies, good popular food from pub classics
up, woodburner in largely stripped-stone
restaurant, quiet lounge and games room
with darts and pool; children welcome (not
in bar after 8pm), dogs in some areas, picnic-
sets on crazy-paved front terrace, more
tables in garden, not far from Pistyll Rhaeadr
(Wales's highest waterfall), well equipped
spacious bedrooms, good breakfast, open
all day. *(Ted and Mary Bates)*

LLANFERRES SJ1860
Druid (01352) 810225
A494 Mold–Ruthin; CH7 5SN Extended
17th-c whitewashed inn set in fine walking
country (Alyn Valley towards Loggerheads

Country Park, or up Offa's Dyke Path to
Moel Famau); views from broad bay window
in civilised plush lounge and from bigger
beamed back bar with two handsome
antique oak settles, pleasant mix of more
modern furnishings and quarry-tiled area
by log fire, Marstons-related ales, 30 malt
whiskies and reasonably priced traditional
food, games room with darts and pool;
background music, quiz nights, TV; children
welcome, dogs in bar (theirs is called Baz),
five bedrooms, open all day Fri-Sun.
(Naomi and Andrew Randall)

LLANFWROG SJ1158
Cross Keys (01824) 308081
B5105 just outside Ruthin; LL15 2AD
Attractively refurbished old pub run by
father and son team; sofas either side of
woodburner in stone fireplace, tartan-
upholstered chairs around wooden tables and
against counter serving Hafod ales and good
wines by the glass, wide choice of well liked
food from sandwiches and sharing boards
up, Mon pie night, restaurant upstairs with
high rafters, whitewashed walls and good
quality furniture; different terrace areas
in garden with fine country views; open all
day Thurs-Sun, closed Mon lunchtime.
(Louise and Simon Peters)

LLANGOLLEN SJ2142
Chainbridge (01978) 860215
2 miles W; LL20 8BS Refurbished 19th-c
hotel in great position overlooking River Dee
rapids, chain bridge and renovated steam
railway; bar, lounge, restaurant and good
outside spaces, decent food from sandwiches
and pubby choices up, two or three well
kept ales including Stonehouse Station
Bitter; children and dogs welcome, plenty of
bedrooms (some with river-view balconies),
good walks, open all day. *(Peter Meister)*

MINERA SJ2651
Tyn-y-Capel (01978) 269347
Church Road; LL11 3DA Ancient
coaching inn under new management, good
food including Tues curry and Thurs pizza
nights, four real ales; regular live music, Sun
quiz, sports TV; children and dogs (in bar)
welcome, lovely hill views from terrace, park
opposite with play area, open (and food) all
day, kitchen shuts 5pm Sun. *(Elizabeth and
Andrew Harvey)*

RUABON SJ3043
Bridge End (01978) 810881
Bridge Street; LL14 6DA Proper old-
fashioned pub serving own McGivern ales
(brewed here) alongside several guests
and ciders, friendly staff and cheerful local
atmosphere, some snacky food, black beams,
open fires; Tues quiz, regular summer live
music, beer festival Aug; children and dogs
welcome, seats in garden, open all day
weekends, from 5pm weekdays (4pm Fri).
(Nicholas and Lucy Sage)

DYFED

ABERAERON   SN4562
Cadwgan (01545) 570149
Market Street; SA46 0AU Small brightly
painted late 18th-c pub opposite the harbour;
fairly basic with friendly regulars, well kept
Hancocks HB and a couple of local guests,
some nautical memorabilia and interesting
old photographs, open fire, no food; sports TV;
children and dogs welcome, pavement seats
and little garden behind, closed Sun evening,
Mon lunchtime, otherwise open all day.
(Fiona and Jack Henderson)

ABERAERON   SN4562
★ Harbourmaster (01545) 570755
Quay Parade; SA46 0BA Charming
small hotel in prime spot by yacht-filled
harbour; cheerful bar with brown leather
wall banquettes and assortment of tables and
chairs on bare boards, a stuffed albatross
(reputed to have collided with a ship
belonging to owner's great-grandfather),
stools by zinc-topped counter serving ales
such as Mantle and Purple Moose, local
cider and 17 good wines by the glass, dining
room has blue leather chairs, sea-blue walls
and seaside-inspired art, much enjoyed food
including local fish/seafood, friendly efficient
staff; children welcome, disabled access,
comfortable bedrooms (most overlook the
harbour), good breakfast, open all day
from 8am. *(Anna and Mark Evans, Mike and
Mary Carter, Mr and Mrs P R Thomas, Harry and
Megan Evans, Jan and Sally Jones)*

ABERCYCH   SN2539
★ Nags Head (01239) 841200
Off B4332 Cenarth–Boncath; SA37 0HJ
Friendly tucked-away riverside pub with
dimly lit beamed bar; woodburner in big
fireplace, stripped-wood tables on flagstones,
clocks showing time around the world and
hundreds of beer bottles on shelves, ales
from local microbreweries and enjoyable
pubby food including daily specials,
various other connecting rooms, one with
a suspended coracle; background music,
darts; children and dogs welcome, benches
(some under cover) in garden overlooking
river (pub has fishing rights), play area with
wooden castle, three comfortable bedrooms,
closed lunchtimes Mon and Tues.
(Michael Cecil)

ABERGORLECH   SN5833
Black Lion (01558) 685271
B4310; SA32 7SN Friendly well looked-
after 16th-c pub in fine rural position;
traditional stripped-stone and beamed
bar, pubby furniture on old flagstones,
woodburner, a couple of local ales and good
home-made food including daily specials,
dining extension/coffee shop with farmhouse
kitchen chairs around mix of tables on
bare boards, local paintings and another

woodburner; background music, free wi-fi;
children and dogs (in bar) welcome, lovely
views of Cothi Valley from riverside garden,
closed Mon, otherwise open all day. *(Elizabeth
and Peter May)*

ABERYSTWYTH   SN6777
Halfway Inn (01970) 880631
*Pisgah – A4120 right out towards Devils
Bridge; SY23 4NE* Panoramic views from
this recently refurbished roadside country
pub; beams and stripped stone, scrubbed
tables, settles and wheelback chairs on
flagstones, open fire and woodburner,
a couple of well kept Montys beers and
enjoyable good value home-cooked food from
fixed-price menu, friendly helpful service;
games part with pool, darts and sports TV;
children welcome (inside play area), dogs in
bar, picnic-sets outside taking in the view,
closed Mon, otherwise open (and food) all
day. *(Graham Swift)*

ANGLE   SM8603
Hibernia (01646) 641517
B4320; SA71 5AT Welcoming village pub
with good reasonably priced home-made food
and well kept changing ales, traditional bar
with coal fire, more modern dining room;
some live music, sports TV, pool; children and
dogs welcome, one bedroom, open all day in
high summer, otherwise closed lunchtimes
Mon-Thurs. *(Ted and Mary Bates)*

BORTH   SN6089
Victoria (01970) 871417
High Street; SY24 5HZ Stone-built pub
backing on to the beach; popular reasonably
priced food and well kept ales such as Sharps
and Wye Valley, good friendly service, more
space upstairs and sea-view balcony; sports
TV; children and dogs (in bar) welcome,
tables on back deck with steps leading
down to the shingle, open all day. *(Sally and
David Champion)*

BOSHERSTON   SR9694
St Govans Country Inn
(01646) 661311   *Off B4319 S of
Pembroke; SA71 5DN* Busy pub with
big modernised open-plan bar, cheery and
simple, with several changing ales and
well priced pubby food, good climbing
photographs and murals of local beauty spots,
log fire in large stone fireplace; background
music, TV, games machine and pool (winter
only); children and dogs welcome, picnic-
sets on small front terrace, four good value
bedrooms (residents' parking), beach and
cliff walks, well placed for water-lily lakes,
open all day in season (all day weekends at
other times). *(Louise and Simon Peters)*

BRECHFA   SN5230
Forest Arms (01267) 202288
Opposite church (B4310); SA32 7RA
Renovated stone-built village inn; well kept
Rhymney General Picton and a summer

guest, enjoyable reasonably priced food including daily specials and good vegetarian/ vegan options, friendly helpful staff, two beamed bars, one with big inglenook and angling theme (pub can arrange fishing on River Cothi), the other in two sections, note Bob the stuffed raven, also dining/ function room with pitched ceiling, chairs from St David's cathedral and another log fire; children and dogs welcome, picnic-sets in back garden, good walks and mountain bike trails, three comfortable bedrooms and self-catering holiday cottage, open all day weekends, closed Mon. *(Jasper)*

BROAD HAVEN   SM8614

★**Druidstone Hotel** (01437) 781221

N on coast road, bear left for about 1.5 miles then follow sign left to Druidstone Haven; SA62 3NE Cheerfully informal country house hotel in grand spot above the sea, individual, relaxed and with terrific views; inventive cooking using fresh local ingredients (best to book), helpful efficient service, cellar bar with a welsh ale tapped from the cask, country wines and other drinks, ceilidhs and folk events, friendly pub dogs (others welcome); attractive high-walled garden, all sorts of sporting activities from boules to sand-yachting, spacious homely bedrooms and five self-catering cottages. *(Bernard Stradling)*

CAIO   SN6739

Brunant Arms (01558) 650483

Off A482 Llanwrda–Lampeter; SA19 8RD Comfortable unpretentious village pub; beams, old settles, china on delft shelving and nice log fire, a couple of ales such as Evan Evans, enjoyable home-made food from regularly changing menu, friendly helpful staff, stripped-stone public bar with games including pool; some live music, sports TV; children and dogs welcome, small Perspex-roofed verandah and lower terrace, bedrooms, handy for Dolaucothi Gold Mines (NT), closed Sun evening, Mon and Tues; new management as we went to press, so there may be changes. *(Alan and Alice Morgan)*

CAREW   SN0403

Carew Inn (01646) 651267

A4075 off A477; SA70 8SL Stone-built pub with appealing cottagey atmosphere; unpretentious small panelled public bar, nice old bentwood stools and mix of tables and chairs on bare boards, small dining area, lounge bar with low tables, warm open fires, two changing beers and enjoyable generously served food including Tues curry and Thurs steak nights, two upstairs dining rooms with leather chairs at black tables; background music, dominoes, darts; children and dogs (in bar) welcome, enclosed back garden with play equipment, view of imposing Carew Castle ruins and remarkable 9th-c celtic cross, self-catering accommodation, open all day. *(Vin Davies)*

CILYCWM   SN7540

Neuadd Fawr Arms (01550) 721644

By church entrance; SA20 0ST Nicely placed 18th-c drovers' inn among lanes to Llyn Brianne above River Gwenlais; eclectic mix of old furniture on huge slate flagstones, woodburners, good seasonal food including interesting specials in bar or smaller dining room (also afternoon and high tea Mar-Sept, must book), one or two changing local ales, friendly helpful service and chatty locals; children and dogs welcome, open all day Sun, closed Mon-Thurs lunchtimes. *(Geoff and Ann Marston)*

COSHESTON   SN0003

Brewery Inn (01646) 686678

Signed E from village crossroads; SA72 4UD Welcoming 17th-c village pub with attractively furnished flagstoned bar; good choice of enjoyable food including vegetarian options, a locally brewed house beer and a guest, good range of gins, helpful friendly service; Weds quiz and some live music; children and dogs welcome, open all day weekends, closed Mon lunchtime. *(Stephen Funnell)*

CRESSWELL QUAY   SN0506

★**Cresselly Arms** (01646) 651210

Village signed from A4075; SA68 0TE Simple unchanging alehouse overlooking tidal creek; plenty of local customers in two old-fashioned linked rooms, built-in wall benches, kitchen chairs and plain tables on red and black tiles, open fire in one room, Aga in the other with lots of china hanging from high beam-and-plank ceiling, third more conventionally furnished red-carpeted room, a house beer from Caffle along with Hancocks, Sharps and a rotating guest; no children or dogs, seats outside making most of the view, you can arrive by boat if tide is right, open all day in summer. *(Jasper)*

CWM GWAUN   SN0333

★**Dyffryn Arms**

Cwm Gwaun and Pontfaen signed off B4313 E of Fishguard; SA65 9SE Classic rural time warp known locally as Bessie's after the much loved veteran landlady (her farming family have run it since 1840 and she's been in charge for well over a third of that time); reopened after fire in 2019 but no updated information as we went to press; well kept Bass served by jug through hatch, low prices, lovely outside view and walks in nearby Preseli Hills, open more or less all day (may close if no customers); news please. *(Giles and Annie Francis)*

DINAS   SN0139

Old Sailors (01348) 811491

Pwllgwaelod; from A487 in Dinas Cross follow Bryn-henllan signpost; SA42 0SE Shack-like building in superb position, snugged down into the sand by isolated cove below Dinas Head; good local fish/seafood (often crab and lobster), also snacks, coffee and summer cream teas, Brains Barry Island IPA, Gwynt Y Ddraig cider and decent wine, maritime bric-a-brac; children welcome, no dogs inside, picnic-sets on grass overlooking beach with views across to Fishguard, bracing walks, open all day Weds-Sat, closed Mon (except bank holidays) and evenings Tues and Sun. *(Alan and Alice Morgan)*

FISHGUARD   SM9537
Fishguard Arms (01348) 872763
Main Street (A487); SA65 9HJ Tiny bay-windowed terrace pub with friendly community atmosphere, front bar with unusually high counter serving well kept/priced Bass direct from the cask, back snug with woodburner, traditional games and sports TV, no food; smokers' area out behind. *(Giles and Annie Francis)*

FISHGUARD   SM9537
Royal Oak (01348) 218632
Market Square, Upper Town; SA65 9HA Welcoming village pub with stripped beams, exposed stonework and slate flagstones, plaque commemorating defeat of bizarre french raid in 1797 (peace treaty was signed in the pub), well kept changing ales and farm cider from carved servery, good choice of popular fairly priced pubby food, friendly efficient service, large picture-window dining extension; folk night Tues; children and dogs welcome, pleasant terrace with view down to Lower Town bay, open all day. *(Darrell Barton)*

FISHGUARD   SM9637
Ship (01348) 874033
Newport Road, Lower Town; SA65 9ND Traditional 18th-c terrace-row pub near the old harbour; dark interior with beams and coal fire, lots of boat pictures, model ships and other memorabilia, well kept Bass, Felinfoel and Hancocks, no food; some live music; children and dogs welcome, front door directly on to the road (careful as you leave), open all day weekends, closed Mon, Tue and lunchtimes Weds-Fri. *(Giles and Annie Francis)*

JAMESTON   SS0699
Tudor Lodge (01834) 871212
A4139, E of Jameston; SA70 7SS Friendly refurbished inn close to the coast; two bars with open fire and woodburner, a couple of well kept ales such as Sharps Doom Bar and several wines by the glass, decent choice of enjoyable food including early bird deal (4-6pm), Tues curry and Thurs steak night, airy dining room with painted beams and high-backed chairs; children welcome, play area and plenty of picnic-sets in large garden, five stylish comfortable bedrooms, open (and food) all day weekends, from 4pm weekdays. *(Jasper)*

LAMPETER   SN5748
Black Lion (01570) 422172
High Street; SA48 7BG Newly reopened/refurbished coaching inn, friendly and relaxed, with enjoyable pub food at reasonable prices, well kept local beers and decent wines by the glass; children welcome, comfortable bedrooms, good breakfast. *(Vin Davies)*

LITTLE HAVEN   SM8512
St Brides Inn (01437) 781266
St Brides Road; SA62 3UN A mere 20 metres from Pembrokeshire Coast Path; neat stripped-stone bar and linked carpeted dining area, traditional furnishings, log fire, interesting well in back corner grotto thought to be partly Roman, Banks's, Marstons and a guest, enjoyable bar food including fresh fish and other local produce, nice staff; background music and TV; children welcome, no dogs inside, seats in sheltered suntrap terrace garden across road, two bedrooms, open all day in summer. *(Simon Rowntree, Bernard Stradling)*

LLANDDAROG   SN5016
★ Butchers Arms (01267) 275330
On back road by church; SA32 8NS Ancient black-beamed local with three intimate eating areas off small central bar, popular food, Felinfoel ales tapped from the cask and nice wines by the glass, conventional pub furniture, gleaming brassware and open woodburner in biggish fireplace; background music; children welcome, tables outside and pretty window boxes, two-bedroom cottage in converted stables, closed Sun, Mon. *(Vin Davies)*

LLANDDAROG   SN5016
White Hart (01267) 275395
Aka Yr Hydd Gwyn; off A48 E of Carmarthen, via B4310; SA32 8NT Ancient thatched pub brewing beers using water from 90-metre borehole, also own ciders and spirits; comfortable lived-in beamed rooms with lots of engaging bric-a-brac and antiques including 17th-c carved settles by huge log fire, interestingly furnished high-raftered dining room with open kitchen, generous if not cheap food, also home-made jams and chutneys for sale; background music; children welcome, no dogs inside, disabled access (ramps provided), picnic-sets on front terrace and in back garden with play area, closed Weds. *(Gareth O'Donovan)*

LLANDEILO   SN6226
Angel (01558) 822765
Rhosmaen Street; SA19 6EN Town-centre local painted a distinctive pale blue; comfortably furnished front bar with ales such as Evan Evans from central counter, step up to popular back restaurant serving very good food at reasonable prices including

daily specials, friendly helpful staff; children welcome, walled beer garden behind, accommodation in refurbished cottage, closed Sun. *(Alan and Alice Morgan)*

LLANDOVERY   SN7634
Castle (01550) 720343
Kings Road; SA20 0AP Popular and welcoming hotel next to castle ruins; good attractively presented food from sandwiches to charcoal grills and daily fresh fish, afternoon teas, courteous efficient service, well kept ales; children and dogs welcome, picnic-sets out in front under parasols, 15 comfortable bedrooms, open all day (till 6pm Sun). *(Darrell Barton)*

LLANDOVERY   SN7634
Kings Head (01550) 720393
Market Square; SA20 0AB Early 18th-c beamed coaching inn; bar with patterned carpet, exposed stonework and large woodburner, three well kept ales including Gower Gold, enjoyable food from snacks and bar meals up, friendly service; children and dogs welcome, nine bedrooms (one on ground floor for disabled guests), open all day. *(Ted and Mary Bates)*

**LLANFIHANGEL-
Y-CREUDDYN**   SN6676
★ **Y Ffarmers** 07890 581568
Village signed off A4120 W of Pisgah; SY23 4LA Popular and welcoming community pub renovated after 2018 fire; highly regarded food (not Sun evening) from pub favourites to more restaurranty dishes, two changing ales, a craft beer, real cider and interesting selection of gins (several from welsh distillers), good friendly service; children and dogs (in bar) welcome, back terrace with steps up to lawn, interesting 13th-c village church opposite, closed Mon and lunchtime Tues. *(Office, B and M Kendall)*

LLANGRANNOG   SN3154
Pentre Arms (01239) 654345
On the front; SA44 6SP Friendly old seafront pub beautifully placed in this pretty coastal village – magnificent sunset sea views from bar's picture window; three well kept ales such as Gales Seafarers and St Austell Tribute, fairly standard food including good steaks and often fresh fish, separate restaurant, pool room with TV and games machines; regular live music; children and dogs (in bar) welcome, seven bedrooms (some directly overlooking the small bay), staff will advise on dolphin-watching, handy for coast path, open all day. *(Alan and Alice Morgan)*

LLANGRANNOG   SN3154
Ship (01239) 654510
Near the front, by pay & display car park entrance; SA44 6SL Just back from the bay with tables out by beachside car park (have to pay); enjoyable food including local

fish/seafood, friendly helpful staff, well kept ales and good selection of gins, bare-boards bar with big woodburner, further spacious upstairs eating area, games room; open mike evenings and other live music; children and dogs welcome, open all day and can get very busy in summer. *(Geoff and Ann Marston)*

LLANSTADWELL   SM9404
Ferry House (01646) 600270
Hazelbeach, Church Road; SA73 1EG Neatly kept, traditionally furnished inn by the Cleddau waterway with great views; good food including local fish, Sharps Doom Bar and a guest, timber-framed dining conservatory making most of the view; children and dogs welcome, picnic-sets on waterside terrace, summer pontoon for visiting boats, six comfortable bedrooms, closed Sun evening. *(Dave Braisted)*

MATHRY   SM8831
Farmers Arms (01348) 831284
Brynamlwg, off A487 Fishguard– St David's; SA62 5HB Popular pub with traditional beamed bar; well kept ales, several gins and ample helpings of enjoyable good value pubby food (all day Sat), friendly staff and locals, large vine-covered dining conservatory; background music, TV, games machine and pool; children welcome, dogs in bar, nearby campsite, open all day. *(Alan and Alice Morgan)*

NEWCHAPEL   SN2239
Ffynnone Arms (01239) 841800
B4332; SA37 0EH Welcoming 18th-c beamed pub with enjoyable traditional food including popular Sun carvery, special diets catered for and some produce home-grown, a couple of changing ales, local cider and afternoon teas in season, two woodburners; darts, pool and table skittles; disabled facilities, picnic-sets in small garden, open all day weekends (from 1pm Sat), closed till 5pm weekdays, no food Mon, Tues. *(Mike Benton)*

NEWPORT   SN0539
Castle (01239) 820742
Bridge Street; SA42 0TB Welcoming old pub with divided bar – one part panelled with open fire, the other with pool, darts, juke box and projector for major sports; wide choice of enjoyable home-made food from lunchtime sandwiches and baguettes up, ales such as Wye Valley, pleasant service, restaurant; some live music; children and dogs welcome, three-bedrooms (one has four-poster), handy for Parrog estuary walk (good for bird-watchers), open all day. *(Darrell Barton)*

NEWPORT   SN0539
Royal Oak (01239) 820632
West Street (A487); SA42 0TA Sizeable 18th-c pub with good traditional food plus lots of authentic curries (takeaway service available, also for fish and chips), well kept Felinfoel and a guest, friendly helpful staff,

lounge with eating areas, separate stone and slate bar with pool, upstairs dining room; children welcome, no dogs, some tables outside, easy walk to beach and coast path, open (and food) all day. *(Heulwen and Neville Pinfield)*

PEMBROKE DOCK SM9603
Shipwright (01646) 682090
Front Street; SA72 6JX Little blue-painted end-of-terrace pub on waterfront overlooking estuary; enjoyable home-made food and a couple of well kept ales, friendly efficient staff, bare-boards interior with nautical and other memorabilia, some booth seating; children welcome, five minutes from Ireland ferry terminal. *(Vin Davies)*

PENRHIWLLAN SN3641
Daffodil (01559) 370343
A475 Newcastle Emlyn–Lampeter; SA44 5NG Contemporary open-plan dining pub with comfortable welcoming bar; sofas and leather tub chairs on pale limestone floor, woodburner, Greene King Abbot, Hancocks HB and maybe a guest from granite-panelled counter, two lower-ceilinged end rooms with big oriental rugs, steps down to a couple of airy dining rooms, open kitchen serving particularly good food (fish dishes and puddings a highlight); background music; children and dogs (in bar) welcome, nicely furnished decked area outside with valley views, closed Mon (except bank holidays), Tues. *(Jasper)*

PONTRHYDFENDIGAID SN7366
Black Lion (01974) 831624
Off B4343 Tregaron–Devils Bridge; SY25 6BE Relaxed country inn run well by friendly landlord; smallish main bar with dark beams and exposed stonework, old country furniture on bare boards, woodburner and big pot-irons in vast fireplace, copper, brass and so forth on mantelpiece, historical photographs, well kept Felinfoel Double Dragon and a guest, several wines by the glass and enjoyable good value home-cooked food, quarry-tiled back restaurant, small games room with pool and darts; background music; children and dogs welcome, back courtyard and tree-shaded garden, bedrooms (some in converted stables), good walking/cycling country and not far from Strata Florida Abbey, open all day Sun, from 4pm other days. *(Liz and Martin Eldon)*

PORTHGAIN SM8132
Sloop (01348) 831449
Off A487 St David's–Fishguard; SA62 5BN Busy tavern (especially holiday times) snuggled down in cove wedged tightly between headlands on Pembrokeshire Coast Path – fine walks in either direction; plank-ceilinged bar with lobster pots and fishing nets, ship clocks, lanterns and some relics from local wrecks, decent-sized eating area with simple furnishings, well liked bar food from sandwiches to good steaks and fresh fish, three real ales including Brains, separate games room; quiz last Thurs of month, summer live music; seats on heated terrace overlooking harbour, self-catering cottage in village, open all day from 9.30am for breakfast, till midnight Sat. *(Heulwen and Neville Pinfield)*

RHANDIRMWYN SN7843
Royal Oak (01550) 760201
7 miles N of Llandovery; SA20 0NY Friendly 17th-c stone-built inn set in remote peaceful walking country; comfortable traditional bar with log fire, three well kept local ales, ciders and perries, good variety of popular sensibly priced food sourced locally, big dining area; children and dogs (in bar) welcome, hill views from garden and five cottagey bedrooms, attached village shop, handy for Brecon Beacons, open all day. *(Darrell Barton)*

ST DAVID'S SM7525
Farmers Arms (01437) 721666
Goat Street; SA62 6RF Bustling old-fashioned low-ceilinged pub by cathedral gate; cheerful and unpretentiously pubby with bar on left and dining room to the right, up to four well kept ales from central servery including Felinfoel Double Dragon and a Hancocks house beer, decent food (summer only) from sandwiches to specials, friendly staff and atmosphere; TV for major sports, pool, free wi-fi; children and dogs welcome, cathedral view from large tables on large back suntrap terrace with own bar, open all day summer, closed weekday lunchtimes in winter. *(Tony Scott)*

ST DOGMAELS SN1646
Ferry (01239) 615172
B4546; SA43 3LF Old whitewashed waterside pub with spectacular views of the Teifi estuary from attractively furnished picture-window dining extension, good freshly made food, Brains ales and several wines by the glass, pleasant attentive staff, character bar with pine tables and leather sofas, interesting old photographs and local artwork; background music; children, walkers and dogs welcome, plenty of room outside on linked decked areas, own jetty/moorings and at start of Pembrokeshire Coast Path, open all day. *(Julie Swift)*

TREFIN SM8332
Ship (01348) 831445
Off A487 at Croes-Goch or via Penparc; Ffordd y Felin; SA62 5AX Well positioned traditional little pub just up from coast path; popular well priced food and a couple of interesting changing beers, friendly service, dining extension; occasional quiz and live music nights; children welcome, lovely view from back garden, open all day. *(Giles and Annie Francis)*

GLAMORGAN

BISHOPSTON   SS5789
Joiners Arms (01792) 232658
Bishopston Road, just off B4436 SW of Swansea; SA3 3EJ Thriving 19th-c stone local with own good value Swansea ales along with well kept guests, ample helpings of enjoyable freshly made pub food (not Sun evening, Mon), friendly staff, unpretentious quarry-tiled bar with massive solid-fuel stove, comfortable lounge; TV for rugby; children and dogs welcome, open all day (from 3pm Mon and Tues). *(Sandra and Miles Spencer)*

BISHOPSTON   SS5889
Plough & Harrow (01792) 234459
Off B4436 Bishopston–Swansea; SA3 3DJ Cleanly modernised and renovated old pub with L-shaped bar and restaurant; good imaginative food from chef-owner from lunchtime sandwiches to tasting menus, ales such as St Austell Tribute and plenty of wines by the glass, helpful courteous service; Sun quiz; open all day Sun (food till 4pm). *(Sandra and Miles Spencer)*

CARDIFF   ST1876
Cambrian Tap (029) 2064 4952
St Mary Street/Caroline Street; CF10 1AD City-centre corner pub popular for its good range of Brains beers plus guests, several more in bottles, friendly knowledgeable staff, nice home-made hot and cold pies; Mon open mike night, Tues comedy; dogs welcome, open all day. *(Tony and Wendy Hobden)*

CARDIFF   ST1876
City Arms (029) 2064 1913
Quay Street; CF10 1EA City-centre alehouse with Brains ales and several guests (some tapped from the cask), tasting trays available, also plenty of draught/bottled continentals and real cider, friendly knowledgeable staff, no food; some live music, darts, free wi-fi; open all day (till 2am Fri, Sat), very busy on rugby match days. *(Gaynor Meades)*

CARDIFF   ST1776
Cricketers (029) 2034 5102
Cathedral Road; CF11 9LL Victorian townhouse in quiet residential area backing on to Glamorgan CC; well kept Evan Evans ales and enjoyable freshly made food (all day Fri and Sat, until 5pm Sun); jazz supper club Thurs; children welcome, sunny back garden, open all day. *(Gaynor Meades)*

COWBRIDGE   SS9974
★ Bear (01446) 774814
High Street, with car park behind off North Street; signed off A48; CF71 7AF Busy Georgian coaching house in smart village; well kept ales, decent house wines and enjoyable food from sandwiches/wraps

up, lunchtime weekday set menu, friendly helpful service; three attractively furnished bars with flagstones, bare boards or carpet, some stripped stone and panelling, big hot open fires, barrel-vaulted cellar restaurant; children and dogs (in one bar and in some bedrooms) welcome, courtyard tables, pétanque and boules pit, disabled parking, open all day. *(Christopher Mannings)*

GWAELOD-Y-GARTH   ST1183
Gwaelod y Garth Inn
(029) 2081 0408 *Main Road; CF15 9HH* Meaning 'foot of the mountain', this stone-built village pub has wonderful valley views and is popular with walkers on the Taff Ely Ridgeway Path; highly thought-of well presented food (all day Fri and Sat, not Sun evening), friendly efficient service, own-brew beer along with Wye Valley and guests from pine-clad bar, log fires, upstairs restaurant (disabled access from back car park); some live music Fri and Sat; table skittles, pool, juke box; children and dogs welcome, three bedrooms, open all day. *(Derek Stafford)*

KENFIG   SS8081
Prince of Wales (01656) 740356
2.2 miles from M4 junction 37; A4229 towards Porthcawl, then right when dual carriageway narrows on bend, signed 'Maudlam, Kenfig'; CF33 4PR Ancient local with plenty of individuality by historic sand dunes; well kept ales including Bass, decent wines and good choice of malts, generous straightforward food served by friendly staff, chatty panelled room off main bar, log fires, stripped stone and lots of wreck pictures, restaurant and upstairs overspill room; TV for rugby; dogs welcome in bar, handy for nature reserve (June orchids), open all day, no food Sun evening. *(Christopher Mannings)*

LLANBLETHIAN   SS9873
Cross (01446) 772995
Church Road; CF71 7JF Welcoming former staging inn; enjoyable freshly made food from pubby choices up in bar or airy split-level restaurant, well kept Wye Valley and guests, good choice of wines, woodburner and open fire; children welcome, dogs in bar, tables out on decking, open till 7pm Sun, closed Mon lunchtime, otherwise open all day. *(Elizabeth and Peter May)*

LLANCARFAN   ST0570
Fox & Hounds (01446) 781287
Signed off A4226; can also be reached from A48 from Bonvilston or B4265 via Llancadle; CF62 3AD Comfortably modernised village pub in charming streamside setting by interesting church; snug bar with woodburner, local ales and nice choice of wines from stone-faced counter, good interesting food including some pub favourites and vegetarian choices, friendly accommodating staff; children and dogs (in

bar) welcome, tables on covered terrace, clean comfortable bedrooms, good breakfast, open all day (from 3pm Mon, Tues). *(Nicholas and Lucy Sage)*

LLANGENNITH
SS4291
Kings Head (01792) 386212
Clos St Cenydd, opposite church; SA3 1HX Extended 17th-c stone-built inn with wide choice of popular food (best to book) including good curries, pizzas and daily specials, local Gower beers, extensive range of gins and malt whiskies, friendly staff; pool and machines in lively public bar – back bar quieter with dining areas; children and dogs welcome, large terrace with village views, good walks, not far from great surfing beach and large campsite, bedrooms in separate buildings to the side and back, open (and food) all day, breakfast for non-residents (8.30-10.30am). *(Liz and Martin Eldon)*

MONKNASH
SS9170
★ Plough & Harrow (01656) 890209
Signposted 'Marcross, Broughton' off B4265 St Brides Major–Llantwit Major – turn left at end of Water Street; OS Sheet 170 map reference 920706; CF71 7QQ Popular historic country pub under new owners; fine range of well kept ales (some tapped from the cask), also local ciders and quite a few gins/whiskies, generous helpings of good traditional food (not Sun evening), friendly efficient service; main bar with its massively thick stone walls used to be the scriptures room and mortuary (this was once part of a monastic grange and dates back nine centuries), heavily beamed ceiling, broad flagstones and log fire in cavernous fireplace with huge bread oven, intriguing arched doorway at the back; some live music; children and dogs welcome, picnic-sets in front garden, can walk from the pub through wooded Cwm Nash valley to spectacular coastline, open all day. *(Audrey and Paul Summers)*

MUMBLES
SS6287
Pilot 07897 895511
Mumbles Road; SA3 4EL Friendly 19th-c seafront local with half a dozen well kept ales including some from own back microbrewery, slate-floored bar with boat suspended from planked ceiling, woodburning stove, no food; TV, free wi-fi; dogs welcome till 9pm, open all day. *(Julian Richardson)*

PENARTH
ST1771
Pilot (029) 2071 0615
Queens Road; CF64 1DJ End-of-terrace pub set high in residential area overlooking Cardiff Bay; good food including pub favourites from blackboard menu, well kept quickly changing ales, friendly welcoming staff; live music Fri evening, summer beer/cider festival; children and dogs allowed, tables out in narrow front area, open (and food) all day. *(Graham Swift)*

PENDERYN
SN9408
Red Lion (01685) 811914
Off A4059 at Lamb, then up Church Road (narrow hill from T junction); CF44 9JR Friendly old stone-built pub (former drovers' inn) set high in lovely walking country; dark beams, flagstones and blazing log fires, antique settles and interesting bits and pieces including some military memorabilia, good range of real ales and ciders tapped from the cask, also whiskies and other spirits from local Penderyn distillery, highly regarded imaginative food (best to book); children and dogs (in bar) welcome, great views from big garden, open all day weekends, closed Mon lunchtime. *(Diana and Bertie Farr)*

PENTYRCH
ST1081
Kings Arms (029) 2089 0202
Church Road; CF15 9QF 16th-c longhouse freshened up under new management; cosy bar with log fire in sizeable brick fireplace, Brains ales, guest beers and 14 wines by the glass, good food (not Sun evening, Mon lunchtime), cooked by chef-owner including blackboard specials, there's also a comfortable lounge and restaurant; quiz nights, sports TV; children and dogs (in bar) welcome, plenty of seats on terrace and lawn, summer barbecues, open all day (till 8pm Sun). *(Sabine and Gerald Grimshaw, Margo and Derek Peters)*

REYNOLDSTON
SS4889
King Arthur (01792) 390775
Higher Green, off A4118; SA3 1AD Cheerful pub-hotel with timbered main bar, country-style restaurant and nautically themed family dining area (games room with pool in winter); good fairly priced food from sandwiches and pub favourites up, Felinfoel and guests kept well, log fires and country house bric-a-brac, buoyant local atmosphere in the evening; background music; tables out on green, play area, bedrooms and self-catering cottage, open (and bar food) all day. *(M and GR)*

ST FAGANS
ST1277
Plymouth Arms (029) 2056 9173
Crofft-y-genau Road; CF5 6DU Stately Victorian pub, now a rambling Vintage Inn with log fires, panelling and local prints in bustling linked areas, enjoyable food including fixed-price and children's menus, well kept Sharps Doom Bar and decent wines by the glass; lots of tables on extensive back lawn, handy for National Museum of History, open (and food) all day. *(Derek Stafford)*

ST HILARY
ST0173
Bush (01446) 776888
Off A48 E of Cowbridge; CF71 7DP Cosily restored 16th-c thatched and beamed pub; flagstoned main bar with inglenook, bare-boards lounge and snug, nice mix of old

furniture, Bass, Greene King, Hancocks and guests, Weston's cider and good wines by the glass, enjoyable food including home-made pies and wellingtons, gluten-free diets catered for, friendly service, restaurant; quiz nights and other events; children and dogs (in bar) welcome, some picnic tables out at front, garden behind, open all day Fri-Sun. *(Jasper)*

SWANSEA SS6492

Brunswick (01792) 465676

Duke Street; SA1 4HS Large rambling local with traditional pubby furnishings, lots of knick-knacks and local artwork, good value popular food all day weekdays till 7.30pm (just lunchtimes weekends), half a dozen well kept ales tapped from the cask, friendly helpful service, regular live music, quiz night Mon; no dogs, open all day. *(Graham Swift)*

TAFFS WELL ST1283

Fagins (029) 2081 1800

Cardiff Road, Glan-y-Llyn; CF15 7QD Terrace-row pub with interesting range of cask-tapped ales, friendly olde-worlde atmosphere, benches, pine tables and other pubby furniture on flagstones, faux black beams, woodburner, good value straightforward food (not Sun evening, Mon, Tues-Fri lunchtimes) from lunchtime baguettes up, restaurant; live music, sports TV; children and dogs welcome, open all day (from 3pm Mon). *(Sally and David Champion)*

THREE CROSSES SS5694

Poundffald Inn (01792) 931061

Tirmynydd Road, NW end; SA4 3PB Refurbished 17th-c beamed and timbered pub; farmhouse, mate's and attractively upholstered chairs around wooden tables on patterned carpet, woodburner, Greene King Abbot and Sharps Doom Bar, enjoyable pubby food from baguettes up; sports TV in separate bar; regular quiz evenings; dogs welcome, picnic-sets under parasols on side terrace, open (and food) all day. *(Liz and Martin Eldon)*

GWENT

ABERGAVENNY SO2914

Angel (01873) 857121

Cross Street, by town hall; NP7 5EN Comfortable late Georgian coaching inn; good local atmosphere in two-level bar, rugs on flagstones, big sofas, armchairs and settles, some lovely bevelled glass behind counter serving real ales such as Wye Valley, proper cider and good choice of wines and malt whiskies, well liked food, friendly helpful staff, attractive lounge (popular afternoon tea 2-4pm) and smart dining room; free wi-fi;

children and dogs (in bar) welcome, pretty candlelit courtyard, 35 bedrooms (some in other buildings), open all day.
(Andrew Vincent)

ABERGAVENNY SO3111

★**Hardwick** (01873) 854220

Hardwick; B4598 SE, off A40 at A465/ A4042 exit – coming from E on A40, go right round the exit system, as B4598 is final road out; NP7 9AA Restaurant-with-rooms and you'll need to book for owner-chef's highly rated imaginative food; drinkers welcome in refurbished bar serving Rhymney and Wye Valley, local perry and a dozen wines by the glass, also a small plates menu, two dining rooms, one with beams, bare boards and huge fireplace, the other in lighter carpeted extension, friendly service; background music; no under-8s in restaurant after 8pm, parasol-shaded teak tables by car park, neat garden, bedrooms, open all day.
(Andrew Vincent)

CAERLEON ST3490

Bell (01633) 420613

Bulmore Road; off M4 junction 24 via B4237 and B4236; NP18 1QQ Old stone coaching inn with good variety of enjoyable food including vegetarian choices and daily specials (some dishes served on boards or slates), three well kept changing ales and ten welsh ciders/perries, friendly service, linked beamed areas, big open fireplace; live singers Sun; children and dogs welcome, pretty back terrace, open all day Fri-Sun, closed Mon and lunchtime Tues (all day Tues in winter). *(Molly and Stewart Lindsay)*

CHEPSTOW ST5394

Three Tuns (01291) 645797

Bridge Street; NP16 5EY Early 17th-c and a pub for much of that time; bare-boards interior with painted farmhouse pine furniture, a couple of sofas by woodburner, plates on dresser, local ales and ciders from nice wooden counter at unusual angle, very reasonably priced lunchtime bar food including speciality pies, friendly staff; background and regular live music, quiz nights; children and dogs welcome, wheelchair access, four bedrooms (one suitable for disabled guests), open all day.
(Tom and Ruth Rees)

GROSMONT SO4024

Angel (01981) 240646

Corner of B4347 and Poorscript Lane; NP7 8EP Small welcoming 17th-c local; rustic interior with simple wooden furniture, Wye Valley Butty Bach, a couple of guests and local cider, reasonably priced traditional food (evenings Thurs, Fri, all Sat, lunchtime Sun), pool room with darts, TV for rugby;

We say if we know a pub has background music.

no lavatories – public ones close by; dogs welcome, seats out by ancient market cross, back garden with boules, good local walks, open all day Sat, closed Sun evening, Tues and weekday lunchtimes. *(Julian Richardson)*

LLANDENNY   SO4103

★**Raglan Arms** (01291) 690800
Centre of village; NP15 1DL Well run dining pub with relaxed informal atmosphere; interesting freshly cooked food, good selection of wines and a changing real ale, friendly welcoming young staff, big pine tables in linked dining rooms leading to conservatory, log fire in flagstoned bar's handsome stone fireplace; children welcome, garden tables, closed Sun and Tues evenings, all day Mon. *(Jasper)*

LLANGATTOCK LINGOED SO3620

Hunters Moon (01873) 821499
Off B4521 just E of Llanvetherine; NP7 8RR Attractive tucked-away pub dating from the 13th c; beams, dark stripped stone and flagstones, woodburner, friendly licensees and locals, welsh ales tapped from the cask and enjoyable straightforward food, separate dining room; children and dogs welcome, tables out on deck and in charming dell with waterfall, glorious country on Offa's Dyke Path, four comfortable bedrooms, open (and food) all day. *(Graham Swift)*

LLANGYBI   ST3797

White Hart (01633) 450258
On main road; NP15 1NP Friendly village dining pub in delightful 12th-c monastic building (part of Jane Seymour's dowry); pubby bar with roaring log fire, steps up to pleasant light restaurant, enjoyable food including daily specials and two-course weekday lunch deal, well kept mainly welsh ales and good choice of wines by the glass, afternoon teas; children welcome, closed Sun evening and Mon, otherwise open all day (best to check winter hours). *(Sandra and Miles Spencer)*

LLANISHEN   SO4703

Carpenters Arms (01600) 860812
B4293 north of Chepstow; NP16 6QH Old cottagey family-run pub with good food including blackboard specials, one changing real ale, friendly welcoming staff, comfortable bar/lounge, coal fire, back games room with pool; flagstoned terrace and little side lawn up steps, self-catering cottage, closed Mon and lunchtime Tues, no food Sun evening. *(Thelma Abbott)*

LLANOVER   SO2907

★**Goose & Cuckoo** (01873) 880277
Upper Llanover signed up track off A4042 S of Abergavenny; after 0.5 miles take first left; NP7 9ER Remote pub looking over picturesque valley just inside Brecon Beacons National Park; essentially one little rustically furnished room with

woodburner in arched stone fireplace, small picture-window extension making most of the view, three well kept ales, 50 whiskies and generous helpings of simple tasty home-cooked food; live music, board games, cribbage and darts; children, walkers and dogs welcome, picnic-sets out on gravel below, bedrooms and self-catering, closed Mon, open all day Fri-Sun. *(Trish James)*

LLANTHONY   SO2827

★**Priory Hotel** (01873) 890487
Aka Abbey Hotel, Llanthony Priory; off A465, back road Llanvihangel Crucorney–Hay; NP7 7NN Magical setting for plain bar in dimly lit vaulted crypt of graceful ruined Norman abbey, lovely in summer with lawns around and the peaceful border hills beyond; well kept Felinfoel Double Dragon and a couple of summer guests, enjoyable good value food (more restaurants in the evening), efficient service; children welcome but not in hotel part (seven non-ensuite bedrooms in restored abbey walls, four reached by spiral staircase), no dogs, open all day weekends Apr-Oct (all day July, Aug), closed in winter apart from Fri evening, Sat and lunchtime Sun. *(Ian Herdman, Mrs J Ekins-Daukes, Peter Meister)*

LLANTRISANT FAWR   ST3997

Greyhound (01291) 672505
Off A449 near Usk; NP15 1LE Prettily set 18th-c country inn with relaxed homely feel in three linked beamed rooms (steps between two), nice mix of furnishings and rustic decorations, well kept Bass, Greene King Abbot and maybe a guest, decent wines and enjoyable home cooking at sensible prices, friendly efficient service, pleasant panelled dining room, log fires; children welcome, muddy boots and dogs in one bar, disabled access, attractive garden with big fountain, hill views, comfortable bedrooms in converted stable block, open (and some food) all day, shuts 9pm Sun. *(Graham Smart)*

**LLANVIHANGEL
CRUCORNEY**   SO3220

Skirrid (01873) 890258
Signed off A465; NP7 8DH One of Britain's oldest pubs, dating partly from 1110 and a former courthouse – plenty of atmosphere and ghostly tales; ancient studded door to high-ceilinged main bar, exposed stone, flagstones and panelling, huge log fire, well kept ales and pubby food, separate dining room; children and dogs (in garden only) welcome, tables on terrace and small sloping back lawn, bedrooms, closed Mon lunchtime. *(Thelma Abbott)*

MAGOR   ST4287

Wheatsheaf (01633) 880608
A mile from M4 junction 23; Newport Road off B4245; NP26 3HN Welcoming white-painted pub with black beams and some exposed stonework, pubby furniture

on wood, flagstone or quarry-tiled floors, woodburner in big fireplace, ales such as Rhymney and Sharps, decent wines and 20 gins, well priced food from bar snacks to full meals (kitchen closes 3pm Sun), good friendly service, carpeted restaurant, pool and darts in tap room; live music Mon, quiz nights; children and dogs welcome, wheelchair access (ramp for restaurant), open all day. *(Fiona and Jack Henderson)*

MAMHILAD   SO3004
Horseshoe (01873) 880542
Old Abergavenny Road; NP4 8QZ Old beamed country pub with slate-floor bar; traditional pubby furniture and a couple of unusual posts acting as elbow tables, original Hancocks pub sign, ornate woodburner in stone fireplace, well kept ales including local Mad Dog and proper ciders, good fairly priced food from lunchtime baguettes to daily specials; children welcome, dogs away from dining area, lovely views particularly from tables by car park over road, open all day Fri-Sun. *(Julian Richardson)*

NEWPORT   ST3188
Olde Murenger House
(01633) 263977 *High Street; NP20 1GA* Fine 16th-c black and white timbered building; carefully restored split-level interior with ancient dark woodwork, leaded windows and traditional furniture on bare boards or carpet, well kept/priced Sam Smiths ales and enjoyable straightforward home-made food (all day Fri, Sat, not Sun evening); open all day Mon-Sat. *(Louise and Simon Peters)*

PANDY   SO3322
Old Pandy (01873) 890208
A465 Abergavenny–Hereford; NP7 8DR Welcoming 17th-c beamed roadside pub on edge of the Black Mountains and popular with walkers; good reasonably priced food from fairly traditional menu, well kept ales including Wye Valley, friendly service; pool and darts; live music; children and dogs welcome, adjacent bunkhouse, open (and food) all day Fri-Sun, closed Mon lunchtime. *(Andrew Davies)*

RAGLAN   SO4107
Beaufort Arms (01291) 690412
High Street; NP15 2DY Pub-hotel (former 16th-c coaching inn) with two character beamed bars, one with big stone fireplace and comfortable seats on slate floor, well kept local ales, carefully sourced food (all starters and mains gluten-free) including good fish/seafood, light airy brasserie, friendly attentive service; background

music, open mike night first Tues of month; children and dogs (in bar) welcome, terrace tables, 16 bedrooms, open all day from 7am. *(Bernard Stradling)*

REDBROOK   SO5309
★Boat (01600) 712615
Car park signed on A466 Chepstow–Monmouth, then 30-metre footbridge over Wye; or very narrow steep car access from Penallt in Wales; NP25 4AJ Beautifully set riverside pub under new management; well kept Wye Valley and guests, real ciders and popular food from baguettes up, friendly helpful staff, stripped-stone walls, flagstones and woodburner; children and dogs welcome, seats in informal tiered suntrap garden with stream spilling down into duck pond, closed Tues in winter, otherwise open all day, no evening food Sun-Tues. *(Molly and Stewart Lindsay)*

SKENFRITH   SO4520
★Bell (01600) 750235
Just off B4521, NE of Abergavenny and N of Monmouth; NP7 8UH Elegant 17th-c coaching inn handy for nearby ruins of Skenfrith Castle (NT); main bar with inglenook fireplace and plenty of seating including comfortable sofas, bleached-oak counter serving ales such as Bespoke, Wickwar and Wye Valley, bottled local cider/perry, 15 wines by the glass and good range of spirits, imaginative modern food using some home-grown produce, friendly helpful staff, restaurant; background music, free wi-fi; children and dogs (in one bar) welcome, disabled access, terrace with good solid tables under parasols, steps up to sloping lawn, orchard area and neat kitchen garden, comfortable well equipped bedrooms named after fishing flies, open all day (closed one week in both Jan and Nov). *(Gerry and Pam Pollard, Jennifer and Nicholas Thompson, Mrs J Ekins-Daukes)*

TALYCOED   SO4115
Warwicks (01600) 780227
B4233 Monmouth–Abergavenny; though its postal address is Llantilio Crossenny, the inn is actually in Talycoed, a mile or two E; NP7 8TL Pretty 17th-c wisteria-clad pub under enthusiastic welcoming management; softly lit beamed bar with friendly locals, good log fire in stone fireplace, settles and mix of other old furniture, horsebrasses and assorted memorabilia, a couple of well kept ales such as Hancocks and Otter, decent wines by the glass and good quality food cooked by

---

Post Office address codings confusingly give the impression that some pubs are in Gwent or Powys, Wales, when they're really in Gloucestershire or Shropshire (which is where we list them).

landlady including daily specials, cosy little dining room; children welcome, dogs in bar, seats on front terrace and in neat garden, lovely countryside and surrounding walks, open all day Sun, closed Mon, Tues and lunchtime Weds. *(Derek Stafford)*

TINTERN   SO5300
Anchor (01291) 689582
Off A466 at brown sign for Tintern Abbey; NP16 6TE Medieval building in wonderful setting next to the magnificent abbey ruins; beams, flagstones and bare stone walls, original horse-drawn cider press (used when the grounds were the abbey's orchards), four real ales such as Otter and Wye Valley, good wines by the glass and well regarded food, restaurant and airy orangery making most of the view (abbey floodlit at night); children and dogs (in bar) welcome, picnic-sets on terrace and lawn, River Wye just behind and lots of surrounding walks, open all day. *(Anna and Mark Evans, Roger and Donna Huggins, Alison and Tony Livesley, Martin and Sue Neville, Ian and Rose Lock, Nigel Salter)*

TRELLECK   SO5005
Lion (01600) 860322
B4293 6 miles S of Monmouth; NP25 4PA Open-plan bar with dining area to the left, one or two low black beams, mix of old furniture and two log fires, ales such as Wye Valley, wide range of enjoyable fair priced food including takeaway pizzas; background music, open mike night first and third Mon of month, traditional games; children and dogs welcome, tables out on grass and side courtyard overlooking church, open (and food) all day, kitchen closes 6pm Sun. *(Julian Richardson)*

TRELLECK GRANGE   SO5001
Fountain (01291) 689303
Minor road Tintern–Llanishen, SE of village; NP16 6QW Welcoming traditional 17th-c country pub; good food cooked by landlady using local produce from pub favourites to game specials, some themed nights, three well kept ales including Glamorgan and Wye Valley, real cider, roomy low-beamed flagstoned bar with log fire; Weds quiz, darts; children and dogs welcome, small walled garden, peaceful spot on small winding road, open all day weekends, closed Mon and lunchtimes Tues-Fri. *(Thelma Abbott)*

USK   SO3700
Kings Head (01291) 672963
Old Market Street; NP15 1AL Popular 16th-c family-run inn, chatty and relaxed, with generously served traditional food and well kept beers such as Fullers, Timothy Taylors and Wye Valley, friendly efficient staff, huge log fire in superb fireplace; sports TV; nine comfortable bedrooms, hearty welsh breakfast, open all day. *(Ian Herdman)*

GWYNEDD

ABERDARON   SH1726
Ty Newydd Hotel (01758) 760207
B4413, by the sea; LL53 8BE Hotel right by the sea with lovely views over Cardigan Bay; good choice of enjoyable food from bar snacks to Sun carvery, four local real ales, friendly helpful staff; panoramic terrace within feet of the waves, 11 bedrooms, traditional welsh breakfast, open all day. *(Steve Parry, Dave Braisted)*

ABERDOVEY   SN6196
★ Penhelig Arms (01654) 767215
Opposite Penhelig station; LL35 0LT Fine harbourside location for this popular 18th-c hotel; traditional bar with warm fire in central stone fireplace, Brains ales and a guest, good choice of wines and malt whiskies, enjoyable reasonably priced food including weekday set lunch, friendly service; children welcome, dogs allowed in bar and comfortable bedrooms (some have balconies overlooking estuary, ones nearest the road can be noisy), open (and food) all day. *(Andrew Vincent)*

BARMOUTH   SH6115
Myrddins (01341) 388060
Church Street; LL42 1EH Micropub-café with good selection of welsh beers (including their own) tapped from the cask and in bottles, generous helpings of enjoyable reasonably priced home-cooked food catering for vegetarian and gluten-free diets; children and dogs welcome, a couple of pavement tables, shuts at 8.30pm, closed Tues and Weds. *(Andrew Bosi)*

BETWS-Y-COED   SH7955
★ Ty Gwyn (01690) 710383
A5 just S of bridge to village; LL24 0SG Family-run restaurant-with-rooms rather than pub (you must eat or stay overnight to be served drinks), but pubby feel in character beamed lounge bar with ancient cooking range, easy chairs, antiques, old prints and bric-a-brac, highly regarded interesting food using local produce including own fruit and vegetables, some themed nights, well kept ales, friendly professional service; background music; children welcome, comfortable bedrooms and holiday cottage, closed Christmas and ten days in Jan. *(Alan and Alice Morgan)*

BLAENAU FFESTINIOG   SH7041
Pengwern Arms (01766) 762200
Church Square, Ffestiniog; LL41 4PB Unpretentious community-owned pub on village square; well kept/priced ales in panelled bar, dining area serving good value food (not Sun evening), friendly local atmosphere; games room, live music; dogs welcome, fine views from back garden, eight

bedrooms, open all day weekends, from 6pm Mon-Thurs, 5pm Fri. *(Julie Swift)*

CAERNARFON SH4762
Bar Bach (01286) 673111
Greengate Street, near the Castle; LL55 2NF Tiny bar opposite Caernarfon Castle; simple furnishings, exposed stonework and small fire, three changing local beers, decent lunchtime food; sports TV; dogs welcome, open all day till 1.30am. *(Peter Meister)*

CAERNARFON SH4762
★ Black Boy (01286) 673604
Northgate Street; LL55 1RW Busy traditional 16th-c inn with cosy beamed lounge bar, sumptuously furnished and packed with tables, additional dining room across corridor and dimly lit atmospheric public bar, well kept welsh beers, nine wines by the glass and extensive selection of whiskies and gins, good generous food from sandwiches up including lunchtime set deal, efficient friendly service and lots of welsh chat; background music, TV, free wi-fi; disabled access (ramps) and loos, tables out on pedestrianised street, bedrooms (some in different buildings), open (and food) all day from 7am. *(Peter Meister, Peter and Anne Hollindale)*

CAPEL CURIG SH7257
Bryn Tyrch (01690) 720223
A5 E; LL24 0EL Family-owned roadside inn perfectly placed for mountains of Snowdonia; bistro-bar with open fire and amazing picture-windows views, Conwy Welsh Pride and a guest, quite a few malt whiskies, comprehensive choice of good well presented food (not Mon lunchtime), second bar with big menu boards, leather sofas and mix of tables on bare boards; free wi-fi; children, walkers and dogs welcome, steep little side garden, more seats on terrace and across road by stream, 11 bedrooms, open all day in summer. *(Stuart Doughty)*

CAPEL CURIG SH7357
Tyn y Coed (01690) 720331
A5 SE of village; LL24 0EE Bustling community inn across from River Llugwy with good surrounding walks; enjoyable home-made food using local produce, well kept Purple Moose and two guests, pleasant quick service, beams and log fires, pool room; children and dogs welcome, small garden either side, restored stagecoach over the road by car park, comfortable bedrooms, cycle storage and drying room, open all day Fri-Sun, from 3pm other days. *(Fiona and Jack Henderson)*

CONWY SH7777
Albion (01492) 582484
Uppergate Street; LL32 8RF Interesting sensitively restored 1920s pub under collective ownership of four welsh brewers – Conwy, Great Orme, Nant and Purple Moose, their beers and guests kept well (tasting trays available), friendly staff, some snacky food including pies, three linked rooms with plenty of well preserved features including stained glass and huge baronial fireplace, back part with serving hatch is quieter; dogs welcome, open all day. *(Stuart Doughty)*

LLANDUDNO SH7882
Cottage Loaf (01492) 870762
Market Street; LL30 2SR Popular former bakery with three linked rooms; dark beams and timbers, rugs on pale flagstones or bare boards, good mix of tables, benches, cushioned settles and dining chairs, woodburners, decent home-made food from sandwiches up, well kept ales (often from local microbreweries), friendly service, big garden room extension; teak furniture on front and back terraces, children welcome, open (and food) all day. *(Mark Lewis)*

LLANFROTHEN SH6141
Brondanw Arms (01766) 770555
Aka Y Ring; A4085 just N of B4410; LL48 6AQ Welsh-speaking village pub at end of short whitewashed terrace; main bar with slate floor and woodburner in large fireplace, pews and window benches, old farm tools on the ceiling, snug with panelled booths and potbelly stove, long spacious dining room behind with contrasting red walls, good home-cooked food including carvery (Weds evening, Sun lunchtime), Robinsons ales and decent range of wines by the glass, friendly helpful staff; free wi-fi; children and dogs welcome, wheelchair access (two long shallow steps at front), Snowdonia National Park views from garden with play area, camping and good walks, handy for Plas Brondanw Gardens, open all day. *(Elizabeth and Andrew Harvey)*

LLANUWCHLLYN SH8730
Eagles (01678) 540278
Aka Eryrod; A494/B4403; LL23 7UB Family-run and welcoming with good reasonably priced food using own farm produce, ales such as Purple Moose; opened-up slate-floor bar with log fire, beams and stripped stone, back picture-window view of mountains with Lake Bala in the distance; sports TV; children welcome, metal tables and chairs on flower-filled back terrace, small shop (from 7.30am), caravan and camping park, open all day. *(Darrell Barton)*

MAENTWROG SH6640
Grapes (01766) 590365
A496; village signed from A470; LL41 4HN Handsome 17th-c village inn; lounge and main bar to the right serving three real ales including Purple Moose, good choice of enjoyable fairly priced pubby food, friendly helpful staff, restaurant on the left and another dining room behind with balcony overlooking church, steps down

to garden; sports TV and pool in separate games room; children welcome, picnic-sets on lawn, play area, eight bedrooms (two in separate cottages), Ffestiniog steam railway nearby, open (and food) all day. *(Geoff and Ann Marston)*

PENMAENPOOL SH6918
George III (01341) 422525
Just off A493, near Dolgellau; LL40 1YD
Attractive recently refurbished inn dating from 1650, delightful views over Mawddach estuary from partly panelled upstairs bar opening into cosy inglenook lounge, beamed and flagstoned downstairs bar, well kept Robinsons ales, more than 20 wines by the glass and some interesting gins, good food from varied menu including sandwiches till 5pm, friendly helpful young staff, restaurant; children and dogs welcome, sheltered terrace, ten bedrooms (some in converted stables – line now a walkway), open (and food) all day. *(David Eberlin)*

PORTH DINLLAEN SH2741
★ Ty Coch (01758) 720498
Beach car park signed from Morfa Nefyn, then 15-minute walk; LL53 6DB
Popular former 19th-c vicarage in idyllic location right on the beach with wonderful views, far from roads and only reached on foot; bar crammed with nautical and other memorabilia, simple furnishings, coal fire, up to three real ales including Purple Moose and a craft beer (served in plastic as worried about glass on the beach), simple lunchtime bar menu, friendly service; children and dogs welcome, open all day in season and school holidays (till 5pm Sun), in winter open all day Fri and Sat, 11-5pm Sun-Thurs. *(Peter Meister)*

PORTHMADOG SH5639
Australia (01766) 515957
(01766) 515957 *High Street; LL49 9LR*
Purple Moose brewery tap with their well kept ales and guests, decent wines by the glass and tasty pub food, chunky contemporary wooden furniture, beer barrel tables and banquettes on bare boards; occasional quiz and live music nights; children welcome, seats outside, open all day. *(Mike and Eleanor Anderson)*

PWLLHELI SH3735
Whitehall (01758) 614091
Gaol Street; LL53 5RG Family-run pub-bistro in centre of this market town; local ales such as Llŷn and good choice of wines, popular freshly made food from lunchtime ciabattas up, friendly staff, spiral stairs to upstairs dining room; TV in bar; children welcome, open all day (till late Fri, Sat). *(Hefina Pritchard, Andrea Watts)*

RHYD DDU SH5652
Cwellyn Arms (01766) 890321
A4085 N of Beddgelert; LL54 6TL

Welcoming 18th-c village pub (same owners for over 30 years) not far below Welsh Highland Railway top terminus; up to half a dozen real ales and good choice of popular seasonal food from home-baked rolls to blackboard specials, friendly helpful staff, two cosy bars with log fires, restaurant with woodburner; children, walkers and dogs welcome, spectacular Snowdon views from garden tables, babbling stream just over wall, bedrooms, self-catering cottages, three bunkhouses, a campsite and a motorhome to rent, open all day. *(Mike and Eleanor Anderson, Adrian Johnson)*

ROWEN SH7571
Ty Gwyn (01492) 650232
Off B5106 S of Conwy; LL32 8YU
Traditional 18th-c whitewashed stone pub in charming village; well kept Lees ales and enjoyable generously served food, friendly service; children and dogs (in bar) welcome, seats out at front and in two gardens (one with stream), good walking country, open all day weekends, closed Tues and till 4pm other weekdays. *(Rick Horsfall)*

TREFRIW SH7863
Old Ship (01492) 640013
B5106; LL27 0JH Well run old pub with nice staff and cheerful local atmosphere; much enjoyed food from interesting daily changing blackboard menu, three well kept local ales, good range of wines/malt whiskies and some 50 gins, log fire and inglenook woodburner; picnic-sets out by stream, children welcome, open (and food) all day weekends, closed Mon except bank holidays. *(Martin Cawley)*

TREMADOG SH5640
Union (01766) 512748
Market Square; LL49 9RB Traditional early 19th-c stone-built pub in terrace overlooking square, cosy and comfortable, with quiet panelled lounge and carpeted public bar, exposed stone walls and woodburner, well kept ales such as Purple Moose, enjoyable pubby food including range of burgers, friendly staff, back restaurant; darts and TV; children and dogs (in bar) welcome, paved terrace behind, closed weekday lunchtimes. *(Liz and Martin Eldon)*

TUDWEILIOG SH2336
Lion (01758) 659724
Nefyn Road (B4417), Llŷn Peninsula; LL53 8ND Cheerful village inn with traditional furnishings in lounge bar and two dining rooms (one for families), enjoyable sensibly priced home-cooked food, changing real ales, decent wines and dozens of malt whiskies, growing gin collection too, quick friendly service; pool and board games in public bar; children and dogs welcome, pleasant front garden, bedrooms, open all day in season. *(Diana and Bertie Farr)*

TY'N-Y-GROES   SH7773
★ **Groes** (01492) 650545
B5106 N of village; LL32 8TN
15th-c pub-hotel in fine setting overlooking
the Vale of Conwy and peaks of Snowdonia;
rambling low-beamed thick-walled rooms
with antique settles, clocks, portraits
and other bits and pieces, big fireplace in
back bar, Lees ales, 14 wines by the glass
and decent range of malt whiskies/gins,
enjoyable food from sandwiches up, can eat
in bar, airy conservatory with its 30-year-old
vine or smart restaurant; background music;
children and dogs welcome, idyllic back
garden with flower-filled hayracks, more
seats on narrow roadside terrace, splendid
views from well equipped bedroom suites
(some have terraces or balconies), open
(and food) all day. *(Dr Martin Owton, Rob
Anderson, Pauline and Mark Evans, Charles
Todd, Hazel Hyde)*

POWYS

BEGUILDY   SO1979
Radnorshire Arms (01547) 510634
B4355 Knighton–Newtown; LD7 1YE
17th-c black and white beamed country pub
with enjoyable good value food (not Sun
evening), Ludlow, Stonehouse and a beer
badged for them, friendly helpful service
inglenook woodburner; quiz last Sun evening
of month, pool; no dogs inside, beer garden,
closed Mon (except bank holidays).
(Julian Richardson)

CILMERY   SO0051
Prince Llewelyn (01982) 552694
A483; LD2 3NU Country pub under
friendly licensees; plush dining chairs and
button-back banquettes in dining room,
woodburner in carpeted bar, a couple of real
ales and enjoyable food including seafood
summer specials; children and dogs welcome,
lovely surrounding walks, closed Sun evening,
Mon and till 6pm Tues. *(Ted and Mary Bates)*

CRICKHOWELL   SO2118
Dragon (01873) 810362
High Street; NP8 1BE Welcoming old
family-owned inn, more hotel-restaurant
than pub, but with neat small bar serving
Rhymney, stone and wood floors, sofas and
armchairs by open fire, enjoyable traditional
food including welsh choices in tidy dining
room, steak night Thurs, good friendly
service; dogs welcome, 15 bedrooms, open
(and food) all day. *(Jan Ivinson)*

CRICKHOWELL   SO1919
Nantyffin Cider Mill
(01873) 810775 *A40/A479 NW; NP8 1SG*
Former 16th-c drovers' inn facing River
Usk in lovely Black Mountains countryside
– charming views from tables on lawn;
bar with solid furniture on tiles or carpet,

woodburner in broad fireplace, a couple of
Felinfoel beers, Thatcher's cider and several
wines by the glass, open-plan main area with
beams, standing timbers and open fire in
grey stonework wall, high-raftered restaurant
with old cider press, good fairly pubby food
at reasonable prices; background music, TV;
children and dogs (in bar) welcome, play area
in garden, handy for Tretower Court and
Castle, closed Mon and Tues (also Weds in
winter), open all day Thurs-Sat, till 6pm Sun.
(Thelma Abbott)

DERWENLAS   SN7299
★ **Black Lion** (01654) 703913
A487 just S of Machynlleth; SY20 8TN
Cosy 16th-c country pub with extensive range
of good well priced food including children's
menu and daily specials, friendly staff coping
well at busy times, Wye Valley Butty Bach and
a guest, decent wines, heavy black beams and
timbering, thick walls, carpet over big slate
flagstones, good log fire; background music;
garden behind with play area and steps
up into woods, limited parking, bedrooms,
closed Mon. *(Sue Griffiths)*

DINAS MAWDDWY   SH8514
Red Lion (01650) 531247
*Dyfi Road; off A470 (N of A458
junction); SY20 9JA* Two small traditional
front bars and more modern back extension,
changing ales and decent food including
popular pies and Sunday carvery, friendly
efficient service, open fire, beams and lots
of brassware; children welcome, six simple
bedrooms (four ensuite); pub named in welsh
(Llew Coch). *(Molly and Stewart Lindsay)*

DOLFOR   SO1187
Dolfor (01686) 626531
*Inn signposted up hill from A483, about
4 miles S of Newtown; SY16 4AA*
Welcoming beamed hillside inn; cosy
carpeted bar with woodburner in stone
fireplace, four well kept ales such as Ludlow
and Wye Valley from brick-faced counter,
dining room with another woodburner in
inglenook, enjoyable generously served
food at fair prices including lunchtime
sandwiches; pool, darts and TV in games
area; children and dogs welcome, good views
from terrace, five comfortable bedrooms
(two sharing bathroom), open all day Thurs-
Sun, closed lunchtimes other days.
(Richard Jones)

FELINFACH   SO0933
Plough & Harrow (01874) 622709
*Village and pub signed from A470,
4 miles N of Brecon; LD3 0UB* Small
village pub under welcoming long-serving
licensees; simple bar, comfortable lounge
area with woodburner and dining room, well
kept Sharps Doom Bar and a guest, good
reasonably priced home-made food; three
bedrooms, open evenings only from 6pm
(7pm Sun). *(Vin Davies)*

GARTHMYL SO1999

Nags Head (01686) 640600

A483; SY15 6RS Attractive Georgian roadside inn with nicely updated interior; good food from sandwiches, sharing plates and pub favourites up, real ales such as Montys, Salopian and Three Tuns, well chosen wines, helpful service from friendly uniformed staff, comfortable slate-floor bar with large two-way woodburner, pitched-roof dining room; children and dogs welcome, tables under parasols on paved back terrace, towpath walks along Montgomery Canal, five good bedrooms, open (and food) all day. *(Ryan Knapton)*

GLADESTRY SO2355

Royal Oak (01544) 370669

B4594; HR5 3NR Friendly old-fashioned village pub on Offa's Dyke Path; simple stripped-stone slate-floored walkers' bar, beams hung with tankards and lanterns, carpeted lounge, open fires, ales such as Wye Valley Butty Bach; may not accept credit cards; children welcome, dogs in bar, sheltered sunny back garden, four bedrooms, camping, only open weekends, food lunchtime. *(Christopher Mannings)*

GLASBURY SO1839

Harp (01497) 847373

B4350 towards Hay, just N of A438; HR3 5NR Welcoming 18th-c pub under new management; good traditional food (not Mon, just pizzas Sun evening) including blackboard specials, two well kept Wye Valley ales, U-shaped beamed interior with woodburner; children and dogs welcome, terrace and garden sloping down to River Wye, four bedrooms, open all day Fri-Sun, closed lunchtimes Mon, Tues. *(Sandra and Miles Spencer)*

HAY-ON-WYE SO2242

Blue Boar (01497) 820884

Castle Street/Oxford Road; HR3 5DF Old ivy-clad pub with character bar: cosy corners, dark panelling, pews and country chairs, open fire in Edwardian fireplace, four well kept ales such as Brains Rev James and Timothy Taylors Landlord, organic bottled cider and several wines by the glass, decent food in long café/dining room with another open fire; background music; children and dogs welcome, tables under parasols in beer garden, open all day from 9am for breakfast. *(Mike Benton)*

HAY-ON-WYE SO2342

Old Black Lion (01497) 820841

Lion Street; HR3 5AD 17th-c inn with comfortable low-beamed bar, country chairs at scrubbed pine tables, painted dados and original fireplace, three real ales such as Evan Evans, Swan and Wye Valley from hop-strewn bar, good range of whiskies too, well liked food from lunchtime sandwiches up,

friendly helpful service; live jazz Fri evening; children and dogs (in one area) welcome, sheltered back terrace, character bedrooms (some above bar) with modern bathrooms, good breakfast, open all day from 8am. *(Rachel Hadley, John Pritchard)*

KNIGHTON SO2872

Horse & Jockey (01547) 520062

Wylcwm Place; LD7 1AE Popular old pub (former 14th-c coaching inn) with good well priced food from traditional choices to daily specials, can eat in bar or adjoining restaurant, cheerful service, well kept changing beers such as Three Tuns and Wye Valley; children and dogs welcome, tables in pleasant courtyard, eight bedrooms, handy for Offa's Dyke Path, open all day. *(Julie Swift)*

LIBANUS SN9926

Tai'r Bull (01874) 622600

A470 SW of Brecon; LD3 8EL Welcoming old roadside village pub; traditional bar with woodburner in large stone fireplace, two well kept ales and a guest, enjoyable home-made food from sharing plates up, airy restaurant with high-backed leather chairs and white tablecloths; children and dogs (in bar) welcome, great views of Pen-y-Fan from small front terrace, five bedrooms, open all day. *(Liz and Martin Eldon)*

LLANBEDR SO2320

Red Lion (01873) 810754

Off A40 at Crickhowell; NP8 1SR Quaint old village local run by charming landlady; heavy beams and log fires, antique settles in lounge and snug, well kept ales and enjoyable fair value home-made food in front dining area; good walking country (porch for muddy boots), open all day weekends, closed Mon and weekday lunchtimes. *(Gillian Longman)*

LLANFIHANGEL-NANT-MELAN SO1958

Red Lion (01544) 350220

A44 10 miles W of Kington; LD8 2TN Beamed and stripped-stone 16th-c roadside pub; roomy main bar with flagstones and woodburner, carpeted restaurant and front sun porch, tasty reasonably priced food cooked by landlord including OAP choices, well kept changing ales, friendly service, back bar with another woodburner; children and dogs welcome, can arrange horse stabling, country views from pleasant garden, five bedrooms (three in annexe), handy for Radnor Forest walks and near impressive waterfall, closed Mon (except bank holidays) and Tues. *(Jasper)*

LLANGATTOCK SO2117

Horseshoe (01873) 268773

Off B4558; NP8 1PA Busy attractively refurbished old inn; bar with flagstones, exposed stonework and some beams, button-back leather wall banquettes and other traditional furniture, two woodburners, more seating in back pitched-ceiling room with bare boards and pine dresser, Wye Valley Butty Bach, Brains Rev James and a guest, well liked food, friendly helpful service; TV; children and dogs welcome, comfortable bedrooms, open all day, no food Sun evening. *(Frank Price)*

LLANGEDWYN   SJ1924
Green Inn (01691) 828234
B4396 E of village; SY10 9JW Old country dining pub with modernised interior, various snug corners and good mix of furnishings including oak settles and comfy sofas, woodburner, real ales such as Three Tuns and enjoyable well priced pubby food (not Mon) including set deal (Tues-Thurs), friendly helpful staff; children and dogs welcome, picnic-sets in garden over road running down towards River Tanat, closed Mon lunchtime, otherwise open all day. *(Geoff and Ann Marston)*

LLANGENNY   SO2417
Dragons Head (01873) 810350
N of village, by bridge; NP8 1HD · Welcoming and popular wisteria-clad pub tucked away in pretty valley; well kept Rhymney, a couple of guests and decent wines by the glass, good freshly cooked food from shortish menu, two-room bar with low beams and mix of traditional seating including leather chesterfields by big woodburner, lots of framed photographs and other bits and pieces, two dining areas; children and dogs welcome, seats in garden and over lane by stream, nearby campsite, closed Mon and lunchtimes Tues-Fri. *(Rachel Pickavance)*

LLANGORSE   SO1327
Castle Inn (01874) 658819
B4560; LD3 7UB Friendly little whitewashed local with good generously served food cooked by landlady including range of pies and burgers, just pizzas Sun evening, Brains Rev James and occasional guest, attentive helpful service; children and dogs welcome, open all day weekends, from 4.30pm weekdays (hours may extend during school holidays). *(Steve Cape)*

LLANGYNIDR   SO1519
Coach & Horses (01874) 730245
Cwm Crawnon Road (B4558 W of Crickhowell); NP8 1LS Flower-decked country dining pub; well kept ales and enjoyable generously served food cooked by chef-owner, beams, stripped stone and big log fire, restaurant; children and dogs (in some areas) welcome, picnic-sets and play area across road in fenced garden by

canal lock, four bedrooms with canal views, open all day. *(Nicholas and Lucy Sage)*

LLANIDLOES   SN9584
Crown & Anchor (01686) 412398
Long Bridge Street; SY18 6EF Friendly largely unspoilt town-centre pub known locally as Ruby's after landlady who ran it for 50 years; well kept Brains Rev James and Wye Valley Bitter, chatty locals' bar, lounge, snug and two other rooms separated by central hallway; pool and games machine; open all day (from 4pm Mon). *(Naomi and Andrew Randall)*

LLANWRTYD WELLS   SN8746
Neuadd Arms (01591) 610236
The Square; LD5 4RB Sizeable 19th-c hotel (friendly and by no means upmarket) brewing its own good value Heart of Wales beers in back stable block (up to ten on at a time), enjoyable straightforward home-made food, log fires in lounge and small tiled public bar still with old service bells, restaurant, games room; well behaved dogs welcome in bars, a few tables out at front, 21 bedrooms (front ones can be noisy), very small town in good walking area, novel events such as bogsnorkelling and man v horse, open all day. *(Louise and Simon Peters)*

MALLWYD   SH8612
Brigands (01650) 511999
A470 by roundabout in village; SY20 9HJ Sizeable 15th-c beamed coaching inn with gently civilised atmosphere; well kept changing ales and enjoyable food from bar snacks up, popular morning and afternoon teas, friendly efficient staff; children and dogs welcome, extensive lawns with lovely views, can arrange fishing on River Dovey, nine bedrooms, open all day. *(Molly and Stewart Lindsay)*

MIDDLETOWN   SJ3012
Breidden (01938) 570880
A458 Welshpool–Shrewsbury; SY21 8EL Cheerful pub with a couple of well kept ales and good chinese restaurant; sports TV, pool; children welcome, decent-sized garden with play area, open from 1pm Fri-Sun, 3pm Tues-Thurs (closed Mon). *(Darrell Barton)*

MONTGOMERY   SO2296
★**Dragon** (01686) 668359
Market Square; SY15 6PA Tall timbered 17th-c hotel (former coaching inn) in quiet little town below ruined Norman castle; beamed back bar on two levels, four well kept ales including local Montys, craft beers and nice choice of wines by the glass, good food from baguettes and pub favourites up, friendly helpful young staff, front bistro-style

---

If you report on a pub that's not a featured entry, please tell us any lunchtimes or evenings when it doesn't serve bar food.

restaurant with central two-way fireplace; unobtrusive background music; children and dogs welcome, 20 comfortable well equipped bedrooms, swimming pool, open all day. *(Steve Whalley)*

PAINSCASTLE SO1646

★**Roast Ox** (01497) 851398
Off A470 Brecon–Builth Wells, or from A438 at Clyro; LD2 3JL Well restored pub with beams, flagstones and stripped-stone walls, appropriate simple furnishings and some rustic bric-a-brac, huge antlers above open fire, ales tapped from the cask and good range of ciders and malt whiskies, popular freshly made food including good fish and chips, friendly quick service; children and dogs welcome, picnic-sets outside, attractive hill country, eight comfortable neat bedrooms; closed Mon, Tues and lunchtimes Weds, Thurs. *(Diana and Bertie Farr)*

PENCELLI SO0925

Royal Oak (01874) 665396
B4558 SE of Brecon; LD3 7LX Unpretentious country pub with two small bars; low beams and log fires, assorted furniture on flagstones, well kept Brains Rev James and a couple of guests, enjoyable home-made food including Sun roasts till 6pm, simple modern dining room; children and dogs welcome, terraces backing on to Monmouth & Brecon Canal (nearby moorings), lovely canalside walks and handy for Taff Trail, open all day. *(Andrew Vincent)*

PENYCAE SN8313

Ancient Briton (01639) 730273
Brecon Road (A4067); SA9 1YY Friendly opened-up roadside pub; nine well kept ales from far and wide, three ciders and enjoyable reasonably priced home-made food; children and dogs welcome, seats outside and play area, four bedrooms, campsite (good facilities including disabled loo and shower), handy for Dan-yr-Ogof caves, Henrhyd Waterfall and Craig-y-Nos Country Park, open all day. *(Julian Richardson)*

RHAYADER SN9668

★**Triangle** (01597) 810537
Cwmdauddwr; B4518 by bridge over River Wye, SW of centre; LD6 5AR Interesting little 16th-c pub with buoyant local atmosphere; good value pubby food (best to book evenings) from shortish menu, well kept Brains Rev James, Hancocks HB and reasonably priced wines, friendly staff, dining area with nice view over to River Wye; darts; children and dogs (in bar) welcome, picnic-sets on small front terrace, self-catering cottage opposite, parking can be difficult, closed Mon in winter (Mon lunchtime summer). *(Darrell Benton)*

A little further afield

Besides the fully inspected pubs, you might like to try these pubs that have been recommended to us and described by readers. Do tell us what you think of them: feedback@goodguides.com

Channel Islands

GUERNSEY

FOREST
Deerhound (01481) 238585
Le Bourg; GY8 0AN Spacious roadside dining pub with modern interior; food can be good, Liberation ales, friendly service; free wi-fi; children welcome, sunny sheltered terrace with parasols, handy for the airport, open all day. *(Alister and Margery Bacon)*

KING'S MILLS
★**Fleur du Jardin** (01481) 257996
King's Mills Road; GY5 7JT Lovely 15th-c country hotel in pretty walled garden; low-beamed bar with log fire, Liberation and guests, local cider and plenty of wines by the glass, very good attractively presented food, afternoon teas, friendly helpful service, restaurant; background music; children and small dogs welcome, plenty of tables on back part-covered terrace, solar-heated swimming pool, 15 stylish, contemporary bedrooms, open all day. *(Simon and Alex Knight)*

ST MARTIN
Les Douvres (01481) 238731
La Fosse; GY4 6ER Sister hotel to the Fleur du Jardin at King's Mills; popular beamed bar with country pub feel, three changing ales and plenty of wines by the glass, decent range of enjoyable fairly priced food including burgers and pizzas, friendly helpful staff; live music Fri; garden with swimming pool, 19 elegant bedrooms, good breakfast, open all day. *(Charlie Walker)*

ST PETER PORT
Ship & Crown (01481) 721368
Opposite Crown Pier, Esplanade; GY1 2NB Bustling old town pub with bay windows overlooking harbour; interesting photographs (especially of World War II occupation, also boats and local shipwrecks), decent bar food from sandwiches up, Liberation ales and guests, welcoming prompt service even when busy, more modern-feel Crow's Nest brasserie upstairs with good views; sports TVs in bar; open all day from 10am (midday Sun) till late. *(Tony Scott)*

VALE
Houmet (01481) 242214
Grande Havre; GY6 8JR Modern building overlooking Grande Havre Bay; front restaurant-bar with conservatory, good choice of reasonably priced food (best to book) including fresh fish/seafood, friendly service, a couple of real ales and several wines by the glass, back public bar with pool, darts and big-screen sports TV (dogs allowed here); children welcome, tables out on sheltered deck, open all day (not Sun evening). *(Simon Sharpe)*

JERSEY

ST AUBIN
Boat House (01534) 747141
North Quay; JE3 8BS Modern steel and timber-clad quayside building with great views (window tables for diners); bar serving well kept local ales and several wines by the glass, good food ranging from small plates to Josper grills, efficient young staff, airy

upstairs restaurant (separate menu) open lunchtimes Fri-Sun and evenings apart from Sun and Mon; balcony and decked terrace overlooking harbour, open all day. *(John Beeken)*

ST AUBIN
⋆Old Court House Inn
(01534) 746433 *Harbour Boulevard; JE3 8AB* Attractively updated and prettily positioned harbourside inn; bustling bar with low beams and open fire, other rambling areas including bistro, popular generously served food from sandwiches and pubby choices to good fresh fish/seafood, well kept Liberation ales and 15 wines by the glass, handsome upstairs restaurant with lovely views across the bay to St Helier, efficient service; children welcome, front deck overlooking harbour, more seats in courtyard behind, ten comfortable well equipped bedrooms, open all day (food all day in summer including breakfasts 7-10am). *(Jeff Davies, Sandra King)*

ST AUBIN
Tenby (01534) 741224
Le Boulevard, towards St Helier; JE3 8AB Randalls pub overlooking the harbour; large bar and several other rooms, decent choice of food (all day Sun) from sandwiches and wraps to good seafood, a couple of real ales such as Skinners and half a dozen gins, helpful service; children welcome, disabled access/loos, seats out on small front deck under awning, more on paved side terrace, open all day. *(Edward and William Johnston)*

ST BRELADE
Old Smugglers (01534) 741510
Ouaisne Bay; OS map reference 595476; JE3 8AW Unpretentious pub just above Ouaisne beach; up to four well kept ales, proper cider and enjoyable traditional food (including vegan choices), friendly service, black beams, built-in settles and log fires, restaurant; occasional live music, sports TV, darts, cribbage and dominoes; children and dogs welcome, sun porch with coast views, open all day in summer (food served all day weekends). *(John Beeken)*

ST HELIER
Cock & Bottle (01534) 722184
Royal Square; JE2 4WA Big lively outside eating area in Royal Square with lovely hanging baskets, rattan tables and chairs under parasols, heaters and blankets for cooler evenings; pleasantly old-fashioned and pubby inside with upholstered settles and small stools in front of large fireplace, wide choice of good food from sandwiches

and wraps through pub favourites and bistro choices to summer seafood menu, well kept Liberation ales; open all day, no evening food Fri-Sun. *(Roger and Donna Huggins)*

ST HELIER
Halkett (01534) 732769
Halkett Place; JE2 4WG Spacious modernised pub-cum-bar close to tree-lined square; two Liberation ales, a guest beer and 17 wines by the glass, fairly priced food from sandwiches/wraps and pubby choices up; DJs Fri and Sat, TVs; sliding door opening on to pavement, open all day, no food Sun evening. *(Roger and Donna Huggins)*

ST HELIER
⋆Lamplighter (01534) 723119
Mulcaster Street; JE2 3NJ Small friendly pub with eight well kept ales, good range of ciders and nearly 200 malt whiskies from long pewter-topped counter, traditional décor with tankards and pump clips on heavy timbers, some old gas light fittings, just snacky food such as pork pies; darts and sports TV; dogs welcome, wheelchair access (no disabled loos), interesting patriotic façade (the only union flag visible during Nazi occupation), open all day. *(Roger and Donna Huggins)*

Isle of Man

DOUGLAS   SC3875
Rovers Return (01624) 676459
Church Street; IM1 3LX Old-fashioned pub tucked down alleyway and popular with good mix of customers; mainly Bushys ales but some mainland guests, generous straightforward lunchtime food (not weekends), friendly staff, several rambling bars, back room filled with Blackburn Rovers memorabilia (landlord is a supporter); rock juke box, TV, pool and darts; no children, tables outside, open all day. *(Chris Stevenson)*

LAXEY   SC4382
Shore (01624) 861509
Old Laxey Hill; IM4 7DA Friendly nautical-themed village pub brewing its own Old Laxey Bosun Bitter, good value wines by the glass and enjoyable pubby food including Tues curry and Thurs steak nights; children welcome, picnic-sets out by lovely stream, nice walk to Laxey waterwheel, two bedrooms, good breakfast, open all day. *(Janet and Tim Dixon)*

PEEL   SC2484
Creek (01624) 842216
Station Place/North Quay; IM5 1AT In lovely setting on the ancient quayside opposite the House of Manannan heritage

centre, very busy at peak times; wide choice of highly thought-of food including fish, crab and lobster fresh from the boats, good local kippers too, up to ten well kept changing ales (always some from Okells), nautical-themed lounge bar with etched mirrors and mainly old woodwork; TVs and weekend live music in public bar; children welcome, tables outside overlooking harbour, open (and food) all day from 10am. *(Dave Samuels)*

PORT ERIN SC1969

Falcon's Nest (01624) 834077

Station Road; IM9 6AF Friendly family-run hotel overlooking the bay, enjoyable food including local fish/seafood and Sun carvery, up to five well kept ales and over 60 malt whiskies, traditional Top Bar with conservatory and open fire, restaurant and separate sports bar (own street entrance) with TV, darts and pool; children welcome, 34 bedrooms, many with sea view, also eight self-catering apartments, handy for steam rail terminus, open all day. *(Jamie Green)*

Pubs that serve food all day

We list here all the pubs (in the Main Entries) that have told us they plan to serve food all day, even if it's only one day of the week. The individual entries for the pubs themselves show the actual details.

Bedfordshire

Ireland, Black Horse

Berkshire

Kintbury, Dundas Arms

Peasemore, Fox

Sonning, Bull

Buckinghamshire

Beaconsfield, White Horse

Forty Green, Royal Standard of England

Cambridgeshire

Peterborough, Brewery Tap

Stilton, Bell

Cheshire

Aldford, Grosvenor Arms

Allostock, Three Greyhounds Inn

Aston, Bhurtpore

Bostock Green, Hayhurst Arms

Bunbury, Dysart Arms

Burleydam, Combermere Arms

Burwardsley, Pheasant

Chester, Architect

Chester, Mill

Chester, Old Harkers Arms

Cholmondeley, Cholmondeley Arms

Delamere, Fishpool

Kelsall, Morris Dancer

Macclesfield, Sutton Hall

Mobberley, Bulls Head

Mobberley, Church Inn

Mobberley, Roebuck

Mottram St Andrew, Bulls Head

Nether Alderley, Wizard

Thelwall, Little Manor

Warmingham, Bears Paw

Cornwall

Mylor Bridge, Pandora

Polgooth, Polgooth Inn

Cumbria

Cartmel Fell, Masons Arms

Crosthwaite, Punch Bowl

Elterwater, Britannia

Ings, Watermill

Levens, Strickland Arms
Lupton, Plough
Ravenstonedale, Black Swan
Threlkeld, Horse & Farrier

Derbyshire

Chelmorton, Church Inn
Fenny Bentley, Coach & Horses
Hathersage, Plough
Hayfield, Royal

Devon

Cockwood, Anchor
Iddesleigh, Duke of York
Postbridge, Warren House

Dorset

Burton Bradstock, Three
    Horseshoes
Weymouth, Red Lion
Worth Matravers, Square &
    Compass

Essex

Feering, Sun
Fyfield, Queens Head
Little Walden, Crown
South Hanningfield, Old Windmill

Gloucestershire

Cheltenham, Old Courthouse
Didmarton, Kings Arms
Nailsworth, Weighbridge
Sheepscombe, Butchers Arms

Hampshire

Bransgore, Three Tuns
Cadnam, White Hart
Eversley, Tally Ho
Littleton, Running Horse
Portsmouth, Old Customs House
Swanwick, Navigator

Hertfordshire

Barnet, Duke of York
St Albans, Prae Wood Arms

Isle of Wight

Bembridge, Spinnaker
Fishbourne, Fishbourne Inn
Seaview, Boathouse

Kent

Chiddingstone Causeway,
    Little Brown Jug
Fordwich, George & Dragon
Langton Green, Hare
Penshurst, Bottle House
Sevenoaks, White Hart
Shipbourne, Chaser
Stalisfield Green, Plough

Lancashire

Bashall Eaves, Red Pump
Bispham Green, Eagle & Child
Formby, Sparrowhawk
Great Mitton, Aspinall Arms
Manchester, Wharf
Nether Burrow, Highwayman
Pleasington, Clog & Billycock
Preston, Haighton Manor
Uppermill, Church Inn

Leicestershire

Swithland, Griffin

Lincolnshire

Kirkby la Thorpe, Queens Head
Stamford, George of Stamford

Norfolk

King's Lynn, Bank House
Larling, Angel
Morston, Anchor

Salthouse, Dun Cow
Thorpe Market, Gunton Arms
Woodbastwick, Fur & Feather

Northumbria

Blanchland, Lord Crewe Arms
Newton, Duke of Wellington

Oxfordshire

Charlbury, Bull
Kingham, Plough
Oxford, Bear
Oxford, Punter
Wolvercote, Jacobs Inn
Woodstock, Woodstock Arms

Shropshire

Baschurch, New Inn
Chetwynd Aston, Fox
Shipley, Inn at Shipley
Shrewsbury, Armoury

Somerset

Dunster, Luttrell Arms
Hinton St George, Lord Poulett
  Arms
Stanton Wick, Carpenters
  Arms
Wedmore, Swan

Staffordshire

Brewood, Oakley
Longdon Green, Red Lion
Salt, Holly Bush
Wrinehill, Hand & Trumpet

Suffolk

Chelmondiston, Butt & Oyster
Southwold, Harbour Inn
Stoke-by-Nayland, Crown
Waldringfield, Maybush

Surrey

Buckland, Pheasant
Chiddingfold, Swan
Chobham, White Hart
Elstead, Mill at Elstead
Englefield Green, Bailiwick
Milford, Refectory
Norwood Hill, Fox Revived

Sussex

Alfriston, George
Bolney, Bolney Stage
Charlton, Fox Goes Free
Eridge Green, Nevill Crest & Gun
Friday Street, Farm at Friday
  Street
Goring-by-Sea, Highdown
Horsham, Black Jug
Ringmer, Cock

Warwickshire

Arrow, Arrow Mill
Birmingham, Old Joint Stock
Birmingham, Physician
Hunningham, Red Lion
Long Compton, Red Lion
Shipston-on-Stour, Black Horse
Shipston-on-Stour, George
Warmington, Falcon
Welford-on-Avon, Bell

Wiltshire

Bradford-on-Avon, Castle

Yorkshire

Beck Hole, Birch Hall
Blakey Ridge, Lion
Bradfield, Strines Inn
Broughton, Bull
Elslack, Tempest Arms
Grinton, Bridge Inn

Halifax, Shibden Mill

Ledsham, Chequers

Linton in Craven, Fountaine

Welburn, Crown & Cushion

Widdop, Pack Horse

York, Judges Lodging

London

Central London, Black Friar

Central London, Coach Makers
Arms

Central London, Old Bank of
England

Central London, Olde Mitre

Central London, Seven Stars

Central London, Thomas Cubitt

North London, Holly Bush

North London, Lighterman

South London, Victoria

West London, Dove

West London, Mute Swan

West London, Old Orchard

Scotland

Applecross, Applecross Inn

Edinburgh, Guildford Arms

Glasgow, Babbity Bowster

Glasgow, Bon Accord

Shieldaig, Tigh an Eilean Hotel

Thornhill, Lion & Unicorn

Scottish Islands

Sligachan, Sligachan Hotel

Wales

Colwyn Bay, Pen-y-Bryn

Gresford, Pant-yr-Ochain

Llandudno Junction, Queens Head

Llanelian-yn-Rhos, White Lion

Llangollen, Corn Mill

Mold, Glasfryn

Overton Bridge, Cross Foxes

Pontypridd, Bunch of Grapes

Pubs near motorway junctions

The number at the start of each line is the number of the junction. Detailed directions are given in the Main Entry for each pub. In this section, to help you find the pubs quickly before you're past the junction, we give the name of the chapter where you'll find the text.

M1

9: Redbourn, Cricketers (Hertfordshire) 3.2 miles

13: Woburn, Birch (Bedfordshire) 3.5 miles

M3

1: Sunbury, Flower Pot (Surrey) 1.6 miles

3: West End, The Inn West End (Surrey) 2.4 miles; Chobham, White Hart (Surrey) 4 miles

5: North Warnborough, Mill House (Hampshire) 1 mile; Hook, Hogget (Hampshire) 1.1 miles; Mattingley, Leather Bottle (Hampshire) 3 miles

M4

9: Bray, Crown (Berkshire) 1.75 miles

13: Curridge, Bunk (Berkshire) 3 miles; Chieveley, Crab & Boar (Berkshire) 3.5 miles; Peasemore, Fox (Berkshire) 4 miles

14: Shefford Woodlands, Pheasant (Berkshire) 0.3 miles

M5

10: Coombe Hill, Gloucester Old Spot (Gloucestershire) 1 mile

13: Eastington, Old Badger (Gloucestershire) 1 mile

M6

16: Barthomley, White Lion (Cheshire) 1 mile

17: Sandbach, Old Hall (Cheshire) 1.2 miles

18: Allostock, Three Greyhounds Inn (Cheshire) 4.7 miles

19: Mobberley, Bulls Head (Cheshire) 4 miles

33: Bay Horse, Bay Horse (Lancashire) 1.2 miles

36: Lupton, Plough (Cumbria) 2 miles; Levens, Strickland Arms (Cumbria) 4 miles

40: Tirril, Queens Head (Cumbria) 3.5 miles

M11

9: Hinxton, Red Lion (Cambridgeshire) 2 miles

10: Whittlesford, Tickell Arms (Cambridgeshire) 2.4 miles

M25

5: Chipstead, George & Dragon (Kent) 1.25 miles

8: Walton on the Hill, Blue Ball (Surrey) 2.5 miles

18: Flaunden, Bricklayers Arms (Hertfordshire) 4 miles

21A: Potters Crouch, Holly Bush (Hertfordshire) 2.3 miles

M27

1: Cadnam, White Hart (Hampshire) 0.5 miles; Fritham, Royal Oak (Hampshire) 4 miles

M40

2: Hedgerley, White Horse (Buckinghamshire) 2.4 miles; Forty Green, Royal Standard of England (Buckinghamshire) 3.5 miles

M42

5: Barston, Malt Shovel (Warwickshire) 3 miles

6: Hampton-in-Arden, White Lion (Warwickshire) 1.25 miles

M50

1: Baughton, Jockey (Worcestershire) 4 miles

3: Kilcot, Kilcot Inn (Gloucestershire) 2.3 miles

M60

13: Worsley, Worsley Old Hall (Lancashire) 1 mile

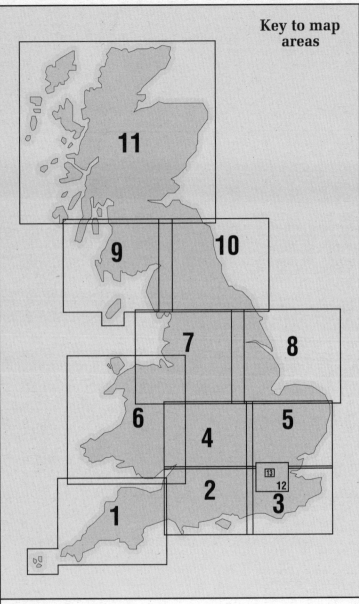

Key to map areas

11

9

10

7

8

6

4

5

13
12

2

3

1

Reference to sectional maps

- ═══ Motorway
- ━━━ Major road
- ----- County boundary

- ● Main Entry
- ◉ Main Entry with accommodation
- ■ Place name to assist navigation

MAPS

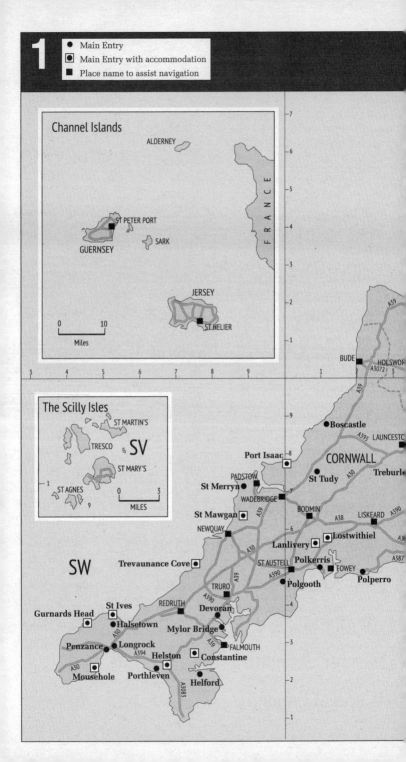

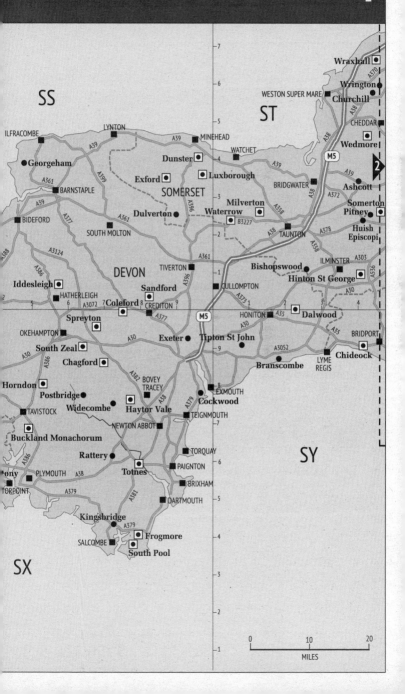

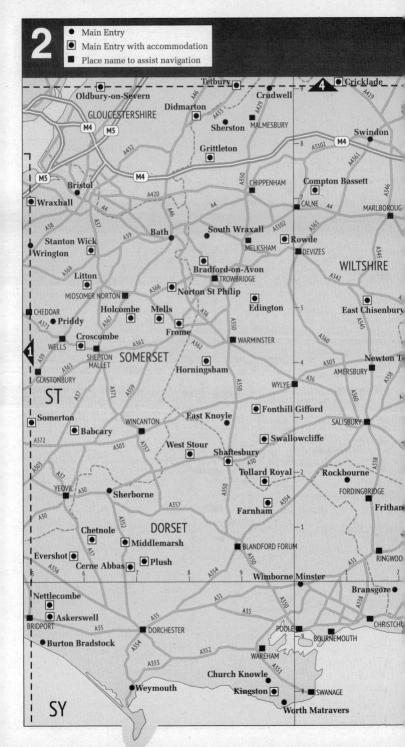

- ● Main Entry
- ◉ Main Entry with accommodation
- ■ Place name to assist navigation

Tetbury
Cricklade
Oldbury-on-Severn
Crudwell
GLOUCESTERSHIRE
Didmarton
M4 M5
Sherston
MALMESBURY
Swindon
Grittleton
M5
CHIPPENHAM
Compton Bassett
Bristol
CALNE
MARLBOROUG
Wraxhall
South Wraxall
Rowde
Stanton Wick
Bath
MELKSHAM
DEVIZES
Wrington
WILTSHIRE
Litton
Bradford-on-Avon
TROWBRIDGE
MIDSOMER NORTON
Norton St Philip
CHEDDAR
Holcombe
Mells
Edington
East Chisenbury
Priddy
Frome
Croscombe
WELLS
WARMINSTER
SHEPTON MALLET
SOMERSET
Horningsham
AMERSBURY
Newton T
GLASTONBURY
WYLYE
ST
Fonthill Gifford
SALISBURY
Somerton
WINCANTON
East Knoyle
Babcary
Swallowcliffe
West Stour
Shaftesbury
Tollard Royal
Rockbourne
YEOVIL
FORDINGBRIDGE
Sherborne
Farnham
Fritham
Chetnole
DORSET
Middlemarsh
BLANDFORD FORUM
RINGWOO
Evershot
Plush
Cerne Abbas
Wimborne Minster
Bransgore
Nettlecombe
CHRISTCH
Askerswell
BRIDPORT
DORCHESTER
POOLE
Burton Bradstock
BOURNEMOUTH
WAREHAM
Church Knowle
Weymouth
Kingston
SWANAGE
SY
Worth Matravers

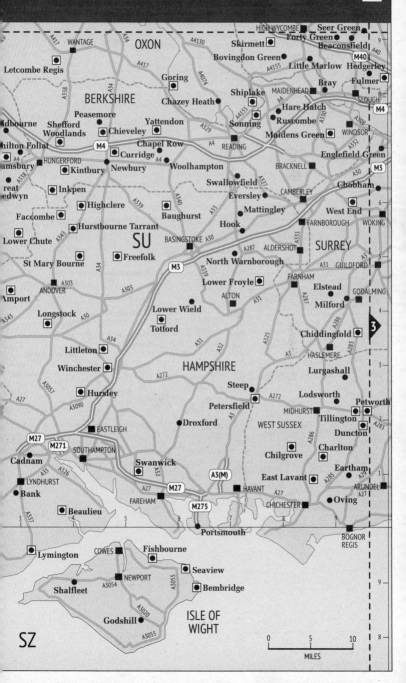

HIGH WYCOMBE ● Seer Green
WANTAGE ● Forty Green
A417 A4130 Skirmett ● Beaconsfield
OXON Bovingdon Green M40
Letcombe Regis A4155 Little Marlow ● Hedgerley
Goring A4074 Bray ● Fulmer
Chazey Heath Shiplake MAIDENHEAD
BERKSHIRE A4155 Hare Hatch SLOUGH M4
Peasemore Yattendon A329 Sonning Ruscombe WINDSOR
dbourne Shefford Chieveley Maidens Green
Woodlands Chapel Row A4 Englefield Green M3
hilton Foliat M4 Curridge READING BRACKNELL A30 Chobham
amsbury HUNGERFORD Newbury A4 Woolhampton Swallowfield CAMBERLEY West End WOKING
Kintbury Highclere A340 Baughurst Mattingley FARNBOROUGH SURREY
reat Inkpen A359 Hook ALDERSHOT GUILDFORD
edwyn Faccombe Hurstbourne Tarrant North Warnborough A31
Lower Chute A345 BASINGSTOKE A30 Lower Froyle FARNHAM Elstead GODALMING
St Mary Bourne A303 M3 ALTON Milford
Amport ANDOVER A34 Lower Wield Chiddingfold
Longstock A303 A30 Totford HAMPSHIRE HASLEMERE Petworth
A345 Littleton A272 Steep Lurgashall
Winchester Hursley Petersfield Lodsworth Tillington
A3057 A3090 Droxford MIDHURST Duncton
Cadnam EASTLEIGH WEST SUSSEX Charlton Eartham
M27 SOUTHAMPTON Swanwick Chilgrove A286 ARUNDEL
M271 Swanwick A3(M) East Lavant CHICHESTER Oving
LYNDHURST M27 FAREHAM HAVANT BOGNOR
Bank M275 CHICHESTER REGIS
Beaulieu Portsmouth
Lymington COWES Fishbourne
NEWPORT Seaview
Shalfleet A3054 Bembridge
Godshill A3020 ISLE OF WIGHT
SZ A3055

SU

0   5   10
MILES

- ● Main Entry
- ◉ Main Entry with accommodation
- ■ Place name to assist navigation

BUCKS

M1   M11   5

Hedgerley   Harefield (see West London section)   M25   A127

M40   GREATER LONDON   Horndon-on-the-Hill

Fulmer   UXBRIDGE   A128

BERKS   M4   TILBURY

M25   A30   GRAVESEND

Englefield   DARTFORD   A2   ROCHESTE

Green   STAINES   A2

A30   Sunbury   Meopham

M3   Esher   M25   M20   A227   A228

Chobham   A3   M26   M2(

A3   Walton on   Chipstead   Chipstead   M20

Ripley   the Hill   A217   A21   MAIDSTON

WOKING   M25   A25   M25   Sevenoaks   TQ

GUILDFORD   Mickleham ◉   Buckland   Oxted   WESTERHAM   Shipbourne

A246   A24   DORKING   A25   A277   A26

Shamley Green   REIGATE   Chiddingstone   TONBRIDGE

SURREY   A217   A23   Penshurst

Norwood Hill   A22   A21

Forest Green   M23   A264   Langton Green   Tunbridge

A281   A24   A23   Copthorne   EAST GRINSTEAD   Wells   A2

Horsham   CRAWLEY   Withyham   Eridge   Mark Cross

A264   West Hoathly   Green   A21

Lower Beeding   Danehill   A22   A26   Ticehurst

A29   Warninglid   A275   CROWBOROUGH   A265   Salehu

Bolney   Fletching   A267

Petworth   A272   HAYWARDS HEATH   Uckfield   Robertsbridge

A283   Dial Post   A23   A22   A267   EAST

A24   BURGESS HILL   A272   SUSSEX

WEST SUSSEX   A273   A275   A26   A271

A29   Ringmer

A283   LEWES   HAILSHAM   A259

ARUNDEL   A27   A27   A26   A27   BEX

A259   WORTHING   BRIGHTON   A259   NEWHAVEN   Alfriston   Friday Stree

Goring-by-Sea   EASTBOURNE

TV

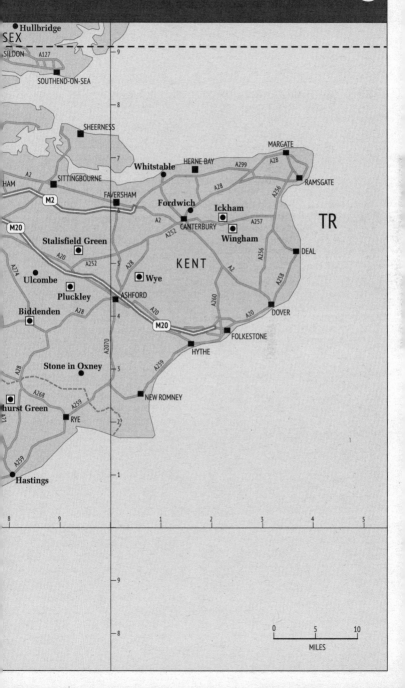

●Hullbridge

SEX

SILDON   A127

SOUTHEND-ON-SEA

SHEERNESS

MARGATE

HERNE BAY   A299   A28

Whitstable

A28   A256   RAMSGATE

HAM   A2

SITTINGBOURNE

M2

FAVERSHAM   **Fordwich**   A28   A257   **TR**

Ickham

M20   A2   CANTERBURY   A252   **Wingham**

A236

Stalisfield Green   DEAL

A20   A252

A28   **KENT**   A2   A256

A274

Ulcombe   ●**Wye**   A258

Pluckley   ASHFORD

Biddenden   A28   A260   DOVER

A20   A20

M20   FOLKESTONE

A2070   HYTHE

Stone in Oxney   A259

A28

A268   A259   NEW ROMNEY

hurst Green

A259   RYE

A259

●**Hastings**

8   9   1   2   3   4   5

9

8   0   5   10

MILES

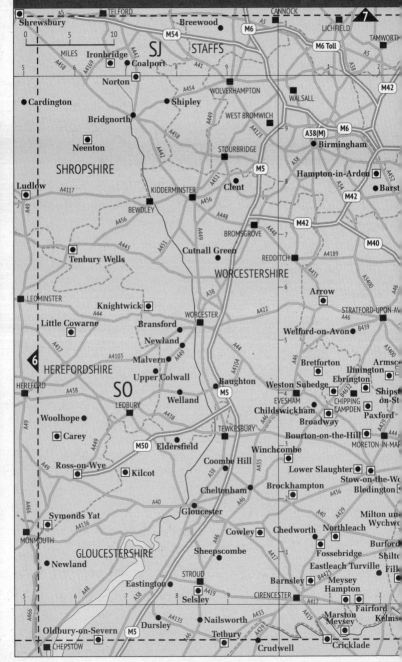

4
- ● Main Entry
- ◉ Main Entry with accommodation
- ■ Place name to assist navigation

Shrewsbury

TELFORD

Breewood

CANNOCK

LICHFIELD

TAMWORTH

A5

M54

M6

M6 Toll

STAFFS

SJ

0   5   10

MILES

Ironbridge

A41

WOLVERHAMPTON

A38

M42

Coalport

Norton

A454

Cardington

Shipley

WALSALL

WEST BROMWICH

A449

A4123

9

M6

A38(M)

Birmingham

Bridgnorth

A458

A442

STOURBRIDGE

A38

M5

Hampton-in-Arden

A452

Neenton

SHROPSHIRE

8

A34

M42

Barst

Ludlow

A4117

A49

KIDDERMINSTER

A451

Clent

A456

A448

M42

M40

BEWDLEY

A456

A443

A451

A449

BROMSGROVE

A448

7

A4189

M40

Tenbury Wells

Cutnall Green

REDDITCH

WORCESTERSHIRE

A435

A3400

A38

6

LEOMINSTER

Arrow

Knightwick

A44

WORCESTER

A422

STRATFORD-UPON-AV

A46

Little Cowarne

A4103

Bransford

5

A44

A46

Bretforton

Armsc

HEREFORDSHIRE

A417

Newland

A449

A4104

Welford-on-Avon

B439

A3400

Ilmington

SO

Malvern

Ebrington

B4632

HEREFORD

Upper Colwall

Baughton

Weston Subedge

Ships

A438

LEDBURY

Welland

M5

EVESHAM

CHIPPING

on-St

Woolhope

A438

Childswickham

CAMPDEN

Paxford

A429

A44

Carey

TEWKESBURY

Broadway

A49

A449

Bourton-on-the-Hill

MORETON-IN-MAR

Ross-on-Wye

M50

Eldersfield

Winchcombe

3

A49

Kilcot

Coombe Hill

A38

A455

Lower Slaughter

Stow-on-the-Wo

MONMOUTH

A40

Cheltenham

A46

Brockhampton

Bledington

Symonds Yat

A4136

Gloucester

2

A436

A40

A429

Milton un

Wychwo

GLOUCESTERSHIRE

Cowley

Chedworth

Northleach

Newland

A46

1

Burford

Sheepscombe

A417

Fossebridge

Shilto

STROUD

Eastleach Turville

Filk

A466

Eastington

A419

Barnsley

B4425

Meysey

Hampton

Selsley

8

9

CIRENCESTER

A417

Oldbury-on-Severn

M5

Dursley

A4135

Nailsworth

A433

A419

Marston

Meysey

Fairford

Kelms

A429

CHEPSTOW

Tetbury

Crudwell

Cricklade

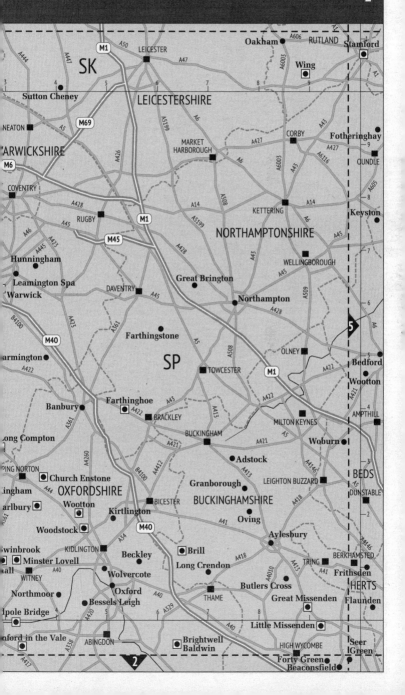

4

SK

M1
A50
LEICESTER
A47
Oakham
A606
RUTLAND
Stamford
A6003
Wing
A1

Sutton Cheney
LEICESTERSHIRE

NEATON
A5
M69
A5199
A6
MARKET HARBOROUGH
A427
CORBY
A43
Fotheringhay

WARWICKSHIRE
A426
A6003
A43
A6116
OUNDLE
A605

M6
COVENTRY
A428
RUGBY
M1
A14
A508
KETTERING
A14
Keyston

M45
A5199
NORTHAMPTONSHIRE
A45

Hunningham
A445
A423
A428
A43
WELLINGBOROUGH
A45

Leamington Spa
DAVENTRY
A45
Great Brington
A509
Northampton
A428

Warwick
A413
A5
A6

M40
A361
Farthingstone
A508
OLNEY
A422
Bedford

armington
A422
SP
TOWCESTER
M1
Wootton
A421

Banbury
A43
Farthinghoe
A422
BRACKLEY
A413
MILTON KEYNES
A5
AMPTHILL

Long Compton
A361
A4260
BUCKINGHAM
A421
A5
Woburn
A146
BEDS

PING NORTON
B4100
A412
Adstock
A413
LEIGHTON BUZZARD
DUNSTABLE

ingham
A44
Church Enstone
OXFORDSHIRE
BICESTER
Granborough
BUCKINGHAMSHIRE
A418

arlbury
Wootton
Kirtlington
Oving
A5

Woodstock
M40
A34
A41
Aylesbury
BERKHAMSTED

winbrook
KIDLINGTON
Beckley
Brill
A418
TRING
A41
Frithsden

Minster Lovell
Long Crendon
A4010
A413
HERTS

all
WITNEY
A40
Wolvercote
Butlers Cross
Great Missenden
Flaunden

Northmoor
Oxford
A40
THAME
Little Missenden

Bessels Leigh
A329

lpole Bridge
A420
Brightwell Baldwin
HIGH WYCOMBE
Seer Green

nford in the Vale
A338
ABINGDON
A40
Forty Green
Beaconsfield

2

5

- Main Entry
- Main Entry with accommodation
- Place name to assist navigation

LINCS

WISBECH

8

DOWNHAM MARKET

Stamford

Ufford

Thorney

TF

Peterborough

Elton

Fotheringhay

Stilton

CAMBRIDGESHIRE

CHATTERIS

OUNDLE

NORTHANTS

A1(M)

ELY

MILDENHALL

Keyston

Huntingdon

Hemingford Grey

4

Horningsea

NEWMARKET

Madingley

Cambridge

TL

Bedford

Balsham

Wootton

BEDFORDSHIRE

Whittlesford

Ireland

ROYSTON

Hinxton

Little Walden

AMPTHILL

Chrishall

SAFFRON WALDEN

Cottered

HERTFORDSHIRE

ESSEX

M1

HITCHIN

STEVENAGE

Ardeley

BRAINTR

DUNSTABLE

Preston

A1(M)

BISHOP'S STORTFORD

Littley Green

LUTON

Watton-at-Stone

Howe Street

Fuller Str

HARPENDEN

HERTFORD

BERKHAMSTED

Redbourn

HATFIELD

Hertford Heath

Fyfield

CHELMSFORD

Frithsden

St Albans

HARLOW

HEMEL HEMPSTEAD

Potters Crouch

Flaunden

EPPING

Sarratt

M1

Barnet

TQ

M25

South Hanningfield

ENFIELD

M25

BRENTWOOD

3

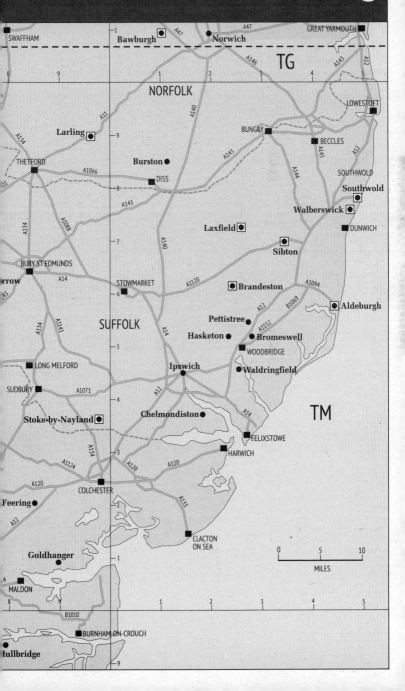

5

SWAFFHAM

Bawburgh ◉

A47

Norwich ●

GREAT YARMOUTH ■

8

9

A146

A47

A143

A12

TG

4

5

NORFOLK

1

2

3

LOWESTOFT ■

A11

A134

Larling ◉

9

A140

BUNGAY ■

BECCLES ■

A143

A145

A12

THETFORD ■

A1066

Burston ●

DISS ■

SOUTHWOLD

A144

Southwold ◉

A11

8

A143

A1008

Walberswick ◉

DUNWICH ■

7

Laxfield ◉

A140

Sibton ◉

BURY ST EDMUNDS ■

A14

STOWMARKET ■

6

A1120

◉ Brandeston

A1094

Aldeburgh ◉

rrow

SUFFOLK

A14

5

Pettistree ●

A12

B1069

A134

A1141

Hasketon ●

A1152

Bromeswell ●

WOODBRIDGE

LONG MELFORD ■

4

Ipswich ■

Waldringfield ●

SUDBURY ■

A1071

A12

TM

Stoke-by-Nayland ◉

Chelmondiston ●

A14

3

A120

A1124

FELIXSTOWE ■

A120

A120

HARWICH ■

A120

Feering ●

COLCHESTER ■

2

A133

A12

0   5   10

CLACTON
ON SEA ■

MILES

Goldhanger ●

1

MALDON ■

4

8

B1010

9

BURNHAM-ON-CROUCH ■

lullbridge ●

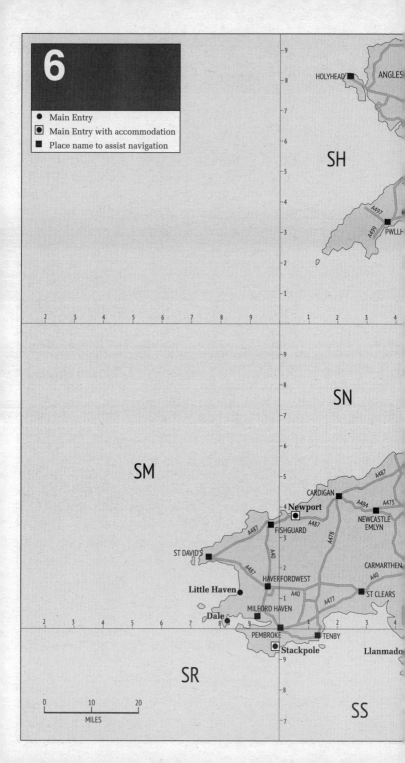

6

- ● Main Entry
- ◉ Main Entry with accommodation
- ■ Place name to assist navigation

HOLYHEAD ■   ANGLES

SH

A497

A499   PWLLH

SN

SM

A487

CARDIGAN   A484   A475

◉ 4 Newport

NEWCASTLE
EMLYN

A487

FISHGUARD   A478

A40

CARMARTHEN

ST DAVID'S

A487

A40

HAVERFORDWEST

Little Haven ●   A40   ST CLEARS

A477

MILFORD HAVEN

Dale ●

PEMBROKE   ■ TENBY

SR   ◉ Stackpole   Llanmado

SS

0   10   20
MILES

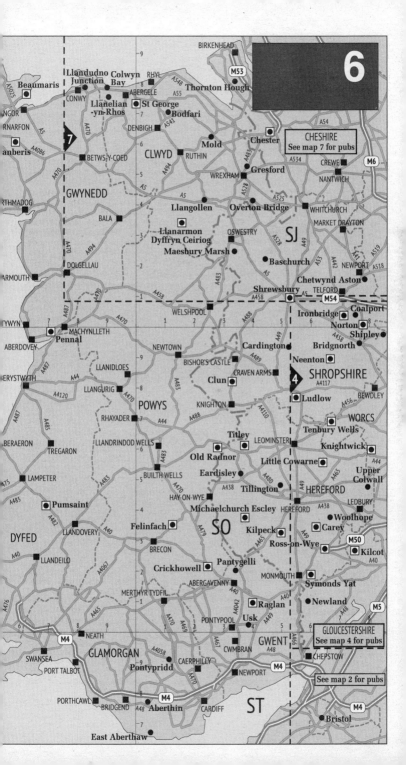

6

BIRKENHEAD

M53

Beaumaris
Llandudno Colwyn RHYL
Junction Bay
CONWY ABERGELE Thornton Hough
A548 A55
Llanelian St George Bodfari
-yn-Rhos
NGOR DENBIGH A541

RNARFON A5 Chester
anberis A4086 Mold CHESHIRE
See map 7 for pubs
BETWS-Y-COED CLWYD RUTHIN
CREWE M6
Gresford NANTWICH
GWYNEDD WREXHAM A534
A528 A525
Llangollen Overton Bridge
BALA WHITCHURCH
OSWESTRY MARKET DRAYTON
Llanarmon
Dyffryn Ceiriog A528 A49 SJ
Maesbury Marsh NEWPORT A518
Baschurch A442
DOLGELLAU A5 Chetwynd Aston
ARMOUTH Shrewsbury TELFORD
A458 M54
Coalport
WELSHPOOL Ironbridge
TYWYN A470 Norton
MACHYNLLETH Shipley
Pennal Cardington Bridgnorth
ABERDOVEY NEWTOWN Neenton
ERYSTWYTH A44 LLANIDLOES Bishop's Castle SHROPSHIRE
A4117
BERAERON LLANGURIG Clun CRAVEN ARMS 4
Ludlow BEWDLEY
POWYS KNIGHTON WORCS
RHAYADER Tenbury Wells
LAMPETER Knightwick
LLANDRINDOD WELLS Titley LEOMINSTER
Pumsaint Old Radnor Little Cowarne Upper
BUILTH WELLS Eardisley Colwall
Felinfach HAY-ON-WYE Tillington HEREFORD
DYFED LEDBURY
LLANDOVERY Michaelchurch Escley Woolhope
SO HEREFORD
Kilpeck Carey
BRECON Ross-on-Wye
LLANDEILO Pantygelli M50
Crickhowell Kilcot
ABERGAVENNY MONMOUTH
MERTHYR TYDFIL Symonds Yat
Raglan Newland M5
PONTYPOOL
NEATH Usk GLOUCESTERSHIRE
See map 4 for pubs
GLAMORGAN CWMBRAN GWENT
SWANSEA CAERPHILLY CHEPSTOW
Pontypridd M4 NEWPORT
PORT TALBOT See map 2 for pubs
PORTHCAWL M4
BRIDGEND Aberthin CARDIFF ST M4
East Aberthaw Bristol

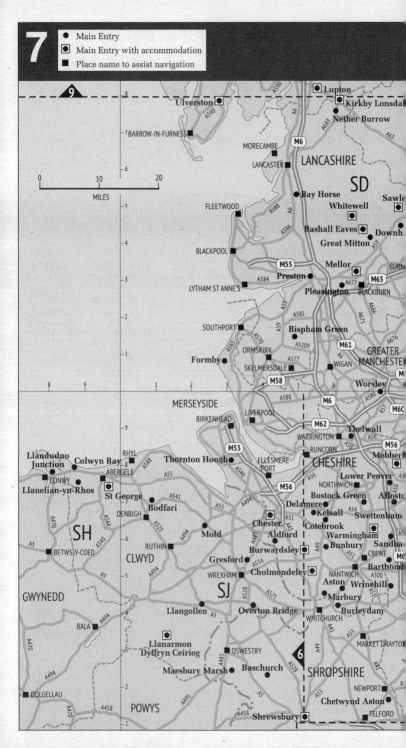

- Main Entry
- Main Entry with accommodation
- Place name to assist navigation

9

Ulverston

Lupton
Kirkby Lonsdale
Nether Burrow

BARROW-IN-FURNESS

MORECAMBE

M6

LANCASTER

LANCASHIRE

SD

Bay Horse
Whitewell
Sawle

FLEETWOOD

Bashall Eaves
Downh
Great Mitton

BLACKPOOL

BURN

Mellor
M65

M55
Preston

LYTHAM ST ANNE'S

Pleasington
BLACKBURN

0   10   20
MILES

SOUTHPORT

Bispham Green

ORMSKIRK
Formby

SKELMERSDALE

WIGAN

GREATER
MANCHESTER

M58

M61

M

Worsley

MERSEYSIDE

M6

M580

M60

LIVERPOOL

BIRKENHEAD

M62

Thelwall

WARRINGTON
RUNCORN

M56

M53

Thornton Hough

ELLESMERE
PORT

CHESHIRE

Mobber

Llandudno
Junction

Colwyn Bay

RHYL

ABERGELE

Lower Peover

NORTHWICH

M56

CONWY
Llanelian-yn-Rhos

St George

A55

Bostock Green
Allosto

Delamere

Bodfari

Swettenham

DENBIGH

Kelsall

Chester

SH

Cotebrook

Aldford

Warmingham

Mold

Burwardsley

Bunbury

Sandba

BETWS-Y-COED

RUTHIN

Gresford

CLWYD

WREXHAM

Cholmondeley

GWYNEDD

SJ

CREWE

M6

Barthom

NANTWICH
Aston
Wrinehill

Marbury

BALA

Llangollen

Overton Bridge

Burleydam

WHITCHURCH

MARKET DRAYTON

Llanarmon
Dyffryn Ceiriog

OSWESTRY

6

DOLGELLAU

Maesbury Marsh

Baschurch

SHROPSHIRE

POWYS

NEWPORT

Chetwynd Aston

TELFORD

Shrewsbury

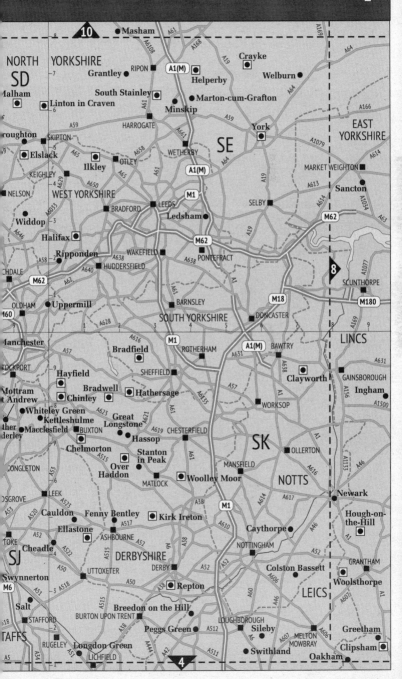

7

10 ● Masham

NORTH YORKSHIRE
SD
Malham   ● RIPON   ● Grantley   A1(M)   Crayke ●
                                                Helperby   Welburn ●
           ● South Stainley
    ● Linton in Craven   ● Marton-cum-Grafton
broughton   Minskip
    SKIPTON   HARROGATE   York ●   EAST
    ● Elslack   WETHERBY   SE   YORKSHIRE
  KEIGHLEY Ilkley OTLEY   MARKET WEIGHTON
● NELSON WEST YORKSHIRE   A1(M)
                            M1   ● Sancton
Widdop   BRADFORD   LEEDS   SELBY ●
          ● Halifax   Ledsham ●   M62
    ● Ripponden   WAKEFIELD   M62
CHDALE M62   HUDDERSFIELD PONTEFRACT   8
OLDHAM ● Uppermill   SCUNTHORPE
160   BARNSLEY   M18   M180
         ● Bradfield SOUTH YORKSHIRE DONCASTER
Manchester   M1   LINCS
TOCKPORT   ROTHERHAM   A1(M) BAWTRY
    ● Hayfield   SHEFFIELD   ● Clayworth GAINSBOROUGH
Mottram ● Bradwell ● Hathersage   ● Ingham
t Andrew ● Chinley
    ● Whiteley Green   ● Great WORKSOP
      ● Kettleshulme   Longstone
ther ● Macclesfield ● BUXTON CHESTERFIELD   SK
derley   ● Chelmorton ● Hassop
CONGLETON   ● Over   ● Stanton   ● OLLERTON
             Haddon in Peak
            MATLOCK ● Woolley Moor MANSFIELD   NOTTS
OSGROVE ● LEEK   ● Newark
    ● Cauldon ● Fenny Bentley ● Kirk Ireton   ● Hough-on-
    ● Ellastone   M1   the-Hill
TOKE ● Cheadle ASHBOURNE   ● Caythorpe
SJ   DERBYSHIRE   NOTTINGHAM   GRANTHAM
Swynnerton UTTOXETER   DERBY   ● Woolsthorpe
M6   ● Repton   ● Colston Bassett
  ● Salt   LEICS
    STAFFORD   Breedon on the Hill LOUGHBOROUGH   ● Greetham
TAFFS   BURTON UPON TRENT   ● Sileby
    RUGELEY ● Longdon Green Peggs Green ● MELTON ● Clipsham
           LICHFIELD   ● Swithland MOWBRAY Oakham ●
                        4

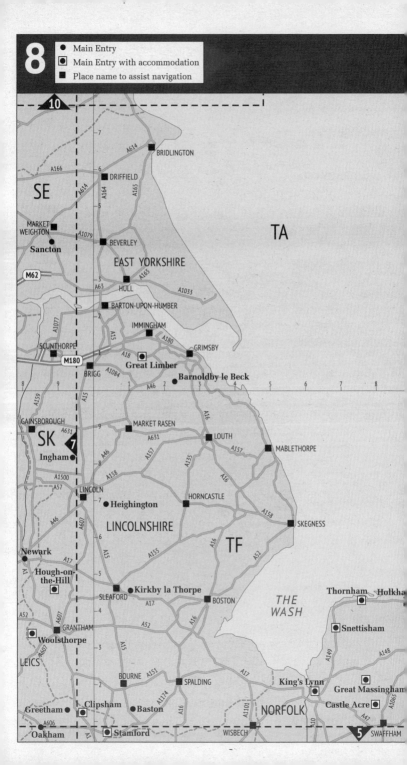

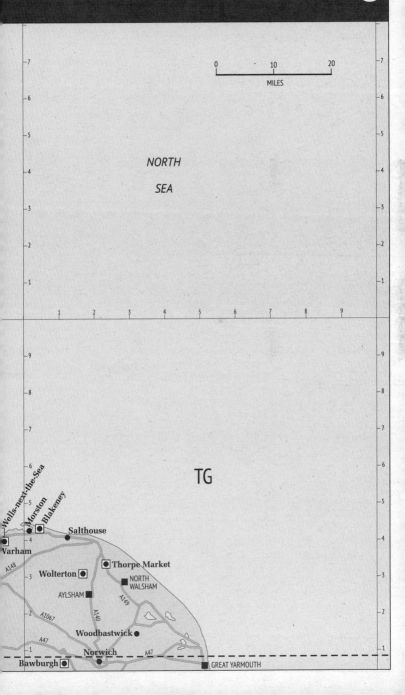

8

0   10   20
MILES

NORTH

SEA

TG

Wells-next-the-Sea

Morston

Blakeney

Salthouse

Varham

A148

Wolterton

☐ **Thorpe Market**

NORTH
WALSHAM

AYLSHAM

A149

A1067

A140

A47

Woodbastwick

Norwich

A47

Bawburgh

GREAT YARMOUTH

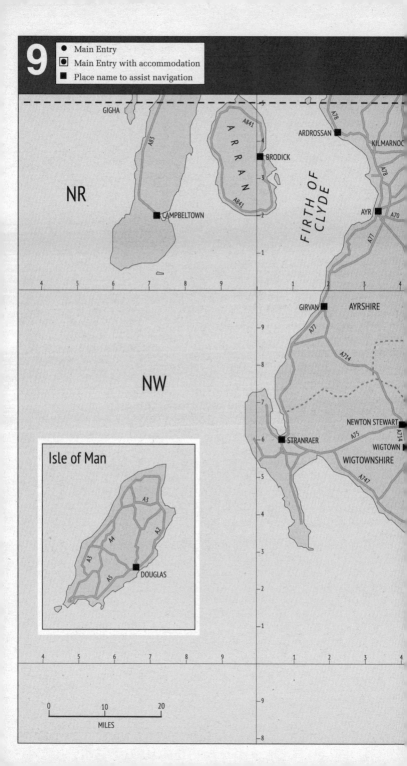

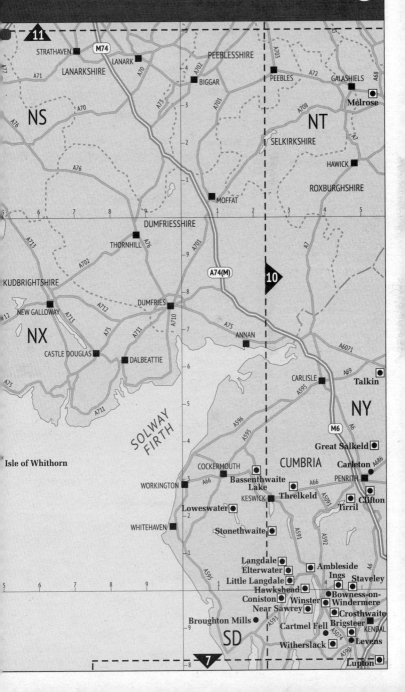

STRATHAVEN
M74
LANARK
LANARKSHIRE
A71
A77
A76
NS
A70
A76

PEEBLESSHIRE
BIGGAR
A701
A702
PEEBLES
A703
GALASHIELS
A68
Melrose
A708
NT
SELKIRKSHIRE
A7
HAWICK
ROXBURGHSHIRE

MOFFAT
DUMFRIESSHIRE
THORNHILL
A76
A702
A713
A701
A74(M)
A7
10

KUDBRIGHTSHIRE
NEW GALLOWAY
A12
A712
A713
A75
A711
DUMFRIES
A710
A75
ANNAN
A6071
A69
NX
CASTLE DOUGLAS
DALBEATTIE
A75
A711
CARLISLE
A595
Talkin
NY

SOLWAY FIRTH

Isle of Whithorn

M6
A6
Great Salkeld
CUMBRIA
Carleton
A686
PENRITH
A66
A6071
A591
A592
Clifton
Tirril

COCKERMOUTH
A66
Bassenthwaite Lake
WORKINGTON
KESWICK
Threlkeld
Loweswater
WHITEHAVEN
Stonethwaite
A595
A596
A595

Langdale
Elterwater
Little Langdale
Hawkshead
Coniston
Near Sawrey
Winster
Ambleside
Ings
Staveley
A6
Bowness-on-Windermere
Crosthwaite
Brigsteer
KENDAL

Broughton Mills
Cartmel Fell
Witherslack
A5074
Levens
A590

SD
A593
A595

7

Lupton

● Main Entry
◉ Main Entry with accommodation
■ Place name to assist navigation

BERWICKSHIRE
Swinton
BERWICK-UPON-TWEED

11

PEEBLES
GALASHIELS
Melrose
COLDSTREAM
KELSO
Seahous

SELKIRKSHIRE
Ancrum
JEDBURGH
NT
WOOLER
Newton-by-the-Sea
Cras

HAWICK
ALNWICK

ROXBURGHSHIRE
NORTHUMBERLAND

DUMFRIESSHIRE
OTTERBURN
Stannersburn
MORPETH

9

Wark
Barrasford
NORTH SHIE

A74(M)
BRAMPTON
Gilsland
HAYDON BRIDGE
Newton
NEWCASTLE UPON TYNE

CARLISLE
Talkin
HEXHAM
CORBRIDGE

NY
Diptonmill
Hedley on the Hill
CONSETT
GATESHEAD

M6
Blanchland
ALSTON
Durham
DURHAM

Great Salkeld

Threlkeld
PENRITH
Carleton
BISHOP AUCKLAND

KESWICK
Clifton
Romaldkirk
Winston

Tirril
BROUGH
Cotherstone
DARLINGTON

Stonethwaite
CUMBRIA
BARNARD CASTLE

Langdale
Elterwater
Ambleside
Ravenstonedale
SCOTCH CORNER
RICHMOND
Moulto

Little Langdale
Ings
Staveley
Grinton
NOR

Hawkshead
Bowness-on-Windermere
Constable Burton

Coniston
Winster
Crosthwaite
KENDAL
Leyburn
Kirkb
Fleeth

Near Sawrey
Brigsteer
SEDBERGH

Cartmel Fell
Levens
East Witton

Witherslack
SD
Thornton Watlass

Lupton
7
Masham

0   10   20

MILES

NU

NORTH

SEA

OUTH SHIELDS

SUNDERLAND   NZ

A19

HARTLEPOOL

MIDDLESBROUGH   A174

A171

WHITBY

A172

A169

A171

Beck Hole

YORKSHIRE   Blakey Ridge

A19   SE   Levisham   TA

A168   Felixkirk   Lockton

HELMSLEY   SCARBOROUGH

THIRSK   A170   PICKERING   A170

A169   A165

8

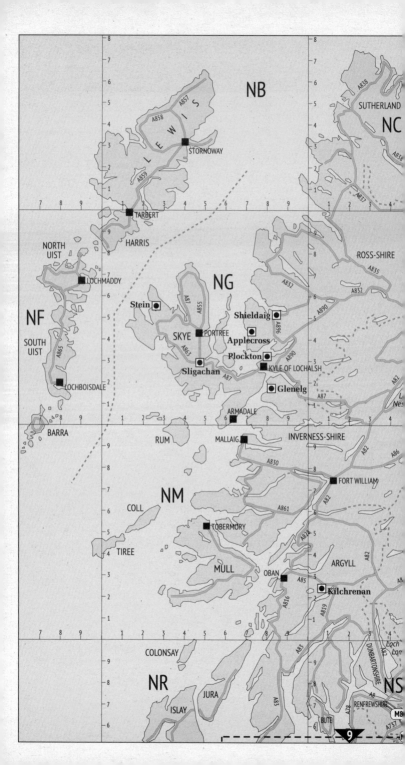

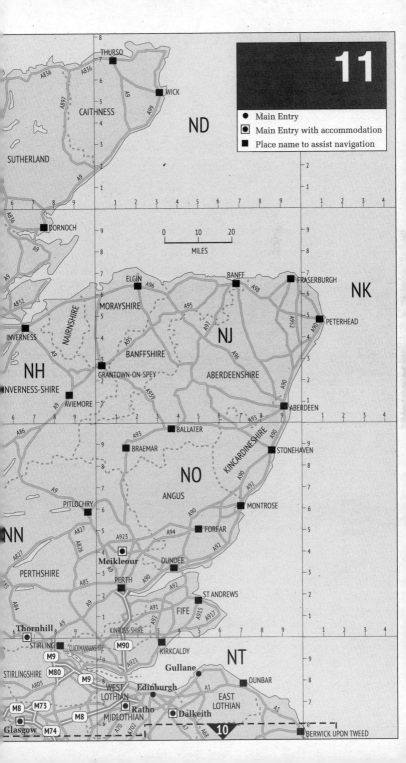

Main Entry
Main Entry with accommodation
Place name to assist navigation

ND

THURSO
WICK
A836 A836 A897 A9 A99
CAITHNESS
SUTHERLAND

DORNOCH
A9
A836
A832

0   10   20
MILES

ELGIN
BANFF
FRASERBURGH
A96 A98
NK
NAIRNSHIRE
MORAYSHIRE
A95
PETERHEAD
A97 A952 A90
NJ
A95
INVERNESS
BANFFSHIRE
A96
NH
GRANTOWN-ON-SPEY
ABERDEENSHIRE
INVERNESS-SHIRE
A939
A9
AVIEMORE
A90
A493
ABERDEEN

A86
BALLATER
A93
KINCARDINESHIRE
BRAEMAR
STONEHAVEN
A90
NO
A92
NN
A9
ANGUS
PITLOCHRY
MONTROSE
A827
A826
A94
FORFAR
A90 A92
A827
A923
A84
A95
MEIKLEOUR
DUNDEE
PERTHSHIRE
PERTH
A85
A90 A92
ST ANDREWS
A91
A915 A917
FIFE
Thornhill
A9
KINROSS-SHIRE
STIRLING
M90
KIRKCALDY
NT
M9
CLACKMANNANSHIRE
A921
Gullane
STIRLINGSHIRE
M80
DUNBAR
M9
WEST
A1
M8 M73
LOTHIAN
Edinburgh
EAST
LOTHIAN
M8
Ratho
A1
Glasgow
M74
MIDLOTHIAN
Dalkeith
A70 A702
A7 A68
10
BERWICK UPON TWEED

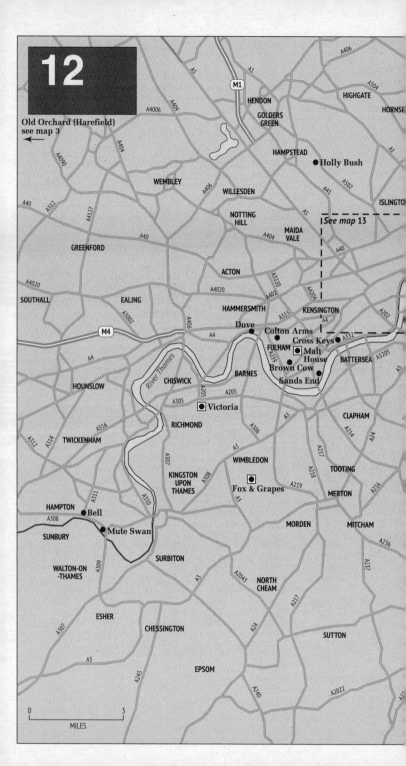

12

Old Orchard (Harefield)
see map 3
←

A406
A5
M1
A504
A1
HIGHGATE
HENDON
HORNSE
GOLDERS
GREEN
A4006
A409
A404
A4090
HAMPSTEAD
● Holly Bush
A502
ISLINGTO
WEMBLEY
A406
WILLESDEN
A41
A312
A40
A4127
NOTTING
HILL
MAIDA
VALE
A5
See map 13
GREENFORD
A40
A404
A40
A4020
A4020
ACTON
A3210
SOUTHALL
EALING
A3002
HAMMERSMITH
A402
A4020
A315
KENSINGTON
A4
A202
M4
A406
A4
Dove
Colton Arms
Cross Keys
A4
A332
A3205
HOUNSLOW
A4
CHISWICK
River Thames
BARNES
FULHAM
A219
Malt
House
BATTERSEA
Brown Cow
Sands End
A305
A205
A205
A306
A5
CLAPHAM
A214
A24
Victoria
RICHMOND
A316
A307
WIMBLEDON
A3
A217
A218
TOOTING
A216
A312
A314
TWICKENHAM
KINGSTON
UPON
THAMES
A308
Fox & Grapes
A219
A3
MERTON
A311
HAMPTON
●Bell
A308
●Mute Swan
MORDEN
MITCHAM
A236
SUNBURY
A310
SURBITON
A237
WALTON-ON
-THAMES
A309
A3
A2043
NORTH
CHEAM
A217
SUTTON
ESHER
CHESSINGTON
A24
A307
A3
EPSOM
A240
A2022
A2

0   3
MILES

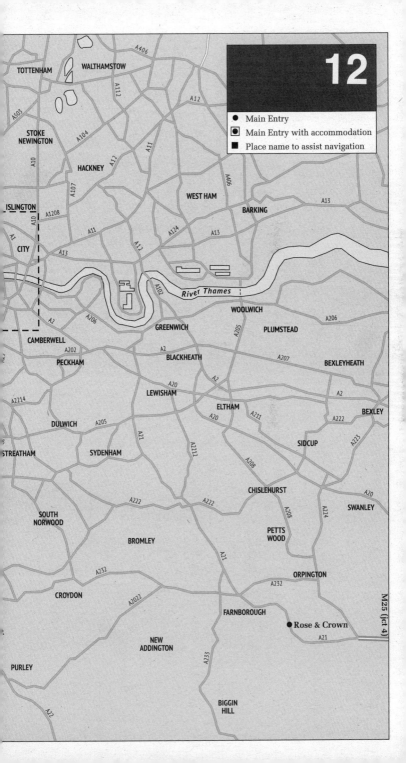

12

- ● Main Entry
- ◉ Main Entry with accommodation
- ■ Place name to assist navigation

TOTTENHAM WALTHAMSTOW
A406
A112
A12
A503
STOKE NEWINGTON
A104
A11
A12
HACKNEY
A10
A107
A11
A406
WEST HAM
ISLINGTON
A1208
BARKING
A13
A10
A11
A124
A13
A1
CITY
A13
A12
River Thames
A102
WOOLWICH
A206
A2
A206
GREENWICH
A205
PLUMSTEAD
CAMBERWELL
A202
A2
BLACKHEATH
A207
BEXLEYHEATH
PECKHAM
A2
A2214
LEWISHAM
A20
A2
ELTHAM
A211
BEXLEY
A222
DULWICH
A205
A21
A112
SIDCUP
A223
STREATHAM
SYDENHAM
A108
A20
CHISLEHURST
SOUTH NORWOOD
A222
A222
A108
A224
SWANLEY
BROMLEY
PETTS WOOD
A21
CROYDON
A232
ORPINGTON
A2022
A232
FARNBOROUGH
● Rose & Crown
M25 (Jct 4)
NEW ADDINGTON
A21
A233
PURLEY
A22
BIGGIN HILL

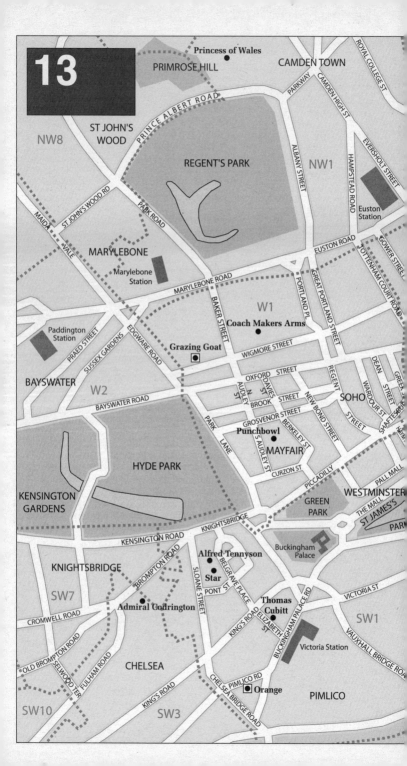

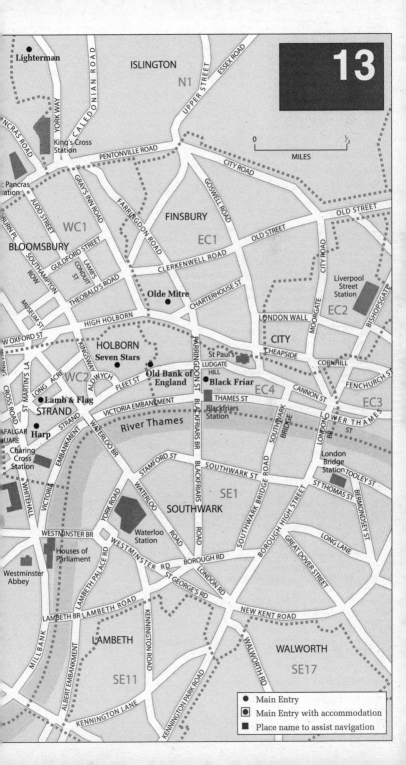

Lighterman

ISLINGTON

N1

CALEDONIAN ROAD

YORK WAY

UPPER STREET

ESSEX ROAD

NCRAS ROAD

King's Cross
Station

Pancras
ation

PENTONVILLE ROAD

CITY ROAD

0   ½

MILES

JUDD STREET

GRAY'S INN ROAD

FARRINGDON ROAD

GOSWELL ROAD

BURN PL

WC1

FINSBURY

EC1

OLD STREET

BLOOMSBURY

GUILDFORD STREET

CONDUIT
ST

LAMB'S
ROAD

THEOBALD'S ROAD

CLERKENWELL ROAD

OLD STREET

CITY ROAD

MOORGATE

BISHOPSGATE

Liverpool
Street
Station

EC2

SOUTHAMPTON

ROW

MUSEUM ST

HIGH HOLBORN

CHARTERHOUSE ST

Olde Mitre

LONDON WALL

W OXFORD ST

HOLBORN

KINGSWAY

Seven Stars

CITY

St Paul's

CHEAPSIDE

CORNHILL

ING

CROSS ROAD

ST MARTIN'S LA

WC2

LONG ACRE

ALDWYCH

Old Bank of
England

FLEET ST

LUDGATE
HILL

FARRINGDON ST

Black Friar

EC4

CANNON ST

FENCHURCH ST

EC3

Lamb & Flag

STRAND

STRAND

VICTORIA EMBANKMENT

WATERLOO BR

BLACKFRIARS BR

THAMES ST

Blackfriars
Station

LOWER THAMES

ST

LONDON BR

FALGAR
UARE

Harp

EMBANKMENT

VICTORIA

River Thames

SOUTHWARK
BRIDGE

London
Bridge
Station

TOOLEY ST

Charing
Cross
Station

STAMFORD ST

BLACKFRIARS ROAD

SOUTHWARK ST

SOUTHWARK BRIDGE ROAD

BOROUGH HIGH STREET

ST THOMAS ST

BERMONDSEY ST

WHITEHALL

WATERLOO ROAD

SE1

SOUTHWARK

LONG LANE

WESTMINSTER BR

Houses of
Parliament

WESTMINSTER

RD

YORK ROAD

Waterloo
Station

BOROUGH RD

LONDON RD

GREAT DOVER STREET

Westminster
Abbey

ST GEORGE'S RD

LAMBETH PALACE RD

LAMBETH BR

LAMBETH ROAD

MILLBANK

ALBERT EMBANKMENT

KENNINGTON ROAD

LAMBETH

SE11

NEW KENT ROAD

WALWORTH

SE17

WALWORTH RD

KENNINGTON PARK ROAD

KENNINGTON LANE

● Main Entry

◉ Main Entry with accommodation

■ Place name to assist navigation

REPORT FORMS

We would very much appreciate hearing about your visits to pubs in this *Guide*, whether you have found them as described and recommend them for continued inclusion or noticed a fall in standards.

We'd also be glad to hear of any new pubs that you think we should know about. Readers' reports are very valuable to us, and sometimes pubs are dropped simply because we have had no up-to-date news on them.

You can use the tear-out forms on the following pages, email us at feedback@goodguides.com or send us comments via our website (www.thegoodpubguide.co.uk) or app. We include two types of forms: one for you to simply list pubs you have visited and confirm that our review is accurate, and the other for you to give us more detailed information on individual pubs. If you would like more forms, please write to us at:

Freepost THE GOOD PUB GUIDE, Random House Publishing,
20 Vauxhall Bridge Road, London SW1V 2SA

We send out thank-you letters to everyone who reports to us, but please understand if there's a delay (particularly in summer, our busiest period).

If you would also like to continue to receive *Good Pub Guide* newsletters and offers from the Random House Group, please tick the box provided on the form.

The end of April is the cut-off date for reports for the next edition. We will, of course, use reports after this date, but your name will not appear in the *Guide* until the following year.

We'll assume we can print your name or initials as a recommender unless you tell us otherwise.

MAIN ENTRY OR 'ALSO WORTH A VISIT'?
Please try to gauge whether a pub should be a Main Entry or in the Also Worth a Visit section (and tick the relevant box). Main Entries need qualities that would make it worth other readers' while to travel some distance to them. If a pub is an entirely new recommendation, the Also Worth a Visit section may be the best place for it to start its career in the *Guide* – to encourage other readers to report on it.

The more detail you can put into your description of a pub, the better. Any information on how good the landlord or landlady is, what it looks like inside, what you like about the atmosphere and character, the quality and type of food, and which real ales are available and whether they're well kept, whether bedrooms are available, and how big/attractive the garden is. Other helpful information includes prices for food and bedrooms, food service and opening hours, and if children or dogs are welcome.

If the food or accommodation are is outstanding, tick the FOOD Award or the STAY Award box.

If you're in a position to gauge a pub's suitability or otherwise for people with disabilities, do please tell us about that.

If you can, give the full address or directions for any pub not currently in the *Guide* – most of all, please give us its postcode. If we can't find a pub's postcode, we don't include it in the *Guide*.

I have been to the following pubs in *The Good Pub Guide 2020* in the last few months, found them as described, and confirm that they deserve continued inclusion:

continued overleaf

PLEASE GIVE YOUR NAME AND ADDRESS ON THE BACK OF THIS FORM

Pubs visited continued..........

I would like to receive Good Pub Guide updates and offers from
The Random House Group. ☐

Your own name and address *(block capitals please)*

....

....

....

Postcode..

Please return to
Freepost THE GOOD PUB GUIDE,
Random House Publishing,
20 Vauxhall Bridge Road,
London SW1V 2SA

IF YOU PREFER, YOU CAN SEND
US REPORTS BY EMAIL:

feedback@goodguides.com

I have been to the following pubs in *The Good Pub Guide 2020* in the last few months, found them as described, and confirm that they deserve continued inclusion:

continued overleaf

PLEASE GIVE YOUR NAME AND ADDRESS ON THE BACK OF THIS FORM

Pubs visited continued..........

I would like to receive Good Pub Guide updates and offers from
The Random House Group. ☐

Your own name and address *(block capitals please)*

....

....

....

Postcode...

Please return to
Freepost THE GOOD PUB GUIDE,
Random House Publishing,
20 Vauxhall Bridge Road,
London SW1V 2SA

IF YOU PREFER, YOU CAN SEND
US REPORTS BY EMAIL:

feedback@goodguides.com

I have been to the following pubs in *The Good Pub Guide 2020* in the last few months, found them as described, and confirm that they deserve continued inclusion:

continued overleaf

PLEASE GIVE YOUR NAME AND ADDRESS ON THE BACK OF THIS FORM

Pubs visited continued..........

I would like to receive Good Pub Guide updates and offers from
The Random House Group. □

Your own name and address *(block capitals please)*

....

....

....

Postcode...

Please return to
Freepost THE GOOD PUB GUIDE,
Random House Publishing,
20 Vauxhall Bridge Road,
London SW1V 2SA

IF YOU PREFER, YOU CAN SEND
US REPORTS BY EMAIL:

feedback@goodguides.com

I have been to the following pubs in *The Good Pub Guide 2020* in the last few months, found them as described, and confirm that they deserve continued inclusion:

continued overleaf

PLEASE GIVE YOUR NAME AND ADDRESS ON THE BACK OF THIS FORM

Pubs visited continued..........

I would like to receive Good Pub Guide updates and offers from The Random House Group. ☐

Your own name and address *(block capitals please)*

....

....

....

Postcode...

Please return to
Freepost THE GOOD PUB GUIDE,
Random House Publishing,
20 Vauxhall Bridge Road,
London SW1V 2SA

IF YOU PREFER, YOU CAN SEND
US REPORTS BY EMAIL:

feedback@goodguides.com

I have been to the following pubs in *The Good Pub Guide 2020* in the last few months, found them as described, and confirm that they deserve continued inclusion:

continued overleaf

PLEASE GIVE YOUR NAME AND ADDRESS ON THE BACK OF THIS FORM

Pubs visited continued..........

I would like to receive Good Pub Guide updates and offers from
The Random House Group. ☐

Your own name and address *(block capitals please)*

....

....

....

Postcode..

Please return to
Freepost THE GOOD PUB GUIDE,
Random House Publishing,
20 Vauxhall Bridge Road,
London SW1V 2SA

IF YOU PREFER, YOU CAN SEND
US REPORTS BY EMAIL:

feedback@goodguides.com

I have been to the following pubs in *The Good Pub Guide 2020* in the last few months, found them as described, and confirm that they deserve continued inclusion:

continued overleaf

PLEASE GIVE YOUR NAME AND ADDRESS ON THE BACK OF THIS FORM

Pubs visited continued..........

I would like to receive Good Pub Guide updates and offers from
The Random House Group. ☐

Your own name and address *(block capitals please)*

....

....

....

Postcode..

Please return to
Freepost THE GOOD PUB GUIDE,
Random House Publishing,
20 Vauxhall Bridge Road,
London SW1V 2SA

IF YOU PREFER, YOU CAN SEND
US REPORTS BY EMAIL:

feedback@goodguides.com

I have been to the following pubs in *The Good Pub Guide 2020* in the last few months, found them as described, and confirm that they deserve continued inclusion:

continued overleaf

PLEASE GIVE YOUR NAME AND ADDRESS ON THE BACK OF THIS FORM

Pubs visited continued..........

I would like to receive Good Pub Guide updates and offers from
The Random House Group. ☐

Your own name and address *(block capitals please)*

....

....

....

Postcode..

Please return to
Freepost THE GOOD PUB GUIDE,
Random House Publishing,
20 Vauxhall Bridge Road,
London SW1V 2SA

IF YOU PREFER, YOU CAN SEND US REPORTS BY EMAIL:
feedback@goodguides.com

I have been to the following pubs in *The Good Pub Guide 2020* in the last few months, found them as described, and confirm that they deserve continued inclusion:

continued overleaf

PLEASE GIVE YOUR NAME AND ADDRESS ON THE BACK OF THIS FORM

Pubs visited continued..........

By returning this form, you confirm your agreement that the information you provide in your review may be used by The Random House Group Ltd (or its assignees and/or licensees) in any media or medium whatsoever. Any personal details which you provide from which we can identify you are held and processed in accordance with the General Data Protection Regulation (GDPR), and details on how we process this personal data can be found in our Privacy Policy (https://www.penguinrandomhouse.co.uk/PrivacyPolicy/). **Your details will not be passed on to any third parties for their marketing purposes.**

I would like to receive Good Pub Guide updates and offers from
The Random House Group. ☐

Your own name and address *(block capitals please)*

....

....

....

Postcode..

Please return to
Freepost THE GOOD PUB GUIDE,
Random House Publishing,
20 Vauxhall Bridge Road,
London SW1V 2SA

IF YOU PREFER, YOU CAN SEND
US REPORTS BY EMAIL:

feedback@goodguides.com

I have been to the following pubs in *The Good Pub Guide 2020* in the last few months, found them as described, and confirm that they deserve continued inclusion:

continued overleaf

PLEASE GIVE YOUR NAME AND ADDRESS ON THE BACK OF THIS FORM

Pubs visited continued..........

I would like to receive Good Pub Guide updates and offers from
The Random House Group.   ☐

Your own name and address *(block capitals please)*

....

....

....

Postcode...

Please return to
Freepost THE GOOD PUB GUIDE,
Random House Publishing,
20 Vauxhall Bridge Road,
London SW1V 2SA

IF YOU PREFER, YOU CAN SEND
US REPORTS BY EMAIL:

feedback@goodguides.com

I have been to the following pubs in *The Good Pub Guide 2020* **in the last few months, found them as described, and confirm that they deserve continued inclusion:**

continued overleaf

PLEASE GIVE YOUR NAME AND ADDRESS ON THE BACK OF THIS FORM

Pubs visited continued..........

I would like to receive Good Pub Guide updates and offers from The Random House Group. ☐

Your own name and address *(block capitals please)*

....

....

....

Postcode..

Please return to
Freepost THE GOOD PUB GUIDE,
Random House Publishing,
20 Vauxhall Bridge Road,
London SW1V 2SA

IF YOU PREFER, YOU CAN SEND
US REPORTS BY EMAIL:

feedback@goodguides.com

I have been to the following pubs in *The Good Pub Guide 2020* in the last few months, found them as described, and confirm that they deserve continued inclusion:

PLEASE GIVE YOUR NAME AND ADDRESS ON THE BACK OF THIS FORM

Pubs visited continued..........

I would like to receive Good Pub Guide updates and offers from
The Random House Group. ☐

Your own name and address *(block capitals please)*

....

....

....

Postcode...

Please return to
Freepost THE GOOD PUB GUIDE,
Random House Publishing,
20 Vauxhall Bridge Road,
London SW1V 2SA

IF YOU PREFER, YOU CAN SEND
US REPORTS BY EMAIL:

feedback@goodguides.com

I have been to the following pubs in *The Good Pub Guide 2020* in the last few months, found them as described, and confirm that they deserve continued inclusion:

continued overleaf

Pubs visited continued..........

I would like to receive Good Pub Guide updates and offers from The Random House Group. ☐

Your own name and address *(block capitals please)*

....

....

....

Postcode..

Please return to
Freepost THE GOOD PUB GUIDE,
Random House Publishing,
20 Vauxhall Bridge Road,
London SW1V 2SA

IF YOU PREFER, YOU CAN SEND
US REPORTS BY EMAIL:

feedback@goodguides.com

Report on   (pub's name)

....

Pub's address

....

☐ YES MAIN ENTRY   ☐ YES WORTH A VISIT   ☐ NO don't include

Please tick one of these boxes to show your verdict, and give reasons, descriptive comments, prices and the date of your visit

☐ Deserves **FOOD Award**   ☐ Deserves **STAY Award**   2020:1

PLEASE GIVE YOUR NAME AND ADDRESS ON THE BACK OF THIS FORM

✂ ....

Report on   (pub's name)

....

Pub's address

....

☐ YES MAIN ENTRY   ☐ YES WORTH A VISIT   ☐ NO don't include

Please tick one of these boxes to show your verdict, and give reasons, descriptive comments, prices and the date of your visit

☐ Deserves **FOOD Award**   ☐ Deserves **STAY Award**   2020:2

PLEASE GIVE YOUR NAME AND ADDRESS ON THE BACK OF THIS FORM

DO NOT USE THIS SIDE OF THE PAGE FOR WRITING ABOUT PUBS

Your own name and address *(block capitals please)*

By returning this form, you confirm your agreement that the information you provide in your review may be used by The Random House Group Ltd (or its assignees and/or licensees) in any media or medium whatsoever. Any personal details which you provide from which we can identify you are held and processed in accordance with the General Data Protection Regulation (GDPR), and details on how we process this personal data can be found in our Privacy Policy (https://www.penguinrandomhouse.co.uk/PrivacyPolicy/). **Your details will not be passed on to any third parties for their marketing purposes.**

I would like to receive Good Pub Guide updates and offers from The Random House Group. ☐

✂ ....

DO NOT USE THIS SIDE OF THE PAGE FOR WRITING ABOUT PUBS

Your own name and address *(block capitals please)*

By returning this form, you confirm your agreement that the information you provide in your review may be used by The Random House Group Ltd (or its assignees and/or licensees) in any media or medium whatsoever. Any personal details which you provide from which we can identify you are held and processed in accordance with the General Data Protection Regulation (GDPR), and details on how we process this personal data can be found in our Privacy Policy (https://www.penguinrandomhouse.co.uk/PrivacyPolicy/). **Your details will not be passed on to any third parties for their marketing purposes.**

I would like to receive Good Pub Guide updates and offers from The Random House Group. ☐

Report on (pub's name)

....

Pub's address

....

☐ YES MAIN ENTRY   ☐ YES WORTH A VISIT   ☐ NO don't include

Please tick one of these boxes to show your verdict, and give reasons,
descriptive comments, prices and the date of your visit

☐ Deserves **FOOD Award**   ☐ Deserves **STAY Award**   2020: 3

PLEASE GIVE YOUR NAME AND ADDRESS ON THE BACK OF THIS FORM

✂ ....

Report on (pub's name)

....

Pub's address

....

☐ YES MAIN ENTRY   ☐ YES WORTH A VISIT   ☐ NO don't include

Please tick one of these boxes to show your verdict, and give reasons,
descriptive comments, prices and the date of your visit

☐ Deserves **FOOD Award**   ☐ Deserves **STAY Award**   2020: 4

PLEASE GIVE YOUR NAME AND ADDRESS ON THE BACK OF THIS FORM

DO NOT USE THIS SIDE OF THE PAGE FOR WRITING ABOUT PUBS

Your own name and address *(block capitals please)*

By returning this form, you confirm your agreement that the information you provide
in your review may be used by The Random House Group Ltd (or its assignees and/or
licensees) in any media or medium whatsoever. Any personal details which you provide
from which we can identify you are held and processed in accordance with the General
Data Protection Regulation (GDPR), and details on how we process this personal data can
be found in our Privacy Policy (https://www.penguinrandomhouse.co.uk/PrivacyPolicy/).
Your details will not be passed on to any third parties for their marketing purposes.

I **would like to receive Good Pub Guide updates and offers from
The Random House Group.**

✂ ....

DO NOT USE THIS SIDE OF THE PAGE FOR WRITING ABOUT PUBS

Your own name and address *(block capitals please)*

By returning this form, you confirm your agreement that the information you provide
in your review may be used by The Random House Group Ltd (or its assignees and/or
licensees) in any media or medium whatsoever. Any personal details which you provide
from which we can identify you are held and processed in accordance with the General
Data Protection Regulation (GDPR), and details on how we process this personal data can
be found in our Privacy Policy (https://www.penguinrandomhouse.co.uk/PrivacyPolicy/).
Your details will not be passed on to any third parties for their marketing purposes.

I **would like to receive Good Pub Guide updates and offers from
The Random House Group.**

Report on (pub's name)

....

Pub's address

....

☐ YES MAIN ENTRY ☐ YES WORTH A VISIT ☐ NO don't include

Please tick one of these boxes to show your verdict, and give reasons,
descriptive comments, prices and the date of your visit

☐ Deserves **FOOD Award** ☐ Deserves **STAY Award** 2020: 5

PLEASE GIVE YOUR NAME AND ADDRESS ON THE BACK OF THIS FORM

✂ ....

Report on (pub's name)

....

Pub's address

....

☐ YES MAIN ENTRY ☐ YES WORTH A VISIT ☐ NO don't include

Please tick one of these boxes to show your verdict, and give reasons,
descriptive comments, prices and the date of your visit

☐ Deserves **FOOD Award** ☐ Deserves **STAY Award** 2020: 6

PLEASE GIVE YOUR NAME AND ADDRESS ON THE BACK OF THIS FORM

DO NOT USE THIS SIDE OF THE PAGE FOR WRITING ABOUT PUBS

Your own name and address *(block capitals please)*

By returning this form, you confirm your agreement that the information you provide in your review may be used by The Random House Group Ltd (or its assignees and/or licensees) in any media or medium whatsoever. Any personal details which you provide from which we can identify you are held and processed in accordance with the General Data Protection Regulation (GDPR), and details on how we process this personal data can be found in our Privacy Policy (https://www.penguinrandomhouse.co.uk/PrivacyPolicy/). **Your details will not be passed on to any third parties for their marketing purposes.**

I **would like to receive Good Pub Guide updates and offers from The Random House Group.**   ☐

✂ ....

DO NOT USE THIS SIDE OF THE PAGE FOR WRITING ABOUT PUBS

Your own name and address *(block capitals please)*

By returning this form, you confirm your agreement that the information you provide in your review may be used by The Random House Group Ltd (or its assignees and/or licensees) in any media or medium whatsoever. Any personal details which you provide from which we can identify you are held and processed in accordance with the General Data Protection Regulation (GDPR), and details on how we process this personal data can be found in our Privacy Policy (https://www.penguinrandomhouse.co.uk/PrivacyPolicy/). **Your details will not be passed on to any third parties for their marketing purposes.**

I **would like to receive Good Pub Guide updates and offers from The Random House Group.**   ☐

Report on (pub's name)

....

Pub's address

....

☐ YES MAIN ENTRY ☐ YES WORTH A VISIT ☐ NO don't include

Please tick one of these boxes to show your verdict, and give reasons,
descriptive comments, prices and the date of your visit

☐ Deserves **FOOD Award** ☐ Deserves **STAY Award** 2020: 7

PLEASE GIVE YOUR NAME AND ADDRESS ON THE BACK OF THIS FORM

✂ ....

Report on (pub's name)

....

Pub's address

....

☐ YES MAIN ENTRY ☐ YES WORTH A VISIT ☐ NO don't include

Please tick one of these boxes to show your verdict, and give reasons,
descriptive comments, prices and the date of your visit

☐ Deserves **FOOD Award** ☐ Deserves **STAY Award** 2020: 8

PLEASE GIVE YOUR NAME AND ADDRESS ON THE BACK OF THIS FORM

DO NOT USE THIS SIDE OF THE PAGE FOR WRITING ABOUT PUBS

Your own name and address *(block capitals please)*

By returning this form, you confirm your agreement that the information you provide in your review may be used by The Random House Group Ltd (or its assignees and/or licensees) in any media or medium whatsoever. Any personal details which you provide from which we can identify you are held and processed in accordance with the General Data Protection Regulation (GDPR), and details on how we process this personal data can be found in our Privacy Policy (https://www.penguinrandomhouse.co.uk/PrivacyPolicy/). **Your details will not be passed on to any third parties for their marketing purposes.**

I would like to receive Good Pub Guide updates and offers from The Random House Group.

✂ ....

DO NOT USE THIS SIDE OF THE PAGE FOR WRITING ABOUT PUBS

Your own name and address *(block capitals please)*

By returning this form, you confirm your agreement that the information you provide in your review may be used by The Random House Group Ltd (or its assignees and/or licensees) in any media or medium whatsoever. Any personal details which you provide from which we can identify you are held and processed in accordance with the General Data Protection Regulation (GDPR), and details on how we process this personal data can be found in our Privacy Policy (https://www.penguinrandomhouse.co.uk/PrivacyPolicy/). **Your details will not be passed on to any third parties for their marketing purposes.**

I would like to receive Good Pub Guide updates and offers from The Random House Group.

Report on (pub's name)

....

Pub's address

....

☐ YES MAIN ENTRY   ☐ YES WORTH A VISIT   ☐ NO don't include

Please tick one of these boxes to show your verdict, and give reasons,
descriptive comments, prices and the date of your visit

☐ Deserves **FOOD Award**   ☐ Deserves **STAY Award**   2020:9

PLEASE GIVE YOUR NAME AND ADDRESS ON THE BACK OF THIS FORM

✂ ....

Report on (pub's name)

....

Pub's address

....

☐ YES MAIN ENTRY   ☐ YES WORTH A VISIT   ☐ NO don't include

Please tick one of these boxes to show your verdict, and give reasons,
descriptive comments, prices and the date of your visit

☐ Deserves **FOOD Award**   ☐ Deserves **STAY Award**   2020:10

PLEASE GIVE YOUR NAME AND ADDRESS ON THE BACK OF THIS FORM

DO NOT USE THIS SIDE OF THE PAGE FOR WRITING ABOUT PUBS

Your own name and address *(block capitals please)*

By returning this form, you confirm your agreement that the information you provide in your review may be used by The Random House Group Ltd (or its assignees and/or licensees) in any media or medium whatsoever. Any personal details which you provide from which we can identify you are held and processed in accordance with the General Data Protection Regulation (GDPR), and details on how we process this personal data can be found in our Privacy Policy (https://www.penguinrandomhouse.co.uk/PrivacyPolicy/). **Your details will not be passed on to any third parties for their marketing purposes.**

I would like to receive Good Pub Guide updates and offers from The Random House Group. ☐

✂ ....

DO NOT USE THIS SIDE OF THE PAGE FOR WRITING ABOUT PUBS

Your own name and address *(block capitals please)*

By returning this form, you confirm your agreement that the information you provide in your review may be used by The Random House Group Ltd (or its assignees and/or licensees) in any media or medium whatsoever. Any personal details which you provide from which we can identify you are held and processed in accordance with the General Data Protection Regulation (GDPR), and details on how we process this personal data can be found in our Privacy Policy (https://www.penguinrandomhouse.co.uk/PrivacyPolicy/). **Your details will not be passed on to any third parties for their marketing purposes.**

I would like to receive Good Pub Guide updates and offers from The Random House Group. ☐

Report on (pub's name)

....

Pub's address

....

☐ YES MAIN ENTRY ☐ YES WORTH A VISIT ☐ NO don't include

Please tick one of these boxes to show your verdict, and give reasons, descriptive comments, prices and the date of your visit

☐ Deserves **FOOD Award** ☐ Deserves **STAY Award** 2020:11

PLEASE GIVE YOUR NAME AND ADDRESS ON THE BACK OF THIS FORM

✂ ....

Report on (pub's name)

....

Pub's address

....

☐ YES MAIN ENTRY ☐ YES WORTH A VISIT ☐ NO don't include

Please tick one of these boxes to show your verdict, and give reasons, descriptive comments, prices and the date of your visit

☐ Deserves **FOOD Award** ☐ Deserves **STAY Award** 2020:12

PLEASE GIVE YOUR NAME AND ADDRESS ON THE BACK OF THIS FORM

DO NOT USE THIS SIDE OF THE PAGE FOR WRITING ABOUT PUBS

Your own name and address *(block capitals please)*

By returning this form, you confirm your agreement that the information you provide in your review may be used by The Random House Group Ltd (or its assignees and/or licensees) in any media or medium whatsoever. Any personal details which you provide from which we can identify you are held and processed in accordance with the General Data Protection Regulation (GDPR), and details on how we process this personal data can be found in our Privacy Policy (https://www.penguinrandomhouse.co.uk/PrivacyPolicy/). **Your details will not be passed on to any third parties for their marketing purposes.**

I **would like to receive Good Pub Guide updates and offers from The Random House Group.** ☐

✂ ....

DO NOT USE THIS SIDE OF THE PAGE FOR WRITING ABOUT PUBS

Your own name and address *(block capitals please)*

By returning this form, you confirm your agreement that the information you provide in your review may be used by The Random House Group Ltd (or its assignees and/or licensees) in any media or medium whatsoever. Any personal details which you provide from which we can identify you are held and processed in accordance with the General Data Protection Regulation (GDPR), and details on how we process this personal data can be found in our Privacy Policy (https://www.penguinrandomhouse.co.uk/PrivacyPolicy/). **Your details will not be passed on to any third parties for their marketing purposes.**

I **would like to receive Good Pub Guide updates and offers from The Random House Group.** ☐

Report on (pub's name)

....

Pub's address

....

☐ YES MAIN ENTRY   ☐ YES WORTH A VISIT   ☐ NO don't include

Please tick one of these boxes to show your verdict, and give reasons, descriptive comments, prices and the date of your visit

☐ Deserves **FOOD Award**   ☐ Deserves **STAY Award**   2020:13

PLEASE GIVE YOUR NAME AND ADDRESS ON THE BACK OF THIS FORM

✂ ....

Report on (pub's name)

....

Pub's address

....

☐ YES MAIN ENTRY   ☐ YES WORTH A VISIT   ☐ NO don't include

Please tick one of these boxes to show your verdict, and give reasons, descriptive comments, prices and the date of your visit

☐ Deserves **FOOD Award**   ☐ Deserves **STAY Award**   2020:14

PLEASE GIVE YOUR NAME AND ADDRESS ON THE BACK OF THIS FORM

DO NOT USE THIS SIDE OF THE PAGE FOR WRITING ABOUT PUBS

Your own name and address *(block capitals please)*

By returning this form, you confirm your agreement that the information you provide in your review may be used by The Random House Group Ltd (or its assignees and/or licensees) in any media or medium whatsoever. Any personal details which you provide from which we can identify you are held and processed in accordance with the General Data Protection Regulation (GDPR), and details on how we process this personal data can be found in our Privacy Policy (https://www.penguinrandomhouse.co.uk/PrivacyPolicy/). **Your details will not be passed on to any third parties for their marketing purposes.**

I w**ould like to receive Good Pub Guide updates and offers from The Random House Group.** ☐

✂ ....

DO NOT USE THIS SIDE OF THE PAGE FOR WRITING ABOUT PUBS

Your own name and address *(block capitals please)*

By returning this form, you confirm your agreement that the information you provide in your review may be used by The Random House Group Ltd (or its assignees and/or licensees) in any media or medium whatsoever. Any personal details which you provide from which we can identify you are held and processed in accordance with the General Data Protection Regulation (GDPR), and details on how we process this personal data can be found in our Privacy Policy (https://www.penguinrandomhouse.co.uk/PrivacyPolicy/). **Your details will not be passed on to any third parties for their marketing purposes.**

I w**ould like to receive Good Pub Guide updates and offers from The Random House Group.** ☐

Report on (pub's name)

....

Pub's address

....

☐ YES MAIN ENTRY　　☐ YES WORTH A VISIT　　☐ NO don't include

Please tick one of these boxes to show your verdict, and give reasons, descriptive comments, prices and the date of your visit

☐ Deserves **FOOD Award**　　☐ Deserves **STAY Award**　　2020:15

PLEASE GIVE YOUR NAME AND ADDRESS ON THE BACK OF THIS FORM

✂ ....

Report on (pub's name)

....

Pub's address

....

☐ YES MAIN ENTRY　　☐ YES WORTH A VISIT　　☐ NO don't include

Please tick one of these boxes to show your verdict, and give reasons, descriptive comments, prices and the date of your visit

☐ Deserves **FOOD Award**　　☐ Deserves **STAY Award**　　2020:16

PLEASE GIVE YOUR NAME AND ADDRESS ON THE BACK OF THIS FORM

DO NOT USE THIS SIDE OF THE PAGE FOR WRITING ABOUT PUBS

Your own name and address *(block capitals please)*

By returning this form, you confirm your agreement that the information you provide in your review may be used by The Random House Group Ltd (or its assignees and/or licensees) in any media or medium whatsoever. Any personal details which you provide from which we can identify you are held and processed in accordance with the General Data Protection Regulation (GDPR), and details on how we process this personal data can be found in our Privacy Policy (https://www.penguinrandomhouse.co.uk/PrivacyPolicy/). **Your details will not be passed on to any third parties for their marketing purposes.**

I **would like to receive Good Pub Guide updates and offers from The Random House Group.**

✂ ....

DO NOT USE THIS SIDE OF THE PAGE FOR WRITING ABOUT PUBS

Your own name and address *(block capitals please)*

By returning this form, you confirm your agreement that the information you provide in your review may be used by The Random House Group Ltd (or its assignees and/or licensees) in any media or medium whatsoever. Any personal details which you provide from which we can identify you are held and processed in accordance with the General Data Protection Regulation (GDPR), and details on how we process this personal data can be found in our Privacy Policy (https://www.penguinrandomhouse.co.uk/PrivacyPolicy/). **Your details will not be passed on to any third parties for their marketing purposes.**

I **would like to receive Good Pub Guide updates and offers from The Random House Group.**

Report on (pub's name)

....

Pub's address

....

☐ YES MAIN ENTRY ☐ YES WORTH A VISIT ☐ NO don't include

Please tick one of these boxes to show your verdict, and give reasons, descriptive comments, prices and the date of your visit

☐ Deserves **FOOD Award** ☐ Deserves **STAY Award** 2020:17

PLEASE GIVE YOUR NAME AND ADDRESS ON THE BACK OF THIS FORM

✂ ....

Report on (pub's name)

....

Pub's address

....

☐ YES MAIN ENTRY ☐ YES WORTH A VISIT ☐ NO don't include

Please tick one of these boxes to show your verdict, and give reasons, descriptive comments, prices and the date of your visit

☐ Deserves **FOOD Award** ☐ Deserves **STAY Award** 2020:18

PLEASE GIVE YOUR NAME AND ADDRESS ON THE BACK OF THIS FORM

DO NOT USE THIS SIDE OF THE PAGE FOR WRITING ABOUT PUBS

Your own name and address *(block capitals please)*

I would like to receive Good Pub Guide updates and offers from The Random House Group.

✂ ....

DO NOT USE THIS SIDE OF THE PAGE FOR WRITING ABOUT PUBS

Your own name and address *(block capitals please)*

I would like to receive Good Pub Guide updates and offers from The Random House Group.

Report on (pub's name)

....

Pub's address

....

☐ YES MAIN ENTRY ☐ YES WORTH A VISIT ☐ NO don't include

Please tick one of these boxes to show your verdict, and give reasons, descriptive comments, prices and the date of your visit

☐ Deserves **FOOD Award** ☐ Deserves **STAY Award** 2020:19

PLEASE GIVE YOUR NAME AND ADDRESS ON THE BACK OF THIS FORM

✂ ....

Report on (pub's name)

....

Pub's address

....

☐ YES MAIN ENTRY ☐ YES WORTH A VISIT ☐ NO don't include

Please tick one of these boxes to show your verdict, and give reasons, descriptive comments, prices and the date of your visit

☐ Deserves **FOOD Award** ☐ Deserves **STAY Award** 2020:20

PLEASE GIVE YOUR NAME AND ADDRESS ON THE BACK OF THIS FORM

DO NOT USE THIS SIDE OF THE PAGE FOR WRITING ABOUT PUBS

Your own name and address *(block capitals please)*

By returning this form, you confirm your agreement that the information you provide in your review may be used by The Random House Group Ltd (or its assignees and/or licensees) in any media or medium whatsoever. Any personal details which you provide from which we can identify you are held and processed in accordance with the General Data Protection Regulation (GDPR), and details on how we process this personal data can be found in our Privacy Policy (https://www.penguinrandomhouse.co.uk/PrivacyPolicy/). **Your details will not be passed on to any third parties for their marketing purposes.**

I would like to receive Good Pub Guide updates and offers from The Random House Group.

✂ ....

DO NOT USE THIS SIDE OF THE PAGE FOR WRITING ABOUT PUBS

Your own name and address *(block capitals please)*

By returning this form, you confirm your agreement that the information you provide in your review may be used by The Random House Group Ltd (or its assignees and/or licensees) in any media or medium whatsoever. Any personal details which you provide from which we can identify you are held and processed in accordance with the General Data Protection Regulation (GDPR), and details on how we process this personal data can be found in our Privacy Policy (https://www.penguinrandomhouse.co.uk/PrivacyPolicy/). **Your details will not be passed on to any third parties for their marketing purposes.**

I would like to receive Good Pub Guide updates and offers from The Random House Group.